Less managing. More teaching. Greater learning.

INSTRUCTORS...

Would you like your **students** to show up for class **more prepared**? *(Let's face it, class is much more fun if everyone is engaged and prepared...)*

Want an **easy way to assign** homework online and track student **progress**? *(Less time grading means more time teaching...)*

Want an **instant view** of student or class performance relative to learning objectives? *(No more wondering if students understand...)*

Need to **collect data and generate reports** required for administration or accreditation? *(Say goodbye to manually tracking student learning outcomes...)*

Want to **record and post your lectures** for students to view online?

With McGraw-Hill's *Connect*™ *Plus Accounting*,

INSTRUCTORS GET:

- Simple **assignment management**, allowing you to spend more time teaching.
- **Auto-graded** assignments, quizzes, and tests.
- **Detailed Visual Reporting** where student and section results can be viewed and analyzed.
- Sophisticated **online testing** capability.
- A **filtering and reporting** function that allows you to easily assign and report on materials that are correlated to accreditation standards, learning outcomes, and Bloom's taxonomy.
- An easy-to-use **lecture capture** tool.
- The option to **upload course documents** for student access.

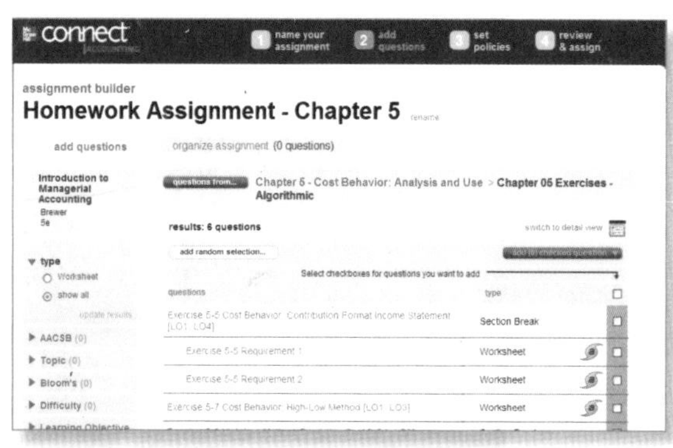

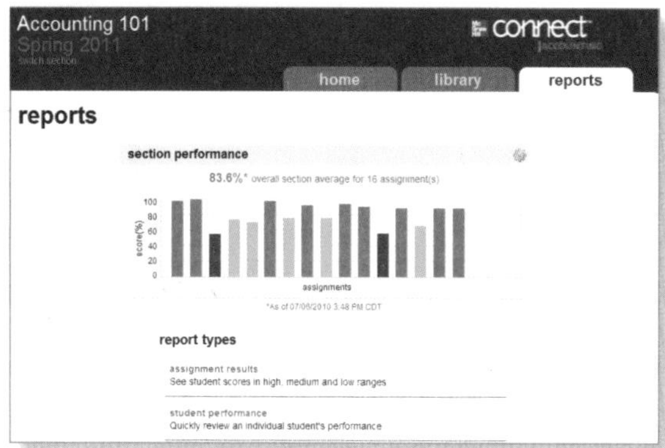

Want an online, **searchable version** of your textbook?

Wish your textbook could be **available online** while you're doing your assignments?

Connect™ *Plus Accounting* eBook

If you choose to use *Connect*™ *Plus Accounting*, you have an affordable and searchable online version of your book integrated with your other online tools.

Connect™ *Plus Accounting* eBook offers features like:

- Topic search
- Direct links from assignments
- Adjustable text size
- Jump to page number
- Print by section

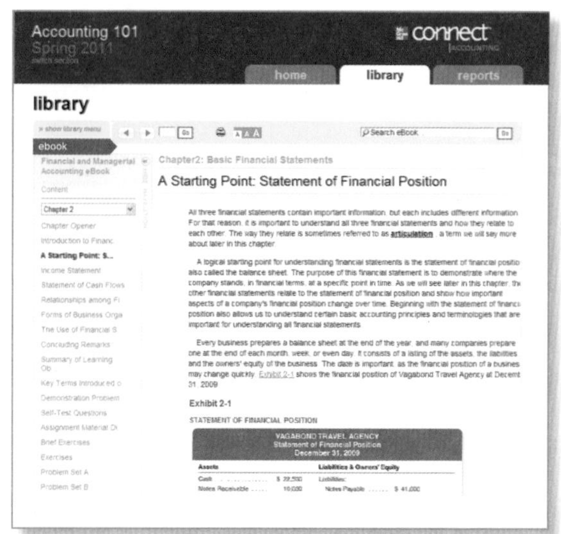

Want to get more **value** from your textbook purchase?

Think learning accounting should be a bit more **interesting**?

Check out the STUDENT RESOURCES section under the *Connect*™ Library tab.

Here you'll find a wealth of resources designed to help you achieve your goals in the course. You'll find things like **quizzes, PowerPoints, and Internet activities** to help you study. Every student has different needs, so explore the STUDENT RESOURCES to find the materials best suited to you.

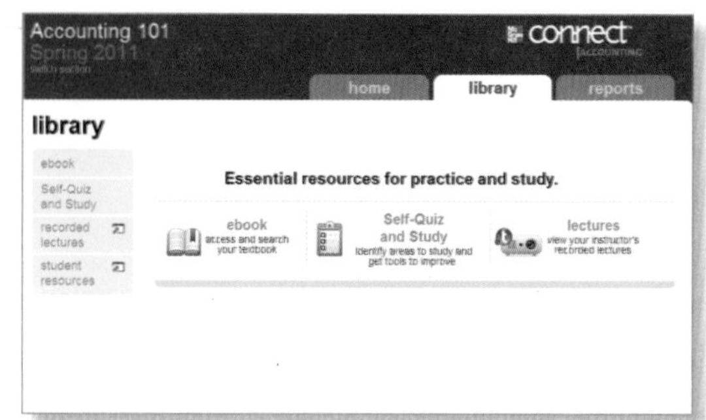

16th Edition

Financial & Managerial Accounting

THE BASIS FOR BUSINESS DECISIONS

Jan R. Williams
University of Tennessee

Susan F. Haka
Michigan State University

Mark S. Bettner
Bucknell University

Joseph V. Carcello
University of Tennessee

The McGraw·Hill Companies

FINANCIAL AND MANAGERIAL ACCOUNTING: THE BASIS FOR BUSINESS DECISIONS

Published by McGraw-Hill/Irwin, a business unit of The McGraw-Hill Companies, Inc., 1221 Avenue of the Americas, New York, NY, 10020.

This book is printed on acid-free paper.

1 2 3 4 5 6 7 8 9 0 DOW/DOW 1 0 9 8 7 6 5 4 3 2 1

ISBN 978-0-07-811104-4
MHID 0-07-811104-8

Vice president and editor-in-chief: *Brent Gordon*
Editorial director: *Stewart Mattson*
Publisher: *Tim Vertovec*
Executive editor: *Steve Schuetz*
Executive director of development: *Ann Torbert*
Developmental editor: *Rebecca Mann*
Vice president and director of marketing: *Robin J. Zwettler*
Marketing director: *Brad Parkins*
Marketing manager: *Michelle Heaster*
Vice president of editing, design, and production: *Sesha Bolisetty*
Managing editor of editing, design, and production: *Lori Koetters*
Managing editor of photo, design, and publishing tools: *Mary Conzachi*
Lead project manager: *Harvey Yep*
Senior buyer: *Michael R. McCormick*
Cover and interior design: *Pam Verros*
Senior photo research coordinator: *Keri Johnson*
Photo researcher: *Ira Roberts*
Senior media project manager: *Allison Souter*
Media project manager: *Ron Nelms*
Cover image: © *Getty Images/Dennis McColeman*
Typeface: *10/12 Times Roman*
Compositor: *Laserwords Private Limited*
Printer: *R. R. Donnelley*

Library of Congress Cataloging-in-Publication Data

Financial & managerial accounting : the basis for business decisions / Jan R. Williams . . . [et al.].
—16th ed.
p. cm.
Includes index.
ISBN-13: 978-0-07-811104-4 (alk. paper)
ISBN-10: 0-07-811104-8 (alk. paper)
1. Accounting. I. Williams, Jan R. II. Title: Financial and managerial accounting.
HF5636.F5314 2012
657—dc22 2010036617

www.mhhe.com

To Ben and Meg Wishart and Asher, Lainey, and Lucy Hunt, who have taught me the joys of being a grandfather.

—Jan R. Williams

For Cliff, Abi, and my mother, Fran.

—Susan F. Haka

To my parents, Fred and Marjorie.

—Mark S. Bettner

To Terri, Stephen, Karen, and Sarah, whose sacrifices enabled me to participate in writing this book. Thank you—I love you!

—Joseph V. Carcello

Jan R. Williams is Dean of the College of Business Administration and the Stokely Foundation Leadership Chair at the University of Tennessee, where he has been a faculty member since 1977. He received a BS degree from George Peabody College, an MBA from Baylor University, and a PhD from the University of Arkansas. He previously served on the faculties at the University of Georgia and Texas Tech University. A CPA in Tennessee and Arkansas, Dr. Williams is also the coauthor of three books and has published over 70 articles on issues of corporate financial reporting and accounting education. He served as president of the American Accounting Association in 1999–2000 and has been actively involved in Beta Alpha Psi, the Tennessee Society of CPAs, the American Institute of CPAs, and AACSB International—the Association to Advance Collegiate Schools of Business—the accrediting organization for business schools and accounting programs worldwide. He currently serves as chair-elect of the Board of Directors of AACSB International.

Susan F. Haka is the Associate Dean for Academic Affairs and Research and the Ernst & Young Professor of Accounting in the Department of Accounting and Information Systems at Michigan State University. Dr. Haka received her PhD from the University of Kansas and a master's degree in accounting from the University of Illinois. She served as president of the American Accounting Association in 2008–2009 and has previously served as president of the Management Accounting Section. Dr. Haka is active in editorial processes and has been editor of *Behavioral Research in Accounting* and an associate editor of *Journal of Management Accounting Research, Accounting Horizons, The International Journal of Accounting,* and *Contemporary Accounting Research.* Dr. Haka has been honored by Michigan State University with several teaching and research awards, including both universitywide Teacher-Scholar and Distinguished Faculty awards.

Meet the **Authors**

Mark S. Bettner is the Christian R. Lindback Chair of Accounting & Financial Management at Bucknell University. Dr. Bettner received his PhD in business administration from Texas Tech University and his MS in accounting from Virginia Tech University. He has received numerous teaching and research awards. In addition to his work on *Financial Accounting* and *Financial & Managerial Accounting*, he has written many ancillary materials, published in scholarly journals, and presented at academic and practitioner conferences. Professor Bettner is also on the editorial advisory boards of several academic journals, including the *International Journal of Accounting and Business Society* and the *Accounting Forum,* and has served as a reviewer for several journals, including *Advances in Public Interest Accounting* and *Hospital and Health Services Administration.*

Joseph V. Carcello is the Ernst & Young and Business Alumni Professor in the Department of Accounting and Information Management at the University of Tennessee. He also is the cofounder and director of research for UT's Corporate Governance Center. Dr. Carcello received his PhD from Georgia State University, his MAcc from the University of Georgia, and his BS from the State University of New York College at Plattsburgh. Dr. Carcello is currently the author or coauthor of four books, more than 60 journal articles, and three monographs. Dr. Carcello serves on the Public Company Accounting Oversight Board's (PCAOB) Investor Advisory Group, and he previously served two terms on the PCAOB's Standing Advisory Group. He also has testified before the U.S. Treasury Department's Advisory Committee on the Auditing Profession and has served as a member of a COSO task force that developed guidance on applying COSO's internal control framework for smaller public companies. Dr. Carcello is active in the American Accounting Association—he serves as an associate editor of *Accounting Horizons* and serves on the editorial boards of *The Accounting Review, Auditing: A Journal of Practice & Theory,* and *Contemporary Issues in Auditing.* Dr. Carcello has consulted with three of the Big Four accounting firms, regional and local accounting firms, and the Securities and Exchange Commission.

REACHING GREAT HEIGHTS BEGINS WITH A SOLID BASE

As our eyes are drawn upward to the skyline of great cities, it's important to remember that these impressive constructions are able to reach such heights only because their foundations are strong. In much the same way, being successful in the business world begins with fundamental courses like financial and managerial accounting. It is only when students have a firm grasp of concepts like the accounting cycle and managerial decision making that they have a base on which to stand, a strong foundation on which to grow.

In this edition, as before, the Williams team has revised the text with a keen eye toward the principle of helping students establish the foundation they will need for future success in business. However, through new coverage of International Financial Reporting Standards and a revised globalization chapter, the Williams book also introduces students to larger themes and evolving concerns. This dual emphasis allows students to keep their eyes trained upward even as they become solidly grounded in accounting fundamentals.

The Williams book continues to rest on a bedrock of four key components:

"This is a well balanced textbook that encompasses many issues, yet provides them in a precise, readable, and orderly fashion to students. The extent of the real-world examples makes this edition clearly a superior choice."

Hossein Noorian, Wentworth Institute

Balanced Coverage. The 16th edition of Williams provides the most balanced coverage of financial and managerial topics on the market. By giving equal weight to financial and managerial topics, the authors emphasize the need for a strong foundation in both aspects of accounting.

"Excellent book! Explains difficult subjects in easy-to-understand terms."

Naser Kamleh, Wallace Community College

Clear Accounting Cycle Presentation. In the first five chapters of *Financial & Managerial Accounting,* the authors present the Accounting Cycle in a clear, graphically interesting four-step process. Central to this presentation is the dedication of three successive chapters to three key components of the cycle: recording entries (Chapter 3), adjusting entries (Chapter 4), and closing entries (Chapter 5). The Williams team places easy-to-read margin notes explaining each equation used in particular journal entries.

Student Motivation. The Williams team has put together a market-leading student package that will not only motivate your students, but help you see greater retention rates in your accounting courses. Vital pieces of technology supplement the core curriculum covered in the book: the Online Learning Center provides supplemental tools for both students and instructors; and McGraw-Hill Connect Accounting uses end-of-chapter material pulled directly from the textbook to create static and algorithmic questions that can be used for homework and practice tests. The full *Financial & Managerial Accounting* package encourages students to apply what they're learning and improve their grades.

"This textbook is current and very interactive. It brings in excellent "real-world" applications for the students to use in applying the concepts. It has excellent student and instructor resources. Some of the resources would be especially valuable for instructors teaching online."

Karen Mozingo, Pitt Community College

"The text is excellent. I wish the texts had been this well written when I was a student!"

Mark Anderson, Bob Jones University

Problem-Solving Skills. *Financial & Managerial Accounting* challenges your students to think about real-world situations and put themselves in the role of the decision maker through Case In Point, Your Turn, and Ethics, Fraud & Corporate Governance boxes. Students reference the Home Depot Financial Statements—included in the text as an appendix—to further hone problem-solving skills by evaluating real world financial data. The authors show a keen attention to detail when creating high-quality end-of-chapter material, such as the Critical Thinking Cases and Problems, ensuring that all homework is tied directly back to chapter learning objectives.

How Does **Williams** Help Students

Step-by-Step Process for the Accounting Cycle

Financial & Managerial Accounting was the FIRST text to illustrate Balance Sheet and Income Statement transactions using the four-step process described below. This hallmark coverage has been further revised and refined in the 16th edition.

The Williams team breaks down the Accounting Cycle into three full chapters to help students absorb and understand this material: recording entries (Chapter 3), adjusting entries (Chapter 4), and closing entries (Chapter 5). Transactions are demonstrated visually to help students conquer recording transactions by showing the four steps in the process:

1. Analysis—shows which accounts are recorded with an increase/decrease.
2. Debit/Credit Rules—helps students to remember whether the account should be debited/credited.
3. Journal Entry—shows the result of the two previous steps.
4. Ledger T-Accounts—shows students what was recorded and where.

The Williams team puts the Accounting Equation (A = L + OE) in the margin by transaction illustrations to show students the big picture!

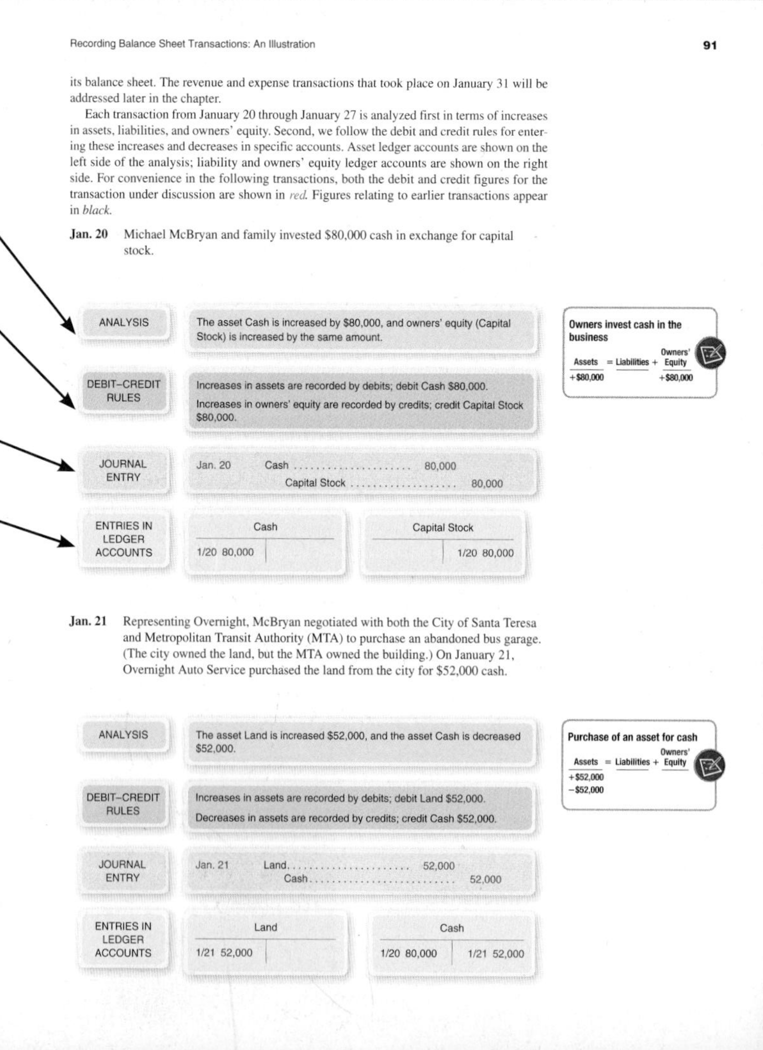

Recording Balance Sheet Transactions: An Illustration 91

its balance sheet. The revenue and expense transactions that took place on January 31 will be addressed later in the chapter.

Each transaction from January 20 through January 27 is analyzed first in terms of increases in assets, liabilities, and owners' equity. Second, we follow the debit and credit rules for entering these increases and decreases in specific accounts. Asset ledger accounts are shown on the left side of the analysis; liability and owners' equity ledger accounts are shown on the right side. For convenience in the following transactions, both the debit and credit figures for the transaction under discussion are shown in *red*. Figures relating to earlier transactions appear in *black*.

Jan. 20 Michael McBryan and family invested $80,000 cash in exchange for capital stock.

ANALYSIS	The asset Cash is increased by $80,000, and owners' equity (Capital Stock) is increased by the same amount.
DEBIT–CREDIT RULES	Increases in assets are recorded by debits; debit Cash $80,000. Increases in owners' equity are recorded by credits; credit Capital Stock $80,000.
JOURNAL ENTRY	Jan. 20 Cash .... 80,000 Capital Stock 80,000
ENTRIES IN LEDGER ACCOUNTS	Cash: 1/20 80,000 | ; Capital Stock: | 1/20 80,000

Owners invest cash in the business

Assets	= Liabilities +	Owners' Equity
+$80,000		+$80,000

Jan. 21 Representing Overnight, McBryan negotiated with both the City of Santa Teresa and Metropolitan Transit Authority (MTA) to purchase an abandoned bus garage. (The city owned the land, but the MTA owned the building.) On January 21, Overnight Auto Service purchased the land from the city for $52,000 cash.

ANALYSIS	The asset Land is increased $52,000, and the asset Cash is decreased $52,000.
DEBIT–CREDIT RULES	Increases in assets are recorded by debits; debit Land $52,000. Decreases in assets are recorded by credits; credit Cash $52,000.
JOURNAL ENTRY	Jan. 21 Land.................... 52,000 Cash.................... 52,000
ENTRIES IN LEDGER ACCOUNTS	Land: 1/21 52,000 | ; Cash: 1/20 80,000 | 1/21 52,000

Purchase of an asset for cash

Assets	= Liabilities +	Owners' Equity
+$52,000		
−$52,000		

Build a Strong Foundation?

Robust End-of-Chapter Material

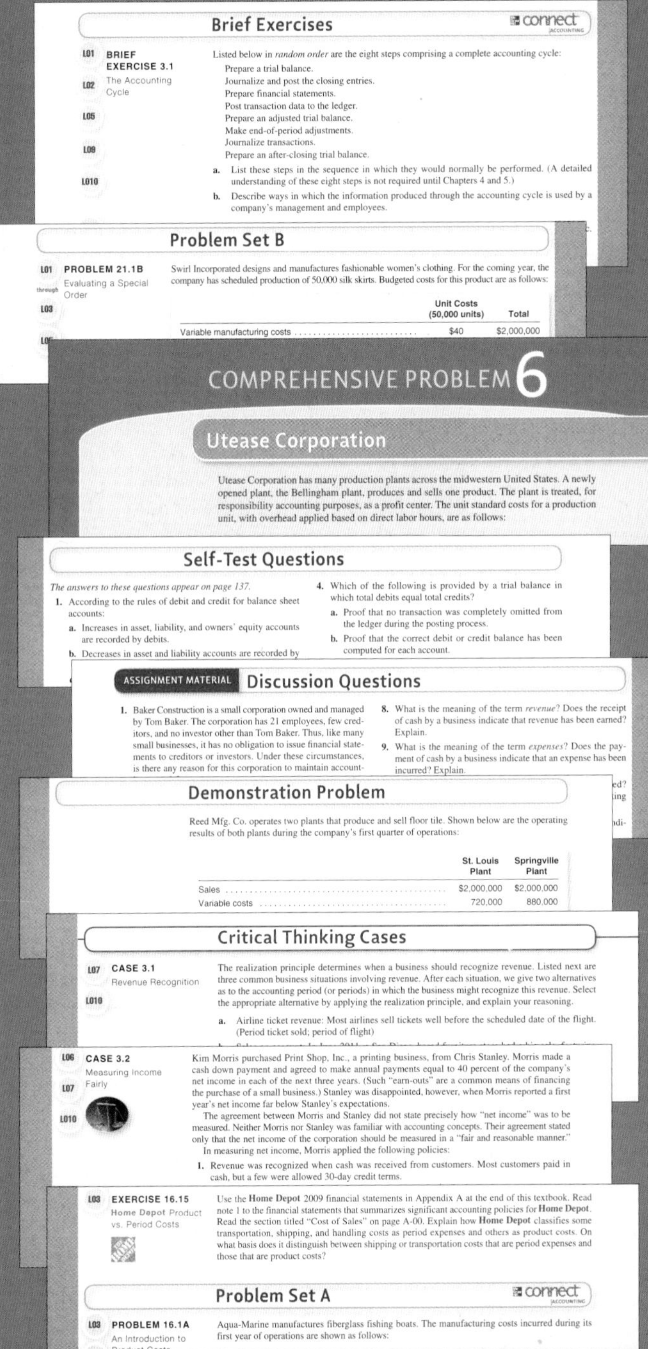

Brief Exercises supplement the exercises with shorter, single-concept exercises that test the basic concepts of each chapter. These brief exercises give instructors more flexibility in their homework assignments.

An Alternate Problem Set provides students with even more practice on important concepts.

Six Comprehensive Problems, ranging from two to five pages in length, present students with real-world scenarios and challenge them to apply what they've learned in the chapters leading up to them.

Defined Key Terms and Self-Test Questions review and reinforce chapter material.

Demonstration Problems and their solutions allow students to test their knowledge of key points in the chapters.

Critical Thinking Cases and Problems put students' analytical skills to the test by having them think critically about key concepts from the chapter and apply them to business decisions. TWO sets of Problems and a full set of Exercises in EACH chapter give *Financial & Managerial Accounting* the edge in homework materials.

Ethics Cases in *each* chapter challenge students to explore the ethical impact of decisions made in business.

The 2009 Home Depot Financial Statements are included in Appendix A. Students are referred to key aspects of the 10-K in the text material and in end-of-chapter material to illustrate actual business applications of chapter concepts.

Excel Templates

Connect Accounting System

Ethical

Group Activities

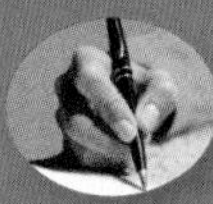

Writing

Internet

International

The Williams Pedagogy Help

High-profile companies frame each chapter discussion through the use of dynamic CHAPTER OPENER vignettes. Students learn to frame the chapter's topic in a real-world scenario.

CHAPTER 12

Income and Changes in Retained Earnings

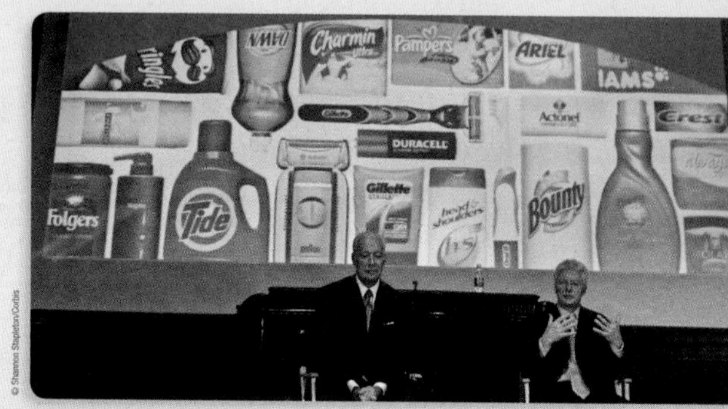

© Shannon Stapleton/Corbis

Learning Objectives

AFTER STUDYING THIS CHAPTER, YOU SHOULD BE ABLE TO:

- LO1 Describe how irregular income items, such as discontinued operations and extraordinary items, are presented in the income statement.
- LO2 Compute earnings per share.
- LO3 Distinguish between basic and diluted earnings per share.
- LO4 Account for cash dividends and stock dividends, and explain the effects of these transactions on a company's financial statements.
- LO5 Describe and prepare a statement of retained earnings.
- LO6 Define *prior period adjustments*, and explain how they are presented in financial statements.
- LO7 Define *comprehensive income*, and explain how it differs from net income.
- LO8 Describe and prepare a statement of stockholders' equity and the stockholders' equity section of the balance sheet.
- LO9 Illustrate steps management might take to improve the appearance of the company's net income.

YOUR TURN boxes challenge students with ethically demanding situations. They must apply what they've learned in the text to situations faced by investors, creditors, and managers in the real world.

YOUR TURN **You as a Team Leader**

Assume you are the leader of the Boards and More product creation team for the new soap box design. At the initial meeting of the cross-organizational team, a serious reservation is raised by the team members from the printing firm about the confidentiality and intellectual printing firm. The reservations of the printing firm representatives are so serious that the viability of the soap box design project is threatened. What should you do?

(See our comments on the Online Learning Center Web site.)

"Lots of eye appeal and in-depth coverage. Students will love it."

James Specht, Concordia College

Exhibit 18–2 PRODUCTION PROCESS FOR METAL PRODUCTS, INC.

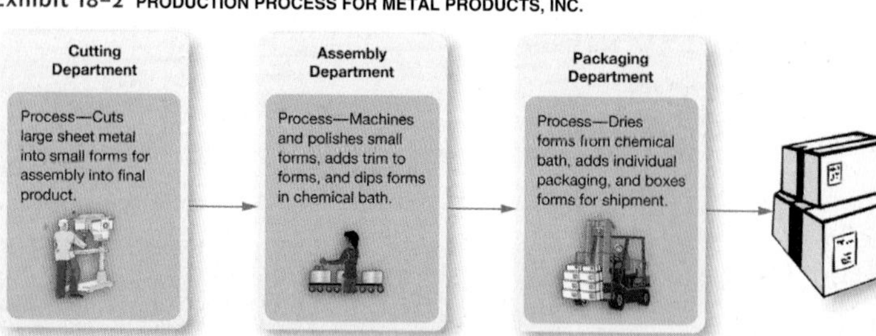

Cutting Department
Process—Cuts large sheet metal into small forms for assembly into final product.
Assembly Department
Process—Machines and polishes small forms, adds trim to forms, and dips forms in chemical bath.
Packaging Department
Process—Dries forms from chemical bath, adds individual packaging, and boxes forms for shipment.

EXHIBITS illustrate key concepts in the text.

Students Reach Great Heights

PROCTER & GAMBLE COMPANY

A company's pattern of sales and net income are important factors in evaluating its financial success. Consider Procter & Gamble Company, for example. Two billion times a day, P&G products are sold around the world. The company has one of the largest and strongest portfolios of recognizable brands, including Pampers, Tide, Ariel, Always, Whisper, Pantene, Bounty, Pringles, Folgers, Charmin, Downy, Lenor, Iams, Crest, Clairol, Actonel, Dawn, and Olay. Ninety-eight thousand people work for P&G in almost 80 countries worldwide.

One of the attributes of financially successful companies like P&G is their consistent strength over time in terms of primary measures of financial performance, such as net sales and net earnings. Net sales, measuring the value of merchandise sold less returns, increased from $74,832 million in 2007 to $81,748 million in 2008 and declined to $78,029 million in 2009. This represents an approximate 9 percent increase in 2008 and a modest 3 percent decline in 2009, for a combined increase for the two years of approximately 6 percent. Net income, which starts with sales and is reduced by various expenses required to generate those sales, increased from $10,340 million in 2007 to $12,075 million in 2008 (an approximate 17 percent increase) and to $13,436 million in 2009 (an approximate 11 percent increase), or a combined increase for the two years of approximately 28 percent. These figures represent impressive financial performance in terms of the company's ability to provide goods to its customers and to operate in a manner that results in a profit that benefits the company's stockholders. ■

"Williams is a great text overall. It provides excellent and accurate coverage of the accounting principles curriculum. Students like it better than any other text I have used. A few years ago I was in a situation where I had to use a different text, since I took over a class for another teacher at the last minute. Students were getting the Williams text on their own and I saw immediate improvement in their understanding and grades across the board. Williams comes through again and again, where other texts fall hopelessly short."

Malcolm E White, Columbia College

CASE IN POINT

Successful companies sometimes experience reductions in cash. Often these reductions are intentional in order to more productively use the company's cash in different ways. For example, in the year ending June 30, 2009, **Microsoft Corporation** reported a *decrease* in cash in excess of $4 billion! Does this mean that the company was experiencing extreme financial difficulty? Not necessarily. That year, operations provided over $19 billion. The overall decline was due to approximately $7.5 billion being used in financing activities, primarily for paying cash dividends to stockholders and purchasing treasury stock. In addition, the company

© ImagineChina via AP Images

CASE IN POINT boxes link accounting concepts in the chapter to their use in the real world. These examples often present an international scenario to expose students to accounting practices around the world.

Ethics, Fraud & Corporate Governance

As discussed in Chapter 2, the Sarbanes-Oxley Act (SOX) substantially increases the civil and criminal penalties associated with securities fraud, including fraudulent financial reporting. The increased penalties are intended to reduce illegal behaviors. Even prior to SOX, the penalties available to the government and the Securities and Exchange Commission for prosecuting securities fraud were substantial. For example, Andrew Fastow, **Enron**'s former chief financial officer, and primary architect of **Enron**'s fraudulent actions, pled guilty to a number of fraud-related criminal charges and has received a 10-year prison sentence. Former chief executive officer of **Enron**, Jeffrey Skilling, also was convicted of numerous criminal charges related to his role at **Enron**.

Businesspeople are sometimes told by their superiors to commit actions that are unethical and in some instances even illegal. The clear message of management is "participate in this behavior or find a job elsewhere." Management pressure and intimidation can make it difficult to resist demands to engage in unethical behavior. Employees sometimes believe that they are insulated from responsibility and liability because "they were just following orders."

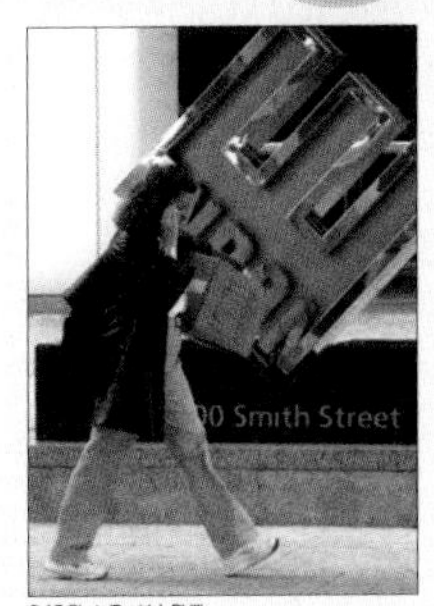

© AP Photo/David J. Phillip

As you encounter ethical dilemmas during your business career, remember that obeying orders from your superiors that are unethical, and certainly those that are illegal, may expose you to serious consequences, including criminal prosecution and incarceration.

ETHICS, FRAUD & CORPORATE GOVERNANCE boxes discuss the accounting scandals of recent years that have sparked such comprehensive legislation as Sarbanes-Oxley. The inclusion of EFCG boxes in each chapter offers instructors the opportunity to bring complex accounting and ethical issues into the classroom.

Setting Standards

McGraw-Hill *Connect Accounting*

Less Managing. More Teaching. Greater Learning.

McGraw-Hill *Connect Accounting* is an online assignment and assessment solution that connects students with the tools and resources needed to achieve success through faster learning, more efficient studying, and higher retention of knowledge.

McGraw-Hill Connect Accounting features

Connect Accounting offers a number of powerful tools and features to make managing assignments easier, so faculty can spend more time teaching. With *Connect Accounting*, students can engage with their coursework anytime and anywhere, making the learning process more accessible and efficient. *Connect Accounting* offers you the features described below.

Simple assignment management

With *Connect Accounting*, creating assignments is easier than ever, so you can spend more time teaching and less time managing. *Connect Accounting* enables you to:

- Create and deliver assignments easily with select end-of-chapter questions and test bank items.
- Go paperless with the eBook and online submission and grading of student assignments.
- Have assignments scored automatically, giving students immediate feedback on their work and side-by-side comparisons with correct answers.

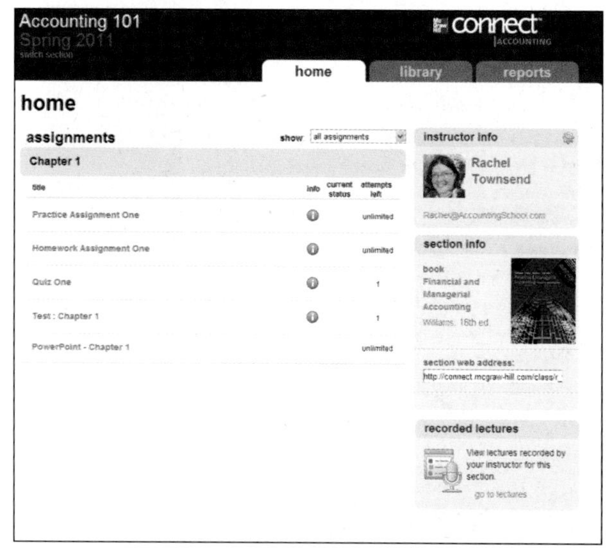

Smart grading

When it comes to studying, time is precious. *Connect Accounting* helps students learn more efficiently by providing feedback and practice material when they need it, where they need it. When it comes to teaching, your time also is precious. The grading function enables you to:

- Have assignments scored automatically, giving students immediate feedback on their work and side-by-side comparisons with correct answers.
- Access and review each response; manually change grades or leave comments for students to review.
- Reinforce classroom concepts with practice tests and instant quizzes.

Instructor library

The *Connect Accounting* Instructor Library is your repository for additional resources to improve student engagement in and out of class. You can select and use any asset that enhances your lecture. The Instructor Library also allows you to upload your own files. Your students can access these files through the student library. The *Connect Accounting* Instructor Library includes

- *eBook*
- *PowerPoint files*
- *Access to all instructor supplements*

in Online Technology

Student library

The *Connect Accounting* Student Library is the place for students to access additional resources. The Student Library:

- Offers students quick access to lectures, practice materials, eBooks, and more.
- Provides instant practice material and study questions, easily accessible on the go.

Assessment and Reporting

Connect Accounting keeps instructors informed about how each student, section, and class is performing, allowing for more productive use of lecture and office hours. The reporting function enables you to:

- View scored work immediately and track individual or group performance with assignment and grade reports.
- Access an instant view of student or class performance relative to learning objectives.
- Collect data and generate reports required by many accreditation organizations, such as AACSB and AICPA.

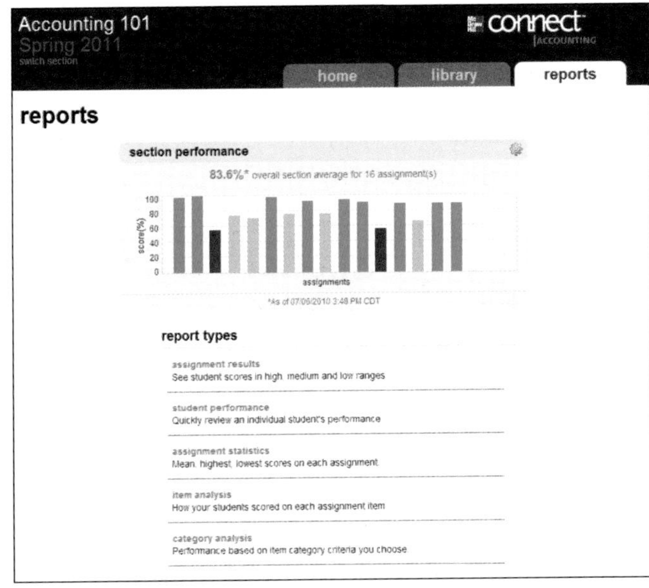

McGraw-Hill *Connect Plus Accounting*

McGraw-Hill reinvents the textbook learning experience for the modern student with *Connect Plus Accounting.* A seamless integration of an eBook and *Connect Accounting, Connect Plus Accounting* provides all of the *Connect Accounting* features plus the following:

- An integrated eBook, allowing for anytime, anywhere access to the textbook.
- Dynamic links between the problems or questions you assign to your students and the location in the eBook where that problem or question is covered.
- A powerful search function to pinpoint and connect key concepts in a snap.

In short, *Connect Accounting* offers you and your students powerful tools and features that optimize your time and energies, enabling you to focus on course content, teaching, and student learning. *Connect Accounting* also offers a wealth of content resources for both instructors and students. This state-of-the-art, thoroughly tested system supports you in preparing students for the world that awaits.

For more information about Connect, go to **www.mcgrawhillconnect.com,** or contact your local McGraw-Hill sales representative.

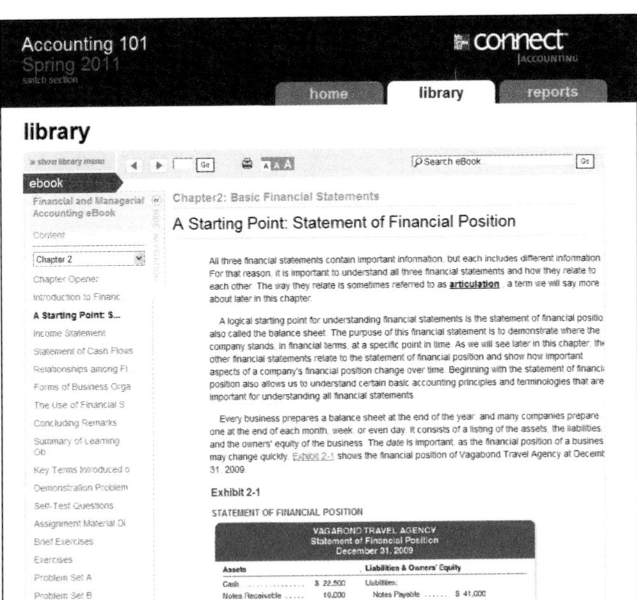

Tegrity Campus: Lectures 24/7

Tegrity campus

Tegrity Campus is a service that makes class time available 24/7 by automatically capturing every lecture in a searchable format for students to review when they study and complete assignments. With a simple one-click start-and-stop process, you capture all computer screens and corresponding audio. Students can replay any part of any class with easy-to-use browser-based viewing on a PC or Mac.

Educators know that the more students can see, hear, and experience class resources, the better they learn. In fact, studies prove it. With Tegrity Campus, students quickly recall key moments by using Tegrity Campus's unique search feature. This search helps students efficiently find what they need, when they need it, across an entire semester of class recordings. Help turn all your students' study time into learning moments immediately supported by your lecture.

To learn more about Tegrity watch a 2-minute Flash demo at **http://tegritycampus.mhhe.com.**

McGraw-Hill Higher Education and Blackboard have teamed up. What does this mean for you?

1. **Your life, simplified.** Now you and your students can access McGraw-Hill's Connect™ and Create™ right from within your Blackboard course—all with one single sign-on. Say goodbye to the days of logging in to multiple applications.
2. **Deep integration of content and tools.** Not only do you get single sign-on with Connect™ and Create™, you also get deep integration of McGraw-Hill content and content engines right in Blackboard. Whether you're choosing a book for your course or building Connect™ assignments, all the tools you need are right where you want them—inside of Blackboard.
3. **Seamless Gradebooks.** Are you tired of keeping multiple gradebooks and manually synchronizing grades into Blackboard? We thought so. When a student completes an integrated Connect™ assignment, the grade for that assignment automatically (and instantly) feeds your Blackboard grade center.
4. **A solution for everyone.** Whether your institution is already using Blackboard or you just want to try Blackboard on your own, we have a solution for you. McGraw-Hill and Blackboard can now offer you easy access to industry leading technology and content, whether your campus hosts it, or we do. Be sure to ask your local McGraw-Hill representative for details.

Do More

ALEKS® Improve Student Learning Outcomes and Save Instructor Time with ALEKS®

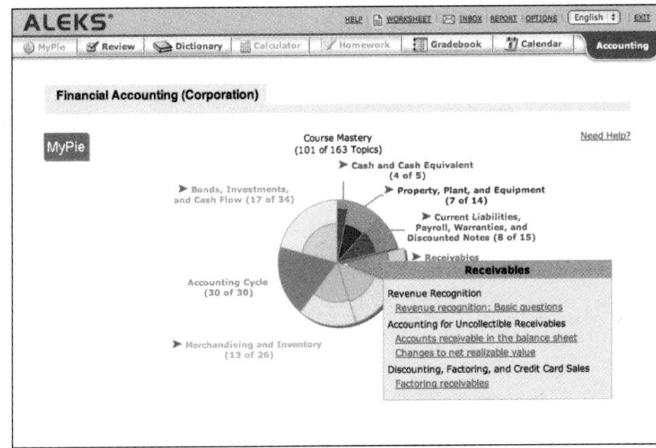

ALEKS is an assessment and learning program that provides individualized instruction in accounting. Available online in partnership with McGraw-Hill/Irwin, ALEKS interacts with students much like a skilled human tutor, with the ability to assess precisely a student's knowledge and provide instruction on the exact topics the student is most ready to learn. By providing topics to meet individual students' needs, allowing students to move between explanation and practice, correcting and analyzing errors, and defining terms, ALEKS helps students to master course content quickly and easily.

ALEKS also includes an Instructor Module with powerful, assignment-driven features and extensive content flexibility. The complimentary Instructor Module provides a course calendar, a customizable gradebook with automatically graded homework, textbook integration, and dynamic reports to monitor student and class progress. ALEKS simplifies course management and allows instructors to spend less time with administrative tasks and more time directing student learning.

To learn more about ALEKS, visit **www.aleks.com/highered/business.**

CourseSmart

Learn Smart. Choose Smart.
CourseSmart is a new way for faculty to find and review eTextbooks. It's also a great option for students who are interested in accessing their course materials digitally and saving money.

CourseSmart offers thousands of the most commonly adopted textbooks across hundreds of courses from a wide variety of higher education publishers. It is the only place for faculty to review and compare the full text of a textbook online, providing immediate access without the environmental impact of requesting a print exam copy.

With the CourseSmart eTextbook, student can save up to 45 percent off the cost of a print book, reduce their impact on the environment, and access powerful Web tools for learning. CourseSmart is an online eTextbook, which means users access and view their textbook online when connected to the Internet. Students can also print sections of the book for maximum portability. CourseSmart eTextbooks are available in one standard online reader with full text search, notes and highlighting, and email tools for sharing notes between classmates.

http://www.coursesmart.com

McGraw-Hill Customer Care Contact Information

At McGraw-Hill, we understand that getting the most from new technology can be challenging. That's why our services don't stop after you purchase our products. You can e-mail our Product Specialists 24 hours a day to get product-training online. Or you can search our knowledge bank of Frequently Asked Questions on our support Web site. For Customer Support, call **800-331-5094**, e-mail **hmsupport@mcgraw-hill.com**, or visit **www.mhhe.com/support**. One of our Technical Support Analysts will be able to assist you in a timely fashion.

Supplements *for Financial & Managerial Accounting*

INSTRUCTOR SUPPLEMENTS

A strong foundation needs support.

Financial & Managerial Accounting authors Williams, Haka, Bettner, and Carcello know that every component of the learning package must be integrated and supported by strong ancillaries. Instructors and students have a wealth of material at their fingertips to help make the most of a challenging course in accounting.

Instructor's CD-ROM

ISBN: 9780077328641

This all-in-one resource contains the Instructor's Resource Manual, Solutions Manual, Testbank Word files, Computerized TB, and PowerPoint® slides.

Online Learning Center (OLC) www.mhhe.com/williams_basis16e

The Online Learning Center (OLC) that accompanies *Financial & Managerial Accounting* provides a wealth of extra material for both instructors and students. With content specific to each chapter of the book, the Williams OLC doesn't require any building or maintenance on your part.

A secure **Instructor Resource Center** stores your essential course materials to save you prep time before class. The **Instructor's Manual, Solutions Manual, PowerPoint presentations,** and **Testbank** are now just a couple of clicks away.

The OLC Web site also serves as a doorway to McGraw-Hill's other technology solutions.

Instructor's Resource Manual

Available on the Instructor's CD and OLC

This manual provides for each chapter: (1) a chapter summary detailing what has changed, new problems that have been added, and author suggestions on how to incorporate new material; (2) brief topical outline; (3) sample "10-minute quizzes" designed to test the basic concepts in each chapter; and (4) suggestions for group, Internet, and other class exercises to supplement the material in the book.

Solutions Manual

Available on the Instructor's CD and OLC

The Solutions Manual includes detailed solutions for every question, exercise, problem, and case in the text.

Testbank

Available on the Instructor's CD and OLC

This comprehensive Testbank contains over 3,000 problems and true/false, multiple-choice, and essay questions. Included in this edition are written explanations to the solutions—making it easier than ever for you to see where students have gone wrong in their calculations.

"A **comprehensive accounting book** that has **more student and instructor resources** than any textbook I have seen thus far. It is well written and very organized by topic."

Terri Meta, Seminole Community College

Assurance of Learning Ready

Many educational institutions today are focused on the notion of assurance of learning, an important element of some accreditation standards. *Financial and Managerial Accounting,* 16e, is designed specifically to support your assurance of learning initiatives with a simple, yet powerful, solution.

Each testbank question for *Financial and Managerial Accounting*, 16e, maps to a specific chapter learning outcome/objective listed in the text. You can use our testbank software, *EZ Test*, and *EZ Test Online*, or in *Connect Accounting* to easily query for learning outcomes/objectives that directly relate to the learning objectives for your course. You can then use the reporting features of *EZ Test* or in *Connect Accounting* to aggregate student results similar fashion, making the collection and presentation of assurance of learning data simple and easy.

AACSB Statement

The McGraw-Hill Companies is a proud corporate member of AACSB International. Understanding the importance and value of AACSB accreditation, *Financial Managerial Accounting*, 16e, recognizes the curricula guidelines detailed in AACSB standards for business accreditation by connecting selected questions in the text and testbank to the six general knowledge and skill guidelines found in the AACSB standards.

The statements contained in *Financial and Managerial Accounting*, 16e, are provided only as a guide for the users of this text. The AACSB leaves content coverage and assessment within the purview of individual schools, the mission of the school, and the faculty. While *Financial and Managerial Accounting*, 16e, and its teaching package make no claim of any specific AACSB qualification or evaluation, we have, within *Financial and Managerial Accounting*, 16e, labeled selected questions according to the six general knowledge and skills areas.

STUDENT SUPPLEMENTS

Study Guide

Volume 1 ISBN: 9780077328665

Volume 2 ISBN: 9780077328672

The Study Guide, written by the text authors, provides chapter summaries, detailed illustrations, and a wide variety of self-study questions, exercises, and multiple-choice problems (with solutions).

Working Papers

Volume 1 ISBN: 9780077328689

Volume 2 ISBN: 9780077328696

Working Papers provide students with formatted templates to aid them in doing homework assignments.

Online Learning Center (OLC) www.mhhe.com/williams_basis16e

The OLC is full of resources for students, including: Online Quizzing, PowerPoint Presentations, Excel Templates, and McGraw-Hill Connect Accounting.

Excel Templates

Available on the OLC

Selected end-of-chapter exercises and problems, marked in the text with an Excel icon, can be solved using these Microsoft Excel templates.

ALEKS for the Accounting Cycle

ALEKS uses assessments in key areas of the accounting cycle to measure student progress. This software has been proven to cut study time on the accounting cycle dramatically by offering students step-by-step progress reports—all of which is available to the instructor to review. **www.business.aleks.com**

What's New about the 16th Edition of *Financial & Managerial Accounting*?

The following list of revisions is a testament to the enthusiastic response of dozens of reviewers who contributed their considerable expertise. In doing so they have helped make the 16th edition of *Financial & Managerial Accounting* the best book of its kind.

Chapter 1

- Updated chapter-opening vignette
- Expanded coverage of support of convergence and global accounting standards
- Updated Case in Point

Chapter 2

- Updated chapter-opening vignette

Chapter 3

- New chapter-opening vignette
- Revised Ethics, Fraud & Corporate Governance section

Chapter 4

- Updated chapter-opening vignette
- Updated Case in Point
- Revised materiality and adjusting entries section

Chapter 5

- New chapter-opening vignette
- Revised Financial Analysis and Decision Making section

Chapter 6

- New chapter-opening vignette
- Updated Case in Point
- Updated Financial Analysis and Decision Making section
- Revised Ethics, Fraud & Corporate Governance section

Chapter 7

- Updated chapter-opening vignette
- Updated cash management section
- Updated Case in Point
- Removed sections on petty cash funds, concentration of credit risk, internal controls for receivables, management of accounts receivable
- Updated nature of interest section
- Updated Financial Analysis and Decision Making section
- Revised Ethics, Fraud & Corporate Governance section

Chapter 8

- Updated chapter-opening vignette
- Removed section on accounting methods affecting financial ratios
- Revised Financial Analysis and Decision Making section
- Revised Ethics, Fraud & Corporate Governance section

Chapter 9

- Updated chapter-opening vignette
- Revised differences in depreciation methods section
- Revised estimates of useful life and residual value section
- Updated Case in Point
- Revised Ethics, Fraud & Corporate Governance section

Chapter 10

- Updated chapter-opening vignette
- Updated Your Turn
- Revised Ethics, Fraud & Corporate Governance section

Chapter 11

- New chapter-opening vignette
- Updated Case in Point
- Revised Financial Analysis and Decision Making section
- Revised Ethics, Fraud & Corporate Governance section

Chapter 12

- Updated chapter-opening vignette
- Revised extraordinary items section
- Updated Financial Analysis and Decision Making section
- Revised Ethics, Fraud & Corporate Governance section

Chapter 13

- New chapter-opening vignette
- Revised introduction to statement of cash flows
- Updated Case in Point
- Revised Financial Analysis and Decision Making section
- Revised Ethics, Fraud & Corporate Governance section

Chapter 14

- Updated chapter-opening vignette
- Revised Ethics, Fraud & Corporate Governance section

Chapter 15

- New chapter-opening vignette
- New Exhibit 15-1 shows location of the world's top multinational companies
- New Case in Point
- Revision of Exhibit 15-5 and Exhibit 15-6
- Revised Ethics, Fraud & Corporate Governance section

Chapter 16

- Updated chapter-opening vignette
- New Case in Point
- Revised Ethics, Fraud & Corporate Governance section

Chapter 18

- Updated chapter-opening vignette

Chapter 19

- Updated chapter-opening vignette
- New Case in Point
- Revised Ethics, Fraud & Corporate Governance section

Chapter 20

- Revised Ethics, Fraud & Corporate Governance section

Chapter 21

- New Case in Point

Chapter 22

- Revision of Exhibit 22-1
- Revised Case in Point

Chapter 23

- New Case in Point

Chapter 24

- Two New Case in Points

Chapter 25

- Updated chapter-opening vignette
- New Case in Point
- Revised Ethics, Fraud & Corporate Governance section

Chapter 26

- New chapter-opening vignette
- Revised Ethics, Fraud & Corporate Governance section

We are grateful . . .

We would like to acknowledge the following individuals for their help authoring some of the text's supplements: Instructor's Manual: David Burba of Bowling Green State University; PowerPoint Presentations: Jon Booker and Charles W. Caldwell, both of Tennessee Technological University, Susan C. Galbreath of Lipscomb University and Cynthia Rooney, University of New Mexico-Los Alamos; Excel Templates: Jack Terry, Comsource Associates; Testbank: Jay Holmen of University of Wisconsin-Eau Claire and Marie Main of Columbia College.

Our special thanks go to Helen Roybark, for accuracy checking the text page proofs, solutions manual proofs and testbank. We appreciate the expert attention given to this project by the staff at McGraw-Hill/Irwin, especially Stewart Mattson, Editorial Director; Tim Vertovec, Publisher; Steve Schuetz, Executive Editor; Rebecca Mann, Development Editor; Michelle Heaster, Marketing Manager; Lori Koetters, Project Manager; Allison Souter, Media Project Manager; Keri Johnson, Photo Research Coordinator; Pam Verros, Designer; and Michael McCormick, Lead Production Supervisor.

Sincerely,

Jan R. Williams, Susan F. Haka, Mark S. Bettner, and Joseph V. Carcello

Acknowledgments

Many of our colleagues reviewed *Financial & Managerial Accounting*. Through their time and effort, we are able to continually improve and update the book to meet the needs of students and professors. We sincerely thank each of you for your valuable time and suggestions.

Sixteenth Edition Reviewers

Susan Borkowski, *La Salle University*
Benoit Boyer, *Sacred Heart University*
Sandra Byrd, *Missouri State University*
Laura DeLaune, *Louisiana State University–Baton Rouge*
David Erlach, *Queens College*
John Gabelman, *Columbus State Community College*
Tony Greig, *Purdue University-West Lafayette*
Betty Habiger, *New Mexico State University at Grants*
Steven Hornik, *University of Central Florida*
Charles Konkol, *University of Wisconsin–Milwaukee*
Marie Main, *Columbia College–Marysville*
Michelle Moshier, *University at Albany*
Chris Rawlings, *Bob Jones University*
Laura Rickett, *Kent State University*
Randall Serrett, *University of Houston–Downtown*
Rajewshwar D. Sharma, *Livingstone College*
Marcia R. Veit, *University of Central Florida*
Malcolm White, *Columbia College–Marysville*
Michael Yampuler, *University of Houston*

Previous Edition Reviewers

Mark Anderson, *Southern Polytechnic State University*
Cynthia Ash, *Davenport University*
Marjorie Ashton, *Truckee Meadows Community College*
Elenito Ayuyao, Los Angeles City College
Walter Baggett, *Manhattan College*
Sharla Bailey, *Southwest Baptist University*
Jill Bale, *Doane College*
Scott Barhight, *Northampton County Area Community College*
William Barze, *St. Petersburg Junior College*
John Bayles, *Oakton Community College*
Janet Becker, *University of Pittsburg*
Rob Beebe, *Morrisville State College*
Kim Belden, *Daytona Beach Community College*
Gerard Berardino, *Community College of Allegheny County*
Teri Bernstein, *Santa Monica College*
Dan Biagi, *Walla Walla Community College*
Margaret Black, *San Jacinto College North*
Cynthia Bolt-Lee, *The Citadel*
Sue Van Boven, *Paradise Valley Community College*
Nancy Boyd, *Middle Tennessee State University*
Sallie Branscom, *Virginia Western Community College*
Russell Bresslauer, *Chabot College*
Nat R. Briscoe, *Northwestern State University*
R. E. Bryson, *University of Alabama*
Bryan Burks, *Harding University*
Priscilla Burnaby, *Bentley College*
Loring Carlson, *Western New England College*
Brenda Catchings, *Augusta Technical College*
James J. Chimenti, *Jamestown Community College*
Steven L. Christian, *Jackson Community College*
David Chu, *College of the Holy Cross*
Stanley Chu, *Borough Manhattan Community College*
Carol Collinsworth, *University of Texas at Brownsville*
Christie L. Comunale, *Long Island University*
Jennie Conn, *Louisiana State University–Alexandria*
Joan Cook, *Milwaukee Area Technical College*
William Cravey, *Jersey City State College*
Chris Crosby, *York Technical College*
Christine M. Cross, *James A. Rhodes State College*
Marcia Croteau, *University of Maryland Baltimore County*
Ana M. Cruz, *Miami–Dade Community College*
Brian Curtis, *Raritan Valley Community College*
Steve Czarsty, *Mary Washington College*
Anthony Daly-Leonard, *Delaware County Community College*
Judy Daulton, *Piedmont Technical College*
Amy David, *Bob Jones University*
Larry Davis, *Southwest Virginia County College*
Mary B. Davis, *University of Maryland Baltimore County*
Scott Davis, *High Point University*
Vaun Day, *Central Arizona College*
Victoria Doby, *Villa Julie College*
Carlton Donchess, *Bridgewater State College*
Jim Dougher, *DeVry University*
Steve Driver, *Horry–Georgetown Tech*
Pamela Druger, *Augustana College*
Anita Ellzey, *Hartford Community College*
Emmanuel Emenyonu, *Sacred Heart University*
David Erlach, *CUNY–Queens College*
Paul Everson, *Northern State University*
Kel-Ann S. Eyler, *Brenau University*
Carla Feinson, *Bethune–Cookman College*
Calvin Fink, *Daytona Beach Community College*
Brother Gerald Fitzgerald, *LaSalle University*
Ralph Fritsch, *Midwestern State University*
Mark Fronke, *Cerritos College*
Mike Fujita, *Leeward Community College*
Mary Lou Gamma, *East Tennessee State University*

Peter Gilbert, *Thomas College*
Penny Hanes, *Mercyhurst College*
Richard Hanna, *Ferris State University*
Stephen Hano, *Rockland Community College*
Heidi Hansel, *Kirkwood Community College*
MAJ Charles V. Hardenbergh, *Virginia Military Institute*
Sara Harris, *Arapahoe Community College*
Carolyn J. Hays, *Mt. San Jacinto College*
Lyle Hicks, *Danville Area Community College*
Jeannelou Hodgens, *Florence-Darlington Technical College*
Merrily Hoffman, *San Jacinto College Central*
Michael Holland, *Valdosta State University*
Mary L. Hollars, *Vincennes University*
Patricia H. Holmes, *Des Moines Area Community College*
Michael Holt, *Eastern Nazarene College*
Evelyn Honaker, *Walters State Community College*
Christine Irujo, *Westfield State College*
Gregory Iwaniuk, *Lake Michigan College*
Jeff Jackson, *San Jacinto College Central*
Dave Jensen, *Bucknell University*
Leo Jubb, *Essex Community College*
David Junnola, *Eastern Michigan University*
Jeffrey Kahn, *Woodbury University*
Naser Kamleh, *Wallace Community College*
Khondkar Karim, *Monmouth University*
James Kennedy, *Texas A&M University*
Jane Kingston, *Piedmont Virginia Community College*
Carol Klinger, *Queens College of CUNY*
Ed Knudson, *Linn Benton Community College*
Samuel Kohn, *Empire State College*
Raymond Krasniewski, *Ohio State University*
Tara Laken, *Joliet Junior College*
Rosemary Lanahan, *Schenectady County Community College*
David Lardie, *Tunxis Community College*
Bill Lasher, *Jamestown Community College*
Dr. Martin Lecker, *Rockland Community College*
Suk Jun Lee, *Chapman University*
Adena Lejune, *Louisiana State University*
Annette M. Leps, *Goucher College*
Eric Lewis, *Union College*
Alexandria Ralph Lindeman, *Kent State University*
Philip Little, *Western Carolina University*
Susan Logorda, *Lehigh Carbon Community College*
J. Thomas Love, *Walters State Community College*
Don Lucy, *Indian River Community College*
Linda L. Mallory, *Central Virginia Community College*
Ken Mark, *Kansas City Kansas Community College*
Dewey Martin, *Husson College*
Nicholas Marudas, *Auburn University Montgomery*
Terri Meta, *Seminole Community College*
Josie Miller, *Mercer Community College*
Merrill Moore, *Delaware Tech & Community College*
Deborah Most, *Dutchess Community College*
Haim Mozes, *Fordham University*
Karen Mozingo, *Pitt Community College*
Tom Nagle, *Northland Pioneer College*
Hossein Noorian, *Wentworth Institute of Technology*
Frank Olive, *Nicholas College*
Bruce Oliver, *Rochester Institute of Technology*
Rudy Ordonez, *LA Mission College*
Ginger Parker, *Creighton University*
Yvonne Phang, *Borough of Manhattan Community College*
Timothy Prindle, *Des Moines Area Community College*
Matthew B. Probst, *Ivy Tech Community College*
Michael Prockton, *Finger Lakes Community College*
Holly Ratwani, *Bridgewater College*
Gary Reynolds, *Ozard Technical College*
Renee Rigoni, *Monroe Community College*
Earl Roberts, *Delaware Tech & Community College*
Julie Rosenblatt, *Delaware Tech & Community College*
Bob Rothenberg, *SUNY-Oneonta*
Victoria Rymer, *University of Maryland*
Benjamin L. Sadler, *Miami-Dade Community College*
Francis A. Sakiey, *Mercer County Community College*
Marcia Sandvold, *Des Moines Area Community College*
Richard Sarkisian, *Camden County College*
Mary Jane Sauceda, *University of Texas at Brownsville*
Linda Schain, *Hofstra University*
Lauran Schmid, *University of Texas at Brownsville*
Mike Schoderbek, *Rutgers University- New Brunswick*
Monica Seiler, *Queensborough Community College*
Joseph W. Sejnoha, *Mount Mary College*
Carlo Silvestini, *Gwynedd-Mercy College*
Kimberly D. Smith, *County College of Morris*
Warren Smock, *Ivy Tech Community College*
James Specht, *Concordia College-Moorhead*
Stan Stanley, *Skagit Valley College*
Jim Stanton, *Mira Costa College*
Robert Stilson, CUNY
Carolyn Strickler, *Ohlone College*
Barbara Sturdevant, *SUNY*
Gene Sullivan, *Liberty University and Central Virginia Community College*
Mary Ann Swindlehurst, *Carroll Community College*
Larry Tartaglino, *Cabrillo College*
Martin Taylor, *University of Texas at Arlington*
Anne Tippett, *Tarrant County College South*
Bruce Toews, *Walla Walla College*
Cynthia Tomes, *Des Moines Area Community College*
Robin D. Turner, *Rowan-Cabarrus Community College*
Don Van Gieson, *Kapiolani Community College*
Shane Warrick, *Southern Arkansas University*
Dr. Michael P. Watters, *Henderson State University*
Malcolm White, *Columbia College-Marysville*
Lisa Wilhite, CPA, *Bevill State Community College*
Andy Williams, *Edmonds Community College*
Harold Wilson, *Middle Tennessee State University*
Steve Wilts, *Bucknell University*
Teri Yohn, *Georgetown University*

Brief **Contents**

Contents

1 Accounting: Information for Decision Making

2 Basic Financial Statements

3 The Accounting Cycle: Capturing Economic Events

4 The Accounting Cycle: Accruals and Deferrals

5 The Accounting Cycle: Reporting Financial Results

COMPREHENSIVE PROBLEM 1

6 Merchandising Activities

7 Financial Assets

8 Inventories and the Cost of Goods Sold

14 Financial Statement Analysis

COMPREHENSIVE PROBLEM 4

15 Global Business and Accounting

16 Management Accounting: A Business Partner

17 Job Order Cost Systems and Overhead Allocations

18 Process Costing

19 Costing and the Value Chain

23 Operational Budgeting

24 Standard Cost Systems

25 Rewarding Business Performance

COMPREHENSIVE PROBLEM 6

26 Capital Budgeting

Financial & Managerial Accounting

THE BASIS FOR BUSINESS DECISIONS

CHAPTER 1

Accounting
Information for Decision Making

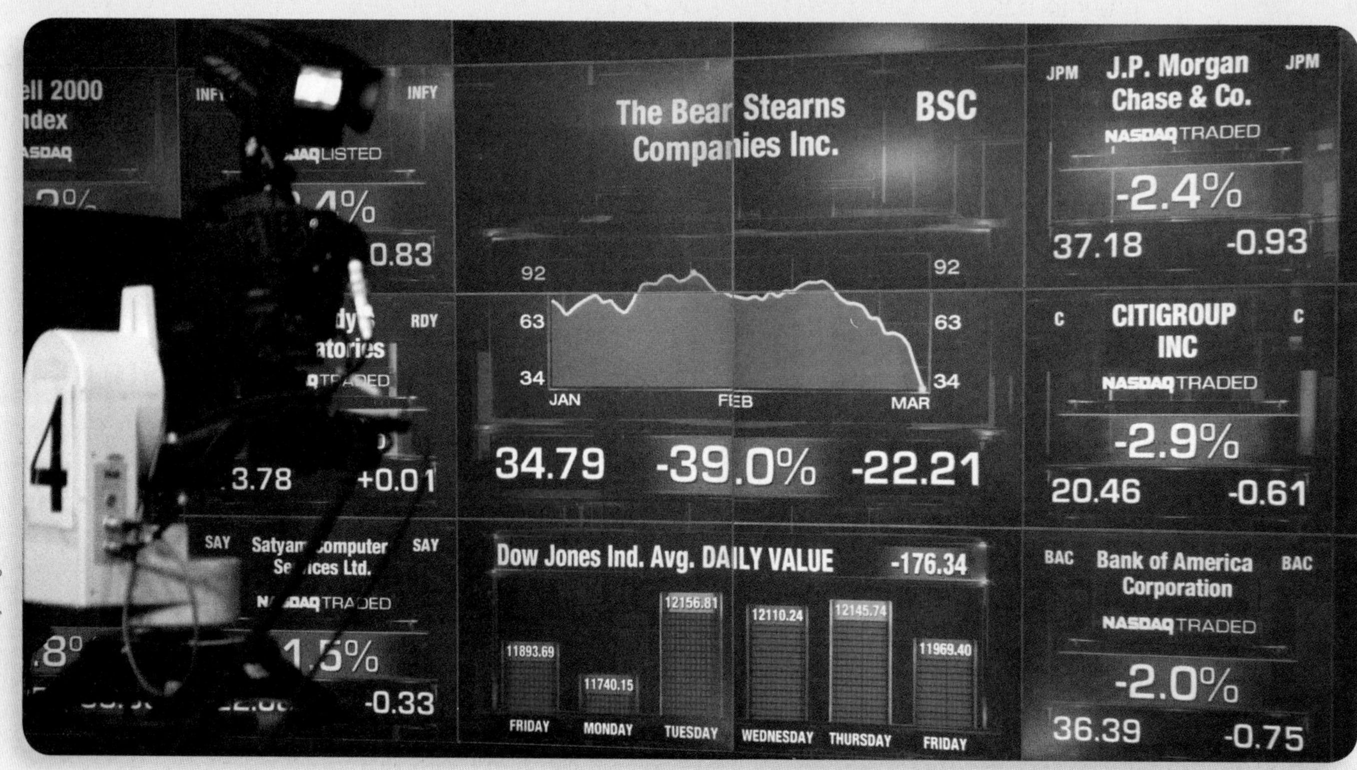

AFTER STUDYING THIS CHAPTER, YOU SHOULD BE ABLE TO:

Learning Objectives

- **LO1** Discuss accounting as the language of business and the role of accounting information in making economic decisions.
- **LO2** Discuss the significance of accounting systems in generating reliable accounting information and understand the five components of internal control.
- **LO3** Explain the importance of financial accounting information for external parties—primarily investors and creditors—in terms of the objectives and the characteristics of that information.
- **LO4** Explain the importance of accounting information for internal parties—primarily management—in terms of the objectives and the characteristics of that information.
- **LO5** Discuss elements of the system of external and internal financial reporting that create integrity in the reported information.
- **LO6** Identify and discuss several professional organizations that play important roles in preparing and communicating accounting information.
- **LO7** Discuss the importance of personal competence, professional judgment, and ethical behavior on the part of accounting professionals.
- **LO8** Describe various career opportunities in accounting.

BEAR STEARNS

Bear Stearns was founded in 1923 as an equity trading house. Bear Stearns grew to become one of the largest global investment banks and brokerage firms in the world. The firm grew rapidly during the early 2000s, and by 2006 the firm reported its fifth consecutive year of record net income and earnings per share. Net income topped $2 billion for the first time, an increase of 40 percent from the prior year. Bear Stearns employed approximately 14,000 people, and was recognized by *Fortune* magazine as the "most admired" securities firm in the United States. Bear Stearns' stock price reached $172 by January 2007, but by March 2008 the firm was forced to sell itself to JP Morgan Chase for $10 per share in order to stave off a bankruptcy filing.

How did a firm that survived the 1929 stock market crash without laying off a single employee see its stock price collapse from $172 to $10 in approximately one year—wiping out billions of dollars of shareholder wealth—and forcing it into a distressed sale?

Bear Stearns had significant investments in subprime mortgage-related securities and had a heavily leveraged capital structure (i.e., a large amount of debt relative to investments by owners). During the latter half of 2007, investors lost confidence in the subprime mortgage market and the value of related securities plunged precipitously. Bear Stearns wrote down investments in subprime mortgage-related securities by billions of dollars, but creditors lost confidence in the firm and were no longer willing to lend it funds. The firm's lack of liquidity forced it to seek a merger partner. The only other option available to Bear Stearns was a bankruptcy filing, but if Bear Stearns had chosen that option shareholders would have received nothing for their shares. As recently as Bear Stearns' 2006 Annual Report, it touted its "dedication to risk evaluation and management that has given us the ability to expand carefully and conservatively." Bear Stearns' risk management controls failed to anticipate and/or adequately protect the firm from the dramatic decline in the value of subprime mortgage-related securities. ■

Source: Bear Stearns 2006 Annual Report, 2007 10-K, and Wikipedia.

Understanding and using accounting information is an important ingredient of any business undertaking. Terms such as sales revenue, net income, cost, expense, operating margin, and cash flow have clearly defined meanings and are commonly used in business-related communications. Although the precise meaning of these terms may be unfamiliar to you at this point, to become an active participant in the business world, you must gain a basic understanding of these and other accounting concepts. Our objective in this book is to provide those who both use and prepare accounting information with that basic understanding.

Information that is provided to external parties who have an interest in a company is sometimes referred to as financial accounting information. Information used internally by management and others is commonly referred to as managerial accounting information. Whereas these two types of information have different purposes and serve different audiences, they have certain attributes in common. For example, both financial and managerial accounting require the use of judgment and information prepared for either purpose should be subject to the company's system of internal control. Financial accounting concepts are critical in order to understand the financial condition of a business enterprise. Determining a company's net income by subtracting its expenses from its revenue is a particularly important part of financial reporting today. This may appear to be a simple process of keeping accounting records and preparing reports from those records, but a great deal of judgment is required. For example, when should the cost of acquiring a resource that is used for several years be recognized as an expense in the company's financial statements? What information is particularly useful for management, but not appropriate for public distribution because of the potential competitive disadvantage that might result? These are among the many complex issues that business faces on a day-to-day basis and which have a critical impact on the company's responsibility to its owners, creditors, the government, and society in general.

As we begin the study of accounting, keep in mind that business does not exist solely to earn a return for its investors and creditors that supply a company's financial resources. Business also has a responsibility to operate in a socially responsible manner and to balance its desire for financial success within this broader social responsibility. We begin our development of these ideas in this chapter, and continue their emphasis throughout this text.

Accounting Information: A Means to an End

The primary objective of accounting is to provide information that is useful for decision-making purposes. From the very start, we emphasize that accounting is *not an end,* but rather it is *a means to an end.* The final product of accounting information is the decision that is enhanced by the use of that information, whether the decision is made by owners, management, creditors, governmental regulatory bodies, labor unions, or the many other groups that have an interest in the financial performance of an enterprise.

Learning Objective
LO1 **Discuss accounting as the language of business and the role of accounting information in making economic decisions.**

Because accounting is widely used to describe all types of business activity, it is sometimes referred to as the *language of business.* Costs, prices, sales volume, profits, and return on investment are all accounting measurements. Investors, creditors, managers, and others who have a financial interest in an enterprise need a clear understanding of accounting terms and concepts if they are to understand and communicate about the enterprise. While our primary orientation in this text is the use of accounting information in business, from time to time we emphasize that accounting information is also used by governmental agencies, nonprofit organizations, and individuals in much the same manner as it is by business organizations.

ACCOUNTING FROM A USER'S PERSPECTIVE

Many people think of accounting as simply a highly technical field practiced only by professional accountants. In reality, nearly everyone uses accounting information daily. Accounting information is the means by which we measure and communicate economic events. Whether you manage a business, make investments, or monitor how you receive and use your money, you are working with accounting concepts and accounting information.

Our primary goal in this book is to develop your ability to understand and use accounting information in making economic decisions. To do this, you need to understand the following:

- The nature of economic activities that accounting information describes.
- The assumptions and measurement techniques involved in developing accounting information.
- The information that is most relevant for making various types of decisions.

Exhibit 1–1 illustrates how economic activities flow into the accounting process. The accounting process produces accounting information used by decision makers in making economic decisions and taking specific actions. These decisions and actions result in economic activities that continue the cycle.

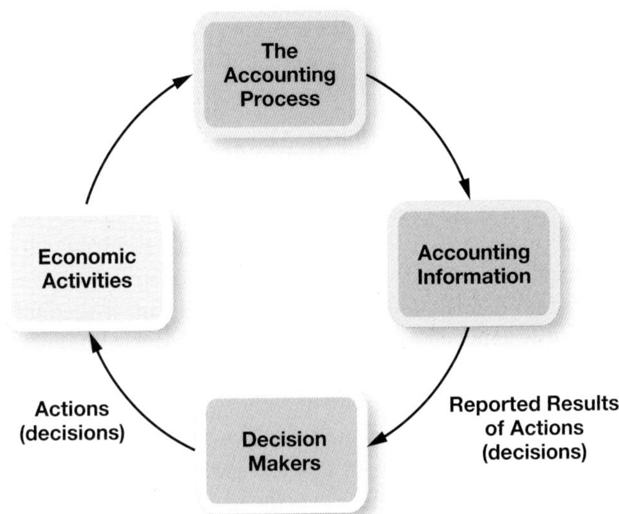

Exhibit 1–1

THE ACCOUNTING PROCESS

Accounting links decision makers with economic activities—and with the results of their decisions

TYPES OF ACCOUNTING INFORMATION

Just as there are many types of economic decisions, there are also many types of accounting information. The terms *financial accounting, management accounting,* and *tax accounting* often are used in describing three types of accounting information that are widely used in the business community.

Financial Accounting

Financial accounting refers to information describing the financial resources, obligations, and activities of an economic entity (either an organization or an individual). Accountants use the term *financial position* to describe an entity's financial resources and obligations at a point in time and the term *results of operations* to describe its financial activities during the year.

CASE IN POINT

In **Sony Corporation**'s 2009 financial statements to owners, financial position is presented as consisting of ¥12,014 trillion in assets (including cash, inventories, property, and equipment), with obligations against those assets of ¥9,049 trillion. This leaves ¥2,965 trillion as the owners' interest in those assets. In the same report, results of operations indicate that Sony had a net loss (expenses exceeded revenues) of ¥99 billion for the year ending March 31, 2009.

Financial accounting information is designed primarily to assist investors and creditors in deciding where to place their scarce investment resources. Such decisions are important to society, because they determine which companies and industries will receive the financial resources necessary for growth.

Financial accounting information also is used by managers and in income tax returns. In fact, financial accounting information is used for so many different purposes that it often is called "general-purpose" accounting information.

Management Accounting **Management** (or managerial) **accounting** involves the development and interpretation of accounting information intended *specifically to assist management* in operating the business. Managers use this information in setting the company's overall goals, evaluating the performance of departments and individuals, deciding whether to introduce a new line of products, and making virtually all types of managerial decisions.

A company's managers and employees constantly need information to run and control daily business operations. For example, they need to know the amount of money in the company's bank accounts; the types, quantities, and dollar amounts of merchandise in the company's warehouse; and the amounts owed to specific creditors. Much management accounting information is financial in nature but is organized in a manner relating directly to the decision at hand.

Tax Accounting The preparation of income tax returns is a specialized field within accounting. To a great extent, tax returns are based on financial accounting information. However, the information often is adjusted or reorganized to conform with income tax reporting requirements. We introduce the idea of tax accounting information to contrast it with financial and management accounting information. Although tax information is important for a company's successful operations and is related to financial and management accounting information, it results from a different system and complies with specialized legal requirements that relate to a company's responsibility to pay an appropriate amount of taxes. Laws and regulations governing taxation are often different from those underlying the preparation of financial and management accounting information, so it should not be a surprise that the resulting figures and reports are different. Because the focus of this text is introductory accounting, and because tax accounting is quite complex, we defer coverage of tax accounting subjects to subsequent accounting courses.

Accounting Systems

Learning Objective
LO2 **Discuss the significance of accounting systems in generating reliable accounting information and understand the five components of internal control.**

An **accounting system** consists of the personnel, procedures, technology, and records used by an organization (1) to develop accounting information and (2) to communicate this information to decision makers. The design and capabilities of these systems vary greatly from one organization to another. In small businesses, accounting systems may consist of little more than a cash register, a checkbook, and an annual trip to an income tax preparer. In large businesses, accounting systems include computers, highly trained personnel, and accounting reports that affect the daily operations of every department. But in every case, the basic purpose of the accounting system remains the same: *to meet the organization's needs for information as efficiently as possible.*

Many factors affect the structure of the accounting system within a particular organization. Among the most important are (1) the company's *needs for accounting information* and (2) the *resources available* for operation of the system.

Describing accounting as an information system focuses attention on the information accounting provides, the users of the information, and the support for financial decisions that is provided by the information. These relationships are depicted in Exhibit 1–2. While some of the terms may not be familiar to you at this early point in your study of business and accounting, you will be introduced to them more completely as we proceed through this textbook and as you undertake other courses in business and accounting. Observe, however, that the information system produces the information presented in the middle of the diagram—financial position, profitability, and cash flows. This information meets the needs of users of the information—investors, creditors, managers, and so on—and supports many kinds of financial decisions—performance evaluation and resource allocation, among others. These relationships are consistent with what we have already learned—namely, that accounting information is intended to be useful for decision-making purposes.

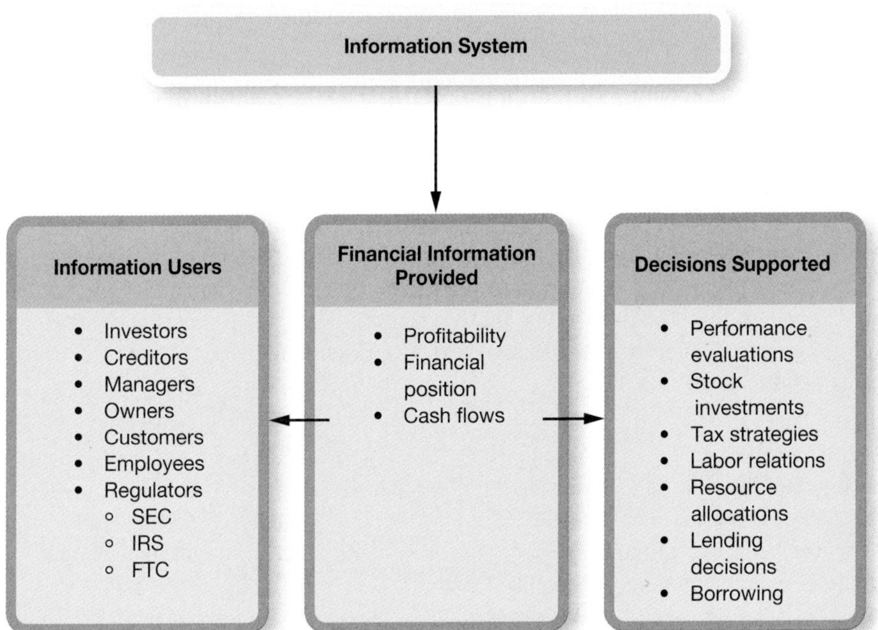

Exhibit 1–2
ACCOUNTING AS AN INFORMATION SYSTEM

DETERMINING INFORMATION NEEDS

The types of accounting information that a company develops vary with such factors as the size of the organization, whether it is publicly owned, and the information needs of management. The need for some types of accounting information may be prescribed by law. For example, income tax regulations require every business to have an accounting system that can measure the company's taxable income and explain the nature and source of every item in the company's income tax return. Federal securities laws require publicly owned companies to prepare financial statements in conformity with generally accepted accounting principles. These statements must be filed with the Securities and Exchange Commission, distributed to stockholders, and made available to the public.

Other types of accounting information are required as matters of practical necessity. For example, every business needs to know the amounts owed to it by each customer and the amounts owed by the company to each creditor. Although much accounting information clearly is essential to business operations, management still has many choices as to the types and amount of accounting information to be developed. For example, should the accounting system of a department store measure separately the sales of each department and of different types of merchandise? The answer to such questions depends on *how useful* management considers the information to be and the *cost* of developing the information.

THE COST OF PRODUCING ACCOUNTING INFORMATION

Accounting systems must be *cost-effective*—that is, the value of the information produced should exceed the cost of producing it. Management has no choice but to produce the types of accounting reports required by law or contract. In other cases, however, management may use *cost-effectiveness* as a criterion for deciding whether or not to produce certain information.

In recent years, the development and installation of computer-based information systems have increased greatly the types and amount of accounting information that can be produced in a cost-effective manner.

BASIC FUNCTIONS OF AN ACCOUNTING SYSTEM

In developing information about the activities of a business, every accounting system performs the following basic functions:

1. *Interpret and record* the effects of business transactions.
2. *Classify* the effects of similar transactions in a manner that permits determination of the various *totals* and *subtotals* useful to management and used in accounting reports.

3. *Summarize and communicate* the information contained in the system to decision makers.

The differences in accounting systems arise primarily in the manner, frequency, and speed with which these functions are performed.

In our illustrations, we often assume the use of a simple manual accounting system. Such a system is useful in illustrating basic accounting concepts, but it is too slow and cumbersome to meet the needs of most business organizations. In a large business, transactions may occur at a rate of several hundred or several thousand per hour. To keep pace with such a rapid flow of information, these companies must use accounting systems that are largely computer-based. The underlying principles within these systems are generally consistent with the basic manual system we frequently refer to in this text. Understanding manual systems allows users to understand the needs that must be met in a computerized system.

WHO DESIGNS AND INSTALLS ACCOUNTING SYSTEMS?

The design and installation of large accounting systems is a specialized field. It involves not just accounting, but expertise in management, information systems, marketing, and—in many cases—computer programming. Thus accounting systems generally are designed and installed by a team of people with many specialized talents.

Large businesses have a staff of systems analysts, internal auditors, and other professionals who work full-time in designing and improving the accounting system. Medium-size companies often hire a CPA firm to design or update their systems. Small businesses with limited resources often purchase one of the many packaged accounting systems designed for small companies in their line of business. These packaged systems are available through office supply stores, computer stores, and software manufacturers.

COMPONENTS OF INTERNAL CONTROL[1]

In developing its accounting system, an organization also needs to be concerned with developing a sound system of internal control. **Internal control** is a process designed to provide reasonable assurance that the organization produces reliable financial reports, complies with applicable laws and regulations, and conducts its operations in an efficient and effective manner. A company's board of directors, its management, and other personnel are charged with developing and monitoring internal control. The five components of internal control, as discussed in *Internal Control–Integrated Framework* (Committee of Sponsoring Organizations of the Treadway Commission), are the *control environment, risk assessment, control activities, information and communication,* and *monitoring.*

An organization's **control environment** is the foundation for all the other elements of internal control, setting the overall tone for the organization. Factors that affect a company's control environment are: (1) the integrity, ethical values, and competence of the company's personnel, (2) management's philosophy and operating style, (3) management's assignment of authority and responsibility, (4) procedures for the hiring and training of personnel, and (5) oversight by the board of directors. The control environment is particularly important because fraudulent financial reporting often results from an ineffective control environment.

Risk assessment involves identifying, analyzing, and managing those risks that pose a threat to the achievement of the organization's objectives. For example, a company should assess the risks that might prevent it from preparing reliable financial reports and then take steps to minimize those risks. The situation described in the chapter opener involving Bear Stearns provides an example of where that firm's risk assessment procedures failed.

Control activities are the policies and procedures that management puts in place to address the risks identified during the risk assessment process. Examples of control activities include approvals, authorizations, verifications, reconciliations, reviews of operating performance, physical safeguarding of assets, and segregation of duties.

Information and communication involves developing information systems to capture and communicate operational, financial, and compliance-related information necessary to run

[1] The information in this section is taken from *Internal Control–Integrated Framework,* Committee of Sponsoring Organizations of the Treadway Commission, September 1992.

the business. Effective information systems capture both internal and external information. In addition, an effective control system is designed to facilitate the flow of information downstream (from management to employees), upstream (from employees to management), and across the organization. Employees must receive the message that top management views internal control as important, and they must understand their role in the internal control system and the roles of others.

All internal control systems need to be monitored. **Monitoring** enables the company to evaluate the effectiveness of its system of internal control over time. Monitoring is generally accomplished through ongoing management and supervisory activities, as well as by periodic separate evaluations of the internal control system. Most large organizations have an internal audit function, and the activities of internal audit represent separate evaluations of internal control.

As a result of the large financial frauds at **Enron** and **WorldCom**, the U.S. Congress passed, and President George W. Bush signed, the **Sarbanes-Oxley Act** (SOX) of 2002. SOX has been described as the most far-reaching securities law since the 1930s. One of the SOX requirements is that public companies issue a yearly report indicating whether they have an effective system of internal control over financial reporting. In essence, management must indicate whether the entity's internal control system provides reasonable assurance that financial statements will be prepared in accordance with laws and regulations governing financial reporting. In addition, the company's external auditor must issue its own report as to whether the auditor believes that the company's internal control system is effective. These requirements are contained in Section 404 of SOX; therefore, many businesspeople describe the above process as the 404 certification and the audit under Section 404. This certification process has been extremely expensive and time-consuming, and some businesspeople believe that the costs associated with this certification requirement exceed the benefits.

Financial Accounting Information

Learning Objective
Explain the importance of financial accounting information for external parties—primarily investors and creditors—in terms of the objectives and the characteristics of that information. **LO3**

Financial accounting is an important subject for students who need only an introduction to the field of accounting, as well as for students who will pursue accounting as a major and take many additional accounting courses. Financial accounting provides information about the financial resources, obligations, and activities of an enterprise that is intended for use primarily by external decision makers—investors and creditors.

EXTERNAL USERS OF ACCOUNTING INFORMATION

What do we mean by *external users* and who are they? **External users** of accounting information are individuals and other enterprises that have a current or potential financial interest in the reporting enterprise, but that are not involved in the day-to-day operations of that enterprise. External users of financial information may include the following:

- Owners
- Creditors
- Potential investors
- Labor unions
- Governmental agencies
- Suppliers
- Customers
- Trade associations
- General public

Each of these groups of external decision makers requires unique information to be able to make decisions about the reporting enterprise. For example, customers who purchase from the enterprise need information to allow them to assess the quality of the products they buy and the faithfulness of the enterprise in fulfilling warranty obligations. Governmental agencies such as the Federal Trade Commission may have an interest in whether the enterprise meets certain governmental regulations that apply. The general public may be interested in the extent to which the reporting enterprise is socially responsible (for example, does not pollute the environment).

Providing information that meets the needs of such a large set of diverse users is difficult, if not impossible, in a single set of financial information. Therefore, external financial reporting is primarily used by two groups—investors and creditors. As you will soon see, investors are individuals and other enterprises that own the reporting enterprise. Creditors, on the other hand, are individuals and other enterprises to whom the reporting entity owes money, goods, or services. For example, a commercial bank may have loaned money to the reporting enterprise, or a supplier may have permitted the reporting enterprise to purchase goods and to pay for those goods later. Our assumption is that by meeting the financial information needs of investors and creditors, we provide information that is also useful to many other users of financial information.

For these reasons, we sometimes refer to investors and creditors as the primary external financial information users. When you see references like these, keep in mind that we are talking about both current investors and creditors and those individuals and other enterprises that may become investors and creditors in the future.

OBJECTIVES OF EXTERNAL FINANCIAL REPORTING

If you had invested in a company, or if you had loaned money to a company, what would be your primary financial interest in the company? You probably would be interested in two things, both of which make up the company's **cash flow prospects.** You would be interested in the return to you at some future date of the amount you had invested or loaned. We refer to this as the **return *of* your investment.** In addition, you would expect the company to pay you something for the use of your funds, either as an owner or a creditor. We refer to this as the **return *on* your investment.** Information that is useful to you in making judgments about the company's ability to provide you with what you expect in terms of the return *of* your funds as well as a return *on* your funds while you do not have use of them is what we mean by information about *cash flow prospects.*

Assume that you have a friend who wants to start a business and needs some help getting the money required to rent space and acquire the needed assets to operate the business (for

YOUR TURN | **You as a Creditor**

You are a loan officer at a bank that makes small loans to individuals to help finance purchases such as automobiles and appliances. You are considering an application from a young woman who needs to purchase a new car. She is requesting a loan of $10,000 which, when combined with the trade-in value of her old car, will allow her to meet her needs. What are your expectations with regard to repayment of the loan, and what information would help you decide whether she is a good credit risk for your bank?

(See our comments on the Online Learning Center Web site.)

example, delivery truck, display fixtures) and pay employees for their work before the doors open and customers begin paying for the products the company plans to sell. You are in a financially strong position and agree to loan your friend $100,000. Your intent is not to be a long-term investor or co-owner of the business, but rather to help your friend start his company and at the same time earn a return on the funds you have loaned him. Assume further that you agree to let your friend have the use of your $100,000 for one year and, if you had not loaned this amount to him, you could have earned an 8 percent return by placing your money in another investment.

In addition to wanting to help a friend, you are interested in knowing how much risk you are taking with regard to your $100,000. You expect your friend to pay that $100,000 back, and to also pay you an additional amount of $8,000 ($100,000 × 8%) for his use of your money. The total return of your investment ($100,000) back to you one year later, added to the amount you expect to receive for his having used your money for a year ($8,000), is shown in Exhibit 1–3.

Providing information for you to assess your friend's ability to meet his cash flow commitment to you is essentially what financial reporting is about. You need information to assess the risk you are taking and the prospects that your friend will be able to deliver $108,000 to you one year from the time you loan him the $100,000. While this is a relatively simple example,

Exhibit 1–3

INVESTMENT ANALYSIS

Cash flow from your original investment

$100,000

Cash flow from a return for allowing another's use of your funds ($100,000 × 8%)

$8,000

Total cash flow expected to be received in one year

$108,000

it sets the stage for your understanding of the kinds of information that will help you make this important investment decision.

The accounting profession has identified certain objectives of external financial reporting to guide its efforts to refine and improve the reporting of information to external decision makers. These general objectives are displayed in Exhibit 1–4 and are best understood if studied from the bottom up—from general to specific.[2]

The first objective is the most general and is to provide information that is useful in making investment and credit decisions. As we indicated earlier, investors and creditors are the primary focus of external financial reporting. We believe that, by meeting the information needs of investors and creditors, we provide general information that is also useful to many other important financial statement users.

The second objective, which is more specific than the first, is to provide information that is useful in assessing the amount, timing, and uncertainty of future cash flows. As we discussed earlier, investors and creditors are interested in future cash flows to them, so an important objective of financial reporting is to provide general information that permits that kind of analysis.

The most specific objective of external financial reporting is to provide information about the enterprise's resources, claims to those resources, and how both the resources and claims to resources change over time. An enterprise's resources are often referred to as *assets,* and the primary claims to those resources are the claims of creditors and owners, known as liabilities and owners equity.

Exhibit 1–4

OBJECTIVES OF FINANCIAL REPORTING: BUILDING FROM THE GENERAL TO THE SPECIFIC

Provide specific information about economic resources, claims to resources, and changes in resources and claims.

Provide information useful in assessing the amount, timing, and uncertainty of future cash flows.

Provide general information useful in making investment and credit decisions.

One of the primary ways investors and creditors assess whether an enterprise will be able to make future cash payments is to examine and analyze the enterprise's financial statements.

[2] FASB *Statement of Financial Accounting Concepts No. 1,* "Objectives of Financial Reporting by Business Enterprises" (Norwalk, Conn.: 1978), p. 4.

In the general sense of the word, a statement is simply a declaration of something believed to be true. A **financial statement,** therefore, is simply a monetary declaration of what is believed to be true about an enterprise. When accountants prepare financial statements, they are describing in financial terms certain attributes of the enterprise that they believe fairly represent its financial activities.

Financial statements prepared for periods of time shorter than one year (for example, for three months or one month) are referred to as *interim financial statements.* Throughout this text, we use both annual and interim financial statements. As you approach a company's financial statements—either as a user or as a preparer—it is important to establish the time period those statements are intended to cover.

The primary financial statements are the following:

- *Statement of financial position (balance sheet).* The **balance sheet** is a position statement that shows where the company stands in financial terms at a specific date.
- *Income statement.* The **income statement** is an activity statement that shows details and results of the company's profit-related activities for a period of time (for example, a month, quarter [three months], or year).
- *Statement of cash flows.* The **statement of cash flows** is an activity statement that shows the details of the company's activities involving cash during a period of time.

The names of the three primary financial statements are descriptive of the information you find in each. The **statement of financial position,** or balance sheet, for example, is sometimes described as a snapshot of the business in financial or dollar terms (that is, what the enterprise looks like at a specific date). An income statement is an activity statement that depicts the profitability of an enterprise for a designated period of time. The statement of cash flows is particularly important in understanding an enterprise for purposes of investment and credit decisions. As its name implies, the statement of cash flows depicts the ways cash has changed during a designated period. While the interest of investors and creditors is in cash flows to themselves rather than to the enterprise, information about cash activity of the enterprise is considered to be an important signal to investors and creditors.

At this early stage in your study of accounting, you are not expected to understand these financial statements or how they precisely help you assess the cash flow prospects of a company. The statement of financial position (balance sheet), income statement, and statement of cash flows are introduced more fully to you in the next chapter. Thereafter, you will learn a great deal about how these statements are prepared and how the information contained in them can be used to help you understand the underlying business activities they represent.

CHARACTERISTICS OF EXTERNALLY REPORTED INFORMATION

Financial information that is reported to investors, creditors, and others external to the reporting enterprise has certain qualities that must be understood for the information to have maximum usefulness. Some of these qualities are discussed in the following paragraphs.

Financial Reporting—A Means As we learned in the introduction to this chapter, financial information is a means to an end, not an end in and of itself. The ultimate outcome of providing financial information is to improve the quality of decision making by external parties. Financial statements themselves are simply a means by which that end is achieved.

Financial Reporting versus Financial Statements Financial reporting is broader than financial statements. Stated another way, financial statements are a subset of the total information encompassed by financial reporting. Investors, creditors, and other external users of financial information learn about an enterprise in a variety of ways in addition to its formal financial statements (for example, press releases sent directly to investors and creditors, articles in *The Wall Street Journal,* and more recently, open communications via the Internet). Serious investors, creditors, and other external users take advantage of many sources of information that are available to support their economic decisions about an enterprise.

Historical in Nature Externally reported financial information is generally historical in nature. It looks back in time and reports the results of events and transactions that already have occurred. While historical information is very useful in assessing the future, the information itself is more about the past than it is about the future. However, in recent years, accounting standard setters are requiring greater use of fair values, rather than historical costs, in measuring assets and liabilities.

Inexact and Approximate Measures Externally reported financial information may have a look of great precision, but in fact much of it is based on estimates, judgments, and assumptions that must be made about both the past and the future. For example, assume a company purchases a piece of equipment for use in its business. To account for that asset and to incorporate the impact of it into the company's externally reported financial information, some assumptions must be made about how long it will be used by the company—how many years it will be used, how many machine-hours it will provide, and so on. The fact that a great deal of judgment underlies most accounting information is a limitation that is sometimes misunderstood.

General-Purpose Assumption As we have already mentioned, we assume that, by providing information that meets the needs of investors and creditors, we also meet the information needs of other external parties. We might be able to provide superior information if we were to treat each potential group of external users separately and prepare different information for each group. This approach is impractical, however, and we instead opt for preparing what is referred to as **general-purpose information** that we believe is useful to multiple user groups (that is, "one size fits all").

Usefulness Enhanced via Explanation The accounting profession believes that the value of externally reported financial information is enhanced by including explanations from management. This information is often nonquantitative and helps to interpret the financial numbers that are presented. For this reason, financial information, including financial statements, is accompanied by a number of notes and other explanations that help explain and interpret the numerical information.

Management Accounting Information

Learning Objective LO4
Explain the importance of accounting information for internal parties—primarily management—in terms of the objectives and the characteristics of that information.

Internal decision makers employed by the enterprise, often referred to as management, create and use internal accounting information not only for exclusive use inside the organization but also to share with external decision makers. For example, in order to meet a production schedule, a producer may design an accounting information system for suppliers detailing its production plans. The producer shares this information with its supplier companies so that they can help the producer meet its objectives. Thus, although the creator and distributor of the accounting information is an internal decision maker, the recipient of the information is, in this case, an external decision maker. Other types of accounting information, however, are not made available to external decision makers. Long-range plans, research and development results, capital budget details, and competitive strategies typically are closely guarded corporate secrets.

USERS OF INTERNAL ACCOUNTING INFORMATION

Every employee of the enterprise uses internal accounting information. From basic labor categories to the chief executive officer (CEO), all employees are paid, and their paychecks are generated by the accounting information system. However, the amount of use and, in particular, the involvement in the design of accounting information systems vary considerably. Examples of **internal users** of accounting information systems are as follows:

- Board of directors
- Chief executive officer (CEO)
- Chief financial officer (CFO)
- Vice-presidents (information services, human resources, ethics, and so forth)
- Business unit managers
- Plant managers
- Store managers
- Line supervisors

Employees have different specific goals and objectives that are designed to help the enterprise achieve its overall strategies and mission. Looking at the typical, simple organization chart in Exhibit 1–5, you can see that the information created and used by various employees

Exhibit 1–5 TYPICAL SIMPLE ORGANIZATION CHART

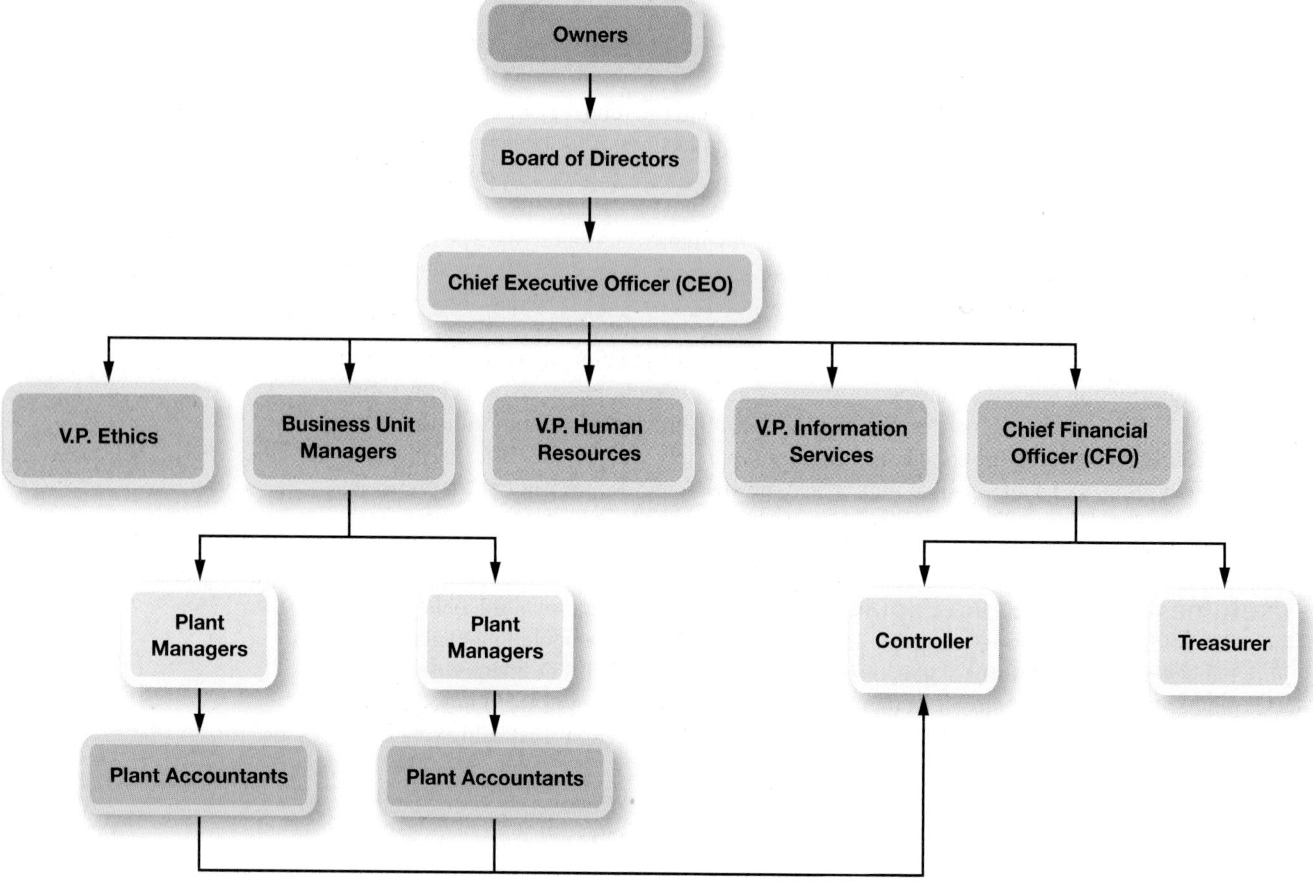

will differ widely. All enterprises follow rules about the design of their accounting information systems to ensure the integrity of accounting information and to protect the enterprise's assets. There are no rules, however, about the type of internal reports or the kind of accounting information that can be generated. A snapshot look inside a firm will demonstrate the diversity of accounting information generated and used in the decision-making processes of employees.

Many enterprises use a database warehousing approach for the creation of accounting information systems. This approach, coupled with user-friendly software, allows management and other designated employees access to information to create a variety of accounting reports, including required external financial reports. For example, detailed cost information about a production process is used by the production line supervisor to help control production costs. A process design engineer, when considering the best configuration of equipment and employees, uses the same information to reduce costs or to increase efficiency. Finally, production-related cost information appears in the external financial statements used by investors and creditors.

OBJECTIVES OF MANAGEMENT ACCOUNTING INFORMATION

Each enterprise has implicit and explicit goals and objectives. Many enterprises have a mission statement that describes their goals. These goals can vary widely among enterprises ranging from nonprofit organizations, where goals are aimed at serving specified constituents, to for-profit organizations, where goals are directed toward maximizing the owners' objectives. For example, the **American Cancer Society**, a nonprofit organization, has the following mission:

> The American Cancer Society is the nationwide community-based voluntary health organization dedicated to eliminating cancer as a major health problem by preventing cancer, saving lives, and diminishing suffering from cancer, through research, education, advocacy, and service.[3]

Procter & Gamble, a for-profit, global producer of consumer products, has the following purpose:

> We will provide branded products and services of superior quality and value that improve the lives of the world's consumers, now and for generations to come.[4]

Procter & Gamble's annual report to shareholders provides more detail on how the company will achieve its mission. **Procter & Gamble**'s design for growth was explained in P&G's annual letter to its shareholders and includes:

- Clear strategies.
- The core strengths required to win in our industry.
- Rigorous cash and cost discipline.
- The most diverse and experienced management team in P&G history.[5]

© Stephanie Bartelt/Alamy

The constituents of these organizations receive external financial information that helps them assess the progress being made in achieving these goals and objectives. In the case of **Procter & Gamble**, quarterly and annual information is provided to shareholders. The **American Cancer Society** is required to report its activities and financial condition to regulators. Providing constituents evaluative information is only one objective of accounting systems.

Enterprises design and use their internal accounting information systems to help them achieve their stated goals and missions. Multiple reports, some as part of the normal reporting process and some that are specially constructed and designed, are produced and distributed regularly. To motivate managers to achieve organizational goals, the internal accounting system is also used to evaluate and reward decision-making performance. When the accounting system compares the plan or budget to the actual outcomes for a period, it creates a signal about the performance of the employee responsible for that part of the budget. In many enterprises management creates a reward system linked to performance as measured by the accounting system.

Thus the objectives of accounting systems begin at the most general level with the objectives and mission of the enterprise. These general organizational goals create a need for information. The enterprise gathers historical and future information from both inside the enterprise and external sources. This information is used by the decision makers who have authority over the firm's resources and who will be evaluated and rewarded based on their decision outcomes.

CHARACTERISTICS OF MANAGEMENT ACCOUNTING INFORMATION

The accounting information created and used by management is intended primarily for planning and control decisions. Because the goal of creating and using management accounting information differs from the reasons for producing externally reported financial information, its characteristics are different.

Both the processes used to create financial accounting reports and the structure of those reports significantly impact management strategy. For example, because external financial reporting standards require companies to include pension-related obligations on their financial statements, management monitors those obligations closely. These pension-related obligations impact labor negotiations and labor-related corporate strategies.

Another example is that the processes necessary to create required external financial reports have historically determined the type of accounting information available inside of companies for internal decision making. Most plants within companies are organized as profit centers where plant-related financial statements mirror those necessary for external reporting purposes.

[3] www.cancer.org

[4] www.pg.com

[5] Procter & Gamble, 2009 Annual Report, Letter to Shareholders.

As you read the chapters of this book, we will remind you about how financial reporting has an impact on and is impacted by management strategies. The following paragraphs identify internal accounting information characteristics.

Importance of Timeliness In order to plan for and control ongoing business processes, accounting information needs to be timely. The competitive environment faced by many enterprises demands immediate access to information. Enterprises are responding to this demand by creating computerized databases that link to external forecasts of industry associations, to their suppliers and buyers, and to their constituents. Time lines for the development and launch of new products and services are becoming shorter and shorter, making quick access to information a priority.

In addition to needing timely information for planning purposes, enterprises are constantly monitoring and controlling ongoing activities. If a process or activity goes out of control, the enterprise can incur significant costs. For example, recalls of products can be very expensive for a company. If the company can monitor processes and prevent low-quality or defective products from reaching its customers, it can experience significant savings.

Identity of Decision Maker Information that is produced to monitor and control processes needs to be provided to those who have decision-making authority to correct problems. Reporting scrap and rework information to line workers without providing them the responsibility for fixing the process is counterproductive. However, a self-directed work team that has been assigned decision-making responsibility over equipment and work-related activities can have a significant impact on rework and scrap if team members control the process causing the problems.

Oriented toward the Future Although some accounting information, like financial accounting information, is historical in nature, the purpose in creating and generating it is to affect the future. The objective is to motivate management to make future decisions that are in the best interest of the enterprise, consistent with its goals, objectives, and mission.

Measures of Efficiency and Effectiveness Accounting information measures the efficiency and effectiveness of resource usage. By comparing the enterprise's resource inputs and outputs with measures of competitors' effectiveness and efficiency, an assessment can be made of how effective management is in achieving the organization's mission. The accounting system uses money as a common unit to achieve these types of comparisons.

Management Accounting Information—A Means As with financial accounting information, management accounting information is a means to an end, not an end in and of itself. The ultimate objective is to design and use an accounting system that helps management achieve the goals and objectives of the enterprise.

Integrity of Accounting Information

What enables investors and creditors to rely on financial accounting information without fear that the management of the reporting enterprise has altered the information to make the company's performance look better than it actually was? How can management be sure that internally generated information is free from bias that might favor one outcome over another? The word **integrity** refers to the following qualities: complete, unbroken, unimpaired, sound, honest, and sincere. Accounting information must have these qualities because of the significance of the information to individuals who rely on it in making important financial decisions.

Learning Objective
LO5 **Discuss elements of the system of external and internal financial reporting that create integrity in the reported information.**

The integrity of accounting information is enhanced in three primary ways. First, certain institutional features add significantly to the integrity of accounting information. These features include standards for the preparation of accounting information, an internal control structure, and audits of financial statements. Second, several professional accounting organizations play unique roles in adding to the integrity of accounting information. Finally, and perhaps most important, is the personal competence, judgment, and ethical behavior of professional accountants. These three elements of the accounting profession come together to ensure that users of accounting information—investors, creditors, managers, and others—can rely on the information to be a fair representation of what it purports to represent.

INSTITUTIONAL FEATURES

Standards for the Preparation of Accounting Information Accounting information that is communicated externally to investors, creditors, and other users must be prepared in accordance with standards that are understood by both the preparers and users of that information. We call these standards **generally accepted accounting principles,** often shortened to GAAP. These principles provide the general framework for determining what information is included in financial statements and how this information is to be prepared and presented. GAAP includes broad principles of measurement and presentation, as well as detailed rules that are used by professional accountants in preparing accounting information and reports.

Accounting principles are not like physical laws; they do not exist in nature waiting to be discovered. Rather, they are developed by people, in light of what we consider to be the most important objectives of financial reporting. In many ways, accounting principles are similar to the rules established for an organized sport, such as baseball or basketball. For example, accounting principles, like sports rules:

- Originate from a combination of tradition, experience, and official decree.
- Require authoritative support and some means of enforcement.
- Are sometimes arbitrary.
- May change over time as shortcomings in the existing rules come to light.
- Must be clearly understood and observed by all participants in the process.

Accounting principles vary somewhat from country to country. The phrase "generally accepted accounting principles (GAAP)" refers to the accounting concepts in use in the United States. The International Accounting Standards Board (IASB) is currently attempting to establish greater uniformity among the accounting principles in use around the world in order to facilitate business activity that increasingly is carried out in more than one country.

In the United States, three organizations are particularly important in establishing accounting principles—the Securities and Exchange Commission (SEC), the Financial Accounting Standards Board (FASB), and the International Accounting Standards Board (IASB).

Securities and Exchange Commission The **Securities and Exchange Commission** is a governmental agency with the *legal power* to establish accounting principles and financial reporting requirements for publicly owned corporations. In the past, the SEC has generally adopted the recommendations of the FASB (discussed below), rather than develop its own set of accounting principles. Thus, accounting principles continue to be developed in the private sector but are given the *force of law* when they are adopted by the SEC.

To ensure widespread acceptance of new accounting standards, the FASB *needs the support* of the SEC. Therefore, the two organizations work closely together in developing new accounting standards. The SEC also reviews the financial statements of publicly owned corporations to ensure compliance with its reporting requirements. In the event that a publicly owned corporation fails to comply with these requirements, the SEC may initiate legal action against the company and the responsible individuals. Thus the SEC enforces compliance with generally accepted accounting principles that are established primarily by the FASB.

Financial Accounting Standards Board Today, the most authoritative source of generally accepted accounting principles is the **Financial Accounting Standards Board.** The FASB is an independent rule-making body, consisting of seven members from the accounting profession, industry, financial statement users, and accounting education. Lending support to these members are an advisory council and a large research staff.

The FASB has compiled all of its standards, and those of its predecessors, in an Accounting Standards Codification. The FASB periodically issues updates to its codification. The codification represents official expressions of generally accepted accounting principles.

In addition to maintaining the Accounting Standards Codification, the FASB has completed a project describing a *conceptual framework* for financial reporting. This conceptual framework sets forth the FASB's views as to the:

- Objectives of financial reporting.
- Desired characteristics of accounting information (such as relevance, reliability, and understandability).
- Elements of financial statements.
- Criteria for deciding what information to include in financial statements.
- Valuation concepts relating to financial statement amounts.

The primary purpose of the conceptual framework is to provide guidance to the FASB in developing new accounting standards, which are issued as updates to the codification. By making each new standard consistent with this framework, the FASB believes that the Accounting Standards Codification resolves accounting problems in a logical and consistent manner.

The FASB is part of the private sector of the economy—*it is not a governmental agency.* The development of accounting principles in the United States traditionally has been carried out in the private sector, although the government, acting through the SEC, exercises considerable influence.

International Accounting Standards Board When an enterprise operates beyond the borders of its own country, differences in financial reporting practices between countries can pose significant problems. For example, when a company buys or sells products in another country, the lack of comparability of accounting information can create uncertainties. Similarly, cross-border financing, where companies sell their securities in the capital markets of another country, is increasingly popular. Business activities that cross borders create the need for more comparable information between companies that reside in different countries.

As a result of increasing cross-border activities, efforts are under way to harmonize accounting standards around the world. The **International Accounting Standards Board (IASB)** is playing a leading role in the harmonization process. The London-based IASB is an elite panel of professionals with deep knowledge of accounting methods used in the most vibrant capital markets.

The IASB issues *International Financial Reporting Standards (IFRSs).* The European Union requires listed companies in its member states to follow IASB standards. In addition, many other countries either require the use of IASB standards or have plans to require their use in the future, including Australia and Canada. Most important, the SEC accepts financial statements prepared using IASB standards from foreign companies that are cross-listed on a U.S. stock exchange, and is considering allowing U.S. companies to prepare their financial statements using either U.S. GAAP (based on FASB standards) or IASB standards. In addition, the AICPA, which essentially has jurisdiction over private company reporting, accepts either FASB standards or IASB standards as authoritative sources of accounting principles.

In early 2010, the SEC issued a Statement in Support of Convergence and Global Accounting Standards. This SEC statement reaffirms the SEC's belief that a single set of high-quality, global accounting standards is in the best interests of investors, and also reaffirms the SEC's belief that IFRS as issued by the IASB is the set of standards best positioned to fill this role. However, the SEC indicates that there remain obstacles to the adoption of IFRS in the United States and until these obstacles are addressed the SEC is reserving its judgment as to whether to require U.S. public companies to prepare their financial statements using IFRS. If the SEC decides to require U.S. public companies to use IFRS, this would be a major development because IASB standards are less detailed and prescriptive than existing FASB standards. The SEC has indicated that if IFRS were to be required in the United States any such change would not occur before 2015.

CASE IN POINT

A movement to IFRS is likely to require significant changes to accounting systems, controls, and procedures. For example, IFRS requires that an entity account for similar transactions in an identical manner regardless of where the transaction occurs in the entity, a requirement that does not exist under U.S. GAAP. Therefore, if IFRS becomes mandatory for U.S. public companies, companies would have to inventory all of their transactions and how they are accounted for throughout the entity.

Public Company Accounting Oversight Board The **Public Company Accounting Oversight Board (PCAOB)** is a quasi-governmental body charged with oversight of the public accounting profession. The Board was created as a result of the Sarbanes-Oxley Act of 2002 and began operations in the spring of 2003.

The PCAOB has extensive powers in overseeing the accounting profession. Any accounting firm wishing to audit a public company must register with the PCAOB. The PCAOB sets auditing standards for audits of publicly traded companies, an activity that previously was performed by the accounting profession. The Board also inspects the quality of audits performed by public accounting firms and conducts investigations and administers penalties when substandard audit work is alleged.

The PCAOB is headquartered in Washington, D.C., and has regional offices in major cities throughout the United States. The PCAOB has five members who serve a five-year term and are eligible to be reappointed once. No more than two members of the Board can be certified public accountants. The Board also maintains a large and well-qualified staff. The PCAOB is funded by a mandatory assessment on publicly traded companies. The assessment is a function of the company's market value relative to overall stock market value in the United States.

Audits of Financial Statements What assurance do outsiders have that the financial statements issued by management provide a complete and reliable picture of the company's financial position and operating results? In large part, this assurance is provided by an *audit* of the company's financial statements, performed by a firm of *certified public accountants (CPAs)*. These auditors are experts in the field of financial reporting and are *independent* of the company issuing the financial statements.

An **audit** is an *investigation* of a company's financial statements, designed to determine the fairness of these statements. Accountants and auditors use the term *fair* in describing financial statements that are reliable and complete, conform to generally accepted accounting principles, and are *not misleading.*

In the auditing of financial statements, generally accepted accounting principles are the standard by which those statements are judged. For the auditor to reach the conclusion that the financial statements are fair representations of a company's financial position, results of operations, and cash flows, the statements must comply in all important ways with generally accepted accounting principles.

Legislation As discussed previously, Congress passed the Sarbanes-Oxley Act in 2002. Among the more important provisions of Sarbanes-Oxley is the creation of the Public Company Accounting Oversight Board described earlier in this chapter. Another important provision of the Act is to ban auditors from providing many nonaudit services for their audit clients on the assumption that those services interfere with the objectivity required of auditors in rendering opinions regarding financial statements upon which investors and creditors rely. Sarbanes-Oxley also places additional responsibilities on corporate boards of directors and audit committees with regard to their oversight of external auditors, and it places responsibility on chief executive officers and chief financial officers of companies to certify the fairness of the company's financial statements.

PROFESSIONAL ORGANIZATIONS

Learning Objective
LO6 **Identify and discuss several professional organizations that play important roles in preparing and communicating accounting information.**

Several professional accounting organizations play an active role in improving the quality of accounting information that is used by investors, creditors, management, and others. In addition to the Securities and Exchange Commission, Financial Accounting Standards Board, and International Accounting Standards Board discussed earlier, the American Institute of CPAs, the Institute of Management Accountants, the Institute of Internal Auditors, the American Accounting Association, and the Committee of Sponsoring Organizations of the Treadway Commission are particularly important.

American Institute of CPAs (AICPA)

The **American Institute of CPAs** is a professional association of certified public accountants. Its mission is to provide members with the resources, information, and leadership to enable them to provide valuable services in the highest professional manner to benefit the public, employers, and clients. The AICPA participates in many aspects of the accounting profession. The AICPA conducts accounting research and works closely with the FASB in the establishment and interpretation of generally accepted accounting principles. In fact, prior to the establishment of the FASB, the AICPA had primary responsibility for the establishment of accounting principles. The AICPA's Auditing Standards Board has developed the standards by which audits of private companies are conducted, and the PCAOB has accepted many of these standards for audits of public companies. The AICPA also issues standards for the conduct of other professional services. Finally, the AICPA is responsible for the preparation and grading of the CPA examination, which is discussed later in this chapter.

Institute of Management Accountants (IMA)

The mission of the **Institute of Management Accountants** is to provide members personal and professional development opportunities through education, association with business professionals, and certification. The IMA is recognized by the financial community as a respected organization that influences the concepts and ethical practice of management accounting and financial management. The IMA sponsors a number of educational activities for its members, including national seminars and conferences, regional and local programs, self-study courses, and in-house and online programs. The IMA offers a certification program—the Certified Management Accountant (CMA). This designation testifies to the individual's competence and expertise in management accounting and financial management.

Institute of Internal Auditors (IIA)

With more than 170,000 members in over 100 countries, the **Institute of Internal Auditors** is the primary international professional association dedicated to the promotion and development of the practice of internal auditing. It provides professional development through the Certified Internal Auditor® Program and leading-edge conferences and seminars; research through the IIA Research Foundation on trends, best practices, and other internal auditing issues; guidance through the *Standards for the Professional Practice of Internal Auditing;* and educational products on virtually all aspects of the profession. The IIA also provides audit specialty services and industry-specific auditing programs, as well as quality assurance reviews and benchmarking services.

American Accounting Association (AAA)

Membership in the **American Accounting Association** is made up primarily of accounting educators, although many practicing accountants are members as well. The mission of the AAA includes advancing accounting education and research, as well as influencing accounting practice. The focus of many of the AAA's activities is on improving accounting education by better preparing accounting professors and on advancing knowledge in the accounting discipline through research and publication. An important contribution of the AAA to the integrity of accounting information is its impact through accounting faculty on the many students who study accounting in college and subsequently become professional accountants.

Committee of Sponsoring Organizations of the Treadway Commission (COSO)

COSO is a voluntary private sector organization dedicated to improving the quality of financial reporting through business ethics, effective internal controls, organizational governance, and enterprise risk management. COSO was originally formed in 1985 to sponsor the National Commission on Fraudulent Financial Reporting (chaired by former SEC

Commissioner James C. Treadway, Jr.). The National Commission on Fraudulent Financial Reporting studied the causal factors that lead to fraudulent financial reporting and made a series of recommendations for improving financial reporting, auditing, and accounting education. The original sponsors of the National Commission on Fraudulent Financial Reporting, and the current sponsors of COSO, are the AAA, the AICPA, Financial Executives International, the IIA, and the IMA.

COSO is best known for its work in developing the standards for evaluating internal control—particularly internal control over financial reporting. As a result of the Sarbanes-Oxley Act, public companies now need to evaluate the effectiveness of their internal control over financial reporting on a yearly basis, as well as have their auditors separately report on the auditors' evaluation of the effectiveness of internal control over financial reporting. The standard for evaluating the effectiveness of internal control over financial reporting is contained in COSO's 1992 publication, *Internal Control–Integrated Framework.* COSO has also issued a document, *Guidance for Smaller Public Companies Reporting on Internal Control over Financial Reporting,* that seeks to provide implementation guidance to smaller businesses in applying the original COSO internal control framework.

COMPETENCE, JUDGMENT, AND ETHICAL BEHAVIOR

Learning Objective
LO7 **Discuss the importance of personal competence, professional judgment, and ethical behavior on the part of accounting professionals.**

Preparing and presenting accounting information is not a mechanical task that can be performed entirely by a computer or even by well-trained clerical personnel. A characteristic common to all recognized professions, including medicine, law, and accounting, is the need for competent individual practitioners to solve problems using their professional judgment and applying strong ethical standards. The problems encountered in the practice of a profession are often complex, and the specific circumstances unique. In many cases, the well-being of others is directly affected by the work of a professional.

To illustrate the importance of competence, professional judgment, and ethical behavior in the preparation of financial statements, consider the following complex issues that must be addressed by the accountant:

- At what point should an enterprise account for transactions that continue over a long period of time, such as a long-term contract to construct an interstate highway?
- What constitutes adequate disclosure of information that would be expected by a reasonably informed user of financial statements?
- At what point are a company's financial problems sufficient to question whether it will be able to remain in business for the foreseeable future, and when should that information be communicated to users of its financial statements?
- When have efforts by management to improve (that is, "window dress") its financial statements crossed a line that is inappropriate, making the financial statements actually misleading to investors and creditors?

Judgment always involves some risk of error. Some errors in judgment result from carelessness or inexperience on the part of the preparer of financial information or the decision maker who uses that information. Others occur simply because future events are uncertain and do not work out as expected when the information was prepared.

If the public is to have confidence in the judgment of professional accountants, these accountants first must demonstrate that they possess the characteristic of *competence.* Both the accounting profession and state governments have taken steps to assure the public of the technical competence of **certified public accountants** (CPAs). CPAs are licensed by the states, in much the same manner as states license physicians and attorneys. The licensing requirements vary somewhat from state to state, but in general, an individual must be of good character, have completed 150 semester hours of college work with a major in accounting, pass a rigorous examination, and have accounting experience. In addition, most states require all CPAs to spend at least 40 hours per year in continuing professional education throughout their careers.

Management accountants are not required to be licensed as CPAs. However, they voluntarily may earn a **Certified Management Accountant** (CMA) or a **Certified Internal Auditor** (CIA) as evidence of their professional competence. These certifications are issued by the

IMA and the IIA, and signify competence in management accounting and internal auditing, respectively. The requirements for becoming a CMA and CIA are similar to those for becoming a CPA.

Integrity in accounting requires honesty and a strong commitment to ethical conduct—doing the right thing. For a professional accountant, ethical behavior is just as important as competence. However, it is far more difficult to test or enforce.

Many professional organizations have codes of ethics or professional conduct that direct the activities of their members. The AICPA, for example, has a code of professional conduct that expresses the accounting profession's recognition of its responsibilities to the public, to clients, and to colleagues. The principles included in the code guide AICPA members in the performance of their professional responsibilities. This code expresses the basic tenets of ethical and professional behavior and is enforced in conjunction with state professional societies of CPAs, although state regulatory boards take precedence in regulating the CPA license.

Exhibit 1–6 contains excerpts from the AICPA code of professional conduct. One of the principles expressed in the AICPA's code of professional conduct is the commitment of CPAs

YOUR TURN **You as a Professional Accountant**

You are a professional accountant working for a public accounting firm and find yourself in a difficult situation. You have discovered some irregularities in the financial records of your firm's client. You are uncertain whether these irregularities are the result of carelessness on the part of the company's employees or represent intentional steps taken to cover up questionable activities. You approach your superior about this and she indicates that you should ignore it. Her response is, "These things happen all of the time and usually are pretty minor. We are on a very tight time schedule to complete this engagement, so let's just keep our eyes on our goal of finishing our work by the end of the month." What would you do?

(See our comments on the Online Learning Center Web site.)

to the public interest, shown in Article II. The public interest is defined as the collective well-being of the community of people and institutions the profession serves. Other principles emphasize the importance of integrity, objectivity, independence, and due care in the performance of one's duties.

Expectations of ethical conduct are also important for other accountants. The IMA has a code of conduct for management accountants, as does the IIA for internal auditors.

Users of accounting information—both external and internal—recognize that the reliability of the information is affected by the competence, professional judgment, and ethical standards of accountants. While the institutional features and professional organizations that were discussed earlier are important parts of the financial reporting system, the personal attributes of competence, professional judgment, and ethical behavior ultimately ensure the quality and reliability of accounting information.

In this text, we address the topic of ethical conduct primarily through questions, exercises, problems, and cases that emphasize the general concepts of honesty, fairness, and adequate disclosure. Most chapters include assignment material in which you are asked to make judgment calls in applying these concepts. (These assignments are identified by the scales of justice logo appearing in the margin.)

Careers in Accounting

Learning Objective
LO8 Describe various career opportunities in accounting.

Accounting—along with such fields as architecture, engineering, law, medicine, and theology—is recognized as a profession. What distinguishes a profession from other disciplines? There is no single recognized definition of a profession, but all of these fields have several characteristics in common.

Exhibit 1–6

EXCERPTS FROM THE AICPA CODE OF PROFESSIONAL CONDUCT

Preamble

These Principles of the Code of Professional Conduct of the American Institute of Certified Public Accountants express the profession's recognition of its responsibilities to the public, to clients, and to colleagues. They guide members in the performance of their professional responsibilities and express the basic tenets of ethical and professional conduct. The Principles call for an unswerving commitment to honorable behavior, even at the sacrifice of personal advantage.

Articles

I. Responsibilities

In carrying out their responsibilities as professionals, members should exercise sensitive professional and moral judgments in all their activities.

II. The Public Interest

Members should accept the obligation to act in a way that will serve the public interest, honor the public trust, and demonstrate commitment to professionalism.

III. Integrity

To maintain and broaden public confidence, members should perform all professional responsibilities with the highest sense of integrity.

IV. Objectivity and Independence

A member should maintain objectivity and be free of conflicts of interest in discharging professional responsibilities. A member in public practice should be independent in fact and appearance when providing auditing and other attestation services.

V. Due Care

A member should observe the profession's technical and ethical standards, strive continually to improve competence and the quality of service, and discharge professional responsibility to the best of the member's ability.

VI. Scope and Nature of Services

A member in public practice should observe the Principles of the Code of Professional Conduct in determining the scope and nature of services to be provided.

First, all professions involve a complex and evolving body of knowledge. In accounting, the complexity and the ever-changing nature of the business world, financial reporting requirements, management's demands for increasingly complex information, and income tax laws certainly meet this criterion.

Second, in all professions, practitioners must use their professional judgment to resolve problems and dilemmas. Throughout this text, we will point out situations requiring accountants to exercise professional judgment.

Of greatest importance, however, is the unique responsibility of professionals *to serve the public's best interest, even at the sacrifice of personal advantage.* This responsibility stems from the fact that the public has little technical knowledge in the professions, yet fair and competent performance by professionals is vital to the public's health, safety, or well-being. The practice of medicine, for example, directly affects public health, while engineering affects public safety. Accounting affects the public's well-being in many ways, because accounting information is used in the allocation of economic resources throughout society. Thus, accountants have a basic social contract to avoid being associated with misleading information.

Accountants tend to specialize in specific fields, as do the members of other professions. Career opportunities in accounting may be divided into four broad areas: (1) public accounting, (2) management accounting, (3) governmental accounting, and (4) accounting education.

PUBLIC ACCOUNTING

Certified public accountants offer a variety of accounting services to the public. These individuals may work in a CPA firm or as sole practitioners.

The work of public accountants consists primarily of auditing financial statements, income tax work, and management advisory services (management consulting).

Management advisory services extend well beyond tax planning and accounting matters; CPAs advise management on such diverse issues as international mergers, manufacturing processes, and the introduction of new products. CPAs assist management because *financial considerations enter into almost every business decision.*

A great many CPAs move from public accounting into managerial positions with organizations. These "alumni" from public accounting often move directly into such top management positions as controller, treasurer, or chief financial officer.

The CPA Examination To become a CPA, a person must meet several criteria, including an extensive university education requirement, passing the CPA examination, and meeting a practice experience requirement. CPA certificates are granted by 55 legal jurisdictions (50 U.S. states, Guam, Puerto Rico, the Virgin Islands, Washington, D.C., and the Mariana Islands). The CPA examination is a rigorous examination that covers a variety of accounting and business subjects that allow candidates to demonstrate their knowledge and skills in areas believed important for protecting the public. The exam is computer based and is offered at many testing centers throughout the United States.

MANAGEMENT ACCOUNTING

In contrast to the public accountant who serves many clients, the management accountant works for one enterprise. Management accountants develop and interpret accounting information designed specifically to meet the various needs of management.

The chief accounting officer of an organization usually is called the *chief accounting officer (CAO)* or *controller.* The term *controller* has been used to emphasize the fact that one basic purpose of accounting data is to aid in controlling business operations. The CAO or controller is part of the top management team, which is responsible for running the business, setting its objectives, and seeing that these objectives are met.

In addition to developing information to assist managers, management accountants are responsible for operating the company's accounting system, including the recording of transactions and the preparation of financial statements, tax returns, and other accounting reports. Because the responsibilities of management accountants are so broad, many areas of specialization have developed. Among the more important are financial forecasting, cost accounting, and internal auditing.

GOVERNMENTAL ACCOUNTING

Governmental agencies use accounting information in allocating their resources and in controlling their operations. Therefore, the need for management accountants in governmental agencies is similar to that in business organizations.

The GAO: Who Audits the Government? The **Government Accountability Office** (GAO) audits many agencies of the federal government, as well as some private organizations doing business with the government. The GAO reports its findings directly to Congress, which, in turn, often discloses these findings to the public.

GAO investigations may be designed either to evaluate the efficiency of an entity's operations or to determine the fairness of accounting information reported to the government.

The IRS: Audits of Income Tax Returns Another governmental agency that performs extensive auditing work is the **Internal Revenue Service** (IRS). The IRS handles the millions of income tax returns filed annually by individuals and business organizations and frequently performs auditing functions to verify data contained in these returns.

The SEC: The "Watchdog" of Financial Reporting The SEC works closely with the FASB in establishing generally accepted accounting principles. Most publicly owned corporations must file audited financial statements with the SEC each year. If the SEC believes that a company's financial statements are deficient in any way, it conducts an investigation. If the SEC concludes that federal securities laws have been violated, it initiates legal action against the reporting entity and responsible individuals.

Many other governmental agencies, including the FBI, the Treasury Department, and the FDIC (Federal Deposit Insurance Corporation), use accountants to audit compliance with governmental regulations and to investigate suspected criminal activity. People beginning their careers in governmental accounting often move into top administrative positions.

ACCOUNTING EDUCATION

Some accountants, including your instructor and the authors of this textbook, have chosen to pursue careers in accounting education. A position as an accounting faculty member offers opportunities for teaching, research, consulting, and an unusual degree of freedom in developing individual skills. Accounting educators contribute to the accounting profession in many ways. One, of course, lies in effective teaching; second, in publishing significant research findings; and third, in influencing top students to pursue careers in accounting.

WHAT ABOUT BOOKKEEPING?

Some people think that the work of professional accountants consists primarily of bookkeeping. Actually, it doesn't. In fact, many professional accountants do *little or no* bookkeeping.

Bookkeeping is the clerical side of accounting—the recording of routine transactions and day-to-day record keeping. Today such tasks are performed primarily by computers and skilled clerical personnel, not by accountants.

Professional accountants are involved more with the *interpretation and use* of accounting information than with its actual preparation. Their work includes evaluating the efficiency of operations, resolving complex financial reporting issues, forecasting the results of future operations, auditing, tax planning, and designing efficient accounting systems. There is very little that is "routine" about the work of a professional accountant.

A person might become a proficient bookkeeper in a few weeks or months. To become a professional accountant, however, is a far greater challenge because this requires more than understanding the bookkeeping systems. It requires years of study, experience, and an ongoing commitment to keeping current.

We will illustrate and explain a number of bookkeeping procedures in this text, particularly in the next several chapters. But teaching bookkeeping skills is *not* our goal; the primary purpose of this text is to develop your abilities to *understand and use* accounting information in today's business world.

ACCOUNTING AS A STEPPING-STONE

We have mentioned that many professional accountants leave their accounting careers for key positions in management or administration. An accounting background is invaluable in such positions, because top management works continuously with issues defined and described in accounting terms and concepts.

An especially useful stepping-stone is experience in public accounting. Public accountants have the unusual opportunity of getting an inside look at many different business organizations, which makes them particularly well suited for top management positions in other organizations.

BUT WHAT ABOUT ME? I'M NOT AN ACCOUNTING MAJOR

Most students who use this book are not accounting majors. However, the study of accounting is still important to you. You need to understand accounting concepts, both for your professional careers and for many aspects of your personal life. Finance students need to understand accounting concepts if they seek positions in investment banking, consulting, or in corporate America as a financial analyst. Approximately 50 percent of the chief financial officers of large U.S. corporations have a background in accounting. A management student seeking a career as a management trainee—with the ultimate goal of running a corporation or a corporate division—needs to understand accounting in order to be able to run, control, and evaluate the performance of a business unit. Accounting is the language of business, and trying to run a business without understanding accounting information is analogous to trying to play sports without understanding the rules. Marketing students often take positions in sales. It is imperative that marketing students understand the principles of revenue recognition, as well as the obligations of a public company under the U.S. securities laws. A lack of this understanding has led many a marketing/sales executive to become involved in improper revenue recognition schemes. Many of these executives have been subject to civil and criminal prosecution.

Ethics, Fraud & Corporate Governance

© AP Photo/Adam Rountree

Dennis Kozlowski, the former CEO of Tyco, leaves court upon his conviction for conspiracy, securities fraud, and falsifying records. Kozlowski was sentenced to 8⅓ to 25 years in prison. A failure to understand and apply securities laws exposes management to great personal and professional risk.

The early 2000s was a time of unprecedented business failures amid allegations of fraudulent financial reporting that include corporations that have now become household names—**Enron, WorldCom, HealthSouth, Adelphia Communications, Tyco,** and **Qwest**, among others. These problems are not exclusively a problem with financial reporting in the United States, as evidenced by fraud allegations at **Parmalat**, a large Italian company.

Fraud typically is perpetrated by senior management; for example, a 2010 study indicates that the company's chief executive officer and/or chief financial officer is involved in 89% of the fraud-related enforcement actions brought by the Securities and Exchange Commission. Committing fraud, an illegal act, obviously suggests a serious lack of ethical awareness and ethical sensitivity on the part of the perpetrators. Another feature of many frauds is that the company where the fraud occurred had a weak corporate governance environment. **Corporate governance** entails corporate structures and processes for overseeing the company's affairs, including oversight by the board of directors of the actions of top management to ensure that the company is being managed with the best interests of shareholders in mind.

In each chapter, we will discuss common fraud-related schemes relevant to the material covered in that chapter, ethical quandaries and challenges faced by businesspeople, or efforts to improve corporate governance and by extension the quality of accounting information in the United States.

Finally, accounting knowledge is helpful in many aspects of your personal lives. Accounting concepts are integral to such everyday decisions as personal budgeting, retirement and college planning, lease versus buy decisions, evaluation of loan terms, and evaluation of investment opportunities. Since accounting skills are designed to help you make better economic decisions, you will be using these skills for the rest of your life. The only question is the degree of skill with which you will apply these concepts.

Concluding Remarks

In this chapter, we have established a framework for your study of accounting. You have learned how financial accounting provides information for external users, primarily investors and creditors, and how accounting provides information for internal management. We have established the importance of integrity in accounting information and have learned about several things that build integrity. Looking ahead, in Chapter 2 we begin to look in greater depth at financial accounting and, more specifically, financial statements. You will be introduced to the details of the three primary financial statements that provide information for investors and creditors. As the text progresses, you will learn more about the important information that these financial statements provide and how that information is used to make important financial decisions.

END-OF-CHAPTER REVIEW

SUMMARY OF LEARNING OBJECTIVES

LO1 Discuss accounting as the language of business and the role of accounting information in making economic decisions. Accounting is the means by which information about an enterprise is communicated and, thus, is sometimes called the language of business. Many different users have need for accounting information in order to make important decisions. These users include investors, creditors, management, governmental agencies, labor unions, and others. Because the primary role of accounting information is to provide useful information for decision-making purposes, it is sometimes referred to as a means to an end, with the end being the decision that is helped by the availability of accounting information.

LO2 Discuss the significance of accounting systems in generating reliable accounting information and understand the five components of internal control. Information systems are critical to the production of quality accounting information on a timely basis and the communication of that information to decision makers. While there are different types of information systems, they all have one characteristic in common—to meet the organization's needs for accounting information as efficiently as possible. Per the COSO framework, the five elements of internal control are: (1) control environment, (2) risk assessment, (3) control activities, (4) information and communication, and (5) monitoring.

LO3 Explain the importance of financial accounting information for external parties—primarily investors and creditors—in terms of the objectives and the characteristics of that information. The primary objectives of financial accounting are to provide information that is useful in making investment and credit decisions; in assessing the amount, timing, and uncertainty of future cash flows; and in learning about the enterprise's economic resources, claims to resources, and changes in claims to resources. Some of the most important characteristics of financial accounting information are: it is a means to an end, it is historical in nature, it results from inexact and approximate measures of business activity, and it is based on a general-purpose assumption.

LO4 Explain the importance of accounting information for internal parties—primarily management—in terms of the objectives and the characteristics of that information. Accounting information is useful to the enterprise in achieving its goals, objectives, and mission; assessing past performance and future directions; and evaluating and rewarding decision-making performance. Some of the important characteristics of internal accounting information are its timeliness, its relationship to decision-making authority, its future orientation, its relationship to measuring efficiency and effectiveness, and the fact that it is a means to an end.

LO5 Discuss elements of the system of external and internal financial reporting that create integrity in the reported information. Integrity of financial reporting is important because of the reliance that is placed on financial information by users both outside and inside the reporting organization. Important dimensions of financial reporting that work together to ensure integrity in information are institutional features (accounting principles, internal structure, audits, and legislation); professional organizations (the AICPA, IMA, IIA, AAA); and the competence, judgment, and ethical behavior of individual accountants.

LO6 Identify and discuss several professional organizations that play important roles in preparing and communicating accounting information. The FASB, IASB, PCAOB, and SEC are important organizations in terms of standard setting in the United States. The FASB and IASB are private-sector organizations that establish accounting standards for public and private companies. The PCAOB sets auditing standards. The SEC is a governmental entity that oversees U.S. public companies and the capital markets.

LO7 Discuss the importance of personal competence, professional judgment, and ethical behavior on the part of accounting professionals. Personal competence and professional judgment are, perhaps, the most important factors in ensuring the integrity of financial information. Competence is demonstrated by one's education and professional certification (CPA, CMA, CIA). Professional judgment is important because accounting information is often based on inexact measurements, and assumptions are required. Ethical behavior refers to the quality of accountants being motivated to "do the right thing."

LO8 Describe various career opportunities in accounting. Accounting opens the door to many career opportunities. Public accounting is the segment of the profession where professionals offer audit, tax, and consulting services. Management, or managerial, accounting refers to that segment of the accounting profession where professional accountants work for individual companies in a wide variety of capacities. Many accountants work for governmental agencies. Some accountants choose education as a career and work to prepare students for future careers in one of the other segments of the accounting profession. While keeping detailed records (that is, bookkeeping) is a part of accounting, it is not a distinguishing characteristic of a career in accounting; in fact, many accounting careers involve little or no bookkeeping. Accounting skills are important to nonaccounting majors and to all students in their personal lives.

Key Terms Introduced or Emphasized in Chapter 1

accounting system (p. 6) The personnel, procedures, devices, and records used by an organization to develop accounting information and communicate that information to decision makers.

American Accounting Association (p. 20) A professional accounting organization consisting primarily of accounting educators that is dedicated to improving accounting education, research, and practice.

American Institute of CPAs (p. 20) A professional accounting organization of certified public accountants that engages in a variety of professional activities, including establishing auditing standards for private companies, conducting research, and establishing industry-specific financial reporting standards.

audit (p. 19) An investigation of financial statements designed to determine their fairness in relation to generally accepted accounting principles.

balance sheet (p. 12) A position statement that shows where the company stands in financial terms at a specific date. (Also called the statement of financial position.)

bookkeeping (p. 25) The clerical dimension of accounting that includes recording the routine transactions and day-to-day record keeping of an enterprise.

cash flow prospects (p. 10) The likelihood that an enterprise will be able to provide an investor with both a return on the investor's investment and the return of that investment.

Certified Internal Auditor (p. 21) A professional designation issued by the Institute of Internal Auditors signifying expertise in internal auditing.

Certified Management Accountant (p. 21) A professional designation issued by the Institute of Management Accountants signifying expertise in management accounting.

Certified Public Accountant (p. 21) An accountant who is licensed by a state after meeting rigorous education, experience, and examination requirements.

Committee of Sponsoring Organizations of the Treadway Commission (COSO) (p. 20) A voluntary private-sector organization dedicated to improving the quality of financial reporting through business ethics, effective internal controls, organizational governance, and enterprise risk management.

control activities (p. 8) Policies and procedures that management puts in place to address the risks identified during the risk assessment process.

control environment (p. 8) The foundation for all the other elements of internal control, setting the overall tone for the organization.

corporate governance (p. 26) Includes the corporate structures and processes for overseeing a company's affairs, for example, the board of directors and the company's internal control processes.

external users (p. 9) Individuals and other enterprises that have a financial interest in the reporting enterprise but that are not involved in the day-to-day operations of that enterprise (e.g., owners, creditors, labor unions, suppliers, customers).

financial accounting (p. 5) Providing information about the financial resources, obligations, and activities of an economic entity that is intended for use primarily by external decision makers—investors and creditors.

Financial Accounting Standards Board (FASB) (p. 17) A private-sector organization that is responsible for determining generally accepted accounting principles in the United States.

financial statement (p. 12) A monetary declaration of what is believed to be true about an enterprise.

general-purpose information (p. 13) Information that is intended to meet the needs of multiple users that have an interest in the financial activities of an enterprise rather than tailored to the specific information needs of one user.

generally accepted accounting principles (GAAP) (p. 17) Principles that provide the framework for determining what information is to be included in financial statements and how that information is to be presented.

Government Accountability Office (p. 24) A federal government agency that audits many other agencies of the federal government and other organizations that do business with the federal government and reports its findings to Congress.

income statement (p. 12) An activity statement that shows details and results of the company's profit-related activities for a period of time.

information and communication (p. 8) The organization's process for capturing operational, financial, and compliance-related information necessary to run the business, and communicating that information downstream (from management to employees), upstream (from employees to management), and across the organization.

Institute of Internal Auditors (p. 20) A professional accounting organization that is dedicated to the promotion and development of the practice of internal auditing.

Institute of Management Accountants (p. 20) A professional accounting organization that intends to influence the concepts and ethical practice of management accounting and financial management.

integrity (p. 16) The qualities of being complete, unbroken, unimpaired, sound, honest, and sincere.

internal control (p. 8) A process designed to provide reasonable assurance that the organization produces reliable financial reports, complies with applicable laws and regulations, and conducts its operations in an efficient and effective manner.

Internal Revenue Service (p. 24) A government organization that handles millions of income tax returns filed by individuals and businesses and performs audit functions to verify the data contained in those returns.

internal users (p. 13) Individuals who use accounting information from within an organization (for example, board of directors, chief financial officer, plant managers, store managers).

International Accounting Standards Board (IASB) (p. 18) The group responsible for creating and promoting *International Financial Reporting Standards (IFRSs)*.

management accounting (p. 6) Providing information that is intended primarily for use by internal management in decision making required to run the business.

monitoring (p. 9) The process of evaluating the effectiveness of an organization's system of internal control over time, including both ongoing management and supervisory activities and periodic separate evaluations.

Public Company Accounting Oversight Board (PCAOB) (p. 19) A quasi-governmental body charged with oversight of the public accounting profession. The PCAOB sets auditing standards for audits of publicly traded companies.

return of investment (p. 10) The repayment to an investor of the amount originally invested in another enterprise.

return on investment (p. 10) The payment of an amount (interest, dividends) for using another's money.

risk assessment (p. 8) A process of identifying, analyzing, and managing those risks that pose a threat to the achievement of the organization's objectives.

Sarbanes-Oxley Act (p. 9) A landmark piece of securities law, designed to improve the effectiveness of corporate financial reporting through enhanced accountability of auditors, boards of directors, and management.

Securities and Exchange Commission (SEC) (p. 17) A governmental organization that has the legal power to establish accounting principles and financial reporting requirements for publicly held companies in the United States.

statement of cash flows (p. 12) An activity statement that shows the details of the company's activities involving cash during a period of time.

statement of financial position (p. 12) Also called the balance sheet.

Demonstration Problem

Find the **Intel Corporation** annual 10-K report from 2009 at the following Internet address (http://www.intc.com/secfiling.cfm?filingID=950123-10-15237) to answer the following questions:

a. Name the titles of the financial reports in the **Intel Corp**. annual report that provide specific information about economic resources, claims to resources, and changes in resources and claims.

b. Name three other sections from **Intel**'s 2009 annual report that provide information useful in assessing the amount, timing, and uncertainty of future cash flows.

c. Which main categories of other general information are useful in making investment and credit decisions?

Solution to the Demonstration Problem

a.
- **Intel Corporation**
  Consolidated Balance Sheets
- **Intel Corporation**
  Consolidated Statements of Stockholders' Equity
- **Intel Corporation**
  Consolidated Statements of Operations
- **Intel Corporation**
  Consolidated Statements of Cash Flows

b.
- Management's Discussion and Analysis of Financial Condition and Results of Operations
- Quantitative and Qualitative Disclosures about Market Risk
- Notes to the Consolidated Financial Statements

c.
- Business Discussion
- Management's Discussion and Analysis of Financial Condition and Results of Operations that contains general discussions about strategy, results of operations, business outlook, and liquidity and capital resources
- Report of the Independent Registered Public Accounting Firm

Self-Test Questions

The answers to these questions appear on page 35.

1. Which of the following does *not* describe accounting?

a. Language of business.

b. Is an end rather than a means to an end.

c. Useful for decision making.

d. Used by business, government, nonprofit organizations, and individuals.

2. To understand and use accounting information in making economic decisions, you must understand:
   a. The nature of economic activities that accounting information describes.
   b. The assumptions and measurement techniques involved in developing accounting information.
   c. Which information is relevant for a particular type of decision that is being made.
   d. All of the above.
3. Purposes of an accounting system include all of the following *except:*
   a. Interpret and record the effects of business transactions.
   b. Classify the effects of transactions to facilitate the preparation of reports.
   c. Summarize and communicate information to decision makers.
   d. Dictate the specific types of business transactions that the enterprise may engage in.
4. External users of financial accounting information include all of the following *except:*
   a. Investors. c. Line managers.
   b. Labor unions. d. General public.
5. Objectives of financial reporting to external investors and creditors include preparing information about all of the following *except:*
   a. Information used to determine which products to produce.
   b. Information about economic resources, claims to those resources, and changes in both resources and claims.
   c. Information that is useful in assessing the amount, timing, and uncertainty of future cash flows.
   d. Information that is useful in making investment and credit decisions.
6. Financial accounting information is characterized by all of the following *except:*
   a. It is historical in nature.
   b. It sometimes results from inexact and approximate measures.
   c. It is factual, so it does not require judgment to prepare.
   d. It is enhanced by management's explanation.
7. Which of the following is *not* a user of internal accounting information?
   a. Store manager.
   b. Chief executive officer.
   c. Creditor.
   d. Chief financial officer.
8. Characteristics of internal accounting information include all of the following *except:*
   a. It is audited by a CPA.
   b. It must be timely.
   c. It is oriented toward the future.
   d. It measures efficiency and effectiveness.
9. Which of the following are important factors in ensuring the integrity of accounting information?
   a. Institutional factors, such as standards for preparing information.
   b. Professional organizations, such as the American Institute of CPAs.
   c. Competence, judgment, and ethical behavior of individual accountants.
   d. All of the above.
10. The code of conduct of the American Institute of Certified Public Accountants includes requirements in which of the following areas?
    a. The Public Interest. c. Independence.
    b. Objectivity. d. All of the above.

ASSIGNMENT MATERIAL Discussion Questions

1. Accounting is sometimes described as the language of business. What is meant by this description?
2. When you invest your savings in a company, what is the difference between the return *on* your investment and the return *of* your investment?
3. Going from general to specific, what are the three primary objectives of financial accounting information?
4. What are the three primary financial statements with which we communicate financial accounting information?
5. Is externally reported financial information always precise and accurate?
6. Is internal accounting information primarily historical or future-oriented? How does that compare with financial accounting information?
7. What is meant by *generally accepted accounting principles,* and how do these principles add to the integrity of financial accounting information?
8. What is the definition of *internal control,* and what are the five components of COSO's internal control framework?
9. What is an *audit,* and how does it add to the integrity of accounting information?
10. What is meant by the professional designations *CPA, CMA,* and *CIA,* and how do these designations add to the integrity of accounting information?
11. Why was the Sarbanes-Oxley legislation passed in 2002, and what are its implications for the accounting profession?
12. What is the Financial Accounting Standards Board (FASB), and what is its role in external financial reporting?

13. What is the Securities and Exchange Commission (SEC), and what is its role in external financial reporting?

14. What is the role of the Public Company Accounting Oversight Board in the audit of financial statements?

15. What is the International Accounting Standards Board (IASB), and what are its objectives?

Brief Exercises

BRIEF EXERCISE 1.1
Users of Information

List four external users of accounting information.

BRIEF EXERCISE 1.2
Components of Internal Control

Match the terms on the left with the descriptions on the right. Each description should be used only once.

Term	Description
______ Control environment	a. Identifying, analyzing, and managing those risks that pose a threat to the achievement of the organization's objectives.
______ Risk assessment	b. A process, involving both ongoing activities and separate evaluations, that enables an organization to evaluate the effectiveness of its system of internal control over time.
______ Control activities	c. The process of capturing and communicating operational, financial, and compliance-related information.
______ Information and communication	d. The foundation for all the other elements of internal control, setting the overall tone for the organization.
______ Monitoring	e. Policies and procedures put in place by management to address the risks identified during the risk assessment process.

BRIEF EXERCISE 1.3
Inexact or Approximate Measures

Why does accounting rely on inexact or approximate measures?

BRIEF EXERCISE 1.4
Standards for the Preparation of Accounting Information

What are the two primary organizations in the U.S. that are responsible for setting standards related to the preparation of accounting information?

BRIEF EXERCISE 1.5
FASB Conceptual Framework

The FASB's conceptual framework sets forth the Board's views on which topics?

BRIEF EXERCISE 1.6
Public Company Accounting Oversight Board (PCAOB)

Use the Web to find the home page of the PCAOB. What are the four primary activities of the PCAOB?

BRIEF EXERCISE 1.7
Committee of Sponsoring Organizations (COSO)

Who are the sponsoring organizations of COSO, and what is COSO best known for doing?

BRIEF EXERCISE 1.8
Professional Certifications in Accounting

List three professional certifications offered in accounting and the organizations that offer them.

BRIEF EXERCISE 1.9
AICPA Code of Professional Conduct

Match the terms on the left with the descriptions on the right. Each description should be used only once.

Term	Description
______ Responsibilities	a. A member should observe the profession's technical and ethical standards, strive continually to improve competence and the quality of service, and discharge professional responsibility to the best of the member's ability.
______ The Public Interest	b. In carrying out their responsibilities as professionals, members should exercise sensitive professional and moral judgments in all their activities.
______ Integrity	c. A member should maintain objectivity and be free of conflicts of interest in discharging professional responsibilities. A member in public practice should be independent in fact and appearance when providing auditing and other attestation services.
______ Objectivity and Independence	d. A member in public practice should observe the Principles of the Code of Professional Conduct in determining the scope and nature of services to be provided.
______ Due Care	e. Members should accept the obligation to act in a way that will serve the public interest, honor the public trust, and demonstrate commitment to professionalism.
______ Scope and Nature of Services	f. To maintain and broaden public confidence, members should perform all professional responsibilities with the highest sense of integrity.

BRIEF EXERCISE 1.10
Personal Benefits of Accounting Skills

List three accounting-related skills that are useful to many people in their personal lives.

Exercises

connect ACCOUNTING

LO1 **EXERCISE 1.1**
You as a User of Accounting Information

Identify several ways in which *you* currently use accounting information in your life as a student. Also identify several situations in which, while you are still a student, you might be required to supply financial information about yourself to others.

LO3 LO4 **EXERCISE 1.2**
Users of Accounting Information

Boeing Company is the largest manufacturer of commercial aircraft in the United States and is a major employer in Seattle, Washington. Explain why each of the following individuals or organizations would be interested in financial information about the company.

a. **California Public Employees Retirement System**, one of the world's largest pension funds.
b. **China Airlines**, a rapidly growing airline serving the Pacific Rim.
c. Henry James, a real estate investor considering building apartments in the Seattle area.
d. **Boeing**'s management.
e. **International Aerospace Machinists**, a labor union representing many **Boeing** employees.

LO3 **EXERCISE 1.3**
What Is Financial Reporting?

A major focus of this course is the process of financial reporting.

a. What is meant by the term *financial reporting*?
b. What are the principal accounting reports involved in the financial reporting process? In general terms, what is the purpose of these reports?
c. Do all business entities engage in financial reporting? Explain.
d. How does society benefit from the financial reporting process?

LO6 **EXERCISE 1.4**
Generally Accepted Accounting Principles

Generally accepted accounting principles play an important role in financial reporting.

a. What is meant by the phrase *generally accepted accounting principles*?
b. What are the major sources of these principles?
c. Is there a single comprehensive list of generally accepted accounting principles? Explain.
d. What types of accounting reports are prepared in conformity with generally accepted accounting principles?

LO6

EXERCISE 1.5

Accounting Organizations

Describe the roles of the following organizations in establishing generally accepted accounting principles:

a. The FASB **b.** The AICPA **c.** The SEC

From which of these organizations can you most easily obtain financial information about publicly owned companies?

LO3

EXERCISE 1.6

Investment Return

You recently invested $12,000 of your savings in a security issued by a large company. The security agreement pays you 7 percent per year and has a maturity two years from the day you purchased it. What is the total cash flow you expect to receive from this investment, separated into the return on your investment and the return of your investment?

LO3 through LO5, LO7

EXERCISE 1.7

Accounting Terminology

Match the terms on the left with the descriptions on the right. Each description should be used only once.

Term	Description
______ Financial accounting	a. The procedural aspect of accounting that involves keeping detailed records of business transactions, much of which is done today by computers.
______ Management accounting	b. A broad term that describes all information provided to external users, including but not limited to financial statements.
______ Financial reporting	c. An important quality of accounting information that allows investors, creditors, management, and other users to rely on the information.
______ Financial statements	d. The segment of the accounting profession that relates to providing audit, tax, and consulting services to clients.
______ General-purpose assumption	e. Procedures and processes within an organization that ensure the integrity of accounting information.
______ Integrity	f. Statement of financial position (balance sheet), income statement, statement of cash flows.
______ Internal control	g. The fact that the same information is provided to various external users, including investors and creditors.
______ Public accounting	h. The area of accounting that refers to providing information to support internal management decisions.
______ Bookkeeping	i. The area of accounting that refers to providing information to support external investment and credit decisions.

LO6

EXERCISE 1.8

Accounting Organizations

Match the organizations on the left with the functions on the right. Each function should be used only once.

Organization	Function
______ Institute of Internal Auditors	a. Government agency responsible for financial reporting by publicly held companies.
______ Securities and Exchange Commission	b. International organization dedicated to the advancement of internal auditing.
______ American Institute of CPAs	c. Organization dedicated to providing members personal and professional development opportunities in the area of management accounting.
______ Institute of Management Accountants	d. The body charged with setting auditing standards for audits of public companies.
______ Financial Accounting Standards Board	e. Organization consisting primarily of accounting educators that encourages improvements in teaching and research.
______ American Accounting Association	f. The group that creates and promotes International Financial Reporting Standards (IFRSs).
______ Public Company Accounting Oversight Board	g. Professional association of Certified Public Accountants.
______ International Accounting Standards Board	h. Private-sector organization that establishes accounting standards.

LO3 LO4 **EXERCISE 1.9**
Financial and Management Accounting

The major focus of accounting information is to facilitate decision making.

a. As an investor in a company, what would be your primary objective?

b. As a manager of a company, what would be your primary objective?

c. Is the same accounting information likely to be equally useful to you in these two different roles?

LO4 **EXERCISE 1.10**
Management Accounting Information

Internal accounting information is used primarily for internal decision making by an enterprise's management.

a. What are the three primary purposes of internal accounting information?

b. Which of these is the most general and which is the most specific?

c. Give several examples of the kinds of decisions that internal accounting information supports.

LO6 **EXERCISE 1.11**
Accounting Organizations

Describe which professional organization(s) would most likely be of greatest value to you if your position involved each of the following independent roles:

a. Accounting educator.

b. Management accountant.

c. Certified public accountant.

LO5 **EXERCISE 1.12**
Purpose of an Audit

Audits of financial statements are an important part of the accounting process to ensure integrity in financial reporting.

a. What is the purpose of an audit?

b. As an external user of accounting information, what meaning would you attach to an audit that concludes that the financial statements are fairly presented in conformity with generally accepted accounting principles?

c. Would your interest in investing in this same company be affected by an auditor's report that concluded the financial statements were *not* fairly presented? Why or why not?

LO5 **EXERCISE 1.13**
Audits of Financial Statements

The annual financial statements of all large, publicly owned corporations are audited.

a. What is an audit of financial statements?

b. Who performs audits?

c. What is the purpose of an audit?

LO7 **EXERCISE 1.14**
Ethics and Professional Judgment

Ethical conduct and professional judgment each play important roles in the accounting process.

a. In general terms, explain why it is important to society that people who prepare accounting information act in an ethical manner.

b. Identify at least three areas in which accountants must exercise *professional judgment,* rather than merely relying on written rules.

LO8 **EXERCISE 1.15**
Careers in Accounting

Four accounting majors, Maria Acosta, Kenzo Nakao, Helen Martin, and Anthony Mandella, recently graduated from Central University and began professional accounting careers. Acosta entered public accounting, Nakao became a management accountant, Martin joined a governmental agency, and Mandella (who had completed a graduate program) became an accounting faculty member.

Assume that each of the four graduates was successful in his or her chosen career. Identify the types of accounting *activities* in which each of these graduates might find themselves specializing several years after graduation.

LO1 LO3 LO5 **EXERCISE 1.16**
Home Depot, Inc.
General and Specific Information

Locate the **Home Depot, Inc.**, 2009 financial statements in Appendix A of this text. Briefly peruse the financial statements and answer the following questions:

a. Name the titles of each of **Home Depot**'s financial statements that provide specific information about economic resources, claims to resources, and changes in resources and claims.

b. Name three other sections from **Home Depot**'s 2009 financial statements that might be useful to a potential investor or creditor.

Due to the introductory nature of this chapter and the conceptual nature of its contents, no items labeled ***Problems*** *are included. In all future chapters, you will find two problem sets, A and B, that generally include computations, are more complex, and generally require more time to complete than the Exercises.*

Critical Thinking Cases

LO5 **CASE 1.1**
Reliability of Financial Statements

In the mid-2000s, **Fannie Mae** was in severe financial difficulty and desperately needed additional capital for the company to survive. What factors prevented **Fannie Mae** from simply providing potential lenders with misleading financial statements to make the company look like a risk-free investment?

LO3 **CASE 1.2**
Objectives of Financial Accounting

Divide into groups as instructed by your professor and discuss the following:

a. How does the description of accounting as the "language of business" relate to accounting as being useful for investors and creditors?

b. Explain how the decisions you would make might differ if you were an external investor or a member of an enterprise's management team.

LO2 **CASE 1.3**
Accounting Systems

You are employed by a business consulting firm as an information systems specialist. You have just begun an assignment with a startup company and are discussing with the owner her need for an accounting system. How would you respond to the following questions from the owner?

a. What is the meaning of the term *accounting system*?

b. What is the purpose of an accounting system and what are its basic functions?

c. Who is responsible for designing and implementing an accounting system?

LO7 **CASE 1.4**
Codes of Ethics

Assume you have recently completed your college degree with a major in accounting and have accepted a position on the accounting staff of a large corporation. Your supervisor suggests that in preparing for your first day on the job, you become familiar with the basic principles included in the code of ethics of the Institute of Management Accountants. Briefly explain what you learn as you study the code and how it might affect your behavior on your new job. (Use the IMA's Web site to obtain access to the IMA's Code of Ethics.)

LO6 LO7 **INTERNET CASE 1.5**
Accessing Information on the Internet

The Internet is a good place to get information that is useful to you in your study of accounting. For example, you can find information about accounting firms, standard setters, and regulators.

Instructions

a. The largest U.S. accounting firms are referred to as the Big 4—Deloitte, Ernst & Young, KPMG, and PricewaterhouseCoopers. Find the Internet sites of these four firms and learn what you can about the types of services provided by the firm.

b. The Public Company Accounting Oversight Board (PCAOB) was created by the Sarbanes-Oxley Act to oversee auditors of public companies. Find the PCAOB's Internet site and learn what you can about the PCAOB's four major activities.

c. The Financial Accounting Standards Board (FASB) is the designated accounting standard setter in the U.S. Find the FASB's Internet site and identify the FASB's board members including a brief description of their backgrounds.

d. The International Accounting Standards Board (IASB) is the body that issues International Financial Reporting Standards. Find the IASB's Internet site and identify the IASB's board members including a brief description of the backgrounds of five board members.

Internet sites are time and date sensitive. It is the purpose of these exercises to have you explore the Internet. You may need to use the Yahoo! search engine http://www.yahoo.com *(or another favorite search engine) to find a company's current Web address.*

Answers to Self-Test Questions

1. b **2.** d **3.** d **4.** c **5.** a **6.** c **7.** c **8.** a
9. d **10.** d

CHAPTER 2

Basic Financial Statements

© Intel Corporation

Learning Objectives

AFTER STUDYING THIS CHAPTER, YOU SHOULD BE ABLE TO:

- **LO1** Explain the nature and general purpose of financial statements.
- **LO2** Explain certain accounting principles that are important for an understanding of financial statements and how professional judgment by accountants may affect the application of those principles.
- **LO3** Demonstrate how certain business transactions affect the elements of the accounting equation: Assets = Liabilities + Owners' Equity.
- **LO4** Explain how the statement of financial position, often referred to as the balance sheet, is an expansion of the basic accounting equation.
- **LO5** Explain how the income statement reports an enterprise's financial performance for a period of time in terms of the relationship of revenues and expenses.
- **LO6** Explain how the statement of cash flows presents the change in cash for a period of time in terms of the company's operating, investing, and financing activities.
- **LO7** Explain how the statement of financial position (balance sheet), income statement, and statement of cash flows relate to each other.
- **LO8** Explain common forms of business ownership—sole proprietorship, partnership, and corporation—and demonstrate how they differ in terms of their presentation in the statement of financial position.
- **LO9** Discuss the importance of financial statements to a company and its investors and creditors and why management may take steps to improve the appearance of the company in its financial statements.

INTEL

Intel supplies the computing and communications industries with chips, boards, and systems building blocks that are the ingredients of computers and servers as well as networking and communications products. These industries use Intel's products to create advanced computing and communications systems. Intel states that its mission is to be the preeminent building block supplier in the worldwide Internet economy.

Technology-based companies like Intel operate in highly competitive markets and continuously introduce new products. Intel's management discusses the company's business strategy in a recent corporate information communication on the company's Web site by explaining the importance of meeting the needs of customers: "Our goal is to be the preeminent provider of semiconductor chips and platforms for the worldwide digital economy. . . We offer products at various levels of integration, to allow our customers flexibility in creating computing and communications systems. The substantial majority of our revenue is from the sale of microprocessors and chipsets."

Modern-day historians indicate that we are rapidly moving from the industrial age, with an emphasis on heavy manufacturing, to the information age. Companies like Intel, Microsoft, Cisco Systems, and others are major players in this transformation of business. For information-age companies the factors of success are quite different than for industrial-age companies. Information-age companies rely more heavily on intellectual capital, research and development, and other intangibles that were less important for companies whose focus was heavy manufacturing or, even earlier in our history, primarily agricultural. ■

If you were a person with considerable wealth who wanted to invest in a forward-looking company in today's information age, how would you know whether **Intel** or any other company is a wise investment? What information would you seek out to help you decide where to place your investment dollars? A primary source of financial information is a company's financial statements. These statements, which are prepared at least once a year and in many cases more frequently, provide insight into the current financial status of the company and how successful the company has been in meeting its financial goals. In this chapter, you are introduced to the three primary financial statements—the statement of financial position (often referred to as the balance sheet), the income statement, and the statement of cash flows. Combined with information presented in notes and other accompanying presentations, these financial statements provide for investors, creditors, and other interested parties a wealth of useful information. In fact, financial information is what this entire textbook is about, and in this chapter you receive your initial introduction to how financial statements come about and how they may be used to better understand a company.

Introduction to Financial Statements

In Chapter 1, we learned that investors and creditors are particularly interested in cash flows that they expect to receive in the future. Creditors, for example, are interested in the ability of an enterprise, to which they have made loans or sold merchandise on credit, to meet its payment obligations, which may include payment of interest. Similarly, investors are interested in the market value of their stock holdings, as well as dividends that the enterprise will pay while they own the stock.

One of the primary ways investors and creditors assess the probability that an enterprise will be able to make future cash payments is to study, analyze, and understand the enterprise's financial statements. As discussed in Chapter 1, a **financial statement** is simply a declaration of what is believed to be true about an enterprise, communicated in terms of a monetary unit, such as the dollar. When accountants prepare financial statements, they are describing in financial terms certain attributes of the enterprise that they believe fairly represent its financial activities.

In this chapter, we introduce three primary financial statements:

- Statement of financial position (commonly referred to as the balance sheet).
- Income statement.
- Statement of cash flows.

In introducing these statements, we use the form of business ownership referred to as a *corporation.* The corporation is a unique form of organization that allows many owners to combine their resources into a business enterprise that is larger than would be possible based on the financial resources of a single or a small number of owners. While businesses of any size may be organized as corporations, most large businesses are corporations because of their need for a large amount of capital that the corporate form of business organization makes possible. Later in this chapter we introduce two other forms of business organization—the sole proprietorship and the partnership—which are alternatives to the corporate form for some business enterprises.

Learning Objective LO1 Explain the nature and general purpose of financial statements.

The names of the three primary financial statements describe the information you find in each. The **statement of financial position,** or **balance sheet,** is a financial statement that describes where the enterprise stands at a specific date. It is sometimes described as a snapshot of the business in financial or dollar terms (that is, what the enterprise "looks like" at a specific date).

As businesses operate, they engage in transactions that create revenues and incur expenses that are necessary to earn those revenues. An **income statement** is an activity statement that shows the revenues and expenses for a designated period of time. Revenues already have resulted in positive cash flows, or are expected to do so in the near future, as a result of transactions with customers. For example, a company might sell a product for $100. This revenue transaction results in an immediate positive cash flow into the enterprise if the customer pays cash at the time of the transaction. An expected future cash flow results if it is a credit transaction in which payment is to be received later. Expenses have the opposite effect in that they result in an immediate cash flow *out* of the enterprise (if a cash transaction) or an expected future flow of cash out of the enterprise (if a credit transaction). For example, if a company incurs a certain expense of $75 and pays it at that time, an immediate cash outflow takes place. If payment is delayed until some future date, the transaction represents an expected future cash outflow. Revenues result in **positive cash flows**—either past, present, or future—while expenses result in **negative cash flows**—either past, present, or future. *Positive* and *negative* indicate the directional impact on cash. The term *net income* (or *net loss*) is simply the difference between all of an enterprise's revenues and expenses for a designated period of time.

The **statement of cash flows** is particularly important in understanding an enterprise for purposes of investment and credit decisions. As its name implies, the statement of cash flows shows the ways cash changed during a designated period—the cash received from revenues and other transactions as well as the cash paid for certain expenses and other acquisitions during the period. While the primary focus of investors and creditors is on cash flows to themselves rather than to the enterprise, information about cash activity of the enterprise is an important signal to investors and creditors about the prospects of future cash flows to them.

A Starting Point: Statement of Financial Position

All three financial statements contain important information, but each includes different information. For that reason, it is important to understand all three financial statements and how they relate to each other. The way they relate is sometimes referred to as **articulation,** a term we will say more about later in this chapter.

A logical starting point for understanding financial statements is the statement of financial position, also called the balance sheet. The purpose of this financial statement is to demonstrate where the company stands, in financial terms, at a specific point in time. As we will see later in this chapter, the other financial statements relate to the statement of financial position and show how important aspects of a company's financial position change over time. Beginning with the statement of financial position also allows us to understand certain basic accounting principles and terminologies that are important for understanding all financial statements.

Every business prepares a balance sheet at the end of the year, and many companies prepare one at the end of each month, week, or even day. It consists of a listing of the assets, the liabilities, and the owners' equity of the business. The *date* is important, as the financial position of a business may change quickly. Exhibit 2–1 shows the financial position of Vagabond Travel Agency at December 31, 2011.

Exhibit 2–1

STATEMENT OF FINANCIAL POSITION

VAGABOND TRAVEL AGENCY
STATEMENT OF FINANCIAL POSITION
DECEMBER 31, 2011

Assets		Liabilities & Owners' Equity		
Cash	$ 22,500	Liabilities:		
Notes Receivable	10,000	Notes Payable	$ 41,000	
Accounts Receivable	60,500	Accounts Payable	36,000	
Supplies	2,000	Salaries Payable	3,000	$ 80,000
Land	100,000	Owners' equity:		
Building	90,000	Capital Stock	$150,000	
Office Equipment	15,000	Retained Earnings	70,000	220,000
Total	$300,000	Total		$300,000

A balance sheet shows financial position at a specific date

Let us briefly describe several features of the statement of financial position, using Exhibit 2–1 as an example. First, the heading communicates three things: (1) the name of the business, (2) the name of the financial statement, and (3) the date. The body of the balance sheet consists of three distinct sections: *assets, liabilities,* and *owners' equity.*

Notice that cash is listed first among the assets, followed by notes receivable, accounts receivable, supplies, and any other assets that will *soon be converted into cash or used up in business operations.* Following these assets are the more permanent assets, such as land, buildings, and equipment.

Moving to the right side of the balance sheet, liabilities are shown before owners' equity. Each major type of liability (such as notes payable, accounts payable, and salaries payable) is listed separately, followed by a figure for total liabilities.

Owners' equity is separated into two parts—capital stock and retained earnings. Capital stock represents the amount that owners originally paid into the company to become owners. It consists of individual shares and each owner has a set number of shares. Notice in this illustration that capital stock totals $150,000. This means that the assigned value of the shares held by owners, multiplied by the number of shares, equals $150,000. For example, assuming an assigned value of $10 per share, there would be 15,000 shares ($10 × 15,000 = $150,000). Alternatively, the assigned value might be $5 per share, in which case there would be 30,000 shares ($5 × 30,000 = $150,000). The retained earnings part of owners' equity is simply the accumulated earnings of previous years that remain within the enterprise. Retained earnings is considered part of the equity of the owners and serves to enhance their investment in the business.

Finally, notice that the amount of total assets ($300,000) is *equal* to the total amount of liabilities and owners' equity (also $300,000). This relationship *always exists*—in fact, the *equality of these totals* is why this financial statement is frequently called a *balance* sheet.

Learning Objective

LO2 Explain certain accounting principles that are important for an understanding of financial statements and how professional judgment by accountants may affect the application of those principles.

The Concept of the Business Entity

Generally accepted accounting principles require that financial statements describe the affairs of a specific economic entity. This concept is called the *entity principle.*

A **business entity** is an economic unit that engages in identifiable business activities. For accounting purposes, the business entity is regarded as *separate from the personal activities of its owners.* For example, Vagabond is a business organization operating as a travel agency. Its owners may have personal bank accounts, homes, cars, and even other businesses. These items are not involved in the operation of the travel agency and do not appear in Vagabond's financial statements.

If the owners were to commingle their personal activities with the transactions of the business, the resulting financial statements would fail to describe clearly the financial activities of the business organization. Distinguishing business from personal activities of the owners may require judgment by the accountant.

ASSETS

Assets are economic resources that are owned by a business and are expected to benefit future operations. In most cases, the benefit to future operations comes in the form of positive future cash flows. The positive future cash flows may come directly as the asset is converted into cash (collection of a receivable) or indirectly as the asset is used in operating the business to create other assets that result in positive future cash flows (buildings and land used to manufacture a product for sale). Assets may have definite physical characteristics such as buildings, machinery, or an inventory of merchandise. On the other hand, some assets exist not in physical or tangible form, but in the form of valuable legal claims or rights; examples are amounts due from customers, investments in government bonds, and patent rights.

One of the most basic and at the same time most controversial problems in accounting is determining the correct dollar amount for the various assets of a business. At present, generally accepted accounting principles call for the valuation of some assets in a balance sheet at *cost,* rather than at their current value. The specific accounting principles supporting cost as the basis for asset valuation are discussed below.

The Cost Principle Assets such as land, buildings, merchandise, and equipment are typical of the many economic resources that are required in producing revenue for the business. The prevailing accounting view is that such assets should be presented at their cost. When we say that an asset is shown in the balance sheet at its *historical cost,* we mean the original amount the business entity paid to acquire the asset. This amount may be different from what it would cost to purchase the same asset today.

For example, let us assume that a business buys a tract of land for use as a building site, paying $100,000 in cash. The amount to be entered in the accounting records for the asset will be the cost of $100,000. If we assume a booming real estate market, a fair estimate of the market value of the land 10 years later might be $250,000. Although the market price or economic value of the land has risen greatly, the amount shown in the company's accounting records and in its balance sheet would continue unchanged at the cost of $100,000. This policy of accounting for many assets at their cost is often referred to as the **cost principle** of accounting.

Exceptions to the cost principle are found in some of the most liquid assets (that is, assets that are expected to soon become cash). Amounts receivable from customers are generally included in the balance sheet at their *net realizable value,* which is an amount that approximates the cash that is expected to be received when the receivable is collected. Similarly, certain investments in other enterprises are included in the balance sheet at their current market value if management's plan includes conversion into cash in the near future.

In reading a balance sheet, it is important to keep in mind that the dollar amounts listed for many assets do not indicate the prices at which the assets could be sold or the prices at which they could be replaced. A frequently misunderstood feature of a balance sheet is that it *does not* show how much the business currently is worth, although it contains valuable information in being able to calculate such a value.

The Going-Concern Assumption *Why* don't accountants change the recorded amounts of assets to correspond with changing market prices for these properties? One reason is that assets like land and buildings are being used to house the business and were acquired for *use* and not for resale; in fact, these assets usually could not be sold without disrupting the business. The balance sheet of a business is prepared on the assumption that the business is a continuing enterprise, or a **going concern.** Consequently, the present estimated prices at which assets like land and buildings could be sold are of less importance than if these properties were intended for sale. These are frequently among the largest dollar amounts of a company's assets. Determining that an enterprise is a going concern may require judgment by the accountant.

The Objectivity Principle Another reason for using cost rather than current market values in accounting for many assets is the need for a definite, factual basis for valuation. The cost of land, buildings, and many other assets that have been purchased can be definitely determined. Accountants use the term *objective* to describe asset valuations that are factual and can be verified by independent experts. For example, if land is shown on the balance sheet at cost, any CPA who performed an audit of the business would be able to find objective evidence that the land was actually measured at the cost incurred in acquiring it. On the other hand, estimated market values for assets such as buildings and specialized machinery are not factual and objective. Market values are constantly changing, and estimates of the prices at which assets could be sold are largely a matter of judgment.

YOUR TURN **You as a Home Owner**

First, assume you have owned your home for 10 years and need to report the value of your home to the city assessor for real estate tax assessment purposes. What information would you provide? Second, assume you are planning to sell your home. What type of information would you provide to potential buyers? What ethical issues arise in these two situations that the objectivity principle helps address?

(See our comments on the Online Learning Center Web site.)

At the time an asset is acquired, the cost and market value are usually the same. With the passage of time, however, the current market value of assets is likely to differ considerably from its historical cost. As you will learn, for some assets we adjust the amount in the balance sheet as the value changes. For other assets, we retain historical cost as the basis of the asset in the balance sheet.

The Stable-Dollar Assumption A limitation of measuring assets at historical cost is that the value of the monetary unit or dollar is not always stable. **Inflation** is a term used to describe the situation where the value of the monetary unit decreases, meaning that it will purchase less than it did previously. **Deflation,** on the other hand, is the opposite situation in which the value of the monetary unit increases, meaning that it will purchase more than it did previously. Typically, countries like the United States have experienced inflation rather than deflation. When inflation becomes severe, historical cost amounts for assets lose their relevance as a basis for making business decisions.

Accountants in the United States prepare financial statements under an assumption that the dollar is a stable unit of measurement, as is the gallon, the acre, or the mile. The cost principle and the **stable-dollar assumption** work well in periods of stable prices but are less satisfactory under conditions of rapid inflation. For example, if a company bought land 20 years ago for $100,000 and purchased a second similar tract of land today for $500,000, the total cost of land shown by the accounting records would be $600,000 following the historical cost principle. This treatment ignores the fact that dollars spent 20 years ago had greater purchasing power than today's dollar. Thus the $600,000 total for the cost of land is a mixture of two "sizes" of dollars with different purchasing power.

INTERNATIONAL CASE IN POINT

Many countries experience prolonged and serious inflation. Inflation can undermine the stable-currency assumption. Accounting rules have been designed in some foreign countries to address the impact of inflation on a company's financial position. For example, Mexican corporate law requires Mexican companies to adjust their balance sheets to current purchasing power by using indexes provided by the government. Because inflation is significant, the indexes are used to devalue the Mexican currency (pesos) to provide a more transparent representation of the company's financial condition.

After much research into this problem, at one time the FASB required on a trial basis that large corporations annually disclose financial data adjusted for the effects of inflation. At the present time, this disclosure is optional, as judged appropriate by the accountant who prepares the financial statements.

LIABILITIES

Liabilities are financial obligations or debts. They represent negative future cash flows for the enterprise. The person or organization to whom the debt is owed is called a **creditor.**

All businesses have liabilities; even the largest and most successful companies often purchase merchandise, supplies, and services "on account." The liabilities arising from such purchases are called *accounts payable.* Many businesses borrow money to finance expansion or the purchase of high-cost assets and pay for them over time. When obtaining a loan, the borrower usually must sign a formal note payable. A *note payable* is a written promise to repay the amount owed by a particular date and usually calls for the payment of interest as well.

Accounts payable, in contrast to notes payable, involve no written promises and generally do not call for interest payments. In essence, a note payable is a *more formal* arrangement than an account payable, but they are similar in that they require the company to make payment in the future.

Liabilities are usually listed in the order in which they are expected to be repaid.[1] Liabilities that are similar may be combined to avoid unnecessary detail in the financial statement. For example, if a company had several expenses payable at the end of the year (for example, wages, interest, taxes), it might combine these into a single line called *accrued expenses.* The word *accrued* is an accounting term communicating that the payment of certain expenses has been delayed or deferred.

Liabilities represent claims against the borrower's assets. As we shall see, the owners of a business *also* have claims on the company's assets. But in the eyes of the law, creditors' claims *take priority* over those of the owners. This means that creditors are entitled to be *paid in full,* even if such payment would exhaust the assets of the business and leave nothing for its owners.

OWNERS' EQUITY

Owners' equity represents the *owners' claims* on the assets of the business. Because liabilities or creditors' claims have legal priority over those of the owners, owners' equity is a *residual amount.* If you are the owner of a business, you are entitled to assets that are left after the claims of creditors have been satisfied in full. Therefore, owners' equity is always equal to *total assets minus total liabilities.* For example, using the data from the illustrated balance sheet of Vagabond Travel Agency (Exhibit 2–1):

Vagabond has total assets of	$300,000
And total liabilities of	(80,000)
Therefore, the owners' equity must be	$220,000

Owners' equity does *not* represent a specific claim to cash or any other particular asset. Rather, it is the owners' overall financial interest in the entire company.

Increases in Owners' Equity

The owners' equity in a business comes from two primary sources:

1. *Investments of cash or other assets* by owners.
2. *Earnings* from profitable operation of the business.

Decreases in Owners' Equity

Decreases in owners' equity also are caused in two ways:

1. *Payments of cash or transfers of other assets* to owners.
2. *Losses* from unprofitable operation of the business.

Accounting for payments to owners and net losses are addressed in later chapters.

THE ACCOUNTING EQUATION

A fundamental characteristic of every statement of financial position is that the total for assets always equals the total of liabilities plus owners' equity. This agreement or balance of total assets with the total of liabilities and owners' equity is the reason for calling this financial statement a *balance sheet.* But *why* do total assets equal the total of liabilities and owners' equity?

The dollar totals on the two sides of the balance sheet are always equal because they represent *two views of the same business.* The listing of assets shows us what things the business owns; the listing of liabilities and owners' equity tells us who supplied these resources to the business and how much each group supplied. Everything that a business owns has been supplied to it either by creditors or by the owners. Therefore, the total claims of the creditors plus the claims of the owners always equal the total assets of the business.

Learning Objective LO3
Demonstrate how certain business transactions affect the elements of the accounting equation: Assets = Liabilities + Owners' Equity.

[1] Short-term liabilities generally are those due within one year. Long-term liabilities are shown separately in the balance sheet, after the listing of all short-term liabilities. Long-term liabilities are addressed in Chapter 10.

The equality of the assets on the one hand and the claims of the creditors and the owners on the other hand is expressed in the following **accounting equation:**

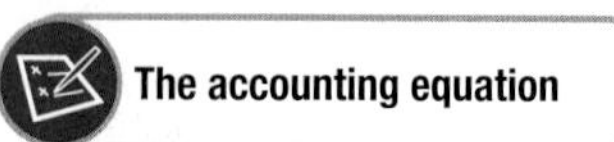

Assets = Liabilities + Owners' Equity
$300,000 = $80,000 + $220,000

The amounts listed in the equation were taken from the balance sheet illustrated in Exhibit 2–1. The balance sheet is simply a detailed statement of this equation. To illustrate this relationship, compare the balance sheet of Vagabond Travel Agency with the above equation.

Every business transaction, no matter how simple or how complex, can be expressed in terms of its effect on the accounting equation. A thorough understanding of the equation and some practice in using it are essential to the student of accounting.

Regardless of whether a business grows or contracts, the equality between the assets and the claims on the assets is always maintained. Any increase in the amount of total assets is necessarily accompanied by an equal increase on the other side of the equation—that is, by an increase in either the liabilities or the owners' equity. Any decrease in total assets is necessarily accompanied by a corresponding decrease in liabilities or owners' equity. The continuing equality of the two sides of the accounting equation can best be illustrated by taking a new business as an example and observing the effects of various transactions.

THE EFFECTS OF BUSINESS TRANSACTIONS: AN ILLUSTRATION

How does a statement of financial position come about? What has occurred in the past for it to exist at any point in time? The statement of financial position is a picture of the results of past business transactions that has been captured by the company's information system and organized into a concise financial description of where the company stands at a point in time. The specific items and dollar amounts are the direct results of the transactions in which the company has engaged. The balance sheets of two separate companies would almost always be different due to the unique nature, timing, and dollar amounts of each company's business transactions.

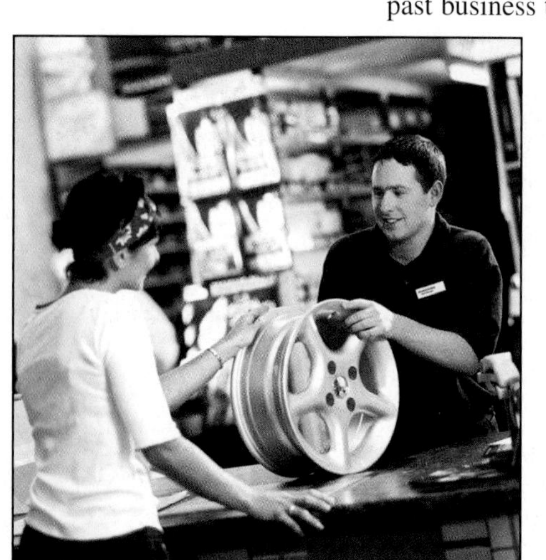
© Getty Images/Stockbyte/DAL

To illustrate how a balance sheet comes about, and later to show how the income statement and statement of cash flows relate to the balance sheet, we use an example of a small auto repair business, Overnight Auto Service.

The Business Entity Assume that Michael McBryan, an experienced auto mechanic, opens his own automotive repair business, Overnight Auto Service. A distinctive feature of Overnight's operations is that all repair work is done at night. This strategy offers customers the convenience of dropping off their cars in the evening and picking them up the following morning.

Operating at night also enables Overnight to minimize labor costs. Instead of hiring full-time employees, Overnight offers part-time work to mechanics who already have day jobs at major automobile dealerships. This eliminates the need for costly employee training programs and for such payroll fringe benefits as group health insurance and employees' pension plans, benefits usually associated with full-time employment.

Overnight's Accounting Policies McBryan has taken several courses in accounting and maintains Overnight's accounting records himself. He knows that small businesses such as his are not required to prepare formal financial statements, but he prepares them anyway. He believes they will be useful to him in running the business. In addition, if Overnight is successful, McBryan plans to open more locations. He anticipates needing to raise substantial amounts of capital from investors and creditors. He believes that the financial history provided by a series of monthly financial statements will be helpful in obtaining investment capital.

The Company's First Transaction McBryan officially started Overnight on January 20, 2011. On that day, he received a charter from the state to begin a small, closely held corporation whose owners consisted of himself and several family members. Capital stock issued to these investors included 8,000 shares at $10 per share. McBryan opened a bank account in the name of Overnight Auto Service, into which he deposited the $80,000 received from the issuance of the capital stock.

This transaction provided Overnight with its first asset—Cash—and also created the initial owners' equity in the business entity. See the balance sheet showing the company's financial position after this initial transaction in Exhibit 2–2.

Exhibit 2–2

BALANCE SHEET, JAN. 20

OVERNIGHT AUTO SERVICE
BALANCE SHEET
JANUARY 20, 2011

Assets		Owners' Equity	
Cash	$80,000	Capital Stock	$80,000

Beginning balance sheet of a new business

Overnight's next two transactions involved the acquisition of a suitable site for its business operations.

Purchase of an Asset for Cash Representing the business, McBryan negotiated with both the City of Santa Teresa and the Metropolitan Transit Authority (MTA) to purchase an abandoned bus garage. (The MTA owned the garage, but the city owned the land.)

On January 21, Overnight purchased the land from the city for *$52,000 cash.* This transaction had two immediate effects on the company's financial position: first, Overnight's cash was reduced by $52,000; and second, the company acquired a new asset—Land. We show the company's financial position after this transaction in Exhibit 2–3.

Exhibit 2–3

BALANCE SHEET, JAN. 21

OVERNIGHT AUTO SERVICE
BALANCE SHEET
JANUARY 21, 2011

Assets		Owners' Equity	
Cash	$28,000	Capital Stock	$80,000
Land	52,000		
Total	$80,000	Total	$80,000

Balance sheet totals unchanged by purchase of land for cash

Purchase of an Asset and Financing Part of the Cost On January 22, Overnight purchased the old garage building from Metropolitan Transit Authority for *$36,000.* Overnight made a cash down payment of *$6,000* and issued a 90-day non-interest-bearing note payable for the *$30,000* balance owed.

As a result of this transaction, Overnight had (1) $6,000 less cash; (2) a new asset, Building, which cost $36,000; and (3) a new liability, Notes Payable, in the amount of $30,000. This transaction is reflected in Exhibit 2–4.

Exhibit 2–4

BALANCE SHEET, JAN. 22

OVERNIGHT AUTO SERVICE
BALANCE SHEET
JANUARY 22, 2011

Assets		Liabilities & Owners' Equity	
Cash	$ 22,000	Liabilities:	
Land	52,000	Notes Payable	$ 30,000
Building	36,000	Owners' equity:	
		Capital Stock	80,000
Total	$110,000	Total	$110,000

Totals increased equally by debt incurred in acquiring assets

Purchase of an Asset on Account On January 23, Overnight purchased tools and automotive repair equipment from Snappy Tools. The purchase price was *$13,800,* due within 60 days. After this purchase, Overnight's financial position is depicted in Exhibit 2–5.

Exhibit 2–5

BALANCE SHEET, JAN. 23

Totals increased equally by debt incurred in acquiring assets

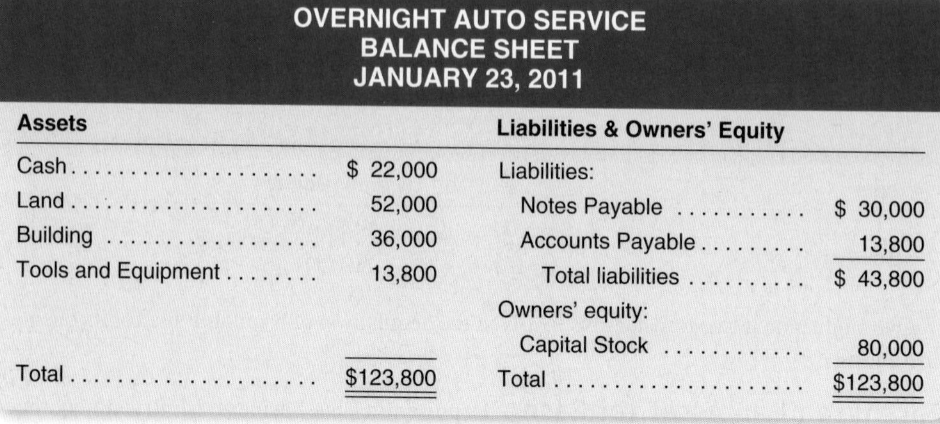

OVERNIGHT AUTO SERVICE
BALANCE SHEET
JANUARY 23, 2011

Assets		Liabilities & Owners' Equity	
Cash	$ 22,000	Liabilities:	
Land	52,000	Notes Payable	$ 30,000
Building	36,000	Accounts Payable	13,800
Tools and Equipment	13,800	Total liabilities	$ 43,800
		Owners' equity:	
		Capital Stock	80,000
Total	$123,800	Total	$123,800

Sale of an Asset After taking delivery of the new tools and equipment, Overnight found that it had purchased more than it needed. Ace Towing, a neighboring business, offered to buy the excess items. On January 24, Overnight sold some of its new tools to Ace for *$1,800,* a price equal to Overnight's cost.[2] Ace made no down payment but agreed to pay the amount due within 45 days. This transaction reduced Overnight's tools and equipment by $1,800 and created a new asset, Accounts Receivable, for that same amount. A balance sheet as of January 24 appears in Exhibit 2–6.

Exhibit 2–6

BALANCE SHEET, JAN. 24

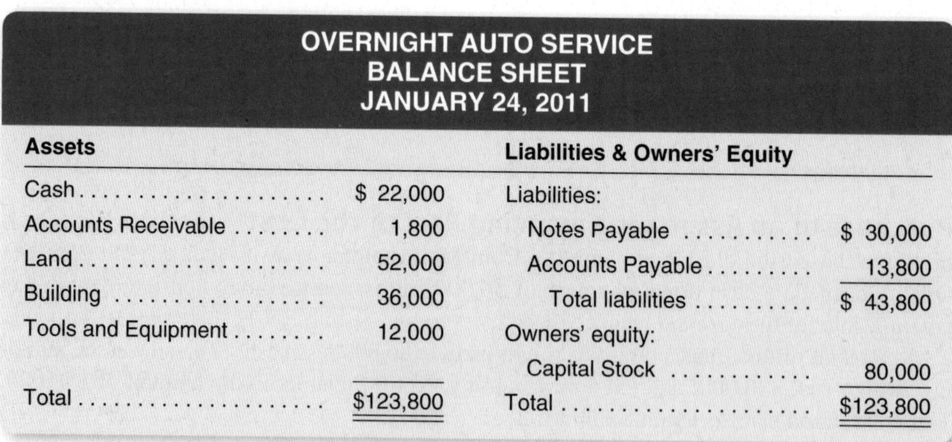

OVERNIGHT AUTO SERVICE
BALANCE SHEET
JANUARY 24, 2011

Assets		Liabilities & Owners' Equity	
Cash	$ 22,000	Liabilities:	
Accounts Receivable	1,800	Notes Payable	$ 30,000
Land	52,000	Accounts Payable	13,800
Building	36,000	Total liabilities	$ 43,800
Tools and Equipment	12,000	Owners' equity:	
		Capital Stock	80,000
Total	$123,800	Total	$123,800

No change in totals by sale of assets at cost

Collection of an Account Receivable On January 26, Overnight received $600 from Ace Towing as partial settlement of its account receivable from Ace. This transaction caused an increase in Overnight's cash but a decrease of the same amount in accounts receivable. This transaction converts one asset into another of equal value; there is no change in the

[2] Sales of assets at prices above or below cost result in gains or losses. Such transactions are discussed in later chapters.

amount of total assets. After this transaction, Overnight's financial position is summarized in Exhibit 2–7.

OVERNIGHT AUTO SERVICE
BALANCE SHEET
JANUARY 26, 2011

Assets		Liabilities & Owners' Equity	
Cash	$ 22,600	Liabilities:	
Accounts Receivable	1,200	Notes Payable	$ 30,000
Land	52,000	Accounts Payable	13,800
Building	36,000	Total liabilities	$ 43,800
Tools and Equipment	12,000	Owners' equity:	
		Capital Stock	80,000
Total	$123,800	Total	$123,800

Exhibit 2–7

BALANCE SHEET, JAN. 26

Totals unchanged by collection of a receivable

Payment of a Liability On January 27, Overnight made a partial payment of $6,800 on its account payable to Snappy Tools. This transaction reduced Overnight's cash and accounts payable by the same amount, leaving total assets and the total of liabilities plus owners' equity in balance. Overnight's balance sheet at January 27 appears in Exhibit 2–8.

OVERNIGHT AUTO SERVICE
BALANCE SHEET
JANUARY 27, 2011

Assets		Liabilities & Owners' Equity	
Cash	$ 15,800	Liabilities:	
Accounts Receivable	1,200	Notes Payable	$ 30,000
Land	52,000	Accounts Payable	7,000
Building	36,000	Total liabilities	$ 37,000
Tools and Equipment	12,000	Owners' equity:	
		Capital Stock	80,000
Total	$117,000	Total	$117,000

Exhibit 2–8

BALANCE SHEET, JAN. 27

Both totals decreased by paying a liability

Earning of Revenue By the last week in January, McBryan had acquired the assets Overnight needed to start operating, and he began to provide repair services for customers. Rather than recording each individual sale of repair services, he decided to accumulate them and record them at the end of the month. Sales of repair services for the last week of January were $2,200, all of which was received in cash.

Earning of revenue represents the creation of value by Overnight. It also represents an increase in the financial interest of the owners in the company. As a result, cash is increased by $2,200 and owners' equity is increased by the same amount. To distinguish owners' equity that is earned from that which was originally invested by the owners, the account *Retained Earnings* is used in the owners' equity section of the balance sheet. The balance sheet in Exhibit 2–9, as of January 31, reflects the increase in assets (cash) and owners' equity (retained earnings) from the revenue earned and received in cash during the last week of January, but before the payment of expenses (see next section).

Exhibit 2–9

BALANCE SHEET, JAN. 31

Revenues increase assets and owners' equity

OVERNIGHT AUTO SERVICE BALANCE SHEET JANUARY 31, 2011				
Assets		**Liabilities & Owners' Equity**		
Cash	$ 18,000	Liabilities:		
Accounts Receivable	1,200	Notes Payable	$ 30,000	
Land	52,000	Accounts Payable	7,000	
Building	36,000	Total liabilities		$ 37,000
Tools and Equipment	12,000	Owners' equity:		
		Capital Stock	$ 80,000	
		Retained Earnings	2,200	$ 82,200
Total	$119,200	Total		$119,200

Learning Objective

LO4 Explain how the statement of financial position, often referred to as the balance sheet, is an expansion of the basic accounting equation.

Payment of Expenses In order to earn the $2,200 of revenue that we have just recorded, Overnight had to pay some operating expenses, namely utilities and wages. McBryan decided to pay all operating expenses at the end of the month. For January, he owed $200 for utilities and $1,200 for wages to his employees, a total of $1,400, which he paid on January 31. Paying expenses has an opposite effect from revenues on the owners' interest in the company—their investment is reduced. Of course, paying expenses also results in a decrease of cash. The January 31 balance sheet, after the payment of utilities and wages, is presented in Exhibit 2–10.

Exhibit 2–10

BALANCE SHEET, JAN. 31

Expenses reduce assets and owners' equity

OVERNIGHT AUTO SERVICE BALANCE SHEET JANUARY 31, 2011				
Assets		**Liabilities & Owners' Equity**		
Cash	$ 16,600	Liabilities:		
Accounts Receivable	1,200	Notes Payable	$ 30,000	
Land	52,000	Accounts Payable	7,000	
Building	36,000	Total liabilities		$ 37,000
Tools and Equipment	12,000	Owners' equity:		
		Capital Stock	$ 80,000	
		Retained Earnings	800	80,800
Total	$117,800	Total		$117,800

Notice that the expenses of $1,400 ($200 for utilities and $1,200 for wages) reduce the amount of retained earnings in the balance sheet. That balance was formerly $2,200, representing the revenues for the last week of January. It is now $800, representing the difference between the revenues for the last week of January and the $1,400 of expenses that Overnight incurred during the same period of time. From this illustration we can see that revenues enhance or increase the financial interest of owners while expenses diminish or reduce the interest of owners. In a corporation, the net effect of this activity is reflected in the balance sheet as retained earnings.

EFFECTS OF THESE BUSINESS TRANSACTIONS ON THE ACCOUNTING EQUATION

As we learned earlier, the statement of financial position, or balance sheet, is a detailed expression of the accounting equation:

Assets = Liabilities + Owners' Equity

As we have progressed through a series of business transactions, we have illustrated the effects of Overnight's January transactions on the balance sheet.

To review, Overnight's transactions during January were as follows, with the resulting balance sheet indicated in parentheses:

Jan. 20 Michael McBryan started the business by depositing $80,000 received from the sale of capital stock in a company bank account (Exhibit 2–2).

Jan. 21 Purchased land for $52,000, paying cash (Exhibit 2–3).

Jan. 22 Purchased a building for $36,000, paying $6,000 in cash and issuing a note payable for the remaining $30,000 (Exhibit 2–4).

Jan. 23 Purchased tools and equipment on account, $13,800 (Exhibit 2–5).

Jan. 24 Sold some of the tools at a price equal to their cost, $1,800, collectible within 45 days (Exhibit 2–6).

Jan. 26 Received $600 in partial collection of the account receivable from the sale of tools (Exhibit 2–7).

Jan. 27 Paid $6,800 in partial payment of an account payable (Exhibit 2–8).

Jan. 31 Received $2,200 of sales revenue in cash (Exhibit 2–9).

Jan. 31 Paid $1,400 of operating expenses in cash—$200 for utilities and $1,200 for wages (Exhibit 2–10).

The expanded accounting equation in Exhibit 2–11 shows the effects of these transactions on the accounting equation. The effect of each transaction is shown in red. Notice that the "balances," shown in black, are the amounts appearing in Overnight's balance sheets in Exhibits 2–2 through 2–10. Notice also that the accounting equation is in balance after each transaction.

While this table represents the impact of Overnight's transactions on the accounting equation, and thus on its financial position as shown in its balance sheet, we can now see how the income statement and statement of cash flows enter the picture. Specifically, the income statement is a separate financial statement that shows how the statement of financial position changed as a result of its revenue and expense transactions. The statement of cash flows shows how the company's cash increased and decreased during the period.

Multiple transactions significantly change the enterprise's financial position

Income Statement

Learning Objective LO5
Explain how the income statement reports an enterprise's financial performance for a period of time in terms of the relationship of revenues and expenses.

The income statement is a summarization of the company's revenue and expense transactions for a period of time. It is particularly important for the company's owners, creditors, and other interested parties to understand the income statement. Ultimately the company will succeed or fail based on its ability to earn revenues in excess of its expenses. Once the company's assets are acquired and business commences, revenues and expenses are important dimensions of the company's operations. **Revenues** are increases in the company's assets from its profit-directed activities, and they result in positive cash flows. **Expenses** are decreases in the company's assets from its profit-directed activities, and they result in negative cash flows. *Net income* is the difference between the revenues and expenses for a specified period of time. Should a company find itself in the undesirable situation of having expenses greater than revenues, we call the difference a *net loss.*

Overnight's income statement for January 20–31 is relatively simple because the company did not have a large number of complex revenue and expense transactions.[3] Taking information directly from the Retained Earnings column in Exhibit 2–11, and separating the total

[3] In this illustration, only revenue and expense transactions change the amount of owners' equity from the original $80,000 investment of the owner. Examples of other events and transactions that affect the amount of owners' equity, but that are *not included in net income,* are the sale of additional shares of capital stock and the payment of dividends to shareholders. These subjects are covered in later chapters.

Exhibit 2–11 EXPANDED ACCOUNTING EQUATION

OVERNIGHT AUTO SERVICE
EXPANDED ACCOUNTING EQUATION
JANUARY 20–31, 2011

	Assets					Liabilities		Owners' Equity	
	Cash	Accounts Receivable	Land	Building	Tools and Equipment	Notes Payable	Accounts Payable	Capital Stock	Retained Earnings
Jan. 20	$80,000							$80,000	
Balances	$80,000							$80,000	
Jan. 21	−52,000		+$52,000						
Balances	$28,000		$52,000					$80,000	
Jan. 22	−6,000			+$36,000		+$30,000			
Balances	$22,000		$52,000	$36,000		$30,000		$80,000	
Jan. 23					+$13,800		+$13,800		
Balances	$22,000		$52,000	$36,000	$13,800	$30,000	$13,800	$80,000	
Jan. 24		+$1,800			−1,800				
Balances	$22,000	$1,800	$52,000	$36,000	$12,000	$30,000	$13,800	$80,000	
Jan. 26	+600	−600							
Balances	$22,600	$1,200	$52,000	$36,000	$12,000	$30,000	$13,800	$80,000	
Jan. 27	−6,800						−6,800		
Balances	$15,800	$1,200	$52,000	$36,000	$12,000	$30,000	$7,000	$80,000	
Jan. 31	+2,200								+$2,200
Jan. 31	−1,400								−1,400
Balances	$16,600	$1,200	$52,000	$36,000	$12,000	$30,000	$7,000	$80,000	$ 800

Statement of Cash Flows

Income Statement

expenses of $1,400 into wages of $1,200 and utilities of $200, we can prepare the company's income statement as shown in Exhibit 2–12.

Exhibit 2–12

INCOME STATEMENT

OVERNIGHT AUTO SERVICE INCOME STATEMENT FOR THE PERIOD JANUARY 20–31, 2011		
Sales Revenues		$2,200
Operating expenses:		
Wages	$1,200	
Utilities	200	1,400
Net Income		$ 800

An income statement displays revenues and expenses for a period of time

Notice that the heading for the income statement refers to a *period* of time rather than a *point* in time, as was the case with the balance sheet. The income statement reports on the financial performance of the company in terms of earning revenue and incurring expenses *over a period of time* and explains, in part, how the company's financial position changed between the beginning and ending of that period.

Statement of Cash Flows

Learning Objective LO6
Explain how the statement of cash flows presents the change in cash for a period of time in terms of the company's operating, investing, and financing activities.

We already have established the importance of cash flows to investors and creditors and that the cash flows of the company are an important consideration in investors' and creditors' assessments of cash flows to them. As a result, a second set of information that is particularly important concerning how a company's financial position changed between two points in time is cash flow information.

We can use the entire Cash column of the analysis in Exhibit 2–11 to create a statement of cash flows for Overnight Auto Service. The statement classifies the various cash flows into three categories—operating, investing, and financing—and relates these categories to the beginning and ending cash balances. Cash flows from **operating activities** are the cash effects of revenue and expense transactions that are included in the income statement.[4] Cash flows from **investing activities** are the cash effects of purchasing and selling assets. Cash flows from **financing activities** are the cash effects of the owners investing in the company and creditors loaning money to the company and the repayment of either or both.

The statement of cash flows for Overnight Auto Service for the period January 20–31 is presented in Exhibit 2–13.

Notice that the operating, investing, and financing categories include both positive and negative cash flows. (The negative cash flows are in parentheses.) Also notice that the combined total of the three categories of the statement (increase of $16,600) explains the total change in cash from the beginning to the end of the period. On January 20, the beginning balance was zero because the company was started on that day. Several transactions and parts of transactions had no cash effects and, therefore, are not included in the statement of cash flows. For example, on January 22, Overnight purchased a building for $36,000, only $6,000 of which was paid in cash. The remaining $30,000 is not included in the statement of cash flows because it did not affect the amount of cash. Similarly, on January 23, Overnight purchased tools and equipment for $13,800, paying no cash at that time. That transaction has no

[4] In this illustration, net cash amounts provided by operating activities and net income are equal. This is because all of Overnight Auto Service's revenues and expenses were cash transactions. This will not always be the case. As we learn more about the accrual method of accounting, you will see that revenues and expenses may be recorded in a different accounting period than the period when cash is received or paid. This will cause net income and net cash from operating activities to be different amounts.

Exhibit 2–13
STATEMENT OF CASH FLOWS

OVERNIGHT AUTO SERVICE STATEMENT OF CASH FLOWS FOR THE PERIOD JANUARY 20–31, 2011		
Cash flows from operating activities:		
Cash received from revenue transactions	$ 2,200	
Cash paid for expenses	(1,400)	
Net cash provided by operating activities		$ 800
Cash flows from investing activities:		
Purchase of land	$(52,000)	
Purchase of building	(6,000)	
Purchase of tools	(6,800)	
Sale of tools	600	
Net cash used by investing activities		(64,200)
Cash flows from financing activities:		
Sale of capital stock		80,000
Increase in cash for the period		$16,600
Beginning cash balance, January 20, 2011		-0-
Ending cash balance, January 31, 2011		$16,600

A statement of cash flows shows how cash changed during the period

CASE IN POINT

It is not unusual for a company to report an increase in cash from operating activities, but a decrease in the total amount of cash. This outcome results from decreases in cash from investing and/or financing activities. For example, one year **Carnival Corporation**, which owns and operates cruise lines, reported cash *provided by* operating activities of almost $1.1 billion but a *decrease* in total cash of almost $3 million. This was due primarily to large expenditures for property and equipment, such as cruise ships, which are presented as investing activities in the company's statement of cash flows.

cash effect on January 23, although the cash payment of $6,800 on January 27, which is a continuation of that transaction, did affect cash and is included in the statement of cash flows. Transactions that did not affect cash are called *noncash investing and financing transactions.* In a formal statement of cash flows, these transactions are required to be noted as we explain later in this text, even though they do not affect the actual flow of cash into and out of the company.

Relationships among Financial Statements

Learning Objective
LO7 Explain how the statement of financial position (balance sheet), income statement, and statement of cash flows relate to each other.

As our discussion of Overnight Auto Service indicates, the statement of financial position (balance sheet), the income statement, and the statement of cash flows are all based on the same transactions, but they present different "views" of the company. They should not be thought of as alternatives to each other; rather, all are important in terms of presenting key financial information about the company.

The diagram in Exhibit 2–14 explains how the three financial statements relate to the period of time they cover. The horizontal line represents time (for example, a month or a year). At the beginning and ending points in time, the company prepares a statement of financial position (balance sheet) that gives a static look in financial terms of where the company stands. The other two financial statements—the income statement and the statement of cash flows—cover the intervening *period of time* between the two balance sheets and help explain important changes that occurred during the period.

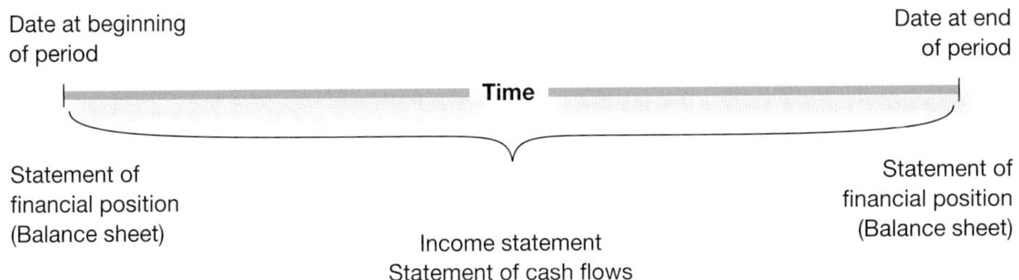

Exhibit 2–14

FINANCIAL REPORTING TIME LINE

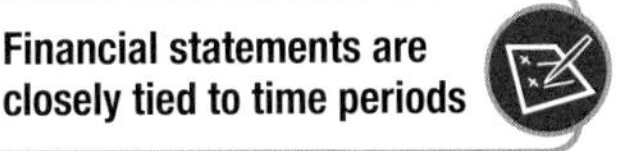

Financial statements are closely tied to time periods

If we understand where a company stands financially at two points in time, and if we understand the changes that occurred during the intervening period in terms of the company's profit-seeking activities (income statement) and its cash activities (statement of cash flows), we know a great deal about the company that is valuable in assessing its future cash flows—information that is useful to investors, creditors, management, and others.

Because the balance sheet, income statement, and statement of cash flows are derived from the same underlying financial information, they are said to "articulate," meaning that they relate closely to each other. The diagram in Exhibit 2–15 indicates relationships that we have discussed in this chapter as we have introduced these three important financial statements. The dollar amounts are taken from the Overnight Auto Service example presented earlier in this chapter. In the balance sheet, the property, plant, and equipment amount of $100,000 represents the total of land ($52,000), building ($36,000), and tools and equipment ($12,000).

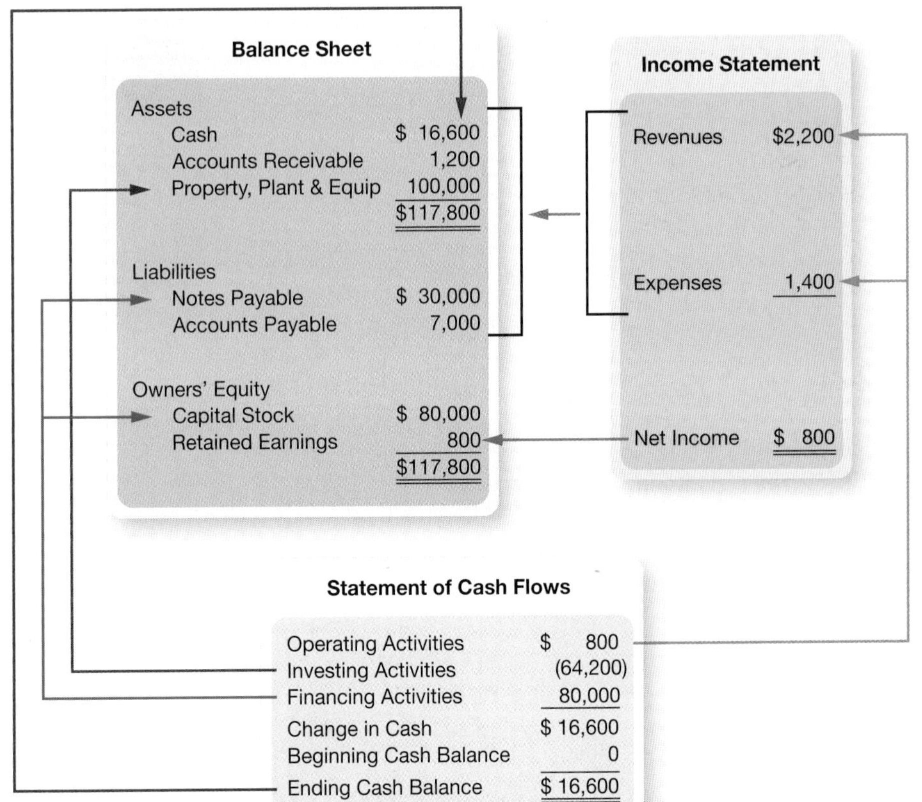

Exhibit 2–15

FINANCIAL STATEMENT ARTICULATION

Financial statements are based on the same underlying transactions

The balance sheet represents an expansion of the accounting equation and explains the various categories of assets, liabilities, and owners' equity. The income statement explains changes in financial position that result from profit-generating transactions in terms of revenue and expense transactions. The resulting number, net income, represents an addition to the owners' equity in the enterprise. The statement of cash flows explains the ways cash increased and decreased during the period in terms of the enterprise's operating, investing, and financing activities.

While these three key financial statements present important information, they do not include all possible information that might be presented about a company. For example, look again at Overnight's activities during the latter part of January. We could have prepared a separate financial statement on how liabilities changed or how the Tools and Equipment asset account changed. There is also important nonfinancial information that underlies the statement of financial position, the income statement, and the statement of cash flows that could be presented and that would benefit users of the statements. Accountants have developed methods of dealing with these other types of information, which we will learn about later in this text. At this point, we have focused our attention on the three primary financial statements that companies most often use to describe the activities that are capable of being captured in financial terms.

Financial reporting, and financial statements in particular, can be thought of as a lens through which you can view a business. (See Exhibit 2–16 .) A lens allows you to see things from a distance that you would not otherwise be able to see; it also allows you to focus in greater detail on certain aspects of what you are looking at. Financial information, and particularly financial statements, allows you to do just that—focus in on certain financial aspects of the enterprise that are of particular interest to you in making important investing and credit decisions. Financial reporting encompasses financial statements, but it is not limited to financial statements.

Exhibit 2–16

FINANCIAL REPORTING AND FINANCIAL STATEMENTS

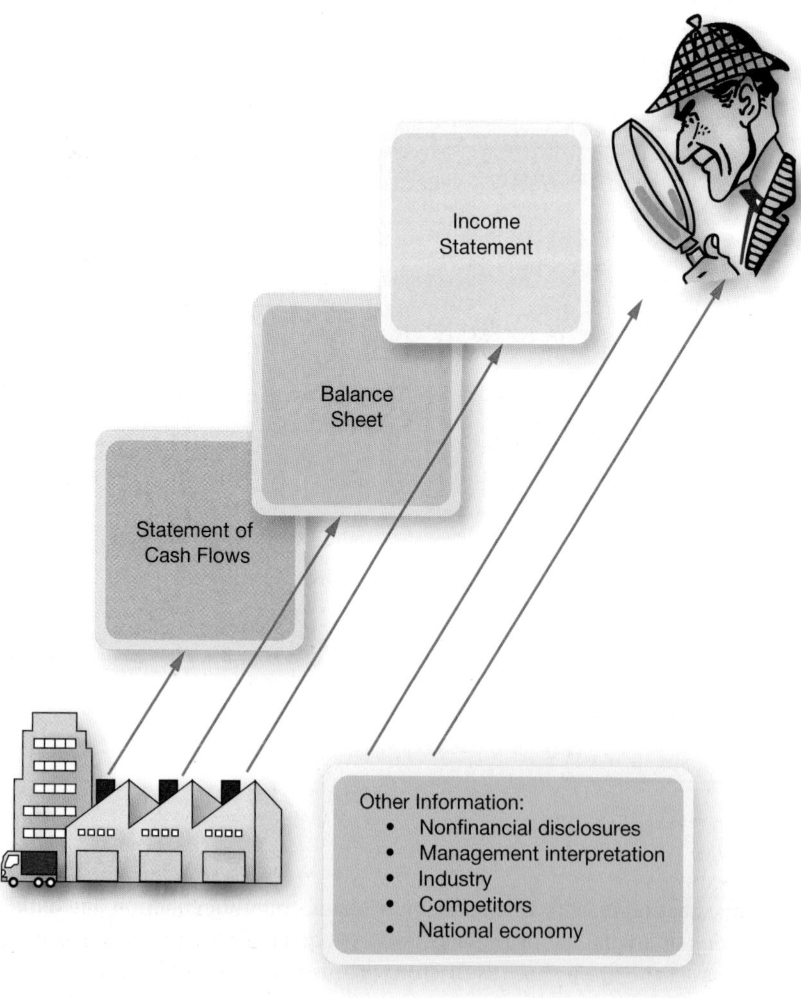

Financial Analysis and Decision Making

Relationships among the three primary financial statements provide the opportunity to learn a great deal about a company by bringing information together in a meaningful way. In fact, some people believe that relationships in the financial statements are as important as the actual dollar figures in those statements.

For example, take another look at the balance sheet in Exhibit 2–10. Notice that the company has $16,600 of cash and $1,200 of accounts receivable, a total of $17,800 in what are sometimes referred to as *current* assets, denoting that they either are cash or will soon become cash. Now look at the liabilities in the balance sheet and notice that the company has notes payable of $30,000 and accounts payable of $7,000 for a total of $37,000 of liabilities. If both types of liabilities are current liabilities, meaning that they will be due in the near future and, therefore, can be expected to require the use of current assets, Overnight Auto Service may have difficulty paying them because it does not have enough liquid assets to cover its liabilities. The relationship of current assets to current liabilities is called the *current ratio.* For Overnight Auto Service it is a low .48 ($17,800 divided by $37,000). This means that Overnight Auto Service has only 48 cents available for every $1 of liabilities that will come due in the near future. On the other hand, if the $30,000 notes payable resulting from the building purchase is not due in the near future, the company's liquidity is much stronger and the company may have sufficient time to bring in enough cash through its operations to pay the note when it is due.

While the above refers exclusively to information found in the balance sheet, key information from one financial statement often is combined with information from another financial statement. For example, we may be interested in knowing the amount of cash provided by operations (cash flow statement) relative to the amount of a company's currently maturing liabilities (balance sheet). Or we might want to compare a company's net income (income statement) with the investment in assets (balance sheet) that were used to generate that income.

Many of the chapters in this text introduce you to various types of financial analysis. We build on those introductory discussions in Chapter 14, Financial Statement Analysis, in which we provide a comprehensive treatment of how financial statements are used to inform investors and creditors.

YOUR TURN **You as a Creditor**

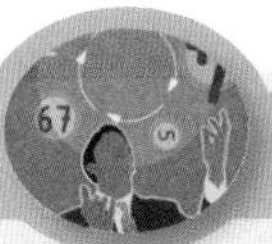

Assume that you are a financial analyst for a potential supplier to Overnight Auto Service. Overnight wants to buy goods from your company on credit. What factors might you consider in deciding whether to extend credit to Overnight?

(See our comments on the Online Learning Center Web site.)

Forms of Business Organization

Learning Objective LO8
Explain common forms of business ownership—sole proprietorship, partnership, and corporation—and demonstrate how they differ in terms of their presentation in the statement of financial position.

In the United States, most business enterprises are organized as *sole proprietorships, partnerships,* or *corporations.* Generally accepted accounting principles can be applied to the financial statements of all three forms of organization.

SOLE PROPRIETORSHIPS

An unincorporated business owned by one person is called a **sole proprietorship.** Often the owner also acts as the manager. This form of business organization is common for small retail stores, farms, service businesses, and professional practices in law, medicine, and accounting. In fact, the sole proprietorship is the most common form of business organization in our economy.

From an accounting viewpoint, a sole proprietorship is regarded as a business entity *separate from the other financial activities of its owner.* From a legal viewpoint, however, the business and its owner are not regarded as separate entities. Thus, *the owner is personally liable* for the debts of the business. If the business encounters financial difficulties, creditors can force the owner to sell his or her personal assets to pay the business debts. While an advantage of the sole proprietorship form of organization is its simplicity, this *unlimited liability* feature is a disadvantage to the owner.

PARTNERSHIPS

An unincorporated business owned by two or more persons voluntarily acting as partners (co-owners) is called a **partnership.** Partnerships, like sole proprietorships, are widely used for small businesses. In addition, some large professional practices, including CPA firms and law firms, are organized as partnerships. As in the case of the sole proprietorship, the owners of a partnership are personally responsible for all debts of the business. From an accounting standpoint, a partnership is viewed as a business entity separate from the personal affairs of its owners.[5] A benefit of the partnership form over the sole proprietorship form is the ability to bring together larger amounts of capital investment from multiple owners.

CORPORATIONS

A **corporation** is a type of business organization that is recognized *under the law* as an entity separate from its owners. Therefore, the owners of a corporation are *not* personally liable for the debts of the business. These owners can lose no more than the amounts they have invested in the business—a concept known as *limited liability.* This concept is one of the principal reasons that corporations are an attractive form of business organization to many investors. Overnight Auto Service, the company used in our illustrations, is a corporation.

Ownership of a corporation is divided into transferable shares of capital stock, and the owners are called **stockholders** or shareholders. Stock certificates are issued by the corporation to each stockholder showing the number of shares that he or she owns. The stockholders are generally free to sell some or all of these shares to other investors at any time. This *transferability of ownership* adds to the attractiveness of the corporate form of organization, because investors can more easily get their money out of the business. Corporations offer an even greater opportunity than partnerships to bring together large amounts of capital from multiple owners.

There are many more sole proprietorships and partnerships than corporations, but most large businesses are organized as corporations. Thus, corporations are the dominant form of business organization in terms of the *dollar volume* of business activity. Of the three types of business, corporations are most likely to distribute financial statements to investors and other outsiders.

REPORTING OWNERSHIP EQUITY IN THE STATEMENT OF FINANCIAL POSITION

Assets and liabilities are presented in the same manner in the statement of financial position of all three types of business organization. Some differences arise, however, in the presentation of the ownership equity.

Sole Proprietorships

A *sole proprietorship* is owned by only one person. Therefore, the owner's equity section of the balance sheet includes only one item—the equity of the owner. If Overnight Auto Service had been organized as a sole proprietorship with Michael McBryan the owner, owner's equity in the January 31 balance sheet would appear as follows:

Ownership equity in a sole proprietorship

Owner's equity:	
Michael McBryan, Capital	$80,800

Partnerships

A *partnership* has two or more owners. Accountants use the term *partners' equity* instead of owners' equity and usually list separately the amount of each partner's equity in the business. If, for example, Michael McBryan had been in partnership with his

[5] Creditors of an unincorporated business often ask to see the *personal* financial statements of the business owners, as these owners ultimately are responsible for paying the debts of the business.

sister, Rebecca McBryan, in Overnight Auto Service, and if each had contributed an equal amount of cash ($40,000) and had shared equally in the net income ($400), the partners' equity section of the balance sheet would have been presented as follows:

. . . in a partnership

Partners' equity:		
Michael McBryan, Capital	$40,400	
Rebecca McBryan, Capital	40,400	
Total partners' equity.		$80,800

Corporations

In a business organized as a *corporation,* it is *not* customary to show separately the equity of each stockholder. In the case of large corporations, this clearly would be impractical because these businesses may have *several million* individual stockholders (owners).

We return to our original assumption that Overnight Auto Service is organized as a corporation. Owners' equity (also referred to as **stockholders' equity** or shareholders' equity) is presented in two amounts—capital stock and retained earnings. This section of the balance sheet appears as follows:

. . . and in a corporation

Owners' equity:		
Capital Stock	$80,000	
Retained Earnings	800	
Total stockholders' equity		$80,800

Capital stock represents the amount that the stockholders originally invested in the business in exchange for shares of the company's stock. **Retained earnings,** in contrast, represents the increase in owners' equity that has accumulated over the years as a result of profitable operations.

The Use of Financial Statements by External Parties

As we learned in Chapter 1, investors and creditors use financial statements in making *financial decisions*—that is, in selecting those companies in which they will invest resources or to which they will extend credit. For this reason, financial statements are designed primarily to meet the needs of creditors and investors. Two factors of particular concern to creditors and investors are the *liquidity* and *profitability* of a business organization.

Creditors are interested in **liquidity**—the ability of the business to pay its debts as they come due. Liquidity is critical to the very survival of a business organization—a business that is not liquid may be forced into bankruptcy by its creditors. Once bankrupt, a business may be forced by the courts to stop its operations, sell its assets (for the purpose of paying its creditors), and eventually go out of existence.

Investors also are interested in the liquidity of a business organization, but often they are even more interested in its profitability. *Profitable operations increase the value of the owners' equity* in the business. A company that continually operates unprofitably will eventually exhaust its resources and be forced out of existence. Therefore, most users of financial statements study these statements carefully for clues to the company's liquidity and future profitability.

The Short Run versus the Long Run

In the short run, liquidity and profitability may be independent of each other. A business may be operating profitably but nevertheless run out of cash needed to meet its obligations. On the other hand, a company may operate unprofitably during a given year yet still have enough cash from previous periods to pay its bills and remain liquid.

Over a longer term, however, liquidity and profitability go hand in hand. If a business is to survive, it must remain liquid and, in the long run, must operate profitably.

Evaluating Short-Term Liquidity As discussed earlier in this chapter, one key indicator of short-term liquidity is the relationship between an entity's *liquid* assets and the liabilities requiring payment *in the near future.* By studying the nature of a company's assets, and the amounts and due dates of its liabilities, users of financial statements often may anticipate whether the company is likely to have difficulty in meeting its upcoming obligations. This simple type of analysis meets the needs of many *short-term* creditors. Evaluating long-term debt-paying ability is a more difficult matter and is discussed in later chapters.

In studying financial statements, users should *always* read the accompanying notes and the auditors' report.

THE NEED FOR ADEQUATE DISCLOSURE

The concept of adequate **disclosure** is an important generally accepted accounting principle. Adequate disclosure means that users of financial statements are informed of all information *necessary for the proper interpretation* of the statements. Adequate disclosure is made in the body of the financial statements and in *notes* accompanying these statements. It is not unusual to find a series of notes to financial statements that are longer than the statements themselves.

Among the events that may require disclosure in notes to the financial statements are occurrences after the date of the financial statements. For example, assume that Overnight Auto Service's building is destroyed by fire on February 2, and that Michael McBryan is using the financial statements to acquire additional financing for the business after that date. Assume also that McBryan has less insurance on the building than will be needed to replace it. Users of the financial statements, such as bankers who might be considering lending money to Overnight, must be informed of this important "subsequent event." This disclosure usually would be done with a note like the following:

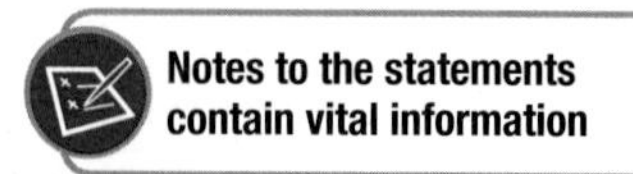
Notes to the statements contain vital information

Note 7: Events occurring after the financial statement date
On February 2, 2011, the building included in the January 31 statement of financial position at $36,000 was destroyed by fire. While the company has insurance on this facility, management expects to recover only approximately $30,000 of the loss.

In addition to important subsequent events, many other situations may require disclosure in notes to the financial statements. Examples include unsettled lawsuits against the company, due dates of major liabilities, assets pledged as collateral to secure loans, amounts receivable from officers or other "insiders," and contractual commitments requiring large future cash outlays.

There is no single comprehensive list of the items and events that may require disclosure. As a general rule, a company should disclose all financial information that a reasonably informed person would consider *necessary for the proper interpretation* of the financial statements. Events that clearly are unimportant *do not* require disclosure. Determining information that should be disclosed in financial statements is another situation that requires significant judgment on the part of the accountant.

MANAGEMENT'S INTEREST IN FINANCIAL STATEMENTS

Learning Objective
LO9 **Discuss the importance of financial statements to a company and its investors and creditors and why management may take steps to improve the appearance of the company in its financial statements.**

While we have emphasized the importance of financial statements to investors and creditors, the management of a business organization is vitally concerned with the financial position of the business and with its profitability and cash flows. Therefore, management is anxious to receive financial statements as frequently and as quickly as possible so that it may take action to improve areas of weak performance. Most large organizations provide managers with financial statements on at least a monthly basis. With modern technology, financial statements prepared on a weekly, daily, or even hourly basis are possible.

Managers have a special interest in the *annual* financial statements, because these statements are used by decision makers outside of the organization. For example, if creditors view the annual financial statements as strong, they will be more willing to extend credit to the business than if they regard the company's financial statements as weak. Management is concerned with its ability to obtain the funds it needs to meet its objectives, so it is particularly interested in how investors and creditors react to the company's financial statements.

A strong statement of financial position is one that shows relatively little debt and large amounts of liquid assets relative to the liabilities due in the near future. A strong income statement is one that shows large revenues relative to the expenses required to earn the revenues. A strong statement of cash flows is one that not only shows a strong cash balance but also indicates that cash is being generated by operations. Demonstrating that these positive characteristics of the company are ongoing and can be seen in a series of financial statements is particularly helpful in creating confidence in the company on the part of investors and creditors. Because of the importance of the financial statements, management may take steps that are specifically intended to improve the company's financial position and financial performance. For example, cash purchases of assets may be delayed until the beginning of the next accounting period so that large amounts of cash will be included in the statement of financial position and the statement of cash flows. On the other hand, if the company is in a particularly strong cash position, liabilities due in the near future may be paid early, replaced with longer-term liabilities, or even replaced by additional investments by owners to communicate that future negative cash flows will not be as great as they might otherwise appear.

These actions are sometimes called **window dressing**—measures taken by management to make the company appear as strong as possible in its financial statements. Users of financial statements should realize that, while the financial statements are fair representations of the financial position at the end of the period and financial performance during the period, they may not necessarily describe the typical financial situation of the business throughout the entire financial reporting period. In its annual financial statements, in particular, management tries to make the company appear as strong as is reasonably possible. As a result, many creditors regard more frequent financial statements (for example, quarterly or even monthly) as providing important additional information beyond that in the annual financial statements. The more frequently financial statements are presented, the less able management is to window-dress and make a company look financially stronger than it actually is.

Ethics, Fraud & Corporate Governance

A major outgrowth from the business failures amid allegations of fraudulent financial reporting discussed in the last chapter was the passage of the Sarbanes-Oxley Act of 2002. This Act was signed into law by President George W. Bush on July 30, 2002. The Sarbanes-Oxley Act (hereafter SOX or the Act) is generally viewed as the most far-reaching piece of securities legislation since the original Securities Acts were passed in the 1930s.

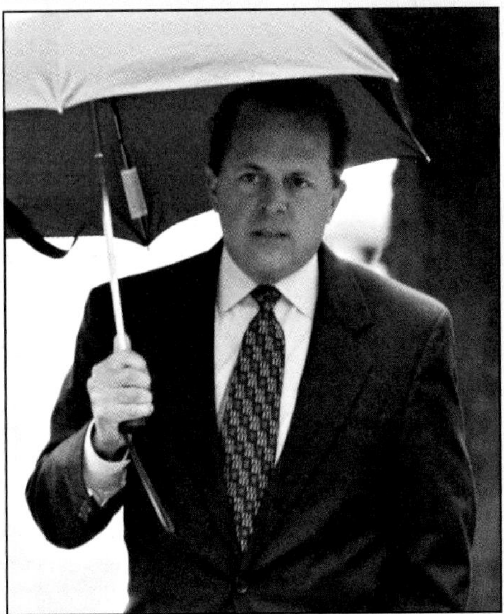

© Gary Tramontinal/Bloomberg via Getty Images

One of the major requirements of this legislation is for CEOs and CFOs to certify the accuracy of their company's financial statements. The CEOs and CFOs of all public companies must certify on an annual and quarterly basis that they (1) have reviewed their company's financial statements, (2) are not aware of any error or omission that would make the financial statements misleading, and (3) believe that the financial statements fairly present in all material respects the company's financial condition (balance sheet) and results of operations (income statement). There is some evidence that this certification requirement is affecting corporate behavior. For example, a former CFO of **HealthSouth** (Weston Smith, shown to the right) contacted federal authorities about the massive (alleged) accounting fraud at that company because he was not willing to certify that **HealthSouth**'s financial statements were materially accurate.

Concluding Remarks

Throughout this text, we emphasize how accounting information is the basis for business decisions. In this chapter, you have been introduced to business transactions and how they are combined and presented in the form of three basic financial statements—the statement of financial position (balance sheet), the income statement, and the statement of cash flows. These financial statements constitute some of the primary products of the accountant's work, and they provide investors, creditors, and other parties with pertinent information that is useful for decision making.

As you continue your study of financial accounting, in Chapter 3 you will learn how business transactions are actually recorded, how they move through an accounting system, and how they eventually lead to the preparation of financial statements. The foundation you have received in Chapter 2 will be helpful to you as we move into a more sophisticated discussion of business transactions and how they impact a company's financial position, results of operations, and cash flows.

END-OF-CHAPTER REVIEW

SUMMARY OF LEARNING OBJECTIVES

LO1 **Explain the nature and general purpose of financial statements.** Financial statements are presentations of information in financial terms about an enterprise that are believed to be fair and accurate. They describe certain attributes of the enterprise that are important for decision makers, particularly investors (owners) and creditors.

LO2 **Explain certain accounting principles that are important for an understanding of financial statements and how professional judgment by accountants may affect the application of those principles.** Accountants prepare financial statements by applying a set of standards or rules referred to as generally accepted accounting principles. Consistent application of these standards permits comparisons between companies and between years of a single company. Generally accepted accounting principles allow for significant latitude in how certain transactions should be accounted for, meaning that professional judgment is particularly important.

LO3 **Demonstrate how certain business transactions affect the elements of the accounting equation: Assets = Liabilities + Owners' Equity.** Business transactions result in changes in the three elements of the basic accounting equation. A transaction that increases total assets must also increase total liabilities and owners' equity. Similarly, a transaction that decreases total assets must simultaneously decrease total liabilities and owners' equity. Some transactions increase one asset and reduce another. Regardless of the nature of the specific transaction, the accounting equation must stay in balance at all times.

LO4 **Explain how the statement of financial position, often referred to as the balance sheet, is an expansion of the basic accounting equation.** The statement of financial position, or balance sheet, presents in detail the elements of the basic accounting equation. Various types of assets are listed and totaled. The enterprise's liabilities are listed, totaled, and added to the owners' equity. The balancing feature of this financial statement is one of its dominant characteristics because the statement is simply an expansion of the basic accounting equation.

LO5 **Explain how the income statement reports an enterprise's financial performance for a period of time in terms of the relationship of revenues and expenses.** Revenues are created as the enterprise provides goods and services for its customers. Many expenses are required to be able to provide those goods and services. The difference between the revenues and expenses is net income or net loss.

LO6 **Explain how the statement of cash flows presents the change in cash for a period of time in terms of the company's operating, investing, and financing activities.** Cash is one of the most important assets, and the statement of cash flows shows in detail how the enterprise's cash balance changed between the beginning and end of the accounting period. Operating activities relate to ongoing revenue and expense transactions. Investing activities relate to the purchase and sale of various types of assets (for example, land, buildings, and equipment). Financing activities describe where the enterprise has received its debt and equity financing. The statement of cash flows combines information about all of these activities into a concise statement of changes in cash that reconciles the beginning and ending cash balances.

LO7 **Explain how the statement of financial position (balance sheet), income statement, and statement of cash flows relate to each other.** The three primary financial statements are based on the same underlying transactions. They are not alternatives to each other, but rather represent three different ways of looking at the financial activities of the reporting enterprise. Because they are based on the same transactions, they "articulate" with each other.

LO8 **Explain common forms of business ownership—sole proprietorship, partnership, and corporation—and demonstrate how they differ in terms of their presentation in the statement of financial position.** Owners' equity is one of three major elements in the basic accounting equation. Regardless of the form of organization, owners' equity represents the interest of the owners in the assets of the reporting enterprise. For a sole proprietorship, owner's equity consists of the interest of a single owner. For a partnership, the ownership interests of all partners are added together to determine the total owners' equity of the enterprise. For a corporation, which may have many owners, the total contribution to the enterprise represents its owners' equity. In all cases, the enterprise's net income is added to owners' equity.

LO9 **Discuss the importance of financial statements to a company and its investors and creditors and why management may take steps to improve the appearance of the company in its financial statements.** Financial statements are particularly important for investors and creditors in their attempts to evaluate future cash flows from the enterprise to them. Management is interested in the enterprise looking as positive as possible in its financial statements and may take certain steps to improve the overall appearance of the enterprise. A fine line, however, exists between the steps management can take and the steps that are unethical, or even illegal.

Key Terms Introduced or Emphasized in Chapter 2

accounting equation (p. 44) Assets are equal to the sum of liabilities plus owners' equity.

articulation (p. 39) The close relationship that exists among the financial statements that are prepared on the basis of the same underlying transaction information.

assets (p. 40) Economic resources owned by an entity.

balance sheet (p. 38) The financial statement showing the financial position of an enterprise by summarizing its assets, liabilities, and owners' equity at a point in time. Also called the statement of financial position.

business entity (p. 40) An economic unit that controls resources, incurs obligations, and engages in business activities.

capital stock (p. 57) Transferable units of ownership in a corporation.

corporation (p. 56) A business organized as a separate legal entity and chartered by a state, with ownership divided into transferable shares of capital stock.

cost principle (p. 41) The widely used principle of accounting for assets at their original cost to the current owner.

creditor (p. 42) A person or organization to whom debt is owed.

deflation (p. 42) A decline in the general price level, resulting in an increase in the purchasing power of the monetary unit.

disclosure (p. 58) The accounting principle of providing with financial statements any financial and other facts that are necessary for proper interpretation of those statements.

expenses (p. 49) Past, present, or future reductions in cash required to generate revenues.

financial statement (p. 38) A declaration of information believed to be true and communicated in monetary terms.

financing activities (p. 51) A category in the statement of cash flows that reflects the results of debt and equity financing transactions.

going-concern assumption (p. 41) An assumption by accountants that a business will operate in the foreseeable future unless specific evidence suggests that this is not a reasonable assumption.

income statement (p. 38) An activity statement that subtracts from the enterprise's revenue those expenses required to generate the revenues, resulting in a net income or a net loss.

inflation (p. 42) An increase in the general price level, resulting in a decline in the purchasing power of the monetary unit.

investing activities (p. 51) A category in the statement of cash flows that reflects the results of purchases and sales of assets, such as land, buildings, and equipment.

liabilities (p. 42) Debts or obligations of an entity that resulted from past transactions. They represent the claims of creditors on the enterprise's assets.

liquidity (p. 57) Having the financial ability to pay debts as they become due.

negative cash flows (p. 39) A payment of cash that reduces the enterprise's cash balance.

operating activities (p. 51) A category in the statement of cash flows that includes the cash effects of all revenues and expenses included in the income statement.

owners' equity (p. 43) The excess of assets over liabilities. The amount of the owners' investment in the business, plus profits from successful operations that have been retained in the business.

partnership (p. 56) An unincorporated form of business organization in which two or more persons voluntarily associate for purposes of carrying out business activities.

positive cash flows (p. 39) Increases in cash that add to the enterprise's cash balance.

retained earnings (p. 57) The portion of stockholders' equity that has accumulated as a result of profitable operations.

revenues (p. 49) Increases in the enterprise's assets as a result of profit-oriented activities.

sole proprietorship (p. 55) An unincorporated business owned by a single individual.

stable-dollar assumption (p. 42) An assumption by accountants that the monetary unit used in the preparation of financial statements is stable over time or changes at a sufficiently slow rate that the resulting impact on financial statements does not distort the information.

statement of cash flows (p. 39) An activity statement that explains the enterprise's change in cash in terms of its operating, investing, and financing activities.

statement of financial position (p. 38) Same as balance sheet.

stockholders (p. 56) Owners of capital stock in a corporation.

stockholders' equity (p. 57) The owners' equity of an enterprise organized as a corporation.

window dressing (p. 59) Measures taken by management specifically intended to make a business look as strong as possible in its balance sheet, income statement, and statement of cash flows.

Demonstration Problem

Account balances for Crystal Auto Wash at September 30, 2011, are shown below. The figure for retained earnings is not given, but it can be determined when all the available information is assembled in the form of a balance sheet.

Accounts Payable	$14,000	Land	$68,000
Accounts Receivable	800	Machinery & Equipment	65,000
Buildings	52,000	Notes Payable (due in 30 days)	29,000
Cash	9,200		
Capital Stock	100,000	Salaries Payable	3,000
Retained Earnings	?	Supplies	400

Instructions

a. Prepare a balance sheet at September 30, 2011.

b. Does this balance sheet indicate that the company is in a strong financial position? Explain briefly.

c. How would an income statement and a statement of cash flows allow you to better respond to part **b**?

Solution to the Demonstration Problem

a.

CRYSTAL AUTO WASH
BALANCE SHEET
SEPTEMBER 30, 2011

Assets		**Liabilities & Owners' Equity**	
Cash	$ 9,200	Liabilities:	
Accounts Receivable	800	Notes Payable	$ 29,000
Supplies	400	Accounts Payable	14,000
Land	68,000	Salaries Payable	3,000
Buildings	52,000	Total liabilities	$ 46,000
Machinery & Equipment	65,000	Owners' equity:	
		Capital Stock	$100,000
		*Retained Earnings	49,400
Total	$195,400	Total	$195,400

*Computed as $195,400 (total assets) − $46,000 (total liabilities) − $149,400 (owners' equity); $149,400 − $100,000 (capital stock) = $49,400.

b. The balance sheet indicates that Crystal Auto Wash is in a *weak* financial position. The only liquid assets—cash and receivables—total only $10,000, but the company has *$46,000* in liabilities due in the near future.

c. An income statement for Crystal Auto Wash would show the company's revenues and expenses for the period (month, quarter, or year) ending on the date of the balance sheet, September 30, 2011. This information would be helpful in determining whether the company is successful in selling its auto wash services at an amount that exceeds its cost of providing those services, something the company must do to remain in business and be successful. The statement of cash flows for the same period as the income statement would show where the company's cash came from and where it went in terms of its operating, investing, and financing activities. This information would be particularly helpful in assessing the strength of the company's ability to satisfy its obligations as they come due in light of the relatively weak balance sheet.

Self-Test Questions

The answers to these questions appear on page 82.

Note: In order to review as many chapter concepts as possible, some self-test questions include *more than one* correct answer. In these cases, you should indicate *all* of the correct answers.

1. A set of financial statements:
   - **a.** Is intended to assist users in evaluating the financial position, profitability, and future prospects of an entity.
   - **b.** Is intended to substitute for filing income tax returns to the Internal Revenue Service in determining the amount of income taxes owed by a business organization.
   - **c.** Includes notes disclosing information necessary for the proper interpretation of the statements.
   - **d.** Is intended to assist investors and creditors in making decisions involving the allocation of economic resources.

2. Which of the following statements is (are) *not* consistent with generally accepted accounting principles relating to asset valuation?
   - **a.** Most assets are originally recorded in accounting records at their cost to the business entity.
   - **b.** Subtracting total liabilities from total assets indicates what the owners' equity in the business is worth under current market conditions.
   - **c.** Accountants assume that assets such as office supplies, land, and buildings will be used in business operations rather than sold at current market prices.
   - **d.** Accountants prefer to base the valuation of assets on objective, verifiable evidence rather than upon appraisals or personal opinions.

3. Waterworld Boat Shop purchased a truck for $12,000, making a down payment of $5,000 cash and signing a $7,000 note payable due in 60 days. As a result of this transaction:
   - **a.** Total assets increased by $12,000.
   - **b.** Total liabilities increased by $7,000.
   - **c.** From the viewpoint of a short-term creditor, this transaction makes the business more liquid.
   - **d.** This transaction had no immediate effect on the owners' equity in the business.
4. A transaction caused a $15,000 *decrease* in both total assets and total liabilities. This transaction could have been:
   - **a.** Purchase of a delivery truck for $15,000 cash.
   - **b.** An asset with a cost of $15,000 destroyed by fire.
   - **c.** Repayment of a $15,000 bank loan.
   - **d.** Collection of a $15,000 account receivable.
5. Which of the following is (are) correct about a company's balance sheet?
   - **a.** Displays sources and uses of cash for the period.
   - **b.** Is an expansion of the basic accounting equation: Assets = Liabilities + Owners' Equity.
   - **c.** Is sometimes referred to as a statement of financial position.
   - **d.** It is unnecessary if both an income statement and statement of cash flows are available.
6. Which of the following would you expect to find in a correctly prepared income statement?
   - **a.** Cash balance at the end of the period.
   - **b.** Revenues earned during the period.
   - **c.** Contributions by the owner during the period.
   - **d.** Expenses incurred during the period to earn revenues.
7. What information would you find in a statement of cash flows that you would not be able to get from the other two primary financial statements?
   - **a.** Cash provided by or used in financing activities.
   - **b.** Cash balance at the end of the period.
   - **c.** Total liabilities due to creditors at the end of the period.
   - **d.** Net income.
8. Which of the following statements relating to the role of professional judgment in the financial reporting process is (are) true?
   - **a.** Different accountants may evaluate similar situations differently.
   - **b.** The determination of which items should be disclosed in notes to financial statements requires professional judgment.
   - **c.** Once a complete list of generally accepted accounting principles is prepared, judgment by accountants will no longer enter into the financial reporting process.
   - **d.** The possibility exists that professional judgment later may prove to have been incorrect.

ASSIGNMENT MATERIAL Discussion Questions

1. In broad general terms, what is the purpose of accounting?
2. Why is a knowledge of accounting terms and concepts useful to persons other than professional accountants?
3. In general terms, what are revenues and expenses? How are they related in the determination of an enterprise's net income or net loss?
4. Why is the statement of financial position, or balance sheet, a logical place to begin a discussion of financial statements?
5. What is the basic accounting equation? Briefly define the three primary elements in the equation.
6. Why is the going-concern assumption an important consideration in understanding financial statements?
7. Can a business transaction cause one asset to increase without affecting any other asset, liability, or owners' equity?
8. Give an example of business transactions that would:
   - **a.** Cause one asset to increase and another asset to decrease, with no effect on either liabilities or owners' equity.
   - **b.** Cause both total assets and liabilities to increase with no effect on owners' equity.
9. What is meant by the terms *positive cash flows* and *negative cash flows*? How do they relate to revenues and expenses?
10. What are the three categories commonly found in a statement of cash flows, and what is included in each category?
11. What is meant by the statement that the financial statements *articulate*?
12. What is meant by the term *adequate disclosure,* and how do accountants fulfill this requirement in the preparation of financial statements?
13. What is meant by the term *window dressing* when referring to financial statements?
14. What are the characteristics of a strong income statement?
15. What are the characteristics of a strong statement of cash flows?

Brief Exercises

LO3 BRIEF EXERCISE 2.1

Recording Transactions

Green Company purchased a piece of machinery on credit for $10,000. Briefly state the way this transaction affects the company's basic accounting equation.

LO3 BRIEF EXERCISE 2.2

Recording Transactions

Foster, Inc., purchased a truck by paying $5,000 and borrowing the remaining $25,000 required to complete the transaction. Briefly state how this transaction affects the company's basic accounting equation.

LO4 BRIEF EXERCISE 2.3

Computing Retained Earnings

Amber Company's assets total $150,000 and its liabilities total $85,000. What is the amount of Amber's retained earnings if its capital stock amounts to $50,000?

LO4 BRIEF EXERCISE 2.4

Computing Total Liabilities

White Company's assets total $780,000 and its owners' equity consists of capital stock of $500,000 and retained earnings of $150,000. Does White Company have any outstanding liabilities and, if so, what is the total amount of its liabilities?

LO5 BRIEF EXERCISE 2.5

Computing Net Income

Wiley Company had total revenues of $300,000 for a recent month. During the month the company incurred operating expenses of $205,000 and purchased land for $45,000. Compute the amount of Wiley's net income for the month.

LO5 BRIEF EXERCISE 2.6

Computing Net Income

Wexler, Inc.'s income statement showed total expenses for the year to be $50,000. If the company's revenues for the year were $125,000 and its year-end cash balance was $35,000, what was Wexler's net income for the year?

LO6 BRIEF EXERCISE 2.7

Computing Change in Cash

Xavier Company had the following transactions during the current year:

- Earned revenues of $100,000 and incurred expenses of $56,000, all in cash.
- Purchased a truck for $20,000.
- Sold land for $10,000.
- Borrowed $15,000 from a local bank.

What was the total change in cash during the year?

LO8 BRIEF EXERCISE 2.8

Alternative Forms of Equity

Solway Company is a sole proprietorship whose owner, Joe Solway, has an equity interest of $50,000. Had Solway been a partnership rather than a sole proprietorship, and the two equal partners were Joe and his brother Tom, how would the $50,000 owners' equity be presented in the company's balance sheet?

LO8 BRIEF EXERCISE 2.9

Alternative Forms of Equity

Repeat Brief Exercise 2.8, except assume that rather than being a sole proprietorship or a partnership, Solway Company is organized as a corporation with capital stock of $40,000. How would the $50,000 of owners' equity be presented in the company's balance sheet?

LO7 BRIEF EXERCISE 2.10

Articulation of Financial Statements

John Franklin, sole owner of Franklin Mattress Company, has an ownership interest in the company of $50,000 at January 1, 2011. During that year, he invests an additional $10,000 in the company and the company reports a net income of $25,000. Determine the balance of owners' equity that will appear in the balance sheet at the end of the year, and explain how the amount of net income articulates with that figure in the balance sheet.

Exercises

LO3 **EXERCISE 2.1**
The Nature of Assets and Liabilities

Assets and liabilities are important elements of a company's financial position.

a. Define *assets.* Give three examples of assets other than cash that might appear in the balance sheet of (1) **American Airlines** and (2) a professional sports team, such as the **Boston Celtics.**

b. Define *liabilities.* Give three examples of liabilities that might appear in the balance sheet of (1) **American Airlines** and (2) a professional sports team, such as the **Boston Celtics.**

LO4 **EXERCISE 2.2**
Preparing a Balance Sheet

The night manager of Dixie Transportation Service, who had no accounting background, prepared the following balance sheet for the company at February 28, 2011. The dollar amounts were taken directly from the company's accounting records and are correct. However, the balance sheet contains a number of errors in its headings, format, and the classification of assets, liabilities, and owners' equity.

DIXIE TRANSPORTATION SERVICE
MANAGER'S REPORT
8 P.M. THURSDAY

Assets		**Owners' Equity**	
Capital Stock	$ 92,000	Accounts Receivable	$ 70,000
Retained Earnings	62,000	Notes Payable	288,000
Cash	69,000	Supplies	14,000
Building	80,000	Land	70,000
Automobiles	165,000	Accounts Payable	26,000
	$468,000		$468,000

Prepare a corrected balance sheet. Include a proper heading.

LO4 **EXERCISE 2.3**
Preparing a Balance Sheet

The balance sheet items of Mercer Company as of December 31, 2011, follow in random order. You are to prepare a balance sheet for the company, using a similar sequence for assets as illustrated in Exhibit 2–9 . You must compute the amount for Retained Earnings.

Land	$90,000	Office Equipment	$ 12,400
Accounts Payable	43,800	Building	210,000
Accounts Receivable	56,700	Capital Stock	75,000
Cash	36,300	Notes Payable	207,000
		Retained Earnings	?

LO2 **EXERCISE 2.4**
Accounting Principles and Asset Valuation

The following cases relate to the valuation of assets. Consider each case independently.

a. World-Wide Travel Agency has office supplies costing $1,700 on hand at the balance sheet date. These supplies were purchased from a supplier that does not give cash refunds. World-Wide's management believes that the company could sell these supplies for no more than $500 if it were to advertise them for sale. However, the company expects to use these supplies and to purchase more when they are gone. In its balance sheet, the supplies were presented at $500.

b. Perez Corporation purchased land in 1957 for $20,000. In 2011, it purchased a similar parcel of land for $300,000. In its 2011 balance sheet, the company presented these two parcels of land at a combined amount of $320,000.

c. At December 30, 2011, Lenier, Inc., purchased a computer system from a mail-order supplier for $14,000. The retail value of the system—according to the mail-order supplier—was $20,000. On January 7, however, the system was stolen during a burglary. In its December 31, 2011, balance sheet, Lenier showed this computer system at $14,000 and made no reference to its retail value or to the burglary. The December balance sheet was issued in February 2012.

In each case, indicate the appropriate balance sheet amount of the asset under generally accepted accounting principles. If the amount assigned by the company is incorrect, briefly explain the accounting principles that have been violated. If the amount is correct, identify the accounting principles that justify this amount.

LO3 **EXERCISE 2.5**

Using the Accounting Equation

Compute the missing amounts in the following table:

	Assets	= Liabilities	+ Owners' Equity
a.	$578,000	$342,000	?
b.	?	562,500	$570,000
c.	307,500	?	187,200

LO3 **EXERCISE 2.6**

The Accounting Equation

A number of business transactions carried out by Smalling Manufacturing Company are as follows:

a. Borrowed money from a bank.

b. Sold land for cash at a price equal to its cost.

c. Paid a liability.

d. Returned for credit some of the office equipment previously purchased on credit but not yet paid for. (Treat this the opposite of a transaction in which you purchased office equipment on credit.)

e. Sold land for cash at a price in excess of cost. (Hint: The difference between cost and sales price represents a gain that will be in the company's income statement.)

f. Purchased a computer on credit.

g. The owner invested cash in the business.

h. Purchased office equipment for cash.

i. Collected an account receivable.

Indicate the effects of each of these transactions on the total amounts of the company's assets, liabilities, and owners' equity. Organize your answer in tabular form, using the following column headings and the code letters **I** for increase, **D** for decrease, and **NE** for no effect. The answer for transaction **a** is provided as an example:

Transaction	Assets	= Liabilities	+ Owners' Equity
(a)	I	I	NE

LO3 **EXERCISE 2.7**

Effects of Business Transactions

For each of the following categories, state concisely a transaction that will have the required effect on the elements of the accounting equation.

a. Increase an asset and increase a liability.

b. Decrease an asset and decrease a liability.

c. Increase one asset and decrease another asset.

d. Increase an asset and increase owners' equity.

e. Increase one asset, decrease another asset, and increase a liability.

LO8 **EXERCISE 2.8**

Forms of Business Organization

Fellingham Software Company has assets of $850,000 and liabilities of $460,000.

a. Prepare the owners' equity section of the company's balance sheet under each of the following *independent* assumptions:

1. The business is organized as a sole proprietorship, owned by Johanna Small.
2. The business is organized as a partnership, owned by Johanna Small and Mikki Yato. Small's equity amounts to $240,000.
3. The business is a corporation with 25 stockholders, each of whom originally invested $10,000 in exchange for shares of the company's capital stock. The remainder of the stockholders' equity has resulted from profitable operation of the business.

b. Assume that you are a loan officer at Security Bank. Fellingham has applied to your bank for a large loan to finance the development of new products. Does it matter to you whether Fellingham is organized as a sole proprietorship, a partnership, or a corporation? Explain.

LO9 **EXERCISE 2.9**

Factors Contributing to Solvency

Explain whether each of the following balance sheet items increases, reduces, or has no direct effect on a company's ability to pay its obligations as they come due. Explain your reasoning.

a. Cash.

b. Accounts Payable.

c. Accounts Receivable.

d. Capital Stock.

LO2 **EXERCISE 2.10**
Professional Judgment

Professional judgment plays a major role in the practice of accounting.

a. In general terms, explain why judgment enters into the accounting process.

b. Identify at least three situations in which accountants must rely on their professional judgment, rather than on official rules.

LO6 **EXERCISE 2.11**
Statement of Cash Flows

During the month of October 2011, Miller Company had the following transactions:

1. Revenues of $10,000 were earned and received in cash.
2. Bank loans of $2,000 were paid off.
3. Equipment of $2,500 was purchased for cash.
4. Expenses of $7,200 were paid.
5. Additional shares of capital stock were sold for $6,000 cash.

Assuming that the cash balance at the beginning of the month was $7,450, prepare a statement of cash flows that displays operating, investing, and financing activities and that reconciles the beginning and ending cash balances.

LO5 **EXERCISE 2.12**
Income Statement

Hernandez, Inc., had the following transactions during the month of March 2011. Prepare an income statement based on this information, being careful to include only those items that should appear in that financial statement.

1. Cash received from bank loans was $10,000.
2. Revenues earned and received in cash were $9,500.
3. Dividends of $4,000 were paid to stockholders.
4. Expenses incurred and paid were $5,465.

LO5 **EXERCISE 2.13**
Income Statement

An inexperienced accountant for Yarnell Company prepared the following income statement for the month of August 2011:

YARNELL COMPANY AUGUST 31, 2011		
Revenues:		
Services provided to customers	$15,000	
Investment by stockholders	5,000	
Loan from bank	15,000	$35,000
Expenses:		
Payments to long-term creditors	$11,700	
Expenses required to provide services to customers	7,800	
Purchase of land	16,000	35,500
Net loss		$ 500

Prepare a revised income statement in accordance with generally accepted accounting principles.

LO6 **EXERCISE 2.14**
Statement of Cash Flows

On the basis of the information for Yarnell Company in Exercise 2.13, prepare a statement of cash flows in a form consistent with generally accepted accounting principles. You may assume all transactions were in cash and that the beginning cash balance was $7,200.

LO9 **EXERCISE 2.15**
Window Dressing Financial Statements

Prepare a two-column analysis that illustrates steps management might take to improve the appearance of its company's financial statements. In the left column, briefly identify three steps that might be taken. In the right column, briefly describe for each step the impact on the balance sheet, income statement, and statement of cash flows. If there is no impact on one or more of these financial statements, indicate that.

LO4 through LO6 **EXERCISE 2.16**
Home Depot, Inc. Financial Statements

Locate the balance sheet, income statement, and statement of cash flows of **Home Depot, Inc.**, in Appendix A of your text. Review those statements and then respond to the following for the year ended January 31, 2010 (fiscal year 2009).

a. Did the company have a net income or net loss for the year? How much?

b. What were the cash balances at the beginning and end of the year? What were the most important causes of the cash decrease during the year? (Treat "cash equivalents" as if they were cash.)

c. What are the two largest assets and liabilities included in the company's balance sheet at the end of the year?

LO5 **EXERCISE 2.17**

Assessing Financial Results

McKesson Corporation's annual report for the year ended March 31, 2009, includes income statements for three years: ending on March 31, 2007, 2008, and 2009. Net income for these three years is as follows (all in millions): $913 (2007), $990 (2008), and $823 (2009). Further analysis of the same income statements reveals that revenues were the following amounts for these same years (all in millions): $92,977 (2007), $101,703 (2008), and $106,632 (2009). State each year's net income as a percentage of revenues and comment briefly on the trend you see over the three-year period.

Problem Set A

LO4 **PROBLEM 2.1A**

Preparing and Evaluating a Balance Sheet

Listed below in random order are the items to be included in the balance sheet of Smokey Mountain Lodge at December 31, 2011:

Equipment	$ 39,200	Buildings	$450,000
Land	425,000	Capital Stock	135,000
Accounts Payable	54,800	Cash	31,400
Accounts Receivable	10,600	Furnishings	58,700
Salaries Payable	33,500	Snowmobiles	15,400
Interest Payable	12,000	Notes Payable	620,000
		Retained Earnings	?

Instructions

a. Prepare a balance sheet at December 31, 2011. Include a proper heading and organize your balance sheet similar to Exhibit 2–9. (After "Buildings," you may list the remaining assets in any order.) You will need to compute the amount to be shown for Retained Earnings.

b. Assume that no payment is due on the notes payable until 2013. Does this balance sheet indicate that the company is in a strong financial position as of December 31, 2011? Explain briefly.

LO3 **PROBLEM 2.2A**

Interpreting the Effects of Business Transactions

The following six transactions of Ajax Moving Company, a corporation, are summarized in equation form, with each of the six transactions identified by a letter. For each of the transactions **(a)** through **(f)** write a separate statement explaining the nature of the transaction. For example, the explanation of transaction **(a)** could be as follows: Purchased equipment for cash at a cost of $3,200.

	Assets					= Liabilities +	Owners' Equity
	Cash +	Accounts Receivable +	Land +	Building +	Equipment =	Accounts Payable +	Capital Stock
Balances	$26,000	$39,000	$45,000	$110,000	$36,000	$42,000	$214,000
(a)	−3,200				+3,200		
Balances	$22,800	$39,000	$45,000	$110,000	$39,200	$42,000	$214,000
(b)	+900	−900					
Balances	$23,700	$38,100	$45,000	$110,000	$39,200	$42,000	$214,000
(c)	−3,500				+13,500	+10,000	
Balances	$20,200	$38,100	$45,000	$110,000	$52,700	$52,000	$214,000
(d)	−14,500					−14,500	
Balances	$ 5,700	$38,100	$45,000	$110,000	$52,700	$37,500	$214,000
(e)	+15,000						+15,000
Balances	$20,700	$38,100	$45,000	$110,000	$52,700	$37,500	$229,000
(f)					+7,500	+7,500	
Balances	$20,700	$38,100	$45,000	$110,000	$60,200	$45,000	$229,000

PROBLEM 2.3A

Recording the Effects of Transactions

Goldstar Communications was organized on December 1 of the current year and had the following account balances at December 31, listed in tabular form:

	Assets				=	Liabilities		+	Owners' Equity
	Cash +	Land +	Building +	Office Equipment	=	Notes Payable +	Accounts Payable	+	Capital Stock
Balances	$37,000	$95,000	$125,000	$51,250		$80,000	$28,250		$200,000

Early in January, the following transactions were carried out by Goldstar Communications:

1. Sold capital stock to owners for $35,000.
2. Purchased land and a small office building for a total price of $90,000, of which $35,000 was the value of the land and $55,000 was the value of the building. Paid $22,500 in cash and signed a note payable for the remaining $67,500.
3. Bought several computer systems on credit for $9,500 (30-day open account).
4. Obtained a loan from Capital Bank in the amount of $20,000. Signed a note payable.
5. Paid the $28,250 account payable due as of December 31.

Instructions

a. List the December 31 balances of assets, liabilities, and owners' equity in tabular form as shown.

b. Record the effects of each of the five transactions in the format illustrated in Exhibit 2–11. Show the totals for all columns after each transaction.

PROBLEM 2.4A

An Alternate Problem on Recording the Effects of Transactions

The items making up the balance sheet of Rankin Truck Rental at December 31 are listed below in tabular form similar to the illustration of the accounting equation in Exhibit 2–11.

	Assets				=	Liabilities		+	Owners' Equity
	Cash +	Accounts Receivable +	Trucks +	Office Equipment	=	Notes Payable +	Accounts Payable	+	Capital Stock
Balances	$9,500	$13,900	$68,000	$3,800		$20,000	$10,200		$65,000

During a short period after December 31, Rankin Truck Rental had the following transactions:

1. Bought office equipment at a cost of $2,700. Paid cash.
2. Collected $4,000 of accounts receivable.
3. Paid $3,200 of accounts payable.
4. Borrowed $10,000 from a bank. Signed a note payable for that amount.
5. Purchased two trucks for $30,500. Paid $15,000 cash and signed a note payable for the balance.
6. Sold additional stock to investors for $75,000.

Instructions

a. List the December 31 balances of assets, liabilities, and owners' equity in tabular form as shown above.

b. Record the effects of each of the six transactions in the preceding tabular arrangement. Show the totals for all columns after each transaction.

LO4 **PROBLEM 2.5A**

Preparing a Balance Sheet; Effects of a Change in Assets

HERE COME THE CLOWNS! is the name of a traveling circus. The ledger accounts of the business at June 30, 2011, are listed here in alphabetical order:

Accounts Payable	$ 26,100	Notes Payable	$180,000
Accounts Receivable	7,450	Notes Receivable	9,500
Animals	189,060	Props and Equipment	89,580
Cages	24,630	Retained Earnings	27,230
Capital Stock	310,000	Salaries Payable	9,750
Cash	?	Tents	63,000
Costumes	31,500	Trucks & Wagons	105,840

Instructions

a. Prepare a balance sheet by using these items and computing the amount of Cash at June 30, 2011. Organize your balance sheet similar to the one illustrated in Exhibit 2–10. (After "Accounts Receivable," you may list the remaining assets in any order.) Include a proper balance sheet heading.

b. Assume that late in the evening of June 30, after your balance sheet had been prepared, a fire destroyed one of the tents, which had cost $14,300. The tent was not insured. Explain what changes would be required in your June 30 balance sheet to reflect the loss of this asset.

LO4 **PROBLEM 2.6A**

Preparing a Balance Sheet—A Second Problem

The following list of balance sheet items are in random order for Wilson Farms, Inc., at September 30, 2011:

Land	$490,000	Fences and Gates	$ 33,570
Barns and Sheds	78,300	Irrigation System	20,125
Notes Payable	330,000	Cash	16,710
Accounts Receivable	22,365	Livestock	120,780
Citrus Trees	76,650	Farm Machinery	42,970
Accounts Payable	77,095	Retained Earnings	?
Property Taxes Payable	9,135	Wages Payable	5,820
Capital Stock	290,000		

Instructions

a. Prepare a balance sheet by using these items and computing the amount for Retained Earnings. Use a sequence of assets similar to that illustrated in Exhibit 2–10. (After "Barns and Sheds," you may list the remaining assets in any order.) Include a proper heading for your balance sheet.

b. Assume that on September 30, immediately after this balance sheet was prepared, a tornado completely destroyed one of the barns. This barn had a cost of $13,700 and was not insured against this type of disaster. Explain what changes would be required in your September 30 balance sheet to reflect the loss of this barn.

LO3 LO4 LO6 **PROBLEM 2.7A**

Preparing a Balance Sheet and Statement of Cash Flows; Effects of Business Transactions

The balance sheet items for The Oven Bakery (arranged in alphabetical order) were as follows at August 1, 2011. (You are to compute the missing figure for Retained Earnings.)

Accounts Payable	$16,200	Equipment and Fixtures	$44,500
Accounts Receivable	11,260	Land	67,000
Building	84,000	Notes Payable	74,900
Capital Stock	80,000	Salaries Payable	8,900
Cash	6,940	Supplies	7,000

During the next two days, the following transactions occurred:

Aug. 2 Additional capital stock was sold for $25,000. The accounts payable were paid in full. (No payment was made on the notes payable or salaries payable.)

Aug. 3 Equipment was purchased at a cost of $7,200 to be paid within 10 days. Supplies were purchased for $1,250 cash from a restaurant supply center that was going out of business. These supplies would have cost $1,890 if purchased through normal channels.

Instructions

a. Prepare a balance sheet at August 1, 2011.

b. Prepare a balance sheet at August 3, 2011, and a statement of cash flows for August 1–3. Classify the payment of accounts payable and the purchase of supplies as operating activities.

c. Assume the notes payable do not come due for several years. Is The Oven Bakery in a stronger financial position on August 1 or on August 3? Explain briefly.

LO4 through LO6

PROBLEM 2.8A

Preparing Financial Statements; Effects of Business Transactions

excel

The balance sheet items of The Sweet Soda Shop (arranged in alphabetical order) were as follows at the close of business on September 30, 2011:

Accounts Payable	$ 8,500	Furniture and Fixtures	20,000
Accounts Receivable	1,250	Land	$55,000
Building	45,500	Notes Payable	?
Capital Stock	50,000	Retained Earnings	4,090
Cash	7,400	Supplies	3,440

The transactions occurring during the first week of October were:

Oct. 3 Additional capital stock was sold for $30,000. The accounts payable were paid in full. (No payment was made on the notes payable.)

Oct. 6 More furniture was purchased on account at a cost of $18,000, to be paid within 30 days. Supplies were purchased for $1,000 cash from a restaurant supply center that was going out of business. These supplies would have cost $1,875 if purchased under normal circumstances.

Oct. 1–6 Revenues of $5,500 were earned and paid in cash. Expenses required to earn the revenues of $4,000 were incurred and paid in cash.

Instructions

a. Prepare a balance sheet at September 30, 2011. (You will need to compute the missing figure for Notes Payable.)

b. Prepare a balance sheet at October 6, 2011. Also prepare an income statement and a statement of cash flows for the period October 1–6, 2011. In your statement of cash flows, treat the purchase of supplies and the payment of accounts payable as operating activities.

c. Assume the notes payable do not come due for several years. Is The Sweet Soda Shop in a stronger financial position on September 30 or on October 6? Explain briefly.

LO4 LO8

PROBLEM 2.9A

Preparing a Balance Sheet; Discussion of Accounting Principles

Helen Berkeley is the founder and manager of Berkeley Playhouse. The business needs to obtain a bank loan to finance the production of its next play. As part of the loan application, Berkeley was asked to prepare a balance sheet for the business. She prepared the following balance sheet, which is arranged correctly but which contains several errors with respect to such concepts as the business entity and the valuation of assets, liabilities, and owner's equity.

BERKELEY PLAYHOUSE
BALANCE SHEET
SEPTEMBER 30, 2011

Assets		Liabilities & Owner's Equity	
Cash	$ 21,900	Liabilities:	
Accounts Receivable	132,200	Accounts Payable	$ 6,000
Props and Costumes	3,000	Salaries Payable	29,200
Theater Building	27,000	Total liabilities	$ 35,200
Lighting Equipment	9,400	Owner's equity:	
Automobile	15,000	Helen Berkeley, Capital	173,300
Total	$208,500	Total	$208,500

In discussions with Berkeley and by reviewing the accounting records of Berkeley Playhouse, you discover the following facts:

1. The amount of cash, \$21,900, includes \$15,000 in the company's bank account, \$1,900 on hand in the company's safe, and \$5,000 in Berkeley's personal savings account.
2. The accounts receivable, listed as \$132,200, include \$7,200 owed to the business by Artistic Tours. The remaining \$125,000 is Berkeley's estimate of future ticket sales from September 30 through the end of the year (December 31).
3. Berkeley explains to you that the props and costumes were purchased several days ago for \$18,000. The business paid \$3,000 of this amount in cash and issued a note payable to Actors' Supply Co. for the remainder of the purchase price (\$15,000). As this note is not due until January of next year, it was not included among the company's liabilities.
4. Berkeley Playhouse rents the theater building from Kievits International at a rate of \$3,000 a month. The \$27,000 shown in the balance sheet represents the rent paid through September 30 of the current year. Kievits International acquired the building seven years ago at a cost of \$135,000.
5. The lighting equipment was purchased on September 26 at a cost of \$9,400, but the stage manager says that it isn't worth a dime.
6. The automobile is Berkeley's classic 1978 Jaguar, which she purchased two years ago for \$9,000. She recently saw a similar car advertised for sale at \$15,000. She does not use the car in the business, but it has a personalized license plate that reads "PLAHOUS."
7. The accounts payable include business debts of \$3,900 and the \$2,100 balance of Berkeley's personal Visa card.
8. Salaries payable include \$25,000 offered to Mario Dane to play the lead role in a new play opening next December and \$4,200 still owed to stagehands for work done through September 30.
9. When Berkeley founded Berkeley Playhouse several years ago, she invested \$20,000 in the business. However, Live Theatre, Inc., recently offered to buy her business for \$173,300. Therefore, she listed this amount as her equity in the above balance sheet.

Instructions

a. Prepare a corrected balance sheet for Berkeley Playhouse at September 30, 2011.

b. For each of the nine numbered items above, explain your reasoning in deciding whether or not to include the items in the balance sheet and in determining the proper dollar valuation.

LO2 LO4

PROBLEM 2.10A

Preparing a Balance Sheet; Discussion of Accounting Principles

Big Screen Scripts is a service-type enterprise in the entertainment field, and its manager, William Pippin, has only a limited knowledge of accounting. Pippin prepared the following balance sheet, which, although arranged satisfactorily, contains certain errors with respect to such concepts as the business entity and asset valuation. Pippin owns all of the corporation's outstanding stock.

BIG SCREEN SCRIPTS
BALANCE SHEET
NOVEMBER 30, 2011

Assets		Liabilities & Owner's Equity	
Cash	\$ 5,150	Liabilities:	
Notes Receivable	2,700	Notes Payable	\$ 67,000
Accounts Receivable	2,450	Accounts Payable	35,805
Land	70,000	Total liabilities	\$102,805
Building	54,320	Owner's equity:	
Office Furniture	8,850	Capital Stock	5,000
Other Assets	22,400	Retained Earnings	58,065
Total	\$165,870	Total	\$165,870

In discussion with Pippin and by inspection of the accounting records, you discover the following facts:

1. The amount of cash, $5,150, includes $3,400 in the company's bank account, $540 on hand in the company's safe, and $1,210 in Pippin's personal savings account.
2. One of the notes receivable in the amount of $500 is an IOU that Pippin received in a poker game several years ago. The IOU is signed by "B.K.," whom Pippin met at the game but has not heard from since.
3. Office furniture includes $2,900 for a Persian rug for the office purchased on November 20. The total cost of the rug was $9,400. The business paid $2,900 in cash and issued a note payable to Zoltan Carpet for the balance due ($6,500). As no payment on the note is due until January, this debt is not included in the liabilities above.
4. Also included in the amount for office furniture is a computer that cost $2,525 but is not on hand because Pippin donated it to a local charity.
5. The "Other Assets" of $22,400 represent the total amount of income taxes Pippin has paid the federal government over a period of years. Pippin believes the income tax law to be unconstitutional, and a friend who attends law school has promised to help Pippin recover the taxes paid as soon as he passes the bar exam.
6. The asset "Land" was acquired at a cost of $39,000 but was increased to a valuation of $70,000 when one of Pippin's friends offered to pay that much for it if Pippin would move the building off the lot.
7. The accounts payable include business debts of $32,700 and the $3,105 balance owed on Pippin's personal MasterCard.

Instructions

a. Prepare a corrected balance sheet at November 30, 2011.

b. For each of the seven numbered items above, use a separate numbered paragraph to explain whether the treatment followed by Pippin is in accordance with generally accepted accounting principles.

Problem Set B

LO4 **PROBLEM 2.1B**

Preparing and Evaluating a Balance Sheet

Listed below in random order are the items to be included in the balance sheet of Deep River Lodge at December 31, 2011:

Equipment	$ 9,000	Buildings	$430,000
Land	140,000	Capital Stock	?
Accounts Payable	27,400	Cash	9,100
Accounts Receivable	3,300	Furnishings	22,600
Salaries Payable	13,200	Notes Payable	217,000
Interest Payable	4,000	Retained Earnings	202,400

Instructions

a. Prepare a balance sheet at December 31, 2011. Include a proper heading and organize your balance sheet similar to the illustrations shown in Chapter 2. (After "Buildings," you may list the remaining assets in any order.) You will need to compute the amount to be shown for Capital Stock.

b. Assume that no payment is due on the notes payable until 2013. Does this balance sheet indicate that the company is in a strong financial position as of December 31, 2011? Explain briefly.

LO3 **PROBLEM 2.2B**

Interpreting the Effects of Business Transactions

Six transactions of Brigal Company, a corporation, are summarized below in equation form, with each of the six transactions identified by a letter. For each of the transactions **(a)** through **(f)** write a separate statement explaining the nature of the transaction. For example, the explanation of transaction **(a)** could be as follows: Purchased furniture for cash at a cost of $800.

	Assets					= Liabilities +	Owners' Equity
	Cash +	Accounts Receivable +	Land +	Building +	Furniture =	Accounts Payable +	Capital Stock
Balances	$ 9,000	$30,000	$40,000	$90,000	$10,000	$30,000	$149,000
(a)	−800				+800		
Balances	$ 8,200	$30,000	$40,000	$90,000	$10,800	$30,000	$149,000
(b)	+500	−500					
Balances	$ 8,700	$29,500	$40,000	$90,000	$10,800	$30,000	$149,000
(c)	−3,000				+5,000	+2,000	
Balances	$ 5,700	$29,500	$40,000	$90,000	$15,800	$32,000	$149,000
(d)	−2,000					−2,000	
Balances	$ 3,700	$29,500	$40,000	$90,000	$15,800	$30,000	$149,000
(e)	+10,000						+10,000
Balances	$13,700	$29,500	$40,000	$90,000	$15,800	$30,000	$159,000
(f)					+3,000	+3,000	
Balances	$13,700	$29,500	$40,000	$90,000	$18,800	$33,000	$159,000

LO3 **PROBLEM 2.3B**

Recording the Effects of Transactions

Delta Corporation was organized on December 1 of the current year and had the following account balances at December 31, listed in tabular form:

	Assets				=	Liabilities	+	Owners' Equity
	Cash +	Land +	Building +	Office Equipment	=	Notes Payable +	Accounts Payable +	Capital Stock
Balances	$12,000	$80,000	$66,000	$41,300		$42,000	$7,300	$150,000

Early in January, the following transactions were carried out by Delta Corporation:

1. Sold capital stock to owners for $40,000.
2. Purchased land and a small office building for a total price of $80,000, of which $30,000 was the value of the land and $50,000 was the value of the building. Paid $10,000 in cash and signed a note payable for the remaining $70,000.
3. Bought several computer systems on credit for $8,000 (30-day open account).
4. Obtained a loan from 2nd Bank in the amount of $12,000. Signed a note payable.
5. Paid the $4,000 account payable due as of December 31.

Instructions

a. List the December 31 balances of assets, liabilities, and owners' equity in tabular form as shown above.

b. Record the effects of each of the five transactions in the format illustrated in Chapter 2 of the text. Show the totals for all columns after each transaction.

LO3 **PROBLEM 2.4B**

An Alternate Problem on Recording the Effects of Transactions

The items making up the balance sheet of Smith Trucking at December 31 are listed below in tabular form similar to the illustration of the accounting equation in Chapter 2 of the text.

	Assets				=	Liabilities	+	Owners' Equity
	Cash +	Accounts Receivable +	Trucks +	Office Equipment	=	Notes Payable +	Accounts Payable +	Capital Stock
Balances	$4,700	$8,300	$72,000	$3,000		$10,000	$8,000	$70,000

During a short period after December 31, Smith Trucking had the following transactions:

1. Bought office equipment at a cost of $2,600. Paid cash.
2. Collected $2,500 of accounts receivable.
3. Paid $2,000 of accounts payable.
4. Borrowed $5,000 from a bank. Signed a note payable for that amount.
5. Purchased three trucks for $60,000. Paid $5,000 cash and signed a note payable for the balance.
6. Sold additional stock to investors for $25,000.

Instructions

a. List the December 31 balances of assets, liabilities, and owners' equity in tabular form as shown above.

b. Record the effects of each of the six transactions in the tabular arrangement illustrated above. Show the totals for all columns after each transaction.

LO4 **PROBLEM 2.5B**

Preparing a Balance Sheet; Effects of a Change in Assets

Circus World is the name of a traveling circus. The ledger accounts of the business at June 30, 2011, are listed here in alphabetical order:

Accounts Payable	$ 25,000	Notes Payable	$115,000
Accounts Receivable	5,600	Notes Receivable	1,200
Animals	310,000	Props and Equipment	108,000
Cages	15,000	Retained Earnings	89,000
Capital Stock	400,000	Salaries Payable	1,250
Cash	?	Tents	40,000
Costumes	16,000	Trucks & Wagons	125,300

Instructions

a. Prepare a balance sheet by using these items and computing the amount of Cash at June 30, 2011. (After "Accounts Receivable," you may list the remaining assets in any order.) Include a proper balance sheet heading.

b. Assume that late in the evening of June 30, after your balance sheet had been prepared, a fire destroyed one of the tents, which had cost $10,000. The tent was not insured. Explain what changes would be required in your June 30 balance sheet to reflect the loss of this asset.

LO4 **PROBLEM 2.6B**

Preparing a Balance Sheet—A Second Problem

Shown below in random order is a list of balance sheet items for Apple Valley Farms at September 30, 2011:

Land	$ 50,000	Fences and Gates	$14,100
Barns and Sheds	19,100	Irrigation System	10,200
Notes Payable	65,000	Cash	9,300
Accounts Receivable	15,000	Livestock	5,000
Apple Trees	84,000	Farm Machinery	20,000
Accounts Payable	8,100	Retained Earnings	?
Property Taxes Payable	4,700	Wages Payable	1,200
Capital Stock	100,000		

Instructions

a. Prepare a balance sheet by using these items and computing the amount for Retained Earnings. Use a sequence of assets similar to that illustrated in Chapter 2 of the text. (After "Barns and Sheds," you may list the remaining assets in any order.) Include a proper heading for your balance sheet.

b. Assume that on September 30, immediately after this balance sheet was prepared, a tornado completely destroyed one of the barns. This barn had a cost of $4,500 and was not insured against this type of disaster. Explain what changes would be required in your September 30 balance sheet to reflect the loss of this barn.

LO3 LO4 LO6

PROBLEM 2.7B

Preparing a Balance Sheet and Statement of Cash Flows; Effects of Business Transactions

The balance sheet items for The City Butcher (arranged in alphabetical order) were as follows at July 1, 2011. (You are to compute the missing figure for Retained Earnings.)

Accounts Payable	$ 7,000	Equipment and Fixtures	$25,000
Accounts Receivable	8,200	Land	50,000
Building	90,000	Notes Payable	40,000
Capital Stock	100,000	Salaries Payable	3,700
Cash	4,100	Supplies	7,000

During the next few days, the following transactions occurred:

July 4 Additional capital stock was sold for $30,000. The accounts payable were paid in full. (No payment was made on the notes payable or salaries payable.)

July 5 Equipment was purchased at a cost of $6,000 to be paid within 10 days. Supplies were purchased for $1,000 cash from a restaurant supply center that was going out of business. These supplies would have cost $2,000 if purchased through normal channels.

Instructions

a. Prepare a balance sheet at July 1, 2011.

b. Prepare a balance sheet at July 5, 2011, and a statement of cash flows for July 1–5. Classify the payment of accounts payable and the purchase of supplies as operating activities.

c. Assume the notes payable do not come due for several years. Is The City Butcher in a stronger financial position on July 1 or on July 5? Explain briefly.

LO4 through LO6

PROBLEM 2.8B

Preparing Financial Statements; Effects of Business Transactions

The balance sheet items of The Candy Shop (arranged in alphabetical order) were as follows at the close of the business on September 30, 2011:

Accounts Payable	$ 6,800	Furniture and Fixtures	$ 9,000
Accounts Receivable	5,000	Land	72,000
Building	80,000	Notes Payable	?
Capital Stock	100,000	Retained Earnings	19,100
Cash	6,900	Supplies	3,000

The transactions occurring during the first week of October were:

Oct. 3 Additional capital stock was sold for $30,000. The accounts payable were paid in full. (No payment was made on the notes payable.)

Oct. 6 More furniture was purchased on account at a cost of $8,000, to be paid within 30 days. Supplies were purchased for $900 cash from a restaurant supply center that was going out of business. These supplies would have cost $2,000 if purchased under normal circumstances.

Oct. 1–6 Revenues of $8,000 were earned and paid in cash. Expenses required to earn the revenues of $3,200 were incurred and paid in cash.

Instructions

a. Prepare a balance sheet at September 30, 2011. (You will need to compute the missing figure for Notes Payable.)

b. Prepare a balance sheet at October 6, 2011. Also prepare an income statement and a statement of cash flows for the period October 1–6, 2011. In your statement of cash flows, treat the purchase of supplies and the payment of accounts payable as operating activities.

c. Assume the notes payable do not come due for several years. Is The Candy Shop in a stronger financial position on September 30 or on October 6? Explain briefly.

LO4 LO8

PROBLEM 2.9B
Preparing a Balance Sheet; Discussion of Accounting Principles

Howard Jaffe is the founder and manager of Old Town Playhouse. The business needs to obtain a bank loan to finance the production of its next play. As part of the loan application, Jaffe was asked to prepare a balance sheet for the business. He prepared the following balance sheet, which is arranged correctly but which contains several errors with respect to such concepts as the business entity and the valuation of assets, liabilities, and owner's equity.

OLD TOWN PLAYHOUSE
BALANCE SHEET
SEPTEMBER 30, 2011

Assets		**Liabilities & Owner's Equity**	
Cash	$ 19,400	Liabilities:	
Accounts Receivable	150,200	Accounts Payable	$ 7,000
Props and Costumes	3,000	Salaries Payable	32,000
Theater Building	26,000	Total Liabilities	$ 39,000
Lighting Equipment	10,000	Owner's Equity:	
Automobile	15,000	Howard Jaffe, Capital	184,600
Total	$223,600	Total	$223,600

In discussions with Jaffe and by reviewing the accounting records of Old Town Playhouse, you discover the following facts:

1. The amount of cash, $19,400, includes $16,000 in the company's bank account, $2,400 on hand in the company's safe, and $1,000 in Jaffe's personal savings account.
2. The accounts receivable, listed as $150,200, include $10,000 owed to the business by Dell, Inc. The remaining $140,200 is Jaffe's estimate of future ticket sales from September 30 through the end of the year (December 31).
3. Jaffe explains to you that the props and costumes were purchased several days ago for $18,000. The business paid $3,000 of this amount in cash and issued a note payable to Ham's Supply Co. for the remainder of the purchase price ($15,000). As this note is not due until January of next year, it was not included among the company's liabilities.
4. Old Town Playhouse rents the theater building from Time International. The $26,000 shown in the balance sheet represents the rent paid through September 30 of the current year. Time International acquired the building seven years ago at a cost of $180,000.
5. The lighting equipment was purchased on September 26 at a cost of $10,000, but the stage manager says that it isn't worth a dime.
6. The automobile is Jaffe's classic 1935 Olds, which he purchased two years ago for $12,000. He recently saw a similar car advertised for sale at $15,000. He does not use the car in the business, but it has a personalized license plate that reads "OTPLAY."
7. The accounts payable include business debts of $6,000 and the $1,000 balance of Jaffe's personal Visa card.
8. Salaries payable include $30,000 offered to Robin Needelman to play the lead role in a new play opening next December and $2,000 still owed to stagehands for work done through September 30.
9. When Jaffe founded Old Town Playhouse several years ago, he invested $20,000 in the business. However, New Theatre, Inc., recently offered to buy his business for $184,600. Therefore, he listed this amount as his equity in the above balance sheet.

Instructions

a. Prepare a corrected balance sheet for Old Town Playhouse at September 30, 2011.

b. For each of the nine numbered items above, explain your reasoning for deciding whether or not to include the items in the balance sheet and in determining the proper dollar valuation.

LO2 LO4

PROBLEM 2.10B

Preparing a Balance Sheet; Discussion of Accounting Principles

Hit Scripts is a service-type enterprise in the entertainment field, and its manager, Joe Russell, has only a limited knowledge of accounting. Joe prepared the following balance sheet, which, although arranged satisfactorily, contains certain errors with respect to such concepts as the business entity and asset valuation. Joe owns all of the corporation's outstanding stock.

HIT SCRIPTS
BALANCE SHEET
NOVEMBER 30, 2011

Assets		Liabilities & Owner's Equity	
Cash	$ 5,000	Liabilities:	
Notes Receivable	4,000	Notes Payable	$ 65,000
Accounts Receivable	3,000	Accounts Payable	32,000
Land	60,000	Total Liabilities	$ 97,000
Building	75,000	Owner's Equity:	
Office Furniture	9,600	Capital Stock	10,000
Other Assets	25,000	Retained Earnings	74,600
Total	$181,600	Total	$181,600

In discussion with Joe and by inspection of the accounting records, you discover the following facts:

1. The amount of cash, $5,000, includes $2,000 in the company's bank account, $1,200 on hand in the company's safe, and $1,800 in Joe's personal savings account.
2. One of the notes receivable in the amount of $600 is an IOU that Joe received in a poker game five years ago. The IOU is signed by "G.W.," whom Joe met at the game but has not heard from since.
3. Office furniture includes $2,500 for an Indian rug for the office purchased on November 15. The total cost of the rug was $10,000. The business paid $2,500 in cash and issued a note payable to Jana Carpet for the balance due ($7,500). As no payment on the note is due until January, this debt is not included in the liabilities above.
4. Also included in the amount for office furniture is a computer that cost $800 but is not on hand because Joe donated it to a local charity.
5. The "Other Assets" of $25,000 represent the total amount of income taxes Joe has paid the federal government over a period of years. Joe believes the income tax law to be unconstitutional, and a friend who attends law school has promised to help Joe recover the taxes paid as soon as he passes the bar exam.
6. The asset "Land" was acquired at a cost of $15,000 but was increased to a valuation of $60,000 when one of Joe's friends offered to pay that much for it if Joe would move the building off the lot.
7. The accounts payable include business debts of $30,000 and the $2,000 balance owed on Joe's personal MasterCard.

Instructions

a. Prepare a corrected balance sheet at November 30, 2011.

b. For each of the seven numbered items above, use a separate numbered paragraph to explain whether the treatment followed by Joe is in accordance with generally accepted accounting principles.

Critical Thinking Cases

LO4

CASE 2.1

Content of a Balance Sheet

You are to prepare a balance sheet for a *hypothetical* business entity of your choosing (or specified by your instructor). Include in your balance sheet the types of assets and liabilities that you think the entity might have, and show these items at what you believe would be realistic dollar amounts. Make reasonable assumptions with regard to the company's capital stock and retained earnings.

Note: The purpose of this assignment is to help you consider the types of assets and liabilities required for the operations of a specific type of business. You should complete this assignment *without* referring to an actual balance sheet for this type of business.

LO4 through LO6

CASE 2.2 Using Financial Statements

Obtain from the library the *annual report* of a well-known company (or a company specified by your instructor).

Instructions

From the balance sheet, income statement, statement of cash flows, and notes to the financial statements, answer the following:

a. What are the largest assets included in the company's balance sheet? Why would a company of this type (size and industry) have a large investment in this particular type of asset?

b. In a review of the company's statement of cash flows:

1. What are the primary sources and uses of cash from investing activities?
2. Did investing activities cause the company's cash to increase or decrease?
3. What are the primary sources and uses of cash from financing activities?
4. Did financing activities cause the company's cash to increase or decrease?

c. In a review of the company's income statement, did the company have a net income or a net loss for the most recent year? What percentage of total revenues was that net income or net loss?

d. Select three items in the notes accompanying the financial statements and explain briefly the importance of these items to people making decisions about investing in, or extending credit to, this company.

e. Assume that you are a lender and this company has asked to borrow an amount of cash equal to 10 percent of its total assets, to be repaid in 90 days. Would you consider this company to be a good credit risk? Explain.

LO4

CASE 2.3 Using a Balance Sheet

Moon Corporation and Star Corporation are in the same line of business and both were recently organized, so it may be assumed that the recorded costs for assets are close to current market values. The balance sheets for the two companies are as follows at July 31, 2011:

MOON CORPORATION
BALANCE SHEET
JULY 31, 2011

Assets		**Liabilities & Owners' Equity**		
Cash	$ 18,000	Liabilities:		
Accounts Receivable	26,000	Notes Payable		
Land	37,200	(due in 60 days)		$ 12,400
Building	38,000	Accounts Payable		9,600
Office Equipment	1,200	Total liabilities		$ 22,000
		Stockholders' equity:		
		Capital Stock	$60,000	
		Retained Earnings	38,400	98,400
Total	$120,400	Total		$120,400

STAR CORPORATION
BALANCE SHEET
JULY 31, 2011

Assets		**Liabilities & Owners' Equity**		
Cash	$ 4,800	Liabilities:		
Accounts Receivable	9,600	Notes Payable		
Land	96,000	(due in 60 days)		$ 22,400
Building	60,000	Accounts Payable		43,200
Office Equipment	12,000	Total liabilities		$ 65,600
		Stockholders' equity:		
		Capital Stock	$72,000	
		Retained Earnings	44,800	116,800
Total	$182,400	Total		$182,400

Instructions

a. Assume that you are a banker and that each company has applied to you for a 90-day loan of $12,000. Which would you consider to be the more favorable prospect? Explain your answer fully.

b. Assume that you are an investor considering purchasing all the capital stock of one or both of the companies. For which business would you be willing to pay the higher price? Do you see any indication of a financial crisis that you might face shortly after buying either company? Explain your answer fully. (For either decision, additional information would be useful, but you are to reach your decision on the basis of the information available.)

LO6 **CASE 2.4**

Using Statements of Cash Flows

John Marshall is employed as a bank loan officer for First State Bank. He is comparing two companies that have applied for loans, and he wants your help in evaluating those companies. The two companies—Morris, Inc., and Walker Company—are approximately the same size and had approximately the same cash balance at the beginning of 2009. Because the total cash flows for the three-year period are virtually the same, John is inclined to evaluate the two companies as equal in terms of their desirability as loan candidates.

Abbreviated information (in thousands of dollars) from Morris, Inc., and Walker Company is as follows:

	Morris, Inc.			Walker Company		
	2009	2010	2011	2009	2010	2011
Cash flows from:						
Operating activities	$10	$13	$15	$ 8	$3	$(2)
Investing activities	(5)	(8)	(10)	(7)	(5)	8
Financing activities	8	(3)	1	12	4	-0-
Net from all activities	$13	$ 2	$ 6	$13	$2	$6

Instructions

a. Do you agree with John's preliminary assessment that the two companies are approximately equal in terms of their strength as loan candidates? Why or why not?

b. What might account for the fact that Walker Company's cash flow from financing activities is zero in 2011?

c. Generally, what would you advise John with regard to using statements of cash flows in evaluating loan candidates?

LO4 **CASE 2.5**

Ethics and Window Dressing

The date is November 18, 2011. You are the chief executive officer of Omega Software—a publicly owned company that is currently in financial difficulty. Omega needs new large bank loans if it is to survive.

You have been negotiating with several banks, but each has asked to see your 2011 financial statements, which will be dated December 31. These statements will, of course, be audited. You are now meeting with other corporate officers to discuss the situation, and the following suggestions have been made:

1. "We are planning to buy WordMaster Software Co. for $8 million cash in December. The owners of WordMaster are in no hurry; if we delay this acquisition until January, we'll have $8 million more cash at year-end. That should make us look a lot more solvent."
2. "At year-end, we'll owe accounts payable of about $18 million. If we were to show this liability in our balance sheet at half that amount—say, $9 million—no one would know the difference. We could report the other $9 million as stockholders' equity and our financial position would appear much stronger."
3. "We owe Delta Programming $5 million, due in 90 days. I know some people at Delta. If we were to sign a note and pay them 12 percent interest, they'd let us postpone this debt for a year or more."
4. "We own land that cost us $2 million but today is worth at least $6 million. Let's show it at $6 million in our balance sheet, and that will increase our total assets and our stockholders' equity by $4 million."

Instructions

Separately evaluate each of these four proposals to improve Omega Software's financial statements. Your evaluations should consider ethical and legal issues as well as accounting issues.

LO4

CASE 2.6
Public Company Accounting Oversight Board

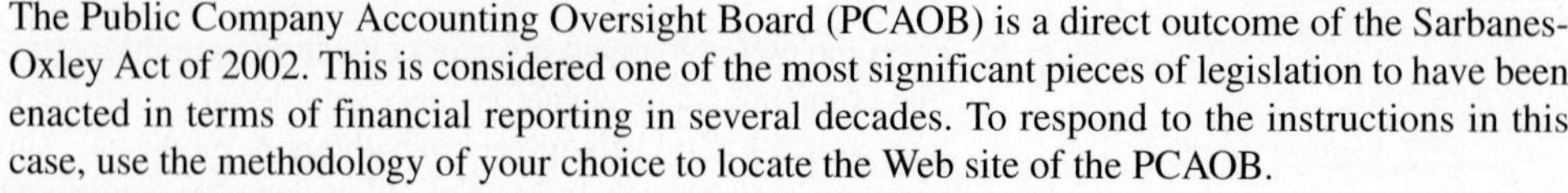

The Public Company Accounting Oversight Board (PCAOB) is a direct outcome of the Sarbanes-Oxley Act of 2002. This is considered one of the most significant pieces of legislation to have been enacted in terms of financial reporting in several decades. To respond to the instructions in this case, use the methodology of your choice to locate the Web site of the PCAOB.

Instructions

a. State the mission of the PCAOB.

b. Access the category "About Us" and list the names of the members of the PCAOB.

c. Access the category "Enforcement" and describe the authority the PCAOB has been granted by the Sarbanes-Oxley Act of 2002.

d. Access the category "Standards" and describe the responsibility of the PCAOB to establish standards that impact corporate financial reporting.

LO4 through LO5

INTERNET CASE 2.7
Gathering Financial Information

This assignment introduces you to EDGAR, the Securities and Exchange Commission's database of financial information about publicly owned companies. The SEC maintains EDGAR to increase the efficiency of financial reporting in the American economy and also to give the public free and easy access to information about publicly owned companies.

Instructions

Access EDGAR at the following Internet address: www.sec.gov. Go to "Filings & Forms."

Click "Search for Company Filings" and then "Companies and Other Filers." Then type Cisco Systems into the search box and click on "Find Companies." Locate the most recent 10Q (quarterly) report.

a. What is the business address of **Cisco Systems**?

b. Locate the balance sheet in Form 10Q and determine whether the amount of the company's cash (and cash equivalents) increased or decreased in the most recent quarter.

c. Locate the income statement (called the "statement of operations"). What was the company's net income for the most recent quarter? Is that amount higher or lower than in the previous quarter?

d. Analyze the statement of cash flows. How much cash was provided by operations to date for the current year?

e. While you are in EDGAR, pick another company that interests you and learn more about it by studying that company's information. Be prepared to tell the class which company you selected and explain what you learned.

Internet sites are time and date sensitive. It is the purpose of these exercises to have you explore the Internet. You may need to use the Yahoo! search engine http://www.yahoo.com *(or another favorite search engine) to find a company's current Web address.*

Answers to Self-Test Questions

1. a, c, d **2.** b **3.** b, d **4.** c **5.** b, c **6.** b, d **7.** a **8.** a, b, d

CHAPTER 3

The Accounting Cycle

Capturing Economic Events

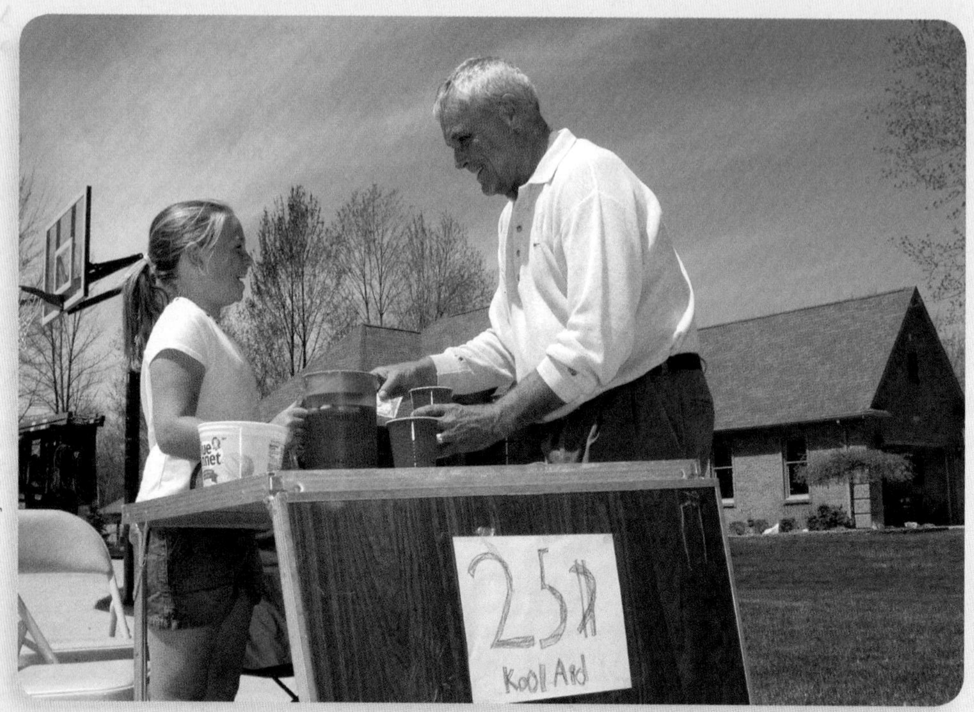

© Dennis MacDonald/Alamy

Learning Objectives

AFTER STUDYING THIS CHAPTER, YOU SHOULD BE ABLE TO:

LO1 Identify the steps in the accounting cycle and discuss the role of accounting records in an organization.

LO2 Describe a ledger account and a ledger.

LO3 Understand how balance sheet accounts are increased or decreased.

LO4 Explain the double-entry system of accounting.

LO5 Explain the purpose of a journal and its relationship to the ledger.

LO6 Explain the nature of *net income, revenue,* and *expenses.*

LO7 Apply the *realization* and *matching* principles in recording revenue and expenses.

LO8 Understand how revenue and expense transactions are recorded in an accounting system.

LO9 Prepare a trial balance and explain its uses and limitations.

LO10 Distinguish between accounting cycle procedures and the *knowledge* of accounting.

KRAFT FOODS, INC.

Capturing the economic events of a *kool-Aid*™ stand is a fairly simple process. In fact, for most *kool-Aid*™ stands, a small notebook, a sharp pencil, and an empty shoebox may serve as a complete information system.

Capturing the economic activities of Kraft Foods, Inc.—the second largest food company in the world and the maker of *kool-Aid*™—is an entirely different matter. This corporate giant controls nearly $70 billion in total assets, earns more than $40 billion in annual revenue, and generates in excess of $5 billion in annual net cash flow from its operating activities. Employing nearly 100,000 people, and managing hundreds of manufacturing facilities and thousands of warehouses and distribution centers, Kraft Foods, Inc., must somehow capture the complex business transactions of its worldwide operations.

From *kool-Aid*™ stands to multinational corporations, efficiently and effectively capturing economic events—such as sales orders and raw material purchases—is absolutely essential for survival. Most enterprises use computer systems to account for these activities. Very few still use paper ledgers and handwritten journals to record daily activities and transactions. ■

Although Overnight Auto Service engaged in several business transactions in the previous chapter, we did not illustrate how these events were captured by Overnight for use by management and other interested parties. This chapter demonstrates how accounting systems record economic events related to a variety of business transactions.

The Accounting Cycle

Learning Objective
LO1 **Identify the steps in the accounting cycle and discuss the role of accounting records in an organization.**

In Chapter 2, we illustrated several transactions of Overnight Auto Service that occurred during the last week in January 2011. We prepared a complete set of financial statements immediately following our discussion of these transactions. For practical purposes, businesses do not prepare new financial statements after every transaction. Rather, they accumulate the effects of individual transactions in their *accounting records.* Then, at regular intervals, the data in these records are used to prepare financial statements, income tax returns, and other types of reports.

The sequence of accounting procedures used to record, classify, and summarize accounting information in financial reports at regular intervals is often termed the **accounting cycle.** The accounting cycle begins with the initial recording of business transactions and concludes with the preparation of a complete set of formal financial statements. The term *cycle* indicates that these procedures must be repeated continuously to enable the business to prepare new, up-to-date financial statements at reasonable intervals.

The accounting cycle generally consists of eight specific steps. In this chapter, we illustrate how businesses (1) journalize (record) transactions, (2) post each journal entry to the appropriate ledger accounts, and (3) prepare a trial balance. The remaining steps of the cycle will be addressed in Chapters 4 and 5. They include (4) making end-of-period adjustments, (5) preparing an adjusted trial balance, (6) preparing financial statements, (7) journalizing and posting closing entries, and (8) preparing an after-closing trial balance.

THE ROLE OF ACCOUNTING RECORDS

The cyclical process of collecting financial information and maintaining accounting records does far more than facilitate the preparation of financial statements. Managers and employees of a business frequently use the information stored in the accounting records for such purposes as:

1. Establishing **accountability** for the assets and/or transactions under an individual's control.
2. Keeping track of routine business activities—such as the amounts of money in company bank accounts, amounts due from credit customers, or amounts owed to suppliers.
3. Obtaining detailed information about a particular transaction.
4. Evaluating the efficiency and performance of various departments within the organization.
5. Maintaining documentary evidence of the company's business activities. (For example, tax laws require companies to maintain accounting records supporting the amounts reported in tax returns.)

The Ledger

Learning Objective
LO2 **Describe a ledger account and a ledger.**

An accounting system includes a separate record for each item that appears in the financial statements. For example, a separate record is kept for the asset cash, showing all increases and decreases in cash resulting from the many transactions in which cash is received or paid. A similar record is kept for every other asset, for every liability, for owners' equity, and for every revenue and expense account appearing in the income statement.

The record used to keep track of the increases and decreases in financial statement items is termed a "ledger account" or, simply, an **account.** The entire group of accounts is kept together in an accounting record called a **ledger.** Exhibit 3–8 on page 108 illustrates the ledger of Overnight Auto Service.

The Use of Accounts

An account is a means of accumulating in one place all the information about changes in specific financial statement items, such as a particular asset or liability. For example, the Cash account provides a company's current cash balance, a record of its cash receipts, and a record of its cash disbursements.

In its simplest form, an account has only three elements: (1) a title; (2) a left side, which is called the *debit* side; and (3) a right side, which is called the *credit* side. This form of an account, illustrated below and on the following page, is called a *T account* because of its resemblance to the letter "T." In a computerized system, of course, the elements of each account are stored and formatted electronically. More complete forms of accounts will be illustrated later.

A T account—a ledger account in its simplest form

Title of Account	
Left or Debit Side	Right or Credit Side

Debit and Credit Entries

An amount recorded on the left, or debit, side of an account is called a **debit,** or a debit entry. Likewise, any amount entered on the right, or credit, side is called a **credit,** or a credit entry. In simple terms, debits refer to the left side of an account, and credits refer to the right side of an account.

To illustrate the recording of debits and credits in an account, let us go back to the eight cash transactions of Overnight Auto Service, described in Chapter 2. When these cash transactions are recorded in the Cash account, the receipts are listed on the debit side, and the payments are listed on the credit side. The dates of the transactions may also be listed, as shown in the following illustration:

Cash transactions entered in ledger account

Cash			
1/20	80,000	1/21	52,000
1/26	600	1/22	6,000
1/31	2,200	1/27	6,800
		1/31	200
		1/31	1,200
1/31 Balance	16,600		

Each debit and credit entry in the Cash account represents a cash receipt or a cash payment. The amount of cash owned by the business at a given date is equal to the *balance* of the account on that date.

Determining the Balance of a T Account

The balance of an account is the difference between the debit and credit entries in the account. If the debit total exceeds the credit total, the account has a *debit balance;* if the credit total exceeds the debit total, the account has a *credit balance.*

In our illustrated Cash account, a line has been drawn across the account following the last cash transaction recorded in January. The total cash receipts (debits) recorded in January amount to $82,800, and the total cash payments (credits) amount to $66,200. By subtracting the credit total from the debit total ($82,800 − $66,200), we determine that the Cash account has a debit balance of *$16,600* on January 31.

This debit balance is entered in the debit side of the account just below the line. In effect, the line creates a "fresh start" in the account, with the month-end balance representing the *net result* of all the previous debit and credit entries. The Cash account now shows the amount of cash owned by the business on January 31. In a balance sheet prepared at this date, Cash in the amount of $16,600 would be listed as an asset.

Debit Balances in Asset Accounts In the preceding illustration of a Cash account, increases were recorded on the left, or debit, side of the account and decreases were recorded on the right, or credit, side. The increases were greater than the decreases and the result was a debit balance in the account.

Learning Objective
LO3 **Understand how balance sheet accounts are increased or decreased.**

All asset accounts *normally have debit balances*. It is hard to imagine an account for an asset such as land having a credit balance, as this would indicate that the business had disposed of more land than it had ever acquired. (For some assets, such as cash, it is possible to acquire a credit balance—but such balances are only *temporary.*)

The fact that assets are located on the *left* side of the balance sheet is a convenient means of remembering the rule that an increase in an asset is recorded on the *left* (debit) side of the account and an asset account normally has a debit *(left-hand)* balance.

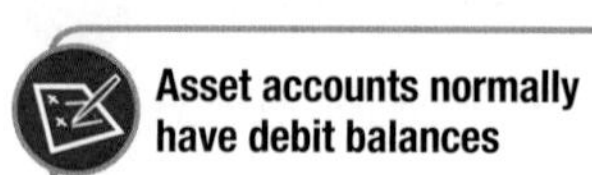
Asset accounts normally have debit balances

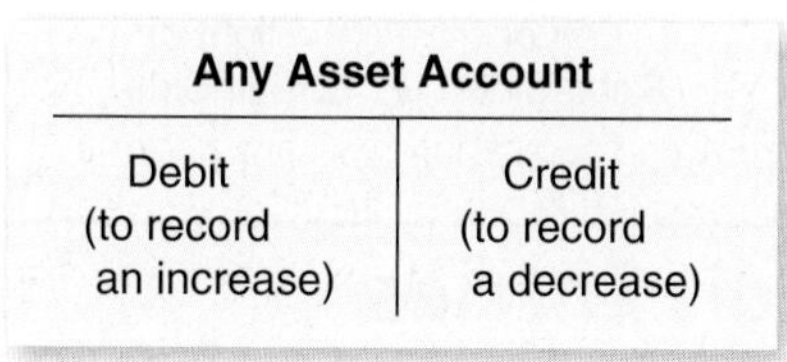

Credit Balances in Liability and Owners' Equity Accounts Increases in liability and owners' equity accounts are recorded by credit entries and decreases in these accounts are recorded by debits. The relationship between entries in these accounts and their position on the balance sheet may be summed up as follows: (1) liabilities and owners' equity belong on the *right* side of the balance sheet, (2) an increase in a liability or an owners' equity account is recorded on the *right* (credit) side of the account, and (3) liability and owners' equity accounts normally have credit *(right-hand)* balances.

Liability and owners' equity accounts normally have credit balances

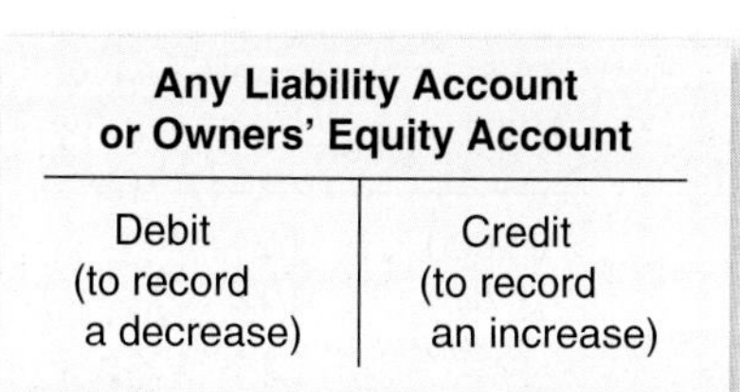

Concise Statement of the Debit and Credit Rules The use of debits and credits to record changes in assets, liabilities, and owners' equity may be summarized as follows:

Debit and credit rules

Asset Accounts	Liability & Owners' Equity Accounts
Normally have debit balances. Thus, increases are recorded by debits and decreases are recorded by credits.	Normally have credit balances. Thus, increases are recorded by credits and decreases are recorded by debits.

DOUBLE-ENTRY ACCOUNTING—THE EQUALITY OF DEBITS AND CREDITS

The rules for debits and credits are designed so that *every transaction is recorded by equal dollar amounts of debits and credits.* The reason for this equality lies in the relationship of the debit and credit rules to the accounting equation:

$$\underbrace{\text{Assets}}_{\textbf{Debit Balances}} = \underbrace{\text{Liabilities} + \text{Owners' Equity}}_{\textbf{Credit Balances}}$$

If this equation is to remain in balance, any change in the left side of the equation (assets) *must be accompanied by an equal change* in the right side (either liabilities or owners' equity). According to the debit and credit rules that we have just described, increases in the left side of the equation (assets) are recorded by *debits,* while increases in the right side (liabilities and owners' equity) are recorded by *credits,* as illustrated below:

Learning Objective **Explain the double-entry system of accounting.** LO4

Assets		=	Liabilities		+	Owners' Equity	
Debit to increase (+)	Credit to decrease (−)		Debit to decrease (−)	Credit to increase (+)		Debit to decrease (−)	Credit to increase (+)

This system is often called **double-entry accounting.** The phrase *double-entry* refers to the need for both *debit entries* and *credit entries,* equal in dollar amount, to record every transaction. Virtually every business organization uses the double-entry system regardless of whether the company's accounting records are maintained manually or by computer. Later in this chapter, we will see that the double-entry system allows us to measure net income at the same time we record the effects of transactions on the balance sheet accounts.

The Journal

Learning Objective **Explain the purpose of a journal and its relationship to the ledger.** LO5

In the preceding discussion we illustrated how the debit and credit rules of double-entry accounting are applied in the recording of economic events. Using T accounts, we stressed the effects that business transactions have on individual asset, liability, and owners' equity accounts that comprise a company's general ledger. It is important to realize, however, that transactions are rarely recorded *directly* in general ledger accounts. In an actual accounting system, the information about each business transaction is *initially* recorded in an accounting record called the **journal.** This information is *later* transferred to the appropriate accounts in the general ledger.

The journal is a chronological (day-by-day) record of business transactions. At convenient intervals, the debit and credit amounts recorded in the journal are transferred (posted) to the accounts in the ledger. The updated ledger accounts, in turn, serve as the basis for preparing the company's financial statements.

To illustrate the most basic type of journal, called a **general journal,** let us examine the very first business transaction of Overnight Auto Service. Recall that on January 20, 2011, the McBryan family invested $80,000 in exchange for capital stock. Thus, the asset Cash increased by $80,000, and the owners' equity account Capital Stock increased by the same amount.

Applying the debit and credit rules discussed previously, we know that increases in assets are recorded by debits, whereas increases in owners' equity are recorded by credits. As such, this event requires a *debit* to Cash and a *credit* to Capital Stock in the amount of $80,000. The transaction is recorded in the company's general journal as illustrated in Exhibit 3–1. Note the basic characteristics of this general journal entry:

1. The name of the account debited (Cash) is written first, and the dollar amount to be debited appears in the left-hand money column.
2. The name of the account credited (Capital Stock) appears below the account debited and is indented to the right. The dollar amount appears in the right-hand money column.
3. A brief description of the transaction appears immediately below the journal entry.

Accounting software packages automate and streamline the way in which transactions are recorded. However, recording transactions manually—without a computer—is an effective way to conceptualize the manner in which economic events are captured by accounting systems and subsequently reported in a company's financial statements.

Exhibit 3–1

RECORDING A TRANSACTION IN THE GENERAL JOURNAL

GENERAL JOURNAL

Date	Account Titles and Explanation	Debit	Credit
2011			
Jan. 20	Cash	80,000	
	Capital Stock		80,000
	Owners invest cash in the business.		

A familiarity with the general journal form of describing transactions is just as essential to the study of accounting as a familiarity with plus and minus signs is to the study of mathematics. The journal entry is a *tool* for *analyzing* and *describing* the impact of various transactions on a business entity. The ability to describe a transaction in journal entry form requires an understanding of the nature of the transaction and its effect on the financial position of the business.

POSTING JOURNAL ENTRIES TO THE LEDGER ACCOUNTS (AND HOW TO "READ" A JOURNAL ENTRY)

We have made the point that transactions are recorded *first* in the journal. Ledger accounts are updated *later,* through a process called **posting.** (In a computerized system, postings often occur instantaneously, rather than later.)

Posting simply means *updating the ledger accounts* for the effects of the transactions recorded in the journal. Viewed as a mechanical task, posting basically amounts to performing the steps you describe when you "read" a journal entry aloud.

Consider the first entry appearing in Overnight's general journal. If you were to read this entry aloud, you would say: "Debit Cash, $80,000; credit Capital Stock, $80,000." That's precisely what a person posting this entry should do: Debit the Cash account for $80,000, and credit the Capital Stock account for $80,000.

The posting of Overnight's first journal entry is illustrated in Exhibit 3–2. Notice that no new information is recorded during the posting process. Posting involves copying into the ledger accounts information that *already has been recorded in the journal.* In manual accounting systems, this can be a tedious and time-consuming process, but in computer-based systems, it is done instantly and automatically. In addition, computerized posting greatly reduces the risk of errors.

Exhibit 3–2

POSTING A TRANSACTION FROM THE JOURNAL TO LEDGER ACCOUNTS

GENERAL JOURNAL

Date	Account Titles and Explanation	Debit	Credit
2011			
Jan. 20	Cash	80,000	
	Capital Stock		80,000
	Owners invest cash in the business.		

GENERAL LEDGER

Cash		Capital Stock	
1/20 80,000			1/20 80,000

Recording Balance Sheet Transactions: An Illustration

To illustrate how to use debits and credits for recording transactions in accounts, we return to the January transactions of Overnight Auto Service. At this point, we discuss only those transactions related to changes in the company's financial position and reported directly in its balance sheet. The revenue and expense transactions that took place on January 31 will be addressed later in the chapter.

Each transaction from January 20 through January 27 is analyzed first in terms of increases in assets, liabilities, and owners' equity. Second, we follow the debit and credit rules for entering these increases and decreases in specific accounts. Asset ledger accounts are shown on the left side of the analysis; liability and owners' equity ledger accounts are shown on the right side. For convenience in the following transactions, both the debit and credit figures for the transaction under discussion are shown in *red*. Figures relating to earlier transactions appear in *black*.

Jan. 20 Michael McBryan and family invested $80,000 cash in exchange for capital stock.

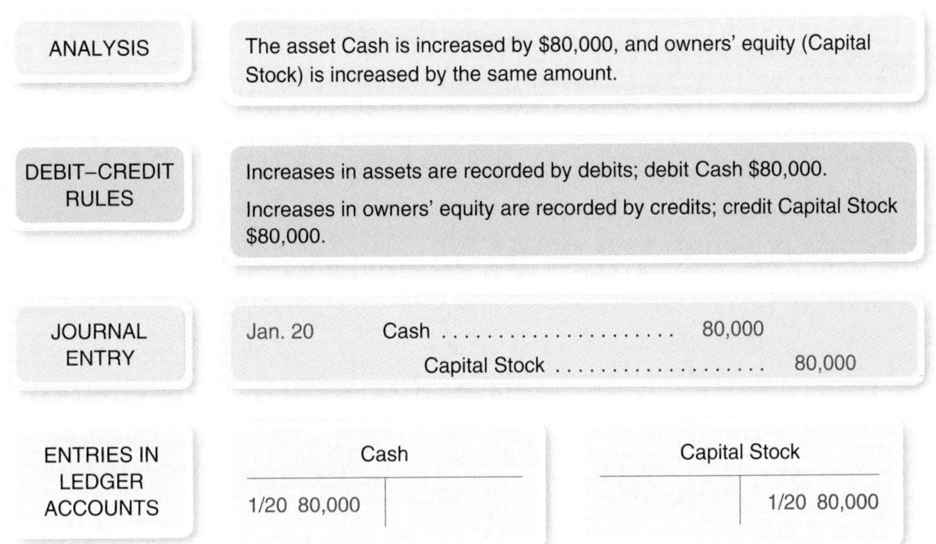

Owners invest cash in the business

Assets	= Liabilities +	Owners' Equity
+$80,000		+$80,000

Jan. 21 Representing Overnight, McBryan negotiated with both the City of Santa Teresa and Metropolitan Transit Authority (MTA) to purchase an abandoned bus garage. (The city owned the land, but the MTA owned the building.) On January 21, Overnight Auto Service purchased the land from the city for $52,000 cash.

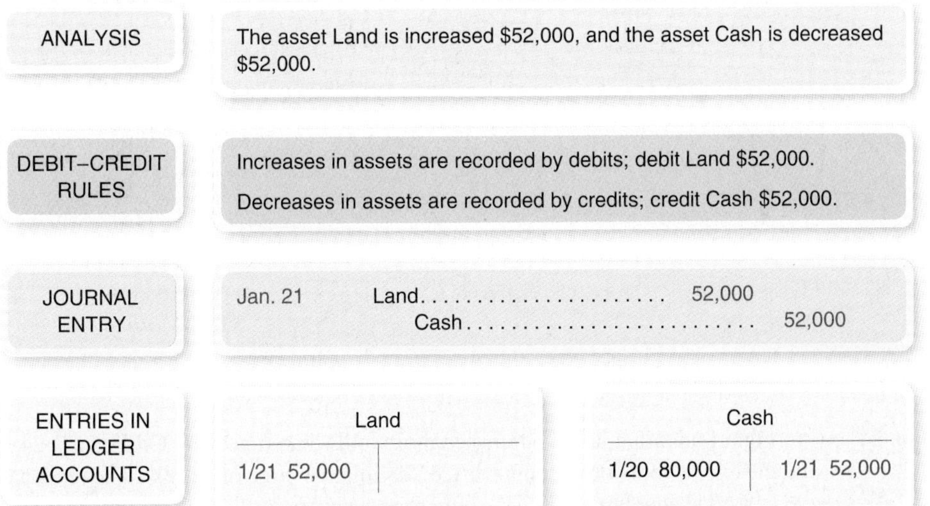

Purchase of an asset for cash

Assets	= Liabilities +	Owners' Equity
+$52,000		
−$52,000		

Jan. 22 Overnight completed the acquisition of its business location by purchasing the abandoned building from the MTA. The purchase price was $36,000; Overnight made a $6,000 cash down payment and issued a 90-day, non-interest-bearing note payable for the remaining $30,000.

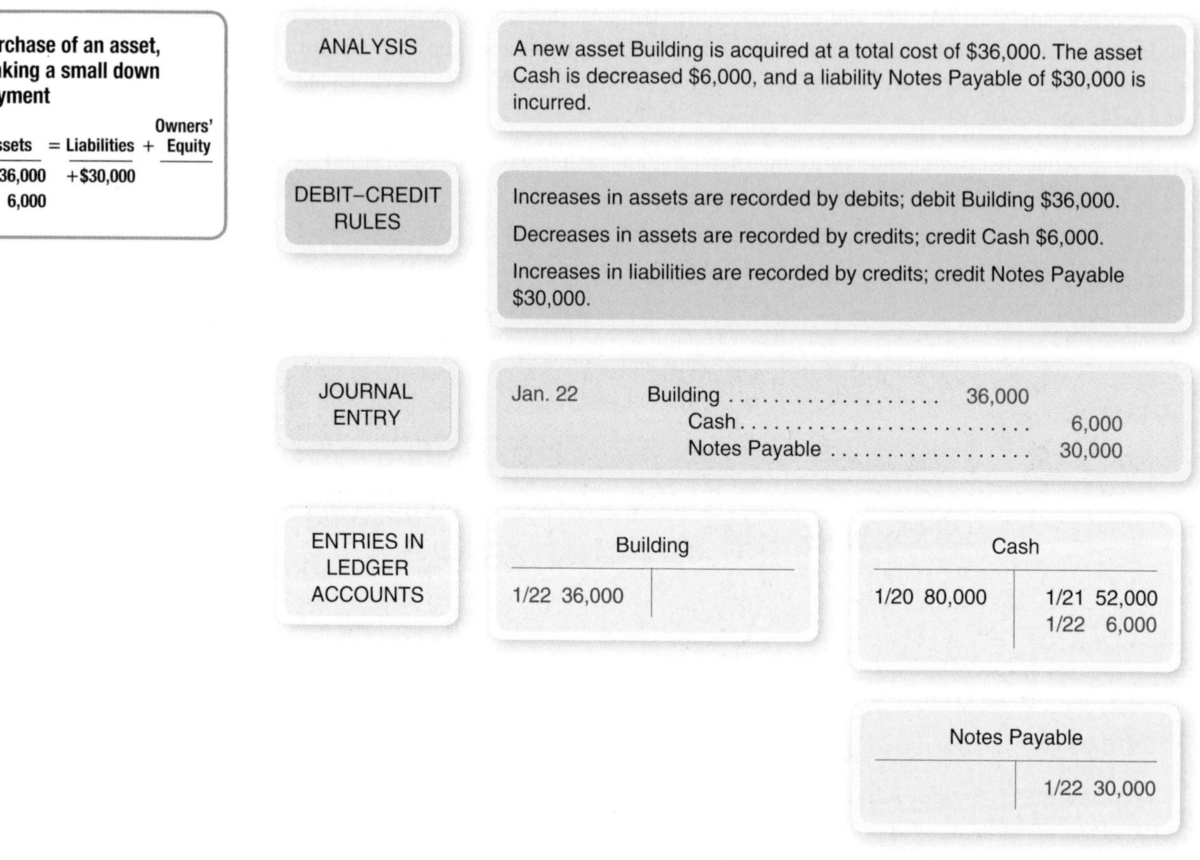

Purchase of an asset, making a small down payment

Assets	= Liabilities +	Owners' Equity
+$36,000	+$30,000	
−$ 6,000		

ANALYSIS
A new asset Building is acquired at a total cost of $36,000. The asset Cash is decreased $6,000, and a liability Notes Payable of $30,000 is incurred.

DEBIT–CREDIT RULES
Increases in assets are recorded by debits; debit Building $36,000.

Decreases in assets are recorded by credits; credit Cash $6,000.

Increases in liabilities are recorded by credits; credit Notes Payable $30,000.

JOURNAL ENTRY

Jan. 22	Building	36,000	
	Cash..........................		6,000
	Notes Payable		30,000

ENTRIES IN LEDGER ACCOUNTS

Building

Debit	Credit
1/22 36,000	

Cash

Debit	Credit
1/20 80,000	1/21 52,000
	1/22 6,000

Notes Payable

Debit	Credit
	1/22 30,000

Jan. 23 Overnight purchased tools and equipment on account from Snappy Tools. The purchase price was $13,800, due in 60 days.

Credit purchase of an asset

Assets	= Liabilities +	Owners' Equity
+$13,800	+$13,800	

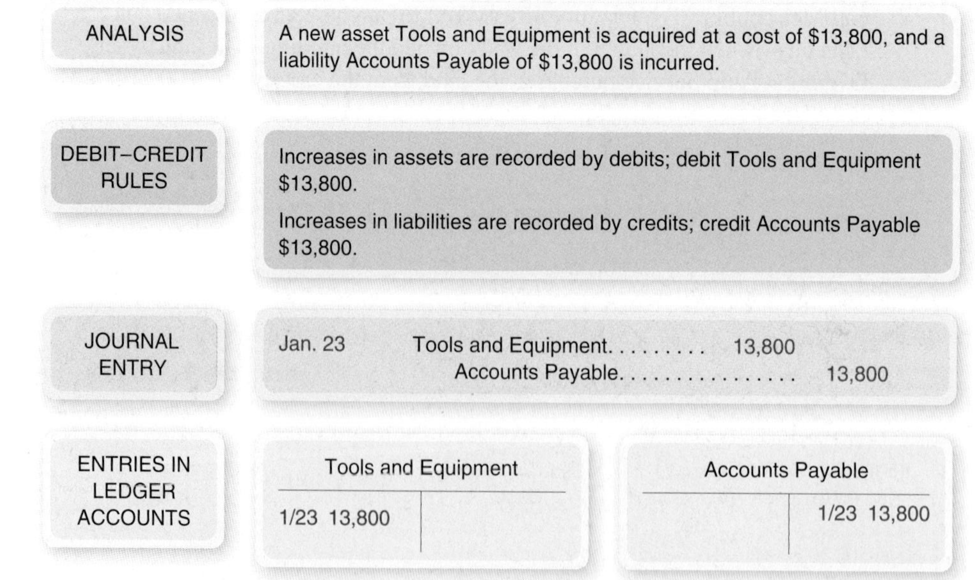

ANALYSIS
A new asset Tools and Equipment is acquired at a cost of $13,800, and a liability Accounts Payable of $13,800 is incurred.

DEBIT–CREDIT RULES
Increases in assets are recorded by debits; debit Tools and Equipment $13,800.

Increases in liabilities are recorded by credits; credit Accounts Payable $13,800.

JOURNAL ENTRY

Jan. 23	Tools and Equipment.........	13,800	
	Accounts Payable................		13,800

ENTRIES IN LEDGER ACCOUNTS

Tools and Equipment

Debit	Credit
1/23 13,800	

Accounts Payable

Debit	Credit
	1/23 13,800

Jan. 24 Overnight found that it had purchased more tools than it needed. On January 24, it sold the excess tools on account to Ace Towing at a price of $1,800. The tools were sold at a price equal to their cost, so there was no gain or loss on this transaction.

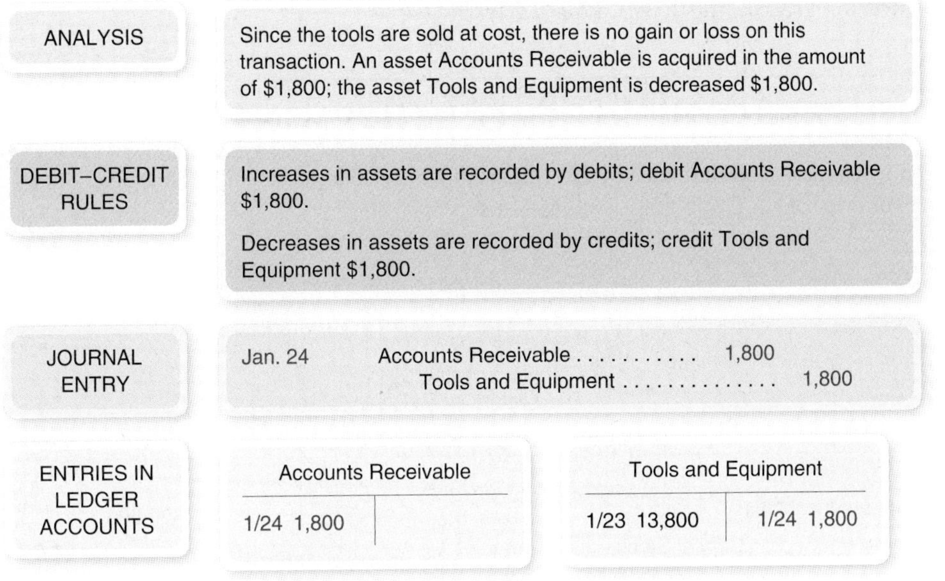

ANALYSIS

Since the tools are sold at cost, there is no gain or loss on this transaction. An asset Accounts Receivable is acquired in the amount of $1,800; the asset Tools and Equipment is decreased $1,800.

DEBIT–CREDIT RULES

Increases in assets are recorded by debits; debit Accounts Receivable $1,800.

Decreases in assets are recorded by credits; credit Tools and Equipment $1,800.

JOURNAL ENTRY

		Debit	Credit
Jan. 24	Accounts Receivable	1,800	
	Tools and Equipment		1,800

ENTRIES IN LEDGER ACCOUNTS

Accounts Receivable	
1/24 1,800	

Tools and Equipment	
1/23 13,800	1/24 1,800

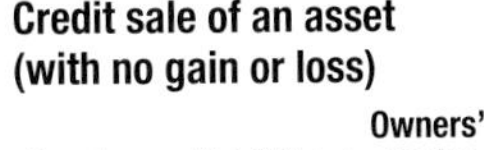

Credit sale of an asset (with no gain or loss)

Assets	=	Liabilities	+	Owners' Equity
+$1,800				
−$1,800				

Jan. 26 Overnight received $600 in partial collection of the account receivable from Ace Towing.

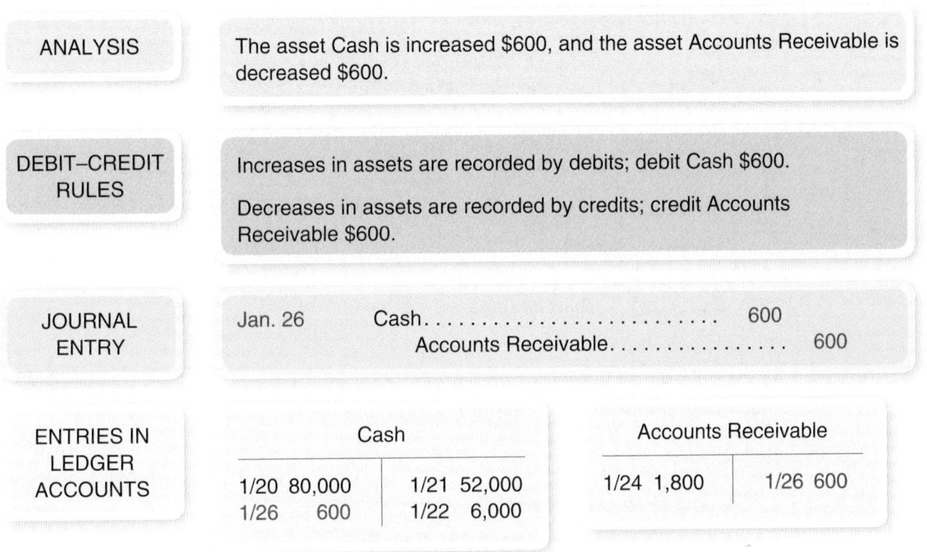

ANALYSIS

The asset Cash is increased $600, and the asset Accounts Receivable is decreased $600.

DEBIT–CREDIT RULES

Increases in assets are recorded by debits; debit Cash $600.

Decreases in assets are recorded by credits; credit Accounts Receivable $600.

JOURNAL ENTRY

		Debit	Credit
Jan. 26	Cash.	600	
	Accounts Receivable.		600

ENTRIES IN LEDGER ACCOUNTS

Cash	
1/20 80,000	1/21 52,000
1/26 600	1/22 6,000

Accounts Receivable	
1/24 1,800	1/26 600

Collection of an account receivable

Assets	=	Liabilities	+	Owners' Equity
+$600				
−$600				

Jan. 27 Overnight made a $6,800 partial payment of its account payable to Snappy Tools.

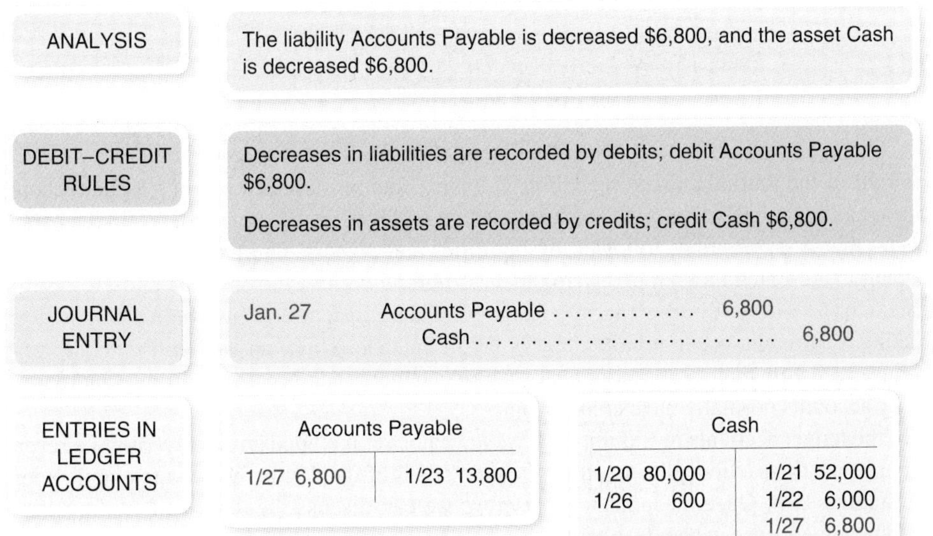

ANALYSIS

The liability Accounts Payable is decreased $6,800, and the asset Cash is decreased $6,800.

DEBIT–CREDIT RULES

Decreases in liabilities are recorded by debits; debit Accounts Payable $6,800.

Decreases in assets are recorded by credits; credit Cash $6,800.

JOURNAL ENTRY

		Debit	Credit
Jan. 27	Accounts Payable	6,800	
	Cash		6,800

ENTRIES IN LEDGER ACCOUNTS

Accounts Payable	
1/27 6,800	1/23 13,800

Cash	
1/20 80,000	1/21 52,000
1/26 600	1/22 6,000
	1/27 6,800

Payment of an account payable

Assets	=	Liabilities	+	Owners' Equity
−$6,800		−$6,800		

Ledger Accounts after Posting

The seven journal entries made by Overnight Auto Service from January 20 through January 27 are summarized in Exhibit 3–3.

Exhibit 3–3
GENERAL JOURNAL ENTRIES: JANUARY 20 THROUGH 27

OVERNIGHT AUTO SERVICE
GENERAL JOURNAL
JANUARY 20–27, 2011

Date	Account Titles and Explanation	Debit	Credit
2011			
Jan. 20	Cash	80,000	
	Capital Stock		80,000
	Owners invest cash in the business.		
21	Land	52,000	
	Cash		52,000
	Purchased land for business site.		
22	Building	36,000	
	Cash		6,000
	Notes Payable		30,000
	Purchased building from the MTA. Paid part cash; balance payable within 90 days.		
23	Tools and Equipment	13,800	
	Accounts Payable		13,800
	Purchased tools and equipment on credit from Snappy Tools. Due in 60 days.		
24	Accounts Receivable	1,800	
	Tools and Equipment		1,800
	Sold unused tools and equipment at cost to Ace Towing.		
26	Cash	600	
	Accounts Receivable		600
	Collected part of account receivable from Ace Towing.		
27	Accounts Payable	6,800	
	Cash		6,800
	Made partial payment of the liability to Snappy Tools.		

After all of the journal entries in Exhibit 3–3 have been posted, Overnight's ledger accounts appear as shown in Exhibit 3–4. The accounts are arranged in the same order as in the balance sheet—that is, assets first, followed by liabilities and owners' equity accounts. Each ledger account is presented in what is referred to as a *running balance* format (as opposed to simple T accounts). You will notice that the running balance format does not indicate specifically whether a particular account has a debit or credit balance. This causes no difficulty, however, because we know that asset accounts normally have debit balances, and liability and owners' equity accounts normally have credit balances.

In the ledger accounts in Exhibit 3–4, we have not yet included any of Overnight's revenue and expense transactions discussed in Chapter 2. All of the company's revenue and expense transactions took place on January 31. Before we can discuss the debit and credit rules for revenue and expense accounts, a more in-depth discussion of *net income* is warranted.

Exhibit 3-4

LEDGER SHOWING TRANSACTIONS

CASH

Date	Debit	Credit	Balance
2011			
Jan. 20	80,000		80,000
21		52,000	28,000
22		6,000	22,000
26	600		22,600
27		6,800	15,800

ACCOUNTS RECEIVABLE

Date	Debit	Credit	Balance
2011			
Jan. 24	1,800		1,800
26		600	1,200

LAND

Date	Debit	Credit	Balance
2011			
Jan. 21	52,000		52,000

BUILDING

Date	Debit	Credit	Balance
2011			
Jan. 22	36,000		36,000

TOOLS AND EQUIPMENT

Date	Debit	Credit	Balance
2011			
Jan. 23	13,800		13,800
24		1,800	12,000

NOTES PAYABLE

Date	Debit	Credit	Balance
2011			
Jan. 22		30,000	30,000

ACCOUNTS PAYABLE

Date	Debit	Credit	Balance
2011			
Jan. 23		13,800	13,800
27	6,800		7,000

CAPITAL STOCK

Date	Debit	Credit	Balance
2011			
Jan. 20		80,000	80,000

What Is Net Income?

Learning Objective
LO6 Explain the nature of *net income, revenue,* and *expenses.*

As previously noted, **net income** is *an increase in owners' equity resulting from the profitable operation of the business.* Net income does not consist of any cash or any other specific assets. Rather, net income is a *computation* of the overall effects of many business transactions on *owners' equity.* The effects of net income on the basic accounting equation are illustrated as follows:

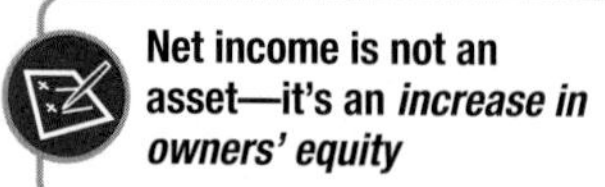
Net income is not an asset—it's an *increase in owners' equity*

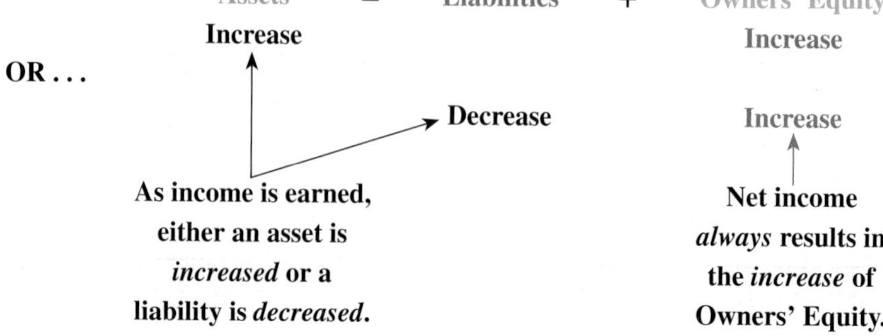
Assets = Liabilities + Owners' Equity
Increase
Increase
OR . . .
Decrease
Increase
As income is earned, either an asset is *increased* or a liability is *decreased.*
Net income *always* results in the *increase* of Owners' Equity.

Our point is that net income represents an *increase in owners' equity* and has no direct relationship to the types or amounts of assets on hand. Even a business operating at a profit may run short of cash.

In the balance sheet, the changes in owners' equity resulting from profitable or unprofitable operations are reflected in the balance of the stockholders' equity account, *Retained Earnings.* The assets and liabilities of the business that change as a result of income-related activities appear in their respective sections of the balance sheet.

RETAINED EARNINGS

As illustrated in Chapter 2, the Retained Earnings account appears in the stockholders' equity section of the balance sheet. Earning net income causes the balance in the Retained Earnings account to increase. However, many corporations follow a policy of distributing to their stockholders some of the resources generated by profitable operations. Distributions of this nature are termed **dividends,** and they reduce both total assets and stockholders' equity. The reduction in stockholders' equity is reflected by decreasing the balance of the Retained Earnings account.

WAL★MART
Always
© The McGraw-Hill Companies, Inc./John Flournoy, photographer/DAL

The balance in the **Retained Earnings** account represents the total net income of the corporation over the *entire lifetime* of the business, less all of the dividends to its stockholders. In short, retained earnings represent the earnings that have been *retained* by the corporation to finance growth. Some of the largest corporations have become large by consistently retaining in the business most of the resources generated by profitable operations. For instance, a recent annual report of **Walmart Stores, Inc.**, shows total stockholders' equity of $65 billion. Of this amount, retained earnings of nearly $64 billion account for over 98 percent of the company's total equity.

THE INCOME STATEMENT: A PREVIEW

An **income statement** is a financial statement that summarizes the profitability of a business entity for a specified period of time. In this statement, net income is determined by comparing *sales prices* of goods or services sold during the period with the *costs* incurred by the business in delivering these goods or services. The technical accounting terms for these components of net income are **revenue** and **expenses.** Therefore, accountants say that net income is equal to *revenue minus expenses.* Should expenses exceed revenue, a **net loss** results.

A sample income statement for Overnight Auto Service for the year ended December 31, 2011, is shown in Exhibit 3–5. In Chapter 5, we show exactly how this income statement was developed from the company's accounting records. For now, however, the illustration will assist us in discussing some of the basic concepts involved in measuring net income.

Exhibit 3–5

A PREVIEW OF OVERNIGHT'S INCOME STATEMENT

OVERNIGHT AUTO SERVICE INCOME STATEMENT FOR THE YEAR ENDED DECEMBER 31, 2011		
Revenue:		
Repair service revenue		$172,000
Rent revenue earned		3,000
Total revenue		$175,000
Expenses:		
Advertising	$ 3,900	
Salaries and wages	58,750	
Supplies	7,500	
Depreciation: building	1,650	
Depreciation: tools and equipment	2,200	
Utilities	19,400	
Insurance	15,000	
Interest	30	108,430
Income before income taxes		$ 66,570
Income taxes		26,628
Net income		$ 39,942

Income Must Be Related to a Specified Period of Time Notice that our sample income statement covers a *period of time*—namely, the year 2011. A balance sheet shows the financial position of a business at a *particular date.* We cannot evaluate net income unless it is associated with a specific time period. For example, if an executive says, "My business earns a net income of $10,000," the profitability of the business is unclear. Does it earn $10,000 per week, per month, or per year?

CASE IN POINT

The late J. Paul Getty, one of the world's first billionaires, was once interviewed by a group of business students. One of the students asked Getty to estimate the amount of his income. As the student had not specified a time period, Getty decided to have some fun with his audience and responded, "About $11,000." He paused long enough to allow the group to express surprise over this seemingly low amount, and then completed his sentence, "an hour." (Incidentally, $11,000 per hour, 24 hours per day, amounts to about $100 million per year.)

Accounting Periods The period of time covered by an income statement is termed the company's **accounting period.** To provide the users of financial statements with timely information, net income is measured for relatively short accounting periods of equal length. This concept, called the **time period principle,** is one of the underlying accounting principles that guide the interpretation of financial events and the preparation of financial statements.

The length of a company's accounting period depends on how frequently managers, investors, and other interested people require information about the company's performance.

Every business prepares annual income statements, and most businesses prepare quarterly and monthly income statements as well. (Quarterly statements cover a three-month period and are prepared by all large corporations for distribution to their stockholders.)

The 12-month accounting period used by an entity is called its **fiscal year.** The fiscal year used by most companies coincides with the calendar year and ends on December 31. Some businesses, however, elect to use a fiscal year that ends on some other date.

For example, **The Walt Disney Company** ends its fiscal year on September 30. Why? For one reason, September and October are relatively slow months at the company's theme parks. Furthermore, September financial statements provide timely information about the preceding summer, which is the company's busiest season. Most large retailers, such as **Walmart** and **JCPenney**, end their fiscal years at the end of January, after the rush of the holiday season. Many choose the last Saturday of January as their cutoff, which results in an exact 52-week reporting period approximately five out of every six years.

Let us now explore the meaning of the accounting terms *revenue* and *expenses* in more detail.

REVENUE

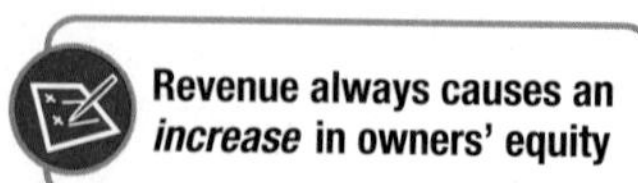
Revenue always causes an *increase* in owners' equity

Revenue is the price of goods sold and services rendered during a given accounting period. Earning revenue causes owners' equity to increase. When a business renders services or sells merchandise to its customers, it usually receives cash or acquires an account receivable from the customer. The inflow of cash and receivables from customers increases the total assets of the company; on the other side of the accounting equation, owners' equity increases to match the increase in total assets. Thus, revenue is the gross *increase in owners' equity* resulting from operation of the business.

Various account titles are used to describe different types of revenue. For example, a business that sells merchandise rather than services, such as **Walmart** or **General Motors**, uses the term *Sales* to describe its revenue. In the professional practices of physicians, CPAs, and attorneys, revenue usually is called *Fees Earned.* A real estate office, however, might call its revenue *Commissions Earned.*

Overnight Auto Service's income statement reveals that the company records its revenue in two separate accounts: (1) *Repair Service Revenue* and (2) *Rent Revenue Earned.* A professional sports team might also have separate revenue accounts for *Ticket Sales, Concessions Revenue,* and *Revenue from Television Contracts.* Another type of revenue common to many businesses is *Interest Revenue* (or Interest Earned), stemming from the interest earned on bank deposits, notes receivable, and interest-bearing investments.

Learning Objective
LO7 **Apply the *realization* and *matching* principles in recording revenue and expenses.**

The Realization Principle: When to Record Revenue

When should revenue be recognized? In most cases, the **realization principle** indicates that revenue should be recognized *at the time goods are sold or services are rendered.* At this point, the business has essentially completed the earnings process, and the sales value of the goods or services can be measured objectively. At any time prior to the sale, the ultimate value of the goods or services sold can only be estimated. After the sale, the only step that remains is to collect from the customer, usually a relatively certain event.

To illustrate, assume that on July 25 a radio station contracts with a car dealership to air a series of one-minute advertisements during August. If all of the agreed-upon ads are aired in August, but payment for the ads is not received until September, in which month should the station recognize the advertising revenue? The answer is August, the month in which it *rendered the services* that earned the advertising revenue. In other words, revenue is recognized when it is *earned,* without regard to when a contract is signed or when cash payment for providing goods or services is received.

EXPENSES

Expenses are the costs of the goods and services used up in the process of earning revenue. Examples include the cost of employees' salaries, advertising, rent, utilities, and the depreciation of buildings, automobiles, and office equipment. All these costs are necessary to attract and serve customers and thereby earn revenue. Expenses are often called the "costs of doing business," that is, the cost of the various activities necessary to carry on a business.

An expense always causes a *decrease in owners' equity.* The related changes in the accounting equation can be either (1) a decrease in assets or (2) an increase in liabilities. An expense reduces assets if payment occurs at the time that the expense is incurred. If the expense will not be paid until later, as, for example, the purchase of advertising services on account, the recording of the expense will be accompanied by an increase in liabilities.

Expenses always cause a *decrease* in owners' equity

The Matching Principle: When to Record Expenses A significant relationship exists between revenue and expenses. Expenses are incurred for the *purpose of producing revenue.* In the measurement of net income for a period, revenue should be offset by *all the expenses incurred in producing that revenue.* This concept of offsetting expenses against revenue on a basis of cause and effect is called the **matching principle.**

Timing is an important factor in matching (offsetting) revenue with the related expenses. For example, in the preparation of monthly income statements, it is important to offset this month's expenses against this month's revenue. We should not offset this month's expenses against last month's revenue because there is no cause and effect relationship between the two.

Assume that the salaries earned by a company's marketing team for serving customers in July are not paid until early August. In which month should these salaries be regarded as expenses—July or August? The answer is July, because July is the month in which the marketing team's services *helped to produce revenue.* Just as revenue and cash receipts are not one and the same, expenses and cash payments are not identical. In fact, the cash payment of an expense may occur before, after, or in the same period that revenue is earned. In deciding when to report an expense in the income statement, the critical question is, "In what period does the cash expenditure help to produce revenue?"—*not,* "When does the payment of cash occur?"

Expenditures Benefiting More than One Accounting Period Many expenditures made by a business benefit two or more accounting periods. Fire insurance policies, for example, usually cover a period of 12 months. If a company prepares monthly income statements, a portion of the cost of such a policy should be allocated to insurance expense each month that the policy is in force. In this case, apportionment of the cost of the policy by months is an easy matter. If the 12-month policy costs $2,400, for example, the insurance expense for each month amounts to $200 ($2,400 cost ÷ 12 months).

Not all transactions can be divided so precisely by accounting periods. The purchase of a building, furniture and fixtures, machinery, a computer, or an automobile provides benefits to the business over all the years in which such an asset is used. No one can determine in advance exactly how many years of service will be received from such long-lived assets. Nevertheless, in measuring the net income of a business for a period of one year or less, accountants must *estimate* what portion of the cost of the building and other long-lived assets is applicable to the current year. Since the allocations of these costs are estimates rather than precise measurements, it follows that income statements should be regarded as useful *approximations* of net income rather than as absolutely correct measurements.

For some expenditures, such as those for employee training programs, it is not possible to estimate objectively the number of accounting periods over which revenue is likely to be produced. In such cases, generally accepted accounting principles require that the expenditure be charged *immediately to expense.* This treatment is based upon the accounting principle of **objectivity** and the concept of **conservatism.** Accountants require *objective evidence* that an expenditure will produce revenue in future periods before they will view the expenditure as creating an asset. When this objective evidence does not exist, they follow the conservative practice of recording the expenditure as an expense. *Conservatism,* in this context, means applying the accounting treatment that results in the *lowest* (most conservative) estimate of net income for the current period.

INTERNATIONAL CASE IN POINT 

International financial reporting standards (IFRSs) differ significantly from U.S. GAAP with respect to costs that are expensed immediately and costs that are capitalized. For example, IFRS 38 allows development costs to be capitalized if certain criteria are met, but under U.S. GAAP these same costs would need to be expensed in the period in which they occur. Alternatively, idle capacity and spoilage costs need to be expensed immediately under IFRS 2, but U.S. GAAP allows these costs to be capitalized in inventory. The FASB and the IASB have made an agreement to work toward eliminating differences between international accounting standards and GAAP over the next several years.

THE ACCRUAL BASIS OF ACCOUNTING

The policy of recognizing revenue in the accounting records when it is *earned* and recognizing expenses when the related goods or services are *used* is called the **accrual basis of accounting.** The purpose of accrual accounting is to measure the profitability of the *economic activities conducted* during the accounting period.

The most important concept involved in accrual accounting is the *matching principle.* Revenue is offset with all of the expenses incurred in generating that revenue, thus providing a measure of the overall profitability of the economic activity.

An alternative to the accrual basis is called *cash basis accounting.* Under cash basis accounting, revenue is recognized when cash is collected from the customer, rather than when the company sells goods or renders services. Expenses are recognized when payment is made, rather than when the related goods or services are used in business operations. The cash basis of accounting measures the amounts of cash received and paid out during the period, but it does *not* provide a good measure of the *profitability of activities* undertaken during the period.

Exhibit 3–6 illustrates that, under the accrual basis of accounting, cash receipts or disbursements may occur *prior to* or *after* revenue is earned or an expense is incurred.

Exhibit 3–6

CASH FLOW VERSUS INCOME STATEMENT RECOGNITION

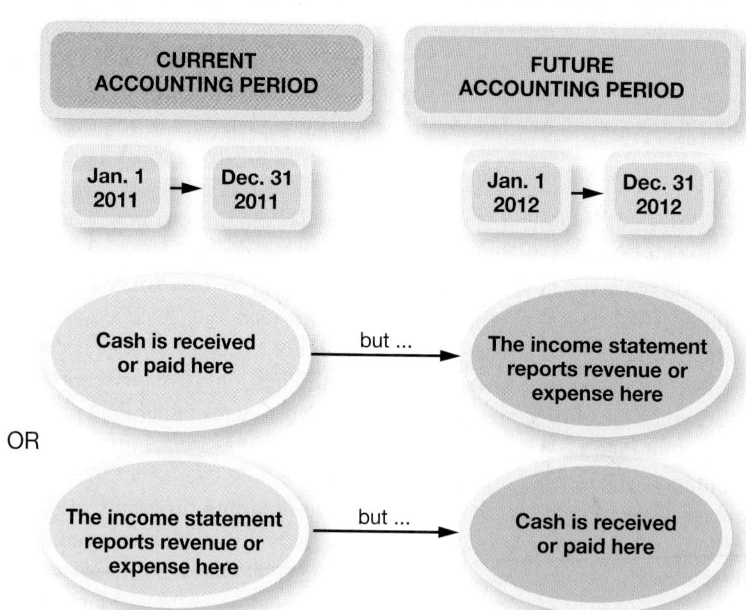

DEBIT AND CREDIT RULES FOR REVENUE AND EXPENSES

We have stressed that revenue increases owners' equity and that expenses decrease owners' equity. The debit and credit rules for recording revenue and expenses in the ledger accounts are a natural extension of the rules for recording changes in owners' equity. The rules previously stated for recording increases and decreases in owners' equity are as follows:

- *Increases* in owners' equity are recorded by *credits.*
- *Decreases* in owners' equity are recorded by *debits.*

This rule is now extended to cover revenue and expense accounts:

- *Revenue* increases owners' equity; therefore, revenue is recorded by *credits.*
- *Expenses* decrease owners' equity; therefore, expenses are recorded by *debits.*

Dividends

A dividend is a distribution of assets (usually cash) by a corporation to its stockholders. In some respects, dividends are similar to expenses—they reduce both the assets and the owners' equity in the business. However, *dividends are not an expense, and they are not deducted from revenue in the income statement.* The reason why dividends are not viewed as an expense is that these payments do not serve to generate revenue. Rather, they are a *distribution of profits* to the owners of the business.

Since the declaration of a dividend reduces stockholders' equity, the dividend could be recorded by debiting the Retained Earnings account. However, a clearer record is created if a separate Dividends account is debited for all dividends to stockholders. The reporting of dividends in the financial statements will be illustrated in Chapter 5.

The debit–credit rules for revenue, expenses, and dividends are summarized below:

Debit–credit rules related to effect on owners' equity

Owners' Equity	
Decreases recorded by Debits	Increases recorded by Credits
Expenses decrease owners' equity	Revenue increases owners' equity
Expenses are recorded by Debits	Revenue is recorded by Credits
Dividends reduce owners' equity	
Dividends are recorded by Debits	

Recording Income Statement Transactions: An Illustration

Learning Objective LO8
Understand how revenue and expense transactions are recorded in an accounting system.

In Chapter 2, we introduced Overnight Auto Service, a small auto repair shop formed on January 20, 2011. Early in this chapter, we journalized and posted all of Overnight's balance sheet transactions through January 27. At this point we will illustrate the manner in which Overnight's January income statement transactions were handled and continue into February with additional transactions.

Three transactions involving revenue and expenses were recorded by Overnight on January 31, 2011. The following illustrations provide an analysis of each transaction.

Jan. 31 Recorded revenue of $2,200, all of which was received in cash.

Revenue earned and collected

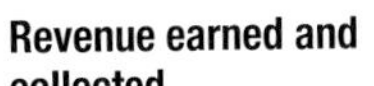

Assets	=	Liabilities	+	Owners' Equity
+$2,200				+$2,200

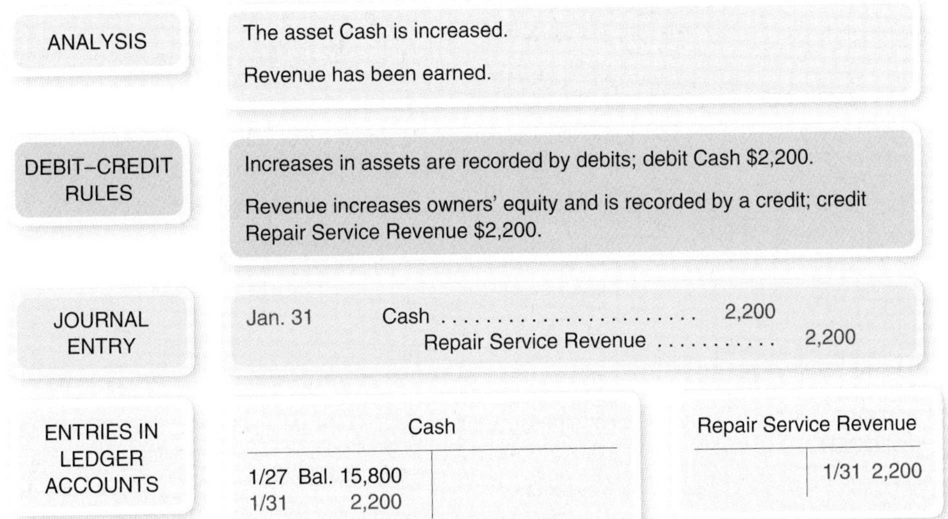

ANALYSIS	The asset Cash is increased. Revenue has been earned.
DEBIT–CREDIT RULES	Increases in assets are recorded by debits; debit Cash $2,200. Revenue increases owners' equity and is recorded by a credit; credit Repair Service Revenue $2,200.
JOURNAL ENTRY	Jan. 31 Cash .... 2,200 Repair Service Revenue 2,200
ENTRIES IN LEDGER ACCOUNTS	**Cash**: 1/27 Bal. 15,800 (debit); 1/31 2,200 (debit) **Repair Service Revenue**: 1/31 2,200 (credit)

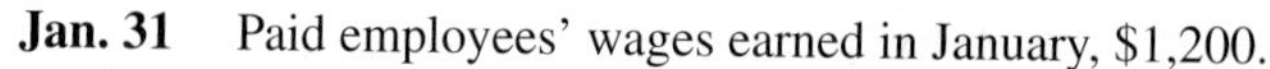

Jan. 31 Paid employees' wages earned in January, $1,200.

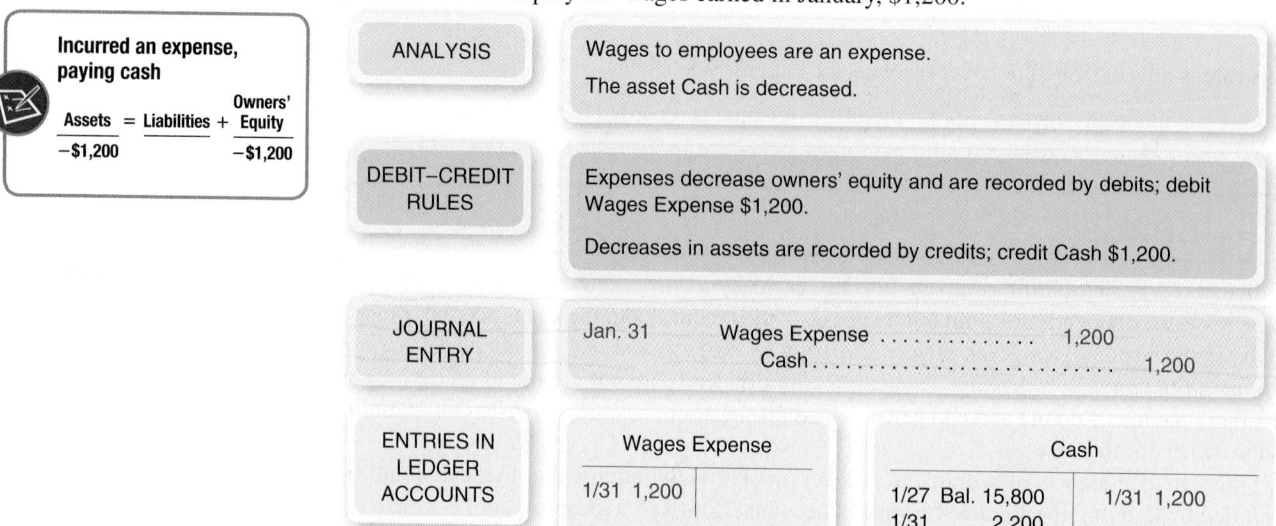

Incurred an expense, paying cash

Assets	=	Liabilities	+	Owners' Equity
−$1,200				−$1,200

ANALYSIS	Wages to employees are an expense. The asset Cash is decreased.
DEBIT–CREDIT RULES	Expenses decrease owners' equity and are recorded by debits; debit Wages Expense $1,200. Decreases in assets are recorded by credits; credit Cash $1,200.
JOURNAL ENTRY	Jan. 31 Wages Expense .... 1,200 Cash.......................... 1,200
ENTRIES IN LEDGER ACCOUNTS	**Wages Expense** Debit: 1/31 1,200 **Cash** Debit: 1/27 Bal. 15,800; 1/31 2,200 Credit: 1/31 1,200

Jan. 31 Paid for utilities used in January, $200.

Incurred an expense, paying cash

Assets	=	Liabilities	+	Owners' Equity
−$200				−$200

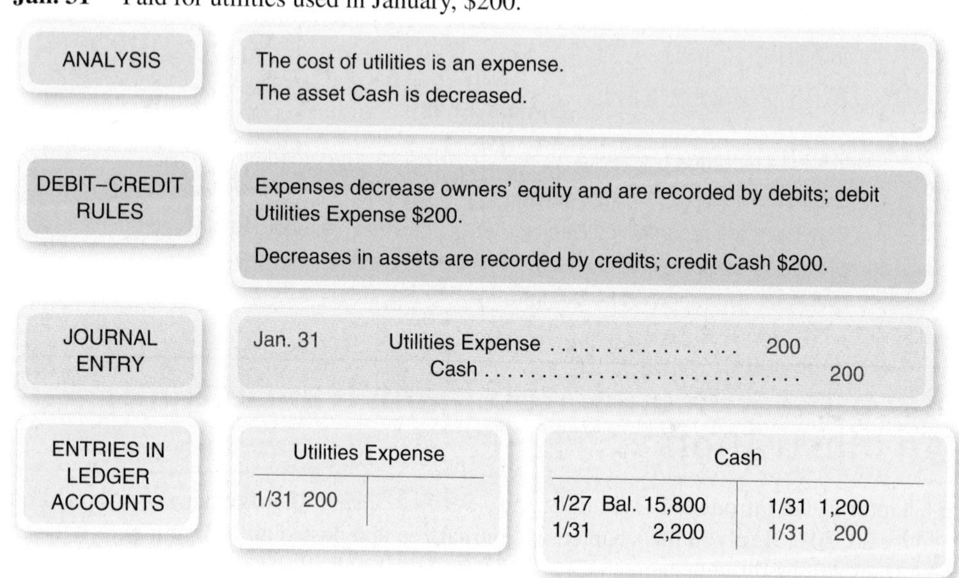

ANALYSIS	The cost of utilities is an expense. The asset Cash is decreased.
DEBIT–CREDIT RULES	Expenses decrease owners' equity and are recorded by debits; debit Utilities Expense $200. Decreases in assets are recorded by credits; credit Cash $200.
JOURNAL ENTRY	Jan. 31 Utilities Expense .... 200 Cash 200
ENTRIES IN LEDGER ACCOUNTS	**Utilities Expense** Debit: 1/31 200 **Cash** Debit: 1/27 Bal. 15,800; 1/31 2,200 Credit: 1/31 1,200; 1/31 200

Having analyzed and recorded all of Overnight's January transactions, next we focus upon the company's February activities. Overnight's February transactions are described, analyzed, and recorded as follows:

Feb. 1 Paid *Daily Tribune* $360 cash for newspaper advertising to be run during February.

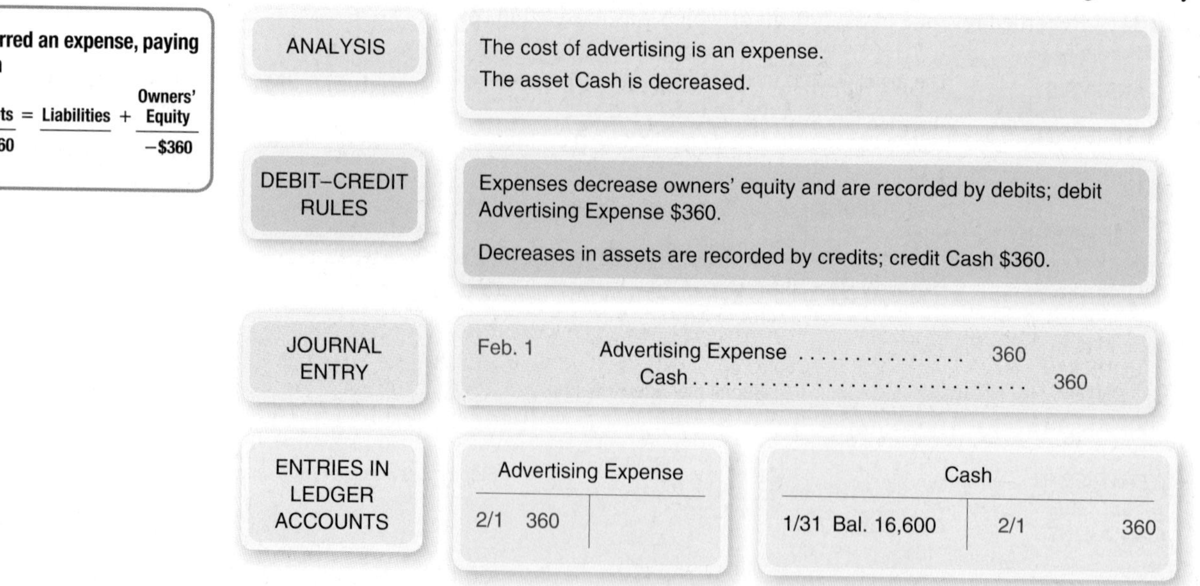

Incurred an expense, paying cash

Assets	=	Liabilities	+	Owners' Equity
−$360				−$360

ANALYSIS	The cost of advertising is an expense. The asset Cash is decreased.
DEBIT–CREDIT RULES	Expenses decrease owners' equity and are recorded by debits; debit Advertising Expense $360. Decreases in assets are recorded by credits; credit Cash $360.
JOURNAL ENTRY	Feb. 1 Advertising Expense .... 360 Cash.............................. 360
ENTRIES IN LEDGER ACCOUNTS	**Advertising Expense** Debit: 2/1 360 **Cash** Debit: 1/31 Bal. 16,600 Credit: 2/1 360

Feb. 2 Purchased radio advertising from KRAM to be aired in February. The cost was $470, payable within 30 days.

ANALYSIS

The cost of advertising is an expense.
The liability Accounts Payable is incurred.

DEBIT–CREDIT RULES

Expenses decrease owners' equity and are recorded by debits; debit Advertising Expense $470.

Increases in liabilities are recorded by credits; credit Accounts Payable $470.

JOURNAL ENTRY

Feb. 2	Advertising Expense	470	
	Accounts Payable		470

ENTRIES IN LEDGER ACCOUNTS

Advertising Expense

2/1	360	
2/2	470	

Accounts Payable

	1/31 Bal.	7,000
	2/2	470

Incurred an expense to be paid later

Assets =	Liabilities +	Owners' Equity
	+$470	−$470

Feb. 4 Purchased various shop supplies (such as grease, solvents, nuts, and bolts) from CAPA Auto Parts; the cost was $1,400, due in 30 days. These supplies are expected to meet Overnight's needs for *three or four months.*

ANALYSIS

As these supplies will last for several accounting periods, they are an asset, not an expense of February.[1]
A liability is incurred.

DEBIT–CREDIT RULES

Increases in assets are recorded by debits; debit Shop Supplies $1,400.

Increases in liabilities are recorded by credits; credit Accounts Payable $1,400.

JOURNAL ENTRY

Feb. 4	Shop Supplies	1,400	
	Accounts Payable		1,400

ENTRIES IN LEDGER ACCOUNTS

Shop Supplies EXPENSE

2/4	1,400	

Accounts Payable

	1/31 Bal.	7,000
	2/2	470
	2/4	1,400

When a purchase clearly benefits future accounting periods, it's an asset, not an expense

Assets =	Liabilities +	Owners' Equity
+$1,400	+$1,400	

[1] If the supplies are expected to be used within the *current* accounting period, their cost may be debited directly to the Supplies Expense account, rather than to an asset account.

Feb. 15 Collected $4,980 cash for repairs made to vehicles of Airport Shuttle Service.

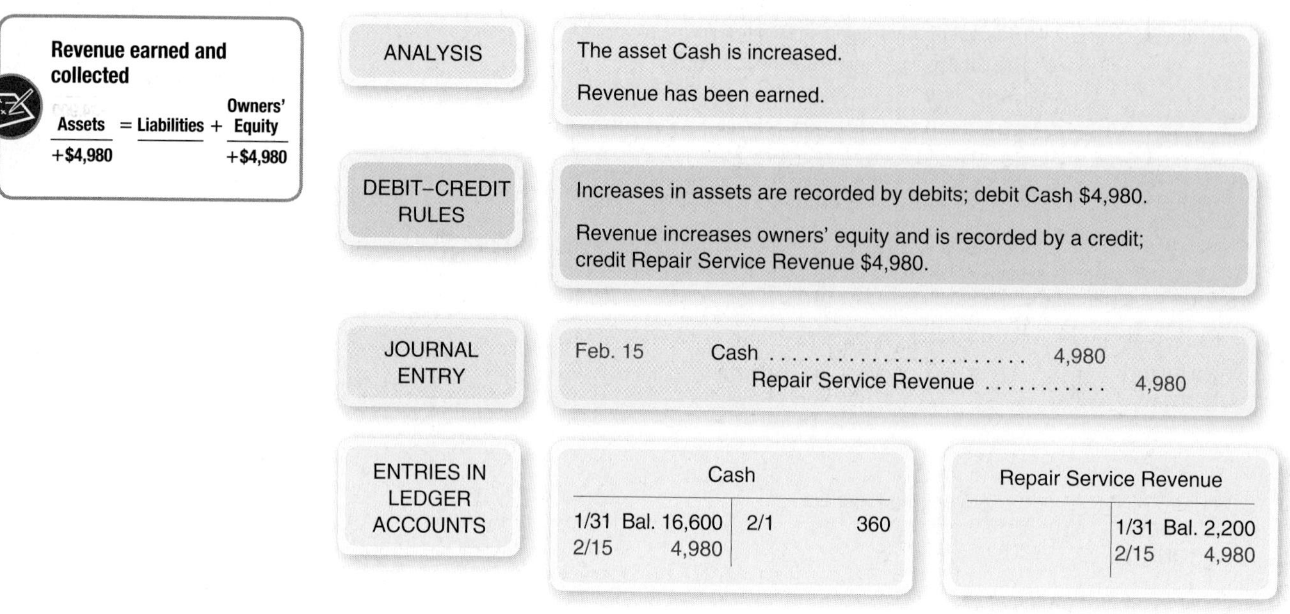

Revenue earned and collected
Assets = Liabilities + Owners' Equity
+$4,980
+$4,980
ANALYSIS
The asset Cash is increased.
Revenue has been earned.
DEBIT–CREDIT RULES
Increases in assets are recorded by debits; debit Cash $4,980.
Revenue increases owners' equity and is recorded by a credit; credit Repair Service Revenue $4,980.
JOURNAL ENTRY
Feb. 15 Cash 4,980
Repair Service Revenue 4,980
ENTRIES IN LEDGER ACCOUNTS
Cash
1/31 Bal. 16,600
2/15 4,980
2/1 360
Repair Service Revenue
1/31 Bal. 2,200
2/15 4,980

Feb. 28 Billed Harbor Cab Co. $5,400 for maintenance and repair services Overnight provided in February. The agreement with Harbor Cab calls for payment to be received by March 10.

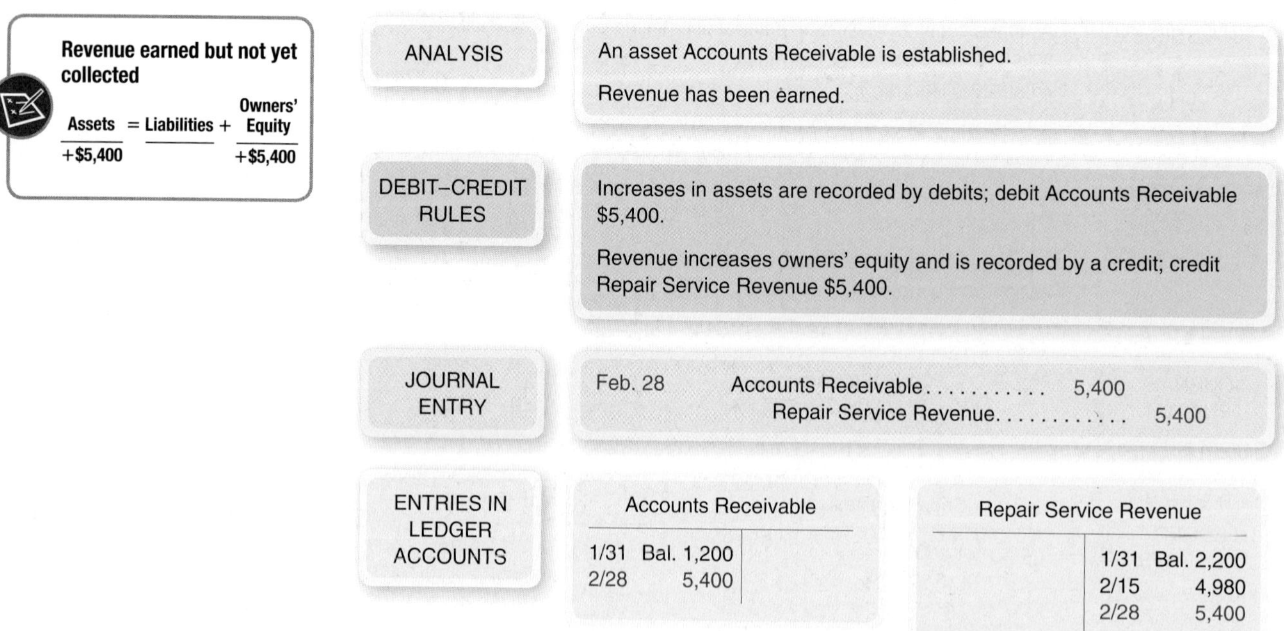

Revenue earned but not yet collected
Assets = Liabilities + Owners' Equity
+$5,400
+$5,400
ANALYSIS
An asset Accounts Receivable is established.
Revenue has been earned.
DEBIT–CREDIT RULES
Increases in assets are recorded by debits; debit Accounts Receivable $5,400.
Revenue increases owners' equity and is recorded by a credit; credit Repair Service Revenue $5,400.
JOURNAL ENTRY
Feb. 28 Accounts Receivable........... 5,400
Repair Service Revenue............ 5,400
ENTRIES IN LEDGER ACCOUNTS
Accounts Receivable
1/31 Bal. 1,200
2/28 5,400
Repair Service Revenue
1/31 Bal. 2,200
2/15 4,980
2/28 5,400

Feb. 28 Paid employees' wages earned in February, $4,900.

ANALYSIS	Wages to employees are an expense. The asset Cash is decreased.
DEBIT–CREDIT RULES	Expenses decrease owners' equity and are recorded by debits; debit Wages Expense $4,900. Decreases in assets are recorded by credits; credit Cash $4,900.
JOURNAL ENTRY	Feb. 28 Wages Expense .... 4,900 Cash 4,900

ENTRIES IN LEDGER ACCOUNTS

Wages Expense

1/31 Bal. 1,200	
2/28 4,900	

Cash

1/31 Bal. 16,600	2/1 360
2/15 4,980	2/28 4,900

Incurred an expense, paying cash

Assets	= Liabilities +	Owners' Equity
−$4,900		−$4,900

YOUR TURN **You as Overnight Auto Service's Accountant**

Your good friend, Fred Jonas, is the manager of Harbor Cab Co. Your family and Fred's family meet frequently outside of your respective workplaces for fun. At a recent barbecue, Fred asked you about the amount of repair services rendered by Overnight Auto to Airport Shuttle Services in February. Airport Shuttle Services competes with Harbor Cab Co. for fares to and from the airport. What should you say to Fred?

(See our comments on the Online Learning Center Web site.)

Feb. 28 Recorded $1,600 utility bill for February. The entire amount is due March 15.

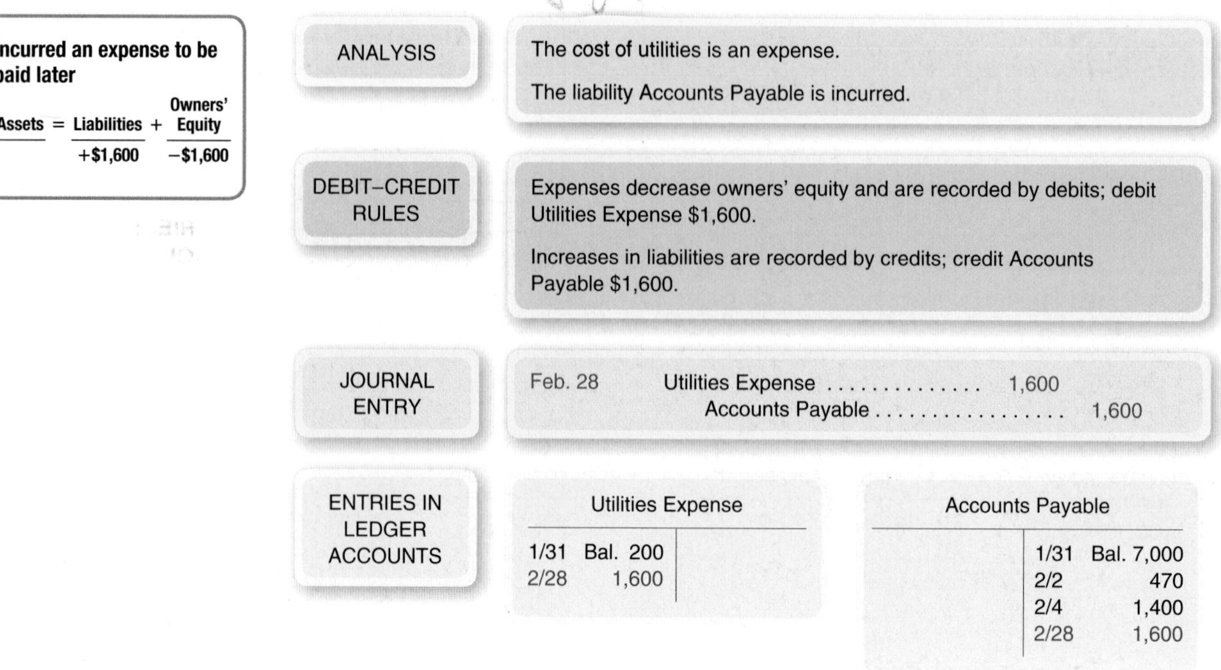

Incurred an expense to be paid later
Assets = Liabilities + Owners' Equity
+$1,600 −$1,600
ANALYSIS
The cost of utilities is an expense.
The liability Accounts Payable is incurred.
DEBIT–CREDIT RULES
Expenses decrease owners' equity and are recorded by debits; debit Utilities Expense $1,600.
Increases in liabilities are recorded by credits; credit Accounts Payable $1,600.
JOURNAL ENTRY
Feb. 28 Utilities Expense 1,600
Accounts Payable 1,600
ENTRIES IN LEDGER ACCOUNTS
Utilities Expense
1/31 Bal. 200
2/28 1,600
Accounts Payable
1/31 Bal. 7,000
2/2 470
2/4 1,400
2/28 1,600

Feb. 28 Overnight Auto Services declares and pays a dividend of 40 cents per share to the owners of its 8,000 shares of capital stock—a total of $3,200.[2]

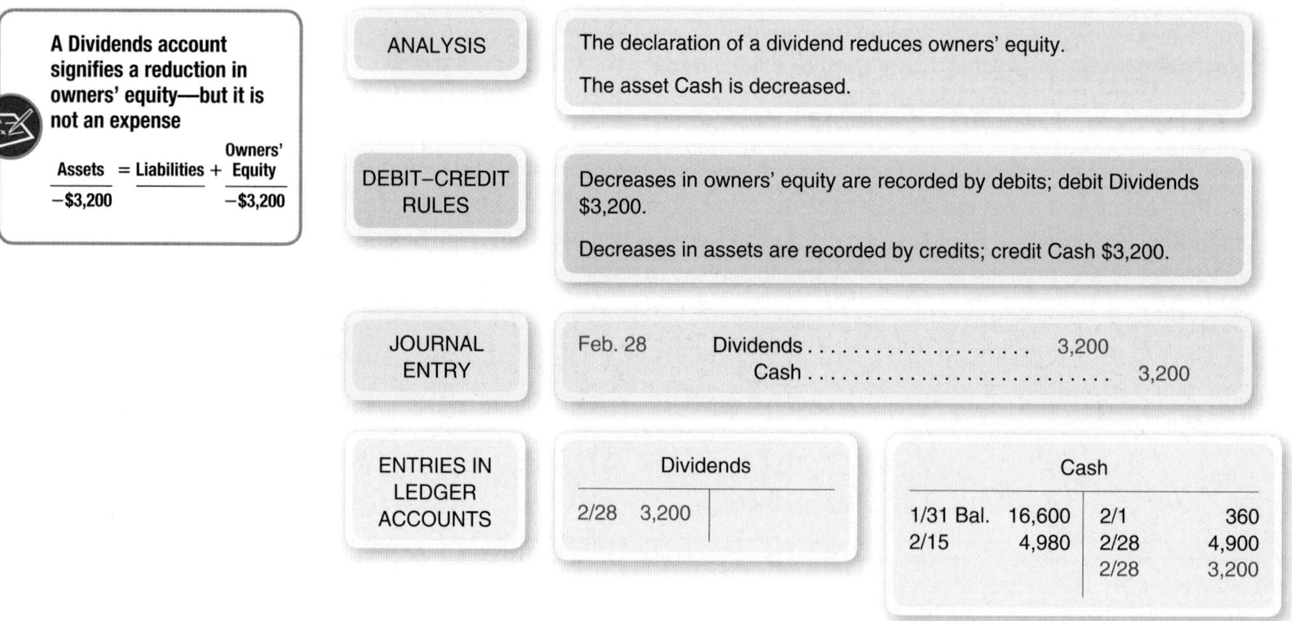

A Dividends account signifies a reduction in owners' equity—but it is not an expense
Assets = Liabilities + Owners' Equity
−$3,200 −$3,200
ANALYSIS
The declaration of a dividend reduces owners' equity.
The asset Cash is decreased.
DEBIT–CREDIT RULES
Decreases in owners' equity are recorded by debits; debit Dividends $3,200.
Decreases in assets are recorded by credits; credit Cash $3,200.
JOURNAL ENTRY
Feb. 28 Dividends 3,200
Cash 3,200
ENTRIES IN LEDGER ACCOUNTS
Dividends
2/28 3,200
Cash
1/31 Bal. 16,600
2/15 4,980
2/1 360
2/28 4,900
2/28 3,200

[2] As explained earlier, dividends are not an expense. In Chapter 5, we will show how the balance in the Dividends account eventually reduces the amount of Retained Earnings reported in the owners' equity section of the balance sheet.

THE JOURNAL

In our illustration, journal entries were shown in a very abbreviated form. The actual entries made in Overnight's journal appear in Exhibit 3–7. Notice that these formal journal entries include short *explanations* of the transactions, which include such details as the terms of credit transactions and the names of customers and creditors.

Exhibit 3–7
GENERAL JOURNAL ENTRIES: JANUARY 31 THROUGH FEBRUARY 28

Journal entries contain more information than just dollar amounts

OVERNIGHT AUTO SERVICE
GENERAL JOURNAL
JANUARY 31–FEBRUARY 28, 2011

Date	Account Titles and Explanation	Debit	Credit
2011			
Jan. 31	Cash	2,200	
	Repair Service Revenue		2,200
	Repair services rendered to various customers.		
31	Wages Expense	1,200	
	Cash		1,200
	Paid all wages for January.		
31	Utilities Expense	200	
	Cash		200
	Paid all utilities for January.		
Feb. 1	Advertising Expense	360	
	Cash		360
	Purchased newspaper advertising from *Daily Tribune* to run in February.		
2	Advertising Expense	470	
	Accounts Payable		470
	Purchased radio advertising on account from KRAM; payment due in 30 days.		
4	Shop Supplies	1,400	
	Accounts Payable		1,400
	Purchased shop supplies on account from CAPA; payment due in 30 days.		
15	Cash	4,980	
	Repair Service Revenue		4,980
	Repair services rendered to Airport Shuttle Service.		
28	Accounts Receivable	5,400	
	Repair Service Revenue		5,400
	Billed Harbor Cab for services rendered in February.		
28	Wages Expense	4,900	
	Cash		4,900
	Paid all wages for February.		
28	Utilities Expense	1,600	
	Accounts Payable		1,600
	Recorded utility bill for February.		
28	Dividends	3,200	
	Cash		3,200
	Paid cash dividend of 40 cents per share on 8,000 shares of capital stock owned by the McBryan family.		

February's Ledger Balances

After posting all of the January and February transactions, Overnight's ledger accounts appear as shown in Exhibit 3–8. To conserve space, we have illustrated the ledger in T account form and have carried forward each account's summary balance from January 31. For convenience,

Exhibit 3–8 OVERNIGHT AUTO SERVICE'S LEDGER ACCOUNTS

OVERNIGHT AUTO SERVICE
THE LEDGER

Asset Accounts

Cash

	Date	Debit	Date	Credit	
	1/31 Bal.	16,600	2/1	360	
	2/15	4,980	2/28	4,900	
Bal. $13,120			2/28	3,200	

Accounts Receivable

	Date	Debit	Date	Credit	
	1/31 Bal.	1,200			
Bal. $6,600	2/28	5,400			

Shop Supplies

	Date	Debit	Date	Credit	
	1/31 Bal.	0			
Bal. $1,400	2/4	1,400			

Land

	Date	Debit	Date	Credit	
Bal. $52,000	1/31 Bal.	52,000			

Building

	Date	Debit	Date	Credit	
Bal. $36,000	1/31 Bal.	36,000			

Tools and Equipment

	Date	Debit	Date	Credit	
Bal. $12,000	1/31 Bal.	12,000			

Liability and Owners' Equity Accounts

Notes Payable

	Date	Debit	Date	Credit	
			1/31 Bal.	30,000	Bal. $30,000

Accounts Payable

	Date	Debit	Date	Credit	
			1/31 Bal.	7,000	
			2/2	470	
			2/4	1,400	
			2/28	1,600	Bal. $10,470

Capital Stock

	Date	Debit	Date	Credit	
			1/31 Bal.	80,000	Bal. $80,000

Dividends

	Date	Debit	Date	Credit	
	1/31 Bal.	0			
Bal. $3,200	2/28	3,200			

Repair Service Revenue

	Date	Debit	Date	Credit	
			1/31 Bal.	2,200	
			2/15	4,980	
			2/28	5,400	Bal. $12,580

Advertising Expense

	Date	Debit	Date	Credit	
	2/1	360			
Bal. $830	2/2	470			

Wages Expense

	Date	Debit	Date	Credit	
	1/31 Bal.	1,200			
Bal. $6,100	2/28	4,900			

Utilities Expense

	Date	Debit	Date	Credit	
	1/31 Bal.	200			
Bal. $1,800	2/28	1,600			

we show in *red* the *February 28 balance* of each account (debit balances appear to the left of the account; credit balances appear to the right).

The accounts in this illustration appear in *financial statement order*—that is, balance sheet accounts first (assets, liabilities, and owners' equity), followed by the income statement accounts (revenue and expenses).

The Trial Balance

Learning Objective
Prepare a trial balance and explain its uses and limitations.
LO9

Since equal dollar amounts of debits and credits are entered in the accounts for every transaction recorded, the sum of all the debits in the ledger must be equal to the sum of all the credits. If the computation of account balances has been accurate, it follows that the total of the accounts with debit balances must be equal to the total of the accounts with credit balances.

Before using the account balances to prepare a balance sheet, it is desirable to *prove* that the total of accounts with debit balances is in fact equal to the total of accounts with credit balances. This proof of the equality of debit and credit balances is called a **trial balance.** A trial balance is a two-column schedule listing the names and balances of all the accounts *in the order in which they appear in the ledger*; the debit balances are listed in the left-hand column and the credit balances in the right-hand column. The totals of the two columns should agree. A trial balance taken from Overnight Auto's ledger accounts on page 108 is shown in Exhibit 3–9.

Exhibit 3–9
OVERNIGHT AUTO SERVICE'S TRIAL BALANCE

OVERNIGHT AUTO SERVICE
TRIAL BALANCE
FEBRUARY 28, 2011

	DEBIT	CREDIT
Cash	$ 13,120	
Accounts receivable	6,600	
Shop supplies	1,400	
Land	52,000	
Building	36,000	
Tools and equipment	12,000	
Notes payable		$ 30,000
Accounts payable		10,470
Capital stock		80,000
Retained earnings		0
Dividends	3,200	
Repair service revenue		12,580
Advertising expense	830	
Wages expense	6,100	
Utilities expense	1,800	
	$133,050	$133,050

A trial balance proves the equality of debits and credits—but it also gives you a feel for how the business stands; but wait—there's more to consider

This trial balance proves the equality of the debit and credit entries in the company's accounting system. Notice that the trial balance contains both balance sheet and income statement accounts. Note also that the Retained Earnings balance is *zero.* It is zero because *no debit or credit entries were made to the Retained Earnings account in January or February.* Overnight, like most companies, updates its Retained Earnings balance only *once each year.* In Chapter 5, we will show how the Retained Earnings account is updated to its proper balance at year-end on December 31.[3]

[3] The balance of $0 in the Retained Earnings account is a highly unusual situation. Because the company is still in its first year of operations, no entries have ever been made to update the account's balance. In any trial balance prepared after the first year of business activity, the Retained Earnings account may be expected to have a balance other than $0.

USES AND LIMITATIONS OF THE TRIAL BALANCE

The trial balance provides proof that the ledger is in balance. The agreement of the debit and credit totals of the trial balance gives assurance that:

1. Equal debits and credits have been recorded for all transactions.
2. The addition of the account balances in the trial balance has been performed correctly.

Suppose that the debit and credit totals of the trial balance do not agree. This situation indicates that one or more errors have been made. Typical of such errors are (1) the posting of a debit as a credit, or vice versa; (2) arithmetic mistakes in determining account balances; (3) clerical errors in copying account balances into the trial balance; (4) listing a debit balance in the credit column of the trial balance, or vice versa; and (5) errors in addition of the trial balance.

The preparation of a trial balance does *not* prove that transactions have been correctly analyzed and recorded in the proper accounts. If, for example, a receipt of cash were erroneously recorded by debiting the Land account instead of the Cash account, the trial balance would still balance. Also, if a transaction were completely omitted from the ledger, the error would not be disclosed by the trial balance. In brief, *the trial balance proves only one aspect of the ledger, and that is the equality of debits and credits.*

Concluding Remarks

THE ACCOUNTING CYCLE IN PERSPECTIVE

Learning Objective
LO10 Distinguish between accounting cycle procedures and the *knowledge* of accounting.

We view the accounting cycle as an efficient means of introducing basic accounting terms, concepts, processes, and reports. This is why we introduce it early in the course. As we conclude the accounting cycle in Chapters 4 and 5, please don't confuse your familiarity with this sequence of procedures with a knowledge of *accounting.* The accounting cycle is but one accounting process—and a relatively simple one at that.

Computers now free accountants to focus upon the more *analytical* aspects of their discipline. These include, for example:

- Determining the information needs of decision makers.
- Designing systems to provide the information quickly and efficiently.
- Evaluating the efficiency of operations throughout the organization.
- Assisting decision makers in interpreting accounting information.
- Auditing (confirming the reliability of accounting information).
- Forecasting the probable results of future operations.
- Tax planning.

We will emphasize such topics in later chapters of this text. But let us first repeat a very basic point from Chapter 1: The need for some familiarity with accounting concepts and processes is not limited to individuals planning careers in accounting. Today, an understanding of accounting information and of the business world go hand in hand. You cannot know much about one without understanding quite a bit about the other.

Ethics, Fraud & Corporate Governance

As discussed in Chapter 2, the Sarbanes-Oxley Act (SOX) substantially increases the civil and criminal penalties associated with securities fraud, including fraudulent financial reporting. The increased penalties are intended to reduce illegal behaviors. Even prior to SOX, the penalties available to the government and the Securities and Exchange Commission for prosecuting securities fraud were substantial. For example, Andrew Fastow, **Enron**'s former chief financial officer, and primary architect of **Enron**'s fraudulent actions, pled guilty to a number of fraud-related criminal charges and has received a 10-year prison sentence. Former chief executive officer of **Enron**, Jeffrey Skilling, also was convicted of numerous criminal charges related to his role at **Enron**.

© AP Photo/David J. Phillip

Businesspeople are sometimes told by their superiors to commit actions that are unethical and in some instances even illegal. The clear message of management is "participate in this behavior or find a job elsewhere." Management pressure and intimidation can make it difficult to resist demands to engage in unethical behavior. Employees sometimes believe that they are insulated from responsibility and liability because "they were just following orders."

As you encounter ethical dilemmas during your business career, remember that obeying orders from your superiors that are unethical, and certainly those that are illegal, may expose you to serious consequences, including criminal prosecution and incarceration.

END-OF-CHAPTER REVIEW

SUMMARY OF LEARNING OBJECTIVES

LO1 **Identify the steps in the accounting cycle and discuss the role of accounting records in an organization.** The accounting cycle generally consists of eight specific steps: (1) journalizing (recording) transactions, (2) posting each journal entry to the appropriate ledger accounts, (3) preparing a trial balance, (4) making end-of-period adjustments, (5) preparing an adjusted trial balance, (6) preparing financial statements, (7) journalizing and posting closing entries, and (8) preparing an after-closing trial balance.

Accounting records provide the information that is summarized in financial statements, income tax returns, and other accounting reports. In addition, these records are used by the company's management and employees for such purposes as:

- Establishing accountability for assets and transactions.
- Keeping track of routine business activities.
- Obtaining details about specific transactions.
- Evaluating the performance of units within the business.
- Maintaining a documentary record of the business's activities. (Such a record is required by tax laws and is useful for many purposes, including audits.)

LO2 **Describe a ledger account and a ledger.** A ledger account is a device for recording the increases or decreases in one financial statement item, such as a particular asset, a type of liability, or owners' equity. The general ledger is an accounting record that includes all the ledger accounts—that is, a separate account for each item included in the company's financial statements.

LO3 **Understand how balance sheet accounts are increased or decreased.** Increases in assets are recorded by debits and decreases are recorded by credits. Increases in liabilities and in owners' equity are recorded by credits and decreases are recorded by debits. Notice that the debit and credit rules are related to an account's *location in the balance sheet.* If the account appears on the *left side* of the balance sheet (asset accounts), increases in the account balance are recorded by *left-side entries* (debits). If the account appears on the *right side* of the balance sheet (liability and owners' equity accounts), increases are recorded by *right-side entries* (credits).

LO4 **Explain the double-entry system of accounting.** The double-entry system of accounting takes its name from the fact that every business transaction is recorded by *two types of entries:* (1) debit entries to one or more accounts and (2) credit entries to one or more accounts. In recording any transaction, the total dollar amount of the debit entries must equal the total dollar amount of the credit entries.

LO5 **Explain the purpose of a journal and its relationship to the ledger.** The journal is the accounting record in which business transactions are initially recorded. The entry in the journal shows which ledger accounts have increased as a result of the transaction and which have decreased. After the effects of the transaction have been recorded in the journal, the changes in the individual ledger accounts are then posted to the ledger.

LO6 **Explain the nature of *net income, revenue,* and *expenses.*** Net income is an increase in owners' equity that results from the profitable operation of a business during an accounting period. Net income also may be defined as revenue minus expenses. Revenue is the price of goods sold and services rendered to customers during the period, and expenses are the costs of the goods and services used up in the process of earning revenue.

LO7 **Apply the *realization* and *matching* principles in recording revenue and expenses.** The realization principle indicates that revenue should be recorded in the accounting records when it is *earned*—that is, when goods are sold or services are rendered to customers. The matching principle indicates that expenses should be offset against revenue on the basis of *cause and effect.* Thus, an expense should be recorded in the period in which the related good or service is consumed in the process of earning revenue.

LO8 **Understand how revenue and expense transactions are recorded in an accounting system.** The debit and credit rules for recording revenue and expenses are based on the rules for recording *changes in owners' equity.* Earning revenue *increases* owners' equity; therefore, revenue is recorded with a credit entry. Expenses *reduce* owners' equity and are recorded with debit entries.

LO9 **Prepare a trial balance and explain its uses and limitations.** In a trial balance, separate debit and credit columns are used to list the balances of the individual ledger accounts. The two columns are then totaled to prove the equality of the debit and credit balances. This process provides assurance that (1) the total of the debits posted to the ledger was equal to the total of the credits and (2) the balances of the individual ledger accounts were correctly computed. While a trial balance proves the equality of debit and credit entries in the ledger, it does *not* detect such errors as failure to record a business transaction, improper analysis of the accounts affected by the transaction, or the posting of debit or credit entries to the wrong accounts.

LO10 **Distinguish between accounting cycle procedures and the *knowledge* of accounting.** Accounting procedures involve the steps and processes necessary to *prepare* accounting information. A knowledge of the discipline enables one to *use* accounting information in evaluating performance, forecasting operations, and making complex business decisions.

Key Terms Introduced or Emphasized in Chapter 3

account (p. 86) A record used to summarize all increases and decreases in a particular asset, such as cash, or any other type of asset, liability, owners' equity, revenue, or expense.

accountability (p. 86) The condition of being held responsible for one's actions by the existence of an independent record of those actions. Establishing accountability is a major goal of accounting records and of internal control procedures.

accounting cycle (p. 86) The sequence of accounting procedures used to record, classify, and summarize accounting information. The cycle begins with the initial recording of business transactions and concludes with the preparation of formal financial statements.

accounting period (p. 97) The span of time covered by an income statement. One year is the accounting period for much financial reporting, but financial statements are also prepared by companies for each quarter of the year and for each month.

accrual basis of accounting (p. 100) Calls for recording revenue in the period in which it is earned and recording expenses in the period in which they are incurred. The effect of events on the business is recognized as services are rendered or consumed rather than when cash is received or paid.

conservatism (p. 99) The traditional accounting practice of resolving uncertainty by choosing the solution that leads to the lower (more conservative) amount of income being recognized in the current accounting period. This concept is designed to avoid overstatement of financial strength or earnings.

credit (p. 87) An amount entered on the right side of a ledger account. A credit is used to record a decrease in an asset or an increase in a liability or in owners' equity.

debit (p. 87) An amount entered on the left side of a ledger account. A debit is used to record an increase in an asset or a decrease in a liability or in owners' equity.

dividends (p. 96) A distribution of resources by a corporation to its stockholders. The resource most often distributed is cash.

double-entry accounting (p. 89) A system of recording every business transaction with equal dollar amounts of both debit and credit entries. As a result of this system, the accounting equation always remains in balance; in addition, the system makes possible the measurement of net income and also the use of error-detecting devices such as a trial balance.

expenses (p. 96) The costs of the goods and services used up in the process of obtaining revenue.

fiscal year (p. 98) Any 12-month accounting period adopted by a business.

general journal (p. 89) The simplest type of journal, it has only two money columns—one for credits and one for debits. This journal may be used for all types of transactions, which are later posted to the appropriate ledger accounts.

income statement (p. 96) A financial statement summarizing the results of operations of a business by matching its revenue and related expenses for a particular accounting period. Shows the net income or net loss.

journal (p. 89) A chronological record of transactions, showing for each transaction the debits and credits to be entered in specific ledger accounts. The simplest type of journal is called a general journal.

ledger (p. 86) An accounting system includes a separate record for each item that appears in the financial statements. Collectively, these records are referred to as a company's ledger. Individually, these records are often referred to as ledger accounts.

matching principle (p. 99) The generally accepted accounting principle that determines when expenses should be recorded in the accounting records. The revenue earned during an accounting period is matched (offset) with the expenses incurred in generating that revenue.

net income (p. 96) An increase in owners' equity resulting from profitable operations. Also, the excess of revenue earned over the related expenses for a given period.

net loss (p. 96) A decrease in owners' equity resulting from unprofitable operations.

objectivity (p. 99) Accountants' preference for using dollar amounts that are relatively factual—as opposed to merely matters of personal opinion. Objective measurements can be verified.

posting (p. 90) The process of transferring information from the journal to individual accounts in the ledger.

realization principle (p. 98) The generally accepted accounting principle that determines when revenue should be recorded in the accounting records. Revenue is realized when services are rendered to customers or when goods sold are delivered to customers.

retained earnings (p. 96) That portion of stockholders' (owners') equity resulting from profits earned and retained in the business.

revenue (p. 96) The price of goods and services charged to customers for goods and services rendered by a business.

time period principle (p. 97) To provide the users of financial statements with timely information, net income is measured for relatively short accounting periods of equal length. The period of time covered by an income statement is termed the company's accounting period.

trial balance (p. 109) A two-column schedule listing the names and the debit or credit balances of all accounts in the ledger.

Demonstration Problem

Epler Consulting Services, Inc., opened for business on January 25, 2011. The company maintains the following ledger accounts:

Cash	Capital Stock
Accounts Receivable	Retained Earnings
Office Supplies	Consulting Revenue
Office Equipment	Rent Expense
Accounts Payable	Utilities Expense

The company engaged in the following business activity in January:

Jan. 20 Issued 5,000 shares of capital stock for $50,000.

Jan. 20 Paid $400 office rent for the remainder of January.

Jan. 21 Purchased office supplies for $200. The supplies will last for several months, and payment is not due until February 15.

Jan. 22 Purchased office equipment for $15,000 cash.

Jan. 26 Performed consulting services and billed clients $2,000. The entire amount will not be collected until February.

Jan. 31 Recorded $100 utilities expense. Payment is not due until February 20.

Instructions

a. Record each of the above transactions in general journal form.

b. Post each entry to the appropriate ledger accounts.

c. Prepare a trial balance dated January 31, 2011.

d. Explain why the Retained Earnings account has a zero balance in the trial balance.

Solution to the Demonstration Problem

a.

EPLER CONSULTING SERVICES, INC.
GENERAL JOURNAL

Date	Account Titles and Explanation	Debit	Credit
2011			
Jan. 20	Cash	50,000	
	Capital Stock		50,000
	To record the issue of 5,000 shares of capital stock at $10 per share.		
20	Rent Expense	400	
	Cash		400
	To record payment of January rent expense.		
21	Office Supplies	200	
	Accounts Payable		200
	To record purchase of office supplies on account.		
22	Office Equipment	15,000	
	Cash		15,000
	To record the purchase of office equipment.		
26	Accounts Receivable	2,000	
	Consulting Revenue		2,000
	Billed clients for consulting services rendered.		
31	Utilities Expense	100	
	Accounts Payable		100
	To record January utilities expense due in February.		

b.

EPLER CONSULTING SERVICES, INC.
THE LEDGER
JANUARY 20–31, 2011

Asset Accounts

Cash

Balance	Date	Debit	Date	Credit
	1/20	50,000	1/20	400
Bal. $34,600			1/22	15,000

Accounts Receivable

Balance	Date	Debit	Date	Credit
Bal. $2,000	1/26	2,000		

Office Supplies

Balance	Date	Debit	Date	Credit
Bal. $200	1/21	200		

Office Equipment

Balance	Date	Debit	Date	Credit
Bal. $15,000	1/22	15,000		

Liability and Owners' Equity Accounts

Accounts Payable

Date	Debit	Date	Credit	Balance
		1/21	200	
		1/31	100	Bal. $300

Capital Stock

Date	Debit	Date	Credit	Balance
		1/20	50,000	Bal. $50,000

Retained Earnings

Date	Debit	Date	Credit	Balance
				Bal. $0

Consulting Revenue

Date	Debit	Date	Credit	Balance
		1/26	2,000	Bal. $2,000

Rent Expense

Balance	Date	Debit	Date	Credit
Bal. $400	1/20	400		

Utilities Expense

Balance	Date	Debit	Date	Credit
Bal. $100	1/31	100		

c.

EPLER CONSULTING SERVIC[illegible]

Cash . . . . [illegible]	$34,600	
Accounts receiv[illegible]	2,000	
Office supplies [illegible]	200	
Office equipmen[illegible]	15,000	
Accounts payabl[illegible]		$ 300
Capital stock . . . [illegible]		50,000
Retained earning[illegible]		0
Consulting revenu[illegible]		2,000
Rent expense . . . [illegible]	400	
Utilities expense . [illegible]	100	
	[illegible]2,300	$52,300

d. Epler's Retained [illegible] [illegible]pany has been in business for only one week [illegible] [illegible]pdated the Retained Earnings account for *any* revenue or expense activities. The periodic adjustment needed to update the Retained Earnings account is discussed in Chapter 5.

Self-Test Questions

The answers to these questions appear on page 137.

1. According to the rules of debit and credit for balance sheet accounts:

a. Increases in asset, liability, and owners' equity accounts are recorded by debits.

b. Decreases in asset and liability accounts are recorded by credits.

c. Increases in asset and owners' equity accounts are recorded by debits.

d. Decreases in liability and owners' equity accounts are recorded by debits.

2. Sunset Tours has a $3,500 account receivable from the Del Mar Rotary. On January 20, the Rotary makes a partial payment of $2,100 to Sunset Tours. The journal entry made on January 20 by Sunset Tours to record this transaction includes:

a. A debit to the Cash Received account of $2,100.

b. A credit to the Accounts Receivable account of $2,100.

c. A debit to the Cash account of $1,400.

d. A debit to the Accounts Receivable account of $1,400.

3. Indicate all of the following statements that correctly describe net income. Net income:

a. Is equal to revenue minus expenses.

b. Is equal to revenue minus the sum of expenses and dividends.

c. Increases owners' equity.

d. Is reported by a company for a specific period of time.

4. Which of the following is provided by a trial balance in which total debits equal total credits?

a. Proof that no transaction was completely omitted from the ledger during the posting process.

b. Proof that the correct debit or credit balance has been computed for each account.

c. Proof that the ledger is in balance.

d. Proof that transactions have been correctly analyzed and recorded in the proper accounts.

5. Which of the following explains the debit and credit rules relating to the recording of revenue and expenses?

a. Expenses appear on the left side of the balance sheet and are recorded by debits; revenue appears on the right side of the balance sheet and is recorded by credits.

b. Expenses appear on the left side of the income statement and are recorded by debits; revenue appears on the right side of the income statement and is recorded by credits.

c. The effects of revenue and expenses on owners' equity.

d. The realization principle and the matching principle.

6. Which of the following is *not* considered an analytical aspect of the accounting profession?

a. Evaluating an organization's operational efficiency.

b. Forecasting the probable results of future operations.

c. Designing systems that provide information to decision makers.

d. Journalizing and posting business transactions.

7. Indicate all correct answers. In the accounting cycle:
   a. Transactions are posted before they are journalized.
   b. A trial balance is prepared after journal entries have been posted.
   c. The Retained Earnings account is not shown as an up-to-date figure in the trial balance.
   d. Journal entries are posted to appropriate ledger accounts.

8. Indicate all correct answers. Dividends:
   a. Decrease owners' equity.
   b. Decrease net income.
   c. Are recorded by debiting the Dividend account.
   d. Are a business expense.

ASSIGNMENT MATERIAL Discussion Questions

1. Baker Construction is a small corporation owned and managed by Tom Baker. The corporation has 21 employees, few creditors, and no investor other than Tom Baker. Thus, like many small businesses, it has no obligation to issue financial statements to creditors or investors. Under these circumstances, is there any reason for this corporation to maintain accounting records?
2. What relationship exists between the position of an account in the balance sheet equation and the rules for recording increases in that account?
3. State briefly the rules of debit and credit as applied to asset accounts and as applied to liability and owners' equity accounts.
4. Does the term *debit* mean increase and the term *credit* mean decrease? Explain.
5. What requirement is imposed by the double-entry system in the recording of any business transaction?
6. Explain the effect of operating profitably on the balance sheet of a business entity.
7. Does net income represent a supply of cash that could be distributed to stockholders in the form of dividends? Explain.
8. What is the meaning of the term *revenue*? Does the receipt of cash by a business indicate that revenue has been earned? Explain.
9. What is the meaning of the term *expenses*? Does the payment of cash by a business indicate that an expense has been incurred? Explain.
10. When do accountants consider revenue to be realized? What basic question about recording revenue in accounting records is answered by the *realization principle*?
11. In what accounting period does the *matching principle* indicate that an expense should be recognized?
12. Explain the rules of debit and credit with respect to transactions recorded in revenue and expense accounts.
13. What are some of the limitations of a trial balance?
14. How do dividends affect owners' equity? Are they treated as a business expense? Explain.
15. List some of the more *analytical* functions performed by professional accountants.

Brief Exercises

LO1 LO2 LO5 LO9 LO10

BRIEF EXERCISE 3.1
The Accounting Cycle

Listed below in *random order* are the eight steps comprising a complete accounting cycle:

Prepare a trial balance.
Journalize and post the closing entries.
Prepare financial statements.
Post transaction data to the ledger.
Prepare an adjusted trial balance.
Make end-of-period adjustments.
Journalize transactions.
Prepare an after-closing trial balance.

a. List these steps in the sequence in which they would normally be performed. (A detailed understanding of these eight steps is not required until Chapters 4 and 5.)
b. Describe ways in which the information produced through the accounting cycle is used by a company's management and employees.

LO3 through LO5

BRIEF EXERCISE 3.2
Recording Transactions in a Journal

Record the following selected transactions in general journal form for Sun Orthopedic Clinic, Inc. Include a brief explanation of the transaction as part of each journal entry.

Oct. 1 The clinic issued 4,000 additional shares of capital stock to Doctor Soges at $50 per share.

Oct. 4 The clinic purchased diagnostic equipment. The equipment cost $75,000, of which $25,000 was paid in cash; a note payable was issued for the balance.

Oct. 12 Issued a check for $9,000 in full payment of an account payable to Zeller Laboratories.

Oct. 19 Purchased surgical supplies for $2,600. Payment is not due until November 28.

Oct. 25 Collected a $24,000 account receivable from Health One Insurance Company.

Oct. 30 Declared and paid a $300,000 cash dividend to stockholders.

LO7 LO8

BRIEF EXERCISE 3.3

Recording Transactions

Brown Consulting Services organized as a corporation on January 18 and engaged in the following transactions during its first two weeks of operation:

Jan. 18 Issued capital stock in exchange for $30,000 cash.

Jan. 22 Borrowed $20,000 from its bank by issuing a note payable.

Jan. 23 Paid $100 for a radio advertisement aired on January 24.

Jan. 25 Provided $1,000 of services to clients for cash.

Jan. 26 Provided $2,000 of services to clients on account.

Jan. 31 Collected $800 cash from clients for the services provided on January 26.

a. Record each of these transactions.

b. Determine the balance in the Cash account on January 31. Be certain to state whether the balance is debit or credit.

LO3 LO8

BRIEF EXERCISE 3.4

Debit and Credit Rules

Five account classifications are shown as column headings in the table below. For each account classification, indicate the manner in which increases and decreases are recorded (i.e., by debits or by credits).

	Revenue	Expenses	Assets	Liabilities	Owners' Equity
Increases recorded by:					
Decreases recorded by:					

LO3 LO6

BRIEF EXERCISE 3.5

Changes in Retained Earnings

Jackson Corporation's Retained Earnings account balance was $75,000 on January 1. During January, the company recorded revenue of $100,000, expenses of $60,000, and dividends of $5,000. The company also purchased land during the period for $20,000 cash.

Determine the company's Retained Earnings account balance on January 31.

LO6 LO7

BRIEF EXERCISE 3.6

Realization and Matching Principles

On May 26, Breeze Camp Ground paid KPRM Radio $500 cash for ten 30-second advertisements. Two of the ads were aired in May, seven in June, and one in July.

a. Apply the realization principle to determine how much advertising revenue KPRM Radio earned from Breeze Camp Ground in May, June, and July.

b. Apply the matching principle to determine how much advertising expense Breeze Camp Ground incurred in May, June, and July.

LO6 LO7

BRIEF EXERCISE 3.7

When Is Revenue Realized?

The following transactions were carried out during the month of May by M. Palmer and Company, a firm of design architects. For each of the five transactions, you are to state whether the transaction represented revenue to the firm during the month of May. Give reasons for your decision in each case.

a. M. Palmer and Company received $25,000 cash by issuing additional shares of capital stock.

b. Collected cash of $2,400 from an account receivable. The receivable originated in April from services rendered to a client.

c. Borrowed $12,800 from Century Bank to be repaid in three months.

d. Earned $83 interest on a company bank account during the month of May. No withdrawals were made from this account in May.

e. Completed plans for guesthouse, pool, and spa for a client. The $5,700 fee for this project was billed to the client in May, but will not be collected until June 25.

LO6 LO7

BRIEF EXERCISE 3.8

When Are Expenses Incurred?

During March, the activities of Evergreen Landscaping included the following transactions and events, among others. Which of these items represented expenses in March? Explain.

a. Purchased a copying machine for $2,750 cash.

b. Paid $192 for gasoline purchases for a delivery truck during March.

c. Paid $2,280 salary to an employee for time worked during March.

d. Paid an attorney $560 for legal services rendered in January.

e. Declared and paid an $1,800 dividend to shareholders.

LO6 LO7

BRIEF EXERCISE 3.9

Realization Principle

Up & Away Airlines has provided the following information regarding cash received for ticket sales in September and October:

Cash received in September for October flights	$500,000
Cash received in October for October flights	300,000
Cash received in October for November flights	400,000

Apply the realization principle to determine how much revenue Up & Away Airlines should report in its October income statement.

LO6 LO7

BRIEF EXERCISE 3.10

Matching Principle

Wilson Consulting has provided the following information regarding cash payments to its employees in May and June:

Salary payments in May for work performed by employees in April	$ 8,000
Salary payments in May for work performed by employees in May	15,000
Salary payments in June for work performed by employees in May	9,000

Apply the matching principle to determine how much salary expense Wilson Consulting should report in its May income statement.

Exercises

LO1 through LO10

EXERCISE 3.1

Accounting Terminology

Listed below are eight technical accounting terms introduced in this chapter:

Realization principle	Credit
Time period principle	Accounting period
Matching principle	Expenses
Net income	Accounting cycle

Each of the following statements may (or may not) describe one of these technical terms. For each statement, indicate the term described, or answer "None" if the statement does not correctly describe any of the terms.

a. The span of time covered by an income statement.

b. The sequence of accounting procedures used to record, classify, and summarize accounting information.

c. The traditional accounting practice of resolving uncertainty by choosing the solution that leads to the lowest amount of income being recognized.

d. An increase in owners' equity resulting from profitable operations.

e. The underlying accounting principle that determines when revenue should be recorded in the accounting records.

f. The type of entry used to decrease an asset or increase a liability or owners' equity account.

g. The underlying accounting principle of offsetting revenue earned during an accounting period with the expenses incurred in generating that revenue.

h. The costs of the goods and services used up in the process of generating revenue.

LO6 LO7

EXERCISE 3.2

The Matching Principle: You as a Driver

The purpose of this exercise is to demonstrate the *matching principle* in a familiar setting. Assume that you own a car that you drive about 15,000 miles each year.

a. List the various costs to you associated with owning and operating this car. Make an estimate of the total annual cost of owning and operating the car, as well as the average cost-per-mile that you drive.

b. Assume also that you have a part-time job. You usually do not use your car in this job, but today your employer asks you to drive 100 miles (round-trip) to deliver some important documents. Your employer offers to "reimburse you for your driving expenses."

You already have a full tank of gas, so you are able to drive the whole 100 miles without stopping and you don't actually spend any money during the trip. Does this mean that you have incurred no "expenses" for which you should be reimbursed? Explain.

LO2 through LO5

EXERCISE 3.3

Relationship between Journal and Ledger Accounts

Transactions are *first* journalized and *then* posted to ledger accounts. In this exercise, however, your understanding of the relationship between the journal and the ledger is tested by asking you to study some ledger accounts and determine the journal entries that probably were made to produce these ledger entries. The following accounts show the first six transactions of Avenson Insurance Company. Prepare a journal entry (including a written explanation) for each transaction.

Cash

Date	Debit	Date	Credit
Nov. 1	120,000	Nov. 8	33,600
		Nov. 25	12,000
		Nov. 30	1,400

Vehicles

Date	Debit	Date	Credit
Nov. 30	9,400		

Land

Date	Debit	Date	Credit
Nov. 8	70,000		

Notes Payable

Date	Debit	Date	Credit
Nov. 25	12,000	Nov. 8	95,000
		Nov. 30	8,000

Building

Date	Debit	Date	Credit
Nov. 8	58,600		

Accounts Payable

Date	Debit	Date	Credit
Nov. 21	480	Nov. 15	3,200

Office Equipment

Date	Debit	Date	Credit
Nov. 15	3,200	Nov. 21	480

Capital Stock

Date	Debit	Date	Credit
		Nov. 1	120,000

LO9

EXERCISE 3.4

Preparing a Trial Balance

Using the information in the ledger accounts presented in Exercise 3.3, prepare a trial balance for Avenson Insurance Company dated November 30.

LO6 LO8

EXERCISE 3.5

Relationship between Net Income and Equity

The following information came from a recent balance sheet of **Apple Computer, Inc.:**

	End of Year	Beginning of Year
Assets	$53.9 billion	$39.6 billion
Liabilities	$26.0 billion	?
Owners' Equity	?	$21.0 billion

a. Determine the amount of total liabilities reported in **Apple Computer**'s balance sheet at the beginning of the year.

b. Determine the amount of total owners' equity reported in **Apple Computer**'s balance sheet at the end of the year.

c. Retained earnings was reported in **Apple Computer**'s year-end balance sheet at $19.5 billion. If retained earnings was $13.8 billion at the beginning of the year, determine net income for the year if no dividends were declared.

LO2 through LO6

EXERCISE 3.6

Effects of Transactions on the Accounting Equation

Satka Fishing Expeditions, Inc., recorded the following transactions in July:

1. Provided an ocean fishing expedition for a credit customer; payment is due August 10.
2. Paid Marine Service Center for repairs to boats performed in June. (In June, Satka Fishing Expeditions, Inc., had received and properly recorded the invoice for these repairs.)

3. Collected the full amount due from a credit customer for a fishing expedition provided in June.
4. Received a bill from Baldy's Bait Shop for bait purchased and used in July. Payment is due August 3.
5. Purchased a new fishing boat on July 28, paying part cash and issuing a note payable for the balance. The new boat is first scheduled for use on August 5.
6. Declared and paid a cash dividend on July 31.

Indicate the effects that each of these transactions will have upon the following six *total amounts* in the company's financial statements for the month of July. Organize your answer in tabular form, using the column headings shown, and use the code letters **I** for increase, **D** for decrease, and **NE** for no effect. The answer to transaction **1** is provided as an example.

	Income Statement			Balance Sheet		
Transaction	Revenue −	Expenses =	Net Income	Assets =	Liabilities +	Owners' Equity
1	I	NE	I	I	NE	I

LO2 through LO6

EXERCISE 3.7

Effects of Transactions on the Accounting Equation

A number of transactions of Claypool Construction are described below in terms of accounts debited and credited:

1. Debit Wages Expense; credit Wages Payable.
2. Debit Accounts Receivable; credit Construction Revenue.
3. Debit Dividends; credit Cash.
4. Debit Office Supplies; credit Accounts Payable.
5. Debit Repairs Expense; credit Cash.
6. Debit Cash; credit Accounts Receivable.
7. Debit Tools and Equipment; credit Cash and Notes Payable.
8. Debit Accounts Payable; credit Cash.

a. Indicate the effects of each transaction upon the elements of the income statement and the balance sheet. Use the code letters **I** for increase, **D** for decrease, and **NE** for no effect. Organize your answer in tabular form using the column headings shown below. The answer for transaction **1** is provided as an example.

	Income Statement			Balance Sheet		
Transaction	Revenue −	Expenses =	Net Income	Assets =	Liabilities +	Owners' Equity
1	NE	I	D	NE	I	D

b. Write a one-sentence description of each transaction.

LO4 LO6 through LO8

EXERCISE 3.8

Preparing Journal Entries for Revenue, Expenses, and Dividends

Shown below are selected transactions of the architectural firm of Baxter, Claxter, and Stone, Inc.

April 5 Prepared building plans for Spangler Construction Company. Sent Spangler an invoice for $900 requesting payment within 30 days. (The appropriate revenue account is entitled Drafting Fees Earned.)

May 17 Declared a cash dividend of $5,000. The dividend will not be paid until June 25.

May 29 Received a $2,000 bill from Bob Needham, CPA, for accounting services performed during May. Payment is due by June 10. (The appropriate expense account is entitled Professional Expenses.)

June 4 Received full payment from Spangler Construction Company for the invoice sent on April 5.

June 10 Paid Bob Needham, CPA, for the bill received on May 29.

June 25 Paid the cash dividend declared on May 17.

a. Prepare journal entries to record the transactions in the firm's accounting records.

b. Identify any of the above transactions that *will not* result in a change in the company's net income.

LO3 LO6 LO7

EXERCISE 3.9

Effects of Transactions on the Financial Statements

Listed below are eight transactions the Foster Corporation made during November:

a. Issued stock in exchange for cash.

b. Purchased land. Made partial payment with cash and issued a note payable for the remaining balance.

c. Recorded utilities expense for November. Payment is due in mid-December.

d. Purchased office supplies with cash.

e. Paid outstanding salaries payable owed to employees for wages earned in October.

f. Declared a cash dividend that will not be paid until late December.

g. Sold land for cash at an amount equal to the land's historical cost.

h. Collected cash on account from customers for services provided in September and October.

Indicate the *effects of the above transactions* on each of the financial statement elements shown in the column headings below. Use the following symbols: **I** = Increase, **D** = Decrease, and **NE** = no effect.

Transaction	Net Income	Assets	Liabilities	Equity
a.				
b.				
c.				
d.				
e.				
f.				
g.				
h.				

LO3 LO5 LO8 LO9

EXERCISE 3.10

Journalizing, Posting, and Preparing a Trial Balance

Trafflet Enterprises incorporated on May 3, 2011. The company engaged in the following transactions during its first month of operations:

May 3 Issued capital stock in exchange for $800,000 cash.

May 4 Paid May office rent expense of $1,000.

May 5 Purchased office supplies for $400 cash. The supplies will last for several months.

May 15 Purchased office equipment for $8,000 on account. The entire amount is due June 15.

May 18 Purchased a company car for $27,000. Paid $7,000 cash and issued a note payable for the remaining amount owed.

May 20 Billed clients $32,000 on account.

May 26 Declared a $5,000 dividend. The entire amount will be distributed to shareholders on June 26.

May 29 Paid May utilities of $200.

May 30 Received $30,000 from clients billed on May 20.

May 31 Recorded and paid salary expense of $14,000.

A partial list of the account titles used by the company includes:

Cash	Dividends Payable
Accounts Receivable	Dividends
Office Supplies	Capital Stock
Office Equipment	Client Revenue
Vehicles	Office Rent Expense
Notes Payable	Salary Expense
Accounts Payable	Utilities Expense

a. Prepare journal entries, including explanations, for the above transactions.

b. Post each entry to the appropriate ledger accounts (use the T account format illustrated in Exhibit 3–8 on page 108).

c. Prepare a trial balance dated May 31, 2011. Assume accounts with zero balances are not included in the trial balance.

LO3 LO5 LO8 LO9

EXERCISE 3.11
Journalizing, Posting, and Preparing a Trial Balance

The McMillan Corporation incorporated on September 2, 2011. The company engaged in the following transactions during its first month of operations:

Sept. 2 Issued capital stock in exchange for $900,000 cash.

Sept. 4 Purchased land and a building for $350,000. The value of the land was $50,000, and the value of the building was $300,000. The company paid $200,000 cash and issued a note payable for the balance.

Sept. 12 Purchased office supplies for $600 on account. The supplies will last for several months.

Sept. 19 Billed clients $75,000 on account.

Sept. 29 Recorded and paid salary expense of $24,000.

Sept. 30 Received $30,000 from clients billed on September 19.

A partial list of the account titles used by the company includes:

Cash	Notes Payable
Accounts Receivable	Accounts Payable
Office Supplies	Capital Stock
Land	Client Revenue
Building	Salary Expense

a. Prepare journal entries, including explanations, for the above transactions.

b. Post each entry to the appropriate ledger accounts (use the T account format illustrated in Exhibit 3–8 on page 108).

c. Prepare a trial balance dated September 30, 2011. Assume accounts with zero balances are not included in the trial balance.

LO3 LO5 LO8 LO9

EXERCISE 3.12
Journalizing, Posting, and Preparing a Trial Balance

Herrold Consulting incorporated on February 1, 2011. The company engaged in the following transactions during its first month of operations:

Feb. 1 Issued capital stock in exchange for $750,000 cash.

Feb. 5 Borrowed $50,000 from the bank by issuing a note payable.

Feb. 8 Purchased land, building, and office equipment for $600,000. The value of the land was $100,000, the value of the building was $450,000, and the value of the office equipment was $50,000. The company paid $300,000 cash and issued a note payable for the balance.

Feb. 11 Purchased office supplies for $600 on account. The supplies will last for several months.

Feb. 14 Paid the local newspaper $400 for a full-page advertisement. The ad will appear in print on February 18.

Feb. 20 Several of the inkjet printer cartridges that Herrold purchased on February 11 were defective. The cartridges were returned and the office supply store reduced Herrold's outstanding balance by $100.

Feb. 22 Performed consulting services for $6,000 cash.

Feb. 24 Billed clients $9,000.

Feb. 25 Paid salaries of $5,000.

Feb. 28 Paid the entire outstanding balance owed for office supplies purchased on February 11.

A partial list of the account titles used by the company includes:

Cash	Notes Payable
Accounts Receivable	Accounts Payable
Office Supplies	Capital Stock
Land	Client Service Revenue
Building	Advertising Expense
Office Equipment	Salaries Expense

a. Prepare journal entries, including explanations, for the above transactions.

b. Post each entry to the appropriate ledger accounts (use the T account format as illustrated in Exhibit 3–8 on page 108).

c. Prepare a trial balance dated February 28, 2011. Assume accounts with zero balances are not included in the trial balance.

LO3 LO6 LO8

EXERCISE 3.13 Analyzing Transactions

Listed below are descriptions of six transactions, followed by a table listing six unique combinations of financial statement effects (**I** is for increase, **D** is for decrease, and **NE** is for no effect). In the blank space to the left of each transaction description, place the appropriate letter from the table that indicates the effects of that transaction on the various elements of the financial statements.

1. ______ Purchased machinery for $5,000, paying $1,000 cash and issuing a $4,000 note payable for the balance.
2. ______ Billed clients $16,000 on account.
3. ______ Recorded a $500 maintenance expense of which $100 was paid in cash and the remaining amount was due in 30 days.
4. ______ Paid an outstanding account payable of $400.
5. ______ Recorded monthly utilities costs of $300. The entire amount is due in 20 days.
6. ______ Declared a $40,000 dividend to be distributed in 60 days.

Transaction	Revenue	Expenses	Assets	Liabilities	Owners' Equity
a.	NE	NE	D	D	NE
b.	NE	I	D	I	D
c.	NE	NE	NE	I	D
d.	NE	I	NE	I	D
e.	NE	NE	I	I	N
f.	I	NE	I	NE	I

LO3 LO6 LO8

EXERCISE 3.14 Analyzing Transactions

Listed below are descriptions of six transactions, followed by a table listing six unique combinations of financial statement effects (**I** is for increase, **D** is for decrease, and **NE** is for no effect). In the blank space to the left of each transaction description, place the appropriate letter from the table that indicates the effects of that transaction on the various elements of the financial statements.

1. ______ Issued capital stock in exchange for $50,000 cash.
2. ______ Billed clients $20,000 on account.
3. ______ Placed a $300 advertisement in the local newspaper. The entire amount is due in 30 days.
4. ______ Collected $100 on account from clients.
5. ______ Recorded and paid a $12,000 dividend.
6. ______ Recorded and paid salaries of $15,000.

Transaction	Revenue	Expenses	Assets	Liabilities	Owners' Equity
a.	NE	I	NE	I	D
b.	NE	I	D	NE	D
c.	NE	NE	D	NE	D
d.	NE	NE	I	NE	I
e.	I	NE	I	NE	I
f.	NE	NE	NE	NE	NE

LO1 through LO3, LO7, LO10

EXERCISE 3.15
Using the Financial Statements of **Home Depot, Inc.**

Throughout this text, we have many assignments based on the financial statements of **Home Depot, Inc.**, in Appendix A. Refer to the financial statements to respond to the following items:

a. Does the company's fiscal year end on December 31? How can you tell?

b. State the company's most recent balance sheet in terms of A = L + E.

c. Did the company post more debits to the Cash account during the year than credits? How can you tell?

Problem Set A

LO3 through LO5

PROBLEM 3.1A
Journalizing Transactions

eXcel

Glenn Grimes is the founder and president of Heartland Construction, a real estate development venture. The business transactions during February while the company was being organized are listed below.

Feb. 1 Grimes and several others invested $500,000 cash in the business in exchange for 25,000 shares of capital stock.

Feb. 10 The company purchased office facilities for $300,000, of which $100,000 was applicable to the land and $200,000 to the building. A cash payment of $60,000 was made and a note payable was issued for the balance of the purchase price.

Feb. 16 Computer equipment was purchased from PCWorld for $12,000 cash.

Feb. 18 Office furnishings were purchased from Hi-Way Furnishings at a cost of $9,000. A $1,000 cash payment was made at the time of purchase, and an agreement was made to pay the remaining balance in two equal installments due March 1 and April 1. Hi-Way Furnishings did not require that Heartland sign a promissory note.

Feb. 22 Office supplies were purchased from Office World for $300 cash.

Feb. 23 Heartland discovered that it paid too much for a computer printer purchased on February 16. The unit should have cost only $359, but Heartland was charged $395. PCWorld promised to refund the difference within seven days.

Feb. 27 Mailed Hi-Way Furnishings the first installment due on the account payable for office furnishings purchased on February 18.

Feb. 28 Received $36 from PCWorld in full settlement of the account receivable created on February 23.

Instructions

a. Prepare journal entries to record the above transactions. Select the appropriate account titles from the following chart of accounts:

Cash	Land
Accounts Receivable	Office Building
Office Supplies	Notes Payable
Office Furnishings	Accounts Payable
Computer Systems	Capital Stock

b. Indicate the effects of each transaction on the company's assets, liabilities, and owners' equity for the month of February. Organize your analysis in tabular form as shown for the February 1 transaction:

Transaction	Assets	=	Liabilities	+	Owners' Equity
Feb. 1	+$500,000 (Cash)		$0		+$500,000 (Capital Stock)

LO3 through LO8

PROBLEM 3.2A
Analyzing and Journalizing Transactions

Environmental Services, Inc., performs various tests on wells and septic systems. A few of the company's business transactions occurring during August are described below:

1. On August 1, the company billed customers $2,500 on account for services rendered. Customers are required to make full payment within 30 days.
2. On August 3, the company purchased testing supplies costing $3,800, paying $800 cash and charging the remainder on the company's 30-day account at Penn Chemicals. The testing supplies are expected to last several months.
3. On August 5, the company returned to Penn Chemicals $100 of testing supplies that were not needed. The return of these supplies reduced by $100 the amount owed to Penn Chemicals.
4. On August 17, the company issued an additional 2,500 shares of capital stock at $8 per share. The cash raised will be used to purchase new testing equipment in September.
5. On August 22, the company received $600 cash from customers it had billed on August 1.
6. On August 29, the company paid its outstanding account payable to Penn Chemicals.
7. On August 30, a cash dividend totaling $6,800 was declared and paid to the company's stockholders.

Instructions

a. Prepare an analysis of each of the above transactions. Transaction 1 serves as an example of the form of analysis to be used.

   1. (a) The asset Accounts Receivable was increased. Increases in assets are recorded by debits. Debit Accounts Receivable $2,500.

      (b) Revenue has been earned. Revenue increases owners' equity. Increases in owners' equity are recorded by credits. Credit Testing Service Revenue $2,500.

b. Prepare journal entries, including explanations, for the above transactions.

c. How does the *realization principle* influence the manner in which the August 1 billing to customers is recorded in the accounting records?

d. How does the *matching principle* influence the manner in which the August 3 purchase of testing supplies is recorded in the accounting records?

LO3 through LO8

PROBLEM 3.3A
Analyzing and Journalizing Transactions

Weida Surveying, Inc., provides land surveying services. During September, its transactions included the following:

Sept. 1 Paid rent for the month of September, $4,400.

Sept. 3 Billed Fine Line Homes $5,620 for surveying services. The entire amount is due on or before September 28. (Weida uses an account entitled Surveying Revenue when billing clients.)

Sept. 9 Provided surveying services to Sunset Ridge Developments for $2,830. The entire amount was collected on this date.

Sept. 14 Placed a newspaper advertisement in the *Daily Item* to be published in the September 20 issue. The cost of the advertisement was $165. Payment is due in 30 days.

Sept. 25 Received a check for $5,620 from Fine Line Homes for the amount billed on September 3.

Sept. 26 Provided surveying services to Thompson Excavating Company for $1,890. Weida collected $400 cash, with the balance due in 30 days.

Sept. 29 Sent a check to the *Daily Item* in full payment of the liability incurred on September 14.

Sept. 30 Declared and paid a $7,600 cash dividend to the company's stockholders.

Instructions

a. Analyze the effects that each of these transactions will have on the following six components of the company's financial statements for the month of September. Organize your answer in tabular form, using the column headings shown. Use **I** for increase, **D** for decrease, and **NE** for no effect. The September 1 transaction is provided for you:

	Income Statement			Balance Sheet		
Transaction	Revenue −	Expenses =	Net Income	Assets =	Liabilities +	Owners' Equity
Sept. 1	**NE**	**I**	**D**	**D**	**NE**	**D**

b. Prepare a journal entry (including explanation) for each of the above transactions.

c. Three of September's transactions involve cash payments, yet only one of these transactions is recorded as an expense. Describe three situations in which a cash payment would *not* involve recognition of an expense.

PROBLEM 3.4A
LO1 through LO10
The Accounting Cycle: Journalizing, Posting, and Preparing a Trial Balance

In June 2011, Wendy Winger organized a corporation to provide aerial photography services. The company, called Aerial Views, began operations immediately. Transactions during the month of June were as follows:

June 1 The corporation issued 60,000 shares of capital stock to Wendy Winger in exchange for $60,000 cash.

June 2 Purchased a plane from Utility Aircraft for $220,000. Made a $40,000 cash down payment and issued a note payable for the remaining balance.

June 4 Paid Woodrow Airport $2,500 to rent office and hangar space for the month.

June 15 Billed customers $8,320 for aerial photographs taken during the first half of June.

June 15 Paid $5,880 in salaries earned by employees during the first half of June.

June 18 Paid Hannigan's Hangar $1,890 for maintenance and repair services on the company plane.

June 25 Collected $4,910 of the amounts billed to customers on June 15.

June 30 Billed customers $16,450 for aerial photographs taken during the second half of the month.

June 30 Paid $6,000 in salaries earned by employees during the second half of the month.

June 30 Received a $2,510 bill from Peatree Petroleum for aircraft fuel purchased in June. The entire amount is due July 10.

June 30 Declared a $2,000 dividend payable on July 15.

The account titles used by Aerial Views are:

Cash	Retained Earnings
Accounts Receivable	Dividends
Aircraft	Aerial Photography Revenue
Notes Payable	Maintenance Expense
Accounts Payable	Fuel Expense
Dividends Payable	Salaries Expense
Capital Stock	Rent Expense

Instructions

a. Analyze the effects that each of these transactions will have on the following six components of the company's financial statements for the month of June. Organize your answer in tabular form, using the column headings shown. Use **I** for increase, **D** for decrease, and **NE** for no effect. The June 1 transaction is provided for you:

	Income Statement			Balance Sheet		
Transaction	Revenue −	Expenses =	Net Income	Assets =	Liabilities +	Owners' Equity
June 1	**NE**	**NE**	**NE**	**I**	**NE**	**I**

b. Prepare journal entries (including explanations) for each transaction.

c. Post each transaction to the appropriate ledger accounts (use a running balance format as illustrated in Exhibit 3–4 on page 95).

d. Prepare a trial balance dated June 30, 2011.

e. Using figures from the trial balance prepared in part **d,** compute total assets, total liabilities, and owners' equity. Are these the figures that the company will report in its June 30 balance sheet? Explain your answer briefly.

LO1 through LO10

PROBLEM 3.5A

The Accounting Cycle: Journalizing, Posting, and Preparing a Trial Balance

Dr. Schekter, DVM, opened a veterinary clinic on May 1, 2011. The business transactions for May are shown below:

May 1 Dr. Schekter invested $400,000 cash in the business in exchange for 5,000 shares of capital stock.

May 4 Land and a building were purchased for $250,000. Of this amount, $70,000 applied to the land, and $180,000 to the building. A cash payment of $100,000 was made at the time of the purchase, and a note payable was issued for the remaining balance.

May 9 Medical instruments were purchased for $130,000 cash.

May 16 Office fixtures and equipment were purchased for $50,000. Dr. Schekter paid $20,000 at the time of purchase and agreed to pay the entire remaining balance in 15 days.

May 21 Office supplies expected to last several months were purchased for $5,000 cash.

May 24 Dr. Schekter billed clients $2,200 for services rendered. Of this amount, $1,900 was received in cash, and $300 was billed on account (due in 30 days).

May 27 A $400 invoice was received for several radio advertisements aired in May. The entire amount is due on June 5.

May 28 Received a $100 payment on the $300 account receivable recorded May 24.

May 31 Paid employees $2,800 for salaries earned in May.

A partial list of account titles used by Dr. Schekter includes:

Cash	Notes Payable
Accounts Receivable	Accounts Payable
Office Supplies	Capital Stock
Medical Instruments	Veterinary Service Revenue
Office Fixtures and Equipment	Advertising Expense
Land	Salary Expense
Building	

Instructions

a. Analyze the effects that each of these transactions will have on the following six components of the company's financial statements for the month of May. Organize your answer in tabular form, using the column headings shown below. Use **I** for increase, **D** for decrease, and **NE** for no effect. The May 1 transaction is provided for you:

	Income Statement			Balance Sheet		
Transaction	Revenue −	Expenses =	Net Income	Assets =	Liabilities +	Owners' Equity
May 1	**NE**	**NE**	**NE**	**I**	**NE**	**I**

b. Prepare journal entries (including explanations) for each transaction.

c. Post each transaction to the appropriate ledger accounts (use the T account format illustrated in Exhibit 3–8 on page 108).

d. Prepare a trial balance dated May 31, 2011.

e. Using figures from the trial balance prepared in part **d,** compute total assets, total liabilities, and owners' equity. Did May appear to be a profitable month?

LO7 through LO9

PROBLEM 3.6A

Short Comprehensive Problem

Donegan's Lawn Care Service began operations in July 2011. The company uses the following general ledger accounts:

Cash	Capital Stock
Accounts Receivable	Retained Earnings
Office Supplies	Mowing Revenue
Mowing Equipment	Salaries Expense
Accounts Payable	Fuel Expense
Notes Payable	

The company engaged in the following transactions during its first month of operations:

July 18 Issued 500 shares of capital stock to Patrick Donegan for $1,500.

July 22 Purchased office supplies on account for $100.

July 23 Purchased mowing equipment for $2,000, paying $400 cash and issuing a 60-day note payable for the remaining balance.

July 24 Paid $25 cash for gasoline. All of this fuel will be used in July.

July 25 Billed Lost Creek Cemetery $150 for mowing services. The entire amount is due July 30.

July 26 Billed Golf View Condominiums $200 for mowing services. The entire amount is due August 1.

July 30 Collected $150 from Lost Creek Cemetery for mowing services provided on July 25.

July 31 Paid $80 salary to employee Teddy Grimm for work performed in July.

a. Record each of the above transactions in general journal form. Include a brief explanation of the transaction as part of each journal entry.

b. Post each entry to the appropriate ledger accounts (use the T account format illustrated in Exhibit 3–8 on page 108).

c. Prepare a trial balance dated July 31, 2011.

d. Explain why the Retained Earnings account has a zero balance in the trial balance.

LO3 through LO9

PROBLEM 3.7A

Short Comprehensive Problem

Sanlucas, Inc., provides home inspection services to its clients. The company's trial balance dated *June 1, 2011,* is shown below:

SANLUCAS, INC.
TRIAL BALANCE
JUNE 1, 2011

Cash	$ 5,100	
Accounts receivable	2,600	
Inspection supplies	800	
Accounts payable		$ 850
Notes payable		2,000
Dividends	600	
Capital stock		3,000
Retained earnings		1,800
Inspection revenue		8,350
Salaries expense	4,900	
Advertising expense	300	
Testing expense	1,700	
	$16,000	$16,000

Sanlucas engaged in the following transactions in June:

June 4 Borrowed cash from Community Bank by issuing a $1,500 note payable.

June 9 Collected a $1,600 account receivable from Nina Lesher.

June 10 Purchased $150 of inspection supplies on account.

June 17 Billed home owners $1,650 for inspection services. The entire amount is due on July 17.

June 25 Paid WLIR Radio $200 for ads to be aired on June 27.

June 28 Recorded and paid $1,300 for testing expenses incurred in June.

June 30 Recorded and paid June salaries of $1,100.

Instructions

a. Record the company's June transactions in general journal form. Include a brief explanation of the transaction as part of each journal entry.

b. Post each entry to the appropriate ledger accounts (use the T account format illustrated in Exhibit 3–8 on page 108).

c. Prepare a trial balance dated June 30, 2011. (Hint: Retained Earnings will be reported at the same amount as on June 1. Accounting for changes in the Retained Earnings account resulting from revenue, expense, and dividend activities is discussed in Chapter 5.)

d. Has the company paid all of the dividends that it has declared? Explain.

LO3 LO8

PROBLEM 3.8A
Analyzing the Effects of Accounting Errors

Home Team Corporation recently hired Steve Willits as its bookkeeper. Mr. Willits is somewhat inexperienced and has made numerous errors recording daily business transactions.

Indicate the *effects of the errors* described below on each of the financial statement elements shown in the column headings. Use the following symbols: **O** for overstated; **U** for understated, and **NE** for no effect.

Error	Net Income	Total Assets	Total Liabilities	Owners' Equity
Recorded the issuance of capital stock by debiting Capital Stock and crediting Service Revenue.				
Recorded the declaration and payment of a dividend by debiting Capital Stock and crediting Cash.				
Recorded the payment of an account payable by debiting Cash and crediting Rent Expense.				
Recorded the collection of an outstanding account receivable by debiting Cash and crediting Service Revenue.				
Recorded client billings on account by debiting Accounts Receivable and crediting Advertising Expense.				
Recorded the cash purchase of land by debiting Supplies Expense and crediting Notes Payable.				
Recorded the purchase of a building on account by debiting Cash and crediting Dividends Payable.				

Problem Set B

LO3 through LO5

PROBLEM 3.1B
Journalizing Transactions

Chris North is the founder and president of North Enterprises, a real estate development venture. The business transactions during April while the company was being organized are listed below.

Apr. 1 North and several others invested $650,000 cash in the business in exchange for 10,000 shares of capital stock.

Apr. 6 The company purchased office facilities for $300,000, of which $60,000 was applicable to the land and $240,000 to the building. A cash payment of $100,000 was made and a note payable was issued for the balance of the purchase price.

Apr. 10 Computer equipment was purchased from Comp Central for $6,000 cash.

Apr. 12 Office furnishings were purchased from Sam's Furniture at a cost of $12,000. A $1,000 cash payment was made at the time of purchase, and an agreement was made to pay the remaining balance in two equal installments due May 1 and June 1. Sam's Furniture did not require that North sign a promissory note.

Apr. 20 Office supplies were purchased from Office Space for $750 cash.

Apr. 25 North discovered that it paid too much for a computer printer purchased on April 10. The unit should have cost only $600, but North was charged $800. Comp Central promised to refund the difference within seven days.

Apr. 28 Mailed Sam's Furniture the first installment due on the account payable for office furnishings purchased on April 12.

Apr. 29 Received $200 from Comp Central in settlement of the account receivable created on April 25.

Instructions

a. Prepare journal entries to record the above transactions. Select the appropriate account titles from the following chart of accounts:

Cash	Land
Accounts Receivable	Office Building
Office Supplies	Notes Payable
Office Furnishings	Accounts Payable
Computer Systems	Capital Stock

b. Indicate the effects of each transaction on the company's assets, liabilities, and owners' equity for the month of April. Organize your analysis in tabular form as shown below for the April 1 transaction:

Transaction	Assets	=	Liabilities	+ Owners' Equity
Apr. 1	+$650,000 (Cash)	=	$0	+$650,000 (Capital Stock)

LO3 through LO8 PROBLEM 3.2B Analyzing and Journalizing Transactions

Lyons, Inc., provides consulting services. A few of the company's business transactions occurring during June are described below:

1. On June 1, the company billed customers $5,000 on account for consulting services rendered. Customers are required to make full payment within 30 days.
2. On June 3, the company purchased office supplies costing $3,200, paying $800 cash and charging the remainder on the company's 30-day account at Office Warehouse. The supplies are expected to last several months.
3. On June 5, the company returned to Office Warehouse $100 of supplies that were not needed. The return of these supplies reduced by $100 the amount owed to Office Warehouse.
4. On June 17, the company issued an additional 1,000 shares of capital stock at $5 per share. The cash raised will be used to purchase new equipment in September.
5. On June 22, the company received $1,200 cash from customers it had billed on June 1.
6. On June 29, the company paid its outstanding account payable to Office Warehouse.
7. On June 30, a cash dividend totaling $1,800 was declared and paid to the company's stockholders.

Instructions

a. Prepare an analysis of each of the above transactions. Transaction 1 serves as an example of the form of analysis to be used.

1. **(a)** The asset Accounts Receivable was increased. Increases in assets are recorded by debits. Debit Accounts Receivable $5,000.

   (b) Revenue has been earned. Revenue increases owners' equity. Increases in owners' equity are recorded by credits. Credit Consulting Revenue $5,000.

b. Prepare journal entries, including explanations, for the above transactions.

c. How does the *realization principle* influence the manner in which the June 1 billings to customers are recorded in the accounting records?

d. How does the *matching principle* influence the manner in which the June 3 purchase of supplies is recorded in the accounting records?

LO3 through LO8

PROBLEM 3.3B Analyzing and Journalizing Transactions

Dana, Inc., provides civil engineering services. During October, its transactions included the following:

Oct. 1 Paid rent for the month of October, $4,000.

Oct. 4 Billed Milton Hotels $8,500 for services. The entire amount is due on or before October 28. (Dana uses an account entitled Service Revenue when billing clients.)

Oct. 8 Provided services to Dirt Valley Development for $4,700. The entire amount was collected on this date.

Oct. 12 Placed a newspaper advertisement in the *Daily Reporter* to be published in the October 25 issue. The cost of the advertisement was $320. Payment is due in 30 days.

Oct. 20 Received a check for $8,500 from Milton Hotels for the amount billed on October 4.

Oct. 24 Provided services to Dudley Company for $3,600. Dana collected $300 cash, with the balance due in 30 days.

Oct. 25 Sent a check to the *Daily Reporter* in full payment of the liability incurred on October 12.

Oct. 29 Declared and paid a $2,600 cash dividend to the company's stockholders.

Instructions

a. Analyze the effects that each of these transactions will have on the following six components of the company's financial statements for the month of October. Organize your answer in tabular form, using the column headings shown below. Use **I** for increase, **D** for decrease, and **NE** for no effect. The October 1 transaction is provided for you:

	Income Statement			Balance Sheet		
Transaction	Revenue −	Expenses =	Net Income	Assets =	Liabilities +	Owners' Equity
Oct. 1	NE	I	D	D	NE	D

b. Prepare a journal entry (including explanation) for each of the above transactions.

c. Three of October's transactions involve cash payments, yet only one of these transactions is recorded as an expense. Describe three situations in which a cash payment would *not* involve recognition of an expense.

LO1 through LO10

PROBLEM 3.4B The Accounting Cycle: Journalizing, Posting, and Preparing a Trial Balance

In March 2011, Mary Tone organized a corporation to provide package delivery services. The company, called Tone Deliveries, Inc., began operations immediately. Transactions during the month of March were as follows:

Mar. 2 The corporation issued 40,000 shares of capital stock to Mary Tone in exchange for $80,000 cash.

Mar. 4 Purchased a truck for $45,000. Made a $15,000 cash down payment and issued a note payable for the remaining balance.

Mar. 5 Paid Sloan Properties $2,500 to rent office space for the month.

Mar. 9 Billed customers $11,300 for services for the first half of March.

Mar. 15 Paid $7,100 in salaries earned by employees during the first half of March.

Mar. 19 Paid Bill's Auto $900 for maintenance and repair services on the company truck.

Mar. 20 Collected $3,800 of the amounts billed to customers on March 9.

Mar. 28 Billed customers $14,400 for services performed during the second half of the month.

Mar. 30 Paid $7,500 in salaries earned by employees during the second half of the month.

Mar. 30 Received an $830 bill from SY Petroleum for fuel purchased in March. The entire amount is due by April 15.

Mar. 30 Declared a $1,200 dividend payable on April 30.

The account titles used by Tone Deliveries are:

Cash	Retained Earnings
Accounts Receivable	Dividends
Truck	Service Revenue
Notes Payable	Maintenance Expense
Accounts Payable	Fuel Expense
Dividends Payable	Salaries Expense
Capital Stock	Rent Expense

Instructions

a. Analyze the effects that each of these transactions will have on the following six components of the company's financial statements for the month of March. Organize your answer in tabular form, using the column headings shown below. Use **I** for increase, **D** for decrease, and **NE** for no effect. The March 2 transaction is provided for you:

	Income Statement			Balance Sheet		
Transaction	Revenue −	Expenses =	Net Income	Assets =	Liabilities +	Owners' Equity
Mar. 2	**NE**	**NE**	**NE**	**I**	**NE**	**I**

b. Prepare journal entries (including explanations) for each transaction.

c. Post each transaction to the appropriate ledger accounts (use a running balance format as shown in Exhibit 3–4, page 95).

d. Prepare a trial balance dated March 31, 2011.

e. Using figures from the trial balance prepared in part **d,** compute total assets, total liabilities, and owners' equity. Are these the figures that the company will report in its March 31 balance sheet? Explain your answer briefly.

LO1 through LO10

PROBLEM 3.5B

The Accounting Cycle: Journalizing, Posting, and Preparing a Trial Balance

Dr. Cravati, DMD., opened a dental clinic on August 1, 2011. The business transactions for August are shown below:

Aug. 1 Dr. Cravati invested $280,000 cash in the business in exchange for 1,000 shares of capital stock.

Aug. 4 Land and a building were purchased for $400,000. Of this amount, $60,000 applied to the land and $340,000 to the building. A cash payment of $80,000 was made at the time of the purchase, and a note payable was issued for the remaining balance.

Aug. 9 Medical instruments were purchased for $75,000 cash.

Aug. 16 Office fixtures and equipment were purchased for $25,000. Dr. Cravati paid $10,000 at the time of purchase and agreed to pay the entire remaining balance in 15 days.

Aug. 21 Office supplies expected to last several months were purchased for $4,200 cash.

Aug. 24 Dr. Cravati billed patients $13,000 for services rendered. Of this amount, $1,000 was received in cash, and $12,000 was billed on account (due in 30 days).

Aug. 27 A $450 invoice was received for several newspaper advertisements placed in August. The entire amount is due on September 8.

Aug. 28 Received a $500 payment on the $12,000 account receivable recorded August 24.

Aug. 31 Paid employees $2,200 for salaries earned in August.

A partial list of account titles used by Dr. Cravati includes:

Cash	Office Fixtures and Equipment
Accounts Receivable	Land
Office Supplies	Building
Notes Payable	Service Revenue
Accounts Payable	Advertising Expense
Capital Stock	Salary Expense
Medical Instruments	

Instructions

a. Analyze the effects that each of these transactions will have on the following six components of the company's financial statements for the month of August. Organize your answer in tabular form, using the column headings shown below. Use **I** for increase, **D** for decrease, and **NE** for no effect. The August 1 transaction is provided for you:

	Income Statement			Balance Sheet		
Transaction	Revenue –	Expenses =	Net Income	Assets =	Liabilities +	Owners' Equity
Aug. 1	**NE**	**NE**	**NE**	**I**	**NE**	**I**

b. Prepare journal entries (including explanations) for each transaction.

c. Post each transaction to the appropriate ledger accounts (use the T account format as illustrated in Exhibit 3–8 on page 108).

d. Prepare a trial balance dated August 31, 2011.

e. Using figures from the trial balance prepared in part **d,** compute total assets, total liabilities, and owners' equity. Did August appear to be a profitable month?

LO7 through LO9

PROBLEM 3.6B

Short Comprehensive Problem

Clown Around, Inc., provides party entertainment for children of all ages. The company's trial balance dated *February 1, 2011,* is shown below.

CLOWN AROUND, INC.
TRIAL BALANCE
FEBRUARY 1, 2011

Cash	$2,850	
Accounts receivable	900	
Accounts payable		$ 800
Capital stock		2,000
Retained earnings		750
Dividends	—	
Party revenue		1,350
Salaries expense	830	
Party food expense	240	
Travel expense	80	
	$4,900	$4,900

Clown Around engaged in the following transactions in February:

Feb. 2 Paid $750 in partial settlement of the outstanding account payable reported in the trial balance dated February 1.

Feb. 6 Collected $900 in full settlement of the outstanding accounts receivable reported in the trial balance dated February 1.

Feb. 18 Billed Sunflower Child Care $175 for clown services. The entire amount is due March 15.

Feb. 26 Billed and collected $480 for performing at several birthday parties.

Feb. 28 Paid clown salaries of $260 for work done in February.

Feb. 28 Recorded and paid $40 for travel expenses incurred in February.

Feb. 28 Declared and paid a $100 dividend to Ralph Jaschob, the company's only shareholder.

a. Record the company's February transactions in general journal form. Include a brief explanation of the transaction as part of each journal entry.

b. Post each entry to the appropriate ledger accounts (use the T account format as illustrated in Exhibit 3–8 on page 108).

c. Prepare a trial balance dated February 28, 2011. (Hint: Retained Earnings will be reported at the same amount as it was on February 1. Accounting for changes in the Retained Earnings account resulting from revenue, expense, and dividend activities is discussed in Chapter 5.)

d. Will the $100 dividend paid February 28 decrease the company's income? Explain.

LO3 through LO9

PROBLEM 3.7B

Short Comprehensive Problem

Ahuna, Inc., provides in-home cooking lessons to its clients. The company's trial balance dated *March 1, 2011,* is shown below:

AHUNA, INC. TRIAL BALANCE MARCH 1, 2011		
Cash	$ 5,700	
Accounts receivable	1,800	
Cooking supplies	800	
Accounts payable		$ 300
Dividends payable		500
Dividends	500	
Capital stock		6,000
Retained earnings		1,400
Client revenue		5,800
Salaries expense	3,100	
Travel expense	1,500	
Printing expense	600	
	$14,000	$14,000

Ahuna engaged in the following transactions in March:

Mar. 3 Collected a $1,200 account receivable from Kim Mitchell.
Mar. 11 Purchased cooking supplies for $700 cash.
Mar. 15 Paid $200 of outstanding accounts payable.
Mar. 20 Issued additional shares of capital stock for $4,000 cash.
Mar. 24 Recorded $6,200 of client revenue on account.
Mar. 27 Paid March salaries of $900.
Mar. 30 Recorded and paid March travel expenses of $400.
Mar. 31 Recorded $300 in printing expenses for recipe books. Payment is due April 12.

Instructions

a. Record the company's March transactions in general journal form. Include a brief explanation of the transaction as part of each journal entry.

b. Post each entry to the appropriate ledger accounts (use the T account format illustrated in Exhibit 3–8 on page 108).

c. Prepare a trial balance dated March 31, 2011. (Hint: Retained Earnings will be reported at the same amount as it was on March 1. Accounting for changes in the Retained Earnings account resulting from revenue, expense, and dividend activities is discussed in Chapter 5.)

d. Has the company paid all of the dividends that it has declared? Explain.

LO3 LO8

PROBLEM 3.8B

Analyzing the Effects of Accounting Errors

Blind River, Inc., recently hired Neil Young as its bookkeeper. Mr. Young is somewhat inexperienced and has made numerous errors recording daily business transactions.

Indicate the *effects of the errors* described below on each of the financial statement elements shown in the column headings. Use the following symbols: **O** for overstated; **U** for understated; and **NE** for no effect.

Error	Net Income	Total Assets	Total Liabilities	Owners' Equity
Recorded the issuance of capital stock by debiting Dividends and crediting Cash.				
Recorded the payment of an account payable by debiting Cash and crediting Accounts Receivable.				
Recorded the collection of an outstanding account receivable by debiting Service Revenue and crediting Cash.				
Recorded client billings on account by debiting Accounts Payable and crediting Cash.				
Recorded the payment of an outstanding dividend payable by debiting Dividends and crediting Cash.				
Recorded the payment of salaries payable by debiting Salaries Expense and crediting Salaries Payable.				
Recorded the purchase of office supplies on account by debiting Rent Expense and crediting Office Supplies.				

Critical Thinking Cases

LO7 LO10

CASE 3.1
Revenue Recognition

The realization principle determines when a business should recognize revenue. Listed next are three common business situations involving revenue. After each situation, we give two alternatives as to the accounting period (or periods) in which the business might recognize this revenue. Select the appropriate alternative by applying the realization principle, and explain your reasoning.

a. Airline ticket revenue: Most airlines sell tickets well before the scheduled date of the flight. (Period ticket sold; period of flight)

b. Sales on account: In June 2011, a San Diego–based furniture store had a big sale, featuring "No payments until 2012." (Period furniture sold; periods that payments are received from customers)

c. Magazine subscriptions revenue: Most magazine publishers sell subscriptions for future delivery of the magazine. (Period subscription sold; periods that magazines are mailed to customers)

LO6 LO7 LO10

CASE 3.2
Measuring Income Fairly

Kim Morris purchased Print Shop, Inc., a printing business, from Chris Stanley. Morris made a cash down payment and agreed to make annual payments equal to 40 percent of the company's net income in each of the next three years. (Such "earn-outs" are a common means of financing the purchase of a small business.) Stanley was disappointed, however, when Morris reported a first year's net income far below Stanley's expectations.

The agreement between Morris and Stanley did not state precisely how "net income" was to be measured. Neither Morris nor Stanley was familiar with accounting concepts. Their agreement stated only that the net income of the corporation should be measured in a "fair and reasonable manner."

In measuring net income, Morris applied the following policies:

1. Revenue was recognized when cash was received from customers. Most customers paid in cash, but a few were allowed 30-day credit terms.
2. Expenditures for ink and paper, which are purchased weekly, were charged directly to Supplies Expense, as were the Morris family's weekly grocery and dry cleaning bills.
3. Morris set her annual salary at $60,000, which Stanley had agreed was reasonable. She also paid salaries of $30,000 per year to her husband and to each of her two teenage children. These family members did not work in the business on a regular basis, but they did help out when things got busy.
4. Income taxes expense included the amount paid by the corporation (which was computed correctly), as well as the personal income taxes paid by various members of the Morris family on the salaries they earned working for the business.

5. The business had state-of-the-art printing equipment valued at $150,000 at the time Morris purchased it. The first-year income statement included a $150,000 equipment expense related to these assets.

Instructions

a. Discuss the fairness and reasonableness of these income-measurement policies. (Remember, these policies do *not* have to conform to generally accepted accounting principles. But they should be *fair* and *reasonable.*)

b. Do you think that the net *cash flow* generated by this business (cash receipts less cash outlays) is higher or lower than the net income as measured by Morris? Explain.

LO6 **CASE 3.3**

Whistle-Blowing

LO7

LO10

Happy Trails, Inc., is a popular family resort just outside Yellowstone National Park. Summer is the resort's busy season, but guests typically pay a deposit at least six months in advance to guarantee their reservations.

The resort is currently seeking new investment capital in order to expand operations. The more profitable Happy Trails appears to be, the more interest it will generate from potential investors. Ed Grimm, an accountant employed by the resort, has been asked by his boss to include $2 million of unearned guest deposits in the computation of income for the current year. Ed explained to his boss that because these deposits had not yet been earned they should be reported in the balance sheet as liabilities, not in the income statement as revenue. Ed argued that reporting guest deposits as revenue would inflate the current year's income and may mislead investors.

Ed's boss then *demanded* that he include $2 million of unearned guest deposits in the computation of income or be fired. He then told Ed in an assuring tone, "Ed, you will never be held responsible for misleading potential investors because you are just following my orders."

Instructions

Should Ed Grimm be forced to knowingly overstate the resort's income in order to retain his job? Is Ed's boss correct in saying that Ed cannot be held responsible for misleading potential investors? Discuss.

LO6 **INTERNET CASE 3.4**

Revenue from Various Sources

Visit the home page of **PC Connection** at the following Internet location: www.pcconnection.com.

Follow links to "Investors and Media" by accessing the "About Us" link at the bottom of the company's home page.

Locate the company's most recent annual report. What percent of the company's total revenue is generated by sales to public sector customers (e.g., governmental agencies, educational institutions, etc.)? Have sales to public sector customers increased or decreased during the past three years? What are the company's other business segments?

Internet sites are time and date sensitive. It is the purpose of these exercises to have you explore the Internet. You may need to use the Yahoo! search engine http://www.yahoo.com *(or another favorite search engine) to find a company's current Web address.*

Answers to Self-Test Questions

1. d **2.** b **3.** a, c, and d **4.** c **5.** c **6.** d **7.** b, c, and d
8. a and c

CHAPTER 4

The Accounting Cycle

Accruals and Deferrals

© Bill Bachmann/Photoedit

Learning Objectives

AFTER STUDYING THIS CHAPTER, YOU SHOULD BE ABLE TO:

- LO1 Explain the purpose of adjusting entries.
- LO2 Describe and prepare the four basic types of adjusting entries.
- LO3 Prepare adjusting entries to convert assets to expenses.
- LO4 Prepare adjusting entries to convert liabilities to revenue.
- LO5 Prepare adjusting entries to accrue unpaid expenses.
- LO6 Prepare adjusting entries to accrue uncollected revenue.
- LO7 Explain how the principles of *realization* and *matching* relate to adjusting entries.
- LO8 Explain the concept of *materiality.*
- LO9 Prepare an adjusted trial balance and describe its purpose.

CARNIVAL CORPORATION

When is revenue actually *earned* by a company? In many cases, revenue is earned when cash is received at the point of sale. For instance, when a taxicab driver takes someone to the airport, revenue is earned when the passenger is dropped off at the appropriate terminal and the fare is collected.

Suppose the same passenger boards a Carnival cruise ship to the Bahamas using a ticket that was purchased six months in advance. At what point should the cruise line recognize that ticket revenue has been earned? A recent Carnival Corporation balance sheet provides the answer to this question.

In its balance sheet, Carnival Corporation reports a $2.6 billion liability account called Customer Deposits. As passengers purchase tickets in advance, Carnival Corporation credits the Customer Deposits account for an amount equal to the cash it receives. It is not until passengers actually *use* their tickets that the company reduces this liability account and records Passenger Revenue in its income statement. ■

For most companies, revenue is *not* always earned as cash is received, nor is an expense necessarily incurred as cash is disbursed. Timing differences between cash flows and the recognition of revenue and expenses are referred to as *accruals* and *deferrals*. In this chapter, we examine how accounting information must be adjusted for accruals and deferrals prior to the preparation of financial statements.

The first three steps of the accounting cycle were discussed in Chapter 3. They included (1) recording transactions, (2) posting transactions, and (3) preparing a trial balance. In this chapter, we focus solely upon the fourth step of the accounting cycle: performing the end-of-period adjustments required to measure business income. The remaining steps of the cycle are covered in Chapter 5.

Adjusting Entries

There is more to the measurement of business income than merely recording simple revenue and expense transactions that affect only a single accounting period. Certain transactions affect the revenue or expenses of *two* or *more* accounting periods. The purpose of adjusting entries is to assign to each accounting period appropriate amounts of revenue and expense. For example, Overnight Auto Service purchased shop supplies that will be used for several months. Thus, an adjusting entry is required to record the expense associated with the shop supplies that Overnight *uses* each month.

THE NEED FOR ADJUSTING ENTRIES

Learning Objective
LO1 Explain the purpose of adjusting entries.

For purposes of measuring income and preparing financial statements, the life of a business is divided into a series of *accounting periods*. This practice enables decision makers to compare the financial statements of successive periods and to identify significant trends.

But measuring net income for a relatively short accounting period—such as a month or even a year—poses a problem because, as mentioned above, some business activities affect the revenue and expenses of *multiple accounting periods*. Therefore, **adjusting entries** are needed at the end of each accounting period to make certain that appropriate amounts of revenue and expense are reported in the company's income statement.

For example, magazine publishers often sell two- or three-year subscriptions to their publications. At the end of each accounting period, these publishers make adjusting entries recognizing the portion of their advance receipts that have been earned during the current period. Most companies also purchase insurance policies that benefit more than one period. Therefore, an adjusting entry is needed to make certain that an appropriate portion of each policy's total cost is reported in the income statement as insurance expense for the period. In short, adjusting entries are needed whenever transactions affect the revenue or expenses of more than one accounting period. These entries assign revenues to the period in which they are *earned,* and expenses to the periods in which related goods or services are *used.*

In theory, a business could make adjusting entries on a daily basis. But as a practical matter, these entries are made *only at the end of each accounting period.* For most companies, adjusting entries are made on a monthly basis.

TYPES OF ADJUSTING ENTRIES

Learning Objective
LO2 Describe and prepare the four basic types of adjusting entries.

The number of adjustments needed at the end of each accounting period depends entirely upon the nature of the company's business activities. However, most adjusting entries fall into one of four general categories:[1]

1. *Converting assets to expenses.* A cash expenditure (or cost) that will benefit more than one accounting period usually is recorded by debiting an asset account (for

[1] A fifth category of adjusting entries consists of adjustments related to the valuation of certain assets, such as marketable securities and accounts receivable. These valuation adjustments are explained and illustrated in Chapter 7.

example, Supplies, Unexpired Insurance, and so on) and by crediting Cash. The asset account created actually represents the *deferral* (or the postponement) of an expense. In each future period that benefits from the use of this asset, an adjusting entry is made to allocate a portion of the asset's cost from the balance sheet to the income statement as an expense. This adjusting entry is recorded by debiting the appropriate expense account (for example, Supplies Expense or Insurance Expense) and crediting the related asset account (for example, Supplies or Unexpired Insurance).

2. *Converting liabilities to revenue.* A business may collect cash in advance for services to be rendered in future accounting periods. Transactions of this nature are usually recorded by debiting Cash and by crediting a liability account (typically called Unearned Revenue). Here, the liability account created represents the *deferral* (or the postponement) of a revenue. In the period that services are actually rendered (or that goods are sold), an adjusting entry is made to allocate a portion of the liability from the balance sheet to the income statement to recognize the revenue earned during the period. The adjusting entry is recorded by debiting the liability (Unearned Revenue) and by crediting *Revenue Earned* (or a similar account) for the value of the services.
3. *Accruing unpaid expenses.* An expense may be incurred in the current accounting period even though no cash payment will occur until a future period. These *accrued* expenses are recorded by an adjusting entry made at the end of each accounting period. The adjusting entry is recorded by debiting the appropriate expense account (for example, Interest Expense or Salary Expense) and by crediting the related liability (for example, Interest Payable or Salaries Payable).
4. *Accruing uncollected revenue.* Revenue may be earned (or *accrued*) during the current period, even though the collection of cash will not occur until a future period. Unrecorded earned revenue, for which no cash has been received, requires an adjusting entry at the end of the accounting period. The adjusting entry is recorded by debiting the appropriate asset (for example, Accounts Receivable or Interest Receivable) and by crediting the appropriate revenue account (for example, Service Revenue Earned or Interest Earned).

ADJUSTING ENTRIES AND TIMING DIFFERENCES

In an accrual accounting system, there are often *timing differences* between cash flows and the recognition of expenses or revenue. A company can pay cash in advance of incurring certain expenses or receive cash before revenue has been earned. Likewise, it can incur certain expenses before paying any cash or it can earn revenue before any cash is received. These timing differences, and the adjusting entries that result from them, are summarized below.

- Adjusting entries to convert assets to expenses result from cash being paid prior to an expense being incurred.
- Adjusting entries to convert liabilities to revenue result from cash being received prior to revenue being earned.
- Adjusting entries to accrue unpaid expenses result from expenses being incurred before cash is paid.
- Adjusting entries to accrue uncollected revenue result from revenue being earned before cash is received.

As illustrated in Exhibit 4–1, adjusting entries provide important linkages between accounting periods related to these timing differences. Specifically, they link: (1) *prior* period cash outflows to *current* period expenses, (2) *prior* period cash inflows to *current* period revenue, (3) *current* period expenses to *future* cash outflows, and (4) *current* period revenue to *future* period cash inflows.

Exhibit 4–1 ADJUSTING ENTRIES PROVIDE LINKS BETWEEN ACCOUNTING PERIODS

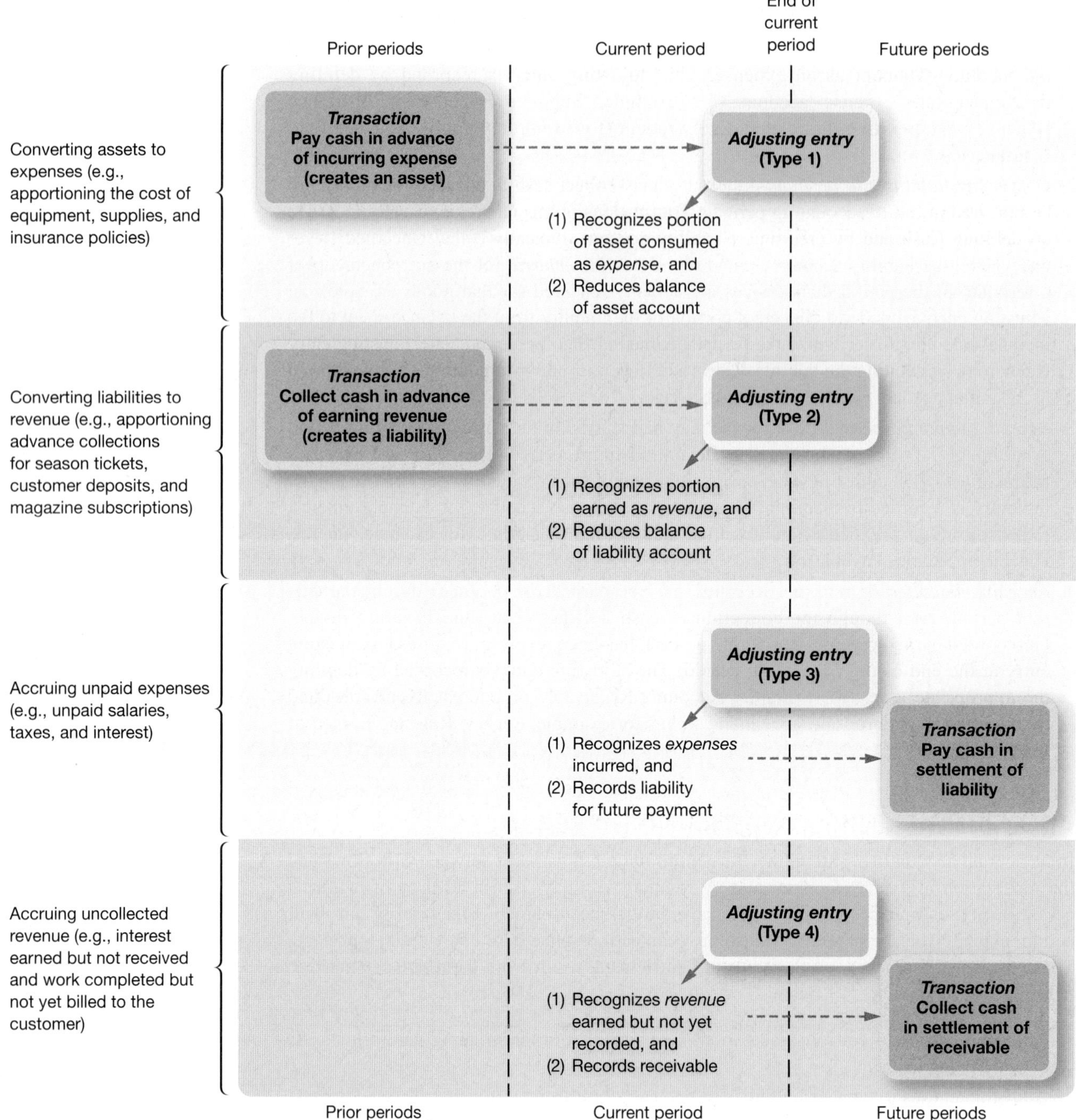

CHARACTERISTICS OF ADJUSTING ENTRIES

Keep in mind two important characteristics of all adjusting entries: First, every adjusting entry *involves the recognition of either revenue or expenses.* Revenue and expenses represent changes in owners' equity. However, owners' equity cannot change by itself; *there also must be a corresponding change in either assets or liabilities.* Thus every adjusting entry affects both an income statement account (revenue or expense) and a balance sheet account (asset or liability). Rarely do adjusting entries include an entry to Cash.

Second, adjusting entries are based on the concepts of accrual accounting, *not upon monthly bills or month-end transactions.* No one sends Overnight Auto Service a bill saying, "Shop Supply Expense for the month is $500." Yet, Overnight must be aware of the need to record the estimated cost of shop supplies consumed if it is to measure income properly for the period. Making adjusting entries requires a greater understanding of accrual accounting concepts than does the recording of routine business transactions. In many businesses, the adjusting process is performed by the controller or by a professional accountant, rather than by the regular accounting staff.

YEAR-END AT OVERNIGHT AUTO SERVICE

To illustrate the various types of adjusting entries, we will again use our example involving Overnight Auto Service. Chapter 3 concluded with Overnight's trial balance dated February 28, 2011 (the end of the company's second month of operations). We will now skip ahead to *December 31, 2011*—the end of Overnight's first *year* of operations. This will enable us to illustrate the preparation of *annual* financial statements, rather than statements that cover only a single month.

Most companies make adjusting entries every *month.* We will assume that Overnight has been following this approach throughout 2011. The company's *unadjusted* trial balance dated December 31, 2011, appears in Exhibit 4–2. It is referred to as an unadjusted trial balance because Overnight last made adjusting entries on *November 30;* therefore, it is still necessary to make adjusting entries for the month of December.

Exhibit 4–2

UNADJUSTED TRIAL BALANCE

OVERNIGHT AUTO SERVICE TRIAL BALANCE DECEMBER 31, 2011		
Cash	$ 18,592	
Accounts receivable	6,500	
Shop supplies	1,800	
Unexpired insurance	4,500	
Land	52,000	
Building	36,000	
Accumulated depreciation: building		$ 1,500
Tools and equipment	12,000	
Accumulated depreciation: tools and equipment		2,000
Notes payable		4,000
Accounts payable		2,690
Income taxes payable		1,560
Unearned rent revenue		9,000
Capital stock		80,000
Retained earnings		0
Dividends	14,000	
Repair service revenue		171,250
Advertising expense	3,900	
Wages expense	56,800	
Supplies expense	6,900	
Depreciation expense: building	1,500	
Depreciation expense: tools and equipment	2,000	
Utilities expense	19,400	
Insurance expense	13,500	
Income taxes expense	22,608	
	$272,000	$272,000

In the next few pages we illustrate several transactions, as well as the related adjusting entries. Both are shown in the format of general journal entries. To help distinguish between transactions and adjusting entries, *transactions* are printed in blue and *adjusting entries* in red.

CONVERTING ASSETS TO EXPENSES

Learning Objective
LO3 **Prepare adjusting entries to convert assets to expenses.**

When a business makes an expenditure that will benefit more than one accounting period, the amount usually is debited to an asset account. At the end of each period benefiting from this expenditure, an adjusting entry is made to transfer an appropriate portion of the cost from the asset account to an expense account. This adjusting entry reflects the fact that part of the asset has been used up—or become an expense—during the current accounting period.

An adjusting entry to convert an asset to an expense consists of a debit to an expense account and a credit to an asset account (or contra-asset account). Examples of these adjustments include the entries to apportion the costs of **prepaid expenses** and entries to record depreciation expense.

Prepaid Expenses

Payments in advance often are made for such items as insurance, rent, and office supplies. If the advance payment (or prepayment) will benefit more than just the current accounting period, the cost *represents an asset* rather than an expense. The cost of this asset will be allocated to expense in the accounting periods in which the services or the supplies are used. In summary, *prepaid expenses are assets;* they become expenses only as the goods or services are used up.

Shop Supplies

To illustrate, consider Overnight's accounting policies for shop supplies. As supplies are purchased, their cost is debited to the asset account Shop Supplies. It is not practical to make journal entries every few minutes as supplies are used. Instead, an estimate is made of the supplies remaining on hand at the end of each month; the supplies that are "missing" are assumed to have been used.

Prior to making adjusting entries at December 31, the balance in Overnight's Shop Supplies account is $1,800. The balance of this asset account represents shop supplies on hand on November 30. The Supplies Expense account shows a balance of $6,900, which represents the cost of supplies used through November 30. Assume that approximately $1,200 of shop supplies remain on hand at December 31. This suggests that supplies costing about $600 have been *used in December;* thus, the following *adjusting entry* is made:

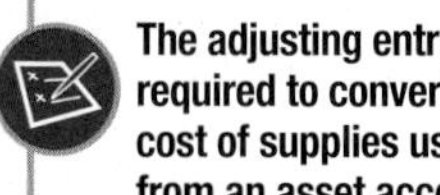

The adjusting entry required to convert the cost of supplies used from an asset account to an expense

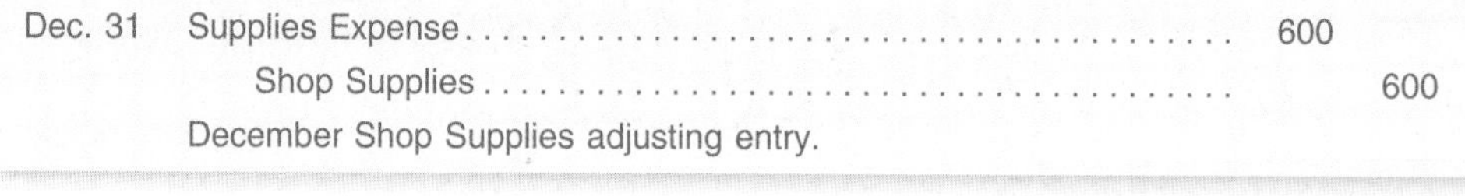

Dec. 31	Supplies Expense	600	
	Shop Supplies		600
	December Shop Supplies adjusting entry.		

This adjusting entry serves two purposes: (1) it charges to expense the cost of supplies used in December, and (2) it reduces the balance of the Shop Supplies account to $1,200—the amount of supplies estimated to be on hand at December 31.

Insurance Policies

Insurance policies also are a prepaid expense. These policies provide a service, insurance protection, over a specific period of time. As the time passes, the insurance policy *expires*—that is, it is used up in business operations.

To illustrate, assume that on March 1, Overnight purchased for $18,000 a one-year insurance policy providing comprehensive liability insurance and insurance against fire and damage to customers' vehicles while in Overnight's facilities. This expenditure (a *transaction*) was debited to an asset account, as follows (again, this is a transaction, *not* an adjusting entry):

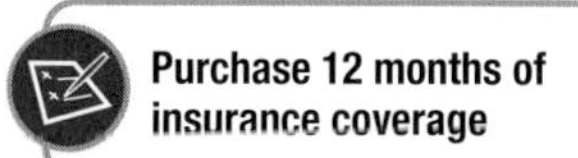

Purchase 12 months of insurance coverage

Mar. 1	Unexpired Insurance	18,000	
	Cash		18,000
	Purchased an insurance policy providing coverage for the next 12 months.		

This $18,000 expenditure provides insurance coverage for a period of one full year. Therefore, 1/12 of this cost, or $1,500, is recognized as insurance expense every month. The $13,500 insurance expense reported in Overnight's trial balance represents the portion of the insurance policy that has expired between March 1 and November 30 ($1,500/mo. × 9 months). The $4,500 amount of unexpired insurance shown in the trial balance is the remaining cost of the 12-month policy still in effect as of November 30 ($1,500/mo. × 3 months). By December 31, another full month of the policy has expired. Thus, the insurance expense for December is recorded by the following *adjusting entry* at month-end:

Dec. 31	Insurance Expense	1,500	
	Unexpired Insurance		1,500
	December Insurance Expense adjusting entry.		

The adjusting entry required to record the cost of insurance coverage expiring in December

Notice the similarities between the *effects* of this adjusting entry and the one that we made previously for shop supplies. In both cases, the entries transfer to expense that portion of an asset used up during the period. This flow of costs from the balance sheet to the income statement is illustrated in Exhibit 4–3.

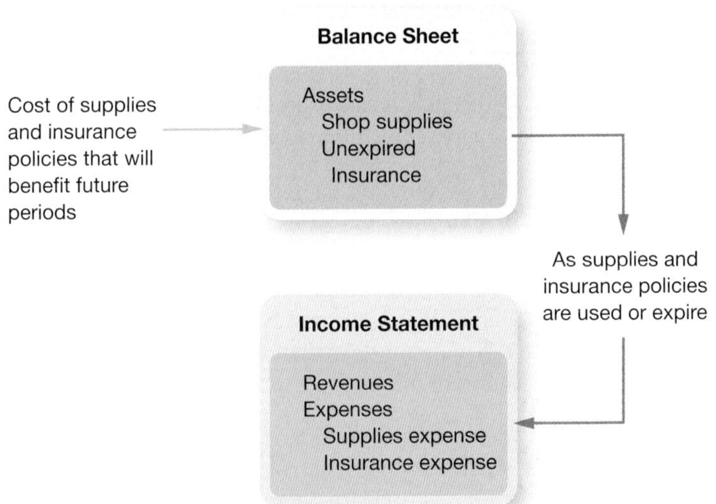

Exhibit 4–3
AN EXPIRED ASSET BECOMES AN EXPENSE

YOUR TURN **You as a Car Owner**

Car owners typically pay insurance premiums six months in advance. Assume that you recently paid your six-month premium of $600 on February 1 (for coverage through July 31). On March 31, you decide to switch insurance companies. You call your existing agent and ask that your policy be canceled. Are you entitled to a refund? If so, why, and how much will it be?

(See our comments on the Online Learning Center Web site.)

Recording Prepayments Directly in the Expense Accounts In our illustration, payments for shop supplies and for insurance covering more than one period were debited to asset accounts. However, some companies follow an alternative policy of debiting such prepayments directly to an expense account, such as Supplies Expense. At the end of the period, the adjusting entry then would be to debit Shop Supplies and credit Supplies Expense for the cost of supplies that had *not* been used.

This alternative method leads to the *same results* as does the procedure used by Overnight. Under either approach, the cost of supplies used during the current period is treated as an *expense,* and the cost of supplies still on hand is carried forward in the balance sheet as an *asset.*

In this text, we will follow Overnight's practice of recording prepayments in asset accounts and then making adjustments to transfer these costs to expense accounts as the assets expire. This approach correctly describes the *conceptual flow of costs* through the elements of financial statements. That is, a prepayment *is* an asset that later becomes an expense. The alternative approach is used widely in practice only because it is an efficient "shortcut," which standardizes the recording of transactions and may reduce the number of adjusting entries needed at the end of the period. Remember, our goal in this course is to develop your ability to understand and use accounting information, not to train you in alternative bookkeeping procedures.

The idea of shop supplies and insurance policies being used up over several months is easy to understand. But the same concept also applies to assets such as buildings and equipment. These assets are converted to expenses through the process of *depreciation.*

THE CONCEPT OF DEPRECIATION

Depreciable assets are *physical objects* that retain their size and shape but that eventually wear out or become obsolete. They are not physically consumed, as are assets such as supplies, but nonetheless their economic usefulness diminishes over time. Examples of depreciable assets include buildings and all types of equipment, fixtures, furnishings—and even railroad tracks. Land, however, is *not* viewed as a depreciable asset, as it has an *unlimited* useful life.

Each period, a portion of a depreciable asset's usefulness *expires.* Therefore, a corresponding portion of its cost is recognized as *depreciation expense.*

What Is Depreciation?

In accounting, the term **depreciation** means the *systematic allocation of the cost of a depreciable asset to expense* over the asset's useful life. This process is illustrated in Exhibit 4–4. Notice the similarities between Exhibit 4–4 and Exhibit 4–3.

Depreciation *is not* an attempt to record changes in the asset's market value. In the short run, the market value of some depreciable assets may even increase, but the process of depreciation continues anyway. The rationale for depreciation lies in the *matching principle.* Our goal is to offset a reasonable portion of the asset's cost against revenue in each period of the asset's **useful life.**

Exhibit 4–4
THE DEPRECIATION PROCESS

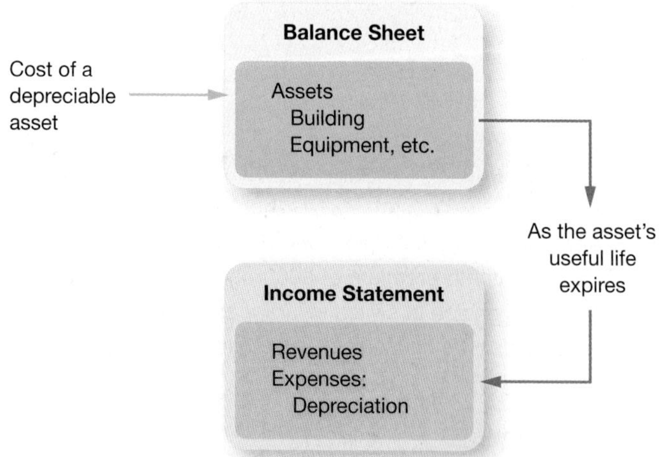

Depreciation expense occurs continuously over the life of the asset, but there are no daily "depreciation transactions." In effect, depreciation expense is paid in advance when the asset is originally purchased. Therefore, *adjusting entries* are needed at the end of each accounting period to transfer an appropriate amount of the asset's cost to depreciation expense.

Depreciation Is Only an Estimate

The appropriate amount of depreciation expense is *only an estimate.* After all, we cannot look at a building or a piece of equipment and determine precisely how much of its economic usefulness has expired during the current period.

The most widely used means of estimating periodic depreciation expense is the **straight-line method of depreciation.** Under the straight-line approach, an *equal portion* of the asset's cost is allocated to depreciation expense in every period of the asset's estimated useful life. The formula for computing depreciation expense by the straight-line method is:[2]

$$\textbf{Depreciation expense (per period)} = \frac{\textbf{Cost of the asset}}{\textbf{Estimated useful life}}$$

The use of an *estimated useful life* is the major reason that depreciation expense is *only an estimate.* In most cases, management does not know in advance exactly how long the asset will remain in use.

CASE IN POINT

© Adam Woolfitt/Corbis

How long does a building last? For purposes of computing depreciation expense, most companies estimate about 30 or 40 years. But the Empire State Building was built in 1931, and it's not likely to be torn down anytime soon. And how about Windsor Castle? While these are not typical examples, they illustrate the difficulty in estimating in advance just how long depreciable assets may remain in use.

Depreciation of Overnight's Building Overnight purchased its building for $36,000 on January 22. Because the building was old, its estimated remaining useful life is only 20 years. Therefore, the building's monthly depreciation expense is $150 ($36,000 cost ÷ 240 months). We will assume that Overnight did *not* record any depreciation expense in January because it operated for only a small part of the month. Thus, the building's $1,500 depreciation expense reported in Overnight's trial balance illustrated in Exhibit 4–2 on page 143 represents 10 *full months* of depreciation recorded in 2011, from February 1 through November 30 ($150/mo. × 10 months). An additional $150 of depreciation expense is still needed on the building for December (bringing the total to be reported in the income statement for the year to $1,650).

The *adjusting entry* to record depreciation expense on Overnight's building for the month of December is:

Dec. 31	Depreciation Expense: Building	150	
	Accumulated Depreciation: Building		150
	December building depreciation adjusting entry ($36,000 ÷ 240 mo.).		

The adjusting entry required to record monthly depreciation on the building

The *Depreciation Expense: Building* account will appear in Overnight's income statement along with other expenses for the year ended December 31, 2011. The balance in the

[2] At this point in our discussion, we are ignoring any possible *residual value* that might be recovered upon disposal of the asset. Residual values are discussed in Chapter 9. We will assume that Overnight Auto Service depreciates its assets using the straight-line method computed without any residual values.

Accumulated Depreciation: Building account will be reported in the December 31 balance sheet as a *deduction* from the Building Account, as shown below.

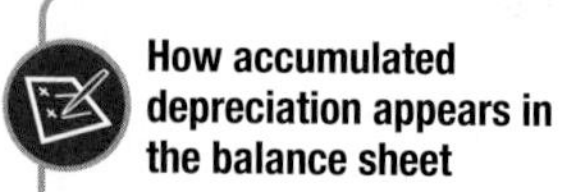
How accumulated depreciation appears in the balance sheet

Building.	$36,000
Less: Accumulated Depreciation: Building	(1,650)
Book Value	$34,350

Accumulated Depreciation: Building is an example of a **contra-asset account** because (1) it has a credit balance, and (2) it is offset against an asset account (Building) to produce the book value for the asset. Accountants often use the term **book value** (or *carrying value*) to describe the net valuation of an asset in a company's accounting records. For depreciable assets, such as buildings and equipment, book value is equal to the cost of the asset, less the related amount of accumulated depreciation. The end result of crediting the Accumulated Depreciation: Building account is much the same as if the credit had been made directly to the Building account; that is, the book value reported in the balance sheet for the building is reduced from $36,000 to $34,350.

Book value is of significance primarily for accounting purposes. It represents costs that will be offset against the revenue of future periods. It also gives users of financial statements an indication of the age of a company's depreciable assets (older assets tend to have larger amounts of accumulated depreciation associated with them than newer assets). It is important to realize that the computation of book value is based upon an asset's *historical* cost. Thus, book value is *not* intended to represent an asset's current *market value.*

Depreciation of Tools and Equipment Overnight depreciates its tools and equipment over a period of five years (60 months) using the straight-line method. The December 31 trial balance shows that the company owns tools and equipment that cost $12,000. Therefore, the *adjusting entry* to record December's depreciation expense is:

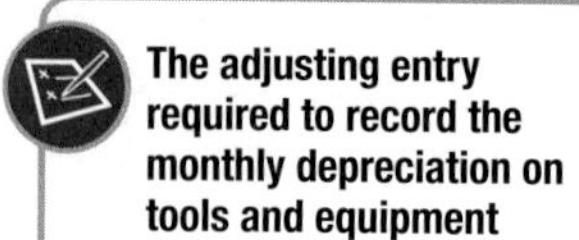
The adjusting entry required to record the monthly depreciation on tools and equipment

Dec. 31	Depreciation Expense: Tools and Equipment.	200	
	Accumulated Depreciation: Tools and Equipment.		200
	December tools and equipment adjusting entry ($12,000 ÷ 60 months = $200/mo.).		

Again, we assume that Overnight did *not* record depreciation expense for tools and equipment in January because it operated for only a small part of the month. Thus, the related $2,000 depreciation expense reported in Overnight's trial balance in Exhibit 4–2 on page 145 represents 10 *full months* of depreciation, from February 1 through November 30 ($200/mo. × 10 months). The tools and equipment still require an additional $200 of depreciation for December (bringing the total to be reported in the income statement for the year to $2,200).

What is the book value of Overnight's tools and equipment at December 31, 2011? If you said *$9,800,* you're right.[3]

Depreciation—A Noncash Expense Depreciation is a *noncash* expense. We have made the point that net income does not represent an inflow of cash or any other asset. Rather, it is a *computation* of the overall effect of certain business transactions on owners' equity. The recognition of depreciation expense illustrates this point. As depreciable assets expire, depreciation expense is recorded, net income is reduced, and owners' equity declines, but there is no corresponding cash outlay in the current period. For this reason, depreciation is called a noncash expense. Often it represents the largest difference between net income and the cash flow from business operations.

[3] Cost, $12,000, less accumulated depreciation, which amounts to $2,200 after the December 31 adjusting entry.

CONVERTING LIABILITIES TO REVENUE

Learning Objective
LO4 **Prepare adjusting entries to convert liabilities to revenue.**

In some instances, customers may *pay in advance* for services to be rendered in later accounting periods. For example, a football team collects much of its revenue in advance through the sale of season tickets. Health clubs collect in advance by selling long-term membership contracts. Airlines sell many of their tickets well in advance of scheduled flights.

For accounting purposes, amounts collected in advance *do not represent revenue,* because these amounts have *not yet been earned.* Amounts collected from customers in advance are recorded by debiting the Cash account and crediting an *unearned revenue* account. **Unearned revenue** also may be called *deferred revenue.*

When a company collects money in advance from its customers, it has an *obligation* to render services in the future. Therefore, the balance of an unearned revenue account is considered to be a liability; *it appears in the liability section of the balance sheet, not in the income statement.* Unearned revenue differs from other liabilities because it usually will be settled by rendering services, rather than by making payment in cash. In short, it will be *worked off* rather than *paid off.* Of course, if the business is unable to render the service, it must discharge this liability by refunding money to its customers.

When a company renders the services for which customers have paid in advance, it is working off its liability to these customers and is earning the revenue. At the end of the accounting period, an adjusting entry is made to transfer an appropriate amount from the unearned revenue account to a revenue account. This adjusting entry consists of a debit to a liability account (unearned revenue) and a credit to a revenue account. For instance, **The New York Times Company** reports a $78 million current liability in its balance sheet called Unexpired Subscriptions. This account represents unearned revenue from selling subscriptions for future newspaper deliveries. The liability is converted to Circulation Revenue and reported in the company's income statement as the actual deliveries occur.

To illustrate these concepts, assume that on December 1, Harbor Cab Co. agreed to rent space in Overnight's building to provide indoor storage for some of its cabs. The agreed-upon rent is $3,000 per month, and Harbor Cab paid for the first three months in advance. The journal entry to record this *transaction* on December 1 was (again, this is a transaction, *not* an adjusting entry):

Dec. 1	Cash	9,000	
	Unearned Rent Revenue		9,000
	Collected in advance from Harbor Cab for rental of storage space for three months.		

Remember that Unearned Rent Revenue is a *liability* account, *not a revenue account.* Overnight will earn rental revenue *gradually* over a three-month period as it provides storage facilities for Harbor Cab. At the end of each of these three months, Overnight will make an *adjusting entry,* transferring $3,000 from the Unearned Rent Revenue account to an earned revenue account, Rent Revenue Earned, which will appear in Overnight's income statement. The first in this series of monthly transfers will be made at December 31 with the following *adjusting entry*:

An "advance"—it's not revenue; it's a liability

Dec. 31	Unearned Rent Revenue	3,000	
	Rent Revenue Earned.		3,000
	December adjusting entry to convert Unearned Rent Revenue to Rent Revenue Earned ($9,000 ÷ 3 mo.).		

An adjusting entry showing that some unearned revenue was earned in December

After this adjusting entry has been posted, the Unearned Rent Revenue account will have a $6,000 credit balance. This balance represents Overnight's obligation to render $6,000 worth of service over the next two months and will appear in the liability section of the company's balance sheet. The Rent Revenue Earned account will appear in Overnight's income statement.

The conversion of unearned revenue to recognize earned revenue is illustrated in Exhibit 4–5.

Exhibit 4–5
UNEARNED REVENUE BECOMES EARNED REVENUE

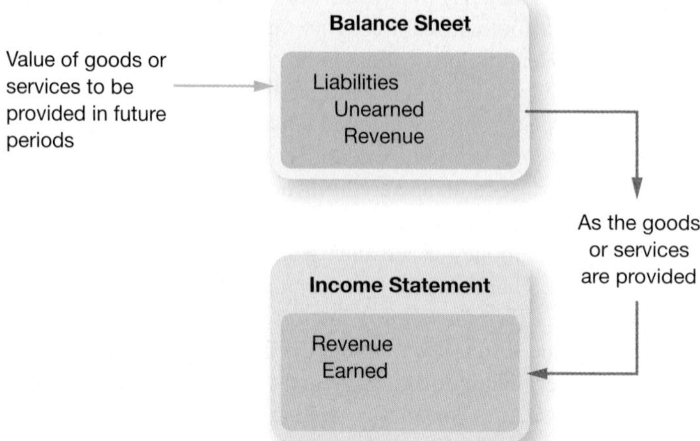

Recording Advance Collections Directly in the Revenue Accounts We have stressed that amounts collected from customers in advance represent liabilities, not revenue. However, some companies follow an accounting policy of crediting these advance collections directly to revenue accounts. The adjusting entry then should consist of a debit to the revenue account and a credit to the unearned revenue account for the portion of the advance payments *not yet earned.* This alternative accounting practice leads to the same results as does the method used in our illustration.

In this text, we will follow the originally described practice of crediting advance payments from customers to an unearned revenue account.

Learning Objective
L05 Prepare adjusting entries to accrue unpaid expenses.

ACCRUING UNPAID EXPENSES

This type of adjusting entry recognizes expenses that will be paid in *future* transactions; therefore, no cost has yet been recorded in the accounting records. Salaries of employees and interest on borrowed money are common examples of expenses that accumulate from day to day but that usually are not recorded until they are paid. These expenses are said to **accrue** over time, that is, to grow or to accumulate. At the end of the accounting period, an adjusting entry should be made to record any expenses that have accrued but that have not yet been recorded. Since these expenses will be paid at a future date, the adjusting entry consists of a debit to an expense account and a credit to a liability account. We shall now use the example of Overnight Auto Service to illustrate this type of adjusting entry.

Accrual of Wages (or Salaries) Expense Overnight, like many businesses, pays its employees every other Friday. This month, however, ends on a Tuesday—three days before the next scheduled payday. Thus Overnight's employees have worked for more than a week in December *for which they have not yet been paid.*

Time cards indicate that since the last payroll date, Overnight's employees have worked a total of 130 hours. Including payroll taxes, Overnight's wage expense averages about $15 per hour. Therefore, at December 31, the company owes its employees approximately *$1,950* for work performed in December.[4] The following *adjusting entry* should be made to record this amount both as wages expense of the current period and as a liability:

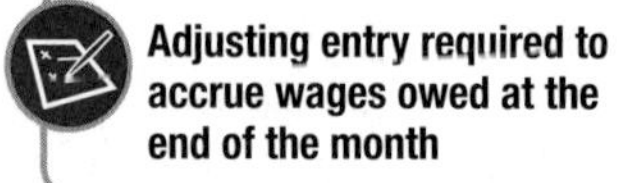
Adjusting entry required to accrue wages owed at the end of the month

Dec. 31	Wages Expense	1,950	
	Wages Payable		1,950
	Adjusting entry to accrue wages owed but unpaid as of December 31.		

[4] In the preparation of a formal payroll, wages and payroll taxes must be computed "down to the last cent." But this is not a payroll; it is an amount to be used in the company's financial statements. Therefore, a reasonable estimate will suffice. The accounting principle of *materiality* is discussed later in this chapter.

This adjusting entry increases Overnight's wages expense for 2011 and also creates a liability—wages payable—that will appear in the December 31 balance sheet.

On Friday, January 3, 2012, Overnight will pay its regular biweekly payroll. Let us assume that this payroll amounts to $2,397. In this case, the *transaction* to record payment is as follows (again, this is a transaction, *not* an adjusting entry):[5]

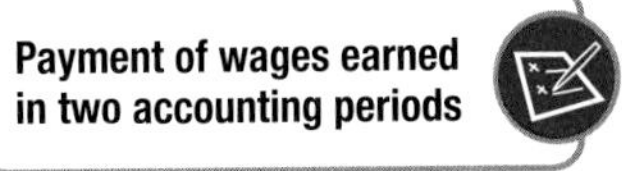

2012			
Jan. 3	Wages Expense (for January)	447	
	Wages Payable (accrued in December)	1,950	
	Cash		2,397
	Biweekly payroll, $1,950 of which had been accrued at December 31, 2011.		

Accrual of Interest Expense On January 22, 2011, Overnight purchased its building, an old bus garage, from the Metropolitan Transit Authority for $36,000. Overnight paid $6,000 cash, and issued a $30,000, 90-day note payable for the balance owed. Overnight paid the $30,000 obligation in April. There was no interest expense to accrue because this note payable was *non-interest-bearing.*

On November 30, 2011, Overnight borrowed $4,000 from American National Bank by issuing an *interest-bearing* note payable. This loan is to be repaid in three months (on February 28, 2012), along with interest computed at an annual rate of 9 percent. The entry made on November 30 to record this borrowing *transaction* is (again, this is a transaction, *not* an adjusting entry):

Nov. 30	Cash	4,000	
	Notes Payable		4,000
	Borrowed cash from American National Bank, issuing a 9%, $4,000 note payable, due in three months.		

On February 28, Overnight must pay the bank $4,090. This represents the $4,000 amount borrowed, *plus $90 interest* ($4,000 × .09 × 3/12). The $90 interest charge covers a period of *three months.* Although no payment is made until February 28, 2012, interest expense is *incurred* (or accrued) at a rate of $30 per month, as shown in Exhibit 4–6.

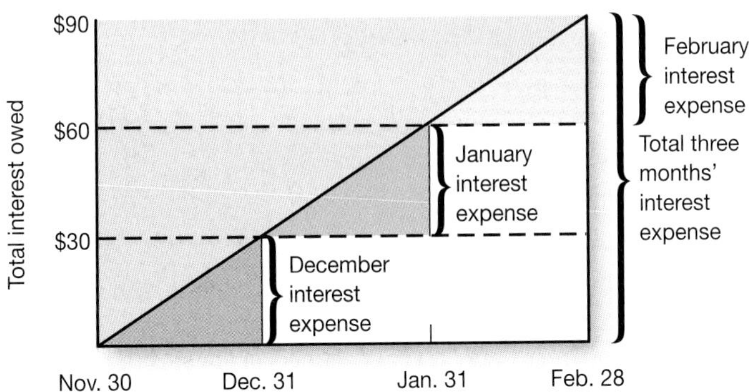

Exhibit 4–6
ACCRUAL OF INTEREST

The following *adjusting entry* is made at December 31 to accrue one month's interest expense and to record the amount of interest owed to the bank at December 31, 2011:

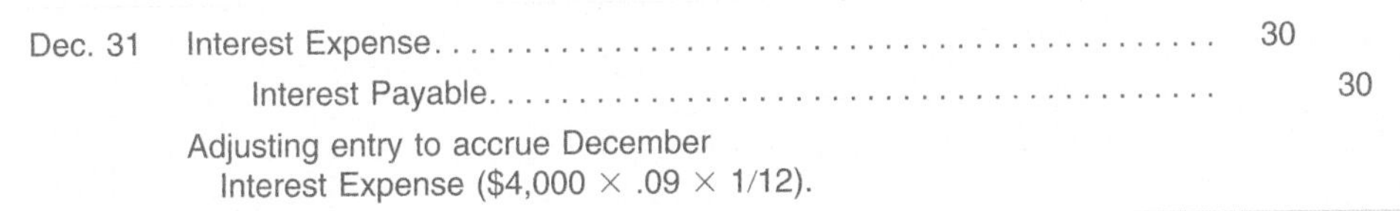

Dec. 31	Interest Expense	30	
	Interest Payable		30
	Adjusting entry to accrue December Interest Expense ($4,000 × .09 × 1/12).		

Adjusting entry required to record interest expense accrued in December

[5] In this illustration, we do not address the details associated with payroll taxes and amounts withheld. These topics are discussed in Chapter 10.

The $30 interest expense that accrued in December will appear in Overnight's 2011 income statement. Both the $30 interest payable and the $4,000 note payable to American National Bank will appear as *liabilities* in the December 31, 2011, balance sheet.

Overnight will make a *second* adjusting entry recognizing another $30 in interest expense on January 31, 2012. The *transaction* on February 28 to record the repayment of this loan, including $90 in interest charges, is (again, this is a transaction, *not* an adjusting entry):

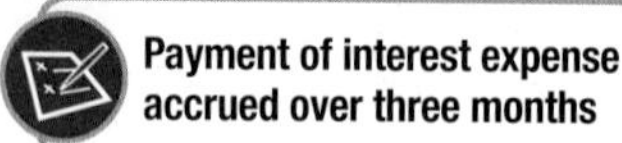
Payment of interest expense accrued over three months

2012			
Feb. 28	Notes Payable	4,000	
	Interest Payable (from December and January)	60	
	Interest Expense (February only)	30	
	Cash		4,090
	Repaid $4,000 note payable to American National Bank, including $90 in interest charges.		

Learning Objective
LO6 **Prepare adjusting entries to accrue uncollected revenue.**

ACCRUING UNCOLLECTED REVENUE

A business may earn revenue during the current accounting period but not bill the customer until a future accounting period. This situation is likely to occur if additional services are being performed for the same customer, in which case the bill might not be prepared until all services are completed. Any revenue that has been *earned but not recorded* during the current accounting period should be recorded at the end of the period by means of an adjusting entry. This adjusting entry consists of a debit to an account receivable and a credit to the appropriate revenue account. The term *accrued revenue* often is used to describe revenue that has been earned during the period but that has not been recorded prior to the closing date.

To illustrate this type of adjusting entry, assume that in December, Overnight entered into an agreement to perform routine maintenance on several vans owned by Airport Shuttle Service. Overnight agreed to maintain these vans for a flat fee of $1,500 per month, payable on the fifteenth of each month.

No entry was made to record the signing of this agreement, because no services had yet been rendered. Overnight began rendering services on *December 15,* but the first monthly payment will not be received until January 15. Therefore, Overnight should make the following *adjusting entry* at December 31 to record the revenue *earned* from Airport Shuttle during the month:

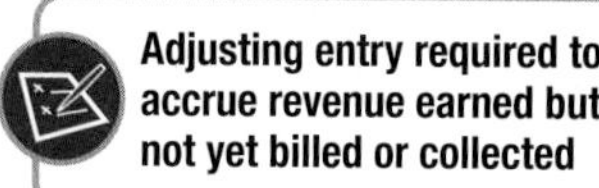
Adjusting entry required to accrue revenue earned but not yet billed or collected

Dec. 31	Accounts Receivable	750	
	Repair Service Revenue		750
	Adjusting entry to record accrued Repair Service Revenue earned in December.		

The collection of the first monthly fee from Airport Shuttle will occur on January 15, 2012. Of this $1,500 cash receipt, half represents collection of the receivable recorded on December 31; the other half represents revenue earned in January. Thus, the *transaction* to record the receipt of $1,500 from Airport Shuttle on January 15 will be (again, this is a transaction, *not* an adjusting entry):

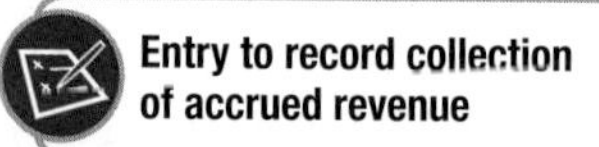
Entry to record collection of accrued revenue

2012			
Jan. 15	Cash	1,500	
	Accounts Receivable		750
	Repair Service Revenue		750
	Cash collected from Airport Shuttle for van maintenance provided December 15 through January 15.		

The net result of the December 31 adjusting entry has been to divide the revenue from maintenance of Airport Shuttle's vans between December and January in proportion to the services rendered during each month.

ACCRUING INCOME TAXES EXPENSE: THE FINAL ADJUSTING ENTRY

As a corporation earns taxable income, it incurs income taxes expense, and also a liability to governmental tax authorities. This liability is paid in four installments called *estimated quarterly payments.* The first three payments normally are made on April 15, June 15, and September 15. The final installment actually is due on *December 15;* but for purposes of our illustration and assignment materials, we will assume the final payment is not due until *January 15* of the following year.[6]

In its unadjusted trial balance (Exhibit 4–2 on page 143), Overnight shows income taxes expense of $22,608. This is the income taxes expense recognized from January 20, 2011, (the date Overnight opened for business) through November 30, 2011. Income taxes accrued through September 30 have already been paid. Thus, the $1,560 liability for income taxes payable represents only the income taxes accrued in *October* and *November.*

The amount of income taxes expense accrued for any given month is only an *estimate.* The actual amount of income taxes cannot be determined until the company prepares its annual income tax return. In our illustrations and assignment materials, we estimate income taxes expense at *40 percent of taxable income.* We also assume that taxable income is equal to *income before income taxes,* a subtotal often shown in an income statement. This subtotal is total revenue less all expenses *other than* income taxes.

INTERNATIONAL CASE IN POINT

Corporate income tax rates vary around the world. A recent survey shows that rates range from 9 percent in Montenegro to 55 percent in the United Arab Emirates. Worldwide, the average tax rate is 25 percent. The average rate in the United States is 40 percent.* In addition to corporate income taxes, some countries also (1) withhold taxes on dividends, interest, and royalties, (2) charge value-added taxes at specified production and distribution points, and (3) impose border taxes such as customs and import duties.

*KPMG Corporate Tax Rate Survey (January 2009).

In 2011, Overnight earned income before income taxes of $66,570 (see the income statement in Exhibit 5–2, page 194, in Chapter 5). Therefore, income taxes expense *for the entire year* is estimated at $26,628 ($66,570 × 40 percent). Given that income taxes expense recognized through November 30 amounts to $22,608 (see the unadjusted trial balance in Exhibit 4–2), an additional $4,020 in income taxes expense must have accrued during *December* ($26,628 − $22,608). The *adjusting entry* to record this expense is:

Dec. 31	Income Taxes Expense	4,020	
	Income Taxes Payable		4,020
	Adjusting entry to record income taxes accrued in December.		

Adjusting entry required to record income taxes accrued in December

[6] This assumption enables us to accrue income taxes in December in the same manner as in other months. Otherwise, income taxes for this month would be recorded as a mid-month transaction, rather than in an end-of-month adjusting entry. The adjusting entry for income taxes is an example of an accrued, but unpaid, expense.

This entry increases the balance in the Income Taxes Expense account to the $26,628 amount required for the year ended December 31, 2011. It also increases the liability for income taxes payable to $5,580 ($1,560 + $4,020). The *transaction* to record the payment of this liability on January 15, 2012, will be (again, this is a transaction, *not* an adjusting entry):

2012			
Jan. 15	Income Taxes Payable	5,580	
	Cash		5,580
	Payment of the remaining 2011 income tax liability.		

Income Taxes in Unprofitable Periods What happens to income taxes expense when *losses* are incurred? In these situations, the company recognizes a "negative amount" of income taxes expense. The adjusting entry to record income taxes at the end of an *unprofitable* accounting period consists of a *debit* to Income Taxes Payable and a *credit* to Income Taxes Expense.

"Negative" income taxes expense means that the company may be able to recover from the government some of the income taxes recognized as expense in prior periods.[7] If the Income Taxes Payable account has a *debit* balance at year-end, it is reclassified as an *asset,* called "Income Tax Refund Receivable." A credit balance in the Income Taxes Expense account is offset against the amount of the before-tax loss, as shown in Exhibit 4–7.

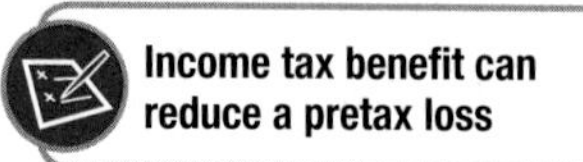
Income tax benefit can reduce a pretax loss

Exhibit 4–7
PARTIAL INCOME STATEMENT

Partial Income Statement—for an *Unprofitable* Period

Income (loss) before income taxes.	$(20,000)
Income tax benefit (recovery of previously recorded taxes)	8,000
Net loss	$(12,000)

We have already seen that income taxes *expense* reduces the amount of before-tax *profits.* Notice now that income tax *benefits*—in the form of tax refunds—can reduce the amount of a pretax *loss.* Thus, income taxes reduce the size of *both* profits and losses. The detailed reporting of profits and losses in the income statement is illustrated in Chapter 5.

Adjusting Entries and Accounting Principles

Learning Objective
LO7 Explain how the principles of *realization* and *matching* relate to adjusting entries.

Adjusting entries are the means by which accountants apply the **realization** and **matching** principles. Through these entries, revenues are recognized as they are *earned,* and expenses are recognized as resources are *used* or consumed in producing the related revenue.

In most cases, the realization principle indicates that revenue should be recognized *at the time goods are sold or services are rendered.* At this point the business has essentially completed the earning process and the sales value of the goods or services can be measured objectively. At any time prior to sale, the ultimate sales value of the goods or services sold can only be estimated. After the sale, the only step that remains is to collect from the customer, and this is usually a relatively certain event.

The matching principle underlies such accounting practices as depreciating plant assets, measuring the cost of supplies used, and amortizing the cost of unexpired insurance policies. All end-of-the-period adjusting entries involving expense recognition are applications of the matching principle.

[7] Tax refunds may be limited to tax payments in recent years. In this introductory discussion, we assume the company has paid sufficient taxes in prior years to permit a full recovery of any "negative tax expense" relating to the loss in the current period.

Costs are matched with revenue in one of two ways:

1. *Direct association of costs with specific revenue transactions.* The ideal method of matching revenue with expenses is to determine the actual amount of expense associated with specific revenue transactions. However, this approach works only for those costs and expenses that can be directly associated with specific revenue transactions. Commissions paid to salespeople are an example of costs that can be *directly associated* with the revenue of a specific accounting period.
2. *Systematic allocation of costs over the useful life of the expenditure.* Many expenditures contribute to the earning of revenue for a number of accounting periods but cannot be directly associated with specific revenue transactions. Examples include the costs of insurance policies and depreciable assets. In these cases, accountants attempt to match revenue and expenses by *systematically allocating the cost to expense* over its useful life. Straight-line depreciation is an example of a systematic technique used to match the cost of an asset with the related revenue that it helps to earn over its useful life.

THE CONCEPT OF MATERIALITY

Learning Objective
Explain the concept of *materiality.*
LO8

Another underlying accounting principle also plays a major role in the making of adjusting entries—the concept of **materiality.** The term *materiality* refers to the *relative importance* of an item or an event. An item is considered material if knowledge of the item might reasonably *influence the decisions* of users of financial statements. Accountants must be sure that all material items are properly reported in financial statements.

However, the financial reporting process should be *cost-effective*—that is, the value of the information should exceed the cost of its preparation. By definition, the accounting treatment accorded to **immaterial** items is of *little or no consequence to decision makers.* Therefore, immaterial items may be handled in the *easiest and most convenient manner.*

Materiality and Adjusting Entries The concept of materiality enables accountants to shorten and simplify the process of making adjusting entries in several ways. For example:

1. Businesses purchase many assets that have a very low cost or that will be consumed quickly in business operations. Examples include wastebaskets, lightbulbs, and janitorial supplies. The materiality concept permits charging such purchases *directly to expense accounts,* rather than to asset accounts. This treatment conveniently eliminates the need to prepare adjusting entries to depreciate these items.
2. Some expenses, such as telephone bills and utility bills, may be charged to expenses as the bills are *paid,* rather than as the services are used. Technically this treatment violates the *matching principle.* However, accounting for utility bills on a cash basis is very convenient, as the monthly cost of utility service is not even known until the utility bill is received. Under this cash basis approach, the amount of utility expense recorded each month is actually based on the *prior* month's bill.
3. Adjusting entries to accrue unrecorded expenses or unrecorded revenue may actually be *ignored* if the dollar amounts are immaterial.

Materiality Is a Matter of Professional Judgment Whether a specific item or event is material is a matter of *professional judgment.* In making these judgments, accountants consider several factors.

First, what constitutes a material amount varies with the size of the organization. For example, a $1,000 expenditure may be material in relation to the financial statements of a small business but not to the statements of a large corporation such as **General Electric**.[8] There are no official rules as to what constitutes a material amount, but most accountants

[8] This point is emphasized by the fact that **General Electric** rounds the dollar amounts shown in its financial statements to the nearest $1 million. This rounding of financial statement amounts is, in itself, an application of the materiality concept.

would consider amounts of less than 2 percent or 3 percent of net income to be immaterial, unless there were other factors to consider. One such other factor is the *cumulative effect* of numerous immaterial events. Each of a dozen items may be immaterial when considered by itself. When viewed together, however, the combined effect of all 12 items may be material.

Finally, materiality depends on the *nature* of the item, as well as its dollar amount. Assume, for example, that several managers systematically have been stealing money from the company that they manage. Stockholders probably would consider this fact important even if the dollar amounts were small in relation to the company's total resources.

YOUR TURN **You as Overnight Auto's Service Department Manager**

You just found out that Betty, one of the best mechanics that you supervise for Overnight Auto, has taken home small items from the company's supplies, such as a screwdriver and a couple of cans of oil. When you talk to Betty, she suggests that these items are immaterial to Overnight Auto because they are not recorded in the inventory and they are expensed when they are purchased. How should you respond to Betty?

(See our comments on the Online Learning Center Web site.)

Note to students: In the assignment material accompanying this textbook, you are to consider all dollar amounts to be material, unless the problem specifically raises the question of materiality.

EFFECTS OF THE ADJUSTING ENTRIES

On pages 140 and 141, we identified four types of adjusting entries, each of which involve one income statement account and one balance sheet account. The effects of these adjustment types on the income statement and balance sheet are summarized in Exhibit 4–8.

Exhibit 4–8 THE EFFECTS OF ADJUSTING ENTRIES ON THE FINANCIAL STATEMENTS

	Income Statement			Balance Sheet		
Adjustment	**Revenue**	**Expenses**	**Net Income**	**Assets**	**Liabilities**	**Owners' Equity**
Type I Converting Assets to Expenses	No effect	Increase	Decrease	Decrease	No effect	Decrease
Type II Converting Liabilities to Revenue	Increase	No effect	Increase	No effect	Decrease	Increase
Type III Accruing Unpaid Expenses	No effect	Increase	Decrease	No effect	Increase	Decrease
Type IV Accruing Uncollected Revenue	Increase	No effect	Increase	Increase	No effect	Increase

The four adjustment types were illustrated and discussed in nine separate *adjusting entries* made by Overnight on December 31. These adjustments appear in the format of general journal entries in Exhibit 4–9. (Overnight also recorded many *transactions* throughout the month of December. These transactions are not illustrated here but were accounted for in the manner described in Chapter 3.)

OVERNIGHT AUTO SERVICE
GENERAL JOURNAL
DECEMBER 31, 2011

Date	Account Titles and Explanation	Debit	Credit
2011			
Dec. 31	Supplies Expense	600	
	Shop Supplies		600
	December shop supplies adjustment.		
31	Insurance Expense	1,500	
	Unexpired Insurance		1,500
	December Insurance adjustment.		
31	Depreciation Expense: Building	150	
	Accumulated Depreciation: Building		150
	December depreciation adjustment on buildings ($36,000 ÷ 240 mo.).		
31	Depreciation Expense: Tools and Equipment	200	
	Accumulated Depreciation: Tools and Equipment		200
	December depreciation adjustment on tools and equipment ($12,000 ÷ 60 mo.).		
31	Unearned Rent Revenue	3,000	
	Rent Revenue Earned		3,000
	December unearned revenue adjustment ($9,000 ÷ 3 mo.).		
31	Wages Expense	1,950	
	Wages Payable		1,950
	December adjustment to accrue wages payable.		
31	Interest Expense	30	
	Interest Payable		30
	December adjustment to accrue interest payable ($4,000 × .09 × 1/12).		
31	Accounts Receivable	750	
	Repair Service Revenue		750
	December adjustment to accrue repair service revenue.		
31	Income Taxes Expense	4,020	
	Income Taxes Payable		4,020
	December adjustment to accrue income taxes payable.		

Exhibit 4–9
ADJUSTING ENTRIES

Adjusting entries are recorded only at the end of the period

After these adjustments are posted to the ledger, Overnight's ledger accounts will be up-to-date (except for the balance in the Retained Earnings account).[9] The company's **adjusted trial balance** at December 31, 2011, appears in Exhibit 4–10. (For emphasis, those accounts affected by the month-end *adjusting entries* are shown in red.)

Learning Objective **Prepare an adjusted trial balance and describe its purpose.** **LO9**

Overnight's financial statements are prepared directly from the adjusted trial balance. Note the order of the accounts: All balance sheet accounts are followed by the statement of retained earnings accounts and then the income statement accounts. In Chapter 5, we illustrate exactly how these three financial statements are prepared.

[9] The balance in the Retained Earnings account will be brought up-to-date during the closing process, discussed in Chapter 5.

Exhibit 4–10

ADJUSTED TRIAL BALANCE

OVERNIGHT AUTO SERVICE
ADJUSTED TRIAL BALANCE
DECEMBER 31, 2011

	Account	Debit	Credit
Balance sheet accounts	Cash	$ 18,592	
	Accounts receivable	7,250	
	Shop supplies	1,200	
	Unexpired insurance	3,000	
	Land	52,000	
	Building	36,000	
	Accumulated depreciation: building		$ 1,650
	Tools and equipment	12,000	
	Accumulated depreciation: tools and equipment		2,200
	Notes payable		4,000
	Accounts payable		2,690
	Wages payable		1,950
	Income taxes payable		5,580
	Interest payable		30
	Unearned rent revenue		6,000
	Capital stock		80,000
Statement of retained earnings accounts	Retained earnings (***Note:*** still must be updated for transactions recorded in the accounts listed below. Closing entries serve this purpose.)		0
	Dividends	14,000	
Income statement accounts	Repair service revenue		172,000
	Rent revenue earned		3,000
	Advertising expense	3,900	
	Wages expense	58,750	
	Supplies expense	7,500	
	Depreciation expense: building	1,650	
	Depreciation expense: tools and equipment	2,200	
	Utilities expense	19,400	
	Insurance expense	15,000	
	Interest expense	30	
	Income taxes expense	26,628	
		$279,100	$279,100

Concluding Remarks

Throughout this chapter, we illustrated end-of-period adjusting entries arising from *timing differences* between cash flows and revenue or expense recognition. In short, the adjusting process helps to ensure that appropriate amounts of revenue and expense are measured and reported in a company's income statement.

In Chapter 5, we continue with our illustration of Overnight Auto Service and demonstrate how adjusting entries are reflected throughout a company's financial statements.

Later chapters explain why accurate income measurement is of critical importance to investors and creditors in estimating the timing and amounts of a company's future cash flows. We also illustrate how understanding certain timing differences enables managers to budget and to plan for future operations.

Ethics, Fraud & Corporate Governance

Improper accounting for operating costs has often resulted in the SEC bringing action against companies for fraudulent financial reporting. Expenditures that are expected only to benefit the year in which they are made should be expensed (deducted from revenue in the determination of net income for the current period). Companies that engage in fraud will often defer these expenditures by capitalizing them (they debit an asset account reported in the balance sheet instead of an expense account reported in the income statement).

Prior to **Enron** and **WorldCom**, one of the largest financial scandals in U.S. history occurred at **Waste Management**. **Waste Management** was the world's largest waste services company. The improper accounting at **Waste Management** lasted for approximately five years and resulted in an overstatement of earnings during this time period of $1.7 billion. Investors lost over $6 billion when **Waste Management**'s improper accounting was revealed.

Waste Management's scheme for overstating earnings was simple. The company deferred recognizing normal operating expenditures as expenses until future periods. These improper deferrals were accomplished in a number of different ways, many of which involved improper accounting for long-term assets. For example, **Waste Management** incurred costs in buying and developing land to be used as landfills (i.e., garbage dumps). Capitalizing these costs—treating them as long-term assets—was proper accounting. However, in certain cases, the company was not able to secure the necessary governmental permits and approvals to use the purchased land as intended. In these cases, the costs that had been capitalized and reported as landfills in the balance sheet should have been expensed immediately, thereby reducing net income for the year in which the company's failure to obtain government permits and approvals occurred.

END-OF-CHAPTER REVIEW

SUMMARY OF LEARNING OBJECTIVES

LO1 **Explain the purpose of adjusting entries.** The purpose of adjusting entries is to allocate revenue and expenses among accounting periods in accordance with the realization and matching principles. These end-of-period entries are necessary because revenue may be earned and expenses may be incurred in periods other than the period in which related cash flows are recorded.

LO2 **Describe and prepare the four basic types of adjusting entries.** The four basic types of adjusting entries are made to (1) convert assets to expenses, (2) convert liabilities to revenue, (3) accrue unpaid expenses, and (4) accrue uncollected revenue. Often a transaction affects the revenue or expenses of *two or more* accounting periods. The related cash inflow or outflow does not always coincide with the period in which these revenue or expense items are recorded. Thus, the need for adjusting entries results from *timing differences* between the receipt or disbursement of cash and the recording of revenue or expenses.

LO3 **Prepare adjusting entries to convert assets to expenses.** When an expenditure is made that will benefit more than one accounting period, an asset account is debited and cash is credited. The asset account is used to *defer* (or postpone) expense recognition until a later date. At the end of each period benefiting from this expenditure, an adjusting entry is made to transfer an appropriate amount from the asset account to an *expense* account. This adjustment reflects the fact that part of the asset's cost has been *matched* against revenue in the measurement of income for the current period.

LO4 **Prepare adjusting entries to convert liabilities to revenue.** Customers sometimes pay in advance for services to be rendered in later accounting periods. For accounting purposes, the cash received does *not* represent revenue until it has been *earned.* Thus, the recognition of revenue must be *deferred* until it is earned. Advance collections from customers are recorded by debiting Cash and by crediting a *liability* account for *unearned* revenue. This liability is sometimes called Customer Deposits, Advance Sales, or Deferred Revenue. As unearned revenue becomes earned, an adjusting entry is made at the end of each period to transfer an appropriate amount from the liability account to a *revenue* account. This adjustment reflects the fact that all or part of the company's obligation to its customers has been fulfilled and that revenue has been realized.

LO5 **Prepare adjusting entries to accrue unpaid expenses.** Some expenses accumulate (or *accrue*) in the current period but are not *paid* until a future period. These accrued expenses are recorded as part of the adjusting process at the end of each period by debiting the appropriate expense (e.g., Salary Expense, Interest Expense, or Income Taxes Expense), and by crediting a liability account (e.g., Salaries Payable, Interest Payable, or Income Taxes Payable). In future periods, as cash is disbursed in settlement of these liabilities, the appropriate liability account is debited and Cash is credited. ***Note:*** Recording the accrued expense in the current period is the adjusting entry. Recording the disbursement of cash in a future period is *not* considered an adjusting entry.

LO6 **Prepare adjusting entries to accrue uncollected revenue.** Some revenues are earned (or *accrued*) in the current period but are not *collected* until a future period. These revenues are normally recorded as part of the adjusting process at the end of each period by debiting an asset account called Accounts Receivable, and by crediting the appropriate revenue account. In future periods, as cash is collected in settlement of outstanding receivables, Cash is debited and Accounts Receivable is credited. ***Note:*** Recording the accrued revenue in the current period is the adjusting entry. Recording the receipt of cash in a future period is *not* considered an adjusting entry.

LO7 **Explain how the principles of *realization* and *matching* relate to adjusting entries.** Adjusting entries are the *tools* by which accountants apply the realization and matching principles. Through these entries, revenues are recognized as they are *earned,* and expenses are recognized as resources are *used* or consumed in producing the related revenue.

LO8 **Explain the concept of *materiality.*** The concept of materiality allows accountants to use estimated amounts and to ignore certain accounting principles if these actions will not have a material effect on the financial statements. A material effect is one that might reasonably be expected to influence the decisions made by the users of financial statements. Thus, accountants may account for immaterial items and events in the easiest and most convenient manner.

LO9 **Prepare an adjusted trial balance and describe its purpose.** The adjusted trial balance reports all of the balances in the general ledger *after* the end-of-period adjusting entries have been made and posted. Generally, all of a company's balance sheet accounts are listed, followed by the statement of retained earnings accounts and, finally, the income statement accounts. The amounts shown in the adjusted trial balance are carried forward directly to the financial statements. The adjusted trial balance is *not* considered one of the four general-purpose financial statements introduced in Chapter 2. Rather, it is simply a *schedule* (or worksheet) used in preparing the financial statements.

Key Terms Introduced or Emphasized in Chapter 4

accrue (p. 150) To grow or accumulate over time; for example, interest expense.

accumulated depreciation (p. 148) A contra-asset account shown as a deduction from the related asset account in the balance sheet. Depreciation taken throughout the useful life of an asset is accumulated in this account.

adjusted trial balance (p. 157) A schedule indicating the balances in ledger accounts *after* end-of-period adjusting entries have been posted. The amounts shown in the adjusted trial balance are carried directly into financial statements.

adjusting entries (p. 140) Entries made at the end of the accounting period for the purpose of recognizing revenue and expenses that are not properly measured as a result of journalizing transactions as they occur.

book value (p. 148) The net amount at which an asset appears in financial statements. For depreciable assets, book value represents cost minus accumulated depreciation. Also called *carrying value.*

contra-asset account (p. 148) An account with a credit balance that is offset against or deducted from an asset account to produce the proper balance sheet amount for the asset.

depreciable assets (p. 146) Physical objects with a limited life. The cost of these assets is gradually recognized as depreciation expense.

depreciation (p. 146) The systematic allocation of the cost of an asset to expense during the periods of its useful life.

immaterial (p. 155) Something of little or no consequence. Immaterial items may be accounted for in the most convenient manner, without regard to other theoretical concepts.

matching (principle) (p. 154) The accounting principle of offsetting revenue with the expenses incurred in producing that revenue. Requires recognition of expenses in the periods that the goods and services are used in the effort to produce revenue.

materiality (p. 155) The relative importance of an item or amount. Items significant enough to influence decisions are said to be *material.* Items lacking this importance are considered *immaterial.* The accounting treatment accorded to immaterial items may be guided by convenience rather than by theoretical principles.

prepaid expenses (p. 144) Assets representing advance payment of the expenses of future accounting periods. As time passes, adjusting entries are made to transfer the related costs from the asset account to an expense account.

realization (principle) (p. 154) The accounting principle that governs the timing of revenue recognition. Basically, the principle indicates that revenue should be recognized in the period in which it is earned.

straight-line method of depreciation (p. 147) The widely used approach of recognizing an equal amount of depreciation expense in each period of a depreciable asset's useful life.

unearned revenue (p. 149) An obligation to deliver goods or render services in the future, stemming from the receipt of advance payment.

useful life (p. 146) The period of time that a depreciable asset is expected to be useful to the business. This is the period over which the cost of the asset is allocated to depreciation expense.

Demonstration Problem

Internet Consulting Service, Inc., adjusts its accounts every month. On the following page is the company's year-end *unadjusted* trial balance dated December 31, 2011. (Bear in mind that adjusting entries already have been made for the first 11 months of 2011, but have *not* been made for December.)

Other Data

1. On December 1, the company signed a new rental agreement and paid three months' rent in advance at a rate of $2,100 per month. This advance payment was debited to the Prepaid Office Rent account.
2. Dues and subscriptions expiring during December amounted to $50.
3. An estimate of supplies on hand was made at December 31; the estimated cost of the unused supplies was $450.
4. The useful life of the equipment has been estimated at five years (60 months) from date of acquisition.
5. Accrued interest on notes payable amounted to $100 at year-end. (Set up accounts for Interest Expense and for Interest Payable.)
6. Consulting services valued at $2,850 were rendered during December to clients who had made payment in advance.

INTERNET CONSULTING SERVICE, INC. UNADJUSTED TRIAL BALANCE DECEMBER 31, 2011		
Cash	$ 49,100	
Consulting fees receivable	23,400	
Prepaid office rent	6,300	
Prepaid dues and subscriptions	300	
Supplies	600	
Equipment	36,000	
Accumulated depreciation: equipment		$ 10,200
Notes payable		5,000
Income taxes payable		12,000
Unearned consulting fees		5,950
Capital stock		30,000
Retained earnings		32,700
Dividends	60,000	
Consulting fees earned		257,180
Salaries expense	88,820	
Telephone expense	2,550	
Rent expense	22,000	
Income taxes expense	51,000	
Dues and subscriptions expense	560	
Supplies expense	1,600	
Depreciation expense: equipment	6,600	
Miscellaneous expenses	4,200	
	$353,030	$353,030

7. It is the custom of the firm to bill clients only when consulting work is completed or, in the case of prolonged engagements, at monthly intervals. At December 31, consulting services valued at $11,000 had been rendered to clients but not yet billed. No advance payments had been received from these clients.
8. Salaries earned by employees but not paid as of December 31 amount to $1,700.
9. Income taxes expense for the year is estimated at $56,000. Of this amount, $51,000 has been recognized as expense in prior months, and $39,000 has been paid to tax authorities. The company plans to pay the $17,000 remainder of its income tax liability on January 15.

Instructions

a. Prepare the necessary adjusting journal entries on December 31, 2011.

b. Determine the amounts to be reported in the company's year-end adjusted trial balance for each of the following accounts:

Consulting Fees Earned	Dues and Subscriptions Expense
Salaries Expense	Depreciation Expense: Equipment
Telephone Expense	Miscellaneous Expenses
Rent Expense	Interest Expense
Supplies Expense	Income Taxes Expense

c. Determine the company's net income for the year ended December 31, 2011. (Hint: Use the amounts determined in part **b** above.)

Solution to the Demonstration Problem

a.

INTERNET CONSULTING SERVICE, INC.
GENERAL JOURNAL
DECEMBER 31, 2011

Date	Account Titles and Explanation	Debit	Credit
Dec. 31			
2011			
1.	Rent Expense	2,100	
	Prepaid Office Rent		2,100
	December rent adjustment.		
2.	Dues and Subscriptions Expense	50	
	Prepaid Dues and Subscriptions		50
	December dues and subscriptions adjustment.		
3.	Supplies Expense	150	
	Supplies		150
	December supplies adjustment.		
4.	Depreciation Expense: Equipment	600	
	Accumulated Depreciation: Equipment		600
	December depreciation adjustment ($36,000 ÷ 60 mos.).		
5.	Interest Expense	100	
	Interest Payable		100
	December interest adjustment.		
6.	Unearned Consulting Fees	2,850	
	Consulting Fees Earned		2,850
	December unearned revenue adjustment.		
7.	Consulting Fees Receivable	11,000	
	Consulting Fees Earned		11,000
	December accrued revenue adjustment.		
8.	Salaries Expense	1,700	
	Salaries Payable		1,700
	December salaries adjustment.		
9.	Income Taxes Expense	5,000	
	Income Taxes Payable		5,000
	December income tax expense adjustment.		

b.

INTERNET CONSULTING SERVICE, INC.
ADJUSTED TRIAL BALANCE
DECEMBER 31, 2011

	Unadjusted Trial Balance Amount	+	Adjustment	=	Adjusted Trial Balance Amount
Consulting Fees Earned	$257,180		(6) $ 2,850		
			(7) $11,000		$271,030
Salaries Expense	$ 88,820		(8) $ 1,700		$ 90,520
Telephone Expense	$ 2,550		None		$ 2,550
Rent Expense	$ 22,000		(1) $ 2,100		$ 24,100
Supplies Expense	$ 1,600		(3) $ 150		$ 1,750
Dues and Subscriptions Expense	$ 560		(2) $ 50		$ 610
Depreciation Expense: Equipment	$ 6,600		(4) $ 600		$ 7,200
Miscellaneous Expenses	$ 4,200		None		$ 4,200
Interest Expense	None		(5) $ 100		$ 100
Income Taxes Expense	$ 51,000		(9) $ 5,000		$ 56,000

c. Using the figures computed in part **b**, net income for the year is computed as follows:

Consulting Fees Earned		$271,030
Salaries Expense	$90,520	
Telephone Expense	2,550	
Rent Expense	24,100	
Supplies Expense	1,750	
Dues and Subscriptions Expense	610	
Depreciation Expense: Equipment	7,200	
Miscellaneous Expenses	4,200	
Interest Expense	100	
Income Taxes Expense	56,000	(187,030)
Net Income		$ 84,000

Self-Test Questions

The answers to these questions appear on page 189.

1. The purpose of adjusting entries is to:
   a. Adjust the Retained Earnings account for the revenue, expense, and dividends recorded during the accounting period.
   b. Adjust daily the balances in asset, liability, revenue, and expense accounts for the effects of business transactions.
   c. Apply the realization principle and the matching principle to transactions affecting two or more accounting periods.
   d. Prepare revenue and expense accounts for recording the transactions of the next accounting period.
2. Before month-end adjustments are made, the January 31 trial balance of Rover Excursions contains revenue of $27,900 and expenses of $17,340. Adjustments are necessary for the following items:

   Portion of prepaid rent applicable to January, $2,700

   Depreciation for January, $1,440

   Portion of fees collected in advance earned in January, $3,300

   Fees earned in January, not yet billed to customers, $1,950

Net income for January is:

a. $10,560 c. $7,770

b. $17,070 d. Some other amount

3. The CPA firm auditing Mason Street Recording Studios found that total stockholders' equity was understated and liabilities were overstated. Which of the following errors could have been the cause?
   - a. Making the adjustment entry for depreciation expense twice.
   - b. Failure to record interest accrued on a note payable.
   - c. Failure to make the adjusting entry to record revenue that had been earned but not yet billed to clients.
   - d. Failure to record the earned portion of fees received in advance.
4. Assume Fisher Corporation usually earns taxable income, but sustains a *loss* in the current period. The entry to record income taxes expense in the current period will most likely (indicate all correct answers):
   - a. Increase the amount of that loss.
   - b. Include a credit to the Income Taxes Expense account.
   - c. Be an adjusting entry, rather than an entry to record a transaction completed during the period.
   - d. Include a credit to Income Taxes Payable.
5. The concept of *materiality* (indicate all correct answers):
   - a. Requires that financial statements be accurate to the nearest dollar, but need not show cents.
   - b. Is based upon what users of financial statements are thought to consider important.
   - c. Permits accountants to ignore generally accepted accounting principles in certain situations.
   - d. Permits accountants to use the easiest and most convenient means of accounting for events that are *immaterial.*

ASSIGNMENT MATERIAL Discussion Questions

1. What is the purpose of making adjusting entries? Your answer should relate adjusting entries to the goals of accrual accounting.
2. Do adjusting entries affect income statement accounts, balance sheet accounts, or both? Explain.
3. Why does the recording of adjusting entries require a better understanding of the concepts of accrual accounting than does the recording of routine revenue and expense transactions occurring throughout the period?
4. Why does the purchase of a one-year insurance policy four months ago give rise to insurance expense in the current month?
5. If services have been rendered to customers during the current accounting period but no revenue has been recorded and no bill has been sent to the customers, why is an adjusting entry needed? What types of accounts should be debited and credited by this entry?
6. What is meant by the term *unearned revenue*? Where should an unearned revenue account appear in the financial statements? As the work is done, what happens to the balance of an unearned revenue account?
7. Briefly explain the concept of *materiality.* If an item is not material, how is the item treated for financial reporting purposes?
8. Discuss the realization principle and how it is applied in the recognition of revenue. Does the receipt of cash for customers necessarily coincide with the recognition of revenue? Explain.
9. Discuss the matching principle and how it is applied in the recognition of expenses. Does the payment of cash necessarily coincide with the recognition of an expense? Explain.
10. Would a $1,000 expenditure be considered material to all businesses? Explain.
11. List various accounts in the balance sheet that represent *deferred expenses.*
12. How is *deferred revenue* reported in the balance sheet?
13. How do accrued but unpaid expenses affect the balance sheet?
14. How does accrued but uncollected revenue affect the balance sheet?
15. Explain how **Carnival Corporation** accounts for customer deposits as passengers purchase cruise tickets in advance.

Brief Exercises

LO3 LO4

BRIEF EXERCISE 4.1

Prepaid Expenses and Unearned Revenue

On November 1, Able Corporation purchased a six-month insurance policy from The Baylor Agency for $3,000.

a. Prepare the necessary adjusting entry for Able Corporation on November 30, assuming it recorded the November 1 expenditure as Unexpired Insurance.

b. Prepare the necessary adjusting entry for The Baylor Agency on November 30, assuming it recorded Able's payment as Unearned Insurance Premiums.

LO3 LO4 **BRIEF EXERCISE 4.2**

Prepaid Expenses and Unearned Revenue

On February 1, Watson Storage agreed to rent Hillbourne Manufacturing warehouse space for $175 per month. Hillbourne Manufacturing paid the first three months' rent in advance.

a. Prepare the necessary adjusting entry for Hillbourne Manufacturing on February 28, assuming it recorded the expenditure on February 1 as Prepaid Rent.

b. Prepare the necessary adjusting entry for Watson Storage on February 28, assuming it recorded Hillbourne Manufacturing's payment as Unearned Rent Revenue.

LO3 **BRIEF EXERCISE 4.3**

Accounting for Supplies

On March 1, Dillmore Corporation had office supplies on hand of $900. During the month, Dillmore purchased additional supplies costing $600. Approximately $400 of unused office supplies remain on hand at the end of the month.

Prepare the necessary adjusting entry on March 31 to account for office supplies.

LO3 **BRIEF EXERCISE 4.4**

Accounting for Depreciation

On January 2, 2006, Hagen Corporation purchased equipment costing $72,000. Hagen performs adjusting entries monthly.

a. Record this equipment's depreciation expense on December 31, 2011, assuming its estimated life was eight years on January 2, 2006.

b. Determine the amount of the equipment's accumulated depreciation reported in the balance sheet dated December 31, 2011.

LO6 **BRIEF EXERCISE 4.5**

Accruing Uncollected Revenue

Marvin's Tax Service had earned—but not yet recorded—the following client service revenue at the end of the current accounting period:

Account Number	Billable Hours	Hourly Billing Rate
Account #4067	10	$85
Account #3940	14	$75
Account #1852	16	$90

Prepare the necessary adjusting entry to record Marvin's unbilled client service revenue

LO4 **BRIEF EXERCISE 4.6**

Unearned Revenue

Jasper's unadjusted trial balance reports Unearned Client Revenue of $3,200 and Client Revenue Earned of $29,000. An examination of client records reveals that $2,800 of previously unearned revenue has now been earned.

a. Prepare the necessary adjusting entry pertaining to these accounts.

b. At what amount will Client Revenue Earned be reported in Jasper's income statement?

LO5 **BRIEF EXERCISE 4.7**

Accruing Unpaid Salaries

Milford Corporation pays its employees on the fifteenth of each month. Accrued, but unpaid, salaries on December 31, 2011, totaled $175,000. Salaries earned by Milford's employees from January 1 through January 15, 2012, totaled $180,000.

a. Prepare the necessary adjusting entry for salaries expense on December 31, 2011.

b. Record the company's payment of salaries on January 15, 2012.

LO5 **BRIEF EXERCISE 4.8**

Accruing Unpaid Interest

Norbert Corporation borrowed $24,000 on December 1, 2011, by issuing a two-month, 8 percent note payable to Service One Credit Union. The entire amount of the loan, plus interest, is due February 1, 2012.

a. Prepare the necessary adjusting entry for interest expense on December 31, 2011.

b. Record the repayment of the loan plus interest on February 1, 2012.

LO5 **BRIEF EXERCISE 4.9**

Accruing Unpaid Income Taxes

Normington's unadjusted trial balance dated December 31, 2011, reports Income Taxes Expense of $57,200, and Income Taxes Payable of $14,300. The company's accountant estimates that income taxes expense for the *entire year* ended December 31, 2011, is $62,800.

a. Prepare the necessary adjusting entry for income taxes expense on December 31, 2011.

b. Determine the amount of income taxes payable reported in the balance sheet dated December 31, 2011.

LO8 **BRIEF EXERCISE 4.10**

Concept of Materiality

The concept of materiality is an underlying principle of financial reporting.

a. Briefly explain the concept of materiality.

b. Is $2,500 a "material" dollar amount? Explain.

c. Describe two ways in which the concept of materiality may save accountants' time and effort in making adjusting entries.

Exercises

connect ACCOUNTING

LO1 through LO9

EXERCISE 4.1
Accounting Terminology

Listed below are nine technical accounting terms used in this chapter:

Unrecorded revenue	Adjusting entries	Accrued expenses
Book value	Matching principle	Accumulated depreciation
Unearned revenue	Materiality	Prepaid expenses

Each of the following statements may (or may not) describe one of these technical terms. For each statement, indicate the accounting term described, or answer "None" if the statement does not correctly describe any of the terms.

a. The net amount at which an asset is carried in the accounting records as distinguished from its market value.

b. An accounting concept that may justify departure from other accounting principles for purposes of convenience and economy.

c. The offsetting of revenue with expenses incurred in generating that revenue.

d. Revenue earned during the current accounting period but not yet recorded or billed, which requires an adjusting entry at the end of the period.

e. Entries made at the end of the period to achieve the goals of accrual accounting by recording revenue when it is earned and by recording expenses when the related goods and services are used.

f. A type of account credited when customers pay in advance for services to be rendered in the future.

g. A balance sheet category used for reporting advance payments of such items as insurance, rent, and office supplies.

h. An expense representing the systematic allocation of an asset's cost over its useful life.

LO1 through LO6, LO9

EXERCISE 4.2
Effects of Adjusting Entries

Security Service Company adjusts its accounts at the end of the month. On November 30, adjusting entries are prepared to record:

a. Depreciation expense for November.

b. Interest expense that has accrued during November.

c. Revenue earned during November that has not yet been billed to customers.

d. Salaries, payable to company employees, that have accrued since the last payday in November.

e. The portion of the company's prepaid insurance that has expired during November.

f. Earning a portion of the amount collected in advance from a customer, Harbor Restaurant.

Indicate the effect of each of these adjusting entries on the major elements of the company's income statement and balance sheet—that is, on revenue, expenses, net income, assets, liabilities, and owners' equity. Organize your answer in tabular form, using the column headings shown and the symbols **I** for increase, **D** for decrease, and **NE** for no effect. The answer for adjusting entry **a** is provided as an example.

	Income Statement			**Balance Sheet**		
Adjusting Entry	Revenue −	Expenses =	Net Income	Assets =	Liabilities +	Owners' Equity
a	NE	I	D	D	NE	D

LO1 through LO7

EXERCISE 4.3
Preparing Adjusting Entries to Convert an Asset to an Expense and to Convert a Liability to Revenue

The Golden Goals, a professional soccer team, prepares financial statements on a monthly basis. The soccer season begins in May, but in April the team engaged in the following transactions:

1. Paid $1,200,000 to the municipal stadium as advance rent for use of the facilities for the five-month period from May 1 through September 30. This payment was initially recorded as Prepaid Rent.
2. Collected $4,500,000 cash from the sale of season tickets for the team's home games. The entire amount was initially recorded as Unearned Ticket Revenue. During the month of May,

the Golden Goals played several home games at which $148,800 of the season tickets sold in April were used by fans.

Prepare the two adjusting entries required on May 31.

LO1 through LO7

EXERCISE 4.4

Preparing Adjusting Entries to Convert an Asset to an Expense and to Convert a Liability to Revenue

Carnival Corporation is the world's largest cruise line company. Its printing costs for brochures are initially recorded as Prepaid Advertising and are later charged to Advertising Expense when they are mailed. Passenger deposits for upcoming cruises are considered unearned revenue and are recorded as Customer Deposits as cash is received. Deposited amounts are later converted to Cruise Revenue as voyages are completed.

a. Where in its financial statements does **Carnival Corporation** report Prepaid Advertising? Where in its financial statements does it report Customer Deposits?

b. Prepare the adjusting entry necessary when brochures costing $18 million are mailed.

c. In its most recent annual report, **Carnival Corporation** reported Customer Deposits in excess of $2.8 billion. Prepare the adjusting entry necessary in the following year as $90 million of this amount is earned.

d. Consider the entire adjusting process at **Carnival Corporation**. Which adjusting entry do you think results in the most significant expense reported in the company's income statement?

LO1 through LO7

EXERCISE 4.5

Preparing Adjusting Entries to Accrue Revenue and Expenses for Which No Cash Has Been Received

The geological consulting firm of Gilbert, Marsh, & Kester prepares adjusting entries on a monthly basis. Among the items requiring adjustment on December 31, 2011, are the following:

1. The company has outstanding a $50,000, 9 percent, two-year note payable issued on July 1, 2010. Payment of the $50,000 note, *plus* all accrued interest for the two-year loan period, is due in full on June 30, 2012.
2. The firm is providing consulting services to Texas Oil Company at an agreed-upon rate of $1,000 per day. At December 31, 10 days of unbilled consulting services have been provided.

a. Prepare the two adjusting entries required on December 31 to record the accrued interest expense and the accrued consulting revenue earned.

b. Assume that the $50,000 note payable plus all accrued interest are paid in full on June 30, 2012. What portion of the total interest expense associated with this note will be reported in the firm's *2012* income statement?

c. Assume that on January 30, 2012, Gilbert, Marsh, & Kester receive $25,000 from Texas Oil Company in full payment of the consulting services provided in December and January. What portion of this amount constitutes revenue earned in *January*?

LO1 LO2 LO4

EXERCISE 4.6

Deferred Revenue

When **American Airlines** sells tickets for future flights, it debits Cash and credits an account entitled Air Traffic Liability (as opposed to crediting Passenger Revenue Earned). This account, reported recently at $4.5 billion, is among the largest liabilities appearing in the company's balance sheet.

a. Explain why this liability is often referred to as a deferred revenue account.

b. What activity normally *reduces* this liability? Can you think of any *other* transaction that would also reduce this account?

c. Assume that, in a recent flight, passengers of the airline used tickets that they had purchased in advance for $200,000. Record the entry **American Airlines** would make upon completion of this flight.

LO1 through LO6 LO9

EXERCISE 4.7

Preparing Various Adjusting Entries

Sweeney & Associates, a large marketing firm, adjusts its accounts at the end of each month. The following information is available for the year ending December 31, 2011:

1. A bank loan had been obtained on December 1. Accrued interest on the loan at December 31 amounts to $1,200. No interest expense has yet been recorded.
2. Depreciation of the firm's office building is based on an estimated life of 25 years. The building was purchased in 2007 for $330,000.
3. Accrued, but unbilled, revenue during December amounts to $64,000.
4. On March 1, the firm paid $1,800 to renew a 12-month insurance policy. The entire amount was recorded as Prepaid Insurance.
5. The firm received $14,000 from King Biscuit Company in advance of developing a six-month marketing campaign. The entire amount was initially recorded as Unearned Revenue. At December 31, $3,500 had actually been *earned* by the firm.

6. The company's policy is to pay its employees every Friday. Since December 31 fell on a Wednesday, there was an accrued liability for salaries amounting to $2,400.

a. Record the necessary adjusting journal entries on December 31, 2011.

b. By how much did Sweeney & Associates's net income increase or decrease as a result of the adjusting entries performed in part **a**? (Ignore income taxes.)

LO1 LO2 LO5

EXERCISE 4.8

Notes Payable and Interest

Ventura Company adjusts its accounts *monthly* and closes its accounts on December 31. On October 31, 2011, Ventura Company signed a note payable and borrowed $120,000 from a bank for a period of six months at an annual interest rate of 9 percent.

a. How much is the total interest expense over the life of the note? How much is the monthly interest expense? (Assume equal amounts of interest expense each month.)

b. In the company's annual balance sheet at December 31, 2011, what is the amount of the liability to the bank?

c. Prepare the journal entry to record issuance of the note payable on October 31, 2011.

d. Prepare the adjusting entry to accrue interest on the note at December 31, 2011.

e. Assume the company prepared a balance sheet at March 31, 2012. State the amount of the liability to the bank at this date.

LO1 through LO7 LO9

EXERCISE 4.9

Relationship of Adjusting Entries to Business Transactions

Among the ledger accounts used by Glenwood Speedway are the following: Prepaid Rent, Rent Expense, Unearned Admissions Revenue, Admissions Revenue, Prepaid Printing, Printing Expense, Concessions Receivable, and Concessions Revenue. For each of the following items, provide the journal entry (if one is needed) to record the initial transaction and provide the adjusting entry, if any, required on May 31, the end of the fiscal year.

a. On May 1, borrowed $300,000 cash from National Bank by issuing a 12 percent note payable due in three months.

b. On May 1, paid rent for six months beginning May 1 at $30,000 per month.

c. On May 2, sold season tickets for a total of $910,000 cash. The season includes 70 racing days: 20 in May, 25 in June, and 25 in July.

d. On May 4, an agreement was reached with Snack-Bars, Inc., allowing that company to sell refreshments at the track in return for 10 percent of the gross receipts from refreshment sales.

LO1 LO3 LO4 LO5 LO7

EXERCISE 4.10

Adjusting Entries and the Balance Sheet

The following information was reported in a recent balance sheet issued by **Microsoft Corporation:**

1. The book value of property and equipment is listed at $3.35 billion (net of depreciation). Related notes to the financial statements reveal that accumulated depreciation on property and equipment totals $5.02 billion.
2. Accrued compensation of $2.33 billion is listed as a liability.
3. Short-term unearned revenue is reported at $10.78 billion, whereas long-term unearned revenue is reported at $1.87 billion. The short-term figure will be converted to revenue within a year. The long-term figure will be converted to revenue over several years. Related notes to the financial statements reveal that the company engages in multiyear leasing of its software products.

a. Determine the original historical cost of the property and equipment reported in **Microsoft Corporation**'s balance sheet.

b. Four types of adjusting entries are illustrated in Exhibit 4–1 (page 142). Explain which type of adjusting entry resulted in the company's accrued compensation figure.

c. Explain why **Microsoft Corporation** reports unearned revenue in its balance sheet. Why might the company report short-term unearned revenue separately from long-term unearned revenue?

LO1 LO4 LO7

EXERCISE 4.11

Reporting of Unearned Revenue

Listed below are seven corporations that receive cash from customers prior to earning revenue:

America West Corporation (airline)

The New York Times Company (newspaper)

Carnival Corporation (cruise company)

Devry, Inc. (for-profit technical college)

Clear Channel Communications, Inc. (radio broadcasting)

AFLAC Incorporated (health insurance)

Bally Total Fitness Corporation (fitness club)

a. Listed below are the accounts used by these corporations to report unearned revenue:

Deferred Advertising Income	Unearned Premiums
Air Traffic Liability	Unexpired Subscriptions
Deferred Member Revenues	Deferred Tuition Revenue
Customer Deposits	

Match each corporation with the account title it uses to report unearned revenue.

b. Apply the *realization* principle to explain when each of these corporations converts unearned revenue to earned revenue.

LO1 through LO7 LO9

EXERCISE 4.12 Preparing Adjusting Entries from a Trial Balance

The *unadjusted* and *adjusted* trial balances for Tinker Corporation on December 31, 2011, are shown below:

TINKER CORPORATION
TRIAL BALANCES
DECEMBER 31, 2011

	Unadjusted		Adjusted	
	Debit	**Credit**	**Debit**	**Credit**
Cash	$ 35,200		$ 35,200	
Accounts receivable	29,120		34,120	
Unexpired insurance	1,200		600	
Prepaid rent	5,400		3,600	
Office supplies	680		380	
Equipment	60,000		60,000	
Accumulated depreciation: equipment		$ 49,000		$ 50,000
Accounts payable		900		900
Notes payable		5,000		5,000
Interest payable		200		250
Salaries payable		—		2,100
Income taxes payable		1,570		2,170
Unearned revenue		6,800		3,800
Capital stock		25,000		25,000
Retained earnings		30,000		30,000
Fees earned		91,530		99,530
Advertising expense	1,500		1,500	
Insurance expense	6,600		7,200	
Rent expense	19,800		21,600	
Office supplies expense	1,200		1,500	
Repairs expense	4,800		4,800	
Depreciation expense: equipment	11,000		12,000	
Salaries expense	26,300		28,400	
Interest expense	200		250	
Income taxes expense	7,000		7,600	
	$210,000	$210,000	$218,750	$218,750

Journalize the nine adjusting entries that the company made on December 31, 2011.

LO1 through LO6

EXERCISE 4.13 Effects of Adjusting Entries

Four types of adjusting entries were identified in this chapter:

Type I	Converting Assets to Expenses
Type II	Converting Liabilities to Revenue
Type III	Accruing Unpaid Expenses
Type IV	Accruing Uncollected Revenue

Complete the following table by indicating the effect of each adjusting entry type on the major elements of the income statement and balance sheet. Use the symbols **I** for increase, **D** for decrease, and **NE** for no effect.

	Income Statement			Balance Sheet		
Adjustment Type	**Revenue**	**Expenses**	**Net Income**	**Assets**	**Liabilities**	**Owners' Equity**
Type I						
Type II						
Type III						
Type IV						

LO1 through LO8

EXERCISE 4.14
Accounting Principles

For each of the situations described below, indicate the underlying accounting principle that is being *violated.* Choose from the following principles:

Matching Materiality
Cost Realization
Objectivity

If you do not believe that the practice violates any of these principles, answer "None" and explain.

a. The bookkeeper of a large metropolitan auto dealership depreciates the $7.20 cost of metal wastebaskets over a period of 10 years.

b. A small commuter airline recognizes no depreciation expense on its aircraft because the planes are maintained in "as good as new" condition.

c. Palm Beach Hotel recognizes room rental revenue on the date that a reservation is received. For the winter season, many guests make reservations as much as a year in advance.

LO1 LO2

EXERCISE 4.15
Using the Financial Statements of **Home Depot, Inc.**

The financial statements of **Home Depot, Inc.**, appear in Appendix A at the end of this textbook. Examine the company's consolidated balance sheet and identify specific accounts that may have required adjusting entries at the end of the year.

Problem Set A

LO1 through LO7

PROBLEM 4.1A
Preparing Adjusting Entries

Florida Palms Country Club adjusts its accounts *monthly.* Club members pay their annual dues in advance by January 4. The entire amount is initially credited to Unearned Membership Dues. At the end of each month, an appropriate portion of this amount is credited to Membership Dues Earned. Guests of the club normally pay green fees before being allowed on the course. The amounts collected are credited to Green Fee Revenue at the time of receipt. Certain guests, however, are billed for green fees at the end of the month. The following information is available as a source for preparing adjusting entries at December 31:

1. Salaries earned by golf course employees that have not yet been recorded or paid amount to $9,600.
2. The Tampa University golf team used Florida Palms for a tournament played on December 30 of the current year. At December 31, the $1,800 owed by the team for green fees had not yet been recorded or billed.
3. Membership dues earned in December, for collections received in January, amount to $106,000.

4. Depreciation of the country club's golf carts is based on an estimated life of 15 years. The carts had originally been purchased for $180,000. The straight-line method is used.

   (*Note:* The clubhouse building was constructed in 1925 and is fully depreciated.)
5. A 12-month bank loan in the amount of $45,000 had been obtained by the country club on November 1. Interest is computed at an annual rate of 8 percent. The entire $45,000, plus all of the interest accrued over the 12-month life of the loan, is due in full on October 31 of the upcoming year. The necessary adjusting entry was made on November 30 to record the first month of accrued interest expense. However, no adjustment has been made to record interest expense accrued in December.
6. A one-year property insurance policy had been purchased on March 1. The entire premium of $7,800 was initially recorded as Unexpired Insurance.
7. In December, Florida Palms Country Club entered into an agreement to host the annual tournament of the Florida Seniors Golf Association. The country club expects to generate green fees of $4,500 from this event.
8. Unrecorded Income Taxes Expense accrued in December amounts to $19,000. This amount will not be paid until January 15.

Instructions

a. For each of the above numbered paragraphs, prepare the necessary adjusting entry (including an explanation). If no adjusting entry is required, explain why.

b. Four types of adjusting entries are described at the beginning of the chapter. Using these descriptions, identify the type of each adjusting entry prepared in part **a** above.

c. Although Florida Palms's clubhouse building is fully depreciated, it is in excellent physical condition. Explain how this can be.

LO1 through LO6

LO9

PROBLEM 4.2A

Preparing and Analyzing the Effects of Adjusting Entries

Enchanted Forest, a large campground in South Carolina, adjusts its accounts *monthly.* Most guests of the campground pay at the time they check out, and the amounts collected are credited to Camper Revenue. The following information is available as a source for preparing the adjusting entries at December 31:

1. Enchanted Forest invests some of its excess cash in certificates of deposit (CDs) with its local bank. Accrued interest revenue on its CDs at December 31 is $400. None of the interest has yet been received. (Debit Interest Receivable.)
2. A six-month bank loan in the amount of $12,000 had been obtained on September 1. Interest is to be computed at an annual rate of 8.5 percent and is payable when the loan becomes due.
3. Depreciation on buildings owned by the campground is based on a 25-year life. The original cost of the buildings was $600,000. The Accumulated Depreciation: Buildings account has a credit balance of $310,000 at December 31, prior to the adjusting entry process. The straight-line method of depreciation is used.
4. Management signed an agreement to let Boy Scout Troop 538 of Lewisburg, Pennsylvania, use the campground in June of next year. The agreement specifies that the Boy Scouts will pay a daily rate of $15 per campsite, with a clause providing a minimum total charge of $1,475.
5. Salaries earned by campground employees that have not yet been paid amount to $1,250.
6. As of December 31, Enchanted Forest has earned $2,400 of revenue from current campers who will not be billed until they check out. (Debit Camper Revenue Receivable.)
7. Several lakefront campsites are currently being leased on a long-term basis by a group of senior citizens. Six months' rent of $5,400 was collected in advance and credited to Unearned Camper Revenue on October 1 of the current year.
8. A bus to carry campers to and from town and the airport had been rented the first week of December at a daily rate of $40. At December 31, no rental payment has been made, although the campground has had use of the bus for 25 days.
9. Unrecorded Income Taxes Expense accrued in December amounts to $8,400. This amount will not be paid until January 15.

Instructions

a. For each of the above numbered paragraphs, prepare the necessary adjusting entry (including an explanation). If no adjusting entry is required, explain why.

b. Four types of adjusting entries are described at the beginning of the chapter. Using these descriptions, identify the type of each adjusting entry prepared in part **a** above.

c. Indicate the effects that each of the adjustments in part **a** will have on the following six *total amounts* in the campground's financial statements for the month of *December*. Organize your answer in tabular form, using the column headings shown below. Use the letters **I** for increase, **D** for decrease, and **NE** for no effect. Adjusting entry **1** is provided as an example.

	Income Statement			Balance Sheet		
Adjusting	Revenue −	Expenses =	Net Income	Assets =	Liabilities +	Owners' Equity
1	I	NE	I	I	NE	I

d. What is the amount of interest expense recognized for the *entire current year* on the $12,000 bank loan obtained September 1?

e. Compute the *book value* of the campground's buildings to be reported in the current year's December 31 balance sheet. (Refer to paragraph **3.**)

LO1 through LO7 LO9

PROBLEM 4.3A
Analysis of Adjusted Data

eXcel

Gunflint Adventures operates an airplane service that takes fishing parties to a remote lake resort in northern Manitoba, Canada. Individuals *must* purchase their tickets at least one month in advance during the busy summer season. The company adjusts its accounts only once each month. Selected balances appearing in the company's June 30 *adjusted* trial balance appear as follows:

	Debit	Credit
Prepaid airport rent	$ 7,200	
Unexpired insurance	3,500	
Airplane	240,000	
Accumulated depreciation: airplane		$36,000
Unearned passenger revenue		90,000

Other Information

1. The airplane is being depreciated over a 20-year life with no residual value.
2. Unearned passenger revenue represents advance ticket sales for bookings in July and August at $300 per ticket.
3. Six months' airport rent had been prepaid on May 1.
4. The unexpired insurance is what remains of a 12-month policy purchased on February 1.
5. Passenger revenue earned in June totaled $75,000.

Instructions

a. Determine the following:
   1. The age of the airplane in months.
   2. The monthly airport rent expense.
   3. The amount paid for the 12-month insurance policy on February 1.

b. Prepare the adjusting entries made on June 30 involving the following accounts:
   1. Depreciation Expense: Airplane
   2. Airport Rent Expense
   3. Insurance Expense
   4. Passenger Revenue Earned

LO1 through LO7, LO9

PROBLEM 4.4A
Preparing Adjusting Entries from a Trial Balance

Campus Theater adjusts its accounts every *month.* Below is the company's *unadjusted* trial balance dated August 31, 2011. Additional information is provided for use in preparing the company's adjusting entries for the month of August. (Bear in mind that adjusting entries *have* already been made for the first seven months of 2011, but *not* for August.)

CAMPUS THEATER
UNADJUSTED TRIAL BALANCE
AUGUST 31, 2011

Account	Debit	Credit
Cash	$ 20,000	
Prepaid film rental	31,200	
Land	120,000	
Building	168,000	
Accumulated depreciation: building		$ 14,000
Fixtures and equipment	36,000	
Accumulated depreciation: fixtures and equipment		12,000
Notes payable		180,000
Accounts payable		4,400
Unearned admissions revenue (YMCA)		1,000
Income taxes payable		4,740
Capital stock		40,000
Retained earnings		46,610
Dividends	15,000	
Admissions revenue		305,200
Concessions revenue		14,350
Salaries expense	68,500	
Film rental expense	94,500	
Utilities expense	9,500	
Depreciation expense: building	4,900	
Depreciation expense: fixtures and equipment	4,200	
Interest expense	10,500	
Income taxes expense	40,000	
	$622,300	$622,300

Other Data

1. Film rental expense for the month is $15,200. However, the film rental expense for several months has been paid in advance.
2. The building is being depreciated over a period of 20 years (240 months).
3. The fixtures and equipment are being depreciated over a period of five years (60 months).
4. On the first of each month, the theater pays the interest that accrued in the prior month on its note payable. At August 31, accrued interest payable on this note amounts to $1,500.
5. The theater allows the local YMCA to bring children attending summer camp to the movies on any weekday afternoon for a fixed fee of $500 per month. On June 28, the YMCA made a $1,500 advance payment covering the months of July, August, and September.
6. The theater receives a percentage of the revenue earned by Tastie Corporation, the concessionaire operating the snack bar. For snack bar sales in August, Tastie owes Campus Theater $2,250, payable on September 10. No entry has yet been made to record this revenue. (Credit Concessions Revenue.)
7. Salaries earned by employees, but not recorded or paid as of August 31, amount to $1,700. No entry has yet been made to record this liability and expense.
8. Income taxes expense for August is estimated at $4,200. This amount will be paid in the September 15 installment payment.

9. Utilities expense is recorded as monthly bills are received. No adjusting entries for utilities expense are made at month-end.

Instructions

a. For each of the numbered paragraphs, prepare the necessary adjusting entry (including an explanation).

b. Refer to the balances shown in the *unadjusted* trial balance at August 31. How many *months* of expense are included in each of the following account balances? (Remember, Campus Theater adjusts its accounts *monthly*. Thus, the accounts shown were last adjusted on July 31, 2011.)
   1. Utilities Expense
   2. Depreciation Expense
   3. Accumulated Depreciation: Building

c. Assume the theater has been operating profitably all year. Although the August 31 trial balance shows substantial income taxes *expense,* income taxes *payable* is a much smaller amount. This relationship is quite normal throughout much of the year. Explain.

LO1 through LO7 LO9

PROBLEM 4.5A
Preparing Adjusting Entries and Determining Account Balances

Terrific Temps fills temporary employment positions for local businesses. Some businesses pay in advance for services; others are billed after services have been performed. Advanced payments are credited to an account entitled Unearned Fees. Adjusting entries are performed on a *monthly* basis. An unadjusted trial balance dated December 31, 2011, follows. (Bear in mind that adjusting entries have already been made for the first 11 months of 2011, but *not* for December.)

TERRIFIC TEMPS
UNADJUSTED TRIAL BALANCE
DECEMBER 31, 2011

Cash	$ 27,020	
Accounts receivable	59,200	
Unexpired insurance	900	
Prepaid rent	3,000	
Office supplies	600	
Equipment	60,000	
Accumulated depreciation: equipment		$ 29,500
Accounts payable		4,180
Notes payable		12,000
Interest payable		320
Unearned fees		6,000
Income taxes payable		4,000
Unearned revenue		20,000
Retained earnings		49,000
Capital stock		25,000
Dividends	3,000	
Fees earned		75,000
Travel expense	5,000	
Insurance expense	2,980	
Rent expense	9,900	
Office supplies expense	780	
Utilities expense	4,800	
Depreciation expense: equipment	5,500	
Salaries expense	30,000	
Interest expense	320	
Income taxes expense	12,000	
	$225,000	$225,000

Other Data

1. Accrued but unrecorded fees earned as of December 31, 2011, amount to $1,500.
2. Records show that $2,500 of cash receipts originally recorded as unearned fees had been earned as of December 31.
3. The company purchased a six-month insurance policy on September 1, 2011, for $1,800.
4. On December 1, 2011, the company paid its rent through February 28, 2012.
5. Office supplies on hand at December 31 amount to $400.
6. All equipment was purchased when the business first formed. The estimated life of the equipment at that time was 10 years (or 120 months).
7. On August 1, 2011, the company borrowed $12,000 by signing a six-month, 8 percent note payable. The entire note, plus six months' accrued interest, is due on February 1, 2012.
8. Accrued but unrecorded salaries at December 31 amount to $2,700.
9. Estimated income taxes expense for the *entire year* totals $15,000. Taxes are due in the first quarter of 2012.

Instructions

a. For each of the numbered paragraphs, prepare the necessary adjusting entry (including an explanation).

b. Determine that amount at which each of the following accounts will be reported in the company's 2011 income statement:
   1. Fees Earned
   2. Travel Expense
   3. Insurance Expense
   4. Rent Expense
   5. Office Supplies Expense
   6. Utilities Expense
   7. Depreciation Expense: Equipment
   8. Interest Expense
   9. Salaries Expense
   10. Income Taxes Expense

c. The unadjusted trial balance reports dividends of $3,000. As of December 31, 2011, have these dividends been paid? Explain.

LO1 **PROBLEM 4.6A**

through LO7 LO9

Preparing Adjusting Entries and Determining Account Balances

Alpine Expeditions operates a mountain climbing school in Colorado. Some clients pay in advance for services; others are billed after services have been performed. Advance payments are credited to an account entitled Unearned Client Revenue. Adjusting entries are performed on a *monthly* basis. An unadjusted trial balance dated December 31, 2011, follows. (Bear in mind that adjusting entries have already been made for the first 11 months of 2011, but *not* for December.)

ALPINE EXPEDITIONS
UNADJUSTED TRIAL BALANCE
DECEMBER 31, 2011

Cash	$ 13,900	
Accounts receivable	78,000	
Unexpired insurance	18,000	
Prepaid advertising	2,200	
Climbing supplies	4,900	
Climbing equipment	57,600	
Accumulated depreciation: climbing equipment		$ 38,400
Accounts payable		1,250
Notes payable		10,000
Interest payable		150
Income taxes payable		1,200
Unearned client revenue		9,600
Capital stock		17,000
Retained earnings		62,400
Client revenue earned		188,000
Advertising expense	7,400	
Insurance expense	33,000	
Rent expense	16,500	
Climbing supplies expense	8,400	
Repairs expense	4,800	
Depreciation expense: climbing equipment	13,200	
Salaries expense	57,200	
Interest expense	150	
Income taxes expense	12,750	
	$328,000	$328,000

Other Data

1. Accrued but unrecorded fees earned as of December 31 amount to $6,400.
2. Records show that $6,600 of cash receipts originally recorded as unearned client revenue had been earned as of December 31.
3. The company purchased a 12-month insurance policy on June 1, 2011, for $36,000.
4. On December 1, 2011, the company paid $2,200 for numerous advertisements in several climbing magazines. Half of these advertisements have appeared in print as of December 31.
5. Climbing supplies on hand at December 31 amount to $2,000.
6. All climbing equipment was purchased when the business first formed. The estimated life of the equipment at that time was four years (or 48 months).
7. On October 1, 2011, the company borrowed $10,000 by signing an eight-month, 9 percent note payable. The entire note, plus eight months' accrued interest, is due on June 1, 2012.
8. Accrued but unrecorded salaries at December 31 amount to $3,100.
9. Estimated income taxes expense for the *entire year* totals $14,000. Taxes are due in the first quarter of 2012.

Instructions

a. For each of the numbered paragraphs, prepare the necessary adjusting entry (including an explanation).

b. Determine that amount at which each of the following accounts will be reported in the company's balance sheet dated December 31, 2011:

1. Cash
2. Accounts Receivable
3. Unexpired Insurance
4. Prepaid Advertising
5. Climbing Supplies
6. Climbing Equipment
7. Accumulated Depreciation: Climbing Equipment
8. Salaries Payable
9. Notes Payable
10. Interest Payable
11. Income Taxes Payable
12. Unearned Client Revenue

c. Which of the accounts listed in part **b** represent *deferred expenses*? Explain.

LO1 through LO7 LO9

PROBLEM 4.7A
Preparing Adjusting Entries from a Trial Balance

Ken Hensley Enterprises, Inc., is a small recording studio in St. Louis. Rock bands use the studio to mix high-quality demo recordings distributed to talent agents. New clients are required to pay in advance for studio services. Bands with established credit are billed for studio services at the end of each month. Adjusting entries are performed on a *monthly* basis. An *unadjusted* trial balance dated December 31, 2011, follows. (Bear in mind that adjusting entries already have been made for the first eleven months of 2011, but *not* for December.)

KEN HENSLEY ENTERPRISES, INC.
UNADJUSTED TRIAL BALANCE
DECEMBER 31, 2011

Cash	$ 43,170	
Accounts receivable	81,400	
Studio supplies	7,600	
Unexpired insurance	500	
Prepaid studio rent	4,000	
Recording equipment	90,000	
Accumulated depreciation: recording equipment		$ 52,500
Notes payable		16,000
Interest payable		840
Income taxes payable		3,200
Unearned studio revenue		9,600
Capital stock		80,000
Retained earnings		38,000
Studio revenue earned		107,000
Salaries expense	18,000	
Supplies expense	1,200	
Insurance expense	2,680	
Depreciation expense: recording equipment	16,500	
Studio rent expense	21,000	
Interest expense	840	
Utilities expense	2,350	
Income taxes expense	17,900	
	$307,140	$307,140

Other Data

1. Records show that $4,400 in studio revenue had not yet been billed or recorded as of December 31.
2. Studio supplies on hand at December 31 amount to $6,900.
3. On August 1, 2011, the studio purchased a six-month insurance policy for $1,500. The entire premium was initially debited to Unexpired Insurance.
4. The studio is located in a rented building. On November 1, 2011, the studio paid $6,000 rent in advance for November, December, and January. The entire amount was debited to Prepaid Studio Rent.
5. The useful life of the studio's recording equipment is estimated to be five years (or 60 months). The straight-line method of depreciation is used.
6. On May 1, 2011, the studio borrowed $16,000 by signing a 12-month, 9 percent note payable to First Federal Bank of St. Louis. The entire $16,000 plus 12 months' interest is due in full on April 30, 2012.
7. Records show that $3,600 of cash receipts originally recorded as Unearned Studio Revenue had been earned as of December 31.
8. Salaries earned by recording technicians that remain unpaid at December 31 amount to $540.
9. The studio's accountant estimates that income taxes expense for the *entire year* ended December 31, 2011, is $19,600. (Note that $17,900 of this amount has already been recorded.)

Instructions

a. For each of the above numbered paragraphs, prepare the necessary adjusting entry (including an explanation).

b. Using figures from the company's unadjusted trial balance in conjunction with the adjusting entries made in part **a,** compute net income for the year ended December 31, 2011.

c. Was the studio's monthly rent for the last 2 months of 2011 more or less than during the first 10 months of the year? Explain your answer.

d. Was the studio's monthly insurance expense for the last five months of 2011 more or less than the average monthly expense for the first seven months of the year? Explain your answer.

e. If the studio purchased all of its equipment when it first began operations, for how many months has it been in business? Explain your answer.

f. Indicate the effect of each adjusting entry prepared in part **a** on the major elements of the company's income statement and balance sheet. Organize your answer in tabular form using the column headings shown. Use the symbols **I** for increase, **D** for decrease, and **NE** for no effect. The answer for the adjusting entry number **1** is provided as an example.

	Income Statement			Balance Sheet		
Adjusting Entry	Revenue −	Expenses =	Net Income	Assets =	Liabilities +	Owners' Equity
1	I	NE	I	I	NE	I

LO1 through LO7, LO9

PROBLEM 4.8A Understanding the Effects of Various Errors

Coyne Corporation recently hired Elaine Herrold as its new bookkeeper. Herrold was not very experienced and made seven recording errors during the last accounting period. The nature of each error is described in the following table.

Instructions

Indicate the effect of the following errors on each of the financial statement elements described in the column headings in the table. Use the following symbols: **O** = overstated, **U** = understated, and **NE** = no effect.

Error	Total Revenue	Total Expenses	Net Income	Total Assets	Total Liabilities	Owners' Equity
a. Recorded a dividend as an expense reported in the income statement.						
b. Recorded the payment of an account payable as a debit to accounts payable and a credit to an expense account.						
c. Failed to record depreciation expense.						
d. Recorded the sale of capital stock as a debit to cash and a credit to retained earnings.						
e. Recorded the receipt of a customer deposit as a debit to cash and a credit to fees earned.						
f. Failed to record expired portion of an insurance policy.						
g. Failed to record accrued interest earned on an outstanding note receivable.						

Problem Set B

LO1 through LO7

PROBLEM 4.1B

Preparing Adjusting Entries

The Georgia Gun Club adjusts its accounts *monthly* and closes its accounts annually. Club members pay their annual dues in advance by January 4. The entire amount is initially credited to Unearned Membership Dues. At the end of each month, an appropriate portion of this amount is credited to Membership Dues Earned. Guests of the club normally pay their fees before being allowed to use the facilities. The amounts collected are credited to Guest Fee Revenue at the time of receipt. Certain guests, however, are billed at the end of the month. The following information is available as a source for preparing adjusting entries at December 31:

1. Salaries earned by the club's employees that have not yet been recorded or paid amount to $13,600.
2. The Georgia State Police used the club's facilities for target practice on December 30 of the current year. At December 31, the $3,200 owed by the state police for guest fees had not yet been recorded or billed.
3. Membership dues earned in December, for collections received at the beginning of the year, amount to $140,000.
4. Depreciation of the furniture and fixtures in the clubhouse is based on an estimated life of eight years. These items had originally been purchased for $120,000. The straight-line method is used. (***Note:*** The clubhouse building was constructed in 1956 and is fully depreciated.)
5. A 12-month bank loan in the amount of $60,000 had been obtained by the club on October 4. Interest is computed at an annual rate of 8 percent. The entire $60,000, plus all of the interest accrued over the 12-month life of the loan, is due in full on September 30 of the upcoming year. The necessary adjusting entry was made on November 30 to record the first two months of accrued interest expense. However, no adjustment has been made to record interest expense accrued in December.
6. A one-year property insurance policy had been purchased on April 30. The entire premium of $10,800 was initially recorded as Unexpired Insurance.
7. In December, the club entered into an agreement to host the annual tournament of the Georgia Junior Rifle Association. The club expects to generate guest fees of $7,200 from this event.
8. Unrecorded Income Taxes Expense accrued in December amounts to $12,600. This amount will not be paid until January 22.

Instructions

a. For each of the above numbered paragraphs, prepare the necessary adjusting entry (including an explanation). If no adjusting entry is required, explain why.

b. Four types of adjusting entries are described at the beginning of the chapter. Using these descriptions, identify the type of each adjusting entry prepared in part **a** above.

c. Although the clubhouse building is fully depreciated, it is in excellent physical condition. Explain how this can be.

LO1 through LO6, LO9

PROBLEM 4.2B

Preparing and Analyzing the Effects of Adjusting Entries

Big Oaks, a large campground in Vermont, adjusts its accounts *monthly* and closes its accounts annually on December 31. Most guests of the campground pay at the time they check out, and the amounts collected are credited to Camper Revenue. The following information is available as a source for preparing the adjusting entries at December 31:

1. Big Oaks invests some of its excess cash in certificates of deposit (CDs) with its local bank. Accrued interest revenue on its CDs at December 31 is $425. None of the interest has yet been received. (Debit Interest Receivable.)
2. An eight-month bank loan in the amount of $12,000 had been obtained on October 1. Interest is to be computed at an annual rate of 8 percent and is payable when the loan becomes due.
3. Depreciation on buildings owned by the campground is based on a 20-year life. The original cost of the buildings was $720,000. The Accumulated Depreciation: Buildings account has a credit balance of $160,000 at December 31, prior to the adjusting entry process. The straight-line method of depreciation is used.
4. Management signed an agreement to let Girl Scouts from Easton, Connecticut, use the campground in June of next year. The agreement specifies that the Girl Scouts will pay a daily rate of $15 per campsite, with a clause providing a minimum total charge of $1,200.
5. Salaries earned by campground employees that have not yet been paid amount to $1,515.

6. As of December 31, Big Oaks has earned $2,700 of revenue from current campers who will not be billed until they check out. (Debit Camper Revenue Receivable.)
7. Several lakefront campsites are currently being leased on a long-term basis by a group of senior citizens. Five months' rent of $7,500 was collected in advance and credited to Unearned Camper Revenue on November 1 of the current year.
8. A bus to carry campers to and from town and the airport had been rented the first week of December at a daily rate of $45. At December 31, no rental payment has been made, although the campground has had use of the bus for 18 days.
9. Unrecorded Income Taxes Expense accrued in December amounts to $6,600. This amount will not be paid until January 15.

Instructions

a. For each of the above numbered paragraphs, prepare the necessary adjusting entry (including an explanation). If no adjusting entry is required, explain why.

b. Four types of adjusting entries are described at the beginning of the chapter. Using these descriptions, identify the type of each adjusting entry prepared in part **a** above.

c. Indicate the effects that each of the adjustments in part **a** will have on the following six *total amounts* in the campground's financial statements for the month of *December*. Organize your answer in tabular form, using the column headings shown below. Use the letters **I** for increase, **D** for decrease, and **NE** for no effect. Adjusting entry **1** is provided as an example.

	Income Statement			Balance Sheet		
Adjusting Entry	Revenue −	Expenses =	Net Income	Assets =	Liabilities +	Owners' Equity
1	I	NE	I	I	NE	I

d. What is the amount of interest expense recognized for the *entire current year* on the $12,000 bank loan obtained October 1?

e. Compute the *book value* of the campground's buildings to be reported in the current year's December 31 balance sheet. (Refer to paragraph **3.**)

LO1 through LO7 LO9

PROBLEM 4.3B
Analysis of Adjusted Data

River Rat, Inc., operates a ferry that takes travelers across the Wild River. The company adjusts its accounts at the end of each month. Selected account balances appearing in the April 30 *adjusted* trial balance are as follows:

	Debit	Credit
Prepaid rent	$12,000	
Unexpired insurance	2,400	
Ferry	96,000	
Accumulated depreciation: ferry		$20,000
Unearned passenger revenue		1,040

Other Data

1. The ferry is being depreciated over an eight-year estimated useful life.
2. The unearned passenger revenue represents tickets good for future rides sold to a resort hotel for $2 per ticket on April 1. During April, 160 of the tickets were used.
3. Five months' rent had been prepaid on April 1.
4. The unexpired insurance is a 12-month fire insurance policy purchased on March 1.

Instructions

a. Determine the following:
   1. The age of the ferry in months.
   2. How many $2 tickets for future rides were sold to the resort hotel on April 1.
   3. The monthly rent expense.
   4. The original cost of the 12-month fire insurance policy.

b. Prepare the adjusting entries that were made on April 30.

LO1 through LO7 LO9

PROBLEM 4.4B

Preparing Adjusting Entries from a Trial Balance

The Off-Campus Playhouse adjusts its accounts every *month.* Below is the company's *unadjusted* trial balance dated September 30, 2011. Additional information is provided for use in preparing the company's adjusting entries for the month of September. (Bear in mind that adjusting entries *have already* been made for the first eight months of 2011, but *not* for September.)

OFF-CAMPUS PLAYHOUSE
UNADJUSTED TRIAL BALANCE
SEPTEMBER 30, 2011

Cash	$ 8,200	
Prepaid costume rental	1,800	
Land	80,000	
Building	150,000	
Accumulated depreciation: building		$ 18,500
Fixtures and equipment	18,000	
Accumulated depreciation: fixtures and equipment		4,500
Notes payable		100,000
Accounts payable		5,700
Unearned admissions revenue (nursing homes)		1,500
Income taxes payable		4,700
Capital stock		9,000
Retained earnings		26,400
Dividends	9,000	
Admissions revenue		180,200
Concessions revenue		19,600
Salaries expense	57,400	
Costume rental expense	2,700	
Utilities expense	7,100	
Depreciation expense: building	4,000	
Depreciation expense: fixtures and equipment	2,400	
Interest expense	8,500	
Income taxes expense	21,000	
	$370,100	$370,100

Other Data

1. Costume rental expense for the month is $600. However, the costume rental expense for several months has been paid in advance.
2. The building is being depreciated over a period of 25 years (300 months).
3. The fixtures and equipment are being depreciated over a period of five years (60 months).
4. On the first of each month, the theater pays the interest which accrued in the prior month on its note payable. At September 30, accrued interest payable on this note amounts to $1,062.
5. The playhouse allows local nursing homes to bring seniors to the plays on any weekday performance for a fixed price of $500 per month. On August 31, a nursing home made a $1,500 advance payment covering the months of September, October, and November.
6. The theater receives a percentage of the revenue earned by Sweet Corporation, the concessionaire operating the snack bar. For snack bar sales in September, Sweet owes Off-Campus Playhouse $4,600, payable on October 14. No entry has yet been made to record this revenue. (Credit Concessions Revenue.)
7. Salaries earned by employees, but not recorded or paid as of September 30, amount to $2,200. No entry has yet been made to record this liability and expense.
8. Income taxes expense for September is estimated at $3,600. This amount will be paid in the October 15 installment payment.
9. Utilities expense is recorded as monthly bills are received. No adjusting entries for utilities expense are made at month-end.

Instructions

a. For each of the numbered paragraphs, prepare the necessary adjusting entry (including an explanation).

b. Refer to the balances shown in the *unadjusted* trial balance at September 30. How many *months* of expense are included in each of the following balances? (Remember, Off-Campus Playhouse adjusts its accounts *monthly*. Thus, the accounts shown were last adjusted on August 31, 2011.)

1. Utilities expense
2. Depreciation expense
3. Accumulated depreciation: building

c. Assume the playhouse has been operating profitably all year. Although the September 30 trial balance shows substantial income taxes *expense*, income taxes *payable* is a much smaller amount. This relationship is quite normal throughout much of the year. Explain.

LO1 through LO7 LO9

PROBLEM 4.5B Preparing Adjusting Entries and Determining Account Balances

Marvelous Music provides music lessons to student musicians. Some students pay in advance for lessons; others are billed after lessons have been provided. Advance payments are credited to an account entitled Unearned Lesson Revenue. Adjusting entries are performed on a *monthly* basis. An unadjusted trial balance dated December 31, 2011, follows. (Bear in mind that adjusting entries have already been made for the first 11 months of 2011, but *not* for December.)

MARVELOUS MUSIC
UNADJUSTED TRIAL BALANCE
DECEMBER 31, 2011

Cash	$ 15,800	
Accounts receivable	2,100	
Unexpired insurance	3,200	
Prepaid rent	6,000	
Sheet music supplies	450	
Music equipment	180,000	
Accumulated depreciation: music equipment		$ 72,000
Accounts payable		3,500
Notes payable		5,000
Dividends payable		1,000
Interest payable		25
Income taxes payable		3,400
Unearned lesson revenue		1,100
Capital stock		20,000
Retained earnings		56,600
Dividends	1,000	
Lesson revenue earned		154,375
Advertising expense	7,400	
Insurance expense	4,400	
Rent expense	16,500	
Sheet music supplies expense	780	
Utilities expense	5,000	
Depreciation expense: music equipment	33,000	
Salaries expense	27,500	
Interest expense	25	
Income taxes expense	13,845	
	$317,000	$317,000

Other Data

1. Accrued but unrecorded lesson revenue earned as of December 31, 2011, amounts to $3,200.
2. Records show that $800 of cash receipts originally recorded as unearned lesson revenue had been earned as of December 31.
3. The company purchased a 12-month insurance policy on August 1, 2011, for $4,800.
4. On October 1, 2011, the company paid $9,000 for rent through March 31, 2012.
5. Sheet music supplies on hand at December 31 amount to $200.
6. All music equipment was purchased when the business was first formed. Its estimated life at that time was five years (or 60 months).
7. On November 1, 2011, the company borrowed $5,000 by signing a three-month, 6 percent note payable. The entire note, plus three months' accrued interest, is due on February 1, 2012.
8. Accrued but unrecorded salaries at December 31 amount to $3,500.
9. Estimated income taxes expense for the *entire year* totals $22,000. Taxes are due in the first quarter of 2012.

Instructions

a. For each of the numbered paragraphs, prepare the necessary adjusting entry (including an explanation).

b. Determine that amount at which each of the following accounts will be reported in the company's 2011 income statement:
   1. Lesson Revenue Earned
   2. Advertising Expense
   3. Insurance Expense
   4. Rent Expense
   5. Sheet Music Supplies Expense
   6. Utilities Expense
   7. Depreciation Expense: Music Equipment
   8. Interest Expense
   9. Salaries Expense
   10. Income Taxes Expense

c. The unadjusted trial balance reports dividends of $1,000. As of December 31, 2011, have these dividends been paid? Explain.

LO1 through LO7 LO9

PROBLEM 4.6B
Preparing Adjusting Entries and Determining Account Balances

Mate Ease is an Internet dating service. All members pay in advance to be listed in the database. Advance payments are credited to an account entitled Unearned Member Dues. Adjusting entries are performed on a *monthly* basis. An unadjusted trial balance dated December 31, 2011, follows. (Bear in mind that adjusting entries have already been made for the first 11 months of 2011, but *not* for December.)

MATE EASE
UNADJUSTED TRIAL BALANCE
DECEMBER 31, 2011

Cash	$169,500	
Unexpired insurance	12,800	
Prepaid rent	14,600	
Office supplies	2,160	
Computer equipment	108,000	
Accumulated depreciation: computer equipment		$ 54,000
Accounts payable		4,300
Notes payable		90,000
Interest payable		6,750
Income taxes payable		7,500
Unearned member dues		36,000
Capital stock		40,000
Retained earnings		28,000
Client fees earned		508,450
Advertising expense	17,290	
Insurance expense	35,200	
Rent expense	80,300	
Office supplies expense	18,400	
Internet connection expense	24,000	
Depreciation expense: computer equipment	33,000	
Salaries expense	239,000	
Interest expense	6,750	
Income taxes expense	14,000	
	$775,000	$775,000

Other Data

1. Records show that $21,000 of cash receipts originally recorded as unearned member dues had been earned as of December 31, 2011.
2. The company purchased a six-month insurance policy on October 1, 2011, for $19,200.
3. On November 1, 2011, the company paid $21,900 for rent through January 31, 2012.
4. Office supplies on hand at December 31 amount to $440.
5. All computer equipment was purchased when the business first formed. The estimated life of the equipment at that time was three years (or 36 months).
6. On March 1, 2011, the company borrowed $90,000 by signing a 12-month, 10 percent note payable. The entire note, plus 12 months' accrued interest, is due on March 1, 2012.
7. Accrued but unrecorded salaries at December 31 amount to $10,500.
8. Estimated income taxes expense for the *entire year* totals $16,000. Taxes are due in the first quarter of 2012.

Instructions

a. For each of the numbered paragraphs, prepare the necessary adjusting entry (including an explanation).

b. Determine that amount at which each of the following accounts will be reported in the company's balance sheet dated December 31, 2011:

1. Cash
2. Unexpired Insurance
3. Prepaid Rent
4. Office Supplies
5. Computer Equipment
6. Accumulated Depreciation: Computer Equipment
7. Accounts Payable
8. Notes Payable
9. Salaries Payable
10. Interest Payable
11. Income Taxes Payable
12. Unearned Member Dues

c. Why doesn't the company immediately record advance payments from customers as *revenue*?

LO1 through LO7 LO9

PROBLEM 4.7B
Preparing Adjusting Entries from a Trial Balance

Clint Stillmore operates a private investigating agency called Stillmore Investigations. Some clients pay in advance for services; others are billed after services have been performed. Advance payments are credited to an account entitled Unearned Retainer Fees. Adjusting entries are performed on a *monthly* basis. An *unadjusted* trial balance dated December 31, 2011, follows. (Bear in mind that adjusting entries have already been made for the first 11 months of 2011, but *not* for December.)

Other Data

1. Accrued but unrecorded client fees earned at December 31 amount to $1,500.
2. Records show that $2,500 of cash receipts originally recorded as Unearned Retainer Fees had been earned as of December 31.
3. Office supplies on hand at December 31 amount to $110.
4. The company purchased all of its office equipment when it first began business. At that time, the equipment's estimated useful life was six years (or 72 months).
5. On October 1, 2011, the company renewed its rental agreement paying $1,800 cash for six months' rent in advance.
6. On March 1 of the current year, the company paid $1,080 cash to renew its 12-month insurance policy.
7. Accrued but unrecorded salaries at December 31 amount to $1,900.
8. On June 1, 2011, the company borrowed money from the bank by signing a $9,000, 8 percent, 12-month note payable. The entire note, plus 12 months' accrued interest, is due on May 31, 2012.
9. The company's CPA estimates that income taxes expense for the *entire year* is $7,500.

STILLMORE INVESTIGATIONS
UNADJUSTED TRIAL BALANCE
DECEMBER 31, 2011

Cash	$ 40,585	
Accounts receivable	2,000	
Office supplies	205	
Prepaid rent	1,200	
Unexpired insurance	270	
Office equipment	54,000	
Accumulated depreciation: office equipment		$ 35,250
Accounts payable		1,400
Interest payable		360
Income taxes payable		1,750
Note payable		9,000
Unearned retainer fees		3,500
Capital stock		30,000
Retained earnings		8,000
Dividends	1,000	
Client fees earned		60,000
Office supplies expense	605	
Depreciation expense: office equipment	8,250	
Rent expense	5,775	
Insurance expense	1,010	
Salaries expense	27,100	
Interest expense	360	
Income taxes expense	6,900	
Totals	$149,260	$149,260

Instructions

a. For each of the above numbered paragraphs, prepare the necessary adjusting entry (including an explanation).

b. Prepare the company's adjusted trial balance dated December 31, 2011.

c. Using figures from the adjusted trial balance prepared in **b,** compute net income for the year ended December 31, 2011.

d. How much was the company's average monthly rent expense in January through September of 2011? Explain your answer.

e. How much was the company's average monthly insurance expense in January and February of 2011? Explain your answer.

f. If the company purchased all of its office equipment when it first began operations, for how many months has it been in business? Explain your answer.

g. Indicate the effect of each adjusting entry prepared in part **a** on the major elements of the company's income statement and balance sheet. Organize your answer in tabular form using the column headings shown. Use the symbols **I** for increase, **D** for decrease, and **NE** for no effect. The answer for adjusting entry number **1** is provided as an example.

	Income Statement			Balance Sheet		
Adjusting Entry	Revenue −	Expenses =	Net Income	Assets =	Liabilities +	Owners' Equity
1	I	NE	I	I	NE	I

LO1 through LO7, LO9

PROBLEM 4.8B Understanding the Effects of Various Errors

Stephen Corporation recently hired Tom Waters as its new bookkeeper. Waters is very inexperienced and has made seven recording errors during the last accounting period. The nature of each error is described in the following table.

Instructions

Indicate the effect of the following errors on each of the financial statement elements described in the column headings in the table. Use the following symbols: **O** = overstated, **U** = understated, and **NE** = no effect

Error	Total Revenue	Total Expenses	Net Income	Total Assets	Total Liabilities	Owners' Equity
a. Recorded a declared but unpaid dividend by debiting dividends and crediting cash.						
b. Recorded a receipt of an account receivable as a debit to cash and a credit to fees earned.						
c. Recorded depreciation expense twice.						
d. Recorded the sale of capital stock as a debit to cash and a credit to revenue.						
e. Purchased equipment and debited supplies expense and credited cash.						
f. Failed to record expired portion of prepaid advertising.						
g. Failed to record accrued and unpaid interest expense.						

Critical Thinking Cases

LO1 through LO7

CASE 4.1
Should This Be Adjusted?

Property Management Professionals provides building management services to owners of office buildings and shopping centers. The company closes its accounts at the *end of the calendar year.* The manner in which the company has recorded several transactions occurring during 2011 is described as follows:

a. On September 1, received advance payment from a shopping center for property management services to be performed over the three-month period beginning September 1. The entire amount received was credited directly to a *revenue* account.

b. On December 1, received advance payment from the same customer described in part **a** for services to be rendered over the three-month period beginning December 1. This time, the entire amount received was credited to an *unearned* revenue account.

c. Rendered management services for many customers in December. Normal procedure is to record revenue on the date the customer is billed, which is early in the month after the services have been rendered.

d. On December 15, made full payment for a one-year insurance policy that goes into effect on January 2, 2012. The cost of the policy was debited to Unexpired Insurance.

e. Numerous purchases of equipment were debited to asset accounts, rather than to expense accounts.

f. Payroll expense is recorded when employees are paid. Payday for the last two weeks of December falls on January 2, 2012.

Instructions

For each item above, explain whether an adjusting entry is needed at *December 31, 2011*, and state the reasons for your answer. If you recommend an adjusting entry, explain the effects this entry would have on assets, liabilities, owners' equity, revenue, and expenses in the 2011 financial statements.

LO8

CASE 4.2
The Concept of Materiality

The concept of materiality is one of the most basic principles underlying financial accounting.

a. Answer the following questions:

 1. Why is the materiality of a transaction or an event a matter of professional judgment?

 2. What criteria should accountants consider in determining whether a transaction or an event is material?

 3. Does the concept of materiality mean that financial statements are not precise, down to the last dollar? Does this concept make financial statements less useful to most users?

b. **Avis Rent-a-Car** purchases a large number of cars each year for its rental fleet. The cost of any individual automobile is immaterial to **Avis**, which is a very large corporation. Would it be acceptable for **Avis** to charge the purchase of automobiles for its rental fleet directly to expense, rather than to an asset account? Explain.

LO3 LO7 LO8

CASE 4.3
Hold the Expenses!

Slippery Slope, Inc., is a downhill ski area in northern New England. In an attempt to attract more ski enthusiasts, Slippery Slope's management recently engaged in an aggressive preseason advertising campaign in which it spent $9,000 to distribute brochures, $17,000 to air broadcast media spots, and $14,000 to run magazine and newspaper ads.

Slippery Slope is now planning to borrow money from a local bank to expand its snowmaking capabilities next season. In preparing financial statements to be used by the bank, Slippery Slope's management capitalized the entire $40,000 of advertising expenditures as Prepaid Advertising in the current year's balance sheet. It decided to defer converting this asset to advertising expense for three years, arguing that it will take a least that long to realize the full benefit of its promotional efforts. Management also contends that it does not matter how the $40,000 advertising expenditure is reported, because the amount is immaterial.

Instructions

a. Does management's decision to defer converting this $40,000 prepayment to advertising expense comply with generally accepted accounting principles? Defend your answer.

b. Could management's decision to defer reporting this expenditure as an expense for three years have any ethical implications? Explain.

LO1 through LO6

INTERNET CASE 4.4

Identifying Accounts Requiring Adjusting Entries

Visit **Hershey's** home page at:

www.hersheys.com

From **Hershey's** home page, access its most recent annual report (see the "Investor Relations" link). Examine the company's balance sheet and identify the accounts most likely to have been involved in the end-of-year adjusting entry process.

Internet sites are time and date sensitive. It is the purpose of these exercises to have you explore the Internet. You may need to use the Yahoo! search engine www.yahoo.com *(or another favorite search engine) to find a company's current Web address.*

Answers to Self-Test Questions

1. c **2.** d, $11,670 ($27,900 − $17,340 − $2,700 − $1,440 + $3,300 + $1,950)

3. d **4.** b, c **5.** b, c, d

CHAPTER 5

The Accounting Cycle

Reporting Financial Results

© Susan Van Etten/Photoedit

AFTER STUDYING THIS CHAPTER, YOU SHOULD BE ABLE TO:

- **LO1** Prepare an income statement, a statement of retained earnings, and a balance sheet.
- **LO2** Explain how the income statement and the statement of retained earnings relate to the balance sheet.
- **LO3** Explain the concept of *adequate disclosure.*
- **LO4** Explain the purposes of *closing entries;* prepare these entries.
- **LO5** Prepare an after-closing trial balance.
- **LO6** Use financial statement information to evaluate profitability and liquidity.
- **LO7** Explain how *interim* financial statements are prepared in a business that closes its accounts only at year-end.
- **LO8** Prepare a worksheet and explain its uses.

**Supplemental Topic,* "The Worksheet."

Learning Objectives

BEST BUY

Best Buy is a national retailer of televisions, video equipment, stereo systems, cellular phones, and an array of other consumer electronic devices and Web-based services.

The company reported an impairment expense in a recent income statement of $111 million—no similar charges appeared in the previous two-year period. Disclosures accompanying Best Buy's financial statements reveal that the company had purchased more than 26 million shares of CPW common stock in a prior period for $183 million. At the end of the most current reporting period, the fair market value of these shares had declined by $111 million. Best Buy's management determined that this decline in value was not temporary; hence, in accordance with accounting standards, it reported the entire amount of the loss as an impairment expense in its income statement.

Disclosures such as these are absolutely essential for the proper interpretation of a company's financial statements. The Best Buy's financial statements also include disclosures about store closings, executive compensation, sources of credit, and many other important issues. ■

In this chapter, we examine how companies prepare general-purpose financial statements used by investors, creditors, and managers. In addition, we discuss how certain events are disclosed in the notes that accompany financial statements. We also illustrate several methods of evaluating liquidity and profitability using financial statement information.

In Chapter 3, we introduced the first of the eight steps in the accounting cycle by illustrating how Overnight Auto Service (1) captured (journalized) economic events, (2) posted these transactions to its general ledger, and (3) prepared an *unadjusted* trial balance from its general ledger account balances. We continued our illustration of the accounting cycle in Chapter 4 by (4) performing the adjusting entries made by Overnight and (5) presenting the company's *adjusted* trial balance at year-end.

In this chapter, we complete the accounting cycle by (6) preparing Overnight's financial statements, (7) performing year-end closing entries, and (8) presenting the company's *after-closing* trial balance.

Preparing Financial Statements

Learning Objective LO1 **Prepare an income statement, a statement of retained earnings, and a balance sheet.**

Publicly owned companies—those with shares listed on a stock exchange—have obligations to release annual and quarterly information to their stockholders and to the public. These companies don't simply prepare financial statements—they publish *annual reports.*

An annual report *includes* comparative financial statements for several years and a wealth of other information about the company's financial position, business operations, and future prospects. (For illustrative purposes, the financial statements of **Home Depot, Inc.** appear in Appendix A.) Before an annual report is issued, the financial statements must be *audited* by a firm of certified public accountants (CPAs). Publicly owned companies must file their audited financial statements and detailed supporting schedules with the Securities and Exchange Commission (SEC).

The activities surrounding the preparation of an annual report become very intense as the new year approaches. Once the fiscal year has ended, it often takes several *months* before the annual report is available for distribution. Thus, many accountants refer to the months of December through March as the "busy season."[1] We cannot adequately discuss all of the activities associated with the preparation of an annual report in a single chapter. Thus, here we focus on the *preparation of financial statements.*

The adjusted trial balance prepared in Chapter 4 is reprinted in Exhibit 5–1. The income statement, statement of retained earnings, and balance sheet can be prepared *directly from the amounts shown in this adjusted trial balance.* For illustrative purposes, we have made marginal notes indicating which accounts appear in which financial statements. Overnight's financial statements for the year ended December 31, 2011, are illustrated in Exhibit 5–2 (page 194).

The income statement is prepared first because it determines the amount of net income to be reported in the statement of retained earnings. The statement of retained earnings is prepared second because it determines the amount of retained earnings to be reported in the balance sheet. Note that we have not included Overnight's statement of cash flows with the other three reports. An in-depth discussion of the statement of cash flows is the primary focus of Chapter 13.

THE INCOME STATEMENT

Learning Objective LO2 **Explain how the income statement and the statement of retained earnings relate to the balance sheet.**

Alternative titles for the income statement include *earnings statement, statement of operations,* and *profit and loss statement.* However, *income statement* is the most popular term for this important financial statement. The income statement is used to summarize the *operating* results of a business by matching the revenue earned during a given period of time with the expenses incurred in generating that revenue.

[1] Some companies elect to end their fiscal year after a seasonal high point in business activity. However, most companies *do* end their fiscal year on December 31.

Exhibit 5–1

ADJUSTED TRIAL BALANCE

OVERNIGHT AUTO SERVICE ADJUSTED TRIAL BALANCE DECEMBER 31, 2011			
Cash	$ 18,592		Balance sheet accounts
Accounts receivable	7,250		
Shop supplies	1,200		
Unexpired insurance	3,000		
Land	52,000		
Building	36,000		
Accumulated depreciation: building		$ 1,650	
Tools and equipment	12,000		
Accumulated depreciation: tools and equipment		2,200	
Notes payable		4,000	
Accounts payable		2,690	
Wages payable		1,950	
Income taxes payable		5,580	
Interest payable		30	
Unearned rent revenue		6,000	
Capital stock		80,000	
Retained earnings (***Note:*** still must be updated for transactions recorded in the accounts listed below. Closing entries serve this purpose.)		0	Statement of retained earnings accounts
Dividends	14,000		
Repair service revenue		172,000	Income statement accounts
Rent revenue earned		3,000	
Advertising expense	3,900		
Wages expense	58,750		
Supplies expense	7,500		
Depreciation expense: building	1,650		
Depreciation expense: tools and equipment	2,200		
Utilities expense	19,400		
Insurance expense	15,000		
Interest expense	30		
Income taxes expense	26,628		
	$279,100	$279,100	

The revenue and expenses shown in Overnight's income statement are taken directly from the company's adjusted trial balance. Overnight's 2011 income statement shows that revenue exceeded expenses for the year, thus producing a net income of $39,942. Bear in mind, however, that this measurement of net income is not absolutely accurate or precise due to the *assumptions and estimates* in the accounting process.

An income statement has certain limitations. For instance, the amounts shown for depreciation expense are based upon estimates of the useful lives of the company's building and equipment. Also, the income statement includes only those events that have been evidenced by actual business transactions. Perhaps during the year, Overnight's advertising has caught the attention of many potential customers. A good "customer base" is certainly an important step toward profitable operations; however, the development of a customer base is not reflected in the income statement because its value cannot be measured *objectively* until actual

Exhibit 5–2

OVERNIGHT AUTO SERVICE'S FINANCIAL STATEMENTS

Amounts are taken directly from the adjusted trial balance

Net income also appears in the statement of retained earnings

The ending balance in the Retained Earnings account also appears in the balance sheet

OVERNIGHT AUTO SERVICE
INCOME STATEMENT
FOR THE YEAR ENDED DECEMBER 31, 2011

Revenue:		
Repair service revenue		$172,000
Rent revenue earned		3,000
Total revenue		$175,000
Expenses:		
Advertising	$ 3,900	
Wages expense	58,750	
Supplies expense	7,500	
Depreciation: building	1,650	
Depreciation: tools and equipment	2,200	
Utilities expense	19,400	
Insurance	15,000	
Interest	30	108,430
Income before income taxes		$ 66,570
Income taxes		26,628
Net income		$ 39,942

OVERNIGHT AUTO SERVICE
STATEMENT OF RETAINED EARNINGS
FOR THE YEAR ENDED DECEMBER 31, 2011

Retained earnings, Jan. 20, 2011	$ 0
Add: Net income	39,942
Subtotal	$39,942
Less: Dividends	14,000
Retained earnings, Dec. 31, 2011	$25,942

OVERNIGHT AUTO SERVICE
BALANCE SHEET
DECEMBER 31, 2011

Assets		
Cash		$ 18,592
Accounts receivable		7,250
Shop supplies		1,200
Unexpired insurance		3,000
Land		52,000
Building	$36,000	
Less: Accumulated depreciation	1,650	34,350
Tools and equipment	$12,000	
Less: Accumulated depreciation	2,200	9,800
Total assets		$126,192
Liabilities & Stockholders' Equity		
Liabilities:		
Notes payable		$ 4,000
Accounts payable		2,690
Wages payable		1,950
Income taxes payable		5,580
Interest payable		30
Unearned rent revenue		6,000
Total liabilities		$ 20,250
Stockholders' equity:		
Capital stock		80,000
Retained earnings		25,942
Total stockholders' equity		$105,942
Total liabilities and stockholders' equity		$126,192

transactions take place. Despite these limitations, the income statement is of vital importance to the users of a company's financial statements.

THE STATEMENT OF RETAINED EARNINGS

Retained earnings is that portion of stockholders' (owners') equity created by earning net income and retaining the related resources in the business. The resources retained from being profitable may include, but are certainly not limited to, *cash.* The statement of retained earnings summarizes the increases and decreases in retained earnings resulting from business operations during the period. Increases in retained earnings result from earning net income; decreases result from net losses and from the declaration of dividends.

Statement of retained earnings

The format of this financial statement is based upon the following relationships:

Retained Earnings at the beginning of the period	+	Net Income	−	Dividends	=	Retained Earnings at the end of the period

The amount of retained earnings at the *beginning* of the period is shown at the top of the statement. Next, the net income for the period is added (or net loss subtracted), and any dividends declared during the period are deducted. This short computation determines the amount of retained earnings at the *end* of the accounting period. The ending retained earnings ($25,942 in our example) appears at the bottom of the statement and also in the company's year-end balance sheet.

Our illustration of the statement of retained earnings for Overnight is unusual in that the beginning balance of retained earnings at the date of the company's formation (January 20, 2011) was *$0.* This occurred only because 2011 was the *first year* of Overnight's business operations. The ending retained earnings ($25,942) becomes the beginning retained earnings for the following year.

A Word about Dividends In Chapter 3, the declaration and payment of a cash dividend were treated as a single event recorded by one journal entry. A small corporation with only a few stockholders may choose to declare and pay a dividend on the same day. In large corporations, an interval of a month or more will separate the date of declaration from the later date of payment. A liability account, Dividends Payable, comes into existence when the dividend is declared and is discharged when the dividend is paid. Because Overnight reports no dividends payable in its adjusted trial balance, we may assume that it declared and paid the entire $14,000 on December 31, 2011.[2]

Finally, it is important to realize that dividends paid to stockholders are *not* reported in the income statement as an expense. In short, dividends represent a decision by a corporation to distribute a portion of its income to stockholders. Thus, the amount of the dividend is not included in the computation of income.

THE BALANCE SHEET

The balance sheet lists the amounts of the company's assets, liabilities, and owners' equity at the *end* of the accounting period. The balances of Overnight's asset and liability accounts are taken directly from the adjusted trial balance in Exhibit 5–1. The amount of retained earnings at the end of the period, $25,942, was determined in the *statement of retained earnings.*

Balance sheets can be presented with asset accounts appearing on the left and liabilities and owners' equity accounts appearing on the right. They may also be presented in *report form,* with liabilities and owners' equity listed *below* (rather than to the right of) the asset section. It is also common for corporations to refer to owners' equity as *stockholders'* equity.

[2] Details related to the declaration and payment of dividends are discussed in Chapter 12.

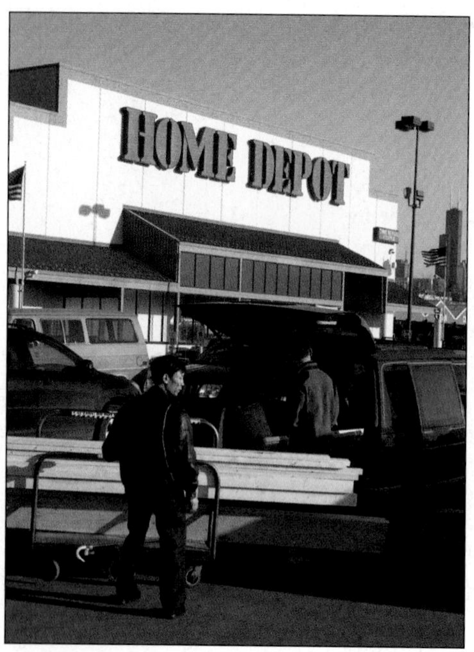

© The McGraw-Hill Companies, Inc./Andrew Resek, photographer/DAL

Separate Balance Sheet Subtotals Many companies group together as separate balance sheet subtotals those assets and liabilities that are considered *current.* To be classified as a **current asset,** an asset must already be cash or must be capable of *being converted into cash* within a relatively short period of time. For most companies, this period of time is usually one year or less. Those assets that get used up quickly (e.g., insurance policies and office supplies) are also classified as current assets. Of Overnight's $126,192 in total assets shown in Exhibit 5–2, the current assets include Cash, Accounts Receivable, Shop Supplies, and Unexpired Insurance. Thus, $30,042 of Overnight's total assets is considered *current.*

A **current liability** is an existing debt or obligation that a company expects to satisfy relatively soon using its current assets. Once again, this period of time is typically one year or less. While not a *debt,* unearned revenue is often considered a current liability also. *All* of Overnight's $20,250 in total liabilities shown in Exhibit 5–2 are considered current liabilities.

Computing separate subtotals for current assets and current liabilities is very useful when evaluating a company's ability to pay its debts as they come due (see this chapter's Financial Analysis discussion). The financial statements of **Home Depot, Inc.**, in Appendix A at the end of this textbook illustrate how subtotals for current assets and current liabilities are presented in the balance sheet. Coverage of several other balance sheet subtotals appears in Chapter 14.

INTERNATIONAL CASE IN POINT 

International Financial Reporting Standard (IFRS) 1 identifies the international reporting requirements for the presentation of the income statement, balance sheet, cash flow statement, and statement showing changes in equity. One very significant difference between the financial reporting requirements under U.S. GAAP and IFRS requirements is that, under the latter, management and auditors are required to depart from compliance with standards when it is necessary to achieve a fair presentation. This "true and fair" override is required if, in the judgment of the management and auditors, compliance is misleading.

Relationships among the Financial Statements

A set of financial statements becomes easier to understand if we recognize that the income statement, statement of retained earnings, and balance sheet all are *related to one another.* These relationships are emphasized by the arrows in the right-hand margin of Exhibit 5–2.

DRAFTING THE NOTES THAT ACCOMPANY FINANCIAL STATEMENTS

Learning Objective
LO3 **Explain the concept of *adequate disclosure.***

To the users of financial statements, **adequate disclosure** is perhaps the most important accounting principle. This principle simply means that financial statements should be accompanied by any information necessary for the statements to be *interpreted properly.*

Most disclosures appear within the numerous pages of **notes** that accompany the financial statements. Drafting these notes can be one of the most challenging tasks confronting accountants at the end of the period. The content of these disclosures often cannot be drawn directly from the accounting records. Rather, they require an *in-depth understanding* of the company and its operations, of accounting principles, and of how accounting information is interpreted by users of financial statements.

Two items always disclosed in the notes to financial statements are the accounting methods in use and the due dates of major liabilities. Thus Overnight's 2011 financial statements should at least include the following notes:

Note 1: Depreciation policies

Depreciation expense in the financial statements is computed by the straight-line method. Estimated useful lives are 20 years for the building and 5 years for tools and equipment.

Note 2: Maturity dates of liabilities

The Company's notes payable consist of a single obligation that matures on February 28 of the coming year. The maturity value of this note, including interest charges, will amount to $4,090.

Note 1 above can be used to help ascertain whether the company may need to replace its depreciable assets in the near future. For instance, given that the estimated useful life of Overnight's building is 20 years, and only $1,650 of its $36,000 initial cost has been depreciated, it is reasonable for one to assume that it will not need to be replaced in the foreseeable future.

The maturity dates reported in Note 2 above should be of particular importance to American National Bank. Specifically, the bank will want to know if Overnight will have enough cash to pay this $4,090 liability in just two months. The company's balance sheet currently reports cash of $18,592; however, several other liabilities will require an outlay of cash in excess of $10,000 in the near future. Furthermore, the company has an $18,000 insurance policy to renew on March 1. Thus, even though Overnight's income statement reports net income of $39,942, the company's balance sheet suggests that the company may not have adequate liquid assets to satisfy all of its upcoming obligations.

WHAT TYPES OF INFORMATION MUST BE DISCLOSED?

There is no comprehensive list of all information that should be disclosed in financial statements. The adequacy of disclosure is based on a combination of official rules, tradition, and accountants' professional judgment.

As a general rule, a company should disclose any facts that an informed user would consider necessary for the statements to be *interpreted properly*. Thus, businesses often disclose such things as:

- Lawsuits pending against the business.
- Scheduled plant closings.
- Significant events occurring *after* the balance sheet date but before the financial statements are actually issued.
- Customers that account for 10 percent or more of the company's revenues.
- Unusual transactions or conflicts of interest between the company and its key officers.

In some cases, companies must disclose information that could have a *damaging effect* on the business. For example, a manufacturer may need to disclose that it is being sued by customers who have been injured by its products. The fact that a disclosure might prove embarrassing—or even damaging to the business—is *not* a valid reason for not disclosing the information. The concept of adequate disclosure demands a *good faith effort* by management to keep the users of financial statements informed about the company's operations. For a look at the types of disclosure made by publicly owned corporations, see the **Home Depot, Inc.**, financial statements, which appear in Appendix A.

YOUR TURN **You as Overnight Auto's Independent Auditor**

Assume that Overnight Auto Service is being sued by a former employee injured while on the job. The person claims that Overnight has been negligent in providing a safe work environment. If the plaintiff prevails, Overnight may have to pay damages well in excess of what is covered by its insurance policies. As Overnight's independent auditor, you have asked that the company disclose information about this lawsuit in the notes that accompany the financial statements. Overnight's management disagrees with your suggestion because in its opinion, the likelihood of the plaintiff prevailing is extremely remote. How should you respond?

(See our comments on the Online Learning Center Web site.)

Closing the Temporary Accounts

Learning Objective
LO4 **Explain the purposes of *closing entries;* prepare these entries.**

As previously stated, revenue increases retained earnings, and expenses and dividends decrease retained earnings. If the only financial statement that we needed was a balance sheet, these changes in retained earnings could be recorded directly in the Retained Earnings account. However, owners, managers, investors, and others need to know amounts of specific revenues and expenses and the amount of net income earned in the period. Therefore, *separate ledger accounts* must be maintained to measure each type of revenue and expense, and to account for dividends declared.

Revenue, expense, and dividends accounts are called *temporary,* or *nominal,* accounts, because they accumulate the transactions of *only one accounting period.* At the end of an accounting period, the changes in retained earnings accumulated in these temporary accounts are transferred into the Retained Earnings account. This process serves two purposes. First, it *updates the balance of the Retained Earnings account* for changes occurring during the accounting period. Second, it *returns the balances of the temporary accounts to zero,* so that they are ready for measuring the revenue, expenses, and dividends of the next accounting period.

Retained Earnings and other balance sheet accounts are called *permanent,* or *real,* accounts, because their balances continue to exist beyond the current accounting period. Transferring the balances of the temporary accounts into the Retained Earnings account is called *the closing process.* The journal entries made for the purpose of closing the temporary accounts are called **closing entries.**

Revenue and expense accounts are closed at the end of each accounting period by *transferring their balances* to an account called the **Income Summary.** After the credit balances of the revenue accounts and the debit balances of the expense accounts have all been transferred to the Income Summary account, its balance will be the *net income* or *net loss* for the period. If revenues (credit balances) exceed expenses (debit balances), the Income Summary account will have a credit balance representing net income. Conversely, if expenses exceed revenues, the Income Summary account will have a debit balance representing a net loss. This is consistent with the rule that increases in owners' equity are recorded by credits and decreases are recorded by debits.

While adjusting entries are usually made on a monthly basis, it is common practice to close accounts only *once each year.* Thus, we will demonstrate the closing of the temporary accounts of Overnight Auto Service at December 31, 2011, the end of its first year of operations.

On the following pages, Overnight's temporary accounts are illustrated in T account form. We have eliminated the detail of every transaction posted to each account throughout the year. Therefore, each account shows only its December 31, 2011, balance as reported in the adjusted trial balance in Exhibit 5–1. The closing process is relatively straightforward and involves just four steps: (1) closing all revenue accounts to the Income Summary, (2) closing all expense accounts to the Income Summary, (3) closing the Income Summary to Retained Earnings, and (4) closing the Dividends account to Retained Earnings.

CLOSING ENTRIES FOR REVENUE ACCOUNTS

Revenue accounts have credit balances. Therefore, closing a revenue account means transferring its credit balance to the Income Summary account. This transfer is accomplished by a journal entry debiting the revenue account in an amount equal to its credit balance, with an offsetting credit to the Income Summary account. The debit portion of this closing entry returns the balance of the revenue account to zero; the credit portion transfers the former balance of the revenue account into the Income Summary account.

Overnight uses two revenue accounts: (1) Repair Service Revenue, which had a credit balance of $172,000 at December 31, 2011, and (2) Rent Revenue Earned, which had a credit balance of $3,000 at December 31, 2011. Two separate journal entries could be made to close these accounts, but the use of one *compound journal entry* is an easier, time-saving method of closing more than one account. The compound closing entry for Overnight's revenue accounts is displayed in Exhibit 5–3.

Exhibit 5–3

CLOSING OF REVENUE ACCOUNTS

OVERNIGHT AUTO SERVICE
GENERAL JOURNAL
DECEMBER 31, 2011

Date	Account Titles and Explanation	Debit	Credit
2011			
Dec. 31	Repair Service Revenue	172,000	
	Rent Revenue Earned	3,000	
	Income Summary		175,000
	To close the Repair Service Revenue and Rent Revenue Earned accounts.		

After this closing entry has been posted, the two revenue accounts each have *zero* balances, whereas Income Summary has a credit balance of $175,000, as illustrated in Exhibit 5–4.

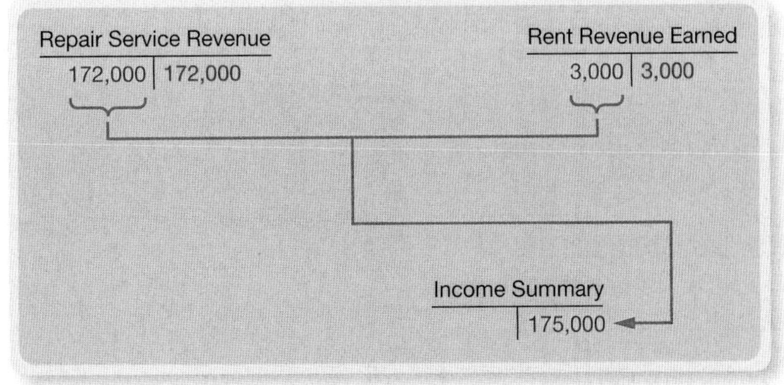

Exhibit 5–4

TRANSFERRING REVENUE ACCOUNT BALANCES TO THE INCOME SUMMARY

CLOSING ENTRIES FOR EXPENSE ACCOUNTS

Expense accounts have debit balances. Closing an expense account means transferring its debit balance to the Income Summary account. The journal entry to close an expense, therefore, consists of a credit to the expense account in an amount equal to its debit balance, with an offsetting debit to the Income Summary account.

There are nine expense accounts in Overnight's ledger (see the adjusted trial balance in Exhibit 5–1). Again, a compound journal entry is used to close each of these accounts. The required closing entry is displayed in Exhibit 5–5.

Exhibit 5–5
CLOSING OF EXPENSE ACCOUNTS

OVERNIGHT AUTO SERVICE
GENERAL JOURNAL
DECEMBER 31, 2011

Date	Account Titles and Explanation	Debit	Credit
2011			
Dec. 31	Income Summary	135,058	
	Advertising Expense		3,900
	Wages Expense		58,750
	Supplies Expense		7,500
	Depreciation Expense: Building		1,650
	Depreciation Expense: Tools and Equipment		2,200
	Utilities Expense		19,400
	Insurance Expense		15,000
	Interest Expense		30
	Income Taxes Expense		26,628
	To close the expense accounts.		

After this closing entry has been posted, the Income Summary account has a *credit balance* of *$39,942* ($175,000 credit posted minus the $135,058 debit posted), and the nine expense accounts each have *zero balances* as shown in Exhibit 5–6. This $39,942 credit balance equals the *net income* reported in Overnight's income statement. Had the company's income statement reported a *net loss* for the year, the Income Summary account would have a *debit balance* equal to the amount of the loss reported.

Exhibit 5–6
TRANSFERRING EXPENSE ACCOUNT BALANCES TO THE INCOME SUMMARY

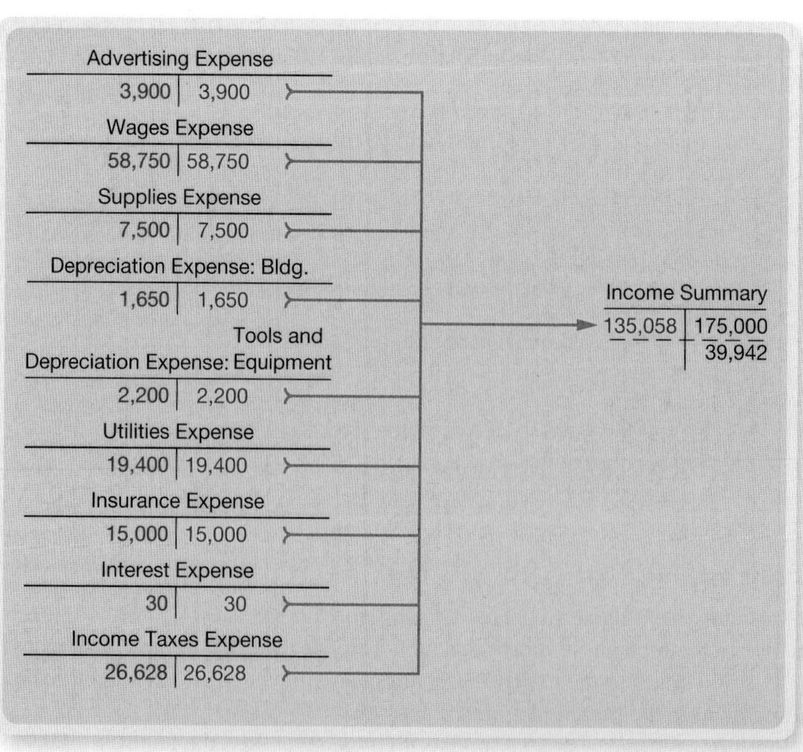

CLOSING THE INCOME SUMMARY ACCOUNT

The net income of $39,942 earned during the year causes an increase in Overnight's owners' equity. Thus, the $39,942 credit balance of the Income Summary account is transferred to the Retained Earnings account by the closing entry in Exhibit 5–7.

Exhibit 5–7
CLOSING THE INCOME SUMMARY ACCOUNT

OVERNIGHT AUTO SERVICE
GENERAL JOURNAL
DECEMBER 31, 2011

Date	Account Titles and Explanation	Debit	Credit
2011			
Dec. 31	Income Summary	39,942	
	Retained Earnings		39,942
	Transferring net income earned in 2011 to the Retained Earnings account.		

After this closing entry has been posted, the Income Summary account has a zero balance, and the net income for the year ended December 31, 2011, appears as an increase (or credit entry) in the Retained Earnings account as shown in Exhibit 5–8.

Exhibit 5–8 INCOME INCREASES RETAINED EARNINGS

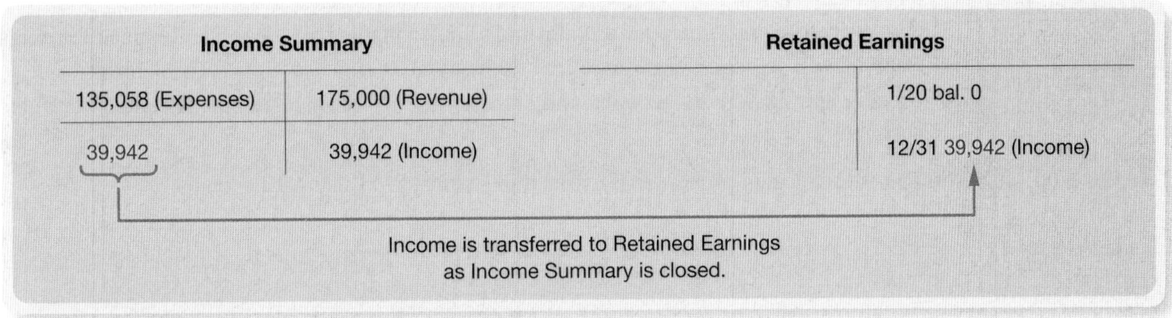

Income Summary
135,058 (Expenses)
175,000 (Revenue)
39,942
39,942 (Income)
Retained Earnings
1/20 bal. 0
12/31 39,942 (Income)
Income is transferred to Retained Earnings as Income Summary is closed.

CLOSING THE DIVIDENDS ACCOUNT

As explained earlier in the chapter, dividends to stockholders are *not* considered an expense of the business; therefore, they are *not* taken into account in determining net income for the period. Since dividends are not an expense, the Dividends account is *not* closed to the Income Summary account. Instead, it is closed directly to the Retained Earnings account, as shown in Exhibit 5–9.

Exhibit 5–9
CLOSING THE DIVIDENDS ACCOUNT

OVERNIGHT AUTO SERVICE
GENERAL JOURNAL
DECEMBER 31, 2011

Date	Account Titles and Explanation	Debit	Credit
2011			
Dec. 31	Retained Earnings.	14,000	
	Dividends		14,000
	To transfer dividends declared in 2011 to the Retained Earnings account.		

After this closing entry has been posted, the Dividends account will have a zero balance, and the Retained Earnings account will have an ending credit balance of $25,942, as shown in Exhibit 5–10.

Exhibit 5–10 DIVIDENDS DECREASE RETAINED EARNINGS

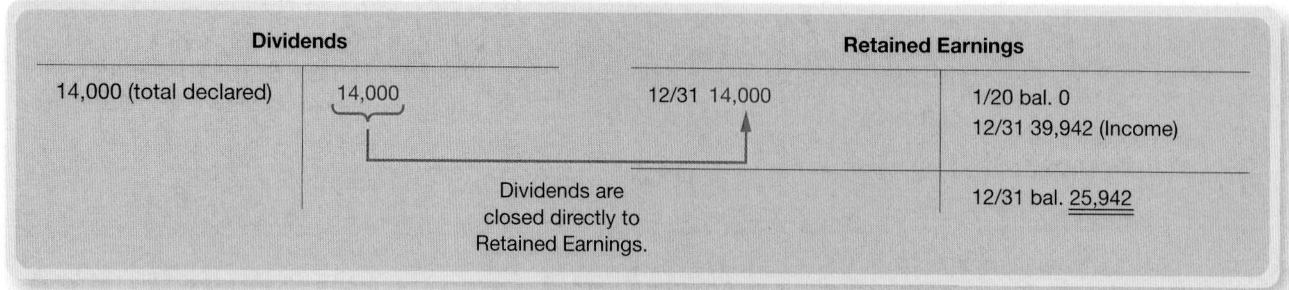

Summary of the Closing Process

As illustrated, the closing process involves four simple steps:

1. Closing the various *revenue* accounts and transferring their balances to the Income Summary account.
2. Closing the various *expense* accounts and transferring their balances to the Income Summary account.
3. Closing the *Income Summary* account and transferring its balance to the Retained Earnings account.
4. Closing the *Dividends* account and transferring its balance to the Retained Earnings account.

The entire closing process is illustrated in Exhibit 5–11 using T accounts.

Exhibit 5–11 FLOWCHART OF THE CLOSING PROCESS

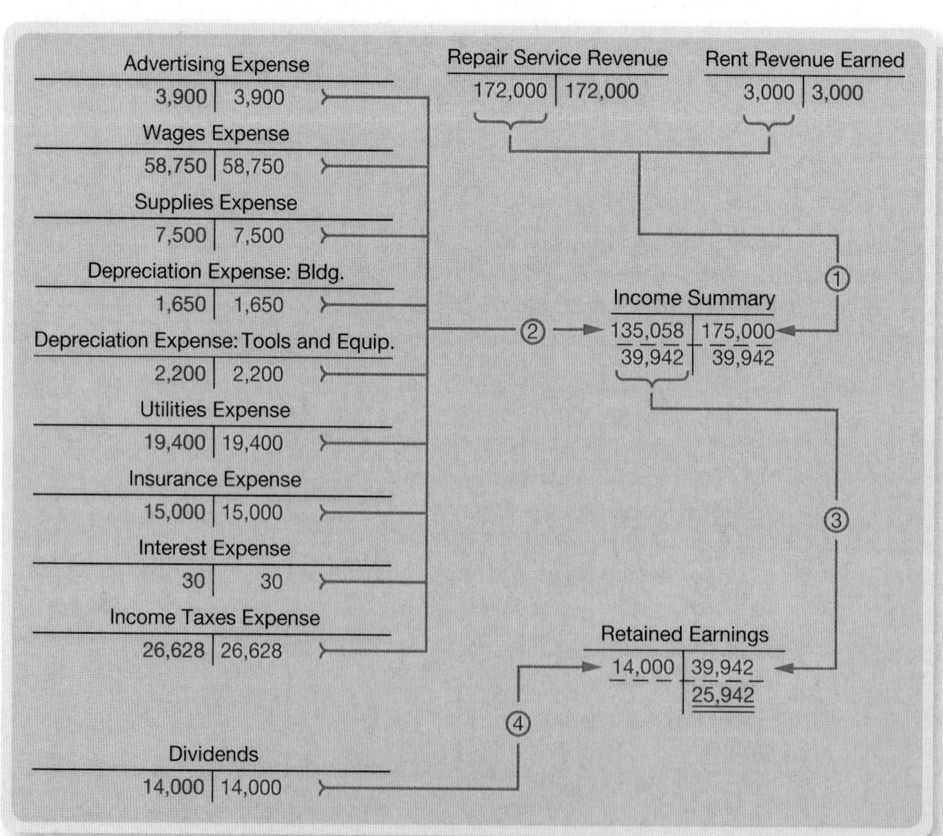

After-Closing Trial Balance

After the revenue and expense accounts have been closed, it is desirable to prepare an **after-closing trial balance** that consists solely of balance sheet accounts. There is always the possibility that an error in posting the closing entries may have upset the equality of debits and credits in the ledger. The after-closing trial balance, or *post-closing trial balance* as it is often called, is prepared from the ledger. It gives assurance that the accounts are in balance and ready for recording transactions in the new accounting period. The after-closing trial balance of Overnight Auto Service is shown in Exhibit 5–12.

Learning Objective Prepare an after-closing trial balance. LO5

Exhibit 5–12
AFTER-CLOSING TRIAL BALANCE

OVERNIGHT AUTO SERVICE AFTER-CLOSING TRIAL BALANCE DECEMBER 31, 2011		
Cash	$ 18,592	
Accounts receivable	7,250	
Shop supplies	1,200	
Unexpired insurance	3,000	
Land	52,000	
Building	36,000	
Accumulated depreciation: building		$ 1,650
Tools and equipment	12,000	
Accumulated depreciation: tools and equipment		2,200
Notes payable		4,000
Accounts payable		2,690
Wages payable		1,950
Income taxes payable		5,580
Interest payable		30
Unearned rent revenue		6,000
Capital stock		80,000
Retained earnings, Dec. 31		25,942
	$130,042	$130,042

In comparison with the adjusted trial balance in Exhibit 5–1, an after-closing trial balance contains only *balance sheet* accounts. Also, the Retained Earnings account no longer has a zero balance. Through the closing of the revenue, expense, and dividends accounts, the Retained Earnings account has been brought *up-to-date*.

A LAST LOOK AT OVERNIGHT: WAS 2011 A GOOD YEAR?

Let us now consider the financial results of Overnight's first fiscal year.

Learning Objective Use financial statement information to evaluate profitability and liquidity. LO6

Evaluating Profitability In 2011, Overnight earned a net income of nearly *$40,000.* Thus, net income for the first year of operations amounts to 50 percent of the stockholders' $80,000 investment. This is a very impressive rate of return for the first year of operations. Of course, Overnight's stockholders (members of the McBryan family) have taken a certain amount of risk by investing their financial resources in this business. Does a 50 percent *return on investment* adequately compensate the stockholders for their risk? Stated differently, could they invest their $80,000 in a less risky venture and still generate a 50 percent rate of return? Probably not.

But in evaluating profitability, the real question is not how the business *did,* but how it is *likely to do in the future.* To generate a substantial return on investment in the first year of operations indicates good profit potential. Overnight's rental contract with Harbor Cab

Company is also promising. In 2011, only $3,000 in revenue was earned by renting storage space to the company for its cabs (December's rent). In 2012, Overnight will earn 12 full months of rent revenue from Harbor Cab ($33,000 more than it earned in 2011). In addition, if Harbor Cab stores its cabs in Overnight's garage, Overnight becomes the likely candidate to perform any necessary maintenance and repairs.

Evaluating Liquidity *Liquidity* refers to a company's ability to meet its cash obligations as they become due. Liquidity, at least in the short term, may be independent of profitability. And in the short term, Overnight appears to have *potential* cash flow problems. In the very near future, Overnight must make cash expenditures for the following items:

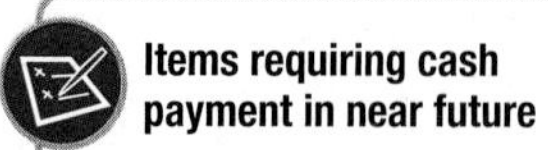

Items requiring cash payment in near future

Note and interest payable	$ 4,030
Accounts payable	2,690
Wages payable	1,950
Income taxes payable	5,580
Insurance policy renewal	18,000
Total expenditures coming due	$32,250

These outlays exceed the company's liquid assets (cash and accounts receivable) reported in its December 31, 2011, balance sheet.

It is important to note that the cash and accounts receivable amounts reported in Overnight's balance sheet represent the balances of those accounts at a *point in time.* Thus, while these liquid assets are currently insufficient to cover the cash expenditures coming due, this may not be the case for long. On the basis of its past performance, Overnight is likely to generate revenue in excess of $40,000 during the next several months. If a substantial amount of this revenue is received in cash, and expenses are kept under control, the company may actually become more liquid than it appears to be now.

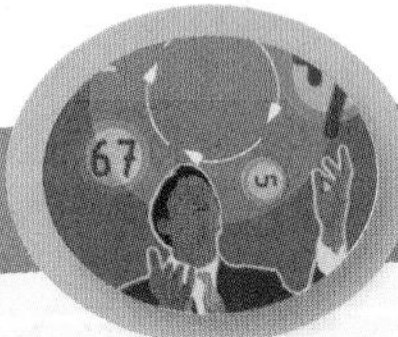

Financial Analysis and Decision Making

Measures of Profitability

The $39,942 net income figure reported in Overnight's income statement is more meaningful when examined in the context of management's ability to control costs or when measured relative to the company's shareholders' equity.

Two commonly used measures of *profitability* that address these issues are the *net income percentage* and *return on equity.* Using data from Overnight's financial statements, these measures are computed as follows:

Net Income Percentage **= Net Income ÷ Total Revenue**
= $39,942 ÷ $175,000 = 22.8%

Return on Equity **= Net Income ÷ Average Stockholders' Equity**
= $39,943 ÷ $92,971 = 43%

All companies must incur costs in order to generate revenue. The *net income percentage* is simply a measure of management's ability to control these costs. In 2011, Overnight was able to convert 22.8 percent of its revenue into net income; thus, it incurred approximately 78 cents in costs for every dollar of revenue it generated.

Return on equity is a measure of net income relative to *average* stockholders' equity throughout the year. In 2011, Overnight's average stockholders' equity was $92,971 (i.e., the average of its beginning stockholders' equity of $80,000, and its ending stockholders' equity of $105,942). Thus, the company earned income of approximately 43 cents on every dollar of equity capital.

Measures of Liquidity

At the end of 2011, Overnight's balance sheet reports liabilities of $20,250, most of which will require payment early in 2012. However, the balance sheet reports cash of only $18,592, which may be an indication of potential liquidity problems.

Two common measures of *liquidity* are a company's *working capital* and its *current ratio.* Using data from Overnight's financial statements, these measures are computed as follows:

Working Capital **= Current Assets − Current Liabilities**
= $30,042 − $20,250 = $9,792

Current Ratio **= Current Assets ÷ Current Liabilities**
= $30,042 ÷ $20,250 = 1.48:1

Working capital is a measure of short-term debt-paying ability expressed in dollars. Current assets represent a company's potential cash *inflows* in the near future, whereas current liabilities represent cash *outlays* coming due soon. Overnight's current assets exceed its current liabilities by $9,792; however, shop supplies and unexpired insurance policies are not truly *liquid* assets. Likewise, unearned rent revenue does not actually represent a future cash *obligation.*

The *current ratio* is simply working capital expressed as a ratio. Thus, Overnight has approximately $1.48 of potential cash inflow for every dollar of current obligations coming due. Again, this figure does not take into account shop supplies and insurance policies will not actually convert into cash, or that unearned revenue will not actually require a future outlay of cash.

Throughout the remainder of this textbook additional measures of performance will be discussed. Chapter 14 is devoted entirely to financial analysis.

PREPARING FINANCIAL STATEMENTS COVERING DIFFERENT PERIODS OF TIME

Learning Objective
LO7
Explain how *interim* financial statements are prepared in a business that closes its accounts only at year-end.

Many businesses prepare financial statements every quarter, as well as at year-end. In addition, they may prepare financial statements covering other time periods, such as one month or the year-to-date.

When a business closes its accounts only at year-end, the revenue, expense, and dividends accounts have balances representing the activities of the *year-to-date.* Thus, at *June 30,* these account balances represent the activities recorded over the past six months. Year-to-date financial statements can be prepared directly from an adjusted trial balance. But how might this business prepare **interim financial statements** covering only the month of June? Or the quarter (three months) ended June 30?

The answer is by doing a little *subtraction.* As an example, assume that the adjusted balance in Overnight's Repair Service Revenue account at the ends of the following months was as shown:

March 31 (end of the first quarter)	$38,000
May 31	67,000
June 30	80,000

Revenue amounts are for the year-to-date

At each date, the account balance represents the revenue earned since January 1. Thus the March 31 balance represents three months' revenue; the May 31 balance, five months' revenue; and the June 30 balance, the revenue earned over a period of six months.

To prepare an income statement for the *six months* ended June 30, we simply use the June 30 balance in the revenue account—*$80,000.* But to prepare an income statement for the *month* ended June 30, we would have to subtract from the June 30 balance of this account its balance as of May 31. The remainder, *$13,000,* represents the amount of revenue recorded in the account during June ($80,000 − $67,000 = $13,000).

To prepare an income statement for the *quarter* ended June 30, we would subtract from the June 30 balance in this revenue account its balance as of March 31. Thus the revenue earned during the second quarter (April 1 through June 30) amounts to *$42,000* ($80,000 − $38,000 = $42,000).

Computations like these are not required for the balance sheet accounts. A balance sheet always is based on the account balances *at the balance sheet date.* Therefore, a June 30 balance sheet looks exactly the same *regardless* of the time period covered by the other financial statements.

Ethics, Fraud & Corporate Governance

As stated previously in this chapter, a company should disclose any facts that an intelligent person would consider necessary for the statements to be *interpreted properly.* Public companies are required to file annual reports with the Securities and Exchange Commission (SEC). These annual reports include a section labeled, "Management Discussion and Analysis" (MD&A). The SEC requires that companies include an MD&A in their annual reports because the financial statements and related notes may be inadequate for assessing the quality and sustainability of a company's earnings.

In the late 1990s, the SEC brought an enforcement action against **Sony Corporation** alleging inadequate disclosure in its MD&A. Although a Japanese corporation, **Sony** lists its stock on the New York Stock Exchange and is therefore subject to SEC oversight. **Sony** had reported only two industry segments in its annual report (electronics and entertainment). The entertainment segment included two separate units, Sony Music Entertainment and Sony Pictures Entertainment. The music group was profitable, whereas the pictures group was losing significant amounts of money. By combining its music and picture units as a single entertainment segment, **Sony** was able to conceal significant losses incurred by Sony Pictures. This decision was at odds with both **Sony**'s external auditor and with its U.S.–based financial staff.

Although **Sony** chose to report only two segments, it could have elaborated on the entertainment segment's performance in its MD&A by separately discussing the results of Sony Music and Sony Pictures. **Sony** did discuss Sony Pictures separately, but not in a manner necessary for an intelligent person to properly interpret the results of Sony Pictures. **Sony**'s MD&A did not discuss the nature and extent of the losses incurred by Sony Pictures. Conversely, **Sony**'s MD&A highlighted certain positive developments at Sony Pictures, including box office receipts, box office market share, and Academy Award nominations.

The SEC concluded that **Sony**'s MD&A disclosures were inadequate. **Sony** consented to an SEC cease-and-desist order without either admitting or denying guilt. In essence, **Sony** did not agree that it did anything wrong, but it promised to never do what it did again. As part of its settlement, **Sony** also agreed to have its external auditor examine the MD&A for the following year and to publicly report the findings. This penalty was meaningful because an examination of the MD&A normally does not fall within the scope of an external audit.

Concluding Remarks

We have now completed the *entire accounting cycle,* the eight steps of which include:

1. *Journalize (record) transactions.* Enter all transactions in the journal, thus creating a chronological record of events.
2. *Post to ledger accounts.* Post debits and credits from the journal to the proper ledger accounts, thus creating a record classified by accounts.
3. *Prepare a trial balance.* Prove the equality of debits and credits in the ledger.
4. *Make end-of-period adjustments.* Make adjusting entries in the general journal and post to ledger accounts.
5. *Prepare an adjusted trial balance.* Prove again the equality of debits and credits in the ledger. (***Note:*** These are the amounts used in the preparation of financial statements.)
6. *Prepare financial statements and appropriate disclosures.* An income statement shows the results of operation for the period. A statement of retained earnings shows changes in retained earnings during the period. A balance sheet shows the financial position of the business at the end of the period. Financial statements should be accompanied by *notes* disclosing facts necessary for the proper interpretation of those statements.
7. *Journalize and post the closing entries.* The closing entries "zero" the revenue, expense, and dividends accounts, making them ready for recording the events of the next accounting period. These entries also bring the balance in the Retained Earnings account up-to-date.
8. *Prepare an after-closing trial balance.* This step ensures that the ledger remains in balance after the posting of the closing entries.

SUPPLEMENTAL TOPIC

The Worksheet

Learning Objective
Prepare a worksheet and explain its uses.
LO8

A **worksheet** illustrates in one place the relationships among the unadjusted trial balance, proposed adjusting entries, and financial statements. A worksheet is prepared at the end of the period, but *before* the adjusting entries are formally recorded in the accounting records. It is not a formal step in the accounting cycle. Rather, it is a *tool* used by accountants to work out the details of the proposed end-of-period adjustments. It also provides them with a preview of how the financial statements will look.

You can see a worksheet for Overnight Auto Service at December 31, 2011, in Exhibit 5–13 on page 209.

ISN'T THIS REALLY A SPREADSHEET?

Yes. The term *worksheet* is a holdover from the days when these schedules were prepared manually on large sheets of columnar paper. Today, most worksheets are prepared using a spreadsheet software or with **general ledger software.**

Since the worksheet is simply a tool used by accountants, it often isn't printed out in hard copy—it may exist only on a computer screen. But the concept remains the same; the worksheet displays *in one place* the unadjusted account balances, proposed adjusting entries, and financial statements as they will appear if the proposed adjustments are made.

HOW IS A WORKSHEET USED?

A worksheet serves several purposes. It allows accountants to *see the effects* of adjusting entries without actually entering these adjustments in the accounting records. This makes it relatively easy for them to correct errors or make changes in estimated amounts. It also enables accountants and management to preview the financial statements before the final drafts are developed. Once the worksheet is complete, it serves as the source for recording adjusting and closing entries in the accounting records and for preparing financial statements.

Another important use of the worksheet is in the preparation of *interim financial statements.* Interim statements are financial statements developed at various points *during* the fiscal year. Most companies close their accounts only once each year. Yet they often need to develop quarterly or monthly financial statements. Through the use of a worksheet, they can develop these interim statements *without* having to formally adjust and close their accounts.

THE MECHANICS: HOW IT'S DONE

Whether done manually or on a computer, the preparation of a worksheet involves five basic steps. We begin by describing these steps as if the worksheet were being prepared manually. Afterward, we explain how virtually all of the mechanical steps can be performed automatically by a computer.

1. *Enter the ledger account balances in the Trial Balance columns.* The worksheet begins with an *unadjusted trial balance.* A few lines should be left blank immediately below the last balance sheet account. It is often necessary to add a few more accounts during the adjusting process. Additional income statement accounts also may be necessary. In our illustration, the unadjusted trial balance appears in *blue.*
2. *Enter the adjustments in the Adjustments columns.* This step is the most important: Enter the appropriate end-of-period adjustments in the Adjustments columns. In our illustration, these adjustments appear in *red.*

   Notice that each adjustment includes both debit and credit entries, which are linked together by the small key letters appearing to the left of the dollar amount. Thus, adjusting entry *a* consists of a $600 debit to Supplies Expense and a $600 credit to Shop Supplies. Because the individual adjusting entries include equal debit and credit amounts, the totals of the debit and credit Adjustments columns should be equal.

Sometimes the adjustments require adding accounts to the original trial balance. (The four ledger account titles printed in *red* were added during the adjusting process.)

3. *Prepare an adjusted trial balance.* The balances in the original trial balance (*blue*) are adjusted for the debit or credit amounts in the Adjustments columns (*red*). The adjusted trial balance is totaled to determine that the accounts remain in balance.

   At this point, the worksheet is almost complete. We have emphasized that financial statements are prepared *directly from the adjusted trial balance.* Thus we have only to arrange these accounts into the format of financial statements.

4. *Extend the adjusted trial balance amounts into the appropriate financial statement columns.* The balance sheet accounts—assets, liabilities, and owners' equity—are extended into the Balance Sheet columns; income statement amounts, into the Income Statement columns. (The "Balance Sheet" and "Income Statement" captions in the original trial balance should simplify this procedure. Notice each amount is extended to only one column. Also, the account retains the same debit or credit balance as shown in the adjusted trial balance.)

5. *Total the financial statement columns; determine and record net income or net loss.* The final step in preparing the worksheet consists of totaling the Income Statement and Balance Sheet columns and then bringing each set of columns into balance. These tasks are performed on the bottom three lines of the worksheet. In our illustration, the amounts involved in this final step are shown in *black.*

When the Income Statement and Balance Sheet columns are first totaled, their respective debit and credit columns will *not* be equal. But each set of columns should be out of balance by the *same amount*—and that amount should be the amount of net income or net loss for the period.

Let us briefly explain *why* both sets of columns initially are out of balance by this amount. First consider the Income Statement columns. The Credit column contains the revenue accounts, and the Debit column, the expense accounts. The difference, therefore, represents the net income (net loss) for the period.

Now consider the Balance Sheet columns. All of the balance sheet amounts are shown at up-to-date amounts *except* for the Retained Earnings account, which still contains the balance from the *beginning* of the period. To bring the Retained Earnings account up-to-date, we must add net income and subtract any dividends. The dividends already appear in the Balance Sheet Debit column. So what's the only thing missing? The net income (or net loss) for the period.

To bring both sets of columns into balance, we enter the net income (or net loss) on the next line. The same amount will appear in both the Income Statement columns and the Balance Sheet columns. But in one set of columns it appears as a debit, and in the other, it appears as a credit.[3] After this amount is entered, each set of columns should balance.

Computers Do the Pencil-Pushing When a worksheet is prepared by computer, accountants perform only *one* of the steps listed above—*entering the adjustments.* The computer automatically lists the ledger accounts in the form of a trial balance. After the accountant has entered the adjustments, it automatically computes the adjusted account balances and completes the worksheet. (Once the adjusted balances are determined, completing the worksheet involves nothing more than putting these amounts in the appropriate column and determining the column totals.)

[3] To bring the Income Statement columns into balance, net *income* is entered in the *Debit column.* This is because the Credit column (revenue) exceeds the Debit column (expenses). But in the balance sheet, net income is an element of owners' equity, which is represented by a credit. In the event of a net *loss,* this situation reverses.

Exhibit 5–13 THE WORKSHEET

OVERNIGHT AUTO SERVICE
WORKSHEET
FOR THE YEAR ENDED DECEMBER 31, 2011

	Trial Balance		Adjustments*		Adjusted Trial Balance		Income Statement		Balance Sheet	
	Dr	Cr	Dr	Cr	Dr	Cr	Dr	Cr	Dr	Cr
Balance sheet accounts:										
Cash	18,592				18,592				18,592	
Accounts Receivable	6,500		(h) 750		7,250				7,250	
Shop Supplies	1,800			(a) 600	1,200				1,200	
Unexpired Insurance	4,500			(b) 1,500	3,000				3,000	
Land	52,000				52,000				52,000	
Building	36,000				36,000				36,000	
Accumulated Depreciation: Building		1,500		(c) 150		1,650				1,650
Tools and Equipment	12,000				12,000				12,000	
Accumulated Depreciation: Tools and Equipment		2,000		(d) 200		2,200				2,200
Notes Payable		4,000				4,000				4,000
Accounts Payable		2,690				2,690				2,690
Income Taxes Payable		1,560		(i) 4,020		5,580				5,580
Unearned Rent Revenue		9,000	(e) 3,000			6,000				6,000
Capital Stock		80,000				80,000				80,000
Retained Earnings		0				0				0
Dividends	14,000				14,000				14,000	
Wages Payable				(f) 1,950		1,950				1,950
Interest Payable				(g) 30		30				30
Income statement accounts:										
Repair Service Revenue		171,250		(h) 750		172,000		172,000		
Advertising Expense	3,900				3,900		3,900			
Wages Expense	56,800		(f) 1,950		58,750		58,750			
Supplies Expense	6,900		(a) 600		7,500		7,500			
Depreciation Expense: Building	1,500		(c) 150		1,650		1,650			
Depreciation Expense: Tools and Equipment	2,000		(d) 200		2,200		2,200			
Utilities Expense	19,400				19,400		19,400			
Insurance Expense	13,500		(b) 1,500		15,000		15,000			
Income Taxes Expense	22,608		(i) 4,020		26,628		26,628			
Rent Revenue Earned				(e) 3,000		3,000		3,000		
Interest Expense			(g) 30		30		30			
	272,000	272,000	12,200	12,200	279,100	279,100	135,058	175,000	144,042	104,100
Net income							39,942			39,942
Totals							175,000	175,000	144,042	144,042

*Adjustments:

(a) Shop supplies used in December.
(b) Portion of insurance cost expiring in December.
(c) Depreciation on building for December.
(d) Depreciation of tools and equipment for December.
(e) Earned one-third of rent revenue collected in advance from Harbor Cab.
(f) Unpaid wages owed to employees at December 31.
(g) Interest payable accrued during December.
(h) Repair service revenue earned in December but not yet billed.
(i) Income taxes expense for December.

WHAT IF: A SPECIAL APPLICATION OF WORKSHEET SOFTWARE

We have discussed a relatively simple application of the worksheet concept—illustrating the effects of proposed *adjusting entries* on account balances. But the same concept can be applied to proposed *future transactions.* The effects of the proposed transactions simply are entered in the "Adjustments" columns. Thus, without disrupting the accounting records, accountants can prepare schedules showing how the company's financial statements might be affected by such events as a merger with another company, a 15 percent increase in sales volume, or the closure of a plant.

There is a tendency to view worksheets as mechanical and old-fashioned. This is not at all the case. Today, the mechanical aspects are handled entirely by computer. The real purpose of a worksheet is to show quickly and efficiently how specific events or transactions will affect the financial statements. This isn't bookkeeping—it's *planning.*

END-OF-CHAPTER REVIEW

SUMMARY OF LEARNING OBJECTIVES

LO1 **Prepare an income statement, a statement of retained earnings, and a balance sheet.** The financial statements are prepared directly from the adjusted trial balance. The income statement is prepared by reporting all revenue earned during the period, less all expenses incurred in generating the related revenue. The retained earnings statement reports any increase to Retained Earnings resulting from net income earned for the period, as well as any decreases to Retained Earnings resulting from dividends declared or a net loss incurred for the period. The balance sheet reveals the company's financial position by reporting its economic resources (assets) and the claims against those resources (liabilities and owners' equity).

LO2 **Explain how the income statement and the statement of retained earnings relate to the balance sheet.** An income statement shows the revenue and expenses of a business for a specified accounting period. In the statement of retained earnings, the net income figure from the income statement is added to the beginning Retained Earnings balance, while dividends declared during the period are subtracted, in arriving at the ending Retained Earnings balance. The ending Retained Earnings balance is then reported in the balance sheet as a component of owners' equity.

LO3 **Explain the concept of *adequate disclosure.*** Adequate disclosure is the generally accepted accounting principle that financial statements should include any information that an informed user needs to interpret the statements properly. The appropriate disclosures usually are contained in several pages of notes that accompany the statements.

LO4 **Explain the purposes of *closing entries;* prepare these entries.** Closing entries serve two basic purposes. The first is to return the balances of the temporary owners' equity accounts (revenue, expense, and dividends accounts) to zero so that these accounts may be used to measure the activities of the next reporting period. The second purpose of closing entries is to update the balance of the Retained Earnings account. Four closing entries generally are needed: (1) close the revenue accounts to the Income Summary account, (2) close the expense accounts to the Income Summary account, (3) close the balance of the Income Summary account to the Retained Earnings account, and (4) close the Dividends account to the Retained Earnings account.

LO5 **Prepare an after-closing trial balance.** After the revenue and expense accounts have been closed, it is desirable to prepare an after-closing trial balance consisting solely of balance sheet accounts. The after-closing trial balance, or post-closing trial balance, gives assurance that the accounts of the general ledger are in balance and ready for recording transactions for the new accounting period.

LO6 **Use financial statement information to evaluate profitability and liquidity.** Profitability is an increase in stockholders' equity resulting from revenue exceeding expenses, whereas liquidity refers to a company's ability to meet its cash obligations as they come due. Liquidity, at least in the short term, may be *independent* of profitability. Financial statements are useful tools for evaluating both profitability and liquidity. In the Financial Analysis feature, we illustrated several measures of profitability and liquidity computed using financial statement information. Throughout the remainder of this text we introduce and discuss many additional measures.

LO7 **Explain how *interim* financial statements are prepared in a business that closes its accounts only at year-end.** When a business closes its accounts only at year-end, the revenue, expense, and dividends accounts have balances representing the activities of the year-to-date. To prepare an income statement for any period shorter than the year-to-date, we subtract from the current balance in the revenue or expense account the balance in the account as of the beginning of the desired period. This process of subtracting prior balances from the current balance is repeated for each revenue and expense account and for the dividends account. No computations of this type are required for the balance sheet accounts, as a balance sheet is based on the account balances at the balance sheet date.

LO8 **Prepare a worksheet and explain its uses.** A worksheet is a "testing ground" on which the ledger accounts are adjusted, balanced, and arranged in the format of financial statements. A worksheet consists of a trial balance, the end-of-period adjusting entries, an adjusted trial balance, and columns showing the ledger accounts arranged as an income statement and as a balance sheet. The completed worksheet is used as the basis for preparing financial statements and for recording adjusting and closing entries in the formal accounting records.

**Supplemental Topic,* "The Worksheet."

Key Terms Introduced or Emphasized in Chapter 5

adequate disclosure (p. 196) The generally accepted accounting principle of providing with financial statements any information that users need to interpret those statements properly.

after-closing trial balance (p. 203) A trial balance prepared after all closing entries have been made. Consists only of accounts for assets, liabilities, and owners' equity.

closing entries (p. 198) Journal entries made at the end of the period for the purpose of closing temporary accounts (revenue, expense, and dividends accounts) and transferring balances to the Retained Earnings account.

current assets (p. 196) Cash and other assets that can be converted into cash or used up within a relatively short period of time without interfering with normal business operations.

current liabilities (p. 196) Existing obligations that are expected to be satisfied with a company's current assets within a relatively short period of time.

general ledger software (p. 207) Computer software used for recording transactions, maintaining journals and ledgers, and preparing financial statements. Also includes spreadsheet capabilities for showing the effects of proposed adjusting entries or transactions on the financial statements without actually recording these entries in the accounting records.

Income Summary (p. 198) The summary account in the ledger to which revenue and expense accounts are closed at the end of the period. The balance (credit balance for a net income, debit balance for a net loss) is transferred to the Retained Earnings account.

interim financial statements (p. 205) Financial statements prepared for periods of less than one year (includes monthly and quarterly statements).

notes (accompanying financial statements) (p. 197) Supplemental disclosures that accompany financial statements. These notes provide users with various types of information considered necessary for the proper interpretation of the statements.

worksheet (p. 207) A multicolumn schedule showing the relationships among the current account balances (a trial balance), proposed or actual adjusting entries or transactions, and the financial statements that would result if these adjusting entries or transactions were recorded. Used both at the end of the accounting period as an aid to preparing financial statements and for planning purposes.

Demonstration Problem

Jan's Dance Studio, Inc., performs adjusting entries every month, but closes its accounts only at year-end. The studio's year-end *adjusted trial balance* dated December 31, 2011, appears below. (Bear in mind, the balance shown for Retained Earnings was last updated on December 31, *2010*.)

JAN'S DANCE STUDIO, INC.
ADJUSTED TRIAL BALANCE
DECEMBER 31, 2011

Cash	$171,100	
Accounts receivable	9,400	
Prepaid studio rent	3,000	
Unexpired insurance	7,200	
Supplies	500	
Equipment	18,000	
Accumulated depreciation: equipment		$ 7,200
Notes payable		10,000
Accounts payable		3,200
Salaries payable		4,000
Income taxes payable		6,000
Unearned studio revenue		8,800
Capital stock		100,000
Retained earnings		40,000
Dividends	6,000	
Studio revenue earned		165,000
Salary expense	85,000	
Supply expense	3,900	
Rent expense	12,000	
Insurance expense	1,900	
Advertising expense	500	
Depreciation expense: equipment	1,800	
Interest expense	900	
Income taxes expense	23,000	
	$344,200	$344,200

Instructions

a. Prepare an income statement and statement of retained earnings for the year ended December 31, 2011. Also prepare the studio's balance sheet dated December 31, 2011.

b. Prepare the necessary closing entries at December 31, 2011.

c. Prepare an after-closing trial balance dated December 31, 2011.

Solution to the Demonstration Problem

a.

JAN'S DANCE STUDIO, INC.
INCOME STATEMENT
FOR THE YEAR ENDED DECEMBER 31, 2011

Revenue:		
Studio revenue earned		$165,000
Expenses:		
Salary expense	$85,000	
Supply expense	3,900	
Rent expense	12,000	
Insurance expense	1,900	
Advertising expense	500	
Depreciation expense: equipment	1,800	
Interest expense	900	106,000
Income before income taxes		$ 59,000
Income taxes expense		23,000
Net income		$ 36,000

JAN'S DANCE STUDIO, INC.
STATEMENT OF RETAINED EARNINGS
FOR THE YEAR ENDED DECEMBER 31, 2011

Retained earnings, January 1, 2011	$40,000
Add: Net income earned in 2011	36,000
Subtotal	$76,000
Less: Dividends declared in 2011	6,000
Retained earnings, December 31, 2011	$70,000

JAN'S DANCE STUDIO, INC.
BALANCE SHEET
DECEMBER 31, 2011

Assets		
Cash		$171,100
Accounts receivable		9,400
Prepaid studio rent		3,000
Unexpired insurance		7,200
Supplies		500
Equipment	$18,000	
Less: Accumulated depreciation: equipment	7,200	10,800
Total assets		$202,000
Liabilities & Stockholders' Equity		
Liabilities:		
Notes payable		$ 10,000
Accounts payable		3,200
Salaries payable		4,000
Income taxes payable		6,000
Unearned studio revenue		8,800
Total liabilities		$ 32,000
Stockholders' equity:		
Capital stock		$100,000
Retained earnings		70,000
Total stockholders' equity		$170,000
Total liabilities and stockholders' equity		$202,000

b.

JAN'S DANCE STUDIO, INC.
GENERAL JOURNAL
DECEMBER 31, 2011

Date	Account Titles and Explanations	Debit	Credit
Dec. 31			
2011			
1.	Studio Revenue Earned	165,000	
	Income Summary		165,000
	To close Studio Revenue Earned.		
2.	Income Summary	129,000	
	Salary Expense		85,000
	Supply Expense		3,900
	Rent Expense		12,000
	Insurance Expense		1,900
	Advertising Expense		500
	Depreciation Expense: Equipment		1,800
	Interest Expense		900
	Income Taxes Expense		23,000
	To close all expense accounts.		
3.	Income Summary	36,000	
	Retained Earnings		36,000
	To transfer net income earned in 2011 to the Retained Earnings account ($165,000 − $129,000 = $36,000).		
4.	Retained Earnings	6,000	
	Dividends		6,000
	To transfer dividends declared in 2011 to the Retained Earnings account.		

c.

JAN'S DANCE STUDIO, INC.
AFTER-CLOSING TRIAL BALANCE
DECEMBER 31, 2011

Cash	$171,100	
Accounts receivable	9,400	
Prepaid studio rent	3,000	
Unexpired insurance	7,200	
Supplies	500	
Equipment	18,000	
Accumulated depreciation: equipment		$ 7,200
Notes payable		10,000
Accounts payable		3,200
Salaries payable		4,000
Income taxes payable		6,000
Unearned studio revenue		8,800
Capital stock		100,000
Retained earnings, December 31		70,000
	$209,200	$209,200

Self-Test Questions

The answers to these questions appear on page 240.

1. For a publicly owned company, indicate which of the following accounting activities are likely to occur at or shortly after year-end. (More than one answer may be correct.)
   - **a.** Preparation of income tax returns.
   - **b.** Adjusting and closing of the accounts.
   - **c.** Drafting of disclosures that accompany the financial statements.
   - **d.** An audit of the financial statements by an independent CPA firm.
2. Which of the following financial statements is generally prepared first?
   - **a.** Income statement.
   - **b.** Balance sheet.
   - **c.** Statement of retained earnings.
   - **d.** Statement of cash flows.
3. Which of the following accounts would *never* be reported in the income statement as an expense?
   - **a.** Depreciation expense.
   - **b.** Income taxes expense.
   - **c.** Interest expense.
   - **d.** Dividends expense.
4. Which of the following accounts would *never* appear in the after-closing trial balance? (More than one answer may be correct.)
   - **a.** Unearned revenue.
   - **b.** Dividends.
   - **c.** Accumulated depreciation.
   - **d.** Income taxes expense.
5. Which of the following journal entries is required to close the Income Summary account of a profitable company?
   - **a.** Debit Income Summary, credit Retained Earnings.
   - **b.** Credit Income Summary, debit Retained Earnings.
   - **c.** Debit Income Summary, credit Capital Stock.
   - **d.** Credit Income Summary, debit Capital Stock.
6. Indicate those items for which generally accepted accounting principles *require* disclosure in notes accompanying the financial statements. (More than one answer may be correct.)
   - **a.** A large lawsuit was filed against the company two days *after* the balance sheet date.
   - **b.** The depreciation method in use, given that several different methods are acceptable under generally accepted accounting principles.
   - **c.** Whether small but long-lived items—such as electric pencil sharpeners and handheld calculators—are charged to asset accounts or to expense accounts.
   - **d.** As of year-end, the chief executive officer had been hospitalized because of chest pains.
7. Ski West adjusts its accounts at the end of each month but closes them only at the end of the calendar year (December 31). The ending balances in the Equipment Rental Revenue account and the Cash account in February and March appear below.

	Feb. 28	Mar. 31
Cash	$14,200	$26,500
Equipment rental revenue	12,100	18,400

   Ski West prepares financial statements showing separately the operating results of each month. In the financial statements prepared for the *month* ended March 31, Equipment Rental Revenue and Cash should appear as follows:
   - **a.** Equipment Rental Revenue, $18,400; Cash, $26,500.
   - **b.** Equipment Rental Revenue, $18,400; Cash, $12,300.
   - **c.** Equipment Rental Revenue, $6,300; Cash, $26,500.
   - **d.** Equipment Rental Revenue, $6,300; Cash, $12,300.
8. Which of the following accounts is *not* closed to the Income Summary account at the end of the accounting period? (More than one answer may be correct.)
   - **a.** Rent Expense.
   - **b.** Accumulated Depreciation.
   - **c.** Unearned Revenue.
   - **d.** Supplies Expense.

ASSIGNMENT MATERIAL Discussion Questions

1. Explain briefly the items generally included in a company's annual report. (You may use the financial statements appearing in Appendix A to support your answer.)
2. Some people think that a company's retained earnings represent *cash* reserved for the payment of dividends. Are they correct? Explain.
3. Discuss the relationship among the income statement, the statement of retained earnings, and the balance sheet.
4. Identify several items that may require disclosure in the notes that accompany financial statements.
5. What type of accounts are referred to as *temporary* or *nominal* accounts? What is meant by these terms?

6. What type of accounts are referred to as *permanent* or *real* accounts? What is meant by these terms?
7. Explain *why* the Dividends account is closed directly to the Retained Earnings account.
8. Which accounts appear in a company's after-closing trial balance? How do these accounts differ from those reported in an adjusted trial balance?
9. Can a company be profitable but not liquid? Explain.
10. What are interim financial statements? Do accounts that appear in a company's interim balance sheet require any special computations to be reported correctly? Explain.
11. Explain the accounting principle of *adequate disclosure.*
12. How does depreciation expense differ from other operating expenses?
13. Explain the need for closing entries and describe the process by which temporary owners' equity accounts are closed at year-end.
14. Explain the significance of measuring a company's *return on equity.*
*15. Explain several purposes that may be served by preparing a worksheet (or using computer software that achieves the goals of a worksheet).

**Supplemental Topic,* "The Worksheet."

Brief Exercises

LO1 LO2 **BRIEF EXERCISE 5.1** Balancing the Accounting Equation

During the current year, the total assets of Mifflinburg Corporation decreased by $60,000 and total liabilities decreased by $300,000. The company issued $100,000 of new stock, and its net income for the year was $250,000. No other changes to stockholders' equity occurred during the year. Determine the dollar amount of dividends declared by the company during the year.

LO1 LO2 **BRIEF EXERCISE 5.2** Income Statement and Balance Sheet Relationships

On December 1, 2011, Millstone Corporation invested $45,000 in a new delivery truck. The truck is being depreciated at a monthly rate of $500. During 2011, the company issued stock for $60,000 and declared dividends of $5,000. Its net income in 2011 was $70,000. Millstone's *ending* Retained Earnings balance as reported in its December 31, 2011, balance sheet was $90,000. Its beginning Capital Stock balance on January 1, 2011, was $200,000. Given this information, determine the total stockholders' equity reported in the company's balance sheet dated December 31, 2011.

LO1 LO2 **BRIEF EXERCISE 5.3** Classifying Balance Sheet Accounts

Indicate in which section of the balance sheet each of the following accounts is *classified.* Use the symbols **CA** for current assets, **NCA** for noncurrent assets, **CL** for current liabilities, **LTL** for long-term liabilities, and **SHE** for stockholders' equity.

a. Prepaid Rent
b. Dividends Payable
c. Salaries Payable
d. Accumulated Depreciation: Equipment
e. Retained Earnings
f. Mortgage Payable (due in 15 years)
g. Unearned Service Revenue
h. Accounts Receivable
i. Land
j. Office Supplies

LO4 **BRIEF EXERCISE 5.4** Identifying and Closing Temporary Accounts

Indicate whether a debit or credit is required to *close* each of the following accounts. Use the symbols **D** if a debit is required, **C** if a credit is required, and **N** if the account is *not* closed at the end of the period.

a. Salary Expense
b. Unexpired Insurance
c. Consulting Fees Earned
d. Depreciation Expense
e. Dividends
f. Retained Earnings
g. Interest Revenue
h. Accumulated Depreciation
i. Income Taxes Expense
j. Unearned Revenue
k. Income Summary (of a *profitable* company)
l. Income Summary (of an *unprofitable* company)

LO4 BRIEF EXERCISE 5.5

Closing Entries of a Profitable Company

The following account balances were taken from Cal Tour Corporation's year-end *adjusted* trial balance (assume these are the company's only *temporary* accounts):

Dividends	$ 600
Service revenue	19,800
Supplies expense	525
Rent expense	3,660
Depreciation expense: equipment	1,200
Salaries expense	12,700
Income taxes expense	615

Prepare the company's necessary closing entries.

LO4 BRIEF EXERCISE 5.6

Closing Entries of an Unprofitable Company

The following account balances were taken from Jachobson Consulting's year-end *adjusted* trial balance (assume these are the company's only *temporary* accounts):

Consulting fees earned	$26,000
Interest revenue	300
Insurance expense	1,900
Rent expense	10,800
Depreciation expense: office equipment	5,600
Salaries expense	16,400
Dividends	400

Prepare the company's necessary closing entries.

LO5 BRIEF EXERCISE 5.7

After-Closing Trial Balance

Indicate whether each of the following accounts appears in the debit column or in the credit column of an *after-closing* trial balance. Use the symbols **D** for debit column, **C** for credit column, and **N** if the account does *not* appear in an after-closing trial balance.

a. Unearned Service Revenue
b. Accumulated Depreciation: Office Equipment
c. Land
d. Consulting Fees Earned
e. Capital Stock
f. Income Summary (of a *profitable* company)
g. Depreciation Expense: Office Equipment
h. Income Taxes Payable
i. Unexpired Insurance
j. Dividends
k. Retained Earnings
l. Dividends Payable

LO6 BRIEF EXERCISE 5.8

Profitability and Liquidity Measures

Dog Daze, Inc., has provided the following information from its most current financial statements:

Total revenue	$60,000
Total expenses	45,000
Total current assets	16,000
Total current liabilities	4,000
Total stockholders' equity, January 1, 2011	37,000
Total stockholders' equity, December 31, 2011	38,000

a. Compute the company's net income percentage in 2011.

b. Compute the company's return on equity in 2011.

c. Compute the company's current ratio at December 31, 2011.

LO7 **BRIEF EXERCISE 5.9**
Measuring Interim Revenue

The following revenue figures were taken from Rosemont Corporation's adjusted trial balance at the end of the following months (adjusting entries are performed *monthly* whereas closing entries are performed *annually*, on December 31):

March 31 (end of the first quarter)	$140,000
September 30 (end of the third quarter)	450,000
December 31 (end of the fourth quarter)	680,000

Compute how much revenue the company earned from:

a. April 1 through September 30.

b. October 1 through December 31 (the fourth quarter).

c. April 1 through December 31.

LO8 ***BRIEF EXERCISE 5.10**
The Worksheet

Accountants at Warner Co. use worksheets similar to the one shown in Exhibit 5–13, on page 209. In the company's most current year-end worksheet, the amounts transferred *from* the adjusted trial balance columns *to* the balance sheet and income statement columns are as follows:

Total amount transferred to the credit column of the balance sheet	$410,000
Total amount transferred to the debit column of the balance sheet	540,000
Total amount transferred to the credit column of the income statement	380,000

a. What was the company's net income for the year?

b. What was the total amount transferred from the adjusted trial balance columns to the debit column of the income statement?

Exercises

connect ACCOUNTING

LO1 through LO7 **EXERCISE 5.1**
Accounting Terminology

Listed below are nine technical terms used in this chapter:

Liquidity	Nominal accounts	Real accounts
Adequate disclosure	After-closing trial balance	Closing entries
Income summary	Interim financial statements	Dividends

Each of the following statements may (or may not) describe one of these technical terms. For each statement, indicate the accounting term described, or answer "None" if the statement does not describe any of the items.

a. The accounting principle intended to assist users in *interpreting* financial statements.

b. A term used to describe a company's ability to pay its obligations as they come due.

c. A term used in reference to accounts that are closed at year-end.

d. A term used in reference to accounts that are not closed at year-end.

e. A document prepared to assist management in detecting whether any errors occurred in posting the closing entries.

f. A policy decision by a corporation to distribute a portion of its income to stockholders.

g. The process by which the Retained Earnings account is updated at year-end.

h. Entries made during the accounting period to correct errors in the original recording of complex transactions.

Supplemental Topic, "The Worksheet."

LO1 LO2 LO6

EXERCISE 5.2

Financial Statement Preparation

Tutors for Rent, Inc., performs adjusting entries every month, but closes its accounts *only at year-end.* The company's year-end *adjusted trial balance* dated December 31, 2011, was:

TUTORS FOR RENT, INC.
ADJUSTED TRIAL BALANCE
DECEMBER 31, 2011

Cash	$ 91,100	
Accounts receivable	4,500	
Supplies	300	
Equipment	12,000	
Accumulated depreciation: equipment		$ 5,000
Accounts payable		1,500
Income taxes payable		3,500
Capital stock		25,000
Retained earnings		45,000
Dividends	2,000	
Tutoring revenue earned		96,000
Salary expense	52,000	
Supply expense	1,200	
Advertising expense	300	
Depreciation expense: equipment	1,000	
Income taxes expense	11,600	
	$176,000	$176,000

a. Prepare an income statement and statement of retained earnings for the year ended December 31, 2011. Also prepare the company's balance sheet dated December 31, 2011.

b. Does the company appear to be liquid? Defend your answer.

c. Has the company been profitable in the past? Explain.

LO1 LO2 LO6

EXERCISE 5.3

Financial Statement Preparation

Wilderness Guide Services, Inc., performs adjusting entries every month, but closes its accounts *only at year-end.* The company's year-end *adjusted trial balance* dated December 31, 2011, follows:

WILDERNESS GUIDE SERVICES, INC.
ADJUSTED TRIAL BALANCE
DECEMBER 31, 2011

Cash	$ 12,200	
Accounts receivable	31,000	
Camping supplies	7,900	
Unexpired insurance policies	2,400	
Equipment	70,000	
Accumulated depreciation: equipment		$ 60,000
Notes payable (due 4/1/12)		18,000
Accounts payable		9,500
Capital stock		25,000
Retained earnings		15,000
Dividends	1,000	
Guide revenue earned		102,000
Salary expense	87,500	
Camping supply expense	1,200	
Insurance expense	9,600	
Depreciation expense: equipment	5,000	
Interest expense	1,700	
	$229,500	$229,500

a. Prepare an income statement and statement of retained earnings for the year ended December 31, 2011. Also prepare the company's balance sheet dated December 31, 2011. (Hint: Unprofitable companies have no income taxes expense.)

b. Does the company appear to be liquid? Defend your answer.

c. Has the company been profitable in the past? Explain.

LO2 LO4 LO5

EXERCISE 5.4
Preparing Closing Entries and an After-Closing Trial Balance

Refer to the adjusted trial balance of Tutors for Rent, Inc., illustrated in Exercise 5.2 to respond to the following items:

a. Prepare all necessary closing entries at December 31, 2011.

b. Prepare an after-closing trial balance dated December 31, 2011.

c. Compare the Retained Earnings balance reported in the after-closing trial balance prepared in part **b** to the balance reported in the adjusted trial balance. Explain *why* the two balances are different. (Include in your explanation why the balance reported in the after-closing trial balance has increased or decreased subsequent to the closing process.)

LO2 LO4 LO5

EXERCISE 5.5
Preparing Closing Entries and an After-Closing Trial Balance

Refer to the adjusted trial balance of Wilderness Guide Services, Inc., illustrated in Exercise 5.3 to respond to the following items:

a. Prepare all necessary closing entries at December 31, 2011.

b. Prepare an after-closing trial balance dated December 31, 2011.

c. Compare the Retained Earnings balance reported in the after-closing trial balance prepared in part **b** to the balance reported in the adjusted trial balance. Explain *why* the two balances are different. (Include in your explanation why the balance reported in the after-closing trial balance has increased or decreased subsequent to the closing process.)

LO3

EXERCISE 5.6
Adequate Disclosure

The following information was taken directly from the footnotes to the financial statements of **Best Buy**:

1. "We recognize revenue at the time the customer takes possession of the merchandise."

2. "We sell gift cards to customers and initially establish an Unredeemed Gift Card Liability for the cash value of the gift card."

3. "Advertising costs are recorded as expenses the first time the advertisement runs."

4. "We compute depreciation using the straight-line method."

a. Discuss what is meant by each of the above footnote items.

b. As noted, **Best Buy** uses a Unredeemed Gift Card Liability account to record the sale of gift cards. Assume that you purchase a $500 gift card from **Best Buy** as a birthday present for a friend. Prepare the journal entries made by **Best Buy** to record (1) your purchase of the gift card and (2) the *use* of the gift card by your friend to purchase a $500 television.

c. Discuss how the *matching principle* relates to **Best Buy**'s treatment of advertising expenditures.

LO2 LO4

EXERCISE 5.7
Closing Entries of a Profitable Company

Gerdes Psychological Services, Inc., closes its temporary accounts once each year on December 31. The company recently issued the following income statement as part of its annual report:

GERDES PSYCHOLOGICAL SERVICES, INC.
INCOME STATEMENT
FOR THE YEAR ENDED DECEMBER 31, 2011

Revenue:		
Counseling revenue		$225,000
Expenses:		
Advertising expense	$ 1,800	
Salaries expense	94,000	
Office supplies expense	1,200	
Utilities expense	850	
Malpractice insurance expense	6,000	
Office rent expense	24,000	
Continuing education expense	2,650	
Depreciation expense: fixtures	4,500	
Miscellaneous expense	6,000	
Income taxes expense	29,400	170,400
Net income		$ 54,600

The firm's statement of retained earnings indicates that a $6,000 cash dividend was declared and paid during 2011.

a. Prepare the necessary closing entries on December 31, 2011.

b. If the firm's Retained Earnings account had a $92,000 balance on January 1, 2011, at what amount should Retained Earnings be reported in the firm's balance sheet dated December 31, 2011?

LO2 LO4 **EXERCISE 5.8**
Closing Entries of an Unprofitable Company

Ferraro Consulting provides risk management services to individuals and to corporate clients. The company closes its temporary accounts once each year on December 31. The company recently issued the following income statement as part of its annual report:

FERRARO CONSULTING
INCOME STATEMENT
FOR THE YEAR ENDED DECEMBER 31, 2011

Revenue:		
Consulting revenue—individual clients		$ 40,000
Consulting revenue—corporate clients		160,000
		$200,000
Expenses:		
Advertising expense	$ 16,000	
Depreciation expense: computers	24,000	
Rent expense	9,600	
Office supplies expense	4,400	
Travel expense	57,800	
Utilities expense	3,300	
Telephone and Internet expense	1,900	
Salaries expense	155,500	
Interest expense	2,500	275,000
Net loss		$ (75,000)

The firm's statement of retained earnings indicates that a $25,000 cash dividend was declared and paid in 2011.

a. Prepare the necessary closing entries on December 31, 2011.

b. If the firm's Retained Earnings account had a $300,000 balance on January 1, 2011, at what amount should Retained Earnings be reported in the firm's balance sheet dated December 31, 2011?

LO2 LO4 **EXERCISE 5.9**
Distinction between the Adjusting and the Closing Process

When Torretti Company began business on August 1, it purchased a one-year fire insurance policy and debited the entire cost of $7,200 to Unexpired Insurance. Torretti *adjusts* its accounts at the end of each month and *closes* its books at the end of the year.

a. Give the *adjusting entry* required at December 31 with respect to this insurance policy.

b. Give the *closing entry* required at December 31 with respect to insurance expense. Assume that this policy is the only insurance policy Torretti had during the year.

c. Compare the dollar amount appearing in the December 31 adjusting entry (part **a**) with that in the closing entry (part **b**). Are the dollar amounts the same? Why or why not? Explain.

LO6 **EXERCISE 5.10**
Measuring and Evaluating Profitability and Liquidity

A recent balance sheet of Oregon Foods is provided below:

OREGON FOODS
BALANCE SHEET
DECEMBER 31, 2011

Assets		
Cash		$ 6,800
Accounts receivable		7,200
Office supplies		300
Prepaid rent		1,700
Equipment	$12,000	
Accumulated depreciation: equipment	(4,800)	$ 7,200
Total assets		$23,200
Liabilities		
Accounts payable		$ 2,200
Income taxes payable		1,800
Total liabilities		$ 4,000
Stockholders' Equity		
Capital stock		$10,000
Retained earnings		9,200
Total stockholders' equity		$19,200
Total liabilities and stockholders' equity		$23,200

Other information provided by the company is as follows:

Total revenue for the year ended December 31, 2011	$25,500
Total expenses for the year ended December 31, 2011	20,400
Total stockholders' equity, January 1, 2011	14,800

Compute and discuss briefly the significance of the following measures as they relate to Oregon Foods:

a. Net income percentage in 2011.
b. Return on equity in 2011.
c. Working capital on December 31, 2011.
d. Current ratio on December 31, 2011.

LO6 **EXERCISE 5.11**
Measuring and Evaluating Profitability and Liquidity

A recent balance sheet of Denver Tours is provided below:

DENVER TOURS
BALANCE SHEET
DECEMBER 31, 2011

Assets		
Cash		$ 75,100
Accounts receivable		14,000
Office supplies		1,500
Prepaid rent		3,400
Buses	$ 240,000	
Accumulated depreciation: buses	(18,000)	$222,000
Total assets		$316,000
Liabilities		
Accounts payable		$140,200
Unearned revenue		94,800
Total liabilities		$235,000
Stockholders' Equity		
Capital stock		$ 80,000
Retained earnings		1,000
Total stockholders' equity		$ 81,000
Total liabilities and stockholders' equity		$316,000

Other information provided by the company is as follows:

Total revenue for the year ended December 31, 2011	$152,000
Total expenses for the year ended December 31, 2011	148,960
Total stockholders' equity, January 1, 2011	79,000

Compute and discuss briefly the significance of the following measures as they relate to Denver Tours:

a. Net income percentage in 2011.
b. Return on equity in 2011.
c. Working capital on December 31, 2011.
d. Current ratio on December 31, 2011.

LO1 LO2 LO7

EXERCISE 5.12

Interim Results

Ski Powder Resort ends its fiscal year on April 30. The business adjusts its accounts monthly, but *closes them only at year-end* (April 30). The resort's busy season is from December 1 through March 31.

Adrian Pride, the resort's chief financial officer, keeps a close watch on Lift Ticket Revenue and Cash. The balances of these accounts at the end of each of the last five months are as follows:

	Lift Ticket Revenue	Cash
November 30	$ 30,000	$ 9,000
December 31	200,000	59,000
January 31	640,000	94,000
February 28	850,000	116,000
March 31	990,000	138,000

Mr. Pride prepares income statements and balance sheets for the resort. Indicate what amounts will be shown in these statements for (1) Lift Ticket Revenue and (2) Cash, assuming they are prepared for:

a. The *month* ended February 28.

b. The entire "busy season to date"—that is, December 1 through March 31.

c. In terms of Lift Ticket Revenue and increases in Cash, which has been the resort's best month? (Indicate the dollar amounts.)

LO1 LO2 LO7

EXERCISE 5.13

Interim Results

Custodian Commandos, Inc., provides janitorial services to public school systems. The business adjusts its accounts monthly, but *closes them only at year-end.* Its fiscal year ends on December 31.

A summary of the company's total revenue and expenses at the end of five selected months is as follows:

	Total Revenue	Total Expenses
March 31	$ 69,000	$ 48,000
June 30	129,000	90,000
August 31	134,000	115,000
September 30	159,000	130,000
December 31	249,000	175,000

a. Rank the company's fiscal quarters from most profitable to least profitable.

b. Compute the company's income for the month of September.

c. Compute the company's net income (or loss) for the first two months of the *third quarter.* Provide a possible explanation why profitability for the first two months of the third quarter differs significantly from profitability achieved in the third month of the quarter (as computed in part **b**).

LO2 LO3

EXERCISE 5.14

Understanding the Effects of Errors on the Financial Statements

Indicate the effect of the following errors on each of the financial statement elements described in the column headings in the table below. Use the following symbols: **O** = overstated, **U** = understated, and **NE** = no effect.

Error	Net Income	Total Assets	Total Liabilities	Retained Earnings
a. Recorded a dividend as an *expense* in the income statement.				
b. Recorded unearned revenue as *earned* revenue in the income statement.				
c. Failed to record accrued wages payable at the end of the accounting period.				
d. Recorded a declared but unpaid dividend by debiting Dividends and crediting Cash.				
e. Failed to disclose a pending lawsuit in the notes accompanying the financial statements.				

LO3 LO6

EXERCISE 5.15

Examining **Home Depot, Inc.**, Financial Statements

The **Home Depot, Inc.**, financial statements appear in Appendix A at the end of this textbook.

a. Does the company use straight-line depreciation? How can you tell?

b. At what point does the company recognize and record revenue from its customers?

c. Using information from the consolidated financial statements, evaluate briefly the company's profitability and liquidity.

Problem Set A

LO1 LO2 LO4 LO6

PROBLEM 5.1A

Correcting Classification Errors

Party Wagon, Inc., provides musical entertainment at weddings, dances, and various other functions. The company performs adjusting entries *monthly,* but prepares closing entries *annually* on December 31. The company recently hired Jack Armstrong as its new accountant. Jack's first assignment was to prepare an income statement, a statement of retained earnings, and a balance sheet using an *adjusted* trial balance given to him by his predecessor, dated December 31, 2011.

From the adjusted trial balance, Jack prepared the following set of financial statements:

PARTY WAGON, INC.
INCOME STATEMENT
FOR THE YEAR ENDED DECEMBER 31, 2011

Revenue:		
Party revenue earned		$130,000
Unearned party revenue		1,800
Accounts receivable		9,000
Total revenue		$140,800
Expenses:		
Insurance expense	$ 1,800	
Office rent expense	12,000	
Supplies expense	1,200	
Dividends	1,000	
Salary expense	75,000	
Accumulated depreciation: van	16,000	
Accumulated depreciation: equipment and music	14,000	
Repair and maintenance expense	2,000	
Travel expense	6,000	
Miscellaneous expense	3,600	
Interest expense	4,400	137,000
Income before income taxes		$ 3,800
Income taxes payable		400
Net income		$ 3,400

PARTY WAGON, INC.
STATEMENT OF RETAINED EARNINGS
FOR THE YEAR ENDED DECEMBER 31, 2011

Retained earnings (per adjusted trial balance)	$15,000
Add: Income	3,400
Less: Income taxes expense	2,000
Retained earnings Dec. 31, 2011	$16,400

PARTY WAGON, INC.
BALANCE SHEET
DECEMBER 31, 2011

Assets		
Cash		$15,000
Supplies		500
Van	$40,000	
Less: Depreciation expense: van	8,000	32,000
Equipment and music	$35,000	
Less: Depreciation expense: music and equipment	7,000	28,000
Total assets		$75,500
Liabilities & Stockholders' Equity		
Liabilities:		
Accounts payable		$ 7,000
Notes payable		39,000
Salaries payable		1,600
Prepaid rent		2,000
Unexpired insurance		4,500
Total liabilities		$54,100
Stockholders' Equity:		
Capital stock		5,000
Retained earnings		16,400
Total stockholders' equity		$21,400
Total liabilities and stockholders' equity		$75,500

Instructions

a. Prepare a corrected set of financial statements dated December 31, 2011. (You may assume that all of the figures in the company's adjusted trial balance were reported correctly except for Interest Payable of $200, which was mistakenly omitted in the financial statements prepared by Jack.)

b. Prepare the necessary year-end closing entries.

c. Using the financial statements prepared in part **a,** briefly evaluate the company's profitability and liquidity.

LO1 LO2 LO4 through LO6

PROBLEM 5.2A
Preparing Financial Statements and Closing Entries of a Profitable Company

Lawn Pride, Inc., provides lawn-mowing services to both commercial and residential customers. The company performs adjusting entries on a *monthly* basis, whereas closing entries are prepared *annually* at December 31. An *adjusted* trial balance dated December 31, 2011, follows.

LAWN PRIDE, INC.
ADJUSTED TRIAL BALANCE
DECEMBER 31, 2011

	Debits	Credits
Cash	$ 58,525	
Accounts receivable	4,800	
Unexpired insurance	8,000	
Prepaid rent	3,000	
Supplies	1,075	
Trucks	150,000	
Accumulated depreciation: trucks		$120,000
Mowing equipment	20,000	
Accumulated depreciation: mowing equipment		12,000
Accounts payable		1,500
Notes payable		50,000
Salaries payable		900
Interest payable		150
Income taxes payable		1,050
Unearned mowing revenue		900
Capital stock		20,000
Retained earnings		30,000
Dividends	5,000	
Mowing revenue earned		170,000
Insurance expense	2,400	
Office rent expense	36,000	
Supplies expense	5,200	
Salary expense	60,000	
Depreciation expense: trucks	30,000	
Depreciation expense: mowing equipment	4,000	
Repair and maintenance expense	3,000	
Fuel expense	1,500	
Miscellaneous expense	5,000	
Interest expense	3,000	
Income taxes expense	6,000	
	$406,500	$406,500

Instructions

a. Prepare an income statement and statement of retained earnings for the year ended December 31, 2011. Also prepare the company's balance sheet dated December 31, 2011.

b. Prepare the necessary year-end closing entries.

c. Prepare an after-closing trial balance.

d. Using the financial statements prepared in part **a,** briefly evaluate the company's profitability and liquidity.

LO1 through LO4 LO6

PROBLEM 5.3A

Preparing Financial Statements and Closing Entries of an Unprofitable Company

eXcel

Mystic Masters, Inc., provides fortune-telling services over the Internet. In recent years the company has experienced severe financial difficulty. Its accountant prepares adjusting entries on a *monthly* basis, and closing entries on an *annual* basis, at December 31. An *adjusted* trial balance dated December 31, 2011, follows.

MYSTIC MASTERS, INC.
ADJUSTED TRIAL BALANCE
DECEMBER 31, 2011

	Debits	Credits
Cash	$ 960	
Accounts receivable	300	
Unexpired insurance	2,000	
Prepaid rent	1,500	
Supplies	200	
Furniture and fixtures	8,400	
Accumulated depreciation: furniture and fixtures		$ 5,200
Accounts payable		6,540
Notes payable		24,000
Salaries payable		1,700
Interest payable		360
Unearned client revenue		200
Capital stock		4,000
Retained earnings		2,600
Client revenue earned		52,000
Insurance expense	6,000	
Office rent expense	9,000	
Supplies expense	440	
Salary expense	48,000	
Depreciation expense: furniture and fixtures	1,400	
Office and telephone expense	3,000	
Internet service expense	4,900	
Legal expense	1,500	
Interest expense	4,000	
Miscellaneous expense	5,000	
	$96,600	$96,600

Instructions

a. Prepare an income statement and statement of retained earnings for the year ended December 31, 2011. Also prepare the company's balance sheet dated December 31, 2011. (Hint: The company incurred no income taxes expense in 2011.)

b. Prepare the necessary year-end closing entries.

c. Prepare an after-closing trial balance.

d. Using the financial statements prepared in part **a,** briefly evaluate the company's performance.

e. Identify information that the company is apt to disclose in the notes that accompany the financial statements prepared in part **a.**

LO1 LO2 LO7

PROBLEM 5.4A
Interim Financial Statements

Guardian Insurance Agency adjusts its accounts monthly but closes them only at the end of the calendar year. Below are the adjusted balances of the revenue and expense accounts at September 30 of the current year and at the ends of two earlier months:

	Sept. 30	Aug. 31	June 30
Commissions earned	$144,000	$128,000	$90,000
Advertising expense	28,000	23,000	15,000
Salaries expense	36,000	32,000	24,000
Rent expense	22,500	20,000	15,000
Depreciation expense	2,700	2,400	1,800

Instructions

a. Prepare a three-column income statement, showing net income for three separate time periods, all of which end on September 30. Use the format illustrated below. Show supporting computations for the amounts of revenue reported in the first two columns.

GUARDIAN INSURANCE AGENCY
INCOME STATEMENT
FOR THE FOLLOWING TIME PERIODS

	Month Ended Sept. 30	Quarter Ended Sept. 30	9 Months Ended Sept. 30
Revenue:			
Commissions earned	$	$	$
Expenses:			

b. Briefly explain how you determined the dollar amounts for each of the three time periods. Would you apply the same process to the balances in Guardian's balance sheet accounts? Explain.

c. Assume that Guardian adjusts *and closes* its accounts at the end of *each month.* Briefly explain how you then would determine the revenue and expenses that would appear in each of the three columns of the income statement prepared in part **a.**

LO1 through LO4 LO6

PROBLEM 5.5A
Short Comprehensive Problem Including Both Adjusting and Closing Entries

Silver Lining, Inc., provides investment advisory services. The company adjusts its accounts *monthly,* but performs closing entries *annually* on December 31. The firm's *unadjusted* trial balance dated December 31, 2011, is shown on the following page.

SILVER LINING, INC.
UNADJUSTED TRIAL BALANCE
DECEMBER 31, 2011

	Debit	Credit
Cash	$ 42,835	
Accounts receivable	2,000	
Office supplies	205	
Prepaid rent	1,200	
Unexpired insurance	270	
Office equipment	54,000	
Accumulated depreciation: office equipment		$ 35,250
Accounts payable		1,400
Interest payable		360
Income taxes payable		1,750
Notes payable		9,000
Unearned consulting services revenue		3,500
Capital stock		30,000
Retained earnings		8,000
Dividends	1,000	
Consulting services revenue		60,000
Office supplies expense	605	
Depreciation expense: office equipment	8,250	
Rent expense	3,525	
Insurance expense	1,010	
Salaries expense	27,100	
Interest expense	360	
Income taxes expense	6,900	
Totals	$149,260	$149,260

Other Data

1. Accrued but *unrecorded* and uncollected consulting services revenue totals $1,500 at December 31, 2011.
2. The company determined that $2,500 of previously unearned consulting services revenue had been earned at December 31, 2011.
3. Office supplies on hand at December 31 total $110.
4. The company purchased all of its equipment when it first began business. At that time, the estimated useful life of the equipment was six years (72 months).
5. The company prepaid its six-month rent agreement on October 1, 2011.
6. The company prepaid its 12-month insurance policy on March 1, 2011.
7. Accrued but *unpaid* salaries total $1,900 at December 31, 2011.
8. On June 1, 2011, the company borrowed $9,000 by signing a nine-month, 8 percent note payable. The entire amount, plus interest, is due on March 1, 2012.
9. The company's CPA estimates that income taxes expense for the *entire year* is $7,500. The unpaid portion of this amount is due early in 2012.

Instructions

a. Prepare the necessary adjusting journal entries on December 31, 2011. Prepare also an *adjusted trial balance* dated December 31, 2011.

b. From the adjusted trial balance prepared in part **a,** prepare an income statement and statement of retained earnings for the year ended December 31, 2011. Also prepare the company's balance sheet dated December 31, 2011.

c. Prepare the necessary year-end closing entries.

d. Prepare an after-closing trial balance.

e. Compute the company's average *monthly* insurance expense for January and February of 2011.

f. Compute the company's average *monthly* rent expense for January through September of 2011.

g. If the company purchased all of its office equipment when it first incorporated, for how long has it been in business as of December 31, 2011?

LO1 through LO4 LO6

PROBLEM 5.6A
Short Comprehensive Problem Including Both Adjusting and Closing Entries

Brushstroke Art Studio, Inc., provides quality instruction to aspiring artists. The business adjusts its accounts *monthly,* but performs closing entries *annually* on December 31. This is the studio's *unadjusted* trial balance dated December 31, 2011.

BRUSHSTROKE ART STUDIO, INC.
UNADJUSTED TRIAL BALANCE
DECEMBER 31, 2011

	Debits	Credits
Cash	$ 22,380	
Client fees receivable	71,250	
Supplies	6,000	
Prepaid studio rent	2,500	
Studio equipment	96,000	
Accumulated depreciation: studio equipment		$ 52,000
Accounts payable		6,420
Note payable		24,000
Interest payable		480
Unearned client fees		8,000
Income taxes payable		5,000
Capital stock		50,000
Retained earnings		20,000
Client fees earned		82,310
Supplies expense	4,000	
Salary expense	17,250	
Interest expense	480	
Studio rent expense	11,250	
Utilities expense	3,300	
Depreciation expense: studio equipment	8,800	
Income taxes expense	5,000	
	$248,210	$248,210

Other Data

1. Supplies on hand at December 31, 2011, total $1,000.
2. The studio pays rent quarterly (every three months). The last payment was made November 1, 2011. The next payment will be made early in February 2012.
3. Studio equipment is being depreciated over 120 months (10 years).

4. On October 1, 2011, the studio borrowed $24,000 by signing a 12-month, 12 percent note payable. The entire amount, plus interest, is due on September 30, 2012.
5. At December 31, 2011, $3,000 of previously unearned client fees had been *earned.*
6. Accrued, but *unrecorded* and uncollected client fees earned total $690 at December 31, 2011.
7. Accrued, but *unrecorded* and unpaid salary expense totals $750 at December 31, 2011.
8. Accrued income taxes expense for the *entire year* ending December 31, 2011, *total* $7,000. The full amount is due early in 2012.

Instructions

a. Prepare the necessary adjusting journal entries on December 31, 2011. Prepare also an *adjusted trial balance* dated December 31, 2011.

b. From the adjusted trial balance prepared in part **a,** prepare an income statement and statement of retained earnings for the year ended December 31, 2011. Also prepare the company's balance sheet dated December 31, 2011.

c. Prepare the necessary year-end closing entries.

d. Prepare an after-closing trial balance.

e. Has the studio's monthly rent remained the same throughout the year? If not, has it gone up or down? Explain.

LO8 ***PROBLEM 5.7A**
Short Comprehensive Problem Including Adjusting Entries, Closing Entries, and Worksheet Preparation

Refer to the Demonstration Problem illustrated in the previous chapter on pages 161–164. Prepare a 10-column worksheet for Internet Consulting Service, Inc., dated December 31, 2011. At the bottom of your worksheet, prepare a brief explanation keyed to each adjusting entry.

LO6 **PROBLEM 5.8A**
Evaluating Profitability and Liquidity

eXcel

A recent annual report issued by **Best Buy** revealed the following data:

	End of Year	Beginning of Year
Current assets	$8.2 billion	$7.3 billion
Current liabilities	$8.4 billion	$6.8 billion
Stockholders' equity	$4.6 billion	$4.5 billion

The company's income statement reported total annual revenue of $45.0 billion and net income for the year of $1.0 billion.

Instructions

a. Evaluate **Best Buy**'s profitability by computing its net income percentage and its return on equity for the year.

b. Evaluate **Best Buy**'s liquidity by computing its working capital and its current ratio at the beginning of the year and at the end of the year.

c. Does **Best Buy** appear to be both profitable and liquid? Explain.

**Supplemental Topic,* "The Worksheet."

Problem Set B

LO1 LO2 LO4 LO6

PROBLEM 5.1B
Correcting Classification Errors

Strong Knot, Inc., a service company, performs adjusting entries *monthly,* but prepares closing entries *annually* on December 31. The company recently hired Sally Addsup as its new accountant. Sally's first assignment was to prepare an income statement, a statement of retained earnings, and a balance sheet using an *adjusted* trial balance given to her by her predecessor, dated December 31, 2011. The statements Sally prepared are as follows:

STRONG KNOT, INC.
INCOME STATEMENT
FOR THE YEAR ENDED DECEMBER 31, 2011

Revenue:		
Service revenue earned		$160,000
Unearned revenue		3,500
Accounts receivable		8,200
Total revenue		$171,700
Expenses:		
Insurance expense	$ 1,800	
Office rent expense	18,000	
Supplies expense	1,200	
Dividends	3,000	
Salary expense	96,000	
Accumulated depreciation: auto	12,000	
Accumulated depreciation: equipment	13,000	
Repair and maintenance expense	1,700	
Travel expense	6,600	
Miscellaneous expense	2,100	
Interest expense	2,800	158,200
Income before income taxes		$ 13,500
Income taxes payable		400
Net income		$ 13,100

STRONG KNOT, INC.
STATEMENT OF RETAINED EARNINGS
FOR THE YEAR ENDED DECEMBER 31, 2011

Retained earnings (per adjusted trial balance)	$17,500
Add: Income	13,100
Less: Income taxes expense	4,000
Retained earnings, Dec. 31, 2011	$26,600

STRONG KNOT, INC.
BALANCE SHEET
DECEMBER 31, 2011

Assets		
Cash		$15,400
Supplies		900
Automobile	$37,000	
Less: Depreciation expense: automobile	4,000	33,000
Equipment and music	$39,000	
Less: Depreciation expense: equipment	3,000	36,000
Total assets		$85,300
Liabilities & Stockholders' Equity		
Liabilities:		
Accounts payable		$ 5,200
Notes payable		45,800
Salaries payable		900
Prepaid rent		800
Unexpired insurance		3,000
Total liabilities		$55,700
Stockholders' Equity:		
Capital stock		3,000
Retained earnings		26,600
Total stockholders' equity		$29,600
Total liabilities and stockholders' equity		$85,300

Instructions

a. Prepare a corrected set of financial statements dated December 31, 2011. (You may assume that all of the figures in the company's adjusted trial balance were reported correctly except for Notes Payable, which is some amount other than $45,800.)

b. Prepare the necessary year-end closing entries.

c. Using the financial statements prepared in part **a,** briefly evaluate the company's profitability and liquidity.

LO1 LO2 LO4 through LO6

PROBLEM 5.2B

Preparing Financial Statements and Closing Entries of a Profitable Company

Garden Wizards provides gardening services to both commercial and residential customers. The company performs adjusting entries on a *monthly* basis, whereas closing entries are prepared *annually* at December 31. An adjusted trial balance dated December 31, 2011, follows.

GARDEN WIZARDS ADJUSTED TRIAL BALANCE DECEMBER 31, 2011	Debits	Credits
Cash	$ 27,800	
Accounts receivable	4,300	
Unexpired insurance	8,700	
Prepaid rent	3,200	
Supplies	1,400	
Trucks	140,000	
Accumulated depreciation: trucks		$ 75,000
Equipment	28,000	
Accumulated depreciation: equipment		14,000
Accounts payable		2,200
Notes payable		38,000
Salaries payable		900
Interest payable		300
Income taxes payable		1,700
Unearned service revenue		2,000
Capital stock		18,000
Retained earnings		21,000
Dividends	3,300	
Service revenue earned		194,000
Insurance expense	1,800	
Office rent expense	28,000	
Supplies expense	5,600	
Salary expense	72,000	
Depreciation expense: trucks	16,000	
Depreciation expense: equipment	4,000	
Repair and maintenance expense	5,300	
Fuel expense	2,200	
Miscellaneous expense	2,700	
Interest expense	3,800	
Income taxes expense	9,000	
	$367,100	$367,100

Instructions

a. Prepare an income statement and statement of retained earnings for the year ended December 31, 2011. Also prepare the company's balance sheet dated December 31, 2011.

b. Prepare the necessary year-end closing entries.

c. Prepare an after-closing trial balance.

d. Using the financial statements prepared in part **a,** briefly evaluate the company's profitability and liquidity.

LO1 through LO6

PROBLEM 5.3B

Preparing Financial Statements and Closing Entries of an Unprofitable Company

Debit Doctors, Inc., provides accounting advice over the Internet. In recent years the company has experienced severe financial difficulty. Its accountant prepares adjusting entries on a *monthly* basis and closing entries on an *annual* basis at December 31. An *adjusted* trial balance dated December 31, 2011, follows.

DEBIT DOCTORS, INC.
ADJUSTED TRIAL BALANCE
DECEMBER 31, 2011

	Debits	Credits
Cash	$ 450	
Accounts receivable	220	
Unexpired insurance	1,600	
Prepaid rent	1,800	
Supplies	900	
Furniture and fixtures	10,000	
Accumulated depreciation: furniture and fixtures		$ 6,600
Accounts payable		7,100
Notes payable		24,000
Salaries payable		2,100
Interest payable		170
Unearned client revenue		600
Capital stock		4,000
Retained earnings		2,000
Client revenue earned		56,700
Insurance expense	6,200	
Office rent expense	12,000	
Supplies expense	300	
Salary expense	48,000	
Depreciation expense: furniture and fixtures	1,200	
Office and telephone expense	4,600	
Internet service expense	7,200	
Legal expense	1,800	
Interest expense	2,700	
Miscellaneous expense	4,300	
	$103,270	$103,270

Instructions

a. Prepare an income statement and statement of retained earnings for the year ended December 31, 2011. Also prepare the company's balance sheet dated December 31, 2011. (Hint: The company incurred no income taxes expense in 2011.)

b. Prepare the necessary year-end closing entries.

c. Prepare an after-closing trial balance.

d. Using the financial statements prepared in part **a,** briefly evaluate the company's performance.

e. Identify information that the company is apt to disclose in the notes that accompany the financial statements prepared in part **a.**

LO1 LO2 LO7

PROBLEM 5.4B
Interim Financial Statements

Silver Real Estate adjusts its accounts monthly but closes them only at the end of the calendar year. Below are the adjusted balances of the revenue and expense accounts at September 30 of the current year and at the ends of two earlier months:

	Sept. 30	Aug. 31	June 30
Commissions earned	$160,000	$145,000	$100,000
Advertising expense	33,000	28,000	18,000
Salaries expense	38,000	35,000	28,000
Rent expense	20,000	18,000	14,000
Depreciation expense	2,200	2,100	1,500

Instructions

a. Prepare a three-column income statement, showing net income for three separate time periods, all of which end on September 30. Use the format illustrated below. Show supporting computations for the amounts of revenue in the first two columns.

SILVER REAL ESTATE
INCOME STATEMENT
FOR THE FOLLOWING TIME PERIODS

	Month Ended Sept. 30	Quarter Ended Sept. 30	Nine Months Ended Sept. 30
Revenue:			
Commissions earned	$	$	$
Expenses:			

b. Briefly explain how you determined the dollar amounts for each of the three time periods. Would you apply the same process to the balances in Silver's balance sheet accounts? Explain.

c. Assume that Silver adjusts *and closes* its accounts at the end of *each month.* Briefly explain how you then would determine the revenue and expenses that would appear in each of the three columns of the income statement prepared in part **a.**

LO1 through LO4 LO6

PROBLEM 5.5B
Short Comprehensive Problem Including Both Adjusting and Closing Entries

Next Job, Inc., provides employment consulting services. The company adjusts its accounts *monthly* but performs closing entries *annually* on December 31. The firm's *unadjusted* trial balance dated December 31, 2011, is shown on the following page.

Other Data

1. Accrued but *unrecorded* and uncollected consulting fees earned total $25,000 at December 31, 2011.
2. The company determined that $15,000 of previously unearned consulting services fees had been earned at December 31, 2011.
3. Office supplies on hand at December 31 total $300.
4. The company purchased all of its equipment when it first began business. At that time, the estimated useful life of the equipment was six years (72 months).
5. The company prepaid its nine-month rent agreement on June 1, 2011.
6. The company prepaid its six-month insurance policy on December 1, 2011.
7. Accrued but *unpaid* salaries total $12,000 at December 31, 2011.
8. On September 1, 2011, the company borrowed $60,000 by signing an eight-month, 4 percent note payable. The entire amount, plus interest, is due on March 1, 2012.
9. The company's accounting firm estimates that income taxes expense for the *entire year* is $50,000. The unpaid portion of this amount is due early in 2012.

NEXT JOB, INC. UNADJUSTED TRIAL BALANCE DECEMBER 31, 2011		
Cash	$276,500	
Accounts receivable	90,000	
Office supplies	800	
Prepaid rent	3,600	
Unexpired insurance	1,500	
Office equipment	72,000	
Accumulated depreciation: office equipment		$ 24,000
Accounts payable		4,000
Notes payable (due 3/1/12)		60,000
Interest payable		600
Income taxes payable		9,000
Dividends payable		3,000
Unearned consulting fees		22,000
Capital stock		200,000
Retained earnings		40,000
Dividends	3,000	
Consulting fees earned		500,000
Rent expense	14,700	
Insurance expense	2,200	
Office supplies expense	4,500	
Depreciation expense: office equipment	11,000	
Salaries expense	330,000	
Utilities expense	4,800	
Interest expense	3,000	
Income taxes expense	45,000	
Totals	$862,600	$862,600

Instructions

a. Prepare the necessary adjusting journal entries on December 31, 2011. Also prepare an *adjusted trial balance* dated December 31, 2011.

b. From the adjusted trial balance prepared in part **a,** prepare an income statement and statement of retained earnings for the year ended December 31, 2011. Also prepare the company's balance sheet dated December 31, 2011.

c. Prepare the necessary year-end closing entries.

d. Prepare an after-closing trial balance.

e. Compute the company's average *monthly* insurance expense for January through November of 2011.

f. Compute the company's average *monthly* rent expense for January through May of 2011.

g. If the company purchased all of its office equipment when it first incorporated, for how long has it been in business as of December 31, 2011?

h. Assume that the company had a note payable outstanding on January 1, 2011, that it paid off on April 1, 2011. How much interest expense accrued on this note in 2011?

LO1 through LO4 LO6

PROBLEM 5.6B

Short Comprehensive Problem Including Both Adjusting and Closing Entries

Tammy Touchtone operates a talent agency called Touchtone Talent Agency. Some clients pay in advance for services; others are billed after services have been performed. Advance payments are credited to an account entitled Unearned Agency Fees. Adjusting entries are performed on a *monthly* basis. Closing entries are performed *annually* on December 31. An *unadjusted* trial balance dated December 31, 2011, follows. (Bear in mind that adjusting entries have already been made for the first 11 months of 2011, but *not* for December.)

TOUCHTONE TALENT AGENCY
UNADJUSTED TRIAL BALANCE
DECEMBER 31, 2011

Cash	$ 14,950	
Fees receivable	35,300	
Prepaid rent	1,200	
Unexpired insurance policies	375	
Office supplies	900	
Office equipment	15,000	
Accumulated depreciation: office equipment		$ 12,000
Accounts payable		1,500
Note payable (due 3/1/12)		6,000
Income taxes payable		3,200
Unearned agency fees		8,000
Capital stock		20,000
Retained earnings		10,800
Dividends	800	
Agency fees earned		46,500
Telephone expense	480	
Office supply expense	1,130	
Depreciation expense: office equipment	2,750	
Rent expense	6,100	
Insurance expense	1,175	
Salaries expense	24,640	
Income taxes expense	3,200	
	$108,000	$108,000

Other Data

1. Office equipment is being depreciated over 60 months (5 years).
2. At December 31, 2011, $2,500 of previously unearned agency fees had been earned.
3. Accrued but *unrecorded* and unpaid salary expense totals $1,360 at December 31, 2011.
4. The agency pays rent quarterly (every three months). The most recent advance payment of $1,800 was made November 1, 2011. The next payment of $1,800 will be made on February 1, 2012.
5. Accrued but *unrecorded* and uncollected agency fees earned total $3,000 at December 31, 2011.
6. Office supplies on hand at December 31, 2011, total $530.
7. On September 1, 2011, the agency purchased a six-month insurance policy for $750.
8. On December 1, 2011, the agency borrowed $6,000 by signing a three-month, 9 percent note payable. The entire amount borrowed, plus interest, is due March 1, 2012.
9. Accrued income taxes payable for the *entire year* ending December 31, 2011, *total* $3,900. The full amount is due early in 2012.

Instructions

a. Prepare the necessary adjusting journal entries on December 31, 2011. Also prepare an *adjusted trial balance* dated December 31, 2011.

b. From the adjusted trial balance prepared in part **a**, prepare an income statement and statement of retained earnings for the year ended December 31, 2011. Also prepare the company's balance sheet dated December 31, 2011.

c. Prepare the necessary year-end closing entries.

d. Prepare an after-closing trial balance.

e. Assume that the agency purchased all of its office equipment when it first began business activities. For how many months has the agency been in operation?

f. Has the agency's monthly office rent remained the same throughout the year? If not, has it gone up or down? Explain.

g. Has the agency's monthly insurance expense remained the same throughout the year? If not, has it gone up or down? Explain.

LO8 ***PROBLEM 5.7B**
Short Comprehensive Problem Including Adjusting Entries, Closing Entries, and Worksheet Preparation

Refer to Problem 4.4A on pages 174–175 in the previous chapter. Prepare a 10-column worksheet for Campus Theater dated August 31, 2011. At the bottom of your worksheet, prepare a brief explanation keyed to each adjusting entry.

LO6 **PROBLEM 5.8B**
Evaluating Profitability and Liquidity

A recent annual report issued by **The Gap, Inc.**, revealed the following data:

	End of Year	Beginning of Year
Current assets	$4.0 billion	$4.1 billion
Current liabilities	$2.2 billion	$2.4 billion
Stockholders' equity	$4.4 billion	$4.3 billion

The company's income statement reported total annual revenue of $14.5 billion and net income for the year of $967 million.

Instructions

a. Evaluate **The Gap**'s profitability by computing its net income percentage and its return on equity for the year.

b. Evaluate **The Gap**'s liquidity by computing its working capital and its current ratio at the beginning of the year and at the end of the year.

c. Does **The Gap, Inc.**, appear to be both profitable and liquid? Explain.

**Supplemental Topic,* "The Worksheet."

Critical Thinking Cases

LO3 **CASE 5.1**
Adequate Disclosure

Listed below are five items that may—or may not—require disclosure in the notes that accompany financial statements.

a. Mandella Construction Co. uses the percentage-of-completion method to recognize revenue on long-term construction contracts. This is one of two acceptable methods of accounting for such projects. Over the life of the project, both methods produce the same overall results, but the annual results may differ substantially.

b. One of the most popular artists at Spectacular Comics is leaving the company and going to work for a competitor.

c. Shortly after the balance sheet date, but before the financial statements are issued, one of Coast Foods's two processing plants was damaged by a tornado. The plant will be out of service for at least three months.

d. The management of Soft Systems believes that the company has developed systems software that will make Windows® virtually obsolete. If they are correct, the company's profits could increase by 10-fold or more.

e. College Property Management (CPM) withheld a $500 security deposit from students who, in violation of their lease, kept a dog in their apartment. The students have sued CPM for this amount in small claims court.

Instructions

For each case, explain what, if any, disclosure is required under generally accepted accounting principles. Explain your reasoning.

LO1 **CASE 5.2**
Working for the Competition

This problem focuses on the following question: *Is it ethical for a CPA (or CPA firm) to provide similar services to companies that compete directly with one another?* These services may include assistance in the preparation of financial statements, income tax services, consulting engagements, and audit work.

Instructions

a. *Before* doing any research, discuss this question as a group. Identify potential arguments on *each side* of the issue.

b. Arrange an interview with a practicing (or retired) public accountant. Learn the accounting profession's position on this issue, and discuss the various arguments developed in part **a.**

c. Develop your group's position on this issue and be prepared to explain it in class. Explain why you have chosen to overlook the conflicting arguments developed in part **a.** (If your group is not in agreement, dissenting members may draft a dissenting opinion.)

LO3 **CASE 5.3**
Certifications by CEOs and CFOs

The Sarbanes-Oxley Act requires that the CEO (chief executive officer) and CFO (chief financial officer) of publicly traded corporations include statements of *personal certification* in the disclosures accompanying the financial reports filed with the SEC. In essence, these statements hold the CEO and CFO personally liable for their company's annual report content. The personal certifications must be signed by both the CEO and the CFO. Each certification requires that the CEO and CFO commit to the following statements:

1. I have reviewed this annual report.
2. On the basis of my knowledge, this report does not contain any untrue statements of material facts or omissions of material facts.
3. On the basis of my knowledge, the financial statements, and other financial information included in this report, fairly present in all material respects the financial condition, results of operations, and cash flows of the business.
4. I am responsible for establishing and maintaining disclosure controls and procedures.
5. I have disclosed any fraud, whether or not material, and have disclosed all significant control deficiencies and material weaknesses involving the company's financial reporting.

Instructions

As a group, discuss the meaning and purpose of the personal certification requirement. How might this requirement contribute to improved investor confidence?

LO3 **INTERNET CASE 5.4**
Annual Report Disclosures

Visit the home page of the **Ford Motor Company** at:

www.ford.com

From **Ford**'s home page, access the company's most recent annual report (select the "About Ford" menu item). Locate the notes to the financial statements and identify the information topics disclosed in these footnotes.

Internet sites are time and date sensitive. It is the purpose of these exercises to have you explore the Internet. You may need to use the Yahoo! search engine **http://www.yahoo.com** *(or another favorite search engine) to find a company's current Web address.*

Answers to Self-Test Questions

1. a, b, c, d **2.** a **3.** d **4.** b, d **5.** a **6.** a, b **7.** c **8.** b, c

COMPREHENSIVE PROBLEM 1

Susquehanna Equipment Rentals

A COMPREHENSIVE ACCOUNTING CYCLE PROBLEM

On December 1, 2011, John and Patty Driver formed a corporation called Susquehanna Equipment Rentals. The new corporation was able to begin operations immediately by purchasing the assets and taking over the location of Rent-It, an equipment rental company that was going out of business. The newly formed company uses the following accounts:

Cash	Income Taxes Payable
Accounts Receivable	Capital Stock
Prepaid Rent	Retained Earnings
Unexpired Insurance	Dividends
Office Supplies	Income Summary
Rental Equipment	Rental Fees Earned
Accumulated Depreciation:	Salaries Expense
Rental Equipment	Maintenance Expense
Notes Payable	Utilities Expense
Accounts Payable	Rent Expense
Interest Payable	Office Supplies Expense
Salaries Payable	Depreciation Expense
Dividends Payable	Interest Expense
Unearned Rental Fees	Income Taxes Expense

The corporation performs adjusting entries monthly. Closing entries are performed annually on December 31. During December, the corporation entered into the following transactions:

Dec. 1 Issued to John and Patty Driver 20,000 shares of capital stock in exchange for a total of $200,000 cash.

Dec. 1 Purchased for $240,000 all of the equipment formerly owned by Rent-It. Paid $140,000 cash and issued a one-year note payable for $100,000. The note, plus all 12-months of accrued interest, are due November 30, 2012.

Dec. 1 Paid $12,000 to Shapiro Realty as three months' advance rent on the rental yard and office formerly occupied by Rent-It.

Dec. 4 Purchased office supplies on account from Modern Office Co., $1,000. Payment due in 30 days. (These supplies are expected to last for several months; debit the Office Supplies asset account.)

Dec. 8 Received $8,000 cash as advance payment on equipment rental from McNamer Construction Company. (Credit Unearned Rental Fees.)

Dec. 12 Paid salaries for the first two weeks in December, $5,200.

Dec. 15 Excluding the McNamer advance, equipment rental fees earned during the first 15 days of December amounted to $18,000, of which $12,000 was received in cash.

Dec. 17 Purchased on account from Earth Movers, Inc., $600 in parts needed to repair a rental tractor. (Debit an expense account.) Payment is due in 10 days.

Dec. 23 Collected $2,000 of the accounts receivable recorded on December 15.

Dec. 26 Rented a backhoe to Mission Landscaping at a price of $250 per day, to be paid when the backhoe is returned. Mission Landscaping expects to keep the backhoe for about two or three weeks.

Dec. 26 Paid biweekly salaries, $5,200.

Dec. 27 Paid the account payable to Earth Movers, Inc., $600.

Dec. 28 Declared a dividend of 10 cents per share, payable on January 15, 2012.

Dec. 29 Susquehanna Equipment Rentals was named, along with Mission Landscaping and Collier Construction, as a co-defendant in a $25,000 lawsuit filed on behalf of Kevin Davenport. Mission Landscaping had left the rented backhoe in a fenced construction site owned by Collier Construction. After working hours on December 26, Davenport had climbed the fence to play on parked construction equipment. While playing on the backhoe, he fell and broke his arm. The extent of the company's legal and financial responsibility for this accident, if any, cannot be determined at this time. (***Note:*** This event does not require a journal entry at this time, but may require disclosure in notes accompanying the statements.)

Dec. 29 Purchased a 12-month public-liability insurance policy for $9,600. This policy protects the company against liability for injuries and property damage caused by its equipment. However, the policy goes into effect on January 1, 2012, and affords no coverage for the injuries sustained by Kevin Davenport on December 26.

Dec. 31 Received a bill from Universal Utilities for the month of December, $700. Payment is due in 30 days.

Dec. 31 Equipment rental fees earned during the second half of December amounted to $20,000, of which $15,600 was received in cash.

Data for Adjusting Entries

a. The advance payment of rent on December 1 covered a period of three months.

b. The annual interest rate on the note payable to Rent-It is 6 percent.

c. The rental equipment is being depreciated by the straight-line method over a period of eight years.

d. Office supplies on hand at December 31 are estimated at $600.

e. During December, the company earned $3,700 of the rental fees paid in advance by McNamer Construction Company on December 8.

f. As of December 31, six days' rent on the backhoe rented to Mission Landscaping on December 26 has been earned.

g. Salaries earned by employees since the last payroll date (December 26) amounted to $1,400 at month-end.

h. It is estimated that the company is subject to a combined federal and state income tax rate of 40 percent of income before income taxes (total revenue minus all expenses *other than* income taxes). These taxes will be payable in 2012.

Instructions

a. Perform the following steps of the accounting cycle for the month of December:

1. Journalize the December transactions. Do *not* record adjusting entries at this point.
2. Post the December transactions to the appropriate ledger accounts.
3. Prepare the *unadjusted* trial balance columns of a 10-column worksheet for the year ended December 31.
4. Prepare the necessary adjusting entries for December.
5. Post the December adjusting entries to the appropriate ledger accounts.
6. Complete the 10-column worksheet for the year ended December 31.

b. Prepare an income statement and statement of retained earnings for the year ended December 31, and a balance sheet (in report form) as of December 31.

c. Prepare required disclosures to accompany the December 31 financial statements. Your solution should include a separate note addressing each of the following areas: (1) depreciation policy, (2) maturity dates of major liabilities, and (3) potential liability due to pending litigation.

d. Prepare closing entries and post to ledger accounts.

e. Prepare an after-closing trial balance as of December 31.

f. During December, this company's cash balance has fallen from $200,000 to $65,000. Does it appear headed for insolvency in the near future? Explain your reasoning.

g. Would it be ethical for Patty Driver to maintain the accounting records for this company, or must they be maintained by someone who is *independent* of the organization?

CHAPTER 6

Merchandising Activities

© AP Photo/Chitose Suzuki

AFTER STUDYING THIS CHAPTER, YOU SHOULD BE ABLE TO:

Learning Objectives

- **LO1** Describe the *operating cycle* of a merchandising company.
- **LO2** Understand the components of a merchandising company's income statement.
- **LO3** Account for purchases and sales of merchandise in a *perpetual* inventory system.
- **LO4** Explain how a *periodic* inventory system operates.
- **LO5** Discuss the factors to be considered in selecting an inventory system.
- **LO6** Account for additional merchandising transactions related to purchases and sales.
- **LO7** Define *special journals* and explain their usefulness.
- **LO8** Measure the performance of a merchandising business.

SAKS INC.

Saks Inc. is a retailer of a wide variety of distinctive luxury fashion apparel, shoes, accessories, jewelry, cosmetics, and gifts. The company operates 108 stores in 28 states, including 53 Saks Fifth Avenue stores and 55 Saks Fifth Avenue Off 5th Street stores. Saks Fifth Avenue stores are located in exclusive shopping destinations or as anchor stores in upscale regional malls. Saks Fifth Avenue Off 5th Street aims to be the premier luxury off-price retailer in the United States.

Saks Inc. tailors the merchandise in each store location to the tastes and lifestyle needs of its local customers. The company has invested in online information technology to provide detailed information about its customers and their purchasing patterns and preferences. In addition, Saks has vendor relationships with leading American and European fashion houses, including Giorgio Armani, Chanel, Gucci, Prada, Louis Vuitton, St. John, Zegna, Cartier, Hugo Boss, Ralph Lauren, Burberry, among many others. Although Saks carries merchandise for both men and women, sales to its female customer base comprise more than 75 percent of total sales.

Saks Inc.'s financial statements are similar to those of the service organizations illustrated in previous chapters. They differ, however, because Saks sells *merchandise* to its customers. Companies that sell merchandise must report information about inventory costs in their financial statements. ■

In this chapter we examine accounting issues related to merchandising businesses, such as clothing retailers and grocery stores. In addition to discussing the unique features of a merchandising company's financial statements, we illustrate ways to use financial information to evaluate the performance of these companies.

Saks Inc.'s retail stores are good examples of merchandising outlets. Managing **inventory** (goods that are purchased for the purpose of resale to customers) is of utmost importance to merchandising businesses. For a luxury chain like **Saks** to be successful, its stores must acquire hundreds of inventory items and sell them quickly at competitive prices.

In most merchandising companies, inventory is a relatively liquid asset—that is, it usually is sold within a few days or weeks. For this reason, inventory appears near the top of the balance sheet, immediately below accounts receivable.

Merchandising Companies

THE OPERATING CYCLE OF A MERCHANDISING COMPANY

Learning Objective
LO1 Describe the *operating cycle* of a merchandising company.

The series of transactions through which a business generates its revenue and its cash receipts from customers is called the **operating cycle.** The operating cycle of a merchandising company consists of the following basic transactions: (1) purchases of merchandise; (2) sales of the merchandise, often on account; and (3) collection of the accounts receivable from customers. As the word *cycle* suggests, this sequence of transactions repeats continuously. Some of the cash collected from the customers is used to purchase more merchandise, and the cycle begins anew. This continuous sequence of merchandising transactions is illustrated in Exhibit 6–1.

Exhibit 6–1
THE OPERATING CYCLE

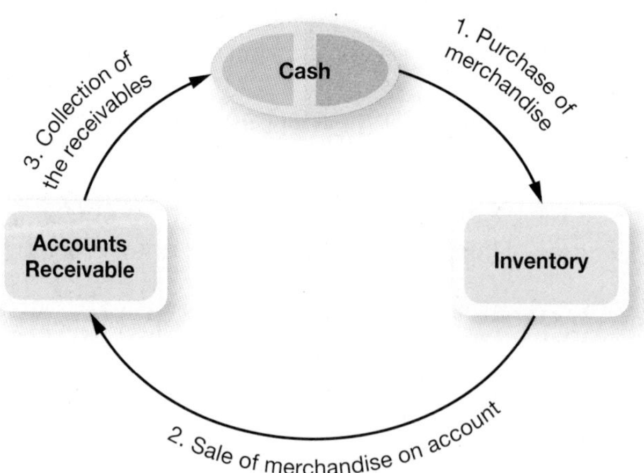

Comparing Merchandising Activities with Manufacturing Activities

Most merchandising companies purchase their inventories from other business organizations in a *ready-to-sell* condition. Companies that manufacture their inventories, such as **General Motors**, **IBM**, and **Boeing Aircraft**, are called *manufacturers,* rather than merchandisers. The operating cycle of a manufacturing company is longer and more complex than that of a merchandising company, because the first transaction—purchasing merchandise—is replaced by the many activities involved in manufacturing the merchandise.

Our examples and illustrations in this chapter are limited to companies that purchase their inventory in a ready-to-sell condition. The basic concepts, however, also apply to manufacturers.

Retailers and Wholesalers Merchandising companies include both retailers and wholesalers. A *retailer* is a business that sells merchandise directly to the public. Retailers may be large or small; they vary in size from national store chains, such as **Saks**, **The Gap**, and **Walmart**, to small neighborhood businesses, such as gas stations and convenience stores. In fact, more businesses engage in retail sales than in any other type of business activity.

The other major type of merchandising company is the *wholesaler*. Wholesalers buy large quantities of merchandise from several different manufacturers and then resell this merchandise to many different retailers. Because wholesalers do not sell directly to the public, even the largest wholesalers are not well known to most consumers. Nonetheless, wholesaling is a major type of merchandising activity.

The concepts discussed in the remainder of this chapter apply equally to retailers and to wholesalers.

INCOME STATEMENT OF A MERCHANDISING COMPANY

Learning Objective **Understand the components of a merchandising company's income statement.** **LO2**

The income statement of a merchandising company differs somewhat from that of a service organization illustrated in previous chapters. Exhibit 6–2 compares the income statement structure of a service company to that of a merchandising company.

Exhibit 6–2

A COMPARISON OF INCOME STATEMENTS USED BY A SERVICE COMPANY AND A MERCHANDISING COMPANY

SERVICE COMPANY'S INCOME STATEMENT

Revenue

minus

Expenses

equals

Net Income

MERCHANDISING COMPANY'S INCOME STATEMENT

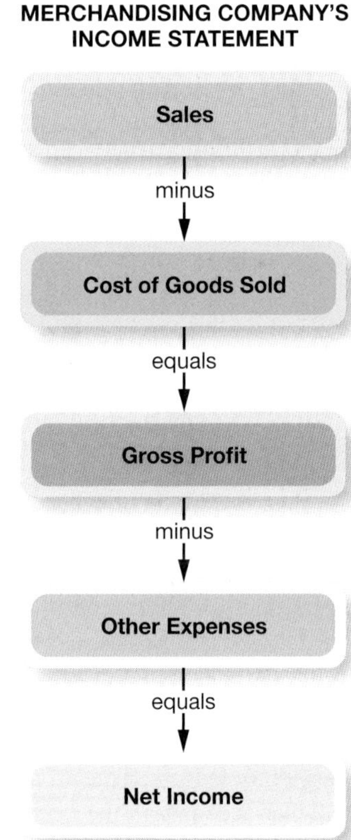

The income statement of Computer City is shown in Exhibit 6–3. The following discussion of its structure and components will illustrate the unique characteristics of income statements prepared by merchandising companies.

Computer City's $900,000 in sales represents the *selling price* of merchandise it sold to customers during the period. Selling merchandise introduces a new and major cost of doing business: the *cost* incurred by Computer City *to acquire* the inventory it sold to customers. As items are sold from inventory, their costs must be removed from the balance sheet and transferred to the income statement to offset sales revenue. This $540,000 cost subtracted from sales revenue in Computer City's income statement is referred to as the **cost of goods sold.** In essence, the cost of goods sold is an *expense;* however, this item is of such importance to a merchandising company that it is shown separately from other expenses in the company's income statement.

Exhibit 6–3

A MERCHANDISING COMPANY'S INCOME STATEMENT

COMPUTER CITY INCOME STATEMENT FOR THE YEAR ENDED DECEMBER 31, 2011		
Sales		$900,000
Less: Cost of goods sold		540,000
Gross profit		$360,000
Operating expenses:		
Wages expense	$150,900	
Advertising expense	6,800	
Insurance expense	9,600	
Utilities expense	6,400	
Office supplies expense	1,700	
Depreciation expense	58,600	234,000
Income before taxes		$126,000
Income taxes expense		36,000
Net income		$ 90,000

The $360,000 difference between sales and the cost of goods sold is Computer City's **gross profit** (or gross margin). Gross profit is a useful means of measuring the profitability of sales transactions, but it does *not* represent the overall profitability of the business. A merchandising company has many expenses in addition to the cost of goods sold. Computer City's $270,000 in other expenses includes wages expense, advertising expense, insurance expense, utilities expense, office supplies expense, depreciation expense, and income taxes expense.[1] A company earns net income only if its gross profit exceeds the sum of its other expenses.

ACCOUNTING SYSTEM REQUIREMENTS FOR MERCHANDISING COMPANIES

In previous chapters, we recorded economic events using only *general ledger* accounts. These accounts, often referred to as **control accounts,** are used to prepare financial statements that *summarize* the financial position of a business and the results of its operations. Although general ledger accounts provide a useful *overview* of a company's financial activities, they do not provide the *detailed information* needed to effectively manage most business enterprises. This detailed information is found in accounting records called *subsidiary ledgers.*

Subsidiary ledgers contain information about specific control accounts in the company's general ledger. Merchandising companies always maintain accounts receivable and accounts payable subsidiary ledgers. Thus, if a company has 500 credit customers, there are 500 individual customer accounts in the *accounts receivable subsidiary ledger* that, in total, add up to the Accounts Receivable general ledger balance reported in the balance sheet. Likewise, if a company has 20 creditors, there are 20 individual records in the *accounts payable subsidiary ledger* that contain detailed information about the amount owed to each creditor. The individual balances of these accounts add up to the Accounts Payable control balance in the general ledger.

Many merchandising companies also maintain an *inventory subsidiary ledger* by creating a separate inventory account for each item that they sell. The inventory subsidiary ledger for a large department store contains thousands of accounts. Each of these accounts tracks information for *one type of product,* showing the quantities and costs of all units purchased, sold, and currently in stock.

---

[1] The income statement presented in Exhibit 6–3 is somewhat condensed. For instance, it is a common practice for companies to subdivide operating expenses into *selling expenses and general and administrative expenses.* A more detailed income statement presentation is developed in Chapter 12.

It may seem that maintaining records for thousands of separate accounts would involve an incredible amount of work. And it would, in a *manual* accounting system. However, in a *computerized* accounting system, subsidiary ledger accounts and general ledger control accounts are posted *automatically* as transactions are recorded. Thus, no significant amount of effort is required.

Throughout the remainder of this chapter we will record various merchandise transactions directly in the general ledger control accounts. To avoid excessive detail, we will *assume* that the specific account information underlying these transactions has been posted to the necessary subsidiary accounts.

TWO APPROACHES USED IN ACCOUNTING FOR MERCHANDISE INVENTORIES

Either of two approaches may be used in accounting for merchandise inventories: (1) a *perpetual inventory system,* or (2) a *periodic inventory system.* In the past, both systems were in widespread use. Today, however, the growing use of computerized accounting systems has made the perpetual approach easy and cost-effective to implement. Thus, the periodic approach is used primarily by very small businesses with manual accounting systems.

Before we examine perpetual and periodic inventory systems, it is important to realize that accounting for inventory is similar to accounting for the *prepaid expenses* we discussed in Chapter 4 (for example, office supplies, unexpired insurance policies, prepaid rent, etc.). As inventory is purchased, it is initially reported as an *asset* in the balance sheet. As it is sold to customers, this asset is converted to an *expense,* specifically, the cost of goods sold.

Both perpetual and periodic inventory systems account for the flow of inventory costs from the balance sheet to the income statement as illustrated in Exhibit 6–4.

Exhibit 6–4

THE FLOW OF INVENTORY COSTS

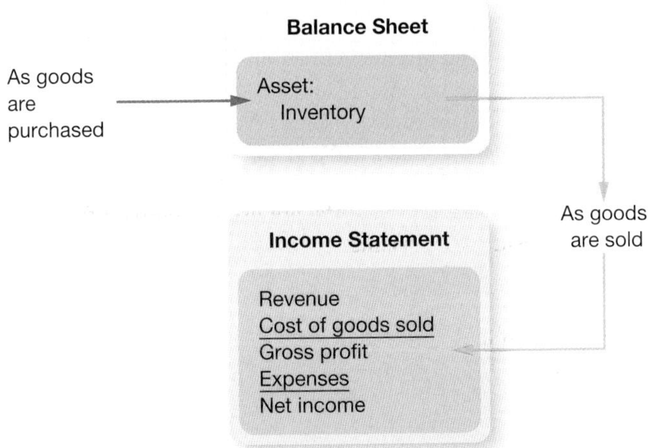

Perpetual Inventory Systems

Learning Objective LO3 Account for purchases and sales of merchandise in a *perpetual* inventory system.

In a **perpetual inventory system,** all transactions involving costs of merchandise are recorded immediately *as they occur.* The system draws its name from the fact that the accounting records are kept perpetually up-to-date. Purchases of merchandise are recorded by debiting an asset account entitled Inventory. When merchandise is sold, two entries are necessary: one to recognize the *revenue earned* and the second to recognize the related *cost of goods sold.* This second entry also reduces the balance of the Inventory account to reflect the sale of some of the company's inventory.

A perpetual inventory system uses an *inventory subsidiary ledger.* This ledger provides company personnel with up-to-date information about each type of product that the company buys and sells, including the per-unit cost and the number of units purchased, sold, and currently on hand.

To illustrate the perpetual inventory system, we follow specific items of merchandise through the operating cycle of Computer City, a retail store. The transactions comprising this illustration are as follows:

Sept. 1 Purchased 10 Regent 21-inch computer monitors on account from Okawa Wholesale Co. The monitors cost $600 each, for a total of $6,000; payment is due in 30 days.

Sept. 7 Sold two monitors on account to RJ Travel Agency at a retail sales price of $1,000 each, for a total of $2,000. Payment is due in 30 days.

Oct. 1 Paid the $6,000 account payable to Okawa Wholesale Co.

Oct. 7 Collected the $2,000 account receivable from RJ Travel Agency.

Purchases of Merchandise Purchases of inventory are recorded at cost. Thus Computer City records its purchase of the 10 computer monitors on September 1 as follows:

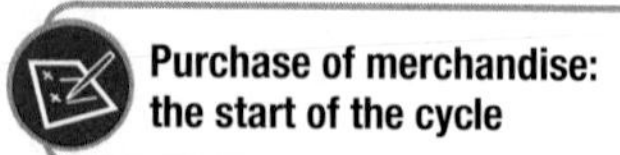

Purchase of merchandise: the start of the cycle

Inventory	6,000	
Accounts Payable (Okawa Wholesale Co.)		6,000
Purchased 10 Regent 21-inch computer monitors for $600 each; payment due in 30 days.		

This entry is posted both to the general ledger control accounts and to the *subsidiary ledgers.* Thus, the debit to Inventory is also posted to the Regent 21-Inch Monitors account in the inventory subsidiary ledger. Information regarding the quantity of monitors purchased and their unit cost is also recorded in this subsidiary ledger. Likewise, the credit to Accounts Payable is posted to the account for Okawa Wholesale Co. in Computer City's accounts payable subsidiary ledger.

Sales of Merchandise The revenue earned in a sales transaction is equal to the *sales price* of the merchandise times the number of units sold, and is credited to a revenue account entitled Sales. Except in rare circumstances, sales revenue is considered realized when the merchandise is *delivered to the customer,* even if the sale is made on account. Therefore, Computer City will recognize the revenue from the sale to RJ Travel Agency on September 7, as follows:

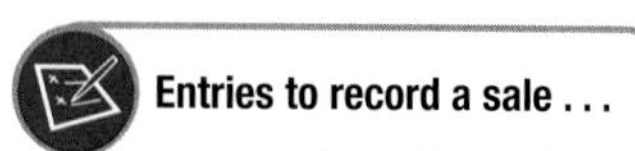

Entries to record a sale . . .

Accounts Receivable (RJ Travel Agency)	2,000	
Sales		2,000
Sold two Regent 21-inch monitors for $1,000 each; payment due in 30 days.		

The *matching principle* requires that revenue be matched (offset) with all of the costs and expenses incurred in producing that revenue. Therefore, a *second journal entry* is required at the date of sale to record the cost of goods sold.

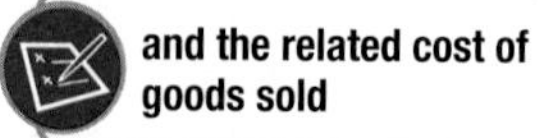

and the related cost of goods sold

Cost of Goods Sold	1,200	
Inventory.		1,200
To transfer the cost of two Regent 21-inch monitors ($600 each) from Inventory to the Cost of Goods Sold account.		

Notice that this second entry is based on the *cost* of the merchandise to Computer City, not on its retail sales price.[2]

Both of the journal entries relating to this sales transaction are posted to Computer City's general ledger. In addition, the $2,000 debit to Accounts Receivable (first entry) is posted to the

[2] In our illustration, all of the Regent monitors were purchased on the same date and have the same unit cost. Often a company's inventory of a given product includes units acquired at several *different* per-unit costs. This situation is addressed in Chapter 8.

account for RJ Travel Agency in the accounts receivable ledger. The credit to Inventory (second entry) also is posted to the Regent 21-Inch Monitors account in the inventory subsidiary ledger.

Payment of Accounts Payable to Suppliers The payment to Okawa Wholesale Co. on October 1 is recorded as follows:

Accounts Payable (Okawa Wholesale Co.)	6,000	
Cash		6,000
Paid account payable.		

Payment of an account payable

Both portions of this entry are posted to the general ledger. In addition, payment of the account payable is entered in the Okawa Wholesale Co. account in Computer City's accounts payable subsidiary ledger.

Collection of Accounts Receivable from Customers On October 7, collection of the account receivable from RJ Travel Agency is recorded as follows:

Cash	2,000	
Accounts Receivable (RJ Travel Agency)		2,000
Collected an account receivable from a credit customer.		

Collection of an account receivable

Both portions of this entry are posted to the general ledger; the credit to Accounts Receivable also is posted to the RJ Travel Agency account in the accounts receivable ledger.

Collection of the cash from RJ Travel Agency completes Computer City's operating cycle with respect to these two units of merchandise.

TAKING A PHYSICAL INVENTORY

The basic characteristic of the perpetual inventory system is that the Inventory account is *continuously updated* for all purchases and sales of merchandise. When a *physical inventory* is taken, management uses the inventory ledger to determine on a product-by-product basis whether a physical count of the inventory on hand corresponds to the amount indicated in the inventory subsidiary ledger. Over time normal inventory shrinkage may cause some discrepancies between the quantities of merchandise shown in the inventory records and the quantities actually on hand. **Inventory shrinkage** refers to unrecorded decreases in inventory resulting from such factors as breakage, spoilage, employee theft, and shoplifting.

In order to ensure the accuracy of their perpetual inventory records, most corporations are required to take a *complete physical count* of the merchandise on hand at least once a year. This procedure is called **taking a physical inventory,** and it usually is performed near year-end.

Once the quantity of merchandise on hand has been determined by a physical count, the per-unit costs in the inventory ledger accounts are used to determine the total cost of the inventory. The Inventory control account and the accounts in the inventory subsidiary ledger then are *adjusted* to the quantities and dollar amounts indicated by the physical inventory.

To illustrate, assume that at year-end both the Inventory control account and inventory subsidiary ledger of Computer City show an inventory with a cost of $72,200. A physical count, however, reveals that some of the merchandise listed in the accounting records is missing; the items actually on hand have a total cost of $70,000. Computer City would make the following adjusting entry to correct its Inventory control account:

Cost of Goods Sold	2,200	
Inventory		2,200
To adjust the perpetual inventory records to reflect the results of the year-end physical count.		

Adjusting for inventory shrinkage

Computer City also will adjust the appropriate accounts in its inventory subsidiary ledger to reflect the quantities indicated by the physical count.

Reasonable amounts of inventory shrinkage are viewed as a normal cost of doing business and simply are debited to the Cost of Goods Sold account, as illustrated above.[3]

INTERNATIONAL CASE IN POINT

International Financial Reporting Standards (IFRSs) for valuing inventory differ in some respects from U.S. GAAP rules. For example, U.S. GAAP does not allow reversals of inventory write-downs, but international standards allow such reversals if certain criteria are met. Thus, the inventory values on the balance sheet and the cost of goods sold on the income statement of a firm could differ depending on whether their financial statements are prepared under GAAP or under IFRSs.

CLOSING ENTRIES IN A PERPETUAL INVENTORY SYSTEM

As explained and illustrated in the previous chapters, revenue and expense accounts are *closed* at the end of each accounting period. A merchandising business with a perpetual inventory system makes closing entries that parallel those of a service-type business. The Sales account is a revenue account and is closed into the Income Summary account along with other revenue accounts. The Cost of Goods Sold account is closed into the Income Summary account in the same manner as the other expense accounts.

YOUR TURN **You as the Inventory Manager for Computer City**

Assume you are the inventory manager for the largest store owned by Computer City. You are very busy one day when Fran Mally, an auditor from the accounting firm employed by Computer City, arrives and asks for assistance in determining the store's physical inventory on hand. You are overwhelmed with work and tell Fran that you do not have the time or the personnel needed to assist her in this task. You are also annoyed because you were not told that she was coming today to complete the physical inventory count. What should you do?

(See our comments on the Online Learning Center Web site.)

Periodic Inventory Systems

A **periodic inventory system** is an *alternative* to a perpetual inventory system. In a periodic inventory system, no effort is made to keep up-to-date records of either the inventory or the cost of goods sold. Instead, these amounts are determined only periodically—usually at the end of each year.

OPERATION OF A PERIODIC INVENTORY SYSTEM

Learning Objective
LO4 Explain how a *periodic* inventory system operates.

A traditional periodic inventory system operates as follows. When merchandise is purchased, its cost is debited to an account entitled *Purchases,* rather than to the Inventory account. When merchandise is sold, an entry is made to recognize the sales revenue, but *no entry* is made to record the cost of goods sold or to reduce the balance of the Inventory account. As the inventory records are not updated as transactions occur, there is no inventory subsidiary ledger.

The foundation of the periodic inventory system is the taking of a *complete physical inventory* at year-end. This physical count determines the amount of inventory appearing in the balance sheet. The cost of goods sold for the entire year then is determined by a short computation.

[3] If a large inventory shortage is caused by an event such as a fire or theft, the cost of the missing or damaged merchandise may be debited to a special loss account, such as Fire Loss. In the income statement, a loss is deducted from revenue in the same manner as an expense.

Data for an Illustration To illustrate, assume that one of Computer City's suppliers, Wagner Office Products, has a periodic inventory system. At December 31, 2011, the following information is available:

1. The inventory on hand at the end of *2010* cost $14,000.
2. During *2011*, purchases of merchandise for resale to customers totaled $130,000.
3. Inventory on hand at the end of *2011* cost $12,000.

The inventories at the end of 2010 and at the end of 2011 were determined by taking a complete physical inventory at (or very near) each year-end. (Because the Inventory account was not updated as transactions occurred during 2011, it still shows a balance of $14,000—the inventory on hand at the *beginning* of the year.)

The $130,000 cost of merchandise purchased during 2011 was recorded in the Purchases account.

Recording Purchases of Merchandise Wagner Office Products made many purchases of merchandise totaling $130,000 during 2011. The entry to record the first of these purchases is as follows:

Jan. 6	Purchases	2,000	
	Accounts Payable (Ink Jet Solutions)		2,000
	Purchased inventory on account; payment due in 30 days.		

This entry was posted to the Purchases and Accounts Payable accounts in the general ledger. The credit portion also was posted to the account for Ink Jet Solutions in Wagner's accounts payable subsidiary ledger. The debit to Purchases was *not* "double-posted," as there is *no inventory subsidiary ledger* in a periodic system.

Computing the Cost of Goods Sold The year-end inventory is determined by taking a complete physical count of the merchandise on hand. Once the ending inventory is known, the cost of goods sold for the entire year can be determined by a short computation. The following computation uses the three information items for Wagner Office Products just presented:

Inventory (beginning of the year) (1)	$ 14,000
Add: Purchases (2)	130,000
Cost of goods available for sale	$144,000
Less: Inventory (end of the year) (3)	12,000
Cost of goods sold	$132,000

Computation of the cost of goods sold

The $132,000 cost of goods sold is made up of two elements: the $130,000 cost of merchandise purchased during the year and the *decrease* in inventory of $2,000 ($14,000 beginning inventory − $12,000 ending inventory).

Recording Inventory and the Cost of Goods Sold Wagner has now determined its inventory at the end of 2011 and its cost of goods sold for the year. But neither of these amounts has yet been recorded in the company's accounting records.

In a periodic system, the ending inventory and the cost of goods sold are recorded during the company's year-end *closing procedures* (The term *closing procedures* refers to the end-of-period adjusting and closing entries.)

CLOSING PROCESS IN A PERIODIC INVENTORY SYSTEM

There are several different ways of recording the ending inventory and cost of goods sold in a periodic system, but they all produce the same results. One approach is to *create* a Cost of Goods Sold account with the proper balance as part of the closing process. Once this account has been created, the company can complete its closing procedures in the same manner as if a perpetual inventory system had been in use.

Creating a Cost of Goods Sold Account A Cost of Goods Sold account is created with two special closing entries. The first entry creates the new account by bringing together the costs contributing toward the cost of goods sold. The second entry adjusts the Cost of Goods Sold account to its proper balance and records the ending inventory in the Inventory account.

The costs contributing to the cost of goods sold include (1) beginning inventory and (2) purchases made during the year. These costs are brought together by closing both the Inventory account (which contains its beginning-of-the-year balance) and the Purchases account into a new account entitled Cost of Goods Sold. This year-end closing entry is:

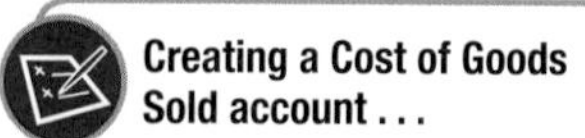

Dec. 31	Cost of Goods Sold	144,000	
	Inventory (beginning balance)		14,000
	Purchases		130,000
	To close the accounts contributing to the cost of goods sold for the year.		

Wagner's Cost of Goods Sold account now includes the cost of all goods *available for sale* during the year. Of course, not all of these goods were sold; the physical inventory taken at the end of 2011 shows that merchandise costing $12,000 is still on hand. Therefore, a second closing entry is made transferring the cost of merchandise still on hand *out* of the Cost of Goods Sold account and *into* the Inventory account. For Wagner, this second closing entry is:

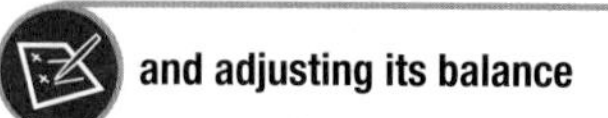

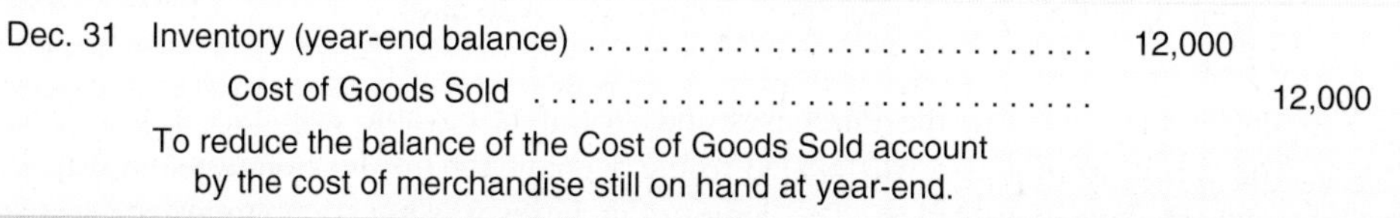

Dec. 31	Inventory (year-end balance)	12,000	
	Cost of Goods Sold		12,000
	To reduce the balance of the Cost of Goods Sold account by the cost of merchandise still on hand at year-end.		

With these two entries, Wagner has created a Cost of Goods Sold account with a balance of $132,000 ($144,000 − $12,000) and has brought its Inventory account up-to-date. Exhibit 6–5 provides a T account presentation of these entries.

Exhibit 6–5

CREATING THE COST OF GOODS SOLD ACCOUNT

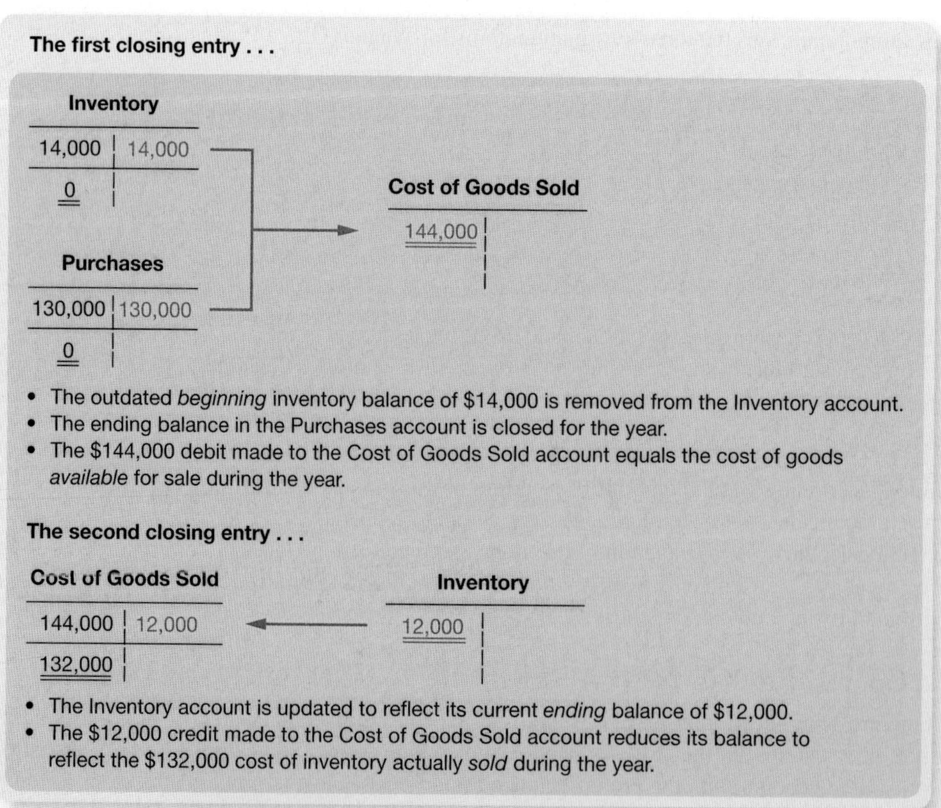

- The outdated *beginning* inventory balance of $14,000 is removed from the Inventory account.
- The ending balance in the Purchases account is closed for the year.
- The $144,000 debit made to the Cost of Goods Sold account equals the cost of goods *available* for sale during the year.

- The Inventory account is updated to reflect its current *ending* balance of $12,000.
- The $12,000 credit made to the Cost of Goods Sold account reduces its balance to reflect the $132,000 cost of inventory actually *sold* during the year.

Completing the Closing Process Wagner may now complete its closing process in the same manner as a company using a perpetual inventory system. The company will make the usual four closing entries, closing the (1) revenue accounts, (2) expense accounts (including Cost of Goods Sold), (3) Income Summary account, and (4) Dividends account.

COMPARISON OF PERPETUAL AND PERIODIC INVENTORY SYSTEMS

Exhibit 6–6 provides a comparison of the way in which various events are recorded in perpetual and periodic systems. Perpetual systems are used when management needs information throughout the year about inventory levels and gross profit. Periodic systems are used when the primary goals are to develop annual data and to minimize record-keeping requirements. A single business may use *different inventory systems* to account for *different types of merchandise.*

Who Uses Perpetual Systems? When management or employees *need up-to-date information about inventory levels,* there is no substitute for a perpetual inventory

Exhibit 6–6 SUMMARY OF THE JOURNAL ENTRIES MADE IN PERPETUAL AND PERIODIC INVENTORY SYSTEMS

Event	Perpetual System			Periodic System		
Acquiring merchandise inventory	Inventory	XXX		Purchases	XXX	
	Accounts Payable (or Cash)		XXX	Accounts Payable (or Cash)		XXX
	To record the purchase of merchandise inventory.			To record the purchase of merchandise inventory.		
Sale of merchandise inventory	Accounts Receivable (or Cash)	XXX		Accounts Receivable (or Cash)	XXX	
	Sales		XXX	Sales		XXX
	To record the sale of merchandise inventory.			To record the sale of merchandise inventory.		
	Cost of Goods Sold	XXX		In a periodic system, no entry at the time of sale is made to update the Cost of Goods Sold and Inventory accounts.		
	Inventory		XXX			
	To update the Cost of Goods Sold and Inventory accounts.					
Settlement of Accounts Payable to suppliers	Accounts Payable	XXX		Accounts Payable	XXX	
	Cash		XXX	Cash		XXX
	To record payment for merchandise inventory purchased on account.			To record payment for merchandise inventory purchased on account.		
Collections from credit customers	Cash	XXX		Cash	XXX	
	Accounts Receivable		XXX	Accounts Receivable		XXX
	To record cash collections from credit customers.			To record cash collections from credit customers.		
Creating year-end balances for Cost of Goods Sold and Inventory accounts	No entry necessary. Cost of Goods Sold and Inventory accounts should both reflect year-end balances in a perpetual system. If a year-end physical count reveals less inventory on hand than reported in the Inventory account, the following entry is needed to record inventory shrinkage:			Cost of Goods Sold	XXX	
				Inventory (beginning bal.)		XXX
				Purchases		XXX
				To close the Purchases and Inventory balances to the Cost of Goods Sold account.		
	Cost of Goods Sold	XXX		Inventory (ending balance)	XXX	
	Inventory (shrinkage amount)		XXX	Cost of Goods Sold		XXX
	To reduce year-end inventory balance for shrinkage.			To create the year-end balance in the Inventory account.		

Note: In a periodic inventory system, the Cost of Goods Sold account is both debited and credited to create its year-end balance.

system. Almost all manufacturing companies use perpetual systems. These businesses need current information to coordinate their inventories of raw materials with their production schedules. Most large merchandising companies—and many small ones—also use perpetual systems.

In the days when all accounting records were maintained by hand, businesses that sold many types of low-cost products had no choice but to use periodic inventory systems. A **Walmart** store, for example, may sell several thousand items *per hour.* Imagine the difficulty of keeping a perpetual inventory system up-to-date if the records were maintained by hand. But with today's *computerized terminals* and *bar-coded merchandise,* many high-volume retailers now use perpetual inventory systems. In fact, **Walmart** has been a leader among retailers in developing perpetual inventory systems.

INTERNATIONAL CASE IN POINT

Walmart, referred to as the company Sam Walton built, is the world's largest retailer. By diversifying from its original discount stores to include **Sam's Club** and its super stores, **Walmart** has fueled its retail engine. International expansion includes 317 stores in Canada, 1,469 in Mexico, 371 in the United Kingdom, 170 Costa Rican stores, 434 stores in Brazil, 279 Chinese stores, 43 stores in Argentina, 371 Japanese stores, and 56 stores in Puerto Rico. According to a recent annual report, 25 percent of total sales came from international locations. **Walmart** employs approximately 1,400,000 associates in the United States and approximately 700,000 internationally.

Source: Walmart stores Inc., 10-K, March 30, 2010.

Perpetual inventory systems are not limited to businesses with computerized inventory systems. Many small businesses with manual systems also use perpetual inventory systems. However, these businesses may update their inventory records on a weekly or a monthly basis, rather than at the time of each sales transaction.

Whether accounting records are maintained manually or by computer, most businesses use perpetual inventory systems in accounting for products with a *high per-unit cost.* Examples include automobiles, heavy machinery, electronic equipment, home appliances, and jewelry. Management has a greater interest in keeping track of inventory when the merchandise is expensive. Also, sales volume usually is low enough that a perpetual system can be used, even if accounting records are maintained by hand.

Who Uses Periodic Systems? Periodic systems are used when the need for current information about inventories and sales *does not justify the cost* of maintaining a perpetual system. In a small retail store, for example, the owner may be so familiar with the inventory that formal perpetual inventory records are unnecessary. Most businesses—large and small—use periodic systems for inventories that are *immaterial* in dollar amount, or when management has little interest in the quantities on hand. As stated previously, businesses that sell many low-cost items and have manual accounting systems sometimes have no choice but to use the periodic method.

SELECTING AN INVENTORY SYSTEM

Learning Objective
LO5 **Discuss the factors to be considered in selecting an inventory system.**

Accountants—and business managers—often must select an inventory system appropriate for a particular situation. Some of the factors usually considered in these decisions are listed in Exhibit 6–7.

The Trend in Today's Business World Advances in technology are quickly extending the use of perpetual inventory systems to more businesses and more types of inventory. This trend is certain to continue. Throughout this textbook, you may assume that a *perpetual inventory system* is in use unless we specifically state otherwise.

Exhibit 6–7

FACTORS INFLUENCING CHOICE OF INVENTORY SYSTEM

Factors Suggesting a Perpetual Inventory System	Factors Suggesting a Periodic Inventory System
Large company with professional management.	Small company, run by owner.
Management and employees wanting information about items in inventory and the quantities of specific products that are selling.	Accounting records of inventories and specific product sales not needed in daily operations; such information developed primarily for use in annual income tax returns.
Items in inventory with a high per-unit cost.	Inventory with many different kinds of low-cost items.
Low volume of sales transactions or a computerized accounting system.	High volume of sales transactions and a manual accounting system.
Merchandise stored at multiple locations or in warehouses separate from the sales sites.	All merchandise stored at the sales site (for example, in the store).

YOUR TURN **You as a Buyer for a Retail Business**

Assume you are in charge of purchasing merchandise for **Ace Hardware Stores**. You are currently making a decision about the purchase of barbecue grills for sale during the upcoming summer season. You must decide how many of each brand and type of grill to order. Describe the types of accounting information that would be useful in making this decision and where this information might be found.

© The McGraw-Hill Companies, Inc./Jill Braaten, photographer/DAL

(See our comments on the Online Learning Center Web site.)

Transactions Relating to Purchases

Learning Objective LO6 **Account for additional merchandising transactions related to purchases and sales.**

In addition to the basic transactions illustrated and explained in this chapter, merchandising companies must account for a variety of additional transactions relating to purchases of merchandise. Examples include discounts offered for prompt payment, merchandise returns, and transportation costs. In our discussion of these transactions, we continue to assume the use of a *perpetual* inventory system.

CREDIT TERMS AND CASH DISCOUNTS

Manufacturers and wholesalers normally sell their products to merchandisers *on account*. The credit terms are stated in the seller's bill, or *invoice*. One common example of credit terms is "net 30 days," or "n/30," meaning full payment is due in 30 days. Another common form of credit terms is "10 eom," meaning payment is due 10 days after the end of the month in which the purchase occurred.

Manufacturers and wholesalers usually allow their customers 30 or 60 days in which to pay for credit purchases. Frequently, however, sellers offer their customers a small discount to encourage earlier payment.

Perhaps the most common credit terms offered by manufacturers and wholesalers are *2/10, n/30*. This expression is read "2, 10, net 30," and means that full payment is due in 30 days, but that the buyer may take a *2 percent discount* if payment is made within 10 days. The period during which the discount is available is termed the *discount period*. Because the discount provides an incentive for the customer to make an early cash payment, it is called a *cash discount*. Buyers, however, often refer to these discounts as *purchase discounts*, while sellers frequently call them *sales discounts*.

Most well-managed companies have a policy of taking advantage of all cash discounts available on purchases of merchandise.[4] These companies initially record purchases of merchandise at the *net cost*—that is, the invoice price *minus* any available discount. After all, this is the amount that the company expects to pay.

To illustrate, assume that on November 3 Computer City purchases 100 spreadsheet programs from PC Products. The cost of these programs is $100 each, for a total of $10,000. However, PC Products offers credit terms of 2/10, n/30. If Computer City pays for this purchase within the discount period, it will have to pay only *$9,800,* or 98 percent of the full invoice price. Therefore, Computer City will record this purchase as follows:

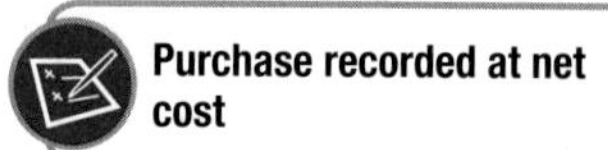
Purchase recorded at net cost

Inventory	9,800	
Accounts Payable (PC Products)		9,800
To record purchase of 100 spreadsheet programs at net cost ($100 × 98% × 100 units).		

If the invoice is paid within the discount period, Computer City simply records payment of a $9,800 account payable.

Through oversight or carelessness, Computer City might fail to make payment within the discount period. In this event, Computer City must pay PC Products the entire invoice price of *$10,000,* rather than the recorded liability of $9,800. The journal entry to record payment *after the discount period*—on, say, December 3—is:

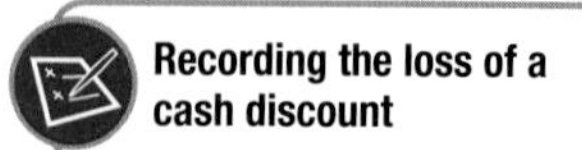
Recording the loss of a cash discount

Accounts Payable (PC Products)	9,800	
Purchase Discounts Lost	200	
Cash		10,000
To record payment of invoice after expiration of the discount period.		

Notice that the $200 paid above the $9,800 recorded amount is debited to an account entitled Purchase Discounts Lost. Purchase Discounts Lost is an *expense account.* The only benefit to Computer City from this $200 expenditure was a *20-day delay* in paying an account payable. Thus the lost purchase discount is basically a *finance charge,* similar to interest expense. In an income statement, finance charges usually are classified as nonoperating expenses.

The fact that purchase discounts *not taken* are recorded in a separate expense account is the primary reason why a company should record purchases of merchandise at *net cost.* The use of a Purchase Discounts Lost account immediately brings to management's attention any failure to take advantage of the cash discounts offered by suppliers.

Recording Purchases at Gross Invoice Price As an alternative to recording purchases at net cost, some companies record merchandise purchases at the gross (total) invoice price. If payment is made within the discount period, these companies must record the amount of the purchase discount *taken.*

To illustrate, assume that Computer City followed a policy of recording purchases at gross invoice price. The entry on November 3 to record the purchase from PC Products would have been:

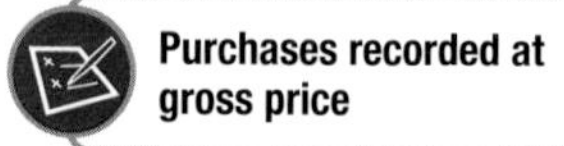
Purchases recorded at gross price

Inventory	10,000	
Accounts Payable (PC Products)		10,000
To record purchase of 100 spreadsheet programs at gross invoice price ($100 × 100 units).		

[4] The terms 2/10, n/30 offer the buyer a 2 percent discount for paying 20 days prior to when the full amount is due. Saving 2 percent over only 20 days is equivalent to earning an annual rate of return of more than 36 percent (2% × 365/20 = 36.5%). Thus, taking cash discounts represents an excellent investment opportunity. Most companies take advantage of all cash discounts, even if they must borrow the necessary cash from a bank to make payment within the discount period.

If payment is made within the discount period, Computer City will discharge this $10,000 account payable by paying only $9,800. The entry will be:

Accounts Payable (PC Products)	10,000	
Cash		9,800
Purchase Discounts Taken		200
To record payment of $10,000 invoice within the discount period; 2% purchase discount taken.		

Buyer records discounts taken 

Purchase Discounts Taken is treated as a reduction in the cost of goods sold.

Both the net cost and gross price methods are widely used and produce substantially the same results in financial statements.[5] A shortcoming of the gross price method as compared to the net cost method for valuing inventory is that it does not direct management's attention to discounts lost. Instead, these discounts are buried in the costs assigned to inventory. Management can use financial reporting policies to motivate the purchasing staff to take advantage of purchase discounts when possible. By recording inventory with the net cost method, management can highlight the success of their purchasing efforts to obtain the lowest possible costs for purchased inventory. Because of the advantage of the net cost method, it is the approach recommended by the authors of this textbook.

RETURNS OF UNSATISFACTORY MERCHANDISE

On occasion, a buyer may find the purchased merchandise unsatisfactory and want to return it to the seller for a refund. Most sellers permit such returns.

To illustrate, assume that on November 9 Computer City returns to PC Products five of the spreadsheet programs purchased on November 3, because these programs were not properly labeled. As Computer City has not yet paid for this merchandise, the return will reduce the amount that Computer City owes PC Products. The gross invoice price of the returned merchandise was $500 ($100 per program). Assume that Computer City records purchases at *net cost.* Therefore, these spreadsheet programs are carried in Computer City's inventory subsidiary ledger at a per-unit cost of *$98,* or $490 for the five programs being returned. The entry to record this purchase return is:

Accounts Payable (PC Products)	490	
Inventory		490
Returned five mislabeled spreadsheet programs to supplier. Net cost of the returned items, $490 ($100 × 98% × 5 units).		

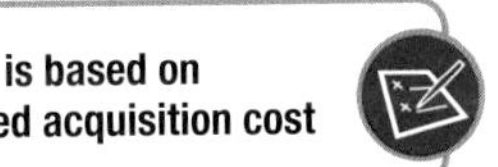

Return is based on recorded acquisition cost

The reduction in inventory must also be recorded in the subsidiary ledger accounts.

TRANSPORTATION COSTS ON PURCHASES

The purchaser sometimes may pay the costs of having the purchased merchandise delivered to its premises. Transportation costs relating to the *acquisition* of inventory, or any other asset, are *not expenses* of the current period; rather, these charges are *part of the cost of the asset* being acquired. If the purchaser is able to associate transportation costs with specific products, these costs should be debited directly to the Inventory account as part of the cost of the merchandise.

Often, many different products arrive in a single shipment. In such cases, it may be impractical for the purchaser to determine the amount of the total transportation cost applicable to each product. For this reason, many companies follow the convenient policy of debiting all transportation costs on inbound shipments of merchandise to an account entitled *Transportation-in.* The dollar amount of transportation-in usually is too small to show separately in the financial statements. Therefore, it is often simply added to the amount reported in the income statement as cost of goods sold.

[5] The net cost method values the ending inventory at net cost, whereas the gross cost method shows this inventory at gross invoice price. This difference, however, is usually *immaterial.*

This treatment of transportation costs is not entirely consistent with the *matching principle.* Some of the transportation costs apply to merchandise still in inventory rather than to goods sold during the current period. We have mentioned, however, that transportation costs are relatively small in dollar amount. The accounting principle of *materiality,* therefore, usually justifies accounting for these costs in the most convenient manner.

Transactions Relating to Sales

Credit terms and merchandise returns also affect the amount of sales revenue earned by the seller. To the extent that credit customers take advantage of cash discounts or return merchandise for a refund, the seller's revenue is reduced. Thus revenue shown in the income statement of a merchandising concern is often called *net sales.*

The term **net sales** means total sales revenue *minus* sales returns and allowances and *minus* sales discounts. The partial income statement in Exhibit 6–8 illustrates this relationship.

Exhibit 6–8
PARTIAL INCOME STATEMENT

COMPUTER CITY
PARTIAL INCOME STATEMENT
FOR THE YEAR ENDED DECEMBER 31, 2011

Revenue:		
Sales		$912,000
Less: Sales returns and allowances	$8,000	
Sales discounts	4,000	12,000
Net sales		$900,000

The details of this computation seldom are shown in an actual income statement. The normal practice is to begin the income statement with the amount of net sales.

SALES RETURNS AND ALLOWANCES

Most merchandising companies allow customers to obtain a refund by returning any merchandise considered to be unsatisfactory. If the merchandise has only minor defects, customers sometimes agree to keep the merchandise if an *allowance* (reduction) is made in the sales price.

Under the perpetual inventory system, two entries are needed to record the sale of merchandise: one to recognize the revenue earned and the other to transfer the cost of the merchandise from the Inventory account to Cost of Goods Sold. If some of the merchandise is returned, both of these entries are partially reversed.

First, let us consider the effects on revenue of granting either a refund or an allowance. Both refunds and allowances have the effect of nullifying previously recorded sales and reducing the amount of revenue earned by the business. This journal entry reduces sales revenue as the result of a sales return (or allowance):

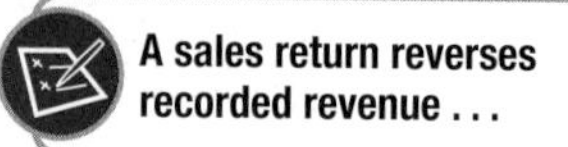
A sales return reverses recorded revenue . . .

Sales Returns and Allowances	1,000	
Accounts Receivable (or Cash)		1,000
Customer returned merchandise purchased on account for $1,000. Allowed customer full credit for returned merchandise.		

Sales Returns and Allowances is a **contra-revenue account**—that is, it is deducted from gross sales revenue as a step in determining net sales.

Why use a separate Sales Returns and Allowances account rather than merely debiting the Sales account? The answer is that using a separate contra-revenue account enables management to see both the total amount of sales *and* the amount of sales returns. The relationship between these amounts gives management an indication of *customer satisfaction* with the merchandise.

If merchandise is returned by the customer, a second entry is made to remove the cost of this merchandise from the Cost of Goods Sold account and restore it to the inventory records. This entry is:

Inventory	600	
Cost of Goods Sold		600
To restore in the Inventory account the cost of merchandise returned by a customer.		

and the recorded cost of goods sold

Notice that this entry is based on the *cost* of the returned merchandise to the seller, *not on its sales price.* (This entry is not necessary when a sales *allowance* is granted to a customer who keeps the merchandise.)

SALES DISCOUNTS

We have explained that sellers frequently offer cash discounts, such as 2/10, n/30, to encourage customers to make early payments for purchases on account.

Sellers and buyers account for cash discounts quite differently. To the seller, the cost associated with cash discounts is not the discounts *lost* when payments are delayed, but rather the discounts *taken* by customers who do pay within the discount period. Therefore, sellers design their accounting systems to measure the sales discounts *taken* by their customers. To achieve this goal, the seller records the sale and the related account receivable at the *gross* (full) invoice price.

To illustrate, assume that Computer City sells merchandise to the Highlander Pub for $1,000, offering terms of 2/10, n/30. The sales revenue is recorded at the full invoice price, as follows:

Accounts Receivable (Highlander Pub)	1,000	
Sales		1,000
Sold merchandise on account. Invoice price, $1,000; terms, 2/10, n/30.		

Sales are recorded at the gross sales price

If the Highlander Pub makes payment after the discount period has expired, Computer City records the receipt of $1,000 cash in full payment of this account receivable. If it pays *within* the discount period, however, the pub will pay only *$980* to settle its account. In this case, Computer City will record the receipt of the pub's payment as follows:

Cash	980	
Sales Discounts	20	
Accounts Receivable (Highlander Pub)		1,000
Collected a $1,000 account receivable from a customer who took a 2% discount for early payment.		

Seller records discounts taken by customers

Sales Discounts is another contra-revenue account. In the computing of net sales, sales discounts are deducted from gross sales along with any sales returns and allowances. (If the customer has returned part of the merchandise, a discount may be taken only on the gross amount owed *after* the return.)

Contra-revenue accounts have much in common with expense accounts; both are deducted from gross revenue in determining net income, and both have debit balances. Thus contra-revenue accounts (Sales Returns and Allowances and Sales Discounts) are closed to the Income Summary account *in the same manner as expense accounts.*

DELIVERY EXPENSES

If the seller incurs any costs in delivering merchandise to the customer, these costs are debited to an expense account entitled Delivery Expense. In an income statement, delivery expense is classified as a regular operating expense, not as part of the cost of goods sold.

ACCOUNTING FOR SALES TAXES

Sales taxes are levied by many states and cities on retail sales.[6] Sales taxes actually are imposed on the consumer, not on the seller. However, the seller must collect the tax, file tax returns at times specified by law, and remit to governmental agencies the taxes collected.

For cash sales, sales tax is collected from the customer at the time of the sales transaction. For credit sales, the sales tax is included in the amount charged to the customer's account. In a computerized accounting system, the liability to the governmental unit for sales taxes is recorded automatically at the time the sale is made, as shown in the following journal entry:

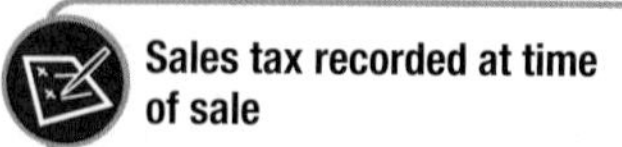
Sales tax recorded at time of sale

Cash (or Accounts Receivable)	1,070	
Sales Tax Payable		70
Sales		1,000
To record sales of $1,000, subject to 7% sales tax.		

Modifying an Accounting System

Learning Objective
LO7 **Define *special journals* and explain their usefulness.**

Throughout this textbook we illustrate the effects of many transactions using the format of a two-column *general journal.* This format is ideal for textbook illustrations, as it allows us to concisely show the effects of *any type* of business transaction.

But while general journal entries are useful for our purposes, they are not the most efficient way for a business to record routine transactions. A supermarket, for example, may sell 10,000 to 15,000 items *per hour.* Clearly, it would not be practical to make a general journal entry to record each of these sales transactions. Therefore, most businesses use *special journals,* rather than a general journal, to record *routine transactions that occur frequently.*

SPECIAL JOURNALS PROVIDE SPEED AND EFFICIENCY

A **special journal** is an accounting record or device designed to record *a specific type of routine transaction quickly and efficiently.*

Some special journals are maintained by hand. An example is the *check register* in your personal checkbook. If properly maintained, this special journal provides an efficient record of all cash disbursements made by check.

But many special journals are highly automated. Consider the **point-of-sale (POS) terminals** that you see in supermarkets and large retail stores. These devices record sales transactions and the related cost of goods sold as quickly as the bar-coded merchandise can be passed over the scanner.

Relative to the general journal, special journals offer the following advantages:

- Transactions are recorded faster and more efficiently.
- Many special journals may be in operation at one time, further increasing the company's ability to handle a large volume of transactions.
- Automation may reduce the risk of errors.
- Employees maintaining special journals generally do not need expertise in accounting.
- The recording of transactions may be an automatic side effect of other basic business activities, such as collecting cash from customers.

Most businesses use separate special journals to record repetitive transactions such as sales of merchandise, cash receipts, cash payments, purchases of merchandise on account, and payrolls. There are no rules for the design or content of special journals. Rather, they are tailored to suit the needs, activities, and resources of the particular business organization.

Let us stress that the *accounting principles* used in special journals are the *same* as those used for transactions recorded in a general journal. The differences lie in the *recording techniques,* not in the information that is recorded.

[6] Sales taxes are applicable only when merchandise is sold to the *final consumer;* thus no sales taxes are normally levied when manufacturers or wholesalers sell merchandise to retailers.

Remember also that special journals are *highly specialized* in terms of the transactions they can record. Thus every business still needs a general journal to record transactions that do not fit into any of its special journals, including, for example, adjusting entries, closing entries, and unusual events such as a loss sustained from a fire.

Management uses information about departments and products for many purposes. These include setting prices, deciding which products to carry and to advertise, and evaluating the performance of departmental managers. By concentrating sales efforts on the products and departments with the *highest margins,* management usually can increase the company's overall gross profit rate.

Financial Analysis and Decision Making

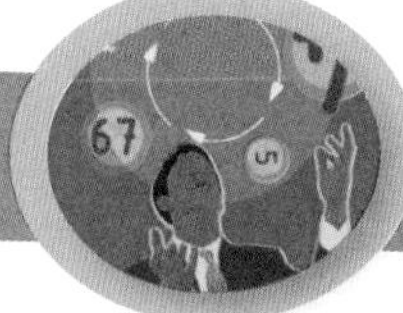

In evaluating the performance of a merchandising business, managers and investors look at more than just net income. Two key measures of past performance and future prospects are trends in the company's *net sales* and *gross profit.*

Net Sales

Learning Objective
Measure the performance of a merchandising business.
LO8

Most investors and business managers consider the *trend* in net sales to be a key indicator of both past performance and future prospects. Increasing sales suggest the probability of larger profits in future periods. Declining sales, on the other hand, may provide advance warning of financial difficulties.

As a measure of performance, the trend in net sales has some limitations, especially when the company is adding new stores. For these companies, an increase in overall net sales in comparison to the prior year may have resulted solely from sales at the new stores. Sales at existing stores may even be declining. Business managers and investors often focus on measures that adjust for changes in the number of stores from period to period, and on measures of space utilization. These measures include:

1. **Comparable store sales.** Net sales at established stores, excluding new stores opened during the period. Indicates whether customer demand is rising or falling at established locations. (Also called *same-store sales.*)
2. **Sales per square foot of selling space.** A measure of how effectively the company is using its physical facilities (such as floor space or, in supermarkets, shelf space).

Gross Profit Margins

Increasing net sales is *not enough* to ensure increasing profitability. Some products are more profitable than others. In evaluating the profitability of sales transactions, managers and investors keep a close eye on the company's **gross profit margin** (also called *gross profit rate*).

Gross profit margin is the dollar amount of gross profit, expressed as a *percentage* of net sales revenue. Gross profit margins can be computed for the business as a whole, for specific sales departments, and for individual products.

To illustrate the computation of gross profit margin, consider selected income statement data for **Home Depot**, **Saks**, and **Walmart**. The sales, cost of sales, and gross profit for these companies are as follows (in thousands of dollars):

	Home Depot	Saks	Walmart
Net sales	$66,176,000	$2,631,532	$405,046,000
Cost of sales	43,764,000	1,668,097	304,657,000
Gross profit	$22,412,000	$ 963,435	$100,389,000

The Overall Gross Profit Margin The average gross profit margin (gross profit rate) is a measure of relative profitability. The gross profit rate is calculated by dividing gross profit (in dollars) by net sales. The gross profit rates for **Home Depot**, **Saks**, and **Walmart** are:

- **Home Depot**: 33.87 percent ($22,412/$66,176)
- **Saks**: 36.61 percent ($963,435/$2,631,532)
- **Walmart**: 24.78 percent ($100,389/$405,046)

Using Information about Gross Profit Margins

Investors usually compute companies' overall gross profit rates from one period to the next. High—or increasing—margins generally indicate popular products and successful marketing strategies. A substandard or declining profit margin, on the other hand, often indicates weak customer demand or intense price competition.[7]

[7] We discuss the interpretation of gross profit in greater depth in Chapter 14.

Ethics, Fraud & Corporate Governance

As discussed previously in this chapter, sales discounts and allowances are contra-revenue accounts. Sales discounts and allowances reduce gross sales. As such, net income will be incorrect if discounts and allowances are not properly recorded. The Securities and Exchange Commission (SEC) brought an enforcement action against **Pepsi-Cola Puerto Rico (Pepsi PR)** alleging that **Pepsi PR** understated its sales discounts and allowances. **Pepsi PR** produces, distributes, and markets **Pepsi Co** beverages throughout Puerto Rico. **Pepsi PR** is a separate company and its stock was listed on the New York Stock Exchange at the time of the SEC enforcement action.

The **Coca-Cola** bottler in Puerto Rico attempted to gain market share by cutting prices. **Pepsi PR** responded by offering more generous sales discounts and allowances. However, offering these additional discounts and allowances would have reduced **Pepsi PR**'s net income. The **Pepsi PR** general manager instructed the company's finance staff not to record some of the sales discounts and allowances given to customers. **Pepsi PR**'s failure to record discounts and allowances resulted in net income for the first quarter being overstated by $3.3 million and net income for the second quarter being overstated by $5.7 million. **Pepsi PR** consented to an SEC cease-and-desist order without either admitting or denying guilt.

Although **Pepsi PR**'s general manager initiated the scheme that led to the misstatement of **Pepsi PR**'s financial statements, the failure to record sales discounts and allowances was carried out by the company's director of finance and other finance department staffers. The individuals who carried out this scheme knew that **Pepsi PR**'s financial results would be misstated if sales discounts and allowances were not recorded correctly. However, these individuals were unwilling to defy their superior, even when their superior was asking them to engage in unethical and illegal behavior. In cases of fraudulent financial reporting, subordinates being pressured by superiors to implement the fraud scheme is relatively common.

The pressure brought to bear on subordinates to implement fraudulent schemes developed by top management can often be intense. Top management can threaten employees with termination if they fail to participate in the fraud. Unfortunately, employees who acquiesce to such pressure face tremendous legal risks. Unlike their superiors, the fingerprints of lower-level employees who actually implement the fraudulent scheme are all over the incriminating documents. For example, a midlevel tax manager who was convicted of participating in a scheme to misstate **Dynergy**'s financial statements was sentenced to 24 years in federal prison (although this sentence was substantially reduced on appeal). This individual's bosses, who were equally implicit in the scheme, pled guilty and testified against their former employee. They received less than five years in prison.

The Sarbanes-Oxley Act provides some protection for lower-level employees who are pressured to participate in an accounting fraud. Public company audit committees must establish procedures (typically company "hotlines") that can be used by employees reporting concerns related to questionable accounting or auditing matters. In addition, Sarbanes-Oxley includes certain "whistle-blower" protections. No public company may discharge, demote, suspend, threaten, harass, or in any other manner discriminate against an employee if the employee provides information or assistance in an investigation involving securities fraud.

Concluding Remarks

The Overnight Auto Service illustration presented in Chapter 2 through Chapter 5 addressed measurement and reporting issues pertaining to a service-type business. Throughout this chapter, we have had an opportunity to see how merchandising companies measure and report the results for their operations. Many of the illustrations and assignments throughout the remainder of this textbook are based upon merchandising enterprises.

In Chapter 7, we examine accounts receivable and other liquid assets common to merchandisers. In Chapter 8, we focus upon issues related to merchandise inventories. Measurement and reporting issues that pertain primarily to manufacturing companies are generally covered in a subsequent course.

END-OF-CHAPTER REVIEW

SUMMARY OF LEARNING OBJECTIVES

LO1 **Describe the *operating cycle* of a merchandising company.** The operating cycle is the repeating sequence of transactions by which a company generates revenue and cash receipts from customers. In a merchandising company, the operating cycle consists of the following transactions: (1) purchases of merchandise, (2) sale of the merchandise—often on account—and (3) collection of accounts receivable from customers.

LO2 **Understand the components of a merchandising company's income statement.** In a merchandising company's income statement, *sales* (or *net sales*) represent the total revenue generated by selling merchandise to its customers. As items are sold from inventory, their costs are transferred from the balance sheet to the income statement, where they appear as the *cost of goods sold.* The cost of goods sold is subtracted from sales to determine the company's *gross profit. Other expenses* (such as wages, advertising, utilities, and depreciation) are subtracted from gross profit in the determination of *net income.* Only if a company's gross profit exceeds the sum of its other expenses will it be profitable.

LO3 **Account for purchases and sales of merchandise in a *perpetual* inventory system.** In a perpetual inventory system, purchases of merchandise are recorded by debiting the Inventory account. Two entries are required to record each sale: one to recognize sales revenue and the second to record the cost of goods sold. This second entry consists of a debit to Cost of Goods Sold and a credit to Inventory.

LO4 **Explain how a *periodic* inventory system operates.** In a periodic system, up-to-date records are *not* maintained for inventory or the cost of goods sold. Thus less record keeping is required than in a perpetual system.

The beginning and ending inventories are determined by taking a complete physical count at each year-end. Purchases are recorded in a Purchases account, and no entries are made to record the cost of individual sales transactions. Instead, the cost of goods sold is determined at year-end by a computation such as the following (dollar amounts are provided only for purposes of example):

Beginning inventory	$ 30,000
Add: Purchases	180,000
Cost of goods available for sale	$210,000
Less: Ending inventory	40,000
Cost of goods sold	$170,000

The amounts of inventory and the cost of goods sold are recorded in the accounting records during the year-end closing procedures.

LO5 **Discuss the factors to be considered in selecting an inventory system.** In general terms, a perpetual system should be used when (1) management and employees need timely information about inventory levels and product sales, and (2) the company has the resources to develop this information at a reasonable cost. A periodic system should be used when the usefulness of current information about inventories does not justify the cost of maintaining a perpetual system.

Perpetual systems are most widely used in companies with computerized accounting systems and in businesses that sell high-cost merchandise. Periodic systems are most often used in small businesses that have manual accounting systems and that sell many types of low-cost merchandise.

LO6 **Account for additional merchandising transactions related to purchases and sales.** Buyers should record purchases at the net cost and record any cash discounts lost in an expense account. Sellers record sales at the gross sales price and record in a contra-revenue account all cash discounts taken by customers.

Assuming a perpetual inventory system, the buyer records a purchase return by crediting the Inventory account for the net cost of the returned merchandise. In recording a sales return, the seller makes two entries: one to record Sales Returns and Allowances (a contra-revenue account) for the amount of the refund and the other to transfer the cost of the returned merchandise from the Cost of Goods Sold account back into the Inventory account.

Buyers record transportation charges on purchased merchandise either as part of the cost of the merchandise or directly as part of the cost of goods sold. Sellers view the cost of delivering merchandise to customers as an operating expense.

Sales taxes are collected by retailers from their customers and paid to state and city governments. Thus collecting sales taxes increases the retailer's assets and liabilities. Paying the sales tax to the government is payment of the liability, not an expense.

LO7 **Define *special journals* and explain their usefulness.** Special journals are accounting records or devices designed to record a specific type of transaction in a highly efficient manner. Because a special journal is used only to record a specific type of transaction, the journal may be located at the transaction site and maintained by employees other than accounting personnel. Thus special journals reduce the time, effort, and cost of recording routine business transactions.

LO8 **Measure the performance of a merchandising business.** There are numerous measures used to evaluate the performance of merchandising businesses. In this chapter, we introduced three of these measures: (1) comparable store sales, which helps determine whether customer demand is rising or falling at established locations, (2) sales per square foot of selling space, which is a measure of how effectively a merchandising business is using its facilities to generate revenue, and (3) gross profit percentages, which help users of financial statements gain insight about a company's pricing policies and the demand for its products.

Key Terms Introduced or Emphasized in Chapter 6

comparable store sales (p. 263) A comparison of sales figures at established stores with existing "track records." (Also called *same-store sales.*)

contra-revenue account (p. 260) A debit balance account that is offset against revenue in the income statement. Examples include Sales Discounts and Sales Returns and Allowances.

control account (p. 248) A general ledger account that summarizes the content of a specific subsidiary ledger.

cost of goods sold (p. 247) The cost to a merchandising company of the goods it has sold to its customers during the period.

gross profit (p. 248) Net sales revenue minus the cost of goods sold.

gross profit margin (p. 263) Gross profit expressed as a percentage of net sales. Also called *gross profit rate*.

inventory (p. 246) Merchandise intended for resale to customers.

inventory shrinkage (p. 251) The loss of merchandise through such causes as shoplifting, breakage, and spoilage.

net sales (p. 260) Gross sales revenue less sales returns and allowances and sales discounts. The most widely used measure of dollar sales volume; usually the first figure shown in an income statement.

operating cycle (p. 246) The repeating sequence of transactions by which a business generates its revenue and cash receipts from customers.

periodic inventory system (p. 252) An alternative to the perpetual inventory system. It eliminates the need for recording the cost of goods sold as sales occur. However, the amounts of inventory and the cost of goods sold are not known until a complete physical inventory is taken at year-end.

perpetual inventory system (p. 249) A system of accounting for merchandising transactions in which the Inventory and Cost of Goods Sold accounts are kept perpetually up-to-date.

point-of-sale (POS) terminals (p. 262) Electronic cash registers used for computer-based processing of sales transactions. The POS terminal identifies each item of merchandise from its bar code and then automatically records the sale and updates the computer-based inventory records. These terminals permit the use of perpetual inventory systems in many businesses that sell a high volume of low-cost merchandise.

sales per square foot of selling space (p. 263) A measure of efficient use of available space.

special journal (p. 262) An accounting record or device designed for recording large numbers of a particular type of transaction quickly and efficiently. A business may use many different kinds of special journals.

subsidiary ledger (p. 248) A ledger containing separate accounts for each of the items making up the balance of a control account in the general ledger. The total of the account balances in a subsidiary ledger are equal to the balance in the general ledger control account.

taking a physical inventory (p. 251) The procedure of counting all merchandise on hand and determining its cost.

Demonstration Problem

STAR-TRACK sells satellite tracking systems for receiving television broadcasts from communications satellites in space. At December 31, 2011, the company's inventory amounted to $44,000. During the first week in January 2012, STAR-TRACK made only one purchase and one sale. These transactions were as follows:

Jan. 3 Sold a tracking system to Mystery Mountain Resort for $20,000 cash. The system consisted of seven different devices, which had a total cost to STAR-TRACK of $11,200.

Jan. 7 Purchased two Model 400 and four Model 800 satellite dishes from Yamaha Corp. The total cost of this purchase amounted to $10,000; terms 2/10, n/30.

STAR-TRACK records purchases of merchandise at net cost. The company has full-time accounting personnel and uses a manual accounting system.

Instructions

a. Briefly describe the operating cycle of a merchandising company.

b. Prepare journal entries to record these transactions, assuming that STAR-TRACK uses a perpetual inventory system.

c. Explain what information in part **b** should be posted to subsidiary ledger accounts.

d. Compute the balance in the Inventory control account at January 7.

e. Prepare journal entries to record the two transactions, assuming that STAR-TRACK uses a *periodic* inventory system.

f. Compute the cost of goods sold for the first week of January, assuming use of the periodic system. As the amount of ending inventory, use your answer to part **d**.

g. Which type of inventory system do you think STAR-TRACK should use? Explain your reasoning.

h. Determine the gross profit margin on the January 3 sales transaction.

Solution to the Demonstration Problem

a. The operating cycle of a merchandising company consists of purchasing merchandise, selling that merchandise to customers (often on account), and collecting the sales proceeds from these customers. In the process, the business converts cash into inventory, the inventory into accounts receivable, and the accounts receivable into cash.

b. Journal entries assuming use of a *perpetual* inventory system:

GENERAL JOURNAL

Date	Account Titles and Explanation	Debit	Credit
2012			
Jan. 3	Cash	20,000	
	Sales		20,000
	Sold tracking system to Mystery Mountain Resort.		
3	Cost of Goods Sold	11,200	
	Inventory		11,200
	To record cost of merchandise sold.		
7	Inventory	9,800	
	Accounts Payable (Yamaha Corp.)		9,800
	Purchased merchandise. Terms, 2/10, n/30; net cost, $9,800 ($10,000, less 2%).		

c. The debits and credits to the Inventory account should be posted to the appropriate accounts in the inventory subsidiary ledger. The information posted would be the costs and quantities of the types of merchandise purchased or sold. The account payable to Yamaha also should be posted to the Yamaha account in STAR-TRACK's accounts payable ledger. No postings are required to the accounts receivable ledger, as this was a cash sale. If STAR-TRACK maintains more than one bank account, however, the debit to cash should be posted to the proper account in the cash subsidiary ledger.

d. $42,600 ($44,000 beginning balance, less $11,200, plus $9,800).

e. Journal entries assuming use of a *periodic* inventory system:

GENERAL JOURNAL

Date	Account Titles and Explanation	Debit	Credit
2012			
Jan. 3	Cash	20,000	
	Sales		20,000
	Sold tracking system to Mystery Mountain Resort.		
7	Purchases	9,800	
	Accounts Payable (Yamaha Corp.)		9,800
	Purchased merchandise. Terms, 2/10, n/30; net cost, $9,800 ($10,000, less 2%).		

f. Computation of the cost of goods sold:

Inventory, January 1	$44,000
Add: Purchases	9,800
Cost of goods available for sale	$53,800
Less: Inventory, January 7 (per part **d**)	42,600
Cost of goods sold	$11,200

g. STAR-TRACK should use a *perpetual* inventory system. The items in its inventory have a high per-unit cost. Therefore, management will want to know the costs of the individual products included in specific sales transactions and will want to keep track of the items in stock. Although the company has a manual accounting system, its volume of sales transactions is low enough that maintaining a perpetual inventory record will not be difficult.

h. Gross profit = Sales revenue − Cost of goods sold
= $20,000 − $11,200
= $8,800

Gross profit margin = Gross profit ÷ Sales revenue
= $8,800 ÷ $20,000
= 44%

Self-Test Questions

The answers to these questions appear on page 285.

1. Mark and Amanda Carter own an appliance store and a restaurant. The appliance store sells merchandise on a 12-month installment plan; the restaurant sells only for cash. Which of the following statements are true? (More than one answer may be correct.)

a. The appliance store has a longer operating cycle than the restaurant.

b. The appliance store probably uses a perpetual inventory system, whereas the restaurant probably uses a periodic system.

c. Both businesses require subsidiary ledgers for accounts receivable and inventory.

d. Both businesses probably have subsidiary ledgers for accounts payable.

2. Which of the following statements about merchandising activities is true? (More than one answer may be correct.)

a. As inventory is purchased, the Inventory Expense account is debited and Cash (or Accounts Payable) is credited.

b. Inventory is recorded as an asset when it is first purchased.

c. As inventory is sold, its cost is transferred from the balance sheet to the income statement.

d. As inventory is sold, its cost is transferred from the income statement to the balance sheet.

3. Marietta Corporation uses a *perpetual* inventory system. All of its sales are made on account. The company sells merchandise costing $3,000 at a sales price of $4,300. In recording this transaction, Marietta will make all of the following entries *except:*

a. Credit Sales, $4,300.

b. Credit Inventory, $4,300.

c. Debit Cost of Goods Sold, $3,000.

d. Debit Accounts Receivable, $4,300.

4. Fashion House uses a *perpetual* inventory system. At the beginning of the year, inventory amounted to $50,000. During the year, the company purchased merchandise for $230,000 and sold merchandise costing $245,000. A physical inventory taken at year-end indicated shrinkage losses of $4,000. *Prior* to recording these shrinkage losses, the year-end balance in the company's Inventory account was:

a. $31,000.

b. $35,000.

c. $50,000.

d. Some other amount.

5. Best Hardware uses a *periodic* inventory system. Its inventory was $38,000 at the beginning of the year and $40,000 at the end. During the year, Best made purchases of merchandise totaling $107,000. Identify all of the correct answers:

a. To use this system, Best must take a complete physical inventory twice each year.

b. Prior to making adjusting and closing entries at year-end, the balance in Best's Inventory account is $38,000.

c. The cost of goods sold for the year is $109,000.

d. As sales transactions occur, Best makes no entries to update its inventory records or to record the cost of goods sold.

6. The two basic approaches to accounting for inventory and the cost of goods sold are the *perpetual* inventory system and the *periodic* inventory system. Indicate which of the following statements are correct. (More than one answer may be correct.)

   a. Most large merchandising companies and manufacturing businesses use periodic inventory systems.

   b. As a practical matter, a grocery store or a large department store could not maintain a perpetual inventory system without the use of point-of-sale terminals.

   c. In a periodic inventory system, the cost of goods sold is not determined until a complete physical inventory is taken.

   d. In a perpetual inventory system, the Cost of Goods Sold account is debited promptly for the cost of merchandise sold.

7. Big Brother, a retail store, purchased 100 television sets from Krueger Electronics on account at a cost of $200 each. Krueger offers credit terms of 2/10, n/30. Big Brother uses a perpetual inventory system and records purchases at *net cost*. Big Brother determines that 10 of these television sets are defective and returns them to Krueger for full credit. In recording this return, Big Brother will:

   a. Debit Sales Returns and Allowances, $1,960.

   b. Debit Accounts Payable, $1,960.

   c. Debit Cost of Goods Sold, $1,960.

   d. Credit Inventory, $2,000.

8. Two of the lawn mowers sold by Garden Products Co. are the LawnMaster and the Mark 5. LawnMasters sell for $250 apiece, which results in a 35 percent gross profit margin. Each Mark 5 costs Garden Products $300 and sells for $400. Indicate all correct answers.

   a. The dollar amount of gross profit is greater on the sale of a Mark 5 than a LawnMaster.

   b. The gross profit margin is higher on Mark 5s than on LawnMasters.

   c. Garden profits relatively more by selling one Mark 5 than by selling one LawnMaster.

   d. Garden profits more by selling $2,000 worth of Mark 5s than $2,000 worth of LawnMasters.

ASSIGNMENT MATERIAL Discussion Questions

1. The income statement of a merchandising company includes a major type of cost that does not appear in the income statement of a service-type business. Identify this cost and explain what it represents.

2. During the current year, Green Bay Company earned a gross profit of $350,000, whereas New England Company earned a gross profit of only $280,000. Both companies had net sales of $900,000. Does this mean that Green Bay is more profitable than New England? Explain.

3. Explain the need for subsidiary ledgers in accounting for merchandising activities.

4. Define the term *inventory shrinkage*. How is the amount of inventory shrinkage determined in a business using a perpetual inventory system, and how is this shrinkage recorded in the accounting records?

5. Briefly contrast the accounting procedures in *perpetual* and *periodic* inventory systems.

6. Evaluate the following statement: "Without electronic point-of-sale terminals, it simply would not be possible to use perpetual inventory systems in businesses that sell large quantities of many different products."

7. Explain the distinguishing characteristics of **(a)** a general journal and **(b)** a special journal.

8. How does a balance arise in the Purchase Discounts Lost account? Why does management pay careful attention to the balance (if any) in this account?

9. European Imports pays substantial freight charges to obtain inbound shipments of purchased merchandise. Should these freight charges be debited to the company's Delivery Expense account? Explain.

10. Outback Sporting Goods purchases merchandise on terms of 4/10, n/60. The company has a line of credit that enables it to borrow money as needed from Northern Bank at an annual interest rate of 13 percent. Should Outback pay its suppliers within the 10-day discount period if it must draw on its line of credit (borrow from Northern Bank) to make these early payments? Explain.

11. TireCo is a retail store in a state that imposes a 6 percent sales tax. Would you expect to find sales tax expense and sales tax payable in TireCo's financial statements? Explain.

12. A seller generally records sales at the full invoice price, but the buyer often records purchases at *net cost*. Explain the logic of the buyer and seller recording the transaction at different amounts.

13. Define the term *gross profit margin*. Explain several ways in which management might improve a company's overall profit margin.

14. Under a perpetual inventory system, a company should know the quantity and price of its inventory at any moment in time. Given this, why do companies that use a perpetual inventory system still take a physical count of their merchandise inventory at least once a year?

15. Under which type of inventory system is an inventory subsidiary ledger maintained?

Brief Exercises

LO2 LO8 **BRIEF EXERCISE 6.1**
Computation of Gross Profit

Office Today is an office supply store. Office Today's revenue in the current year is $800 million and its cost of goods sold is $640 million. Compute Office Today's gross profit and its gross profit percentage.

LO7 **BRIEF EXERCISE 6.2**
Accounts Receivable Subsidiary Ledger

The accounts receivable subsidiary ledger for Ranalli's Lawn Care has the following customer accounts and balances at the end of the current year. What should be the Accounts Receivable balance in the general ledger? [Hint: Customer accounts with a credit balance are not considered in determining the total balance in the Accounts Receivable account; rather these amounts are reclassified as Accounts Payable.

Customer Name	Balance	Debit or Credit
Peter Gurney	$200	Dr
Robert King	150	Dr
Bruce Landis	50	Cr
Robert McNeil	100	Dr
Mark Noakes	50	Dr
Frank Rimshaw	300	Dr
Michael Sangster	50	Dr
Lawrence Williams	100	Cr

LO2 LO3 LO8 **BRIEF EXERCISE 6.3**
Perpetual Inventory System—Computation of Income

Alberto & Sons, Inc., a retailer of antique figurines, engages in the following transactions during October of the current year:

Oct. 1 Purchases 100 Hummels at $50 each.

Oct. 5 Sells 50 of the Hummels at $80 each.

Compute Alberto & Sons's gross profit for October.

LO2 LO4 LO8 **BRIEF EXERCISE 6.4**
Periodic Inventory System—Inventory Balance during Year

Neel & Neal Inc. is a retailer of fine leather goods. The company's inventory balance at the beginning of the year was $300,000; Neel & Neal purchased $250,000 of goods during January, and sales during January were $400,000. What is the balance that would appear in Neel & Neal's inventory account on February 1 assuming use of a periodic inventory system?

LO2 LO4 LO8 **BRIEF EXERCISE 6.5**
Periodic Inventory System—Determine Cost of Goods Sold

Murphy Co. is a high-end retailer of fine fashions for men. Murphy's inventory balance at the beginning of the year is $300,000, and Murphy purchases $600,000 of goods during the year. Its inventory balance at the end of the year is $250,000. What is the cost of goods sold for the year?

LO2 LO4 LO8 **BRIEF EXERCISE 6.6**
Periodic Inventory System—Working Backward through the COGS Section

Yang & Min Inc. is a retailer of contemporary furniture. You are told that Yang & Min's ending inventory is $200,000 and its cost of goods sold is $500,000. Yang & Min had $100,000 of inventory at the beginning of the year. What was the dollar amount of goods purchased by Yang & Min during the year?

LO2 LO4 BRIEF EXERCISE 6.7
Periodic Inventory System—Closing Process

Bronson Inc. is a retailer of sporting goods. Bronson's beginning inventory is $80,000 and its purchases during the year are $250,000. Its ending inventory is $30,000. Make the closing entries necessary given that Bronson uses a periodic inventory system.

LO6 BRIEF EXERCISE 6.8
Benefit of Taking a Purchase Discount

Pag Inc. is a clothing retailer and it has terms from one of its vendors of *1/10, n/30.* Compute the equivalent annual rate of return that Pag earns by always paying its bills within the discount period.

LO6 BRIEF EXERCISE 6.9
Sales Returns and Allowances

Inamra Inc. is a clothing manufacturer. The firm uses a periodic inventory system. Inamra shipped $20,000 of defective goods to a retailer. The retailer and Inamra agreed that the retailer would keep the goods in exchange for a $2,000 allowance. The cost of the goods was $1,000. What journal entry (or entries) would Inamra record?

LO7 BRIEF EXERCISE 6.10
Special Journals

List three special journals often used in accounting to facilitate the recording of repetitive transactions.

LO8 BRIEF EXERCISE 6.11
Ethics, Fraud, and Corporate Governance

You are the assistant controller for a public company. Wall Street stock analysts are projecting an earnings per share figure of $0.25 for your company. On December 29, a large customer returns a very large shipment of your goods that were defective. You tell the controller about the customer return and that the debit to sales returns and allowances will have the effect of reducing earnings per share from $0.25 to $0.24. The controller indicates that failing to meet the consensus earnings expectations of the analyst community will result in a large stock price decline. The controller suggests waiting until January 2 (your company operates on a calendar year-end basis) to record the customer return. What should you do?

Exercises

LO1 LO6 EXERCISE 6.1
You as a Student

As a fund-raiser, the pep band at Melrose University sells T-shirts fans can wear when attending the school's 12 home basketball games. As the band's business manager, you must choose among several options for ordering and selling the T-shirts.

1. Place a single order in October large enough to last the entire season. The band must pay for the shirts in full when the order is placed. A 5 percent quantity discount applies to this option.
2. Place a series of small orders, as needed, throughout the season. Again, payment in full is due when the order is submitted. No discount applies to this option.
3. Have band members sell shirts directly to members of the student body. Cash is collected immediately as sales are made.
4. Sell all of the T-shirts through the university bookstore. The bookstore would receive a 6 percent commission on total sales and would remit to the band its share of the proceeds in a lump-sum payment at the end of the season.

a. Describe which combination of options would give the pep band the shortest operating cycle.

b. Describe which combination of options would give the pep band the longest operating cycle.

c. Discuss briefly the advantages and disadvantages of each option.

LO1 EXERCISE 6.2
Effects of Basic Merchandising Transactions

Shown below are selected transactions of Konshock's, a retail store that uses a perpetual inventory system.

a. Purchased merchandise on account.

b. Recognized the revenue from a sale of merchandise on account. (Ignore the related cost of goods sold.)

c. Recognized the cost of goods sold relating to the sale in transaction **b**.

d. Collected in cash the account receivable from the customer in transaction **b**.

e. Following the taking of a physical inventory at year-end, made an adjusting entry to record a normal amount of inventory shrinkage.

Indicate the effects of each of these transactions on the elements of the company's financial statements shown below. Organize your answer in tabular form, using the column headings shown below. (Notice that the cost of goods sold is shown separately from all other expenses.) Use the code letters **I** for increase, **D** for decrease, and **NE** for no effect.

	Income Statement				Balance Sheet		
Transaction	Net Sales –	Cost of Goods Sold –	All Other Expenses =	Net Income	Assets =	Liabilities +	Owners' Equity
a	____	____	____	____	____	____	____

LO2 LO5 LO8 **EXERCISE 6.3** Understanding Inventory Cost Flows

PC Connection is a leading mail order retailer of personal computers. A recent financial report issued by the company revealed the following information:

Merchandise inventory (beginning of the year)	$69 million
Merchandise inventory (end of the year)	$57 million
Net sales for the year	$1.2 billion
Gross profit margin	11%

a. Compute the company's cost of goods sold for the year.

b. Approximately how much inventory did **PC Connection** *purchase* during the year?

c. What factors might contribute to the company's low gross profit margin?

d. Discuss reasons why **PC Connection** uses a perpetual inventory system.

LO3 LO8 **EXERCISE 6.4** Perpetual Inventory Systems

Ranns Supply uses a perpetual inventory system. On January 1, its inventory account had a beginning balance of $6,450,000. Ranns engaged in the following transactions during the year:

1. Purchased merchandise inventory for $9,500,000.
2. Generated net sales of $26,000,000.
3. Recorded inventory shrinkage of $10,000 after taking a physical inventory at year-end.
4. Reported gross profit for the year of $15,000,000 in its income statement.

a. At what amount was Cost of Goods Sold reported in the company's year-end income statement?

b. At what amount was Merchandise Inventory reported in the company's year-end balance sheet?

c. Immediately prior to recording inventory shrinkage at the end of the year, what was the balance of the Cost of Goods Sold account? What was the balance of the Merchandise Inventory account?

LO6 LO8 **EXERCISE 6.5** Evaluating Performance

These selected statistics are from recent annual reports of two well-known retailers:

	Walmart	Target
Percentage increase (decrease) in net sales	1%	1%
Percentage increase (decrease) in gross profit rate	2.4%	2.6%
Percentage increase (decrease) in comparable store net sales	−0.8%	−2.5%

a. Explain the significance of each of these three measures.

b. Evaluate briefly the performance of each company on the basis of these three measures.

LO3 **EXERCISE 6.6**
Taking a Physical Inventory

Frisbee Hardware uses a perpetual inventory system. At year-end, the Inventory account has a balance of $250,000, but a physical count shows that the merchandise on hand has a cost of only $246,000.

a. Explain the probable reason(s) for this discrepancy.

b. Prepare the journal entry required in this situation.

c. Indicate all the accounting records to which your journal entry in part **b** should be posted.

LO4 **EXERCISE 6.7**
Periodic Inventory Systems

Boston Bait Shop uses a periodic inventory system. At December 31, Year 2, the accounting records include the following information:

Inventory (as of December 31, Year 1)	$ 2,800
Net sales	79,600
Purchases	30,200

A complete physical inventory taken at December 31, Year 2, indicates merchandise costing $3,000 remains in stock.

a. How were the amounts of beginning and ending inventory determined?

b. Compute the amount of the cost of goods sold in Year 2.

c. Prepare two closing entries at December 31, Year 2: the first to create a Cost of Goods Sold account with the appropriate balance and the second to bring the Inventory account up-to-date.

d. Prepare a partial income statement showing the shop's gross profit for the year.

e. Describe why a company such as Boston Bait Shop would use a periodic inventory system rather than a perpetual inventory system.

LO4 **EXERCISE 6.8**
Relationships within Periodic Inventory Systems

This exercise stresses the relationships between the information recorded in a periodic inventory system and the basic elements of an income statement. Each of the five lines represents a separate set of information. You are to fill in the missing amounts. A net loss in the right-hand column is to be indicated by placing brackets around the amount, as for example in line **e** <15,000>.

Net Sales	Beginning Inventory	Net Purchases	Ending Inventory	Cost of Goods Sold	Gross Profit	Expenses	Net Income or (Loss)
a. 240,000	76,000	104,000	35,200	?	95,200	72,000	?
b. 480,000	72,000	272,000	?	264,000	?	?	20,000
c. 630,000	207,000	?	166,500	441,000	189,000	148,500	?
d. 810,000	?	450,000	135,000	?	234,000	270,000	?
e. ?	156,000	?	153,000	396,000	135,000	?	<15,000>

LO5 LO8 **EXERCISE 6.9**
Selecting an Inventory System

Year after year two huge supermarket chains—**Publix Super Markets, Inc.**, and **Safeway, Inc.**—consistently report gross profit rates between 26 percent and 29 percent. Each uses a sophisticated perpetual inventory system to account for billions of dollars in inventory transactions.

a. Discuss reasons why these firms consistently report such similar and stable gross profit rates.

b. What technologies make it possible for these retailing giants to use perpetual inventory systems?

LO6 **EXERCISE 6.10**

Cash Discounts

Golf World sold merchandise to Mulligans for $10,000, offering terms of 1/15, n/30. Mulligans paid for the merchandise within the discount period. Both companies use perpetual inventory systems.

a. Prepare journal entries in the accounting records of Golf World to account for this sale and the subsequent collection. Assume the original cost of the merchandise to Golf World had been $6,500.

b. Prepare journal entries in the accounting records of Mulligans to account for the purchase and subsequent payment. Mulligans records purchases of merchandise at *net cost.*

c. Assume that, because of a change in personnel, Mulligans failed to pay for this merchandise within the discount period. Prepare the journal entry in the accounting records of Mulligans to record payment *after* the discount period.

LO8 **EXERCISE 6.11**

Evaluating Performance

This selected information is from recent annual reports of the two largest retail pharmaceutical companies in the United States. (Dollar amounts are stated in billions.)

	Walgreen Company	Rite Aid Corporation
Net sales	$63.3	$26.3
Cost of goods sold	?	19.3
Gross profit	?	?
Gross profit margin (or rate)	27.8%	?%
Total square feet of selling space	79 million	49 million
Sales per square foot of selling space	?	?

a. Fill in the missing amounts and percentages. (Round all amounts to one decimal place.)

b. On the basis of the information provided above, do you expect Walgreen or Rite Aid to be more profitable and why?

LO3 through LO5 **EXERCISE 6.12**

Comparison of Inventory Systems

Sky Probe sells state-of-the-art telescopes to individuals and organizations interested in studying the solar system. At December 31 last year, the company's inventory amounted to $250,000. During the first week of January this year, the company made only one purchase and one sale. These transactions were as follows:

Jan. 2 Sold one telescope costing $90,000 to Central State University for cash, $117,000.

Jan. 5 Purchased merchandise on account from Lunar Optics, $50,000. Terms, net 30 days.

a. Prepare journal entries to record these transactions assuming that Sky Probe uses the perpetual inventory system. Use separate entries to record the sales revenue and the cost of goods sold for the sale on January 2.

b. Compute the balance of the Inventory account on January 7.

c. Prepare journal entries to record the two transactions, assuming that Sky Probe uses the periodic inventory system.

d. Compute the cost of goods sold for the first week of January assuming use of a periodic inventory system. Use your answer to part **b** as the ending inventory.

e. Which inventory system do you believe that a company such as Sky Probe would probably use? Explain your reasoning.

LO4 LO5 **EXERCISE 6.13**

The Periodic Inventory System

Mountain Mabel's is a small general store located just outside of Yellowstone National Park. The store uses a periodic inventory system. Every January 1, Mabel and her husband close the store and take a complete physical inventory while watching the Rose Bowl Parade on television. The inventory balance on January 1 of the prior year was $6,240, and the inventory balance on December 31 was $4,560. Sales were $150,000 during the prior year, and purchases were $74,400.

a. Compute the cost of goods sold for the prior year.

b. Explain why a small business such as this might use the periodic inventory system.

c. Explain some of the *disadvantages* of the periodic system to a larger business, such as a **Sears** store.

LO8 **EXERCISE 6.14** Difference between Income and Cash Flow

State College Technology Store (SCTS) is a retail computer store in the university center of a large midwestern university. SCTS engaged in the following transactions during November of the current year:

Nov. 1 Purchased 20 Nopxe laptop computers on account from Led Inc. The laptop computers cost $800 each, for a total of $16,000. Payment is due in 30 days.

Nov. 6 Sold four Nopxe laptop computers on account to the Department of Microbiology at State College at a retail sales price of $1,200 each, for a total of $4,800. Payment is due in 30 days.

Dec. 1 Paid the $16,000 account payable to Led Inc.

Dec. 6 Collected the $4,800 account receivable from State College's Department of Microbiology.

Assume that the other expenses incurred by SCTS during November and December were $1,000, and assume that all of these expenses were paid in cash. SCTS is not subject to income tax because it is a wholly-owned unit of a nonprofit organization. Compute the net income of SCTS during November and December using accrual accounting principles. Also, compute what SCTS's net income would have been had it used the cash basis of accounting. Explain the difference.

LO8 **EXERCISE 6.15** Using **Home Depot, Inc.**, Financial Statements

The **Home Depot, Inc.**, financial statements appear in Appendix A at the end of this textbook. Use the statements to complete the following requirements:

a. Calculate the gross profit percentage of **Home Depot, Inc.**, for each of the years shown in the company's income statements.

b. Evaluate the company's trend in sales and gross profit.

Problem Set A

LO1 LO3 LO8 **PROBLEM 6.1A** Evaluating Profitability

Claypool Hardware is the only hardware store in a remote area of northern Minnesota. Some of Claypool's transactions during the current year are as follows:

Nov. 5 Sold lumber on account to Bemidji Construction, $13,390. The inventory subsidiary ledger shows the cost of this merchandise was $9,105.

Nov. 9 Purchased tools on account from Owatonna Tool Company, $3,800.

Dec. 5 Collected in cash the $13,390 account receivable from Bemidji Construction.

Dec. 9 Paid the $3,800 owed to Owatonna Tool Company.

Dec. 31 Claypool's personnel counted the inventory on hand and determined its cost to be $182,080. The accounting records, however, indicate inventory of $183,790 and a cost of goods sold of $695,222. The physical count of the inventory was observed by the company's auditors and is considered correct.

Instructions

a. Prepare journal entries to record these transactions and events in the accounting records of Claypool Hardware. (The company uses a perpetual inventory system.)

b. Prepare a partial income statement showing the company's gross profit for the year. (Net sales for the year amount to $1,024,900.)

c. Claypool purchases merchandise inventory at the same wholesale prices as other hardware stores. Due to its remote location, however, the company must pay between $18,000 and $20,000 per year in extra transportation charges to receive delivery of merchandise. (These additional charges are included in the amount shown as cost of goods sold.)

Assume that an index of key business ratios in your library shows hardware stores of Claypool's approximate size (in total assets) average net sales of $1 million per year and a gross profit margin of 25 percent.

Is Claypool able to pass its extra transportation costs on to its customers? Does the business appear to suffer or benefit financially from its remote location? Explain your reasoning and support your conclusions with specific accounting data comparing the operations of Claypool Hardware with the industry averages.

LO1 through LO3, LO6, LO8

PROBLEM 6.2A
Preparation and Interpretation of a Merchandising Company's Income Statement

eXcel

Hendry's Boutique is a retail clothing store for women. The store operates out of a rented building in Storm Lake, Iowa. Shown below is the store's *adjusted* year-end trial balance dated December 31, 2011.

HENDRY'S BOUTIQUE
ADJUSTED TRIAL BALANCE
DECEMBER 31, 2011

Cash	$ 15,200	
Accounts receivable	2,600	
Merchandise inventory	17,500	
Prepaid rent	1,800	
Office supplies	900	
Office equipment	41,000	
Accumulated depreciation: office equipment		$ 12,000
Accounts payable		12,750
Sales taxes payable		3,200
Capital stock		18,000
Retained earnings		21,050
Sales		226,000
Sales returns and allowances	2,500	
Cost of goods sold	100,575	
Purchase discounts lost	250	
Utilities expense	4,120	
Office supply expense	520	
Depreciation expense: office equipment	2,750	
Rent expense	6,100	
Insurance expense	900	
Salaries expense	88,095	
Income taxes expense	8,190	
	$293,000	$293,000

Instructions

a. Prepare an income statement for Hendry's Boutique dated December 31, 2011.

b. Compute the store's gross profit margin as a percentage of *net sales*.

c. Do the store's customers seem to be satisfied with their purchases? Defend your answer.

d. Explain how you can tell that the business records inventory purchases *net* of any purchase discounts.

e. The store reports sales taxes payable of $3,200 in its adjusted trial balance. Explain why it does not report any *sales taxes expense*.

f. Which accounts appearing in the store's adjusted trial balance comprise its *operating cycle*?

LO8

PROBLEM 6.3A
Trend Analysis

Shown below is information from the financial reports of Knauss Supermarkets for the past few years.

	2011	2010	2009
Net sales (in millions)	$5,495	$5,184	$4,800
Number of stores	448	445	430
Square feet of selling space (in millions)	11.9	11.1	10.0
Average net sales of comparable stores (in millions)	$ 10.8	$ 11.0	$ 11.4

Instructions

a. Calculate the following statistics for Knauss Supermarkets (round your answers to one decimal place):

1. The percentage change in net sales from 2009 to 2010 and 2010 to 2011. Hint: The percentage change is computed by dividing the dollar amount of the change between years by the amount of the base year. For example, the percentage change in net sales from 2009 to 2010 is computed by dividing the difference between 2009 to 2010 net sales by the amount of 2009 net sales, or ($5,184 − $4,800) ÷ $4,800 = 8% increase.
2. The percentage change in net sales per square foot of selling space from 2009 to 2010 and 2010 to 2011.
3. The percentage change in comparable store sales from 2009 to 2010 and 2010 to 2011.

b. Evaluate the sales performance of Knauss Supermarkets.

LO3 LO6 **PROBLEM 6.4A**
Comparison of Net Cost and Gross Price Methods

Lamprino Appliance uses a perpetual inventory system. The following are three recent merchandising transactions:

June 10 Purchased 10 televisions from Mitsu Industries on account. Invoice price, $300 per unit, for a total of $3,000. The terms of purchase were 2/10, n/30.

June 15 Sold one of these televisions for $450 cash.

June 20 Paid the account payable to Mitsu Industries within the discount period.

Instructions

a. Prepare journal entries to record these transactions assuming that Lamprino records purchases of merchandise at:

1. Net cost
2. Gross invoice price

b. Assume that Lamprino did *not* pay Mitsu Industries within the discount period but instead paid the full invoice price on July 10. Prepare journal entries to record this payment assuming that the original liability had been recorded at:

1. Net cost
2. Gross invoice price

c. Assume that you are evaluating the efficiency of Lamprino's bill-paying procedures. Which accounting method—net cost or gross invoice price—provides you with the most *useful* information? Explain.

LO3 LO6 **PROBLEM 6.5A**
Merchandising Transactions
eXcel

The following is a series of related transactions between Siogo Shoes, a shoe wholesaler, and Sole Mates, a chain of retail shoe stores:

Feb. 9 Siogo Shoes sold Sole Mates 100 pairs of hiking boots on account, terms 1/10, n/30. The cost of these boots to Siogo Shoes was $60 per pair, and the sales price was $100 per pair.

Feb. 12 United Express charged $80 for delivering this merchandise to Sole Mates. These charges were split evenly between the buyer and seller and were paid immediately in cash.

Feb. 13 Sole Mates returned 10 pairs of boots to Siogo Shoes because they were the wrong size. Siogo Shoes allowed Sole Mates full credit for this return.

Feb. 19 Sole Mates paid the remaining balance due to Siogo Shoes within the discount period.

Both companies use a perpetual inventory system.

Instructions

a. Record this series of transactions in the general journal of Siogo Shoes. (The company records sales at gross sales price.)

b. Record this series of transactions in the general journal of Sole Mates. (The company records purchases of merchandise at *net cost* and uses a Transportation-in account to record transportation charges on inbound shipments.)

c. Sole Mates does not always have enough cash on hand to pay for purchases within the discount period. However, it has a line of credit with its bank, which enables Sole Mates to easily borrow money for short periods of time at an annual interest rate of 11 percent. (The bank charges interest only for the number of days until Sole Mates repays the loan.) As a matter of general policy, should Sole Mates take advantage of 1/10, n/30 cash discounts even if it must borrow the money to do so at an annual rate of 11 percent? Explain fully—and illustrate any supporting computations.

LO2 LO3 LO6

PROBLEM 6.6A

Correcting Errors—Recording of Merchandising Transactions

King Enterprises is a book wholesaler. King hired a new accounting clerk on January 1 of the current year. The new clerk does not understand accrual accounting and recorded the transactions below based on when cash receipts and disbursements changed hands rather than when the transaction occurred. King uses a perpetual inventory system, and its accounting policy calls for inventory purchases to be recorded net of any discounts offered.

Jan. 10 Paid Aztec Enterprises \$9,800 for books that it received on December 15. (This purchase was recorded as a debit to Inventory and a credit to Accounts Payable on December 15 of last year, but the accounting clerk ignores that fact.)

Dec. 27 Received books from McSaw Inc. for \$20,000; terms 2/10, n/30.

Dec. 30 Sold books to Booksellers Unlimited for \$30,000; terms 1/10, n/30. The cost of these books to King was \$24,500.

Instructions

a. As a result of the accounting clerk's errors, compute the amount by which the following accounts are overstated or understated.

1. Accounts Receivable
2. Inventory
3. Accounts Payable
4. Sales
5. Cost of Goods Sold

b. Compute the amount by which net income is overstated or understated.

c. Prepare a single journal entry to correct the errors that the accounting clerk has made. (Assume that King has yet to close its books for the current year.)

d. Assume that King has already closed its books for the current year. Make a single journal entry to correct the errors that the accounting clerk has made.

e. Assume that the ending inventory balance is correctly stated based on adjustments resulting from a physical inventory count. (Cost of Goods Sold was debited or credited based on the inventory adjustment.) Assume that King has already closed its books for the current year, and make a single journal entry to correct the errors that the accounting clerk has made.

LO1 LO3 LO6

PROBLEM 6.7A

Accrual Accounting, Cash Flow, and Fair Value

Genuine Accessories Inc. is a wholesaler of automobile and truck accessories. Genuine Accessories began operations in November of the current year and engaged in the following transactions during November and December of this year. Genuine Accessories uses a perpetual inventory system.

Nov. 3 Purchased \$400,000 of automotive accessories, terms n/30.

Nov. 15 Sold \$300,000 of automotive accessories, terms n/60. The cost of the accessories sold is \$200,000.

Nov. 28 Purchased \$600,000 of automotive accessories, terms n/45.

Dec. 3 Settled the \$400,000 purchase of November 3.

Dec. 15 Sold \$750,000 of automotive accessories, terms n/60. The cost of the accessories sold is \$500,000.

Dec. 27 Purchased \$900,000 of automotive accessories, terms n/30.

Instructions

a. Compute the gross profit on Genuine Accessories's transactions during November and December.

b. Compute the gross profit on Genuine Accessories's transactions during November and December if a cash-basis accounting system was used.

c. Explain the difference between the results in **a** and **b**.

d. Assume that the fair value of Genuine Accessories's inventory at December 31 is $1,500,000. A potential lender asks Genuine Accessories to prepare a fair-value–based balance sheet. Prepare the journal entry to reflect inventory at fair value. Comment on how a wholesaler might determine fair value for inventory items. [Hint: Increase the Inventory account by the difference between fair value and book value with the offset to an account titled Revaluation of Inventory to Market Value.]

LO1 through LO8

PROBLEM 6.8A
A Comprehensive Problem

CPI sells computer peripherals. At December 31, 2011, CPI's inventory amounted to $500,000. During the first week in January 2012, the company made only one purchase and one sale. These transactions were as follows:

Jan. 2 Purchased 20 modems and 80 printers from Sharp. The total cost of these machines was $25,000, terms 3/10, n/60.

Jan. 6 Sold 30 different types of products on account to Pace Corporation. The total sales price was $10,000, terms 5/10, n/90. The total cost of these 30 units to CPI was $6,100 (net of the purchase discount).

CPI has a full-time accountant and a computer-based accounting system. It records sales at the gross sales price and purchases at net cost and maintains subsidiary ledgers for accounts receivable, inventory, and accounts payable.

Instructions

a. Briefly describe the operating cycle of a merchandising company. Identify the assets and liabilities directly affected by this cycle.

b. Prepare journal entries to record these transactions, assuming that CPI uses a *perpetual* inventory system.

c. Compute the balance in the Inventory account at the close of business on January 6.

d. Prepare journal entries to record the two transactions, assuming that CPI uses a *periodic* inventory system.

e. Compute the cost of goods sold for the first week of January assuming use of the periodic system. (Use your answer to part **c** as the ending inventory.)

f. Which type of inventory system do you think CPI most likely would use? Explain your reasoning.

g. Compute the gross profit margin on the January 6 sales transaction.

Problem Set B

LO1 LO3 LO8

PROBLEM 6.1B
Evaluating Profitability

Big Oak Lumber is a lumber yard on Angel Island. Some of Big Oak's transactions during the current year are as follows:

Apr. 15 Sold lumber on account to Hard Hat Construction, $19,700. The inventory subsidiary ledger shows the cost of this merchandise was $10,300.

Apr. 19 Purchased lumber on account from LHP Company, $3,700.

May 10 Collected in cash the $19,700 account receivable from Hard Hat Construction.

May 19 Paid the $3,700 owed to LHP Company.

Dec. 31 Big Oak's personnel counted the inventory on hand and determined its cost to be $114,000. The accounting records, however, indicate inventory of $116,500 and a cost of goods sold of $721,000. The physical count of the inventory was observed by the company's auditors and is considered correct.

Instructions

a. Prepare journal entries to record these transactions and events in the accounting records of Big Oak Lumber. (The company uses a perpetual inventory system.)

b. Prepare a partial income statement showing the company's gross profit for the year. (Net sales for the year amount to $1,422,000.)

c. Big Oak purchases merchandise inventory at the same wholesale prices as other lumber yards. Because of its remote location the company must pay between $8,000 and $18,000 per year in extra transportation charges to receive delivery of merchandise. (These additional charges are included in the amount shown as cost of goods sold.)

Assume that an index of key business ratios in your library shows lumber yards of Big Oak's approximate size (in total assets) average net sales of $1 million per year and a gross profit rate of 22 percent.

Is Big Oak able to pass its extra transportation costs on to its customers? Does the business appear to suffer or benefit financially from its remote location? Explain your reasoning and support your conclusions with specific accounting data comparing the operations of Big Oak Lumber with the industry averages.

LO1 through LO3, LO6, LO8

PROBLEM 6.2B Preparation and Interpretation of a Merchandising Company's Income Statement

Harry's Haberdashery is a retail clothing store for men. The store operates out of a rented building in Albertsville, Virginia. Shown below is the store's *adjusted* year-end trial balance dated December 31, 2011.

HARRY'S HABERDASHERY
ADJUSTED TRIAL BALANCE
DECEMBER 31, 2011

Cash	$ 39,270	
Accounts receivable	4,400	
Merchandise inventory	29,700	
Prepaid rent	3,100	
Office supplies	1,500	
Office equipment	70,000	
Accumulated depreciation: office equipment		$ 20,000
Accounts payable		22,000
Sales taxes payable		5,000
Capital stock		31,000
Retained earnings		36,000
Sales		384,000
Sales returns and allowances	4,000	
Cost of goods sold	157,630	
Purchase discounts lost	400	
Utilities expense	7,000	
Office supply expense	900	
Depreciation expense: office equipment	4,700	
Rent expense	10,000	
Insurance expense	1,500	
Salaries expense	150,000	
Income tax expense	13,900	
	$498,000	$498,000

Instructions

a. Prepare an income statement for Harry's Haberdashery dated December 31, 2011.

b. Compute the store's gross profit margin as a percentage of *net sales.*

c. Do the store's customers seem to be satisfied with their purchases? Defend your answer.

d. Explain how you can tell that the business records inventory purchases *net* of any purchase discounts.

e. The store reports sales taxes payable of $5,000 in its adjusted trial balance. Explain why it does not report any *sales taxes expense.*

f. What is meant by the term "operating cycle" and which accounts in the trial balance comprise Harry's Haberdashery's operating cycle?

LO8 **PROBLEM 6.3B**
Trend Analysis

Shown below is information from the financial reports of Jill's Department Stores for the past few years.

	2011	2010	2009
Net sales (in millions)	$9,240	$8,810	$8,140
Number of stores	133	122	115
Square feet of selling space (in millions)	6.0	5.7	5.1
Average net sales of comparable stores (in millions)	$ 70.2	$ 72.3	$ 75.0

Instructions

a. Calculate the following statistics for Jill's Department Stores (round all computations to one decimal place):

1. The percentage change in net sales from 2009 to 2010 and 2010 to 2011. Hint: The percentage change is computed by dividing the dollar amount of the change between years by the amount of the base year. For example, the percentage change in net sales from 2009 to 2010 is computed by dividing the difference between 2010 and 2009 net sales by the amount of 2009 net sales, or ($8,810 − $8,140) ÷ $8,140 = 8.2% increase.
2. The percentage change in net sales per square foot of selling space from 2009 to 2010 and 2010 to 2011.
3. The percentage change in comparable store sales from 2009 to 2010 and 2010 to 2011.

b. Evaluate the sales performance of Jill's Department Stores.

LO3 LO6 **PROBLEM 6.4B**
Comparison of Net Cost and Gross Price Methods

Mary's TV uses a perpetual inventory system. The following are three recent merchandising transactions:

Mar. 6 Purchased eight TVs from Whosa Industries on account. Invoice price, $350 per unit, for a total of $2,800. The terms of purchase were 2/10, n/30.

Mar. 11 Sold two of these televisions for $600 cash.

Mar. 16 Paid the account payable to Whosa Industries within the discount period.

Instructions

a. Prepare journal entries to record these transactions assuming that Mary's records purchases of merchandise at:

1. Net cost
2. Gross invoice price

b. Assume that Mary's did *not* pay Whosa Industries within the discount period but instead paid the full invoice price on April 6. Prepare journal entries to record this payment assuming that the original liability had been recorded at:

1. Net cost
2. Gross invoice price

c. Assume that you are evaluating the efficiency of Mary's bill-paying procedures. Which accounting method—net cost or gross invoice price—provides you with the most *useful* information? Explain.

LO3 LO6 **PROBLEM 6.5B**
Merchandising Transactions

The following is a series of related transactions between Hip Pants and Sleek, a chain of retail clothing stores:

Oct. 12 Hip Pants sold Sleek 300 pairs of pants on account, terms 1/10, n/30. The cost of these pants to Hip Pants was $20 per pair, and the sales price was $60 per pair.

Oct. 15 Wings Express charged $50 for delivering this merchandise to Sleek. These charges were split evenly between the buyer and the seller and were paid immediately in cash.

Oct. 16 Sleek returned four pairs of pants to Hip Pants because they were the wrong size. Hip Pants allowed Sleek full credit for this return.

Oct. 22 Sleek paid the remaining balance due to Hip Pants within the discount period.

Both companies use a perpetual inventory system.

Instructions

a. Record this series of transactions in the general journal of Hip Pants. (The company records sales at gross sales price.)

b. Record this series of transactions in the general journal of Sleek. (The company records purchases of merchandise at *net cost* and uses a Transportation-in account to record transportation charges on inbound shipments.)

c. Sleek does not always have enough cash on hand to pay for purchases within the discount period. However, it has a line of credit with its bank, which enables Sleek to easily borrow money for short periods of time at an annual interest rate of 12 percent. (The bank charges interest only for the number of days until Sleek repays the loan.) As a matter of general policy, should Sleek take advantage of 1/10, n/30 cash discounts even if it must borrow the money to do so at an annual rate of 12 percent? Explain fully—and illustrate any supporting computations.

PROBLEM 6.6B

LO2 LO3 LO6

Correcting Errors—Recording of Merchandising Transactions

Queen Enterprises is a furniture wholesaler. Queen hired a new accounting clerk on January 1 of the current year. The new clerk does not understand accrual accounting and recorded the transactions below based on when cash receipts and disbursements changed hands rather than when the transaction occurred. Queen uses a perpetual inventory system, and its accounting policy calls for inventory purchases to be recorded net of any discounts offered.

Jan. 7 Paid Hardwoods Forever Inc. $4,900 for furniture that it received on December 20. (This purchase was recorded as a debit to Inventory and a credit to Accounts Payable on December 20 of last year, but the accounting clerk ignores that fact.)

Dec. 23 Received furniture from Koos Hoffwan Co. for $10,000; terms 2/10, n/30.

Dec. 26 Sold furniture to Beige Chipmunk Inc. for $15,000; terms 1/10, n/30. The cost of the furniture to Queen was $12,250.

Instructions

a. As a result of the accounting clerk's errors, compute the amount by which the following accounts are overstated or understated:

1. Accounts Receivable
2. Inventory
3. Accounts Payable
4. Sales
5. Cost of Goods Sold

b. Compute the amount by which net income is overstated or understated.

c. Prepare a single journal entry to correct the errors that the accounting clerk has made. (Assume that Queen has yet to close its books for the current year.)

d. Assume that Queen has already closed its books for the current year. Make a single journal entry to correct the errors that the accounting clerk has made.

e. Assume that the ending inventory balance is correctly stated based on adjustments resulting from a physical inventory count. (Cost of Goods Sold was debited or credited based on the inventory adjustment.) Assume that Queen has already closed its books for the current year, and make a single journal entry to correct the errors that the accounting clerk has made.

PROBLEM 6.7B

LO1 LO3 LO6

Accrual Accounting, Cash Flow, and Fair Value

Computer Resources Inc. is a computer retailer. Computer Resources began operations in December of the current year and engaged in the following transactions during that month. Computer Resources uses a perpetual inventory system.

Dec. 5 Purchased $100,000 of computer equipment, terms n/30.

Dec. 12 Sold $100,000 of computer equipment, terms n/30. The cost of the equipment sold is $50,000.

Dec. 26 Purchased $200,000 of computer equipment, terms n/30.

Instructions

a. Compute the gross profit on Computer Resources's transactions during December.

b. Compute the gross profit on Computer Resources's transactions during December if a cash-basis accounting system was used.

c. Explain the difference between the results in **a** and **b**.

d. Assume that the fair value of Computer Resources's inventory at December 31 is $375,000. A potential lender asks Computer Resources to prepare a fair-value–based balance sheet. Prepare the journal entry to reflect inventory at fair value. Comment on how a retailer might determine fair value for inventory items. [Hint: Increase the Inventory account by the difference between fair value and book value with the offset to an account titled Revaluation of Inventory to Market Value.]

LO1 through LO8

PROBLEM 6.8B
A Comprehensive Problem

SUI sells presses. At December 31, 2011, SUI's inventory amounted to $500,000. During the first week of January 2012, the company made only one purchase and one sale. These transactions were as follows:

Jan. 5 Purchased 60 machines from Double, Inc. The total cost of these machines was $40,000, terms 3/10, n/60.

Jan. 10 Sold 30 different types of products on account to Air Corporation. The total sales price was $28,000, terms 5/10, n/90. The total cost of these 30 units to SUI was $10,000 (net of the purchase discount).

SUI has a full-time accountant and a computer-based accounting system. It records sales at the gross sales price and purchases at net cost and maintains subsidiary ledgers for accounts receivable, inventory, and accounts payable.

Instructions

a. Briefly describe the operating cycle of a merchandising company. Identify the assets and liabilities directly affected by this cycle.

b. Prepare journal entries to record these transactions, assuming SUI uses a *perpetual* inventory system.

c. Explain the information in part **b** that should be posted to subsidiary ledger accounts.

d. Compute the balance in the Inventory control account at the close of business on January 10.

e. Prepare journal entries to record the two transactions, assuming that SUI uses a *periodic* inventory system.

f. Compute the cost of goods sold for the two weeks of January assuming use of the periodic system. (Use your answer to part **d** as the ending inventory.)

g. Which type of inventory system do you think SUI most likely would use? Explain your reasoning.

h. Compute the gross profit margin on the January 10 sales transaction. [Round your answer to one decimal place.]

Critical Thinking Cases

LO5

CASE 6.1
Selecting an Inventory System

In each of the following situations, indicate whether you would expect the business to use a periodic inventory system or a perpetual inventory system. Explain the reasons for your answer.

a. The Frontier Shop is a small retail store that sells boots and Western clothing. The store is operated by the owner, who works full-time in the business, and by one part-time salesclerk. Sales transactions are recorded on an antique cash register. The business uses a manual accounting system, which is maintained by ACE Bookkeeping Service. At the end of each month, an employee of ACE visits The Frontier Shop to update its accounting records, prepare sales tax returns, and perform other necessary accounting services.

b. Allister's Corner is an art gallery in the Soho district of New York. All accounting records are maintained manually by the owner, who works in the store on a full-time basis. The store sells three or four paintings each week, at sales prices ranging from about $5,000 to $50,000 per painting.

c. A publicly owned corporation publishes about 200 titles of college-level textbooks. The books are sold to college bookstores throughout the country. Books are distributed to these bookstores from four central warehouses located in California, Texas, Ohio, and Virginia.

d. Toys-4-You operates a national chain of 86 retail toy stores. The company has a state-of-the-art computerized accounting system. All sales transactions are recorded on electronic point-of-sale terminals. These terminals are tied into a central computer system that provides the national headquarters with information about the profitability of each store on a weekly basis.

e. Mr. Jingles is an independently owned and operated ice cream truck.

f. TransComm is a small company that sells very large quantities of a single product. The product is a low-cost spindle of recordable compact disks (CDRs) manufactured by a large Japanese company. Sales are made only in large quantities, primarily to chains of computer stores and large discount stores. This year, the average sales transaction amounted to $14,206 of merchandise. All accounting records are maintained by a full-time employee using commercial accounting software and a personal computer.

LO4 LO8

CASE 6.2 A Cost-Benefit Analysis

Village Hardware is a retail store selling hardware, small appliances, and sporting goods. The business follows a policy of selling all merchandise at exactly twice the amount of its cost to the store and uses a *periodic* inventory system.

At year-end, the following information is taken from the accounting records:

Net sales	$580,000
Inventory, January 1	58,000
Purchases	$297,250

A physical count indicates merchandise costing $49,300 is on hand at December 31.

Instructions

a. Prepare a partial income statement showing computation of the gross profit for the year.

b. On seeing your income statement, the owner of the store makes the following comment: "Inventory shrinkage losses are really costing me. If it weren't for shrinkage losses, the store's gross profit would be 50 percent of net sales. I'm going to hire a security guard and put an end to shoplifting once and for all."

Determine the amount of loss from inventory shrinkage stated (1) at cost and (2) at retail sales value. (Hint: Without any shrinkage losses, the cost of goods sold and the amount of gross profit would each amount to 50 percent of net sales.)

c. Assume that Village Hardware could virtually eliminate shoplifting by hiring a security guard at a cost of $1,800 per month. Would this strategy be profitable? Explain your reasoning.

LO3 through LO5

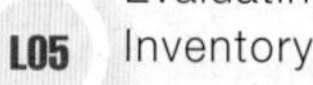

LO7

CASE 6.3 Group Assignment—Evaluating an Inventory System

Identify one local business that uses a perpetual inventory system and another that uses a periodic system. Interview an individual in each organization who is familiar with the inventory system and the recording of sales transactions.

Instructions

Separately for each business organization:

a. Describe the procedures used in accounting for sales transactions, keeping track of inventory levels, and determining the cost of goods sold.

b. Explain the reasons offered by the person interviewed as to *why* the business uses this type of system.

c. Indicate whether your group considers the system in use appropriate under the circumstances. If not, recommend specific changes. *Explain your reasoning.*

LO8 **CASE 6.4**
Manipulating Income

You have recently taken a position with Albers, Inc., a wholesale company that relies heavily on sales outside the United States. In order to facilitate sales worldwide, the company has warehouses at several non–U.S. locations from which it services important markets in different parts of the world.

You are in the midst of year-end closings, and your supervisor approaches you about what can be done to improve the appearance of the company's performance for the current year. His idea is to intentionally overstate year-end inventory at locations outside the United States, thereby reducing cost of goods sold and improving gross profit and net income. Because of the remote locations where much of the inventory is housed, he reasons that it is unlikely that the overstatement will be discovered. You are aware that his compensation includes a bonus based, in part, on reported income. He has also indicated that he will "take care of you" in the future if you are supportive in taking steps to improve the company's reported financial performance, such as the inventory overstatement he currently proposes.

Instructions

a. Once you get over the shock of being asked to engage in this activity, how will you deal with this situation? What are the implications to you of going along with your supervisor's plan? If you are not inclined to cooperate, how will you deal with this situation?

b. Besides being unethical, what other implications does your supervisor's plan have for your company's reported performance in future years?

LO8 **INTERNET CASE 6.5**
Exploring the Annual Report of **Gap, Inc.**

You can find a large amount of information on the Internet to evaluate the performance of companies. Many firms provide links to this information on their home pages.

Access the home page of **The Gap, Inc.**, at the following Internet location:

www.gapinc.com

Instructions

a. What links to financial information are available on the company's home page?

b. Download the company's most recent annual report and use it to answer the following questions:

1. By what percentage amounts did net sales increase or decrease in each of the three years reported?
2. What was the company's gross profit rate for each of the three years reported?
3. What were the company's sales per square foot of selling space for each of the three years reported?
4. For the most recent year reported, how many new stores were opened? How many existing stores, if any, were closed?
5. By what percentage amounts did comparable store sales increase or decrease in each of the three years reported?
6. What dollar amount of inventory does the company report in its most recent balance sheet?

Internet sites are time and date sensitive. It is the purpose of these exercises to have you explore the Internet. You may need to use the Yahoo! search engine http://www.yahoo.com *(or another favorite search engine) to find a company's current Web address.*

Answers to Self-Test Questions

1. a, b, d **2.** b, c **3.** b **4.** b **5.** b, d **6.** b, c, d **7.** b **8.** a, c

CHAPTER 7

Financial Assets

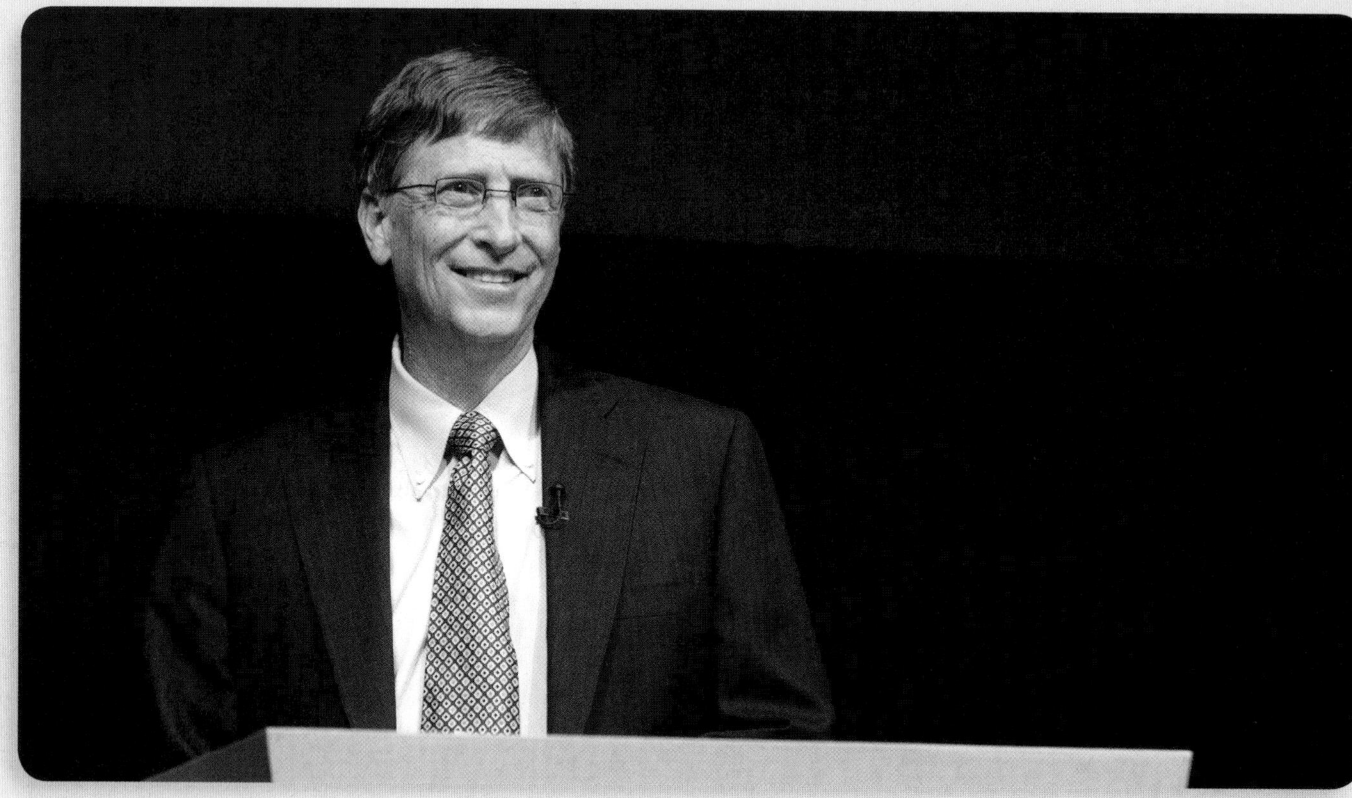

© Keizo Moi/UPI Photo/Newscom

AFTER STUDYING THIS CHAPTER, YOU SHOULD BE ABLE TO:

Learning Objectives

- **LO1** Define financial assets and explain their valuation in the balance sheet.
- **LO2** Describe the objectives of cash management and internal controls over cash.
- **LO3** Prepare a bank reconciliation and explain its purpose.
- **LO4** Describe how short-term investments are reported in the balance sheet and account for transactions involving marketable securities.
- **LO5** Account for uncollectible receivables using the allowance and direct write-off methods.
- **LO6** Explain, compute, and account for notes receivable and interest revenue.
- **LO7** Evaluate the liquidity of a company's accounts receivable.

MICROSOFT CORPORATION

Microsoft Corporation is a multibillion-dollar company that develops, manufactures, licenses, and supports a wide range of software products. The company operates facilities in Ireland, Singapore, and the Greater Seattle area.

You might think that Microsoft would have most of its resources tied up in plant assets. In fact, the company's balance sheet recently reported property and equipment of $7.5 billion. The same balance sheet, however, shows total assets of nearly $78 billion. Thus, property and equipment comprise only 9.6 percent of Microsoft's total assets.

Financial assets of $42 billion account for 54 percent of Microsoft's total assets. Financial assets are a company's most liquid resources. They include cash, cash equivalents, certain investments in marketable securities, accounts receivable, and notes receivable.

Microsoft is fortunate to have an abundance of liquid resources. As the most devastating credit crisis in recent history escalated, access to short-term financing in the commercial paper market became restricted, leaving many companies unable to borrow funds, buy inventory, pay bills, or honor commitments to employees. Even with the passage of a Congressional bailout package of nearly $1 trillion, investments in marketable securities remain volatile.

Our coverage of financial assets throughout this chapter directly relates to the recent turmoil in financial markets. Topics we address include commercial paper (and other cash equivalents), the volatility of investment portfolios, and the inability of companies to collect outstanding accounts receivable. ■

Financial assets are a company's most liquid (or cashlike) resources. The ability of a company to service its debt, purchase inventory, pay taxes, and cover payroll obligations hinges on the availability of these highly liquid assets. In this chapter, we will examine how companies determine and report the *current values* of financial assets, and how effective companies quickly convert certain financial assets into cash.

HOW MUCH CASH SHOULD A BUSINESS HAVE?

In response to this question, most businesspeople would say, "As little as necessary." In a well-managed company, daily cash receipts are deposited promptly in the bank. Often, a principal source of these daily receipts is the collection of accounts receivable. If the daily receipts exceed routine cash outlays, the company can meet its obligations while maintaining relatively low balances in its bank accounts.

Cash that will not be needed in the immediate future often is invested in highly liquid, short-term securities. These investments are more productive than cash because they earn revenue in the forms of interest and dividends. If the business should need more cash than it has in its bank accounts, it can easily convert some of its investments back into cash.

Learning Objective
LO1 Define financial assets and explain their valuation in the balance sheet.

The term **financial assets** describes not just cash but also those assets easily and directly *convertible into known amounts of cash.* These assets include cash, short-term investments (also called **marketable securities**), and receivables. We address these three types of financial assets in a single chapter because they are so closely related. All of these assets represent *forms of money;* financial resources flow quickly among these asset categories.

In summary, businesses "store" money in three basic forms: cash, short-term investments, and receivables. The flow of cash among these types of financial assets is illustrated in Exhibit 7–1.

Exhibit 7–1
MONEY FLOWS AMONG THE FINANCIAL ASSETS

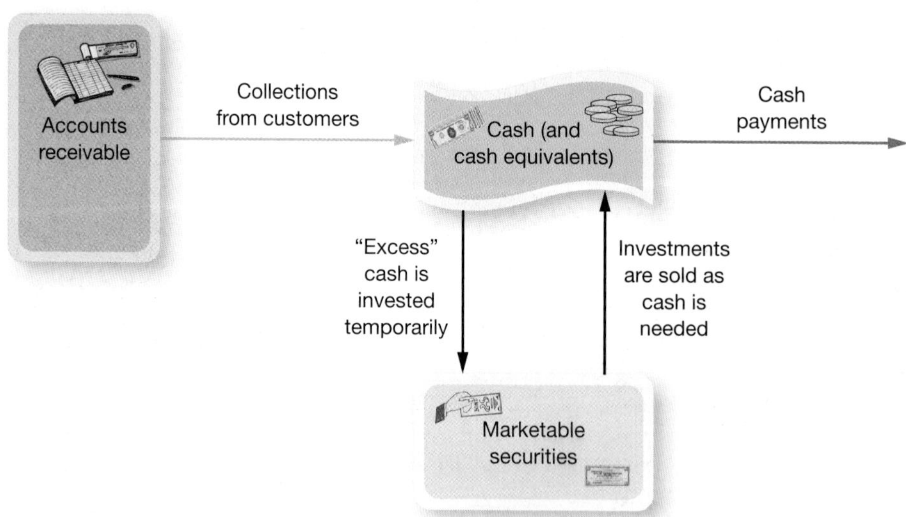

THE VALUATION OF FINANCIAL ASSETS

In the balance sheet, financial assets are shown at their *current values,* meaning the amounts of cash that these assets represent. Interestingly, current value is measured differently for each type of financial asset.

The current value of cash is simply its face amount. But the current value of marketable securities may change daily, based on fluctuations in stock prices, interest rates, and other factors. Therefore, most short-term investments appear in the balance sheet at their current *market values.* (Notice that the valuation of these investments represents an exception to the cost principle.)

Accounts receivable, like cash, have stated face amounts. But large companies usually do not expect to collect every dollar of their accounts receivable. Some customers simply will be unable to make full payment. Therefore, receivables appear in the balance sheet at the estimated *collectible* amount—called **net realizable value.**

The three methods of measuring the current value of financial assets are summarized in Exhibit 7–2.

Type of Financial Asset	Basis for Valuation in the Balance Sheet
Cash (and cash equivalents)	Face amount
Short-term investments (marketable securities)	Fair market value
Receivables	Net realizable value

Exhibit 7–2

METHODS OF MEASURING THE CURRENT VALUE OF FINANCIAL ASSETS

Cash

Accountants define *cash* as money on deposit in banks and any items that banks will accept for deposit. These items include not only coins and paper money, but also checks, money orders, and travelers' checks. Banks also accept drafts signed by customers using bank credit cards, such as **Visa** and **MasterCard**. Thus sales to customers using bank cards are considered *cash sales,* not credit sales, to the enterprise that makes the sale.

Most companies maintain several bank accounts as well as keep a small amount of cash on hand. Therefore, the Cash account in the general ledger is often a *control account.* A cash subsidiary ledger includes separate accounts corresponding to each bank account and each supply of cash on hand within the organization.

REPORTING CASH IN THE BALANCE SHEET

Cash is listed first in the balance sheet because it is the most liquid of all assets. For purposes of balance sheet presentation, the balance in the Cash control account is combined with that of the control account for **cash equivalents.**

Cash Equivalents

Some short-term investments are so liquid that they are termed *cash equivalents.* Examples include money market funds, U.S. Treasury bills, and high-grade commercial paper (very short-term notes payable that are issued by large, creditworthy corporations). These assets are considered so similar to cash that they are combined with the amount of cash in the balance sheet. Therefore, the first asset listed in the balance sheet often is called Cash and Cash Equivalents.

To qualify as a cash equivalent, an investment must be very safe, have a very stable market value, and mature within 90 days of the date of acquisition. Investments in even the highest quality stocks and bonds of large corporations are *not* viewed as meeting these criteria. Short-term investments that do not qualify as cash equivalents are listed in the balance sheet as Marketable Securities.

Restricted Cash

Some bank accounts are restricted as to their use, so they are not available to meet the normal operating needs of the company. For example, a bank account may contain cash specifically earmarked for the repayment of a noncurrent liability, such as a bond payable. Restricted cash should be presented in the balance sheet as part of the section entitled "Investments and Restricted Funds."

As a condition for granting a loan, banks often require the borrower to maintain a **compensating balance** (minimum average balance) on deposit in a non-interest-bearing checking account. This agreement does not actually prevent the borrower from using the cash, but it does mean the company must quickly replenish this bank account. Compensating balances are included in the amount of cash listed in the balance sheet, but these balances should be disclosed in the notes accompanying the financial statements.

Lines of Credit Many businesses arrange **lines of credit** with their banks. A line of credit means that the bank has agreed *in advance* to lend the company any amount of money up to a specified limit. The company can borrow this money at any time simply by drawing checks on a special bank account. A liability to the bank arises as soon as a portion of the credit line is used.

The *unused* portion of a line of credit is neither an asset nor a liability; it represents only the *ability* to borrow money quickly and easily. Although an unused line of credit does not appear as an asset or a liability in the balance sheet, it increases the company's liquidity. Thus unused lines of credit usually are *disclosed* in notes accompanying the financial statements. For example, **Wet Seal, Inc.**, recently included the following information in the footnotes accompanying its financial statements:

> We maintain a $35 million line of credit that can be increased up to $50 million in absence of any defaults. To date, $7.4 million of this amount has been used for the purchase of inventory.

CASH MANAGEMENT

Learning Objective
LO2 Describe the objectives of cash management and internal controls over cash.

The term **cash management** refers to planning, controlling, and accounting for cash transactions and cash balances. Because cash moves so readily between bank accounts and other financial assets, cash management really means the management of *all financial resources.* Efficient management of these resources is essential to the success—even to the survival—of every business organization. The basic objectives of cash management are as follows:

- Provide accurate accounting for cash receipts, cash disbursements, and cash balances.
- Prevent or minimize losses from theft or fraud.
- Anticipate the need for borrowing and assure the availability of adequate amounts of cash for conducting business operations.
- Prevent unnecessarily large amounts of cash from sitting idle in bank accounts that produce no revenue.

INTERNAL CONTROL OVER CASH

Internal control over cash is sometimes regarded merely as a means of preventing fraud and theft. A good system of internal control, however, will also aid in achieving the other objectives of efficient cash management, including accurate accounting for cash transactions, anticipating the need for borrowing, and the maintenance of adequate but not excessive cash balances.

The major steps in achieving internal control over cash transactions and cash balances include the following:

- Separate the function of handling cash from the maintenance of accounting records. Employees who handle cash *should not have access to the accounting records,* and accounting personnel should not have access to cash.
- Prepare *cash budgets* (or forecasts) of planned cash receipts, cash payments, and cash balances, scheduled month-by-month for the coming year.
- Prepare a *control listing* of cash receipts at the time and place the money is received.

- Require that all cash receipts be *deposited daily* in the bank.
- Make all payments *by check.* The only exception should be for small payments to be made in cash from a *petty cash fund.* (Petty cash funds are discussed later in this chapter.)
- Require that every expenditure be verified *before* a check is issued in payment. Separate the function of approving expenditures from the function of signing checks.
- Promptly reconcile bank statements with the accounting records. The person who reconciles the bank statements should not have any opportunities to physically handle cash. (Bank statement reconciliations are discussed later in this chapter.)

Cash Over and Short In the handling of daily cash transactions, a few minor errors inevitably will occur. These errors may cause a cash shortage or overage at the end of the day when the cash is counted and compared with the reading on the cash registers.

For example, assume that total cash sales recorded during the day amount to $4,500. However, the cash receipts in the register drawers total only $4,485. The following entry would be made to adjust the accounting records for this $15 shortage in the cash receipts:

Cash Over and Short	15	
Cash		15
To record a shortage in cash receipts for the day.		

The account entitled Cash Over and Short is debited for shortages and credited with overages. If the account has a debit balance, it appears in the income statement as a miscellaneous expense; if it has a credit balance, it is shown as a miscellaneous revenue.

BANK STATEMENTS

Each month the bank provides the depositor with a statement of the depositor's account.[1] As illustrated in Exhibit 7–3, a bank statement shows the account balance at the beginning of the month, the deposits, the checks paid, any other additions and subtractions during the month, and the new balance at the end of the month. (To keep the illustration short, we have shown a limited number of deposits rather than one for each business day in the month.)

RECONCILING THE BANK STATEMENT

Learning Objective
Prepare a bank reconciliation and explain its purpose. **LO3**

A **bank reconciliation** is a schedule *explaining any differences* between the balance shown in the bank statement and the balance shown in the depositor's accounting records. The bank and the depositor maintain independent records of the deposits, the checks, and the current balance of the bank account. Each month, the depositor should prepare a bank reconciliation to verify that these independent sets of records are in agreement. This reconciliation may disclose internal control failures, such as unauthorized cash disbursements or failures to deposit cash receipts, as well as errors in either the bank statement or the depositor's accounting records. In addition, the reconciliation identifies certain transactions that must be recorded in the depositor's accounting records and helps to determine the actual amount of cash on deposit.

Normal Differences between Bank Records and Accounting Records

The balance shown in a monthly bank statement seldom equals the balance appearing in the depositor's accounting records. Certain transactions recorded by the depositor may not have been recorded by the bank. The most common examples are:

[1] Large businesses may receive bank statements on a weekly basis.

Exhibit 7–3

A BANK STATEMENT

Western National Bank
100 Olympic Boulevard
Los Angeles, CA

Customer Account No. 501390
Parkview Company
109 Parkview Road
Los Angeles, CA

Bank Statement for the Month Ended July 31, 2011

Date				Amount
June 30	Previous statement balance			$ 5,029.30
	Deposits and Other Increases (Credits)			
July 1		300.00		
July 2		1,250.00		
July 8		993.60		
July 12		1,023.77		
July 18		1,300.00		
July 22		500.00	CM	
July 24		1,083.25		
July 30		711.55		
July 31		24.74	INT	
	Total deposits and other increases (credits)			7,186.91
	Checks Written and Other Decreases (Debits)			
July 2	Ck. 882	1,100.00		
July 3	Ck. 883	415.20		
July 3	Ck. 884	10.00		
July 10	Ck. 885	96.00		
July 10	Ck. 886	400.00		
July 12	Ck. 887	1,376.57		
July 15	Ck. 889	425.00		
July 18	Ck. 892	2,095.75		
July 22	Ck. 893	85.00		
July 22		5.00	DM	
July 24	Ck. 894	1,145.27		
July 30		50.25	NSF	
July 31		12.00	SC	
	Total checks written and other decreases (debits)			(7,216.04)
July 31	Balance this statement			$5,000.17

Explanation of Symbols

CM	Credit Memoranda
DM	Debit Memoranda
INT	Interest Earned on Average Balance
NSF	Not Sufficient Funds
SC	Service Charge

- *Outstanding checks.* Checks issued and recorded by the company but not yet presented to the bank for payment.
- *Deposits in transit.* Cash receipts recorded by the depositor that reached the bank too late to be included in the bank statement for the current month.

In addition, certain transactions appearing in the bank statement may not have been recorded by the depositor. For example:

- *Service charges.* Banks often charge a fee for handling small accounts. The amount of this charge usually depends on both the average balance of the account and the number of checks paid during the month.
- *Charges for depositing NSF checks.* **NSF** stands for "Not Sufficient Funds." When checks from customers are deposited, the bank generally gives the depositor immediate credit. On occasion, one of these checks may prove to be uncollectible, because the customer who wrote the check did not have sufficient funds in his or her account. In such cases, the bank will reduce the depositor's account by the amount of this uncollectible item and return

the check to the depositor marked "NSF." The depositor should view an NSF check as an account receivable from the customer, not as cash.

- *Credits for interest earned.* The checking accounts of *unincorporated* businesses often earn interest. At month-end, this interest is credited to the depositor's account and reported in the bank statement. (Current law prohibits interest on corporate checking accounts.)
- *Miscellaneous bank charges and credits.* Banks charge for services—such as printing checks, handling collections of notes receivable, and processing NSF checks. The bank *deducts* these charges from the depositor's account and notifies the depositor by including a debit memorandum in the monthly bank statement. If the bank collects a note receivable on behalf of the depositor, it credits the depositor's account and issues a credit memorandum.[2]

In a bank reconciliation, the balances shown in the bank statement and in the accounting records are both *adjusted for any unrecorded transactions.* Additional adjustments may be required to correct any errors discovered in the bank statement or in the accounting records.

Steps in Preparing a Bank Reconciliation The specific steps in preparing a bank reconciliation are as follows:

1. Compare deposits listed in the bank statement with the deposits shown in the accounting records. Any deposits not yet recorded by the bank are deposits in transit and should be added to the balance shown in the bank statement.
2. Compare checks paid by the bank with the corresponding entries in the accounting records. Any checks issued but not yet paid by the bank should be listed as outstanding checks to be deducted from the balance reported in the bank statement.
3. Add to the balance per the depositor's accounting records any credit memoranda issued by the bank that have not been recorded by the depositor.
4. Deduct from the balance per the depositor's records any debit memoranda issued by the bank that have not been recorded by the depositor.
5. Make appropriate adjustments to correct any errors in either the bank statement or the depositor's accounting records.
6. Determine that the adjusted balance of the bank statement is equal to the adjusted balance in the depositor's records.
7. Prepare journal entries to record any items in the bank reconciliation listed as adjustments to the balance per the depositor's records.

Illustration of a Bank Reconciliation The July bank statement sent by the bank to Parkview Company was illustrated in Exhibit 7–3. This statement shows a balance of cash on deposit at July 31 of *$5,000.17.* Assume that on July 31, Parkview's ledger shows a bank balance of *$4,262.83.* The employee preparing the bank reconciliation has identified the following reconciling items:

1. A deposit of $410.90 made after banking hours on July 31 does not appear in the bank statement.
2. Four checks issued in July have not yet cleared the bank. These checks are:

Check No.	Date	Amount
881	July 1	$100.00
888	July 14	10.25
890	July 16	402.50
891	July 17	205.00

[2] Banks view each depositor's account as a *liability.* Debit memoranda are issued for transactions that reduce this liability, such as bank service charges. Credit memoranda are issued to recognize an increase in this liability, as results, for example, from interest earned by the depositor.

3. Two credit memoranda were included in the bank statement:

Date	Amount	Explanation
July 22	$500.00	Proceeds from collection of a non-interest-bearing note receivable from J. David. The bank's collection department collected this note for Parkview Company.
July 31	24.74	Interest earned on average account balance during July.

4. Three debit memoranda accompanied the bank statement:

Date	Amount	Explanation
July 22	$ 5.00	Fee charged by bank for handling collection of note receivable.
July 30	50.25	Check from customer J. B. Ball deposited by Parkview Company charged back as NSF.
July 31	12.00	Service charge by bank for the month of July.

5. Check no. 893 was issued to the telephone company in the amount of $85 but was erroneously recorded in the cash payments journal as $58. The check, in payment of telephone expense, was paid by the bank and correctly listed at $85 in the bank statement. In Parkview's ledger, the Cash account is *overstated* by $27 because of this error ($85 − $58 = $27).

The July 31 bank reconciliation for Parkview Company is shown in Exhibit 7–4. (The numbered arrows coincide both with the steps in preparing a bank reconciliation and with the reconciling items just listed.)

Exhibit 7–4
THE BANK RECONCILIATION

PARKVIEW COMPANY
BANK RECONCILIATION
JULY 31, 2011

Step			
	Balance per bank statement, July 31, 2011		$5,000.17
①	Add: Deposit of July 31 not recorded by bank		410.90
			$5,411.07
②	Deduct: Outstanding checks:		
	No. 881	$100.00	
	No. 888	10.25	
	No. 890	402.50	
	No. 891	205.00	717.75
	Adjusted cash balance		$4,693.32
	Balance per depositor's records, July 31, 2011		$4,262.83
③	Add: Note receivable collected for us by bank	$500.00	
	Interest earned during July	24.74	524.74
			$4,787.57
④	Deduct: Collection fee	$ 5.00	
④	NSF check of J. B. Ball	50.25	
④	Service charge	12.00	
⑤	Error on check stub no. 893	27.00	94.25
	Adjusted cash balance (as above)		$4,693.32

⑥ (arrows linking the two adjusted cash balances)

Updating the Accounting Records The last step in reconciling a bank statement is to update the depositor's accounting records for any unrecorded cash transactions brought to light. In the bank reconciliation, every adjustment to the *balance per depositor's records* is a cash receipt or a cash payment that has not been recorded in the depositor's accounts. Therefore, *each of these items should be recorded.*

In this illustration and in our assignment material, we follow a policy of making one journal entry to record the unrecorded cash receipts and another to record the unrecorded cash reductions. (Acceptable alternatives would be to make separate journal entries for each item or to make one compound entry for all items.) On the basis of our recording policy, the entries to update the accounting records of Parkview Company are:

Cash	524.74	
Notes Receivable		500.00
Interest Revenue		24.74
To record collection of note receivable from J. David collected by bank and interest earned on bank account in July.		
Bank Service Charges	17.00	
Accounts Receivable (J. B. Ball)	50.25	
Telephone Expense	27.00	
Cash		94.25
To record bank charges (service charge, $12; collection fee, $5); to reclassify NSF check from customer J. B. Ball as an account receivable; and to correct understatement of cash payment for telephone expense.		

Per bank credit memoranda

Per bank debit memoranda (and correction of an error)

Short-Term Investments

Learning Objective
LO4 **Describe how short-term investments are reported in the balance sheet and account for transactions involving marketable securities.**

Companies with large amounts of liquid resources often hold most of these resources in the form of marketable securities rather than cash.

Marketable securities consist primarily of investments in bonds and in the capital stocks of publicly owned corporations. These marketable securities are traded (bought and sold) daily on organized securities exchanges, such as the **New York Stock Exchange**, the **Tokyo Stock Exchange**, and **Mexico's Bolsa**. A basic characteristic of all marketable securities is that they are *readily marketable*—meaning that they can be purchased or sold quickly and easily *at quoted market prices.*

Investments in marketable securities earn a return for the investor in the form of interest, dividends, and—if all goes well—an increase in market value. Meanwhile, these investments are *almost as liquid as cash itself.* They can be sold immediately over the telephone, simply by placing a "sell order" with a brokerage firm such as **Merrill Lynch** or **Morgan Stanley**, or on the Internet, by using an online brokerage firm such as **E*TRADE Financial**.

Due to their liquidity, investments in marketable securities usually are listed immediately after Cash in the balance sheet and are most often classified as *available for sale* securities.[3]

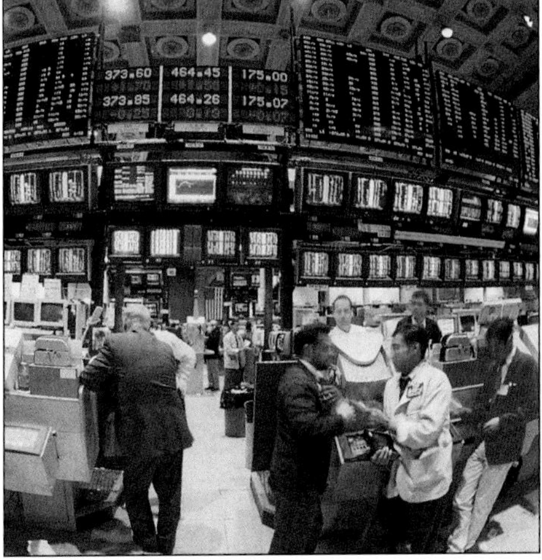

© Digital Vision/Getty Images/DAL

[3] Other investment classifications include *trading* securities and *held-to-maturity* securities. These classifications are discussed in more advanced courses.

CASE IN POINT

It is common for enterprises to invest a portion of their excess cash in marketable securities in anticipation of earning higher returns than they would by keeping these funds in the form of cash and cash equivalents. The following sample taken from recently issued balance sheets illustrates the willingness of companies to invest millions, even billions, of dollars in marketable securities:

	Amount Invested
Best Buy	$ 11 million
Dell Computer Corporation	$ 331 million
Ford Motor Company	$15.1 billion
Pfizer, Inc.	$ 24 billion
Microsoft Corporation	$25.3 billion

Accounting for Marketable Securities

There are four basic events relating to investments in marketable securities: (1) the purchase of investments, (2) the receipt of dividends or interest revenue, (3) the sale of investments, and (4) end-of-period adjustments.

PURCHASE OF MARKETABLE SECURITIES

Investments in marketable securities are originally recorded at cost, which includes any brokerage commissions. To illustrate, assume that Foster Corporation purchases as a short-term investment 4,000 shares of **The Coca-Cola Company** on December 1. Foster paid *$48.98 per share,* plus a brokerage commission of $80. The entry to record the purchase of these shares is:

Marketable Securities	196,000	
Cash		196,000

Purchased 4,000 shares of **Coca-Cola** capital stock. Total cost $196,000 ($48.98 × 4,000 shares + $80); cost per share, $49 ($196,000 ÷ 4,000 shares).

Marketable Securities is a control account used to report *all* of a company's short-term investments. If Foster Corporation invests in other companies it will make an entry similar to the one shown above; however, it will also create a marketable securities *subsidiary ledger* to maintain a separate record of each security owned.

Notice that the $49 cost per share computed in the explanation of the above journal entry includes a portion of the total brokerage commission. The $49 per share *cost basis* will be used in computing any gains or losses when Foster Corporation sells these securities.

RECOGNITION OF INVESTMENT REVENUE

Entries to recognize interest and dividend revenue typically involve a debit to Cash and a credit to either Interest Revenue or Dividend Revenue. To illustrate, assume that on December 15,

Foster Corporation receives a $0.30 per share dividend on its 4,000 shares of **Coca-Cola**. The entry to record this receipt is:

Cash	1,200	
Dividend Revenue		1,200
Received a quarterly dividend on shares of **Coca-Cola** capital stock ($0.30 per share × 4,000 shares).		

Dividend and interest revenue is reported in the income statement as a component of a company's net income. It most often appears near the bottom of the income statement in the computation of income before taxes. The reporting of investment revenue is discussed further in Chapter 11.

SALE OF INVESTMENTS

When an investment is sold, a gain or a loss often results. If an investment is sold for more than its cost basis a **gain** is recorded, whereas selling an investment for an amount less than its cost basis results in a **loss.** These items appear in the "Other Income/Expense" section of the income statement.

Investments Sold at a Gain To illustrate, assume that Foster Corporation sells 500 shares of its **Coca-Cola** stock on December 18 for $50.04 per share, less a $20 brokerage commission. Recall that Foster's cost basis, as computed on December 1, is $49 per share. Thus, the entry to record the sale and the $500 gain is as follows:

Cash	25,000	
Marketable Securities		24,500
Gain on Sale of Investments		500
Sold 500 shares of **Coca-Cola** stock at a gain:		
Sale proceeds ($50.04 × 500 shares − $20 commission)	$25,000	
Cost basis ($49 × 500 shares)	24,500	
Gain on sale	$ 500	

This transaction results in a gain because Foster Corporation sold the shares at an amount above their cost basis. The gain on the sale increases the company's net income for the period and is reported in the income statement in similar fashion to interest and dividend revenue. At the end of the period, the credit balance in the Gain on Sale of Investments account is closed to the Income Summary account, along with the credit balances of the other revenue accounts.

Investments Sold at a Loss Assume that Foster Corporation sells an additional 2,500 shares of its **Coca-Cola** stock on December 27 for $48.01 per share, less a $25 brokerage commission. The entry to record the sale and the $2,500 loss is recorded as follows:

Cash	120,000	
Loss on Sale of Investments	2,500	
Marketable Securities		122,500
Sold 2,500 shares of **Coca-Cola** stock at a loss:		
Cost basis ($49 × 2,500 shares)	$122,500	
Sale proceeds ($48.01 × 2,500 shares − $25 commission)	120,000	
Loss on sale	$ 2,500	

This loss reduces Foster Corporation's net income and is reported near the bottom of the income statement. The debit balance in the Loss on Sale of Investments account is closed to the Income Summary account at the end of the period, along with the debit balances of the other expense accounts.

ADJUSTING MARKETABLE SECURITIES TO MARKET VALUE

Securities classified as available for sale are presented in the balance sheet at their *current market value* as of the balance sheet date. Hence, this valuation principle is often called **fair value accounting.** The adjustment of marketable securities to their current market value requires the use of an account entitled **Unrealized Holding Gain (or Loss) on Investments.** This account appears as a stockholders' equity item in the balance sheet.[4]

To illustrate, let us assume that Foster Corporation's 1,000 remaining shares of **Coca-Cola** capital stock have a current market value of $47,000 on December 31 (1,000 shares at a market price of $47 per share). Prior to any adjustment, the company's Marketable Securities account has a balance of $49,000 (1,000 shares at $49 per share). Thus, Foster Corporation must make the following fair value adjustment on December 31:

Unrealized Holding Loss on Investments	2,000	
Marketable Securities		2,000
To adjust the balance sheet valuation of marketable securities from $49,000 (1,000 shares × $49) to the December 31 market value of $47,000 (1,000 shares × $47).		

Exhibit 7–5 illustrates Foster Corporation's condensed balance sheet following its marketable securities valuation adjustment.

Exhibit 7–5
PRESENTATION OF MARKETABLE SECURITIES IN THE BALANCE SHEET

FOSTER CORPORATION
BALANCE SHEET
AS OF DECEMBER 31 OF THE CURRENT YEAR

Assets		**Liabilities & Stockholders' Equity**	
Current assets:		**Liabilities:**	
Cash	$ 50,000	(Detail not shown)...........	$350,000
Marketable securities (cost, $49,000; market value, $47,000)....................	47,000	**Stockholders' equity:**	
Accounts receivable	23,000	Capital stock	$400,000
Total current assets	$120,000	Retained earnings	152,000
Other assets:		**Unrealized holding loss on investments**	**(2,000)**
		Total stockholders' equity	$550,000
(Detail not shown)	$780,000		
Total........................	$900,000	Total	$900,000

Although the $49,000 cost of Foster Corporation's marketable securities is *disclosed* in the balance sheet, the $47,000 market value is used in the computation of total assets. The difference between the cost and market value also appears as an *element of stockholders'*

[4] Unrealized holding gains and losses are often combined with other activities and reported in a stockholders' equity account entitled Accumulated Other Comprehensive Income. Comprehensive income is discussed in Chapter 12.

equity, entitled Unrealized Holding Loss on Investments. When the market value of investment falls *below* cost, as in the case just presented, this special equity account is a *subtraction* from equity, representing a holding *loss.* But if the market value is *above* cost, this account is an *addition* to equity, representing a holding *gain.* Thus, if Foster's 1,000 shares of **Coca-Cola** had a market value on December 31 of $51 per share, the investment would have been reported in the asset section of the balance sheet at $51,000, and the stockholders' equity section of the balance sheet would have included the addition of a $2,000 unrealized holding *gain* on investments.

Unrealized holding gains and losses are *not* subject to income taxes. Income taxes are levied only upon *realized* gains and losses recognized when investments are sold. Nonetheless, unrealized holding gains and losses are actually reported in the balance sheet net of expected *future* income tax effects. The computation of future tax effects is beyond the scope of our introductory discussion and is addressed in more advanced accounting courses. In the assignment material at the end of this chapter, unrealized holding gains and losses simply represent the difference between the cost and the current market value of the securities owned.

INTERNATIONAL CASE IN POINT

Fair value accounting is not always used internationally for valuing short-term investments. Germany and Japan continue to use the lower of cost or market valuation techniques because their accounting standards setters (Ministry of Finance for Japan and the German government) believe the techniques are more conservative. *International Financial Reporting Standards* (IFRS) account for available-for-sale marketable securities in similar fashion to U.S. GAAP.

Accounts Receivable

One of the key factors underlying the growth of the American economy is the trend toward selling goods and services on credit. Accounts receivable comprise the largest financial asset of many merchandising companies.

Accounts receivable are relatively liquid assets, usually converting into cash within a period of 30 to 60 days. Therefore, accounts receivable from customers usually appear in the balance sheet immediately after cash and short-term investments in marketable securities.

In Chapter 5, we explained that assets capable of being converted quickly into cash are classified in the balance sheet as current assets. The period used to define current assets is typically one year or the company's operating cycle, whichever is longer. The operating cycle was defined in Chapter 6 as the normal period of time required to convert cash into inventory, inventory into accounts receivable, and accounts receivable back into cash. Some companies sell merchandise on long-term installment plans that require accounts receivable be outstanding for 12, 24, or even 48 months before being collected. These receivables are part of the company's normal operating cycle. Therefore, *all* accounts receivable arising from normal sales activity are generally classified as current assets, even if the credit terms extend beyond one year.

UNCOLLECTIBLE ACCOUNTS

Learning Objective
Account for uncollectible receivables using the allowance and direct write-off methods. **LO5**

We have stated that accounts receivable are shown in the balance sheet at the estimated collectible amount—called *net realizable value.* No business wants to sell merchandise on account to customers who will be unable to pay. Nonetheless, if a company makes credit sales to hundreds—perhaps thousands—of customers, some accounts inevitably will turn out to be uncollectible.

A limited amount of uncollectible accounts is not only expected—it is evidence of a sound credit policy. If the credit department is overly cautious, the business may lose many sales opportunities by rejecting customers who should have been considered acceptable credit risks.

Reflecting Uncollectible Accounts in the Financial Statements An account receivable that has been determined to be uncollectible is no longer an asset. The loss of this asset represents an *expense,* termed Uncollectible Accounts Expense.

In measuring business income, one of the most fundamental principles of accounting is that revenue should be *matched* with (offset by) the expenses incurred in generating that revenue. Uncollectible accounts expense is *caused by selling goods on credit* to customers who fail to pay their bills. Therefore, this expense is estimated and recorded in the time period in which the *related sales* are made, even though specific accounts receivable may not be determined to be uncollectible until a later accounting period. Thus an account receivable that originates from a credit sale in January and is determined to be uncollectible in June represents an expense in *January.* Exhibit 7–6 illustrates how uncollectible accounts expense is matched to revenue in the period in which the credit sale is made.

Exhibit 7–6
MATCHING UNCOLLECTIBLE ACCOUNTS EXPENSE TO THE PERIOD IN WHICH THE CREDIT SALE IS MADE

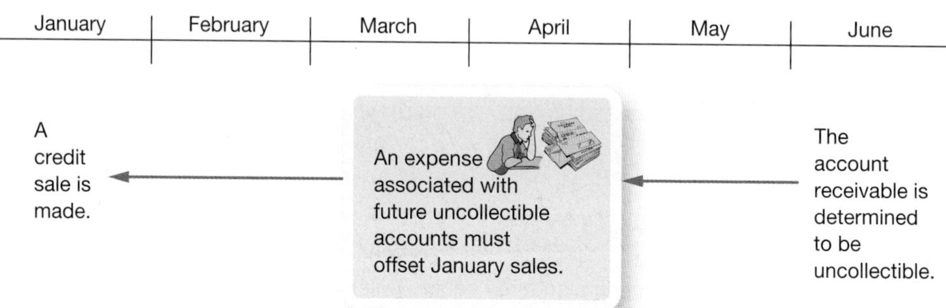

To illustrate the matching process, assume that World Famous Toy Co. begins business on January 1, 2011, and makes most of its sales on account. At January 31, accounts receivable amount to $250,000. On this date, the credit manager reviews the accounts receivable and *estimates* that approximately $10,000 of these accounts will prove to be uncollectible. The following adjusting entry should be made at January 31:

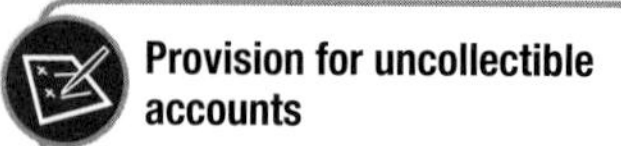

Uncollectible Accounts Expense	10,000	
Allowance for Doubtful Accounts		10,000
To record the portion of total accounts receivable estimated to be uncollectible.		

The Uncollectible Accounts Expense account created by the debit part of this entry is closed into the Income Summary account in the same manner as any other expense account. The Allowance for Doubtful Accounts that was credited in the above journal entry appears in the balance sheet as a deduction from the face amount of the accounts receivable. It reduces the accounts receivable to their *net realizable value* in the balance sheet, as shown in Exhibit 7–7.

Exhibit 7–7
REPORTING ACCOUNTS RECEIVABLE AT ESTIMATED NET REALIZABLE VALUE

WORLD FAMOUS TOY CO.
PARTIAL BALANCE SHEET
JANUARY 31, 2011

Current assets:		
Cash and cash equivalents		$ 75,000
Marketable securities		25,000
Accounts receivable	$250,000	
Less: Allowance for doubtful accounts	10,000	240,000
Inventory		300,000
Total current assets		$640,000

THE ALLOWANCE FOR DOUBTFUL ACCOUNTS

There is no way of telling in advance *which* accounts receivable will prove to be uncollectible. It is therefore not possible to credit the accounts of specific customers for our estimate of probable uncollectible accounts. A practical solution, therefore, is to credit a separate account called **Allowance for Doubtful Accounts** with the amount estimated to be uncollectible.

The Allowance for Doubtful Accounts often is described as a *contra-asset* account or a *valuation* account. The Allowance for Doubtful Accounts has a credit balance which offsets the Accounts Receivable control account to produce a more useful and reliable measure of a company's liquidity. Because the Allowance for Doubtful Accounts is merely an estimate and not a precise calculation, *professional judgment* plays a considerable role in determining the size of this valuation account.

Monthly Adjustments of the Allowance Account In the adjusting entry made by World Famous Toy Co. at January 31, the amount of the adjustment ($10,000) was equal to the estimated amount of uncollectible accounts. This is true only because January was the first month of operations and this was the company's first estimate of its uncollectible accounts. In future months, the amount of the adjusting entry will depend on two factors: (1) the *estimate* of uncollectible accounts and (2) the *current balance* in the Allowance for Doubtful Accounts. Before we illustrate the adjusting entry for a future month, let us see why the balance in the allowance account may change during the accounting period.

WRITING OFF AN UNCOLLECTIBLE ACCOUNT RECEIVABLE

Whenever an account receivable from a specific customer is determined to be uncollectible, it no longer qualifies as an asset and should be written off. To *write off* an account receivable is to reduce the balance of the customer's account to zero. The journal entry to accomplish this consists of a credit to the Accounts Receivable control account in the general ledger (and to the customer's account in the subsidiary ledger) and an offsetting debit to the Allowance for Doubtful Accounts.

To illustrate, assume that, early in February, World Famous Toy Co. learns that Discount Stores has gone out of business and that the $4,000 account receivable from this customer is now worthless. The entry to write off this uncollectible account receivable is:

Allowance for Doubtful Accounts	4,000	
Accounts Receivable (Discount Stores)		4,000
To write off the account receivable from Discount Stores as uncollectible.		

Writing off a receivable "against the allowance"

The important thing to note in this entry is that the debit is made to the Allowance for Doubtful Accounts and *not* to the Uncollectible Accounts Expense account. The estimated expense of credit losses is charged to the Uncollectible Accounts Expense account at the end of each accounting period. When a specific account receivable is later determined to be worthless and is written off, this action does not represent an additional expense but merely confirms our previous estimate of the expense.

Notice also that the entry to write off an uncollectible account receivable reduces both the asset account and the contra-asset account by the same amount. Thus writing off an uncollectible account *does not change* the net realizable value of accounts receivable in the balance sheet. The net realizable value of World Famous Toy Co.'s accounts receivable before and after the write-off of the account receivable from Discount Stores is:

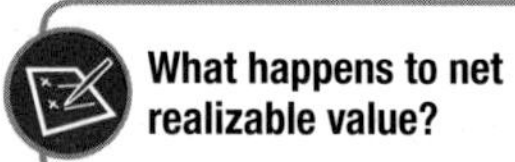
What happens to net realizable value?

Before the Write-off		After the Write-off	
Accounts receivable	$250,000	Accounts receivable	$246,000
Less: Allowance for doubtful accounts	10,000	Less: Allowance for doubtful accounts	6,000
Net realizable value	$240,000	Net realizable value	$240,000

Let us repeat the point that underlies the allowance approach. Credit losses are recognized as an expense in the period in which the *sale occurs,* not the period in which the account is determined to be uncollectible. The reasoning for this position is based on the *matching principle.*

Write-offs Seldom Agree with Previous Estimates The total amount of accounts receivable actually written off will seldom, if ever, be exactly equal to the estimated amount previously credited to the Allowance for Doubtful Accounts.

If the amounts written off as uncollectible turn out to be less than the estimated amount, the Allowance for Doubtful Accounts will continue to show a credit balance. If the amounts written off as uncollectible are greater than the estimated amount, the Allowance for Doubtful Accounts will acquire a *temporary debit balance,* which will be eliminated by the adjustment at the end of the period.

MONTHLY ESTIMATES OF CREDIT LOSSES

At the end of each month, management should again estimate the probable amount of uncollectible accounts and adjust the Allowance for Doubtful Accounts to this new estimate.

To illustrate, assume that at the end of February the credit manager of World Famous Toy Co. analyzes the accounts receivable and estimates that approximately *$11,000* of these accounts will prove uncollectible. Currently, the Allowance for Doubtful Accounts has a credit balance of only *$6,000,* determined as follows:

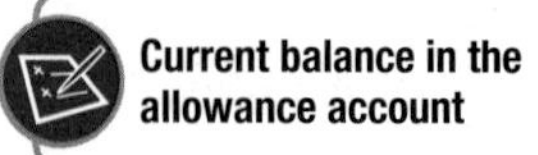
Current balance in the allowance account

Balance at January 31 (credit)	$10,000
Less: Write-off of account considered worthless (Discount Stores)	4,000
Credit balance at February 28 (prior to adjustment)	$ 6,000

To increase the balance in the allowance account to $11,000 at February 28, the month-end adjusting entry must add $5,000 to the allowance. The entry will be:

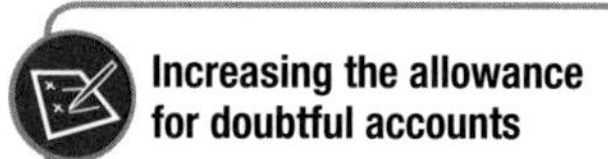
Increasing the allowance for doubtful accounts

Uncollectible Accounts Expense		5,000	
Allowance for Doubtful Accounts.			5,000
To increase the Allowance for Doubtful Accounts to $11,000, computed as follows:			
Required allowance at Feb. 28	$11,000		
Credit balance prior to adjustment	6,000		
Required adjustment	$ 5,000		

In the World Famous Toy illustration, estimates of the required allowance for doubtful accounts at January 31 and February 28 were simply given. There are actually two general approaches to estimating credit losses: (1) a *balance sheet approach,* and (2) an *income statement approach.*

Estimating Credit Losses—The Balance Sheet Approach The most widely used method of estimating the probable amount of uncollectible accounts is based on **aging the accounts receivable.** This method is sometimes called the *balance sheet* approach because the method emphasizes the proper balance sheet valuation of accounts receivable.

"Aging" accounts receivable means classifying each receivable according to its age. An aging schedule for the accounts receivable of Valley Ranch Supply is illustrated in Exhibit 7–8.

Exhibit 7–8

ACCOUNTS RECEIVABLE AGING SCHEDULE

VALLEY RANCH SUPPLY
ANALYSIS OF ACCOUNTS RECEIVABLE BY AGE
DECEMBER 31, 2011

	Total	Not Yet Due	1–30 Days Past Due	31–60 Days Past Due	61–90 Days Past Due	Over 90 Days Past Due
Animal Care Center	$ 9,000	$ 9,000				
Butterfield, John D.	2,400			$ 2,400		
Citrus Groves, Inc.	4,000	3,000	$ 1,000			
Dairy Fresh Farms	1,600				$ 600	$1,000
Eastlake Stables	13,000	7,000	6,000			
(Other customers)	70,000	32,000	22,000	9,600	2,400	4,000
Totals	$100,000	$51,000	$29,000	$12,000	$3,000	$5,000

An aging schedule is useful to management in reviewing the status of individual accounts receivable and in evaluating the overall effectiveness of credit and collection policies. In addition, the schedule is used as the basis for estimating the amount of uncollectible accounts.

The longer an account is past due, the greater the likelihood that it will not be collected in full. On the basis of past experience, the credit manager estimates the percentage of credit losses likely to occur in each age group of accounts receivable. This percentage, when applied to the total dollar amount in the age group, gives the estimated uncollectible portion for that group. By adding together the estimated uncollectible portions for all age groups, the *required balance* in the Allowance for Doubtful Accounts is determined. Exhibit 7–9 provides a schedule listing the group totals from the aging schedule and shows how the estimated total amount of uncollectible accounts is computed.

Exhibit 7–9

ESTIMATED DOLLAR AMOUNT OF UNCOLLECTIBLE ACCOUNTS

VALLEY RANCH SUPPLY
ESTIMATED UNCOLLECTIBLE ACCOUNTS RECEIVABLE
DECEMBER 31, 2011

	Age Group Total		Percentage Considered Uncollectible*		Estimated Uncollectible Accounts
Not yet due	$ 51,000	×	1%	=	$ 510
1–30 days past due	29,000	×	3	=	870
31–60 days past due	12,000	×	10	=	1,200
61–90 days past due	3,000	×	20	=	600
Over 90 days past due	5,000	×	50	=	2,500
Totals	$100,000				$5,680

*These percentages are estimated each month by the credit manager, based on recent experience and current economic conditions.

At December 31, Valley Ranch Supply has total accounts receivable of $100,000, of which $5,680 are estimated to be uncollectible. Thus, an adjusting entry is needed to increase the Allowance for Doubtful Accounts from its present level to $5,680. If the allowance account currently has a credit balance of *$4,000,* the month-end adjusting entry should be in the amount of *$1,680,* determined as follows:[5]

[5] If accounts receivable written off during the period *exceed* the Allowance for Doubtful Accounts at the last adjustment date, the allowance account temporarily acquires a *debit balance.* This situation seldom occurs if the allowance is adjusted each month but often occurs if adjusting entries are made only at year-end.

If Valley Ranch Supply makes only an annual adjustment for uncollectible accounts, the allowance account might have a debit balance of $10,000. In this case, the year-end adjusting entry should be for *$15,680* in order to offset the $10,000 debit balance and to bring the allowance up to the required credit balance of $5,680.

Regardless of how often adjusting entries are made, the balance in the allowance account of Valley Ranch Supply should be *$5,680 at year-end.*

Determine the difference between the current balance and the required balance

Credit balance at December 31 (prior to adjustment)	$4,000
Credit adjustment required	1,680
Credit balance required at December 31 (per aging schedule)	$5,680

Thus, the following adjusting entry is made at December 31:

The difference between the current balance and the required balance is the Uncollectible Accounts Expense matched to the period

Uncollectible Accounts Expense	1,680	
Allowance for Doubtful Accounts		1,680
To increase the Allowance for Doubtful Accounts to its required balance of $5,680.		

Estimating Credit Losses—The Income Statement Approach An alternative method of estimating and recording credit losses is called the *income statement* approach. This method focuses on estimating the uncollectible accounts *expense* to be reported in the income statement for the period. On the basis of past experience, the uncollectible accounts expense is estimated at some percentage of net credit sales. The adjusting entry is made in the *full amount of the estimated expense,* without regard for the current balance in the Allowance for Doubtful Accounts.

To illustrate, assume that a company's past experience indicates that about 2 percent of its credit sales will prove to be uncollectible. If credit sales for September amount to $150,000, the month-end adjusting entry to record uncollectible accounts expense is:

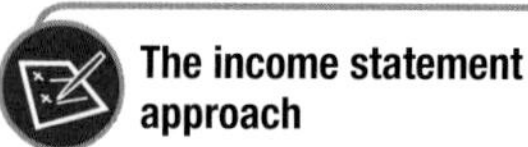

The income statement approach

Uncollectible Accounts Expense	3,000	
Allowance for Doubtful Accounts		3,000
To record uncollectible accounts expense, estimated at 2% of credit sales ($150,000 × 2% = $3,000).		

This approach is fast and simple—no aging schedule is required and no consideration is given to the existing balance in the Allowance for Doubtful Accounts. The aging of accounts receivable, however, provides a more reliable estimate of uncollectible accounts because of the consideration given to the age and collectibility of specific accounts receivable at the balance sheet date.

In past years, many small companies used the income statement approach in preparing monthly financial statements but used the balance sheet method in annual financial statements. Most businesses today have computer software that quickly and easily prepares monthly aging schedules of accounts receivable. Thus most businesses now use the *balance sheet approach* in both their monthly and annual financial statements.

RECOVERY OF AN ACCOUNT RECEIVABLE PREVIOUSLY WRITTEN OFF

Occasionally a receivable that has been written off as worthless will later be collected in full or in part. Such collections are often referred to as *recoveries* of bad debts. Collection of an account receivable previously written off is evidence that the write-off was an error; the receivable should therefore be reinstated as an asset.

Let us assume, for example, that a company wrote off a $500 account receivable from Brad Wilson on February 16. The write-off of this account was recorded as follows:

Wilson account considered uncollectible

Allowance for Doubtful Accounts	500	
Accounts Receivable (Brad Wilson)		500
To write off the account receivable from Brad Wilson as uncollectible.		

If the customer, Brad Wilson, pays the account in full on February 27, the entry to reverse the previous write-off is as follows:

Accounts Receivable (Brad Wilson)	500	
Allowance for Doubtful Accounts		500
To reinstate as an asset an account receivable previously written off.		

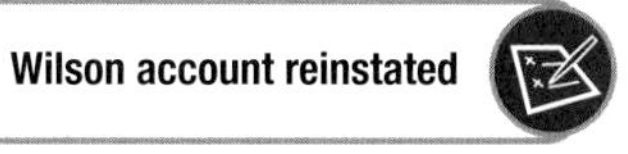

Notice that this entry is *exactly the opposite* of the entry made when the account was written off as uncollectible. A separate entry will be made to record the cash collected from Brad Wilson and to remove his reinstated account from the system.

Cash	500	
Accounts Receivable (Brad Wilson)		500
To record the collection of account receivable from Brad Wilson.		

Wilson account previously reinstated is finally collected

DIRECT WRITE-OFF METHOD

Some companies do not use any valuation allowance for accounts receivable. Instead of making end-of-period adjusting entries to record uncollectible accounts expense on the basis of estimates, these companies recognize no uncollectible accounts expense until specific receivables are determined to be worthless. This method makes no attempt to match revenue with the expense of uncollectible accounts.

When a particular customer's account is determined to be uncollectible, it is written off directly to Uncollectible Accounts Expense, as follows:

Uncollectible Accounts Expense	250	
Accounts Receivable (Bell Products)		250
To write off the account receivable from Bell Products as uncollectible.		

When the **direct write-off method** is used, the accounts receivable will be listed in the balance sheet at their gross amount, and *no valuation allowance* will be used. The receivables, therefore, are not stated at estimated net realizable value.

The allowance method is preferable to the direct write-off method because the allowance method does a better job of matching revenues and expenses. In some situations, however, use of the direct write-off method is acceptable. If a company makes most of its sales for cash, the amount of its accounts receivable will be small in relation to other assets. The expense from uncollectible accounts should also be small. Consequently, the direct write-off method is acceptable because its use does not have a *material* effect on the reported net income.

It is important to note that current income tax regulations *require* taxpayers to use the direct write-off method in determining the uncollectible accounts expense used in computing *taxable income.* From the standpoint of accounting theory, the allowance method is better because it enables expenses to be *matched* with the related revenue and thus provides a more logical measurement of net income. Therefore, most companies use the allowance method in their financial statements.[6]

FACTORING ACCOUNTS RECEIVABLE

The term **factoring** describes transactions in which a business sells its accounts receivable to a financial institution (often called a *factor*). These arrangements enable a business to obtain cash immediately instead of having to wait until the receivables can be collected.

[6] An annual survey of the accounting practices of 600 publicly owned corporations consistently shows more than 500 of these companies use the allowance method in their financial statements. All of these companies, however, use the direct write-off method in their income tax returns.

Factoring accounts receivable is a popular practice among small business organizations that do not have well-established credit. Large and liquid organizations often can borrow money using unsecured lines of credit.

YOUR TURN **You as a Used Car Purchaser**

Assume you purchased a car from John's Used Cars for $500 down and 24 payments of $150 per month. After making three months of payments to John's Used Cars, you are notified that John's plans to factor your account receivable to the Barb Smith Collection Agency. You are concerned about owing money to this particular collection agency because you have heard it uses very aggressive tactics to collect overdue payments. You call the car lot and speak directly with John. You question the legality and ethics of factoring accounts receivable. You state that you entered into a contract with him and not a collection agency. You state that you did not give permission to sell your receivable and that selling the receivable to another organization eliminates your obligation to pay it. John says factoring accounts receivable is legal and suggests that you consult the Uniform Commercial Code. What would you do?

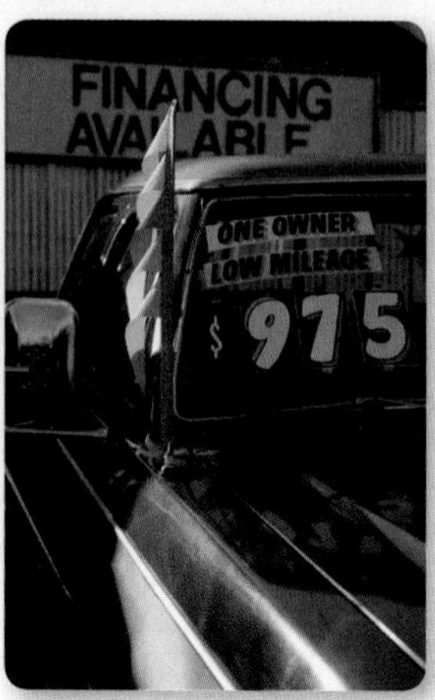

© Photodisc Green/Getty Images/DAL

(See our comments on the Online Learning Center Web site.)

CREDIT CARD SALES

By making sales through credit card companies, merchants receive cash more quickly from credit sales and avoid uncollectible accounts expense. They also avoid the expenses of investigating customers' credit, maintaining an accounts receivable subsidiary ledger, and making collections from customers.

Bank Credit Cards Some widely used credit cards (such as **Visa** and **MasterCard**) are issued by banks. When the credit card company is a bank, the retailing business may deposit the signed credit card drafts directly in its bank account. Because banks accept these credit card drafts for immediate deposit, sales to customers using bank credit cards are recorded as *cash sales.*

In exchange for handling the credit card drafts, the bank makes a monthly service charge that usually runs between 1¼ percent and 3½ percent of the amount of the drafts. This monthly service charge is deducted from the merchant's bank account and appears with other bank service charges in the merchant's monthly bank statement.

Other Credit Cards When customers use nonbank credit cards (such as **American Express**), the retailing business cannot deposit the credit card drafts directly in its bank account. Instead of debiting Cash, the merchant records an account receivable from the credit card company. Periodically, the credit card company reimburses the merchant. Businesses, however, are not reimbursed for the full amount of the outstanding receivable. The agreement between the credit card company and merchants usually allows the credit card company to discount the amount reimbursed by 3½ percent to 5 percent.

To illustrate, assume that Bradshaw Camera Shop sells a camera for $1,200 to a customer who uses a Quick Charge credit card. The entry would be:

Accounts Receivable (Quick Charge Co.)	1,200	
Sales		1,200
To record sale to customer using Quick Charge credit card.		

This receivable is from the credit card company

At the end of the week, Bradshaw Camera Shop mails the $1,200 credit card draft to Quick Charge Company, which redeems the draft after deducting a 5 percent discount. When payment is received by Bradshaw, the entry is:

Cash	1,140	
Credit Card Discount Expense	60	
Accounts Receivable (Quick Charge Co.)		1,200
To record collection of account receivable from Quick Charge Co., less 5% discount.		

The expense account, Credit Card Discount Expense, is included among the selling expenses in the income statement of Bradshaw Camera Shop.

Notes Receivable and Interest Revenue

Learning Objective
Explain, compute, and account for notes receivable and interest revenue. LO6

Accounts receivable usually do not bear interest. When interest will be charged, creditors usually require the debtor to sign a formal promissory note. A promissory note is an unconditional promise in writing to pay on demand or at a future date a definite sum of money.

The person who signs the note and thereby promises to pay is called the *maker* of the note. The person to whom payment is to be made is called the *payee* of the note. In Exhibit 7–10, Pacific Rim Corp. is the maker of the note and First National Bank is the payee.

Exhibit 7–10
SIMPLIFIED FORM OF PROMISSORY NOTE

$200,000 **Los Angeles, California** **July 10, 2011**

One year **AFTER DATE** **Pacific Rim Corp.** **PROMISES TO PAY**

TO THE ORDER OF **First National Bank**

---Two hundred thousand and no/100--- **DOLLARS**

PLUS INTEREST COMPUTED AT THE RATE OF **6% per annum**

SIGNED *G. R. Smith*

TITLE **Treasurer**

From the viewpoint of the maker, Pacific Rim, the illustrated note is a liability and is recorded by crediting the Notes Payable account. However, from the viewpoint of the payee, First National Bank, this same note is an asset and is recorded by debiting the Notes Receivable account. The maker of a note expects to pay cash at the *maturity date* (or due date); the payee expects to receive cash at that date.

NATURE OF INTEREST

Interest is a charge made for the use of money. A borrower incurs interest expense. A lender earns interest revenue. When you see notes payable in a company's financial statements, you know that the company has borrowed money, so you should expect to find interest expense in its income statement. If you see notes receivable, you know that the company has loaned money, so you should expect its income statement to report interest revenue.

Computing Interest In Chapter 4, we introduced the following formula to compute interest:

Interest = Principal × Rate of Interest × Time

(This formula is often expressed as I = P × R × T.)

Interest rates usually are stated on an *annual basis.* For example, the total interest charge on a $200,000, one-year, 6 percent note receivable is computed as follows:

P × R × T = $200,000 × .06 × 1 = $12,000

If the term of the note were only *four months* instead of one year, the total interest revenue earned in the life of the note would be $4,000, computed as follows:

P × R × T = $200,000 × .06 × 4⁄12 = $4,000

It should be noted that these computations illustrate *simple* interest, meaning no interest accrues on the unpaid interest amounts each month. We will introduce *compound* interest in Chapter 10.

ACCOUNTING FOR NOTES RECEIVABLE

In some fields of business, notes receivable are seldom encountered; in other fields they occur frequently and may constitute an important part of total assets. In banks and financial institutions, for example, notes receivable often represent the company's largest asset category and generate most of the company's revenue. Some retailers that sell on installment plans, such as **Sears Roebuck & Co.**, also own large amounts of notes receivable from customers.

All notes receivable are usually posted to a single account in the general ledger. The amount debited to Notes Receivable is always the *face amount* of the note, regardless of whether the note bears interest. When an interest-bearing note is collected, the amount of cash received may be larger than the face amount of the note. The interest collected is credited to an Interest Revenue account, and only the face amount of the note is credited to the Notes Receivable account.

Illustrative Entries Assume that on December 1, a 3-month, 6 percent note receivable is acquired from a customer, Marvin White, in settlement of an existing account receivable of $60,000. The entry for acquisition of the note is as follows:

Note received to replace account receivable

Notes Receivable	60,000	
Accounts Receivable (Marvin White)		60,000
Accepted 3-month, 6% note in settlement of account receivable.		

At December 31, the end of the company's fiscal year, the interest earned to date on notes receivable should be accrued by an adjusting entry as follows:

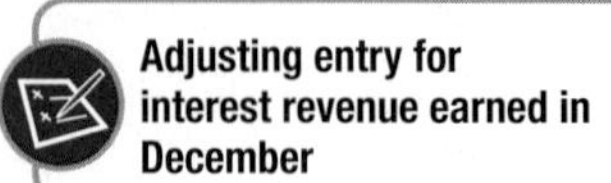
Adjusting entry for interest revenue earned in December

Interest Receivable	300	
Interest Revenue		300
To accrue interest for the month of December on Marvin White note ($60,000 × 6% × 1⁄12 = $300).		

To simplify this illustration, we will assume our company makes adjusting entries *only at year-end.* Therefore, no entries are made to recognize the interest revenue accruing during January and February.

On March 1 (3 months after the date of the note), the note matures. The entry to record collection of the note will be:

Cash	60,900	
Notes Receivable		60,000
Interest Receivable		300
Interest Revenue		600
Collected 90-day, 6% note from Marvin White ($60,000 × 6% × 3⁄12 = $900 interest, of which $600 was earned in current year).		

Collection of principal and interest

The preceding three entries show that interest is being earned throughout the term of the note and that the interest should be apportioned between years on a time basis. The revenue of each year will then include the interest actually earned in that year.

If the Maker of a Note Defaults A note receivable that cannot be collected at maturity is said to have been **defaulted** by the maker. Immediately after the default of a note, an entry should be made by the holder to transfer the amount due from the Notes Receivable account to an account receivable from the debtor.

To illustrate, assume that on March 1, our customer, Marvin White, had defaulted on the note used in the preceding example. In this case, the entry on March 1 would have been:

Accounts Receivable (Marvin White)	60,900	
Notes Receivable		60,000
Interest Receivable		300
Interest Revenue		600
To record default by Marvin White on 3-month, 6% note.		

Notice that the interest earned on the note is recorded through the maturity date and is included in the account receivable from the maker. The interest receivable on a defaulted note is just as valid a claim against the maker as is the principal amount of the note.

Learning Objective LO7
Evaluate the liquidity of a company's accounts receivable.

Financial Analysis and Decision Making

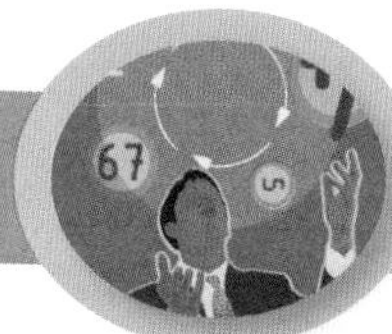

Collecting accounts receivable *on time* is important; it spells the success or failure of a company's credit and collection policies. A past-due receivable is a candidate for write-off as a credit loss. To help us judge how good a job a company is doing in granting credit and collecting its receivables, we compute the ratio of net sales to average receivables. This **accounts receivable turnover rate** tells us how many times the company's average investment in receivables was converted into cash during the year. The ratio is computed by dividing annual net sales by average accounts receivable. The higher the turnover rate, the more liquid the company's receivables. Dividing 365 days by the turnover rate provides an estimate of the average number of *days* an account receivable remains outstanding before it is collected. High turnover rates result in shorter collection periods than low turnover rates.

In some companies, such as restaurants, hotels, and public utilities, turnover rates are relatively high. For other enterprises, such as large manufacturing firms, turnover rates are relatively low, making the average time it takes to collect an outstanding receivable much longer.

To illustrate, Exhibit 7–11 contains information taken from recent financial statements issued by **Allete, Inc.** (an electric utility company), and **3M (Minnesota Mining and Manufacturing Company)**.

Exhibit 7–11

ACCOUNTS RECEIVABLE COLLECTION PERFORMANCE

	Allete, Inc.	3M
a. Net sales	$842 billion	$24.5 billion
Accounts receivable (beginning of year)	$ 70 million	$ 3.2 billion
Accounts receivable (end of year)	$ 80 million	3.4 billion
	$150 million	$ 6.6 billion
	÷ 2	÷ 2
b. Average accounts receivable	$ 75 million	$ 3.3 billion
c. Accounts receivable turnover rate **(a ÷ b)**	11.3 times	7.4 times
Average days outstanding **(365 days ÷ c)**	32 days	49 days

As shown in Exhibit 7–11, **Allete**'s accounts receivable turnover rate is *11.3 times* compared to **3M**'s turnover rate of only *7.4 times*. Thus, **Allete**'s accounts receivable remain outstanding an average of *32 days* before being collected, whereas **3M**'s accounts receivable remain outstanding an average of *49 days* prior to collection.

YOUR TURN — You as a Credit Manager

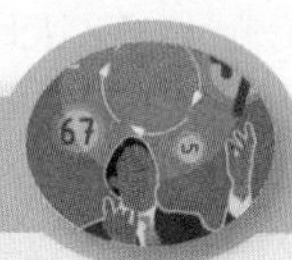

Assume that you were hired by Regis Department Stores in 2008 to develop and implement a new credit policy. At the time of your hire, the average collection period for an outstanding receivable was in excess of 90 days (far greater than the industry average). Thus the primary purpose of the new policy was to better screen credit applicants in an attempt to improve the quality of the company's accounts receivable.

Shown below are sales and accounts receivable data for the past four years (in thousands):

	2011	2010	2009	2008
Sales	$17,000	$14,580	$9,600	$9,000
Average accounts receivable	1,700	1,620	1,600	1,800

Based on the above data, was the credit policy you developed successful? Explain.

(See our comments on the Online Learning Center Web site.)

Ethics, Fraud & Corporate Governance

As discussed previously in this chapter, accounts receivable is a significant account for many companies. Accounts receivable is particularly prone to misrepresentation because revenue often increases when accounts receivable increase. Manipulating accounts receivable can result in the overstatement of both revenue and income, which is the objective of many fraudulent financial reporting schemes. Management often has an incentive to overstate income because bonus plans may be tied to this figure, and the values of the stock and stock options that managers hold in the company are sensitive to reported earnings. A study sponsored by **COSO** (a joint undertaking of the **AICPA**, **IIA**, **IMA**, **FEI**, and **AAA**—see Chapter 1 for a discussion of these groups), found that improper revenue recognition was the most common scheme in fraud-related SEC enforcement actions.

In the annual audit of a company by a CPA firm, the independent auditors will verify receivables by communicating directly with a random sample of those people who owe money. This confirmation process is designed to provide evidence that customers and other debtors actually exist. The CPA firm may also verify the credit rating of major debtors.

Concluding Remarks

This is the first of three chapters in which we explore the issues involved in accounting for assets. The central theme in these chapters is the *valuation* of assets. In Exhibit 7–2 (page 289), we have summarized how a company's financial assets are reported in the balance sheet.

We have illustrated numerous transactions involving the financial assets throughout this chapter. In addition to addressing balance sheet valuation issues, we have also determined whether these transactions are reported in the income statement and the statement of cash flows.

In the next two chapters, we explore the valuation of inventories and of plant assets. For each of these assets, you will see that several *alternative* valuation methods are acceptable. These different methods, however, may produce *significantly different results.* An understanding of these alternative accounting methods is essential to the proper use and interpretation of financial statements and in the preparation of income tax returns.

END-OF-CHAPTER REVIEW

SUMMARY OF LEARNING OBJECTIVES

LO1 **Define financial assets and explain their valuation in the balance sheet.** Financial assets are cash and other assets that convert directly into *known amounts* of cash. The three basic categories are cash, marketable securities, and receivables. In the balance sheet, financial assets are listed at their *current value.* For cash, this means the face amount; for marketable securities, current market value; and for receivables, net realizable value.

LO2 **Describe the objectives of cash management and internal controls over cash.** The objectives of cash management are accurate accounting for cash transactions, the prevention of losses through theft or fraud, and maintaining adequate—but not excessive—cash balances. The major steps in achieving internal control over cash transactions are as follows: (1) separate cash handling from the accounting function, (2) prepare departmental cash budgets, (3) prepare a control listing of all cash received through the mail and from over-the-counter cash sales, (4) deposit all cash receipts in the bank daily, (5) make all payments by check, (6) verify every expenditure before issuing a check in payment, and (7) promptly reconcile bank statements.

LO3 **Prepare a bank reconciliation and explain its purpose.** The cash balance shown in the month-end bank statement usually will differ from the amount of cash shown in the depositor's ledger. The difference is caused by items that have been recorded by either the depositor or the bank, but not recorded by both. Examples are outstanding checks and deposits in transit. The bank reconciliation adjusts the cash balance per the books and the cash balance per the bank statement for any unrecorded items and thus produces the correct amount of cash to be included in the balance sheet at the end of the month.

The purpose of a bank reconciliation is to achieve the control inherent in the maintenance of two independent records of cash transactions: one record maintained by the depositor and the other by the bank. When these two records are reconciled (brought into agreement), we gain assurance of a correct accounting for cash transactions.

LO4 **Describe how short-term investments are reported in the balance sheet and account for transactions involving marketable securities.** Short-term investments (marketable securities) are adjusted to their *market value* at each balance sheet date (a valuation principle often referred to as *fair value accounting*). If the value of a company's marketable securities has increased above their original cost, an *unrealized holding gain* is reported as a component of stockholders' equity. If the value of its marketable securities has fallen below their original cost, an *unrealized holding loss* is reported as a component of stockholders' equity.

Interest and dividends generally are recognized as revenue when they are received. When securities are sold, the cost is compared to the sales price, and the difference is recorded as a gain or a loss in the income statement.

LO5 **Account for uncollectible receivables using the allowance and direct write-off methods.** Under the allowance method, the portion of each period's credit sales expected to prove uncollectible is *estimated.* This estimated amount is recorded by a debit to the Uncollectible Accounts Expense account and a credit to the contra-asset account Allowance for Doubtful Accounts. When specific accounts are determined to be uncollectible, they are written off by debiting Allowance for Doubtful Accounts and crediting Accounts Receivable.

Under the direct write-off method, uncollectible accounts are charged to expense in the period that they are determined to be worthless.

The allowance method is theoretically preferable because it is based on the matching principle. However, only the direct write-off method may be used in income tax returns.

LO6 **Explain, compute, and account for notes receivable and interest revenue.** Accounts receivable usually do not bear interest. When interest will be charged, creditors usually require the debtor to sign a formal, legally binding promissory note. Promissory notes appear in the balance sheet as assets designated as notes receivable.

Interest on a note receivable is a contractual amount that accumulates (accrues) over time. The amount of interest accruing over a time period may be computed by the formula **Principal × Rate × Time.**

LO7 **Evaluate the liquidity of a company's accounts receivable.** The most liquid financial asset is cash, followed by cash equivalents, marketable securities, and receivables. The liquidity of receivables varies depending on their collectibility and maturity dates.

The Allowance for Doubtful Accounts should provide for those receivables that may prove to be uncollectible. However, users of financial statements may also want to evaluate the concentrations-of-credit-risk disclosure and, perhaps, the credit ratings of major debtors. The accounts receivable turnover rate provides insight as to how quickly receivables are being collected.

Key Terms Introduced or Emphasized in Chapter 7

accounts receivable turnover rate (p. 309) A ratio used to measure the liquidity of accounts receivable and the reasonableness of the accounts receivable balance. Computed by dividing net sales by average receivables.

aging the accounts receivable (p. 302) The process of classifying accounts receivable by age groups such as current, 1–30 days past due, 31–60 days past due, etc. A step in estimating the uncollectible portion of the accounts receivable.

Allowance for Doubtful Accounts (p. 301) A valuation account or contra-asset account relating to accounts receivable and showing the portion of the receivables estimated to be uncollectible.

bank reconciliation (p. 291) An analysis that explains the difference between the balance of cash shown in the bank statement and the balance of cash shown in the depositor's records.

cash equivalents (p. 289) Very short-term investments that are so liquid that they are considered equivalent to cash. Examples include money market funds, U.S. Treasury bills, certificates of deposit, and commercial paper. These investments must mature within 90 days of acquisition.

cash management (p. 290) Planning, controlling, and accounting for cash transactions and cash balances.

compensating balance (p. 290) A minimum average balance that a bank may require a borrower to leave on deposit in a non-interest-bearing account.

default (p. 309) Failure to pay interest or principal of a promissory note at the due date.

direct write-off method (p. 305) A method of accounting for uncollectible receivables in which no expense is recognized until individual accounts are determined to be worthless. At that point the account receivable is written off, with an offsetting debit to uncollectible accounts expense. Fails to match revenue and related expenses and is used primarily for tax accounting.

factoring (p. 305) Transactions in which a business either sells its accounts receivable to a financial institution (often called a *factor*) or borrows money by pledging its accounts receivable as collateral.

fair value accounting (p. 298) The balance sheet valuation standard applied to investments in marketable securities. Involves adjusting the securities to market value at each balance sheet date. (Represents an exception to the cost principle.)

financial assets (p. 288) Cash and assets convertible directly into known amounts of cash (such as marketable securities and receivables).

gain (p. 297) An increase in owners' equity resulting from a transaction other than earning revenue or investment by the owners. The most common example is the sale of an asset at a price above book value.

line of credit (p. 290) A prearranged borrowing agreement in which a bank stands ready to advance the borrower without delay any amount up to a specified credit limit. Once used, a line of credit becomes a liability. The unused portion of the line represents the ability to borrow cash without delay.

loss (p. 297) A decrease in owners' equity resulting from any transaction other than an expense or a distribution to the owners. The most common example is the sale of an asset at a price below book value.

marketable securities (p. 288) Highly liquid investments, primarily in stocks and bonds, that can be sold at quoted market prices in organized securities exchanges.

net realizable value (p. 289) The balance sheet valuation standard applied to receivables. Equal to the gross amount of accounts and notes receivable, less an estimate of the portion that may prove to be uncollectible.

NSF check (p. 292) A customer's check that was deposited but returned because of a lack of funds (Not Sufficient Funds) in the account on which the check was drawn.

Unrealized Holding Gain (or Loss) on Investments (p. 298) A stockholders' equity account representing the difference between the cost of investments owned and their market value at the balance sheet date. In short, gains or losses on these investments that have not been "realized" through the sale of the securities.

Demonstration Problem

Shown below are selected transactions of Gulf Corp. during the month of December 2011.

Dec. 1 Accepted a one-year, 8 percent note receivable from a customer, Glenn Holler. The note is in settlement of an existing $1,500 account receivable. The note, plus interest, is due in full on November 30, 2012.

Dec. 8 An account receivable from S. Willis in the amount of $700 is determined to be uncollectible and is written off against the Allowance for Doubtful Accounts.

Dec. 15 Unexpectedly received $200 from F. Hill in full payment of her account. The $200 account receivable from Hill previously had been written off as uncollectible.

Dec. 31 The month-end bank reconciliation includes the following items: outstanding checks, $12,320; deposit in transit, $3,150; check from customer T. Jones returned "NSF," $358; bank service charges, $10; bank collected $20,000 in maturing U.S. Treasury bills (a cash equivalent) on the company's behalf. (These Treasury bills had cost $19,670, so the amount collected includes $330 interest revenue.)

Data for Adjusting Entries

1. An aging of accounts receivable indicates probable uncollectible accounts totaling $9,000. Prior to the month-end adjustment, the Allowance for Doubtful Accounts had a credit balance of $5,210.
2. Prior to any year-end adjustment, the balance in the Marketable Securities account was $213,800. At year-end, marketable securities owned had a cost of $198,000 and a market value of $210,000.
3. Accrued interest revenue on the note receivable from Glenn Holler dated December 1.

Instructions

a. Prepare entries in general journal entry form for the December transactions. In adjusting the accounting records from the bank reconciliation, make one entry to record any increases in the Cash account and a separate entry to record any decreases.

b. Prepare the month-end adjustments indicated by the data for adjusting entries given above.

c. What is the adjusted balance in the Unrealized Holding Gain (or Loss) on Investments account at December 31? Where in the financial statements does this account appear?

Solution to the Demonstration Problem

a.

GENERAL JOURNAL

Date	Account Titles and Explanation	Debit	Credit
Dec. 1	Notes Receivable	1,500	
	Accounts Receivable (Glenn Holler)		1,500
	Accepted a one-year, 8% note in settlement of a $1,500 account receivable.		
8	Allowance for Doubtful Accounts	700	
	Accounts Receivable (S. Willis)		700
	To write off receivable from S. Willis as uncollectible.		
15	Accounts Receivable (F. Hill)	200	
	Allowance for Doubtful Accounts		200
	To reinstate account receivable previously written off as uncollectible.		
15	Cash	200	
	Accounts Receivable (F. Hill)		200
	To record collection of account receivable.		
31	Cash	20,000	
	Cash Equivalents		19,670
	Interest Revenue		330
	To record collection of maturing T-bills by bank.		
31	Accounts Receivable (T. Jones)	358	
	Bank Service Charges	10	
	Cash		368
	To record bank service charge and to reclassify NSF check from T. Jones as an account receivable.		

GENERAL JOURNAL				
b.	**Adjusting Entries**			
Dec. 31	Uncollectible Accounts Expense		3,790	
	Allowance for Doubtful Accounts			3,790
	To increase Allowance for Doubtful Accounts to $9,000 ($9,000 − $5,210 = $3,790).			
31	Unrealized Holding Gain (or Loss) on Investments		3,800	
	Marketable Securities			3,800
	To reduce the balance in the Marketable Securities account to a market value of $210,000.			
31	Interest Receivable		10	
	Interest Revenue			10
	Accrued one-month interest revenue on note receivable: $1,500 × 8% × 1/12 = $10.			

c. The Unrealized Holding Gain (or Loss) on Investments account has a *$12,000 credit balance*, representing the unrealized gain on securities owned as of December 31. (The unrealized gain is equal to the $210,000 market value of these securities, less their $198,000 cost.) The account appears in the stockholders' equity section of Gulf Corp.'s balance sheet.

Self-Test Questions

The answers to these questions appear on page 337.

1. In general terms, financial assets appear in the balance sheet at:

- **a.** Face value.
- **b.** Current value.
- **c.** Cost.
- **d.** Estimated future sales value.

2. Which of the following practices contributes to efficient cash management?

- **a.** Never borrow money—maintain a cash balance sufficient to make all necessary payments.
- **b.** Record all cash receipts and cash payments at the end of the month when reconciling the bank statements.
- **c.** Prepare monthly forecasts of planned cash receipts, payments, and anticipated cash balances up to a year in advance.
- **d.** Pay each bill as soon as the invoice arrives.

3. Each of the following measures strengthens internal control over cash receipts *except:*

- **a.** Factoring accounts receivable.
- **b.** Preparation of a daily listing of all checks received through the mail.
- **c.** The deposit of cash receipts in the bank on a daily basis.
- **d.** The use of cash registers.

Use the following data for questions 4 and 5:
Quinn Company's bank statement at January 31 shows a balance of $13,360, while the ledger account for Cash in Quinn's ledger shows a balance of $12,890 at the same date. The only reconciling items are the following:

- Deposit in transit, $890.
- Bank service charge, $24.
- NSF check from customer Greg Denton in the amount of $426.
- Error in recording check no. 389 for rent: check was written in the amount of $1,320, but was recorded improperly in the accounting records as $1,230.
- Outstanding checks, $?????

4. What is the total amount of outstanding checks at January 31?

a. $1,048. **b.** $868. **c.** $1,900. **d.** $1,720.

5. Assuming a single journal entry is made to adjust Quinn Company's accounting records at January 31, the journal entry includes:

- **a.** A debit to Rent Expense for $90.
- **b.** A credit to Accounts Receivable, G. Denton, for $426.
- **c.** A credit to Cash for $450.
- **d.** A credit to Cash for $1,720.

6. Which of the following best describes the application of generally accepted accounting principles to the valuation of accounts receivable?

- **a.** Realization principle—Accounts receivable are shown at their net realizable value in the balance sheet.
- **b.** Matching principle—The loss due to an uncollectible account is recognized in the period in which the sale is

made, not in the period in which the account receivable is determined to be worthless.

c. Cost principle—Accounts receivable are shown at the initial cost of the merchandise to customers, less the cost the seller must pay to cover uncollectible accounts.

d. Principle of conservatism—Accountants favor using the lowest reasonable estimate for the amount of uncollectible accounts.

7. On January 1, Dillon Company had a $3,100 credit balance in the Allowance for Doubtful Accounts. During the year, sales totaled $780,000, and $6,900 of accounts receivable were written off as uncollectible. A December 31 aging of accounts receivable indicated the amount probably uncollectible to be $5,300. (No recoveries of accounts previously written off were made during the year.) Dillon's financial statements for the current year should include:

a. Uncollectible accounts expense of $9,100.

b. Uncollectible accounts expense of $5,300.

c. Allowance for Doubtful Accounts with a credit balance of $1,500.

d. Allowance for Doubtful Accounts with a credit balance of $8,400.

8. Under the *direct write-off* method of accounting for uncollectible accounts:

a. The current year uncollectible accounts expense is less than the expense would be under the allowance approach.

b. The relationship between the current period net sales and current period uncollectible accounts expense illustrates the matching principle.

c. The Allowance for Doubtful Accounts is debited when specific accounts receivable are determined to be worthless.

d. Accounts receivable are not stated in the balance sheet at net realizable value, but at the balance of the Accounts Receivable control account.

9. Which of the following actions is *least* likely to increase a company's accounts receivable turnover?

a. Encouraging customers to use bank credit cards, such as **Visa** and **MasterCard**, rather than other national credit cards, such as **American Express**.

b. Offer customers larger cash discounts for making early payments.

c. Reduce the interest rate charged to credit customers.

d. Sell accounts receivable to a factor.

10. On October 1, *2011*, Coast Financial loaned Barr Corporation $300,000, receiving in exchange a nine-month, 12 percent note receivable. Coast ends its fiscal year on December 31 and makes adjusting entries to accrue interest earned on all notes receivable. The interest earned on the note receivable from Barr Corporation during *2012* will amount to:

a. $9,000. b. $18,000.
c. $27,000. d. $36,000.

11. Puget Sound Co. sold marketable securities costing $80,000 for $92,000 cash. In the company's income statement and statement of cash flows, respectively, this will appear as:

a. A $12,000 gain and a $92,000 cash receipt.

b. A $92,000 gain and an $8,000 cash receipt.

c. A $12,000 gain and an $80,000 cash receipt.

d. A $92,000 sale and a $92,000 cash receipt.

ASSIGNMENT MATERIAL Discussion Questions

1. Briefly describe the flow of cash among receivables, cash, and marketable securities.

2. Different categories of financial assets are valued differently in the balance sheet. These different valuation methods have one common goal. Explain.

3. What are *cash equivalents*? Provide two examples. Why are these items often combined with cash for the purpose of balance sheet presentation?

4. What are lines of credit? From the viewpoint of a short-term creditor, why do lines of credit increase a company's liquidity? How are the unused portions of these lines presented in financial statements?

5. Why are cash balances in *excess* of those needed to finance business operations viewed as relatively nonproductive assets? Suggest several ways in which these excess cash balances may be utilized effectively.

6. List two items often encountered in reconciling a bank statement that may cause cash per the bank statement to be *larger* than the balance of cash shown in the depositor's accounting records.

7. Why are investments in marketable securities shown separately from cash equivalents in the balance sheet?

8. Explain the *fair value adjustment procedure* for short-term investments classified as available-for-sale securities.

9. What does the account Unrealized Holding Gain (or Loss) on Investment represent? How is this account presented in the financial statements for short-term investments classified as available-for-sale securities?

10. Explain the relationship between the *matching principle* and the need to estimate uncollectible accounts receivable.

11. In making the annual adjusting entry for uncollectible accounts, a company may utilize a *balance sheet approach*

to make the estimate, or it may use an *income statement approach*. Explain these two alternative approaches.

12. Must companies use the same method of accounting for uncollectible accounts receivable in their financial statements and in their income tax returns? Explain.

13. What are the advantages to a retailer of making credit sales only to customers who use nationally recognized credit cards?

14. Explain how each of the following is presented in (1) a multiple-step income statement and (2) a statement of cash flows.

    a. Sale of marketable securities at a loss.

    b. Adjusting entry to create (or increase) the allowance for doubtful accounts.

    c. Entry to write off an uncollectible account against the allowance.

    d. Adjusting entry to increase the balance in the Marketable Securities account to a higher market value (assume these investments are classified as available-for-sale securities).

15. What is the formula for computing interest on a note receivable, and what does each term mean?

Brief Exercises

LO1 LO2 BRIEF EXERCISE 7.1
Cash and Cash Equivalents

The following footnote appeared in a recent financial statement of **Westinghouse Electric**:

> The Corporation considers all investment securities with a maturity of three months or less when acquired to be cash equivalents. All cash and temporary investments are placed with high-credit-quality financial institutions, and the amount of credit exposure to any one financial institution is limited. At December 31, cash and cash equivalents include restricted funds of $42 million.

a. Are the company's cash equivalents debt or equity securities? How do you know?

b. Explain what is meant by the statement that "the credit exposure to any one financial institution is limited."

c. Explain what is meant by the term *restricted funds* used in the footnote.

LO2 LO3 BRIEF EXERCISE 7.2
Bank Reconciliation and Cash Equivalents

The Cash account in the general ledger of Lyco Corporation showed a balance of $21,749 at December 31 (but prior to performing a bank reconciliation). The company's bank statement showed a balance of $22,000 at the same date. The only reconciling items consisted of: (1) a $5,000 deposit in transit, (2) a bank service charge of $200, (3) outstanding checks totaling $9,000, (4) a $3,000 check marked "NSF" from Susque Company, one of Lyco's customers, and (5) a check written for office supplies in the amount of $1,832, recorded by the company's bookkeeper as a debit to Office Supplies of $1,283, and a credit to Cash of $1,283.

In addition to the above information, Lyco owned the following financial assets at December 31: (1) a money market account of $60,000, (2) $3,000 of high-grade, 120-day commercial paper, and (3) $5,000 of highly liquid stock investments.

a. Prepare the company's December 31 bank reconciliation.

b. Determine the amount at which cash and cash equivalents will be reported in the company's balance sheet dated December 31.

c. Prepare the necessary journal entry to update the accounting records.

LO1 LO4 BRIEF EXERCISE 7.3
Fair Value Adjustment

Weis Markets accumulates large amounts of excess cash throughout the year. It typically invests these funds in marketable securities until they are needed. The company's most recent financial statements revealed a nearly $14 million unrealized gain on short-term investments. Footnotes to the financial statements disclosed that **Weis** reports its short-term investments at fair value.

a. Explain the meaning of the company's unrealized gain on short-term investments.

b. How does the unrealized gain impact the company's financial statements?

c. Is the unrealized gain included in the computation of the company's taxable income? Explain.

d. Evaluate fair value accounting from the perspective of the company's creditors.

LO1 LO4 BRIEF EXERCISE 7.4
Accounting for Marketable Securities

Mumford Corporation invested $30,000 in marketable securities on December 4. On December 9, it sold some of these investments for $10,000, and on December 18, it sold more of these investments for $5,000. The securities sold on December 9 had cost the company $7,000, whereas the securities sold on December 18 had cost the company $6,000.

a. Record the purchase of marketable securities on December 4.

b. Record the sale of marketable securities on December 9.

c. Record the sale of marketable securities on December 18.

d. Record the necessary fair value adjustment on December 31, assuming that the market value of the company's remaining unsold securities was $20,000.

LO1 LO5

BRIEF EXERCISE 7.5

Accounting for Uncollectible Accounts: A Balance Sheet Approach

Pachel Corporation reports the following information pertaining to its accounts receivable:

	Days Past Due			
Current	**1–30**	**31–60**	**61–90**	**Over 90**
$60,000	$40,000	$25,000	$12,000	$2,000

The company's credit department provided the following estimates regarding the percent of accounts expected to eventually be written off from each category listed above:

Current receivables outstanding	2%
Receivables 1–30 days past due	4
Receivables 31–60 days past due	16
Receivables 61–90 days past due	40
Receivables over 90 days past due	90

The company uses a *balance sheet* approach to estimate credit losses.

a. Record the company's uncollectible accounts expense, assuming it has a *$1,400 credit balance* in its Allowance for Doubtful Accounts *prior* to making the necessary adjustment.

b. Record the company's uncollectible accounts expense, assuming it has a *$1,600 debit balance* in its Allowance for Doubtful Accounts *prior* to making the necessary adjustment.

LO1 LO5

BRIEF EXERCISE 7.6

Accounting for Uncollectible Accounts: An Income Statement Approach

Wilson Corporation uses an *income statement* approach to estimate credit losses. Its *gross* Accounts Receivable of $5,000,000 at the *beginning* of the period had a *net realizable value* of $4,925,000. During the period, the company *wrote off* actual accounts receivable of $100,000 and collected $7,835,000 from credit customers. Credit sales for the year amounted to $9,000,000. Of its credit sales, 1 percent was estimated to eventually be uncollectible.

Determine the *net realizable value* of the company's accounts receivable at the *end* of the period.

LO1 LO5 LO7

BRIEF EXERCISE 7.7

Analyzing Accounts Receivable

Following are the average accounts receivable and net sales reported recently by two large beverage companies (dollar amounts are stated in millions):

	Average Accounts Receivable	Net Sales
Molson Coors Brewing Co.	$720	$ 8,320
Anheuser-Busch Companies, Inc.	900	17,400

a. Compute the accounts receivable turnover rate for each company (round your results to one decimal place).

b. Compute the average number of days that it takes for each company to collect its accounts receivable (round your results to the nearest whole day).

c. Based upon your computations in **a** and **b,** which company's accounts receivable appear to be most liquid? Defend your answer.

LO6 **BRIEF EXERCISE 7.8**

Notes Receivable and Interest

On September 1, 2011, Health Wise International acquired a 12 percent, nine-month note receivable from Herbal Innovations, a credit customer, in settlement of a $22,000 account receivable. Prepare journal entries to record the following:

a. The receipt of the note on September 1, 2011, in settlement of the account receivable.

b. The adjustment to record accrued interest revenue on December 31, 2011.

c. The collection of the principal and interest on May 31, 2012.

LO5 **BRIEF EXERCISE 7.9**

LO7 Industry Characteristics and Allowances for Doubtful Accounts

The following percentages were computed using figures from recent annual reports of **Weis Markets**, a large grocery store chain, and **Sprint Nextel Corporation**, a provider of telecommunication services:

	Weis	Sprint
Allowance for doubtful accounts as a percentage of net sales	0.04%	1.1%
Accounts receivable as a percentage of net sales	2.1	10.5

Explain why **Sprint**'s percentages are so much larger than **Weis Markets'** percentages.

LO7 **BRIEF EXERCISE 7.10**

Analyzing Accounts Receivable

Cromley Corporation reports annual sales of $1,500,000. Its accounts receivable throughout the year averaged $125,000.

a. Compute the company's accounts receivable turnover rate.

b. Compute the average days outstanding of the company's accounts receivable.

Exercises

LO3 **EXERCISE 7.1**

You as a Student

Assume that the following information relates to your most recent bank statement dated September 30:

Balance per bank statement at September 30	$3,400

Checks written that had not cleared the bank as of September 30:

#203	University tuition	$1,500
#205	University bookstore	350
#208	Rocco's Pizza	25
#210	Stereo purchase	425
#211	October apartment rent	500

Interest amounting to $4 was credited to your account by the bank in September. The bank's service charge for the month was $5. In addition to your bank statement, you received a letter from your parents informing you that they had made a $2,400 electronic funds transfer directly into your account on October 2. After reading your parents' letter, you looked in your checkbook and discovered its balance was $601. Adding your parents' deposit brought that total to $3,001.

Prepare a bank reconciliation to determine your correct checking account balance. Explain why neither your bank statement nor your checkbook shows this amount.

LO1 **EXERCISE 7.2**

Financial Assets

LO2

The following financial assets appeared in a recent balance sheet of **Apple Computer, Inc.** (dollar amounts are stated in millions):

Cash and cash equivalents	$ 5,263
Marketable securities (short-term investments)	18,201
Accounts receivable (net of allowance for doubtful accounts of $52)	3,361

a. Define *financial assets*.

b. A different approach is used in determining the balance sheet value for each category of **Apple Computer**'s financial assets, although each approach serves a common goal. Explain.

c. Why do companies like **Apple Computer** hold so much of their financial assets in the form of marketable securities and receivables?

d. What types of investments might **Apple Computer** own that are considered cash equivalents?

e. Explain what is meant by the balance sheet presentation of **Apple Computer**'s Accounts Receivable as shown in the table.

LO2 **EXERCISE 7.3**
Grandmother's Secret

The former bookkeeper of **White Electric Supply** is serving time in prison for embezzling nearly $416,000 in less than five years. She describes herself as "an ordinary mother of three kids and a proud grandmother of four." Like so many other "ordinary" employees, she started out by taking only small amounts. By the time she was caught, she was stealing lump sums of $5,000 and $10,000.

Her method was crude and simple. She would write a check for the correct amount payable to a supplier for, say, $15,000. However, she would record in the company's check register an amount significantly greater, say, $20,000. She would then write a check payable to herself for the $5,000 difference. In the check register, next to the number of each check she had deposited in her personal bank account, she would write the word "void," making it appear as though the check had been destroyed. This process went undetected for nearly five years.

a. What controls must have been lacking at **White Electric Supply** to enable the bookkeeper to steal nearly $416,000 before being caught?

b. What the bookkeeper did was definitely unethical. But *what if* one of her grandchildren had been ill and needed an expensive operation? If this had been the case, would it have been ethical for her to take company funds to pay for the operation if she intended to pay the company back in full? Defend your answer.

LO2 **EXERCISE 7.4**
Embezzlement Issues

D. J. Fletcher, a trusted employee of Bluestem Products, found himself in personal financial difficulties and decided to "borrow" $3,000 from the company and to conceal his theft.

As a first step, Fletcher removed $3,000 in currency from the cash register. This amount represented the bulk of the cash received in over-the-counter sales during the three business days since the last bank deposit. Fletcher then removed a $3,000 check from the day's incoming mail; this check had been mailed in by a customer, Michael Adams, in full payment of his account. Fletcher made no journal entry to record the $3,000 collection from Adams, but deposited the check in Bluestem Products's bank account in place of the $3,000 over-the-counter cash receipts he had stolen.

In order to keep Adams from protesting when his month-end statement reached him, Fletcher made a journal entry debiting Sales Returns and Allowances and crediting Accounts Receivable—Michael Adams. Fletcher posted this entry to the two general ledger accounts affected and to Adams's account in the subsidiary ledger for accounts receivable.

a. Did these actions by Fletcher cause the general ledger to be out of balance or the subsidiary ledger to disagree with the control account? Explain.

b. Assume that Bluestem Products prepares financial statements at the end of the month without discovering the theft. Would any items in the balance sheet or the income statement be in error? Explain.

c. Several weaknesses in internal control apparently exist in Bluestem Products. Indicate three specific changes needed to strengthen internal control over cash receipts.

LO3 **EXERCISE 7.5**
Bank Reconciliation

Shown below is the information needed to prepare a bank reconciliation for Warren Electric at December 31:

1. At December 31, cash per the bank statement was $15,200; cash per the company's records was $17,500.
2. Two debit memoranda accompanied the bank statement: service charges for December of $25, and a $775 check drawn by Jane Jones marked "NSF."
3. Cash receipts of $10,000 on December 31 were not deposited until January 4.
4. The following checks had been issued in December but were not included among the paid checks returned by the bank: no. 620 for $1,000, no. 630 for $3,000, and no. 641 for $4,500.

a. Prepare a bank reconciliation at December 31.

b. Prepare the necessary journal entry or entries to update the accounting records.

c. Assume that the company normally is *not* required to pay a bank service charge if it maintains a minimum average daily balance of $1,000 throughout the month. If the company's average daily balance for December had been $8,000, why did it have to pay a $25 service charge?

LO1 LO2 **EXERCISE 7.6**
Evaluating Cash Equivalents

Tyson Furniture has $100,000 in excess cash that it wants to invest in one or more cash equivalents. The treasurer has researched two money market accounts and two certificates of deposit (CDs) offered by four major banks. This is the information she gathered:

Investment Institution	Investment Type	Minimum Investment	Interest Rate	Penalty for Early Withdrawal?	Financial Risk
Nexity Bank	Money market account	$ 1,000	0.5%	No	Very low
Bank of America	Money market account	50,000	1.0	No	Very low
Discover Bank	90-day CD	2,500	1.3	Yes	Very low
Commerce Bank	90-day CD	100,000	1.4	Yes	Very low

The two 90-day certificates of deposit are FDIC insured for up to $100,000. The money market accounts are not FDIC insured.

Suggest how Tyson Furniture might allocate its $100,000 cash among these four opportunities. Discuss the trade-offs that management must consider.

LO1 LO4 **EXERCISE 7.7**
The Nature of Marketable Securities

Many companies hold a significant portion of their financial assets in the form of marketable securities. For example, **Microsoft Corporation** recently reported investments in marketable securities totaling $25.3 billion, an amount equal to 59 percent of its total financial assets. In contrast, only 26 percent of its financial assets were in the form of accounts receivable.

a. Define *marketable securities* (also referred to as short-term investments). What characteristics of these securities justify classifying them as financial assets?

b. What is the basic advantage of **Microsoft Corporation** keeping financial assets in the form of marketable securities instead of cash? Is there any disadvantage?

c. Explain how **Microsoft Corporation** values these investments in its balance sheet.

d. Discuss whether the valuation of marketable securities represents a departure from (1) the cost principle and (2) the objectivity principle.

e. Explain how *fair value accounting* benefits the *users* of **Microsoft Corporation**'s financial statements.

LO1 LO5 **EXERCISE 7.8**
Reporting Uncollectible Accounts

The credit manager of Montour Fuel has gathered the following information about the company's accounts receivable and credit losses during the current year:

Net credit sales for the year		$8,000,000
Accounts receivable at year-end		1,750,000
Uncollectible accounts receivable:		
Actually written off during the year	$96,000	
Estimated portion of year-end receivables expected to prove uncollectible (per aging schedule)	84,000	180,000

Prepare one journal entry summarizing the recognition of uncollectible accounts expense for the entire year under each of the following independent assumptions:

a. Uncollectible accounts expense is estimated at an amount equal to 2.5 percent of net credit sales.

b. Uncollectible accounts expense is recognized by adjusting the balance in the Allowance for Doubtful Accounts to the amount indicated in the year-end aging schedule. The balance in the allowance account at the *beginning* of the current year was $25,000. (Consider the effect of the write-offs during the year on the balance in the Allowance for Doubtful Accounts.)

c. The company uses the direct write-off method of accounting for uncollectible accounts.

d. Which of the three methods gives investors and creditors the most accurate assessment of a company's liquidity? Defend your answer.

LO7 **EXERCISE 7.9** Industry Characteristics and Collection Performance

The following information was taken from recent annual reports of **Goodyear Tire & Rubber**, and **PPL Energy Co.**, a public utility:

	Goodyear	PPL
Net sales	$19.6 billion	$ 5.1 billion
Average accounts receivable	3.1 billion	$376 million

a. Compute for each company the accounts receivable turnover rate for the year.

b. Compute for each company the average number of days required to collect outstanding receivables (round answers to nearest whole day).

c. Explain why the figures computed for **Goodyear** in parts **a** and **b** are so different from those computed for **PPL**.

LO1 through LO5 **EXERCISE 7.10** Analyzing the Effects of Transactions

Six events pertaining to financial assets are described as follows:

a. Invested idle cash in marketable securities and classified them as available for sale.

b. Collected an account receivable.

c. Sold marketable securities at a loss (proceeds from the sale were equal to the market value reflected in the last balance sheet).

d. Determined a particular account receivable to be uncollectible and wrote it off against the Allowance for Doubtful Accounts.

e. Received interest earned on an investment in marketable securities (company policy is to recognize interest as revenue *when received*).

f. Made a fair value adjustment increasing the balance in the Marketable Securities account to reflect a rise in the market value of securities owned.

Indicate the effects of each transaction or adjusting entry upon the financial measurements in the four column headings listed below. Use the code letters **I** for increase, **D** for decrease, and **NE** for no effect. Cash flow classifications were discussed in Chapter 2.

Transaction	Total Assets	Net Income	Operating Cash Flow	Nonoperating Cash Flow
a				

LO1 **EXERCISE 7.11** Reporting Financial Assets

Explain how each of the following items is reported in a complete set of financial statements, including the accompanying notes. (In one or more cases, the item may not appear in the financial statements.) The answer to the first item is provided as an example.

a. Cash equivalents.

b. Cash in a special fund being accumulated as legally required for the purpose of retiring a specific long-term liability.

c. Compensating balances.

d. The amount by which the current market value of securities classified as available for sale exceeds their cost.

e. The Allowance for Doubtful Accounts.

f. The accounts receivable turnover rate.

g. Realized gains and losses on investments sold during the period.

h. Proceeds from converting cash equivalents into cash.

i. Proceeds from converting investments in marketable securities into cash.

Example: **a.** Cash equivalents normally are *not* shown separately in financial statements. Rather, they are combined with other types of cash and reported under the caption "Cash and Cash Equivalents." A note to the statements often shows the breakdown of this asset category.

LO1 LO5 LO7

EXERCISE 7.12

Effects of Accounting Errors

Indicate the effects of *the following errors* on each of the items listed in the column headings below. Use the following symbols: **O** = overstated, **U** = understated, and **NE** = no effect. Assume that the company does *not* use the direct write-off method to account for uncollectible accounts.

Transaction	Gross Profit	Current Ratio	Receivables Turnover Rate	Net Income	Retained Earnings	Working Capital
a. Recorded uncollectible accounts expense by debiting Sales and crediting Accounts Receivable.						
b. Wrote off an account receivable deemed uncollectible by debiting Uncollectible Accounts Expense and crediting Accounts Receivable.						
c. Collected cash from credit customers in settlement of outstanding accounts receivable by debiting Cash and crediting Sales.						

- Gross Profit = Sales − Cost of Goods Sold
- Current Ratio = Current Assets ÷ Current Liabilities
- Receivables Turnover Rate = Sales ÷ Average Accounts Receivable (net)
- Working Capital = Current Assets − Current Liabilities

LO1 LO4

EXERCISE 7.13

Accounting for Marketable Securities

McGoun Industries pays income taxes on capital gains at a rate of 30 percent. At December 31, *2011,* the company owns marketable securities that cost $90,000 but have a current market value of $260,000.

a. How will users of McGoun's financial statements be made aware of this substantial increase in the market value of the company's investments?

b. As of December 31, 2011, what income taxes has McGoun paid on the increase in value of these investments? Explain.

c. Prepare a journal entry at January 4, 2012, to record the cash sale of these investments at $260,000.

d. What effect will the sale recorded in part **c** have on McGoun's tax obligation for 2012?

LO6

EXERCISE 7.14

Notes and Interest

On August 1, 2011, Hampton Construction received a 9 percent, six-month note receivable from Dusty Roads, one of Hampton Construction's problem credit customers. Roads had owed $36,000 on an outstanding account receivable. The note receivable was taken in settlement of this amount. Assume that Hampton Construction makes adjusting entries for accrued interest revenue *once each year* on December 31.

a. Journalize the following four events on the books of Hampton Construction.

1. Record the receipt of the note on August 1 in settlement of the account receivable.
2. Record accrued interest at December 31, 2011.
3. Assume that Dusty Roads pays the note plus accrued interest in full. Record the collection of the principal and interest on January 31, 2012.
4. Assume that Dusty Roads did *not* make the necessary principal and interest payment on January 31, 2012. Rather, assume that he defaulted on his obligation. Record the default on January 31, 2012.

b. Indicate the effects of each of the four transactions journalized in part **a** on the elements of the financial statement shown below. Use the code letters **I** for increase, **D** for decrease, and **NE** for no effect.

Transaction	Revenue − Expenses = Net Income	Assets = Liabilities + Equity
1		

LO1 LO4 LO5 LO7

EXERCISE 7.15
Using the Financial Statements of **Home Depot, Inc.**

The **Home Depot, Inc.**, financial statements appear in Appendix A at the end of this textbook. Use these statements to answer the following questions:

a. What is the total dollar value of the company's financial assets for the most current year reported?

b. Does the company report any investments in marketable securities? If so, how does it report unrealized gains and losses?

c. What is the company's allowance for uncollectible accounts for the most current year reported? (Hint: Examine the footnotes to the financial statements.)

d. On average, for how many days do the company's accounts receivable remain outstanding before collection?

Problem Set A

LO1 LO3

PROBLEM 7.1A
Bank Reconciliation

The cash transactions and cash balances of Banner, Inc., for July were as follows:

1. The ledger account for Cash showed a balance at July 31 of $125,568.
2. The July bank statement showed a closing balance of $114,828.
3. The cash received on July 31 amounted to $16,000. It was left at the bank in the night depository chute after banking hours on July 31 and therefore was not recorded by the bank on the July statement.
4. Also included with the July bank statement was a debit memorandum from the bank for $50 representing service charges for July.
5. A credit memorandum enclosed with the July bank statement indicated that a non-interest-bearing note receivable for $4,000 from Rene Manes, left with the bank for collection, had been collected and the proceeds credited to the account of Banner, Inc.
6. Comparison of the paid checks returned by the bank with the entries in the accounting records revealed that check no. 821 for $519, issued July 15 in payment for office equipment, had been erroneously entered in Banner's records as $915.
7. Examination of the paid checks also revealed that three checks, all issued in July, had not yet been paid by the bank: no. 811 for $314; no. 814 for $625; no. 823 for $175.
8. Included with the July bank statement was a $200 check drawn by Howard Williams, a customer of Banner, Inc. This check was marked "NSF." It had been included in the deposit of July 27 but had been charged back against the company's account on July 31.

Instructions

a. Prepare a bank reconciliation for Banner, Inc., at July 31.

b. Prepare journal entries (in general journal form) to adjust the accounts at July 31. Assume that the accounts have not been closed.

c. State the amount of cash that should be included in the balance sheet at July 31.

d. Explain why the balance per the company's bank statement is often larger than the balance shown in its accounting records.

LO2 **PROBLEM 7.2A**
Protecting Cash

LO3

Osage Farm Supply had poor internal control over its cash transactions. Facts about the company's cash position at November 30 are described below.

The accounting records showed a cash balance of $35,400, which included a deposit in transit of $1,245. The balance indicated in the bank statement was $20,600. Included in the bank statement were the following debit and credit memoranda:

Debit Memoranda:	
Check from customer G. Davis, deposited by Osage Farm Supply, but charged back as NSF.	$ 130
Bank service charges for November.	15
Credit Memorandum:	
Proceeds from collection of a note receivable from Regal Farms, which Osage Farm Supply had left with the bank's collection department	$6,255

Outstanding checks were as follows:

Check No.	Amount
8231	$ 400
8263	524
8288	176
8294	5,000

Bev Escola, the company's cashier, has been taking portions of the company's cash receipts for several months. Each month, Escola prepares the company's bank reconciliation in a manner that conceals her thefts. Her bank reconciliation for November was as follows:

Balance per bank statement, Nov. 30		$20,600
Add: Deposits in transit.	$2,145	
Collection of note from Regal Farms	6,255	8,400
Subtotal		$30,000
Less: Outstanding checks:		
No. 8231	$ 400	
8263	524	
8288	176	1,000
Adjusted cash balance per bank statement		$29,000
Balance per accounting records, Nov. 30.		$35,400
Add: Credit memorandum from bank		6,255
Subtotal		$29,145
Less: Debit memoranda from bank:		
NSF check of G. Davis	$ 130	
Bank service charges	15	145
Adjusted cash balance per accounting records		$29,000

Instructions

a. Determine the amount of the cash shortage that has been concealed by Escola in her bank reconciliation. (As a format, we suggest that you prepare the bank reconciliation correctly. The amount of the shortage then will be the difference between the adjusted balances per the bank statement and per the accounting records. You can then list this unrecorded cash shortage as the final adjustment necessary to complete your reconciliation.)

b. Carefully review Escola's bank reconciliation and explain in detail how she concealed the amount of the shortage. Include a listing of the dollar amounts that were concealed in various ways. This listing should total the amount of the shortage determined in part **a.**

c. Suggest some specific internal control measures that appear to be necessary for Osage Farm Supply.

LO1 LO5 **PROBLEM 7.3A** Aging Accounts Receivable; Write-offs

Super Star, a Hollywood publicity firm, uses the balance sheet approach to estimate uncollectible accounts expense. At year-end, an aging of the accounts receivable produced the following five groupings:

a. Not yet due	$500,000
b. 1–30 days past due	210,000
c. 31–60 days past due	80,000
d. 61–90 days past due	15,000
e. Over 90 days past due	30,000
Total	$835,000

On the basis of past experience, the company estimated the percentages probably uncollectible for the above five age groups to be as follows: Group a, 1 percent; Group b, 3 percent; Group c, 10 percent; Group d, 20 percent; and Group e, 50 percent.

The Allowance for Doubtful Accounts before adjustment at December 31 showed a credit balance of $11,800.

Instructions

a. Compute the estimated amount of uncollectible accounts based on the above classification by age groups.

b. Prepare the adjusting entry needed to bring the Allowance for Doubtful Accounts to the proper amount.

c. Assume that on January 10 of the following year, Super Star learned that an account receivable that had originated on September 1 in the amount of $8,250 was worthless because of the bankruptcy of the client, April Showers. Prepare the journal entry required on January 10 to write off this account.

d. The firm is considering the adoption of a policy whereby clients whose outstanding accounts become more than 60 days past due will be required to sign an interest-bearing note for the full amount of their outstanding balance. What advantages would such a policy offer?

LO1 LO5 **PROBLEM 7.4A** Accounting for Uncollectible Accounts

Wilcox Mills is a manufacturer that makes all sales on 30-day credit terms. Annual sales are approximately $30 million. At the end of *2010*, accounts receivable were presented in the company's balance sheet as follows:

Accounts receivable from clients	$3,100,000
Less: Allowance for doubtful accounts	80,000

During *2011*, $165,000 of specific accounts receivable were written off as uncollectible. Of these accounts written off, receivables totaling $15,000 were subsequently collected. At the end of 2011, an aging of accounts receivable indicated a need for a $90,000 allowance to cover possible failure to collect the accounts currently outstanding.

Wilcox Mills makes adjusting entries for uncollectible accounts *only at year-end*.

Instructions

a. Prepare the following general journal entries:

   1. One entry to summarize all accounts written off against the Allowance for Doubtful Accounts during 2011.
   2. Entries to record the $15,000 in accounts receivable that were subsequently collected.
   3. The adjusting entry required at December 31, 2011, to increase the Allowance for Doubtful Accounts to $90,000.

b. Notice that the Allowance for Doubtful Accounts was only $80,000 at the end of 2010, but uncollectible accounts during 2011 totaled $150,000 ($165,000 less the $15,000 reinstated). Do these relationships appear reasonable, or was the Allowance for Doubtful Accounts greatly understated at the end of 2010? Explain.

LO1 LO4

PROBLEM 7.5A

Accounting for Marketable Securities

At December 31, *2010,* Weston Manufacturing Co. owned the following investments in capital stock of publicly traded companies (classified as available-for-sale securities):

	Cost	Current Market Value
Footlocker, Inc. (5,000 shares: cost, $17 per share; market value, $20).	$ 85,000	$100,000
The Gap, Inc. (4,000 shares: cost, $17 per share; market value, $15)	68,000	60,000
	$153,000	$160,000

In *2011,* Weston engaged in the following two transactions:

Apr. 10 Sold 1,000 shares of its investment in **Footlocker, Inc.**, at a price of $21 per share, less a brokerage commission of $50.

Aug. 7 Sold 2,000 shares of its investment in **The Gap, Inc.**, at a price of $14 per share, less a brokerage commission of $60.

At December 31, 2011, the market values of these stocks were: **Footlocker, Inc.**, $18 per share; and **The Gap, Inc.**, $16 per share.

Instructions

a. Illustrate the presentation of marketable securities and the unrealized holding gain or loss in Weston's balance sheet at December 31, *2010.* Include a caption indicating the section of the balance sheet in which each of these accounts appears.

b. Prepare journal entries to record the transactions on April 10 and August 7.

c. Prior to making a fair value adjustment at the end of 2011, determine the unadjusted balance in the Marketable Securities control account and the Unrealized Holding Gain (or Loss) on Investments account. (Assume that no unrealized gains or losses have been recognized since last year.)

d. Prepare a schedule showing the cost and the market values of securities owned at the end of 2011. (Use the same format as the schedule illustrated above.)

e. Prepare the fair value adjusting entry required at December 31, 2011.

f. Illustrate the presentation of the marketable securities and unrealized holding gain (or loss) in the balance sheet at December 31, *2011.* (Follow the same format as in part **a.**)

g. Illustrate the presentation of the net *realized* gains (or losses) in the 2011 income statement. Assume a multiple-step income statement and show the caption identifying the section in which this amount would appear.

h. Explain how both the realized and unrealized gains and losses will affect the company's 2011 income tax return.

LO6 **PROBLEM 7.6A**
Notes Receivable

Eastern Supply sells a variety of merchandise to retail stores on account, but it insists that any customer who fails to pay an invoice when due must replace their account receivable with an interest-bearing note. The company adjusts and closes its accounts at December 31. Among the transactions relating to notes receivable were the following:

Sept. 1 Received from a customer (Party Plus) a nine-month, 10 percent note for $75,000 in settlement of an account receivable due today.

June 1 Collected in full the nine-month, 10 percent note receivable from Party Plus, including interest.

Instructions

a. Prepare journal entries (in general journal form) to record: (1) the receipt of the note on September 1; (2) the adjustment for interest on December 31; and (3) collection of principal and interest on June 1. (To better illustrate the allocation of interest revenue between accounting periods, we will assume Eastern Supply makes adjusting entries *only at year-end.*)

b. Assume that instead of paying the note on June 1, the customer (Party Plus) had defaulted. Give the journal entry by Eastern Supply to record the default. Assume that Party Plus has sufficient resources that the note eventually will be collected.

c. Explain why the company insists that any customer who fails to pay an invoice when due must replace it with an interest-bearing note.

LO1 LO3 through LO7 **PROBLEM 7.7A**
Short Comprehensive Problem

The Scooter Warehouse provided the following information at December 31, 2011:

Bank Reconciliation

General ledger cash balance, 12/31/11	$17,566	Bank statement balance, 12/31/11	$16,306
Bank service charge	(25)	Deposits in transit	2,450
Returned customer checks marked NSF	(375)	Outstanding checks	(1,356)
Error in recording of office supplies	234		
Adjusted cash balance, 12/31/11	$17,400	Adjusted cash balance, 12/31/11	$17,400

Marketable Securities

The company invested $26,000 in a portfolio of marketable securities on December 22, 2011. The portfolio's market value on December 31, 2011, had increased in value to $28,500.

Notes Receivable

On November 1, 2011, The Scooter Warehouse sold 25 scooters to Bermuda Fantasy Resort for $65,000. The resort paid $5,000 at the point of sale and issued a one-year, $60,000, 5 percent note for the remaining balance. The note, plus accrued interest, is due in full on October 31, 2012. The Scooter Warehouse adjusts for accrued interest revenue monthly.

Accounts Receivable

The Scooter Warehouse uses a *balance sheet* approach to account for uncollectible accounts expense. Outstanding accounts receivable on December 31, 2011, total $450,000. After aging these accounts, the company estimates that their *net realizable value* is $435,000. Prior to making any adjustment to record uncollectible accounts expense, The Scooter Warehouse's Allowance for Doubtful Accounts has a *credit balance* of $4,000.

Instructions

a. Prepare the journal entry necessary to update the company's accounts immediately after performing its bank reconciliation on December 31, 2011.

b. Prepare the journal entry necessary to adjust the company's marketable securities to market value at December 31, 2011.

c. Prepare the journal entry necessary to accrue interest in December 2011.

d. Prepare the journal entry necessary to report the company's accounts receivable at their net realizable value at December 31, 2011.

e. Discuss briefly how the entry performed in part **d** affects the accounts receivable turnover rate. Does the *write-off* of an account receivable affect the accounts receivable turnover rate differently than the entry performed in part **d**? Explain.

LO1 LO3 through LO7

PROBLEM 7.8A

Short Comprehensive Problem

The Cash account in the general ledger of Hendry Corporation shows a balance of $96,990 at December 31, 2011 (prior to performing a bank reconciliation). The company's bank statement shows a balance of $100,560 at the same date. An examination of the bank statement reveals the following:

1. Deposits in transit amount to $24,600.
2. Bank service charges total $200.
3. Outstanding checks total $31,700.
4. A $3,600 check marked "NSF" from Kent Company (one of Hendry Corporation's customers) was returned to Hendry Corporation by the bank. This was the only NSF check that Hendry Corporation received during 2011.
5. A canceled check (no. 244) written by Hendry Corporation in the amount of $1,250 for office equipment was incorrectly recorded in the general ledger as a debit to Office Equipment of $1,520, and a credit to Cash of $1,520.

In addition to the above information, Hendry Corporation owns the following assets at December 31, 2011: (1) money market accounts totaling $75,000, (2) $3,000 of high-grade, 90-day, commercial paper, and (3) highly liquid stock investments valued at $86,000 at December 31, 2011 (these investments originally cost Hendry Corporation $116,000).

On December 1, 2011, Hendry Corporation sold an unused warehouse to Moran Industries for $100,000. Hendry accepted a six-month, $100,000, 6 percent note receivable from Moran. The note, plus accrued interest, is due in full on May 31, 2012. Hendry Corporation adjusts for accrued interest revenue *monthly*.

Hendry Corporation uses the *income statement approach* to compute its uncollectible accounts expense. The general ledger had reported Accounts Receivable of $2,150,000 at *January 1, 2011*. At that time, the Allowance for Doubtful Accounts had a credit balance of $40,000. Throughout 2011, the company *wrote off* actual accounts receivable of $140,000 and collected $21,213,600 on account from credit customers (this amount includes the $3,600 NSF check received from Kent Company). Credit sales for the year ended December 31, 2011, totaled $20,000,000. Of these credit sales, 2 percent were estimated to eventually become uncollectible.

Instructions

a. Prepare Hendry Corporation's bank reconciliation dated December 31, 2011, and provide the journal entry necessary to update the company's general ledger balances.

b. Compute cash and cash equivalents to be reported in Hendry Corporation's balance sheet dated December 31, 2011.

c. Prepare the adjusting entry necessary to account for the note receivable from Moran Industries at December 31, 2011.

d. Determine the net realizable value of Hendry Corporation's accounts receivable at December 31, 2011.

e. Determine the total dollar amount of financial assets to be reported in Hendry Corporation's balance sheet dated December 31, 2011.

f. Assume that it is normal for firms similar to Hendry Corporation to take an average of 45 days to collect an outstanding receivable. Is Hendry Corporation's collection performance above or below this average?

Problem Set B

LO1 LO3

PROBLEM 7.1B
Bank Reconciliation

The cash transactions and cash balances of Dodge, Inc., for November were as follows:

1. The ledger account for Cash showed a balance at November 30 of $6,750.
2. The November bank statement showed a closing balance of $4,710.
3. The cash received on November 30 amounted to $3,850. It was left at the bank in the night depository chute after banking hours on November 30 and therefore was not recorded by the bank on the November statement.
4. Also included with the November bank statement was a debit memorandum from the bank for $15 representing service charges for November.
5. A credit memorandum enclosed with the November bank statement indicated that a non-interest-bearing note receivable for $4,000 from Wright Sisters, left with the bank for collection, had been collected and the proceeds credited to the account of Dodge, Inc.
6. Comparison of the paid checks returned by the bank with the entries in the accounting records revealed that check no. 810 for $430, issued November 15 in payment for computer equipment, had been erroneously entered in Dodge's records as $340.
7. Examination of the paid checks also revealed that three checks, all issued in November, had not yet been paid by the bank: no. 814 for $115; no. 816 for $170; no. 830 for $530.
8. Included with the November bank statement was a $2,900 check drawn by Steve Dial, a customer of Dodge, Inc. This check was marked "NSF." It had been included in the deposit of November 27 but had been charged back against the company's account on November 30.

Instructions

a. Prepare a bank reconciliation for Dodge, Inc., at November 30.

b. Prepare journal entries (in general journal form) to adjust the accounts at November 30. Assume that the accounts have not been closed.

c. State the amount of cash that should be included in the balance sheet at November 30.

LO2 LO3

PROBLEM 7.2B
Protecting Cash

Jason Chain Saws, Inc., had poor internal control over its cash transactions. Facts about the company's cash position at April 30 are described below.

The accounting records showed a cash balance of $20,325, which included a deposit in transit of $5,000. The balance indicated in the bank statement was $14,300. Included in the bank statement were the following debit and credit memoranda:

Debit Memoranda:	
Check from customer, deposited but charged back as NSF	$ 125
Bank service charges for April	50
Credit Memorandum:	
Proceeds from collection of a note receivable on company's behalf	$6,200

Outstanding checks as of April 30 were as follows:

Check No.	Amount
836	$ 500
842	440
855	330
859	1,300

Tom Crook, the company's cashier, has been taking portions of the company's cash receipts for several months. Each month, Crook prepares the company's bank reconciliation in a manner that conceals his thefts. His bank reconciliation for April is illustrated as follows:

Balance per bank statement, April 30		$14,300
Add: Deposits in transit	$7,120	
Collection of note	6,200	13,320
Subtotal		$27,620
Less: Outstanding checks:		
No. 836	$ 500	
No. 842	440	
No. 855	330	1,270
Adjusted cash balance per bank statement		$26,350
Balance per accounting records, April 30		20,325
Add: Credit memorandum from bank		6,200
Subtotal		$26,525
Less: Debit memoranda from bank:		
NSF check	$ 125	
Bank service charges	50	175
Adjusted cash balance per accounting records		$26,350

Instructions

a. Determine the amount of cash shortage that has been concealed by Crook in his bank reconciliation. (As a format, we suggest that you prepare the bank reconciliation correctly. The amount of the shortage then will be the difference between the adjusted balances per the bank statement and per the accounting records. You can then list this unrecorded cash shortage as the final adjustment necessary to complete your reconciliation.)

b. Carefully review Crook's bank reconciliation and explain in detail how he concealed the amount of the shortage. Include a listing of the dollar amounts that were concealed in various ways. This listing should total the amount of shortage determined in part **a.**

c. Suggest some specific internal control measures that appear to be necessary for Jason Chain Saws, Inc.

LO1 LO5

PROBLEM 7.3B

Aging Accounts Receivable; Write-offs

Starlight, a Broadway media firm, uses the balance sheet approach to estimate uncollectible accounts expense. At year-end an aging of the accounts receivable produced the following five groupings:

a. Not yet due	$500,000
b. 1–30 days past due	110,000
c. 31–60 days past due	50,000
d. 61–90 days past due	30,000
e. Over 90 days past due	60,000
Total	$750,000

On the basis of past experience, the company estimated the percentages probably uncollectible for the above five age groups to be as follows: Group a, 1 percent; Group b, 3 percent; Group c, 10 percent; Group d, 20 percent; and Group e, 50 percent.

The Allowance for Doubtful Accounts before adjustments at December 31 showed a credit balance of $4,700.

Instructions

a. Compute the estimated amount of uncollectible accounts based on the above classification by age groups.

b. Prepare the adjusting entry needed to bring the Allowance for Doubtful Accounts to the proper amount.

c. Assume that on January 18 of the following year, Starlight learned that an account receivable that had originated on August 1 in the amount of $1,600 was worthless because of the bankruptcy of the client, May Flowers. Prepare the journal entry required on January 18 to write off this account.

d. The firm is considering the adoption of a policy whereby clients whose outstanding accounts become more than 60 days past due will be required to sign an interest-bearing note for the full amount of their outstanding balance. What advantages would such a policy offer?

LO1 LO5

PROBLEM 7.4B
Accounting for Uncollectible Accounts

Walc Factory is a manufacturer that makes all sales on 30-day credit terms. Annual sales are approximately $20 million. At the end of *2010*, accounts receivable were presented in the company's balance sheet as follows:

Accounts receivable from clients	$1,800,000
Less: Allowance for doubtful accounts	40,000

During 2011, $115,000 of specific accounts receivable were written off as uncollectible. Of these accounts written off, receivables totaling $9,000 were subsequently collected. At the end of 2011, an aging of accounts receivable indicated a need for a $75,000 allowance to cover possible failure to collect the accounts currently outstanding.

Walc Factory makes adjusting entries for uncollectible accounts *only at year-end.*

Instructions

a. Prepare the following general journal entries:

1. One entry to summarize all accounts written off against the Allowance for Doubtful Accounts during 2011.
2. Entries to record the $9,000 in accounts receivable that were subsequently collected.
3. The adjusting entry required at December 31, 2011, to increase the Allowance for Doubtful Accounts to $75,000.

b. Notice that the Allowance for Doubtful Accounts was only $40,000 at the end of 2010, but uncollectible accounts during 2011 totaled $106,000 ($115,000 less the $9,000 reinstated). Do these relationships appear reasonable, or was the Allowance for Doubtful Accounts greatly understated at the end of 2010? Explain.

LO1 LO4

PROBLEM 7.5B
Accounting for Marketable Securities

At December 31, *2010,* Westport Manufacturing Co. owned the following investments in the capital stock of publicly owned companies (all classified as available-for-sale securities):

	Cost	Current Market Value
Lamb Computer, Inc. (1,000 shares: cost, $30 per share; market value, $50)	$30,000	$50,000
Dry Foods (5,000 shares: cost, $9 per share; market value, $8)	45,000	40,000
Totals	$75,000	$90,000

In *2011,* Westport engaged in the following two transactions:

Apr. 6 Sold 100 shares of its investment in Lamb Computer at a price of $55 per share, less a brokerage commission of $20.

Apr. 20 Sold 2,500 shares of its Dry Foods stock at a price of $7 per share, less a brokerage commission of $20.

At December 31, 2011, the market values of these stocks were: Lamb Computer, $40 per share; Dry Foods, $7.

Instructions

a. Illustrate the presentation of marketable securities and the unrealized holding gain or loss in Westport's balance sheet at December 31, *2010*. Include a caption indicating the section of the balance sheet in which each of these accounts appears.

b. Prepare journal entries to record the transactions on April 6 and April 20.

c. Prior to making a fair value adjustment at the end of 2011, determine the unadjusted balance in the Marketable Securities controlling account and the Unrealized Holding Gain (or Loss) on Investments account. (Assume that no unrealized gains or losses have been recognized since last year.)

d. Prepare a schedule showing the cost and market values of securities owned at the end of 2011. (Use the same format as the schedule illustrated above.)

e. Prepare the fair value adjusting entry required at December 31, 2011.

f. Illustrate the presentation of the marketable securities and unrealized holding gain (or loss) in the balance sheet at December 31, *2011*. (Follow the same format as in part **a.**)

g. Illustrate the presentation of the net *realized* gains (or losses) in the 2011 income statement. Assume a multiple-step income statement and show the caption identifying the section in which this amount would appear.

h. Explain how both the realized and the unrealized gains and losses will affect the company's 2011 income tax return.

LO6 **PROBLEM 7.6B**
Notes Receivable

Southern Supply sells a variety of merchandise to retail stores on account, but it insists that any customer who fails to pay an invoice when due must replace their account receivable with an interest-bearing note. The company adjusts and closes its accounts at December 31. Among the transactions relating to notes receivable were the following:

Nov. 1 Received from a customer (LCC) a nine-month, 12 percent note for $60,000 in settlement of an account receivable due today.

Aug. 1 Collected in full the nine-month, 12 percent note receivable from LCC, including interest.

Instructions

a. Prepare journal entries (in general journal form) to record: (1) the receipt of the note on November 1; (2) the adjustment for interest on December 31; and (3) the collection of principal and interest on August 1. (To better illustrate the allocation of interest revenue between accounting periods, we will assume Southern Supply makes adjusting entries *only at year-end.*)

b. Assume that instead of paying the note on August 1, the customer (LCC) had defaulted. Give the journal entry by Southern Supply to record the default. Assume that LCC has sufficient resources that the note eventually will be collected.

c. Explain why the company insists that any customer who fails to pay an invoice when due must replace it with an interest-bearing note.

LO1 **PROBLEM 7.7B**
Short Comprehensive Problem
LO3 through LO7

Data Management, Inc., provided the following information at December 31, 2011:

Bank Reconciliation

General ledger cash balance, 12/31/11	$44,637	Bank statement balance, 12/31/11	$37,960
Bank service charge	(125)	Deposits in transit	18,800
Returned customer checks marked NSF	(2,350)	Outstanding checks	(15,560)
Error in recording of office supplies	(962)		
Adjusted cash balance, 12/31/11	$41,200	Adjusted cash balance, 12/31/11	$41,200

Marketable Securities

The company invested $75,000 in a portfolio of marketable securities on December 9, 2011. The portfolio's market value on December 31, 2011, had decreased in value to $68,000.

Notes Receivable

On October 1, 2011, Data Management sold 50 laptop computers to the Mifflinburg School District for $74,500. The school district paid $2,500 at the point of sale and issued a one-year, $72,000, 6 percent note for the remaining balance. The note, plus accrued interest, is due in full on September 30, 2012. Data Management adjusts for accrued interest revenue monthly.

Accounts Receivable

Data Management uses a *balance sheet* approach to account for uncollectible accounts expense. Outstanding accounts receivable on December 31, 2011, total $900,000. After aging these accounts, the company estimates that their *net realizable value* is $860,000. Prior to making any adjustment to record uncollectible accounts expense, Data Management's Allowance for Doubtful Accounts has a *debit balance* of $9,000.

Instructions

a. Prepare the journal entry necessary to update the company's accounts immediately after performing its bank reconciliation on December 31, 2011.

b. Prepare the journal entry necessary to adjust the company's marketable securities to market value at December 31, 2011.

c. Prepare the journal entry necessary to accrue interest revenue in December 2011.

d. Prepare the journal entry necessary to report the company's accounts receivable at their net realizable value at December 31, 2011.

e. Discuss briefly why the company's Allowance for Doubtful Accounts had a *debit balance* prior to the adjustment made in part **d.** How might the company change the percentages it applies to the accounts receivable aging categories to avoid future debit balances in its Allowance for Doubtful Accounts?

LO1 LO3 through LO7

PROBLEM 7.8B
Short Comprehensive Problem

The Cash account in the general ledger of Ciavarella Corporation shows a balance of $112,000 at December 31, 2011 (prior to performing a bank reconciliation). The company's bank statement shows a balance of $104,100 at the same date. An examination of the bank statement reveals the following:

1. Deposits in transit amount to $16,800.
2. Bank service charges total $100.
3. Outstanding checks total $12,400.
4. A $2,500 check marked "NSF" from Needham Company (one of Ciavarella's customers) was returned to Ciavarella Corporation by the bank. This was the only NSF check that Ciavarella received during 2011.
5. Check no. 550 was actually written by Ciavarella in the amount of $3,200 for computer equipment but was incorrectly recorded in the general ledger as a debit to Computer Equipment of $2,300, and a credit to Cash of $2,300.

In addition to the above information, Ciavarella owns the following assets at December 31, 2011: (1) money market accounts totaling $150,000, (2) $5,000 of high-grade, 60-day commercial paper, and (3) highly liquid stock investments valued at $245,000 at December 31, 2011 (these investments originally cost Ciavarella $225,000).

On December 1, 2011, Ciavarella sold a used truck to Ritter Industries for $18,000. Ciavarella accepted a three-month, $18,000, 9 percent note receivable from Ritter. The note, plus accrued interest, is due in full on March 1, 2012. Ciavarella adjusts for accrued interest revenue monthly.

Ciavarella uses the *income statement approach* to compute uncollectible accounts expense. The general ledger had reported Accounts Receivable of $540,000 at *January 1, 2011*. At that time, the Allowance for Doubtful Accounts had a credit balance of $12,000. Throughout 2011, the company *wrote off* actual accounts receivable of $14,000 and collected $5,252,500 on account from credit customers (this amount includes the $2,500 NSF check received from Needham Company). Credit sales for the year ended December 31, 2011, totaled $6,480,000. Of these credit sales, 1 percent were estimated to eventually become uncollectible.

Instructions

a. Prepare Ciavarella's bank reconciliation dated December 31, 2011, and provide the journal entry necessary to update the company's general ledger balances.

b. Compute cash and cash equivalents to be reported in Ciavarella's balance sheet dated December 31, 2011.

c. Prepare the adjusting entry necessary to account for the note receivable from Ritter Industries at December 31, 2011.

d. Determine the net realizable value of Ciavarella's accounts receivable at December 31, 2011.

e. Determine the total dollar amount of financial assets to be reported in Ciavarella's balance sheet dated December 31, 2011.

f. Assume that it is normal for firms similar to Ciavarella to take an average of 60 days to collect an outstanding receivable. Is Ciavarella Corporation's collection performance above or below this average?

Critical Thinking Cases

LO1 LO5 LO6

CASE 7.1
Accounting Principles

In each of the situations described below, indicate the accounting principles or concepts, if any, that have been violated and explain briefly the nature of the violation. If you believe the practice is *in accord* with generally accepted accounting principles, state this as your position and defend it.

a. A small business in which credit sales fluctuate greatly from year to year uses the direct write-off method both for income tax purposes and in its financial statements.

b. Computer Systems often sells merchandise in exchange for interest-bearing notes receivable, maturing in 6, 12, or 24 months. The company records these sales transactions by debiting Notes Receivable for the maturity value of the notes, crediting Sales for the sales price of the merchandise, and crediting Interest Revenue for the balance of the maturity value of the note. The cost of goods sold also is recorded.

c. A company has $400,000 in unrestricted cash, $1 million in a bank account specifically earmarked for the construction of a new factory, and $2 million in cash equivalents. In the balance sheet, these amounts are combined and shown as "Cash and cash equivalents . . . $3.4 million."

LO2 LO5 LO7

CASE 7.2
If Things Get Any Better, We'll Be Broke

Rock, Inc., sells stereo equipment. Traditionally, the company's sales have been in the following categories: cash sales, 25 percent; customers using national credit cards, 35 percent; sales on account (due in 30 days), 40 percent. With these policies, the company earned a modest profit, and monthly cash receipts exceeded monthly cash payments by a comfortable margin. Uncollectible accounts expense was approximately 1 percent of net sales. (The company uses the direct write-off method in accounting for uncollectible accounts receivable.)

Two months ago, the company initiated a new credit policy, which it calls "Double Zero." Customers may purchase merchandise on account, with no down payment and no interest charges. The accounts are collected in 12 monthly installments of equal amounts.

The plan has proven quite popular with customers, and monthly sales have increased dramatically. Despite the increase in sales, however, Rock is experiencing cash flow problems—it hasn't been generating enough cash to pay its suppliers, most of which require payment within 30 days.

The company's bookkeeper has prepared the following analysis of monthly operating results:

Sales	Before Double Zero	Last Month
Cash	$12,500	$ 5,000
National credit card	17,500	10,000
30-day accounts	20,000	-0-
Double Zero accounts	-0-	75,000
Total monthly sales	$50,000	$ 90,000
Cost of goods sold and expenses	40,000	65,000
Net income	$10,000	$ 25,000
Cash receipts		
Cash sales	$12,500	$ 5,000
National credit card companies	17,500	10,000
30-day accounts	19,500	-0-
Double Zero accounts	-0-	11,250
Total monthly cash receipts	$49,500	$ 26,250
Accounts written off as uncollectible	$ 500	$ -0-
Accounts receivable at month-end	$20,000	$135,000

The bookkeeper offered the following assessment: "Double Zero is killing us. Since we started that plan, our accounts receivable have increased nearly sevenfold, and they're still growing. We can't afford to carry such a large nonproductive asset on our books. Our cash receipts are down to nearly half of what they used to be. If we don't go back to more cash sales and receivables that can be collected more quickly, we'll become insolvent."

In reply Maxwell "Rock" Swartz, founder and chief executive officer, shouted out: "Why do you say that our accounts receivable are nonproductive? They're the most productive asset we have! Since we started Double Zero, our sales have nearly doubled, our profits have more than doubled, and our bad debt expense has dropped to nothing!"

Instructions

a. Is it logical that the Double Zero plan is causing sales and profits to increase while also causing a decline in cash receipts? Explain.

b. Why has the uncollectible accounts expense dropped to zero? What would you expect to happen to the company's uncollectible accounts expense in the future—say, next year? Why?

c. Do you think that the reduction in monthly cash receipts is permanent or temporary? Explain.

d. In what sense are the company's accounts receivable a "nonproductive" asset?

e. Suggest several ways that Rock may be able to generate the cash it needs to pay its bills without terminating the Double Zero plan.

f. Would you recommend that the company continue offering Double Zero financing, or should it return to the use of 30-day accounts? Explain the reasons for your answer, and identify any unresolved factors that might cause you to change this opinion in the future.

LO1 through LO5 LO7

CASE 7.3 "Improving" the Balance Sheet

Affections manufactures candy and sells only to retailers. It is not a publicly owned company and its financial statements are not audited. But the company frequently must borrow money. Its creditors insist that the company provide them with unaudited financial statements at the end of each quarter.

In October, management met to discuss the fiscal year ending next December 31. Due to a sluggish economy, Affections was having difficulty collecting its accounts receivable, and its cash position was unusually low. Management knew that if the December 31 balance sheet did not look good, the company would have difficulty borrowing the money it would need to boost production for Valentine's Day.

Thus the purpose of the meeting was to explore ways in which Affections might improve its December 31 balance sheet. Some of the ideas discussed are as follows:

1. Offer customers purchasing Christmas candy a 10 percent discount if they make payment within 30 days.
2. Allow a 30-day grace period on all accounts receivable overdue at the end of the year. As these accounts will no longer be overdue, the company will not need an allowance for overdue accounts.
3. For purposes of balance sheet presentation, combine all forms of cash, including cash equivalents, compensating balances, and unused lines of credit.
4. Require officers who have borrowed money from the company to repay the amounts owed at December 31. This would convert into cash the "notes receivable from officers," which now appear in the balance sheet as noncurrent assets. The loans could be renewed immediately after year-end.
5. Present investments in marketable securities at their market value, rather than at cost.
6. Treat inventory as a financial asset and show it at current sales value.
7. On December 31, draw a large check against one of the company's bank accounts and deposit it in another of the company's accounts in a different bank. The check won't clear the first bank until after year-end. This will substantially increase the amount of cash in bank accounts at year-end.

Instructions

a. Separately evaluate each of these proposals. Consider ethical issues as well as accounting issues.

b. Do you consider it ethical for management to hold this meeting in the first place? That is, should management plan in advance how to improve financial statements that will be distributed to creditors and investors?

LO1 LO2

INTERNET CASE 7.4

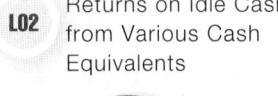

Returns on Idle Cash from Various Cash Equivalents

Prudent cash management is an important function in any business. Large amounts of cash sitting idle in non-interest-bearing checking accounts can cost a company thousands—even millions—of dollars annually in foregone revenue. Thus, many businesses invest large amounts of idle cash in Treasury bills, certificates of deposit (CDs), and money market accounts.

Visit the **Bankrate.com** home page at the following address:

www.bankrate.com

Search the site for information on CDs, money market accounts, and other interest-bearing products. Look for links under the "Compare Rates" menu.

Instructions

a. Prepare a table showing the current interest rates on Treasury bills, various CDs, and money market accounts.

b. If you were in charge of investing $1 million among the cash equivalents identified in part **a,** how would you make your allocation? Defend your answer.

Internet sites are time and date sensitive. It is the purpose of these exercises to have you explore the Internet. You may need to use the Yahoo! search engine http://www.yahoo.com *(or another favorite search engine) to find a company's current Web address.*

Answers to Self-Test Questions

1. b **2.** c **3.** a **4.** c **5.** a **6.** b **7.** a **8.** d **9.** c
10. b ($300,000 × 12% × 6/12) **11.** a

CHAPTER 8

Inventories and the Cost of Goods Sold

© AP Photo/David Kohl

AFTER STUDYING THIS CHAPTER, YOU SHOULD BE ABLE TO:

Learning Objectives

- **LO1** In a perpetual inventory system, determine the cost of goods sold using (a) specific identification, (b) average cost, (c) FIFO, and (d) LIFO. Discuss the advantages and shortcomings of each method.
- **LO2** Explain the need for taking a physical inventory.
- **LO3** Record shrinkage losses and other year-end adjustments to inventory.
- **LO4** In a periodic inventory system, determine the ending inventory and the cost of goods sold using (a) specific identification, (b) average cost, (c) FIFO, and (d) LIFO.
- **LO5** Explain the effects on the income statement of errors in inventory valuation.
- **LO6** Estimate the cost of goods sold and ending inventory by the gross profit method and by the retail method.
- **LO7** Compute the inventory turnover and explain its uses.

KROGER CO.

Having the right merchandise available at the right time and in the right place is critically important to all companies that sell products to their customers. These businesses include chain stores such as grocery stores, drugstores, and department stores.

Consider the case of Kroger Co.—a giant retailer that spans many states with store formats that include grocery and multidepartment stores, convenience stores, and mall jewelry stores. Kroger operates under nearly two dozen banners or names and is one of the country's largest grocery retailers with 2,468 grocery retail stores and 2009 sales of $76.7 million. Kroger also operates food-processing or manufacturing facilities that produce private-label products, supermarket fuel centers, and pharmacies located in its combination food and drugstores. Imagine the challenges this complex retailer faces in having product at the right place, at the right time, and in the needed quantities. To meet these objectives, a company's inventory is constantly changing.

Accounting for the movement of inventory into and out of a company like Kroger also presents a significant challenge. Inventory is often one of the largest assets in a company's statement of financial position (balance sheet), one of its most important determinants of the results of its operation (income statement), and one of its most significant cash flows (statement of cash flows). ■

Accounting for merchandise inventory presents one of the greatest challenges for companies that sell products. These companies must maintain not only a record of inventory items for sale but also the prices at which these items are purchased and sold, both of which change over time. This adds a significant complication to accounting for inventory and the expense included in the income statement when inventory is sold to customers. You learn how to account for inventory and its cost in this chapter.

INVENTORY DEFINED

In a merchandising company, inventory consists of all goods owned and held for sale to customers. Inventory is expected to be converted into cash within the company's *operating cycle.*[1] In the balance sheet, inventory is listed immediately after accounts receivable, because it is just one step farther removed from conversion into cash than customer receivables.

The Flow of Inventory Costs

Inventory is a nonfinancial asset and usually is shown in the balance sheet at its cost.[2] As items are sold from inventory, their costs are removed from the balance sheet and transferred to the cost of goods sold, which is offset against sales revenue in the income statement. This flow of costs is illustrated in Exhibit 8–1.

Exhibit 8–1 THE FLOW OF COSTS THROUGH FINANCIAL STATEMENTS

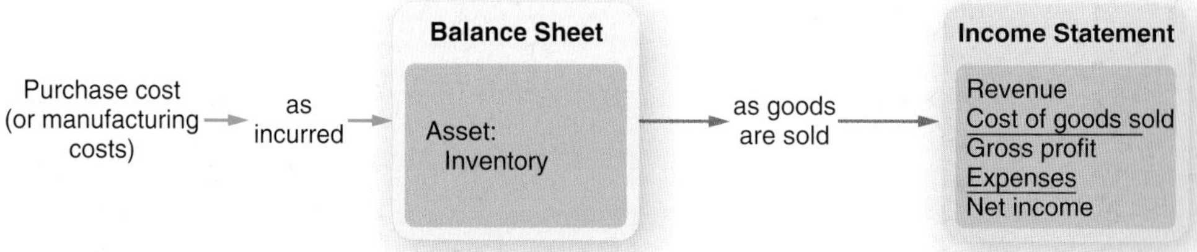

In a perpetual inventory system, entries in the accounting records parallel this flow of costs. When merchandise is purchased, its cost (net of allowable cash discounts) is added to the asset account Inventory. As the merchandise is sold, its cost is removed from the Inventory account and transferred to the Cost of Goods Sold account.

The valuation of inventory and cost of goods sold is of critical importance to managers and to external users of financial statements. In many cases, inventory is a company's largest asset, and the cost of goods sold is its largest expense. These two accounts have a significant effect on the financial statement subtotals and ratios used in evaluating the liquidity and profitability of the business.

Several different methods of pricing inventory and of measuring the cost of goods sold are acceptable under generally accepted accounting principles. These different methods may

[1] As explained in Chapter 6, the *operating cycle* of a merchandising business is the period of time required to convert cash into inventory, inventory into accounts receivable, and accounts receivable into cash. Assets expected to be converted into cash within one year or the operating cycle, whichever is longer, are regarded as current assets.

[2] Some companies deal in inventories that can be sold in a worldwide market at quoted market prices. Examples include mutual funds, stock brokerages, and companies that deal in commodities such as agricultural crops or precious metals. Often these companies value their inventories at market price rather than at cost. Our discussions in this chapter are directed to the more common situation in which inventories are valued at cost.

produce significantly different results, both in a company's financial statements and in its income tax returns. Therefore, managers and investors should understand the effects of the different inventory valuation methods.

WHICH UNIT DID WE SELL?

Purchases of merchandise are recorded in the same manner under all of the inventory valuation methods. The differences in these methods lie in determining *which costs* should be removed from the Inventory account when merchandise is sold.

We illustrated the basic entries relating to purchases and sales of merchandise in Chapter 6. In that introductory discussion, however, we made a simplifying assumption: All of the units in inventory had been acquired at the same unit cost. In practice, a company often has in its inventory identical units of a given product that were acquired at *different costs.* Acquisition costs may vary because the units were purchased at different dates, from different suppliers, or in different quantities.

When identical units of inventory have different unit costs, a question arises as to *which of these costs* should be used in measuring the cost of goods sold.

DATA FOR AN ILLUSTRATION

To illustrate the alternative methods of measuring the cost of goods sold, assume that Mead Electric Company sells electrical equipment and supplies. Included in the company's inventory are five Elco AC-40 generators. These generators are identical; however, two were purchased on January 5 at a per-unit cost of *$1,000,* and the other three were purchased a month later, shortly after Elco had announced a price increase, at a per-unit cost of *$1,200.* These purchases are reflected in Mead's inventory subsidiary ledger in Exhibit 8–2.

Exhibit 8–2

INVENTORY SUBSIDIARY LEDGER

Item Elco AC-40 **Primary supplier** Elco Manufacturing
Description Portable generator **Secondary supplier** Vegas Wholesale Co.
Location Daily St. warehouse **Inventory level: Min:** 2 **Max:** 5

	Purchased			Sold			Balance		
Date	**Units**	**Unit Cost**	**Total**	**Units**	**Unit Cost**	**Cost of Goods Sold**	**Units**	**Unit Cost**	**Total**
Jan. 5	2	$1,000	$2,000				2	$1,000	$2,000
Feb. 5	3	1,200	3,600				2	1,000	
							3	1,200	5,600

Notice that, on February 5, the Balance columns contain two "layers" of unit cost information, representing the units purchased at the two different unit costs. A new **cost layer** is created whenever units are acquired at a different per-unit cost. (As all units comprising a cost layer are sold, the layer is eliminated from the inventory. Therefore, a business is unlikely to have more than three or four cost layers in its inventory at any given time.)

Now assume that, on March 1, Mead sells one of these Elco generators to Boulder Construction Company for $1,800 cash. What cost should be removed from the Inventory account and recognized as the cost of goods sold—$1,000 or $1,200?

In answering such questions, accountants may use an approach called **specific identification,** or they may adopt a **cost flow assumption.** Either of these approaches is acceptable. Once an approach has been selected, however, it should be *applied consistently* in accounting for all sales of this particular type of merchandise.

SPECIFIC IDENTIFICATION

Learning Objective

LO1 In a perpetual inventory system, determine the cost of goods sold using (a) specific identification, (b) average cost, (c) FIFO, and (d) LIFO. Discuss the advantages and shortcomings of each method.

The specific identification method can be used only when the actual costs of individual units of merchandise can be determined from the accounting records. For example, each of the generators in Mead's inventory may have an identification number, and these numbers may appear on the purchase invoices. With this identification number, Mead's accounting department can determine whether the generator sold to Boulder Construction cost $1,000 or $1,200. The *actual cost* of this particular unit then is used in recording the cost of goods sold.

COST FLOW ASSUMPTIONS

If the items in inventory are *homogeneous* in nature (identical, except for insignificant differences), it is *not necessary* for the seller to use the specific identification method. Rather, the seller may follow the more convenient practice of using a *cost flow assumption.* Using a cost flow assumption, often referred to as simply a flow assumption, is particularly common where the company has a large number of identical inventory items that were purchased at different prices.

When a cost flow assumption is in use, the seller makes an *assumption* as to the sequence in which units are withdrawn from inventory. For example, the seller might assume that the oldest merchandise always is sold first or that the most recently purchased items are the first to be sold.

Three cost flow assumptions are in widespread use:

1. *Average cost.* This assumption values all merchandise—units sold and units remaining in inventory—at the *average* per-unit cost. (In effect, the average-cost method assumes that units are withdrawn from the inventory in random order.)
2. *First-in, first-out (FIFO).* As the name implies, FIFO involves the assumption that goods sold are the *first* units that were purchased—that is, the *oldest* goods on hand. Thus the remaining inventory is comprised of the most recent purchases.
3. *Last-in, first-out (LIFO).* Under LIFO, the units sold are assumed to be those *most recently* acquired. The remaining inventory, therefore, is assumed to consist of the earliest purchases.

The cost flow assumption selected by a company *need not* correspond to the actual physical movement of the company's merchandise. When the units of merchandise are identical (or nearly identical), it *does not matter* which units are delivered to the customer in a particular sales transaction. Therefore, in measuring the income of a business that sells units of identical merchandise, accountants consider the flow of *costs* to be more important than the physical flow of the merchandise.

The use of a cost flow assumption *eliminates the need for separately identifying each unit sold and looking up its actual cost.* Experience has shown that these cost flow assumptions provide useful and reliable measurements of the cost of goods sold, as long as they are applied consistently to all sales of the particular type of merchandise.

AVERAGE-COST METHOD

When the **average-cost method** is in use, the *average cost* of all units in inventory is computed after every purchase. This average cost is computed by dividing the total cost of goods available for sale by the number of units in inventory. Because the average cost may change following each purchase, this method also is called the **moving average method** when a perpetual inventory system is used.

As of January 5, Mead had only two Elco generators in its inventory, each acquired at a purchase cost of $1,000. Therefore, the average cost is $1,000 per unit. After the purchase on February 5, Mead had five Elco generators in inventory, acquired at a total cost of $5,600 (2 units @ $1,000, plus 3 units @ $1,200 = $5,600). Therefore, the *average* per-unit cost now is *$1,120* ($5,600 ÷ 5 units = $1,120).

On March 1, two entries are made to record the sale of one of these generators to Boulder Construction Company. The first recognizes the revenue from this sale, and the second recognizes the cost of the goods sold. These entries follow, with the cost of goods sold measured by the average-cost method:

Cash	1,800	
Sales		1,800
To record the sale of one Elco AC-40 generator.		
Cost of Goods Sold	1,120	
Inventory		1,120
To record the cost of one Elco AC-40 generator sold to Boulder Construction Co. Cost determined by the average-cost method.		

(The entry to recognize the $1,800 in sales revenue is the same, regardless of the inventory method in use. Therefore, we will not repeat this entry in our illustrations of the other cost flow assumptions.)

When the average-cost method is in use, the inventory subsidiary ledger is modified slightly from the format in Exhibit 8–2. Following the sale on March 1, Mead's subsidiary ledger for Elco generators would be modified to show the average unit cost as in Exhibit 8–3.

Exhibit 8–3

INVENTORY SUBSIDIARY LEDGER—AVERAGE-COST BASIS

	Purchased			Sold			Balance		
Date	Units	Unit Cost	Total	Units	Unit Cost	Cost of Goods Sold	Units	Unit Cost	Total
Jan. 5	2	$1,000	$2,000				2	$1,000*	$2,000
Feb. 5	3	1,200	3,600				5	$1,120**	5,600
Mar. 1				1	$1,120	$1,120	4	$1,120	4,480

*$2,000 total cost ÷ 2 units = $1,000.
**$5,600 total cost ÷ 5 units = $1,120.

Notice that the Unit Cost column for purchases still shows actual unit costs—$1,000 and $1,200. The Unit Cost columns relating to sales and to the remaining inventory, however, show the *average unit cost* ($5,600 total ÷ 5 units = $1,120).

Under the average-cost assumption, all items in inventory are assigned the *same* per-unit cost (the average cost). Hence, it does not matter which units are sold; the cost of goods sold always is based on the current average unit cost. When one generator is sold on March 1, the cost of goods sold is $1,120; if three generators had been sold on this date, the cost of goods sold would have been $3,360 (3 units × $1,120 per unit).

FIRST-IN, FIRST-OUT METHOD

The **first-in, first-out method,** often called *FIFO,* is based on the assumption that the *first merchandise purchased is the first merchandise sold.* Thus, the accountant for Mead Electric would assume that the generator sold on March 1 was one of those purchased on *January 5.* The entry to record the cost of goods sold would be:

Cost of Goods Sold	1,000	
Inventory		1,000
To record the cost of one Elco AC-40 generator sold to Boulder Construction Co. Cost determined by the FIFO flow assumption.		

Following this sale, Mead's inventory ledger would appear as shown in Exhibit 8–4.

Exhibit 8-4

INVENTORY SUBSIDIARY LEDGER—FIFO BASIS

	Purchased			Sold			Balance		
Date	Units	Unit Cost	Total	Units	Unit Cost	Cost of Goods Sold	Units	Unit Cost	Total
Jan. 5	2	$1,000	$2,000				2	$1,000	$2,000
Feb. 5	3	1,200	3,600				2	1,000	
							3	1,200	5,600
Mar. 1				1	$1,000	$1,000	1	1,000	
							3	1,200	4,600

Notice that FIFO uses actual purchase costs, rather than an average cost. Thus, if merchandise has been purchased at several different costs, the inventory will include several different cost layers. The cost of goods sold for a given sales transaction also may involve several different cost layers. To illustrate, assume that Mead had sold *four* generators to Boulder Construction, instead of only one. Under the FIFO flow assumption, Mead would assume that it first sold the two generators purchased on January 5 and then two of those purchased on February 5. Thus the total cost of goods sold ($4,400) would include items at *two different unit costs,* as shown here:

2 generators from Jan. 5 purchase @ $1,000	$2,000
2 generators from Feb. 5 purchase @ $1,200	$2,400
Total cost of goods sold (4 units)	$4,400

As the cost of goods sold always is recorded at the oldest available purchase costs, the units remaining in inventory are valued at the more recent acquisition costs.

LAST-IN, FIRST-OUT METHOD

The **last-in, first-out method,** commonly known as *LIFO,* is among the most widely used methods of determining the cost of goods sold and valuing inventory. As the name suggests, the *most recently* purchased merchandise (the last in) is assumed to be sold first. If Mead were using the LIFO method, it would assume that the generator sold on March 1 was one of those acquired on *February 5,* the most recent purchase date. Thus, the cost transferred from inventory to the cost of goods sold would be *$1,200.*

The journal entry to record the cost of goods sold is shown below. The inventory subsidiary ledger record after this entry has been posted is shown in Exhibit 8–5.

Cost of Goods Sold	1,200	
Inventory		1,200
To record the cost of one Elco AC-40 generator sold to Boulder Construction Co. Cost determined by the LIFO flow assumption.		

Exhibit 8–5

INVENTORY SUBSIDIARY LEDGER—LIFO BASIS

	Purchased			Sold			Balance		
Date	Units	Unit Cost	Total	Units	Unit Cost	Cost of Goods Sold	Units	Unit Cost	Total
Jan. 5	2	$1,000	$2,000				2	$1,000	$2,000
Feb. 5	3	1,200	3,600				2	1,000	
							3	1,200	5,600
Mar. 1				1	$1,200	$1,200	2	1,000	
							2	1,200	4,400

Like FIFO, the LIFO method uses actual purchase costs, rather than an average cost. Thus, the inventory may have several different cost layers. If a sale includes more units than are included in the most recent cost layer, some of the goods sold are assumed to come from the next most recent layer. For example, if Mead had sold four generators (instead of one) on March 1, the cost of goods sold determined under the LIFO assumption would be $4,600:

3 generators from Feb. 5 purchase @ $1,200	$3,600
1 generator from Jan. 5 purchase @ $1,000	$1,000
Total cost of goods sold (4 units)	$4,600

As LIFO transfers the most recent purchase costs to the cost of goods sold, the goods remaining in inventory are valued at the oldest acquisition costs.

EVALUATION OF THE METHODS

All three of the cost flow assumptions just described are acceptable for use in financial statements and in income tax returns. As we have explained, it is not necessary that the physical flow of merchandise correspond to the cost flow assumption. Different flow assumptions may be used for different types of inventory or for inventories in different geographical locations.

The only requirement for using a flow assumption is that the units to which the assumption is applied should be *homogeneous* in nature—that is, virtually identical to one another. If each unit is unique, such as the sale of portraits by an art studio, only the specific identification method can properly match sales revenue with the cost of goods sold.

Each inventory valuation method has certain advantages and shortcomings. In the final analysis, the selection of inventory valuation methods is a managerial decision. However, the method (or methods) used in financial statements always should be disclosed in notes accompanying the statements.

Specific Identification The specific identification method is best suited to inventories of high-priced, low-volume items. This is the only method that exactly parallels the physical flow of the merchandise. If each item in the inventory is unique, as in the case of valuable paintings, custom jewelry, and most real estate, specific identification is clearly the logical choice.

The specific identification method has an intuitive appeal, because it assigns actual purchase costs to the specific units of merchandise sold or in inventory. However, when the units in inventory are identical (or nearly identical), the specific identification method may produce *misleading results* by implying differences in value that—under current market conditions—do not exist. There is also the potential to manipulate the company's financial statement numbers by selecting which items (and as a result which costs) are sold.

As an example, assume that a coal dealer has purchased 100 tons of coal at a cost of $90 per ton. A short time later, the company purchases another 100 tons of the *same grade* of coal—but this time, the cost is $120 per ton. The two purchases are in separate piles; thus it would be possible for the company to use the specific identification method in accounting for sales.

Assume now that the company has an opportunity to sell 10 tons of coal at a retail price of $180 per ton. Does it really matter from which pile this coal is removed? The answer is *no;* the coal is a homogeneous product. Under current market conditions, the coal in each pile is equally valuable. To imply that it is more profitable to sell coal from one pile rather than the other is an argument of questionable logic.

Average Cost Identical items will have the same accounting values only under the average-cost method. Assume, for example, that a hardware store sells a given size nail for 65 cents per pound. The hardware store buys the nails in 100-pound quantities at different times at prices ranging from 40 to 50 cents per pound. Several hundred pounds of nails are always on hand, stored in a large bin. The average-cost method properly recognizes that when a customer buys a pound of nails it is not necessary to know exactly which nails the customer selected from the bin in order to measure the cost of goods sold. Therefore, the average-cost method avoids the shortcomings of the specific identification method. It is not necessary to keep track of the specific items sold and of those still in inventory. Also, it is not possible to manipulate income merely by selecting the specific items to be delivered to customers.

A shortcoming of the average-cost method is that changes in current replacement costs of inventory are concealed because these costs are averaged with older costs. Thus neither the valuation of ending inventory nor the cost of goods sold will quickly reflect changes in the current replacement cost of merchandise.

First-In, First-Out The distinguishing characteristic of the FIFO method is that the oldest purchase costs are transferred to the cost of goods sold, while the most recent costs remain in inventory.

Over the past 50 years, we have lived in an inflationary economy, which means that most prices rise over time. When purchase costs are rising, the FIFO method assigns *lower* (older) costs to the cost of goods sold and the higher (more recent) costs to the goods remaining in inventory.

By assigning lower costs to the cost of goods sold, FIFO usually causes a business to report *higher profits* than would be reported under the other inventory valuation methods. Some companies favor the FIFO method for financial reporting purposes, because their goal is to report the highest net income possible. For income tax purposes, however, reporting more income than necessary results in paying more income taxes than necessary.

Some accountants and decision makers believe that FIFO tends to *overstate* a company's profitability in periods of rising prices. Revenue is based on current market conditions. By offsetting this revenue with a cost of goods sold based on older (and lower) prices, gross profits may be overstated consistently.

A conceptual advantage of the FIFO method is that in the balance sheet inventory is valued at recent purchase costs. Therefore, this asset appears in the balance sheet at an amount more closely approximating its current replacement cost.

Last-In, First-Out The LIFO method is one of the most interesting and controversial flow assumptions. The basic assumption in the LIFO method is that the most recently purchased units are sold first and that the older units remain in inventory. This assumption is *not* in accord with the physical flow of merchandise in most businesses. Yet there are strong logical arguments in support of the LIFO method, in addition to income tax considerations.

For the purpose of measuring income, most accountants consider the *flow of costs* more important than the physical flow of merchandise. Supporters of the LIFO method contend that the measurement of income should be based on *current market conditions.* Therefore, current sales revenue should be offset by the *current* cost of the merchandise sold. By the LIFO method, the costs assigned to the cost of goods sold are relatively current because they reflect the most recent purchases.

There is one significant shortcoming to the LIFO method. The valuation of the asset inventory is based on the company's oldest inventory acquisition costs. After the company has been in business for many years, these oldest costs may greatly understate the current replacement cost of the inventory. Thus, when an inventory is valued by the LIFO method, the company also should disclose the current replacement cost of the inventory in a note to the financial statements.

During periods of rising inventory replacement costs, the LIFO method results in the lowest valuation of inventory and measurement of net income. Therefore, LIFO is regarded as the most *conservative* of the inventory pricing methods. FIFO, on the other hand, is the least conservative method.[3]

Income tax considerations are the principal strategic reason for the popularity of the LIFO method. Remember that the LIFO method assigns the most recent inventory purchase costs to the cost of goods sold. In the common situation of rising prices, these most recent costs are also the highest costs. By reporting a higher cost of goods sold than results from other inventory valuation methods, the LIFO method usually results in *lower taxable income.* In short, if inventory costs are rising, a company can reduce the amount of its income tax obligation by using the LIFO method in its income tax return.

It may seem reasonable that a company would use the LIFO method in its tax return to reduce taxable income and use the FIFO method in its financial statements to increase the amount of net income reported to investors and creditors. However, income tax regulations allow a corporation to use LIFO in its income tax return *only* if the company also uses LIFO in its financial statements. Thus, income tax considerations often provide the overriding strategic reason for selecting the LIFO method.

DO INVENTORY METHODS REALLY AFFECT PERFORMANCE?

Except for their effects on income taxes, the answer to this question is *no.*

During a period of rising prices, a company might *report* higher profits by using FIFO instead of LIFO. But the company would not really *be* any more profitable. An inventory valuation method affects only the *allocation of costs* between the Inventory account and the Cost of Goods Sold account. It has *no effect* on the total costs actually *incurred* in purchasing or manufacturing inventory. Except for the amount of income taxes paid, differences in the profitability reported under different inventory methods exist only on paper.

The inventory method in use *does* affect the amount of income taxes owed. To the extent that an inventory method reduces these taxes, it *does* increase profitability. In Exhibit 8–6 we summarize characteristics of the basic inventory valuation methods.

THE PRINCIPLE OF CONSISTENCY

The principle of **consistency** is one of the basic concepts underlying reliable financial statements. This principle means that, once a company has adopted a particular accounting method, it must *follow that method consistently,* rather than switch methods from one year to the next. Thus, once a company has adopted a particular inventory flow assumption (or the specific identification method), it should continue to apply that assumption to all sales of that type of merchandise.

The principle of consistency does *not* prohibit a company from *ever* changing its accounting methods. If a change is made, however, the reasons for the change must be explained, and the effects of the change on the company's net income must be fully disclosed.

JUST-IN-TIME (JIT) INVENTORY SYSTEMS

In recent years, much attention has been paid to the **just-in-time (JIT) inventory system** in manufacturing operations. The phrase "just-in-time" usually means that purchases of raw materials and component parts arrive just in time for use in the manufacturing process—often within a few hours of the time they are scheduled for use. A second application of the just-in-time concept is completing the manufacturing process just in time to ship the finished goods to customers.

[3] During a prolonged period of *declining* inventory replacement costs, this situation reverses: FIFO becomes the most conservative method, and LIFO the least conservative.

Exhibit 8–6 SUMMARY OF INVENTORY VALUATION METHODS

	Costs Allocated to:		
Valuation Method	**Cost of Goods Sold**	**Inventory**	**Comments**
Specific identification	Actual costs of the units sold	Actual cost of units remaining	• Parallels physical flow • Logical method when units are unique • May be misleading when the units are identical
Flow assumptions (acceptable only for an inventory of *homogeneous units*):			
Average cost	Number of units sold times the *average unit cost*	Number of units on hand times the *average unit cost*	• Assigns all units the same *average unit cost* • Current costs are averaged in with older costs
First-in, first-out (FIFO)	Costs of *earliest purchases* on hand at the time of the sale (first-in, first-out)	Cost of *most recently* purchased units	• Cost of goods sold is based on older costs • Inventory valued at most recent costs • May overstate income during periods of rising prices; may increase income taxes due
Last-in, first-out (LIFO)	Cost of *most recently purchased* units (last-in, first-out)	Costs of *earliest* purchases (assumed *still* to be in inventory)	• Cost of goods sold shown at most recent prices • Inventory shown at old (and perhaps out-of-date) costs • Most conservative method during periods of rising prices; often results in lower income taxes due

Although a just-in-time system reduces the size of a company's inventories, it does not eliminate them entirely. The February 1, 2008, balance sheet of **Dell Computer Corporation**, for example, shows inventories of *almost $1.2 billion* (**Dell** reports its inventories by the FIFO method).

CASE IN POINT

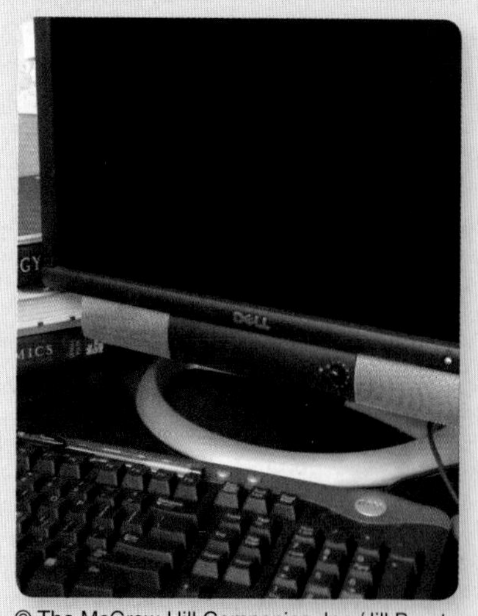

© The McGraw-Hill Companies, Inc./Jill Braaten, photographer/DAL

Dell Computer Corporation generates millions in revenue each day by selling computers on the Internet. The company has long been a model of just-in-time manufacturing. **Dell** doesn't start ordering components or assembling computers until an order has been booked. Most of its suppliers keep components warehoused in close proximity to **Dell**'s factories. The JIT philosophy applies to suppliers, assemblers, and distributors. A customer order placed Monday morning can be on a delivery truck by Tuesday evening.

The concept of minimizing inventories applies more to manufacturing operations than to retailers. Ideally, manufacturers have buyers lined up for their merchandise even before the goods are produced. Many retailers, in contrast, want to offer their customers a large selection of in-stock merchandise—which means a big inventory.

The just-in-time concept actually involves much more than minimizing the size of inventories. It has been described as the philosophy of constantly working to increase efficiency throughout the organization. One basic goal of an accounting system is to provide management with useful information about the efficiency—or inefficiency—of operations.

Taking a Physical Inventory

Learning Objective **Explain the need for taking a physical inventory.** **LO2**

In Chapter 6 we explained the need for businesses to make a complete physical count of the merchandise on hand at least once a year. The primary reason for this procedure of "taking inventory" is to adjust the perpetual inventory records for unrecorded **shrinkage losses,** such as theft, spoilage, or breakage.

The **physical inventory** usually is taken at (or near) the end of the company's fiscal year.[4] Often a business selects a fiscal year ending after a period of high activity. For example, many large retailers use a fiscal year that starts February 1 and ends January 31.

RECORDING SHRINKAGE LOSSES

Learning Objective **Record shrinkage losses and other year-end adjustments to inventory.** **LO3**

In most cases, the year-end physical count of the inventory reveals some shortages or damaged merchandise. The costs of missing or damaged units are removed from the inventory records using the same flow assumption as is used in recording the costs of goods sold.

To illustrate, assume that a company's inventory subsidiary ledger shows the following 158 units of a particular product in inventory at year-end:

8 units purchased Nov. 2 @ $100	$ 800
150 units purchased Dec. 10 @ $115	17,250
Total (158 units)	$18,050

A year-end physical count, however, discloses that only *148* of these units actually are on hand. On the basis of this physical count, the company should adjust its inventory records to reflect the loss of 10 units.

The inventory flow assumption in use affects the measurement of shrinkage losses in the same way it affects the cost of goods sold. If the company uses *FIFO,* for example, the missing units will be valued at the oldest purchase costs shown in the inventory records. Thus 8 of the missing units will be assumed to have cost $100 per unit and the other 2, $115 per unit. Under FIFO, the shrinkage loss amounts to *$1,030* (8 units @ $100 + 2 units @ $115). But if this company uses *LIFO,* the missing units all will be assumed to have come from the most recent purchase (on December 10). Therefore, the shrinkage loss amounts to *$1,150* (10 units @ $115).

If shrinkage losses are small, the costs removed from inventory may be charged (debited) directly to the Cost of Goods Sold account. If these losses are *material* in amount, the offsetting debit should be entered in a special loss account, such as Inventory Shrinkage Losses. In the income statement, a loss account is deducted from revenue in the same manner as an expense account.

LCM AND OTHER WRITE-DOWNS OF INVENTORY

In addition to shrinkage losses, the value of inventory may decline because the merchandise has become obsolete or is unsalable for other reasons. If inventory has become obsolete or is otherwise unsalable, its carrying amount in the accounting records should be *written down*

[4] The reason for taking a physical inventory near year-end is to ensure that any shrinkage losses are reflected in the annual financial statements. The stronger the company's system of internal control over inventories, the farther away this procedure may be moved from the balance sheet date.

to zero (or to its "scrap value," if any). A **write-down** of inventory reduces both the carrying amount of the inventory in the balance sheet and the net income of the current period. The reduction in income is handled in the same manner as a shrinkage loss. If the write-down is relatively small, the loss is debited directly to the Cost of Goods Sold account. If the write-down is *material in amount,* however, it is charged to a special loss account, perhaps entitled Loss from Write-Down of Inventory.

The Lower-of-Cost-or-Market (LCM) Rule An asset is an economic resource. It may be argued that no economic resource is worth more than it would cost to *replace* that resource in the open market. For this reason, accountants traditionally have valued inventory in the balance sheet at the lower of its (1) cost or (2) market value. In this context, "market value" usually means *current replacement cost.* Thus the inventory is valued at the lower of its historical cost or its current replacement cost. This accounting convention is referred to as the **lower-of-cost-or-market (LCM) rule.**

The LCM rule can be used in conjunction with any cost flow assumption. It may also be applied on the basis of individual inventory items, major inventory categories, or the entire inventory. To illustrate, assume that Joel's Ski Shop uses the FIFO cost flow assumption. The store sells various lines of merchandise with costs and market values shown in Exhibit 8–7.

Exhibit 8–7

APPLYING THE LCM RULE BY INDIVIDUAL ITEM, BY CATEGORY, AND BY TOTAL INVENTORY

			LCM Applied on the Basis of . . .		
	FIFO Cost	Market Value	Individual Items	Inventory Category	Total Inventory
Ski equipment					
Downhill skis	$16,000	$18,000	$16,000		
Cross-country skis	4,000	3,000	3,000		
Total ski equipment	$20,000	$21,000		$20,000	
Ski accessories					
Ski boots	$ 2,400	$ 1,500	1,500		
Ski jackets	6,600	6,000	6,000		
Total ski accessories	$ 9,000	$ 7,500		7,500	
Total inventory	$29,000	$28,500	**$26,500**	**$27,500**	**$28,500**

Measured at its FIFO cost, the inventory of Joel's Ski Shop is currently recorded at $29,000 in the general ledger. If management applies the LCM rule on the basis of *individual items,* the inventory must be written down to its market value of $26,500. This is accomplished by crediting the Merchandise Inventory account for $2,500 ($29,000 – $26,500). The offsetting debit is charged to either the Cost of Goods Sold or to the Loss from Write-Down of Inventory account, depending on the materiality of the dollar amount.

If management applies the LCM rule on the basis of *inventory category,* it would write down the $29,000 FIFO cost by $1,500 ($29,000 – $27,500). Likewise, if the LCM rule is applied on the basis of *total inventory,* a write-down of only $500 is required ($29,000 – $28,500).

In their financial statements, most companies state that inventory is valued at the lower-of-cost-or-market. In an inflationary economy, however, the lower of these two amounts is usually cost, especially for companies using LIFO.[5]

THE YEAR-END CUTOFF OF TRANSACTIONS

Making a proper *cutoff* of transactions is an essential step in the preparation of reliable financial statements. A proper cutoff simply means that the transactions occurring near year-end are *recorded in the correct accounting period.*

[5] A notable exception is the petroleum industry, in which the replacement cost of inventory can fluctuate very quickly and in either direction. Large oil companies occasionally report LCM adjustments of several hundred million dollars in a single year.

One aspect of a proper cutoff is determining that all purchases of merchandise through the end of the period are recorded in the inventory records and included in the physical count of merchandise on hand at year-end. Of equal importance is determining that the cost of all merchandise sold through the end of the period has been removed from the inventory accounts and charged to the Cost of Goods Sold. This merchandise should *not* be included in the year-end physical count.

If some sales transactions have not been recorded as of year-end, the quantities of merchandise shown in the inventory records will exceed the quantities actually on hand. When the results of the physical count are compared with the inventory records, these unrecorded sales easily could be mistaken for inventory shortages.

Making a proper cutoff may be difficult if sales transactions are occurring while the merchandise is being counted. For this reason, many businesses count their physical inventory during nonbusiness hours, even if they must shut down their sales operations for a day.

Matching Revenue and the Cost of Goods Sold Accountants must determine that both the sales revenue and the cost of goods sold relating to sales transactions occurring near year-end are recorded in the *same* accounting period. Otherwise, the revenues and expenses from these transactions will not be properly matched in the company's income statements.

Goods in Transit A sale should be recorded *when title to the merchandise passes to the buyer.* In making a year-end cutoff of transactions, questions may arise when goods are in transit between the seller and the buyer as to which company owns the merchandise. The answer to such questions lies in the terms of shipment. If these terms are **F.O.B.** (free on board) **shipping point,** title passes at the point of shipment and the goods are the property of the buyer while in transit. If the terms of the shipment are **F.O.B. destination,** title does not pass until the shipment reaches its destination and the goods belong to the seller while in transit.

Many companies ignore these distinctions, because goods in transit usually arrive within a day or two. In such cases, the amount of merchandise in transit usually is *not material* in dollar amount, and the company may follow the *most convenient* accounting procedures. It usually is most convenient to record all purchases when the inbound shipments arrive and all sales when the merchandise is shipped to the customer.

In some industries, however, goods in transit may be very material. Oil companies, for example, often have millions of dollars of inventory in transit in pipelines and supertankers. In these situations, the company must consider the terms of each shipment in recording its purchases and sales.

YOUR TURN **You as a Sales Manager**

As sales manager for Tempto Co., a producer of fine home furnishings, you have responsibility for the northeast region of the country. Assume you have just returned from the company's annual sales managers' conference in New Orleans. At the conference, in casual conversation with some of the regional managers, you became aware that several managers report sales that are scheduled for shipment in early January as if they were shipped in late December. What should you do?

(See our comments on the Online Learning Center Web site.)

PERIODIC INVENTORY SYSTEMS

Learning Objective LO4
In a periodic inventory system, determine the ending inventory and the cost of goods sold using (a) specific identification, (b) average cost, (c) FIFO, and (d) LIFO.

In our preceding discussions, we have emphasized the perpetual inventory system—that is, inventory records that are kept continuously up-to-date. With the extensive use of technology, today most large business organizations use perpetual inventory systems.

Some small businesses, however, use *periodic* inventory systems. In a periodic inventory system, the cost of merchandise purchased during the year is debited to a *Purchases* account, rather than to the Inventory account. When merchandise is sold to a customer, an entry is made recognizing the sales revenue, but no entry is made to reduce the inventory account or to recognize the cost of goods sold.

The inventory on hand and the cost of goods sold for the year are not determined until year-end. At the end of the year, all goods on hand are counted and priced at cost. The cost assigned to this ending inventory is then used to compute the cost of goods sold. (The dollar amounts are assumed for the purpose of completing this illustration.)

Inventory at the beginning of the year	$10,000
Add: Purchases during the year	80,000
Cost of goods available for sale during the year	$90,000
Less: Inventory based on year-end count	7,000
Cost of goods sold	$83,000

The only item in this computation that is kept continuously up-to-date in the accounting records is the Purchases account. The amounts of inventory at the beginning and end of the year are determined by annual physical observation.

Determining the cost of the year-end inventory involves two distinct steps: counting the merchandise and pricing the inventory—that is, determining the cost of the units on hand. Together, these procedures determine the proper valuation of inventory and the cost of goods sold.

Applying Flow Assumptions in a Periodic System In our discussion of perpetual inventory systems, we have emphasized the costs that are transferred from inventory *to the cost of goods sold* as the sales occur. In a periodic system, the emphasis shifts to determining the costs that should be assigned *to inventory* at the end of the period.

To illustrate, assume that The Kitchen Counter, a retail store, uses a periodic inventory system. The year-end physical inventory indicates that 12 units of a particular model food processor are on hand. Purchases of these food processors during the year are listed in Exhibit 8–8.

Exhibit 8–8
SUMMARY OF INVENTORY PURCHASES

	Number of Units	Cost per Unit	Total Cost
Beginning inventory	10	$ 80	$ 800
First purchase (Mar. 1)	5	90	450
Second purchase (July 1)	5	100	500
Third purchase (Oct. 1)	5	120	600
Fourth purchase (Dec. 1)	5	130	650
Available for sale	30		$3,000
Units in ending inventory	12		
Units sold	18		

In Exhibit 8–8, note that of the 30 food processors available for sale in the course of the year, 12 are still on hand. Thus, 18 of these food processors apparently were sold.[6] We will now use these data to determine the cost of the year-end inventory and the cost of goods sold using the specific identification method and the average-cost, FIFO, and LIFO flow assumptions.

Specific Identification If specific identification is used, the company must identify the 12 food processors on hand at year-end and determine their actual costs from purchase invoices. Assume that these 12 units have an actual total cost of $1,240. The cost of goods

[6] The periodic inventory method does not distinguish between merchandise sold and shrinkage losses. Shrinkage losses are included automatically in the cost of goods sold.

sold then is determined by subtracting this ending inventory from the cost of goods available for sale as shown below:

Cost of goods available for sale	$3,000
Less: Ending inventory (specific identification)	1,240
Cost of goods sold	$1,760

Average Cost The average cost is determined by dividing the total cost of goods available for sale during the year by the total number of units available for sale. Thus the average per-unit cost is *$100* ($3,000 ÷ 30 units). Under the average-cost method, the ending inventory would be priced at $1,200 (12 units × $100 per unit), and the cost of goods sold would be *$1,800* ($3,000 cost of goods available for sale, less $1,200 in costs assigned to the ending inventory).

FIFO Under the FIFO flow assumption, the oldest units are assumed to be the first sold. The ending inventory, therefore, is assumed to consist of the *most recently* acquired goods. (Remember, we are now talking about the goods *remaining in inventory,* not the goods sold.) Thus the inventory of 12 food processors would be valued at the following costs:
The cost of goods sold would be *$1,550* ($3,000 – $1,450).

5 units from the Dec. 1 purchase @ $130	$ 650
5 units from the Oct. 1 purchase @ $120	600
2 units from the July 1 purchase @ $100	200
Ending inventory, 12 units at FIFO cost	$1,450

Notice that the FIFO method results in an inventory valued at relatively recent purchase costs. The cost of goods sold, however, is based on the older acquisition costs.

LIFO Under LIFO, the last units purchased are considered to be the first goods sold. Therefore, the ending inventory is assumed to contain the *earliest* purchases. The 12 food processors in inventory would be valued as:
The cost of goods sold under the LIFO method is *$2,020* ($3,000 – $980).

10 units from the beginning inventory @ $80	$800
2 units from the Mar. 1 purchase @ $90	180
Ending inventory, 12 units at LIFO cost	$980

Notice that the cost of goods sold under LIFO is *higher* than that determined by the FIFO method ($2,020 under LIFO, as compared with $1,550 under FIFO). LIFO always results in a higher cost of goods sold when purchase costs are rising. Thus LIFO tends to minimize reported net income and income taxes during periods of rising prices in both perpetual and periodic systems.

Notice also that the LIFO method may result in an ending inventory that is priced *well below* its current replacement cost. In this illustration, ending inventory is determined at $80 and $90 per unit, but the most recent purchase price is $130 per unit.

INTERNATIONAL CASE IN POINT

Although FIFO techniques are allowed for financial reporting in nearly all countries, LIFO is more controversial in international settings. International accounting standards prohibit LIFO because it leads to outdated inventory numbers in the balance sheet. Thus, to make inventory amounts between U.S. companies using LIFO and non–U.S. companies using FIFO (or weighted-average methods) comparable, a financial analyst must revalue inventory numbers.

Receiving the Maximum Tax Benefit from the LIFO Method Many companies that use LIFO in a perpetual inventory system *restate* their year-end inventory at the costs indicated by the *periodic* LIFO costing procedures illustrated above. This restatement is accomplished by either debiting or crediting the Inventory account and making an offsetting entry to the Cost of Goods Sold account.

Often, restating ending inventory using periodic costing procedures results in older (and lower) unit costs than those shown in the perpetual inventory records. When less cost is assigned to the ending inventory, it follows that more of these costs will be assigned to the cost of goods sold. A higher cost of goods sold, in turn, means lower taxable income.

Why would applying LIFO on a periodic basis at year-end result in a lower valuation of inventory than does applying LIFO on a perpetual basis? Consider the last purchase in our example. This purchase of five food processors was made on December 1, at the relatively high unit cost of $130. Assuming that no additional units were sold in December, they would be included in the year-end inventory in perpetual inventory records, even if these records were maintained on a LIFO basis. When the ending inventory is priced using "periodic LIFO," however, a last-minute purchase is *not* included in inventory, but rather is transferred to the income statement as part of cost of goods sold.

Both the LIFO and average-cost methods produce different valuations of inventory under perpetual and periodic costing procedures. Only companies using LIFO, however, usually adjust their perpetual records to indicate the unit costs determined by periodic costing procedures. When FIFO is in use, the perpetual and periodic costing procedures result in the same valuation of inventory.

Pricing the Year-End Inventory by Computer If purchase records are maintained by computer, as is now the case for most companies, the value of the ending inventory can be computed automatically using any of the flow assumptions that have been discussed. Only the number of units must be entered at year-end. A computer also can apply the specific identification method, but the system requires an identification number for each unit in the ending inventory. This is one reason why the specific identification method usually is not used for inventories consisting of a large number of low-cost items.

INTERNATIONAL FINANCIAL REPORTING STANDARDS

To introduce this chapter we covered the importance of establishing the cost of inventory and the movement of that cost to the income statement as cost of goods sold. The general principles upon which this important feature of financial reporting are based are essentially the same in U.S. generally accepted accounting principles and in international financial reporting standards. There are differences, however, in how those principles are applied.

One major difference is that international standards do not recognize the LIFO method of accounting for the cost of inventory. Only the first-in, first-out (FIFO) or weighted average cost methods are acceptable under international standards. This is a major difference because of the widespread use of LIFO in the United States due to its income tax benefits. Remember that the conformity requirement under U.S. tax law requires a company that uses LIFO for tax purposes to also use that method in its financial statements.

An effort is currently under way to bring U.S. generally accepted accounting principles and international financial reporting standards closer together. This effort is often referred to as "convergence" of the two. The facts that international standards do not permit the use of LIFO, and LIFO is the most popular inventory method for companies reporting under U.S. generally accepted accounting principles are difficult to reconcile. In the authors' opinion, to change U.S. standards to preclude the use of LIFO or to include LIFO as an acceptable method in international standards are both unlikely. The most logical approach appears to be to eliminate the conformity requirement, thereby allowing companies accounting by U.S. standards to use LIFO in its income tax filings, but not require that LIFO be used in its financial statements. LIFO would, in effect, become a tax method that is not used in a company's financial statements. The current conformity requirement has been in place for many years and any change in it would require a significant change in the U.S. tax law. The political process that would be required for such a change is unlikely to happen quickly, but may eventually be the outcome as we seek conformity between U.S. and *International Financial Reporting Standards.*

There are other areas where accounting for inventories differs between U.S. and international standards. One of those is accounting for the lower-of-cost-or-market. Under U.S. generally accepted accounting standards, once an inventory is written down to a lower market value, recovery of that value before the inventory is sold is not permitted. Under international standards, however, the subsequent recovery of market value is treated as a reduction in cost of goods sold in the period of the recovery.

IMPORTANCE OF AN ACCURATE VALUATION OF INVENTORY

The most important liquid assets in the balance sheets of most companies are cash, accounts receivable, and inventory. Of these assets, inventory often is the largest. It also is the only one of these assets for which alternative valuation methods are acceptable.

Because of the relatively large size of inventory, and because many different products may be stored in different locations, an error in inventory valuation may not be readily apparent. Even a small error in the valuation of inventory may have a material effect on net income. Therefore, care must be taken in counting and pricing the inventory at year-end.

An error in the valuation of inventory will affect several balance sheet measurements, including assets and total owners' equity. It also will affect key figures in the *income statement,* including the cost of goods sold, gross profit, and net income. And remember that the ending inventory of one year is the beginning inventory of the next. Thus an error in inventory valuation will *carry over* into the financial statements of the following year.

Effects of an Error in Valuing Ending Inventory To illustrate, assume that some items of merchandise in a company's inventory are overlooked during the year-end physical count. As a result of this error, the ending inventory will be *understated.* The costs of the uncounted merchandise erroneously will be transferred out of the Inventory account and included in the cost of goods sold. This overstatement of the cost of goods sold, in turn, results in an understatement of gross profit and net income.[7]

Inventory Errors Affect Two Years An error in the valuation of ending inventory affects not only the financial statements of the current year but also the income statement for the *following* year.

Learning Objective
Explain the effects on the income statement of errors in inventory valuation. **LO5**

Assume that the ending inventory in 2011 is *understated* by $10,000. As we have described above, the cost of goods sold in 2011 is overstated by this amount, and both gross profit and net income are *understated.*

The ending inventory in 2011, however, becomes the *beginning inventory* in 2012. An understatement of the beginning inventory results in an understatement of the cost of goods sold and, therefore, an *overstatement* of gross profit and net income in 2012.

Notice that the original error has exactly the *opposite effects* on the net incomes of the two successive years. Net income was *understated* by the amount of the error in 2011 and *overstated* by the same amount in 2012. For this reason, inventory errors are said to be "counterbalancing" or "self-correcting" over a two-year period.

The fact that offsetting errors occur in the financial statements of two successive years does not lessen the consequences of errors in inventory valuation. Rather, it *exaggerates* the misleading effects of the error on *trends* in the company's performance from one year to the next.

Effects of Errors in Inventory Valuation: A Summary In Exhibit 8–9 we summarize the effects of an error in the valuation of ending inventory over two successive years. In this exhibit we indicate the effects of the error on various financial statement measurements using the code letters **U** (understated), **O** (overstated), and **NE** (no effect). The effects of errors in the valuation of inventory are the same regardless of whether the company uses a perpetual or a periodic inventory system. The **NE** for owners' equity at year-end in the Following Year column results from the offsetting of the first-year error in the second year.

[7] If income tax effects are ignored, the amount of the error is exactly the same in inventory, gross profit, and net income. If tax effects are considered, the amount of the error may be lessened in the net income figure.

Exhibit 8–9
EFFECTS OF INVENTORY ERRORS

Original Error: Ending Inventory Understated	Year of the Error	Following Year
Beginning inventory	NE	U
Cost of goods available for sale	NE	U
Ending inventory	U	NE
Cost of goods sold	O	U
Gross profit	U	O
Net income	U	O
Owners' equity at year-end	U	NE

Original Error: Ending Inventory Overstated	Year of the Error	Following Year
Beginning inventory	NE	O
Cost of goods available for sale	NE	O
Ending inventory	O	NE
Cost of goods sold	U	O
Gross profit	O	U
Net income	O	U
Owners' equity at year-end	O	NE

TECHNIQUES FOR ESTIMATING THE COST OF GOODS SOLD AND THE ENDING INVENTORY

Taking a physical inventory every month would be expensive and time-consuming. Therefore, if a business using a periodic inventory system prepares monthly or quarterly financial statements, it may *estimate* the amounts of its inventory and cost of goods sold except at the end of its annual period. One approach to making these estimates is called the gross profit method; another—used primarily by retail stores—is the retail method.

THE GROSS PROFIT METHOD

Learning Objective
LO6 Estimate the cost of goods sold and ending inventory by the gross profit method and by the retail method.

The **gross profit method** is a quick and simple technique for estimating the cost of goods sold and the amount of inventory on hand. Using this method assumes that the rate of gross profit earned in the preceding year (or several years) will remain the same for the current year. When we know the rate of gross profit, we can divide the dollar amount of net sales into two elements: (1) the gross profit and (2) the cost of goods sold. We view net sales as 100 percent. If the gross profit rate, for example, is 40 percent of net sales, the cost of goods sold must be 60 percent. The cost of goods sold percentage (or **cost ratio**) is determined by deducting the gross profit rate from 100 percent.

When the gross profit rate is known, the ending inventory can be estimated by the following procedures:

1. Determine the *cost of goods available for sale* from the general ledger records of beginning inventory and net purchases.
2. Estimate the *cost of goods sold* by multiplying the net sales by the cost ratio.
3. Deduct the estimated *cost of goods sold* from the *cost of goods available for sale* to find the estimated ending inventory.

To illustrate, assume that Metro Hardware has a beginning inventory of $50,000 on January 1. During the month of January, net purchases amount to $20,000 and net sales total $30,000. Assume that the company's normal gross profit rate is 40 percent of net sales; it follows that the cost ratio is *60 percent.* Using these facts, the inventory on January 31 may be estimated as indicated at the top of the following page.

The gross profit method of estimating inventory has several uses apart from the preparation of interim financial statements. For example, if an inventory is destroyed by fire, the company must estimate the amount of the inventory on hand at the date of the fire to file an insurance claim. A convenient way to determine this inventory amount may be the gross profit method.

The gross profit method is also used at year-end after the taking of a physical inventory to confirm the overall reasonableness of the amount determined by the counting and pricing

Goods available for sale:		
Beginning inventory, Jan. 1		$50,000
Purchases		20,000
Cost of goods available for sale		$70,000
Deduct: Estimated cost of goods sold:		
Net sales	$30,000	
Cost ratio (100% − 40%)	60%	
Estimated cost of goods sold ($30,000 × 60%)		18,000
Estimated ending inventory, Jan. 31		$52,000

When gross profit rate is known:

Step 1 Determine cost of goods available for sale (COGAS);
Step 2 Estimate the cost of goods sold (COGS) (multiply net sales by cost ratio); and
Step 3 Deduct estimated COGS from the COGAS to find estimated ending inventory.

process. The gross profit method is not, however, a satisfactory substitute for periodically taking an actual physical inventory.

THE RETAIL METHOD

The **retail method** of estimating inventory and the cost of goods sold is similar to the gross profit method. The basic difference is that the retail method requires that management determine the value of ending inventory at *retail* prices. The retail value of ending inventory is then converted to its approximate cost using a cost ratio.

To determine the cost ratio, a business must keep track of goods available for sale at both cost and at retail prices. To illustrate, assume that Ski Valley has merchandise available for sale costing $450,000 for the year, and that management offers this merchandise for sale to customers at *retail* prices totaling $1,000,000. Thus Ski Valley's cost ratio for the year is 45 percent ($450,000 ÷ $1,000,000). Ski Valley can use this ratio to convert the retail value of its ending merchandise inventory to its estimated *cost.*

Assume that Ski Valley's employees determine that inventory on hand at the end of the year has a total *retail* value of $300,000. This amount is converted to *cost* using the 45 percent cost ratio as follows:

a	Goods available for sale at *cost*	$ 450,000
b	Goods available for sale at *retail*	1,000,000
c	Cost ratio [**a** ÷ **b**]	45%
d	Physical count of ending inventory priced at *retail*	300,000
e	Estimated ending inventory at cost [**c** × **d**]	$ 135,000

This application of the retail method approximates a valuation of ending inventory at its average cost. A widely used variation of this method enables management to estimate a LIFO valuation of ending inventory.

"TEXTBOOK" INVENTORY SYSTEMS CAN BE MODIFIED . . . AND THEY OFTEN ARE

In this chapter we have described the basic characteristics of the most common inventory systems. In practice, businesses often modify these systems to suit their particular needs. Some businesses also use *different inventory systems for different purposes.*

We described one modification in Chapter 6—a company that maintains little inventory may simply charge (debit) all purchases directly to the cost of goods sold. Another common modification is to maintain perpetual inventory records showing only the *quantities* of merchandise bought and sold, with no dollar amounts. Such systems require less record keeping than a full-blown perpetual system, and they still provide management with useful information about sales and inventories. To generate the dollar amounts needed in financial statements and tax returns, these companies might use the gross profit method, the retail method, or a periodic inventory system.

Businesses such as restaurants often update their inventory records by physically counting products on a daily or weekly basis. In effect, they use frequent periodic counts as the basis for maintaining a perpetual inventory system.

In summary, real-world inventory systems often differ from the illustrations in a textbook. But the underlying principles remain the same.

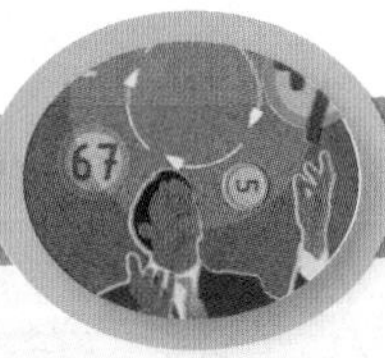

Financial Analysis and Decision Making

Inventory often is the largest of a company's current assets. But how liquid is this asset? How quickly will it be converted into cash? As a step toward answering these questions, short-term creditors often compute the **inventory turnover.**

Inventory Turnover

The inventory turnover is equal to the cost of goods sold divided by the average amount of inventory (beginning inventory plus ending inventory, divided by 2). This ratio indicates how many *times* in the course of a year the company is able to sell the amount of its average inventory. The higher this rate, the more quickly the company sells its inventory.

Learning Objective
LO7 Compute the inventory turnover and explain its uses.

© Roberts Publishing Services/Joshua Roberts

To illustrate, a recent annual report of **Target** shows a cost of goods sold of $44,157 million and average inventory of $6,743 million. The inventory turnover rate for **Target**, therefore, is 6.55 ($44,157 million ÷ $6,743 million). We may compute the number of *days* required for the company to sell its inventory by dividing 365 days by the turnover rate. Thus **Target** requires *56 days* to turn over (sell) the amount of its average inventory. The computation of **Target**'s inventory turnover and the average number of days required to sell its inventory is summarized as follows:

Inventory Turnover

$$\frac{\text{Cost of Goods Sold}}{\text{Average Inventory*}} = \frac{\$44{,}157 \text{ million}}{\$6{,}743 \text{ million}} = 6.55 \text{ times}$$

Average Number of Days to Sell Inventory

$$\frac{\text{Days in the Year}}{\text{Inventory Turnover}} = \frac{365 \text{ days}}{6.55 \text{ times}} = 56 \text{ days}$$

*Average Inventory = (Beginning Inventory + Ending Inventory) ÷ 2

Users of financial statements find the inventory turnover useful in evaluating the liquidity of the company's inventory. Managers and independent auditors may use this computation to help identify inventory that is not selling well and that may have become obsolete. A declining turnover indicates that merchandise is not selling as quickly as in the past. Comparing a company's inventory turnover with that of competitors is particularly useful in evaluating how effective a company is at managing its inventory, often one of its largest assets.

Receivables Turnover

Most businesses sell merchandise on account. Therefore, the sale of inventory often does not provide an immediate source of cash. To determine how quickly inventory is converted into cash, the number of days required to *sell the inventory* must be combined with the number of days required to *collect the accounts receivable.*

The number of days required to collect accounts receivable depends on a company's *accounts receivable turnover.* This figure is computed by dividing net sales by the average accounts receivable. The number of days required to collect these receivables then is determined by dividing 365 days by the turnover rate. Data for the **Target** annual report indicate that the company needed approximately *5 days* (on average) for receivables to convert to cash.

Length of the Operating Cycle The *operating cycle* of a merchandising company is the average time period between the purchase of merchandise and the conversion of this merchandise back into cash. In other words, the merchandise acquired as inventory gradually is converted into

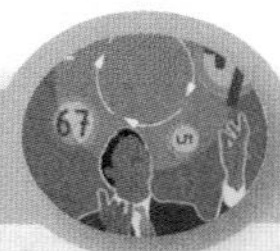

YOUR TURN **You as a Credit Analyst**

Assume that you are employed by **GE Capital** as a credit analyst, and that **Target** is seeking to borrow money using its merchandise inventory as collateral. You have determined that the company's inventory turnover is 3.46 times, and that the average time to sell its inventory is 100 days (see previous computations). Assume that **Target**'s inventory reported at *cost* is currently $3.2 billion, and that its gross profit as a percentage of sales is approximately 37 percent. Estimate the *market value* of the company's inventory for use as collateral.

(See our comments on the Online Learning Center Web site.)

accounts receivable by sale of the goods on account, and these receivables are converted into cash through the process of collection.

The operating cycle of **Target** was approximately *105 days,* computed by adding the average *100 days* required to sell its inventory and the *5 days* required to collect cash from customers. From the viewpoint of short-term creditors, the shorter the operating cycle, the higher the quality of the company's liquid assets because they will be converted into cash more quickly.

Ethics, Fraud & Corporate Governance

As discussed previously in this chapter, the valuation of inventory and the cost of goods sold is of critical importance to managers and to users of the company's financial statements. The two primary issues with regard to inventory valuation are existence and valuation.

In a well-known case of inventory fraud, the Securities and Exchange Commission (SEC) brought an enforcement action against an officer of **MiniScribe Corporation** related to his involvement in overstating inventory reported in the company's balance sheet. The overstatement of inventory resulted in an understatement of cost of goods sold and an overstatement of profits reported in the company's income statement (**MiniScribe**'s net income was actually inflated by $22 million, or *244 percent*).

Prior to being acquired by **Maxtor Corporation**, **MiniScribe** manufactured computer disk drives and its stock was quoted on NASDAQ. The company had discovered a material shortfall in its inventory balance. Reporting this shortfall would have increased the cost of goods sold and reduced the company's net income significantly. So **MiniScribe** concealed the shortfall from its independent auditors by taking a number of actions to inappropriately overstate its actual inventory balance. First, it recorded a fictitious transfer of nonexistent inventory from its headquarters to an overseas subsidiary. Second, it repackaged scrap items and obsolete inventory as if they were "good" inventory items. Third, it packed *bricks* into computer disk drive boxes and shipped them to its distributors (these shipments were still counted as inventory by **MiniScribe** until the distributors sold the boxes).

Concluding Remarks

Throughout this chapter we have learned about different inventory valuation methods. Each method is based upon a particular assumption about cost flows and does not necessarily parallel the physical movement of merchandise. Moreover, the choice of valuation by management can have significant effects on a company's income statement, balance sheet, and tax returns.

In the following chapter, we will see that a similar situation exists with respect to alternative methods used to account for plant and equipment.

END-OF-CHAPTER REVIEW

SUMMARY OF LEARNING OBJECTIVES

LO1 In a perpetual inventory system, determine the cost of goods sold using (a) specific identification, (b) average cost, (c) FIFO, and (d) LIFO. Discuss the advantages and shortcomings of each method. By the *specific identification method,* the actual costs of the specific units sold are transferred from inventory to the cost of goods sold. (Debit Cost of Goods Sold: credit Inventory.) This method achieves the proper matching of sales revenue and cost of goods sold when the individual units in the inventory are unique. However, the method becomes cumbersome and may produce misleading results if the inventory consists of homogeneous items.

The remaining three methods are flow assumptions, which should be applied only to an inventory of homogeneous items.

By the *average-cost method,* the average cost of all units in the inventory is computed and used in recording the cost of goods sold. This is the only method in which all units are assigned the same (average) per-unit cost.

FIFO (first-in, first-out) is the assumption that the first units purchased are the first units sold. Thus, inventory is assumed to consist of the most recently purchased units. FIFO assigns current costs to inventory but older (and often lower) costs to the cost of goods sold.

LIFO (last-in, first-out) is the assumption that the most recently acquired goods are sold first. This method matches sales revenue with relatively current costs. In a period of inflation, LIFO usually results in lower reported profits and lower income taxes than the other methods. However, the oldest purchase costs are assigned to inventory, which may result in inventory becoming grossly understated in terms of current replacement costs.

LO2 Explain the need for taking a physical inventory. In a perpetual inventory system, a physical inventory is taken to adjust the inventory records for shrinkage losses. In a periodic inventory system, the physical inventory is the basis for determining the cost of the ending inventory and for computing the cost of goods sold.

LO3 Record shrinkage losses and other year-end adjustments to inventory. Shrinkage losses are recorded by removing from the Inventory account the cost of the missing or damaged units. The offsetting debit may be to Cost of Goods Sold, if the shrinkage is normal in amount, or to a special loss account. If inventory is found to be obsolete and unlikely to be sold, it is written down to zero (or its scrap value, if any). If inventory is valued at the lower-of-cost-or-market, it is written down to its current replacement cost, if at year-end this amount is substantially below the cost shown in the inventory records.

LO4 In a periodic inventory system, determine the ending inventory and the cost of goods sold using (a) specific identification, (b) average cost, (c) FIFO, and (d) LIFO. The cost of goods sold is determined by combining the beginning inventory with the purchases during the period and subtracting the cost of the ending inventory. Thus, the cost assigned to ending inventory also determines the cost of goods sold.

By the specific identification method, the ending inventory is determined by the specific costs associated with the units on hand. By the average-cost method, the ending inventory is determined by multiplying the number of units on hand by the average cost of the units available for sale during the year. By FIFO, the units in inventory are priced using the unit costs from the most recent cost layers. By the LIFO method, inventory is priced using the unit costs in the oldest cost layers.

LO5 Explain the effects on the income statement of errors in inventory valuation. In the current year, an error in the costs assigned to ending inventory will cause an opposite error in the cost of goods sold and, therefore, a repetition of the original error in the amount of gross profit. For example, understating ending inventory results in an overstatement of the cost of goods sold and an understatement of gross profit.

The error has exactly the opposite effect on the cost of goods sold and the gross profit of the following year, because the error is now in the cost assigned to *beginning* inventory.

LO6 Estimate the cost of goods sold and ending inventory by the gross profit method and by the retail method. Both the gross profit and retail methods use a cost ratio to estimate the cost of goods sold and ending inventory. The cost of goods sold is estimated by multiplying net sales by this cost ratio; ending inventory then is estimated by subtracting this cost of goods sold from the cost of goods available for sale.

In the gross profit method, the cost ratio is 100 percent minus the company's historical gross profit rate. In the retail method, the cost ratio is the percentage of cost to the retail prices of merchandise available for sale.

LO7 Compute the inventory turnover and explain its uses. The inventory turnover rate is equal to the cost of goods sold divided by the average inventory. Users of financial statements find the inventory turnover rate useful in evaluating the liquidity of the company's inventory. In addition, managers and independent auditors use this computation to help identify inventory that is not selling well and that may have become obsolete.

Key Terms Introduced or Emphasized in Chapter 8

average-cost method (p. 342) A method of valuing all units in inventory at the same average per-unit cost, which is recomputed after every purchase.

consistency (in inventory valuation) (p. 347) An accounting principle that calls for the use of the same method of inventory pricing from year to year, with full disclosure of the effects of any change in method. Intended to make financial statements comparable.

cost flow assumption (p. 342) Assumption as to the sequence in which units are removed from inventory for the purpose of sale. Is not required to parallel the physical movement of merchandise if the units are homogeneous.

cost layer (p. 341) Units of merchandise acquired at the same unit cost. An inventory comprised of several cost layers is characteristic of all inventory valuation methods except *average cost.*

cost ratio (p. 356) The cost of merchandise expressed as a percentage of its retail selling price. Used in inventory estimating techniques, such as the gross profit method and the retail method.

first-in, first-out (FIFO) method (p. 343) A method of computing the cost of inventory and the cost of goods sold based on the assumption that the first merchandise acquired is the first merchandise sold and that the ending inventory consists of the most recently acquired goods.

F.O.B. destination (p. 351) A term meaning the seller bears the cost of shipping goods to the buyer's location. Title to the goods remains with the seller while the goods are in transit.

F.O.B. shipping point (p. 351) The buyer of goods bears the cost of transportation from the seller's location to the buyer's location. Title to the goods passes at the point of shipment, and the goods are the property of the buyer while in transit.

gross profit method (p. 356) A method of estimating the cost of the ending inventory based on the assumption that the rate of gross profit remains approximately the same from year to year. Used for interim valuations and for estimating losses.

inventory turnover (p. 358) The cost of goods sold divided by the average amount of inventory. Indicates how many times the average inventory is sold during the course of the year.

just-in-time (JIT) inventory system (p. 347) A technique designed to minimize a company's investment in inventory. In a manufacturing company, this means receiving purchases of raw materials just in time for use in the manufacturing process and completing the manufacture of finished goods just in time to fill sales orders. Just-in-time also may be described as the philosophy of constantly striving to become more efficient by purchasing and storing less inventory.

last-in, first-out (LIFO) method (p. 344) A method of computing the cost of goods sold by use of the prices paid for the most recently acquired units. Ending inventory is valued on the basis of prices paid for the units first acquired.

lower-of-cost-or-market (LCM) rule (p. 350) A method of inventory pricing in which goods are valued at original cost or replacement cost (market), whichever is lower.

moving average method (p. 342) A method of valuing all units of inventory at the same average per-unit cost, recalculating this cost after each purchase. This method is used in a perpetual inventory system.

physical inventory (p. 349) A systematic count of all goods on hand, followed by the application of unit prices to the quantities counted and development of a dollar valuation of the ending inventory.

retail method (p. 357) A method of estimating the cost of goods sold and ending inventory. Similar to the gross profit method, except that the cost ratio is based on current cost-to-retail price relationships rather than on those of the prior year.

shrinkage losses (p. 349) Losses of inventory resulting from theft, spoilage, or breakage.

specific identification (p. 342) Recording as the cost of goods sold the actual costs of the specific units sold. Necessary if each unit in inventory is unique, but not if the inventory consists of homogeneous products.

write-down (of an asset) (p. 350) A reduction in the carrying amount of an asset because it has become obsolete or its usefulness has otherwise been impaired. Involves a credit to the appropriate asset account, with an offsetting debit to a loss account.

Demonstration Problem

The Audiophile sells high-performance stereo equipment. Massachusetts Acoustic recently introduced the Carnegie-440, a state-of-the-art speaker system. During the current year, The Audiophile purchased nine of these speaker systems at the following dates and acquisition costs:

Date	Units Purchased	Unit Cost	Total Cost
Oct. 1	2	$3,000	$ 6,000
Nov. 17	3	3,200	9,600
Dec. 1	4	3,250	13,000
Available for sale during the year	9		$28,600

On *November 21,* The Audiophile sold four of these speaker systems to the Boston Symphony. The other five Carnegie-440s remained in inventory at December 31.

Instructions

Assume that The Audiophile uses a *perpetual inventory system.* Compute (1) the cost of goods sold relating to the sale of Carnegie-440 speakers to the Boston Symphony and (2) the ending inventory of these speakers at December 31, using each of the following flow assumptions:

a. Average cost.

b. First-in, first-out (FIFO).

c. Last-in, first-out (LIFO).

Show the number of units and the unit costs of the cost layers comprising the cost of goods sold and the ending inventory.

Solution to the Demonstration Problem

a.	**1.**	Cost of goods sold (at average cost):		
		Average unit cost at Nov. 21 [($6,000 + $9,600) ÷ 5 units]	$ 3,120	
		Cost of goods sold (4 units × $3,120 per unit)		$12,480
	2.	Inventory at Dec. 31 (at average cost):		
		Units remaining after sale of Nov. 21 (1 unit @ $3,120)	$ 3,120	
		Units purchased on Dec. 1 (4 units @ $3,250)	13,000	
		Total cost of 5 units in inventory	$16,120	
		Average unit cost at Dec. 31 ($16,120 ÷ 5 units)	$ 3,224	
		Inventory at Dec. 31 (5 units × $3,224 per unit)		$16,120
b.	**1.**	Cost of goods sold (FIFO basis):		
		(2 units @ $3,000 + 2 units @ $3,200)		$12,400
	2.	Inventory at Dec. 31 (4 units @ $3,250 + 1 unit @ $3,200)		$16,200
c.	**1.**	Cost of goods sold (LIFO basis):		
		(3 units @ $3,200 + 1 unit @ $3,000)		$12,600
	2.	Inventory at Dec. 31 (4 units @ $3,250 + 1 unit @ $3,000)		$16,000

Self-Test Questions

The answers to these questions appear on page 380.

1. The primary purpose for using an inventory cost flow *assumption* is to:

a. Parallel the physical flow of units of merchandise.

b. Offset against revenue an appropriate cost of goods sold.

c. Minimize income taxes.

d. Maximize the reported amount of net income.

2. Ace Auto Supply uses a perpetual inventory system. On March 10, the company sells two Shelby four-barrel carburetors. Immediately prior to this sale, the perpetual inventory records indicate three of these carburetors on hand, as follows:

Date	Quantity Purchased	Unit Cost	Units on Hand	Total Cost
Feb. 4	1	$220	1	$220
Mar. 2	2	235	3	690

With respect to the sale on March 10: (More than one of the following answers may be correct.)

a. If the average-cost method is used, the cost of goods sold is $460.

b. If these carburetors have identification numbers, Ace must use the specific identification method to determine the cost of goods sold.

c. If the company uses LIFO, the cost of goods sold will be $15 higher than if it were using FIFO.

d. If the company uses LIFO, the carburetor *remaining* in inventory after the sales will be assumed to have cost $220.

3. T-Shirt City uses a *periodic* inventory system. During the first year of operations, the company made four purchases of a particular product. Each purchase was for 500 units and the prices paid were $9 per unit in the first purchase, $10 per unit in the second purchase, $12 per unit in the third purchase, and $13 per unit in the fourth purchase. At year-end,

650 of these units remained unsold. Compute the cost of goods sold under the FIFO method and LIFO method, respectively.

a. $13,700 (FIFO) and $16,000 (LIFO).

b. $8,300 (FIFO) and $6,000 (LIFO).

c. $16,000 (FIFO) and $13,700 (LIFO).

d. $6,000 (FIFO) and $8,300 (LIFO).

4. Trent Department Store uses a perpetual inventory system but adjusts its inventory records at year-end to reflect the results of a complete physical inventory. In the physical inventory taken at the ends of 2010 and 2011, Trent's employees failed to count the merchandise in the store's window displays. The cost of this merchandise amounted to $13,000 at the end of 2010 and $19,000 at the end of 2011. As a result of these errors, the cost of goods sold for 2011 will be:

a. Understated by $19,000.

b. Overstated by $6,000.

c. Understated by $6,000.

d. None of the above.

5. In July 2011, the accountant for LBJ Imports is in the process of preparing financial statements for the quarter ended June 30, 2011. The physical inventory, however, was last taken on June 5, and the accountant must establish the approximate cost at June 30 from the following data:

Physical inventory, June 5, 2011	$900,000
Transactions for the period June 5–June 30:	
Sales	700,000
Purchases	400,000

The gross profit on sales has consistently averaged 40 percent of sales. Using the gross profit method, compute the approximate inventory cost at June 30, 2011.

a. $420,000.

b. $880,000.

c. $480,000.

d. $1,360,000.

6. Allied Products maintains a large inventory. The company has used the LIFO inventory method for many years, during which the purchase costs of its products have risen substantially. (More than one of the following answers may be correct.)

a. Allied would have reported a *higher* net income in past years if it had been using the average-cost method.

b. Allied's financial statements imply a *lower* inventory turnover rate than they would if the company were using FIFO.

c. If Allied were to let its inventory fall far below normal levels, the company's gross profit rate would *decline*.

d. Allied would have paid more income taxes in past years if it had been using the FIFO method.

ASSIGNMENT MATERIAL Discussion Questions

1. Briefly describe the advantages of using a cost flow assumption, rather than the specific identification method, to value an inventory.

2. Under what circumstances do generally accepted accounting principles permit the use of an inventory cost flow assumption? Must a cost flow assumption closely parallel the physical movement of the company's merchandise?

3. A large art gallery has in inventory more than 100 paintings. No two are alike. The least expensive is priced at more than $1,000 and the higher-priced items carry prices of $100,000 and more. Which of the four methods of inventory valuation discussed in this chapter would you consider to be most appropriate for this business? Give reasons for your answer.

4. During a period of steadily increasing purchase costs, which inventory flow assumption results in the highest reported profits? The lowest taxable income? The valuation of inventory that is closest to current replacement cost? Briefly explain your answers.

5. What are the characteristics of a *just-in-time* inventory system? Briefly explain some advantages and risks of this type of system.

6. Why do companies that use perpetual inventory systems also take an annual *physical inventory*? When is this physical inventory usually taken? Why?

7. Under what circumstances might a company write down its inventory to carrying value below cost?

8. What is meant by the year-end *cutoff* of transactions? If merchandise in transit at year-end is material in dollar amount, what determines whether these goods should be included in the inventory of the buyer or the seller? Explain.

9. Explain why errors in the valuation of inventory at the end of the year are sometimes called "counterbalancing" or "self-correcting."

10. Briefly explain the *gross profit method* of estimating inventories. In what types of situations is this technique likely to be useful?

11. A store using the *retail inventory method* takes its physical inventory by applying current retail prices as marked on the merchandise to the quantities counted. Does this procedure mean that the inventory will appear in the financial statements at retail selling price? Explain.

12. How is the *inventory turnover* computed? Why is this measurement of interest to short-term creditors?

13. Baxter Corporation has been using FIFO during a period of rising costs. Explain whether you would expect each of the following measurements to be higher or lower if the company had been using LIFO.
    a. Net income.
    b. Inventory turnover rate.
    c. Income taxes expense.
14. In anticipation of *declining* inventory replacement costs, the management of Computer Products Co. elects to use the *FIFO* inventory method rather than LIFO. Explain how this decision should affect the company's future:
    a. Rate of gross profit.
    b. Net cash flow from operating activities.
15. Notes to the financial statements of two clothing manufacturers follow:

    Inventories: The inventories are stated at the lower of cost, determined principally by the LIFO method, or market.

    Inventories: Inventories are stated at the lower of cost (first-in, first-out method) or market value, assuming a period of rising prices.

    a. Which company is using the more conservative method of pricing its inventories? Explain.
    b. On the basis of the inventory methods in use in their financial statements, which company is in the better position to minimize the amount of income taxes that it must pay? Explain.
    c. Could either company increase its cash collections from customers or reduce its cash payments to suppliers of merchandise by switching from FIFO to LIFO, or from LIFO to FIFO? Explain.

Brief Exercises

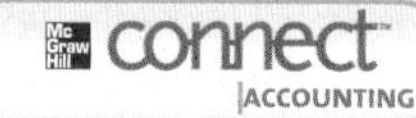

LO1 LO4 **BRIEF EXERCISE 8.1**
FIFO Inventory

Smalley, Inc., purchased items of inventory as follows:

Jan. 4 100 units @ $2.00
Jan. 23 120 units @ $2.25

Smalley sold 50 units on January 28. Compute the cost of goods sold for the month under the FIFO inventory method.

LO1 LO4 **BRIEF EXERCISE 8.2**
LIFO Inventory

Wasson Company purchased items of inventory as follows:

Dec. 2 50 units @ $20
Dec. 12 12 units @ $21

Wasson sold 15 units on December 20. Determine the cost of goods sold for the month under the LIFO inventory method.

LO4 **BRIEF EXERCISE 8.3**
Average-Cost Inventory

Fox Company purchased items of inventory as follows:

May 3 100 units @ $3.05
May 10 150 units @ $3.10
May 15 120 units @ $3.15

By the end of the month of May, Fox had sold 125 units. If the company uses the average-cost method of accounting for inventory, what is the amount of the ending inventory?

LO4 **BRIEF EXERCISE 8.4**
FIFO and LIFO Inventory

Murray, Inc., purchased a new inventory item two times during the month of April, as follows:

Apr. 5 100 units @ $5.00
Apr. 15 100 units @ $5.05

a. What is the amount of the ending inventory of this item on April 30 if the company has sold 75 units and uses the LIFO inventory method?
b. How would this amount differ if the company used the FIFO inventory method?

LO4 **BRIEF EXERCISE 8.5**
FIFO and Average-Cost Inventory

United Co. had 10 units of an inventory item on hand at the beginning of the current year, each of which had a per-unit cost of $10. During the year, 20 additional units were purchased at $11, and 25 units were sold. What is the amount of the ending inventory under the LIFO and the average-cost methods of accounting for inventory?

LO3 **BRIEF EXERCISE 8.6**
Inventory Shrinkage

Wexler Company's inventory is subject to shrinkage via evaporation. At the end of the current financial reporting period, the company's inventory had a cost of $100,000. Management estimates that evaporation has resulted in a 5 percent inventory loss. Assuming that loss is recorded in a separate inventory loss account, prepare the general journal entry to record the inventory shrinkage for the year.

LO5 **BRIEF EXERCISE 8.7**
Inventory Error

Black and Blue, Inc., overlooked $100,000 of inventory at the end of the current year because it was stored temporarily in a warehouse owned by another company. Before discovering this error, the company's income statement showed the following:

Sales	$990,000
Cost of goods sold	(560,000)
Gross profit	$430,000

Restate these figures to reflect the inclusion of the overlooked inventory.

LO5 **BRIEF EXERCISE 8.8**
Inventory Error

Due to ineffective controls while counting its inventory, Walker & Comer, Inc., double-counted $50,000 of inventory at the end of the current year. Before discovering this error, the company's ending inventory was $670,000. How will correction of this error affect the company's inventory and cost of goods sold figures?

LO7 **BRIEF EXERCISE 8.9**
Inventory Turnover

Miller & Miller Company recorded sales, cost of goods sold, and ending inventory for the current year in the following amounts: $650,000, $500,000, and $128,000, respectively. Calculate the amount of the company's inventory turnover for the year. What is the company's average number of days to sell inventory?

LO7 **BRIEF EXERCISE 8.10**
Inventory Turnover

Rouse Incorporated reported sales, cost of sales, and inventory figures for 2010 and 2011 as follows (all dollars in thousands):

	Sales	Cost of Goods Sold	Inventory
2010	$100	$85	$27
2011	110	90	35

What is the amount of inventory turnover for each year, and in which year did Rouse manage its inventory most efficiently?

Exercises

LO1 through LO7 **EXERCISE 8.1**
Accounting Terminology

Listed below are eight technical accounting terms introduced in this chapter.

Retail method	FIFO method	Lower-of-cost-or-market
Gross profit method	LIFO method	Specific identification
Flow assumption	Average-cost method	

Each of the following statements may (or may not) describe one of these technical terms. For each statement, indicate the term described, or answer "None" if the statement does not correctly describe any of the terms.

a. A pattern of transferring unit costs from the Inventory account to the Cost of Goods Sold that may (or may not) parallel the physical flow of merchandise.

b. The only flow assumption in which all units of merchandise are assigned the same per-unit cost.

c. The method used to record the cost of goods sold when each unit in the inventory is unique.

d. The most conservative of the flow assumptions during a period of sustained inflation.

e. The flow assumption that provides the most current valuation of inventory in the balance sheet.

f. A technique for estimating the cost of goods sold and the ending inventory that is based on the relationship between cost and sales price during the *current* accounting period.

LO1 **EXERCISE 8.2**
Cost Flow Assumptions

On May 10, Hudson Computing sold 90 Millennium laptop computers to Apex Publishers. At the date of this sale, Hudson's perpetual inventory records included the following cost layers for the Millennium laptops:

Purchase Date	Quantity	Unit Cost	Total Cost
Apr. 9	70	$1,500	$105,000
May 1	30	$1,600	48,000
Total on hand	100		$153,000

Prepare journal entries to record the cost of the 90 Millennium laptops sold on May 10, assuming that Hudson Computing uses the:

a. Specific identification method (62 of the units sold were purchased on April 9, and the remaining units were purchased on May 1).

b. Average-cost method.

c. FIFO method.

d. LIFO method.

e. Discuss briefly the financial reporting differences that may arise from choosing the FIFO method over the LIFO method.

LO4 **EXERCISE 8.3**
Physical Flow versus Cost Flow Assumptions

The Warm-Up Shop sells heating oil, coal, and kerosene fuel to residential customers. Heating oil is kept in large storage tanks that supply the company's fleet of delivery trucks. Coal is kept in huge bins that are loaded and emptied from the top by giant scooping machines. Kerosene is sold "off the shelf" in five-gallon containers at the company's retail outlet. Separate inventory records are maintained for each fuel type.

a. Which of the cost flow assumptions (average-cost, FIFO, or LIFO) best describes the *physical flow* of:

1. The heating oil inventory? Explain.
2. The coal inventory? Explain.
3. The kerosene inventory? Explain.

b. Which of these cost flow assumptions is likely to result in the *lowest* income tax liability for the company? Explain.

c. Explain why management keeps separate inventory records for its heating oil, coal, and kerosene inventories.

LO4 **EXERCISE 8.4**
Effects of Different Flow Assumptions

Lollar, Inc., is a giant provider of home furnishings. The company uses the FIFO inventory method. The following information was taken from the company's recent financial statements (dollar amounts are in thousands):

Cost of goods sold	$1,850,000
Income before taxes	125,000
Income taxes expense (and payments)	52,500
Net income	72,500
Net cash provided by operating activities	123,250

The financial statements also revealed that had Lollar been using *LIFO,* its cost of goods sold would have been $1,865,000. The company's income taxes and payments amount to approximately 40 percent of income before taxes.

a. Explain how LIFO can result in a higher cost of goods sold. Would you expect LIFO to result in a greater or lesser valuation of the company's ending inventories? Defend your answer.

b. Assuming that Lollar had been using *LIFO,* compute the following amounts for the current year. Show your supporting computations, with dollar amounts in thousands.

1. Income before taxes
2. Income taxes expense (which are assumed equal to income taxes actually paid)
3. Net income
4. Net cash provided by operating activities

LO2 **EXERCISE 8.5**
Transfer of Title

Jensen Tire had two large shipments in transit at December 31. One was a $125,000 inbound shipment of merchandise (shipped December 28, F.O.B. shipping point), which arrived at Jensen's receiving dock on January 2. The other shipment was a $95,000 outbound shipment of merchandise to a customer, which was shipped and billed by Jensen on December 30 (terms F.O.B. shipping point) and reached the customer on January 3.

In taking a physical inventory on December 31, Jensen counted all goods on hand and priced the inventory on the basis of average cost. The total amount was $600,000. No goods in transit were included in this figure.

What amount should appear as inventory on the company's balance sheet at December 31? Explain. If you indicate an amount other than $600,000, state which asset or liability other than inventory also would be changed in amount.

LO3 **EXERCISE 8.6**
Inventory Write-Downs

Late in the year, Software City began carrying WordCrafter, a new word processing software program. At December 31, Software City's perpetual inventory records included the following cost layers in its inventory of WordCrafter programs:

Purchase Date	Quantity	Unit Cost	Total Cost
Nov. 14	8	$400	$3,200
Dec. 12	20	310	6,200
Total available for sale at Dec. 31	28		$9,400

a. At December 31, Software City takes a physical inventory and finds that all 28 units of WordCrafter are on hand. However, the current replacement cost (wholesale price) of this product is only $250 per unit. Prepare the entries to record:

1. This write-down of the inventory to the lower-of-cost-or-market at December 31. (Company policy is to charge LCM adjustments of less than $2,000 to Cost of Goods Sold and larger amounts to a separate loss account.)
2. The cash sale of 15 WordCrafter programs on January 9, at a retail price of $350 each. Assume that Software City uses the FIFO flow assumption.

b. Now assume that the current replacement cost of the WordCrafter programs is $405 each. A physical inventory finds only 25 of these programs on hand at December 31. (For this part, return to the original information and ignore what you did in part **a.**)

1. Prepare the journal entry to record the shrinkage loss assuming that Software City uses the FIFO flow assumption.
2. Prepare the journal entry to record the shrinkage loss assuming that Software City uses the LIFO flow assumption.
3. Which cost flow assumption (FIFO or LIFO) results in the lowest net income for the period? Would using this assumption really mean that the company's operations are less efficient? Explain.

LO4 **EXERCISE 8.7**

Costing Inventory in a Periodic System

Pemberton Products uses a *periodic* inventory system. The company's records show the beginning inventory of PH4 oil filters on January 1 and the purchases of this item during the current year to be as follows:

Jan. 1	Beginning inventory	9 units @ $3.00	$ 27.00
Feb. 23	Purchase	12 units @ $3.50	42.00
Apr. 20	Purchase	30 units @ $3.80	114.00
May 4	Purchase	40 units @ $4.00	160.00
Nov. 30	Purchase	19 units @ $5.00	95.00
	Totals	110 units	$438.00

A physical count indicates 20 units in inventory at year-end.

Determine the cost of the ending inventory on the basis of each of the following methods of inventory valuation. (Remember to use *periodic* inventory costing procedures.)

a. Average cost

b. FIFO

c. LIFO

d. Which of the above methods (if any) results in the same ending inventory valuation under *both* periodic and perpetual costing procedures? Explain.

LO5 **EXERCISE 8.8**

Effects of Errors in Inventory Valuation

Boswell Electric prepared the following condensed income statements for two successive years:

	2011	2010
Sales	$2,000,000	$1,500,000
Cost of goods sold	1,250,000	900,000
Gross profit on sales	$ 750,000	$ 600,000
Operating expenses	400,000	350,000
Net income	$ 350,000	$ 250,000

At the end of 2010 (right-hand column above), the inventory was understated by $40,000, but the error was not discovered until after the accounts had been closed and financial statements prepared at the end of 2011. The balance sheets for the two years showed owner's equity of $500,000 at the end of 2010 and $580,000 at the end of 2011. (Boswell is organized as a sole proprietorship and does not incur income taxes expense.)

a. Compute the corrected net income figures for 2010 and 2011.

b. Compute the gross profit amounts and the gross profit percentages for each year on the basis of corrected data.

c. What correction, if any, should be made in the amounts of the company's owner's equity at the end of 2010 and at the end of 2011?

LO6 **EXERCISE 8.9**

Estimating Inventory by the Gross Profit Method

When Laura Rapp arrived at her store on the morning of January 29, she found empty shelves and display racks; thieves had broken in during the night and stolen the entire inventory. Rapp's accounting records showed that she had inventory costing $50,000 on January 1. From January 1 to January 29, she had made net sales of $70,000 and net purchases of $80,000. The gross profit during the past several years had consistently averaged 45 percent of net sales. Rapp wishes to file an insurance claim for the theft loss.

a. Using the gross profit method, estimate the cost of Rapp's inventory at the time of the theft.

b. Does Rapp use the periodic inventory method or does she account for inventory using the perpetual method? Defend your answer.

LO6 **EXERCISE 8.10**

Estimating Inventory by the Retail Method

Phillips Supply uses a periodic inventory system but needs to determine the approximate amount of inventory at the end of each month without taking a physical inventory. Phillips has provided the following inventory data:

	Cost Price	Retail Selling Price
Inventory of merchandise, June 30	$300,000	$500,000
Purchases during July	222,000	400,000
Goods available for sale during July	$522,000	$900,000
Net sales during July		$600,000

a. Estimate the cost of goods sold and the cost of the July 31 ending inventory using the retail method of evaluation.

b. Was the cost of Phillips's inventory, as a percentage of retail selling prices, higher or lower in July than it was in June? Explain.

LO1 LO7 **EXERCISE 8.11**

Evaluating Cost Flow Assumptions

An annual report issued by **General Motors Corporation** included the following information:

Inventories are valued using various cost methods. The percentage of year-end inventories valued using each of these methods is:

LIFO	50%
FIFO and Average Cost	50%

If the LIFO method of valuation had not been used, total inventories would have been $1.4 billion *more* than reported.

a. Does the company's use of three different inventory methods violate the accounting principle of consistency? Defend your answer.

b. Had the LIFO method *not* been used, would the company's gross profit reported in its income statement have been higher or lower? Explain.

c. On the basis of the information from the company's annual report, do its inventory replacement costs appear to be rising or falling? Explain.

LO1 LO7 **EXERCISE 8.12**

FIFO versus LIFO: A Challenging Analysis

Ford Motor Company uses LIFO to account for all of its domestic inventories. A note to the company's financial statements indicated that:

> If the FIFO method had been used instead of the LIFO method, inventories would have been higher by over a billion dollars.

a. Indicate whether each of the following financial measurements would have been *higher, lower,* or *unaffected* had **Ford Motor Company** used FIFO instead of LIFO. Explain the reasoning behind your answers.
   1. Gross profit rate.
   2. Reported net income.
   3. Current ratio (**Ford**'s current ratio is greater than 1 to 1).
   4. Inventory turnover rate.
   5. Accounts receivable turnover rate.
   6. Cash payments made to suppliers.
   7. Net cash flow from operations (**Ford**'s operating cash flows are positive).

b. Provide *your own* assessment of whether using LIFO has made **Ford Motor Company** more or less (1) liquid and (2) well-off. Defend your answers.

LO7 **EXERCISE 8.13**
Inventory Turnover

A recent annual report of **Kraft Foods, Inc.**, reveals the following information (dollar amounts are stated in millions):

Cost of goods sold	$24,651
Inventory (beginning of year)	3,506
Inventory (end of year)	4,096
Average time required to collect accounts receivable	45 days

a. Compute **Kraft**'s inventory turnover for the year (round to nearest tenth).

b. Compute the number of days required by **Kraft** to sell its average inventory (round to the nearest day).

c. What is the length of **Kraft**'s *operating cycle*?

d. What comparative information would you want to be able to evaluate **Kraft**'s operating cycle figure?

LO7 **EXERCISE 8.14**
Inventory Analysis

A recent income statement of **Walmart** reports sales of $405,046 million and cost of goods sold of $304,657 million for the year ended January 31, 2010. The comparable sales and cost of goods sold figures for the year ended one year earlier were $401,087 million and $304,056 million, respectively. As you would expect, to be able to achieve this high level of sales, a great deal of inventory must be maintained so that customers will find what they want to buy when they shop in **Walmart** stores. In fact, in the January 31, 2010, balance sheet, inventory is presented at $33,160 million and the comparable figure for a year earlier is $34,511 million.

a. Compute the inventory turnover for **Walmart** for both years.

b. Compute the average number of days required by **Walmart** to sell its inventory for the same years.

c. In which year was the company more efficient in its management of inventory? Explain your answer.

LO7 **EXERCISE 8.15**
Using the Financial Statements of **Home Depot, Inc.**

The **Home Depot, Inc.**, financial statements appear in Appendix A at the end of this textbook. Using figures from the income statement and balance sheet, answer the following questions:

a. What was the company's inventory turnover for the most recent year reported?

b. Using your answer from part **a,** what was the average number of days that merchandise remained in inventory before it was sold?

c. Is the company's operating cycle influenced significantly by its accounts receivable turnover rate? Explain.

Problem Set A

LO1 PROBLEM 8.1A
Four Methods of Inventory Valuation
eXcel

On January 15, 2011, BassTrack sold 1,000 Ace-5 fishing reels to Angler's Warehouse. Immediately prior to this sale, BassTrack's perpetual inventory records for Ace-5 reels included the following cost layers:

Purchase Date	Quantity	Unit Cost	Total Cost
Dec. 12, 2010	600	$29	$17,400
Jan. 9, 2011	900	32	28,800
Total on hand	1,500		$46,200

Instructions

Note: We present this problem in the normal sequence of the accounting cycle—that is, journal entries before ledger entries. However, you may find it helpful to work part **b** first.

a. Prepare a separate journal entry to record the cost of goods sold relating to the January 15 sale of 1,000 Ace-5 reels, assuming that BassTrack uses:

1. Specific identification (500 of the units sold were purchased on December 12, and the remaining 500 were purchased on January 9).

2. Average cost.

3. FIFO.

4. LIFO.

b. Complete a subsidiary ledger record for Ace-5 reels using each of the four inventory valuation methods listed above. Your inventory records should show both purchases of this product, the sale on January 15, and the balance on hand at December 12, January 9, and January 15. Use the formats for inventory subsidiary records illustrated on pages 343–345 of this chapter.

c. Refer to the cost of goods sold figures computed in part **a.** For financial reporting purposes, can the company use the valuation method that resulted in the *lowest* cost of goods sold if, for tax purposes, it used the method that resulted in the *highest* cost of goods sold? Explain.

Problems 8.2A and 8.3A are based on the following data:

Speed World Cycles sells high-performance motorcycles and motocross racers. One of Speed World's most popular models is the Kazomma 900 dirt bike. During the current year, Speed World purchased eight of these cycles at the following costs:

Purchase Date	Units Purchased	Unit Cost	Total Cost
July 1	2	$4,950	$ 9,900
July 22	3	5,000	15,000
Aug. 3	3	5,100	15,300
	8		$40,200

On *July 28,* Speed World sold four Kazomma 900 dirt bikes to the Vince Wilson racing team. The remaining four bikes remained in inventory at September 30, the end of Speed World's fiscal year.

LO1 PROBLEM 8.2A
Alternative Cost Flow Assumptions in a Perpetual System

Assume that Speed World uses a *perpetual inventory system.* (See the data given above.)

Instructions

a. Compute the cost of goods sold relating to the sale on July 28 and the ending inventory of Kazomma 900 dirt bikes at September 30, using the following cost flow assumptions:

1. Average cost.

2. FIFO.

3. LIFO.

Show the number of units and the unit costs of each layer comprising the cost of goods sold and ending inventory.

b. Using the cost figures computed in part **a,** answer the following questions:

1. Which of the three cost flow assumptions will result in Speed World Cycles reporting the *highest net income* for the current year? Would this always be the case? Explain.
2. Which of the three cost flow assumptions will *minimize the income taxes owed* by Speed World Cycles for the year? Would you expect this usually to be the case? Explain.
3. May Speed World Cycles use the cost flow assumption that results in the highest net income for the current year in its financial statements, but use the cost flow assumption that minimizes taxable income for the current year in its income tax return? Explain.

LO4 **PROBLEM 8.3A**

Alternative Cost Flow Assumptions in a Periodic System

Assume that Speed World uses a *periodic inventory system.* (See the data given before Problem 8.2A.)

Instructions

a. Compute the cost of goods sold relating to the sale on July 28 and the ending inventory of Kazomma 900 dirt bikes at September 30, using the following cost flow assumptions:

1. Average cost.
2. FIFO.
3. LIFO.

Show the number of units and unit costs in each cost layer of the *ending inventory.* You may determine the cost of goods sold by deducting ending inventory from the cost of goods available for sale.

b. If Speed World Cycles uses the LIFO cost flow assumption for financial reporting purposes, can it use the FIFO method for income tax purposes? Explain.

LO1 through LO3 **PROBLEM 8.4A**

Year-End Adjustments; Shrinkage Losses and LCM

Mario's Nursery uses a perpetual inventory system. At December 31, the perpetual inventory records indicate the following quantities of a particular blue spruce tree:

	Quantity	Unit Cost	Total Cost
First purchase (oldest)	130	$25.00	$ 3,250
Second purchase	120	28.50	3,420
Third purchase	100	39.00	3,900
Total	350		$10,570

A year-end physical inventory, however, shows only 310 of these trees on hand.

In its financial statements, Mario's values its inventories at the lower-of-cost-or-market. At year-end, the per-unit replacement cost of this tree is $40. (Use $3,500 as the "level of materiality" in deciding whether to debit losses to Cost of Goods Sold or to a separate loss account.)

Instructions

Prepare the journal entries required to adjust the inventory records at year-end, assuming that:

a. Mario's uses:

1. Average cost.
2. Last-in, first-out.

b. Mario's uses the first-in, first-out method. However, the replacement cost of the trees at year-end is $20 apiece, rather than the $40 stated originally. [Make separate journal entries to record (1) the shrinkage losses and (2) the restatement of the inventory at a market value lower than cost. Record the shrinkage losses first.]

c. Assume that the company had been experiencing monthly inventory shrinkage of 30 to 60 trees for several months. In response, management placed several hidden security cameras throughout the premises. Within days, an employee was caught on film loading potted trees into his pickup truck. The employee's attorney asked that the case be dropped because the company had "unethically used a hidden camera to entrap his client." Do you agree with the attorney? Defend your answer.

L04 **PROBLEM 8.5A**
Periodic Inventory Costing Procedures

Mach IV Audio uses a periodic inventory system. One of the store's most popular products is an MP3 car stereo system. The inventory quantities, purchases, and sales of this product for the most recent year are as follows:

	Number of Units	Cost per Unit	Total Cost
Inventory, Jan. 1	10	$299	$ 2,990
First purchase (May 12)	15	306	4,590
Second purchase (July 9)	20	308	6,160
Third purchase (Oct. 4)	8	315	2,520
Fourth purchase (Dec. 18)	19	320	6,080
Goods available for sale	72		$22,340
Units sold during the year	51		
Inventory, Dec. 31	21		

Instructions

a. Using *periodic* costing procedures, compute the cost of the December 31 inventory and the cost of goods sold for the MP3 systems during the year under each of the following cost flow assumptions:

1. First-in, first-out.
2. Last-in, first-out.
3. Average cost (round to nearest dollar, except unit cost).

b. Which of the three inventory pricing methods provides the most realistic balance sheet valuation of inventory in light of the current replacement cost of the MP3 units? Does this same method also produce the most realistic measure of income in light of the costs being incurred by Mach IV Audio to replace the MP3 systems when they are sold? Explain.

L05 **PROBLEM 8.6A**
Effects of Inventory Errors on Earnings

The owners of Hexagon Health Foods are offering the business for sale. The partial income statements of the business for the three years of its existence are summarized below.

	2011	2010	2009
Net sales	$875,000	$840,000	$820,000
Cost of goods sold	481,250	487,200	480,000
Gross profit on sales	$393,750	$352,800	$340,000
Gross profit percentage	45%	42%	41%

In negotiations with prospective buyers of the business, the owners of Hexagon are calling attention to the rising trends of the gross profit and the gross profit percentage as very favorable elements.

Assume that you are retained by a prospective purchaser of the business to make an investigation of the fairness and reliability of the enterprise's accounting records and financial statements. You find everything in order except for the following: (1) An arithmetic error in the computation of inventory at the end of 2009 had caused a $40,000 understatement in that inventory, and (2) a duplication of figures in the computation of inventory at the end of 2011 had caused an overstatement of $81,750 in that inventory. The company uses the periodic inventory system, and these errors had not been brought to light prior to your investigation.

Instructions

a. Prepare a revised three-year partial income statement summary.

b. Comment on the trends of gross profit and gross profit percentage before and after the revision.

LO2 LO3 LO6

PROBLEM 8.7A
Retail Method

Between The Ears (BTE.com) is a popular Internet music store. During the current year, the company's cost of goods available for sale amounted to $462,000. The retail sales value of this merchandise amounted to $840,000. Sales for the year were $744,000.

Instructions

a. Using the retail method, estimate (1) the cost of goods sold during the year and (2) the inventory at the end of the year.

b. At year-end, BTE.com takes a physical inventory. The general manager walks through the warehouse counting each type of product and reading its retail price into a tape recorder. From the recorded information, another employee prepares a schedule listing the entire ending inventory at retail sales prices. The schedule prepared for the current year reports ending inventory at $84,480 at retail sales prices.

   1. Use the cost ratio computed in part **a** to reduce the inventory counted by the general manager from its retail value to an estimate of its cost.
   2. Determine the estimated shrinkage losses (measured at cost) incurred by BTE.com during the year.
   3. Compute BTE.com's gross profit for the year. (Include inventory shrinkage losses in the cost of goods sold.)

c. What controls might BTE.com implement to reduce inventory shrinkage?

LO1 LO7

PROBLEM 8.8A
FIFO versus LIFO Comparisons

Wal-Mart uses LIFO to account for its inventories. Recent financial statements were used to compile the following information (dollar figures are in millions):

Average inventory (throughout the year)	$ 33,835
Current assets (at year-end)	48,949
Current liabilities (at year-end)	55,390
Net sales	401,244
Cost of goods sold	306,158
Gross profit	95,086
Average time required to collect outstanding receivables (approximate)	10 days

Instructions

a. Using the information provided, compute the following measures based upon the *LIFO* method:

   1. Inventory turnover.
   2. Current ratio (see Chapter 5 for a discussion of this ratio).
   3. Gross profit rate (see Chapter 6 for a discussion of this statistic).

b. Assuming cost of goods sold would be lower under FIFO, what circumstances must the company have encountered to cause this situation? (Were replacement costs, on average, rising or falling?)

c. How would you expect these ratios to differ (i.e., what direction) had the company used FIFO instead of LIFO?

d. Explain why the average number of days required by **Walmart** to collect its accounts receivable is so low. (See Chapter 7 for a discussion of the accounts receivable turnover rate.)

Problem Set B

LO1 PROBLEM 8.1B
Four Methods of Inventory Valuation

On January 22, 2011, Dome, Inc., sold 700 toner cartridges to Maxine Supplies. Immediately prior to this sale, Dome's perpetual inventory records for these units included the following cost layers:

Purchase Date	Quantity	Unit Cost	Total Cost
Dec. 12, 2010	400	$20	$ 8,000
Jan. 16, 2011	1,200	22	26,400
Total on hand	1,600		$34,400

Instructions

Note: We present this problem in the normal sequence of the accounting cycle—that is, journal entries before ledger entries. However, you may find it helpful to work part **b** first.

a. Prepare a separate journal entry to record the cost of goods sold relating to the January 22 sale of 700 toner cartridges, assuming that Dome uses:

1. Specific identification (300 of the units sold had been purchased on December 12, and the remaining 400 had been purchased on January 16).

2. Average cost.

3. FIFO.

4. LIFO.

b. Complete a subsidiary ledger record for the toner cartridges using each of the four inventory valuation methods listed above. Your inventory records should show both purchases of this product, the sale on January 22, and the balance on hand at December 12, January 16, and January 22. Use the formats for inventory subsidiary records illustrated on pages 343–345 of this chapter.

c. Refer to the cost of goods sold figures computed in part **a.** For financial reporting purposes, can the company use the valuation method that resulted in the *highest* cost of goods sold if, for tax purposes, it used the method that resulted in the *lowest* cost of goods sold? Explain.

Problems 8.2B and 8.3B are based on the following data:

Sea Travel sells motor boats. One of Sea Travel's most popular models is the Wing. During the current year, Sea Travel purchased 12 of these boats at the following costs:

Purchase Date	Units Purchased	Unit Cost	Total Cost
Apr. 1	4	$8,000	$32,000
Apr. 19	5	8,200	41,000
May 8	3	8,500	25,500
	12		$98,500

On *April 28,* Sea Travel sold five Wings to the Jack Sport racing team. The remaining seven boats remained in inventory at June 30, the end of Sea Travel's fiscal year.

LO1 PROBLEM 8.2B
Alternative Cost Flow Assumptions in a Perpetual System

Assume that Sea Travel uses a *perpetual inventory system.* (See the data given above.)

Instructions

a. Compute (a) the cost of goods sold relating to the sale on April 28 and (b) the ending inventory of Wing boats at June 30, using the following cost flow assumptions:

1. Average cost (round cost to nearest whole dollar).

2. FIFO.

3. LIFO.

Show the number of units and the unit costs of each layer comprising the cost of goods sold and ending inventory.

b. Using the cost figures computed in part **a,** answer the following questions:

1. Which of the three cost flow assumptions will result in Sea Travel reporting the *lowest net income* for the current year? Would this always be the case? Explain.
2. Which of the three cost flow assumptions will result in the *highest* income tax expense for the year? Would you expect this usually to be the case? Explain.
3. May Sea Travel use the cost flow assumption that results in the *lowest* net income for the current year in its financial statements, but use the cost flow assumption that *maximizes* taxable income for the current year in its income tax return? Explain.

LO4 **PROBLEM 8.3B**

Alternative Cost Flow Assumptions in a Periodic System

Assume that Sea Travel uses a *periodic inventory system.* (Refer to the data that precede Problem 8.2B.)

Instructions

a. Compute the cost of goods sold relating to the sale on April 28 and the ending inventory of Wing boats at June 30, using the following cost flow assumptions:

1. Average cost (round cost to nearest whole dollar).
2. FIFO.
3. LIFO.

Show the number of units and the unit costs of each layer comprising the *ending inventory.* You may determine the cost of goods sold by deducting ending inventory from the cost of goods available for sale.

b. If Sea Travel uses the LIFO cost flow assumption for income tax purposes, can it use the FIFO method for financial reporting purposes? Explain.

LO1 through LO3 **PROBLEM 8.4B**

Year-End Adjustments; Shrinkage Losses and LCM

Sam's Lawn Mowers uses a perpetual inventory system. At December 31, the perpetual inventory records indicate the following quantities of a particular mower.

	Quantity	Unit Cost	Total Cost
First purchase (oldest)	80	$100	$ 8,000
Second purchase	100	110	11,000
Third purchase	20	120	2,400
Total	200		$21,400

A year-end physical inventory, however, shows only 199 of these lawn mowers on hand.

In its financial statements, Sam's values its inventories at the lower-of-cost-or-market. At year-end, the per-unit replacement cost of this particular model is $125.

Instructions

Prepare the journal entries required to adjust the inventory records at year-end assuming that:

a. Sam's uses:

1. Average cost.
2. Last-in, first-out.

b. Sam's uses the first-in, first-out method. However, the replacement cost of the lawn mowers at year-end is $90 apiece, rather than the $125 stated originally. Make separate journal entries to record (1) the shrinkage loss and (2) the restatement of the inventory at a market value lower than cost. Record the shrinkage loss first.

c. Assume that the company had been experiencing monthly inventory shrinkage of one to four lawn mowers for several months. In response, management placed several hidden security cameras throughout the premises. Within days, an employee was caught on film loading lawn mowers into his pickup truck. The employee's attorney asked that the case be dropped because the company had "unethically used a hidden camera to entrap his client." Do you agree with the attorney? Defend your answer.

LO4 **PROBLEM 8.5B**

Periodic Inventory Costing Procedures

Roman Sound uses a periodic inventory system. One of the store's products is a wireless headphone. The inventory quantities, purchases, and sales of this product for the most recent year are as follows:

	Number of Units	Cost per Unit	Total Cost
Inventory, Jan. 1	10	$100	$ 1,000
First purchase	30	101	3,030
Second purchase	40	104	4,160
Third purchase	5	106	530
Fourth purchase	15	110	1,650
Goods available for sale	100		$10,370
Units sold during the year	80		
Inventory, Dec. 31	20		

Instructions

a. Using *periodic* costing procedures, compute the cost of the December 31 inventory and the cost of goods sold for the year under each of the following cost assumptions:

1. First-in, first-out.

2. Last-in, first-out.

3. Average cost (round to the nearest dollar, except unit cost).

b. Which of the three inventory pricing methods provides the most realistic balance sheet valuation of inventory in light of the current replacement cost of these headphones? Does this same method also produce the most realistic measure of income in light of the costs being incurred by Roman Sound to replace these units when they are sold? Explain.

LO5 **PROBLEM 8.6B**

Effects of Inventory Errors on Earnings

The owners of City Software are offering the business for sale. The income statements of the business for the three years of its existence are summarized below.

	2011	2010	2009
Net sales	$1,000,000	$920,000	$840,000
Cost of goods sold	600,000	570,400	546,000
Gross profit on sales	$ 400,000	$349,600	$294,000
Gross profit percentage	40%	38%	35%

In negotiations with prospective buyers of the business, the owners are calling attention to the rising trends of the gross profit and the gross profit percentage as very favorable elements.

Assume that you are retained by a prospective purchaser of the business to make an investigation of the fairness and reliability of the enterprise's accounting records and financial statements. You find everything in order except for the following: (1) An arithmetic error in the computation of inventory at the end of 2009 has caused a $20,000 understatement in that inventory, and (2) an error in the computation of inventory at the end of 2011 has caused an overstatement of $80,000 in that inventory. The company uses the periodic inventory system, and these errors have not been brought to light prior to your investigation.

Instructions

a. Prepare a revised three-year partial income statement summary.

b. Comment on the trends of gross profit and gross profit percentage before and after the revision.

LO2 LO3 LO6

PROBLEM 8.7B
Retail Method

Sing Along is a popular music store. During the current year, the company's cost of goods available for sale amounted to $330,000. The retail sales value of this merchandise amounted to $600,000. Sales for the year were $520,000.

Instructions

a. Using the retail method, estimate (1) the cost of goods sold during the year and (2) the inventory at the end of the year.

b. At year-end, Sing Along takes a physical inventory. The general manager walks through the store counting each type of product and reading its retail price into a tape recorder. From the recorded information, another employee prepares a schedule listing the entire ending inventory at retail sales prices. The schedule prepared for the current year reports ending inventory of $75,000 at retail sales prices.

   1. Use the cost ratio computed in part **a** to reduce the inventory counted by the general manager from its retail value to an estimate of its cost.
   2. Determine the estimated shrinkage losses (measured at cost) incurred by Sing Along during the year.
   3. Compute Sing Along's gross profit for the year. (Include inventory shrinkage losses in the cost of goods sold.)

c. What controls might Sing Along implement to reduce inventory shrinkage?

LO1 LO7

PROBLEM 8.8B
FIFO versus LIFO Comparisons

JC Penney Company uses LIFO in applying the lower-of-cost-or-market. Recent financial statements were used to compile the following information (dollar figures in millions):

Average inventory (throughout the year)	$ 3,142
Current assets (at year-end)	6,652
Current liabilities (at year-end)	3,249
Net sales	17,556
Cost of goods sold	10,646
Gross profit	6,910
Average time required to collect outstanding receivables (approximate)	5 days

Instructions

a. Using the information provided, compute the following measures based upon the *LIFO* method:

   1. Inventory turnover.
   2. Current ratio (see Chapter 5 for a discussion of this ratio).
   3. Gross profit rate (see Chapter 6 for a discussion of this statistic).

b. Assuming the cost of goods sold would be lower under FIFO, what circumstances must the company have encountered to cause this situation? (Were replacement costs, on average, rising or falling?)

c. How would you expect these ratios to differ (i.e., what direction) had the company used FIFO instead of LIFO?

d. Explain why the average number of days required by **JC Penney** to collect its accounts receivable is so low. (See Chapter 7 for a discussion of the accounts receivable turnover.)

Critical Thinking Cases

LO5 **CASE 8.1**

It's Not Right, but at Least It's Consistent

Our Little Secret is a small manufacturer of swimsuits and other beach apparel. The company is closely held and has no external reporting obligations, other than payroll reports and income tax returns. The company's accounting system is grossly inadequate. Accounting records are maintained by clerical employees with little knowledge of accounting and with many other job responsibilities. Management has decided that the company must hire a competent controller, who can establish and oversee an adequate accounting system.

Amy Lee, CPA, has applied for this position. During a recent interview, Dean Frost, the company's director of personnel, said, "Amy, the job is yours. But you should know that we have a big inventory problem here.

"For some time now, it appears that we have been understating our ending inventory in income tax returns. No one knows when this all got started, or who was responsible. We never even counted our inventory until a few months ago. But the problem is pretty big. In our latest tax return—that's for 2010—we listed inventory at only about half its actual cost. That's an understatement of, maybe, $400,000.

"We don't know what to do. We sure don't want a big scandal—tax evasion, and all that. Maybe the best thing is to continue understating inventory by the same amount as we did in 2010. That way, taxable income will be correctly stated in future years. Anyway, this is just something I thought you should know about."

Instructions

a. Briefly identify the ethical issues raised for Lee by Frost's disclosure.

b. From Lee's perspective, evaluate the possible solution proposed by Frost.

c. Identify and discuss the alternative ethical courses of action that are open to Lee.

LO4 **CASE 8.2**

LIFO Liquidation

Jackson Specialties has been in business for more than 50 years. The company maintains a perpetual inventory system, uses a LIFO flow assumption, and ends its fiscal year at December 31. At year-end, the cost of goods sold and inventory are adjusted to reflect periodic LIFO costing procedures.

A railroad strike has delayed the arrival of purchases ordered during the past several months of 2011, and Jackson Specialties has not been able to replenish its inventories as merchandise is sold. At December 22, one product appears in the company's perpetual inventory records at the following unit costs:

Purchase Date	Quantity	Unit Cost	Total Cost
Nov. 14, 1958	3,000	$6	$18,000
Apr. 12, 1959	2,000	8	16,000
Available for sale at Dec. 22, 2011	5,000		$34,000

Jackson Specialties has another 8,000 units of this product on order at the current wholesale cost of $30 per unit. Because of the railroad strike, however, these units have not yet arrived (the terms of purchase are F.O.B. destination). Jackson Specialties also has an order from a customer who wants to purchase 4,000 units of this product at the retail sales price of $47 per unit. Jackson Specialties intends to make this sale on December 30, regardless of whether the 8,000 units on order arrive by this date. (The 4,000-unit sale will be shipped by truck, F.O.B. shipping point.)

Instructions

a. Are the units in inventory really more than 50 years old? Explain.

b. Prepare a schedule showing the sales revenue, cost of goods sold, and gross profit that will result from this sale on December 30, assuming that the 8,000 units currently on order (1) arrive before year-end and (2) do not arrive until some time in the following year. (In each computation, show the number of units comprising the cost of goods sold and their related per-unit costs.)

c. Comment on these results.

d. Might management be wise to delay this sale by a few days? Explain.

LO3 CASE 8.3
Dealing with the Bank

Avery Frozen Foods owes the bank $50,000 on a line of credit. Terms of the agreement specify that Avery must maintain a minimum current ratio of 1.2 to 1, or the entire outstanding balance becomes immediately due in full. To date, the company has complied with the minimum requirement. However, management has just learned that a failed warehouse freezer has ruined thousands of dollars of frozen foods inventory. If the company records this loss, its current ratio will drop to approximately 0.8 to 1.

Whether any or all of this loss may be covered by insurance currently is in dispute and will not be known for at least 90 days—perhaps much longer. There are several reasons why the insurance company may have no liability.

In trying to decide how to deal with the bank, management is considering the following options: (1) postpone recording the inventory loss until the dispute with the insurance company is resolved, (2) increase the current ratio to 1.2 to 1 by making a large purchase of inventory on account, (3) explain to the bank what has happened, and request that it be flexible until things get back to normal.

Instructions

a. Given that the company hopes for at least partial reimbursement from the insurance company, is it really unethical for management to postpone recording the inventory loss in the financial statements it submits to the bank?

b. Is it possible to increase the company's current ratio from 0.8 to 1 to 1.2 to 1 by purchasing more inventory on account? Explain.

c. What approach do you think the company should follow in dealing with the bank?

LO7 INTERNET CASE 8.4
Inventory Turnover

A company's inventory turnover is one measure of its potential to convert inventory into cash. But what is considered a good inventory turnover? The answer to that question depends on a variety of industry and company characteristics.

Access the EDGAR database at the following Internet address:

www.sec.gov

Locate the most recent 10-K reports of **Safeway, Inc.**, and **Staples, Inc.** Compute the inventory turnover of each company. Does the higher turnover computed for **Safeway** mean that the company manages its inventory more effectively than **Staples**? Explain.

Internet sites are time and date sensitive. It is the purpose of these exercises to have you explore the Internet. You may need to use the Yahoo! search engine http://www.yahoo.com *(or another favorite search engine) to find a company's current Web address.*

Answers to Self-Test Questions

1. b **2.** a, c, d **3.** a **4.** b **5.** b **6.** a, d

COMPREHENSIVE PROBLEM 2

Guitar Universe, Inc.

Guitar Universe, Inc., is a popular source of musical instruments for professional and amateur musicians. The company's accountants make necessary adjusting entries *monthly,* and they make all closing entries *annually*. Guitar Universe is growing rapidly and prides itself on having no long-term liabilities.

The company has provided the following *trial balance* dated *December 31, 2011:*

GUITAR UNIVERSE, INC. TRIAL BALANCE DECEMBER 31, 2011		
Cash	$ 45,000	
Marketable securities	25,000	
Accounts receivable	125,000	
Allowance for doubtful accounts		$ 5,000
Merchandise inventory	250,000	
Office supplies	1,200	
Prepaid insurance	6,600	
Building and fixtures	1,791,000	
Accumulated depreciation		800,000
Land	64,800	
Accounts payable		70,000
Unearned customer deposits		8,000
Income taxes payable		75,000
Capital stock		1,000,000
Retained earnings		240,200
Unrealized holding gain on investments		6,000
Sales		1,600,000
Cost of goods sold	958,000	
Bank service charges	200	
Uncollectible accounts expense	9,000	
Salary and wages expense	395,000	
Office supplies expense	400	
Insurance expense	6,400	
Utilities expense	3,600	
Depreciation expense	48,000	
Income tax expense	75,000	
	$3,804,200	$3,804,200

Other information pertaining to Guitar Universe's trial balance is shown below:

1. The company's most recent bank statement reports a balance of $46,975. Included with the bank statement was a $2,500 check from Iggy Bates, a professional musician, charged back to Guitar Universe as NSF. The bank's monthly service charge was $25. Three checks written by Guitar Universe to suppliers of merchandise inventory had not yet cleared the bank for payment as of the statement date. These checks included: no. 507, $4,000; no. 511, $9,000; and no. 521, $8,000. Deposits made by Guitar Universe of $16,500 had reached the bank too late for inclusion in the current statement. The company prepares a bank reconciliation at the end of each month.
2. Guitar Universe has a portfolio of marketable securities. The initial investment in the portfolio was $19,000. As of December 31, the market value of these securities was $27,500. Management classifies all short-term investments as "available for sale."
3. During December, $6,400 of accounts receivable were written off as uncollectible. A recent aging of the company's accounts receivable helped management to conclude that an allowance for doubtful accounts of $8,500 was needed at December 31, 2011.

4. The company uses a perpetual inventory system. A year-end physical count revealed that several guitars reported in the inventory records were missing. The cost of the missing units amounted to $1,350. This amount is not considered significant relative to the total cost of inventory on hand.
5. At December 31, approximately $900 in office supplies remained on hand.
6. The company pays for its insurance policies 12 months in advance. Its most recent payment was made on November 1, 2011. The cost of this policy was slightly higher than the cost of coverage for the previous 12 months.
7. Depreciation expense related to the company's building and fixtures is $5,000 for the month ending December 31, 2011.
8. Although Guitar Universe carries an extensive inventory, it is not uncommon for musicians to order custom guitars made to their exact specifications. Manufacturers do not allow any sales returns of custom-made guitars. Thus, all customers must pay in advance for these special orders. The entire sales amount is collected at the time a custom order is placed, and it is credited to an account entitled "Unearned Customer Deposits." As of December 31, $4,800 of these deposits remained unearned. Assume that the cost of goods sold and the reduction in inventory associated with all custom orders is recorded when the custom merchandise is delivered to customers. Thus, the adjusting entry requires only a decrease to unearned customer deposits and an increase to sales.
9. Accrued income taxes payable for the *entire year ending* December 31, 2011, total $81,000. No income tax payments are due until early in 2012.

Instructions

a. Prepare a bank reconciliation and make the necessary journal entries to update the accounting records of Guitar Universe as of December 31, 2011.

b. Prepare the necessary adjusting entry to update the company's marketable securities portfolio to its mark-to-market value.

c. Prepare the adjusting entry at December 31, 2011, to report the company's accounts receivable at their net realizable value.

d. Prepare the entry to account for the guitars missing from the company's inventory at the end of the year.

e. Prepare the adjusting entry to account for the office supplies used during December.

f. Prepare the adjusting entry to account for the expiration of the company's insurance policies during December.

g. Prepare the adjusting entry to account for the depreciation of the company's building and fixtures during December.

h. Prepare the adjusting entry to report the portion of unearned customer deposits that were earned during December.

i. Prepare the adjusting entry to account for income tax expense that accrued during December.

j. On the basis of the adjustments made to the accounting records in parts **a** through **i** above, prepare the company's adjusted trial balance at December 31, 2011.

k. Using the adjusted trial balance prepared in part **j** above, prepare an *annual* income statement, statement of retained earnings, and a balance sheet dated December 31, 2011.

l. Using the financial statements prepared in part **k** above, determine approximately how many days an account receivable remains outstanding before it is collected. You may assume that the company's ending accounts receivable balance on December 31 is a close approximation of its average accounts receivable balance throughout the year.

m. Using the financial statements prepared in part **k,** determine approximately how many days an item of merchandise remains in stock before it is sold. You may assume that the company's ending merchandise inventory balance on December 31 is a close approximation of its average merchandise inventory balance throughout the year.

n. Using the financial statements prepared in part **k,** determine approximately how many days it takes to convert the company's inventory into cash. Stated differently, what is the length of the company's operating cycle?

o. Comment briefly upon the company's financial condition from the perspective of a short-term creditor.

CHAPTER 9

Plant and Intangible Assets

United Parcel Service of America, Inc.

Learning Objectives

AFTER STUDYING THIS CHAPTER, YOU SHOULD BE ABLE TO:

LO1 Determine the cost of plant assets.

LO2 Distinguish between capital expenditures and revenue expenditures.

LO3 Compute depreciation by the straight-line and declining-balance methods.

LO4 Account for depreciation using methods other than straight-line or declining-balance.

LO5 Account for the disposal of plant assets.

LO6 Explain the nature of intangible assets, including goodwill.

LO7 Account for the depletion of natural resources.

LO8 Explain the cash effects of transactions involving plant assets.

UNITED PARCEL SERVICE

What kind of plant and intangible assets would you expect United Parcel Service to have? Probably the first thing you would think of is vehicles, primarily trucks, because you are used to seeing UPS trucks on the streets and highways virtually every day. In addition, UPS has a very large investment in aircraft. In fact, property, plant, and equipment make up over 56 percent of UPS's total assets ($17,979 of $31,883 million), according to the company's 2009 consolidated balance sheet. Of the $17,979 million, aircraft is the largest single type of asset and another large category is vehicles.

How do the amount of plant assets and percentage of plant assets to total assets for UPS compare with other companies? These amounts vary considerably from company to company as evidenced by the following examples:

Intel—$17,225 million or 32 percent of total assets; Kimberly-Clark—$8,033 million or 42 percent of total assets; Carnival Corporation—$29,870 or 81 percent of total assets.

Plant assets are important for a company such as United Parcel Service to be successful in its daily operations. The exact types and amount of plant assets used by a particular company depend on the nature of the company and its operations. Virtually all companies need some type of plant assets to operate efficiently and be successful. In addition, some companies require certain intangible assets to do business. Intangibles are rights and privileges that have been developed or acquired, such as trade names and patents; these may be as important to a business as its equipment, buildings, and land. ■

In earlier chapters, we introduced the idea of plant assets and depreciation and stressed the importance of such assets to the successful functioning of businesses. In this chapter, we explore in greater depth the accounting issues surrounding plant assets and discuss intangible assets. Together, plant and intangible assets make up a significant part of corporate balance sheets because they represent major investments of resources. The future of many business enterprises depends on their investment in plant and intangible assets.

PLANT ASSETS AS A "STREAM OF FUTURE SERVICES"

Plant assets represent a bundle of future services and, thus, can be thought of as long-term prepaid expenses. Ownership of a delivery truck, for example, may provide about 100,000 miles of transportation. The cost of the truck is entered in an asset account, which in essence represents the *advance purchase* of these transportation services. Similarly, a building represents the advance purchase of many years of housing services. As the years go by, these services are utilized by the business, and the cost of the plant asset gradually is transferred to depreciation expense to reflect the cost of using the asset to generate revenue.

MAJOR CATEGORIES OF PLANT ASSETS

Plant and equipment items are often classified into the following groups:

1. **Tangible plant assets.** The term *tangible* refers to an asset's physical characteristics, as exemplified by land, a building, or a machine. This category may be further separated into two distinct classifications:
   a. *Property subject to depreciation.* Included are plant assets of limited useful life such as buildings and office equipment.
   b. *Land.* The only plant asset not subject to depreciation is land, which has an unlimited term of existence and whose usefulness does not decline over time.
2. **Intangible assets.** The term *intangible assets* is used to describe assets that are used in the operation of the business but have no physical characteristics and are noncurrent. Examples include patents, copyrights, trademarks, franchises, and goodwill. Current assets such as accounts receivable or prepaid rent are not included in the intangible classification, even though they also are lacking in physical substance.
3. **Natural resources.** A site acquired for the purpose of extracting or removing some valuable resource such as oil, minerals, or timber is classified as a *natural resource,* not as land. This type of plant asset is gradually converted into *inventory* as the natural resource is extracted from the site.

ACCOUNTABLE EVENTS IN THE LIVES OF PLANT ASSETS

For all categories of plant assets, there are three primary *accountable events:* (1) acquisition, (2) allocation of the acquisition cost to expense over the asset's useful life (depreciation), and (3) sale or disposal.

Acquisitions of Plant Assets

Learning Objective
LO1 Determine the cost of plant assets.

The cost of a **plant asset** includes all expenditures that are *reasonable* and *necessary* for getting the asset to the desired location and *ready for use.* Thus many incidental costs may be included in the cost assigned to a plant asset. These include, for example, sales taxes on the purchase price, delivery costs, and installation costs.

Only reasonable and necessary costs should be included. Assume, for example, that a machine is dropped and damaged while it is being unloaded. The cost of repairing this damage should be recognized as an expense of the current period, *not* added to the cost of the machine. Although it is necessary to repair the machine, it was not necessary to drop it—and that's what brought about the need for the repairs.

Companies often purchase plant assets on an installment plan or by issuing a note payable. Interest charges after the asset is ready for use are recorded as interest expense, not as part of the cost of the asset. But if a company constructs a plant asset for its own use, the interest charges *during the construction period* are viewed as part of the asset's cost.

DETERMINING COST: AN EXAMPLE

The concept of including in the cost of a plant asset all of the incidental charges necessary to put the asset in use is illustrated by the following example. A factory in Mississippi orders a machine from a Colorado tool manufacturer at a list price of $10,000. Payment will be made in 48 monthly installments of $250, which include $2,000 in interest charges. Sales taxes of $600 must be paid, as well as freight charges of $1,350. Installation and other set-up costs amount to $500. The cost of this machine to be established in the Machinery account is computed as follows:

List price*	$10,000
Sales taxes	600
Transportation charges	1,350
Cost of installation and set-up	500
Total	$12,450

All reasonable and necessary costs are capitalized

*The $2,000 in interest charges on the installment purchase will be recognized as interest expense over the next 48 months. (Accounting for installment notes payable is discussed in the next chapter.)

SOME SPECIAL CONSIDERATIONS

Land When land is purchased, various incidental costs are often incurred in addition to the purchase price. These additional costs may include commissions to real estate brokers, escrow fees, legal fees for examining and insuring the title, delinquent taxes paid by the purchaser, and fees for surveying, draining, clearing, and grading the property. All these expenditures become part of the cost of the land.

Sometimes land purchased as a building site has on it an old building that is not suitable for the buyer's use. In this case, the only useful asset being acquired is the land. Therefore, the entire purchase price is charged to the Land account, as well as the costs of tearing down and removing the unusable building.

Land Improvements Improvements to real estate such as driveways, fences, parking lots, landscaping, and sprinkler systems have a limited life and are therefore subject to depreciation. For this reason, they should be recorded in a separate account entitled Land Improvements.

Buildings Buildings are sometimes purchased with the intention of remodeling them prior to placing them in use. Costs incurred under these circumstances are charged to the Buildings account. After the building has been placed in use, however, ordinary repairs are considered to be maintenance expense when incurred.

Equipment When equipment is purchased, all of the sales taxes, delivery costs, and costs of getting the equipment in good running order are treated as part of the cost of the asset. Once the equipment has been placed in operation, maintenance costs (including interest, insurance, and property taxes) are treated as expenses of the current period.

Allocation of a Lump-Sum Purchase Several different types of plant assets may be purchased at one time. Separate control accounts are maintained for each type of plant asset, such as land, buildings, and equipment.[1]

[1] Each control account is supported by a subsidiary ledger providing information about the cost, annual depreciation, and book value of each asset (or group of similar assets).

When land and buildings (and perhaps other assets) are purchased for a lump sum, the purchase price must be *allocated* among the types of assets acquired. An appraisal may be needed for this purpose. Assume, for example, that Exercise-for-Health, Inc., purchases a complete fitness center from Golden Health Spas. Exercise-for-Health purchases the entire facility at a bargain price of $800,000. The allocation of this cost on the basis of an appraisal is illustrated as follows:

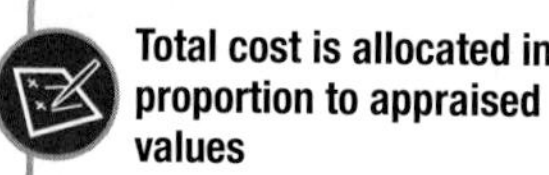

Total cost is allocated in proportion to appraised values

	Value per Appraisal	Percentage of Total Appraised Value	Allocation of $800,000 Cost
Land	$ 250,000	25%	$200,000
Land improvements	50,000	5	40,000
Building	300,000	30	240,000
Equipment	400,000	40	320,000
Total	$1,000,000	100%	$800,000

Assuming that Exercise-for-Health purchased this facility for cash, the journal entry to record this acquisition would be:

The journal entry allocating the total cost

Land	200,000	
Land Improvements	40,000	
Building	240,000	
Equipment	320,000	
Cash		800,000
To record purchase of fitness center from Golden Health Spas for cash.		

YOUR TURN **You as the New Facility Manager for Exercise-for-Health**

Assume you have been hired as manager of the new Golden Health Spas facility that was recently purchased by Exercise-for-Health. One of your responsibilities as manager is to show that the facility is profitable. In fact, your contract specifies a bonus if the profits are at least 10 percent above the budgeted amount each year. In a recent conversation with the appraiser, it becomes clear to you that some of the items classified as land in the appraisal were really building improvements. No one at Exercise-for-Health is aware of this misclassification. As a result, the appraised value for the building asset account should be $350,000 instead of $300,000. When budgeted profits for the Golden Health Spas facility are computed each year, a charge for depreciation on the building is deducted from the profits. What impact does the improper appraisal have on your ability to achieve the bonus? What should you do?

(See our comments on the Online Learning Center Web site.)

Learning Objective
LO2 Distinguish between capital expenditures and revenue expenditures.

CAPITAL EXPENDITURES AND REVENUE EXPENDITURES

Expenditures for the purchase or expansion of plant assets are called **capital expenditures** and are recorded in asset accounts. Accountants often use the verb **capitalize** to mean charging an expenditure to an asset account rather than to an expense account. Expenditures for ordinary repairs, maintenance, fuel, and other items necessary to the ownership and use of plant and equipment are called **revenue expenditures** and are recorded in expense accounts. The charge to an expense account is based on the assumption that the benefits from the expenditure will be used up in the current period, and therefore the cost should be deducted from the revenue of the period in determining the net income. Charging an expenditure directly to an expense account is often called "expensing" the item.

A business may purchase many small items that will benefit several accounting periods but that have a relatively low cost. Examples of such items include auto batteries, wastebaskets, and pencil sharpeners. Such items are theoretically capital expenditures, but if they are recorded as assets in the accounting records, it will be necessary to compute and record the related depreciation expense in future periods. We have previously mentioned the idea that the extra work involved in developing more precise accounting information should be weighed against the benefits that result. Thus, for reasons of convenience and economy, expenditures that are *not material* in dollar amount are treated in the accounting records as expenses of the current period.

In brief, any material expenditure that will benefit several accounting periods is considered a *capital expenditure*. Any expenditure that will benefit only the current period or that is not material in amount is treated as a *revenue expenditure*.

Many companies develop formal policies defining capital and revenue expenditures as a guide toward consistent accounting practice from year to year. These policy statements often set a minimum dollar amount (such as $500) for expenditures that are to be capitalized.

Depreciation

We first introduced the concept of depreciation in Chapter 4. Now we expand that discussion to address such topics as residual values and alternative depreciation methods.

ALLOCATING THE COST OF PLANT AND EQUIPMENT OVER THE YEARS OF USE

Tangible plant assets, with the exception of land, are of use to a company for only a limited number of years. **Depreciation,** as the term is used in accounting, is the *allocation of the cost of a tangible plant asset to expense in the periods in which services are received from the asset.* The basic purpose of depreciation is to offset the revenue of an accounting period with the costs of the goods and services being consumed in the effort to generate that revenue. (See Exhibit 9–1.)

Earlier in this chapter, we described a delivery truck as a stream of transportation services to be received over the years that the truck is owned and used. The cost of the truck initially is added to an asset account, because the purchase of these transportation services will benefit several future accounting periods. As these services are received, however, the cost of the truck gradually is removed from the balance sheet and becomes an expense, through the process of depreciation.

Depreciation: a process of allocating the cost of an asset to expense over the asset's useful life

Exhibit 9–1 THE DEPRECIATION PROCESS

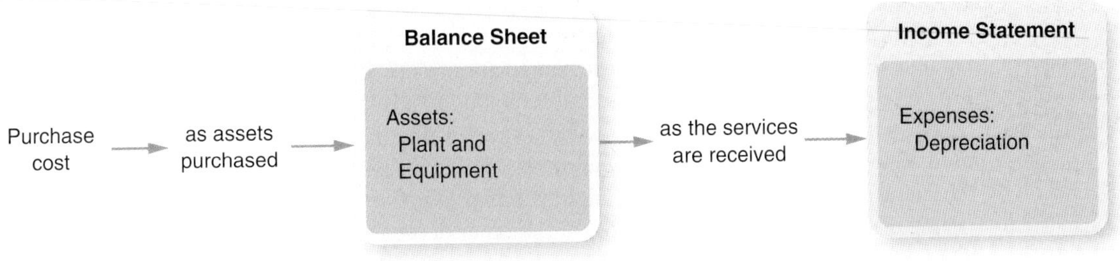

The journal entry to record depreciation expense consists of a debit to Depreciation Expense and a credit to Accumulated Depreciation. The credit portion of the entry removes from the balance sheet that portion of the asset's cost estimated to have been used up during the current period. The debit portion of the entry allocates this expired cost to expense.

Separate Depreciation Expense and Accumulated Depreciation accounts are maintained for different types of depreciable assets, such as factory buildings, delivery equipment, and office equipment. These separate accounts help accountants to measure separately the costs of different business activities, such as manufacturing, sales, and administration.

Depreciation Is Not a Process of Valuation Depreciation is a process of *cost allocation,* not a process of asset valuation. Accounting records do not attempt to show the current market values of plant assets. The market value of a building, for example, may increase during some accounting periods within the building's useful life. The recognition of depreciation expense continues, however, without regard to such temporary increases in market value. Accountants recognize that the building will render useful services only for a limited number of years and that the full cost of the building should be *systematically allocated to expense* during these years.

Depreciation differs from most other expenses in that it does not depend on cash payments at or near the time the expense is recorded. For this reason, depreciation often is called a "non-cash" expense. Bear in mind, however, that large cash payments usually are required at the time depreciable assets are purchased.

Book Value Plant assets are shown in the balance sheet at their book values (or *carrying values*). The **book value** of a plant asset is its *cost minus the related accumulated depreciation*. Accumulated depreciation is a contra-asset account, representing that portion of the asset's cost that has *already* been allocated to expense. Thus, book value represents the portion of the asset's cost that remains to be allocated to expense in future periods.

CAUSES OF DEPRECIATION

The need to systematically allocate plant asset costs over multiple accounting periods arises from two major causes: (1) physical deterioration and (2) obsolescence.

Physical Deterioration Physical deterioration of a plant asset results from use, as well as from exposure to sun, wind, and other climatic factors. When a plant asset has been carefully maintained, it is not uncommon for the owner to claim that the asset is as "good as new." Such statements are not literally true. Although a good repair policy may lengthen the useful life of a machine, every machine eventually reaches the point at which it must be discarded. Making repairs does not eliminate the need for recognition of depreciation.

Obsolescence The term *obsolescence* means the process of becoming out of date because improved, more efficient assets become available. An airplane, for example, may become obsolete even though it is in excellent physical condition; it becomes obsolete because better planes of superior design and performance become available.

METHODS OF COMPUTING DEPRECIATION

Learning Objective LO3 Compute depreciation by the straight-line and declining-balance methods.

In Chapter 4, we computed depreciation only by the **straight-line depreciation** method. Companies actually may use several depreciation methods. Generally accepted accounting principles require only that a depreciation method result in a *rational and systematic* allocation of cost over the asset's useful life. The straight-line method is by far the most commonly used depreciation method for financial reporting purposes.

The straight-line method allocates an *equal portion* of depreciation expense to each period of the asset's useful life. Most of the other depreciation methods are various forms of accelerated depreciation. The term **accelerated depreciation** means that larger amounts of depreciation are recognized in the early years of the asset's life, and smaller amounts are recognized in the later years. Over the entire life of the asset, however, both the straight-line method and accelerated methods recognize the same *total* amount of depreciation.

The differences between the straight-line method and accelerated methods are illustrated in Exhibit 9–2.

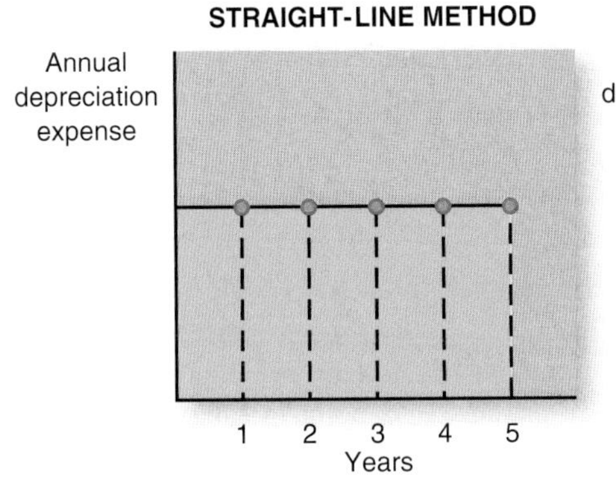

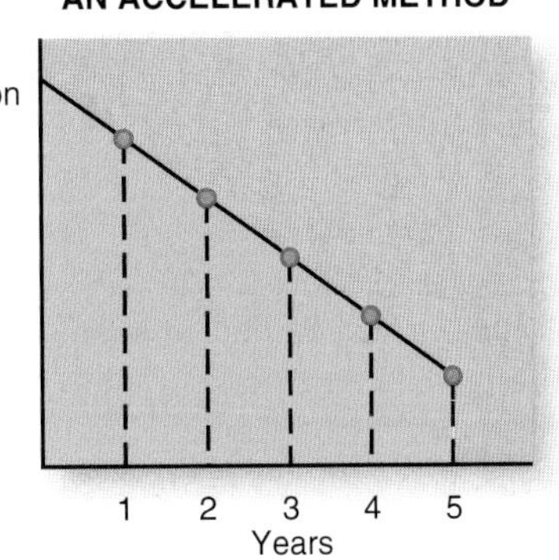

Exhibit 9–2

STRAIGHT-LINE AND ACCELERATED DEPRECIATION METHODS

Both methods recognize the same total depreciation

There are several accelerated methods, each producing slightly different results. Different depreciation methods may be used for different assets. The depreciation methods in use should be disclosed in notes accompanying the financial statements.

In this section, we illustrate and explain straight-line depreciation and one variation of the most widely used accelerated method, which is called *fixed-percentage-of-declining-balance,* or simply the *declining-balance* method. Other depreciation methods are discussed briefly in the section that follows.

© David Young Wolff/PhotoEdit

Data for Our Illustrations Our illustrations of depreciation methods are based on the following data: On January 2, S&G Wholesale Grocery acquires a new delivery truck. The data and estimates needed for the computation of the annual depreciation expense are:

Cost	$17,000
Estimated residual value	$ 2,000
Estimated useful life	5 years

THE STRAIGHT-LINE METHOD

Under the straight-line method, an *equal portion* of the asset's cost is recognized as depreciation expense in each period of the asset's useful life. Annual depreciation expense is computed by deducting the estimated **residual value** (or **salvage value**) from the cost of the asset and dividing the remaining *depreciable cost* by the years of estimated useful life. Using the data in our example, the annual straight-line depreciation is computed as follows:

$$\frac{\textbf{Cost} - \textbf{Residual Value}}{\textbf{Years of Useful Life}} = \frac{\$17{,}000 - \$2{,}000}{5\ \textbf{years}} = \$3{,}000\ \textbf{per year}$$

In Exhibit 9–3, the schedule summarizes the effects of straight-line depreciation over the entire life of the asset.

Exhibit 9–3

STRAIGHT-LINE DEPRECIATION SCHEDULE

Depreciation Schedule: Straight-Line Method

Year	Computation	Depreciation Expense	Accumulated Depreciation	Book Value
				$17,000
First	$15,000 × ⅕	$ 3,000	$ 3,000	14,000
Second	15,000 × ⅕	3,000	6,000	11,000
Third	15,000 × ⅕	3,000	9,000	8,000
Fourth	15,000 × ⅕	3,000	12,000	5,000
Fifth	15,000 × ⅕	3,000	15,000	2,000
Total		$15,000		

(We present several depreciation schedules in this chapter. In each schedule we highlight in red those features that we want to emphasize.)

The term "book value" in Exhibit 9–3 is the amount of the depreciable cost of the asset that has not yet been recognized as depreciation expense at a point in time. For example, book value at the end of the third year after depreciation for that year has been recognized is $8,000, computed as follows:

Cost	$17,000
Accumulated depreciation at end of third year	(9,000)
Book value	$ 8,000

Notice that the depreciation expense over the life of the truck totals *$15,000*—the cost of the truck *minus the estimated residual value.* The residual value is *not* part of the cost "used up" in business operations. Instead, the residual value is expected to be recovered in cash upon disposal of the asset.

In practice, residual values may be ignored if they are not expected to be *material* in amount. Office equipment, furniture, fixtures, and special-purpose equipment seldom are considered to have significant residual values. Assets such as vehicles, aircraft, and construction equipment, in contrast, often do have residual values that are material in amount.

It often is convenient to state the portion of an asset's depreciable cost that will be written off during the year as a percentage, called the *depreciation rate.* When straight-line depreciation is in use, the depreciation rate is simply *1* divided by the *life* (in years) of the asset. The delivery truck in our example has an estimated life of 5 years, so the depreciation expense each year is ⅕, or 20 percent, of the depreciable amount. Similarly, an asset with a 10-year life has a depreciation rate of ⅒, or 10 percent; and an asset with an 8-year life, a depreciation rate of ⅛, or 12½ percent.

Depreciation for Fractional Periods When an asset is acquired during an accounting period, it is not necessary to compute depreciation expense to the nearest day or week. In fact, such a computation would give a misleading impression of great precision. Since depreciation is based on an estimated useful life of many years, the depreciation applicable to any one year is *only an approximation.*

One widely used method of computing depreciation for part of a year is to round the calculation to the nearest whole month. In our example, S&G acquired the delivery truck on January 2. Therefore, we computed a full year's depreciation for the year of acquisition. Assume, however, that the truck had been acquired later in the year on *October 1.* Thus the truck would have been in use for only 3 months (or 3⁄12) of the first year. In this case, depreciation expense for the first year would be only *$750,* or 3⁄12 of a full year's depreciation ($3,000 × 3⁄12 = $750).

Another widely used approach, called the **half-year convention,** is to record one-half year's depreciation on all assets acquired during the year. This approach is based on the assumption that the actual purchase dates will average out to approximately midyear. The half-year convention is widely used for assets such as office equipment, automobiles, and machinery. To complete the depreciation process for an asset by the half-year convention, a one-half-year's depreciation is also taken in the last year of the asset's life.

Assume that S&G Wholesale Grocery uses straight-line depreciation with the half-year convention. In Exhibit 9–4, we summarize depreciation on the $17,000 delivery truck with the 5-year life.

Exhibit 9–4

STRAIGHT-LINE DEPRECIATION SCHEDULE

Depreciation Schedule
Straight-Line Method with Half-Year Convention

Year	Computation	Depreciation Expense	Accumulated Depreciation	Book Value
				$17,000
First	$15,000 × ⅕ × ½	$ 1,500	$ 1,500	15,500
Second	15,000 × ⅕	3,000	4,500	12,500
Third	15,000 × ⅕	3,000	7,500	9,500
Fourth	15,000 × ⅕	3,000	10,500	6,500
Fifth	15,000 × ⅕	3,000	13,500	3,500
Sixth	15,000 × ⅕ × ½	1,500	15,000	2,000
Total		$15,000		

When the half-year convention is in use, we ignore the date on which the asset was actually purchased. We simply recognize *one-half year's depreciation* in both the first year and the last year of the depreciation schedule. Notice that our depreciation schedule now includes depreciation expense in the sixth year. Taking only a partial year's depreciation in the first year always extends the recognition of depreciation into one additional year.

The half-year convention enables us to treat similar assets acquired at different dates during the year as a single group. For example, assume that an insurance company purchases hundreds of desktop computers throughout the current year at a total cost of $600,000. The company depreciates these computers by the straight-line method, assuming a 5-year life and no residual value. Using the half-year convention, the depreciation expense on all of the computers purchased during the year may be computed as follows: $600,000 ÷ 5 years × 6/12 = $60,000. If we did not use the half-year convention, depreciation would have to be computed separately for computers purchased in different months.

THE DECLINING-BALANCE METHOD

The most widely used accelerated depreciation method is called **fixed-percentage-of-declining-balance depreciation.** However, the method is used primarily in *income tax returns,* rather than financial statements.[2]

Under the declining-balance method, an accelerated *depreciation rate* is computed as a specified percentage of the straight-line depreciation rate. Annual depreciation expense then is computed by applying this accelerated depreciation rate to the undepreciated cost (book value) of the asset. This computation may be summarized as follows:

$$\textbf{Depreciation Expense} = \textbf{Remaining Book Value} \times \textbf{Accelerated Depreciation Rate}$$

[2] In 1986, Congress adopted an accelerated method of depreciation called the *Modified Accelerated Cost Recovery System* (or MACRS). Companies may use straight-line depreciation for federal income tax purposes, but most prefer to use MACRS because of its favorable income tax consequences. MACRS is the *only* accelerated depreciation method that may be used in federal income tax returns.

The accelerated depreciation rate *remains constant* throughout the life of the asset. Hence, the rate represents the "fixed-percentage" described in the name of this depreciation method. The book value (cost minus accumulated depreciation) *decreases every year* and represents the "declining-balance."

Thus far, we have described the accelerated depreciation rate as a "specified percentage" of the straight-line rate. Most often, this specified percentage is 200 percent, meaning that the accelerated rate is exactly twice the straight-line rate. As a result, the declining-balance method of depreciation often is called *double-declining-balance* (or 200 percent declining-balance). Tax rules, however, often specify a *lower* percentage, such as 150 percent of the straight-line rate. This version of the declining-balance method may be described as "150 percent declining-balance."[3]

Double-Declining-Balance To illustrate the double-declining-balance method, consider our example of the $17,000 delivery truck. The estimated useful life is 5 years; therefore, the straight-line depreciation rate is 20 percent (1 ÷ 5 years). Doubling this straight-line rate indicates an accelerated depreciation rate of 40 percent. Each year, we will recognize as depreciation expense 40 percent of the truck's book value, as we show in Exhibit 9–5.

Exhibit 9–5

200% DECLINING-BALANCE DEPRECIATION SCHEDULE

Depreciation Schedule: 200% Declining-Balance Method

Year	Computation	Depreciation Expense	Accumulated Depreciation	Book Value
				$17,000
First	$17,000 × 40%	$ 6,800	$ 6,800	10,200
Second	10,200 × 40%	4,080	10,880	6,120
Third	6,120 × 40%	2,448	13,328	3,672
Fourth	3,672 × 40%	1,469	14,797	2,203
Fifth	2,203 − $2,000	203	15,000	2,000
Total		$15,000		

As with the straight-line method illustrated earlier, the asset's book value is computed by subtracting depreciation recognized to date from the asset's cost. For example, from Exhibit 9–5, the book value of the asset at the end of the third year is computed as follows:

Cost	$ 17,000
Accumulated depreciation at end of third year	(13,328)
Book value	$ 3,672

Recall that book value at the end of the third year by the straight-line method was $8,000. The difference between that figure and the $3,672 computed above is due to the more rapid depreciation recognized by the declining-balance method compared with the straight-line method.

Notice that the estimated residual value of the delivery truck *does not* enter into the computation of depreciation expense until the end. This is because the declining-balance method provides an "*automatic*" residual value. As long as each year's depreciation expense is equal

[3] The higher the specified percentage of the straight-line rate, the more accelerated this depreciation becomes. Experience and tradition have established 200 percent of the straight-line rate as the maximum level. For federal income tax purposes, MACRS (see footnote 2) is based upon a 200 percent declining-balance for some assets, and a 150 percent declining-balance for others. The 150 percent declining-balance slows down the rates at which taxpayers may depreciate specific types of assets in their income tax returns.

to only a portion of the undepreciated cost of the asset, the asset *will never be entirely written off.* However, if the asset has a significant residual value, depreciation should *stop at this point.* Since our delivery truck has an estimated residual value of *$2,000,* the depreciation expense for the fifth year is *limited to $203,* rather than the $881 indicated by taking 40 percent of the remaining book value (40% × $2,203 = $881). With the last year's depreciation expense limited in this manner, the book value of the truck at the end of the fifth year is equal to its $2,000 estimated residual value.

In Exhibit 9–5 we computed a full year's depreciation in the first year because the asset was acquired on January 2. But if the half-year convention were in use, depreciation in the first year would be *reduced by half,* to $3,400. The depreciation in the second year would be ($17,000 − $3,400) × 40%, or *$5,440.*

150 Percent Declining-Balance Now assume that we wanted to depreciate this truck using 150 percent of the straight-line rate. In this case, the depreciation rate will be 30 percent, instead of 40 percent (a 20% straight-line rate × 150% = 30%). This depreciation schedule is in Exhibit 9–6.

Exhibit 9–6

150% DECLINING-BALANCE DEPRECIATION SCHEDULE

Depreciation Schedule: 150% Declining-Balance Method

Year	Computation	Depreciation Expense	Accumulated Depreciation	Book Value
				$17,000
First	$17,000 × 30%	$ 5,100	$ 5,100	11,900
Second	11,900 × 30%	3,570	8,670	8,330
Third	8,330 × 30%	2,499	11,169	5,831
Fourth	(5,831 − 2,000) ÷ 2	1,916*	13,085	3,915
Fifth	3,915 − 2,000	1,915*	15,000	2,000
Total		$15,000		

*Switched to the straight-line method for Years 4 and 5.

Notice that we switched to straight-line depreciation in the last two years. The undepreciated cost of the truck at the end of Year 3 was *$5,831.* To depreciate the truck to an estimated residual value of $2,000 at the end of Year 5, $3,831 in depreciation expense must be recognized over the next two years. At this point, *larger depreciation charges* can be recognized if we simply allocate this $3,831 by the straight-line method, rather than continuing to compute 30 percent of the remaining book value. (In our table, we round the allocation of this amount to the nearest dollar.)

Allocating the remaining book value over the remaining life by the straight-line method does *not* represent a change in depreciation methods. Rather, a switch to straight-line when this will result in larger depreciation is *part of the declining-balance method.* This is the way in which we arrive at the desired residual value.

WHICH DEPRECIATION METHODS DO MOST BUSINESSES USE?

Many businesses use the straight-line method of depreciation in their financial statements and accelerated methods in their income tax returns. The reasons for these choices are easy to understand.

Accelerated depreciation methods result in higher charges to depreciation expense early in the asset's life and, therefore, lower reported net income than straight-line depreciation. Most publicly owned companies want to appear as profitable as possible—certainly as profitable as their competitors. Therefore, the majority of publicly owned companies use straight-line depreciation in their financial statements.

For income tax purposes, it's a different story. Management wants to report the *lowest* possible taxable income in the company's income tax returns. Accelerated depreciation methods can substantially reduce both taxable income and tax payments for a period of years.[4]

Accounting principles and income tax laws both permit companies to use *different depreciation methods* in their financial statements and their income tax returns. Therefore, many companies use straight-line depreciation in their financial statements and accelerated methods (variations of the declining-balance method) in their income tax returns.

The Differences in Depreciation Methods: Are They "Real"? Using the straight-line depreciation method will cause a company to *report* higher profits than would be reported if an accelerated method were in use in the early years of the asset's life. But *is* the company better off than if it had used an accelerated method? The answer is *no!* Depreciation—no matter how it is computed—*is only an estimate.* The amount of this estimate has *no effect* on the actual financial strength of the business. Thus, a business that uses an accelerated depreciation method in its financial statements is simply measuring its net income *more conservatively* than a business that uses straight-line. However, the benefits of using an accelerated method for income tax purposes *are* real because the amount of depreciation claimed affects the amount of taxes owed. Lower income taxes translate directly into increased cash availability in the early years of the asset's life.

In the preceding chapter, we made the point that if a company wants to use LIFO in its income tax return, it *must* use LIFO in its financial statements. *No similar requirement exists for depreciation methods.* A company may use an accelerated method in its income tax returns and the straight-line method in its financial statements—and most companies do.

FINANCIAL STATEMENT DISCLOSURES

A company must *disclose* in notes to its financial statements the methods used to depreciate plant assets. This disclosure is located in a note describing various accounting policies and methods used in preparing the financial statements. Readers of the statements should recognize that accelerated depreciation methods transfer the costs of plant assets to expense more quickly than the straight-line method. Thus, accelerated methods result in more *conservative* (lower) balance sheet amounts of plant assets and measurements of net income in the early years of an asset's life. These differences eventually reverse as assets more later into their life cycle.

Estimates of Useful Life and Residual Value Estimating the useful lives and residual values of plant assets is the *responsibility of management.* These estimates usually are based on the company's past experience with similar assets, but they also reflect the company's current circumstances and management's future plans. The estimated lives of similar assets may vary from one company to another.

The estimated lives of plant assets affect the amount of net income reported each period. The longer the estimated useful life, the smaller the amount of cost transferred each period to depreciation expense and the larger the amount of reported net income. Bear in mind, however, that all large corporations are *audited* annually by a firm of independent public accountants. One of the responsibilities of these auditors is to determine that management's estimates of the useful lives of plant assets are reasonable under the circumstances.

Automobiles typically are depreciated over relatively short estimated lives—say, from 3 to 5 years. Other types of equipment are generally depreciated over a period of 5 to 15 years. Buildings are depreciated over much longer lives—perhaps 30 to 50 years for a new building and 15 years or more for a building acquired used.

The Principle of Consistency The *consistent* application of accounting methods is a fundamental concept underlying generally accepted accounting principles. With respect to depreciation methods, this means that a company *does not change* from year to year the method used in computing the depreciation expense for a given plant asset. However,

[4] For a *growing* business, the use of accelerated depreciation in income tax returns may reduce taxable income *every* year. This is because a growing business may always have more assets in the early years of its recovery periods than in the later years.

management *may* use different methods in computing depreciation for different assets. Also, as we have stressed repeatedly, a company may—and often *must*—use different depreciation methods in its financial statements and income tax returns.

Revision of Estimated Useful Lives What should be done if, after a few years of using a plant asset, management decides that the asset actually is going to last for a longer or shorter period than was originally estimated? When this situation arises, a *revised estimate* of useful life should be made and the periodic depreciation expense decreased or increased accordingly.

The procedure for changing the depreciation schedule is to spread the remaining undepreciated cost of the asset *over the years of remaining useful life.* This change affects only the amount of depreciation expense that will be recorded in the current and future periods. The financial statements of past periods are *not* revised to reflect changes in the estimated useful lives of depreciable assets.

To illustrate, assume that a company acquires a $10,000 asset estimated to have a 5-year useful life and no residual value. Under the straight-line method, the annual depreciation expense is $2,000. At the end of the third year, accumulated depreciation is $6,000, and the asset has an undepreciated cost (or book value) of $4,000.

At the beginning of the fourth year, management decides that the asset will last for 5 *more* years. The revised estimate of useful life is, therefore, a total of 8 years. The depreciation expense to be recognized for the fourth year and for each of the remaining years is $800, computed as follows:

Undepreciated cost at end of third year ($10,000 − $6,000)	$4,000
Revised estimate of remaining years of useful life	5 years
Revised amount of annual depreciation expense ($4,000 ÷ 5)	$ 800

THE IMPAIRMENT OF PLANT ASSETS

Sometimes, it becomes apparent that a company cannot reasonably expect to recover the carrying amount of certain plant assets, either through use or through sale. For example, a computer manufacturer may have paid a high price to acquire specialized production equipment. If new technology renders the equipment obsolete, however, it may become apparent that it is worth less than the amount at which the equipment is carried in the accounting records.

If the carrying amount of an asset cannot be recovered through future use or sale, the asset should be *written down* to its fair value. The offsetting debit is to an **impairment loss** account.

CASE IN POINT

The 2009 annual report of **JCPenney** indicates that the company evaluates long-lived assets, such as store property and equipment and other corporate assets, for impairment whenever events or changes in circumstances indicate that the carrying amount of those assets may not be recoverable. Factors that may trigger an impairment review include significant underperformance relative to historical or projected operating results, significant changes in the manner of use of the assets, and changes in the company's overall business strategies. The amount of the impairment loss represents the excess of the carrying value (i.e., book value) of the asset over its fair value.

Other Depreciation Methods

Learning Objective
Account for depreciation using methods other than straight-line or declining-balance.
LO4

Most companies that prepare financial statements in conformity with generally accepted accounting principles use the straight-line method of depreciation. However, any rational and systematic method is acceptable, as long as costs are allocated to expense in a reasonable manner. Several such methods are discussed here.

THE UNITS-OF-OUTPUT METHOD

Under the **units-of-output** method, depreciation is based on some measure of output *rather than* on the passage of time. When depreciation is based on units of output, more depreciation is recognized in the periods in which the assets are most heavily used.

To illustrate this method, consider S&G's delivery truck, which cost \$17,000 and has an estimated salvage value of \$2,000. Assume that S&G plans to retire this truck after it has been driven 100,000 miles. The depreciation rate *per mile of operation is 15 cents,* computed as follows:

$$\frac{\textbf{Cost} - \textbf{Residual Value}}{\textbf{Estimated Units of Output (Miles)}} = \begin{array}{c}\textbf{Cost per}\\ \textbf{Unit of Output (Mile)}\end{array}$$

$$\frac{\$17{,}000 - \$2{,}000}{100{,}000 \text{ miles}} = \$0.15 \text{ Depreciation per Mile}$$

At the end of each year, the amount of depreciation to be recorded is determined by multiplying the 15-cent rate by the number of miles the truck has been driven during the year. After the truck has gone 100,000 miles, it is fully depreciated, and the depreciation process is stopped.

This method provides an excellent matching of expense with revenue. However, the method should be used only when the total units of output can be estimated with reasonable accuracy. Also, this method is used only for assets such as vehicles and certain types of machinery. Assets such as buildings, computers, and furniture do not have well-defined "units of output" and ordinarily do not use this method.

In many cases, units-of-output is an *accelerated method.* Often assets are used more extensively in the earlier years of their useful lives than in the later years.

MACRS

Most businesses use a depreciation method called **MACRS** (Modified Accelerated Cost Recovery System) in their federal income tax returns. Some small businesses also use this method in their financial statements, so they do not have to compute depreciation in several different ways. MACRS is based on the declining-balance method, but should be considered for use in financial statements only if the *designated "recovery periods"* and the *assumption of no salvage value* are reasonable. For publicly traded companies, the use of MACRS in financial statements is usually not considered to be in conformity with generally accepted accounting principles.

SUM-OF-THE-YEARS' DIGITS

Sum-of-the-years' digits, or **SYD,** is a form of accelerated depreciation. It generally produces results that lie between the double-declining-balance and 150 percent-declining-balance methods.

SYD is a traditional topic that is included in many accounting textbooks. But it is the most complex of the accelerated methods—especially when partial years are involved. SYD is rarely used in today's business world. Because of its complexity, it is even less frequently used in small businesses. SYD is seldom used for income tax purposes, because tax laws usually define allowable depreciation rates in terms of the declining-balance method. For these reasons, we defer coverage of the mechanics of this method to later accounting courses.

DECELERATED DEPRECIATION METHODS

Depreciation methods exist that recognize *less* depreciation expense in the early years of an asset's useful life and *more in the later years.* Such methods may achieve a reasonable matching of depreciation expense and revenue when the plant asset is expected to become *increasingly productive* over time. Utility companies, for example, may use these methods for new power plants that will be more fully utilized as the population of the area increases.

These depreciation methods are rarely used; thus we defer coverage to later accounting courses.

DEPRECIATION METHODS IN USE: A SURVEY

Every year the American Institute of Certified Public Accountants (AICPA) conducts a survey of 600 publicly owned companies to determine the accounting methods most widely used in financial statements. The number of methods in use exceeds 600 because some companies use different depreciation methods for different types of assets.

For many consecutive years, the straight-line method has consistently been by far the most widely used method of depreciation in financial statements. In fact, in most years the straight-line method accounts for approximately 90 percent of the depreciation methods used by these 600 companies. Other methods covered in this chapter—units-of-output and various accelerated methods—are used relatively infrequently.

Straight-line is clearly the method most widely used in financial statements

Bear in mind this survey indicates only the depreciation methods used in financial statements. In income tax returns, most companies use accelerated depreciation methods such as MACRS.

Disposal of Plant and Equipment

Learning Objective
Account for the disposal of plant assets.
LO5

When depreciable assets are disposed of at any date other than the end of the year, an entry should be made to record depreciation for the *fraction of the year* ending with the date of disposal. If the half-year convention is in use, six months' depreciation should be recorded on all assets disposed of during the year. In the following illustrations of the disposal of items of plant and equipment, it is assumed that any necessary entries for fractional-period depreciation already have been recorded.

As units of plant and equipment wear out or become obsolete, they must be scrapped, sold, or traded in on new equipment. Upon the disposal or retirement of a depreciable asset, the cost of the property is removed from the asset account, and the accumulated depreciation is removed from the related contra-asset account. Assume, for example, that office equipment purchased 10 years ago at a cost of $20,000 has been fully depreciated and is no longer useful. The entry to record the scrapping of the worthless equipment is as follows:

Accumulated Depreciation: Office Equipment	20,000	
Office Equipment		20,000
To remove from the accounts the cost and the accumulated depreciation on fully depreciated office equipment now being scrapped. No salvage value.		

Scrapping a fully depreciated asset

Once an asset has been fully depreciated, no more depreciation should be recorded on it, even though the property may be in good condition and still in use. The objective of depreciation is to spread the *cost* of an asset over the periods of its usefulness; in no case can depreciation expense be greater than the cost of the asset. When a fully depreciated asset remains in use beyond the original estimate of useful life, the asset account and the Accumulated Depreciation account should remain in the accounting records without further entries until the asset is retired.

GAINS AND LOSSES ON THE DISPOSAL OF PLANT AND EQUIPMENT

Since the residual values and useful lives of plant assets are only estimates, it is not uncommon for a plant asset to be disposed of at an amount that differs from its book value at the date of disposal. When plant assets are sold, any gain or loss on the disposal is computed by comparing the *book value with the amount received from the sale.* A sales price in excess of the book value produces a gain; a sales price below the book value produces a loss. These gains or losses, if material in amount, should be shown separately in the income statement following the computation of income from operations, usually in a section titled "other income."

Disposal at a Price above Book Value Assume that a machine costing $10,000 had accumulated depreciation of $8,000 and a book value of $2,000 at the time it was sold for $3,000 cash. The journal entry to record this disposal is as follows:

Gain on disposal of plant asset

Cash	3,000	
Accumulated Depreciation: Machinery	8,000	
Machinery		10,000
Gain on Disposal of Plant Assets		1,000
To record sale of machinery at a price above book value.		

In this situation, the gain on the disposal is calculated as follows:

Cost	$10,000
Accumulated depreciation at time of disposal	(8,000)
Book value at time of disposal	$ 2,000
Cash received	3,000
Gain on disposal	$ 1,000

Disposal at a Price below Book Value Now assume instead that the same machine is sold for $500. The journal entry in this case would be as follows:

Loss on disposal of plant asset

Cash	500	
Accumulated Depreciation: Machinery	8,000	
Loss on Disposal of Plant Assets	1,500	
Machinery		10,000
To record sale of machinery at a price below book value.		

In this situation, the loss on the disposal is calculated as follows:

Cost	$10,000
Accumulated depreciation at time of disposal	(8,000)
Book value at time of disposal	$ 2,000
Cash received	500
Loss on disposal	$ 1,500

The disposal of a depreciable asset at a price *equal to* book value results in neither a gain nor a loss. The entry for such a transaction consists of a debit to Cash for the amount received, a debit to Accumulated Depreciation for the balance accumulated, and a credit to the asset account for the original cost.

TRADING IN USED ASSETS FOR NEW ONES

Certain types of depreciable assets, such as automobiles and trucks, sometimes are traded in for new assets of the same kind. In most instances, a trade-in is viewed as both a *sale* of the old asset and a purchase of a new one. Transactions of this type are usually considered to have "commercial substance," and give rise to the recognition of a gain or loss.

To illustrate, assume that Rancho Landscape has an old pickup truck that originally cost $10,000 but that now has a book value (and tax basis) of $2,000. Rancho trades in this old truck for a new one with a fair market value of $25,000. The truck dealership grants Rancho a trade-in allowance of $3,500 for the old truck, and Rancho pays the remaining $21,500 cost of the new truck in cash. Rancho Landscape should record this transaction as follows:

Vehicles (new truck)	25,000	
Accumulated Depreciation: Trucks (old truck)	8,000	
Vehicles (old truck)		10,000
Cash		21,500
Gain on Disposal of Plant Assets		1,500
Traded in old truck for a new one costing $15,000. Received $3,500 trade-in allowance on the old truck, which had a book value of $2,000.		

Entry to record a typical trade-in

Notice that Rancho treats the $3,500 trade-in allowance granted by the truck dealership as the *sales price* of the old truck. Thus Rancho recognizes a *$1,500 gain* on the disposal (trade-in) of this asset ($3,500 trade-in allowance − $2,000 book value = $1,500 gain).

For financial reporting purposes, gains and losses on routine trade-ins are recorded in the accounting records whenever the transaction also involves the payment of a significant amount of cash (or the creation of debt). Income tax rules do *not* permit recognition of gains or losses on exchanges of assets that are used for similar purposes. Thus, the $1,500 gain recorded in our example is not regarded as taxable income.[5]

INTERNATIONAL FINANCIAL REPORTING STANDARDS

In discussing plant assets and depreciation, we have emphasized the use of historical cost and that depreciation is a process of allocating or spreading that cost over the useful life of the asset. Under U.S. generally accepted accounting principles, this emphasis on cost and depreciation is due primarily to the importance of including as an expense a portion of the cost of the plant assets which contributed to the earning of a company's income. Cost reduced by accumulated depreciation is the amount shown in the statement of financial position (balance sheet) and generally does not reflect the current value of the asset other than situations where an impairment in value is recorded as described earlier.

Under international accounting standards, companies have an option to follow a revaluation process rather than continuing to use historical cost throughout the asset's useful life. This revaluation alternative requires that an asset's fair value can be reliably measured and it must be applied to an entire class of plant assets. Revaluation is not required every financial reporting period, but must be frequent enough to ensure that the carrying amount of the asset (i.e., its revalued amount less accumulated depreciation) does not differ materially from what it would be if determined by fair value at the end of the financial reporting period.

If an asset's carrying amount is increased as a result of a revaluation, the increase is recorded in other comprehensive income and accumulated equity. This subject is covered in greater depth in Chapter 12 of this textbook.

Intangible Assets

CHARACTERISTICS

Learning Objective **Explain the nature of intangible assets, including goodwill.** **LO6**

As the word *intangible* suggests, assets in this classification have no physical characteristics. Common examples are patents, trademarks, and goodwill. Intangible assets are classified in the balance sheet as a subgroup of plant assets. However, not all assets that lack physical substance are regarded as intangible assets. An account receivable, for example, has no physical attributes but is classified as a current asset and is not regarded as an intangible. In brief, *intangible assets are assets that are used in the operation of the business but that have no physical substance and are noncurrent.*

The basis of valuation for intangible assets is cost. In some companies, however, certain intangible assets such as trademarks may be of great importance but may have been acquired without incurring any significant cost. These intangible assets appear in the balance sheet at their *cost,* regardless of their value to the company. Intangible assets are listed only if significant costs are incurred in their acquisition or development. If these costs are *insignificant,* they are treated as revenue expenditures (ordinary expenses).

[5] Had the trade-in allowance been less than book value, the resulting loss would *not be deductible* in the determination of taxable income.

OPERATING EXPENSES VERSUS INTANGIBLE ASSETS

For an expenditure to qualify as an intangible asset, there must be reasonable evidence of future benefits. Many expenditures offer some prospects of yielding benefits in subsequent years, but the existence and life span of these benefits are so uncertain that most companies treat these expenditures as operating expenses. Examples are the expenditures required to reorganize a business and the expense of training employees to work with new types of machinery or office equipment. There is little doubt that some benefits from these outlays continue beyond the current period, but because of the uncertain duration of the benefits, it is almost universal practice to treat expenditures of this nature as an expense of the current period.

AMORTIZATION

The term **amortization** describes the systematic write-off to expense of the cost of an intangible asset over its useful life. Amortization of an intangible asset is essentially the same as depreciation for a tangible asset. The usual accounting entry for amortization consists of a debit to Amortization Expense and a credit to the intangible asset account. There is no theoretical objection to crediting an accumulated amortization account rather than the intangible asset account, but this method is seldom encountered in practice.

Although it is difficult to estimate the useful life of an intangible such as a trademark, it is probable that such an asset will not contribute to future earnings on a permanent basis. The cost of the intangible asset should, therefore, be deducted from revenue during the years in which it may be expected to aid in producing revenue. The straight-line method normally is used for amortizing intangible assets.

GOODWILL

The intangible asset **goodwill** is often found in corporate balance sheets. While this word has a variety of meanings in our general vocabulary, it has a specific and specialized meaning in financial reporting. Goodwill represents an amount that a company has paid to acquire certain favorable intangible attributes as part of an acquisition of another company. For example, assume a company purchases another company that has a favorable reputation for high-quality customer service. The purchasing company might be willing to pay a price to acquire this favorable attribute because of the positive impact this customer service is expected to have on future profitability. Even though an intangible asset such as a favorable reputation for customer service lacks the physical qualities of land, buildings, and equipment, such service may be just as important for the future success of a company.

Goodwill is a general term that encompasses a wide variety of favorable attributes expected to permit the acquiring company to operate at a greater-than-normal level of profitability. Positive attributes often included in goodwill are:

- Favorable reputation.
- Positive market share.
- Positive advertising image.
- Reputation for high quality and loyal employees.
- Superior management.
- Manufacturing and other operating efficiency.

All of these attributes can be expected to contribute to positive future cash flows of the acquiring company. The **present value** of future cash flows is the amount that a knowledgeable investor would pay today for the right to receive those future cash flows. (The present value concept is discussed further in later chapters and in Appendix B.)

Goodwill is sometimes described and measured as the price paid to receive an *above-normal return* on the purchase of another company's net identifiable assets. This requires that we explain the phrase *normal return on the net identifiable assets. Net assets* refers to assets minus liabilities, or owners' equity. Goodwill is not a separately identifiable asset, however, and the existence of goodwill is implied by the ability of a business to earn an above-average return. The term, **net identifiable assets,** is used to mean all assets except goodwill, minus liabilities.

A *normal return* on net identifiable assets is the rate of return that investors demand in a particular industry to justify their buying a business at the fair value of its net identifiable assets. A business has goodwill when investors will pay a *higher* price because the business earns *more* than the normal rate of return.

Assume that two similar restaurants are offered for sale and that the normal return on the fair market value of the net identifiable assets of restaurants of this type is 15 percent a year. The relative earning power of the two restaurants during the past five years is as follows:

	Mandarin Coast	Golden Dragon
Fair market value of net identifiable assets	$1,000,000	$1,000,000
Normal rate of return on net assets	15%	15%
Normal earnings, computed as 15% of net identifiable assets	150,000	150,000
Average actual net income for past five years	$ 150,000	$ 200,000
Earnings in excess of normal	$ -0-	$ 50,000

Which business is worth more?

An investor presumably would be willing to pay $1,000,000 to buy Mandarin Coast, because this restaurant earns the normal 15 percent return that justifies the fair market value of its net identifiable assets. Although Golden Dragon has the same amount of net identifiable assets, an investor should be willing to pay *more* for Golden Dragon than for Mandarin Coast, because Golden Dragon has a record of superior earnings. The *extra amount* that a buyer pays to purchase Golden Dragon represents the value of this business's *goodwill.*

Estimating Goodwill How much will an investor pay for goodwill? Above-average earnings in past years are of significance to prospective purchasers only if they believe that these earnings *will continue* after they acquire the business. Investors' appraisals of goodwill, therefore, will vary with their estimates of the *future earning power* of the business. Few businesses, however, are able to maintain above-average earnings indefinitely. Consequently, the purchaser of a business will usually limit any amount paid for goodwill to not more than four or five times the amount by which annual earnings exceed normal earnings.

Estimating an amount for goodwill in the purchase of a business is a difficult and speculative process. In attempting to make such an estimate, you are essentially trying to look into the future and predict the extent to which purchasing another business will add so much value to your current business that you are willing to pay a price greater than the value of the identifiable net assets of the business you are acquiring. For example, in the previous example, how much more than $1,000,000 would you be willing to pay for Golden Dragon in comparison with Mandarin Coast? History indicates that Golden Dragon is more profitable, and thus worth more, than Mandarin Coast, but whether that extra profitability will continue in the future requires considerable judgment.

Several methods exist for placing a monetary value on the amount of goodwill in the purchase of a business. A widely used method that is consistent with the description of goodwill is to value the business as a whole and then subtract the current value of the net identifiable assets to estimate the amount of goodwill. For example, assume that successful restaurants sell at about 6½ times annual earnings.[6] This suggests that Golden Dragon is worth about $1,300,000, which is the company's $200,000 average net income times 6.5. Because the company's net identifiable assets have a fair value of only $1,000,000, a reasonable estimate of the positive attributes of Golden Dragon, such as positive reputation or market share, is $300,000, determined as follows:

Estimated value of the business as a whole ($200,000 × 6.5)	$1,300,000
Fair market value of net identifiable assets	1,000,000
Estimated value of goodwill	$ 300,000

[6] Investments in small businesses involve more risk and less liquidity than investments in publicly owned companies. For these reasons, the price-earnings ratios of small businesses tend to be substantially lower than those of publicly owned corporations.

If a buyer of Golden Dragon pays $1,300,000 to purchase the business, $300,000 of goodwill would be recorded. On the other hand, if the buyer is able to purchase Golden Dragon for less than $1,300,000, say, $1,250,000, only $250,000 of goodwill would be recorded ($1,250,000 − $1,000,000 = $250,000), even though the estimated value of goodwill is more than the amount paid.

Recording Goodwill in the Accounts Because of the difficulties in objectively estimating the value of goodwill, this asset is recorded only when it is purchased. Goodwill is purchased when one company buys another. The purchaser records the identifiable assets it has purchased at their fair values and then establishes any additional amount paid to an asset account entitled Goodwill.

Many businesses never purchase goodwill but develop goodwill attributes like good customer relations, superior management, or other factors that result in above-average earnings. Because there is no objective way of determining the value of these qualities unless the business is sold, internally generated goodwill is *not recorded* in the accounting records. The absence of internally generated goodwill is one of the principal reasons why a balance sheet does not indicate a company's current market value.

For many years, generally accepted accounting principles required that purchased goodwill be amortized over a period not exceeding 40 years. Goodwill is no longer required to be amortized, but is now subject to assessment for impairment in value, similar to that for plant assets as explained earlier in this chapter. When the recorded amount of goodwill is no longer recoverable, an impairment loss must be recorded by reducing the asset amount and including a loss in the income statement of the same accounting period.

INTERNATIONAL CASE IN POINT

Goodwill was identified as a topic for harmonization efforts when the FASB and the International Accounting Standards Board (IASB) agreed to work toward convergence of reporting requirements in 2002, an effort that continues today and will undoubtedly continue for years to come. U.S. GAAP requires capitalization of goodwill but no amortization. Instead, goodwill is reviewed annually and its value is adjusted if subject to impairment. Until March 2004, international standards required goodwill to be capitalized and amortized over its estimated useful life (20 years or less). In 2004, the IASB changed international standards for goodwill to be consistent with the U.S. GAAP approach by requiring an impairment test rather than amortization for goodwill.

PATENTS

A patent is an exclusive right granted by the federal government for manufacture, use, and sale of a particular product. The purpose of this exclusive grant is to encourage the invention of new products and processes. When a company acquires a patent by purchase from the inventor or other holder, the purchase price is recorded in an intangible asset account Patents.

Patents are granted for 20 years, and the period of amortization should not exceed that period. However, if the patent is likely to lose its usefulness in less than 20 years, amortization should be based on the shorter estimated useful life. Assume that a patent is purchased from the inventor at a cost of $100,000 after five years of the legal life have expired. The remaining *legal* life is, therefore, 15 years. But if the estimated *useful* life is only four years, amortization should be based on this shorter period. The entry to record the annual amortization expense would be:

Amortization Expense: Patents	25,000	
Patents		25,000
To amortize cost of patent on a straight-line basis over an estimated useful life of 4 years.		

Entry for amortization of patent 

TRADEMARKS AND TRADE NAMES

Coca-Cola's famous name, usually printed in a distinctive typeface, is a classic example of a trademark known around the world. A trademark is a name, symbol, or design that identifies a product or group of products. A permanent exclusive right to use a trademark, brand name, or commercial symbol may be obtained by registering it with the federal government.

The costs of developing a trademark or brand name often consist of advertising campaigns, which should be treated as expenses when incurred. If a trademark or brand name is *purchased,* however, the cost may be substantial. Such cost should be capitalized and amortized to expense over the time period the trademark or brand name is expected to be used. If the use of the trademark is discontinued or its contribution to earnings becomes doubtful, any unamortized cost should be written off immediately.

FRANCHISES

A franchise is a right granted by a company or a governmental unit to conduct a certain type of business in a specific geographical area. An example of a franchise is the right to operate a **McDonald's** restaurant in a specific geographic region. The cost of franchises varies greatly and often is quite substantial. When the cost of a franchise is small, it may be charged immediately to expense or amortized over a short period such as five years. When the cost is material, amortization is based on the life of the franchise (if defined by the franchise agreement); the amortization period, however, should not exceed the period the franchise is expected to generate revenue.

COPYRIGHTS

A copyright is an exclusive right granted by the federal government to protect the production and sale of literary or artistic materials for the life of the creator plus 70 years. The cost of obtaining a copyright may be minor and therefore is chargeable to expense when paid. Only when a copyright is *purchased* from an existing owner will the expenditure be *material enough* to warrant its being capitalized and spread over the useful life. The revenue from copyrights is usually limited to only a few years, and the purchase cost should be amortized over the years in which the revenue is expected.

OTHER INTANGIBLES AND DEFERRED CHARGES

Among the other intangibles found in the published balance sheets of large corporations are moving costs, plant rearrangement costs, formulas, processes, name lists, and film rights. Some companies group items of this type under the title of Deferred Charges, meaning expenditures that will provide benefits beyond the current year and that will be written off to expense over their useful economic lives. It is also common practice to combine these items under the heading of Other Assets, which is listed at the bottom of the asset section of the balance sheet.

RESEARCH AND DEVELOPMENT (R&D) COSTS

Billions of dollars are spent each year on research and development of new products. In fact, expenditures for R&D are a striking characteristic of U.S. industry. The annual research and development expenditures of some companies often exceed $1 billion and account for a substantial percentage of their total costs and expenses.

In the past, some companies treated all research and development costs as expenses in the year incurred; other companies in the same industry recorded these costs as intangible assets to be amortized over future years. This diversity of practice prevented financial statements of different companies from being comparable.

The Financial Accounting Standards Board standardized accounting for R&D when it ruled that as a general rule research and development expenditures should be charged to expense *when incurred.* This action by the FASB had the beneficial effect of reducing the number of alternative accounting practices and helping to make financial statements of different companies more comparable.

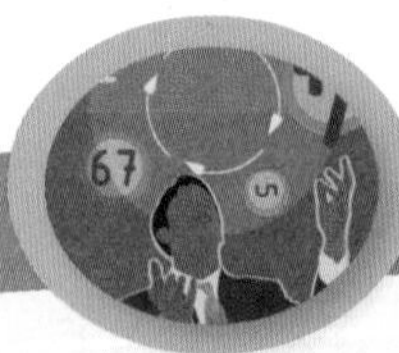

Financial Analysis and Decision Making

The success of many businesses depends on research and development activities (R&D). To better understand a company's commitment to funding R&D, users of financial statements often examine the level of, and trends in, a company's R&D expenditures as a percentage of net sales:

R&D to Sales = R&D Costs ÷ Net Sales

R&D expenditures as a percentage of net sales are naturally higher in some industries than in others. To illustrate this point, see the R&D figures for a recent year for well-known companies from four industries in Exhibit 9–7.

Exhibit 9–7
COMPARATIVE R&D EXPENDITURES

	R&D Costs (in millions)	Net Sales (in millions)	R&D (%)
Chemical Products			
DuPont	1,349	26,996	5.00
Dow Chemical	981	32,632	3.01
Computer Hardware			
Sun Microsystems	1,837	11,434	16.07
Silicon Graphics	177	1,341	13.20
Pharmaceuticals			
Eli Lilly & Co.	2,350	12,583	18.68
Pfizer	7,131	45,188	15.78
Computer Software			
Oracle	1,180	9,475	12.45
Microsoft	4,379	25,296	17.31

YOUR TURN **You as a Financial Analyst**

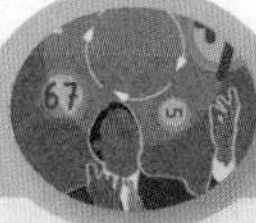

You are working as an equity analyst on Wall Street and a college intern asks you to explain why companies can differ greatly in the R&D expense to net sales ratio. How do you respond?

(See our comments on the Online Learning Center Web site.)

Natural Resources

ACCOUNTING FOR NATURAL RESOURCES

Learning Objective
Account for the depletion of natural resources. **LO7**

Mining properties, oil and gas reserves, and tracts of standing timber are examples of natural resources. The distinguishing characteristic of these assets is that they are physically removed from their natural environment and are converted into inventory. Theoretically, a coal mine might be regarded as an underground inventory of coal; however, such an inventory is certainly not a current asset. In the balance sheet, mining property and other natural resources are classified as property, plant, and equipment. Once the coal is removed from the ground, however, this coal *does* represent inventory.

We have explained that plant assets such as buildings and equipment depreciate because of physical deterioration or obsolescence. A mine or an oil reserve does not depreciate for these reasons, but it is gradually *depleted* as the natural resource is removed from the ground. Once all of the coal has been removed from a coal mine, for example, the mine is "fully depleted" and will be abandoned or sold for its residual value.

To illustrate the **depletion** of a natural resource, assume that Rainbow Minerals pays $45 million to acquire the Red Valley Mine, which is believed to contain 10 million tons of coal. The residual value of the mine after all of the coal is removed is estimated to be $5 million. The depletion that will occur over the life of the mine is the original cost minus the residual value, or $40 million. This depletion will occur at the rate of *$4 per ton* ($40 million ÷ 10 million tons) as the coal is removed from the mine. If we assume that 2 million tons are mined during the first year of operations, the entry to record the depletion of the mine would be as follows:

Recording depletion

Inventory.	8,000,000	
Accumulated Depletion: Red Valley Mine.		8,000,000
To record depletion of the Red Valley Mine for the year; 2,000,000 tons mined @ $4 per ton.		

Once removed from the mine, coal becomes available for sale. Therefore, the estimated cost of this coal is added to the Inventory account. As the coal is sold, this cost is transferred from the Inventory account to the Cost of Goods Sold account.

Accumulated Depletion is a *contra-asset account* similar to the Accumulated Depreciation account; it represents the portion of the mine that has been used up (depleted) to date. In Rainbow Minerals's balance sheet, the Red Valley Mine now appears as follows:

The mine gradually is turned into inventory

Property, Plant, & Equipment:		
Mining properties: Red Valley Mine.	$45,000,000	
Less: Accumulated depletion.	8,000,000	$37,000,000

Depreciation of Buildings and Equipment Closely Related to Natural Resources Buildings and equipment installed at a mine or drilling site may be useful only at that particular location. Consequently, such assets should be depreciated over their normal useful lives or over the life of the natural resource, *whichever is shorter.* Often depreciation on such assets is computed using the units-of-output method, which was discussed earlier in the chapter, based on the quantity of the natural resource removed.

DEPRECIATION, AMORTIZATION, AND DEPLETION—A COMMON GOAL

The processes of depreciation, amortization, and depletion discussed in this chapter all have a common goal. That goal is to *allocate the acquisition cost of long-lived assets to expense over the years in which the asset contributes to revenue.* Allocating the acquisition cost of long-lived assets over the years that benefit from the use of these assets is an important application of the *matching principle.* The determination of income requires matching revenue with the expenses incurred to produce that revenue.

Plant Transactions and the Statement of Cash Flows

Learning Objective
LO8 Explain the cash effects of transactions involving plant assets.

The cash effects of plant and equipment transactions are different from the effects reported in the income statement. Cash payments for plant assets occur when those assets are *purchased*—or, more precisely, when payment is made. Cash receipts often occur when assets are sold. (These receipts are equal to the *total proceeds* received from the sale, not just the amount of any gain.) Cash flows relating to acquisitions and disposals of plant assets appear in the statement of cash flows, classified as *investing activities.*

Depreciation and amortization expense both *reduce net income,* but they have *no effect on cash flows.* As a result, both tend to make net income *less* than the net cash flows from operating activities. Likewise, the write-down of impaired assets is another example of a **noncash charge or expense** against income having no immediate effect on cash flows.

Noncash Investing Activities Not all purchases and sales of plant assets result in cash payments or cash receipts during the current accounting period. For example, a company may finance the purchase of plant assets by issuing notes payable, or it may sell plant assets

Ethics, Fraud & Corporate Governance

A learning objective for this chapter is to distinguish between capital expenditures and revenue expenditures (a revenue expenditure is an operating expense). A capital expenditure is charged to an asset account rather than to an expense account. The largest instance of fraudulent financial reporting in U.S. history was largely due to improper capitalization of operating expenditures. **WorldCom Inc.** (**WorldCom**) from as early as 1999 through the first quarter of 2002 overstated its reported income by approximately $11 billion, including approximately $7 billion of ordinary operating expenses that were improperly capitalized. The revelation of the fraud led to **WorldCom**'s filing for protection from its creditors under the provisions of the U.S. Bankruptcy Code. Although the fraud at **Enron** had prompted congressional interest in auditing, financial reporting, and corporate governance, by the spring of 2002 congressional efforts to draft a law in response to the **Enron** fraud had stalled due to disagreements between the two houses of Congress. The fraud at **WorldCom** broke this congressional logjam and resulted in the passage of the Sarbanes-Oxley Act less than two months after the revelation of the **WorldCom** fraud.

Almost immediately after the revelation of the **WorldCom** fraud—in June 2002—the Securities and Exchange Commission (SEC) brought an enforcement action against **WorldCom**. **WorldCom** is a major global telecommunications provider, providing services in more than 65 countries. At the time of the fraud, **WorldCom** was traded on NASDAQ.

As the economy began to cool in 1999, demand for **WorldCom**'s telecommunications services was reduced, leading to a decline in profits. The slowing economy made it difficult for **WorldCom** to continue to meet the expectations of Wall Street analysts for reported profitability.

WorldCom's senior management directed subordinates to take steps to hide the deterioration in **WorldCom**'s profitability from analysts and other external parties. A primary means of carrying out the fraud was to transfer ordinary operating expenses, line costs, to a capital asset account, fixed assets. This accounting treatment resulted in the understatement of operating expenses and an increase in income.

The fraud at **WorldCom** has numerous ethical and corporate governance implications. Although the fraud at **WorldCom** was directed by top management, much of the implementation was carried out by midlevel finance and accounting personnel.

WorldCom did not have a code of ethics. Attempts to develop such a code were met by the CEO's description of a code of ethics as a "colossal waste of time." The Sarbanes-Oxley Act and related SEC interpretations require public companies to disclose whether they have a code of ethics that applies to the CEO, CFO, and chief accounting officer and, if not, why not. Moreover, the NYSE and NASDAQ now require companies listed on these exchanges to have a code of ethics. Although these requirements are a step in the right direction, they will fail to have their intended effect if senior management doesn't fully embrace the written code.

in exchange for notes receivable. The noncash aspects of investing and financing activities are summarized in a special schedule that accompanies a statement of cash flows. This schedule is illustrated and explained in Chapter 13.

Concluding Remarks

This chapter completes our discussion of accounting for various types of assets. To briefly review, we have seen that cash is reported in the financial statements at its face value, marketable securities at their market value, accounts receivable at their net realizable value (i.e., net amount of cash expected to be collected), inventories at the lower-of-cost-or-market, and plant assets at cost less accumulated depreciation.

Two ideas that have been consistently reflected in each of these valuation bases are the matching principle and conservatism. A major determinant of the amount at which many assets are accounted for in the balance sheet is the future amount to be released as an expense into the income statement. Closely related to this is the objective of not overstating the current and future expectations of a company's financial activities by overstating assets and understating current expenses.

In the next chapter, we turn our attention to the measurement and presentation of liabilities.

END-OF-CHAPTER REVIEW

SUMMARY OF LEARNING OBJECTIVES

LO1 Determine the cost of plant assets. Plant assets are long-lived assets acquired for use in the business and not for resale to customers. The matching principle requires that we include in the plant and equipment accounts those costs that will provide services over a period of years. During these years, the use of the plant assets contributes to the earning of revenue. The cost of a plant asset includes all expenditures reasonable and necessary in acquiring the asset and placing it in a position and condition for use in the operations of the business.

LO2 Distinguish between capital expenditures and revenue expenditures. Capital expenditures include any material expenditure that will benefit several accounting periods. Therefore, these expenditures are charged to asset accounts (capitalized) and are recognized as expense in future periods.

Revenue expenditures are charged directly to expense accounts because either (1) there is no objective evidence of future benefits or (2) the amounts are immaterial.

LO3 Compute depreciation by the straight-line and declining-balance methods. Straight-line depreciation assigns an equal portion of an asset's cost to expense in each period of the asset's life. Declining-balance depreciation is an accelerated method. Each year, a fixed (and relatively high) depreciation rate is applied to the remaining book value of the asset. There are several variations of declining-balance depreciation.

LO4 Account for depreciation using methods other than straight-line or declining-balance. Most companies that prepare financial statements in conformity with generally accepted accounting principles use the straight-line method of depreciation. Other accepted methods include the units-of-output method, sum-of-the-years' digits, and, in rare circumstances, decelerated depreciation methods.

LO5 Account for the disposal of plant assets. When plant assets are disposed of, depreciation should be recorded to the date of disposal. The cost is then removed from the asset account and the total recorded depreciation is removed from the Accumulated Depreciation account. The sale of a plant asset at a price above or below book value results in a gain or loss to be reported in the income statement.

Because different depreciation methods are used for income tax purposes, the gain or loss reported in income tax returns may differ from that shown in the income statement. The gain or loss shown in the financial statement is recorded in the company's general ledger accounts.

LO6 Explain the nature of intangible assets, including goodwill. Intangible assets are assets owned by the business that have no physical substance, are noncurrent, and are used in business operations. Examples include trademarks and patents.

Among the most interesting intangible assets is goodwill. Goodwill is the present value of future earnings in excess of a normal return on net identifiable assets. It stems from such factors as a good reputation, loyal customers, and superior management. Any business that earns significantly more than a normal rate of return actually has goodwill. But goodwill is recorded in the accounts only if it is *purchased* by acquiring another business at a price higher than the fair market value of its net identifiable assets.

LO7 Account for the depletion of natural resources. Natural resources (or wasting assets) include mines, oil fields, and standing timber. Their cost is converted into inventory as the resource is mined, pumped, or cut. This allocation of the cost of a natural resource to inventories is called depletion. The depletion rate per unit extracted equals the cost of the resource (less residual value) divided by the estimated number of units it contains.

LO8 Explain the cash effects of transactions involving plant assets. Depreciation is a noncash expense; cash expenditures for the acquisition of plant assets are independent of the amount of depreciation for the period. Cash payments to acquire plant assets (and cash receipts from disposals) appear in the statement of cash flows, classified as investing activities.

Write-downs of plant assets also are noncash charges, which do not involve cash payments.

Key Terms Introduced or Emphasized in Chapter 9

accelerated depreciation (p. 391) Methods of depreciation that call for recognition of relatively large amounts of depreciation in the early years of an asset's useful life and relatively small amounts in the later years.

amortization (p. 402) The systematic write-off to expense of the cost of an intangible asset over the periods of its economic usefulness.

book value (p. 390) The cost of a plant asset minus the total recorded depreciation, as shown by the Accumulated Depreciation account. The remaining undepreciated cost is also known as *carrying value.*

capital expenditures (p. 388) Costs incurred to acquire a long-lived asset. Expenditures that will benefit several accounting periods.

capitalize (p. 388) A verb with two different meanings in accounting. The first is to debit an expenditure to an asset account, rather than directly to expense. The second is to estimate the value of an investment by dividing the annual return by the investor's required rate of return.

depletion (p. 407) Allocating the cost of a natural resource to the units removed as the resource is mined, pumped, cut, or otherwise consumed.

depreciation (p. 389) The systematic allocation of the cost of an asset to expense over the years of its estimated useful life.

fixed-percentage-of-declining-balance depreciation (p. 393) An accelerated method of depreciation in which the rate is a multiple of the straight-line rate and is applied each year to the undepreciated cost of the asset. The most commonly used rate is double the straight-line rate.

goodwill (p. 402) The present value of expected future earnings of a business in excess of the earnings normally realized in the industry. Recorded when a business entity is purchased at a price in excess of the fair value of its net identifiable assets less liabilities.

half-year convention (p. 393) The practice of taking six months' depreciation in the year of acquisition and in the year of disposition, rather than computing depreciation for partial periods to the nearest month. This method is widely used and is acceptable for both income tax reporting and financial reports, as long as it is applied to all assets of a particular type acquired during the year. The half-year convention generally is not used for buildings.

impairment loss (p. 397) Writing down a long-lived asset for the difference between its carrying amount less its fair value.

intangible assets (p. 386) Those assets that are used in the operation of a business but that have no physical substance and are noncurrent.

MACRS (p. 398) The Modified Accelerated Cost Recovery System. The accelerated depreciation method permitted in federal income tax returns for assets acquired after December 31, 1986. Depreciation is based on prescribed recovery periods and depreciation rates.

natural resources (p. 386) Mines, oil fields, standing timber, and similar assets that are physically consumed and converted into inventory.

net identifiable assets (p. 402) The total of all assets minus liabilities.

noncash charge or expense (p. 408) A charge against earnings—either an expense or a loss—that does not require a cash expenditure at or near the time of recognition. Thus, the charge reduces net income but does not affect cash flows (except, perhaps, for income tax payments). Examples are depreciation and the write-off of asset values because an asset has become impaired.

plant assets (p. 386) Long-lived assets that are acquired for use in business operations rather than for resale to customers.

present value (p. 402) The amount that a knowledgeable investor would pay today for the right to receive future cash flows. The present value is always less than the sum of the future cash flows because the investor requires a return on the investment.

residual (salvage) value (p. 391) The portion of an asset's cost expected to be recovered through sale or trade-in of the asset at the end of its useful life.

revenue expenditures (p. 389) Expenditures that will benefit only the current accounting period.

straight-line depreciation (p. 390) A method of depreciation that allocates the cost of an asset (minus any residual value) equally to each year of its useful life.

sum-of-the-years' digits (SYD) depreciation (p. 398) A long-established but seldom-used method of accelerated depreciation. Usually produces results that lie in between the 200 percent- and 150 percent-declining-balance methods.

tangible plant assets (p. 386) Plant assets that have physical substance but that are not natural resources. Examples include land, buildings, and all types of equipment.

units-of-output (p. 398) A depreciation method in which cost (minus residual value) is divided by the estimated units of lifetime output. The unit depreciation cost is multiplied by the actual units of output each year to compute the annual depreciation expense.

Demonstration Problem

On April 1, 2011, Mattson Industries purchased new equipment at a cost of $325,000. The useful life of this equipment was estimated at five years, with a residual value of $25,000.

Instructions

Compute the annual depreciation expense for each year until this equipment becomes fully depreciated under each depreciation method listed below. Because you will record depreciation for only a fraction of a year in 2011, depreciation will extend into 2016 for both methods. Show supporting computations.

a. Straight-line, with depreciation for fractional years rounded to the nearest whole month.

b. 200 percent declining-balance, with the half-year convention. Limit depreciation in 2016 to an amount that reduces the undepreciated cost to the estimated residual value.

c. Assume that the equipment is sold at the end of December 2013 for $176,250 cash. Record the necessary gain or loss resulting from the sale under the straight-line method.

Solution to the Demonstration Problem

Expense under Each Method of Depreciation

Year	a. Straight-Line	b. 200% Declining-Balance
2011	$ 45,000	$ 65,000
2012	60,000	104,000
2013	60,000	62,400
2014	60,000	37,440
2015	60,000	22,464
2016	15,000	8,696
Totals	$300,000	$300,000

c. Entry to record sale of equipment in 2013:

Cash	176,250	
Accumulated Depreciation: Equipment	165,000	
Equipment		325,000
Gain on Sale of Equipment		16,250

Supporting computations:

a. 2011: ($325,000 − $25,000) × ⅕ × 9⁄12 = $45,000

2012–2015: $300,000 × ⅕ = $60,000

2016: $300,000 × ⅕ × 3⁄12 = $15,000

b.

Year	Undepreciated Cost		Rate		Depreciation Expense
2011	$325,000	×	40% × ½	=	$ 65,000
2012	260,000	×	40%	=	104,000
2013	156,000	×	40%	=	62,400
2014	93,600	×	40%	=	37,440
2015	56,160	×	40%	=	22,464
2016	33,696	−	$25,000	=	8,696

c. Accumulated depreciation at the end of 2013:

Depreciation expense, 2011	$ 45,000
Depreciation expense, 2012	60,000
Depreciation expense, 2013	60,000
Accumulated depreciation at the end of 2013	$165,000
Original cost of equipment in 2011	$325,000
Less: Accumulated depreciation at the end of 2013	(165,000)
Book value of equipment at time of disposal	$160,000
Cash proceeds from sale	$176,250
Less: Book value of equipment at time of disposal	(160,000)
Gain on sale of disposal	$ 16,250

Self-Test Questions

The answers to these questions appear on page 427.

1. In which of the following situations should the named company *not* record any depreciation expense on the asset described?
   - a. Commuter Airline is required by law to maintain its aircraft in "as good as new" condition.
   - b. Metro Advertising owns an office building that has been increasing in value each year since it was purchased.
   - c. Computer Sales Company has in inventory a new type of computer, designed "never to become obsolete."
   - d. None of the above answers is correct—in each case, the named company should record depreciation on the asset described.
2. Which of the following statements is (are) correct?
   - a. Accumulated depreciation represents a cash fund being accumulated for the replacement of plant assets.
   - b. The cost of a machine includes the cost of repairing damage to the machine during the installation process.
   - c. A company may use different depreciation methods in its financial statements and its income tax return.
   - d. The use of an accelerated depreciation method causes an asset to wear out more quickly than does use of the straight-line method.
3. On April 1, 2010, Sanders Construction paid $10,000 for equipment with an estimated useful life of 10 years and a residual value of $2,000. The company uses the double-declining-balance method of depreciation and applies the half-year convention to fractional periods. In 2011, the amount of depreciation expense to be recognized on this equipment is:
   - a. $1,600.
   - b. $1,440.
   - c. $1,280.
   - d. Some other amount.
4. Evergreen Mfg. is a rapidly growing company that acquires equipment every year. Evergreen uses straight-line depreciation in its financial statements and an accelerated method in its tax returns. Identify all correct statements:
   - a. Using straight-line depreciation in the financial statements instead of an accelerated method reduces Evergreen's reported net income.
   - b. Using straight-line depreciation in the financial statements instead of an accelerated method increases Evergreen's annual net cash flow.
   - c. Using an accelerated method instead of straight-line depreciation in income tax returns increases Evergreen's cash flow from operating activities.
   - d. As long as Evergreen keeps growing, it will probably report more depreciation in its income tax returns *each year* than it does in its financial statements.
5. Ladd Company sold a plant asset that originally cost $50,000 for $22,000 cash. If Ladd correctly reports a $5,000 gain on this sale, the *accumulated depreciation* on the asset at the date of sale must have been:
   - a. $33,000.
   - b. $28,000.
   - c. $23,000.
   - d. Some other amount.
6. In which of the following situations would Martinez Industries include goodwill in its balance sheet?
   - a. The fair market value of Martinez's net identifiable assets amounts to $2,000,000. Normal earnings for this industry are 15 percent of net identifiable assets. Net income for the past five years has averaged $390,000.
   - b. Martinez spent $800,000 during the current year for research and development for a new product that promises to generate substantial revenue for at least 10 years.
   - c. Martinez acquired Baxter Electronics at a price in excess of the fair market value of Baxter's net identifiable assets.
   - d. A buyer wishing to purchase Martinez's entire operation has offered a price in excess of the fair market value of the company's net identifiable assets.

ASSIGNMENT MATERIAL Discussion Questions

1. **Coca-Cola**'s distinctive trademark is more valuable to the company than its bottling plants. But the company's bottling plants are listed in the balance sheet, and the famous trademark isn't. Explain.
2. Identify the basic "accountable events" in the life of a depreciable plant asset. Which of these events directly affect the net income of the current period? Which directly affect cash flows (other than income tax payments)?
3. The following expenditures were incurred in connection with a new machine acquired by a metals manufacturing company. Identify those that should be included in the cost of the asset. (a) Freight charges, (b) sales tax on the machine, (c) payment to a passing motorist whose car was damaged by the equipment used in unloading the machine, (d) wages of employees for time spent in installing and testing the machine before it was placed in service, (e) wages of employees assigned to lubricate and make minor adjustments to the machine one year after it was placed in service.
4. What is the distinction between a *capital expenditure* and a *revenue expenditure*?

5. If a capital expenditure is erroneously treated as a revenue expenditure, will the net income of the current year be overstated or understated? Will this error have any effect on the net income reported in future years? Explain.
6. Shoppers' Market purchased for $245,000 a site on which it planned to build a new store. The site consisted of three acres of land and included an old house and two barns. County property tax records showed the following appraised values for this property: land, $160,000; buildings, $40,000. Indicate what Shoppers' should do with this $245,000 cost in its financial statements, and explain your reasoning.
7. Should depreciation continue to be recorded on a building when ample evidence exists that the current market value is greater than original cost and that the rising trend of market values is continuing? Explain.
8. Explain what is meant by an *accelerated* depreciation method. Are accelerated methods more widely used in financial statements or in income tax returns? Explain.
9. One accelerated depreciation method is called *fixed-percentage-of-declining-balance.* Explain what is meant by the terms "fixed-percentage" and "declining-balance." For what purpose is this method most widely used?
10. Criticize the following quotation: "We shall have no difficulty in paying for new plant assets needed during the coming year because our estimated outlays for new equipment amount to only $80,000, and we have more than twice that amount in our accumulated depreciation account at present."
11. Explain two approaches to computing depreciation for a fractional period in the year in which an asset is purchased. (Neither of your approaches should require the computation of depreciation to the nearest day or week.)
12. Over what period of time should the cost of various types of intangible assets be amortized by regular charges against revenue? (Your answer should be in the form of a principle or guideline rather than a specific number of years.) What method of amortization is generally used?
13. Mineral World recognizes $20 depletion for each ton of ore mined. During the current year the company mined 600,000 tons but sold only 500,000 tons, as it was attempting to build up inventories in anticipation of a possible strike by employees. How much depletion should be deducted from revenue of the current year?
14. Explain the meaning of an *impairment* of an asset. Provide several examples. What accounting event should occur when an asset has become substantially impaired?
15. Several years ago Walker Security purchased for $120,000 a well-known trademark for padlocks and other security products. After using the trademark for three years, Walker Security discontinued it altogether when the company withdrew from the lock business and concentrated on the manufacture of aircraft parts. Amortization of the trademark at the rate of $3,000 a year is being continued on the basis of a 20-year life, which the owner says is consistent with accounting standards. Do you agree? Explain.

Brief Exercises

LO1 LO2 **BRIEF EXERCISE 9.1**
Cost of Plant Asset

Padre, Inc., purchased a used piece of heavy equipment for $25,000. Delivery of the equipment to Padre's business site cost $750. Expenditures to recondition the equipment and prepare it for use totaled $2,230. The maintenance for the first year Padre owned the equipment was $1,200. Determine the cost that is the basis for calculating annual depreciation on the equipment.

LO3 **BRIEF EXERCISE 9.2**
Straight-Line Depreciation

Twin-Cities, Inc., purchased a building for $400,000. Straight-line depreciation was used for each of the first two years using the following assumptions: 25-year estimated useful life, with a residual value of $100,000.

a. Calculate the annual depreciation for the first two years that Twin-Cities owned the building.
b. Calculate the book value of the building at the end of the second year.

LO3 **BRIEF EXERCISE 9.3**
Straight-Line and Declining-Balance Depreciation

Waller Company purchased equipment for $24,000. The company is considering whether to determine annual depreciation using the straight-line method or the declining-balance method at 150 percent of the straight-line rate. Waller expects to use the equipment for 10 years, at the end of which it will have an estimated salvage value of $4,000. Prepare a comparison of these two alternatives for the first two years Waller will own the equipment.

LO3 **BRIEF EXERCISE 9.4**
Declining-Balance Depreciation

Equipment costing $76,000 was purchased by Spence, Inc., at the beginning of the current year. The company will depreciate the equipment by the declining-balance method, but it has not determined whether the rate will be at 150 percent or 200 percent of the straight-line rate. The estimated useful life of the equipment is eight years. Prepare a comparison of the two alternative rates for management for the first two years Spence owns the equipment.

LO3 LO4

BRIEF EXERCISE 9.5

Straight-Line and Units-of-Output Depreciation

Finx, Inc., purchased a truck for $35,000. The truck is expected to be driven 15,000 miles per year over a five-year period and then sold for approximately $5,000. Determine depreciation for the first year of the truck's useful life by the straight-line and units-of-output methods if the truck is actually driven 16,000 miles.

LO3 LO5

BRIEF EXERCISE 9.6

Disposal of Plant Asset

Alexander Company purchased a piece of equipment for $12,000 and depreciated it for three years over a five-year estimated life with an expected residual value at the end of five years of $2,000. At the end of the third year, Alex decided to upgrade to equipment with increased capacity and sold the original piece of equipment for $7,200. Calculate the gain or loss on the disposal at the end of the third year.

LO3 LO5

BRIEF EXERCISE 9.7

Disposal of Plant Asset

Tullahoma Company purchased equipment for $27,500. It depreciated the equipment over a five-year life by the double-declining-balance method until the end of the second year, at which time the asset was sold for $8,500. Calculate the gain or loss on the sale at the end of the second year.

LO6

BRIEF EXERCISE 9.8

Goodwill

Hunt Company is considering purchasing a competing company in order to expand its market share. Estimates of the excess of the value of the individual assets, less liabilities to be assumed, range from $50,000 to $60,000, depending on the manner in which that excess is calculated. Hunt believes it can purchase the competitor for a direct cash outlay of $700,000, which is only $25,000 more than the value of the individual assets less the liabilities that Hunt will assume. Assuming Hunt makes the purchase for $700,000, at what amount should goodwill be recorded? Briefly explain your answer.

LO7

BRIEF EXERCISE 9.9

Natural Resources

Miller Mining acquired rights to a tract of land with the intent of extracting from the land a valuable mineral. The cost of the rights was $2,500,000 and an estimated 10,000 tons of the mineral are expected to be extracted. Assuming that 1,600 tons of the mineral are actually extracted in the first year, determine the amount of depletion expense that should be recognized for that year.

LO4

BRIEF EXERCISE 9.10

Alternative Depreciation Methods

R. C. Smith purchased a truck for $30,500 to be used in his business. He is considering depreciating the truck by two methods: units-of-output (assuming total miles driven of 80,000) and double-declining balance (assuming a five-year useful life). The truck is expected to be sold for approximately $6,500 at the end of its useful life. Prepare a comparison of the first year's depreciation expense that will be recognized under these methods, assuming the truck was actually driven 10,000 miles in the first year. Briefly state why the difference between the two is so great.

Exercises

LO2 LO3

EXERCISE 9.1

You as a Student

Assume that you recently applied for a student loan to go to graduate school. As part of the application process, your bank requested a list of your assets. Aside from an extensive CD collection, your only other asset is a pickup truck. You purchased the truck six years ago for $15,000. Its current fair value is approximately $5,000.

a. What factors caused your pickup truck to depreciate $10,000 in value?

b. Assume that the bank is willing to lend you money for graduate school. Even with the loan, however, you still need to raise an additional $5,000. Do you think that the bank will lend you $5,000 more for graduate school if you agree to use your truck as collateral? Explain.

c. Assume that the truck has been used solely in a delivery service business that you operated while in college. Would your balance sheet necessarily show $10,000 in accumulated depreciation related to the truck? Explain.

LO1 LO2 **EXERCISE 9.2** Distinguishing Capital Expenditures from Revenue Expenditures

Identify the following expenditures as capital expenditures or revenue expenditures:

a. Immediately after acquiring a new delivery truck, paid $195 to have the name of the store and other advertising material painted on the vehicle.

b. Painted delivery truck at a cost of $450 after two years of use.

c. Purchased new battery at a cost of $40 for two-year-old delivery truck.

d. Installed an escalator at a cost of $17,500 in a three-story building that had been used for some years without elevators or escalators.

e. Purchased a pencil sharpener at a cost of $15.00.

f. Original life of the delivery truck had been estimated at four years, and straight-line depreciation of 25 percent yearly had been recognized. After three years' use, however, it was decided to recondition the truck thoroughly, including adding a new engine.

LO3 **EXERCISE 9.3** Depreciation for Fractional Years

On August 3, Srini Construction purchased special-purpose equipment at a cost of $1,000,000. The useful life of the equipment was estimated to be eight years, with a residual value of $50,000.

a. Compute the depreciation expense to be recognized each calendar year for financial reporting purposes under the straight-line depreciation method (half-year convention).

b. Compute the depreciation expense to be recognized each calendar year for financial reporting purposes under the 200 percent declining-balance method (half-year convention) with a switch to straight-line when it will maximize depreciation expense.

c. Which of these two depreciation methods (straight-line or double-declining-balance) results in the highest net income for financial reporting purposes during the first two years of the equipment's use? Explain.

LO3 **EXERCISE 9.4** Depreciation Methods

On January 2, 2011, Jansing Corporation acquired a new machine with an estimated useful life of five years. The cost of the equipment was $40,000 with a residual value of $5,000.

a. Prepare a complete depreciation table under the three depreciation methods listed below. Use a format similar to the illustrations in Exhibits 9–4, 9–5, and 9–6. In each case, assume that a full year of depreciation was taken in 2011.

   1. Straight-line.
   2. 200 percent declining-balance.
   3. 150 percent declining-balance with a switch to straight-line when it will maximize depreciation expense.

b. Comment on significant differences or similarities that you observe among the patterns of depreciation expense recognized under each of these methods.

LO3 **EXERCISE 9.5** Evaluation of Disclosures in Annual Reports

A recent annual report of **H. J. Heinz Company** includes the following note:

Depreciation: For financial reporting purposes, depreciation is provided on the straight-line method over the estimated useful lives of the assets, which generally have the following ranges: buildings—40 years or less; machinery and equipment—15 years or less; computer software—3–7 years; and lease hold improvements—over the life of the lease, not to exceed 15 years. Accelerated depreciation methods are generally used for income tax purposes.

a. Is the company violating the accounting principle of consistency by using different depreciation methods in its financial statements than in its income tax returns? Explain.

b. *Why* do you think that the company uses accelerated depreciation methods in its income tax returns?

c. Would the use of accelerated depreciation in the financial statements be more conservative or less conservative than the current practice of using the straight-line method? Explain.

LO3 **EXERCISE 9.6** Revision of Depreciation Estimates

Swindall Industries uses straight-line depreciation on all of its depreciable assets. The company records annual depreciation expense at the end of each calendar year. On January 11, 2007, the company purchased a machine costing $90,000. The machine's useful life was estimated to be 12 years with a residual value of $18,000. Depreciation for partial years is recorded to the nearest full month.

In 2011, after almost five years of experience with the machine, management decided to revise its estimated life from 12 years to 20 years. No change was made in the estimated residual value. The revised estimate of the useful life was decided *prior* to recording annual depreciation expense for the year ended December 31, 2011.

a. Prepare journal entries in chronological order for the above events, beginning with the purchase of the machinery on January 11, 2007. Show separately the recording of depreciation expense in 2007 through 2011.

b. What factors may have caused the company to revise its estimate of the machine's useful life?

LO5 **EXERCISE 9.7**
Accounting for Trade-ins

Mathews Bus Service traded in a used bus for a new one. The original cost of the old bus was $52,000. Accumulated depreciation at the time of the trade-in amounted to $34,000. The new bus cost $65,000, but Mathews was given a trade-in allowance of $10,000.

a. What amount of cash did Mathews have to pay to acquire the new bus?

b. Compute the gain or loss on the disposal for financial reporting purposes.

c. Explain how the gain or loss would be reported in the company's income statement.

LO6 **EXERCISE 9.8**
Estimating Goodwill

During the past several years the annual net income of Avery Company has averaged $540,000. At the present time the company is being offered for sale. Its accounting records show the book value of net assets (total assets minus all liabilities) to be $2,800,000. The fair value of Avery's net identifiable assets, however, is $3,000,000.

An investor negotiating to buy the company offers to pay an amount equal to the fair value for the net identifiable assets and to assume all liabilities. In addition, the investor is willing to pay for goodwill an amount equal to the above-average earnings for five years.

On the basis of this agreement, what price should the investor offer? A normal return on the fair value of net assets in this industry is 15 percent.

LO5 **EXERCISE 9.9**
LO8 The Write-Down of Impaired Assets

For several years, a number of **Food Lion, Inc.**, grocery stores were unprofitable. The company closed some of these locations. It was apparent that the company would not be able to recover the cost of the assets associated with the closed stores. Thus, the current value of these impaired assets had to be written down.

A note in the financial statements indicated that the company tests assets for impairment when circumstances indicate that an impairment may exist. For impairment testing, each store is considered a cash-generating unit. Stores with potential impairments are tested by comparing their carrying value with their recoverable amounts.

a. Explain why **Food Lion** wrote down the current carrying value of its unprofitable stores.

b. Explain why the write-down of impaired assets is considered a noncash expense.

LO1 **EXERCISE 9.10**
LO6 Ethics: "Let the Buyer Beware"

Bill Gladstone has owned and operated Gladstone's Service Station for over 30 years. The business, which is currently the town's only service station, has always been extremely profitable. Gladstone recently decided that he wanted to sell the business and retire. His asking price exceeds the fair market value of its net identifiable assets by nearly $50,000. Gladstone attributes this premium to the above-normal returns that the service station has always generated.

Gladstone recently found out about two issues that could have a profound effect upon the future of the business: (1) A well-known service station franchise will be built across the street from his station in approximately 18 months, and (2) one of his underground fuel tanks *may* have developed a very slow leak.

a. How might these issues affect the $50,000 in goodwill that Gladstone included in his selling price?

b. Assume that Gladstone is *not* disclosing this information to potential buyers. Does he have an ethical obligation to do so? Defend your answer.

LO7 **EXERCISE 9.11**
Depletion of Natural Resources

Salter Mining Company purchased the Northern Tier Mine for $21 million cash. The mine was estimated to contain 2.5 million tons of ore and to have a residual value of $1 million.
During the first year of mining operations at the Northern Tier Mine, 50,000 tons of ore were mined, of which 40,000 tons were sold.

a. Prepare a journal entry to record depletion during the year.

b. Show how the Northern Tier Mine, and its accumulated depletion, would appear in Salter Mining Company's balance sheet after the first year of operations.

c. Will the entire amount of depletion computed in part **a** be deducted from revenue in the determination of income for the year? Explain.

d. Indicate how the journal entry in part **a** affects the company's current ratio (its current assets divided by its current liabilities). Do you believe that the activities summarized in this entry do, in fact, make the company any more or less liquid? Explain.

LO6 LO8 **EXERCISE 9.12** Researching a Real Company

Locate an annual report in your library (or some other source) that includes a large gain or loss on the disposal of fixed assets. Report to the class the amount of the gain or loss and where in the company's income statement it is reported. Describe how the gain or loss is reported in the company's statement of cash flows. Summarize any discussion in the footnotes concerning the cause of the disposal.

LO4 **EXERCISE 9.13** Units-of-Output Method

During the current year, Airport Auto Rentals purchased 60 new automobiles at a cost of $14,000 per car. The cars will be sold to a wholesaler at an estimated $5,000 each as soon as they have been driven 50,000 miles. Airport Auto Rentals computes depreciation expense on its automobiles by the units-of-output method, based on mileage.

a. Compute the amount of depreciation to be recognized for each mile that a rental automobile is driven.

b. Assuming that the 60 rental cars are driven a total of 1,770,000 miles during the current year, compute the total amount of depreciation expense that Airport Auto Rentals should recognize on this fleet of cars for the year.

c. In this particular situation, do you believe the units-of-output depreciation method achieves a better matching of expenses with revenue than would the straight-line method? Explain.

LO4 **EXERCISE 9.14** Units-of-Production Depreciation Method

Dasher Company acquired a truck for use in its business for $25,500 in a cash transaction. The truck is expected to be used over a five-year period, will be driven approximately 18,000 miles per year, and is expected to have a value at the end of the five years of $4,500.

a. Compute the amount of depreciation that will be taken in the first two years of the truck's useful life if the actual miles driven are 16,000 and 18,200, respectively. Round the depreciation per mile to the nearest full cent.

b. How does the amount of accumulated depreciation at the end of the second year compare with what it would have been had the company chosen the straight-line depreciation method?

LO1 LO3 **EXERCISE 9.15** Using the **Home Depot, Inc.,** Financial Statements to Determine Depreciation Methods Used

The **Home Depot** financial statements appear in Appendix A at the end of this textbook. Use these statements to answer the following questions and indicate where in the financial statements you found the information.

a. What depreciation method does **Home Depot** use for buildings, furniture, fixtures, and equipment? What are the useful lives over which these assets are depreciated?

b. From the notes to **Home Depot**'s financial statements, what can you learn about the company's policy regarding impairment of plant assets?

c. Locate **Home Depot**'s balance sheet and find the section entitled "Property and Equipment, at cost." As of January 31, 2010, determine the amount of the company's investment in property and equipment and the amount of depreciation taken to date on those assets. Are these assets, taken as a whole, near the beginning or end of their estimated useful lives? Explain your answer.

Problem Set A

connect ACCOUNTING

LO1 through LO3 **PROBLEM 9.1A** Determining the Cost of Plant Assets

Wilmet College recently purchased new computing equipment for its library. The following information refers to the purchase and installation of this equipment:

1. The list price of the equipment was $275,000; however, Wilmet College qualified for an "education discount" of $25,000. It paid $50,000 cash for the equipment, and issued a three-month, 9 percent note payable for the remaining balance. The note, plus accrued interest charges of $4,500, was paid promptly at the maturity date.
2. In addition to the amounts described in **1**, Wilmet paid sales taxes of $15,000 at the date of purchase.
3. Freight charges for delivery of the equipment totaled $1,000.
4. Installation costs related to the equipment amounted to $5,000.

5. During installation, one of the computer terminals was accidentally damaged by a library employee. It cost the college $500 to repair this damage.
6. As soon as the computers were installed, the college paid $4,000 to print admissions brochures featuring the library's new, state-of-the-art computing facilities.

Instructions

a. In one sentence, make a general statement summarizing the nature of expenditures that qualify for inclusion in the cost of plant assets such as computing equipment.

b. For each of the six numbered paragraphs, indicate which items should be included by Wilmet College in the total cost debited to its Computing Equipment account. Also briefly indicate the proper accounting treatment of those items that *are not* included in the cost of the equipment.

c. Compute the total cost debited to the college's Computing Equipment account.

d. Prepare a journal entry at the end of the current year to record depreciation on the computing equipment. Wilmet College will depreciate this equipment by the straight-line method (half-year convention) over an estimated useful life of five years. Assume a zero residual value.

LO3 LO5 **PROBLEM 9.2A**
Comparison of Straight-Line and Accelerated Methods

Swanson & Hiller, Inc., purchased a new machine on September 1, 2008 at a cost of $108,000. The machine's estimated useful life at the time of the purchase was five years, and its residual value was $8,000.

Instructions

a. Prepare a complete depreciation schedule, beginning with calendar year 2008, under each of the methods listed below (assume that the half-year convention is used):
   1. Straight-line.
   2. 200 percent declining-balance.
   3. 150 percent declining-balance, switching to straight-line when that maximizes the expense.

b. Which of the three methods computed in part **a** is most common for financial reporting purposes? Explain.

c. Assume that Swanson & Hiller sells the machine on December 31, 2011, for $28,000 cash. Compute the resulting gain or loss from this sale under each of the depreciation methods used in part **a.** Does the gain or loss reported in the company's income statement have any direct cash effects? Explain.

LO1 through LO3 LO5 **PROBLEM 9.3A**
Issues Involving Alternative Depreciation Methods

Smart Hardware purchased new shelving for its store on April 1, 2011. The shelving is expected to have a 20-year life and no residual value. The following expenditures were associated with the purchase:

Cost of the shelving	$12,000
Freight charges	520
Sales taxes	780
Installation of shelving	2,700
Cost to repair shelf damaged during installation	400

Instructions

a. Compute depreciation expense for the years 2011 through 2013 under each depreciation method listed below:
   1. Straight-line, with fractional years rounded to the nearest whole month.
   2. 200 percent declining-balance, using the half-year convention.
   3. 150 percent declining-balance, using the half-year convention.

b. Smart Hardware has two conflicting objectives. Management wants to report the highest possible earnings in its financial statements, yet it also wants to minimize its taxable income reported to the IRS. Explain how both of these objectives can be met.

c. Which of the depreciation methods applied in part **a** resulted in the lowest reported book value at the end of 2014? Is book value an estimate of an asset's fair value? Explain.

d. Assume that Smart Hardware sold the old shelving that was being replaced. The old shelving had originally cost $9,000. Its book value at the time of the sale was $400. Record the sale of the old shelving under the following conditions:

1. The shelving was sold for $1,200 cash.
2. The shelving was sold for $200 cash.

LO5 **PROBLEM 9.4A**
Disposal of Plant Assets

During the current year, Ramirez Developers disposed of plant assets in the following transactions:

Feb. 10 Office equipment costing $26,000 was given to a scrap dealer at no charge. At the date of disposal, accumulated depreciation on the office equipment amounted to $25,800.

Apr. 1 Ramirez sold land and a building to Claypool Associates for $900,000, receiving $100,000 cash and a five-year, 9 percent note receivable for the remaining balance. Ramirez's records showed the following amounts: Land, $50,000; Building, $550,000; Accumulated Depreciation: Building (at the date of disposal), $250,000.

Aug. 15 Ramirez traded in an old truck for a new one. The old truck had cost $26,000, and its accumulated depreciation amounted to $18,000. The list price of the new truck was $39,000, but Ramirez received a $10,000 trade-in allowance for the old truck and paid only $29,000 in cash. Ramirez includes trucks in its Vehicles account.

Oct. 1 Ramirez traded in its old computer system as part of the purchase of a new system. The old system had cost $15,000, and its accumulated depreciation amounted to $11,000. The new computer's list price was $8,000. Ramirez accepted a trade-in allowance of $500 for the old computer system, paying $1,500 down in cash and issuing a one-year, 8 percent note payable for the $6,000 balance owed.

Instructions

a. Prepare journal entries to record each of the disposal transactions. Assume that depreciation expense on each asset has been recorded up to the date of disposal. Thus, you need not update the accumulated depreciation figures stated in the problem.

b. Will the gains and losses recorded in part **a** above affect the *gross profit* reported in Ramirez's income statement? Explain.

c. Explain how the financial reporting of gains and losses on plant assets differs from the financial reporting of *unrealized* gains and losses on marketable securities discussed in Chapter 7.

LO6 **PROBLEM 9.5A**
Accounting for Intangible Assets under GAAP

During the current year, Black Corporation incurred the following expenditures which should be recorded either as operating expenses or as intangible assets:

a. Expenditures were made for the training of new employees. The average employee remains with the company for five years, but is trained for a new position every two years.

b. Black purchased a controlling interest in a vinyl flooring company. The expenditure resulted in the recording of a significant amount of goodwill. Black expects to earn above-average returns on this investment indefinitely.

c. Black incurred large amounts of research and development costs in developing a dirt-resistant carpet fiber. The company expects that the fiber will be patented and that sales of the resulting products will contribute to revenue for at least 25 years. The legal life of the patent, however, will be only 20 years.

d. Black made an expenditure to acquire the patent on a popular carpet cleaner. The patent had a remaining legal life of 14 years, but Black expects to produce and sell the product for only six more years.

e. Black spent a large amount to sponsor the televising of the Olympic Games. Black's intent was to make television viewers more aware of the company's name and its product lines.

Instructions

Explain whether each of the above expenditures should be recorded as an operating expense or an intangible asset. If you view the expenditure as an intangible asset, indicate the number of years over which the asset should be amortized, if any. Explain your reasoning.

LO6 **PROBLEM 9.6A**
Accounting for Goodwill

Kivi Service Stations is considering expanding its operations to include the greater Dubuque area. Rather than build new service stations in the Dubuque area, management plans to acquire existing service stations and convert them into Kivi outlets.

Kivi is evaluating two similar acquisition opportunities. Information relating to each of these service stations is presented below:

	Joe's Garage	Gas N' Go
Estimated normal rate of return on net assets	20%	20%
Fair value of net identifiable assets	$950,000	$980,000
Actual average net income for past five years	220,000	275,000

Instructions

a. Compute an estimated fair value for any goodwill associated with Kivi purchasing Joe's Garage. Base your computation upon an assumption that successful service stations typically sell at about 9.25 times their annual earnings.

b. Compute an estimated fair value for any goodwill associated with Kivi purchasing Gas N' Go. Base your computation upon an assumption that Kivi's management expects excess earnings to continue for four years.

c. Many of Kivi's existing service stations are extremely profitable. If Kivi acquires Joe's Garage or Gas N' Go, should it also record the goodwill associated with its existing locations? Explain.

LO4 **PROBLEM 9.7A**
Alternative Depreciation Methods

Millar, Inc., purchased a truck to use for deliveries and is attempting to determine how much depreciation expense would be recognized under three different methods. The truck cost $20,000 and is expected to have a value of $4,000 at the end of its five-year life. The truck is expected to be used at the rate of 10,000 miles in the first year, 20,000 miles in the second and third years, and 15,000 miles in the fourth and fifth years.

Instructions

a. Determine the amount of depreciation expense that will be recognized under each of the following depreciation methods in the first and second years of the truck's useful life. A full year's depreciation will be recognized in the first year the truck is used.

1. Straight-line.

2. Double-declining-balance.

3. Units-of-output (based on miles).

b. Prepare the plant assets section of the balance sheet at the end of the second year of the asset's useful life under the double-declining-balance method, assuming the truck is the only plant asset owned by Millar, Inc.

c. By which of the three methods is it *not* possible to determine the actual amount of depreciation expense prior to the end of each year? What uncertainty causes this to be true?

LO2 **PROBLEM 9.8A**
LO3 Disposal of Plant and Intangible Assets
LO5

During the current year, Rothchild, Inc., purchased two assets that are described as follows:

Heavy Equipment

Purchase price, $275,000.

Expected to be used for 10 years, with a residual value at the end of that time of $50,000.

Expenditures required to recondition the equipment and prepare it for use, $75,000.

Patent

Purchase price, $75,000.

Expected to be used for five years, with no value at the end of that time.

Rothchild depreciates heavy equipment by the declining-balance method at 150 percent of the straight-line rate. It amortizes intangible assets by the straight-line method. At the end of two years, because of changes in Rothchild's core business, it sold the patent to a competitor for $35,000.

Instructions

a. Compute the amount of depreciation expense on the heavy equipment for each of the first three years of the asset's life.

b. Compute the amount of amortization on the patent for each of the two years it was owned by Rothchild.

c. Prepare the plant and intangible assets section of Rothchild's balance sheet at the end of the first and second years. Also, calculate the amount of the gain or loss on the patent that would be included in the second year's income statement.

Problem Set B

LO1 through LO3

PROBLEM 9.1B
Determining the Cost of Plant Assets

Walker Motel recently purchased new exercise equipment for its exercise room. The following information refers to the purchase and installation of this equipment:

1. The list price of the equipment was $40,000; however, Walker qualified for a "special discount" of $5,000. It paid $10,000 cash for the equipment, and issued a three-month, 12 percent note payable for the remaining balance. The note, plus accrued interest charges of $750, was paid promptly at the maturity date.
2. In addition to the amounts described in **1**, Walker paid sales taxes of $2,100 at the date of purchase.
3. Freight charges for delivery of the equipment totaled $600.
4. Installation and training costs related to the equipment amounted to $900.
5. During installation, one of the pieces of equipment was accidentally damaged by an employee. It cost the motel $400 to repair this damage.
6. As soon as the equipment was installed, the motel paid $3,200 to print brochures featuring the exercise room's new, state-of-the-art exercise facilities.

Instructions

a. In one sentence, make a general statement summarizing the nature of expenditures that qualify for inclusion in the cost of plant assets such as exercise equipment.

b. For each of the six numbered paragraphs, indicate which items should be included by Walker in the total cost debited to its Equipment account. Also briefly indicate the proper accounting treatment of those items that *are not* included in the cost of the equipment.

c. Compute the total cost debited to the motel's Equipment account.

d. Prepare a journal entry at the end of the current year to record depreciation on the exercise equipment. Walker Motel will depreciate this equipment by the straight-line method (half-year convention) over an estimated useful life of five years. Assume a zero residual value.

LO3 LO5

PROBLEM 9.2B
Comparison of Straight-Line and Accelerated Methods

R&R, Inc., purchased a new machine on September 1, 2009, at a cost of $180,000. The machine's estimated useful life at the time of the purchase was five years, and its residual value was $10,000.

Instructions

a. Prepare a complete depreciation schedule, beginning with calendar year 2009, under each of the methods listed below (assume that the half-year convention is used):
   1. Straight line.
   2. 200 percent declining-balance.
   3. 150 percent declining-balance (not switching to straight-line).

b. Which of the three methods computed in part **a** is most common for financial reporting purposes? Explain.

c. Assume that R&R sells the machine on December 31, 2012, for $55,000 cash. Compute the resulting gain or loss from this sale under each of the depreciation methods used in part **a.** Does the gain or loss reported in the company's income statement have any direct cash effects? Explain.

LO1 through LO3, LO5

PROBLEM 9.3B

Issues Involving Alternative Depreciation Methods

Davidson, DDS, purchased new furniture for its store on May 1, 2011. The furniture is expected to have a 10-year life and no residual value. The following expenditures were associated with the purchase:

Cost of the furniture	$11,000
Freight charges	375
Sales taxes	550
Installation of furniture	75
Cost to repair furniture damaged during installation	400

Instructions

a. Compute depreciation expense for the years 2011 through 2014 under each depreciation method listed below:

1. Straight-line, with fractional years rounded to the nearest whole month.
2. 200 percent declining-balance, using the half-year convention.
3. 150 percent declining-balance, using the half-year convention.

b. Davidson, DDS, has two conflicting objectives. Management wants to report the highest possible earnings in its financial statements, yet it also wants to minimize its taxable income reported to the IRS. Explain how both of these objectives can be met.

c. Which of the depreciation methods applied in part **a** resulted in the lowest reported book value at the end of 2014? Is book value an estimate of an asset's fair value? Explain.

d. Assume that Davidson, DDS, sold the old furniture that was being replaced. The old furniture had originally cost $3,000. Its book value at the time of the sale was $400. Record the sale of the old furniture under the following conditions:

1. The furniture was sold for $600 cash.
2. The furniture was sold for $300 cash.

LO5

PROBLEM 9.4B

Disposal of Plant Assets

During the current year, Blake Construction disposed of plant assets in the following transactions:

Jan. 6 Equipment costing $18,000 was given to a scrap dealer at no charge. At the date of disposal, accumulated depreciation on the office equipment amounted to $16,800.

Mar. 3 Blake sold land and a building for $800,000, receiving $100,000 cash and a five-year, 12 percent note receivable for the remaining balance. Blake's records showed the following amounts: Land, $50,000; Buildings, $680,000; Accumulated Depreciation: Building (at the date of disposal), $250,000.

Jul. 10 Blake traded in an old truck for a new one. The old truck had cost $26,000, and its accumulated depreciation amounted to $22,000. The list price of the new truck was $37,000, but Blake received a $12,000 trade-in allowance for the old truck and paid only $25,000 in cash. Blake includes trucks in its Vehicles account.

Sept. 3 Blake traded in its old computer system as part of the purchase of a new system. The old system had cost $12,000, and its accumulated depreciation amounted to $9,000. The new computer's list price was $10,000. Blake accepted a trade-in allowance of $400 for the old computer system, paying $1,000 down in cash and issuing a one-year, 10 percent note payable for the $8,600 balance owed.

Instructions

a. Prepare journal entries to record each of the disposal transactions. Assume that depreciation expense on each asset has been recorded up to the date of disposal. Thus you need not update the accumulated depreciation figures stated in the problem.

b. Will the gains and losses recorded in part **a** above affect the *gross profit* reported in Blake's income statement? Explain.

c. Explain how the financial reporting of gains and losses on plant assets differs from the financial reporting of *unrealized* gains and losses on marketable securities discussed in Chapter 7.

LO6 **PROBLEM 9.5B**
Accounting for Intangible Assets under GAAP

During the current year, Omega Products Corporation incurred the following expenditures which should be recorded either as operating expenses or as intangible assets:

a. Expenditures were made for the training of new employees. The average employee remains with the company for five years, but is trained for a new position every two years.

b. Omega purchased a controlling interest in a wallpaper company. The expenditure resulted in recording a significant amount of goodwill. Omega expects to earn above-average returns on this investment indefinitely.

c. Omega incurred large amounts of research and development costs in developing a superior product. The company expects that it will be patented and that sales of the resulting products will contribute to revenue for at least 40 years. The legal life of the patent, however, will be only 20 years.

d. Omega made an expenditure to acquire the patent on a whatsa. The patent had a remaining legal life of 10 years, but Omega expects to produce and sell the product for only four more years.

e. Omega spent a large amount to sponsor the televising of the World Series. Omega's intent was to make television viewers more aware of the company's name and product lines.

Instructions

Explain whether each of the above expenditures should be recorded as an operating expense or an intangible asset. If you view the expenditure as an intangible asset, indicate the number of years over which the asset should be amortized. Explain your reasoning.

LO6 **PROBLEM 9.6B**
Accounting for Goodwill

Jell Stores is considering expanding its operations to include the greater Boston area. Rather than build new stores in the Boston area, management plans to acquire existing stores and convert them into Jell outlets.

Jell is evaluating two similar acquisition opportunities. Information relating to each of these stores is presented below:

	Carnie's	Mell's
Estimated normal rate of return on net assets	20%	20%
Fair market value of net identifiable assets	$900,000	$980,000
Actual average net income for past five years	250,000	280,000

Instructions

a. Compute an estimated fair value for any goodwill associated with Jell purchasing Carnie's. Base your computation upon an assumption that successful stores of this type typically sell at about 10 times their annual earnings.

b. Compute an estimated fair value for any goodwill associated with Jell purchasing Mell's. Base your computation upon an assumption that Jell's management wants to generate a target return on investment of 35 percent.

c. Many of Jell's existing stores are extremely profitable. If Jell acquires Carnie's or Mell's, should it also record the goodwill associated with its existing locations? Explain.

LO4 **PROBLEM 9.7B**
Alternative Depreciation Methods

Wilson, Inc., purchased a truck to use for deliveries and is attempting to determine how much depreciation expense would be recognized under three different methods. The truck cost $24,000 and is expected to have a value of $6,000 at the end of its six-year life. The truck is expected to be used at the rate of 15,000 miles in the first year, 20,000 miles in the second and third years, and 12,000 miles in the fourth, fifth, and sixth years.

Instructions

a. Determine the amount of depreciation expense that will be recognized under each of the following depreciation methods in the first and second years of the truck's useful life. A full year's depreciation will be recognized in the first year the truck is used.

1. Straight-line.
2. Double-declining-balance.
3. Units-of-output (based on miles).

b. Prepare the plant assets section of the balance sheet at the end of the second year in the asset's useful life under the units-of-output method, assuming the truck is the only plant asset owned by Wilson, Inc.

c. By which of the three methods is it *not* possible to determine the actual amount of depreciation expense prior to the end of each year? What uncertainty causes this to be true?

LO2 LO3 LO5

PROBLEM 9.8B
Disposal of Plant and Intangible Assets

During the current year, Rodgers Company purchased two assets that are described as follows:

Heavy Equipment

Purchase price, $550,000.
Expected to be used for 10 years, with a residual value at the end of that time of $70,000.
Expenditures required to recondition the equipment and prepare it for use, $120,000.

Patent

Purchase price, $80,000.
Expected to be used for six years, with no value at the end of that time.

Rodgers depreciates heavy equipment by the declining-balance method at 200 percent of the straight-line rate. It amortizes intangible assets by the straight-line method. At the end of two years, because of changes in Rodgers's core business, it sold the patent to a competitor for $40,000.

Instructions

a. Compute the amount of depreciation expense on the heavy equipment for each of the first three years of the asset's life.

b. Compute the amount of amortization on the patent for each of the two years it was owned by Rodgers.

c. Prepare the plant and intangible assets section of Rodgers's balance sheet at the end of the first and second years. Also, calculate the amount of the gain or loss on the patent that would be included in the second year's income statement.

Critical Thinking Cases

LO3

CASE 9.1
Are Useful Lives "Flexible"?

Mickey Gillespie is the controller of Print Technologies, a publicly owned company. The company is experiencing financial difficulties and is aggressively looking for ways to cut costs.
Suzanne Bedell, the CEO, instructs Gillespie to lengthen from 5 to 10 years the useful life used in computing depreciation on certain special-purpose machinery. Bedell believes that this change represents a substantial cost savings, as it will reduce the depreciation expense on these assets by nearly one-half.

Note: The proposed change affects only the depreciation expense recognized in financial statements. Depreciation deductions in income tax returns will not be affected.

Instructions

a. Discuss the extent to which Bedell's idea will, in fact, achieve a cost savings. Consider the effects on both net income and cash flows.

b. Who is responsible for estimating the useful lives of plant assets?

c. Discuss any ethical issues that Gillespie should consider with respect to Bedell's instructions.

LO1

CASE 9.2
Departures from GAAP—Are They Ethical?

Martin Myers owns Myers Construction Co. The company maintains accounting records for the purposes of exercising control over its construction activities and meeting its reporting obligations regarding payrolls and income tax returns. As it has no other financial reporting obligations, Myers does not prepare formal financial statements.

The company owns land and several other assets with current market values well in excess of their historical costs. Martin Myers directs the company's accountant, Maureen O'Shaughnessey, to prepare a balance sheet in which assets are shown at estimated market values. Myers says this type of balance sheet will give him a better understanding of where the business stands. He also thinks it will be useful in obtaining bank loans, as loan applications always ask for the estimated market values of real estate owned.

Instructions

a. Would the financial statements requested by Martin Myers be in conformity with generally accepted accounting principles?

b. Is Myers Construction under any legal or ethical obligation to prepare financial statements that *do* conform to generally accepted accounting principles?

c. Discuss any ethical issues that O'Shaughnessey should consider with respect to Myers's request.

LO3 LO4 CASE 9.3
Depreciation Policies in Annual Reports

The following is a note accompanying a recent financial statement of **International Paper Company**:

Plant, Properties, and Equipment
Plant, properties, and equipment are stated at cost less accumulated depreciation. Expenditures for betterments are capitalized, whereas normal repairs and maintenance are expensed as incurred. The units-of-production method of depreciation is used for major pulp and paper mills, and the straight-line method is used for other plants and equipment. Annual straight-line depreciation rates are, for buildings—2½ percent to 8½ percent, and for machinery and equipment—5 percent to 33 percent.

Instructions

a. Are the depreciation methods used in the company's financial statements determined by current income tax laws? If not, who is responsible for selecting these methods? Explain.

b. Does the company violate the consistency principle by using different depreciation methods for its paper mills and wood products facilities than it uses for its other plant and equipment? If not, what does the principle of consistency mean? Explain.

c. What is the estimated useful life of the machinery and equipment being depreciated with a straight-line depreciation rate of:

 1. 5 percent.

 2. 33 percent (round to the nearest year).

 Who determines the useful lives over which specific assets are to be depreciated?

d. Why do you think the company uses accelerated depreciation methods for income tax purposes, rather than using the straight-line method?

LO2 CASE 9.4
Capitalization vs. Expense

One of your responsibilities as division manager of an important component of Roxby Industries is to oversee accounting for the division. One of the issues you grapple with on an almost continuous basis is whether particular costs should be expensed immediately or whether they should be capitalized. The company has an accounting policy manual that includes a section on this topic, but it is rather vague in this regard. It simply says that if a cost benefits multiple accounting periods, the cost should be capitalized; otherwise, that cost should be expensed immediately. It also makes a brief reference to *materiality* by stating that, if a cost is sufficiently small, it should be immediately expensed despite the fact that it may benefit multiple accounting periods. No additional guidance is provided with regard to how these general concepts should be applied.

Over several years you have noticed a tendency of your staff to capitalize rather than expense more costs. While you and your coworkers in the division do not receive a bonus or other direct compensation that is tied to your division's performance, you know that upper management monitors carefully the financial performance of divisions. From time to time in various meetings and in written correspondence, comments are made praising individuals and divisions of the company for their positive financial performance. In fact, within your division you have done the same when you meet with your employees and either compliment them for strong financial performance or express concern about weak financial performance.

Roxby Industries has a code of professional conduct that is shown to employees when they are hired. Within that code are references to personal integrity and the responsibility of employees to carry out company policy and not engage in activities that benefit themselves at the expense of the company. Like the accounting policies referred to above, there is no guidance on how this general principle might be carried out.

Instructions

a. What behavior may your comments in meetings with your employees, or the comments made to you from upper management, be motivating in terms of the continuous decisions that are being made about capitalizing and expensing costs?

b. What steps might you take to ensure that you and the employees in your division are not taking actions that they should not take in light of the company's accounting policies and code of professional conduct?

LO2 INTERNET CASE 9.5

R&D in the Pharmaceutical Industry

The pharmaceutical industry spends billions of dollars each year on research and development. Rather than capitalize these R&D expenditures as intangible assets, companies are required to charge them to expense in the year incurred.

Perform a keyword search of Pharmaceutical Companies using the search engine of your choice (e.g., Yahoo, Google).

Your search will result in a list of companies that research and develop pharmaceutical products. Select three of these companies and obtain their 10-K reports using the SEC's EDGAR system or going directly to the Web sites of the companies you choose.

Instructions

a. For each of the companies you selected, determine:

1. Total R&D expense for the most current year.
2. Total R&D expense as a percentage of total operating costs and expenses.
3. Total R&D expense as a percentage of net sales.
4. The percentage by which operating income would have increased had the entire R&D expenditure been recorded as an intangible asset instead of being charged to expense.

b. Using information from the 10-K reports, summarize briefly the kinds of drugs being researched and developed by each of these companies. To a potential investor, which company appears to be the most innovative and promising? Explain.

Internet sites are time and date sensitive. It is the purpose of these exercises to have you explore the Internet. You may need to use the Yahoo! search engine http://www.yahoo.com *(or another favorite search engine) to find a company's current Web address.*

Answers to Self-Test Questions

1. c (Depreciation is not recorded on inventory.) **2.** c **3.** d, $1,800 [2010 depreciation = $10,000 × 20% × ½ = $1,000; 2011 depreciation = ($10,000 − $1,000) × 20% = $1,800] **4.** c, d **5.** a ($22,000 selling price − $17,000 book value = $5,000 gain; $50,000 cost − $17,000 book value = $33,000 accumulated depreciation) **6.** c

CHAPTER 10

Liabilities

© ThinkStock/PunchStock/DAL

AFTER STUDYING THIS CHAPTER, YOU SHOULD BE ABLE TO:

- **LO1** Define *liabilities* and distinguish between current and long-term liabilities.
- **LO2** Account for notes payable and interest expense.
- **LO3** Describe the costs and the basic accounting activities relating to payrolls.
- **LO4** Prepare an amortization table allocating payments between interest and principal.
- **LO5** Describe corporate bonds and explain the tax advantage of debt financing.
- **LO6** Account for bonds issued at a discount or premium.
- **LO7** Explain the concept of present value as it relates to bond prices.
- **LO8** Explain how estimated liabilities, loss contingencies, and commitments are disclosed in financial statements.
- **LO9** Evaluate the safety of creditors' claims.
- **LO10** Describe reporting issues related to leases, postretirement benefits, and deferred taxes.

Learning Objectives

DuPont

Buying items on credit has never been easier. Each day, large retailers and credit card companies seem to encourage consumers to go deeper and deeper into debt. Add to credit card debt other long-term obligations—such as home mortgages and automobile loans—and it's no wonder that payments on total household debt consume the majority of total disposable income in the United States.

Large corporations also have jumped on the bandwagon in recent years by issuing more debt than ever to finance expansion and acquisitions. The tremendous debt service costs associated with corporate borrowing can require a significant portion of a company's operating cash flows.

Consider, for example, DuPont. In the 2009 balance sheet, DuPont reports total liabilities over $30.5 billion in comparison to total stockholders' equity of only approximately $7.7 billion. The company's heavy reliance on debt financing burdens the company with billions of dollars in debt service costs annually. Notes accompanying DuPont's recent financial statements indicate management's intent to reduce current debt levels to improve the company's overall financial flexibility. Other major corporations are likely to do the same. ■

Creditors and investors evaluate carefully the liabilities appearing in financial reports. Understanding short-term versus long-term debt is important for managers choosing how to finance their businesses. This chapter provides a basic understanding of concepts related to liabilities and describes how liabilities are recorded and later presented in the financial statements. In addition, the impact of debt on various financial ratios is illustrated.

THE NATURE OF LIABILITIES

Learning Objective
LO1 **Define *liabilities* and distinguish between current and long-term liabilities.**

Liabilities may be defined as *debts or obligations arising from past transactions or events* that require settlement at a future date. All liabilities have certain characteristics in common; however, the specific terms of different liabilities, and the rights of the creditors, vary greatly.

Distinction between Debt and Equity Businesses have two basic sources of financing: liabilities and owners' equity. Liabilities differ from owners' equity in several respects. The feature that most clearly distinguishes the claims of creditors from owners' equity is that all liabilities eventually *mature*—that is, they come due. Owners' equity does not mature. The date on which a liability comes due is called the **maturity date.**[1]

Although all liabilities eventually mature, their maturity dates vary. Some liabilities are so short in term that they are paid before the financial statements are prepared. Long-term liabilities, in contrast, may not mature for many years. The maturity dates of key liabilities may be a critical factor in the solvency of a business.

The providers of borrowed capital are *creditors* of the business, not owners. As creditors, they have financial claims against the business but usually do *not* have the right to control business operations. The traditional roles of owners, managers, and creditors may be modified, however, in an *indenture contract.* Creditors sometimes insist on being granted some control over business operations as a condition of making a loan, particularly if the business is in poor financial condition. Indenture contracts may impose such restrictions as limits on management salaries and on dividends, and may require the creditor's approval for additional borrowing or for large capital expenditures.

The claims of creditors have *legal priority* over the claims of owners. If a business ceases operations and liquidates, creditors must be *paid in full* before any distributions are made to the owners. The relative security of creditors' claims, however, can vary among the creditors. Sometimes the borrower pledges title to specific assets as **collateral** for a loan. If the borrower defaults on a secured loan, the creditor may foreclose on the pledged assets. Assets that have been pledged as security for loans should be identified in notes accompanying the borrower's financial statements.

Liabilities that are not secured by specific assets are termed *general credit obligations.* The priorities of general credit obligations vary with the nature of the liability and the terms of indenture contracts.

Many Liabilities Bear Interest Many long-term liabilities, and some short-term ones, require the borrower to pay interest. Only interest accrued *as of the balance sheet date* appears as a liability in the borrower's balance sheet. The borrower's obligation to pay interest in *future* periods sometimes is disclosed in the notes to the financial statements, but it is not shown as an existing liability.

Estimated Liabilities Most liabilities are for a definite dollar amount, clearly stated by contract. Examples include notes payable, accounts payable, and accrued expenses, such as interest payable and salaries payable. In some cases, however, the dollar amount of a liability must be *estimated* at the balance sheet date.

[1] Some liabilities are *due on demand,* which means that the liability is payable upon the creditor's request. Liabilities due on demand may come due at any time and are classified as current liabilities.

Estimated liabilities have two basic characteristics: The liability is *known to exist,* but the precise dollar amount cannot be determined until a later date. For instance, the automobiles sold by most automakers are accompanied by a warranty obligating the automaker to replace defective parts for a period of several years. As each car is sold, the automaker *incurs a liability* to perform any work that may be required under the warranty. The dollar amount of this liability, however, can only be estimated.

Current Liabilities

Current liabilities are obligations that must be paid within one year or within the operating cycle, whichever is longer. Another requirement for classification as a current liability is the expectation that the debt will be paid from current assets (or through the rendering of services). Liabilities that do not meet these conditions are classified as long-term or noncurrent liabilities.

The time period used in defining current liabilities parallels that used in defining current assets. The amount of *working capital* (current assets less current liabilities) and the *current ratio* (current assets divided by current liabilities) are valuable indicators of a company's ability to pay its debts in the near future.

Among the most common examples of current liabilities are accounts payable, short-term notes payable, the current portion of long-term debt, accrued liabilities (such as interest payable, income taxes payable, and payroll liabilities), and unearned revenue.

ACCOUNTS PAYABLE

Accounts payable often are subdivided into the categories of *trade* accounts payable and *other* accounts payable. Trade accounts payable are short-term obligations to suppliers for purchases of merchandise. Other accounts payable include liabilities for any goods and services other than merchandise.

Technically, the date at which a trade account payable comes into existence depends on whether goods are purchased F.O.B. (free on board) shipping point or F.O.B. destination. Under F.O.B. shipping point, a liability arises and title to the goods transfers when the merchandise is *shipped* by the supplier. Under F.O.B. destination, a liability does not arise and title of ownership does not transfer until the goods are *received* by the buyer. However, unless *material* amounts of merchandise are purchased on terms F.O.B. shipping point, most companies follow the convenient practice of recording trade accounts payable when merchandise is received.

NOTES PAYABLE

Learning Objective
Account for notes payable and interest expense.
LO2

Notes payable are issued whenever bank loans are obtained. Other transactions that may give rise to notes payable include the purchase of real estate or costly equipment, the purchase of merchandise, and the substitution of a note for a past-due account payable.

Notes payable usually require the borrower to pay an interest charge. Normally, the interest rate is stated separately from the **principal amount** of the note.[2]

To illustrate, assume that on November 1, Porter Company borrows $10,000 from its bank for a period of six months at an annual interest rate of 12 percent. Six months later on May 1, Porter Company will have to pay the bank the principal amount of $10,000, plus $600 interest ($\$10,000 \times .12 \times 6/12$). As evidence of this loan, the bank will require Porter Company to issue a note payable similar to the one in Exhibit 10–1.

[2] An alternative is to include the interest charges in the face amount of the note. This form of note is seldom used today, largely because of the disclosure requirements under "truth-in-lending" laws.

Exhibit 10–1
A NOTE PAYABLE

Miami, Florida		November 1, 20__
Six months	**AFTER THIS DATE**	Porter Company

PROMISES TO PAY TO SECURITY NATIONAL BANK THE SUM OF $ $10,000

WITH INTEREST AT THE RATE OF 12% **PER ANNUM.**

SIGNED *John Caldwell*

TITLE Treasurer

The journal entry in Porter Company's accounting records for this November 1 borrowing is:

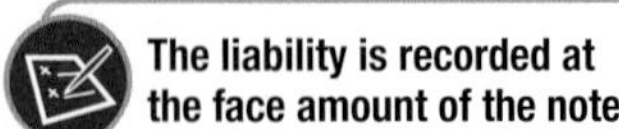
The liability is recorded at the face amount of the note

Cash	10,000	
Notes Payable		10,000
Borrowed $10,000 for 6 months at 12% interest per year.		

Notice that no liability is recorded for the interest charges when the note is issued. At the date that money is borrowed, the borrower has a liability *only for the principal amount of the loan;* the liability for interest accrues day by day over the life of the loan. At December 31, two months' interest expense has accrued, and the following year-end adjusting entry is made:

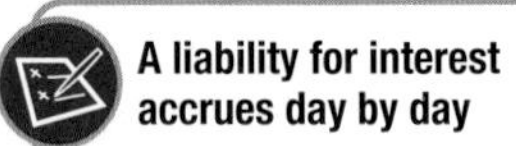
A liability for interest accrues day by day

Interest Expense	200	
Interest Payable		200
To record interest expense incurred through year-end on 12%, 6-month note dated Nov. 1 ($10,000 × 12% × 2/12 = $200).		

For simplicity, we will assume that Porter Company makes adjusting entries *only at year-end.* Thus, the entry on May 1 to record payment of the note will be:

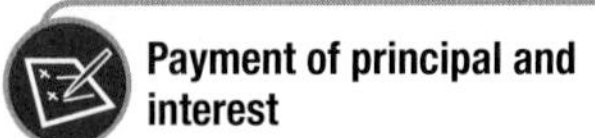
Payment of principal and interest

Notes Payable	10,000	
Interest Payable	200	
Interest Expense	400	
Cash		10,600
To record payment of 12%, 6-month note on maturity date and to recognize interest expense accrued since Jan. 1 ($10,000 × 12% × 4/12 = $400).		

If Porter Company paid this note *prior* to May 1, interest charges usually would be computed only through the date of early payment.[3]

THE CURRENT PORTION OF LONG-TERM DEBT

Some long-term debts, such as mortgage loans, are payable in a series of monthly or quarterly installments. In these cases, the *principal* amount due within one year (or the operating

[3] Computing interest charges only through the date of payment is the normal business practice. However, some notes are written in a manner requiring the borrower to pay interest for the full term of the note even if payment is made early. Borrowers should look carefully at these terms.

cycle) is regarded as a current liability, and the remainder of the obligation is classified as a long-term liability.

As the maturity date of a long-term liability approaches, the obligation eventually becomes due within the current period. Long-term liabilities that become payable within one year of the balance sheet date are *reclassified* in the balance sheet as current liabilities.[4] Changing the classification of a liability does not require a journal entry; the obligation is simply shown in a different section of the balance sheet.

ACCRUED LIABILITIES

Accrued liabilities arise from the recognition of expenses for which payment will be made in a future period. Thus accrued liabilities also are called *accrued expenses.* Examples of accrued liabilities include interest payable, income taxes payable, and a number of liabilities relating to payrolls. As accrued liabilities stem from the recording of expenses, the *matching* principle governs the timing of their recognition.

All companies incur accrued liabilities. In most cases, however, these liabilities are paid at frequent intervals. Therefore, they usually do not accumulate to large amounts. In a balance sheet, small amounts of accrued liabilities are sometimes included in the amount shown as accounts payable.

PAYROLL LIABILITIES

Learning Objective LO3
Describe the costs and the basic accounting activities relating to payrolls.

The preparation of a payroll is a specialized accounting function beyond the scope of this text. But we believe that every student should have some understanding of the various costs associated with payrolls. Employers must compute, record, and pay a number of costs in addition to the wages and salaries owed to employees. In fact, the total wages and salaries expense (or gross pay) represents only the starting point of payroll computations.

To illustrate, assume that Fulbright Medical Lab employs 20 highly skilled employees. If monthly wages for this workforce in January were $100,000, the *total* payroll costs incurred by this employer would actually be much higher, as shown in Exhibit 10–2.

Exhibit 10–2
THE COMPUTATION OF TOTAL PAYROLL COSTS

Gross pay (wages expense)	$100,000
Social Security and Medicare taxes	7,650
Federal and state unemployment taxes	6,200
Workers' Compensation Insurance	4,000
Group health and life insurance benefits	6,000
Employee pension plan benefits	9,500
Total payroll costs for January	$133,350

The amounts in Exhibit 10–2 shown in red are **payroll taxes** and insurance premiums required by law. Costs shown in green currently are not required by law but often are included in the total compensation package provided to employees at the discretion of the employer.

In our example, total payroll-related costs exceed wages expense *by more than 30 percent.* This relationship will vary from one employer to another, but our illustration is typical of many payrolls.

Payroll Taxes and Mandated Costs

All employers must pay Social Security and Medicare taxes on the wages or salary paid to each employee. The percentages of the employee's earnings subject to these taxes vary from year to year. Federal unemployment taxes apply only to the *first* set dollar amount earned by each employee during the year (state unemployment taxes may vary). Thus these taxes tend to drop off dramatically as the year progresses.

[4] Exceptions are made to this rule if the liability will be *refinanced* (that is, extended or renewed) on a long-term basis and certain specific conditions are met or if a special *sinking fund* has been accumulated for the purpose of repaying this obligation. In these cases, the debt remains classified as a long-term liability, even though it will mature within the current period.

Workers' compensation is a state-mandated program that provides insurance to employees against job-related injury. Like most other insurance policies, the premiums are generally paid *in advance* by debiting a current asset account, Prepaid Workers' Compensation Insurance, and by crediting Cash. The premiums vary greatly by state and by occupational classification. In some high-risk industries (for example, roofers), workers' compensation premiums may exceed 50 percent of the employees' wages.

Other Payroll-Related Costs Many employers pay some or all of the costs of health and life insurance for their employees and their family members, as well as make contributions to employee pension plans. Contributions to employee pension plans, if any, vary greatly among employers.

Amounts Withheld from Employees' Pay Thus far, our illustration has specified only those taxes and other mandated costs levied on the *employer.* Employees, too, incur taxes on their earnings. In addition to federal and state income taxes, employees share in paying Social Security and Medicare taxes.[5] Employers must withhold these amounts from their employees' pay and forward them directly to the appropriate tax authorities.[6] (The net amount of cash actually paid to employees after all required withholdings have been made is often referred to as the employees' *take-home pay.*)

In our illustration, Fulbright Medical Lab's 20 employees earned gross wages of $100,000 in January. Their take-home pay will be significantly less than the gross amount, as shown in Exhibit 10–3, using assumed numbers for state and federal income tax withholdings.

Exhibit 10–3
COMPUTATION OF EMPLOYEE TAKE-HOME PAY

Gross pay (wages expense)	$100,000
Less:	
State income tax withholdings	(2,350)
Federal income tax withholdings	(22,500)
Social Security and Medicare tax withholdings	(7,650)
Employee take-home pay for January	$ 67,500

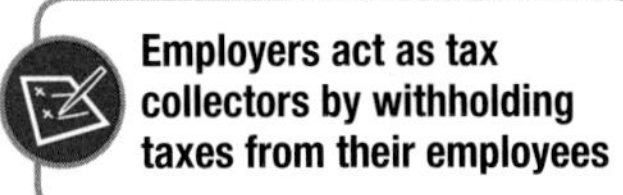

Employers act as tax collectors by withholding taxes from their employees

It is important to realize that amounts withheld from employees' pay do *not* represent taxes on the *employer.* The amounts withheld are simply a portion of the gross wages and salaries expense that must be sent directly to the tax authorities, rather than paid to the employees. In essence, the employer is required by law to act as the tax *collector.* In the employer's balance sheet, these withholdings represent current liabilities until they are forwarded to the proper tax authorities, but they do not represent payroll taxes of the employer.

Recording Payroll Activities Let us conclude our illustration of Fulbright Medical Lab by making the necessary entries to record its payroll activities. In Exhibit 10–2, the lab's *total* payroll costs for January were computed as $133,350. Of this amount, $100,000 represented gross wages earned by employees, $17,850 represented employer payroll taxes and other mandated costs (shown in red), and $15,500 represented other employee benefits paid for by the employer (shown in green). The accounting for these three amounts by Fulbright Medical Lab is summarized in Exhibit 10–4.

[5] Social Security and Medicare taxes are levied on *employees* at the same percentage rate as levied upon *employers.* Thus, total Social Security and Medicare taxes amount to more than 15 percent of gross wages and salaries. There is a cap on the portion of an employee's earnings that is subject to Social Security taxes. There is no cap on employee wages or salaries subject to Medicare taxes.

[6] In many companies, employers make additional withholdings when their employees share in paying for the cost of health insurance, life insurance, retirement contributions, and other fringe benefits.

Exhibit 10–4

PAYROLL ACTIVITIES RECORDED BY THE EMPLOYER

A. Record gross wages, employee withholdings, and employee take-home pay (withholdings and take-home pay figures taken from Exhibit 10–3).

Wages Expense	100,000	
State Income Tax Payable		2,350
Federal Income Tax Payable		22,500
Social Security and Medicare Taxes Payable		7,650
Cash (or Wages Payable)		67,500
To record gross wages, employee withholdings, and employee take-home pay.		

B. Record employer's payroll tax expense (red figures taken from Exhibit 10–2).

Payroll Tax Expense	17,850	
Social Security and Medicare Taxes Payable		7,650
Federal and State Unemployment Taxes Payable		6,200
Prepaid Workers' Compensation Insurance		4,000
To record employer payroll tax expense, $4,000 of which is the expiration of prepaid workers' compensation insurance premiums.		

C. Record employee benefit expenses (green figures taken from Exhibit 10–2).

Employee Health and Life Insurance Expense	6,000	
Pension Fund Expense	9,500	
Prepaid Employee Health and Life Insurance		6,000
Cash (or Pension Benefits Payable)		9,500
To record employee benefit expenses, $6,000 of which is the expiration of prepaid employee health and life insurance premium.		

UNEARNED REVENUE

A liability for unearned revenue arises when a customer pays in advance. Upon receipt of an advance payment from a customer, the company debits Cash and credits a liability account such as Unearned Revenue or Customers' Deposits. As the services are rendered to the customer, an entry is made debiting the liability account and crediting a revenue account. Notice that the liability for unearned revenue normally is satisfied by rendering services to the creditor, rather than by making cash payments.

Unearned revenue ordinarily is classified as a current liability because activities involved in earning revenue are part of the business's normal operating cycle.

Long-Term Liabilities

Long-term obligations usually arise from major expenditures, such as acquisitions of plant assets, the purchase of another company, or refinancing an existing long-term obligation that is about to mature. Thus, transactions involving long-term liabilities are relatively few in number but often involve large dollar amounts. In contrast, current liabilities usually arise from routine operating transactions.

Many businesses regard long-term liabilities as an alternative to owners' equity as a source of permanent financing. Although long-term liabilities eventually mature, they often are *refinanced*—that is, the maturing obligation simply is replaced with a new long-term liability. As a result, the financing becomes a permanent part of the financing of the business.

MATURING OBLIGATIONS INTENDED TO BE REFINANCED

One special type of long-term liability is an obligation that will mature in the current period but that is expected to be refinanced on a long-term basis. For example, a company may have a bank loan that comes due each year but is routinely extended for the following year. Both the company and the bank may intend for this arrangement to continue on a long-term basis.

If management has both the *intent* and the *ability* to refinance soon-to-mature obligations on a long-term basis, these obligations are classified as long-term liabilities. In this situation, the accountant looks to the *economic substance* of the situation rather than to its legal form.

When the economic substance of a transaction differs from its legal form or its outward appearance, financial statements should reflect the *economic substance.* Accountants summarize this concept with the phrase *"Substance takes precedence over form."* Today's business world is characterized by transactions of ever-increasing complexity. Recognizing those situations in which the substance of a transaction differs from its form is one of the greatest challenges confronting the accounting profession.

INTERNATIONAL CASE IN POINT

It is typical in Japan for short-term debt to have lower interest rates than long-term debt. Thus, Japanese managers find short-term debt more attractive than long-term debt. In addition, banks are happy to renew these loans because this allows them to adjust the interest rates to changing market conditions. Thus, short-term debt in Japan works like long-term debt elsewhere. In fact, the use of short-term debt to finance long-term assets appears to be the rule, not the exception, in Japan.

INSTALLMENT NOTES PAYABLE

Purchases of real estate and certain types of equipment often are financed by the issuance of long-term notes that call for a series of installment payments. These payments (often called **debt service**) may be due monthly, quarterly, semiannually, or at any other interval. If these installments continue until the debt is completely repaid, the loan is said to be "fully amortizing." Often, however, installment notes contain a due date at which the remaining unpaid balance is to be repaid in a single "balloon" payment.

Some installment notes call for installment payments equal to the periodic interest charges (an "interest only" note). Under these terms, the principal amount of the loan is payable at a specified maturity date. More often, however, the installment payments are *greater* than the amount of interest accruing during the period. Thus, only a portion of each installment payment represents interest expense, and the remainder of the payment reduces the principal amount of the liability. As the amount owed is reduced by each payment, the portion of each successive payment representing interest expense *decreases,* and the portion going toward repayment of principal *increases.*

Allocating Installment Payments between Interest and Principal

In accounting for an installment note, the accountant must determine the portion of each payment that represents interest expense and the portion that reduces the principal amount of the liability. This distinction is made in advance by preparing an **amortization table.**

Learning Objective
LO4 Prepare an amortization table allocating payments between interest and principal.

To illustrate, assume that on October 15, Year 1, King's Inn purchases furnishings at a total cost of $16,398. In payment, the company issues an installment note payable for this amount, plus interest at 12 percent per annum (or 1 percent per month). This note will be paid in 18 monthly installments of $1,000 each, beginning on November 15. An amortization table for this installment note payable is shown in Exhibit 10–5 (amounts of interest expense are *rounded to the nearest dollar*).

Preparing an Amortization Table

Let us explore the content of Exhibit 10–5. First, notice that the payments are made on a *monthly* basis. Therefore, the amounts of the payments (column A), interest expense (column B), and reduction in the unpaid balance (column C) are all *monthly amounts.*

Exhibit 10–5

AMORTIZATION TABLE FOR A NOTE PAYABLE

AMORTIZATION TABLE (12% NOTE PAYABLE FOR $16,398; PAYABLE IN 18 MONTHLY INSTALLMENTS OF $1,000)

Interest Period	Payment Date	(A) Monthly Payment	(B) Interest Expense (1% of the Last Unpaid Balance)	(C) Reduction in Unpaid Balance (A) − (B)	(D) Unpaid Balance
Issue date	Oct. 15, Year 1	—	—	—	$16,398
1	Nov. 15	$1,000	$164	$836	15,562
2	Dec. 15	1,000	156	844	14,718
3	Jan. 15, Year 2	1,000	147	853	13,865
4	Feb. 15	1,000	139	861	13,004
5	Mar. 15	1,000	130	870	12,134
6	Apr. 15	1,000	121	879	11,255
7	May 15	1,000	113	887	10,368
8	June 15	1,000	104	896	9,472
9	July 15	1,000	95	905	8,567
10	Aug. 15	1,000	86	914	7,653
11	Sept. 15	1,000	77	923	6,730
12	Oct. 15	1,000	67	933	5,797
13	Nov. 15	1,000	58	942	4,855
14	Dec. 15	1,000	49	951	3,904
15	Jan. 15, Year 3	1,000	39	961	2,943
16	Feb. 15	1,000	29	971	1,972
17	Mar. 15	1,000	20	980	992
18	Apr. 15	1,000	8*	992	-0-

*In the last period, interest expense is equal to the amount of the final payment minus the remaining unpaid balance. This compensates for the cumulative effect of rounding interest amounts to the nearest dollar.

The interest rate used in the table is of special importance; this rate must coincide with the period of time *between payment dates*—in this case, one month. Thus, if payments are made monthly, column B must be based on the *monthly* rate of interest. If payments were made quarterly, this column would use the quarterly rate of interest.

An amortization table begins with the original amount of the liability ($16,398) listed at the top of the Unpaid Balance column. The amounts of the monthly payments, shown in column A, are specified by the installment contract. The monthly interest expense, shown in column B, is computed for each month by applying the monthly interest rate to the unpaid balance at the *beginning of that month*. The portion of each payment that reduces the amount of the liability (column C) is simply the remainder of the payment (column A minus column B). Finally, the unpaid balance of the liability (column D) is reduced each month by the amount indicated in column C.

Rather than continuing to make monthly payments, King's Inn could settle this liability at any time by paying the amount currently shown as the unpaid balance.

Notice that the amount of interest expense listed in column B decreases each month, because the unpaid balance is continually decreasing.[7]

Preparing each horizontal line in an amortization table involves making the same computations, based on a new unpaid balance. Thus an amortization table of any length can be easily

[7] If the monthly payments were *less* than the amount of the monthly interest expense, the unpaid balance of the note would *increase* each month. This, in turn, would cause the interest expense to increase each month. This pattern, termed *negative amortization*, occurs temporarily in some "adjustable-rate" home mortgages.

and quickly prepared by computer software. (Most "money management" software includes a program for preparing amortization tables.) Only three items of data need to be entered into such a program: (1) the original amount of the liability, (2) the amount of periodic payments, and (3) the interest rate (per payment period).

Using an Amortization Table Once an amortization table has been prepared, the entries to record each payment are taken directly from the amounts shown in the table. For example, the entry to record the first monthly payment (November 15, Year 1) is:

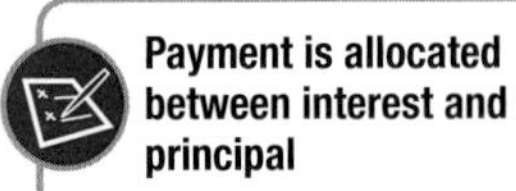

Payment is allocated between interest and principal

Interest Expense	164	
Installment Note Payable	836	
Cash		1,000
Made Nov. payment on installment note payable.		

Similarly, the entry to record the *second* payment, made on *December 15, Year 1,* is:

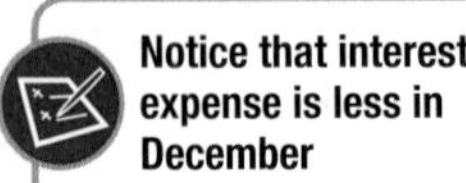

Notice that interest expense is less in December

Interest Expense	156	
Installment Note Payable	844	
Cash		1,000
Made Dec. payment on installment note payable.		

At December 31, Year 1, King's Inn should make an adjusting entry to record one-half month's accrued interest on this liability. The amount of this adjusting entry is based on the unpaid balance shown in the amortization table as of the last payment (December 15). This entry is:

Year-end adjusting entry

Interest Expense	74	
Interest Payable		74
Adjusting entry to record interest expense on installment note for the last half of Dec.: $14,718 × 1% × ½ = $74.		

The Current Portion of Long-Term Debt Notice that as of December 31, Year 1, the unpaid balance of this note is $14,718. As of December 31, *Year 2,* however, the unpaid balance will be only $3,904. Thus the principal amount of this note will be reduced by *$10,814* during Year 2 ($14,718 − $3,904 = $10,814). In the balance sheet prepared at December 31, Year 1, the $10,814 portion of this debt that is scheduled for repayment within the *next 12 months* is classified as a *current liability.* The remaining $3,904 is classified as a long-term liability.

BONDS PAYABLE

Learning Objective
LO5 **Describe corporate bonds and explain the tax advantage of debt financing.**

Financially sound corporations may arrange limited amounts of long-term financing by issuing notes payable to banks or to insurance companies. But to finance a large project, such as developing an oil field or purchasing a controlling interest in the capital stock of another company, a corporation may need more capital than any single lender can supply. When a corporation needs to raise large amounts of long-term capital—perhaps 50, 100, or 500 million dollars (or more)—it generally sells additional shares of capital stock or issues **bonds payable.**

WHAT ARE BONDS?

The issuance of bonds payable is a technique for splitting a very large loan into many transferable units, called bonds. Each bond represents a *long-term, interest-bearing note payable,* usually in the face amount (or par value) of $1,000 or some multiple of $1,000. The bonds are sold to the investing public, enabling many different investors (bondholders) to participate in the loan.

Bonds usually are very long-term notes, maturing in perhaps 15 or 30 years. The bonds are transferable, however, so individual bondholders may sell their bonds to other investors at any time. Most bonds call for quarterly or semiannual interest payments to the bondholders, with interest computed at a specified *contract rate* throughout the life of the bond. Thus investors often describe bonds as "fixed income" investments.

An example of a corporate bond issue is the 8½ percent bonds of **Pacific Bell** (a Pacific Telesis company, known as **PacBell**), due August 15, 2031. Interest on these bonds is payable semiannually on February 15 and August 15. With this bond issue, **PacBell** borrowed $225 million by issuing 225,000 bonds of $1,000 each.

PacBell did not actually print and issue 225,000 separate notes payable. Each bondholder is issued a single *bond certificate* indicating the number of bonds purchased. Each certificate is in the face amount of $25,000 and, therefore, represents ownership of 25 bonds. Investors such as mutual funds, banks, and insurance companies often buy thousands of bonds at one time.

The Issuance of Bonds Payable When bonds are issued, the corporation usually utilizes the services of an investment banking firm, called an **underwriter.** The underwriter guarantees the issuing corporation a specific price for the entire bond issue and makes a profit by selling the bonds to the investing public at a higher price. The corporation records the issuance of the bonds at the net amount received from the underwriter. The use of an underwriter assures the corporation that the entire bond issue will be sold without delay and that the entire amount of the proceeds will be available at a specific date.

Transferability of Bonds Corporate bonds, like capital stocks, are traded daily on organized securities exchanges, such as the *New York Bond Exchange.* The holders of a 25-year bond issue need not wait 25 years to convert their investments into cash. By placing a telephone call to a broker, an investor may sell bonds within a matter of minutes at the going market price. This *liquidity* is one of the most attractive features of an investment in corporate bonds.

© Digital Vision/Getty Images/DAL

Quoted Market Prices Bond prices are quoted as a *percentage* of their face value or *maturity* value, which is usually $1,000. The maturity value is the amount the issuing company must pay to redeem the bond at the date it matures (becomes due). A $1,000 bond quoted at *102* would therefore have a market price of $1,020 (102 percent of $1,000). Bond prices are quoted at the nearest one-eighth of a percentage point. The following line for a hypothetical company illustrates the type of information available in print or on the Internet summarizing the previous day's trading in bonds.

Bonds	Sales	High	Low	Close	Net Change
Alvaro, Inc. 8½ 14	175	97½	95½	97	+1

This line of condensed information indicates that 175 of Alvaro's 8½ percent, $1,000 bonds maturing in 2014 were traded during the day. The highest price is reported as 97½, or $975 for a bond of $1,000 face value. The lowest price was 95½, or $955 for a $1,000 bond. The closing price (last sale of the day) was 97, or $970. This was one point above the closing price of the previous day, an increase of $10 in the price of a $1,000 bond.

Types of Bonds Bonds secured by the pledge of specific assets are called *mortgage bonds.* An unsecured bond is called a *debenture bond;* its value rests on the general credit of the corporation. A debenture bond issued by a large and strong corporation may have a higher investment rating than a secured bond issued by a corporation in less satisfactory financial condition.

Bond interest is paid semiannually by transferring to each bondholder a check for six months' interest on the bonds he or she owns.[8] Many bonds are *callable,* which means that the corporation has the right to redeem the bonds *in advance* of the maturity date by paying a specified *call price.* To compensate bondholders for being forced to give up their investments, the call price usually is somewhat higher than the face value of the bonds.

Traditionally, bonds have appealed to conservative investors, interested primarily in a reliable income stream from their investments. To make a bond issue more attractive to these investors, some corporations create a bond **sinking fund,** designated for repaying the bonds at maturity. At regular intervals, the corporation deposits cash into this sinking fund. A bond sinking fund is not classified as a current asset, because it is not available for the payment of current liabilities. Such funds are shown in the balance sheet under the caption "Long-Term Investments," which appears below the current asset section.

As an additional attraction to investors, corporations sometimes include a conversion privilege in the bond indenture. A **convertible bond** is one that may be exchanged at the option of the bondholder for a specified number of shares of capital stock. Thus the market value of a convertible bond tends to fluctuate with the market value of an equivalent number of shares of capital stock.

Junk Bonds In recent years, some corporations have issued securities that have come to be known as **junk bonds.** This term describes a bond issue that involves a substantially greater risk of default than normal. A company issuing junk bonds usually has so much long-term debt that its ability to meet interest and principal repayment obligations is questionable. To compensate bondholders for this unusual level of risk, junk bonds promise a substantially higher rate of interest than do "investment quality" bonds.

TAX ADVANTAGE OF BOND FINANCING

A principal advantage of raising money by issuing bonds instead of stock is that interest payments are *deductible* in determining income subject to corporate income taxes. Dividends paid to stockholders, however, are *not deductible* in computing taxable income.

To illustrate, assume that a corporation pays income taxes at a rate of *30 percent* on its taxable income. If this corporation issues $10 million of 10 percent bonds payable, it will incur interest expense of $1 million per year. This interest expense, however, will reduce taxable income by $1 million, thus reducing the corporation's annual income taxes by $300,000. As a result, the *after-tax* cost of borrowing the $10 million is only *$700,000:*

Interest expense ($10,000,000 × 10%)	$1,000,000
Less: Income tax savings ($1,000,000 deduction × 30%)	300,000
After-tax cost of borrowing	$ 700,000

This effectively reduces the cost of borrowing to 7 percent ($700,000/$10,000,000).

A shortcut approach to computing the after-tax cost of borrowing is simply multiplying the interest expense by *1 minus the company's tax rate,* as follows: $1,000,000 × (1 − .30) = $700,000.

ACCOUNTING FOR BONDS PAYABLE

Accounting for bonds payable closely parallels accounting for notes payable. The accountable events for a bond issue usually are (1) issuance of the bonds, (2) semiannual interest

[8] In recent years, corporations have issued only *registered* bonds, for which interest is paid by mailing a check to the registered owners of the bonds. In past decades, some companies issued *coupon bonds* or *bearer bonds,* which had a series of redeemable coupons attached. At each interest date, the bondholder had to "clip" the coupon and present it to a bank to collect the interest. These bonds posed a considerable hazard to investors—if the investor lost the coupon, or forgot about an interest date, he or she received no interest. In many states, issuing coupon bonds now is illegal.

payments, (3) accrual of interest payable at the end of each accounting period, and (4) retirement of the bonds at maturity.[9]

To illustrate these events, assume that on March 1, 2011, Wells Corporation issues $1 million of 12 percent, 20-year bonds payable.[10] These bonds are dated March 1, 2011, and interest is computed from this date. Interest on the bonds is payable semiannually, each September 1 and March 1. If all of the bonds are sold at par value (also referred to as face value), the issuance of the bonds on March 1 will be recorded by the following entry:

Cash	1,000,000	
Bonds Payable		1,000,000
Issued 12%, 20-year bonds payable at a price of 100.		

Entry at the issuance date 

Every September 1 during the term of the bond issue, Wells Corporation must pay $60,000 to the bondholders ($1,000,000 × .12 × ½ = $60,000). This semiannual interest payment will be recorded as shown below:

Bond Interest Expense	60,000	
Cash		60,000
Semiannual payment of bond interest.		

Entry to record semiannual interest payments 

Every December 31, Wells Corporation must make an adjusting entry to record the four months' interest that has accrued since September 1:

Bond Interest Expense	40,000	
Bond Interest Payable		40,000
To accrue bond interest payable for four months ended Dec. 31 ($1,000,000 × .12 × 4⁄12 = $40,000).		

Adjusting entry at year-end 

The accrued liability for bond interest payable will be paid within a few months and, therefore, is classified as a current liability.

Two months later, on March 1, a semiannual interest payment is made to bondholders. This transaction represents payment of the four months' interest accrued at December 31 and the two months' interest that has accrued since year-end. Thus the entry to record the semiannual interest payments every March 1 will be:

Bond Interest Expense	20,000	
Bond Interest Payable	40,000	
Cash		60,000
To record semiannual interest payment to bondholders, and to recognize two months' interest expense accrued since year-end ($1,000,000 × .12 × 2⁄12 = $20,000).		

Interest payment following the year-end adjusting entry 

[9] To simplify our illustrations, we assume in all of our examples and assignment material that adjusting entries for accrued bond interest payable are made *only at year-end.* In practice, these adjustments usually are made on a monthly basis.

[10] The amount of $1 million is used only for purposes of illustration. As explained earlier, actual bond issues are for many millions of dollars.

When the bonds mature 20 years later on March 1, 2031, two entries are required: one to record the regular semiannual interest payment and a second to record the retirement of the bonds. The entry to record the retirement of the bond issue is:

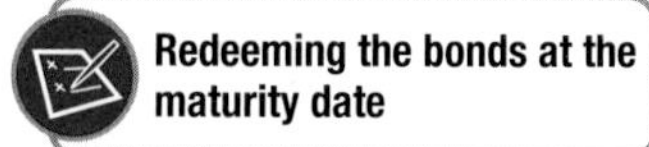
Redeeming the bonds at the maturity date

Bonds Payable	1,000,000	
Cash		1,000,000
Paid face amount of bonds at maturity.		

Bonds Issued between Interest Dates The semiannual interest dates (such as January 1 and July 1, or April 1 and October 1) are printed on the bond certificates. However, bonds are often issued between the specified interest dates. The *investor* is then required to pay the interest accrued to the date of issuance *in addition* to the stated price of the bond. This practice enables the corporation to pay a full six months' interest on all bonds outstanding at the semiannual interest payment date. The accrued interest collected from investors who purchase bonds between interest payment dates is thus returned to them on the next interest payment date.

To illustrate, let us modify our illustration to assume that Wells Corporation issues $1 million of 12 percent bonds at par value on *May 1*—two months *after* the March interest date printed on the bonds. The amount received from the bond purchasers now will include two months' accrued interest, as follows:

Bonds issued between interest dates

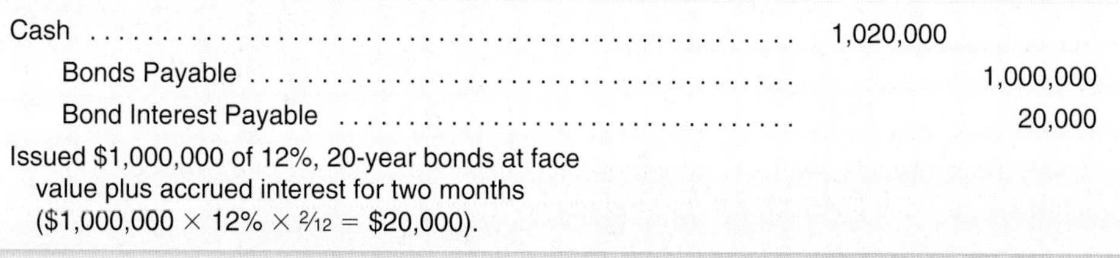

Cash	1,020,000	
Bonds Payable		1,000,000
Bond Interest Payable		20,000
Issued \$1,000,000 of 12%, 20-year bonds at face value plus accrued interest for two months (\$1,000,000 × 12% × 2⁄12 = \$20,000).		

Four months later on the regular September 1 semiannual interest payment date, a full six months' interest ($60 per $1,000 bond) will be paid to all bondholders, *regardless of when they purchased their bonds.* The entry for the semiannual interest payment is illustrated below:

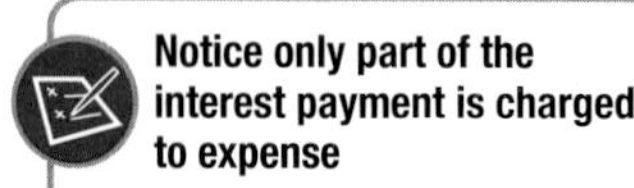
Notice only part of the interest payment is charged to expense

Bond Interest Payable	20,000	
Bond Interest Expense	40,000	
Cash		60,000
Paid semiannual interest on \$1,000,000 face value of 12% bonds.		

Now consider these interest transactions from the standpoint of the *investors.* They paid for two months' accrued interest at the time of purchasing the bonds and then received checks for six months' interest after holding the bonds for only four months. They have, therefore, been reimbursed properly for the use of their money for four months.

When bonds are subsequently sold by one investor to another, they sell at the quoted market price *plus accrued interest* since the last interest payment date. This practice enables the issuing corporation to pay all the interest for an interest period to the investor owning the bond at the interest date. Otherwise, the corporation would have to make partial payments to every investor who bought or sold the bond during the interest period.

The amount that investors will pay for bonds is the *present value* of the principal and interest payments they will receive. The concept of present value is discussed on pages 448–449. A more in-depth coverage of present value appears in Appendix B at the end of this textbook.

BONDS ISSUED AT A DISCOUNT OR A PREMIUM

Learning Objective
LO6 Account for bonds issued at a discount or premium.

Underwriters normally sell corporate bonds to investors either at face value or at a price very close to face value. Therefore, the underwriter usually purchases these bonds from the issuing corporation at a discount—that is, at a price below face value. The discount generally is quite small—perhaps 1 percent or 2 percent of the face amount of the bonds.

When bonds are issued, the borrower records a liability equal to the *amount received.* If the bonds are issued at a small discount—which is the normal case—this liability is smaller than the face value of the bond issue. At the maturity date, of course, the issuing corporation must redeem the bonds at full face value. Thus, over the term of the bond issue, the borrower's liability gradually *increases* from the original issue price to the maturity value.

ACCOUNTING FOR A BOND DISCOUNT: AN ILLUSTRATION

To illustrate, assume that on March 1, 2011, Wells Corporation sells $1 million of 12 percent, 20-year bonds payable to an underwriter at a price of *97* (meaning that the bonds were sold to the underwriter at 97 percent of their face value). On March 1, 2011, Wells Corporation receives $970,000 cash from the underwriter and records a *net* liability of this amount. When these bonds mature in 20 years, however, Wells will owe its bondholders the *full* $1 million face value of the bond issue. Thus, the company's liability must somehow be *increased* by $30,000 over the 20 years that the bonds are outstanding.

The gradual growth in the company's liability is illustrated in Exhibit 10–6. Notice that the liability increases at an average rate of $1,500 per year ($30,000 total increase ÷ 20-year life of the bond issue).

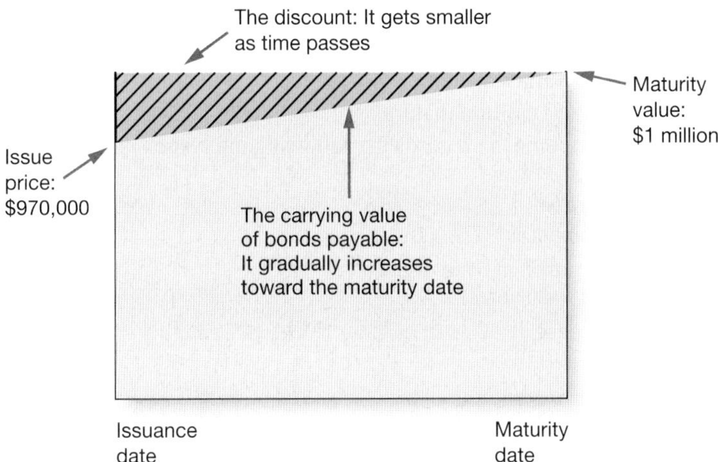

Exhibit 10–6

THE CARRYING VALUE OF A BOND DISCOUNT

Bond Discount: Part of the Cost of Borrowing When bonds are issued at a discount, the borrower must repay more than the amount originally borrowed. Thus any discount in the issuance price becomes an additional cost of the overall borrowing transaction.

In terms of cash outlays, the additional cost represented by the discount is not paid until the bonds mature. But the *matching principle* generally requires the borrower to recognize this cost gradually over the life of the bond issue.[11]

When the bonds are issued, the amount of any discount is debited to an account entitled *Discount on Bonds Payable.* Thus, Wells Corporation will record the March 1 issuance as follows:

Cash	970,000	
Discount on Bonds Payable	30,000	
Bonds Payable		1,000,000
Issued 20-year bonds with $1,000,000 face value to an underwriter at a price of 97.		

[11] If the amount of the discount is immaterial, it may be charged directly to expense as a matter of convenience. In this text, the straight-line method of amortizing bond discounts and premiums is used. The effective interest method is more common and conceptually correct and is covered in more advanced accounting textbooks.

Wells Corporation's liability at the date of issuance appears in the balance sheet as follows:

Long-Term Liabilities	
Bonds payable	$1,000,000
Less: Discount on bonds payable	30,000
Net carrying value of bonds payable	$ 970,000

The Discount on Bonds Payable account has a debit balance and is treated as a *contra-liability account.* As illustrated, it is shown in the balance sheet as a *reduction* in the face or par value of bonds payable. Thus, the net carrying value of the bonds payable on the date of issuance is equal to the *amount borrowed.*

Amortization of the Discount On March 1, 2011, Wells Corporation received $970,000 from the underwriter. When the bonds mature 20 years later on March 1, 2031, the company must pay its bondholders the *full* $1 million face value of the bond issue. This additional $30,000 represents *interest expense* that is amortized over the 20-year life of the bond. At each interest payment date, an adjusting entry is made to transfer a portion of the balance in the Discount on Bonds Payable account into interest expense. Thus, over time, the discount declines and the carrying value of the bonds—the face amount less the remaining discount balance—rises toward the $1 million maturity value of the bond issue.

Each September 1, the company records the following interest expense of *$60,750:*

Semiannual interest *payment* ($1,000,000 × 12% × ½)	$60,000
Add: Semiannual amortization of bond discount [($30,000 discount ÷ 20 years) × ½]	750
Semiannual interest expense	$60,750

The entry to record interest expense on September 1 throughout the life of the bond issue is:

Bond Interest Expense	60,750	
Cash		60,000
Discount on Bonds Payable		750
To record semiannual interest expense and to recognize six months' amortization of the $30,000 discount on 20-year bonds payable.		

Notice that the amortization of the discount increases Wells Corporation's semiannual interest expense by $750. It does not, however, require any immediate cash outlay. The $30,000 interest expense represented by the *entire* amortized discount will not be paid until the bonds mature on March 1, 2031.

Every December 31, Wells Corporation must make an adjusting entry to record four months' interest expense that has accrued since September 1. The computation of this $40,500 accrual is computed as follows:

Four months' accrued interest *payable* ($1,000,000 × 12% × 4⁄12)	$40,000
Add: Four months' amortization of bond discount [($30,000 discount ÷ 20 years) × 4⁄12]	500
Interest accrued from September 1 through December 31	$40,500

Thus, the adjusting entry required on December 31 throughout the life of the bond issue is as follows:

Bond Interest Expense	40,500	
Bond Interest Payable		40,000
Discount on Bonds Payable		500
To record four months' interest expense and to recognize four months' amortization of the discount on 20-year bonds payable.		

Two months later, on every March 1, a *full* semiannual interest payment is made to the company's bondholders, and an additional two months' amortization of the discount is recognized. The $20,250 interest expense recorded on this date is computed as:

Two months' accrued interest *payable* ($1,000,000 × 12% × 2⁄12)	$20,000
Add: Two months' amortization of bond discount [($30,000 discount ÷ 20 years) × 2⁄12]	250
Interest accrued from January 1 through March 1	$20,250

The semiannual interest payment recorded on March 1 throughout the life of the bond issue is:

Bond Interest Expense	20,250	
Bond Interest Payable	40,000	
Cash		60,000
Discount on Bonds Payable		250
To record two months' interest expense, to recognize two months' amortization of the discount on 20-year bonds payable, and to record semiannual interest payment to bondholders.		

When the bonds mature 20 years later on March 1, 2031, two entries are required: one to record the regular semiannual interest payment, and a second to record the retirement of the bonds. At this date, the original $30,000 discount will be *fully amortized* (that is, the Discount on Bonds Payable account will have a zero balance). Thus the carrying value of the bond issue will be $1 million, and the entry required to record the retirement of the bond issue will be:

Bonds Payable	1,000,000	
Cash		1,000,000
Paid the face amount of bonds at maturity.		

It is important to realize that over the life of this bond issue, Wells Corporation recognized *total* interest expense of $2,430,000 (40 semiannual interest payments of $60,000, plus the $30,000 discount amortized).

ACCOUNTING FOR A BOND PREMIUM: AN ILLUSTRATION

As noted previously, underwriters normally purchase bonds from the issuing corporation at a slight discount. Under some circumstances, however, an underwriter may actually pay a slight premium to the issuer—that is, a price above par.

To illustrate, assume that on March 1, 2011, Wells Corporation sells $1 million of 12 percent, 20-year bonds payable to an underwriter at a price of *103* (meaning that the bonds were sold to the underwriter at 103 percent of their face value). On March 1, 2011, Wells Corporation receives $1,030,000 cash from the underwriter and records a liability equal to this amount. When these bonds mature in 20 years, however, Wells will owe its bondholders only the $1 million *face value* of the bond issue. Thus, the company's initial liability must somehow be *reduced* by $30,000 over the 20 years that the bonds are outstanding.

The gradual decrease in the company's liability is illustrated in Exhibit 10–7. Notice that the liability decreases at an average rate of $1,500 per year ($30,000 total increase ÷ 20-year life of the bond issue).

Exhibit 10–7

THE CARRYING VALUE OF A BOND PREMIUM

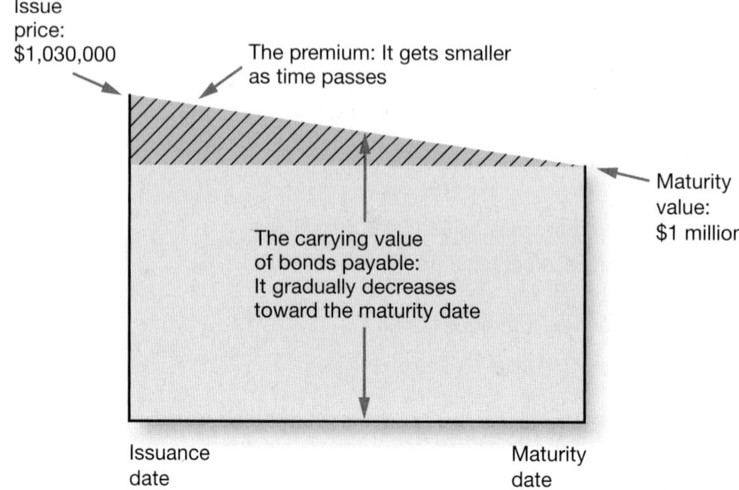

Bond Premium: A Reduction in the Cost of Borrowing When bonds are issued at a premium, the borrower repays less than the amount originally received at the date of issuance. Thus, any premium actually represents a reduction in the overall cost of borrowing. Unlike bonds issued at a discount, the interest expense associated with bonds issued at a premium will be *less* than the semiannual cash payment made to bondholders.

When the bonds are issued, the amount of any premium is credited to an account entitled *Premium on Bonds Payable.* Thus, Wells Corporation will record the March 1 issuance as follows:

Cash	1,030,000	
Premium on Bonds Payable		30,000
Bonds Payable		1,000,000
Issued 20-year bonds with $1,000,000 face value to an underwriter at a price of 103.		

Wells Corporation's liability at the date of issuance will appear in the balance sheet as follows:

Long-Term Liabilities	
Bonds payable	$1,000,000
Add: Premium on bonds payable	30,000
Carrying value of bonds payable	$1,030,000

Note that, because the Premium on Bonds Payable account has a credit balance, it is shown in the balance sheet as an *increase* in the face or par value of bonds payable.

Amortization of the Premium On March 1, 2011, Wells Corporation received $1,030,000 from the underwriter. When the bonds mature 20 years later on March 1, 2031, the company must pay back its bondholders only the $1 million *face value* of the bond issue. This $30,000 reduction in the amount owed represents *interest savings* that is amortized over the 20-year life of the bond. Thus, over time, the premium declines, and the carrying value of the bonds—the face amount plus the remaining premium balance—also declines toward the $1 million maturity value of the bond issue.

Each September 1, the company records interest expense of *$59,250,* computed as:

Semiannual interest *payment* ($1,000,000 × 12% × ½)	$60,000
Less: Semiannual amortization of bond premium [($30,000 premium ÷ 20 years) × ½]	750
Semiannual interest expense	$59,250

The entry to record interest expense on September 1 throughout the life of the bond issue is:

Bond Interest Expense	59,250	
Premium on Bonds Payable	750	
Cash		60,000
To record semiannual interest expense and to recognize six months' amortization of the $30,000 premium on 20-year bonds payable.		

Notice that the $60,000 semiannual interest payment is the same regardless of whether the bonds are issued at face value, at a discount, or at a premium. The amortization of the premium does, however, reduce the amount of interest expense recognized by the company over the life of the bond issue.

Every December 31, Wells Corporation must make an adjusting entry to record four months' interest expense that has accrued since September 1. The $39,500 accrual is computed as follows:

Four months' accrued interest *payable* ($1,000,000 × 12% × 4⁄12)	$40,000
Less: Four months' amortization of bond premium [($30,000 premium ÷ 20 years) × 4⁄12]	500
Interest accrued from September 1 through December 31	$39,500

Thus, the following adjusting entry is required on December 31 throughout the life of the bond issue:

Bond Interest Expense	39,500	
Premium on Bonds Payable	500	
Bond Interest Payable		40,000
To record four months' interest expense and to recognize four months' amortization of the premium on 20-year bonds payable.		

Two months later, on every March 1, a *full* semiannual interest payment is made to the company's bondholders, and an additional two months' amortization of the premium is recognized. The $19,750 interest expense recorded on this date is computed as:

Two months' accrued interest *payable* ($1,000,000 × 12% × 2⁄12)	$20,000
Less: Two months' amortization of bond premium [($30,000 premium ÷ 20 years) × 2⁄12]	250
Interest accrued from January 1 through March 1	$19,750

The semiannual interest payment recorded on March 1 throughout the life of the bond issue is:

Bond Interest Expense	19,750	
Bond Interest Payable	40,000	
Premium on Bonds Payable	250	
Cash		60,000
To record two months' interest expense, to recognize two months' amortization of the premium on 20-year bonds payable, and to record semiannual interest payment to bondholders.		

When the bonds mature 20 years later on March 1, 2031, two entries are required: one to record the regular semiannual interest payment, and a second to record the retirement of the bonds. At this date, the original $30,000 premium will be *fully amortized* (that is, the Premium on Bonds Payable account will have a zero balance). Thus the carrying value of the bond issue will be $1 million, and the entry required to record the retirement of the bond issue will be as follows:

Bonds Payable	1,000,000	
Cash		1,000,000
Paid the face amount of bonds at maturity.		

In the previous illustration involving a bond discount, Wells Corporation recognized total interest expense of $2,430,000 over the life of the bonds. Had these same bonds been issued at a premium of 103, however, we see that the company would have incurred total interest expense of $2,370,000 (40 semiannual interest payments of $60,000, less the $30,000 premium amortized).

BOND DISCOUNT AND PREMIUM IN PERSPECTIVE

From a conceptual point of view, investors might pay a premium price to purchase bonds that pay an *above-market* rate of interest. If the bonds pay a *below-market* rate, investors will buy them only at a discount.

But these concepts seldom come into play when bonds are first issued. Most bonds are issued *at* the market rate of interest. Corporate bonds are rarely issued at a premium. Bonds often are issued at a small discount, but this discount represents only the underwriter's profit margin, not investors' response to a below-market interest rate.[12] The annual effects of amortizing bond discounts or premiums are diluted further because these amounts are amortized over the entire life of the bond issue—usually 20 years or more.

In summary, bond discounts and premiums *seldom have a material effect* on a company's annual interest expense or its financial position. For this reason, we defer further discussion of this topic to more advanced accounting courses.[13]

THE CONCEPT OF PRESENT VALUE

Learning Objective
LO7 Explain the concept of present value as it relates to bond prices.

The concept of present value is based on the time value of money—the idea that receiving money today is preferable to receiving money at some later date. Assume, for example, that an investment promises to pay $1,000 five years from today and will pay no interest in the meantime. Investors would not pay $1,000 for this opportunity today, because they would receive no return on their investment over the next five years. There are prices less than $1,000, however, at which investors would be interested. For example, if the investment could be purchased for $600, the investor could expect a return (interest) of $400 over the five-year period.

[12] A study of 685 bond issues indicates that none were issued at a premium, and over 95 percent were issued at par or at a discount of less than 2 percent of face value.

[13] Some companies issue *zero-coupon* bonds, which pay *no* interest but are issued at huge discounts. In these situations, amortization of the discount *is* material and may comprise much of the company's total interest expense. Zero-coupon bonds are a specialized form of financing that will be discussed in later accounting courses and courses in corporate finance.

The **present value** of a future cash receipt is the amount that a knowledgeable investor will pay *today* for the right to receive that future payment. The exact amount of the present value depends on (1) the amount of the future payment, (2) the length of time until the payment will be received, and (3) the rate of return required by the investor. However, the present value will always be *less* than the future amount. This is because money received today can be invested to earn interest and grow to a larger amount in the future.

The rate of interest that will cause a given present value to grow to a given future amount is called the *discount rate* or *effective rate.* The effective interest rate required by investors at any given time is regarded as the going *market rate* of interest. (The procedures for computing the present value of a future amount are illustrated in Appendix B at the end of this textbook. The concept of present value is very useful in managing your personal financial affairs. We suggest that you read Appendix B—even if it has not been assigned.)

The Present Value Concept and Bond Prices The price at which bonds sell is the present value to investors of the future principal and interest payments. If the bonds sell at face value, the market rate is equal to the *contract interest rate* (also referred to as the stated or nominal rate) printed on the bonds. The *higher* the effective interest rate that investors require, the *less* they will pay underwriters for bonds with a given contract rate of interest. For example, if investors insist on a 10 percent return, they will pay less than $1,000 for a 9 percent, $1,000 bond. Thus, if investors require an effective interest rate *greater* than the contract rate of interest, the bonds will be sold by underwriters at a *discount* (a price less than their face value). On the other hand, if market conditions support an effective interest rate of *less* than the contract rate, the bonds will sell at a *premium* (a price above their face value). Since market rates of interest fluctuate constantly, it must be expected that the contract rate of interest may vary somewhat from the market rate at the date the bonds are issued.

BOND PRICES AFTER ISSUANCE

Bond prices move inversely with market interest rates

As stated earlier, many corporate bonds are traded daily on organized securities exchanges at quoted market prices. After bonds are issued, their market prices vary *inversely* with changes in market interest rates. As interest rates rise, investors will be willing to pay less money to own a bond that pays a given contract rate of interest. Conversely, as interest rates decline, the market prices of bonds rise.

CASE IN POINT

This is a historical case on the impact of interest rates on the price of bonds. **IBM** sold to underwriters $500 million of 9⅜ percent, 25-year debenture bonds. The underwriters planned to sell the bonds to the public at a price of 99⅝. Just as the bonds were offered for sale, however, a change in Federal Reserve credit policy started an upward surge in interest rates. The underwriters encountered great difficulty selling the bonds. Within one week, the market price of the bonds had fallen to 94½. The underwriters dumped their unsold inventory at this price and sustained one of the largest underwriting losses in Wall Street history.

During the months that followed, interest rates soared to record levels. Within five months, the price of the bonds had fallen to 76⅜. Thus nearly one-fourth of the market value of these bonds evaporated in less than half a year. At this time, the financial strength of **IBM** was never in question; this dramatic loss in market value was caused entirely by rising interest rates.

Changes in the current level of interest rates are not the only factors influencing the market prices of bonds. The length of time remaining until the bonds mature is another major force. As a bond nears its maturity date, its market price normally moves closer and closer to the maturity value. This trend is dependable because the bonds are redeemed at face value on the maturity date.

Volatility of Short-Term and Long-Term Bond Prices When interest rates fluctuate, the market prices of long-term bonds are affected to a far greater extent than are the market prices of bonds due to mature in the near future. To illustrate, assume that market interest rates suddenly soar from 9 percent to 12 percent. A 9 percent bond scheduled to mature in a few days will still have a market value of approximately $1,000—the amount to be collected in a few days from the issuing corporation. However, the market price of a 9 percent bond maturing in 10 years will drop significantly. Investors who must accept these below-market interest payments for many years will buy the bonds only at a discounted price.

In summary, fluctuations in interest rates have a far greater effect on the market prices of long-term bonds than on the prices of short-term bonds.

Remember that, after bonds have been issued, they belong to the bondholder, *not to the issuing corporation.* Therefore, changes in the market price of bonds subsequent to their issuance *do not* affect the amounts shown in the financial statements of the issuing corporation, and these changes are not recorded in the company's accounting records.

YOUR TURN **You as a Financial Advisor**

Assume that you are the financial advisor for a recently retired couple. Your clients want to invest their savings in such a way as to receive a stable stream of cash flow every year throughout their retirement. They have expressed their concerns to you regarding the volatility of long-term bond prices when interest rates fluctuate.

If your clients invest their savings in a variety of long-term bonds and hold these bonds until maturity, will interest rate fluctuations affect their annual cash flow during their retirement years?

(See our comments on the Online Learning Center Web site.)

EARLY RETIREMENT OF BONDS PAYABLE

Bonds are sometimes retired before the maturity date. The principal reason for retiring bonds early is to relieve the issuing corporation of the obligation to make future interest payments. If interest rates decline to the point that a corporation can borrow at an interest rate below that being paid on a particular bond issue, the corporation may benefit from retiring those bonds and issuing new bonds at a lower interest rate.

Most bond issues contain a call provision, permitting the corporation to redeem the bonds by paying a specified price, usually a few points above face value. Even without a call provision, the corporation may retire its bonds before maturity by purchasing them in the open market. If the bonds can be purchased by the issuing corporation at less than their carrying value, a *gain* is realized on the retirement of the debt. If the bonds are reacquired by the issuing corporation at a price in excess of their carrying value, a *loss* must be recognized.

For example, assume that Briggs Corporation has outstanding a 13 percent, $10 million bond issue, callable on any interest date at a price of 104. Assume also that the bonds were issued at par and will not mature for nine years. Recently, however, market interest rates have declined to less than 10 percent, and the market price of Briggs's bonds has increased to 106.[14]

Regardless of the market price, Briggs can call these bonds at 104. If the company exercises this call provision for 10 percent of the bonds ($1,000,000 face value), the entry will be:

Bonds Payable	1,000,000	
Loss on Early Retirement of Bonds	40,000	
Cash		1,040,000
To record the call of $1 million in bonds payable at a call price of 104.		

[14] Falling interest rates cause bond prices to rise. On the other hand, falling interest rates also provide the issuing company with an incentive to call the bonds and, perhaps, replace them with bonds bearing a lower rate of interest. For this reason, call prices often serve as an approximate "ceiling" on market prices.

Notice that Briggs *called* these bonds, rather than repurchasing them at market prices. Therefore, Briggs is able to retire these bonds at their call price of 104. (Had the market price of the bonds been *below* 104, Briggs might have been able to retire the bonds at less cost by purchasing them in the open market.)

Estimated Liabilities, Loss Contingencies, and Commitments

ESTIMATED LIABILITIES

Learning Objective
Explain how estimated liabilities, loss contingencies, and commitments are disclosed in financial statements. **LO8**

The term *estimated liabilities* refers to *liabilities that appear in financial statements at estimated dollar amounts.* Let us consider the example of the automaker's liability to honor its new car warranties. A manufacturer's liability for warranty work is recorded by an entry debiting Warranty Expense and crediting Liability for Warranty Claims. The *matching principle* requires that the expense of performing warranty work be recognized in the period in which the products are *sold,* in order to offset this expense against the related sales revenue. As the warranty may extend several years into the future, the dollar amount of this liability (and expense) must be estimated. Because of the uncertainty regarding when warranty work will be performed, accountants traditionally have classified the liability for warranty claims as a current liability.

By definition, estimated liabilities involve some degree of uncertainty. However, (1) the liabilities are known to exist, and (2) the uncertainty as to dollar amount is *not so great* as to prevent the company from making a reasonable estimate and recording the liability.

LOSS CONTINGENCIES

Loss contingencies are similar to estimated liabilities but may involve even more uncertainty. A loss contingency is a *possible loss* (or expense), stemming from *past events,* that is expected to be resolved in the future.

Central to the definition of a loss contingency is the element of *uncertainty*—uncertainty as to the amount of loss and, in some cases, uncertainty as to *whether or not any loss actually has been incurred.* A common example of a loss contingency is a lawsuit pending against a company. The lawsuit is based on past events, but until the suit is resolved, uncertainty exists as to the amount (if any) of the company's liability.

Loss contingencies differ from estimated liabilities in two ways. First, a loss contingency may involve a *greater degree of uncertainty.* Often the uncertainty extends to whether any loss or expense actually has been incurred. In contrast, the loss or expense relating to an estimated liability is *known to exist.*

Second, the concept of a loss contingency extends not only to possible liabilities but also to possible *impairments of assets.* Assume, for example, that a bank has made large loans to a foreign country now experiencing political instability. Uncertainty exists as to the amount of loss, if any, associated with this loan. From the bank's point of view, this loan is an asset that may be impaired, not a liability.

Loss Contingencies in Financial Statements The manner in which loss contingencies are presented in financial statements depends on the *degree of uncertainty involved.*

Loss contingencies are *recorded* in the accounting records only when both of the following criteria are met: (1) It is *probable* that a loss has been incurred, and (2) the amount of loss can be *reasonably estimated.* An example of a loss contingency that usually meets these criteria and is recorded in the accounts is the obligation a company has for product warranties and defects.

When these criteria are *not* met, loss contingencies are *disclosed* in notes to the financial statements if there is a *reasonable possibility* that a material loss has been incurred. Pending lawsuits, for example, usually are disclosed in notes accompanying the financial statements, but the loss, if any, is not recorded in the accounting records until the lawsuit is settled. Companies are not required to disclose loss contingencies if the risk of a material loss having occurred is considered *remote.*

Notice the *judgmental nature* of the criteria used in accounting for loss contingencies. These criteria involve assessments as to whether the risk of material loss is "probable," "reasonably possible," or "remote." Thus the collective *professional judgment* of the company's management, accountants, legal counsel, and auditors is the deciding factor in accounting for loss contingencies. Loss contingencies relate only to possible losses from *past events*. The risk that losses may result from *future* events is *not* a loss contingency.

When loss contingencies are disclosed in notes to the financial statements, the note should describe the nature of the contingency and, if possible, provide an estimate of the amount of possible loss. If a reasonable estimate of the amount of possible loss cannot be made, the disclosure should include the range of possible loss or a statement that an estimate cannot be made. The following note is typical of the disclosure of the loss contingency arising from pending litigation:

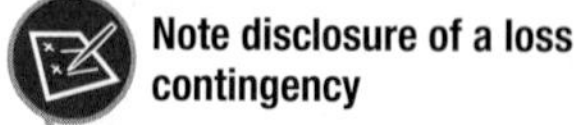
Note disclosure of a loss contingency

Note 8: Contingencies
In October of 2010, the Company was named as defendant in a $400 million patent infringement lawsuit. The Company denies all charges and is preparing its defense against them. It is not possible at this time to determine the ultimate legal or financial responsibility that may arise as a result of this litigation.

Sometimes a *portion* of a loss contingency qualifies for immediate recognition, whereas the remainder only meets the criteria for disclosure. Assume, for example, that a company is required by the Superfund Act to clean up an environmental hazard over a 10-year period. The company cannot predict the total cost of the project but considers it probable that it will lose at least $1 million. The company should recognize a $1 million expected loss and record it as a liability. In addition, it should disclose in the notes to the financial statements that the actual cost ultimately may exceed the recorded amount.

COMMITMENTS

Contracts for future transactions are called **commitments.** They are not liabilities, but, if material, they are disclosed in notes to the financial statements. For example, a professional baseball club may issue a three-year contract to a player at an annual salary of, say, $5 million. This is a commitment to pay for services to be rendered in the future. There is no obligation to make payment until the services are received. As liabilities stem only from *past transactions,* this commitment has not yet created a liability.

Other examples of commitments include a corporation's long-term employment contract with a key officer, a contract for construction of a new plant, and a contract to buy or sell inventory at future dates. The common quality of all these commitments is an intent to enter into transactions *in the future.* Commitments that are material in amount should be disclosed in notes to the financial statements.

Evaluating the Safety of Creditors' Claims

Learning Objective
LO9 **Evaluate the safety of creditors' claims.**

Creditors, of course, want to be sure that their claims are safe—that is, that they will be paid on time. Actually, *everyone* associated with a business—management, owners, employees—should be concerned with the company's ability to pay its debts. If a business becomes *illiquid* (unable to pay its obligations), it may be forced into **bankruptcy.**[15]

Not only does management want the business to remain liquid, but it also wants the company to maintain a high *credit rating* with agencies such as **Moody's** and **Standard & Poor's**. A high credit rating helps a company borrow money more easily and at lower interest rates.

In evaluating debt-paying ability, short-term creditors and long-term creditors look at different relationships. Short-term creditors are interested in the company's *immediate* liquidity. Long-term creditors, in contrast, are interested in the company's ability to meet its interest

[15] Bankruptcy is a legal status under which the company's fate is determined largely by the U.S. Bankruptcy Court. Sometimes the company is reorganized and allowed to continue its operations. In other cases, the business is closed and its assets are sold. Often managers and other employees lose their jobs. In almost all bankruptcies, the company's creditors and owners incur legal costs and sustain financial losses.

obligations over a *period of years,* as well as its ability to repay or refinance large obligations as they come due.

In previous chapters we introduced several measures of short-term liquidity and long-term credit risk. These measures are summarized in Exhibit 10–8—along with the *interest coverage ratio,* which is discussed below.

METHODS OF DETERMINING CREDITWORTHINESS

Interest Coverage Ratio Creditors, investors, and managers all feel more comfortable when a company has enough income to cover its interest payments by a wide margin. One widely used measure of the relationship between earnings and interest expense is the **interest coverage ratio.**

The interest coverage ratio is computed by dividing *operating income* by the annual interest expense. From a creditor's point of view, the higher this ratio, the better. In past years, most companies with good credit ratings had interest coverage ratios of, perhaps, 4 to 1 or more.

Less Formal Means of Determining Creditworthiness Not all decisions to extend credit involve formal analysis of the borrower's financial statements. Most suppliers of goods or services, for example, will sell on account to almost any long-established business—unless they know the customer is in severe financial difficulty. If the customer is not a well-established business, these suppliers may investigate the customer's credit history by contacting a credit-rating agency.

In lending to small businesses organized as corporations, lenders may require key stockholders to *personally guarantee* repayment of the loan.

HOW MUCH DEBT SHOULD A BUSINESS HAVE?

All businesses incur some debts as a result of normal business operations. These include, for example, accounts payable and accrued liabilities. But many businesses aggressively use long-term debt, such as mortgages and bonds payable, to finance growth and expansion. Is this wise? Does it benefit the stockholders? The answer hinges on another question: *Can the borrowed funds be invested to earn a return higher than the rate of interest paid to creditors?*

Using borrowed money to finance business operations is called applying **leverage.** Extensive use of leverage—that is, a great deal of debt—sometimes benefits a business dramatically. But if things don't work out, it can "wipe out" the borrower.

If borrowed money can be invested to earn a rate of return *higher* than the interest rates paid to the lenders, net income and the return on stockholders' equity will *increase.*[16] For example, if you borrow money at an interest rate of 9 percent and invest it to earn 15 percent, you will benefit from "the spread."

But leverage is a double-edged sword—the effects may be favorable *or unfavorable.* If the rate of return earned on the borrowed money falls *below* the rate of interest being paid, the use of borrowed money *reduces* net income and the return on equity. Companies with large amounts of debt sometimes become victims of their own debt-service requirements.

The effects of leverage may be summarized as follows:

Relationship of Return on Assets to Interest Rate on Borrowed Funds	Effect on Net Income and Return on Equity
Return on Assets > Interest Rates Being Paid	Increase
Return on Assets < Interest Rates Being Paid	Decrease

The more leverage a company applies, the greater the effects on net income and the return on equity. Using more leverage simply means having more debt. Therefore, the *debt ratio* is a basic measure of the amount of leverage being applied.

[16] The rate of return earned on invested capital usually is viewed as the overall *return on assets*—that is, operating income divided by average total assets. *Return on equity* is net income expressed as a percentage of average stockholders' equity. Both of these return on investment measures are discussed in Chapter 14.

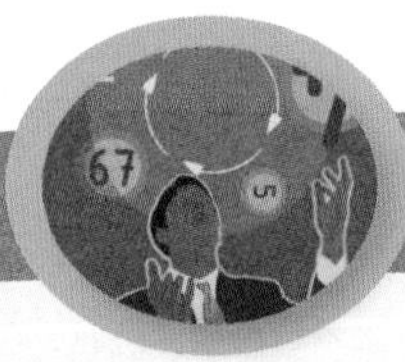

Financial Analysis and Decision Making

Exhibit 10–8 provides a summary of common measures used by creditors and investors to evaluate a company's *short-term and long-term debt-paying ability.*

Exhibit 10-8
MEASURES OF DEBT-PAYING ABILITY

Short-Term	Long-Term
Quick ratio—Most liquid assets divided by current liabilities; a stringent measure of liquidity.	Debt ratio—Total liabilities divided by total assets. Measures percentage of capital structure financed by creditors.
Current ratio—Current assets divided by current liabilities; the most common measure of liquidity, but less stringent than the quick ratio.	Interest coverage ratio—Operating income divided by interest expense. Shows how many times the company earns its annual interest obligations.
Working capital—Current assets less current liabilities; the "uncommitted" liquid resources.	Trend in net cash flows from operating activities—Indicates trend in cash-generating ability. Determined from comparative statements of cash flows.
Turnover rates—Measures of how quickly receivables are collected or inventory is sold. (Computed separately for receivables and inventory.)	Trend in net income—Less related to debt-paying ability than cash flow, but still an excellent measure of long-term financial health.
Operating cycle—The period of time required to convert inventory into cash.	
Net cash flows from operating activities—Measures a company's ability to generate cash. (Shown in the statement of cash flows.)	
Lines of credit—Indicates ready access to additional cash should the need arise.	

YOUR TURN — You as a Credit Analyst

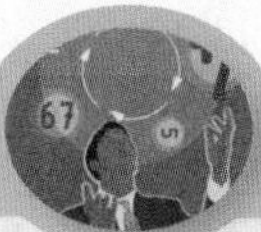

Assume that you are a credit analyst at a bank. **Dell Inc.** wants to borrow from your bank on a short-term basis. You assign the task of reviewing **Dell**'s short-term creditworthiness to a college intern working for your bank. The intern remembers that working capital (current assets minus current liabilities) and the current ratio (current assets divided by current liabilities) are useful tools for evaluating short-term liquidity. Selected financial information for **Dell** is as follows (all items are in millions):

	Recent Year	Prior Year
Cash and cash equivalents	$ 10,635	$ 8,352
Short-term investments	373	740
Accounts receivable (net)	5,837	4,731
Financing Receivables	2,706	1,712
Inventories	1,051	867
Other	3,643	3,749
Total current liabilities	18,960	14,859
Cash provided by operations	3,906	2,894
Net income	1,433	2,478

The intern is concerned about lending **Dell** money because working capital is $5,285. As a result, **Dell**'s current ratio is only 1.28. Do you agree with the intern's assessment?

(See our comments on the Online Learning Center Web site.)

Ethics, Fraud & Corporate Governance

The most infamous financial fraud in U.S. history occurred at **Enron** and was revealed in the fall of 2001. A major part of the **Enron** fraud involved the understatement of debt. **Enron** understated its debt by at least $550 million each year from 1997 to 2000. **Enron**'s management was motivated to understate debt in order to maintain a high credit rating from **Moody's** and **Standard & Poor's**.

Enron was engaged in the energy business and was also a trader of contracts to buy and sell commodities. At the time of the fraud, **Enron** was traded on the New York Stock Exchange. The revelation of the financial improprieties at **Enron** in October 2001 ultimately led to a collapse in **Enron**'s credit rating. Without access to ongoing financing, **Enron** was forced to file for bankruptcy in December 2001. At the time of **Enron**'s bankruptcy filing, it was the seventh-largest corporation in the United States.

Enron understated its liabilities by transferring debt to **special purpose entities (SPEs).** SPEs are separate entities established by corporations to accomplish specific purposes. Often, the economic objective of an SPE is to borrow money and then transfer it to the sponsoring corporation without the sponsoring corporation having to report the SPE's debt in its balance sheet.

These SPEs were organized as partnerships, and **Enron**'s chief financial officer, Andrew Fastow, was the managing general partner of a number of them. Fastow and other **Enron** employees were among the parties providing equity capital to the SPEs. **Enron** guaranteed these investors that they would not only get back what they had invested, but that they would also receive substantial returns.

The fraud at **Enron** has numerous ethical and corporate governance implications. Given the complexity of **Enron**'s fraudulent activity, it could not have been accomplished without the cooperation of outside professionals (e.g., attorneys, auditors, credit rating agencies, and investment bankers). The external auditor, **Arthur Andersen**, issued unqualified audit opinions on **Enron**'s financial statements despite severe doubt that **Enron**'s filings conformed with GAAP. Credit rating agencies maintained investment grade credit ratings on **Enron**'s debt throughout the entire period of the fraud and did not downgrade **Enron**'s debt until a few weeks before the bankruptcy filing. Finally, major Wall Street investment banks created the SPE structures, including numerous transactions that resulted in debt being transferred from **Enron**'s books to the SPEs.

The unethical conduct of **Enron**'s outside professionals has not been without severe consequences. **Arthur Andersen** was convicted of a felony for its role in shredding its working papers related to the **Enron** audit. The felony indictment and conviction led to the dissolution of this former large, international accounting firm. A number of major Wall Street investment banks have paid the U.S. government multimillion-dollar settlements stemming from their **Enron** involvement. Private litigation related to the **Enron** debacle is ongoing and is likely to remain active for a number of years.

Special Types of Liabilities

Learning Objective L10
Describe reporting issues related to leases, postretirement benefits, and deferred taxes.

The types of liabilities discussed up to this point have been those short-term and long-term obligations encountered by most organizations. Here we examine three special types of liabilities most common to large organizations: (1) leases, (2) postretirement benefits, and (3) deferred taxes.

LEASE PAYMENT OBLIGATIONS

A company may purchase the assets needed in its business operations or, as an alternative, it may lease them. A *lease* is a contract in which the lessor gives the lessee the right to use an asset for a specified period of time in exchange for periodic rental payments. The **lessor** is the owner of the property; the **lessee** is a tenant or renter. Examples of assets frequently acquired by lease include automobiles, building space, computers, and equipment.

OPERATING LEASES

When the lessor gives the lessee the right to use leased property for a limited period of time but retains the usual risks and rewards of ownership, the contract is known as an **operating lease.** An example of an operating lease is a contract leasing office space in an office building. If the building increases in value, the *lessor* can receive the benefits of this increase by either selling the building or increasing the rental rate once the initial lease term has expired. Likewise, if the building declines in value, the lessor bears the loss.

In accounting for an operating lease, the lessor views the monthly lease payments received as rental revenue, and the lessee regards these payments as rental expense. No asset or liability (other than a short-term liability for accrued rent payable) relating to the lease appears in the lessee's balance sheet. Thus, operating leases are sometimes termed **off-balance sheet financing** and disclosure is required of the amounts due in each of the next five years, plus the balance thereafter.

CAPITAL LEASES

Some lease contracts are intended to provide financing to the lessee for the eventual purchase of the property or to provide the lessee with use of the property over most of its useful life. These lease contracts are called **capital leases** (or financing leases). In contrast to an operating lease, a capital lease transfers most of the risks and rewards of ownership from the lessor to the *lessee.*

From an accounting viewpoint, capital leases are regarded as *equivalent to a sale* of the property by the lessor to the lessee, even though title to the leased property has not been transferred. Thus a capital lease should be recorded by the *lessor as a sale* of property and by the *lessee as a purchase.*

When equipment is acquired through a capital lease, the lessee *debits an asset account,* Leased Equipment, and *credits a liability account,* Lease Payment Obligation, for the present value of the future lease payments. Lease payments made by the lessee are allocated between Interest Expense and a reduction in the liability Lease Payment Obligation. The portion of the lease payment obligation that will be repaid within the next year is classified as a current liability, and the remainder is classified as long-term.

No rent expense is recorded by the lessee in a capital lease. The asset account Leased Equipment is usually depreciated by the lessee over the life of the equipment rather than the term of the lease. Disclosure of future payments on the lease is also required. Accounting for capital leases is illustrated in Appendix B at the end of this textbook.

Distinguishing between Capital Leases and Operating Leases The Financial Accounting Standards Board (FASB) has identified certain criteria that qualify a lease as a capital lease. For example, if the lease transfers ownership of the property to the lessee at the end of the lease term, the lease is a capital lease. Similarly, if the lease term is equal to 75 percent or more of the estimated economic life of the leased property, the lease is a capital lease. Leases that do not meet any of specified criteria are accounted for as operating leases.

LIABILITIES FOR PENSIONS AND OTHER POSTRETIREMENT BENEFITS

Many employers agree to pay their employees a pension; that is, monthly cash payments for life, beginning at retirement. Pensions are not an expense of the years in which cash payments are made to retired workers. Employees earn the right to receive the pension *while they are working for their employer.* Therefore, the employer's cost of future pension payments *accrues* over the years that each employee is on the payroll.

The amounts of the retirement benefits that will be paid to today's workers after they retire are not known with certainty. Among other things, these amounts depend on how long retired employees live. Therefore, the employer's obligation for future pension payments arising during the current year *must be estimated.*

Employers do not usually pay retirement pensions directly to retired employees. Most employers meet their pension obligations by making periodic payments to a **pension fund** (or pension plan) throughout the years of each worker's employment.

A pension fund is an *independent entity* managed by a trustee (usually a bank or an insurance company). As the employer makes payments to the pension fund, the trustee invests the money in securities such as stocks and bonds. Over time, the pension fund earns investment income and normally accumulates to a balance far in excess of the employer's deposits. The *pension fund*—not the employer—disburses monthly pension benefits to retired workers.

If the employer meets *all* of its estimated pension obligations by promptly paying cash in a pension fund, the pension fund is said to be *fully funded.* If a pension plan is fully funded, *no liability* for pension payments appears in the employer's balance sheet. The employer's obligation is discharged in the *current period* through the payments made to the pension fund. The employer records each payment to this fund by debiting Pension Expense and crediting Cash.

Determining Pension Expense From a conceptual point of view, the pension expense of a given period is the *present value* of the future pension rights granted to employees as a result of their services during the period. The computation of annual pension expense is complex and involves many assumptions. The amount of this expense is computed not by accountants, but rather by an **actuary,** who considers these factors:

- Average age, retirement age, and life expectancy of employees.
- Employee turnover rates.
- Compensation levels and estimated rate of pay increases.
- Expected rate of return to be earned on pension fund assets.

For example, assume that the actuarial firm of Gibson & Holt computes a pension expense for Cramer Cable Company of $400,000 for the current year. This amount represents the present value of pension rights granted to Cramer's employees for the work they performed during the year. To fully fund this obligation, Cramer transfers $400,000 to National Trust Co., the trustee of the company's pension plan.

The following entry summarizes Cramer's fully funded pension expense for the year:

Pension Expense	400,000	
Cash		400,000
Pension expense for the year as determined by actuarial firm of Gibson & Holt; fully funded by payments to National Trust Co.		

Postretirement Benefits Other than Pensions In addition to pension plans, many companies have promised their employees other types of **postretirement benefits,** such as continuing health insurance. In most respects, these nonpension postretirement benefits are accounted for in the same manner as are pension benefits. Most companies, however, do not fully fund their obligations for nonpension postretirement benefits. Thus recognition of the annual expense often includes a credit to an unfunded liability for part of the cost.

Continuing with our illustration of Cramer Cable Company, assume that Gibson & Holt computes for the company a $250,000 nonpension postretirement benefits expense for the current year. Unlike its pension expense, however, Cramer does *not* fully fund its nonpension obligations.

Only $140,000 of the total amount was paid in cash. The entry to summarize this expense for the year is:

Postretirement Benefits Expense	250,000	
Cash		140,000
Unfunded Liability for Postretirement Benefits		110,000
To record nonpension postretirement benefits expense per report of Gibson & Holt, actuaries; expense funded to the extent of $140,000.		

Any portion of the unfunded liability that the company intends to fund during the next year is classified as a *current liability;* the remainder is classified as a *long-term liability.*

Unfunded Postretirement Costs Are Noncash Expenses Postretirement costs are recognized as expenses as workers earn the right to receive these benefits. If these costs are fully funded, the company makes cash payments to a trustee within the current period equal to this expense. But if these benefits are *not* funded, the cash payments are not made until after the employees retire.

Unfunded retirement benefits often are called a noncash expense. That is, the expense is charged against current earnings, but there are no corresponding cash payments in the period. In the journal entry above, notice that the expense exceeds the cash outlays by $110,000 ($250,000 − $140,000 = $110,000). This amount corresponds to the growth in the unfunded liability.

Unfunded Liabilities for Postretirement Costs: Are They Significant Amounts? Many of America's largest and best-known corporations have obligations for unfunded postretirement benefits that are large relative to their total assets and other liabilities. Let us suggest several things to consider in evaluating a company's ability to pay its unfunded liability for postretirement costs. First, this liability represents only the *present value* of the estimated future payments. The future payments are expected to be *substantially more* than the amount shown in the balance sheet. Next, this liability may *continue to grow,* especially if the company has more employees today than in the past. On the other hand, this liability does *not* have to be paid all at once. It will be paid over a *great many years*—the life span of today's workforce.

In evaluating a company's ability to meet its postretirement obligations, we suggest looking to the *statement of cash flows* in addition to the balance sheet and income statement. In the statement of cash flows, payments of postretirement costs are classified as operating activities. Thus, if a company has a steadily increasing net cash flow from operating activities, it is in a stronger position to handle retirement costs as they come due. But if the net cash flow from operating activities starts to decline, the company may have no choice but to reduce the benefits it provides to retired employees. Often these benefits are *not* contractual and can be reduced at management's discretion.

DEFERRED INCOME TAXES

We have seen in earlier chapters that differences sometimes exist between the way certain types of revenue or expense are recognized in financial statements and the way these same items are reported in income tax returns. For example, most companies use the straight-line method of depreciation in their financial reports but use an accelerated method in their income tax returns. Because of such differences between accounting principles and tax rules, income appearing in the income statement today may not be subject to income taxes until future years. However, the *matching principle* requires that the income shown in an income statement be offset by all related income taxes expense, regardless of when these taxes will be paid. Thus the entry to record a corporation's income tax expense might appear as follows:

Income Tax Expense	1,000,000	
Income Tax Payable		800,000
Deferred Income Taxes.		200,000
To record corporate income taxes applicable to the income of the current year.		

Payment of income taxes expense often can be deferred

Income Tax Payable is a current liability representing the portion of the income taxes expense that must be paid when the company files its income tax return for the current year. The portion of income taxes expense that is deferred to future tax returns is credited to a liability account entitled **Deferred Income Taxes.**

Deferred Income Taxes in Financial Statements How deferred income taxes are classified in the balance sheet depends on the classification of the assets and liabilities that *caused* the tax deferrals. Although deferred taxes often appear as liabilities, certain conditions may require that they be classified as assets. Accounting for deferred taxes involves a number of complex issues that are addressed in more advanced accounting courses.

Concluding Remarks

Businesses have two basic sources of financing their assets: liabilities and owners' equity. Throughout this chapter, we have studied current liabilities, long-term liabilities, and estimated liabilities common to most large businesses. We have learned that liabilities differ from owners' equity in several respects. The feature that most clearly distinguishes the claims of creditors from those of owners is that virtually all liabilities eventually mature and become due. We have also learned that the claims of creditors have legal priority over the claims of owners.

In the next two chapters, we turn our attention to owners' equity. We will examine many important topics including treasury stock transactions, cash dividends, stock dividends, stock splits, and the differences between common and preferred stockholders.

END-OF-CHAPTER REVIEW

SUMMARY OF LEARNING OBJECTIVES

LO1 **Define *liabilities* and distinguish between current and long-term liabilities.** Liabilities are debts arising from past transactions or events that require payment (or the rendering of services) at some future date. Current liabilities are those maturing within one year or the company's operating cycle (whichever is longer) and that are expected to be paid from current assets. Liabilities classified as long-term include obligations maturing more than one year in the future and shorter-term obligations that will be refinanced or paid from noncurrent assets.

LO2 **Account for notes payable and interest expense.** Initially, a liability is recorded only for the principal amount of a note—that is, the amount owed *before* including any interest charges. Interest expense accrues over time. Any accrued interest expense is recognized at the end of an accounting period by an adjusting entry that records both the expense and a short-term liability for accrued interest payable.

LO3 **Describe the costs and the basic accounting activities relating to payrolls.** The basic cost of payrolls is, of course, the salaries and wages earned by employees. However, all employers also incur costs for various payroll taxes, such as the employer's share of Social Security and Medicare, workers' compensation premiums, and unemployment insurance. Many employers also incur costs for various employee benefits, such as health insurance and postretirement benefits. (These additional payroll-related costs often amount to 30 percent to 40 percent of the basic wages and salaries expense.)

LO4 **Prepare an amortization table allocating payments between interest and principal.** An amortization table includes four money columns, showing (1) the amount of each payment, (2) the portion of the payment representing interest expense, (3) the portion of the payment that reduces the principal amount of the loan, and (4) the remaining unpaid balance (or principal amount). The table begins with the original amount of the loan listed in the unpaid balance column. A separate line then is completed showing the allocation of each payment between interest and principal reduction and indicating the new unpaid balance subsequent to the payment.

LO5 **Describe corporate bonds and explain the tax advantage of debt financing.** Corporate bonds are transferable long-term notes payable. Each bond usually has a face value of $1,000 (or a multiple of $1,000), calls for interest payments at a contractual rate, and has a stated maturity date. By issuing thousands of bonds to the investing public at one time, the corporation divides a very large and long-term loan into many transferable units.

The principal advantage of issuing bonds instead of capital stock is that interest payments to bondholders are deductible in determining taxable income, whereas dividend payments to stockholders are not.

LO6 **Account for bonds issued at a discount or premium.** When bonds are issued at a discount, the borrower must repay more than the amount originally borrowed. Thus, any discount in the issuance price represents additional cost in the overall borrowing transaction. The matching principle requires that the borrower recognize this cost gradually over the life of the bond issue as interest expense.

If bonds are issued at a premium, the borrower will repay an amount less than the amount originally borrowed. Thus the premium serves to reduce the overall cost of the borrowing transaction. Again, the matching principle requires that this reduction in interest expense be recognized gradually over the life of the bond issue.

LO7 **Explain the concept of present value as it relates to bond prices.** The basic concept of present value is that an amount of money that will not be paid or received until some future date is equivalent to a smaller amount of money today. This is because the smaller amount available today could be invested to earn interest and thereby accumulate over time to the larger future amount.

The amount today considered equivalent to the future amount is termed the present value of that future amount. The concept of present value is used in the valuation of most long-term liabilities. It also is widely used in investment decisions. Readers who are not familiar with this concept are encouraged to read Appendix B at the end of this textbook.

LO8 **Explain how estimated liabilities, loss contingencies, and commitments are disclosed in financial statements.** Estimated liabilities, such as an automobile manufacturer's responsibility to honor new car warranties, appear in the financial statements at their estimated dollar amounts. Loss contingencies appear as liabilities *only* when it is probable that a loss has been incurred *and* the amount can be reasonably estimated. Unless both these conditions are met, loss contingencies are simply disclosed in the notes to the financial statements. Commitments are contracts for future transactions; they are *not* liabilities. However, if considered material, they are often disclosed in the notes to the financial statements.

LO9 **Evaluate the safety of creditors' claims.** Short-term creditors may evaluate the safety of their claims using such measures of liquidity as the current ratio, the quick ratio, the available lines of credit, and the debtor's credit rating. Long-term creditors look more to signs of stability and long-term financial health, including the debt ratio, interest coverage ratio, and trends in net income and net cash flow from operating activities.

LO10 **Describe reporting issues related to leases, postretirement benefits, and deferred taxes.** Leases that are essentially equivalent to a sale of property by the lessor to the lessee are regarded as capital leases. Under a capital lease arrangement, the lessee reports in its balance sheet the present values of both an asset (for example, leased equipment) and a liability (lease payment obligations). Lease arrangements that do not qualify as capital leases are treated as operating leases, requiring that lease payments be treated as expenses when paid.

Unfunded postretirement costs are reported in the balance sheet at their discounted present values as long-term liabilities. Unfunded postretirement benefits are often called a noncash expense. That is, the expense is charged against current earnings without a corresponding outlay of cash.

Deferred income taxes result because timing differences exist between financial accounting principles and tax rules. Thus, income appearing in the income statement today may not be subject to income taxes until future years. Likewise, income subject to income taxes today may not appear in the company's income statement until future periods. Depending on the circumstances, deferred taxes may appear in the balance sheet as liabilities and/or assets (both current and long-term).

Key Terms Introduced or Emphasized in Chapter 10

accrued liabilities (p. 433) The liability to pay an expense that has accrued during the period. Also called *accrued expenses.*

actuary (p. 457) A statistician who performs computations involving assumptions as to human life spans. One function is computing companies' liabilities for pensions and postretirement benefits.

amortization table (p. 436) A schedule that indicates how installment payments are allocated between interest expense and repayments of principal.

bankruptcy (p. 452) A legal status in which the financial affairs of an illiquid business (or individual) are managed, in large part, by the U.S. Bankruptcy Court.

bonds payable (p. 438) Long-term debt securities that subdivide a very large and long-term corporate debt into transferable increments of $1,000 or multiples thereof.

capital lease (p. 456) A lease contract that finances the eventual purchase by the lessee of leased property. The lessor accounts for a capital lease as a sale of property; the lessee records an asset and a liability equal to the present value of the future lease payments. Also called a *financing lease.*

collateral (p. 430) Assets that have been pledged to secure specific liabilities. Creditors with secured claims can foreclose on (seize title to) these assets if the borrower defaults.

commitments (p. 452) Agreements to carry out future transactions. Although they are not a liability (because the transaction has not yet been performed), they may be disclosed in notes to the financial statements.

convertible bond (p. 440) A bond that may be exchanged (at the bondholder's option) for a specified number of shares of the company's capital stock.

debt service (p. 436) The combined cash outlays required for repayment of principal amounts borrowed and for payments of interest expense during the period.

deferred income taxes (p. 459) A liability account to pay income taxes that have been postponed to a future year's income tax return. In some cases, this account can also be an asset account representing income taxes to be saved in a future year's income tax return.

estimated liabilities (p. 431) Liabilities known to exist, but that must be recorded in the accounting records at estimated dollar amounts.

interest coverage ratio (p. 453) Operating income divided by interest expense. Indicates the number of times that the company was able to earn the amount of its interest charges.

junk bonds (p. 440) Bonds payable that involve a greater than normal risk of default and, therefore, must pay higher than normal rates of interest in order to be attractive to investors.

lessee (p. 455) The tenant, user, or renter of leased property.

lessor (p. 455) The owner of property leased to a lessee.

leverage (p. 453) The use of borrowed money to finance business operations.

loss contingencies (p. 451) Situations involving uncertainty as to whether a loss has occurred. The uncertainty will be resolved by a future event. An example of a loss contingency is the possible loss relating to a lawsuit pending against a company. Although loss contingencies are sometimes recorded in the accounts, they are more frequently disclosed only in notes to the financial statements.

maturity date (p. 430) The date on which a liability becomes due.

off-balance sheet financing (p. 456) An arrangement in which the use of resources is financed without the obligation for future payments appearing as a liability in the balance sheet. An operating lease is a common example of off-balance sheet financing.

operating lease (p. 456) A lease contract which is in essence a rental agreement. The lessee has the use of the leased property, but the lessor retains the usual risks and rewards of ownership. The periodic lease payments are accounted for as rent expense by the lessee and as rental revenue by the lessor.

payroll taxes (p. 433) Taxes levied on an employer based on the amount of wages and salaries being paid to employees during the period. They include the employer's share of Social Security and Medicare taxes, unemployment taxes, and (though not called a "tax") workers' compensation premiums.

pension fund (p. 457) A fund managed by an independent trustee into which an employer-company makes periodic payments. The fund is used to make pension payments to retired employees.

postretirement benefits (p. 457) Benefits that will be paid to retired workers. The present value of the future benefits earned by workers during the current period is an expense of the period. If not fully funded, this expense results in a liability for unfunded postretirement benefits. (For many companies, these liabilities have become very large.)

present value (of a future amount) (p. 449) The amount of money that an informed investor would pay today for the right to receive the future amount, based on a specific rate of return required by the investor.

principal amount (p. 431) The unpaid balance of an obligation, exclusive of any interest charges for the current period.

sinking fund (p. 440) Cash set aside by a corporation at regular intervals (usually with a trustee) for the purpose of repaying a bond issue at its maturity date.

special purpose entities (p. 455) SPEs are separate entities established by corporations to accomplish specific purposes. SPEs are often used to borrow money and then transfer it to the sponsoring corporation as an off-balance sheet financing arrangement.

underwriter (p. 439) An investment banking firm that handles the sale of a corporation's stocks or bonds to the public.

workers' compensation (p. 434) A state-mandated insurance program insuring workers against job-related injuries. Premiums are charged to employers as a percentage of the employees' wages and salaries. The amounts vary by state and by the employees' occupations but, in some cases, can be very substantial.

Demonstration Problem

Listed below are selected items from the financial statements of G & H Pump Mfg. Co. for the year ended December 31, 2011.

Note payable to Porterville Bank	$ 99,000
Income taxes payable	63,000
Loss contingency relating to lawsuit	200,000
Accounts payable and accrued expenses	163,230
Mortgage note payable	240,864
Bonds payable	2,200,000
Premium on bonds payable	1,406
Accrued bond interest payable	110,000
Pension expense	61,400
Unearned revenue	25,300

Other Information

1. The note payable owed to Porterville Bank is due in 30 days. G & H has arranged with this bank to renew the note for an additional two years.
2. G & H has been sued for $200,000 by someone claiming the company's pumps are excessively noisy. It is reasonably possible, but not probable, that a loss has been sustained.
3. The mortgage note is payable at $8,000 per month over the next three years. During the next 12 months, the principal amount of this note will be reduced to $169,994.
4. The bonds payable mature in seven months. A sinking fund has been accumulated to repay the full maturity of this bond issue.

Instructions

a. Using this information, prepare the current liabilities and long-term liabilities sections of a classified balance sheet at December 31, 2011.

b. Explain briefly how the information in each of the four numbered paragraphs affected your presentation of the company's liabilities.

Solution to the Demonstration Problem

a.

G & H PUMP MFG. CO.
PARTIAL BALANCE SHEET
DECEMBER 31, 2011

Liabilities:		
Current liabilities:		
Accounts payable and accrued expenses		$ 163,230
Income taxes payable		63,000
Accrued bond interest payable		110,000
Unearned revenue		25,300
Current portion of long-term debt		70,870
Total current liabilities		$ 432,400
Long-term liabilities:		
Note payable to Porterville Bank		$ 99,000
Mortgage note payable		169,994
Bonds payable	$2,200,000	
Add: Premium on bonds payable	1,406	2,201,406
Total long-term liabilities		$2,470,400
Total liabilities		$2,902,800

b.

1. Although the note payable to Porterville Bank is due in 30 days, it is classified as a long-term liability as it will be refinanced on a long-term basis.

2. The pending lawsuit is a loss contingency requiring disclosure, but it is not included in the liability section of the balance sheet.

3. The $70,870 of the mortgage note that will be repaid within the next 12 months ($240,864 − $169,994) is a current liability; the remaining balance, due after December 31, 2012, is long-term debt.

4. Although the bonds payable mature in seven months, they will be repaid from a sinking fund, rather than from current assets. Therefore, these bonds retain their long-term classification.

Self-Test Questions

The answers to these questions appear on page 481.

1. Which of the following is characteristic of liabilities rather than of equity? (More than one answer may be correct.)

a. The obligation matures.

b. Interest paid to the provider of the capital is deductible in the determination of taxable income.

c. The capital providers' claims are *residual* in the event of liquidation of the business.

d. The capital providers normally have the right to exercise control over business operations.

2. On October 1, Dalton Corp. borrows $100,000 from National Bank, signing a six-month note payable for that amount, plus interest to be computed at a rate of 9 percent per annum. Indicate all correct answers.

a. Dalton's liability at October 1 is only $100,000.

b. The maturity value of this note is $104,500.

c. At December 31, Dalton will have a liability for accrued interest payable in the amount of $4,500.

d. Dalton's total liability for this loan at November 30 is $101,500.

3. Identify all correct statements concerning payrolls and related payroll costs.

   a. Both employers and employees pay Social Security and Medicare taxes.

   b. Workers' compensation premiums are withheld from employees' wages.

   c. An employer's total payroll costs usually exceed total wages expense by about 7½ percent.

   d. Under current law, employers are required to pay Social Security taxes on employees' earnings, but they are not required to pay for health insurance.

4. Identify the types of information that can readily be determined from an amortization table for an installment loan. (More than one answer may be correct.)

   a. Interest expense on this liability for the current year.

   b. The present value of the future payments under changing market conditions.

   c. The unpaid balance remaining after each payment.

   d. The portion of the unpaid balance that is a current liability.

5. Which of the following statements is (are) correct? (More than one statement may be correct.)

   a. A bond issue is a technique for subdividing a very large loan into many small, transferable units.

   b. Bond interest payments are contractual obligations, whereas the board of directors determines whether or not dividends will be paid.

   c. As interest rates rise, the market prices of bonds fall; as interest rates fall, bond prices tend to rise.

   d. Bond interest payments are deductible in determining income subject to income taxes, whereas dividends paid to stockholders are not deductible.

6. Identify all statements that are *consistent* with the concept of present value. (More than one answer may be correct.)

   a. The present value of a future amount always is *less* than that future amount.

   b. An amount of money available today is considered *more* valuable than the *same sum* that will not become available until a future date.

   c. A bond's issue price is equal to the present value of its future cash flows.

   d. The liability for an installment note payable is recorded at only the *principal* amount, rather than the sum of the scheduled future payments.

7. Identify those trends that are *unfavorable* from the viewpoint of a bondholder. (More than one answer may be correct.)

   a. Market interest rates are steadily rising.

   b. The issuing company's interest coverage ratio is steadily rising.

   c. The issuing company's net cash flow from operating activities is steadily declining.

   d. The issuing company's debt ratio is steadily declining.

8. A basic difference between *loss contingencies* and "real" liabilities is:

   a. Liabilities stem from past transactions; loss contingencies stem from future events.

   b. Liabilities always are recorded in the accounting records, whereas loss contingencies never are.

   c. The extent of uncertainty involved.

   d. Liabilities can be large in amount, whereas loss contingencies are immaterial.

9. Which of the following situations require recording a liability in 2011? (More than one answer may be correct.)

   a. In 2011, a company manufactures and sells stereo equipment that carries a three-year warranty.

   b. In 2011, a theater group receives payments in advance from season ticket holders for productions to be performed in 2012.

   c. A company is a defendant in a legal action. At the end of 2011, the company's attorney feels it is possible the company will lose and that the amount of the loss might be material.

   d. During 2011, a Midwest agricultural cooperative is concerned about the risk of loss if inclement weather destroys the crops.

10. Silverado maintains a fully funded pension plan. During 2011, $1 million was paid to retired workers, and workers currently employed by the company earned a portion of the right to receive pension payments expected to total $6 million *over their lifetimes.* Silverado's pension *expense* for 2011 amounts to:

    a. $1 million.

    b. $6 million.

    c. $7 million.

    d. Some other amount.

11. Deferred income taxes result from:

    a. The fact that bond interest is deductible in the computation of taxable income.

    b. Depositing income taxes due in future years in a special fund managed by an independent trustee.

    c. Differences between certain revenue and expense items recognized in financial statements but not in income tax returns.

    d. The inability of a bankrupt company to pay its income tax liability on schedule.

ASSIGNMENT MATERIAL Discussion Questions

1. Define *liabilities*. Identify several characteristics that distinguish liabilities from owners' equity.
2. Explain the relative priority of the claims of owners and of creditors to the assets of a business. Do all creditors have equal priority? Explain.
3. Define *current liabilities* and *long-term liabilities*. Under what circumstances might a 10-year bond issue be classified as a current liability? Under what circumstances might a note payable maturing 30 days after the balance sheet date be classified as a long-term liability?
4. Explain why an employer's "total cost" of a payroll may exceed by a substantial amount the total wages and salaries earned by employees.
5. A friend of yours has just purchased a house and has taken out a $50,000, 11 percent mortgage, payable at $476.17 per month. After making the first monthly payment, he received a receipt from the bank stating that only $17.84 of the $476.17 had been applied to reducing the principal amount of the loan. Your friend computes that, at the rate of $17.84 per month, it will take over 233 years to pay off the $50,000 mortgage. Do you agree with your friend's analysis? Explain.
6. Briefly explain the income tax advantage of raising capital by issuing bonds rather than by selling capital stock.
7. Tampa Boat Company pays federal income taxes at a rate of 30 percent on taxable income. Compute the company's annual *after-tax* cost of borrowing on a 10 percent, $5 million bond issue. Express this after-tax cost as a percentage of the borrowed $5 million.
8. Why do bond prices vary inversely with interest rates?
9. Some bonds now being bought and sold by investors on organized securities exchanges were issued when interest rates were much higher than they are today. Would you expect these bonds to be trading at prices above or below their face values? Explain.
10. There is an old business saying that "You shouldn't *be* in business if your company doesn't earn higher than bank rates." This means that if a company is to succeed, its return on assets should be *significantly higher* than its cost of borrowing. Why is this so important?
11. Identify two characteristics of *estimated liabilities*. Provide at least two examples of estimated liabilities.
12. What is the meaning of the term *loss contingency*? Give several examples. How are loss contingencies presented in financial statements? Explain.
13. Explain how the lessee accounts for an operating lease and a capital lease. Why is an operating lease sometimes called *off-balance sheet financing*?
14. When are the costs of postretirement benefits recognized as an expense? When are the related cash payments made?
15. What are *deferred income tax liabilities*? How are these items presented in financial statements?

Brief Exercises

LO2 BRIEF EXERCISE 10.1
Cash Effects of Borrowing

Jacobs Company borrowed $10,000 on a one-year, 8 percent note payable from the local bank on April 1. Interest was paid quarterly, and the note was repaid one year from the time the money was borrowed. Calculate the amount of cash payments Jacobs was required to make in each of the two calendar years that were affected by the note payable.

LO5 BRIEF EXERCISE 10.2
Effective Interest Rate

One of the advantages of borrowing is that interest is deductible for income tax purposes.

a. If a company pays 8 percent interest to borrow $500,000, but is in an income tax bracket that requires it to pay 40 percent income tax, what is the actual net-of-tax interest cost that the company incurs?

b. What is the effective interest rate that is paid by the company?

LO6 BRIEF EXERCISE 10.3
Bonds Issued at a Discount

Cronan, Inc., sells $1,000,000 general obligation bonds for 98. The interest rate on the bonds, paid quarterly, is 6 percent. Calculate (**a**) the amount that the company will actually receive from the sale of the bonds, and (**b**) the amount of both the quarterly and the total annual cash interest that the company will be required to pay.

LO6 **BRIEF EXERCISE 10.4**
Bonds Issued at a Premium

Pearl Company sells $1,000,000 general obligation bonds for 101. The interest rate on the bonds, paid quarterly, is 5 percent. Calculate (**a**) the amount that the company will actually receive from the sale of the bonds, and (**b**) the amount of both the quarterly and the total annual cash interest that the company will be required to pay.

LO6 **BRIEF EXERCISE 10.5**
Recording Bonds Issued at a Discount

Red & Blue Company sold bonds at 97 on an interest payment date for $500,000. Assuming the bonds will be retired in 10 years and interest is paid annually, calculate the amount of cash that will be received and paid by Red & Blue in the first year, as well as the interest expense that will be recognized in that year. The bonds carry a stated interest rate of 5 percent.

LO6 **BRIEF EXERCISE 10.6**
Recording Bonds Issued at a Premium

Purple & Orange, Inc., sold $700,000 of bonds on an interest payment date at 102. Assuming the bonds will be retired in 10 years and interest is paid annually, calculate the amount of cash that will be received and paid by Purple & Orange in the first full year, as well as the amount of interest expense that will be recognized in that year. The bonds carry a stated interest rate of 6.5 percent.

LO9 **BRIEF EXERCISE 10.7**
Debt Ratio

Fox Company has debt totaling $2,000,000 and total stockholders' equity of $4,000,000. Wolfe Company has debt totaling $3,000,000 and stockholders' equity of $5,000,000.

a. Calculate the debt ratio for each company. (Hint: You will find an explanation of the debt ratio and how it is computed in Exhibit 10–8.)

b. Briefly explain the meaning of the debt ratio.

LO6 **BRIEF EXERCISE 10.8**
Early Retirement of Bonds

Joseph Max, Inc., sold 10-year, 7 percent bonds for $1,000,000 at 98. On the interest payment date at the end of the 5th year the bonds were outstanding, 50 percent of the bonds were retired by Max at 101 under an early retirement option that was written into the bond agreement. Determine the gain or loss that Max will incur as a result of retiring the bonds.

LO10 **BRIEF EXERCISE 10.9**
Deferred Income Taxes

Gosling Company determines its annual income tax expense to be $459,000. Of that amount, $300,000 has already been paid during the year (on a quarterly basis) and charged to the Income Taxes Expense account. The company has determined that, of the amount that has not yet been paid or recorded, $75,000 will be deferred into future years under certain favorable income tax provisions available to the company. Prepare the end-of-year general journal entry to recognize income taxes accrued.

LO10 **BRIEF EXERCISE 10.10**
Pension and Other Postretirement Benefit Costs

Grammar, Inc., offers its full-time employees pension and other postretirement benefits, primarily health insurance. During the current year, pension benefits for the employees totaled $250,000. Other postretirement benefits totaled $140,000. The pension benefits are fully funded by the company by transferring cash to a trustee that administers the plan. The other postretirement benefits are similarly funded, but only at the 50 percent level. Determine the total amount that Grammar will need to transfer to its trustee for both benefit plans during the current year.

Exercises

LO4 **EXERCISE 10.1**
You as a Student

Assume that you will have a 10-year, $10,000 loan to repay to your parents when you graduate from college next month. The loan, plus 8 percent annual interest on the unpaid balance, is to be repaid in 10 annual installments of $1,490 each, beginning one year after you graduate. You have accepted a well-paying job and are considering an early settlement of the entire unpaid balance in just three years (immediately after making the third annual payment of $1,490).

Prepare an amortization schedule showing how much money you will need to save to pay your parents the entire unpaid balance of your loan three years after your graduation. (Round amounts to the nearest dollar.)

LO1 through LO6 **EXERCISE 10.2**
Effects of Transactions on the Accounting Equation

Listed below are eight events or transactions of GemStar Corporation.

a. Made an adjusting entry to record interest on a short-term note payable.

b. Made a monthly installment payment of a fully amortizing, six-month, interest-bearing installment note payable.

c. Recorded a regular biweekly payroll, including the amounts withheld from employees, the issuance of paychecks, and payroll taxes on the employer.

d. Came within 12 months of the maturity date of a note payable originally issued for a period of 18 months.

e. Deposited employee tax withholdings with proper tax authorities.

f. Issued bonds payable at face value.

g. Recognized semiannual interest expense on bonds payable described in part **f** and paid bondholders the full interest amount.

h. Recorded the necessary adjusting entry on December 31, 2011, to accrue three months' interest on bonds payable that had been issued at a discount several years prior. The next semiannual interest payment will occur March 31, 2012.

Indicate the effects of each of these transactions on the following financial statement categories. Organize your answer in tabular form, using the illustrated column headings. Use the following code letters to indicate the effects of each transaction on the accounting element listed in the column heading: **I** for increase, **D** for decrease, and **NE** for no effect.

	Income Statement			Balance Sheet			
Transaction	Revenue −	Expenses =	Net Income	Assets =	Current Liab. +	Long-Term Liab. +	Owners' Equity
a							

LO1 LO2 LO4 through LO6 LO8

EXERCISE 10.3

Effects of Transactions on Various Financial Measurements

Six events relating to liabilities follow:

a. Paid the liability for interest payable accrued at the end of the last accounting period.

b. Made the current monthly payment on a 12-month installment note payable, including interest and a partial repayment of principal.

c. Issued bonds payable at 98 on March 1, 2011. The bonds pay interest March 1 and September 1.

d. Recorded September 1, 2011, interest expense and made semiannual interest payment on bonds referred to in part **c.**

e. Recorded necessary adjusting entry on December 31, 2011, for bonds referred to in part **c**.

f. Recorded estimated six-month warranty expense on December 31, 2011.

Indicate the effects of each transaction or adjusting entry on the financial measurements in the five column headings listed below. Use the code letters **I** for increase, **D** for decrease, and **NE** for no effect.

Transaction	Current Liabilities	Long-Term Liabilities	Net Income	Net Cash Flow from Operating Activities	Net Cash Flow (from All Sources)
a					

LO3

EXERCISE 10.4

Employees—What Do They Really Cost?

Magnum Plus, Inc., is a manufacturer of hunting supplies. The following is a summary of the company's annual payroll-related costs:

Wages and salaries expense (of which $2,200,000 was withheld from employees' pay and forwarded directly to tax authorities)	$7,200,000
Payroll taxes	580,000
Workers' compensation premiums	250,000
Group health insurance premiums	725,000
Contributions to employees' pension plan	450,000

a. Compute Magnum's total payroll-related costs for the year.

b. Compute the net amount of cash actually paid to employees (their take-home pay).

c. Express total payroll-related costs as a percentage of (1) total wages and salaries expense, and (2) employees' take-home pay. (Round computations to the nearest 1 percent.)

LO3 **EXERCISE 10.5**
Accounting for Payroll Activities

Gruver Corporation reported the following payroll-related costs for the month of February:

Gross pay (wages expense)	$250,000
Social Security and Medicare taxes	19,125
Federal and state unemployment taxes	15,500
Workers' compensation insurance	8,500
Group health and life insurance benefits	10,000
Employee pension plan benefits	22,875
Total payroll costs for February	$326,000

Gruver's insurance premiums for workers' compensation and group health and life insurance were paid for in a prior period and recorded initially as prepaid insurance expense. Withholdings from employee wages in February were as follows:

State income tax withholdings	$ 5,875
Federal income tax withholdings	56,000
Social Security and Medicare tax withholdings	19,125

a. Record Gruver's gross wages, employee withholdings, and employee take-home pay for February.

b. Record Gruver's payroll tax expense for February.

c. Record Gruver's employee benefit expenses for February.

d. Do the amounts withheld from Gruver's employees represent taxes levied on Gruver Corporation? Explain.

LO4 **EXERCISE 10.6**
Use of an Amortization Table

Glen Pool Club, Inc., has a $150,000 mortgage liability. The mortgage is payable in monthly installments of $1,543, which include interest computed at an annual rate of 12 percent (1 percent monthly).

a. Prepare a partial amortization table showing (**1**) the original balance of this loan, and (**2**) the allocation of the first two monthly payments between interest expense and the reduction in the mortgage's unpaid balance. (Round to the nearest dollar.)

b. Prepare the journal entry to record the second monthly payment.

c. Will monthly interest increase, decrease, or stay the same over the life of the loan? Explain your answer.

LO5 **EXERCISE 10.7**
After-Tax Cost of Borrowing

DuPont reports in a recent balance sheet $598 million of 5.25 percent notes payable due in 2016. The company's income tax rate is approximately 19 percent.

a. Compute the company's after-tax cost of borrowing on this bond issue stated as a total dollar amount.

b. Compute the company's after-tax cost of borrowing on this bond issue stated as a percentage of the amount borrowed.

c. Describe briefly the advantage of raising funds by issuing bonds as opposed to stocks.

LO5 **EXERCISE 10.8**
Bond Interest on Bonds Issued at Face Value

On March 31, 2011, Gardner Corporation received authorization to issue $50,000 of 9 percent, 30-year bonds payable. The bonds pay interest on March 31 and September 30. The entire issue was dated March 31, 2011, but the bonds were not issued until April 30, 2011. They were issued at face value.

a. Prepare the journal entry at April 30, 2011, to record the sale of the bonds.

b. Prepare the journal entry at September 30, 2011, to record the semiannual bond interest payment.

c. Prepare the adjusting entry at December 31, 2011, to record bond interest expense accrued since September 30, 2011. (Assume that no monthly adjusting entries to accrue interest expense had been made prior to December 31, 2011.)

d. Explain why the issuing corporation charged its bond investors for interest accrued in April 2011, prior to the issuance date (see part **b** above).

LO5 LO6 **EXERCISE 10.9**

Accounting for Bonds Issued at a Premium: Issuance, Interest Payments, and Retirement

Swanson Corporation issued $8 million of 20-year, 8 percent bonds on April 1, 2011, at 102. Interest is due on March 31 and September 30 of each year, and all of the bonds in the issue mature on March 31, 2031. Swanson's fiscal year ends on December 31. Prepare the following journal entries:

a. April 1, 2011, to record the issuance of the bonds.

b. September 30, 2011, to pay interest and to amortize the bond premium.

c. March 31, 2031, to pay interest, amortize the bond premium, and retire the bonds at maturity (make two separate entries).

d. Briefly explain the effect of amortizing the bond premium upon (1) annual net income and (2) annual net cash flow from operating activities. (Ignore possible income tax effects.)

LO5 LO6 **EXERCISE 10.10**

Accounting for Bonds Issued at a Discount: Issuance, Interest Payments, and Retirement

Mellilo Corporation issued $5 million of 20-year, 9.5 percent bonds on July 1, 2011, at 98. Interest is due on June 30 and December 31 of each year, and all of the bonds in the issue mature on June 30, 2031. Mellilo's fiscal year ends on December 31. Prepare the following journal entries:

a. July 1, 2011, to record the issuance of the bonds.

b. December 31, 2011, to pay interest and amortize the bond discount.

c. June 30, 2031, to pay interest, amortize the bond discount, and retire the bonds at maturity (make two separate entries).

d. Briefly explain the effect of amortizing the bond discount upon (1) annual net income and (2) annual net cash flow from operating activities. (Ignore possible income tax effects.)

LO9 **EXERCISE 10.11**

Safety of Creditors' Claims

Shown below are data from recent reports of two toy makers. Dollar amounts are stated in thousands.

	Toyco	Playco
Total assets	$615,132	$2,616,388
Total liabilities	349,792	1,090,776
Interest expense	28,026	37,588
Operating income	13,028	304,672

a. Compute for each company (1) the debt ratio and (2) the interest coverage ratio. (Round the debt ratio to the nearest percent and the interest coverage ratio to two decimal places.)

b. In your opinion, which of these companies would a long-term creditor probably view as the safer investment? Explain.

LO10 **EXERCISE 10.12**

Accounting for Leases

On July 1, Pine Region Dairy leased equipment from Farm America for a period of three years. The lease calls for monthly payments of $2,500 payable in advance on the first day of each month, beginning July 1.

Prepare the journal entry needed to record this lease in the accounting records of Pine Region Dairy on July 1 under each of the following independent assumptions:

a. The lease represents a simple rental arrangement.

b. At the end of three years, title to this equipment will be transferred to Pine Region Dairy at no additional cost. The present value of the 36 monthly lease payments is $76,021, of which $2,500 is paid in cash on July 1. None of the initial $2,500 is allocated to interest expense.

c. Why is situation **a**, the operating lease, sometimes called off-balance sheet financing?

d. Would it be acceptable for a company to account for a capital lease as an operating lease to report rent expense rather than a long-term liability?

LO10 **EXERCISE 10.13**
Pension Plans

At the end of the current year, Western Electric received the following information from its actuarial firm:

Pension expense	$2,500,000
Postretirement benefits expense	750,000

The pension plan is fully funded. Western Electric has funded only $50,000 of the nonpension postretirement benefits this year.

a. Prepare the journal entry to summarize pension expense for the entire year.

b. Prepare the journal entry to summarize the nonpension postretirement benefits expense for the entire year.

c. If the company becomes illiquid in future years, what prospects, if any, do today's employees have of receiving the pension benefits that they have earned to date?

d. Does the company have an ethical responsibility to fully fund its nonpension postretirement benefits?

LO10 **EXERCISE 10.14**
Deferred Income Taxes

The following journal entry summarizes for the current year the income tax expense of Wilson's Software Warehouse:

Income Tax Expense	1,500,000	
Cash		960,000
Income Tax Payable		340,000
Deferred Income Tax		200,000
To record income tax expense for the current year.		

Of the deferred income taxes, only $30,000 is classified as a current liability.

a. Define the term *deferred income tax.*

b. What is the amount of income tax that the company has paid or expects to pay in conjunction with its income tax return for the current year?

c. Illustrate the allocation of the liabilities shown in the above journal entry between the classifications of current liabilities and long-term liabilities.

LO9 **EXERCISE 10.15**
Examining **Home Depot**'s Capital Structure

To answer the following questions use the financial statements for **Home Depot, Inc.**, in Appendix A at the end of the textbook:

a. Compute the company's current ratio and quick ratio for the most recent year reported. Do these ratios provide support that **Home Depot** is able to repay its current liabilities as they come due? Explain.

b. Compute the company's debt ratio. Does **Home Depot** appear to have excessive debt? Explain.

c. Examine the company's statement of cash flows. Does **Home Depot**'s cash flow from operating activities appear adequate to cover its current liabilities as they come due? Explain.

Problem Set A

LO1 through LO6, LO8 **PROBLEM 10.1A**
Effects of Transactions on Financial Statements

Fifteen transactions or events affecting Computer Specialists, Inc., are as follows:

a. Made a year-end adjusting entry to accrue interest on a note payable.

b. A liability classified for several years as long-term becomes due within the next 12 months.

c. Recorded the regular biweekly payroll, including payroll taxes, amounts withheld from employees, and the issuance of paychecks.

d. Earned an amount previously recorded as unearned revenue.

e. Made arrangements to extend a bank loan due in 60 days for another 18 months.

f. Made a monthly payment on a fully amortizing installment note payable. (Assume this note is classified as a current liability.)

g. Called bonds payable due in seven years at a price above the carrying value of the liability in the accounting records.

h. Issued bonds payable at 97 on May 1, 2011. The bonds pay interest May 1 and November 1.

i. Recorded November 1, 2011, interest expense and made semiannual interest payment on bonds referred to in part **h.**

j. Recorded necessary adjusting entry on December 31, 2011, for bonds referred to in part **h.**

k. Issued bonds payable at 102 on July 31, 2011. The bonds pay interest July 31 and January 31.

l. Recorded necessary adjusting entry on December 31, 2011, for bonds referred to in part **k.**

m. Recorded an estimated liability for warranty claims.

n. Entered into a two-year commitment to buy all hard drives from a particular supplier at a price 10 percent below market.

o. Received notice that a lawsuit has been filed against the company for $7 million. The amount of the company's liability, if any, cannot be reasonably estimated at this time.

Instructions

Indicate the effects of each of these transactions upon the following elements of the company's financial statements. Organize your answer in tabular form, using the column headings shown below. Use the following code letters to indicate the effects of each transaction on the accounting element listed in the column headings: **I** for increase, **D** for decrease, and **NE** for no effect.

	Income Statement			Balance Sheet			
Transaction	Revenue –	Expenses =	Net Income	Assets =	Current Liab. +	Long-Term Liab. +	Owners' Equity
a							

LO1 LO2 LO4 LO8

PROBLEM 10.2A

Balance Sheet Presentation of Liabilities

The following are selected items from the accounting records of Seattle Chocolates for the year ended December 31, 2011:

Note payable to Northwest Bank	$500,000
Income taxes payable	40,000
Accrued expenses and payroll taxes	60,000
Mortgage note payable	750,000
Accrued interest on mortgage note payable	5,000
Trade accounts payable	250,000
Unearned revenue	15,000
Potential liability in pending lawsuit	100,000

Other Information

1. The note payable to Northwest Bank is due in 60 days. Arrangements have been made to renew this note for an additional 12 months.
2. The mortgage requires payments of $6,000 per month. An amortization table shows that its balance will be paid down to $739,000 by December 31, 2012.
3. Accrued interest on the mortgage note payable is paid monthly. The next payment is due near the end of the first week in January 2012.
4. Seattle Chocolates has been sued for $100,000 in a contract dispute. It is not possible at this time, however, to make a reasonable estimate of the possible loss, if any, that the company may have sustained.

Instructions

a. Using the information provided, prepare the current and long-term liability sections of the company's balance sheet dated December 31, 2011. (Within each classification, items may be listed in any order.)

b. Explain briefly how the information in each of the four numbered paragraphs above influenced your presentation of the company's liabilities.

LO2 **PROBLEM 10.3A**
Notes Payable: Accruing Interest

During the fiscal year ended December 31, Swanson Corporation engaged in the following transactions involving notes payable:

Aug. 6 Borrowed $12,000 from Maple Grove Bank, signing a 45-day, 12 percent note payable.

Sept. 16 Purchased office equipment from Seawald Equipment. The invoice amount was $18,000, and Seawald agreed to accept, as full payment, a 10 percent, three-month note for the invoice amount.

Sept. 20 Paid Maple Grove Bank the note plus accrued interest.

Nov. 1 Borrowed $250,000 from Mike Swanson, a major corporate stockholder. The corporation issued Swanson a $250,000, 15 percent, 90-day note payable.

Dec. 1 Purchased merchandise inventory in the amount of $5,000 from Gathman Corporation. Gathman accepted a 90-day, 14 percent note as full settlement of the purchase. Swanson Corporation uses a perpetual inventory system.

Dec. 16 The $18,000 note payable to Seawald Equipment matured today. Swanson paid the accrued interest on this note and issued a new 30-day, 16 percent note payable in the amount of $18,000 to replace the note that matured.

Instructions

a. Prepare journal entries (in general journal form) to record the above transactions. Use a 360-day year in making the interest calculations.

b. Prepare the adjusting entry needed at December 31, prior to closing the accounts. Use one entry for all three notes (round to the nearest dollar).

c. Provide a possible explanation why the new 30-day note payable to Seawald Equipment pays 16 percent interest instead of the 10 percent rate charged on the September 16 note.

LO4 **PROBLEM 10.4A**
Preparation and Use of an Amortization Table

On September 1, 2011, Quick Lube signed a 30-year, $1,080,000 mortgage note payable to Mifflinburg Bank and Trust in conjunction with the purchase of a building and land. The mortgage note calls for interest at an annual rate of 12 percent (1 percent per month). The note is fully amortizing over a period of 360 months.

The bank sent Quick Lube an amortization table showing the allocation of monthly payments between interest and principal over the life of the loan. A small part of this amortization table is illustrated below. (For convenience, amounts have been rounded to the nearest dollar.)

AMORTIZATION TABLE (12%, 30-YEAR MORTGAGE NOTE PAYABLE FOR $1,080,000; PAYABLE IN 360 MONTHLY INSTALLMENTS OF $11,110)

Interest Period	Payment Date	Monthly Payment	Interest Expense	Principal Reduction	Unpaid Balance
Issue date	Sept. 1, 2011	—	—	—	$1,080,000
1	Oct. 1	$11,110	$10,800	$310	1,079,690
2	Nov. 1	11,110	10,797	313	1,079,377

Instructions

a. Explain whether the amounts of interest expense and the reductions in the unpaid principal are likely to change in any predictable pattern from month to month.

b. Prepare journal entries to record the first two monthly payments on this mortgage.

c. Complete this amortization table for two more monthly installments—those due on December 1, 2011, and January 1, 2012. (Round amounts to the nearest dollar.)

d. Will any amounts relating to this 30-year mortgage be classified as current liabilities in Quick Lube's December 31, 2011, balance sheet? Explain, but you need not compute any additional dollar amounts.

LO5 **PROBLEM 10.5A**
Bond Interest (Bonds Issued at Face Value)

Blue Mountain Power Company obtained authorization to issue 20-year bonds with a face value of $10 million. The bonds are dated May 1, 2011, and have a contract rate of interest of 10 percent. They pay interest on November 1 and May 1. The bonds were issued on August 1, 2011, at 100 plus three months' accrued interest.

Instructions

Prepare the necessary journal entries in general journal form on:

a. August 1, 2011, to record the issuance of the bonds.

b. November 1, 2011, to record the first semiannual interest payment on the bond issue.

c. December 31, 2011, to record interest expense accrued through year-end. (Round to the nearest dollar.)

d. May 1, 2012, to record the second semiannual interest payment. (Round to the nearest dollar.)

e. What was the prevailing market rate of interest on the date that the bonds were issued? Explain.

LO5 LO6 **PROBLEM 10.6A**
Amortization of a Bond Discount and Premium

On September 1, 2011, Park Rapids Lumber Company issued $80 million in 20-year, 10 percent bonds payable. Interest is payable semiannually on March 1 and September 1. Bond discounts and premiums are amortized at each interest payment date and at year-end. The company's fiscal year ends at December 31.

Instructions

a. Make the necessary adjusting entries at December 31, 2011, and the journal entry to record the payment of bond interest on March 1, 2012, under each of the following assumptions:

  1. The bonds were issued at 98. (Round to the nearest dollar.)

  2. The bonds were issued at 101. (Round to the nearest dollar.)

b. Compute the net bond liability at December 31, 2012, under assumptions **1** and **2** above. (Round to the nearest dollar.)

c. Under which of the above assumptions, **1** or **2,** would the investor's effective rate of interest be higher? Explain.

LO1 LO5 LO6 LO10 **PROBLEM 10.7A**
Reporting Liabilities in a Balance Sheet

eXcel

The following items were taken from the accounting records of Minnesota Satellite Telephone Corporation (MinnSat) for the year ended December 31, 2011 (dollar amounts are in thousands):

Accounts payable	$ 65,600
Accrued expenses payable (other than interest)	11,347
6¾% Bonds payable, due Feb. 1, 2012	100,000
8½% Bonds payable, due June 1, 2012	250,000
Discount on bonds payable (8½% bonds of 2012)	260
11% Bonds payable, due June 1, 2021	300,000
Premium on bonds payable (11% bonds of 2021)	1,700
Accrued interest payable	7,333
Bond interest expense	61,000
Other interest expense	17,000
Notes payable (short-term)	110,000
Lease obligations—capital leases	23,600
Pension obligation	410,000
Unfunded obligations for postretirement benefits other than pensions	72,000
Deferred income taxes	130,000
Income tax expense	66,900
Income tax payable	17,300
Operating income	280,800
Net income	134,700
Total assets	2,093,500

Other Information

1. The 6¾ percent bonds due in February 2012 will be refinanced in January 2012 through the issuance of $150,000 in 9 percent, 20-year bonds payable.
2. The 8½ percent bonds due June 1, 2012, will be repaid entirely from a bond sinking fund.
3. MinnSat is committed to total lease payments of $14,400 in 2012. Of this amount, $7,479 is applicable to operating leases, and $6,921 to capital leases. Payments on capital leases will be applied as follows: $2,300 to interest expense and $4,621 to reduction in the capitalized lease payment obligation.
4. MinnSat's pension plan is fully funded with an independent trustee.
5. The obligation for postretirement benefits other than pensions consists of a commitment to maintain health insurance for retired workers. During 2012, MinnSat will fund $18,000 of this obligation.
6. The $17,300 in income tax payable relates to income taxes levied in 2011 and must be paid on or before March 15, 2012. No portion of the deferred tax liability is regarded as a current liability.

Instructions

a. Using this information, prepare the current liabilities and long-term liabilities sections of a classified balance sheet as of December 31, 2011. (Within each classification, items may be listed in any order.)

b. Explain briefly how the information in each of the six numbered paragraphs affected your presentation of the company's liabilities.

c. Compute as of December 31, 2011, the company's **(1)** debt ratio and **(2)** interest coverage ratio.

d. Solely on the basis of information stated in this problem, indicate whether this company appears to be an outstanding, medium, or poor long-term credit risk. State specific reasons for your conclusion.

LO1 LO5 LO6 LO8 LO10

PROBLEM 10.8A
Financial Statement Presentation of Liabilities

As of December 31 of the current year, Chernin Corporation has prepared the following information regarding its liabilities and other obligations:

Notes payable, of which $10,000 will be repaid within the next 12 months . . .	$ 80,000
Interest expense that will result from existing liabilities over the next 12 months . . .	125,000
Lawsuit pending against the company, in which $500,000 is claimed in damages. Legal counsel can make no reasonable estimate of the company's ultimate liability at this time . . .	500,000
20-year bond issue that matures in two years. The entire amount will be repaid from a bond sinking fund . . .	900,000
Accrued interest on the 20-year bond issue as of the balance sheet date . . .	36,000
Three-year commitment to John Higgins as chief financial officer at a salary of $250,000 per year . . .	750,000
Note payable due within 90 days (but that is expected to be extended for an additional 18 months) . . .	75,000
Cash deposits from customers for goods and services to be delivered over the next nine months . . .	300,000
Income taxes, of which $100,000 are currently payable and the remainder deferred indefinitely . . .	185,000

Instructions

a. Prepare a listing of the company's current and long-term liabilities as they should be presented in the company's December 31 balance sheet.

b. Briefly explain why you have excluded any of the listed items in your listing of current and long-term liabilities.

Problem Set B

LO1 through LO6 LO8

PROBLEM 10.1B
Effects of Transactions on Financial Statements

Fifteen transactions or events affecting Westmar, Inc., are as follows:

a. Made a year-end adjusting entry to accrue interest on a note payable that has the interest rate stated separately from the principal amount.

b. A liability classified for several years as long-term becomes due within the next 12 months.

c. Recorded the regular weekly payroll, including payroll taxes, amounts withheld from employees, and the issuance of paychecks.

d. Earned an amount previously recorded as unearned revenue.

e. Made arrangements to extend a bank loan due in 60 days for another 36 months.

f. Made a monthly payment on a fully amortizing installment note payable. (Assume this note is classified as a current liability.)

g. Called bonds payable due in 10 years at a price below the carrying value of the liability in the accounting records.

h. Issued bonds payable at 101 on January 31, 2011. The bonds pay interest on January 31 and July 31.

i. Recorded July 31, 2011, interest expense and made semiannual interest payment on bonds referred to in part **h.**

j. Recorded necessary adjusting entry on December 31, 2011, for bonds referred to in part **h.**

k. Issued bonds payable at 98 on August 31, 2011. The bonds pay interest August 31 and February 28.

l. Recorded the necessary adjusting entry on December 31, 2011, for bonds referred to in part **k.**

m. Recorded an estimated liability for warranty claims.

n. Entered into a five-year commitment to buy all supplies from a particular supplier at a price 20 percent below market.

o. Received notice that a lawsuit has been filed against the company for $8 million. The amount of the company's liability, if any, cannot be reasonably estimated at this time.

Instructions

Indicate the effects of each of these transactions upon the following elements of the company's financial statements. Organize your answer in tabular form, using the column headings shown below. Use the following code letters to indicate the effects of each transaction on the accounting elements listed in the column headings: **I** for increase, **D** for decrease, and **NE** for no effect.

	Income Statement			Balance Sheet			
Transaction	Revenue −	Expenses =	Net Income	Assets =	Current Liabilities +	Long-Term Liabilities +	Owners' Equity
a							

LO1 LO2 LO4 LO8

PROBLEM 10.2B
Balance Sheet Presentation of Liabilities

The following are selected items from the accounting records of Atlanta Peach for the year ended December 31, 2011:

Note payable to Southern Bank	$ 250,000
Income taxes payable	15,000
Accrued expenses and payroll taxes	26,000
Mortgage note payable	750,000
Accrued interest on mortgage note payable	15,000
Trade accounts payable	275,000
Unearned revenue	33,000
Potential liability in pending lawsuit	2,000,000

Other Information

1. The note payable to Southern Bank is due in 60 days. Arrangements have been made to renew this note for an additional 24 months.
2. The mortgage requires payments of $10,000 per month. An amortization table shows that its balance will be paid down to $733,000 by December 31, 2012.
3. Accrued interest on the mortgage note payable is paid monthly. The next payment is due near the end of the first week in January 2012.
4. Atlanta Peach has been sued for $2,000,000 in a product damage case. It is not possible at this time, however, to make a reasonable estimate of the possible loss, if any, that the company may have sustained.

Instructions

a. Using the information provided, prepare the current and long-term liability sections of the company's balance sheet dated December 31, 2011. (Within each classification, items may be listed in any order.)

b. Explain briefly how the information in each of the four numbered paragraphs above influenced your presentation of the company's liabilities.

LO2 PROBLEM 10.3B
Notes Payable: Accruing Interest

During the fiscal year ended December 31, Swanlee Corporation engaged in the following transactions involving notes payable:

July 1 Borrowed $20,000 from Weston Bank, signing a 90-day, 12 percent note payable.

Sept. 16 Purchased office equipment from Moontime Equipment. The invoice amount was $30,000, and Moontime agreed to accept, as full payment, a 10 percent, three-month note for the invoice amount.

Oct. 1 Paid Weston Bank the note plus accrued interest.

Dec. 1 Borrowed $100,000 from Jean Will, a major corporate stockholder. The corporation issued Will a $100,000, 9 percent, 120-day note payable.

Dec. 1 Purchased merchandise inventory in the amount of $10,000 from Listen Corporation. Listen accepted a 90-day, 12 percent note as a full settlement of the purchase. Swanlee Corporation uses a perpetual inventory system.

Dec. 16 The $30,000 note payable to Moontime Equipment matured today. Swanlee paid the accrued interest on this note and issued a new 60-day, 16 percent note payable in the amount of $30,000 to replace the note that matured.

Instructions

a. Prepare journal entries (in general journal form) to record the above transactions. Use a 360-day year in making the interest calculations.

b. Prepare the adjusting entry needed at December 31, prior to closing the accounts. Use one entry for all three notes (round to the nearest dollar).

c. Provide a possible explanation why the new 60-day note payable to Moontime Equipment pays 16 percent interest instead of the 10 percent rate charged on the September 16 note.

LO4 PROBLEM 10.4B
Preparation and Use of an Amortization Table

On October 1, 2011, Walla signed a 4-year, $100,000 note payable to Vicksburg National Bank in conjunction with the purchase of equipment. The note calls for interest at an annual rate of 12 percent (1 percent per month). The note is fully amortizing over a period of 48 months.

The bank sent Walla an amortization table showing the allocation of monthly payments between interest and principal over the life of the loan. A small part of this amortization table is illustrated below. (For convenience, amounts have been rounded to the nearest dollar.)

Interest Period	Payment Date	Monthly Payment	Interest Expense	Principal Reduction	Unpaid Balance
AMORTIZATION TABLE (12%, 4-YEAR NOTE PAYABLE FOR $100,000; PAYABLE IN 48 MONTHLY INSTALLMENTS OF $2,633)					
Issue date	Oct. 1, 2011	—	—	—	$100,000
1	Nov. 1	$2,633	$1,000	$1,633	98,367
2	Dec. 1	2,633	984	1,649	96,718

Instructions

a. Explain whether the amounts of interest expense and the reductions in the unpaid principal are likely to change in any predictable pattern from month to month.

b. Prepare journal entries to record the first two monthly payments on this note.

c. Complete this amortization table for two more monthly installments.

d. Will any amounts relating to this 4-year note be classified as current liabilities in Walla's December 31, 2011, balance sheet? Explain, but you need not compute any additional dollar amounts.

LO5

PROBLEM 10.5B

Bond Interest (Bonds Issued at Face Value)

Lake Company obtained authorization to issue 10-year bonds with a face value of $5 million. The bonds are dated June 1, 2011, and have a contract rate of interest of 6 percent. They pay interest on December 1 and June 1. The bonds are issued on September 1, 2011, at 100 plus three months' accrued interest.

Instructions

Prepare the necessary journal entries in general journal form on:

a. September 1, 2011, to record the issuance of the bonds.

b. December 1, 2011, to record the first semiannual interest payment on the bond issue.

c. December 31, 2011, to record interest expense accrued through year-end.

d. June 1, 2012, to record the second semiannual interest payment.

e. What was the prevailing market rate of interest on the date that the bonds were issued? Explain.

LO5 LO6

PROBLEM 10.6B

Amortization of a Bond Discount and Premium

On September 1, 2011, Bella Company issued $5 million in 10-year, 12 percent bonds payable. Interest is payable semiannually on March 1 and September 1. Bond discounts and premiums are amortized at each interest payment date and at year-end. The company's fiscal year ends at December 31.

Instructions

a. Make the necessary adjusting entries at December 31, 2011, and the journal entry to record the payment of bond interest on March 1, 2012, under each of the following assumptions:

 1. The bonds were issued at 98. (Round to the nearest dollar.)

 2. The bonds were issued at 104. (Round to the nearest dollar.)

b. Compute the net bond liability at December 31, 2012, under assumptions **1** and **2** above. (Round to the nearest dollar.)

c. Under which of the above assumptions, **1** or **2,** would the investor's effective rate of interest be higher? Explain.

LO1 LO5 LO6 LO10

PROBLEM 10.7B
Reporting Liabilities in a Balance Sheet

The following items were taken from the accounting records of Delaware Utility Company for the year ended December 31, 2011 (dollar amounts are in thousands):

Accounts payable	$ 48,000
Accrued expenses payable (other than interest)	7,200
10% Bonds payable, due April 1, 2012	100,000
8% Bonds payable, due October 1, 2012	150,000
Unamortized bond discount (8% bonds of 2012)	270
12% Bonds payable, due April 1, 2024	300,000
Unamortized bond premium (12% bonds of 2024)	2,000
Accrued interest payable	3,650
Bond interest expense	57,000
Other interest expense	8,000
Notes payable (short-term)	75,000
Lease obligations—capital leases	18,000
Pension obligation	410,000
Unfunded obligations for postretirement benefits other than pensions	60,000
Deferred income taxes	110,000
Income tax expense	42,000
Income tax payable	8,000
Operating income	341,250
Net income	210,000
Total assets	2,203,950

Other Information

1. The 10 percent bonds due in April 2012 will be refinanced in March 2012 through the issuance of $125,000 in 9 percent, 20-year bonds payable.
2. The 8 percent bonds due October 1, 2012, will be repaid entirely from a bond sinking fund.
3. Delaware Utility is committed to total lease payments of $11,000 in 2012. Of this amount, $6,000 is applicable to operating leases, and $5,000 to capital leases. Payments on capital leases will be applied as follows: $2,000 to interest expense and $3,000 to reduction in the capitalized lease payment obligation.
4. Delaware Utility's pension plan is fully funded with an independent trustee.
5. The obligation for postretirement benefits other than pensions consists of a commitment to maintain health insurance for retired workers. During 2012, Delaware Utility will fund $16,000 of this obligation.
6. The $8,000 in income taxes payable relates to income taxes levied in 2011 and must be paid on or before March 15, 2012. No portion of the deferred tax liability is regarded as a current liability.

Instructions

a. Using this information, prepare the current liabilities and long-term liabilities sections of a classified balance sheet as of December 31, 2011. (Within each classification, items may be listed in any order.)

b. Explain briefly how the information in each of the six numbered paragraphs affected your presentation of the company's liabilities.

c. Compute as of December 31, 2011, the company's (**1**) debt ratio and (**2**) interest coverage ratio.

d. Solely on the basis of information stated in this problem, indicate whether this company appears to be an outstanding, medium, or poor long-term credit risk. State specific reasons for your conclusion.

LO1 LO5 LO6 LO8 LO10

PROBLEM 10.8B

Financial Statement Presentation of Liabilities

As of December 31 of the current year, Fernandez Company has prepared the following information regarding its liabilities and other obligations:

Notes payable, of which $20,000 will be repaid within the next 12 months	$150,000
Interest expense that will result from existing liabilities over the next 12 months	175,000
Lawsuit pending against the company, in which $500,000 is claimed in damages. Legal counsel can make no reasonable estimate of the company's ultimate liability at this time	400,000
20-year bond issue that matures in two years. The entire amount will be repaid from a bond sinking fund	750,000
Accrued interest on the 20-year bond issue as of the balance sheet date	22,500
Three-year commitment to John Higgins as chief financial officer at a salary of $170,000 per year	510,000
Note payable due within 90 days (but that is expected to be extended for an additional 18 months)	90,000
Cash deposits from customers for goods and services to be delivered over the next nine months	268,000
Income taxes, of which $145,000 are currently payable and the remainder deferred indefinitely	260,000

Instructions

a. Prepare a listing of the company's current and long-term liabilities as they should be presented in the company's December 31 balance sheet.

b. Briefly explain why you have excluded any of the listed items in your listing of current and long-term liabilities.

Critical Thinking Cases

LO1 LO10

CASE 10.1

The Nature of Liabilities

Listed below are seven publicly owned corporations and a liability that regularly appears in each corporation's balance sheet:

a. **Wells Fargo & Company** (banking): Deposits: interest bearing

b. **The New York Times Company**: Unexpired subscriptions

c. **The Hollywood Park Companies** (horse racing): Outstanding mutuel tickets

d. **American Greetings** (greeting cards and gift wrap products manufacturer): Sales returns

e. **Wausau Paper Mills Company**: Current maturities of long-term debt

f. **Club Med., Inc.** (resorts): Amounts received for future vacations

g. **Apple Computer, Inc.**: Accrued marketing and distribution

Instructions

Briefly explain what you believe to be the nature of each of these liabilities, including how the liability arose and the manner in which it is likely to be discharged.

LO5 through LO7

CASE 10.2

Factors Affecting Bond Prices

In the past, **Abbott Labs** had two bond issues outstanding with the following characteristics:

Issue	Interest Rate	Maturity	Current Price
A	6%	2008	115
B	6%	2012	118

Instructions

Answer the following questions regarding these bond issues:

a. Which issue, A or B, has the higher effective rate of interest? How can you tell?

b. Assume that the bonds of both issues had face values of $1,000 each. How much total interest did each bond from *issue A* provide investors in *12 months*? How much total interest did each bond from *issue B* provide investors in *12 months*?

c. Note that both issues are by the same company, have the same contract rate of interest, and have identical credit ratings. In view of these facts, explain the current price difference of each issue.

LO8 **CASE 10.3**
Loss Contingencies

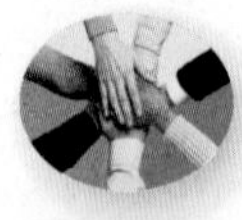

Discuss each of the following situations, indicating whether the situation is a loss contingency that should be recorded or disclosed in the financial statements of Aztec Airlines. If the situation is not a loss contingency, explain how (if at all) it should be reported in the company's financial statements. (Assume that all dollar amounts are material.)

Instructions

a. 1. Aztec estimates that $700,000 of its accounts receivable will prove to be uncollectible.
   2. The company's president is in poor health and has previously suffered two heart attacks.
   3. As with any airline, Aztec faces the risk that a future airplane crash could cause considerable loss.
   4. Aztec is being sued for $10 million for failing to adequately provide for passengers whose reservations were canceled as a result of the airline's overbooking certain flights. This suit will not be resolved for a year or more.

b. Make a general statement that summarizes management's ethical responsibility regarding reporting loss contingencies in its financial statements.

LO1 LO10 **CASE 10.4**
Off-Balance Sheet Financing

Airlines AMR (American Airlines) leases most of its commercial aircraft and is currently committed to pay over $11 billion in future lease obligations. However, the company's 2009 financial statement reported only $689 million of these commitments as long-term capital lease obligations in the liability section of its balance sheet. The remaining commitments are structured as operating leases. Obligations to pay future operating lease obligations are not reported in the balance sheet as liabilities. Instead, cash outlays for operating leases appear only in the income statement as expenses as the obligations come due.

American's recent balance sheet reports assets totaling $25.5 billion. The company's long-term debt, including its capital lease obligations, total approximately $10.5 billion, and the stockholders' equity section of its balance sheet reveals a deficit (negative) balance in retained earnings.

Instructions

a. If **American Airlines** had structured its aircraft commitments as capital leases instead of operating leases, how would the appearance and potential interpretation of its balance sheet have changed?

b. Is it ethical for **American Airlines** to structure less than $1 billion of its aircraft commitments as capital leases and the remaining as off-balance sheet financing? Defend your answer.

c. With regard to **American Airlines**'s lease obligations, why is it important for investors and creditors to read and understand the footnotes accompanying the airline's financial statements?

LO5 LO6 LO9 **INTERNET CASE 10.5**
Credit Ratings on Bonds

The Internet provides a wealth of information concerning long-term liabilities, bond ratings, and credit markets. Visit the home page of **BondsOnline** at the following Internet address:

www.BondsOnline.com

Instructions

a. Go to the "Chart Center" section of the Web site. Define in your own words the term "yield curve." Why is the yield curve relevant to you as a bond investor?

b. Return to the home page. On thc left side of the screen, locate the heading that provides current market information. Summarize two things you learned about the current financial markets by studying this information.

c. Again return to the home page. Select the option "Financial Career Center" and select the job classification that interests you the most. Browse the jobs listed under that classification and select a specific job you would apply for were you currently qualified. Write a brief description why this job interests you.

Internet sites are time and date sensitive. It is the purpose of these exercises to have you explore the Internet. You may need to use the Yahoo! search engine http://www.yahoo.com *(or another favorite search engine) to find a company's current Web address.*

Answers to Self-Test Questions

1. a, b **2.** a, b, d **3.** a, d **4.** a, c, d **5.** a, b, c, d **6.** a, b, c, d
7. a, c **8.** c **9.** a, b **10.** d **11.** c

CHAPTER 11

Stockholders' Equity: Paid-In Capital

© AP Photo/Pat Sullivan

AFTER STUDYING THIS CHAPTER, YOU SHOULD BE ABLE TO:

Learning Objectives

- **LO1** Discuss the advantages and disadvantages of organizing a business as a corporation.
- **LO2** Distinguish between publicly owned and closely held corporations.
- **LO3** Explain the rights of stockholders and the roles of corporate directors and officers.
- **LO4** Account for paid-in capital and prepare the equity section of a corporate balance sheet.
- **LO5** Contrast the features of common stock with those of preferred stock.
- **LO6** Discuss the factors affecting the market price of preferred stock and common stock.
- **LO7** Explain the significance of book value and market value of capital stock.
- **LO8** Explain the purpose and effects of a stock split.
- **LO9** Account for treasury stock transactions.

TARGET CORPORATION

Stockholders' equity is a major source of resources for corporations. As we learn in Chapter 11, stockholders' equity comes from two primary sources: the original contributions of stockholders when they purchase shares of common or preferred stock directly from the company. The second source is the company's accumulated earnings, less dividends and other adjustments, that have been achieved since the company's inception.

How important is stockholders' equity as a source of funds for a company like Target Corporation? The answer is very important. In Target's 2009 statement of financial position (balance sheet), stockholders' equity totals $15,347 million which represents more than 34% of total assets. Of the total stockholders' equity of $15,347 million, $2,974 million came from the original investments of stockholders and the remainder from profitable operations. Clearly the original investment of owners has been enhanced via profitable operations of the company.

Companies like Target carefully manage their relationship of debt to stockholders' equity. Unlike debt, equity has no maturity date. If a stockholder in a company like Target wants to sell his or her investment, the shares owned are offered for sale on a stock exchange or over-the-counter market in which sellers and buyers come together in exchange transactions. The numbers you often see in the business news about stock prices usually represent transactions between willing buyers and sellers, not between buyers and the issuing corporation. ■

In this chapter we explore issues related to stockholders' equity, including treasury stock transactions, preferred stock, and stock splits. We also discuss why businesses incorporate and describe the factors that influence the price of their stock in the open market.

Corporations

The corporate form is the organization of choice for many businesses—large and small. The owners of a corporation are called **stockholders.** In many small corporations, there are only one or two stockholders. But in large corporations, such as **IBM** and **AT&T**, there are literally millions of stockholders.

A **corporation** is a form of business organization that is recognized under the law as a *separate legal entity,* with rights and responsibilities *apart from those of its owners.* The assets of a corporation belong to the corporation *itself,* not to the stockholders. The corporation is responsible for its own debts and must pay income taxes on its earnings. As a separate legal entity, a corporation has status in court; it may enter into contracts, and it may sue and be sued as if it were a person. The major advantages and disadvantages of this form of business organization are summarized in Exhibit 11–1.

Learning Objective
LO1 Discuss the advantages and disadvantages of organizing a business as a corporation.

Exhibit 11–1
ADVANTAGES AND DISADVANTAGES OF THE CORPORATE FORM

Advantages	Disadvantages
1. *Stockholders are not personally liable for the debts of a corporation.* This concept is called *limited personal liability* and often is cited as the greatest advantage of the corporate form of organization.	1. *Heavy taxation.* Corporate earnings are subject to **double taxation**. First, the corporation must pay *corporate income taxes* on its earnings. Second, stockholders must pay *personal income taxes* on any portion of these earnings that they receive as *dividends.*
2. *Transferability of ownership.* Ownership of a corporation is evidenced by *transferable shares of stock,* which may be sold by one investor to another.	2. *Greater regulation.* Corporations are affected by state and federal laws to a far greater extent than are unincorporated businesses.
3. *Professional management.* The stockholders own a corporation, but they do not manage it on a daily basis. To administer the affairs of the corporation, the stockholders elect a *board of directors.* The directors, in turn, hire professional managers to run the business.	3. *Cost of formation.* An unincorporated business can be formed at little or no cost. Forming a corporation, however, normally requires the services of an attorney.
4. *Continuity of existence.* Changes in the names and identities of stockholders do not directly affect the corporation. Therefore, the corporation may continue its operations *without disruption,* despite the retirement or death of individual stockholders.	4. *Separation of ownership and management.* If stockholders do not approve of the manner in which management runs the business, they may find it difficult to take the united action necessary to remove that management group.

What types of businesses choose the corporate form of organization? The answer, basically, is *all kinds.* When we think of corporations, we often think of large, well-known companies such as **ExxonMobil**, **General Motors**, and **Procter & Gamble**. Indeed, almost all large businesses are organized as corporations. Limited shareholder liability, transferability of ownership, professional management, and continuity of existence make the corporation the best form of organization for pooling the resources of a great many equity investors. Not all corporations, however, are large and publicly owned. Many small businesses are organized as corporations.

WHY BUSINESSES INCORPORATE

Businesses incorporate for many reasons, but the two of greatest importance are (1) limited shareholder liability and (2) transferability of ownership.

We have previously discussed the concept of **limited personal liability.** This simply means that shareholders are not personally responsible for the debts of the corporation. Thus, if the corporation has financial problems, the most that a stockholder usually can lose is the amount of his or her equity investment.

Another special feature of the corporation is the *transferability of ownership*—that is, ownership is represented by shares of **capital stock** that can be bought and sold. For a small, family-owned business, this provides a convenient means of gradually transferring ownership and control of the business from one generation to the next. For a large company, it makes ownership of the business a *highly liquid investment,* which can be purchased and sold in organized securities exchanges.[1]

YOUR TURN **You as a Loan Officer**

GOTCHA! is a small business that manufactures board games. It is one of the many business ventures of Gayle Woods, who is very wealthy and one of your bank's most valued customers. She has done business with your bank for more than 20 years, and the balance in her personal checking, savings, and money market accounts normally exceeds $500,000. GOTCHA! is organized as a corporation, and Woods is the only stockholder.

GOTCHA! has applied for a $200,000 line of credit, which it intends to use to purchase copyrights to additional board games. Although the company is profitable, its most recent balance sheet shows total assets of only $52,000, including $47,000 in copyrights. The corporation has just under $3,000 in liabilities and over $49,000 in stockholders' equity.

Do you consider GOTCHA! a good credit risk? Would you make the loan? Under what conditions?

(See our comments on the Online Learning Center Web site.)

PUBLICLY OWNED CORPORATIONS

The capital stock of many large corporations is bought and sold (traded) through organized securities exchanges. As these shares are available for purchase by the general public, these large corporations are said to be **publicly owned.**

Far more people have a financial interest in the shares of publicly owned companies than one might expect. If you purchase the stock of such a corporation, you become a stockholder with a *direct* ownership interest—that is, *you* are a stockholder. But mutual funds and pension funds invest heavily in the stocks of many publicly owned corporations. Thus, if you invest in a mutual fund or you are covered by a pension plan, you have an *indirect* financial interest in the stocks of many publicly owned corporations.

Corporations whose shares are *not* traded on any organized stock exchanges are said to be **closely held.** Because there is no organized market for buying and selling their shares, these corporations usually have relatively few stockholders. Often, a closely held corporation is owned by one individual or by the members of one family.

Learning Objective
Distinguish between publicly owned and closely held corporations. **LO2**

Publicly Owned Corporations Face Different Rules

The government seeks to protect the interests of the public. Therefore, publicly owned corporations are subject to more regulation than those that are closely held. For example, publicly owned corporations are *required by law* to:

- Prepare and issue quarterly and annual financial statements in conformity with generally accepted accounting principles. (These statements are **public information.**)
- Have their annual financial statements audited by an independent firm of certified public accountants.
- Comply with federal securities laws, which include both criminal penalties and civil liability for deliberately or carelessly distributing misleading information to the public.
- Submit much of their financial information to the Securities and Exchange Commission for review.

[1] These securities exchanges include, among others, the New York Stock Exchange, the National Association of Securities Dealers' Automated Quotations (NASDAQ), the Tokyo Stock Exchange, and Mexico's Bolsa. Collectively, stock exchanges often are described simply as *the stock market.*

Closely held corporations normally are exempt from these requirements. Our discussions will focus primarily on the accounting and reporting issues confronting *publicly owned companies.*

Formation of a Corporation

In the United States, a corporation is brought into existence under the laws of a particular state. The state in which the corporation is formed is called the **state of incorporation.**

The state of incorporation is not necessarily where the corporation does business. Rather, a state often is selected because of the leniency of its laws regulating corporate activities. Indeed, many corporations conduct most—sometimes all—of their business activities *outside* the state in which they are incorporated.

The first step in forming a corporation is to obtain a *corporate charter* from the state of incorporation. To obtain this charter, the organizers of the corporation submit an application called the *articles of incorporation.* Once the charter is obtained, the stockholders in the new corporation hold a meeting to elect a *board of directors* and to pass *bylaws* that will govern the corporation's activities. The directors in turn hold a meeting at which the top corporate officers and managers are appointed.

Organization Costs

Forming a corporation is more costly than starting a sole proprietorship. The costs may include, for example, attorneys' fees, incorporation fees paid to the state, and other outlays necessary to bring the corporation into existence. Conceptually, organization costs are an *intangible asset* that will benefit the corporation over its entire life. As a practical matter, however, most corporations expense those costs immediately, even though they are often spread over a five-year period for income tax purposes.

Thus you will seldom see organization costs in the balance sheet of a publicly owned corporation. They have long since been recognized as an expense.

Learning Objective
LO3 **Explain the rights of stockholders and the roles of corporate directors and officers.**

Rights of Stockholders

A corporation is owned collectively by its stockholders. Each stockholder's ownership interest is determined by the number of *shares* that he or she owns. Assume that a corporation issues 10,000 shares of capital stock. If you own 1,000 of these shares, you own *10 percent* of the corporation. If you acquire another 500 shares from another stockholder, you will own *15 percent.*

Each stockholder, or the stockholder's brokerage firm, receives from the corporation a **stock certificate** indicating the number of shares he or she owns.

The ownership of capital stock in a corporation usually carries the following basic rights:

1. *To vote for directors and on certain other key issues.* A stockholder has one vote for each share owned. The issues on which stockholders may vote are specified in the corporation's bylaws. Any stockholder—or group of stockholders—that owns *more than 50 percent* of the capital stock has the power to elect the board of directors and to set basic corporate policies. Therefore, these stockholders control the corporation.
2. *To participate in any dividends declared by the board of directors.* Stockholders in a corporation *may not* make withdrawals of company assets, as may the owners of unincorporated businesses. However, the directors may elect to distribute some or all of the earnings of a profitable corporation to its stockholders in the form of cash *dividends.* Dividends can be distributed only after they have been formally *declared* (authorized) by the board of directors. Dividends are paid to all shareholders in proportion to the number of shares owned.
3. *To share in the distribution of assets if the corporation is liquidated.* When a corporation ends its existence, the creditors must first be paid in full. The shareholders have a residual interest, and any remaining assets are divided among the shareholders in proportion to the number of shares owned.

Stockholders' meetings usually are held once each year. At these meetings, stockholders may ask questions of management and vote on certain issues. In large corporations, these meetings usually are attended by relatively few people—often less than 1 percent of the company's stockholders. Prior to these meetings, however, the management group requests that stockholders who do not plan to attend send in *proxy statements,* granting management the voting rights associated with their shares.

Functions of the Board of Directors The primary functions of the **board of directors** are to set corporate policies and to protect the interests of the stockholders. Specific duties of the directors include hiring corporate officers and setting those officers' salaries, declaring dividends, and reviewing the findings of both internal auditors and independent auditors.

The board of a large corporation always includes several members of top management. In recent years, increasing importance has been attached to the inclusion of "outside" directors. The term *outside directors* refers to individuals who are *not* officers of the corporation and, therefore, bring an *independent perspective* to the board.

Functions of the Corporate Officers The top management of a corporation is appointed (hired) by the board of directors. These individuals are called the *corporate officers.* Individual stockholders *do not* have the right to transact corporate business *unless they have been properly appointed to a managerial position.*

The top level of management usually includes a chief executive officer (CEO) or president, a chief financial officer (CFO) or controller, a treasurer, and a secretary. In addition, a vice president usually oversees each functional area, such as sales, personnel, and production.

The responsibilities of the CFO (controller), treasurer, and secretary are most directly related to the accounting phase of business operation. The CFO is responsible for the maintenance of adequate internal control and for the preparation of accounting records and financial statements. Such specialized activities as budgeting, tax planning, and preparation of tax returns are usually placed under the CFO's jurisdiction. The *treasurer* has custody of the company's funds and is generally responsible for planning and controlling the company's cash position. The treasurer's department also has responsibility for relations with the company's financial institutions and major creditors.

The *secretary* represents the corporation in many contractual and legal matters and maintains minutes of the meetings of directors and stockholders. Other responsibilities of the secretary are to coordinate the preparation of the annual report and to manage the investor relations department. In small corporations, one officer frequently acts as both secretary and treasurer.

The organization chart in Exhibit 11–2 indicates lines of authority extending from stockholders to the directors to the CEO and other officers.

Exhibit 11–2 CORPORATE ORGANIZATION CHART

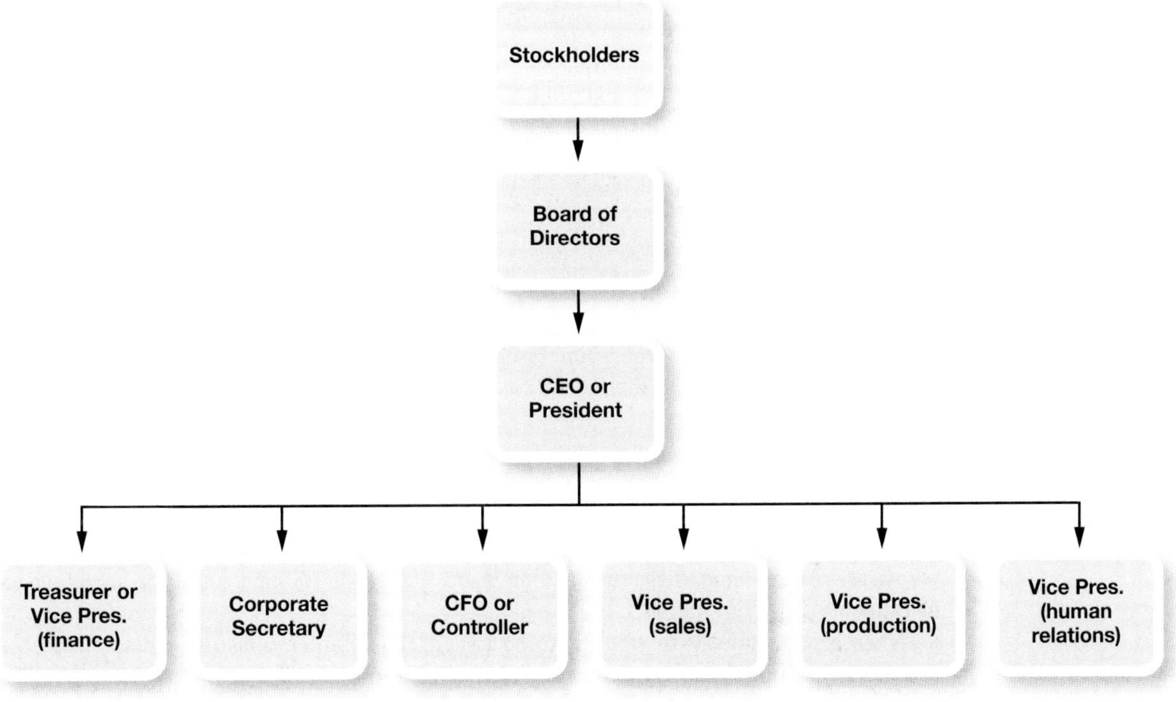

STOCKHOLDER RECORDS IN A CORPORATION

Many corporations with shares listed on the New York Stock Exchange have millions of shares outstanding and hundreds of thousands of stockholders. Each day many stockholders sell their shares; the buyers of these shares become new members of the company's family of stockholders.

A corporation must have an up-to-date record of the names and addresses of this constantly changing group of stockholders so that it can send dividend checks, financial statements, and voting forms to the right people.

Stockholders Subsidiary Ledger When there are numerous stockholders, it is not practical to include a separate account for each stockholder in the general ledger. Instead, a single controlling account entitled Capital Stock appears in the general ledger, and a **stockholders subsidiary ledger** is maintained. This ledger contains an account for each individual stockholder. Entries in the stockholders subsidiary ledger are made in *number of shares,* rather than in dollars. Thus each stockholder's account shows the number of shares owned and the dates of acquisitions and sales. This record enables the corporation to send each stockholder a single dividend check, even though the stockholder may have acquired shares on different dates.

Stock Transfer Agent and Stock Registrar Many large, publicly owned corporations use an independent **stock transfer agent** and a **stock registrar** to maintain their stockholder records and to establish strong internal control over the issuance of stock certificates. These transfer agents and registrars are usually banks or trust companies. When stock certificates are transferred from one owner to another, the old certificates are sent to the transfer agent, who cancels them, makes the necessary entries in the stockholders subsidiary ledger, and prepares a new certificate for the new owner of the shares. This new certificate then must be registered with the stock registrar before it represents valid and transferable ownership of stock in the corporation.

Small, closely held corporations generally do not use the services of independent registrars and transfer agents. In these companies, the stockholder records usually are maintained by a corporate officer. To prevent the accidental or fraudulent issuance of an excessive number of stock certificates, the corporation should require that each certificate be signed by at least two designated corporate officers.

Paid-In Capital of a Corporation

Learning Objective
LO4 Account for paid-in capital and prepare the equity section of a corporate balance sheet.

Stockholders' equity of a corporation is normally increased in one of two ways: (1) from contributions by investors in exchange for capital stock—called **paid-in capital** or **contributed capital**—and (2) from the retention of profits earned by the corporation over time—called **retained earnings.** As previously noted, our focus in this chapter is primarily on issues related to paid-in capital. In Chapter 12, we shift our attention to issues concerning retained earnings.

AUTHORIZATION AND ISSUANCE OF CAPITAL STOCK

The articles of incorporation specify the number of shares that a corporation is *authorized* to issue by the state of incorporation. Issues of capital stock that will be sold to the general public must be approved by the federal Securities and Exchange Commission, as well as by state officials.

Corporations normally obtain authorization for more shares than they initially plan to issue. This way, if more capital is needed later, the corporation already has the authorization to issue additional shares.

Shares that have been *issued* and are in the hands of stockholders are called the *outstanding* shares. At any time, these outstanding shares represent 100 percent of the stockholders' investment in the corporation.

When a large amount of stock is to be issued, most corporations use the services of an investment banking firm, frequently referred to as an **underwriter.** The underwriter guarantees the issuing corporation a specific price for the stock and earns a profit by selling the shares to the investing public at a slightly higher price. The corporation records the issuance of the stock at the net amount received from the underwriter. The use of an underwriter assures the corporation that the entire stock issue will be sold without delay and that the entire amount of funds to be raised will be available on a specific date.

The price that a corporation will seek for a new issue of stock is based on such factors as (1) expected future earnings and dividends, (2) the financial strength of the company, and (3) the current state of the investment markets. If the corporation asks too high a price, it simply will not find an underwriter or other buyers willing to purchase the shares.

State Laws Affect the Balance Sheet Presentation of Stockholders' Equity The number of different accounts that a corporation must use in the stockholders' equity section of its balance sheet is determined largely by state laws. We have seen that corporations use separate stockholders' equity accounts to represent (1) contributed capital, or paid-in capital, and (2) earned capital, or retained earnings. Up to this point, we have assumed that all paid-in capital is presented in a single account entitled Capital Stock. But this often is not the case.

Some corporations issue several *different types* (or classes) of capital stock. In these situations, a separate account is used to indicate each type of stock outstanding. A legal concept called *par value* also affects the balance sheet presentation of paid-in capital.

Par Value **Par value** (or **stated value**) represents the **legal capital** per share—the amount below which stockholders' equity cannot be reduced, except by losses from business operations (or by special legal action). Par value, therefore, may be regarded as a minimum cushion of equity capital existing for the protection of creditors.

Because of the legal restrictions associated with par value, state laws require corporations to show separately in the stockholders' equity section of the balance sheet the par value of shares issued. This special balance sheet presentation has led some people to believe that par value has some special significance. In many corporations, however, the par value of the shares issued is a small portion of total stockholders' equity.

A corporation may set the par value of its stock at $1 per share, $5 per share, or any other amount that it chooses. Most large corporations set the par value of their common stocks at nominal amounts, such as 1 cent per share or $1 per share. The par value of the stock is *not an indication of its market value;* the par value merely indicates the amount per share to be entered in the Capital Stock account. The stock of **Ford** has a par value of $.01 and **Microsoft**'s stock has a par value of only one-tenth of a cent. The market value of each of these securities is far above its par value.

Issuance of Par Value Stock Authorization of a stock issue does not bring an asset into existence, nor does it give the corporation any capital. The obtaining of authorization from the state for a stock issue merely affords a legal opportunity to obtain assets through the sale of stock. Additional capital is created for the company only when that stock is sold to stockholders.

When par value stock is *issued,* the Capital Stock account is credited with the par value of the shares issued, regardless of whether the issuance price is more or less than par. Assuming that 50,000 shares of $2 par value stock have been authorized and that 10,000 of these authorized shares are sold at a price of $2 each, Cash is debited and Capital Stock is credited for $20,000. When stock is sold for more than par value, the Capital Stock account is credited with the par value of the shares issued, and a separate account, **Additional Paid-in Capital,** is credited for the excess of selling price over par. If, for example, our 10,000 shares were issued at a price of $10 per share, the entry would be:

Cash	100,000	
Capital Stock		20,000
Additional Paid-in Capital		80,000
Issued 10,000 shares of $2 par value stock at a price of $10 a share.		

Stockholders' investment in excess of par value

The additional paid-in capital does not represent a profit to the corporation. It is part of the *invested capital,* and it is added to the capital stock in the balance sheet to show the total paid-in capital. The stockholders' equity section of the balance sheet follows. (The $150,000 in retained earnings is assumed in order to have a complete illustration.)

Stockholders' equity:	
Capital stock, $2 par value; authorized, 50,000 shares; issued and outstanding, 10,000 shares	$ 20,000
Additional paid-in capital	80,000
Total paid-in capital	$100,000
Retained earnings	150,000
Total stockholders' equity	$250,000

If stock is issued by a corporation for *less* than par, the account Discount on Capital Stock should be debited for the difference between the issuance price and the par value. A discount on capital stock reduces, rather than increases, the amount of stockholders' equity in the balance sheet. The issuance of stock at a discount is seldom encountered because it is illegal in many states.

In some cases, stock is issued in exchange for assets other than cash. When this occurs, the appropriate asset account is debited (for example, Inventory or Land) and the stock accounts are credited as if the stock had been sold for cash. Establishing a value for recording a transaction of this type is sometimes difficult, but should be based on either the fair value of the assets received or the stock issued, whichever can be more objectively determined.

No-Par Stock Some states allow corporations to issue stock without designating a par or stated value. When this "no-par" stock is issued, the *entire issue price* is credited to the Capital Stock account and is viewed as legal capital not subject to withdrawal.

COMMON STOCK AND PREFERRED STOCK

The account title Capital Stock is widely used when a corporation has issued only *one type* of stock. In order to appeal to as many investors as possible, however, some corporations issue several types (or classes) of capital stock, each providing investors with different rights and opportunities.

Learning Objective
LO5 Contrast the features of common stock with those of preferred stock.

The basic type of capital stock issued by every corporation often is called **common stock.** Common stock possesses the traditional rights of ownership—voting rights, participation in dividends, and a residual claim to assets in the event of liquidation. When the rights of stockholders are modified, the term **preferred stock** is normally used to describe the resulting type of capital stock. A few corporations issue two or more classes of preferred stock, with each class having distinctive features designed to appeal to a particular type of investor.

The following stockholders' equity section illustrates the balance sheet presentation for a corporation having both preferred and common stock. As before, a retained earnings amount is assumed so we can provide a complete example.

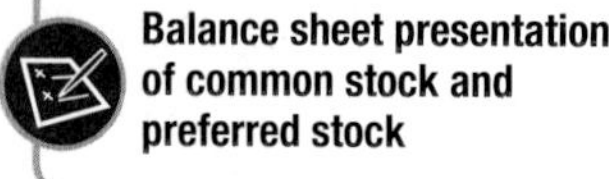

Balance sheet presentation of common stock and preferred stock

Stockholders' equity:	
9% cumulative preferred stock, $100 par value, authorized 100,000 shares, issued and outstanding 50,000 shares	$ 5,000,000
Common stock, $5 par value, authorized 3 million shares, issued and outstanding 2 million shares	10,000,000
Additional paid-in capital:	
Preferred stock	500,000
Common stock	20,000,000
Total paid-in capital	$35,500,000
Retained earnings	14,000,000
Total stockholders' equity	$49,500,000

CHARACTERISTICS OF PREFERRED STOCK

Most preferred stocks have the following distinctive features:

1. Preference over common stock as to dividends.
2. Cumulative dividend rights.
3. Preference over common stock as to assets in event of the liquidation of the company.
4. Callable at the option of the corporation.
5. No voting power.

Another important but less common feature of some preferred stocks is a clause permitting the *conversion* of preferred stock into common stock at the option of the holder. Preferred stocks vary widely with respect to the special rights and privileges granted. Careful study of the terms of the individual preferred stock contract is a necessary step in the evaluation of any preferred stock.

INTERNATIONAL CASE IN POINT

Specific preferred stock characteristics can affect the reporting location on the balance sheet. For example, preferred stock that is mandatorily redeemable by the issuing company is required by international accounting standards to be classified as a liability (rather than an equity) on the balance sheet. In 2003, the FASB changed U.S. GAAP reporting requirements from allowing redeemable preferred stock to be reported in the equity section to requiring it to be reported in the liability section, consistent with international standards.

Stock Preferred as to Dividends Corporations often make periodic cash payments, called **dividends,** to stockholders.[2] Dividends normally involve a distribution of cash that represents accumulated earnings and therefore cannot exceed the amount of a corporation's retained earnings.

Preferred stock is said to have dividend preference because preferred stock investors are entitled to receive a specified amount each year before any dividend is paid to common stock investors. The specified dividend may be stated as a dollar amount, such as $5 per share. Some preferred stocks, however, state the specified dividend as a *percentage of par value.* For example, a share of preferred stock with a par value of $100 and a dividend preference of *9 percent* must provide a $9 dividend ($100 × 9 %) each year to each share of preferred stock before any dividends can be paid on the common shares.

The holders of preferred stock have no guarantee that they will always receive the indicated dividend. A corporation is obligated to pay dividends to stockholders only when cash is available and the board of directors declares a dividend. Dividends must be paid on preferred stock before anything is paid to the common stockholders, but if the corporation is not prospering, it may decide not to pay any dividends at all. For a corporation to pay dividends, profits must be earned and cash must be available.

Cumulative Preferred Stock The dividend preference carried by most preferred stocks is *cumulative.* If all or any part of the regular dividend on the preferred stock is omitted in a given year, the amount omitted is said to be *in arrears* and must be paid in a subsequent year before any dividend can be paid on the common stock.

Assume that a corporation is organized on January 1, 2009, with 10,000 shares of $8 preferred stock and 50,000 shares of common stock. If the preferred stock is *noncumulative,*

[2] In Chapter 12, we will discuss specific accounting issues related to cash dividends and other forms of distributions to stockholders. For the purposes of this chapter, dividends may be viewed simply as the distribution to stockholders of accumulated profits that reduce both cash and retained earnings.

the $8 per share dividend does not carry forward if it is not paid each year. On the other hand, if the preferred stock is *cumulative,* the $8 per share dividend carries forward to future years if it is not paid and the accumulated amount must be paid before any dividend can be paid on common stock. Assume that the $8 preferred dividend is paid in 2009, a partial dividend of $2 per share is paid on preferred stock in 2010, and no preferred dividend is paid in 2011. Following is an analysis of the status of the preferred dividend at the end of 2011.

	2009	2010	2011
If preferred stock is noncumulative			
Dividend paid	$80,000	$20,000	—
Dividend in arrears		Not applicable	
If preferred stock is cumulative			
Dividend paid	$80,000	$20,000	—
Dividends in arrears	—	$60,000	$140,000

In the case of noncumulative preferred stock, the unpaid dividend does *not* carry forward to future years and has no effect on the company's ability to pay dividends on common stock in the future. In the case of cumulative preferred stock, however, any unpaid dividend on preferred stock carries forward and must be paid before dividends can be paid on common stock. In 2010, the partial unpaid dividend of $60,000 would have to have been paid before any dividend could have been paid on common stock. At the end of 2011, this amount has grown to $140,000 (the $60,000 carried forward from 2010, plus the $80,000 that was not paid in 2011). Before a dividend could have been paid on common stock in 2011, the $60,000 preferred dividend *in arrears* from 2010 and the current preferred dividend of $80,000 for 2011 would have to have been paid.

Dividends in arrears are not included among the liabilities of a corporation, because no liability exists until a dividend is declared by the board of directors. The amount of any dividends in arrears on preferred stock is an important factor to investors, however, and should always be *disclosed.* This disclosure is usually made by a note accompanying the balance sheet such as the following:

Note 6: Dividends in arrears
As of December 31, 2011, dividends on the $8 cumulative preferred stock were in arrears to the extent of $14 per share and amounted in total to $140,000.

In 2012, we shall assume that the company earned large profits, has available cash, and wished to pay dividends on both the preferred and common stocks. Before paying a dividend on the common, the corporation must pay the $140,000 in arrears on the cumulative preferred stock *plus* the regular $8 per share applicable to the current year. The preferred stockholders would, therefore, receive a total of $220,000 in dividends in 2012 ($22 per share); the board of directors would then be free to declare dividends on the common stock.

Other Features of Preferred Stock To add to the attractiveness of preferred stock as an investment, corporations sometimes offer a *conversion privilege* that entitles the preferred stockholders to exchange their shares for common stock at a stipulated ratio. If the corporation prospers, its common stock will probably rise in market value, and dividends on the common stock will probably increase. The investor who buys a convertible preferred stock rather than common stock has greater assurance of regular dividends. In addition, through the conversion privilege, the investor is assured of an opportunity to share in any substantial increase in value of the company's common stock.

The three primary elements of stockholders' equity for most companies are common stock, preferred stock, and retained earnings. While important, other elements that we learn about later in this chapter, as well as in Chapter 12, are typically smaller in amount than these three primary elements. The relationship of common stock, preferred stock, and retained earnings is depicted in Exhibit 11–3.

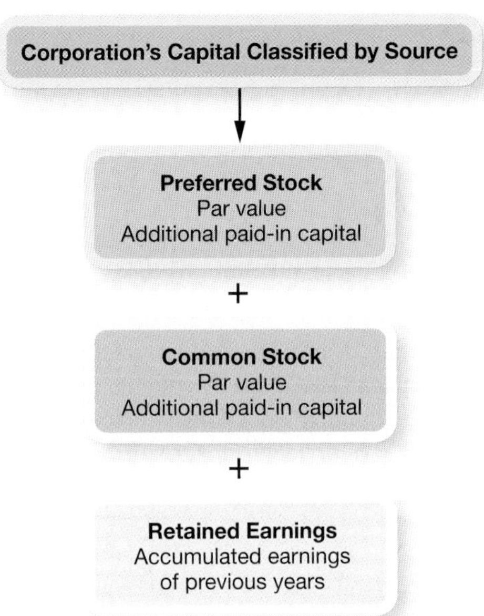

Exhibit 11–3
PRIMARY SOURCES OF CORPORATE EQUITY

BOOK VALUE PER SHARE OF COMMON STOCK

Because the equity of each stockholder in a corporation is determined by the number of shares he or she owns, an accounting measurement of interest to some stockholders is book value per share of common stock. **Book value per share** is the amount of net assets represented by each share of stock. The term *net assets* means total assets minus total liabilities; in other words, net assets are equal to *total stockholders' equity*. Thus, in a corporation that has issued common stock only, the book value per share is computed by dividing total stockholders' equity by the number of shares outstanding.

For example, assume that a corporation has 4,000 shares of common stock outstanding and the stockholders' equity section of the balance sheet is as follows:

Stockholders' equity:	
Common stock, $1 par value (4,000 shares issued and outstanding)	$ 4,000
Additional paid-in capital	40,000
Retained earnings	76,000
Total stockholders' equity	$120,000

The book value per share is *$30;* it is computed by dividing the stockholders' equity of $120,000 by the 4,000 shares of outstanding stock.

Book Value When a Company Has Both Preferred and Common Stock Book value is usually computed only for common stock. If a company has both preferred and common stock outstanding, the computation of book value per share of common stock requires two steps. First, the amount assigned to preferred stock and any *dividends in arrears* are deducted from total stockholders' equity. Second, the remaining amount of stockholders' equity is divided by the number of common shares outstanding to determine book value per common share. This procedure reflects the fact that the common stockholders are the *residual owners* of the corporate entity.

How much is book value per share?

To illustrate the computation of book value per share when preferred stock is outstanding, assume that the stockholders' equity of Hart Company at December 31 is as follows:

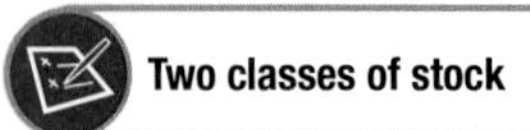

Stockholders' equity:	
8% preferred stock, $100 par value, 10,000 shares authorized, issued, and outstanding	$1,000,000
Common stock, $10 stated value, authorized 100,000 shares, issued and outstanding 50,000 shares	500,000
Additional paid-in capital: common stock	750,000
Total paid-in capital	$2,250,000
Retained earnings	130,000
Total stockholders' equity	$2,380,000

Because of a weak cash position, Hart Company has paid no dividends during the current year. As of December 31, dividends in arrears on the cumulative preferred stock total *$80,000.*

All the equity belongs to the common stockholders, except the $1,000,000 applicable to the preferred stock and the $80,000 of dividends in arrears on preferred stock. The calculation of book value per share of common stock is as follows:

Total stockholders' equity		$2,380,000
Less: Equity of preferred stockholders:		
Par value of preferred stock	$1,000,000	
Dividends in arrears	80,000	1,080,000
Equity of common stockholders		$1,300,000
Number of common shares outstanding		50,000
Book value per share of common stock ($1,300,000 ÷ 50,000 shares)		$26

In a statement of cash flows, transactions with the stockholders of a corporation are classified as *financing activities.* Thus, the issuance of capital stock for cash represents a *receipt* from financing activities. Distributions of cash to stockholders—including the payment of cash dividends—represent a cash *outlay,* which is also classified under financing activities.

Transactions with owners do not always have an immediate effect on cash flows. Consider an exchange of the corporation's capital stock for a noncash asset, such as land. Cash is not increased or decreased by this event. These types of noncash transactions are described in a special schedule that accompanies the statement of cash flows.

Market Value

After shares of stock have been issued, they may be sold by one investor to another. The price at which these shares change hands represents the *market price* of the stock. This market price may differ substantially from such amounts as par value, the original issue price, and the current book value. Which is the most relevant amount? That depends on your point of view.

After shares are issued, they belong to the stockholder, not to the issuing corporation. Thus, changes in the market price of these shares directly affect the financial position of the stockholder, but not that of the issuing company. This concept explains why the issuing company and stockholders apply different accounting principles to the same outstanding shares.

Accounting by the Issuer From the viewpoint of the issuing company, outstanding stock represents an amount invested in the company by its owners at a particular date. While the market value of the stockholders' investment may change, the amount of resources that they originally invested in the company does not change.

Thus the company issuing stock records the issue price—that is, the proceeds received from issuing the stock—in its paid-in capital accounts. The balances in these accounts remain unchanged unless (1) more shares are issued or (2) outstanding shares are permanently retired (for example, preferred stock is called or stock is purchased on the open market and then retired).

Accounting by the Investor From the investor's point of view, shares owned in a publicly owned company are an asset, usually called Marketable Securities.

To the investor, the current market value of securities owned is more relevant than the original issue price—or than the securities' par values or book values. The market value indicates what the securities are worth today. Changes in market value directly affect the investor's liquidity and financial position. For these reasons, investors show investments in marketable securities at current market value in their balance sheets.

CASE IN POINT

In a single day, the market price of **IBM**'s capital stock dropped over $31 per share, falling from $135 to $103.25. Of course, this was not a typical day. The date, October 19, 1987, will long be remembered as "Black Monday." On this day, stock prices around the world suffered the greatest one-day decline in history.

Stocks listed on the New York Stock Exchange lost about 20 percent of their value in less than six hours. Given that the annual dividends on these stocks averaged about 2 percent of their market value, this one-day market loss was approximately equal to the loss by investors of all dividend revenue for about 10 years.

How did this disastrous decline in **IBM**'s stock price affect the balance sheet of **IBM**? Actually, it didn't. **IBM**'s stock isn't owned by **IBM**—it is owned by the company's stockholders.

Because market prices are of such importance to investors, we will briefly discuss the factors that most affect the market prices of preferred and common stocks.

MARKET PRICE OF PREFERRED STOCK

Learning Objective **Discuss the factors affecting the market price of preferred stock and common stock.** **LO6**

Investors buy preferred stocks primarily to receive the dividends that these shares pay. Thus, dividend rate is one important factor in determining the market price of a preferred stock. A second important factor is *risk*. In the long run, a company must be profitable enough to pay dividends. If there is a distinct possibility that the company will *not* operate profitably and pay dividends, the price of its preferred stock will probably decline.

A third factor greatly affecting the value of preferred stocks is the level of *interest rates*. What happens to the market price of an 8 percent preferred stock, originally issued at a par value of $100, if government policies and other factors cause long-term interest rates to rise to, say, 15 percent or 16 percent? If investments offering a return of 16 percent with the same level of risk are readily available, investors will no longer pay $100 for a share of preferred stock that provides a dividend of only $8 per year. Thus the market price of the preferred stock will fall to about half of its original issue price, or about $50 per share. At this market price, the stock offers a 16 percent return (called the **dividend yield**) to an investor purchasing the stock.

However, if the prevailing long-term interest rates should again decline to the 8 percent range, the market price of an 8 percent preferred stock should rise to approximately par value. In summary, the market price of preferred stock *varies inversely with interest rates*. As interest rates rise, preferred stock prices decline; as interest rates fall, preferred stock prices rise.

MARKET PRICE OF COMMON STOCK

Prevailing interest rates also affect the market price of common stock. However, dividends paid to common stockholders are not fixed in amount. Both the amount of the dividend and the market price of the stock may increase dramatically if the corporation is successful.

Alternatively, if the company is unsuccessful, the common stockholders may not even recover their original investment. Therefore, the most important factors in the market price of common stock are *investors' expectations* as to the future profitability of the business and the *risk* that this level of profitability may not be achieved.

BOOK VALUE AND MARKET PRICE

To some extent, *book value* is used in evaluating the reasonableness of the market price of a stock. However, it must be used with caution; the fact that a stock is selling at less than book value does not necessarily indicate a bargain.

Learning Objective LO7 Explain the significance of book value and market value of capital stock.

Book value is a historical concept, representing the amounts invested by stockholders plus the amounts earned and retained by the corporation. If a stock is selling at a price *above* book value, investors believe that management has created a business worth more than the historical cost of the resources entrusted to its care. This, in essence, is the sign of a successful corporation.

On the other hand, if the market price of a stock is *less than* book value, investors believe that the company's resources are worth less than their cost while under the control of current management. Thus the relationship between book value and market price is one measure of investors' *confidence in a company's management.*

STOCK SPLITS

Learning Objective LO8 Explain the purpose and effects of a stock split.

Over time, the market price of a corporation's common stock may increase in value so much that it becomes too expensive for many investors. When this happens, a corporation may *split* its stock by increasing the number of its common shares outstanding. The purpose of a **stock split** is to reduce substantially the market price of the company's common stock, with the intent of making it more affordable to investors.

For example, assume that Felix Corporation has outstanding 1 million shares of $10 par value common stock. The market price is currently $90 per share. To make the stock more affordable, the corporation decides to increase the number of outstanding shares from 1 million to 2 million. This action is called a *2-for-1 stock split.* A stockholder who owned 100 shares of the stock before the split will own 200 shares after the split. Since the number of outstanding shares has doubled without any change in total assets or total stockholders' equity, the market price of the stock should drop from $90 to approximately $45 per share. In splitting its stock, a corporation is required to reduce the par value per share in proportion to the size of the split. As this was a 2-for-1 split, the company must reduce the par value of the stock from $10 to $5 per share. Had it been a 4-for-1 split, the par value would have been reduced from $10 to $2.50 per share and the stock price would have declined to approximately 25 percent of its former amount.

A stock split does not change the balance of any accounts in the balance sheet; consequently, the transaction is recorded merely by a *memorandum entry.* For Felix Corporation, this memorandum entry might read as follows:

Memorandum entry to record a stock split

Sept. 30 Memorandum: Issued additional 1 million shares of common stock in a 2-for-1 stock split. Par value reduced from $10 per share to $5 per share.

The description of common stock also is changed in the balance sheet to reflect the lower par value and the greater number of shares outstanding.

Another form of stock distribution to current stockholders is a stock dividend. While stock dividends are similar to stock splits in some respects, they are much smaller in size and have a different intent. Because they are important considerations in a company's dividend policy, we defer the detailed coverage of stock dividends to Chapter 12.

Treasury Stock

Learning Objective LO9 Account for treasury stock transactions.

Treasury stock is defined as shares of a corporation's own capital stock that have been issued and later *reacquired by the issuing company* but that have not been canceled or permanently retired. Treasury shares may be held indefinitely or may be issued again at any time. Shares of capital stock held in the treasury ordinarily are not entitled to receive dividends, to vote, or to share in assets upon dissolution of the company.

Stock option plans are an important part of employee compensation for many companies. They permit employees to purchase stock in the company, often at advantageous prices, and are a means of creating employee loyalty to the company. Treasury stock purchases are one means by which the company can have available the shares of stock needed to satisfy the requirement of stock option plans to issue shares of stock to employees. Rather than increasing the total number of outstanding shares, thereby reducing or diluting the ownership of each share, the company purchases shares of stock from the current owners and then sells the same shares a second time to its employees.

RECORDING PURCHASES OF TREASURY STOCK

Purchases of treasury stock are usually recorded by debiting the Treasury Stock account with the cost of the stock. For example, if Riley Corporation reacquires 1,600 shares of its own $5 par stock at a price of $90 per share, the entry is as follows:

Treasury Stock	144,000	
Cash		144,000
Purchased 1,600 shares of $5 par treasury stock at $90 per share.		

Note that the Treasury Stock account is debited for the *cost* of the shares purchased, not their par value. Treasury stock is a *contra-equity* account. When treasury stock is purchased, the corporation is eliminating part of its stockholders' equity by a payment to one or more stockholders. The purchase of treasury stock should be regarded as a *reduction of stockholders' equity,* not as the acquisition of an asset. For this reason, the Treasury Stock account appears in the balance sheet as a deduction in the stockholders' equity section. Treasury shares are both authorized and issued, but while they are held by the issuing company, they are *not* outstanding.

The presentation of treasury stock in Riley Corporation's balance sheet appears as follows, based on assumed numbers (except for treasury stock):

Stockholders' equity:	
Common stock, $5 par value, authorized 250,000 shares, issued 100,000 shares (of which 1,600 are held in treasury)	$ 500,000
Additional paid-in capital: common stock	900,000
Total paid-in capital	$1,400,000
Retained earnings	600,000
Subtotal	$2,000,000
Less: Treasury stock (1,600 shares of common, at $90 cost)	144,000
Total stockholders' equity	$1,856,000

REISSUANCE OF TREASURY STOCK

When treasury shares are reissued, the Treasury Stock account is credited for the cost of the shares reissued and Additional Paid-in Capital from Treasury Stock Transactions is debited or credited for any *difference* between cost and the reissue price. To illustrate, assume that 1,000 of the treasury shares acquired by Riley Corporation at a cost of $90 per share are now reissued at a price of $115 per share. The entry to record the reissuance of these shares at a price above cost is:

Cash	115,000	
Treasury Stock		90,000
Additional Paid-in Capital: Treasury Stock		25,000
Sold 1,000 shares of treasury stock, which cost $90,000, at a price of $115 per share.		

Treasury stock reissued at a price above cost

The $25,000 of additional paid-in capital resulting from the reissuance of Riley's treasury stock is reported in the stockholders' equity section of the company's balance sheet. It appears immediately after additional paid-in capital from common stock, as shown here:

Stockholders' equity:	
Common stock, $5 par value, authorized 250,000 shares, issued 100,000 shares (of which 600 are held in treasury)	$ 500,000
Additional paid-in capital:	
Common stock	900,000
Treasury stock	25,000
Total paid-in capital	$1,425,000
Retained earnings	600,000
Subtotal	$2,025,000
Less: Treasury stock (600 shares of common, at $90 cost)	54,000
Total stockholders' equity	$1,971,000

If treasury stock is reissued at a price below cost, additional paid-in capital from previous treasury stock transactions is reduced (debited) by the excess of cost over the reissue price. To illustrate, assume that Riley Corporation reissues its remaining 600 shares of treasury stock (acquired at a cost of $90 per share) at a price of $75 per share. The entry is:

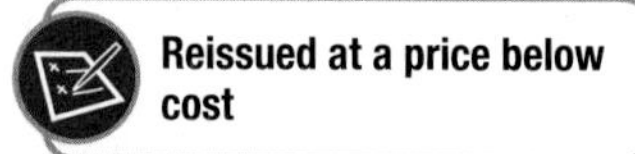
Reissued at a price below cost

Cash	45,000	
Additional Paid-in Capital: Treasury Stock	9,000	
Treasury Stock		54,000
Sold 600 shares of treasury stock, which cost $54,000, at a price of $75 each.		

If there is no additional paid-in capital from previous treasury stock transactions, the excess of the cost of the treasury shares over the reissue price is recorded as a debit to the Additional Paid-in Capital: Common Stock account. If that account is not sufficient, Retained Earnings is debited.

Notice that *no gain or loss is recognized on treasury stock transactions,* even when the shares are reissued at a price above or below cost. A corporation earns profits by selling goods and services to outsiders, not by issuing or reissuing shares of its own capital stock. When treasury shares are reissued at a price above cost, the corporation receives from the new stockholder an amount of paid-in capital that is larger than the reduction in stockholders' equity that occurred when the corporation acquired the treasury shares. Conversely, if treasury shares are reissued at a price below cost, the corporation has less paid-in capital as a result of the purchase and reissuance of the shares.

STOCK BUYBACK PROGRAMS

Historically, most treasury stock transactions involved relatively small dollar amounts. Hence, the topic was not of great importance to investors or other users of financial statements. Some corporations have buyback programs, in which they repurchase large amounts of their own common stock. As a result of these programs, treasury stock has become a material item in the balance sheets of many corporations.

Transactions between the corporation and its stockholders are classified in the statement of cash flows as *financing activities.* When treasury stock is purchased, a financing cash *outflow* is reported in the statement of cash flows. When treasury stock is reissued, the amount of cash received is reported as a financing cash *inflow* in the statement of cash flows.

Because treasury stock transactions do not give rise to gains or losses, they have no effect on the corporation's net income. Any difference between the purchase price of the treasury stock and the cash received when it is reissued is reported as an increase or decrease in the corporation's paid-in capital.

Financial Analysis and Decision Making

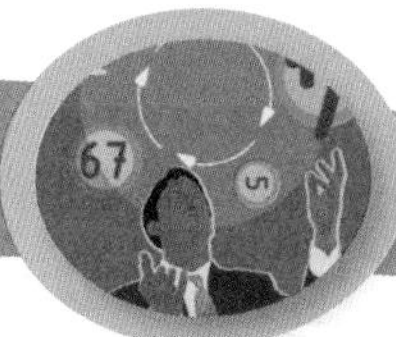

The following information was taken from a recent annual report of **Verizon Communications** (in millions):

Net income	$ 6,428
Average total assets	$194,656
Average common stockholders' equity	$ 46,144

Several frequently used measures of profitability that are based, in part, on capital stock concepts covered in this chapter can be derived from the above figures:

Profitability Measure	Computation	Significance
Return on total assets	$\frac{\text{Net Income}}{\text{Average Total Assets}}$	The rate of return on the total asset investment used to earn that return
Return on common stockholders' equity	$\frac{\text{Net Income}}{\text{Average Common Stockholders' Equity}}$	The rate of return earned on the common stockholders' equity when the company has only common stock

Using the figures provided, **Verizon**'s profitability measures would be:

Return on total assets:	$6,428 ÷ $194,656 = 3.3%
Return on common shareholders' equity:	$6,428 ÷ $ 46,144 = 13.9%

YOUR TURN **You as a Financial Analyst**

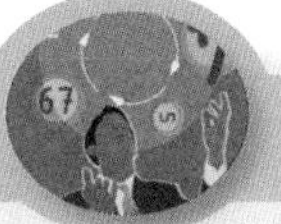

You are working for a stock market research firm and your boss has asked you to assess **Verizon**'s return on assets and on common shareholders' equity. How might you proceed?

(See our comments on the Online Learning Center Web site.)

Ethics, Fraud & Corporate Governance

A learning objective for this chapter is to understand the advantages of organizing a business as a corporation. Corporations often choose to go public in order to raise equity capital from many investors.

Unfortunately, the process of going public can be abused and can result in the defrauding of investors. A common scheme is the use of "shell companies" in a "pump-and-dump scheme." The Securities and Exchange Commission (SEC) proposes to define a shell company as a company with little or no operating activities, little or no assets, or assets consisting solely of cash and cash equivalents. Most commonly, a private operating business is combined with the public shell company in a reverse merger. In a reverse merger, the public shell company is the surviving entity but it is controlled by the shareholders of the previously private business. The rest of the "pump-and-dump scheme" works as follows: (1) the owners (promoters) of the company claim that the previously private business has high growth potential, (2) limited financial and other information on the combined company is filed with the SEC, (3) the owners (promoters) "pump" the stock through unduly positive press releases and other manipulative devices, (4) high-pressure sales tactics are often employed to get individuals to buy the stock, and (5) the owners (promoters) "dump" their stock at artificially high prices.

An example of a stock manipulation scheme using a shell company occurred in the case of **2DoTrade, Inc. 2DoTrade** was a public shell company when a group of promoters secretly acquired over 99 percent of its shares. The promoters merged

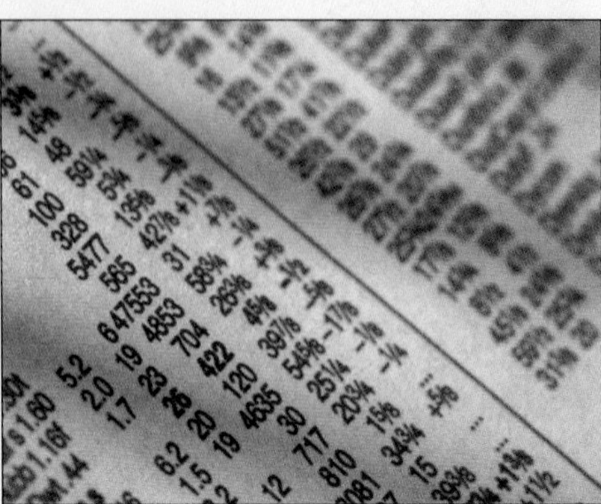

© Royalty-Free/Corbis/DAL

2DoTrade with a private company controlled by a convicted felon. The promoters "pumped" the stock by claiming that the company had import/export contracts worth more than $300 million and that the company was developing an antianthrax compound. In reality, the contracts were worthless because no antianthrax compound was in development, and one was never seriously contemplated. At one point during the "pump" campaign the market value of the company exceeded $46 million, yet the company had no assets and no revenue. The promoters then "dumped" their shares, reaping almost $2 million in profits.

The SEC has brought civil enforcement actions against the promoters of **2DoTrade**, and the FBI has arrested a number of the promoters as criminal charges have also been filed by the U.S. Justice Department.

Concluding Remarks

In this chapter, we covered the aspects of stockholders' equity that result primarily from various transactions between the company and its stockholders, including the sale and repurchase of capital stock. We explored different characteristics of stock, including the unique features of preferred stock.

Another major source of stockholders' equity is the accumulated earnings of previous years that have been retained for purposes of expansion and meeting other business objectives. This is the subject of Chapter 12, which follows. While paid-in capital and retained earnings are two distinct aspects of stockholders' equity, they are closely related and, therefore, are virtually impossible to discuss totally independently of each other. For that reason, in this chapter there were occasional references to retained earnings. Similarly, in Chapter 12 you will find references to common and preferred stock, additional paid-in capital, treasury stock, and other aspects of stockholders' equity that we covered primarily in this chapter. Combining the content of Chapters 11 and 12, you will have a good working knowledge of stockholders' equity and how it fits together with assets and liabilities to form the basis for a company's balance sheet.

END-OF-CHAPTER REVIEW

SUMMARY OF LEARNING OBJECTIVES

LO1 Discuss the advantages and disadvantages of organizing a business as a corporation. The primary advantages are no personal liability of stockholders for the debts of the business, the transferability of ownership shares, continuity of existence, the ability to hire professional management, and the relative ease of accumulating large amounts of capital. The primary disadvantages are double taxation of earnings and greater governmental regulation.

LO2 Distinguish between publicly owned and closely held corporations. The stock of publicly owned corporations is available for purchase by the general public, usually on an organized stock exchange. Stock in a closely held corporation, in contrast, is not available to the public.

Publicly owned corporations tend to be so large that individual stockholders seldom control the corporation; in essence, most stockholders in publicly owned companies are investors, rather than owners in the traditional sense. Closely held corporations usually are quite small, and one or two stockholders often do exercise control. Publicly owned corporations are subject to more government regulation than are closely held companies, and they must disclose to the public much information about their business operations.

LO3 Explain the rights of stockholders and the roles of corporate directors and officers. Stockholders in a corporation normally have the right to elect the board of directors, to share in dividends declared by the directors, and to share in the distribution of assets if the corporation is liquidated.

The directors formulate company policies, review the actions of the corporate officers, and protect the interests of the company's stockholders. Corporate officers are professional managers appointed by the board of directors to manage the business on a daily basis.

LO4 Account for paid-in capital and prepare the equity section of a corporate balance sheet. When capital stock is issued, appropriate asset accounts are debited for cash or the market value of the goods or services received in exchange for the stock. A capital stock account (which indicates the type of stock issued) is credited for the par value of the issued shares. Any excess of the market value received over the par value of the issued shares is credited to an Additional Paid-in Capital account.

The equity section of a corporate balance sheet shows for each class of capital stock outstanding (1) the total par value (legal capital) and (2) any additional paid-in capital. Together, these amounts represent the corporation's total paid-in capital. In addition, the equity section shows separately any earned capital—that is, retained earnings.

LO5 Contrast the features of common stock with those of preferred stock. Common stock represents the residual ownership of a corporation. These shares have voting rights and cannot be called. Also, the common stock dividend is not fixed in dollar amount—thus it may increase or decrease based on the company's performance.

Preferred stock has preference over common stock with respect to dividends and to distributions in the event of liquidation. This preference means that preferred stockholders must be paid in full before any payments are made to holders of common stock. The dividends on preferred stock usually are fixed in amount. In addition, the stock often has no voting rights. Preferred stocks sometimes have special features, such as being convertible into shares of common stock.

LO6 Discuss the factors affecting the market price of preferred stock and common stock. The market price of preferred stock varies inversely with interest rates. As interest rates rise, preferred stock prices decline; as interest rates fall, preferred stock prices rise. If a company's ability to continue the preferred dividend is in doubt, this may affect preferred stock prices.

Interest rates also affect the market price of common stock. However, common stock dividends are not fixed in amount. Both the amount of the dividend and the market value of the stock may fluctuate, based on the prosperity of the company. Therefore, the principal factor in the market price of common stock is investors' expectations as to the future profitability of the company.

LO7 Explain the significance of book value and market value of capital stock. Par value has the least significance. It is a legal concept, representing the amount by which stockholders' equity cannot be reduced except by losses. Intended as a buffer for the protection of creditors, it usually is so low as to be of little significance.

Book value per share is the net assets per share of common stock. This value is based on amounts invested by stockholders, plus retained earnings. It often provides insight into the reasonableness of market price.

To investors, market price is the most relevant of the three values. This is the price at which they can buy or sell the stock today. Changes in market price directly affect the financial position of the stockholder, but not of the issuing company. Therefore, market values do not appear in the equity section of the issuing company's balance sheet—but they are readily available in the daily newspaper and on the Internet.

LO8 Explain the purpose and effects of a stock split. When the market price of a corporation's common stock appreciates in value significantly, it may become too expensive for many investors. When this happens, the corporation may split its stock by increasing the number of its common shares outstanding. The purpose of a stock split is to reduce the market price of the company's common stock, with the intent of making it more affordable to investors. A stock split does not change the balance of any ledger account; consequently, the transaction is recorded merely by a memorandum entry.

LO9 **Account for treasury stock transactions.** Purchases of treasury stock are recorded by establishing a contra-equity account, Treasury Stock. No profit or loss is recorded when the treasury shares are reissued at a price above or below cost. Rather, any difference between the reissuance price and the cost of the shares is debited or credited to a paid-in capital account. While treasury stock transactions may affect cash flow, they have no effect on the net income of the corporation.

Key Terms Introduced or Emphasized in Chapter 11

Additional Paid-in Capital (p. 489) An account showing the amounts invested in a corporation by stockholders in excess of par value or stated value. In short, this account shows paid-in capital in excess of legal capital.

board of directors (p. 487) Persons elected by common stockholders to direct the affairs of a corporation.

book value per share (p. 493) The stockholders' equity represented by each share of common stock, computed by dividing common stockholders' equity by the number of common shares outstanding.

capital stock (p. 485) Transferable units of ownership in a corporation. A broad term that can refer to common stock, preferred stock, or both.

closely held corporation (p. 485) A corporation owned by a small group of stockholders. Not publicly owned.

common stock (p. 490) A type of capital stock that possesses the basic rights of ownership, including the right to vote. Represents the residual element of ownership in a corporation.

contributed capital (p. 488) The stockholders' equity that results from capital contributions by investors in exchange for shares of common or preferred stock. Also referred to as paid-in capital.

corporation (p. 484) A business organized as a legal entity separate from its owners. Chartered by the state with ownership divided into shares of transferable stock. Stockholders are not liable for debts of the corporation.

dividend yield (p. 495) The annual dividend paid to a share of stock, expressed as a percentage of the stock's market value. Indicates the rate of return represented by the dividend.

dividends (p. 491) Distribution of assets (usually cash) by a corporation to its stockholders. Normally viewed as a distribution of profits, dividends cannot exceed the amount of retained earnings. Must be formally declared by the board of directors and distributed on a per-share basis. ***Note:*** Stockholders *cannot* simply withdraw assets from a corporation at will.

double taxation (p. 484) The fact that corporate income is taxed to the corporation when earned and then again taxed to the stockholders when distributed as dividends.

legal capital (p. 489) Equal to the par value or stated value of capital stock issued. This amount represents a permanent commitment of capital by the owners of a corporation and cannot be removed without special legal action. Of course, it may be eroded by losses.

limited personal liability (p. 484) The concept that the owners of a corporation are not personally liable for the debts of the business. Thus stockholders' potential financial losses are limited to the amount of their equity investment.

paid-in capital (p. 488) The amounts invested in a corporation by its stockholders.

par value (or stated value) (p. 489) The legal capital of a corporation. Represents the minimum amount per share invested in the corporation by its owners and cannot be withdrawn except by special legal action.

preferred stock (p. 490) A class of capital stock usually having preferences as to dividends and in the distribution of assets in the event of liquidation.

public information (p. 485) Information that, by law, must be made available to the general public. Includes the quarterly and annual financial statements—and other financial information—about publicly owned corporations.

publicly owned corporation (p. 485) Any corporation whose shares are offered for sale to the general public.

retained earnings (p. 488) The element of owners' equity in a corporation that has accumulated through profitable business operations. Net income increases retained earnings; net losses and dividends reduce retained earnings.

state of incorporation (p. 486) The state in which the corporation is legally formed. This may or may not be the state in which the corporation conducts most or any of its business.

stock certificate (p. 486) A document issued by a corporation (or its transfer agent) as evidence of the ownership of the number of shares stated on the certificate.

stock registrar (p. 488) An independent fiscal agent, such as a bank, retained by a corporation to provide assurance against overissuance of stock certificates.

stock split (p. 496) An increase in the number of shares outstanding with a corresponding decrease in par value per share. The additional shares are distributed proportionately to all common shareholders. The purpose of a stock split is to reduce market price per share and encourage wider public ownership of the company's stock. A 2-for-1 stock split will give each stockholder twice as many shares as previously owned.

stock transfer agent (p. 488) A bank or trust company retained by a corporation to maintain its records of capital stock ownership and make transfers from one investor to another.

stockholders (p. 484) The owners of a corporation. The name reflects the fact that their ownership is evidenced by transferable shares of capital stock.

stockholders subsidiary ledger (p. 488) A record showing the number of shares owned by each stockholder.

treasury stock (p. 496) Shares of a corporation's stock that have been issued and then reacquired, but not canceled.

underwriter (p. 488) An investment banking firm that handles the sale of a corporation's stock to the public.

Demonstration Problem

The stockholders' equity section of Elmwood Corporation's balance sheet appears as follows:

Stockholders' equity:		
8% preferred stock, $100 par value, 200,000 shares authorized		$12,000,000
Common stock, $5 par value, 5,000,000 shares authorized		14,000,000
Additional paid-in capital:		
Preferred stock	$ 360,000	
Common stock	30,800,000	31,160,000
Retained earnings		2,680,000
Total stockholders' equity		$59,840,000

Instructions

On the basis of this information, answer the following questions and show any necessary supporting computations:

a. How many shares of preferred stock have been issued?

b. What is the total annual dividend requirement on the outstanding preferred stock?

c. How many shares of common stock have been issued?

d. What was the average price per share received by the corporation for its common stock?

e. What is the total amount of legal capital?

f. What is the total paid-in capital?

g. What is the book value per share of common stock? (Assume no dividends in arrears.)

Solution to the Demonstration Problem

a. 120,000 shares ($12,000,000 total par value, divided by $100 par value per share)

b. $960,000 (120,000 shares outstanding × $8 per share)

c. 2,800,000 shares ($14,000,000 total par value, divided by $5 par value per share)

d.

Par value of common shares issued	$14,000,000
Additional paid-in capital on common shares	30,800,000
Total issue price of common shares	$44,800,000
Number of common shares issued (part **c**)	2,800,000
Average issue price per share ($44,800,000 ÷ 2,800,000 shares)	$ 16

e. $26,000,000 ($12,000,000 preferred, $14,000,000 common)

f. $57,160,000 ($26,000,000 legal capital, plus $31,160,000 additional paid-in capital)

g.

Total stockholders' equity	$59,840,000
Less: Claims of preferred stockholders (120,000 shares × $100)	12,000,000
Equity of common stockholders	$47,840,000
Number of common shares outstanding (part **c**)	2,800,000
Book value per share ($47,840,000 ÷ 2,800,000 shares)	$ 17.09

Self-Test Questions

The answers to these questions appear on page 518.

1. When a business is organized as a corporation, which of the following statements is true?
   - a. Stockholders are liable for the debts of the business in proportion to their percentage ownership of capital stock.
   - b. Stockholders do *not* have to pay personal income taxes on dividends received, because the corporation is subject to income taxes on its earnings.
   - c. Fluctuations in the market value of outstanding shares of capital stock do *not* affect the amount of stockholders' equity shown in the balance sheet.
   - d. Each stockholder has the right to bind the corporation to contracts and to make other managerial decisions.
2. Western Moving Corporation was organized with authorization to issue 100,000 shares of $1 par value common stock. Forty thousand shares were issued to Tom Morgan, the company's founder, at a price of $5 per share. No other shares have yet been issued. Which of the following statements is true?
   - a. Morgan owns *40 percent* of the stockholders' equity of the corporation.
   - b. The corporation should recognize a $160,000 gain on the issuance of these shares.
   - c. If the balance sheet includes retained earnings of $50,000, total *paid-in* capital amounts to $250,000.
   - d. In the balance sheet, the Additional Paid-in Capital account will have a $160,000 balance, regardless of the profits earned or losses incurred since the corporation was organized.
3. Which of the following is *not* a characteristic of the *common stock* of a large, publicly owned corporation?
   - a. The shares may be transferred from one investor to another without disrupting the continuity of business operations.
   - b. Voting rights in the election of the board of directors.
   - c. A cumulative right to receive dividends.
   - d. After issuance, the market value of the stock is unrelated to its par value.
4. Tri-State Electric is a profitable utility company that has increased its dividend to *common* stockholders every year for 42 consecutive years. Which of the following is *least* likely to affect the market price of the company's *preferred* stock by a significant amount?
   - a. A decrease in long-term interest rates.
   - b. An increase in long-term interest rates.
   - c. The board of directors announces its intention to increase common stock dividends in the current year.
   - d. Whether or not the preferred stock carries a conversion privilege.
5. The following information is taken from the balance sheet and related disclosures of Maxwell, Inc.:

Total paid-in capital	$5,400,000
Outstanding shares:	
Common stock, $5 par value	100,000 shares
6% preferred stock, $100 par value . . .	10,000 shares
Preferred dividends in arrears	2 years
Total stockholders' equity	$4,700,000

   Which of the following statements is (are) true? (For this question, more than one answer may be correct.)
   - a. The preferred dividends in arrears amount to $120,000 and should appear as a liability in the corporate balance sheet.
   - b. The book value per share of common stock is $35.
   - c. The stockholders' equity section of the balance sheet should indicate a deficit (negative amount in retained earnings) of $700,000.
   - d. The company has paid no dividend on its *common* stock during the past two years.
6. On December 10, 2010, Smitty Corporation reacquired 2,000 shares of its own $5 par value common stock at a price of $60 per share. In 2011, 500 of the treasury shares are reissued at a price of $70 per share. Which of the following statements is correct?
   - a. The treasury stock purchased is recorded at cost and is shown in Smitty's December 31, 2010, balance sheet as an asset.
   - b. The two treasury stock transactions result in an overall net reduction in Smitty's stockholders' equity of $85,000.
   - c. Smitty recognizes a gain of $10 per share on the reissuance of the 500 treasury shares in 2011.
   - d. Smitty's stockholders' equity was increased by $110,000 when the treasury stock was acquired.

ASSIGNMENT MATERIAL Discussion Questions

1. Why are large corporations often said to be *publicly owned*?
2. Distinguish between corporations and sole proprietorships in terms of the following characteristics:
   - a. Owners' liability for debts of the business.
   - b. Transferability of ownership interest.
   - c. Continuity of existence.
   - d. Federal taxation on income.
3. Distinguish between *paid-in capital* and *retained earnings* of a corporation. Why is such a distinction useful?
4. Explain the significance of *par value.* Does par value indicate the reasonable market price for a share of stock? Explain.
5. Describe the usual nature of the following features as they apply to a share of preferred stock: (a) cumulative, and (b) convertible.

6. Why is noncumulative preferred stock often considered an unattractive form of investment?
7. State the balance sheet or income statement classification (asset, liability, stockholders' equity, revenue, or expense) of each of the following accounts:
   a. Cash (received from the issuance of capital stock).
   b. Organization Costs.
   c. Preferred Stock.
   d. Retained Earnings.
   e. Additional Paid-in Capital.
   f. Income Taxes Payable.
8. What does *book value per share* of common stock represent? Does it represent the amount common stockholders would receive in the event of liquidation of the corporation? Explain briefly.
9. What would be the effect, if any, on book value per share of common stock as a result of each of the following independent events: (**a**) a corporation obtains a bank loan; (**b**) a dividend is declared (to be paid in the next accounting period)?
10. In the stock market crash of October 19, 1987, the market price of **IBM**'s capital stock fell by over $31 per share. Explain the effects, if any, of this decline in share price on **IBM**'s balance sheet.
11. What is the purpose of a *stock split*?
12. What is *treasury stock*? Why do corporations purchase their own shares? Is treasury stock an asset? How should it be reported in the balance sheet?
13. In many states, corporation law requires that retained earnings be restricted for dividend purposes to the extent of the cost of treasury shares. What is the reason for this legal rule?
14. The basic accounting equation for a corporation is **Assets = Liabilities + Stockholders' Equity.** Stockholders' equity is further divided into two categories: paid-in capital and retained earnings. What are the major transactions and other financial activities that impact the amount of paid-in capital of a corporation? Identify for each major type of transaction or activity whether it increases or decreases the amount of paid-in capital.
15. If you were going to start a corporation and expected to need to raise capital from several investors, would you include preferred stock in your capital structure? Why or why not? If your answer is that you would include preferred stock, what features would you incorporate into this class of stock?

Brief Exercises

LO4 BRIEF EXERCISE 11.1
Stockholders' Equity

Alpha Co. sold 10,000 shares of common stock, which has a par value of $10, for $13 per share. The company's balance in retained earnings is $75,000. Prepare the stockholders' equity section of the company's balance sheet.

LO4 BRIEF EXERCISE 11.2
Stockholders' Equity

Beta Co. sold 10,000 shares of common stock, which has a par value of $25, for $27 per share. The company also sold 1,000 shares of $100 par value preferred stock for $110. Assume the balance in retained earnings is $100,000. Prepare the stockholders' equity section of Beta's balance sheet.

LO5 BRIEF EXERCISE 11.3
Dividends on Preferred Stock

Zeta Co. has outstanding 100,000 shares of $100 par value cumulative preferred stock which has a dividend rate of 6 percent. The company has not declared any cash dividends on the preferred stock for the last three years. Calculate the amount of dividends in arrears on Zeta's preferred stock and briefly explain how this amount will be known to investors and creditors who may use the company's financial statements.

LO5 BRIEF EXERCISE 11.4
Dividends on Common and Preferred Stock

Mega, Inc., has common and 6 percent preferred stock outstanding as follows:
Preferred stock: 10,000 shares, $100 par value, cumulative
Common stock: 50,000 shares, $50 par value
The company declares a total dividend of $200,000. If the dividends on preferred stock are one year in arrears (in addition to the current year), how will the total dividend be divided between the common and preferred stock?

LO5 BRIEF EXERCISE 11.5
Dividends on Common and Preferred Stock

Walla Company has common and preferred stock outstanding as follows:

Common stock:	100,000 shares, $30 par value
8 percent preferred stock:	10,000 shares, $100 par value

Dividends on preferred stock have not been paid for the last three years (in addition to the current year). If the company pays a total of $120,000 in dividends, how much will the common stockholders receive per share if the preferred stock is not cumulative? How will your answer differ if the preferred stock is cumulative?

LO7 **BRIEF EXERCISE 11.6**
Book Value

Menza Company has stockholders' equity accounts as follows:

Common stock (100,000 shares @ $10 par value)	$1,000,000
Additional paid-in capital on common stock	750,000
Retained earnings	600,000

Calculate the amount of book value per share for common stock and summarize briefly what that figure means in relation to the current market value of the stock.

LO7 **BRIEF EXERCISE 11.7**
Book Value

Smalley, Inc., has preferred and common stock outstanding as follows:

$5 preferred stock, 40,000 shares @ $100 par value	$4,000,000
Common stock, 500,000 shares at $10 par value	5,000,000
Additional paid-in capital on common stock	800,000
Retained earnings	1,750,000

Calculate the book value on common stock, assuming preferred dividends are cumulative and are currently one year in arrears.

LO8 **BRIEF EXERCISE 11.8**
Stock Split

Smelling Company declared a 2-for-1 stock split on its common stock in order to intentionally reduce the market value of its stock so that it would be an attractive investment for a larger set of investors. The company's common stock is described as follows:

> Common stock: 100,000 shares outstanding, $10 par value, originally sold at $12.50, current market price $50.

Describe the likely impact, if any, that the 2-for-1 stock split will have on **(a)** the number of shares outstanding, **(b)** the market price of the stock, and **(c)** the total stockholders' equity attributable to common stock.

LO4 LO9 **BRIEF EXERCISE 11.9**
Treasury Stock

Melcher, Inc., originally sold 100,000 shares of its $10 par value common stock at $25 per share. Several years later the company repurchased 10,000 of these shares at $55 per share. Melcher currently holds those shares in treasury. Prepare the company's stockholders' equity section of the balance sheet to reflect this information.

LO4 LO9 **BRIEF EXERCISE 11.10**
Treasury Stock

Reeves, Inc., sold 1,000,000 shares of $25 par value common stock at $30. It subsequently repurchased 100,000 of those shares at $50 per share and then sold 70,000 of those shares at $55. Calculate the total amount of stockholders' equity given the above transactions.

Exercises

LO1 through LO3 **EXERCISE 11.1**
Form of Organization

Assume that you have recently obtained your scuba instructor's certification and have decided to start a scuba diving school.

a. Describe the advantages and disadvantages of organizing your scuba diving school as a:
   1. Sole proprietorship
   2. Corporation

b. State your opinion about which form of organization would be best and explain the basis for your opinion.

LO1 through LO9 **EXERCISE 11.2**
Accounting Terminology

Listed below are 12 technical accounting terms discussed in this chapter:

Par value	Board of directors	Double taxation
Book value	Paid-in capital	Dividends in arrears

Market value	Preferred stock	Closely held corporation
Retained earnings	Common stock	Publicly owned corporation

Each of the following statements may (or may not) describe one of these technical terms. For each statement, indicate the term described, or answer "None" if the statement does not correctly describe any of the terms.

a. A major *disadvantage* of the corporate form of organization.

b. From investors' point of view, the most important value associated with capital stock.

c. Cash available for distribution to the stockholders.

d. The class of capital stock that normally has the most voting power.

e. A distribution of assets that may be made in future years to the holders of common stock.

f. A corporation whose shares are traded on an organized stock exchange.

g. Equity arising from investments by owners.

h. The element of stockholders' equity that is increased by net income.

i. Total assets divided by the number of common shares outstanding.

j. The class of stock for which market price normally rises as interest rates increase.

LO4 LO5

EXERCISE 11.3
Stockholders' Equity Section of a Balance Sheet

When Resisto Systems, Inc., was formed, the company was authorized to issue 5,000 shares of $100 par value, 8 percent cumulative preferred stock, and 100,000 shares of $2 stated value common stock.

Half of the preferred stock was issued at a price of $103 per share, and 70,000 shares of the common stock were sold for $13 per share. At the end of the current year, Resisto has retained earnings of $382,000.

a. Prepare the stockholders' equity section of the company's balance sheet at the end of the current year.

b. Assume Resisto Systems's common stock is trading at $24 per share and its preferred stock is trading at $107 per share at the end of the current year. Would the stockholders' equity section prepared in part **a** be affected by this additional information?

LO4 LO5

EXERCISE 11.4
Dividends: Preferred and Common

A portion of the stockholders' equity section from the balance sheet of Walland Corporation appears as follows:

Stockholders' equity:	
Preferred stock, 9% cumulative, $50 par, 40,000 shares authorized, issued, and outstanding	$2,000,000
Preferred stock, 12% noncumulative, $100 par, 8,000 shares authorized, issued, and outstanding	800,000
Common stock, $5 par, 400,000 shares authorized, issued, and outstanding	2,000,000
Total paid-in capital	$4,800,000

Assume that all the stock was issued on January 1 and that no dividends were paid during the first two years of operation. During the third year, Walland Corporation paid total cash dividends of $736,000.

a. Compute the amount of cash dividends paid during the third year to each of the three classes of stock.

b. Compute the dividends paid *per share* during the third year for each of the three classes of stock.

c. What was the average issue price of each type of preferred stock?

LO4 through LO7

EXERCISE 11.5
Analyzing Stockholders' Equity

The year-end balance sheet of Jackson Products, Inc., includes the following stockholders' equity section (with certain details omitted):

Stockholders' equity:	
Capital stock:	
7% cumulative preferred stock, $100 par value	$ 15,000,000
Common stock, $5 par value, 5,000,000 shares authorized, 4,000,000 shares issued and outstanding	20,000,000
Additional paid-in capital:	
Common stock	44,000,000
Retained earnings	64,450,000
Total stockholders' equity	$143,450,000

From this information, compute answers to the following questions:

a. How many shares of preferred stock have been issued?

b. What is the total amount of the annual dividends to which preferred stockholders are entitled?

c. What was the average issuance price per share of common stock?

d. What is the amount of legal capital and the amount of total paid-in capital?

e. What is the book value per share of common stock?

f. Is it possible to determine the fair market value per share of common stock from the stockholders' equity section above? Explain.

LO5 LO6

EXERCISE 11.6
Preferred Stock Alternatives

Walker, Inc., has the following capital structure:

Preferred stock—$25 par value, 10,000 shares authorized, 7,000 shares issued and outstanding	$175,000
Common stock—$10 par value, 100,000 shares authorized, 80,000 shares issued and outstanding	800,000
Total paid-in capital	$975,000
Retained earnings	550,000
Total stockholders' equity	$1,525,000

The number of issued and outstanding shares of both preferred and common stock have been the same for the last two years. Dividends on preferred stock are 8 percent of par value and have been paid each year the stock was outstanding except for the immediate past year. In the current year, management declares a total dividend of $50,000. Indicate the amount that will be paid to both preferred and common stockholders assuming (**a**) the preferred stock is not cumulative and (**b**) the preferred stock is cumulative.

LO4 LO7

EXERCISE 11.7
Reporting the Effects of Transactions

Three events pertaining to Lean Manufacturing Co. are described below.

a. Issued common stock for cash.

b. The market value of the corporation's stock increased.

c. Declared and paid a cash dividend to stockholders.

Indicate the immediate effects of the events on the financial measurements in the four columnar headings listed below. Use the code letters **I** for increase, **D** for decrease, and **NE** for no effect.

Event	Current Assets	Stockholders' Equity	Net Income	Net Cash Flow (from any source)
a				

LO4 through LO7

EXERCISE 11.8
Computing Book Value

The following information is necessary to compute the net assets (stockholders' equity) and book value per share of common stock for Rothchild Corporation:

8% cumulative preferred stock, $100 par	$200,000
Common stock, $5 par, authorized 100,000 shares, issued 60,000 shares	300,000
Additional paid-in capital	452,800
Deficit (negative amount in retained earnings)	146,800
Dividends in arrears on preferred stock, 1 full year	16,000

a. Compute the amount of net assets (stockholders' equity).

b. Compute the book value per share of common stock.

c. Is book value per share (answer to part **b**) the amount common stockholders should expect to receive if Rothchild Corporation were to cease operations and liquidate? Explain.

LO9 **EXERCISE 11.9** Recording Treasury Stock Transactions

Johnston, Inc., engaged in the following transactions involving treasury stock:

Feb. 10 Purchased for cash 17,000 shares of treasury stock at a price of $25 per share.

June 4 Reissued 6,000 shares of treasury stock at a price of $33 per share.

Dec. 22 Reissued 4,000 shares of treasury stock at a price of $22 per share.

a. Prepare general journal entries to record these transactions.

b. Compute the amount of retained earnings that should be restricted because of the treasury stock still owned at December 31.

c. Does a restriction on retained earnings affect the dollar amount of retained earnings reported in the balance sheet? Explain briefly.

LO8 **EXERCISE 11.10** Effects of a Stock Split

The common stock of Fido Corporation was trading at $45 per share on October 15, 2010. A year later, on October 15, 2011, it was trading at $80 per share. On this date, Fido's board of directors decided to split the company's common stock.

a. If the company decides on a 2-for-1 split, at what price would you expect the stock to trade immediately after the split goes into effect?

b. If the company decides on a 4-for-1 split, at what price would you expect the stock to trade immediately after the split goes into effect?

c. Why do you think Fido's board of directors decided to split the company's stock?

LO9 **EXERCISE 11.11** Treasury Stock Presentation

Albert Company was experiencing financial difficulty late in the current year. The company's income was sluggish, and the market price of its common stock was tumbling. On December 21, the company began to buy back shares of its own stock in an attempt to boost its market price per share and to improve its earnings per share.

a. Is it unethical for a company to purchase shares of its own stock to improve measures of financial performance? Defend your answer.

b. Assume that the company classified the shares of treasury stock as short-term investments in the current asset section of its balance sheet. Is this appropriate? Explain.

LO4 **EXERCISE 11.12** Authorized Stock

The 2009 balance sheet for **Carnival Corporation** indicates that the company has 1,960 million shares of common stock authorized, of which approximately 620 million were outstanding.

a. How many additional shares of common stock could **Carnival Corporation** sell?

b. How are the shares that have not yet been issued included in the company's balance sheet? Do they represent an asset of the company?

LO4 LO9 **EXERCISE 11.13** Accounting Terminology

Smiley, Inc., is authorized to sell 1,000,000 shares of $10 par value common stock and 50,000 shares of $100 par value 6 percent preferred stock. As of the end of the current year, the company has actually sold 550,000 shares of common stock at $12 per share and 40,000 shares of preferred stock at $110 per share. In addition, of the 550,000 shares of common that have been sold, 40,000 shares have been repurchased at $60 per share and are currently being held in treasury to be used to meet the future requirements of a stock option plan that the company intends to implement.

a. Prepare the general journal entries required to record all of the above transactions.

b. Prepare the stockholders' equity section of Smiley's balance sheet to reflect the transactions you have recorded.

LO8 LO9 **EXERCISE 11.14** Treasury Stock and Stock Split

Twin Towns, Inc., was authorized to issue 200,000 shares of common stock and originally issued 100,000 shares of $10 par value stock at $18 per share. Subsequently, 25,000 shares were repurchased at $20, of which 10,000 were subsequently resold at $23.

Assume the company's retained earnings balance is $120,000.

a. Prepare the stockholders' equity section of Twin Towns's balance sheet, including all appropriate disclosures.

b. Briefly explain how the declaration and distribution of a 2-for-1 stock split subsequent to the above transactions would affect the stockholders' equity section you have prepared.

LO4 LO7 **EXERCISE 11.15** Using the **Home Depot, Inc.**, Financial Statements

The financial statements of **Home Depot, Inc.**, appear in Appendix A of this text. These statements contain information describing the details of the company's stockholders' equity.

a. What is the par value of the company's common stock? Did the common stock originally sell at, above, or below par value? How do you know this?

b. For the most current year shown, how many shares of common stock are authorized? What is the meaning of "authorized shares"?

c. What is the total stockholders' equity amount for **Home Depot** for the most recent year reported? Does this figure mean that the total outstanding stock is actually worth this amount? Explain your answer.

Problem Set A

LO4 through LO6 **PROBLEM 11.1A** Stockholders' Equity in a Balance Sheet

Early in 2008, Robbinsville Press was organized with authorization to issue 100,000 shares of $100 par value preferred stock and 500,000 shares of $1 par value common stock. Ten thousand shares of the preferred stock were issued at par, and 170,000 shares of common stock were sold for $15 per share. The preferred stock pays an 8 percent cumulative dividend.

During the first four years of operations (2008 through 2011), the corporation earned a total of $1,085,000 and paid dividends of 75 cents per share in each year on its outstanding common stock.

Instructions

a. Prepare the stockholders' equity section of the balance sheet at December 31, 2011. Include a supporting schedule showing your computation of the amount of retained earnings reported. (Hint: Income increases retained earnings, whereas dividends decrease retained earnings.)

b. Are there any dividends in arrears on the company's preferred stock at December 31, 2011? Explain your answer.

LO4 through LO6 **PROBLEM 11.2A** Stockholders' Equity Section

Waller Publications was organized early in 2006 with authorization to issue 20,000 shares of $100 par value preferred stock and 1 million shares of $1 par value common stock. All of the preferred stock was issued at par, and 300,000 shares of common stock were sold for $20 per share. The preferred stock pays a 10 percent cumulative dividend.

During the first five years of operations (2006 through 2010) the corporation earned a total of $4,460,000 and paid dividends of $1 per share each year on the common stock. In 2011, however, the corporation reported a net loss of $1,750,000 and paid no dividends.

Instructions

a. Prepare the stockholders' equity section of the balance sheet at December 31, 2011. Include a supporting schedule showing your computation of retained earnings at the balance sheet date. (Hint: Income increases retained earnings, whereas dividends and net losses decrease retained earnings.)

b. Draft a note to accompany the financial statements disclosing any dividends in arrears at the end of 2011.

c. Do the dividends in arrears appear as a liability of the corporation as of the end of 2011? Explain.

LO4 through LO6 **PROBLEM 11.3A** Stockholders' Equity in a Balance Sheet

Maria Martinez organized Manhattan Transport Company in January 2008. The corporation immediately issued at $8 per share one-half of its 200,000 authorized shares of $2 par value common stock. On January 2, 2009, the corporation sold at par value the entire 5,000 authorized shares of 8 percent, $100 par value cumulative preferred stock. On January 2, 2010, the company again needed money and issued 5,000 shares of an authorized 10,000 shares of no-par cumulative preferred stock for a total of $512,000. The no-par shares have a stated dividend of $9 per share.

The company declared no dividends in 2008 and 2009. At the end of 2009, its retained earnings were $170,000. During 2010 and 2011 combined, the company earned a total of $890,000. Dividends of 50 cents per share in 2010 and $1.60 per share in 2011 were paid on the common stock.

Instructions

a. Prepare the stockholders' equity section of the balance sheet at December 31, 2011. Include a supporting schedule showing your computation of retained earnings at the balance sheet date. (Hint: Income increases retained earnings, whereas dividends decrease retained earnings.)

b. Assume that on January 2, 2009, the corporation could have borrowed $500,000 at 8 percent interest on a long-term basis instead of issuing the 5,000 shares of the $100 par value cumulative preferred stock. Identify two reasons a corporation may choose to issue cumulative preferred stock rather than finance operations with long-term debt.

LO4 LO5

PROBLEM 11.4A

Stockholders' Equity: A Short Comprehensive Problem

eXcel

Early in the year Bill Barnes and several friends organized a corporation called Barnes Communications, Inc. The corporation was authorized to issue 50,000 shares of $100 par value, 10 percent cumulative preferred stock and 400,000 shares of $2 par value common stock. The following transactions (among others) occurred during the year:

Jan. 6 Issued for cash 20,000 shares of common stock at $14 per share. The shares were issued to Barnes and 10 other investors.

Jan. 7 Issued an additional 500 shares of common stock to Barnes in exchange for his services in organizing the corporation. The stockholders agreed that these services were worth $7,000.

Jan. 12 Issued 2,500 shares of preferred stock for cash of $250,000.

June 4 Acquired land as a building site in exchange for 15,000 shares of common stock. In view of the appraised value of the land and the progress of the company, the directors agreed that the common stock was to be valued for purposes of this transaction at $15 per share.

Nov. 15 The first annual dividend of $10 per share was declared on the preferred stock to be paid December 20. (Hint: Record the dividend by debiting Dividends and crediting Dividends Payable.)

Dec. 20 Paid the cash dividend declared on November 15.

Dec. 31 After the revenue and expenses were closed into the Income Summary account, that account indicated a net income of $147,200.

Instructions

a. Prepare journal entries in general journal form to record the above transactions. Include entries at December 31 to close the Income Summary account and the Dividends account.

b. Prepare the stockholders' equity section of the Barnes Communications, Inc., balance sheet at December 31.

LO4 LO5

PROBLEM 11.5A

Analysis of an Equity Section of a Balance Sheet

The year-end balance sheet of Smithfield Products includes the following stockholders' equity section (with certain details omitted):

Stockholders' equity:	
7½% cumulative preferred stock, $100 par value, 100,000 shares authorized	$ 2,400,000
Common stock, $2 par value, 900,000 shares authorized	900,000
Additional paid-in capital: common stock	8,325,000
Retained earnings	2,595,000
Total stockholders' equity	$14,220,000

Instructions

From this information, compute answers to the following questions:

a. How many shares of preferred stock have been issued?

b. What is the total amount of the annual dividends paid to preferred stockholders?

c. How many shares of common stock are outstanding?

d. What was the average issuance price per share of common stock?

e. What is the amount of legal capital?

f. What is the total amount of paid-in capital?

g. What is the book value per share of common stock? (There are no dividends in arrears.)

h. Assume that retained earnings at the beginning of the year amounted to $717,500 and that net income for the year was $3,970,000. What was the dividend declared during the year on *each share* of common stock? (Hint: Net income increases retained earnings, whereas dividends decrease retained earnings.)

LO1 through LO7

PROBLEM 11.6A Analysis of an Equity Section—More Comprehensive

Parsons, Inc., is a publicly owned company. The following information is excerpted from a recent balance sheet. Dollar amounts (except for per share amounts) are stated in thousands.

Stockholders' equity:	
Convertible $17.20 preferred stock, $250 par value, 1,000,000 shares authorized; 345,000 shares issued and outstanding	$ 86,250
Common stock, par value $0.50; 25,000,000 shares authorized	6,819
Additional paid-in capital	87,260
Retained earnings	57,263
Total stockholders' equity	$237,592

Instructions

From this information, answer the following questions:

a. How many shares of common stock have been issued?

b. What is the total amount of the annual dividends paid to preferred stockholders?

c. What is the total amount of paid-in capital?

d. What is the book value per share of common stock?

e. Briefly explain the advantages and disadvantages to Parsons of being publicly owned rather than operating as a closely held corporation.

f. What is meant by the term *convertible* used in the caption of the preferred stock? Is there any more information that investors need to know to evaluate this conversion feature?

g. Assume that the preferred stock currently is selling at *$248* per share. Does this provide a higher or lower dividend yield than an 8 percent, $50 par value preferred with a market price of $57 per share? Show computations (round to the nearest tenth of 1 percent). Explain why one preferred stock might yield less than another.

LO4 LO7

PROBLEM 11.7A Par, Book, and Market Values

Techno Corporation is the producer of popular business software. Recently, an investment service published the following per-share amounts relating to the company's only class of stock:

Par value	$ 0.001
Book value (estimated)	6.50
Market value	$65.00

Instructions

a. Without reference to dollar amounts, explain the nature and significance of *par value, book value,* and *market value.*

b. Comment on the *relationships,* if any, among the per-share amounts shown for the company. What do these amounts imply about Techno Corporation and its operations? Comment on what these amounts imply about the security of *creditors'* claims against the company.

LO4 LO5 LO7 LO9

PROBLEM 11.8A
Reporting Stockholders' Equity with Treasury Stock

Early in 2009, Feller Corporation was formed with authorization to issue 50,000 shares of $1 par value common stock. All shares were issued at a price of $8 per share. The corporation reported net income of $82,000 in 2009, $25,000 in 2010, and $78,000 in 2011. No dividends were declared in any of these three years.

In 2010, the company purchased its own shares for $35,000 in the open market. In 2011, it reissued all of its treasury stock for $40,000.

Instructions

a. Prepare the stockholders' equity section of the balance sheet at December 31, 2011. Include a supporting schedule showing your computation of retained earnings at the balance sheet date. (Hint: Income increases retained earnings.)

b. As of December 31, compute the company's book value per share of common stock.

c. Explain how the treasury stock transactions in 2010 and 2011 were reported in the company's statement of cash flows.

LO4 LO5 LO7 through LO9

PROBLEM 11.9A
Reporting Stockholders' Equity with Treasury Stock and Stock Splits

Early in 2007, Herndon Industries was formed with authorization to issue 200,000 shares of $10 par value common stock and 30,000 shares of $100 par value cumulative preferred stock. During 2007, all the preferred stock was issued at par, and 120,000 shares of common stock were sold for $16 per share. The preferred stock is entitled to a dividend equal to 10 percent of its par value before any dividends are paid on the common stock.

During its first five years of business (2007 through 2011), the company earned income totaling $3,700,000 and paid dividends of 50 cents per share each year on the common stock outstanding.

On January 2, 2009, the company purchased 20,000 shares of its own common stock in the open market for $400,000. On January 2, 2011, it reissued 10,000 shares of this treasury stock for $250,000. The remaining 10,000 were still held in treasury at December 31, 2011.

Instructions

a. Prepare the stockholders' equity section of the balance sheet for Herndon Industries at December 31, 2011. Include supporting schedules showing (1) your computation of any paid-in capital on treasury stock and (2) retained earnings at the balance sheet date. (Hint: Income increases retained earnings, whereas dividends reduce retained earnings. Dividends are not paid on shares of stock held in treasury.)

b. As of December 31, compute Herndon's book value per share of common stock. (Hint: Book value per share is computed only on the shares of stock outstanding.)

c. At December 31, 2011, shares of the company's common stock were trading at $30. Explain what would have happened to the market price per share had the company split its stock 3-for-1 at this date. Also explain what would have happened to the par value of the common stock and to the number of common shares outstanding.

Problem Set B

LO4 through LO6

PROBLEM 11.1B
Stockholders' Equity in a Balance Sheet

Early in 2008, Septa, Inc., was organized with authorization to issue 1,000 shares of $100 par value preferred stock and 200,000 shares of $1 par value common stock. Five hundred shares of the preferred stock were issued at par, and 80,000 shares of common stock were sold at $15 per share. The preferred stock pays a 10 percent cumulative dividend.

During the first four years of operations (2008 through 2011), the corporation earned a total of $1,800,000 and paid dividends of 40 cents per share in each year on its outstanding common stock.

Instructions

a. Prepare the stockholders' equity section of the balance sheet at December 31, 2011. Include a supporting schedule showing your computation of the amount of retained earnings reported. (Hint: Income increases retained earnings, whereas dividends decrease retained earnings.)

b. Are there any dividends in arrears on the company's preferred stock at December 31, 2011? Explain your answer.

c. Assume that interest rates increase steadily from 2008 through 2011. Would you expect the market price of the company's preferred stock to be higher or lower than its call price of $110 at December 21, 2011? (The call price is the amount the company must pay to repurchase the shares from the stockholders.)

LO4 through LO6

PROBLEM 11.2B
Stockholders' Equity Section

Banner Publications was organized early in 2006 with authorization to issue 10,000 shares of $100 par value preferred stock and 1 million shares of $1 par value common stock. All of the preferred stock was issued at par, and 400,000 shares of common stock were sold for $15 per share. The preferred stock pays a 10 percent cumulative dividend.

During the first five years of operations (2006 through 2010) the corporation earned a total of $4,100,000 and paid dividends of $.80 per share each year on the common stock. In 2011, however, the corporation reported a net loss of $1,100,000 and paid no dividends.

Instructions

a. Prepare the stockholders' equity section of the balance sheet at December 31, 2011. Include a supporting schedule showing your computation of retained earnings at the balance sheet date. (Hint: Income increases retained earnings, whereas dividends and net losses decrease retained earnings.)

b. Draft a note to accompany the financial statements disclosing any dividends in arrears at the end of 2011.

c. Do the dividends in arrears appear as a liability of the corporation as of the end of 2011? Explain.

LO4 through LO6

PROBLEM 11.3B
Stockholders' Equity in a Balance Sheet

Joy Sun organized Ray Beam, Inc., in January 2008. The corporation immediately issued at $15 per share one-half of its 260,000 authorized shares of $1 par value common stock. On January 2, 2009, the corporation sold at par value the entire 10,000 authorized shares of 10 percent, $100 par value cumulative preferred stock. On January 2, 2010, the company again needed money and issued 5,000 shares of an authorized 8,000 shares of no-par cumulative preferred stock for a total of $320,000. The no-par shares have a stated dividend of $6 per share.

The company declared no dividends in 2008 and 2009. At the end of 2009, its retained earnings were $530,000. During 2010 and 2011 combined, the company earned a total of $1,400,000. Dividends of 90 cents per share in 2010 and $2 per share in 2011 were paid on the common stock.

Instructions

a. Prepare the stockholders' equity section of the balance sheet at December 31, 2011. Include a supporting schedule showing your computation of retained earnings at the balance sheet date. (Hint: Income increases retained earnings, whereas dividends and net losses decrease retained earnings.)

b. Assume that on January 2, 2009, the corporation could have borrowed $1,000,000 at 10 percent interest on a long-term basis instead of issuing the 10,000 shares of the $100 par value cumulative preferred stock. Identify two reasons a corporation may choose to issue cumulative preferred stock rather than finance operations with long-term debt.

LO4 LO5

PROBLEM 11.4B
Stockholders' Equity: A Short Comprehensive Problem

Early in the year Debra Deal and several friends organized a corporation called Markup, Inc. The corporation was authorized to issue 100,000 shares of $100 par value, 5 percent cumulative preferred stock and 100,000 shares of $1 par value common stock. The following transactions (among others) occurred during the year:

Jan. 7 Issued for cash 30,000 shares of common stock at $10 per share. The shares were issued to Deal and four other investors.

Jan. 12 Issued an additional 1,000 shares of common stock to Deal in exchange for her services in organizing the corporation. The stockholders agreed that these services were worth $12,000.

Jan. 18 Issued 4,000 shares of preferred stock for cash of $400,000.

July 5 Acquired land as a building site in exchange for 10,000 shares of common stock. In view of the appraised value of the land and the progress of the company, the directors agreed that the common stock was to be valued for purposes of this transaction at $12 per share.

Nov. 25 The first annual dividend of $5 per share was declared on the preferred stock to be paid December 11.

Dec. 11 Paid the cash dividend declared on November 25.

Dec. 31 After the revenue and expenses were closed into the Income Summary account, that amount indicated a net income of $810,000.

Instructions

a. Prepare journal entries in general journal form to record the above transactions. Include entries at December 31 to close the Income Summary account and the Dividends account.

b. Prepare the stockholders' equity section of the Markup, Inc., balance sheet at December 31.

LO4 LO5 **PROBLEM 11.5B**

Analysis of an Equity Section of a Balance Sheet

The year-end balance sheet of Manor, Inc., includes the following stockholders' equity section (with certain details omitted):

Stockholders' equity:	
10% cumulative preferred stock, $100 par value, authorized 100,000 shares	$ 4,400,000
Common stock, $2 par value, authorized 2,000,000 shares	3,400,000
Additional paid-in capital: common stock	6,800,000
Donated capital	400,000
Retained earnings	3,160,000
Total stockholders' equity	$18,160,000

Instructions

From this information, compute answers to the following questions:

a. How many shares of preferred stock have been issued?

b. What is the total amount of the annual dividends paid to preferred stockholders?

c. How many shares of common stock are outstanding?

d. What was the average issuance price per share of common stock?

e. What is the amount of legal capital?

f. What is the total amount of paid-in capital?

g. What is the book value per share of common stock? (There are no dividends in arrears.)

h. Assume that retained earnings at the beginning of the year amounted to $1,200,000 and the net income for the year was $4,800,000. What was the dividend declared during the year on *each share* of common stock? (Hint: Net income increases retained earnings, whereas dividends decrease retained earnings.)

LO1 through LO7 **PROBLEM 11.6B**

Analysis of an Equity Section—More Comprehensive

Toasty Corporation is a publicly owned company. The following information is taken from a recent balance sheet. Dollar amounts (except for per-share amounts) are stated in thousands.

Stockholders' equity:	
Convertible $10 preferred stock, no par value, 1,000,000 shares authorized, 250,000 shares issued and outstanding, $200 per share liquidation preference	$ 50,000
Common stock, $3 par value, 40,000,000 shares authorized	9,600
Additional paid-in capital	76,800
Retained earnings	50,600
Total stockholders' equity	$187,000

Instructions

From this information, compute answers to the following questions:

a. How many shares of common stock have been issued?

b. What is the total amount of the annual dividends paid to preferred stockholders?

c. What is the total amount of paid-in capital?

d. What is the book value per share of common stock?

e. Briefly explain the advantages and disadvantages to Toasty of being publicly owned rather than operating as a closely held corporation.

f. What is meant by the term *convertible* used in the caption of the preferred stock? Is there any more information that investors need to know to evaluate this conversion feature?

g. Assume that the preferred stock currently is selling at *$190* per share. Does this provide a higher or lower dividend yield than a 6 percent, $50 par value preferred with a market price of $52 per share? Show computations. Explain why one preferred stock might yield less than another.

LO4 LO7

PROBLEM 11.7B
Par, Book, and Market Values

Brain Corporation is the producer of popular video games. Recently, an investment service published the following per-share amounts relating to the company's only class of stock:

Par value	$ 0.05
Book value (estimated)	10.00
Market value	96.00

Instructions

a. Without reference to dollar amounts, explain the nature and significance of *par value, book value,* and *market value.*

b. Comment on the *relationships,* if any, among the per-share accounts shown for the company. What do these amounts imply about Brain and its operations? Comment on what these amounts imply about the security of *creditors'* claims against the company.

LO4 LO5 LO7 LO9

PROBLEM 11.8B
Reporting Stockholders' Equity with Treasury Stock

Early in 2009, Tin Corporation was formed with authorization to issue 50,000 shares of $3 par value common stock. All shares were issued at a price of $10 per share. The corporation reported net income of $150,000 in 2009, $80,000 in 2010, and $100,000 in 2011. No dividends were declared in any of these three years.

In 2010, the company purchased its own shares for $30,000 in the open market. In 2011, it reissued all of its treasury stock for $40,000.

Instructions

a. Prepare the stockholders' equity section of the balance sheet at December 31, 2011. Include a supporting schedule showing your computation of retained earnings at the balance sheet date. (Hint: Income increases retained earnings.)

b. As of December 31, compute the company's book value per share of common stock.

c. Explain how the treasury stock transactions in 2010 and 2011 were reported in the company's statement of cash flows.

LO4 LO5 LO7 through LO9

PROBLEM 11.9B
Reporting Stockholders' Equity with Treasury Stock and Stock Splits

Early in 2007, Parker Industries was formed with authorization to issue 100,000 shares of $20 par value common stock and 10,000 shares of $100 par value cumulative preferred stock. During 2007, all the preferred stock was issued at par, and 80,000 shares of common stock were sold for $35 per share. The preferred stock is entitled to a dividend equal to 6 percent of its par value before any dividends are paid on the common stock.

During its first five years of business (2007 through 2011), the company earned income totaling $3,800,000 and paid dividends of 60 cents per share each year on the common stock outstanding.

On January 2, 2009, the company purchased 1,000 shares of its own common stock in the open market for $40,000. On January 2, 2011, it reissued 600 shares of this treasury stock for $30,000. The remaining 400 shares were still held in treasury at December 31, 2011.

Instructions

a. Prepare the stockholders' equity section of the balance sheet at December 31, 2011. Include a supporting schedule showing (1) your computation of any paid-in capital on treasury stock and (2) retained earnings at the balance sheet date. (Hint: Income increases retained earnings, whereas dividends reduce retained earnings. Dividends are not paid on shares of stock held in treasury.)

b. As of December 31, 2011, compute the company's book value per share of common stock. (Hint: Book value per share is computed only on the shares of stock outstanding.)

c. At December 31, 2011, shares of the company's common stock were trading at $56. Explain what would have happened to the market price per share had the company split its stock 2-for-1 at this date. Also explain what would have happened to the par value of the common stock and to the number of common shares outstanding.

Critical Thinking Cases

LO5 LO7 **CASE11.1**

Factors Affecting the Market Prices of Preferred and Common Stocks

ADM Labs is a publicly owned company with several issues of capital stock outstanding. Over the past decade, the company has consistently earned modest profits and has increased its common stock dividend annually by 5 or 10 cents per share. Recently the company introduced several new products that you believe will cause future sales and profits to increase dramatically. You also expect a gradual increase in long-term interest rates from their present level of about 11 percent to, perhaps, 12 percent to 12¼ percent.

Instructions

On the basis of these forecasts, explain whether you would expect to see the market prices of the following issues of ADM capital stock increase or decrease. Explain your reasoning in each answer.

a. 10 percent, $100 par value preferred stock (currently selling at $90 per share).

b. $5 par value common stock (currently paying an annual dividend of $2.50 and selling at $40 per share).

c. 7 percent, $100 par value convertible preferred stock (currently selling at $125 per share).

LO7 **CASE 11.2**

Factors Affecting the Market Prices of Common Stocks

Each of the following situations describes an event that affected the stock market price of a particular company.

a. The price of a common share of **McDonnell Douglas, Inc.**, increased by over $5 per share in the several days after it was announced that Saudia Airlines would order $6 billion of commercial airliners from **Boeing** and **McDonnell Douglas**.

b. **Citicorp**'s common stock price fell by over $3.50 per share shortly after the Federal Reserve Board increased the discount rate by ¼ percent. The discount rate is the rate charged to banks for short-term loans they need to meet their reserve requirements.

c. The price of a common share of **Ventitex, Inc.**, a manufacturer of medical devices, fell over $10 (27.7 percent) after it was announced that representatives of the Federal Drug Administration paid a visit to the company.

Instructions

For each of the independent situations described, explain the likely underlying rationale for the change in market price of the stock.

LO1 through LO3 **CASE 11.3**

Selecting a Form of Business Organization

Interview the owners of two local small businesses. One business should be organized as a corporation and the other as either a sole proprietorship or a partnership. Inquire as to:

- *Why* this form of entity was selected.
- Have there been any unforeseen complications with this form of entity?
- Is the form of entity likely to be changed in the foreseeable future? And if so, why?

LO1 through LO3 **CASE 11.4**

SEC Enforcement Division

The Enforcement Division of the Securities and Exchange Commission (SEC) is an important aspect of the corporate governance structure in the United States that is intended to protect investors. Locate the home page of the SEC by doing a general search on the title "Securities and Exchange Commission," and answer the following.

Instructions

a. Identify the four divisions of the SEC.

b. Access the category "Enforcement Division," and write a one-sentence description of the purpose of this division.

c. Access the subcategory "Investor Alerts," and locate the SEC publication that deals with pump-and-dump schemes on the Internet.

d. Write a concise description of a pump-and-dump scheme, and list the suggestions of the SEC to investors to avoid these schemes.

LO4 LO5 LO7 LO9

INTERNET CASE 11.5

Stockholders' Equity Items

WWW

Visit the home page of **Staples, Inc.**, at the following Internet address:

www.staples.com

Locate the company's most current balance sheet by selecting "Investor Information."

Instructions

Answer the following questions:

a. Does the company report preferred stock in its balance sheet? If so, how many shares are currently outstanding?

b. How much common stock does the company report in its most recent balance sheet? What is the par value of each share?

c. Does the company report any treasury stock? Has this amount changed since the previous year?

Internet sites are time and date sensitive. It is the purpose of these exercises to have you explore the Internet. You may need to use the Yahoo! search engine **http://www.yahoo.com** *(or another favorite search engine) to find a company's current Web address.*

Answers to Self-Test Questions

1. c **2.** d **3.** c **4.** c **5.** c, d **6.** b [(2,000 × $60) − (500 × $70)]

COMPREHENSIVE PROBLEM 3

McMinn Retail, Inc.

McMinn Retail, Inc., is a retailer that has engaged you to assist in the preparation of its financial statements at December 31, 2011. Following are the correct adjusted account balances, in alphabetical order, as of that date. Each balance is the "normal" balance for that account. (Hint: The "normal" balance is the same as the debit or credit side that increases the account.)

Accounts payable	$ 12,750
Accounts receivable	2,600
Accumulated depreciation: office equipment	12,000
Additional paid-in capital (common stock)	7,000
Bonds payable (due December 31, 2014)	22,500
Cash	15,200
Common stock (1,800 shares, $10 par value)	18,000
Cost of goods sold	100,575
Deferred income taxes	5,750
Depreciation expense: office equipment	2,750
Dividends declared	5,000
Income tax expense	8,190
Insurance expense	900
Land	37,500
Merchandise inventory	17,500
Notes payable (due December 31, 2012)	2,500
Office equipment	41,000
Office supplies	900
Office supplies expense	520
Preferred stock (250 shares, $20 par value)	5,000
Premium on bonds payable	1,750
Prepaid rent	1,800
Rent expense	6,100
Retained earnings (January 2011)	21,050
Salaries expense	88,095
Sales	226,000
Sales returns and allowances	2,500
Sales taxes payable	3,200
Treasury stock (200 common shares at cost)	2,250
Utilities expense	4,120

Instructions

a. Prepare an income statement for the year ended December 31, 2011, which includes amounts for gross profit, income before income taxes, and net income. List expenses (other than cost of goods sold and income tax expense) in order, from the largest to the smallest dollar balance. You may ignore earnings per share.

b. Prepare a statement of retained earnings for the year ending December 31, 2011.

c. Prepare a statement of financial position (balance sheet) as of December 31, 2011, following these guidelines:

- Include separate asset and liability categories for those assets which are "current."
- Include and label amounts for total assets, total liabilities, total stockholders' equity, and total liabilities and stockholders' equity.
- Present deferred income taxes as a noncurrent liability.
- To the extent information is available that should be disclosed, include that information in your statement.

CHAPTER 12

Income and Changes in Retained Earnings

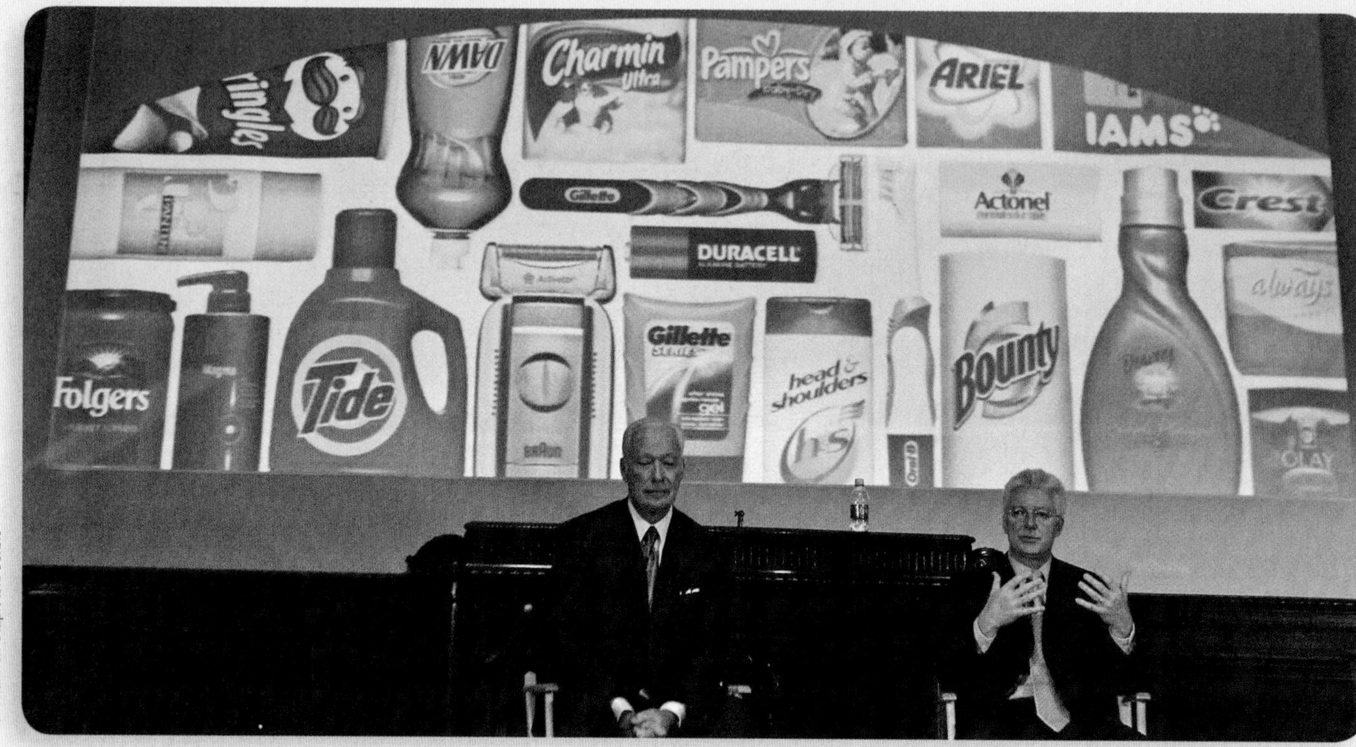

© Shannon Stapleton/Corbis

AFTER STUDYING THIS CHAPTER, YOU SHOULD BE ABLE TO:

Learning Objectives

LO1 Describe how irregular income items, such as discontinued operations and extraordinary items, are presented in the income statement.

LO2 Compute earnings per share.

LO3 Distinguish between basic and diluted earnings per share.

LO4 Account for cash dividends and stock dividends, and explain the effects of these transactions on a company's financial statements.

LO5 Describe and prepare a statement of retained earnings.

LO6 Define *prior period adjustments,* and explain how they are presented in financial statements.

LO7 Define *comprehensive income,* and explain how it differs from net income.

LO8 Describe and prepare a statement of stockholders' equity and the stockholders' equity section of the balance sheet.

LO9 Illustrate steps management might take to improve the appearance of the company's net income.

PROCTER & GAMBLE COMPANY

A company's pattern of sales and net income are important factors in evaluating its financial success. Consider Procter & Gamble Company, for example. Two billion times a day, P&G products are sold around the world. The company has one of the largest and strongest portfolios of recognizable brands, including Pampers, Tide, Ariel, Always, Whisper, Pantene, Bounty, Pringles, Folgers, Charmin, Downy, Lenor, Iams, Crest, Clairol, Actonel, Dawn, and Olay. Ninety-eight thousand people work for P&G in almost 80 countries worldwide.

One of the attributes of financially successful companies like P&G is their consistent strength over time in terms of primary measures of financial performance, such as net sales and net earnings. Net sales, measuring the value of merchandise sold less returns, increased from $74,832 million in 2007 to $81,748 million in 2008 and declined to $78,029 million in 2009. This represents an approximate 9 percent increase in 2008 and a modest 3 percent decline in 2009, for a combined increase for the two years of approximately 6 percent. Net income, which starts with sales and is reduced by various expenses required to generate those sales, increased from $10,340 million in 2007 to $12,075 million in 2008 (an approximate 17 percent increase) and to $13,436 million in 2009 (an approximate 11 percent increase), or a combined increase for the two years of approximately 28 percent. These figures represent impressive financial performance in terms of the company's ability to provide goods to its customers and to operate in a manner that results in a profit that benefits the company's stockholders. ■

For investors seeking companies in which to place their funds, a pattern of increases in key performance figures such as sales and net income is very attractive. In this chapter, we look more closely at the income statement and learn about the useful information available in that financial statement for making important investment and credit decisions. In addition to learning more about how an income statement is prepared, you will learn about earnings per share, dividends, and other key factors that indicate the financial success of a company.

Reporting the Results of Operations

The most important aspect of corporate financial reporting, in the view of many investors, is periodic income. Both the market price of common stock and the amount of cash dividends per share depend on the current and future earnings of the corporation.

DEVELOPING PREDICTIVE INFORMATION

Revenue is a measure of the value of products and services that have been sold to customers. Revenue represents the increases in the company's assets that result from its profit-directed activities. Generally, revenue increases cash either at the time it is included in the income statement or at an earlier or later date. Expenses are measures of the cost of producing and distributing the products and services that are sold to customers. They represent decreases in the company's assets that result from its profit-directed activities. Expenses decrease cash at the time they are incurred, or at an earlier or later date. An income statement presents a company's revenue and expenses for a stated period of time, such as a quarter or year.

As this brief description of revenue and expenses indicates, the income statement provides important information for investors and creditors as they attempt to make estimates of future cash flows. Because of the importance of income reporting in making assessments about the future, events and transactions that are irregular require careful attention in the preparation and interpretation of an income statement.

For information about financial performance to be of maximum usefulness to investors, creditors, and other financial statement users, the results of items that are unusual and not likely to recur should be presented separately from the results of the company's normal, recurring activities. Two categories of unusual, nonrecurring events that require special treatment are (1) the results of *discontinued operations* and (2) the impact of *extraordinary items*. One of the challenges that has faced the accounting profession is to define these terms with sufficient clarity that users of financial statements can reliably compare the information provided by different companies and by the same company over time.

REPORTING IRREGULAR ITEMS: AN ILLUSTRATION

To illustrate the presentation of irregular items in an income statement, assume that Farmer Corporation operates both a small chain of retail stores and two motels. Near the end of the current year, the company sells both motels to a national hotel chain. In addition, Farmer Corporation reports two "extraordinary items." An income statement illustrating the correct format for reporting these events appears in Exhibit 12–1.

CONTINUING OPERATIONS

The first section of the Farmer Corporation income statement contains only the results of *continuing business activities*—that is, the retail stores. Notice that the income tax expense shown in this section ($300,000) relates *only to continuing operations.* The income taxes relating to the irregular items are shown separately in the income statement as adjustments to the amounts of these items.

Income from Continuing Operations The subtotal *income from continuing operations* measures the profitability of the ongoing operations. This subtotal should be helpful in making predictions of the company's future earnings. For example, if we predict no

FARMER CORPORATION INCOME STATEMENT FOR THE YEAR ENDED DECEMBER 31, 2011		
Net sales		$8,000,000
Cost and expenses:		
Cost of goods sold	$4,500,000	
Selling expenses	1,500,000	
General and administrative expenses	920,000	
Loss on settlement of lawsuit	80,000	
Income tax (on continuing operations)	300,000	7,300,000
Income from continuing operations		$ 700,000
Discontinued operations:		
Operating loss on motels (net of $90,000 income tax benefit)	$ (210,000)	
Gain on sale of motels (net of $195,000 income tax)	455,000	245,000
Income before extraordinary items		$ 945,000
Extraordinary items:		
Gain on condemnation of land by State Highway Department (net of $45,000 income tax)	$ 105,000	
Loss from earthquake damage to New York store (net of $75,000 income tax benefit)	(175,000)	(70,000)
Net income		$ 875,000

Exhibit 12–1

INCOME STATEMENT WITH NONRECURRING ITEMS

Notice the order in which the irregular items are reported

significant change in the profitability of its retail stores, we would expect Farmer Corporation to earn a net income of approximately $700,000 next year.

DISCONTINUED OPERATIONS

Learning Objective LO1
Describe how irregular income items, such as discontinued operations and extraordinary items, are presented in the income statement.

When management enters into a formal plan to sell or discontinue a **segment of the business,** the results of that segment's operations are shown separately in the income statement. Excluding that part of the business that will no longer be part of the company's operations enables users of the financial statements to better evaluate the performance of the company's ongoing (continuing) operations.

Two items are included in the **discontinued operations** section of the income statement: (1) the income or loss from *operating* the segment prior to its disposal and (2) the gain or loss on *disposal* of the segment. The income taxes relating to the discontinued operations are *shown separately* from the income tax expense relating to continuing business operations.

EXTRAORDINARY ITEMS

The second category of irregular events requiring disclosure in a separate section of the income statement is extraordinary items. An **extraordinary item** is a gain or loss that is (1) *unusual in nature* and (2) *not expected to recur in the foreseeable future.* An example of an extraordinary item is the loss of a company's plant due to an earthquake in a geographic location where earthquakes rarely occur.

When a gain or loss qualifies as an extraordinary item, it appears after the section on discontinued operations (if any), following the subtotal *income before extraordinary items.* This subtotal is necessary to show investors what the net income *would have been* if the extraordinary gain or loss *had not occurred.* Extraordinary items are shown net of any related income tax effects.

Over the years, the Financial Accounting Standards Board has continued to refine the definition of extraordinary items in a manner that restricts the transactions companies can classify in this manner. As a result, today few extraordinary items are found in the financial statements of publicly held companies.

Other Unusual Gains and Losses Some transactions are not typical of normal operations but also do not meet the stringent criteria for separate presentation as extraordinary items. Among such events are losses incurred because of labor strikes and the gains or losses resulting from sales of plant assets. Such items, if material, should be individually listed as items of revenue or expense, rather than being combined with other items in broad categories such as sales revenue or general and administrative expenses.

In the income statement of Farmer Corporation (Exhibit 12–1), the $80,000 loss resulting from the settlement of a lawsuit is listed separately in the income statement but is *not* shown as an extraordinary item. This loss is important enough to bring to the attention of readers of the income statement by presenting it as a separate item, but it is not considered sufficiently unusual or infrequent enough to be an extraordinary item.

Restructuring Charges One important type of unusual loss relates to the restructuring of operations. The restructuring of operations has become a common aspect of the American economy. As companies struggle to meet the competitive challenges of a global economy, they incur significant costs to close plants, reduce workforces, and consolidate operating facilities.

Restructuring charges consist of items such as losses from write-downs or sales of plant assets, severance pay for terminated workers, and expenses related to the relocation of operations and remaining personnel. In determining operating income, they are presented in the company's income statement as a single item like the loss incurred in the settlement of a lawsuit in the Farmer Corporation income statement in Exhibit 12–1. If the restructuring involves discontinuing a segment of the business, the expenses related to that aspect of the restructuring are presented as discontinued operations.

Distinguishing between the Unusual and the Extraordinary In the past, some corporate managements had a tendency to classify many *losses* as extraordinary, while classifying many *gains* as a part of normal, recurring operations. This resulted in

YOUR TURN **You as an Investor**

One of the most important determinants of a company's stock price is expected future earnings. Assume that you are considering investing in Worsham Corporation and are evaluating the company's profitability in the current year. The net income of the corporation, which amounted to $4,000,000, includes the following items:

Loss on a discontinued segment of the business (net of income tax benefit)	$750,000
Extraordinary gain (net of income tax paid)	300,000

Adjust net income to develop a number that represents a good starting point for predicting the future net income of Worsham Corporation. Explain the reason for each of the adjustments. Explain how this adjusted number may help you predict future earnings for the company.

(See our comments on the Online Learning Center Web site.)

reporting higher income before extraordinary items, but the final net income figure was not affected. To counter this potentially misleading practice, the accounting profession now strictly defines extraordinary items and intends for them to be quite rare. There is no comprehensive list of extraordinary items. Thus the classification of a specific event is a matter of *judgment.*

EARNINGS PER SHARE (EPS)

Learning Objective LO2
Compute earnings per share.

One of the most widely used accounting statistics is **earnings per share** on common stock. Investors who buy or sell stock in a corporation need to know the annual earnings per share. Stock market prices are quoted on a per-share basis. If you are considering investing in a company's stock at a price of $50 per share, you need to know the earnings per share and the annual dividend per share to decide whether this price is reasonable.

To compute earnings per share, the common stockholders' share of the company's net income is divided by the average number of common shares outstanding. Earnings per share applies only to *common stock;* preferred stockholders have no claim to earnings beyond the stipulated preferred stock dividends.

Computing earnings per share is easiest when the corporation has issued only common stock and the number of outstanding shares has not changed during the year. In this case, earnings per share is equal to net income divided by the number of shares outstanding.

In many companies, the number of shares of stock outstanding changes during the year. If additional shares are sold, or if shares of common stock are retired (repurchased from the shareholders), the computation of earnings per share is based on the *weighted-average* number of shares outstanding.[1]

The weighted-average number of shares for the year is determined by multiplying the number of shares outstanding by the fraction of the year that number of shares outstanding remained unchanged. For example, assume that 80,000 shares of common stock were outstanding during the first nine months of 2011 and 140,000 shares were outstanding during the last three months. The increase in shares outstanding resulted from the sale of 60,000 shares for cash. The weighted-average number of shares outstanding during 2011 is *95,000,* determined as follows:

80,000 shares × 9⁄12 of a year	60,000
140,000 shares × 3⁄12 of a year	35,000
Weighted-average number of common shares outstanding	95,000

By using the weighted-average number of shares in calculating earnings per share, we recognize that the cash received from the sale of the 60,000 additional shares was available to generate earnings only during the last three months of the year.

Preferred Dividends and Earnings per Share

When a company has preferred stock outstanding, the preferred stockholders participate in net income only to the extent of the preferred stock dividends. To determine the earnings *applicable to the common stock,* we first deduct from net income the amount of current year preferred dividends. The annual dividend on *cumulative* preferred stock is *always* deducted, even if not declared by the board of directors for the current year. When there are preferred dividends in arrears,

[1] When the number of shares outstanding changes as a result of a stock split or a stock dividend (discussed later in this chapter), the computation of the weighted-average number of shares outstanding should be adjusted *retroactively* rather than weighted for the period the new shares were outstanding. This makes earnings per share data for prior years consistent in terms of the current capital structure.

only the *current year's* cumulative preferred stock dividend is deducted in the earnings per share computation. Noncumulative preferred dividends are deducted only if they have been declared.

To illustrate, let us assume that Perry Corporation has 200,000 shares of common stock and 12,000 shares of $6 cumulative preferred stock outstanding throughout the year. Net income for the year totals $595,000. Earnings per share of common stock would be computed as follows:

Net income	$595,000
Less: Dividends on preferred stock (12,000 shares × $6)	72,000
Earnings applicable to common stock	$523,000
Weighted-average number of common shares outstanding	200,000
Earnings per share of common stock ($523,000 ÷ 200,000 shares)	$2.62

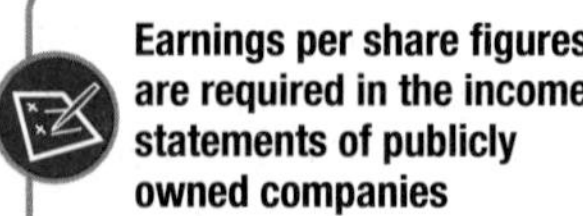

Earnings per share figures are required in the income statements of publicly owned companies

Presentation of Earnings per Share in the Income Statement All publicly owned corporations are *required* to present earnings per share figures in their income statements.[2] If an income statement includes subtotals for income from continuing operations, or for income before extraordinary items, per-share figures are shown for these amounts as well as for net income. These additional per-share amounts are computed by substituting the amount of the appropriate subtotal for the net income figure in the preceding calculation.

To illustrate all of the potential per-share computations, we will expand our Perry Corporation example to include income from continuing operations and income before extraordinary items. We should point out, however, that all of these figures seldom appear in the same income statement. The condensed income statement shown in Exhibit 12–2 is intended to illustrate the proper format for presenting earnings per share figures and to provide a review of the calculations.

Exhibit 12–2
EARNINGS PER SHARE PRESENTATION

PERRY CORPORATION
CONDENSED INCOME STATEMENT
FOR THE YEAR ENDED DECEMBER 31, 2011

Net sales	$9,115,000
Costs and expenses (including tax on continuing operations)	8,310,000
Income from continuing operations	$ 805,000
Loss from discontinued operations (net of income tax benefits)	(90,000)
Income before extraordinary items	$ 715,000
Extraordinary loss (net of income tax benefit)	$ (120,000)
Net income	$ 595,000
Earnings per share of common stock:	
Earnings from continuing operations	$3.67[a]
Loss from discontinued operations	(0.45)
Earnings before extraordinary items	$3.22[b]
Extraordinary loss	(0.60)
Net earnings	$2.62[c]

[a]($805,000 − $72,000 preferred dividends) ÷ 200,000 shares
[b]($715,000 − $72,000) ÷ 200,000 shares
[c]($595,000 − $72,000) ÷ 200,000 shares

[2] The FASB has exempted closely held corporations (those not publicly owned) from the requirement of computing and reporting earnings per share, although some do it voluntarily.

Financial Analysis and Decision Making

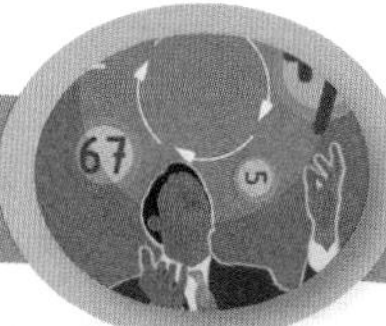

The relationship between earnings per share and stock price is expressed by the **price-earnings (p/e) ratio.** This ratio is simply the current stock price divided by the earnings per share for the year. Price-earnings ratios are of such interest to investors that they are published daily in the financial pages of major newspapers. Price-earnings ratios and other measures useful for evaluating financial performance are covered in Chapter 14.

Stock prices actually reflect investors' expectations of *future* earnings. The p/e ratio, however, is based on the earnings over the *past* year. Thus, if investors expect earnings to *increase* substantially from current levels, the p/e ratio may be quite high—perhaps 20, 30, or even more. But if investors expect earnings to *decline* from current levels, the p/e ratio may be quite low, say, 8 or less. A mature company with stable earnings usually sells between 10 and 12 times earnings. Thus the p/e ratio reflects *investors' expectations* of the company's future prospects.[3]

When using per-share information, it is important to know exactly *which* per-share statistic is being presented. For example, the price-earnings ratios (market price divided by earnings per share) for common stocks listed on major stock exchanges are reported daily in *The Wall Street Journal* and other financial publications. Which earnings per share figures are used in computing these ratios? If a company reports an extraordinary gain or loss, the price-earnings ratio is computed using the per-share *earnings before the extraordinary item.* Otherwise, the ratio is based on *net earnings.*

INTERNATIONAL CASE IN POINT

Valuation multiples such as price-earnings ratios are often used to estimate a firm's value. The use of price multiples to compare firms from different countries is challenging for many reasons. One important reason is that national differences in accounting principles are a source of cross-country differences. For example, research has shown that such differences in accounting principles cause p/e ratios in Japan to be generally lower than in the United States for comparable companies with similar financial results.

YOUR TURN — You as a Financial Analyst

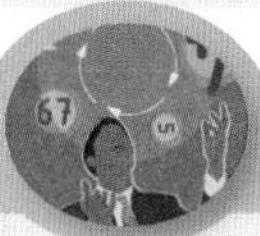

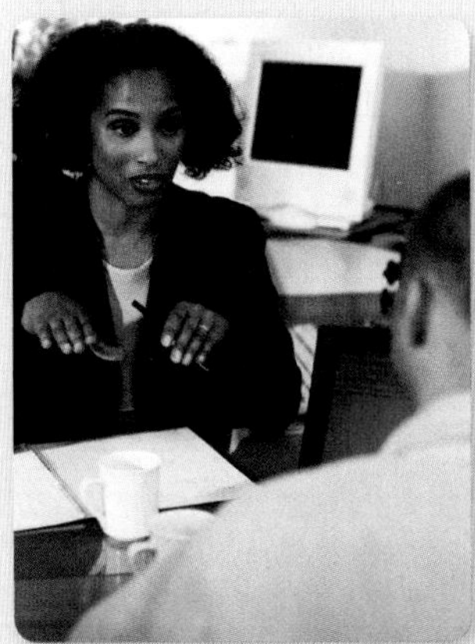

© Ryan McVay/Getty Images/DAL

You are working for a stock market research firm and your boss asks you to present an analysis of Foster, Inc.'s performance, focusing primarily on earnings per share. Her primary purpose for having you do this analysis is to consider whether Foster, Inc., is a good investment in terms of the company's expectations for future profitability. In analyzing Foster, Inc.'s income statement you determine the following:

[3] A word of caution—if current earnings are *very low,* the p/e ratio tends to be quite high *regardless* of whether future earnings are expected to rise or fall. In such situations, the p/e ratio is not a meaningful measurement.

(continued)

	2011	2010	2009
Basic earnings per share on:			
Income from continuing operations	$3.02	$2.56	$1.75
Discontinued operations	(1.90)	(1.05)	(0.15)
Net income	$1.12	$1.51	$1.60

On the basis of only the limited information presented above, what is your recommendation to your boss regarding Foster, Inc.'s prospects for future profitability? Justify your conclusion.

(See our comments on the Online Learning Center Web site.)

Basic and Diluted Earnings per Share

Learning Objective
LO3 **Distinguish between basic and diluted earnings per share.**

Let us assume that a company has an outstanding issue of preferred stock that is convertible into shares of common stock at a rate of two shares of common stock for each share of preferred stock. The conversion of this preferred stock would increase the number of common shares outstanding and might *dilute* (reduce) earnings per share. Any common stockholder interested in the trend of earnings per share needs to know what effect the conversion of the preferred stock would have on earnings per share of common stock. Keep in mind that the decision to convert the preferred shares into common shares is made by the stockholders, not the corporation.

To inform investors of the potential dilution that might occur, two figures are presented for each income number from the income statement. The first figure, called **basic earnings per share,** is based on the weighted-average number of common shares *actually outstanding* during the year. This figure excludes the potential dilution represented by the convertible preferred stock. The second figure, called **diluted earnings per share,** incorporates the *impact that conversion* of the preferred stock would have on basic earnings per share.[4]

Convertible preferred stock is not the only potential diluter of earnings per share. Convertible debt instruments (e.g., convertible bonds) are another type of financial instrument that may reduce earnings per share if the holders choose to redeem them. Similarly, stock options may reduce earnings per share if the holders choose to exercise them and purchase additional shares of stock.

[4] If the preferred stock had been issued during the current year, we would assume that it was converted into common stock on the date it was issued.

To informed users of financial statements, each of these figures has a different significance. Earnings per share from continuing operations represents the results of continuing and ordinary business activity. This figure is the most useful one for predicting future operating results. *Net earnings* per share, on the other hand, shows the overall operating results of the current year, including any discontinued operations and extraordinary items.

Other Transactions Affecting Retained Earnings

CASH DIVIDENDS

Learning Objective
LO4 **Account for cash dividends and stock dividends, and explain the effects of these transactions on a company's financial statements.**

Investors buy stock in a corporation with the expectation of getting their original investment back as well as earning a reasonable return on that investment. The return on a stock investment is a combination of two forms: (1) the increase in value of the stock (stock appreciation) and (2) **cash dividends.**

Some profitable corporations do not pay dividends. Generally, these corporations are in an early stage of development and must conserve cash for the purchase of plant and equipment or for other needs of the company. These so-called growth companies cannot obtain sufficient financing at reasonable interest rates to finance their operations, so they must rely on their earnings. Often only after a significant number of years of profitable operations does the board of directors decide that paying cash dividends is appropriate.

The preceding discussion suggests three requirements for the payment of a cash dividend. These are:

1. *Retained earnings.* Since dividends are a distribution of assets that represent earnings to stockholders, the theoretical maximum for dividends is the total undistributed net income of the company, represented by the credit balance of the Retained Earnings account. As a practical matter, many corporations limit dividends to amounts significantly less than annual net income, on the basis that a major portion of the net income must be retained in the business if the company is to grow and keep pace with its competitors.
2. *An adequate cash position.* The fact that the company reports earnings does not necessarily mean that it has a large amount of cash on hand. Cash generated from earnings may have been invested in new plant and equipment, or it may have already been used to pay off debts or to acquire a larger inventory. There is no necessary relationship between the balance in the Retained Earnings account and the balance in the Cash account. The common expression of "paying dividends out of retained earnings" is misleading. Cash dividends can be paid only out of cash.
3. *Dividend action by the board of directors.* Even though a company's net income is substantial and its cash position seemingly satisfactory, dividends are not paid automatically. A formal action by the board of directors is necessary to declare a dividend.

DIVIDEND DATES

Four significant dates are involved in the distribution of a dividend. These are:

1. *Date of declaration.* On the day on which the dividend is declared by the board of directors, a liability to make the payment comes into existence.
2. *Ex-dividend date.* The **ex-dividend date** is significant for investors in companies whose stocks trade on stock exchanges. To permit the compilation of the list of stockholders as of the record date, it is customary for the stock to go *ex-dividend* three business days before the date of record (see following discussion). A person who buys the stock before the ex-dividend date is entitled to receive the dividend that has already been declared; conversely, a stockholder who sells shares before the ex-dividend date does not receive the dividend. A stock is said to be selling ex-dividend on the day that it *loses* the right to receive the latest declared dividend.
3. *Date of record.* The **date of record** follows the date of declaration, usually by two or three weeks, and is always stated in the dividend declaration. To be eligible to receive the dividend, a person must be listed in the corporation's records as the owner of the stock on this date.
4. *Date of payment.* The declaration of a dividend always includes announcement of the date of payment as well as the date of record. Usually the date of payment comes two to four weeks after the date of record.

Journal entries are required only on the dates of declaration and of payment, as these are the only transactions affecting the corporation declaring the dividend. These entries are illustrated below:

Dec. 15	Dividends	125,000	
	Dividends Payable		125,000
	To record declaration of a cash dividend of $1 per share on the 125,000 shares of common stock outstanding. Payable Jan. 25 to stockholders of record on Jan. 10.		

Entries made on declaration date and . . .

Jan. 25	Dividends Payable	125,000	
	Cash		125,000
	To record payment of $1 per share dividend declared Dec. 15 to stockholders of record on Jan. 10.		

on payment date

No entries are made on either the ex-dividend date or the date of record. These dates are of importance only in determining *to whom* the dividend checks will be sent. From the stockholders' point of view, it is the *ex-dividend date* that determines who receives the dividend. The date of record is of significance primarily to the stock transfer agent and the stock registrar.

At the end of the accounting period, a closing entry is required to transfer the debit balance of the Dividends account into the Retained Earnings account. (Some companies follow the alternative practice of debiting Retained Earnings when the dividend is declared instead of using a Dividends account. Under either method, the balance of the Retained Earnings account ultimately is reduced by all dividends declared during the period.)

LIQUIDATING DIVIDENDS

A *liquidating dividend* occurs when a corporation pays a dividend that *exceeds the balance in the Retained Earnings account.* Thus the dividend returns to stockholders all or part of their paid-in capital investment. Liquidating dividends usually are paid only when a corporation is going out of existence or is making a permanent reduction in the size of its operations. Stockholders may assume that a dividend represents a distribution of profits unless they are notified by the corporation that the dividend is a return of invested capital.

STOCK DIVIDENDS

Stock dividend is a term used to describe a distribution of *additional shares of stock* to a company's stockholders in proportion to their present holdings. In other words, the dividend is payable in additional shares of stock rather than in cash. Most stock dividends consist of additional shares of common stock distributed to holders of common stock. Therefore, our discussion focuses on this type of stock dividend.

An important distinction exists between a cash dividend and a stock dividend. A *cash dividend* is a distribution of cash by a corporation to its stockholders. A cash dividend reduces both assets and stockholders' equity. In a *stock dividend,* however, *no assets are distributed.* Thus a stock dividend causes *no change* in assets, liabilities, or in total stockholders' equity. Each stockholder receives additional shares, but his or her percentage ownership in the corporation is *no larger than before,* and the company receives no assets in the transaction.

To illustrate this point, assume that a corporation with 2,000 shares of stock is owned equally by James Davis and Susan Miller, each owning 1,000 shares of stock. The corporation declares a stock dividend of 10 percent and distributes 200 additional shares (10 percent of 2,000 shares), with 100 shares going to each of the two stockholders. Davis and Miller now hold 1,100 shares apiece, but each *still owns one-half of the business.* Furthermore, the corporation has not changed in size; its assets and liabilities and its total stockholders' equity are exactly the same as before the dividend.

Now let us consider the logical effect of this stock dividend on the *market price* of the company's stock. Assume that, before the stock dividend, the outstanding 2,000 shares in our example had a market price of $110 per share. This price indicates a total market value for the corporation of $220,000 (2,000 shares × $110 per share). Because the stock dividend does not change total assets or total stockholders' equity, the total market value of the corporation *should remain $220,000* after the stock dividend. As 2,200 shares are now outstanding, the market price of each share *should fall* to $100 ($220,000 ÷ 2,200 shares). In other words, the market value of the stock *should fall in proportion* to the number of new shares issued. Whether the market price per share *will* fall in proportion to a small increase in the number of outstanding shares is another matter.

Entries to Record a Stock Dividend

In accounting for relatively *small* stock dividends (say, less than 20 percent), the *market value* of the new shares is transferred from the Retained Earnings account to the paid-in capital accounts. This process sometimes is called *capitalizing* retained earnings. The overall effect is the same as if the dividend had been paid in cash, and the stockholders had immediately reinvested the cash in the business in exchange for additional shares of stock. Of course, no cash actually changes hands—the new shares of stock are simply sent directly to the stockholders.

To illustrate, assume that on June 1, Aspen Corporation has outstanding 100,000 shares of $5 par value common stock with a market value of $25 per share. On this date, the company declares a 10 percent stock dividend, distributable on July 15 to stockholders of record on June 20. The entry at June 1 to record the *declaration* of this dividend is:

Retained Earnings	250,000	
Stock Dividend to Be Distributed		50,000
Additional Paid-in Capital: Stock Dividends		200,000
Declared a 10% stock dividend consisting of 10,000 shares (100,000 shares × 10%) of $5 par value common stock, market price $25 per share. Distributable July 15 to stockholders of record on June 20.		

Stock dividend declared; use market price of stock

The Stock Dividend to Be Distributed account is *not a liability* because there is no obligation to distribute cash or any other asset. If a balance sheet is prepared between the date of declaration of a stock dividend and the date of distribution of the shares, this account, as well as the Additional Paid-in Capital: Stock Dividends account, should be presented in the stockholders' equity section of the balance sheet.

Notice that the Retained Earnings account was reduced by the *market value* of the shares to be issued (10,000 shares × $25 per share = $250,000). Notice also that *no change* occurs in the total amount of stockholders' equity. The amount removed from the Retained Earnings account was simply transferred into two other stockholders' equity accounts.

On July 15, the entry to record the *distribution* of the dividend shares is:

Stock Dividend to Be Distributed	50,000	
Common Stock		50,000
Distributed 10,000-share stock dividend declared June 1.		

Stock dividend distributed

Reasons for Stock Dividends Although stock dividends cause *no change* in total assets, liabilities, or stockholders' equity, they are popular both with management and with stockholders. Management often finds stock dividends appealing because they allow management to distribute something of perceived value to stockholders while conserving cash which may be needed for other purposes like expanding facilities and introducing new product lines.

Stockholders like stock dividends because they receive more shares, often the stock price does *not* fall proportionately, and the dividend is not subject to income taxes (until the shares received are sold). Also, *large* stock dividends tend to keep the stock price down in a trading range that appeals to most investors.

CASE IN POINT

An investor who purchased 100 shares of **Home Depot, Inc.**, in 1985 would have paid about $1,700. Fifteen years later, that stock was worth about $273,000!

Does this mean that each share increased in value from $17 to more than $2,730? No—in fact, this probably couldn't happen. Investors like to buy stock in lots of 100 shares. At $2,730 per share, who could afford 100 shares? Certainly not the average small investor.

Home Depot's board of directors *wanted* to attract small investors. These investors help create more demand for the company's stock—and in many cases, they also become loyal customers.

So as the price of **Home Depot**'s stock rose, the board declared several stock splits and stock dividends. An investor who had purchased 100 shares in 1985 owned over *3,900* shares 15 years later without ever having had to purchase additional shares. Each share had a market value of $70, a price considered affordable to the average investor.

Distinction between Stock Splits and Stock Dividends What is the difference between a stock dividend and a stock split (discussed in Chapter 11)? In some respects the two are similar. Both involve the distribution of shares of a company's own stock to its present stockholders without payment by those stockholders to the company. Both stock dividends and stock splits increase the number of outstanding shares of stock in the company's stockholders' equity. The difference between a stock dividend and a stock split lies in the intent of management and the size of the distribution. A stock dividend usually is intended to substitute for a cash dividend and is small enough that the market price of the stock is relatively unaffected. Stock dividends typically increase the number of outstanding shares by 2, 5, or 10 percent. Stock splits, on the other hand, are intended to reduce the market price of the stock to bring it down to a desired trading range. Stock splits typically represent much larger increases in the number of outstanding shares, such as 100 percent (2:1 split) or 200 percent (3:1 split).

The previous discussion focuses on the purposes and management intent of stock dividends and stock splits. Accounting for the two also varies. Stock dividends do not result in a change in the par value of the stock, and usually an amount equal to the market value of the shares issued is transferred from retained earnings to the par value and additional paid-in capital accounts. Stock splits, on the other hand, result in a pro rata reduction in the par value of the stock and no change in the actual dollar balances of the stockholders' equity accounts. Both stock dividends and stock splits are integral parts of management strategy with regard to the company's ownership, and the accounting differences parallel these differences in management intent.

STATEMENT OF RETAINED EARNINGS

Learning Objective
LO5 Describe and prepare a statement of retained earnings.

The term *retained earnings* refers to the portion of stockholders' equity derived from profitable operations. Retained earnings is increased by earning net income and is reduced by incurring net losses and by the declaration of dividends. Prior period adjustments, discussed later in this chapter, may increase or decrease retained earnings.

In addition to a balance sheet, an income statement, and a statement of cash flows, some companies present a **statement of retained earnings,** as in Exhibit 12–3.

Exhibit 12–3
STATEMENT OF RETAINED EARNINGS FOR SALT LAKE CORPORATION

SALT LAKE CORPORATION STATEMENT OF RETAINED EARNINGS FOR THE YEAR ENDED DECEMBER 31, 2011		
Retained earnings, Dec. 31, 2010		$ 750,000
Net income for 2011		280,000
Subtotal		$1,030,000
Less dividends:		
Cash dividends on preferred stock ($5 per share)	$ 15,000	
Cash dividends on common stock ($2 per share)	59,600	
10% stock dividend	140,000	214,600
Retained earnings, Dec. 31, 2011		$ 815,400

Notice that the 2011 net income is added to the beginning balance of retained earnings. Earlier in this text when we studied the accounting cycle, we learned that, as part of the end-of-period process of closing the books and preparing financial statements, the revenue and expense accounts are brought to a zero balance, and the net amount of these items (either net income or net loss) is added to or subtracted from owners' equity. For a corporation, net income or loss is added to or subtracted from retained earnings. The addition of net income in the statement of retained earnings is a reflection of this closing process. Notice, also, that in the statement of retained earnings the balance is reduced by the amounts of cash dividends declared during the year, as well as the amount of the stock dividend that was declared.

PRIOR PERIOD ADJUSTMENTS

Learning Objective LO6
Define *prior period adjustments*, and explain how they are presented in financial statements.

On occasion, a company may discover that a *material error* was made in the measurement of net income in a prior year. Because net income is closed into the Retained Earnings account, an error in reported net income will cause an error in the amount of retained earnings shown in all subsequent balance sheets. When such errors are discovered, they should be corrected. The correction, called a **prior period adjustment,** is shown in the *statement of retained earnings* as an adjustment to the balance of retained earnings at the beginning of the current year. The amount of the adjustment is shown net of any related income tax effects.

To illustrate, assume that late in 2011 Salt Lake Corporation discovers that it failed to record depreciation on certain assets in 2010. After considering the income tax effects of this error, the company finds that the net income reported in 2010 was overstated by $35,000. Thus, the beginning 2011 balance of the Retained Earnings account ($750,000 at December 31, 2010) also is *overstated by $35,000.* The statement of retained earnings in *2011* must include a *correction* of the retained earnings at the beginning of the year. (See the illustration in Exhibit 12–4.)

Exhibit 12–4
STATEMENT OF RETAINED EARNINGS WITH PRIOR PERIOD ADJUSTMENT

SALT LAKE CORPORATION
STATEMENT OF RETAINED EARNINGS
FOR THE YEAR ENDED DECEMBER 31, 2011

Retained earnings, Dec. 31, 2010		
As originally reported		$750,000
Less: Prior period adjustment for error in recording 2010 depreciation expense (net of $15,000 income taxes)		35,000
As restated		$715,000
Net income for 2011		280,000
Subtotal		$995,000
Less dividends:		
Cash dividends on preferred stock ($5 per share)	$ 15,000	
Cash dividends on common stock ($2 per share)	59,600	
10% stock dividend	140,000	214,600
Retained earnings, Dec. 31, 2011		$780,400

Adjust beginning retained earnings for correction

Prior period adjustments rarely appear in the financial statements of large, publicly owned corporations. The financial statements of these corporations are audited annually by certified public accountants and are not likely to contain material errors that subsequently will require correction by prior period adjustments. Such adjustments are much more likely to appear in the financial statements of closely held corporations that are not audited on an annual basis.

Restrictions of Retained Earnings Some portion of retained earnings may be restricted because of various contractual agreements. A restriction of retained earnings prevents a company from declaring a dividend that would cause retained earnings to fall below a designated level. Most companies disclose restrictions of retained earnings in notes accompanying the financial statements. For example, a company with total retained earnings of $10 million might include the following note in its financial statements:

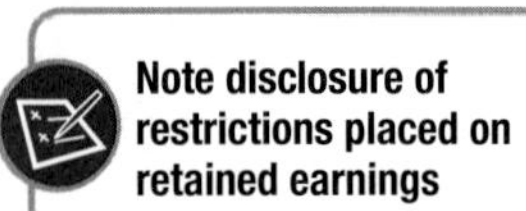

Note disclosure of restrictions placed on retained earnings

Note 7: Restriction of retained earnings
As of December 31, 2011, certain long-term debt agreements prohibited the declaration of cash dividends that would reduce the amount of retained earnings below $5,200,000. Retained earnings in excess of this restriction total $4,800,000.

COMPREHENSIVE INCOME

Learning Objective
LO7 **Define *comprehensive income*, and explain how it differs from net income.**

The Financial Accounting Standards Board (FASB) has identified certain changes in financial position that should be recorded but should not enter into the determination of net income. One way to describe these events is that they are *recognized* (that is, recorded and incorporated in the financial statements) but not *realized* (that is, not included in the determination of the company's net income). We have studied one of these items earlier in this text—the change in market value of available-for-sale debt and equity investments.

Recall from Chapter 7 the way changes in value for various types of investments are recorded. Those investments identified as available for sale are revalued to their current market value at the end of each accounting period. These changes in value are accumulated and reported in a separate stockholders' equity account. The change in value does *not* enter into the determination of net income as it would had investments been sold. The change in market value of available-for-sale investments adds to the amount of stockholders' equity if the value has gone up; it reduces the amount of stockholders' equity if the value has gone down. This adjustment is described as an element of *other comprehensive income.*

Comprehensive income is a term that identifies the total of net income plus or minus the elements of other comprehensive income. Comprehensive income may be displayed to users of financial statements in any of the following ways:

- *As a second income statement.* One income statement displays the components of net income and the other displays the components of comprehensive income, one element of which is net income.
- *As a single income statement* that includes both the components of net income and the components of other comprehensive income.
- *As an element in the changes in stockholders' equity* displayed as a column in the statement of stockholders' equity (discussed later in this chapter).

In addition to the presentation of each year's changes in the elements of other comprehensive income, the accumulated amount of these changes is an element in the stockholders' equity section of the balance sheet. The components of comprehensive income are presented net of income tax, much like an extraordinary item.

Home Depot, Inc., whose financial statements for the year ended January 31, 2010, are included in Appendix A of this text, follows the third of these alternatives and presents comprehensive income as a column in its Consolidated Statements of Stockholders' Equity and Comprehensive Income. For each of the three years presented, the primary adjustments to Comprehensive Income, other than the company's annual net earnings, relate to the company's foreign operations. These are considered part of the company's overall income history, but are not part of its net income that is presented in the income statement. The majority of publicly held companies present the elements of other comprehensive income in a manner similar to **Home Depot, Inc.**

STATEMENT OF STOCKHOLDERS' EQUITY

Learning Objective
LO8 **Describe and prepare a statement of stockholders' equity and the stockholders' equity section of the balance sheet.**

Many corporations expand their statement of retained earnings to show the changes during the year in *all* of the stockholders' equity accounts. This expanded statement, called a **statement of stockholders' equity,** is illustrated in Exhibit 12–5 for Salt Lake Corporation.

The top line of the statement includes the beginning balance of each major category of stockholders' equity. Notice that the fourth column, Retained Earnings, includes the same information as the statement of retained earnings for Salt Lake Corporation that was presented in Exhibit 12–4. We have added several other stock transactions to illustrate the full range of information you will typically find in a statement of stockholders' equity:

- Issuance of common stock for $260,000 (resulting in an increase in both common stock and additional paid-in capital).
- Conversion of shares of preferred stock into common stock at $100,000, resulting in a decrease in 5 percent convertible preferred stock and an increase in common stock and additional paid-in capital.
- Purchase of $47,000 of treasury stock, increasing the amount of treasury stock and decreasing the total of stockholders' equity (as discussed in Chapter 11).

STOCKHOLDERS' EQUITY SECTION OF THE BALANCE SHEET

The stockholders' equity section of Salt Lake Corporation's balance sheet for the year ended December 31, 2011, is shown in Exhibit 12–6. Note that these figures are taken directly from the last line of the statement of stockholders' equity as illustrated in Exhibit 12–5. You should be able to explain the nature and origin of each account and disclosure printed in red as a result of having studied this chapter.

The published financial statements of leading corporations indicate that there is no one standard arrangement for the various items making up the stockholders' equity section. Variations occur in the selection of titles, in the sequence of items, and in the extent of detailed classification. Many companies, in an effort to avoid excessive detail in the balance sheet, combine several related ledger accounts into a single balance sheet item.

Exhibit 12–5 STATEMENT OF STOCKHOLDERS' EQUITY

SALT LAKE CORPORATION
STATEMENT OF STOCKHOLDERS' EQUITY
FOR THE YEAR ENDED DECEMBER 31, 2011

	5% Convertible Preferred Stock ($100 par value)	Common Stock ($10 par value)	Additional Paid-in Capital	Retained Earnings	Treasury Stock	Total Stockholders' Equity
Balances, Dec. 31, 2010	$400,000	$200,000	$300,000	$750,000	$ -0-	$1,650,000
Prior period adjustment (net of $15,000 taxes)				(35,000)		(35,000)
Issued 5,000 common shares @ $52		50,000	210,000			260,000
Conversion of 1,000 preferred into 3,000 common shares	(100,000)	30,000	70,000			
Distributed 10% stock dividend (2,800 shares at $50; market price)		28,000	112,000	(140,000)		
Purchased 1,000 shares of common stock held in treasury at $47 a share					(47,000)	(47,000)
Net income				280,000		280,000
Cash dividends:						
Preferred ($5 a share)				(15,000)		(15,000)
Common ($2 a share)				(59,600)		(59,600)
Balances, Dec. 31, 2011	$300,000	$308,000	$692,000	$780,400	$(47,000)	$2,033,400

Note: The numbers that are not bracketed represent positive stockholders' equity amounts. The bracketed numbers represent negative stockholders' equity amounts.

Exhibit 12-6
STOCKHOLDERS' EQUITY SECTION OF BALANCE SHEET

Stockholders' Equity		
Capital stock:		
5% convertible preferred, $100 par value, 3,000 shares authorized and issued		$ 300,000
Common stock, $10 par value, 100,000 shares authorized, issued 30,800 (of which 1,000 are held in treasury)		308,000
Additional paid-in capital:		
From issuance of common stock	$580,000	
From stock dividends	112,000	692,000
Total paid-in capital		$1,300,000
Retained earnings		780,400
Subtotal		$2,080,400
Less: Treasury stock (1,000 shares at $47 per share)		47,000
Total stockholders' equity		$2,033,400

Ethics, Fraud & Corporate Governance

As discussed in this chapter, the most important aspect of periodic reporting for many investors is the reporting of net income. Investors often are attracted to companies that report increasing income each year. As a result, overstating net income is the most common practice for engaging in inappropriate financial reporting.

The Securities and Exchange Commission (SEC) brought a series of enforcement actions against **Just for Feet, Inc.**, its former employees, and employees of former vendors related to the overstatement of **Just for Feet**'s reported income. Although **Just for Feet** overstated its income through a number of different techniques, two prominent techniques used to overstate income related to fictitious co-op revenue and fictitious "booth" income.

Learning Objective LO9
Illustrate steps management might take to improve the appearance of the company's net income.

Just for Feet was a national retailer of athletic and outdoor footwear and apparel. **Just for Feet** filed for bankruptcy protection, and it began the process of liquidating its assets and settling its liabilities.

Just for Feet incurred large amounts of advertising expenses. A vendor (e.g., **Adidas**, **Fila**, **Nike**) would often reduce the amount that **Just for Feet** owed for merchandise purchases if a particular advertisement featured the vendor's products. These reductions in amounts owed were referred to as "advertising co-op" or "vendor allowances." These vendor allowances were unwritten and not guaranteed. **Just for Feet** sent vendors copies of advertisements placed, and the vendor determined whether to grant an advertising allowance.

In one fiscal year, **Just for Feet** recorded $19.4 million in co-op receivables (and recognized revenue as a result of recording the receivables) that was not earned. The fictitious revenue of over $19 million was a substantial percentage of **Just for Feet**'s reported income of $43 million.

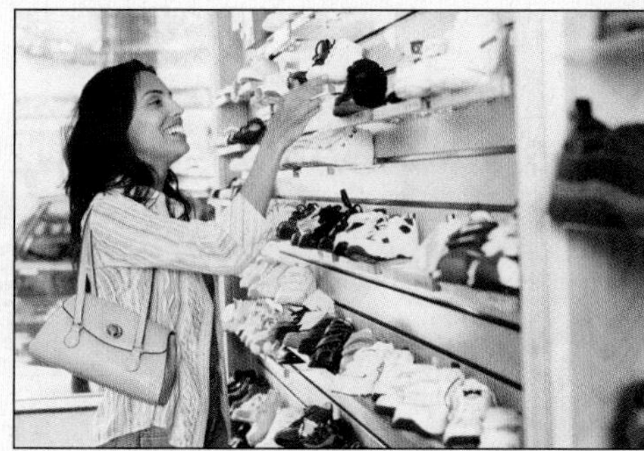

© Blend Images/Getty Images/DAL

One important facet of the **Just for Feet** fraud is that the SEC brought enforcement actions against a number of vendor representatives for providing false confirmations to **Just for Feet**'s auditor. When fraud exists, management at the company committing the fraud often tries to convince customers to falsely confirm to the auditors that they owe amounts that are in fact not owed. Such behavior represents a crime. It is worth noting that the criminal penalties for lying to external auditors have been substantially increased under the Sarbanes-Oxley Act, and that the SEC and the U.S. Justice Department are more likely to prosecute individuals for this type of behavior than was true in the past. Individuals in sales and marketing positions are often targets for requests to falsely confirm facts to external auditors (i.e., to lie). They should be aware of the substantial civil and criminal penalties that can result from lying to auditors.

Concluding Remarks

We discussed various aspects of stockholders' equity, focusing first on paid-in capital in Chapter 11 and then on earned capital in Chapter 12. These discussions complete our detailed coverage of assets, liabilities, and stockholders' equity, which began in Chapter 7 and included financial assets, inventories, plant and intangible assets, liabilities, and, finally, stockholders' equity. While these chapters generally follow a balance sheet organization, in Chapter 12 we also covered the income statement, including the presentation of irregular income items and earnings per share.

In the next chapter, we turn our attention to the statement of cash flows. Recall that companies present three primary financial statements to their stockholders, creditors, and other interested parties—a statement of financial position or balance sheet, an income statement, and a statement of cash flows. We delayed the detailed coverage of the statement of cash flows to this point in this textbook because of the importance of the material we have now covered, particularly in Chapters 7 to 12, for a full understanding of that financial statement.

END-OF-CHAPTER REVIEW

SUMMARY OF LEARNING OBJECTIVES

LO1 **Describe how irregular income items, such as discontinued operations and extraordinary items, are presented in the income statement.** Each of these irregular items is shown in a separate section of the income statement, following income or loss from ordinary and continuing operations. Each special item is shown net of any related income tax effects.

LO2 **Compute earnings per share.** Earnings per share is computed by dividing the income applicable to the common stock by the weighted-average number of common shares outstanding. If the income statement includes subtotals for income from continuing operations, or for income before extraordinary items, per-share figures are shown for these amounts, as well as for net income.

LO3 **Distinguish between basic and diluted earnings per share.** Diluted earnings per share is computed for companies that have outstanding securities convertible into shares of common stock. In such situations, the computation of basic earnings per share is based on the number of common shares actually outstanding during the year. The computation of diluted earnings per share, however, is based on the potential number of common shares outstanding if the various securities were converted into common shares. The purpose of showing diluted earnings is to alert investors to the extent to which conversions of securities could reduce basic earnings per share.

LO4 **Account for cash dividends and stock dividends, and explain the effects of these transactions on a company's financial statements.** Cash dividends reduce retained earnings at the time the company's board of directors declares the dividends. At that time, the dividends become a liability for the company. Stock dividends generally are recorded by transferring the market value of the additional shares to be issued from retained earnings to the appropriate paid-in capital accounts. Stock dividends increase the number of shares outstanding but do not change total stockholders' equity, nor do they change the relative amount of the company owned by each individual stockholder.

LO5 **Describe and prepare a statement of retained earnings.** A statement of retained earnings shows the changes in the balance of the Retained Earnings account during the period. In its simplest form, this financial statement shows the beginning balance of retained earnings, adds the net income for the period, subtracts any dividends declared, and thus computes the ending balance of retained earnings.

LO6 **Define *prior period adjustments*, and explain how they are presented in financial statements.** A prior period adjustment corrects errors in the amount of net income reported in a *prior* year. Because the income of the prior year has already been closed into retained earnings, the error is corrected by increasing or decreasing the Retained Earnings account. Prior period adjustments appear in the statement of retained earnings as adjustments to beginning retained earnings. They are *not* reported in the income statement for the current period.

LO7 **Define *comprehensive income*, and explain how it differs from net income.** Net income is a component of comprehensive income. Comprehensive income is broad and includes the effect of certain transactions that are recognized in the financial statements but that are not included in net income because they have not yet been realized. An example is the change in market value of available-for-sale investments. Net income is presented in the income statement. Comprehensive income may be presented in a combined statement with net income, in a separate statement of comprehensive income, or as a part of the statement of stockholders' equity.

LO8 **Describe and prepare a statement of stockholders' equity and the stockholders' equity section of the balance sheet.** This expanded version of the statement of retained earnings explains the changes during the year in each stockholders' equity account. It is not a required financial statement but is often prepared instead of a statement of retained earnings. The statement lists the beginning balance in each stockholders' equity account, explains the nature and the amount of each change, and computes the ending balance in each equity account.

LO9 **Illustrate steps management might take to improve the appearance of the company's net income.** Companies may take certain steps that are intended to improve the appearance of the company's financial performance in its financial statements. The Securities and Exchange Commission brought a series of enforcement actions against **Just for Feet** for taking steps to artificially enhance the appearance of the company's performance.

Key Terms Introduced or Emphasized in Chapter 12

basic earnings per share (p. 528) Net income applicable to the common stock divided by the weighted-average number of common shares outstanding during the year.

cash dividend (p. 528) A distribution of cash by a corporation to its stockholders.

comprehensive income (p. 534) Net income plus or minus certain changes in financial position that are recorded as direct adjustments to stockholders' equity (for example, changes in the value of available-for-sale investments) rather than as elements in the determination of net income.

date of record (p. 529) The date on which a person must be listed as a shareholder to be eligible to receive a dividend. Follows the date of declaration of a dividend by two or three weeks.

diluted earnings per share (p. 528) Earnings per share computed under the assumption that all convertible securities were converted into additional common shares at the beginning of the current year. The purpose of this pro forma computation is to alert common stockholders to the risk that future earnings per share might be reduced by the conversion of other securities into common stock.

discontinued operations (p. 523) The net operating results (revenue and expenses) of a segment of a company that has been or is being sold, as well as the gain or loss on disposal.

earnings per share (p. 525) Net income applicable to the common stock divided by the weighted-average number of common shares outstanding during the year.

ex-dividend date (p. 529) A date three days prior to the date of record specified in a dividend declaration. A person buying a stock prior to the ex-dividend date also acquires the right to receive the dividend. The three-day interval permits the compilation of a list of stockholders as of the date of record.

extraordinary items (p. 523) Transactions and events that are unusual in nature and occur infrequently—for example, most large earthquake losses. Such items are shown separately in the income statement after the determination of income before extraordinary items.

price-earnings (p/e) ratio (p. 527) Market price of a share of common stock divided by annual earnings per share.

prior period adjustment (p. 533) A correction of a material error in the earnings reported in the financial statements of a prior year. Prior period adjustments are recorded directly in the Retained Earnings account and are not included in the income statement of the current period.

restructuring charges (p. 524) Costs related to reorganizing and downsizing the company to make the company more efficient. These costs are presented in the income statement as a single line item in determining operating income.

segment of the business (p. 523) Those elements of a business that represent a separate and distinct line of business activity or that service a distinct category of customers.

statement of retained earnings (p. 532) A financial statement explaining the change during the year in the amount of retained earnings. May be expanded into a statement of stockholders' equity.

statement of stockholders' equity (p. 534) An expanded version of a statement of retained earnings. Summarizes the changes during the year in all stockholders' equity accounts. Not a required financial statement, but widely used as a substitute for the statement of retained earnings.

stock dividend (p. 530) A distribution of additional shares to common stockholders in proportion to their holdings.

Demonstration Problem

The stockholders' equity of Embassy Corporation at December 31, 2010, is shown below.

Stockholders' equity:	
Common stock, $10 par, 100,000 shares authorized,	
40,000 shares issued and outstanding	$ 400,000
Additional paid-in capital: common stock	200,000
Total paid-in capital	$ 600,000
Retained earnings	1,700,000
Total stockholders' equity	$2,300,000

Transactions affecting stockholders' equity during 2011 are as follows:

Mar. 31 A 5-for-4 stock split proposed by the board of directors was approved by vote of the stockholders. The 10,000 new shares were distributed to stockholders.

Apr. 1 The company purchased 2,000 shares of its common stock on the open market at $37 per share.

July 1 The company reissued 1,000 shares of treasury stock at $48 per share.

July 1 The company issued for cash 20,000 shares of previously unissued $8 par value common stock at a price of $47 per share.

Dec. 1 A cash dividend of $1 per share was declared, payable on December 30, to stockholders of record at December 14.

Dec. 22 A 10 percent stock dividend was declared; the dividend shares are to be distributed on January 15 of the following year. The market price of the stock on December 22 was $48 per share.

The net income for the year ended December 31, 2011, amounted to $173,000, after an extraordinary loss of $47,400 (net of related income tax benefits).

Instructions

a. Prepare journal entries (in general journal form) to record the transactions affecting stockholders' equity that took place during the year.

b. Prepare the lower section of the income statement for 2011, beginning with *income before extraordinary items* and showing the extraordinary loss and the net income. Also illustrate the presentation of earnings per share in the income statement, assuming that earnings per share is determined on the basis of the *weighted-average* number of shares outstanding during the year.

c. Prepare a statement of retained earnings for the year ending December 31, 2011.

Solution to the Demonstration Problem

a.

GENERAL JOURNAL — **Page 1**

Date		Account Titles and Explanations	Debit	Credit
Mar.	31	Memorandum: A 5-for-4 stock split increased the number of shares of common stock outstanding from 40,000 to 50,000 and reduced the par value from $10 to $8 per share. The 10,000 new shares were distributed.		
Apr.	1	Treasury Stock	74,000	
		Cash		74,000
		Acquired 2,000 shares of treasury stock at $37.		
July	1	Cash	48,000	
		Treasury Stock		37,000
		Additional Paid-in Capital: Treasury Stock Transactions		11,000
		Sold 1,000 shares of treasury stock at $48 per share.		
July	1	Cash	940,000	
		Common Stock, $8 par		160,000
		Additional Paid-in Capital: Common Stock		780,000
		Issued 20,000 shares at $47.		
Dec.	1	Dividends	69,000	
		Dividends Payable		69,000
		To record declaration of cash dividend of $1 per share on 69,000 shares of common stock outstanding (1,000 shares in treasury are not entitled to receive dividends).		
		Note: Entry to record the payment of the cash dividend is not shown here because the action does not affect the stockholders' equity.		
Dec.	22	Retained Earnings	331,200	
		Stock Dividends to Be Distributed		55,200
		Additional Paid-in Capital: Stock Dividends		276,000
		To record declaration of 10% stock dividend (10% × 69,000 shares outstanding): 6,900 shares of $8 par value common stock to be distributed on Jan. 15 of next year. Market price at date of issuance, $48.		
Dec.	31	Income Summary	173,000	
		Retained Earnings		173,000
		To close Income Summary account.		
Dec.	31	Retained Earnings	69,000	
		Dividends		69,000
		To close Dividends account.		

b.

EMBASSY CORPORATION
PARTIAL INCOME STATEMENT
FOR THE YEAR ENDED DECEMBER 31, 2011

Income before extraordinary items	$220,400
Extraordinary loss (net of income tax benefit)	(47,400)
Net income	$173,000
Earnings per share:*	
Income before extraordinary items	$3.73
Extraordinary loss	(0.80)
Net income	$2.93

*The 59,000 weighted-average number of shares of common stock outstanding during 2011 determined as follows:

Jan. 1–Mar. 31: (40,000 + 10,000 shares issued pursuant to a 5-for-4 split) × ¼ of year	12,500
Apr. 1–June 30: (50,000 − 2,000 shares of treasury stock) × ¼ of year	12,000
July 1–Dec. 31: (50,000 + 20,000 shares of new stock − 1,000 shares of treasury stock) × ½ of year	34,500
Weighted-average number of shares outstanding	59,000

c.

EMBASSY CORPORATION
STATEMENT OF RETAINED EARNINGS
FOR THE YEAR ENDED DECEMBER 31, 2011

Retained earnings, Dec. 31, 2010		$1,700,000
Net income for 2011		173,000
Subtotal		$1,873,000
Less: Cash dividends ($1 per share)	$ 69,000	
10% stock dividend	331,200	400,200
Retained earnings, Dec. 31, 2011		$1,472,800

Self-Test Questions

The answers to these questions appear on page 561.

1. The primary purpose of showing special types of events separately in the income statement is to:
   - **a.** Increase earnings per share.
   - **b.** Assist users of the income statement in evaluating the profitability of normal, ongoing operations.
   - **c.** Minimize the income taxes paid on the results of ongoing operations.
   - **d.** Prevent unusual losses from recurring.
2. Which of the following situations would *not* be presented in a separate section of the current year's income statement of Hamilton Corporation? During the current year:
   - **a.** Hamilton's Los Angeles headquarters are destroyed by a tornado.
   - **b.** Hamilton sells its entire juvenile furniture operations and concentrates on its remaining children's clothing segment.
   - **c.** Hamilton's accountant discovers that the entire price paid several years ago to purchase company offices in Texas had been charged to a Land account; consequently, no depreciation has ever been taken on these buildings.
   - **d.** As a result of labor union contract changes, Hamilton paid increased compensation expense during the year.
3. When a corporation has outstanding both common and preferred stock:
   - **a.** Basic and diluted earnings per share are reported only if the preferred stock is cumulative.
   - **b.** Earnings per share is reported for each type of stock outstanding.
   - **c.** Earnings per share is computed without regard to the amount of the annual preferred dividends.
   - **d.** Earnings per share is computed without regard to the amount of dividends declared on common stock.

4. Which of the following is (are) *not* true about a stock dividend?
   a. Total stockholders' equity does not change when a stock dividend is declared but does change when it is distributed.
   b. Between the time a stock dividend is declared and when it is distributed, the company's commitment is presented in the balance sheet as a current liability.
   c. Stock dividends do not change the relative portion of the company owned by individual stockholders.
   d. Stock dividends have no impact on the amount of the company's assets.

5. The statement of retained earnings:
   a. Includes prior period adjustments, cash dividends, and stock dividends.
   b. Indicates the amount of cash available for the payment of dividends.
   c. Need not be prepared if a separate statement of stockholders' equity accompanies the financial statements.
   d. Shows revenue, expenses, and dividends for the accounting period.

ASSIGNMENT MATERIAL Discussion Questions

1. What is the purpose of arranging an income statement to show subtotals for *income from continuing operations* and *income before extraordinary items*?

2. Frank's Fun Company owns 30 pizza parlors and a minor league baseball team. During the current year, the company sold three of its pizza parlors and closed another when the lease on the building expired. Should any of these events be classified as discontinued operations in the company's income statement? Explain.

3. Define *extraordinary items.* How are extraordinary items distinguished from items that are presented as separate line items in an income statement, but are not extraordinary?

4. In an effort to make the company more competitive, Fast-Guard, Inc., incurred significant expenses related to a reduction in the number of employees, consolidation of offices and facilities, and disposition of assets that are no longer productive. Explain how these costs should be presented in the financial statements of the company, and describe how an investor should view these costs in predicting future earnings of the company.

5. A *prior period adjustment* relates to the income of past accounting periods. Explain how such an item is shown in the financial statements.

6. In evaluating the potential future profitability of a company, how would you consider irregular income items, such as extraordinary items, discontinued operations, and prior period adjustments?

7. Explain how each of the following is computed:
   a. Price-earnings ratio.
   b. Basic earnings per share.
   c. Diluted earnings per share.

8. Throughout the year, Baker Construction Company had 3 million shares of common stock and 150,000 shares of convertible preferred stock outstanding. Each share of preferred is convertible into two shares of common. What number of shares should be used in the computation of (**a**) basic earnings per share and (**b**) diluted earnings per share?

9. A financial analyst notes that Collier Corporation's earnings per share have been rising steadily for the past five years. The analyst expects the company's net income to continue to increase at the same rate as in the past. In forecasting future basic earnings per share, what special risk should the analyst consider if Collier's basic earnings are significantly larger than its diluted earnings?

10. Distinguish between a *stock split* and a *stock dividend.* Is there any reason for the difference in accounting treatment of these two events?

11. What are *restructuring charges*? How are they presented in financial statements?

12. If a company's total stockholders' equity is unchanged by the distribution of a stock dividend, how is it possible for a stockholder who received shares in the distribution of the dividend to benefit?

13. What is a liquidating dividend, and how does it relate to a regular (nonliquidating) dividend?

14. In discussing stock dividends and stock splits in an investments class you are taking, one of the students says, "Stock splits and stock dividends are exactly the same—both are distributions of a company's stock to existing owners without payment to the company." Do you agree? Why or why not?

15. A *statement of stockholders' equity* sometimes is described as an "expanded" statement of retained earnings. Why?

Brief Exercises

LO1 BRIEF EXERCISE 12.1
Extraordinary Loss

Fellups, Inc., had net income for the year just ended of $75,000, without considering the following item or its tax effects. During the year, a tornado damaged one of the company's warehouses and its contents. Tornado damage is quite rare in Fellups's location. The estimated amount of the loss from the tornado is $100,000 and the related tax effect is 40 percent. Prepare the final section of Fellups's income statement, beginning with income before extraordinary items.

LO1 BRIEF EXERCISE 12.2
Extraordinary Gain

Walker Company had total revenue and expense numbers of $1,500,000 and $1,200,000, respectively, in the current year. In addition, the company had a gain of $230,000 that resulted from the passage of new legislation, which is considered unusual and infrequent for financial reporting purposes. The gain is expected to be subject to a 35 percent income tax rate. Prepare an abbreviated income statement for Walker for the year.

LO1 BRIEF EXERCISE 12.3
Discontinued Operations

Wabash, Inc., had revenue and expenses from ongoing business operations for the current year of $480,000 and $430,000, respectively. During the year, the company sold a division which had revenue and expenses (not included in the previous figures) of $100,000 and $75,000, respectively. The division was sold at a loss of $55,000. All items are subject to an income tax rate of 40 percent. Prepare an abbreviated income statement for Wabash for the year.

LO4 BRIEF EXERCISE 12.4
Cash and Stock Dividends

Gannon, Inc., had 100,000 shares of common stock outstanding. During the current year, the company distributed a 10 percent stock dividend and subsequently paid a $0.50 per share cash dividend. Calculate the number of shares outstanding at the time of the cash dividend and the amount of cash required to fund the cash dividend.

LO5 BRIEF EXERCISE 12.5
Statement of Retained Earnings

Messer Company had retained earnings at the beginning of the current year of $590,000. During the year, the following activities occurred:

- Net income of $88,000 was earned.
- A cash dividend of $1.20 per share was declared and distributed on the 50,000 shares of common stock outstanding.

Prepare a statement of retained earnings for the year.

LO5 LO6 BRIEF EXERCISE 12.6
Statement of Retained Earnings

Salt & Pepper, Inc., had retained earnings at the beginning of the current year of $460,000. During the year the company earned net income of $250,000 and declared dividends as follows:

- $1 per share for the current-year dividend on the 10,000 shares of preferred stock outstanding.
- $1 per share for the dividend in arrears for one year on the 10,000 shares of preferred stock outstanding.
- $0.50 per share for the current-year dividend on the 200,000 shares of common stock outstanding.

In addition, the company discovered an overstatement in the prior year's net income of $65,000 and corrected that error in the current year. Prepare a statement of retained earnings for the year.

LO4 BRIEF EXERCISE 12.7
Cash Dividend Journal Entries

Gammon, Inc., declared dividends during the current year as follows:

- The current year's cash dividend on the 6 percent, $100 par value preferred stock. 100,000 shares were outstanding at the time of the declaration.
- A cash dividend of $0.75 per share on the $10 par value common stock. 750,000 shares were outstanding at the time of the declaration.

Prepare the general journal entries to record the declaration and payment of these dividends, assuming the declaration is recorded directly to retained earnings.

LO4 **BRIEF EXERCISE 12.8**
Stock Dividend Journal Entries

WOW! Inc. declared a 5 percent stock dividend on its 500,000 shares of common stock. The $10 par value common stock was originally sold for $12 and was selling at $15 at the time the stock dividend was declared. Prepare the general journal entries to record and distribute the stock dividend.

LO4 LO8 **BRIEF EXERCISE 12.9**
Stockholders' Equity Section of Balance Sheet

Alexander, Inc., declared and distributed a 10 percent stock dividend on its 700,000 shares of outstanding $5 par value common stock when the stock was selling for $12 per share. The outstanding shares had originally been sold at $8 per share. The balance in retained earnings before the declaration of the stock dividend, but after the addition of the current year's net income, was $995,000. Prepare the stockholders' section of Alexander's balance sheet to reflect these facts.

LO7 **BRIEF EXERCISE 12.10**
Comprehensive Income

Crasher Company had net income in the current year of $500,000. In addition, the company had an unrealized gain on its portfolio of available-for-sale investments of $20,000, net of related income taxes. Assuming the company uses the two-income statement approach for presenting elements of other comprehensive income to its investors and creditors, prepare the statement of comprehensive income for the current year.

Exercises

LO4 **EXERCISE 12.1**
Stock Dividends and Stock Splits

Assume that when you were in high school you saved $1,000 to invest for your college education. You purchased 200 shares of Smiley Incorporated, a small but profitable company. Over the three years that you have owned the stock, the corporation's board of directors have taken the following actions:

1. Declared a 2-for-1 stock split.
2. Declared a 20 percent stock dividend.
3. Declared a 3-for-1 stock split.

The current price of the stock is $12 per share.

a. Calculate the current number of shares and the market value of your investment.

b. Explain the likely reason the board of directors of the company has not declared a cash dividend.

c. State your opinion as to whether or not you would have been better off if the board of directors had declared a cash dividend instead of the stock dividend and stock splits.

LO1 through LO4, LO6, LO7 **EXERCISE 12.2**
Accounting Terminology

The following are 10 technical accounting terms introduced or emphasized in Chapters 11 and 12:

P/e ratio	Treasury stock	Discontinued operations
Stock dividend	Extraordinary item	Prior period adjustment
Basic earnings per share	Additional paid-in capital	Diluted earnings per share
Comprehensive income		

Each of the following statements may (or may not) describe one of these technical terms. For each statement, indicate the term described, or answer "None" if the statement does not correctly describe any of the terms.

a. A gain or loss that is unusual in nature and not expected to recur in the foreseeable future.

b. The asset represented by shares of capital stock that have not yet been issued.

c. A distribution of additional shares of stock that reduces retained earnings but causes no change in total stockholders' equity.

d. The amount received when stock is sold in excess of par value.

e. An adjustment to the beginning balance of retained earnings to correct an error previously made in the measurement of net income.

f. A statistic expressing a relationship between the current market value of a share of common stock and the underlying earnings per share.

g. A separate section sometimes included in an income statement as a way to help investors evaluate the profitability of ongoing business activities.

h. A pro forma figure indicating what earnings per share would have been if all securities convertible into common stock had been converted at the beginning of the current year.

i. A broadly defined measure of financial performance that includes, but is not limited to, net income.

LO1 LO2

EXERCISE 12.3

Discontinued Operations

During the current year, Sports +, Inc., operated two business segments: a chain of surf and dive shops and a small chain of tennis shops. The tennis shops were not profitable and were sold near year-end to another corporation. Sports + operations for the current year are summarized below. The first two captions, "Net sales" and "Costs and expenses," relate only to the company's continuing operations.

Net sales	$12,500,000
Costs and expenses (including applicable income tax)	8,600,000
Operating loss from tennis shops (net of income tax benefit)	192,000
Loss on sale of tennis shops (net of income tax benefit)	348,000

The company had 182,000 shares of a single class of capital stock outstanding throughout the year.

a. Prepare a condensed income statement for the year. At the bottom of the statement, show any appropriate earnings per share figures. (A condensed income statement is illustrated in Exhibit 12–2.)

b. Which earnings per share figure in part **a** do you consider most useful in predicting future operating results for Sports +, Inc.? Why?

LO1 LO2

EXERCISE 12.4

Reporting an Extraordinary Item

For the year ended December 31, Global Exports had net sales of $7,750,000, costs and other expenses (including income tax) of $6,200,000, and an extraordinary gain (net of income tax) of $420,000.

a. Prepare a condensed income statement (including earnings per share), assuming that 910,000 shares of common stock were outstanding throughout the year. (A condensed income statement is illustrated in Exhibit 12–2.)

b. Which earnings per share figure is used in computing the price-earnings ratio for Global Exports reported in financial publications such as *The Wall Street Journal*? Explain briefly.

LO2

EXERCISE 12.5

Computing Earnings per Share: Effect of Preferred Stock

The net income of Foster Furniture, Inc., amounted to $1,920,000 for the current year.

a. Compute the amount of earnings per share assuming that the shares of capital stock outstanding throughout the year consisted of:

1. 400,000 shares of $1 par value common stock and no preferred stock.

2. 100,000 shares of 8 percent, $100 par value preferred stock and 300,000 shares of $5 par value common stock.

b. Is the earnings per share figure computed in part **a(2)** considered to be basic or diluted? Explain.

LO2 LO4

EXERCISE 12.6

Restating Earnings per Share after a Stock Dividend

The 2010 annual report of Software City, Inc., included the following comparative summary of earnings per share over the last three years:

	2010	2009	2008
Earnings per share	$3.15	$2.40	$1.64

In 2011, Software City, Inc., declared and distributed a 100 percent stock dividend. Following this stock dividend, the company reported earnings per share of $1.88 for 2011.

a. Prepare a three-year schedule similar to the one above, but compare earnings per share during the years 2011, 2010, and 2009. (Hint: All per-share amounts in your schedule should be based on the number of shares outstanding *after* the stock dividend.)

b. In preparing your schedule, which figure (or figures) did you have to restate? Why? Explain the logic behind your computation.

LO4

EXERCISE 12.7

Cash Dividends, Stock Dividends, and Stock Splits

HiTech Manufacturing Company has 1,000,000 shares of $1 par value capital stock outstanding on January 1. The following equity transactions occurred during the current year:

Apr. 30 Distributed additional shares of capital stock in a 2-for-1 stock split. Market price of stock was $35 per share.

June 1 Declared a cash dividend of $0.60 per share.

July 1 Paid the $0.60 cash dividend to stockholders.

Aug. 1 Declared a 5 percent stock dividend. Market price of stock was $19 per share.

Sept. 10 Issued shares resulting from the 5 percent stock dividend declared on August 1.

a. Prepare journal entries to record the above transactions.

b. Compute the number of shares of capital stock outstanding at year-end.

c. What is the par value per share of HiTech Manufacturing stock at the end of the year?

d. Determine the effect of each of the following on *total* stockholders' equity: stock split, declaration and payment of a cash dividend, declaration and distribution of a stock dividend. (Your answers should be either *increase, decrease,* or *no effect.*)

LO4

EXERCISE 12.8

Effect of Stock Dividends on Stock Price

Express, Inc., has a total of 80,000 shares of common stock outstanding and no preferred stock. Total stockholders' equity at the end of the current year amounts to $5 million and the market value of the stock is $66 per share. At year-end, the company declares a 10 percent stock dividend—one share for each 10 shares held. If all parties concerned clearly recognize the nature of the stock dividend, what should you expect the market price per share of the common stock to be on the ex-dividend date?

LO8

EXERCISE 12.9

Reporting the Effects of Transactions

Five events pertaining to Lubbock Manufacturing Co. are described below.

a. Declared and paid a cash dividend.

b. Issued a 10 percent stock dividend.

c. Issued a 2-for-1 stock split.

d. Purchased treasury stock.

e. Reissued the treasury stock at a price greater than the purchase price.

Indicate the immediate effects of the events on the financial measurements in the four columnar headings listed below. Use the code letters **I** for increase, **D** for decrease, and **NE** for no effect.

Event	Current Assets	Stockholders' Equity	Net Income	Net Cash Flow (from any source)

LO2 LO4

EXERCISE 12.10

Effects of Various Transactions on Earnings per Share

Explain the immediate effects, if any, of each of the following transactions on a company's earnings per share:

a. Split the common stock 3-for-1.

b. Realized a gain from the sale of a discontinued operation.

c. Declared and paid a cash dividend on common stock.

d. Declared and distributed a stock dividend on common stock.

e. Acquired several thousand shares of treasury stock.

LO1 LO5 LO8

EXERCISE 12.11
Where to Find Financial Information

You have now learned about the following financial statements issued by corporations: balance sheet, income statement, statement of retained earnings, statement of stockholders' equity, and statement of cash flows. Listed below are various items frequently of interest to a corporation's owners, potential investors, and creditors, among others. You are to specify which of the above corporate financial statements, if any, reports the desired information. If the listed item is not reported in any formal financial statement issued by a corporation, indicate an appropriate source for the desired information.

a. Number of shares of stock outstanding as of year-end.

b. Total dollar amount of cash dividends declared during the current year.

c. Market value per share at balance sheet date.

d. Cumulative dollar effect of an accounting error made in a previous year.

e. Detailed disclosure of why the number of shares of stock outstanding at the end of the current year is greater than the number of shares of stock outstanding at the end of the prior year.

f. Earnings per share of common stock.

g. Book value per share.

h. Price-earnings (p/e) ratio.

i. The total amount the corporation paid to buy back shares of its own stock, which it now holds.

LO7

EXERCISE 12.12
Comprehensive Income

Minor, Inc., had revenue of $572,000 and expenses (other than income taxes) of $282,000 for the current year. The company is subject to a 35 percent income tax rate. In addition, available-for-sale investments, which were purchased for $17,500 early in the year, had a market value at the end of the year of $19,200.

a. Determine the amount of Minor's net income for the year.

b. Determine the amount of Minor's comprehensive income for the year.

c. How would your answers to parts **a** and **b** differ if the market value of Minor's investments at the end of the year had been $14,200?

LO4

EXERCISE 12.13
Cash and Stock Dividends

Kosmier Company has outstanding 500,000 shares of $50 par value common stock that originally sold for $60 per share. During the three most recent years, the company carried out the following activities in the order presented: declared and distributed a 10 percent stock dividend, declared and paid a cash dividend of $1 per share, declared and distributed a 2-for-1 stock split, and declared and paid a $0.60 per share cash dividend.

a. Determine the number of shares of stock outstanding after the four transactions described above.

b. Determine the amount of cash that the company paid in the four transactions described above.

c. If you were a stockholder who held 100 shares of stock that you purchased four years ago when the market value of the shares was $65, how many shares would you own after the four transactions described above? If the market value of the stock was $40 after the four transactions, would you be better or worse off than before the four transactions?

LO3 LO5

EXERCISE 12.14
EPS and Dividends Using **Home Depot, Inc.**, Financial Statements

Home Depot, Inc.'s income statements for 2007, 2008, and 2009 show basic earnings per share of $2.38, $1.34, and $1.58, respectively. Diluted earnings per share figures are slightly lower than these numbers, indicating the impact of potential capital stock activity that could reduce earnings per share for current stockholders.

The company paid cash dividends of $0.90 per share in each of 2007, 2008, and 2009.

a. Why do you think **Home Depot** is paying out only about 38 percent to 67 percent of its net income to stockholders in the form of cash dividends?

b. If you were an investor in **Home Depot**'s stock, would you be unhappy because your dividends represented such a small percentage of the company's net income?

LO1 LO8 **EXERCISE 12.15**
Analysis of Stock Information using **Home Depot, Inc.**, Financial Statements

Use the financial statements of **Home Depot, Inc.**, in Appendix A of this text to answer these questions:

a. Study the income statements of **Home Depot, Inc.**, for the three years ending on or about February 1, 2010, 2009, and 2008. Do these statements include any irregular items that might affect your use of the information to project future earnings?

b. Review the stockholders' equity section of the company's balance sheet at January 31, 2010. What type of capital stock is in the capital structure, and how many shares are authorized, issued, and outstanding, and held in treasury on that date?

c. Locate the statement of stockholders' equity and comprehensive income. What treasury stock transactions has **Home Depot** engaged in during the three-year period presented? Has any additional stock (other than treasury stock) been issued during the period reported? If so, what were the circumstances in which that stock was issued?

Problem Set A

LO1 LO2 **PROBLEM 12.1A**
Reporting Unusual Events; Using Predictive Subtotals

Atlantic Airlines operated both an airline and several motels located near airports. During the year just ended, all motel operations were discontinued and the following operating results were reported:

Continuing operations (airline):	
Net sales	$55,120,000
Costs and expenses (including income taxes on continuing operations)	43,320,000
Other data:	
Operating income from motels (net of income tax)	864,000
Gain on sale of motels (net of income tax)	4,956,000
Extraordinary loss (net of income tax benefit)	3,360,000

The extraordinary loss resulted from the destruction of an airliner by an earthquake. Atlantic Airlines had 1,000,000 shares of capital stock outstanding throughout the year.

Instructions

a. Prepare a condensed income statement, including proper presentation of the discontinued motel operations and the extraordinary loss. Include all appropriate earnings per share figures.

b. Assume that you expect the profitability of Atlantic Airlines operations to *decline by 5 percent* next year, and the profitability of the motels to decline by 10 percent. What is your estimate of the company's net earnings per share next year?

LO1 LO2 LO5 LO6 **PROBLEM 12.2A**
Format of an Income Statement and a Statement of Retained Earnings

The following data relate to the operations of Slick Software, Inc., during 2011.

Continuing operations:	
Net sales	$19,850,000
Costs and expenses (including applicable income tax)	16,900,000
Other data:	
Operating income during 2011 on segment of the business discontinued near year-end (net of income tax)	140,000
Loss on disposal of discontinued segment (net of income tax benefit)	550,000
Extraordinary loss (net of income tax benefit)	900,000
Prior period adjustment (increase in 2010 depreciation expense, net of income tax benefit)	350,000
Cash dividends declared	950,000

Instructions

a. Prepare a condensed income statement for 2011, including earnings per share figures. Slick Software, Inc., had 200,000 shares of $1 par value common stock and 80,000 shares of $6.25, $100 par value preferred stock outstanding throughout the year.

b. Prepare a statement of retained earnings for the year ended December 31, 2011. As originally reported, retained earnings at December 31, 2010, amounted to $7,285,000.

c. Compute the amount of cash dividend *per share of common stock* declared by the board of directors for 2011. Assume no dividends in arrears on the preferred stock.

d. Assume that 2012 earnings per share is a single figure and amounts to $8.00. Assume also that there are no changes in outstanding common or preferred stock in 2012. Do you consider the $8.00 earnings per share figure in 2012 to be a favorable or unfavorable statistic in comparison with 2011 performance? Explain.

LO1 LO2 LO5 LO6

PROBLEM 12.3A
Reporting Unusual Events: A Comprehensive Problem

The income statement below was prepared by a new and inexperienced employee in the accounting department of Phoenix, Inc., a business organized as a corporation.

PHOENIX, INC. INCOME STATEMENT FOR THE YEAR ENDED DECEMBER 31, 2011		
Net sales		$10,800,000
Gain on sale of treasury stock		62,000
Excess of issuance price over par value of capital stock		510,000
Prior period adjustment (net of income tax)		60,000
Extraordinary gain (net of income tax)		36,000
Total revenue		$11,468,000
Less:		
Cost of goods sold	$6,000,000	
Selling expenses	1,104,000	
General and administrative expenses	1,896,000	
Loss from settlement of litigation	24,000	
Income tax on continuing operations	720,000	
Operating loss on discontinued operations (net of income tax benefit)	252,000	
Loss on disposal of discontinued operations (net of income tax benefit)	420,000	
Dividends declared on common stock	350,000	
Total costs and expenses		10,766,000
Net income		$ 702,000

Instructions

a. Prepare a corrected income statement for the year ended December 31, 2011, using the format illustrated in Exhibit 12–2. Include at the bottom of your income statement all appropriate earnings-per-share figures. Assume that throughout the year the company had outstanding a weighted average of 180,000 shares of a single class of capital stock.

b. Prepare a statement of retained earnings for 2011. (As originally reported, retained earnings at December 31, 2010, amounted to $2,175,000.)

c. What does the $62,000 "gain on sale of treasury stock" represent? How would you report this item in Phoenix's financial statements at December 31, 2011?

PROBLEM 12.4A
Effects of Stock Dividends, Stock Splits, and Treasury Stock Transactions

At the beginning of the year, Albers, Inc., has total stockholders' equity of $840,000 and 40,000 outstanding shares of a single class of capital stock. During the year, the corporation completes the following transactions affecting its stockholders' equity accounts:

Jan. 10 A 5 percent stock dividend is declared and distributed. (Market price, $20 per share.)

Mar. 15 The corporation acquires 2,000 shares of its own capital stock at a cost of $21.00 per share.

May 30 All 2,000 shares of the treasury stock are reissued at a price of $31.50 per share.

July 31 The capital stock is split 2-for-1.

Dec. 15 The board of directors declares a cash dividend of $1.10 per share, payable on January 15.

Dec. 31 Net income of $525,000 is reported for the year ended December 31.

Instructions

Compute the amount of total stockholders' equity, the number of shares of capital stock outstanding, and the book value per share following each successive transaction. Organize your solution as a three-column schedule with these separate column headings: (1) Total Stockholders' Equity, (2) Number of Shares Outstanding, and (3) Book Value per Share.

LO8

PROBLEM 12.5A
Preparing a Statement of Stockholders' Equity

A summary of the transactions affecting the stockholders' equity of Strait Corporation during the current year follows:

Prior period adjustment (net of income tax benefit)	$ (80,000)
Issuance of common stock: 10,000 shares of $10 par value capital stock at $34 per share	340,000
Declaration and distribution of 5% stock dividend (6,000 shares, market price $36 per share)	(216,000)
Purchased 1,000 shares of treasury stock at $35	(35,000)
Reissued 500 shares of treasury stock at a price of $36 per share	18,000
Net income	845,000
Cash dividends declared	(142,700)

Note: Parentheses ( ) indicate a reduction in stockholders' equity.

Instructions

a. Prepare a statement of stockholders' equity for the year. Use these column headings and beginning balances. (Notice that all additional paid-in capital accounts are combined into a single column.)

	Capital Stock ($10 par value)	Additional Paid-in Capital	Retained Earnings	Treasury Stock	Total Stock-holders' Equity
Balances, Jan. 1	$1,100,000	$1,765,000	$950,000	$ -0-	$3,815,000

b. What was the overall effect on total stockholders' equity of the 5 percent stock dividend of 6,000 shares? What was the overall effect on total stockholders' equity of the cash dividends declared? Do these two events have the same impact on stockholders' equity? Why or why not?

LO4 LO8 **PROBLEM 12.6A**

Recording Stock Dividends and Treasury Stock Transactions

At the beginning of 2011, Thompson Service, Inc., showed the following amounts in the stockholders' equity section of its balance sheet:

Stockholders' equity:	
Capital stock, $1 par value, 500,000 shares authorized, 382,000 issued and outstanding	$ 382,000
Additional paid-in capital: capital stock	4,202,000
Total paid-in capital	$4,584,000
Retained earnings	2,704,600
Total stockholders' equity	$7,288,600

The transactions relating to stockholders' equity during the year are as follows:

Jan. 3 Declared a dividend of $1 per share to stockholders of record on January 31, payable on February 15.

Feb. 15 Paid the cash dividend declared on January 3.

Apr. 12 The corporation purchased 6,000 shares of its own capital stock at a price of $40 per share.

May 9 Reissued 4,000 shares of the treasury stock at a price of $44 per share.

June 1 Declared a 5 percent stock dividend to stockholders of record at June 15, to be distributed on June 30. The market price of the stock at June 1 was $42 per share. (The 2,000 shares remaining in the treasury do not participate in the stock dividend.)

June 30 Distributed the stock dividend declared on June 1.

Aug. 4 Reissued 600 of the 2,000 remaining shares of treasury stock at a price of $37 per share.

Dec. 31 The Income Summary account, showing net income for the year of $1,928,000, was closed into the Retained Earnings account.

Dec. 31 The $382,000 balance in the Dividends account was closed into the Retained Earnings account.

Instructions

a. Prepare in general journal form the entries to record the above transactions.

b. Prepare the stockholders' equity section of the balance sheet at December 31, 2011. Use the format illustrated in Exhibit 12–6. Include a supporting schedule showing your computation of retained earnings at that date.

c. Compute the maximum cash dividend per share that legally could be declared at December 31, 2011, without impairing the paid-in capital of Thompson Service. (Hint: The availability of retained earnings for dividends is restricted by the cost of treasury stock owned.)

LO8 **PROBLEM 12.7A**

Effects of Transactions

Tech Process, Inc., manufactures a variety of computer peripherals, such as tape drives and printers. Listed below are five events that occurred during the current year.

1. Declared a $1.00 per share cash dividend.
2. Paid the cash dividend.
3. Purchased 1,000 shares of treasury stock for $20.00 per share.
4. Reissued 500 shares of the treasury stock at a price of $18.00 per share.
5. Declared a 15 percent stock dividend.

Instructions

a. Indicate the effects of each of these events on the financial measurements listed in the four columnar headings listed below. Use the following code letters: **I** for increase, **D** for decrease, and **NE** for no effect

Event	Current Assets	Stockholders' Equity	Net Income	Net Cash Flow (from any source)

b. For each event, *explain* the reasoning behind your answers. Be prepared to explain this reasoning in class.

LO4 LO8

PROBLEM 12.8A
Preparing the Stockholders' Equity Section: A Challenging Case

The Mandella family decided early in 2010 to incorporate their family-owned vineyards under the name Mandella Corporation. The corporation was authorized to issue 500,000 shares of a single class of $10 par value capital stock. Presented below is the information necessary to prepare the stockholders' equity section of the company's balance sheet at the end of 2010 and at the end of 2011.

2010. In January the corporation issued to members of the Mandella family 150,000 shares of capital stock in exchange for cash and other assets used in the operation of the vineyards. The fair market value of these assets indicated an issue price of $30 per share. In December, Joe Mandella died, and the corporation purchased 10,000 shares of its own capital stock from his estate at $34 per share. Because of the large cash outlay to acquire this treasury stock, the directors decided not to declare cash dividends in 2010 and instead declared a 10 percent stock dividend to be distributed in January 2011. The stock price at the declaration date was $35 per share. (The treasury shares do not participate in the stock dividend.) Net income for 2010 was $940,000.

2011. In January the corporation distributed the stock dividend declared in 2010, and in February, the 10,000 treasury shares were sold to Maria Mandella at $39 per share. In June, the capital stock was split 2-for-1. (Approval was obtained to increase the authorized number of shares to 1 million.) On December 15, the directors declared a cash dividend of $2 per share, payable in January 2012. Net income for 2011 was $1,080,000.

Instructions

Using the format illustrated in Exhibit 12–6, prepare the stockholders' equity section of the balance sheet at:

a. December 31, 2010.

b. December 31, 2011.

Show any necessary computations in supporting schedules.

LO1 LO2

PROBLEM 12.9A
Format of an Income Statement; EPS

The following information is excerpted from the financial statements in a recent annual report of Esper Corporation. (Dollar figures and shares of stock are in thousands.)

Extraordinary loss on extinguishment of debt	$ (8,490)
Loss from continuing operations	$(16,026)
Income from discontinued operations	$ 6,215
Preferred stock dividend requirements	$ (2,778)
Weighted-average number of shares of common stock outstanding	39,739

Instructions

a. Rearrange the items to present in good form the last portion of the income statement for Esper Corporation, beginning with "Loss from continuing operations."

b. Calculate the amount of *net loss* per share for the period. (Do *not* calculate per-share amounts for subtotals, such as income from continuing operations, loss before extraordinary items, etc. You are required to compute only a single earnings per share amount.)

Problem Set B

LO1 LO2 **PROBLEM 12.1B**

Reporting Unusual Events: Using Predictive Subtotals

Pacific Airlines operated both an airline and several rental car operations located near airports. During the year just ended, all rental car operations were discontinued and the following operating results were reported:

Continuing operations (airline):	
Net sales	$61,440,000
Costs and expenses (including income taxes on continuing operations)	53,980,000
Other data:	
Operating income from car rentals (net of income tax)	670,000
Gain on sale of rental car business (net of income tax)	4,330,000
Extraordinary loss (net of income tax benefit)	3,120,000

The extraordinary loss resulted from the destruction of an airliner by terrorists. Pacific Airlines had 4,000,000 shares of capital stock outstanding throughout the year.

Instructions

a. Prepare a condensed income statement, including proper presentation of the discontinued rental car operations and the extraordinary loss. Include all appropriate earnings per share figures.

b. Assume that you expect the profitability of Pacific's airline operations to *decline by 10 percent* next year and the profitability of the rental car operation to decline by 10 percent. What is your estimate of the company's net earnings per share next year?

LO1 LO2 LO5 LO6 **PROBLEM 12.2B**

Format of an Income Statement and a Statement of Retained Earnings

Shown below are data relating to the operations of Beach, Inc., during 2011.

Continuing operations:	
Net sales	$37,400,000
Costs and expenses (including applicable income taxes)	21,500,000
Other data:	
Operating income during 2011 on segment of the business discontinued near year-end (net of income taxes)	205,000
Loss on disposal of discontinued segment (net of income tax benefit)	510,000
Extraordinary loss (net of income tax benefit)	930,000
Prior period adjustment (increase in 2010 amortization expense, net of income tax benefit)	310,000
Cash dividends declared	2,000,000

Instructions

a. Prepare a condensed income statement for 2011, including earnings per share statistics. Beach, Inc., had 200,000 shares of $1 par value common stock and 100,000 shares of $6, $100 par value preferred stock outstanding throughout the year.

b. Prepare a statement of retained earnings for the year ended December 31, 2011. As originally reported, retained earnings at December 31, 2010, amounted to $10,700,000.

c. Compute the amount of cash dividend *per share of common stock* declared by the board of directors for 2011. Assume no dividends in arrears on the preferred stock.

d. Assume that 2012 earnings per share is a single figure and amounts to $75. Assume also that there are no changes in outstanding common or preferred stock in 2012. Do you consider the $75 earnings per share figure in 2012 to be a favorable or unfavorable statistic in comparison with 2011 performance? Explain.

LO1 LO2 LO5 LO6

PROBLEM 12.3B
Reporting Unusual Events: A Comprehensive Problem

The income statement below was prepared by a new and inexperienced employee in the accounting department of Dexter, Inc., a business organized as a corporation:

DEXTER, INC. INCOME STATEMENT FOR THE YEAR ENDED DECEMBER 31, 2011		
Net sales		$10,200,000
Gain on sale of treasury stock		56,000
Excess of issuance price over par value of capital stock		710,000
Prior period adjustment (net of income tax)		80,000
Extraordinary gain (net of income tax)		110,000
Total revenue		$11,156,000
Less:		
Cost of goods sold	$4,000,000	
Selling expenses	1,050,000	
General and administrative expenses	840,000	
Loss from settlement of litigation	10,000	
Income tax on continuing operations	612,000	
Operating loss on discontinued operations (net of income tax benefit)	180,000	
Loss on disposal of discontinued operations (net of income tax benefit)	240,000	
Dividends declared on common stock	300,000	
Total costs and expenses		7,232,000
Net income		$ 3,924,000

Instructions

a. Prepare a corrected income statement for the year ended December 31, 2011, using the format illustrated in Exhibit 12–2. Include at the bottom of your income statement all appropriate earnings per share figures. Assume that throughout the year the company had outstanding a weighted average of 500,000 shares of a single class of capital stock.

b. Prepare a statement of retained earnings for 2011. (As originally reported, retained earnings at December 31, 2010, amount to $3,200,000.)

c. What does the $56,000 "Gain on sale of treasury stock" represent? How would you report this item in Dexter's financial statements at December 31, 2011?

LO4

PROBLEM 12.4B
Effects of Stock Dividends, Stock Splits, and Treasury Stock Transactions

At the beginning of the year, Jessel, Inc., has total stockholders' equity of $600,000 and 20,000 outstanding shares of a single class of capital stock. During the year, the corporation completes the following transactions affecting its stockholders' equity accounts:

Jan. 16 A 5 percent stock dividend is declared and distributed. (Market price, $50 per share.)

Feb. 9 The corporation acquires 300 shares of its own capital stock at a cost of $55 per share.

Mar. 3 All 300 shares of the treasury stock are reissued at a price of $65 per share.

Jul. 5 The capital stock is split 2-for-1.

Nov. 22 The board of directors declares a cash dividend of $6 per share, payable on January 22.

Dec. 31 Net income of $87,000 is reported for the year ended December 31.

Instructions

Compute the amount of total stockholders' equity, the number of shares of capital stock outstanding, and the book value per share following each successive transaction. Organize your solution as a three-column schedule with these separate column headings: (1) "Total Stockholders' Equity," (2) "Number of Shares Outstanding," and (3) "Book Value per Share."

LO4 LO8 **PROBLEM 12.5B** Preparing a Statement of Stockholders' Equity

The following is a summary of the transactions affecting the stockholders' equity of Dry Wall, Inc., during the current year:

Prior period adjustment (net of income tax benefit)	$ (47,000)
Issuance of common stock: 20,000 shares of $1 par value capital stock at $15 per share	300,000
Declaration and distribution of 10% stock dividend (15,000 shares, market price $17 per share)	255,000*
Purchased 3,000 shares of treasury stock at $16	(48,000)
Reissued 1,000 shares of treasury stock at a price of $18 per share	18,000
Net income	1,200,000
Cash dividends declared ($1 per share)	(163,000)

Note: Parentheses ( ) indicate a reduction in stockholders' equity. Asterisk * indicates no change in total shareholders' equity.

Instructions

a. Prepare a statement of stockholders' equity for the year. Use the column headings and beginning balances shown below. (Notice that all additional paid-in capital accounts are combined into a single column.)

	Capital Stock ($1 par value)	Additional Paid-in Capital	Retained Earnings	Treasury Stock	Total Stockholders' Equity
Balances, Jan. 1	$130,000	$1,170,000	$1,400,000	–0–	$2,700,000

b. What was the overall effect on total stockholders' equity of the 10 percent stock dividend of 15,000 shares? What was the overall effect on total stockholders' equity of the cash dividends declared? Do these two events have the same impact on stockholders' equity? Why or why not?

LO4 LO8 **PROBLEM 12.6B** Recording Stock Dividends and Treasury Stock Transactions

At the beginning of 2011, Greene, Inc., showed the following amounts in the stockholders' equity section of its balance sheet:

Stockholders' equity:	
Capital stock, $1 par value, 1,000,000 shares authorized, 560,000 issued and outstanding	$ 560,000
Additional paid-in capital: capital stock	4,480,000
Total paid-in capital	5,040,000
Retained earnings	3,000,000
Total stockholders' equity	$8,040,000

The transactions relating to stockholders' equity during the year are as follows:

Jan. 5 Declared a dividend of $1 per share to stockholders of record on January 31, payable on February 18.

Feb. 18 Paid the cash dividend declared on January 5.

Apr. 20 The corporation purchased 1,000 shares of its own capital stock at a price of $10 per share.

May 25 Reissued 500 shares of the treasury stock at a price of $12 per share.

June 15 Declared a 5 percent stock dividend to stockholders of record at June 22, to be distributed on June 30. The market price of the stock at June 15 was $11 per share. (The 500 shares remaining in the treasury do not participate in the stock dividend.)

June 30 Distributed the stock dividend declared on June 15.

Aug. 12 Reissued 300 of the 500 remaining shares of treasury stock at a price of $9.75 per share.

Dec. 31 The Income Summary account, showing net income for the year of $1,750,000, was closed into the Retained Earnings account.

Dec. 31 The $560,000 balance in the Dividends account was closed into the Retained Earnings account.

Instructions

a. Prepare in general journal form the entries to record the above transactions.

b. Prepare the stockholders' equity section of the balance sheet at December 31, 2011. Use the format illustrated in Exhibit 12–6. Include a supporting schedule showing your computation of retained earnings at that date.

c. Compute the maximum cash dividend per share that legally could be declared at December 31, 2011, without impairing the paid-in capital of Greene, Inc. (Hint: The availability of retained earnings for dividends is restricted by the cost of treasury stock owned.)

LO8 PROBLEM 12.7B
Effects of Transactions

Hot Water, Inc., manufactures a variety of dry cleaning equipment. Listed below are five events that occurred during the current year:

1. Declared a $5 per share cash dividend.
2. Paid the cash dividend.
3. Purchased 1,000 shares of treasury stock for $37 per share.
4. Reissued 600 shares of the treasury stock at a price of $36 per share.
5. Declared a 5 percent stock dividend.

Instructions

a. Indicate the effects of each of these events on the financial measurements listed in the four column headings listed below. Use the following code letters: **I** for increase, **D** for decrease, and **NE** for no effect.

Event	Current Assets	Stockholders' Equity	Net Income	Net Cash Flow (from any source)

b. For each event, *explain* the reasoning behind your answers. Be prepared to explain this reasoning in class.

LO4 LO8 PROBLEM 12.8B
Preparing the Stockholders' Equity Section: A Challenging Case

The Adams family decided early in 2010 to incorporate their family-owned farm under the name Adams Corporation. The corporation was authorized to issue 100,000 shares of a single class of $1 par value capital stock. Presented below is the information necessary to prepare the stockholders' equity section of the company's balance sheet at the end of 2010 and at the end of 2011.

2010. In January the corporation issued to members of the Adams family 20,000 shares of capital stock in exchange for cash and other assets used in the operation of the farm. The fair market value of these assets indicated an issue price of $25 per share. In December, George Adams died and the corporation purchased 4,000 shares of its own capital stock from his estate at $30 per share. Because of the large cash outlay to acquire this treasury stock, the directors decided not to declare cash dividends in 2010 and instead declared a 10 percent stock dividend to be distributed in January 2011. The stock price at the declaration date was $31 per share. (The treasury shares do not participate in the stock dividend.) Net income for 2010 was $850,000.

2011. In January the corporation distributed the stock dividend declared in 2010, and in February, the 4,000 treasury shares were sold to Joan Adams at $35 per share. In June, the capital stock was split 2-for-1. (Approval was obtained to increase the authorized number of shares to 200,000.) On December 11, the directors declared a cash dividend of $1 per share, payable in January 2012. Net income for 2011 was $810,000.

Instructions

Using the format illustrated in Exhibit 12–6, prepare the stockholders' equity section of the balance sheet at:

a. December 31, 2010.

b. December 31, 2011.

Show any necessary computations in supporting schedules.

LO1 LO2

PROBLEM 12.9B

Format of an Income Statement EPS

The following information is excerpted from the financial statements in a recent annual report of Blue Jay Manufacturing Corporation. (Dollar figures and shares of stock are in thousands.)

Extraordinary loss on extinguishment of debt	$ (8,750)
Loss from continuing operations	(19,470)
Income from discontinued operations	12,000
Preferred stock dividend requirements	(3,100)
Weighted-average number of shares of common stock outstanding	10,000

Instructions

a. Rearrange the items to present in good form the last portion of the income statement for Blue Jay Manufacturing Corporation, beginning with "Loss from continuing operations."

b. Calculate the amount of *net loss* per share for the period. (Do *not* calculate per-share amounts for subtotals, such as income from continuing operations, loss before extraordinary items, and so forth. You are required to compute only a single earnings per share amount.)

Critical Thinking Cases

LO1

CASE 12.1

What's This?

The following events were reported in the financial statements of large, publicly owned corporations:

a. **Atlantic Richfield Company (ARCO)**, previously a separate company that is now owned by BP America, sold or abandoned the entire noncoal minerals segment of its operations. In the year of disposal, this segment had an operating loss. **ARCO** also incurred a loss of $514 million on disposal of its noncoal minerals segment of the business.

b. **American Airlines** increased the estimated useful life used in computing depreciation on its aircraft. If the new estimated life had always been in use, the net income reported in prior years would have been substantially higher.

c. **Union Carbide Corp.** sustained a large loss as a result of the explosion of a chemical plant.

d. **Georgia-Pacific Corporation** realized a $10 million gain as a result of condemnation proceedings in which a governmental agency purchased assets from the company in a "forced sale."

Instructions

Indicate whether each event should be classified as a discontinued operation, or an extraordinary item, or included among the revenue and expenses of normal and recurring business operations. Briefly explain your reasons for each answer.

LO1 **CASE 12.2**

Is There Life without Baseball?

Jackson Publishing, Inc. (JPI), publishes two newspapers and, until recently, owned a professional baseball team. The baseball team had been losing money for several years and was sold at the end of 2011 to a group of investors who plan to move it to a larger city. Also in 2011, JPI suffered an extraordinary loss when its Raytown printing plant was damaged by a tornado. The damage has since been repaired. A condensed income statement follows:

JACKSON PUBLISHING, INC.
INCOME STATEMENT
FOR THE YEAR ENDED DECEMBER 31, 2011

Net revenue		$41,000,000
Costs and expenses		36,500,000
Income from continuing operations		$ 4,500,000
Discontinued operations:		
Operating loss on baseball team	$(1,300,000)	
Gain on sale of baseball team	4,700,000	3,400,000
Income before extraordinary items		$ 7,900,000
Extraordinary loss:		
Tornado damage to Raytown printing plant		(600,000)
Net income		$ 7,300,000

Instructions

On the basis of this information, answer the following questions. Show any necessary computations and explain your reasoning.

a. What would JPI's net income have been for 2011 if it *had not* sold the baseball team?

b. Assume that for 2012 you expect a 7 percent increase in the profitability of JPI's newspaper business but had projected a $2,000,000 operating loss for the baseball team if JPI had continued to operate the team in 2012. What amount would you forecast as JPI's 2012 net income *if the company had continued to own and operate the baseball team*?

c. Given your assumptions in part **b,** but given that JPI *did* sell the baseball team in 2011, what would you forecast as the company's estimated net income for 2012?

d. Assume that the expenses of operating the baseball team in 2011 amounted to $32,200,000, net of any related income tax effects. What was the team's *net revenue* for the year?

LO1 through LO3 **CASE 12.3**

Using Earnings per Share Statistics

For many years New York Studios has produced television shows and operated several FM radio stations. Late in the current year, the radio stations were sold to Times Publishing, Inc. Also during the current year, New York Studios sustained an extraordinary loss when one of its camera trucks caused an accident in an international grand prix auto race. Throughout the current year, the company had 3 million shares of common stock and a large quantity of convertible preferred stock outstanding. Earnings per share reported for the current year were as follows:

	Basic	Diluted
Earnings from continuing operations	$8.20	$6.80
Earnings before extraordinary items	$6.90	$5.50
Net earnings	$3.60	$2.20

Instructions

a. Briefly explain why New York Studios reports diluted earnings per share amounts as well as basic earnings per share. What is the purpose of showing investors the diluted figures?

b. What was the total dollar amount of the extraordinary loss sustained by New York Studios during the current year?

c. Assume that the price-earnings ratio shown in the morning newspaper for New York Studios's common stock indicates that the stock is selling at a price equal to 10 times the reported earnings per share. What is the approximate market price of the stock?

d. Assume that you expect both the revenue and expenses involved in producing television shows to increase by 10 percent during the coming year. What would you forecast as the company's basic earnings per share for the coming year under each of the following independent assumptions? (Show your computations and explain your reasoning.)

1. *None* of the convertible preferred stock is converted into common stock during the coming year.
2. *All* of the convertible preferred stock is converted into common stock at the beginning of the coming year.

LO8 CASE 12.4

Interpreting a Statement of Stockholders' Equity

The following information has been excerpted from the statement of stockholders' equity included in a recent annual report of Thompson Supply Company. (Dollar figures are in millions.)

	Common Stock		Additional Paid-in Capital	Retained Earnings	Treasury Stock	
	Shares	Amount			Shares	Amount
Balances, beginning of year	82,550,000	$425.0	$29.5	$ 950.2	4,562,500	$(135.9)
Net income				200.0		
Cash dividends declared on common stock				(95.7)		
Common stock issued for stock option plans			(1.4)		(601,300)	16.7
Repurchases of common stock					1,235,700	(78.6)
Balances, year-end	82,550,000	$425.0	$28.1	$1,054.5	5,196,900	$(197.8)

Instructions

Use the information about Thompson Supply to answer the following questions.

a. How many shares of common stock are outstanding at the *beginning* of the year? At the *end* of the year?

b. What was the total common stock dividend declared during the presented year? Thompson's annual report disclosed that the common stock dividend during that year was $1.23 per share. Approximately how many shares of common stock were entitled to the $1.23 per share dividend during the year? Is this answer compatible with your answers in part **a**?

c. The statement presented indicates that common stock was both issued and repurchased during the year, yet the number of common shares shown and the common stock amount (first and second columns) did not change from the beginning to the end of the year. Explain.

d. What was the average price per share Thompson paid to acquire the treasury shares held at the *beginning* of the year?

e. Was the aggregate issue price of the 601,300 treasury shares issued during the year for stock option plans higher or lower than the cost Thompson paid to acquire those treasury shares? (Hint: Analyze the impact on Additional Paid-in Capital.)

f. What was the average purchase price per share paid by Thompson to acquire treasury shares *during the current year*?

g. In its annual report, Thompson disclosed that the (weighted) average number of common shares outstanding during the year was 77,500,000. In part **a** above, you determined the number of common shares outstanding as of the end of the year. Which figure is used in computing *earnings per share*? Which is used in computing *book value per share*?

LO1 LO2 LO8

CASE 12.5 Classification of Unusual Items—and the Potential Financial Impact

Elliot-Cole is a publicly owned international corporation, with operations in over 90 countries. Net income has been growing at approximately 15 percent per year, and the stock consistently trades at about 20 times earnings.

To attract and retain key management leadership, the company has developed a compensation plan in which managers receive earnings in the form of bonuses as well as opportunities to purchase shares of the company's stock at a reduced price. In general, the higher the company's net income each year, the greater the benefit to management in terms of their personal compensation.

During the current year, political unrest and economic upheaval threatened Elliot-Cole's business operations in three foreign countries. At year-end, the company's auditors insisted that management write off the company's assets in these countries, stating that these assets were "severely impaired." Said one corporate official, "We can't argue with that. Each of these countries is a real trouble spot. We might be pulling out of these places at any time, and any assets probably would just be left behind."

Management agreed that the carrying value of Elliot-Cole's assets in these three countries should be reduced to "scrap value"—which was nothing. These write-downs amounted to approximately 18 percent of the company's income *prior* to recognition of these losses. (These write-offs are for financial reporting purposes only; they have *no effect* on the company's income tax obligations.)

At the meeting with the auditors, one of Elliot-Cole's officers states, "There's no doubt we should write these assets off. But of course, this is an extraordinary loss. A loss of this size can't be considered a routine matter."

Instructions

a. Explain the logic behind writing down the book values of assets that are still in operation.

b. Evaluate the officer's statement concerning the classification of these losses. Do you agree that they should be classified as an extraordinary item? Explain.

c. Explain the effect that the classification of these losses—that is, as ordinary or extraordinary—will have in the current period on Elliot-Cole's:

1. Net income.
2. Income before extraordinary items.
3. Income from continuing operations.
4. Net cash flow from operating activities.

d. Explain how the classification of these losses will affect the p/e ratio reported in newspapers such as *The Wall Street Journal.*

e. Does management appear to have any self-interest in the classification of these losses? Explain.

f. Explain how (if at all) these write-offs are likely to affect the earnings of *future* periods.

g. What "ethical dilemma" confronts management in this case?

LO9

CASE 12.6 Managing Profitability

You are a staff accountant for Pearce, Pearce, and Smith, CPAs, and have worked for several years on the audit of a major client of the firm, Flexcom, Inc. Flexcom sells its products in a highly competitive market and relies heavily on the careful management of inventory because of the unique nature of the products sold and the importance of minimizing the company's investment in inventory. Flexcom sells cellular phones, personal handheld computers, and other communications devices that are particularly sensitive to changes in consumer demands and changes in technology, which are both frequent and significant in terms of their impact on the attractiveness of Flexcom's products to buyers.

In the course of your work, you have noticed several trends related to inventory that interest you and that have caused you to explore further the underlying details. Specifically, you have determined the following:

- Despite sluggish sales volume, the company's net income has steadily increased for each of the last three years.
- Inventory has been increasing at a higher-than-normal rate.
- The allowance to reduce inventory for obsolescence has dramatically declined during the last three years, going from nearly 10 percent of inventory three years ago to approximately 2 percent at the end of the most recent year.

You are aware that, within Flexcom, profitability is a major factor in the evaluation of management and has been cited in at least two recent situations as the basis for replacing individuals in leadership positions.

Instructions

Prepare a brief report to your supervisor explaining why you are bothered by these trends and offer one or more explanations that may underlie what is actually going on within Flexcom.

LO2 **INTERNET CASE 12.7**

Analyzing Stockholders' Equity and EPS

Important information concerning a company's operating performance can be found in its income statement and statement of financial position (balance sheet). Using the search mechanism of your choice, locate the most recent annual report of **Martin Marietta Materials, Inc.** and respond to the following.

Instructions

a. For the most recent day indicated, what were the highest and lowest prices at which the company's common stock sold?

b. Find the company's balance sheet and determine the following: the number of outstanding shares of common stock and the average price at which those shares were originally sold.

c. What is the relationship between the current market price and the amount you have calculated in part **b** as the average price at which the stock originally sold?

d. Find the company's income statement and identify the trend in basic earnings per share, including discontinued operations. Did discontinued operations have a significant impact on EPS?

e. For the most recent year, what is the average number of shares of common stock that was used to compute basic earnings per share? Why is that number different from the number outstanding in the company's balance sheet?

Internet sites are time and date sensitive. It is the purpose of these exercises to have you explore the Internet. You may need to use the Yahoo! search engine http://www.yahoo.com *(or another favorite search engine) to find a company's current Web address.*

Answers to Self-Test Questions

1. b **2.** c, d **3.** d **4.** a, b **5.** a, c

CHAPTER 13

Statement of Cash Flows

© AP Photo/mark Lennihan

Learning Objectives

AFTER STUDYING THIS CHAPTER, YOU SHOULD BE ABLE TO:

LO1 Explain the purposes and uses of a statement of cash flows.

LO2 Describe how cash transactions are classified in a statement of cash flows.

LO3 Compute the major cash flows relating to operating activities.

LO4 Compute the cash flows relating to investing and financing activities.

LO5 Distinguish between the direct and indirect methods of reporting operating cash flows.

LO6 Explain why net income differs from net cash flows from operating activities.

LO7 Compute net cash flows from operating activities using the *indirect* method.

LO8 Discuss the likely effects of various business strategies on cash flows.

LO9 Explain how a worksheet may be helpful in preparing a statement of cash flows.

LOWE'S

Cash is sometimes referred to as the "lifeblood" of a company, implying that companies require cash to be successful and to even continue to exist. Cash is required on a daily basis to meet current obligations and to position the company for future success. Cash requirements include activities as broad ranging as meeting payroll requirements for employees, purchasing inventory to meet the shopping needs of customers, repaying debt when it is due, paying dividends to stockholders, and from time to time expanding the business by acquiring plant assets or even entire other businesses.

Cash flow is particularly important for large companies like Lowe's as it continuously seeks to expand its markets. Lowe's 2009 annual report includes three-year comparative statements of cash flows for 2009, 2008, and 2007. These statements are presented in three major categories: operating activities, investing activities, and financing activities. Lowe's shows over $4 billion from operating cash flows for each year presented. This cash was used for many purposes, including major acquisitions, repurchasing the company's common stock, paying dividends to stockholders, and retiring debt.

Efficiently managing cash flows of this magnitude is an important responsibility of the company's leadership and is critical for the company's continued success. ■

Cash flow information about a company is helpful to investors and creditors in judging future cash flows. If the company itself does not have strong cash flow, it is unlikely that the company will be in a cash position to provide strong cash flows to its investors and creditors. We introduced in Chapter 2 the idea of a financial statement that describes cash flows, and in Chapter 13 we go into greater depth regarding this important financial statement. The statement of cash flows shows how the company's cash changed during the period and explains how the company managed its cash in terms of its operating, investing, and financing activities.

Statement of Cash Flows

PURPOSES OF THE STATEMENT

Learning Objective
LO1 **Explain the purposes and uses of a statement of cash flows.**

The objective of a statement of cash flows is to provide information about the *cash receipts* and *cash payments* of a business entity during the accounting period. The term **cash flows** includes both cash receipts and payments. In a statement of cash flows, information about cash receipts and cash payments is classified in terms of the company's operating activities, investing activities, and financing activities. The statement of cash flows assists investors, creditors, and others in assessing such factors as:

- The company's ability to generate positive cash flows in future periods.
- The company's ability to meet its obligations and to pay dividends.
- The company's need for external financing.
- Reasons for differences between the amount of net income and the related net cash flows from operating activities.
- Both the cash and noncash aspects of the company's investment and financing transactions for the period.
- Causes of the change in the amount of cash and cash equivalents between the beginning and the end of the accounting period.

Stated simply, a statement of cash flows helps users of financial statements evaluate a company's ability to have sufficient cash—both on a short-run and on a long-run basis. For this reason, the statement of cash flows is useful to virtually everyone interested in the company's financial health: short- and long-term creditors, investors, management—and both current and prospective competitors.

EXAMPLE OF A STATEMENT OF CASH FLOWS

An example of a statement of cash flows appears in Exhibit 13–1. Cash outflows are shown in parentheses.[1]

CLASSIFICATION OF CASH FLOWS

Learning Objective
LO2 **Describe how cash transactions are classified in a statement of cash flows.**

The cash flows shown in the statement are presented in three major categories: (1) **operating activities,** (2) **investing activities,** and (3) **financing activities.**[2] We will now look briefly at the way cash flows are classified among these three categories.

Operating Activities The operating activities section shows the *cash effects* of revenue and expense transactions. Stated another way, the operating activities section of the statement of cash flows includes the cash effects of those transactions reported in the continuing operations section of the income statement. To illustrate this concept, consider the effects

[1] In this illustration, net cash flows from operating activities are determined by the *direct method.* An alternative approach, called the *indirect method,* is illustrated later in this chapter.

[2] To reconcile to the ending cash balance, "effects of changes in exchange rates on cash" is used in the cash flow statements of companies with foreign currency holdings. This classification, as well as other complexities, is discussed in more advanced accounting courses.

Exhibit 13-1

ALLISON CORPORATION STATEMENT OF CASH FLOWS

ALLISON CORPORATION STATEMENT OF CASH FLOWS FOR THE YEAR ENDED DECEMBER 31, 2011		
Cash flows from operating activities:		
Cash received from customers	$ 870,000	
Interest and dividends received	10,000	
Cash provided by operating activities		$880,000
Cash paid to suppliers and employees	$(764,000)	
Interest paid	(28,000)	
Income taxes paid	(38,000)	
Cash disbursed for operating activities		(830,000)
Net cash flows from operating activities		$ 50,000
Cash flows from investing activities:		
Purchases of marketable securities	$ (65,000)	
Proceeds from sales of marketable securities	40,000	
Loans made to borrowers	(17,000)	
Collections on loans	12,000	
Purchases of plant assets	(160,000)	
Proceeds from sales of plant assets	75,000	
Net cash flows from investing activities		(115,000)
Cash flows from financing activities:		
Proceeds from short-term borrowing	$ 45,000	
Payments to settle short-term debts	(55,000)	
Proceeds from issuing bonds payable	100,000	
Proceeds from issuing capital stock	50,000	
Dividends paid	(40,000)	
Net cash flows from financing activities		100,000
Net increase (decrease) in cash		$ 35,000
Cash and cash equivalents, Jan. 1, 2011		20,000
Cash and cash equivalents, Dec. 31, 2011		$ 55,000

of credit sales. Credit sales are reported in the income statement in the period when the sales occur. But the cash effects occur later—when the receivables are collected in cash. For many credit sales, cash will be received in the same financial reporting period. If these events occur in different accounting periods, however, the income statement and the operating activities section of the statement of cash flows will differ. Similar differences may exist between the recognition of an expense and the related cash payment. Consider, for example, the expense of postretirement benefits earned by employees during the current period. If this expense is not funded with a trustee, the cash payments may not occur for many years—after today's employees have retired.

Cash flows from operating activities include:

Cash Receipts	Cash Payments
Collections from customers for sales of goods and services	Payments to suppliers of merchandise and services, including payments to employees
Interest and dividends received	Payments of interest
Other receipts from operations; for example, proceeds from settlement of litigation	Payments of income taxes
	Other expenditures relating to operations; for example, payments in settlement of litigation

Notice that receipts of *interest and dividends* and payments of *interest* are classified as operating activities, not as investing or financing activities.

Investing Activities Cash flows relating to investing activities present the cash effects of transactions involving plant assets, intangible assets, and investments. They include:

Cash Receipts	Cash Payments
Cash proceeds from selling investments and plant and intangible assets	Payments to acquire investments and plant and intangible assets
Cash proceeds from collecting principal amounts on loans	Amounts advanced to borrowers

Financing Activities Cash flows classified as financing activities include the following items that result from debt and equity financing transactions:

Cash Receipts	Cash Payments
Proceeds from both short-term and long-term borrowing	Repayment of amounts borrowed (excluding interest payments)
Cash received from owners (for example, from issuing stock)	Payments to owners, such as cash dividends

Repayment of amounts borrowed refers to repayment of *loans,* not to payments made on accounts payable or accrued liabilities. Payments of accounts payable and of accrued liabilities are payments to suppliers of merchandise and services related to revenues and expenses and are classified as cash outflows from operating activities. Also, remember that all interest payments are classified as operating activities.

Why Are Receipts and Payments of Interest Classified as Operating Activities? A case can be made that interest and dividend receipts are related to investing activities, and that interest payments are related to financing activities. The Financial Accounting Standards Board (FASB) considered this point of view but decided instead to require companies to present interest and dividend receipts and interest payments as operating activities. The FASB position reflects the view that cash flows from operating activities should include the cash effects of the revenue and expense transactions entering into the determination of net income. Because dividend and interest revenue and interest expense enter into the determination of net income, the FASB decided that the related cash flows should be presented as operating activities in the statement of cash flows. Payments of dividends, however, *do not* enter into the determination of net income. Therefore, dividend payments are classified as financing activities.

INTERNATIONAL CASE IN POINT

Both the Financial Accounting Standards Board in the United States and the International Accounting Standards Board require companies to present a statement of cash flows organized into three categories: operating activities, investing activities, and financing activities. One difference in these two sets of financial reporting standards is the classification of interest received on investments and interest paid on debt financing. As you have learned in this chapter, the FASB requires these to be presented as part of operating cash flows. IASB standards, on the other hand, allow interest received to be classified as either operating or investing and interest paid to be classified as either operating or financing.

Cash and Cash Equivalents

For purposes of preparing a statement of cash flows, cash is defined as including *both cash and cash equivalents.* **Cash equivalents** are short-term, highly liquid investments, such as money market funds, commercial paper, and Treasury bills that will mature within 90 days from the acquisition date.

If an item is determined to not be a cash equivalent, its cash flows are presented in the investing activities section of the statement of cash flows. The amount shown as *cash and cash equivalents* in the balance sheet must be the same as the amount shown on the statement of cash flows. Transfers of money between a company's bank accounts and these cash equivalents are *not viewed as cash receipts or cash payments.* Money is considered cash regardless of whether it is held in currency, in a bank account, or in the form of cash equivalents. Interest received from holding cash equivalents is included in cash receipts from operating activities.

Marketable securities, such as investments in the stocks and bonds of other companies, *do not qualify as cash equivalents.* Therefore, purchases and sales of marketable securities *do* result in cash flows that are reported in the statement of cash flows as investing activities.

In the long run, a company must have a strategy that generates positive net cash flows from its operating activities if it is to be successful. A business with negative cash flows from operations will not be able to raise cash from other sources indefinitely. In fact, the ability of a business to raise cash through financing activities is highly dependent on its ability to generate cash from its normal business operations. Creditors and stockholders are reluctant to invest in a company that does not generate enough cash from operating activities to ensure prompt payment of maturing liabilities, interest, and dividends.

Similarly, companies cannot expect to survive indefinitely on cash provided by investing activities. At some point, plant assets, investments, and other assets available for sale will be depleted.

Cash versus Accrual Information

The items in an income statement and a balance sheet represent the balances of specific general ledger accounts. Notice, however, that the captions used in the statement of cash flows *do not* correspond to specific ledger accounts. A statement of cash flows summarizes *cash transactions* during the accounting period. The general ledger, however, is maintained on the **accrual basis** of accounting, not the cash basis. Thus an amount such as "Cash received from customers . . . $870,000" does not appear as the balance in a specific ledger account, but it is derived from one or more such accounts.

In a small business, it may be practical to prepare a statement of cash flows directly from the special journals for cash receipts and cash payments. For most businesses, however, it is easier to prepare the statement of cash flows by examining the income statement and the *changes* during the period in all of the balance sheet accounts *except for* Cash. This approach is based on the double-entry system of accounting; any transaction affecting cash must also affect some other asset, liability, or owners' equity account.[3] The change in these *other accounts* determines the nature of the cash transaction, as we see in the example that follows.

Preparing a Statement of Cash Flows

Earlier in this chapter we illustrated the statement of cash flows of Allison Corporation. We will now show how this statement was developed from the company's accrual-basis accounting records.

Basically, a statement of cash flows can be prepared from the information contained in an income statement and *comparative* balance sheets at the beginning and end of the period. It is also necessary, however, to have some detailed information about the *changes* occurring during the period in certain balance sheet accounts. Shown in Exhibit 13–2 is Allison's income statement, and in Exhibit 13–3 the firm's comparative balance sheets for the current year are presented.

Additional Information

An analysis of changes in the balance sheet accounts of Allison Corporation provides the following information about the company's activities in the current

[3] Revenue, expenses, and dividends represent changes in owners' equity and, therefore, may be regarded as owners' equity accounts.

Exhibit 13–2
ALLISON CORPORATION INCOME STATEMENT

ALLISON CORPORATION INCOME STATEMENT FOR THE YEAR ENDED DECEMBER 31, 2011		
Revenue and gains:		
Net sales		$900,000
Dividend revenue		3,000
Interest revenue		6,000
Gain on sales of plant assets		31,000
Total revenue and gains		$940,000
Costs, expenses, and losses:		
Cost of goods sold	$500,000	
Operating expenses (including depreciation of $40,000)	300,000	
Interest expense	35,000	
Income tax expense	36,000	
Loss on sales of marketable securities	4,000	
Total costs, expenses, and losses		875,000
Net income		$ 65,000

year. To assist in the preparation of a statement of cash flows, we have classified this information into the categories of operating activities, investing activities, and financing activities.

OPERATING ACTIVITIES

1. Accounts receivable increased by $30,000 during the year.
2. Dividend revenue is recognized on the cash basis, but interest revenue is recognized on the accrual basis. Accrued interest receivable decreased by $1,000 during the year.
3. Inventory increased by $10,000 and accounts payable increased by $15,000 during the year.
4. During the year, short-term prepaid expenses increased by $3,000 and accrued expenses payable (other than for interest or income taxes) decreased by $6,000. Depreciation for the year amounted to $40,000.
5. The accrued liability for interest payable increased by $7,000 during the year.
6. The accrued liability for income taxes payable decreased by $2,000 during the year.

INVESTING ACTIVITIES

7. Analysis of the Marketable Securities account shows debit entries of $65,000, representing the cost of securities purchased, and credit entries of $44,000, representing the cost of securities sold. (No marketable securities are classified as cash equivalents.)
8. Analysis of the Notes Receivable account shows $17,000 in debit entries, representing cash loaned by Allison Corporation to borrowers during the year, and $12,000 in credit entries, representing collections of notes receivable. (Collections of interest were recorded in the Interest Revenue account and are considered cash flows from operating activities.)
9. Allison's plant asset accounts increased by $116,000 during the year. An analysis of the underlying transactions indicates the following:

	Effect on Plant Asset Accounts
Purchased $200,000 in plant assets, paying $160,000 cash and issuing a long-term note payable for the $40,000 balance	$200,000
Sold for $75,000 cash plant assets with a book value of $44,000	(44,000)
Recorded depreciation expense for the period	(40,000)
Net change in plant asset controlling accounts	$116,000

Exhibit 13–3
ALLISON CORPORATION BALANCE SHEETS

ALLISON CORPORATION COMPARATIVE BALANCE SHEETS DECEMBER 31, 2011 AND 2010	2011	2010
Assets		
Current assets:		
Cash and Cash Equivalents	$ 55,000	$ 20,000
Marketable Securities	85,000	64,000
Notes Receivable	17,000	12,000
Accounts Receivable	110,000	80,000
Accrued Interest Receivable	2,000	3,000
Inventory	100,000	90,000
Prepaid Expenses	4,000	1,000
Total current assets	$373,000	$270,000
Plant and Equipment (net of accumulated depreciation)	616,000	500,000
Total assets	$989,000	$770,000
Liabilities & Stockholders' Equity		
Current liabilities:		
Notes Payable (short-term)	$ 45,000	$ 55,000
Accounts Payable	76,000	61,000
Interest Payable	22,000	15,000
Income Taxes Payable	8,000	10,000
Other Accrued Expenses Payable	3,000	9,000
Total current liabilities	$154,000	$150,000
Long-term liabilities:		
Notes Payable (long-term)	40,000	–0–
Bonds Payable	400,000	300,000
Total liabilities	$594,000	$450,000
Stockholders' equity:		
Capital Stock	$ 60,000	$ 50,000
Additional Paid-in Capital	140,000	100,000
Retained Earnings	195,000	170,000
Total stockholders' equity	$395,000	$320,000
Total liabilities & stockholders' equity	$989,000	$770,000

FINANCING ACTIVITIES

10. During the year, Allison Corporation borrowed $45,000 cash by issuing short-term notes payable to banks. Also, the company repaid $55,000 in principal amounts due on these loans and other notes payable. (Interest payments are classified as operating activities.)
11. The company issued bonds payable for $100,000 cash.
12. The company issued 1,000 shares of $10 par value capital stock for cash at a price of $50 per share.
13. Cash dividends declared and paid to stockholders amounted to $40,000 during the year.

CASH AND CASH EQUIVALENTS

14. Cash and cash equivalents as shown in Allison Corporation's balance sheets amounted to $20,000 at the beginning of the year and $55,000 at year-end—a net increase of $35,000.

Using this information, we will now illustrate the steps in preparing Allison Corporation's statement of cash flows and a supporting schedule disclosing the noncash investing and financing activities. In our discussion, we will often refer to these items of additional information by citing the paragraph numbers shown in the list just described.

The distinction between accrual-basis measurements and cash flows is fundamentally important in understanding financial statements and other accounting reports. To assist in making this distinction, we use two colors in our illustrated computations. We show in blue the accrual-based data from Allison Corporation's income statement and the preceding numbered paragraphs. The cash flows that we compute from these data are shown in red.

CASH FLOWS FROM OPERATING ACTIVITIES

Learning Objective
LO3 Compute the major cash flows relating to operating activities.

As shown in our statement of cash flows in Exhibit 13–1, the net cash flows from operating activities are determined by combining certain cash inflows and subtracting certain cash outflows. The inflows are cash received from customers and interest and dividends received; the outflows are cash paid to suppliers and employees, interest paid, and income taxes paid.

In computing each of these cash flows, our starting point is an income statement amount, such as net sales, cost of goods sold, or interest expense. As you study each computation, be sure that you *understand why* the income statement amount must be increased or decreased to determine the related cash flows. You will find that an understanding of these computations will do more than show you how to compute cash flows; it will also strengthen your understanding of the income statement and the balance sheet.

Cash Received from Customers

To the extent that sales are made for cash, there is no difference between the amount of cash received from customers in the statement of cash flows and the amount recorded as sales revenue in the income statement. Differences arise, however, when sales are made on account. If accounts receivable increase during the year, credit sales will have exceeded collections of cash from accounts receivable. Therefore, we *deduct the increase* in accounts receivable from net sales to determine the amount of cash received during the year. If accounts receivable decrease, collections of these accounts will have exceeded credit sales. Therefore, we *add the decrease* in accounts receivable to net sales to determine the amount of cash received during the year. The relationship between cash received from customers and net sales is summarized below:

$$\text{Cash Received from Customers} = \text{Net Sales} \begin{Bmatrix} + \text{ Decrease in Accounts Receivable} \\ \text{or} \\ - \text{ Increase in Accounts Receivable} \end{Bmatrix}$$

In our Allison Corporation example, paragraph **1** of the additional information tells us that accounts receivable *increased* by $30,000 during the year. The income statement shows net sales for the year of $900,000. Therefore, the amount of cash received from customers is computed as follows:

Net sales (accrual basis)	$900,000
Less: Increase in accounts receivable	30,000
Cash received from customers	$870,000

Interest and Dividends Received

Our next step is to determine the amounts of cash received during the year from dividends and interest on the company's investments. As explained in paragraph **2** of the additional information, dividend revenue is recorded on the cash basis. Therefore, the $3,000 shown in the income statement also represents the amount of cash received as dividends.

Interest revenue, on the other hand, is recognized on the accrual basis. We have already shown how to convert one type of revenue, net sales, from the accrual basis to the cash basis. We use the same approach to convert interest revenue from the accrual basis to the **cash basis.** Our formula for converting net sales to the cash basis may be modified to convert interest revenue to the cash basis as follows:

$$\textbf{Interest Received} = \text{Interest Revenue} \begin{Bmatrix} + \text{ Decrease in Interest Receivable} \\ \text{or} \\ - \text{ Increase in Interest Receivable} \end{Bmatrix}$$

The income statement for Allison Corporation shows interest revenue of $6,000, and paragraph **2** states that the amount of accrued interest receivable *decreased* by $1,000 during the year. Thus the amount of cash received as interest is computed as follows:

Interest revenue (accrual basis)	$6,000
Add: Decrease in accrued interest receivable	1,000
Interest received (cash basis)	$7,000

The amounts of interest and dividends received in cash are combined for presentation in the statement of cash flows:

Interest received (cash basis)	$ 7,000
Dividends received (cash basis)	3,000
Interest and dividends received	$10,000

CASH PAYMENTS FOR MERCHANDISE AND FOR EXPENSES

The next item in the statement of cash flows, "Cash paid to suppliers and employees," includes all cash payments for purchases of merchandise and for operating expenses (excluding interest and income taxes). Payments of interest and income taxes are listed as separate items in the statement. The amounts of cash paid for purchases of merchandise and for operating expenses are computed separately.

Cash Paid for Purchases of Merchandise An accrual basis income statement reflects the *cost of goods sold* during the year, regardless of whether the merchandise was acquired or paid for in that period. The statement of cash flows, on the other hand, reports the *cash paid* for merchandise during the year, even if the merchandise was acquired in a previous period or remains unsold at year-end. The relationship between cash payments for merchandise and the cost of goods sold depends on the changes during the period in *two* related balance sheet accounts: inventory and accounts payable to suppliers of merchandise. This relationship may be stated as follows:

$$\textbf{Cash Payments for Purchases} = \text{Cost of Goods Sold} \begin{Bmatrix} + \text{ Increase in Inventory} \\ \text{or} \\ - \text{ Decrease in Inventory} \end{Bmatrix} \text{and} \begin{Bmatrix} + \text{ Decrease in Accounts Payable} \\ \text{or} \\ - \text{ Increase in Accounts Payable} \end{Bmatrix}$$

Using information from the Allison Corporation income statement and paragraph **3,** the cash payments for purchases may be computed as follows:

Cost of goods sold	$500,000
Add: Increase in inventory	10,000
Net purchases (accrual basis)	$510,000
Less: Increase in accounts payable to suppliers	15,000
Cash payments for purchases of merchandise	$495,000

Here is the logic behind this computation: If a company is increasing its inventory, it is *buying more merchandise than it sells* during the period. If the company is increasing its accounts payable to merchandise creditors, it is *not paying cash* for all of these purchases in the current period. Some portion of the purchases will be paid for in the next period.

Cash Payments for Expenses Expenses, as shown in the income statement, represent the cost of goods and services used up during the period. However, the amounts shown as expenses may differ from the cash payments made during the period. Consider, for example, depreciation expense. Recording depreciation expense *requires no cash payment,* but it does increase total expenses measured on the accrual basis. Thus, in converting accrual-basis expenses to the cash basis, we deduct depreciation expense and any other noncash expenses from our accrual-basis operating expenses. Other noncash expenses—expenses not requiring cash outlays—include amortization of intangible assets, any unfunded portion of postretirement benefits expense, and amortization of bond discount.

A second type of difference arises from short-term *timing differences* between the recognition of expenses and the actual cash payments. Expenses are recorded in accounting records when the related goods or services are used. However, the cash payments for these expenses might occur (1) in an earlier period, (2) in the same period, or (3) in a later period. Let us briefly consider each case.

1. If payment is made in advance, the payment creates an asset, termed a prepaid expense, or, in our formula, a "prepayment." Thus, to the extent that prepaid expenses increase over the year, cash payments *exceed* the amount recognized as expense.
2. If payment is made in the same period, the cash payment is equal to the amount of expense.
3. If payment is made in a later period, the payment reduces a liability for an accrued expense payable. Thus, to the extent that accrued expenses payable decrease over the year, cash payments exceed the amount recognized as expense.

The relationship between cash payments for expenses and accrual-basis expenses is summarized below:

$$\text{Cash Payments for Expenses} = \text{Expenses} \left\{ - \begin{array}{c}\text{Depreciation}\\ \text{and Other}\\ \text{Noncash}\\ \text{Expenses}\end{array} \right\} \text{and} \left\{ \begin{array}{l} + \text{Increase in Related Prepayments} \\ \text{or} \\ - \text{Decrease in Related Prepayments} \end{array} \right\} \text{and} \left\{ \begin{array}{l} + \text{Decrease in Related Accrued Liabilities} \\ \text{or} \\ - \text{Increase in Related Accrued Liabilities} \end{array} \right\}$$

In a statement of cash flows, cash payments for interest and for income taxes are shown separately from cash payments for operating expenses. Using information from Allison Corporation's income statement and from paragraph **4,** we may compute the company's cash payments for operating expenses as follows:

Operating expenses (including depreciation)		$300,000
Less: Noncash expenses (depreciation)		40,000
Subtotal		$260,000
Add: Increase in short-term prepayments	$3,000	
Decrease in accrued liabilities	6,000	9,000
Cash payments for operating expenses		$269,000

Cash Paid to Suppliers and Employees The caption used in our cash flow statement, "Cash paid to suppliers and employees," includes cash payments for both purchases of merchandise and for operating expenses. This cash outflow may now be computed by combining the two previous calculations:

Cash payments for purchases of merchandise	$495,000
Cash payments for operating expenses	269,000
Cash payments to suppliers and employees	$764,000

Cash Payments for Interest and Taxes Interest expense and income taxes expense may be converted to cash payments with the same formula we used to convert operating expenses. Allison Corporation's income statement shows interest expense of $35,000, and paragraph **5** states that the liability for interest payable increased by $7,000 during the year. The fact that the liability for unpaid interest *increased* over the year means that *not all of the interest expense shown in the income statement was paid in cash* in the current year. To determine the amount of interest actually paid, we *subtract* from total interest expense the portion that has been financed through an increase in the liability for interest payable. The computation is as follows:

Interest expense	$35,000
Less: Increase in related accrued liability	7,000
Interest paid	$28,000

Similar reasoning is used to determine the amount of income tax paid by Allison Corporation during the year. The accrual-based income tax expense reported in the income statement amounts to $36,000. However, paragraph **6** states that the company has reduced its liability for income taxes payable by $2,000 over the year. Incurring income tax expense increases the tax liability; making cash payments to tax authorities reduces it. Thus, if the liability *decreased* over the year, cash payments to tax authorities *must have been greater* than the income tax expense for the current year. The amount of the cash payments is determined as follows:

Income tax expense	$36,000
Add: Decrease in related accrued liability	2,000
Income tax paid	$38,000

A Quick Review We have now shown the computation of each cash flow relating to Allison Corporation's operating activities. In Exhibit 13–1 we illustrated a complete statement of cash flows for the company. For your convenience, we again show the operating activities section of that statement, illustrating the information developed in the preceding paragraphs.

Cash flows from operating activities:		
Cash received from customers	$ 870,000	
Interest and dividends received	10,000	
Cash provided by operating activities		$ 880,000
Cash paid to suppliers and employees	$(764,000)	
Interest paid	(28,000)	
Income taxes paid	(38,000)	
Cash disbursed for operating activities		(830,000)
Net cash flows from operating activities		$ 50,000

CASH FLOWS FROM INVESTING ACTIVITIES

Learning Objective LO4 **Compute the cash flows relating to investing and financing activities.**

Paragraphs **7** through **9** in the additional information for our Allison Corporation example provide most of the information necessary to determine the cash flows from investing activities. In the following discussion, we illustrate the presentation of these cash flows and explain the sources of the information contained in the numbered paragraphs.

Much information about investing activities can be obtained simply by looking at the changes in the related asset accounts during the year. Debit entries in these accounts represent purchases of the assets, or cash outlays. Credit entries represent sales of the assets, or cash receipts. However, credit entries in asset accounts represent the *cost* (or *book value*) of the assets sold. To determine the cash proceeds from these transactions, we must adjust the amount of the credit entries for any gains or losses recognized on the sales.

Purchases and Sales of Securities To illustrate, consider paragraph **7,** which summarizes the debit and credit entries to the Marketable Securities account. As explained earlier in this chapter, the $65,000 in debit entries represents purchases of marketable securities. The $44,000 in credit entries represents the *cost* of marketable securities sold during the period. However, the income statement shows that these securities were sold at a *$4,000 loss*. Thus the cash proceeds from these sales amounted to only *$40,000* ($44,000 cost, minus $4,000 loss on sale). In the statement of cash flows, these investing activities are summarized as follows:

Purchases of marketable securities	$(65,000)
Proceeds from sales of marketable securities	40,000

Loans Made and Collected Paragraph **8** provides all the information necessary to summarize the cash flows from making and collecting loans:

Loans made to borrowers	$(17,000)
Collections on loans	12,000

This information comes directly from the Notes Receivable account. Debit entries in the account represent new loans made during the year; credit entries indicate collections of the *principal* amount on outstanding notes (loans). (Interest received is credited to the Interest Revenue account and is included among the cash receipts from operating activities.)

YOUR TURN **You as a Sales Manager**

Assume you are a regional sales manager for Wiggins Foods, Inc., a distributor of bulk food products to schools, nursing homes, hospitals, prisons, and other institutions. Recently, the purchasing agent for Baggins Preschools, Inc., tells you the company will likely have to forgo its normal monthly order because of cash flow problems. The purchasing agent tells you other companies are helping it through the cash flow squeeze and asks if your company could loan the payment to Baggins. The purchasing agent suggests you could record the sale as revenue and increase notes receivable (rather than accounts receivable) by the same amount. Baggins is one of your largest customers. Without its order, you will not meet your sales goals for the month—so you are tempted to say yes. However, on reflection you wonder if it might be unethical for the company to lend its customer money to finance purchases. What should you do?

(See our comments on the Online Learning Center Web site.)

Cash Paid to Acquire Plant Assets Paragraph **9** states that Allison Corporation purchased plant assets during the year for $200,000, paying $160,000 in cash and issuing a long-term note payable for the $40,000 balance. Notice that *only the $160,000 cash payment* appears in the statement of cash flows. However, one objective of this financial statement is to show all of the company's *investing and financing activities* during the year. Therefore, the *noncash aspects* of these transactions are shown in a supplementary schedule, as follows:

Supplementary Schedule of Noncash Investing and Financing Activities	
Purchases of plant assets	$200,000
Less: Portion financed through issuance of long-term debt	40,000
Cash paid to acquire plant assets	$160,000

This supplementary schedule accompanies the statement of cash flows.

Proceeds from Sales of Plant Assets Assume that an analysis of the plant asset accounts shows net credit entries totaling $44,000 in the year. ("Net credit entries" means all credit entries, net of related debits to accumulated depreciation when assets were sold.) These net credit entries represent the *book value* of plant assets sold during the year. However, the income statement shows that these assets were sold at a *gain of $31,000.* Therefore, the *cash proceeds* from sales of plant assets amounted to $75,000, as follows:

Book value of plant assets sold	$44,000
Add: Gain on sales of plant assets	31,000
Proceeds from sales of plant assets	$75,000

The amount credited to the Accumulated Depreciation account during the year is not a cash flow and is not included in the statement of cash flows.

A Quick Review We have now shown the computation of each cash flow related to Allison Corporation's investing activities. In Exhibit 13–1 we illustrated a complete statement of cash flows for the company. For your convenience, we again show the investing activities section of that statement, illustrating the information developed in the preceding paragraphs.

Cash flows from investing activities:		
Purchases of marketable securities	$ (65,000)	
Proceeds from sales of marketable securities	40,000	
Loans made to borrowers	(17,000)	
Collections on loans	12,000	
Purchases of plant assets	(160,000)	
Proceeds from sales of plant assets	75,000	
Net cash flows from investing activities		$(115,000)

An important feature of the investing activities section of a statement of cash flows is that increases and decreases in cash from similar transactions are presented separately rather than being combined and netted against each other. For example, in this illustration the negative cash flow from purchasing marketable securities ($65,000) is shown separately from the positive cash flow from the sales of marketable securities ($40,000) rather than netting the two to a single negative figure of $25,000 ($65,000 − $40,000).

CASH FLOWS FROM FINANCING ACTIVITIES

Cash flows from financing activities are determined by analyzing the debit and credit changes recorded during the period in the related liability and stockholders' equity accounts. Cash flows from financing activities are more easily determined than those relating to investing activities, because financing activities seldom involve gains or losses.[4] Thus the debit or credit changes in the balance sheet accounts usually are equal to the amounts of the related cash flows.

Credit changes in such accounts as Notes Payable and the accounts for long-term debt and paid-in capital usually indicate cash receipts; debit changes indicate cash payments.

Short-Term Borrowing Transactions To illustrate, consider paragraph **10,** which provides the information supporting the following cash flows:

Proceeds from short-term borrowing	$45,000
Payments to settle short-term debts	(55,000)

[4] An early retirement of debt is an example of a financing transaction that may result in a gain or a loss.

Both the proceeds from short-term borrowing of $45,000 (a positive cash flow) and the payments to settle short-term debts of $55,000 (a negative cash flow) are presented in the statement of cash flows. Presenting both directions of the changes in cash, rather than combining the two and presenting a net amount of $10,000 ($55,000 − $45,000), is an important feature of the statement of cash flows. Presenting both positive and negative cash flows is referred to as presenting *gross* cash flows rather than presenting *net* cash flows.

Is it possible to determine the proceeds of short-term borrowing transactions throughout the year without carefully reviewing each cash receipt? The answer is yes—the proceeds from short-term borrowing are equal to the *sum of the credit entries* in the short-term *Notes Payable* account. Payments to settle short-term debts are equal to the *sum of the debit entries* in this account.

Proceeds from Issuing Bonds Payable and Capital Stock Paragraph **11** states that Allison Corporation received cash of $100,000 by issuing bonds payable. This amount was determined by summing the credit entries in the Bonds Payable account. The Bonds Payable account included no debit entries during the year; thus, no bonds were retired.

Paragraph **12** states that during the year Allison Corporation issued capital stock for $50,000. The proceeds from issuing stock are equal to the sum of the credit entries made in the Capital Stock and Additional Paid-in Capital accounts ($10,000 + $40,000).

Cash Dividends Paid to Stockholders Paragraph **13** states that Allison Corporation declared and paid cash dividends of $40,000 during the year. If dividends are both declared and paid during the same year, the cash payments are equal to the related debit entries in the Retained Earnings account.

If the balance sheet includes a liability for dividends payable, the amounts debited to Retained Earnings represent dividends *declared* during the period, which may differ from the amount of dividends *paid*. To determine cash dividends paid, we adjust the amount of dividends declared by adding any decrease (or subtracting any increase) in the Dividends Payable account over the period.

A Quick Review We have now shown the computation of each cash flow related to Allison Corporation's financing activities. In Exhibit 13–1 we illustrated a complete statement of cash flows for the company. For your convenience, we again show the financing activities section of that statement, illustrating the information developed in the preceding paragraphs.

Cash flows from financing activities:		
Proceeds from short-term borrowing	$ 45,000	
Payments to settle short-term debts	(55,000)	
Proceeds from issuing bonds payable	100,000	
Proceeds from issuing capital stock	50,000	
Dividends paid	(40,000)	
Net cash flows from financing activities		$100,000

RELATIONSHIP BETWEEN THE STATEMENT OF CASH FLOWS AND THE BALANCE SHEET

The first asset appearing in the balance sheet is Cash and Cash Equivalents. The statement of cash flows explains in some detail the change in this asset from one balance sheet date to the next. The last three lines in the statement of cash flows illustrate this relationship, as shown in our Allison Corporation example:

Net increase (decrease) in cash and cash equivalents	$35,000
Cash and cash equivalents, beginning of year	20,000
Cash and cash equivalents, end of year	$55,000

This is referred to as a reconciliation of the beginning and ending cash balances.

CASE IN POINT

Successful companies sometimes experience reductions in cash. Often these reductions are intentional in order to more productively use the company's cash in different ways. For example, in the year ending June 30, 2009, **Microsoft Corporation** reported a *decrease* in cash in excess of $4 billion! Does this mean that the company was experiencing extreme financial difficulty? Not necessarily. That year, operations provided over $19 billion. The overall decline was due to approximately $7.5 billion being used in financing activities, primarily for paying cash dividends to stockholders and purchasing treasury stock. In addition, the company used almost $16 billion in investing activities, primarily to purchase investments in other companies. In fact, that year the company did very well, with a net income of more than $14 billion. By comparison, the previous year resulted in a cash *increase* of $4,228 million.

© ImagineChina via AP Images

Lessons to be learned from this example are twofold. First, a decrease in cash does not necessarily signal financial problems, and second, a company's cash position may change in ways very different from its net income.

REPORTING OPERATING CASH FLOWS BY THE INDIRECT METHOD

In determining cash flows from operating activities for Allison Corporation, we have followed what is commonly referred to as the direct method. To this point in our study of the statement of cash flows, we have emphasized the direct method because we consider it to be the more informative and more readily understood approach. The direct method is recommended by the FASB, although companies are permitted to use either the direct or indirect method. Before completing our Allison Corporation illustration of preparing a statement of cash flows, we first look more carefully at the indirect method.

Exhibit 13–4 includes a comparison of the direct and indirect methods of determining net cash provided by operating activities for Allison Corporation. The direct method is the same as discussed earlier in this chapter. The two methods are more similar than it may appear at first glance. Both methods are based on the same underlying information and they result in the same net cash flow amount—in Allison Corporation's case, $50,000. Both methods convert information originally prepared on the accrual basis to information prepared on the cash basis. In Exhibit 13–4, accrual-based data appear in blue: cash flows are shown in red.

To illustrate the similarity in the computations, look briefly at the formulas for computing the cash inflows and outflows shown under the direct method (pages 570–572). Each formula begins with an income statement amount and then adds or subtracts the change during the period in related balance sheet accounts. Now look at our illustration of the indirect method in Exhibit 13–4. Notice that this computation also focuses on the net changes during the period in balance sheet accounts.

The difference between the two methods lies only in approach. However, the two approaches provide readers of the statement of cash flows with different types of information. The direct method informs these readers of the nature and dollar amounts of the *specific cash inflows and outflows* comprising the operating activities of the business. The indirect method, in contrast, *explains why* the net cash flows from operating activities differ from another measurement of performance—net income.

Exhibit 13–4

COMPARISON OF DIRECT AND INDIRECT METHODS

Direct Method

Cash flows from operating activities:		
Cash received from customers	$ 870,000	
Interest and dividends received	10,000	
Cash provided by operating activities		$880,000
Cash paid to suppliers and employees	$(764,000)	
Interest paid	(28,000)	
Income taxes paid	(38,000)	
Cash disbursed for operating activities		(830,000)
Net cash provided by operating activities		$ 50,000

Indirect Method

Net income		$ 65,000
Add: Depreciation expense		40,000
Decrease in accrued interest receivable		1,000
Increase in accounts payable		15,000
Increase in accrued interest liabilities		7,000
Nonoperating loss on sales of marketable securities		4,000
Subtotal		$132,000
Less: Increase in accounts receivable	$30,000	
Increase in inventory	10,000	
Increase in prepaid expenses	3,000	
Decrease in accrued operating expenses payable	6,000	
Decrease in accrued income taxes payable	2,000	
Nonoperating gain on sales of plant assets	31,000	82,000
Net cash provided by operating activities		$ 50,000

Learning Objective
LO5 **Distinguish between the direct and indirect methods of reporting operating cash flows.**

RECONCILING NET INCOME WITH NET CASH FLOWS

Learning Objective
LO6 **Explain why net income differs from net cash flows from operating activities.**

To further your understanding of the indirect method, we now discuss common adjustments required to reconcile net income with net cash flows from operating activities. The nature and dollar amounts of these adjustments are determined by an accountant using a worksheet or a computer program; they are *not* entered in the company's accounting records.

1. *Adjusting for Noncash Expenses*

   Depreciation is an example of a noncash expense—that is, depreciation expense reduces net income but does not require any cash outlay during the period. (The cash outflow related to depreciation resulted when the asset was purchased and was presented as an investing activity at that time—before any depreciation was ever recognized.) Depreciation causes expenses on the accrual basis to exceed cash payments, and net income for the period is less than net cash flows. To reconcile net income with net cash flows, we add back to net income the amount of depreciation and any other noncash expenses. (Other noncash expenses included unfunded pension expense, amortization of intangible assets, depletion of natural resources, and amortization of bond discount.)

2. *Adjusting for Timing Differences*

   Timing differences between elements of net income and net cash flows arise whenever revenue or expenses are recognized by debiting or crediting an account *other than* Cash. Changes over the period in the balances of these asset and liability accounts represent differences between the amount of revenue or expenses recognized in the income statement on the accrual basis and the net cash flows from operating activities. The balance sheet accounts that give rise to these timing differences include Accounts Receivable, Inventories, Prepaid Expenses, Accounts Payable, and Accrued Expenses Payable.

3. *Adjusting for Nonoperating Gains and Losses*

   Nonoperating gains and losses include gains and losses from sales of investments, plant assets, and discontinued operations (which relate to investing activities); and gains and losses on early retirement of debt (which relate to financing activities).

In a statement of cash flows, cash flows are classified as operating activities, investing activities, or financing activities. Nonoperating gains and losses, by definition, do not affect *operating activities*. However, these gains and losses do enter into the determination of net income. Therefore, in converting net income to net cash flows from operating activities, we *add back any nonoperating losses* and *deduct any nonoperating gains* included in net income. The full cash effect of the transaction is then presented as an investing activity (for example, sale of a building) or as a financing activity (for example, retirement of debt) in the statement of cash flows.

THE INDIRECT METHOD: A SUMMARY

The adjustments to net income explained in our preceding discussion are summarized as follows:

Net income
Add: Depreciation
Decrease in accounts receivable
Decrease in inventories
Decrease in prepaid expenses
Increase in accounts payable
Increase in accrued expenses payable
Increase in deferred income taxes payable
Nonoperating losses deducted in computing net income
Deduct: Increase in accounts receivable
Increase in inventories
Increase in prepaid expenses
Decrease in accounts payable
Decrease in accrued expenses payable
Decrease in deferred income taxes payable
Nonoperating gains added in computing net income
Net cash provided by (used in) operating activities

Learning Objective **LO7** Compute net cash flows from operating activities using the *indirect* method.

INDIRECT METHOD MAY BE REQUIRED IN A SUPPLEMENTARY SCHEDULE

The FASB recommends use of the *direct method* in presenting net cash flows from operating activities. The majority of companies, however, elect to use the indirect method. One reason is that the FASB requires companies opting for the direct method to meet an additional reporting requirement.

Companies using the direct method are required to provide a *supplementary schedule* showing the computation of net cash flows from operating activities by the indirect method. However, no supplementary computations are required of companies that present the indirect method computations in their cash flow statements because this same information is already presented in the body of the statement.

THE STATEMENT OF CASH FLOWS: A SECOND LOOK

We have now completed our explanation of Allison Corporation's statement of cash flows. We have analyzed each type of cash flow by reconciling amounts included in the other two financial statements—the income statement and the balance sheet—to determine the amounts of individual operating, investing, and financing cash flows. In computing cash flows from operating activities, we began by using the direct method, in which major categories of both positive and negative cash flows were determined and presented.

We also illustrated the indirect method to determine the amount of operating cash flows. Rather than adjusting each individual operating cash flow category for changes in balance sheet accounts, these same adjustments were made to net income.

Exhibit 13–5 includes an expanded statement of cash flows for Allison Corporation. This statement uses the direct method for operating activities and includes two supplementary schedules.

Supplementary Schedule A in Exhibit 13–5 illustrates the determination of net cash flows from operating activities by the *indirect method. Supplementary Schedule B* in Exhibit 13–5

Exhibit 13–5

ALLISON CORPORATION (EXPANDED) STATEMENT OF CASH FLOWS

ALLISON CORPORATION
STATEMENT OF CASH FLOWS
FOR THE YEAR ENDED DECEMBER 31, 2011

Cash flows from operating activities:		
Net cash provided by operating activities (see Supplementary Schedule A)		$ 50,000
Cash flows from investing activities:		
Purchases of marketable securities	$ (65,000)	
Proceeds from sales of marketable securities	40,000	
Loans made to borrowers	(17,000)	
Collections on loans	12,000	
Cash paid to acquire plant assets (see Supplementary Schedule B)	(160,000)	
Proceeds from sales of plant assets	75,000	
Net cash used in investing activities		(115,000)
Cash flows from financing activities:		
Proceeds from short-term borrowing	$ 45,000	
Payments to settle short-term debts	(55,000)	
Proceeds from issuing bonds payable	100,000	
Proceeds from issuing capital stock	50,000	
Dividends paid	(40,000)	
Net cash provided by financing activities		100,000
Net increase (decrease) in cash		$ 35,000
Cash and cash equivalents, Jan. 1, 2011		20,000
Cash and cash equivalents, Dec. 31, 2011		$ 55,000

Supplementary Schedule A: Net Cash Provided by Operating Activities

Net income		$ 65,000
Add: Depreciation expense		40,000
Decrease in accrued interest receivable		1,000
Increase in accounts payable		15,000
Increase in accrued liabilities		7,000
Nonoperating loss on sales of marketable securities		4,000
Subtotal		$ 132,000
Less: Increase in accounts receivable	$ 30,000	
Increase in inventory	10,000	
Increase in prepaid expenses	3,000	
Decrease in accrued liabilities	8,000	
Nonoperating gain on sales of plant assets	31,000	82,000
Net cash provided by operating activities		$ 50,000

Supplementary Schedule B: Noncash Investing and Financing Activities

Purchases of plant assets	$ 200,000
Less: Portion financed through issuance of long-term debt	40,000
Cash paid to acquire plant assets	$ 160,000

Notice this supplementary schedule illustrates the indirect method of determining cash flows from operations

discloses any noncash aspects of the company's investing and financing activities. This type of supplementary schedule is required whenever some aspects of the company's investing and financing activities do not coincide with cash flows occurring within the current period.

How would the statement of cash flows in Exhibit 13–5 differ if the indirect method were used? The information included in Supplementary Schedule A would be moved up into the "Cash flows from operating activities" section of the financial statement and would no longer be required as a supplemental disclosure. In fact, this is one reason for the popularity of the indirect method. Because the indirect method calculation is required to be disclosed if the direct method is used, many companies simply prefer to include the reconciliation of net income to net cash from operating activities in the body of the statement of cash flows and avoid the need for the supplemental disclosure of that same information.

Financial Analysis and Decision Making

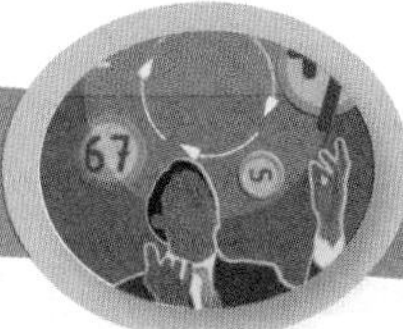

The users of a statement of cash flows are particularly interested in the *net cash flows from operating activities*. Is the amount large enough to provide for necessary replacements of plant assets and maturing liabilities? And if so, is there enough left for the current dividend to look secure—or even be increased?

Consider two competitors in the import craft supplies business, Gonzalez, Inc., and Alvarez Company. These companies have approximately the same size assets, liabilities, and sales. Selected information from their most recent statements of cash flows follows:

	Beginning Cash Balance	Net Cash Flow from (in thousands) Operating Activities	Investing Activities	Financing Activities	Ending Cash Balance
Gonzalez	$150	$600	$(500)	$400	$650
Alvarez	150	50	500	(50)	650

Which company is in the stronger cash flow position? Although both have the same beginning and ending cash balances ($150,000 and $650,000, respectively), Gonzalez is in the stronger position because of its strong operating cash flows of $600,000. Gonzalez has been able to invest $500,000 in operating assets, while financing only $400,000, and still has a $650,000 ending cash balance. Alvarez, on the other hand, has generated only a small amount of cash from operations ($50,000) and has sold assets to generate cash ($500,000) to support its ending cash balance. Whether Alvarez will be able to sustain its cash position over time, and be able to meet its recurring obligations in the future, is questionable.

Even more important than net cash flows from operating activities in any one year is the *trend* in cash flows over a period of years—and the *consistency* of that trend from year to year. The best results are net cash flows from operating activities that increase each year by a substantial—but also predictable—percentage.[5]

Free Cash Flow Many analysts compute an amount called **free cash flow.** Free cash flow represents the cash flow available to management for discretionary purposes, *after* the company has met all of its basic obligations relating to business operations. The term *free cash flow* is widely cited within the business community. Different analysts compute this measure in different ways. For example, are all expenditures for plant assets "basic obligations," or only those expenditures made to maintain the current level of productive capacity?

One common method of computing free cash flow is to deduct from the net cash flows from operating activities net cash used to purchase plant assets and any dividends paid. This computation follows, using information from the Allison Corporation statement of cash flows shown earlier.

This computation suggests that Allison Corporation *did not* generate enough cash from operations to meet its basic obligations. Thus, management had to raise cash from other sources. But, of course, an analyst always should look behind the numbers. For example, was Allison's purchase of plant assets during the year a basic obligation, or did it represent a discretionary expansion of the business?

Net cash flows from operating activities		$ 50,000
Less: Net cash used for acquiring plant assets ($160,000 − $75,000 proceeds)	$85,000	
Dividends paid	40,000	125,000
Free cash flow		$(75,000)

What's left for discretionary purposes?

[5] Percentage change is the dollar amount of change from one year to the next, expressed as a percentage of (divided by) the amount from the *earlier* of the two years. For example, if net cash provided by operating activities was $100,000 in the first year and $120,000 in the second year, the percentage increase is 20 percent, computed as follows: ($120,000 − $100,000) ÷ $100,000.

(continued)

YOUR TURN **You as a Financial Analyst**

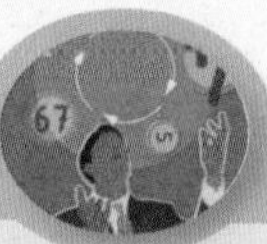

You are working for the same stock market research firm as in Chapter 12, but unlike your previous boss (who tended to focus on growth and relative value, both based on reported earnings), your new boss focuses primarily on free cash flow and dividends in choosing stocks.

Your new boss is interested in stocks where free cash flow equals at least 50 percent of cash flow from operations. He also wants dividends to be 25 percent or more of cash flow from operations. You are considering the same stocks as before: **Home Depot**, **Intel**, **Coca-Cola**, and **Amazon**. Your new boss provides you with the following information and asks you to recommend which stocks are consistent with his investment criteria.

	In Millions		
Company	**Cash Flow from Operations (CFO)**	**Net Capital Expenditures**	**Dividends**
Home Depot	$ 5,125	$ 966	$1,525
Intel	11,170	4,515	3,108
Coca-Cola	8,186	1,993	3,800
Amazon	3,293	373	—

He also tells you that a potential new client is going to be calling you this afternoon. This potential client is an elderly widow who is quite wealthy, and she is curious as to why the relative levels of free cash flow and dividends are important metrics. She also doesn't understand why all firms don't pay dividends. Your boss tells you to answer this prospective client's questions.

(See our comments on the Online Learning Center Web site.)

Managing Cash Flows

Management can do much to influence the cash flows of a particular period. In fact, it has a responsibility to manage cash flows. No business can afford to run out of cash and default on its obligations. Even being a few days late in meeting payrolls, or paying suppliers or creditors, can severely damage important business relationships. Thus, one of management's most basic responsibilities is to ensure that the business has enough cash to meet its obligations as they come due.

BUDGETING: THE PRIMARY CASH MANAGEMENT TOOL

The primary tool used by management to anticipate and shape future cash flows is a *cash budget*. A **cash budget** is a *forecast* of future cash receipts and payments. This budget is *not* a financial statement and is not widely distributed to people outside of the organization. To managers, however, it is among the most useful of all accounting reports.

In many ways, a cash budget is similar to a statement of cash flows. However, the budget shows the results *expected in future periods,* rather than those achieved in the past. Also, the cash budget is more *detailed,* usually showing expected cash flows month-by-month and separately for every department within the organization.

Cash budgets serve many purposes. Among the most important are:

- Encouraging managers to plan and coordinate the activities of their departments in advance.
- Providing managers with advance notice of the resources at their disposal and the results they are expected to achieve.
- Providing targets useful in evaluating departmental performance.
- Providing advance warnings of potential cash shortages.

WHAT PRIORITY SHOULD MANAGERS GIVE TO INCREASING NET CASH FLOWS?

Learning Objective
Discuss the likely effects of various business strategies on cash flows. **LO8**

Creditors and investors look to a company's cash flows to protect their investment and provide future returns. Trends in key cash flows (such as from operations and free cash flow) affect a company's credit rating, stock price, and access to additional investment capital. For these reasons, management is under constant pressure to improve the key measures of cash flow. Unfortunately, the pressure to report higher cash flows in the current period may *conflict* with managers' long run responsibilities.

Short-Term Results versus Long-Term Growth Often, short-term operating results can be improved at the expense of long-term growth. For example, reducing expenditures for developing new products will increase earnings and net cash flows in the current period. But over time, this strategy may lessen the company's competitiveness and long-term profitability.

One-Time Boosts to Cash Flows Some strategies can increase the net cash flows of the current period, but *without having much effect* on future cash flows. Such strategies include collecting receivables more quickly and reducing the size of inventory.

Assume, for example, that a company offers 60-day terms to its credit customers. Thus credit sales made in January are collected in March, and credit sales made in February are collected in April. Notice that in each month, the company is collecting about *one month's amount* of credit sales.

Now assume that on March 1 the company changes its policies to allow only *30-day* credit terms. In April, the company will collect *two months* of credit sales—those made in February (under the former 60-day terms) *and* those made in March (under the new 30-day terms).

This significantly increases the cash received from customers for the month of April. But it does not signal higher cash flows for the months ahead. In May, the company will collect only those credit sales made in April. Thus it quickly returns to the pattern of collecting about *one month's* credit sales in the current month. Shortening the collection period provided only a one-time boost in cash receipts.

A similar one-time boost may be achieved by reducing the size of inventory. This reduces the need for purchasing merchandise, *but only while inventory levels are falling.* Once the company stabilizes the size of its inventory at the new and lower level, its monthly purchases must return to approximately the quantity of goods sold during the period.

SOME STRATEGIES FOR PERMANENT IMPROVEMENTS IN CASH FLOW

Several strategies may improve cash flows in *both* the short and long term. These are *deferring income taxes, peak pricing,* and developing an *effective product mix.*

Deferring Income Taxes *Deferring* income taxes means using accounting methods for income tax purposes that legally postpone the payment of income taxes. An example is using an *accelerated depreciation method* for income tax purposes.

Deferring taxes may benefit a growing business *every year.* Thus, it is an effective and popular cash management strategy.[6]

[6] The Modified Accelerated Cost Recovery System (MACRS) is an accelerated method widely used for income tax purposes. Deferred income taxes were discussed briefly in Chapter 10. The reason a growing business can benefit from deferred taxes *every year* is that each year it defers a *greater amount* than comes due from the past.

Peak Pricing Some businesses have more customers than they can handle—at least at certain times of the day or year. Examples of such businesses include popular restaurants, resort hotels, telephone companies, and providers of electricity.

Peak pricing is a strategy of using sales prices both to increase revenue and to ration goods and services when total demand exceeds supply (or capacity). A higher price is charged during the peak periods of customer demand and a lower price during off-peak periods. Peak pricing has two related goals. First, it *increases the seller's revenue* during the periods of greatest demand. Second, it *shifts* some of the demand to off-peak periods, when the business is better able to service additional customers.

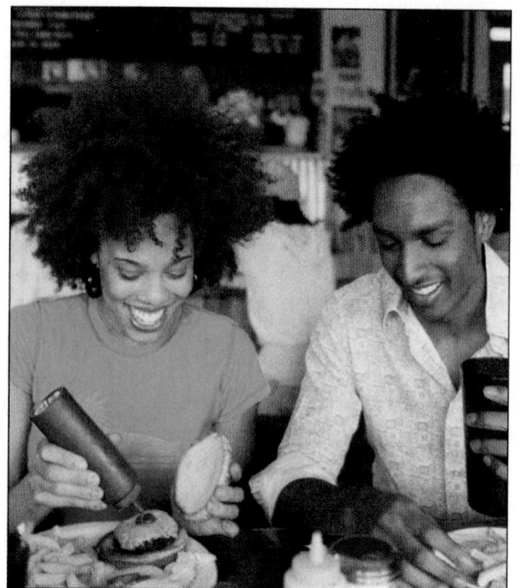

© PunchStock/Brand X Pictures/DAL

Peak pricing may make goods and services available to customers who otherwise could not afford them. Also, peak pricing may prevent systems, such as cellular telephones, from becoming so overloaded that they simply cannot function. Peak pricing is *not always appropriate*. For example, we would not expect hospitals or physicians to raise their prices during epidemics or natural disasters. The alternative to peak pricing is a single price all the time.

Develop an Effective Product Mix Another tool for increasing revenue and cash receipts is the mix of products offered for sale. The dual purposes of an effective **product mix** are to (1) increase total sales and (2) increase gross margins (that is, the excess of the selling price over the cost of the product).

Some products complement one another, meaning the customer who buys one product often may purchase the other. Common examples of **complementary products** include french fries at a hamburger restaurant, snacks at a movie theater, and a car wash connected to a gas station.

Ethics, Fraud & Corporate Governance

As discussed in this chapter, cash flow from operations is the subtotal on the statement of cash flows that is most closely scrutinized by financial statement readers. A large and growing cash flow from operations is viewed positively for at least three reasons. First, companies pay bills with cash, not with earnings. Second, a company with significant cash flows from operations is better positioned to fund future growth with its own cash flows rather than having to borrow additional monies or issue more stock. Third, the quality of a company's earnings is viewed as better if cash flow from operations closely matches reported net income.

Although it may be difficult to manipulate cash flows from operations, it is not impossible, as the Securities and Exchange Commission (SEC) enforcement action involving **Dynergy, Inc.**, illustrates. **Dynergy** produces and delivers energy, including natural gas, electricity, and coal, to customers throughout North America and Europe, and its shares are traded on the New York Stock Exchange. **Dynergy** entered into a structured transaction (hereafter referred to as Project Alpha) that resulted in **Dynergy** reporting $300 million in cash flow from operations that should have been reported as cash flow from financing activities. A primary motivation for **Dynergy**'s involvement with Project Alpha was to bring cash flow from operations closer to reported net income.

Project Alpha had a five-year term and worked as follows. **Dynergy** sponsored a special-purpose entity, **ABG Supply**, to sell **Dynergy** natural gas. In the first year of the five-year term of Project Alpha, **ABG Supply** sold **Dynergy** gas at below-market prices. **Dynergy** then sold this gas at a $300 million profit and reported the resulting cash flow in the operating activities portion of the statement of cash flows. In the remaining four years of Project Alpha's life, **Dynergy** was obligated to buy gas from **ABG Supply** at above-market prices. These purchases at above-market prices would be sufficient to pay back the $300 million, plus interest. In substance, the original sale of gas to **Dynergy** in year 1 at $300 million below market prices represented a loan, and transactions in years 2 to 5 would result in the loan being repaid with interest. As such, the $300 million cash flow in Year 1 should have been reported in the financing activities portion of the statement of cash flows—not in the operating activities portion of the statement.

Three midlevel **Dynergy** tax executives were largely responsible for Project Alpha's structure, and they

(continued)

participated in an active scheme to hide the details of the structure from **Dynergy**'s outside auditors. Two of these executives pled guilty to federal *criminal* charges and testified against the third executive. The third executive, Jamie Olis, was convicted of criminal charges and was sentenced to over 20 years in federal prison (although this sentence was reduced substantially on appeal). This case clearly illustrates the personal risk of violating securities laws, particularly when there is an active scheme to hide the true nature of transactions from auditors, investors, and other outside parties.

Some complementary products are *essential* to satisfying the customer. (Would you be happy at a sports stadium that didn't sell food?) Others increase sales by *attracting customers* who also purchase other types of merchandise.

Some complementary products appear to be only incidental to the company's main product lines. But, in reality, these incidental items may *be* the company's most important products.

A Worksheet for Preparing a Statement of Cash Flows

Learning Objective
Explain how a worksheet may be helpful in preparing a statement of cash flows. LO9

A statement of cash flows is developed by *systematically analyzing all changes in the noncash balance sheet accounts.* This process can be formalized and documented through the preparation of a specially designed worksheet. The worksheet also provides the accountant with visual assurance that the changes in balance sheet accounts have been fully explained.

DATA FOR AN ILLUSTRATION

We will illustrate the worksheet approach using the 2011 financial data of Auto Supply Co.[7] Shown in Exhibit 13–6 are the balances in Auto's balance sheet accounts at the beginning and

Exhibit 13–6
AUTO SUPPLY CO. BALANCE SHEETS

AUTO SUPPLY CO.
COMPARATIVE BALANCE SHEETS

	December 31, 2010	December 31, 2011
Assets		
Cash	$ 50,000	$ 45,000
Marketable Securities	40,000	25,000
Accounts Receivable	320,000	330,000
Inventory	240,000	235,000
Plant and Equipment (net of accumulated depreciation)	600,000	640,000
Totals	$1,250,000	$1,275,000
Liabilities & Stockholders' Equity		
Accounts Payable	$ 150,000	$ 160,000
Accrued Expenses Payable	60,000	45,000
Mortgage Note Payable (long-term)	–0–	70,000
Bonds Payable (due in 2020)	500,000	350,000
Capital Stock (no par value)	160,000	160,000
Retained Earnings	380,000	490,000
Totals	$1,250,000	$1,275,000

Changes in the noncash accounts are the key to identifying cash flows

[7] Our example involving Allison Corporation was quite comprehensive. Therefore, a worksheet for Allison Corporation would be too long and detailed for use as an introductory illustration of a worksheet for the statement of cash flows.

end of 2011. (Notice in this illustration that the account balances at the end of the current year appear in the *right-hand* column. This format also is used in the worksheet.)

Additional Information The following information also is used in the preparation of the worksheet. (Accrual-based measurements appear in **blue**, cash flows in **red**.)

1. Net income for the year amounted to *$250,000*. Cash dividends of ***$140,000*** were declared and paid.
2. Auto's only noncash expense was depreciation, which totaled *$60,000*.
3. Marketable securities costing *$15,000* were sold for ***$35,000*** cash, resulting in a *$20,000* nonoperating gain.
4. The company purchased plant assets for *$100,000*, making a ***$30,000*** cash down payment and issuing a *$70,000* mortgage note payable for the balance of the purchase price.

THE WORKSHEET

Auto Supply Co. reports cash flows from operating activities by the *indirect method.*[8] A worksheet for preparing a statement of cash flows appears in Exhibit 13–7.

To set up the worksheet, the company's balance sheet accounts are listed in the top portion of the worksheet, with the beginning balances in the first column and the year-end balances in the last (right-hand) column. (For purposes of illustration, we have shown these accounts and account balances in **black.**)

The two middle columns are used to (1) explain the changes in each balance sheet account over the year and (2) indicate how each change affected cash.

Entries in the Two Middle Columns The entries in the *top portion of the worksheet* summarize the transactions recorded in the account over the year. (Because these entries summarize transactions recorded on the accrual basis, they are shown in blue.)

For each summary entry in the top portion of the worksheet, we make an offsetting entry (in the opposite column) in the *bottom portion* of the worksheet indicating the *cash effects* of the transactions. These cash effects are classified as operating, investing, or financing activities and are explained with a descriptive caption. (Entries representing the *cash effects* of transactions and the related descriptive captions appear in red.)

Entries in the two middle columns may be made in any sequence, but we recommend the following approach:

1. Explain the change in the Retained Earnings account.
2. Account for depreciation expense (and any other noncash expenses).
3. Account for timing differences between net income and cash flows from operating activities.
4. Explain any remaining changes in balance sheet accounts *other than Cash.* (Hint: Changes in asset accounts represent investing activities; changes in liability and equity accounts represent financing activities.)
5. Compute and record the net increase or decrease in cash.

Using this approach, we next explain the entries in our illustrated worksheet.

ENTRY

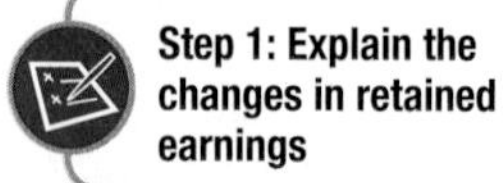
Step 1: Explain the changes in retained earnings

1. Auto's net income explains a $250,000 *credit* to the Retained Earnings account. In the bottom portion of the working paper, an offsetting entry is made in the *Sources* column and is classified as an operating activity.[9]
2. Cash dividends of $140,000 caused a *debit* to the Retained Earnings account during 2011. The offsetting entry falls into the *Uses* column; payments of dividends are classified as a financing activity.

---

[8] If the worksheet utilizes the direct method, numerous subclassifications are required within the operating activities section. Such worksheets are illustrated in more advanced accounting courses.

[9] When the *indirect method* is used, net income serves as the *starting point* for computing net cash flows from operating activities.

AUTO SUPPLY CO.
WORKSHEET FOR A STATEMENT OF CASH FLOWS
FOR THE YEAR ENDED DECEMBER 31, 2011

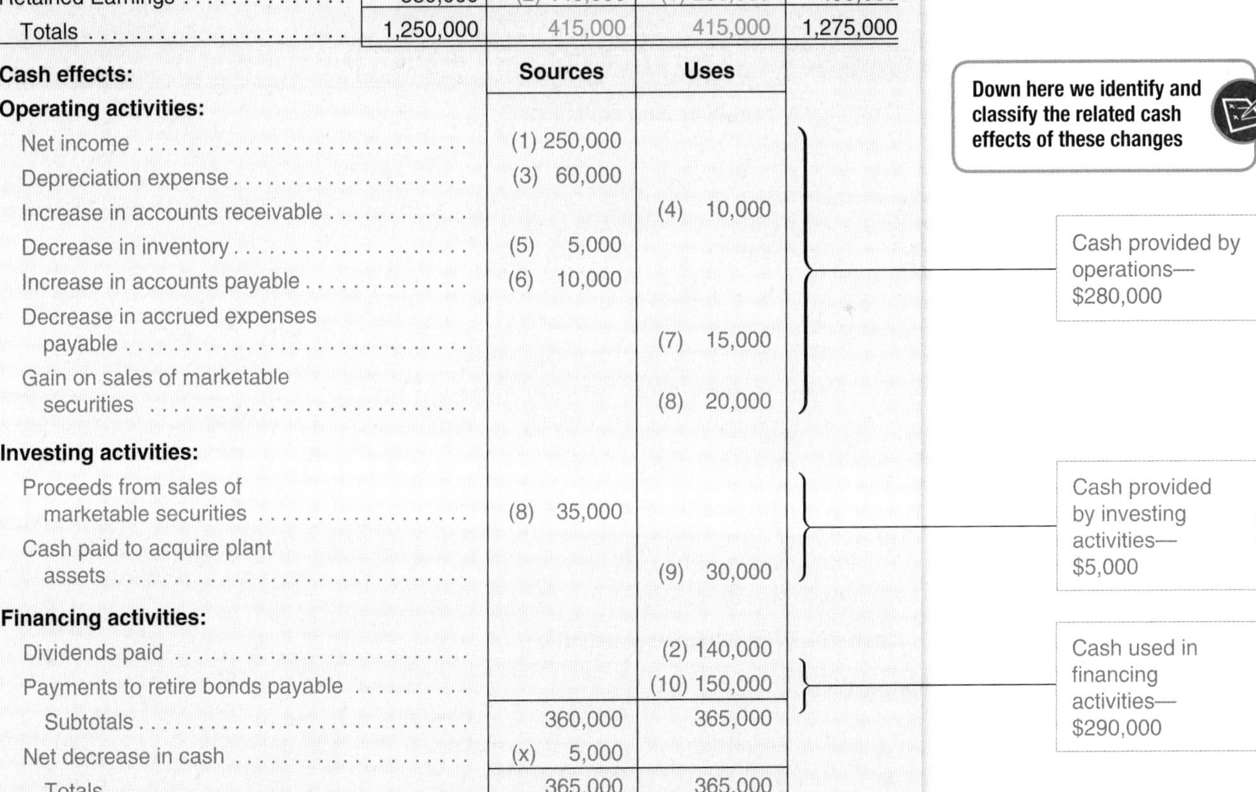

		Effects of Transactions		
Balance sheet effects:	**Beginning Balance**	**Debit Changes**	**Credit Changes**	**Ending Balance**
Assets				
Cash and Cash Equivalents	50,000		(x) 5,000	45,000
Marketable Securities	40,000		(8) 15,000	25,000
Accounts Receivable	320,000	(4) 10,000		330,000
Inventory	240,000		(5) 5,000	235,000
Plant and Equipment (net of accumulated depreciation)	600,000	(9) 100,000	(3) 60,000	640,000
Totals	1,250,000			1,275,000
Liabilities & Stockholders' Equity				
Accounts Payable.	150,000		(6) 10,000	160,000
Accrued Expenses Payable	60,000	(7) 15,000		45,000
Mortgage Note Payable	–0–		(9) 70,000	70,000
Bonds Payable	500,000	(10) 150,000		350,000
Capital Stock	160,000			160,000
Retained Earnings	380,000	(2) 140,000	(1) 250,000	490,000
Totals	1,250,000	415,000	415,000	1,275,000
Cash effects:		**Sources**	**Uses**	
Operating activities:				
Net income		(1) 250,000		
Depreciation expense.		(3) 60,000		
Increase in accounts receivable			(4) 10,000	
Decrease in inventory.		(5) 5,000		
Increase in accounts payable		(6) 10,000		
Decrease in accrued expenses payable			(7) 15,000	
Gain on sales of marketable securities			(8) 20,000	
Investing activities:				
Proceeds from sales of marketable securities		(8) 35,000		
Cash paid to acquire plant assets			(9) 30,000	
Financing activities:				
Dividends paid			(2) 140,000	
Payments to retire bonds payable			(10) 150,000	
Subtotals.		360,000	365,000	
Net decrease in cash		(x) 5,000		
Totals		365,000	365,000	

Cash provided by operations—$280,000

Cash provided by investing activities—$5,000

Cash used in financing activities—$290,000

Exhibit 13–7

WORKSHEET FOR A STATEMENT OF CASH FLOWS

Up here we summarize the changes in each noncash account

Down here we identify and classify the related cash effects of these changes

With these first two entries, we have explained how Auto's Retained Earnings account increased during 2011 from $380,000 to $490,000.

3. Auto's only noncash expense was depreciation. In the top portion of the worksheet, depreciation explains a $60,000 credit (decrease) in Plant and Equipment (which includes the Accumulated Depreciation accounts). The offsetting entry in the

Step 2: Account for noncash expenses

bottom of the worksheet is placed in the Sources column. We have explained that depreciation is not really a source of cash, but that it *is added back* to net income as a step in computing the cash flows from operating activities.

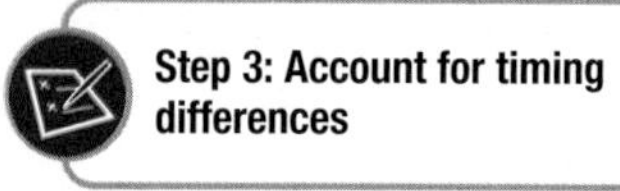

Step 3: Account for timing differences

4–7. Fluctuations in current assets and current liabilities create *timing differences* between net income and the net cash flows from operating activities. In the top portion of the worksheet, entries (4) through (7) summarize the changes in these current asset and current liability accounts. In the bottom portion, they show how these changes affect the computation of cash flows from operating activities.

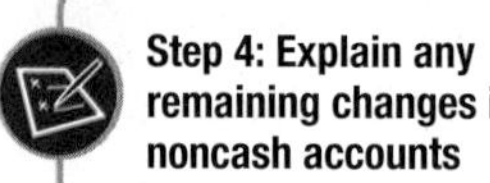

Step 4: Explain any remaining changes in noncash accounts

8. In 2011, Auto sold marketable securities with a cost of $15,000 for $35,000 cash, resulting in a $20,000 nonoperating gain. In the top portion of the worksheet, the entry explains the $15,000 credit change in the Marketable Securities account. In the bottom portion, it reports cash proceeds of $35,000. The difference? The $20,000 nonoperating gain, which is *removed from the Operating Activities section* of the worksheet and included instead within the amount reported as "Proceeds from sales of marketable securities" in the Investing Activities category.
9. Auto purchased $100,000 in plant assets, paying $30,000 cash and issuing a $70,000 note payable. These events explain a $100,000 debit in Plant and Equipment and the $70,000 credit change in Mortgage Note Payable; they involved a cash outlay of $30,000, which is classified as an investing activity. (The $70,000 financed by issuance of a note payable is a *noncash* investing and financing activity.)

Exhibit 13–8

AUTO SUPPLY CO. STATEMENT OF CASH FLOWS

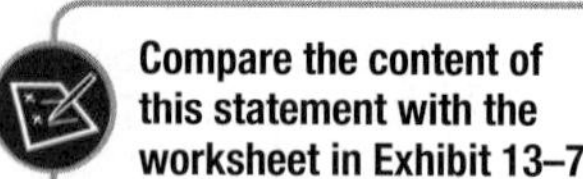

Compare the content of this statement with the worksheet in Exhibit 13–7

AUTO SUPPLY CO.
STATEMENT OF CASH FLOWS
FOR THE YEAR ENDED DECEMBER 31, 2011

Cash flows from operating activities:		
Net income		$ 250,000
Add: Depreciation expense		60,000
Decrease in inventory		5,000
Increase in accounts payable		10,000
Subtotal		$ 325,000
Less: Increase in accounts receivable	$ 10,000	
Decrease in accrued expenses payable	15,000	
Gain on sales of marketable securities	20,000	45,000
Net cash provided by operating activities		$ 280,000
Cash flows from investing activities:		
Proceeds from sales of marketable securities	$ 35,000	
Cash paid to acquire plant assets (see supplementary schedule below)	(30,000)	
Net cash provided by investing activities		5,000
Cash flows from financing activities:		
Dividends paid	$ (140,000)	
Payments to retire bonds payable	(150,000)	
Net cash used for financing activities		(290,000)
Net decrease in cash		$ (5,000)
Cash and cash equivalents, Jan. 1, 2011		50,000
Cash and cash equivalents, Dec. 31, 2011		$ 45,000

Supplementary Schedule: Noncash Investing and Financing Activities

Purchases of plant assets	$ 100,000
Less: Portion financed through issuance of long-term debt	70,000
Cash paid to acquire plant assets	$ 30,000

10. The $150,000 debit change in Auto's Bonds Payable account indicates that this amount of the liability has been repaid—that is, $150,000 in bonds has been retired. This is included in the financing activities category.

At this point, we should check to determine that our entries in the two middle columns *fully explain* the differences between the beginning and ending balance of each noncash balance sheet account. If the top portion of the worksheet explains the changes in every noncash account, the bottom section should include all of the cash flows for the year.

(x) We now total the Sources (cash increases) and Uses (cash decreases) columns in the bottom portion of the worksheet. The difference between these column subtotals represents the *net increase or decrease* in cash. In our example, the Sources column totals $360,000, while the Uses column totals $365,000, indicating a *$5,000 decrease* in cash over the period. Notice that this is exactly the amount by which Cash decreased during 2011: $50,000 − $45,000 = $5,000. Our last entry, labeled *(x)*, explains the credit change in the Cash account at the top of the worksheet and brings the bottom of the worksheet into balance.

Step 5: Compute and record the net change in cash

The formal statement of cash flows, reporting the cash flows from operating activities by the indirect method, can be prepared directly from the bottom portion of this worksheet. In Exhibit 13–8, amounts appearing in accrual-based accounting records are shown in blue; cash flows appear in red.

Concluding Remarks

In this chapter, we have discussed the importance of cash flow information for investors and creditors and how that information is arranged and presented in the statement of cash flows. We delayed in-depth coverage of this important topic to this point because of the importance of understanding accounting for assets, liabilities, and stockholders' equity as a forerunner to understanding how cash flow information differs from accrual accounting information.

As stated earlier, companies have an option of presenting cash flow from operations information by either the direct or the indirect method. Although we have presented both in this chapter, our emphasis has been on the direct method despite the fact that most companies employ the indirect method in their financial reporting. We have done this for two reasons. First, we believe the direct method is more readily understood by students and others who are learning for the first time how cash-based and accrual-based information relate. Second, and perhaps more important, investors appear to generally favor the direct method, as evidenced by the following quote from the former chief accountant of the Securities and Exchange Commission, speaking to a group of certified public accountants:

> I've heard many investors express a strong preference for use of the direct method of preparing the statement of cash flows. It's widely understood and believed by many to be a more informative presentation. We are not requiring a change, but it is an action you could consider to promote transparency given the importance to investors of cash flow information.[10]

In the next chapter, we take a broader look at financial statement analysis, including how information about cash flows is combined with information from the other financial statements, to better understand a company's financial activities. Managers and investors alike must look beyond short-term changes in earnings and cash flows from one period to the next. They must consider factors that cause these changes and how they may affect future operations. Throughout this text, we have introduced simple financial analysis techniques that are useful in analyzing a company. In Chapter 14, we bring those techniques together into a comprehensive model for analyzing financial statements in a way that assists informed decision makers in understanding a company's business activities and in anticipating the long-term effects of business strategies.

[10] Donald T. Nicolaisen in a speech entitled, "Remarks before the 2003 Thirty-First AICPA National Conference on Current SEC Developments," December 11, 2003.

END-OF-CHAPTER REVIEW

SUMMARY OF LEARNING OBJECTIVES

LO1 **Explain the purposes and uses of a statement of cash flows.** The primary purpose of a statement of cash flows is to provide information about the cash receipts and cash payments of the entity and how they relate to the entity's operating, investing, and financing activities. Readers of financial statements use this information to assess the liquidity of a business and to evaluate its ability to generate positive cash flows in future periods, pay dividends, and finance growth.

LO2 **Describe how cash transactions are classified in a statement of cash flows.** Cash flows are classified as (1) operating activities, (2) investing activities, or (3) financing activities. Receipts and payments of interest are classified as operating activities.

LO3 **Compute the major cash flows relating to operating activities.** The major operating cash flows are (1) cash received from customers, (2) cash paid to suppliers and employees, (3) interest and dividends received, (4) interest paid, and (5) income taxes paid. These cash flows are computed by converting the income statement amounts for revenue, cost of goods sold, and expenses from the accrual basis to the cash basis. This is done by adjusting the income statement amounts for changes occurring over the period in related balance sheet accounts.

LO4 **Compute the cash flows relating to investing and financing activities.** Cash flows from investing and financing activities are determined by examining the entries in the related asset and liability accounts, along with any related gains or losses shown in the income statement. Debit entries in asset accounts represent purchases of assets (an investing activity). Credit entries in asset accounts represent the cost of assets sold. The amount of these credit entries must be adjusted by any gains or losses recognized on these sales transactions.

Debit entries to liability accounts represent repayment of debt, while credit entries represent borrowing. Both types of transactions are classified as financing activities. Other financing activities include the issuance of stock (indicated by credits to the paid-in capital accounts) and payment of dividends (indicated by a debit change in the Retained Earnings account).

LO5 **Distinguish between the direct and indirect methods of reporting operating cash flows.** The direct and indirect methods are alternative formats for reporting net cash flows from operating activities. The *direct* method shows the specific cash inflows and outflows comprising the operating activities of the business. By the *indirect* method, the computation begins with accrual-based net income and then makes adjustments necessary to arrive at net cash flows from operating activities. Both methods result in the same dollar amount of net cash flows from operating activities. When the direct method is used, the indirect method must also be disclosed.

LO6 **Explain why net income differs from net cash flows from operating activities.** Net income differs from net operating cash flows for several reasons. One reason is noncash expenses, such as depreciation and the amortization of intangible assets. These expenses, which require no cash outlays when they are recognized, reduce net income but do not require cash payments. Another reason is the many timing differences existing between the recognition of revenue and expense and the occurrence of the underlying cash flows. Finally, nonoperating gains and losses enter into the determination of net income, but the related cash flows are classified as investing or financing activities, not operating activities.

LO7 **Compute net cash flows from operating activities using the *indirect* method.** The indirect method uses net income (as reported in the income statement) as the starting point in the computation of net cash flows from operating activities. Adjustments to net income necessary to arrive at net cash flows from operating activities are described in three categories: noncash expenses, timing differences, and nonoperating gains and losses. Adjustments reconcile net income (accrual basis) to net cash flows from operating activities. Specific adjustments from each category are illustrated in the summary analysis of the indirect method on page 579.

LO8 **Discuss the likely effects of various business strategies on cash flows.** It is difficult to predict the *extent* to which a business strategy will affect cash flows. However, an informed decision maker should understand the *direction* in which a strategy is likely to affect cash flows—both in the short term and over a longer term.

LO9 **Explain how a worksheet may be helpful in preparing a statement of cash flows.** A worksheet can be used to analyze the changes in balance sheet accounts other than Cash and, thereby, determine the related cash flows. In the top portion of the worksheet, entries are made summarizing the changes in each noncash account. In the bottom half, offsetting entries are made to represent the cash effects of the transactions summarized in the top portion. The entries in the bottom half of the worksheet are classified into the same categories as in a statement of cash flows—operating, investing, and financing. The statement of cash flows then is prepared from the data in the bottom portion of the worksheet.

Key Terms Introduced or Emphasized in Chapter 13

accrual basis (p. 567) A method of summarizing operating results in terms of revenue earned and expenses incurred, rather than cash receipts or cash payments.

cash basis (p. 570) The practice of summarizing operating results in terms of cash receipts and cash payments, rather than revenue earned or expenses incurred.

cash budget (p. 582) A detailed forecast of expected future cash receipts, usually organized department by department and month by month for the coming year.

cash equivalents (p. 567) Highly liquid short-term investments, such as Treasury bills, money market funds, and commercial paper. For purposes of preparing a statement of cash flows, money held in cash equivalents is considered the same as cash. Thus transfers between a bank account and cash equivalents are not considered receipts or disbursements of cash.

cash flows (p. 564) A term describing both cash receipts (inflows) and cash payments (outflows).

complementary products (p. 584) Products that "fit together"—that tie in with a company's other products. As a result, customers attracted to one product may also purchase others.

financing activities (p. 564) Transactions such as borrowing, repaying borrowed amounts, raising equity capital, or making distributions to owners. The cash effects of these transactions are reported in the financing activities section of the statement of cash flows. Noncash aspects of these transactions are disclosed in a supplementary schedule.

free cash flow (p. 581) The portion of the annual net cash flows from operating activities that remains available for discretionary purposes after the basic obligations of the business have been met. Can be computed in several different ways.

investing activities (p. 564) Transactions involving acquisitions or sales of investments or plant assets and making or collecting loans. The cash aspects of these transactions are shown in the investing activities section of the statement of cash flows. Noncash aspects of these transactions are disclosed in a supplementary schedule to this financial statement.

operating activities (p. 564) Transactions entering into the determination of net income, with the exception of gains and losses relating to financing or investing activities. The category includes such transactions as selling goods or services, earning investment income, and incurring costs and expenses, such as payments to suppliers and employees, interest, and income taxes. The cash effects of these transactions are reflected in the operating activities section of the statement of cash flows.

peak pricing (p. 584) The strategy of charging a higher price during periods of high demand, and a lower price during periods of slack demand. Intended to both maximize revenue and shift excess demand to periods in which it can be more easily accommodated.

product mix (p. 584) The variety and relative quantities of goods and services that a company offers for sale.

Demonstration Problem

You are the chief accountant for Electro Products, Inc. Your assistant has prepared an income statement for the current year and has developed the following additional information by analyzing changes in the company's balance sheet accounts.

ELECTRO PRODUCTS, INC.
INCOME STATEMENT
FOR THE YEAR ENDED DECEMBER 31, 2011

Revenue:		
Net sales		$9,500,000
Interest income		320,000
Gain on sales of marketable securities		70,000
Total revenue and gains		$9,890,000
Costs and expenses:		
Cost of goods sold	$4,860,000	
Operating expenses (including depreciation of $700,000)	3,740,000	
Interest expense	270,000	
Income tax expense	300,000	
Loss on sales of plant assets	90,000	
Total costs, expenses, and losses		9,260,000
Net income		$ 630,000

Changes in the company's balance sheet accounts over the year are summarized as follows:

1. Accounts Receivable decreased by $85,000.
2. Accrued Interest Receivable increased by $15,000.
3. Inventory decreased by $280,000, and Accounts Payable to suppliers of merchandise decreased by $240,000.
4. Short-term prepayments of operating expenses decreased by $18,000, and accrued liabilities for operating expenses increased by $35,000.
5. The liability for Accrued Interest Payable decreased by $16,000 during the year.
6. The liability for Accrued Income Taxes Payable increased by $25,000 during the year.
7. The following schedule summarizes the total debit and credit entries during the year in other balance sheet accounts:

	Debit Entries	Credit Entries
Marketable Securities	$ 120,000	$ 210,000
Notes Receivable (cash loans made to others)	250,000	190,000
Plant Assets (see paragraph **8**)	3,800,000	360,000
Notes Payable (short-term borrowing)	620,000	740,000
Bonds Payable		1,100,000
Capital Stock		50,000
Additional Paid-in Capital (from issuance of stock)		840,000
Retained Earnings (see paragraph **9**)	320,000	630,000

8. The $360,000 in credit entries to the Plant Assets account is net of any debits to accumulated depreciation when plant assets were retired. Thus, the $360,000 in credit entries represents the *book value* of all plant assets sold or retired during the year.
9. The $320,000 debit to Retained Earnings represents dividends declared and paid during the year. The $630,000 credit entry represents the net income for the year.
10. All investing and financing activities were cash transactions.
11. Cash and cash equivalents amounted to $448,000 at the beginning of the year and to $330,000 at year-end.

Instructions

You are to prepare a statement of cash flows for the current year, following the format illustrated in Exhibit 13–1. Cash flows from operating activities are to be determined by the *direct method.* Place brackets around dollar amounts representing cash outlays. Show separately your computations of the following amounts:

a. Cash received from customers.

b. Interest received.

c. Cash paid to suppliers and employees.

d. Interest paid.

e. Income taxes paid.

f. Proceeds from sales of marketable securities.

g. Proceeds from sales of plant assets.

h. Proceeds from issuing capital stock.

Solution to the Demonstration Problem

ELECTRO PRODUCTS, INC.
STATEMENT OF CASH FLOWS
FOR THE YEAR ENDED DECEMBER 31, 2011

Cash flows from operating activities:		
Cash received from customers **(a)**	$ 9,585,000	
Interest received **(b)**	305,000	
Cash provided by operating activities		$9,890,000
Cash paid to suppliers and employees **(c)**	$(7,807,000)	
Interest paid **(d)**	(286,000)	
Income taxes paid **(e)**	(275,000)	
Cash disbursed for operating activities		(8,368,000)
Net cash provided by operating activities		$1,522,000
Cash flows from investing activities:		
Purchases of marketable securities	$ (120,000)	
Proceeds from sales of marketable securities **(f)**	280,000	
Loans made to borrowers	(250,000)	
Collections on loans	190,000	
Cash paid to acquire plant assets	(3,800,000)	
Proceeds from sales of plant assets **(g)**	270,000	
Net cash used for investing activities		(3,430,000)
Cash flows from financing activities:		
Proceeds from short-term borrowing	$ 740,000	
Payments to settle short-term debts	(620,000)	
Proceeds from issuing bonds payable	1,100,000	
Proceeds from issuing capital stock **(h)**	890,000	
Dividends paid	(320,000)	
Net cash provided by financing activities		1,790,000
Net increase (decrease) in cash		$ (118,000)
Cash and cash equivalents, Jan. 1, 2011		448,000
Cash and cash equivalents, Dec. 31, 2011		$ 330,000

Supporting computations:

a. Cash received from customers:	
Net sales	$9,500,000
Add: Decrease in accounts receivable	85,000
Cash received from customers	$9,585,000
b. Interest received:	
Interest income	$ 320,000
Less: Increase in accrued interest receivable	15,000
Interest received	$ 305,000
c. Cash paid to suppliers and employees:	
Cash paid for purchases of merchandise:	
Cost of goods sold	$4,860,000
Less: Decrease in inventory	280,000
Net purchases	$4,580,000
Add: Decrease in accounts payable to suppliers	240,000
Cash paid for purchases of merchandise	$4,820,000

ELECTRO PRODUCTS, INC. (continued)
STATEMENT OF CASH FLOWS
FOR THE YEAR ENDED DECEMBER 31, 2011

Cash paid for operating expenses:		
Operating expenses		$3,740,000
Less: Depreciation (a "noncash" expense)	$700,000	
Decrease in prepayments	18,000	
Increase in accrued liabilities for operating expenses	35,000	753,000
Cash paid for operating expenses		$2,987,000
Cash paid to suppliers and employees ($4,820,000 + $2,987,000)		$7,807,000
d. Interest paid:		
Interest expense		$ 270,000
Add: Decrease in accrued interest payable		16,000
Interest paid		$ 286,000
e. Income taxes paid:		
Income tax expense		$ 300,000
Less: Increase in accrued income taxes payable		25,000
Income taxes paid		$ 275,000
f. Proceeds from sales of marketable securities:		
Cost of marketable securities sold (credit entries to the Marketable Securities account)		$ 210,000
Add: Gain reported on sales of marketable securities		70,000
Proceeds from sales of marketable securities		$ 280,000
g. Proceeds from sales of plant assets:		
Book value of plant assets sold (paragraph **8**)		$ 360,000
Less: Loss reported on sales of plant assets		90,000
Proceeds from sales of plant assets		$ 270,000
h. Proceeds from issuing capital stock:		
Amounts credited to the Capital Stock account		$ 50,000
Add: Amounts credited to Additional Paid-in Capital account		840,000
Proceeds from issuing capital stock		$ 890,000

Self-Test Questions

The answers to these questions appear on page 618.

1. The statement of cash flows is designed to assist users in assessing each of the following, *except:*

a. The ability of a company to remain liquid.

b. The major sources of cash receipts during the period.

c. The company's profitability.

d. The reasons why net cash flows from operating activities differ from net income.

2. Which of the following is *not* included in the statement of cash flows, or in a supplementary schedule accompanying the statement of cash flows?

a. Disclosure of investing or financing activities that did not involve cash.

b. A reconciliation of net income to net cash flows from operating activities.

c. Disclosure of the amount of cash invested in money market funds during the accounting period.

d. The amount of cash and cash equivalents owned by the business at the end of the accounting period.

3. Cash flows are grouped in the statement of cash flows into the following major categories:

a. Operating activities, investing activities, and financing activities.

b. Cash receipts, cash disbursements, and noncash activities.

c. Direct cash flows and indirect cash flows.

d. Operating activities, investing activities, and collecting activities.

4. The following is a list of various cash payments and cash receipts:

Cash paid to suppliers and employees	$420,000
Dividends paid	18,000
Interest paid	12,000
Purchases of plant assets	45,000
Interest and dividends received	17,000
Payments to settle short-term bank loans	29,000
Income taxes paid	23,000
Cash received from customers	601,000

Based only on the above items, net cash flows from operating activities are:

a. $138,000
b. $91,000
c. $120,000
d. $163,000

5. During the current year, two transactions were recorded in the Land account of Duke Industries. One involved a debit of $320,000 to the Land account; the second was a $210,000 credit to the Land account. Duke's income statement for the year reported a loss on sale of land in the amount of $25,000. All transactions involving the Land account were cash transactions. These transactions would be shown in the statement of cash flows as:

a. $320,000 cash provided by investing activities, and $210,000 cash disbursed for investing activities.
b. $185,000 cash provided by investing activities, and $320,000 cash disbursed for investing activities.
c. $235,000 cash provided by investing activities, and $320,000 cash disbursed for investing activities.
d. $210,000 cash provided by investing activities, and $320,000 cash disbursed for investing activities.

6. Which of the following business strategies is *most likely* to increase the net cash flows of a software developer in the short run but *reduce* them over a longer term?

a. Develop software that is more costly to create but easier to update and improve.
b. Lower the price of existing versions of products as customer demand begins to fall.
c. Reduce expenditures for the purpose of developing new products.
d. Purchase the building in which the business operates (assume the company currently rents this location).

ASSIGNMENT MATERIAL Discussion Questions

1. Briefly state the purposes of a statement of cash flows.
2. Does a statement of cash flows or an income statement best measure the profitability of a financially sound business? Explain.
3. Give two examples of cash receipts and two examples of cash payments that fit into each of the following classifications:
   a. Operating activities.
   b. Investing activities.
   c. Financing activities.
4. Why are payments and receipts of interest classified as operating activities rather than as financing or investing activities?
5. In the long run, is it more important for a business to have positive cash flows from its operating activities, investing activities, or financing activities? Why?
6. Of the three types of business activities summarized in a statement of cash flows, which type is *least* likely to show positive net cash flows in a successful, growing business? Explain your reasoning.
7. Identify three factors that may cause net income to differ from net cash flows from operating activities.
8. Briefly explain the difference between the *direct* and *indirect methods* of computing net cash flows from operating activities. Which method results in higher net cash flows?
9. Moss, Inc., acquired land by issuing $665,000 of capital stock. No cash changed hands in this transaction. Will the transaction be disclosed in the company's statement of cash flows? Explain.
10. The only transaction recorded in the plant assets account of Pompei Company in the current year was a $220,000 credit to the Land account. Assuming that this credit resulted from a cash transaction, does this entry indicate a cash receipt or a cash payment? Should this $220,000 appear in the statement of cash flows, or is some adjustment necessary?
11. During the current year, the following credit entries were posted to the paid-in capital accounts of Crawford Shipyards:

Capital Stock	$12,000,000
Additional Paid-in Capital	43,500,000

Explain the type of cash transaction that probably caused these credit changes, and illustrate the presentation of this transaction in a statement of cash flows.

12. At the beginning of the current year, Callifax Corporation had dividends payable of $1,500,000. During the current year, the company declared cash dividends of $4,300,000, of which $900,000 appeared as a liability at year-end. Determine the amount of cash dividends *paid* during this year.
13. Define the term *free cash flow*. Explain the significance of this measurement to (1) short-term creditors, (2) long-term creditors, (3) stockholders, and (4) management.
14. Explain the concept of *peak pricing* and provide an example from your own experience.
15. Explain why speeding up the collection of accounts receivable provides only a one-time increase in cash receipts.

Brief Exercises

LO3 BRIEF EXERCISE 13.1
Cash Flows from Operations (Direct)

Olympic, Inc., had the following positive and negative cash flows during the current year:

Positive cash flows:	
Received from customers	$240,000
Interest and dividends	50,000
Sale of plant assets	330,000
Negative cash flows:	
Paid to suppliers and employees	$127,000
Purchase of investments	45,000
Purchase of treasury stock	36,000

Determine the amount of cash provided by or used for operating activities by the direct method.

LO7 BRIEF EXERCISE 13.2
Cash Flows from Operations (Indirect)

Garagiola Company had net income in the current year of $430,000. Depreciation expense for the year totaled $67,000. During the year the company experienced an increase in accounts receivable (all from sales to customers) of $35,000 and an increase in accounts payable (all to suppliers) of $56,000. Compute the amount of cash provided by or used for operating activities by the indirect method.

LO3 BRIEF EXERCISE 13.3
Cash Flows from Operations (Direct)

Georgia Products Co. had the following positive cash flows during the current year: received cash from customers of $750,000; received bank loans of $35,000; and received cash from the sale of common stock of $145,000. During the same year, cash was paid out to purchase inventory for $335,000, to employees for $230,000, and for the purchase of plant assets of $190,000. Calculate the amount of cash provided by or used for operating activities by the direct method.

LO7 BRIEF EXERCISE 13.4
Cash Flows from Operations (Indirect)

Patterson Company reported net income for the current year of $666,000. During the year the company's accounts receivable increased by $50,000, inventory decreased by $23,000, accounts payable decreased by $55,000, and accrued expenses payable increased by $14,000. Determine the amount of cash provided by or used for operating activities by the indirect method.

LO4 BRIEF EXERCISE 13.5
Cash Flows from Investing

Old Alabama Company purchased investments for $45,000 and plant assets for $127,000 during the current year, during which it also sold plant assets for $66,000, at a gain of $6,000. The company also purchased treasury stock for $78,000 and sold a new issue of common stock for $523,000. Determine the amount of cash provided by or used for investing activities for the year.

LO4 BRIEF EXERCISE 13.6
Cash Flows from Financing Activities

Texas, Inc., sold common stock for $560,000 and preferred stock for $36,000 during the current year. In addition, the company purchased treasury stock for $35,000 and paid dividends on common and preferred stock for $24,000. Determine the amount of cash provided by or used for financing activities during the year.

LO3 BRIEF EXERCISE 13.7
Cash Payment for Merchandise

Dane, Inc., reported cost of goods sold of $100,100 during the current year. Following are the beginning and ending balances of merchandise inventory and accounts payable for the year:

	Beginning	Ending
Merchandise inventory	$35,000	$43,000
Accounts payable	23,000	30,000

Determine the amount of cash payments for purchases during the year.

LO2 **BRIEF EXERCISE 13.8**

Determining Beginning Cash Balance

Tyler, Inc.'s cash balance at December 31, 2011, the end of its financial reporting year, was $155,000. During 2011, cash provided by operations was $145,000, cash used in investing activities was $67,000, and cash provided by financing activities was $10,000. Calculate the amount of Tyler's beginning cash balance at January 1, 2011.

LO6 **BRIEF EXERCISE 13.9**

Reconciling Net Income to Cash from Operations

Zephre Company reported net income for the year of $56,000. Depreciation expense for the year was $12,000. During the year, accounts receivable increased by $4,000, inventory decreased by $6,000, accounts payable increased by $3,000, and accrued expenses payable decreased by $2,000. Reconcile the amount of net income to the amount of cash provided by or used for operating activities.

LO2 **BRIEF EXERCISE 13.10**

Preparing Statement of Cash Flows

Watson, Inc., had a cash balance at the beginning of the year of $89,000. During the year, the following cash flows occurred:

From operating activities	$136,000
From investing activities	(56,000)
From financing activities	(34,000)

Prepare an abbreviated statement of cash flows, including a reconciliation of the beginning and ending cash balances for the year.

Exercises

connect ACCOUNTING

LO1 **EXERCISE 13.1**

LO2 Using a Statement of Cash Flows

Wallace Company's statement of cash flows for the current year is summarized as follows:

Cash provided by operating activities	$200,000
Cash used in investing activities	(120,000)
Cash provided by financing activities	88,000
Increase in cash during the year	$168,000
Cash balance, beginning of the year	75,000
Cash balance, end of the year	$243,000

a. Briefly explain what is included in each of the first three categories listed (i.e., the cash from operating, investing, and financing activities categories).

b. On the basis of the limited information presented above, describe the company's change in cash position during the year and your interpretation of the strength of the company's current (end-of-year) cash position.

LO1 **EXERCISE 13.2**

LO2 Using a Statement of Cash Flows

LO6

Auto Supply Company's 2011 statement of cash flows appears in Exhibit 13–8. Study the statement and respond to the following questions:

a. What was the company's free cash flow in 2011?

b. What were the major sources and uses of cash from financing activities during 2011? Did the net effect of financing activities result in an increase or a decrease in cash during the year?

c. What happened to the total amount of cash and cash equivalents during the year? Assuming 2011 was a typical year, is the firm in a position to continue its dividend payments in the future? Explain.

d. Look at the reconciliation of net income to net cash provided by operating activities, and explain the following:

1. Net loss (gain) from the sale of marketable securities.
2. Increase in accounts receivable.

LO4 **EXERCISE 13.3**
Computing Cash Flows

An analysis of the Marketable Securities control account of Prosper Products, Inc., shows the following entries during the year:

Balance, Jan. 1	$ 290,000
Debit entries	125,000
Credit entries	(140,000)
Balance, Dec. 31	$ 275,000

In addition, the company's income statement includes a $35,000 loss on sales of marketable securities. None of the company's marketable securities is considered a cash equivalent.

Compute the amounts that should appear in the statement of cash flows as:

a. Purchases of marketable securities.

b. Proceeds from sales of marketable securities.

LO3 **EXERCISE 13.4**
Comparing Net Sales and Cash Receipts
LO6

During the current year, Tachnic, Inc., made cash sales of $285,000 and credit sales of $460,000. During the year, accounts receivable decreased by $32,000.

a. Compute for the current year the amounts of:
1. Net sales reported as revenue in the income statement.
2. Cash received from collecting accounts receivable.
3. Cash received from customers.

b. Write a brief statement explaining *why* cash received from customers differs from the amount of net sales.

LO3 **EXERCISE 13.5**
Computing Cash Paid for Purchases of Merchandise

The general ledger of MPX, Inc., provides the following information relating to purchases of merchandise:

	End of Year	Beginning of Year
Inventory	$820,000	$780,000
Accounts payable to merchandise suppliers	430,000	500,000

The company's cost of goods sold during the year was $2,975,000. Compute the amount of cash payments made during the year to suppliers of merchandise.

LO3 **EXERCISE 13.6**
Reporting Lending Activities and Interest Revenue
LO6

During the current year, Maine Savings and Loan Association made new loans of $15 million. In addition, the company collected $36 million from borrowers, of which $30 million was interest revenue. Explain how these cash flows will appear in the company's statement of cash flows, indicating the classification and the dollar amount of each cash flow.

LO2 **EXERCISE 13.7**
Format of a Statement of Cash Flows

The accounting staff of Wyoming Outfitters, Inc., has assembled the following information for the year ended December 31, 2011:

Cash and cash equivalents, Jan. 1	$ 35,800
Cash and cash equivalents, Dec. 31	74,800
Cash paid to acquire plant assets	21,000
Proceeds from short-term borrowing	10,000
Loans made to borrowers	5,000
Collections on loans (excluding interest)	4,000
Interest and dividends received	27,000
Cash received from customers	795,000
Proceeds from sales of plant assets	9,000
Dividends paid	55,000
Cash paid to suppliers and employees	635,000
Interest paid	19,000
Income taxes paid	71,000

Using this information, prepare a statement of cash flows. Include a proper heading for the financial statement, and classify the given information into the categories of operating activities, investing activities, and financing activities. Determine net cash flows from operating activities by the direct method. Place brackets around the dollar amounts of all cash disbursements.

LO8

EXERCISE 13.8

Effects of Business Strategies

Indicate how you would expect the following strategies to affect the company's net cash flows from *operating activities* (1) in the near future and (2) in later periods (after the strategy's long-term effects have "taken hold"). *Fully explain your reasoning.*

a. A successful pharmaceutical company substantially reduces its expenditures for research and development.

b. A restaurant that previously sold only for cash adopts a policy of accepting bank credit cards, such as Visa and MasterCard.

c. A manufacturing company reduces by 50 percent the size of its inventories of raw materials (assume no change in inventory storage costs).

d. Through tax planning, a rapidly growing real estate developer is able to defer significant amounts of income taxes.

e. A rapidly growing software company announces that it will stop paying cash dividends for the foreseeable future and will instead distribute stock dividends.

LO6 LO7

EXERCISE 13.9

An Analysis of Possible Reconciling Items

An analysis of the annual financial statements of Conner Corporation reveals the following:

a. The company had a $5 million extraordinary loss from insurance proceeds received due to a tornado that destroyed a factory building.

b. Depreciation for the year amounted to $8 million.

c. During the year, $2 million in cash was transferred from the company's checking account into a money market fund.

d. Accounts receivable from customers increased by $4 million over the year.

e. Cash received from customers during the year amounted to $167 million.

f. Prepaid expenses decreased by $1 million over the year.

g. Dividends declared during the year amounted to $7 million; dividends paid during the year amounted to $6 million.

h. Accounts payable (to suppliers of merchandise) increased by $2.5 million during the year.

i. The liability for accrued income taxes payable amounted to $5 million at the beginning of the year and $3 million at year-end.

In the computation of net cash flows from operating activities by the *indirect method,* explain whether each of the above items should be *added to net income, deducted from net income,* or *omitted from the computation.* Briefly explain your reasons for each answer.

LO7 **EXERCISE 13.10**

Computation of Net Cash Flows from Operating Activities—Indirect Method

The following data are taken from the income statement and balance sheet of Keaner Machinery, Inc.:

	Dec. 31, 2011	Jan. 1, 2011
Income statement:		
Net Income	$385,000	
Depreciation Expense	125,000	
Amortization of Intangible Assets	40,000	
Gain on Sale of Plant Assets	90,000	
Loss on Sale of Investments	35,000	
Balance sheet:		
Accounts Receivable	$335,000	$380,000
Inventory	503,000	575,000
Prepaid Expenses	22,000	10,000
Accounts Payable (to merchandise suppliers)	379,000	410,000
Accrued Expenses Payable	180,000	155,000

Using this information, prepare a partial statement of cash flows for the year ended December 31, 2011, showing the computation of net cash flows from operating activities by the *indirect* method.

LO2 **EXERCISE 13.11**

Classifying Cash Flows

Among the transactions of Beeler, Inc., were the following:

a. Made payments on accounts payable to merchandise suppliers.

b. Paid the principal amount of a note payable to First Bank.

c. Paid interest charges relating to a note payable to First Bank.

d. Issued bonds payable for cash; management plans to use this cash in the near future to expand manufacturing and warehouse capabilities.

e. Paid salaries to employees in the finance department.

f. Collected an account receivable from a customer.

g. Transferred cash from the general bank account into a money market fund.

h. Used the cash received in **d,** above, to purchase land and a building suitable for a manufacturing facility.

i. Made a year-end adjusting entry to recognize depreciation expense.

j. At year-end, purchased for cash an insurance policy covering the next 12 months.

k. Paid the quarterly dividend on preferred stock.

l. Paid the semiannual interest on bonds payable.

m. Received a quarterly dividend from an investment in the preferred stock of another corporation.

n. Sold for cash an investment in the preferred stock of another corporation.

o. Received cash upon the maturity of an investment in cash equivalents. (Ignore interest.)

Instructions

Most of the preceding transactions should be included among the activities summarized in a statement of cash flows. For each transaction that should be included in this statement, indicate whether the transaction should be classified as an operating activity, an investing activity, or a financing activity. If the transaction *should not be included* in the current year's statement of cash flows, briefly explain why not. (Assume that net cash flows from operating activities are determined by the *direct method.*)

LO2 **EXERCISE 13.12**

Classifying Cash Flows

Among the transactions of Marvel Manufacturing were the following:

1. Made payments on accounts payable to office suppliers.
2. Paid the principal amount of a mortgage to Seventh Bank.
3. Paid interest charges relating to a mortgage to Seventh Bank.
4. Issued preferred stock for cash; management plans to use this cash in the near future to purchase another company.

5. Paid salaries to employees in the finance department.
6. Collected an account receivable from a customer.
7. Transferred cash from the general bank account into a money market fund.
8. Used the cash received in **4**, above, to purchase Moran Manufacturing Co.
9. Made a year-end adjusting entry to recognize amortization expense.
10. At year-end, purchased for cash an advertising spot on a local radio station for the next eight months.
11. Paid the annual dividend on preferred stock.
12. Paid the semiannual interest on bonds payable.
13. Received a semiannual dividend from an investment in the common stock of another corporation.
14. Sold for cash an investment in the common stock of another corporation.
15. Received cash upon the maturity of an investment in cash equivalents. (Ignore interest.)

Instructions

Most of the preceding transactions should be included among the activities summarized in a statement of cash flows. For each transaction that should be included in this statement, indicate whether the transaction should be classified as an operating activity, an investing activity, or a financing activity. If the transaction *should not be included* in the current year's statement of cash flows, briefly explain why not. (Assume that net cash flows from operating activities are determined by the *direct method.*)

LO4 **EXERCISE 13.13**
Cash Flows from Investing Activities

Wofford Company provides the following information related to its investing and financing activities for the current year:

Cash receipts:	
Sale of common stock	$250,000
Sale of equipment (at $34,000 loss)	156,000
Sale of land (at $50,000 gain)	160,000
Cash payments:	
Purchase of equipment	$178,000
Purchase of treasury stock	45,000
Retirement of debt	36,500
Dividends on preferred and common stock	75,000

a. Calculate the net amount of cash provided by or used for investing activities for the year.

b. What impact, if any, do the following facts have on your calculation? (**1**) Equipment was sold at a loss, and (**2**) land was sold at a gain.

c. Briefly explain your decision to exclude any of the items listed above if they were not included in your calculation in part **a.**

LO4 **EXERCISE 13.14**
Cash Flows from Financing Activities

Shepherd Industries had the following cash flows by major categories during the current year:

Cash provided by:	
Receipts from customers	$560,000
Sale of bonds	400,000
Sale of treasury stock	34,000
Interest and dividends received	56,000
Sale of equipment (at a $56,000 loss)	236,000
Cash used for:	
Payments to employees	$135,000
Payments to purchase inventory	190,000
Dividends on common stock	60,000
Purchase of treasury stock	20,000
Interest expense	78,000

a. Calculate the net amount of cash provided by or used for financing activities for the year.

b. Briefly justify why you excluded any of the above items in your calculation in part **a.**

c. Briefly explain your treatment of interest expense in your calculation in part **a.**

LO1 LO2 LO4 **EXERCISE 13.15**

Home Depot, Inc.

Using a Statement of Cash Flows

Statements of cash flow for **Home Depot, Inc.**, for 2009, 2008, and 2007 are included in Appendix A of this text.

a. Focus on the information for 2009 (year ending January 31, 2010). How does net earnings compare with net cash provided by or used in operations, and what accounts for the primary difference between the two amounts?

b. What are the major uses of cash, other than operations, and how have these varied over the three-year period presented?

c. Cash flows from both investing and financing activities have been mostly negative for all three years presented. Considering **Home Depot**'s overall cash flows, including its cash flows from operations, would you say that this leads to a negative interpretation of **Home Depot**'s cash position at January 31, 2010? Why or why not?

d. Calculate the amount of free cash flow for each of 2007, 2008, and 2009, and comment briefly on your conclusion concerning this information.

Problem Set A

LO2 through LO4 **PROBLEM 13.1A**

Format of a Statement of Cash Flows

The accounting staff of Harris Company has assembled the following information for the year ended December 31, 2011:

Cash sales	$ 800,000
Credit sales	2,500,000
Collections on accounts receivable	2,200,000
Cash transferred from the money market fund to the general bank account	250,000
Interest and dividends received	100,000
Purchases (all on account)	1,800,000
Payments on accounts payable to merchandise suppliers	1,500,000
Cash payments for operating expenses	1,050,000
Interest paid	180,000
Income taxes paid	95,000
Loans made to borrowers	500,000
Collections on loans (excluding receipts of interest)	260,000
Cash paid to acquire plant assets	3,100,000
Book value of plant assets sold	660,000
Loss on sales of plant assets	80,000
Proceeds from issuing bonds payable	2,500,000
Dividends paid	120,000
Cash and cash equivalents, Jan. 1	489,000

Instructions

Prepare a statement of cash flows in the format illustrated in Exhibit 13–1. Place brackets around amounts representing cash outflows. Use the *direct method* of reporting cash flows from operating activities.

Some of the items above will be listed in your statement without change. However, you will have to combine certain given information to compute the amounts of (1) collections from customers, (2) cash paid to suppliers and employees, and (3) proceeds from sales of plant assets. (Hint: Not every item listed is used in preparing a statement of cash flows.)

LO4 **PROBLEM 13.2A**

Reporting Investing Activities

An analysis of the income statement and the balance sheet accounts of Headrick, Inc., at December 31, 2011, provides the following information:

Income statement items:	
Gain on Sale of Marketable Securities	$ 42,000
Loss on Sales of Plant Assets	33,000
Analysis of balance sheet accounts:	
Marketable Securities account:	
Debit entries	$ 75,000
Credit entries	90,000
Notes Receivable account:	
Debit entries	210,000
Credit entries	162,000
Plant and Equipment accounts:	
Debit entries to plant asset accounts	196,000
Credit entries to plant asset accounts	120,000
Debit entries to accumulated depreciation accounts	75,000

Additional Information

1. Except as noted in **4** below, payments and proceeds relating to investing transactions were made in cash.
2. The marketable securities are not cash equivalents.
3. All notes receivable relate to cash loans made to borrowers, not to receivables from customers.
4. Purchases of new equipment during the year ($196,000) were financed by paying $60,000 in cash and issuing a long-term note payable for $136,000.
5. Debits to the accumulated depreciation accounts are made whenever depreciable plant assets are retired. Thus, the book value of plant assets retired during the year was $45,000 ($120,000 − $75,000).

Instructions

a. Prepare the investing activities section of a statement of cash flows. Show supporting computations for the amounts of (1) proceeds from sales of marketable securities and (2) proceeds from sales of plant assets. Place brackets around numbers representing cash outflows.

b. Prepare the supporting schedule that should accompany the statement of cash flows in order to disclose the noncash aspects of the company's investing and financing activities.

c. Assume that Headrick's management expects approximately the same amount of cash to be used for investing activities next year. In general terms, explain how the company might generate cash for this purpose.

LO4 **PROBLEM 13.3A**
Reporting Investing Activities

An analysis of the income statement and the balance sheet accounts of Hayes Export Co. at December 31, 2011 provides the following information:

Income statement items:	
Gain on Sale of Plant Assets	$ 12,000
Loss on Sales of Marketable Securities	16,000
Analysis of balance sheet accounts:	
Marketable Securities account:	
Debit entries	$ 78,000
Credit entries	62,000
Notes Receivable account:	
Debit entries	55,000
Credit entries	60,000
Plant and Equipment accounts:	
Debit entries to plant asset accounts	150,000
Credit entries to plant asset accounts	140,000
Debit entries to accumulated depreciation accounts	100,000

Additional Information

1. Except as noted in **4** below, payments and proceeds relating to investing transactions were made in cash.
2. The marketable securities are not cash equivalents.
3. All notes receivable relate to cash loans made to borrowers, not to receivables from customers.
4. Purchases of new equipment during the year ($150,000) were financed by paying $50,000 in cash and issuing a long-term note payable for $100,000.
5. Debits to the accumulated depreciation accounts are made whenever depreciable plant assets are sold or retired. Thus, the book value of plant assets sold or retired during the year was $40,000 ($140,000 − $100,000).

Instructions

a. Prepare the investing activities section of a statement of cash flows. Show supporting computations for the amounts of (1) proceeds from sales of marketable securities and (2) proceeds from sales of plant assets. Place brackets around amounts representing cash outflows.

b. Prepare the supplementary schedule that should accompany the statement of cash flows in order to disclose the noncash aspects of the company's investing and financing activities.

c. Does management have *more* control or *less* control over the timing and amount of cash outlays for investing activities than for operating activities? Explain.

LO3 LO8 **PROBLEM 13.4A**
Reporting Operating Cash Flows by the Direct Method

The following income statement and selected balance sheet account data are available for Treece, Inc., at December 31, 2011:

TREECE, INC.
INCOME STATEMENT
FOR THE YEAR ENDED DECEMBER 31, 2011

Revenue:		
Net sales		$2,850,000
Dividend income		104,000
Interest income		70,000
Gain on sales of marketable securities		4,000
Total revenue and gains		$3,028,000
Costs and expenses:		
Cost of goods sold	$1,550,000	
Operating expenses	980,000	
Interest expense	185,000	
Income tax expense	90,000	
Total costs and expenses		2,805,000
Net income		$ 223,000

	End of Year	Beginning of Year
Selected account balances:		
Accounts receivable	$ 650,000	$ 720,000
Accrued interest receivable	9,000	6,000
Inventories	800,000	765,000
Short-term prepayments	20,000	15,000
Accounts payable (merchandise suppliers)	570,000	562,000
Accrued operating expenses payable	65,000	94,000
Accrued interest payable	21,000	12,000
Accrued income taxes payable	22,000	35,000

Additional Information

1. Dividend revenue is recognized on the cash basis. All other income statement amounts are recognized on the accrual basis.
2. Operating expenses include depreciation expense of $115,000.

Instructions

a. Prepare a partial statement of cash flows, including only the *operating activities* section of the statement and using the *direct method*. Place brackets around numbers representing cash payments. Show supporting computations for the following:
   1. Cash received from customers
   2. Interest and dividends received
   3. Cash paid to suppliers and employees
   4. Interest paid
   5. Income taxes paid

b. Management of Treece, Inc., is exploring ways to increase the cash flows from operations. One way that cash flows could be increased is through more aggressive collection of receivables. Assuming that management has already taken all the steps possible to increase revenue and reduce expenses, describe two other ways that cash flows from operations could be increased.

LO6 LO7

PROBLEM 13.5A

Reporting Operating Cash Flows by the Indirect Method

Using the information presented in Problem **13.4A,** prepare a partial statement of cash flows for the current year, showing the computation of net cash flows from operating activities by the *indirect method.* Explain why the decline in accounts receivable over the year was *added* to net income in computing the cash flows from operating activities.

LO2 through LO4 LO6 LO8

PROBLEM 13.6A

Preparing a Statement of Cash Flows: A Comprehensive Problem without a Worksheet

excel

You are the controller for 21st Century Technologies. Your staff has prepared an income statement for the current year and has developed the following additional information by analyzing changes in the company's balance sheet accounts.

21st CENTURY TECHNOLOGIES
INCOME STATEMENT
FOR THE YEAR ENDED DECEMBER 31, 2011

Revenue:		
Net sales		$3,200,000
Interest revenue		40,000
Gain on sales of marketable securities		34,000
Total revenue and gains		$3,274,000
Costs and expenses:		
Cost of goods sold	$1,620,000	
Operating expenses (including depreciation of $150,000)	1,240,000	
Interest expense	42,000	
Income tax expense	100,000	
Loss on sales of plant assets	12,000	
Total costs, expenses, and losses		3,014,000
Net income		$ 260,000

Additional Information

1. Accounts receivable increased by $60,000.
2. Accrued interest receivable decreased by $2,000.

3. Inventory decreased by $60,000, and accounts payable to suppliers of merchandise decreased by $16,000.
4. Short-term prepayments of operating expenses increased by $6,000, and accrued liabilities for operating expenses decreased by $8,000.
5. The liability for accrued interest payable increased by $4,000 during the year.
6. The liability for accrued income taxes payable decreased by $14,000 during the year.
7. The following schedule summarizes the total debit and credit entries during the year in other balance sheet accounts:

	Debit Entries	Credit Entries
Marketable Securities	$ 60,000	$ 38,000
Notes Receivable (cash loans made to borrowers)	44,000	28,000
Plant Assets (see paragraph **8**)	500,000	36,000
Notes Payable (short-term borrowing)	92,000	82,000
Capital Stock		20,000
Additional Paid-in Capital—Capital Stock		160,000
Retained Earnings (see paragraph **9**)	120,000	260,000

8. The $36,000 in credit entries to the Plant Assets account is net of any debits to Accumulated Depreciation when plant assets were retired. Thus, the $36,000 in credit entries represents the book value of all plant assets sold or retired during the year.
9. The $120,000 debit to Retained Earnings represents dividends declared and paid during the year. The $260,000 credit entry represents the net income shown in the income statement.
10. All investing and financing activities were cash transactions.
11. Cash and cash equivalents amounted to $244,000 at the beginning of the year and to $164,000 at year-end.

Instructions

a. Prepare a statement of cash flows for the current year. Use the *direct method* of reporting cash flows from operating activities. Place brackets around dollar amounts representing cash outflows. Show separately your computations of the following amounts:
   1. Cash received from customers
   2. Interest received
   3. Cash paid to suppliers and employees
   4. Interest paid
   5. Income taxes paid
   6. Proceeds from sales of marketable securities
   7. Proceeds from sales of plant assets
   8. Proceeds from issuing capital stock

b. Explain the *primary reason* why:
   1. The amount of cash provided by operating activities was substantially greater than the company's net income.
   2. There was a net decrease in cash over the year, despite the substantial amount of cash provided by operating activities.

c. As 21st Century's controller, you think that through more efficient cash management, the company could have held the increase in accounts receivable for the year to $10,000, without affecting net income. Explain how holding down the growth in receivables affects cash. Compute the effect that limiting the growth in receivables to $10,000 would have had on the company's net increase or decrease in cash (and cash equivalents) for the year.

LO1 through LO9

PROBLEM 13.7A

Prepare and Analyze a Statement of Cash Flows with a Worksheet

Satellite 2010 was founded in 2010 to apply a new technology for efficiently transmitting closed-circuit (cable) television signals without the need for an in-ground cable. The company earned a profit of $115,000 in 2010, its first year of operations, even though it was serving only a small test market. In 2011, the company began dramatically expanding its customer base. Management expects both sales and net income to more than triple in each of the next five years.

Comparative balance sheets at the end of 2010 and 2011, the company's first two years of operations, follow. (Notice that the balances at the end of the current year appear in the right-hand column.)

Additional Information

The following information regarding the company's operations in 2011 is available in either the company's income statement or its accounting records:

1. Net income for the year was $440,000. The company has never paid a dividend.
2. Depreciation for the year amounted to $147,000.
3. During the year the company purchased plant assets costing $2,200,000, for which it paid $1,850,000 in cash and financed $350,000 by issuing a long-term note payable. (Much of the cash used in these purchases was provided by short-term borrowing, as described below.)
4. In 2011, Satellite 2010 borrowed $1,450,000 against a $6 million line of credit with a local bank. In its balance sheet, the resulting obligations are reported as notes payable (short-term).
5. Additional shares of capital stock (no par value) were issued to investors for $500,000 cash.

SATELLITE 2010
COMPARATIVE BALANCE SHEETS

	December 31, 2010	2011
Assets		
Cash and cash equivalents	$ 80,000	$ 37,000
Accounts receivable	100,000	850,000
Plant and equipment (net of accumulated depreciation)	600,000	2,653,000
Totals	$780,000	$3,540,000
Liabilities & Stockholders' Equity		
Notes payable (short-term)	$ -0-	$1,450,000
Accounts payable	30,000	63,000
Accrued expenses payable	45,000	32,000
Notes payable (long-term)	390,000	740,000
Capital stock (no par value)	200,000	700,000
Retained earnings	115,000	555,000
Totals	$780,000	$3,540,000

Instructions

a. Prepare a worksheet for a statement of cash flows, following the general format illustrated in Exhibit 13–7. (***Note:*** If this problem is completed as a group assignment, each member of the group should be prepared to explain in class all entries in the worksheet, as well as the group's conclusions in parts **c** and **d.**)

b. Prepare a formal statement of cash flows for 2011, including a supplementary schedule of noncash investing and financing activities. (Follow the format illustrated in Exhibit 13–8. Cash provided by operating activities is to be presented by the *indirect method.*)

c. Briefly explain how operating activities can be a net *use* of cash when the company is operating so profitably.

d. Because of the expected rapid growth, management forecasts that operating activities will be an even greater use of cash in the year 2012 than in 2011. If this forecast is correct, does Satellite 2010 appear to be heading toward illiquidity? Explain.

LO1 through LO9

PROBLEM 13.8A

Prepare and Analyze a Statement of Cash Flows; Involves Preparation of a Worksheet

Miracle Tool, Inc., sells a single product (a combination screwdriver, pliers, hammer, and crescent wrench) exclusively through television advertising. The comparative income statements and balance sheets are for the past two years.

Additional Information

The following information regarding the company's operations in 2011 is available from the company's accounting records:

1. Early in the year the company declared and paid a $4,000 cash dividend.
2. During the year marketable securities costing $15,000 were sold for $14,000 cash, resulting in a $1,000 nonoperating loss.
3. The company purchased plant assets for $20,000, paying $2,000 in cash and issuing a note payable for the $18,000 balance.
4. During the year the company repaid a $10,000 note payable, but incurred an additional $18,000 in long-term debt as described in **3.**
5. The owners invested $15,000 cash in the business as a condition of the new loans described in paragraph **4.**

MIRACLE TOOL, INC.
COMPARATIVE INCOME STATEMENT
FOR THE YEARS ENDED DECEMBER 31, 2010 AND 2011

	2010	2011
Sales	$500,000	$350,000
Less: Cost of goods sold	200,000	140,000
Gross profit on sales	$300,000	$210,000
Less: Operating expenses (including depreciation of $34,000 in 2010 and $35,000 in 2011)	260,000	243,000
Loss on sale of marketable securities	–0–	1,000
Net income (loss)	$ 40,000	($ 34,000)

MIRACLE TOOL, INC.
COMPARATIVE BALANCE SHEETS

	December 31, 2010	December 31, 2011
Assets		
Cash and cash equivalents	$ 10,000	$ 60,000
Marketable securities	20,000	5,000
Accounts receivable	40,000	23,000
Inventory	120,000	122,000
Plant and equipment (net of accumulated depreciation)	300,000	285,000
Totals	$490,000	$495,000
Liabilities & Stockholders' Equity		
Accounts payable	$ 50,000	$ 73,000
Accrued expenses payable	17,000	14,000
Note payable	245,000	253,000
Capital stock (no par value)	120,000	135,000
Retained earnings	58,000	20,000
Totals	$490,000	$495,000

Instructions

a. Prepare a worksheet for a statement of cash flows, following the general format illustrated in Exhibit 13–7. (***Note:*** If this problem is completed as a group assignment, each member of the group should be prepared to explain in class all entries in the worksheet, as well as the group's conclusions in parts **c, d,** and **e.**)

b. Prepare a formal statement of cash flows for 2011, including a supplementary schedule of noncash investing and financing activities. (Use the format illustrated in Exhibit 13–8. Cash provided by operating activities is to be presented by the *indirect method.*)

c. Explain how Miracle Tool, Inc., achieved positive cash flows from operating activities, despite incurring a net loss for the year.

d. Does the company's financial position appear to be improving or deteriorating? Explain.

e. Does Miracle Tool, Inc., appear to be a company whose operations are growing or contracting? Explain.

f. Assume that management *agrees* with your conclusions in parts **c, d,** and **e.** What decisions should be made and what actions (if any) should be taken? Explain.

Problem Set B

LO2 through LO4

PROBLEM 13.1B

Format of a Statement of Cash Flows

The accounting staff of Best Company has assembled the following information for the year ended December 31, 2011:

Cash sales	$ 230,000
Credit sales	3,450,000
Collections on accounts receivable	2,810,000
Cash transferred from the money market fund to the general bank account	200,000
Interest and dividends received	40,000
Purchases (all on account)	1,822,000
Payments on accounts payable to merchandise suppliers	1,220,000
Cash payments for operating expenses	930,000
Interest paid	130,000
Income taxes paid	65,000
Loans made to borrowers	690,000
Collections on loans (excluding receipts of interest)	300,000
Cash paid to acquire plant assets	1,700,000
Book value of plant assets sold	520,000
Loss on sales of plant assets	30,000
Proceeds from issuing bonds payable	2,000,000
Dividends paid	250,000
Cash and cash equivalents, Jan. 1	115,000

Instructions

Prepare a statement of cash flows in the format illustrated in Exhibit 13–1. Place brackets around amounts representing cash outflows. Use the *direct method* of reporting cash flows from operating activities.

Some of the items above will be listed in your statement without change. However, you will have to combine certain given information to compute the amounts of (1) collections from customers, (2) cash paid to suppliers and employees, and (3) proceeds from sales of plant assets. (Hint: Not every item listed above is used in preparing a statement of cash flows.)

LO4

PROBLEM 13.2B

Reporting Investing Activities

An analysis of the income statement and the balance sheet accounts of Schmatah Fashions at December 31, 2011, provides the following information:

Income statement items:	
Gain on Sales of Marketable Securities	$ 15,000
Loss on Sales of Plant Assets	10,000
Analysis of balance sheet accounts:	
Marketable Securities account:	
Debit entries	65,000
Credit entries	74,000
Notes Receivable account:	
Debit entries	175,000
Credit entries	50,000
Plant and Equipment accounts:	
Debit entries to plant asset accounts	220,000
Credit entries to plant asset accounts	150,000
Debit entries to accumulated depreciation accounts	60,000

Additional Information

1. Except as noted in **4,** payments and proceeds relating to investing transactions were made in cash.
2. The marketable securities are not cash equivalents.
3. All notes receivable relate to cash loans made to borrowers, not to receivables from customers.
4. Purchases of new equipment during the year ($220,000) were financed by paying $70,000 in cash and issuing a long-term note payable for $150,000.
5. Debits to the accumulated depreciation accounts are made whenever depreciable plant assets are retired. Thus, the book value of plant assets retired during the year was $90,000 ($150,000 − $60,000).

Instructions

a. Prepare the investing activities section of a statement of cash flows. Show supporting computations for the amounts of (1) proceeds from sales and marketable securities and (2) proceeds from sales from plant assets. Place brackets around numbers representing cash outflows.

b. Prepare the supporting schedule that should accompany the statement of cash flows in order to disclose the noncash aspects of the company's investing and financing activities.

c. Assume that Schmatah Fashions's management expects approximately the same amount of cash to be used for investing activities next year. In general terms, explain how the company might generate cash for this purpose.

LO4 **PROBLEM 13.3B**
Reporting Investing Activities

An analysis of the income statement and the balance sheet accounts of RPZ Imports at December 31, 2011, provides the following information:

Income statement items:	
Gain on Sales of Plant Assets	$ 6,000
Loss on Sales of Marketable Securities	8,000
Analysis of balance sheet accounts:	
Marketable Securities account:	
Debit entries	59,000
Credit entries	60,000
Notes Receivable account:	
Debit entries	40,000
Credit entries	31,000
Plant and Equipment accounts:	
Debit entries to plant asset accounts	140,000
Credit entries to plant asset accounts	100,000
Debit entries to accumulated depreciation accounts	75,000

Additional Information

1. Except as noted in **4,** payments and proceeds relating to investing transactions were made in cash.
2. The marketable securities are not cash equivalents.
3. All notes receivable relate to cash loans made to borrowers, not to receivables from customers.
4. Purchases of new equipment during the year ($140,000) were financed by paying $50,000 in cash and issuing a long-term note payable for $90,000.
5. Debits to the accumulated depreciation accounts are made whenever depreciable plant assets are retired. Thus, the book value of plant assets sold or retired during the year was $25,000 ($100,000 − $75,000).

Instructions

a. Prepare the investing activities section of a statement of cash flows. Show supporting computations for the amounts of (1) proceeds from sales and marketable securities and (2) proceeds from sales from plant assets. Place brackets around numbers representing cash outflows.

b. Prepare the supplementary schedule that should accompany the statement of cash flows in order to disclose the noncash aspects of the company's investing and financing activities.

c. Does management have *more* control or *less* control over the timing and amount of cash outlays for investing activities than for operating activities? Explain.

LO3 LO8

PROBLEM 13.4B

Reporting Operating Cash Flows by the Direct Method

The following income statement and selected balance sheet account data are available for Royce Interiors, Inc., at December 31, 2011:

ROYCE INTERIORS, INC.
INCOME STATEMENT
FOR THE YEAR ENDED DECEMBER 31, 2011

Revenue:		
Net sales		$2,600,000
Dividend income		55,000
Interest income		40,000
Gain on sales of marketable securities		3,000
Total revenue and gains		$2,698,000
Costs and expenses:		
Cost of goods sold	$1,300,000	
Operating expenses	300,000	
Interest expense	60,000	
Income tax expense	110,000	
Total costs and expenses		$1,770,000
Net income		$ 928,000

	End of Year	Beginning of Year
Selected account balances:		
Accounts receivable	$ 450,000	$ 440,000
Accrued interest receivable	7,000	3,000
Inventories	575,000	550,000
Short-term prepayments	9,000	8,000
Accounts payable (merchandise suppliers)	415,000	410,000
Accrued operating expenses payable	86,000	90,000
Accrued interest payable	10,000	8,000
Accrued income taxes payable	20,000	22,000

Additional Information

1. Dividend revenue is recognized on the cash basis. All other income statement amounts are recognized on the accrual basis.
2. Operating expenses include depreciation expense of $49,000.

Instructions

a. Prepare a partial statement of cash flows, including only the *operating activities* section of the statement and using the *direct method.* Place brackets around numbers representing cash payments. Show supporting computations for the following:
   1. Cash received from customers
   2. Interest and dividends received
   3. Cash paid to suppliers and employees
   4. Interest paid
   5. Income taxes paid

b. Management of Royce Interiors, Inc., is exploring ways to increase the cash flows from operations. One way that cash flows could be increased is through more aggressive collection of receivables. Assuming that management has already taken all the steps possible to increase revenue and reduce expenses, describe two other ways that cash flows from operations could be increased.

LO6 LO7

PROBLEM 13.5B
Reporting Operating Cash Flows by the Indirect Method

Using the information presented in Problem **13.4B,** prepare a partial statement of cash flows for the current year, showing the computation of net cash flows from operating activities using the *indirect method.* Explain why the increase in accounts receivable over the year was *subtracted* from net income in computing the cash flows from operating activities.

LO2 through LO4 LO6 LO8

PROBLEM 13.6B
Preparing a Statement of Cash Flows: A Comprehensive Problem without a Worksheet

You are the controller for Foxboro Technologies. Your staff has prepared an income statement for the current year and has developed the following additional information by analyzing changes in the company's balance sheet accounts.

FOXBORO TECHNOLOGIES
INCOME STATEMENT
FOR THE YEAR ENDED DECEMBER 31, 2011

Revenue:		
Net sales		$3,400,000
Interest income		60,000
Gain on sales of marketable securities		25,000
Total revenue and gains		$3,485,000
Costs and expenses:		
Cost of goods sold	$1,500,000	
Operating expenses (including depreciation of $75,000)	900,000	
Interest expense	27,000	
Income tax expense	115,000	
Loss on sales of plant assets	8,000	
Total costs, expenses, and losses		2,550,000
Net income		$ 935,000

Additional Information

1. Accounts receivable increased by $60,000.
2. Accrued interest receivable decreased by $5,000.
3. Inventory decreased by $30,000, and accounts payable to suppliers of merchandise decreased by $22,000.
4. Short-term prepayments of operating expenses increased by $8,000, and accrued liabilities for operating expenses decreased by $9,000.
5. The liability for accrued interest payable increased by $4,000 during the year.
6. The liability for accrued income taxes payable decreased by $10,000 during the year.
7. The following schedule summarizes the total debit and credit entries during the year in other balance sheet accounts:

	Debit Entries	Credit Entries
Marketable Securities	$ 50,000	$ 40,000
Notes Receivable (cash loans made to borrowers)	30,000	27,000
Plant Assets (see paragraph **8**)	350,000	30,000
Notes Payable (short-term borrowing)	70,000	56,000
Capital Stock		60,000
Additional Paid-in Capital—Capital Stock		100,000
Retained Earnings (see paragraph **9**)	300,000	935,000

8. The $30,000 in credit entries to the Plant Assets account is net of any debits to Accumulated Depreciation when plant assets were retired. Thus the $30,000 in credit entries represents the book value of all plant assets sold or retired during the year.
9. The $300,000 debit to Retained Earnings represents dividends declared and paid during the year. The $935,000 credit entry represents the net income shown in the income statement.
10. All investing and financing activities were cash transactions.
11. Cash and cash equivalents amount to $20,000 at the beginning of the year and to $473,000 at year-end.

Instructions

a. Prepare a statement of cash flows for the current year. Use the *direct method* of reporting cash flows from operating activities. Place brackets around dollar amounts representing cash outflows. Show separately your computations of the following amounts:
   1. Cash received from customers
   2. Interest received
   3. Cash paid to suppliers and employees
   4. Interest paid
   5. Income taxes paid
   6. Proceeds from sales of marketable securities
   7. Proceeds from sales of plant assets
   8. Proceeds from issuing capital stock

b. Explain why cash paid to suppliers is so much higher than cost of goods sold.

c. Does the fact that Foxboro's cash flows from both investing and financing activities are negative indicate that the company is in a weak cash position?

LO1 through LO9

PROBLEM 13.7B

Prepare and Analyze a Statement of Cash Flows

LGIN was founded in 2010 to apply a new technology for the Internet. The company earned a profit of $190,000 in 2010, its first year of operations. Management expects both sales and net income to more than double in each of the next four years.

Comparative balance sheets at the end of 2010 and 2011, the company's first two years of operations, appear below. (Notice that the balances at the end of the current year appear in the right-hand column.)

LGIN
COMPARATIVE BALANCE SHEETS

	December 31, 2010	2011
Assets		
Cash and cash equivalents	$ 45,000	$ 42,000
Accounts receivable	15,000	880,000
Plant and equipment (net of accumulated depreciation)	680,000	3,140,000
Totals	$740,000	$4,062,000
Liabilities and Stockholders' Equity		
Notes payable (short-term)	$ 0	$1,490,000
Accounts payable	45,000	82,000
Accrued expenses payable	55,000	38,000
Notes payable (long-term)	200,000	785,000
Capital stock (no par value)	250,000	915,000
Retained earnings	190,000	752,000
Totals	$740,000	$4,062,000

Additional Information

The following information regarding the company's operations in 2011 is available in either the company's income statement or its accounting records:

1. Net income for the year was $562,000. The company has never paid a dividend.
2. Depreciation for the year amounted to $125,000.
3. During the year the company purchased plant assets costing $2,585,000, for which it paid $2,000,000 in cash and financed $585,000 by issuing a long-term note payable. (Much of the cash used in these purchases was provided by short-term borrowing, as described below.)
4. In 2011, LGIN borrowed $1,490,000 against a $5 million line of credit with a local bank. In its balance sheet, the resulting obligations are reported as notes payable (short-term).
5. Additional shares of capital stock (no par value) were issued to investors for $665,000 cash.

Instructions

a. Prepare a formal statement of cash flows for 2011, including a supplementary schedule of noncash investing and financing activities. (Follow the format illustrated in Exhibit 13–8. Cash provided by operating activities is to be presented by the *indirect method.*)

b. Briefly explain how operating activities can be a net *use* of cash when the company is operating so profitably.

c. Because of the expected rapid growth, management forecasts that operating activities will include an even greater use of cash in the year 2012 than in 2011. If this forecast is correct, does LGIN appear to be heading toward insolvency? Explain.

LO1 through LO9

PROBLEM 13.8B

Prepare and Analyze a Statement of Cash Flows; Involves Preparation of a Worksheet

Extra-Ordinaire, Inc., sells a single product (Pulsa) exclusively through newspaper advertising. The comparative income statements and balance sheets are for the past two years.

EXTRA-ORDINAIRE, INC.
COMPARATIVE INCOME STATEMENT
FOR THE YEARS ENDED DECEMBER 31, 2010 AND 2011

	2010	2011
Sales	$640,000	$ 410,000
Less: Cost of goods sold	310,000	190,000
Gross profit on sales	330,000	220,000
Less: Operating expenses (including depreciation of $28,000 in 2010 and $29,000 in 2011)	260,000	250,000
Loss on sale of marketable securities	0	4,000
Net income (loss)	$ 70,000	$ (34,000)

EXTRA-ORDINAIRE, INC.
COMPARATIVE BALANCE SHEETS

	December 31, 2010	2011
Assets		
Cash and cash equivalents	$ 22,000	$ 60,000
Marketable securities	27,000	12,000
Accounts receivable	40,000	35,000
Inventory	120,000	128,000
Plant and equipment (net of accumulated depreciation)	250,000	241,000
Totals	$459,000	$476,000
Liabilities & Stockholders' Equity		
Accounts payable	50,000	70,000
Accrued expenses payable	16,000	14,000
Notes payable	235,000	237,000
Capital stock (no par value)	108,000	143,000
Retained earnings	50,000	12,000
Totals	$459,000	$476,000

Additional Information

The following information regarding the company's operations in 2011 is available from the company's accounting records:

1. Early in the year the company declared and paid a $4,000 cash dividend.
2. During the year marketable securities costing $15,000 were sold for $11,000 cash, resulting in a $4,000 nonoperating loss.
3. The company purchased plant assets for $20,000, paying $8,000 in cash and issuing a note payable for the $12,000 balance.
4. During the year the company repaid a $10,000 note payable, but incurred an additional $12,000 in long-term debt as described in **3,** above.
5. The owners invested $35,000 cash in the business as a condition of the new loans described in paragraphs **3** and **4,** above.

Instructions

a. Prepare a worksheet for a statement of cash flows, following the example shown in Exhibit 13–7.

b. Prepare a formal statement of cash flows for 2011, including a supplementary schedule of noncash investing and financing activities. (Use the format illustrated in Exhibit 13–8. Cash provided by operating activities is to be presented by the *indirect method.*)

c. Explain how Extra-Ordinaire, Inc., achieved positive cash flows from operating activities, despite incurring a net loss for the year.

d. Does the company's financial position appear to be improving or deteriorating? Explain.

e. Does Extra-Ordinaire, Inc., appear to be a company whose operations are growing or contracting? Explain.

f. Assume that management *agrees* with your conclusions in parts **c, d,** and **e.** What decisions should be made and what actions (if any) should be taken? Explain.

Critical Thinking Cases

LO1

CASE 13.1
Another Look at Allison Corporation

This case is based on the statement of cash flows for Allison Corporation, illustrated in Exhibit 13–1. Use this statement to evaluate the company's ability to continue paying the current level of dividends—$40,000 per year. The following information also is available:

1. The net cash flows from operating activities shown in the statement are relatively normal for Allison Corporation. Net cash flows from operating activities have not varied by more than a few thousand dollars in any of the past three years.
2. The net outflow for investing activities was unusually high, because the company modernized its production facilities during the year. The normal investing cash outflow is about $45,000 per year, the amount required to replace existing plant assets as they are retired. Over the long run, marketable securities transactions and lending transactions have a very small impact on Allison's net cash flows from investing activities.
3. The net cash flows from financing activities were unusually large in the current year because of the issuance of bonds payable and capital stock. These securities were issued to finance the modernization of the production facilities. In a typical year, financing activities include only short-term borrowing transactions and payments of dividends.

Instructions

a. Solely on the basis of the company's past performance, do you believe that the $40,000 annual dividend payments are secure? That is, does the company appear able to pay this amount in dividends every year without straining its cash position? Do you think it more likely that Allison Corporation will increase or decrease the amount of dividends that it pays? Explain fully.

b. Should any of the unusual events appearing in the statement of cash flows for the current year affect your analysis of the company's ability to pay future dividends? Explain.

LO1 LO8

CASE 13.2
Cash Budgeting for You as a Student

Individuals generally do not prepare statements of cash flows concerning their personal activities. But they do engage in cash budgeting—if not on paper, then at least in their heads.

Assume it is December 29—a Monday. While you are in school, you share a small apartment with another student and work part-time, both near your school to minimize expenses. In two days your rent for January, $200, will be due. You now have $140 in the bank; every Friday you receive a paycheck for $100. You probably see the problem. And it probably doesn't look too serious; you can find a way to deal with it. That's what *budgeting* is all about.

Let's take this example a step further. In addition to the facts given above, your weekly cash payments include meals, $30; entertainment, $20; and gasoline, $10.

Instructions

a. Using the following cash budget, compute your cash balance at the end of weeks 2, 3, and 4.

	Week			
	1	2	3	4
Beginning cash balance	$ 140	$(20)	$?	$?
Expected cash receipts	100	100	100	100
Less: Expected cash outlays:				
Monthly rent	(200)			
Meals	(30)			
Entertainment	(20)			
Gasoline	(10)			
Ending cash balance	$ (20)	$?	$?	$?

b. Evaluate your financial situation.

LO1 LO4 LO8

CASE 13.3
Lookin' Good?

It is late summer and General Wheels, Inc., an auto manufacturer, is facing a financial crisis. A large issue of bonds payable will mature next March, and the company must issue stock or new bonds to raise the money to retire this debt. Unfortunately, profits and cash flows have been declining over recent years. Management fears that if cash flows and profits do not improve in the current year, the company will not be able to raise the capital needed to replace the maturing bonds. Therefore, members of management have made the following proposals to improve the cash flows and profitability that will be reported in the financial statements dated this coming December 31.

1. Switch from the LIFO method to the FIFO method of valuing inventories. Management estimates that the FIFO method will result in a lower cost of goods sold but in higher income taxes for the current year. However, the additional income taxes will not actually be paid until early next year.
2. Switch from the 150 percent declining-balance method of depreciation to the straight-line method and lengthen the useful lives over which assets are depreciated. (These changes would be made only for financial reporting purposes, not for income tax purposes.)
3. Pressure dealers to increase their inventories—in short, to buy more cars. (The dealerships are independently owned; thus dealers are the customers to whom General Wheels sells automobiles.) Management estimates that this strategy could increase sales for the current year by 5 percent. However, any additional sales in the current year would be almost entirely offset by fewer sales in the following year.
4. Require dealers to pay for purchases more quickly. Currently, dealers must pay for purchases of autos within 60 days. Management is considering reducing this period to 30 days.
5. Pass up cash discounts offered by suppliers for prompt payment (that is, 2/10, n/30), and do not pay any bills until the final due date.
6. Borrow at current short-term interest rates (about 10 percent) and use the proceeds to pay off long-term debt bearing an interest rate of 13 percent.
7. Substitute stock dividends for the cash dividends currently paid on capital stock.

Instructions

a. Prepare a schedule with four columns. The first column is to be headed "Proposals" and is to contain the paragraph numbers of the seven proposals listed above. The next three columns are to be headed with the following financial statement captions: (1) "Net Income," (2) "Net Cash Flows from Operating Activities," and (3) "Cash."

For each of the seven proposals in the left-hand column, indicate whether you expect the proposal to "Increase," "Decrease," or have "No Effect" in the current year on each of the financial statement captions listed in the next three columns. (***Note:*** Only a few months remain in the current year. Therefore, you are to determine the *short-term* effects of these proposals.)

b. For each of the seven proposals, write a short paragraph explaining the reasoning behind your answers to part **a.**

LO8

CASE 13.4
Peak Pricing

"Peak pricing is unfair. It makes goods and services available only to the wealthy and prices the average person out of the market."

Instructions

a. Comment on the extent to which you agree or disagree with the preceding statement.

b. What is the alternative to peak pricing?

c. Explain how peak pricing might be applied by:

1. A hotel in Palm Springs, California. (Palm Springs is a winter resort in southern California with wonderful golf facilities. In the summer months, however, temperatures are well over 100 degrees and the tourist business slows dramatically.)
2. Movie theaters.

d. Both in general terms and using specific examples, describe the conditions (if any) under which you might regard peak pricing as *unethical.*

CASE 13.5
Improving the Statement of Cash Flows

The Securities and Exchange Commission (SEC) is an important governmental organization that exists primarily for the protection of the interests of investors in the U.S. securities markets. The SEC provides a wealth of information through its Web site, www.sec.gov.

Instructions

a. Access the SEC's Web site at the above address. Generally review the site to become familiar with the types of information provided.

b. Enter the section of the Web site identified as "About the SEC," then proceed to the section on "Commissioners." Within that section, maneuver around until you are able to access speeches made by the SEC and its staff.

c. Locate the following speech given by Scott A. Taub, former Deputy Chief Accountant, Office of the Chief Accountant of the SEC, in the second quarter of 2004: "Remarks at the University of Southern California, Leventhal School of Accounting, SEC and Financial Reporting Conference."

d. Peruse that entire speech, and then read carefully Mr. Taub's conclusion. Write a paragraph that captures what Mr. Taub had to say about how financial reporting could be improved in general, and how he specifically believes the statement of cash flows could be improved.

INTERNET CASE 13.6
Comparing Cash Flow Information from Two Companies

In the long run, a company must generate positive net cash flows from operating activities to survive. A business that has negative cash flows from operations will not be able to raise cash indefinitely from other sources and will eventually cease existing. Many creditors and stockholders are reluctant to invest in companies that do not generate positive cash flows from operations. However, some investors will invest in companies with negative cash flows from operations due to an optimistic future outlook for the company. Thus, investors have invested millions of dollars in Internet companies that have negative cash flows from operations.

Instructions

a. Visit **Coca-Cola**'s Internet site (www.coke.com) and select "Investors." Under "Financial Information," select the most recent SEC 10K filing or annual report. View the Consolidated Statements of Cash Flows.

b. Visit **Amazon.com**'s Internet site (www.amazon.com) and select "Investor Relations" at the bottom of the page, then click "SEC Filings." Select the most recent SEC 10K filing or annual report and view the Cash Flow Statement.

c. Compare the Net Cash Provided by Operating Activities for each company. Which company has higher Net Cash Provided by Operating Activities? Speculate why one company has much higher Net Cash Provided by Operating Activities than the other.

d. What type of company may have Negative Net Cash Provided from Operating Activities?

e. What type of company may have large Positive Net Cash Provided from Operating Activities?

Internet sites are time and date sensitive. It is the purpose of these exercises to have you explore the Internet. You may need to use the Yahoo! search engine http://www.yahoo.com *(or another favorite search engine) to find a company's current Web address.*

Answers to Self-Test Questions

1. c **2.** c **3.** a **4.** d ($601,000 − $420,000 − $12,000 + $17,000 − $23,000)
5. b **6.** c

CHAPTER 14

Financial Statement Analysis

© BananaStock/PictureQuest/DAL

Learning Objective

AFTER STUDYING THIS CHAPTER, YOU SHOULD BE ABLE TO:

- **LO1** Explain the uses of dollar and percentage changes, trend percentages, component percentages, and ratios.
- **LO2** Discuss the quality of a company's earnings, assets, and working capital.
- **LO3** Explain the nature and purpose of classifications in financial statements.
- **LO4** Prepare a classified balance sheet and compute widely used measures of liquidity and credit risk.
- **LO5** Prepare a multiple-step and a single-step income statement and compute widely used measures of profitability.
- **LO6** Put a company's net income into perspective by relating it to sales, assets, and stockholders' equity.
- **LO7** Compute the ratios widely used in financial statement analysis and explain the significance of each.
- **LO8** Analyze financial statements from the viewpoints of common stockholders, creditors, and others.

JOHNSON & JOHNSON

Johnson & Johnson is the world's most comprehensive and broadly based manufacturer of health care products and related services. In 2009 it had over $50 billion in sales. Other measures of Johnson & Johnson's size include the facts that it has over $94 billion in assets and conducts business in virtually all countries of the world.

How does one get a handle on the financial performance of a huge company such as Johnson & Johnson? Financial statements, including the balance sheet, income statement, and statement of cash flows, provide a wealth of information that is helpful in performing this significant task. Financial statement analysis involves taking key items from these financial statements and gleaning as much useful information as possible from them. For example, we can determine that the amount of Johnson & Johnson's 2009 net income ($12,266 million) represented a return of approximately 13 percent on the total assets used to generate that income. Is a return on assets of 13 percent satisfactory or unsatisfactory? This is a difficult question to answer. To make this judgment we would need more information than we have at this point. For example, we would like to know the trend in various financial measures for Johnson & Johnson for several years. We would also like to know comparative information about other companies with similar operating characteristics (i.e., in the same industry). We will study all of this and more in this chapter as we look at the interesting and challenging subject of financial statement analysis. ■

Financial measures are used often to evaluate corporate performance. As a result, the Securities and Exchange Commission, the Financial Accounting Standards Board, the financial press, and the accounting profession are committed to high-quality financial reporting. Throughout this text, we emphasize the importance of integrity in financial reporting as a means of protecting the interests of investors and creditors. This chapter explores financial statement analysis in depth, building on the introductory sections of this important subject in preceding chapters.

Our discussion of financial statement analysis is presented in three sections. First, we consider general tools of analysis that emphasize comparing information about enterprises with relevant benchmarks. Second, we consider measures of liquidity and credit risk, followed by a consideration of profitability. Third, we present and discuss a comprehensive illustration in which we analyze a company's financial statements from the perspective of three important users of information—common stockholders, long-term creditors, and short-term creditors. Throughout this chapter, we draw on information that was covered in earlier chapters and we use new information that is presented here for the first time.

FINANCIAL STATEMENTS ARE DESIGNED FOR ANALYSIS

In today's global economy, investment capital is always on the move. Through organized capital markets such as the New York Stock Exchange, investors each day shift billions of investment dollars among different companies, industries, and nations. Capital flows to those areas in which investors expect to earn the greatest returns with the least risk. How do investors forecast risk and potential returns? One of the most important ways is by analyzing accounting information for a specific company in the context of its unique industry setting.

The goal of accounting information is to provide economic decision makers with useful information. The financial statements generated through the accounting process are designed to assist users in identifying key relationships and trends. The financial statements of most publicly owned companies are classified and are presented in comparative form. Often, the word *consolidated* appears in the headings of the statements. Users of financial statements should have a clear understanding of these terms.

Most business organizations prepare **classified financial statements,** meaning that items with certain characteristics are placed together in a group, or classification. The purpose of these classifications is to *develop useful subtotals* that will assist users of the statements in their analyses. These classifications and subtotals are standardized throughout most of American business, a practice that assists decision makers in comparing the financial statements of different companies. An example of a classified financial statement is a balance sheet that separates assets and liabilities into current and noncurrent categories.

© AP Photo/Steven Senne

In **comparative financial statements,** the financial statement amounts *for several time periods* appear side by side in vertical columns. This assists investors in identifying and evaluating significant changes and trends.

Most large corporations own other companies through which they conduct some of their business activities. A corporation that owns other businesses is the **parent company,** and the owned companies are called divisions or **subsidiaries.** For example, **PepsiCo**, which makes Pepsi-Cola, also owns and operates the companies that make **Frito-Lay**, **Quaker Foods**, **Gatorade**, and **Tropicana** products. In essence, these subsidiaries are part of the organization generally known as **PepsiCo**. **Consolidated financial statements** present the financial position and operating results of the parent company and its subsidiaries *as if they were a single business organization.*

For Example . . . At this point, take a brief look at the financial statements of **Home Depot, Inc.**, which appear in Appendix A at the end of the text. These financial statements illustrate all of the concepts discussed; they are classified and presented in comparative form, and they describe a consolidated business entity. These financial statements also have been *audited* by **KPMG LLP**, an international public accounting firm.

Tools of Analysis

Significant changes in financial data are easier to see when financial statement amounts for two or more years are placed side by side in adjacent columns. Such a statement is called a *comparative financial statement.* The amounts for the most recent year are usually placed in the left-hand money column, closest to the words that describe the item. The balance sheet, income statement, and statement of cash flows are often prepared in the form of comparative statements. A highly condensed comparative income statement covering three years is shown in Exhibit 14–1.

Exhibit 14–1

COMPARATIVE INCOME STATEMENT

BENSON CORPORATION
COMPARATIVE INCOME STATEMENT
FOR THE YEARS ENDED DECEMBER 31, 2011, 2010, 2009
(IN THOUSANDS OF DOLLARS)

	2011	2010	2009
Net sales	$600	$500	$400
Cost of goods sold	370	300	235
Gross profit	$230	$200	$165
Expenses	194	160	115
Net income	$ 36	$ 40	$ 50

Comparative statements place important financial information in a context that is useful for gaining better understanding. For example, knowing that Benson Corporation had sales of $600,000 in 2011 after years in which sales were $500,000 (2010) and $400,000 (2009) is helpful in understanding Benson's sales trend.

Few figures in a financial statement are highly significant in and of themselves. It is their relationship to other quantities or the amount and direction of change that is important. Analysis is largely a matter of establishing significant relationships and identifying changes and trends. Four widely used analytical techniques are (1) dollar and percentage changes, (2) trend percentages, (3) component percentages, and (4) ratios.

DOLLAR AND PERCENTAGE CHANGES

Learning Objective **Explain the uses of dollar and percentage changes, trend percentages, component percentages, and ratios.** LO1

The dollar amount of change from year to year is significant, and expressing the change in percentage terms adds perspective. For example, if sales this year have increased by $100,000, the fact that this is an increase of 10 percent over last year's sales of $1 million puts it in a different perspective than if it represented a 1 percent increase over sales of $10 million for the prior year.

The dollar amount of any change is the difference between the amount for a *comparison* year and the amount for a *base* year. The percentage change is computed by dividing the amount of the dollar change between years by the amount for the base year. This is illustrated in the following tabulation, using data from the comparative income statement shown in Exhibit 14–1.

	In Thousands			Increase or (Decrease)			
				2011 over 2010		2010 over 2009	
	Year 2011	Year 2010	Year 2009	Amount	%	Amount	%
Net sales	$600	$500	$400	$100	20%	$100	25%
Net income	36	40	50	(4)	(10)	(10)	(20)

Dollar and percentage changes 

Although net sales increased $100,000 in both 2010 and 2011, the percentage change differs because of the change in the base from 2009 to 2010. These calculations present no problems when the figures for the base year are positive amounts. If a negative amount or a zero amount appears in the base year, however, a percentage change cannot be computed. Thus, if Benson Corporation had incurred a net loss in 2010, the percentage change in net income from 2010 to 2011 could not have been calculated.

Evaluating Percentage Changes in Sales and Earnings Computing the percentage changes in sales, gross profit, and net income from one year to the next gives insight into a company's rate of growth. If a company is experiencing growth in its economic activities, sales and earnings should increase at *more than the rate of inflation.* Assume, for example, that a company's sales increase by 6 percent while the general price level rises by 10 percent. The entire increase in the dollar amount of sales may be explained by inflation, rather than by an increase in sales volume (the number of units sold). In fact, the company may well have sold *fewer* goods than in the preceding year.

In measuring the dollar or percentage change in *quarterly* sales or earnings, it is customary to compare the results of the current quarter with those of the *same quarter in the preceding year.* Use of the same quarter of the preceding year as the base period prevents our analysis from being distorted by seasonal fluctuations in business activity.

Percentages Become Misleading When the Base Is Small Percentage changes may create a misleading impression when the dollar amount used as a base is unusually small. Occasionally we hear a television newscaster say that a company's profits have increased by a very large percentage, such as 900 percent. The initial impression created by such a statement is that the company's profits must now be excessively large. But assume, for example, that a company had net income of $100,000 in its first year, that in the second year net income drops to $10,000, and that in the third year net income returns to the $100,000 level. In this third year, net income has increased by $90,000, representing a 900 percent increase over the profits of the second year. What needs to be added to the news commentary is that this 900 percent increase in profits in the third year follows a very small profit in the second year and *exactly offsets* the 90 percent decline in profits in the second year.

TREND PERCENTAGES

The changes in financial statement items from a base year to following years are often expressed as *trend percentages* to show the extent and direction of change. Two steps are necessary to compute trend percentages. First, a base year is selected and each item in the financial statements for the base year is given a weight of 100 percent. The second step is to express each item in the financial statements for following years as a percentage of its base-year amount. This computation consists of dividing an item such as sales in the years after the base year by the amount of sales in the base year.

For example, assume that 2006 is selected as the base year and that sales in the base year amounted to $300,000, as shown in the following table. The trend percentages for sales are computed by dividing the sales amount of each following year by $300,000. Also shown in the illustration are the yearly amounts of net income. The trend percentages for net income are computed by dividing the net income amount for each following year by the base-year amount of $15,000.

Dollar Amounts	**2011**	**2010**	**2009**	**2008**	**2007**	**2006**
Sales.	$450,000	$360,000	$330,000	$321,000	$312,000	$300,000
Net income	22,950	14,550	21,450	19,200	15,600	15,000
Trend Percentages	**2011**	**2010**	**2009**	**2008**	**2007**	**2006**
Sales.	150%	120%	110%	107%	104%	100%
Net income	153	97	143	128	104	100

These trend percentages indicate a modest growth in sales in the early years and accelerated growth in 2010 and 2011. Net income also shows an increasing growth trend with the exception of the year 2010, when net income declined despite a solid increase in sales. The problem was overcome in 2011 with a sharp rise in net income. Overall the trend percentages give a picture of a profitable, growing enterprise.

COMPONENT PERCENTAGES

Component percentages indicate the *relative size* of each item included in a total. For example, each item in a balance sheet could be expressed as a percentage of total assets. This shows quickly the relative importance of each type of asset as well as the relative amount of financing obtained from current creditors, long-term creditors, and stockholders. By computing component percentages for several successive balance sheets, we can see which items are increasing in importance and which are becoming less significant.

Another application of component percentages is to express all items in an income statement as a percentage of net sales. Such a statement is called a *common size income statement.* See the condensed income statement in dollars and in common size form in Exhibit 14–2.

Exhibit 14-2
COMPONENT PERCENTAGES

Income Statement

	Dollars		Component Percentages	
	2011	**2010**	**2011**	**2010**
Net sales	$1,000,000	$600,000	100.0%	100.0%
Cost of goods sold	700,000	360,000	70.0	60.0
Expenses (including income taxes)	250,000	180,000	25.0	30.0
Net income	$ 50,000	$ 60,000	5.0%	10.0%

Are the year-to-date changes favorable?

Looking only at the component percentages, we see that the increase in cost of goods sold (60 percent to 70 percent) was only partially offset by the decrease in expenses as a percentage of net sales, causing net income to decrease from 10 percent to 5 percent of net sales.

RATIOS

A ratio is a simple mathematical expression of the relationship of one item to another. Every percentage may be viewed as a ratio—that is, one number expressed as a percentage of another.

Ratios may be stated in several ways. To illustrate, let us consider the current ratio, which expresses the relationship between a company's most liquid assets (current) and its liabilities that require payment soon (current). If current assets are $240,000 and current liabilities are $80,000, we may say either that the current ratio is 3 to 1 (which is written as 3:1) or that current assets are 300 percent of current liabilities. Either statement correctly summarizes the relationship—that is, that current assets are three times as large as current liabilities.

Ratios are particularly important in understanding financial statements because they permit us to compare information from one financial statement with information from another financial statement. For example, we might compare net income (taken from the income statement) with total assets (taken from the balance sheet) to see how effectively management is using available resources to earn a profit. For a ratio to be useful, however, the two amounts being compared must be logically related. In subsequent sections of this chapter, we will make extensive use of ratios to better demonstrate important dimensions of an enterprise's financial activities.

STANDARDS OF COMPARISON

In using dollar and percentage changes, trend percentages, component percentages, and ratios, financial analysts constantly search for some standard of comparison against which to judge whether the relationships they have found are favorable or unfavorable. Two such standards are (1) the past performance of the company and (2) the performance of other companies in the same industry. For internal management purposes, another important comparison is with expected or budgeted numbers.

Past Performance of the Company Comparing financial information for a current period with similar information for prior years affords some basis for judging whether the condition of the business is improving or worsening. This comparison of data over time is sometimes called *horizontal analysis,* to express the idea of reviewing data for a number of consecutive periods. It is distinguished from *vertical,* or *static,* analysis, which refers to the review of the financial information within a single accounting period.

In addition to determining whether the situation is improving or becoming worse, horizontal analysis may aid in making estimates of future prospects. Because changes may reverse their direction at any time, however, projecting past trends into the future always involves risk.

A weakness of horizontal analysis is that comparison with the past does not afford any basis for evaluation in absolute terms. The fact that net income was 2 percent of sales last year and is 3 percent of sales this year indicates improvement, but if there is evidence that net income *should be* 7 percent of sales, the record for both years is unfavorable.

Industry Standards The limitations of horizontal analysis may be overcome to some extent by finding appropriate benchmarks against which to measure a particular company's performance. The benchmarks used by most analysts are the performance of comparable companies and the average performance of several companies in the same industry.[1]

Assume, for example, that the revenue of Alpha Airlines drops by 8 percent during the current year. If the revenue for the airlines industry had dropped an average of 15 percent during this year, Alpha's 8 percent decline might be viewed as a *favorable* performance. As another example, assume that Omega Co. earns a net income equal to 3 percent of net sales. This would be substandard if Omega were a pharmaceutical company, but it would be satisfactory performance if it were a retail grocery chain because of the difference in earnings expected in the two industries.

When we compare a given company with its competitors or with industry averages, our conclusions are valid only if the companies in question are comparable. Because of the large number of diversified companies formed in recent years, the term *industry* is difficult to define, and even companies that fall roughly within the same industry may not be comparable in many respects. For example, one company may engage only in the marketing of oil products; another may be a fully integrated producer from the well to the gas pump; yet both are said to be in the oil industry.

QUALITY OF EARNINGS

Learning Objective LO2 Discuss the quality of a company's earnings, assets, and working capital.

Profits are the lifeblood of a business entity. No entity can survive indefinitely and accomplish its other goals unless it is profitable. Continuous losses drain assets from the business, consume owners' equity, and leave the company at the mercy of creditors. In assessing the prospects of a company, we are interested not only in the total *amount* of earnings but also in the *rate* of earnings on sales, on total assets, and on owners' equity. In addition, we must look at the *stability* and *source* of earnings. An erratic earnings performance over a period of years, for example, is less desirable than a steady level of earnings. A history of increasing earnings is preferable to a flat earnings record.

A breakdown of sales and earnings by *major product lines* may be useful in evaluating the future performance of a company. Publicly owned companies include with their financial statements supplementary schedules showing sales and profits by product line and by geographical area. These schedules assist financial analysts in forecasting the effect on the company of changes in consumer demand for particular types of products.

[1] Industry data are available from a number of sources. For example, Robert Morris Associates publishes *Annual Statement Studies,* which includes data from many thousands of annual reports, grouped into several hundred industry classifications. Industry classifications are subdivided further by company size. Dun & Bradstreet, Inc., annually publishes *Key Business Ratios* for more than 800 lines of business.

Financial analysts often express the opinion that the earnings of one company are of higher quality than the earnings of other similar companies. This concept of *quality of earnings* arises because each company's management can choose from a variety of accounting principles and methods, all of which are considered generally acceptable. A company's management often is under pressure to report rising earnings or to meet previously stated earnings projections, and accounting policies may be tailored toward these objectives. We have already pointed out the impact on current reported earnings of the choice between the LIFO and FIFO methods of inventory valuation and the choice of depreciation policies. In judging the quality of earnings, the financial analyst should consider whether the accounting principles and methods selected by management lead to a conservative measurement of earnings (high quality) or tend to inflate reported earnings (low quality).

QUALITY OF ASSETS AND THE RELATIVE AMOUNT OF DEBT

Although a satisfactory level of earnings may be a good indication of the company's long-run ability to pay its debts and dividends, we must also look at the composition of assets, their condition and liquidity, the timing of repayment of liabilities, and the total amount of debt outstanding. A company may be profitable and yet be unable to pay its liabilities on time; sales and earnings may appear satisfactory, but plant and equipment may be deteriorating because of poor maintenance policies; valuable patents may be expiring; substantial losses may be imminent due to slow-moving inventories and past-due receivables. Companies with large amounts of debt often are vulnerable to increases in interest rates and are particularly vulnerable to declines in profitability and operating cash flows.

Measures of Liquidity and Credit Risk

Liquidity refers to a company's ability to meet its continuing obligations as they arise. For example, a company that has borrowed money must make interest and principal payments to a financial institution. A company that has purchased its inventory and other necessities on credit may be required to pay the seller within 30 days of the purchase date. Transactions like these require a company to maintain a close watch on its liquidity.

We emphasize throughout this text the importance to investors, creditors, and other users of financial statements of information that permits them to assess the amount, timing, and uncertainty of future cash flows from the enterprise to them. As a result, analyzing an enterprise's liquidity and its credit risk is very important and is a natural place for us to start our study of analyzing financial statements.

In this section we learn about ways to assess liquidity, starting with the classified balance sheet and then looking at a number of ratios commonly used to glean information about liquidity from the financial statements.

A CLASSIFIED BALANCE SHEET

Learning Objective
Explain the nature and purpose of classifications in financial statements. **LO3**

In a classified balance sheet, assets usually are presented in three groups: (1) current assets, (2) plant and equipment, and (3) other assets. Liabilities are classified into two categories: (1) current liabilities and (2) long-term or noncurrent liabilities. A classified balance sheet for Computer City appears in Exhibit 14–3.

The classifications *current assets* and *current liabilities* are especially useful in evaluating a company's liquidity.

Current Assets **Current assets** represent relatively liquid resources. This category includes cash, investments in marketable securities, receivables, inventories, and prepaid expenses. To qualify as a current asset, an asset must already be cash or must be capable of *being converted into cash* or used up within a relatively short period of time, without interfering with normal business operations.

Current assets are tied to an enterprise's **operating cycle.** Most companies have several operating cycles within a year. This means that they take cash and purchase inventory, sell the inventory, and collect the receivable in cash several times within a year. For these companies, the time period used to identify current assets is one year, so any asset that is expected to be

Exhibit 14–3

COMPUTER CITY CLASSIFIED BALANCE SHEET

COMPUTER CITY BALANCE SHEET DECEMBER 31, 2011			
Assets			
Current assets:			
Cash			$ 30,000
Marketable securities			11,000
Notes receivable			5,000
Accounts receivable			60,000
Inventory			70,000
Prepaid expenses			4,000
Total current assets			$180,000
Plant and equipment:			
Land		$151,000	
Building	$120,000		
Less: Accumulated depreciation	9,000	111,000	
Sales Fixtures and equipment	$ 45,000		
Less: Accumulated depreciation	27,000	18,000	
Total plant and equipment			280,000
Other assets:			
Land held as a future building site			170,000
Total assets			$630,000
Liabilities & Stockholders' Equity			
Current liabilities:			
Notes payable (due in 6 months)			$ 10,000
Accounts payable			62,000
Income taxes payable			13,000
Sales taxes payable			3,000
Accrued expenses payable			8,000
Unearned revenue and customer deposits			4,000
Total current liabilities			$100,000
Long-term liabilities:			
Mortgage payable (due in 10 years)			110,000
Total liabilities			$210,000
Stockholders' equity:			
Capital stock (15,000 shares issued and outstanding)		$150,000	
Retained earnings		270,000	
Total stockholders' equity			420,000
Total liabilities & stockholders' equity			$630,000

Learning Objective

LO4 **Prepare a classified balance sheet and compute widely used measures of liquidity and credit risk.**

converted into cash within one year is classified as a current asset in the enterprise's balance sheet. Some enterprises, however, have relatively long operating cycles. For example, a company that constructs very large items (for example, airplanes or ships) may have a production period that extends well beyond one year. In these cases, the length of the company's operating cycle is used to define those assets that are classified as current. While most current assets are expected to be converted into cash, we also include as current assets those that will be used up or consumed during the year or operating cycle, if longer. For example, prepaid expenses are classified as current assets on the basis that their having been paid in advance preserves cash that otherwise would have to be paid in the current period. Combining these ideas, we can define current assets as assets that are already cash, or are expected to be converted into cash or used up within the next year or operating cycle, whichever is longer.

In a balance sheet, current assets are listed in order of liquidity. (The closer an asset is to becoming cash, the greater its liquidity.) Thus cash always is listed first among the current assets, usually followed by investments in marketable securities, receivables, inventory, and prepaid expenses, in that order.

Current Liabilities **Current liabilities** are *existing obligations* that are expected to be paid by using the enterprise's current assets. Among the most common current liabilities are notes payable (due within one year), accounts payable, unearned revenue, and accrued expenses, such as income taxes payable, salaries payable, or interest payable. In the balance sheet, notes payable usually are listed first, followed by accounts payable; other types of current liabilities may be listed in any sequence.

The *relationship* between current assets and current liabilities is as important as the total dollar amount in either category. Current liabilities must be paid in the near future, and the cash to pay these liabilities is expected to come from current assets. Thus, decision makers evaluating the liquidity of a business often compare the relative amounts of current assets and current liabilities, whereas an evaluation of *long-term* credit risk requires a comparison of total assets to total liabilities.

We will now use Computer City's classified balance sheet to examine some widely applied measures of short-term liquidity and long-term credit risk.

WORKING CAPITAL

Working capital is a measurement sometimes used to express the relationship between current assets and current liabilities. **Working capital** is the *excess* of current assets over current liabilities. Computer City's working capital is *$80,000,* computed as follows:

Current assets	$180,000
Less: Current liabilities	100,000
Working capital	$ 80,000

Working capital varies by industry and company size

Recall that current assets are expected to convert into cash (or be used up) within a relatively short period of time, and that current liabilities require a prompt cash payment. Thus, working capital measures a company's potential excess *sources* of cash over its upcoming *uses* of cash.

The amount of working capital that a company needs to satisfy its liabilities as they come due varies with the size of the organization and the nature of its business activities. An analyst familiar with the nature of a company's operations usually can determine from the amount of working capital whether the company is in a sound financial position or is heading for financial difficulties.

CURRENT RATIO

A widely used measure of short-term debt-paying ability is the **current ratio.** This ratio is computed by *dividing* total current assets by total current liabilities.

In the illustrated balance sheet of Computer City, current assets amount to $180,000 and current liabilities total $100,000. Therefore, Computer City's current ratio is *1.8 to 1,* computed as follows:

Current assets	$180,000
Current liabilities	$100,000
Current ratio ($180,000 ÷ $100,000)	1.8 to 1

A widely used measure of liquidity

A current ratio of 1.8 to 1 means that the company's current assets are 1.8 times as large as its current liabilities.

The *higher* the current ratio, the more liquid the company appears to be. Historically, some bankers and other short-term creditors have believed that a company should have a current ratio of 2 to 1 or higher to qualify as a good credit risk. Such rules of thumb are questionable, however, because many successful businesses have current ratios of less than 2 to 1 because their receivables and inventory convert into cash quickly relative to the amount and timing of their payables. Likewise, it is possible for financially weak businesses to have high current ratios as a result of slow turnover in receivables and inventory. In other words, care must be taken in interpreting all ratios, including the current ratio, to ensure that inappropriate conclusions are not reached as a result of superficial analysis. Confirming the information communicated via one ratio by looking at other financial measures is often a good way to help ensure a valid interpretation.

QUICK RATIO

Inventory and prepaid expenses are the *least liquid* of the current assets. In a business with a long operating cycle, it may take several months to convert inventory into cash. Therefore, some short-term creditors prefer the **quick ratio** (sometimes called the acid-test ratio) to the current ratio as a measure of short-term liquidity.

The quick ratio compares only the *most liquid* current assets—called **quick assets**—with current liabilities. Quick assets include cash, marketable securities, and receivables—the current assets that can be converted most quickly into cash. Computer City's quick ratio is *1.06 to 1,* computed as follows:

Quick assets (cash, marketable securities, and receivables)	$106,000
Current liabilities	$100,000
Quick ratio ($106,000 ÷ $100,000)	1.06 to 1

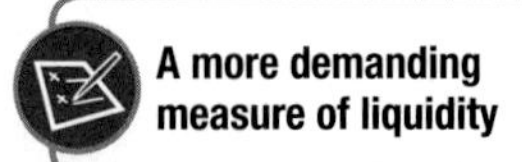
A more demanding measure of liquidity

Quick ratios are especially useful in evaluating the liquidity of companies that have inventories of slow-moving merchandise (such as real estate) or inventories that have become excessive in size.

DEBT RATIO

If a business fails and must be liquidated, the claims of creditors take priority over those of the owners. But if the business has a great deal of debt, there may not be enough assets even to make full payment to all creditors.

A basic measure of the safety of creditors' claims is the **debt ratio,** which states total liabilities as a *percentage* of total assets. A company's debt ratio is computed by dividing total liabilities by total assets, as shown below for Computer City:

Total liabilities	$210,000
Total assets	$630,000
Debt ratio ($210,000 ÷ $630,000)	33⅓%

The debt ratio is not a measure of short-term liquidity. Rather, it is a measure of creditors' *long-term* risk. The smaller the portion of total assets financed by creditors, the smaller the risk that the business may become unable to pay its debts. From the creditors' point of view, the *lower* the debt ratio, the *safer* their position.

Many financially sound American companies traditionally have maintained debt ratios under 50 percent. But again, the financial analyst must be familiar with industry characteristics. Banks, for example, may have very high debt ratios—often over 90 percent.

EVALUATING FINANCIAL RATIOS

We caution users of financial statements *against* placing too much emphasis on rules of thumb, such as *a current ratio should be at least 2 to 1, a quick ratio should be at least 1 to 1,* or *a debt ratio should be under 50 percent.* To interpret any financial ratio properly, the decision maker must first understand the characteristics of the company and the industry in which it operates.

Retailers, for example, tend to have higher current ratios than do wholesalers or manufacturing companies. Service-type businesses—which have no inventory—generally have lower current ratios than merchandising or manufacturing companies. Large businesses with good credit ratings and reliable sources of cash receipts are able to operate with lower current ratios than are small companies whose continuous inflow of cash may be less predictable.

Although a high current ratio is one indication of strong debt-paying ability, an extremely high ratio—say, 4 or 5 to 1—may indicate that *too much* of the company's resources are tied up in current assets. In maintaining such a highly liquid position, the company may be using its financial resources inefficiently and not earning the return that could be earned if the assets were invested in a more productive way.

Standards for Comparison Financial analysts generally use two criteria in evaluating the reasonableness of a financial ratio. One criterion is the *trend* in the ratio over a period of years. By reviewing this trend, analysts are able to determine whether a company's performance or financial position is improving or deteriorating. Second, analysts often compare a company's financial ratios with those of *similar companies* and with *industrywide averages*. These comparisons assist analysts in evaluating a particular ratio in light of the company's current business environment.

Annual Reports Publicly owned corporations issue **annual reports** that provide a great deal of information about the company. For example, annual reports include comparative financial statements that have been audited by a firm of independent public accountants. They also include 5- or 10-year *summaries* of key financial data and **management's discussion and analysis** of the company's operating results, liquidity, and financial position. This is where management identifies and discusses favorable and unfavorable trends and events that may affect the company in the future.

Annual reports are mailed directly to all stockholders of the corporation. They are also available to the public either through the Internet, in libraries, or by writing or calling the stockholder relations department of the corporation.

Industry Information Financial information about *entire industries* is available through financial publications (such as **Dun & Bradstreet, Inc.**) and through online databases (such as **Media General Financial Services**). Such information allows investors and creditors to compare the financial health of an individual company with the industry in which that company operates.

Usefulness and Limitations of Financial Ratios A financial ratio expresses the relationship of one amount to another. Most users of financial statements find that certain ratios assist them in quickly evaluating the financial position, profitability, and future prospects of a business. A comparison of key ratios for several successive years usually indicates whether the business is becoming stronger or weaker. Ratios also provide a way to compare quickly the financial strength and profitability of different companies.

Users of financial statements should recognize, however, that ratios have several limitations. For example, management may enter into year-end transactions that temporarily improve key ratios—a process called **window dressing.**

INTERNATIONAL CASE IN POINT

Two issues confront accountants analyzing international companies. First, there is great variation in accounting measurement, disclosure, and audit quality across countries. Second, obtaining the information necessary to conduct cross-border accounting analyses is frequently difficult and sometimes not possible. Financial reporting in China is a case in point. Until recent years China did not have active stock markets requiring financial reporting. In addition, there was no external auditing in forms that would be familiar to Westerners. Dealing with these differences is one of the primary objectives of establishing international financial accounting standards.

To illustrate, the December 31, 2011, balance sheet of Computer City (Exhibit 14–3) includes current assets of $180,000 and current liabilities of $100,000, indicating a current ratio of *1.8 to 1*. What would happen if, shortly before year-end, management used $20,000 of the company's cash to pay accounts payable that are not due until January 2012? This transaction would reduce current assets to $160,000 ($180,000 − $20,000) and current liabilities to $80,000 ($100,000 − $20,000), resulting in an increase in the current ratio to a more impressive 2 to 1 ($160,000 ÷ $80,000). Is the company really better off as a result of having simply paid $20,000 of liabilities a few days early? The answer is probably no, although looking only at the current ratio one might think it is stronger after paying the $20,000 than before. Such steps to improve the company's appearance in its financial statements are common and, within reason, are a natural part of financial reporting. The astute reader of financial statements needs to be aware of this, however, and should look for instances where there is evidence that steps have been taken to artificially improve a company's appearance. Usually this can be done by looking at multiple financial measures rather than focusing on a single financial measure.

Financial statement ratios contain the same limitations as do the dollar amounts used in financial statements. For example, some assets are reported at historical cost rather than current market value. Also, financial statement ratios express only *financial* relationships. They give no indication of a company's progress in achieving nonfinancial goals, such as improving customer satisfaction or worker productivity. A thorough analysis of investment opportunities involves more than merely computing and comparing financial ratios.

LIQUIDITY, CREDIT RISK, AND THE LAW

Accountants view a business entity as separate from the other economic activities of its owners, regardless of how the business is organized. The law, however, draws an important distinction between *corporations* and *unincorporated* business organizations. Users of financial statements should understand this legal distinction, as it may affect both creditors and owners.

Under the law, the owners of unincorporated businesses (sole proprietorships and partnerships) are *personally liable* for any and all debts of the business organization. Therefore, creditors of unincorporated businesses often base their lending decisions on the financial position of the *owners,* rather than the financial strength of the business entity.[2]

If a business is organized as a corporation, however, the owners (stockholders) are *not* personally responsible for the liabilities of the business. Creditors may look *only to the business entity* in seeking payment of their claims. Therefore, the liquidity of the business entity becomes much more important if the business is organized as a corporation.

Small Corporations and Loan Guarantees Small corporations often do not have sufficient financial resources to qualify for the credit they need. In such cases, creditors may require that one or more of the company's stockholders personally guarantee (or co-sign) specific debts of the business entity. By co-signing debts of the corporation, the individual stockholders *do* become personally liable for the debt if the corporation fails to make payment.

Measures of Profitability

Measures of a company's *profitability* are of interest to equity investors and management and are drawn primarily from the income statement. The measures that we discuss in this chapter include percentage changes in key measurements, gross profit rates, operating income, net income as a percentage of sales, earnings per share, return on assets, and return on equity.

[2] In a *limited* partnership, only the *general partners* are personally responsible for the debts of the business. Every limited partnership must have one or more general partners.

Public opinion polls show that many people believe that most businesses earn a profit equal to 30 percent or more of the sales price of their merchandise. Actually, this is far from true. Most successful companies earn a net income that is between 5 percent and, in unusual cases, 15 percent of sales revenue.

CLASSIFICATIONS IN THE INCOME STATEMENT

An income statement may be prepared in either the *multiple-step* or the *single-step* format. The multiple-step income statement is more useful in illustrating accounting concepts because it provides more detailed information than the single-step format. A multiple-step income statement for Computer City is shown in Exhibit 14–4.

Exhibit 14–4

COMPUTER CITY INCOME STATEMENT (MULTIPLE-STEP)

COMPUTER CITY INCOME STATEMENT FOR THE YEAR ENDED DECEMBER 31, 2011			
Net sales			$900,000
Less: Cost of goods sold (including transportation-in)			540,000
Gross profit			$360,000
Less: Operating expenses:			
Selling expenses:			
Sales salaries and commissions	$64,800		
Advertising	42,000		
Delivery service	14,200		
Depreciation: store equipment	9,000		
Other selling expenses	6,000		
Total selling expenses		$136,000	
General and administrative expenses:			
Administrative and office salaries	$93,000		
Utilities	3,100		
Depreciation: building	3,000		
Other general and administrative expenses	4,900		
Total general and administrative expenses		104,000	
Total operating expenses			240,000
Operating income			$120,000
Less (add): Nonoperating items:			
Interest expense	$12,000		
Purchase discounts lost	1,200		
Interest revenue	(3,200)		10,000
Income before income taxes			$110,000
Income tax expense			38,000
Net income			$ 72,000
Earnings per share			$4.80

A knowledge of accounting does not enable you to say what the level of corporate earnings *should be;* however, it does enable you to read audited financial statements that show what corporate earnings *actually are*. Moreover, you are aware that the information in published financial statements of corporations has been audited by CPA firms and has been periodically reviewed in detail by government agencies, such as the Securities and Exchange Commission (SEC). Consequently, you have some assurance that the profits reported in these published financial statements are reliable; they have been determined in accordance with generally accepted accounting principles and verified by independent experts.

YOUR TURN — **You as a Member of the House of Representatives**

Assume you are a member of the U.S. House of Representatives. Because of the financial frauds at **Enron**, **WorldCom**, and other public companies, the Congress passed, and President Bush signed, the Sarbanes-Oxley Act of 2002. The Sarbanes-Oxley Act significantly expanded the compliance burden, particularly related to financial reporting, on public companies. Certain of your business constituents argue that the compliance burden is excessive and that smaller public companies will go private, and that private businesses that need capital to expand will not go public because of the increased compliance burden. Your constituents also argue that the economy will grow more slowly, creating fewer jobs for your constituents, if companies are excluded from the capital markets because of the compliance burden imposed by the Sarbanes-Oxley Act. How would you respond?

(See our comments on the Online Learning Center Web site.)

MULTIPLE-STEP INCOME STATEMENTS

Learning Objective
LO5 **Prepare a multiple-step and a single-step income statement and compute widely used measures of profitability.**

A multiple-step income statement draws its name from the *series of steps* in which costs and expenses are deducted from revenue and other nonoperating items are incorporated into the income statement. As a first step, the cost of goods sold is deducted from net sales to determine the subtotal *gross profit.* As a second step, operating expenses are deducted to obtain a subtotal called **operating income** (or income from operations). As a final step, income tax expense and other nonoperating items are taken into consideration to arrive at *net income.*

Notice that the income statement is divided into four major sections: (1) revenue, (2) cost of goods sold, (3) operating expenses, and (4) nonoperating items. Multiple-step income statements are noted for their numerous sections and the development of significant subtotals.

The Revenue Section

In a merchandising company, the revenue section of the income statement usually contains only one line, entitled *net sales.* (Other types of revenue, if any, appear in the final section of the statement.)

Investors and managers are vitally interested in the *trend* in net sales. As one means of evaluating this trend, they often compute the percentage change in net sales from year to year. As discussed earlier in this chapter, a **percentage change** is the dollar amount of the *change* in a financial measurement, expressed as a percentage. It is computed by dividing the dollar amount of increase or decrease by the dollar amount of the measurement *before* the change occurred. (Dollar changes *cannot* be expressed as percentages if the financial statement amount in the earlier period is zero or has changed from a negative amount to a positive amount.)

In our economy, most prices increase over time. The average increase in prices during the year is called the *rate of inflation.* Because of inflation, a company's net sales may increase slightly from year to year even if the company is not selling greater amounts of merchandise. If a company's physical sales volume is increasing, net sales usually will grow faster than the rate of inflation.

If a company's sales grow faster than the *industry average,* the company increases its **market share**—that is, its share of total industry sales.

Publicly owned corporations include in their annual reports schedules summarizing operating data—such as net sales—for a period of 5 or 10 years. This information is also readily available through several online databases.

The Cost of Goods Sold Section

The second section of a merchandising company's income statement shows cost of goods sold for the period. Cost of goods sold usually appears as a single dollar amount, which includes such incidental items as freight costs and normal shrinkage losses.

Gross Profit: A Key Subtotal

In a multiple-step income statement, gross profit appears as a subtotal. This makes it easy for users of the income statement to compute the company's *gross profit rate* (or profit margin).

The gross profit rate is gross profit expressed as a *percentage of net sales.* In 2011, Computer City earned an average gross profit rate of *40 percent,* computed as follows:

Dollar amount of gross profit	$360,000
Net sales	$900,000
Gross profit rate ($360,000 ÷ $900,000)	40%

In evaluating the gross profit rate of a particular company, the analyst should consider the rates earned in prior periods, as well as the rates earned by *other companies* in the same industry. For most merchandising companies, gross profit rates are often between 20 percent and 50 percent, depending on the types of products they sell. These rates usually are lowest on fast-moving merchandise, such as groceries, and highest on specialty and novelty products.

Under normal circumstances, a company's gross profit rate tends to remain *reasonably stable* from one period to the next. Significant changes in this rate may provide investors with an early indication of changing consumer demand for the company's products.

The Operating Expenses Section Operating expenses are incurred for the purpose of *producing revenue.* These expenses often are subdivided into the classifications of *selling expenses* and *general and administrative expenses.* Subdividing operating expenses into functional classifications aids management and other users of the statements in separately evaluating different aspects of the company's operations. For example, selling expenses often rise and fall in concert with changes in net sales. Administrative expenses, on the other hand, usually remain more constant from one period to the next.

Operating Income: Another Key Subtotal Some of the revenue and expenses of a business result from activities other than the company's basic business operations. Common examples include interest earned on investments and income tax expense.

Operating income (or income from operations) shows the relationship between revenue earned from customers and expenses incurred in producing this revenue. In effect, operating income measures the profitability of a company's *basic or core business operations* and leaves out other types of revenue and expenses.

Nonoperating Items Revenue and expenses that are not directly related to the company's primary business activities are listed in a final section of the income statement following operating income.

Two significant nonoperating items are interest expense and income tax expense. Interest expense results from the manner in which assets are *financed,* not the manner in which these assets are used in business operations. Income tax expense is not included among the operating expenses because paying income taxes *does not directly contribute to the production of revenue.* Nonoperating revenues, such as interest and dividends earned on investments, also are listed in this section of the income statement.

Net Income Many equity investors consider net income (or net loss) to be the most important figure in a company's financial statements. This amount usually represents the overall increase (or decrease) in owners' equity resulting from all profit-directed activities during the period.

Financial analysts often compute net income as a *percentage of net sales* (net income divided by net sales). This measurement provides an indication of management's *ability to control expenses* and to retain a reasonable portion of its revenue as profit.

The normal ratio of net income to net sales varies greatly by industry. In some industries, companies may be successful by earning a net income equal to only 2 percent or 3 percent of net sales. In other industries, net income may be much higher. In 2011, Computer City's net income amounts to *8 percent* of net sales.

Learning Objective LO6
Put a company's net income into perspective by relating it to sales, assets, and stockholders' equity.

Net income	$ 72,000
Net sales	$900,000
Net income as a percentage of net sales ($72,000 ÷ $900,000)	8%

EARNINGS PER SHARE

Ownership of a corporation is evidenced by *shares* of capital stock. What does the net income of a corporation mean to someone who owns, say, 100 shares of a corporation's capital stock? To assist individual stockholders in relating the corporation's net income to *their ownership shares,* public companies compute **earnings per share** and show these amounts at the bottom of their income statements.[3]

In the simplest case, earnings per share is net income, expressed on a per-share basis. For example, the balance sheet in Exhibit 14–3 indicates that Computer City has 15,000 shares of capital stock outstanding.[4] Assuming these shares had been outstanding all year, earnings per share amounts to *$4.80:*

Net income	$72,000
Shares of capital stock outstanding	15,000
Earnings per share ($72,000 ÷ 15,000 shares)	$4.80

Earnings per share is one of the most widely used of all accounting ratios. The *trend* in earnings per share and the expected earnings in future periods are *major factors* affecting the market value of a company's shares.

PRICE-EARNINGS RATIO

Learning Objective
LO7 Compute the ratios widely used in financial statement analysis and explain the significance of each.

Financial analysts express the relationship between the market price of a company's stock and the underlying earnings per share as a **price-earnings (p/e) ratio.** This ratio is computed by dividing the current market price per share of the company's stock by annual earnings per share. (A p/e ratio cannot be computed for a period in which the company incurs a net loss.)

To illustrate, assume that, at the end of 2011, Computer City's capital stock is trading among investors at a market price of *$96* per share. The p/e ratio of the company's stock is computed as follows:

Current market price per share of stock	$96
Earnings per share (for the last 12 months)	$4.80
Price-earnings ratio ($96 ÷ $4.80)	20

Technically, this ratio is 20 to 1. But it is common practice to omit the "to 1" and merely describe a p/e ratio by the first number. The p/e ratios of many publicly owned corporations are quoted daily in the financial pages of many newspapers.

The p/e ratio reflects *investors' expectations* concerning the company's *future performance.* The more optimistic these expectations, the higher the p/e ratio is likely to be.

A p/e ratio of 10 or less often indicates that investors expect earnings to *decline* from the current level. It could also mean, however, that the stock is *undervalued.* Likewise, a stock with a p/e ratio of 30 or more usually means that investors expect earnings to *increase* from the current level. However, it may also signal that the stock is *overvalued.*

One word of caution. If earnings decline to *very low levels,* the price of the stock usually does not follow the earnings all the way down. Therefore, a company with *very low earnings* may have a *high p/e ratio* even if investors are not optimistic about future earnings. From this discussion, it should be obvious that significant judgment is required in interpreting the p/e and other financial statement ratios.

[3] Only publicly held corporations are *required* to report earnings on a per-share basis. For small businesses, such as Computer City, the reporting of earnings per share is optional.

[4] Assume that all 15,000 shares have been outstanding throughout the year. Computation of earnings per share in more complex situations is addressed in Chapter 12.

SINGLE-STEP INCOME STATEMENTS

In their annual reports, many publicly owned corporations present their financial statements in a highly condensed format. For this reason, the *single-step* income statement is widely used in annual reports. The 2011 income statement of Computer City in Exhibit 14–5 has been revised to a single-step format.

Exhibit 14–5
COMPUTER CITY INCOME STATEMENT (SINGLE-STEP)

COMPUTER CITY INCOME STATEMENT FOR THE YEAR ENDED DECEMBER 31, 2011		
Revenue:		
Net sales		$900,000
Interest earned		3,200
Total revenue		$903,200
Less: Costs and expenses:		
Cost of goods sold	$540,000	
Selling expenses	136,000	
General and administrative expenses	104,000	
Interest expense	12,000	
Purchase discounts lost	1,200	
Income tax expense	38,000	
Total costs and expenses		831,200
Net income		$ 72,000
Earnings per share		$4.80

The single-step form of income statement takes its name from the fact that all costs and expenses are deducted from total revenue in a single step. No subtotals are shown for gross profit or for operating income, although the statement provides investors with enough information to compute these subtotals on their own. Notice that the amounts of net income and earnings per share are the same in the multiple-step and single-step income statements.

EVALUATING THE ADEQUACY OF NET INCOME

How much net income must a business earn to be considered successful? Obviously, the dollar amount of net income that investors consider adequate depends on the *size of the business*. An annual net income of $1 million might seem impressive for an automobile dealership but would represent poor performance for a company the size of **Ford**, **Procter & Gamble**, or **Home Depot**.

© Stone/Getty Images

Investors usually consider two factors in evaluating a company's profitability: (1) the trend in earnings and (2) the amount of current earnings in relation to the amount of the resources needed to produce the earnings.

Some investors regard the *trend* in earnings from year to year as more important than the amount of net income in the current period. Equity investors stand to benefit from the company's performance over the long run. Years of steadily increasing earnings may increase the value of the stockholders' investment manyfold.

In evaluating the current level of earnings, many investors use *return on investment* analysis.

RETURN ON INVESTMENT (ROI)

We have emphasized throughout this text that a basic purpose of accounting is to assist decision makers in efficiently allocating and using economic resources. In deciding where to invest their money, equity investors want to know how efficiently companies utilize resources. A common method of evaluating the efficiency with which financial resources are employed is to compute the rate of return earned on these resources. This rate of return is called the *return on investment,* or *ROI,* and is sometimes referred to as return on assets.

Mathematically, computing return on investment is simple: the annual return (or profit) generated by the investment is stated as a *percentage* of the average amount invested throughout the year. The basic idea is illustrated by the following formula:

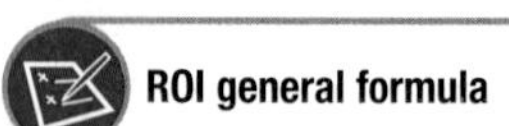

ROI general formula

$$\textbf{Return on Investment (ROI)} = \frac{\textbf{Return}}{\textbf{Average Amount Invested}}$$

The return is earned throughout the period. Therefore, it is logical to express this return as a percentage of the *average* amount invested during the period, rather than the investment at year-end. The average amount invested usually is computed by adding the amounts invested as of the beginning and end of the year, and dividing this total by 2. If the investment is relatively stable over time, the year-end balance may be used instead of an average.

The concept of ROI is applied in many different situations, such as evaluating the profitability of a business, a branch location, or a specific investment opportunity. As a result, a number of variations in the basic ROI ratio have been developed, each suited to a particular type of analysis. These ratios differ in the manner in which return and average amount invested are defined. We will discuss two common applications of the ROI concept: *return on assets* and *return on equity.*

RETURN ON ASSETS (ROA)

This ratio is used in evaluating whether management has earned a reasonable return with the assets under its control. In this computation, return usually is defined as *operating income,* since interest expense and income taxes are determined by factors other than the manner in which assets are used. The **return on assets** is computed as follows:

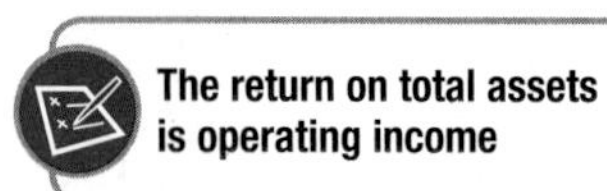

The return on total assets is operating income

$$\textbf{Return on Assets (ROA)} = \frac{\textbf{Operating Income}}{\textbf{Average Total Assets}}$$

Let us now determine the return on assets earned by the management of Computer City in 2011. Operating income, as shown in the income statement in Exhibit 14–4, amounts to *$120,000.* Assume that Computer City's assets at the beginning of 2011 totaled $570,000. The illustrated balance sheet in Exhibit 14–3 shows total assets of $630,000 at year-end. Therefore, the company's *average* total assets during the year amounted to *$600,000* [($570,000 + $630,000) ÷ 2]. The return on assets in 2011 is *20 percent,* determined as follows:

$$\frac{\textbf{Operating Income}}{\textbf{Average Total Assets}} = \frac{\textbf{\$120,000}}{\textbf{\$600,000}} = \textbf{20\%}$$

Most successful businesses earn a return on average total assets of, perhaps, 15 percent or more. At this writing, businesses must pay interest rates of between 3 percent and 8 percent to borrow money. However, interest rates are at historic lows in the United States and are likely to rise in the future. If a business is well managed and has good future prospects, management should be able to earn a return on assets that is higher than the company's cost of borrowing.

RETURN ON EQUITY (ROE)

The return on assets that we calculated above measures the efficiency with which management has utilized the assets under its control, regardless of whether these assets were financed with debt or equity capital. The **return on equity** ratio, in contrast, looks only at the return earned by management on the stockholders' investment—that is, on *owners' equity.*

The return to stockholders is *net income,* which represents the return from all sources, both operating and nonoperating. Thus, return on equity is computed as follows:

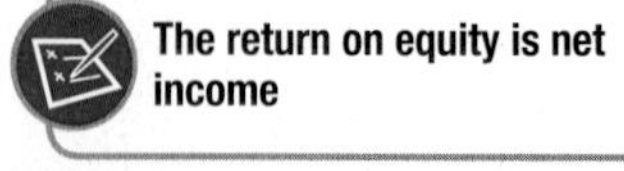

The return on equity is net income

$$\textbf{Return on Equity (ROE)} = \frac{\textbf{Net Income}}{\textbf{Average Total Stockholders' Equity}}$$

To illustrate, let us again turn to the 2011 financial statements of Computer City. The company earned net income of *$72,000.* The year-end balance sheet (Exhibit 14–3) shows total stockholders' equity of $420,000. To enable us to complete our computation, we will assume that the stockholders' equity at the *beginning* of the year amounted to $380,000. Therefore, the *average* stockholders' equity for the year amounts to *$400,000* [($380,000 + $420,000) ÷ 2]. The return on stockholders' equity in 2011 is *18 percent,* computed as follows:

$$\frac{\textbf{Net Income}}{\textbf{Average Total Stockholders' Equity}} = \frac{\$72{,}000}{\$400{,}000} = 18\%$$

Traditionally, stockholders have expected to earn an average annual return of 12 percent or more from equity investments in large, financially strong companies. Annual returns on equity of 30 percent or more are not uncommon, especially in rapidly growing companies with new or highly successful products.

The return on equity may be higher or lower than the overall return on assets, depending on how the company has financed its assets and on the amounts of its nonoperating revenue and expenses. A company that suffers a net loss provides its stockholders with a *negative* return on stockholders' equity.

Comprehensive Illustration: Seacliff Company

Now that we have presented several techniques that are useful in better understanding an enterprise's financial statements, we will show the comprehensive analysis of a company. This illustration draws from material presented in this chapter as well as from information presented earlier in the text. We take a comprehensive look at the analysis of financial statements from the perspectives of three important groups: common stockholders, long-term creditors, and short-term creditors.

The basic information for our analysis is contained in a set of condensed two-year comparative financial statements for Seacliff Company shown in Exhibits 14–6 through 14–10. Summarized statement data, together with computations of dollar increases and decreases, and component percentages where applicable, have been compiled. For convenience in this illustration, relatively small dollar amounts have been used in the Seacliff Company financial statements.

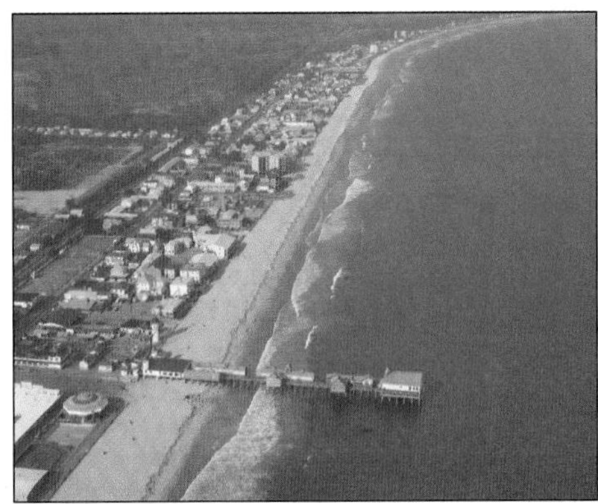

© Digital Vision/Getty Images/DAL

Exhibit 14–6 SEACLIFF INCOME STATEMENTS

SEACLIFF COMPANY
COMPARATIVE INCOME STATEMENT
FOR THE YEARS ENDED DECEMBER 31, 2011, AND DECEMBER 31, 2010

			Increase or (Decrease)		Percentage of Net Sales	
	2011	2010	Dollars	%	2011	2010
Net sales	$900,000	$750,000	$150,000	20.0	100.0	100.0
Cost of goods sold	530,000	420,000	110,000	26.2	58.9	56.0
Gross profit on sales	$370,000	$330,000	$ 40,000	12.1	41.1	44.0
Operating expenses:						
Selling expenses	$117,000	$ 75,000	$ 42,000	56.0	13.0	10.0
General and administrative expenses	126,000	95,000	31,000	32.6	14.0	12.7
Total operating expenses	$243,000	$170,000	$ 73,000	42.9	27.0	22.7
Operating income	$127,000	$160,000	$ (33,000)	(20.6)	14.1	21.3
Interest expense	24,000	30,000	(6,000)	(20.0)	2.7	4.0
Income before income tax	$103,000	$130,000	$ (27,000)	(20.8)	11.4	17.3
Income tax expense	28,000	40,000	(12,000)	(30.0)	3.1	5.3
Net income	$ 75,000	$ 90,000	$ (15,000)	(16.7)	8.3	12.0
Earnings per share of common stock	$ 13.20	$ 20.25	$ (7.05)	(34.8)		

Exhibit 14–7 SEACLIFF STATEMENTS OF RETAINED EARNINGS

SEACLIFF COMPANY
STATEMENT OF RETAINED EARNINGS
FOR THE YEARS ENDED DECEMBER 31, 2011, AND DECEMBER 31, 2010

			Increase or (Decrease)	
	2011	**2010**	**Dollars**	**%**
Retained earnings, beginning of year	$176,000	$115,000	$ 61,000	53.0
Net income	75,000	90,000	(15,000)	(16.7)
	$251,000	$205,000	$ 46,000	22.4
Less: Dividends on common stock ($5.00 per share in 2010, $4.80 per share in 2011)	$ 24,000	$ 20,000	$ 4,000	20.0
Dividends on preferred stock ($9 per share)	9,000	9,000		
	$ 33,000	$ 29,000	$ 4,000	13.8
Retained earnings, end of year	$218,000	$176,000	$ 42,000	23.9

Exhibit 14–8 SEACLIFF BALANCE SHEETS

SEACLIFF COMPANY
CONDENSED COMPARATIVE BALANCE SHEET*
DECEMBER 31, 2011, AND DECEMBER 31, 2010

			Increase or (Decrease)		Percentage of Total Assets	
Assets	**2011**	**2010**	**Dollars**	**%**	**2011**	**2010**
Current assets	$390,000	$288,000	$102,000	35.4	41.1	33.5
Plant and equipment (net)	500,000	467,000	33,000	7.1	52.6	54.3
Other assets (loans to officers)	60,000	105,000	(45,000)	(42.9)	6.3	12.2
Total assets	$950,000	$860,000	$ 90,000	10.5	100.0	100.0
Liabilities & Stockholders' Equity						
Liabilities:						
Current liabilities	$112,000	$ 94,000	$ 18,000	19.1	11.8	10.9
12% long-term note payable (due in 7 years)	200,000	250,000	(50,000)	(20.0)	21.1	29.1
Total liabilities	$312,000	$344,000	$ (32,000)	(9.3)	32.9	40.0
Stockholders' equity:						
9% preferred stock, $100 par	$100,000	$100,000	—	—	10.5	11.6
Common stock, $50 par	250,000	200,000	$ 50,000	25.0	26.3	23.2
Additional paid-in capital	70,000	40,000	30,000	75.0	7.4	4.7
Retained earnings	218,000	176,000	42,000	23.9	22.9	20.5
Total stockholders' equity	$638,000	$516,000	$122,000	23.6	67.1	60.0
Total liabilities & stockholders' equity	$950,000	$860,000	$ 90,000	10.5	100.0	100.0

*In order to focus attention on important subtotals, this statement is highly condensed and does not show individual asset and liability items. These details will be introduced as needed in the text discussion. For example, a list of Seacliff Company's current assets and current liabilities appears in Exhibit 14–18.

Exhibit 14–9 SEACLIFF STATEMENT OF CASH FLOWS

SEACLIFF COMPANY
CONDENSED COMPARATIVE STATEMENT OF CASH FLOWS
FOR THE YEARS ENDED DECEMBER 31, 2011, AND DECEMBER 31, 2010

			Increase or (Decrease)	
	2011	**2010**	**Dollars**	**%**
Cash flows from operating activities:				
Net cash flows from operating activities	$ 19,000	$ 95,000	$(76,000)	(80.0)
Cash flows from investing activities:				
Purchases of plant assets	(63,000)	(28,000)	(35,000)	125.0
Collections of loans from officers	45,000	(35,000)	80,000	N/A*
Net cash used by investing activities	$(18,000)	$(63,000)	$ 45,000	(71.4)
Cash flows from financing activities:				
Dividends paid	$(33,000)	$(29,000)	$ (4,000)	13.8
Repayment of long-term debt	(50,000)	–0–	(50,000)	N/A*
Proceeds from issuing capital stock	80,000	–0–	80,000	N/A*
Net cash used by financing activities	$ (3,000)	$(29,000)	$ 26,000	(89.7)
Net increase (decrease) in cash and cash equivalents	$ (2,000)	$ 3,000	$ (5,000)	N/A*
Cash and cash equivalents, January 1, 2011	40,000	37,000	3,000	8.1
Cash and cash equivalents, December 31, 2011	$ 38,000	$ 40,000	$ (2,000)	(5.0)

*N/A indicates that computation of the percentage change is not appropriate. Percentage changes cannot be determined if the base year is zero or if a negative amount (cash outflow) changes to a positive amount (cash inflow).

Exhibit 14–10

SEACLIFF NOTES TO FINANCIAL STATEMENTS

SEACLIFF COMPANY
NOTES TO FINANCIAL STATEMENTS
FOR THE YEARS ENDED DECEMBER 31, 2011, AND DECEMBER 31, 2010

Note 1—Accounting Policies

Inventories Inventories are determined by the LIFO method.

Depreciation Depreciation is computed by the straight-line method. Buildings are depreciated over 40 years, and equipment and fixtures over periods of 5 or 10 years.

Note 2—Unused Lines of Credit

The company has a confirmed line of credit in the amount of $35,000. None was in use at December 31, 2011.

Note 3—Contingencies and Commitments

As of December 31, 2011, the company has no material commitments or noncancellable obligations. There currently are no loss contingencies known to management.

Note 4—Current Values of Financial Instruments

All financial instruments appear in the financial statements at dollar amounts that closely approximate their current values.

Note 5—Concentrations of Credit Risk

The company engages in retail sales to the general public from a single location in Seattle, Washington. No individual customer accounts for more than 2% of the company's total sales or accounts receivable. Accounts receivable are unsecured.

ANALYSIS BY COMMON STOCKHOLDERS

Learning Objective
LO8 Analyze financial statements from the viewpoints of common stockholders, creditors, and others.

Common stockholders and potential investors in common stock look first at a company's earnings record. Their investment is in shares of stock, so *earnings per share* and *dividends per share* are of particular interest.

Earnings per Share of Common Stock As indicated in Chapter 12, earnings per share of common stock are computed by dividing the income applicable to the common stock by the weighted-average number of shares of common stock outstanding during the year. Any preferred dividend requirements must be subtracted from net income to determine income applicable to common stock, as shown in the computations for Seacliff Company in Exhibit 14–11.

Exhibit 14–11
EARNINGS PER SHARE OF COMMON STOCK

Earnings related to number of common shares outstanding

	2011	2010
Net income	$75,000	$90,000
Less: Preferred dividend requirements	9,000	9,000
Income applicable to common stock	(a) $66,000	$81,000
Shares of common stock outstanding, during the year	(b) 5,000	4,000
Earnings per share of common stock (a ÷ b)	$ 13.20	$ 20.25

Notice that earnings per share have decreased by *$7.05* in 2011, representing a decline of nearly *35 percent* from their level in 2010 ($7.05 ÷ $20.25 = 34.8%). Common stockholders consider a decline in earnings per share to be an unfavorable development. A decline in earnings per share generally represents a decline in the profitability of the company and creates uncertainty as to the company's prospects for future growth.

With such a significant decline in earnings per share, we should expect to see a decline in the market value of Seacliff's common stock during 2011. [For purposes of our illustration, we assume the common stock had a market value of *$160* at December 31, 2010, and of *$132* at the end of 2011. This drop of $28 per share represents a *17½ percent* decline in the market value of every common stockholder's investment ($28 decline ÷ $160 = 17.5%).]

Price-Earnings Ratio As we mentioned earlier in this chapter, the relationship between the market price of common stock and earnings per share is widely recognized and is expressed as a ratio, called the *price-earnings ratio* (or *p/e ratio*). The p/e ratio is determined by dividing the market price per share by the annual earnings per share.

The outlook for future earnings is the major factor influencing a company's p/e ratio. Companies with track records of rapid growth may sell at p/e ratios of perhaps 30 to 1, or even higher. Companies with "flat" earnings or earnings expected to decline in future years often sell at price-earnings ratios below 10 to 1.

At the end of 2010, Seacliff's p/e ratio was approximately *8 to 1* ($160 ÷ $20.25 = 7.9), suggesting that investors *were expecting* earnings to decline in 2011. At December 31, 2011, the price-earnings ratio was *10 to 1* ($132 ÷ $13.20 = 10.0). A p/e ratio in this range suggests that investors expect future earnings to stabilize around the current level.

Dividend Yield Dividends are of prime importance to some stockholders, but a secondary factor to others. Some stockholders invest primarily to receive regular cash income, while others invest in stocks principally with the expectation of rising market prices. If a corporation is profitable and retains its earnings for expansion of the business, the expanded operations should produce an increase in the net income of the company and thus tend to make each share of stock more valuable.

In comparing the merits of alternative investment opportunities, we should relate earnings and dividends per share to the *market value* of the stock at a particular date. Dividends per share divided by market price per share determine the *yield* rate of a company's stock. Dividend yield is especially important to those investors whose objective is to maximize the dividend revenue from their investments. For Seacliff, the dividend yield on its common stock was 3.1 percent in 2010 ($5 ÷ $150) and 3.6 percent in 2011 ($4.80 ÷ $132).

Summary of Earnings and Dividend Data for Seacliff The relationships of Seacliff's per-share earnings and dividends to its year-end stock prices are summarized in Exhibit 14–12.

Exhibit 14–12
EARNINGS AND DIVIDENDS PER SHARE OF COMMON STOCK

Date	Market Value per Share	Earnings per Share	Price-Earnings Ratio	Dividends per Share	Dividend Yield, %
Dec. 31, 2010	$160	$20.25	8	$5.00	3.1
Dec. 31, 2011	132	13.20	10	4.80	3.6

Earnings and dividends related to market price of common stock

The decline in market value during 2011 presumably reflects the decreases in both earnings and dividends per share. Investors appraising this stock at December 31, 2011, should consider whether a price-earnings ratio of 10 and a dividend yield of 3.6 percent meet their expectations in light of alternative investment opportunities. These investors will also place considerable weight on estimates of the company's prospective future earnings and the probable effect of such estimated earnings on the market price of the stock and on dividend payments.

Revenue and Expense Analysis The trend of earnings of Seacliff Company is unfavorable, and stockholders will want to know the reasons for the decline in net income. The comparative income statements in Exhibit 14–6 show that despite a 20 percent increase in net sales, net income fell from $90,000 in 2010 to $75,000 in 2011, a decline of 16.7 percent. As a percentage of net sales, net income fell from 12 percent to only 8.3 percent. The primary causes of this decline were the increases in selling expenses (56.0 percent), general and administrative expenses (32.6 percent), and the cost of goods sold (26.2 percent), all of which exceeded the 20 percent increase in net sales.

Let us assume that further investigation reveals Seacliff Company decided in 2011 to reduce its sales prices in an effort to generate greater sales volume. This would explain the decrease in the gross profit rate from 44 percent to 41.1 percent of net sales. Since the dollar amount of gross profit increased $40,000 in 2011, the strategy of reducing sales prices to increase volume would have been successful if there had been little or no increase in operating expenses. However, operating expenses rose by $73,000, resulting in a $33,000 decrease in operating income.

The next step is to find which expenses increased and why. An investor may be limited here, because detailed operating expenses are not usually shown in published financial statements. Some conclusions, however, can be reached on the basis of even the condensed information available in the comparative income statements for Seacliff Company shown in Exhibit 14–6.

The substantial increase in selling expenses presumably reflects greater selling effort during 2011 in an attempt to improve sales volume. However, the fact that selling expenses increased $42,000 while gross profit increased only $40,000 indicates that the cost of this increased sales effort was not justified in terms of results. Even more bothersome is the increase in general and administrative expenses. Some growth in administrative expenses might be expected to accompany increased sales volume, but because some of the expenses are fixed, the growth generally should be *less than proportional* to any increase in sales. The increase in general and administrative expenses from 12.7 percent to 14 percent of sales should be of concern to informed investors.

Management generally has greater control over operating expenses than over revenue. The *operating expense ratio* is often used as a measure of management's ability to control its operating expenses. We show the unfavorable trend in this ratio for Seacliff Company in Exhibit 14–13.

Exhibit 14–13
OPERATING EXPENSE RATIO

	2011	2010
Operating expenses	(a) $243,000	$170,000
Net sales	(b) $900,000	$750,000
Operating expense ratio (a ÷ b)	27.0%	22.7%

Does a higher operating expense ratio indicate higher net income?

If management were able to increase the sales volume while at the same time increasing the gross profit rate and decreasing the operating expense ratio, the effect on net income could

be dramatic. For example, if in the year 2012 Seacliff Company can increase its sales by approximately 11 percent, to $1,000,000, increase its gross profit rate from 41.1 to 44 percent, and reduce the operating expense ratio from 27 to 24 percent, its operating income will increase from $127,000 to $200,000 ($1,000,000 − $560,000 − $240,000), an increase of over 57 percent.

RETURN ON INVESTMENT (ROI)

The rate of return on investment (often called ROI) is a measure of management's efficiency in using available resources. Regardless of the size of the organization, capital is a scarce resource and must be used efficiently. In judging the performance of branch managers or of companywide management, it is reasonable to raise the question: What rate of return have you earned on the resources under your control?

Return on Assets An important test of management's ability to earn a return on funds supplied from all sources is the rate of return on total assets.

As noted previously, the income figure used in computing this ratio should be *operating income,* since interest expense and income taxes are determined by factors other than the efficient use of resources. Operating income is earned throughout the year and therefore should be related to the *average* investment in assets during the year. In Exhibit 14–14, the computation of this ratio of Seacliff Company assumes total assets at the beginning of 2010 were $820,000.

Exhibit 14–14

PERCENTAGE RETURN ON ASSETS

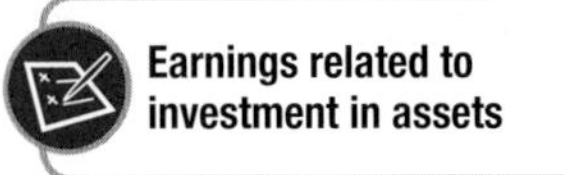
Earnings related to investment in assets

	2011	2010
Operating income	(a) $127,000	$160,000
Total assets, beginning of year	(b) $860,000	$820,000
Total assets, end of year	(c) $950,000	$860,000
Average investment in assets [(b + c) ÷ 2]	(d) $905,000	$840,000
Return on assets (a ÷ d)	14%	19%

This ratio shows that the rate of return earned on the company's assets fell in 2011. Before drawing conclusions as to the effectiveness of Seacliff's management, however, we should consider the trend in the return on assets earned by other companies of similar kind and size.

Return on Common Stockholders' Equity We introduced the concept of return on equity using a company that had only one class of capital stock. Therefore, the return on equity was simply net income divided by average stockholders' equity. But Seacliff has issued both preferred stock *and* common stock. The preferred stock does not participate fully in the company's earnings; rather, the return to preferred stockholders is limited to their dividend. Thus, we must adjust the return on equity computation to reflect the return on *common* stockholders' equity.

The return to common stockholders is equal to net income *less* any preferred dividends. Thus, the return on common stockholders' equity, assuming common stockholders' equity at the beginning of 2010 was $355,000, is computed in Exhibit 14–15.

Exhibit 14–15

RETURN ON COMMON STOCKHOLDERS' EQUITY

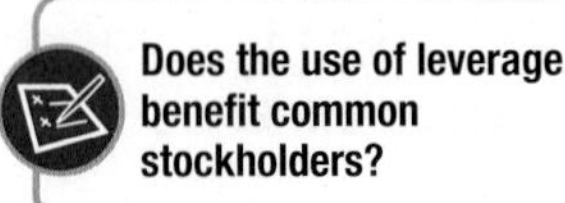
Does the use of leverage benefit common stockholders?

	2011	2010
Net income	$ 75,000	$ 90,000
Less: Preferred dividend requirements	9,000	9,000
Net income applicable to common stock	(a) $ 66,000	$ 81,000
Common stockholders' equity, beginning of year	(b) $416,000	$355,000
Common stockholders' equity, end of year	(c) $538,000	$416,000
Average common stockholders' equity [(b + c) ÷ 2]	(d) $477,000	$385,500
Return on common stockholders' equity (a ÷ d)	13.8%	21.0%

In both years, the rate of return on common stockholders' equity was higher than the 12 percent rate of interest paid to long-term creditors or the 9 percent dividend rate paid to preferred stockholders. This result was achieved through the favorable use of leverage.

LEVERAGE

Applying leverage means using borrowed money to earn a return *greater* than the cost of borrowing, increasing net income and the return on common stockholders' equity. In other words, if you can borrow money at 12 percent and use it to earn 20 percent, you will benefit by doing so. However, leverage can act as a double-edged sword; the effects may be favorable or unfavorable to the holders of common stock.

If the rate of return on total assets should fall *below* the average rate of interest on borrowed capital, leverage will *reduce* the return on common stockholders' equity. In this situation, paying off the loans that carry high interest rates would appear to be a logical move. However, many companies do not have enough cash to retire long-term debt on short notice. Therefore, the common stockholders may become locked in to the unfavorable effects of leverage.

In deciding how much leverage is appropriate, the common stockholders should consider the *stability* of the company's return on assets as well as the relationship of this return to the average cost of borrowed capital. If a business incurs so much debt that it becomes unable to meet the required interest and principal payments, the creditors may force liquidation or reorganization of the business.

Debt Ratio One indicator of the amount of leverage used by a business is the debt ratio. This ratio measures the proportion of the total assets financed by creditors, as distinguished from stockholders. It is computed by dividing total liabilities by total assets. A *high* debt ratio indicates an extensive use of leverage, that is, a large proportion of financing provided by creditors. A low debt ratio, on the other hand, indicates that the business is making little use of leverage.

The debt ratio at year-end for Seacliff is determined as shown in Exhibit 14–16.

Exhibit 14–16
DEBT RATIO

	2011	2010
Total liabilities	(a) $312,000	$344,000
Total assets (or total liabilities & stockholders' equity)	(b) $950,000	$860,000
Debt ratio (a ÷ b)	32.8%	40.0%

Proportion of assets financed by creditors

Seacliff Company has a lower debt ratio in 2011 than in 2010. Is this favorable or unfavorable?

From the viewpoint of the common stockholder, a high debt ratio produces maximum benefits if management is able to earn a rate of return on assets greater than the rate of interest paid to creditors. However, a high debt ratio can be *unfavorable* if the return on assets falls *below* the rate of interest paid to creditors. Since the return on total assets earned by Seacliff Company has declined from 19 percent in 2010 to a relatively low 14 percent in 2011, the common stockholders probably would *not* want to risk a high debt ratio. The action by management in 2011 of retiring $50,000 in long-term liabilities will help to protect the common stockholders from the unfavorable effects of leverage if the rate of return on assets continues to decline.

CASE IN POINT

A historical example from **Dell Inc.** provides an interesting case study in how financial leverage can be used to greatly increase the returns earned by common stockholders without appreciably increasing the company's risk profile. **Dell**'s 2004 return on assets was an impressive 20 percent, and its return on common equity was an eye-popping 47 percent. Clearly **Dell** benefited from favorable financial leverage.

Moreover, **Dell** benefited from favorable financial leverage without increasing its risk profile. That is, most of **Dell**'s leverage was in the form of *non-interest*-bearing liabilities. Although liabilities comprised 67.5 percent of **Dell**'s assets, *interest-bearing* liabilities represented only 2.6 percent of assets. Approximately 84 percent of **Dell**'s liabilities were current, representing either trade credit (accounts payable) or accrued liabilities (e.g., unpaid salaries and benefits). In essence, much of **Dell**'s financing was being provided by its trade creditors and employees, which are essentially free sources of financing.

ANALYSIS BY LONG-TERM CREDITORS

Bondholders and other long-term creditors are primarily interested in three factors: (1) the rate of return on their investment, (2) the firm's ability to meet its interest requirements, and (3) the firm's ability to repay the principal of the debt when it falls due.

Yield Rate on Bonds The yield rate on bonds or other long-term indebtedness cannot be computed in the same manner as the yield rate on shares of stock, because bonds, unlike stocks, have a definite maturity date and amount. The ownership of a 12 percent, 10-year, \$1,000 bond represents the right to receive \$120 each year for 10 years plus the right to receive \$1,000 at the end of 10 years. If the market price of this bond is \$950, the yield rate on an investment in the bond is the rate of interest that will make the *present value* of these two contractual rights equal to the \$950 market price.

When bonds sell at maturity value, the yield rate is equal to the bond interest rate. *The yield rate varies inversely with changes in the market price of the bond.* If interest rates rise, the market price of existing bonds will fall; if interest rates decline, the price of bonds will rise. If the price of a bond is above maturity value, the yield rate is less than the bond interest rate; if the price of a bond is below maturity value, the yield rate is higher than the bond interest rate.

Interest Coverage Ratio Bondholders feel that their investments are relatively safe if the issuing company earns enough income to cover its annual interest obligations by a comfortable margin.

A common measure of creditors' safety is the ratio of operating income available for the payment of interest to the annual interest expense, called the *interest coverage ratio* or *times interest earned.* See this computation for Seacliff Company in Exhibit 14–17.

Exhibit 14–17
INTEREST COVERAGE RATIO

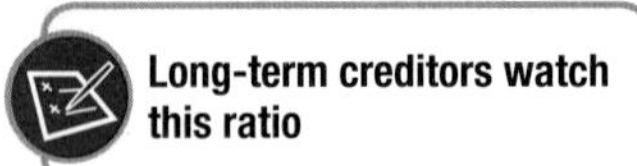
Long-term creditors watch this ratio

	2011	2010
Operating income (before interest and income taxes)	(a) \$127,000	\$160,000
Annual interest expense.	(b) \$ 24,000	\$ 30,000
Interest coverage (a ÷ b)	5.3 times	5.3 times

The ratio remained unchanged at a satisfactory level during 2011. Generally an interest coverage ratio above 2.0 is considered strong.

Debt Ratio Long-term creditors are interested in the percentage of total assets financed by debt, as distinguished from the percentage financed by stockholders. The percentage of total assets financed by debt is measured by the debt ratio, which was computed in Exhibit 14–16.

From a creditor's viewpoint, the lower the debt ratio, the better, since this means that stockholders have contributed a higher percentage of the funds to the business, and therefore the margin of protection to creditors against a shrinkage of the assets is high.

As shown in Exhibit 14–16, the debt ratio, or the percentage of assets financed by debt, decreased from 2010 to 2011 from 40 percent to 32.8 percent. This would generally be considered by long-term creditors to be a favorable change because the debt burden, including required interest payments, is less in 2011 than in 2010, thereby making the claim of each creditor more secure.

Secured Claims Sometimes the claims of long-term creditors are secured with specific collateral, such as the land and buildings owned by the borrower. In these situations, the secured creditors may look primarily to the *value of the collateral* in assessing the safety of their claims.

Assets pledged as collateral to secure specific liabilities are disclosed in notes to the financial statements. As Seacliff makes no such disclosures, we may assume that none of its assets have been pledged as collateral to secure specific liabilities.

ANALYSIS BY SHORT-TERM CREDITORS

Bankers and other short-term creditors share the interest of stockholders and bondholders in the profitability and long-run stability of a business. Their primary interest, however, is in the current position of the company—its ability to generate sufficient funds (working capital) to meet current operating needs and to pay current debts promptly. Thus, the analysis of financial statements by a banker considering a short-term loan, or by a trade creditor investigating the credit status of a customer, is likely to center on the working capital position of the prospective debtor.

Amount of Working Capital Working capital is the excess of current assets over current liabilities. It represents the cash and near-cash assets that provide a "cushion" of liquidity over the amount expected to be needed in the near future to satisfy maturing obligations. The details of the working capital of Seacliff Company are shown in Exhibit 14–18.

Exhibit 14–18 SEACLIFF SCHEDULE OF WORKING CAPITAL

SEACLIFF COMPANY
COMPARATIVE SCHEDULE OF WORKING CAPITAL
AS OF DECEMBER 31, 2011, AND DECEMBER 31, 2010

			Increase or (Decrease)		Percentage of Total Current Items	
	2011	**2010**	**Dollars**	**%**	**2011**	**2010**
Current assets:						
Cash	$ 38,000	$ 40,000	$ (2,000)	(5.0)	9.7	13.9
Accounts receivable (net)	117,000	86,000	31,000	36.0	30.0	29.9
Inventories	180,000	120,000	60,000	50.0	46.2	41.6*
Prepaid expenses	55,000	42,000	13,000	31.0	14.1	14.6
Total current assets	$390,000	$288,000	$102,000	35.4	100.0	100.0
Current liabilities:						
Notes payable to creditors	$ 14,600	$ 10,000	$ 4,600	46.0	13.1*	10.7*
Accounts payable	66,000	30,000	36,000	120.0	58.9	31.9
Accrued liabilities	31,400	54,000	(22,600)	(41.9)	28.0	57.4
Total current liabilities	$112,000	$ 94,000	$ 18,000	19.1	100.0	100.0
Working capital	$278,000	$194,000	$ 84,000	43.3		

*Amounts adjusted so that totals equal 100.0.

This schedule shows that current assets increased $102,000, while current liabilities rose by only $18,000. As a result, working capital increased $84,000.

Quality of Working Capital In evaluating the debt-paying ability of a business, short-term creditors should consider the quality of working capital as well as the total dollar amount. The principal factors affecting the quality of working capital are (1) the nature of the current assets and (2) the length of time required to convert those assets into cash.

The schedule in Exhibit 14–18 shows an unfavorable shift in the composition of Seacliff Company's working capital during 2011: cash decreased from 13.9 percent to 9.7 percent of current assets, while inventory rose from 41.6 percent to 46.2 percent. Inventory is a less liquid resource than cash. Therefore, the quality of working capital is not as liquid as in 2010. *Turnover rates* (or *ratios*) may be used to assist short-term creditors in estimating the time required to turn assets such as receivables and inventory into cash.

Accounts Receivable Turnover Rate As explained in Chapter 7, the accounts receivable turnover rate indicates how quickly a company converts its accounts receivable into cash. The accounts receivable turnover *rate* is determined by dividing net sales by the average balance of accounts receivable.[5] The number of *days* required (on average) to collect accounts receivable then may be determined by dividing the number of days in a year (365) by the turnover rate. The computations in Exhibit 14–19 use the data in our Seacliff example, assuming accounts receivable at the beginning of 2010 were $80,000.

Exhibit 14–19
ACCOUNTS RECEIVABLE TURNOVER

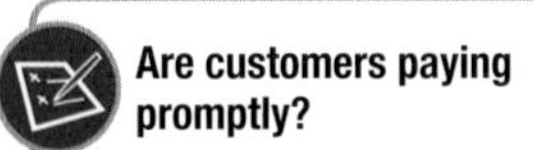
Are customers paying promptly?

	2011	2010
Net sales	(a) $900,000	$750,000
Accounts receivable, beginning of year	$ 86,000	$ 80,000
Accounts receivable, end of year	$117,000	$ 86,000
Average accounts receivable	(b) $101,500	$ 83,000
Accounts receivable turnover per year (a ÷ b)	8.9 times	9.0 times
Average number of days to collect accounts receivable (divide 365 days by accounts receivable turnover)	41 days	41 days

There has been no change in the average time required to collect receivables. The interpretation of the average age of receivables depends upon the company's credit terms and the seasonal activity immediately before year-end. For example, if the company grants 30-day credit terms to its customers, the analysis in Exhibit 14–19 indicates that accounts receivable collections are lagging. If the terms are for 60 days, however, collections are being made ahead of schedule.

Inventory Turnover Rate The inventory turnover rate indicates how many times during the year the company is able to sell a quantity of goods equal to its average inventory. Mechanically, this rate is determined by dividing the cost of goods sold for the year by the average amount of inventory on hand during the year. The number of days required to sell this amount of inventory may be determined by dividing 365 days by the turnover rate. These computations were explained in Chapter 8 and are demonstrated in Exhibit 14–20 using the information for Seacliff Company, assuming inventory at the beginning of 2010 was $100,000. The trend indicated by this analysis is unfavorable, since the length of time required for Seacliff to turn over (sell) its inventory is increasing.

Exhibit 14–20
INVENTORY TURNOVER

	2011	2010
Cost of goods sold	(a) $530,000	$420,000
Inventory, beginning of year	$120,000	$100,000
Inventory, end of year	$180,000	$120,000
Average inventory	(b) $150,000	$110,000
Average inventory turnover per year (a ÷ b)	3.5 times	3.8 times
Average number of days to sell inventory (divide 365 days by inventory turnover)	104 days	96 days

Companies that have low gross profit rates often need high inventory turnover rates in order to operate profitably. This is another way of saying that if the gross profit rate is low, a high volume of transactions is necessary to produce a satisfactory amount of profits. Companies that sell high markup items, such as jewelry stores and art galleries, can operate successfully with much lower inventory turnover rates.

Operating Cycle The inventory turnover rate indicates how quickly inventory *sells,* but not how quickly this asset converts into *cash.* Short-term creditors, of course, are interested primarily in the company's ability to generate cash.

The period of time required for a merchandising company to convert its inventory into cash is called the *operating cycle.* The illustration appeared in Chapter 6 and is repeated in Exhibit 14–21 for your convenience.

[5] Ideally, the accounts receivable turnover is computed by dividing net *credit* sales by the *monthly* average of receivables. Such detailed information, however, generally is not provided in annual financial statements.

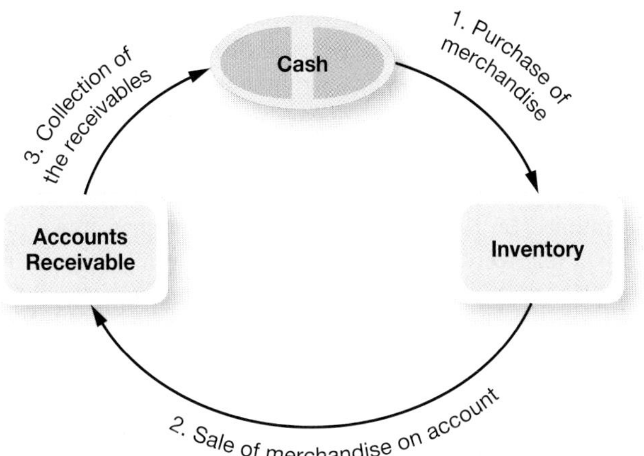

Exhibit 14–21
OPERATING CYCLE

The operating cycle repeats continuously 

Seacliff's operating cycle in 2011 was approximately 145 days, computed by adding the 104 days required to turn over inventory and the average 41 days required to collect receivables. This compares with an operating cycle of only 137 days in 2010, computed as 96 days to dispose of the inventory plus 41 days to collect the resulting receivables. From the viewpoint of short-term creditors, the *shorter* the operating cycle, the *higher the quality* of the borrower's working capital. Therefore, these creditors would regard the lengthening of Seacliff Company's operating cycle as an unfavorable trend.

Current Ratio The current ratio expresses the relationship between current assets and current liabilities. A strong current ratio provides considerable evidence that a company will be able to meet its obligations coming due in the near future. The current ratio for Seacliff Company is computed in Exhibit 14–22.

Exhibit 14–22
CURRENT RATIO

	2011	2010
Total current assets	(a) $390,000	$288,000
Total current liabilities	(b) $112,000	$ 94,000
Current ratio (a ÷ b)	3.5	3.1

Does this indicate satisfactory debt-paying ability? 

Quick Ratio Because inventories and prepaid expenses are further removed from conversion into cash than other current assets, the *quick ratio* is sometimes computed as a supplement to the current ratio. The quick ratio compares the most liquid current assets (cash, marketable securities, and receivables) with current liabilities. Seacliff Company has no marketable securities; its quick ratio is computed in Exhibit 14–23.

Exhibit 14–23
QUICK RATIO

	2011	2010
Quick assets (cash and accounts receivable)	(a) $155,000	$126,000
Current liabilities	(b) $112,000	$ 94,000
Quick ratio (a ÷ b)	1.4	1.3

A measure of liquidity 

Here again the analysis reveals a favorable trend and a strong position. If the credit periods extended to customers and granted by creditors are roughly equal, a quick ratio of 1.0 or better is considered satisfactory.

Unused Lines of Credit From the viewpoint of a short-term creditor, a company's unused lines of credit represent a resource almost as liquid as cash. An unused line of credit means that a bank has agreed in advance to lend the company any amount, up to the specified limit. As long as this line of credit remains available, creditors know that the business can borrow cash quickly and easily for any purpose, including payments of creditors' claims.

Existing unused lines of credit are *disclosed* in notes accompanying the financial statements. See Note 2 to the financial statements in Exhibit 14–10. Short-term creditors would view Seacliff's $35,000 line of credit as enhancing the company's liquidity.

CASH FLOW ANALYSIS

We often have stressed the importance of a company's being able to generate sufficient cash flows from its operations. In 2010, Seacliff generated net cash flows of $95,000 from its operating activities—a relatively "normal" amount, considering that net income for the year was $90,000. This $95,000 remained *after* payment of interest to creditors and amounted to more than three times the dividends paid to stockholders. Thus, in 2010 the net cash flows from operating activities appeared quite sufficient to ensure that Seacliff could pay its interest obligations and also pay dividends.

In 2011, however, net cash flows from operating activities declined to $19,000, an amount far below the company's $75,000 net income and only approximately 58 percent of the amount of dividends paid. Stockholders and creditors would view this dramatic decline in cash flows as a negative and potentially dangerous development.

A reconciliation of Seacliff's net income in 2011 with its net cash flows from operating activities is shown in Exhibit 14–24. For purposes of this analysis, we assume that the notes payable to creditors resulted from purchases from suppliers rather than loans from a financial institution. Therefore, the increase in notes payable is treated in the same way as the increase in accounts payable as part of the reconciliation of net income to net cash from operating activities. Had the notes payable resulted from borrowing activities, the change would be classified as a financing activity and not as an adjustment to net income in determining net cash from operating activities.

Exhibit 14–24

SEACLIFF RECONCILIATION OF NET INCOME TO NET CASH FROM OPERATING ACTIVITIES

Net income		$ 75,000
Add:		
Depreciation expense	$30,000	
Increase in notes payable to creditors	4,600	
Increase in accounts payable	36,000	70,600
		$145,600
Less:		
Increase in accounts receivable	$31,000	
Increase in inventories	60,000	
Increase in prepaid expenses	13,000	
Decrease in accrued liabilities	22,600	126,600
Net cash flows from operating activities		$ 19,000

As explained in Chapter 13, the FASB requires companies to provide this reconciliation either in the body of the statement of cash flows or in a supplemental schedule.

The primary reasons for Seacliff's low net operating cash flows appear to be the growth in uncollected accounts receivable and inventories, combined with the substantial reduction in accrued liabilities. Given the significant increase in sales during 2011, the increase in accounts receivable is to be expected. The large reduction in accrued liabilities may be a one-time event that will not necessarily recur next year. The large increase in inventory, however, may have reduced Seacliff's liquidity unnecessarily.

Seacliff's financial position, particularly its short-term liquidity, would appear considerably stronger if its increased sales volume were supported by a higher *inventory turnover rate,* instead of a larger inventory.

Cash Flows from Operations to Current Liabilities An additional measure of liquidity that is sometimes computed, based in part on information from the statement of cash flows, is the ratio of cash flows from operations to current liabilities. This measure provides evidence of the company's ability to cover its currently maturing liabilities from normal operations. For 2010 and 2011, the ratio is computed for Seacliff Corporation in Exhibit 14–25.

	2011	2010
Cash flows from operations	(a) $ 19,000	$95,000
Current liabilities	(b) $112,000	$94,000
Cash flows from operations to current liabilities (a ÷ b)	0.17	1.01

Exhibit 14–25

CASH FLOWS FROM OPERATIONS TO CURRENT LIABILITIES

As you can see from this measure, Seacliff was much stronger in 2010 than in 2011. In 2010, operating cash flows were slightly more than current liabilities at year-end, indicating an ability to cover current obligations from normal operations without regard to the amount of existing current assets. In 2011, however, operations provided only 17 percent as much cash as needed to meet current obligations, implying a need to rely more heavily on existing current assets than in 2010. Some analysts consider a ratio of cash flows from operations to current liabilities of 0.40 or higher to be strong.

USEFULNESS OF NOTES TO FINANCIAL STATEMENTS

A set of financial statements normally is accompanied by several *notes,* disclosing information useful in *interpreting* the statements. Users should view these notes as an *integral part* of the financial statements.

In preceding chapters we have identified many items that are disclosed in notes accompanying the financial statements. Among the most useful are the following:

- Accounting policies and methods
- Unused lines of credit
- Significant commitments and loss contingencies
- Current values of financial instruments (if different from the carrying values shown in the statements)
- Dividends in arrears
- Concentrations of credit risk
- Assets pledged to secure specific liabilities

In Exhibit 14–10 the notes accompanying Seacliff's financial statements are quite clean—that is, they contain no surprises or cause for concern. Of course, the unused line of credit disclosed in Note 2 would be of interest to anyone evaluating the company's short-term debt-paying ability.

You as a Financial Analyst

Assume that you are a financial analyst and that two of your clients are requesting your advice on certain companies as potential investments. Both clients are interested in purchasing common stock. One is primarily interested in the dividends to be received from the investment. The second is primarily interested in the growth of the market value of the stock. What information would you advise your clients to focus on in their respective analyses?

(See our comments on the Online Learning Center Web site.)

INTERNATIONAL FINANCIAL REPORTING STANDARDS

As you have learned throughout this text, an effort is currently under way to standardize financial reporting practices worldwide. During this period of transition, which is expected to require several years, analyzing financial statements that originate in different countries poses a significant challenge due to differences in reporting practices. There exist many different local standards, as in the United States, and there are emerging international standards which are rapidly being accepted in various countries.

Two areas of particular interest in analyzing financial statements are consolidated statements and segment reporting. Earlier in this chapter, we briefly covered consolidated financial statements; where there are strong financial connections (e.g., overlapping ownership) between or among two or more companies, those companies typically present consolidated financial statements. This means that they report as a single entity rather than as separate entities, although legally they may be recognized as separate entities. At the present time, there is no single agreed-upon criterion for when consolidated financial statements should be prepared. This makes comparisons difficult because of the significant impact preparing consolidated statements has on the information provided when compared with presenting information about each separate entity.

Segment reporting refers to the presentation of information about parts of a business, usually along industry or product lines and geographic areas. Because risks that companies take vary considerably by industry and location, accounting standards require companies to provide supplemental information that informs investors and creditors of the extent of contribution a company's operations in different industries and in different geographic areas to the totals found in the primary financial statements. Some of the differences that exist around the world among individual country standards and between those standards and international standards deal with the definitions used in presenting segment information, the criteria used to identify segments for which disclosure is required, and the specific information that must be presented when disclosure is required.

Policies regarding consolidated financial statements and segment reporting are only two of the many areas the financial statement analyst must be aware of in approaching financial statements from different parts of the world. The authors are confident that, over time, we will move toward greater standardization for these and other aspects of financial reporting so that, in the future, we will be able to place even greater reliance than today on the comparability of financial statements worldwide.

SUMMARY OF ANALYTICAL MEASUREMENTS

The financial ratios and other measurements introduced in this textbook thus far, including this chapter—and their significance—are summarized in Exhibit 14–26.

Exhibit 14–26 SUMMARY OF ANALYTICAL MEASURES

Ratios or Other Measurements	Method of Computation	Significance
Measures of short-term liquidity		
Current ratio	Current Assets / Current Liabilities	A measure of short-term debt-paying ability
Quick ratio	Quick Assets / Current Liabilities	A measure of short-term debt-paying ability
Working capital	Current Assets − Current Liabilities	A measure of short-term debt-paying ability
Net cash provided by operating activities	Appears in the statement of cash flows	Indicates the cash generated by operations after allowing for cash payment of expenses and operating liabilities
Cash flow from operations to current liabilities	Cash Flows from Operating Activities / Current Liabilities	Indicates ability to cover currently maturing obligations from recurring operations
Accounts receivable turnover rate	Net Sales / Average Accounts Receivable	Indicates how quickly receivables are collected
Days to collect average accounts receivable	365 Days / Accounts Receivable Turnover Rate	Indicates in days how quickly receivables are collected
Inventory turnover rate	Cost of Goods Sold / Average Inventory	Indicates how quickly inventory sells

(continued on next page)

Exhibit 14–26 continued

Ratios or Other Measurements	Method of Computation	Significance
Days to sell the average inventory	365 Days / Inventory Turnover Rate	Indicates in days how quickly inventory sells
Operating cycle	Days to Sell Inventory + Days to Collect Receivables	Indicates in days how quickly cash invested in inventory converts back into cash
Free cash flow	Net Cash from Operating Activities − Cash Used for Investing Activities and Dividends	Excess of operating cash flow over basic needs
Measures of long-term credit risk		
Debt ratio	Total Liabilities / Total Assets	Percentage of assets financed by creditors; indicates relative size of the equity position
Trend in net cash provided by operating activities	Appears in comparative statements of cash flows	Indicator of a company's ability to generate the cash necessary to meet its obligations
Interest coverage ratio	Income before Interest and Taxes / Annual Interest Expense	Indicator of a company's ability to meet its interest payment obligations
Measures of profitability		
Percentage changes; that is, in net sales and net income	Dollar Amount of Change / Financial Statement Amount in the Earlier Year	The rate at which a key measure is increasing or decreasing; the "growth rate"
Gross profit rate	Gross Profit / Net Sales	A measure of the profitability of the company's products
Operating expense ratio	Operating Expenses / Net Sales	A measure of management's ability to control expenses
Operating income	Gross Profit − Operating Expenses	The profitability of a company's basic business activities
Net income as a percentage of net sales	Net Income / Net Sales	An indicator of management's ability to control costs
Earnings per share	Net Income − Preferred Dividends / Average Number of Common Shares Outstanding	Net income applicable to each share of common stock
Return on assets	Operating Income / Average Total Assets	A measure of the productivity of assets, regardless of how the assets are financed
Return on equity	Net Income / Average Total Equity	The rate of return earned on the stockholders' equity in the business
Return on common stockholders' equity	Net Income − Preferred Dividends / Average Common Stockholders' Equity	The rate of return earned on the common stockholders' equity; appropriate when company has both common and preferred stock
Measures for evaluating the current market price of common stock		
Market value of financial instruments	Quoted in financial press or disclosed in financial statements	Reflects both investors' expectations and current market conditions
Price-earnings ratio	Current Stock Price / Earnings per Share	A measure of investors' expectations about the company's future prospects
Dividend yield	Annual Dividend / Current Stock Price	Dividends expressed as a rate of return on the market price of the stock
Book value per share	Common Stockholders' Equity / Shares of Common Stock Outstanding	The recorded value of net assets underlying each share of common stock

Ethics, Fraud & Corporate Governance

The tools discussed in this chapter involve using financial statement numbers to help make investment and credit decisions. Given the high-profile accounting frauds of the early 2000s and the resulting focus on corporate governance, a new type of tool has arisen to help investors and creditors make investment decisions. This new tool involves ratings of the quality of a company's corporate governance. Many investors and creditors believe that better-governed firms are better managed, and that these firms will either offer superior performance (returns) over time and/or will offer returns comparable to less well governed firms but with less risk.

A number of organizations provide ratings of corporate governance quality for public companies. Two of the most prominent of these organizations are **ISS Governance Services**, a unit of **Risk Metrics Group**, and **The Corporate Library** (**TCL**) (Portland, Maine).

ISS Governance Services describes itself as "a leader in proxy voting and corporate governance matters." **ISS** provides coverage of over 38,000 shareholder meetings across 100 markets, serving institutional and corporate clients. These clients hire **ISS** to analyze corporate proxy statements and to make recommendations on the manner in which these institutional and corporate clients should vote on matters subject to shareholder ratification.

ISS rates the quality of a company's corporate governance by computing a Corporate Governance Quotient (CGQ). **ISS** computes CGQs for more than 7,500 companies worldwide. A company's CGQ is based on its ratings in these eight core categories: (1) board structure and composition, (2) audit issues, (3) charter and bylaw provisions, (4) laws of the state of incorporation, (5) executive and director compensation, (6) progressive practices, (7) D&O stock ownership, and (8) director education.

The Corporate Library (TCL) is a more recent entrant into the market for rating governance effectiveness. Unlike **ISS**, **TCL** claims that its proprietary dynamic indicators go beyond conventional benchmarks for good corporate governance. Many rating systems are based on a company's compliance with governance practices perceived as best practices; **TCL** attempts to differentiate its rating system by focusing only on those board characteristics that its proprietary research has found to be associated with preserving and enhancing shareholder wealth. **TCL** considers a company's governance in four key areas: (1) board composition and succession planning, (2) CEO compensation practices, (3) takeover defenses, and (4) board level accounting concerns.

Concluding Remarks

For the most part, our discussion in this chapter has been limited to the kinds of analysis that can be performed by external users who do not have access to the company's accounting records. Investors and creditors must rely to a considerable extent on the financial statements published in annual and quarterly reports. In the case of publicly owned corporations, additional information is filed with the Securities and Exchange Commission (SEC) and is available to the public in hard copy, as well as on the Internet. In fact, the Internet is the fastest growing source of *free* information available to decision makers in this information age.

Many financial analysts who evaluate the financial statements and future prospects of publicly owned companies sell their conclusions and investment recommendations for a fee. For example, detailed financial analyses of most large companies are available from **Standard & Poor's**, **Moody's Investors Service**, and **The Value Line Investment Survey**. Anyone may subscribe to these investment services.

Bankers and major creditors usually are able to obtain detailed financial information from borrowers simply by requesting it as a condition for granting a loan. Suppliers and other trade creditors may obtain some financial information about almost any business from credit-rating agencies, such as **Dun & Bradstreet**.

Stock prices, like p/e ratios, are a *measure of investors' expectations.* A company may be highly profitable and growing fast. But if investors had expected even better performance, the market price of its stock may decline. Similarly, if a troubled company's losses are smaller than expected, the price of its stock may rise.

In financial circles, evaluating stock price by looking at the underlying profitability of the company is termed **fundamental analysis.** This approach to investing works better in the long run than in the short run. In the short run, stock prices can be significantly affected by many factors, including short-term interest rates, current events, political events, fads, and rumors. But in the long run, good companies increase in value.

END-OF-CHAPTER REVIEW

SUMMARY OF LEARNING OBJECTIVES

LO1 **Explain the uses of dollar and percentage changes, trend percentages, component percentages, and ratios.** An important aspect of financial statement analysis is determining relevant relationships among specific items of information. Companies typically present financial information for more than one time period, which permits users of the information to make comparisons that help them understand changes over time. Dollar and percentage changes and trend percentages are tools for comparing information from successive time periods. Component percentages and ratios, on the other hand, are tools for establishing relationships and making comparisons within an accounting period. Both types of comparisons are important in understanding an enterprise's financial position, results of operations, and cash flows.

LO2 **Discuss the quality of a company's earnings, assets, and working capital.** Assessing the quality of information is an important aspect of financial statement analysis. Enterprises have significant latitude in the selection of financial reporting methods within generally accepted accounting principles. Assessing the quality of a company's earnings, assets, and working capital is done by evaluating the accounting methods selected for use in preparing financial statements. Management's choice of accounting principles and methods that are in the best long-term interests of the company, even though they may currently result in lower net income, reported total assets, or working capital, leads to a conclusion of high quality in reported accounting information.

LO3 **Explain the nature and purpose of classifications in financial statements.** In classified financial statements, items with certain common characteristics are placed together in a group, or classification. The purpose of these classifications is to develop subtotals that will assist users in analyzing the financial statements.

LO4 **Prepare a classified balance sheet and compute widely used measures of liquidity and credit risk.** In a classified balance sheet, assets are subdivided into the categories of current assets, plant and equipment, and other assets. Liabilities are classified either as current or long-term.

The liquidity measures derived from the balance sheet are as follows:

Working capital. Current assets minus current liabilities.

Current ratio. Current assets divided by current liabilities.

Quick ratio. Quick assets divided by current liabilities.

A measure of long-term credit risk is the debt ratio, which is total liabilities expressed as a percentage of (divided by) total assets.

LO5 **Prepare a multiple-step and a single-step income statement and compute widely used measures of profitability.** In a multiple-step income statement, the cost of goods sold is deducted from net sales to provide the subtotal, gross profit. Operating expenses then are deducted to arrive at income from operations. As a final step, nonoperating items are added together and subtracted from income from operations to arrive at net income. In a single-step income statement, all revenue items are listed first, and then all expenses are combined and deducted from total revenue.

The profitability measures discussed in this chapter are as follows:

Percentage change. The dollar amount of change in a financial statement item from one period to the next, expressed as a percentage of (divided by) the item value in the earlier of the two periods being compared.

Gross profit rate. Dollar amount of gross profit divided by net sales. A measure of the profitability of a company's products.

Net income as a percentage of sales. Net income divided by net sales. A measure of management's ability to control expenses.

Earnings per share. In the simplest case, net income divided by shares of capital stock outstanding. Indicates the earnings applicable to each share of stock.

Price-earnings ratio. Market price of the stock divided by earnings per share. A measure of investors' expectations regarding future profitability.

Return on assets. Operating income divided by average total assets. Measures the return generated by assets, regardless of how the assets are financed.

Return on equity. Net income divided by average total equity. Indicates the rate of return earned on owners' equity.

LO6 **Put a company's net income into perspective by relating it to sales, assets, and stockholders' equity.** Financial accounting information is most useful if viewed in comparison with other relevant information. Net income is an important measure of the financial success of an enterprise. To make the amount of net income even more useful than if it were viewed simply in isolation, it is often compared with the sales from which net income results, the assets used to generate the income, and the amount of stockholders' equity invested by owners to earn the net income.

LO7 **Compute the ratios widely used in financial statement analysis and explain the significance of each.** Ratios are mathematical calculations that compare one financial statement item with another financial statement item. The two items may come from the same financial statement, such as the current ratio, which compares the amount of current assets with the amount of current liabilities, both of which appear in the statement of financial position (balance sheet). On the other hand, the items may come from two different financial statements, such as the return on stockholders' equity, which compares net income from the income statement with the amount of stockholders' equity from the statement of financial position (balance sheet). Accountants and financial analysts have developed many ratios that place information from a company's financial statements in a context to permit better understanding to support decision making.

LO8 **Analyze financial statements from the viewpoints of common stockholders, creditors, and others.** Different groups of users of financial statements are interested in different aspects of a company's financial activities. Short-term creditors are interested primarily in the company's ability to make cash payments in the short term; they focus their attention on operating cash flows and current assets and liabilities. Long-term creditors, on the other hand, are more interested in the company's long-term ability to pay interest and principal and would not limit their analysis to the company's ability to make cash payments in the immediate future. The focus of common stockholders can vary from one investor to another, but generally stockholders are interested in the company's ability to pay dividends and increase the market value of the stock of the company. Each group may focus on different information in the financial statements to meet its unique objectives.

Key Terms Introduced or Emphasized In Chapter 14

annual report (p. 631) A document issued annually by publicly owned companies to their stockholders. Includes audited comparative financial statements, management's discussion and analysis of performance and liquidity, and other information about the company.

classified financial statements (p. 622) Financial statements in which similar items are arranged in groups, and subtotals are shown to assist users in analyzing the statements.

comparative financial statements (p. 622) Financial statements of one company for two or more years presented in a side-by-side format to facilitate comparison.

consolidated financial statements (p. 622) Financial statements that show the combined activities of a parent company and its subsidiaries.

current assets (p. 627) Cash and other assets that can be converted into cash or used up within one year or the operating cycle (whichever is longer) without interfering with normal business operations.

current liabilities (p. 629) Existing liabilities that are expected to be satisfied by using the enterprise's current assets.

current ratio (p. 629) Current assets divided by current liabilities. A measure of short-term debt-paying ability.

debt ratio (p. 630) Total liabilities divided by total assets. Represents the portion of total assets financed by debt, rather than by equity capital.

earnings per share (p. 636) Net income expressed on a per-share basis.

fundamental analysis (p. 655) Evaluating the reasonableness of a company's stock price by evaluating the performance and financial strength of the company.

management's discussion and analysis (p. 631) A discussion by management of the company's performance during the current year and its financial position at year-end. These discussions are included in the annual reports of publicly owned companies.

market share (p. 634) A company's percentage share of total dollar sales within its industry.

operating cycle (p. 627) The time required to invest cash in inventory, sell the inventory, and collect the receivable, resulting in an increase in cash.

operating income (p. 634) A subtotal in a multiple-step income statement representing the income resulting from the company's principal business activities.

parent company (p. 622) A corporation that does portions of its business through other companies that it owns (termed *subsidiaries*).

percentage change (p. 634) The change in a dollar amount between two accounting periods, expressed as a percentage of the amount in an earlier period. Used in evaluating rates of growth (or decline).

price-earnings (p/e) ratio (p. 636) The current market price of a company's capital stock, expressed as a multiple of earnings per share. Reflects investors' expectations regarding future earnings.

quick assets (p. 630) The most liquid current assets, which include only cash, marketable securities, and receivables.

quick ratio (p. 630) Quick assets (cash, marketable securities, and receivables) divided by current liabilities. A measure of short-term debt-paying ability. (Sometimes referred to as the acid-test ratio.)

return on assets (p. 638) Operating income expressed as a percentage of average total assets. A measure of the efficiency with which management utilizes the assets of a business.

return on equity (p. 638) Net income expressed as a percentage of average total stockholders' equity. A measure of the rate of return earned on the stockholders' equity in the business.

subsidiary (p. 622) A company that is owned and operated by a parent company. In essence, the subsidiary is a part of the parent organization.

window dressing (p. 631) Measures taken by management to make a business look as strong as possible at the balance sheet date.

working capital (p. 629) Current assets less current liabilities. A measure of short-term debt-paying ability.

Demonstration Problem

The following data are adapted from a recent annual report of **Walgreen Drug Stores** (dollar amounts are stated in millions):

	2009	2008
Balance sheet data:		
Quick assets	$ 5,083	$ 2,970
Current assets	12,049	10,433
Current liabilities	6,769	6,644
Stockholders' equity	14,376	12,869
Total assets	25,142	22,410
Income statement data:		
Net sales	$63,335	$59,034
Gross profit	17,613	16,643
Operating income	3,247	3,441
Net earnings	2,006	2,157

Instructions

a. Compute the following for 2009 and 2008. (Round to one decimal place.)

1. Working capital

2. Current ratio

3. Quick ratio

b. Comment on the trends in the liquidity measures and state whether **Walgreen** appears to be able to satisfy its liabilities at the end of 2009.

c. Compute the percentage changes for 2009 in the amounts of net sales and net income. (Round to one-tenth of 1 percent.)

d. Compute the following for 2009 and 2008. (Round to one-tenth of 1 percent. For items **3** and **4,** use the year-end amounts stated above as substitutes for average assets and average stockholders' equity.)

1. Gross profit rate

2. Net income as a percentage of sales

3. Return on assets

4. Return on stockholders' equity

e. Comment on the trends in the profitability measures computed in parts **c** and **d.**

Solution to the Demonstration Problem

a.

		2009	2008
1.	**Working capital:**		
	$12,049 − $6,769	$5,280	
	$10,433 − $6,644		$3,789
2.	**Current ratio:**		
	$12,049 ÷ $6,769	1.78 to 1	
	$10,433 ÷ $6,644		1.57 to 1
3.	**Quick ratio:**		
	$5,083 ÷ $6,769	0.75 to 1	
	$2,970 ÷ $6,644		0.45 to 1

b. Working capital during 2009 increased by $1,491 million, from $3,789 million to $5,280 million. The current ratio increased from 1.57 to 1.78. The quick ratio increased from 0.45 to 0.75. The relatively low quick ratio may be of some concern in terms of the company's ability to satisfy its future obligations.

c. Percentage change from 2008:

	2009
Net sales: [($63,335 − $59,034) ÷ $59,034]	+7.3%
Net income: [($2,006 − $2,157) ÷ $2,157]	−7.0%

d.

		2009	2008
1.	**Gross profit rate:**		
	$17,613 ÷ $63,335	27.8%	
	$16,643 ÷ $59,034		28.2%
2.	**Net income as a percentage of sales:**		
	$2,006 ÷ $63,335	3.2%	
	$2,157 ÷ $59,034		3.7%
3.	**Return on assets:**		
	$2,006 ÷ $25,142	8.0%	
	$2,157 ÷ $22,410		9.6%
4.	**Return on equity:**		
	$2,006 ÷ $14,376	14.0%	
	$2,157 ÷ $12,869		16.8%

e. Profitability indicators are generally negative.

- Net sales increased, but net earnings decreased.
- The gross profit rate decreased by 0.4% (28.2% to 27.8%).
- Net income as a percentage of sales decreased by 0.5% (3.7% to 3.2%).
- Return on assets decreased by 1.6% (9.6% to 8.0%).
- Return on equity decreased by 2.8% (16.8% to 14.0%).

While the percentage changes are relatively small, they are applied to very large dollar amounts, resulting in relatively large dollar changes. Small percentage improvements in these key financial statement numbers can render significant improvements in the company's financial performance.

Self-Test Questions

The answers to these questions appear on page 679.

1. Which of the following usually is *least* important as a measure of short-term liquidity?
   a. Quick ratio.
   b. Debt ratio.
   c. Current ratio.
   d. Cash flows from operating activities.
2. In each of the past five years, the net sales of Plaza Co. have increased at about half the rate of inflation, but net income has increased at approximately *twice* the rate of inflation. During this period, the company's total assets, liabilities, and equity have remained almost unchanged; dividends are approximately equal to net income. These relationships suggest (indicate all correct answers):
   a. Management is successfully controlling costs and expenses.
   b. The company is selling more merchandise every year.
   c. The annual return on assets has been increasing.
   d. Financing activities are likely to result in a net use of cash.

3. From the viewpoint of a stockholder, which of the following relationships do you consider of *least* significance?
   a. The return on assets consistently is higher than the industry average.
   b. The return on equity has increased in each of the past five years.
   c. Net income is greater than the amount of working capital.
   d. The return on assets is greater than the rate of interest being paid to creditors.

4. The following information is available from the annual report of Frixell, Inc.:

Current assets	$ 480,000	Current liabilities	$300,000
Average total assets	2,000,000	Operating income	240,000
Average total equity	800,000	Net income	80,000

Which of the following statements are correct? (More than one statement may be correct.)
   a. The return on equity exceeds the return on assets.
   b. The current ratio is 0.625 to 1.
   c. Working capital is $1,200,000.
   d. None of the above answers is correct.

5. Hart Corporation's net income was $400,000 in 2010 and $160,000 in 2011. What percentage increase in net income must Hart achieve in 2012 to offset the decline in profits in 2011?
   a. 60%.
   b. 150%.
   c. 600%.
   d. 67%.

6. If a company's current ratio declined in a year during which its quick ratio improved, which of the following is the most likely explanation?
   a. Inventory is increasing.
   b. Inventory is declining.
   c. Receivables are being collected more rapidly than in the past.
   d. Receivables are being collected more slowly than in the past.

7. In financial statement analysis, the most difficult of the following items to predict is whether:
   a. The company will be liquid in six months.
   b. The company's market share is increasing or declining.
   c. Profits have increased since the previous year.
   d. The market price of capital stock will rise or fall over the next two months.

ASSIGNMENT MATERIAL Discussion Questions

1. In financial statement analysis, what is the basic objective of observing trends in data and ratios? Suggest some other standards of comparison.
2. In financial statement analysis, what information is produced by computing a ratio that is not available in a simple observation of the underlying data?
3. Distinguish between *trend percentages* and *component percentages*. Which would be better suited for analyzing the change in sales over a term of several years?
4. Differentiate between *horizontal* and *vertical* analysis.
5. What is the basic purpose of *classifications* in financial statements? Identify the classifications widely used in a balance sheet, a multiple-step income statement, and a statement of cash flows.
6. Distinguish between the terms *classified, comparative,* and *consolidated* as they apply to financial statements. May a given set of financial statements have more than one of these characteristics?
7. What is the characteristic common to all *current assets*? Many retail stores regularly sell merchandise on installment plans, calling for payments over a period of 24 or 36 months. Do such receivables qualify as current assets? Explain.
8. Identify four ratios or other analytical tools used to evaluate profitability. Explain briefly how each is computed.
9. Distinguish between *operating income* and *net income.*
10. Why might earnings per share be more significant to a stockholder in a large corporation than the total amount of net income?
11. Assume that Congress announces its intention to limit the prices and profits of pharmaceutical companies as part of an effort to control health care costs. What effect would you expect this announcement to have on the p/e ratios and stock prices of pharmaceutical companies such as **Merck** and **Bristol-Myers Squibb**? Explain.
12. Under what circumstances might a company have a high p/e ratio even when investors are *not* optimistic about the company's future prospects?
13. Spencer Company earned a 16 percent return on its total assets. Current liabilities are 10 percent of total assets.

Long-term bonds carrying an 11 percent coupon rate are equal to 30 percent of total assets. There is no preferred stock. Is this application of leverage favorable or unfavorable from the viewpoint of Spencer's stockholders?

14. Ahi Co. has a current ratio of 3 to 1. Ono Corp. has a current ratio of 2 to 1. Does this mean that Ahi's operating cycle is longer than Ono's? Why?

15. An investor states, "I bought this stock for $50 several years ago and it now sells for $100. It paid $5 per share in dividends last year so I'm earning 10 percent on my investment." Evaluate this statement.

Brief Exercises

LO1 BRIEF EXERCISE 14.1

Dollar and Percentage Change

Wofford Company had net sales of $150,000 in its first year and $187,500 in its second year. Calculate the amount of change in terms of both dollars and percentage.

LO1 BRIEF EXERCISE 14.2

Trend Percentages

White, Inc., had depreciation expenses on its plant assets as follows for 2009, 2010, and 2011, respectively: $267,000, $289,000, and $357,000. Compute the trend percentages for these years, assuming 2009 is the base year.

LO1 BRIEF EXERCISE 14.3

Component Percentages

Yankee Doodle, Inc., had the following income statement figures:

Sales	$560,000
Cost of sales	(340,000)
Gross margin	$220,000
Operating expenses	(150,000)
Net income	$ 70,000

Calculate component percentages for this information.

LO4 BRIEF EXERCISE 14.4

Working Capital and Current Ratio

Harrisonburg Company had current and total assets of $450,000 and $1,000,000, respectively. The company's current and total liabilities were $267,000 and $600,000, respectively. Calculate the amount of working capital and the current ratio using this information.

LO4 BRIEF EXERCISE 14.5

Current and Quick Ratio

Garrett Company had current assets and current liabilities as follows:

Current assets:	
Cash	$ 50,000
Accounts receivable	75,000
Inventory	125,000
Current liabilities:	
Accrued expenses	$ 25,000
Accounts payable	110,000
Current portion of long-term debt	45,000

Calculate the current and quick ratios using the information provided.

LO4 **BRIEF EXERCISE 14.6**
Debt Ratio

Maxey Company had current and noncurrent liabilities of $50,000 and $150,000, respectively. The company's current assets were $76,000, out of a total asset figure of $424,000. Calculate the company's debt ratio.

LO6 **BRIEF EXERCISE 14.7**
Net Income as Percentage of Sales

Lone Star, Inc., reported sales of $560,000, cost of sales of $240,000, and operating expenses of $130,000 for the current year. Using this information, calculate the amount of net income and net income as a percentage of sales.

LO6 **BRIEF EXERCISE 14.8**
Earnings Per Share

Multi-Star, Inc., had sales of $890,000, cost of sales and operating expenses of $450,000 and $200,000, respectively, and 10,000 shares of common stock outstanding. Calculate the amount of earnings per share.

LO7 **BRIEF EXERCISE 14.9**
Return on Assets

Walland Company's operating income for the current year was $450,000. The company's average total assets for the same period were $3,500,000, and its total liabilities were $1,000,000. Calculate the company's return on assets.

LO7 **BRIEF EXERCISE 14.10**
Return on Equity

Fillips Company had net income of $36,700 in a year when its stockholders' equity averaged $450,000 and its total assets averaged $2,500,000. Calculate the company's return on equity for the period.

Exercises

connect ACCOUNTING

LO1 **EXERCISE 14.1**
Percentage Changes

Selected information taken from the financial statements of Maxum Company for two successive years follows. You are to compute the percentage change from 2010 to 2011 whenever possible. Round all calculations to the nearest whole percentage.

	2011	2010
a. Accounts receivable	$126,000	$160,000
b. Marketable securities	–0–	250,000
c. Retained earnings	80,000	(80,000)
d. Notes receivable	120,000	–0–
e. Notes payable	870,000	800,000
f. Cash	84,000	80,000
g. Sales	970,000	910,000

LO1 **EXERCISE 14.2**
Trend Percentages

Compute *trend percentages* for the following items taken from the financial statements of Lopez Plumbing over a five-year period. Treat 2007 as the base year. State whether the trends are favorable or unfavorable. (Dollar amounts are stated in thousands.)

	2011	2010	2009	2008	2007
Sales	$81,400	$74,000	$61,500	$59,000	$50,000
Cost of goods sold	58,500	48,000	40,500	37,000	30,000

LO1 **EXERCISE 14.3**
Common Size Income Statements

Prepare *common size* income statements for Pellum Company, a sole proprietorship, for the two years shown below by converting the dollar amounts into percentages. For each year, sales will appear as 100 percent and other items will be expressed as a percentage of sales. (Income taxes are not involved as the business is not incorporated.) Comment on whether the changes from 2010 to 2011 are favorable or unfavorable.

	2011	2010
Sales	$500,000	$400,000
Cost of goods sold	330,000	268,000
Gross profit	$170,000	$132,000
Operating expenses	130,000	116,000
Net income	$ 40,000	$ 16,000

LO3 LO4 **EXERCISE 14.4**
Measures of Liquidity

Roy's Toys is a manufacturer of toys and children's products. The following are selected items appearing in a recent balance sheet (dollar amounts are in millions):

Cash and short-term investments	$ 47.3
Receivables	159.7
Inventories	72.3
Prepaid expenses and other current assets	32.0
Total current liabilities	130.1
Total liabilities	279.4
Total stockholders' equity	344.0

a. Using the information above, compute the amounts of Roy's Toys (**1**) quick assets and (**2**) total current assets.

b. Compute for Roy's Toys the (**1**) quick ratio, (**2**) current ratio, and (**3**) dollar amount of working capital. (Round ratios to one decimal place.)

c. Discuss whether Roy's Toys appears liquid from the viewpoint of a short-term creditor.

LO5 **EXERCISE 14.5**
Multiple-Step Income Statements

LINK, INC. STATEMENT OF EARNINGS FOR THE YEAR ENDED DECEMBER 31, 2011	
Net sales	$4,395,253
Costs and expenses:	
Cost of goods sold	(2,821,455)
Operating expenses	(1,004,396)
Interest revenue	15,797
Earnings before income tax	$ 585,199
Income tax expense	(204,820)
Net earnings	$ 380,379
Earnings per share	$1.70

Comparative balance sheets report average total assets for the year of *$2,450,000* and average total equity of *$1,825,000* (dollar amounts in thousands, except earnings per share).

a. Prepare an income statement for the year in a multiple-step format.

b. Compute the (**1**) gross profit rate, (**2**) net income as a percentage of net sales, (**3**) return on assets, and (**4**) return on equity for the year. (Round computations to the nearest one-tenth of 1 percent.)

c. Explain why interest revenue is not included in the company's gross profit computation.

LO6 **EXERCISE 14.6**
ROI

Shown below are selected data from a recent annual report of **Kimberly-Clark Corporation**, a large consumer products provider. (Dollar amounts are in millions.)

	Beginning of the Year	End of the Year
Total assets	$17,660	$18,840
Total stockholders' equity	4,280	5,690
Operating income		3,210
Net income		1,880

a. Compute for the year **Kimberly-Clark**'s return on average total assets. (Round computations to the nearest two-tenths of 1 percent.)

b. Compute for the year **Kimberly-Clark**'s return on average total stockholders' equity. (Round computations to the nearest two-tenths of 1 percent.)

c. What is the most likely explanation why **Kimberly-Clark**'s total stockholders' equity for the year increased?

LO1 LO6 **EXERCISE 14.7**
Computing and Interpreting Rates of Change

Selected information from the financial statements of Rochet, Inc., includes the following:

	2011	2010
Net sales	$2,200,000	$2,000,000
Total expenses	1,998,000	1,800,000

a. Compute the percentage change in 2011 for the amounts of (**1**) net sales and (**2**) total expenses.

b. Using the information developed in part **a,** express your opinion as to whether the company's *net income* for 2011:

1. Increased at a greater or lower percentage rate than did net sales.
2. Represented a larger or smaller percentage of net sales revenue than in 2010. For each answer, explain your reasoning *without* making any computations or references to dollar amounts.

LO6 **EXERCISE 14.8**
Research Problem

Obtain from your library, the Internet, or other source the most recent annual report of a publicly owned company.

a. Using the annual report data, compute the basic measures of liquidity, long-term credit risk, and profitability summarized in Exhibit 14–26. Compare these measures with the appropriate industry norms available in your library. Briefly comment on your findings.

b. Using the financial pages of a daily newspaper (such as *The Wall Street Journal*), determine (**1**) the current market price of your company's common stock, (**2**) its 52-week high and low market prices, and (**3**) its p/e ratio. Briefly comment on your findings.

c. On the basis of your analysis in parts **a** and **b,** make a recommendation as to whether investors should buy shares of the stock, hold the shares they currently own, or sell the shares they currently own. Defend your position.

LO3 LO4 LO6 **EXERCISE 14.9**
Home Depot, Inc., Management's Discussion and Analysis

The financial statements of large public companies are often accompanied by a multiple-year summary of key financial and other information that is helpful in understanding the company. Appendix A of this text includes the financial statements of **Home Depot, Inc.**, and selected other information from the company's annual report. Included is a ten-year Summary of Financial and Operating Results for the period 2000–2009. Locate this summary in Appendix A and respond to the following.

a. Considering the "store data" section of the ten-year summary, what conclusions can you draw about the change in size of **Home Depot, Inc.**, during the ten-year period?

b. Comment on the ten-year trend in net earnings as a percentage of sales and what this trend means to you as an investor in the company.

c. Has the company's liquidity improved or diminished over the 10-year period? Justify your answer.

LO4 LO6 **EXERCISE 14.10**

Evaluating Employment Opportunities

Assume that you will soon graduate from college and that you have job offers with two pharmaceutical firms. The first offer is with Alpha Research, a relatively new and aggressive company. The second is with Omega Scientific, a very well established and conservative company.

Financial information pertaining to each firm, and to the pharmaceutical industry as a whole, is as follows:

Financial Measure	Alpha	Omega	Industry Average
Current ratio	2.2 to 1	4.5 to 1	2.5 to 1
Quick ratio	1.2 to 1	2.8 to 1	1.5 to 1
Return on assets	17%	8%	10%
Return on equity	28%	14%	16%
P/e ratio	20 to 1	10 to 1	12 to 1

The Omega offer is for $36,000 per year. The Alpha offer is for $32,000. However, unlike Omega, Alpha awards its employees a stock option bonus based on profitability for the year. Each option enables the employee to purchase shares of Alpha's common stock at a significantly reduced price. The more profitable this company is, the more stock each employee can buy at a discount.

Show how the above information may help you justify accepting the Alpha Research offer, even though the starting salary is $4,000 lower than the Omega Scientific offer.

LO7 **EXERCISE 14.11**

Ratios for a Retail Store

Selected financial data for SellFast, Inc., a retail store, appear as follows:

	2011	2010
Sales (all on account)	$750,000	$610,000
Cost of goods sold	495,000	408,000
Average inventory during the year	110,000	102,000
Average receivables during the year	150,000	100,000

a. Compute the following for both years:

1. Gross profit percentage
2. Inventory turnover
3. Accounts receivable turnover

b. Comment on favorable and unfavorable trends.

LO7 **EXERCISE 14.12**

Computing Ratios

A condensed balance sheet for Bradford Corporation prepared at the end of the year appears as follows:

Assets		Liabilities & Stockholders' Equity	
Cash	$ 95,000	Notes payable (due in 6 months)	$ 40,000
Accounts receivable	155,000	Accounts payable	110,000
Inventory	270,000	Long-term liabilities	360,000
Prepaid expenses	60,000	Capital stock, $5 par	300,000
Plant & equipment (net)	570,000	Retained earnings	430,000
Other assets	90,000		
Total	$1,240,000	Total	$1,240,000

During the year the company earned a gross profit of $1,116,000 on sales of $2,950,000. Accounts receivable, inventory, and plant assets remained almost constant in amount throughout the year.

Compute the following:

a. Current ratio.

b. Quick ratio.

c. Working capital.

d. Debt ratio.

e. Accounts receivable turnover (all sales were on credit).

f. Inventory turnover.

g. Book value per share of capital stock.

LO6 LO7

EXERCISE 14.13
Current Ratio, Debt Ratio, and Earnings per Share

Selected items from successive annual reports of Carey, Inc., appear as follows:

	2011	2010
Total assets (40% of which are current)	$400,000	$325,000
Current liabilities	$ 80,000	$100,000
Bonds payable, 12%	100,000	50,000
Capital stock, $5 par value	100,000	100,000
Retained earnings	120,000	75,000
Total liabilities & stockholders' equity	$400,000	$325,000

Dividends of $16,000 were declared and paid in 2011.

Compute the following:

a. Current ratio for 2011 and 2010.

b. Debt ratio for 2011 and 2010.

c. Earnings per share for 2011.

LO7

EXERCISE 14.14
Ratio Analysis for Two Similar Companies

Selected data from the financial statements of Italian Marble Co. and Brazil Stone Products for the year just ended follow. Assume that for both companies dividends declared were equal in amount to net earnings during the year and therefore stockholders' equity did not change. The two companies are in the same line of business.

	Italian Marble Co.	Brazil Stone Products
Total liabilities	$ 200,000	$ 100,000
Total assets	800,000	400,000
Sales (all on credit)	1,800,000	1,200,000
Average inventory	240,000	140,000
Average receivables	200,000	100,000
Gross profit as a percentage of sales	40%	30%
Operating expenses as a percentage of sales	36%	25%
Net income as a percentage of sales	3%	5%

Compute the following for each company and state a brief conclusion about which company is in the stronger financial position.

a. Net income.

b. Net income as a percentage of stockholders' equity.

c. Accounts receivable turnover.

d. Inventory turnover.

LO6 LO7 **EXERCISE 14.15**
Ratio Analysis for Feature Company

Johnson & Johnson's 2009 financial statements include the following items (all dollars in millions):

	2009	2008
Balance sheet		
Current assets	$39,541	$34,377
Current liabilities	21,731	20,852
Total assets	94,682	84,912
Income statement		
Sales	$61,897	$63,747
Gross profit	43,450	45,231
Net earnings (income)	12,266	12,949

Compute the following ratios and comment on the trend you can observe from the limited two years of data you have available.

a. Gross profit rate

b. Net income as a percentage of sales

c. Current ratio

Problem Set A

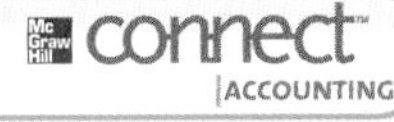

LO1 LO5 **PROBLEM 14.1A**
Comparing Operating Results with Average Performance in the Industry

Campers, Inc., manufactures camping equipment. Shown below for the current year are the income statement for the company and a common size summary for the industry in which the company operates. (Notice that the percentages in the right-hand column are *not* for Campers, Inc., but are average percentages for the industry.)

	Campers, Inc.	Industry Average
Sales (net)	$20,000,000	100%
Cost of goods sold	9,800,000	57
Gross profit on sales	$10,200,000	43%
Operating expenses:		
Selling	$ 4,200,000	16%
General and administrative	3,400,000	20
Total operating expenses	$ 7,600,000	36%
Operating income	$ 2,600,000	7%
Income tax expense	1,200,000	3
Net income	$ 1,400,000	4%
Return on assets	23%	14%

Instructions

a. Prepare a two-column common size income statement. The first column should show for Campers, Inc., all items expressed as a percentage of net sales. The second column should show the equivalent industry average for the data given in the problem. The purpose of this common size statement is to compare the operating results of Campers, Inc., with the average for the industry.

b. Comment specifically on differences between Campers, Inc., and the industry average with respect to gross profit on sales, selling expenses, general and administrative expenses, operating income, net income, and return on assets. Suggest possible reasons for the more important disparities.

LO3 LO5

PROBLEM 14.2A
Analysis to Identify Favorable and Unfavorable Trends

The following information was developed from the financial statements of Darwin, Inc. At the beginning of 2011, the company's former supplier went bankrupt, and the company began buying merchandise from another supplier.

	2011	2010
Gross profit on sales	$1,008,000	$1,134,000
Income before income tax	230,400	252,000
Net income	172,800	189,000
Net income as a percentage of net sales	6.0%	7.5%

Instructions

a. Compute the net sales for each year.

b. Compute the cost of goods sold in dollars and as a percentage of net sales for each year.

c. Compute operating expenses in dollars and as a percentage of net sales for each year. (Income taxes expense is not an operating expense.)

d. Prepare a condensed comparative income statement for 2010 and 2011. Include the following items: net sales, cost of goods sold, gross profit, operating expenses, income before income tax, income taxes expense, and net income. Omit earnings per share statistics.

e. Identify the significant favorable and unfavorable trends in the performance of Darwin, Inc. Comment on any unusual changes.

LO3 LO4

PROBLEM 14.3A
Measures of Liquidity

Some of the accounts appearing in the year-end financial statements of Roger Grocery, Inc., appear below. This list includes all of the company's current assets and current liabilities.

Sales	$1,880,000
Accumulated depreciation: equipment	370,000
Notes payable (due in 90 days)	70,000
Retained earnings	241,320
Cash	67,600
Capital stock	150,000
Marketable securities	175,040
Accounts payable	127,500
Mortgage payable (due in 15 years)	320,000
Salaries payable	7,570
Dividends	25,000
Income taxes payable	14,600
Accounts receivable	230,540
Inventory	179,600
Unearned revenue	10,000
Unexpired insurance	4,500

Instructions

a. Prepare a schedule of the company's current assets and current liabilities. Select the appropriate items from the preceding list.

b. Compute the current ratio and the amount of working capital. Explain how each of these measurements is computed. State, with reasons, whether you consider the company to be in a strong or weak current position.

LO3 LO4 LO7

PROBLEM 14.4A

Liquidity of **Kroger**

The Kroger Company is one of the world's largest supermarket chains. These selected items were adapted from a recent **Kroger** balance sheet. (Dollar amounts are in millions.)

Cash (including deposit-in-transit)	$1,078
Receivables	909
Merchandise inventories	4,902
Other current assets	561
Property, plant and equipment (net of depreciation)	13,929
Retained earnings	7,344
Total current liabilities	7,714

Instructions

a. Using the information above, compute the amounts of **Kroger**'s total current assets and total quick assets.

b. Compute the company's (**1**) current ratio, (**2**) quick ratio, and (**3**) working capital. (Round to two decimal points.)

c. From these computations, are you able to conclude whether **Kroger** is a good credit risk for short-term creditors or on the brink of bankruptcy? Explain.

d. Is there anything unusual about the operating cycle of supermarkets that would make you think that they normally would have lower current ratios than, say, large department stores?

e. What *other types of information* could you utilize in performing a more complete analysis of **Kroger**'s liquidity?

LO3 LO4 LO7

PROBLEM 14.5A

Balance Sheet Measures of Liquidity and Credit Risk

A recent balance sheet of Sweet Tooth, Inc., included the following items, among others. (Dollar amounts are stated in thousands.)

Cash	$ 49,625
Marketable securities (short-term)	55,926
Accounts receivable	23,553
Inventories	32,210
Prepaid expenses	5,736
Retained earnings	121,477
Notes payable to banks (due within one year)	20,000
Accounts payable	5,912
Dividends payable	1,424
Accrued liabilities (short-term)	21,532
Income taxes payable	6,438

The company also reported total assets of $353,816 thousand, total liabilities of $81,630 thousand, and a return on total assets of *18.1 percent.*

Instructions

a. Compute Sweet Tooth's (**1**) quick assets, (**2**) current assets, and (**3**) current liabilities.

b. Compute Sweet Tooth's (**1**) quick ratio, (**2**) current ratio, (**3**) working capital, and (**4**) debt ratio. (Round to one decimal place.)

c. Discuss the company's liquidity from the viewpoints of (1) short-term creditors, (2) long-term creditors, and (3) stockholders.

LO4 **PROBLEM 14.6A**

Financial Statement Analysis

LO5 

LO7

Shown below is selected information from the financial statements of Downing, Inc., a retail furniture store.

From the balance sheet:		
Cash		$ 30,000
Accounts receivable		150,000
Inventory		200,000
Plant assets (net of accumulated depreciation)		500,000
Current liabilities		150,000
Total stockholders' equity		300,000
Total assets		1,000,000
From the income statement:		
Net sales		$1,500,000
Cost of goods sold		1,080,000
Operating expenses		315,000
Interest expense		84,000
Income tax expense		6,000
Net income		15,000
From the statement of cash flows:		
Net cash provided by operating activities (including interest paid of $79,000)		$ 40,000
Net cash used in investing activities		(46,000)
Financing activities:		
Amounts borrowed	$ 50,000	
Repayment of amounts borrowed	(14,000)	
Dividends paid	(20,000)	
Net cash provided by financing activities		16,000
Net increase in cash during the year		$ 10,000

Instructions

a. Explain how the interest expense shown in the income statement could be $84,000, when the interest payment appearing in the statement of cash flows is only $79,000.

b. Compute the following (round to one decimal place):

1. Current ratio
2. Quick ratio
3. Working capital
4. Debt ratio

c. Comment on these measurements and evaluate Downing, Inc.'s short-term debt-paying ability.

d. Compute the following ratios (assume that the year-end amounts of total assets and total stockholders' equity also represent the average amounts throughout the year):

1. Return on assets
2. Return on equity

e. Comment on the company's performance under these measurements. Explain *why* the return on assets and return on equity are so different.

f. Discuss (**1**) the apparent safety of long-term creditors' claims and (**2**) the prospects for Downing, Inc., continuing its dividend payments at the present level.

LO4 LO5 LO7

PROBLEM 14.7A
Basic Ratio Analysis

Medtronics is a world leader in medical technology. The following selected data are adapted from a recent annual report. (Dollar amounts are stated in millions.)

	Beginning of the Year	End of the Year
Total current assets	$ 7,322	$ 7,460
Total current liabilities	3,535	3,147
Total assets	22,198	23,661
Total stockholders' equity	11,536	12,851
Operating income		2,594
Net income		2,169

The company has long-term liabilities that bear interest at annual rates ranging from 6 percent to 8 percent.

Instructions

a. Compute the company's current ratio at (**1**) the *beginning* of the year and (**2**) the *end* of the year. (Carry to two decimal places.)

b. Compute the company's working capital at (**1**) the beginning of the year and (**2**) the end of the year. (Express dollar amounts in thousands.)

c. Is the company's short-term debt-paying ability improving or deteriorating?

d. Compute the company's (**1**) return on average total assets and (**2**) return on average stockholders' equity. (Round average assets and average equity to the nearest dollar and final computations to the nearest 1 percent.)

e. As an equity investor, do you think that **Medtronic**'s management is utilizing the company's resources in a reasonably efficient manner? Explain.

LO5 LO7

PROBLEM 14.8A
Ratios; Consider Advisability of Incurring Long-Term Debt

At the end of the year, the following information was obtained from the accounting records of Zachery, Inc.

Sales (all on credit)	$2,750,000
Cost of goods sold	1,755,000
Average inventory	375,000
Average accounts receivable	290,000
Interest expense	45,000
Income tax expense	84,000
Net income	159,000
Average investment in assets	1,800,000
Average stockholders' equity	895,000

Instructions

a. From the information given, compute the following:

1. Inventory turnover.
2. Accounts receivable turnover.
3. Total operating expenses.
4. Gross profit percentage.
5. Return on average stockholders' equity.
6. Return on average assets.

b. Zachery has an opportunity to obtain a long-term loan at an annual interest rate of 12 percent and could use this additional capital at the same rate of profitability as indicated by the given data. Would obtaining the loan be desirable from the viewpoint of the stockholders? Explain.

LO5 LO7 LO8

PROBLEM 14.9A
Ratios: Evaluation of Two Companies

Shown below are selected financial data for Another World and Imports, Inc., at the end of the current year:

	Another World	Imports, Inc.
Net credit sales	$675,000	$560,000
Cost of goods sold	504,000	480,000
Cash	51,000	20,000
Accounts receivable (net)	75,000	70,000
Inventory	84,000	160,000
Current liabilities	105,000	100,000

Assume that the year-end balances shown for accounts receivable and for inventory approximate the average balances of these items throughout the year.

Instructions

a. For each of the two companies, compute the following:

1. Working capital.
2. Current ratio.
3. Quick ratio.
4. Number of times inventory turned over during the year and the average number of days required to turn over inventory (round computation to the nearest day).
5. Number of times accounts receivable turned over during the year and the average number of days required to collect accounts receivable (round computation to the nearest day).
6. Operating cycle.

b. From the viewpoint of a short-term creditor, comment on the *quality* of each company's working capital. To which company would you prefer to sell $20,000 in merchandise on a 30-day open account?

Problem Set B

LO1 LO5

PROBLEM 14.1B
Comparing Operating Results with Average Performance in the Industry

Bathrooms, Inc., manufactures bathroom equipment. Shown below for the current year are the income statements for the company and a common size summary for the industry in which the company operates. (Notice that the percentages in the right-hand column are *not* for Bathrooms, Inc., but are average percentages for the industry.)

	Bathrooms, Inc.	Industry Average
Sales (net)	$12,000,000	100%
Cost of goods sold	7,320,000	70
Gross profit on sales	$ 4,680,000	30%
Operating expenses:		
Selling	$ 1,800,000	10%
General and administrative	720,000	14
Total operating expenses	$ 2,520,000	24%
Operating income	$ 2,160,000	6%
Income tax expense	120,000	2
Net income	$ 2,040,000	4%
Return on assets	20%	12%

Instructions

a. Prepare a two-column common size income statement for Bathrooms, Inc. The first column should show for Bathrooms, Inc., all items expressed as a percentage of net sales. The second column should show the equivalent industry average for the data given in the problem. The purpose of this common size statement is to compare the operating results of Bathrooms, Inc., with the average for the industry. (Round to the nearest percent.)

b. Comment specifically on differences between Bathrooms, Inc., and the industry average with respect to gross profit on sales, selling expenses, general and administrative expenses, operating income, net income, and return on assets. Suggest possible reasons for the more important disparities.

LO3 LO5

PROBLEM 14.2B
Analysis to Identify Favorable and Unfavorable Trends

The following information was developed from the financial statements of Slow Time, Inc. At the beginning of 2011, the company's former supplier went bankrupt, and the company began buying merchandise from another supplier.

	2011	2010
Gross profit on sales	$720,000	$800,000
Income before income tax	200,000	220,000
Net income	150,000	170,000
Net income as a percentage of net sales	8%	10%

Instructions

a. Compute the net sales for each year.

b. Compute the cost of goods sold in dollars and as a percentage of net sales for each year.

c. Compute operating expenses in dollars and as a percentage of net sales for each year. (Income taxes expense is not an operating expense.)

d. Prepare a condensed comparative income statement for 2010 and 2011. Include the following items: net sales, cost of goods sold, gross profit, operating expenses, income before income tax, income tax expense, and net income. Omit earnings per share statistics.

e. Identify the significant favorable and unfavorable trends in the performance of Slow Time, Inc. Comment on any unusual changes.

LO3 LO4

PROBLEM 14.3B
Measures of Liquidity

Some of the accounts appearing in the year-end financial statements of Gino, Inc., appear below. This list includes all of the company's current assets and current liabilities.

Sales	$2,500,000
Accumulated depreciation: equipment	180,000
Notes payable (due in 120 days)	85,000
Retained earnings	240,000
Cash	61,000
Capital stock	250,000
Marketable securities	160,000
Accounts payable	105,000
Mortgage payable (due in 20 years)	650,000
Salaries payable	5,800
Dividends	20,000
Income taxes payable	14,400
Accounts receivable	217,000
Inventory	195,000
Unearned revenue	15,000
Unexpired insurance	8,000

Instructions

a. Prepare a schedule of the company's current assets and current liabilities. Select the appropriate items from the above list.

b. Compute the current ratio and the amount of working capital. Explain how each of these measurements is computed. State, with reasons, whether you consider the company to be in a strong or weak current position.

LO3 LO4 LO7

PROBLEM 14.4B
Liquidity of Cheese, Inc.

Cheese, Inc., is one of the world's largest cheese store chains. Shown below are selected items adapted from a recent Cheese, Inc., balance sheet. (Dollar amounts are in the millions.)

Cash	$ 72.4
Receivables	150.4
Merchandise inventories	1,400.0
Prepaid expenses	91.0
Fixtures and equipment	3,150.0
Retained earnings	295.0
Total current liabilities	2,500.0

Instructions

a. Using the information above, compute the amounts of Cheese's total current assets and total quick assets.

b. Compute the company's (**1**) current ratio, (**2**) quick ratio, and (**3**) working capital. (Round to two decimal places.)

c. From these computations, are you able to conclude whether Cheese is a good credit risk for short-term creditors or on the brink of bankruptcy? Explain.

d. Is there anything unusual about the operating cycle of cheese stores that would make you think that they normally would have lower current ratios than, say, large department stores?

e. What *other types of information* could you utilize in performing a more complete analysis of Cheese's liquidity?

LO3 LO4 LO7

PROBLEM 14.5B
Balance Sheet Measures of Liquidity and Credit Risk

A recent balance sheet of Sweet as Sugar included the following items, among others. (Dollar amounts are stated in thousands.)

Cash	$ 49,630
Marketable securities (short-term)	65,910
Accounts receivable	25,330
Inventories	44,000
Prepaid expenses	5,850
Retained earnings	350,000
Notes payable to banks (due within one year)	28,000
Accounts payable	4,900
Dividends payable	1,800
Accrued liabilities (short-term)	21,500
Income taxes payable	8,500

The company also reported total assets of $600,000, total liabilities of $90,000, and a return on total assets of 20 percent.

Instructions

a. Compute Sweet as Sugar's: (**1**) quick assets, (**2**) current assets, and (**3**) current liabilities.

b. Compute Sweet as Sugar's: (**1**) quick ratio, (**2**) current ratio, (**3**) working capital, and (**4**) debt ratio. (Round to one decimal place.)

c. Discuss the company's liquidity from the viewpoints of (**1**) short-term creditors, (**2**) long-term creditors, and (**3**) stockholders.

LO4 LO5 LO7

PROBLEM 14.6B
Financial Statement Analysis

Shown below are selected data from the financial statements of Hamilton Stores, a retail lighting store.

From the balance sheet:		
Cash		$ 35,000
Accounts receivable		175,000
Inventory		225,000
Plant assets (net of accumulated depreciation)		550,000
Current liabilities		190,000
Total stockholders' equity		500,000
Total assets		1,300,000
From the income statement:		
Net sales		$2,400,000
Cost of goods sold		1,800,000
Operating expenses		495,000
Interest expense		80,000
Income tax expense		4,000
Net income		21,000
From the statement of cash flows:		
Net cash provided by operating activities (including interest paid of $72,000)		$ 50,000
Net cash used in investing activities		(54,000)
Financing activities:		
Amounts borrowed	$ 56,000	
Repayment of amounts borrowed	(25,000)	
Dividends paid	(24,000)	
Net cash provided by financing activities		7,000
Net increase in cash during the year		$ 3,000

Instructions

a. Explain how the interest expense shown in the income statement could be $80,000, when the interest payment appearing in the statement of cash flows is only $72,000.

b. Compute the following (round to one decimal place):

1. Current ratio **3.** Working capital

2. Quick ratio **4.** Debt ratio

c. Comment on these measurements and evaluate Hamilton's short-term debt-paying ability.

d. Compute the following ratios (assume that the year-end amounts of total assets and total stockholders' equity also represent the average amounts throughout the year):

1. Return on assets

2. Return on equity

e. Comment on the company's performance under these measurements. Explain *why* the return on assets and return on equity are so different.

f. Discuss (**1**) the apparent safety of long-term creditors' claims and (**2**) the prospects for Hamilton Stores continuing its dividend payments at the present level.

LO4 LO5 LO7

PROBLEM 14.7B
Basic Ratio Analysis

Balsum Corporation is engaged primarily in the business of manufacturing raincoats. Shown below are selected information from a recent annual report. (Dollar amounts are stated in thousands.)

	Beginning of the Year	End of the Year
Total current assets	$ 43,000	$ 82,000
Total current liabilities	54,000	75,000
Total assets	230,000	390,000
Total stockholders' equity	120,000	205,000
Operating income		74,000
Net income		51,000

The company has long-term liabilities that bear interest at annual rates ranging from 8 percent to 12 percent.

Instructions

a. Compute the company's current ratio at (**1**) the beginning of the year and (**2**) the end of the year. (Carry to two decimal places.)

b. Compute the company's working capital at (**1**) the beginning of the year and (**2**) the end of the year. (Express dollar amounts in thousands.)

c. Is the company's short-term debt-paying ability improving or deteriorating?

d. Compute the company's (**1**) return on average total assets and (**2**) return on average stockholders' equity. (Round average assets and average equity to the nearest dollar and final computations to the nearest 1 percent.)

e. As an equity investor, do you think that Balsum's management is utilizing the company's resources in a reasonably efficient manner? Explain.

LO5 LO7

PROBLEM 14.8B

Ratios: Consider Advisability of Incurring Long-Term Debt

At the end of the year, the following information was obtained from the accounting records of Clips Systems, Inc.:

Sales (all on credit)	$4,800,000
Cost of goods sold	3,000,000
Average inventory	420,000
Average accounts receivable	380,000
Interest expense	50,000
Income tax expense	80,000
Net income	280,000
Average investment in assets	2,600,000
Average stockholders' equity	1,000,000

Instructions

a. From the information given, compute the following:

1. Inventory turnover.
2. Accounts receivable turnover.
3. Total operating expenses.
4. Gross profit percentage.
5. Return on average stockholders' equity.
6. Return on average assets.

b. Clips Systems has an opportunity to obtain a long-term loan at an annual interest rate of 8 percent and could use this additional capital at the same rate of profitability as indicated by the given data. Would obtaining the loan be desirable from the viewpoint of the stockholders? Explain.

LO5 LO7 LO8

PROBLEM 14.9B

Ratios: Evaluation of Two Companies

Shown below are selected financial data for THIS Star, Inc., and THAT Star, Inc., at the end of the current year:

	THIS Star, Inc.	THAT Star, Inc.
Net credit sales	$900,000	$840,000
Cost of goods sold	700,000	640,000
Cash	90,000	40,000
Accounts receivable (net)	100,000	90,000
Inventory	50,000	160,000
Current liabilities	120,000	110,000

Assume that the year-end balances shown for accounts receivable and for inventory also represent the average balances of these items throughout the year.

Instructions

a. For each of the two companies, compute the following:

1. Working capital.
2. Current ratio.

3. Quick ratio.
4. Number of times inventory turned over during the year and the average number of days required to turn over inventory (round computation to the nearest day).
5. Number of times accounts receivable turned over during the year and the average number of days required to collect accounts receivable (round computation to the nearest day).
6. Operating cycle.

b. From the viewpoint of a short-term creditor, comment on the *quality* of each company's working capital. To which company would you prefer to sell $50,000 in merchandise on a 30-day open account?

Critical Thinking Cases

LO1 **CASE 14.1**
Season's Greetings

Holiday Greeting Cards is a local company organized late in July of 2010. The company's net income for each of its first six calendar quarters of operations is summarized below. (Amounts are stated in thousands of dollars.)

	2011	2010
First quarter (Jan. through Mar.)	$ 253	–0–
Second quarter (Apr. through June)	308	–0–
Third quarter (July through Sept.)	100	$ 50
Fourth quarter (Oct. through Dec.)	450	500
Total for the calendar year	$1,111	$550

Glen Wallace reports the business and economic news for a local radio station. On the day that Holiday Greeting Cards released the above financial information, you heard Wallace make the following statement during his broadcast: "Holiday Greeting Cards enjoyed a 350 percent increase in its profits for the fourth quarter, and profits for the entire year were up by over 100 percent."

Instructions

a. Show the computations that Wallace probably made in arriving at his statistics. (Hint: Wallace did not make his computations in the manner recommended in this chapter. His figures, however, can be developed from these financial data.)

b. Do you believe that Wallace's percentage changes present a realistic impression of Holiday Greeting Cards's rate of growth in 2011? Explain.

c. What figure would you use to express the percentage change in Holiday's fourth-quarter profits in 2011? Explain why you would compute the change in this manner.

LO3 through LO5 **CASE 14.2**
Evaluating Debt-Paying Ability

You are a loan officer with Third Texas Bank. Dan Scott owns two successful restaurants, each of which has applied to your bank for a $250,000 one-year loan for the purpose of opening a second location. Condensed balance sheets for the two business entities are shown below.

TEXAS STEAK RANCH
BALANCE SHEET
DECEMBER 31, 2011

Assets		Liabilities & Stockholders' Equity	
Current assets	$ 75,000	Current liabilities	$ 30,000
Plant and equipment	300,000	Long-term liabilities	200,000
		Capital stock	100,000
		Retained earnings	45,000
Total assets	$375,000	Total liabilities & stockholders' equity	$375,000

THE STOCKYARDS
BALANCE SHEET
DECEMBER 31, 2011

Assets		Liabilities & Owners' Equity	
Current assets	$ 24,000	Current liabilities	$ 30,000
Plant and equipment	301,000	Long-term liabilities	200,000
		Capital, Dan Scott	95,000
Total assets	$325,000	Total liabilities & owners' equity	$325,000

Both restaurants are popular and have been successful over the past several years. Texas Steak Ranch has been slightly more profitable, but the operating results for the two businesses have been quite similar. You think that either restaurant's second location should be successful. On the other hand, you know that restaurants are a very "faddish" type of business and that their popularity and profitability can change very quickly.

Dan Scott is one of the wealthiest people in Texas. He made a fortune—estimated at more than $2 billion—as the founder of Micro Time, a highly successful manufacturer of computer software. Scott now is retired and spends most of his time at Second Life, his 50,000-acre cattle ranch. Both of his restaurants are run by experienced professional managers.

Instructions

a. Compute the current ratio and working capital of each business entity.

b. On the basis of the information provided in this case, which of these businesses do you consider to be the better credit risk? Explain fully.

c. What simple measure might you insist upon that would make the other business as good a credit risk as the one you identified in part **b?** Explain.

LO5 CASE 14.3
Strategies to Improve the Current Ratio

Nashville Do-It-Yourself owns a chain of nine retail stores that sell building materials, hardware, and garden supplies. In early October, the company's current ratio is 1.7 to 1. This is about normal for the company, but it is lower than the current ratios of several large competitors. Management feels that, to qualify for the best credit terms from its suppliers, the company's year-end balance sheet should indicate a current ratio of at least 2 to 1.

Instructions

a. Indicate whether taking each of the following actions would increase or decrease the company's current ratio. Explain your reasoning.

1. Pay some of the company's current liabilities.
2. Purchase large amounts of inventory on account.
3. Offer credit customers a special discount if they pay their account balance prior to year-end.

b. Propose several other ethical steps that management might take to increase the company's current ratio prior to year-end.

LO5 CASE 14.4
Evaluating Corporate Governance Quality

Assume that you are an intern working for the **California Public Employees Retirement System (CALPERS)** in its investments office and you have been asked to evaluate a number of companies for possible investment by **CALPERS**. You prepare an analysis of each company's prospects using the tools of financial statement analysis (e.g., trend analysis, common size statements, ratio analysis). Thinking you are done, you present your analysis to your boss. She tells you that, although your analysis of each company's financial information is fine, she is also interested in the quality of each company's corporate governance. Pick a public company, download their most recent proxy statement in support of the annual meeting of shareholders, and write a brief report on the quality of each company's board of directors in terms of board composition and structure, size, committees, and expertise.

LO7 **INTERNET CASE 14.5**

LO8 Evaluating Liquidity and Profitability

Use the Internet search engine of your choice and do a general search on the name of a company of interest to you (e.g., **General Motors**, **Johnson & Johnson**, **Coca-Cola**, etc.). Explore the Web site of the company you choose and locate that company's most recent financial statements. You may need to look under a category that provides general information about the company and/or investor information.

Instructions

a. Find and read the description of the company, including the type of business it is in. Why is gaining an understanding of the industry and type of business an important starting point for financial statement analysis?

b. Locate the company's primary financial statements. Find the summary table of ratios in this chapter in Exhibit 14–26. Calculate three of the listed ratios under each of the following categories: "Measures of short-term liquidity" and "Measures of profitability." Show your work in calculating these ratios. Write a brief statement describing what you have learned about your company's liquidity and profitability.

c. Why do you think the Internet has become such a widely used source of financial information by investors and creditors?

Internet sites are time and date sensitive. It is the purpose of these exercises to have you explore the Internet. You may need to use the Yahoo! search engine http://www.yahoo.com *(or another favorite search engine) to find a company's current Web address.*

Answers to Self-Test Questions

1. b **2.** a, c, d **3.** c **4.** d (see below) **5.** b (see below) **6.** b **7.** d

Why answers a, b, and c in question **4** are incorrect:

a. The return on assets, 12 percent ($240,000 ÷ $2,000,000), exceeds the return on equity, which is 10 percent ($80,000 ÷ $800,000).

b. The current ratio is 1.6 to 1 ($480,000 ÷ $300,000).

c. Working capital amounts to $180,000 ($480,000 − $300,000).

Increase in net income required in question **5** : ($400,000 − $160,000) ÷ $160,000 = 150%

COMPREHENSIVE PROBLEM 4

Home Depot, Inc.

ANALYSIS OF THE FINANCIAL STATEMENTS OF A PUBLICLY OWNED CORPORATION

This Comprehensive Problem is to acquaint you with the content of the 2009 financial statements of **Home Depot, Inc.**, reproduced in Appendix A of this textbook. (The 2009 financial statements are for the fiscal year ended January 31, 2010.) The problem contains three major parts, which are independent of one another: *Part I* is designed to familiarize you with the general contents of a company's financial statements; *Part II* involves analysis of the company's liquidity; and *Part III* analyzes the trend in its profitability.

If you work this problem as a group assignment, each group member should be prepared to discuss the group's findings and conclusions in class.

A good starting point for understanding the financial statements of a company such as **Home Depot, Inc.**, is to understand the accounting policies used in preparing those statements. The first note accompanying the financial statements provides a brief description of the major accounting policies the company used. Most of the areas discussed in this note have been covered in this text.

Part I Annual reports include not only comparative financial statements but also other sources of information, such as:

- A multiyear summary of financial highlights, a summary of key statistics for the past 5 or 10 years.
- Several pages of *Notes* that accompany the financial statements.
- Reports by management and by the independent auditors in which they express their respective responsibilities for the financial statements.

Instructions

Answer each of the following questions and briefly explain *where* in the statements, notes, or other sections of the annual report you located the information used in your answer.

a. How many years are covered in each of the primary comparative financial statements? Were all of these statements audited? Name the auditors. What were the auditors' conclusions concerning these statements?

b. **Home Depot, Inc.**, combines its statement of retained earnings with another financial statement. Where are details about changes in the amount of retained earnings found?

c. Over the three years presented, have the company's annual net cash flows been positive or negative from (**1**) operating activities, (**2**) investing activities, and (**3**) financing activities? Has the company's cash balance increased or decreased during each of these three years?

Part II Assume that you are the credit manager of a medium-size supplier of building supplies. **Home Depot** wants to make credit purchases from your company, with payment due in 60 days.

Instructions

a. As general background, read the first note to the financial statements, "Summary of Significant Accounting Policies." Next, compute the following for the fiscal years ending January 31, 2010, and February 1, 2009 (round percentages to the nearest tenth of 1 percent, and other computations to one decimal place):

1. Current ratio.
2. Quick ratio.
3. Amount of working capital.

4. Percentage change in working capital from the prior year.
5. Percentage change in cash and cash equivalents from the prior year.

b. On the basis of your analysis in part **a,** does the company's liquidity appear to have *increased* or *decreased* during the most recent fiscal year? Explain.

c. Other than the ability of **Home Depot** to pay for its purchases, do you see any major considerations that should enter into your company's decision? Explain.

d. Your company assigns each customer one of the four credit ratings listed below. Assign a credit rating to **Home Depot, Inc.**, and write a memorandum explaining your decision. (In your memorandum, you may refer to any of your computations or observations in parts **a** through **c,** and to any information contained in the annual report.)

Possible Credit Ratings

A Outstanding Little or no risk of inability to pay. For customers in this category, we fill any reasonable order without imposing a credit limit. The customer's credit is reevaluated annually.

B Good Customer has good debt-paying ability but is assigned a credit limit that is reviewed every 90 days. Orders above the credit limit are accepted only on a cash basis.

C Marginal Customer appears sound, but credit should be extended only on a 30-day basis and with a relatively low credit limit. Creditworthiness and credit limit are reevaluated every 90 days.

D Unacceptable Customer does not qualify for credit.

Part III As general background, study the "10-Year Summary of Financial and Operating Results."

Instructions

a. Compute the following for the fiscal years ending January 31, 2010, and February 1, 2009 (round percentages to the nearest tenth of 1 percent):

1. Percentage change in net sales (relative to the prior year).
2. Percentage change in net earnings.
3. Gross profit rate.
4. Net income as a percentage of sales.
5. Return on average total assets.
6. Return on average total equity.

b. Write a statement that describes your conclusion(s) concerning trends in **Home Depot**'s profitability during the period covered in your analysis in part **a** above. Justify your conclusion(s).

CHAPTER 15

Global Business and Accounting

© Chris Kleponis/Bloomberg via Getty Images

AFTER STUDYING THIS CHAPTER, YOU SHOULD BE ABLE TO:

- **LO1** Define four mechanisms companies use to globalize their business activities.
- **LO2** Identify how global environmental forces—(a) political and legal systems, (b) economic systems, (c) culture, and (d) technology and infrastructure—affect accounting practices.
- **LO3** Explain why there is demand for harmonization of global financial reporting standards.
- **LO4** Demonstrate how to convert an amount of money from one currency to another.
- **LO5** Compute gains or losses on receivables or payables that are stated in a foreign currency when exchange rates fluctuate.
- **LO6** Describe techniques for "hedging" against losses from fluctuations in exchange rates.
- **LO7** Discuss how global sourcing increases product cost complexity.
- **LO8** Explain the importance of the Foreign Corrupt Practices Act.

Learning Objectives

INTERNATIONAL ACCOUNTING STANDARDS BOARD

Sir David Tweedie was appointed chairman of the International Accounting Standards Board (IASB) in 2001. Over the last decade, Sir David and other board members have worked tirelessly promoting and engaging the world community with International Financial Reporting Standards (IFRS). Their goal is the creation of a globally accepted single set of high-quality financial reporting standards.

In fulfilling its standard-setting duties the IASB engages with stakeholders around the world, including investors, analysts, regulators, business leaders, accounting standard-setters, and the accountancy profession. In the determining of standards, it is paramount that the board members understand the diversity of businesses, cultures, economic conditions, political and legal structures, and infrastructures around the world. Recent interest in IFRS from the G-20 leaders[1] demonstrates the importance of considering global political and economic ramifications of creating and changing International Financial Reporting Standards. ■

[1] Group of Twenty (G-20) was established in 1999 to bring together systemically important industrialized and developing economies to discuss key issues in the global economy. The G-20 consists of 19 countries plus the European Union and represent 85 percent of global gross national product, 80 percent of world trade, and two-thirds of the world population.

The London-based International Accounting Standards Board began a mission in 1993 to develop financial reporting rules that all countries could use. The board has made significant progress. In this chapter we describe that progress and provide you with a foundation for understanding the richness and complexity of international accounting issues.

Accounting rules, procedures, and standards in almost any chosen country developed differently from those in the United States and those in other countries. Countries such as the United Kingdom, Japan, and Germany establish their own accounting rules, procedures, and standards. The goal of the International Accounting Standards Board is to identify a set of accounting standards that will be acceptable to all governments and their related securities markets. This is a very ambitious goal because accounting rules, procedures, and standards are affected by the political, legal, economic, and cultural systems in which they are embedded. Thus, the variations in these systems from country to country have a significant impact on how investors, creditors, and managers understand and use accounting information.

The objective of this chapter is to introduce you to the complexity of global business and to explore some of the accounting issues associated with global business. This is only a brief introduction. As your business education progresses, additional details will be added to the ideas introduced here.

Globalization

Globalization occurs as managers become aware of and engage in cross-border trade and operations. Think of globalization as a continuous process where at the most basic level a purely domestic company's managers become aware that changes in foreign exchange rates,

Exhibit 15-1

LOCATION OF THE WORLD'S LARGEST MULTINATIONALS IN 2009

Country/Block	Number of Companies	Percentage
European Union	163	33%
United States	140	28%
Japan	68	14%
China	37	7%
Switzerland	15	3%
Canada	14	3%
South Korea	14	3%
Central/South America /	11	2%
Australia	9	2%
Russia	8	1%
India	7	1%
Others	14	3%

Source: Adapted from "The Fortune Global 500," **http:/money.cnn.com/magazines/fortune/global500/2009/countries**.
In 2005, more than 450 of the largest multinationals were headquartered in Europe (195), the United States (176), and Japan (80).

international technological advances, cultural diversity, or international political and economic issues will have an impact on their firm's ability to compete. An example of a higher level of globalization is a multinational enterprise that begins with raw material extraction and ends with final product assembly and sales in multiple foreign locations. In Exhibit 15–1 we show the location of the world's top multinational companies. The top 10 companies include seven oil companies, one automobile company (Toyota), one retailer (Walmart), and one banking corporation (ING Group).

Learning Objective
Define four mechanisms companies use to globalize their business activities. **LO1**

Globalization typically progresses through a series of stages that include exporting, licensing, joint ventures, wholly owned subsidiaries, and, finally, global sourcing. **Exporting** is, at the simplest level, selling a good or service to a foreign customer. While *exporting* maintains control over product creation, *licensing* gives up some control for a monetary return. **International licensing** is a contractual agreement between a company and a foreign party allowing the use of trademarks, patents, technology, designs, processes, intellectual property, or other proprietary advantage. Most major multinational food manufacturing companies are involved in some form of international product licensing. An **international joint venture** is a company owned by two or more companies from different countries. A **wholly owned international subsidiary** is created when a company uses its own funds to construct or purchase 100 percent equity control of a foreign subsidiary. Finally, **global sourcing** is the close coordination of R&D, manufacturing, and marketing across national boundaries and typically includes exporting, licensing, joint ventures, and wholly owned subsidiaries in cross-border operations.

As shown in Exhibit 15–2, companies typically engage in globalization through an outward growth path. Those companies wishing to globalize typically progress through the following stages: (1) exporting domestically produced products, (2) establishing licensing and joint venture arrangements, (3) creating wholly owned subsidiaries, and (4) full-scale global sourcing. In practice, there are many subcategories that are not shown in the exhibit, and companies may pursue multiple globalization processes simultaneously.

Exhibit 15–2
PROCESSES FOR INCREASING GLOBALIZATION

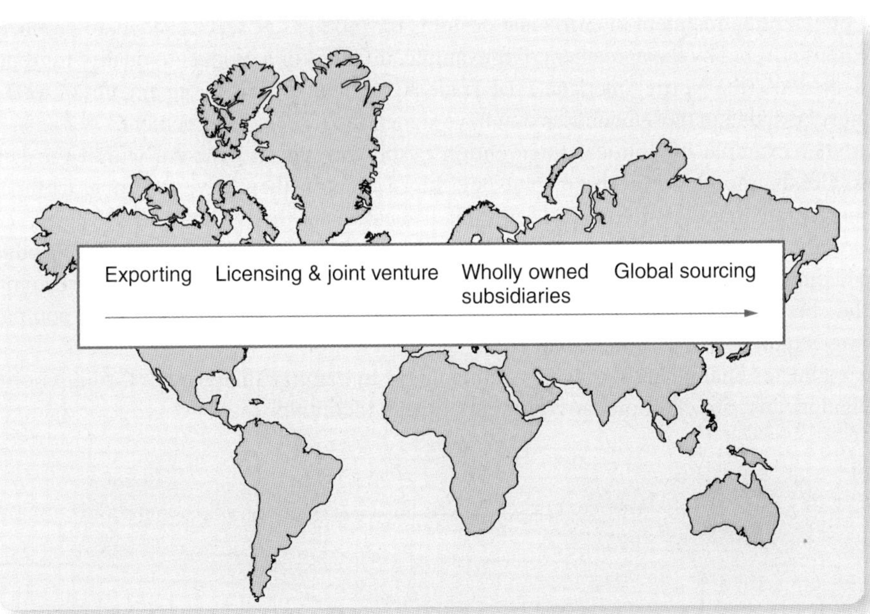

Globalization has implications for the type of accounting information gathered, created, and reported. U.S. GAAP requirements for exporting, licensing, joint ventures, and wholly owned subsidiaries are very different. In addition, differences in currency exchange rates create financial reporting issues. Management decisions about how to globalize clearly impact a firm's accounting outputs, processes, and procedures.

Environmental Forces Shaping Globalization

Learning Objective
LO2 Identify how global environmental forces—(a) political and legal systems, (b) economic systems, (c) culture, and (d) technology and infrastructure—affect accounting practices.

To help you understand how international environmental forces affect the accounting information measured, reported, and created, we consider environmental forces in four categories: (1) political and legal systems, (2) economic systems, (3) culture, and (4) technology and infrastructure.

These categories are not independent. A country's economy and culture have an influence on its political and legal structures. Culture affects and is affected by economics. As illustrated in Exhibit 15–3, the technological position of a country is dependent on political, demographic, and cultural issues.

POLITICAL AND LEGAL SYSTEMS

Learning Objective
LO2a Identify how political and legal systems affect accounting practices.

Managers operating in or planning operations in foreign settings must monitor associated political risks. Political risk occurs because governments have the ability to shift asset ownership from the company to the government or because the company may be asked to relinquish control over operations due to government intervention. For example, when Iran nationalized its oil industry in the late 1970s, many companies lost ownership of their Iranian assets invested in oil exploration, drilling, and oil delivery. United States GAAP requires companies to include in their financial reports discussions about political risk that may significantly impair assets or profits.

Laws enacted by foreign governments often have an impact on the net profits earned from international activities. Taxes, tariffs, and licensing fees vary substantially from country to country. Laws restricting the flow of currency can affect the amounts of foreign-earned profits that can be transferred out and used elsewhere. Ownership requirements are a common form of governmental control. For example, governments in China and India have ownership restrictions on subsidiaries and joint ventures in their countries.

Other types of political intervention include content or value-added requirements and sourcing requirements. Trade agreements often specify the source of raw materials or labor content to allow preferential treatment in tariffs and customs for products or services that are produced in the regions covered by the agreement. For example, in order for a product to qualify for reduced tariffs, NAFTA (the North American Free Trade Agreement) specifies the amount of total cost that must be added in those countries that have signed the free trade agreement.

Another example of political intervention is the **foreign trade zone** within the United States. Goods imported into these zones are duty-free until they leave the zone. Companies that import raw materials frequently set up their factories in these trade zones. These companies are not required to pay duty on the imported raw materials until the finished product is shipped out of the zone. Using foreign trade zones can have an impact on revenue recognition and the cost of goods sold. In addition, a delay in paying the duty enlarges the company's working capital as discussed in Chapter 14.

As countries change and grow, governments try to manage that growth through political and legal means. For example, governments use tax incentives that encourage or discourage

Exhibit 15–3
ENVIRONMENTAL FORCES IMPACTING GLOBALIZATION

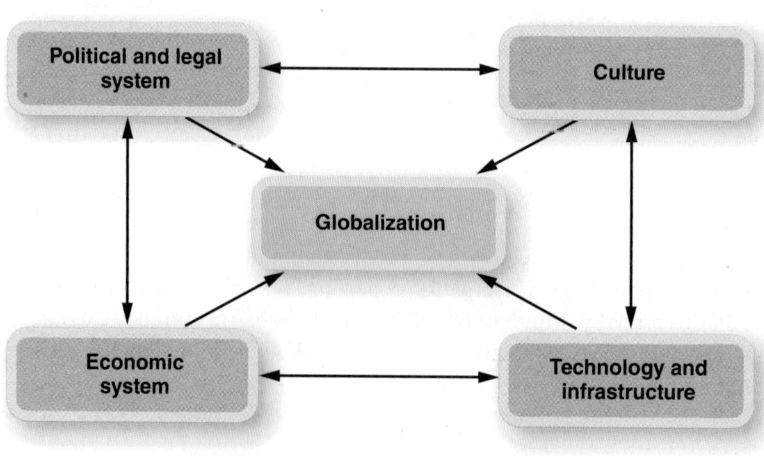

ownership of stocks. Policies also affect the level of individual savings, which impacts the availability of capital. Educational policies impact the literacy rate, the extent of formal education and training, and the number of accounting professionals. The political and legal structures of each country provide the framework for their economic structures.

ECONOMIC SYSTEMS

Learning Objective LO2b
Identify how economic systems affect accounting practices.

The economic systems under which businesses operate significantly affect the form and availability of accounting information. For example, in a **planned economy** the government uses central planning to allocate resources and determine output among various segments of the economy. Land and production facilities are government owned and controlled. The former Soviet Union and Soviet Eastern Bloc countries used central planning and had planned economies. China continues to use central planning extensively. Alternatively, in **market economies,** ownership of land and the means of production are private, and markets dictate the allocation of resources and the output among segments of the economy. Companies formerly operating in a planned economy can encounter significant difficulties when attempting to operate in a market economy. The reverse can also be true.

In some countries, businesses arrange themselves into **industrial organizations** as one method of raising capital. In South Korea and Japan, companies group themselves into conglomerates representing different industries. South Korean conglomerates, called *chaebol,* and Japanese conglomerates, called *keiretsu,* consist of companies that are grouped as customers and suppliers, and they usually contain a bank. Within these cartels of companies, suppliers receive loans, investment capital, technology, and long-term supply agreements from customers higher up on the pyramid. Suppliers integrate their operations with other suppliers and with their customers. Transactions between suppliers and customers are not arm's-length as in most U.S. transactions. In the United States, antitrust and price-fixing laws preclude the type of organized business groups found in Japan and South Korea.

INTERNATIONAL CASE IN POINT

Samsung, **Hyundai**, **LG**, and other Korean *chaebol* have reported impressive jumps in sales and profits in recent years. However, while the big Korean companies expand, the smaller- and medium-sized firms in the Korean economy are struggling. While the *chaebol* unquestionably have fueled the country's growth in recent decades, they're so powerful that they may be hampering innovation from smaller- and medium-sized companies that may harm Korea's long-run economic success. Economists worry that the *chaebol*'s deepening influence is hurting fair competition with suppliers and start-ups.

CULTURE

Learning Objective LO2c
Identify how culture affects accounting practices.

Think of culture as the mental mind-set that affects the way individuals in a society act and perceive each others' actions.[2] U.S. cultural practices have a significant effect on the way foreign companies conduct business in the United States. Likewise, certain forms of advertising, methods of acquiring business, and hierarchical organizational structures, which are common practices in the United States, would not be culturally preferred elsewhere. Ignoring cultural variables can create significant business problems.

Experts have identified four cultural mindsets that significantly differ among international locations.

- *Individualism versus collectivism.* The degree of interdependence that a society maintains among individuals, where high interdependence connotes collectivism. Citizens of Asian countries typically score higher on collectivism than those in the United States.

[2] For a more detailed discussion of the information in this section, see G. Hofstede, *Cultures and Organizations: Software of the Mind* (Berkshire, England: McGraw-Hill, 1991), or www.geert-hofstede.com.

- *Uncertainty avoidance.* The extent to which members of a society feel uncomfortable or threatened by unknown or uncertain situations. Citizens of South American countries score high on uncertainty avoidance.
- *Short-term versus long-term orientation.* With a long-term orientation, perseverance, thriftiness, maintaining of order, and lasting relationships are highly valued. A short-term orientation focuses on the past and the present, ignores the future, and values personal stability.
- *Large versus small power distance.* Large power distance cultures accept unequally distributed power within and across institutions and organizations. The idea that everyone is created equal or should have an equal voice is more highly valued in small power distance societies.

Exhibit 15–4 provides a rough measure of the relative differences between selected countries.

Exhibit 15-4
CULTURAL MINDSETS

Country	Individualism	Uncertainty Avoidance	Long-Term Orientation	High Power Distance
Japan	L	H	H	M
South Korea	L	H	H	H
Brazil	L	H	M	H
Italy	M	H	*	M
Germany	M	M	L	L
United States	H	M	L	M
Great Britain	H	L	L	L
Sweden	M	L	L	L

H = High, M = Medium, L = Low.
*Not available.

We can use Exhibit 15–4 to understand how cultural variables can affect both the type of accounting information that is produced and how that information is used. Studies have shown that in South Korea and Japan, where collectivism is high, less emphasis is placed on the transparency of financial statements for investors. The needs of creditors are given preference over the needs of investors. Thus, because financing for companies comes primarily from a bank in the keiretsu or chaebol, most accounting information is kept within the collectivist group. In addition, because of the strict government control of accounting regulations, the accounting profession in Asian countries has been slow to develop. The relative number of independent accountants is small, but increasing in many Asian countries.

TECHNOLOGY AND INFRASTRUCTURE

Learning Objective LO2d Identify how technology and infrastructure affect accounting practices.

Other cross-border differences create global business challenges because of variations in infrastructure and education level. The ability to transfer information and knowledge between and among various geographic locations and peoples can be difficult. Frequently companies that create joint ventures or start wholly owned operations in foreign locations find few employees with the education and technical training available in the U.S. workforce.

INTERNATIONAL CASE IN POINT

Western-style management training is a recent development in many countries. Budapest has one of the oldest graduate management programs in eastern Europe, and it was founded in 1988. More specifically, because companies in formerly planned economies used centrally determined accounts and procedures, accounting as a profession did not exist in eastern Europe prior to 1988. Thus, companies establishing business operations in eastern European locations have difficulty locating trained accounting personnel. In addition, prior business records are unreliable. Before the early 1990s, there were no independent auditors, public accountants, or management accountants in most eastern European countries.

Differences in internal accounting systems can also create challenges for international business dealings. Culture, education, language, and software differences hinder the free flow of information. Potential benefits from acquired international operations are sometimes lost because of the inability to transfer valuable information within and between international companies.

© AP Photo/Manish Swarup

Infrastructure impediments also pose problems for globalization. Poor access to communication equipment (for example, telephones, faxes, and computers), a lack of necessary R&D facilities (for example, specialized laboratory equipment, computer-aided design, or manufacturing), and fluctuating or unreliable power sources create significant hurdles to establishing international business in some locations. Manufacturing plants in many developing countries are not heated or cooled, which can create adverse operating environments for equipment that relies on lubricants and coolants. Inadequate transportation systems can slow the transfer of goods in and out of an international location. When estimating costs for inventory balance sheet items or cost of goods sold, accountants need to incorporate these unexpected costs into their computations to properly compute the cost of globally sourced products.

Harmonization of Financial Reporting Standards

Learning Objective LO3
Explain why there is demand for harmonization of global financial reporting standards.

Cross-border differences in financial reporting standards create problems for analyzing and comparing accounting information. For example, financial reporting in the United States is based primarily on the principle of historical cost without adjustment for changes in general price levels. South and Central American countries such as Brazil or Mexico, on the other hand, have experienced such high rates of inflation that inflation-adjusted information is required. These differences cause the financial statements of a U.S. company and a Mexican company to be very different and difficult to compare.

As long as an enterprise operates solely within its own borders, differences in financial reporting practices between countries are not as significant a problem as they are if business activity extends across borders. For example, **cross-border financing,** in which a company sells its securities in the capital markets of another country, has become increasingly popular. Business activities that cross borders create the need for more comparable information between companies that reside in different countries.

The need for comparable information has led to an interest in the **harmonization of accounting standards,** a term used to describe the globalization of similar accounting methods and principles throughout the world. The **International Accounting Standards Board (IASB)** is particularly interested in harmonization and is charged with the responsibility of establishing and gaining acceptance of international financial reporting standards (IFRSs). This committee represents over 150 professional organizations from more than 120 countries and over 2 million accounting professionals worldwide. While the IASB has no regulatory authority in any country, it uses its influence to move the reporting standards of all countries closer together in hopes of better harmonizing those standards. For countries that do not have well-developed capital markets, the IASB standards provide a model that often has a significant influence on their early attempts to develop standardized accounting practices.

INTERNATIONAL FINANCIAL REPORTING STANDARDS: ADOPTION OR CONVERGENCE

Countries and jurisdictions have taken two approaches to implementing international accounting standards to achieve harmonization. First, some countries have chosen to adopt international financial reporting standards exactly as written and promulgated by the IASB. **Adoption** means abandoning the country's current financial reporting standards and replacing them with IFRS. The adoption approach was agreed to by the European Union in 2005 when all companies trading on European Union securities markets were required to adopt IFRS for their annual reports. Exhibit 15–5 shows that Chile, Mexico, and Canada have chosen to adopt IFRS.

Alternatively, Exhibit 15–5 shows that some countries or jurisdictions have chosen to converge their existing standards to IFRS. **Convergence** means changing the countries' existing standards so that they will produce IFRS "equivalent" financial reports. Convergence has been described as an ongoing process because, as IFRS changes, converging countries must reconsider whether their standards continue to be equivalent, or need to be changed. China, Japan, and Australia have chosen to amend their current financial reporting standards so that they will converge with IFRS.

Exhibit 15–5
IFRS GLOBAL ADOPTION AND CONVERGENCE

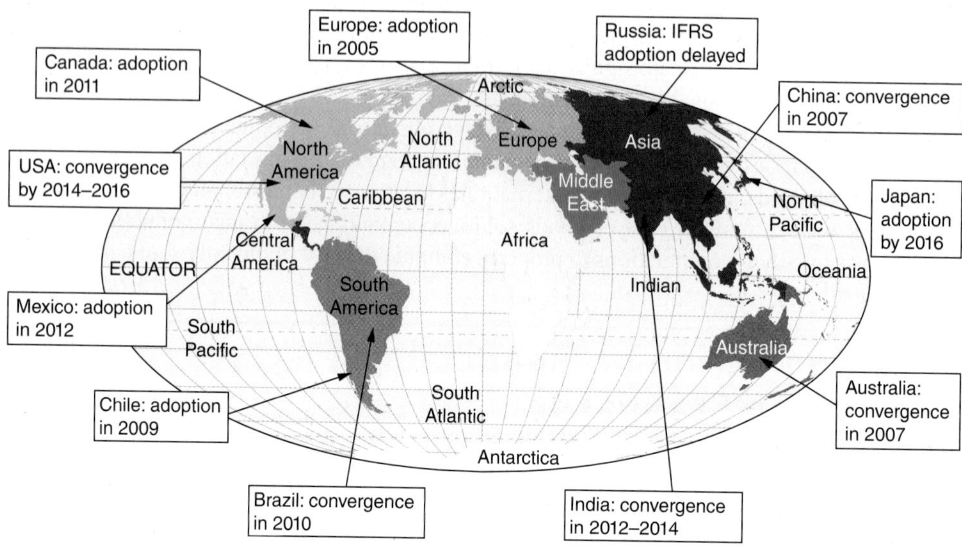

The United States has been working toward convergence of U.S. GAAP and IFRS for several years. However, progress has been slow and some companies and audit firms have called for the outright adoption of IFRS. The SEC suggested in 2010 that a small number of U.S. domestic companies might be allowed to use IFRS by 2015. The SEC is currently debating the best approach to moving U.S. GAAP to be compliant with international standards.

Exhibit 15–6 provides a flavor of the differences that currently exist among financial reporting requirements around the world. The first column shows that the number of available auditors in any particular country varies significantly. This variation is a direct result of the environmental variables discussed earlier. The United States and the United Kingdom have the most highly developed capital markets in the world and the related auditing demands are evident in the table. Column two shows that fixed asset revaluations are only allowed under IFRS and U.K. GAAP. Variations in inventory valuation and goodwill practices are illustrated in columns three and four. The final column in Exhibit 15–6 displays differences in segment disclosure. Segment information has been in demand from investors in recent years. Countries such as Germany and Brazil, where capital is typically provided by banks, require lower levels of segment disclosure. These banks usually have access to inside information from their

Exhibit 15–6 GLOBAL VARIATION IN ACCOUNTING PRACTICES

Country GAAP	Auditors per 100,000	Fixed Asset Revaluation Allowed	LIFO Allowed	Goodwill Impairment Test or Amortize	Depreciation Basis	Segment Disclosure Required
IFRS	—	Yes	No	Impairment	Economic	Yes
United States	93	No	Yes	Impairment	Economic	Yes
United Kingdom	211	Yes	No	Impairment	Economic	Yes
Japan	16	No	Yes	Amortize (20 yr)	Tax	Yes
Germany	15	No	No	Amortize (4 yr)	Tax	Limited
China	15	No	Yes	Impairment	Economic/tax	No
Brazil	1	No	Yes	Impairment	Economic	No
Russia	?	No	Yes	Amortized (20 yr)	Tax	No

borrowers. Thus, demand for segment information to be included on required statutory financial reports is much lower in these countries.

Foreign Currencies and Exchange Rates

In addition to the environmental characteristics described above, companies with international business dealings encounter financial measurement challenges that result from using multiple currencies. Consider, for example, a Japanese company that sells merchandise to a U.S. corporation. The Japanese company will want to be paid in Japanese currency—yen—but the U.S. company's bank account contains U.S. dollars. Thus one currency must be converted into another.

Most banks participate in an international currency exchange that enables them to buy foreign currencies at the prevailing *exchange rate.* Thus, a U.S. corporation can pay a liability to a Japanese company through the international banking system. The U.S. company will pay its bank in dollars. The bank will then use these dollars to purchase the required amount of yen on the international currency exchange and will arrange for delivery of the yen to the Japanese company's bank.[3]

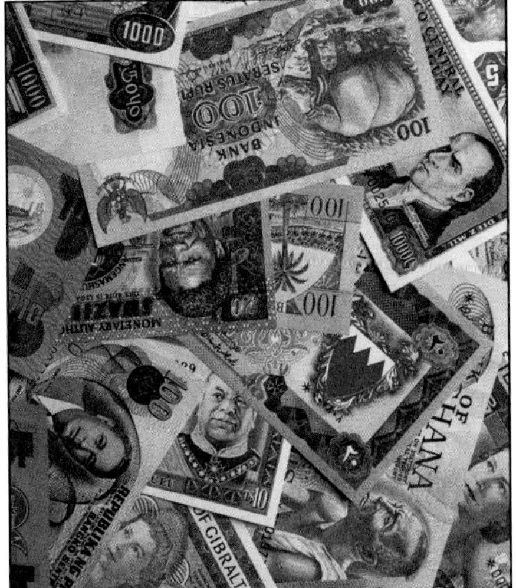

© Royalty-Free/Corbis/DAL

EXCHANGE RATES

A currency **exchange rate** is the amount it costs to purchase one unit of currency with another currency. Thus the exchange rate may be viewed as the "price" of buying one unit of a foreign currency, stated in terms of the domestic currency (which for our purpose is U.S. dollars). Exchange rates fluctuate daily, based on the worldwide supply and demand for particular currencies. The current exchange rate between the dollar and most major currencies is published daily in the financial press. For example, a few of the exchange rates in *The Wall Street Journal* are shown in Exhibit 15–7.

Exhibit 15–7

U.S. DOLLAR EQUIVALENTS FOR FIVE FOREIGN CURRENCIES

Country/Region	Currency	Exchange Rate (in dollars)	Exchange Rate (in foreign currency)
Britain	Pound (£)	$1.7425	0.534
Europe*	Euro (€)	1.4758	0.678
Japan	Yen (¥)	0.00764	130.9
Mexico	Peso ($)	0.10946	9.136
India	Rupee (Rs)	0.02045	48.889

*Many European countries, such as Austria, Belgium, Finland, France, Germany, Greece, Ireland, Italy, Luxembourg, the Netherlands, Portugal, and Spain, are using the euro.

Learning Objective LO4
Demonstrate how to convert an amount of money from one currency to another.

Exchange rates may be used to determine how much of one currency is equivalent to a given amount of another currency. Assume that a U.S. company owes a Japanese company 1 million yen (expressed ¥1,000,000). How many dollars are needed to settle this obligation, assuming that the current exchange rate is $0.00764 per yen? To restate an amount of foreign currency in terms of the equivalent amount of U.S. dollars, we multiply the foreign currency amount by the exchange rate, as follows:[4]

Amount Stated in Foreign Currency	× Exchange Rate (in dollars)	= Equivalent Number of U.S. Dollars
¥1,000,000	× $0.00764 per yen =	$7,640

[3] Alternatively, the U.S. company may send the Japanese company a check (or a bank draft) stated in dollars. The Japanese company can then arrange to have the dollars converted into yen through its bank in Japan.

[4] To convert an amount of dollars into the equivalent amount of a foreign currency, we would *divide* the dollar amount by the exchange rate. For example, $7,640 ÷ $0.00764 per yen = ¥1,000,000.

Alternatively, consider that a Japanese company agrees to pay a U.S. company $10,000 for imported goods. To determine the equivalent amount of yen, the Japanese company needs to know the number of yen per dollar. The yen per dollar can be computed by dividing one dollar by the number of dollars per yen. Thus, $1 ÷ $.00764/yen = ¥130.9/dollar. Using the yen per dollar exchange rate, we can convert the dollars to yen as follows:

Amount Stated in U.S. Dollars	×	Exchange Rate (in yen)	=	Amount Stated in Foreign Currency (yen)
$10,000	×	**¥130.9 per dollar**	=	**¥1,309,000**

This process of restating an amount of foreign currency in terms of the equivalent number of dollars or restating a dollar amount into an equivalent amount of foreign currency is called *translating* the currency.

Exchange Rate Jargon In the financial press, currencies are often described as "strong" or "weak," or as rising or falling against one another. For example, an evening newscaster might say, "A strong dollar rose sharply against the weakening British pound, but fell slightly against the Japanese yen and the Swiss franc." What does this tell us about exchange rates?

To understand such terminology, we must remember that an exchange rate is simply the price of one currency *stated in terms of another currency.* Throughout this chapter, we refer to the prices of various foreign currencies stated in terms of *U.S. dollars.* In other countries, however, the U.S. dollar is a foreign currency, and its price is stated in terms of the local (domestic) currency.

To illustrate, consider the table from *The Wall Street Journal* shown in Exhibit 15–7. The exchange rate for the Japanese yen is $0.00764. At this exchange rate, $1 is equivalent to ¥130.9 (as shown above). Thus, while we would say that the exchange rate for the Japanese yen is *$0.00764,* the Japanese would say that the exchange rate for the U.S. dollar is *¥130.9.*

Now let us assume that the exchange rate for the yen (stated in dollars) rises to $0.0109. At this exchange rate, $1 is equivalent to only ¥92 ($1 ÷ $.0109 = ¥92). In the United States, we would say that the exchange rate for the yen has *risen* from $0.00764 to $0.0109. In Japan, however, they would say that the exchange rate for the dollar has *fallen* from ¥130.9 to ¥92. In the financial press, it might be said that "the yen has risen against the dollar" or that "the dollar has fallen against the yen." The two statements mean the same thing—that the yen has become more valuable relative to the dollar.

Now let us return to our original phrase, "A strong dollar rose sharply against the weakening British pound, but fell slightly against the Japanese yen and the Swiss franc." When exchange rates are stated in terms of U.S. dollars, this statement means that the price (exchange rate) of the British pound fell sharply, but the prices of the Japanese yen and the Swiss franc rose slightly. A currency is described as "strong" when its exchange rate is rising relative to most other currencies and as "weak" when its exchange rate is falling. Exchange rates fluctuate because of changes in the environmental forces discussed earlier in this chapter.

ACCOUNTING FOR TRANSACTIONS WITH FOREIGN COMPANIES

Learning Objective
LO5 Compute gains or losses on receivables or payables that are stated in a foreign currency when exchange rates fluctuate.

When a U.S. company buys or sells merchandise in a transaction with a foreign company, the transaction price may be stipulated either in U.S. dollars or in units of the foreign currency. If the price is stated in *dollars,* the U.S. company encounters no special accounting problems. The transaction may be recorded in the same manner as are similar transactions with domestic suppliers or customers.

If the transaction price is stated in terms of the *foreign currency,* the company encounters two accounting problems. First, as the U.S. company's accounting records are maintained in dollars, the transaction price must be *translated* into dollars before the transaction can be recorded. The second problem arises when (1) the purchase or sale is made *on account* and (2) the exchange rate *changes* between the date of the transaction and the date that the account is paid. This fluctuation in the exchange rate will cause the U.S. company to experience either a *gain* or a *loss* in the settlement of the transaction.

Credit Purchases with Prices Stated in a Foreign Currency Assume that on August 1 a U.S. company buys merchandise from a British company at a price of 10,000 British pounds (£10,000), with payment due in 60 days. The exchange rate on August 1 is *$1.63* per British pound. The entry on August 1 to record this purchase (assuming use of a perpetual inventory system) would be:

Inventory	16,300	
Accounts Payable		16,300
To record the purchase of merchandise from a British company for £10,000 when the exchange rate is $1.63 per pound (£10,000 × $1.63 = $16,300).		

The amount of a foreign currency credit purchase is determined by using the exchange rate on the date it is journalized

Let us now assume that by September 30, when the £10,000 account payable must be paid, the exchange rate has fallen to *$1.61* per British pound. If the U.S. company had paid for the merchandise on August 1, the cost would have been $16,300. On September 30, however, only *$16,100* is needed to pay the £10,000 liability (£10,000 × $1.61 = $16,100). Thus, *the decline in the exchange rate has saved the company $200.* This savings is recorded in the accounting records as a *Gain on Fluctuations in Foreign Exchange Rates.* The entry on September 30 to record payment of the liability and recognition of this gain would be:

Accounts Payable		16,300	
Cash			16,100
Gain on Fluctuations in Foreign Exchange Rates			200
To record payment of £10,000 liability to British company and to recognize gain from decline in exchange rate:			
Original liability (£10,000 × $1.63)	$16,300		
Amount paid (£10,000 × $1.61)	16,100		
Gain from decline in exchange rate	$ 200		

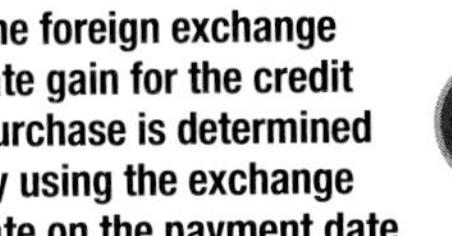
The foreign exchange rate gain for the credit purchase is determined by using the exchange rate on the payment date

Now let us assume that instead of declining, the exchange rate had *increased* from $1.63 on August 1 to *$1.66* on September 30. Under this assumption, the U.S. company would have to pay *$16,600* to pay off the £10,000 liability on September 30. Thus, the company would be paying *$300 more* than if the liability had been paid on August 1. This additional $300 cost was caused by the increase in the exchange rate and should be recorded as a loss. The entry on September 30 would be:

Accounts Payable		16,300	
Loss on Fluctuations in Foreign Exchange Rates		300	
Cash			16,600
To record payment of £10,000 liability to British company and to recognize loss from increase in exchange rate:			
Original liability (£10,000 × $1.63)	$16,300		
Amount paid (£10,000 × $1.66)	16,600		
Loss from increase in exchange rate	$ 300		

A foreign exchange rate loss occurs if the exchange rate increases between the purchase date and the collection date

In summary, having a liability that is fixed in terms of a foreign currency results in a gain for the debtor if the exchange rate declines between the date of the transaction and the date of payment. The gain results because fewer dollars will be needed to repay the debt than had originally been owed. An increase in the exchange rate, on the other hand, causes the debtor to incur a loss. In this case, the debtor will have to spend more dollars than had originally been owed in order to purchase the foreign currency needed to pay the debt.

Credit Sales with Prices Stated in a Foreign Currency A company that makes credit *sales* at prices stated in a foreign currency also will experience gains or losses from fluctuations in the exchange rate. To illustrate, let us change our preceding example to assume that the U.S. company *sells* merchandise on August 1 to the British company at a price of £10,000. We shall again assume that the exchange rate on August 1 is \$1.63 per British pound and that payment is due in 60 days. The entry on August 1 to record this sale would be:

Accounts Receivable	16,300	
Sales		16,300
To record sale to British company with sales price set at £10,000 (£10,000 × \$1.63) = \$16,300. To be collected in 60 days.		

In 60 days (September 30), the U.S. company will collect from the British company the U.S. dollar equivalent of £10,000. If the exchange rate on September 30 has fallen to \$1.61 per pound, the U.S. company will collect only \$16,100 (£ 10,000 × \$1.61 = \$16,100) in full settlement of its account receivable. Since the receivable had originally been equivalent to \$16,300, the decline in the exchange rate has caused a loss of \$200 to the U.S. company. The entry to be made on September 30 would be:

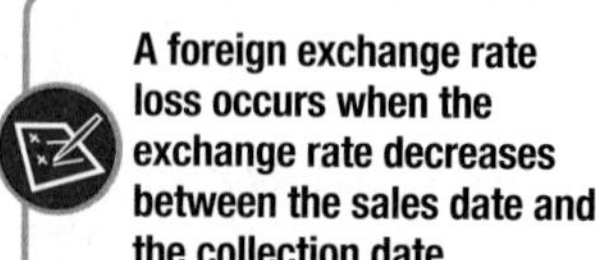

A foreign exchange rate loss occurs when the exchange rate decreases between the sales date and the collection date

Cash		16,100	
Loss on Fluctuations in Foreign Exchange Rates		200	
Accounts Receivable			16,300
To record collection of £10,000 receivable from British company and to recognize loss from fall in exchange rate since date of sale:			
Original sales price (£10,000 × \$1.63)	\$16,300		
Amount received (£10,000 × \$1.61)	16,100		
Loss from decline in exchange rate	\$ 200		

Now consider the alternative case, in which the exchange rate rises from \$1.63 at August 1 to \$1.66 at September 30. In this case, the British company's payment of £10,000 will convert into \$16,600, creating a gain for the U.S. company. The entry on September 30 would then be:

Cash		16,600	
Accounts Receivable			16,300
Gain on Fluctuations in Foreign Exchange Rates			300
To record collection of £10,000 receivable from British company and to recognize gain from increase in exchange rate:			
Original sales price (£10,000 × \$1.63)	\$16,300		
Amount received (£10,000 × \$1.66)	16,600		
Gain from increase in exchange rate	\$ 300		

Adjustment of Foreign Receivables and Payables at the Balance Sheet Date We have seen that fluctuations in exchange rates may cause gains or losses for companies with accounts payable or receivable in foreign currencies. Exchange rates fluctuate on a daily basis. For convenience, however, the company usually waits until the account is paid or collected before recording the related gain or loss. An exception to this convenient practice occurs at the end of the accounting period. An *adjusting entry* is made to recognize any gains or losses that have accumulated on any foreign payables or receivables through the balance sheet date.

To illustrate, assume that the transaction illustrated in Exhibit 15–8 occurs on November 10 when a U.S. company buys equipment from a Japanese company at a price of 10 million yen (¥10,000,000), payable on January 10 of the following year. If the exchange rate is \$0.0100 per yen on November 10, the entry for the U.S. company to record the purchase would be:

Equipment	100,000	
Accounts Payable		100,000
To record purchase of equipment from Japanese company at a price of ¥10,000,000, payable January 10 (¥10,000,000 × \$0.0100 = \$100,000).		

Assets purchased on account must be recorded in dollars using the exchange rate on the date of purchase

Exhibit 15–8

FOREIGN EXCHANGE TRANSACTION: U.S. COMPANY BUYS EQUIPMENT FROM A JAPANESE COMPANY

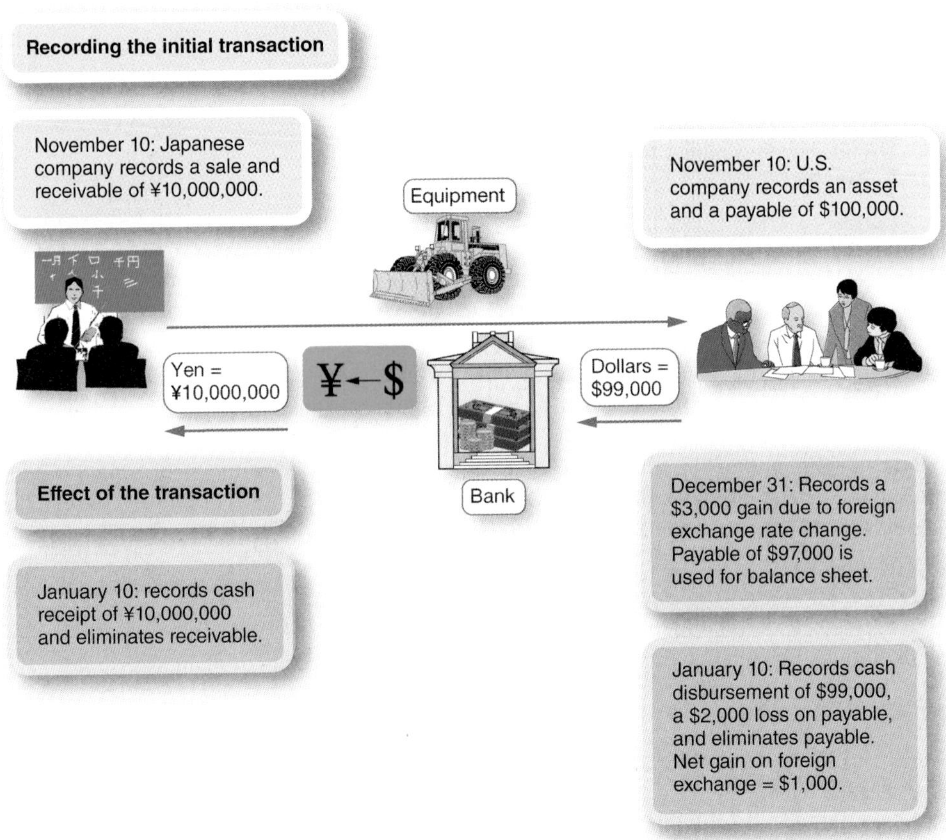
Recording the initial transaction
November 10: Japanese company records a sale and receivable of ¥10,000,000.
Equipment
November 10: U.S. company records an asset and a payable of \$100,000.
Yen = ¥10,000,000
¥←\$
Dollars = \$99,000
Bank
Effect of the transaction
December 31: Records a \$3,000 gain due to foreign exchange rate change. Payable of \$97,000 is used for balance sheet.
January 10: records cash receipt of ¥10,000,000 and eliminates receivable.
January 10: Records cash disbursement of \$99,000, a \$2,000 loss on payable, and eliminates payable. Net gain on foreign exchange = \$1,000.

Now assume that on December 31, the exchange rate has fallen to \$0.0097 per yen. At this exchange rate, the U.S. company's account payable is equivalent to only \$97,000 (¥10,000,000 × \$0.0097). Gains and losses from changes in exchange rates are recognized in the period *in which the change occurs.* Therefore, the American company should make an adjusting entry to restate its liability at the current dollar-equivalent and to recognize any related gain or loss. This entry, dated December 31, would be:

Accounts Payable	3,000	
Gain on Fluctuations in Foreign Exchange Rates		3,000
To adjust balance of ¥10,000,000 account payable to amount indicated by year-end exchange rate:		
Original account balance	\$100,000	
Adjusted balance (¥10,000,000 × \$0.0097)	97,000	
Required adjustment	\$ 3,000	

The foreign exchange rate gain on accounts payable is included in year-end statements

Similar adjustments should be made for any other accounts payable or receivable at year-end that are fixed in terms of a foreign currency.

If the exchange rate changes again between the date of this adjusting entry and the date that the U.S. company pays the liability, an additional gain or loss must be recognized. Assume, for example, that on January 10 the exchange rate has risen to $0.0099 per yen. As shown in Exhibit 15–8, the U.S. company must now spend $99,000 to buy the ¥10,000,000 needed to pay its liability to the Japanese company. Thus, the rise in the exchange rate has caused the U.S. company a $2,000 loss since year-end. The entry to record payment of the account on January 10 would be:

Accounts Payable.	97,000	
Loss on Fluctuations in Foreign Exchange Rates	2,000	
Cash		99,000
To record payment of ¥10,000,000 payable to Japanese company and to recognize loss from rise in exchange rate since year-end:		
Account payable, December 31	$97,000	
Amount paid, January 10	99,000	
Loss from increase in exchange rate	$ 2,000	

Notice the *overall effect* of entering into this credit transaction stated in yen was a $1,000 gain due to fluctuations in the exchange rate for the yen between November 10 and the date of payment (January 10). The U.S. company recognized a $3,000 gain on fluctuations in the exchange rate from November 10 through the balance sheet date (December 31). This was partially offset in the next fiscal year by a $2,000 loss on fluctuations in the exchange rate between December 31 and January 10. The overall effect can be computed directly by multiplying the amount of the foreign currency times the *change* in exchange rates between the transaction date and the payment date (¥10,000,000 × [$0.0100 − $0.0099] = $1,000 gain). The $3,000 gain recorded at the balance sheet date and the $2,000 loss recorded at the date of payment have no associated cash flow effects.

Gains and losses from fluctuations in exchange rates on transactions carried out in a foreign currency should be included in the income statement. They typically are presented in a manner much like interest expense and gains and losses on the sale of plant assets.

CURRENCY FLUCTUATIONS—WHO WINS AND WHO LOSES?

Gains and losses from fluctuations in exchange rates are sustained by companies (or individuals) that have either payables or receivables that are *fixed in terms of a foreign currency.* United States companies that import foreign products usually have large foreign liabilities. Companies that export U.S. products to other countries are likely to have large receivables stated in foreign currencies.

As foreign exchange rates (stated in dollars) *fall,* U.S.-based importers will gain and exporters will lose. When a foreign exchange rate falls, the foreign currency becomes *less expensive.* Therefore, importers will have to spend fewer dollars to pay their foreign liabilities. Exporters, on the other hand, will have to watch their foreign receivables become worth fewer and fewer dollars.

When foreign exchange rates *rise,* this situation reverses. Importers will lose, because more dollars are required to pay the foreign debts. Exporters will gain, because their foreign receivables become equivalent to an increasing number of dollars.

Strategies to Avoid Losses from Rate Fluctuations There are two basic approaches to avoiding losses from fluctuations in foreign exchange rates. One approach is to insist that receivables and payables be settled at specified amounts of domestic currency. The other approach is called *hedging* and can be accomplished in a number of ways.

To illustrate the first approach, assume that a U.S. company makes large credit sales to companies in Mexico, but anticipates that the exchange rate for the Mexican peso will gradually decline. The U.S. company can avoid losses by setting its *sales prices in dollars.* Then, if the exchange rate does decline, the Mexican companies will have to spend more pesos to pay for their purchases, but the U.S. company will not receive fewer dollars. On the other hand, the U.S. company will benefit from making credit *purchases* from Mexican companies at *prices stated in pesos,* because a decline in the exchange rate will reduce the number of dollars needed to pay for these purchases.

The interests of the Mexican companies, however, are exactly the opposite of those of the U.S. company. If the Mexican companies anticipate an increase in the exchange rate for the U.S. dollar, they will want to buy at prices stated in pesos and sell at prices stated in dollars. Ultimately, the manner in which the transactions will be priced simply depends on which company is in the better bargaining position.

Learning Objective
Describe techniques for "hedging" against losses from fluctuations in exchange rates. LO6

Hedging

Hedging refers to the strategy of "sitting on both sides of the fence"—that is, of taking offsetting positions so that your gains and losses tend to offset one another. To illustrate the concept, assume that you make a large bet on a football game. Later you have second thoughts about the bet, and you want to eliminate your risk of incurring a loss. You could "hedge" your original bet by making a similar bet on the other team. In this way, you will lose one bet, but you will win the other—your loss will be offset by a corresponding gain.

A company that has similar amounts of accounts receivable and accounts payable in the same foreign currency automatically has a hedged position. A decrease in the foreign exchange rate will cause losses on the foreign receivables and gains on the foreign payables. If the exchange rate rises, the gains on the foreign receivables will be offset by losses on the foreign payables.

Most companies, of course, do *not* have similar amounts of receivables and payables in the same foreign currency. However, they may create this situation by buying or selling foreign currency **future contracts.** These contracts, commonly called *futures,* are the right to receive a specified quantity of foreign currency at a future date. In short, they are accounts receivable in foreign currency. Thus, for example, a company that has only foreign accounts payable may hedge its position by purchasing a similar dollar amount of foreign currency future contracts. Then, if the exchange rate rises, any losses on the foreign payables will be offset by a gain in the value of the future contracts.

Exchange Rates and Competitive Prices

Up to this point, we have discussed only the gains and losses incurred by companies that have receivables or payables stated in a foreign currency. However, fluctuations in exchange rates change the *relative prices* of goods produced in different countries. Exchange rate fluctuations may make the prices of a country's products more or less competitive both at home and to customers throughout the world. Even a small store with no foreign accounts receivable or payable may find its business operations greatly affected by fluctuations in foreign exchange rates.

Consider, for example, a small store in Kansas that sells a U.S.-made brand of television sets. If foreign exchange rates fall, which happens when the dollar is strong, the price of foreign-made television sets will decline. Thus, the store selling U.S.-made television sets may have to compete with stores selling imported television sets at lower prices. Also, a strong dollar makes U.S. goods *more expensive to customers in foreign countries.* Thus, a U.S. television manufacturer will find it more difficult to sell its products abroad.

The situation reverses when the dollar is weak—that is, when foreign exchange rates are relatively high. A weak dollar makes foreign imports more expensive to U.S. consumers. Also, a weak dollar makes U.S. products less expensive to customers in foreign countries.

YOUR TURN **You as a Consumer**

Assume you are in the market for a new racing bicycle. You are considering buying an Italian, British, or U.S. racing bicycle. You have recently heard that the dollar is strengthening against the euro and is falling against the British pound. These trends are expected to continue for another month. How would this news affect your assessment of choices among racing bicycles?

(See our comments on the Online Learning Center Web site.)

In summary, we may say that a strong U.S. dollar *helps companies that sell foreign-made goods in the U.S. market.* A weak dollar, on the other hand, *gives a competitive advantage to companies that sell U.S. products both at home and abroad.*

CONSOLIDATED FINANCIAL STATEMENTS THAT INCLUDE FOREIGN SUBSIDIARIES

In Chapter 14, we discussed the concept of *consolidated* financial statements. These statements view the operations of the parent company and its subsidiaries as if the affiliated companies were a single business entity. Several special accounting problems arise in preparing consolidated financial statements when subsidiaries operate in foreign countries. First, the accounting records of the foreign subsidiaries must be translated into U.S. dollars. Second, the accounting principles in use in the foreign countries may differ significantly from U.S. generally accepted accounting principles.

These problems pose interesting challenges to professional accountants and will be addressed in later accounting courses. Readers of the financial statements of U.S.-based corporations, however, should know that the consolidated financial statements of these companies are expressed in U.S. dollars and conform to U.S. generally accepted accounting principles.

Global Sourcing

Learning Objective
LO7 Discuss how global sourcing increases product cost complexity.

Differences in exchange rates can create significant complexities for firms practicing global sourcing. An article in the *Los Angeles Times* illustrated the additional problems associated with determining the cost of producing a doll using inputs from several countries. Exhibit 15–9

Exhibit 15–9
GLOBAL SOURCING FOR MATTEL INC.'S BARBIE™ DOLL

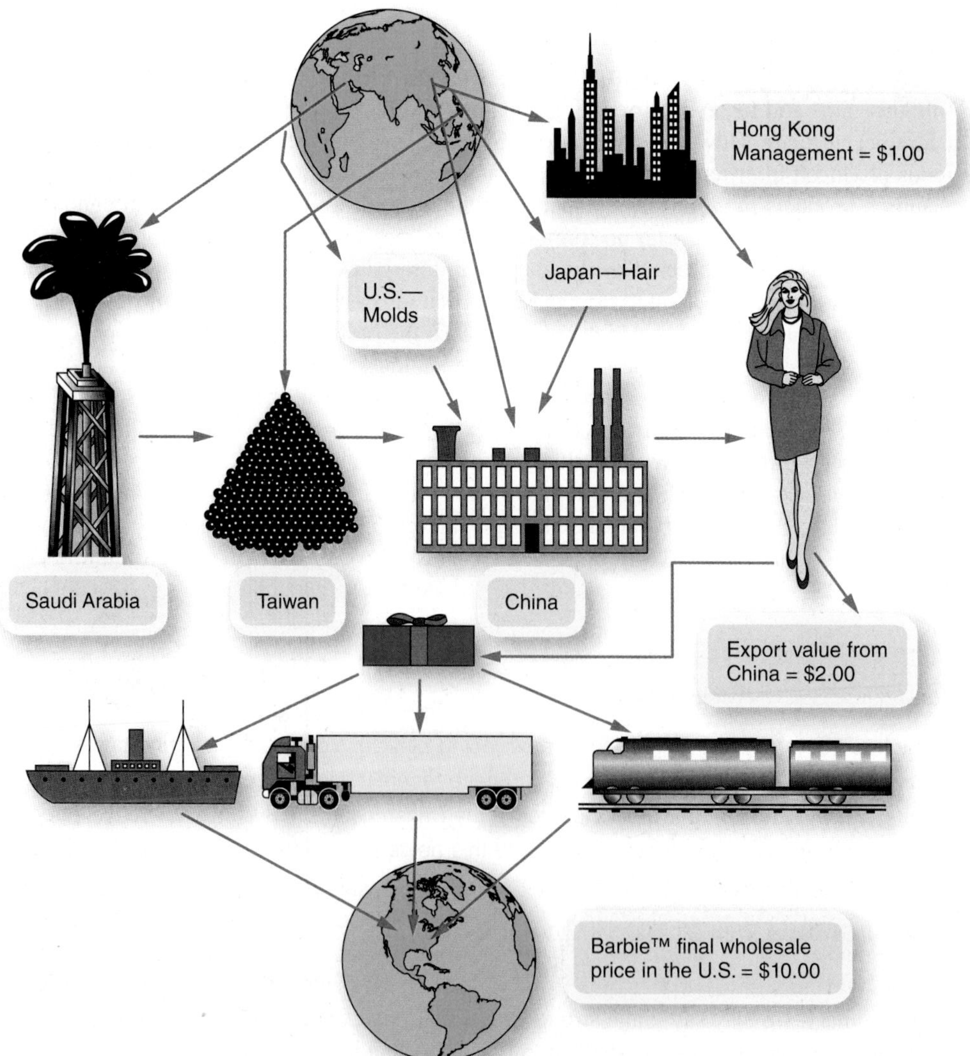

traces the multicountry path of a Barbie™ doll from its raw materials source in a Saudi Arabian oil field to U.S. toy stores. After the oil is refined to produce ethylene, Taiwan uses the ethylene to produce vinyl pellets that are shipped to Dongguan in China's Guangdong province. At the Chinese joint-venture factory, 5,500 workers, paid between $30 and $40 per month, make the plastic doll and her clothes. However, most of the machinery and tools, including the plastic mold injection machines, are imported from the United States, Europe, and Japan. The molds themselves come directly from the United States. Japan contributes Barbie's nylon hair. Hong Kong manages the entire process, arranging banking and insurance, supervising exporting and importing, and overseeing transportation back to the United States. Finally, U.S. domestic packaging, trucking, advertising, and other functions that employ thousands of U.S. workers result in a $10.00 Barbie™ wholesale price. **Mattel Inc.** has indicated that its typical profit from the sale of a Barbie™ is about $1.00.

Exhibit 15–10 illustrates the costs and exchange rate issues involved in the production of a Barbie™ doll. Panel A provides the currency exchange rates for the countries involved in global sourcing for the Barbie™ doll. Panel B includes estimated product export costs for the **Mattel Inc.** Barbie™ made at the Meitai factory in Dongguan, China. The estimated costs in the exhibit are based on a single day's reported exchange rates. Companies must choose a representative exchange rate to compute the cost buildup in their domestic currency.

Exhibit 15–10

EXCHANGE RATES AND ESTIMATED PRODUCT COST FOR BARBIE™ DOLLS

Estimated Product Cost for Barbie™*

Panel A: Exchange Rates†

Country	Currency	U.S. $ Equivalent
Saudi Arabia	Riyal	.2667
Taiwan	Taiwanese dollar	.0326
Hong Kong	Hong Kong dollar	.1286
Japan	Yen	.0095
China	Yuan	.1225

Panel B: Estimated Product Cost Buildup

Input	Foreign Currency Value	U.S. $ Equivalent
Raw materials:		
Saudi Arabia	0.6374 riyal	$0.17
Taiwan	4.908 Taiwanese dollars	0.16
Japan	22.11 yen	0.21
China	0.898 yuan	0.11
Direct labor:		
China	2.857 yuan	0.35
Overhead:		
Hong Kong	7.776 Hong Kong dollars	1.00
Total export cost		$2.00

*Estimates based on information provided in R. Tempest, "Barbie and the World Economy," *Los Angeles Times*, September 22, 1999, p. 1.

†Based on exchange rates from www.xe.com/ucc.

The information in the exhibit does not provide details about customs duties, import and export fees, multicountry tax laws, and tax treaties. These are also costs of doing business in a global environment. Many companies underestimate the cost of globalizing their business operations because they are not familiar with the environmental characteristics discussed at the beginning of this chapter. Making accurate estimates of costs for global sourcing is a challenge for companies wishing to become more global.

FOREIGN CORRUPT PRACTICES ACT

In many countries, product costs also include expenses incurred to expedite official paperwork. Kenyan business executives refer to *kitu kidogo* ("something small"), the Chinese pay *huilu,* Russians shell out *vzyatka,* and Middle Easterners pay *baksheesh.* In dozens of countries around the world, bribery is part of doing business. In many countries, this officially sanctioned corruption is not viewed as wrong or unethical. However, U.S.-based businesses are prohibited from influence peddling. The **Foreign Corrupt Practices Act** (FCPA), passed in 1977 and amended in 1986 and 1998 by the U.S. Congress, prescribes fines and jail time for managers violating its rules. For over 20 years, U.S. companies have complained about the advantage experienced by international competitors who are not bound by the FCPA.

Experiences in the past 5 to 10 years have changed international attitudes about the impact of corrupt practices on economic viability. In particular, the 1997–1998 Asian crisis was blamed partly on graft and influence peddling. According to some estimates, corruption associated with doing business in China can add 5 percent to operating costs. Corruption can be so rampant that companies refuse to operate in some foreign locations, causing countries to lose valuable direct foreign investment.

The International Monetary Fund and the World Bank instituted policies in the late 1990s to cut off funding to countries ignoring corrupt practices. In 1997, $292 million in loans to Kenya were suspended until policies and procedures to prevent corruption were instituted. Many of the recommended policies and procedures are modeled after the FCPA. The scope of the FCPA is very broad. Under FCPA rules, it is illegal for all U.S. companies and foreign companies operating in the United States, their affiliates, and their agents to bribe a government official. Criminal and civil prosecution can lead to fines of up to $2 million for the company and $100,000 for executives involved, with prison terms of up to five years.

YOUR TURN | **You as a Head of International Acquisitions**

Assume you are the head of international acquisitions for a large multinational toy company traded on the New York Stock Exchange. You have been involved for several months in a deal to acquire a large facility in a midsize city in central China. This building will be remodeled by your company to produce a range of toy products for the Chinese market. For a variety of reasons, progress has been extremely slow on completing the acquisition. In particular, city administrators have continually delayed issuing the necessary paperwork. You decide to fly to China to meet with the city's top three officials. During your meeting it becomes clear that the three city officials would guarantee processing the associated paperwork much faster if your company would provide a significant payment to each of them to help expedite the necessary work. These administrators point out that a German company that acquired a facility in the city the previous year was willing to pay extra to expedite paperwork.

Your CEO has made it clear to you that the China project is very important and expediting it is critical for its long-run success. What should you do?

(See our comments on the Online Learning Center Web site.)

Learning Objective
LO8 Explain the importance of the Foreign Corrupt Practices Act.

The FCPA has implications for accounting in two specific areas: record keeping and internal control procedures. The act requires that all payments, including improper payments, be recorded and disclosed. Further, the act requires an adequate system of internal controls that maintains the integrity of the company's assets, allowing only authorized personnel to have access to them. The 1986 amendment to the FCPA distinguished between *influence peddling,* to

Ethics, Fraud & Corporate Governance

The Foreign Corrupt Practices Act (FCPA) applies to U.S. companies and foreign companies operating in the U.S., their affiliates, and their agents. Violations of the FCPA expose companies and individuals to both civil and criminal liability. For example, the Securities and Exchange Commission (SEC) brought an enforcement action against **InVision Technologies, Inc. (InVision)**, alleging that **InVision** violated the FCPA. The SEC alleged that **InVision** authorized improper payments to government officials in China, Thailand, and the Philippines in connection with sales activities.

InVision's sales agent in China provided $95,000 of foreign travel and other benefits to airport officials in Guangzhou. The sales agent notified **InVision**'s regional sales manager, who notified the senior sales executive of these payments. These payments were improperly recorded by **InVision** as cost of goods sold.

InVision paid its sales agent in the Philippines $108,000 to be used to make gifts and pay cash to government officials in order to generate sales. **InVision** improperly recorded this payment as a sales commission.

InVision violated the following provisions of the FCPA: (1) illegal offers and payments, (2) books and records (e.g., improperly recording gifts and other payments as cost of goods sold or sales commissions), and (3) internal controls. **InVision** agreed to disgorge $589,000 in profits from sales where the FCPA was violated, pay $28,700 in prejudgment interest, and pay a $500,000 civil penalty. In addition, **InVision** agreed to retain an independent consultant to develop a corporate compliance program designed to prevent and detect future violations of the FCPA.

motivate the awarding of business that would not otherwise have been awarded, and *facilitating payments,* to motivate officials to undertake actions more rapidly than they might otherwise. A facilitating payment might be given to a customs official to expedite imported merchandise through customs. This latter type of payment is not illegal under the act. Companies engaging in globalization must ensure that their cross-border employees comply with the FCPA.

Concluding Remarks

In this chapter we have established a framework to help you understand international financial reporting issues. You have learned how global environmental differences create demand for different types of financial information. However, other global forces, particularly global securities markets and large international firms, are pushing for a uniform set of international accounting standards for financial reporting. What does the development of international accounting standards foreshadow? We believe that significant progress toward harmonization is occurring. However, users of international financial statements should expect wide variation in disclosure levels and financial reporting practices for several years to come.

END-OF-CHAPTER REVIEW

SUMMARY OF LEARNING OBJECTIVES

LO1 Define four mechanisms companies use to globalize their business activities. Companies globalize their business activities through exporting, licensing, joint ventures, and wholly owned subsidiaries. Multinational companies use a global sourcing approach.

LO2 Identify how global environmental forces—(a) political and legal systems, (b) economic systems, (c) culture, and (d) technology and infrastructure—affect accounting practices. Countries use their political and legal systems to transfer and control business assets. Market versus centrally planned economic systems create different demands for financial reporting. Culture influences business relationships through beliefs and expectations of customers and business associates. The technology and infrastructure of each global location will affect the type and costs of business activities and related financial accounting reports.

LO3 Explain why there is demand for harmonization of global financial reporting standards. Cross-border differences in accounting and reporting create analysis and comparability problems between and among companies. The need for comparable information has led to the demand for harmonization.

LO4 Demonstrate how to convert an amount of money from one currency to another. To convert a foreign currency to an equivalent dollar amount, multiply the foreign currency by the foreign exchange rate. To convert a dollar amount into an equivalent amount of foreign currency, divide the dollar amount by the exchange rate.

LO5 Compute gains or losses on receivables or payables that are stated in a foreign currency when exchange rates fluctuate. The receivable or payable is recorded on the date the transaction is agreed to using the prevailing exchange rate. When exchanging cash completes the transaction, the exchange rate at the completion date is used to record the cash flow; the difference between the cash exchanged and the receivable or payable is recorded as a foreign exchange gain or loss.

LO6 Describe techniques for "hedging" against losses from fluctuations in exchange rates. Hedging is offsetting the potential for losses from foreign exchange rate fluctuations. It can be accomplished by having offsetting receivables and payables in the foreign currency or by buying or selling foreign currency future contracts.

LO7 Discuss how global sourcing increases product cost complexity. When some of the activities of designing, developing, producing, marketing, and servicing a product or service occur in more than one country, then global considerations affect product costs. These considerations include foreign exchange gains and losses, taxes, import and export duties, trade agreements, foreign trade zones, and limitations on currency flows.

LO8 Explain the importance of the Foreign Corrupt Practices Act. The FCPA prohibits influence peddling through bribery in international locations. The act requires companies engaged in global business activities to maintain good record keeping and adequate internal controls to safeguard company assets.

Key Terms Introduced or Emphasized in Chapter 15

adoption of IFRS (p. 689) Means abandoning the country's financial reporting standards and replacing them with *International Financial Reporting Standards* (IFRS).

convergence with IFRS (p. 690) A process by which a country's financial reporting standards are changed so that the use of their country GAAP standards will produce IFRS "equivalent" financial reports.

cross-border financing (p. 689) Occurs when a company sells its securities in the capital markets of another country.

exchange rate (p. 691) The amount it costs to purchase one unit of currency with another currency.

exporting (p. 685) Selling a good or service to a foreign customer in a foreign country.

Foreign Corrupt Practices Act (p. 700) Passed in 1977 and amended in 1986 and 1998 by the U.S. Congress, prescribes fines and jail time for managers violating its rules. It distinguishes between illegal influence peddling to motivate awarding of business that would not otherwise have been awarded and legal facilitating payments made to motivate officials to undertake actions more rapidly than they might otherwise.

foreign trade zones (p. 686) Goods imported into these designated U.S. areas are duty free until they leave the zone.

future contracts (p. 697) A contract giving the right to receive a specified quantity of foreign currency at a future date.

global sourcing (p. 685) The close coordination of R&D, manufacturing, and marketing across national boundaries.

globalization (p. 684) Occurs as managers become aware of and engage in cross-border trade and operations.

harmonization of accounting standards (p. 689) The globalization of similar accounting methods and principles used throughout the world.

hedging (p. 697) The practice of minimizing or eliminating risk of loss associated with foreign currency fluctuations.

industrial organizations (p. 687) Exist when companies group themselves into conglomerates representing different industries. South Korean conglomerates, called *chaebol,* and Japanese conglomerates, called *keiretsu,* consist of companies that are grouped as customers and suppliers and usually contain a bank.

infrastructure (p. 689) Access to communication, transportation, and utilities provided to businesses in each global location.

International Accounting Standards Board (IASB) (p. 689) Charged with the responsibility of creating and promulgating international standards.

international joint venture (p. 685) A company owned by two or more companies from different countries.

international licensing (p. 685) A contractual agreement between a company and a foreign party allowing the use of trademarks, patents, technology, designs, processes, intellectual property, or other proprietary advantage.

market economy (p. 687) Exists when ownership of land and the means of production are private and markets dictate the allocation of resources and the output among segments of the economy.

planned economy (p. 687) Exists when the government uses central planning to allocate resources and determine output among various segments of the economy. Government ownership of land and the means of production characterize planned economies.

wholly owned international subsidiary (p. 685) Created through a company's foreign direct investment; involves using domestically generated funds in another country to purchase 100 percent equity control of a foreign subsidiary.

Demonstration Problem

IronMan, Inc., is a U.S. company that manufactures exercise machines and distributes several lines of imported bicycles. Selected transactions of the company were as follows:

Oct. 4 Purchased manufacturing equipment from Rhine Mfg. Co., a German company. The purchase price was €400,000, due in 60 days. Current exchange rate, $0.7020 per euro. (Debit the Equipment account.)

Oct. 18 Purchased 2,500 racing bicycles from Ninja Cycles, a Japanese company, at a price of ¥60,000,000. Payment is due in 90 days; the current exchange rate is $0.0110 per yen. (IronMan uses the perpetual inventory system.)

Nov. 15 Purchased 1,000 touring bicycles from Royal Lion Ltd., a British corporation. The purchase price was £192,500, payable in 30 days. Current exchange rate, $1.65 per British pound.

Dec. 3 Issued a check to First Bank for the U.S. dollar-equivalent of €400,000 in payment of the account payable to Rhine Mfg. Co. Current exchange rate, $0.7110 per euro.

Dec. 15 Issued a check to First Bank for dollar-equivalent of £192,500 in payment of the account payable to Royal Lion Ltd. Current exchange rate, $1.60 per British pound.

Instructions

a. Prepare entries in general journal form to record the preceding transactions.

b. Prepare the December 31 adjusting entry relating to the account payable to Ninja Cycles. The year-end exchange rate is $0.0113 per Japanese yen.

c. Identify some methods that IronMan, Inc., could use to decrease its exposure to foreign exchange rate fluctuations.

d. Discuss environmental characteristics of Japan, Germany, and the United Kingdom that influence their exchange rate fluctuations.

Solution to the Demonstration Problem

a. The general journal entries to record the transactions are as follows:

GENERAL JOURNAL

Date	Account Titles and Explanation	Debit	Credit
Oct. 4	Equipment	280,800	
	Accounts Payable (Rhine Mfg. Co.)		280,800
	To record purchase of equipment from Rhine Mfg. Co. for €400,000, exchange rate $0.7020 per euro (€400,000 × $0.7020 = $280,800).		
Oct. 18	Inventory	660,000	
	Accounts Payable (Ninja Cycles)		660,000
	Purchased 2,500 bicycles from Ninja Cycles for ¥60,000,000, exchange rate $0.0110 (¥60,000,000 × $0.0110 = $660,000).		
Nov. 15	Inventory	317,625	
	Accounts Payable (Royal Lion Ltd.)		317,625
	Purchased 1,000 bicycles from Royal Lion Ltd. for £192,500, due in 30 days. Exchange rate $1.65 per pound (£192,500 × $1.65 = $317,625).		
Dec. 3	Accounts Payable (Rhine Mfg. Co.)	280,800	
	Loss on Fluctuations of Foreign Exchange Rates	3,600	
	Cash		284,400
	Paid €400,000 liability to Rhine Mfg. Co. (Original balance less amount paid equals loss: $280,800 − (€400,000 × $0.7110) = −$3,600).		
Dec. 15	Accounts Payable (Royal Lion Ltd.)	317,625	
	Gain on Fluctuations of Foreign Exchange Rates		9,625
	Cash		308,000
	Paid £192,500 liability to Royal Lion Ltd. (Original balance less amount paid equals gain: $317,625 − (£192,500 × $1.60) = $9,625).		

b. The December 31 adjusting entry for the account payable to Ninja Cycles:

GENERAL JOURNAL

Date	Account Titles and Explanation	Debit	Credit
Dec. 31	Loss on Fluctuations in Foreign Exchange Rates	18,000	
	Accounts Payable (Ninja Cycles)		18,000
	To adjust balance of ¥60,000,000 liability to amount indicated by year-end exchange rate: (Original balance less adjusted balance equals loss: $660,000 − (¥60,000,000 × $0.0113) = −$18,000).		

c. IronMan could use offsetting payables and receivables to control potential foreign exchange rate losses. For example, if IronMan could export its exercise equipment to Japan, then it would have a receivable to offset its payable. IronMan could also purchase future contracts maturing at the same time the liabilities were due. Gains and losses on the future contracts would offset gains and losses resulting from foreign currency fluctuations.

d. Germany has a lower volume and smaller capitalized equities market. Germany uses the euro and is part of the European Union. Banks are a major provider of capital to businesses in Germany. Japan has *keiretsu* organizations for many of its industrial groups. These organizations include manufacturers, distributors, wholesalers, retailers, and suppliers who work together and share resources. The accounting profession is much weaker in both Germany and Japan than in the United States. The United Kingdom is most like the United States, with active equity markets, a strong accounting profession, and similar accounting rules.

Self-Test Questions

The answers to these questions appear on page 719.

1. Which of the following statements are *true* about globalization methods?

- **a.** International licensing involves the creation of a new company that is owned by two or more firms from different countries.
- **b.** Exporting involves contracts that allow a foreign company to use a domestic company's trademarks, patents, processes, or technology.
- **c.** Global sourcing involves the close coordination of research and development, purchasing, marketing, and manufacturing across national boundaries.
- **d.** A wholly owned international subsidiary is created when a foreign government owns 100 percent of the equity in a U.S.-based firm.

2. Which of the following environmental factors can affect the cost of doing business in a foreign country? (Identify all correct answers.)

- **a.** The educational level of the workforce.
- **b.** Laws regulating the transfer of profits out of a country.
- **c.** Tax and tariff regulations.
- **d.** Restricted access to communication and transportation networks.

3. A country whose citizens are highly group oriented and who accept unequal power distributions between and within organizations would be considered:

- **a.** Individualistic and low power distance.
- **b.** Collectivist and high power distance.
- **c.** Individualistic and high power distance.
- **d.** Collectivist and low power distance.

4. On March 1, Laton Products (a U.S. firm) purchased manufacturing inputs from a Mexican supplier for 20,000 pesos, payable on June 1. The exchange rate for pesos on March 1 was $0.17. If the exchange rate increases to $0.19 on June 1, what amount of gain or loss would be reported by Laton related to the currency exchange?

- **a.** $400 gain.
- **b.** $200 loss.
- **c.** $400 loss.
- **d.** $200 gain.

5. On January 1, a German company purchased merchandise from a U.S. firm for $50,000, payable on March 1. The exchange rate for the euro on January 1 was $1.10. If the exchange rate increases to $1.12 on March 1, what amount of gain or loss would the U.S. firm report related to currency fluctuations?

- **a.** $1,000 gain.
- **b.** $1,000 loss.
- **c.** $500 gain.
- **d.** No gain or loss would be reported.

ASSIGNMENT MATERIAL

Discussion Questions

1. In general terms, identify several factors that prompt different countries to develop different accounting principles.

2. What is the International Accounting Standards Board? Why has the board been unable to obtain uniform global application of its standards?

3. An American company is considering entering into a joint venture with a Japanese firm. Describe what cultural differences each party should consider.

4. Consider Exhibit 15–4. Explain the cultural differences between the United States and Brazil.

5. Why is it important to understand the economic system under which a company operates *before* entering into a business relationship?

6. Provide an example showing how the following environmental forces affect accounting practices:

- **a.** Political and legal systems
- **b.** Economic systems
- **c.** Culture
- **d.** Technology and infrastructure

7. Discuss two ways in which the Foreign Corrupt Practices Act has affected U.S. companies.

8. Explain two ways in which a company that makes purchases on account from foreign companies can protect itself against the losses that would arise from a sudden increase in the foreign exchange rate.

9. What does the *globalization* of business mean? Think of two companies with which you are familiar. How would you describe their level of globalization?

10. You've just read in *The Wall Street Journal* that the U.S. dollar has weakened relative to the euro. All else equal, what would you expect to happen to the quantity of Italian leather jackets sold in the United States? Why?

11. What is the difference between an international licensing agreement and an international joint venture?

12. To maintain a high level of control over production operations and final product quality, what types of globalization activities could a company engage in?
13. How might the required financial reports differ between countries that are individualistic and countries that are collectivist?
14. A French furniture maker agrees to purchase wood stain from a U.S. paint manufacturer. If all payments are to be made in U.S. dollars, which company bears the risk of exchange rate gains and losses?
15. What is meant by the phrase *natural hedging against exchange rate risk*?

Brief Exercises

LO4

BRIEF EXERCISE 15.1

Foreign Currency Translations

Translate the following amounts of foreign currency into an equivalent number of U.S. dollars using the exchange rates in Exhibit 15.7.

a. £800,000

b. ¥350,000

c. €50,000

LO4 LO5

BRIEF EXERCISE 15.2

Purchases in a Foreign Currency

Assume that a U.S. company makes a purchase from a British company and agrees to pay a price of £2 million.

a. How will the U.S. company determine the cost of this purchase for the purpose of recording it in its accounting records?

b. Briefly explain how the U.S. company can arrange for the payment of pounds to the British company.

LO4

BRIEF EXERCISE 15.3

Currency Strength

A recent newspaper shows the exchange rate for the British pound at $1.44 and the yen at $0.0108. Does this indicate that the pound is stronger than the yen? Explain.

LO5

BRIEF EXERCISE 15.4

Exchange Rate Fluctuations

Explain how an increase in a foreign exchange rate will affect a U.S. company that makes:

a. Credit sales to a foreign company at prices stated in the foreign currency.

b. Credit purchases from a foreign company at prices stated in the foreign currency.

c. Credit sales to a foreign company at prices stated in U.S. dollars.

LO5 LO6

BRIEF EXERCISE 15.5

Currency Choice

You are the purchasing agent for a U.S. business that purchases merchandise on account from companies in Mexico. The exchange rate for the Mexican peso has been falling against the U.S. dollar and the trend is expected to continue for at least several months. Would you prefer that the prices for purchases from the Mexican companies be specified in U.S. dollars or in Mexican pesos? Explain.

LO4

BRIEF EXERCISE 15.6

Currency Strength and Gains and Losses

CompuTech is a U.S.-based multinational corporation. Foreign sales are made at prices set in U.S. dollars, but foreign purchases are often made at prices stated in foreign currencies. If the exchange rate for the U.S. dollar has risen against most foreign currencies throughout the year, would **CompuTech** have recognized primarily gains or losses as a result of exchange rate fluctuations? Explain.

LO2

BRIEF EXERCISE 15.7

Culture Effects on Business

When business transactions are conducted internationally, cultural differences must be taken into consideration. Geert Hofstede is a leading researcher on how cultural variables can affect such international arrangements. Hofstede has a Web site where he is quoted as saying:

> For those who work in international business, it is sometimes amazing how different people in other cultures behave. We tend to have a human instinct that "deep inside" all people are the same—but they are not. Therefore, if we go into another country and make decisions based on how we operate in our own home country—the chances are we'll make some very bad decisions.

Go to Hofstede's Web site (http://www.geert-hofstede.com) and find an example of how business dealings can be hindered by a lack of understanding of cultural differences.

LO5 LO6 **BRIEF EXERCISE 15.8**
Currency Fluctuation Effects

Bell Corporation has a receivable denominated in British pounds and a payable in Mexican pesos resulting from imports from Mexico. Bell recorded foreign exchange gains related to both its pound-related receivable and its peso-denominated payable. Did the foreign currencies increase or decrease in dollar value from the date of the transaction to the settlement date?

LO8 **BRIEF EXERCISE 15.9**
Foreign Corrupt Practices Act

In 1995, **Lockheed** was prosecuted by the U.S. government for allegedly paying $1 million to a member of the Egyptian parliament in order to sell its military jets to Egypt's armed forces. The company paid a $24.5 million fine and a vice president was fined $125,000 and sentenced to 18 months in prison. What U.S. law was violated and why?

LO4 **BRIEF EXERCISE 15.10**
Exchange Rate Computation

A U.S. company purchased a shipment of fabrics from Bahrain for 3,500,000 dinars. According to the current exchange rate, what is the value of this contract in U.S. dollars?

Exercises

LO1 through LO8 **EXERCISE 15.1**
Global Business Terminology

The following are nine global business terms used in this chapter:

Hedging	Foreign exchange risk	International Accounting Standards Board
Foreign Corrupt Practices Act	Planned economy	Harmonization
Globalization	International licensing	Exporting

Each of the following statements may describe one of these terms. For each statement, indicate the global business term described, or answer "None" if the statement does not correctly describe any of the terms.

a. The amount it costs to purchase one unit of currency with another currency.

b. Selling a good or service to a foreign customer.

c. A cross-border contractual agreement allowing one company to use the trademarks, patents, or technology of another company.

d. Distinguishes between illegal influence peddling and legal facilitating payments.

e. The practice of minimizing or eliminating risk of loss associated with foreign currency fluctuations.

f. Markets dictate the allocation of resources and output among segments of the economy.

g. The group charged with the responsibility of creating and encouraging the use of international financial reporting standards.

LO1 LO2 **EXERCISE 15.2**
External Financial Reports and Globalization

With a group of two or three students, choose a publicly traded global company that you think you might want to invest in some time in the future. Use the Internet or annual report data to answer the following questions.

a. In which geographical regions does the company operate?

b. What is the proportion of total sales represented by foreign sales? How has this changed over the past five years?

c. What efforts has the company recently undertaken to increase/decrease globalization (for example, joint ventures, licensing agreements, etc.)?

d. What are the company's hedging practices/policies?

e. Have any overseas activities been unsuccessful, discontinued, or resulted in asset losses? If so, what happened?

f. Overall, how aggressively do you feel this company is pursuing globalization?

LO4

EXERCISE 15.3

Understanding Exchange Rate Conversions

For each of the following scenarios, use the current exchange rates in *The Wall Street Journal* or from an Internet site such as www.xe.com/ucc to compute the required amount:

a. A Citroën automobile is advertised in France for 15,000 euros. What is the dollar equivalent of 15,000 euros?

b. Jackk's food emporium is importing foreign hot sauce from Brazil for 7,000 reals. What is the dollar equivalent?

c. You are traveling on safari in South Africa and have brought $3,000 in spending money. How many South African rand will you receive for spending money?

d. While traveling in Europe, you cross the border between Germany and Switzerland. You have 150 euros left from your German travels when you spot a souvenir in a Swiss shop for 250 Swiss francs. Do you have enough spending money to buy the souvenir if you convert your euros to Swiss francs?

LO2 LO7 LO8

EXERCISE 15.4

Location International Business Information

The State Department of the U.S. government maintains an Internet site containing information on various countries (www.state.gov). The site includes a database under the countries and regions tab. Use the data or other publicly available data to answer the following questions about Indonesia.

a. What are the country's main exports and imports?

b. What is the educational and job classification composition of the labor force?

c. How would you describe the infrastructure and technology base of the country?

d. What are the political and legal risks of doing business there?

e. If you were advising a U.S. company that wanted to locate a wholly owned subsidiary in Indonesia, what aspects of the country would you stress that management take into account when deciding whether to invest there and how to organize the subsidiary's manufacturing process?

LO2 LO5

EXERCISE 15.5

Currency Fluctuations: Who Wins and Who Loses?

Indicate whether each of the companies or individuals in the following independent cases would benefit more from a strong U.S. dollar (relatively low foreign exchange rates) or a weak U.S. dollar (relatively high foreign exchange rates). Provide a brief explanation of your reasoning.

a. **Boeing** (a U.S. aircraft manufacturer that sells many planes to foreign customers).

b. A **Nikon** camera store in Beverly Hills, California (Nikon cameras are made in Japan).

c. **Citroën** (made by **Peugot**, an auto manufacturer in France).

d. The Mexico City dealer for **Caterpillar** tractors (made in the United States).

e. A U.S. tourist visiting England.

f. A small store that sells U.S.-made video recorders in Toledo, Ohio (the store has no foreign accounts receivable or payable).

LO4 LO5

EXERCISE 15.6

Foreign Currency Transactions

The following table summarizes the facts of five independent cases (labeled **a** through **e**) of U.S. companies engaging in credit transactions with foreign corporations while the foreign exchange rate is fluctuating:

	Column			
Case	Type of Credit Transaction 1	Currency Used in Contract 2	Exchange Rate Direction 3	Effect on Income 4
a	Sales	Foreign currency	Falling	______
b	Purchases	U.S. dollars	Rising	______
c	______	Foreign currency	Rising	Loss
d	Sales	______	Falling	No effect
e	Purchases	Foreign currency	______	Gain

You are to fill in each blank space after evaluating the information about the case provided in the other three columns. The content of each column and the word or words that you should enter in the blank spaces are described as follows:

Column 1 indicates the type of credit transaction in which the U.S. company engaged with the foreign corporations. The answer entered in this column should be either *Sales* or *Purchases.*

Column 2 indicates the currency in which the invoice price is stated. The answer may be either *U.S. dollars* or *Foreign currency.*

Column 3 indicates the direction in which the foreign currency exchange rate has moved between the date of the credit transaction and the date of settlement. The answer entered in this column may be either *Rising* or *Falling.*

Column 4 indicates the effect of the exchange rate fluctuation on the income of the American company. The answers entered in this column are to be selected from the following: *Gain, Loss,* or *No effect.*

LO3 **EXERCISE 15.7**
Harmonization around the World

Visit the IASB Web site at www.iasplus.com/country/useias.htm

a. Name three governments that require companies to prepare their financial reports *only* in accordance with IFRS in order to list their stocks on the country's securities markets.

b. Name three governments that will not allow companies that prepare their financial reports *only* in accordance with IFRS list their stocks on the country's securities markets.

LO4 LO5 **EXERCISE 15.8**
Foreign Currency Sale Journal Entries

Assume that on May 1, Zavior Corporation (a U.S. company) sells goods to a Portuguese corporation at a price of 100,000 euros, with payment due within three months. At the date of the sale, the exchange rate is $1.20 per euro. The Portuguese customer waits until the three months have passed and pays for the purchase on July 31, when the exchange rate is $1.18 per euro. What is the gain or loss on the transaction for Zavior? Show the journal entries that Zavior would record on May 1 and on July 31.

LO1 LO2 **EXERCISE 15.9**
Home Depot's International Expansion

In the **Home Depot** 2009 financial statements in Appendix A at the end of this textbook, read note 1. Find the information about **Home Depot**'s international store locations.

a. In what countries (other than the U.S.) does **Home Depot** have stores?

b. What environmental factors does it need to consider when expanding to foreign countries and why?

LO5 **EXERCISE 15.10**
Matching Foreign Exchange Gains and Losses

Match the following transactions, which are denominated in a foreign currency, with the appropriate foreign currency and exchange gain or loss effects.

Transaction	Matching Transaction Letter	Foreign Currency Effect	Foreign Exchange Gain or Loss
a. Export sale	?	Appreciates	Loss
b. Import purchase	?	Appreciates	Gain
c. Foreign currency receivable	?	Depreciates	Gain
d. Payable in foreign currency	?	Depreciates	Loss

LO6 **EXRCISE 15.11**
Foreign Currency Translation Effects

Find the Consolidated Statement of Stockholders' Equity and Comprehensive Income section of the **Home Depot** 2009 financial statements in Appendix A. Locate the translation adjustment for 2009. Was the effect of the adjustment positive or negative on Comprehensive Income? What is the implication of the translation adjustment?

LO4 LO7 **EXERCISE 15.12**
Global Sourcing Costs for **Mattel Inc.**

Reconsider Exhibit 15–10, panel B, in the chapter. Use current exchange rates to estimate the global costs of making a Barbie™ doll. Has the total cost increased or decreased as a result of changes in exchange rates?

LO2 LO3

EXERCISE 15.13 Financial Statement Harmonization

Refer to Exhibit 15–6 in this chapter. Assume a United Kingdom company, Brits International, lists on both the London Exchange using U.K. GAAP and the New York Stock Exchange. Brits International must prepare a reconciliation from U.K. GAAP to U.S. GAAP. This reconciliation shows the following difference associated with revaluations of fixed assets:

	Net Income	Shareholder's Equity
U.K. balances	$783,200	$4,767,900
U.S. GAAP adjustments:		
a. Additional depreciation charges that result from revaluation of assets	47,600	326,533
b. Reversal of revaluation of fixed assets	——	(523,740)
U.S. GAAP restatement	$830,800	$4,570,693

Required:

a. Explain why the adjustment to U.S. GAAP resulted in additions to net income.

b. Explain why there are additions to shareholders' equity and why those additions are greater than the additions to net income.

c. Explain why there is a deduction to shareholders' equity.

LO3

EXERCISE 15.14 **Honda Motor Company**'s Use of IFRS or U.S. GAAP

Honda Motor Company reports that it has manufacturing facilities in over twenty locations around the world. Only four of those locations are in Japan. Several are in the U.S., Europe, and South America. Identify the advantages and disadvantages for **Honda Motor Company** of reporting its financial results using either IFRS or U.S. GAAP.

LO2

EXERCISE 15.15 Comparing Environmental Factors

Research China and write a brief comparison of Chinese political-legal, economic, cultural, and infrastructure factors as contrasted to those in the U.S. Explain how these factors might affect accounting practices in the two countries.

Problem Set A

LO4 LO5 LO7

PROBLEM 15.1A Exchange Rates and Export Decision

Crackle Cookie Company is a relatively new company and so far has sold its products only in its home country, Denmark. In December, Crackle determined that it had excess capacity to produce more of its special Christmas cookies. It is trying to decide whether to use that capacity to ship a batch of cookies overseas. The marketing department has determined that the United States and Great Britain are the two most viable markets. Crackle has enough excess capacity to produce only one batch, which can be shipped to either country. The materials and labor cost to produce the batch amount to 8,500 kroner. The marketing department, which located a U.S. shipping company that could deliver to either location, also provided the following information:

	United States	Great Britain
Shipping cost	3,000 U.S. dollars	2,000 U.S. dollars
Duties/customs charges and miscellaneous selling expenses	400 U.S. dollars	480 British pounds
Total sales revenue	5,200 U.S. dollars	2,800 British pounds
Exchange rate data	1 krone = 0.166 U.S. dollars	1 krone = 0.115 British pounds

Instructions

a. If Crackle exports the batch to the United States, what is its estimated profit/loss in Danish kroner?

b. If Crackle exports the batch to Great Britain, what is its estimated profit/loss in Danish kroner?

c. If the British pound has exhibited rather large fluctuations relative to the Danish kroner recently, how might this impact Crackle's decision as to which country to ship to?

LO1 LO4 through LO6

PROBLEM 15.2A
Gains and Losses Journalizing Exchange Rate

Global Motors is a U.S. corporation that purchases automobiles from European manufacturers for distribution in the United States. A recent purchase involved the following events:

Nov. 12 Purchased automobiles from Stockholm Motors in Swedish kronor for Sk20,000,000, payable in 60 days. Current exchange rate, $0.1286 per krona. (Global uses the perpetual inventory system.)

Dec. 31 Made year-end adjusting entry relating to the Sk20,000,000 account payable to Stockholm Motors. Current exchange rate, $0.1288 per krona.

Jan. 11 Issued a check to World Bank for $2,566,800 in full payment of the account payable to Stockholm Motors.

Instructions

a. Prepare in general journal form the entries necessary to record the preceding events.

b. Compute the exchange rate (price) of the krona in U.S. dollars on January 11.

c. Explain a hedging technique that Global might have used to protect itself from the possibility of losses resulting from a significant increase in the exchange rate for the krona.

LO4 through LO7

PROBLEM 15.3A
Exchange Rates and Income Effects

Wallerton, Inc., is a U.S. company that has business operations in Canada. Wallerton's Canadian operation exports the majority of its output to customers in the U.S. and sells only a small portion of its output to Canadian customers. The following budgeted income statement for Wallerton separates the revenue and costs that are in Canadian dollars from those in U.S. dollars. Wallerton wants to know the impact of three possible exchange rate scenarios for the Canadian dollar on its budgeted income statement (assume one Canadian dollar is equivalent to either $.72, $.77, or $.82 in U.S. dollars).

WALLERTON, INC.
BUDGETED INCOME STATEMENT
FOR THE PERIOD ENDING DECEMBER 31, 2011

	Currency in Millions	
	U.S.	**Canadian**
Sales	$304.00	C$ 4
Cost of goods sold	50.00	200
Gross profit	**$254.00**	**C$(196)**
Operating expenses:		
Fixed	30.00	–0–
Variable	30.72	–0–
Total	$ 60.72	–0–
Operating earnings	$193.28	C$(196)
Interest expenses	3.00	10
Earnings before tax	**$190.28**	**C$(206)**

Additional Information

Possible Exchange Rate	Projected U.S. Sales
$.72	$300
.77	304
.82	307

Instructions

a. Complete the chart in the working papers related to Wallerton's budgeted income statement in U.S. dollars:

	C$ = $.72	C$ = $.77	C$ = $.82
Sales:			
(1) U.S.			
(2) Canadian			
(3) Total			
Cost of goods sold:			
(4) U.S.			
(5) Canadian			
(6) Total			
(7) Gross profit		**$103.08**	
Operating expenses:			
(8) U.S. fixed			
(9) U.S. variable			
10% of sales			
(10) Total			
(11) Operating earnings			**$35.252**
Interest expenses:			
(12) U.S.			
(13) Canadian			
(14) Total			
Earnings before tax	**$38.392**		

b. Explain the impact of a stronger Canadian dollar on budgeted earnings before tax.

LO4 LO7 **PROBLEM 15.4A**
Exchange Rates and Production Decisions

Ulsa Company has manufacturing subsidiaries in Malaysia and Malta. It is considering shipping the subcomponents of Product Y to one or the other of these countries for final assembly. The final product will be sold in the country where it is assembled. Other information is as follows:

	Malaysia	Malta
Average exchange rate	$1 = 4.30 ringgits	$1 = 0.40 lira
Import duty	5%	15%
Income tax rate	20%	10%
Unit selling price of Product Y	645 ringgits	70 liri
Price of subcomponent	215 ringgits	20 liri
Final assembly costs	200 ringgits	25 liri
Number of units to be sold	12,000 units	8,000 units

In both countries, the import duties are based on the value of the incoming goods in the receiving country's currency.

Instructions

a. For each country, prepare an income statement on a per-unit basis denominated in that country's currency.

b. In which country would the highest profit per unit (in dollars) be earned?

c. In which country would the highest total profit (in dollars) be earned?

LO2 LO7

PROBLEM 15.5A

NAFTA vs. ASEAN

Form a group of students and research the ASEAN Initiative. A government Web site, www.ustr.gov, provides information on various trade agreements. Prepare a short presentation or a paper that explains how the North American Free Trade Agreement (NAFTA) differs from the ASEAN. Explain how trade agreements help businesses and people in various countries.

LO4 through LO6

PROBLEM 15.6A

A Comprehensive Problem: Journalizing Exchange Rate Effects

Wolfe Computer is a U.S. company that manufactures portable personal computers. Many of the components for the computer are purchased abroad, and the finished product is sold in foreign countries as well as in the United States. Among the recent transactions of Wolfe are the following:

Oct. 28 Purchased from Mitsutonka, a Japanese company, 20,000 disk drives. The purchase price was ¥180,000,000, payable in 30 days. Current exchange rate, $0.0105 per yen. (Wolfe uses the perpetual inventory method; debit the Inventory of Raw Materials account.)

Nov. 9 Sold 700 personal computers to the Bank of England for £604,500 due in 30 days. The cost of the computers, to be debited to the Cost of Goods Sold account, was $518,000. Current exchange rate, $1.65 per British pound. (Use one compound journal entry to record the sale and the cost of goods sold. In recording the cost of goods sold, credit Inventory of Finished Goods.)

Nov. 27 Issued a check to Inland Bank for $1,836,000 in *full payment* of account payable to Mitsutonka.

Dec. 2 Purchased 10,000 gray-scale monitors from German Optical for €1,200,000, payable in 60 days. Current exchange rate, $0.7030 per euro. (Debit Inventory of Raw Materials.)

Dec. 9 Collected dollar-equivalent of £604,500 from the Bank of England. Current exchange rate, $1.63 per British pound.

Dec. 11 Sold 10,000 personal computers to Computique, a Swiss retail chain, for SFr23,750,000, due in 30 days. Current exchange rate, $0.6000 per Swiss franc. The cost of the computers, to be debited to Cost of Goods Sold and credited to Inventory of Finished Goods, is $7,400,000.

Instructions

a. Prepare in general journal form the entries necessary to record the preceding transactions.

b. Prepare the adjusting entries needed at December 31 for the €1,200,000 account payable to German Optical and the SFr23,750,000 account receivable from Computique. Year-end exchange rates, $0.7000 per euro and $0.5980 per Swiss franc. (Use a separate journal entry to adjust each account balance.)

c. Compute (to the nearest dollar) the unit sales price of computers in U.S. dollars in either the November 9 or December 11 sales transaction. (The sales price is the same in each transaction.)

d. Compute the exchange rate for the yen, stated in U.S. dollars, on November 27.

e. Explain how Wolfe Computer could have hedged its position to reduce the risk of loss from exchange rate fluctuations on (**1**) its foreign payables and (**2**) its foreign receivables.

LO8

PROBLEM 15.7A

FCPA Violations

Company A, a U.S. company, has a subsidiary located in Country Z, where various forms of bribery are accepted and expected. To oversee the operations of the subsidiary, Company A sent one of its top U.S. managers to Country Z. Manager M engaged in the following activities while in Country Z during recent months of operation:

a. Paid the equivalent of $200 to a government inspector to reschedule the inspection date of a new manufacturing facility from April 15 to February 15.

b. Paid an average of $50 each to four local police officers who are in charge of patrolling the area around the new manufacturing facility. The officers have agreed to increase the number of times they check the area.

c. Company N, a domestic company, is in competition with Company A for a government contract. Company A has learned that N has given approximately $5,000 to the official who will make the final contract decision. To remain in the running, Manager M authorized Company A to pay an equal amount to the official.

d. The electric utilities are government owned and operated. Due to the frequency of severe storms, there are often power outages due to downed lines. Manager M has paid the official in charge of coordinating repair crews $200 to ensure that the manufacturing plant's power is one of the first restored.

Under the Foreign Corrupt Practices Act, as amended, which of the above activities do you think would be considered illegal? From an operations standpoint, which of the above activities would be considered bad management practice? Are there solutions other than bribery?

LO1 LO2 LO6 LO7

PROBLEM 15.8A
Home Depot's Globalization

Consider note 1 to the 2009 financial statements of **Home Depot, Inc.**, in Appendix A at the end of this textbook. Use this report to assess the globalization of **Home Depot** by answering the following questions:

a. What are the locations of **Home Depot**'s international stores? What other global operations does **Home Depot** undertake?

b. Refer to note 1 under "Segment Information." What percentages of total assets and net sales revenue were associated with international operations in 2009? in 2008?

c. Read note 1 under "Foreign Currency Translation." What exchange rate is used to translate foreign assets and liabilities for reporting purposes?

d. Read note 1 under "Derivatives." Is there any evidence that management undertakes any formal hedging to attempt to reduce the impact of currency exchange risk?

e. **Home Depot**'s provision for taxes for 2009 and 2008 was $1,362 and $1,278 million, respectively. Of the total taxes each year, $166 and $62 million, respectively, were paid to foreign governments. What percentage of taxes was paid to foreign countries each year?

f. Do you believe **Home Depot, Inc.**, is a multinational company? Why or why not?

Problem Set B

LO4 LO5 LO7

PROBLEM 15.1B
Exchange Rates and Export Decisions

Monster Cookie Company is located in Denmark. It is a relatively new company and so far has sold its products only in its home country. In December, Monster determined that it had excess capacity to produce more of its special Halloween cookies. It is trying to decide whether to use that capacity to ship a batch of cookies overseas. The marketing department has determined that the United States and Great Britain are the two most viable markets. Monster has enough excess capacity to produce only one batch, which can be shipped to either country. The materials and labor cost to produce the batch amount to 9,000 kroner. The marketing department, which located a U.S. shipping company that could deliver to either location, also provided the following information:

	United States	Great Britain
Shipping cost	2,800 U.S. dollars	1,900 U.S. dollars
Duties/customs charges and miscellaneous selling expenses	420 U.S. dollars	500 British pounds
Total sales revenue	6,000 U.S. dollars	2,600 British pounds
Exchange rate data	1 krone = 0.16 U.S. dollars	1 krone = 0.09 British pounds

Instructions

a. If Monster exports the batch to the United States, what is its estimated profit/loss in Danish kroner?

b. If Monster exports the batch to Great Britain, what is its estimated profit/loss in Danish kroner?

c. If the British pound has exhibited rather large fluctuations relative to the Danish krone recently, how might this impact Monster's decision as to which country to ship to?

LO1 LO4 through LO6

PROBLEM 15.2B

Gains and Losses Journalizing Exchange Rate

Euroam is a U.S. corporation that purchases motors from European manufacturers for distribution in the United States. A recent purchase involved the following events:

Dec. 1 Purchased tractors from WMB Motors for SFr4,000,000, payable in 45 days. Current exchange rate, $0.75 per Swiss franc. (Euroam uses the perpetual inventory system.)

Dec. 31 Made year-end adjusting entry relating to the SFr4,000,000 account payable to WMB Motors. Current exchange rate, $0.78 per Swiss franc.

Jan. 15 Issued a check to World Bank for $3,080,000 in full payment of the account payable to WMB Motors.

Instructions

a. Prepare in general journal form the entries necessary to record the preceding events.

b. Compute the exchange rate (price) of the Swiss franc in U.S. dollars on January 15.

c. Explain a hedging technique that Euroam might have used to protect itself from the possibility of losses resulting from a significant increase in the exchange rate for the Swiss franc.

LO4 through LO7

PROBLEM 15.3B

Exchange Rates and Income Effects

Jelton, Inc., is a U.S. company that has some business operations in Canada. The Canadian operation exports most of its output to the U.S., but incurs most of its costs in Canadian dollars. The budgeted income statement for next year is shown below. Jelton wants to know the impact of three possible exchange rate scenarios for the Canadian dollar on its budgeted income statement (assume one Canadian dollar is equivalent to either $0.70, $0.80, or $0.90 in U.S. dollars).

JELTON, INC.
BUDGETED INCOME STATEMENT
FOR THE PERIOD ENDING DECEMBER 31, 2011

	U.S.	Canadian
Sales	$400.00	C$ 5
Cost of goods sold	100.00	100
Gross profit	**$300.00**	**C$ (95)**
Operating expenses:		
Fixed	30.00	–0–
Variable	40.00	–0–
Total	$ 70.00	–0–
Operating earnings	$230.00	C$ (95)
Interest expenses	5.00	10
Earnings before tax	**$225.00**	**C$(105)**

Additional Information

Possible Exchange Rate	Projected U.S. Sales
$0.70	$395
0.80	400
0.90	405

Instructions

a. Complete the chart in the working papers related to Jelton's budgeted income statement in U.S. dollars:

	C$ = $0.70	C$ = $0.80	C$ = 0.90
Sales:			
(1) U.S.			
(2) Canadian			
(3) Total			
Cost of goods sold			
(4) U.S.			
(5) Canadian			
(6) Total			
(7) Gross profit		**$224.00**	
Operating expenses:			
(8) U.S. fixed			
(9) U.S. variable			
10% of sales			
(10) Total			
(11) Operating earnings			**$148.55**
Interest expenses:			
(12) U.S.			
(13) Canadian			
(14) Total			
Earnings before tax	**$146.65**		

b. Explain the impact of a stronger Canadian dollar on earnings before tax.

LO4 LO7

PROBLEM 15.4B
Exchange Rates and Product Decisions

Haliday Company has manufacturing subsidiaries in Thailand and Mexico. It is considering shipping the subcomponents of Product X to one or the other of these countries for final assembly. The final product will be sold in the country where it is assembled. Other information is as follows:

	Thailand	Mexico
Average exchange rate	$1 = 32.5 bhats	$1 = 12 pesos
Import duty	4%	12%
Income tax rate	30%	28%
Unit selling price of Product X	5055 bhats	2250 pesos
Price of subcomponent	1444 bhats	540 pesos
Final assembly costs	1805 bhats	900 pesos
Number of units to be sold	14,000 units	10,000 units

In both countries, the import duties are based on the value of the incoming goods in the receiving country's currency.

Instructions

a. For each country, prepare an income statement on a per-unit basis denominated in that country's currency.

b. In which country would the highest profit per unit (in dollars) be earned?

c. In which country would the highest total profit (in dollars) be earned?

LO2 LO7 **PROBLEM 15.5B**
NAFTA vs. CAFTA-DR

Form a group of students and research Dominican Republic–Central America–United States (CAFTA-DR) trade agreement for central America. A government Web site, www.ustr.gov, provides information on various trade agreements. Prepare a short presentation or a paper that explains how requirements for CAFTA-DR differ from those of the North American Free Trade Agreement (NAFTA). Explain how trade agreements help businesses and people in various countries.

LO4 through LO6 **PROBLEM 15.6B**
A Comprehensive Problem: Journalizing Exchange Rate Effects

Fox Games is a U.S. company that manufacturers computer game consoles. Many of the components for the consoles are purchased abroad, and the finished product is sold in foreign countries as well as in the United States. Among the recent transactions of Fox are the following:

Oct. 25 Purchased from Sutaki, a Japanese company, 15,000 parts. The purchase price was ¥120,000,000, payable in 30 days. Current exchange rate, $0.01 per yen. (Fox uses the perpetual inventory method; debit the Inventory of Raw Materials account.)

Nov. 15 Sold 500 consoles to British Vibes for £200,000, due in 30 days. The cost of the consoles, to be debited to the Cost of Goods Sold account, was $160,000. Current exchange rate, $1.60 per British pound. (Use one compound journal entry to record the sale and the cost of goods sold. In recording the cost of goods sold, credit Inventory of Finished Goods.)

Nov. 24 Issued a check to Inland Bank for $1,150,000 in *full payment* of account payable to Sutaki.

Dec. 4 Purchased 5,000 black cases from Swiss Plastics for SFr80,000, payable in 60 days. Current exchange rate, $0.70 per Swiss franc. (Debit Inventory of Raw Materials.)

Dec. 15 Collected dollar-equivalent of £200,000 from British Vibes. Current exchange rate, $1.55 per British pound.

Dec. 21 Sold 6,000 game consoles to Sounds, a Norwegian retail chain, for NOK40,000,000, due in 30 days. Current exchange rate, $0.20 per Norwegian krone. The cost of the consoles, to be debited to Cost of Goods Sold and credited to Inventory of Finished Goods, is $5,000,000.

Instructions

a. Prepare in general journal form the entries necessary to record the preceding transactions.

b. Prepare the adjusted entries needed at December 31 for the SFr80,000 account payable to Swiss Plastics and the NOK40,000,000 account receivable from Sounds. Year-end exchange rates, $0.68 per Swiss franc and $0.18 per Norwegian krone. (Use a separate journal entry to adjust each account balance.)

c. Compute (to the nearest dollar) the unit sales price of consoles in U.S. dollars in both the November 15 and the December 21 sales transaction. (The sales price may not be the same in each transaction.)

d. Compute the exchange rate for the yen, stated in U.S. dollars, on November 24.

e. Explain how Fox Games could have hedged its position to reduce the risk of loss from exchange rate fluctuations on (**1**) its foreign payables and (**2**) its foreign receivables.

LO8 **PROBLEM 15.7B**
FCPA Violations

Company P, a U.S. company, has a foreign subsidiary in Country Q, where various forms of bribery are accepted and expected. Company P sent one of its top U.S. managers to oversee operations in its subsidiary in Country Q. That manager engaged in the following activities while in Country Q:

a. Paid the equivalent of $200,000 to a government official to win the bid for a new manufacturing facility that opened on April 15.

b. Paid about $80 each to four local clerks at the import agency who agreed to move the company's import inspection process to expedite status, saving the company one week of inspection time.

c. The streets and sanitation department in Country Q is government owned and operated. Because of many hurricanes, downed trees and other debris frequently block access to the roads leading to the plant. The manager paid the official in charge of streets an additional $200 to ensure quick clearing of the streets leading to the plant.

d. After learning that a competing foreign company paid a government official in Country Q $10,000 to have priority consideration on a new contract to supply the military, the manager of Company P offered the official $20,000 for priority consideration for the same contract.

Under the Foreign Corrupt Practices Act as amended, which of the above activities would be considered illegal? From an operations standpoint, which of the above activities would be considered bad management practice? What alternative actions could you suggest for the manager?

Critical Thinking Cases

LO1 LO2

CASE 15.1 Decisions to Globalize Are Complex

Bristow Inc. is interested in establishing a presence in Country Y. Bristow is expecting demand for several of its products to increase in that country because a major customer, Kale Enterprises, is building a large manufacturing plant in Y. Bristow has been supplying Kale's other foreign manufacturing operations mainly through exporting. However, shipping costs and long delivery times have been somewhat troublesome to both companies in the past. Bristow has also identified several other companies native to Country Y as potential customers.

Bristow currently has operations only in the United States. Kale Enterprises is a successful global company with operations in over 20 countries. Bristow's managers have identified the following possible options:

a. Simply export to Country Y.

b. A company in Y has expressed an interest in licensing Bristow's technology and has the capability and capacity to produce the products used by Kale.

c. A joint venture with Kale may be possible, but managers for Kale would be willing to enter into an agreement only if substantial control for Bristow's operations is given to Kale managers.

d. Bristow's managers have located a company that could be purchased and operated as a subsidiary. The company currently produces products similar to Bristow, but it is using outdated technology.

Instructions

Discuss what factors should be considered when choosing among the above options. Develop a list of additional information you believe would be useful in making the decision.

LO2 LO3 LO5

CASE 15.2 Disclosure Requirements

The International Organization of Securities Commissions (IOSCO) is a group of top securities administrators from about 50 countries. The Securities and Exchange Commission (SEC) is a member of IOSCO. IOSCO is a primary supporter of the internationalization of financial reporting standards through the International Accounting Standards Board (IASB). At a recent meeting, a discussion of the pros and cons of internationalizing financial reporting standards included the following arguments:

Pro:

Having the same accounting standards for external financial reporting for all securities markets will reduce misunderstandings and create comparable information. For example, investors will be able to compare the financial reports of similar companies located in the United States with those located in China and decide where best to allocate their investments. One set of accounting standards will also save corporations money because they will not need multiple sets of books to track their international operations.

Con:

Requiring companies that list on all global securities exchanges to use the same external reporting requirements will mislead investors. For example, in countries where the majority of investment funds come from banks in the form of long-term borrowing, debt to equity ratios will look very different than those of comparable U.S. firms. Accounting information must reflect its environment. Besides, as all business becomes global, reporting requirements will naturally evolve to what investors demand.

Instructions

Write a one-page summary reflecting your opinion about the value of harmonizing accounting standards for global equity markets. Support your opinions by referencing comparable cross-country companies you have located on the Internet.

LO1 LO2 LO7

INTERNET CASE 15.3
U.S. Foreign Trade Zones

The National Association of Foreign Trade Zones (FTZs) maintains an Internet site containing information on U.S. foreign trade zones. Locate the site by searching under "foreign trade zone," or go to:

www.naftz.org

Instructions

a. What is the difference between a zone and a subzone?

b. Identify an FTZ in your state. Where is it located? What types of business use it?

c. Other information is available at the site. Use that information to answer the following:

1. How are FTZs created?

2. What businesses utilize FTZs?

3. What benefits can firms obtain from operating in FTZs?

LO2 LO3

CASE 15.4
International Demand for Corporate Governance

The international business community has been calling for stronger corporate governance for companies around the globe. As a result, in 1999 the Organization for Economic Cooperation and Development (OECD) issued some principles that deal with the ethical and fair treatment of shareholders, the importance of transparency, and adequate disclosure. These OECD principles were revised in 2004. The World Bank and the International Monetary Fund support these efforts. In particular, principle number five, called Disclosure and Transparency, states:

> The corporate governance framework should ensure that timely and accurate disclosure is made on all material matters regarding the corporation, including the financial situation, performance, ownership and governance of the company (see www.oecd.org).

Required

Form a group of four students. Visit the OECD Web site and use the information to write a one-page paper that explains why OECD corporate governance principle number five is important for international capital flows.

Internet sites are time and date sensitive. It is the purpose of these exercises to have you explore the Internet. You may need to use the Yahoo! search engine http://www.yahoo.com *(or another favorite search engine) to find a company's current Web address.*

Answers to Self-Test Questions

1. c **2.** a, b, c, d **3.** b **4.** c (.17 − .19) × 20,000
5. d (the transaction was denominated in dollars)

CHAPTER 16

Management Accounting

A Business Partner

© Imagestate Media Partners Limited-Impact Photos/Alamy

AFTER STUDYING THIS CHAPTER, YOU SHOULD BE ABLE TO:

- **LO1** Explain the three principles guiding the design of management accounting systems.
- **LO2** Describe the three basic types of manufacturing costs.
- **LO3** Distinguish between product costs and period costs.
- **LO4** Describe how manufacturing costs flow through perpetual inventory accounts.
- **LO5** Distinguish between direct and indirect costs.
- **LO6** Prepare a schedule of the cost of finished goods manufactured.

Learning Objective

COCA-COLA COMPANY

The secret syrup formula for Coca-Cola® was created in 1886 by Dr. John S. Pemberton, a pharmacist in Atlanta, Georgia.[1] Dr. Pemberton's partner, Frank Robinson, a management accountant, penned the famous trademark symbol *Coca-Cola.*® In 1891, when Asa Candler purchased the Coca-Cola business from Pemberton for $2,300, he also recognized the value of the management accounting skills of Frank Robinson. In 1892, Candler and Robinson, along with three other associates, formed the Georgia corporation now known as the Coca-Cola Company.

Today, the Coca-Cola Company produces more than 3,300 products in over 200 countries. Seventy-four percent of Coca-Cola's income is derived from sales outside the United States. To help manage its global business, the Coca-Cola Company employs thousands of management accountants in hundreds of countries. ■

[1] For more details, see **www.thecoca-colacompany.com/heritage/chronicle_birth_refreshing_idea.html**.

Management Accounting: Basic Framework

Because accounting information is critical for assessing an organization's output, performance measurement and reporting are key activities frequently coordinated through accounting. In this chapter, you will learn how management accounting becomes an important business partner. Management accounting information links decision-making authority with the information necessary to make decisions. It also provides a means to assess decision performance. This chapter introduces the foundations of management accounting.

The opening story describes a management accountant at **Coca-Cola Company**. **Management accounting** is the design and use of accounting information systems inside the company to achieve the company's objectives. Three principles govern how management accounting systems are designed. First, management accounting systems help to decide who has decision-making authority over company assets. Second, accounting information produced by or created from the management accounting system supports planning and decision making. Finally, management accounting reports provide a means of monitoring, evaluating, and rewarding performance.

MANAGEMENT ACCOUNTING'S ROLE IN ASSIGNING DECISION-MAKING AUTHORITY

Learning Objective
LO1 Explain the three principles guiding the design of management accounting systems.

To achieve organizational goals, managers are assigned decision-making authority for some of the firm's assets. For example, plant managers typically are responsible for decisions about equipment in the plant, employees at the plant, the physical plant layout, and sources of raw materials, among other things. Within the plant, the materials inventory manager may be delegated decision-making responsibility for reordering materials, and the production supervisor may be delegated decision-making responsibility for assigning employees to jobs on the production line. The point is that all members of an organization have some decision-making authority.

Employees within a corporation know their decision-making responsibilities because they are outlined in a variety of ways, such as in job descriptions, verbal instructions from their supervisors, and management accounting system documents and reports. Just as you have received a course syllabus that outlines your instructor's standards for you to follow to earn an A or B in this course, managers receive management accounting reports that outline expected outcomes to help achieve the organization's goals. Just as you have decision-making responsibility over the "assets" necessary to achieve an A or B (the time you allocate to studying), managers have decision-making responsibility over the assets included in their management accounting reports.

MANAGEMENT ACCOUNTING'S ROLE IN DECISION MAKING

Managers need reliable and timely information on which to base their decisions. For example, the plant manager needs information to help assess if equipment is inefficient or if certain work arrangements and plant layouts are more productive than others. Thus, managers need both historical information (for example, the current equipment's cost and productivity) and projected information (for example, the productivity and cost of other available equipment). They need information oriented both toward their specific operations and toward other parts of the organization's value chain. A **value chain** is the linked set of activities and resources necessary to create and deliver the product or service to the customer. Therefore, plant managers will require information from other parts of the value chain such as engineering or sales. They need information from both internal operations and externally oriented benchmark sources.

More and more organizations are sharing information. It is very common for organizations to participate in and undertake **benchmark studies.** Independent consulting companies often create benchmark reports by collecting information from companies in the same industry. These studies show an organization how its costs and processes compare with others in its industry. Organizations also share information with customers and suppliers in their value chain. For example, in order for shipments from suppliers to arrive at the exact time they are needed for use in production, buyers and suppliers share their production information. Customers often require or are voluntarily provided quality information. As shown in Exhibit 16–1, the management accounting system provides past-, current-, and future-oriented information for users both inside and outside the firm.

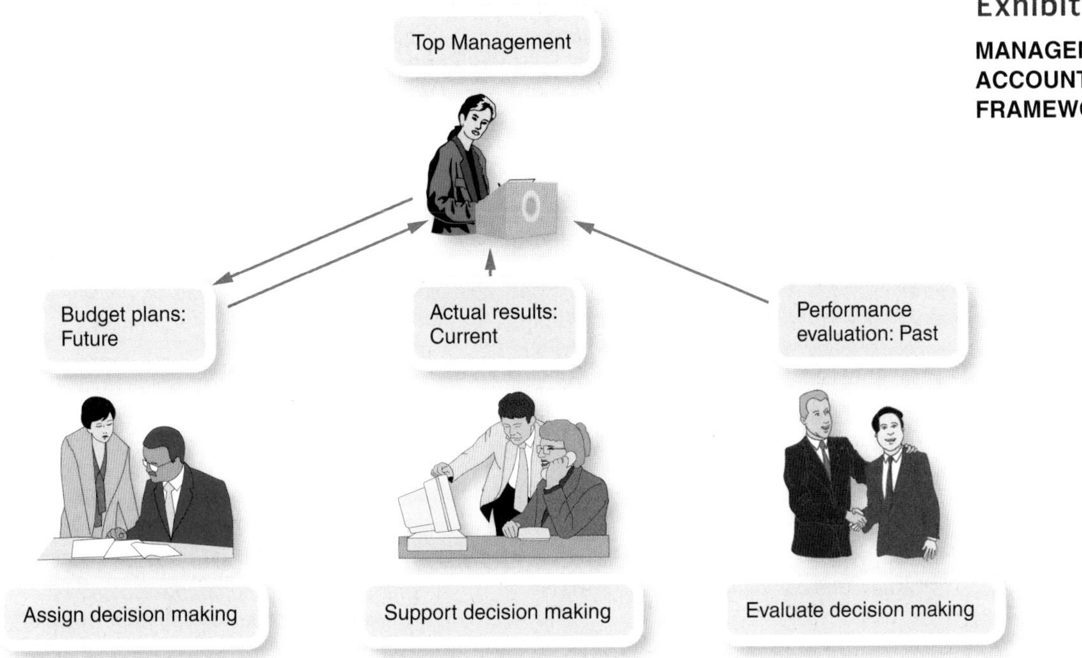

Exhibit 16–1

MANAGEMENT ACCOUNTING SYSTEM FRAMEWORK

MANAGEMENT ACCOUNTING'S ROLE IN PERFORMANCE EVALUATION AND REWARDS

The assets over which managers have decision-making authority do not belong to these managers. The corporation owns these assets, and the returns from these assets belong to the corporation. To make sure the assets are earning a good return, the corporation monitors the outcomes of the decisions made by the managers. When the corporation is owned by shareholders, the external financial statements discussed in previous chapters serve this monitoring role for the corporation as a whole. Parallel monitoring systems are designed to serve similar functions inside corporations. For example, many companies prepare plant-level income statements. Headquarters' executives compare these plant-level financial statements with budgets to monitor the decisions made by plant managers. Frequently, managerial rewards and bonuses are related to the outcomes of these internally prepared financial statements.

Exhibit 16–1 shows that the accounting system must be designed to fulfill all of the three roles described above simultaneously. The system must clearly allocate decision-making authority, provide information for decision making, and furnish information for evaluating and rewarding performance. The accounting system must be constantly monitored and adjusted to make sure all three roles are being supported.

ACCOUNTING SYSTEMS: A BUSINESS PARTNER

Creating accounting information systems that can satisfy the demands of both external users (shareholders, creditors, IRS, SEC) and internal users (plant managers, marketing managers, human resource personnel, CFO, CEO) is very challenging. Exhibit 16–2 outlines the demands placed on accounting information systems. Users want accounting information for different, sometimes conflicting, reasons. Information necessary for planning and decision making is likely to be future oriented, and information for monitoring is likely to be historical. Shareholders, creditors, and the IRS do not expect information that is as timely, or at the same level of detail, as the information needed by a plant manager. Yet, the same accounting information system usually serves multiple sets of users. Employees use it across a multitude

Exhibit 16-2

DEMAND FOR ACCOUNTING INFORMATION

THE ACCOUNTING SYSTEM

Financial Accounting	Management Accounting
Purpose	Purpose
To provide investors, creditors, and other external parties with useful information about the financial position, financial performance, and cash flow prospects of an enterprise.	*To provide managers with information useful for planning, evaluating and rewarding performance, and sharing with other outside parties. To apportion decision-making authority over firm resources.*
Types of Reports	Types of Reports
Primarily financial statements (statement of financial position or balance sheet, income statement, statement of cash flows) and related notes and supplemental disclosures that provide investors, creditors, and other users information to support external decision-making processes.	*Many different types of reports, depending on the nature of the business and the specific information needs of management. Examples include budgets, financial projections, benchmark studies, activity-based cost reports, and cost-of-quality assessment.*
Standards for Presentation	Standards for Presentation
Generally accepted accounting principles, including those formally established in the authoritative accounting literature and standard industry practice.	*Rules are set within each organization to produce information most relevant to the needs of management. Management needs include reporting to both external constituents and internal users.*
Reporting Entity	Reporting Entity
Usually the company viewed as a whole.	*A component of the company's value chain, such as a business segment, supplier, customer, product line, department, or product.*
Time Periods Covered	Time Periods Covered
Usually a year, quarter, or month. Most reports focus on completed periods. Emphasis is placed on the current (latest) period, with prior periods often shown for comparison.	*Any period—year, quarter, month, week, day, even a work shift. Some reports are historical in nature; others focus on estimates of results expected in future periods.*

Financial Accounting	Management Accounting
Users of Information	Users of Information
Outsiders as well as managers. For financial statements, these outsiders include stockholders, creditors, prospective investors, regulatory authorities, and the general public.	*Management (different reports to different managers), customers, auditors, suppliers, and others involved in an organization's value chain.*

of organizational levels and job responsibilities, and it spreads over numerous geographic areas with different cultures, languages, currencies, and economic environments. Companies such as **Coca-Cola Company** are much better than they were 15 years ago at designing cost-efficient accounting information systems to serve multiple users. One of the primary reasons for better accounting information systems is the advance in these systems' technological capabilities.

Due to rapidly evolving changes in technology and information needs, business managers study management accounting throughout their professional careers. In fact, many companies require employees to complete training in a variety of accounting techniques. Professional certification is available to individuals who plan to make their career in management accounting. The Institute of Certified Management Accountants sponsors two certification exams, the Certified Management Accountant (CMA) exam and the Certified Financial Manager (CFM) exam. To become either a CMA or a CFM, an individual must meet educational and experience requirements as well as pass a rigorous examination.

CASE IN POINT

As the tech industry shifted from the PC to the Internet, the company Michael Dell started in his college dorm to efficiently build and sell personal computers fell on hard times. For example, in 2005 **Dell** was valued at $100 billion, but by 2009 its value fell to $30 billion.[2] It seems clear that **Dell** had stayed with its old playbook of cranking out PCs as efficiently as possible for too long.

© Keith Eng 2007/DAL

Michael Dell returned to the chief executive roll in 2007 with the objective of remaking the company. However, lack of structure at the massive company including a lack of management accounting processes, tools, and culture didn't support a new way of doing business. To get executives to seize new business opportunities and take more risks, Dell needed to change the company's management structure and culture. He arranged for leaders of each division to be *responsible for meeting financial targets and have broad authority to figure out how to reach them.* Dell thought that by focusing outward and giving top managers more responsibility and more flexibility, the company would be more responsive to clients. Results are supporting his claims. By late 2009, **Dell** was beginning to show improvement in its financial results.

As you progress through the remaining chapters, keep in mind the three principles of management accounting systems: assigning decision-making authority, making and supporting decisions, and evaluating and rewarding performance. The procedures and techniques discussed in the remaining chapters are aimed at one or more of these principles. In addition, you will encounter many familiar terms and concepts because of the overlap of management and financial accounting. After all, a single accounting system serves both sets of users. It is common for managers to use information about revenue, expenses, and assets in their daily decision making. Managers receive customized accounting information (for example, by product line or customer) as needed to make decisions.

Accounting for Manufacturing Operations

A merchandising company buys its inventory in a ready-to-sell condition. Therefore, its cost of goods is mostly composed of the purchase price of the products it sells. A *manufacturing* company, however, *produces* the goods that it sells. As a consequence, its cost of goods sold consists of various **manufacturing costs,** including the cost of materials, wages earned by production workers, and a variety of other costs relating to the operation of a production facility.[3]

Manufacturing operations are an excellent example of how managerial and financial accounting overlap because manufacturing costs are of vital importance to both financial and managerial accountants. Financial accountants use manufacturing costs to determine the cost of goods sold and inventory values reported in financial statements. Management accountants also rely on prompt and reliable information about manufacturing costs to help answer such questions as:

[2] "Dell's Do-Over," *BusinessWeek,* Iss. 4152, October 26, 2009, p. 36.

[3] Manufacturing costs are the cost of producing inventory, which is an asset. Therefore, these expenditures are termed *costs* rather than *expenses.* Unexpired costs are assets; expired costs are expenses.

- What sales price must we charge for our products to earn a reasonable profit?
- Is it possible to lower the cost of producing a particular product line in order to be more price competitive?
- Is it less expensive to buy certain parts used in our products or to manufacture these parts ourselves?
- Should we automate our production process with a robotic assembly line?

CLASSIFICATIONS OF MANUFACTURING COSTS

Learning Objective LO2 **Describe the three basic types of manufacturing costs.**

A typical manufacturing company purchases raw materials and converts these materials into finished goods through the process of production. The costs of converting raw materials into finished goods, specifically the direct labor and overhead costs, are called **conversion costs.** In contrast, the direct materials and direct labor that are consumed in production are referred to as **prime costs.** Thus, direct labor is both a prime cost and a conversion cost. These cost classifications are illustrated in Exhibit 16–3 and described below. The manufacturing costs are often divided into three broad categories:

1. **Direct materials**—the raw materials and component parts used in production whose costs are directly traceable to the products manufactured.
2. **Direct labor**—wages and other payroll costs of employees whose efforts are directly traceable to the products they manufacture.
3. **Manufacturing overhead**—a catchall classification, which includes all manufacturing costs *other than* the costs of direct materials and direct labor. Examples include factory utilities, supervisor salaries, equipment repairs, and depreciation on production machinery.

Exhibit 16–3 **FLOW OF PHYSICAL GOODS IN PRODUCTION**

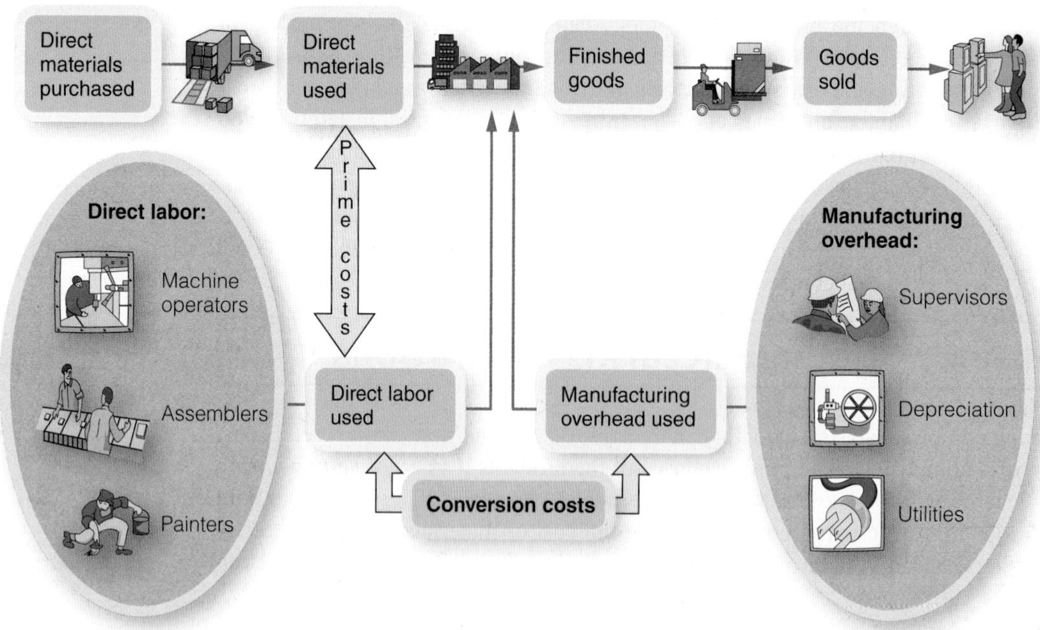

Note that manufacturing costs are *not* immediately recorded as current period expenses. Rather, they are costs of *creating inventory,* and they remain on the balance sheet until the inventory is sold. For this reason, manufacturing costs are often called *product costs* (or inventoriable costs).

PRODUCT COSTS VERSUS PERIOD COSTS

Learning Objective LO3 **Distinguish between product costs and period costs.**

The terms *product costs* and *period costs* are helpful in explaining the difference between manufacturing costs and operating expenses. In a manufacturing environment, **product costs** are those costs incurred to manufacture inventory. Thus, until the related goods are sold, product costs *represent inventory.* As such, they are reported in the balance sheet as an asset. When the goods are ultimately sold, product costs are transferred from the balance sheet to the income statement, where they are deducted from revenue as the cost of goods sold.

Operating expenses associated with *time periods,* rather than with the production of inventory, are referred to as **period costs.** Period costs are charged directly to expense accounts on the assumption that their benefit is recognized entirely in the period when the cost is incurred. Period costs include all selling expenses, general and administrative expenses, interest expense, and income tax expense. In short, period costs are classified in the income statement separately from cost of goods sold, as deductions from a company's gross profit.

The flow of product costs and period costs through the financial statements is shown in Exhibit 16–4.

Exhibit 16–4 "FLOW" OF COSTS THROUGH FINANCIAL STATEMENTS

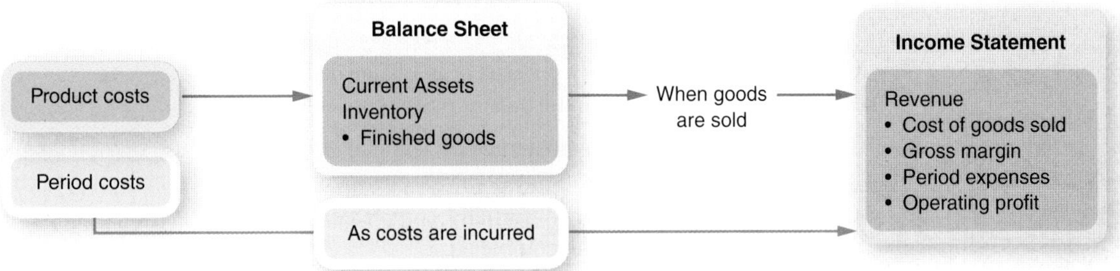

To further illustrate the distinction between product and period costs, consider two costs that, on the surface, appear quite similar: the depreciation of a warehouse used to store raw materials versus depreciation of a warehouse used to store finished goods. Depreciation of the raw materials warehouse is considered a *product cost* (a component of manufacturing overhead) because the building is part of the manufacturing process. Once the manufacturing process is complete and the finished goods are available for sale, all costs associated with their storage are considered selling expenses. Thus, the depreciation of the finished goods warehouse is a *period cost.*

Ethics, Fraud & Corporate Governance

A company can artificially inflate reported income by improperly capitalizing period costs. Capitalizing period costs violates GAAP. For example, the Securities and Exchange Commission (SEC) brought an enforcement action against **Winners Internet Network, Inc. (Winners)**, its former chairman/CEO/president, and its former auditing firm for filing materially misleading financial statements with the SEC, due at least in part to the improper capitalization of period costs.

Winners capitalized wages, payroll taxes, rent, travel, marketing, and consulting costs—all period costs that were related to the employment of **Winners**'s chairman/CEO/president. These costs were unrelated to the development of **Winners**'s software asset. As such, these costs should have been expensed as incurred. **Winners**'s improper capitalization of period costs resulted in an overstatement of its total assets by 416 percent.

The SEC sought and received a permanent injunction barring **American Television and Film Company** (the successor company to **Winners**) from further violations of the securities laws, in addition to issuing other sanctions against **Winners**'s former chairman/CEO/president and **Winners**'s former accounting firm.

PRODUCT COSTS AND THE MATCHING PRINCIPLE

Underlying the distinction between product costs and period costs is a familiar accounting concept—the *matching principle.* In short, product costs should be reported in the income statement only when they can be matched against product revenue. To illustrate, consider a real estate developer who starts a tract of 10 homes in May of the current year. During the year, the developer incurs material, labor, and overhead costs amounting to $1 million (assume $100,000 per house). By the end of December, none of the houses has been sold. How much of the $1 million in construction costs should appear in the developer's income statement for the current year?

The answer is *none.* These costs are not related to any revenue earned by the developer during the current year. Instead, they are related to future revenue the developer will earn when the houses are eventually sold. Therefore, at the end of the current year, the $1 million of product costs should appear in the developer's balance sheet as *inventory.* As each house is sold, $100,000 will be deducted from sales revenue as cost of goods sold. This way, the developer's income statements in future periods will properly match sales revenue with the cost of each sale.

INVENTORIES OF A MANUFACTURING BUSINESS

In the preceding example, assume all 10 houses were completed by the end of the year. In this case, the developer's inventory consists only of finished goods. Most manufacturing companies, however, typically account for *three types* of inventory:

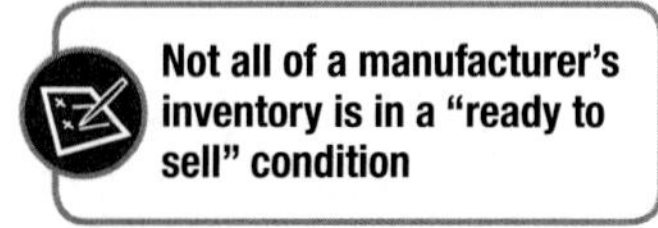

Not all of a manufacturer's inventory is in a "ready to sell" condition

1. **Materials inventory**—raw materials on hand and available for use in the manufacturing process.
2. **Work in process inventory**—partially completed goods on which production activities have been started but not yet completed.
3. **Finished goods inventory**—unsold finished products available for sale to customers.

All three of these inventories are classified on the balance sheet as current assets. The cost of the materials inventory is based in its purchase price. The work in process and finished goods inventories are based on the costs of direct material, direct labor, and manufacturing overhead assigned to them.

INTERNATIONAL CASE IN POINT

In many countries such as Argentina and Greece, inventory valuation does not conform to the lower of cost or market value rules used in the United States. In addition, many countries, including Korea, Mexico, Nigeria, Poland, and Taiwan, allow upward revaluation of property and equipment. These differences in accounting methods make comparing inventory values of companies from different parts of the world very difficult.

Manufacturing companies may use either a perpetual or a periodic inventory system. Perpetual systems have many advantages, however, such as providing managers with up-to-date information about the amounts of inventory on hand and the per-unit costs of manufacturing products. For these reasons, virtually all large manufacturing companies use *perpetual inventory systems.* Also, the flow of manufacturing costs through the inventory accounts and into the cost of goods sold is most easily illustrated in a perpetual inventory system. Therefore, we will assume the use of a perpetual inventory system in our discussion of manufacturing activities.

THE FLOW OF COSTS PARALLELS THE FLOW OF PHYSICAL GOODS

When a perpetual inventory system is in use, the flow of manufacturing costs through the company's general ledger accounts closely parallels the physical flow of goods through the production process. This relationship is illustrated in Exhibit 16–5. The numbered boxes in the exhibit represent six *general ledger accounts* used by manufacturing companies to account for their production activities: (1) Materials Inventory, (2) Direct Labor, (3) Manufacturing Overhead, (4) Work in Process Inventory, (5) Finished Goods Inventory, and (6) Cost of Goods Sold.

Learning Objective
Describe how manufacturing costs flow through perpetual inventory accounts.
LO4

Exhibit 16–5 **FLOW OF COST ASSOCIATED WITH PRODUCTION**

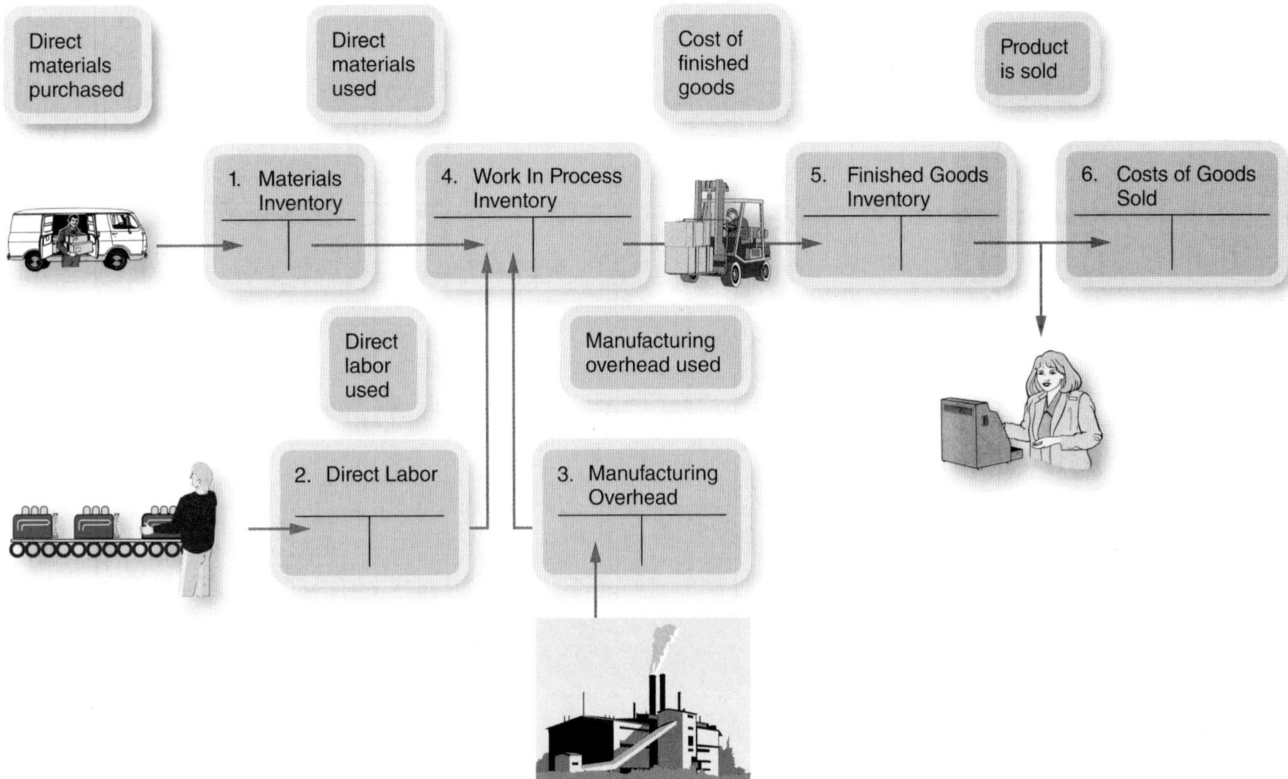

ACCOUNTING FOR MANUFACTURING COSTS: AN ILLUSTRATION

To illustrate accounting for manufacturing costs, we will assume that Conquest, Inc., manufactures high-quality mountain bikes in Bend, Oregon. The company relies on cost information to monitor its production efficiency, set prices, and maintain control over its inventories.

Conquest carefully tracks the flow of manufacturing costs through its general ledger accounts as illustrated in Exhibit 16–6 on the following page. The figures shown represent all of Conquest's manufacturing costs for the current year. The debit and credit entries summarize the numerous transactions recorded by the company throughout the year.

Our use of several colors in this illustration will help you follow the flow of manufacturing costs through these accounts. The beginning balances in the three inventory accounts are shown in black. Manufacturing costs, and the arrows showing the transfer of these costs from one account to another, are shown in red. Account balances at year-end, which will appear in the company's financial statements, are shown in blue.

Let us now look more closely at exactly how the company's manufacturing costs flow through these general ledger accounts.

DIRECT MATERIALS

Direct materials are the raw materials and component parts that become an integral part of finished products and can be traced directly and conveniently to products manufactured. Conquest's direct materials include lightweight alloy tubing for cycle frames, brakes, shifting levers, pedals, sprockets, tires, and so on. The mountain bikes assembled from these components are Conquest's *finished goods.*

The terms *direct materials* and *finished goods* are defined from the viewpoint of individual manufacturing companies. For example, Conquest views brake components as a direct

Exhibit 16–6 ACCOUNTING FOR MANUFACTURING COSTS

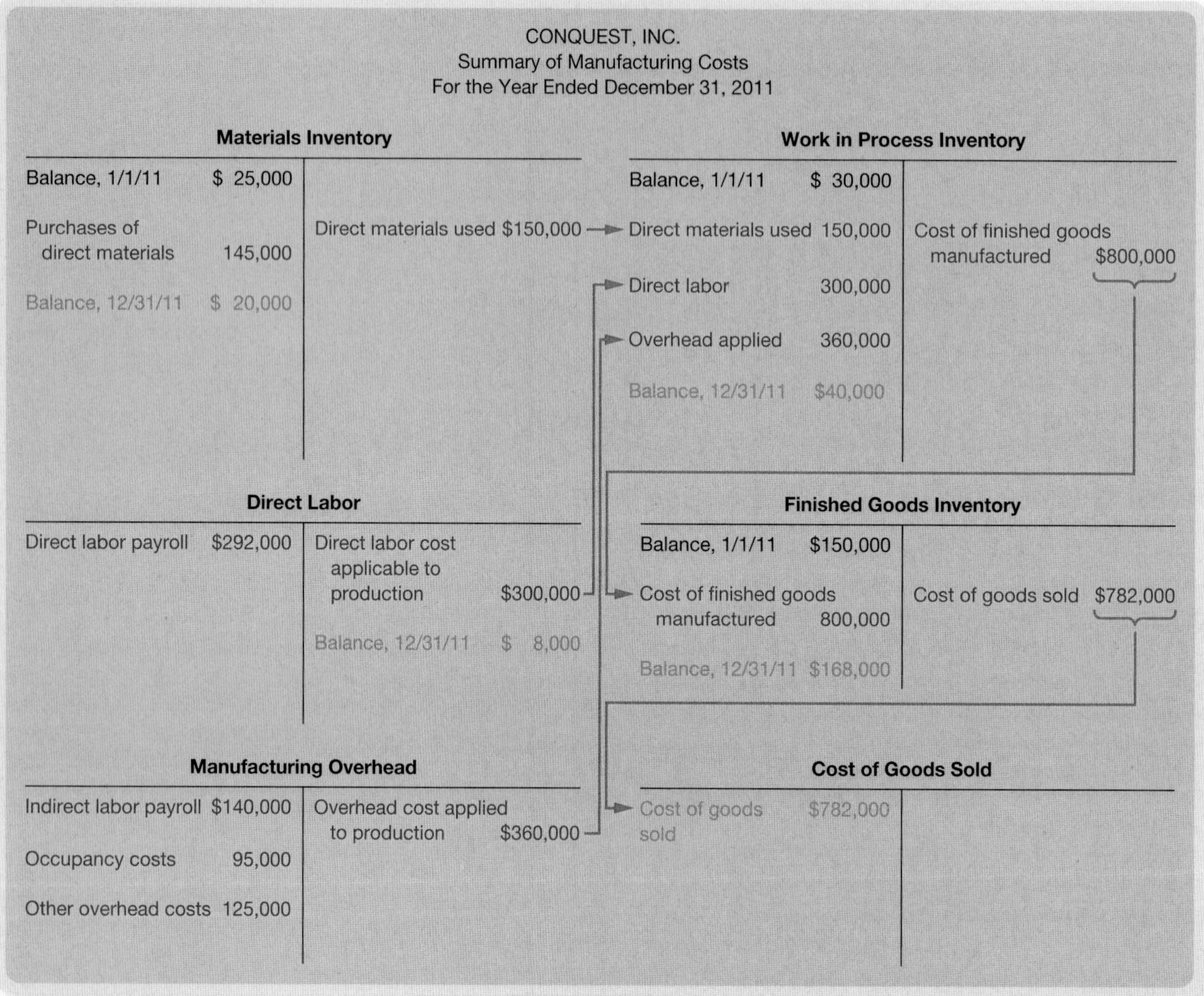

material. However, the **Shimano Company** (a brake manufacturer) views the brake components it sells to Conquest as finished goods.

CONQUEST, INC.
Summary of Manufacturing Costs
For the Year Ended December 31, 2011
Materials Inventory
Balance, 1/1/11 $ 25,000
Purchases of direct materials 145,000
Balance, 12/31/11 $ 20,000
Direct materials used $150,000
Work in Process Inventory
Balance, 1/1/11 $ 30,000
Direct materials used 150,000
Direct labor 300,000
Overhead applied 360,000
Balance, 12/31/11 $40,000
Cost of finished goods manufactured $800,000
Direct Labor
Direct labor payroll $292,000
Direct labor cost applicable to production $300,000
Balance, 12/31/11 $ 8,000
Finished Goods Inventory
Balance, 1/1/11 $150,000
Cost of finished goods manufactured 800,000
Balance, 12/31/11 $168,000
Cost of goods sold $782,000
Manufacturing Overhead
Indirect labor payroll $140,000
Occupancy costs 95,000
Other overhead costs 125,000
Overhead cost applied to production $360,000
Cost of Goods Sold
Cost of goods sold $782,000

Conquest uses a perpetual inventory system. Accordingly, the costs of direct materials purchased are debited directly to the Materials Inventory account. As these materials are placed into production, their costs are transferred from the Materials Inventory account to the Work in Process Inventory account by debiting Work in Process Inventory and crediting Materials Inventory. The balance remaining in the Materials Inventory account at year-end represents the cost of direct materials on hand and ready for use.

Some materials used in the production process cannot be traced conveniently or directly to the finished goods manufactured. For Conquest, examples include bearing grease, welding materials, and material used in factory maintenance such as cleaning compounds. These items are referred to as **indirect materials** and are classified as part of manufacturing overhead.

DIRECT LABOR

The Direct Labor account is used to record the payroll cost of direct workers and assign this cost to the goods they help manufacture.[4] Direct workers are those employees who work directly on the bicycles being manufactured, either by hand or by using machines.

[4] As explained in Chapter 10, payroll costs include such factors as payroll taxes and "fringe benefits" as well as the wages earned by employees. Some companies classify fringe benefits as overhead because they are not proportionally related to hourly wages.

Conquest employs five classifications of direct laborers. Each classification and its corresponding job description are as follows:

Classification	Job Description
Cutters	Cut alloy tubing into appropriate lengths.
Welders	Transform the cut pieces of alloy tubing into bicycle frames.
Painters	Prime and paint each frame.
Assemblers	Partially assemble each bicycle in preparation for packing.
Packers	Pack the partially assembled bicycles in boxes.

There are two separate and distinct aspects of accounting for direct labor costs. The first involves the *payment* of cash made to the direct workers at the end of each pay period. At each payroll date, the Direct Labor account is debited for the total direct labor payroll, and an offsetting credit is made to Cash. The second aspect involves the *application* of direct labor costs to the goods being produced. As direct labor employees contribute to the production process during the period, the cost of their labor is *applied* to production by debiting the Work in Process Inventory account and crediting the Direct Labor account.

In our T accounts in Exhibit 16–6, the flow of direct labor costs looks similar to the flow of direct materials costs. There is, however, one significant difference. Materials are purchased *before* they are used; therefore, the Materials Inventory account has a *debit* balance equal to the cost of unused materials on hand. The services of employees, however, are used before the employees are paid. Thus, the credits to the Direct Labor account are recorded *throughout* the payroll period, but the debits are not recorded until the *end* of the payroll period. If the balance sheet date falls between payroll dates and before adjusting entries are made, the Direct Labor account will have a *credit* balance representing the amount owed to employees for work already performed. This credit balance should be listed in the balance sheet as *wages payable,* a current liability.

Many employees in a manufacturing plant do not work directly on the goods being manufactured. Examples at Conquest include factory supervisors, maintenance personnel, forklift drivers, and security guards. These **indirect labor** costs, which are handled in a fashion similar to that used for indirect materials costs, are considered part of Conquest's manufacturing overhead.

MANUFACTURING OVERHEAD

All manufacturing costs, *other than* direct materials and direct labor, are classified as *manufacturing overhead.* The Manufacturing Overhead account is used to (1) record all costs classified as "overhead" and (2) assign these costs to products being manufactured.

There are many types of overhead costs. Consequently, Manufacturing Overhead is treated as a *control account* for which subsidiary records are typically maintained to keep track of various overhead classifications.

Because of the diverse nature of manufacturing companies, it simply isn't possible to prepare a complete list of all overhead cost types. However, specific examples at Conquest include the following:

1. *Indirect materials costs*
   a. Factory supplies that do not become an integral part of finished goods, such as oil used to lubricate the cutting machines and solvents used to clean the painting machines.
   b. Materials that become an integral part of finished goods but whose cost would require great effort to actually trace to finished goods. These items include grease used in each bike's bearing assembly and the nuts and bolts used to attach shift levers and other component parts.
2. *Indirect labor costs*
   a. Supervisors' salaries.
   b. Salaries of factory maintenance workers, forklift drivers, receiving clerks in the materials warehouse, and factory security personnel.

3. *Plant occupancy costs*
   a. Depreciation of the factory and the materials warehouse.
   b. Insurance and property taxes on land and buildings.
   c. Maintenance and repairs on buildings.
   d. Utilities and telephone costs.
4. *Machinery and equipment costs*
   a. Depreciation of machinery.
   b. Maintenance of machinery.
5. *Cost of regulatory compliance*
   a. Meeting factory safety requirements.
   b. Disposal of waste materials such as empty paint canisters.
   c. Control over factory emissions (meeting clean air standards).

Selling expenses and general and administrative expenses do *not* relate to the manufacturing process and are *not* included in manufacturing overhead. Certain costs, such as insurance, property taxes, and utilities, sometimes apply in part to manufacturing operations and in part to selling and administrative functions. In such cases, these costs are *apportioned* among manufacturing overhead, general and administrative expenses, and selling expenses.

Recording Overhead Costs The Manufacturing Overhead account is debited to record any cost classified as overhead. Examples of costs debited to this account include the payment of indirect labor payrolls, the payment of factory utilities, the recording of depreciation on factory assets, and the purchase of indirect materials.[5] The account credited will vary depending on the nature of the overhead cost. For example, in recording the purchase of indirect materials, the account credited is usually Accounts Payable. In recording depreciation on machinery, however, the account credited is Accumulated Depreciation.

As the items included in total overhead costs are consumed by production activities, the related costs are transferred from the Manufacturing Overhead account into the Work in Process Inventory account (debit Work in Process Inventory, credit Manufacturing Overhead). In the course of the year, all the overhead costs incurred should be assigned to units of product manufactured. Thus, at year-end, the Manufacturing Overhead account should have a zero balance.

DIRECT AND INDIRECT MANUFACTURING COSTS

Learning Objective
LO5 Distinguish between direct and indirect costs.

The costs of direct materials and direct labor may be traced conveniently and directly to specific units of product. At Conquest, for example, it is relatively easy to determine the cost of the metal tubing and the cost of the direct labor that go into making a particular bicycle. For this reason, accountants call these items **direct manufacturing costs.**

Overhead, however, is an **indirect manufacturing cost.** Consider, for example, the types of costs that Conquest classifies as overhead. These costs include property taxes on the factory, depreciation on tools and equipment, supervisors' salaries, and repairs to equipment. How much of these indirect costs should be assigned to each bicycle?

There is no easy answer to this question. By definition, indirect costs *cannot* be traced easily and directly to specific units of production. While these costs are often easier to view *as a whole* than on a per-unit basis, we will see that both financial and management accountants require unit cost information. Therefore, manufacturing companies must develop methods of allocating an appropriate portion of total manufacturing overhead to each product manufactured. These methods will be discussed in detail in Chapter 17.

WORK IN PROCESS INVENTORY, FINISHED GOODS INVENTORY, AND THE COST OF GOODS SOLD

We have devoted much of this chapter to discussing the three types of manufacturing costs—direct materials, direct labor, and manufacturing overhead. We will now shift our attention to

[5] Some companies record the purchase of indirect materials in the Materials Inventory account or in a separate inventory account. Our approach is commonly used when the quantity of indirect materials purchased does not differ significantly from the quantity of indirect materials used during each period.

the three accounts that provide the structure for the flow of these costs—the Work in Process Inventory account, the Finished Goods Inventory account, and the Cost of Goods Sold account.

The Work in Process Inventory account is used (1) to record the accumulation of manufacturing costs associated with the units of product worked on during the period and (2) to allocate these costs between those units completed during the period and those that are only partially completed.

Because direct materials, direct labor, and manufacturing overhead are consumed in production, their related costs are debited to the Work in Process Inventory account. The flow of costs into this inventory account (rather than into a corresponding expense account) is consistent with the idea that manufacturing costs are *product costs,* not period costs.

As specific units are completed, the cost of manufacturing them is transferred from the Work in Process Inventory account to the Finished Goods Inventory account. Thus, the balance in the Work in Process account represents only the manufacturing costs associated with units still "in process."

It is important to realize that once products are classified as finished goods, *no additional costs are allocated to them.* Therefore, the costs of storing, marketing, or delivering finished goods are regarded as *selling expenses,* not manufacturing costs. When units of finished goods are sold, their related costs must "flow" from the balance sheet through the income statement in compliance with the matching principle. Accordingly, as products are sold, their costs are transferred from the Finished Goods Inventory account to the Cost of Goods Sold account.

YOUR TURN **You as a Chief Financial Officer**

Assume that you are CFO of Conquest, Inc., and that you have just received an income statement and balance sheet from plant accountant Jim Sway in Bend, Oregon. In your conversations with Jim you learn that, in the recent reporting period, plant manager Darlene Cosky asked that inventory transportation cost, the cost of repairing the plant parking lot, and the newly installed plant landscaping costs all be allocated to cost of production. In addition, when these allocations took place, the plant produced many more bicycles than were sold, creating significant increases in the amount of inventory on hand. As a result, most of the costs described by Jim have been assigned to the inventory on hand (included as part of inventory costs in the balance sheet) but have not been assigned to cost of goods sold expenses (included on the income statement). Furthermore, during the recent reporting period both Darlene and Jim earned significant bonuses based on plant profitability. What, if anything, would you do as the CFO?

(See our comments on the Online Learning Center Web site.)

THE NEED FOR PER-UNIT COST DATA

Transferring the cost of specific units from one account to another requires knowledge of each unit's *per-unit cost*—that is, the total manufacturing costs assigned to specific units. The determination of unit cost is one of the primary goals of every cost accounting system and will be explained and illustrated more completely in Chapter 17.

Unit costs are of importance to both financial and management accountants. Financial accountants use unit costs in recording the transfer of completed goods from Work in Process to Finished Goods and from Finished Goods to Cost of Goods Sold. Management accountants use the same information to make pricing decisions, evaluate the efficiency of current operations, and plan for future operations.

DETERMINING THE COST OF FINISHED GOODS MANUFACTURED

Learning Objective **Prepare a schedule of the cost of finished goods manufactured.** LO6

Most manufacturing companies prepare a **schedule of the cost of finished goods manufactured** to provide managers with an overview of manufacturing activities during the period.

Using the information from Exhibit 16–6, a schedule of Conquest's cost of finished goods manufactured is shown in Exhibit 16–7.

Exhibit 16–7
SCHEDULE OF MANUFACTURING ACTIVITIES AT CONQUEST, INC., FOR 2011

CONQUEST, INC. SCHEDULE OF THE COST OF FINISHED GOODS MANUFACTURED FOR THE YEAR ENDED DECEMBER 31, 2011		
Work in process inventory, beginning of the year		$ 30,000
Manufacturing cost assigned to production:		
Direct materials used	$150,000	
Direct labor	300,000	
Manufacturing overhead	360,000	
Total manufacturing costs		810,000
Total cost of all work in process during the year		$840,000
Less: Work in process inventory, end of the year		(40,000)
Cost of finished goods manufactured		$800,000

Notice that all of the figures in this schedule were obtained from Conquest's Work in Process Inventory account illustrated in Exhibit 16–6. In short, Exhibit 16–7 summarizes the flow of manufacturing costs into and out of the Work in Process Inventory account.

Purpose of the Schedule A schedule of the cost of finished goods manufactured is *not* a formal financial statement and generally does not appear in the company's annual report. Rather, it is intended primarily to assist managers in understanding and evaluating the overall cost of manufacturing products. By comparing these schedules for successive periods, for example, managers can determine whether direct labor or manufacturing overhead is rising or falling as a percentage of total manufacturing costs. In addition, the schedule is helpful in developing information about unit costs.

If a company manufactures only a single product line, its cost per unit simply equals its *cost of finished goods manufactured* divided by the *number of units produced.* For example, if Conquest produces only one line of mountain bikes, its average cost per unit would be *$80* had it produced *10,000* finished units during 2011 ($800,000 divided by 10,000 units). If Conquest produced multiple lines of mountain bikes, it would prepare a separate schedule of the cost of finished goods manufactured for each product line.

FINANCIAL STATEMENTS OF A MANUFACTURING COMPANY

Let us now illustrate how the information used in our example will be reported in the 2011 income statement and balance sheet of Conquest, Inc.

The company's 2011 income statement is presented in Exhibit 16–8.

Notice that no manufacturing costs appear among the company's operating expenses. In fact, manufacturing costs appear in only two places in a manufacturer's financial statements. First, costs associated with units *sold* during the period appear in the income statement as the *cost of goods sold.* The $782,000 cost of goods sold figure reported in Conquest's income statement was taken directly from the company's perpetual inventory records. However, this amount may be verified as follows:

Beginning finished goods inventory (1/1/11)	$150,000
Add: Cost of finished goods manufactured during the year	800,000
Cost of finished goods available for sale	$950,000
Less: Ending finished goods inventory (12/31/11)	168,000
Cost of goods sold	$782,000

Exhibit 16–8

REPORTED INCOME AT CONQUEST, INC., FOR 2011

CONQUEST, INC. INCOME STATEMENT FOR THE YEAR ENDED DECEMBER 31, 2011		
Sales		$1,300,000
Cost of goods sold		782,000
Gross profit on sales		$ 518,000
Operating expenses:		
Selling expenses	$135,000	
General and administrative expenses	265,000	
Total operating expenses		400,000
Income from operations		$ 118,000
Less: Interest expense		18,000
Income before income taxes		$ 100,000
Income taxes expense		30,000
Net income		$ 70,000

Second, all manufacturing costs associated with goods *still on hand* are classified as *inventory* and appear in the balance sheet. The balance sheet presentation of Conquest's three types of inventory is illustrated in Exhibit 16–9.

Exhibit 16–9

CONQUEST, INC.'S CURRENT ASSET BALANCE AT THE END OF 2011

CONQUEST, INC. PARTIAL BALANCE SHEET DECEMBER 31, 2011		
Current assets:		
Cash and Cash Equivalents		$ 60,000
Accounts Receivable (net of allowance for doubtful accounts)		190,000
Inventories:		
Materials	$ 20,000	
Work in Process	40,000	
Finished Goods	168,000	
Total Inventories		228,000
Total current assets		$478,000

Notice the three types of inventory

As previously mentioned, Conquest's balance sheet includes a current liability for wages payable equal to the unadjusted $8,000 credit balance in the Direct Labor account.

INTERNATIONAL FINANCIAL REPORTING STANDARDS AND INVENTORIES

U.S. generally accepted accounting principles (GAAP) allows a variety of inventory methods for financial statement presentation including the average cost approach discussed in this chapter (others are specific identification, LIFO, FIFO, or average cost). However, international accounting standards are not consistent with several U.S. GAAP methods. For example, as discussed in Chapter 8, LIFO methods are allowed by U.S. GAAP, but not allowed under IFRS. Further, when impairment of inventory occurs then both U.S. GAAP and IFRS require companies to write inventories down. However, IFRS requires revaluation under certain circumstances, but U.S. GAAP does not allow such a revaluation. As the members of the FASB and the IASB work to reconcile differences and converge their financial reporting standards, consideration of internal management accounting activities are brought to their attention from such organizations as the Institute of Management Accountants, mentioned earlier in this chapter.

Concluding Remarks

This chapter provides a framework to help you think about the role of management accounting in business. The framework says management accounting information, tools, and techniques help (1) assign decision-making responsibility, (2) support the decision-making process, and (3) evaluate decision outcomes. Past, current, and future information is collected by the management accounting system to support various decisions. Much of what you will learn in later chapters is based on this initial framework and on the management accounting terminology introduced in this chapter. These ideas will be useful to you whether you currently (or in the future will) work for a business or if you someday (or now) own your own business.

END-OF-CHAPTER REVIEW

SUMMARY OF LEARNING OBJECTIVES

LO1 **Explain the three principles guiding the design of management accounting systems.** First, management accounting systems help to decide who has the decision-making authority over company assets. Second, accounting information produced or created from the management accounting system supports planning and decision making. Finally, management accounting reports provide a means of monitoring, evaluating, and rewarding performance.

LO2 **Describe the three basic types of manufacturing costs.** Direct materials used consist of the parts and materials that become part of the finished products. Direct labor cost consists of the wages paid to factory employees who work directly on the products being manufactured. Manufacturing overhead includes all manufacturing costs other than the cost of materials used and direct labor. Examples of manufacturing overhead include depreciation of machinery and the plant security service.

LO3 **Distinguish between product costs and period costs.** Product costs are the costs of creating inventory. They are treated as assets until the related goods are sold, at which time the product costs are deducted from revenue as the cost of goods sold. Thus, goods manufactured this year but not sold until next year are deducted from next year's revenue.

Period costs are charged to expense in the accounting period in which they are incurred. Period costs are not related to production of goods; consequently, they are deducted from revenue on the assumption that the benefits obtained from the expenditures are received in the same period as the costs are incurred. Period costs include general and administrative expense, selling expense, and income taxes expense.

LO4 **Describe how manufacturing costs flow through perpetual inventory accounts.** Manufacturing costs originally are recorded in three controlling accounts: Materials Inventory, Direct Labor, and Manufacturing Overhead. As these costs become applicable to goods placed into production, they are transferred from these manufacturing cost accounts to the Work in Process Inventory account. As units are completed, their cost is transferred from the Work in Process account to Finished Goods Inventory. Then, when units are sold, their costs are transferred from Finished Goods Inventory to the Cost of Goods Sold account.

LO5 **Distinguish between direct and indirect costs.** Direct manufacturing costs (direct materials and direct labor) can be identified with specific products. Indirect manufacturing costs are the many elements of manufacturing overhead that apply to factory operations as a whole and cannot be traced to specific products.

LO6 **Prepare a schedule of the cost of finished goods manufactured.** This schedule summarizes the flow of manufacturing costs into and out of the Work in Process Inventory account. Its purpose is to assist management in understanding and evaluating manufacturing costs incurred in the period.

To prepare this schedule, start by listing the work in process inventory at the beginning of the year. To this amount, add the materials used, direct labor costs, and overhead for the period. Combining these four items indicates the total cost of all work in process during the period. A final step is deducting the cost of work still in process at the end of the period. This gives us the cost of finished goods manufactured during the period.

Key Terms Introduced or Emphasized in Chapter 16

benchmark study (p. 722) A study designed to show an organization how its costs and processes compare to others in the industry.

conversion costs (p. 726) The direct labor and overhead costs required to convert raw materials into finished goods.

direct labor (p. 726) Payroll costs for employees who work directly on the products being manufactured, either by hand or with machines.

direct manufacturing cost (p. 732) A manufacturing cost that can be traced conveniently and directly into the quantity of finished goods manufactured. Examples include direct materials and direct labor.

direct materials (p. 726) Materials and component parts that become an integral part of the manufactured goods and can be traced directly to the finished products.

finished goods inventory (p. 728) The completed units that have emerged from the manufacturing process and are on hand available for sale.

indirect labor (p. 731) Payroll costs relating to factory employees who do not work directly on the goods being manufactured. Examples are wages of security guards and maintenance personnel. Indirect labor costs are classified as manufacturing overhead.

indirect manufacturing cost (p. 732) A manufacturing cost that cannot be conveniently traced to the specific products being manufactured. Examples include property taxes, depreciation on machinery, and other types of manufacturing overhead.

indirect materials (p. 730) Materials used in the manufacturing process that cannot be traced conveniently to specific units of production. Examples include lubricating oil, maintenance supplies, and glue. Indirect materials are accounted for as part of manufacturing overhead.

management accounting (p. 722) The design and use of accounting information systems inside the firm to achieve the firm's objectives.

manufacturing costs (p. 725) The cost of manufacturing the goods that will be sold to customers. The basic types of manufacturing costs are direct materials, direct labor, and manufacturing overhead.

manufacturing overhead (p. 726) A "catchall" category including all manufacturing costs other than the costs of direct materials used and direct labor.

materials inventory (p. 728) The cost of direct materials on hand and available for use in the manufacturing process.

period costs (p. 727) Costs that are charged to expense accounts in the period that the costs are incurred. Includes all items classified as "expense."

prime costs (p. 726) The direct materials and direct labor consumed in the production of goods and services.

product costs (p. 726) The costs of purchasing or manufacturing inventory. Until the related goods are sold, these product costs represent an asset—inventory. Once the goods are sold, these costs are deducted from revenue as the cost of goods sold.

schedule of the cost of finished goods manufactured (p. 733) A schedule summarizing the flow of manufacturing costs into and out of the Work in Process Inventory account. Intended to assist managers in evaluating manufacturing costs.

value chain (p. 722) The linked set of activities and resources necessary to create and deliver a product or service to customers.

work in process inventory (p. 728) Goods at any stage of the manufacturing process short of completion. As these units are completed, they become finished goods.

Demonstration Problem

The following T accounts summarize the flow of manufacturing costs during the current year through the ledger accounts of Marston Manufacturing Company:

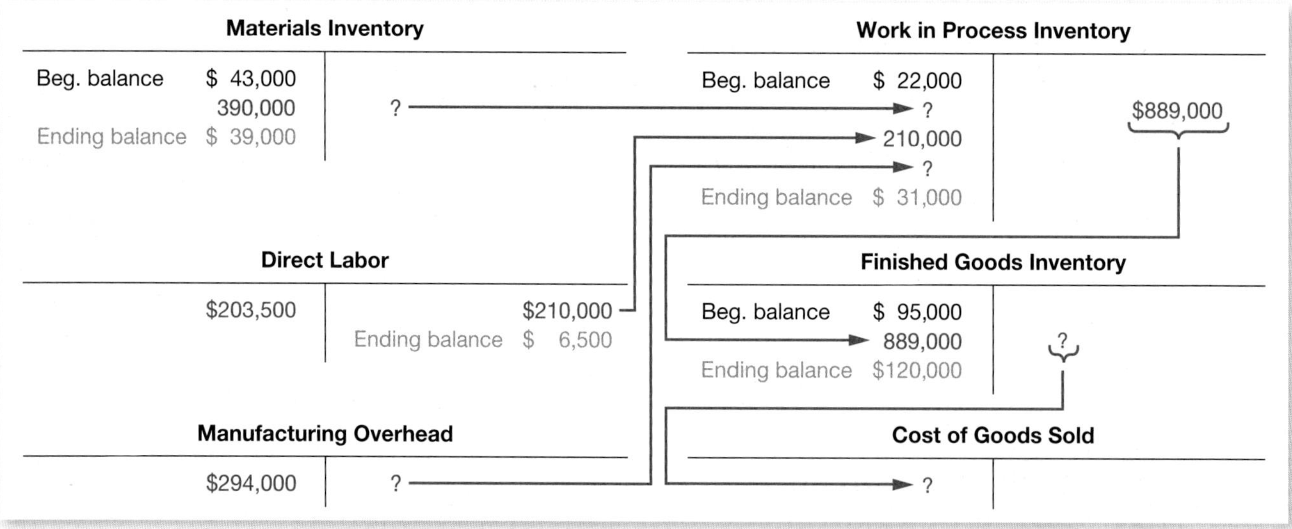

Instructions

Using the data above, determine the following amounts. Some amounts already appear in the T accounts; others require short computations.

a. Purchases of direct materials.

b. Direct materials used during the year.

c. Direct labor costs assigned to production.

d. The year-end liability to direct workers for wages payable.

e. The overhead costs assigned to production during the year.

f. Total manufacturing costs charged to production during the year.

g. The cost of finished goods manufactured.

h. The cost of goods sold.

i. The total costs classified as inventory in the year-end balance sheet.

Solution to the Demonstration Problem

a.	Purchases of direct materials	$390,000
b.	Computation of direct materials used:	
	Materials inventory, beginning of year	$ 43,000
	Purchases of direct materials	390,000
	Direct materials available for use	$433,000
	Less: Materials inventory, end of year	39,000
	Direct materials used	$394,000
c.	Direct labor costs assigned to production	$210,000
d.	Year-end liability for direct wages payable	$ 6,500
e.	Overhead costs during the year:	
	Cost transferred out of work in process	$889,000
	Ending work in process	31,000
	Total cost to account for	$920,000
	Less: Direct materials used (part **b**)	394,000
	Direct labor used	210,000
	Beginning work in process	22,000
	Overhead assigned	$294,000
f.	Total manufacturing costs charged to production:	
	Direct materials used (part **b**)	$394,000
	Direct labor costs assigned to production	210,000
	Manufacturing overhead assigned (part **e**)	294,000
	Total manufacturing costs charged to production	$898,000
g.	Cost of finished goods manufactured	$889,000
h.	Computation of cost of goods sold:	
	Beginning inventory of finished goods	$ 95,000
	Cost of finished goods manufactured	889,000
	Cost of goods available for sale	$984,000
	Less: Ending inventory of finished goods	120,000
	Cost of goods sold	$864,000
i.	Total year-end inventory:	
	Materials	$ 39,000
	Work in process	31,000
	Finished goods	120,000
	Total inventory	$190,000

Self-Test Questions

The answers to these questions appear on page 757.

1. Indicate which of the following statements are more descriptive of management accounting than of financial accounting. (More than one answer may be appropriate.)

a. Recognized standards are used for presentation.

b. Information is tailored to the needs of individual decision makers.

c. Information is more widely distributed.

d. Emphasis is on expected future results.

2. In a manufacturing company, the costs debited to the Work in Process Inventory account represent:

a. Direct materials used, direct labor, and manufacturing overhead.

b. Cost of finished goods manufactured.

c. Period costs and product costs.

d. None of the above; the types of costs debited to this account will depend on the type of products being manufactured.

3. The Work in Process Inventory account had a beginning balance of $4,200 on February 1. During February, the cost of direct materials used was $29,000 and direct labor cost assigned to production was $3,000. $3,600 of overhead was assigned. If the cost of finished goods manufactured was $34,100, compute the balance in the Work in Process Inventory account at the *end* of February.

a. $9,900.
b. $1,500.
c. $2,100.
d. $5,700.

4. Manufacturing overhead costs would include:

a. Marketing costs related to selling the product.
b. The salary of the production line supervisor.
c. The chief executive officer's salary.
d. Research and development costs for a new product.

5. The accounting records of Newport Mfg. Co. include the following information for the most recent year ended December 31:

	Dec. 31	Jan. 1
Inventory of work in process	$ 20,000	$10,000
Inventory of finished goods	80,000	60,000
Direct materials used	200,000	
Direct labor	120,000	
Manufacturing overhead	180,000	
Selling expenses	150,000	

Indicate which of the following are correct. (More than one answer may be correct.)

a. Amount debited to the Work in Process Inventory account during the year, $500,000.
b. Cost of finished goods manufactured, $490,000.
c. Cost of goods sold, $470,000.
d. Total manufacturing costs for the year, $650,000.

ASSIGNMENT MATERIAL Discussion Questions

1. Briefly distinguish between management and financial accounting information in terms of (**a**) the intended users of the information and (**b**) the purpose of the information.

2. Describe the three principles guiding the design of management accounting systems.

3. Is management accounting information developed in conformity with generally accepted accounting principles or some other set of prescribed standards? Explain.

4. A manufacturing firm has three inventory control accounts. Name each of the accounts, and describe briefly what the balance in each at the end of any accounting period represents.

5. Is the cost of disposing of hazardous waste materials resulting from factory operations a product cost or a period cost? Explain.

6. An important focus of management accounting is decision-making authority. Everyone within an organization has some decision-making authority. How do employees and managers know what decision-making authority they have regarding firm assets?

7. What amounts are *debited* to the Materials Inventory account? What amounts are *credited* to this account? What type of balance (debit or credit) is this account likely to have at year-end? Explain.

8. Briefly explain what accounting benchmark studies are and why they are important for an organization's management accounting system.

9. What amounts are debited to the Direct Labor account during the year? What amounts are credited to this account? What type of balance (debit or credit) is this account likely to have at year-end? Explain.

10. Exhibit 16–6 includes six ledger accounts. Which of these six accounts often have balances at year-end that appear in the company's formal financial statements? Briefly explain how these balances will be classified in the financial statements.

11. Argo Mfg. Co. uses approximately $1,200 in janitorial supplies to clean the work area and factory equipment each month. Should this $1,200 be included in the cost of direct materials used? Explain.

12. What amounts are *debited* to the Work in Process Inventory account during the year? What amounts are *credited* to this account? What does the year-end balance in this account represent?

13. What amounts are *debited* to the Finished Goods Inventory account during the year? What amounts are *credited* to this account? What type of balance (debit or credit) is this account likely to have at year-end?

14. Briefly describe the computation of the cost of finished goods manufactured as it appears in a schedule of the cost of finished goods manufactured.

15. A schedule of the cost of finished goods manufactured is a helpful tool in determining the per-unit cost of manufactured products. Explain several ways in which information about per-unit manufacturing costs is used by (**a**) management accountants and (**b**) financial accountants.

Brief Exercises

LO3 BRIEF EXERCISE 16.1
Product vs. Period Costs

During the year, Coronado Boat Yard has incurred manufacturing costs of $420,000 in building three large sailboats. At year-end, each boat is about 70 percent complete. How much of these manufacturing costs should be recognized as expense in Coronado Boat Yard's income statement for the current year? Explain.

LO4 BRIEF EXERCISE 16.2
Direct Materials Used

During the current year, the cost of direct materials purchased by a manufacturing firm was $510,000, and the direct materials inventory increased by $40,000. What was the cost of direct materials used during the year?

LO3 LO4 BRIEF EXERCISE 16.3
Cost of Goods Sold

A company that assembles trucks produces 60 trucks during the current year and incurs $3 million of material, labor, and overhead costs. Fifty-three trucks were sold during the year and each is allocated the same amount of costs. How much of the $3 million assembly costs should appear on the company's income statement for the current year?

LO4 BRIEF EXERCISE 16.4
Materials Inventory

Hula's Heavyweights, Inc., is a company that manufactures forklifts. During the year, Hula's purchased $1,450,000 of direct materials and placed $1,525,000 worth of direct materials into production. Hula's beginning balance in the Materials Inventory account was $320,000. What is the ending balance in Hula's Materials Inventory account?

LO2 LO4 BRIEF EXERCISE 16.5
Direct Labor Journal Entries

A.J.'s Cooling Systems, Inc., assigns $230,000 of direct labor costs to production during the current period. A.J.'s also pays employees $200,000 during the period. What are the two journal entries used to record these transactions?

LO4 LO5 BRIEF EXERCISE 16.6
Manufacturing Overhead Assigned

During the current year, CF Manufacturing Co. incurred $370,000 of indirect labor costs, $15,000 of indirect materials costs, $125,000 of rent costs, and $163,000 of other overhead costs. How much did CF Manufacturing assign to the Work in Process Inventory account from the Manufacturing Overhead account?

LO4 BRIEF EXERCISE 16.7
Inventory Balances

Ardvark Pets, Inc., has three stores in the state. The owner, Ms. Perkins, is having trouble tracking inventory costs in the three pet stores. Ms. Perkins knows about your skill in tracking and understanding cost flows and asks you to find the following missing items for the three stores:

	Midwest Ardvark	Northern Ardvark	Eastern Ardvark
Beginning inventory	$ 30,000	?	?
Transferred in	100,000	$200,000	$160,000
Transferred out	110,000	180,000	150,000
Ending Inventory	?	60,000	40,000

LO4 BRIEF EXERCISE 16.8
Work in Process Balances

The Work in Process Inventory account had a beginning balance of $16,200 on April 1. During April, the cost of direct materials used was $408,000 and direct labor cost assigned to production was $56,000. A total of $72,000 of overhead was assigned to production in April. If the cost of finished goods manufactured was $523,500, what was the balance in the Work in Process Inventory account on April 30?

LO3 through LO5 BRIEF EXERCISE 16.9
Prime vs. Conversion Costs

Hapless Repairs Co. does all the repair work for a medium-sized manufacturer of handheld computer games. The games are sent directly to Hapless, and after the games are repaired, Hapless bills the game manufacturer for cost plus a 30 percent markup. In the month of February, purchases of parts (replacement parts) by Hapless amounted to $90,000, the beginning inventory of parts was $40,500, and the ending inventory of parts was $15,250. Payments to repair technicians during the month of February totaled $63,000. Overhead incurred was $113,000.

a. What was the cost of materials used for repair work during the month of February?

b. What was the prime cost for February?

c. What was the conversion cost for February?

d. What was the total repair cost for February?

LO3 **BRIEF EXERCISE 16.10**
Partial Balance Sheet

At the end of the year, Kyler Electronic Corporation had the following balances:

Work in process	$ 43,600
Cash and cash equivalents	532,000
Finished goods	85,700
Raw materials	25,400
Accounts receivable	237,000

Prepare a partial balance sheet for Kyler's showing the above accounts.

Exercises

connect ACCOUNTING

LO1 through LO5 **EXERCISE 16.1**
Accounting Terminology

Listed below are eight technical accounting terms introduced or emphasized in this chapter:

Work in Process Inventory	Cost of finished goods manufactured
Conversion costs	Cost of Goods Sold
Period costs	Management accounting
Product costs	Manufacturing overhead

Each of the following statements may (or may not) describe one of these technical terms. For each statement, indicate the accounting term described, or answer "None" if the statement does not correctly describe any of the terms.

a. The preparation and use of accounting information designed to assist managers in planning and controlling the operations of a business.

b. All manufacturing costs other than direct materials used and direct labor.

c. Direct materials and direct labor used in manufacturing a product.

d. A manufacturing cost that can be traced conveniently and directly to manufactured units of product.

e. The account debited at the time that the Manufacturing Overhead account is credited.

f. The amount transferred from the Work in Process Inventory account to the Finished Goods Inventory account.

g. Costs that are debited directly to expense accounts when the costs are incurred.

LO2 **EXERCISE 16.2**
Basic Types of Manufacturing Costs

Into which of the three elements of manufacturing cost would each of the following be classified?

a. Tubing used in manufacturing bicycles.

b. Wages paid by an automobile manufacturer to employees who test-drive completed automobiles.

c. Property taxes on machinery.

d. Gold bullion used by a jewelry manufacturer.

e. Wages of assembly-line workers who package frozen food.

f. Salary of plant superintendent.

g. Electricity used in factory operations.

h. Salary of a nurse in a factory first-aid station.

LO3 LO5 **EXERCISE 16.3**
Product Costs and Period Costs

Indicate whether each of the following should be considered a *product cost* or a *period cost.* If you identify the item as a product cost, also indicate whether it is a *direct* or an *indirect* cost. For example, the answer to item **0** is "indirect product cost." Begin with item **a.**

0. Property taxes on factory building.

a. Cost of disposal of hazardous waste materials to a chemical plant.

b. Amounts paid by a mobile home manufacturer to a subcontractor who installs plumbing in each mobile home.

c. Depreciation on sales showroom fixtures.

d. Salaries of security guards in an administrative office building.

e. Salaries of factory security guards.

f. Salaries of office workers in the credit department.

g. Depreciation on the raw materials warehouse.

h. Income taxes on a profitable manufacturing company.

LO4 **EXERCISE 16.4**

Flow of Costs through Manufacturing Accounts

The following information was taken from the accounting records of Reliable Tool Corporation:

Work in process inventory, beginning of the year	$ 35,000
Cost of direct materials used	245,000
Direct labor cost applied to production	120,000
Cost of finished goods manufactured	675,000

Overhead is assigned to production at $300,000. Compute the amount of the work in process inventory on hand at year-end.

LO6 **EXERCISE 16.5**

Preparing a Schedule of the Cost of Finished Goods Manufactured

The accounting records of NuTronics, Inc., include the following information for the year ended December 31, 2011.

	Dec. 31	Jan. 1
Inventory of materials	$ 24,000	$20,000
Inventory of work in process	8,000	12,000
Inventory of finished goods	90,000	80,000
Direct materials used	210,000	
Direct labor	120,000	
Selling expenses	170,000	
General and administrative expenses	140,000	

Overhead is assigned to production at $192,000.

a. Prepare a schedule of the cost of finished goods manufactured. (Not all of the data given above are used in this schedule.)

b. Assume that the company manufactures a single product and that 20,000 units were completed during the year. What is the average per-unit cost of manufacturing this product?

LO3 through LO5 **EXERCISE 16.6**

Flow of Costs through Manufacturing Accounts

The Bags and Luggage Company had the following account balances as of January 1:

Direct Materials Inventory	$ 9,200
Work in Process Inventory	78,400
Finished Goods Inventory	53,600
Manufacturing Overhead	–0–

During the month of January, all of the following occurred:

1. Direct labor costs were $42,000 for 1,800 hours worked.
2. Direct materials costing $35,750 and indirect materials costing $3,500 were purchased.
3. Sales commissions of $16,500 were earned by the sales force.
4. $26,000 worth of direct materials were used in production.
5. Advertising costs of $6,300 were incurred.
6. Factory supervisors earned salaries of $12,000.
7. Indirect labor costs for the month were $3,000.
8. Monthly depreciation on factory equipment was $4,500.

9. Utilities expense of $7,800 was incurred in the factory.
10. Luggage with manufacturing costs of $70,100 were transferred to finished goods.
11. Monthly insurance costs for the factory were $4,200.
12. $5,000 in property taxes on the factory were incurred and paid.
13. Luggage with manufacturing costs of $89,000 were sold for $145,000.

Instructions

a. If Bags and Luggage assigns manufacturing overhead of $34,400, what will be the balances in the Direct Materials, Work in Process, and Finished Goods Inventory accounts at the end of January?
b. As of January 31, what will be the balance in the Manufacturing Overhead account?
c. What was Bags and Luggage's operating income for January?

LO1 **EXERCISE 16.7** Manipulating Accounting Figures

Joe Felan is the production manager at Utex Corporation. He was recently quoted as saying, "Since management reports aren't subject to generally accepted accounting principles, and they aren't directly used by outside investors and creditors, it's really okay for managers to manipulate the reports as they see fit." Do you agree with Felan's statement? Defend your answer.

LO1 **EXERCISE 16.8** Design of Management Accounting Systems

Sheila Lufty manages the plant that produces dining room furniture for Bastile Furniture Company. Sheila's annual performance is evaluated based on how well she manages all the costs incurred to run the plant and produce the furniture. For her annual evaluation, the costs incurred for the year are compared to the budgeted costs that were established at the beginning of the year. Sheila receives a large bonus if the total costs are less than those budgeted at the beginning of the year.

Recently, Sheila provided the following end-of-year explanation to her boss, the division head, Rose Pantle:

> Rose, I know that the plant costs were over budget again this year. However, during the year I only receive four reports from accounting about the plant costs. These quarterly reports from accounting tell me what the actual plant costs are each quarter. Because the budget is based on yearly totals, it is difficult to tell from the accounting reports if we are falling behind budget. In addition, the sales department decides how many sets of dining room furniture we will produce during the year. This year, sales demanded 1,000 more dining room sets than budgeted at the beginning of the year. These extra sets increased the plant costs significantly.

On the basis of the three principles of management accounting system design discussed in this chapter, identify three problems with Bastile Furniture Company's management accounting system. What would you recommend that Bastile do to fix the problems?

LO4 LO6 **EXERCISE 16.9** Preparing an Income Statement Using the Cost of Finished Goods Manufactured

The Anthony Company, a sole proprietorship, reports the following information pertaining to its operating activities:

	Ending Balance	Beginning Balance
Materials Inventory	$10,000	$40,000
Work in Process Inventory	29,000	60,000
Finished Goods Inventory	52,000	42,000

During the year, the company purchased $40,000 of direct materials and incurred $21,000 of direct labor costs. Total manufacturing overhead costs for the year amounted to $18,000. Selling and administrative expenses amounted to $60,000, and the company's annual sales amounted to $250,000.

a. Prepare Anthony's schedule of the cost of finished goods manufactured.
b. Prepare Anthony's income statement (ignore income taxes).

LO4 LO6 **EXERCISE 16.10** Preparing an Income Statement Using the Cost of Finished Goods Manufactured

Ridgeway Company reports the following information pertaining to its operating activities:

	Ending Balance	Beginning Balance
Materials Inventory	$70,000	$60,000
Work in Process Inventory	41,000	29,000
Finished Goods Inventory	16,000	21,000

During the year, the company purchased $35,000 of direct materials and incurred $22,000 of direct labor costs. Total manufacturing overhead costs for the year amounted to $19,000. Selling and administrative expenses amounted to $30,000, and the company's annual sales amounted to $80,000.

a. Prepare Ridgeway's schedule of the cost of finished goods manufactured.

b. Prepare Ridgeway's income statement (ignore income taxes).

LO1 **EXERCISE 16.11** Management Accounting Systems Design

Boeing Company has had its financial ups and downs. Recently, the CFO for **Boeing** helped turn its problems around by analyzing the amount of value each product was providing to the company's bottom line. The analysis ultimately determined which programs were making or losing money for **Boeing**. Based on the analysis, key operational metrics were established and reported to managers on a regular basis. These performance metrics detailed the company's progress toward reducing inventory, reducing costs, and streamlining operations. Managers were evaluated based on these metrics.

Explain how the above description of activities at **Boeing Company** is consistent with the three principles that govern how management accounting systems are designed and used in companies.

LO3 LO4 LO6 **EXERCISE 16.12** Costs at Hobart Industries

The accounting records of Hobart Industries show the following information for the most recent year ended December 31:

	Dec. 31	Jan. 1
Inventory of work in process	$ 40,000	$18,000
Inventory of finished goods	60,000	68,000
Direct materials used	250,000	
Direct labor	120,000	
Manufacturing overhead	145,000	
Selling expenses	135,000	

a. Find the amount debited to the Work In Process Inventory account during the year.

b. What is the cost of goods manufactured for the year?

c. What is the cost of goods sold for the year?

d. What are the total manufacturing costs for the year?

LO2 LO3 LO5 **EXERCISE 16.13** Classifying Costs

Classify each of the following costs as a *product cost* or *period cost*. If it is a product cost, classify it as *direct* (or *indirect*) *materials*, *direct* (or *indirect*) *labor*, or *overhead*.

a. Wheat used to make flour at **General Mills**.

b. Sales commissions paid to sales personnel at **Gap** retail stores.

c. Costs incurred by **General Motors** to ship automobile seats purchased from the **Lear Corporation** to GM assembly plants.

d. Insurance paid on the **Target** retail stores in Michigan.

e. Insurance paid on the **Target** warehouse holding merchandise inventory.

f. Bonus paid to all production employees of **General Motors** at the end of a profitable fiscal year.

g. Health care costs for the office workers at the headquarters of **Johnson & Johnson Company**.

h. Bolts used by **Trek Bicycle Corporation** to secure the bike parts to the frame.

LO2 LO5 **EXERCISE 16.14**
Manufacturing Costs at **Coca-Cola**

Go to the following Web site for the **Coca-Cola Company:**
http://www.worldofcoca-cola.com
Select the "Virtual Tour" from the list of activities on the left-hand side of the screen. Choose "Bottle work" to see the bottling operation.

a. Determine five direct materials that are used to create Coca-Cola.®

b. Identify at least three types of labor. For each type of labor, identify it as *direct* or *indirect.*

c. Identify at least three types of overhead costs.

LO3 **EXERCISE 16.15**
Home Depot Product vs. Period Costs

Use the **Home Depot** 2009 financial statements in Appendix A at the end of this textbook. Read note 1 to the financial statements that summarizes significant accounting policies for **Home Depot**. Read the section titled "Cost of Sales" on page A-9. Explain how **Home Depot** classifies some transportation, shipping, and handling costs as period expenses and others as product costs. On what basis does it distinguish between shipping or transportation costs that are period expenses and those that are product costs?

Problem Set A

LO3 LO4 **PROBLEM 16.1A**
An Introduction to Product Costs

Aqua-Marine manufactures fiberglass fishing boats. The manufacturing costs incurred during its first year of operations are shown as follows:

Direct materials purchased	$225,000
Direct materials used	216,000
Direct labor	200,000
Manufacturing overhead	350,000
Cost of finished goods manufactured (112 boats)	728,000

During the year, 112 completed boats were manufactured, of which 100 were sold. (Assume that the amount of the ending inventory of finished goods and the cost of goods sold are determined using the average per-unit cost of manufacturing a completed boat.)

Instructions

a. Compute each of the following and show all computations:

1. The average per-unit cost of manufacturing a completed boat during the current year.
2. The year-end balances of the inventories of materials, work in process, and finished goods.
3. The cost of goods sold during the year.

b. For the current year, the costs of direct materials purchased, direct labor assigned to production, and actual manufacturing overhead total $775,000. Is this the amount of manufacturing costs deducted from revenue in the current year? Explain fully.

LO2 through LO4 **PROBLEM 16.2A**
An Introduction to Product Costs

Road Warrior Corporation began operations early in the current year, building luxury motor homes. During the year, the company started and completed 45 motor homes at a cost of $55,000 per unit. Of these, 43 were sold for $105,000 each and two remain in finished goods inventory. In addition, the company had six partially completed units in its factory at year-end. Total costs for the year (summarized alphabetically) were as follows:

Direct materials used	$ 750,000
Direct labor	800,000
Income tax expense	100,000
General and administrative expenses	500,000
Manufacturing overhead	1,200,000
Selling expenses	500,000

Instructions

Compute the following for the current year:

a. Total manufacturing costs charged to work in process during the period.

b. Cost of finished goods manufactured.

c. Cost of goods sold.

d. Gross profit on sales.

e. Ending inventories of (**1**) work in process and (**2**) finished goods.

LO4 PROBLEM 16.3A

The Flow of Manufacturing Costs through Ledger Accounts

The flow of manufacturing costs through the ledger accounts of Superior Locks, Inc., in the current year is illustrated below in summarized form.

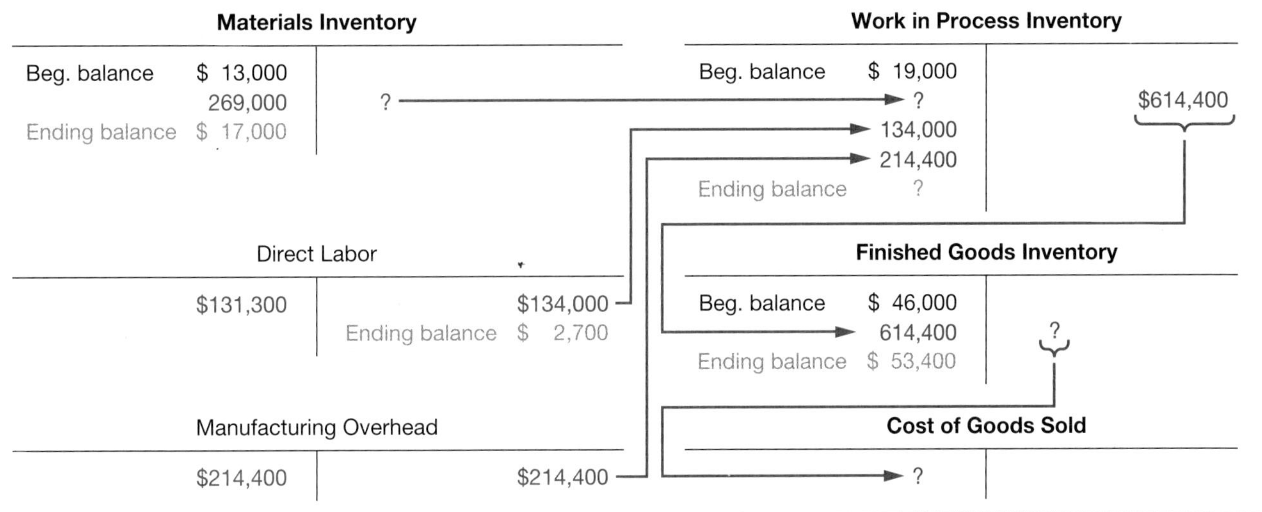

Instructions

Indicate the amounts requested below. Some amounts are shown in the illustrated T accounts; others require short computations. (Show all computations.)

a. Purchases of direct materials.

b. The cost of direct materials used.

c. Direct labor costs assigned to production.

d. The year-end liability for direct wages payable.

e. Total manufacturing costs charged to the Work in Process Inventory account during the current year.

f. The cost of finished goods manufactured.

g. The year-end balance in the Work in Process Inventory account.

h. The cost of goods sold.

i. The total amount of inventory listed in the year-end balance sheet.

LO4 PROBLEM 16.4A

The Flow of Manufacturing Costs through Perpetual Inventory Records

The following T accounts summarize the flow of manufacturing costs during the current year through the ledger accounts of Double Bar Corporation:

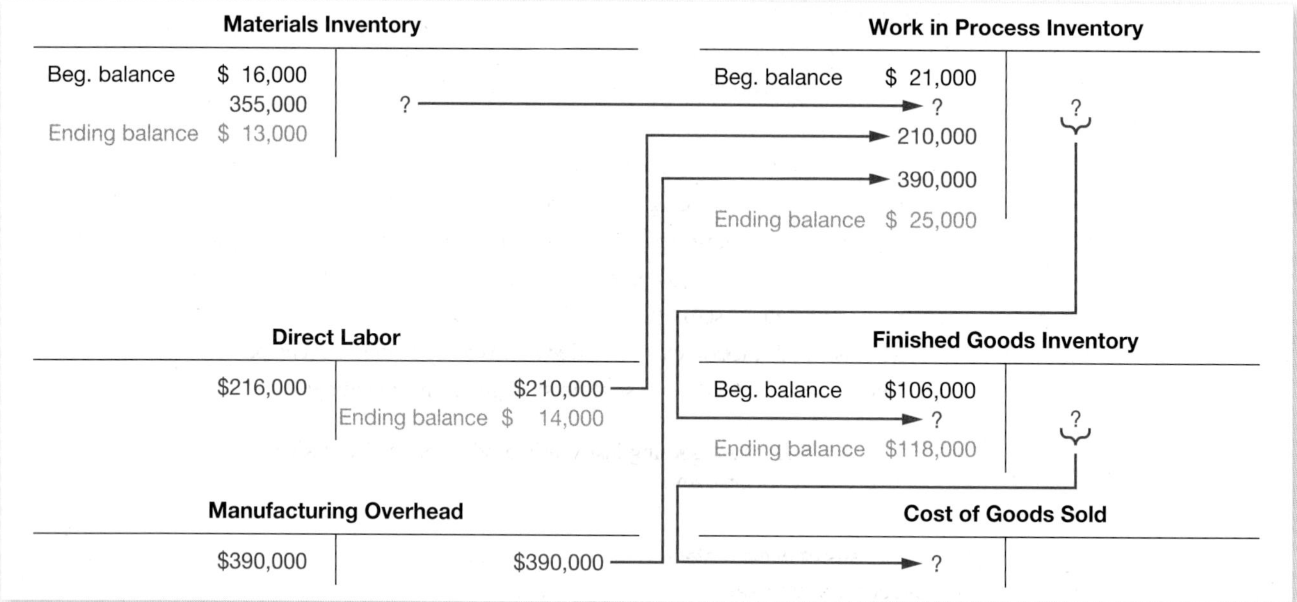

Instructions

From the data supplied above, indicate the following amounts. Some amounts are shown in the T accounts; others require short computations. (Show all computations.)

a. Purchases of direct materials during the year.

b. The cost of direct materials used.

c. Direct labor payrolls paid during the year.

d. Direct labor costs assigned to production.

e. Total manufacturing costs charged to the Work in Process Inventory account during the year.

f. The cost of finished goods manufactured.

g. The cost of goods sold.

h. The total costs to be classified as inventory in the year-end balance sheet.

LO3 LO4 LO6

PROBLEM 16.5A
The Flow of Manufacturing Costs: A Comprehensive Problem

The balances in the perpetual inventory accounts of Hillsdale Manufacturing Corporation at the beginning and end of the current year are as follows:

	End of Year	Beginning of Year
Inventory accounts:		
Materials	$26,000	$22,000
Work in Process	9,000	5,000
Finished Goods Inventory	25,000	38,000

The total dollar amounts debited and credited during the year to the accounts used in recording manufacturing activities are as follows:

	Debit Entries	Credit Entries
Account:		
Materials Inventory	$410,000	$?
Direct Labor Payable	189,000	192,000
Manufacturing Overhead	393,600	393,600
Work in Process Inventory	?	?
Finished Goods Inventory	?	?

Instructions

a. Using these data, state or compute for the year the following amounts:

1. Direct materials purchased.
2. Direct materials used.
3. Payments of direct labor payrolls.
4. Direct labor cost assigned to production.
5. Total manufacturing costs charged to the Work in Process Inventory account during the year.
6. The cost of finished goods manufactured.
7. Cost of goods sold.
8. The total amount to be classified as inventory in the year-end balance sheet.

b. Prepare a schedule of the cost of finished goods manufactured.

LO4 LO6 **PROBLEM 16.6A** Determining and Reporting Product Cost Information

The following are data regarding last year's production of Dicer Ricer, one of the major products of Kitchen Gadget Company:

Purchases of direct materials	$332,000
Direct materials used	333,600
Direct labor payrolls (paid during the year)	176,700
Direct labor costs assigned to production	180,000
Manufacturing overhead	288,000

During the year, 61,000 units of this product were manufactured and 62,100 units were sold. Selected information concerning inventories during the year follows:

	End of Year	Beginning of Year
Materials	$?	$12,800
Work in Process	4,700	3,000
Finished Goods, Jan. 1 (3,000 units @ $13)	?	39,000

Instructions

a. Prepare a schedule of the cost of finished goods manufactured for the Dicer Ricer product.

b. Compute the average cost of a Dicer Ricer per finished unit for last year.

c. Compute the cost of goods sold associated with the sale of Dicer Ricer. Assume that there is a first-in, first-out (FIFO) flow through the Finished Goods Inventory account and that all units completed during the year are assigned the per-unit costs determined in part **b.**

d. Compute the amount of inventory relating to Dicer Ricer that will be listed in the company's balance sheet at December 31. Show supporting computations for the year-end amounts of materials inventory and finished goods inventory.

e. Explain how the $180,000 in direct labor costs assigned to production affect the company's income statement and balance sheet.

LO4 LO6 **PROBLEM 16.7A** Determining Unit Costs Using the Cost of Finished Goods Manufactured

The accounting records of Idaho Paper Company include the following information relating to the current year:

	Dec. 31	Jan. 1
Materials inventory	$ 20,000	$ 25,000
Work in process inventory	37,500	40,000
Finished goods inventory, Jan. 1 (10,000 units @ $21 per unit)	?	210,000
Purchases of direct materials during year	330,000	
Direct labor costs assigned to production	375,000	
Manufacturing overhead	637,500	

The company manufactures a single product; during the current year, *45,000* units were manufactured and *40,000* units were sold.

Instructions

a. Prepare a schedule of the cost of finished goods manufactured for the current year. (Show a supporting computation of the cost of direct materials *used* during the year.)

b. Compute the average per-unit cost of production during the current year.

c. Compute the cost of goods sold during the year, assuming that the FIFO (first-in, first-out) method of inventory costing is used.

d. Compute the cost of the inventory of finished goods at December 31 of the current year, assuming that the FIFO (first-in, first-out) method of inventory costing is used.

LO3 LO4 LO6

PROBLEM 16.8A
Measuring Unit Cost

Early in the year, John Raymond founded Raymond Engineering Co. for the purpose of manufacturing a special flow control valve that he had designed. Shortly after year-end, the company's accountant was injured in a skiing accident, and no year-end financial statements were prepared. However, the accountant had correctly determined the year-end inventories at the following amounts:

Materials	$46,000
Work in process	31,500
Finished goods (3,000 units)	88,500

As this was the first year of operations, there were no beginning inventories.

While the accountant was in the hospital, Raymond improperly prepared the following income statement from the company's accounting records:

Net sales		$610,600
Cost of goods sold:		
Purchases of direct materials	$181,000	
Direct labor costs	110,000	
Manufacturing overhead	170,000	
Selling expenses	70,600	
Administrative expenses	132,000	
Total costs		663,600
Net loss for year		$ (53,000)

Raymond was very disappointed in these operating results. He stated, "Not only did we lose more than $50,000 this year, but look at our unit production costs. We sold 10,000 units this year at a cost of $663,600; that amounts to a cost of $66.36 per unit. I know some of our competitors are able to manufacture similar valves for about $35 per unit. I don't need an accountant to know that this business is a failure."

Instructions

a. Prepare a schedule of the cost of finished goods manufactured for the year. (As there were no beginning inventories, your schedule will start with "Manufacturing costs assigned to production:".) Show a supporting computation for the cost of direct materials used during the year.

b. Compute the average cost per unit manufactured.

c. Prepare a corrected income statement for the year, using the multiple-step format. If the company has earned any operating income, assume an income tax rate of 30 percent. (Omit earnings per share figures.)

d. Explain whether you agree or disagree with Raymond's remarks that the business is unprofitable and that its unit cost of production ($66.36, according to Raymond) is much higher than that of competitors (around $35). If you disagree with Raymond, explain any errors or shortcomings in his analysis.

Problem Set B

LO3 LO4

PROBLEM 16.1B
An Introduction to Product Costs

Pinning, Inc., manufactures dowhats. The manufacturing costs incurred during its first year of operations are as follows:

Direct materials purchased	$415,000
Direct materials used	385,000
Direct labor	335,000
Manufacturing overhead	430,000
Cost of finished goods manufactured (100 dowhats)	880,000

During the year, 110 completed dowhats were manufactured, of which 90 were sold. (Assume that the amount of the ending inventory of finished goods and the cost of goods sold are determined using the average per-unit cost of manufacturing a completed dowhat.)

Instructions

a. Compute each of the following and show all computations:
   1. The average per-unit cost of manufacturing a completed dowhat during the current year.
   2. The year-end balances of the following inventories: materials, work in progress, and finished goods.
   3. The cost of goods sold during the year.

b. For the current year, the costs of direct materials purchased, direct labor, and manufacturing overhead total $1,180,000. Is this the amount of manufacturing costs deducted from revenue in the current year? Explain fully.

LO2 through LO4

PROBLEM 16.2B
An Introduction to Product Costs

River Queen Corporation began operations early in the current year, building luxury boats. During the year, the company started and completed 40 boats at a cost of $80,000 per unit. Of these, 30 were sold for $130,000 each and 10 remain in finished goods inventory. In addition, the company had five partially completed units in its factory at year-end. Total costs for the year (summarized alphabetically) were as follows:

Direct materials used	$ 800,000
Direct labor	1,000,000
Income tax expense	80,000
General and administrative expenses	600,000
Manufacturing overhead	2,000,000
Selling expenses	400,000

Instructions

Compute the following for the current year:

a. Total manufacturing costs charged to work in process during the period.
b. Cost of finished goods manufactured.
c. Cost of goods sold.
d. Gross profit on sales.
e. Ending inventories of (**1**) work in process and (**2**) finished goods.

LO4

PROBLEM 16.3B
The Flow of Manufacturing Costs through Ledger Accounts

The flow of manufacturing costs through the ledger accounts of ISP, Inc., in the current year is illustrated below in summarized form:

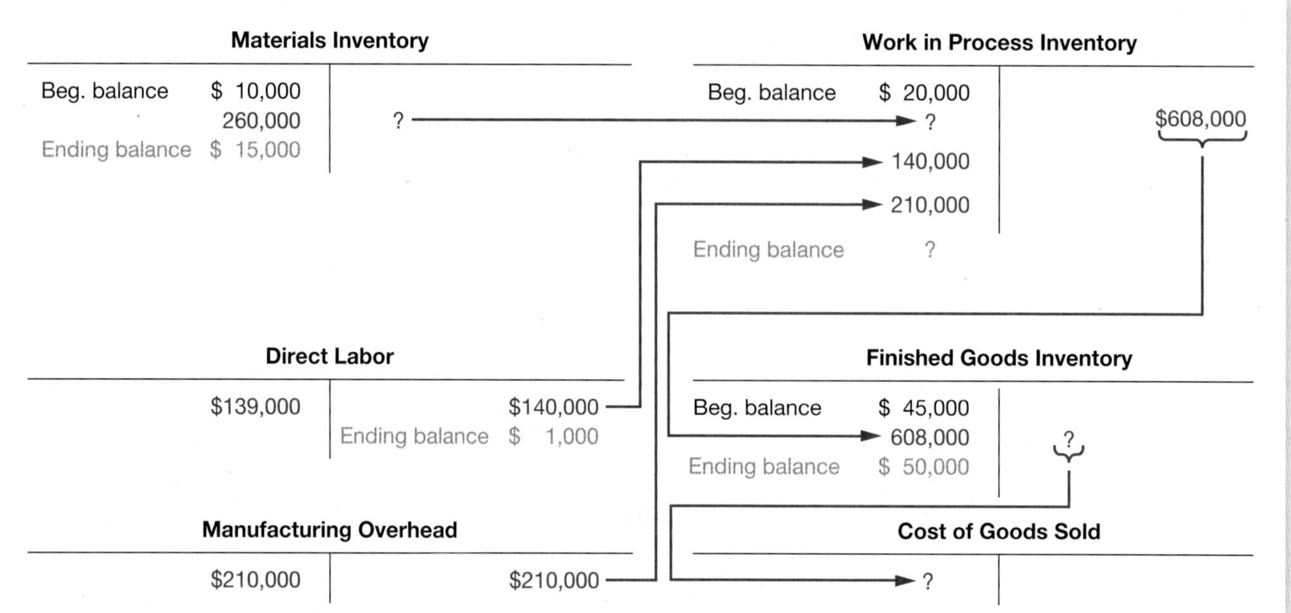

Instructions

Indicate the amounts requested below. Some amounts are shown in the T accounts above; others require short computations. (Show all computations.)

a. Purchases of direct materials.
b. The cost of direct materials used.
c. Direct labor costs assigned to production.
d. The year-end liability for direct wages payable.
e. The overhead as a percentage of direct labor costs.
f. Total manufacturing costs charged to the Work in Process Inventory account during the current year.
g. The cost of finished goods manufactured.
h. The year-end balance in the Work in Process Inventory account.
i. The cost of goods sold.
j. The total amount of inventory listed in the year-end balance sheet.

LO4 **PROBLEM 16.4B**
The Flow of Manufacturing Costs through Perpetual Inventory Records

The following T accounts summarize the flow of manufacturing costs during the current year through the ledger accounts of Payback Corporation:

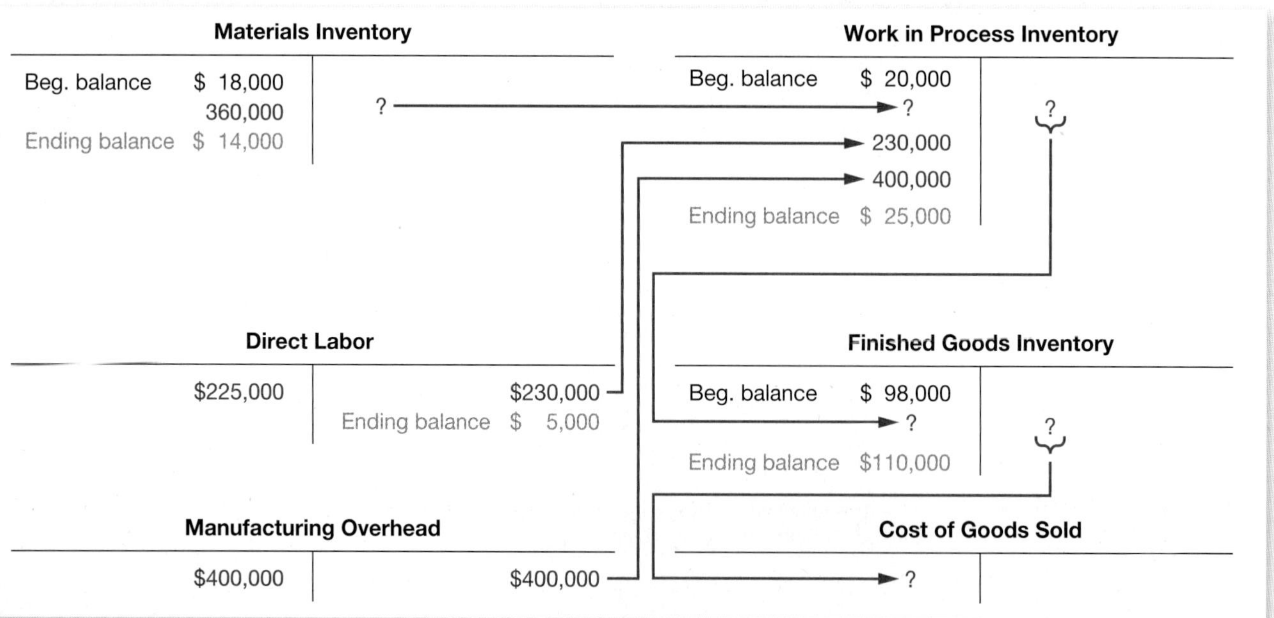

Instructions

From the data supplied above, indicate the following amounts. Some amounts are shown in the T accounts above; others require short computations. (Show all computations.)

a. Purchases of direct materials during the year.

b. The cost of direct materials used.

c. Direct labor payrolls paid during the year.

d. Direct labor costs assigned to production.

e. The overhead assigned to production as a percentage of direct labor costs.

f. Total manufacturing costs charged to the Work in Process Inventory account during the current year.

g. The cost of finished goods manufactured.

h. The cost of goods sold.

i. The total costs to be classified as inventory in the year-end balance sheet.

LO3 LO4 LO6

PROBLEM 16.5B

The Flow of Manufacturing Costs: A Comprehensive Problem

The balances in the perpetual inventory accounts of Valleyview Manufacturing Corporation at the beginning and end of the current year are as follows:

	End of Year	Beginning of Year
Inventory accounts:		
Materials	$15,000	$25,000
Work in Process	10,000	8,000
Finished Goods Inventory	24,000	30,000

Total dollar amounts debited and credited during the year to the accounts used in recording manufacturing activities are as follows:

	Debit Entries	Credit Entries
Account:		
Materials Inventory	$225,000	$?
Direct Labor	200,000	210,000
Manufacturing Overhead	420,000	420,000
Work in Process Inventory	?	?
Finished Goods Inventory	?	?

Instructions

a. Using these data, state or compute for the year the following amounts:

1. Direct materials purchased.
2. Direct materials used.
3. Payments of direct labor payrolls.
4. Direct labor cost assigned to production.
5. The overhead assigned to production stated as a percentage of direct labor costs.
6. Total manufacturing costs charged to the Work in Process Inventory account during the year.
7. The cost of finished goods manufactured.
8. The cost of goods sold.
9. The total amount to be classified as inventory in the year-end balance sheet.

b. Prepare a schedule of the cost of finished goods manufactured.

LO4 LO6

PROBLEM 16.6B

Determining and Reporting Product Cost Information

The following are data regarding last year's production of Old Joe, one of the major products of Columbus Toy Company:

Purchases of direct materials	$400,000
Direct materials used	402,000
Direct labor payrolls (paid during the year)	180,000
Direct labor costs assigned to production	220,000
Manufacturing overhead (incurred and applied)	330,000

During the year, 50,000 units of this product were manufactured and 51,500 units were sold. Selected information concerning inventories during the year follows:

	End of Year	Beginning of Year
Materials	$?	$15,000
Work in Process	6,000	5,000
Finished Goods, Jan. 1 (4,000 units @ $19)	?	76,000

Instructions

a. Prepare a schedule of the cost of finished goods manufactured for the Old Joe product.

b. Compute the average cost of Old Joe per finished unit.

c. Compute the cost of goods sold associated with the sale of Old Joe. Assume that there is a first-in, first-out (FIFO) flow through the Finished Goods Inventory account and that all units completed are assigned the per-unit costs determined in part **b.**

d. Compute the amount of inventory relating to Old Joe that will be listed in the company's balance sheet at December 31. Show supporting computations for the year-end amounts of materials inventory and finished goods inventory.

e. Explain how the $220,000 in direct labor costs assigned to production affect the company's income statement and balance sheet.

LO4 LO6

PROBLEM 16.7B

Determining Unit Costs Using the Cost of Finished Goods Manufactured

The accounting records of Maine Products Company include the following information relating to the current year:

	Dec. 31	Jan. 1
Materials inventory	$ 22,000	$ 30,000
Work in process inventory	39,000	39,000
Finished goods inventory, Jan. 1 (8,000 units @ $22 per unit)	?	176,000
Purchases of direct materials during year	290,000	
Direct labor costs assigned to production	350,000	
Manufacturing overhead assigned to production	552,000	

The company manufactures a single product; during the current year, *60,000* units were manufactured and *50,000* units were sold.

Instructions

a. Prepare a schedule of the cost of finished goods manufactured for the current year. (Show a supporting computation of the cost of direct materials *used* during the year.)

b. Compute the average per-unit cost of production during the current year.

c. Compute the cost of goods sold during the year, assuming that the FIFO (first-in, first-out) method of inventory costing is used.

d. Compute the cost of the inventory of finished goods at December 31 of the current year, assuming that the FIFO (first-in, first-out) method of inventory costing is used.

L03 L04 L06

PROBLEM 16.8B
Measuring Unit Cost

Early in the year, Jane Jackson founded Jackson Engineering Co. for the purpose of manufacturing a special plumbing device that she had designed. Shortly after year-end, the company's accountant was injured in an auto accident, and no year-end financial statements were prepared. However, the accountant had correctly determined the year-end inventories at the following amounts:

Materials	$51,000
Work in process	32,000
Finished goods (4,000 units)	108,000

As this was the first year of operations, there were no beginning inventories.

While the accountant was in the hospital, Jackson improperly prepared the following income statement from the company's accounting records:

Net sales		$625,000
Cost of goods sold:		
Purchases of direct materials	$188,000	
Direct labor costs assigned to production	113,000	
Manufacturing overhead applied to production	160,000	
Selling expenses	75,000	
Administrative expenses	135,000	
Total costs		671,000
Net loss for year		$ (46,000)

Jackson was very disappointed in these operating results. She stated, "Not only did we lose more than $40,000 this year, but look at our unit production costs. We sold 10,000 units this year at a cost of $671,000; that amounts to a cost of $67.10 per unit. I know some of our competitors are able to manufacture similar plumbing devices for about $30 per unit. I don't need an accountant to know that this business is a failure."

Instructions

a. Prepare a schedule of the cost of finished goods manufactured for the year. (As there were no beginning inventories, your schedule will start with "Manufacturing costs assigned to production:".) Show a supporting computation for the cost of direct materials used during the year.

b. Compute the average cost per-unit manufactured. (Round your answer to two decimal places.)

c. Prepare a corrected income statement for the year, using the multiple-step format. If the company has earned any operating income, assume an income tax rate of 20 percent. (Omit earnings per share figures.)

d. Explain whether you agree or disagree with Jackson's remarks that the business is unprofitable and that its unit cost of production ($67.10, according to Jackson) is much higher than that of competitors (around $30). If you disagree with Jackson, explain any errors or shortcomings in her analysis.

Critical Thinking Cases

L03 L04 L06

CASE 16.1
Effect on Income Statement of Errors in Handling Manufacturing Costs

William Nelson, the chief accountant of West Texas Guitar Company, was injured in an automobile accident shortly before the end of the company's first year of operations. At year-end, a clerk with a very limited understanding of accounting prepared the following income statement, which is unsatisfactory in several respects:

WEST TEXAS GUITAR COMPANY INCOME STATEMENT FOR THE YEAR ENDED DECEMBER 31, 20__		
Net sales		$ 1,300,000
Cost of goods sold:		
Purchases of direct materials	$460,000	
Direct labor	225,000	
Indirect labor	90,000	
Depreciation on machinery—factory	50,000	
Rent	144,000	
Insurance	16,000	
Utilities	28,000	
Miscellaneous manufacturing overhead	34,600	
Other operating expenses	273,800	
Dividends declared on capital stock	46,000	
Cost of goods sold		$(1,367,400)
Loss for year		$ (67,400)

You are asked to help management prepare a corrected income statement for the first year of operations. Management informs you that 60 percent of the rent, insurance, and utilities applies to factory operations, and that the remaining 40 percent should be classified as period expenses. Also, the correct ending inventories are as follows:

Material	$ 38,000
Work in process	10,000
Finished goods	110,400

As this is the first year of operations, there were no beginning inventories.

Instructions

a. Identify the shortcomings and errors in the above income statement. On the basis of the shortcomings you have identified, explain whether you would expect the company's actual net income for the first year of operations to be higher or lower than the amount shown.

b. Prepare schedules to determine:

  1. The cost of direct materials used.

  2. Total manufacturing overhead.

c. Prepare a schedule of cost of finished goods manufactured during the year. (Use the amounts computed in part **b** as the costs of direct materials used and manufacturing overhead.)

d. Prepare a corrected income statement for the year, using a multiple-step format. Assume that income tax expense amounts to 30 percent of income before income taxes.

LO2 through LO4 LO6

CASE 16.2 The Meadowbrooke Miracle

Prescott Manufacturing operates several plants, each of which produces a different product. Early in the current year, John Walker was hired as the new manager of the Meadowbrooke Plant. At year-end, all the plant managers are asked to summarize the operations of their plants at a meeting of the company's board of directors. John Walker displayed the following information on a chart as he made his presentation:

	Current Year	Last Year
Inventories of finished goods:		
Beginning of the year (30,000 units in the current year and 10,000 units last year)	$255,000	$ 85,000
End of the year (20,000 units in the current year and 30,000 units last year)	202,000	255,000
Cost of finished goods manufactured	909,000	1,020,000

Walker made the following statements to the board: "As you know, sales volume has remained constant for the Meadowbrooke Plant. Both this year and last, our sales amounted to 100,000 units. We have made real gains, however, in controlling our manufacturing costs. Through efficient plant operations, we have reduced our cost of finished goods manufactured by over \$100,000. These economies are reflected in a reduction of the manufacturing cost per unit sold from \$10.20 last year (\$1,020,000 ÷ 100,000 units) to \$9.09 in the current year (\$909,000 ÷ 100,000 units)."

Father Alan Carter is president of St. Mary's University and is a member of Prescott Manufacturing's board of directors. However, Father Carter has little background in the accounting practices of manufacturing companies, and he asks you for assistance in evaluating Walker's statements.

Instructions

a. As a preliminary step to your analysis, compute the following for the Meadowbrooke Plant in each of the two years:

1. Cost of goods sold.
2. Number of finished units manufactured.
3. Average cost per unit manufactured.
4. Average cost per unit sold.

b. Evaluate the statements made by Walker. Comment specifically on Walker's computation of the manufacturing cost of units sold and on whether it appears that the reduction in the cost of finished goods sold was in fact achieved through more efficient operations.

LO4 LO6

INTERNET CASE 16.3

Calculating Cost of Goods Manufactured

Pfizer, Inc., develops and manufactures various pharmaceutical products. Visit its home page at the following address:

www.pfizer.com

From the home page, access the most recent annual report by clicking on the investors' tab.

Instructions

a. What categories of inventory does **Pfizer** show in its inventories footnote under "Notes to Consolidated Financial Statements"?

b. Using the income statement and inventory information from the footnote, calculate the cost of finished goods manufactured for the most recent year.

c. What elements of manufacturing overhead can you identify using the annual report?

LO1 LO3

INTERNET CASE 16.4

Code of Conduct at **Coca-Cola**

Many companies have established business codes of conduct that outline procedures for employees, suppliers, and customers to alert management about suspected accounting, internal control, or auditing problems. As discussed in this chapter, one potential violation of GAAP would be to capitalize period costs, inflating the value of inventory and understating the expenses on the income statement for the period. **Coca-Cola Company** provides a "Code of Business Conduct" at http://www.thecoca-colacompany.com/ourcompany/pdf/COBC_English.pdf that identifies the code and what constitutes a violation. Also provided are examples of what employees and others can do if they suspect ethics or fraud violations at **Coca-Cola**. Go to the above Web site and find the following information:

a. Identify the accounting-related components of the code.

b. Review the section titled "Administration of the Code." Identify the steps that an employee would take if he or she wanted to report capitalization of period costs by a bottling plant manager.

c. Identify the types of disciplinary actions the company can impose on employees who are found to be in violation of the company's code of conduct.

d. Identify how the violation might be recorded and who would be notified about the violation.

Internet sites are time and date sensitive. It is the purpose of these exercises to have you explore the Internet. You may need to use the Yahoo! search engine http://www.yahoo.com *(or another favorite search engine) to find a company's current Web address.*

Answers to Self-Test Questions

1. b, d **2.** a **3.** d (4,200 + 29,000 + 3,000 + 3,600 − 34,100)
4. b **5.** a, b, c

CHAPTER 17

Job Order Cost Systems and Overhead Allocations

© Lon C. Diehl/PhotoEdit

Learning Objectives

AFTER STUDYING THIS CHAPTER, YOU SHOULD BE ABLE TO:

LO1 Explain the purposes of cost accounting systems.

LO2 Identify the processes for creating goods and services that are suited to job order costing.

LO3 Explain the purpose and computation of overhead application rates for job order costing.

LO4 Describe the purpose and the content of a job cost sheet.

LO5 Account for the flow of costs when using job order costing.

LO6 Define overhead-related *activity cost pools* and provide several examples.

LO7 Demonstrate how activity bases are used to assign activity cost pools to units produced.

GM GOODWRENCH

Either because of general wear and tear or because of an accident, almost every driver, sooner or later, visits a vehicle service garage. With over 7,000 locations nationwide, the GM Goodwrench network is the industry's largest service provider. GM Goodwrench has been able to maintain its extensive service network because it provides GM Goodwrench dealers with the latest GM vehicle technical information, the most advanced equipment, and GM parts, and because dealers service all types of GM vehicles.

GM Goodwrench service providers use a system called job order costing to track repairs and maintenance costs to specific automobiles or trucks. Because each repair or maintenance job on a vehicle is unique, service providers must have a costing system that is able to trace the specific work and cost of that work to the associated vehicle. When customers arrive to pay for the service work on their vehicles, the service provider can give them an accurate record of the actual work performed, including the cost of parts, labor, and overhead for their vehicles. ■

Cost Accounting Systems

An organization's accounting system must provide a good "map" that links costs to the processes used in creating goods and/or services. An effective cost accounting system matches processes that consume resources with associated costs so that managers can decide how to best provide products or services to customers. Moreover, cost accounting systems are essential for maintaining competitive advantage.

Learning Objective
LO1 **Explain the purpose of cost accounting systems.**

Cost accounting systems are the methods and techniques used by enterprises to track resources consumed in creating and delivering products and services to customers. Management uses the information produced by cost accounting systems to monitor resource consumption and to evaluate and reward employee performance. In addition, the information produced by cost accounting systems is used for external reporting requirements. Inventories, cost of goods sold, and period costs are tracked by cost accounting systems and are reported in the balance sheet and income statement.

In manufacturing and service companies, cost accounting systems help attain two important management objectives: (1) to determine unit manufacturing costs and (2) to provide managers with useful information for planning and cost control functions. As we saw in Chapter 16, *unit costs* are determined by tracing direct materials, direct labor, and overhead to specific units of production.

A unit of product is defined differently in different industries. It is easy to think of units as individual products, such as automobiles or television sets. In some industries, however, units of production may be stated in tons, gallons, kilowatt hours, board-feet, passenger miles flown, or any other appropriate unit of output. Regardless of how they are stated, unit costs provide a basis for inventory valuation and determination of the cost of goods sold. They also provide managers with information for setting prices, deciding what products to manufacture or services to provide, evaluating the efficiency of operations, and controlling costs.

Cost control refers to keeping costs at reasonable levels. When cost accounting systems provide timely information about unit costs, managers can react quickly should costs begin to rise to unacceptable levels. By comparing current unit costs with budgeted costs and other target measures, managers are able to identify those areas in which corrective actions are most needed.

JOB ORDER COST SYSTEMS AND THE CREATION OF GOODS AND SERVICES

Cost accounting systems are typically designed to accommodate the specific needs of individual companies. In this chapter, we demonstrate a widely used accounting system for measuring and tracking resource consumption: job order costing.

Learning Objective
LO2 **Identify the processes for creating goods and services that are suited to job order costing.**

Job order costing is typically used by companies that tailor their goods or services to the specific needs of individual customers. In job order costing, the costs of direct materials, direct labor, and overhead are accumulated separately for each job. A "job" represents the goods manufactured or services provided to fill a particular order, or the production of a batch of a particular product. If a job contains multiple units of a product, unit costs are determined by dividing the total cost charged to the job by the number of units manufactured.

Construction companies use job order cost systems because each construction project is unique. Job order cost systems are also used by shipbuilders, motion picture studios, defense contractors, print shops, and custom furniture makers. In addition, these systems are widely used in service organizations, such as automotive repair shops, accounting firms, law firms, doctors' offices, and hospitals.

To summarize, job order costing is appropriate for environments characterized by customized jobs that require differing amounts and types of direct labor, direct materials, and overhead. Other costing methods are used for production processes that produce mass quantities of identical units that use the same amounts and types of direct labor, direct materials, and overhead. The type of cost accounting system best suited to a particular company *depends on the nature of the company's operations.* In fact, a company that is involved in diverse activities may use many cost accounting methods concurrently. In the following sections of this chapter, we will illustrate and explain job order cost accounting systems.

OVERHEAD APPLICATION RATES

Learning Objective
Explain the purpose and computation of overhead application rates for job order costing.
LO3

Before we begin the discussion of job order costing in detail, it is important to have a clear understanding of how and why overhead costs are allocated to products and services using an estimated overhead application rate. There are at least three reasons why overhead isn't applied to products by simply dividing the company's annual actual overhead cost by the actual number of units produced or services provided during the year. First, total overhead costs and total units produced are not known until the end of the year. Because the amount of overhead assigned to a unit of service or product is important information for setting prices to charge customers at the time of sale, an estimated amount is necessary. Second, not all products and services consume an equal amount of overhead. Third, an expected amount of overhead per product or service helps managers make decisions about whether too much overhead is being used in production.

Thus, estimated overhead application rates are used to assign overhead costs to specific units of production as services are being provided or as units are being produced throughout the accounting period. The rate expresses an expected relationship between overhead costs and some *activity base* related to the production process (direct labor hours, machine hours, and so forth). Overhead is then assigned to products *in proportion* to this activity base. For example, a company using direct labor hours as an activity base would allocate the greatest proportion of its overhead costs to those products or services requiring the most direct labor hours.

The **overhead application rate** is determined at the *beginning* of the period and is based on *estimated* amounts. The rate is typically computed as follows:

$$\textbf{Overhead Application Rate} = \frac{\textbf{Estimated Overhead Costs}}{\textbf{Estimated Units in the Activity Base}}$$

The mechanics of computing and using an overhead application rate are quite simple. The challenging problems for accountants are (1) selecting an appropriate activity base and (2) making reliable estimates at the beginning of the accounting period regarding the total of the overhead costs to be incurred and the total units in the activity base that will be required.

Computation and Use of Overhead Application Rates

Consider, for example, Compuline Corporation, a company that creates individualized software programs for other companies. Assume that, at the beginning of 2011, Compuline's management makes the following estimates relating to software development for the coming year:

Estimated total overhead costs for the year	$360,000
Estimated total direct labor hours for the year	30,000 hours
Estimated total lines of code for the year	1,000,000 lines

Using the above estimates, we will illustrate the use of an overhead application rate using two independent assumptions.

Assumption 1: Compuline Uses Direct Labor Hours as Its Activity Base

If Compuline uses direct labor hours to apply overhead costs, the application rate will be *$12 per direct labor hour* ($360,000 of estimated overhead costs, divided by 30,000 estimated direct labor hours). Throughout the year, manufacturing overhead costs will be assigned in direct proportion to the *actual* direct labor hours required to create a software product for a company. For example, if creating a particular piece of software uses 200 direct labor hours, then $2,400 of manufacturing overhead will be assigned as a part of that software's costs (200 direct labor hours used, multiplied by the $12 application rate). The assignment will be made by debiting the Work in Process Inventory account and crediting the Manufacturing Overhead account for $2,400.

Assumption 2: Compuline Uses Lines of Code as Its Activity Base If Compuline chooses to use lines of code to apply overhead costs, its application rate will be $0.36 per line of code ($360,000 of estimated overhead costs divided by 1,000,000 estimated lines of code). Using this approach, overhead costs will be assigned to software jobs based on the number of lines of code required to create the software package. If 1,000 lines were required for a particular piece of software, that software would be assigned $360 of overhead costs (1,000 lines times $0.36 per line). Again, the assignment is made by debiting the Work in Process Inventory account and crediting the Overhead account for $360.

YOUR TURN **You as a Manager**

Assume you are the manager of the engineering group at Compuline that creates the software code. Also assume that Compuline is using lines of code as the activity base to apply overhead costs to the software packages created. One of the engineers in your group has just approached you suggesting that if the lines of code used for software packages could be reduced by 10 percent in general, the company could reduce overhead costs by $36,000 per year (10% × $360,000). How would you respond?

(See our comments on the Online Learning Center Web site.)

WHAT "DRIVES" OVERHEAD COSTS?

For overhead application rates to provide reliable results, any activity base chosen to compute an application rate must be a significant "driver" of overhead costs. To be a **cost driver,** an activity base must be a *causal factor* in the incurrence of overhead costs. In other words, an increase in the number of activity base units (for example, direct labor hours worked) must cause a proportional increase in the actual overhead costs incurred.

Historically, direct labor hours (or direct labor costs) were viewed as the primary driver of overhead costs—and for good reason. Products that required more direct labor often required more indirect labor (supervision), resulted in more wear and tear on machinery (maintenance costs), and consumed a greater amount of supplies. Therefore, manufacturing companies often followed the practice of applying all manufacturing overhead costs in proportion to direct labor hours or direct labor costs.

As factories have become more highly automated, direct labor has become much less of a causal factor in driving many overhead costs. Today, many manufacturing companies find that activity bases such as machine hours, computer time, or the time required to set up a production run result in a better matching of overhead costs and activities.

The Use of Multiple Overhead Application Rates In an attempt to gain a better understanding of what it costs to manufacture different types of products, many companies have begun to implement techniques that rely on the use of *multiple* allocation bases. One such approach, **activity-based costing,** is illustrated later in this chapter.

In essence, activity-based costing uses multiple allocation bases that represent different types of manufacturing overhead costs. For instance, machine maintenance costs may be allocated using machine hours as an activity base, whereas supervision costs may be allocated using direct labor hours. Different application rates may also be used in each production department and in applying overhead costs to different types of products.

The key point is that each manufactured product should be charged with the overhead costs *generated by* the creation of that product. If the activity base used to apply overhead costs is *not* a primary cost driver, the relative production cost of different products and services may become *significantly distorted.*

The Increasing Importance of Proper Overhead Allocation In today's global economy, competition among companies is greater than ever before. If a company is to determine whether it can compete effectively in the marketplace, it must first know with some degree of precision its costs on a per-unit basis. In highly automated factories, overhead is often the largest of the three basic categories of manufacturing costs. Therefore, the allocation of overhead costs is one of the major challenges facing management accountants.

Job Order Costing

Overhead allocations are particularly important for job order costing because the distinguishing characteristic of job order costing is that costs are accumulated separately for each job. Thus, overhead must be assigned separately to each job. As explained in Chapter 16, all product or service costs are charged (debited) to the Work in Process Inventory account as incurred. In job costing, Work in Process Inventory is a control (or summary) account, supported by **job cost sheets** for each job. Collectively, the job cost sheets serve as a subsidiary ledger showing the details of costs charged to each job.

If a company is using an accounting software package, job cost information is recorded in computer-based files. However, the form and content of most job cost records are basically the same, regardless of whether they are maintained manually or by computer.

THE JOB COST SHEET

Learning Objective
Describe the purpose and the content of a job cost sheet.
L04

Job cost sheets are the heart of job order costing. A separate job cost sheet is prepared for each job and is used to accumulate a record of all manufacturing costs charged to the job. Once the job is finished, the job cost sheet indicates the cost of the finished goods and provides the information necessary to compute the unit costs of production.

Direct manufacturing costs (direct materials used and direct labor) are recorded on the job cost sheet as quickly as these costs can be traced to the job. Simultaneously, overhead costs are applied using an overhead application rate. Exhibit 17–1 is a completed job cost sheet of Oak & Glass Furniture Co. Job no. 831. This job involved the manufacture of 100 dining tables of a particular style.

Exhibit 17–1
COMPLETED JOB COST SHEET

OAK & GLASS FURNITURE CO.
JOB COST SHEET

831

Product French Court dining tables **Date started** 1/03/11

Number of units manufactured 100 **Date completed** 1/21/11

COSTS CHARGED TO THIS JOB

MANUFACTURING DEPARTMENT	DIRECT MATERIALS	DIRECT LABOR		MANUFACTURING OVERHEAD	
		HOURS	COST	RATE	COST APPLIED
Milling & Carving	$10,000	70	$14,000	150%	$21,000
Finishing	15,000	300	6,000	150%	9,000

COST SUMMARY AND UNIT COSTS

	Total Costs	Unit Costs
Direct materials used	$25,000	$250
Direct labor	20,000	200
Manufacturing overhead applied	30,000	300
Cost of finished goods manufactured (100 tables)	$75,000	$750

Throughout the production process, manufacturing costs traceable to the job were accumulated in the "Costs Charged to This Job" section of the job cost sheet. The "Cost Summary" section was filled in when the job was completed.

The total cost of completing job no. 831 was *$75,000.* Upon completion, this amount should be transferred from the Work in Process Inventory account to the Finished Goods Inventory account. The unit cost figures shown in the job cost sheet were determined by dividing the total manufacturing costs by the 100 units manufactured.

Learning Objective
LO5 **Account for the flow of costs when using job order costing.**

FLOW OF COSTS IN JOB COSTING: AN ILLUSTRATION

Exhibit 17–2a and b on pages 766 and 767 illustrates the flow of costs for Oak & Glass Furniture Co. This flowchart summarizes the company's manufacturing operations during the month of January. Notice that each of the inventory accounts (Materials, Work in Process, and Finished Goods) is supported by a subsidiary ledger.

In our flowchart, all subsidiary ledger accounts are shown in T account form to conserve space. In practice, the individual job cost sheets serve as the subsidiary ledger for the Work in Process Inventory account. Also, the subsidiary ledger accounts for direct materials and finished goods would have additional columns providing detailed information as to quantities on hand and unit costs.

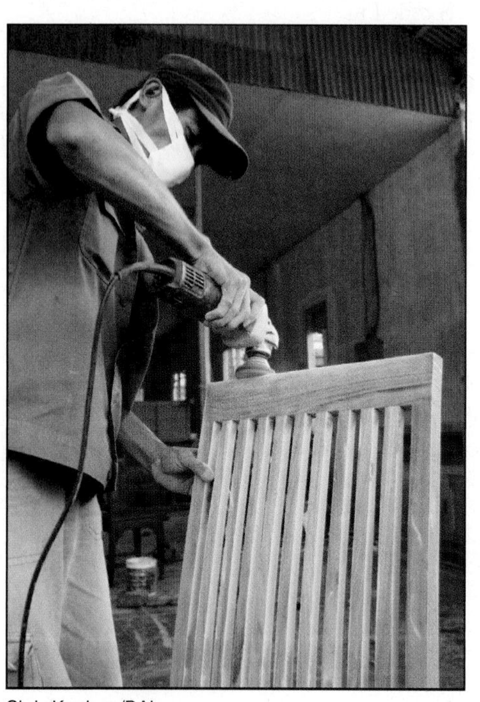
Chris Kerrigan/DAL

We will now use Oak & Glass Furniture Co. to explain the flow of manufacturing costs when using job order costing.

ACCOUNTING FOR DIRECT MATERIALS

In a perpetual inventory system, purchases of direct materials are posted from the purchases journal to the accounts in the materials subsidiary ledger. The entries in the subsidiary ledger indicate the type, quantity, and cost of the material purchased. As shown in Exhibit 17–2a, at the end of each month, a summary entry is made debiting the Materials Inventory account for the total cost of direct materials *purchased* during the period. (The offsetting credit normally is to Accounts Payable.)

Likewise, at month-end, all the materials used during the month are totaled, and the following summary entry is made in the accounts:

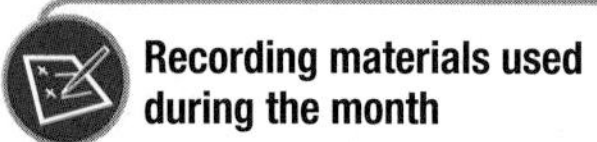
Recording materials used during the month

Work in Process Inventory	50,000	
Materials Inventory		50,000
To record the cost of all direct materials placed into production during Jan.		

INTERNATIONAL CASE IN POINT

Multinational companies frequently source their direct materials from many countries. Because suppliers of direct materials are located in different countries, the costs of those materials are affected by international differences that do not affect direct materials sourced from domestic suppliers. Such factors as import duties, exchange rate fluctuations, and foreign taxes have an impact on the cost of direct materials, making the purchasing function more complex for companies sourcing internationally.

ACCOUNTING FOR DIRECT LABOR COSTS

Debits to the Direct Labor account arise from making payments to direct factory workers; the offsetting credit is to the Cash account.[1] Payments to *indirect* factory workers (such as supervisors and security guards) are debited to Manufacturing Overhead, not to the Direct Labor account.

The Direct Labor account is credited as direct labor is *used*—that is, as employees work on specific jobs. A number of mechanical and computerized means have been developed for determining the direct labor cost applicable to each job. One common method is to prepare *time cards* for each employee, showing the number of hours worked on each job, the employee's rate of pay, and the direct labor cost chargeable to each job.

As shown in Exhibit 17–2a and b, at the end of each month, a summary entry is made debiting Work in Process Inventory and crediting the Direct Labor account for all direct labor costs assigned to jobs during the month. For Oak & Glass, this entry is as follows:

Work in Process Inventory	60,000	
Direct Labor		60,000
To record in the general ledger all direct labor costs charged to jobs during Jan.		

Recording direct labor costs 

Notice that the Direct Labor account is debited (with an offsetting credit to Cash) when employees are *paid,* but it is credited for the cost of work *performed* on jobs. Work is performed on a daily basis, but employees are paid only at periodic intervals, such as every two weeks. Thus, the direct labor cost charged to jobs does not necessarily equal the amount paid to employees during the month. In our example, $60,000 of direct labor was assigned to the three jobs in process, but payments to employees totaled only $52,000. Thus, the unadjusted $8,000 credit balance of the Direct Labor account at month-end represents a *liability for accrued wages payable* and is reported in the balance sheet.

ACCOUNTING FOR OVERHEAD COSTS

Manufacturing overhead includes all manufacturing costs *other than* the costs of direct materials and direct labor. Manufacturing Overhead is a control account; the details of the many different types of overhead costs are kept in a subsidiary ledger.

The Manufacturing Overhead account is debited for the *actual* amount of overhead costs incurred during the period. As shown in Exhibit 17–2a, actual overhead costs in January total $93,000. These costs are posted to the overhead account from several sources. Indirect labor costs, for example, come from payroll records; purchases of indirect materials and payments of utility bills come from invoices and receipts; and depreciation of plant assets comes from end-of-period adjusting entries in the general journal.

Application of Overhead Costs to Jobs Overhead is an *indirect* cost and cannot be traced conveniently to specific jobs or units. As discussed previously, a predetermined overhead application rate is used to assign overhead costs to work in process. Oak & Glass uses an overhead application rate equal to *150 percent of direct labor cost.* Therefore, each job cost sheet is charged with overhead costs equal to 150 percent of the direct labor cost relating to the job.

On the bottom of the page 766 is the summary entry made in the general ledger to record all overhead costs applied to jobs during the period.

[1] To the extent that amounts are withheld from employees' pay for such purposes as income taxes and Social Security taxes, the offsetting credits are to various current liability accounts. Accounting for payrolls was discussed in Chapter 10.

Exhibit 17–2a **FLOW OF COSTS FOR OAK & GLASS FURNITURE CO.**

Direct Labor

Direct labor payroll	52,000	Direct labor used	60,000
		(Bal., $8,000)	

Manufacturing Overhead

Indirect labor payroll	40,000	Applied (150% of direct labor)	90,000
Other	53,000		
(Bal., $3,000*)			
*Underapplied overhead			

Materials Inventory

Beg. balance	13,000	Materials used	50,000
Purchases	54,000		
(Bal., $17,000)			

(For detail, see subsidiary ledger below.)

Materials Subsidiary Ledger
Woods

Beg. balance	6,000	Used: Job no. 830	8,000
		Job no. 831	10,000
Purchases	29,000	Job no. 832	12,000
(Bal., $5,000)			

Glass

Beg. balance	7,000	Used: Job no. 831	15,000
		Job no. 832	5,000
Purchases	25,000		
(Bal., $12,000)			

Postings to Job Cost Sheets
Direct labor, per time tickets:

Job no. 830	*$24,000*
Job no. 831	*20,000*
Job no. 832	*16,000*
Total	*$60,000*

Overhead ($90,000) at predetermined rate of 150% of direct labor

Direct materials, per requisitions:

Job no. 830	*$ 8,000*
Job no. 831	*25,000*
Job no. 832	*17,000*
Total	*$50,000*

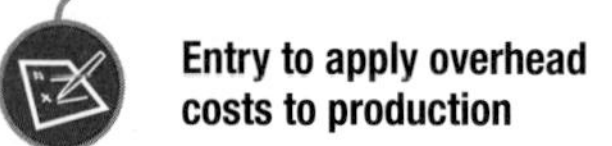
Entry to apply overhead costs to production

Work in Process Inventory	90,000	
Manufacturing Overhead		90,000

To charge the Work in Process account with overhead costs applied to jobs during the month (150% of direct labor costs for the month; $60,000 × 150% = $90,000).

Over- or Underapplied Overhead In our example, actual overhead costs incurred during January amounted to $93,000, while the overhead applied to jobs using the overhead application rate totaled only $90,000. We should not expect that applied overhead will

Exhibit 17–2b FLOW OF COSTS FOR OAK & GLASS FURNITURE CO. (CONTINUED)

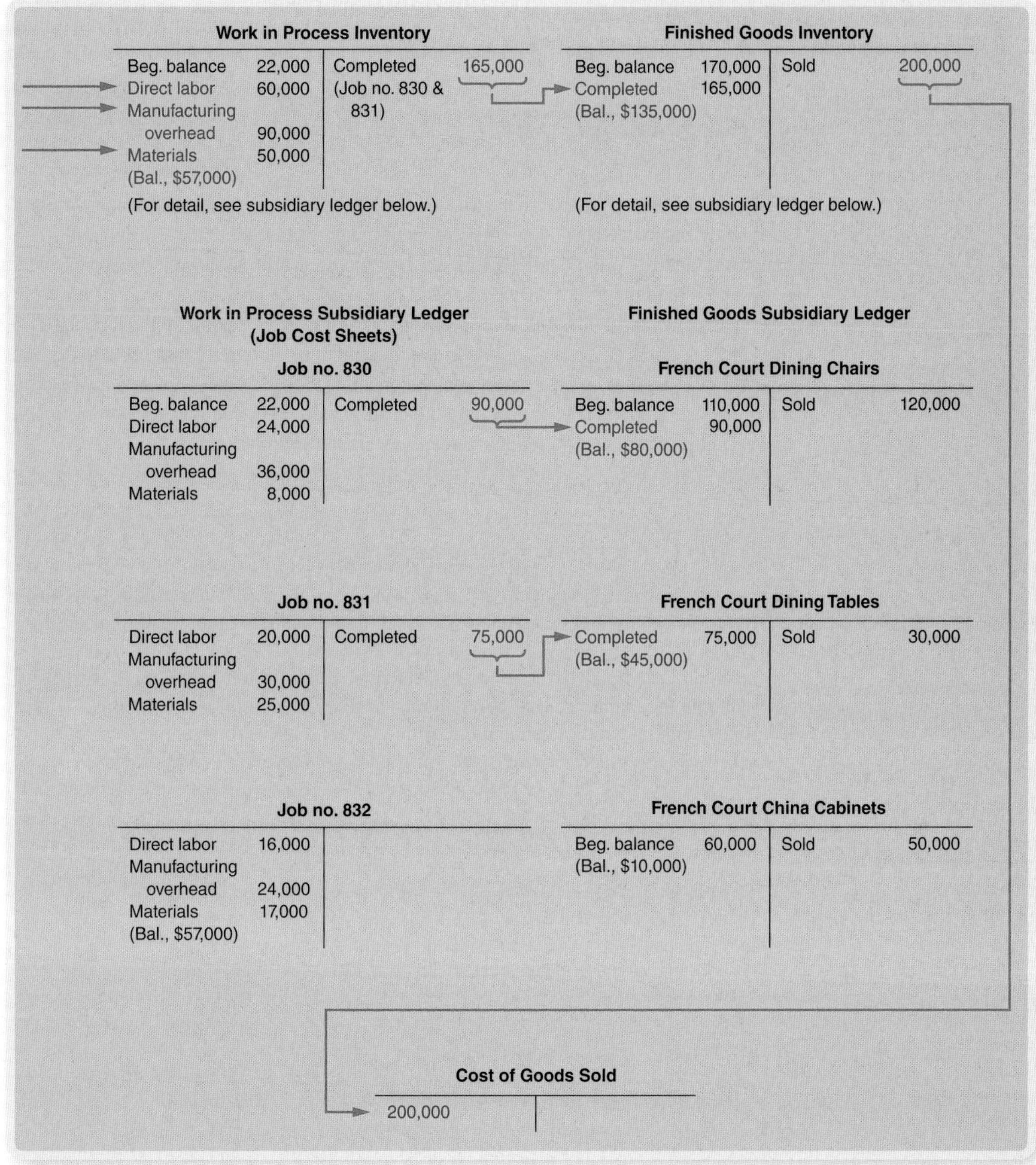

exactly equal actual overhead because the predetermined overhead application rate is based on *estimates*.

A debit balance in the Manufacturing Overhead account at month-end indicates that overhead applied to jobs was *less* than the actual overhead costs incurred during the month. Therefore, a debit balance remains in the Manufacturing Overhead account and it is called **underapplied overhead.** A credit balance remaining in the account indicates that overhead applied to jobs *exceeded* actual overhead costs; thus a credit balance is termed **overapplied overhead.**

The month-end balances remaining in the Manufacturing Overhead account normally are allowed to accumulate throughout the year. These amounts tend to balance out from month to month, and the amount of overapplied or underapplied overhead at year-end usually *is not material* in dollar amount. In this case, the year-end balance in the Manufacturing Overhead account may be closed *directly to the Cost of Goods Sold,* on the grounds that most of the remaining balance is applicable to goods sold during the year. If the year-end balance in the overhead account *is material* in dollar amount, it should be apportioned among the Work in Process Inventory, Finished Goods Inventory, and Cost of Goods Sold accounts.

YOUR TURN **You as a Treasurer**

Assume you are the treasurer of ABI, Inc., a manufacturer of industrial lasers. Among your many responsibilities is supervising preparation of the company's tax returns. The assistant treasurer has pointed out to you that the controller is allocating a significantly large and material amount of underapplied overhead from last period among the Work in Process Inventory, Finished Goods Inventory, and Cost of Goods Sold accounts. The assistant suggests that assigning the entire amount of underapplied overhead to Cost of Goods Sold would have advantageous tax consequences. She says the result would be a higher cost of goods sold expense on the income statement and resulting lower profits. Lower profits would, in turn, reduce taxes. How should you respond?

(See our comments on the Online Learning Center Web site.)

ACCOUNTING FOR COMPLETED JOBS

We have now explained how manufacturing costs are charged (debited) to the Work in Process Inventory account and how the costs of specific jobs are separately accumulated on job cost sheets.

As each job is completed, the job cost sheet is removed from the work in process subsidiary ledger and the manufacturing costs on the sheet are totaled to determine the cost of finished goods manufactured. As shown in Exhibit 17–2b, this cost then is transferred from the Work in Process Inventory account to the Finished Goods Inventory account.

During January, Oak & Glass completed work on job nos. 830 and 831. The entries to record completion of these jobs appear as follows:

Entries to record completed jobs

Finished Goods Inventory	90,000	
Work in Process Inventory		90,000
To record completion of job no. 830, consisting of 600 French Court dining chairs (unit cost, $150).		
Finished Goods Inventory	75,000	
Work in Process Inventory		75,000
To record completion of job no. 831, consisting of 100 French Court dining tables (unit cost, $750).		

As sales of the finished units occur, the unit cost figure will be used in determining the cost of goods sold. For example, the sale of 40 of the French Court dining tables at a total sales price of $48,000 is recorded as follows:

Accounts Receivable (Anthony's Fine Furniture)	48,000	
Sales		48,000
Sold 40 French Court dining tables on account.		
Cost of Goods Sold	30,000	
Finished Goods Inventory		30,000
To record the cost of the 40 French Court dining tables sold to Anthony's Fine Furniture (40 × $750 cost per unit = $30,000).		

JOB ORDER COSTING IN SERVICE INDUSTRIES

In the preceding example, we have emphasized the use of job order costing in a manufacturing company. However, many service industries also use this method to accumulate the costs of servicing a particular customer.

In a hospital, for example, each patient represents a separate "job," and the costs of caring for the patient are accumulated on a job cost sheet. Costs of such items as medicine, blood transfusions, and x-rays represent the usage of direct materials; services rendered by doctors are direct labor. The costs of nursing, meals, linen service, and depreciation of the hospital building and equipment all are part of the hospital's overhead. In a hospital, overhead often is applied to each patient's account at a predetermined daily rate.

Activity-Based Costing (ABC)

For Oak & Glass Furniture Co. discussed above, we illustrated how manufacturing overhead costs may be applied to production using an overhead application rate based on a single cost driver (such as direct labor hours). This approach works well for many companies, especially if all products are manufactured in a similar manner.

But now consider a company that uses *very different processes* in manufacturing different products. The factors that drive overhead costs may vary greatly among different product lines. Such companies may benefit from *activity-based costing.* Activity-based costing (ABC) is an overhead allocation method that uses multiple overhead rates to track indirect costs by the *activities* that consume those costs. Examples of activities that consume overhead resources include purchasing and storing materials for production, supervising direct labor, number of machine runs, consuming electricity, or maintenance work on equipment.

In ABC, *many different* activity bases (or cost drivers) are used in applying overhead costs to products. Thus, ABC recognizes the special overhead considerations of each product line. As a result, overhead allocations tend to be more useful. In addition, ABC provides management with information about the cost of performing various overhead activities.

CASE IN POINT

Ford Motor Company used ABC techniques to cut costs by 20 percent in its accounts payable department. The process was so successful that it led to a wholesale reworking of **Ford**'s procurement system. Previously, when a supplier shipped an ordered part, a clerk attempted to reconcile three documents—the purchase order, the receiving document, and the vendor's invoice. When all three agreed, payment was issued. Now orders are entered into a database. When the part arrives, the receiving department checks the database for agreement and approves payment. The payment is automatically issued to the supplier upon approval.

© AP Photo/David Zalubowki

Learning Objective LO6
Define overhead-related *activity cost pools* and provide several examples.

How ABC Works

Activity-based costing consists of two stages. The first stage in ABC is to subdivide overhead costs into a number of **activity cost pools.** Each cost pool represents a type of overhead activity, such as building maintenance, purchasing materials, heating of the factory, and machinery repairs. In the second ABC stage, the overhead costs in each pool are applied to production separately. In short, ABC separately identifies and makes use of the most appropriate cost driver for applying each category of overhead costs.

The Benefits of ABC Measurement of unit costs may assist managers in several ways. For example, it helps them in setting sales prices and in evaluating the profitability of each product line. ABC also helps managers to better understand what activities drive overhead costs. This understanding may inspire them to develop new operating procedures that may reduce overhead costs.

ABC VERSUS A SINGLE APPLICATION RATE: A COMPARISON

Assume that Master File, Inc., makes two lines of file cabinets: (1) metal file cabinets, sold through office supply outlets for commercial use, and (2) wooden file cabinets, sold through fine furniture stores for home use.

In a typical year, the company produces and sells approximately 42,000 metal cabinets and 9,000 wooden cabinets. Total manufacturing overhead at this level of production is expected to average *$249,600 per year* and is currently allocated to products at a rate of *$1.60 per direct labor hour (DLH),* as computed below.

Step 1: Compute total direct labor hours at normal levels of production.

Overhead rate using direct labor hours

Metal cabinets (42,000 units per year × 2 DLH per unit)	84,000 DLH
Wooden cabinets (9,000 units per year × 8 DLH per unit)	72,000 DLH
Total DLH at normal production levels	156,000 DLH

Step 2: Compute the overhead application rate per DLH.

Overhead application rate ($249,600 ÷ 156,000 DLH)	$1.60 per DLH

Using direct labor hours as a single activity base, the company's total manufacturing costs per unit average *$38.20* for metal cabinets and *$117.80* for wooden cabinets, as shown below.

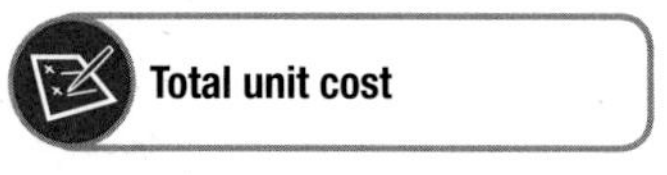

Total unit cost

	Metal Cabinets	Wooden Cabinets
Direct materials	$15.00	$ 25.00
Direct labor (at $10.00 per hour)	20.00	80.00
Manufacturing overhead (at $1.60 per DLH)	3.20	12.80
Total manufacturing costs per unit	$38.20	$117.80

Master File sets its selling prices at *160 percent* of total manufacturing costs. Thus, the company sells its metal cabinets for *$61.12* (total unit cost of $38.20 × 160%) and its wooden cabinets for *$188.48* (total unit cost of $117.80 × 160%). At these prices, the metal cabinets sell for about *$3 less* per unit than comparable cabinets sold by Master File's competitors. However, the price of wooden cabinets averages *$10 more* per unit than comparable products available on the market.

Glen Brown, Master File's marketing director, believes that sales of the wooden cabinets have suffered as a result of the company's pricing policy. He recently hired a consultant, Lisa Scott, to evaluate how prices are set. Scott drafted the memo in Exhibit 17–3 summarizing her findings:

Exhibit 17–3

MEMO ABOUT OVERHEAD ALLOCATIONS

MEMO

DATE: January 16

TO: Glen Brown, Marketing Director, Master File, Inc.

FROM: Lisa Scott, Consultant, Scott & Associates

Having carefully examined Master File's pricing policy, I find it consistent with pricing policies used throughout the office furniture industry. Therefore, I recommend that you continue setting prices at 160% of total manufacturing costs.

I do, however, strongly encourage management to change the method currently used to allocate manufacturing overhead to products. The use of direct labor hours as an activity base is causing an excessive share of total overhead costs to be allocated to the wooden cabinet line. Let me explain what is happening.

The wooden product line is very labor intensive in comparison to the metal cabinet line (that is, it takes an average of eight direct labor hours to manufacture a wooden cabinet, compared to an average of two direct labor hours to manufacture a metal cabinet). Because manufacturing overhead is allocated on the basis of direct labor hours, each wooden cabinet receives a far greater cost allocation than each metal cabinet. This would be appropriate if direct labor hours were the primary overhead *cost driver.* The fact is, however, that direct labor hours are not a significant driver of your overhead costs.

My analysis of manufacturing overhead at Master File, Inc., reveals that the most significant cost drivers are activities most closely associated with the metal cabinet line. Thus, it would make sense if your company selected activity bases that allocate more overhead costs to the metal cabinets. This would indicate a lower cost for the wooden cabinets and provide justification for lowering their selling prices, making them more in line with the competition.

I suggest that we make an appointment to discuss using *activity-based costing* at Master File, Inc.

Assume that Master File decides to implement ABC as suggested by the consultant. Remember that the company's expected *total overhead costs* at normal levels of production average *$249,600 per year*. Let us assume that these overhead costs fall into two broad categories: (1) Maintenance Department costs and (2) utilities costs. Recall that ABC is typically undertaken in two stages—first, identify separate activity cost pools and, second, allocate each cost pool to the product with an appropriate cost driver. We will create an ABC system for Master File, Inc., by using these two stages. Exhibit 17–4 illustrates stage 1 of the ABC system for Master File.

STAGE 1: SEPARATE ACTIVITY COST POOLS

Maintenance Department Costs The Maintenance Department incurs approximately *$180,000* of Master File's total overhead costs. The department has five full-time employees. Three employees are responsible for repair work, such as fixing the large cutting and bending machines used to manufacture metal file cabinets. The other two employees are responsible for set-up activities, such as adjusting machinery prior to each production run.

Using ABC, Master File identifies repair activities and set-up activities as separate *activity cost pools.* Thus each pool is assigned a portion of the department's $180,000 in total costs. Management believes that the *number of employees* engaged in each activity is the most significant *cost driver* of the Maintenance Department's total costs. As shown in Exhibit 17–4, by using the number of employees as an *activity base, $108,000* is assigned to the *repair cost pool,* and *$72,000* is assigned to the *set-up cost pool*. These computations are shown beneath Exhibit 17–4 on the following page.

Exhibit 17–4 **STAGE 1: CREATING ACTIVITY COST POOLS**

ACTIVITY COST POOLS
MASTER FILE, INC.

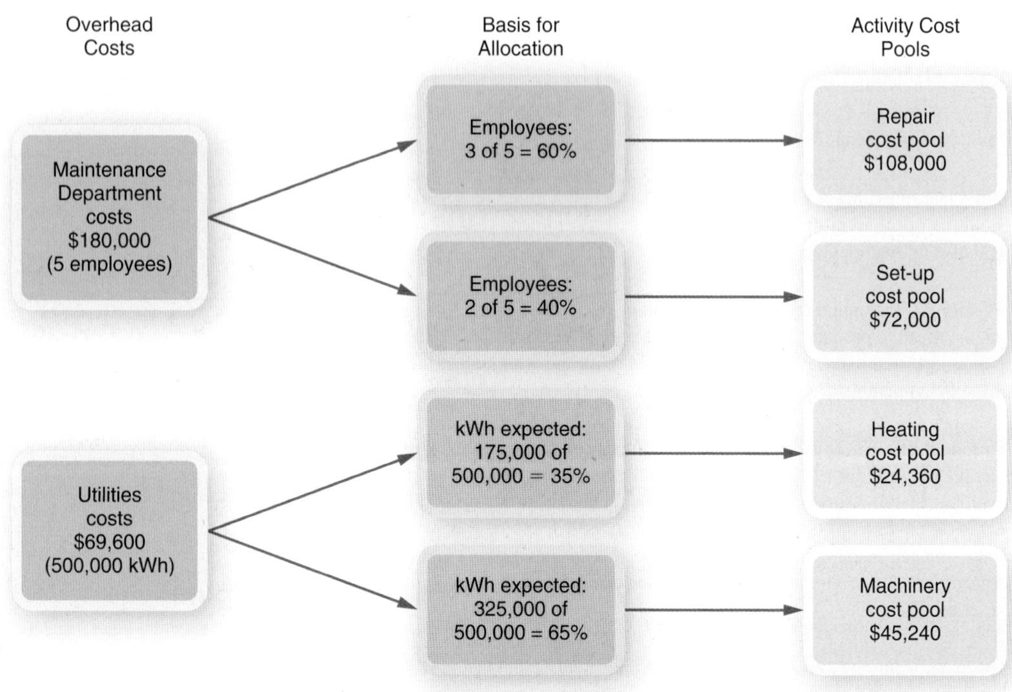

Assigning Maintenance Department Costs to Activity Pools

Step 1: Establish the percentage of total Maintenance Department costs to be assigned to each activity cost pool using the number of employees as an activity base.

		% of total
Employees engaged in repair activities	3	60%
Employees engaged in set-up activities	2	40%
Employees in the Maintenance Department	5	100%

Step 2: Assign total Maintenance Department costs of $180,000 to each activity cost pool based on the percentages computed in step 1.

Costs assigned to the repair cost pool ($180,000 × 60%)	$108,000
Costs assigned to the set-up cost pool ($180,000 × 40%)	72,000
Total Maintenance Department costs assigned	$180,000

Utilities Costs Utilities costs account for nearly $69,600 of Master File's total manufacturing overhead costs. A large portion of this amount is incurred to heat the factory and supply power to the large machines used in manufacturing the metal cabinet line.

Thus, using ABC, Master File identifies heating demands and machinery power demands as separate *activity cost pools.* As shown in Exhibit 17–4, each of these pools is assigned a portion of the $69,600 utilities costs. Management believes that the *number of kilowatt hours (kWh)* required for each activity is the most significant driver of utilities costs. With kilowatt hours as an *activity base, $24,360* is assigned to the *heating cost pool,* whereas *$45,240* is assigned to the *machinery cost pool,* as computed at the top of the following page.

Assigning Utilities Costs to Activity Pools

Step 1: Establish the percentage of total utilities costs to be assigned to each activity cost pool using the number of kilowatt hours as an activity base.

		% of total
kWh per year for heating requirements	175,000	35%
kWh per year for machinery requirements	325,000	65%
kWh required per year	500,000	100%

Step 2: Assign total utilities costs of $69,600 to each activity cost pool based on the percentages computed in step 1.

Costs assigned to the heating cost pool ($69,600 × 35%)	$24,360
Costs assigned to the machinery cost pool ($69,600 × 65%)	45,240
Total utilities costs assigned	$69,600

Utilities costs assigned to cost pools

STAGE 2: ALLOCATE ACTIVITY COST POOLS TO THE PRODUCTS

The costs assigned to each cost pool must now be allocated to Master File's two product lines. Exhibit 17–5 shows that management has determined that the *number of repair work orders* is the most appropriate activity base for allocating the *repair cost pool* to each product line. The Maintenance Department receives approximately *250* repair work orders each year. Of these, about *200* are related to the metal cabinet line, and *50* are related to the wooden cabinet line. In a typical year, the metal cabinets are allocated approximately *$86,400* from the repair costs pool, whereas wooden cabinets are allocated approximately *$21,600,* as computed below.

Allocation of Repair Cost Pool to Each Product Line

Step 1: Establish the percentage of repair cost pool to be allocated to each product line using the number of work orders as an activity base.

		% of total
Work orders related to metal cabinet line per year	200	80%
Work orders related to wooden cabinet line per year	50	20%
Total work orders per year	250	100%

Step 2: Allocate $108,000 from the repair cost pool to each product line based on the percentages computed in step 1.

Costs allocated to the metal cabinet line ($108,000 × 80%)	$ 86,400
Costs allocated to the wooden cabinet line ($108,000 × 20%)	21,600
Total repair costs allocated to both product lines	$108,000

Repair cost pool allocated to each product line

The *number of production runs* is determined to be the most significant driver of set-up costs. Thus, production runs will serve as the activity base for allocating the *set-up cost pool* to each product line. Master File schedules approximately *200* production runs each year. Of these, about *150* are for metal cabinets, and *50* are for wooden cabinets. Thus, in a typical year, the metal cabinets are allocated approximately *$54,000* from the set-up cost pool, whereas wooden cabinets are allocated about *$18,000,* as shown in Exhibit 17–5 and computed beneath Exhibit 17–5 on the following page.

Allocation of Set-up Cost Pool to Each Product Line

Step 1: Establish the percentage of set-up cost pool to be allocated to each product line using the number of production runs as an activity base.

		% of total
Production runs of metal cabinets per year	150	75%
Production runs of wooden cabinets per year	50	25%
Total production runs per year	200	100%

Exhibit 17-5 STAGE 2: ALLOCATION OF COST POOLS TO EACH PRODUCT

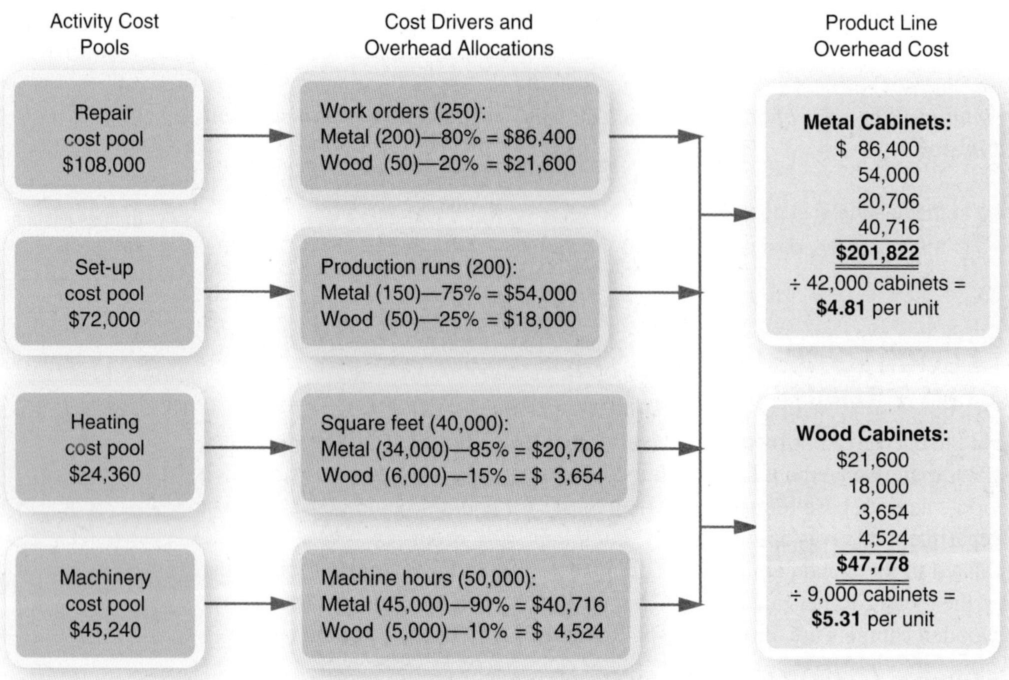

Step 2: Allocate $72,000 from the set-up cost pool to each product line based on the percentages computed in step 1.

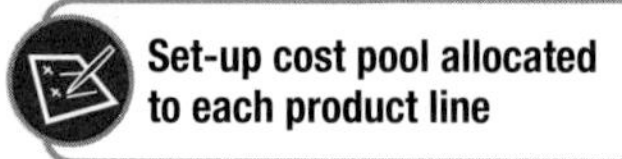

Costs allocated to the metal cabinet line ($72,000 × 75%)	$54,000
Costs allocated to the wooden cabinet line ($72,000 × 25%)	18,000
Total set-up costs allocated to both product lines.	$72,000

In summary, the Maintenance Department averages $108,000 in repair-related costs and $72,000 in set-up costs each year (or total costs of $180,000). Thus, at normal levels of production, ABC allocates $86,400 in repair costs to the metal cabinet line and $21,600 in repair costs to the wooden cabinet line. In addition, ABC allocates $54,000 in set-up costs to the metal cabinet line and $18,000 in set-up costs to the wooden cabinet line.

The costs assigned to each heating and machinery cost pool must now be allocated to the metal and wooden product lines. Management believes that *square feet* of production space occupied by each product line is the most appropriate activity base for allocating the *heating cost pool*. Of the company's 40,000 square feet of production space, about *34,000* is dedicated to the metal cabinet line, and *6,000* is dedicated to the wooden cabinet line. Thus, in a typical year, the metal cabinets are allocated *$20,706* of heating pool costs, whereas wooden cabinets are allocated only *$3,654,* as computed at the top of the following page.

Allocation of Heating Cost Pool to Each Product Line

Step 1: Establish the percentage of heating cost pool to be allocated to each product line using square feet of production space as an activity base.

		% of total
Square feet occupied by the metal cabinet line	34,000	85%
Square feet occupied by the wooden cabinet line	6,000	15%
Square feet of total production space occupied	40,000	100%

Step 2: Allocate $24,360 in the heating cost pool to each product line based on the percentages computed in step 1.

Costs allocated to the metal cabinet line ($24,360 × 85%)	$20,706
Costs allocated to the wooden cabinet line ($24,360 × 15%)	3,654
Total heating costs allocated to both product lines	$24,360

Heating cost pool allocated to each product line

The *number of machine hours* is determined to be the most significant driver of machinery power costs. Thus, machine hours will serve as the activity base for allocating the *machinery cost pool* to each product line. The company utilizes approximately *50,000* machine hours each year. Of these, about *45,000* pertain to machinery used to manufacture metal cabinets, and *5,000* pertain to machines used for making wooden cabinets. Thus, in a typical year, the metal cabinets are allocated approximately *$40,716* of machinery pool costs, whereas wooden cabinets are allocated approximately *$4,524,* as shown in Exhibit 17–5 and computed below.

Allocation of Machinery Cost Pool to Each Product Line

Step 1: Establish the percentage of machinery cost pool to be allocated to each product line using the number of machine hours as an activity base.

		% of total
Machine hours used for metal cabinets per year	45,000	90%
Machine hours used for wooden cabinets per year	5,000	10%
Total machine hours per year	50,000	100%

Step 2: Allocate $45,240 in the machinery cost pool to each product line based on the percentages computed in step 1.

Costs allocated to the metal cabinet line ($45,240 × 90%)	$40,716
Costs allocated to the wooden cabinet line ($45,240 × 10%)	4,524
Total machinery costs allocated to both product lines	$45,240

Machinery cost pool allocated to each product line

In summary, annual utilities costs average $24,360 for heating and $45,240 for powering machinery (for a total of $69,600). At normal levels of production, ABC allocates approximately $20,706 of heating costs to the metal cabinet line and $3,654 of heating costs to the wooden cabinet line. In addition, it allocates $40,716 of machinery power costs to the metal cabinet line and $4,524 to the wooden cabinet line.

DETERMINING UNIT COSTS USING ABC

Learning Objective
Demonstrate how activity bases are used to assign activity cost pools to units produced. **LO7**

We may now compute Master File's overhead costs on a *per-unit* basis. At normal levels of activity, the company produces and sells 42,000 metal file cabinets and 9,000 wooden file cabinets per year. Thus, the unit manufacturing overhead cost of each metal cabinet is *$4.81,* compared to *$5.31* for each wooden cabinet. These unit costs are computed below.

Unit costs using ABC

	Metal Cabinets	Wooden Cabinets
Maintenance Department costs:		
Allocated from the repair cost pool	$ 86,400	$21,600
Allocated from the set-up cost pool	54,000	18,000
Utilities costs:		
Allocated from the heating cost pool	20,706	3,654
Allocated from the machinery cost pool	40,716	4,524
Total manufacturing costs allocated to each line	$201,822	$47,778
Total units produced and sold per year	42,000	9,000
Manufacturing overhead costs per unit	$ 4.81	$ 5.31

Two observations should be made regarding these figures. First, at normal levels of activity, Master File's ABC process allocates the entire $249,600 in annual overhead costs to each product line ($201,822 to the metal cabinet line and $47,778 to the wooden cabinet line). Second, the amount of manufacturing overhead allocated to each product is significantly *different* than what was allocated using a single activity base, as shown below.

	Metal Cabinets	Wooden Cabinets
Manufacturing overhead allocated using ABC	$4.81	$ 5.31
Manufacturing overhead applied using direct labor hours (DLH):		
Metal cabinets (2 DLH × $1.60 per DLH)	3.20	
Wooden cabinets (8 DLH × $1.60 per DLH)		12.80
Differences in overhead application per unit	$1.61	$(7.49)

As indicated, manufacturing overhead applied to the metal file cabinets using ABC is *$1.61 more* than it was when a single activity base of direct labor hours was used. However, the amount applied to the wooden cabinets using ABC is *$7.49 less* than it was previously. As a consequence, Master File is likely to *raise* the selling price of its metal file cabinets and *lower* the selling price of its wooden file cabinets, as shown below.

	Metal Cabinets	Wooden Cabinets
Direct materials	$15.00	$ 25.00
Direct labor (at $10.00 per hour)	20.00	80.00
Manufacturing overhead (using the ABC system)	4.81	5.31
Total manufacturing costs per unit	$39.81	$110.31
Sales price as a percentage of total manufacturing cost	160%	160%
Selling prices indicated by the ABC system	$63.70	$176.50
Selling prices indicated by the single activity base system	61.12	188.48
Price increase (reduction) indicated by the ABC system	$ 2.58	$ (11.98)

If Master File maintains its current pricing policy, it will raise the price of metal file cabinets by *$2.58* per unit and lower the price of its wooden file cabinets by *$11.98* per unit.[2]

You will recall that Master File currently is selling its metal filing cabinets for about *$3 less* than competitive products. Therefore, the metal cabinet prices will remain competitive even if their sales price is raised by $2.58 per unit. However, the company's wooden file cabinets have been priced at *$10.00 more* than competitive products. Thus, by the lowering of the unit selling price by $11.98, Master File's wooden cabinets can now be priced competitively *without sacrificing product quality.*

The Trend toward More Informative Cost Accounting Systems

Today's global economy is fiercely competitive. To a large extent, competitive means cost-efficient. If you cannot produce quality products efficiently, you may lose out to Japanese, German, or Korean companies, or a company down the street.

Up to this point, we have discussed job order and activity-based costing methods. Job order costing has two advantages: (1) it measures the costs of products produced in "batches," and

[2] To keep our illustration short, we assumed that maintenance and utilities costs were Master File's *only* manufacturing overhead costs. Consequently, overhead costs are relatively low in comparison to the cost of direct materials and direct labor. In many companies, overhead represents a much larger component of total manufacturing costs. Thus, cost distortions often are significantly greater than those shown here.

(2) unit costs are determined as soon as the job is complete. In an ABC system, the allocation of manufacturing overhead is based on the specific activities that drive overhead costs. Thus, ABC should provide a more useful measure of each product's cost. Many companies today have "hybrid" cost systems, designed to realize the advantages of many costing approaches.

Ethics, Fraud & Corporate Governance

In addition to allocating manufacturing overhead costs to products (as discussed in this chapter), many companies allocate general corporate overhead charges to their segments or divisions. However, failure to do so properly can result in misleading financial statement information and potentially jeopardize the careers of those responsible.

The Securities and Exchange Commission (SEC) brought an enforcement action against the former chief accounting officer (CAO) and controller of **Vivendi Universal, S.A.** **Vivendi** is a French entertainment conglomerate, and its stock was cross-listed in Paris and New York. **Vivendi**'s shares were traded on the New York Stock Exchange.

The former CAO and controller was involved in making improper allocations of corporate overhead to **Vivendi**'s music division, **Universal Music Group (UMG)**. **Vivendi**'s senior management had established a €250 million target number for **UMG**'s earnings before interest, taxes, depreciation, and amortization (EBITDA) for the third quarter of operations. In October, **Vivendi**'s CAO and controller temporarily reduced the amount of corporate overhead charged to **UMG** by €7 million, exactly the reduction needed for **UMG** to report €250 million in EBITDA for the third quarter.

The change in the allocation of corporate overhead to **UMG** was made without proper supporting documentation and was not in conformity with U.S. GAAP. GAAP requires that accounting allocations be distributed according to a plan or a formula, and that allocated amounts affecting the reporting of a segment's performance be allocated in a reasonable manner. **Vivendi**'s former CAO and controller did not reasonably allocate corporate overhead in accordance with a plan or formula; rather, the allocation was based on a desire to report a predetermined EBITDA amount.

The SEC permanently barred **Vivendi**'s CAO and controller from appearing or practicing before the SEC as an accountant. Even if a reinstatement request is granted, the SEC will require this individual's work to be reviewed by the independent audit committee of any future employer or in some other manner acceptable to the SEC for as long as this individual works for a public company.

There are three important takeaways from this case. First, metrics other than net income are often important to investors and creditors; therefore, misstatements of other metrics valued by the capital markets can attract SEC scrutiny. Second, investors and creditors often are interested in the performance of different parts of the business (i.e., segments). As a result, GAAP requires the disclosure of segment information in the notes to the financial statements. Misstatement of the financial statement notes can attract regulatory scrutiny. Third, sanctions against individuals for violations of the securities laws can be severe. Although the SEC does not have criminal enforcement power, the ability to bar an individual from practicing before it as an accountant, as well as the SEC's ability to bar an individual from serving as an officer or director of a public company, can have severe economic consequences for individuals subject to these sanctions.

Concluding Remarks

Job order costing is ideal for companies that create unique products or services. Many professional service firms such as medical, law, or accounting firms rely on job order costing techniques to determine the price to charge for their services. However, job order costing alone does not provide the detail that many companies need to sufficiently track overhead to jobs. Activity-based costing, used simultaneously with job order costing, gives managers and their customers a clearer understanding of how a particular service or product uses up indirect overhead costs. In coming chapters, we will see how understanding the significant activities that cause costs to vary can provide a basis for planning future activities and managing the costs of current activities.

END-OF-CHAPTER REVIEW

SUMMARY OF LEARNING OBJECTIVES

LO1 **Explain the purposes of cost accounting systems.** Cost accounting systems provide information useful for managing the activities that consume resources. Managers use the information to evaluate and reward employee performance. In addition, the cost information is reported on external financial statements as, for example, inventories, cost of goods sold, and period expenses.

LO2 **Identify the processes for creating goods and services that are suited to job order costing.** Job order costing methods are appropriate for businesses and companies producing customized jobs that require differing amounts and types of direct labor, direct materials, and overhead.

LO3 **Explain the purpose and computation of overhead application rates for job order costing.** An overhead application rate is a device used to assign appropriate amounts of overhead costs to specific services, products, or jobs that are in progress. The overhead application rate expresses the relationship between the overhead costs and some activity base that can be used to trace costs directly to each specific job. An overhead application rate is computed by dividing the expected or estimated overhead costs for the period by the expected amount of activity (for example, machine hours, labor hours, etc.) related to the activity base.

LO4 **Describe the purpose and the content of a job cost sheet.** The purpose of a job cost sheet is to keep track of all manufacturing costs relating to a particular job. Each job cost sheet shows the cost of all the materials, direct labor, and factory overhead charged to the job. The job cost sheets of all jobs in process serve as a subsidiary ledger supporting the balance of the Work in Process Inventory account.

LO5 **Account for the flow of costs when using job order costing.** Costs flow from the Direct Labor account, the Direct Materials Inventory account, and the Manufacturing Overhead account into the Work in Process Inventory account. As jobs are completed, the accumulated costs are transferred to the Finished Goods Inventory account. As units are sold, their costs flow from the Finished Goods Inventory account to the Cost of Goods Sold account.

LO6 **Define overhead-related *activity cost pools* and provide several examples.** Activity cost pools are the costs of resources consumed by an activity that is necessary to produce a good or service. Types of overhead activity cost pools include building maintenance, utilities, purchasing activities, and machinery repairs, among others.

LO7 **Demonstrate how activity bases are used to assign activity cost pools to units produced.** Activity bases are the measures of the activity that consumes the associated resource cost pool. Thus, for the purchasing activities cost pool, the activity base is the number of purchase orders processed. Dividing the activity cost pool by the activity base provides the cost per unit of activity. Activity costs are assigned to the product by tracking the activity base associated with the product and multiplying it by the appropriate cost per unit of activity.

Key Terms Introduced or Emphasized in Chapter 17

activity-based costing (p. 762) Cost accounting method that tracks indirect costs to the activities that consume resources.

activity cost pools (p. 769) Overhead categories that represent the costs associated with an activity that consumes overhead resources.

cost accounting systems (p. 760) The methods and techniques used by enterprises to track resources consumed in creating and delivering products and services to customers.

cost driver (p. 762) An activity base that can be traced directly to units produced and that serves as a causal factor in the incurrence of overhead costs. Serves as an activity base in an overhead application rate.

job cost sheet (p. 763) A record used in job order costing to summarize the manufacturing costs (materials, labor, and overhead) applicable to each job or batch of production. Job cost sheets may be viewed as a subsidiary ledger supporting the balance of the Work in Process Inventory control account.

job order costing (p. 760) A cost accounting method under which the focal point of costing is a quantity of product known as a *job* or *lot*. Costs of direct materials, direct labor, and manufacturing overhead applicable to each job are compiled to arrive at average unit cost.

over- or underapplied overhead (p. 767) The difference between the actual manufacturing overhead incurred during the period and the amount applied to work in process by use of a predetermined overhead application rate.

overhead application rate (p. 761) A device used to apply a normal amount of overhead costs to work in process. The rate is predetermined at the beginning of the year and expresses the percentage relationship between estimated total overhead for the year and the estimated total of some cost driver, such as direct labor hours, direct labor costs, or machine hours. Use of the overhead application rate causes overhead to be charged to work in process in proportion to the amount of "cost driver" traceable to those units.

Demonstration Problem

Oceanview Enterprises is a print shop that uses job order costing. Overhead is applied to individual jobs at a predetermined rate based on direct labor costs. The job cost sheet for job no. 21 appears below.

JOB COST SHEET

JOB NUMBER: 21 DATE STARTED: Feb. 1

PRODUCT: Income Tax Handbook DATE COMPLETED: Feb. 6

UNITS COMPLETED: 2,500

Direct materials used	$3,200
Direct labor	400
Manufacturing overhead applied	1,200
Total cost of job no. 21	$4,800
Unit cost ($4,800 ÷ 2,500 units)	$ 1.92

Instructions

Prepare general journal entries to:

a. Summarize the manufacturing costs charged to job no. 21. (Use one compound entry.)

b. Record the completion of job no. 21.

c. Record the credit sale of 2,000 units from job no. 21 at a unit sales price of $4. Record in a separate entry the related cost of goods sold.

Solution to the Demonstration Problem

GENERAL JOURNAL

a. Work in Process Inventory	4,800	
Materials Inventory		3,200
Direct Labor		400
Manufacturing Overhead		1,200
Manufacturing costs incurred on job no. 21.		
b. Finished Goods Inventory	4,800	
Work in Process Inventory		4,800
To record completion of job no. 21.		
c. Accounts Receivable	8,000	
Sales		8,000
To record credit sale of 2,000 units from job no. 21 @ $4 per unit.		
Cost of Goods Sold	3,840	
Finished Goods Inventory		3,840
To record cost of sales for 2,000 units from job no. 21 (2,000 × $1.92 per unit).		

Self-Test Questions

The answers to these questions appear on page 801.

1. If CustomCraft uses *job order* costing, each of the following is true, *except:*

a. Individual job cost sheets accumulate all manufacturing costs applicable to each job and together constitute a subsidiary ledger for the Work in Process Inventory account.

b. Direct labor cost applicable to individual jobs is recorded when paid by a debit to Work in Process Inventory and a credit to Cash, as well as by entering the amount on the job cost sheets.

c. The amount of direct materials used in individual jobs is recorded by debiting the Work in Process Inventory account and crediting the Materials Inventory account, as well as by entering the amount used on job cost sheets.

d. The manufacturing overhead applied to each job is transferred from the Manufacturing Overhead account to the Work in Process Inventory account, as well as entered on the individual job cost sheets.

2. When job costing is in use, *underapplied* overhead:

a. Represents the cost of manufacturing overhead that relates to unfinished jobs.

b. Is indicated by a credit balance remaining at year-end in the Manufacturing Overhead account.

c. Is closed out at year-end into the Cost of Goods Sold account if the amount is not material.

d. Results when actual overhead costs incurred during a year are less than the amounts applied to individual jobs.

3. Which of the following businesses would most likely use *job order* costing?

a. A print shop that specializes in wedding invitations.

b. A company that makes frozen pizzas.

c. A brewery.

d. An oil refinery.

4. The purpose of an overhead application rate is to:

a. Assign a portion of indirect manufacturing costs to each product manufactured.

b. Determine the type and amount of costs to be debited to the Manufacturing Overhead account.

c. Charge the Work in Process Inventory account with the appropriate amount of direct manufacturing costs.

d. Allocate manufacturing overhead to expense in proportion to the number of units manufactured during the period.

5. Which of the following are *true* regarding activity-based costing?

a. A primary goal of using ABC is a more useful allocation of manufacturing overhead to product lines.

b. Under ABC, direct labor hours are never used to allocate overhead costs to activity pools or product lines.

c. The use of ABC is indicated when it is suspected that each of a firm's product lines consumes approximately the same amount of overhead resources but the current allocation scheme assigns each line a substantially different amount.

d. ABC can be used in conjunction with job order costing.

6. Which of the following would be the most appropriate basis for allocating the costs of plant insurance that covers equipment theft and damage?

a. Direct labor hours.

b. Value of equipment.

c. Machine hours.

d. Square feet of plant space.

7. Using ABC to allocate manufacturing overhead can help managers to:

a. Identify what activities drive overhead costs.

b. Set product prices.

c. Locate inefficiencies in the production process.

d. Do all of the above.

ASSIGNMENT MATERIAL Discussion Questions

1. What is a cost accounting system?

2. What are the major objectives of a cost accounting system in a manufacturing company?

3. What factors should be taken into account in deciding whether to use job order costing in any given manufacturing situation?

4. What is meant by the term *overhead application rate*?

5. What is meant by the term *overhead cost driver*? How does the cost driver enter into the computation of an overhead application rate?

6. What is meant by underapplied overhead? By overapplied overhead?

7. Gerox Company applies manufacturing overhead on the basis of machine-hours, using a predetermined overhead rate. At the end of the current year, the Manufacturing Overhead account has a credit balance. What are the possible explanations for this? What disposition should be made of this balance?

8. Taylor & Malone is a law firm. Would the concepts of job order costing be appropriate for this type of service business? Explain.

9. Define the term *activity base*.
10. Define the term *cost driver*.
11. Why is the use of a single activity base inappropriate for some companies?
12. Describe how activity-based costing can improve overhead cost allocations in companies that produce a diverse line of products.
13. What is an *activity cost pool*?
14. Why is the use of direct labor hours as an activity base likely to be inappropriate in a highly mechanized production facility?
15. Discuss the potential benefits associated with using activity-based costing.

Brief Exercises

LO5 **BRIEF EXERCISE 17.1**

Accounting for Overhead

Newton Corporation uses a job order costing system and allocates manufacturing overhead at a rate of $25 per machine hour. During the period, the company used 600 machine hours and actually incurred manufacturing overhead costs of $14,500.

a. Prepare a summary journal entry to record total manufacturing overhead allocated to jobs during the period.

b. Prepare a summary journal entry to record actual overhead costs incurred during the period (make the credit portion of the entry to "Various Accounts").

c. Prepare the journal entry to close the Manufacturing Overhead account directly to Cost of Goods Sold at the end of the period.

LO5 **BRIEF EXERCISE 17.2**

Transferring Costs in a Job Order System

Mayfield Corporation finished job no. 314 on June 1. On June 10, the company sold job no. 314 for $10,000, cash. Total manufacturing costs allocated to this job at the time of the sale amounted to $6,500.

a. Record the transfer of job no. 314 from Work in Process to Finished Goods on June 1.

b. Record the sale of job no. 314, and the transfer of its costs from Finished Goods, on June 10.

LO3 **BRIEF EXERCISE 17.3**

Overhead Application Rates

Munson Manufacturing applies manufacturing overhead at a rate of $30 per direct labor hour.

a. When during the year was this rate computed?

b. Describe briefly how this rate was computed.

c. Identify the shortcomings of this rate that will cause overhead applied during the period to differ from the actual overhead costs incurred during the period.

LO3 **BRIEF EXERCISE 17.4**

LO5 Actual Overhead versus Applied Overhead

Swanson Corporation applies manufacturing overhead to jobs at a rate of $30 per direct labor hour. During the current period, actual overhead costs totaled $175,000, and 6,000 direct labor hours were worked by the company's employees.

a. Record the journal entry to close the Manufacturing Overhead account directly to Cost of Goods Sold at the end of the period.

b. Was manufacturing overhead overapplied, or was it underapplied?

LO1 **BRIEF EXERCISE 17.5**

LO2 Types of Cost Accounting Systems

Indicate whether job order costing is appropriate for each of the following businesses. Explain why.

a. Old Home Bakery, Inc. (a bakery that produces to order).

b. Baxter, Claxter, and Stone, CPAs.

c. Thompson Construction Company.

d. Satin Wall Paints, Inc.

e. Apache Oil and Gas Refinery.

f. Dr. Carr's Auto Body Shoppe.

g. Health-Rite Vitamins.

h. Shampoo Products International.

LO5 **BRIEF EXERCISE 17.6**

Applying Direct Labor Costs

Willoughby Manufacturing pays its direct labor employees $20 per hour. During the current period, 300 direct labor hours were recorded on employee time cards, and the company actually paid its direct labor employees $5,400.

a. Record the summary journal entry to apply direct labor costs to all jobs during the period.

b. Prepare the summary journal entry to record direct labor wages paid during the period.

c. What is the balance of the Direct Labor account at the end of the period? How is it reported in the company's financial statements?

LO5 **BRIEF EXERCISE 17.7**

Applying Direct Materials Costs

Zappe Industries purchased direct materials costing $500,000 during the current period. It actually used only $350,000 of direct materials on jobs during the period.

a. Prepare the summary journal entry to record direct materials purchased during the period. Assume that all purchases are made on account.

b. Prepare the summary journal entry to record all direct materials used during the period.

LO5 **BRIEF EXERCISE 17.8**

Recording Manufacturing Costs

For each of the accounts listed below, prepare *two* summary journal entries. In the first entry, illustrate a transaction that would cause the account to be *debited.* In the second entry, illustrate a transaction that would cause the account to be *credited.* Assume that perpetual inventory records are maintained. Include a brief written explanation with each journal entry and use "XXX" in place of dollar amounts.

a. Materials Inventory

b. Direct Labor

c. Manufacturing Overhead

d. Finished Goods Inventory

LO6 **BRIEF EXERCISE 17.9**

Selecting Activity Bases

Listed below are the eight activity cost pools used by Charvez Corporation.

Production set-up costs	Maintenance costs
Heating costs	Design and engineering costs
Machinery power costs	Materials warehouse costs
Purchasing department costs	Product inspection costs

Suggest an appropriate activity base for allocating each of the above activity cost pools to products. (Consider each cost pool independently.)

LO6 **BRIEF EXERCISE 17.10**

Allocations in an ABC System

Leah, Inc., applies manufacturing overhead to production using an activity-based costing system. The company's utilities cost pool has accumulated $150,000, its maintenance cost pool has accumulated $200,000, and its set-up cost pool has accumulated $50,000. The company has two product lines, Deluxe and Basic. The utilities cost pool is allocated to these product lines on the basis of machine hours. The maintenance pool is allocated on the basis of work orders. The set-up pool is allocated on the basis of production runs.

a. Allocate the utilities cost pool to each product line assuming the Deluxe model used 4,000 machine hours and the Basic model used 1,000 machine hours.

b. Allocate the maintenance pool to each product line assuming the Deluxe model required 25 work orders and the Basic model required 75 work orders.

c. Allocate the set-up pool to each product line assuming the Deluxe model required 9 production runs and the Basic model required 21 production runs.

Exercises

LO1 through LO4 LO6 LO7 **EXERCISE 17.1**

Accounting Terminology

Listed below are seven technical accounting terms introduced or emphasized in this chapter.

Job order costing	Cost driver
Overhead application rate	Cost of finished goods manufactured
Overapplied overhead	Job cost sheet
Activity-based costing	

Each of the following statements may (or may not) describe these technical terms. For each statement, indicate the term described, or answer "None" if the statement does not correctly describe any of the terms.

a. An activity base that can be traced directly to units produced and can be used as a denominator in computing an overhead application rate.

b. The total of all direct labor, direct materials, and manufacturing overhead transferred from work in process to finished goods.

c. A means of assigning indirect product costs to work in process during the period.

d. A debit balance remaining in the Manufacturing Overhead account at the end of the period.

e. The type of cost accounting system likely to be used by a construction company.

f. The type of cost accounting method likely to be used for overhead costs.

LO1 through LO5

EXERCISE 17.2

Flow of Costs in Job Order Costing

The information below was taken from the job cost sheets of Bates Company.

Job Number	Manufacturing Costs as of June 30	Manufacturing Costs in July
101	$4,200	
102	3,240	
103	900	$2,000
104	2,250	4,000
105		6,000
106		3,700

During July, jobs no. 103 and 104 were completed, and jobs no. 101, 102, and 104 were delivered to customers. Jobs no. 105 and 106 are still in process at July 31. From this information, compute the following:

a. The work in process inventory at June 30.

b. The finished goods inventory at June 30.

c. The cost of goods sold during July.

d. The work in process inventory at July 31.

e. The finished goods inventory at July 31.

LO1 through LO5

EXERCISE 17.3

Journal Entries in Job Order Costing

Riverside Engineering is a machine shop that uses job order costing. Overhead is applied to individual jobs at a predetermined rate based on direct labor costs. The job cost sheet for job no. 321 appears below.

JOB COST SHEET

JOB NUMBER: 321 DATE STARTED: May 10

PRODUCT: 2" Brass Check Valves DATE COMPLETED: May 21

UNITS COMPLETED: 4,000

Direct materials used	$ 7,720
Direct labor	1,400
Manufacturing overhead applied	3,080
Total cost of job no. 321	$12,200
Unit cost ($12,200 ÷ 4,000 units)	$ 3.05

Prepare general journal entries to:

a. Summarize the manufacturing costs charged to job no. 321. (Use one compound entry.)

b. Record the completion of job no. 321.

c. Record the credit sale of 2,100 units from job no. 321 at a unit sales price of $5. Record in a separate entry the related cost of goods sold.

LO3 LO6

EXERCISE 17.4

Overhead Cost Drivers; Determination and Use of Unit Cost

During June, Assembly Department no. 4 of Riverview Electronics produced 12,000 model 201 computer keyboards. Assembly of these units required 1,476 hours of direct labor at a cost of $26,400, direct materials costing $318,960, and 2,880 hours of machine time. Based on an analysis of overhead costs at the beginning of the year, overhead is applied to keyboards using the following formula:

Overhead = 75% of Direct Labour Cost + $32 per Machine Hour

a. Compute the total amount of overhead cost applied to the 12,000 keyboards.

b. Compute the *per-unit cost* of manufacturing these keyboards.

c. Briefly explain *why* the department might use *two separate activity bases* in applying overhead costs to one type of product.

d. Identify at least two types of overhead cost pools that might be "driven" by each of the two cost drivers indicated in this situation.

e. What appears to be the *primary* driver of overhead costs in the manufacture of keyboards?

f. Compute the gross profit that will result from the sale of 2,000 of these keyboards at a sales price of $75 each.

LO2

EXERCISE 17.5

Cost Classifications

Identify whether each of the following costs of **Granite Construction, Inc.**, would be classified as direct labor, direct materials, manufacturing overhead, or as selling, general, and administrative costs.

a. Hourly wages paid to backhoe operators.

b. Crankcase oil used in construction machinery.

c. PVC pipes used in a municipal sewer construction project.

d. Depreciation of bulldozers and other construction equipment.

e. Advertising costs.

f. Steel beams used in the construction of an office building.

g. Salaries paid to foremen responsible for supervising multiple construction projects.

h. Legal costs.

i. Gasoline used in trucks that haul construction equipment to various job sites.

j. Hourly wages paid to masons and carpenters.

k. Costs for accounting and tax services.

l. The CEO's salary.

m. Rivets, screws, nuts, and bolts.

LO3 through LO5

EXERCISE 17.6

Cost Flows and Financial Statements

Conklin Corporation recorded the following activities during its first month of operations:

- Purchased materials costing $250,000.
- Used direct materials in production costing $230,000.
- Incurred direct labor costs of $300,000, of which $275,000 had actually been paid at the end of the month.
- Applied manufacturing overhead at a rate of $15 per direct labor hour. (Direct labor workers earn $25 per hour.)
- Incurred actual manufacturing overhead costs of $175,000.
- Transferred completed jobs costing $520,000 to finished goods.
- Sold completed jobs for $700,000. The cost applied to the jobs sold totaled $480,000.

- Closed the Manufacturing Overhead account directly to Cost of Goods Sold at the end of the month.
- Incurred selling and administrative costs of $100,000 during the month.

a. Prepare Conklin Corporation's income statement for its first month of operations. Ignore income taxes.

b. Determine the company's inventory balances at the end of its first month of operations.

LO3 through LO5

EXERCISE 17.7

Journal Entries, Cost Flows, and Determining Account Balances

Zelda Manufacturing organized in June and recorded the following transactions during June, its first month of operations:

1. Purchased materials costing $800,000.
2. Used direct materials in production costing $485,000.
3. Applied direct labor costs of $500,000 to various jobs.
4. Applied manufacturing overhead at a rate of $10 per direct labor hour. (Direct labor workers earn $20 per hour.)
5. Incurred actual manufacturing overhead costs of $245,000 (credit "Various Accounts").
6. Transferred completed jobs costing $745,000 to finished goods.
7. Sold completed jobs for $1,000,000 on account. The cost applied to the jobs sold totaled $615,000.
8. Closed the Manufacturing Overhead account directly to Cost of Goods Sold on June 30.

a. Prepare a journal entry for each of the eight transactions listed above.

b. Compute the balance of the Cost of Goods Sold account at June 30.

c. Determine the company's inventory balances at the end of June.

LO3 through LO5

EXERCISE 17.8

Journal Entries, Cost Flows, and Financial Reporting

Blue Plate Construction organized in December and recorded the following transactions during its first month of operations:

Dec. 2 Purchased materials on account for $400,000.

Dec. 3 Used direct materials costing $100,000 on job no. 100.

Dec. 9 Used direct materials costing $150,000 on job no. 101.

Dec. 15 Used direct materials costing $30,000 on job no. 102.

Dec. 28 Applied the following direct labor costs to jobs: job no. 100, $9,000; job no. 101, $11,000; job no. 102, $5,000.

Dec. 28 Applied manufacturing overhead to all jobs at a rate of 300% of direct labor dollars.

Dec. 29 Completed and transferred job no. 100 and job no. 101 to the finished goods warehouse.

Dec. 30 Sold job no. 100 on account for $200,000.

Dec. 31 Recorded and paid actual December manufacturing overhead costs of $78,000, cash.

Dec. 31 Closed the Manufacturing Overhead account directly to Cost of Goods Sold.

a. Record each of the above transactions as illustrated on pages 764–768.

b. Compute the amount at which Cost of Goods Sold is reported in the company's income statement for the month ended December 31.

c. Determine the inventory balances reported in the company's balance sheet dated December 31.

d. Was manufacturing overhead in December overapplied, or was it underapplied? Explain.

LO3 through LO5

EXERCISE 17.9

Journal Entries, Cost Flows, and Financial Reporting

Schmeltz Industries organized in January and recorded the following transactions during its first month of operations:

Jan. 5 Purchased materials on account for $800,000.

Jan. 9 Used materials costing $450,000 on job no. 1001.

Jan. 14 Used materials costing $200,000 on job no. 1002.

Jan. 18 Used materials costing $100,000 on job no. 1003.

Jan. 25 Applied the following direct labor costs to jobs: job no. 1001, $3,600; job no. 1002, $5,400; job no. 1003, $1,350. (Direct labor workers earn $18 per hour.)

Jan. 27 Applied manufacturing overhead to all jobs at a rate of $450 per direct labor hour.

Jan. 28 Completed and transferred job no. 1001 and job no. 1002 to the finished goods warehouse.

Jan. 29 Sold job no. 1001 on account for $725,000.

Jan. 31 Recorded and paid actual January manufacturing overhead costs of $250,000, cash.

Jan. 31 Closed the Manufacturing Overhead account directly to Cost of Goods Sold.

a. Prepare journal entries for each of the above transactions.

b. Compute the balance of the Cost of Goods Sold account at January 31.

c. Determine the company's inventory balances at January 31.

d. Was manufacturing overhead in January overapplied, or was it underapplied? Explain.

LO3 through LO5

EXERCISE 17.10

Journal Entries, Cost Flows, and Financial Reporting

Crenshaw uses a job order costing system to account for projects. It applies manufacturing overhead to jobs on the basis of direct labor hours and pays its direct labor workers $25 per hour. The following relates to activity for the month of December:

Manufacturing overhead budgeted (estimated on December 1)	$133,000
Budgeted driver activity (DLH) (estimated on December 1)	1,900 DLH
Direct materials purchased in December	$125,000
Direct materials used in December	100,000
Actual direct labor costs in December	50,000
Actual manufacturing overhead in December	150,000
Cost of jobs completed in December	275,000
Revenue earned in December	600,000
Cost of goods sold in December (prior to adjusting for overhead)	325,000
Selling and administrative costs in December	250,000
Materials Inventory, December 1	20,000
Work in Process Inventory, December 1	75,000
Finished Goods Inventory, December 1	105,000

a. Record the purchase of direct materials in December. Assume all purchases are made on account.

b. Record the cost of direct materials applied to jobs in December.

c. Record the cost of direct labor applied to jobs in December.

d. Record the *actual* cost of manufacturing overhead incurred in December. Assume all overhead costs were paid in cash.

e. Record the cost of manufacturing overhead *applied* to jobs in December.

f. Record revenue and the related cost of jobs sold in December. Assume all sales are made on account.

g. Record December selling and administrative costs. Assume all selling and administrative costs were paid in cash.

h. Close the Manufacturing Overhead account directly to Cost of Goods Sold on December 31.

i. Compute the company's December income. Ignore taxes.

LO3 through LO5

EXERCISE 17.11

Solving for Missing Amounts in a Job Costing System

Rush Company budgeted that it would incur $180,000 of manufacturing overhead costs in the upcoming period. By the end of the period, Rush had actually incurred manufacturing overhead costs totaling $192,000. Other information from the company's accounting records is provided below:

- Beginning Work in Process Inventory was $30,000, whereas ending Work in Process Inventory was $25,000.
- Total manufacturing costs of $470,000 were charged to Work in Process Inventory during the period. This amount included direct materials costs of $200,000.
- Workers logged 5,400 direct labor hours during the period.

- Beginning Finished Goods Inventory was $50,000.
- The Manufacturing Overhead account had a $30,000 debit balance immediately prior to closing at the end of the period. Manufacturing overhead was applied to jobs throughout the period on the basis of direct labor hours.
- Prior to any adjustment to account for overapplied or underapplied manufacturing overhead, Cost of Goods Sold had a $520,000 debit balance.
- Sales for the period totaled $1,050,000, whereas selling and administrative expenses totaled $400,000.

a. Determine how much manufacturing overhead was *applied* to jobs during the period.

b. Determine the company's manufacturing overhead *application rate* per direct labor hour.

c. How many direct labor hours were *budgeted* at the beginning of the period?

d. What was the average hourly wage rate earned by direct labor workers?

e. What was the company's ending Finished Goods Inventory balance?

f. What was the company's net income for the period? Ignore taxes.

LO3 through LO5

EXERCISE 17.12

Solving for Missing Amounts in a Job Costing System

Fenwick Corporation's manufacturing and finished goods warehouse facilities burned to the ground on January 31. The loss was fully covered by insurance. The insurance company wanted to know the cost of the inventories destroyed in the fire. The company's accountants gathered the following information:

Direct materials purchased in January	$160,000
Work in Process Inventory, January 1	34,000
Materials Inventory, January 1	16,000
Finished Goods Inventory, January 1	30,000
Direct labor costs incurred in January	190,000
Prime costs charged to jobs in January	294,000
Cost of finished goods available for sale in January	450,000
Sales revenue earned in January	500,000
Gross profit as a percentage of January sales	25%
Manufacturing overhead applied to jobs in January as a percentage of total conversion costs	60%

Assume that actual manufacturing overhead was exactly equal to the amount applied to production at the time of the fire.

On the basis of the information shown above, compute the cost of the following inventories lost in the fire. (Hint: Prime costs and conversion costs were discussed in Chapter 16.)

a. Materials inventory (assume materials inventory is comprised entirely of direct materials).

b. Work in process inventory.

c. Finished goods inventory.

LO3 through LO5

EXERCISE 17.13

Determining Balance Sheet Amounts from Job Sheets

Robinson International began operations in early February. The company has provided the following summary of total manufacturing costs assigned to the job sheets of its entire client base during its first three months of operations:

Job Number	February	March	April	Total Costs Assigned
1000	$12,400	$ 6,800		$19,200
1001	15,000	7,400	$1,400	23,800
1002	2,000			2,000
1003		16,000	4,000	20,000
1004		9,000	6,000	15,000

Job no. 1002 was completed in February and sold in March. Job no. 1000 was completed and sold in March. Job no. 1001 was completed and sold in April. Job no.1003 was completed in April, but won't be delivered until early May. Only job no. 1004 remains in process at April 30. The selling prices are set at 175 percent of the manufacturing costs assigned to each job.

a. Determine the Work in Process Inventory balance at the end of February, March, and April.

b. Determine the Finished Goods Inventory balance at the end of February, March, and April.

c. Compute the company's *total gross profit* for the three months ended April 30.

LO6 LO7

EXERCISE 17.14

Allocating Activity Cost Pool

Costume Kings has two product lines: machine-made costumes and hand-made costumes. The company assigns $80,000 in manufacturing overhead costs to two cost pools: power costs and inspection costs. Of this amount, the power cost pool has been assigned $32,000 and the inspection cost pool has been assigned $48,000. Additional information about each product line is shown below.

	Machine-Made	Hand-Made
Sales revenue	$240,000	$160,000
Direct labor and materials costs	$120,000	$ 96,000
Units produced and sold	48,000	16,000
Machine hours	96,000	4,000
Square feet of production space	1,200	800
Material orders received	150	100
Quality control inspection hours	2,000	500

a. Allocate the manufacturing overhead from the activity cost pools to each product line. Use what you believe are the most significant cost drivers from the information provided.

b. Compute the cost per unit of machine-made costumes and hand-made costumes.

c. On a per-unit basis, which product line appears to be the most profitable? Explain.

LO6 LO7

EXERCISE 17.15

Using ABC to Determine a Bid Price

Spear Custom Furniture uses an activity-based cost accounting system to apply overhead to production. The company maintains four overhead cost pools. The four cost pools, and their budgeted amounts for the upcoming period, are as follows:

Maintenance	$40,000
Materials handling	20,000
Set-ups	10,000
Quality control	45,000

Four cost drivers are used by Spear to allocate its overhead cost pools to production. The four cost drivers, and their budgeted total levels of activity for the upcoming period, are shown below:

Machine hours (to allocate maintenance costs)	600 hours
Material moves (to allocate materials handling costs)	400 moves
Set-ups (to allocate set-up costs)	100 set-ups
Number of inspections (to allocate quality control costs)	300 inspections

The company has been asked by Cosmopolitan University to submit a bid for tables to be used in a new computer lab. The plant manager feels that obtaining this job would result in new business in future years. Estimates for the Cosmopolitan University project are as follows:

Direct materials	$14,000
Direct labor (500 hours)	$15,000
Number of machine hours	60
Number of material moves	20
Number of set-ups	4
Number of inspections	2

a. Estimate the *total cost* of manufacturing the tables for Cosmopolitan University.

b. Determine the company's bid price if bids are based upon the total estimated manufacturing cost of a particular project, plus 75 percent.

Problem Set A

LO1 through LO5 PROBLEM 17.1A
Job Order Costing: Computations and Journal Entries

Chesapeake Sailmakers uses job order costing. Manufacturing overhead is charged to individual jobs through the use of a predetermined overhead rate based on direct labor costs. The following information appears in the company's Work in Process Inventory account for the month of June:

Debits to account:	
Balance, June 1	$ 7,200
Direct materials	12,000
Direct labor	9,000
Manufacturing overhead (applied to jobs as 150% of direct labor cost)	13,500
Total debits to account	$41,700
Credits to account:	
Transferred to Finished Goods Inventory account	33,200
Balance, June 30	$ 8,500

Instructions

a. Assuming that the direct labor charged to the jobs still in process at June 30 amounts to $2,100, compute the amount of manufacturing overhead and the amount of direct materials that have been charged to these jobs as of June 30.

b. Prepare general journal entries to summarize:
   1. The manufacturing costs (direct materials, direct labor, and overhead) charged to production during June.
   2. The transfer of production completed during June to the Finished Goods Inventory account.
   3. The cash sale of 90 percent of the merchandise completed during June at a total sales price of $46,500. Show the related cost of goods sold in a separate journal entry.

LO1 through LO5 PROBLEM 17.2A
Job Order Costing: Journal Entries and Cost Flows

The following information relates to the manufacturing operations of O'Shaughnessy Mfg. Co. during the month of March. The company uses job order costing.

a. Purchases of direct materials during the month amount to $59,700. (All purchases were made on account.)

b. Materials requisitions issued by the Production Department during the month total $56,200.

c. Time cards of direct workers show 2,000 hours worked on various jobs during the month, for a total direct labor cost of $30,000.

d. Direct workers were paid $26,300 in March.

e. Actual overhead costs for the month amount to $34,900 (for simplicity, you may credit Accounts Payable).

f. Overhead is applied to jobs at a rate of $18 per direct labor hour.

g. Jobs with total accumulated costs of $116,000 were completed during the month.

h. During March, units costing $128,000 were sold for $210,000. (All sales were made on account.)

Instructions

Prepare general journal entries to summarize each of these transactions in the company's general ledger accounts.

LO1 through LO5

PROBLEM 17.3A Job Order Costing: A Comprehensive Problem

Georgia Woods, Inc., manufactures furniture to customers' specifications and uses job order costing. A predetermined overhead rate is used in applying manufacturing overhead to individual jobs. In Department One, overhead is applied on the basis of machine-hours, and in Department Two, on the basis of direct labor hours. At the beginning of the current year, management made the following budget estimates to assist in determining the overhead application rate:

	Department One	Department Two
Direct labor cost	$300,000	$225,000
Direct labor hours	20,000	15,000
Manufacturing overhead	$420,000	$337,500
Machine-hours	12,000	7,500

Production of a batch of custom furniture ordered by City Furniture (job no. 58) was started early in the year and completed three weeks later on January 29. The records for this job show the following cost information:

	Department One	Department Two
Job order for City Furniture (job no. 58):		
Direct materials cost	$10,100	$ 7,600
Direct labor cost	$16,500	$11,100
Direct labor hours	1,100	740
Machine-hours	750	500

Selected additional information for January is as follows:

	Department One	Department Two
Direct labor hours—month of January	1,600	1,200
Machine-hours—month of January	1,100	600
Manufacturing overhead incurred in January	$39,010	$26,540

Instructions

a. Compute the predetermined overhead rate for each department.

b. What is the total cost of the furniture produced for City Furniture?

c. Prepare the entries required to record the sale (on account) of the furniture to City Furniture. The sales price of the order was $147,000.

d. Determine the over- or underapplied overhead for each department at the end of January.

LO1 through LO5

PROBLEM 17.4A Job Order Costing: A Comprehensive Problem

eXcel

Precision Instruments, Inc., uses job order costing and applies manufacturing overhead to individual jobs by using predetermined overhead rates. In Department A, overhead is applied on the basis of machine-hours, and in Department B, on the basis of direct labor hours. At the beginning of the current year, management made the following budget estimates as a step toward determining the overhead application rates:

	Department A	Department B
Direct labor	$420,000	$300,000
Manufacturing overhead	$540,000	$412,500
Machine-hours	18,000	1,900
Direct labor hours	28,000	25,000

Production of 4,000 tachometers (job no. 399) was started in the middle of January and completed two weeks later. The cost records for this job show the following information:

	Department A	Department B
Job no. 399 (4,000 units of product):		
Cost of materials used on job	$6,800	$4,500
Direct labor cost	$8,100	$7,200
Direct labor hours	540	600
Machine-hours	250	100

Instructions

a. Determine the overhead rate that should be used for each department in applying overhead costs to job no. 399.

b. What is the total cost of job no. 399, and what is the unit cost of the product manufactured on this production order?

c. Prepare the journal entries required to record the sale (on account) of 1,000 of the tachometers to SkiCraft Boats. The total sales price was $19,500.

d. Assume that actual overhead costs for the year were $517,000 in Department A and $424,400 in Department B. Actual machine-hours in Department A were 17,000, and actual direct labor hours in Department B were 26,000 during the year. On the basis of this information, determine the over- or underapplied overhead in each department for the year.

LO1 through LO5

PROBLEM 17.5A
Poor Drivers Are Cost Drivers

Ye Olde Bump & Grind, Inc., is an automobile body and fender repair shop. Repair work is done by hand and with the use of small tools. Customers are billed based on time (direct labor hours) and materials used in each repair job.

The shop's overhead costs consist primarily of indirect materials (welding materials, metal putty, and sandpaper), rent, indirect labor, and utilities. Rent is equal to a percentage of the shop's gross revenue for each month. The indirect labor relates primarily to ordering parts and processing insurance claims. The amount of indirect labor, therefore, tends to vary with the size of each job.

Henry Lee, manager of the business, is considering using either direct labor hours or number of repair jobs as the basis for allocating overhead costs. He has estimated the following amounts for the coming year:

Estimated total overhead	$123,000
Estimated direct labor hours	10,000
Estimated number of repair jobs	300

Instructions

a. Compute the overhead application rate based on (**1**) direct labor hours and (**2**) number of repair jobs.

b. Shown below is information for two repair jobs:

Job 1 Repair a dented fender. Direct material used, $25; direct labor hours, 5; direct labor cost, $75.

Job 2 Repair an automobile involved in a serious collision. Direct materials used, $3,800; direct labor hours, 200; direct labor cost, $3,000.

Determine the *total cost* of each repair job, assuming that overhead costs are applied to each job based on:

1. Direct labor hours.
2. Number of repair jobs.

c. Discuss the results obtained in part **b.** Which overhead application method appears to provide the more realistic results? Explain the reasoning behind your answer, addressing the issue of what "drives" overhead costs in this business.

PROBLEM 17.6A
Applying Overhead Costs Using ABC

Norton Chemical Company produces two products: Amithol and Bitrite. The company uses activity-based costing (ABC) to allocate manufacturing overhead to these products. The costs incurred by Norton's Purchasing Department average \$80,000 per year and constitute a major portion of the company's total manufacturing overhead.

Purchasing Department costs are assigned to two activity cost pools: (1) the order cost pool and (2) the inspection cost pool. Costs are assigned to the pools based on the number of employees engaged in each activity. Of the department's five full-time employees, one is responsible for ordering raw materials, and four are responsible for inspecting incoming shipments of materials.

Costs assigned to the order pool are allocated to products based on the total number of purchase orders generated by each product line. Costs assigned to the inspection pool are allocated to products based on the number of inspections related to each product line.

For the upcoming year, Norton estimates the following activity levels:

	Total	Amithol	Bitrite
Purchase orders generated	10,000	2,000	8,000
Inspections conducted	2,400	1,800	600

In a normal year, the company conducts 2,400 inspections to sample the quality of raw materials. The large number of Amithol-related inspections is due to quality problems experienced in the past. The quality of Bitrite materials has been consistently good.

Instructions

a. Assign the Purchasing Department's costs to the individual cost pools.

b. Allocate the order cost pool to the individual product lines.

c. Allocate the inspection cost pool to the individual product lines.

d. Suggest how Norton might reduce manufacturing costs incurred by the Purchasing Department.

PROBLEM 17.7A
ABC versus Use of a Single Activity Base

Dixon Robotics manufactures three robot models: the A3B4, the BC11, and the C3PO. Dixon allocates manufacturing overhead to each model based on machine hours. A large portion of the company's manufacturing overhead costs is incurred by the Maintenance Department. This year, the department anticipates that it will incur \$100,000 in total costs. The following estimates pertain to the upcoming year:

Model	Estimated Machine-Hours	Estimated Units of Production
A3B4	20,000	6,250
BC11	15,000	5,000
C3PO	5,000	2,500

Ed Smith, Dixon's cost accountant, suspects that unit costs are being distorted by using a single activity base to allocate Maintenance Department costs to products. Thus, he is considering the implementation of activity-based costing (ABC).

Under the proposed ABC method, the costs of the Maintenance Department would be allocated to the following activity cost pools using the number of work orders as an activity base: (1) the repairs pool and (2) the janitorial pool. Of the 2,000 work orders filed with the Maintenance Department each year, approximately 400 relate to repair activities, and 1,600 relate to janitorial activities.

Machinery repairs correlate with the number of production runs of each robot model. Thus, the repairs pool would be allocated to robots based on each model's corresponding number of production runs. Janitorial services correlate with square feet of production space. Thus, the janitorial pool would be allocated to products based on the square feet of production space devoted to each robot model. The following table provides a summary of annual production run activity and square footage requirements:

Model	Estimated Number of Production Runs	Estimated Square Feet of Production Space Used
A3B4	50	5,000
BC11	150	10,000
C3PO	200	25,000

Instructions

a. Calculate the amount of Maintenance Department costs that would be allocated to each robot model (on a per-unit basis) using machine-hours as a single activity base.

b. Calculate the amount of Maintenance Department costs that would be allocated to each robot model (on a per-unit basis) using the proposed ABC method.

c. Are cost allocations distorted using machine-hours as a single activity base? Explain your answer.

LO6 LO7 **PROBLEM 17.8A**
ABC versus Use of a Single Activity Base

Healthy Hound, Inc., makes two lines of dog food: (1) Basic Chunks, and (2) Custom Cuts. The Basic Chunks line is a dry food that is processed almost entirely by an automated process. Custom Cuts is a canned food made with real horsemeat. The slabs of meat are cut and trimmed by hand before being shoveled into a automated canning machine. Basic Chunks sells very well and is priced significantly below competitive brands. Sales of Custom Cuts have been on the decline, as the company has failed to keep the brand price competitive. Other information concerning each product line is provided below.

	Basic Chunks	Custom Cuts
Number of units* produced and sold per month	50,000	20,000
Direct materials cost per unit	$2	$4
Direct labor cost per hour	$12	$12
Direct labor hours per unit	0.01	0.10

*Units for Basic Chunks refer to *bags*; units for Custom Cuts refer to *cases*.

The company currently allocates manufacturing overhead to each product line on the basis of direct labor hours. Budgeted manufacturing overhead per month is $24,600, whereas budgeted direct labor hours amount to 2,500 per month.

Healthy Hound recently hired a consultant to examine its cost accounting system. The consultant recommends that the company adopt activity-based costing to allocate manufacturing overhead. She proposes that the following cost pools and cost drivers be used:

Cost Pool	Amount Allocated	Cost Driver	Total Driver Volume
Utilities	$ 8,000	Kilowatt-hours	100,000 kWh
Maintenance	1,000	Machine-hours	200 mh
Depreciation of plant and equipment	15,000	Square feet occupied	80,000 sq. ft.
Miscellaneous	600	Direct labor hours	2,500 DLH
Total allocation	$24,600		

The amount of driver activity corresponding to each product line is as follows:

Cost Driver	Basic Chunks	Custom Cuts
Kilowatt-hours	90,000 kWh	10,000 kWh
Machine-hours	160 mh	40 mh
Square feet occupied	60,000 sq. ft.	20,000 sq. ft.
Direct labor hours	500 DLH	2,000 DLH

Instructions

a. Allocate *manufacturing overhead* costs to each product line using direct labor hours as a single cost driver.

b. Allocate *manufacturing overhead* costs to each product line using the activity-based costing approach recommended by the consultant.

c. Compute the *total monthly manufacturing costs* assigned to each product line when activity-based costing is used to allocate manufacturing overhead.

d. Assume that the company sets selling prices as a fixed percentage above the total manufacturing costs allocated to each product line. On the basis of your results from parts **a** and **b,** discuss a possible reason why sales of the Custom Cuts product line are currently experiencing a decline.

e. Discuss reasons why the company should adopt the recommendation of the consultant and implement an activity-based costing system.

Problem Set B

LO1 through LO5

PROBLEM 17.1B Job Order Costing: Computations and Journal Entries

Hastings International uses job order costing. Manufacturing overhead is charged to individual jobs through the use of a predetermined overhead rate based on direct labor costs. The following information appears in the company's Work in Process Inventory account for the month of April:

Debits to account:	
Balance, April 1	$12,000
Direct materials	18,000
Direct labor	15,000
Manufacturing overhead (applied to jobs as 160% of direct labor cost)	24,000
Total debits to account	$69,000
Credits to account:	
Transferred to Finished Goods Inventory account	55,000
Balance, April 30	$14,000

Instructions

a. Assuming that the direct labor charged to the jobs still in process at April 30 amounts to $3,750, compute the amount of manufacturing overhead and the amount of direct materials that have been charged to these jobs as of April 30.

b. Prepare general journal entries to summarize:

1. The manufacturing costs (direct materials, direct labor, and overhead) charged to production during April.
2. The transfer of production completed during April to the Finished Goods Inventory account.
3. The cash sale of 90 percent of the merchandise completed during April at a total sales price of $77,000. Show the related cost of goods sold in a separate journal entry.

LO1 through LO5

PROBLEM 17.2B Job Order Costing: Journal Entries and Cost Flows

The following information relates to the manufacturing operations of Fargo Development Co. during the month of July. The company uses job order costing.

a. Purchases of direct materials during the month amount to $100,000. (All purchases were made on account.)

b. Materials issued for various jobs in process during the month total $98,000.

c. Time cards of direct workers show 1,800 hours worked on various jobs during the month, for a total direct labor cost of $54,000.

d. Direct workers were paid $50,000 in July.

e. Actual overhead costs for the month amount to $110,000 (for simplicity, you may credit Accounts Payable).

f. Overhead is applied to jobs at a rate of $60 per direct labor hour.

g. Jobs with total accumulated costs of $222,000 were completed during the month.

h. During July, units costing $180,000 were sold for $288,000. (All sales were made on account.)

Instructions

Prepare general journal entries to summarize each of these transactions in the company's general ledger accounts.

LO1 through LO5

PROBLEM 17.3B
Job Order Costing: A Comprehensive Problem

Lincoln Estates manufactures log homes to customers' specifications and uses job order costing. A predetermined overhead rate is used in applying manufacturing overhead to individual jobs. In the Cutting Department, overhead is applied on the basis of machine-hours. In the Assembly Department, overhead is applied on the basis of direct labor hours. At the beginning of the current year, management made the following estimates to assist in determining the overhead application rates:

Annual Estimates	Cutting Department	Assembly Department
Direct labor cost	$800,000	$960,000
Direct labor hours	40,000	32,000
Manufacturing overhead	$600,000	$480,000
Machine-hours	30,000	15,000

Production of a home ordered by Cliff Newton (job no. 80) was started early in the year and completed at the end of the first quarter, on March 31. The records for this job show the following cost information:

	Cutting Department	Assembly Department
Job order for Cliff Newton (job no. 80):		
Direct materials cost	$100,000	$150,000
Direct labor cost	$10,000	$108,000
Direct labor hours	500	3,600
Machine-hours	400	300

Selected additional information for the first quarter is as follows:

	Cutting Department	Assembly Department
Direct labor hours—first quarter	8,000	6,000
Machine-hours—first quarter	7,000	3,000
Manufacturing overhead incurred in first quarter	$142,000	$87,000

Instructions

a. Compute the predetermined overhead rate for each department.

b. What is the total cost of the home produced for Cliff Newton?

c. Prepare the entries required to record the sale (on account) of the home to Cliff Newton. The sales price of the order was $602,000.

d. Determine the over- or underapplied overhead for each department at the end of the first quarter.

LO1 through LO5

PROBLEM 17.4B
Job Order Costing: A Comprehensive Problem

Monark Electronics uses job order costing and applies manufacturing overhead to individual jobs by using predetermined overhead rates. In Department A, overhead is applied on the basis of machine hours, and in Department B, on the basis of direct labor hours. At the beginning of the current year, management made the following budget estimates as a step toward determining the overhead application rates:

Annual Estimates	Department A	Department B
Direct labor	$630,000	$450,000
Manufacturing overhead	$810,000	$620,000
Machine-hours	16,200	3,000
Direct labor hours	25,200	24,800

Production of 1,000 circuit boards (job no. 652) was started in the middle of January and completed two weeks later. The cost records for this job show the following information:

	Department A	Department B
Job no. 652 (1,000 units of product):		
Cost of materials used on job	$19,000	$1,750
Direct labor cost	$1,500	$750
Direct labor hours	60	40
Machine-hours	180	120

Instructions

a. Determine the overhead rate that should be used for each department in applying overhead costs to job no. 652.

b. What is the total cost of job no. 652, and what is the unit cost of the product manufactured on this production order?

c. Prepare the journal entries required to record the sale (on account) of all 1,000 circuit boards to Computex Computers. The total sales price was $50,000.

d. Assume that actual overhead costs for the year were $800,000 in Department A and $615,000 in Department B. Actual machine-hours in Department A were 16,500, and actual direct labor hours in Department B were 24,000 during the year. On the basis of this information, determine the over- or underapplied overhead in each department for the year.

LO1 through LO5

PROBLEM 17.5B
Drivers for Drivers

Big Boomers makes custom clubs for golfers. The company also provides repair services for golfers with broken clubs. Most of the work is done by hand and with small tools used by craftsmen. Customers are quoted a price in advance of their clubs being manufactured or repaired. To produce and repair clubs at a profit, management must have a thorough understanding of product costs.

Jeff Ranck, manager of the business, is considering using either direct labor hours or the number of jobs as the basis for allocating overhead costs. He has estimated the following amounts for the coming year:

Estimated total overhead	$180,000
Estimated direct labor hours	15,000
Estimated number of jobs	2,500

Instructions

a. Compute the overhead application rate based on **(1)** direct labor hours and **(2)** the number of jobs.

b. Shown below is information for two customer orders:

Job 1 Manufacture a full set of custom clubs. Direct materials used, $300; direct labor hours, 12; direct labor cost, $276.

Job 2 Repair broken putter and replace grips on a full set of irons. Direct materials used, $100; direct labor hours, 3; direct labor cost, $60.

Determine the *total cost* of each job assuming that overhead costs are applied on the basis of:

1. Direct labor hours
2. Number of jobs

c. Discuss the results obtained in part **b**. Which overhead application method appears to provide more realistic results? Explain the reasoning behind your answer.

LO6 LO7 **PROBLEM 17.6B**
Applying Overhead Costs Using ABC

Logan Pharmaceutical produces two products: Caltrate and Dorkamine. The company uses activity-based costing (ABC) to allocate manufacturing costs to each product line. The costs incurred by the Quality Control Department average $5 million per year and constitute one of the largest components of the company's total manufacturing overhead.

The Quality Control Department conducts routine inspections at two critical points. First, all raw materials are inspected before they are entered into the production process. Second, all completed batches of product are inspected before being shipped to the finished goods warehouse. The department's costs are assigned to two activity cost pools: (1) preproduction inspections, and (2) postproduction inspections. Costs are assigned to the pools based on the number of employees engaged in each activity. Of the department's 16 full-time employees, 4 are responsible for preproduction inspections and 12 are responsible for postproduction inspections.

Costs assigned to the preproduction pool are allocated to products based on the number of materials shipments received for each product line. Costs assigned to the postproduction pool are allocated to products based on the number of batches of each product produced.

For the upcoming year, Logan Pharmaceutical estimates the following activity levels:

	Total	Caltrate	Dorkamine
Shipments received	1,200	900	300
Batches produced	2,000	400	1,600

The materials used to produce Caltrate can be ordered only in small quantities and therefore must be ordered frequently. The company's four preproduction inspectors devote a disproportionate amount of their time inspecting the 900 shipments of Caltrate materials. Dorkamine can be produced only in small batches and therefore must be produced frequently. Most of the problems associated with completed batches of Dorkamine can be traced to poor-quality materials. Very few problems are associated with the quality of Caltrate materials.

Instructions

a. Assign the Quality Control Department's costs to the individual cost pools.

b. Allocate the preproduction cost pool to each product line.

c. Allocate the inspection cost pool to each product line.

d. Suggest how Logan Pharmaceutical might reassign responsibilities to make better use of its quality control inspectors.

LO6 LO7 **PROBLEM 17.7B**
ABC versus Use of a Single Activity Base

Downhill Fast manufactures three ski products: boots, poles, and helmets. The company allocates manufacturing costs to each product line based on machine-hours. A large portion of its manufacturing overhead cost is incurred by the Maintenance Department. This year, the department anticipates that it will incur $250,000 in total costs. The following estimates pertain to the upcoming year:

Product	Estimated Machine-Hours	Estimated Units of Production
Boots	5,000	50,000
Poles	10,000	200,000
Helmets	35,000	20,000

Carol Safooma, the company's cost accountant, suspects that unit costs are being distorted by using a single activity base to allocate Maintenance Department costs to products. She is considering the implementation of an activity-based costing system (ABC).

Under the proposed ABC system, the maintenance costs would be allocated to the following activity cost pools using the number of work orders as an activity base: (1) the equipment set-up pool, and (2) the custodial pool. Of the 2,400 work orders filed with the Maintenance Department each year, approximately 600 relate to equipment set-up activities, whereas 1,800 relate to custodial functions.

Equipment set-ups correlate with the number of production runs associated with each product line. Thus, the equipment set-up pool would be allocated based on the number of production runs required for each product. Custodial services correlate with square feet of production space and would be allocated based on the space required to produce each product line. The following table provides a summary of annual production activity and square footage requirements:

Product	Estimated Production Runs	Estimated Square Feet of Production Space
Boots	500	9,000
Poles	300	15,000
Helmets	200	6,000

Instructions

a. Calculate the amount of Maintenance Department costs that would be allocated to each product line (on a per-unit basis) using machine-hours as a single activity base.

b. Calculate the amount of Maintenance Department costs that would be allocated to each product line (on a per-unit basis) using the proposed ABC system.

c. Are cost allocations currently being distorted using machine-hours as a single activity base? Defend your answer.

LO6 LO7

PROBLEM 17.8B
ABC versus Use of a Single Activity Base

Happy Cat, Inc., makes two lines of cat food: (1) Tabby Treat, and (2) Fresh n' Fishy. The Tabby Treat line is a dry food that is processed almost entirely by an automated process. Fresh n' Fishy is a canned food made with real carp from the Mississippi River. Each carp is filleted by hand before being tossed into an automated grinding and canning machine. Tabby Treat sells very well and is priced significantly below competitive brands. Sales of Fresh n' Fishy have been on the decline, as the company has failed to keep the brand price competitive. Other information concerning each product line is provided below.

	Tabby Treat	Fresh n' Fishy
Number of units* produced and sold per month	75,000	48,000
Direct materials cost per unit	$1	$3
Direct labor cost per hour	$16	$16
Direct labor hours per unit	0.04	0.25

*Units for Tabby Treat refer to *bags*. Units for Fresh n' Fishy refer to *cases*.

The company currently allocates manufacturing overhead to each product line on the basis of direct labor hours. Budgeted manufacturing overhead per month is $60,000, whereas budgeted direct labor hours amount to 15,000 per month.

Happy Cat recently hired a consultant to examine its cost accounting system. The consultant recommends that the company adopt activity-based costing to allocate manufacturing overhead. He proposes that the following cost pools and cost drivers be used:

Cost Pool	Amount Allocated	Cost Driver	Total Driver Volume
Utilities	$26,000	Kilowatt-hours	250,000 kWh
Maintenance	19,000	Machine set-ups	100 set-ups
Depreciation of plant and equipment	12,000	Square feet occupied	50,000 sq. ft.
Miscellaneous	3,000	Direct labor hours	15,000 DLH
Total allocation	$60,000		

The amount of driver activity corresponding to each product line is as follows:

Cost Driver	Tabby Treat	Fresh n' Fishy
Kilowatt-hours	200,000 kWh	50,000 kWh
Machine set-ups	70 mh	30 mh
Square feet occupied	42,000 sq. ft.	8,000 sq. ft.
Direct labor hours	3,000 DLH	12,000 DLH

Instructions

a. Allocate *manufacturing overhead* costs to each product line using direct labor hours as a single cost driver.

b. Allocate *manufacturing overhead* costs to each product line using the activity-based costing approach recommended by the consultant.

c. Compute the *total monthly manufacturing costs* assigned to each product line when activity-based costing is used to allocate manufacturing overhead.

d. Assume that the company sets selling prices as a fixed percentage above the total manufacturing costs allocated to each product line. On the basis of your results from parts **a** and **b,** discuss a possible reason why sales of the Fresh n' Fishy product line are currently experiencing a decline.

e. Discuss reasons why the company should adopt the recommendation of the consultant to implement an activity-based costing system.

Critical Thinking Cases

LO1 LO3 LO6 LO7

CASE 17.1

Effect of Overhead Application on Performance Evaluation

Classic Cabinets has one factory in which it produces two product lines. Walter manages the Wood Division, which produces wood cabinets, and Mary manages the Metal Division, which produces metal cabinets. Estimated unit production costs for the two types of cabinets are as follows:

	Wood	Metal
Direct materials	$50.00	$35.00
Direct labor cost	20.00	30.00
Manufacturing overhead	16.30	24.45
Total production cost per unit	$86.30	$89.45
Selling price per unit	$180	$160
Direct labor hours required per unit	2	3
Direct labor cost per hour	$10	$10

At the end of the year, total overhead costs are allocated to each division based on direct labor hours used. A breakdown of estimated yearly overhead costs is as follows:

Salaries:	
Walter	$ 50,000
Mary	50,000
Maintenance	20,000
Utilities	16,000
Property taxes	10,000
Annual straight-line depreciation:	
Equipment, Wood Division	80,000
Equipment, Metal Division	120,000
Total overhead	$346,000

Demand for cabinets over the past several years has been steady and is not expected to change. The Marketing Department estimates that approximately 10,000 wood cabinets and 7,500 metal cabinets will be sold each year for the foreseeable future. Each manager's performance evaluation is based on the total production cost per unit for his or her product line. The manager that succeeds in reducing unit costs by the greatest amount from those estimated will earn a bonus.

Mary is considering purchasing a new machine for $500,000 that will last approximately 10 years and have no salvage value. If the machine is purchased, the direct labor hours required to produce a metal cabinet will be reduced to 2.5 hours.

Instructions

a. If the machine is purchased, what will be the total unit costs of production for each type of cabinet, assuming all other cost and production estimates are correct?

b. From Mary's point of view, should the machine be purchased? Discuss whether Mary and Walter should be given sole authority over which equipment to purchase for their respective divisions.

c. What information do you think is necessary to decide whether to purchase the machine?

d. If the machine is purchased, do you think the performance evaluation of Walter and Mary will be accurate and fair under the current system?

LO6 LO7

CASE 17.2
Implementing ABC

Dave Miller is the controller of Mica Corporation. Mica produces five industrial cleaning products. Miller recently decided to implement activity-based costing at Mica. In designing the system, he decided to identify heating costs as a separate cost pool. These costs will be allocated to products using the square feet of production space as a cost driver. Thus, the more square footage a particular product line requires, the greater its allocation of heating costs will be.

Miller has asked each production manager to submit an estimate of the production space occupied by their respective product lines. The figures he receives will be used to allocate the heating cost pool. The five production managers at Mica are paid an annual bonus based on their ability to control production costs traceable to their respective product lines.

Instructions

a. What ethical concern do you have regarding the method used to gather information about space utilization at Mica?

b. What suggestions do you have regarding how this information should be gathered?

LO1 LO2 LO4

CASE 17.3
The Bidding Wars

Kendahl Plastics Corporation contracts with **NASA** to manufacture component parts used in communications satellites. **NASA** reimburses Kendahl on the basis of the actual manufacturing costs it incurs, plus a fixed percentage. Prior to being awarded a contract, Kendahl must submit a bid that details the estimated costs associated with each project. An examination of Kendahl's job cost sheets reveals that actual costs consistently exceed cost estimates quoted during the bidding process. As a consequence, **NASA** ends up paying considerably more than the bids Kendahl submits.

A Kendahl representative was recently quoted as saying, "We really aren't overcharging **NASA** for the work that we do. The actual costs shown on our job cost sheets seem high only because we are forced to understate our bid estimates in order to be awarded contracts. It's a common practice, and everybody does it. The truth of the matter is companies that quote realistic bid prices are not awarded contracts."

Instructions

Let us assume that it is common practice to purposely underestimate bids in order to win **NASA** contracts. Is it wrong for Kendahl to take part in this activity as long as it does not overstate the actual costs it incurs?

LO1 LO2 LO4 LO7

INTERNET CASE 17.4
Costing Construction Work

C. Erickson and Sons, Inc., is a Philadelphia-based construction company. Visit its home page at the following address:

www.cerickson.com

Instructions

a. Identify three projects and/or services provided by the company.

b. For each project or service identified, explain how cost accounting information would be useful to the company in providing the service or creating the project.

c. Which projects or services that you have identified would be most likely to benefit from job order costing and/or activity-based costing? Explain why.

Internet sites are time and date sensitive. It is the purpose of these exercises to have you explore the Internet. You may need to use the Yahoo! search engine http://www.yahoo.com *(or another favorite search engine) to find a company's current Web address.*

Answers to Self-Test Questions

1. b **2.** c **3.** a **4.** a **5.** a, c, d **6.** b **7.** d

CHAPTER 18

Process Costing

AFTER STUDYING THIS CHAPTER, YOU SHOULD BE ABLE TO:

Learning Objectives

- **LO1** Distinguish production procedures that match with process costing from those that correspond with job order costing.
- **LO2** Account for the physical flows and related cost flows when using process costing.
- **LO3** Demonstrate how to calculate equivalent units.
- **LO4** Use the costs of resources consumed to calculate the cost per equivalent unit of production.
- **LO5** Use the cost per equivalent unit to assign costs to the work completed during the period.
- **LO6** Create a process costing production report and use the report for decision making.

KELLOGG COMPANY

Located in Battle Creek, Michigan, Kellogg Company uses production methods that are ideal for process costing. William Kellogg's accidental discovery of cereal in 1894 illustrates these methods. While experimenting with different food production techniques at the Battle Creek Sanatorium in Michigan, William and his brother, Dr. John Kellogg, decided to run boiled wheat dough through rollers, which enabled them to produce thin sheets of wheat. After a sudden interruption in their laboratory activities left cooked wheat exposed to the air for more than a day, the Kellogg brothers decided to run the wheat through the rollers despite the fact it was no longer fresh. To their amazement, instead of a single, large sheet of wheat, the rollers discharged a single flake for each wheat berry—and cereal flakes were born.

With net sales in excess of $12.5 billion, Kellogg Company is the world's leading producer of cereal and a leading producer of convenience foods, including cookies, crackers, toaster pastries, cereal bars, frozen waffles, meat alternatives, pie crusts, and ice cream cones. Kellogg products are manufactured in 19 countries and marketed in more than 160 countries around the world. ■

Production of Goods and Services and Costing Systems

Business owners and managers rely heavily upon information provided by **cost accounting systems.** Costing systems provide information that is used for a large variety of business decisions, including planning production of goods and services, pricing products, and controlling associated costs of production. Thus, the choice of an appropriate costing system is a key underlying foundation for good decision making. In choosing the appropriate cost systems, managers carefully consider how products and services are created. The production procedures for goods and services are matched to the appropriate costing system.

A production procedure that results in a large number of identical products, such as described for Kellogg's cornflakes in the chapter opener, is a candidate for process costing procedures. **Process costing** is a method for accumulating the direct and indirect costs of a production process and averaging those costs over the identical units produced by that process. Process costing differs from **job order costing** because job order costing traces specific direct costs, that is, direct labor and direct materials, to the specific job being created. In addition, job order costing applies overhead to jobs using an activity base representing resources consumed by the job. However, process costing averages direct and indirect costs across mass-produced identical units.

Learning Objective
LO1 **Distinguish production procedures that match with process costing from those that correspond with job order costing.**

As we discussed in the previous chapter, processes that result in unique services, products, or batches are well suited to job order costing. Thus, automobile repair, furniture creation, lawn services, and accounting services are examples of production processes consistent with job order costing. Alternatively, packaged food products, oil and gas, paint, compact disks, television sets, textiles, and hand tools are examples of products that are created by production procedures suited for process costing. Exhibit 18–1 compares the production characteristics that help managers decide if job order or process costing is appropriate for their businesses.

Exhibit 18–1
DISTINGUISHING JOB ORDER AND PROCESS COSTING OPERATIONS

Job Order Costing	Process Costing
Product characteristics: • Use different amounts of direct materials • Use different amounts of direct labor • Tend to be unique • Are typically low volume • Are often custom-ordered	Product characteristics: • Are high volume • Are identical • Use identical amounts of direct materials • Use identical amounts of direct labor • Are created with repetitive operations

Of course, we know that many businesses have multiple operations associated with creating goods and services. Some of these operations may be consistent with a job order costing system and some of these operations may be better suited to process costing procedures. For example, consider **Dell Computer**'s goal of custom designing computer systems to customer-ordered specifications. Customer specifications differ widely and create unique products delivered to the customer's door. However, most of the system components, such as monitors and keyboards, are the product of mass production processes. Process costing systems are useful to track costs associated with the manufacture of the keyboard, but job order costing procedures are useful to track the specific combination of components ordered by individual customers. Thus, it is not uncommon to find companies that use both types of costing systems simultaneously. Surveys show that job order costing is more widely used than process costing, but that a majority of companies use both types of systems.

INTERNATIONAL CASE IN POINT 

A survey* of 141 manufacturers shows that 51 percent use job order costing, 14 percent use process costing, and another 11 percent use combinations of costing methods. The same survey shows that direct materials costs are 47 percent of the total manufacturing costs, followed by overhead costs (38 percent) and direct labor (15 percent). As companies become more automated, and as labor is continually outsourced to countries with lower wage rates, overhead costs will increase as direct labor costs decrease. Such trends in overhead and automation frequently require the use of process costing procedures.

*See E. Shim and J. Larkin, "A Survey of Current Managerial Accounting Practices: Where Do We Stand?" *Ohio CPA Journal* 53(1), pp. 21–27.

Process Costing

Many companies produce a *continuous stream of identical units,* such as bottles of beer, gallons of gasoline, or kilowatt-hours of electricity. When identical products are produced in a continuous stream, there are no distinct "jobs." Therefore, companies engaging in mass production often use *process costing* rather than job order costing.

Mass production usually involves a series of specific steps, or manufacturing *processes.* Process costing measures separately the cost of performing *each process* and then allocates these costs to the units processed during the month.

Process costing serves two related purposes. First, it measures the cost of goods manufactured on both a total and per-unit basis. This information is used in valuing inventories and in recording the cost of goods sold. But process costing also provides management with information about the *per-unit cost of performing each step* in the production process. This information is useful in evaluating the *efficiency* of production departments and often draws attention to potential cost savings.

CASE IN POINT

Large bottles of **Heinz** ketchup used to have two labels—one in front and one on the back. Through a careful analysis of manufacturing costs, production managers found that **Heinz** could save several hundred thousand dollars per year by applying only one label.

TRACKING THE PHYSICAL FLOW AND RELATED PRODUCTION COSTS

Understanding Physical Flows Because process costing involves averaging costs across products produced, it is very important to know the actual units worked on and those transferred out during the period. Therefore, one of the first steps in process costing is to make sure there is a clear understanding of the physical flow of products during the period in which costs are being assigned to products.

We use the company Metal Products, Inc., to illustrate the steps in process costing. Metal Products produces small metal souvenir products such as key rings and bottle openers. Production of these souvenirs occurs in three sequential departments, the Cutting Department, the Assembly Department, and the Packaging Department. Each department is considered to be a separate process in the production of the final product. Exhibit 18–2 describes the processes that occur in each department.

Exhibit 18–2 PRODUCTION PROCESS FOR METAL PRODUCTS, INC.

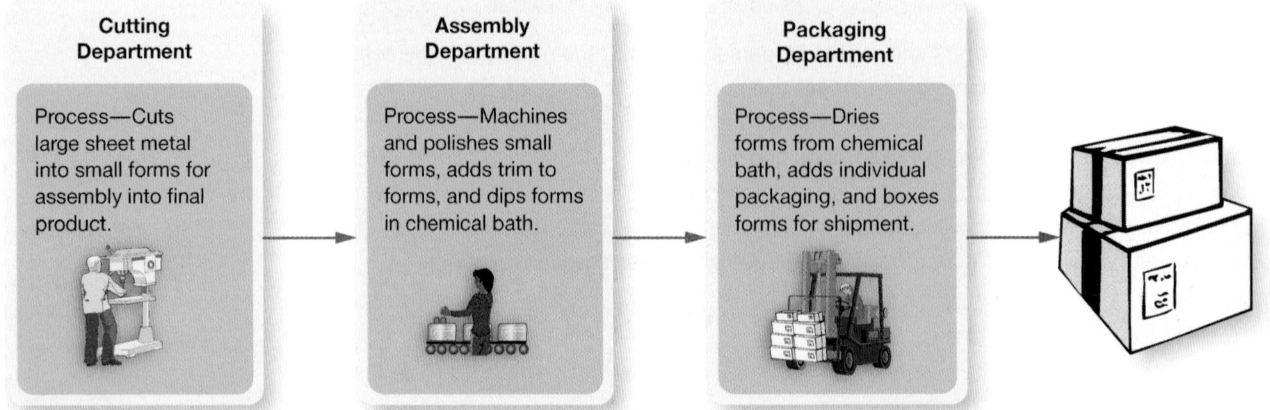

Learning Objective

LO2 Account for the physical flows and related cost flows when using process costing.

Production begins at Metal Products when rolled sheet metal is shipped into the Cutting Department and put into production. The Cutting Department tracks usage of the sheet metal by pounds until cutting produces the souvenir form (for example, a key chain or bottle opener). When the forms are transferred to the Assembly Department they become units. Throughout the remainder of the production process, units are used to track and assign costs of production. Exhibit 18–3 shows the typical physical flow of units and costs associated with Metal Products, Inc., for one month. Notice in the exhibit that it is important to know the number of units that are in four categories: (1) beginning work in process, (2) the number of units started during the period, (3) the number of units transferred to the next department during the period, and (4) the number of units in ending work in process. When you know where all units are during a period, then you know the physical flow.

Exhibit 18–3 PHYSICAL FLOWS AND COST FLOWS FOR PROCESS COSTING

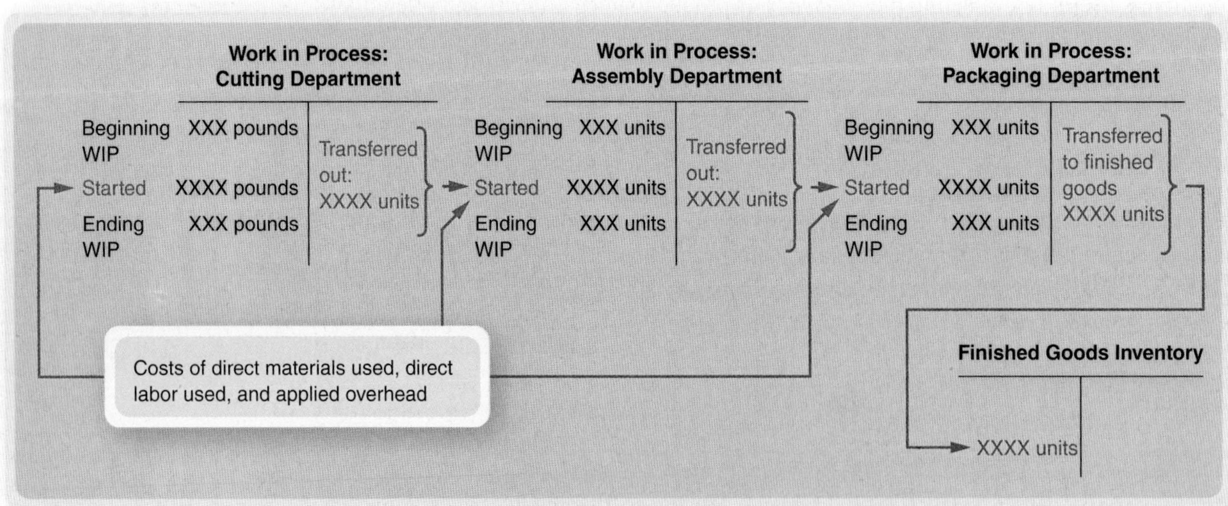

Understanding Cost Flows Process costing uses a separate Work in Process Inventory account to measure the costs incurred in *each production process.* Costs flow through these accounts *in sequence,* just as the units on an assembly line move from one production process to the next. Only when the units complete the *final* production process are their costs transferred to the Finished Goods Inventory account.

Accounting for Material, Labor, and Applied Overhead Each Work in Process account is charged (debited) for the materials used, direct labor, and overhead that relate to *that specific process.* For example, only those materials that require cutting are charged to the Cutting Department. Component parts sent directly to the Assembly Department are charged to the Assembly Department's Work in Process account. Direct labor and overhead costs related to the work done in that department also are applied separately to each Work in Process account.

Costs Flow from One Process to the Next Units in production pass from one process to the next. Process costing parallels this physical flow of units by transferring their *cost* from one Work in Process account to the next.

Assume that during the current month, $200,000 in manufacturing costs (including direct materials, direct labor, and overhead) were charged to the Cutting Department. Assume also that this department cut enough material to manufacture 10,000 units of product, and that the cut materials were transferred to the Assembly Department. At month-end, the following journal entry would be made to summarize the transfer of cut materials during the month:

Work in Process: Assembly Department	200,000	
Work in Process: Cutting Department		200,000
To transfer cost of processed units from the Cutting Department to the Assembly Department. Cutting cost per unit, $20 ($200,000 ÷ 10,000 units).		

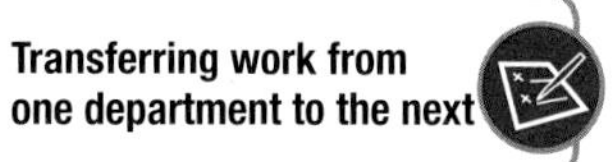

In essence, the output of the Cutting Department is a form of "direct materials" charged to the Assembly Department.

Notice that we transferred *all $200,000* of the Cutting Department's production costs to the Assembly Department. In effect, we assumed that all of the Cutting Department's costs are applicable to the *units completed and transferred during the month.*

PROCESS COSTING AND EQUIVALENT UNITS

Although some companies do not have significant ending work in process inventories, others that do must assign production costs to unfinished units. Consider the Assembly Department of Metal Products, Inc. As illustrated previously in Exhibit 18–2, the Assembly Department receives cut materials from the Cutting Department and processes them further by consuming additional direct labor, direct materials, and overhead.

Assume that the cut materials transferred in from the Cutting Department are first machined and polished. Let's say that this step represents 30 percent of the assembly process. Next, additional trim material is added to the polished cut units. Assume that this step represents 50 percent of the assembly process. Finally, before being transferred to the Packaging Department, the nearly completed units must be washed in a chemical bath. This step represents the final 20 percent of the assembly process. Because direct labor and overhead costs are incurred uniformly throughout the period, they are lumped together for convenience and referred to as **conversion costs.** Exhibit 18–4 illustrates the three steps of the production process in the Assembly Department.

Assume that, at the end of March, the Assembly Department has 3,000 units in process that are 80 percent finished (that is, they have not yet undergone step 3, the chemical bath). As discussed in previous chapters, any significant costs incurred in creating partially finished units should be assigned to work in process inventories.

In process costing systems, unfinished units are restated in terms of **equivalent units.** An equivalent unit is a percentage measure of a completed unit's resource requirements present in a partially finished unit. Thus, the Assembly Department's work in process that is 80 percent complete on March 31 is considered *100 percent* complete with respect to the cut material transferred in from the Cutting Department and the trim material added in the Assembly Department. In other words, the materials used to partially complete these units are *equivalent* to the materials needed to produce 3,000 *finished* units. These same units are only 80 percent complete with respect to their conversion requirements (direct labor and overhead). The conversion required to make 3,000 units 80 percent complete is *equivalent* to the conversion required to make 2,400 units 100 percent complete (3,000 units × 80%). Thus, we can say

Exhibit 18-4

STEPS IN THE PRODUCTION PROCESS AT METAL PRODUCTS, INC.

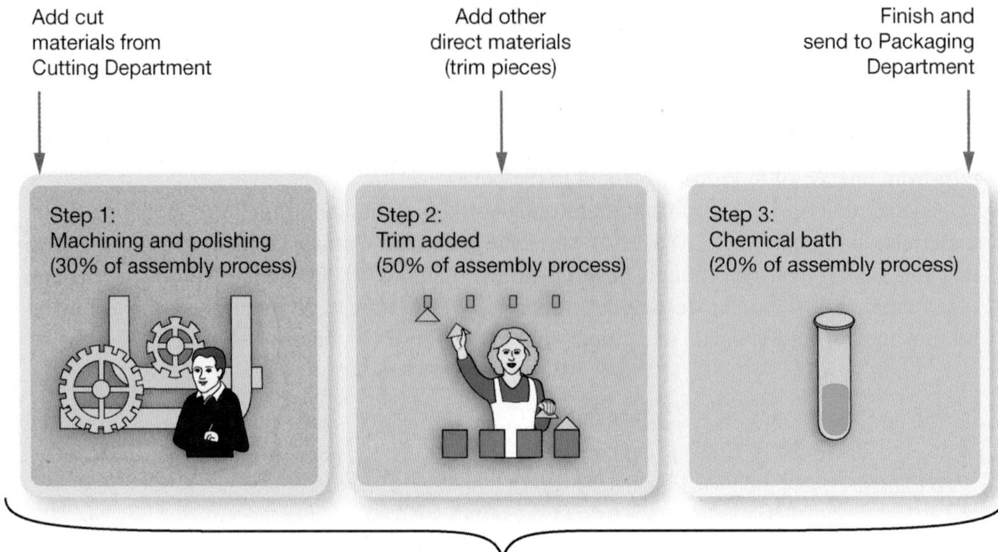

that ending inventory in the Assembly Department is comprised of 1,000 equivalent units of cut material transferred in from the Cutting Department, 1,000 equivalent units of trim material added in step 2, and 2,400 equivalent units of conversion added throughout the period. We will see that expressing resources consumed in terms of equivalent units enables companies to better understand the costs of production.

To illustrate process costing more fully, consider a typical month in the Assembly Department. Let's assume that on March 1, 1,000 units were in process. These units were 30 percent complete (they had not yet been through step 2 or step 3). During March, 10,000 units of cut materials were transferred from the Cutting Department to the Assembly Department. On March 31, there were 3,000 units in process. These units were 80 percent complete with respect to their conversion (they had not yet been through step 3). Exhibit 18–5 summarizes the costs accounted for by the Assembly Department in March.

Exhibit 18-5

MARCH COSTS IN THE ASSEMBLY DEPARTMENT

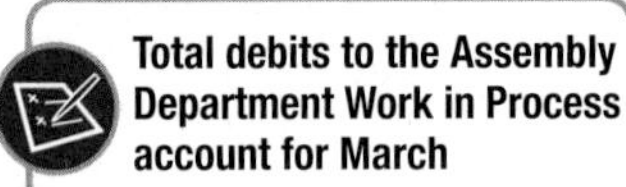
Total debits to the Assembly Department Work in Process account for March

Beginning work in process (March 1)	$ 29,500
Cut materials transferred from Cutting Department in March	200,000
Trim materials added in March	44,000
Direct labor incurred in March	105,000
Overhead incurred in March	147,500
Total costs to account for in March	$526,000

During March, the Assembly Department transferred 8,000 completed units to the Packaging Department. Of the units transferred, 1,000 were the units of beginning inventory carried forward from February, and 7,000 were units *started and completed* in March. Assuming a first-in, first-out (FIFO) physical flow of units, these amounts can be computed as follows:

Computing started and completed units is an important step in tracking equivalent units of production

Beginning inventory, March 1	1,000
Add: Units started in March (units transferred in from the Cutting Department)	10,000
Total units in process	11,000
Less: Ending inventory, March 31	3,000
Units transferred to the Packaging Department in March	8,000
Less: Beginning inventory	1,000
Units started and completed in March	7,000

Given the physical flow of units shown above, Exhibit 18–6 summarizes the equivalent units of resource inputs consumed by the Assembly Department in March.

Exhibit 18-6
EQUIVALENT UNITS OF RESOURCE INPUTS IN MARCH

	Equivalent Units of Resource Inputs in March		
Resources Used to:	**Cut Materials Transferred in**	**Trim Materials**	**Conversion**
Finish beginning work in process, 1,000 units . . .	–0–	1,000	700
Start and complete 7,000 new units	7,000	7,000	7,000
Start (but not complete) 3,000 new units	3,000	3,000	2,400
Total equivalent units of input in March.	10,000	11,000	10,100

Learning Objective
Demonstrate how to calculate equivalent units. LO3

The first row of figures in Exhibit 18–6 represents the equivalent units of resource inputs required to *finish* the 1,000 units of beginning inventory carried forward from February. Zero equivalent units of cut materials were required in March to complete these units because all of their cut material was transferred to the Assembly Department in February. These 1,000 units had only gone through step 1 of the assembly process (machining and polishing), so to finish them required 100 percent of their trim materials, or 1,000 equivalent units. Having completed step 1 of the assembly process, the units in beginning inventory had received 30 percent of their conversion requirements in February. Thus, they required an additional 70 percent of their conversion resource inputs, or 700 equivalent units to complete them in March (1,000 units × 70 percent conversion added in March).

The second row of figures in Exhibit 18–6 reveals that the 7,000 units started and completed in March required 100 percent of each resource input, or 7,000 equivalent units of cut materials, 7,000 units of trim materials, and 7,000 units of conversion.

The third row of figures in Exhibit 18–6 indicates the equivalent units of resource inputs required to *start but not finish* the 3,000 units in ending inventory on March 31. These units were fully processed through step 1 and step 2 of the assembly process. Thus, they had received 100 percent of their cut materials and trim materials in March, or 3,000 equivalent units of each. However, because these units had not undergone step 3 of the assembly process (the chemical bath), they had received only 80 percent of their conversion resource inputs, or 2,400 equivalent units (3,000 units × 80 percent conversion added in March).

COST PER EQUIVALENT UNIT

Learning Objective
Use the costs of resources consumed to calculate the cost per equivalent unit of production. LO4

To determine the amount of cost to assign to the four types of work completed—beginning work in process, ending work in process, started and completed, and transferred out—managers compute the cost per equivalent unit. This simple averaging technique divides the cost accumulated for each resource in a given time frame by the associated total equivalent units for each resource. For example, divide the total trim materials cost for March, $44,000, by the total equivalent units for trim, 11,000 (shown in Exhibit 18–6), to get $4 of trim cost per equivalent unit. Exhibit 18–7 provides the details of the computation of the cost per equivalent unit of each resource input used in March by the Assembly Department.

Exhibit 18-7 COST PER EQUIVALENT UNIT OF RESOURCE INPUTS IN MARCH

	Cut Materials Transferred in	Trim Materials	Conversion
Total cost of resources used in March (from Exhibit 18–5)	$200,000	$44,000	$252,500
Equivalent units of resource inputs in March (from Exhibit 18–6)	10,000	11,000	10,100
Cost per equivalent unit of resource inputs in March	$ 20	$ 4	$ 25

The total per-unit cost of the started and completed units in March is $49 ($20 + $4 + $25). The costs of the resource inputs and the associated units transferred in March for the Assembly Department are shown in the Work in Process T account in Exhibit 18–8.

Exhibit 18-8
ASSIGN COST TO PRODUCTION

Details for the Assembly Department Work in Process Inventory for March

Beg. balance (1,000 units)	$ 29,500	Cost transferred to Packaging: (8,000 units)	
		(1) From beg. work in process:	
Direct labor	105,000	Beg. balance	$ 29,500
		Work in March	
Direct materials:		Trim (1,000 × $4)	4,000
From Cutting Dept.	200,000	Conversion	
Trim	44,000	(700 × $25)	17,500
		(2) Started and completed	
Overhead	147,500	(7,000 × $49)	343,000
Total to account for:	$526,000	Total transferred out (8,000 units)	$394,000
Ending balance			
Direct materials:			
Cut (3,000 equivalent units × $20)	$ 60,000		
Trim (3,000 equivalent units × $4)	12,000		
Conversion (2,400 equivalent units × $25)	60,000		
Total ending work in process (3,000 units)	$132,000		

Learning Objective
LO5 Use the cost per equivalent unit to assign costs to the work completed during the period

The 3,000 units in ending work in process are assigned $132,000, which will be the April beginning Work in Process balance. During the month of March, $394,000 of costs are transferred from Assembly to Packaging. The following journal entry would be made to summarize the transfer of costs from Assembly to Packaging:

Transfer costs of units completed from one department to the next

Work in Process: Packaging.	394,000	
Work in Process: Assembly.		394,000
To transfer cost of completely processed units from the Assembly Department to the Packaging Department.		

Notice that the $394,000 transferred from Assembly to Packaging includes a portion of the $200,000 previously transferred from Cutting to Assembly. Eventually, all of the company's manufacturing costs will be transferred to Cost of Goods Sold in the income statement.

YOUR TURN **You as a Cost Accountant**

Assume that you have been hired as the cost accountant of a large candy manufacturer. The company currently uses a process costing system to assign costs to several work in process accounts. You observe that units of production pass very quickly through the various phases of production, often in a matter of hours. To simplify the accounting system, you propose that all manufacturing costs be charged directly to Finished Goods Inventory, thereby eliminating the need to report any work in process in the company's balance sheet. Is this practice ethical? Defend your answer.

(See our comments on the Online Learning Center Web site.)

TRACKING COSTS USING A PROCESS COSTING PRODUCTION REPORT

© Neil Beer/Getty Images/DAL

In this section we will illustrate how a production cost report is used in a process costing system to help managers track costs. Assume that RainTree Cola produces a bottled soft drink. The company has two production departments: the Syrup Department, which mixes the cola syrup; and the Bottling Department, which bottles a mixture of the syrup and carbonated water.

Assume that on June 1, there were 1,000 gallons of syrup mix in the Syrup Department inventory. Costs associated with the mix carried forward from May 31 totaled $4,400. The mix was 100 percent complete with respect to its direct materials, but only 40 percent complete with respect to its conversion requirements. During June, the Syrup Department started 76,000 new gallons of mix and transferred 75,000 gallons of finished mix to the Bottling Department. June production costs in the Syrup Department were comprised of $304,000 of direct materials and $75,000 of conversion (of which $32,000 was direct labor and $43,000 was manufacturing overhead). At June 30, there were 2,000 gallons of partially processed syrup mix remaining in inventory. The mix was 100 percent complete with respect to its direct materials, but only 20 percent complete with respect to conversion.

Exhibit 18–9 provides a summary of the activity in the Syrup Department for the month of June. This information will later be used to complete the department's production cost report for the month of June.

Exhibit 18-9
SUMMARY OF SYRUP DEPARTMENT ACTIVITY IN JUNE

Physical Goods Flow in Units (gallons)		
Beginning work in process, June 1	1,000	
Units (gallons) started in June	76,000	
Total units in production	77,000	
Less: Ending work in process, June 30	2,000	
Gallons of mix transferred to the Bottling Department	75,000	
Less: Beginning work in process, June 1	1,000	
Units (gallons) started and completed in June	74,000	
Equivalent Units of Resource Inputs (gallons)	**Direct Materials**	**Conversion**
Finish 1,000 units of beginning work in process inventory:		
Direct materials (100% complete; require 0%)	0	
Conversion (40% complete; requires 60%)		600
Units started and completed in June:	74,000	74,000
Start 2,000 units of ending work in process inventory:		
Direct materials (100% complete)	2,000	
Conversion (20% complete)		400
Total equivalent units of resource inputs in June	76,000	75,000
Cost per Equivalent Unit of Resource Input in June	**Direct Materials**	**Conversion**
Costs incurred in June	$304,000	$ 75,000
Total equivalent units of resource inputs in June	÷ 76,000	÷ 75,000
Cost per equivalent unit of input in June	$ 4	$ 1

The flow of manufacturing costs through RainTree's entire process costing system is illustrated in Exhibit 18–10. The entries in red represent the costs of materials, direct labor, and manufacturing overhead charged to production in June. The entries made to record materials used and direct labor were made *throughout the period,* based on materials requisitions and employee time cards. Overhead was applied at month-end, using a separate overhead application rate for each department. The entries shown in *green* and in *blue* are the entries made at month-end to transfer the cost of units processed during the period from one department to the next.

Exhibit 18–10
PROCESS COSTING UNIT COST FLOWS

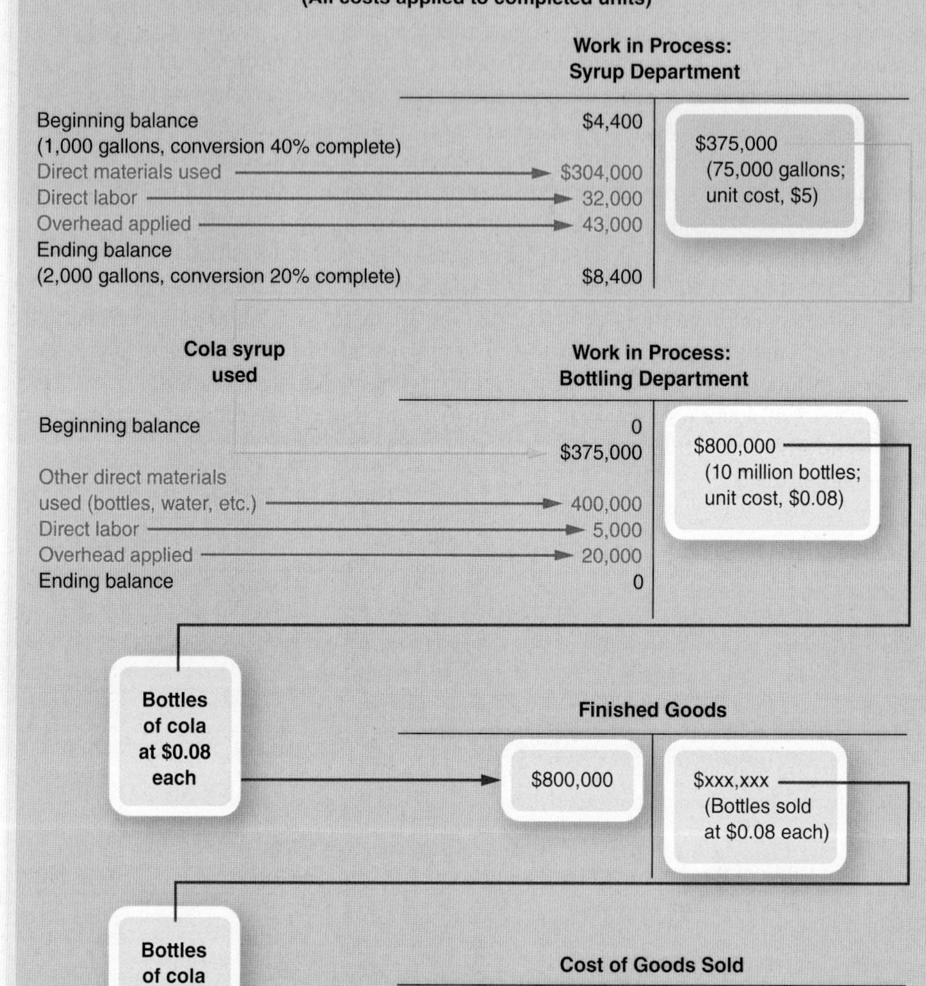

Syrup is transferred to Bottling Department as if it were a direct material

Finished bottles transferred to Finished Goods

Per-unit processing costs are easily computed using process costing methods—not just for the finished products but also for the output of each department. For example, the cost of finished goods emerging from the Bottling Department this month was *$0.08 per bottle* ($800,000 ÷ 10 million bottles produced); the cost of syrup produced in the Syrup Department was *$5 per gallon* ($375,000 ÷ 75,000 gallons).[1]

Learning Objective LO6 Create a process costing production report and use the report for decision making

Production Cost Report for Process Costing Companies frequently present the results of operations for a period, typically a month, with a production cost report. The **production cost report** is a summary of the work completed during the period and of the related cost, both per-unit and total costs. Exhibit 18–11 displays the June production cost report for RainTree

[1] Notice that, in each of our two departments, "units" of output are defined differently. In the Syrup Department, units are expressed in *gallons of syrup,* whereas in the Bottling Department, units are defined as *bottles of cola.*

Cola's Syrup Department. Because companies design their cost reports to help manage each individual production process, these reports can look different from company to company. However, several common pieces of information are typically contained in these reports.[2]

Exhibit 18–11

JUNE PRODUCTION COST REPORT FOR RAINTREE COLA SYRUP DEPARTMENT

Part I. Physical Flow	**Total Units**		
Inputs:			
• Beginning WIP	1,000		
• Started	76,000		
Gallons to account for	77,000		
Outputs:			
• Gallons completed	75,000		
• Ending WIP	2,000		
Gallons accounted for	77,000		
Part II. Equivalent Units		**Direct Materials**	**Conversion**
Based on monthly input:			
• Finish beginning WIP		–0–	600
• Start new units in June		76,000	74,400
Equivalent units of input		76,000	75,000
Based on monthly output:			
• Units transferred		74,000	74,600
• Ending WIP		2,000	400
Equivalent units of output		76,000	75,000
Part III. Cost per Equivalent Unit	**Total Unit Cost**	**Direct Materials**	**Conversion Costs**
Cost of input resources, June		$304,000	$75,000
Equivalent units, June		÷76,000	÷75,000
Cost per equivalent unit, June	$5.00	$4.00	$1.00
Part IV. Total Cost Assignment	**Total Costs**	**Direct Materials**	**Conversion Costs**
Costs to account for:			
• Cost of beginning WIP, June 1	$ 4,400		
• Cost added in June	379,000		
Total cost to account for, June	$383,400		
Costs accounted for:			
• Cost of goods transferred in June:			
Beginning WIP costs, June 1	$ 4,400	$ 4,000[a]	$ 400[b]
Cost to complete beginning WIP	600	–0–	600[c]
Cost of units started and completed	370,000	296,000[d]	74,000[e]
Total cost transferred in June	$375,000	$300,000	$75,000
• Add ending WIP, June 30	8,400	8,000[f]	400[g]
Total cost accounted for in June	$383,400	$308,000	$75,400

Supporting calculations (figures taken from Exhibit 18–9):
[a]1,000 equivalent units × $4 = $4,000.
[b]1,000 equivalent units × 40% complete × $1 = $400.
[c]1,000 equivalent units × 60% required × $1 = $600.
[d]74,000 equivalent units × $4 = $296,000.
[e]74,000 equivalent units × $1 = $74,000.
[f]2,000 equivalent units × $4 = $8,000.
[g]2,000 equivalent units × 20% complete × $1 = $400.

[2] The production cost report shown in Exhibit 18–11 is typically referred to as a FIFO-based report. That is, physical units and costs are traced on a first-in, first-out basis. Another widely used method is referred to as the weighted-average process costing method. This method averages costs each period over the units transferred out and the ending work in process. The weighted-average method assumes that the difference between beginning and ending work in process is not material in any given month. More advanced accounting courses provide details on both methods.

One function of the production cost report is to trace the physical flow of equivalent units during the period. Notice that the arrows on the side of column 1 in Exhibit 18–11 show that the physical flow is accounted for by identifying both the physical inputs and outputs during the period. This tells management that all inflows during the period are accounted for by matching outflows. Another function of the production cost report is to match cost flows in and out during the period. For example, use the third set of arrows outside column 1 from Exhibit 18–11 to find *Total cost to account for, June,* and *Total cost accounted for in June.* Observe that all costs, including beginning work in process costs and costs added during the period, must be accounted for by assigning those costs to either the units transferred out or the ending work in process.

The production cost report in Exhibit 18–11 also shows that the equivalent unit outcomes are identical when focusing either on the resources consumed by the inputs or the work needed to complete the outputs during the month (second set of arrows). The inputs to the Syrup Department during the current month are direct materials and conversion. For the direct materials resources, all 76,000 gallons started during the month consumed materials (sugar, corn syrup, water, etc.) and are counted as equivalent units of work. On the other hand, for the beginning work in process units, direct materials were added in the previous month and thus, no equivalent units are used for materials.

However, beginning work in process gallons are in need of additional conversion. In fact, 600 equivalent units were needed to finish beginning work in process units. Finally, 74,400 equivalent units of conversion work were completed on the units started during the month including (1) 74,000 started and completed and (2) another 400 equivalent units from 2,000 ending work in process units that were 20 percent complete at the end of the month.

The existence of beginning and ending work in process makes equivalent unit computations one of the more difficult concepts for students. It is helpful, when considering the equivalent units associated with the physical flow of outputs, to remember that the 75,000 gallons transferred from the Syrup Department to the Bottling Department includes 1,000 gallons from beginning work in process and 74,000 gallons out of the 76,000 gallons started during the month.

Exhibit 18–12 provides a more detailed illustration of the equivalent units computations for RainTree Cola's Syrup Department. As shown in the last column of Exhibit 18–12, 600 equivalent units of conversion were needed to finish the beginning work in process gallons and 74,000 conversion equivalent units were needed to finish the remaining gallons transferred out. As shown in column 3 of Exhibit 18–12, 74,000 direct materials equivalent units were needed to finish the gallons started and completed during the month. Because direct materials were added to the beginning work in process in the previous month, no equivalent units of direct materials were used for beginning work in process during the current month. Finally, as shown in the fourth row of Exhibit 18–12, resources were consumed to create the ending work in process gallons. Those resources include 2,000 equivalent units of direct materials added in the current month, but only 400 equivalent units of conversion because ending work in process gallons are only 20 percent processed at month-end.

Exhibit 18–12

RAINTREE COLA SYRUP DEPARTMENT ACCOUNTING FOR EQUIVALENT UNITS

	Matching Physical Flow	Direct Materials Equivalent Units	Conversion Equivalent Units
Beginning WIP, June 1	1,000 gallons (40% complete)	–0–	600
Started and completed in June:	74,000 gallons (100% complete)	74,000	74,000
Total equivalent units transferred out:	75,000 gallons	74,000	74,600
Add ending WIP, June 30	2,000 gallons (20% complete)	2,000	400
Total equivalent units during June		76,000	75,000

In summary, a typical production cost report contains the four parts that are shown in bold print in Exhibit 18–11: (1) accounting for the physical flow, (2) determining equivalent units, (3) finding the cost per equivalent unit, and (4) assigning costs to the production for the period. These four parts help management make several decisions related to the production process.

RainTree's management will use the unit cost data provided by process costing for many purposes, including the following:

- Setting sales prices.
- Evaluating the efficiency of manufacturing departments.
- Forecasting future manufacturing costs.
- Valuing inventories and measuring the cost of goods sold, in both financial statements and income tax returns.

YOUR TURN **You as a Product-Line Manager**

Assume you are the manager of the RainTree Cola product line. As one of your responsibilities, you must motivate, evaluate, and reward the performance of the managers of the Syrup Department and the Bottling Department. How could you use process costing information to help with these management responsibilities?

(See our comments on the Online Learning Center Web site.)

EVALUATING DEPARTMENTAL EFFICIENCY

One of management's key concerns is whether the costs of resource inputs consumed in the current period have risen, fallen, or stayed the same as in prior months. For instance, June unit costs in the Syrup Department were \$4 per gallon for direct labor and \$1 per gallon for conversion (see Exhibit 18–9 and Exhibit 18–11). These amounts are *exactly the same* as those carried forward from May in the Syrup Department's beginning inventory (1,000 equivalent units of direct materials × \$4, plus 400 equivalent units of conversion × \$1, equals the Syrup Department's \$4,400 beginning inventory balance on June 1). Thus, management may conclude that unit costs in the Syrup Department have held steady from May through June.

In evaluating the efficiency of a production department, management should consider only those costs incurred as a result of *that department's activities.* Costs transferred in from other processing departments should not be allowed to "cloud the picture." To illustrate, consider the Bottling Department in our example. As shown in Exhibit 18–10, a total of \$800,000 was charged to the Bottling Department during June. But \$375,000 of this cost was 75,000 gallons transferred in from the Syrup Department at \$5 per gallon. This amount represents the cost of *making syrup,* not the cost of bottling cola.

Manufacturing costs resulting from *bottling activities* include only the direct materials, direct labor, and overhead charged to the Bottling Department. For RainTree's Bottling Department, these costs total *\$425,000,* or *\$0.0425 per unit* (\$425,000 ÷ 10 million bottles produced).

In summary, total unit costs *accumulate* as the product passes from one processing department to the next. These total unit costs are used in valuing inventory, measuring the cost of goods sold, and evaluating the overall efficiency of manufacturing operations. But in evaluating the efficiency of a particular processing department, management should look primarily at the costs incurred *within that department.*

Of course, managers can also compute the per-unit costs of the materials, direct labor, and overhead incurred within each department. This detailed cost information should assist them in quickly identifying the *cause of any change* in a product's total unit cost.

Ethics, Fraud & Corporate Governance

Using a process costing system requires ethics and judgment in computing equivalent units of production. By deliberately overstating equivalent units of resources in ending inventory, managers can understate cost of goods sold and thereby overstate net income. Equivalent units of production can easily be overstated by inflating the application of direct labor and overhead to work in process. Given the complexity of many manufacturing processes, company employees are often in the best position to know if management has overstated the equivalent units of production. The Sarbanes-Oxley Act (SOX) contains provisions to increase the likelihood that employees will come forward with concerns they may have about possible fraudulent financial reporting.

SOX requires publicly traded companies to develop procedures to encourage employees to report questionable accounting or auditing matters. The audit committees of these companies must establish procedures to ensure that employees have a confidential, anonymous mechanism by which they can report concerns regarding questionable practices (often referred to as a whistleblower hotline). In addition, employees who make allegations in good faith are granted certain protections. The protections apply if the allegations are made to criminal investigators, federal regulators, Congress, or an employee's supervisor (or other appropriate individuals within the company). When good faith allegations are made through these appropriate channels, the company is prohibited from discharging, demoting, suspending, threatening, harassing, or in any other manner discriminating against the employee. Employers who violate this provision can be held liable to reinstate the employee with back pay (including interest), and to pay for all litigation costs.

Although SOX provides protection from retaliation, employees still take some risks when making allegations. In short, the protections provided under SOX are only as effective as their enforcement. Employees who believe that they have been retaliated against because they expressed a concern about the company's potential violation of securities law can file a complaint with the U.S. Department of Labor (DOL). One criticism of this well-intentioned provision is that the DOL lacks the resources and expertise to effectively investigate potential retaliation by an employer against an employee for alleging securities law violations. Notwithstanding this possible concern, employees now have a better means by which to expose questionable accounting and auditing practices and better protection against potential retaliation.

Concluding Remarks

In this chapter and the previous chapter, we have emphasized the measurement of unit costs. In upcoming chapters we will see how managers identify, measure, and employ related cost information for allocating decision-making authority, planning, and controlling costs. Unit cost information is ever present in business settings. We will see that having a thorough understanding of how unit costs are created provides a sturdy foundation for running a profitable business.

END-OF-CHAPTER REVIEW

SUMMARY OF LEARNING OBJECTIVES

LO1 **Distinguish production procedures that match with process costing from those that correspond with job order costing.** Job order costing methods are appropriate for businesses and companies producing customized jobs that require differing amounts and types of direct labor, direct materials, and overhead. Process costing is used for production processes that produce mass quantities of identical units that use the same amounts and types of direct labor, direct materials, and overhead.

LO2 **Account for the physical flows and related cost flows when using process costing.** The physical flow associated with a production process includes the beginning work in process, the units started during the period, the ending work in process, and the units transferred out during the period. Costs in process costing flow through the accounts in a manner similar to job order costing. Throughout the period, the costs of direct labor, direct materials, and overhead are charged to the appropriate work in process accounts. At the end of each period, costs in each Work in Process account are transferred to the next Work in Process account (or to a Finished Goods account).

LO3 **Demonstrate how to calculate equivalent units.** Equivalent units are measures of productive activity that include work performed on partially completed units. The basic idea is that performing, say, 50 percent of the processing on 500 units is equivalent to performing all of the processing on 250 units.

LO4 **Use the costs of resources consumed to calculate the cost per equivalent unit of production.** Costs associated with work done in the current period and added to work in process for the current period are pooled for each significant input. Dividing total costs by total equivalent units provides cost per equivalent unit for each input.

LO5 **Use the cost per equivalent unit to assign costs to the work completed during the period.** The equivalent units associated with the units transferred out are multiplied by the cost per equivalent unit for each input. The units transferred out will typically contain some units in process at the start of the period. The remaining transferred units will be started and completed during the current period. Beginning work in process units will have some cost attached to them from the previous period and some costs added during the current period. Both costs must be transferred out with the completed units.

LO6 **Create a process costing production report and use the report for decision making.** The process costing production report is a summary of the work completed during the period and the related cost, both per-unit and total costs. A typical production cost report contains four parts: (1) accounting for the physical flow, (2) determining equivalent units, (3) finding the cost per equivalent unit, and (4) assigning costs to the production for the period. The report is used to help management make several decisions related to the production process.

Key Terms Introduced or Emphasized in Chapter 18

conversion costs (p. 807) The direct labor and overhead costs associated with converting direct materials into the units transferred out.

cost accounting systems (p. 804) The method and techniques used by enterprises to track resources consumed in creating and delivering products and services to customers.

equivalent units (p. 807) A measure of the work done during an accounting period. Includes work done on beginning and ending inventories of work in process as well as work on units completely processed during the period.

job order costing (p. 804) A cost accounting method under which the focal point of costing is a quantity of product known as a job or a lot. Costs of direct materials, direct labor, and overhead applicable to each job are compiled to arrive at average unit costs.

process costing (p. 804) A cost accounting method used in enterprises with processes characterized by continuous mass production. Costs are assigned to a manufacturing process or department before being averaged over units produced.

production cost report (p. 812) A detailed production report for a specified process and time period that details (1) the physical flow, (2) equivalent units, (3) cost per equivalent unit, and (4) total costs assigned.

Demonstration Problem

Magna Bin, Inc., manufactures large metal waste containers that are purchased by local sanitation departments. Containers are produced in two processing departments, Fabricating and Painting. In the Fabricating Department, all of the direct materials are added at the beginning of the process, overhead is applied evenly throughout the entire process, and labor is added evenly only during the last 50 percent of the process. In the Painting Department, materials and labor are added evenly throughout the first half of the process, while overhead is applied evenly throughout the entire process. Magna Bin uses process costing and had the following cost and production information available for the month of January:

	Fabricating Department	Painting Department
Direct materials costs	$ 7,740	$13,752
Direct labor costs	18,060	8,022
Manufacturing overhead applied	27,090	12,033
Units in beginning work in process	0	0
Units started during Jan.	750	600
Units completed and transferred out	600	510

At the end of January, units remaining in work in process in the Fabricating Department were 30 percent complete, while units in ending work in process in the Painting Department were 70 percent complete. During the month, 450 containers were sold at an average selling price of $180 each.

Instructions

a. Calculate the number of equivalent units produced for each cost category in each of the two departments during January.

b. Based on equivalent units, what were the fabricating cost, painting cost, and total cost of producing a container in January?

c. Prepare the journal entries summarizing the manufacturing costs charged to the Fabricating Department and the Painting Department.

d. Prepare the month-end journal entries to transfer the costs of containers moved from the Fabricating Department to the Painting Department and from the Painting Department to Finished Goods Inventory.

e. Prepare the entries to record the sales made in January and the corresponding reduction of Finished Goods Inventory.

f. Using T accounts, calculate the ending balances in the Work in Process accounts and Finished Goods Inventory.

Solution to Demonstration Problem

a. **Equivalent Units of Production—Fabricating Department**

	Direct Materials	Labor	Overhead
Beginning work in process	0	0	0
Started and completed	600	600	600
Ending work in process	150	0	45 (150 × 0.3)
Total equivalent units	750	600	645

Note: Since the units in ending work in process are 30 percent complete, all direct materials have been added, no direct labor has been used, and 30 percent of the overhead has been applied.

Equivalent Units of Production—Painting Department

	Direct Materials	Labor	Overhead
Beginning work in process	0	0	0
Started and completed	510	510	510
Ending work in process	90	90	63 (90 × 0.7)
Total equivalent units	600	600	573

Note: Since the units in ending work in process are 70 percent complete, all direct materials and labor have been added, while only 70 percent of the overhead has been applied.

b. Fabricating costs per container produced during January:

Direct materials costs ($7,740 ÷ 750 equivalent units)	$10.32
Direct labor costs ($18,060 ÷ 600 equivalent units)	30.10
Manufacturing overhead ($27,090 ÷ 645 equivalent units)	42.00
Fabricating costs per container	$82.42

Painting costs per container produced during January:

Direct materials costs ($13,752 ÷ 600 equivalent units)	$ 22.92
Direct labor costs ($8,022 ÷ 600 equivalent units)	13.37
Manufacturing overhead ($12,033 ÷ 573 equivalent units)	21.00
Painting costs per container	$ 57.29
Total cost per container ($82.42 + $57.29)	$139.71

c.

Work in Process—Fabricating	52,890.00	
Direct Materials Inventory		7,740.00
Direct Labor		18,060.00
Manufacturing Overhead Applied		27,090.00
Summary of costs incurred during January by the Fabricating Department.		
Work in Process—Painting	33,807.00	
Direct Materials Inventory		13,752.00
Direct Labor		8,022.00
Manufacturing Overhead Applied		12,033.00
Summary of costs incurred during January by the Painting Department.		

d.

Work in Process—Painting (600 units transferred × $82.42 cost/unit)	49,452.00	
Work in Process—Fabricating		49,452.00
To transfer the cost of completely processed units from the Fabricating Department to the Painting Department.		
Finished Goods Inventory (510 units transferred × $139.71 cost/unit)	71,252.10	
Work in Process—Painting		71,252.10
To transfer the cost of completely processed units from the Painting Department to Finished Goods Inventory.		

e.

Cash, Accounts Receivable	81,000.00	
Sales Revenue (450 units sold × $180/unit)		81,000.00
To record sales made during Jan.		
Cost of Goods Sold (450 units sold × $139.71 cost/unit)	62,869.50	
Finished Goods Inventory		62,869.50
To record the cost of goods sold during Jan.		

f.

	Work in Process—Fabricating		
Direct materials	7,740.00		
Direct labor	18,060.00		
Manufacturing overhead applied	27,090.00	49,452.00	Transferred to Painting
Ending balance	3,438.00		

	Work in Process—Painting		
From Fabricating	49,452.00		
Direct materials	13,752.00		
Direct labor	8,022.00		
Manufacturing overhead applied	12,033.00	71,252.10	Transferred to Finished Goods Inventory
Ending balance	12,006.90		

	Finished Goods Inventory		
From Painting	71,252.10		
		62,869.50	Transferred to Cost of Goods Sold
Ending balance	8,382.60		

Self-Test Questions

The answers to these questions appear on page 838.

1. If Power Products uses *process costing,* which of the following are likely to be true:
   a. The production processes are high volume.
   b. The products use different amounts of direct labor.
   c. The products are created with repetitive processes.
   d. The products are created to customer specifications.
2. Which of the following businesses would most likely use *process* costing?
   a. A law firm.
   b. A maker of frozen orange juice.
   c. A hospital.
   d. An auto repair shop.
3. Nut House manufactures and sells jars of peanut butter. All of the company's output passes through five production processes, which are performed in sequential order. Identify all correct answers, assuming that process costing is in use.
   a. The processing departments may define "units of output" differently.
   b. Costs transferred from one processing department are charged to the next processing department (or to finished goods).
   c. The cost accounting system separately measures the per-unit cost of each manufacturing process.
   d. No manufacturing overhead is charged to each processing department.
4. Indicate which of the following phrases correctly completes this sentence: "Equivalent units of production . . ." (Indicate all correct answers.)
   a. Are a measure of productive activity.
   b. Represent work done on units still in process, as well as those completed during the period.
   c. Are used as the basis for computing per-unit costs in most process cost accounting systems.
   d. Are computed separately for each significant input consumed in the production process.
5. A production cost report contains which of the following parts? (Identify all correct answers.)
   a. Equivalent units for each significant category of resources consumed in making the product.
   b. The total cost to account for.
   c. The physical flow of production.
   d. The overhead costs applied to each completed job.
   e. The total costs accounted for.

ASSIGNMENT MATERIAL Discussion Questions

1. Why would a company use multiple cost accounting systems?
2. What factors should be taken into account in deciding whether to use job order costing or process costing in any given production situation?

3. Rodeo Drive Jewelers makes custom jewelry for celebrities. Would you expect the company to use job order or process costing? Explain.
4. Describe at least two products or production processes that might use both process and job order costing methods to determine the cost of a finished unit.
5. What are the four significant parts of the production cost report for process costing?
6. Taylor & Malone is a law firm. Would the concepts of job order or process costing be more appropriate for this type of service business? Explain.
7. Briefly explain the operation of process costing, including the manner in which the unit costs of finished goods are determined.
8. Some companies that use process costing simply assign the entire cost of production to those units completed and transferred during the month, even if some units remain in process at the end of the period. Is this practice reasonable?
9. Discuss how managers use information they obtain from process costing.
10. Explain the term *equivalent units*. In a fast-moving, assembly-line operation, are the equivalent units likely to differ significantly from the number of units completed during a month? Explain.
11. Identify various product characteristics that distinguish job costing systems from process costing systems.
12. In a process costing system, what condition must be present in order for accountants to combine direct labor and manufacturing overhead costs and treat them simply as conversion costs?
13. Why is the combination of direct labor and manufacturing overhead referred to as a conversion cost?
14. Why might the unit cost of those items started and completed during the period differ from the unit cost of all items completed and transferred during the period?
15. In a process costing system that uses a FIFO cost flow assumption, how is the number of units started and completed during the period computed?

Brief Exercises

LO1 **BRIEF EXERCISE 18.1**

Selecting Cost Accounting Systems

Determine whether each of the following companies is best suited for a job order cost system, a process costing system, or both.

a. **C. Erickson & Sons, Inc.** (a construction company with multiple job sites).
b. **Apple Computer** (a manufacturer of computers for individual and institutional clients).
c. **PlayWorld Systems, Inc.** (a provider of custom-designed playground equipment for city parks and schools districts).
d. **Strong Industries** (a manufacturer of injection-molded plastic doghouses).
e. **Nature Made Nutritional Products** (a maker of vitamins and nutritional supplements).

LO1 **BRIEF EXERCISE 18.2**

Matching Cost Systems and Business Activities

Match the business with the appropriate cost system(s) for that business using the number of the cost system where 1 = job order costing, 2 = process costing, and 3 = activity-based costing.

a. Ketcher, Tryer, and Friar, attorneys-at-law
b. **Walmart Inc.**
c. **Johnson & Johnson Company**
d. Handyman Special, Inc.
e. Carpet Makers Corporation

LO2 **BRIEF EXERCISE 18.3**

Flow of Costs in a Cost Accounting System

For each of the four accounts listed below, prepare an example of a journal entry that would cause the account to be (1) debited and (2) credited using a process costing system. Assume perpetual inventory records are maintained. Include written explanations with your journal entries and use "XXX" in place of dollar amounts.

a. Materials Inventory
b. Direct Labor
c. Manufacturing Overhead
d. Finished Goods Inventory

LO2 **BRIEF EXERCISE 18.4**

Journal Entries in Process Costing Systems

Morning Glow Corporation uses a process costing system for its two production departments: Mixing and Packaging. The company provided the following manufacturing cost information for the month of May:

	Mixing	Packaging
Beginning work in process	$ 500	$ 900
Costs transferred in	?	?
Costs incurred in May	3,000	5,000
Ending work in process	1,200	1,500

a. Record the transfer of costs from the Mixing Department to the Packaging Department in May.

b. Record the transfer of costs from the Packaging Department to Finished Goods Inventory in May.

LO3 **BRIEF EXERCISE 18.5**

Computing Equivalent Units of Resource Inputs

Dittmar Products has provided the following information pertaining to equivalent units of production in its Cutting Department for the month of September:

	Direct Materials	Conversion
Units in beginning work in process, September 1	5,000	?
Units started and completed in September	?	15,000
Units in ending work in process, September 30	2,000	?

All of the direct materials used in the Cutting Department are added at the beginning of the process. On September 1, beginning inventory was 20 percent complete with respect to conversion. On September 30, ending inventory was 60 percent complete with respect to conversion.

Compute equivalent units of direct materials and conversion used by the Cutting Department in September.

LO3 LO4 **BRIEF EXERCISE 18.6**

Determining the Cost per Equivalent Unit of Input Resource

On March 1, Lesher Manufacturing had 2,000 units in its Molding Department. These units were 90 percent complete with respect to direct materials requirements and 30 percent complete with respect to their conversion requirements. During March, the Molding Department started and completed 20,800 units. Direct materials costs in March incurred in the Molding Department totaled $152,600, whereas March conversion costs totaled $203,400. On March 31, there remained 1,000 units in ending inventory that were 80 percent complete with respect to direct materials, and 40 percent complete with respect to conversion.

a. Compute the Molding Department's cost per equivalent unit of direct materials in March.

b. Compute the Molding Department's cost per equivalent unit of conversion in March.

LO3 LO4 **BRIEF EXERCISE 18.7**

Solving for Missing Information

Green Dragon Corporation had 5,000 units of beginning inventory in its Forming Department on July 1. The units were 100 percent complete with respect to direct materials requirements but only 30 percent complete with respect to conversion requirements. On July 31, the company had 4,000 units of inventory remaining in its Forming Department. These units were 100 percent complete with respect to their direct materials requirements but only 40 percent complete with respect to conversion. The Forming Department's direct materials cost for July totaled $380,000, or $20 per equivalent unit consumed. Its conversion costs for July totaled $603,000, or $30 per equivalent unit.

Determine how many units were started and completed in the Forming Department during July.

LO5 **BRIEF EXERCISE 18.8**

Determining Departmental Manufacturing Costs

On September 1, the Blending Department of Jordan Bakery had costs carried forward from August totaling $30,000. Resources consumed to complete the beginning inventory totaled $20,000. The total cost of units started in the Blending Department during September was $400,000. On September 30, costs assigned to the department's ending inventory totaled $40,000.

Compute the costs transferred out of the Blending Department during September.

LO6 **BRIEF EXERCISE 18.9**

Interpreting a Production Cost Report

The following equivalent unit figures were taken from the December production cost report of the Distillation Department of Meadow Brook Lubricants:

Equivalent Units	Direct Materials	Conversion
Equivalent units to finish beginning inventory	0	800
Equivalent units to start new units in December	48,000	47,000
Equivalent units of input in December	48,000	47,800

a. At what point in the production process are direct materials added in the company's Distillation Department? Explain your answer.

b. If the Distillation Department's ending inventory on December 31 is comprised of 5,000 equivalent units of direct materials and 4,000 equivalent units of conversion, how many units were started and completed by the department during December?

LO6 **BRIEF EXERCISE 18.10**

Interpreting a Production Cost Report

Iverson Industrial's production cost report for its Packaging Department reveals that the cost per equivalent unit started and completed in November was $148. The same report reveals that the cost per equivalent unit transferred out of the Packaging Department in November was $150.

Were November manufacturing costs per equivalent unit higher than, lower than, or the same as October costs per equivalent unit? Explain your answer.

Exercises

LO1 through LO3 LO6 **EXERCISE 18.1**

Accounting Terminology

Listed below are six technical accounting terms introduced or emphasized in this chapter.

Job order costing	Equivalent units
Process costing	Cost of finished goods manufactured
Conversion costs	Production cost report

Each of the following statements may (or may not) describe these technical terms. For each statement, indicate the term described, or answer "None" if the statement does not correctly describe any of the terms.

a. The type of cost accounting method likely to be used in a **Coca-Cola** bottling plant.

b. Direct labor and overhead consumed in a production process.

c. A measure of the *quantity* of production work done during a time period, including work on partially completed units.

d. Process cost information for the period, including physical flow and total cost to account for.

e. The type of cost accounting method likely to be used by a construction company.

LO2 LO3 **EXERCISE 18.2**

Calculating Equivalent Units

Starr Scopes, Inc., produces telescopes for use by high school students. All direct materials used in the production of telescopes are added at the beginning of the manufacturing process. Labor and overhead are added evenly thereafter, as each unit is assembled, adjusted, and tested. Starr Scopes uses process costing and had the following unit production information available for the months of January and February:

	Jan.	Feb.
Number of units in beginning work in process inventory	0	50
Number of units started during the month	200	300
Total number of units transferred to finished goods	150	250

The units remaining in work in process at the end of January were approximately 40 percent complete. During the month of February, all of the beginning work in process units was completed and the units remaining in work in process at the end of the month were approximately 75 percent complete.

a. For the month of January, calculate the equivalent units produced for each of the two cost categories—direct materials *and* labor and overhead.

b. For the month of February, calculate the equivalent units produced for each of the two cost categories—direct materials *and* labor and overhead.

LO2 through LO5

EXERCISE 18.3

Process Costing

Shamrock Industries uses process costing. All of the company's manufacturing activities take place in a single processing department. The following information was available for the month of June:

Direct materials	$ 89,750
Direct labor	28,975
Manufacturing overhead applied	40,275
Total costs to account for in June	$159,000

The amounts of work in process at the beginning and end of the month were immaterial and assigned no dollar value. During June, 13,250 units were completed, of which 10,000 were sold on account at $25 per unit.

a. Prepare a journal entry to summarize the total manufacturing costs applied to production in June.

b. Prepare the journal entry to transfer completed units from work in process to the finished goods warehouse in June.

c. Prepare the journal entries to record the sale of 10,000 units manufactured during the period and the related cost of goods sold.

LO6

EXERCISE 18.4

Production Cost Report

Use the information from Exercise 18.3 to complete a production cost report for Shamrock Industries for the month of June.

LO2 through LO5

EXERCISE 18.5

Computing Costs per Equivalent Unit

Old Victrola, Inc., produces top-quality stereos and uses process costing. The manufacture of stereos is such that direct materials, labor, and overhead are all added evenly throughout the production process. Due to the smooth production process, only one cost category—manufacturing costs—is used for equivalent unit calculations. Old Victrola had the following cost and production information available for the months of March and April:

	March	April
Direct materials costs	$ 978,460	$1,168,310
Direct labor costs	2,562,260	3,041,940
Manufacturing overhead applied	3,438,640	3,571,030
Total manufacturing costs	$6,979,360	$7,781,280
Units in beginning work in process	7,000	4,800
Units transferred to finished goods	18,500	23,000
Units in ending work in process	4,800	6,400

Beginning work in process was 30 percent complete in March and 60 percent complete in April. Ending work in process was 60 percent complete in March and 35 percent complete in April.

a. For each of the two months, calculate the equivalent units of production.

b. Based on equivalent units produced, did total manufacturing costs per unit increase or decrease between March and April?

c. Did the direct materials cost per equivalent unit increase or decrease between March and April?

LO2 through LO5

EXERCISE 18.6

Process Costing with No Beginning Inventories: Part I

Ogden Office Outfitters began making high-quality office furniture in January. The company's executive desks are produced in two departments: Cutting and Finishing. Component kits are produced in the Cutting Department and then transferred to the Finishing Department for trimming and assembly. During its first month of operations, the Cutting Department started 10,000 executive desk kits. January direct materials costs in the Cutting Department totaled $200,000, and conversion costs totaled $258,000. Ending inventory on January 31 consisted of 2,000 partially processed component kits. These units were 100 percent complete with respect to direct materials, but only 30 percent complete with respect to conversion.

a. Compute the number of component kits transferred from the Cutting Department to the Finishing Department in January.

b. Compute the equivalent units of input resources for the Cutting Department in January.

c. Compute the cost per equivalent unit of input resource for the Cutting Department in January.

d. Prepare the summary journal entry required to transfer finished component kits from the Cutting Department to the Finishing Department in January.

e. Compute the total cost assigned to the Cutting Department's ending inventory on January 31.

LO2 through LO5

EXERCISE 18.7

Process Costing with No Beginning Inventories: Part II

Exercise 18.7 is an extension of Exercise 18.6.

Assume that on January 31 the Finishing Department of Ogden Office Outfitters had 1,000 partially trimmed and assembled executive desks in ending inventory. These units were, of course, 100 percent complete with respect to components transferred in from the Cutting Department, but only 20 percent complete with respect to direct trim materials, and 40 percent complete with respect to conversion. During January, the Finishing Department incurred direct materials costs (for trim) of $43,200, and conversion costs of $81,400.

a. Compute how many units were started in the Finishing Department during January.

b. Compute the number of executive desks transferred out of the Finishing Department in January.

c. Compute the equivalent units of input resources for the Finishing Department in January.

d. Compute the cost per equivalent unit of input resource for the Finishing Department in January.

e. Prepare the summary journal entry required to transfer the cost of executive desks from the Finishing Department's Work in Process Inventory to the company's Finished Goods Inventory in January.

f. Compute the total cost assigned to the Finishing Department's ending inventory in process on January 31.

LO2 through LO5

EXERCISE 18.8

Process Costing with Beginning Inventories: Part I

Dahl's Treats makes institutional cakes. Finished cakes must pass through two departments: Mixing and Baking. Vats of cake batter are processed in the Mixing Department and then transferred to the Baking Department, where individual cakes are baked, cooled, and frosted. There were 200 gallons of partially mixed batter in the Mixing Department's inventory on August 1. The batter was 100 percent complete with respect to direct materials, but only 20 percent complete with respect to conversion. Manufacturing costs assigned to the inventory carried forward from July totaled $440. During August, the Mixing Department started 8,000 new gallons of batter. August direct materials costs in the Mixing Department totaled $16,000, and conversion costs totaled $8,120. Ending inventory on August 31 consisted of 100 partially mixed gallons of batter. These units were 100 percent complete with respect to direct materials, but only 60 percent complete with respect to conversion.

a. Prepare a schedule showing: (1) gallons of mix transferred from the Mixing Department to the Baking Department in August, and (2) gallons of mix started and completed by the Mixing Department in August.

b. Compute the equivalent units of input resources for the Mixing Department in August.

c. Compute the cost per equivalent unit of input resource for the Mixing Department in August.

d. Prepare the summary journal entry required to transfer the cost of fully mixed batter from the Mixing Department to the Baking Department in August.

e. Compute the total cost assigned to the Mixing Department's ending inventory on August 31.

LO2 through LO5

EXERCISE 18.9

Process Costing with Beginning Inventories: Part II

Exercise 18.9 is an extension of Exercise 18.8.

Dahl's Treats uses one gallon of mix for each cake produced by the Baking Department. On August 1, the Baking Department had 500 cakes in process. These units were 100 percent complete with respect to batter transferred in from the Mixing Department during July, but only 70 percent complete with respect to direct (frosting) materials, and 80 percent complete with respect to conversion. Costs applied to these units carried forward from July totaled $2,600. Costs incurred by the Baking Department during August included $8,040 of direct materials and $31,900 of conversion. The ending inventory in the Baking Department on August 31 consisted of 300 cakes in process. These units were 100 percent complete with respect to batter transferred in from the Mixing Department, but only 30 percent complete with respect to direct (frosting) materials, and 25 percent complete with respect to conversion.

a. Compute how many cakes were started in the Baking Department during August.

b. Prepare a schedule showing: (1) cakes transferred out of the Baking Department in August, and (2) cakes *started and completed* by the Baking Department in August.

c. Compute the equivalent units of input resources for the Baking Department in August.

d. Compute the cost per equivalent unit of input resource for the Baking Department in August.

e. Prepare the summary journal entry required to transfer the cost of baked cakes from the Baking Department's Work in Process Inventory to the company's Finished Goods Inventory in August.

f. Compute the total cost assigned to the Baking Department's ending inventory in process on August 31.

LO2 through LO5

EXERCISE 18.10

Process Costing through Two Departments: Department I

Accessory World makes floor mats for the automobile industry. Finished sets of mats must pass through two departments: Cutting and Coating. Large sheets of synthetic material are cut to size in the Cutting Department and then transferred to the Coating Department, where each set is sprayed with a chemical coating for improved durability. The following information pertains to May activity in the Cutting Department:

Cost data:	
Total cost of beginning inventory on May 1	$ 44,800
Direct materials costs incurred in May	200,000
Conversion costs incurred in May	87,200
Physical units data:	
Units in process, May 1	8,000 sets
Units started in May	50,000 sets
Units in process, May 31	10,000 sets
Percentage of completion data:	
Direct materials, May 1	100%
Conversion, May 1	80
Direct materials, May 31	100%
Conversion, May 31	20

a. Prepare a schedule showing: (1) the number of mat sets transferred from the Cutting Department to the Coating Department in May, and (2) the number of mat sets *started and completed* by the Cutting Department in May.

b. Compute the equivalent units of input resources for the Cutting Department in May.

c. Compute the cost per equivalent unit of input resource for the Cutting Department in May.

d. Prepare the summary journal entry required to transfer the cost of completed mat sets from the Cutting Department to the Coating Department in May.

e. Compute the total cost assigned to the Cutting Department's ending inventory on May 31.

LO2 through LO5

EXERCISE 18.11

Process Costing through Two Departments: Department II

Exercise 18.11 is an extension of Exercise 18.10.

The following information pertains to May activity in Accessory World's Coating Department:

Cost data:	
Total cost of beginning inventory on May 1	$45,300
Direct materials costs incurred in May	11,925
Conversion costs incurred in May	84,525
Cut sets transferred in during May	?
Physical units data:	
Units in process, May 1	6,000 sets
Units started in May	? sets
Units in process, May 31	9,000 sets
Percentage of completion data:	
Direct materials, May 1	60%
Conversion, May 1	80
Cut sets transferred in, May 1	?
Direct materials, May 31	70%
Conversion, May 31	90
Cut sets transferred in, May 31	?

a. Compute how many cut mat sets were started in the Coating Department during May.

b. Prepare a schedule showing: (1) the number of mat sets transferred out of the Coating Department in May, and (2) the number of mat sets *started and completed* by the Coating Department in May.

c. Compute the equivalent units of input resources for the Coating Department in May.

d. Compute the cost per equivalent unit of input resource for the Coating Department in May.

e. Prepare the summary journal entry required to transfer the cost of finished mat sets from the Coating Department's Work in Process Inventory to the company's Finished Goods Inventory in May.

f. Compute the total cost assigned to the Coating Department's ending inventory in process on May 31.

LO2 through LO5

EXERCISE 18.12

Solving for Missing Account Information

Comas Corporation manufactures metal roofing in two departments: Pressing and Painting. Sheets of metal material are formed in the Pressing Department before being transferred to the Painting Department. The following information was taken from the company's general ledger and cost accounting records on June 30:

Work in Process: Pressing Department

6/1	Beginning balance	$ 6,000	6/30	Transferred to Painting	?
6/30	Direct materials	25,500			
6/30	Direct labor	8,200			
6/30	Manufacturing overhead	32,800			
6/30	Ending balance	?			

Physical Units: Pressing Department	
Units in process, June 1	300 sheets
Units transferred to Painting Department in June	1,500 sheets
Units in process, June 30	500 sheets
Percentages of Completion: Pressing Department	
Direct materials, June 1	100%
Conversion, June 1	20
Direct materials, June 30	100%
Conversion, June 30	40

a. Compute the number of sheets *started* by the Pressing Department in June.

b. Compute the number of units *started and completed* by the Pressing Department in June.

c. Compute the equivalent units of input resources for the Pressing Department in June.

d. Compute the cost per equivalent unit of input resource for the Pressing Department in June.

e. Prepare the summary journal entry required to transfer pressed sheets from the Pressing Department to the Painting Department in June.

f. Compute the total cost assigned to the Pressing Department's ending inventory on June 30.

LO1 through LO6

EXERCISE 18.13

Assessing the Need for Process Costing

Goodwater Corporation mass-produces pencils through several processing departments. The company currently uses a process costing system and traces manufacturing costs from one process department to the next. The company produces over 90 million pencils per year. The number of pencils in production at any single point in time never exceeds 40,000.

Rick Brintnall has just been hired as the company's cost accountant. Given the company's annual output relative to production activity at any single point in time, Brintnall suspects that the cost of maintaining a process costing system outweighs the benefit. Therefore, Brintnall recommends that the company's current work in process inventory accounts be eliminated, and that all manufacturing costs be charged directly to the Finished Goods Inventory account.

Defend Brintnall's recommendation.

LO2 through LO6

EXERCISE 18.14

Interpreting Information from a Production Cost Report

Lavalear Corporation uses a process costing system and traces costs through several processing departments, starting with the Bonding Department. Shown below is information taken from the Bonding Department's September production cost report:

Cost Data: Bonding Department	
Direct materials costs in beginning inventory, September 1	$ 50,400
Conversion costs in beginning inventory, September 1	36,000
Direct materials costs incurred in September	789,750
Conversion costs incurred in September	787,500
Physical Units: Bonding Department	
Units in process, September 1	300
Units transferred out during September	1,500
Units in process, September 30	500
Percentages of Completion: Bonding Department	
Direct materials, September 1	40%
Conversion, September 1	25
Direct materials, September 30	75%
Conversion, September 30	30

a. Compute the cost per equivalent unit of direct materials and conversion carried forward from *August* and assigned to the Bonding Department's beginning inventory on September 1.

b. Compute the cost per equivalent unit of direct materials and conversion incurred by the Bonding Department in *September*.

c. Discuss how the cost figures computed in parts **a** and **b** would be useful to the company's management.

LO2 through LO6

EXERCISE 18.15

Finding Missing Information for a Production Cost Report

Newton Corporation uses a process costing system to trace costs through several phases of production, starting with the Blending Department and ending with the Packaging Department. Recent computer problems have caused some of the company's accounting records to be destroyed. Shown below is a partial summary of information retrieved by accountants from the Blending Department's February production cost report:

Cost Data: Blending Department	
Direct materials costs in beginning inventory, February 1	$ 12,000
Conversion costs in beginning inventory, February 1	25,200
Direct materials costs incurred in February	162,000
Conversion costs incurred in February	271,000
Cost per equivalent unit of conversion in February	5
Physical Units: Blending Department	
Units in process, February 1	?
Units transferred out during February	58,000
Units started in February	54,000
Units in process, February 28	2,000
Percentage of Completion: Blending Department	
Direct materials, February 1	100%
Conversion, February 1	?
Direct materials, February 28	100%
Conversion, February 28	20

a. Compute the number of units that were in the Blending Department's beginning inventory on February 1.

b. Compute the number of units that were *started and completed* by the Blending Department in February.

c. Compute the cost per equivalent unit of direct materials and conversion carried forward from *January* and assigned to the Blending Department's beginning inventory on February 1.

d. Compute the Blending Department's cost per equivalent unit of *direct materials* consumed in *February*.

Problem Set A

LO2 LO3 PROBLEM 18.1A
Calculating Equivalent Units
eXcel

Superior Lighting, Inc., mass-produces reading lamps. Materials used in constructing the body of the lamp are added at the start of the process, while the materials used in wiring the lamps are added at the halfway point. All labor and overhead are added evenly throughout the manufacturing process. Superior uses process costing and had the following unit production information available for the months of June and July:

	June	July
Number of lamps in beginning work in process	850	1,200
Lamps transferred to finished goods	3,500	3,300
Number of lamps in ending work in process	1,200	900

In June, the lamps in beginning work in process were approximately 80 percent complete, while those in ending work in process were only 30 percent complete. In July, the units remaining in ending work in process were 60 percent complete. All lamps in ending work in process are finished during the next month.

Instructions

a. For the month of June, calculate the equivalent units of production for the three major cost categories—body materials, wiring materials, and labor and overhead.

b. For the month of July, calculate the equivalent units of production for the three major cost categories—body materials, wiring materials, and labor and overhead.

LO2 through LO5 PROBLEM 18.2A
Computing and Using Unit Costs

One of Sun Appliance's products is a dishwasher. Two processing departments are involved in the dishwasher's manufacture. The tub is assembled in one department, and a second department assembles and installs the motor. There is no beginning or ending work in process in either department. During March, the company incurred the following costs in the manufacture of 4,000 dishwashers.

	Tub Department	Motor Department
Direct materials	$150,000	$96,000
Direct labor	12,000	18,000
Manufacturing overhead	18,000	6,000

Instructions

a. Compute the following *per-unit* costs for the month of March:
   1. A tub assembly transferred to the Motor Department.
   2. Assembling a motor and installing it.
   3. A completed dishwasher.
   4. Materials used in assembling a tub.
   5. Direct labor cost of assembling and installing a motor.

b. Which of these unit costs would be most useful to management in evaluating the overall monthly efficiency of the Motor Department? Explain your reasoning.

LO6 PROBLEM 18.3A
Production Cost Report

Refer to the information from Problem 18.2A.

Instructions

Complete a production cost report for the Motor Department of Sun Appliance for March.

LO2 through LO5

PROBLEM 18.4A

Process Costing with No Beginning or Ending Inventories

Toll House makes chocolate chip cookies. The cookies pass through three production processes: mixing the cookie dough, baking, and packaging. Toll House uses process costing.

The following are data concerning the costs incurred in each process during May, along with the number of units processed:

	Mixing	Baking	Packaging
Direct materials	$3,600	$ 0	$1,020
Direct labor	3,000	1,800	2,100
Manufacturing overhead	6,000	12,000	1,200
Output	14,000 lbs.	4,000 gross*	48,000 boxes

*A gross is 12 dozen.

To ensure freshness, cookies are baked and packaged on the same day that the dough is mixed. Thus, the company has no inventory still in process at the end of a business day.

Instructions

a. Prepare a separate journal entry summarizing the costs incurred by the Mixing Department in preparing 14,000 pounds of cookie dough in May. In the explanation of your entry, indicate the department's unit cost.

b. Prepare the month-end entry recording the transfer of cookie dough to the Baking Department during May.

c. Prepare a journal entry summarizing the costs incurred by the Baking Department in May (excluding the costs transferred from the Mixing Department). In the explanation, indicate the *cost per gross* of the baking process.

d. Prepare the month-end entry recording the transfer of cookies from the Baking Department to the Packaging Department in May.

e. Prepare a journal entry summarizing the costs incurred by the Packaging Department in May. In the explanation, indicate the packaging cost per box.

f. Prepare the month-end entry to record the transfers in May of boxes of cookies from the Packaging Department to the finished goods warehouse. In the explanation, indicate the total cost per box transferred.

g. Briefly explain how management will use the unit cost information appearing in entries **a, c, e,** and **f.**

LO2 through LO4

PROBLEM 18.5A

Calculate Cost per Equivalent Unit

Badgersize Company has the following information for its Forming Department for the month of August:

Work in Process Inventory, August 1: 20,000 units	
Direct materials: 100% complete	$ 80,000
Conversion: 20% complete	24,000
Balance in work in process, August 1	$104,000
Units started during August	50,000
Units completed and transferred in August	60,000
Work in process (70% complete), August 31	?
Costs charged to Work in Process in August	
Direct materials	$150,000
Conversion costs:	
Direct labor	$120,000
Overhead applied	132,000
Total conversion	$252,000

Assume materials are added at the start of processing.

Instructions

a. Calculate the equivalent units for the Forming Department for the month of August.

b. Find the cost per equivalent unit of the transferred units.

LO5 LO6 PROBLEM 18.6A
Production Cost Report

Refer to the information in Problem 18.5A.

Instructions

a. Complete a production cost report for the Badgersize Company Forming Department for the month of August.

b. Discuss how management might use the production cost report to help manage costs.

LO2 through LO5 PROBLEM 18.7A
Process Costing through Two Departments

Hound Havens produces plastic doghouses as part of a continuous process through two departments: Molding and Finishing. Direct materials and conversion are added throughout the month in both departments, but at different rates. The information presented below was compiled at the end of April:

	Molding Department	Finishing Department
Beginning Inventories (on April 1):		
Physical units in production carried forward from March 31 . . .	2,800	5,000
Costs:		
Transferred Molding costs carried forward from March 31 . .		$125,000
Direct materials costs carried forward from March 31	$ 33,340	15,000
Conversion costs carried forward from March 31	11,180	6,000
Current Production (in April):		
Units started during April	48,200	?
Units in ending inventories as of April 30	3,400	2,000
Costs:		
Molding costs transferred to Finishing during April		?
Direct materials costs incurred in April	$669,200	$496,000
Conversion costs incurred in April	521,840	147,600
Percentage of Completion:		
Inventories with respect to direct materials on April 1	90%	30%
Inventories with respect to conversion on April 1	30	40
Inventories with respect to direct materials on April 30	80%	25%
Inventories with respect to conversion on April 30	20	30

Instructions

a. Complete the following requirements for the *Molding Department:*

1. Prepare a schedule showing units *started and completed* in the Molding Department during April.
2. Compute the equivalent units of direct materials and conversion for the Molding Department in April.
3. Determine the cost per equivalent unit of input resource for the Molding Department during April.
4. Prepare the summary journal entry required to transfer units from the Molding Department to the Finishing Department during April.
5. Compute the costs assigned to ending inventory in the Molding Department on April 30.

b. Complete the following requirements for the *Finishing Department:*

1. Prepare a schedule showing units *started and completed* in the Finishing Department during April.
2. Compute the equivalent units of direct materials and conversion for the Finishing Department in April. Direct materials include both those transferred in from the Molding Department and those added by the Finishing Department.
3. Determine the cost per equivalent unit of input resource for the Finishing Department during April.

4. Prepare the summary journal entry required to transfer units from the Finishing Department to Finished Goods Inventory during April.
5. Compute the costs assigned to ending inventory in the Finishing Department on April 30.

LO2 through LO5

PROBLEM 18.8A
Process Costing through Two Departments

Wilson Dynamics makes flanges in a continuous process through two departments: Forging and Assembly. All direct materials are added at the *beginning* of the process in the Forging Department, whereas all direct materials are added at the *end* of the process in the Assembly Department. Conversion costs are incurred uniformly over time in both departments. As units are completed in the Forging Department they are transferred to the Assembly Department. The costs associated with the transferred units are included in the computation of the Assembly Department's total costs. The information presented below was compiled at the end of July:

	Forging Department	Assembly Department
Beginning Inventories (on July 1):		
Physical units in production carried forward from June 30	5,000	4,000
Costs:		
Transferred Forging costs carried forward from June 30		$ 68,000
Direct materials costs carried forward from June 30	$ 45,000	?
Conversion costs carried forward from June 30	16,000	3,000
Current Production (in July):		
Units started during July	75,000	?
Units in ending inventories as of July 31	8,000	16,000
Costs:		
Forging costs transferred to Assembly during July		?
Direct materials costs incurred in July	$675,000	$720,000
Conversion costs incurred in July	608,000	191,400
Percentage of Completion:		
Inventories with respect to conversion on July 1	40%	25%
Inventories with respect to conversion on July 31	75	30

Instructions

a. Complete the following requirements for the *Forging Department:*

1. Prepare a schedule showing units *started and completed* in the Forging Department during July.
2. Compute the equivalent units of direct materials and conversion for the Forging Department in July.
3. Determine the cost per equivalent unit of input resource for the Forging Department during July.
4. Prepare the summary journal entry required to transfer units from the Forging Department to the Assembly Department during July.
5. Compute the costs assigned to ending inventory in the Forging Department on July 31.

b. Complete the following requirements for the *Assembly Department:*

1. Prepare a schedule showing units *started and completed* in the Assembly Department during July.
2. Compute the equivalent units of direct materials and conversion for the Assembly Department in July. Direct materials include both those transferred in from the Forging Department and those added by the Assembly Department.
3. Determine the cost per equivalent unit of input resource for the Assembly Department during July.
4. Prepare the summary journal entry required to transfer units from the Assembly Department to Finished Goods Inventory during July.
5. Compute the costs assigned to ending inventory in the Assembly Department on July 31.

Problem Set B

LO2 LO3 **PROBLEM 18.1B**
Calculating Equivalent Units

Morgan Industries, Inc., mass-produces street lights. Materials used in constructing the body of the lights are added at the start of the process, while the materials used in wiring the lights are added at the halfway point. All labor and overhead are added evenly throughout the manufacturing process. Morgan uses process costing and had the following unit production information available for the months of March and April:

	March	April
Number of lights in beginning work in process	600	1,600
Lights transferred to finished goods	4,200	4,000
Number of lights in ending work in process	1,600	700

In March, the lights in beginning work in process were approximately 60 percent complete, while those in ending work in process were only 20 percent complete. In April, the units remaining in ending work in process were 70 percent complete. All lights in ending work in process are finished during the next month.

Instructions

a. For the month of March, calculate the equivalent units of production for the three major cost categories—body materials, wiring materials, and labor and overhead.

b. For the month of April, calculate the equivalent units of production for the three major cost categories—body materials, wiring materials, and labor and overhead.

LO2 through LO5 **PROBLEM 18.2B**
Computing and Using Unit Costs

One of MowTown Manufacturing's products is a small lawnmower. Two processing departments are involved in the mower's production. The deck is assembled in one department, and a second department assembles and installs the engine. There is no beginning or ending work in process in either department. During May, the company incurred the following costs in the manufacture of 6,000 lawnmowers:

	Deck Department	Engine Department
Direct materials	$192,000	$480,000
Direct labor	48,000	108,000
Manufacturing overhead	54,000	66,000

Instructions

a. Compute the following *per-unit* costs for the month of May.
1. A deck assembly transferred to the Engine Department.
2. Assembling an engine and installing it.
3. A completed lawnmower.
4. Materials used in assembling a deck.
5. Direct labor cost of assembling and installing an engine.

b. Which of these unit costs would be most useful to management in evaluating the overall monthly efficiency of the Engine Department? Explain your reasoning.

LO6 **PROBLEM 18.3B**
Production Cost Report

Refer to the information from Problem 18.2B.

Instructions

Complete a production cost report for the Engine Department of MowTown Manufacturing for May.

LO2 through LO5

PROBLEM 18.4B
Process Costing with No Beginning or Ending Inventories

Snack Happy makes chocolate brownies. The brownies pass through three production processes: mixing the batter, baking, and packaging. The company uses process costing.

The following are data concerning the costs incurred in each process during August, along with the number of units processed:

	Mixing	Baking	Packaging
Direct materials	$25,000	$ 0	$ 3,000
Direct labor	60,000	40,000	14,000
Manufacturing overhead	35,000	50,000	7,000
Output	20,000 lbs.	5,000 gross*	12,000 cases

*A gross is 12 dozen.

To ensure freshness, brownies are baked and packaged on the same day that the batter is mixed. Thus, the company has no inventory still in process at the end of a business day.

Instructions

a. Prepare a separate journal entry summarizing the costs incurred by the Mixing Department in preparing 20,000 pounds of batter in August. In the explanation of your entry, indicate the department's unit cost.

b. Prepare the month-end entry recording the transfer of batter to the Baking Department during August.

c. Prepare a journal entry summarizing the costs incurred by the Baking Department in August (excluding the costs transferred from the Mixing Department). In the explanation, indicate the *cost per gross* of the baking process.

d. Prepare the month-end entry recording the transfer of brownies from the Baking Department to the Packaging Department in August.

e. Prepare a journal entry summarizing the costs incurred by the Packaging Department in August. In the explanation, indicate the packaging cost per case.

f. Prepare the month-end entry to record the transfers in August of cases of brownies from the Packaging Department to the finished goods warehouse. In the explanation, indicate the total cost per case transferred.

g. Briefly explain how management will use the unit cost information appearing in entries **a, c, e,** and **f.**

LO2 through LO4

PROBLEM 18.5B
Calculate Cost per Equivalent Unit

Balfanz Company has the following information for its Finishing Department for the month of September:

Work in Process Inventory, September 1: 50,000 units	
Direct materials: 100% complete	$ 150,000
Conversion: 40% complete	120,000
Balance in work in process, September 1	$ 270,000
Units started during September	300,000
Units completed and transferred in September	280,000
Work in process (80% complete), September 30	?
Costs charged to Work in Process in September	
Direct materials	$1,200,000
Conversion costs:	
Direct labor	$1,000,000
Overhead applied	$1,212,000
Total conversion	$2,212,000

Assume materials are added at the start of processing.

Instructions

a. Calculate the equivalent units for the Finishing Department for the month of September.

b. Find the cost per equivalent unit of the transferred units.

LO5 LO6 **PROBLEM 18.6B** Production Cost Report

Refer to the information in Problem 18.5B.

Instructions

a. Complete a production cost report for the Balfanz Company Finishing Department for the month of September.

b. Discuss how management might use the production cost report to help manage costs.

LO2 through LO5 **PROBLEM 18.7B** Process Costing through Two Departments

Delray Industries manufactures plastic wading pools as part of a continuous process through two departments: Molding and Finishing. Direct materials and conversion are added throughout the month in both departments, but at different rates. The information presented below was compiled at the end of June:

	Molding Department	Finishing Department
Beginning Inventories (on June 1):		
Physical units in production carried forward from May 31	3,000	5,000
Costs:		
Transferred Molding costs carried forward from May 31.		$150,000
Direct materials costs carried forward from May 31	$ 37,800	4,000
Conversion costs carried forward from May 31.	14,400	24,000
Current Production (in June):		
Units started during June	50,000	?
Units in ending inventories as of June 30.	1,000	2,000
Costs:		
Molding costs transferred to Finishing during June.		?
Direct materials costs incurred in June	$912,600	$222,000
Conversion costs incurred in June	612,000	430,400
Percentage of Completion:		
Inventories with respect to direct materials on June 1	70%	20%
Inventories with respect to conversion on June 1.	40	60
Inventories with respect to direct materials on June 30	80%	75%
Inventories with respect to conversion on June 30.	20	90

Instructions

a. Complete the following requirements for the *Molding Department:*

1. Prepare a schedule showing units *started and completed* in the Molding Department during June.
2. Compute the equivalent units of direct materials and conversion for the Molding Department in June.
3. Determine the cost per equivalent unit of input resource for the Molding Department during June.
4. Prepare the summary journal entry required to transfer units from the Molding Department to the Finishing Department during June.
5. Compute the costs assigned to ending inventory in the Molding Department on June 30.

b. Complete the following requirements for the *Finishing Department:*

1. Prepare a schedule showing units *started and completed* in the Finishing Department during June.
2. Compute the equivalent units of direct materials and conversion for the Finishing Department in June. Direct materials include both those transferred in from the Molding Department and those added by the Finishing Department.
3. Determine the cost per equivalent unit of input resource for the Finishing Department during June.
4. Prepare the summary journal entry required to transfer units from the Finishing Department to Finished Goods Inventory during June.
5. Compute the costs assigned to ending inventory in the Finishing Department on June 30.

LO2 through LO5

PROBLEM 18.8B Process Costing through Two Departments

Thompson Tools produces dampers in a continuous process through two departments: Assembly and Packaging. All direct materials are added at the *beginning* of the process in the Assembly Department, whereas all direct materials are added at the *end* of the process in the Packaging Department. Conversion costs are incurred uniformly over time in both departments. As units are completed in the Assembly Department, they are transferred to the Packaging Department. The costs associated with the transferred units are included in the computation of the Packaging Department's total costs. The information presented below was compiled at the end of March:

	Assembly Department	Packaging Department
Beginning Inventories (on March 1):		
Physical units in production carried forward from February 28	5,000	4,000
Costs:		
Transferred Assembly costs carried forward from February 28		$ 60,000
Direct materials costs carried forward from February 28	$ 45,000	?
Conversion costs carried forward from February 28	9,000	3,200
Current Production (in March):		
Units started during March	80,000	?
Units in ending inventories as of March 31	9,000	20,000
Costs:		
Assembly costs transferred to Packaging during March		?
Direct materials costs incurred in March	$720,000	$840,000
Conversion costs incurred in March	490,200	260,800
Percentage of Completion:		
Inventories with respect to conversion on March 1	30%	20%
Inventories with respect to conversion on March 31	80	30

Instructions

a. Complete the following requirements for the *Assembly Department:*

1. Prepare a schedule showing units *started and completed* in the Assembly Department during March.
2. Compute the equivalent units of direct materials and conversion for the Assembly Department in March.
3. Determine the cost per equivalent unit of input resource for the Assembly Department during March.
4. Prepare the summary journal entry required to transfer units from the Assembly Department to the Packaging Department during March.
5. Compute the costs assigned to ending inventory in the Assembly Department on March 31.

b. Complete the following requirements for the *Packaging Department:*

1. Prepare a schedule showing units *started and completed* in the Packaging Department during March.
2. Compute the equivalent units of direct materials and conversion for the Packaging Department in March. Direct materials include both those transferred in from the Assembly Department and those added by the Packaging Department.
3. Determine the cost per equivalent unit of input resource for the Packaging Department during March.
4. Prepare the summary journal entry required to transfer units from the Packaging Department to Finished Goods Inventory during March.
5. Compute the costs assigned to ending inventory in the Packaging Department on March 31.

Critical Thinking Cases

LO1 through LO3

CASE 18.1
Evaluation of a Cost System: Does It Meet the Company's Needs?

Viking Beer is a microbrewery that produces one type of beer. The production level is 18,000 gallons per month, which is bottled in 192,000 twelve-ounce bottles. The beer is brewed in batches of 3,600 gallons, which is the capacity of the fermenting tanks. Each batch requires six days of processing, during which it passes through six separate production processes.

Viking uses process costing. All manufacturing costs incurred during the month are assigned to the 192,000 bottles produced; no valuation is assigned to the 3,600 gallons currently sitting in the fermenting tanks.

Viking has hired Matt Brown, a recent college graduate, as a cost analyst. After learning about the company's cost accounting system, Brown sent the following memo to Viking's controller:

> I have two suggestions as to how we might improve our cost accounting system. First, our beer is processed in identifiable batches; so we could use *job order*, rather than process, costing. This would enable us to determine separately the cost of each batch.
>
> Second, we always have 3,600 gallons of beer in the fermenting tanks. But our cost accounting system assigns all manufacturing costs during the period to the finished goods produced. Some of these costs should be assigned to the beer in the fermenting tanks and identified as "work in process inventory." This can be done by computing the *equivalent units* that these 3,600 gallons represent.

Instructions

As Viking's controller, draft a memo responding to Brown's suggestions.

LO2 through LO6

CASE 18.2
Interpreting and Using Process Costing Information

Assume that you are the production manager of the Assembly Department illustrated on pages 807–810 of this chapter (Metal Products, Inc.). One of your responsibilities is to determine whether costs are remaining relatively stable from month to month. Assume that the $29,500 associated with the 1,000 units in process on *March 1* (see Exhibit 18–5, page 808) is comprised of the following:

Cut materials transferred from the Cutting Department in *February*	$25,000
Direct materials added in the Assembly Department in *February*	0
Conversion added in the Assembly Department in *February*	4,500
Total cost associated with beginning inventory on *March 1*	$29,500

The *cost per equivalent unit* of input resource used by the Assembly Department in March is as follows (see Exhibit 18–7, page 809):

Cut materials transferred from the Cutting Department in *March*	$20
Direct materials added in the Assembly Department in *March*	4
Conversion added in the Assembly Department in *March*	25
Cost per equivalent unit of input resource used in *March*	$49

Instructions

a. By how much did the cost per equivalent unit of cut material transferred in from the Cutting Department in *February* differ from the cost per equivalent unit of cut material transferred to the Assembly Department in *March*?

b. By how much did the cost per equivalent unit of conversion for the Assembly Department in *February* differ from the cost per equivalent unit of conversion for the Assembly Department in *March*?

c. Speculate as to why the cost per equivalent unit of input resource (cut materials and conversion) may have changed from February to March.

LO1 LO2 **CASE 18.3**
Processes and Product Costs at **PepsiCo**

Visit the **PepsiCo** Web site at:

http://www.pepsiusa.com/faqs.php/

Follow the link to "How Pepsi is Made" (under "Product Information") for parts **a.**, **b.**, and **c.** Follow the links under "Community Information" for part **d.**

Instructions

a. Identify and discuss briefly the processes involved in manufacturing Pepsi.

b. What are Pepsi's direct materials?

c. Of the company's conversion costs, does labor or manufacturing overhead comprise the larger component of manufacturing costs? Defend your answer.

d. View the **PepsiCo**'s charitable, educational, and environmental initiatives. Would it be improper for **PepsiCo** to report these initiatives as product costs? Do you believe that it is ethical for **PepsiCo** to report only the positive impacts of its community-oriented efforts throughout the world? Defend your answer.

LO1 LO2 **INTERNET CASE 18.4**
Manufacturing Processes

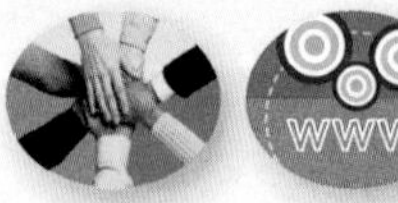

Wrigley Company manufactures chewing gum. Visit its home page at the following address:

www.wrigley.com

From the home page, click on the choices labeled "About Us," then "About Gum,"and then "How Gum Is Made."

Instructions

a. Prepare a simple flowchart that illustrates the major steps in the manufacture of chewing gum.

b. If **Wrigley** uses process costing, how many separate processing departments might be used and what would you label them?

c. What do you think are the major types of manufacturing overhead at **Wrigley**? What activity bases could be used to assign each type of overhead to the processing departments you listed in part **b?**

Internet sites are time and date sensitive. It is the purpose of these exercises to have you explore the Internet. You may need to use the Yahoo! search engine **http://www.yahoo.com** *(or another favorite search engine) to look for a company's current Web address.*

Answers To Self-Test Questions

1. a, c **2.** b **3.** a, b, c **4.** a, b, c, d **5.** a, b, c, e

CHAPTER 19

Costing and the Value Chain

AFTER STUDYING THIS CHAPTER, YOU SHOULD BE ABLE TO:

Learning Objectives

- **LO1** Define the value chain and describe its basic components.
- **LO2** Distinguish between non-value-added and value-added activities.
- **LO3** Explain how activity-based management is related to activity-based costing (ABC).
- **LO4** Describe the target costing process and list its components.
- **LO5** Identify the relationship between target costing and the value chain.
- **LO6** Explain the nature and goals of a just-in-time (JIT) manufacturing system.
- **LO7** Identify the components of the cost of quality.
- **LO8** Describe the characteristics of quality measures.

KIMBERLY-CLARK CORPORATION

For nearly 140 years, Kimberly-Clark has helped improve the quality of life for millions of people by developing some of the world's most trusted and recognized health and hygiene brands. Kimberly-Clark is a recognized leader in sustainable resource initiatives. In its annual sustainability report,[1] Kimberly-Clark shares its vision to reduce product packaging by 5 percent by 2013, while continuing to work toward recycling 100 percent of nonhazardous solid waste from operations. In a recent sustainability report, Kimberly-Clark reports that they produced 1.48 million tons of total waste, of which 293,000 tons were sent to landfills. . . . Approximately 423,000 tons were recycled, composted, or incinerated and 762,000 tons were reused directly or in other products or processes.

By identifying non-value-added activities in its value chain, like sending waste to a landfill rather than recycling or reusing that waste, Kimberly-Clark was able to save more than $10 million. ■

[1] http://www.kimberly-clark.com/aboutus/sus_2010/sustainability_pg41.aspx.

The Value Chain

Learning Objective
LO1 **Define the value chain and describe its basic components.**

To focus on core operations, management begins by identifying components of the organization's value chain. In Chapter 16, we defined the **value chain** as the set of activities and resources necessary to create and deliver the product or service valued by customers.

Obviously, the details of each organization's value chain will look different. Further, the value chain for each particular product or service within an organization can be very different. Consider **Kimberly-Clark Corporation**, the company discussed in the chapter opener. On its Web site, **Kimberly-Clark** lists some of its products and services for the consumer, health care, and professional markets. These categories represent different markets with different types of suppliers and customers. For example, product characteristics that are valued by a typical consumer will differ significantly from those valued by a health care customer. In addition, the suppliers for health care and consumer products differ significantly. Creating a value chain to satisfy diverse customer needs is a major challenge for most businesses.

For each of a company's products and services, the following components of the value chain (as also shown in Exhibit 19–1) are active:

- *Research and development (R&D) and design activities* include the creation of ideas and the development of prototype products, processes, and services.
- *Suppliers and production-related activities* include the procurement of raw materials and supplies and the activities needed to convert them into finished goods and services.
- *Marketing and distribution activities* are designed to provide information to potential customers and make the products and services accessible to customers.
- *Customer service activities* are those resources consumed by supporting the product or service after it is sold to the customer.

INTERNATIONAL FINANCIAL REPORTING STANDARDS AND THE VALUE CHAIN

Several reporting differences between U.S. generally accepted accounting principles (GAAP) and IFRS are value chain related. Two examples are accounting for R&D and creating multiple sets of financial statements. First, IFRS requires some research and development activities to be capitalized while U.S. GAAP requires them to be expensed. This difference may affect R&D investment decision making.

Second, companies with operations in countries where IFRS is the accepted standard may need to file financial reports that meet both local GAAP and IFRS standards. They may also need to reconcile to U.S. GAAP to meet reporting requirements of the U.S. parent company. Similarly, a U.S. company that's a subsidiary of a publicly traded international firm headquartered in an IFRS reporting country must prepare IFRS financial statements. Or it must be able to reconcile its U.S. GAAP statement to IFRS for inclusion in the parent company's consolidated financial statement. These additional reporting requirements add costs to the value chain.

VALUE- AND NON-VALUE-ADDED ACTIVITIES

Learning Objective
LO2 **Distinguish between non-value-added and value-added activities.**

Organizations attempt to identify and eliminate the **non-value-added activities** in their value chains. **Value-added activities** add to the product's or service's desirability in the eyes of the consumer. Non-value-added activities do not add to the product's desirability. Thus, an organization can decrease its costs if a non-value-added activity that consumes resources can be eliminated without changing the product's desirability. Examples of value-added and non-value-added activities are included in Exhibit 19–1. One example of a non-value-added activity is having large amounts of raw materials, work in process, or finished goods inventory. **Kimberly-Clark**'s management recognizes the non-value-added cost associated with holding inventories because a part of its operating plan is to focus on tight inventory control. Just-in-time inventory management processes, discussed later in this chapter, have been developed to reduce the consumption of non-value-added resources associated with large amounts of inventories.

YOUR TURN **You as a Raw Materials Inventory Manager**

Assume you are the manager of raw materials for a lumber mill. What types of resources are being consumed when a large amount of redwood logs sits idle, waiting to be put through the mill?

(See our comments on the Online Learning Center Web site.)

Exhibit 19–1 VALUE-ADDED AND NON-VALUE-ADDED ACTIVITIES IN THE VALUE CHAIN

Value-added activities in the value chain:
- Designs that meet customer specifications
- Use of suppliers that provide timely high-quality inputs
- Production process that provides just-in-time output for customer
- Timely distribution and easy access to customer
- Clear and truthful marketing
- Competent and timely after-sales customer help

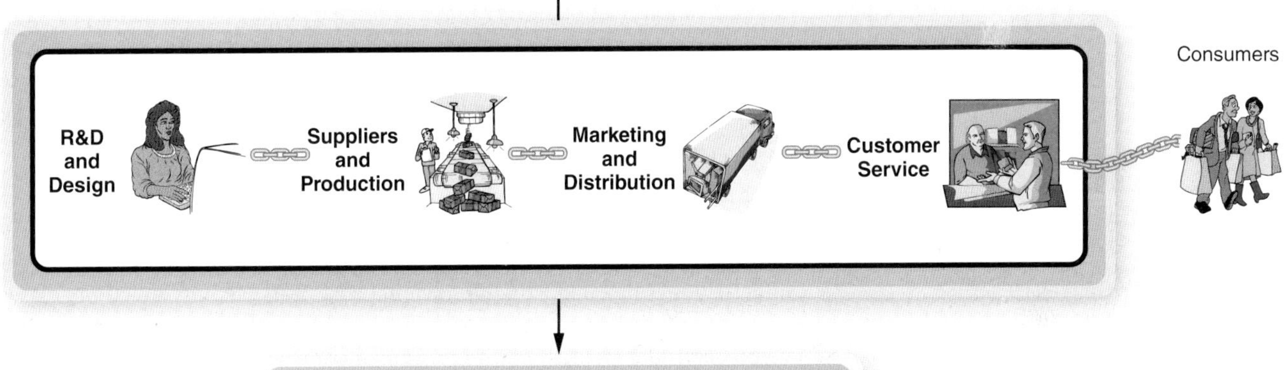

Non-value-added activities in the value chain:
- Designs that meet engineering specifications but not customer needs
- Supplier deliveries that are poor quality or not timely, causing delays in production
- Production processes that create rework, scrap, and significant work in process inventories
- Delayed distribution to customer
- Deceptive or misleading marketing
- After-sales customer help that is not valued by customers

In the previous three chapters, we concentrated our cost analysis only on the production phase of the value chain. However, resources are consumed across the value chain. Organizations attempt to minimize resource consumption at all points on the value chain while simultaneously providing the products and services desired by consumers at competitive prices. In this chapter, we will consider other cost accounting procedures and techniques that have been developed to assess resource use and costs in all parts of the value chain. These procedures include *activity-based management,* which is effective over the entire value chain; *target costing,* designed for the R&D and design phase of the value chain; *just-in-time manufacturing procedures;* and, finally, *total quality management,* which is also relevant over the entire value chain.

Activity-Based Management

Previously, when we introduced activity-based costing (ABC), we provided an ABC example focused on production overhead. You may remember that the basic procedures related to ABC include the following:

1. Identify the *activity.*
2. Create an associated *activity cost pool.*
3. Identify an *activity measure.*
4. Create the *cost per unit of activity.*

Our earlier focus was on using ABC to assign cost to units of the product. However, activity-based cost information is also important in management decision making. Remember that management is trying to eliminate non-value-added activities from the value chain. For example, if the downtime needed for equipment repair can be eliminated from the value chain *without increasing the cost associated with the total value chain,* then it is a non-value-added activity. The process of using activity-based costs to help reduce and eliminate non-value-added activities is **activity-based management.** Redesigning equipment layout, acquiring higher-quality materials as inputs, buying new equipment, outsourcing repair work, or some combination of these management decisions may reduce or eliminate activity cost and associated resource use.

ACTIVITY-BASED MANAGEMENT ACROSS THE VALUE CHAIN

While activity-based cost information is very important in the production portion of the value chain, it is also very useful for assessing activities associated with most period expenses such as R&D, distribution, administration, finance, marketing, and customer service. In many organizations, period expenses are more significant to overall profitability than product expenses.

© Ryan McVay/Getty Images/DAL

Managing Activities: An Illustration Management uses ABC information to identify activities and processes that are non-value-added or where the added costs of those activities and processes outweigh their benefits to the customer. One way that managers compare the costs and benefits of activities is by contrasting the internal cost of the activity to the purchased external cost for that activity. To illustrate how activity-based management works, consider Boards and More, Inc., a company that sells lumber, paper, and packaging products. Boards and More's chief financial officer (CFO) has been approached by a software vendor selling software called "Transaction Reduction." The software is designed to reduce the cost of processing transactions. In order to determine the cost savings for Boards and More, the CFO decides to undertake an ABC study of the activities of his Accounting and Finance (A&F) Department.

The activities performed by the A&F Department include:

1. Transaction-related activities.
2. External financial reporting.
3. Annual planning and budgeting.
4. Specially requested analyses.

In addition, the labor cost pool and associated wages are:

1. Twelve clerks at $20 per hour.
2. Five finance analysts at a salary of $45,000 each.
3. Six budget analysts at a salary of $39,000 each.
4. Three senior analysts at $75,000 each and the CFO at $185,000.

The CFO, with the help of the employees, completes an extensive activity analysis of the labor time consumed for the four identified activities. The CFO then determines the percentage of time devoted to each of the four activities by each of the four labor categories. Please study Exhibit 19–2 carefully. It shows the related percentages, cost pools, and activities for the A&F Department.

Remember that the objective of the ABC analysis is to compare the internal cost of processing transactions with the external cost of the proposed software. Thus, the next step in the activity analysis is to calculate the detailed cost for each activity. Exhibit 19–3 breaks out the cost of each activity by using the percentages from Exhibit 19–2 and the cost of each type of labor. The ABC analysis in Exhibit 19–2 will help the CFO manage his own activities and those of the 26 employees in the A&F Department. In particular, the CFO can consider whether the internal transaction-related activity costs are non-value-added in comparison to the external cost of the Transaction Reduction software.

Exhibit 19–2 IDENTIFYING COST POOLS AND ACTIVITIES

Boards and More, Inc.
Department of Accounting and Finance

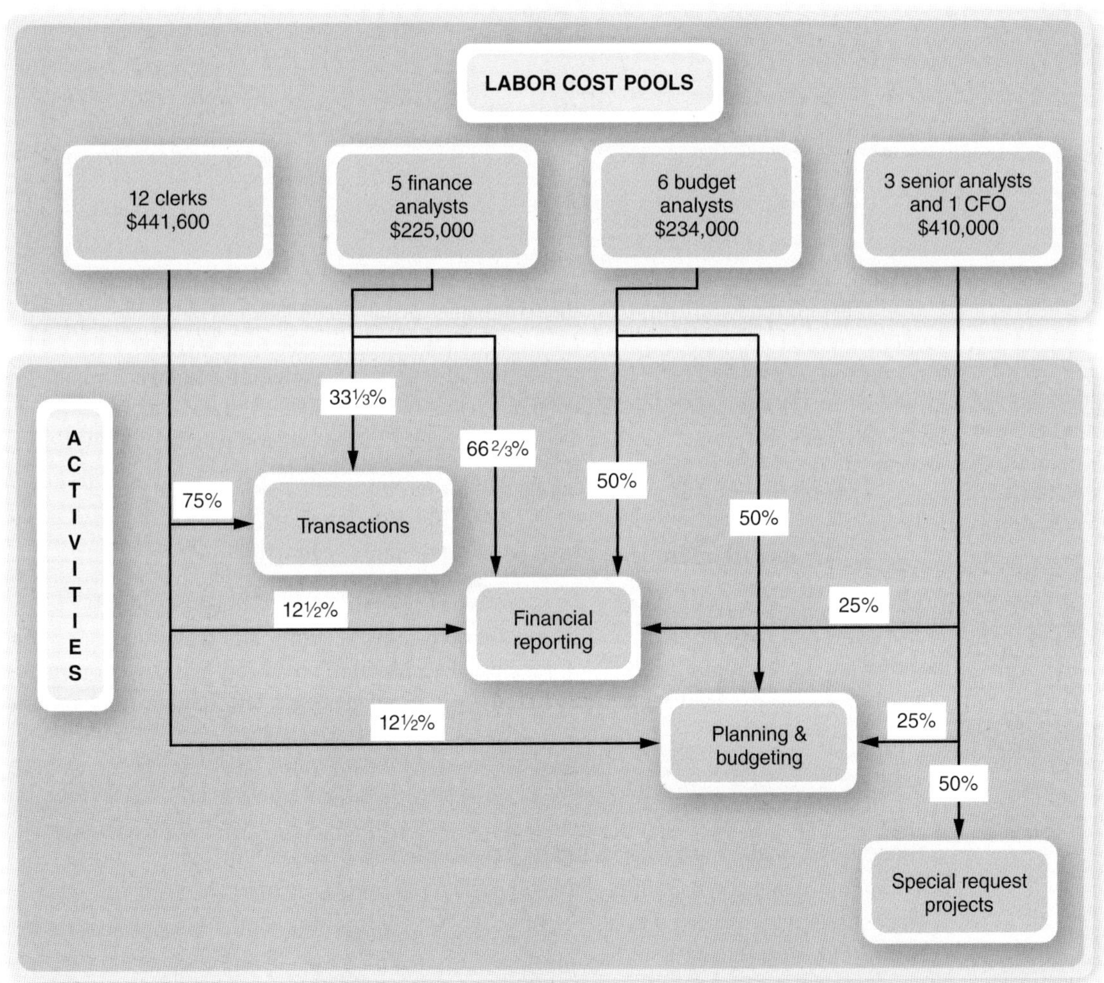

Examine the transaction-related activity costs in the first column in Exhibit 19–3. These costs are required to make sure basic journal entries are properly recorded and monitored throughout the firm to safeguard the firm's assets. Account clerks complete much of the detailed work. However, financial analysts are also involved in assessing transactions and undertaking analysis in order to complete their financial reporting responsibilities. As a result of the ABC analysis, the CFO estimates $406,200 of the total labor cost pool of $1,310,600 is associated with transaction-related activities.

Exhibit 19–3 ACTIVITY COST ANALYSES

Labor Category	Activity Category: Transaction-Related	Financial Reporting	Planning and Budgeting	Special Analyses	Total Labor Resources
Clerks	¾ (75%)	⅛ (12.5%)	⅛ (12.5%)	0	22,080 hours = (12 clerks, 46 weeks @ 40 hrs. per week @ $20/hr) =
	$331,200	$55,200	$55,200	$0	$441,600
Finance analysts	⅓ (33.33%)	⅔ (66.67%)	0	0	5 salaried analysts @$45,000 each =
	$75,000	$150,000	$0	$0	$225,000
Budget analysts	0	½ (50%)	½ (50%)	0	6 salaried analysts @ $39,000 =
	$0	$117,000	$117,000	$0	$234,000
Senior analysts and CFO	0	¼ (25%)	¼ (25%)	½ (50%)	3 seniors @$75,000 each and 1 CFO @$185,000 =
	$0	$102,500	$102,500	$205,000	$410,000
Total activity resources	$406,200	$424,700	$274,700	$205,000	**$1,310,600**

The software vendor affirms that other companies installing and using Transaction Reduction have experienced a 50 percent per year reduction in transaction-related costs. Transaction Reduction's quoted price is $450,000 for the fully installed package, including employee training and customer support services. If the CFO purchases the software and the vendor's savings estimates are correct, the software will recover its initial cost after 2.22 years, computed as follows:

Transaction Activities Cost Pool = $406,200 × 50% savings per year
= $203,100 per year
"Transaction Reduction" Costs = $450,000 ÷ $203,100 per year
= 2.22 years to recover

We know that the CFO will have many other concerns in addition to the cost savings from the software. For example, since ¾ of the clerks (9 clerks) are engaged in transaction-related activities, would 4½ need to be fired? If so, what are the legal and human implications?

INTERNATIONAL CASE IN POINT 

These days, value chain activities such as drawing up detailed architectural blueprints, slicing and dicing a company's financial disclosures, or designing a revolutionary microprocessor are often outsourced overseas. That's why **Intel Inc.** and **Texas Instruments Inc.** are furiously hiring Indian and Chinese engineers, many with graduate degrees, to design chip circuits. Dutch consumer electronics giant **Philips** has shifted research and development on most televisions, cell phones, and audio products to Shanghai. **Procter & Gamble Co.** has employees in Manila, most of whom have business and finance degrees, to help prepare **P&G** 's tax returns around the world.

One of the biggest trends reshaping the global economy is in process. The driving forces are digitization, the Internet, and high-speed data networks that girdle the globe. Now, all kinds of knowledge work can be done almost anywhere. Predictions are that at least 3.3 million white-collar jobs and $136 billion in wages will be added to low-cost countries by 2015.

The CFO may also be concerned that a longer time to recover the initial investment would be undesirable given rapid change in software technology. In order to determine the exact resources (clerks versus analysts) that might be affected by the new software, a more detailed analysis than that just displayed must be undertaken.

ABC: A SUBSET OF ACTIVITY-BASED MANAGEMENT

ABC information must be created before management of the activity can occur. To see this, consider the ABC data from Boards and More, Inc. Suppose the external auditors for Boards and More proposed to the CFO that an independent consulting firm could perform the financial analysts' function for $190,000. At the simplest level, this might be considered a cost reduction because the five financial analysts consume $225,000 in resources and the proposed outsourcing consumes $190,000 in resources. This suggests that a savings of $35,000 per year ($225,000 − $190,000) would result from hiring the outside firm. Closer inspection of the external auditors' proposal, however, reveals that the activities under consideration are restricted to those in the financial reporting area. The ABC data, however, tell the CFO that these activities comprise only two-thirds of the total financial analysts' activities (⅔ × $225,000 = $150,000). Thus, the true resource cost from the external auditors' proposal would be a loss of $40,000 ($150,000 − $190,000), rather than the $35,000 yearly savings. Thus, the CFO should reject the external auditors' proposal.

Managing the activities at Boards and More requires a clear understanding of what consumes resources *and* the costs associated with these resources. In addition, having benchmark information about competitive practices can help the company identify non-value-added activities. This benchmark information can be in the form of industry studies, competitive outside bids, or internal prototyping. Thus, ABC is a critical component of activity-based management, but managing the activities also requires benchmark information. Exhibit 19–4 captures the details of activity-based management.

Learning Objective LO3
Explain how activity-based management is related to activity-based costing (ABC).

Exhibit 19–4 ABC IS A SUBSET OF ACTIVITY-BASED MANAGEMENT

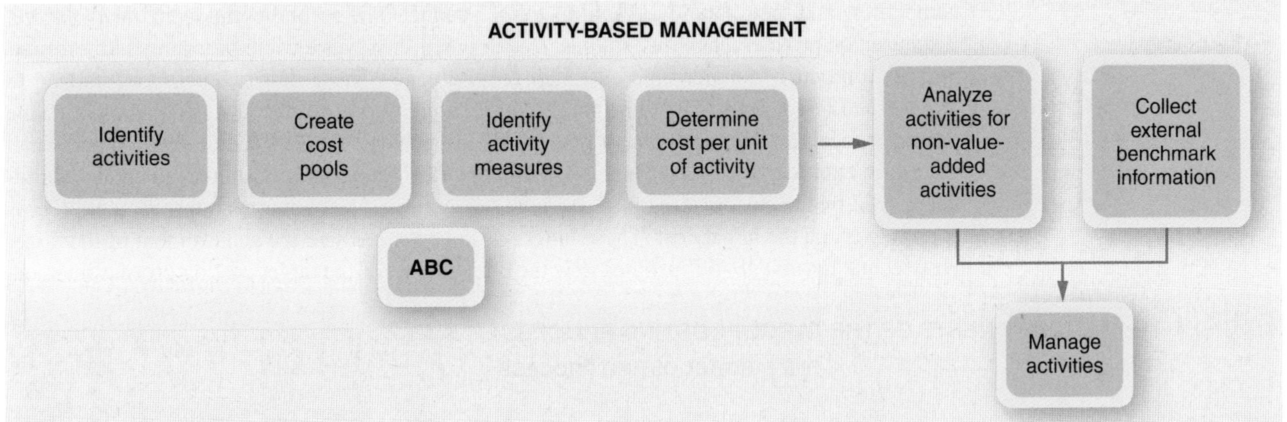

The Target Costing Process

The previous example based on Boards and More, Inc., is aimed at considering activities of existing, established processes. **Target costing** is a business process aimed at the earliest stages of new product and service development, before creation and design of production methods. It is a process driven by the customer, focused on design, and encompassing the entire life of the product. The objective is to create a production process that provides adequate profits. By focusing simultaneously on profit and cost planning over the entire value chain, organizations are able to tap synergies among the various value chain parts. Consideration of the entire value chain at the product development phase is critical because research demonstrates that 80 percent of production-related expenses are committed once the production process begins. These committed resources cannot be changed later without great cost to the company.

Learning Objective
LO4 **Describe the target costing process and list its components.**

The target costing process begins with the customer. Customer desires about functionality, quality, and, most important, price drive the analysis. Having a clear understanding of customer needs is critical. There are likely to be functional requirements that must be present to meet customer needs. Further, the customer may be unwilling to trade off functional requirements for lower price or lower quality. Knowing customer requirements also means understanding competitor offerings. Consumers do not operate in a vacuum. They demand product characteristics based on what is available in the marketplace. If a competitor offers a higher-quality product with a similar functionality at a lower price, then companies attempt to reengineer their processes to meet that competition.

COMPONENTS OF THE TARGET COSTING PROCESS

At the most basic level, the *desired* target cost is the cost of resources that should be consumed to create a product that can be sold at a target price. The target costing process begins with identifying the target price. The target price is determined through interaction with consumers. However, management must determine an acceptable profit margin for the product to compute the desired target cost. That profit margin, although not considered in detail here, is a function of the type of business and the demands of the marketplace. The basic target cost formula is as follows:

Target Cost = Target Price − Profit Margin

Target costing can be best understood by considering its four components:

- Planning and market analysis.
- Concept development.
- Production design and value engineering.
- Production and continuous improvement.

First, significant resources are consumed in *planning and market analysis.* During planning, the customer niche is identified and thoroughly documented. Market analysts carefully consider competitors and their potential reactions to the product. The second component, *development,* is focused on product feasibility studies. Development involves a cycle of testing and reformulating the product to understand customer requirements. These first two components lead to an expected target price. The third phase, *production design,* follows the establishment of the product concept in the development phase. Engineering and experienced production personnel use **value engineering** to determine the least costly combination of resources to create a product desired by the customer. Finally, *production* begins and a continuous improvement process is used to attain the target cost. These latter two stages are where the achievement of the target cost occurs. Exhibit 19–5 illustrates how the components of the target costing process interact.

Exhibit 19–5 COMPONENTS OF THE TARGET COSTING PROCESS

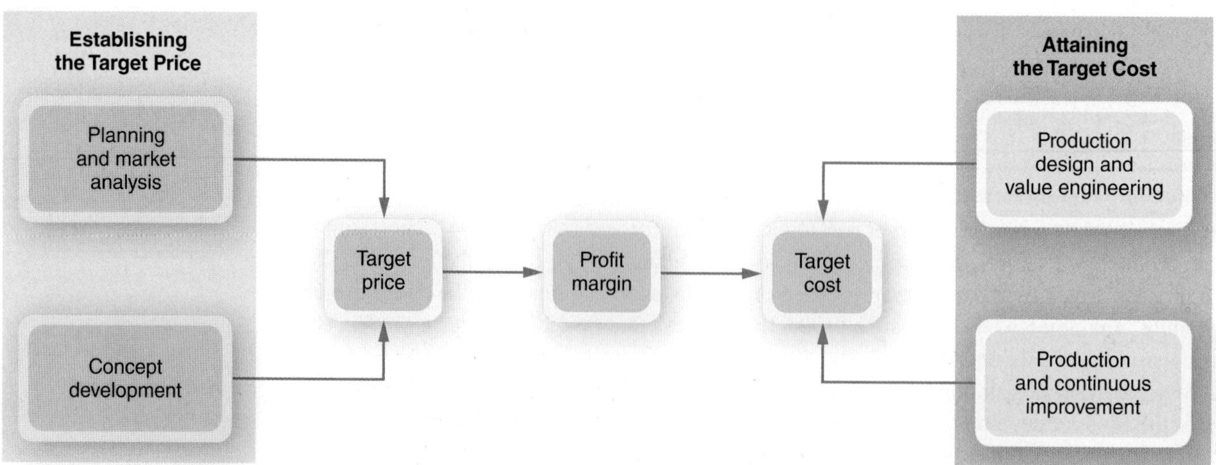

TARGET COSTING: AN ILLUSTRATION

To illustrate the target costing process, we will use Boards and More, Inc., the company previously discussed. One of Boards and More's product lines is creating paper packaging for various products. The company bids on packaging jobs for such products as laundry soap, cereal boxes, and pancake mix. The typical value chain for the cardboard boxes is shown in Exhibit 19–6. The value chain for these packaging materials includes the research and development objective of creating cardboard with superior quality and strength at the lowest possible weight. Boards and More produces the cardboard in large rolls that are shipped to suppliers for printing and box formation before the boxes are shipped to, in this example, the soap manufacturer.

Exhibit 19–6 TARGET COSTING ACROSS THE VALUE CHAIN

VALUE CHAIN FOR CARDBOARD PACKAGING

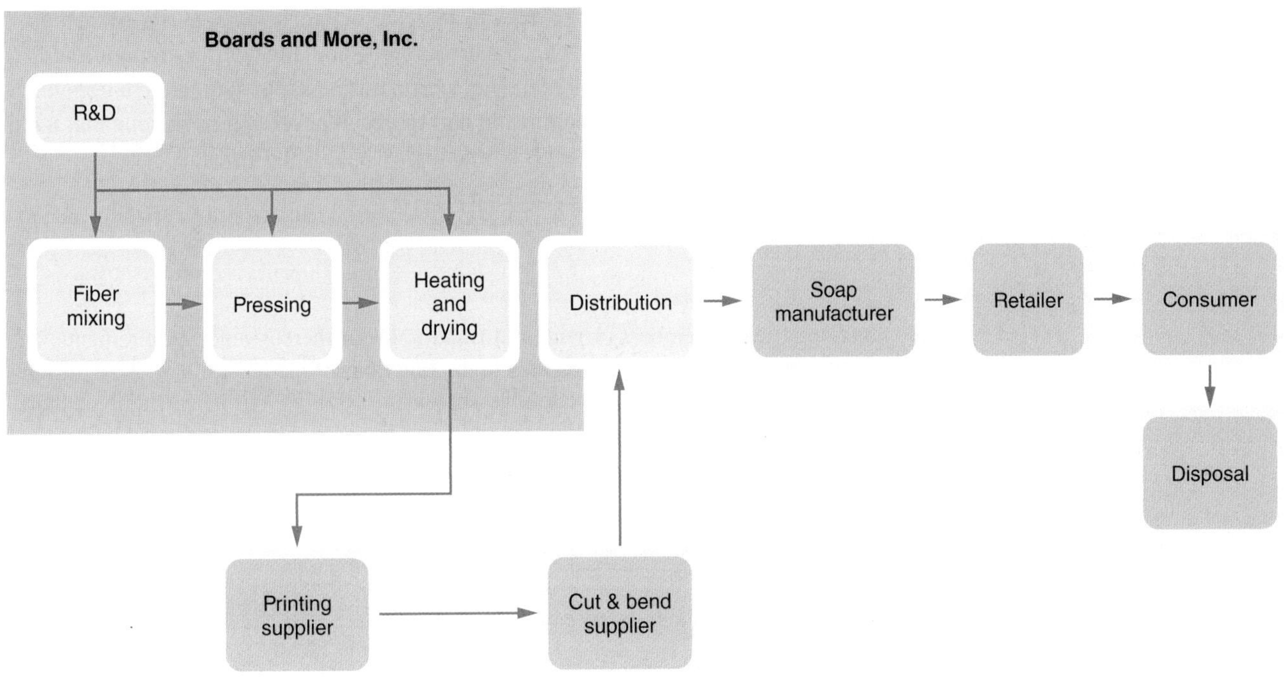

In a recent survey of the soap box market by Boards and More's Marketing and Planning Department, customers expressed dissatisfaction with currently available packaging. Further analysis reveals soap manufacturers believe the packaging is too heavy, increasing their shipping costs. Soap consumers are also unhappy with the ink used because, when the boxes get wet, the printing bleeds or rubs off.

The customer affects target costs

A cross-functional, cross-organizational team is assembled to create a product to satisfy customer needs. Notice that two sets of customers, both in the value chain, are important: the soap manufacturer and the soap consumer. The product creation team consists of marketing, design engineering, accounting, and production engineering personnel from Boards and More and similar personnel from the printing firm and the soap company. The charge to the team is to create new paperboard for the cardboard soap boxes that satisfies customers' needs.

The entire value chain affects target costs

Observe that, although Boards and More leads the new product team, all members of the value chain should participate in new product creation. If the new cardboard created by Boards and More is of a lighter weight but cannot properly absorb ink, then the solution is not viable. Similarly, if the cardboard is lightweight but its strength does not allow proper filling by the machinery at the soap manufacturer, then the solution is not feasible. Finally, in addition to the design changes that Boards and More considers undertaking, other team members from the printing or soap companies may want to modify or change their processes to satisfy the ultimate customer, the soap consumer.

YOUR TURN **You as a Team Leader**

Assume you are the leader of the Boards and More product creation team for the new soap box design. At the initial meeting of the cross-organizational team, a serious reservation is raised by the team members from the printing firm about the confidentiality and intellectual properties of any new designs created by the overall team. The printing firm has a policy of keeping all printing formulas and processes secret to protect its competitive advantage in the marketplace. The printing firm team members point out that five years ago Boards and More engineers used an idea that they got while talking with the engineers from the printing firm. The reservations of the printing firm representatives are so serious that the viability of the soap box design project is threatened. What should you do?

(See our comments on the Online Learning Center Web site.)

The marketing team members provide information about the customer requirements, and the design engineers link those requirements to the functions of the paperboard. A small sample of relevant requirements and functions is shown in Exhibit 19–7. The "high" or "low" indicates the importance of the function in satisfying the requirement and the "+" or "−" indicates if the function and requirement are positively or negatively associated.

Exhibit 19–7
PRODUCT FUNCTION ANALYSIS

		Cardboard Function	
	Requirements	**Ability to Bend and Cut**	**Absorption Rate**
Soap consumer requirements	Box is easy to pour	High (+)	Low
	Ink does not bleed when wet	Low	High (+)
Soap manufacturer requirements	Box is lightweight for shipping	High (+)	High (+)
	Box is strong for filling	High (−)	Low

The requirements/functions table helps the design engineers to focus on product functions that can best meet the needs of the customers. In this case, the ability to bend and cut the cardboard is very important for how easy the box is to pour, its weight, and its strength. Unfortunately, the current technology in paperboard implies that, although lightweight cardboard is easier to bend and cut and is easier for the consumer to pour, it is not strong enough to meet the soap manufacturer's requirements. It seems clear from Exhibit 19–7 that if the box could be made stronger while simultaneously maintaining light weight and high absorption, several consumer requirements could be met. Of course, the problem of the additional cost associated with the lighter weight paperboard must be considered.

The marketing members of the team must determine the target price consumers are willing to pay to gain the desired requirements. After market surveys, it becomes clear that soap consumers are unwilling to pay more than the current price of $4.50 per box for the desired requirements. The soap manufacturer is thus unwilling to increase the amount it pays to Boards and More, $2.30, for the printed soap boxes.

Competitors' actions affect target costs

Additional investigation reveals competitors are about to release new packaging designed to solve some of these problems—plastic bottles. The plastic bottles are lightweight and strong and have labels that eliminate the printing problems. Although this new packaging approach does not require a price increase, the head marketing and engineering managers at Boards and More are skeptical of its acceptance by soap consumers because of pouring problems. The narrow neck of the plastic jug causes the powdered soap to clump together as it pours, creating problems for the consumer. It is clear, however, that competitors are working to solve these problems.

The design engineers, working with the accountants who have gathered ABC information, have come up with a potential solution to meet customer requirements as illustrated in Exhibit 19–8.

The design engineers propose an initial target cost of $1.77. Lowering the wood fiber content of the paperboard and using microscopic plastic fibers that reduce weight and increase strength generates this initial target cost. The new mixture would require fewer pounds of pressure when being rolled but would require longer drying time and higher heat during drying. The paperboard would then be ready for printing. However, the printing company determines the new paperboard would require new printing technology because of absorption problems created by the plastic fibers. The new paperboard would increase printing costs by $0.03 and the total cost by $0.05 per box ($1.72 to $1.77).

Exhibit 19–8

VALUE ENGINEERING TO MEET TARGET COST

	Cardboard—Cost per Box		
Solutions	**Current ABC-Based Cost**	**Initial Target Cost**	**Value Engineered Target Cost**
Fiber mix	$0.52	$0.55	$0.55
Pressing requirements	0.08	0.05	0.05
Drying time	0.04	0.06	0.05
Bend and cut—outsourced	0.33	0.33	0.30
Printing—outsourced	0.75	0.78	0.77
Total	**$1.72**	**$1.77**	**$1.72**

Suppliers affect target costs

Because the initial target cost of $1.77 is too high to maintain previous margins, value engineering becomes critical. Cost must be driven out of the value chain or the proposed solution will not be acceptable. One piece of the value chain not yet considered is the bending and cutting used to create the box. Boards and More approaches the supplier that bends and cuts the boxes before they are shipped to the soap manufacturer. Boards and More asks for a price cut of $0.03 from the current price because the bending and cutting process should be easier and less costly, and the supplier agrees. Then Boards and More suggests splitting the remaining $0.02 of the total cost increase with the printer to achieve the target of $1.72, the price the soap producer is willing to pay. The printer agrees to the $0.01 reduction and Boards and More finds a way to cut $0.01 out of its heating and drying costs. Through value engineering across the value chain, suppliers and producers are able to arrive at the desired target cost.

One aspect of target costing not yet discussed is consideration of product costs over the life of the product. **Life-cycle costing** is the consideration of all potential resources consumed by the product over its entire life. These costs stretch from product development and R&D costs through warranty and disposal costs. In the Boards and More case, if the new paperboard mix for the soap boxes creates additional disposal costs for the soap consumer, these costs must be considered. For example, Boards and More needs to understand the impact of the new paperboard mix that contains plastic fibers on the ability of consumers to recycle the soap boxes and on their own potential environmental costs. These additional product life-cycle considerations are a formal part of the target costing process.

CHARACTERISTICS OF THE TARGET COSTING PROCESS

Learning Objective
LO5 Identify the relationship between target costing and the value chain.

Notice several characteristics in our illustration of the target costing process. First, the entire value chain is involved in driving cost out while satisfying customer needs. Second, process understanding is the cornerstone of target costing. A clear understanding of the connection between the key components of the process and the associated costs is critical for focusing value engineering efforts. Third, target costing requires an emphasis on the product's functional characteristics and their importance to the customer. Fourth, a primary objective of the target costing process is to reduce development time. The cross-functional, cross-organizational team approach allows for simultaneous, rather than sequential, consideration of possible solutions, speeding up new product development time. Finally, ABC information is very useful in determining which process changes will drive costs out of the activities necessary to achieve the target cost.

Just-in-Time Inventory Procedures

One approach used to drive cost out of the production process is a **just-in-time (JIT) manufacturing system.** The phrase "just in time" refers to acquiring materials and manufacturing goods only as needed to fill customer orders. JIT systems are sometimes described as *demand pull* manufacturing because production is totally driven by customer demand. This contrasts with more traditional *supply push* systems in which manufacturers simply produce as many goods as possible.

A JIT system is characterized by extremely small or nonexistent inventories of materials, work in process, and finished goods. As shown in Exhibit 19–9 materials are scheduled to

Exhibit 19–9

JIT CHARACTERISTICS ACROSS THE VALUE CHAIN

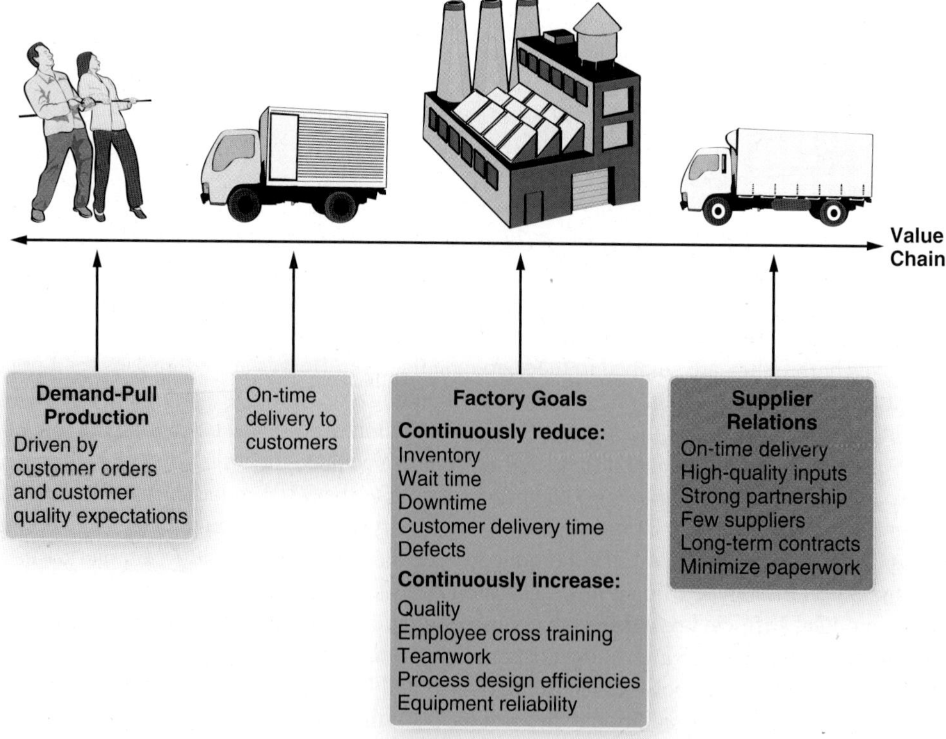

arrive only as needed, and products flow quickly from one production process to the next without wait time or downtime. Finished goods in excess of existing customer orders are not produced. One goal of a JIT system is to reduce or eliminate costs associated with storing inventory, most of which *do not add value* to the product.[2]

JIT is part of a philosophy of *eliminating non-value-added activities* and *increasing product quality* throughout the manufacturing process. As discussed previously, the term *non-value-added activities* refers to those functions that *do not* directly increase the worth of a product to a customer. Examples of non-value-added activities include storing direct materials, setting up machinery, and time during which machinery or employees stand idle.

Just-in-time strives to eliminate non-value-added activities

JIT, SUPPLIER RELATIONSHIPS, AND PRODUCT QUALITY

Learning Objective
Explain the nature and goals of a just-in-time (JIT) manufacturing system. LO6

Perhaps the most important goal of a successful JIT system is to control product costs without sacrificing product quality. This goal is achieved, in part, by cultivating strong and lasting relationships with a limited number of select suppliers. Reliable vendor relationships are essential for achieving long-term quality, even if vendor prices are not the lowest available. In fact, slightly higher prices related to higher quality may actually result in *quality improvement and cost savings* in the long run because a JIT manufacturer can then reduce the time devoted to inspecting and testing materials received.

Exhibit 19–9 shows that implementing a successful JIT system involves much more than reliable vendor relationships. The workers in a JIT system must be extremely versatile. Since products are produced only as needed, workers must be able to shift quickly from the production of one product to another. To do so, they must learn to perform various tasks and operate different machines. Many companies have found that this concept of *flexible manufacturing* improves employee morale, skill, and productivity.

In order to accommodate the demands of flexible manufacturing within a JIT system, an efficient plant layout is critical. Machines used in sequential order must be close to each other to achieve a smooth and rapid flow of work in process. Since machinery downtime can interrupt the entire production process, *equipment reliability* is also a vital concern. To help ensure reliability, workers in JIT systems are often trained to perform *preventive maintenance* on the machinery they use and make many routine repairs themselves.

MEASURES OF EFFICIENCY IN A JIT SYSTEM

Timing is of critical importance in a JIT system. Therefore, time measurements are essential for scheduling production activities in a manner that avoids bottlenecks and ensures that jobs are completed "just in time."

The length of time required for a product to pass completely through a manufacturing process is called the **cycle time.** The cycle time is often viewed as containing four separate elements: (1) processing time, (2) storage and waiting time, (3) movement time, and (4) inspection time. *Only during processing time, however, is value added to the product.* Ideally, the other elements of a product's cycle time should be reduced as much as possible.

A widely used measure of efficiency in a JIT system is the **manufacturing efficiency ratio** (or throughput ratio). This measure expresses the time spent in value-added activities (processing activities) as a percentage of total cycle time. The ratio is calculated as follows:

$$\textbf{Manufacturing Efficiency Ratio} = \frac{\textbf{Value-Added Time}}{\textbf{Cycle Time}}$$

The optimal efficiency ratio is *100 percent,* which indicates that *no* time is being spent on non-value-added activities. In practice, however, this ratio is always considerably less than 100 percent. But in many cases, this ratio should provide managers with a wake-up call. Companies that have not made concerted efforts to improve efficiency sometimes have manufacturing efficiency ratios *less than 10 percent.* Improvements in efficiency often translate directly into cost savings for a company.

[2] Factors considered in determining the optimal size of inventories were discussed in Chapter 8.

Measuring Quality Accounting systems in JIT companies measure *quality,* as well as costs and cycle times. One widely used measure of production quality is *defects per million* units produced. In some companies, defect rates have been reduced to less than one defective part per million units of production. Other measures of quality include merchandise returns, number of warranty claims, customer complaints, and the results of customer satisfaction surveys.

A JIT system does not, in itself, ensure quality. Rather, it establishes *striving for quality* as a basic goal of the organization.

Total Quality Management and the Value Chain

The widespread adoption of JIT techniques demonstrates that current global competitive market conditions require firms to compete on quality and costs. The cost of ignoring quality is very high, most notably from lost sales. Companies that are able to compete globally on quality and cost inevitably have well-developed **total quality management (TQM)** processes. Total quality management includes assigning responsibility for managing quality, providing good quality measures for decision making, and evaluating and rewarding quality performance. Accountants participate in this measurement and reporting process by designing systems that can track quality and assign cost to quality failures.

Learning Objective
LO7 Identify the components of the cost of quality.

COMPONENTS OF THE COST OF QUALITY

Four components of quality are typically considered when designing a measurement system to track quality costs:

- *Prevention costs* refer to the cost of resources consumed in activities that prevent defects from occurring. Examples include employee training, quality process audits, quality concern issues embedded in target costing processes for new products, and supplier quality evaluations.
- *Appraisal costs* are incurred to determine whether products conform to quality standards. Examples include inspection of incoming supplies and materials, in-process inventories, and finished goods; inspection and monitoring of production processes; and inspection of testing equipment to ensure quality.
- *Internal failure costs* include additional production-related costs incurred to correct low-quality output. Examples include rework, downtime, engineering change orders, scrap, retesting, and reinspection.
- *External failure costs* are the largest and most difficult to measure. These costs are incurred because quality failures are allowed to enter the market. They include lost sales, costs due to returns and allowances, warranty costs, product liability costs, and lost goodwill.

These four types of quality costs are not independent. Obviously, if more time and effort are spent ensuring that defective goods do not leave the firm, lower external failure costs are likely. In fact, these quality cost trade-offs have been identified and are represented by the graph in Exhibit 19–10.

The graph demonstrates that, as more resources are consumed in the prevention and appraisal categories, the costs associated with external and internal failures will decline. Designing processes to produce high-quality units through prevention of failures pays off in lower rework, higher customer satisfaction, more repeat business, and lower warranty costs, among other benefits. A focus on prevention occurs during the target costing process described earlier. But prevention also includes identifying high-quality suppliers, as discussed in the section about just-in-time inventory procedures.

The arrows in Exhibit 19–10 show a phenomenon that has been occurring over the past 20 years. Prior to computerized equipment becoming commonplace in manufacturing plants and offices, quality had to be inspected into the product through the consumption of labor resources. Using labor to inspect all incoming raw materials, work in process on the shop floor, and finished goods is very expensive and not as reliable as might be desired. The use of computerized technology to perform quality inspections has reduced appraisal costs and improved appraisal reliability. The reduction in appraisal and prevention costs has shifted the cost curves, making high quality a less costly option.

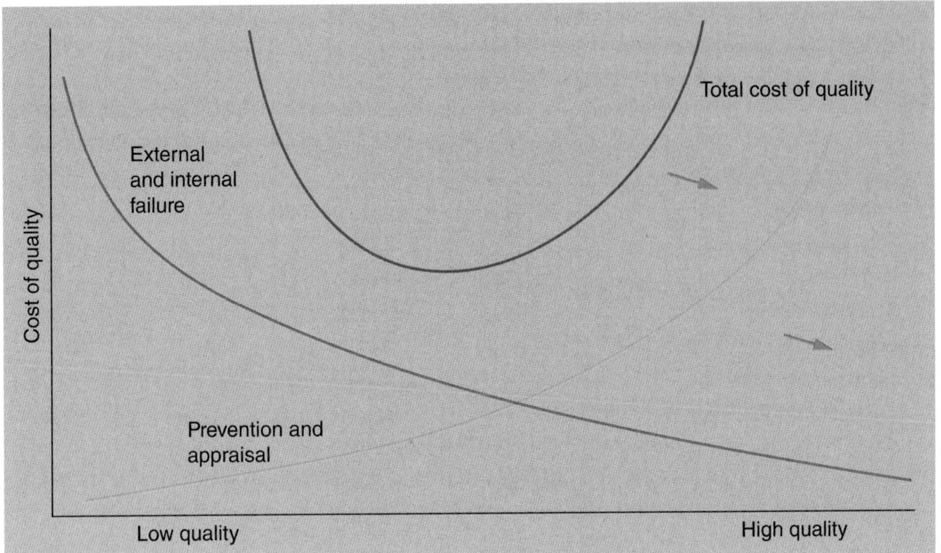

Exhibit 19–10
GRAPH ILLUSTRATING QUALITY COSTS

A second, important development leading to the prominence of TQM is the recognition of the interconnectedness of the value chain. If quality is low in one part of the value chain, quality costs can increase for all components in that chain. A supplier providing low-quality inputs can cause the buyer to incur rework and warranty expenses. A retailer that provides low-quality access for the consumer will hurt sales and affect the entire value chain. Therefore, the entire value chain must participate in a total quality management approach.

CASE IN POINT

Six Sigma is a complementary process many companies use with total quality management. Six Sigma, a business management strategy originally developed by **Motorola**, has been described as TQM on steroids. The central idea behind Six Sigma is that if you can measure how many "defects" you have in a process, you can systematically figure out how to eliminate defects getting as close to "zero defects" as possible. In Six Sigma, a defect is defined as any process output that does not meet customer specifications, or that could lead to creating an output that does not meet customer specifications. To achieve Six Sigma quality, a process must produce no more than 3.4 defects per million opportunities (i.e., 99.99966% error-free).

Many companies use Six Sigma techniques to improve business and manufacturing processes. For example, **General Electric Company** has made Six Sigma part of its corporate culture because they believe their competitive environment leaves no room for error. However, critics of the approach suggest that it can stifle creativity by focusing too many resources on existing processes rather than on new business opportunities.

MEASURING THE COST OF QUALITY

Learning Objective **Describe the characteristics of quality measures.** **LO8**

Quality is a multidimensional concept. Multiple measures are necessary to capture the varied aspects of quality. Most firms begin by creating a cost of quality report based on the four components of quality discussed previously. Exhibit 19–11 shows an example of such a quarterly report for Boards and More, Inc.

Simply reporting quality costs is only the first step in managing the associated activities. Twenty thousand dollars in lost sales is a significant non-value-added cost that Boards and More would like to eliminate. In order to eliminate these costs, management must understand and track the activities that created them. In other words, management must determine the

Exhibit 19-11

A QUALITY COST REPORT

BOARDS AND MORE, INC. QUALITY COST REPORT FOR QUARTER ENDED SEPTEMBER 30, 2011			
	Cost	**TQM Category Cost**	**Percentage of Sales**
Prevention costs:			
Training	$12,000		
Maintenance	10,000		
Quality planning	8,000	$30,000	3.2%
Appraisal costs:			
Inspections—Materials	6,000		
Inspections—Equipment	2,000		
Inspections—Work in process	4,000		
Testing equipment	5,000	17,000	1.8
Internal failure costs:			
Rework	5,000		
Downtime	7,000		
Scrap	8,000	20,000	2.1
External failure costs:			
Warranty	4,500		
Lost sales	20,000		
Repairs	6,500	31,000	3.3
Totals		$98,000	10.4%

cost drivers of lost sales, rework, warranty costs, and so on. Measuring and managing quality requires multiple measures of these cost drivers. Customer satisfaction surveys, vendor rating systems, measures of manufacturing defect rates, downtime, on-time deliveries, and so on are tracked and measured by companies using total quality management approaches.

PRODUCTIVITY AND QUALITY

Measuring quality without simultaneous concern for productivity can be a recipe for bankruptcy. Quality and productivity are ultimately linked, and managers prefer to undertake activities that reduce the costs associated with low quality *and* increase productivity. Fortunately, this is often possible. Managers frequently find that activities that reduce scrap and rework also increase productivity.

Ethics, Fraud & Corporate Governance

In order to increase the likelihood that public companies prepare accurate and reliable financial statements, the Sarbanes-Oxley Act requires public companies and their auditors to issue separate reports on the effectiveness of their internal control structures. The internal control structure includes all measures used by an organization to guard against errors, waste, and fraud (non-value-added activities), with the objective of ensuring the quality and reliability of accounting information. Because a company's value chain typically includes transactions recorded in accounting records, the internal control structure must take into account the reliability of the entire value chain.

The requirement that companies issue audited reports on the effectiveness of their internal control structures has been expensive. As a result, it has been very unpopular with some segments of the business community, who question whether these audited reports are value-added. In particular, smaller public companies have complained that the costs of internal control reporting place a disproportionate burden on them given their smaller size.

Productivity is usually measured by comparing inputs and outputs. Quality improvements are evident when the amount of input is reduced for a given, fixed level of output. In the quality cost report, the column labeled "Percentage of Sales" is a productivity measure. The outputs are sales dollars and the inputs are the resources consumed by quality-related activities. Increases in quality for Boards and More are signaled by a decrease in the total quality cost as a percentage of sales dollars. Earlier in this chapter, we discussed another productivity measure—the JIT manufacturing efficiency ratio. It compares the input, value-added time, and the output, cycle time, to obtain a measure of productivity throughput.

Concluding Remarks

We have identified four techniques commonly used by organizations to manage costs over their value chain. The underlying objective of these four techniques—activity-based management, the target costing process, just-in-time procedures, and total quality management—is to eliminate non-value-added activities from the value chain. This objective is achieved by assigning employees the responsibility for managing these non-value-added activities, providing information about the cost of these activities, and rewarding managers who eliminate these activities. The customer ultimately defines non-value-added activities. It is true that, in determining the shape and structure of the value chain, the customer is king.

END-OF-CHAPTER REVIEW

SUMMARY OF LEARNING OBJECTIVES

LO1 Define the value chain and describe its basic components. We define the value chain as the set of activities and resources necessary to create and deliver the product or service valued by customers. Its basic components include research and development, production and supplier relations, marketing and distribution, and customer service activities.

LO2 Distinguish between non-value-added and value-added activities. Value-added activities add to the product's or service's desirability in the eyes of the consumer. Non-value-added activities do not add to the product's desirability.

LO3 Explain how activity-based management is related to activity-based costing (ABC). Activity-based management requires an understanding of the link between activities that consume resources and the costs associated with those resources. The objective of ABC is to create the cost per unit of a measured cost driver. The objective of activity-based management is to manage the activities that drive those costs.

LO4 Describe the target costing process and list its components. Target costing is a business process aimed at the earliest stages of new product and service development. The components of target costing consist of concept development through planning and market analysis; product development using value engineering; and production with continuous improvement goals.

LO5 Identify the relationship between target costing and the value chain. The entire value chain is involved in the target costing process to identify activities that drive cost out while satisfying customer needs. A primary objective of the target costing process is to reduce development time. The cross-functional, cross-organizational value chain approach allows for simultaneous, rather than sequential, consideration of possible solutions, speeding up new product development time.

LO6 Explain the nature and goals of a just-in-time (JIT) manufacturing system. In a JIT system, materials are acquired and goods are produced just in time to meet sales requirements. Thus, production is pulled by customer demand, rather than pushed by an effort to produce inventory. The goals of a JIT system are to eliminate (minimize) non-value-added activities and to increase the focus on product quality throughout the production process.

LO7 Identify the components of the cost of quality. Quality costs are classified into four groups: (1) costs associated with preventing poor quality from occurring, (2) costs of appraising and inspecting quality into the product, (3) internal failure costs that are incurred to correct quality problems before the customer receives the good or service, and (4) external failure costs that happen when an unsatisfactory good or service is delivered to a customer.

LO8 Describe the characteristics of quality measures. Quality measures must be customer focused because quality failures can be identified only by customers. These measures should be multidimensional, including both financial and nonfinancial components, to help management focus on activities that drive quality costs.

Key Terms Introduced or Emphasized in Chapter 19

activity-based management (p. 844) The process of using activity-based costs to help reduce and eliminate non-value-added activities.

cycle time (p. 853) The length of time for a product to pass completely through a specific manufacturing process or the manufacturing process viewed as a whole. Used as a measure of efficiency in JIT systems.

just-in-time (JIT) manufacturing system (p. 852) An approach to manufacturing that reduces or eliminates non-value-added activities, such as maintenance of inventories. Focuses on both efficiency and product quality.

life-cycle costing (p. 851) The consideration of all potential resources consumed by the product over its entire life. It is an important part of the target costing process where target costing teams estimate all potential costs to the consumer over the product's life.

manufacturing efficiency ratio (p. 853) Processing time stated as a percentage of cycle time. Used as a measure of efficiency in JIT systems.

non-value-added activity (p. 842) An activity within the value chain that does not make the product or service more valuable to the customer.

Six Sigma (p. 855) A process used by companies to eliminate defects in a process with a goal of as close to zero defects as possible.

target costing (p. 847) A business process aimed at the earliest stages of new product and service development, before creation and design of production methods. It is a process driven by the customer, focused on design, and encompassing the entire life of the product.

total quality management (TQM) (p. 854) An approach to eliminating wasteful activities and improving quality throughout the value chain by assigning quality management responsibility, monitoring quality costs, and rewarding low-cost, high-quality results.

value-added activity (p. 842) An activity within the value chain that makes the product or service more valuable to the customer.

value chain (p. 842) The set of activities necessary to create and distribute a desirable product or service to a customer.

value engineering (p. 848) The methods used by engineers and production personnel to determine the least costly combination of resources to create a product desired by the customer.

Demonstration Problem

At the beginning of 2011, Suskin, Inc., initiated a quality improvement program. Considerable effort was expended to reduce the number of defective units produced. By the end of 2012, reports from the production manager revealed that scrap and rework had both decreased. The CFO was pleased to hear of the success but wanted some assessment of the financial impact of the improvements. To make this assessment, the following financial data were collected for the current and preceding two years:

	2010	2011	2012
Sales	$10,000,000	$10,000,000	$10,000,000
Scrap	450,000	400,000	300,000
Rework	625,000	600,000	400,000
Product inspection	100,000	120,000	125,000
Product warranty	875,000	800,000	600,000
Quality training	20,000	40,000	80,000
Materials inspection	80,000	40,000	40,000

Instructions

a. Classify the costs as prevention, appraisal, internal failure, and external failure.

b. Compute total quality cost as a percentage of sales for each of the three years. By how much has profit increased because of quality improvements between 2010, 2011, and 2012?

c. Graph the prevention and appraisal costs versus the internal and external failure costs for 2010, 2011, and 2012. Extrapolate the curves to show the optimal quality point.

d. Consider the quality costs as non-value-added activities. Describe how these activities might be eliminated.

Solution to the Demonstration Problem

a.

	Prevention	Appraisal	Internal Failure	External Failure	
	Quality Training	Product and Materials Inspection	Scrap and Rework	Product Warranty	Totals
2010	$20,000	$180,000	$1,075,000	$875,000	$2,150,000
2011	40,000	160,000	1,000,000	800,000	2,000,000
2012	80,000	165,000	700,000	600,000	1,545,000
Change in cost 2010–2011	+20,000	−20,000	−75,000	−75,000	−150,000
Change in cost 2011–2012	+40,000	+5,000	−300,000	−200,000	−455,000

b.

Year	Total Quality Cost ÷ Sales	Profit Increase = Cost Decrease
2010	$2,150,000 ÷ $10,000,000 = 21.5%	
2011	$2,000,000 ÷ $10,000,000 = 20.00%	$2,150,000 − 2,000,000 = $150,000
2012	$1,545,000 ÷ $10,000,000 = 15.45%	$2,000,000 − 1,545,000 = $455,000

c.

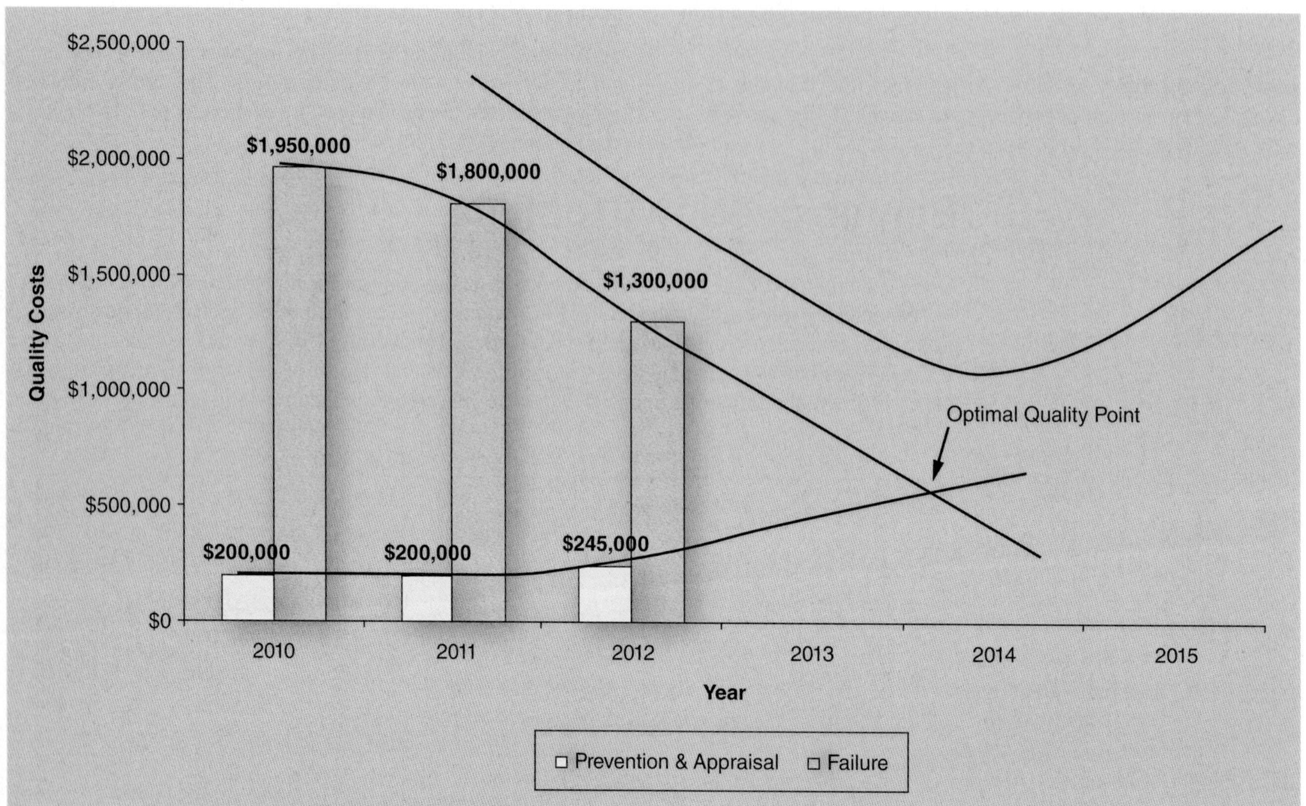

d. Non-value-added activities are those that can be eliminated without reducing the value (that is, increasing the cost or lowering the quality) of the product to the customer. The following example solutions assume that costs to the customer will not increase and quality will be maintained. Many other activities may drive these costs, and other solutions are viable.

Quality Category	Activity	Example Solution
Scrap	Machine problem	New equipment/better maintenance
	Labor problem	Quality training and/or incentives
Rework	Too many parts	Value engineering
	Employee carelessness	Quality training and/or incentives
Product inspection	Poor-quality raw materials	Supplier quality certification programs
	Poor testing equipment	New testing equipment
Product warranty	Inspection failures	Buy more reliable equipment
	Too many parts	Value engineering
Materials inspections	Transportation-in problem	Quality certification for shippers
	Supplier ships poor-quality goods	Quality certification for suppliers

Self-Test Questions

The answers to these questions appear on page 877.

1. Which of the following would be considered non-value-added activities by a bakery's bread customers?

   a. The mixing of flour, eggs, milk, and other ingredients into bread dough.

   b. Baking the bread.

   c. Shipping the loaves to a warehouse to await distribution to local stores.

   d. Delivering loaves to local stores.

   e. Rotating bread stock in the stores so that older loaves are sold first.

2. Premo Pens, Inc., is in the process of developing a new pen to replace its existing top-of-the-line Executive Model. Market research has identified the critical features the pen must have, and it is estimated that customers would be willing to pay $30 for a pen with these features. Premo's production manager estimates that with existing equipment it will cost $26 to produce the proposed model. The current Executive Model sells for $24 and has a total production cost of $20. A competitor sells a pen similar to the proposed model, but without Premo's patented easy retract feature, for $28. It is estimated to cost the competitor $25 to produce. If Premo seeks to earn a 20 percent return on sales on the new model, which of the following represents the target cost for the new pen?
   - **a.** $26.00.
   - **b.** $22.40.
   - **c.** $24.00.
   - **d.** $19.80.
3. JIT inventory systems strive to:
   - **a.** Cultivate long-term relationships with a select group of reliable suppliers.
   - **b.** Keep inventories at minimal levels.
   - **c.** Improve overall product quality.
   - **d.** All of the above.
4. Which of the following would *not* be considered a cost of quality?
   - **a.** Lost sales due to bad publicity generated by product failures.
   - **b.** The cost of repairing merchandise that was dropped by a forklift in the factory.
   - **c.** The amount of a bonus paid to the work team producing the fewest defective units.
   - **d.** The cost of the external audit.
5. Which of the following would *not* be classified as an external failure cost?
   - **a.** Extra shipping charges incurred to rush a customer an order that was delayed for rework.
   - **b.** Costs incurred for a product recall.
   - **c.** The cost of product liability insurance.
   - **d.** The cost of maintaining a customer complaint hotline.

ASSIGNMENT MATERIAL Discussion Questions

1. What are three important criteria for successful business process management?
2. Suppose you are interested in opening up a new restaurant in your area. What specific activities would you undertake in the research and development and design stage of the value chain for the restaurant?
3. What activities would make up the marketing and distribution component of the value chain of a local fire department?
4. Distinguish between value-added and non-value-added activities and provide an example of each.
5. Assume you are the manager of the finished goods warehouse of a stereo manufacturer. What costs are being incurred as stereos are stored while awaiting shipment to retail stores?
6. Why is target costing most effectively applied at the research and development and production process design stage of the value chain?
7. What is the objective of activity-based management and how does it differ from activity-based costing?
8. Why is the output of a JIT system likely to contain fewer defective units than the output of a traditional manufacturing system?
9. Why is JIT often described as a "philosophy," rather than as an inventory management technique?
10. List and describe the four components of the cost of quality and provide examples of each.
11. What is life-cycle costing and why should it be used in the target costing process?
12. Explain why the selection of cost drivers is an important part of identifying non-value-added activities.
13. Some managers believe machine performance is more important in a JIT environment than in a non-JIT environment. Do you agree or disagree? Explain your answer.
14. Why is it so important that target costing procedures focus on the customer?
15. What are the four components of target costing? Why are each of these components important for target costing?

Brief Exercises

LO1 BRIEF EXERCISE 19.1
Value Chain Components

SailRight Boat Company builds and sells small sailboats. Identify at least four specific components of SailRight's value chain. For each component describe what activities might take place in that part of the value chain.

LO4 BRIEF EXERCISE 19.2
Capturing Market Share with Target Prices

Assume Bracy's, a retail establishment, wants to capture a 30 percent share of the evening gown market. In order to capture that share, it has determined that the average price of an evening gown should be $450.00. Bracy's requires a 25 percent markup on all clothing lines. What is the target cost for the average evening gown?

LO7 BRIEF EXERCISE 19.3
Cost of Quality

Identify a restaurant where you have dined. Identify some of the types of costs that the restaurant incurs in each of the four cost-of-quality categories. Consider how those costs are related to each other.

LO2 BRIEF EXERCISE 19.4
Cost Reduction Non-Value-Added Activities

Identify a non-value-added activity at a grocery store, a bank, and a hotel. Explain how each organization might be able to eliminate the non-value-added activity identified.

LO6 BRIEF EXERCISE 19.5
Manufacturing Efficiency in a JIT System

Bronigan's, a maker of handheld video games, recently analyzed its manufacturing process to identify value-added and non-value-added activities. Bronigan's found that the total non-value-added manufacturing time associated with producing the average game was 12 hours and the total time to produce the average game was 16 hours. What is the manufacturing efficiency ratio for game production at Bronigan's?

LO2 LO3 LO7 BRIEF EXERCISE 19.6
Activity-Based Management Cost Savings

An activity analysis at Loaf's End Bread Company found the following activities for its bread makers: 10 percent of time, adding ingredients; 60 percent of time, mixing and kneading dough; 10 percent of time, shaping into loaves; and 10 percent of time, cleaning up. The total salary and benefits cost pool for bread makers is $850,000 per year. Loaf's End is considering buying new equipment that would reduce the time required to mix and knead by 80 percent. What is the potential savings to Loaf's End per year if it acquires the new equipment? What other value chain and quality issues, besides cost savings, should be considered?

LO4 BRIEF EXERCISE 19.7
Target Costing

Assume you've just started a new business to manufacture **Weed Be-Gone**, a new electronic gizmo that zaps weeds. Your business analyst tells you that in the long run **Weed Be-Gone** will sell for $12.50 because, after a few years pass, similar products will be introduced by your competitors. Assume that, in the long run, you want to earn $2.50 on each unit of **Weed Be-Gone** sold. What is the target price? What is the target profit? What is the target cost?

LO7 BRIEF EXERCISE 19.8
Cost of Quality

Mark each of the following as true or false:

a. Total quality costs are covered by external failure and appraisal costs.
b. Traditional job order costing systems identify and account for quality costs.
c. A rise in internal failures means higher appraisal costs.
d. Quality can pay for itself.
e. As the amount of rework rises, the internal failure costs rise, but external failure costs should fall.
f. Higher quality often leads to higher productivity.
g. Just-in-time manufacturing typically requires tracking of quality costs.
h. Internal and external failure costs are independent.

LO8 BRIEF EXERCISE 19.9
Characteristics of Quality

Acme International hired a consulting firm to determine if it had any quality-related problems. The consulting firm spent two months reviewing all processes at Acme and suggested that Acme buy new equipment to reduce throughput time. Then the consulting firm billed Acme $50,000 for services rendered. Should Acme be happy with the consulting firm's work related to product quality? Why or why not?

LO5 BRIEF EXERCISE 19.10
Target Costing Cash Flows

Team members involved in the target costing process should consider the current and *future* effects of their proposed solutions to arrive at the proposed target cost. Assume in the Boards and More example illustrated in Exhibit 19–8 that one proposed solution is to acquire new heating and drying equipment for the new paperboard mix. Assume the new equipment has a purchase price of $500,000 and is expected to increase the annual depreciation expense from $100,000 to $150,000 per year. What are the cash flow consequences to paperboard in the current year? In future years?

Exercises

LO2 through LO6 **EXERCISE 19.1** Accounting Terminology

The following are eight technical accounting terms introduced or emphasized in this chapter:

Activity-based management	Total quality management
Just-in-time manufacturing system	Target costing
Life-cycle costing	Value-added activity
Non-value-added activity	Value engineering

Each of the following statements may (or may not) describe one of these terms. For each statement, indicate the accounting term described, or answer "none" if the statement does not correctly describe any of these terms.

a. Can be eliminated without changing a product's desirability in the eyes of consumers.

b. The focus of this costing method is to assign manufacturing costs to final products.

c. The process of determining the least costly combination of resources needed to create a product desired by customers.

d. This method considers all costs borne by the consumer from purchase to disposal of a product.

e. If eliminated, the product's desirability to consumers is decreased.

f. The process of using activity-based costs to help reduce and eliminate non-value-added activities.

g. A method in which a product's selling price is determined by adding a fixed amount to the product's current production cost.

h. An approach that explicitly monitors quality costs and rewards quality-enhancing behavior.

i. An important aspect of this method is the reduction of unnecessary inventories.

LO1 **EXERCISE 19.2** Value-Chain Activities

Assume you have just been hired as the management accountant in charge of providing your firm's managers with product cost information. Identify the activities you might undertake for the following four value chain components:

a. Research and development

b. Production

c. Marketing

d. Customer service

LO2 LO3 **EXERCISE 19.3** Value-Added versus Non-Value-Added Activities

Dainty Diners, Inc., produces various types of bird feeders. The following is a detailed description of the steps involved in the production of wooden bird feeders:

1. Raw materials, such as wood, nails, and clear plastic are purchased.
2. The raw materials are unloaded from the delivery truck into a raw materials storage area.
3. The purchase order is checked for accuracy by an employee doing a visual count of the items.
4. The materials are inspected for defects such as rotting, excessive knots, and scratches.
5. The Cutting Department orders raw materials by sending a requisition form to the raw materials storage area.
6. When a requisition is received, raw materials are moved from the storage area to the Cutting Department.
7. The wood and plastic are cut into properly sized pieces.
8. The cut pieces are stacked and moved to a work in process warehouse.
9. The Assembly Department orders cut pieces when they are needed by sending a requisition form to the work in process warehouse.
10. When a requisition is received, cut pieces are moved from the work in process warehouse to the Assembly Department.
11. The cut pieces are assembled into a bird feeder.

a. For each of the above steps, indicate whether it is a value-added or non-value-added activity.

b. For each of the non-value-added activities, determine whether it can be eliminated; if it cannot be eliminated, suggest ways in which the costs could be minimized or productive efficiency increased.

LO3 **EXERCISE 19.4**
Activity-Based Management

Blake Furniture, Inc., maintains an Accounts Receivable Department that currently employs eight people. Blake is interested in doing an activity analysis because an outside firm has offered to take over a portion of the activities currently handled by the Accounts Receivable Department. The four main activities handled by the department are (1) billing and recording payments, (2) customer service activities, (3) financial reporting and analysis, and (4) collecting delinquent accounts.

The salaries paid to the department's employees are as follows:

Manager, 1 @ $65,000 per year	$ 65,000
Clerks, 5 @ $30,000 per year	150,000
Account specialists, 2 @ $38,000 per year	76,000
Total	$291,000

It is estimated that the manager of the Accounts Receivable Department spends an equal amount of her time supervising the four main activities. The clerks spend approximately half of their time on billing and recording payments. Their remaining time is divided equally between reporting activities and customer service. The two account specialists spend half of their time on delinquent account activities, and the rest of their time is split equally between financial analysis activities and customer service activities that the clerks are not qualified to perform.

Paypro, Inc., has proposed that it can perform all the activities related to collecting delinquent accounts for a fee of $50,000 per year. The manager of Paypro argues that Blake can save $26,000 because the $76,000 in salaries paid to the specialists who currently handle all delinquent accounts can be eliminated. If the contract is accepted, it is estimated that the manager of the Accounts Receivable Department would need to devote a quarter of her time to dealing with Paypro employees.

a. Using the information given, prepare an activity table such as that in Exhibit 19–3 on page 846 to calculate the labor cost for personnel devoted to each of the four main activities of the Accounts Receivable Department.

b. Should Blake accept Paypro's offer to take over its delinquent account activities?

LO4 LO5 **EXERCISE 19.5**
Target Costing

On Point, Inc., is interested in producing and selling a deluxe electric pencil sharpener. Market research indicates that customers are willing to pay $40 for such a sharpener and that 20,000 units could be sold each year at this price. The cost to produce the sharpener is currently estimated to be $34.

a. If On Point requires a 20 percent return on sales to undertake production of a product, what is the target cost for the new pencil sharpener?

b. If a competitor sells basically the same sharpener for $36, what would On Point's target cost be to maintain a 20 percent return on sales?

c. At a price of $36, On Point estimates that it can sell 21,000 sharpeners per year. Assuming target costs are reached, would On Point earn more or less profit per year at the $36 selling price compared to the original estimated selling price of $40?

LO6 **EXERCISE 19.6**
Just-in-Time Manufacturing

Nanner Corporation is trying to determine how long it takes for one product to pass through the production process. The following information was gathered regarding how many days the product spent in various production activities:

Activity	Number of Days
Inspection	5
Storage	6
Assembly	3
Handling	2
Painting	3
Packaging	1

a. Which of the above activities are value-added?

b. What is Nanner's total cycle time?

c. Determine Nanner's manufacturing efficiency ratio.

d. If Nanner implements a total quality management program and a just-in-time inventory system, which of the above activities could be eliminated? What would be the change in Nanner's manufacturing efficiency ratio?

LO7 LO8

EXERCISE 19.7

Cost of Quality

Chris Hines is the manager of Lumble Manufacturing and is interested in doing a cost of quality analysis. The following cost and revenue data are available for the most recent year ended December 31:

Sales revenue	$250,000
Cost of goods sold	140,000
Warranty expense	22,000
Inspection costs	12,000
Scrap and rework	8,000
Product returns due to defects	6,000
Depreciation expense	10,000
Machine maintenance expense	2,000
Wage expense	35,000
Machine breakdown costs	4,000
Estimated lost sales due to poor quality	5,000

a. Classify each of the above costs into the four quality cost categories and prepare a cost of quality report for Lumble.

b. What percentage of sales revenue is being spent on prevention and appraisal activities?

c. What percentage of sales revenue is being spent on internal and external failure costs?

LO2 LO7

EXERCISE 19.8

Value-Added and Non-Value-Added Activity Costs

The three activities described below were part of the production process in November at Foundry & Bellows, Inc. Describe how each activity creates additional costs and whether it is value-added or non-value-added. If it is non-value-added, identify the associated cost of quality category.

a. The Purchasing Department acquired cheaper materials at a big discount but, in order to get the discount, it had to accept delivery of a six-month supply.

b. When materials were issued to production, they were found to be of low quality and products required extensive rework. As a result, overtime pay was required for 50 employees.

c. The production schedule fell behind because of the additional rework. To meet the production schedule for November, workers were transferred from inspection to direct labor and inspection activities were curtailed.

LO3

EXERCISE 19.9

Activity-Based Management at First Bank

First Bank Corporation is using activity-based cost information to determine whether it can save money by reassigning activities in its bank branches. The following information has been gathered:

	Annual Salary	% Time on Checking Account Customers	% Time on Loan Applicants	% Time Idle
Tellers—8	$25,000	80	5	10
Loan officers—5	$32,000	20	60	15

In its activity analysis, First Bank found that tellers have about 10 percent idle time while they wait for customers to enter the bank. The analysis also showed that tellers are able to help loan applicants complete initial paperwork. Furthermore, the analysis suggested that about 5 percent of loan officers' time is spent helping loan applicants complete initial paperwork.

Could First Bank reduce the number of loan officers at the bank branches if the loan application activity were transferred to the tellers? What other considerations should the bank investigate before assigning the loan application task to the tellers?

LO1 LO2 LO7

EXERCISE 19.10 Quality Costs and Value Chain Decisions

Dust Buster's Inc. manufactures two types of small hand-operated vacuum cleaners. Dust Busters is concerned about quality issues and has compiled the following information for the past year associated with the two vacuums.

	Heavy Duty	Regular	Activity Costs
Units produced	160,000	320,000	
Warranty work (units)	1,200	620	$118,300
Recalled units	1,600	450	112,750
Reworked units	1,900	520	55,660
Inspection hrs. (incoming materials)	1,530	680	30,940
Inspection hrs. (completed units)	1,720	820	40,640
Quality training hrs.	110	100	31,500
Total Activity Costs			**$389,790**

Find the quality cost per unit for each product. (Round your answer to two decimal places.) Which product has higher quality costs? How might a manager use this quality information to make decisions (e.g., about the production process or about suppliers) related to the value chain?

LO6

EXERCISE 19.11 Just-in-Time Efficiency Measures

The following information is related to manufacturing office furniture at Outreach, Inc.:

a. Accept and arrange raw materials in inventory—1 day.

b. Store raw materials in inventory—5 days.

c. Issue raw materials to various points in the production process—1 day.

d. Use raw materials to manufacture finished goods—3 days.

e. Store finished goods—8 days.

f. Prepare finished goods for shipping—1 day.

Compute the manufacturing efficiency ratio at Outreach.

LO4 LO5

EXERCISE 19.12 Target Costing at Pizza Pies Limited

Pizza Pies Limited has the following value chain for its pizzas. Boxes are designed by Shala Designers Inc. and printed and delivered by Rodoes Printing Co. for $.95 per box. The pizzas are made in the stores with fresh ingredients and baked in the ovens for a total cost of $3.80, including labor, ingredients, and overhead. The pizza delivery costs $1.35. Pizza Pies needs to reduce the price of its pizza to $6.50 to meet local demand. However, it desires a 10 percent markup for profit.

a. What is the target cost? By how much will Pizza Pies need to cut costs in order to achieve the target cost?

b. Identify places in the Pizza Pies Limited value chain where possible savings could be achieved to meet the target cost.

LO2 LO7

EXERCISE 19.13 Classifying Activities

Classify each of the following activities into one of the four cost of quality categories and/or identify it as a value-added or a non-value-added activity.

a. Rework, due to poor materials, on bicycles at **Trek**.

b. Inspection costs incurred by **Walmart** on merchandise purchased from **Mattel, Inc.**

c. Costs incurred by **Walmart** when merchandise, purchased from **Grocers, Inc.**, spoils in its warehouse before shipping to its stores.

d. Work in process inventory wait-and-move time between the lathing and finishing stages in a furniture manufacturing facility.

e. Training for line workers on proper operation of equipment.

f. Recording the number of defects produced each month.

g. Offering customer refunds due to defective products.

h. Waste disposal costs at **Kimberly-Clark**.

LO7 **EXERCISE 19.14**
Quality Cost Trade-offs

Flip Flop's To Go has gathered the following data on its quality costs for the past two years:

	Year 1	Year 2
Prevention costs:		
Quality training	$ 8,000	$10,500
Quality technology	7,500	9,000
Quality production design	4,000	9,000
Failure costs:		
Warranty handling	$15,000	$10,000
Customer reimbursements	11,000	7,200
Customer returns handling	7,000	4,000

a. Compute the percentage change in the total quality costs from year 1 to year 2.

b. Explain what you think caused the change.

LO3 **EXERCISE 19.15**
Home Depot Non-Value-Added Costs

In the **Home Depot** 2009 financial statements in Appendix A at the end of this textbook, find note 1 to the financial statements. Note 1 summarizes significant accounting policies for **Home Depot**. Read the section in Note 1 titled " Merchandise Inventories."

a. Identify **Home Depot**'s definition of "shrink."

b. What are the causes of inventory shrink mentioned by **Home Depot**? Classify those causes as value-added or non-value-added.

c. What methods does **Home Depot** use to measure shrink?

d. How does **Home Depot** account for shrink?

Problem Set A

LO2 LO6 **PROBLEM 19.1A**
Identifying Value-Added and Non-Value-Added Activities

Castner Corporation is considering implementation of a JIT inventory system. The company's industrial engineer recently conducted a study to determine the average number of days spent in each activity of the production process. The following table summarizes her findings:

Production Activity	Number of Days
Inspecting materials	3
Storing materials	17
Moving materials into production	3
Setting up production equipment	2
Cutting materials	6
Bending materials	5
Assembling finished products	9
Painting finished products	5

Instructions

a. Identify Castner's value-added production activities.

b. Identify Castner's non-value-added production activities.

c. Calculate Castner's total cycle time.

d. Determine Castner's manufacturing efficiency ratio.

e. Which of the above activities might be reduced or eliminated if Castner implemented a JIT system?

f. What ethical issues might be related to eliminating some of the non-value-added activities?

LO2 through LO5

PROBLEM 19.2A Activity-Based Management and Target Costing

Kallapur Company manufactures two products: KAP1, which sells for $120; and QUIN, which sells for $220. Estimated cost and production data for the current year are as follows:

	KAP1	QUIN
Direct materials cost	$30	$45
Direct labor cost (@ $12/hr)	$24	$60
Estimated production (units)	25,000	15,000

In addition, fixed manufacturing overhead is estimated to be $2,000,000 and variable overhead is estimated to equal $3 per direct labor hour. Kallapur desires a 15 percent return on sales for all of its products.

Instructions

a. Calculate the target cost for both KAP1 and QUIN.

b. Estimate the total manufacturing cost per unit of each product if fixed overhead costs are assigned to products on the basis of estimated production in units. Which of the products is earning the desired return?

c. Recalculate the total manufacturing cost per unit if fixed overhead costs are assigned to products on the basis of direct labor hours. Which of the products is earning the desired return?

d. On the basis of the confusing results of parts **b** and **c,** Kallapur's manager decides to perform an activity analysis of fixed overhead. The results of the analysis are as follows:

			Demands	
Activity	**Costs**	**Driver**	**KAP1**	**QUIN**
Machine set-ups	$ 400,000	# of set-ups	100	400
Purchase orders	600,000	# of orders	200	100
Machining	500,000	# of machine-hours	2,000	6,000
Inspection	200,000	# of batches	50	30
Shipping to customers	300,000	# of shipments	300	200
Total fixed overhead	$2,000,000			

Estimate the total manufacturing cost per unit of each product if activity-based costing is used for assigning fixed overhead costs. Under this method, which product is earning the desired return?

e. What proportion of fixed overhead is value-added? In attempting to reach the target cost for QUIN, which activity would you look to improving first and why?

f. Kallapur's production manager believes that design changes would reduce the number of set-ups required for QUIN to 25. Fixed overhead costs for set-ups would remain unchanged. What will be the impact of the design changes on the manufacturing costs of both products? Which of the products will earn the desired return?

g. An alternative to the design change is to purchase a new machine that will reduce the number of set-ups for KAP1 to 20 and the number of set-ups for QUIN to 80. The machine will also reduce fixed set-up costs to $200,000. Calculate the manufacturing costs for each product if the machine is purchased. Should QUIN be redesigned or should the machine be purchased? Why?

LO4 LO5

PROBLEM 19.3A Target Costing

Meiger Mining, Inc., has just discovered two new mining sites for iron ore. Geologists and engineers have come up with the estimates on the following page regarding costs and ore yields if the mines are opened:

	Site A	Site B
Variable extraction costs per ton	$3.80	$4.00
Fixed costs over the life of the mine:		
Blasting	$150,000	$185,000
Construction	225,000	240,000
Maintenance	25,000	20,000
Restoration costs	40,000	35,000
Total fixed costs	$440,000	$480,000
Total tons of ore that can be extracted over the life of the mine:	200,000	160,000

Meiger's owners currently demand a return of 20 percent of the market price of iron ore.

Instructions

a. If the current market price of iron ore is $8 per ton, what is Meiger's target cost per ton?

b. Given the $8 market price, should either of the mines be opened?

c. The engineer working on Site B believes that if a custom conveyor system is installed, the variable extraction cost could be reduced to $3 per ton. The purchase price of the system is $25,000, but the costs to restore the site will increase to $45,000 if it is installed. Given the current $8 market price, should Meiger install the conveyor and open Site B?

LO7 LO8

PROBLEM 19.4A
Cost of Quality

eXcel

Arusetta Inc. produces a popular brand of air conditioner that is backed by a five-year warranty. In Year 1, Arusetta began implementing a total quality management program that has resulted in significant changes in its cost of quality. Listed below is Arusetta's financial information relating to sales and quality for Years 1 and 2.

	Year 1	Year 2
Sales revenue	$500,000	$500,000
Warranty expense	22,000	18,500
Product design	5,000	15,000
Scrap	2,000	1,200
Process reengineering	8,000	12,000
Raw materials inspections	4,800	2,300
Product liability claims	5,000	8,500
Rework	3,100	2,800
Returns resulting from defects	7,000	4,500
Supplier certification costs	500	2,500
Preventive maintenance on equipment	1,300	2,600
Final inspection costs	10,000	7,000
Employee quality training	1,200	4,000
Equipment breakdown repair costs	8,500	3,000
Estimate of lost sales due to quality problems	10,000	10,000

Instructions

a. Prepare a cost of quality report for Arusetta covering Year 1 and Year 2. Your report should divide the above costs into the four categories of quality costs and include total dollar amounts for each category.

b. How have the total amounts of prevention and external failure costs changed over the two years? What are some possible explanations for these changes?

c. At Arusetta, preventive maintenance has a direct effect on the repair costs associated with equipment breakdowns. Did the decrease in repair costs justify the increase in maintenance costs?

d. Why might Arusetta's estimate of lost sales remain the same despite the adoption of the total quality management program?

LO1 through LO7

PROBLEM 19.5A
Home Depot's Value Chain

Read note 1 in **Home Depot**'s 2009 financial statements in Appendix A at the end of this textbook. With a group of students identified by your instructor, list answers to the following.

Instructions

a. List the specific categories in note 1 (cite the page and section) that discuss parts of its value chain. Use the value chain categories discussed at the beginning of the chapter to organize your answer.

b. Identify information in note 1 that shows management cares about the cost categories discussed in this chapter: non-value-added costs, ABC and ABM, JIT, quality cost, and/or target costing.

LO7 LO8

PROBLEM 19.6A
Kare Company's Quality Improvement Program

At the beginning of Year 1, Kare Company initiated a quality improvement program. Considerable effort was expended over two years to reduce the number of defective units produced. By the end of the second year, reports from the production manager revealed that scrap and rework had both decreased. The president of the company was pleased to hear of the success but wanted some assessment of the financial impact of the improvements. To make this assessment, the following financial data were collected for the two years.

	Year 1	Year 2
Sales	$10,000,000	$10,000,000
Scrap	400,000	300,000
Rework	600,000	400,000
Product inspection	100,000	125,000
Product warranty	800,000	600,000
Quality training	40,000	80,000
Materials inspection	60,000	40,000

Instructions

a. Classify the costs as prevention, appraisal, internal failure, and external failure.

b. Compute total quality cost as a percentage of sales for each of the two years. By how much has profit increased because of quality improvements between Year 1 and Year 2?

c. Graph the prevention and appraisal costs versus the internal and external failure costs for Year 1 and Year 2.

d. Several individuals are critical of the cost–benefit quality model. Identify and explain at least two criticisms. Identify measures, other than cost numbers, that companies can use to track quality.

LO2 LO3

PROBLEM 19.7A
Activity-Based Management at BookWeb, Inc.

BookWeb, Inc., sells books and software over the Internet. A recent article in a trade journal has caught the attention of management because the company has experienced soaring inventory handling costs. The article notes that similar firms have purchasing, warehousing, and distribution costs that average 13 percent of sales. Thirteen percent is attractive to BookWeb management when compared to its results for the past year, shown in the following table:

Activity (cost)	Cost Driver	Cost Driver Quantity	% of Cost Driver for Books	% of Cost Driver for Software
Incoming receipts ($300,000)	Number of purchase orders	2,000	70%	30%
Warehousing ($360,000)	Number of inventory moves	9,000	80	20
Shipments ($225,000)	Number of shipments	15,000	25	75

Book sales revenue totaled $3,900,000 and software sales revenue totaled $2,600,000. A review of the company's activities found various inefficiencies with respect to the warehousing of books and the outgoing shipments of software. In particular, book misplacements resulted in an extra 550 moves and software had 250 incorrect shipments.

a. What is activity-based management (as opposed to cost-based management, for example) and under what circumstances is it useful? What is a non-value-added activity?

b. How much did non-value-added activities cost BookWeb this past year?

c. Cite at least two examples of situations that may have given rise to non-value-added activities at BookWeb.

d. Will the elimination of non-value-added activities allow BookWeb to achieve 13 percent as a cost percentage of sales for each of the product lines? (Show all calculations to support your answer.)

e. Do either of the product lines require additional cost cutting to achieve the target percentages? How much additional cost cutting is needed and what tools (or methods) might the company use to achieve the cuts? Briefly describe them.

LO1 through LO8 PROBLEM 19.8A
Value Chain, Quality, and Efficiency at **Kimberly-Clark**

In a recent annual report the chief executive officer of **Kimberly-Clark** outlined his plans as follows:

> We continue to address the elements under our control, focusing on areas critical to delivering long-term, sustainable growth and returns to our shareholders. Specifically we:
>
> - . . . placed our near-term emphasis on realizing higher selling prices in order to improve margins.
> - . . . took advantage of growth opportunities in developing and emerging (D&E) markets. We also concentrated on further extending our portfolio in higher margin segments such as the workplace and safety gear in our K-C Professional business and medical devices in Health Care.
> - . . . make substantial investments in our brands and in the key capabilities—innovation, marketing and customer development—that support long-term growth.
> - . . . kept our attention firmly fixed on the needs of shoppers and users of all ages worldwide. . . .

*See http://rkconline.net/AR/KimberlyClark08/.

Instructions

For each critical area identified by **Kimberly-Clark**, match the area with one or more of the concepts documented in the learning objectives for this chapter. Use every learning objective at least once. Explain how each concept highlighted in the learning objectives would help **Kimberly-Clark** with their critical area.

Problem Set B

LO2 LO6 PROBLEM 19.1B
Identifying Value-Added and Non-Value-Added Activities

Smit Corporation is considering implementation of a JIT inventory system. The company's industrial engineer recently conducted a study to determine the average number of days spent in each activity of the production process. The following table summarizes her findings:

Production Activity	Number of Days
Cutting materials	13
Rework	5
Warranty repairs	7
Quality training	14
Painting finished goods	15
Bending materials	10
Purchasing raw materials	3
Assembling finished products	19

Instructions

a. Identify Smit's value-added production activities.

b. Identify Smit's non-value-added production activities.

c. Calculate Smit's total cycle time.

d. Determine Smit's manufacturing efficiency ratio.

e. Which of the above activities might be reduced or eliminated if Smit implemented a JIT system?

f. List some of the positive and negative consequences of eliminating some of the non-value-added activities.

LO2 through LO5

PROBLEM 19.2B Activity-Based Management and Target Costing

Parvee Company manufactures two products: PAR, which sells for $100; and VEE, which sells for $200. Estimated cost and production data for the current year are as follows:

	PAR	VEE
Direct materials cost	$25	$40
Direct labor cost (@ $10/hr.)	$20	$50
Estimated production (units)	30,000	10,000

In addition, fixed manufacturing overhead is estimated to be $2,500,000 and variable overhead is estimated to equal $2.50 per direct labor hour. Parvee desires a 10 percent return on sales for all of its products.

Instructions

a. Calculate the target cost for both PAR and VEE.

b. Estimate the total manufacturing cost per unit of each product if fixed overhead costs are assigned to products on the basis of estimated production in units. Which of the products is earning the desired return?

c. Recalculate the total manufacturing cost per unit if fixed overhead costs are assigned to products on the basis of direct labor hours. Which of the products is earning the desired return? (Round to the nearest penny.)

d. Given the confusing results of parts **b** and **c**, Parvee's production manager decides to perform an activity analysis of fixed overhead. The results of the analysis are as follows:

			Demands	
Activity	**Costs**	**Driver**	**PAR**	**VEE**
Machine set-ups	$ 350,000	# of set-ups	100	300
Purchase orders	650,000	# of orders	300	100
Machining	500,000	# of machine-hours	3,000	4,000
Inspection	300,000	# of batches	40	20
Shipping to customers	200,000	# of shipments	400	100
Total fixed overhead	$2,000,000			

Estimate the total manufacturing cost per unit of each product if activity-based costing is used for assigning fixed overhead costs. Under this method, which product is earning the desired return?

e. What proportion of fixed overhead is value-added? In attempting to reach the target cost for VEE, which activity would you look to improving first and why?

f. Parvee's production manager believes that design changes would reduce the number of set-ups required for VEE to 75. Fixed overhead costs for set-up would remain unchanged. What will be the impact of the design changes on the manufacturing costs of both products? Which of the products will earn the desired return?

g. An alternative to the design change is to purchase a new machine that will reduce the number of set-ups for PAR to 50 and the number of set-ups for VEE to 140. The machine also will reduce fixed set-up costs to $275,500. Calculate the manufacturing costs for each product if the machine is purchased. Should VEE be redesigned or should the machine be purchased? Why?

LO4 LO5

PROBLEM 19.3B
Target Costing

Oro Mining, Inc., has just discovered two new mining sites for copper. Geologists and engineers have come up with the following estimates regarding costs and copper yields if the mines are opened:

	Site A	Site Z
Variable extraction costs per ton	$4.20	$4.50
Fixed costs over the life of the mine:		
Blasting	$160,000	$200,000
Construction	240,000	260,000
Maintenance	30,000	30,000
Restoration costs	50,000	10,000
Total fixed costs	$480,000	$500,000
Total tons of copper that can be extracted over the life of the mine:	240,000	200,000

Oro's owners currently demand a return of 18 percent of the market price of copper.

Instructions

a. If the current market price of copper is $10 per ton, what is Oro's target cost per ton?

b. Given the $10 market price, should either of the mines be opened?

c. The engineer working on Site Z believes that if a custom conveyor system is installed, the variable extraction cost could be reduced to $3.50 per ton. The purchase price of the system is $20,000, but the costs to restore the site will increase to $30,000 if it is installed. Given the current $10 market price, should Oro install the conveyor and open Site Z?

LO7 LO8

PROBLEM 19.4B
Cost of Quality

Nazu, Inc., produces a popular brand of humidifier that is backed by a five-year warranty. In Year 1, Nazu began implementing a total quality management program that has resulted in significant changes in its cost of quality. Listed below is Nazu's financial information relating to sales and quality for the past two years.

	Year 1	Year 2
Sales revenue	$600,000	$600,000
Warranty expense	25,000	23,000
Product design	4,000	16,000
Scrap	3,000	1,000
Process reengineering	7,000	15,000
Raw materials inspections	5,200	2,000
Product liability claims	6,200	7,000
Rework	3,000	2,800
Returns resulting from defects	6,400	5,000
Supplier certification costs	600	2,000
Preventive maintenance on equipment	1,200	2,000
Final inspection costs	12,000	8,000
Employee quality training	1,400	3,000
Equipment breakdown repair costs	9,000	6,000
Estimate of lost sales due to quality problems	12,000	12,000

Instructions

a. Prepare a cost of quality report for Nazu covering Year 1 and Year 2. Your report should divide the above costs into the four categories of quality costs and include total dollar amounts for each category.

b. How have the total amounts of prevention and external failure costs changed over the two years? What are some possible explanations for these changes?

c. At Nazu, preventive maintenance has a direct effect on the repair costs associated with equipment breakdowns. Did the decrease in repair costs justify the increase in maintenance costs?

d. Why might Nazu's estimate of lost sales remain the same despite the adoption of the total quality management program?

Critical Thinking Cases

LO2 through LO7

CASE 19.1
Activity-Based Management and Target Costing

Dana Martin, president of Mays Electronics, is concerned about the end-of-the-year marketing report. According to Mary O'Brien, marketing manager, a price decrease for the coming year is again needed to maintain the company's market share of integrated circuit boards (CBs). The current selling price of $18 per unit is producing a $2 per-unit profit—half the customary $4 per-unit profit. Foreign competitors keep reducing their prices, and to match their latest reduction, the price must drop from $18 to $14. This price drop would put Mays's price below the cost to produce and sell a CB. How could other firms sell for such a low price?

Determined to find out if there are problems with the company's operations, Dana has decided to hire a consultant to evaluate the way in which the CBs are produced and sold. After two weeks, the consultant has identified the following activities and costs associated with producing 120,000 CBs:

Activity	Cost
Set-ups	$ 125,000
Materials handling	180,000
Inspection	122,000
Customer support	120,000
Customer complaints	100,000
Warranty expense	170,000
Storage	80,000
Rework	75,000
Direct materials	500,000
Utilities	48,000
Manual insertion labor*	250,000
Other direct labor	150,000
Total costs	$1,920,000

*Diodes, resistors, and integrated circuits are inserted manually into the circuit board.

The consultant indicates that some preliminary activity analysis shows that per-unit costs can be reduced by at least $7. The marketing manager indicates that the market share for the CBs could be increased by 50 percent if the price could be reduced to $12.

Instructions

a. For each activity, determine whether it is value-added or non-value-added.

b. If all the non-value-added activities could be eliminated, by how much would the cost per CB decrease? Was the consultant correct in her preliminary cost reduction assessment?

c. Compute the target cost required to maintain Mays's current market share while earning the usual profit of $4 per unit. Also compute the target cost required to expand sales by 50 percent. By how much would the cost per unit need to be reduced to achieve each target?

d. The consultant also revealed the following: switching to automated insertion would save $90,000 of direct labor, $20,000 in rework, and $40,000 in warranty costs. The yearly cost of the necessary machinery would be $50,000. With this additional information, what is the potential cost reduction per unit available? Can Mays achieve the target cost to maintain its current market share?

e. In an effort to reach the target cost, Mays solicited suggestions from customers, suppliers, employees, and other consultants. The following were found to be feasible:

- Mays's production manager believes that the factory can be redesigned so that materials handling costs can be reduced by $100,000—which would in turn result in a $10,000 savings in rework costs. The cost to redesign the factory would be $20,000.
- A supplier suggests leasing a machine that would reduce set-up costs by $80,000. The yearly cost to lease the machine is $15,000.
- A customer, KD, Inc., proposes setting up a just-in-time delivery system between Mays, KD, and Mays's largest raw materials supplier. This would reduce Mays's storage costs by $45,000, while increasing shipping costs by only $5,000.
- An employee suggests that Mays train all its employees in quality control measures and then offer a bonus for meeting quality targets. An outside consultant estimates that the cost of the training and bonus would be $35,000. In return, inspections could be eliminated and rework, customer complaint costs, and warranty work could be reduced by $120,000.

If all of the above suggestions are implemented, including the automation of the insertion process, would Mays reach the target cost needed to maintain its current market share?

LO1 LO2 LO6

CASE 19.2
Just-in-Time Frozen Dinners

Healthy Times produces four types of frozen TV dinners that it sells to supermarkets and independent grocery stores. The company operates from two locations: a manufacturing plant and a refrigerated warehouse located a few blocks away. (Administrative offices are located in the manufacturing plant.)

The types of dinners to be produced each week are scheduled a week in advance, based on customer orders. The *number* of dinners produced, however, is always the same. The company runs its production facilities at full capacity—20,000 units per day—to minimize fixed manufacturing costs per unit.

Every Friday, local suppliers deliver to Healthy Times's factory the fresh vegetables, chicken, fish, and other ingredients required for the following week's production. (Materials are abundant in the region.) These ingredients then are cut into meal-sized portions, "fresh frozen" using special equipment, and transported by truck to the refrigerated warehouse. The company maintains an inventory of frozen ingredients equal to approximately two weeks' production.

Every day, ingredients for 20,000 dinners are brought by truck from the warehouse to the factory. All dinners produced in a given production run must be of the same type. However, production workers can make the machinery "set-up" changes necessary to produce a different type of frozen dinner in about 10 minutes.

Monday through Thursday, Healthy Times produces one type of dinner each day. On Friday, it manufactures whatever types of dinners are needed to balance its inventories. Completed frozen dinners are transported back to the refrigerated warehouse on a daily basis.

Frozen dinners are shipped daily from the warehouse to customers. All shipments are sent by independent carriers. Healthy Times usually maintains about a 10-day inventory of frozen dinners in the warehouse. Recently, however, daily sales have been averaging about 2,000 units less than the level of production, and the finished goods inventory has swelled to a 25-day supply.

Marsha Osaka, the controller of Healthy Times, recently read about the JIT inventory system used by **Toyota** in its Japanese production facilities. She is wondering whether a JIT system might benefit Healthy Times.

Instructions

With a group of students write a report to Marsha Osaka that covers the following issues:

a. In *general terms,* describe a JIT manufacturing system. Identify the basic goals of a JIT manufacturing system and any basic conditions that must exist for the system to operate efficiently.

b. Identify any non-value-added activities in Healthy Times's operations that might be reduced or eliminated in a JIT system. Also identify specific types of costs that might be reduced or eliminated.

c. Assume that Healthy Times *does* adopt a JIT manufacturing system. Prepare a description of the company's operations under such a system. (Your description should be consistent with the details provided above.)

d. Explain whether or not you think that a JIT system would work for Healthy Times. Identify any ethical concerns that Osaka should consider and provide specific reasons supporting your conclusion.

LO2 LO6

CASE 19.3
JIT and Economywide Impacts

A book called *End of the Line: The Rise and Coming Fall of the Global Corporation,* by Barry C. Lynn suggests that global corporations have become globally lean by using JIT, identifying and eliminating non-value-added activities through outsourcing, and taking advantage of deregulation by countries around the world. However, Lynn contends that the systems are so specialized that a relatively small glitch in production on the far side of the world has the potential to be devastating to the American economy. He suggests that laws are needed that would require companies to triple-source supplies and services from two or more nations.

Instructions

Write a paragraph that explains whether you agree or disagree with the premise of the book and provide at least three reasons why or why not.

LO1 through LO7

INTERNET CASE 19.4
Lean Manufacturing Solutions

Manufacturing Engineering, Inc., is a leading provider of lean manufacturing solutions. Its Web site is at the following address:

www.mfgeng.com

On its Web site, **Manufacturing Engineering** lists several categories of projects. With a team of students choose a category from the list and answer the following questions:

Instructions

a. What part of the value chain is targeted by the category?

b. What benefits can be identified from the category?

c. Do you believe target costing, activity-based management, cost of quality management, or just-in-time inventory was useful in the category your team looked at? Why?

Internet sites are time and date sensitive. It is the purpose of these exercises to have you explore the Internet. You may need to use the Yahoo! search engine http://www.yahoo.com *(or another favorite search engine) to find a company's current Web address.*

LO1 through LO3

CASE 19.5
Internal Controls and through Non-Value-Added Activities

Section 404 of the Sarbanes-Oxley Act (SOX) is designed to nip accounting problems in the bud, before they can blossom into fraud, by focusing on internal controls. Many companies, in complying with Section 404, have discovered—to their surprise—that reviewing internal controls can in fact result in benefits beyond unmasking accounting problems. For example, **Pitney Bowes** used the internal audit review process to consolidate four accounts receivable offices into one, saving more than $500,000 in one year alone. **Cisco Systems, Inc.**, which spent $50 million and 240,000 hours complying with SOX, found opportunities to streamline steps for ordering products and services, making it easier for customers to do business with **Cisco**.

Despite reports suggesting that individual companies benefited by eliminating non-value-added costs as a result of SOX Section 404, many CFOs believe the costs are not worth the benefits to their individual companies.

a. Discuss with your classmates the cost–benefit outcomes of Section 404 of the Sarbanes-Oxley Act. What types of societywide benefits are being overlooked by CFOs?

b. Would those societywide benefits ultimately provide benefits to each individual firm? How?

Answers to Self-Test Questions

1. c, e **2.** c [$30 − (.2 × $30)] **3.** d **4.** d **5.** a (rework is an internal failure)

CHAPTER 20

Cost-Volume-Profit Analysis

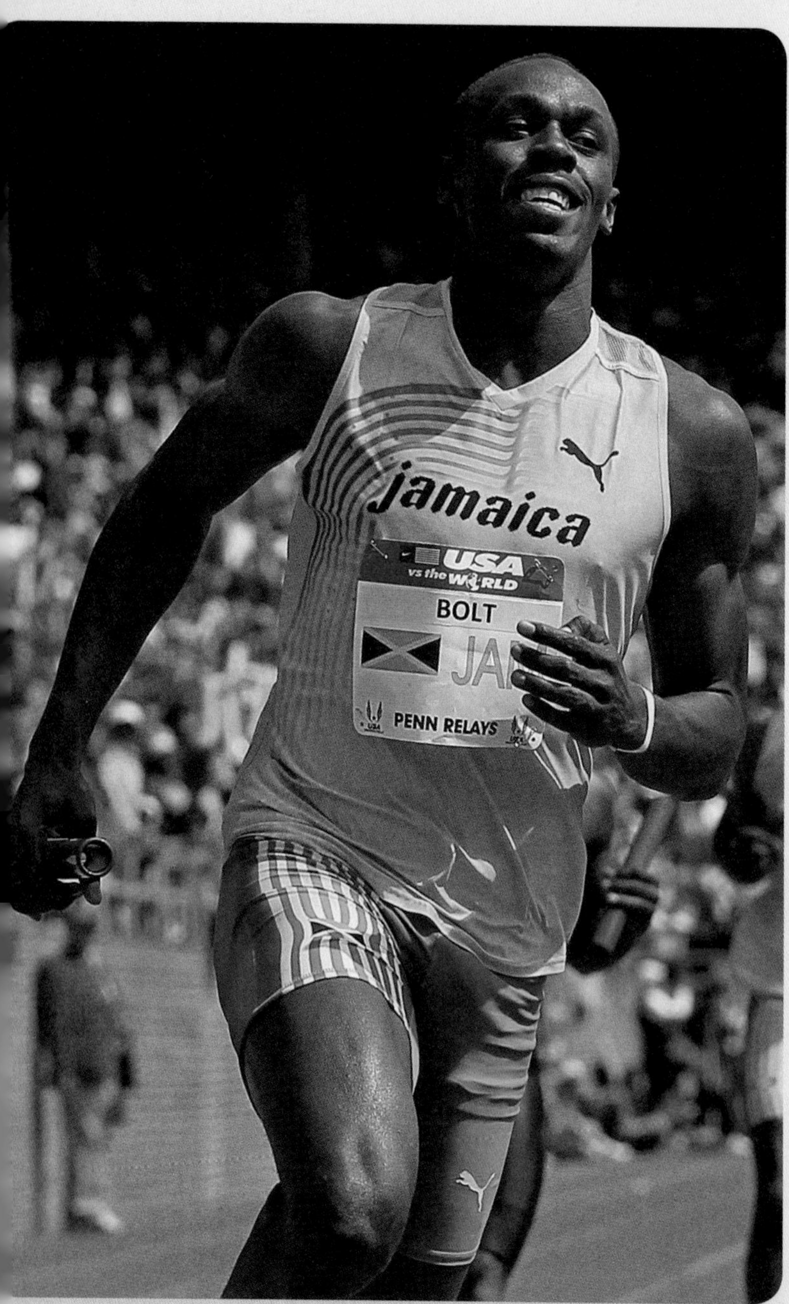

© Chris McGrath/Getty Images

AFTER STUDYING THIS CHAPTER, YOU SHOULD BE ABLE TO:

- **LO1** Explain how fixed, variable, and semivariable costs respond to changes in the volume of business activity.
- **LO2** Explain how economies of scale can reduce unit costs.
- **LO3** Prepare a cost-volume-profit graph.
- **LO4** Compute contribution margin and explain its usefulness.
- **LO5** Determine the sales volume required to earn a desired level of operating income.
- **LO6** Use the contribution margin ratio to estimate the change in operating income caused by a change in sales volume.
- **LO7** Use CVP relationships to evaluate a new marketing strategy.
- **LO8** Use CVP when a company sells multiple products.
- **LO9** Determine semivariable cost elements.

Learning Objectives

PUMA AG

Many companies have gotten very serious about controlling costs. At Puma AG, executives are also keenly aware of the strategic importance of product mix management. By gathering information about market demand and combining it with a marketing strategy that focuses on higher margin products, Puma has been able to survive in a crowded marketplace by reinventing itself.

Puma executives understand the economic consequences of cost structure, contribution margin, and break-even sensitivity on the company's profitability and strategic decision making. Moreover, they realize that Puma's continued success depends, in large part, on their handling of resource constraints, production bottlenecks, and an array of complex nonfinancial issues. ■

Companies like **Puma** can maintain and improve their profitability by understanding the profitability of each product line. A clear understanding of the link between product costs, volume, and profitability can help managers build strategies that improve corporate earnings. This chapter will help you understand cost-volume-profit (CVP) relationships and how they can be useful for business decisions.

CVP analysis is a means of learning how costs and profits behave in response to changes in the level of business activity. An understanding of these relationships is essential in developing plans and budgets for future business operations.

Cost-volume-profit analysis may be used by managers to answer questions such as the following:

- What level of sales must be reached to cover all expenses, that is, to break even?
- How many units of a product must be sold to earn a specific operating income?
- What will happen to our profitability if we expand capacity?
- What will be the effect of changing salespeople's compensation from fixed monthly salaries to a commission of 10 percent on sales?
- If we increase our spending on advertising to $100,000 per month, what increase in sales volume will be required to maintain our current level of income from operations?

The concepts of cost-volume-profit analysis may be applied to the business as a whole; to individual segments of the business such as a division, a branch, or a department; or to a particular product line.

Cost-Volume Relationships

To illustrate the relationships between costs and activity levels, we examine the operation of McKinley Airlines, a small charter service based in Fairbanks, Alaska. Assume that the *average* monthly cost of operating the airline is $66,000. Obviously, in any given month, it would be mere coincidence if the company's *actual* total cost exactly equaled $66,000. Indeed, many factors may cause its actual expenses to be more or less than the average. Throughout this chapter, we will discover the importance of determining which factors drive costs and how managers can use this information to improve their planning and control activities.

Managers using CVP analysis begin by identifying the activities that cause costs to vary. For each activity the manager seeks some measurable base that allows increases or decreases in that activity to be matched with increases or decreases in costs. For example, one activity that causes costs to vary is the use of machines. Machine-hours is a measurable base that can be used to match the use of machines with the costs of electricity and maintenance associated with the machines.

An activity base may be expressed in a variety of ways, depending on the nature of the company's operations. For example, in retail environments, an activity base may be defined in terms of *output,* such as units sold or dollars of sales revenue. In manufacturing operations, it is sometimes more appropriate to select key elements of production *input* as an activity base, such as direct labor hours or machine-hours. Airlines often consider *passenger miles flown* to be their most significant cost driver. Accordingly, we will use this measurement for studying the behavior of costs at McKinley Airlines.

Having identified passenger miles as an appropriate activity base, we will next classify each of the airline's operating costs into one of three broad categories: fixed costs, variable costs, and semivariable costs.

FIXED COSTS (AND FIXED EXPENSES)

Learning Objective
LO1 **Explain how fixed, variable, and semivariable costs respond to changes in the volume of business activity.**

Fixed costs are those costs and expenses that *do not change* significantly in response to changes in an activity base. McKinley's depreciation expense is an example of a fixed cost, as the monthly depreciation expense does not vary with the number of passenger miles flown. Depending on the nature of a particular business, fixed costs can also include administrative and executive salaries, property taxes, rents and leases, and many types of insurance protection.

Variable Costs (and Variable Expenses) A **variable cost** is one whose total rises or falls in approximate proportion to changes in an activity base. McKinley's fuel expense is an example of a variable cost, as it changes in approximate proportion to the number of passenger miles flown. For instance, if total passenger miles were to increase by 10 percent in a given month, we would expect to see a similar increase in fuel expense.

Semivariable Costs (and Semivariable Expenses) **Semivariable costs** are sometimes called *mixed costs* because they contain both a *fixed* and a *variable* component. The monthly fee McKinley pays to the Fairbanks airport is a good example of a semivariable cost, since it contains both a fixed base rate and an added charge for each passenger mile flown. The fixed portion pertains to the rental of hangar space for McKinley's aircraft, which remains constant regardless of its flight activity. The variable portion pertains to the airline's use of the passenger terminal. The more passenger miles McKinley flies during a given month, the higher the terminal usage fee charged by the airport.

The concept of semivariable costs often applies when a variety of different costs are combined in one broad category. In manufacturing, for example, overhead includes a variety of fixed and variable costs. The fixed costs may include property taxes, supervisor salaries, and depreciation expense. The variable costs may include supplies, electricity, and machinery repairs.

INTERNATIONAL CASE IN POINT

Identifying and separating fixed and variable costs is not easy. This task is significantly more complicated when products are manufactured in and transferred between international locations. For example, in Jordan, because of cultural and legal differences, some costs that might be classified as fixed costs in the United States are classified as variable costs in Jordanian accounts or vice versa. Examples of the costs impacted are product warranty, freight expenses, interest expenses, and wages. Culturally acceptable methods for delaying payments, bargaining for lower sales prices, and bureaucratic delays may transform a cost thought of as variable in the United States into a fixed recurring expense in an international location. In Jordan, for instance, clearing items through customs takes inordinate numbers of repeat visits to airports or seaports and is frequently mentioned as an additional cost of doing business in Jordan.

COST-VOLUME RELATIONSHIPS: A GRAPHIC ANALYSIS

To illustrate cost-volume behavior, we shall examine the somewhat simplified data pertaining to McKinley's fixed, variable, and semivariable costs given in Exhibit 20–1.

Exhibit 20–1

COST INFORMATION FOR MCKINLEY AIRLINES

Type of Cost	Amount
Fixed costs	
Insurance	$11,000 per month
Depreciation	$ 8,000 per month
Salaries	$20,000 per month
Variable costs	
Fuel and maintenance	8 cents per mile
Semivariable costs	
Airport usage fees	$3,000 per month + 2 cents per passenger mile

We have expressed these cost-volume relationships graphically in Exhibit 20–2 (for each cost type and in total). Carefully note the relationship between volume (monthly passenger miles flown) and cost in each diagram.

Exhibit 20–2 COST BEHAVIOR AT MCKINLEY AIRLINES

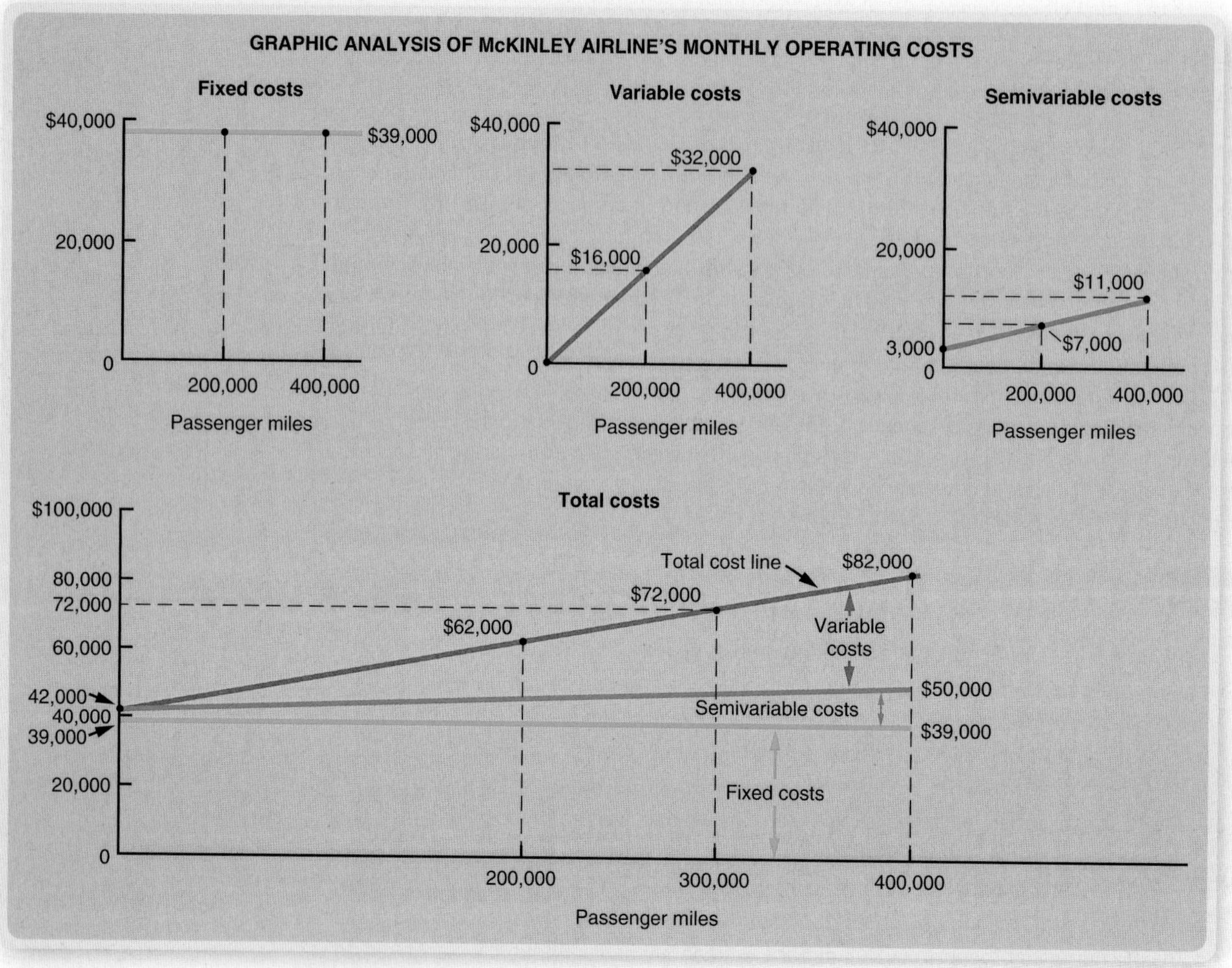

GRAPHIC ANALYSIS OF McKINLEY AIRLINE'S MONTHLY OPERATING COSTS

Fixed costs

$40,000
20,000
0
$39,000
200,000 400,000
Passenger miles

Variable costs

$40,000
20,000
0
$32,000
$16,000
200,000 400,000
Passenger miles

Semivariable costs

$40,000
20,000
3,000
0
$11,000
$7,000
200,000 400,000
Passenger miles

Total costs

$100,000
80,000
72,000
60,000
42,000
40,000
39,000
20,000
0
Total cost line
$82,000
$72,000
$62,000
Variable costs
$50,000
Semivariable costs
$39,000
Fixed costs
200,000 300,000 400,000
Passenger miles

We can read from the total cost graph in Exhibit 20–2 the estimated monthly cost for any assumed volume of passenger miles. As shown, if McKinley anticipates a volume of 300,000 passenger miles in any given month, its estimated total cost is $72,000, or 24 cents per passenger mile. By separating all fixed and variable cost elements, we can generalize McKinley's cost-volume relationship and simply state that the monthly cost of operating the airline, for any given number of passenger miles, is approximately *$42,000 plus 10 cents for each passenger mile flown.*

The effect of volume on McKinley's *total unit cost* (its cost per passenger mile) can be observed by converting its total cost figures to average cost figures, as shown in Exhibit 20–3. Note that the average total cost per passenger mile decreases as passenger miles increase.

Exhibit 20–3

AVERAGE COST PER PASSENGER MILE AT MCKINLEY AIRLINES

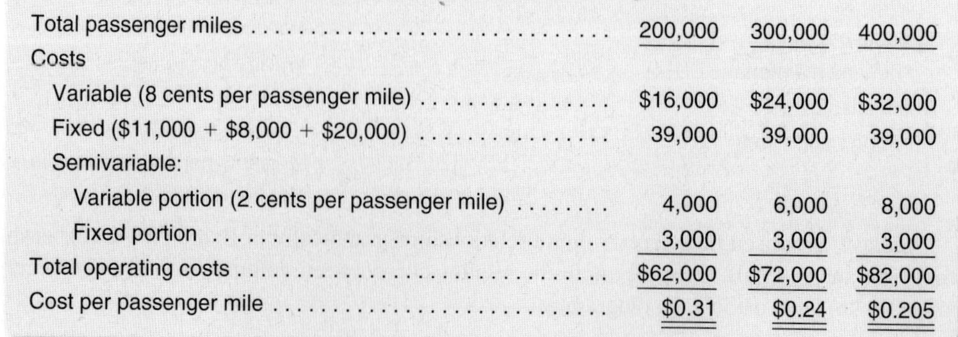

McKinley Airlines's Cost per Passenger Mile

Total passenger miles	200,000	300,000	400,000
Costs			
Variable (8 cents per passenger mile)	$16,000	$24,000	$32,000
Fixed ($11,000 + $8,000 + $20,000)	39,000	39,000	39,000
Semivariable:			
Variable portion (2 cents per passenger mile)	4,000	6,000	8,000
Fixed portion	3,000	3,000	3,000
Total operating costs	$62,000	$72,000	$82,000
Cost per passenger mile	$0.31	$0.24	$0.205

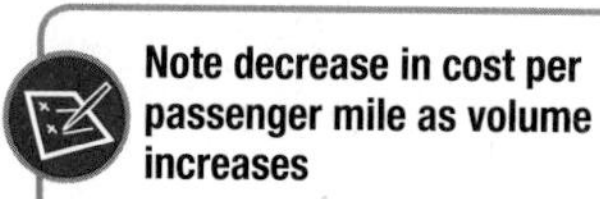

Note decrease in cost per passenger mile as volume increases

McKinley's unit cost behavior is presented graphically in Exhibit 20–4 for both total cost and fixed cost. You can see that the distance between the two cost curves (representing variable costs of 10 cents per passenger mile) *remains constant* across a range of activity base volumes.

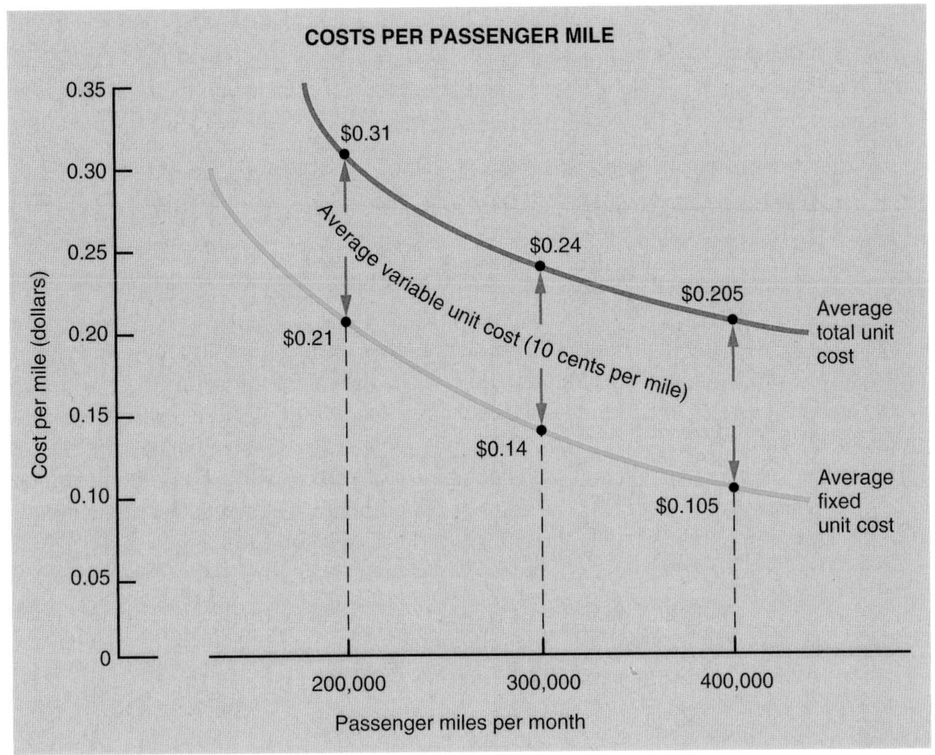

Exhibit 20–4

AVERAGE COST PER PASSENGER MILE OF OPERATING MCKINLEY AIRLINES

THE BEHAVIOR OF PER-UNIT COSTS

In our example, note that the *variable cost per passenger mile* remains constant at 10 cents, regardless of the number of passenger miles flown. However, on a *per-passenger mile basis,* the fixed cost component gets smaller as passenger miles increase and larger as passenger miles decrease. This is because total fixed costs do not vary with changes in the activity base. As illustrated in Exhibit 20–4, fixed costs per unit decrease when volume increases. For McKinley Airlines, fixed per-unit costs decrease from 21 cents per passenger mile to 10.5 cents per passenger mile as monthly activity increases from 200,000 passenger miles to 400,000 passenger miles. Study Exhibit 20–5 to make sure you understand how costs change when volume increases or decreases.

As Volume Increases (Decreases):

	Variable Costs	Fixed Costs
Per-Unit Costs	Stay the same	Decrease
	(Stay the same)	(Increase)
Total Costs	Increase	Stay the same
	(Decrease)	(Stay the same)

Exhibit 20–5

VOLUME VARIATION AND CHANGES IN FIXED AND VARIABLE COSTS

YOUR TURN **You as a Manager**

Assume that you are the manager of ground operations for **Northwest Airlines** at Detroit Metro Airport. You have just been informed that the plane size between Philadelphia and Detroit will be increased from a Boeing 737 to a 747 and is expected to generate 50 additional passengers per flight. What ground operations costs do you think will increase because of the additional 50 passengers per flight? What ground operations costs will not be affected?

(See our comments on the Online Learning Center Web site.)

ECONOMIES OF SCALE

Learning Objective
LO2 **Explain how economies of scale can reduce unit costs.**

The decrease in McKinley's fixed cost per unit at higher levels of activity represents a more efficient use of the company's productive assets—its aircraft. In general, *most businesses can reduce unit costs by using their facilities more intensively.*[1] These savings are called **economies of scale.**

To illustrate, assume that an automobile plant incurs fixed costs of $8.4 million per month and has the capacity to produce 7,000 automobiles per month. The fixed cost per unit manufactured is shown in Exhibit 20–6 at three different levels of production.

Exhibit 20–6
FIXED COSTS AT AN AUTOMOBILE PLANT

Fixed Costs per Month	Level of Production	Fixed Cost per Unit
$8,400,000	4,000 cars	$2,100
8,400,000	6,000 cars	1,400
8,400,000	7,000 cars	1,200

Notice that by producing 7,000 cars per month the automaker's manufacturing costs are *$900 less* per automobile than if the automaker produces only 4,000 cars each month ($2,100 − $1,200 = $900). This cost advantage results from fully utilizing the company's production facilities and, therefore, spreading the company's fixed costs over as many units as possible.

Economies of scale are most apparent in businesses with *high fixed costs*, such as airlines, oil refineries, steel mills, and utility companies. Most large companies automatically realize some economies of scale. This is one of the reasons why it is difficult for a small company to compete with a much larger one. But smaller companies also can realize their own economies of scale by *using their facilities as intensively as possible.*

CASE IN POINT

Many airlines, including some of the nation's largest, have been losing money in recent years. But relatively small **Southwest Airlines** has been doing very well. Why? Because **Southwest** operates *at or near full capacity*—that is, with a paying passenger in almost every seat.

As a result, **Southwest** incurs lower fixed costs per passenger mile than its competitors. This enables **Southwest** to earn a higher profit margin than most airlines and to offer very competitive fares—which keep those seats full.

[1] Increasing the level of activity can increase certain per-unit costs, such as direct labor—especially if overtime rates must be paid. Seldom, however, do such cost increases fully offset the economies achieved from a higher level of output.

ADDITIONAL COST BEHAVIOR PATTERNS

Cost relationships are seldom as simple as those in our example involving the operation of McKinley Airlines. However, the operating costs of all businesses exhibit variable, semivariable, and fixed characteristics.

In addition to the cost behaviors we have described thus far, some business costs increase in lump-sum steps as shown in graph (**a**) in Exhibit 20–7. For example, when production reaches a point where another supervisor and crew must be added, a lump-sum addition to labor costs occurs. Other costs may vary along a curve rather than a straight line, as shown in graph (**b**). For example, when a production schedule requires employees to work overtime, labor costs per unit may rise more rapidly than volume because of the overtime premium.

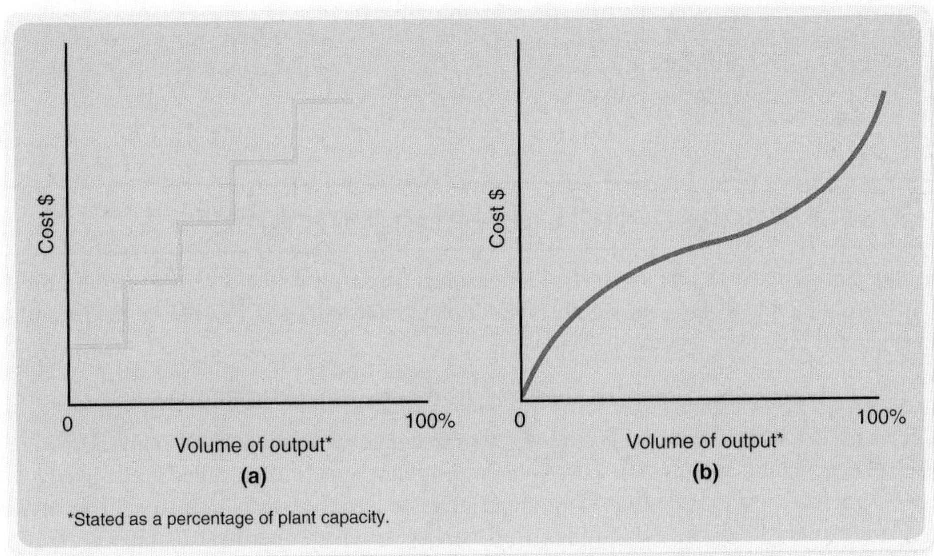

Exhibit 20–7
SEMIVARIABLE COSTS

Stair-step and curvilinear costs

Taking all the possible variations of cost behavior into account would add greatly to the complexity of cost-volume analysis. How far from reality are the assumed straight-line relationships shown at the beginning of this chapter in Exhibit 20–2? Fortunately, there are two factors that make straight-line approximations of cost behavior useful for analytical purposes.

First, unusual patterns of cost behavior tend to offset one another. If we were to plot actual total costs incurred by a business over a time period in which volume changes occurred, the result might appear as in the cost-volume graph (**a**) in Exhibit 20–8. Notice that the cost pattern approximates a straight line, even though the actual points do not fall on the line itself.

Second, unusual patterns of cost behavior are most likely to occur at extremely high or extremely low levels of volume. For example, if output were increased to near 100 percent of plant capacity, variable costs would curve sharply upward because of payments for overtime. An extreme decline in volume, on the other hand, might require shutting down plants and extensive layoffs, thereby reducing some expenditures that are usually considered fixed costs. Most businesses, however, operate somewhere between perhaps 45 percent and 80 percent of capacity and try to avoid large fluctuations in volume. For a given business, the probability that volume will vary outside of a fairly narrow range is usually remote. The range over which output may be expected to vary is called the **relevant range,** as shown in graph (**b**) in Exhibit 20–8. Within this relevant range, the assumption that total costs vary in straight-line relation to changes in volume is reasonably realistic for most companies.

Exhibit 20–8

IDENTIFYING THE RELEVANT RANGE

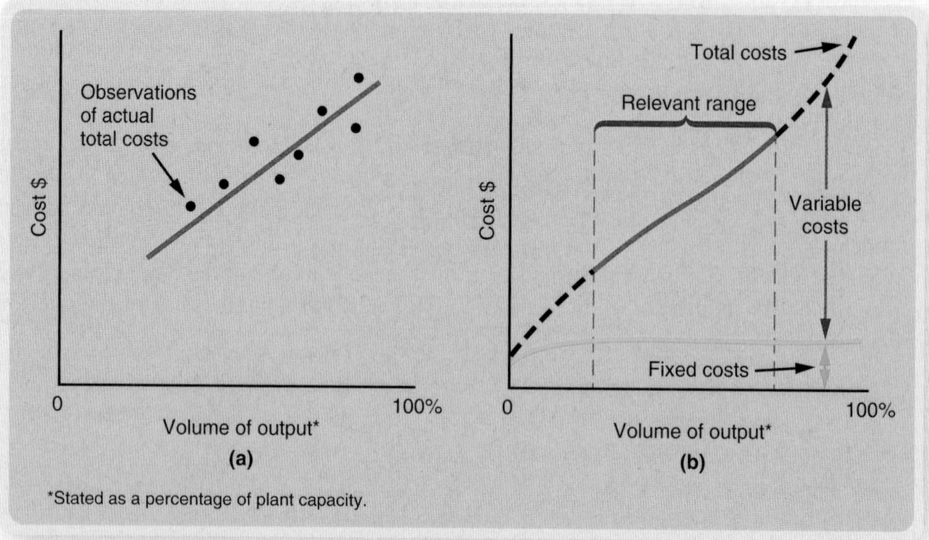

Cost Behavior and Operating Income

Having gained an understanding of various cost behaviors, we can now expand our discussion to include the relationships among costs (both manufacturing costs *and* operating expenses), revenue, and operating income as follows:

Revenue − Variable Costs − Fixed Costs = Operating Income

This basic relationship sets the stage for introducing cost-volume-profit analysis, a widely used management planning tool. Cost-volume-profit analysis is often called *break-even analysis,* in reference to the point at which total revenue exactly equals total cost. The **break-even point** may be defined as the level of activity at which operating income is equal to *zero.* Its computation often serves as a starting point in decisions involving cost-volume-profit relationships.

© Steve Mason/Getty Images/DAL

Before we proceed with an illustration, two final points must be emphasized. First, the term *profit* in cost-volume-profit analysis refers to *operating income,* not *net income.* This is because income taxes and nonoperating gains and losses do not possess the characteristics of variable or fixed costs. Second, cost-volume-profit analysis conveys very little information about *cash flows.* Revenue, for example, often results from both cash and credit sales, whereas expenses often result from both cash payments and charges made on account. Thus, if sales of a particular product are expected to result in long-term holdings of accounts receivable, managers may decide to include in their cost-volume-profit analysis the lost opportunity to earn a return on the cash tied up in accounts receivable.

COST-VOLUME-PROFIT ANALYSIS: AN ILLUSTRATION

Assume that SnowGlide Company manufactures entry-level snowboards. The company currently sells its product to wholesale distributors in Colorado, Washington, and Oregon. Because of the popularity of snowboarding, the company is considering distributing to several East Coast wholesalers as well. Although wholesale prices vary depending on the quantity of boards purchased by a distributor, revenue consistently *averages* \$90 per board sold. SnowGlide's monthly operating statistics are shown in Exhibit 20–9.

Exhibit 20–9
SNOWGLIDE'S OPERATING INFORMATION

	Dollars	Percentage of Sales Price
Average selling price per board	$90.00	100%
Variable expenses per board		
Direct labor cost	2.25	2.5
Direct materials cost	28.25	31.4
Variable manufacturing overhead	3.10	3.4
Variable administrative expenses	2.40	2.7
Total variable cost per board	36.00	40.0%
Unit contribution margin and contribution margin ratio (discussed on following pages)	$54.00	60.0%
Fixed costs		
Administrative salaries	$23,000	
Insurance	1,300	
Depreciation	5,000	
Advertising	8,500	
Total fixed cost per month	$37,800	

Note variable and fixed cost elements

Notice that income taxes are not included among the monthly operating expenses. Income taxes are neither fixed nor variable because they depend on the amount of taxable income, rather than sales volume.

CVP analysis may be performed either by stating the cost-volume-profit relationships in the form of mathematical formulas or by illustrating them visually in a graph. Let us begin with a graph.

PREPARING AND USING A COST-VOLUME-PROFIT GRAPH

The *cost-volume-profit* (or *break-even*) graph in Exhibit 20–10 is based on SnowGlide's cost and revenue statistics. The graph shows the reader, at a glance, the break-even point in units and in dollars.

Exhibit 20–10
GRAPHING PROFITS AT SNOWGLIDE

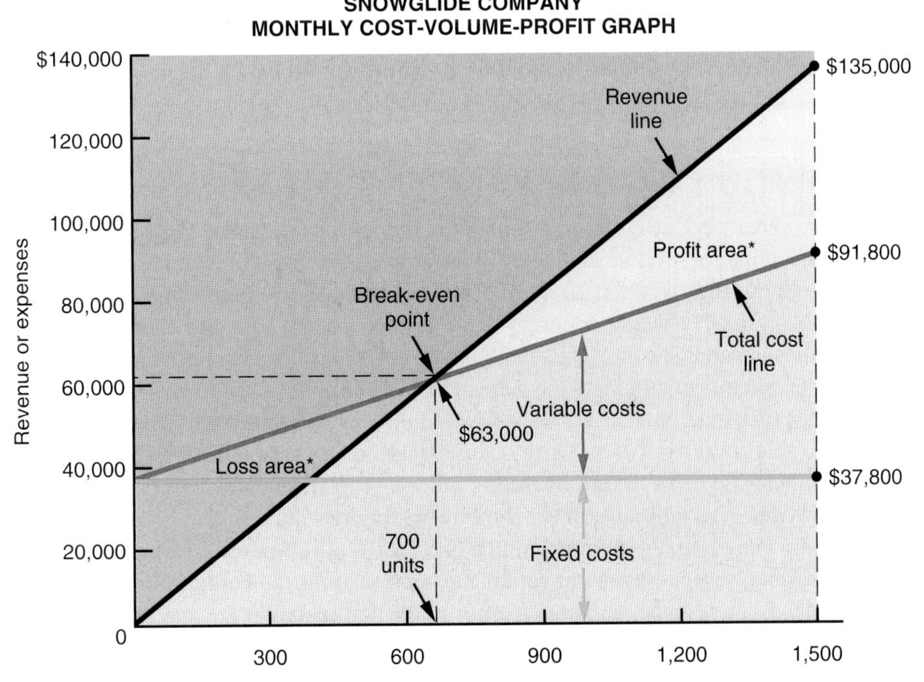

*Profit and loss represent income or loss before income taxes.

Learning Objective
LO3 Prepare a cost-volume-profit graph.

The horizontal axis represents the activity base, which for SnowGlide is boards sold per month. Since the company is not equipped to manufacture more than 1,500 units per month, this is assumed to be the upper limit of the relevant range. The vertical axis of the graph represents dollars of revenue and costs corresponding to various levels of unit sales activity. The steps in drawing this graph are as follows:

1. Draw the total revenue line. This line runs from $0 to $135,000 in total revenue, which is the maximum revenue that the company can currently generate, given its monthly production capacity of 1,500 units. Note that the slope of the total revenue line equals the average selling price per unit of $90.
2. Draw the fixed cost line. This is a horizontal line representing a constant $37,800 monthly fixed cost at all volumes within the company's relevant range of activity.
3. Draw the total cost line. Starting where the fixed cost line intercepts the vertical axis at $37,800, the total cost line will rise by $54,000 to a total cost of $91,800. This is the maximum total cost the company expects to incur, given its monthly production capacity of 1,500 units. Note that, for any level of activity, the distance from the fixed cost line to the total cost line represents the company's *total variable cost* and that the slope of the total cost line equals the company's *variable cost per unit* of $36. Thus, for each additional snowboard that the company sells, its total cost will increase by $36.
4. Label the point at which the revenue line intersects the total cost line as the *break-even point.* Note that SnowGlide's break-even point is at 700 units, which corresponds to $63,000 in total revenue.

The operating profit or loss expected at any sales volume equals the distance between the total revenue line and the total cost line. Since this distance is zero at the break-even point, operating income at the break-even point must be zero, verified as follows:

Computation verifying the break-even point in our graph

Revenue (700 boards × $90 per board)		$63,000
Costs and expenses:		
Fixed	$37,800	
Variable (700 boards × $36 per board)	25,200	63,000
Operating income		$ -0-

If SnowGlide is able to operate at its monthly capacity of 1,500 units, its monthly operating income will amount to $43,200 ($135,000 in revenue, less $91,800 in total costs).

CONTRIBUTION MARGIN: A KEY RELATIONSHIP

Learning Objective
LO4 Compute contribution margin and explain its usefulness.

We have shown that variable costs change in direct proportion to revenue. Thus, the generation of an additional dollar of revenue will result in an additional amount of variable cost. The operating data for SnowGlide (Exhibit 20–9) indicate that variable costs account for 40 percent of every sales dollar. In other words, for every $1 in revenue that the company earns, it can expect to incur 40 cents in variable costs. The remaining 60 cents is called the **contribution margin.**

The contribution margin is simply the *amount by which revenue exceeds variable costs.* Prior to reaching the break-even point, every $1 of SnowGlide's revenue generates 60 cents in contribution margin to help cover *fixed costs.* Once sales pass the break-even point, every $1 in additional revenue contributes 60 cents toward *operating income.* The allocation of every revenue dollar between SnowGlide's variable costs and contribution margin is illustrated in Exhibit 20–11.

Contribution margin may be expressed as a percentage of revenue, as a total dollar amount for the period (total revenue less total variable expenses), or as the **contribution margin per unit** (unit sales price less the variable cost per unit). For example, the average contribution margin *per snow board* sold by SnowGlide is *$54,* computed as follows:

Unit Contribution Margin	=	Unit Selling Price	−	Variable Cost per Unit
$54	=	$90	−	$36

REVENUE DOLLAR
40¢ of each revenue dollar is consumed by variable expenses relating to the sale.
60¢ of each revenue dollar is available to cover fixed expenses up to the break-even point and contributes 60¢ to operating income thereafter. This is called the **contribution margin**.

Exhibit 20–11

CONTRIBUTION MARGIN AT SNOWGLIDE

Contribution Margin Ratio When contribution margin is expressed as a *percentage of revenue,* it is termed **contribution margin ratio.** This ratio may be computed either by dividing the total contribution margin for the period by total revenue, or on a per-unit basis as follows:

$$\textbf{Contribution Margin Ratio} = \frac{\textbf{Contribution Margin per Unit}}{\textbf{Unit Sales Price}}$$

Using SnowGlide's per-unit data from Exhibit 20–9, we can compute the contribution margin ratio as follows:

$$\textbf{Contribution Margin Ratio} = \frac{\$54}{\$90} = 60\%$$

Once again, prior to breaking even, a contribution margin ratio of 60 percent means that 60 cents of every sales dollar helps to cover fixed costs. Once the break-even point is reached, every additional sales dollar provides a 60-cent increase in operating profit.

We will now examine how the important concept of contribution margin can be used to answer some fundamental questions about a company's operations.

HOW MANY UNITS MUST WE SELL?

Learning Objective
Determine the sales volume required to earn a desired level of operating income. **LO5**

The concept of contribution margin provides a quick means of determining the *unit sales volume* required for a business to break even or earn any desired level of operating income. Knowing the break-even sales volume can be of vital importance, especially to companies deciding whether to introduce a new product line, build a new plant or, in some cases, remain in business.

To illustrate the relationship between sales volume and contribution margin, assume that we want to compute how many snowboards SnowGlide must sell in a month to break even. From the cost-volume-profit graph in Exhibit 20–10, we can see that the answer is 700 units. We will now prove that this is so. At the break-even point, the company must generate a total contribution exactly equal to its fixed costs. The data from Exhibit 20–9 show that monthly fixed costs amount to *$37,800.* Given a contribution margin of *$54* from each board, the company must sell 700 pairs per month to break even, as follows:

$$\textbf{Sales Volume (in units)} = \frac{\$37{,}800}{\$54} = \textbf{700 units per month}$$

This reasoning can be taken one step further to find not only the unit sales volume needed to break even but also the unit sales volume needed to achieve *any desired level of operating income.* The following formula enables us to do this:

$$\textbf{Sales Volume (in units)} = \frac{\textbf{Fixed Costs + Target Operating Income}}{\textbf{Contribution Margin per Unit}}$$

For example, how many snowboards must SnowGlide sell to earn a monthly operating income of *$5,400*?

$$\textbf{Sales Volume (in units)} = \frac{\$37{,}800 + \$5{,}400}{\$54} = \textbf{800 units per month}$$

HOW MANY DOLLARS IN SALES MUST WE GENERATE?

To find the *dollar sales volume* a company must generate for a given target of operating income, we could first compute the required sales volume in units and then multiply our answer by the average selling price per unit. Thus, SnowGlide would have to generate approximately *$72,000* in revenue (800 snowboards × $90) to earn a monthly operating income of $5,400.

Taking a more direct approach to compute the required sales volume, we can simply substitute the *contribution margin ratio* for the contribution margin per unit in our CVP formula, as follows:

$$\textbf{Sales Volume (in dollars)} = \frac{\textbf{Fixed Costs + Target Operating Income}}{\textbf{Contribution Margin Ratio}}$$

To illustrate, let us again compute the sales volume required for SnowGlide to earn a monthly operating income of $5,400:

$$\textbf{Sales Volume (in dollars)} = \frac{\$37{,}800 + \$5{,}400}{60\%} = \textbf{\$72,000 per month}$$

WHAT IS OUR MARGIN OF SAFETY?

The dollar amount by which actual sales volume *exceeds* the break-even sales volume is called the **margin of safety.** It also represents the dollar amount by which sales can *decline* before an operating loss is incurred. In today's volatile economy, it is important for managers to understand the extent to which their companies can endure a downturn in sales. SnowGlide's monthly sales volume required to break even is:

$$\textbf{Sales Volume (in dollars)} = \frac{\$37{,}800}{60\%} = \textbf{\$63,000 per month}$$

Thus, if monthly sales total *$73,000,* the margin of safety for that month is *$10,000* ($73,000 − $63,000).

The margin of safety can provide a quick means of estimating operating income at any projected sales level. This relationship is summarized as follows:

Operating Income = Margin of Safety × Contribution Margin Ratio

The rationale for this formula stems from the fact that the margin of safety represents sales dollars *in excess* of the break-even point. Therefore, if fixed costs have already been covered, the *entire contribution margin of these sales increases operating income.*

To illustrate, let us assume that we estimate SnowGlide's sales to be $72,000 next month. Given that its break-even sales volume is $63,000, its estimated margin of safety is $9,000. Thus, the projected operating income is *$5,400* ($9,000 × 60%).

WHAT CHANGE IN OPERATING INCOME DO WE ANTICIPATE?

Learning Objective
LO6 Use the contribution margin ratio to estimate the change in operating income caused by a change in sales volume.

As stated, the contribution margin ratio in our example is 60 percent. Thus, once break-even is reached, every additional dollar of sales increases SnowGlide's operating income by 60 cents. Conversely, a $1 sales decline lowers profitability by 60 cents. This relationship may be summarized as follows:

$$\textbf{Change in Operating Income} = \textbf{Change in Sales Volume} \times \textbf{Contribution Margin Ratio}$$

Therefore, if SnowGlide estimates a $5,000 increase in monthly sales, it would anticipate a corresponding increase in operating income of $3,000 ($5,000 × 60%).

BUSINESS APPLICATIONS OF CVP

The use of cost-volume-profit analysis is not limited to accountants. On the contrary, it provides valuable information to many individuals throughout an organization. Cost-volume-profit relationships are widely used during the budget process to set sales targets, estimate costs, and provide information for a variety of decisions.

To illustrate, let us consider several ways in which cost-volume-profit relationships might be used by the management of SnowGlide Company. As previously mentioned, the popularity of snowboarding has prompted SnowGlide to consider distribution to East Coast wholesalers. Different managers within the company will naturally have different, yet interrelated, planning concerns regarding the implementation of this new market strategy.

We now will examine the concerns of three SnowGlide executives.

Learning Objective
Use CVP relationships to evaluate a new marketing strategy. LO7

Director of Advertising Assume that SnowGlide is currently selling approximately *900 snowboards* each month. In response to the new market strategy, the company's director of advertising is asking for an increase of $1,500 in her monthly budget. She plans to use these funds to advertise in several East Coast trade publications. From her experience, she is confident that the advertisements will result in monthly orders from East Coast distributors for 500 boards. She wishes to emphasize the impact of her request on the company's *operating income.*

Analysis We begin by calculating the company's current monthly income based on current sales of 900 units. We will then compute estimated monthly income based on 1,400 units, taking into account the additional advertising costs of $1,500 (an increase in total fixed costs from $37,800 to $39,300 per month). This will enable us to estimate the impact of the proposed advertising expenditures on monthly operating income.

Using the company's operating statistics shown in Exhibit 20–9 (page 887), its current operating income is computed in Exhibit 20–12.

Exhibit 20–12
OPERATING INCOME AT SNOWGLIDE

Sales (900 units @ $90)	$81,000
Variable costs (40% of sales)	(32,400)
Contribution margin (60% of sales)	48,600
Current monthly fixed costs	(37,800)
Current monthly operating income	$10,800

As the proposed advertising is viewed as a fixed cost, this expenditure does not affect SnowGlide's contribution margin ratio of *60 percent.* Based on projected monthly sales of *$126,000* (1,400 units × $90), the projected monthly operating income can be determined as follows:

$$\textbf{Projected Sales} = \frac{\textbf{Fixed Costs + Projected Operating Income}}{\textbf{Contribution Margin Ratio}}$$

$$\$126{,}000 = \frac{\$39{,}300 + \text{Projected Operating Income}}{60\%}$$

$$\text{Projected Operating Income} = 60\%\ (\$126{,}000) - \$39{,}300$$
$$= \$36{,}300 \text{ per month}$$

The target income figure is $25,500 higher than the present monthly figure of $10,800 ($36,300 − $10,800 = $25,500). Thus, the director of advertising believes that her request for an additional $1,500 is well justified.

Plant Manager SnowGlide's plant manager does not completely agree with the advertising director's projections. He believes that the increased demand for the company's product will initially put pressure on the plant's production capabilities. To cope with the pressure, he asserts that many factory workers will be required to work excessive overtime hours, causing an increase in direct labor costs of approximately *$1.80 per unit.* Assuming that he is correct, he wants to know the *sales volume in units* required to achieve the advertising director's projected monthly income figure of $36,300.

Analysis Holding the selling price at $90 per unit, the $1.80 overtime premium will reduce SnowGlide's current contribution margin from $54 per unit to $52.20 per unit as follows:

$$\begin{aligned}\textbf{Unit Contribution Margin} &= \textbf{Selling Price} - \textbf{Unit Variable Cost}\\ &= \$90.00 - (\$36.00 + \$1.80)\\ &= \$52.20\end{aligned}$$

If the director of advertising receives a monthly increase of $1,500 in her budget, and if a $36,300 income target is established, the number of units that must be sold is computed as follows:

$$\begin{aligned}\textbf{Projected Unit Sales} &= \frac{\textbf{Fixed Costs} + \textbf{Target Operating Income}}{\textbf{Unit Contribution Margin}}\\ &= \frac{\$39{,}300 + \$36{,}300}{\$52.20}\\ &= \textbf{1,448 units per month}\end{aligned}$$

Given that 1,448 units is approaching the upper limit of SnowGlide's 1,500 unit production capacity, the plant manager remains cautiously optimistic regarding the company's ability to market its product through East Coast distributors. Accordingly, he recommends that the company begin planning to increase plant capacity as soon as possible.

YOUR TURN **You as a Plant Accountant**

Assume you are the plant accountant and that you have a budgeted fixed overhead of $20,800 per month for a production level at normal capacity of 1,000 units per month. Thus, your overhead application rate has been set at $20,800/1,000 units, or $20.80 per unit. You realize that a production increase to 1,500 units per month will result in over applying fixed overhead to the tune of $10,400 per month (500 units × $20.80). You are hesitant to bring up the problem of the overhead application rate with the plant manager because both of you receive a yearly bonus based on plant profitability. If overhead is being overapplied because production is at 1,500 units, the application rate is too high ($20.80 versus $20,800/1,500 = $13.87 per unit). If the projected sales volume of 1,500 units does not occur, significant fixed overhead costs will be assigned to the unsold inventories. As a result, plant income will be larger and your bonus—as well as the plant manager's—will be larger. What should you do?

(See our comments on the Online Learning Center Web site.)

Vice President of Sales The vice president of sales isn't convinced that an increase in the monthly advertising budget of $1,500 will yield sales of 500 units per month in the East Coast region. Her estimate is more conservative, at 350 units per month (for total monthly sales of *1,250 units*). Assume that the monthly advertising budget is increased by $1,500, and that direct labor costs actually do increase by $1.80 per unit because of the overtime premium required to meet increased production demands. If the vice president of sales is correct regarding her 1,250 unit projection, she wants to know the extent to which the company would have to *raise its selling prices* (above the current price of $90 per unit) to achieve a target monthly income figure of $36,300.

Analysis If 1,250 units are sold each month instead of 1,400 units, the contribution margin per unit must increase in order for the company to achieve the same target income (taking the increases in advertising and direct labor costs into consideration). Once again, we use the following formula:

$$\text{Projected Unit Sales} = \frac{\text{Fixed Costs} + \text{Target Operating Income}}{\text{Contribution Margin per Unit}}$$

$$\text{1,250 units} = \frac{\$39{,}300 + \$36{,}300}{\text{Contribution Margin per Unit}}$$

$$\text{Contribution Margin per Unit} = \frac{\$39{,}300 + \$36{,}300}{\text{1,250 units}}$$

$$= \$60.48$$

Recall that the unit contribution margin is computed as follows:

Unit Contribution Margin = Unit Selling Price − Unit Variable Cost

Thus, given a required unit contribution margin of \$60.48 and a variable cost per unit of \$37.80, we can easily solve for the required unit selling price as follows:

\$60.48 = Unit Selling Price − \$37.80
Unit Selling Price = \$60.48 + \$37.80
= \$98.28

Faced with an extremely competitive wholesale sporting goods market, the vice president of sales is worried that a 9.2 percent price increase (from \$90.00 per unit to \$98.28 per unit) is likely to have an adverse effect on the company's total sales. Therefore, she recommends that the price remain at \$90 per unit and that the company's target monthly income figure be lowered accordingly.

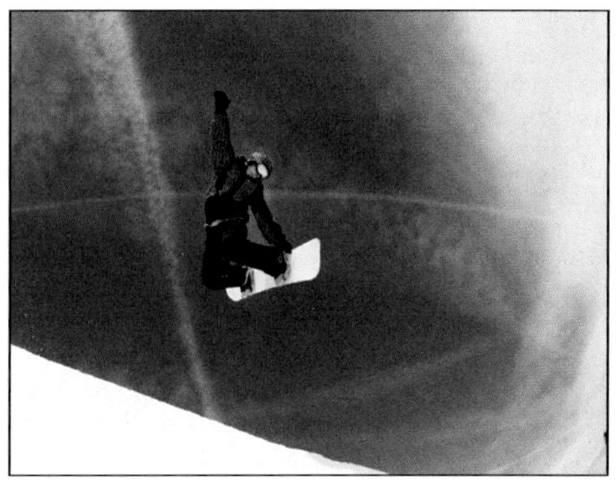
© Robert Michael/Corbis/DAL

ADDITIONAL CONSIDERATIONS IN CVP

In practice, the application of cost-volume-profit analysis is often complicated by various operating factors, including (1) different products with different contribution margins, (2) determining semivariable cost elements, and (3) complying with the assumptions of cost-volume-profit analysis. Let us address such considerations.

CVP ANALYSIS WHEN A COMPANY SELLS MANY PRODUCTS

SnowGlide sells only a single product. Most companies, however, sell a mix of many different products. In fact, the term **sales mix** often is used to describe the relative percentages of total sales provided by different products.

Different products usually have different contribution margin ratios. In many cases, decisions are based on the contribution margin of a particular product. But often managers apply cost-volume relationships to the business *viewed as a whole*. For this purpose, they use the *average* contribution margin ratio, reflecting the company's current sales mix.

The average contribution margin ratio may be computed by *weighting* the contribution margin ratios of each product line by the *percentage of total sales* which that product represents.

To illustrate, assume that, in addition to snowboards, SnowGlide sells goggles. Contribution margin ratios for the two product lines are snowboards, 60 percent, and goggles, 80 percent. Snowboards account for 90 percent of total sales, and goggles, the other 10 percent. The *average* contribution margin ratio for SnowGlide's sales "mix" is computed in Exhibit 20–13.

Learning Objective
Use CVP when a company sells multiple products. LO8

Exhibit 20–13
COMPUTING THE AVERAGE CONTRIBUTION MARGIN RATIO

	Product CM Ratio		Percentage of Sales	
Snowboards	60%	×	90%	= 54%
Goggles	80%	×	10%	= 8%
Average contribution margin ratio				62%

Improving the "Quality" of the Sales Mix Notice that goggles have a higher contribution margin ratio than snowboards. A business can improve its average contribution ratio, and its overall profitability, by shifting its sales mix to include more products with *high contribution margin ratios.* This is the strategy used by **Puma** and described in the chapter opener.

Sales of products with the high contribution margins often are described as *quality sales* because they contribute so greatly to the company's profitability. SnowGlide management should be thinking of ways to *sell more goggles.* Almost every business encourages its salespeople to aggressively market the high-margin products.

DETERMINING SEMIVARIABLE COST ELEMENTS: THE HIGH-LOW METHOD

Learning Objective
LO9 Determine semivariable cost elements.

As previously discussed, semivariable costs have both a fixed portion and a variable portion. Throughout this chapter we have simplified the handling of semivariable costs by providing the fixed and variable components for you. In practice, you must estimate the fixed and variable elements of semivariable costs. Several mathematical techniques may be used to accomplish this task. We will focus on one approach called the **high-low method.**[2]

To illustrate the high-low method, assume that some portion of SnowGlide's total administrative cost is fixed and that some portion varies with the level of production. Information pertaining to production and administrative costs for the first six months of the year is shown in Exhibit 20–14.

Exhibit 20–14
PRODUCTION AND ADMINISTRATION COSTS AT SNOWGLIDE

	Total Units Produced	Total Administrative Costs
Jan.	900	$25,060
Feb.	850	25,040
Mar.	925	25,183
Apr.	950	25,280
May	875	25,140
June	910	25,194

To find the *variable portion* of total administrative costs, we relate the change in cost to the change in *the activity base* between the highest and the lowest months of production activity as shown in Exhibit 20–15.

Exhibit 20–15
USING HIGHEST AND LOWEST PRODUCTION TO FIND VARIABLE ADMINISTRATION COSTS

	Total Units Produced	Total Administrative Costs
Apr. (highest)	950	$25,280
Feb. (lowest)	850	25,040
Changes	100	$ 240

Notice that a 100-unit increase in production results in a $240 increase in administrative costs. Therefore, the variable element of this cost may be estimated at $240 per 100 units, or *$2.40 per unit.*

To determine the fixed portion of the monthly administrative cost, we take the *total monthly cost* at either the high point or the low point, and deduct the *variable* administrative cost from that amount. The following computation uses the highest level of activity to determine the fixed cost portion:

Fixed Cost = Total Cost − Variable Cost
= $25,280 − ($2.40 per unit × 950 units)
= $25,280 − $2,280
= $23,000 per month

[2] Other approaches to determining the fixed and variable elements of semivariable costs include the least squares method and regression analysis. These techniques are typically discussed in a cost accounting course.

Note that the variable and fixed administrative costs correspond to those reported in SnowGlide's monthly summary of average operating statistics in Exhibit 20–9.

We have now developed a **cost formula** for monthly administrative costs: *$23,000 + $2.40 per unit.* In addition to helping the company evaluate the reasonableness of administrative costs incurred in a given month, this formula is also valuable in forecasting administrative costs likely to be incurred in the future. For example, what amount of administrative cost should SnowGlide expect in a month in which it has scheduled 930 units of production? The answer is approximately *$25,232,* determined as follows:

Monthly fixed administrative cost	$23,000
Variable costs ($2.40 × 930 units)	2,232
Total estimated administrative cost	$25,232

Calculating semivariable administrative costs

ASSUMPTIONS UNDERLYING COST-VOLUME-PROFIT ANALYSIS

Throughout the chapter we have relied on certain assumptions that have simplified the application of cost-volume-profit analysis. In practice, however, some of these assumptions may not always hold true. These assumptions include:

1. Sales price per unit is assumed to remain constant.
2. If more than one product is sold, the proportion of the various products sold (the sales mix) is assumed to remain constant.
3. Fixed costs (expenses) are assumed to remain constant at all levels of sales within a relevant range of activity.
4. Variable costs (expenses) are assumed to remain constant as a percentage of sales revenue.
5. For manufacturing companies, the number of units produced is assumed to equal the number of units sold each period.

Even if some of these assumptions are violated, cost-volume-profit analysis can still be a useful planning tool for management. As changes take place in selling prices, sales mix, expenses, and production levels, management should update and revise its analysis.

SUMMARY OF BASIC COST-VOLUME-PROFIT RELATIONSHIPS

In this chapter, we have demonstrated a number of ratios and mathematical relationships that are useful in cost-volume-profit analysis. For your convenience, these relationships are summarized in Exhibit 20–16.

Exhibit 20–16

COST-VOLUME-PROFIT MATHEMATICAL RELATIONSHIPS

Measurement	Method of Computation
Contribution Margin	Sales Revenue − Total Variable Costs
Unit Contribution Margin	Unit Sales Price − Variable Costs per Unit
Contribution Margin Ratio	$\frac{\text{Unit Sales Price} - \text{Variable Costs per Unit}}{\text{Unit Sales Price}}$ or $\frac{\text{Sales} - \text{Total Variable Costs}}{\text{Sales}}$
Sales Volume (in units)	$\frac{\text{Fixed Costs} + \text{Target Operating Income}}{\text{Unit Contribution Margin}}$
Sales Volume (in dollars)	$\frac{\text{Fixed Costs} + \text{Target Operating Income}}{\text{Contribution Margin Ratio}}$
Margin of Safety	Actual Sales Volume − Break-Even Sales Volume
Operating Income	Margin of Safety × Contribution Margin Ratio
Change in Operating Income	Change in Sales Volume × Contribution Margin Ratio

Ethics, Fraud & Corporate Governance

As discussed in this chapter, some industries are characterized by high fixed costs. Examples of industries characterized by high fixed costs include airlines, automobile manufacturers, and telecommunications companies. Companies in these industries purchase or self-construct different types of fixed assets—for example, airplanes, production equipment, fiber optic cable, and so on. A company's heavy reliance on fixed assets may result in: (1) an airline contracting with **Boeing** or **Airbus** to purchase or lease new planes, (2) an automobile manufacturer's decision to close a production facility and lay off workers covered by its pension plan, or (3) a telecommunications company investing in a technology that later becomes obsolete or unproductive and thereby makes the investment impaired. All of these events are potentially of interest to investors and creditors. And although these events (or the effects thereof) would be reflected in quarterly and annual financial statements filed with the Securities and Exchange Commission (SEC), the Sarbanes-Oxley Act (SOX) requires a more rapid disclosure of these events to the capital markets.

Section 409 of SOX requires public companies to disclose, by filing a Form 8-K, certain material events within four business days after they occur. Such events include entering into, or terminating, material agreements. For example, if an airline enters into an agreement to purchase or lease additional planes, the airline must disclose the date of the agreement, the parties to the agreement, any relationship between the company and the parties, and the terms and conditions of the agreement. Companies must also file a Form 8-K if management is committed to disposing of long-lived assets or terminating employees covered under a pension plan. These disclosures must include all relevant dates and costs associated with these actions. Finally, a Form 8-K must be filed if a fixed asset or intangible asset has become materially impaired.

Section 409 of SOX identifies other events that require disclosure on a Form 8-K on a rapid and current basis. Examples of these events include: (1) company bankruptcy or receivership, (2) buying another business or disposing of the company's own assets, (3) delisting from a stock exchange, (4) a change in the company's audit firm, (5) the departure/election/appointment of board members or principal officers, and (6) amendments to the company's code of ethics or waivers of provisions of the code of ethics. The goal of requiring disclosure of certain material events on a rapid and current basis is to provide more timely information to market participants of material information.

Concluding Remarks

An understanding of cost behavior—the manner in which costs normally respond to changes in the level of activity—is required in each remaining chapter of this textbook. In these chapters, we will explore the use of accounting information in evaluating the performance of managers and departments, in planning future business operations, and in making numerous types of management decisions. The concepts and terminology introduced in Chapter 20 will be used extensively in these discussions.

END-OF-CHAPTER REVIEW

SUMMARY OF LEARNING OBJECTIVES

LO1 **Explain how fixed, variable, and semivariable costs respond to changes in the volume of business activity.** Fixed costs (fixed expenses) remain unchanged despite changes in sales volume, while variable costs (or expenses) change in direct proportion to changes in sales volume. With a semivariable cost, part of the cost is fixed and part is variable. Semivariable costs change in response to a change in the level of activity, but they change by less than a proportionate amount.

LO2 **Explain how economies of scale can reduce unit costs.** Economies of scale are reductions in unit cost that can be achieved through a higher volume of activity. One economy of scale is fixed costs that are spread over a larger number of units, thus reducing unit cost.

LO3 **Prepare a cost-volume-profit graph.** The vertical axis on a break-even graph is dollars of revenue or costs, and the horizontal axis is unit sales. Lines are plotted on the graph showing revenue and total costs at different sales volumes. The vertical distance between these lines represents the amount of operating income (or loss). The lines intersect at the break-even point.

LO4 **Compute contribution margin and explain its usefulness.** Contribution margin is the excess of revenue over variable costs. Thus, it represents the amount of revenue available to cover fixed costs and to provide an operating profit. Contribution margin is useful in estimating the sales volume needed to achieve earnings targets, or the income likely to result from a given sales volume.

LO5 **Determine the sales volume required to earn a desired level of operating income.** The sales volume (in units) required to earn a target profit is equal to the sum of the fixed costs plus the target profit, divided by the unit contribution margin. To determine the sales volume in dollars, the sum of the fixed costs plus the target profit is divided by the contribution margin ratio.

LO6 **Use the contribution margin ratio to estimate the change in operating income caused by a change in sales volume.** Multiplying the expected dollar change in sales volume by the contribution margin ratio indicates the expected change in operating income.

LO7 **Use CVP relationships to evaluate a new marketing strategy.** An understanding of CVP relationships assists managers in estimating the changes in revenue and costs which are likely to accompany a change in sales volume. Thus, they are able to estimate the likely effects of marketing strategies on overall profitability.

LO8 **Use CVP when a company sells multiple products.** For companies that sell multiple products, CVP analysis is performed using a *weighted-average* contribution margin. The weighted-average contribution margin is based on each product's individual contribution margin and the percentage it comprises of the company's overall sales mix.

LO9 **Determine semivariable cost elements.** Semivariable costs have both a fixed component and a variable component. Separating semivariable costs into their fixed and variable components is a constant challenge faced by managers. The high-low method is a simple approach used by managers to better understand the structure of semivariable costs.

Key Terms Introduced or Emphasized In Chapter 20

break-even point (p. 886) The level of sales at which a company neither earns an operating profit nor incurs a loss. Revenue exactly covers costs and expenses.

contribution margin (p. 888) Sales minus variable costs. The portion of sales revenue that is not consumed by variable costs and, therefore, is available to cover fixed costs and contribute to operating income.

contribution margin per unit (p. 888) The excess of unit sales price over variable cost per unit; the dollar amount contributed by the sale of each unit toward covering fixed costs and generating operating income.

contribution margin ratio (p. 889) The contribution margin expressed as a percentage of sales price. Represents the percentage of each revenue dollar that is available to cover fixed costs or to provide an operating profit.

cost formula (p. 895) A mathematical statement expressing the expected amount of a cost in terms of the fixed element of the cost and/or the portion of the cost that varies in response to changes in some activity base. For example, the cost formula for a semivariable cost might be $2,500 per month, plus 5 percent of net sales.

economies of scale (p. 884) A reduction in unit cost achieved through a higher volume of output.

fixed costs (p. 880) Costs and expenses that remain unchanged despite changes in the level of the activity base.

high-low method (p. 894) A method of dividing a semivariable (or mixed) cost into its fixed and variable elements by relating the change in the cost to the change in the activity base between the highest and lowest levels of observed activity.

margin of safety (p. 890) Amount by which actual sales exceed the break-even point.

relevant range (p. 885) The span or range of output over which output is likely to vary and assumptions about cost behavior are generally valid. Excludes extreme volume variations.

sales mix (p. 893) The relative percentages of total sales generated by each type of product that a business sells.

semivariable costs (p. 881) Costs and expenses that respond to changes in the level of the activity base by less than a proportionate amount.

variable costs (p. 881) Costs and expenses that vary directly and proportionately with changes in the level of the activity base.

Demonstration Problem

The management of Fresno Processing Company has engaged you to assist in the development of information to be used for management decisions.

The company has the capacity to process 20,000 tons of cottonseed per year. This processing results in several salable products, including oil, meal, hulls, and lint.

A marketing study indicates that the company can sell its output for the coming year at $200 per ton processed.

You have determined the company's cost structure to be as follows:

Cost of cottonseed	$80 per ton
Processing costs:	
Variable	$26 per ton
Fixed	$340,000 per year
Marketing costs	All variable, $44 per ton
Administrative costs	All fixed, $300,000 per year

Instructions

a. Compute (**1**) the contribution margin and (**2**) the contribution margin ratio per ton of cottonseed processed.

b. Compute the break-even sales volume in (**1**) dollars and (**2**) tons of cottonseed.

c. Assume that the company's budget calls for an operating income of $240,000. Compute the sales volume required to reach this profit objective, stated (**1**) in dollars and (**2**) in tons of cottonseed.

d. Compute the maximum amount that the company can afford to pay per ton of raw cottonseed and still break even by processing and selling 16,000 tons during the current year.

Solution to the Demonstration Problem

a. (**1**) Total revenue per ton of cottonseed		$200
Less: Variable costs:		
Cottonseed	$80	
Processing	26	
Marketing	44	150
Unit contribution margin ($200 − $150)		$ 50
(**2**) Contribution margin ratio ($50 ÷ $200)		25%
b. (**1**) Break-even dollar sales volume:		
Fixed costs ($340,000 + $300,000)		$ 640,000
Contribution margin ratio (part **a**)		25%
Break-even dollar sales volume ($640,000 ÷ 0.25)		$2,560,000
(**2**) Break-even unit sales volume (in tons):		
Fixed costs (per previous)		$ 640,000
Unit contribution margin (part **a**)		$ 50
Break-even unit sales volume, stated in tons of cottonseed products ($640,000 ÷ $50)		12,800

(Alternative computation: Break-even dollar sales volume, $2,560,000, divided by unit sales price, $200, equals 12,800 tons.)

c. **(1)** Required dollar sales volume:

Fixed expenses	$ 640,000
Add: Target operating income	240,000
Required contribution margin	$ 880,000
Contribution margin ratio (part **a**)	25%
Required dollar sales volume ($880,000 ÷ 0.25)	$3,520,000

(2) Required unit sales volume:

Required dollar sales volume [from (**1**)]	$3,520,000
Unit sales price	$ 200
Required unit sales volume, in tons ($3,520,000 ÷ $200)	17,600

(Alternative computation: Required contribution margin to cover fixed expenses and target operating income, $880,000, [part **c**(**1**)], divided by unit contribution margin, $50 per ton, equals 17,600 tons.)

d.

Total revenue (16,000 tons × $200)		$3,200,000
Less: Costs other than cottonseed:		
Processing (16,000 tons × $26)	$416,000	
Marketing (16,000 tons × $44)	704,000	
Fixed costs	640,000	1,760,000
Maximum amount that can be paid for 16,000 tons of cottonseed, while allowing company to break even		$1,440,000
Maximum amount that can be paid per ton of cottonseed, while allowing company to break even ($1,440,000 ÷ 16,000 tons)		$90

Self-Test Questions

The answers to these questions appear on page 915.

1. During the current year, the net sales of Ridgeway, Inc., were 10 percent below last year's level. You should expect Ridgeway's semivariable costs to:
   a. Decrease in total, but increase as a percentage of net sales.
   b. Increase in total and increase as a percentage of net sales.
   c. Decrease in total and decrease as a percentage of net sales.
   d. Increase in total, but decrease as a percentage of net sales.
2. Marston Company sells a single product at a sales price of $50 per unit. Fixed costs total $15,000 per month, and variable costs amount to $20 per unit. If management reduces the sales price of this product by $5 per unit, the sales volume needed for the company to break even will:
   a. Increase by $5,000. **c.** Increase by $2,000.
   b. Increase by $4,500. **d.** Remain unchanged.
3. Olsen Auto Supply typically earns a contribution margin ratio of 40 percent. The store manager estimates that by spending an additional $5,000 per month for radio advertising the store will be able to increase its operating income by $3,000 per month. The manager is expecting the radio advertising to increase monthly dollar sales volume by:
   a. $12,500. **c.** $7,500.
   b. $8,000. **d.** Some other amount.
4. Shown below are the monthly high and low levels of direct labor hours and total manufacturing overhead for Apex Mfg. Co.

	Direct Labor Hours	Total Manufacturing Overhead
Highest observed level	6,000	$17,000
Lowest observed level	4,000	14,000

   In a month in which 5,000 direct labor hours are used, the *fixed element* of total manufacturing overhead costs should be approximately:
   a. $15,500. **c.** $7,500.
   b. $8,000. **d.** $8,000 plus $1.50 per unit.
5. Driver Company manufactures two products. Data concerning these products are shown below:

	Product A	Product B
Total monthly demand (in units)	1,000	200
Sales price per unit	$400	$500
Contribution margin ratio	30%	40%
Relative sales mix	80%	20%

   If fixed costs are equal to $320,000, what amount of total sales revenue is needed to break even?
   a. $914,286. **c.** $320,000.
   b. $457,143. **d.** $1,000,000.

ASSIGNMENT MATERIAL

Discussion Questions

1. Why is it important for management to understand cost-volume-profit relationships?
2. What is an *activity base* and why is it important in analyzing cost behavior?
3. What is the effect of an increase in activity on the following items?
   a. Total variable costs.
   b. Variable costs per unit of activity.
   c. Total fixed costs.
   d. Fixed costs per unit of activity.
4. The simplifying assumption that costs and volume vary in straight-line relationships makes the analysis of cost behavior much easier. What factors make this a reasonable and useful assumption in many cases?
5. Define the *relevant range* of activity.
6. Explain how the high-low method determines:
   a. The variable portion of a semivariable cost.
   b. The fixed portion of a semivariable cost.
7. Define (**a**) *contribution margin,* (**b**) *contribution margin ratio,* and (**c**) *average contribution margin ratio.*
8. What important relationships are shown on a cost-volume-profit (break-even) graph?
9. Explain how the unit contribution margin can be used to determine the unit sales required to break even.
10. Define *margin of safety.*
11. An executive of a large American steel company put the blame for lower net income for a recent fiscal period on the "shift in product mix to a higher proportion of export sales." Sales for the period increased slightly while net income declined by 28 percent. Explain how a change in product (sales) mix to a higher proportion in export sales could result in a lower level of net income.
12. Explain why businesses normally can reduce unit costs by utilizing their facilities more intensively.
13. Why does cost-volume-profit analysis focus upon *operating income* instead of *net income*?
14. A regional airline and a furniture manufacturer each generate annual revenue of $120 million and earn net income of $10 million. Which company probably has the higher break-even point? Explain.
15. List the assumptions that underlie cost-volume-profit analysis.

Brief Exercises

LO1 **BRIEF EXERCISE 20.1**

Patterns of Cost Behavior

Explain the effects of an increase in the volume of activity on the following costs. (Assume volume remains within the relevant range.)

a. Total variable costs
b. Variable cost per unit
c. Total fixed cost
d. Fixed cost per unit
e. Total semivariable costs
f. Semivariable cost per unit

LO1 **BRIEF EXERCISE 20.2**

Classification of Various Costs

Explain whether you regard each of the following costs or categories of costs as fixed, variable, or semivariable with respect to net sales. Briefly explain your reasoning. If you do not believe that a cost fits into any of these classifications, explain.

a. The cost of goods sold.
b. Salaries to salespeople (these salaries include a monthly minimum amount, plus a commission on all sales).
c. Income taxes expense.
d. Property taxes expense.
e. Depreciation expense on a sales showroom, based on the straight-line method of depreciation.
f. Depreciation expense on a sales showroom, based on the double-declining-balance method of depreciation.

LO1 LO9 **BRIEF EXERCISE 20.3**

Using a Cost Formula

City Ambulance Service estimates the monthly cost of responding to emergency calls to be $19,500, plus $110 per call.

a. In a month in which the company responds to 125 emergency calls, determine the estimated:
   1. Total cost of responding to emergency calls.
   2. Average cost of responding to emergency calls.
b. Assume that in a given month, the number of emergency calls was unusually low. Would you expect the average cost of responding to emergency calls during this month to be higher or lower than in other months? Explain.

LO1 LO4 LO5 LO9

BRIEF EXERCISE 20.4

Using a Cost Formula

Through using the high-low method, Regency Hotels estimates the total costs of providing room service meals to amount to $5,950 per month, plus 30 percent of room service revenue.

a. What is the contribution margin ratio of providing room service meals?

b. What is the break-even point for room service operations in terms of total room service revenue?

c. What would you expect to be the total cost of providing room service in a month in which room service revenue amounts to $15,000?

LO4 through LO6

BRIEF EXERCISE 20.5

Computing Sales Volume

Porter Corporation has fixed costs of $660,000, variable costs of $24 per unit, and a contribution margin ratio of 40 percent.

Compute the following:

a. Unit sales price and unit contribution margin for the above product.

b. The sales volume in units required for Porter Corporation to earn an operating income of $300,000.

c. The dollar sales volume required for Porter Corporation to earn an operating income of $300,000.

LO4 through LO6

BRIEF EXERCISE 20.6

Computing Sales Volume

Jackson Company recently calculated its break-even sales revenue to be $15,000. For each dollar of sales revenue, $0.70 goes to cover variable costs.

Compute the following:

a. The contribution margin ratio.

b. Total fixed costs.

c. The sales revenue that would have to be generated to earn an operating income of $9,000.

LO1 LO4 through LO6

BRIEF EXERCISE 20.7

Relating Contribution Margin Ratio to Sales Price

Firebird Mfg. Co. has a contribution margin ratio of 45 percent and must sell 25,000 units at a price of $80 each in order to break even.

a. Compute total fixed costs.

b. Compute variable cost per unit.

c. Develop the company's *cost formula.*

LO7

BRIEF EXERCISE 20.8

Evaluating a Marketing Strategy

Chaps & Saddles, a retailer of tack and Western apparel, earns an average contribution margin of 45 percent on its sales volume. Recently, the advertising manager of a local "country" radio station offered to run numerous radio advertisements for Chaps & Saddles at a monthly cost of $1,800.

Compute the amount by which the proposed radio advertising campaign must increase Chaps & Saddles's monthly sales volume to:

a. Pay for itself.

b. Increase operating income by $1,000 per month. (Round computations to the nearest dollar.)

LO1

BRIEF EXERCISE 20.9

Selecting an Activity Base

You have been hired as a consultant to assist the following companies with cost-volume-profit analysis:

Freeman's Retail Floral Shop

Susquehanna Trails Bus Service

Wilson Pump Manufacturers

McCauley & Pratt, Attorneys-at-Law

Suggest an appropriate activity base for each of these clients.

LO8

BRIEF EXERCISE 20.10

CVP with Multiple Products

Glow Worm Corporation makes flashlights and batteries. Its monthly fixed costs average $3,680,000. The company has provided the following information about its two product lines:

	Contribution Margin Ratio	Percentage of Total Sales
Flashlights	40%	15%
Batteries	20	85

a. Determine the company's monthly break-even point in *sales dollars.*

b. How much revenue must the company generate in the upcoming month for a monthly operating income of $1,380,000?

Exercises

LO1 LO2 LO4

EXERCISE 20.1

Accounting Terminology

Listed below are nine technical accounting terms introduced in this chapter:

Variable costs	Relevant range	Contribution margin
Break-even point	Fixed costs	Semivariable costs
Economies of scale	Sales mix	Unit contribution margin

Each of the following statements may (or may not) describe one of these technical terms. For each statement, indicate the accounting term described, or answer "None" if the statement does not correctly describe any of the terms.

a. The level of sales at which revenue exactly equals costs and expenses.

b. Costs that remain unchanged despite changes in sales volume.

c. The span over which output is likely to vary and assumptions about cost behavior generally remain valid.

d. Sales revenue less variable costs and expenses.

e. Unit sales price minus variable cost per unit.

f. The reduction in unit cost achieved from a higher level of output.

g. Costs that respond to changes in sales volume by less than a proportionate amount.

h. Operating income less variable costs.

LO1 LO9

EXERCISE 20.2

High-Low Method of Cost Analysis

The following information is available regarding the total manufacturing overhead of Bursa Mfg. Co. for a recent four-month period:

	Machine-Hours	Manufacturing Overhead
Jan.	5,500	$311,500
Feb.	3,200	224,000
Mar.	4,900	263,800
Apr.	2,800	184,600

a. Use the high-low method to determine:

1. The variable element of manufacturing overhead costs per machine-hour.

2. The fixed element of monthly overhead cost.

b. Bursa expects machine-hours in May to equal 5,300. Use the cost relationships determined in part **a** to forecast May's manufacturing overhead costs.

c. Suppose Bursa had used the cost relationships determined in part **a** to estimate the total manufacturing overhead expected for the months of February and March. By what amounts would Bursa have over- or underestimated these costs?

LO4 LO5

EXERCISE 20.3 Computing Required Sales Volume

The following is information concerning a product manufactured by Ames Brothers:

Sales price per unit	$ 70
Variable cost per unit	43
Total fixed manufacturing and operating costs (per month)	405,000

Determine the following:

a. The unit contribution margin.

b. The number of units that must be sold each month to break even.

c. The unit sales level that must be reached to earn an operating income of $270,000 per month.

LO4 through LO6

EXERCISE 20.4 Computing the Break-Even Point

Malibu Corporation has monthly fixed costs of $63,000. It sells two products for which it has provided the following information:

	Sales Price	Contribution Margin
Product 1	$10	$6
Product 2	10	3

a. What total monthly sales revenue is required to break even if the relative sales mix is 40 percent for Product 1 and 60 percent for Product 2?

b. What total monthly sales revenue is required to earn a monthly operating income of $12,000 if the relative sales mix is 25 percent for Product 1 and 75 percent for Product 2?

LO1 LO4

EXERCISE 20.5 Cost-Volume-Profit Relationships

For each of the six independent situations below, compute the missing amounts.

a. Using contribution margin per unit:

	Sales	Variable Costs	Contribution Margin per Unit	Fixed Costs	Operating Income	Units Sold
(1)	$______	$120,000	$20	$______	$25,000	4,000
(2)	180,000	______	___	45,000	30,000	5,000
(3)	600,000	______	30	150,000	90,000	____

b. Using the contribution margin ratio:

	Sales	Variable Costs	Contribution Margin Ratio	Fixed Costs	Operating Income
(1)	$900,000	$720,000	__%	$______	$95,000
(2)	600,000	______	40%	______	75,000
(3)	______	______	30%	90,000	60,000

LO5 through LO7

EXERCISE 20.6 Ethical and Behavioral Implications of CVP

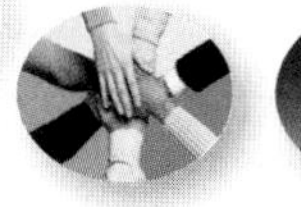

Tom Klem is the controller of Watson Manufacturing, Inc. He estimates that the company's break-even point in sales dollars is $2 million. However, he recently told all of the regional sales managers that sales of $3 million were needed to break even. He also told them that if the company failed to break even, the sales force would be reduced in size by 40 percent. Klem believes that his tactics will motivate the sales force to generate record profits for the upcoming year.

Is his approach to motivating employees ethical? What other approaches might he use?

LO4 through LO6

EXERCISE 20.7 Using Cost-Volume-Profit Formulas

MURDER TO GO! writes and manufactures murder mystery parlor games that it sells to retail stores. The following is per-unit information relating to the manufacture and sale of this product:

Unit sales price	$ 28
Variable cost per unit	7
Fixed costs per year	240,000

Determine the following, showing as part of your answer the formula that you used in your computation. For example, the formula used to determine the contribution margin ratio (part **a**) is:

$$\textbf{Contribution Margin Ratio} = \frac{\textbf{Unit Sales Price} - \textbf{Variable Costs per Unit}}{\textbf{Unit Sales Price}}$$

a. Contribution margin ratio.

b. Sales volume (in dollars) required to break even.

c. Sales volume (in dollars) required to earn an annual operating income of $450,000.

d. The margin of safety sales volume if annual sales total 40,000 units.

e. Operating income if annual sales total 40,000 units.

LO4 through LO6

EXERCISE 20.8 Using Cost-Volume-Profit Formulas

Arrow Products typically earns a contribution margin ratio of 25 percent and has current fixed costs of $80,000. Arrow's general manager is considering spending an additional $20,000 to do one of the following:

1. Start a new ad campaign that is expected to increase sales revenue by 5 percent.

2. License a new computerized ordering system that is expected to increase Arrow's contribution margin ratio to 30 percent.

Sales revenue for the coming year was initially forecast to equal $1,200,000 (that is, without implementing either of the above options).

a. For each option, how much will projected operating income increase or decrease relative to initial predictions?

b. By what percentage would sales revenue need to increase to make the ad campaign as attractive as the ordering system?

LO1 LO2 LO4 through LO6

EXERCISE 20.9 Understanding Break-Even Relationships

EasyWriter manufactures an erasable ballpoint pen, which sells for $1.75 per unit. Management recently finished analyzing the results of the company's operations for the current month. At a break-even point of 40,000 units, the company's total variable costs are $50,000 and its total fixed costs amount to $20,000.

a. Calculate the contribution margin per unit.

b. Calculate the company's margin of safety if monthly sales total 45,000 units.

c. Estimate the company's monthly operating loss if it sells only 38,000 units.

d. Compute the total cost per unit at a production level of (**1**) 40,000 pens per month and (**2**) 50,000 pens per month. Explain the reason for the change in unit costs.

LO4 LO5

EXERCISE 20.10 Computing Contribution Margin Ratio and Margin of Safety

The following information relates to the only product sold by Harper Company:

Sales price per unit	$ 24
Variable cost per unit	18
Fixed costs per year	240,000

a. Compute the contribution margin ratio and the dollar sales volume required to break even.

b. Assuming that the company sells 75,000 units during the current year, compute the margin of safety sales volume (dollars).

LO1 LO2 LO4 through LO6

EXERCISE 20.11 Applying CVP Concepts

Mathias Corporation manufactures and sells wire rakes. The rakes sell for $16 each. Information about the company's costs is as follows:

Variable manufacturing cost per unit	$ 8
Variable selling and administrative cost per unit	4
Fixed manufacturing overhead per month	$150,000
Fixed selling and administrative cost per month	350,000

a. Determine the company's monthly break-even point in units.

b. Determine the sales volume (in dollars) required for a monthly operating income of $100,000.

c. Compute the company's margin of safety if its current monthly sales level is $3,800,000.

d. Estimate the amount by which monthly operating income will increase if the company anticipates a $200,000 increase in monthly sales volume.

LO5 LO6

EXERCISE 20.12 Finding Missing Information

Palomus Controls currently produces and sells 20,000 regulators monthly. At this level, its variable cost per regulator is $26 and its fixed cost *per regulator* is $7. The company's monthly break-even point is 10,000 regulators.

Determine the company's current *selling price* per regulator.

LO1 LO4 through LO6

EXERCISE 20.13 Determining a Bid Price Using CVP Relationships

Douglas Company has been asked to submit a bid on supplying gas masks to the Pentagon. The company's current cost structure *per mask* is as follows:

Direct materials	$9
Direct labor	8
Variable manufacturing overhead	7
Variable sales commissions	6

a. Assume that there would be *no variable sales commission* on this special order. Determine the *lowest* unit price that Douglas can bid without reducing its current level of operating income.

b. Assume the company desires a 36 percent contribution margin ratio from this sale and that a special sales commission of 4 percent of the bid price will be applied to the order *instead of* its normal $6 variable sales commission. Determine the bid price per unit given these unique circumstances.

LO7 LO8

EXERCISE 20.14 CVP with Multiple Products

Water World sells three products: ski vests, slalom skis, and ski ropes. Information related to each product line is provided below:

	Ski Vests	Slalom Skis	Ski Ropes
Unit selling price	$120	$300	$50
Unit variable cost	60	210	10
Sales mix percentage	20%	70%	10%

The company's annual fixed costs are approximately $741,000.

a. Compute total annual sales that the company must generate to *break even.*

b. Compute total annual sales that the company must generate to earn *operating income* of $234,000.

c. As Water World's marketing manager, what marketing strategy would you pursue to help the company maximize its profit potential?

LO9

EXERCISE 20.15 Estimating Semivariable Costs

Dinklemyer Corporation uses direct labor hours as its single cost driver. Actual overhead costs and actual direct labor hours for the first five months of the current year are as follows:

Month	Actual Total Overhead	Actual Direct Labor Hours
January	$980,000	19,200
February	950,000	18,400
March	860,000	17,000
April	752,500	12,700
May	760,000	13,200

a. Compute the company's estimated *variable* manufacturing overhead cost *per direct labor hour.*

b. Estimate the company's total monthly *fixed* manufacturing overhead cost.

c. Estimate the company's *total* manufacturing overhead for *June through August* if 50,000 total direct labor hours are budgeted for that specific three-month period.

Problem Set A

LO4 through LO7

PROBLEM 20.1A Setting Sales Price and Computing the Break-Even Point

Thermal Tent, Inc., is a newly organized manufacturing business that plans to manufacture and sell 50,000 units per year of a new product. The following estimates have been made of the company's costs and expenses (other than income taxes):

	Fixed	Variable per Unit
Manufacturing costs:		
Direct materials		$47
Direct labor		32
Manufacturing overhead	$340,000	4
Period costs:		
Selling expenses		1
Administrative expenses	200,000	
Totals	$540,000	$84

Instructions

a. What should the company establish as the sales price per unit if it sets a target of earning an operating income of $260,000 by producing and selling 50,000 units during the first year of operations? (Hint: First compute the required contribution margin per unit.)

b. At the unit sales price computed in part **a,** how many units must the company produce and sell to break even? (Assume all units produced are sold.)

c. What will be the margin of safety (in dollars) if the company produces and sells 50,000 units at the sales price computed in part **a**? Using the margin of safety, compute operating income at 50,000 units.

d. Assume that the marketing manager thinks that the price of this product must be no higher than $94 to ensure market penetration. Will setting the sales price at $94 enable Thermal Tent to break even, given the plans to manufacture and sell 50,000 units? Explain your answer.

LO1 LO4 LO5

PROBLEM 20.2A Estimating Costs and Profits

Blaster Corporation manufactures hiking boots. For the coming year, the company has budgeted the following costs for the production and sale of 30,000 pairs of boots:

	Budgeted Costs	Budgeted Costs per Pair	Percentage of Costs Considered Variable
Direct materials	$ 630,000	$21	100%
Direct labor	300,000	10	100
Manufacturing overhead (fixed and variable)	720,000	24	25
Selling and administrative expenses	600,000	20	20
Totals	$2,250,000	$75	

Instructions

a. Compute the sales price per unit that would result in a budgeted operating income of $900,000, assuming that the company produces and sells 30,000 pairs. (Hint: First compute the budgeted sales revenue needed to produce this operating income.)

b. Assuming that the company decides to sell the boots at a unit price of $121 per pair, compute the following:

1. Total fixed costs budgeted for the year.
2. Variable cost per unit.
3. The unit contribution margin.
4. The number of pairs that must be produced and sold annually to break even at a sales price of $121 per pair.

LO3 through LO6 LO9

PROBLEM 20.3A
Preparing a "Break-Even" Graph

Stop-n-Shop operates a downtown parking lot containing 800 parking spaces. The lot is open 2,500 hours per year. The parking charge per car is 50 cents per hour; the average customer parks two hours. Stop-n-Shop rents the lot from a development company for $7,250 per month. The lot supervisor is paid $24,000 per year. Five employees who handle the parking of cars are paid $300 per week for 50 weeks, plus $600 each for the two-week vacation period. Employees rotate vacations during the slow months when four employees can handle the reduced load of traffic. Lot maintenance, payroll taxes, and other costs of operating the parking lot include fixed costs of $3,000 per month and variable costs of 5 cents per parking-space hour.

Instructions

a. Draw a cost-volume-profit graph for Stop-n-Shop on an annual basis. Use thousands of parking-space hours as the measure of volume of activity. [Stop-n-Shop has an annual capacity of 2 million parking-space hours (800 spaces × 2,500 hours per year).]

b. What is the contribution margin ratio? What is the annual break-even point in dollars of parking revenue?

c. Suppose that the five employees were taken off the hourly wage basis and paid 30 cents per car parked, with the same vacation pay as before. (**1**) How would this change the contribution margin ratio and total fixed costs? (Hint: The variable costs per parking-space hour will now include 15 cents, or one-half of the 30 cents paid to employees per car parked, because the average customer parks for two hours.) (**2**) What annual revenue would be necessary to produce operating income of $300,000 under these circumstances?

LO3 LO4 LO6 LO9

PROBLEM 20.4A
Drawing a Cost-Volume-Profit Graph

Rainbow Paints operates a chain of retail paint stores. Although the paint is sold under the Rainbow label, it is purchased from an independent paint manufacturer. Guy Walker, president of Rainbow Paints, is studying the advisability of opening another store. His estimates of monthly costs for the proposed location are:

Fixed costs:	
Occupancy costs	$3,160
Salaries	3,640
Other	1,200
Variable costs (including cost of paint)	$6 per gallon

Although Rainbow stores sell several different types of paint, monthly sales revenue consistently averages $10 per gallon sold.

Instructions

a. Compute the contribution margin ratio and the break-even point in dollar sales and in gallons sold for the proposed store.

b. Draw a monthly cost-volume-profit graph for the proposed store, assuming 3,000 gallons per month as the maximum sales potential.

c. Walker thinks that the proposed store will sell between 2,200 and 2,600 gallons of paint per month. Compute the amount of operating income that would be earned per month at each of these sales volumes.

LO3 through LO7 LO9

PROBLEM 20.5A
Cost-Volume-Profit Analysis; Preparing a Graph

Simon Teguh is considering investing in a vending machine operation involving 20 vending machines located in various plants around the city. The machine manufacturer reports that similar vending machine routes have produced a sales volume ranging from 800 to 1,000 units per machine per month. The following information is made available to Teguh in evaluating the possible profitability of the operation.

1. An investment of $45,000 will be required, $9,000 for merchandise and $36,000 for the 20 machines.
2. The machines have a service life of five years and no salvage value at the end of that period. Depreciation will be computed on the straight-line basis.
3. The merchandise (candy and soft drinks) retails for an average of 75 cents per unit and will cost Teguh an average of 25 cents per unit.
4. Owners of the buildings in which the machines are located are paid a commission of 5 cents per unit of candy and soft drinks sold.

5. One person will be hired to service the machines. The salary will be $1,500 per month.
6. Other expenses are estimated at $600 per month. These expenses do not vary with the number of units sold.

Instructions

a. Determine the unit contribution margin and the break-even volume in units and in dollars per month.

b. Draw a monthly cost-volume-profit graph for sales volume up to 1,000 units per machine per month.

c. What sales volume in units and in dollars per month will be necessary to produce an operating income equal to a 30 percent annual return on Teguh's $45,000 investment? (Round to the nearest unit.)

d. Teguh is considering offering the building owners a flat rental of $30 per machine per month in lieu of the commission of 5 cents per unit sold. What effect would this change in commission arrangement have on his *monthly* break-even volume in terms of units?

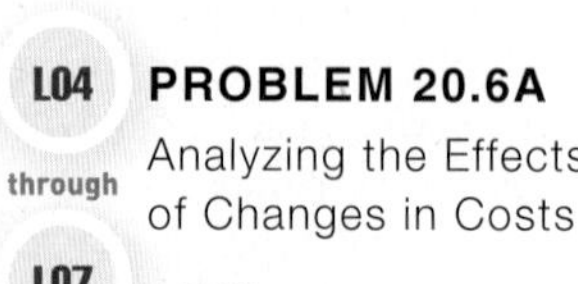

PROBLEM 20.6A
Analyzing the Effects of Changes in Costs

eXcel

Precision Systems manufactures CD burners and currently sells 18,500 units annually to producers of laptop computers. Jay Wilson, president of the company, anticipates a 15 percent increase in the cost per unit of direct labor on January 1 of next year. He expects all other costs and expenses to remain unchanged. Wilson has asked you to assist him in developing the information he needs to formulate a reasonable product strategy for next year.

You are satisfied that volume is the primary factor affecting costs and expenses and have separated the semivariable costs into their fixed and variable segments. Beginning and ending inventories remain at a level of 1,000 units. Current plant capacity is 20,000 units.

Below are the current-year data assembled for your analysis:

Sales price per unit		$100
Variable costs per unit:		
Direct materials	$10	
Direct labor	20	
Manufacturing overhead and selling and administrative expenses	30	60
Contribution margin per unit (40%)		$ 40
Fixed costs		$390,000

Instructions

a. What increase in the selling price is necessary to cover the 15 percent increase in direct labor cost and still maintain the current contribution margin ratio of 40 percent?

b. How many units must be sold to maintain the current operating income of *$350,000* if the sales price remains at $100 and the 15 percent wage increase goes into effect? (Hint: First compute the unit contribution margin.)

c. Wilson believes that an additional $700,000 of machinery (to be depreciated at 20 percent annually) will increase present capacity (20,000 units) by 25 percent. If all units produced can be sold at the present price of $100 per unit and the wage increase goes into effect, how would the estimated operating income before capacity is increased compare with the estimated operating income after capacity is increased? Prepare schedules of estimated operating income at full capacity *before* and *after* the expansion.

LO4 LO6

PROBLEM 20.7A
Analyzing the Effects of Changes in Costs and Volume

Percula Farms raises marine fish for sale in the aquarium trade. Each year, Percula obtains a batch of approximately 1 million eggs from a local supplier. Percula's manager is trying to decide whether to use the farm's facilities to raise Maroon Clownfish or Queen Angelfish. Clownfish eggs cost $5,500 per batch, while angelfish eggs cost $9,500 per batch. Due to differences in needs, only one species may be raised at a time and only one batch of fish can be raised in any 52-week period.

With current facilities, approximately 10 percent of clownfish eggs and 5 percent of angelfish eggs can be successfully raised to maturity. Clownfish take approximately 35 weeks to grow to a salable size, while angelfish take 50 weeks. Angelfish also require more care than clownfish. Each week, angelfish need two complete water changes and 20 feedings, while clownfish need only one water change and 15 feedings. Each feeding costs $150 and each water change costs $1,000. Heating and lighting costs equal $400 per week of rearing, regardless of which type of fish is being raised. Fixed overhead costs for the year amount to $80,000. Percula can sell clownfish for $4 each and angelfish for $10 each.

Instructions

a. Which species should Percula raise to earn the highest operating income for the year?

b. Other than fixed costs, which factors or categories of costs seem to have the greatest influence on operating income?

c. Percula's manager is considering the following improvements, each of which will cost an additional $8,000 for the year. Due to resource limitations, only one can be implemented.

   1. Purchasing a higher quality filter material that will significantly improve water conditions in the rearing tanks. The higher water quality will increase the survival rates to 12 percent for clownfish and 6 percent for angelfish. The need for water changes will also be reduced to one each week for angelfish. Due to the higher yields, feeding costs will increase to $160 each.
   2. Installing newer, more efficient equipment that will reduce heating and lighting costs to $300 per week of rearing. The new equipment will promote more stable conditions, increasing the survival rates of clownfish to 10.5 percent and of angelfish to 5.5 percent. The slight change in survival rates is not expected to increase feeding costs.

   Using your answers to part **b** above (with no calculations), which option do you think will be more beneficial?

d. Perform the necessary calculations to check if your answer to part **c** was correct. Should either of the investments be undertaken, and if so, which fish species should be raised?

LO4 through LO8 PROBLEM 20.8A
CVP with Multiple Products

Lifefit Products sells running shoes and shorts. The following is selected per-unit information for these two products:

	Shoes	Shorts
Sales price	$50	$5
Variable costs and expenses	35	1
Contribution margin	$15	$4

Fixed costs and expenses amount to *$378,000* per month.

Lifefit has total sales of $1 million per month, of which 80 percent result from the sale of running shoes and the other 20 percent from the sale of shorts.

Instructions

a. Compute separately the contribution margin ratio for each line of products.

b. Assuming the current sales mix, compute:
   1. Average contribution margin ratio of total monthly sales.
   2. Monthly operating income.
   3. The monthly break-even sales volume (stated in dollars).

c. Assume that through aggressive marketing Lifefit is able to *shift its sales mix* toward more sales of shorts. Total sales remain $1 million per month, but now 30 percent of this revenue stems from sales of shorts. Using this new sales mix, compute:
   1. Average contribution margin ratio of total monthly sales.
   2. Monthly operating income.
   3. The monthly break-even sales volume (stated in dollars).

d. Explain *why* the company's financial picture changes so significantly with the new sales mix.

Problem Set B

LO4 through LO7 PROBLEM 20.1B
Setting Sales Price and Computing the Break-Even Point

Satka, Inc., is a newly organized manufacturing business that plans to manufacture and sell 30,000 units per year of a new product. The following estimates have been made of the company's costs and expenses (other than income taxes):

	Fixed	Variable per Unit
Manufacturing costs:		
Direct materials		$ 38
Direct labor		47
Manufacturing overhead	$440,000	9
Period costs:		
Selling expenses		6
Administrative expenses	360,000	
Totals	$800,000	$100

Instructions

a. What should the company establish as the sales price per unit if it sets a target of earning an operating income of $400,000 by producing and selling 30,000 units during the first year of operations? (Hint: First compute the required contribution margin per unit.)

b. At the unit sales price computed in part **a,** how many units must the company produce and sell to break even? (Assume all units produced are sold.)

c. What will be the margin of safety (in dollars) if the company produces and sells 30,000 units at the sales price computed in part **a**?

d. Assume that the marketing manager thinks that the price of this product must be no higher than $132 to ensure market penetration. Will setting the sales price at $132 enable Satka to break even, given the plans to manufacture and sell 30,000 units? Explain your answer.

PROBLEM 20.2B Estimating Costs and Profits

LO1 LO4 LO5

Snug-As-A-Bug manufactures sleeping bags. For the coming year, the company has budgeted the following costs for the production and sale of 80,000 units:

	Budgeted Costs	Budgeted Costs per Unit	Percentage of Costs Considered Variable
Direct materials	$1,440,000	$18	100%
Direct labor	160,000	2	100
Manufacturing overhead (fixed and variable)	2,400,000	30	10
Selling and administrative expenses	800,000	10	40
Totals	$4,800,000	$60	

Instructions

a. Compute the sales price per unit that would result in a budgeted operating income of $560,000, assuming that the company produces and sells 80,000 bags. (Hint: First compute the budgeted sales revenue needed to produce this operating income.)

b. Assuming that the company decides to sell the sleeping bags at a unit price of $71 per unit, compute the following:

1. Total fixed costs budgeted for the year.
2. Variable cost per unit.
3. The unit contribution margin.
4. The number of bags that must be produced and sold annually to break even at a sales price of $71 per unit.

PROBLEM 20.3B Preparing a "Break-Even" Graph

LO3 through LO6 LO9

Moor-n-More operates a boat mooring service in the downtown harbor with 80 docking spaces. The business is open 3,000 hours per year. The mooring charge per boat is $5 per hour; the average boater docks for two hours. Moor-n-More rents the harbor space from the Harbor Authority for $5,000 per month. The general manager is paid $32,940 per year. Three employees assist in the operations and are paid $250 per week for 50 weeks, plus $500 each for a two-week vacation period. Employees rotate their vacations. Other costs include fixed city taxes of $1,500 per month and variable costs of 10 cents per occupied mooring-space hour (a usage tax charged by the Harbor Authority).

Instructions

a. Draw a cost-volume-profit graph for Moor-n-More on an annual basis. Use thousands of mooring-space hours as the measure of volume of activity. [Moor-n-More has an annual capacity of 240,000 mooring-space hours (80 spaces × 3,000 hours per year).]

b. What is the contribution margin ratio? What is the annual break-even point in dollars of mooring revenue?

c. Suppose that the three employees were taken off the hourly wage basis and paid 40 cents per boat moored, with the same vacation pay as before. (**1**) How would this change the contribution margin ratio and total fixed costs? (Hint: The variable costs per mooring-space hour will now include 20 cents, or one-half of the 40 cents paid to employees per occupied mooring space, because the average boater stays for two hours.) (**2**) What annual revenue would be necessary to produce operating income of $112,560 under these circumstances?

LO3 LO4 LO6 LO9

PROBLEM 20.4B
Drawing a Cost-Volume-Profit Graph

Green Thumb operates a chain of lawn fertilizer stores. Although the fertilizer is sold under the Green Thumb label, it is purchased from an independent manufacturer. Sue Smith, president of Green Thumb, is studying the advisability of opening another store. Her estimates of monthly costs for the proposed location are:

Fixed costs:	
Occupancy costs	$5,000
Salaries	2,400
Other	1,600
Variable costs (including cost of fertilizer)	$ 12 per bag

Although Green Thumb stores sell several different types of fertilizer, monthly sales revenue consistently averages $20 per bag sold.

Instructions

a. Compute the contribution margin ratio and the break-even point in dollar sales and in bags sold for the proposed store.

b. Draw a monthly cost-volume-profit graph for the proposed store, assuming 2,000 bags per month as the maximum sales potential.

c. Smith thinks that the proposed store will sell between 1,500 and 1,800 bags of fertilizer per month. Compute the amount of operating income that would be earned per month at each of these sales volumes.

LO3 through LO7 LO9

PROBLEM 20.5B
Cost-Volume-Profit Analysis; Preparing a Graph

Ed Winslow is considering investing in a sandwich machine operation involving 50 sandwich machines located in various locations throughout the city. The machine manufacturer reports that similar sandwich machine routes have produced a sales volume ranging from 40 to 60 units per machine per month. The following information is made available to Winslow in evaluating the possible profitability of the operation.

1. An investment of $70,000 will be required, $10,000 for merchandise and $60,000 for the 50 machines.
2. The machines have a service life of five years and no salvage value at the end of that period. Depreciation will be computed on the straight-line basis.
3. Sandwiches sell for an average of $3.20 and will cost Winslow an average of $1.10 per unit to prepare.
4. Owners of the buildings in which the machines are located are paid a commission of 10 cents per sandwich sold.
5. One person will be hired to service the machines. The salary will be $1,800 per month.
6. Other expenses are estimated at $200 per month. These expenses do not vary with the number of units sold.

Instructions

a. Determine the unit contribution margin and the break-even volume in units and in dollars per month.

b. Draw a monthly cost-volume-profit graph for sales volume up to 60 units per machine per month.

c. What sales volume in units and in dollars per month will be necessary to produce an operating income equal to a 12 percent annual return on Winslow's $70,000 investment? (Round to the nearest unit.)

d. Winslow is considering offering the building owners a flat rental of $45 per machine per month in lieu of the commission of 10 cents per unit sold. What effect would this change in commission arrangement have on his *monthly* break-even volume in terms of units?

LO4 through LO7 LO9

PROBLEM 20.6B

Analyzing the Effects of Changes in Costs

Electro Systems manufactures relays and currently sells 200,000 units annually to producers of electronic equipment. Mac Scott, president of the company, anticipates a 20 percent increase in the cost per unit of direct labor on January 1 of next year. He expects all other costs and expenses to remain unchanged. Scott has asked you to assist him in developing the information he needs to formulate a reasonable product strategy for next year.

You are satisfied that volume is the primary factor affecting costs and expenses and have separated the semivariable costs into their fixed and variable segments. Beginning and ending inventories remain at a level of 3,000 units. Current plant capacity is 210,000 units.

Below are the current-year data assembled for your analysis:

Sales price per unit		$15
Variable costs per unit:		
Direct materials	$3	
Direct labor	1	
Manufacturing overhead and selling and administrative expenses	2	6
Contribution margin per unit (60%)		$ 9
Fixed costs		$1,000,000

Instructions

a. What increase in the selling price is necessary to cover the 20 percent increase in direct labor cost and still maintain the current contribution margin ratio of 60 percent?

b. Approximately how many units must be sold to maintain the current operating income of *$800,000* if the sales price remains at $15 and the 20 percent wage increase goes into effect? (Hint: First compute the unit contribution margin.)

c. Scott believes that an additional $500,000 of machinery (to be depreciated at 20 percent annually) will increase present capacity (210,000 units) by 5 percent. If all units produced can be sold at the present price of $15 per unit and the wage increase goes into effect, how would the estimated operating income before capacity is increased compare with the estimated operating income after capacity is increased? Prepare schedules of estimated operating income at full capacity *before* and *after* the expansion.

LO4 LO6 LO7

PROBLEM 20.7B

Analyzing the Effects of Changes in Costs and Volume

Dorsal Ranch raises fish for sale in the restaurant industry. The company can obtain batches of 2 million eggs from its supplier. Management is trying to decide whether to raise cod or salmon. Cod eggs cost $14,000 per batch, while salmon eggs cost $18,000 per batch. Due to differences in needs, only one species can be raised during a 52-week period.

With current facilities, approximately 15 percent of cod eggs and 10 percent of salmon eggs can be raised to maturity. Cod take approximately 40 weeks to grow to a marketable size, while salmon take 50 weeks. Salmon also require more care than cod. Each week, salmon require two water treatments and 35 feedings. Each feeding costs $400 and each water treatment costs $600. Cod require only 21 feedings and a single water treatment. Heat and light regulation costs average $300 per week for either species. The company can sell cod for $5 apiece and salmon for $9 a piece. Annual fixed costs, regardless of which species is raised, total $900,000.

Instructions

a. Which species should Dorsal Ranch raise to earn the highest operating income for the year?

b. Other than fixed costs, which factors or categories of costs seem to have the greatest influence on operating income?

c. Management is considering one of the following improvements, each of which will cost an additional $20,000 for the year. Due to resource constraints, only one can be implemented.

1. Installing a new filtration system to improve water quality. This will increase the survival rates to 20 percent for cod and 14 percent for salmon. The need for water treatments will be reduced to one per week for salmon. Due to higher yields, feeding costs will increase by $80 weekly.
2. Installing an environment regulation system that will reduce heating and lighting costs to $250 per week. The equipment will increase the survival rate for cod to 16 percent and the survival rate for salmon to 11 percent. This slight change in survival rates is not expected to increase either water changing requirements or feeding costs.

Using your answers to part **b** above (with no calculations), which option do you think will be most beneficial?

d. Perform the necessary calculations to check if your answer to part **c** was correct. Should either of these investments be undertaken, and if so, which species should be raised?

LO4 through LO8

PROBLEM 20.8B
CVP with Multiple Products

HomeTeam Sports sells hats and shirts licensed by the NFL and the NBA. The following is selected per-unit information for these two product lines:

	Hats	Shirts
Sales price	$20	$28
Variable costs and expenses	14	7
Contribution margin	$ 6	$21

Fixed costs and expenses amount to *$684,000* per month.

HomeTeam has total sales of $1.5 million per month, of which 60 percent result from the sale of shirts and the other 40 percent from the sale of hats.

Instructions

a. Compute separately the contribution margin ratio for each line of products.

b. Assuming the current sales mix, compute:

1. Average contribution margin ratio of total monthly sales.
2. Monthly operating income.
3. The monthly break-even sales volume (stated in dollars).

c. Assume that because of consumer trends, the company's *sales mix* shifts to a higher demand for hats. Total sales remain $1.5 million per month, but now 60 percent of this revenue stems from sales of hats. Using this new sales mix, compute:

1. Average contribution margin ratio of total monthly sales.
2. Monthly operating income.
3. The monthly break-even sales volume (stated in dollars).

d. Explain *why* the company's financial picture changes so significantly with the new sales mix.

Critical Thinking Cases

LO1

CASE 20.1
CVP from Different Points of View

Assume that you are preparing a seminar on cost-volume-profit analysis for nonaccountants. Several potential attendees have approached you and have asked why they should be interested in learning about your topic. The individuals include:

1. A factory worker who serves as her company's labor union representative in charge of contract negotiations.
2. A purchasing agent in charge of ordering raw materials for a large manufacturing company.
3. A vice president of sales for a large automobile company.
4. A director of research and development for a pharmaceutical company.

Instructions

What unique reasons would you give each of these individuals to motivate them to come to your seminar?

LO1 LO4 through LO7

CASE 20.2
Evaluating Marketing Strategies

Purple Cow operates a chain of drive-ins selling primarily ice cream products. The following information is taken from the records of a typical drive-in now operated by the company:

Average selling price of ice cream per gallon		$14.80
Number of gallons sold per month		3,000
Variable costs per gallon:		
Ice cream	$4.60	
Supplies (cups, cones, toppings, etc.)	2.20	
Total variable expenses per gallon		$6.80
Fixed costs per month:		
Rent on building		$ 2,200.00
Utilities and upkeep		760.00
Wages, including payroll taxes		4,840.00
Manager's salary, including payroll taxes but excluding any bonus		2,500.00
Other fixed expenses		1,700.00
Total fixed costs per month		$12,000.00

Based on these data, the monthly break-even sales volume is determined as follows:

$$\frac{\textbf{\$12,000 (fixed costs)}}{\textbf{\$8.00 (contribution margin per unit)}} = \textbf{1,500 gallons (or \$22,200)}$$

Instructions

a. Currently, all store managers have contracts calling for a bonus of 20 cents per gallon for each gallon sold *beyond* the break-even point. Compute the number of gallons of ice cream that must be sold per month in order to earn a monthly operating income of $10,000 (round to the nearest gallon).

b. To increase operating income, the company is considering the following two alternatives:

1. Reduce the selling price by an average of $2.00 per gallon. This action is expected to increase the number of gallons sold by 20 percent. (Under this plan, the manager would be paid a salary of $2,500 per month without a bonus.)

2. Spend $3,000 per month on advertising without any change in selling price. This action is expected to increase the number of gallons sold by 10 percent. (Under this plan, the manager would be paid a salary of $2,500 per month without a bonus.)

Which of these two alternatives would result in the higher monthly operating income? How many gallons must be sold per month under each alternative for a typical outlet to break even? Provide schedules in support of your answers.

c. Draft a memo to management indicating your recommendations with respect to these alternative marketing strategies.

LO1

CASE 20.3
What They Don't Know Won't Hurt 'Em

Floyd Christianson is the chief executive officer of Murango Pharmaceuticals. The company has been struggling in recent years to break even and its stock price has been on the decline. The company's Jacksonville plant manufactures a prescription drug that has lost significant market share to alternative drugs marketed by its competitors. On February 1, management decided that it would close the Jacksonville plant at the end of June.

On February 3, Susan Lohmar, Murango's chief financial officer, asked Christianson to review the Form 8-K she was about to file with the SEC (see this chapter's Ethics, Fraud & Corporate Governance feature on page 896). Christianson read the document and immediately instructed Lohmar not to file it, saying:

> There's no need to cause alarm in the marketplace. Our stock price is depressed enough the way it is. What people don't know won't hurt 'em. Besides, the charge to income you're proposing will cause us to operate in the red, and that won't go over well with shareholders.

Instructions

a. What is a Form 8-K?

b. What charge to income was disclosed in the Form 8-K prepared by Susan Lohmar?

c. Why would filing a Form 8-K cause the company to appear unprofitable?

d. Do you agree with Floyd Christianson's argument against filing a Form 8-K? Defend your answer.

LO8 **INTERNET CASE 20.4**

Sales Mix

Visit the home page of **The Securities & Exchange Commission** at the following address:

www.sec.gov

Use EDGAR to locate the most recent 10-K of **Ford Motor Company**. Locate the tables in the 10-K that provide information about the U.S. vehicle mix of sales, and **Ford**'s vehicle mix of sales.

Instructions

a. In the most recent year reported, which vehicle type has contributed most to **Ford**'s sales mix?

b. In the most recent year reported, which vehicle type has contributed most to the U.S. automobile industry's sales mix?

c. Has **Ford**'s sales mix over the past several years changed?

d. Has the U.S. automobile industry's sales mix, in general, changed over the past several years?

e. How does a company's sales mix influence its profitability?

Internet sites are time and date sensitive. It is the purpose of these exercises to have you explore the Internet. You may need to use the Yahoo! search engine http://www.yahoo.com *(or another favorite search engine) to find a company's current Web address.*

Answers to Self-Test Questions

1. a **2.** c (from $25,000 to $27,000) **3.** d ($20,000) **4.** b **5.** d

CHAPTER 21

Incremental Analysis

AFTER STUDYING THIS CHAPTER, YOU SHOULD BE ABLE TO:

Learning Objective

- **LO1** Explain what makes information relevant to a particular business decision.
- **LO2** Discuss the relevance of opportunity costs, sunk costs, and out-of-pocket costs in making business decisions.
- **LO3** Use incremental analysis in common business decisions.
- **LO4** Discuss how contribution margin can be maximized when one factor limits productive capacity.
- **LO5** Identify nonfinancial considerations and creatively search for better courses of action.

MARS INCORPORATED

Mars is one of the world's largest family-owned companies. It was started by Frank C. Mars with butter creams made in his Tacoma, Washington, kitchen in 1911. Mars now operates in 66 countries with global sales of over $22 billion. The MILKY WAY®, SNICKERS®, MARS® bars, and M&M'S® are Mars brands. In 1995 Mars introduced a new color for their M&M'S® brand and lit the New York City Chrysler Building blue as a means to advertise the change in their product. In 2004, Mars introduced Internet sales of M&M'S® that allow customers to print their own messages on the shell.

Changing products, introducing new products, choosing to produce in various locations, or closing a manufacturing facility are ongoing business decisions that are made regularly by companies. Many of these types of decisions are short term in nature, other decisions, such as acquiring another business, have long-run impacts and are not considered in this chapter. This chapter focuses on short-run decisions that are compatible with incremental analysis, such as changing the color of a product or introducing a new marketing channel on the Internet. ■

The Challenge of Changing Markets

Short-run business decisions are inherently different from future-oriented, long-run strategic plans. Short-run decisions are made with a fixed set of resources and must meet the demands of the current marketplace. There is no time to create demand or acquire a significantly different resource base. This chapter's opening story shows that **Mars** made long-run, strategic decisions while simultaneously making short-run decisions. All organizations engage in long-run strategic planning and short-run decision making simultaneously.

This chapter focuses on short-run decisions sometimes referred to as the result of *incremental decision making.* We focus on common concepts used for short-run decisions such as sunk costs, opportunity costs, out-of-pocket costs, and incremental costs and revenues. Costs identified as important for a particular business decision are called relevant costs. Financial information relevant for some business decisions is likely to be irrelevant for other decisions. We cannot overemphasize the importance of using a decision focus when identifying relevant information. Exhibit 21–1 illustrates that good judgment about relevant information occurs by looking through the lens of the particular decision under consideration. These concepts are important in several universal business decision settings and are illustrated here for these specific decisions: special order decisions, product mix decisions, make or buy decisions, and joint product decisions.

Exhibit 21–1

RELEVANT FINANCIAL INFORMATION

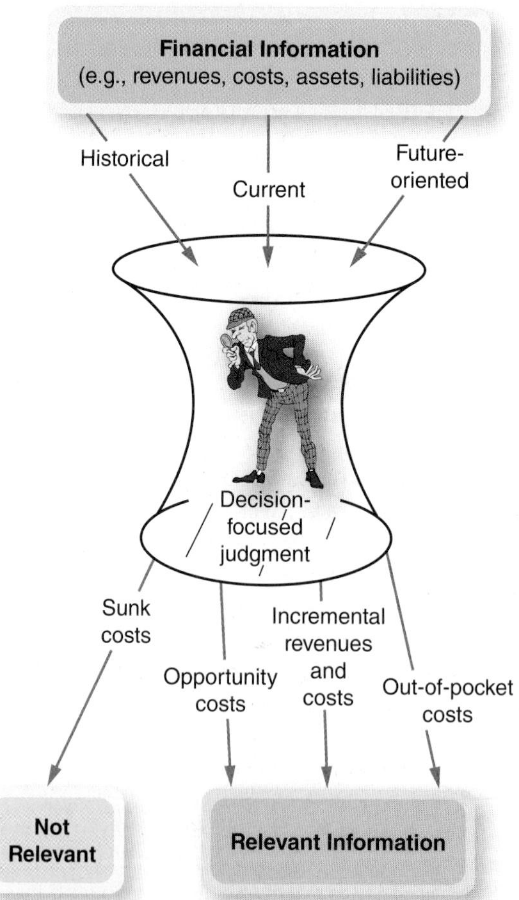

The Concept of Relevant Cost Information

We begin with a very simple but familiar decision setting to allow you to become familiar with the ideas and terminology.

Kevin Anderson is a sophomore at the **University of Minnesota** in Minneapolis. Following the most brutal winter ever recorded in the state's history, Anderson is faced with an extremely important decision: Should he drive to Miami for spring break, or should he fly?

If he drives, he will leave on Saturday, stay in a roadside motel Saturday night, and arrive in Miami late Sunday evening allowing him to enjoy five full days in Miami (Monday through Friday). However, he would have to leave the following Saturday, and spend another Saturday night in a motel, to arrive back in Minneapolis late Sunday evening. If he flies, he will simply leave on Saturday morning and arrive in Miami late that night allowing him to relax on the beach for seven full days before having to fly back to Minnesota Sunday.

To help make his decision as objective as possible, Kevin has compiled a list of the most relevant factors affecting his decision as shown in Exhibit 21–2.

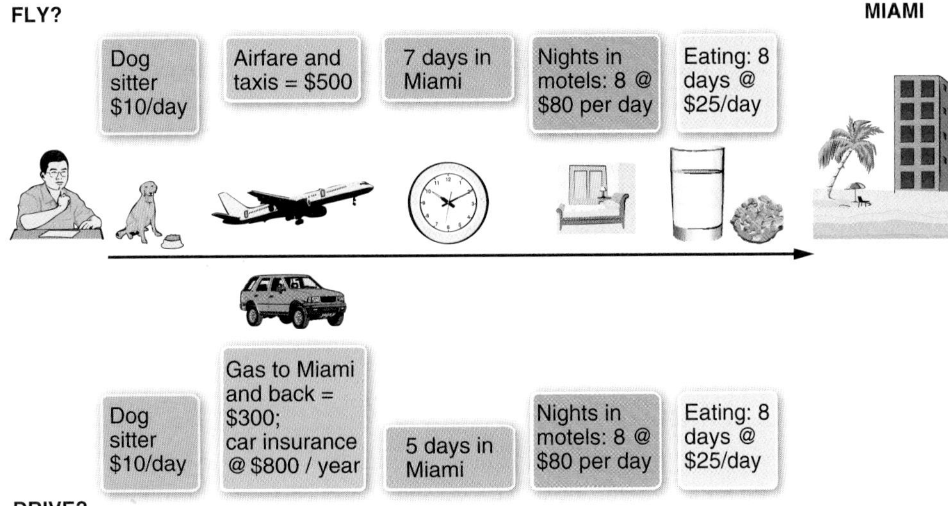

Exhibit 21–2
IDENTIFYING RELEVANT INFORMATION

Let's help Kevin analyze this information and make a decision regarding his vacation plans.

If he decides to drive to Florida, he must stay a total of eight nights in a motel (two nights on the interstate and six nights in Miami). If he decides to fly, he must also stay eight nights in a motel (from Saturday through Saturday in Miami). Thus, if we assume that the cost of a room in Miami does not differ significantly from the cost of a room along the interstate, motel charges are not relevant in deciding between driving or flying.

The same logic applies to the dog sitting cost and the cost of Kevin's meals. Regardless of how Kevin gets to Miami, he will be away from Minneapolis a total of nine days and eight nights. Thus the dog will require the same amount of care, and Kevin's total food costs will be about the same, whether he drives or flies.

How about the $800 Kevin spent for car insurance? This cost has already been incurred and will not be affected by whether Kevin drives or flies. Such past costs, which cannot be affected by future decisions, are termed **sunk costs.** Sunk costs, as shown in Exhibit 21–1, are *not relevant* to making decisions about the future.

In financial terms, Kevin's decision can be made by comparing the $300 he would spend for gasoline if he drives to the $500 he would spend for a round-trip airline ticket and taxi if he flies. Thus we may be tempted to tell him to drive and save $200.

However, there are other nonfinancial factors Kevin may wish to consider. For instance, how much does he value the two extra days he can spend on the beach if he flies? What physical condition will he be in if he decides to drive? How much wear-and-tear must his car endure if he drives? Might his car break down and spoil his plans? Which mode of transportation is the safest?

In the remainder of this chapter we will learn how to identify and use information relevant to specific types of business decisions. Although our discussion will take place in a business context, many of the fundamental concepts involved are similar to those faced by Kevin Anderson.

RELEVANT INFORMATION IN BUSINESS DECISIONS

Identifying all of the information relevant to a particular business decision is a challenging task, because relevance is a broad concept. The process requires an understanding of quantitative and *qualitative* information, a grasp of legal issues, sensitivity to ethical concerns, and an ability to discern fact from opinion. In short, identifying the information relevant to a decision, as shown in Exhibit 21–1, requires *judgment*—and more careful thought than first meets the eye. To simplify matters, our discussion will focus primarily on relevant *financial information*—namely, costs and revenues.

Learning Objective
LO1 **Explain what makes information relevant to a particular business decision.**

Virtually all business decisions involve choosing among alternative courses of action. The only information relevant to a decision is that *which varies among the possible courses of action being considered.* Costs, revenues, and other factors that *do not vary* among possible courses of action *are not relevant* to the decision.

INTERNATIONAL FINANCIAL REPORTING STANDARDS AND RELEVANT COSTS

Reporting differences between U.S. generally accepted accounting principles (GAAP) and IFRS can impact a decision maker's assessment of costs as relevant or irrelevant. For example, international accounting standards allowed borrowing costs on assets that require a substantial period to bring them to a marketable condition to be expensed immediately rather than capitalized as required by U.S. GAAP. Immediate expensing of borrowing costs may cause decision makers to consider borrowing costs to be relevant for some decisions because immediate expensing decreases current earnings and ultimately decreases current period income tax expenses. As part of the FASB/IASB convergence project, IASB changed their standard so that after January 1, 2009, borrowing costs are required to be capitalized in a manner consistent with U.S. GAAP requirements.

A SIMPLE ILLUSTRATION OF RELEVANT COSTS

To illustrate the concept of relevant information, assume that Redstar Ketchup Company is closed for a labor strike. During the strike, Redstar is incurring costs of approximately $15,000 per week for utilities, interest, and salaries of nonstriking employees. A major film company has offered to rent the ketchup factory for a week at a price of $10,000 to shoot several scenes of a new Robocop movie. If the factory is rented, Redstar's management estimates that its cleanup costs will amount to nearly $2,000. Solely on the basis of this information, would it be profitable to rent the ketchup factory to the film company?

If the factory is rented, Redstar's profitability for the week may be measured as follows:

Revenue		$10,000
Costs and expenses:		
Weekly factory expenses	$15,000	
Cleanup costs	2,000	17,000
Operating income (loss)		$ (7,000)

Does an anticipated operating loss of $7,000 mean that Redstar should refuse the film company's offer? A closer examination reveals that not all of the information in this income statement is *relevant* to the decision at hand. Indeed, the $15,000 in weekly factory expenses will continue *whether or not* the factory is rented to the film company.

Thus the relevant factors in this decision are the *differences* in the costs incurred and the revenue earned under the alternative courses of action (renting or not renting). These differences are referred to often as **incremental (or differential) costs** and **revenues.** The analysis in Exhibit 21–3 focuses upon these incremental revenues and costs.

Our analysis shows that accepting the film company's offer will result in $10,000 of incremental revenue but only $2,000 in incremental costs. Thus renting the ketchup factory to the film company will benefit Redstar by reducing its operating loss for the week by $8,000.

Before we begin to examine relevant information related to specific types of business decisions, it is appropriate to examine three important cost concepts: (1) opportunity costs, (2) sunk costs, and (3) out-of-pocket costs.

	Reject Offer	Accept Offer	Incremental Analysis
Revenue	$ 0	$10,000	$10,000
Costs and expenses:			
Weekly factory expenses	(15,000)	(15,000)	0
Estimated cleanup costs	0	(2,000)	(2,000)
Operating income (loss)	$(15,000)	$ (7,000)	$ 8,000

Exhibit 21–3
INCREMENTAL ANALYSIS

OPPORTUNITY COSTS

Learning Objective
Discuss the relevance of opportunity costs, sunk costs, and out-of-pocket costs in making business decisions. **LO2**

An **opportunity cost** is the benefit that *could have been obtained* by pursuing an alternative course of action. For example, assume that you pass up a summer job that pays $4,000 and instead attend summer school. The $4,000 may be viewed as an opportunity cost of attending summer school.

Although opportunity costs are *not recorded* in a company's accounting records, they are important factors to consider in many business decisions. Unfortunately, they sometimes are *not known* at the time a decision is made. To illustrate, consider the previous example involving Redstar Ketchup Company.

We concluded that Redstar could reduce its operating loss by $8,000 if it were to rent its factory to the film company. Assume, however, that the labor strike ends *just before filming begins*. As a consequence, Redstar must forego any profit that the factory could have earned during the week that filming is in process. Thus, if operating profit for the week could have totaled $25,000, the *opportunity cost* of renting to the film company is the $25,000 foregone.

SUNK COSTS VERSUS OUT-OF-POCKET COSTS

As mentioned earlier, a *sunk cost* is one that has *already been incurred* and cannot be changed by future actions. For example, Redstar's investment in its ketchup factory is a sunk cost. This cost will not change regardless of whether Redstar rents the factory, resumes operations, or lets the building stand vacant.

The only costs *relevant* to a decision are those that *vary* among the courses of action being considered. Sunk costs are *not relevant* because they *cannot be changed,* regardless of what decision is made.

In contrast to sunk costs, the term **out-of-pocket cost** is often used to describe costs that have *not yet* been incurred and that *may vary* among the possible courses of action. For example,

The Sarbanes-Oxley Act (SOX) and subsequent changes to New York Stock Exchange and NASDAQ listing standards impose a number of new requirements for improving the quality and authority of a company's board of directors, particularly its audit committee. SOX and the new exchange-listing standards require public companies to have at least one financial expert on their audit committees. The Securities and Exchange Commission (SEC) defines an "audit committee financial expert" as an individual who possesses these traits: (1) an understanding of generally accepted accounting principles (GAAP) and financial statements, (2) experience applying GAAP in connection with the accounting for estimates, accruals, and reserves, (3) experience preparing or auditing financial statements, (4) experience with internal controls and procedures for financial reporting, and (5) an understanding of audit committee functions.

Although the requirement for a financial expert on the audit committee imposes incremental costs on firms, it helps firms avoid situations with significant opportunity costs. Because audit committee financial experts often have backgrounds as current or former chief financial officers or former accounting firm partners, they are better able to spot significant internal control or financial issues before those issues can create significant opportunity costs for a company. In addition to providing enhanced oversight of the financial reporting process, these audit committee financial experts should help the boards on which they sit identify and analyze relevant information in making incremental business decisions.

Redstar's estimated cleanup expenditures are considered out-of-pocket costs. Out-of-pocket costs are normally identified as relevant in most business decisions.

Cash effects differ among the concepts of opportunity costs, sunk costs, and out-of-pocket costs. Sunk costs represent cash outflows that have already occurred. No cash flow effects are associated with opportunity costs. They do not represent cash outflows or inflows. Out-of-pocket costs usually refer to planned cash outflows. Considering the cash effects of short-run business decisions is critical in an ongoing enterprise. Many small businesses fail because of poor, short-run cash planning.

Incremental Analysis in Common Business Decisions

Let us now see how incremental analysis can be used in a variety of business decisions.

SPECIAL ORDER DECISIONS

Companies sometimes receive large special orders to provide merchandise at less than the regular price. Typically, these orders are not from a company's regular customers.

Learning Objective
LO3 Use incremental analysis in common business decisions.

To illustrate, assume that Par Four manufactures golf balls that it distributes exclusively through professional golf shops in the United States. Although the company has the capacity to manufacture 2 million balls per month, its current sales volume requires that only 800,000 units be produced. At this level of output, monthly manufacturing costs average approximately $480,000, or *$0.60* per ball as follows:

Average cost per ball

Manufacturing costs:	
Variable ($0.20 per ball × 800,000 balls)	$160,000
Fixed	320,000
Total cost of manufacturing 800,000 balls per month	$480,000
Average manufacturing cost per ball ($480,000 ÷ 800,000 balls)	$ 0.60

Assume that Par Four receives a special order from NGC, a company that sells golf products in Japan, for 500,000 "special label" golf balls per month. The balls would be imprinted with the NGC name and logo and would not in any way be identified with Par Four.

To avoid direct competition with Par Four's regular customers, NGC has agreed not to sell these balls outside of Japan. However, it is willing to pay Par Four only *$250,000* per month for the special order, which amounts to *$0.50* per ball. Would it be profitable for Par Four to accept this order?

At first glance, the order appears to be unprofitable. Not only is NGC's offer of $0.50 per ball much less than the regular sales price of $1.25, it is even less than Par Four's *$0.60* per-unit manufacturing cost. However, before we decide to reject NGC's order, let us first perform an incremental analysis of the costs and revenue relevant to this decision.

Exhibit 21–4 indicates that accepting NGC's special order would generate incremental revenue of $250,000 and incremental costs of $100,000. Therefore, the order would *increase* Par Four's monthly gross profit on sales by *$150,000.*

Exhibit 21–4
INCREMENTAL ANALYSIS FOR A SPECIAL ORDER

	Production Level		
	Without Special Order (800,000 balls)	With Special Order (1,300,000 balls)	Incremental Analysis
Sales:			
Regular sales @ $1.25	$1,000,000	$1,000,000	$ –0–
Special order @ $0.50	–0–	250,000	250,000
Manufacturing costs:			
Variable @ $0.20 per ball	(160,000)	(260,000)	(100,000)
Fixed manufacturing costs per month	(320,000)	(320,000)	–0–
Gross profit on sales	$ 520,000	$ 670,000	$ 150,000

The relevant factors in this type of decision are the incremental (additional) revenue that will be earned and the incremental costs that will be incurred by accepting the order. Only the additional variable costs of $0.20 per unit are relevant to this decision, because the fixed costs remain $320,000 regardless of whether the order is accepted or not. Thus, the $0.60 average manufacturing cost, which includes fixed costs per unit, is *not relevant* to this decision.[1]

We can reach the same conclusion regarding this special order by returning to the concept of *contribution margin* discussed in Chapter 20. Recall that a product's contribution margin per unit is its selling price per unit less its unit variable cost. In our example, the unit selling price of the special order is $0.50, and the unit variable cost is $0.20. That means the contribution margin associated with the special order is *$0.30 per unit.* In other words, each golf ball sold to NGC *contributes $0.30 to Par Four's operating profit. The special order should increase operating income by $150,000 per month* (500,000 balls × $0.30 per unit).

In evaluating the merits of a special order such as the one received by Par Four, managers should consider the effect that filling the order might have on the company's regular sales volume and selling prices. Obviously, it would not be wise for Par Four to sell golf balls at $0.50 apiece to a domestic company, which might then try to sell the balls to Par Four's regular customers for less than Par Four's normal selling price of $1.25 per ball. Par Four's management should also consider how the company's regular customers might react if word gets out about the special order. These customers may also demand a $0.50-per-ball selling price!

YOUR TURN **You as a Sales Representative**

Assume that you are a sales representative for Par Four. One of your best customers, Clubs & Caddies, a chain of retail golf shops, has heard about the special order shipment to NGC in Japan. Clubs & Caddies has been paying $0.80 per ball and would like the same special order price given to NGC. In fact, the purchasing manager at Clubs & Caddies says it is unethical for you not to sell at the same price per ball that you are charging NGC. How should you respond?

(See our comments on the Online Learning Center Web site.)

In summary, incremental analysis is a useful tool for evaluating the effects of expected short-term changes in revenue and costs. Managers should always be alert, however, to the long-run implications of their actions.

PRODUCTION CONSTRAINT DECISIONS

Learning Objective **Discuss how contribution margin can be maximized when one factor limits productive capacity.** **LO4**

In the discussion above, we demonstrated how a contribution margin approach can be used in incremental analyses. The contribution margin approach often applies when the availability of a particular production input (such as a raw material, skilled labor, floor space, etc.) is limited. An understanding of contribution margin concepts enables managers to decide what products to manufacture (or purchase for resale) and what products to eliminate in order to *maximize the contribution margin per unit of the limited input.*

Assume that you are offered two equally satisfactory jobs, one paying $8 per hour and one paying $12 per hour. If you are able to work only 40 hours per week and you wish to maximize the amount you earn per hour of your time, you would naturally choose the job paying $12 per hour. For the same reason, if a company's output is limited by a particular resource, such as labor or machine-hours, management should use this resource in a way that maximizes total contribution margin.

To illustrate this concept, assume that Fran's Studio creates three products: (1) watercolor paintings, (2) oil paintings, and (3) custom frames. Total output, however, is limited to what

[1] In our discussion, we evaluate only the *profitability* of accepting this order. Some countries have "antidumping" laws that legally prohibit a foreign company from selling its products in that country at a price below the average full manufacturing cost (variable *and* fixed costs) per unit. Par Four should, of course, consider the legal as well as the economic implications of accepting this special order.

can be produced in 6,000 hours of direct labor. The contribution margin per direct labor hour required to complete each of the studio's products is as follows:

Product	Unit Selling Price	−	Unit Variable Costs	=	Unit Contribution Margin	÷	Direct Labor Hours Required per Unit	=	Contribution Margin per Hour
Watercolor paintings	$ 90		$30		$ 60		2		$30
Oil paintings	160		60		100		4		25
Custom frames...	35		15		20		1		20

Notice that oil paintings generate the highest contribution margin on a per-unit basis ($100). However, watercolors are the studio's most profitable product in terms of their *contribution margin per direct labor hour.*

In general, when capacity is constrained by the limited availability of a particular input, a company should attempt to maximize its contribution margin per unit *of that input.* Exhibit 21–5 shows the total contribution margin Fran's Studio would earn if it used all 6,000 of its annual labor hours to create a single product line. The studio can maximize its total contribution margin and, therefore, its operating income, by creating only *watercolor paintings.*

Exhibit 21–5

MOST PROFITABLE USE OF CONSTRAINED RESOURCES

	Total Capacity (Hours)	×	Contribution Margin per Hour of Direct Labor	=	Total Contribution Margin If Only One Product Is Created
Watercolors	6,000		$30		$180,000
Oil paintings	6,000		25		150,000
Custom frames	6,000		20		120,000

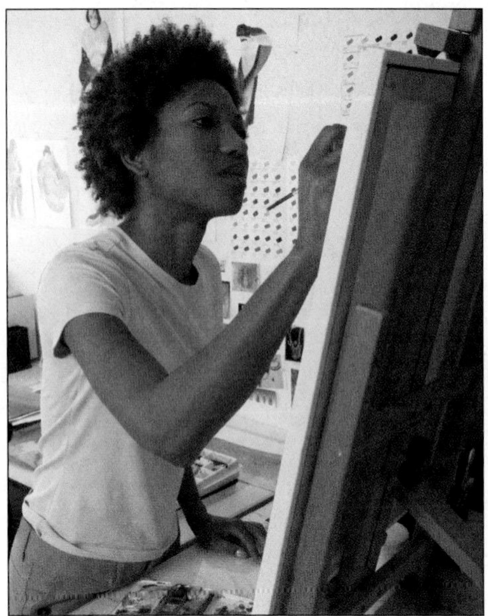

© John Lund/Drew Kelly/age fotostock/DAL

In most cases, however, a company cannot simply manufacture the single product that is most profitable. For example, the demand for watercolors may not be sufficient to allow Fran's Studio to sell all of the watercolor paintings it is capable of producing. In this case, operating income would be maximized by creating oil paintings once the demand for water-colors is satisfied. If the demand for oil paintings is also met, any remaining direct labor hours would be devoted to producing custom frames.

Another important consideration is that some of the studio's labor hours may have to be used to produce custom frames that *support the sale of paintings.* Even though frames contribute less to the studio's operating income than paintings do, many customers may wish to have the studio frame the paintings they purchase. Thus, in addition to understanding the contribution margins of its products, a company must also attempt to understand the complementary nature of its products. That is, does the sale of one product contribute to the sale of another? Products for which sales of one contribute to the sales of another are called **complementary products**.

YOUR TURN **You as a Store Manager**

Assume that you are the store manager of Fran's Studio. Fran would like you to expand the store by selling posters and prints in addition to the watercolors and oil paintings currently produced by the studio. Do you think the posters and prints are complementary with the other products sold at Fran's Studio? Explain why or why not.

(See our comments on the Online Learning Center Web site.)

MAKE OR BUY DECISIONS

In many manufacturing operations, a company must decide whether to produce a certain part required in the assembly of its finished products or to buy the part from outside suppliers. If the company is currently producing a part that could be purchased at a lower cost from outsiders, profits may be increased by a decision to buy the part and utilize the company's own manufacturing resources for other purposes.

For example, if a company can buy for $5 per unit a part that costs the company $6 per unit to produce, the choice seems to be clearly in favor of buying. But the astute reader will quickly raise the question, "What is included in the cost of $6 per unit?" Assume that the $6 unit cost of producing a normal required volume of 10,000 units per month was determined as follows:

Manufacturing costs:	
Direct materials	$ 8,000
Direct labor	12,500
Variable overhead	10,000
Fixed overhead per month	29,500
Total cost of manufacturing 10,000 units per month	$60,000
Average manufacturing cost per unit ($60,000 ÷ 10,000 units)	$6

Assume that a review of operations indicates that if the production of this part were discontinued, all of the cost of direct materials and direct labor plus $9,000 of variable overhead would be eliminated. In addition, $2,500 of the fixed overhead would be eliminated. These, then, are the *relevant costs* in producing the 10,000 units of the component part, and we can summarize them as shown in Exhibit 21–6.

	Make the Part	Buy the Part	Incremental Analysis
Manufacturing costs for 10,000 units:			
Direct materials	$ 8,000		$ 8,000
Direct labor	12,500		12,500
Variable overhead	10,000	$ 1,000	9,000
Fixed overhead	29,500	27,000	2,500
Purchase price of part, $5 per unit		50,000	(50,000)
Total cost to acquire part	$60,000	$78,000	$(18,000)

Exhibit 21–6

INCREMENTAL ANALYSIS FOR A MAKE OR BUY DECISION

Our analysis shows that making the part will cost $60,000 per month, while buying the part will cost $78,000. Thus the company will save $18,000 per month by continuing to make the part.

In our example, we assumed that only $9,000 of the variable overhead incurred in producing the part would be eliminated if the part were purchased. We also assumed that $2,500 of the fixed overhead could be eliminated if the part were purchased. The purpose of these assumptions was to show that not all variable costs are incremental and that some fixed costs may be incremental in a given situation.

What if management wanted to know the price (or volume) where they would be indifferent between buying and producing the part? Knowing the purchase price where they are indifferent between making and buying would allow management to search for a supplier that meets their need to outsource, yet maintain current profitability. The company will be indifferent between buying and making the part when the total incremental cost of making the part equals the total incremental cost of buying the part, illustrated by the following equation (where **P** is price and **V** is volume):

$$\mathbf{P} \times \mathbf{V} = [\mathbf{V} \times (\text{incremental variable costs per unit})] + \text{total incremental fixed costs.}$$

The incremental variable costs (direct materials, direct labor, and variable overhead) shown in the last column of Exhibit 21–6 can be used to find the incremental variable costs per unit based on 10,000 units. Thus the following equation can be solved to find the price where management would be indifferent between buying and making the part:

$$\mathbf{P} \times (10{,}000) = [10{,}000 \times (\$0.80 + \$1.25 + \$0.90)] + \$2{,}500$$

The price where management would be indifferent between buying and making the part for a volume level of 10,000 units would be $3.20 per unit.

Note that it is important to understand how incremental costs vary when the volume level varies. For example, if the volume being considered for outsourcing were only 5,000 units rather than 10,000 units, then it is possible that there would be no saving of any fixed overhead costs. That is, outsourcing production of only 5,000 units would have no effect on fixed overhead costs. Alternatively, perhaps at a volume of 5,000 units direct materials cost per unit would increase because the company might lose its volume discount from suppliers. It is clear that understanding how costs change as volume changes is critical for understanding make or buy decisions.

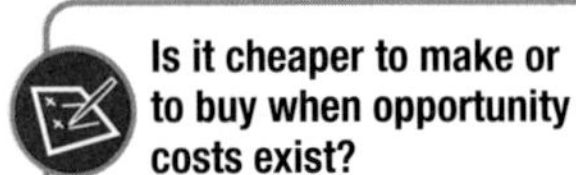

Is it cheaper to make or to buy when opportunity costs exist?

Finally, what if the company could have used its production facilities to manufacture a new product line that would increase overall profitability by $25,000 per month? If this were the case, the $25,000 profit would be viewed as the *opportunity cost* of using the company's production facilities to manufacture a component part. Obviously, the company should not forego a $25,000 profit to save $18,000. Thus, when the opportunity cost is considered, it becomes evident that the company should buy the part and use its production facilities to manufacture the new product.

In addition to evaluating the opportunity costs associated with a make or buy decision, managers must evaluate other important concerns that are nonfinancial in nature. For instance, does the decision to make or buy involve issues of product quality? Are there questions regarding the decision's impact on production scheduling and flexibility? Have certain long-term implications been considered, such as product availability and maintaining reliable supplier relationships? Ignoring important questions such as these is a common source of error in incremental analyses.

INTERNATIONAL CASE IN POINT

Until recently many automobile companies in Japan produced their autos in Japan and exported them to markets in the United States and Asia. In the early 1990s, foreign exchange fluctuations between the U.S. dollar and the Japanese yen made it difficult for Japan to sell products in the United States at a profit. In the 1990s, Japanese auto companies changed their strategies and began building assembly plants in the countries where they sold their products. In addition, Japanese auto makers now choose to buy many auto parts from U.S. suppliers rather than make the parts themselves. With this strategy, the Japanese auto companies pay for the cost of production using the same currency that they receive from customers when they sell their product. This strategy allows these companies to avoid the incremental costs associated with foreign exchange fluctuation.

SELL, SCRAP, OR REBUILD DECISIONS

Another problem companies face is what to do with obsolete or defective products. Management must decide whether to devote the resources to rebuild these units, sell them at a reduced price, or simply scrap them.

To illustrate, assume that Computex, Inc., has in its inventory 500 laptop computers that cost $325,000 to produce. Unfortunately, their processors are technologically obsolete. Consequently management must decide what to do with these machines. It is considering the following options:

1. Sell the laptop computers "as is" to Television Shopping Network (TSN) for $250,000.
2. Sell them for $235,000 to surrounding school districts for use in their computer labs.

3. Scrap the existing processor in each machine and replace it with faster, state-of-the-art equipment at a total cost of $190,000. If this option is selected, the rebuilt laptops could be sold for $450,000.

Regardless of which option Computex chooses, the $325,000 originally incurred to manufacture these laptops is a *sunk cost* and is therefore *irrelevant* to the decision at hand. The only relevant costs and revenue are those that *vary* among the alternatives under consideration. An incremental analysis of the three options appears in Exhibit 21–7.

	Sell to TSN	Sell to Schools	Rebuild
Incremental revenue	$250,000	$235,000	$450,000
Incremental costs	0	0	190,000
Incremental income	$250,000	$235,000	$260,000

Exhibit 21–7

INCREMENTAL ANALYSIS FOR SELL, SCRAP, OR REBUILD DECISIONS

Notice that no matter which option Computex selects, it will *not be able* to fully recover the $325,000 that it already has invested in these laptop computers.

Rebuilding the computers with state-of-the-art equipment appears to be the company's most profitable course of action. However, management may wish to consider several other factors. For example, does Computex have *sufficient plant capacity* to rebuild these laptops without reducing its production of other products?

If rebuilding these laptops interferes with the production of other products, the "rebuild" option involves an *opportunity cost*—the profit foregone on the products that could have been manufactured instead. If this opportunity cost exceeds *$10,000,* Computex would maximize its income by selling these computers to TSN and using its production facilities to manufacture other products.

Next, there may be a long-term advantage in selling the laptops to schools, even though this appears to be the *least* profitable alternative. Relative to selling the computers to TSN, selling to the schools involves a $15,000 opportunity cost. But management may consider this opportunity cost to be *cost-effective advertising.* The students who use these laptops—and their parents—may become customers of other Computex products.

Incremental analysis provides an excellent starting point for many business decisions. Seldom, however, does this analysis tell the whole story.

© Creatas/PunchStock/DAL

CASE IN POINT

Acro Industries Inc., a full-service manufacturer of metal processing jobs, purchased a used 500-ton hydraulic press from **Kodak**. The press was about 15 years old and in very good condition. The press performed well for years after its acquisition. Eventually, however, the control system components for the press were no longer available. With no direct source for upgrades, spare parts, and other support, the press control system became more obsolete and unreliable. **Acro** was faced with a decision to scrap the press or try to rebuild the press.

Because the press was still in excellent hydraulic and mechanical shape except for the control system, **Acro** chose to rebuild the press. For about one-quarter the cost of a new press, **Acro** was able to rejuvenate an obsolete press by providing it with contemporary levels of control and productivity.

JOINT PRODUCT DECISIONS

Many companies produce multiple products from common raw materials and a shared production process. Examples include oil refineries, lumber and steel mills, and meat processing companies. Products resulting from a shared manufacturing process are termed **joint products,** and the manufacturing costs that relate to these products as a group are called **joint costs**.

In such manufacturing processes, two business issues arise. One is how to allocate joint costs among the various types of products manufactured. The second incremental type of decision is whether some types of products should be *processed further* to create an even more valuable finished good.

Joint Costs

Let us first address the issue of joint costs. Assume that Char-Core mixes together wood chips and pine oil. After joint manufacturing costs of *\$2,000* have been incurred, this mixture separates into two salable products: granulated charcoal and methyl alcohol. How should the \$2,000 in joint costs be allocated between these products?

There is no "right" way to allocate joint costs, but the most common method is in proportion to the *relative sales value* of the products produced. Assume that the quantity of charcoal produced by CharCore's \$2,000 in joint manufacturing costs has a sales value of *\$5,000* and that the alcohol has a sales value of *\$9,000.* Thus the batch of products collectively has a sales value of *\$14,000.*

The \$2,000 in joint costs could be allocated between these products as follows:

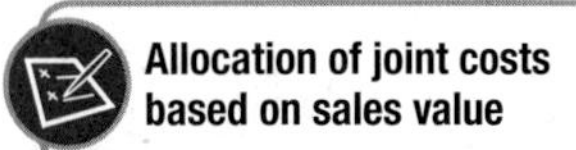

Charcoal [\$2,000 in joint costs × (\$5,000/\$14,000)]	\$ 714
Alcohol [\$2,000 in joint costs × (\$9,000/\$14,000)]	1,286

Decisions after the Split-Off Point

Once joint products can be separated, they have reached what is called the **split-off point.** At this point, each product may be sold *independently of the other,* or it may be processed further.

Again consider CharCore. The company may sell its charcoal and alcohol after the split-off point without further processing, or it may continue processing either of these products. CharCore can use the granulated charcoal to manufacture air filters and the methyl alcohol to make cleaning solvent. Exhibit 21–8 illustrates CharCore's options and reflects current sales prices and manufacturing costs.

Exhibit 21–8 CHARCORE'S PRODUCTION PROCESS, COSTS, AND REVENUE

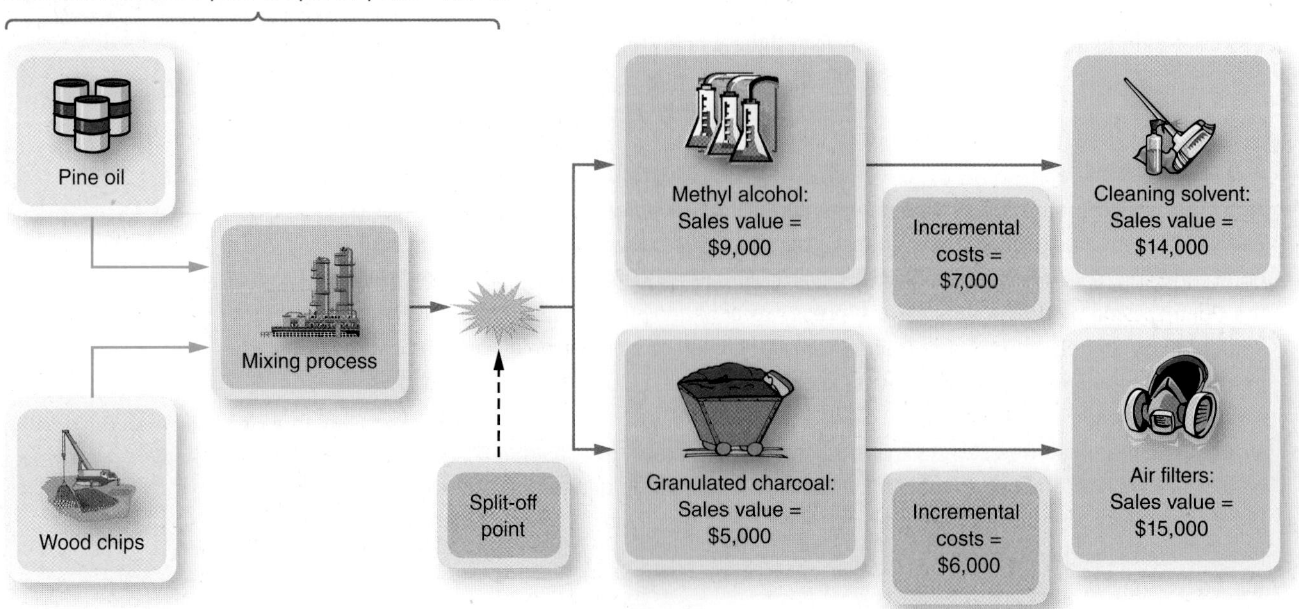

The decision of whether to sell the charcoal and alcohol or to continue processing is based on the incremental costs and revenue expected *after* the split-off point. An analysis of these cost and revenue considerations appears in Exhibit 21–9.

Exhibit 21–9

INCREMENTAL ANALYSIS OF A DECISION TO PROCESS FURTHER

CharCore Analysis after Split-off	
Revenue if charcoal is used to make air filters	$15,000
Less: Revenue if charcoal is sold at split-off point	5,000
Incremental revenue from air filters	10,000
Less: Incremental cost to produce air filters	6,000
Net increase (decrease) in operating income from air filters	$ 4,000
Revenue if alcohol is used to make cleaning solvent	$14,000
Less: Revenue if alcohol is sold at split-off point	9,000
Incremental revenue from solvent	5,000
Less: Incremental cost to produce cleaning solvent	7,000
Net increase (decrease) in operating income from solvent	$(2,000)

Going by this analysis, CharCore currently should use its charcoal to produce air filters, but it should sell its alcohol at the split-off point. The optimal course of action may change, however, with fluctuations in the prices of these products or in incremental manufacturing costs.

Concluding Remarks

We have merely scratched the surface in discussing the possible kinds of analyses that might be prepared in making business decisions. Our coverage in this chapter, however, has been sufficient to establish the basic principles that lie behind such analyses. The profitability of a course of action depends on the *incremental* revenue and expenses. However, *opportunity costs* may play a major role in the decision.

Learning Objective **Identify nonfinancial considerations and creatively search for better courses of action.** **LO5**

We also have stressed that, in addition to quantitative information, many *nonfinancial* factors must be taken into consideration. It would be irresponsible and short-sighted for managers to seek solutions and base decisions entirely on revenue and cost figures. Indeed, as shown in Exhibit 21–10, most business decisions also require an examination of legal issues, a sensitivity to ethical implications, and an ability to distinguish fact from opinion. Thus, while incremental analysis is an excellent tool for evaluating alternative courses of action, managers should not automatically follow the first course of action that holds a promise of increased profitability. Rather, they should always be alert to the possibility that a more satisfactory, and perhaps more creative, solution exists.

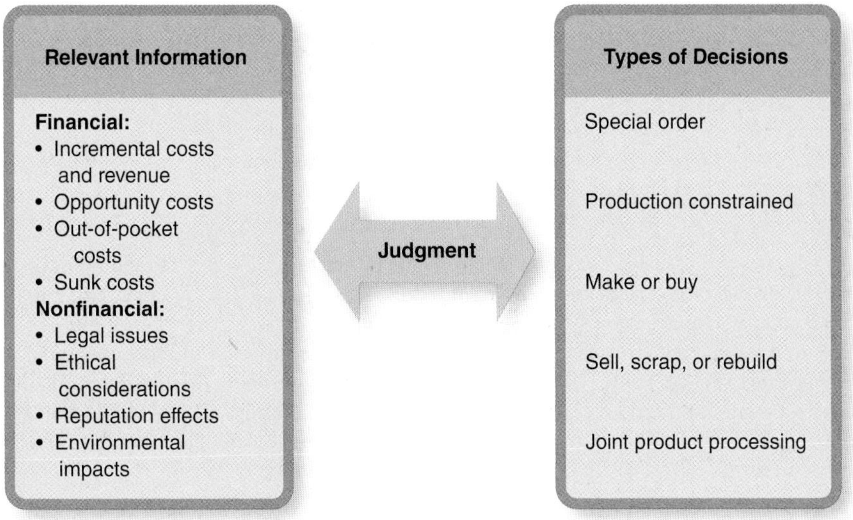

Exhibit 21–10

DECISION-FOCUSED JUDGMENTS

Relevant Information

Financial:
- Incremental costs and revenue
- Opportunity costs
- Out-of-pocket costs
- Sunk costs

Nonfinancial:
- Legal issues
- Ethical considerations
- Reputation effects
- Environmental impacts

Judgment

Types of Decisions

Special order

Production constrained

Make or buy

Sell, scrap, or rebuild

Joint product processing

END-OF-CHAPTER REVIEW

SUMMARY OF LEARNING OBJECTIVES

LO1 **Explain what makes information relevant to a particular business decision.** Only information that varies among the alternative courses of action being considered is relevant to the decision. Costs or revenue that do not vary among the alternative courses of action are not relevant to the decision.

LO2 **Discuss the relevance of opportunity costs, sunk costs, and out-of-pocket costs in making business decisions.** An opportunity cost is the benefit that could have been obtained by pursuing another course of action. Opportunity costs often are subjective, but they are important considerations in any business decision. Sunk costs, on the other hand, have already been incurred as a result of past actions. These costs cannot be changed regardless of the action taken and are not relevant to the decision at hand. Out-of-pocket costs will be incurred in the future and are relevant if they will vary among the possible courses of action.

LO3 **Use incremental analysis in common business decisions.** Incremental analysis is the technique of comparing one course of action to another by determining the differences expected to arise in revenue and in costs.

LO4 **Discuss how contribution margin can be maximized when one factor limits productive capacity.** Identify the production input factor that limits the amount of output. Then determine the output mix that maximizes the contribution margin per unit of the limiting factor.

LO5 **Identify nonfinancial considerations and creatively search for better courses of action.** Examples of relevant nonfinancial information include legal and ethical considerations and the long-run effects of decisions on company image, employee morale, and the environment. Also, managers should search creatively for alternative courses of action. Unless a company selects the best possible course of action, it incurs an opportunity cost. Opportunity costs are not recorded in the accounting records, but they may determine the success or failure of a business enterprise.

Key Terms Introduced or Emphasized in Chapter 21

complementary products (p. 924) Those products for which the sales of one may contribute to the sales of another.

incremental (or differential) cost (p. 920) The increase or decrease in total costs incurred by selecting one course of action over another.

incremental (or differential) revenue (p. 920) The increase or decrease in total revenue earned by selecting one course of action over another.

joint costs (p. 928) Costs incurred in manufacturing processes that produce several different products. Joint costs cannot be traced directly to the individual types of products manufactured and, therefore, must be allocated in a more or less arbitrary manner.

joint products (p. 928) Products that share, in part, common materials and production processes.

opportunity cost (p. 921) The benefit foregone by not pursuing an alternative course of action. Opportunity costs are not recorded in the accounting records but are important in making many types of business decisions.

out-of-pocket costs (p. 921) Costs that have not yet been incurred and that may vary among alternative courses of action.

split-off point (p. 928) The point at which separate and distinct joint products emerge from common materials and a shared production process.

sunk cost (p. 919) A cost that has been incurred as a result of past actions. Sunk costs are irrelevant to decisions involving future actions.

Demonstration Problem

Calkist Mfg. is a multiple product manufacturer. One product line consists of motors for lawnmowers, and the company produces three different models. Calkist is currently considering a proposal from a supplier who wants to sell the company blades for the lawnmower motor line.

The company currently produces all the blades it requires. In order to meet customers' needs, Calkist currently produces three different blades for each motor model (nine different blades). The supplier is offering to provide five varieties of blades for each model. A total of 15 blades would considerably expand the variety of cutting ability for the motors available to customers. The supplier would charge Calkist $25 per blade, regardless of blade type.

For the coming year Calkist has projected the costs of its own blade production as follows (based on projected volume of 10,000 units):

Direct materials	$ 75,000
Direct labor	65,000
Variable overhead	55,000
Fixed overhead	
Depreciation	50,000
Property taxes	15,000
Factory supervision	35,000
Total production costs	$295,000

Assume (1) the equipment utilized to produce the blades has no alternative use and no market value, (2) the space occupied by blade production will remain idle if the company purchases rather than makes the blades, and (3) factory supervision costs reflect the salary of a production supervisor who would be dismissed from the firm if blade production ceased.

Instructions

a. Determine the net monetary advantage or disadvantage of purchasing (rather than manufacturing) the blades required for motor production in the coming year.

b. Determine the volume of motor production where Calkist would be indifferent between buying and producing the blades. If the future volume level is predicted to decrease, would that influence Calkist's decision?

c. For this part only, assume that the space presently occupied by blade production could be leased to another firm for $45,000 per year. How would this affect the make or buy decision?

d. Name at least four other factors Calkist should take into account in making the decision.

Solution to the Demonstration Problem

a. This is a make or buy decision, so compare the incremental cost to make with the incremental cost to buy.

Incremental Costs Per Unit	Make the Blades
Direct materials ($75,000 ÷ 10,000 units)	$ 7.50
Direct labor ($65,000 ÷ 10,000 units)	6.50
Variable overhead ($55,000 ÷ 10,000 units)	5.50
Supervision ($35,000 ÷ 10,000 units)	3.50
Total cost	$23.00

Compare the cost to make the blades for 10,000 motors, $23.00, with the cost to buy, $25.00. There is a net $2.00 disadvantage if Calkist chooses to buy the blades.

b. Calkist will be indifferent between buying and making the blades when the total incremental costs are equal. Total incremental costs for making and buying will be equal at the volume level where the variable costs per unit times the volume, plus the fixed avoidable costs, are equal to the supplier's offered cost of $25.00 per unit times the volume.

[(Direct materials + Direct labor + Variable overhead) × Volume] + Supervision = Price to buy × Volume. Let volume in units = V.

$$[(\$7.50 + \$6.50 + \$5.50) \times V] + \$35{,}000 = \$25.00 \times V$$
$$(\$19.50 \times V) + \$35{,}000 = \$25.00 \times V$$
$$\$35{,}000 = (\$25.00 \times V) - (\$19.50 \times V)$$
$$\$35{,}000 = \$5.50 \times V$$
$$V = 6{,}364 \text{ units of blades}$$

As volume of production decreases, Calkist's average per-unit cost of in-house production increases. If the volume falls below 6,364 blades, then Calkist will want to buy the blades from the supplier.

c. If the space presently occupied by blade production could be leased to another firm for $45,000 per year, Calkist would face an opportunity cost associated with in-house blade production for the 10,000 units of $4.50 per unit. Add that to the original cost:

$23.00 + $4.50 = $27.50 New Cost to Make

Now Calkist should buy because the cost to make, $27.50, is higher than the cost to buy, $25.00.

d. Other factors that Calkist should consider before choosing to buy from the outside supplier include the following:

- The quality of the supplier's products.
- The shipping reliability of the supplier.
- Alternative uses of production capacity.
- The impact on the current workforce if employees are laid off.
- The long-term financial stability of the supplier.
- Other suppliers' ability to provide the blades.
- The ability to generate new sales from the increased variety of blades.

Self-Test Questions

The answers to these questions appear on page 948.

The following data relate to questions 1 and 2.

One of Phoenix Computer's products is WizardCard. The company currently produces and sells 30,000 WizardCards per month, although it has the plant capacity to produce 50,000 units per month. At the 30,000 units-per-month level of production, the average per-unit cost of manufacturing WizardCards is $45, consisting of $15 in variable costs and $30 in fixed costs. Phoenix sells WizardCards to retail stores for $90 each. Computer Marketing Corp. has offered to purchase 10,000 WizardCards per month at a reduced price. Phoenix can manufacture these additional units with no change in fixed manufacturing costs.

1. In deciding whether to accept this special order from Computer Marketing Corp., Phoenix should be *least* concerned with:

a. What Computer Marketing Corp. intends to do with the WizardCards.

b. The $45 average cost of manufacturing WizardCards.

c. The opportunity cost of not accepting the order.

d. The incremental cost of manufacturing an additional 10,000 WizardCards per month.

2. Assume that Phoenix decides to accept the special order at a unit sales price that will add $400,000 per month to its operating income. The unit price of the special order will be:

a. $85. **c.** $55.

b. $70. **d.** Some other amount.

3. When faced with a limited availability of machine-hours, management should consider producing those products that:

a. Have the highest contribution margin per unit.

b. Have the highest contribution margin ratios.

c. Require the fewest machine-hours to produce.

d. Contribute the highest contribution margin per machine-hour.

4. Consultant Frank Alvarez recently commented that the most common error made by his clients is ignoring opportunity costs associated with business decisions. The costs Alvarez was referring to are:

a. Benefits foregone by selecting one course of action over another.

b. The out-of-pocket costs of implementing a particular business decision.

c. Costs that make future opportunities possible.

d. Costs that have made past opportunities possible.

5. Which of the following questions would *not* be relevant to a make or buy decision?

a. Will the supplier make a product that is equal in quality to our own?

b. Will the supplier meet our specified delivery dates?

c. For how long will the supplier be committed to the quoted price?

d. All of the above questions are relevant.

ASSIGNMENT MATERIAL

Discussion Questions

1. What is the difference between short-run business decisions and long-run strategic plans?
2. Discuss the importance of incremental costs and revenue when considering alternative courses of action.
3. Define *opportunity costs* and explain why they represent a common source of error in making cost analyses.
4. What is the difference between a *sunk cost* and an *out-of-pocket cost*?
5. What nonfinancial considerations should be taken into account when deciding whether to accept a special order?
6. Harvey Corporation produces several joint products from common materials and shared production processes. Why are costs incurred up to the split-off point not relevant in deciding which products Harvey sells at the split-off point and which products it processes further?
7. **Procter and Gamble** sells **Gillette** razors near or below their manufacturing cost. It also sells razor blades that have a relatively high contribution margin. Explain why **P & G** does not eliminate its unprofitable razor line and sell only blades.
8. Assume **Harley-Davidson Motorcycle Company** is analyzing an offer to buy from a supplier a component that would replace a component it currently makes for its motorcycles. What additional factors beyond price should **Harley-Davidson** take into account in this make or buy decision?
9. Wolvo Company has defective products in inventory. It has the opportunity to either sell, scrap, or rebuild the defective products. Identify several factors Wolvo Company should consider before making a decision.
10. How do cash effects differ among out-of-pocket costs, sunk costs, and opportunity costs?
11. Why is the contribution margin an important concept for incremental decision making?
12. Harry Haney, manager of the Eastern Division of Mertock Co., made the following comment to the manager of the Central Division:

    It's all well and good for you to say that I should disregard sunk costs when I consider whether to replace the old, inefficient equipment with new, more efficient equipment. But my performance evaluation is based on net operating profits divided by total assets. The new equipment will increase my total asset base and lower the ratio of profits to assets, hurting my performance. Thus, I will not sell the old equipment.

    Do you agree with Haney's statement? Why or why not?
13. Traditional accounting systems record only actual transactions. As a result, how can opportunity costs be important in incremental decisions?
14. "When special orders are accepted that are below full product cost (variable cost plus fixed costs), companies run the risk of filling up their capacity with products that do not provide enough contribution to cover fixed costs such as rent and management salaries." Do you agree or disagree with this statement (explain why)?
15. Explain the concept of complementary products and why this concept is important in incremental decisions about individual products.

Brief Exercises

LO1 LO3 **BRIEF EXERCISE 21.1** Using Average Unit Costs

A company regularly sells 100,000 washing machines at an average price of $250. The average cost of producing these machines is $180. Under what circumstances might the company accept a special order for 20,000 washing machines at $175 per machine?

LO2 through LO4 **BRIEF EXERCISE 21.2** Make or Buy Decision

Wilson Corporation produces a large number of fishing products. The costs per unit of a particular fishing reel are as follows:

Direct materials and direct labor	$7.00
Variable factory overhead	4.00
Fixed factory overhead	2.00

The company recently decided to buy 10,000 fishing reels from another manufacturer for $12.50 per unit because "it was cheaper than our cost of $13.00 per unit." Evaluate the decision made by Wilson's management based on the data given.

LO1 LO2 LO4

BRIEF EXERCISE 21.3

Joint Cost Allocations

Two products, wood chips and fiberboard, come out of a joint process costing $420,000 per year. The sales value of the wood chips is $260,000 per year. The sales value of the fiberboard is $780,000 per year. Use the relative sales value method to allocate the joint costs of the joint process to the products. (Round your answer.)

LO2 LO4 LO5

BRIEF EXERCISE 21.4

Outsourcing a Product

Sounds, Inc., is a company that produces sound systems for car stereos. It is considering outsourcing its customer service operation. It has a bid of $2.50 per call from Callers Service Company. Its current costs to service customers are estimated to be $2.00 per call, but it could use the idle space currently occupied by the customer service operation to earn an additional $3,500 per year. Sounds, Inc., currently receives about 200 customer calls per month. Should Sounds, Inc., outsource its customer service operation? What nonfinancial factors should be considered?

LO2

BRIEF EXERCISE 21.5

Opportunity Costs

A friend offers you a ticket to a Chicago Cubs baseball game for $50. You know you can sell the ticket to another friend for $75. What is the opportunity cost of buying the ticket but then choosing to go to the game?

LO2

BRIEF EXERCISE 21.6

Identifying Costs

Which of the following are sunk, out-of-pocket, or opportunity costs:

a. The amount you will pay to go to the movies next week.

b. The insurance payment on your car last year.

c. The amount of rent you could receive if you were to sublet your apartment and live in a tent for spring term.

d. The difference between the price of a 12-pack of soda at the convenience store versus the price of the same product at the discount warehouse.

e. Tuition payments made this term.

f. Book costs for next semester.

LO4

BRIEF EXERCISE 21.7

Allocating Productive Capacity

The local gym has stationary bicycles. Assume these are available for use 500 hours per week. These bicycles are used in two different exercise programs. First, the cycling class takes two hours and earns a $15 contribution margin per customer. Second, the combo class uses bicycles and floor routines and lasts for 1.5 hours and generates a $12 contribution margin per customer. Which type of class generates the highest contribution margin per constrained resource? If demand for combo classes could be restricted to 200 hours per week, how much contribution margin could the gym generate on both types of classes?

LO1 LO3 LO4

BRIEF EXERCISE 21.8

Matching Decisions to All Relevant Costs or Revenue

Match the following decisions in column 1 (**a** through **e**) to all relevant costs or revenue in column 2 (**1** through **5**):

a. Reject a special order.	**1.** Contribution margin per unit of limited resource.
b. Production-constrained decision.	**2.** Interference with other production.
c. Make or buy a component.	**3.** Selling price of supplier.
d. Sell, scrap, or rebuild.	**4.** Sales revenue at split-off point.
e. Continue processing a joint product.	**5.** Contribution margin of product.

LO2 through LO4

BRIEF EXERCISE 21.9

Selling at Split-off or Processing Further

A variety of products—chicken wings, drumsticks, thighs, and so on—are the result of a joint production process of butchering a chicken that costs $0.25 per pound. The wings can be sold at the split-off point for $0.35 per pound, or they can be processed further by cooking them in barbecue sauce and selling them as buffalo wings for $0.46 per pound. The cooking process can accommodate 1,300 pounds of wings at a time and costs $90 for sauce, cooking time, and labor. Should the wings be processed further to make buffalo wings?

LO2 through LO4 BRIEF EXERCISE 21.10
Scrap or Rebuild Decision

Vickery Machining Company is nearly finished constructing a specially designed piece of machining equipment when the customer declares bankruptcy and cannot pay for the equipment. Vickery estimates that the cost associated with making the uncompleted equipment was $1,693,000. Since the machining equipment was specially designed for the customer, there are no other buyers for the equipment unless it is rebuilt. The cost to rebuild is $450,000, after which the product can be sold for $500,000, or the equipment can be scrapped for $30,000. Identify each of the costs in this scenario as sunk, out-of-pocket, or incremental. What should Vickery do?

Exercises

LO1 through LO5 EXERCISE 21.1
Accounting Terminology

Listed below are seven technical accounting terms introduced or emphasized in this chapter.

Opportunity cost	Sunk cost
Out-of-pocket cost	Split-off point
Joint products	Relevant information
Incremental analysis	

Each of the following statements may (or may not) describe one of these terms. For each statement, indicate the accounting term or terms described, or answer "none" if the statement does not correctly describe any of these terms.

a. Examination of differences between costs to be incurred and revenue to be earned under different courses of action.

b. A cost incurred in the past that cannot be changed as a result of future actions.

c. Costs and revenue that are expected to vary, depending on the course of action decided on.

d. The benefit foregone by not pursuing an alternative course of action.

e. Products made from common raw materials and shared production processes.

f. A cost yet to be incurred that will require future payment and may vary among alternative courses of action.

g. The point at which manufacturing costs are split equally between ending inventory and cost of goods sold.

LO1 LO2 EXERCISE 21.2
Home Depot's Financial Statements: Incremental, Sunk, and Opportunity Costs

Read the paragraph in Appendix A, note 1, under item "3. RATIONALIZATION CHARGES." The paragraph describes a series of business decisions made by **Home Depot** to close some of its stores, including 15 underperforming stores, and invest more in their existing stores. Write a short paragraph identifying the type of costs that would be considered incremental, sunk, or opportunity costs for a decision to invest in remodeling (or close) a current store.

LO1 through LO3 EXERCISE 21.3
Incremental Analysis: Accepting a Special Order

Sutherland manufactures and sells 110,000 laser printers each month. A principal component part in each printer is its paper feed drive. Sutherland's plant currently has the monthly capacity to produce 150,000 drives. The unit costs of manufacturing these drives (up to 150,000 per month) are as follows:

Variable costs per unit:	
Direct materials	$45
Direct labor	25
Variable manufacturing overhead	5
Fixed costs per month:	
Fixed manufacturing overhead	$1,430,000

Desk-Mate Printers has offered to buy 20,000 paper feed drives from Sutherland to be used in its own printers. Compute the following:

a. The average unit cost of manufacturing each paper feed drive assuming that Sutherland manufactures only enough drives for its own laser printers.

b. The incremental unit cost of producing an additional paper feed drive.

c. The per-unit sales price that Sutherland should charge Desk-Mate to earn $500,000 in monthly pretax profit on the sale of drives to Desk-Mate.

LO1 through LO4

EXERCISE 21.4 Scarce Resources

Texteriles Company creates different types of bolts of cloth. These bolts of cloth are made on the same machinery. The textile machines have the capacity of 3,600 hours per month. Texteriles is considering producing three different types of cloth: denim, chenille, and gauze, with contribution margins per bolt of $14, $22, and $9, respectively. Texteriles knows it can sell only a total of 6,000 bolts of denim, 2,000 bolts of chenille, and/or 1,200 bolts of gauze. A bolt of each type of cloth requires a different amount of machine time as follows: denim takes .5 machine-hours, chenille takes 1 machine-hour, and gauze takes .3 machine-hours. What combination of products will maximize the profits of Texteriles?

LO1 through LO4

EXERCISE 21.5 Special Order Decisions and Opportunity Costs

Poppycrock, Inc., manufactures large crates of microwaveable popcorn that are typically sold to distributors. Its main factory has the capacity to manufacture and sell 35,000 crates per month. The following information is available for the factory:

Sales price per crate	$26.00
Variable cost per crate:	
Direct materials	5.50
Direct labor	10.50
Variable overhead	3.50
Fixed costs per month	$122,000.00

Boys and Girls of Canada is a not-for-profit organization that raises funds each year by selling popcorn door-to-door. It offers to pay Poppycrock $22 per crate for a special-order batch of 5,000 crates. The special-order popcorn would include a unique label with information about the Boys and Girls of Canada. The additional cost of the label is estimated at $1.00 per crate. In addition, the variable overhead for these special-order crates would decrease by $.50 because there would be no distribution costs.

a. What is the incremental cost of creating a normal crate of popcorn? A special-order crate of popcorn?

b. Show the impact on Poppycrock's monthly operating profit if it accepts the offer and it is producing and distributing 30,000 normal crates per month. What is the opportunity cost of not accepting the offer?

c. Show the impact on Poppycrock's monthly operating profit if it accepts the offer and it is producing and selling 35,000 normal crates per month. What is the opportunity cost of accepting the offer?

LO1 through LO4

EXERCISE 21.6 Incremental Analysis: Make or Buy Decision

The cost to Swank Company of manufacturing 20,000 units of a particular part is $255,000, of which $100,000 is fixed and $155,000 is variable. The company can buy the part from an outside supplier for $8 per unit. Fixed costs will remain the same regardless of Swank's decision. Should the company buy the part or continue to manufacture it? Prepare a comparative schedule in the format illustrated in Exhibit 21–6.

LO1 through LO4

EXERCISE 21.7 Make or Buy Decision

Bacrometer, Inc., makes part no. 566 on one of its production lines. Each month Bacrometer makes 60,000 of part no. 566 at a variable cost of $2.50 per part. The fixed costs for the production line are $180,000, or $3.00 per part. Bacrometer has been provided a bid for part no. 566 from another manufacturer that will make the part for $2.65 per part. Bacrometer knows the production line could be rented to another manufacturer for $5,000 per month. Should Bacrometer continue to make part no. 566 or should it buy the part and rent the production line?

LO1 through LO4

EXERCISE 21.8
Sunk Costs: Scrap or Rework Decision

Road Master Shocks has 20,000 units of a defective product on hand that cost \$123,500 to manufacture. The company can either sell this product as scrap for \$4.18 per unit or it can sell the product for \$10 per unit by reworking the units and correcting the defects at a cost of \$119,200. What should the company do? Prepare a schedule in support of your recommendation.

LO1 through LO4

EXERCISE 21.9
Scarce Resources

Gunst Company produces three video games: Android, Bio-Mutant, and Cyclops. Cost and revenue data pertaining to each product are as follows:

	Android	Bio-Mutant	Cyclops
Selling price	\$100	\$60	\$125
Direct labor	48	24	60
Direct materials	9	8	16
Variable overhead	7	4	9

At the present time, demand for each of the company's products far exceeds its capacity to produce them. Thus, management is trying to determine which of its games to concentrate on next week in filling its backlog of orders. Gunst's direct labor rate is \$12 per hour, and only 1,000 hours of direct labor are available each week. Determine the maximum total contribution margin the company can make by its best use of the 1,000 available hours.

LO1 through LO4

EXERCISE 21.10
Joint Products

Treadwell Pharmaceuticals produces two medications in a joint process: Amoxiphore and Benidrate. With each production run, Treadwell incurs \$4,000 in common costs up to the split-off point.

Amoxiphore can be sold for \$2,700 at the split-off point or be processed further at a cost of \$1,600, at which time it can be sold for \$4,200. However, if Amoxiphore is sold at the split-off point, its side effects include nausea and headaches. If it is processed further, these side effects are diminished. Demand for Amoxiphore far exceeds Treadwell's production capacity.

Benidrate can be sold for \$2,400 at the split-off point or be processed further at a cost of \$3,700, at which time it can be sold for \$6,000.

a. Determine which product is more profitable to process beyond the split-off point.

b. With a group of three students identify and discuss the ethical issues the company faces regarding its processing decisions.

LO1 through LO4

EXERCISE 21.11
Joint Processes: Sell or Process Further

Chemy Corporation produces three products in a monthly joint production process. During the first stage of the process liquids and chemicals costing \$60,000 are heated and three different compounds emerge: 3,000 gallons of Molecue worth \$22 per gallon are created from the steam; 10,000 gallons of Borphue worth \$15 are drained from the tank; and 1,000 gallons of the tank residue, labeled as Polygard, are sold as fertilizer for \$5.50 per gallon. Before Molecue is sold, it must be purified in another process that costs \$10,000, and before the Polygard fertilizer is sold, it must be bottled at a price of \$1.50 per gallon.

a. What is the profitability of the joint process?

b. Is it profitable to process Molecue further if it can be sold at split-off for \$5 per gallon?

c. BioMorphs has an offer to buy Polygard bulk at the split-off point without bottling for \$3,500 per month. What is the incremental profit (loss) to BioMorphs if it accepts the offer?

d. What are the sunk costs related to the decision to accept the Polygard offer?

LO1 through LO3

EXERCISE 21.12
Pricing a Special Order

Mazeppa Corporation sells relays at a selling price of \$28 per unit. The company's cost per unit, based on full capacity of 160,000 units, is as follows:

Direct materials	\$6
Direct labor	4
Overhead (⅔ of which is variable)	9

Mazeppa has been approached by a distributor in Montana offering to buy a special order consisting of 30,000 relays. Mazeppa has the capacity to fill the order. However, it will incur an additional shipping cost of $2 for each relay it sells to the distributor.

a. Assume that Mazeppa is currently operating at a level of 100,000 units. What unit price should it charge the distributor if it wishes to increase operating income by $2 for each unit included in the special order?

b. Assume that Mazeppa is currently operating at full capacity. To fill the special order, regular customers will have to be turned away. Now what unit price should it charge the distributor if it wishes to increase total operating income by $60,000 more than it would be without accepting the special order?

LO1 through LO3

EXERCISE 21.13
Evaluating a Special Order

Visionary Game Company sells 600,000 units per year of a particular video game cartridge at $12 each. The current unit cost of the game is broken down as follows:

Direct materials	$3.00
Direct labor	1.00
Variable factory overhead	3.50
Fixed factory overhead	1.50
Total	$9.00

At the beginning of the current year, Visionary received a special order for 10,000 of these game cartridges per month, *for one year only,* at a sales price of $8 per unit. To fill the order, Visionary will have to rent additional assembly space at a cost of $12,000 ($1,000 per month).

Compute the estimated increase or decrease in annual operating income that will result from accepting this special order.

LO1 through LO5

EXERCISE 21.14
Scarce Resources

Gulf Breeze Corporation produces three products for water skiing enthusiasts: life vests, tow ropes, and water skis. Information relating to each product line is as follows:

	Life Vests	Tow Ropes	Water Skis
Selling price	$58	$25	$175
Direct materials	12	3	75
Direct labor	20	10	80
Variable overhead	6	2	4

Gulf Breeze pays its direct labor workers an average of $10 per hour. At full capacity, 65,000 direct labor hours are available per year. The marketing department has just released the following sales estimates for the upcoming year: life vests (25,000 units), tow ropes (15,000 units), and water skis (5,000 units). Based on these figures, demand for the current year is expected to exceed the company's direct labor capacity.

a. What products should Gulf Breeze produce to maximize its operating income?

b. The company's marketing manager believes that the production of the least profitable product is needed to "support" the demand for the most profitable products. How may this influence management's decision regarding the company's production schedule?

LO1 through LO3

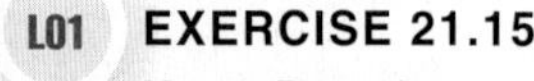

EXERCISE 21.15
Home Depot's Charitable Contribution

On the **Home Depot** Web site, the company describes an initiative where **Home Depot** donates employee time and materials to help local communities through an associated charity, KaBoom!. Extensive community relations programs bring together volunteerism, do-it-yourself expertise, product donations, and monetary grants to meet critical needs and build affordable community playgrounds.

Use Exhibit 21–1 to identify the types of relevant costs and revenue that **Home Depot**'s management might consider when engaging in a service program like KaBoom!.

Problem Set A

LO1 through LO3, LO5

PROBLEM 21.1A Evaluating a Special Order

D. Lawrance designs and manufactures fashionable men's clothing. For the coming year, the company has scheduled production of 40,000 suede jackets. Budgeted costs for this product are as follows:

	Unit Costs (40,000 units)	Total
Variable manufacturing costs	$50	$2,000,000
Variable selling expenses	20	800,000
Fixed manufacturing costs	10	400,000
Fixed operating expenses	5	200,000
Total costs and expenses	$85	$3,400,000

The management of D. Lawrance is considering a special order from Discount Apparel for an additional 10,000 jackets. These jackets would carry the Discount Apparel label, rather than the D. Lawrance label. In all other respects, they would be identical to the regular D. Lawrance jackets.

Although D. Lawrance regularly sells its jackets to retail stores at a price of $150 each, Discount Apparel has offered to pay only $80 per jacket. However, because no sales commissions would be involved with this special order, D. Lawrance will incur variable selling expenses of only $5 per unit on these sales, rather than the $20 it normally incurs. Accepting the order would cause no change in the company's fixed manufacturing costs or fixed operating costs. D. Lawrance has enough plant capacity to produce 55,000 jackets per year.

Instructions

a. Using incremental revenue and incremental costs, compute the expected effect of accepting this special order on D. Lawrance's operating income.

b. Briefly discuss any other factors that you believe D. Lawrance's management should consider in deciding whether to accept the special order. Include nonfinancial as well as financial considerations.

LO1 through LO4

PROBLEM 21.2A Make or Buy Decision

eXcel

Easyuse Tool Co. manufactures an electric motor that it uses in several of its products. Management is considering whether to continue manufacturing the motors or to buy them from an outside source. The following information is available:

1. The company needs 12,000 motors per year. The motors can be purchased from an outside supplier at a cost of $21 per unit.
2. The unit cost of manufacturing the motors is $35, computed as follows:

Direct materials	$ 96,000
Direct labor	120,000
Factory overhead:	
Variable	90,000
Fixed	114,000
Total manufacturing costs	$420,000
Cost per unit ($420,000 ÷ 12,000 units)	$35

3. Discontinuing the manufacture of motors will eliminate all the raw materials and direct labor costs but will eliminate only 75 percent of the variable factory overhead costs.
4. If the motors are purchased from an outside source, machinery used in the production of motors will be sold at its book value. Accordingly, no gain or loss will be recognized. The sale

of this machinery would also eliminate $6,000 in fixed costs associated with depreciation and taxes. No other reductions in fixed factory overhead will result from discontinuing the production of motors.

Instructions

a. Prepare a schedule in the format illustrated in Exhibit 21–6 to determine the incremental cost or benefit of buying the motors from the outside supplier. Using this schedule, would you recommend that the company manufacture the motors or buy them from the outside source?

b. Assume that if the motors are purchased from the outside source, the factory space previously used to produce motors can be used to manufacture an additional 4,000 power trimmers per year. Power trimmers have an estimated contribution margin of $8 per unit. The manufacture of the additional power trimmers would have no effect on fixed factory overhead. Would this new assumption change your recommendation as to whether to make or buy the motors? In support of your conclusion, prepare a schedule showing the incremental cost or benefit of buying the motors from the outside source and using the factory space to produce additional power trimmers.

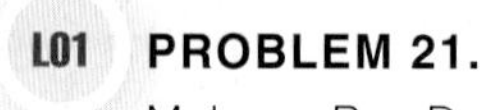

LO1 through LO4

PROBLEM 21.3A
Make or Buy Decision

Parsons Plumbing & Heating manufactures thermostats that it uses in several of its products. Management is considering whether to continue manufacturing the thermostats or to buy them from an outside source. The following information is available:

1. The company needs 80,000 thermostats per year. Thermostats can be purchased from an outside supplier at a cost of $6 per unit.
2. The cost of manufacturing thermostats is $7.50 per unit, computed as follows:

Direct materials	$156,000
Direct labor	132,000
Manufacturing overhead:	
Variable	168,000
Fixed	144,000
Total manufacturing costs	$600,000
Cost per unit ($600,000 ÷ 80,000 units)	$7.50

3. Discontinuing the manufacture of the thermostats will eliminate all of the direct materials and direct labor costs but will eliminate only 60 percent of the variable overhead costs.
4. If the thermostats are purchased from an outside source, certain machinery used in the production process would no longer have to be leased. Accordingly, $9,200 of fixed overhead costs could be avoided. No other reductions will result from discontinuing production of the thermostats.

Instructions

a. Prepare a schedule to determine the incremental cost or benefit of buying thermostats from the outside supplier. On the basis of this schedule, would you recommend that the company manufacture thermostats or buy them from the outside source?

b. Assume that if thermostats are purchased from the outside source, the factory space previously used to produce thermostats can be used to manufacture an additional 6,000 heat-flow regulators per year. These regulators have an estimated contribution margin of $18 per unit. The manufacture of the additional heat-flow regulators would have no effect on fixed overhead.

   Would this new assumption change your recommendation as to whether to make or buy thermostats? In support of your conclusion, prepare a schedule showing the incremental cost or benefit of buying thermostats from the outside source and using the factory space to produce additional heat-flow regulators.

LO1 through LO4

PROBLEM 21.4A

Determining the Most Profitable Product Given Scarce Resources

Insiteful Instruments produces two models of binoculars. Information for each model is as follows:

	Model 100		Model 101	
Sales price per unit		$200		$215
Costs and expenses per unit:				
Direct materials	$51		$38	
Direct labor	33		30	
Manufacturing overhead (applied at the rate of $18 per machine-hour, ⅓ of which is fixed and ⅔ variable)	36		72	
Variable selling expenses	30		15	
Total costs and expenses per unit		150		155
Profit per unit		$ 50		$ 60
Machine-hours required to produce one unit		2		4

Total manufacturing overhead amounts to $180,000 per month, one-third of which is fixed. The demand for either product is sufficient to keep the plant operating at full capacity (10,000 machine-hours per month). Assume that *only one product is to be produced in the future.*

Instructions

a. Prepare a schedule showing the contribution margin per machine-hour for each product.

b. Explain your recommendation as to which of the two products should be discontinued.

LO1 through LO5

PROBLEM 21.5A

Decision to Sell or Rebuild Deficient Units

BestView manufactures sophisticated digital cameras. The company's new models are very popular, but it has an inventory of 1,000 old models for which there is little demand. BestView is considering the following options for disposing of these old models:

1. Sell them to a discount mail-order company at a total price of $150,000. The mail-order firm would then sell these old models at a unit price of $399.
2. Convert them to new models at a remanufacturing cost of $700 per unit. These new models then could be sold to camera stores for $1,200 each.

The old models had been manufactured at a cost of $450 per unit. The cost of manufacturing new models of the same size, however, normally amounts to $800 per unit.

Instructions

a. Perform an incremental analysis of the revenue, costs, and profit resulting from converting the old models to new models as compared with selling them to the mail-order firm.

b. Identify any sunk costs, out-of-pocket costs, and possible opportunity costs.

c. Indicate which of these options you would select and explain your reasoning, assuming that BestView currently:

1. Has substantial excess capacity.
2. Is operating at full capacity manufacturing new models.

LO1 through LO5

PROBLEM 21.6A

Sell or Rebuild Decision

Silent Sentry manufactures gas leak detectors that are sold to homeowners throughout the United States at $25 apiece. Each detector is equipped with a sensory cell that is guaranteed to last two full years before needing to be replaced. The company currently has 50,000 gas leak detectors in its inventory that contain sensory cells that had been purchased from a discount vendor. Silent Sentry engineers estimate that these sensory cells will last only 18 months before needing to be replaced. The company has incurred the following unit costs related to the 50,000 detectors:

Direct materials	$10
Direct labor	2
Variable overhead	3
Fixed overhead	1
Total	$16

Silent Sentry is currently evaluating three options regarding the 50,000 detectors:

1. Scrap the inferior sensory cell in each unit and replace it with a new one at a cost of $8 each. The units could then be sold at their full unit price of $25.
2. Sell the units with the inferior sensory cells at a discounted unit price of $24. This option would also involve changing the packaging of each unit to inform the buyer that the estimated life of the sensory cell is 18 months. The estimated out-of-pocket cost associated with the packaging changes is $3 per unit.
3. Sell each unit "as is" with its current packaging to a discount buyer in a foreign country. The buyer has offered to pay Silent Sentry a unit price of $22.

Instructions

a. Perform an incremental analysis of these options. Based on the analysis, which option should Silent Sentry choose?

b. What nonfinancial concerns should the company take into consideration?

LO1 through LO4

PROBLEM 21.7A

Joint Products

excel

Kelp Company produces three joint products from seaweed. At the split-off point, three basic products emerge: Sea Tea, Sea Paste, and Sea Powder. Each of these products can either be sold at the split-off point or be processed further. If they are processed further, the resulting products can be sold as delicacies to health food stores. Cost and revenue information is as follows:

			Sales Value and Additional Costs If Processed Further	
Product	Pounds Produced	Sales Value at Split-Off	Final Sales Value	Additional Cost
Sea Tea	9,000	$60,000	$ 90,000	$35,000
Sea Paste	4,000	80,000	160,000	50,000
Sea Powder	2,000	70,000	85,000	14,000

Instructions

a. Which products should Kelp process beyond the split-off point?

b. At what price per pound would it be advantageous for Kelp Company to sell Sea Paste at the split-off point rather than process it further?

LO1 through LO3 LO5

PROBLEM 21.8A

Pay Off or Pay Up?

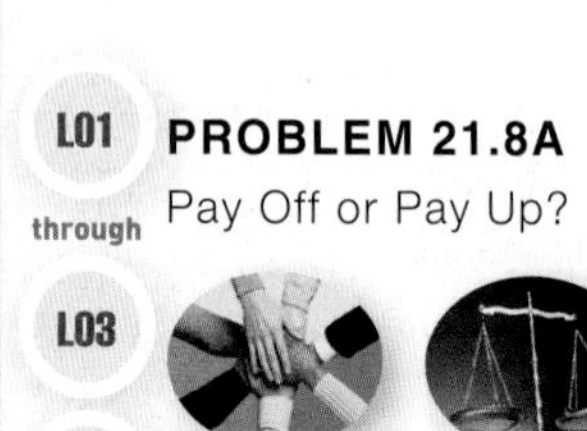

McKay Chemical Company is based in the town of Swampton. The company is Swampton's "economic lifeblood," generating annual income of $100 million and employing nearly 75 percent of its workforce. McKay produces many hazardous wastes as byproducts of its manufacturing processes. Proper disposal of these by-products in compliance with environmental regulations would cost McKay in excess of $10 million per year. Rather than comply, McKay has chosen for two decades to dump its hazardous wastes in a field at the outskirts of Swampton's city limits. For doing so, it pays a fine of $100,000 per year. The following information also pertains to McKay Chemical Company and the town of Swampton:

1. A reporter has threatened to expose McKay Chemical Company on a 60-minute, prime-time television news program. The story could result in a national boycott of the company's products and fines of up to $50 million. A boycott could reduce the company's income by as much as $25 million per year. However, the reporter has agreed not to air the story if McKay pays her a consulting fee of $1 million per year.
2. The townspeople are becoming increasingly concerned that the illegal dumping may eventually pollute the groundwater and present a serious health hazard. However, most are equally concerned that if the company's practices are exposed, Swampton and its inhabitants would face financial ruin.
3. The judge who hands down the $100,000 fine each year is also a major shareholder of McKay Chemical Company and serves on its board of directors. The town board invests the annual fine in a scholarship fund available on the basis of need to children of McKay's employees. Over the years, many of the scholarship recipients have gone on to become successful doctors, teachers, scientists, and other productive members of society.

Assume that you have just been appointed as the new chief executive officer of McKay Chemical. You have been presented with the facts described in this case, along with the following incremental analysis performed by an assistant:

	Pay the Consulting Fee	Risk Public Exposure	Incremental Analysis
Consulting fee	$(1,000,000)		$ 1,000,000
Potential fines	0	$(50,000,000)	(50,000,000)
Reduction in current fines	0	100,000	100,000
Additional disposal costs	0	(10,000,000)	(10,000,000)
Potential cost of boycott	0	(25,000,000)	(25,000,000)
Net cost of options	$(1,000,000)	$(84,900,000)	$(83,900,000)

Instructions

a. Identify any shortcomings in the preceding incremental analysis.

b. Draft a memorandum to the board of directors summarizing what you intend to do about this situation.

Problem Set B

LO1 through LO3, LO5

PROBLEM 21.1B
Evaluating a Special Order

Swirl Incorporated designs and manufactures fashionable women's clothing. For the coming year, the company has scheduled production of 50,000 silk skirts. Budgeted costs for this product are as follows:

	Unit Costs (50,000 units)	Total
Variable manufacturing costs	$40	$2,000,000
Variable selling expenses	15	750,000
Fixed manufacturing costs	12	600,000
Fixed operating expenses	10	500,000
Total costs and expenses	$77	$3,850,000

The management of Swirl is considering a special order from Discount Fashions for an additional 18,000 skirts. These skirts would carry the Discount Fashions label, rather than the Swirl label. In all other respects, they would be identical to the regular Swirl skirts.

Although Swirl regularly sells its skirts to retail stores at a price of $180 each, Discount Fashions has offered to pay only $55 per skirt. However, because no sales commissions would be involved with this special order, Swirl will incur variable selling expenses of only $5 per unit on these sales, rather than the $15 it normally incurs. Accepting the order would cause no change in the company's fixed manufacturing costs or fixed operating costs. Swirl has enough plant capacity to produce 70,000 skirts per year.

Instructions

a. Using incremental revenue and incremental costs, compute the expected effect of accepting this special order on Swirl's operating income.

b. Briefly discuss any other factors that you believe Swirl's management should consider in deciding whether to accept the special order. Include nonfinancial as well as financial considerations.

LO1 through LO4

PROBLEM 21.2B
Make or Buy Decision

Matchless Corp. manufactures radios that it uses in several of its products. Management is considering whether to continue manufacturing the radios or to buy them from an outside source. The following information is available:

1. The company needs 20,000 radios per year. The radios can be purchased from an outside supplier at a cost of $50 per unit.

2. The unit cost of manufacturing the radios is $85, computed as follows:

Direct materials	$ 400,000
Direct labor	500,000
Factory overhead:	
Variable	350,000
Fixed	450,000
Total manufacturing costs	$1,700,000
Cost per unit ($1,700,000 ÷ 20,000 units)	$85

3. Discontinuing the manufacture of radios will eliminate all the raw materials and direct labor costs but will eliminate only 80 percent of the variable factory overhead costs.
4. If the radios are purchased from an outside source, machinery used in the production of radios will be sold at its book value. Accordingly, no gain or loss will be recognized. The sale of this machinery would also eliminate $5,000 in fixed costs associated with depreciation and taxes. No other reductions in fixed factory overhead will result from discontinuing the production of radios.

Instructions

a. Prepare a schedule in the format illustrated in Exhibit 21–6 of the text to determine the incremental cost or benefit of buying the radios from the outside supplier. On the basis of this schedule, would you recommend that the company manufacture the radios or buy them from the outside source?

b. Assume that if the radios are purchased from the outside source, the factory space previously used to produce radios can be used to manufacture an additional 8,000 timepieces per year. Timepieces have an estimated contribution margin of $15 per unit. The manufacture of the additional timepieces would have no effect on fixed factory overhead. Would this new assumption change your recommendation as to whether to make or buy the radios? In support of your conclusion, prepare a schedule showing the incremental cost or benefit of buying the radios from the outside source and using the factory space to produce additional timepieces.

LO1 through LO4

PROBLEM 21.3B
Make or Buy Decision

James Lighting manufactures switches that it uses in several of its products. Management is considering whether to continue manufacturing the switches or to buy them from an outside source. The following information is available:

1. The company needs 100,000 switches per year. Switches can be purchased from an outside supplier at a cost of $4 per unit.
2. The cost of manufacturing switches is $5 per unit, computed as follows:

Direct materials	$150,000
Direct labor	100,000
Manufacturing overhead:	
Variable	200,000
Fixed	50,000
Total manufacturing costs	$500,000
Cost per unit ($500,000 ÷ 100,000 units)	$5.00

3. Discontinuing the manufacture of the switches will eliminate all of the direct materials and direct labor costs but will eliminate only 70 percent of the variable overhead costs.
4. If the switches are purchased from an outside source, certain machinery used in the production process would no longer have to be leased. Accordingly, $19,000 of fixed overhead costs could be avoided. No other reduction will result from discontinuing production of the switches.

Instructions

a. Prepare a schedule to determine the incremental cost or benefit of buying switches from the outside supplier. On the basis of this schedule, would you recommend that the company manufacture the switches or buy them from the outside source?

b. Assume that if switches are purchased from the outside source, the factory space previously used to produce switches can be used to manufacture an additional 10,000 dimmers per year. These dimmers have an estimated contribution margin of $14 per unit. The manufacture of the additional dimmers would have no effect on fixed overhead. Would this new assumption change your recommendation as to whether to make or buy switches? In support of your conclusion, prepare a schedule showing the incremental cost or benefit of buying switches from the outside source and using the factory space to produce additional dimmers.

LO1 through LO4

PROBLEM 21.4B
Determining the Most Profitable Product Given Scarce Resources

Superior Instruments produces two models of instruments. Information for each model is as follows:

	Model A		Model B	
Sales price per unit		$300		$150
Costs and expenses per unit:				
Direct materials	$60		$50	
Direct labor	40		20	
Manufacturing overhead (applied at the rate of $24 per machine-hour, ⅓ of which is fixed and ⅔ variable)	72		24	
Variable selling expenses	62		25	
Total costs and expenses per unit		234		119
Profit per unit		$ 66		$ 31
Machine-hours required to produce one unit		3		1

The demand for either product is sufficient to keep the plant operating at full capacity (15,000 machine-hours per month). Assume that *only one product is to be produced in the future.*

Instructions

a. Prepare a schedule showing the contribution margin per machine-hour for each product.

b. Explain your recommendation as to which of the two products should be discontinued.

LO1 through LO5

PROBLEM 21.5B
Decision to Sell or Rebuild Deficient Units

Bold Face manufactures TVs. The company's high-definition TVs are very popular, but it has an inventory of 500 large-screen, standard-definition TVs for which there is little demand. Bold Face is considering the following options for disposing of these TVs:

1. Sell them to a discount mail-order company at a total price of $40,000. The mail-order firm would then sell these large-screen, standard-definition TVs at a unit price of $200.
2. Convert them to high-definition TVs at a remanufacturing cost of $400 per unit. These converted TVs then could be sold to TV stores for $1,000 each.

The standard-definition TVs were manufactured at a cost of $300 per unit. The cost of manufacturing high-definition TVs of the same size, however, normally amounts to $410 per unit.

Instructions

a. Perform an incremental analysis of the revenue, costs, and profit resulting from converting the standard-definition TVs to high definition as compared with selling them to the mail-order firm.

b. Identify any sunk costs, out-of-pocket costs, and possible opportunity costs.

c. Indicate which of these options you would select and explain your reasoning, assuming that Bold Face currently:
   1. Has substantial excess capacity.
   2. Is operating at full capacity manufacturing high-definition TVs.

LO1 through LO5

PROBLEM 21.6B
Sell or Rebuild Decision

Fire Code manufactures smoke detectors that are sold to homeowners throughout the United States at $20 apiece. Each detector is equipped with a sensory cell that is guaranteed to last two full years before needing to be replaced. The company currently has 80,000 smoke detectors in its inventory, which contain sensory cells that had been purchased from a discount vendor. Fire Code engineers estimate that these sensory cells will last only 18 months before needing to be replaced. The company has incurred the following unit costs related to the 80,000 detectors:

Direct materials	$ 8
Direct labor	1
Variable overhead	2
Fixed overhead	1
Total	$12

Fire Code is currently evaluating three options regarding the 80,000 detectors:

1. Scrap the inferior sensory cell in each unit and replace it with a new one at a cost of $6 each. The units could then be sold at their full unit price of $20.
2. Sell the units with the inferior sensory cells at a discounted unit price of $18. This option would also involve changing the packaging of each unit to inform the buyer that the estimated life of the sensory cell is 18 months. The estimated out-of-pocket cost associated with the packaging changes is $2 per unit.
3. Sell each unit "as is" with its current packaging to a discount buyer in a foreign country. The buyer has offered to pay Fire Code a unit price of $17.

Instructions

a. Perform an incremental analysis of these options. Based on your analysis, which option should Fire Code choose?

b. What nonfinancial concerns should the company take into consideration?

LO1 through LO4

PROBLEM 21.7B
Joint Products

Vitamin Bits Co. produces three joint products from mint leaves. At the split-off point, three basic products emerge: B_1, B_3, and B_{15}. Each of these products can be either sold at the split-off point or processed further. If they are processed further, the resulting products can be sold to high-end health food stores. Cost and revenue information is as follows:

			Sales Value and Additional Costs If Processed Further	
	Pounds Produced	Sales Value at Split-Off	Final Sales Value	Additional Cost
B_1	10,000	$110,000	$200,000	$50,000
B_3	5,000	100,000	180,000	60,000
B_{15}	3,000	90,000	110,000	21,000

Instructions

a. Which products should Vitamin Bits process beyond the split-off point?

b. At what price per pound would it be advantageous for Vitamin Bits to sell B_3 at the split-off point rather than process it further?

LO1 through LO5

PROBLEM 21.8B
Scarce Resources

Home Run Corporation produces three products for baseball enthusiasts: bats, gloves, and balls. Information relating to each product line is as follows:

	Bats	Gloves	Balls
Selling price	$48	$80	$12
Direct materials	14	10	1
Direct labor	8	24	4
Variable overhead	1	1	1

Home Run pays its direct labor workers an average of $8 per hour. At full capacity, 60,000 direct labor hours are available per year. The marketing department has just released the following sales estimates for the upcoming year: bats (60,000 units), gloves (20,000 units), and balls (100,000 units). Based on these figures, demand for the current year is expected to exceed the company's direct labor capacity.

Instructions

a. What products should Home Run produce to maximize its operating income?

b. The company's marketing manager believes that the production of the least profitable product is needed to "support" the demand for the most profitable products. How may this influence management's decision regarding the company's production schedule?

Critical Thinking Cases

LO4 **CASE 21.1**
Factors That Limit Capacity

We have made the point that managers often attempt to maximize the contribution margin per unit of a particular resource that limits output capacity. The following are five familiar types of businesses:

1. Small medical or dental practice
2. Restaurant
3. Supermarket
4. Builder of residential housing
5. Auto dealer's service department

Instructions

With a group of students:

a. For each type of business, identify the factor that you believe is most likely to limit potential output capacity.

b. Suggest several ways (other than raising prices) the business can maximize the contribution margin per unit of this limiting resource. (Hint: These businesses often *do* implement the types of strategies you are likely to suggest. Thus, your solution to this case may explain basic characteristics of businesses that you personally have observed.)

LO1 through LO3, LO5 **CASE 21.2**
Relevant Information and Opportunity Costs

McFriendly Software recently developed new spreadsheet software, Easy-Calc, which it intends to market by mail through ads in computer magazines. Just prior to introducing Easy-Calc, McFriendly receives an unexpected offer from Jupiter Computer to buy all rights to the software for $10 million cash.

Instructions

a. Is the $10 million offer "relevant" financial information?

b. Describe McFriendly's opportunity cost if it (1) accepts Jupiter's offer and (2) turns down the offer and markets Easy-Calc itself. Would these opportunity costs be recorded in McFriendly's accounting records? If so, explain the journal entry to record these costs.

c. Briefly describe the extent to which the dollar amounts of the two opportunity costs described in part **b** are known to management at the time the decision is made to accept or reject Jupiter's offer.

d. Might there be any other opportunity costs to consider at the time of making this decision? If so, explain briefly.

LO3 through LO5 **INTERNET CASE 21.3**

Dow Corporation produces a wide variety of products ranging from raw chemicals that are used as inputs by other firms to final goods that are sold to consumers. Access **Dow**'s home page at the following address:

www.dow.com

Instructions

a. Choose two or three product areas to explore on the Web site. Based on your investigations, what types of incremental decisions are most likely to be made for each of the product areas?

b. What do you think **Dow**'s limiting resources might be?

c. In addition to profit considerations, what other qualitative factors might be considered in **Dow**'s incremental decision making?

Internet sites are time and date sensitive. It is the purpose of these exercises to have you explore the Internet. You may need to use the Yahoo! search engine http://www.yahoo.com *(or another favorite search engine) to find a company's current Web address.*

LO1 through LO3

CASE 21.4
SEC Enforcement Fines

Until recently, the SEC was reluctant to hit companies with big fines for wrongdoing because the penalties hurt shareholders whose stock prices had already been hammered by scandal. But the Sarbanes-Oxley Act now lets the SEC use the fine funds to repay stockholders. For example, accounting frauds cost **WorldCom** (now **MCI Inc.**) $750 million and **Adelphia** $715 million in fines. Recent pressure from Congress has encouraged the SEC to try to create some objective measures for fines so there can be continuity from case to case. The SEC has been trying to define which behaviors should get which punishments.

The SEC wants a series of objective measures so there can be continuity from case to case. Many believe a good starting point is whether a company benefited from its wrongdoing, in which case fines would be higher. Commissioners also debated how much credit a company should get for cooperating with the SEC, in which case fines would be lower. Some individuals argue that any signposts will be better than today's unmarked landscape.

Instructions

With a group of students identified by your instructor, write a one-page discussion that uses Exhibit 21–1 to identify how SEC policies have the potential to change managers' decision processes. In particular, focus on decisions managers make when considering whether to commit fraud. Consider the relevant costs and earnings that managers might consider in making this type of decision. Use the ideas in this chapter that are related to what is relevant to a particular decision to help with your analysis. In the conclusion of your paper, state whether your group thinks objective measures for fines will change the decision processes of managers who are considering fraud.

Answers to Self-Test Questions

1. b **2.** c [$15 + ($400,000 ÷ 10,000 cards)] **3.** d **4.** a **5.** d

COMPREHENSIVE PROBLEM 5

The Gilster Company

The Gilster Company, a machine tooling firm, has several plants. One plant, located in St. Falls, Minnesota, uses a job order costing system for its batch production processes. The St. Falls plant has two departments through which most jobs pass. Plantwide overhead, which includes the plant manager's salary, accounting personnel, cafeteria, and human resources, is budgeted at $200,000. During the past year, actual plantwide overhead was $190,000. Each department's overhead consists primarily of depreciation and other machine-related expenses. Selected budgeted and actual data from the St. Falls plant for the past year are as follows:

	Department A	Department B
Budgeted department overhead (excludes plantwide overhead)	$100,000	$500,000
Actual department overhead	110,000	520,000
Expected activity:		
Direct labor hours	50,000	10,000
Machine-hours	10,000	50,000
Actual activity:		
Direct labor hours	51,000	9,000
Machine-hours	10,500	52,000

For the coming year, the accountants at St. Falls are in the process of helping the sales force create bids for several jobs. Projected data pertaining to job no. 110 are as follows:

Direct materials	$20,000
Direct labor cost:	
Department A (2,000 hr)	30,000
Department B (500 hr)	6,000
Machine-hours projected:	
Department A	100
Department B	1,200
Units produced	10,000

Instructions

(Round overhead rates and unit costs to 2 decimal places and round other cost calculations to the nearest dollar.)

a. Assume the St. Falls plant uses a single plantwide overhead rate to assign *all* overhead (plantwide and department) costs to jobs. Use expected direct labor hours to compute the overhead rate. Find the overhead rate and determine the projected amount of total manufacturing costs per unit for the units in job no. 110.

b. Recalculate the projected manufacturing costs for job no. 110 using three separate rates: one rate for plantwide overhead and two separate department overhead rates, all based on machine-hours.

c. The sales policy at St. Falls dictates that job bids be calculated by adding 30 percent to total manufacturing costs. What would be the bid for job no. 110 using (**1**) the overhead rate from part **a** and (**2**) the overhead rate from part **b**? Explain why the bids differ. Which of the overhead allocation methods would you recommend and why?

d. Using the allocation rates in part **b,** compute the under- or overapplied overhead for the St. Falls plant for the year. Explain the impact on net income of assigning the under- or overapplied overhead to cost of goods sold rather than prorating the amount between inventories and cost of goods sold.

e. A St. Falls subcontractor has offered to produce the parts for job no. 110 for a price of $8 per unit. Assume the St. Falls sales force has already committed to the bid price based on the calculations in part **b.** Should St. Falls buy the $8 per unit part from the subcontractor or continue to make the parts for job no. 110 itself?

f. Would your response to part **e** change if the St. Falls plant could use the facilities necessary to produce parts for job no. 110 for another job that could earn an incremental profit of $15,000?

g. If the subcontractor mentioned in part **e** is located in Mexico, what additional international environmental issues, other than price, will Gilster and St. Falls management need to evaluate?

h. If Gilster Company management decides to undertake a target costing approach to pricing its jobs, what types of changes will it need to make for such an approach to be successful?

CHAPTER 22

Responsibility Accounting and Transfer Pricing

© Ben Blankenberg/Corbis/DAL

Learning Objectives

AFTER STUDYING THIS CHAPTER, YOU SHOULD BE ABLE TO:

- **LO1** Distinguish among cost centers, profit centers, and investment centers.
- **LO2** Explain the need for responsibility center information and describe a responsibility accounting system.
- **LO3** Prepare an income statement showing contribution margin and responsibility margin.
- **LO4** Distinguish between *traceable* and *common* fixed costs.
- **LO5** Explain the usefulness of contribution margin and responsibility margin in making short-term and long-term decisions.
- **LO6** Describe three transfer pricing methods and explain when each is useful.

COLUMBIA SPORTSWEAR COMPANY

All people are held accountable for their actions throughout their lives. Companies hold their managers and businesses accountable for outcomes by using responsibility centers. For example, Columbia Sportswear Company engages in the design, sourcing, marketing, and distribution of active outdoor apparel. Columbia's Web site identifies the following product lines on its investors relations page:

- **Outerwear**—products designed to protect the wearer from inclement weather in everyday use in a variety of outdoor activities.
- **Sportswear**—durable, functional, value-priced, authentic, active outdoor apparel.
- **Footwear**—seasonal outdoor footwear for adults and youth in cold weather, hiking, trail, sandal, outdoor casual, and rugged comfort styles.
- **Accessories**—hats, caps, scarves, gloves, mittens, and headbands that complement the outerwear and sportswear lines.
- **Equipment**—technically advanced tents and sleeping systems for mountaineering, ultralight backpacking, and camping.

Companies like Columbia often segment their businesses into responsibility centers by product line and hold those responsibility centers accountable by using accounting information. ■

An organization's employees need guidelines that determine their responsibilities for organizational resources. These guidelines are in the form of job descriptions, work rules, union agreements, and organizational hierarchies. By creating profit centers and business units, companies are designing an organizational hierarchy of responsibility centers that determines decision-making authority. Profit center managers are responsible for decisions to create short-run profits. Business unit managers have more significant responsibilities for strategic business decisions.

Once the authority for decision making has been assigned, organizations must evaluate and reward decision outcomes. Giving profit-related, decision-making authority to profit center managers is typically linked with merit-based pay and performance reviews for those managers. Performance evaluation mechanisms are necessary to make sure decision outcomes are consistent with an organization's long-term strategic goals and objectives.

In this chapter we identify common organizational responsibility structures and their related accounting implications for performance evaluation and rewards. We show how decision-making authority over organizational resources must be linked, through a responsibility accounting system, to performance evaluation and rewards. Understanding how businesses organize decision-making responsibility will help you clarify your own responsibilities within organizations you currently work for or will work for in the future.

Responsibility Centers

Most businesses are organized into a number of different subunits that perform different functions. For example, a manufacturing company typically has departments specializing in purchasing, production, sales, shipping, accounting, finance, and personnel. Production departments and sales departments often are further subdivided along different product lines or geographical areas. Organizing a business in this manner enables managers and employees to specialize in specific types of business activity. This type of organization also helps to establish clear lines of management responsibility.

Companies use many different names to describe their internal operating units, including divisions, departments, branches, product lines, and sales territories. In our discussion, we generally will use the term **responsibility center** to describe a subunit within a business organization. A designated manager is responsible for directing the activities of each such center.

In most business organizations, large responsibility centers are further subdivided into smaller ones. Consider, for example, a retail store within a chain such as **Sears** or **Walmart**. Each store is a responsibility center under the control of a store manager. Each store is further divided into many separate sales departments, such as appliances, automotive products, and sporting goods. Each sales department also is a responsibility center, under the control of a department manager. These department managers report to, and are supervised by, the store manager.

THE NEED FOR INFORMATION ABOUT RESPONSIBILITY CENTER PERFORMANCE

An income statement measures the overall profit performance of a business entity. However, managers also need accounting information measuring the performance of *each center* within the business organization. This information assists managers in the following tasks:

1. *Planning and allocating resources.* Management needs to know how well various sections of the business are performing to set future performance goals and to allocate resources to those responsibility centers offering the greatest profit potential. If one product line is more

profitable than another, for example, the company's overall profitability may increase by allocating more production capacity to the more profitable product.

2. *Controlling operations.* One use of responsibility center data is to identify those portions of the business that are performing inefficiently or below expectations. When revenue lags, or costs become excessive, center information helps to focus management's attention on those areas responsible for the poor performance. If a part of the business is unprofitable, perhaps it should be discontinued.
3. *Evaluating the performance of center managers.* As each center is an area of management responsibility, the performance of the center provides one basis for evaluating the skills of the center manager.

Thus, measuring the performance of each center in the business organization is an important function of any accounting system designed to meet the needs of management.

COST CENTERS, PROFIT CENTERS, AND INVESTMENT CENTERS

Learning Objective
Distinguish among cost centers, profit centers, and investment centers. LO1

Business responsibility centers are usually classified as cost centers, profit centers, or investment centers. To illustrate, assume that NuTech Electronics owns and manages a Mail-Order facility and several retail stores located throughout the greater Chicago area. Each store is equipped with its own sales area and repair facilities.

On the following page, Exhibit 22–1 displays a responsibility hierarchy for NuTech showing how decision responsibility is delegated downward throughout an organization (see the **black** arrows). Although responsibility is delegated down in organizations, accounting information flows up through the organization from the smallest responsibility center up to top management and the board of directors (see the **red** arrows).

Cost Centers

A **cost center** is a business section that incurs costs (or expenses) but does not directly generate revenue.[1] NuTech views its administrative departments—accounting, finance, data processing, and legal services—as cost centers. In addition, it also views maintenance and janitorial functions as cost centers. Each cost center provides services to other NuTech centers. The bottom of Exhibit 22–1 shows that the cost centers provide services to other responsibility centers. However, none of the cost centers sells goods or services directly to NuTech's customers.

© Kent Knudson/PhotoLink/Getty Images/DAL

The decision-making responsibility assigned to cost center managers includes decisions about input resources. For a janitorial cost center manager at NuTech, input-related decisions would include hiring of personnel, assignment of personnel, obtaining the right equipment, and monitoring the use of janitorial resources. However, the janitorial cost center manager would not try to sell the department's services to other customers. Therefore, output-related decisions—such as pricing, type of service to offer, and choice of target markets—are not typically the responsibility of cost center managers.

Cost centers are evaluated primarily on (1) their ability to control costs and (2) the *quantity* and the *quality* of the services that they provide. Because cost centers do not directly generate revenue, income statements are not prepared for them. However, accounting systems must accumulate separately the costs incurred by each cost center.

In some cases, costs serve as an objective basis for evaluating the performance of a cost center. For example, NuTech's janitorial service can be evaluated primarily on the basis of its cost per square foot per day.

[1] Cost centers sometimes generate insignificant amounts of revenue, but the direct generation of revenue is incidental to the basic purpose of the center.

Evaluating the performance of NuTech's accounting department is more subjective. Here, management must compare the department's costs with the "value" of services provided to the organization. Such services include meeting the financial and tax reporting requirements, as well as providing managers with information necessary to run the business.

Exhibit 22–1 RESPONSIBILITY HIERARCHY AT NUTECH

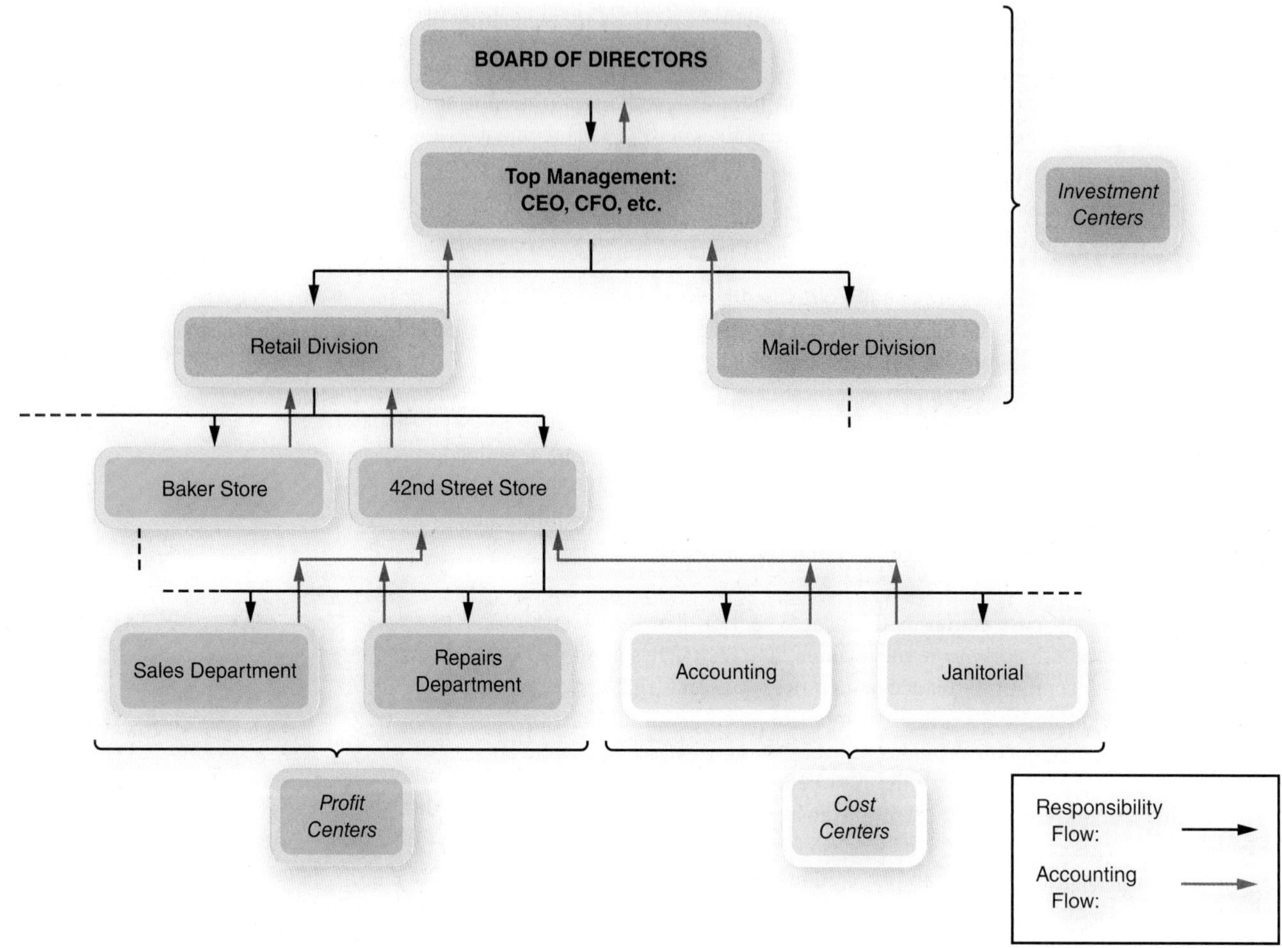

Profit Centers A **profit center** is a part of a business that generates *both revenue and costs.*[2] At NuTech, the retail stores are primary profit centers. Within the retail stores, the Sales and Repairs Departments are viewed as profit centers.[3] See Exhibit 22–1 for an illustration of NuTech's profit centers. Examples of profit centers in other types of organizations might include product lines, sales territories, retail outlets, and specific sales departments within each retail outlet.

In a profit center, managers have decision-making responsibility over both input- and output-related resources. They are responsible for using the center's resources in the least costly method possible to generate the highest revenue for an ongoing business. At NuTech, the manager of the repairs department must compete for business with other repairs departments

[2] In this chapter, we continue the convenient practice of using the term *costs* to describe both unexpired costs (such as finished goods inventory) and expired costs (such as the cost of goods sold).

[3] Repairs is considered a profit center in our example because it is assumed that NuTech customers are billed separately for repairs.

at other electronic-related facilities. The repairs manager may choose to expend resources on advertising the repair department's services to local customers as a means of generating more revenue. However, profit center managers do not have authority or responsibility for major capital acquisitions. If the manager of the repairs department wanted new equipment, responsibility to make such a capital expenditure would belong to NuTech's CEO or the Retail Division's top manager.

Profit centers are evaluated primarily on their profitability. Thus, NuTech prepares *responsibility income statements* that show separately the revenue and expenses of each profit center within the company. These results are compared with budgeted amounts, prior period performance, and, most important, the profitability of other profit centers.

Assume, for example, each of the repair departments in NuTech's retail stores is profitable. On a square-foot basis, however, the sales departments are far *more profitable.* In this case, management might consider closing some repair departments and using the space for additional sales facilities. (If repairs are closed, repair work could be provided by independent companies).

INTERNATIONAL CASE IN POINT 

A **revenue center** is a business unit that focuses primarily on the accumulation of sales. A revenue center manager is evaluated on the generation of sales revenue and has responsibility for pricing and market choice decisions. Although there are some instances of revenue centers in the United States (primarily marketing departments), revenue centers are more frequent in other parts of the world. In particular, Japanese companies have historically had a strong strategic emphasis on gaining market share. Surveys show that Japanese companies are more likely to emphasize revenue growth by using return on sales as their primary performance measure.

Investment Centers Some profit centers also qualify as investment centers. An **investment center** is a profit center for which management has been given decision-making responsibility for making significant capital investments related to the center's business activities. As shown in Exhibit 22–1, at NuTech, the Mail-Order and Retail Divisions are considered investment centers as well as profit centers because the manager of each division is responsible for making profit *and* for related capital investment choices. Thus, the Retail and Mail-Order managers could make major investment-related decisions such as repaving the parking areas or purchasing new equipment. However, very large strategic capital investments usually are reserved for the board of directors. Deciding to build a new retail store or considering a merger with another company are decisions reserved for collaboration between top management and the board.

To evaluate the performance of an investment center, it is necessary to measure objectively the cost of assets used in the center's operations. The performance of each investment center is evaluated using return on investment measurements. These return on investment performance measures are discussed in Chapter 25.

Not all profit centers can be evaluated as investment centers. For example, if a profit center shares common facilities with other parts of the business, it may be difficult to determine the precise "amount of assets invested" in the profit center. Thus, while profit centers that share common facilities can be evaluated with respect to their *profitability,* they usually are not evaluated in terms of their *return on investment.*

As previously mentioned, NuTech's Retail Division has several profit centers—e.g., the Baker and 42nd Street Stores. The stores share many common costs, such as advertising, and mainframe computer support. The allocation of these shared assets to each profit center is typically highly arbitrary. Thus, we cannot objectively evaluate these segments as investment centers. Similarly, even though each store's sales and repairs departments are separate profit centers, they are not considered investment centers because they also share many common costs, e.g., a parking lot or janitorial services.

YOUR TURN **You as a NuTech Manager**

You are the manager of the Mail-Order investment center at NuTech. You report directly to the CEO, and the Compensation Committee of the board evaluates your performance and decides on your raises and bonuses. The Compensation Committee has gathered performance information for each of the divisions, including ROA (return on assets). The committee plans to divide a bonus pool among the division managers based on these performance numbers. Given that the Mail-Order operation is only two years old and the other retail stores are, on average, 10 years old, how do you feel about the committee's plan? What other information should the board consider?

(See our comments on the Online Learning Center Web site.)

Responsibility Accounting Systems

Learning Objective
LO2 **Explain the need for responsibility center information and describe a responsibility accounting system.**

An accounting system designed to measure the performance of each center within a business is referred to as a **responsibility accounting system**. Measuring performance along the lines of management responsibility is an important function. A responsibility accounting system holds individual managers accountable for the performance of the business centers under their control. In addition, such systems provide top management with information useful in identifying strengths and weaknesses among units throughout the organization.

The successful operation of a responsibility accounting system requires three basic characteristics. First, *budgets* are prepared for each responsibility center. Budgets serve as performance targets for each subunit in an organization. Second, the accounting system *measures the performance* of each responsibility center. Third, timely *performance reports* are prepared that compare the actual performance of each center with the amounts budgeted. Frequent performance reports help center managers keep their performance "on target." They also assist top management in evaluating the performance of each manager.

In this chapter, we emphasize the second characteristic in the operation of a responsibility accounting system—measuring the performance of each responsibility center. (The use of budgets and of performance reports is discussed in more depth in the following three chapters.)

RESPONSIBILITY ACCOUNTING: AN ILLUSTRATION

Learning Objective
LO3 **Prepare an income statement showing contribution margin and responsibility margin.**

The key to a responsibility accounting system is the ability to measure separately the operating results of each *responsibility center* within the organization. These results can then be summarized in a series of *responsibility income statements.*

A **responsibility income statement** shows not only the operating results of a particular part of a business but also the revenue and expenses *of each profit center* within that part. Such income statements enable managers to review quickly the performance of the various profit centers under their control.

To illustrate, consider NuTech Electronics' two divisions: Retail and Mail-Order. As we have seen, the Retail Division consists of many retail stores; each retail store, in turn, has several profit centers. For illustration we will focus on two, a Sales Department and a Repairs Department. A partial diagram[4] of NuTech's responsibility income statements for March appears in Exhibit 22–2.

As you read down the NuTech illustration, you are looking at smaller and smaller parts of the company. The recording of revenue and costs must begin at the *bottom* of the illustration—that is, for the *smallest* areas of management responsibility. If income statements are to be prepared for each profit center in the 42nd Street store, for example, NuTech's chart of accounts must be sufficiently detailed to measure separately the revenue and costs of these departments. The income statements for larger responsibility centers then may be prepared primarily by

[4] NuTech also prepares responsibility income statements showing the profit centers in the Mail-Order Division and in the Baker Street store and its other stores. To conserve space, these statements are not included in our illustration.

Exhibit 22–2

MONTHLY RESPONSIBILITY INCOME STATEMENTS

NUTECH ELECTRONICS RESPONSIBILITY ACCOUNTING STATEMENT FOR MARCH

	Entire Company	Investment Centers: Retail Division	Investment Centers: Mail-Order Division
Sales	$900,000	$500,000	$400,000
Variable costs	400,000	240,000	160,000
Contribution margin	$500,000	$260,000	$240,000
Fixed costs traceable to divisions	360,000	170,000	190,000
Division responsibility margin	$140,000	$ 90,000	$ 50,000
Common fixed costs	40,000		
Operating income	$100,000		
Income tax expense	35,000		
Net income	$ 65,000		

Divisions designated as investment centers

	Retail Division	Profit Centers: 42nd Street Store	Profit Centers: Baker Street Store
Sales	$500,000	$200,000	$300,000
Variable costs	240,000	98,000	142,000
Contribution margin	$260,000	$102,000	$158,000
Fixed costs traceable to stores	140,000	60,000	80,000
Store responsibility margin	$120,000	$ 42,000	$ 78,000
Common fixed costs	30,000		
Responsibility margin for division	$ 90,000		

Stores designated as profit centers

	42nd Street Store	Profit Centers: Sales Department	Profit Centers: Repairs Department
Sales	$200,000	$180,000	$ 20,000
Variable costs	98,000	90,000	8,000
Contribution margin	$102,000	$ 90,000	$ 12,000
Fixed costs traceable to departments	32,000	18,000	14,000
Departmental responsibility margin	$ 70,000	$ 72,000	$ (2,000)
Common fixed costs	28,000		
Responsibility margin for store	$ 42,000		

Departments designated as profit centers

combining the amounts appearing in the income statements of the smaller subunits. Notice, for example, that the total monthly sales of the 42nd Street store ($200,000) are equal to the sum of the sales reported by the two profit centers within the store ($180,000 and $20,000).

ASSIGNING REVENUE AND COSTS TO RESPONSIBILITY CENTERS

In responsibility income statements, revenue is assigned first to the profit center responsible for earning that revenue. Assigning revenue to the proper department is relatively easy. Automated cash registers, for example, classify sales revenue by the department of origin.

In assigning costs to parts of a business, two concepts generally are applied:

1. *Costs are classified into the categories of variable costs and fixed costs.*[5] When costs are classified in this manner, a subtotal may be developed in the income statement showing the *contribution margin* of the business center. Arranging an income statement in this manner is termed the *contribution margin approach* and is widely used in preparing reports for use by managers.
2. *Each center is charged with only those costs that are "directly traceable" to that center.* A cost is directly traceable to a particular center if that center is *solely responsible* for the cost being incurred. Thus, traceable costs should *disappear if the center is discontinued.*

The question of whether a cost is traceable to a particular center is not always clear-cut. In assigning costs to centers, accountants must often exercise professional judgment.

YOUR TURN **You as a Department Manager**

Assume that the Mail-Order Division of NuTech consists of two departments, Sales and Packaging. Also, assume that you are the manager of the Sales Department. To meet the profit goals and expectations of your division head, you have been promising customers that their orders will be expedited. The manager of the Packaging Department came to your office and was very angry. She said that expedited orders are causing her budget overruns because of labor overtime and special packaging requirements. She said that the Packaging Department would no longer be able to guarantee expedited sales orders. She also suggested that it was unethical for you to meet your budgeted goals by causing the Packaging Department to be unable to meet its budgeted goals. How would you respond?

(See our comments on the Online Learning Center Web site.)

In the following discussion, we examine the various elements of NuTech's performance reports that are shown in Exhibit 22–2 using the contribution margin approach.

VARIABLE COSTS

In responsibility income statements, variable costs are those costs that change in approximate proportion to changes in the center's sales volume. For NuTech, variable costs include the cost of goods sold, sales commissions paid to salespeople for each system they sell, parts and labor costs incurred by each store's Repairs Department, and numerous other operating expenses that vary with sales volume.

Because variable costs are related to specific revenue dollars, they are usually traced directly to the profit center responsible for generating that revenue. For instance, the cost of a home stereo system sold at NuTech's 42nd Street store is directly traceable to the Sales Department of that store. In a similar fashion, parts and labor costs incurred in repairs are directly traceable to the Repairs Department. If a particular profit center were eliminated, all of its variable costs normally would disappear.

CONTRIBUTION MARGIN

Contribution margin (revenue minus variable costs) is an important tool for cost-volume-profit analysis. For example, the effect of a change in sales volume on operating income may be estimated by either (1) multiplying the change in unit sales by the contribution margin per unit or (2) multiplying the dollar change in sales volume by the contribution margin ratio.

[5] In Chapter 20, we discussed techniques such as the "high-low method" for separating semivariable costs into their variable and fixed elements.

(To assist in this type of analysis, responsibility income statements often include percentages as well as dollar amounts. A monthly responsibility income statement for NuTech with percentage columns is illustrated later in this chapter.)

Contribution margin expresses the relationship between revenue and variable costs but ignores fixed costs. Thus, contribution margin is primarily a *short-run* planning tool. It is useful in decisions relating to price changes, short-run promotional campaigns, or changes in the level of output that will not significantly affect fixed costs. As we discussed in Chapter 21, for longer-term decisions, such as whether to build a new plant or close a particular profit center, managers must consider *fixed costs* as well as contribution margin.

FIXED COSTS

For a business to be profitable, total contribution margin must exceed total fixed costs. However, many fixed costs cannot be easily traced to specific parts of a business. Thus, a distinction is often drawn in responsibility income statements between *traceable fixed costs* and *common fixed costs.*

TRACEABLE FIXED COSTS

Learning Objective **Distinguish between *traceable* and *common* fixed costs.** LO4

Traceable fixed costs are those that are easily traced to a specific business center. In short, traceable fixed costs arise because of a center's existence and *could be eliminated* if the related center were closed. Examples of traceable fixed costs include salaries of the center's employees and depreciation of buildings and equipment used exclusively by that center.

In determining the extent to which a specific center adds to the profitability of the business, traceable fixed costs are typically subtracted from the contribution margin. In a responsibility income statement, the contribution margin less traceable fixed costs is termed the **responsibility margin.**

COMMON FIXED COSTS

© AP Photo/Rich Kareckas

Common fixed costs (or indirect fixed costs) *jointly benefit several parts of the business.* The level of these fixed costs usually would not change significantly even if one of the centers deriving benefits from these costs were discontinued.

Consider, for example, a large department store, such as a **Macy's** or a **Nordstrom**. Every department in the store derives some benefit from the store building. However, such costs as depreciation and property taxes on the store will continue at current levels even if one or more of the departments within the store are discontinued. Thus, from the viewpoint of the centers within the store, depreciation on the building is a common fixed cost.

Common fixed costs cannot be assigned to specific subunits except by arbitrary means, such as in proportion to relative sales volume or square feet of space occupied. In an attempt to measure the "overall profitability" of each profit center, some businesses allocate common fixed costs to subunits along with traceable costs. A common approach, however, is to charge each profit center only with those costs *directly traceable* to that part of the business. In this text, we follow this latter approach.

Common Fixed Costs Include Costs Traceable to Service Departments

In a responsibility income statement, the category of traceable fixed costs usually includes only those fixed costs *traceable to profit centers.* Costs traceable to *service departments,* such as the accounting department, benefit many parts of the business. Thus, the costs of operating service departments are classified in a responsibility income statement as common fixed costs. For example, in Exhibit 22–3 on the following page the $28,000 in common fixed costs shown in the income statement of NuTech's 42nd Street store includes the monthly costs of operating the store's accounting, security, and maintenance departments, as well as other storewide costs such as depreciation, utilities expense, and the store manager's salary.

Exhibit 22–3

EMPHASIZING FIXED COSTS IN MONTHLY RESPONSIBILITY REPORTS

NUTECH MARCH RESPONSIBILITY REPORT

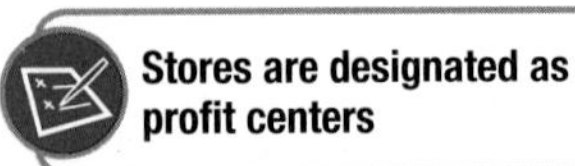

Stores are designated as profit centers

	Retail Division	Profit Centers: 42nd Street Store	Profit Centers: Baker Street Store
Sales	$500,000	$200,000	$300,000
Variable costs	240,000	98,000	142,000
Contribution margin	$260,000	$102,000	$158,000
Fixed costs traceable to stores	140,000	60,000	80,000
Store responsibility margin	$120,000	$ 42,000	$ 78,000
Common fixed costs	30,000		
Responsibility margin for division	$ 90,000		

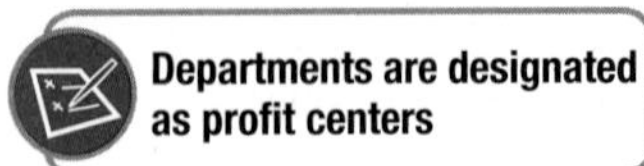

Departments are designated as profit centers

	42nd Street Store	Profit Centers: Sales Department	Profit Centers: Repairs Department
Sales	$200,000	$180,000	$ 20,000
Variable costs	98,000	90,000	8,000
Contribution margin	$102,000	$ 90,000	$ 12,000
Fixed costs traceable to departments	32,000	18,000	14,000
Departmental responsibility margin	$ 70,000	$ 72,000	$ (2,000)
Common fixed costs	28,000		
Responsibility margin for store	$ 42,000		

Most service departments are evaluated as cost centers. Therefore, the responsibility accounting system should accumulate separately the costs traceable to each service department.

Common Fixed Costs Are Traceable to Larger Responsibility Centers All costs are traceable to *some level* of the organization. To illustrate this concept, a portion of the March responsibility accounting system of NuTech Electronics is repeated in Exhibit 22–3, with emphasis on the monthly fixed costs in the 42nd Street store.

We have made the point that certain storewide costs, such as the operation of the maintenance department and the store manager's salary, are not traceable to the specific profit centers within the store. These costs are, however, easily traceable to the 42nd Street store. Therefore, whether these costs are classified as traceable or "common" depends on whether we define the centers as stores or as departments within the stores.

As we move up a responsibility reporting system to broader and broader areas of responsibility, common costs at the lower levels of management responsibility *become traceable costs* as they fall under the control of the managers of larger responsibility centers. The fact that common costs become traceable at higher responsibility center levels is emphasized by using red in Exhibit 22–3.

RESPONSIBILITY MARGIN

Learning Objective

LO5 Explain the usefulness of contribution margin and responsibility margin in making short-term and long-term decisions.

We have mentioned that contribution margin provides an excellent tool for evaluating the effects of short-run decisions on profitability. Such decisions typically do not involve changes in a company's fixed costs. Unlike short-run decisions, long-run decisions often have fixed cost implications. Thus, responsibility margin is considered a more useful *longer-run* measure of profitability than contribution margin because it takes into consideration changes in fixed costs traceable to a particular business center. Examples of such long-run decisions include whether to expand current capacity, add a new profit center, or eliminate a profit center that is performing poorly.

To illustrate how the responsibility margin of a profit center can be used to measure performance, we will examine NuTech's Retail and Mail-Order divisions. The company's monthly income statement for these two divisions is shown in Exhibit 22–4. (The format is identical to that shown in Exhibit 22–2, except for the inclusion of *component percentages* which accompany the dollar amounts.)

Exhibit 22–4 CONTRIBUTION MARGIN RESPONSIBILITY REPORTS

	Entire Company		Business Center: Retail Division		Business Center: Mail-Order Division	
	Dollars	**%**	**Dollars**	**%**	**Dollars**	**%**
Sales	$900,000	100.0%	$500,000	100.0%	$400,000	100.0%
Variable costs	400,000	44.4	240,000	48.0	160,000	40.0
Contribution margin	$500,000	55.6%	$260,000	52.0%	$240,000	60.0%
Fixed costs traceable to divisions	360,000	40.0	170,000	34.0	190,000	47.5
Division responsibility margin	$140,000	15.6%	$ 90,000	18.0%	$ 50,000	12.5%
Common fixed costs	40,000	4.4				
Operating income	$100,000	11.1%*				
Income tax expense	35,000	3.9				
Net income	$ 65,000	7.2%				

*Small errors may appear in adding or subtracting percentage amounts due to rounding.

Which of NuTech's two divisions is most profitable? The answer depends on whether you are making short-run decisions, in which fixed costs do not change, or long-run decisions, in which changes to fixed costs become important factors.

First, let us consider a short-run decision. Assume that NuTech's management has recently budgeted $5,000 for a radio advertising campaign. However, it is not certain whether to use the $5,000 to promote its Retail Division or its Mail-Order Division.

Assume that management believes that the $5,000 in radio advertising will result in approximately $20,000 in additional sales for whichever division is advertised. In this case, management should spend its advertising dollars promoting the *Mail-Order Division,* because this division has the higher contribution margin ratio. An additional $20,000 in mail-order sales generates *$12,000* in contribution margin ($20,000 × 60%), whereas $20,000 in retail sales generates a contribution margin of only $10,400 ($20,000 × 52%).[6]

Now let us take a longer-run view. Assume that NuTech has decided to downsize and continue operating only one of its divisions. Given that current revenue and cost relationships are expected to remain relatively stable over time, which division would you recommend that NuTech continue to operate? The answer is the *Retail Division.*

After considering fixed costs, we see in Exhibit 22–4 that the Retail Division contributes *$90,000* to NuTech's net income, but the Mail-Order Division contributes only *$50,000.* Stated another way, if the Mail-Order Division is discontinued, all of the revenue, variable costs, and traceable fixed costs relating to it should disappear. In short, the company would lose the $50,000 monthly *responsibility margin* now produced by this division. This, of course, is preferable to losing the $90,000 monthly margin currently provided by the Retail Division.

[6] Notice that the additional contribution margin generated in *either* division is expected to exceed the cost of the advertising. This suggests that management should aggressively advertise *both* of NuTech's divisions. Creative decision making should not "come to an end" with the identification of the best of the proposed alternatives.

In summary, when making short-run decisions that do not affect fixed costs, managers should attempt to generate the greatest *contribution margin* for the additional costs incurred. This usually means emphasizing those centers with the highest contribution margin ratios. When making long-run decisions, however, managers must consider fixed cost implications. This requires a shift in focus to *responsibility margins* and *responsibility margin ratios.*

WHEN IS A RESPONSIBILITY CENTER "UNPROFITABLE"?

In deciding whether a specific profit center is "unprofitable," numerous factors must be considered. Responsibility margin, however, is a good starting point. As we've seen, this margin indicates the extent to which a profit center earns an adequate contribution margin to cover its traceable fixed costs.

To illustrate, consider the monthly responsibility income statement prepared for NuTech's 42nd Street store and shown in Exhibit 22–5.

Exhibit 22–5

RESPONSIBILITY INCOME STATEMENT FOR 42ND STREET STORE

		Profit Centers	
	42nd Street Store	Sales Department	Repairs Department
Sales	$200,000	$180,000	$ 20,000
Variable costs	98,000	90,000	8,000
Contribution margin	$102,000	$ 90,000	$ 12,000
Fixed costs traceable to departments	32,000	18,000	14,000
Departmental responsibility margin	$ 70,000	$ 72,000	$ (2,000)
Common fixed costs	28,000		
Responsibility margin for store	$ 42,000		

According to these data, discontinuing the Repairs Department would eliminate $20,000 in revenue and $22,000 in costs ($8,000 in variable costs and $14,000 in traceable fixed costs). Thus, closing this department might well increase the profitability of the store by *$2,000*—its negative margin.

However, as we learned in Chapter 21, NuTech's management should take into consideration many other factors. For example, is the Repairs Department consistently unprofitable, or was this an unusual month? Does the existence of the Repairs Department contribute to the store's ability to sell merchandise? What alternative use could be made of the space now used by the Repairs Department? Thus, even though the Repairs Department is unprofitable, there may be other factors to consider before deciding that this department should be closed.

EVALUATING RESPONSIBILITY CENTER MANAGERS

Some fixed costs traceable to a center are simply beyond the manager's immediate control. If a center is saddled with high costs that are beyond the manager's control, the center's reported performance may not be indicative of its manager's individual performance. This can be an extremely sensitive issue, especially when a manager's compensation or bonus is affected.

To illustrate, assume that NuTech's 42nd Street store has been open since 1956, whereas its Baker Street store has been in operation for only three years. Consequently, the depreciation and property taxes applicable to the Baker Street store far exceed those incurred at the 42nd Street store. If the bonus paid to the manager of the Baker Street store is based solely on the store's responsibility margin, this manager will be unjustly penalized for serving at the newer location.

In response to this type of problem, some companies subdivide traceable fixed costs as *controllable fixed costs* or *committed fixed costs.* **Controllable fixed costs** are those under the manager's immediate control, such as salaries and advertising. **Committed fixed costs** are those that the manager cannot readily change, such as depreciation and property taxes. In the responsibility income statement, controllable fixed costs can be deducted from the contribution margin to arrive at a subtotal called **performance margin.** Committed fixed costs then can be deducted from the performance margin to determine the *responsibility margin.*

Subdividing traceable costs in this manner draws a distinction between the performance of a center manager and the profitability of a center as a long-term investment. The performance margin includes only the revenue and costs *under the manager's direct control,* making it useful in evaluating the manager's ability to control costs. The responsibility margin, however, is used for measuring and evaluating the long-term profitability of the *center* viewed as a whole.

ARGUMENTS AGAINST ALLOCATING COMMON FIXED COSTS TO BUSINESS CENTERS

We have mentioned that some companies follow a policy of allocating common fixed costs among the business centers benefiting from those costs. The bases used for allocating common costs are necessarily arbitrary, such as relative sales volume or square feet of floor space occupied by the center. In a responsibility income statement, responsibility margin less common fixed costs is called "operating income."

We do *not* recommend this practice, for several reasons:

1. *Common fixed costs often would not change even if a business center were eliminated.* Therefore, an allocation of these costs only distorts the amount contributed by each center to the income of the company.

   To illustrate this point, assume that $10,000 in common costs are allocated to a center that has a responsibility margin of only $4,000. Also assume that total common costs would not change even if the center were eliminated. The allocation of common costs makes the center *appear* to be unprofitable, showing an operating loss of $6,000 ($4,000 responsibility margin less $10,000 in allocated common fixed costs). However, closing the center would actually *reduce* the company's income by *$4,000,* as the center's $4,000 margin would be lost, but common fixed costs would not change.
2. *Common fixed costs are not under the direct control of the center's managers.* Therefore, allocating these costs to the center does not assist in evaluating the performance of managers.
3. *Allocation of common fixed costs may imply changes in profitability that are unrelated to the center's performance.* To illustrate this point, assume that $50,000 in monthly common fixed costs are allocated equally to each of five profit centers. Thus, each profit center is charged with *$10,000* of these costs. Now assume that one of the profit centers is discontinued but that the monthly level of common fixed costs does not change. Each of the four remaining profit centers will now be charged with *$12,500* in common fixed costs ($50,000 ÷ 4). As a result, the continuing profit centers are made to appear less profitable because of an event (closure of the fifth profit center) that is *unrelated* to their activities.

TRANSFER PRICES

All of NuTech's profit centers sell products or services to customers *outside* of the organization. In addition many responsibility centers supply some of their output to other parts of the business.

When products (either goods or services) are transferred from one department to another, *transfer prices* play an important role in the evaluation of departmental performance. A **transfer price** is the dollar amount used in recording this interdepartmental transfer.

Learning Objective LO6
Describe three transfer pricing methods and explain when each is useful.

Exhibit 22–6, on the following page, illustrates a transfer of goods between the Retail and Mail-Order Divisions of NuTech. If a product requested from a mail-order customer is not in stock in the warehouse, a transfer of that product from a retail store can be requested. Retail stores, as profit centers, will want to transfer the product to mail-order at the market price that could be obtained from a retail customer. Because retail market prices tend to be higher than mail-order prices, the mail-order manager will want to negotiate a lower price. Alternatively, NuTech's upper management may simply declare an appropriate transfer price based on the cost of the product plus some appropriate markup. Exhibit 22–6 shows the three types of transfer prices we will discuss in this section.

Exhibit 22–6 **TRANSFER PRICING AT NUTECH**

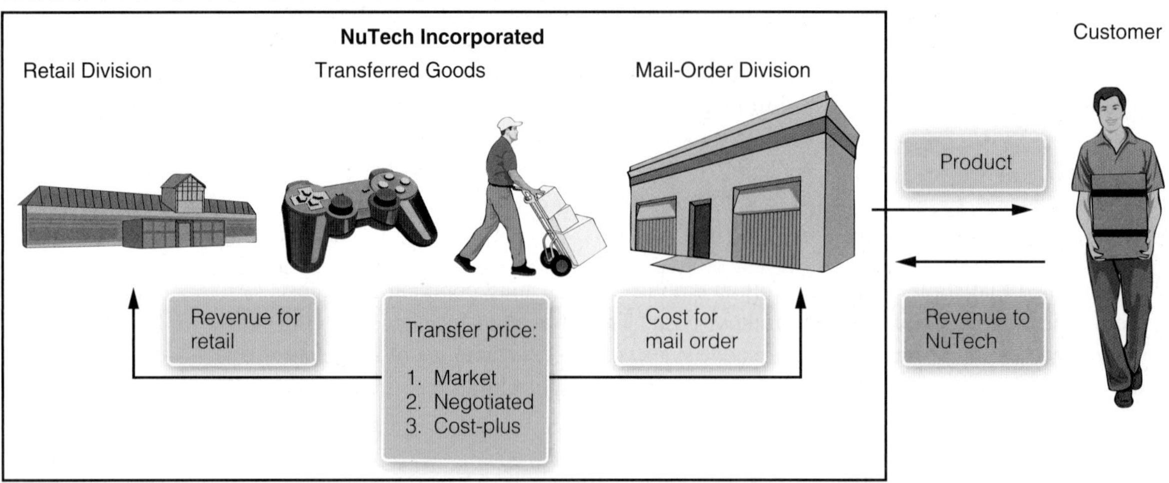

Transfer Prices for Profit Centers Profit centers normally *sell* their output to organizations outside of the firm. But some profit centers also provide a portion of their output to other business units within the business organization.

If cost were used as a transfer price, the profit center would be using some of its resources in a manner that *produces no profit.* Supplying more product to internal parts of the business at cost, rather than to outside customers at a profit, would *reduce* the department's contribution margin, responsibility margin, and other measures of departmental performance.

On the other hand, the department receiving the transferred goods at cost would be getting a bargain. Presumably, this transferred cost would be well below external market prices, making that department look unusually profitable. In short, using cost as a transfer price would *shift margin* from the department that *originated* the product to the departments that eventually sell that product to outside customers.

For this reason, many companies now use **market value** as the transfer price of products produced in profit centers. In this way, the departmental profit winds up in the profit center that *originated* the product, rather than in the center to which the product is transferred.

Transfer Prices When Market Prices Don't Exist Unfortunately, well-defined markets for transferred products do not always exist. When market prices do not exist for the good or service being transferred, companies use other types of transfer prices. We discuss two types of transfer prices, a negotiated transfer price and a cost-plus transfer price.

Many companies ask their division managers to negotiate an acceptable transfer price, generally referred to as a **negotiated transfer price.** During the negotiation process, the supplying and buying divisions agree on a transfer price. That negotiated transfer price *allocates the profits* associated with the transferred product between the two divisions.

As an example, assume Division A supplies a component that Division B includes in an assembled finished product sold by B. The total per-unit cost of creating the component in Division A is $42.00. Division B adds other components to the product transferred by A and builds them into the finished product that sells for $150.00. Assume the costs added by Division B equal $78.00 per unit. Profit on the finished product is shown in Exhibit 22–7.

Exhibit 22–7

PRODUCT PROFIT FOR THE FIRM

Assembled Finished Product Sold by Division B	
Outside of firm sales price	$150.00
Less:	
Costs in Division A	42.00
Costs in Division B	78.00
Product profit	$ 30.00

Divisions A and B divide the $30 total profits for the finished product by agreeing on a transfer price. For example, if they agree on a negotiated transfer price of $53, then the profits for Division A will be $11 ($53 − $42) and the profits for Division B will be $19 [$150 − ($53 + $78)]. As shown in Exhibit 22–8 under the Negotiated columns, with this profit allocation, Division A's return on sales is 20.75 percent on each sales dollar ($11/$53) and Division B's is 12.67 percent on each sales dollar ($19/$150). The red arrows in Exhibit 22–8 show that the transfer price is a revenue for Division A and a cost for Division B.

A second approach to determining a transfer price when no market price exists is to add a predetermined markup to the total cost of the product transferred. This second type of transfer price is called a **cost-plus transfer price**. For example, some companies may want responsibility managers to transfer products internally, but they may not want to use negotiation. By requiring a 15 percent or 20 percent markup over cost, companies automatically allocate some profit to the supplying division. As shown in Exhibit 22–8 under the Cost-plus columns, with a 20 percent markup, Division A would transfer the component to Division B at $50.40 = $42 + (.2 × $42). Profits for Division A would be $8.40 and profits for Division B would be $21.60 = ($30 − $8.40). With this allocation, Division A earns 16.7 percent profit on each sales dollar ($8.40/$50.40) and Division B earns 14.4 percent of profit on each sales dollar ($21.60/$150). As shown in the final column of Exhibit 22–8, transfer prices are eliminated when companies compute total firm profits to eliminate double counting.

Exhibit 22–8

TRANSFER PRICE IMPACT ON DIVISION PROFITS

Two Types of Transfer Prices When No Market Price Exists

	Division A		Division B		
	Negotiated	**Cost-plus**	**Negotiated**	**Cost-plus**	**Total Firm**
Revenues:					
Division A	$53.00	$50.40	—	—	—
Division B	—	—	$150.00	$150.00	$150.00
Component costs	42.00	42.00	—	—	42.00
Costs from A	—		53.00	50.40	
Other costs	—		78.00	78.00	78.00
Gross profits	$11.00	$ 8.40	$ 19.00	$ 21.60	$ 30.00
Return on sales	20.75%	16.67%	12.67%	14.4%	20%

Transfer prices are eliminated when computing total firm profits.

Exhibit 22–8 suggests that the manager of Division A would prefer the negotiated transfer price and the manager of Division B would prefer the cost-plus transfer price. Because the transfer price allocates profits between the two divisions and because significant portions of these managers' evaluations are based on their division profits, determining a fair transfer price can be very controversial. Frequently, central administration must step in and provide guidance to resolve transfer pricing issues.

Transfer Prices for Multinational Companies Setting appropriate transfer prices becomes much more complicated if parts of a business are located in different countries. If goods are shipped across international borders, the transfer price may be affected by taxes, duties and tariffs, and international trade agreements. In addition, the market value of the goods may be quite different in the country in which they are manufactured and in the country to which they are shipped.

Intercompany transfer price entries are eliminated when companywide financial statements are constructed. Transfer prices are not revenue for a firm and they do not mean additional cost to the firm. However, international transfer prices between a firm's subsidiaries in two countries with different tax rates can have cash flow implications for the overall firm.

As a simple example, consider ABC Company where Division A transfers a component to Division B. B uses the component to make widgets that sell to the public for $10. The production costs are $3 in Division A and $4 in Division B. Thus, the profit per widget is $3 [$10 − ($3 + $4)]. If the transfer price between A and B is set at $4.50, then the $3 profit per widget is divided equally ($1.50 each) between the two divisions. This transfer price has no cash flow effects if the divisions are subject to the same tax and tariff structures. However, if Division B is located in a high-tax country (50 percent) and Division A is located in a low-tax country (10 percent), then ABC will experience cash flow tax effects. The $4.50 transfer price will cause Division B to record taxable profits of $1.50 per unit and be taxed at a rate of 50 percent, or $0.75 per unit. Profits for Division A will be taxed at 10 percent, or $0.15 per unit. ABC Company could save taxes, lower costs, and increase cash flows by using a $6 transfer price where all profits are allocated to Division A and the low-tax country.

This simple example illustrates the potential tax effects of international transfers. The actual laws and regulations governing international transfer pricing are complex and vary from country to country.

Some Concluding Comments on Transfer Prices Transfer prices usually are not paid in cash; neither are they considered incremental revenue or costs to the company. They are only *entries made in the accounting records* to record the "flow" of goods and services among departments within the business.[7]

In essence, the transfer price may be viewed as revenue earned by the segment supplying the products and as a cost (or expense) to the segments receiving them. As these departmental revenue and cost amounts are equal, transfer prices have no direct effect on the company's *overall* pre-tax operating income.

NONFINANCIAL OBJECTIVES AND INFORMATION

Thus far, we have emphasized measuring only the *financial* performance of responsibility centers within a business organization. In addition to financial criteria, many firms specify *nonfinancial* objectives that they consider important to their basic goals. A responsibility accounting system can be designed to gather both financial and nonfinancial information about each of its centers. Shown in Exhibit 22–9 are some common nonfinancial measures that managers often evaluate. These concepts are discussed more fully in Chapter 25.

Exhibit 22–9
COMMON NONFINANCIAL PERFORMANCE MEASURES

Nonfinancial Performance Measures

Product Quality	Personnel
Number of defective parts	Number of sick days taken
Number of customer returns	Employee turnover
Number of customer complaints	Number of grievances filed
Marketing	**Efficiency and Capacity**
Number of new customers	Cycle time (manufacturing businesses)
Number of sales calls initiated	Occupancy rates (hotels and motels)
Market share	Passenger miles flown (airline industry)
Number of product stockouts	Patient-days (hospitals)
	Transactions processed (banking)

[7] If the transfer of products is between subsidiary corporations, the transfer prices may, in fact, be paid in cash.

Ethics, Fraud & Corporate Governance

As discussed in this chapter, nonfinancial objectives are important to many companies in evaluating their performance. For example, many retailers closely monitor sales per square foot and same store sales. Investors and creditors are interested in nonfinancial performance measures as well, and companies often disclose key nonfinancial performance measures in press releases, interactions with stock analysts, and financial reports filed with the Securities and Exchange Commission (SEC).

In fact, some companies believe that their performance is best portrayed by excluding certain GAAP items from the computation of income. For example, companies often suggest that EBITDA (earnings before interest, taxes, depreciation, and amortization) is a better measure of periodic operating performance than is net income. Companies that present financial results (often in press releases) that are calculated on a non-GAAP basis refer to these results as *pro forma.* The SEC believes that such pro forma reporting has often been abused because the pro forma earnings number is typically higher than comparable GAAP-based earnings.

The Sarbanes-Oxley Act (SOX) attempts to reduce or eliminate the abuses associated with pro forma reporting. SOX requires public companies to provide a reconciliation of the difference between any non-GAAP financial measure provided to investors and creditors and the comparable GAAP-based result. In addition, SOX prohibits the publication of pro forma results that are misleading or that contain untrue statements. The objective of this SOX requirement is to enable investors and creditors to simultaneously compare non-GAAP pro forma measures with the comparable GAAP numbers.

Responsibility Center Reporting in Financial Statements

In this chapter, we have focused on responsibility centers from the *perspective of management.* From this perspective, centers are defined along areas of management responsibility, beginning with the very smallest units of the business, such as departments or each salesperson's "territory."

A large corporation may have literally thousands of centers for which information is developed. This information is intended to assist management in planning and controlling *every aspect* of business operations.

The Financial Accounting Standards Board (FASB) requires large corporations to disclose certain "segment information" in notes to their financial statements. This disclosure includes the net sales, operating income, and identifiable assets of the major industries and geographic regions in which the company operates.

The segment information appearing in financial statements is *far less detailed* than the responsibility center information developed for management. But of course it serves a very different purpose. The users of an annual report are evaluating the overall profitability and future prospects of the company *viewed as a whole,* not the efficiency of every department, store, and production process. For financial reporting purposes, some publicly owned corporations subdivide their operations into only two "segments"; few (if any) show more than 10.

INTERNATIONAL FINANCIAL REPORTING STANDARDS AND RESPONSIBILITY CENTER REPORTING

Both U.S. generally accepted accounting principles (GAAP) and IFRS require publicly traded companies to report operating segment information in their financial statements. However, IFRS requirements are more extensive than U.S. GAAP, compelling the disclosure of a measure of segment liabilities if that measure is provided regularly to the chief operating decision maker. U.S. GAAP requires companies to report a measure of segment profit or loss, certain specific revenue and expense items, and segment assets, but not segment liabilities.

Concluding Remarks

One purpose of this chapter is to "tie together" many of the concepts introduced in the preceding management accounting chapters. Notice, for example, how such concepts as the distinction between variable costs and fixed costs, cost-volume-profit relationships, the nature of period costs and product costs, and the flow of manufacturing costs through an accounting system have played major roles in our evaluation of a responsibility center's performance. In the next chapter, we introduce the topic of budgeting. The budget provides one of the major standards with which current performance is compared.

END-OF-CHAPTER REVIEW

SUMMARY OF LEARNING OBJECTIVES

LO1 Distinguish among cost centers, profit centers, and investment centers. A cost center is a responsibility center that incurs costs (or expenses) but does not directly generate revenue. A profit center is a business center that generates both revenue and costs. Some profit centers are also considered investment centers. An investment center is a profit center for which management is able to measure objectively the cost of assets used in the center's operations.

LO2 Explain the need for responsibility center information and describe a responsibility accounting system. Responsibility center information presents separately the operating results of each business center within an organization. A responsibility accounting system shows the performance of the center under each manager's control.

LO3 Prepare an income statement showing contribution margin and responsibility margin. In responsibility income statements, revenue is assigned to the profit center responsible for generating that revenue. Two concepts are used in assigning and classifying expenses. First, each center is charged only with those costs directly traceable to the center. Second, costs charged to the center are subdivided between the categories of variable costs and fixed costs. Subtracting variable costs from revenue indicates the center's contribution margin; subtracting traceable fixed costs indicates the responsibility margin.

LO4 Distinguish between *traceable* and *common* fixed costs. A cost is traceable to a particular center if that center is solely responsible for the cost being incurred. Traceable costs should disappear if the center is discontinued. Common costs are not traceable to a particular center. Thus, common costs will not disappear if the center is discontinued.

LO5 Explain the usefulness of contribution margin and responsibility margin in making short-term and long-term decisions. Fixed costs generally cannot be changed in the short run. Therefore, the effects of short-run strategies on operating income are equal to the change in contribution margin (revenue less variable costs). In the long run, however, strategies may affect changes in the fixed costs traceable to a business center. Therefore, the profitability of long-run strategies may be evaluated in terms of changes in responsibility margin (revenue less variable costs and less traceable fixed costs).

LO6 Describe three transfer pricing methods and explain when each is useful. Transfer prices are the dollar amounts used by the supplying and buying divisions within a company to record the exchange of a good or service. When an external market exists for the product or service, then most companies use the market price as the transfer price. When no external market exists, then companies use either negotiated transfer prices or cost-plus transfer prices. Negotiated transfer prices are used when the buying and supplying divisions can agree on a transfer price. Where negotiation is too costly or not possible, many companies add a predetermined markup to the supplying division's total cost to determine the transfer price.

Key Terms Introduced or Emphasized in Chapter 22

committed fixed costs (p. 964) Fixed costs that are traceable to a responsibility center but that, in the short run, cannot readily be changed by the center's manager.

common fixed costs (p. 961) Fixed costs that are of joint benefit to several responsibility centers. These common costs cannot be traced to the centers deriving the benefit, except by arbitrary means.

contribution margin (p. 960) Revenue less variable costs; also, the amount of revenue available to contribute toward fixed costs and operating income (or responsibility margin). The key statistic for most types of cost-volume-profit analysis.

controllable fixed costs (p. 964) Fixed costs that are under the direct control of the center's manager.

cost center (p. 955) The part of a business that incurs costs but that does not directly generate revenue.

cost-plus transfer price (p. 967) The transfer price that results from adding a predetermined markup to the total cost of the product transferred.

investment center (p. 957) A profit center for which management has been given decision-making responsibility for making significant capital investments related to the center's business activities.

market value (p. 966) The transfer price that is based on existing external market prices for the product or service being transferred.

negotiated transfer price (p. 966) The transfer price that results when the supplying and buying divisions negotiate and agree on a transfer price.

performance margin (p. 964) A subtotal in a responsibility income statement designed to assist in evaluating the performance of a manager based solely on revenue and expenses under the manager's control. Consists of contribution margin less the controllable fixed costs traceable to the department.

profit center (p. 956) The part of a business that directly generates revenue as well as incurs costs.

responsibility accounting system (p. 958) An accounting system that separately measures the performance of each responsibility center in the organization.

responsibility center (p. 954) The part of a business a particular manager is in charge of and held responsible for.

responsibility income statement (p. 958) An income statement that subdivides the operating results of a business segment among the profit centers comprising that segment.

responsibility margin (p. 961) Revenue less variable costs and traceable fixed costs. A long-run measure of the profitability of a profit center. Consists of the revenue and costs likely to disappear if the responsibility center were eliminated.

revenue center (p. 957) A business unit that focuses on the accumulation of sales revenue.

traceable fixed costs (p. 961) Fixed costs that are directly traceable to a specific center. These costs usually would be eliminated if the center were discontinued.

transfer price (p. 965) The dollar amount used in recording products (either goods or services) supplied to one part of a business by another.

Demonstration Problem

Reed Mfg. Co. operates two plants that produce and sell floor tile. Shown below are the operating results of both plants during the company's first quarter of operations:

	St. Louis Plant	Springville Plant
Sales	$2,000,000	$2,000,000
Variable costs	720,000	880,000
Traceable fixed costs	750,000	550,000

During the quarter, common fixed costs relating to both plants amounted to $500,000.

Instructions

a. Prepare a partial income statement for Reed with responsibility by plant. Conclude with the company's income from operations.

b. At which plant would a $200,000 increase in sales contribute the most to Reed's operating income?

c. What types of costs and expenses might be included in the company's $500,000 common fixed costs?

Solution to the Demonstration Problem

a. Responsibility income statement:

		Profit Centers	
	Reed Mfg. Co.	St. Louis Plant	Springville Plant
Sales	$4,000,000	$2,000,000	$2,000,000
Variable costs	1,600,000	720,000	880,000
Contribution margin	$2,400,000	$1,280,000	$1,120,000
Traceable fixed costs	1,300,000	750,000	550,000
Responsibility margin	$1,100,000	$ 530,000	$ 570,000
Common fixed costs	500,000		
Income from operations	$ 600,000		

b. The St. Louis plant has a contribution margin ratio of 64 percent ($1,280,000 ÷ $2,000,000). Thus, should its sales increase by $200,000, the company's operating income would increase by $128,000 ($200,000 × 64%). The Springville plant has a contribution margin ratio of 56 percent ($1,120,000 ÷ $2,000,000). Should its sales increase by $200,000, the company's operating income would increase by only $112,000 ($200,000 × 56%).

c. The $500,000 would include fixed costs not directly traceable to either plant. Such items might include charges related to legal fees, corporate accounting and personnel departments, centralized computer facilities, and the salaries of corporate officers.

Self-Test Questions

The answers to these questions appear on page 989.

1. Which of the following is a common fixed cost to the sales departments in a department store?
   a. Salaries of store security personnel.
   b. Salaries of sales department managers.
   c. Cost of goods sold.
   d. Depreciation on fixtures used exclusively in a specific sales department.
2. In preparing an income statement that measures contribution margin and responsibility margin for a responsibility center, two concepts are applied in classifying costs. One is whether the costs are variable or fixed. The other is whether the costs are:
   a. Product costs or period costs.
   b. Traceable to the responsibility center.
   c. Under the control of the manager.
   d. Transfer prices.
3. A subtotal used in evaluating the performance of a responsibility center manager, as distinct from the performance of the center, is:
   a. Contribution margin, less traceable fixed costs.
   b. Sales, less committed costs.
   c. Contribution margin, plus fixed costs deferred into inventory.
   d. Contribution margin, less controllable fixed costs.
4. The Knuckles and Brackets Division transfers a component product to the Assembly Division. Both divisions are part of Automakers Inc. and are organized as profit centers. Automakers has a general policy of using a 10 percent markup for cost-based transfer prices. Knuckles and Brackets also can sell the component product in the open market to other automobile companies for \$75. The cost to make the component is \$55. By transferring the component internally, the Knuckles and Brackets Division saves \$5 in sales expenses and transportation costs. The manager of the Knuckles and Brackets Division wants the transfer price to be \$75 and the manager of the Assembly Division wants the transfer price to be \$70. Which of the following are *not* true (select all appropriate answers):
   a. If the transfer price is \$75, then the divisions are using a market-based transfer price.
   b. If the transfer price is \$40, then the divisions are using a cost-based transfer price.
   c. If the transfer price is \$70, then the divisions are using a negotiated transfer price.
   d. If the transfer price is \$70, then both divisions are sharing the profits.
   e. If the transfer price is \$55, then the Knuckles and Brackets Division is keeping all the profits.
5. Assume the U.S. corporate income tax rate is 40 percent and the Mexican corporate income tax rate is 30 percent. Jacques International Apparel Company has subsidiaries in both the U.S. and Mexico. Jacques is trying to decide what transfer price to use for its famous French frock, which is being transferred from the U.S. subsidiary to the Mexican subsidiary. It could ship the frock at the market price of \$75 or at cost plus 20 percent. The cost of the frock is \$40. Which transfer price would minimize Jacques's tax burden?
   a. \$75.
   b. \$48.
   c. \$90.
   d. \$75 − \$40 = \$35.

ASSIGNMENT MATERIAL Discussion Questions

1. What are some of the uses that management may make of accounting information about individual responsibility centers of the business?
2. Distinguish among a *cost center*, a *profit center*, and an *investment center*, and give an example of each for a multi-hospital corporation.
3. Name three types of transfer prices and explain when each type of transfer price would be used.
4. In a responsibility accounting system, should the recording of revenue and costs begin at the largest areas of responsibility or the smallest? Explain.
5. Distinguish between *traceable* and *common* fixed costs. Give an example of each type of fixed cost for an auto dealership with a sales department and a service department.
6. How do the costs of operating *service departments* (organized as cost centers) appear in a responsibility income statement?
7. DeskTop, Inc., operates a national sales organization. The income statements prepared for each sales territory are created by product line. In these income statements, the sales territory manager's salary is treated as a common fixed cost. Will this salary be viewed as a common fixed cost at all levels of the organization? Explain.
8. Explain why transfer pricing decisions between divisions in separate countries may involve tax or tariff issues.
9. Criticize the following statement: "In our business, we maximize profits by closing any department that does not show a responsibility margin ratio of at least 15 percent."

10. What is the relationship between contribution margin and responsibility margin? Explain how each of these measurements is useful in making management decisions.
11. What does a consistently negative responsibility margin imply will happen to the operating income of the business if the center is closed? Why? Identify several other factors that should be considered in deciding whether or not to close the center.
12. Briefly explain the distinction between *controllable* fixed costs and *committed* fixed costs. Also explain the nature and purpose of performance margin in a responsibility income statement.
13. The controller of Fifties, a chain of drive-in restaurants, is considering modifying the monthly income statements by charging all costs relating to operations of the corporate headquarters to the individual restaurants in proportion to each restaurant's gross revenue. Do you think that this would increase the usefulness of the responsibility income statement in evaluating the performance of the restaurants or the restaurant managers? Explain.
14. Explain why using cost as a transfer price is *inappropriate* when the center producing the product is evaluated as a *profit center.*
15. Even though transfer prices have no direct effect on a company's overall net income, these transfer prices still matter to managers of responsibility centers. Explain why.

Brief Exercises

LO5 BRIEF EXERCISE 22.1
Contribution Margin Effects

Assume that Department A has a higher contribution margin ratio but a lower responsibility margin ratio than Department B. If $10,000 in advertising is expected to increase the sales of either department by $50,000, in which department would the advertising dollars be spent to the best advantage?

LO2 LO3 BRIEF EXERCISE 22.2
Contribution Margin versus Responsibility Margin

Marshall's grocery store has a small bakery that sells a variety of baked goods. The manager of the bakery responsibility center has decided to sell a cup of coffee and doughnut combo at the low price of $1.75, as a means of attracting customers. The incremental cost of labor per combo sale has been calculated as $0.89, the variable cost of the doughnut is $0.37, and the variable cost of the coffee (including cup) is $0.42. What is the contribution margin for the combo? How does the manager think the combo will affect the bakery's responsibility margin?

LO1 LO2 BRIEF EXERCISE 22.3
Responsibility Center Design

Kraxton Chemie Company consists of seven divisions. Divisions One through Five make products that are sold in the competitive market. Divisions Two and Three make their own investment and transfer pricing decisions. Twenty-five percent of Division Two's output is devoted to a component that is transferred to Division Three as part of the subassembly of Division Three's main product. Divisions Six and Seven provide services to the other divisions. Eighty percent of Division Six's output is environmental cleanup services provided to Divisions One and Two. The remaining twenty percent is sold to external customers. Finally, Division Seven is devoted to R&D activities that support the entire company. What type of responsibility center design would you recommend for Kraxton Chemie Company?

LO6 BRIEF EXERCISE 22.4
Transfer Prices

Porcus Corporation manufactures and sells bicycles. The Wheel & Frame Division creates parts that are both sold externally and transferred internally to the Assembly Division for assembly. Wheel #606 sells externally for $35 and the variable cost to make it is $27. What would you recommend as the transfer price between Wheels & Frames and Assembly if there is a competitive external market for #606? Would your answer change if there were no external market for #606? Why? What would the transfer price be if upper management required cost plus 20 percent as the transfer price?

LO2 LO3 BRIEF EXERCISE 22.5
Contribution Margin Ratio and Responsibility Center Margin

The contribution margin ratio of the Furniture Department at Glad's Mercantile is 0.75. The traceable fixed costs for the Furniture Department are estimated at $188,000 per year. Sales in the Furniture Department next year are expected to be $300,000. What is the expected responsibility margin for the Furniture Department next year?

LO6 BRIEF EXERCISE 22.6
Identifying Transfer Prices

Categorize the following transfer prices as being market-based, negotiated, or cost-based:

a. The market price of a widget is $25, the cost is $15, and the actual transfer price is $22, the market price less cost of sales commissions.
b. The manager of the packaging responsibility center agrees to package a special order for the shipping department for the cost of the packaging materials.

c. The Wilton Ball Division sells baseballs to the Wilton Combo Division for $5.00 each. The Ball Division sells a two-ball package to **Dick's Sporting Goods** for $10.

d. After consulting with stand-alone accounting firms, the Accounting Division charges each of the 13 manufacturing plants in the company $545 per month for accounting services.

LO4 **BRIEF EXERCISE 22.7**
Tracing Common Costs

Hilgen Hotel & Spa is located in beautiful Sydney, Australia. Hilgen operates three profit centers: the Hotel, Restaurant, and Spa. The complex occupies 15,000 square feet and has 220 employees. The complex's general upkeep costs (e.g. insurance, utilities, etc.) are $450,000 per month and the human resource department costs are $118,000 per month. If the Spa occupies 1,800 square feet and has 6 employees, show how upkeep and human resource costs could be assigned to the Spa.

LO1 LO4 **BRIEF EXERCISE 22.8**
Common or Traceable Costs

For each of the following costs associated with a chain of bicycle stores, decide if the cost is common or traceable to: 1) the store departments (Repairs and Sales), 2) each store, or 3) the company.

a. $25,000 in rent paid for store space.

b. Store manager's salary.

c. Delivery charges for bicycles and parts.

d. National advertising costs.

e. Audit costs for the company.

f. Insurance on the headquarters building.

LO2 **BRIEF EXERCISE 22.9**
Responsibility Accounting System Characteristics

The president of Cold Moo Ice Cream Company, a chain of ice cream stores in the Midwest, was unhappy with the actual six-month profit figures for the company recently prepared by the CFO. The president asked the CFO for a profit breakdown, by store, of the actual six-month results. When the president received the report, he was extremely upset and called the CFO into his office. The president stated, "These reports show that each store in the chain is profitable, but our company results are unprofitable! How can this be?" The CFO pointed out that each store was allowed to set prices for ice cream based on its cost structure. However, the stores' cost structures did not include headquarters costs or the costs of advertising and delivery of products.

What are the three characteristics for operating a successful responsibility accounting system? Consider whether the accounting system at Cold Moo Ice Cream Company includes the three characteristics of a successful responsibility accounting system. How could the responsibility accounting system at Cold Moo be improved?

LO4 LO5 **BRIEF EXERCISE 22.10**
Common Costs and Responsibility Centers

Janice Black, manager of the Produce Department at Spanky's Grocery, has a monthly responsibility margin of $4,000. The store manager has decided to allocate storewide common costs to each department. After the allocation, Ms. Black's responsibility margin is −$1,200 per month. Identify the disadvantages of allocating common costs to responsibility centers.

Exercises

LO1 LO4 LO6 **EXERCISE 22.1**
Accounting Terminology

The following are nine technical accounting terms introduced or emphasized in this chapter:

Responsibility margin	Transfer price	Common fixed costs
Contribution margin	Cost-plus transfer price	Traceable fixed costs
Performance margin	Product costs	Committed fixed costs

Each of the following statements may (or may not) describe one of these technical terms. For each statement, indicate the accounting term described, or answer "None" if the statement does not correctly describe any of the terms.

a. The costs deducted from contribution margin to determine responsibility margin.

b. Cost to produce plus a predetermined markup.

c. Fixed costs that are readily controllable by the manager.

d. A subtotal in a responsibility income statement, equal to responsibility margin plus committed fixed costs.

e. The subtotal in a responsibility income statement that is most useful in evaluating the short-run effect of various marketing strategies on the income of the business.

f. The subtotal in a responsibility income statement that comes closest to indicating the change in income from operations that would result from closing a particular part of the business.

g. The amount used in recording products or services supplied by one business unit to another.

LO1 **EXERCISE 22.2**

Types of Responsibility Centers

Video World owns and operates a national chain of video game arcades. Indicate whether Video World would evaluate each of the following as an investment center, a profit center (other than an investment center), or a cost center. Briefly explain the reason for your answer.

a. An individual video arcade within a chain of video arcades.

b. A snack bar within one of the company's arcades.

c. A particular video game within one of the company's arcades.

d. The security officers at each arcade location.

LO4 **EXERCISE 22.3**

Classification of Costs in an Income Statement

The controller of Maxwell Department Store is preparing an income statement divided by sales departments and including subtotals for contribution margin, performance margin, and responsibility margin. Indicate the appropriate classification of the seven items (**a** through **g**) listed below. Select from the following cost classifications:

Variable costs
Traceable fixed costs—controllable
Traceable fixed costs—committed
Common fixed costs
None of the above

a. Cost of operating the store's accounting department.

b. Cost of advertising specific product lines (classify as a fixed cost).

c. Sales taxes on merchandise sold.

d. Depreciation on the sewing machinery used in the Alterations Department.

e. Salaries of departmental sales personnel.

f. Salary of the store manager.

g. Cost of merchandise sold in the Sportswear Department.

LO1 LO2 **EXERCISE 22.4**

Evaluating **Home Depot**'s Responsibility Centers

Consider the **Home Depot** "10-Year Summary of Financial and Operating Resuluts" shown at the end of Appendix A. Assume that **Home Depot** designates each of the countries in which it operates as an investment center (i.e., the United States with 1,976, Canada with 179, Mexico with 79, and China with 10 stores, respectively). In addition, assume each individual store is a profit center. Within each store, assume that inventory and janitorial are designated as cost centers. For each type of responsibility center described choose as many measures from those listed in the 10-Year Summary that seem appropriate to help evaluate the given center. Explain why the measures you have chosen are appropriate for the type of responsibility center (investment-country level, profit-store level, or cost center substore level).

LO1 through LO5 **EXERCISE 22.5**

Preparing a Responsibility Income Statement

Gemini Technologies has two product lines: lasers and integrated circuits. During the current month, the two product lines reported the following results:

	Lasers	Circuits
Sales	$600,000	$900,000
Variable costs (as a percentage of sales)	40%	60%
Traceable fixed costs	$275,000	$225,000

In addition, fixed costs common to both product lines amounted to $80,000.

Prepare an income statement showing percentages as well as dollar amounts. Conclude your statement with income from operations for the business and with the responsibility margin for each product line.

Exercises 22.6, 22.7, and 22.8 are based on the following data:
Shown below is a segmented income statement for Drexel-Hall during the current month:

	Drexel-Hall		Profit Centers					
			Store 1		Store 2		Store 3	
	Dollars	%	Dollars	%	Dollars	%	Dollars	%
Sales	$1,800,000	100%	$600,000	100%	$600,000	100%	$600,000	100%
Variable costs	1,080,000	60	372,000	62	378,000	63	330,000	55
Contribution margin	$ 720,000	40%	$228,000	38%	$222,000	37%	$270,000	45%
Traceable fixed costs: controllable	432,000	24	120,000	20	102,000	17	210,000	35
Performance margin	$ 288,000	16%	$108,000	18%	$120,000	20%	$ 60,000	10%
Traceable fixed costs: committed	180,000	10	48,000	8	66,000	11	66,000	11
Store responsibility margin	$ 108,000	6%	$ 60,000	10%	$ 54,000	9%	$ (6,000)	(1)%
Common fixed costs	36,000	2						
Income from operations	$ 72,000	4%						

All stores are similar in size, carry similar products, and operate in similar neighborhoods. *Store 1* was established first and was built at a lower cost than were Stores 2 and 3. This lower cost results in less depreciation expense for Store 1. *Store 2* follows a policy of minimizing both costs and sales prices. *Store 3* follows a policy of providing extensive customer service and charges slightly higher prices than the other two stores.

LO1 LO2

EXERCISE 22.6

Evaluation of Responsibility Centers and Center Managers

Use the data presented above for Drexel-Hall to answer the following questions:

a. Assume that by spending an additional $15,000 per month in advertising a particular store, Drexel-Hall can increase the sales of that store by 10 percent. Which store should the company advertise to receive the maximum benefit from this additional advertising expenditure? Explain.

b. From the viewpoint of top management, which is the most profitable of the three stores? Why?

c. Which store manager seems to be pursuing the most effective strategy in managing his or her store? Why?

LO1 through LO3, LO5

EXERCISE 22.7

Closing an Unprofitable Business Unit

Top management of Drexel-Hall is considering closing Store 3. The three stores are close enough together that management estimates closing Store 3 would cause sales at Store 1 to increase by $60,000, and sales at Store 2 to increase by $120,000. Closing Store 3 is not expected to cause any change in common fixed costs.

Compute the increase or decrease that closing Store 3 should cause in:

a. Total monthly sales for Drexel-Hall stores.

b. The monthly responsibility margin of Stores 1 and 2.

c. The company's monthly income from operations.

LO1 through LO4

EXERCISE 22.8

Cost-Volume-Profit Analysis

The marketing manager of Drexel-Hall is considering two alternative advertising strategies, each of which would cost $15,000 per month. One strategy is to advertise the name Drexel-Hall, which is expected to increase the monthly sales at all stores by 5 percent. The other strategy is to emphasize the low prices available at Store 2, which is expected to increase monthly sales at Store 2 by $150,000, but to reduce sales by $30,000 per month at Stores 1 and 3.

Determine the expected effect of each strategy on the company's overall income from operations.

LO1 LO2 LO6

EXERCISE 22.9

Transfer Pricing

Delmar Foods has two divisions: (1) a Processed Meat Division and (2) a Frozen Pizza Division. Delmar's frozen pizzas use processed meat as a topping. The company's Processed Meat Division supplies the Frozen Pizza Division with all of its meat toppings. Delmar managers are paid bonuses based on their division's profitability.

The manager of the Processed Meat Division argues for a transfer price based on a market value approach. The manager of the Frozen Pizza Division favors a transfer price based on a cost approach. Explain how Delmar's bonus system may influence each manager's opinion regarding which approach to use in establishing a transfer price.

LO1 through LO3

EXERCISE 22.10

Types of Responsibility Centers and Basis for Evaluation

Listed below are parts of various well-known businesses:

1. The bookstore of **Northern Jersey University**.
2. The billing department of **Rhode Island Life Insurance Co.**
3. The Norwalk Factory of **Melvin's Chocolates**.

4. The jewelry department of **Bloomingdale's**.
5. The gift shop at the **Museum of Natural History**.
6. The legal department of **Sears**.

Indicate whether each part represents an investment center, a profit center (other than an investment center), or a cost center. Why are business organizations divided into responsibility centers? Explain how revenue and costs are assigned to a responsibility center using a responsibility center income statement.

LO2 LO4

EXERCISE 22.11
Corporate Costs: Traceable or Common?

The following discussion occurred between two division managers, Bob and Jalenne, and the chief operating officer, Harry.

Bob: "Jalenne's division has twice as many employees as my division, yet corporate headquarters costs, which include human resource costs, are allocated to our two divisions equally, hurting my bottom line."

Jalenne: "You know Bob is right to be upset about the human resource cost allocation. However, the CEO and the CFO devote much more time and attention to Bob's division because it is in financial difficulty. Perhaps we should track consumption of corporate time and allocate the corporate headquarters costs to divisions on the basis of corporate time devoted to each division."

Harry: "In my 25 years working at corporate, I have heard these arguments year after year. Tracking time spent on activities related to divisions would be expensive and nearly impossible for central management. Furthermore, there are many corporate costs that are not related to human time spent on divisional issues. Allocating an equal portion of these costs to each division is the only practical method."

Use your understanding of common and traceable costs to discuss the appropriateness of Harry's response. Is there a method that could be used so that Jalenne and Bob would be less concerned about the allocation of corporate headquarters costs?

LO3 LO5 LO6

EXERCISE 22.12
Transfer Prices and Responsibility Margins

Consider Exhibit 22–5, which shows the responsibility margins for the Sales Department and Repairs Department profit centers at the 42nd Street store of NuTech Electronics. Assume that 25 percent of the Repairs Department repair work is done for the Sales Department and that the Repairs Department has been transferring its services to Sales at variable cost as the transfer price. Because the Repairs Department has a negative responsibility profit, assume the Repairs Department has asked the manager of the 42nd Street store to allow a transfer price that will earn the normal contribution margin that is earned on repair services to external customers. Compute the new responsibility margins for the Sales and Repairs Departments if the store manager allows the new transfer price.

LO6

EXERCISE 22.13
Transfer Price and International Taxes

Cristina's Crafts has two operating divisions: one in the U.S. and one in Mexico. The Mexican Division produces product X, which is a component used in the production process of the U.S. Division. If the U.S. Division purchases product X from the Mexican Division, a transfer price of $650,000 is charged. However, if the U.S. Division were to purchase product X from an outside supplier, the cost would be $750,000. The operating expenses for the Mexican and U.S. Divisions are, respectively, $200,000 and $350,000 (not including the cost of goods transferred from the Mexican Division). The U.S. Division has revenue amounting to $1,500,000. Cristina, the CEO of the company, is trying to decide which amount should be used for the transfer price ($650,000 or $750,000).

a. Assume that the marginal tax rates for Mexico and the U.S. are 30 percent and 40 percent, respectively. What is the tax liability of each division for each of the transfer pricing alternatives?

b. Which transfer pricing alternative will produce the lowest tax liability for the company as a whole? Show your computations.

LO1 LO2

EXERCISE 22.14
Responsibility Centers in a Golf Resort

Jasper Golf Resort has a full-service hotel and three golf courses. The hotel, in addition to having over 100 hotel rooms, has two dining areas and a catering service for weddings and meetings. The hotel has a housekeeping staff and a repairs and maintenance group. In addition, there is a meetings coordinator with a technical staff to support meetings.

The golf courses have a superintendent that oversees a grounds and maintenance staff. Each course has a pro shop that includes apparel and golf supplies and a lunch counter. In addition, there is a golf cart center that provides carts to each course. Design a responsibility center chart like Exhibit 22–1 for Jasper Golf Resort.

LO1 through LO3

EXERCISE 22.15
Home Depot's Responsibility Centers 

Use the first paragraph in note 1 in Appendix A to create a responsibility center design for **Home Depot**. Your design should be similar to Exhibit 22–1 and show investment, profit, and cost centers for **Home Depot**.

Problem Set A

LO3 through LO5

PROBLEM 22.1A
Preparing and Using Responsibility Income Statements

Mixers, Inc., produces two products: soda water and seltzer juice. Cost and revenue data for each product line for the current month are as follows:

	Product Lines	
	Soda Water	**Seltzer Juice**
Sales	$750,000	$970,000
Contribution margin as a percentage of sales	35%	60%
Fixed costs traceable to product lines	$175,000	$150,000

In addition, fixed costs that are common to both product lines amount to $75,000.

Instructions

a. Prepare Mixers, Inc.'s responsibility income statement for the current month. Report the responsibility margin for each product line and income from operations for the company as a whole. Also include columns showing all dollar amounts as percentages of sales.

b. According to the analysis performed in part **a,** which product line is more profitable? Should the common fixed costs be considered when determining the profitability of individual product lines? Why or why not?

c. Mixers, Inc., has $15,000 to be used in advertising for one of the two product lines and expects that this expenditure will result in additional sales of $50,000. How should the company decide which product line to advertise?

LO3 through LO5

PROBLEM 22.2A
Preparing and Using Responsibility Income Statements

Regal Flair Enterprises has two product lines: jewelry and women's apparel. Cost and revenue data for each product line for the current month are as follows:

	Product Lines	
	Jewelry	**Apparel**
Sales.	$800,000	$450,000
Variable costs as a percentage of sales.	55%	28%
Fixed costs traceable to product lines	$200,000	$250,000

In addition to the costs shown above, the company incurs monthly fixed costs of $100,000 common to both product lines.

Instructions

a. Prepare Regal Flair Enterprises's responsibility income statement for the current month. Report the responsibility margin for each product line and income from operations for the company as a whole. Also include columns showing all dollar amounts as percentages of sales.

b. Assume that a marketing survey shows that a $75,000 monthly advertising campaign focused on either product line should increase that product line's monthly sales by approximately $150,000. Do you recommend this additional advertising for either or both product lines? Show computations to support your conclusions.

c. Management is considering expanding one of the company's two product lines. An investment of a given dollar amount is expected to increase the sales of the expanded product line by $300,000. It is also expected to increase the traceable fixed costs of the expanded product line by 75 percent. On the basis of this information, which product line do you recommend expanding? Explain the basis for your conclusion.

LO3 through LO5

PROBLEM 22.3A
Preparing and Using a Responsibility Income Statement

Giant Chef Equipment Company is organized into two divisions: Commercial Sales and Home Products. During June, sales for the Commercial Sales Division totaled $1,500,000, and its contribution margin ratio averaged 34 percent. Sales generated by the Home Products Division totaled $900,000, and its contribution margin ratio averaged 50 percent. Monthly fixed costs traceable to each division are $180,000. Common fixed costs for the month amount to $120,000.

Instructions

a. Prepare Giant Chef Equipment's responsibility income statement for the current month. Be certain to report responsibility margin for each division and income from operations for the company as a whole. Also include columns showing all dollar amounts as percentages of sales.

b. Compute the dollar sales volume required for the Home Products Division to earn a monthly responsibility margin of *$500,000.*

c. A marketing study indicates that sales in the Home Products Division would increase by *5* percent if advertising expenditures for the division were increased by *$15,000* per month. Would you recommend this increase in advertising? Show computations to support your decision.

LO3 through LO5

PROBLEM 22.4A
Preparing Responsibility Income Statements in a Responsibility Accounting System

Muscle Bound Co. sells home exercise equipment. The company has two sales territories, Eastern and Western. Two products are sold in each territory: FasTrak (a Nordic ski simulator) and RowMaster (a stationary rowing machine).

During January, the following data are reported for the Eastern territory:

	FasTrak	RowMaster
Sales	$600,000	$750,000
Contribution margin ratios	55%	40%
Traceable fixed costs	$ 80,000	$150,000

Common fixed costs in the Eastern territory amounted to $120,000 during the month.

During January, the Western territory reported total sales of $600,000, variable costs of $270,000, and a responsibility margin of $200,000. Muscle Bound also incurred $180,000 of common fixed costs that were not traceable to either sales territory.

In addition to being profit centers, each territory is also evaluated as an investment center. Average assets utilized by the Eastern and Western territories amount to $14,000,000 and $12,000,000, respectively.

Instructions

a. Prepare the January income statement for the Eastern territory by product line. Include columns showing percentages as well as dollar amounts.

b. Prepare the January income statement for the company showing profits by sales territories. Conclude your statement with income from operations for the company and with responsibility margins for the two territories. Show percentages as well as dollar amounts.

c. Compute the rate of return on average assets earned in each sales territory during the month of January.

d. In part **a,** your income statement for the Eastern territory included $120,000 in common fixed costs. What happened to these common fixed costs in the responsibility income statement shown in part **b**?

e. The manager of the Eastern territory is authorized to spend an additional $50,000 per month to advertise one of the products. On the basis of past experience, the manager estimates that additional advertising will increase the sales of either product by $120,000. On which product should the manager focus this advertising campaign? Explain.

f. Top management is considering investing several million dollars to expand operations in one of its two sales territories. The expansion would increase the traceable fixed costs to the expanded territory in proportion to its increase in sales. Which territory would be the best candidate for this investment? Explain.

LO3 through LO5

PROBLEM 22.5A
Analysis of Responsibility Income Statements

Shown on the following page are responsibility income statements for Butterfield, Inc., for the month of March.

	Investment Centers					
	Butterfield, Inc.		Division 1		Division 2	
	Dollars	%	Dollars	%	Dollars	%
Sales	$450,000	100%	$300,000	100%	$150,000	100%
Variable costs	225,000	50	180,000	60	45,000	30
Contribution margin	$225,000	50%	$120,000	40%	$105,000	70%
Fixed costs traceable to divisions	135,000	30	63,000	21	72,000	48
Division responsibility margin	$ 90,000	20%	$ 57,000	19%	$ 33,000	22%
Common fixed costs	45,000	10				
Income from operations	$ 45,000	10%				

			Profit Centers			
	Division 1		Product A		Product B	
	Dollars	%	Dollars	%	Dollars	%
Sales	$300,000	100%	$100,000	100%	$200,000	100%
Variable costs	180,000	60	52,000	52	128,000	64
Contribution margin	$120,000	40%	$ 48,000	48%	$ 72,000	36%
Fixed costs traceable to products	42,000	14	26,000	26	16,000	8
Product responsibility margin	$ 78,000	26%	$ 22,000	22%	$ 56,000	28%
Common fixed costs	21,000	7				
Responsibility margin for division	$ 57,000	19%				

Instructions

a. The company plans to initiate an advertising campaign for one of the two products in Division 1. The campaign would cost $10,000 per month and is expected to increase the sales of whichever product is advertised by $30,000 per month. Compute the expected increase in the responsibility margin of Division 1 assuming that **(1)** product A is advertised and **(2)** product B is advertised.

b. Assume that the sales of both products by Division 1 are equal to total manufacturing capacity. To increase sales of either product, the company must increase manufacturing facilities, which means an increase in traceable fixed costs in approximate proportion to the expected increase in sales. In this case, which product line would you recommend expanding? Explain.

c. The income statement for Division 1 includes $21,000 in common fixed costs. What happens to these fixed costs in the income statement for Butterfield, Inc.?

d. Assume that in April the monthly sales in Division 2 increase to $200,000. Compute the expected effect of this change on the operating income of the company (assume no other changes in revenue or cost behavior).

e. Prepare an income statement for Butterfield, Inc., by division, under the assumption stated in part **d.** Organize this income statement in the format illustrated above, including columns for percentages.

LO3 through LO5 **PROBLEM 22.6A** Evaluating an Unprofitable Business Center

FlyWiz, Inc., is a small manufacturer of professional fishing equipment. The company has two divisions: the Rod Division and the Reel Division. Data for the month of January are shown on the following page.

		Profit Centers	
	Entire Company	Rod Division	Reel Division
Sales	$64,000	$26,000	$38,000
Variable costs	29,000	13,000	16,000
Contribution margin	$35,000	$13,000	$22,000
Traceable fixed costs	27,000	17,000	10,000
Division responsibility margin	$ 8,000	$ (4,000)	$12,000
Common fixed costs	3,000		
Monthly operating income	$ 5,000		

Nick Fulbright, the company's chief financial officer since January 1 of the current year, wants to close the unprofitable Rod Division. He believes that doing so will benefit FlyWiz and benefit him, given that his end-of-year bonus is to be based on the company's overall operating income. In a recent interview, Fulbright summarized his business philosophy as follows: "A company is only as strong as its least profitable segment. As long as I'm at the financial helm, only the strongest shall survive at FlyWiz."

Instructions

a. Had the Rod Division been closed on *January 1,* what would the company's operating income for the month have been?

b. After learning about Fulbright's business philosophy, the Rod Division's director of marketing made the following statement: "Nick Fulbright may understand numbers, but he doesn't understand the complementary relationship between rods and reels, nor the seasonal nature of our business." What did the director of marketing mean by this statement? How might such information influence Fulbright's assessment of the company's Rod Division?

c. By how much would the Rod Division's monthly sales have to increase for it to generate a positive responsibility margin of $4,000 in any given month? Show all of your computations.

PROBLEM 22.7A

LO1 LO6 Transfer Pricing Decisions

Rhinesch Corporation has two divisions: the Motor Division and the Pump Division. The Motor Division supplies the motors used by the Pump Division. The Pump Division produces approximately 10,000 pumps annually. Thus, it receives 10,000 motors from the Motor Division each year. The market price of these motors is $320. The total variable cost of the motor is $195 per unit. The market price of the pumps is $500. The unit variable cost of each pump, excluding the cost of the motor, is $75.

The Motor Division is currently operating at full capacity, producing 20,000 motors per year (10,000 of which are transferred to the Pump Division). The demand for the motors is so great that all 20,000 units could be sold to outside customers if the Pump Division acquired its motors elsewhere. The Motor Division uses the full market price of $320 as the transfer price charged to the Pump Division.

The manager of the Pump Division asserts that the Motor Division benefits from the intercompany transfers because of reduced shipping costs. As a result, he wants to negotiate a lower transfer price of $310 per unit.

Instructions

a. Compute the contribution margin earned annually by each division and by the company as a whole using the current transfer price.

b. Compute the contribution margin that would be earned annually by each division and by the company as a whole if the discounted transfer price were used.

c. What issues and concerns should be considered in setting a transfer price for intercompany transfers of motors?

PROBLEM 22.8A

LO1 LO6 Transfer Pricing Decisions

Sparta and Associates produces trophies and has two divisions: the Green Division and the White Division. The Green Division produces the trophy base, which it can sell to outside markets for $150. A trophy base has variable costs per unit of $65 and fixed costs of $100,000, based on monthly production of 2,000 bases. Each trophy base could be sold to outside customers by the Green Division, as bases are in high demand. The Green Division has no idle capacity.

The White Division uses the base in the production of championship trophies. The market price of a championship trophy is $300. The White Division can acquire trophy bases from outside suppliers for $160. The manager of the White Division is interested in purchasing 1,500 trophy bases from the Green Division, but she wants to negotiate for a lower transfer price of $135. The current transfer price for a trophy base is the full market price of $150. The fixed costs in producing championship trophies are $57,500, and the variable cost of producing a championship trophy is $75, excluding the cost of the trophy base.

Instructions

a. What is the operating profit before tax for each division using the market transfer price of $150?

b. What is the operating profit before tax for each division using the transfer price of $135, as suggested by the manager of the White Division?

c. How is the company's net income affected under the two transfer pricing scenarios?

d. Would it be more beneficial to the company if the Green Division sold trophy bases externally and the White Division purchased trophy bases from an outside supplier? Show your calculations.

Problem Set B

LO3 through LO5

PROBLEM 22.1B

Preparing and Using Responsibility Income Statements

Fasteners, Inc., produces two products: zippers and buckles. Cost and revenue data for each product line for the current month are as follows:

	Product Lines	
	Zippers	**Buckles**
Sales	$135,000	$220,000
Variable costs as a percentage of sales	20%	45%
Fixed costs traceable to product lines	$ 90,000	$ 66,000

In addition, fixed costs that are common to both product lines amount to $35,000.

Instructions

a. Prepare Fasteners, Inc.'s responsibility income statement for the current month. Report the responsibility margin for each product line and income from operations for the company as a whole. Also include columns showing all dollar amounts as percentages of sales.

b. According to the analysis performed in part **a,** which product line is more profitable? Should the common fixed costs be considered when determining the profitability of individual product lines? Why or why not?

c. Use the contribution margin ratios for each product line. Assume Fasteners, Inc., has $12,000 to be used for advertising one of the two product lines, with the expectation that this expenditure will result in additional sales of $40,000. Show the contribution associated with the $12,000 advertising expenditure for each product line. To which product line should the advertising be devoted?

LO3 through LO5

PROBLEM 22.2B

Preparing and Using Responsibility Income Statements

Brown Enterprises has two product lines: bags and shoes. Cost and revenue data for each product line for the current month are as follows:

	Product Lines	
	Bags	**Shoes**
Sales	$1,000,000	$500,000
Variable costs as a percentage of sales	60%	30%
Fixed costs traceable to product lines	$ 250,000	$275,000

In addition to the costs shown above, the company incurs monthly fixed costs of $75,000 common to both product lines.

Instructions

a. Prepare Brown Enterprises's responsibility income statement for the current month. Report the responsibility margin for each product line and income from operations for the company as a whole. Also include columns showing all dollar amounts as percentages of sales.

b. Assume that a marketing survey shows that a $50,000 monthly advertising campaign focused on either product line should increase that product line's monthly sales by approximately $100,000. Do you recommend this additional advertising for either or both product lines? Show computations to support your conclusions.

c. Management is considering expanding one of the company's two product lines. An investment of a given dollar amount is expected to increase the sales of the expanded product line by $250,000. It is also expected to increase the traceable fixed costs of the expanded product line by 60 percent. On the basis of this information, which product line do you recommend expanding? Explain the basis for your conclusion.

LO3 through LO5

PROBLEM 22.3B
Preparing and Using a Responsibility Income Statement

Robinns Company is organized into two divisions: Deluxe and Standard. During August, sales for the Deluxe Division totaled $2,000,000, and its contribution margin ratio averaged 35 percent. Sales generated by the Standard Division totaled $1,200,000, and its contribution margin ratio averaged 50 percent. Monthly fixed costs traceable to each division are $200,000. Common fixed costs for the month amount to $100,000.

Instructions

a. Prepare Robinns Company's responsibility income statement for the current month. Be certain to report the responsibility margin for each division and income from operations for the company as a whole. Also include columns showing all dollar amounts as percentages of sales.

b. Compute the dollar sales volume required for the Standard Division to earn a monthly responsibility margin of $600,000.

c. A marketing study indicates that sales in the Standard Division would increase by 4 percent if advertising expenditures for the division were increased by $12,000 per month. Would you recommend this increase in advertising? Show computations to support your decision.

LO3 through LO5

PROBLEM 22.4B
Preparing a Responsibility Income Statement in a Responsibility Accounting System

Freeze, Inc., sells air conditioners. The company has two sales territories, Northern and Southern. Two products are sold in each territory: Economy and Efficiency.

During January, the following data are reported for the Northern territory:

	Economy	Efficiency
Sales	$500,000	$1,000,000
Contribution margin ratios	70%	30%
Traceable fixed costs	$ 90,000	$ 200,000

Common fixed costs in the Northern territory amount to $125,000 during the month.

During January, the Southern territory reports total sales of $800,000, variable costs of $352,000, and a responsibility margin of $158,000. Freeze also incurs $140,000 of common fixed costs that are not traceable to either sales territory.

In addition to being profit centers, each territory is also evaluated as an investment center. Average assets utilized by the Northern and Southern territories amount to $16,000,000 and $10,000,000, respectively.

Instructions

a. Prepare the January income statement for the Northern territory by product line. Include columns showing percentages as well as dollar amounts.

b. Prepare the January income statement for the company showing profits by sales territories. Conclude your statement with income from operations for the company and with responsibility margins for the two territories. Show percentages as well as dollar amounts.

c. Compute the rate of return on average assets earned in each sales territory during the month of January.

d. In part **a,** your income statement for the Northern territory included $125,000 in common fixed costs. What happened to these common fixed costs in the responsibility income statement shown in part **b**?

e. The manager of the Northern territory is authorized to spend an additional $40,000 per month to advertise one of the two products. On the basis of past experience, the manager estimates that additional advertising will increase the sales of either product by $100,000. On which product should the manager focus this advertising campaign? Explain.

f. Top management is considering investing several million dollars to expand operations in one of its two sales territories. The expansion would increase the traceable fixed costs to the expanded territory in proportion to its increase in sales. Which territory would be the best candidate for this investment? Explain.

LO3 through LO5

PROBLEM 22.5B
Analysis of Responsibility Income Statements

Shown below are responsibility income statements for Sotheby, Inc., for the month of June.

	Investment Centers					
	Sotheby, Inc.		Division 1		Division 2	
	Dollars	%	Dollars	%	Dollars	%
Sales	$500,000	100%	$340,000	100%	$160,000	100%
Variable costs	302,000	60	238,000	70	64,000	40
Contribution margin	$198,000	40%	$102,000	30%	$ 96,000	60%
Fixed costs traceable to divisions	132,000	26	68,000	20	64,000	40
Division responsibility margin	$ 66,000	13%	$ 34,000	10%	$ 32,000	20%
Common fixed costs	46,000	9				
Income from operations	$ 20,000	4%				

	Profit Centers					
	Division 1		Product C		Product D	
	Dollars	%	Dollars	%	Dollars	%
Sales	$340,000	100%	$120,000	100%	$220,000	100%
Variable costs	238,000	70	60,000	50	178,000	81
Contribution margin	$102,000	30%	$ 60,000	50%	$ 42,000	19%
Fixed costs traceable to products	48,000	14	28,000	23	20,000	9
Product responsibility margin	$ 54,000	16%	$ 32,000	27%	$ 22,000	10%
Common fixed costs	20,000	6				
Responsibility margin for division	$ 34,000	10%				

Instructions

a. The company plans to initiate an advertising campaign for one of the two products in Division 1. The campaign would cost $8,000 per month and is expected to increase the sales of whichever product is advertised by $25,000 per month. Compute the expected increase in the responsibility margin of Division 1 assuming (**1**) that product C is advertised, and (**2**) that product D is advertised.

b. Assume that the sales of both products by Division 1 are equal to total manufacturing capacity. To increase sales of either product, the company must increase manufacturing facilities, which means an increase in traceable fixed costs in approximate proportion to the expected increase in sales. In this case, which product line would you recommend expanding? Explain.

c. The income statement for Division 1 includes $20,000 in common fixed costs. What happens to these fixed costs in the income statements for Sotheby, Inc.?

d. Assume that in November the monthly sales in Division 2 increase to $200,000. Prepare an income statement for Sotheby, Inc., by division in the format illustrated above. What is the expected effect of this change on the operating income of the company?

LO3 through LO5

PROBLEM 22.6B
Evaluating an Unprofitable Business Center

Foot B, Inc., is a small manufacturer of professional football equipment. The company has two divisions: the Pad Division and the Helmet Division. Data for the month of June are as follows:

	Profit Centers		
	Entire Company	Pad Division	Helmet Division
Sales	$70,000	$30,000	$40,000
Variable costs	30,000	15,000	15,000
Contribution margin	$40,000	$15,000	$25,000
Traceable fixed costs	30,000	18,000	12,000
Division responsibility margin	$10,000	$ (3,000)	$13,000
Common fixed costs	4,000		
Monthly operating income	$ 6,000		

Jacques, the company's chief financial officer since June 1 of the current year, wants to close the unprofitable Pad Division. He believes that doing so will benefit Foot B and benefit him, given that his end-of-year bonus is to be based on the company's overall operating income. In a recent interview, Jacques summarized his business philosophy as follows: "A company is only as strong as its least profitable segment. As long as I'm at the financial helm, only the strongest shall survive at Foot B."

Instructions

a. Had the Pad Division been closed on June 1, what would the company's operating income for the month have been?

b. After learning about Jacques's business philosophy, the Pad Division's director of marketing made the following statement: "Jacques may understand numbers, but he doesn't understand the complementary relationship between pads and helmets, nor the seasonal nature of our business." What did the director of marketing mean by this statement? How might such information influence Jacques's assessment of the company's Pad Division?

c. By how much would the Pad Division's monthly sales have to increase for it to generate a positive responsibility margin of $2,000 in any given month? Show all your computations.

LO1 LO6

PROBLEM 22.7B
Transfer Pricing Decisions

Eastrise Corporation has two divisions: the Motor Division and the Mower Division. The Motor Division supplies the motors used by the Mower Division. The Mower Division produces approximately 10,000 mowers annually. Thus, it receives 10,000 motors from the Motor Division each year. The market price of these motors is $400. The total variable cost of the mower is $220 per unit. The market price of the mower is $600. The unit variable cost of each mower, excluding the cost of the motor, is $100.

The Motor Division is currently operating at full capacity, producing 30,000 motors per year (10,000 of which are transferred to the Mower Division). The demand for the motors is so great that all 30,000 units could be sold to outside customers if the Mower Division acquired its motors elsewhere. The Motor Division uses the full market price of $400 as the transfer price charged to the Mower Division.

The manager of the Mower Division asserts that the Motor Division benefits from the inter-company transfers because of reduced advertising costs. As a result, he wants to negotiate a lower transfer price of $380 per unit.

Instructions

a. Compute the contribution margin earned annually by each division and by the company as a whole using the current transfer price.

b. Compute the contribution margin that would be earned annually by each division and by the company as a whole if the discounted transfer price were used.

c. The transfer price charged to the Mower Division is $400, which is the market price of the motor. Why is manufacturing cost not a satisfactory transfer price for the Motor Division?

LO1 LO6

PROBLEM 22.8B
Transfer Pricing Decisions

Westminster Inc. produces clocks and has two divisions: the Frames Division and the Works Division. The Frames Division produces the outside casings for clocks, which it sells to the outside market. The casing for the desktop grandfather clock sells for $135. The casing has variable costs per unit of $72 and fixed costs of $280,000, based on monthly production of 5,500 casings. Each casing could be sold to outside customers by the Frames Division, as casings are in high demand. The Frames Division has no idle capacity.

The Works Division uses the casing in the production of the desktop grandfather clock, one of its most popular clocks. The market price of a desktop grandfather clock is $275. The Works Division can acquire casings from outside suppliers for $140. The manager of the Works Division is interested in purchasing 3,000 casings from the Frames Division, but he wants to negotiate for a lower transfer price of $130. The current transfer price for a casing is the full market price of $135. The fixed costs in producing desktop grandfather clocks are $104,000, and the variable cost of producing a clock is $85, excluding the cost of the casing.

Instructions

a. What is the operating profit before tax for each division using the market transfer price of $135?

b. What is the operating profit before tax for each division using the transfer price of $130, as suggested by the manager of the Works Division?

c. How is the company's net income affected under the two transfer pricing scenarios?

d. Would it be more beneficial to the company if the Frames Division sold casings externally and the Works Division purchased casings from an outside supplier? Show your calculations.

Critical Thinking Cases

LO1 LO2 LO4

CASE 22.1
Allocating Fixed Costs to Responsibility Centers

You have just been hired as the controller of Land's End Hotel. The hotel prepares monthly responsibility income statements in which all fixed costs are allocated among the various profit centers in the hotel, based on the relative amounts of revenue generated by each profit center.

Robert Chamberlain, manager of the hotel dining room, argues that this approach understates the profitability of his department. "Through developing a reputation as a fine restaurant, the dining room has significantly increased its revenue. Yet the more revenue we earn, the larger the percentage of the hotel's operating costs that are charged against our department. Also, whenever vacancies go up, rental revenue goes down, and the dining room is charged with a still greater percentage of overall operating costs. Our strong performance is concealed by poor performance in departments responsible for keeping occupancy rates up." Chamberlain suggests that fixed costs relating to the hotel should be allocated among the profit centers based on the number of square feet occupied by each department.

Debra Mettenburg, manager of the Sunset Lounge, objects to Chamberlain's proposal. She points out that the lounge is very big, because it is designed for hotel guests to read, relax, and watch the sunset. Although the lounge does serve drinks, the revenue earned in the lounge is small in relation to its square footage. Many guests just come to the lounge for the free hors d'oeuvres and don't even order a drink. Chamberlain's proposal would cause the lounge to appear unprofitable, yet a hotel must have some "open space" for its guests to sit and relax.

Instructions

With a group of students:

a. Separately evaluate the points raised by each of the two managers.

b. Suggest an approach to allocating the hotel's fixed costs among the various profit centers.

LO1 LO3 LO6

CASE 22.2
An Ethical Dilemma

Osborn Diversified Products, Inc., is a billion-dollar manufacturing company with headquarters in Dayton, Ohio. The company has 15 divisions, two of which are the Battery Division and the Golf Cart Division. The company's Battery Division supplies the Golf Cart Division with batteries used to power electric carts.

Jim Peterson, age 45, is the general manager of the Battery Division. Jim has been with the company for 18 years and has done a remarkable job managing his operations. Unfortunately, due to health reasons, his physician has ordered that he take early retirement effective immediately. Jim is the single parent of a daughter who is currently a sophomore at a private university in Boston.

Sara Morrison, age 65, is the general manager of the Golf Cart Division. She has been with the company for 40 years and has been subjected to intense ridicule regarding her performance. In a fit of rage, the company's CEO recently told Sara: "I regret the day I ever promoted a woman to division manager." Sara and her husband, Rob, are independently wealthy with a net worth in excess of $20 million. She will happily retire from the company with a full pension in several months.

Both Jim and Sara receive bonuses based on the responsibility margins earned by their respective divisions. However, Jim's contract specifies that his bonus is to be calculated *net of any intercompany transactions.* Thus, his bonus is based on the Battery Division's segment margin less that portion earned from selling batteries to the Golf Cart Division.

Due to an undetected computer error, Jim's recent bonus was *not* calculated net of intercompany transactions. As such, the bonus was approximately $40,000 *more* than it should have been. Jim is the only division manager affected by the error. No one else in the company is aware that the error occurred. In view of Jim's personal situation, his attorney has advised him—off the record—to keep the money because the probability of the mistake being detected is *extremely remote.* Due to the design of the company's responsibility accounting system, the only person likely to ever detect the error is Sara, and the chance that she will do so prior to her retirement is slim.

Instructions

Have a group discussion and come to an agreement on the following issues:

a. Will this billion-dollar company be significantly damaged by the error in computing Jim's bonus? If you were in Jim's situation, what would you do? Defend your answer.

b. Assume that Sara becomes aware of the error one week prior to her retirement. She remains bitter over the criticism and sexist remarks she has received from the company's CEO, yet she is basically an honest person. What would you do if you were Sara?

c. Is it ethical for Jim's attorney to suggest—albeit off the record—that Jim keep the money? What would you do if you were Jim's attorney?

d. Assume that you are Jim's daughter, who attends a private Boston university. You have learned that the only chance your father has of keeping you enrolled at this prestigious institution is to subsidize your tuition with the excess $40,000 he received from his company. However, if you were to transfer back to Ohio and live at home, there would be sufficient funds to pay for your education. What would you do in this situation? Defend your answer.

LO1 LO2 LO5

CASE 22.3 Hospital Profit Centers

Researchers suggest that many angioplasties and implanted cardiac pacemaker surgeries done in the United States each year are medically unwarranted. The additional risk to patients' health posed by these surgeries and the high cost of health care that result are an obvious concern to those who are trying to balance the risks and benefits in health care decisions. However, the financial stakes are very high because **Boston Scientific Corp.** and **Johnson & Johnson** and other companies that make pacemakers and the stents for angioplasties earn significant profits on them. In addition, these cardiac-related surgeries help make cardiac units some of the most profitable responsibility centers in hospitals.

Instructions

a. The paragraph above states that cardiac surgery is a profit center for hospitals. List three or four other profit centers that might be found in a hospital. List at least three cost centers.

b. Write a short paragraph identifying the ethical issues that are related to designating a surgery procedure as a "profit center." Consider how these problems could be avoided within the responsibility center framework.

LO1 through LO3

INTERNET CASE 22.4 Comparing Responsibility Center Structure

General Mills produces and sells a variety of food products in numerous countries. Access its home page and look at the company overview at the following address:

www.generalmills.com

Now consider **Kirby Company**. It manufactures and sells one product line—vacuum cleaners and their accessories. Access its home page at the following address:

www.kirby.com

Instructions

a. On the basis of information from the Web site, how would you divide **General Mills** into responsibility centers? Give examples of possible investment centers, profit centers, and cost centers.

b. On the basis of information from the Web site, how would you divide **Kirby** into responsibility centers? Give examples of possible investment centers, profit centers, and cost centers.

c. What organizational factors might account for the differences between the two firms' responsibility center systems?

Internet sites are time and date sensitive. It is the purpose of these exercises to have you explore the Internet. You may need to use the Yahoo! search engine http://www.yahoo.com *(or another favorite search engine) to find a company's current Web address.*

LO1 LO2

CASE 22.5
University Ethics

Ethical dilemmas often face university and college administrators as they attempt to provide students with services and products to make college life easier. For example, the **University of Minnesota** issues "U Cards" to students. U Cards are a multipurpose ID that serves as a library and security card. Students have the option to open a checking account and use the U Card's debit and ATM features. The University of Minnesota has a contract with **TCF** Financial Corporation where **TCF** pays for the cards and also makes other contributions to the university (the new football stadium is named the **TCF** Bank Stadium).

Critics contend these types of deals are fraught with potential conflicts of interest. For example, recent scandals have occurred in which university financial aid officers were caught accepting free meals, tips, and shares of company stock. Some university and college administrators believe there is a problem that stems from considering every point of contact with students as a potential profit center.

Answers to Self-Test Questions

1. a **2.** b **3.** d **4.** b, e **5.** b

CHAPTER 23

Operational Budgeting

© AP Photo/Ed Reinke

Learning Objectives

AFTER STUDYING THIS CHAPTER, YOU SHOULD BE ABLE TO:

- **LO1** Explain how a company can be "profit rich, yet cash poor."
- **LO2** Discuss the benefits that a company may derive from a formal budgeting process.
- **LO3** Explain two philosophies that may be used in setting budgeted amounts.
- **LO4** Describe the elements of a master budget.
- **LO5** Prepare the budgets and supporting schedules included in a master budget.
- **LO6** Prepare a flexible budget and explain its uses.

HILLERICH & BRADSBY COMPANY

The family-owned company that makes the famous Louisville Slugger® baseball bat, Hillerich & Bradsby Co., began as a woodworking shop in 1856, making everything from balustrades to bedposts. By 1875, the little company was employing 20 people. According to company legend, the first pro bat was turned in 1884 for Pete Browning, a star on Louisville's professional American Association team—the Eclipse. One of Browning's nicknames was "The Louisville Slugger."

Hillerich & Bradsby increased the success of the Louisville Slugger® bat by allowing amateur baseball players to purchase the bat model of their favorite big-league player. In 1915 the Louisville Slugger first appeared in a youth-size model and in 1919 the company launched its first national advertising campaign. Just four years later, the company was producing one million bats a year.

In 1954, Hillerich & Bradsby purchased a Pennsylvania timber company to ensure an adequate supply of high-quality white ash for their bats. In 1970, the company began making aluminum baseball bats and, in 1975, they began selling baseball and softball gloves. In 2009, Hillerich & Bradsby celebrated the 125th anniversary of the Louisville Slugger®.

The above discussion shows the challenges firms face when they evolve from a small enterprise to a large company. Ensuring sources of supply and introducing new products require careful planning. The focus of this chapter, budgeting, is a key component of successful company growth. Operational budgeting is critical for long-term company viability. ■

Companies such as **Hillerich & Bradsby** use the budget (1) to assign decision-making authority over the company's resources, (2) to coordinate and implement plans, and (3) to hold employees accountable for the results of their decision making.

In this chapter, we show you how to *construct* responsibility budgets and *use* those budgets to assign decision-making authority and hold employees accountable for their decisions. After describing the master budget and its many components in detail, we go on to explain how to use the master budget as a means to implement planning and control through flexible budgeting. By the time you finish studying this chapter, you should appreciate the role of budgeting as a cornerstone of successful business activity.

Profit Rich, Yet Cash Poor

Learning Objective
LO1 Explain how a company can be "profit rich, yet cash poor."

In January 2010, Nancy Conrad founded Network Technologies, Inc. (NTI). NTI manufactures a screening device designed to safeguard personal computers against viruses transmitted through networks. Unlike disinfectant programs that remove viruses from infected hard drives, the NTI product actually screens all incoming network transmissions. If a virus is detected, it is destroyed *before* it can infect a computer's hard drive and cause damage to files.

Operating from a small manufacturing facility in Baltimore, NTI struggled through its first nine months of operations. However, the company experienced a very strong fourth quarter and managed to finish the year with total sales of $900,000 and a net income of $144,000.

The following profitability measures were taken from NTI's financial report for the year ended December 31, 2010:

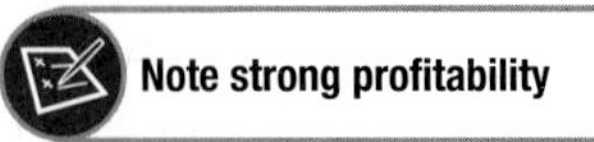

Selected Profitability Measures	NTI	Industry Average
Gross profit percentage (gross profit ÷ sales)	60%	45%
Net income percentage (net income ÷ sales)	16	12
Return on equity (net income ÷ average shareholders' equity)	29	18
Return on assets (net income ÷ average total assets)	15	14

Even though NTI appears to be *profitable* relative to industry averages, it is plagued by severe *cash flow problems.* In fact, for the year ending December 31, 2010, NTI reported a *$250,000 negative cash flow from operations.* Unable to obtain additional bank credit, Conrad loaned her company $36,000 on January 1, 2011, so that payroll checks would clear.

The liquidity measures presented below were also taken from NTI's December 31, 2010, financial report. Unlike the profitability measures, these measures are all well *below* industry averages.

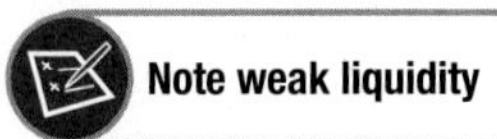

Selected Liquidity Measures	NTI	Industry Average
Current ratio (current assets ÷ current liabilities)	1.4	2.4
Quick ratio (quick assets ÷ current liabilities)	0.6	1.5
Inventory turnover (cost of goods sold ÷ average inventory)	2.2	7.3
Accounts receivable turnover (net sales ÷ average receivables)	4.5	8.0

What we see happening at NTI is a dilemma common to many businesses. In short, the company is *profit rich, yet cash poor.* How can a profitable business experience cash flow problems? Surprisingly, we will see that this condition often stems from *rapid growth.*

OPERATING CASH FLOWS: THE LIFEBLOOD OF SURVIVAL

In response to a surge in demand experienced in the fourth quarter of 2010, NTI disbursed large sums of cash to manufacture goods available for sale. NTI's cash was literally *tied up* in direct materials, work in process, and finished goods inventories as units were produced. Furthermore, as these goods were sold, cash remained tied up in accounts receivable. Exhibit 23–1 shows NTI's **operating cycle** and illustrates the cause and severity of its cash flow problems.[1]

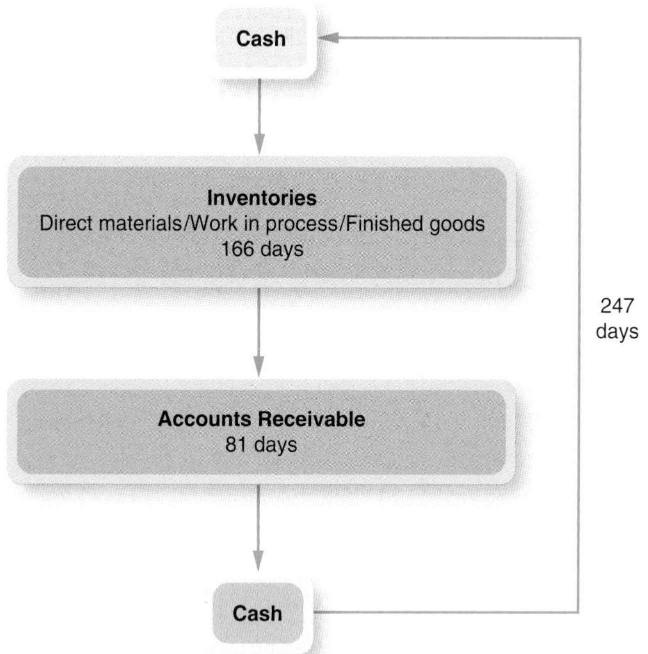

Exhibit 23–1
NTI'S OPERATING CYCLE

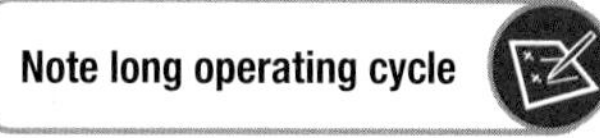

As shown, NTI's operating cycle during 2010 averaged 247 days.[2] In other words, *cash was tied up in inventory and receivables for 247 days before converting back into cash.* Throughout its operating cycle, however, payrolls, materials purchases, debt service, and overhead costs all required disbursements of cash on a timely basis (for example, 30 days). No wonder NTI's 2010 statement of cash flows reported a $250,000 negative cash flow from operations!

Fortunately, if NTI develops a comprehensive plan to control its operating activities, it may be possible to correct these cash flow problems. Such a plan is referred to as a *master budget.* In the sections that follow, we will introduce and discuss the budgeting process in detail. Then, later in the chapter, we will return to the NTI illustration and develop a master budget for its operations in 2011.

Budgeting: The Basis for Planning and Control

A **budget** is a comprehensive *financial plan* setting forth the expected route for achieving the financial and operational goals of an organization. Budgeting is an essential step in effective financial planning. Even the smallest business will benefit from preparing a formal written plan for its future operations, including the expected levels of sales, expenses, net income, cash receipts, and cash outlays.

The use of a budget is a key element of financial planning and it assists managers in controlling costs. Managers compare actual costs with the budgeted amounts and take corrective action as necessary. Thus, controlling costs means keeping actual costs in line with the financial plan.

[1] The *operating cycle* of a manufacturing firm is the average time period between the purchase of direct materials and the conversion of these materials back into cash.

[2] NTI's operating cycle of 247 days is equal to the number of days required to turn over inventory (365 days ÷ 2.2 inventory turnover = 166 days) plus the number of days required to turn over accounts receivable (365 days ÷ 4.5 accounts receivable turnover = 81 days).

Virtually all economic entities—businesses, governmental agencies, universities, churches, and individuals—engage in some form of budgeting. For example, a college student with limited financial resources may prepare a list of expected monthly cash payments to see that she does not exceed expected monthly cash receipts. This list is a simple form of a cash budget.

While all businesses engage in some degree of planning, the extent to which plans are formalized in written budgets varies from one business to another. Large, well-managed companies generally have carefully developed budgets for every aspect of their operations. Inadequate or sloppy budgeting is a characteristic of companies with weak or inexperienced management.

INTERNATIONAL CASE IN POINT

Operational budgeting for multinational companies can be very complex. For example, **Yahoo!** has global operations in more than 25 worldwide locations and offerings are available in more than 30 languages. Because **Yahoo!** collects revenue and pays expenses in foreign currencies, **Yahoo!** experiences foreign exchange rate fluctuation risks. Managers try to forecast exchange rates during the budgeting period and undertake measures that manage the impact of the exchange rate changes on the revenue, assets, liabilities, and expenses incurred in these foreign currencies.

BENEFITS DERIVED FROM BUDGETING

A budget is a forecast of future events. In fact, the process of budgeting is often called *financial forecasting.* Careful planning and preparation of a formal budget benefit a company in many ways, including the following:

Learning Objective
LO2 Discuss the benefits that a company may derive from a formal budgeting process.

1. *Enhanced management responsibility.* On a day-to-day basis, most managers focus their attention on the routine problems of running the business. In preparing a budget, however, managers are forced to consider all aspects of a company's internal activities and to make estimates of future economic conditions, including costs, interest rates, demand for the company's products, and the level of competition. Thus, budgeting increases management's awareness of the company's external economic environment.
2. *Assignment of decision-making responsibilities.* Because the budget shows the expected results of future operations, management is forewarned of and responsible for financial problems. If, for example, the budget shows that the company will run short of cash during the summer months, the responsible manager has advance warning to hold down expenditures or obtain additional financing.
3. *Coordination of activities.* Preparation of a budget provides management with an opportunity to coordinate the activities of the various departments within the business. For example, the production department should be budgeted to produce approximately the same quantity of goods the sales department is budgeted to sell. A written budget shows department managers in quantitative terms exactly what is expected of their departments during the upcoming period.
4. *Performance evaluation.* Budgets show the expected costs and expenses for each department as well as the expected output, such as revenue to be earned or units to be produced. Thus, the budgets provide a yardstick with which each department's actual performance may be measured.

ESTABLISHING BUDGETED AMOUNTS

Comparisons of actual performance with budgeted amounts are widely used in evaluating the performance of departments and department managers. Two basic philosophies prevail today that dictate the levels at which budgeted amounts should be set. We identify these philosophies as

(1) the *behavioral* approach and (2) the *total quality management* approach. We first discuss the behavioral approach, which currently is the more widely used budgeting philosophy.

The Behavioral Approach The assumption underlying the behavioral approach is that managers will be most highly motivated if they view the budget as a *fair* basis for evaluating a responsibility center's performance. Therefore, budgeted amounts are set at *reasonable and achievable levels;* that is, at levels that *can be achieved* through reasonably efficient operations. A department that operates in a highly efficient manner should be able to *exceed* the budgeted level of performance. Failure to stay within the budget, in contrast, is viewed as an unacceptable level of performance.

YOUR TURN **You as Vice President of Production and Sales**

Assume that you are vice president for production and sales at NTI. Your department is a profit center and is evaluated on profits. Profit goals are set for each quarter during the year. You, your sales manager, Bob Poole, and your production manager, Joe Reco, share a $1,500 bonus each quarter you are able to meet your profit goal. Halfway through the second quarter of 2011, it becomes clear that the department will not be able to meet its profit goal for the second quarter. Bob suggests that he could "move" the booking of some sales from quarter two to quarter three to increase the likelihood of earning the quarter-three bonus. Joe also suggests using some additional resources during the second quarter to get a head start on meeting the third-quarter profit goals. Joe states, "If we use overtime labor during the second quarter to increase inventory of finished goods, then our costs in quarter three will be lower and we will be more likely to meet our profit goal and earn the quarter-three bonus." What will you say to Joe and Bob?

(See our comments on the Online Learning Center Web site.)

The Total Quality Management Approach A basic premise of total quality management is that every individual and segment of the organization should strive for improvement constantly. The entire organization is committed to the goal of *completely eliminating* inefficiency and non-value-added activities. In short, the organization strives to achieve *perfection* across its entire value chain.

As a step toward achieving this goal, budgeted amounts may be set at levels representing *absolute efficiency.* Departments generally will fall somewhat short of achieving this level of performance. However, even small failures to achieve the budgeted performance serve to direct management's attention toward those areas in which there is room for improvement.

Selecting and Using a Budgeting Approach The approach used in setting budgeted amounts reflects the philosophy and goals of top management. Under either approach, however, managers should *participate actively* in the budgeting process. Department managers generally are the best source of information about the levels of performance that can be achieved within their departments. These managers also should understand both the intended purpose of the budget and the philosophy underlying the development of budgeted amounts.

Learning Objective **Explain two philosophies that may be used in setting budgeted amounts.** **LO3**

In comparing actual performance with budgeted amounts, top management should consider the philosophy used in developing the budgeted amounts. If a behavioral approach is employed, a highly efficient unit may *exceed* the budgeted level of performance. If a total quality management approach is used, a highly efficient unit should fall *slightly short* of the budget standards.

In the remainder of this chapter and in our assignment material, we will assume that budgeted amounts are set at *reasonable and achievable levels* (that is, the behavioral approach). Using this approach enables us to illustrate and discuss actual levels of performance both above and below budgeted levels.

Ethics, Fraud & Corporate Governance

Although we discuss budgets within the context of for-profit entities, the budgeting process is just as important for governmental and not-for-profit entities. Budgets are often included in documents given to investors when governmental or not-for-profit entities seek to obtain debt financing. Material misstatements in these budgets act as a fraud upon the purchasers of bonds issued by governmental or not-for-profit entities and expose both individuals and organizations to civil and criminal prosecution.

The Securities and Exchange Commission (SEC) brought an enforcement action against the former chief administrative officer (i.e., the city manager) of the city of Miami for including fraudulent budgetary numbers in bond offering documents provided to potential investors. In preparing its 1995 general fund budget, the city of Miami was initially facing a $15.8 million budget deficit. The city was able to reduce this preliminary deficit by $6.8 million through increases in property taxes, asset sales, and additional revenue from various licenses and permits. The city was not able to reduce the remaining $9 million deficit through additional revenue and was unwilling to reduce city operating expenses (i.e., cut services to constituents). The city ostensibly balanced its budget by including an expected payment of $9 million from the federal government under the Violent Crime Control and Law Enforcement Act of 1994.

The Violent Crime Control and Law Enforcement Act (VCCLEA), as initially drafted, would have provided lump sum grants in fiscal year 1995 to local governments for fighting crime. A report issued by a municipal lobbying group projected that the city of Miami would receive $9 million in 1995 under the VCCLEA. However, the final version of the VCCLEA reduced funding to local governments, provided for funding over five years rather than in a lump sum, and delayed the initial year of funding to fiscal year 1996. The city manager of Miami was aware of these changes to the final version of the VCCLEA. Yet he submitted his 1995 budget to Miami's city commission for approval with the $9 million still included in the budget. The city commission approved the budget, and the city's general fund budget was included in offering documents provided to potential bond investors. The general fund budget included in these debt offering documents was materially misstated, as the city of Miami did not have a balanced budget for fiscal year 1995; rather 57 percent—$9 million of the city's $15.8 million of projected revenue—was based on a source of funds that the city manager knew, or was reckless in not knowing, that the city of Miami would not receive.

The SEC settled these charges with the city manager by entering into a cease-and-desist order. The city manager of Miami agreed to cease and desist (stop) from any future violations of the securities laws. The penalty meted out in this case by the SEC was relatively mild, but future violations of the cease-and-desist order will be quite serious and will expose violators to more severe legal consequences.

THE BUDGET PERIOD

As a general rule, the period covered by a budget should be long enough to show the effect of management policies but short enough so that estimates can be made with reasonable accuracy. This suggests that different types of budgets should be made for different time spans.

Capital expenditures budgets, which summarize plans for major investments in plant and equipment, might be prepared to cover plans for as long as 5 to 10 years. Projects such as building a new factory or an oil refinery require many years of planning and expenditures before the new facilities are ready for use.

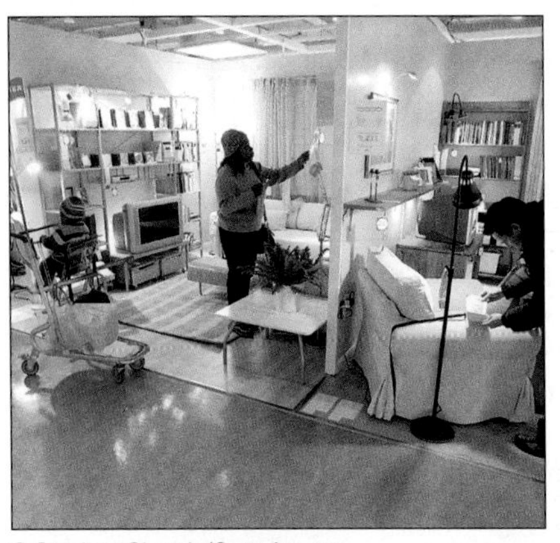

© Stephen Chernin/Getty Images

Most operating budgets and financial budgets cover a period of one fiscal year. Companies often divide these annual budgets into four quarters, with budgeted figures for each quarter. The first quarter is then subdivided into budget targets for each month, while only quarterly figures are shown for the next three quarters. As the end of each quarter nears, the budget for the next quarter is reviewed, revised for any changes in economic conditions, and divided into monthly budget targets. This process assures that the budget is reviewed at least several times each year and that the budgeted figures for the months just ahead are based on current conditions and estimates. In addition, budgeted figures for relatively short periods of time enable managers to compare actual performance to the budget without waiting until year-end.

An increasing number of companies, like **IKEA**, use **rolling budgeting,** whereby a new quarter or month is added to the end of the budget as the current quarter or month draws to a close. Thus, the budget always covers the upcoming 12 months. One advantage of rolling budgeting is that it stabilizes the planning horizon at one year ahead. Under the fiscal year approach, the planning period becomes shorter as the year progresses. Also, rolling budgeting forces managers into a continuous review and reassessment of the budget estimates and the company's current progress.

THE MASTER BUDGET: A PACKAGE OF RELATED BUDGETS

The "budget" is not a single document. Rather, the **master budget** consists of a number of interrelated budgets that collectively summarize all the planned activities of the business. The elements of a master budget vary depending on the size and nature of the business. A typical master budget for a manufacturing company would include the following:

Learning Objective **Describe the elements of a master budget.** **LO4**

1. Operating budgets
   a. Sales budget
   b. Production budgets including
      - Units to produce
      - Direct materials
      - Direct labor
      - Overhead
   c. Cost of goods manufactured and sold budget
   d. Selling and administrative expense budget
      - Marketing
      - Administrative expenses
      - Research and development
   e. Cash budget
2. Financial budgets
   a. Budgeted income statement
   b. Budgeted balance sheet
   c. Budgeted cash flows statement[3]
   d. Capital expenditures budget

Some elements of the master budget are *organized by responsibility center.* The budgeted income statement, for example, indicates the budgeted revenue and expenses of each profit center. The cash budget shows the budgeted cash flows for each cost center as well as each revenue center. The production schedule and manufacturing cost budget indicate the unit production and manufacturing costs budgeted for each production process. The portion of the budget relating to an individual responsibility center is called a **responsibility budget.** As explained in Chapter 22, responsibility budgets are an important element of a responsibility accounting system.

The many budgets and schedules making up the master budget are closely interrelated. Some of these relationships are illustrated in Exhibit 23–2 on the following page. Our discussion relates to two categories of budgets, operating and financial. Operating budgets are internal working budgets used by employees of the company. On the other hand, financial budget information is more externally focused and more likely to be shared with creditors, investors, customers, labor unions, and so forth. Exhibit 23–2 shows that operating and financial budgets are closely linked. As we discuss NTI's 2011 budgets, you will see specifically how the operating and financial budgets link together. To help you follow our discussion in the remainder of this chapter, operating or financial budget exhibits will have either a blue or green background, respectively, the same colors shown in Exhibit 23–2.

STEPS IN PREPARING A MASTER BUDGET

Some parts of the master budget should not be prepared until other parts have been completed. For example, the budgeted financial statements are not prepared until the sales, manufacturing, and operating expense budgets are available. This is the logical sequence of steps for preparing the annual elements of the master budget:

1. *Prepare a sales forecast.* The sales forecast is the starting point in the preparation of a master budget. This forecast is based on a business strategic plan, past experience, estimates of

[3] The budgeted cash flows statement and capital expenditures budget are not covered in this chapter. The focus in this chapter is on operational budgets and their relationships to the budgeted income statement and balance sheet. Capital expenditures are discussed in Chapter 26 and budgeted cash flows statements are covered in more advanced accounting courses.

Exhibit 23–2 ORGANIZATIONAL BUDGETING

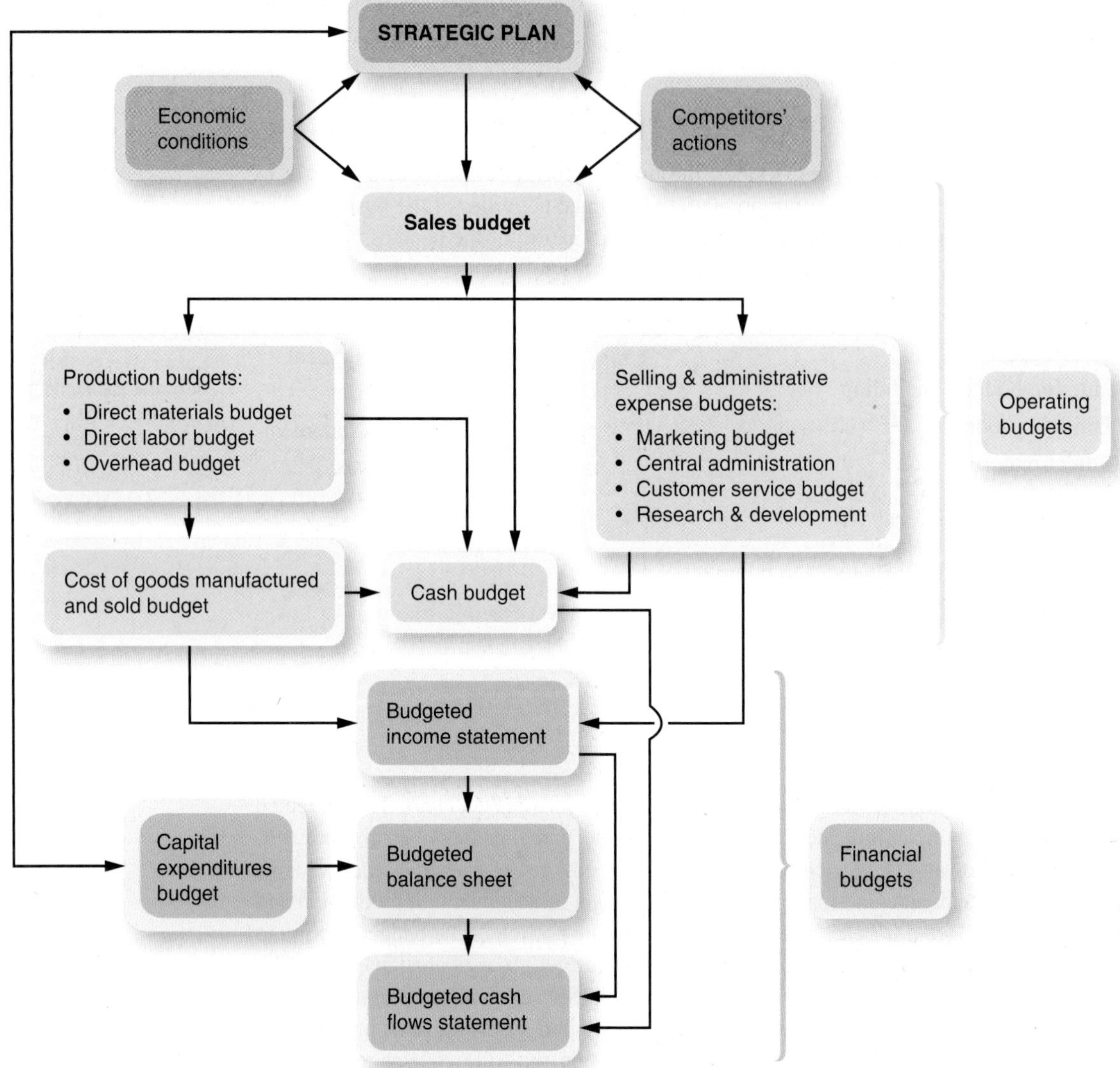

general business and economic conditions, and expected levels of competition. A forecast of the expected level of sales is a prerequisite to scheduling production and to budgeting revenue and variable costs. The arrows in Exhibit 23–2 indicate that information flows from this forecast into several other budgets.

2. *Prepare budgets for production, manufacturing costs, and operating expenses.* Once the level of sales has been forecast, production may be scheduled and estimates made of the expected manufacturing costs and operating expenses for the year. These elements of the master budget depend on both the level of sales and cost-volume relationships.
3. *Prepare a budgeted income statement.* The budgeted income statement is based on the sales forecast, the manufacturing costs comprising the cost of goods sold, and the budgeted operating expenses.
4. *Prepare a cash budget.* The cash budget is a forecast of the cash receipts and cash payments for the budget period. The cash budget is affected by many of the other budget estimates.

The budgeted level of cash receipts depends on the sales forecast, credit terms offered by the company, and the company's experience in collecting accounts receivable from customers. Budgeted cash payments depend on the forecasts of manufacturing costs, operating expenses, and capital expenditures, as well as the credit terms offered by suppliers. Anticipated borrowing, debt repayment, cash dividends, and issuance of capital stock also are reflected in the cash budget.

5. *Prepare a budgeted balance sheet.* A projected balance sheet cannot be prepared until the effects of cash transactions on various asset, liability, and owners' equity accounts have been determined. In addition, the balance sheet is affected by budgeted capital expenditures and budgeted net income.

The capital expenditures budget covers a span of many years. This budget is continuously reviewed and updated, but usually it is not prepared anew on an annual basis.

PREPARING THE MASTER BUDGET: AN ILLUSTRATION

Let us now return to the NTI illustration introduced at the beginning of the chapter. Even though the company's first year of operations was profitable, NTI experienced significant cash flow problems due to rapid sales growth in the fourth quarter of 2010.

Learning Objective
Prepare the budgets and supporting schedules included in a master budget. LO5

We will now develop NTI's master budget for 2011. A primary objective of this process is to help NTI avoid the cash flow problems experienced during 2010. Shown in Exhibit 23–3 is the company's balance sheet, dated January 1, 2011.

Exhibit 23–3
NTI'S BALANCE SHEET AT THE BEGINNING OF 2011

NTI BALANCE SHEET JANUARY 1, 2011		
Assets		
Current assets:		
Cash		$ 10,000
Receivables		225,000
Inventories (FIFO method)		
Direct Materials (8,000 units)	$ 60,000	
Finished Goods (8,000 units)	240,000	300,000
Prepayments		5,000
Total current assets		$540,000
Plant and equipment:		
Buildings and Equipment	$420,000	
Less: Accumulated Depreciation (straight line method)	20,000	
Total plant and equipment		400,000
Total assets		$940,000
Liabilities & Stockholders' Equity		
Current liabilities:		
Notes Payable, to officer (12 months @ 12%)		$ 36,000
Notes Payable, to bank (3 months @ 14%)		246,000
Other Current Payables		50,000
Income Taxes Payable		64,000
Total current liabilities		$396,000
Stockholders' equity:		
Capital Stock, no par, 10,000 shares outstanding	$400,000	
Retained Earnings	144,000	544,000
Total liabilities & stockholders' equity		$940,000

Sales of NTI's product are expected to increase throughout 2011. However, the company will drastically cut back production during the first quarter to liquidate some of the finished goods inventory currently on hand. As of January 1, there is no work in process inventory. No capital expenditures are planned for 2011.

OPERATING BUDGET ESTIMATES

The first step in preparing NTI's master budget is to develop each of its operating budgets for 2011. Information from these budgets will be used to prepare budgeted quarterly income statements. All of the information needed to estimate budgeted *income from operations* comes from the operating budget estimates.

Manufacturing Cost Estimates In preparation for the budget process, Lisa Scott, NTI's cost accountant, has thoroughly analyzed the company's variable and fixed manufacturing costs. Lisa determines that direct materials consist of two specially coated disks that cost $7.50 each. Variable overhead is primarily the cost of burning the programs onto the disks, packaging the disks, and insurance on the unfinished product. Direct labor is one-eighth hour per disk or one-quarter hour per finished unit. She is confident that variable manufacturing costs per unit will not increase during 2011. Lisa also analyzes fixed overhead costs and finds they consist of factory rent plus $3,500 per quarter of depreciation expense on equipment. She also believes that fixed manufacturing overhead will hold steady at approximately $15,000 per quarter. On the basis of her analysis, she compiled the following manufacturing cost estimates:

Manufacturing Cost Estimates for 2011	
Variable costs per unit manufactured:	
Direct materials (2 disks @ $7.50/disk)	$ 15
Direct labor (¼ hour per finished unit @ $20/hour)	5
Variable manufacturing overhead (per finished unit)	7
Fixed manufacturing overhead (per quarter)	$15,000

The Sales Budget Bob Poole, NTI's marketing director, is optimistic that demand for the company's product will continue to grow in 2011. He estimates that sales will reach 8,000 units in the first quarter and 10,000 units in the second quarter. Sales estimates for the third and fourth quarters are 30,000 units and 40,000 units, respectively. To keep its product affordable to a wide range of users, NTI is committed to holding its selling price per unit at $75 throughout the year. On the basis of this information, the sales budget shown in Exhibit 23–4 is prepared.

Production Budgets Upon examining performance reports for 2010, Joe Reco, NTI's production manager, concluded that he had overreacted to the rapid sales growth experienced in the fourth quarter. As a consequence, the company was carrying an excessive inventory of finished goods at the start of 2011. He immediately adopted a new policy for 2011 to increase inventory turnover and improve operating cash flows. The number of units in the finished goods inventory will be reduced and will depend on unit sales volume anticipated in the following quarter.

Joe decides that, for a given sales forecast of 10,000 units for the second quarter, the desired finished goods inventory at the end of the first quarter is 1,000 units. Likewise, given a sales forecast of 30,000 units for the third quarter, the desired finished goods inventory at the end of the second quarter is 3,000 units. Beginning in the third quarter, Joe has negotiated some delivery agreements that will allow the ending inventory to remain constant at 5,000 units in the third and fourth quarters. Based on these projections, the unit production budget shown in Exhibit 23–5, Schedule A1, is created.

Manufacturing Cost Budgets Combining the production unit estimates in Exhibit 23–5, Schedule A1, with the manufacturing cost estimates prepared by Lisa Scott, the manufacturing cost budgets shown in Exhibit 23–5, Schedules A2 through A4, are created.

Notice the arrow between the sales budget and the production budget that shows the dependence between the budgets. Projected unit sales are the key element for constructing Schedule A1, which shows budgeted units of production. On the other hand, budgeted units of production provide the key information for constructing the remaining manufacturing cost budgets for direct materials, direct labor, and overhead in Schedules A2 through A4. Notice the arrows that show the flow of information between the parts of the production budget. For example, ending inventory amounts in quarter two are the beginning inventory amounts in quarter three.

Exhibit 23-4

NTI'S SALES BUDGET FOR 2011

NTI
SALES BUDGET FOR 2011

	1st Quarter	2nd Quarter	3rd Quarter	4th Quarter
Projected unit sales	**8,000**	**10,000**	**30,000**	**40,000**
Sales price per unit	$75	$75	$75	$75
Projected revenue	$600,000	$750,000	$2,250,000	$3,000,000

Exhibit 23-5

NTI'S PRODUCTION BUDGETS FOR 2011

NTI
PRODUCTION BUDGETS FOR 2011

SCHEDULE A1: Units of Production

	1st Quarter	2nd Quarter	3rd Quarter	4th Quarter
Projected unit sales	8,000	10,000	30,000	40,000
Add desired ending inventory	1,000	3,000	5,000	5,000
Units available for sale	9,000	13,000	35,000	45,000
Less beginning inventory	8,000	1,000	3,000	5,000
Budgeted production in units	**1,000**	**12,000**	**32,000**	**40,000**

SCHEDULE A2: Direct Materials Budget

	1st Quarter	2nd Quarter	3rd Quarter	4th Quarter
Disks needed for production (two disks per unit)	2,000	24,000	64,000	80,000
Add desired ending inventory of disks	8,000	8,000	8,000	8,000
Disks available for production	10,000	32,000	72,000	88,000
Less beginning inventory	8,000	8,000	8,000	8,000
Budgeted unit purchases of direct materials disks	**2,000**	**24,000**	**64,000**	**80,000**
Purchase price per unit	× $7.50	× $7.50	× $7.50	× $7.50
Budgeted cost of purchased materials	$15,000	$180,000	$480,000	$600,000

SCHEDULE A3: Direct Labor Budget

	1st Quarter	2nd Quarter	3rd Quarter	4th Quarter
Budgeted production	1,000	12,000	32,000	40,000
Labor hours per unit	× .25	× .25	× .25	× .25
Total hours needed	250	3,000	8,000	10,000
Multiply by cost per hour	× $20	× $20	× $20	× $20
Budgeted direct labor cost	$5,000	$60,000	$160,000	$200,000

SCHEDULE A4: Overhead Budget

	1st Quarter	2nd Quarter	3rd Quarter	4th Quarter
Budgeted production	1,000	12,000	32,000	40,000
Variable overhead cost	× $7	× $7	× $7	× $7
Budgeted variable overhead cost	$7,000	$84,000	$224,000	$280,000
Add budgeted fixed overhead	$15,000	$15,000	$ 15,000	$ 15,000
Total budgeted overhead	$22,000	$99,000	$239,000	$295,000

Exhibit 23–6 NTI'S COST OF GOODS MANUFACTURED AND SOLD BUDGET FOR 2011

NTI
BUDGETED COST OF GOODS MANUFACTURED AND SOLD
FOR 2011

	1st Quarter		2nd Quarter		3rd Quarter		4th Quarter	
Finished goods, beginning inventory		$240,000		$ 42,000		$ 84,750		$ 137,344
Add cost of goods manufactured (from Exhibit 23–5):								
Direct materials used	$15,000		$180,000		$480,000		$600,000	
Direct labor used	5,000		60,000		160,000		200,000	
Variable overhead	7,000		84,000		224,000		280,000	
Fixed overhead	15,000	42,000	15,000	339,000	15,000	879,000	15,000	1,095,000
Total cost of goods available for sale		$282,000		$381,000		$963,750		$1,232,344
Less: Ending finished goods (see supplemental schedule below)		42,000		84,750		137,344		136,875
Cost of goods sold		$240,000		$296,250		$826,406		$1,095,469

Supplemental Schedule
Finished Goods Inventory

	1st Quarter	2nd Quarter	3rd Quarter	4th Quarter
Cost of goods manufactured	$42,000	$339,000	$879,000	$1,095,000
Divide by: Units of production (Exhibit 23–5, Schedule A1)	÷ 1,000	÷ 12,000	÷ 32,000	÷ 40,000
Production cost per unit	$ 42.00	$ 28.25	$27.4688	$ 27.375
Multiply by ending inventory (Schedule A1)	× 1,000	× 3,000	× 5,000	× 5,000
Cost of ending finished goods	$42,000	$ 84,750	$137,344	$ 136,875

Cost of Goods Manufactured and Sold Budget A manufacturing company's cost of goods sold is equal to its beginning finished goods inventory, plus the cost of goods manufactured during the period, less its ending finished goods inventory.

Consequently, the budget estimates for cost of goods sold in Exhibit 23–6 are computed using the beginning finished goods inventory figure from the balance sheet in Exhibit 23–3 and information from the production budgets in Exhibit 23–5. Make sure you can match up the cost of goods manufactured amounts in Exhibit 23–6 with those computed for the production budget shown in Exhibit 23–5.

© Royalty-Free/Corbis/DAL

Finished Goods Inventory As mentioned, NTI recently adopted a policy to reduce the number of units in finished goods inventory at the end of each quarter depending on the sales volume anticipated in the following quarter.

Thus, applying this policy in conjunction with the production costs shown in Exhibit 23–5, Schedules A2 to A4, ending inventory estimates are shown in the supplemental schedule in Exhibit 23–6.

Note that the budgeted manufacturing costs in the first quarter total *$42.00 per unit,* compared to *$28.25 per unit* in the second quarter. These amounts differ due to a *decrease in fixed manufacturing costs per unit* anticipated in the second quarter. During the first quarter, $15,000 in fixed manufacturing costs is allocated to 1,000 units produced (or *$15.00 per unit*). During the second quarter, however, $15,000 is allocated to 12,000 units produced (or *$1.25 per unit*).

Selling and Administrative Expense Budget NTI's variable operating expenses amount to $7.50 per unit. Most of this cost applies to sales commissions. The company's quarterly fixed operating expenses of $175,000 pertain primarily to the salaries of its officers. Based on this information, the operating expense budget in Exhibit 23–7 was prepared.

Exhibit 23–7 NTI'S SELLING AND ADMINISTRATIVE EXPENSE BUDGET FOR 2011

NTI
SELLING AND ADMINISTRATIVE EXPENSE BUDGET
FOR 2011

	1st Quarter	2nd Quarter	3rd Quarter	4th Quarter
Variable operating expenses ($7.50 per unit sold)	$ 60,000	$ 75,000	$225,000	$300,000
Fixed operating expenses (per quarter)	175,000	175,000	175,000	175,000
Total selling and administrative expenses	$235,000	$250,000	$400,000	$475,000

BUDGETED INCOME STATEMENT

NTI's budgeted income statements are based on estimates from Exhibits 23–4, 23–6, and 23–7. In addition, they include budgeted amounts for interest expense and income tax expense. Interest expense and income taxes are also reported in Exhibits 23–11 and 23–12, which are discussed later in the chapter. The following discussion explains how these figures were determined.

The $36,000 note payable reported in the January 1, 2011, balance sheet (Exhibit 23–3) is the loan from NTI's president, Nancy Conrad. The note is payable in four quarterly installments of $9,000, *plus* accrued interest on the outstanding balance at the end of each quarter. The note's interest rate is 12 percent (or 3 percent quarterly). Thus, interest due at the end of the first quarter is $1,080 ($36,000 × 3%), whereas interest due at the end of the second quarter is only $810 ($27,000 × 3%).

The $246,000 note payable is the remaining principal owed on a loan that originated in late December 2010. The note's interest rate is 14 percent (or 3.5 percent quarterly). The entire $246,000, plus $8,610 in accrued interest ($246,000 × 3.5%), is due at the end of the first quarter of 2011. Thus, total interest expense budgeted on notes payable for the first quarter is $9,690 ($1,080 plus $8,610).

Income tax expense is budgeted at 40 percent of income before income taxes.

On the basis of this information, we prepared the budgeted income statement shown in Exhibit 23–8.

Exhibit 23–8 NTI'S 2011 BUDGETED INCOME STATEMENT

NTI
BUDGETED INCOME STATEMENT
FOR EACH QUARTER IN 2011

		1st Quarter		2nd Quarter		3rd Quarter		4th Quarter
Sales (Exhibit 23–4)		$600,000		$750,000		$2,250,000		$3,000,000
Cost of goods sold (Exhibit 23–6) . .		240,000		296,250		826,406		1,095,469
Gross profit		$360,000		$453,750		$1,423,594		$1,904,531
Less operating expenses:								
Selling and administrative (Exhibit 23–7)	$235,000		$250,000		$400,000		$475,000	
Interest (Exhibit 23–11)	9,690	244,690	810	250,810	540	400,540	270	475,270
Operating income before tax		$115,310		$202,940		$1,023,054		$1,429,261
Income tax (40%) (Exhibit 23–12) . .		46,124		81,176		409,222		571,704
Net income		$ 69,186		$121,764		$ 613,832		$ 857,557

The budgeted income statement shows the effects that budgeted activities are expected to have on NTI's revenue, expenses, and net income. However, it is not indicative of the company's cash flow expectations for 2011. *Recall that during 2010 the company was profit rich, yet it remained cash poor.*

Now we must prepare *cash budget estimates* to formulate NTI's quarterly cash flow expectations. These estimates will also help us to prepare the company's budgeted balance sheets each quarter.

CASH BUDGET ESTIMATES

The estimates and data necessary to prepare the cash budget and budgeted balance sheets are called ***cash budget estimates***. These include budgeted disbursements for payables, prepayments, debt service, and taxes. In addition, NTI must budget cash receipts from collection of receivables. To avoid confusing these figures with the *operating budget estimates* used to prepare the budgeted income statement, the amounts in Exhibits 23–9 through 23–13 to be used in the preparation of NTI's cash budget are highlighted in ***red***.

Current Payables Budget Our preparation of a cash budget begins with estimating the portion of budgeted costs and expenses that will require *cash payment in the near future.* Certain expenses will *not* require an outlay of cash. These include (1) expenses that result from the expiration of prepaid items (such as insurance policies) and (2) the depreciation of plant assets. However, *only* those costs and expenses financed by *current payables* (which include immediate *cash* payments as well as accounts payable and accrued expenses) will require cash payments.

Exhibit 23–9 separates the costs and expenses financed by NTI's current payables from those related to the expiration of prepayments and depreciation. The last row, labeled "Cash payments for current payables," indicates the portion of current costs and expenses that requires cash disbursements in the near future. Examples of these items include purchases of direct materials (whether for cash or on account), factory payrolls, and various overhead costs. The amounts shown under the rows labeled "Prepayments for Insurance" and "Depreciation" are reported as *expenses* in the company's budgeted income statement. However, these amounts do not call for future disbursements of cash. We will assume that the expired prepayment estimates were made based on an evaluation of the company's insurance policies.

Exhibit 23–9 NTI'S BUDGET FOR CURRENT PAYABLES AND DISBURSEMENTS FOR PAYABLES FOR 2011

NTI
BUDGETED CURRENT PAYABLES AND CASH DISBURSEMENTS FOR CURRENT PAYABLES
FOR 2011

	1st Quarter		2nd Quarter		3rd Quarter		4th Quarter	
Beginning balance of payables		$ 50,000		$ 75,000		$ 100,000		$ 225,000
Add (from Exhibits 23–5 and 23–7):								
Direct materials purchased	$ 15,000		$180,000		$480,000		$600,000	
Direct labor used	5,000		60,000		160,000		200,000	
Overhead	22,000		99,000		239,000		295,000	
Selling and administrative	235,000	277,000	250,000	589,000	400,000	1,279,000	475,000	1,570,000
Less: Prepayments for Insurance (Exhibit 23–10)	$4,000		$5,500		$10,500		$12,000	
Depreciation	5,000	(9,000)	5,000	(10,500)	5,000	(15,500)	5,000	(17,000)
Total current payables		$318,000		$653,500		$1,363,500		$1,778,000
Less: Estimated ending balance in accounts payable		75,000		100,000		225,000		350,000
Cash payments for current payables		$243,000		$553,500		$1,138,500		$1,428,000

The starting point in Exhibit 23–9 is the $50,000 beginning payables balance appearing in NTI's January 1, 2011, balance sheet (see Exhibit 23–3). To this amount, we add the total payables budgeted in Exhibits 23–5 and 23–7. The balance of current payables at the end of the first quarter was estimated by Paul Foss, NTI's treasurer, after making a thorough analysis of suppliers' credit terms. Note, as shown by the arrows, that the beginning balance of current payables for the second quarter is simply the ending balance from the first quarter.

Prepayments Budget Exhibit 23–10 budgets the expected cash payments for prepayments made during the year. For NTI, these payments involve its insurance policies. Thus, preparation of the schedule called for an analysis of all policies reported on the January 1, 2011, balance sheet and the anticipated expiration of prepayments. Based on this analysis, the prepayments budget in Exhibit 23–10 was prepared.

Exhibit 23–10 PREPAYMENTS BUDGET FOR NTI IN 2011

NTI
PREPAYMENTS BUDGET
FOR 2011

	1st Quarter	2nd Quarter	3rd Quarter	4th Quarter
Balance at beginning of quarter	$ 5,000	→ $ 7,000	→ $ 8,000	→ $ 9,500
Estimated cash expenditure during quarter	6,000	6,500	12,000	15,000
Total prepayments	$11,000	$13,500	$20,000	$24,500
Less: Expiration of prepayments	4,000	5,500	10,500	12,000
Prepayments at end of quarter	$ 7,000	$ 8,000	$ 9,500	$12,500

Debt Service Budget The purpose of this schedule is to summarize the cash payments (both principal and interest) required to service NTI's debt each quarter. NTI has two notes payable outstanding on January 1, 2011.

The 12 percent, $36,000 note payable is the loan from Nancy Conrad, NTI's president. The loan agreement calls for quarterly payments of $9,000 plus interest accrued on the outstanding balance at a quarterly rate of 3 percent. The debt service on this note in the first quarter equals $9,000 in principal plus interest of $1,080 ($36,000 × 3%), or a cash outlay of *$10,080*. The note's debt service in the second quarter equals $9,000 in principal plus interest of $810 ($27,000 × 3%), or a cash outlay of *$9,810*.

The 14 percent, $246,000 note payable is to NTI's bank. The loan agreement calls for payment of the entire $246,000 at the end of the first quarter of 2011, plus interest accrued at a quarterly rate of 3.5 percent. Thus, the debt service on this note in the first quarter equals $246,000 plus interest of $8,610 ($246,000 × 3.5%), or a cash outlay of *$254,610*. There is no debt service cost associated with this note in the second quarter.

As shown in Exhibit 23–11, the total debt service cash outflow is budgeted at *$264,690* in the first quarter, *$9,810* in the second quarter, and, by the end of 2011, notes payable declines to $0.

Exhibit 23–11 NTI'S DEBT SERVICE BUDGET FOR 2011

NTI
DEBT SERVICE BUDGET
FOR 2011

	1st Quarter	2nd Quarter	3rd Quarter	4th Quarter
Notes payable at the beginning of the quarter	$282,000	→ $27,000	→ $18,000	→ $9,000
Interest expense for the quarter	9,690	810	540	270
Total principal plus accrued interest	$291,690	$27,810	$18,540	$9,270
Less: Cash payments (principal and interest)	264,690	9,810	9,540	9,270
Notes payable at the end of the quarter	$ 27,000	$18,000	$ 9,000	$ 0

Budgeted Income Taxes The budgeted cash payments for income tax expense are summarized in Exhibit 23–12. Each quarter, NTI makes income tax payments equal to its income tax liability at the beginning of that quarter. NTI's $64,000 liability at the beginning of the first quarter was taken from its January 1, 2011, balance sheet. The $46,124 liability at the beginning of the second quarter is simply the income tax liability at the end of the first quarter. These tax liabilities are shown on the budgeted income statement in Exhibit 23–8.

Exhibit 23–12 NTI'S INCOME TAX BUDGET FOR 2011

NTI BUDGETED INCOME TAXES FOR 2011	1st Quarter	2nd Quarter	3rd Quarter	4th Quarter
Income tax liability at beginning of quarter	$ 64,000	$ 46,124	$ 81,176	$409,222
Estimated income taxes for the quarter (per budgeted income statement, Exhibit 23–8)	46,124	81,176	409,222	571,704
Total accrued income tax liability	$110,124	$127,300	$490,398	$980,926
Cash payment of amount owed at beginning of quarter	64,000	46,124	81,176	409,222
Income tax liability at end of quarter	$ 46,124	$ 81,176	$409,222	$571,704

Estimated Cash Receipts from Customers All of NTI's sales are made on account. As such, the sole source of cash receipts is the collection of accounts receivable. NTI's operating cycle in Exhibit 23–1 shows that NTI turned over its accounts receivable 4.5 times during 2010. Thus, the average account was outstanding for *81 days* (365 days ÷ 4.5 = 81).

In an attempt to improve cash flow performance in 2009, NTI's credit manager, Richard Baker, set the following goals for his department: (1) to collect the entire $225,000 of accounts receivable reported on the January 1, 2011, balance sheet by the end of the first quarter, and (2) to collect 75 percent of quarterly sales during the quarter in which they are made and collect the remaining 25 percent in the subsequent quarter. If successful, Baker estimates that NTI's average collection period will be reduced from 81 days to 30 days.

Exhibit 23–13 on the following page shows the budgeted cash collections under the new collection policy. Losses for uncollectible accounts are ignored in our example. As shown in Exhibit 23–13, the beginning accounts receivable balance, plus credit sales and minus collections on account, equals the estimated ending balance of accounts receivable. The arrows show that the ending balance of accounts receivable in a quarter is the beginning balance in the next quarter.

YOUR TURN **You as Manager of the Credit Department**

Assume you are the manager of NTI's credit department. Nancy Conrad, the founder of NTI, has asked you to manage receivables and payables by leading and lagging. Leading receivables implies collecting cash from customers more quickly than previously. Lagging payables means delaying payment to creditors. You are concerned that what Conrad is suggesting is unethical. What should you do?

(See our comments on the Online Learning Center Web site.)

THE CASH BUDGET

We use NTI's cash flow budget estimates from Exhibits 23–9 through 23–13 to create the 2011 cash budget shown in Exhibit 23–14. This cash budget demonstrates that NTI expects to have enough cash to service its debt, particularly in the first quarter.

Exhibit 23–13 NTI'S BUDGET FOR ACCOUNTS RECEIVABLE AND COLLECTIONS OF RECEIVABLES FOR 2011

NTI
BUDGETED ACCOUNTS RECEIVABLE AND CASH COLLECTIONS FROM CUSTOMERS
FOR 2011

	1st Quarter		2nd Quarter		3rd Quarter		4th Quarter	
Beginning balance of receivables		$225,000		$150,000		$ 187,500		$ 562,500
Add: Sales on account from sales budget (Exhibit 23–4)		600,000		750,000		2,250,000		3,000,000
Total accounts receivable during the month		$825,000		$900,000		$2,437,500		$3,562,500
Less total cash receipts from customers:								
Previous quarter	$225,000		$150,000		$ 187,500		$ 562,500	
This quarter	450,000	675,000	562,500	712,500	1,687,500	1,875,000	2,250,000	2,812,500
Estimated ending balance in accounts receivable		$150,000		$187,500		$ 562,500		$ 750,000

Exhibit 23–14 NTI'S CASH BUDGET FOR 2011

NTI
CASH BUDGET
FOR 2011

	1st Quarter		2nd Quarter		3rd Quarter		4th Quarter	
Cash balance at beginning of quarter . . .		$ 10,000		$107,310		$ 203,876		$ 837,660
Add: Cash receipts (Exhibit 23–13)		675,000		712,500		1,875,000		2,812,500
Total cash available		$685,000		$819,810		$2,078,876		$3,650,160
Less: Cash payments for								
Current payables (Exhibit 23–9).	$243,000		$553,500		$1,138,500		$1,428,000	
Prepayments (Exhibit 23–10).	6,000		6,500		12,000		15,000	
Debt service (Exhibit 23–11)	264,690		9,810		9,540		9,270	
Income tax (Exhibit 23–12)	64,000	577,690	46,124	615,934	81,176	1,241,216	409,222	1,861,492
Cash balance at end of quarter		$107,310		$203,876		$ 837,660		$1,788,668

NTI's budgeted cash position at the end of 2011 is a vast improvement over its actual cash position at the end of 2010. We have discussed two primary reasons for the anticipated turnaround. First, a new policy was developed to improve control of inventory management and production scheduling. Second, ambitious goals were established to tighten credit policies. Keep in mind that these cash figures are based completely on budget *estimates.* Only if management's estimates and expectations are *realistic* will the company's cash flow problems be resolved.

BUDGETED BALANCE SHEETS

We now have the necessary information to forecast NTI's financial position at the end of each quarter in 2011. The company's quarterly budgeted balance sheets are shown in Exhibit 23–15. The budget exhibits used to derive various figures are indicated parenthetically.

Exhibit 23–15 NTI'S BUDGETED BALANCE SHEET FOR 2011

NTI
BUDGETED BALANCE SHEET
AT THE END OF EACH QUARTER IN 2011

	1st Quarter	2nd Quarter	3rd Quarter	4th Quarter
Current assets:				
Cash (Exhibit 23–14)	$107,310	$203,876	$ 837,660	$1,788,668
Receivables (Exhibit 23–13)	150,000	187,500	562,500	750,000
Inventories:				
Direct materials (Exhibit 23–5, Schedule A2, 8,000 units @ $7.50 each)	60,000	60,000	60,000	60,000
Finished goods (Exhibit 23–6)	42,000	84,750	137,344	136,875
Prepayments (Exhibit 23–10)	7,000	8,000	9,500	12,500
Total current assets	$366,310	$544,126	$1,607,004	$2,748,043
Plant and equipment:				
Buildings and equipment	$420,000	$420,000	$ 420,000	$ 420,000
Less: Accumulated depreciation	(25,000)	(30,000)	(35,000)	(40,000)
Total plant and equipment	$395,000	$390,000	$ 385,000	$ 380,000
Total assets	$761,310	$934,126	$1,992,004	$3,128,043
Current liabilities:				
Notes payable to officer (Exhibit 23–11)	$ 27,000	$ 18,000	$ 9,000	$ -0-
Other current payables (Exhibit 23–9)	75,000	100,000	225,000	350,000
Income taxes payable (Exhibit 23–12)	46,124	81,176	409,222	571,704
Total current liabilities	$148,124	$199,176	$ 643,222	$ 921,704
Stockholders' equity:				
Capital stock, no par, 10,000 shares	$400,000	$400,000	$ 400,000	$ 400,000
Retained earnings, beginning of quarter	144,000	→ 213,186	→ 334,950	→ 948,782
Quarterly income (Exhibit 23–8)	69,186	121,764	613,832	857,557
Total stockholders' equity	$613,186	$734,950	$1,348,782	$2,206,339
Total liabilities & stockholders' equity	$761,310	$934,126	$1,992,004	$3,128,043

INTERNATIONAL FINANCIAL REPORTING: STANDARDS AND BUDGETING

For many companies, U.S. generally accepted accounting principles (GAAP) requirements are embedded in their operating budget computations. The adoption of, or convergence with, IFRS is likely to require significant revision in the budgeting processes of U.S. companies. For example, regarding revenue recognition, IFRS and U.S. GAAP generally agree at the principles level. However, U.S. GAAP contains extensive supporting literature that provides detailed and industry-specific guidance for revenue recognition. U.S. publicly traded companies are required to follow that specific guidance in creating their external financial statements. There are other areas where U.S. GAAP, with over 20,000 pages of supporting authoritative guidance, has specific and detailed recommendations that are not embodied in the 4,000 pages of authoritative IFRS guidance. Standard setters are currently considering whether the additional guidance provided with U.S. GAAP will become a part of the IFRS guidance in future years.

USING BUDGETS EFFECTIVELY

In preparing a budget, managers are forced to consider carefully all aspects of the company's activities. This study and analysis should, in itself, enable managers to do a better job of managing.

The primary benefits of budgeting, however, result from how the budgeted information is used. Among these benefits are:

1. *Advance warning of and assignment of responsibility for conditions that require corrective action.* For example, NTI now knows that one result of the expected increase in sales between the first and fourth quarters (8,000 units to 40,000 units) is a large increase in needed direct labor hours from the 400 hours in the first quarter to 10,000 hours by the fourth quarter. Hiring additional skilled labor and training them will be assigned to human resources personnel.
2. *Coordination of activities among all departments within the organization.* The increased demand for direct labor, described above, will require significant coordination between the administration (particularly human resources, payroll, etc.) and the manufacturing department. Also, NTI might need to add one or two work shifts and/or find additional production space to accommodate the additional workers.
3. *The creation of standards for evaluating performance.* Because Lisa Scott, NTI's cost accountant, analyzed the direct labor required to produce a finished unit, the company now has an expected or standard amount of time to produce a finished unit (one-quarter hour). This standard allows for planning the number of employees to hire and allows for an evaluation of the efficiency of current employees.

Let us now consider in more detail how NTI's master budget serves these functions.

Advance Warning of and Responsibility for Decision Making Earlier in this chapter, we described NTI's financial condition as *profit rich, yet cash poor.* We attributed this condition to the rapid sales growth experienced in the fourth quarter of 2010. In short, a sudden surge in demand for NTI's product caused excessive amounts of cash to become *tied up* in inventories and receivables. As a result, one of management's major responsibilities at the start of 2011 is generating enough cash flow from operations to meet obligations as they become due. Had a master budget been prepared in 2010, management would have been *forewarned* of this condition, thereby making the severity of the current situation less threatening to the company's survival.

Coordination of the Activities of Departments The budget provides a comprehensive plan enabling all of the departments to work together in a coordinated manner. For example, the Production Department knows the quantity of goods to produce to meet the expected needs of the Sales Department. The Purchasing Department, in turn, is informed of the quantities of direct materials that must be ordered to meet the requirements of the Production Department. The budgeting process requires that managers of departments and other segments of the organization *communicate with each other.*

A Yardstick for Evaluating Management Performance The comparison of actual results with budgeted amounts is a common means of evaluating performance in organizations. As discussed in Chapter 22, the evaluation of performance should be based only on the revenue and costs that are *under the control* of the person being evaluated. Therefore, for the purposes of evaluation, budgeted fixed costs should be subdivided into the categories of *controllable costs* and *committed costs.*

FLEXIBLE BUDGETING

Learning Objective
LO6 Prepare a flexible budget and explain its uses.

Performance may become difficult to evaluate if the actual level of activity (either sales or production) differs substantially from the level originally budgeted. A **flexible budget** is one that can be adjusted easily to show budgeted revenue, costs, and cash flows at *different levels* of activity. Thus, if a change in volume lessens the usefulness of the original budget, a new budget may be prepared quickly to reflect the actual level of activity for the period.

To illustrate the usefulness of a flexible budget, assume that on March 31, 2011, Joe Reco (NTI's production manager) is presented with the **performance report** shown in Exhibit 23–16. The report compares the manufacturing costs originally budgeted for the quarter (Exhibit 23–5) with his department's actual performance for the period.

Exhibit 23–16
NTI'S PRODUCTION DEPARTMENT PERFORMANCE REPORT FOR THE FIRST QUARTER OF 2011

NTI
PERFORMANCE REPORT OF THE PRODUCTION DEPARTMENT
FOR THE 1ST QUARTER ENDED MARCH 31, 2011

	Amount Budgeted	Actual	Over (Under) Budget
Manufacturing costs:			
Direct materials used	$15,000	$21,000	$ 6,000
Direct labor	5,000	7,000	2,000
Variable manufacturing overhead	7,000	9,500	2,500
Fixed manufacturing overhead	15,000	15,750	750
Total manufacturing costs—first quarter	$42,000	$53,250	$11,250

At first glance, it appears that Reco's performance is quite poor, as all production costs exceed the amounts budgeted. However, we have deliberately omitted one piece of information from this performance report. To meet a higher-than-expected customer demand for NTI's product, the production department produced *1,500 units* instead of the *1,000 units* originally budgeted for the first quarter.

Under these circumstances, we should reevaluate our conclusions concerning Reco's ability to control manufacturing costs. At this higher level of production, variable manufacturing costs should naturally exceed the amounts originally budgeted. In order to evaluate his performance, the budget must be adjusted to indicate the levels of cost that would have been budgeted to manufacture 1,500 units.

Flexible budgeting may be viewed as combining the concepts of budgeting and cost-volume-profit analysis. Using the variable and fixed cost estimates prepared by Lisa Scott (page 1000), the manufacturing cost budget for NTI can be revised to reflect any level of production. For example, in Exhibit 23–17, these relationships are used to forecast quarterly manufacturing costs at three different levels of production:

	Level of Production (in units)		
	500	1,000	1,500
Manufacturing cost estimates:			
Variable costs:			
Direct materials ($15 per unit)	$ 7,500	$15,000	$22,500
Direct labor ($5 per unit)	2,500	5,000	7,500
Variable manufacturing overhead ($7 per unit)	3,500	7,000	10,500
Fixed costs:			
Manufacturing overhead ($15,000 per quarter)	15,000	15,000	15,000
Total manufacturing costs—first quarter	$28,500	$42,000	$55,500

Exhibit 23–17

NTI'S BUDGETED PRODUCTION COSTS AT VARIOUS PRODUCTION VOLUMES FOR 2011

Notice that budgeted *variable* manufacturing costs change with the level of production, whereas budgeted *fixed costs* remain the same.

We can now modify the performance report for NTI's production department to reflect the actual *1,500* unit level of production achieved during the first quarter of 2011. The modified report is presented in Exhibit 23–18.

NTI
PERFORMANCE REPORT OF THE PRODUCTION DEPARTMENT
FOR THE 1ST QUARTER ENDED MARCH 31, 2011

	Level of Production (in units)			
	Originally Budgeted 1,000	Flexible Budget 1,500	Actual Cost 1,500	Actual Costs Over (Under) Flexible Budget
Manufacturing costs:				
Direct materials used	$15,000	$22,500	$21,000	$(1,500)
Direct labor	5,000	7,500	7,000	(500)
Variable overhead	7,000	10,500	9,500	(1,000)
Fixed overhead	15,000	15,000	15,750	750
Total manufacturing costs	$42,000	$55,500	$53,250	$(2,250)

Exhibit 23–18

FLEXIBLE BUDGET-BASED PERFORMANCE REPORT AT NTI FOR 2011

This comparison paints quite a different picture from the report presented in Exhibit 23–16. Considering the actual level of production, the production manager has kept all manufacturing costs below budgeted amounts, with the exception of fixed overhead (most of which may be committed costs).

The techniques of flexible budgeting may also be applied to profit centers by applying cost-volume-profit relationships to the actual level of *sales* achieved.

Computers and Flexible Budgeting Adjusting the entire budget to reflect a different level of sales or production would be a sizable task in a manual system. In a computer-based system, however, it can be done quickly and easily. Once the cost-volume-profit relationships have been entered into a budgeting program, the computer instantly performs the computations necessary to generate a complete master budget for any level of business activity. There are numerous budgeting software programs available on the market. However, many managers choose to develop their own budgeting programs using spreadsheet packages.

Managers often use their budgeting software to generate complete budgets under many different assumptions. These managers use a standard cost system to provide the costs of resources consumed. We will discuss standard cost systems in the next chapter. For managers using standard costs, software becomes a valuable planning tool with which to assess the expected impact of changes in sales, production, and other key variables on all aspects of their operations.

Concluding Remarks

Chapter 23 serves as a link between the preceding several chapters and the next chapters. The preparation of a master budget closely relates to the use of standard costs, covered in the next chapter, and draws heavily on concepts regarding cost flows, product costing, cost-volume-profit analysis, and responsibility accounting. In our next chapters, we will see how managers select and use budget information for controlling operations and when making decisions pertaining to investments in long-term assets.

END-OF-CHAPTER REVIEW

SUMMARY OF LEARNING OBJECTIVES

LO1 **Explain how a company can be "profit rich, yet cash poor."** Companies must often tie up large sums of cash in direct materials, work in process, and finished goods inventories. As finished goods are sold, cash continues to remain tied up in accounts receivable. Thus, a company may be reporting record profits, yet still experience cash flow problems.

LO2 **Discuss the benefits that a company may derive from a formal budgeting process.** The benefits of budgeting are the benefits that come from thinking ahead. Budgeting helps to coordinate the activities of the different departments, provides a basis for evaluating department performance, and provides managers with responsibility for future decision making. In addition, budgeting forces management to estimate future economic conditions, including costs of materials, demand for the company's products, and interest rates.

LO3 **Explain two philosophies that may be used in setting budgeted amounts.** The most widely used approach is to set budgeted amounts at levels that are reasonably achievable under normal operating conditions. The goal in this case is to make the budget a fair and reasonable basis for evaluating performance.

An alternative is to budget an ideal level of performance. Under this approach, departments normally fall somewhat short of budgeted performance, but the variations may identify areas in which improvement is possible.

LO4 **Describe the elements of a master budget.** A "master budget" is a group of related budgets and forecasts that together summarize all the planned activities of the business. A master budget usually includes a sales forecast, production schedule, manufacturing costs budget, operating expense budget, cash budget, capital expenditures budget, and projected financial statements. The number and type of individual budgets and schedules that make up the master budget depend on the size and nature of the business.

LO5 **Prepare the budgets and supporting schedules included in a master budget.** A logical sequence of steps in preparing a master budget begins with a sales forecast. The operating budget estimates are used primarily in preparing a budgeted income statement, whereas the cash flow estimates are used in preparing the cash budget and budgeted balance sheets.

LO6 **Prepare a flexible budget and explain its uses.** A flexible budget shows budgeted revenue, costs, and profits for different levels of business activity. Thus, a flexible budget can be used to evaluate the efficiency of departments throughout the business, even if the actual level of business activity differs from management's original estimates. The amounts included in a flexible budget at any given level of activity are based on cost-volume-profit relationships.

Key Terms Introduced or Emphasized in Chapter 23

budget (p. 993) A plan or forecast for a future period expressed in quantitative terms. Establishes objectives and aids in evaluating subsequent performance.

flexible budget (p. 1012) A budget that can be readily revised to reflect budgeted amounts given the actual levels of activity (sales and production) achieved during the period. Makes use of cost-volume-profit relationships to restate the master budget for the achieved level of activity.

master budget (p. 997) An overall financial and operating plan, including budgets for all aspects of business operations and for all responsibility centers.

operating cycle (p. 993) The average time required for the cash invested in inventories to be converted into the cash ultimately collected on sales made to customers.

performance report (p. 1012) A schedule comparing the actual and budgeted performance of a particular responsibility center.

responsibility budget (p. 997) A portion of the master budget showing the budgeted performance of a particular responsibility center within the organization.

rolling budgeting (p. 996) A technique of extending the budget period by one month as each month passes. Therefore, the budget always covers the upcoming 12 months.

Demonstration Problem

Gertz Corporation is completing its master budget for the first two quarters of the current year. The following financial budget estimates (labeled *E1* through *E5*) have been prepared:

Payments on Current Payables (E1)

	1st Quarter	2nd Quarter
Balance at beginning of quarter	$244,000	$ 80,000
Budgeted increase in payables during the quarter	300,000	320,000
Total payables during quarter	$544,000	$400,000
Less: Estimated balance at end of quarter	80,000	90,000
Payments on current payables during quarter	$464,000	$310,000

Prepayments Budget (E2)

	1st Quarter	2nd Quarter
Balance at beginning of quarter	$ 5,000	$ 7,000
Estimated cash expenditure during quarter	8,000	9,000
Total prepayments	$13,000	$16,000
Less: Expiration of prepayments	6,000	8,000
Prepayments at end of quarter	$ 7,000	$ 8,000

Debt Service Budget (E3)

	1st Quarter	2nd Quarter
Notes payable at the beginning of the quarter	$50,000	$49,000
Interest expense for the quarter	1,500	1,470
Total principal plus accrued interest	$51,500	$50,470
Less: Cash payments (principal and interest)	2,500	2,500
Notes payable at the end of the quarter	$49,000	$47,970

Budgeted Income Taxes (E4)

	1st Quarter	2nd Quarter
Income tax liability at beginning of quarter	$25,000	$30,000
Estimated income taxes for the quarter (per budgeted income statement)	30,000	40,000
Total accrued income tax liability	$55,000	$70,000
Cash payment of amount owed at beginning of quarter	25,000	30,000
Income tax liability at end of quarter	$30,000	$40,000

Estimated Receipts from Customers (E5)

	1st Quarter	2nd Quarter
Balance of receivables at beginning of year	$150,000	
Collections on first quarter sales of $500,000—60% in first quarter and 40% in the second quarter	300,000	$200,000
Collections on second quarter sales of $600,000—60% in the second quarter and 40% in the third quarter		360,000
Cash receipts from customers	$450,000	$560,000

Instructions

a. Prepare a cash budget for Gertz Corporation for the first two quarters of the current year. Assume that the company's cash balance at the beginning of the first quarter is $50,000.

b. Discuss any cash flow problems revealed by your budget.

Solution to the Demonstration Problem

a. The following cash budget can be prepared using the financial budget estimates provided:

GERTZ CORPORATION
CASH BUDGET
FIRST TWO QUARTERS OF CURRENT YEAR

	1st Quarter	2nd Quarter
Cash balance at beginning of quarter	$ 50,000	$ 500
Cash receipts:		
Cash received from customers (E5)	450,000	560,000
Total cash available	$500,000	$560,500
Cash payments:		
Payment of current payables (E1)	$464,000	$310,000
Prepayments (E2)	8,000	9,000
Debt service, including interest (E3)	2,500	2,500
Income tax payments (E4)	25,000	30,000
Total disbursements	$499,500	$351,500
Cash balance at end of the quarter	$ 500	$209,000

b. The cash budget reveals that Gertz expects to disburse more cash than it will collect during the first quarter. As a result, a cash balance of only $500 is budgeted for the end of that quarter. Because these figures are estimates, it is possible that its cash balance may actually be less than the amount budgeted. Thus, Gertz should arrange for a line of credit now, in the event that a short-term loan becomes necessary. It does not appear that the company will have any cash flow problems during the second quarter.

Self-Test Questions

The answers to these questions appear on page 1035.

1. Which of the following statements correctly describes relationships within the master budget? (More than one answer may be correct.)
   - **a.** The production budgets are based in large part on the sales forecast.
   - **b.** In many elements of the master budget, the amounts budgeted for the upcoming quarter are reviewed and subdivided into monthly budget figures.
   - **c.** The operating budgets affect the budgeted income statement, the cash budget, and the budgeted balance sheet.
   - **d.** The capital expenditures budget affects the direct materials budget.

2. During the first quarter of its operations, Morris Mfg. Co. expects to sell 50,000 units and create an ending inventory of 20,000 units. Variable manufacturing costs are budgeted at $10 per unit, and fixed manufacturing costs at $100,000 per quarter. The company's treasurer expects that 80 percent of the variable manufacturing costs will require cash payment during the quarter and that 20 percent will be financed through accounts payable and accrued liabilities. Only 50 percent of the fixed manufacturing costs are expected to require cash payments during the quarter. In the cash budget, payments for manufacturing costs during the quarter will total:
   - **a.** $800,000.
   - **b.** $610,000.
   - **c.** $600,000.
   - **d.** $450,000.

3. Rodgers Mfg. Co. prepares a flexible budget. The original budget forecasts sales of 100,000 units @ $20 and operating expenses of $300,000 fixed, plus $2 per unit. Production was budgeted at 100,000 units. Actual sales and production for the period totaled 110,000 units. When the budget is adjusted to reflect these new activity levels, which of the following budgeted amounts will increase, but by *less than* 10 percent?
   - **a.** Sales revenue.
   - **b.** Variable manufacturing costs.

c. Fixed manufacturing costs.

d. Total operating expenses.

4. Lamberton Manufacturing Company has just completed its master budget. The budget indicates that the company's operating cycle needs to be shortened. Thus, the company will likely attempt:

   a. Stocking larger inventories.

   b. Reducing cash discounts for prompt payment.

   c. Tightening credit policies.

   d. None of the above selections is correct.

5. Which of the following is *not* an element of the master budget?

   a. The capital expenditures budget.

   b. The production schedule.

   c. The operating expense budget.

   d. All of the above are elements of the master budget.

6. Which of the following is *not* a potential benefit of using budgets?

   a. Enhanced coordination of firm activities.

   b. More motivated managers.

   c. More accurate external financial statements.

   d. Improved interdepartmental communication.

ASSIGNMENT MATERIAL Discussion Questions

1. Explain the relationship between the management functions of *planning* and *controlling costs.*
2. Briefly explain at least three ways in which a business may expect to benefit from preparing a formal budget.
3. Criticize the following quotation:

   "At our company, budgeted revenue is set so high and budgeted expenses so low that no department can ever meet the budget. This way, department managers can never relax; they are motivated to keep working harder no matter how well they are already doing."
4. Why is the preparation of a sales forecast one of the earliest steps in preparing a master budget?
5. What are *responsibility budgets*? What responsibility centers would serve as the basis for preparing responsibility sales budgets in a large retail store, such as **Sears** or **Nordstrom**?
6. What is a *flexible budget*? Explain how a flexible budget increases the usefulness of budgeting as a means of evaluating performance.
7. An article in *BusinessWeek* stated that approximately one-third of the total federal budget is considered "controllable." What is meant by a budgeted expenditure being controllable? Give two examples of government expenditures that may be considered "noncontrollable."
8. Explain why companies that undergo periods of rapid growth often experience cash flow problems.
9. Explain how to compute the average collection period and why it is a critical factor in creating the collections of receivables budget (see Exhibit 23–13).
10. List and briefly explain the two budget philosophies described in the chapter.
11. Some expenses that appear in the income statement do not require a direct cash payment during the period. List at least two such expenses.
12. Explain why it is necessary to distinguish between cash budget estimates and operating budget estimates.
13. When evaluating the performance of a manager, why should fixed costs be divided into the categories of controllable costs and committed costs?
14. What is a rolling budget? Why do some companies choose to use rolling budgets?
15. Frequently, the disadvantages of budgeting are not discussed in textbooks. Go to the Web site www.bbrt.org. Click on Beyond Budgeting to find some disadvantages to budgeting.

Brief Exercises

BRIEF EXERCISE 23.1

Budgeting Philosophies

Renaldo's Boutiques, Inc., has 14 stores located in a midwestern part of the United States. Renaldo, the president of the company, has set budgets for each store that do not allow for lost, stolen, or misplaced merchandise (inventory shrinkage). Research shows the disappearance of store merchandise is attributed to a combination of internal and external causes:

Customer theft—35 percent

Employee theft—40 percent

Administrative errors—18 percent

Vendor dishonesty—7 percent

This chapter discussed two types of budgeting philosophies. Which philosophy do you believe Renaldo is following? Use information in this problem to support your answer.

LO1 LO5 **BRIEF EXERCISE 23.2**
Cash Flow at Body Builders

Body Builders Corporation is opening a chain of five health clubs in the Minneapolis area. Body Builders's marketing manager has suggested a marketing plan designed to generate new memberships. The plan would allow new members to delay payment for the first three months' membership and pay at the end of the first quarter. Thus, the cash flow from membership fees will not occur for three months.

Discuss the implications of this marketing approach for the cash flows of Body Builders.

LO4 **BRIEF EXERCISE 23.3**
Production Budget

Expected sales for tents at Sandy's Camping Gear are 4,200, 6,100, 2,200, 3,400, and 5,300 for the next five quarters. At the end of the current year, inventory of finished tents on hand is 500 tents. Sandy's has a desired ending inventory of 10 percent of next quarter's sales.

Create the production budget in numbers of tents for quarters one through four for the coming year.

LO4 **BRIEF EXERCISE 23.4**
Estimating Direct Materials Inventory

On January 1, Salter Corporation determined that its direct materials inventory needs to contain 6,500 pounds of materials by March 31. To achieve this goal, Salter will have to use 10 pounds of direct materials for every pound that it purchases during the upcoming quarter. On the basis of the company's budgeted sales volume, management estimates that 10,000 pounds of direct materials need to be purchased by March 31.

Determine the number of pounds in Salter's beginning direct materials inventory on January 1.

LO2 **BRIEF EXERCISE 23.5**
Benefits of Budgeting

Cheri Standish, the controller at Harmonics International, overheard the following conversation among two of her product line department heads, Bob, manager of Pianos and Keyboards, and Fran, manager of Horns and Stringed Instruments.

Fran: "This budgeting process is consuming an inordinate amount of time. Each time I prepare a budget and send it to the controller's office, it comes back for revision. This is the third time I have had to reallocate funds for my budget requests.

Bob: "I know what you mean. And because we are evaluated on our ability to stay in budget, it is critical to have a cushion in case the economy turns south and sales of musical instruments do not meet projections."

What comments should the controller make to these two department heads about the benefits and the importance of the budgeting process?

LO4 LO5 **BRIEF EXERCISE 23.6**
Elements of the Budget

Match each budget in column A with the corresponding budget(s) in column B that represent **key** elements in its construction:

Column A	Column B
1. Budgeted income statement	**a.** Direct materials budget
2. Budgeted balance sheet	**b.** Cost of goods sold budget
3. Cash flow budget	**c.** Production budget
4. Cost of goods sold budget	**d.** Payables budget
5. Production budget	**e.** Sales budget
	f. Budgeted income statement

LO6 **BRIEF EXERCISE 23.7**
Flexible Budgets

Falstags Brewery has estimated \$63,375, \$68,625, and \$73,875 budgeted costs for the manufacture of 3,500, 4,500, and 5,500 gallons of beer, respectively, next quarter.

What are the variable and fixed manufacturing costs in the flexible budget for Falstags Brewery?

LO4 LO5 **BRIEF EXERCISE 23.8**
Operating Expense Budget

Last month, Widner Corporation generated sales of \$800,000 and incurred selling and administrative expenses of \$320,000, half of which were variable. This month, the company estimates that it will generate sales of \$900,000. Management does not anticipate any changes in unit variable costs. However, it does expect fixed selling and administrative costs to increase by \$5,000.

Compute Widner's total selling and administrative expense budget for the upcoming month.

LO2 LO3 **BRIEF EXERCISE 23.9**
Costs of Budgeting Systems

Many managers complain about the budgeting process. They claim it takes too long, requires too much management time, encourages managers to "pad the budget" because of uncertainties, and creates unnecessary tension among managers. As a result of these charges, some managers and business leaders have called for an abandonment of traditional budgeting practices. However, regardless of budgeting's failures, it continues to be widely used across all types of businesses and not-for-profit enterprises. One reason for the continued use of budgeting is the belief that a competent management team can plan for, manage, and control in large measure the relevant variables that dominate the life of a business. Managers must grapple with uncertainties regardless of whether or not they have a budget.

Do you think that managers' complaints about the budgeting process are realistic? Do these complaints create costs for organizations? If so, why do organizations continue to use budgets?

LO6 **BRIEF EXERCISE 23.10**

Evaluating Managers with Flexible Budgets

Harry Blackmun, manager of the Dry Goods Department at Goodright's Grocery, has a budget of $6,000 per month for the current year. This budget includes the allocation of $500 of storewide common costs based on the square feet occupied by Dry Goods. Recently, Dry Goods expanded its total store space to include household items that had not previously been included in the store. During the current month, Mr. Blackmun was over budget by $700. The store manager was upset with the manager of Dry Goods and asked for an explanation.

What could be causing the budget overage? What budget tool could Goodright's use to better evaluate its department managers?

Exercises

connect ACCOUNTING

LO4 LO5 **EXERCISE 23.1**

Budgeting Purchases and Cash Payments

The following information is from the manufacturing budget and the budgeted financial statements of Fabor Fabrication:

Direct materials inventory, Jan. 1	$ 68,000
Direct materials inventory, Dec. 31	80,000
Direct materials budgeted for use during the year	255,000
Accounts payable to suppliers of materials, Jan. 1	50,000
Accounts payable to suppliers of materials, Dec. 31	79,000

Compute the budgeted amounts for:

a. Purchases of direct materials during the year.

b. Cash payments during the year to suppliers of materials.

LO4 LO5 **EXERCISE 23.2**

Budgeting Labor Costs

Deep Valley Foods manufactures a product that is first smoked and then packed for shipment to customers. During a normal month the product's direct labor cost per pound is budgeted using the following information:

	Direct Labor Hours (per pound)	Budgeted Direct Labor Cost (per hour)
Process:		
Smoking	.04	$10.00
Packing	.01	8.00

The budget for March calls for the production of 500,000 pounds of product. However, March's direct labor costs for smoking are expected to be 5 percent above normal due to anticipated scheduling inefficiencies. Yet direct labor costs in the packing room are expected to be 3 percent below normal because of changes in equipment layout.

Prepare a budget for direct labor costs in March using three column headings: Total, Smoking, and Packing.

LO4 LO5

EXERCISE 23.3
Production Budgets

Mercury Bag Company produces cases of grocery bags. The managers at Mercury are trying to develop budgets for the upcoming quarter. The following data have been gathered:

Projected sales in units	1,200 cases
Selling price per case	$240
Inventory at the beginning of the quarter	150 cases
Target inventory at the end of the quarter	100 cases
Direct labor hours needed to produce one case	2 hours
Direct labor wages	$10 per hour
Direct materials cost per case	$8
Variable manufacturing overhead cost per case	$6
Fixed overhead costs for the upcoming quarter	$220,000

a. Using the above information, develop Mercury's sales forecast in dollars and production schedule in units.

b. What is Mercury's budgeted variable manufacturing cost per case?

c. Prepare Mercury's manufacturing cost budget.

d. What is the projected ending value of the Inventory account?

LO4 LO5

EXERCISE 23.4
Production and Direct Materials Budget

Lock Tight, Inc., produces outside doors for installation on homes. The following information was gathered to prepare budgets for the upcoming year beginning January 1:

Sales forecast in units	6,500 doors
Finished goods inventory, Jan. 1	720 doors
Target finished goods inventory, Dec. 31	680 doors
Raw materials inventory—steel, Jan. 1	40,000 pounds
Target inventory—steel, Dec. 31	80,000 pounds
Raw materials inventory—glass, Jan. 1	6,000 square feet
Target inventory—glass, Dec. 31	4,000 square feet
Budgeted purchase price—steel	$4 per pound
Budgeted purchase price—glass	$2 per square foot

The manufacture of each door requires 20 pounds of steel and 6 square feet of glass.

a. Prepare the production schedule in units for Lock Tight.

b. Using the production schedule, develop the direct materials purchase budgets for steel and glass.

c. Why might Lock Tight's target level of steel inventory be higher than last year's ending balance and its target level of glass inventory be lower than last year's ending balance?

LO4 LO5

EXERCISE 23.5
Budgeting for Prepayments

Springfield Company's master budget includes estimated costs and expenses of $325,000 for its third quarter of operations. Of this amount, $300,000 is expected to be financed with current payables. Depreciation expense for the quarter is budgeted at $20,000. Springfield's prepayments balance at the end of the third quarter is expected to be twice that of its prepayments balance at the beginning of the quarter. The company estimates it will prepay expenses totaling $8,000 in the third quarter. What is Springfield's budgeted prepayments balance at the end of the third quarter?

LO4 LO5

EXERCISE 23.6
Budgeting for Interest Expense

On February 1, 2011, Willmar Corporation borrowed $100,000 from its bank by signing a 12 percent, 15-year note payable. The note calls for 180 monthly payments of $1,200. Each payment includes an interest and a principal component.

a. Compute the interest expense in February.

b. Compute the portion of Willmar's March 31, 2011, $1,200 payment that will be applied to the principal of the note.

c. Compute the carrying value of the note on April 30, 2011 (round to the nearest dollar).

LO6 **EXERCISE 23.7**

Preparing a Flexible Overhead Budget

Razmon's Jewelers has accumulated the following budgeted overhead information (dollar amounts may include both fixed and variable costs):

	Direct Labor Hours	
	1,000 hours	**2,000 hours**
Maintenance	$10,000	$16,000
Depreciation	5,000	5,000
Supervision	15,000	15,000
Indirect supplies	1,400	2,800
Utilities	750	1,500
Other	8,100	8,200

Use this information to create the overhead budget for 1,500 direct labor employee hours.

LO4 LO5 **EXERCISE 23.8**

Budgeting Cash Receipts

Sales on account for the first two months of the current year are budgeted as follows:

Jan.	$700,000
Feb.	750,000

All sales are made on terms of 2/10, n/30 (2% discount if paid in 10 days, full amount by 30 days); collections on accounts receivable are typically made as follows:

Collections within the month of sale:	
Within discount period	60%
After discount period	15
Collections within the month following sale:	
Within discount period	15
After discount period	7
Returns, allowances, and uncollectibles	3
Total	100%

Compute the estimated cash collections on accounts receivable for the month of *February.*

LO4 LO5 **EXERCISE 23.9**

Budgeting an Ending Cash Balance

On March 1 of the current year, Spicer Corporation compiled information to prepare a cash budget for March, April, and May. All of the company's sales are made on account. The following information has been provided by Spicer's management:

Month	**Credit Sales**
Jan.	$300,000 (actual)
Feb.	400,000 (actual)
Mar.	600,000 (estimated)
Apr.	700,000 (estimated)
May	800,000 (estimated)

The company's collection activity on credit sales historically has been as follows:

Collections in the month of the sale	50%
Collections one month after the sale	30
Collections two months after the sale	15
Uncollectible accounts	5

Spicer's total cash expenditures for March, April, and May have been estimated at $1,200,000 (an average of $400,000 per month). Its cash balance on March 1 of the current year is $500,000. No financing or investing activities are anticipated during the second quarter.

Compute Spicer's budgeted cash balance at the ends of March, April, and May.

LO6 **EXERCISE 23.10** Preparing a Flexible Budget

Outdoor Outfitters has created a flexible budget for the 70,000-unit and the 80,000-unit levels of activity as shown below.

	70,000 Units	80,000 Units	90,000 Units
Sales	$1,400,000	$1,600,000	$
Cost of goods sold	840,000	960,000	
Gross profit on sales	$ 560,000	$ 640,000	$
Operating expenses ($90,000 fixed)	370,000	410,000	
Operating income	$ 190,000	$ 230,000	$
Income taxes (30% of operating income)	57,000	69,000	
Net income	$ 133,000	$ 161,000	$

Complete Outdoor Outfitters's flexible budget at the 90,000-unit level of activity. Assume that the cost of goods sold and variable operating expenses vary directly with sales and that income taxes remain at 30 percent of operating income.

LO6 **EXERCISE 23.11** More on Flexible Budgeting

The cost accountant for Upload Games Company prepared the following monthly performance report relating to the Packaging Department:

	Budgeted Production (10,000 units)	Actual Production (11,000 units)	Variances	
			Favorable	Unfavorable
Direct materials used	$310,000	$320,000		$10,000
Direct labor	110,000	115,000		5,000
Variable manufacturing overhead	20,000	21,500		1,500
Fixed manufacturing overhead	150,000	149,200	$800	

Prepare a revised performance report in which the variances are computed by comparing the actual costs incurred with estimated costs *using a flexible budget* for 11,000 units of production.

LO2 **EXERCISE 23.12** Budget Estimates

LO3

William George is the marketing manager at Crunchy Cookie Company. Each quarter, he is responsible for submitting a sales forecast to be used in the formulation of the company's master budget. George consistently understates the sales forecast because, as he puts it, "I am reprimanded if actual sales are less than I've projected, and I look like a hero if actual sales exceed my projections."

a. What would you do if you were the marketing manager at Crunchy Cookie Company? Would you also understate sales projections? Defend your answer.

b. What measures might be taken by the company to discourage the manipulation of sales forecasts?

LO4 **EXERCISE 23.13** Budgeting Manufacturing Overhead

LO5

Wells Enterprises manufactures a component that is processed successively by Department I and Department II. Manufacturing overhead is applied to units produced at the following budget costs:

	Manufacturing Overhead per Unit		
	Fixed	Variable	Total
Department I	$15	$8	$20
Department II	12	6	15

These budgeted overhead costs per unit are based on the normal volume of production of 5,000 units per month. In January, variable manufacturing overhead in Department II is expected to be 25 percent above budget because of major scheduled repairs to equipment. The company plans to produce 8,000 units during January.

Prepare a budget for manufacturing overhead costs in January using three column headings: Total, Department I, and Department II.

LO2 LO3 **EXERCISE 23.14**
Establishing Budget Amounts

Budgets are essential for the successful operation of an organization. Finding the resources to implement budget goals requires extensive use of human resources. How managers perceive their roles in the budgeting process is important to the successful and effective use of the budget as a tool for planning, communicating, and controlling operations.

Discuss the implications for planning and control when a company's management employs an imposed budgetary approach where managers do not actively participate in setting the budget. Contrast this approach with a participative budgetary approach. How does communication work differently when using an imposed versus a participative budgetary approach?

LO2 LO3 **EXERCISE 23.15**
Home Depot's Budget Goals

Locate the table titled "10-Year Summary of Financial and Operating Results" in the **Home Depot** 2009 Financial Information in Appendix A. Assume **Home Depot** identifies each store as a profit center. Identify the categories of information in the "Store Data" section of the table that would provide useful goals to be included in each store's annual budget. Explain why these categories would be useful and how each associated storewide goal could be used for performance evaluation of a store.

Problem Set A

LO4 LO5 **PROBLEM 23.1A**
Budgeting Production, Inventories, and Cost of Sales

Renfrow International manufactures and sells a single product. In preparing its master budget for the current quarter, the company's controller has assembled the following information:

	Units	Dollars
Sales (budgeted)	150,000	$7,500,000
Finished goods inventory, beginning of quarter	38,000	975,000
Finished goods inventory, end of quarter	28,000	?
Cost of finished goods manufactured (assume a budgeted manufacturing cost of $28 per unit)	?	?

Renfrow International used the average cost method of pricing its inventory of finished goods.

Instructions

Compute the following budgeted quantities or dollar amounts:

a. Planned production of finished goods (in units).

b. Cost of finished goods manufactured.

c. Ending finished goods inventory. (Remember that in using the average cost method you must first compute the average cost of units available for sale.)

d. Cost of goods sold.

LO4 LO5 **PROBLEM 23.2A**
Short Budgeting Problem

Harmony Corporation manufactures and sells a single product. In preparing the budget for the first quarter, the company's cost accountant has assembled the following information:

	Units	Dollars
Sales (budgeted)	150,000	$12,150,000
Finished goods inventory, Jan. 1 (actual)	30,000	1,080,000
Finished goods inventory, Mar. 31 (budgeted)	20,000	?
Cost of finished goods manufactured (budgeted manufacturing cost is $39 per unit)	?	?

The company uses the first-in, first-out method of pricing its inventory of finished goods.

Instructions

Compute the following budgeted quantities or dollar amounts:

a. Planned production of finished goods (in units).

b. Cost of finished goods manufactured.

c. Finished goods inventory, March 31. (Remember to use the first-in, first-out method in pricing the inventory.)

d. Cost of goods sold.

LO4 LO5

PROBLEM 23.3A
Budgeting for Cash

Barnum Distributors wants a projection of cash receipts and cash payments for the month of November. On November 28, a note will be payable in the amount of $98,500, including interest. The cash balance on November 1 is $29,600. Accounts payable to merchandise creditors at the end of October were $217,000.

The company's experience indicates that 70 percent of sales will be collected during the month of sale, 20 percent in the month following the sale, and 7 percent in the second month following the sale; 3 percent will be uncollectible. The company sells various products at an average price of $11 per unit. Selected sales figures are as follows:

	Units
Sept.—actual	40,000
Oct.—actual	60,000
Nov.—estimated	80,000
Dec.—estimated	50,000
Total estimated for the current year	800,000

Because purchases are payable within 15 days, approximately 50 percent of the purchases in a given month are paid in the following month. The average cost of units purchased is $7 per unit. Inventories at the end of each month are maintained at a level of 2,000 units plus 10 percent of the number of units that will be sold in the following month. The inventory on October 1 amounted to 8,000 units.

Budgeted operating expenses for November are $220,000. Of this amount, $90,000 is considered fixed (including depreciation of $35,000). All operating expenses, other than depreciation, are paid in the month in which they are incurred.

The company expects to sell fully depreciated equipment in November for $8,400 cash.

Instructions

Prepare a cash budget for the month of November, supported by schedules of cash collections on accounts receivable and cash payments for purchases of merchandise.

LO1 LO2 LO4 LO5

PROBLEM 23.4A
Estimating Borrowing Requirements

Former Corporation sells office supplies to government agencies. At the beginning of the current quarter, the company reports the following selected account balances:

Cash	$ 10,000
Accounts receivable	210,000
Current payables	88,000

Former's management has made the following budget estimates regarding operations for the current quarter:

Sales (estimated)	$500,000
Total costs and expenses (estimated)	400,000
Debt service payment (estimated)	145,000
Tax liability payment (estimated)	45,000

Of Former's total costs and expenses, $20,000 is quarterly depreciation expense, and $20,000 represents the expiration of prepayments. The remaining $360,000 is to be financed with current payables. The company's ending prepayments balance is expected to be the same as its beginning prepayments balance. Its ending current payables balance is expected to be $22,000 more than its beginning balance.

All of Former's sales are on account. Approximately 65 percent of its sales are collected in the quarter in which they are made. The remaining 35 percent are collected in the following quarter. Because all of the company's sales are made to government agencies, it experiences virtually no uncollectible accounts.

Former's minimum cash balance requirement is $10,000. Should the balance fall below this amount, management negotiates a short-term loan with a local bank. The company's debt ratio (liabilities ÷ assets) is currently 80 percent.

Instructions

a. Compute Former's budgeted cash receipts for the quarter.

b. Compute Former's payments of current payables budgeted for the quarter.

c. Compute Former's cash prepayments budgeted for the quarter.

d. Prepare Former's cash budget for the quarter.

e. Estimate Former's short-term borrowing requirements for the quarter.

f. Discuss problems Former might encounter in obtaining short-term financing.

LO1 LO2 LO4 LO5

PROBLEM 23.5A
Budgeted Income Statement and Cash Budget

Rizzo's has been in business since January of the current year. The company buys frozen pizza crusts and resells them to large supermarket chains in five states. The following information pertains to Rizzo's first four months of operations:

	Purchases	Sales
Jan.	$40,000	$62,000
Feb.	32,000	49,000
Mar.	44,000	65,000
Apr.	24,000	42,000

Rizzo's expects to open several new sales territories in May. In anticipation of increased volume, management forecasts May sales at $72,000. To meet this demand, purchases in May are budgeted at $42,000. The company maintains a gross profit margin of approximately 40 percent.

All of Rizzo's sales are on account. Due to strict credit policies, the company has no bad debt expense. The following collection performance is anticipated for the remainder of the year:

Percent collected in month of sale	30%
Percent collected in month following sale	60
Percent collected in the second month following sale	10

Rizzo's normally pays for 80 percent of its purchases in the month that the purchases are made. The remaining amount is paid in the following month. The company's fixed selling and administrative expenses average $12,000 per month. Of this amount, $4,000 is depreciation expense. Variable selling and administrative expenses are budgeted at 5 percent of sales. The company pays all of its selling and administrative expenses in the month that they are incurred.

Rizzo's debt service is $5,000 per month. Of this amount, approximately $4,500 represents interest expense, and $500 is payment on the principal. The company's tax rate is approximately 35 percent. Quarterly tax payments are made at the end of March, June, September, and December.

Instructions

a. Prepare Rizzo's budgeted income statement for May.

b. Prepare Rizzo's cash budget for May. Assume that the company's cash balance on May 1 is $25,000.

c. Explain why Rizzo's budgeted cash flow in May differs from its budgeted net income.

LO1 LO2 LO4 LO5

PROBLEM 23.6A
Preparing a Cash Budget

eXcel

Jake Marley, owner of Marley Wholesale, is negotiating with the bank for a $200,000, 90-day, 12 percent loan effective July 1 of the current year. If the bank grants the loan, the proceeds will be $194,000, which Marley intends to use on July 1 as follows: pay accounts payable, $150,000; purchase equipment, $16,000; add to bank balance, $28,000.

The current working capital position of Marley Wholesale, according to financial statements as of June 30, is as follows:

Cash in bank	$ 20,000
Receivables (net of allowance for doubtful accounts)	160,000
Merchandise inventory	90,000
Total current assets	$270,000
Accounts payable (including accrued operating expenses)	150,000
Working capital	$120,000

The bank loan officer asks Marley to prepare a forecast of his cash receipts and cash payments for the next three months to demonstrate that the loan can be repaid at the end of September.

Marley has made the following estimates, which are to be used in preparing a three-month cash budget: Sales (all on account) for July, $300,000; August, $360,000; September, $270,000; and October, $200,000. Past experience indicates that 80 percent of the receivables generated in any month will be collected in the month following the sale, 19 percent will be collected in the second month following the sale, and 1 percent will prove uncollectible. Marley expects to collect $120,000 of the June 30 receivables in July and the remaining $40,000 in August.

Cost of goods sold consistently has averaged about 65 percent of sales. Operating expenses are budgeted at $36,000 per month plus 8 percent of sales. With the exception of $4,400 per month depreciation expense, all operating expenses and purchases are on account and are paid in the month following their incurrence.

Merchandise inventory at the end of each month should be sufficient to cover the following month's sales.

Instructions

a. Prepare a monthly cash budget showing estimated cash receipts and cash payments for July, August, and September, and the cash balance at the end of each month. Supporting schedules should be prepared for estimated collections on receivables, estimated merchandise purchases, and estimated payments for operating expenses and of accounts payable for merchandise purchases.

b. On the basis of this cash forecast, write a brief report to Marley explaining whether he will be able to repay the $200,000 bank loan at the end of September.

LO2 LO4 through LO6

PROBLEM 23.7A
Preparing and Using a Flexible Budget

Snells is a retail department store. The following cost-volume relationships were used in developing a flexible budget for the company for the current year:

	Yearly Fixed Expenses	Variable Expenses per Sales Dollar
Cost of merchandise sold		$0.600
Selling and promotion expense	$ 210,000	0.082
Building occupancy expense	186,000	0.022
Buying expense	150,000	0.041
Delivery expense	111,000	0.008
Credit and collection expense	72,000	0.002
Administrative expense	531,000	0.003
Totals	$1,260,000	$0.758

Management expected to attain a sales level of $12 million during the current year. At the end of the year, the actual results achieved by the company were as follows:

Net sales	$10,500,000
Cost of goods sold	6,180,000
Selling and promotion expense	1,020,000
Building occupancy expense	420,000
Buying expense	594,000
Delivery expense	183,000
Credit and collection expense	90,000
Administrative expense	564,000

Instructions

a. Prepare a schedule comparing the actual results with flexible budget amounts developed for the actual sales volume of $10,500,000. Organize your schedule as a partial multiple-step income statement, ending with operating income. Include separate columns for (1) flexible budget amounts, (2) actual amounts, and (3) any amount over (under) budget. Use the cost-volume relationships given in the problem to compute the flexible budget amounts.

b. Write a statement evaluating the company's performance in relation to the plan reflected in the flexible budget.

LO2 **PROBLEM 23.8A**
Flexible Budgeting
LO4 eXcel
through
LO6

Braemar Saddlery uses department budgets and performance reports in planning and controlling its manufacturing operations. The following annual performance report for the custom saddle production department was presented to the president of the company:

	Budgeted Costs for 5,000 Units		Actual Costs Incurred	Over (Under) Budget
	Per Unit	Total		
Variable manufacturing costs:				
Direct materials	$ 30.00	$150,000	$171,000	$21,000
Direct labor	48.00	240,000	261,500	21,500
Indirect labor	15.00	75,000	95,500	20,500
Indirect materials, supplies, etc.	9.00	45,000	48,400	3,400
Total variable manufacturing costs	$102.00	$510,000	$576,400	$66,400
Fixed manufacturing costs:				
Lease rental	$ 9.00	$ 45,000	$ 45,000	–0–
Salaries of foremen	24.00	120,000	125,000	$ 5,000
Depreciation and other	15.00	75,000	78,600	3,600
Total fixed manufacturing costs	$ 48.00	$240,000	$248,600	$ 8,600
Total manufacturing costs	$150.00	$750,000	$825,000	$75,000

Although a production volume of 5,000 saddles was originally budgeted for the year, the actual volume of production achieved for the year was *6,000* saddles. Direct materials and direct labor are charged to production at actual cost. Factory overhead is applied to production at the predetermined rate of 150 percent of the actual direct labor cost.

After a quick glance at the performance report showing an unfavorable manufacturing cost variance of $75,000, the president said to the accountant: "Fix this thing so it makes sense. It looks as though our production people really blew the budget. Remember that we exceeded our budgeted production schedule by a significant margin. I want this performance report to show a better picture of our ability to control costs."

Instructions

a. Prepare a revised performance report for the year on a flexible budget basis. Use the same format as the production report above, but revise the budgeted cost figures to reflect the actual production level of *6,000* saddles.

b. Briefly comment on Braemar's ability to control its variable manufacturing costs.

c. What is the amount of over- or underapplied manufacturing overhead for the year?

Problem Set B

LO4 **PROBLEM 23.1B**
LO5 Budgeting Production, Inventories, and Cost of Sales

Frowren Domestic manufactures and sells a single product. In preparing its master budget for the current quarter, the company's controller has assembled the following information:

	Units	Dollars
Sales (budgeted)	200,000	$8,000,000
Finished goods inventory, beginning of quarter	30,000	750,000
Finished goods inventory, end of quarter	25,000	?
Cost of finished goods manufactured (assume a budgeted manufacturing cost of $26 per unit)	?	?

Frowren Domestic used the average cost method of pricing its inventory of finished goods.

Instructions

Compute the following budgeted quantities or dollar amounts:

a. Planned production of finished goods (in units).

b. Cost of finished goods manufactured.

c. Ending finished goods inventory. (Remember that in using the average cost method you first must compute the average cost of units available for sale.)

d. Cost of goods sold.

LO4 LO5 **PROBLEM 23.2B**
Short Budgeting Problem

Melody Corporation manufactures and sells a single product. In preparing the budget for the first quarter, the company's cost accountant has assembled the following information:

	Units	Dollars
Sales (budgeted)	200,000	$15,000,000
Finished goods inventory, Jan. 1 (actual)	40,000	1,440,000
Finished goods inventory, Mar. 31 (budgeted)	30,000	?
Cost of finished goods manufactured (budgeted manufacturing cost is $38 per unit)	?	?

The company uses the first-in, first-out method of pricing its inventory of finished goods.

Instructions

Compute the following budgeted quantities or dollar amounts:

a. Planned production of finished goods (in units).

b. Cost of finished goods manufactured.

c. Finished goods inventory, March 31. (Remember to use the first-in, first-out method in pricing the inventory.)

d. Cost of goods sold.

LO4 LO5 **PROBLEM 23.3B**
Budgeting for Cash

Barley, Inc., wants a projection of cash receipts and cash payments for the month of November. On November 28, a note will be payable in the amount of $102,250, including interest. The cash balance on November 1 is $37,200. Accounts payable to merchandise creditors at the end of October were $206,000.

The company's experience indicates that 70 percent of sales will be collected during the month of sale, 25 percent in the month following the sale, and 3 percent in the second month following the sale; 2 percent will be uncollectible. The company sells various products at an average price of $10 per unit. Selected sales figures are as follows:

	Units
Sept.—actual	50,000
Oct.—actual	70,000
Nov.—estimated	90,000
Dec.—estimated	60,000
Total estimated for the current year	900,000

Because purchases are payable within 15 days, approximately 50 percent of the purchases in a given month are paid in the following month. The average cost of units purchased is $6 per unit. Inventories at the end of each month are maintained at a level of 2,000 units plus 10 percent of the number of units that will be sold in the following month. The inventory on October 1 amounted to 9,000 units.

Budgeted operating expenses for November are $225,000. Of this amount, $100,000 is considered fixed (including depreciation of $40,000). All operating expenses, other than depreciation, are paid in the month in which they are incurred.

The company expects to sell fully depreciated equipment in November for $9,000 cash.

Instructions

Prepare a cash budget for the month of November, supported by schedules of cash collections on accounts receivable and cash payments for purchases of merchandise.

LO1 LO2 LO4 LO5

PROBLEM 23.4B
Estimating Borrowing Requirements

Peter Corporation sells its products to a single customer. At the beginning of the current quarter, the company reports the following selected account balances:

Cash	$ 10,000
Accounts receivable	250,000
Current payables	90,000

Peter's management has made the following budget estimates regarding operations for the current quarter:

Sales (estimated)	$700,000
Total costs and expenses (estimated)	500,000
Debt service payment (estimated)	260,000
Tax liability payment (estimated)	50,000

Of Peter's total costs and expenses, $40,000 is quarterly depreciation expense, and $18,000 represents the expiration of prepayments. The remaining $442,000 is to be financed with current payables. The company's ending prepayments balance is expected to be the same as its beginning prepayments balance. Its ending current payables balance is expected to be $15,000 more than its beginning balance.

All of Peter's sales are on account. Approximately 70 percent of its sales are collected in the quarter in which they are made. The remaining 30 percent are collected in the following quarter. Because all of the company's sales are made to a single customer, it experiences virtually no uncollectible accounts.

Peter's minimum cash balance requirement is $10,000. Should the balance fall below this amount, management negotiates a short-term loan with a local bank. The company's debt ratio (liabilities ÷ assets) is currently 90 percent.

Instructions

a. Compute Peter's budgeted cash receipts for the quarter.

b. Compute Peter's payments of current payables budgeted for the quarter.

c. Compute Peter's cash prepayments budgeted for the quarter.

d. Prepare Peter's cash budget for the quarter.

e. Estimate Peter's short-term borrowing requirements for the quarter.

f. Discuss problems Peter might encounter in obtaining short-term financing.

LO1 LO2 LO4 LO5

PROBLEM 23.5B
Budgeted Income Statement and Cash Budget

Synder's has been in business since January of the current year. The company buys fresh pasta and resells it to large supermarket chains in five states. The following information pertains to Synder's first four months of operations:

	Purchases	Sales
Jan.	$50,000	$80,000
Feb.	40,000	60,000
Mar.	55,000	90,000
Apr.	25,000	40,000

Synder's expects to open several new sales territories in May. In anticipation of increased volume, management forecasts May sales at $100,000. To meet this demand, purchases in May are budgeted at $60,000. The company maintains a gross profit margin of approximately 40 percent.

All of Synder's sales are on account. Due to strict credit policies, the company has no bad debt expense. The following collection performance is anticipated for the remainder of the year:

Percent collected in month of sale	40%
Percent collected in month following sale	50
Percent collected in the second month following sale	10

Synder's normally pays for 75 percent of its purchases in the month that the purchases are made. The remaining amount is paid in the following month. The company's fixed selling and administrative expenses average $10,000 per month. Of this amount, $3,000 is depreciation expense. Variable selling and administrative expenses are budgeted at 5 percent of sales. The company pays all of its selling and administrative expenses in the month that they are incurred.

Synder's debt service is $4,000 per month. Of this amount, approximately $3,000 represents interest expense, and $1,000 is payment on the principal. The company's tax rate is approximately 25 percent. Quarterly tax payments are made at the end of March, June, September, and December.

Instructions

a. Prepare Synder's budgeted income statement for May.

b. Prepare Synder's cash budget for May. Assume that the company's cash balance on May 1 is $30,000.

c. What are the primary benefits that Synder's will gain from preparing and using a budget?

LO1 LO2 LO4 LO5

PROBLEM 23.6B Preparing a Cash Budget

Ann Hoffman, owner of Hoffman Industries, is negotiating with the bank for a $250,000, 90-day, 15 percent loan effective July 1 of the current year. If the bank grants the loan, the net proceeds will be $240,000, which Hoffman intends to use on July 1 as follows: pay accounts payable, $200,000; purchase equipment, $25,000; and add to bank balance, $15,000.

The current working capital position of Hoffman Industries, according to financial statements as of June 30, is as follows:

Cash in bank	$ 18,000
Receivables (net of allowance for doubtful accounts)	200,000
Merchandise inventory	80,000
Total current assets	$298,000
Accounts payable (including accrued operating expenses)	160,000
Working capital	$138,000

The bank loan officer asks Hoffman to prepare a forecast of her cash receipts and cash payments for the next three months to demonstrate that the loan can be repaid at the end of September.

Hoffman has made the following estimates, which are to be used in preparing a three-month cash budget: Sales (all on account) for July, $340,000; August, $360,000; September, $300,000; and October, $220,000. Past experience indicates that 75 percent of the receivables generated in any month will be collected in the month following the sale, 24 percent will be collected in the second month following the sale, and 1 percent will prove uncollectible. Hoffman expects to collect $160,000 of the June 30 receivables in July and the remaining $40,000 in August.

Cost of goods sold consistently has averaged about 65 percent of sales. Operating expenses are budgeted at $40,000 per month plus 10 percent of sales. With the exception of $5,000 per month depreciation expense, all operating expenses and purchases are on account and are paid in the month following their incurrence.

Merchandise inventory at the end of each month should be sufficient to cover the following month's sales.

Instructions

a. Ann Hoffman has contacted you to prepare a cash budget showing estimated cash receipts and cash payments for July, August, and September. First, you must prepare the following schedules:

1. Estimated cash collections on receivables.
2. Estimated merchandise purchases.
3. Estimated cash payments for operating expenses.
4. Estimated cash payments on accounts payable (including operating expenses).

b. Once the schedules have been prepared, complete the cash budgets for July, August, and September showing the cash balance at the end of each month.

LO2 LO4 through LO6

PROBLEM 23.7B Preparing and Using a Flexible Budget

Eight Flags is a retail department store. The following cost-volume relationships were used in developing a flexible budget for the company for the current year:

	Yearly Fixed Expenses	Variable Expenses per Sales Dollar
Cost of merchandise sold		$0.65
Selling and promotion expense	$160,000	0.09
Building occupancy expense	120,000	0.02
Buying expense	100,000	0.05
Delivery expense	110,000	0.01
Credit and collection expense	60,000	0.01
Administrative expense	300,000	0.02
Totals	$850,000	$0.85

Management expected to attain a sales level of $20 million during the current year. At the end of the year, the actual results achieved by the company were as follows:

Net sales	$18,000,000
Cost of goods sold	11,160,000
Selling and promotion expense	800,000
Building occupancy expense	450,000
Buying expense	720,000
Delivery expense	200,000
Credit and collection expense	100,000
Administrative expense	360,000

Instructions

a. Prepare a schedule comparing the actual results with flexible budget amounts developed for the actual sales volume of $18,000,000. Organize your schedule as a partial multiple-step income statement, ending with operating income. Include separate columns for (**1**) flexible budget amounts, (**2**) actual amounts, and (**3**) any amount over (under) budget. Use the cost-volume relationships given in the problem to compute the flexible budget amounts.

b. Write a statement evaluating the company's performance in relation to the plan reflected in the flexible budget.

c. Why is a flexible budget useful in evaluating the performance of the Eight Flags store?

d. Do fixed costs and variable costs always change in a flexible budget?

LO2 LO4 through LO6

PROBLEM 23.8B Flexible Budgeting

XL Industries uses department budgets and performance reports in planning and controlling its manufacturing operations. The following annual performance report for the widget production department was presented to the president of the company:

	Budgeted Costs for 4,000 Units		Actual Costs Incurred	Over (Under) Budget
	Per Unit	Total		
Variable manufacturing costs:				
Direct materials	$ 25.00	$100,000	$120,000	$20,000
Direct labor	50.00	200,000	210,000	10,000
Indirect labor	12.00	48,000	50,000	2,000
Indirect materials, supplies, etc.	10.00	40,000	43,000	3,000
Total variable manufacturing costs	$ 97.00	$388,000	$423,000	$35,000
Fixed manufacturing costs:				
Lease rental	$ 10.00	$ 40,000	$ 40,000	–0–
Salaries of foremen	25.00	100,000	104,000	$ 4,000
Depreciation and other	18.00	72,000	75,000	3,000
Total fixed manufacturing costs	$ 53.00	$212,000	$219,000	$ 7,000
Total manufacturing costs	$150.00	$600,000	$642,000	$42,000

Although a production volume of 4,000 widgets was originally budgeted for the year, the actual volume of production achieved for the year was *5,000* widgets. Direct materials and direct labor are charged to production at actual costs. Factory overhead is applied to production at the predetermined rate of 150 percent of the actual direct labor cost.

After a quick glance at the performance report showing an unfavorable manufacturing cost variance of $42,000, the president said to the accountant: "Fix this thing so it makes sense. It looks as though our production people really blew the budget. Remember that we exceeded our budgeted production schedule by a significant margin. I want this performance report to show a better picture of our ability to control costs."

Instructions

a. Prepare a revised performance report for the year on a flexible budget basis. Use the same format as the production report above, but revise the budgeted cost figures to reflect the actual production level of *5,000* widgets.

b. Briefly comment on XL's ability to control its variable manufacturing costs.

c. What is the amount of over- or underapplied manufacturing overhead for the year?

Critical Thinking Cases

LO2 LO5 **CASE 23.1**

Budgeting in a Nutshell

The purpose of this problem is to demonstrate some of the interrelationships in the budgeting process. Shown below is a very simple balance sheet at January 1, along with a simple budgeted income statement for the month. (Assume dollar amounts are stated in thousands; you also may state dollar amounts in this manner.)

NUTSHELL BALANCE SHEET JANUARY 1

Assets		Liabilities & Equity	
Cash	$ 40	Accounts payable	$ 30
Accounts receivable	120	Owners' equity	180
Inventory	50		
Total	$210	Total	$210

NUTSHELL BUDGETED INCOME STATEMENT FOR JANUARY

Sales	$100
Cost of goods sold	60
Gross profit	$ 40
Expenses	25
Net income	$ 15

As Nutshell has no plant assets, there is no depreciation expense. Prepare a cash budget for January and a budgeted balance sheet as of January 31.

These budgets are to reflect *your own assumptions* as to the amounts of cash and credit sales, collections of receivables, purchases of inventory, and payments to suppliers. We require only that the cash balance be *$50* at January 31, that receivables and inventory *change* from the January 1 levels, and that the company engage in *no* "financing" or "investing" activities (as these terms are used in a statement of cash flows).

Clearly state your assumptions as part of your solution, and be prepared to explain in class how they result in the amounts shown in your budgets.

LO1 through LO3 **CASE 23.2**

An Ethical Dilemma

Beta Computers is experiencing financial difficulties attributed to declining sales of its mainframe computer systems. Several years ago, the company obtained a large loan from Midland State Bank. The covenants of the loan agreement strictly state that if Beta is unable to maintain a current ratio of 3:1, a quick ratio of 1:1, and a return on assets of 12 percent, the bank will exercise its right to liquidate the company's assets in settlement of the loan. To monitor Beta's performance, the bank demands quarterly financial statements that have been reviewed by an independent CPA.

Nick Price, Beta's CEO, has just reviewed the company's master budget projections for the first two quarters of the current year. What he has learned is disturbing. If sales trends continue, it appears that Beta will be in violation of its loan covenants by the end of the second quarter. If these projections are correct, the bank might foreclose on the company's assets. As a consequence, Beta's 750 employees will join the ranks of the unemployed.

In February of the current year, Rembrant International contacted Beta to inquire about purchasing a custom-configured mainframe computer system. Not only would the sale generate over a million dollars in revenue, it would put Beta back in compliance with its loan covenants. Unfortunately, Rembrant International is an extremely bad credit risk, and the likelihood of collecting on the sale is slim. Nonetheless, Nick Price approved the sale on February 1, which resulted in the recording of a $1.4 million receivable.

On March 31, Edgar Gamm, CPA, arrived at Beta's headquarters. In Gamm's opinion, the $1.4 million receivable from Rembrant International should immediately be written off as uncollectible. Of course, if the account is written off, Beta will be in violation of its loan covenants and the bank will soon foreclose. Gamm told Price that it is his professional duty to prevent any material misstatement of the company's assets.

Price reminded Gamm that if the account is written off, 750 employees will be out of work, and that Gamm's accounting firm probably could not collect its fee for this engagement. Price then showed Gamm Beta's master budget for the third and fourth quarters of the current year. The budget indicated a complete turnaround for the company. Gamm suspected, however, that most of the budget's estimates were overly optimistic.

Instructions

With a group of students answer the following questions:

a. Should Gamm insist that the Rembrant International account be classified as uncollectible? Should the optimistic third and fourth quarter master budget projections influence his decision? What would you do if you were in his position? Defend your actions.

b. If you were the president of Midland State Bank, what would you do if you discovered that the Rembrant International account constituted a large portion of Beta's reported liquid assets and sales activity for the quarter? How would you react if Edgar Gamm's accounting firm had permitted Beta to classify the account as collectible?

LO1 LO2 CASE 23.3 Cash Budgeting

The importance of cash budgets for all types of businesses and individuals cannot be overemphasized. The following six steps to cash flow control are critical.

1. Create a monthly cash flow budget. Determine the amount you need to achieve your business and personal financial goals, including enough to pay taxes and fund your retirement.
2. At the end of each month compare cash infows and outflows to make necessary adjustments to cash spending or saving.
3. Accounting software can help automate the process.
4. Set aside cash each month to pay your taxes on time.
5. Make quarterly contributions to a retirement account.
6. Establish a line of credit with a bank, or investigate other short-term financing sources, well before you think you'll need the extra cash.

Instructions

a. Assume for item number 2 that a business's actual cash flows are not enough to achieve its business goals and some necessary adjustments must be made. Name at least four adjustment procedures that businesses can use to equalize cash flows.

b. Write a short paragraph discussing how cash budgeting can be critical for your ongoing success.

LO2 LO6 INTERNET CASE 23.4 Budgeting Shareware

Medlin Accounting Shareware produces accounting programs that Internet users can download and try for free. Access the **Medlin** Web site at:

www.medlin.com/budget.htm

Investigate the **Medlin** budgeting package.

Instructions

a. What features are provided with the budgeting software?

b. Explain how the features can be used for (**1**) advance warning and assignment of responsibility for corrective action, (**2**) coordination of activities among all departments within the organization, or (**3**) the creation of standards for evaluating performance.

Internet sites are time and date sensitive. It is the purpose of these exercises to have you explore the Internet. You may need to use the Yahoo! search engine http://www.yahoo.com *(or another favorite search engine) to find a company's current Web address.*

LO4 **CASE 23.5**
Budgeting and Internal Controls

Under the Public Company Accounting Oversight Board (PCAOB) procedures, companies are required to disclose "material weaknesses" in their internal controls. A material weakness means a company's deficiencies are so bad that there's more than a remote chance of a material misstatement in its financial reports. An example is when a bank does not regularly check for errors in estimating loan-loss expenses. This type of undetected error, for instance, could be rooted in a formula in a computer spreadsheet that budgets how lending will be affected by interest rate changes. Fannie Mae, the mortgage finance company, reported a $1.3 billion error from its computer models prior to a large accounting scandal. Some auditors are reporting that the material weaknesses they are seeing are the result of flawed checks on formulas used to figure, for example, income tax expense.

Instructions

Consider how errors in formulas, embedded in linked budgeting spreadsheets and used to estimate sales each quarter, can impact the budgeting process.

a. Use Exhibit 23–2 to trace how errors can permeate the various budgets of a company. Explain how an error that causes a material overstatement of budgeted sales will affect other budgets for the organization.

b. Explain how the PCAOB requirements to evaluate internal controls can improve the budgeting process at a company.

Answers to Self-Test Questions

1. a, b, c **2.** b (70,000 units × $10 per unit × 80%) + ($100,000 × 50%) = $610,000
3. d **4.** c **5.** d **6.** c

CHAPTER 24

Standard Cost Systems

© Royalty-Free/Corbis/DAL

Learning Objectives

AFTER STUDYING THIS CHAPTER, YOU SHOULD BE ABLE TO:

LO1 Define standard costs and explain how they assist managers in controlling costs.

LO2 Explain the difference between setting ideal standards and setting reasonably achievable standards.

LO3 Compute direct materials and direct labor variances and explain the meaning of each.

LO4 Compute overhead variances and explain the meaning of each.

LO5 Discuss the causes of specific cost variances.

UNITED STATES NAVY

The U.S. Navy was founded on October 13, 1775, and the Department of the Navy was established on April 30, 1798. Today, the Navy has nearly 300 ships and over 4,000 operational aircraft. You can imagine that the amount of materials and supplies purchased by the Navy in any given year is quite large. To help the Navy and other branches of the armed services with procurement of ships, planes, missiles, rockets, tanks, and supporting equipment and supplies, the Office of Management and Budget operates the Cost Accounting Standards Board.

The five-member Cost Accounting Standards Board (CASB) is an independent, legislatively established board. The board has the exclusive authority to make, promulgate, and amend cost accounting standards and interpretations designed to achieve uniformity and consistency in the cost accounting practices governing the measurement, assignment, and allocation of costs to contracts with the United States. The standards are mandatory for use by all branches of the armed services and by contractors and subcontractors in estimating, accumulating, and reporting costs in connection with pricing and all negotiated prime contract and subcontract procurement with the United States in excess of $500,000. The CASB recommendations include the use of standard costing systems for all government contractors. ■

Hundreds of companies have discovered the importance of cost control as a means of survival in fiercely competitive markets. By implementing an organized, companywide process for controlling costs, a firm can reverse its sinking earnings trend and recover its market position. One important tool companies use to control ongoing operating costs is a standard cost system.

The managers who have decision-making authority over company resources compare their actual results with the standard costs embedded in the budgets. When the actual results and the standard costs are significantly different, managers take corrective action to control the costs that have strayed from the standard.

Standard Cost Systems

A cost accounting system becomes more useful when it includes the *budgeted* or *expected* costs to serve as standards for comparison with the costs actually incurred. These budgeted amounts are called *standard costs* (or *cost standards*). An accounting system that accumulates costs using standard input prices and quantities is a **standard cost system.** Standard costs are used with job order and process cost systems and with activity-based costing.

Learning Objective LO1 Define standard costs and explain how they assist managers in controlling costs.

A **standard cost** is the per-unit cost *expected* to be incurred under normal (but efficient) operating conditions. Standard costs are estimated separately for the materials, direct labor, and overhead relating to each type of product that the company manufactures. Comparison of the actual costs with these cost standards quickly directs management's attention to situations in which actual costs differ from expected levels.

Differences between actual and standard input prices or quantities are called **variances.** A variance is said to be *favorable* when actual input costs or quantities are *less* than standard. When actual input costs or quantities *exceed* the standard, the variance is said to be *unfavorable.*

A standard cost system is illustrated in Exhibit 24–1. The exhibit shows that standard cost systems make use of *both* actual and standard costs. The actual costs are recorded in the Direct Materials, Direct Labor, and Overhead accounts in the manner described in prior chapters. However, the amounts charged to the Work in Process accounts are the *standard costs* for the number of units produced. Any differences between the actual costs incurred and the standard costs charged to the Work in Process accounts are recorded in special *cost variance accounts.*

A separate cost variance account is maintained for each type of cost variance. Thus, the cost accounting system provides managers with detailed information as to the *nature and amount* of the differences between actual and expected (standard) manufacturing costs.

Standard costs and variance accounts assist management in controlling costs by quickly bringing differences in actual and expected costs to management's attention. Otherwise, these cost differences might flow unnoticed into the Finished Goods Inventory and Cost of Goods Sold accounts.

ESTABLISHING AND REVISING STANDARD COSTS

Learning Objective LO2 Explain the difference between setting ideal standards and setting reasonably achievable standards.

Standard costs are established and revised each period during the budgeting process. Standard costs are continually reviewed and periodically revised if significant changes occur in production methods or in the prices paid for materials, labor, and overhead.

What should the expectations of management be as it establishes standard cost targets? This is an important question. Under *ideal* conditions, management would leave no room for any inefficiencies in the production process—there would be no waste, spoilage, fatigue, breakdowns, cost overruns, etc. However, ideal expectations are unrealistic and would result in cost standards impossible to achieve. Hence, management's level of expectation must be something *less than ideal.*

The level of production output plays an important role in determining cost standards. For instance, grossly underutilized production facilities often experience varying degrees of cost inefficiency. Conversely, the stress and demands imposed on production facilities operating at full capacity can cause cost overruns. Thus, as previously stated, standards should correspond to what costs should be under *normal* operating conditions for a particular company. However, costs of idle capacity should not be part of standard product costs.

Exhibit 24–1 A STANDARD COST SYSTEM WITH ACTUAL AND STANDARD QUANTITIES AND COSTS

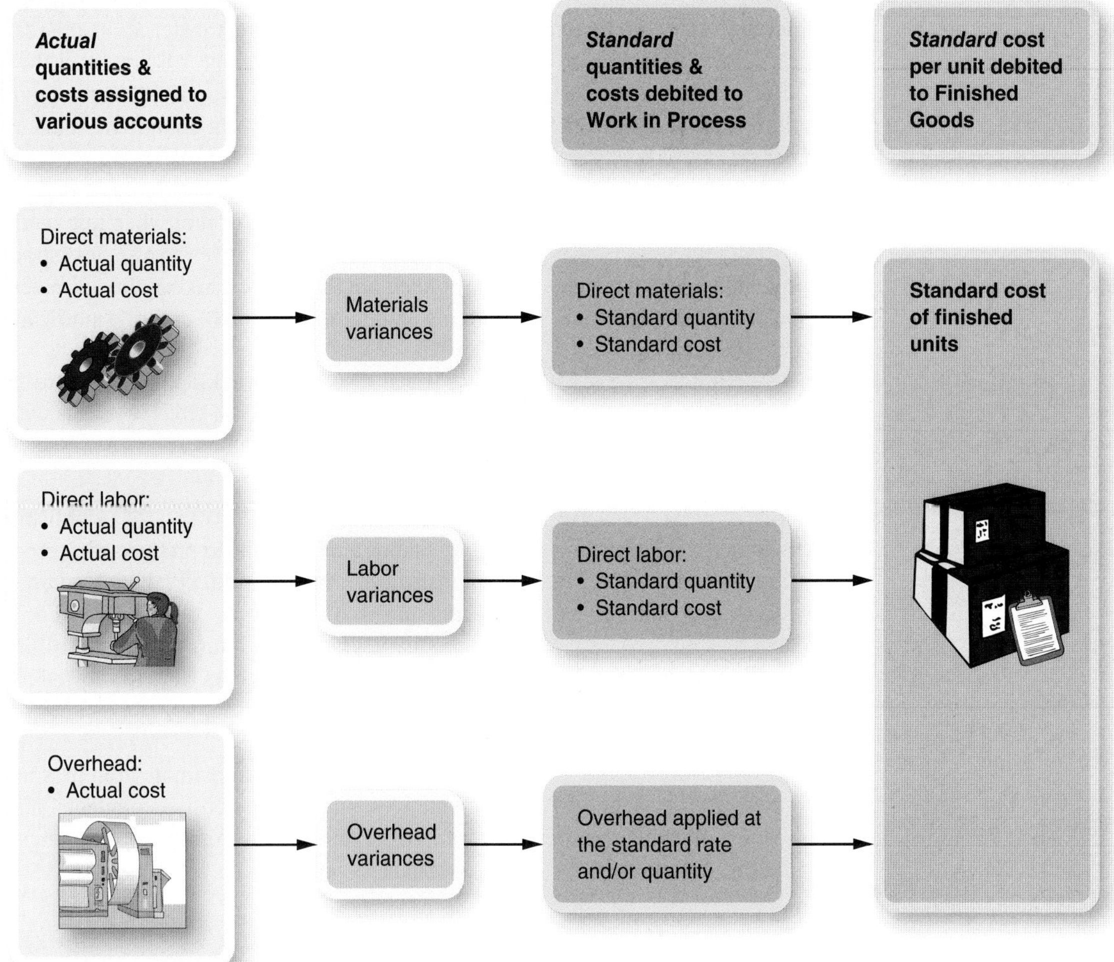

YOUR TURN — You as a Production Manager

Assume you supervise the production line for a product called Wingdits. Over several previous years, the average demand for Wingdits has required about 80 percent of production capacity, but during the current year demand has required the production line to be run at 100 percent capacity.

Your production line has been designated as a responsibility cost center and you have the authority to make input-related decisions such as ordering raw materials, hiring employees to work on the production line, and maintaining the equipment used to produce Wingdits. During the current year, the plant manager has been questioning your management ability because the actual costs of producing Wingdits are significantly higher than the expected standard costs. What could explain the significant difference between the actual and standard costs of the recently produced Wingdits? What related ethical issues should you raise with the plant manager?

(See our comments on the Online Learning Center Web site.)

DIRECT MATERIALS STANDARDS

The first step in establishing standard costs for direct materials is identifying the specific materials required to produce each product. The setting of direct materials standards involves both the *cost* and the *quantity* of each material used. For example, assume that the standard cost of mozzarella cheese used in the production of frozen pizzas is $2.40 per pound. If the standard quantity of cheese allowed per pizza is one-quarter of a pound, the standard cost of cheese per pizza is $0.60 ($2.40 per pound times ¼ pound).

The setting of direct materials standards also involves assessing relationships among cost, quality, and selling prices. High-quality materials generally cost more than low-quality materials. However, the use of high-quality materials often results in less waste, less spoilage, and fewer product defects. In Chapter 19 we pointed out that the cost and quality of materials used in production are key factors in determining selling prices, which, in turn, significantly influence customer demand.

Issues relating to storage, availability, waste disposal, and shipping costs also should be taken into consideration.

DIRECT LABOR STANDARDS

Establishing standard costs for direct labor is similar to the process of establishing direct materials standards. First, the specific direct labor requirements to produce each product must be identified. Once this has been accomplished, the setting of direct labor standards involves both the *wage rate* and the amount of *time allowed* to produce each product. For example, assume that the standard wage rate of a production worker in a furniture manufacturing company is $15 per hour. If the standard number of direct labor hours (DLH) allowed to produce a particular table is three hours, the standard direct labor cost per table is $45 ($15 per DLH times 3 DLH).

The setting of reasonable direct labor standards often requires input from personnel managers, industrial engineers, union representatives, supervisors, cost accountants, and factory employees. Establishing realistic cost standards requires input from many different sources—often including people from outside of the business organization.

CASE IN POINT

Several automobile companies—including **General Motors**, **Toyota**, and **Ford**—let manufacturing workers take part in establishing their own standards. The reason? When managers or industrial engineers set standards, they often are ignored, and both efficiency and motivation suffer. These companies have discovered that when individual work teams are allowed to set their own target standards, and are encouraged to compare their actual performances with the acheivements of other teams on other shifts, efficiency and motivation tend to improve significantly.

MANUFACTURING OVERHEAD STANDARDS

Standard overhead cost per unit is based on an estimate of total overhead at the *normal* level of production. Various cost drivers and, perhaps, activity-based costing may be used in developing the standard overhead cost per unit. Once this standard has been established, however, overhead is applied to production at the standard cost per unit.

STANDARD COSTS AND VARIANCE ANALYSIS: AN ILLUSTRATION

To illustrate the use of standard costs and the computation of variances, we will examine the operations of Brice Mills in Moscow, Idaho. Among the company's major products are laminated wooden beams used in the construction industry. The production process involves two steps. First, 2-inch by 12-inch boards of varying lengths are cut from rough white pine lumber supplied by wholesalers from throughout the Pacific Northwest. These boards are then glued together, like a sandwich, to form a laminated beam. The more 2-inch by 12-inch boards used in the lamination, the stronger the beam. One of the most common beams that Brice manufactures on a regular basis is 20 feet long and requires six layers of pine boards. At normal capacity, the company produces *700* of these beams each month.

When finished, each beam contains 240 board-feet of lumber. However, because of waste caused by knots, warps, cracks, and blade cuts, Brice allows *264 board-feet* as the standard quantity for each 20-foot beam manufactured. The company's standard cost of rough white pine is $0.25 per board-foot. Therefore, the standard cost of direct materials is $66 per beam (264 board-feet × $0.25 per foot).

Converting rough lumber into boards suitable for finished beams requires a variety of direct labor tasks. For instance, boards must be cut and planed, glued together, pressed, and coated with a protective sealant. Brice has established a standard of 1.5 direct labor hours for each beam it produces. Its standard labor rate is $12 per hour, resulting in a standard direct labor cost of $18 per beam.

Let us now consider the standard *overhead* cost per beam. Manufacturing overhead includes both *fixed* and *variable* costs. **Fixed manufacturing costs** are those that *are not affected* by short-term changes in the level of production. Examples include supervisors' salaries, depreciation on machinery, and property taxes on the factory. **Variable manufacturing costs,** on the other hand, rise and fall in *approximate proportion* to changes in production volume. The best examples of variable production costs are direct materials and direct labor. However, certain overhead costs also are variable, including machinery repairs and the amounts of electricity and indirect materials (such as glue) used in production.

Brice budgets total fixed overhead relating to the production of beams at $5,600 per month. At the normal production level of 700 beams per month, this amounts to *$8* per beam ($5,600 ÷ 700 beams). In addition, the company *applies* variable manufacturing overhead to beams using direct labor hours as an activity base. Its *application rate* is $4 per direct labor hour allowed per beam. Given that 1.5 direct labor hours are allowed per 20-foot beam, Brice expects to incur *$6* per beam in variable overhead. Thus, the company's standard cost for overhead is estimated at *$14 per unit.*

The following table summarizes the standard costs Brice expects to incur in the manufacture of its 20-foot beams. (Throughout this illustration, we show standard costs in ***red,*** actual costs in ***blue,*** and cost variances in ***black.***)

Direct materials (264 board-feet at $0.25 per board-foot)		$66
Direct labor (1.5 DLH at $12 per DLH)		18
Manufacturing overhead:		
Fixed ($5,600 per month ÷ 700 units)	$8	
Variable ($4 per DLH × 1.5 DLH allowed per unit)	6	14
Standard cost per unit		$98

Standard costs for direct labor, direct materials, and overhead

During March, Brice experienced several production delays. As a result of these delays, only 600 beams were produced (or 100 fewer than "normal" monthly output). There were no units in process either at the beginning or at the end of March. *Total* manufacturing costs *actually incurred* to produce 600 beams during the month were as follows:

Direct materials (180,000 board-feet at $0.20 per board-foot)		$36,000
Direct labor (1,080 DLH at $13 per DLH)		14,040
Manufacturing overhead:		
Fixed	$5,000	
Variable	3,680	8,680
Actual total cost of finished goods manufactured		$58,720

By comparing the actual costs incurred in March to the standard costs allowed to actually produce 600 beams, we can determine the *total cost variance* for the month as follows:

Actual total costs for March (from above)	$58,720
Standard costs allowed for producing 600 units (600 units × $98)	58,800
Total favorable cost variance (actual costs are less than standard)	$ 80

As shown above and in Exhibit 24–2, total costs incurred to manufacture 600 20-foot beams during the month *were actually $80 less than* the standard cost allowed. Thus, the *total variance* from standard is said to be *favorable.* Because it is favorable, one might jump to the conclusion that operating efficiency is slightly better than expected and that no corrective actions are necessary. We will see, however, that the $80 total variance from standard does not provide enough detailed information to adequately assess manufacturing efficiency. Only by comparing actual costs of direct materials, direct labor, and overhead to their related standard costs can we begin to understand the dynamics of the numerous relationships illustrated in Exhibit 24–2. Let us begin by determining the portion of the company's total variance attributable to the price and quantity of direct materials used in March.

Exhibit 24–2 RELATIONSHIPS AMONG MATERIALS AND LABOR VARIANCES AT BRICE

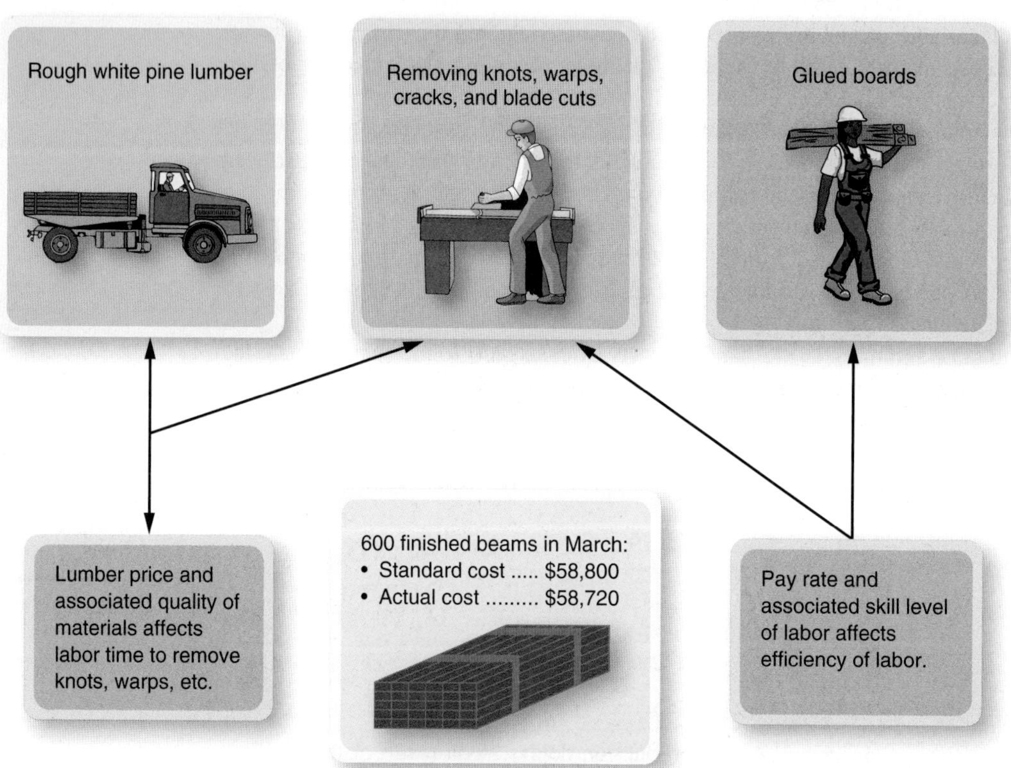

MATERIALS PRICE AND QUANTITY VARIANCES

Learning Objective LO3 **Compute direct materials and direct labor variances and explain the meaning of each.**

In establishing the standard materials cost for each unit of product, two factors are considered: (1) the *quantity* of materials required and (2) the *prices* that should be paid to acquire these materials. Therefore, a total cost variance for materials can result from differences in the quantities used, in the prices paid to suppliers, or a combination of these factors.

Let us compute the total materials variance incurred by Brice in the production of *600* laminated beams in March. As we have stated, a cost variance is the *difference* between the actual cost and the standard cost of the unit produced. Thus, Brice had a $3,600 favorable materials variance for the 600 beams produced in March:

Standard quantity at standard price:	
158,400 board-feet × $0.25 per board-foot	$39,600
Actual quantity at actual price:	
180,000 board-feet × $0.20 per board-foot	36,000
Total materials cost variance (favorable)	$ 3,600

This cost variance is *favorable* because the actual costs were *less* than standard.

We will now see, however, that this $3,600 favorable variance has two distinct components: (1) a $9,000 favorable *materials price variance* and (2) a $5,400 unfavorable *materials quantity variance.*

The favorable **materials price variance** resulted from the purchasing agent acquiring lumber for *5 cents less* than the standard cost of $0.25 per square foot. The formula for computing the materials price variance is as follows:

Materials Price Variance = Actual Quantity Used × (**Standard Price** − Actual Price)
= 180,000 board-feet × (**$0.25** − $0.20)
= **$9,000 (Favorable)**

(***Note:*** The formulas for computing all of the cost variances discussed in this chapter are summarized in Exhibit 24–9 at the end of this chapter.)

The unfavorable **materials quantity variance** resulted from the production department using more lumber than the cost standard allows. The production department actually used 180,000 board-feet of pine in producing 600 beams. But the standard cost allows only 264 board-feet per beam, or *158,400* for the production of 600 beams. Therefore, the production department has used *21,600 more board-feet of lumber* than the materials cost standard allows. The computation of the materials quantity variance is as follows:

Materials Quantity Variance = **Standard Price** × (**Standard Quantity** − Actual Quantity)
= **$0.25** × (**158,400 board-feet** − 180,000 board-feet)
= **−$5,400 (or $5,400 Unfavorable)**

(***Note:*** All of our variance formulas result in a *negative number* when the variance is *unfavorable* and in a *positive number* when the variance is *favorable.*)

Exhibit 24–3 illustrates how the two materials cost variances explain the *difference* between the standard materials cost for producing 600 beams and the actual costs incurred by Brice.

Exhibit 24–3

MATERIALS VARIANCES AT BRICE IN MARCH

Actual Quantity at Actual Price	Actual Quantity at Standard Price	Standard Quantity Allowed at Standard Price
180,000 Board-Feet × $0.20	180,000 Board-Feet × $0.25	158,400 Board-Feet × $0.25
$36,000	**$45,000**	**$39,600**

Materials Price Variance $9,000 Favorable — **Materials Quantity Variance $5,400 Unfavorable**

Total Materials Variance, $3,600 Favorable

The following journal entry is made to record the cost of materials used during March and the related cost variances:

Work in Process Inventory (at standard cost)	39,600	
Materials Quantity Variance (unfavorable)	5,400	
Materials Price Variance (favorable)		9,000
Direct Materials Inventory (at actual cost)		36,000
To record the cost of direct materials used in March.		

Record materials costs and related variances 

Notice that the Work in Process Inventory account is debited for the *standard cost* of materials used, and the Direct Materials Inventory account is credited for the *actual cost* of materials used. The difference between the standard and actual total cost is recorded in the two *cost variance accounts.*[1] Unfavorable variances are recorded by debit entries because they represent costs in excess of the budgeted standards. Favorable variances, however, are recorded by credit entries because they represent cost savings relative to standard amounts.

LABOR RATE AND EFFICIENCY VARIANCES

Brice incurred actual direct labor costs of $14,040 in March. The standard labor cost allowed for manufacturing 600 beams is only $10,800 (600 units × 1.5 hours per unit × $12 per hour). Thus, the company is faced with an unfavorable labor variance of *$3,240* ($10,800 − $14,040). We can gain additional insight regarding the reasons for this overrun by separating the total variance amount into two elements—a *labor rate variance* and a *labor efficiency variance.*

Actual labor costs are a function of: (1) the wage rate paid to direct labor workers and (2) the number of direct labor hours worked. A **labor rate variance** shows the extent to which hourly wage *rates* contributed to deviations from standard costs. The **labor efficiency variance** indicates the extent to which the number of *labor hours* worked during the period contributed to deviations from standard costs.

The labor rate variance is equal to the actual number of hours worked multiplied by the difference between the standard wage rate and the actual wage rate. Time cards show that 1,080 direct labor hours were used in March. The average wage rate for the month was $13 per hour. Thus, the labor rate variance for Brice is computed as follows:

Labor Rate Variance = Actual Labor Hours × (**Standard Rate** − Actual Rate)
= 1,080 hours × (**$12** − $13)
= **−$1,080 (or $1,080 Unfavorable)**

An *unfavorable* labor rate variance can result from using highly paid employees to perform lower-payscale jobs, poor scheduling, or excessive overtime costs.[2] Since the production manager is usually responsible for assigning employees to production activities, he or she normally is responsible for labor rate variances. (But, as we will see in our example, this is not always the case.)

The *labor efficiency variance* (also called the *labor usage variance*) is a measure of worker productivity. This variance is favorable when workers are able to complete the scheduled production in fewer hours than allowed by the standard. It is unfavorable when wasted time or low productivity causes actual hours to exceed the standard. The labor efficiency variance is computed by multiplying the standard hourly wage rate by the difference between the standard hours allowed and actual hours used. Brice allows *900* direct labor hours to produce 600 beams (600 units × 1.5 hours per unit). Given that *1,080* hours were actually required, the company's *unfavorable* labor efficiency variance for March is computed as follows:

Labor Efficiency Variance = **Standard Hourly Rate** × (**Standard Hours** − Actual Hours)
= **$12 per hour** × (**900 hours** − 1,080 hours)
= **−$2,160 (or $2,160 Unfavorable)**

The *unfavorable* labor efficiency variance indicates that direct labor workers were unable to manufacture the 600 beams in the standard time allowed. Once again, the production manager is responsible for worker productivity and usually is held accountable for the labor efficiency variance.

The labor efficiency variance and the labor rate variance are closely related. For instance, excessive direct labor hours may cause both the labor efficiency variance and the

[1] An alternative is to record the materials price variance at the time the materials are purchased. Such alternatives are discussed in cost accounting courses.

[2] If the standard level of production requires overtime even with efficient scheduling, the overtime wage rate should be reflected in the standard cost.

labor rate variance to be unfavorable if, due to the excess hours, workers must be paid at overtime rates.

INTERNATIONAL CASE IN POINT

Creating low-cost standards for direct labor may involve a trade-off between wage rates and assembly times allowed. For example, many international high-tech companies such as **Cisco Systems, Inc.**, and **Hewlett-Packard** rely heavily upon offshore assembly plants for low labor costs. Yet offshore labor often is less efficient than the more skilled workforce available in the United States. Even so, the low labor rates in countries such as Hungary and the Czech Republic more than offset labor inefficiencies, enabling these companies to compete in a global marketplace.

© Ingram Publishing/AGE Fotostock/DAL

The two labor cost variances are summarized in Exhibit 24–4.

Exhibit 24–4
LABOR VARIANCES AT BRICE IN MARCH

Actual Hours at Actual Rate	Actual Hours at Standard Rate	Standard Hours at Standard Rate
1,080 DLH × $13	1,080 DLH × $12	900 DLH × $12
$14,040	$12,960	$10,800

Labor Rate Variance $1,080 Unfavorable | **Labor Efficiency Variance $2,160 Unfavorable**

Total Labor Variance, $3,240 Unfavorable

The following journal entry is made to record the cost of direct labor charged to production during March:

Record labor costs and related variances

Work in Process Inventory (at standard cost)	10,800	
Labor Rate Variance (unfavorable)	1,080	
Labor Efficiency Variance (unfavorable)	2,160	
Direct Labor (at actual cost)		14,040
To record the cost of direct labor charged to production in March.		

In similar fashion to the way direct materials costs were charged to production, the Work in Process Inventory account is debited for the *standard labor cost* allowed, and the Direct Labor account is credited for the *actual labor cost* incurred. The unfavorable labor rate and efficiency variances are recorded by debit entries, because they both represent costs in excess of the budgeted standards.

MANUFACTURING OVERHEAD VARIANCES

The difference between actual manufacturing overhead costs incurred and the standard overhead costs charged to production is called the *overhead variance.* Whereas direct materials and direct labor are *variable costs,* manufacturing overhead is comprised of both variable and fixed cost components. Therefore, the analysis of the overhead cost variance differs somewhat from the analysis of materials and labor variances. We will now examine two elements of the overhead cost variance—the *spending variance* and the *volume variance.*[3]

[3] "Three-way" and "four-way" analyses of the overhead variances are covered in more advanced cost accounting courses.

Learning Objective
LO4 Compute overhead variances and explain the meaning of each.

The Overhead Spending Variance The most important element of the overhead cost variance is the **spending variance.** This variance is the difference between the *standard overhead allowed* for a given level of output and the actual overhead costs incurred during the period. The overhead spending variance for Brice Mills in March may be computed as follows:

Standard overhead costs allowed at 600 units of production:		
Fixed overhead costs	$5,600	
Variable overhead ($6 per beam × 600 beams)	3,600	$9,200
Actual overhead costs incurred in March:		
Fixed overhead costs	$5,000	
Variable overhead	3,680	8,680
Overhead spending variance (favorable)		$ 520

The spending variance is typically the responsibility of the production manager. In many cases, much of the spending variance involves *controllable* overhead costs. For this reason, it sometimes is called the *controllable* variance. At Brice, the production manager has kept variable overhead costs very close to standard and has kept fixed costs well below the $5,600 amount budgeted.

The Overhead Volume Variance The **volume variance** represents the difference between the overhead *applied to work in process* (at standard cost) and the overhead expected at the actual level of production. We will see that the volume variance is caused simply by the difference between the *normal volume* of output (*700 units* per month) and the *actual volume* of output (*600 units* in March).

In a standard cost system, overhead is charged to work in process using standard unit costs. As shown on page 1041, we determined that Brice's standard manufacturing overhead cost was $14 per unit. Thus, its Work in Process Inventory account was debited with $14 in overhead costs for each unit produced during the month. The more units produced during the month, the more overhead costs are charged to production.

In essence, a standard cost system treats all overhead as a *variable cost.* In reality, however, manufacturing overhead includes many fixed costs. Treating manufacturing overhead as a variable cost *automatically* causes a cost variance whenever the level of production varies from the normal volume.

To illustrate the variances that result from applying overhead to production in a standard cost system, in Exhibit 24–5 we compare the overhead costs that Brice would apply to production of its 20-foot beams at three different levels of monthly output.

Exhibit 24–5
OVERHEAD APPLIED TO VARIOUS VOLUMES

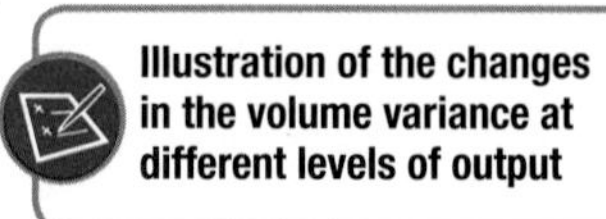
Illustration of the changes in the volume variance at different levels of output

	Actual Production (in units)		
	600	700	800
Overhead applied to work in process using a $14 standard rate	$8,400	$9,800	$11,200
Budgeted overhead:			
Fixed	$5,600	$5,600	$ 5,600
Variable ($6 per unit)	3,600	4,200	4,800
Total	$9,200	$9,800	$10,400
Volume variances—favorable (unfavorable)	$ (800)	$ –0–	$ 800

Notice that at an actual level of production of 700 beams per month, the normal level of output, there is no volume variance. This is because our $14 standard cost figure *assumes* that 700 units will actually be produced each month. As shown on page 1041, the $14 unit cost *includes $8 per unit in fixed costs* ($5,600 of budgeted fixed overhead ÷ 700 units).

Whenever actual production is less than 700 units, less than $5,600 in fixed overhead costs will be applied to production. In March, for example, only *600 beams* were actually produced. Thus, use of a standard cost that includes *$8* in fixed costs applies only *$4,800* in fixed overhead costs to production. The remaining *$800* in fixed overhead is recorded as an *unfavorable* volume variance. It is viewed as an unfavorable variance because actual production volume (600) is below normal production volume (700) and, as a result, fixed overhead has been *underapplied.* When fixed overhead is underapplied, additional overhead costs must be charged to the units produced.

The situation reverses whenever actual production *exceeds* the normal level. Had Brice's actual output in March been *800* units, the application of overhead using a standard rate of $14 per unit would have applied *more than* $5,600 in fixed overhead costs to production ($8 of fixed cost per unit × 800 units = $6,400). Here, the $800 volume variance is viewed as *favorable.* It is favorable because the cost standard has charged production with *too much* fixed overhead, making the actual costs look low by comparison.

The key point is that volume variances *occur automatically* whenever actual output differs from the level of output assumed in computing the standard overhead cost per unit. Over time, average production levels should equal the normal level used in developing the standard cost. Thus, the favorable and unfavorable volume variances should balance out during the year.

As long as the production department is producing the desired number of units, volume variances do *not* indicate either efficient or inefficient performance. Volume variances are simply the natural result of fluctuations in the level of production from month to month. These fluctuations often occur because of seasonal sales demand, efforts to increase or decrease inventory levels, or holidays and vacations. Thus, unless the production department fails to produce a scheduled number of units, no manager should be considered responsible for a volume variance.

Summary of the Overhead Cost Variances The overhead spending and volume variances experienced by Brice Mills in March are summarized in Exhibit 24–6.

Exhibit 24–6
OVERHEAD VARIANCES AT BRICE IN MARCH

Actual Overhead		Budgeted Overhead @ 600 Units		Overhead Applied at Standard Cost
Fixed	$5,000	Fixed	$5,600	600 × $14 per unit
Variable	3,680	Variable	3,600	
Total	$8,680	Total	$9,200	$8,400

Spending Variance $520 Favorable — Volume Variance $800 Unfavorable

Total Overhead Variance, $280 Unfavorable

As shown, the $8,680 in overhead costs that Brice actually incurred is *$520 less* than the budgeted overhead at the 600 units level of production. Thus, Brice's overhead spending variance is favorable. Its $800 volume variance is a direct result of actual output being *100 units less* than normal.

The following journal entry is made to apply overhead costs to production during March:

	Debit	Credit
Work in Process Inventory (at standard cost)	8,400	
Overhead Volume Variance (unfavorable)	800	
Overhead Spending Variance (favorable)		520
Manufacturing Overhead (at actual cost)		8,680
To apply overhead to production in March.		

Record overhead costs and related variances

VALUATION OF FINISHED GOODS

We have seen that, in a standard cost system, costs are charged to the Work in Process Inventory account at standard. Thus, finished goods also are valued at standard as their costs are transferred to the Finished Goods Inventory account and to the Cost of Goods Sold account. The entry made at the end of March to record the completion of 600 beams is:

Transfer costs to finished goods

Finished Goods Inventory: 20-Foot Beams	58,800	
Work in Process Inventory: 20-Foot Beams		58,800
To record completion during March of 600 20-foot beams at standard cost (600 units × $98 per unit = $58,800).		

Notice that the inventory of finished goods is valued at *standard cost.* As beams are sold, their standard cost ($98 per beam) will be transferred into the Cost of Goods Sold account.

What About the Cost Variance Accounts? The balances in the variance accounts represent *differences* between actual manufacturing costs and the standard costs used to value the finished goods inventory and cost of goods sold. These balances are typically allowed to accumulate in the variance accounts from month to month.

Often, the favorable and the unfavorable variances will balance out during the year, leaving only a small amount in each variance account at year-end. In this case, the variance accounts are simply closed into the Cost of Goods Sold account. However, if the balances in the variance accounts at the end of the year represent *a material dollar amount,* the amount should be apportioned among the Work in Process Inventory, Finished Goods Inventory, and Cost of Goods Sold accounts.

EVALUATING COST VARIANCES FROM DIFFERENT PERSPECTIVES

Learning Objective
LO5 Discuss the causes of specific cost variances.

Early in April, Brice's cost accountant prepared cost variance summary reports on each of the company's product lines for distribution at the monthly staff meeting. Among those attending the meeting were (1) the director of purchasing, (2) the production manager, (3) the quality control inspector, (4) the employee grievance representative, and (5) the sales manager. The report they were given pertaining to the production of 20-foot beams is shown in Exhibit 24–7.

Exhibit 24–7
VARIANCE SUMMARY REPORT

BRICE MILLS
COST VARIANCE SUMMARY REPORT
FOR 20-FOOT LAMINATED BEAMS
FOR THE MONTH ENDING MARCH 31

Total Variance to Be Explained		
Standard manufacturing costs allowed (600 units × $98)		$58,800
Actual manufacturing costs incurred in March		58,720
Total manufacturing cost variance—favorable		$ 80
Breakdown of Individual Variances		
Materials price variance—favorable	$ 9,000	
Materials quantity variance—unfavorable	(5,400)	
Total materials variance—favorable		$ 3,600
Labor rate variance—unfavorable	$(1,080)	
Labor efficiency variance—unfavorable	(2,160)	
Total labor variance—unfavorable		(3,240)
Overhead spending variance—favorable	$ 520	
Overhead volume variance—unfavorable	(800)	
Total overhead variance—unfavorable		(280)
Total manufacturing cost variance—favorable		$ 80

Let us now consider these cost variances from the perspectives of various department managers.

Accounting The cost accountant opened the meeting by announcing that she had a combination of "good news" and "bad news." On the bright side, she was encouraged that the company's total manufacturing cost variance for 20-foot beams was favorable for the first time in many months (albeit only $80). She was especially pleased about the successful effort to control manufacturing overhead costs associated with this product, as revealed by the $520 favorable overhead spending variance. However, she immediately expressed concern regarding several unfavorable variances experienced across the beams product line during the month. She displayed a PowerPoint slide containing the graphs shown in Exhibit 24–8 on the following page to make her point. In particular, she was troubled by the consistent pattern of unfavorable labor rate, labor efficiency, and materials quantity variances shown by the hatched areas in the graph. The remainder of her presentation was spent stressing the severity of these unfavorable variances.

Purchasing The first person to respond to the cost accountant's comments was the purchasing agent. Taking a defensive posture, he stressed that none of the unfavorable variances experienced during the month were under his control. In fact, he bragged that the $9,000 favorable price variance for 20-foot beams "saved the company from financial disaster in March." He pointed at the Graph for Direct Materials displayed in Exhibit 24–8 and suggested that his favorable price variance compensated for the unfavorable usage materials variance created by the production department. He pounded the table, exclaiming that he had "shopped for price" in three different states, getting what he believed to be the best bargain possible for rough white pine lumber.

Production The production manager stood up and confronted the purchasing agent. He verbally attacked the purchasing department, accusing it of acquiring materials of "grossly inferior quality." He told the group that the lumber he and his crew had been issued was green and full of knots, warps, and cracks. In his opinion, these defects were the direct cause of the unfavorable materials usage variance for the laminated beams. He also believed that numerous production bottlenecks resulting from poor quality materials had caused production output in March to be significantly less than normal.

Quality Control The quality control inspector concurred with the production manager's assessment. She noted that many of the company's product lines, especially its 20-foot beams, either failed to pass inspection or did so only marginally. Never in recent history had there been a month in which she rejected so many beams.

Factory Workers The employee grievance representative is a member of the production crew elected to communicate grievances to management. His comments provided a unique perspective to what had become an emotionally heated meeting. He conveyed to the group that factory morale in March had hit an all-time low. He admitted that every member of the production crew knew productivity was way down (as reflected by the unfavorable labor efficiency variances), yet added that everyone thought the inferior materials were the cause of the problem. He concluded by saying that the only good thing about inferior materials is "the overtime pay we earn working extra hours." (The $1,080 unfavorable labor rate variance for laminated beams resulted primarily from the overtime pay rates.)

© Dave Thompson/Life File/Getty Image

Marketing The sales manager argued that, even with overtime and extra shifts, demand during March still exceeded output. He told the company's cost accountant that this was one of those occasions when an unfavorable volume variance had severe implications. To illustrate his point, he noted that the unfavorable volume variance associated with the production of 20-foot beams (caused by producing 600 units instead of the normal 700 units) translated directly into $16,000 of lost sales in March. He also worried that

Exhibit 24-8

GRAPHICAL ILLUSTRATION OF VARIANCES

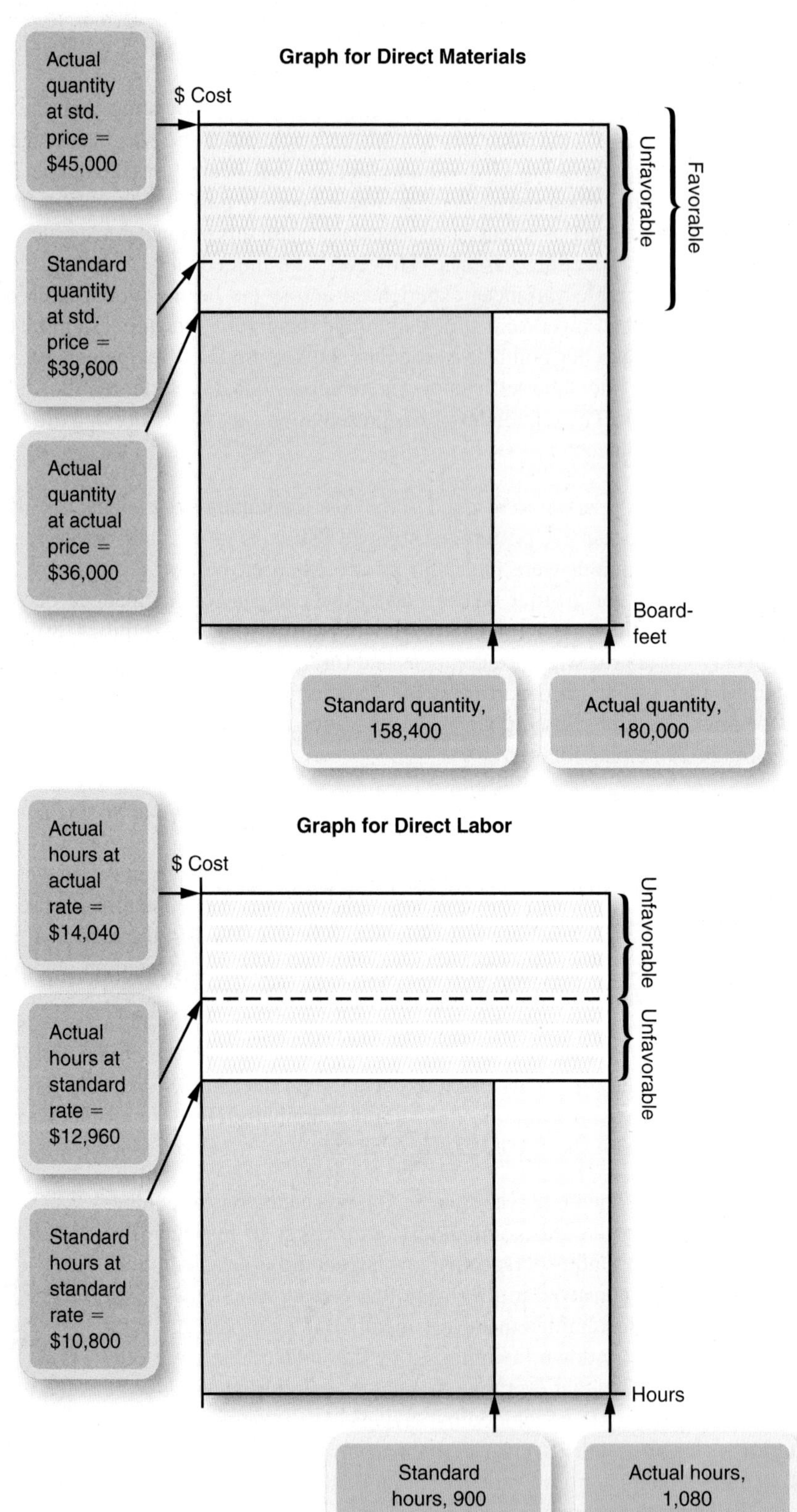

the beams that were sold may not have been of the quality customers had come to expect. His remarks raised questions regarding the company's legal liability should a beam fail because of structural defects.

YOUR TURN **You as a Plant Manager**

You are the plant manager for Brice. You have recently implemented a bonus system for your employees that provides a 10 percent bonus for favorable variances. What are the potential benefits, costs, and ethical concerns of such a bonus system?

(See our comments on the Online Learning Center Web site.)

A FINAL NOTE: JIT SYSTEMS AND VARIANCE ANALYSIS

A just-in-time (JIT) approach combined with total quality management (TQM), as discussed in Chapter 19, can reduce or eliminate many unfavorable cost variances. For instance, long-term pricing agreements with a select group of suppliers can virtually eliminate materials price variances. Materials usage variances caused by defective materials also may be minimized. Should a batch of inferior materials be encountered, the production process is halted and the supplier is contacted to resolve the problem immediately. Thus, rather than discovering quality control problems after the fact, using JIT and total quality control makes it possible to detect and correct quality problems *as they occur.*

Workers in a JIT system must be able to shift production quickly from one product to another. Adherence to carefully planned production schedules reduces idle time and eliminates non-value-added activities. As a consequence, labor efficiency variances often are improved under a JIT approach.

Well-trained employees, *working smarter and more efficiently,* can minimize the need for overtime hours. Thus, JIT systems may reduce or eliminate unfavorable labor rate variances. Finally, by cutting overhead costs associated with non-value-added activities, JIT and TQM systems also help management avoid unfavorable overhead spending variances.

Concluding Remarks

We have illustrated that cost information is not just for cost accountants. Indeed, it affects virtually every aspect of business operations. At Brice, the savings from purchasing inexpensive materials made the purchasing department look good but created cost overruns and other problems throughout the organization.

While a cost accounting system does not solve such problems, it can bring the many dimensions of the problem *promptly to management's attention.*

Summary of Cost Variances For your convenience, the six cost variances discussed in this chapter are summarized in Exhibit 24–9.

Exhibit 24–9 SUMMARY OF VARIANCE COMPUTATIONS AND MANAGER RESPONSIBILITIES

Variance	Computation	Manager Responsible
Materials:		
Price variance	Actual Quantity × (Standard Price − Actual Price)	Purchasing agent
Quantity variance	Standard Price × (Standard Quantity − Actual Quantity)	Production manager
Labor:		
Rate variance	Actual Hours × (Standard Hourly Rate − Actual Hourly Rate)	Production manager Human resource manager
Efficiency variance	Standard Hourly Rate × (Standard Hours − Actual Hours)	Production manager
Overhead:		
Spending variance	Budgeted Overhead (at Actual Production Level) − Actual Overhead	Production manager (to extent variance relates to controllable costs)
Volume variance	Applied Overhead (at Standard Rate) − Budgeted Overhead (at Actual Production Level)	None—this variance results from scheduling production at any level other than "normal"

Ethics, Fraud & Corporate Governance

For companies that use standard costing systems, the accuracy of the inventory and cost of goods sold figures reported in their financial statements depends upon the reliability of these standard cost numbers. A company's financial statements can be materially misstated when standard costs do not accurately represent the actual manufacturing costs incurred.

The Securities and Exchange Commission (SEC) brought an enforcement action against **NCI Building Systems, Inc.**, in regard to a material overstatement of reported income that was largely due to erroneous standard cost amounts assigned to inventory. NCI is a manufacturer and distributor of metal building components and engineered building systems, and its stock is traded on the New York Stock Exchange.

NCI's senior management noted an unusually high inventory balance in its Components Division. Even though senior management instructed the Components Division to stop purchasing steel, NCI's inventory balance did not decrease by the expected amount. NCI took a physical inventory to compare the actual inventory on hand with the inventory balance per the accounting records. The inventory balance per the accounting records was \$15–\$18 million greater than the physical inventory amount. This overstatement of inventory had the effect of *understating* cost of goods sold and, therefore, *overstating* net income.

The overstatement of inventory was largely due to problems with NCI's standard cost system. NCI's manufacturing process generated a nontrivial amount of scrap, but NCI's standard cost was inadequate to account for all of the scrap material that was generated during the manufacturing process. As a result, the value of scrap material was included as usable inventory, which had the effect of overstating the inventory balance.

An interesting side note to this case is how NCI's management handled these accounting problems. First, NCI retained its outside accounting firm to investigate the large difference between the book and physical inventory amounts. Second, NCI promptly restated its previously issued financial statements. Third, significant remedial measures were put in place to reduce the likelihood of such errors in the future. Fourth, a number of NCI's accounting personnel were terminated. Finally, NCI cooperated fully with the SEC in its investigation of this matter. As a result of these factors, which were specifically referred to by the SEC in its written enforcement release, the sanction imposed on NCI for its violation of the securities laws was relatively mild.

END-OF-CHAPTER REVIEW

SUMMARY OF LEARNING OBJECTIVES

LO1 Define standard costs and explain how they assist managers in controlling costs. Standard costs are the expected (or budgeted) costs per unit. When standard costs are used in a cost accounting system, differences between actual costs and standard costs are promptly brought to management's attention using a schedule of differences called variances.

LO2 Explain the difference between setting ideal standards and setting reasonably achievable standards. The most widely used approach is to set budgeted amounts at levels that are reasonably achievable under normal operating conditions. The goal in this case is to make the cost standard a fair and reasonable basis for evaluating performance.

An alternative is to budget an ideal level of performance. Under this approach, departments normally fall somewhat short of budgeted performance, but the variations may identify areas in which improvement is possible.

LO3 Compute direct materials and direct labor variances and explain the meaning of each. Cost variances are computed by comparing actual costs to standard costs and explaining the reasons for any differences. Differences in the cost of materials used may be caused either by variations in the price paid to purchase materials or in the quantity of materials used. Differences in the cost of direct labor may be caused by variations in wage rates or in the number of hours worked.

LO4 Compute overhead variances and explain the meaning of each. To compute overhead cost variances, compare the actual overhead to the budgeted overhead and compare the budgeted overhead to the applied overhead. Cost variances can result from spending more than budgeted or from a difference between the projected volume used to create the overhead application rate and the actual production used to apply overhead.

LO5 Discuss the causes of specific cost variances. Materials variances may be caused by the quality and price of materials purchased and by the efficiency with which those materials are used. Labor variances stem from workers' productivity, pay scales of workers placed on the job, and the quality of the materials with which they work. Overhead variances result both from actual spending and from differences between actual and normal levels of production.

Key Terms Introduced or Emphasized in Chapter 24

fixed manufacturing cost (p. 1041) A manufacturing cost that, in the short run, does not vary in response to changes in the level of production.

labor efficiency variance (p. 1044) The portion of the total labor variance caused by a difference between the standard and actual number of labor hours required to complete the task. Computed as Standard Hourly Rate × (Standard Hours − Actual Hours). Also called *labor usage variance.*

labor rate variance (p. 1044) The portion of the total labor variance caused by a difference between the standard hourly wage rate and the rate actually paid to workers. Usually stems from overtime or using workers at a different pay scale than assumed in developing the standard cost. Computed as Actual Hours × (Standard Hourly Rate − Actual Hourly Rate).

materials price variance (p. 1043) The portion of the total materials variance caused by paying a different price to purchase materials than was assumed in the standard cost. Computed as Actual Quantity × (Standard Unit Price − Actual Unit Price).

materials quantity variance (p. 1043) The portion of the total materials variance caused by using more or less material in the production process than is called for in the standard. Computed as Standard Unit Price × (Standard Quantity − Actual Quantity).

spending variance (p. 1046) The portion of the total overhead variance caused by incurring more overhead costs than are allowed for the actual level of activity achieved.

standard cost (p. 1038) The budgeted cost that should be incurred under normal, efficient conditions.

standard cost system (p. 1038) A system that accumulates product, service, or process costs using standard input prices and quantities.

variable manufacturing cost (p. 1041) A manufacturing cost that varies in approximate proportion to the number of units produced.

variance (p. 1038) A difference between the actual level of cost incurred and the standard (budgeted) level for the cost. The total cost variance may be subdivided into separate cost variances indicating the amount of variance attributable to specific causal factors.

volume variance (p. 1046) The portion of the total overhead variance that results from a difference between the actual level of production and the "normal" level assumed in computing the standard unit cost. In effect, the volume variance is a misallocation of fixed overhead costs and often is not relevant in evaluating performance.

Demonstration Problem

Krueger Corporation recently implemented a standard cost system. The company's cost accountant has gathered the following information needed to perform a variance analysis at the end of the month:

Standard Cost Information	
Direct materials	$5 per pound
Quantity allowed per unit	100 pounds per unit
Direct labor rate	$20.00 per hour
Hours allowed per unit	2 hours per unit
Fixed overhead budgeted	$12,000 per month
Normal level of production	1,200 units
Variable overhead application rate	$ 2.00 per unit
Fixed overhead application rate ($12,000 ÷ 1,200 units)	10.00 per unit
Total overhead application rate	$12.00 per unit
Actual Cost Information	
Cost of materials purchased and used	$468,000
Pounds of materials purchased and used	104,000 pounds
Cost of direct labor	$46,480
Hours of direct labor	2,240 hours
Cost of variable overhead	$2,352
Cost of fixed overhead	$12,850
Volume of production	1,000 units

Instructions

a. Compute the direct materials price variance, given an actual price of $4.50 per pound ($468,000 ÷ 104,000 pounds).

b. Compute the materials quantity variance, given a standard quantity of 100,000 pounds allowed to produce 1,000 units (1,000 units × 100 pounds per unit).

c. Prepare a journal entry summarizing the cost of direct materials charged to production.

d. Compute the labor rate variance, given an actual labor rate of $20.75 per hour ($46,480 ÷ 2,240 hours).

e. Compute the labor efficiency variance.

f. Prepare a journal entry summarizing the cost of direct labor charged to production.

g. Compute the overhead spending variance.

h. Compute the overhead volume variance.

i. Prepare a journal entry summarizing the application of overhead costs to production.

Solution to the Demonstration Problem

a. Materials Price Variance = Actual Quantity Used × (Standard Price − Actual Price)
= 104,000 pounds × ($5.00 − $4.50)
= $52,000 Favorable

b. Materials Quantity Variance = Standard Price × (Standard Quantity − Actual Quantity)
= $5.00 per pound × (100,000 − 104,000)
= −$20,000 (or $20,000 Unfavorable)

c.

Work in Process Inventory (at standard cost)	500,000*	
Materials Quantity Variance (unfavorable)	20,000	
Materials Price Variance (favorable)		52,000
Direct Materials Inventory (at actual cost)		468,000
To record the cost of direct materials charged to production.		

*1,000 actual units × 100 pounds allowed per unit × $5 per pound = $500,000.

d. Labor Rate Variance = Actual Labor Hours × (Standard Rate − Actual Rate)
= 2,240 hours × ($20.00 − $20.75)
= −$1,680 (or $1,680 Unfavorable)

e. Labor Efficiency Variance = Standard Rate × (Standard Hours − Actual Hours)
= $20 × (2,000 hours* − 2,240 hours)
= −$4,800 (or $4,800 Unfavorable)

*1,000 units × 2 hours per unit.

f.

Work in Process Inventory (at standard cost)	40,000*	
Labor Rate Variance (unfavorable)	1,680	
Labor Efficiency Variance (unfavorable)	4,800	
Direct Labor (at actual cost)		46,480
To record the cost of direct labor charged to production.		

*1,000 actual units × 2 hours allowed per unit × $20.00 per hour = $40,000.

g.

Standard overhead costs allowed at 1,000 units of production:		
Fixed overhead costs	$12,000	
Variable overhead ($2 per unit × 1,000 units)	2,000	$14,000
Actual overhead costs incurred in March:		
Fixed overhead costs	$12,850	
Variable overhead	2,352	15,202
Overhead spending variance (unfavorable)		$(1,202)

h.

Overhead *applied* to work in process (1,000 units × $12)		$12,000
Standard overhead *allowed* (at 1,000 units):		
Fixed	$12,000	
Variable ($2 per unit)	2,000	
Total overhead *allowed* at standard		14,000
Overhead volume variance (unfavorable)		$(2,000)

i.

Work in Process Inventory (at standard cost)	12,000	
Overhead Spending Variance (unfavorable)	1,202	
Overhead Volume Variance (unfavorable)	2,000	
Manufacturing Overhead (at actual cost)		15,202
To apply overhead to production.		

Self-Test Questions

The answers to these questions appear on page 1074.

1. The labor rate variance is determined by multiplying the difference between the actual labor rate and the standard labor rate by:
   a. The standard labor hours allowed for a given level of output.
   b. The standard labor rate.
   c. The actual hours worked during the period.
   d. The actual labor rate.
2. Which of the following is *not* a possible cause of an unfavorable direct labor efficiency variance?
   a. Lack of motivation.
   b. Low-quality materials.

   c. Poor supervision.
   d. All of the above could be considered possible causes of an unfavorable labor efficiency variance.

3. An unfavorable overhead volume variance indicates that:
   a. Total fixed overhead has exceeded the standard amount budgeted.
   b. Variable overhead per unit has exceeded the standard amount budgeted.
   c. Actual production was less than the normal volume of output.
   d. Actual production was more than the normal volume of output.
4. A favorable overhead spending variance means that:
   a. Overhead has been overapplied.
   b. Overhead has been underapplied.
   c. Actual production was less than the normal volume of output.
   d. None of the above.
5. Modern Art, Inc., produces handpainted foam mouse pads. The following budgeted and actual results are for a recent month in which actual production was equal to budgeted production.

	Budgeted Amount	Actual Result
Direct materials: Foam		
Usage	1.5 square feet per pad	1.3 square feet per pad
Price	$0.15 per square foot	$0.18 per square foot
Direct labor:		
Usage	.25 hours per pad	.30 hours per pad
Rate	$15 per hour	$13 per hour

Which of the following are *true*? (There may be more than one response.)

   a. The materials price variance is favorable.
   b. The direct labor rate variance is favorable.
   c. The materials quantity variance is unfavorable.
   d. The direct labor efficiency variance is unfavorable.

ASSIGNMENT MATERIAL Discussion Questions

1. Define *standard costs* and briefly indicate how they may be used by management in planning and control.
2. Identify what is wrong with the following statement: "There are three basic kinds of cost accounting systems: job order, process, and standard."
3. Once standard costs are established, what conditions would require that standards be revised?
4. Identify the variances from standard cost that are generally computed for direct materials, direct labor, and manufacturing overhead.
5. Would a production manager be equally responsible for an unfavorable materials price variance and an unfavorable materials quantity variance? Explain.
6. What is meant by a favorable labor efficiency variance? How is the labor efficiency variance computed?
7. Why is an unfavorable overhead volume variance usually not considered in evaluating the performance of the production department manager?
8. Why do overtime hours usually result in unfavorable direct labor rate variances?
9. How do direct materials variances and direct labor cost variances differ from overhead cost variances?
10. At the end of the year, when closing the books, what is the treatment for immaterial standard variance account balances? What is the treatment for standard variance account balances that are material in amount?
11. How can operating at 100 percent of capacity create unfavorable variances?
12. Why is it important to consider the relationships among cost, quality, and selling prices when establishing standards for direct materials?
13. Who might a plant accountant consult with when establishing direct labor quantity or rate standards?
14. Why are unfavorable variances recorded by using debit entries and favorable variances recorded by using credit entries?
15. Explain how efficiency and price or rate variances for direct labor can be closely interrelated.

Brief Exercises

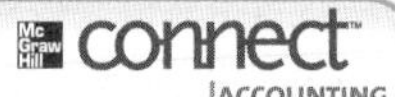

LO2 Variances and Normal Capacity

LO5

The production manager at Bramford Industries is investigating the cause of unfavorable materials and labor variances that occurred in the previous month. Standards are based on normal or expected production of 400 units per month at Bramford. The manager has discovered that 500 units were needed the previous month to meet shipment needs as ordered by headquarters. During the previous month, 100 units were spoiled, so production last month was actually 600 units.

Use your judgment to speculate as to why the variances occurred at Bramford last month.

LO3 **BRIEF EXERCISE 24.2**

Standard Cost Applied to Production

At Franklis Incorporated, during the month of January, the direct labor rate variance was $2,500 unfavorable, and the direct labor efficiency variance was $5,000 favorable. Actual direct labor costs during January were $87,000. What was the standard direct labor applied to production at Franklis during the month of January?

LO4 **BRIEF EXERCISE 24.3**

Expected Volume Variance

Use the information in Exhibit 24–5 on page 1046 to compute the expected volume variance at 750 units.

LO4 **BRIEF EXERCISE 24.4**

LO5 Volume and Spending Variances

Jesse is the office manager of a large firm called Law & Legal Services, Inc. At Law & Legal Services, overhead is allocated to client accounts using hours billed. Jesse found the following information related to overhead for the previous month:

- Spending variance = $14,000 unfavorable
- Volume variance = $6,000 favorable
- Actual overhead = $56,000
- Actual hours billed = 4,000 hours

Are the normal or expected hours for billing each month higher or lower than the actual hours billed last month? Were the actual expenditures of office supplies, equipment, indirect labor, and so on, higher or lower than expected?

LO2 **BRIEF EXERCISE 24.5**

LO5 Normal versus Ideal Standard Costs

	Normal or Expected Standards	Ideal Standards
Direct materials quantity per unit	2 lbs. per unit	1.8 lbs. per unit
Direct materials price per pound	$8 per lb.	$7.75 per lb.
Direct labor hours per unit	3 hours per unit	2.8 hours per unit
Direct labor rate per hour	$22 per hour	$21.50 per hour

Compute the standard cost per finished unit for the normal or expected standards and for the ideal standards. Explain how both normal and ideal standards would be used by managers.

LO1 **BRIEF EXERCISE 24.6**

LO3 Computing Labor Cost Variances

LO5

A popular product of Loring Glassworks is a hand-decorated vase. The company's standard cost system calls for 0.75 hours of direct labor per vase, at a standard wage rate of $8.25. During September, Loring produced 4,000 vases at an actual direct labor cost of $24,464 for 2,780 direct labor hours.

What is the actual wage rate per hour? Compute the labor rate and efficiency variances for the month. Was paying workers the actual wage rather than the standard wage an efficient strategy for Loring?

LO3 **BRIEF EXERCISE 24.7**

Journal Entry for Direct Labor

See Brief Exercise 24.6. Provide the journal entry for direct labor usage for the month of September for Loring Glassworks.

LO3 **BRIEF EXERCISE 24.8**

Computing Materials Cost Variances

One of the products of Hearts & Flowers is a one-pound box of chocolate candy, packaged in a box bearing the customer's logo (minimum order, 100 boxes). The standard cost of the chocolate candy used is $2 per pound. During November, 20,000 of these one-pound boxes were produced, requiring 20,800 pounds of chocolate candy at a total direct materials cost of $42,640.

Determine the materials price and quantity variances for November with respect to the candy used in producing this product.

LO3 **BRIEF EXERCISE 24.9**

Journal Entry for Direct Materials

See Brief Exercise 24.8. Provide the journal entry for direct materials usage for the month of November for Hearts & Flowers.

LO4 **BRIEF EXERCISE 24.10**

Overhead Cost Variances

Ringo Corporation applied $7,200 of manufacturing overhead to production during the month. Its actual overhead costs for the month were $8,000. The cost accountant reports that Ringo's unfavorable spending variance for the month totals $1,500.

Did Ringo produce more or less than its normal output for the month? Defend your answer.

Exercises

LO1 through LO5 **EXERCISE 24.1**

Accounting Terminology

The following are seven technical terms introduced in this chapter:

Spending variance	Materials price variance	Standard costs
Labor rate variance	Materials quantity variance	Volume variance
Labor efficiency variance		

Each of the following statements may (or may not) describe one of these technical terms. For each statement, indicate the accounting term discussed, or answer "None" if the statement does not correctly describe any of the terms.

a. The budgeted costs of producing a product under normal conditions.

b. The dollar amount associated with the difference between the actual direct labor hours required and the standard number of direct labor hours allowed for a given level of production under normal conditions.

c. A variance that is always favorable when actual production levels exceed normal levels.

d. The portion of the total materials variance caused by using more or less material than allowed for a given level of output.

e. The portion of the total overhead variance caused by incurring more overhead costs than allowed for a given level of production.

f. The portion of the total materials variance for which a company's purchasing agent is often responsible.

g. The portion of the total labor variance that is related to the differences between the actual hourly wages paid and the budgeted standard wage.

LO3 LO4 **EXERCISE 24.2**

Relationships among Standard Costs, Actual Costs, and Cost Variances

The standard costs and variances for direct materials, direct labor, and factory overhead for the month of May are as follows:

		Variances	
	Standard Cost	**Unfavorable**	**Favorable**
Direct materials	$ 90,000		
Price variance		$4,500	
Quantity variance			$2,700
Direct labor	180,000		
Rate variance			1,800
Efficiency variance		5,400	
Manufacturing overhead	270,000		
Spending variance			3,600
Volume variance			2,400

Determine the *actual costs* incurred during the month of May for direct materials, direct labor, and manufacturing overhead.

LO3 LO5 **EXERCISE 24.3** Understanding Materials Cost Variances

The cost accountant for Blue Pharmaceuticals has informed you that the company's materials quantity variance for the drug Allegro was exactly equal to its materials price variance for the year. The company's normal level of production is 50 batches of Allegro per year. However, due to uncertainties regarding foundation funding, it produced only 25 batches during the current year. Other cost information regarding Allegro's direct materials is as follows:

Standard price per gram of material	$60
Actual kilograms purchased and used during the year	100 kg
Actual cost of materials purchased during the period	$6,000,000
Number of grams per kilogram	1,000 grams

a. Compute Blue's materials price variance.

b. Compute the standard quantity of materials allowed per batch of Allegro produced.

c. Why would you *not* expect Blue to have a large materials quantity variance?

LO3 through LO5 **EXERCISE 24.4** Computing Materials Cost Variances and Volume Variance

Gumchara Corporation reported the following information with respect to the materials required to manufacture amalgam florostats during the current month:

Standard price per gram of materials	$1.25
Standard quantity of materials per amalgam florostat	4 grams
Actual materials purchased and used in production	2,800 grams
Actual amalgam florostats produced during the month	520 units
Actual cost of materials purchased	$3,920
Normal monthly output	550 units

a. Determine Gumchara's materials price variance.

b. Determine Gumchara's materials quantity variance.

c. Will Gumchara's overhead volume variance be favorable or unfavorable? Why?

LO4 LO5 **EXERCISE 24.5** Manufacturing Overhead Variances

Chasman Corporation estimated overhead for the year as follows: fixed = $330,000, variable = $2.50 per unit. Chasman expected to produce 60,000 units for the year.

a. Compute the rate that will be used to apply overhead costs to products.

b. During the year, Chasman incurred actual overhead costs of $430,000 and produced 65,000 units. Compute the overhead applied to units produced.

c. Compute the amount of under- or overapplied overhead and the spending and volume variances.

d. What caused the applied overhead to be different from the actual overhead?

LO1 LO3 LO5 **EXERCISE 24.6** Computing Labor Cost Variances

Marlo Enterprises produces radon mitigation pumps. Information pertaining to the company's monthly direct labor usage is provided below:

Standard labor rate per hour	$16
Standard hours allowed per radon mitigation pump	0.5 hours
Actual pumps produced during the current month	9,000
Actual labor hours worked during the current month	3,600
Actual labor cost for the current month	$64,800

a. Compute the company's labor rate variance.

b. Compute the company's labor efficiency variance.

c. An extremely large order of radon mitigation pumps was filled during the month for exportation to Saudi Arabia. Filling this order resulted in extended hours for many of the company's workers. Which labor variance reflects the extra hours worked by Marlo's employees? Was their time well utilized? Explain.

LO3 **EXERCISE 24.7**
Elements of the Materials Cost Variances

The following computation of the materials variances of Weitzen Foods is incomplete. The missing data are labeled (**a**) through (**d**).

Materials price variance = 3,640 pounds × [(**a**) standard price − $9.00 actual price]	$910 Unfavorable
Materials quantity variance = (**b**) × [3,800 pounds − (**c**) actual quantity]	$ (**d**)

Supply the missing data for items (**a**) through (**d**). Prepare a caption describing the item, as well as indicating the dollar amount and physical quantity. Briefly explain each answer, including how you determined the amount.

LO5 **EXERCISE 24.8**
Interpreting Variances

The manager of a manufacturing firm received the following information related to the last period's direct materials and direct labor variances:

Direct materials price variance	Favorable
Direct materials quantity variance	Favorable
Direct labor rate variance	Unfavorable
Direct labor efficiency variance	Favorable

a. Ignoring all other variances, what are possible reasons for a favorable direct materials price variance?

b. Given that the quality of direct materials purchased was exactly as expected, how would you explain the above combination of the four variances?

LO4 **EXERCISE 24.9**
Computing Overhead Cost Variances

From the following information for Alfred Industries, compute the overhead spending variance and the volume variance.

Standard manufacturing overhead based on normal monthly volume:		
Fixed ($300,000 ÷ 20,000 units)	$15.00	
Variable ($100,000 ÷ 20,000 units)	5.00	$20.00
Units actually produced in current month		18,000 units
Actual overhead costs incurred (including $300,000 fixed)		$383,800

LO4 **EXERCISE 24.10**
Overhead Journal Entries

Use the information in Exercise 24.9 to prepare the journal entry to record the overhead at Alfred Industries.

LO4 LO5 **EXERCISE 24.11**
Overhead Cost Variances

Zeta, Inc., produces handwoven rugs. Budgeted production is 5,000 rugs per month and the standard direct labor required to make each rug is 2 hours. All overhead is allocated based on direct labor hours. Zeta's manager is interested in what caused the recent month's $3,000 unfavorable overhead variance. The following information was available to aid in the analysis:

	Budgeted Amounts	Actual Results
Production in units	5,000	4,500
Total labor hours	10,000	9,000
Total variable overhead	$ 60,000	$55,000
Total fixed overhead	40,000	38,000
Total overhead	$100,000	$93,000

a. What was the overhead spending variance for the month?

b. What was the overhead volume variance?

c. What corrective actions should Zeta's manager undertake related to the unfavorable overhead variance?

LO4 **EXERCISE 24.12**

Understanding Overhead Variances

McGill's overhead spending variance is unfavorable by $600. The company's accountant credited the Cost of Goods Sold account for $4,200 to close out any over- or underapplied overhead at the end of the current period.

Compute McGill's overhead volume variance.

LO3 **EXERCISE 24.13**

Computing Materials and Labor Variances

Nolan Mills uses a standard cost system. During May, Nolan manufactured 15,000 pillowcases, using 27,000 yards of fabric costing $3.05 per yard and incurring direct labor costs of $19,140 for 3,300 hours of direct labor. The standard cost per pillowcase assumes 1.75 yards of fabric at $3.10 per yard, and 0.20 hours of direct labor at $5.95 per hour.

a. Compute both the price variance and quantity variance relating to direct materials used in the manufacture of pillowcases in May.

b. Compute both the rate variance and efficiency variance for direct labor costs incurred in manufacturing pillowcases in May.

LO1 LO3 LO5 **EXERCISE 24.14**

Causes of Cost Variances

For each of the following variances, briefly explain at least one probable cause and indicate the department manager (if any) responsible for the variance.

a. A favorable materials price variance.

b. An unfavorable labor rate variance.

c. A favorable volume variance.

d. An unfavorable materials quantity variance.

LO1 LO5 **EXERCISE 24.15**

Standards for **Home Depot**

It may be easier to think about setting standards to help manage manufacturing businesses, like the lumber business of Brice, Inc., discussed in this chapter, than to help manage retail establishments. For a company like **Home Depot**, main inputs (direct labor and overhead) are sales personnel and store space. **Home Depot**'s main outputs are sales of retail items. Look at the **Home Depot** financial information in Appendix A. Locate the "10-Year Summary of Financial and Operating Results" that includes a section titled: "Store Sales and Other Data" with six categories of information. Identify at least two of these categories that could be used to create standards per employee for direct labor (sales personnel) in a typical **Home Depot** store. Explain how the direct labor standards you are considering would help a store manager control costs.

Problem Set A

LO3 through LO5 **PROBLEM 24.1A**

Understanding Materials Cost Variances and Volume Variance

Wilson's materials quantity variance for the current month was exactly one-half of its materials price variance. Both variances were unfavorable. The company's cost accountant has supplied the following standard cost information:

Standard price per pound of materials	$15
Actual pounds purchased and used during the month	600 pounds
Actual cost per pound of materials purchased and used	$16
Actual units manufactured during the month	500 units
Normal productive output per month	550 units

Instructions

a. Compute Wilson's materials price variance.

b. Compute the standard quantity of materials allowed for producing 550 units of product.

c. Record the journal entry to charge Work in Process for the cost of materials used during the month.

d. Assume Wilson's overhead volume variance is twice the amount of its materials quantity variance. Is the volume variance favorable or unfavorable? How do you know?

LO3 LO4 **PROBLEM 24.2A**

Computing and Journalizing Cost Variances

AgriChem Industries manufactures fertilizer concentrate and uses cost standards. The fertilizer is produced in 500-pound batches; the normal level of production is 250 batches of fertilizer per month. The standard costs per batch are as follows:

		Standard Costs per Batch
Direct materials:		
Various chemicals (500 pounds per batch at $0.60/pound)		$300
Direct labor:		
Preparation and blending (25 hours per batch at $7.00/hour)		175
Manufacturing overhead:		
Fixed ($50,000 per month ÷ 250 batches)	$200	
Variable (per batch)	25	225
Total standard cost per batch of fertilizer		$700

During January, the company temporarily reduced the level of production to 200 batches of fertilizer. Actual costs incurred in January were as follows:

Direct materials (102,500 pounds at $0.57/pound)	$ 58,425
Direct labor (4,750 hours at $6.80/hour)	32,300
Manufacturing overhead	54,525
Total actual costs (200 batches)	$145,250
Standard cost of 200 batches (200 batches × $700 per batch)	140,000
Net unfavorable cost variance	$ 5,250

Instructions

You have been engaged to explain in detail the elements of the $5,250 net unfavorable cost variance and to record the manufacturing costs for January in the company's standard cost accounting system.

a. As a first step, compute the materials price and quantity variances, the labor rate and efficiency variances, and the overhead spending and volume variances for the month.

b. Prepare journal entries to record the flow of manufacturing costs through the standard cost system and the related cost variances. Make separate entries to record the costs of direct materials used, direct labor, and manufacturing overhead. Work in Process Inventory is to be debited only with standard costs.

LO3 LO4 **PROBLEM 24.3A** Computing and Journalizing Cost Variances

American Hardwood Products uses standard costs in a process cost system. At the end of the current month, the following information is prepared by the company's cost accountant:

	Direct Materials	Direct Labor	Manufacturing Overhead
Actual costs incurred	$96,000	$82,500	$123,240
Standard costs	90,000	84,000	115,500
Materials price variance (favorable)	2,400		
Materials quantity variance (unfavorable)	8,400		
Labor rate variance (favorable)		3,000	
Labor efficiency variance (unfavorable)		1,500	
Overhead spending variance (unfavorable)			3,240
Overhead volume variance (unfavorable)			4,500

The total standard cost per unit of finished product is $30. During the current month, 9,000 units were completed and transferred to the finished goods inventory and 8,800 units were sold. The inventory of work in process at the end of the month consists of 1,000 units that are 65 percent complete. There was no inventory in process at the beginning of the month.

Instructions

a. Prepare journal entries to record all variances and the costs incurred (at standard) in the Work in Process account as separate compound entries for (1) direct materials, (2) direct labor, and (3) manufacturing overhead.

b. Prepare journal entries to record (1) the transfer of units finished to the Finished Goods Inventory account and (2) the Cost of Goods Sold (at standard) for the month.

c. Assuming that the company operated at 90 percent of its normal capacity during the current month, what is the amount of the budgeted fixed manufacturing overhead per month?

LO3 LO4

PROBLEM 24.4A
Computing and Journalizing Cost Variances

Sven Enterprises is a large producer of gourmet pet food. During April, it produced 147 batches of puppy meal. Each batch weighs 1,000 pounds. To produce this quantity of output, the company purchased and used 148,450 pounds of direct materials at a cost of $593,800. It also incurred direct labor costs of $17,600 for the 2,200 hours worked by employees on the puppy meal crew. Manufacturing overhead incurred at the puppy meal plant during April totaled $3,625, of which $2,450 was considered fixed. Sven's standard cost information for 1,000-pound batches of puppy meal is as follows:

Direct materials standard price	$4.20 per pound
Standard quantity allowed per batch	1,020 pounds
Direct labor standard rate	$8.50 per hour
Standard hours allowed per batch	14 direct labor hours
Fixed overhead budgeted	$2,800 per month
Normal level of production	140 batches per month
Variable overhead application rate	$ 9.00 per batch
Fixed overhead application rate ($2,800 ÷ 140 batches)	20.00 per batch
Total overhead application rate	$29.00 per batch

Instructions

a. Compute the materials price and quantity variances.

b. Compute the labor rate and efficiency variances.

c. Compute the manufacturing overhead spending and volume variances.

d. Record the journal entry to charge materials (at standard) to Work in Process.

e. Record the journal entry to charge direct labor (at standard) to Work in Process.

f. Record the journal entry to charge manufacturing overhead (at standard) to Work in Process.

g. Record the journal entry to transfer the 147 batches of puppy meal produced in April to Finished Goods.

h. Record the journal entry to close any over- or underapplied overhead to Cost of Goods Sold.

LO3 LO4

PROBLEM 24.5A
Computing and Journalizing Cost Variances

Slick Corporation is a small producer of synthetic motor oil. During May, the company produced 5,000 cases of lubricant. Each case contains twelve quarts of synthetic oil. To achieve this level of production, Slick purchased and used 16,500 gallons of direct materials at a cost of $20,625. It also incurred average direct labor costs of $15 per hour for the 4,200 hours worked in May by its production personnel. Manufacturing overhead for the month totaled $9,950, of which $2,200 was considered fixed. Slick's standard cost information for each case of synthetic motor oil is as follows:

Direct materials standard price	$1.30 per gallon
Standard quantity allowed per case	3.25 gallons
Direct labor standard rate	$16 per hour
Standard hours allowed per case	0.75 direct labor hours
Fixed overhead budgeted	$2,600 per month
Normal level of production	5,200 cases per month
Variable overhead application rate	$1.50 per case
Fixed overhead application rate ($2,600 ÷ 5,200 cases)	0.50 per case
Total overhead application rate	$2.00 per case

Instructions

a. Compute the materials price and quantity variances.

b. Compute the labor rate and efficiency variances.

c. Compute the manufacturing overhead spending and volume variances.

d. Prepare the journal entries to:

1. Charge materials (at standard) to Work in Process.
2. Charge direct labor (at standard) to Work in Process.
3. Charge manufacturing overhead (at standard) to Work in Process.
4. Transfer the cost of the 5,000 cases of synthetic motor oil produced in May to Finished Goods.
5. Close any over- or underapplied overhead to Cost of Goods Sold.

LO3 LO4 **PROBLEM 24.6A** Computing and Journalizing Cost Variances

The accountants for Polyglaze, Inc., have developed the following information regarding the standard cost and the actual cost of a product manufactured in June:

	Standard Cost	Actual Cost
Direct materials:		
Standard: 10 ounces at $0.15 per ounce	$1.50	
Actual: 11 ounces at $0.16 per ounce		$1.76
Direct labor:		
Standard: 0.50 hours at $10.00 per hour	5.00	
Actual: 0.45 hours at $10.40 per hour		4.68
Manufacturing overhead:		
Standard: $5,000 fixed cost and $5,000 variable cost for 10,000 units normal monthly volume	1.00	
Actual: $5,000 fixed cost and $4,600 variable cost for 8,000 units actually produced in June		1.20
Total unit cost	$7.50	$7.64

Instructions

a. Compute the materials price variance and the materials quantity variance, indicating whether each is favorable or unfavorable. Prepare the journal entry to record the cost of direct materials used during June in the Work in Process account (at standard).

b. Compute the labor rate variance and the labor efficiency variance, indicating whether each is favorable or unfavorable. Prepare the journal entry to record the cost of direct labor used during June in the Work in Process account (at standard).

c. Compute the overhead spending variance and the overhead volume variance, indicating whether each is favorable or unfavorable. Prepare the journal entry to assign overhead cost to production in June.

LO3 through LO5 **PROBLEM 24.7A** Computing, Journalizing, and Analyzing Cost Variances

Heritage Furniture Co. uses a standard cost system. One of the company's most popular products is an oak entertainment center that looks like an old icebox but houses a television, stereo, or other electronic components. The per-unit standard costs of the entertainment center, assuming a "normal" volume of 1,000 units per month, are as follows:

Direct materials, 100 board-feet of wood at $1.30 per foot		$130.00
Direct labor, 5 hours at $8.00 per hour		40.00
Manufacturing overhead (applied at $22 per unit)		
Fixed ($15,000 ÷ 1,000 units of normal production)	$15.00	
Variable	7.00	22.00
Total standard unit cost		$192.00

During July, 800 entertainment centers were scheduled and produced at the following actual unit costs:

Direct materials, 110 feet at $1.20 per foot	$132.00
Direct labor, 5½ hours at $7.80 per hour	42.90
Manufacturing overhead, $18,480 ÷ 800 units	23.10
Total actual unit cost	$198.00

Instructions

a. Compute the following cost variances for the month of July:

1. Materials price variance
2. Materials quantity variance
3. Labor rate variance
4. Labor efficiency variance
5. Overhead spending variance
6. Volume variance

b. Prepare journal entries to assign manufacturing costs to the Work in Process Inventory account and to record cost variances for July. Use separate entries for (**1**) direct materials, (**2**) direct labor, and (**3**) overhead costs.

c. Comment on any significant problems or areas of cost savings revealed by your computation of cost variances. Also comment on any possible causal relationships between significant favorable and unfavorable cost variances.

LO1 LO3 LO4

PROBLEM 24.8A

Understanding Cost Variances: Solving for Missing Data

Ripley Corporation has supplied the following information obtained from its standard cost system in June:

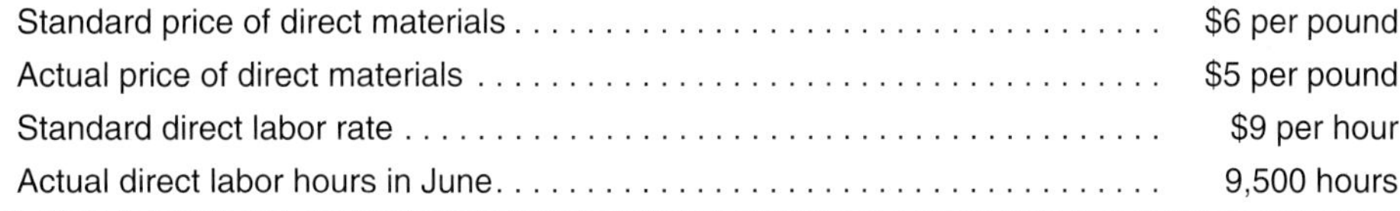

Standard price of direct materials	$6 per pound
Actual price of direct materials	$5 per pound
Standard direct labor rate	$9 per hour
Actual direct labor hours in June	9,500 hours

The following journal entries were made during June with respect to Ripley's standard cost system:

Work in Process Inventory (at standard cost)	48,000	
Materials Quantity Variance	1,200	
Direct Materials Inventory (at actual cost)		41,000
Materials Price Variance		8,200
To record the cost of direct materials used in June.		

Work in Process Inventory (at standard cost)	81,000	
Labor Rate Variance	950	
Labor Efficiency Variance	4,500	
Direct Labor (at actual cost)		86,450
To record the cost of direct labor charged to production in June.		

Work in Process Inventory (at standard cost)	25,000	
Overhead Spending Variance	2,000	
Overhead Volume Variance		5,000
Manufacturing Overhead (at actual cost)		22,000
To apply overhead to production in June.		

Instructions

a. Determine the actual quantity of materials purchased and used in production during June.

b. Determine the standard quantity of materials allowed for the productive output achieved during June.

c. Determine the actual average direct labor rate in June.

d. Determine the standard direct labor hours allowed for the production output achieved during June.

e. Determine the total overhead costs allowed for the production output achieved during June.

f. Prepare a journal entry to record the transfer of all work in process to finished goods at the end of June.

g. Close all cost variances directly to the Cost of Goods Sold account at the end of June.

h. Was Ripley's production output in June more or less than its normal level of output? How can you tell?

LO3 LO4

PROBLEM 24.9A
Understanding Variance Calculations

Anton Company manufactures wooden magazine stands. An accountant for Anton just completed the variance report for the current month. After printing the report, his computer's hard drive crashed, effectively destroying most of the actual results for the month. All that the accountant remembers is that actual production was 220 stands and that all materials purchased were used in production. The following information is also available:

Current Month: Budgeted Amounts		
Budgeted production: 200 magazine stands		
Direct materials: Wood		
Usage	3 square feet per stand	
Price	$0.25 per square foot	
Direct labor:		
Usage	0.5 hours per stand	
Rate	$10 per hour	
Variable overhead (allocated based on direct labor hours):		
Rate per labor hour	$4	
Rate per stand	$2	
Fixed overhead (allocated based on direct labor hours):		
Rate per labor hour	$6	
Rate per stand	$3	
Current Month: Variances		
Direct materials price variance	$ 33	Unfavorable
Direct materials quantity variance	–0–	
Direct labor rate variance	231	Favorable
Direct labor efficiency variance	550	Unfavorable
Overhead volume variance	60	Favorable
Overhead spending variance	210	Unfavorable

Instructions

Using the budget for the current month and the variance report, construct the items below.

a. What was the actual purchase price per square foot of wood?

b. How many labor hours did it actually take to produce each stand?

c. What was the actual wage rate paid per hour?

d. What was actual total overhead for the month?

Problem Set B

LO3 through LO5 PROBLEM 24.1B
Understanding Materials Cost Variances and Volume Variance

Denton's materials quantity variance for the current month was exactly one-half of its materials price variance. Both variances were unfavorable. The company's cost accountant has supplied the following standard cost information:

Standard price per pound of materials	$12
Actual pounds purchased and used during the month	800 pounds
Actual cost per pound of materials purchased and used	$15
Actual units manufactured during the month	600 units
Normal productive output per month	700 units

Instructions

a. Compute Denton's materials price variance.

b. Compute the standard quantity of materials allowed for producing 700 units of product.

c. Record the journal entry to charge work in process for the cost of materials used during the month.

d. Assume Denton's overhead volume variance is twice the amount of its materials quantity variance. Is the volume variance favorable or unfavorable? How do you know?

LO3 LO4 PROBLEM 24.2B
Computing and Journalizing Cost Variances

Dyelot Industries manufactures dyes and uses cost standards. The dye is produced in 1,000 pound batches; the normal level of production is 500 batches of dye per month. The standard costs per batch are as follows:

		Standard Costs per Batch
Direct materials:		
Various chemicals (1,000 pounds per batch at $0.80/pound)		$ 800
Direct labor:		
Preparation and blending (20 hours per batch at $8.00/hour)		160
Manufacturing overhead:		
Fixed ($150,000 per month ÷ 500 batches)	$300	
Variable (per batch)	20	320
Total standard cost per batch of fertilizer		$1,280

During January, the company temporarily reduced the level of production to 400 batches of dye. Actual costs incurred in January were as follows:

Direct materials (410,000 pounds at $0.75)	$307,500
Direct labor (7,950 hours at $7.80/hour)	62,010
Manufacturing overhead	150,490
Total actual costs (400 batches)	$520,000
Standard cost of 400 batches (400 batches × $1,280 per batch)	512,000
Net unfavorable cost variance	$ 8,000

Instructions

You have been engaged to explain in detail the elements of the $8,000 net unfavorable cost variance and to record the manufacturing costs for January in the company's standard cost accounting system.

a. As a first step, compute the materials price and quantity variances, the labor rate and efficiency variances, and the overhead spending and volume variances for the month.

b. Prepare journal entries to record the flow of manufacturing costs through the standard cost system and the related cost variances. Make separate entries to record the costs of direct materials used, direct labor, and manufacturing overhead. Work in Process Inventory is to be debited only with standard costs.

LO3 LO4 **PROBLEM 24.3B**
Computing and Journalizing Cost Variances

Latin Silk Products uses standard costs in a process cost system. At the end of the current month, the following information is prepared by the company's cost accountant:

	Direct Materials	Direct Labor	Manufacturing Overhead
Actual costs incurred	$108,000	$96,000	$120,000
Standard costs	100,000	94,000	112,800
Materials price variance (favorable)	2,000		
Materials quantity variance (unfavorable)	10,000		
Labor rate variance (favorable)		6,000	
Labor efficiency variance (unfavorable)		8,000	
Overhead spending variance (unfavorable)			1,200
Overhead volume variance (unfavorable)			6,000

The total standard cost per unit of finished product is $15. During the current month, 20,000 units were completed and transferred to the finished goods inventory and 18,000 units were sold. The inventory of work in process at the end of the month consists of 3,000 units that are 70 percent complete. There was no inventory in process at the beginning of the month.

Instructions

a. Prepare journal entries to record all variances and the costs incurred (at standard) in the Work in Process account as separate compound entries for (**1**) direct materials, (**2**) direct labor, and (**3**) manufacturing overhead.

b. Prepare journal entries to record (**1**) the transfer of units finished to the Finished Goods Inventory account and (**2**) the Cost of Goods Sold (at standard) for the month.

c. Assuming that the company operated at 80 percent of its normal capacity during the current month, what is the amount of the budgeted fixed manufacturing overhead per month?

LO3 LO4 **PROBLEM 24.4B**
Computing and Journalizing Cost Variances

Hans Enterprises is a large producer of birdseed. During June, the company produced 160 batches of crow bait. Each batch weighs 1,000 pounds. To produce this quantity of output, the company purchased and used 170,000 pounds of direct materials at a cost of $816,000. It also incurred direct labor costs of $20,000 for the 2,500 hours worked by employees on the crow bait crew. Manufacturing overhead incurred at the crow bait plant during June totaled $4,200, of which $3,100 was considered fixed. Hans's standard cost information for each 1,000-pound batch of crow bait is as follows:

Direct materials standard price	$5.00 per pound
Standard quantity allowed per batch	1,025 pounds
Direct labor standard rate	$8.25 per hour
Standard hours allowed per batch	15 direct labor hours
Fixed overhead budgeted	$3,200 per month
Normal level of production	150 batches per month
Variable overhead application rate	$10.00 per batch
Fixed overhead application rate ($3,300 ÷ 150 batches)	22.00 per batch
Total overhead application rate	$32.00 per batch

Instructions

a. Compute the materials price and quantity variances.

b. Compute the labor rate and efficiency variances.

c. Compute the manufacturing overhead spending and volume variances.

d. Record the journal entry to charge materials (at standard) to Work in Process.

e. Record the journal entry to charge direct labor (at standard) to Work in Process.

f. Record the journal entry to charge manufacturing overhead (at standard) to Work in Process.

g. Record the journal entry to transfer the 160 batches of crow bait produced in June to Finished Goods.

h. Record the journal entry to close any over- or underapplied overhead to Cost of Goods Sold.

LO3 LO4 **PROBLEM 24.5B**

Computing and Journalizing Cost Variances

Smooth Corporation is a small producer of paint. During June, the company produced 10,000 cases of paint. Each case contains twelve quarts of paint. To achieve this level of production, Smooth purchased and used 34,000 gallons of direct materials at a cost of $43,520. It also incurred average direct labor costs of $14 per hour for the 8,300 hours worked in June by its production personnel. Manufacturing overhead for the month totaled $21,000, of which $4,500 was considered fixed. Smooth's standard cost information for each case of paint is as follows:

Direct materials standard price	$1.32 per gallon
Standard quantity allowed per case	3.00 gallons
Direct labor standard rate	$15 per hour
Standard hours allowed per case	0.80 direct labor hours
Fixed overhead budgeted	$5,252 per month
Normal level of production	10,100 cases per month
Variable overhead application rate	$1.60 per case
Fixed overhead application rate ($5,252 ÷ 10,100 cases)	0.52 per case
Total overhead application rate	$2.12 per case

Instructions

a. Compute the materials price and quantity variances.

b. Compute the labor rate and efficiency variances.

c. Compute the manufacturing overhead spending and volume variances.

d. Prepare the journal entries to:

1. Charge materials (at standard) to Work in Process.
2. Charge direct labor (at standard) to Work in Process.
3. Charge manufacturing overhead (at standard) to Work in Process.
4. Transfer the cost of the 10,000 cases of paint produced in June to Finished Goods.
5. Close any over- or underapplied overhead to Cost of Goods Sold.

LO3 LO4 **PROBLEM 24.6B**
Computing and Journalizing Cost Variances

The accountants for Monoglut, Inc., have developed the following information regarding the standard cost and the actual cost of a product manufactured in March:

	Standard Cost	Actual Cost
Direct materials:		
Standard: 12 ounces at $0.20 per ounce	$ 2.40	
Actual: 13 ounces at $0.22 per ounce		$ 2.86
Direct labor:		
Standard: 0.60 hours at $12.00 per hour	7.20	
Actual: 0.50 hours at $13.00 per hour		6.50
Manufacturing overhead:		
Standard: $6,000 fixed cost and $4,000 variable cost for 10,000 units normal monthly volume	1.00	
Actual: $6,000 fixed cost and $2,540 variable cost for 7,000 units actually produced in March		1.22
Total unit cost	$10.60	$10.58

Instructions

a. Compute the materials price variance and the materials quantity variance, indicating whether each is favorable or unfavorable. Prepare the journal entry to record the cost of direct materials used during March in the Work in Process account (at standard).

b. Compute the labor rate variance and the labor efficiency variance, indicating whether each is favorable or unfavorable. Prepare the journal entry to record the cost of direct labor used during March in the Work in Process account (at standard).

c. Compute the overhead spending variance and the overhead volume variance, indicating whether each is favorable or unfavorable. Prepare the journal entry to assign overhead cost to production in March.

LO3 through LO5 **PROBLEM 24.7B**
Computing, Journalizing, and Analyzing Cost Variances

Colonial Furniture Co. uses a standard cost system. One of the company's most popular products is a cherrywood desk. The per-unit standard costs of the desk, assuming a "normal" volume of 2,000 units per month, are as follows:

Direct materials, 100 board-feet of wood at $1.50 per foot		$150.00
Direct labor, 4 hours at $10.00 per hour		40.00
Manufacturing overhead (applied at $18 per unit)		
Fixed ($20,000 ÷ 2,000 units of normal production)	$10.00	
Variable	8.00	18.00
Total standard unit cost		$208.00

During May, 1,800 desks were scheduled and produced at the following actual unit costs:

Direct materials, 105 feet at $1.40 per foot	$147.00
Direct labor, 4½ hours at $9.00 per hour	40.50
Manufacturing overhead, $34,200 ÷ 1,800 units	19.00
Total actual unit cost	$206.50

Instructions

a. Compute the following cost variances for the month of May:

1. Materials price variance
2. Materials quantity variance
3. Labor rate variance

4. Labor efficiency variance
5. Overhead spending variance
6. Volume variance

b. Prepare journal entries to assign manufacturing costs to the Work in Process Inventory account and to record cost variances for May. Use separate entries for (**1**) direct materials, (**2**) direct labor, and (**3**) overhead costs.

c. Comment on any significant problems or areas of cost savings revealed by your computation of cost variances. Also comment on any possible causal relationships between significant favorable and unfavorable cost variances.

LO1 LO3 LO4

PROBLEM 24.8B

Understanding Cost Variances: Solving for Missing Data

Foding Corporation has supplied the following information obtained from its standard cost system in May:

Standard price of direct materials	$7 per pound
Actual price of direct materials	$6 per pound
Standard direct labor rate	$10 per pound
Actual direct labor hours in May	4,000 hours

The following journal entries were made during May with respect to Foding's standard cost system:

Work in Process Inventory (at standard cost)	9,500	
Materials Quantity Variance	1,000	
Direct Materials Inventory (at actual cost)		9,000
Materials Price Variance		1,500
To record the cost of direct materials used in May.		

Work in Process Inventory (at standard cost)	35,000	
Labor Rate Variance	8,000	
Labor Efficiency Variance	5,000	
Direct Labor (at actual cost)		48,000
To record the cost of direct labor charged to production in May.		

Work in Process Inventory (at standard cost)	28,000	
Overhead Spending Variance	3,000	
Overhead Volume Variance		6,000
Manufacturing Overhead (at actual cost)		25,000
To apply overhead to production in May.		

Instructions

a. Determine the actual quantity of materials purchased and used in production during May.

b. Determine the standard quantity of materials allowed for the production output achieved during May.

c. Determine the actual average direct labor rate in May.

d. Determine the standard direct labor hours allowed for the production output achieved during May.

e. Determine the total overhead costs allowed for the production output achieved during May.

f. Prepare a journal entry to record the transfer of all work in process to finished goods at the end of May.

g. Close all cost variances directly to the Cost of Goods Sold account at the end of May.

h. Was Foding's production output in May more or less than its normal level of output? How can you tell?

LO3 LO4

PROBLEM 24.9B
Understanding Variance Calculations

Ninna Company manufactures wooden shelves. An accountant for Ninna just completed the variance report for the current month. After printing the report, his computer's hard drive crashed, effectively destroying most of the actual results for the month. The accountant remembers that actual production was 250 shelves and that all materials purchased were used in production. The following information is also available:

Current Month: Budgeted Amounts

Budgeted production: 225 shelves	
Direct materials: Wood	
Usage	4 square feet per shelf
Price	$0.20 per square foot
Direct labor:	
Usage	0.4 hours per shelf
Rate	$12 per hour
Variable overhead (allocated based on direct labor hours):	
Rate per labor hour	$5
Rate per shelf	$2
Fixed overhead (allocated based on direct labor hours):	
Rate per labor hour	$10
Rate per shelf	$4

Current Month: Variances

Direct materials price variance	$ 40	Unfavorable
Direct materials quantity variance	–0–	
Direct labor rate variance	200	Favorable
Direct labor efficiency variance	300	Unfavorable
Overhead volume variance	50	Favorable
Overhead spending variance	100	Unfavorable

Instructions

Using the budget for the current month and the variance report, construct the items below:

a. What was the actual purchase price per square foot of wood?

b. How many labor hours did it actually take to produce each shelf?

c. What was the actual wage rate paid per hour?

d. What was the actual total overhead for the month?

Critical Thinking Cases

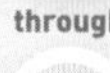

LO1 LO3 through LO5

CASE 24.1
It's Not My Fault

Cabinets, Inc., is a large manufacturer of modular kitchen cabinets, sold primarily to builders and developers. The company uses a standard cost system. Standard production costs have been developed for each type of cabinet; these costs, and any cost variances, are charged to the production department. A budget also has been developed for the sales department. The sales department is credited with the gross profit on sales (measured at standard cost) and is charged with selling expenses and any variations between budgeted and actual selling expenses.

In early April, the manager of the sales department asked the production department to fill a rush order of kitchen cabinets for a tract of 120 homes. The sales manager stated that the entire order must be completed by May 31. The manager of the production department argued that an order of this size would take 12 weeks to produce. The sales manager answered, "The customer needs it on May 31, or we don't get the business. Do you want to be responsible for our losing a customer who makes orders of this size?"

Of course, the production manager did not want to take that responsibility. Therefore, he gave in and processed the rush order by having production personnel work overtime through April and May. As a result of the overtime, the performance reports for the production department in those months showed large, unfavorable labor rate variances. The production manager, who in the past had prided himself on coming in under budget, now has very ill feelings toward the sales manager. He also has stated that the production department will never again accept a rush order.

Instructions

a. Identify any problem that you see in the company's standard cost system or in the manner in which cost variances are assigned to the responsible managers.

b. Make recommendations for changing the cost accounting system to reduce or eliminate any problems that you have identified.

LO1 LO3 through LO5

CASE 24.2

Determination and Use of Standard Costs

Armstrong Chemical began operations in January. The company manufactures an acrylic car wax called Tough-Coat. The following standard cost estimates were developed several months before the company began operations, based on an estimated production of 1,000,000 units (pints):

Material X-1 (1 ounce)	$1.00
Material X-2 (1 pound)	0.50
Direct labor	0.80
Manufacturing overhead ($1,400,000 ÷ 1,000,000 units)	1.40
Total estimated standard cost per pint	$3.70

During the year, 1,000,000 pints of Tough-Coat were actually produced, of which 900,000 were sold. Actual costs incurred during the year were:

Material X-1 purchased, 1,200,000 ounces @ $0.70	$ 840,000
Material X-2 purchased, 1,150,000 pounds @ $0.50	575,000
Direct labor	880,000
Manufacturing overhead	1,400,000
Total production cost incurred during the year	$3,695,000

The company's inventories at the end of the year consisted of the following, with the Finished Goods inventory stated at standard cost:

Direct materials:		
Material X-1: 200,000 ounces @ $0.70	$140,000	
Material X-2: 100,000 pounds @ $0.50	50,000	$190,000
Finished Goods:		
Tough-Coat: 100,000 pints @ $3.70 standard cost		370,000
Total inventory at December 31		$560,000

The independent certified public accountant who has been engaged to audit the company's financial statements wants to adjust the valuation of Finished Goods inventory to "a revised standard cost" that would take into account the favorable price variance on material X-1 ($0.30 per ounce) and the 10 percent wage increase early in the year. (An unfavorable quantity variance on material X-2 was caused by spoilage in production; the CPA feels no adjustment to the standard should be made for this type of item.)

The president of the company objects on the following grounds: "Such a revision is not necessary because the cost of material X-1 already shows signs of going up and the wage increase was not warranted because the productivity of workers did not increase one bit. Furthermore, if we revise our inventory figure of $560,000, our operating income will be reduced from the current level of $50,000." You are called in by the president to help resolve the controversy.

Instructions

a. Do you agree with the president that revision of the $3.70 standard cost figure is not necessary?

b. Assume that you conclude that the standards for this first year of operations should be revised. Compute a "revised standard cost per unit" and determine the value to be assigned to the ending inventory of finished units using this revised standard cost.

c. What effect would this revaluation of Finished Goods inventory have on the company's operating income?

d. Using the *original* standards, compute the following:

1. Materials price variance and quantity variance for material X-1.
2. Materials price variance and quantity variance for material X-2.
3. Total direct labor variance (do not separate into rate variance and usage variance).
4. Total manufacturing overhead variance.

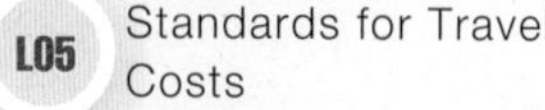

LO2 LO5

INTERNET CASE 24.3

Standards for Travel Costs

Each year, a large clothing store in New York City sends its top five salespersons on a five-day retreat in Orlando, Florida. The retreat begins on the first Monday in February and ends the following Friday afternoon. The company must purchase five coach-class airline tickets from New York City to Orlando, Florida. The total budgeted airfare for the trip is $1,400 for five tickets.

As the assistant in charge of purchasing the tickets, visit the following Web address:

www.travelocity.com

Find the lowest fare between the two airlines for a round-trip flight leaving the first Monday morning in February and returning Friday evening.

Instructions

a. On the basis of the lowest fare, calculate the total spending variance related to the ticket purchase. Is it favorable or unfavorable?

b. Does the standard seem reasonable given current ticket prices? What factors might determine whether the price variance is favorable or unfavorable?

LO4

CASE 24.4

Standard Cost System and Inventory Misstatement

Jams and Jellies, Inc., uses a standard cost system to track inventories and cost of goods sold. The blueberry factory that produces blueberry jams and jellies increased its standard product costs at the beginning of the fourth quarter of its operations for the current year. At the end of the year, the blueberry factory had a large favorable standard cost variance account balance. Buck, the manager of the blueberry factory, receives a large bonus based on the annual factory profits.

Buck has told Sheila, the factory accountant, to close the favorable variance account to Cost of Goods Sold. Sheila remembers that materials variance account balances should be allocated between the Inventory accounts and the Cost of Goods Sold account. However, Buck says that, although the total variance might seem material for the factory, in the grand scheme of the entire company the blueberry factory total variance is not material and Sheila should do as he has suggested.

Instructions

a. Why do you think Buck wants to close the entire variance balance to Cost of Goods Sold? If the variance account balance is closed to Cost of Goods Sold, will the ending finished goods inventory be overstated or understated?

b. Consult the Institute of Management Accountants's (IMA) Web site at http://www.imanet.org and select "About IMA" to search the "Ethics Center." Find the IMA "Statement of Ethical Professional Practice" and read the Resolution of Professional Conflict. Based on your reading, what do you think Sheila should do?

Internet sites are time and date sensitive. It is the purpose of these exercises to have you explore the Internet. You may need to use the Yahoo! search engine http://www.yahoo.com *(or another favorite search engine) to find a company's current Web address.*

Answers to Self-Test Questions

1. c **2.** d **3.** c **4.** d **5.** b and d

CHAPTER 25

Rewarding Business Performance

© AP Photo/Ben Margot

AFTER STUDYING THIS CHAPTER, YOU SHOULD BE ABLE TO:

Learning Objectives

- **LO1** Explain the importance of incentive systems for motivating performance.
- **LO2** Use the DuPont system to evaluate business performance.
- **LO3** Identify and explain the criticisms of using return on investment (ROI) as the only performance measure.
- **LO4** Calculate and explain residual income (RI) and economic value added (EVA).
- **LO5** Use the balanced scorecard to identify, evaluate, and reward business performance.
- **LO6** Identify and explain the components of management compensation and the trade-offs that compensation designers make.

GOOGLE

Two computer science graduate students, Larry Page and Sergey Brin, met in 1995 and went on to create a formula for rank ordering random Internet search results by relevancy. In 1997, the two graduate students adopted the name Google for their findings, and by 1999, the two students had raised almost $30 million in funding to launch the Google Web site. To generate revenue and increase profitability, Google launched AdWords and AdSense, two search-based advertising services, in 2001 and 2002, respectively. By 2004, Page and Brin realized the company's business performance was sufficient to go public for capital. The once highly secretive company became a public company by launching one of the most highly anticipated initial public offerings (IPO) of stock ever, raising $1.6 billion in capital on the NYSE.

One of the challenges faced by both the Google founders and its existing and potential investors is evaluating the business performance of the company and its management. This chapter focuses on measuring and rewarding business performance. ■

Motivation and Aligning Goals and Objectives

Your goals and objectives for this course might be to get a high grade and learn important accounting tools that will help you in the future. Alternatively, you or other students might view this as a required course and you may not be interested in accounting. In such a case, a goal might be to simply pass the course with the least amount of effort. Your instructor also has goals and objectives for this course. The instructor's goals for you and the other students are that you master the subject matter and understand its importance for business. The instructor's goals may or may not be consistent with any individual student's goals.

Even when your goals are consistent with your instructor's goals, it can be difficult for you to determine how to achieve the goals. For example, students encounter many demands that compete for their time, such as working at a job, reading a good novel, bowling, other course work, or snowboarding. You and your fellow students must determine how to allocate your resources (time and effort in this instance) among competing activities to achieve your goals.

COMMUNICATING GOALS AND OBJECTIVES

An instructor's goals are communicated to students by the course syllabus and through assignments, class discussions, and periodic examinations. The course syllabus directs your attention to the topics that the instructor decides are important. Periodic feedback also provides a mechanism that helps align students' goals with those of the instructor. For example, to measure progress toward the instructor's goals, you receive periodic grades for exercises, class participation, and/or examinations. This feedback is both an attempt to steer you toward the goals that the instructor has for the course and an indication of whether you are making progress in achieving those goals.

This periodic feedback is an attention-getting device that helps students allocate their valuable resources—time and effort. If the feedback suggests you are not allocating enough time and effort to accounting to learn the material and/or earn the grade that is one of your goals for the course, you will be likely to allocate more time and effort to studying accounting.

ACCOUNTING INFORMATION AND FEEDBACK ABOUT GOAL ACHIEVEMENT

Learning Objective
LO1 Explain the importance of incentive systems for motivating performance.

Just as you have objectives and goals you are trying to achieve by studying accounting, most organizations have objectives and goals they are trying to achieve in their operations. Just as you make choices about what to do with the resources under your control, an organization's employees must make choices about the resources for which they are responsible. Accounting information can align employees' goals with the organization's and provide feedback and incentives that guide employees in using the resources under their control to achieve the organization's goals.

Consider, for example, that your course syllabus is similar to an organization's annual budget (see Chapter 23) because both provide guidance about important goals. Such goals could include which chapters to study for your course and production quota figures for employees in an organization. Further, similar to the grading feedback that helps direct your attention and resources, periodically comparing accounting results of actual outcomes against budgeted accounting information helps employees understand how well they have allocated their resources and suggests how to reallocate resources in the future.

REWARDING GOAL ACHIEVEMENT

This chapter focuses on motivating business employees, customers, suppliers, and others in and outside of the company to help the organization achieve its goals and objectives. Exhibit 25–1 shows how accounting information plays an important role in aligning employee and organizational goals and in motivating employees to achieve those goals.

Exhibit 25–1 THE ROLE OF THE ACCOUNTING SYSTEM IN GOAL ACHIEVEMENT

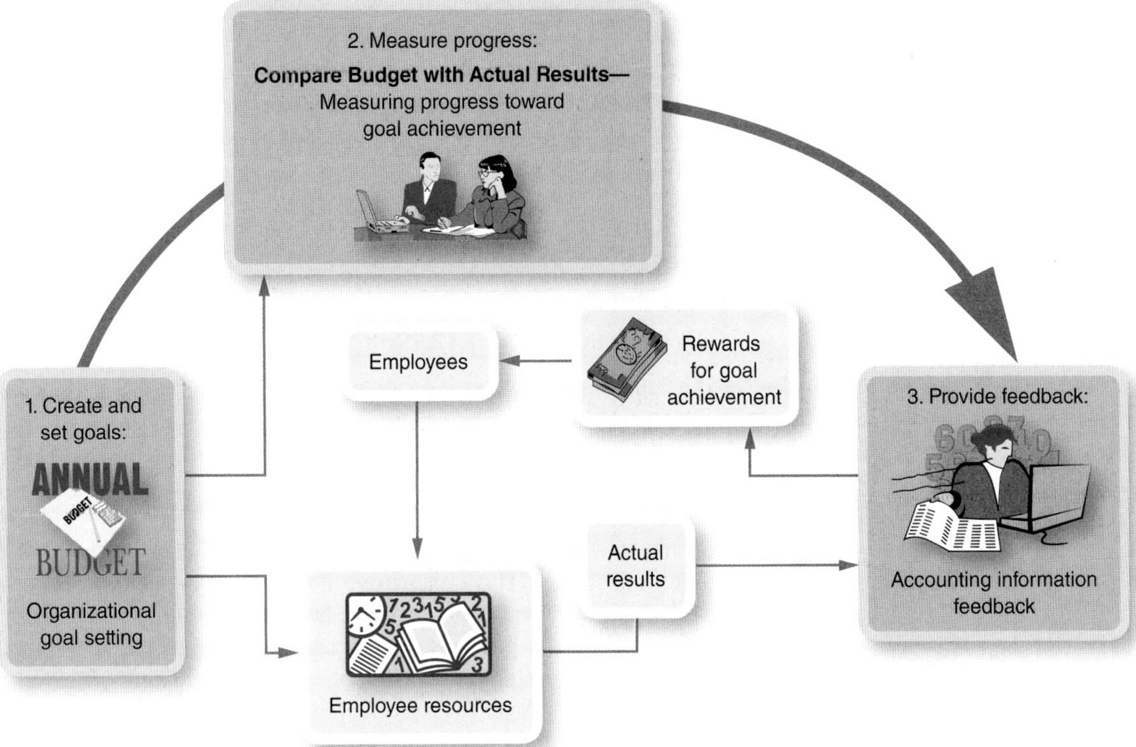

Generating motivation requires three actions from accounting systems. **First,** the accounting system helps *create and set goals* and objectives through planning information such as budgeting. **Second,** the accounting system *measures progress* toward the goals and provides *feedback* about that progress. And **third,** accounting-based information is instrumental in allocating *rewards* for progress toward goal achievement. Exhibit 25–1 shows the role of the accounting system in motivating employees to achieve the organization's goals. Accounting systems are an important management tool for generating and focusing employee motivation.

The DuPont System

One of the first systems to focus on business performance measurement was created during the early 1900s by managers at the **DuPont de Nemours Powder Company**. Managers at **DuPont** wanted a method to help them set goals and measure progress toward achieving objectives. These managers began by experimenting with a performance evaluation system that still has many advocates around the world. Because **DuPont**'s owners received significant bank loans for their business, the owners and their managers needed a system to control and evaluate their operations that would ensure repayment of the loans.

RETURN ON INVESTMENT

After tracing the costs and revenue associated with their products, **DuPont**'s managers soon realized that product line profits were an incomplete performance measure. The profit computations included no measure of the amount of invested capital for each product line. Two product lines could be returning the same profit, for example, $250,000, but one product line might require twice as many assets (say, $4 million versus $2 million) to produce the same profit. Thus, the **DuPont** managers created the idea of **return on investment** or **ROI.**

ROI, also often referred to as return on assets (ROA), was introduced in Chapter 14 and is calculated as shown in Exhibit 25–2.

Exhibit 25–2
CALCULATION OF RETURN ON INVESTMENT

$$\text{ROI} = \frac{\textbf{Operating Income}}{\textbf{Average Total Assets}}$$

Although ROI is usually discussed as a percent, it basically tells managers the amount of earnings expected for the average invested dollar. In the example discussed at the bottom of the previous page, the ROI of the two product lines is:

Product line 1 ROI = 6.25% = \$250,000 ÷ \$4,000,000
Product line 2 ROI = 12.5% = \$250,000 ÷ \$2,000,000

For the first product line, managers earned \$.0625 on the average invested dollar. For the second product line, however, they earned \$.125 per average invested dollar. If a company financed its assets with bank loans carrying an interest rate of 8 percent, then the first product line would not provide a large enough return on invested capital to repay the interest on the loans.

The **DuPont** managers wanted to assess ROI for different segments of their business as well as for different product lines. This broader use of ROI requires careful measures of the invested capital for each segment and/or product line. Invested capital in a segment or product line refers to expenditures made to purchase plant assets, develop new product lines, acquire subsidiary companies, purchase equipment, pay for significant training costs, etc. These investments commit financial resources to projects, products, buildings, equipment, and so on, with the expectation that the investment will benefit the firm by producing income over long periods of time. Firms want invested capital to produce income by increasing sales and/or reducing costs. Thus, firms want to *predict* (before committing financial resources) and *measure* (after committing those resources) return on investment. Please note that ROI is used for both planning and control purposes. Tracking plant, properties, and inventories to each segment and product line is challenging work.

Not satisfied with knowing only the ROI, the **DuPont** managers developed a system to help them understand the component parts of ROI so that they could determine what causes ROI to change. Exhibit 25–3 shows the definitions of the two component parts of ROI, capital turnover (CT = Sales ÷ Total Investment) and return on sales (ROS = Earnings ÷ Sales):

$$\textbf{ROI} = \textbf{CT} \times \textbf{ROS}$$

Exhibit 25–3 DUPONT SYSTEM OF PERFORMANCE MEASUREMENT

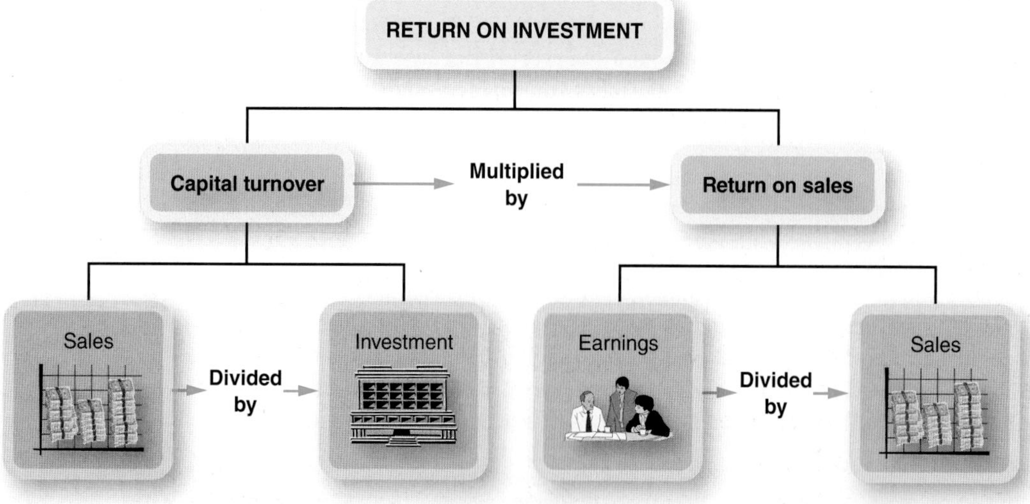

THE COMPONENTS OF RETURN ON INVESTMENT

Learning Objective
Use the DuPont system to evaluate business performance. LO2

The component parts of ROI, capital turnover and return on sales, give managers a way to compare product line ROIs and a way to evaluate changes in ROI over time. **Capital turnover (CT)** tells managers about how the invested capital is generating (or "turning over") sales dollars, that is, the amount of monetary sales that can be expected from a dollar of invested capital. **Return on sales (ROS)** indicates the operating earnings or profitability that can be expected from one dollar of sales. Operating earnings rather than net income is used to compute return on sales because operating earnings better reflect the resources that managers can control. Thus, the **DuPont system of performance measurement** analyzes business performance by considering both the earnings per sales dollar and the investment in assets used to generate those sales dollars.

To better understand how the components of ROI can help evaluate and assess business processes, we will use the information for two product lines of Bastille Company, a producer of fine French dining products, shown in Exhibit 25–4 on the following page.

Although the ROI is significantly higher for the Cookware product line, additional analysis will clarify the role of the components of ROI. To explain their roles, we analyze the ROI component information computed for Bastille Company.

© Getty Images/Stockbyte/DAL

RETURN ON SALES

In Exhibit 25–4 results for the Fine China Division in Year 1 show that the return on sales was 30 percent or, alternatively, each sales dollar generated $0.30 of earnings. For the Cookware Division, however, each sales dollar generated $0.525 of earnings. To have an impact on return on sales in Year 2, a division manager would need to *reduce* cost of goods sold or operating expenses without any impact on revenue or *increase* revenue without a proportional impact on expenses.

In Year 2, the manager of the Fine China Division was able to increase revenue from $1,500,000 to $1,700,000 without a proportional increase in cost of goods sold. Although cost of goods sold did increase, the percentage increase was smaller than the percentage increase in revenue, as shown below.

Revenue increase = 13.3% = ($1,700,000 − $1,500,000) ÷ $1,500,000
Cost of goods sold increase = 12% = ($840,000 − $750,000) ÷ $750,000

In addition, the manager of the Fine China Division kept the percentage increase in other operating expenses below the 13.3 percent increase in revenue [($330,000 − $300,000) ÷ $300,000 = 10%]. The return on sales increase of 1 percent from Year 1 to Year 2 shows that the combination of efforts to increase revenue and have a smaller increase in cost resulted in increased earnings of more than $.01 for each dollar of sales revenue.

The Cookware Division manager did not fare as well with return on sales between Years 1 and 2 as the manager of the Fine China Division. By comparing return on sales in Year 1 and Year 2 from Exhibit 25–4, you can see that the Cookware Division showed a drop of $.01 of earnings (52.5% − 51.5% = 1%) for each sales dollar. Using our DuPont method to analyze the Cookware Division shows that revenue remained constant while cost of goods sold and operating expenses increased.

Constant revenue = 0% = ($400,000 − $400,000)
Cost of goods sold increase = 2.5% = [($100,000 − $102,500) ÷ $100,000]
Operating expenses increase = 1.7% = [($90,000 − $91,500) ÷ $90,000]

YOUR TURN **You as Cookware Division Manager**

Assume you are the manager of the Cookware Division at Bastille Company. Your boss has criticized your division's performance in Year 2, specifically targeting the return on sales. When planning your operating budget for Year 3, what strategies might you consider that could improve your division's return on sales?

(See our comments on the Online Learning Center Web site.)

Exhibit 25–4 ACCOUNTING INFORMATION IN YEARS 1 & 2 FOR BASTILLE COMPANY

Year 1

	Fine China	Cookware
Sales	$1,500,000	$ 400,000
Cost of goods sold	750,000	100,000
Operating expenses	300,000	90,000
Operating earnings	$ 450,000	$ 210,000
Average invested capital	$6,000,000	$1,400,000
ROI	**(450,000 ÷ 6,000,000) = 7.5%**	**(210,000 ÷ 1,400,000) = 15%**
Return on sales	**(450,000 ÷ 1,500,000) = 30%**	**(210,000 ÷ 400,000) = 52.5%**
Capital turnover	**(1,500,000 ÷ 6,000,000) = 25%**	**(400,000 ÷ 1,400,000) = 28.57%**

Year 2

	Fine China	Cookware
Sales	$1,700,000	$ 400,000
Cost of goods sold	840,000	102,500
Operating expenses	330,000	91,500
Operating earnings	$ 530,000	$ 206,000
Average invested capital	$6,200,000	$1,300,000
ROI	**(530,000 ÷ 6,200,000) = 8.55%**	**(206,000 ÷ 1,300,000) = 15.85%**
Return on sales	**(530,000 ÷ 1,700,000) = 31.18%**	**(206,000 ÷ 400,000) = 51.5%**
Capital turnover	**(1,700,000 ÷ 6,200,000) = 27.42%**	**(400,000 ÷ 1,300,000) = 30.77%**

CAPITAL TURNOVER

The capital turnover ratio in Exhibit 25–4 for the Cookware Division in Year 1 shows $0.286 of sales for each dollar of invested capital. The Cookware Division's capital turnover increased in Year 2 to $0.308 of sales per dollar of capital. How was the Cookware manager able to increase capital turnover despite total sales revenue that remained flat from Year 1 to Year 2? The manager reduced the average amount of invested capital by $100,000 ($1,400,000 – $1,300,000). Managers can reduce invested capital by selling equipment, warehouse space, and such. Generating constant sales using a smaller amount of invested capital is one method that managers can use to improve capital turnover.

The turnover ratio for Fine China in Year 1 tells us that this division is creating $0.25 of sales for each dollar of invested capital. The turnover ratio improved significantly in Year 2 to $0.274 per dollar of invested capital. How was the manager of Fine China able to achieve this increase? By increasing sales without a proportional increase in average invested capital, as shown below. Evidently the additional capital expenditures made by the manager of the Fine China Division significantly improved sales revenue.

Sales increase = 13.3% = [($1,700,000 – $1,500,000) ÷ $1,500,000]
Capital increase = 3.3% = [($6,200,000 – $6,000,000) ÷ $6,000,000]

INTERNATIONAL CASE IN POINT

Surveys comparing Australian and Japanese companies' use of divisional performance measures show that fewer Japanese companies use ROI compared to Australian and U.S. companies. In contrast, many more Japanese companies use return on sales (ROS) compared to U.S. and Australian companies. The Japanese emphasis on ROS is characteristic of a strong focus on growing market share. The Australian and U.S. emphasis on ROI is more consistent with a focus on pleasing stockholders.

Criticisms of ROI

The primary reason for using any performance measurement criteria such as ROI is to motivate employees to make decisions consistent with the goals and objectives of the organization. ROI motivates managers to earn the highest possible profits while using the minimum amount of average invested capital. Thus, managers who are measured and rewarded only on their divisions' ROI may decide to increase profits and decrease capital in their divisions in ways that are inconsistent with the best interests of the whole company. There are three primary criticisms of using ROI and the DuPont system as the only business performance measurement.

Learning Objective
Identify and explain the criticisms of using return on investment (ROI) as the only performance measure. LO3

THE SHORT HORIZON PROBLEM

The first criticism is the short horizon problem that occurs because managers frequently move from one job to another. As a result, many people believe ROI encourages a short-term orientation to the detriment of longer-term planning. For example, the Cookware Division manager in the example discussed above might know that he will soon be transferred to another job assignment. By selling assets to reduce the average invested capital, he can improve his ROI now. Even though those assets may be critical for the long-term success of the division, he is not concerned about long-run issues because he will not be managing the division in the long run.

Alternatively, the same manager might reduce cost of goods sold expenses by purchasing inferior-quality merchandise from suppliers at a lower price. The reduction in cost of goods sold expense increases the annual operating earnings for this period. However, the long-run impact of the poor-quality inputs could be reflected in the firm's overall reputation. Poor-quality cookware could have serious reputation repercussions for the entire Bastille Company, including the Fine China Division.

FAILING TO UNDERTAKE PROFITABLE INVESTMENTS

A second problem with using ROI as the only business performance measure is that, under some circumstances, it presents an incentive for a manager to reject a good project that would increase the ROI for the firm as a whole. The project rejection occurs when investing in the project would reduce the division's ROI. Reconsider the information for Bastille Company in Year 1. Notice that the average ROI for Bastille Company is 8.9 percent, as shown below:

Division—Year 1	Operating Earnings	Average Capital	ROI
Fine China	$450,000	$6,000,000	7.5%
Cookware	210,000	1,400,000	15
Bastille Company—Total	$660,000	$7,400,000	8.9%

If an opportunity arose in Year 2 for the Cookware Division to undertake an investment of $500,000 with expected annual operating earnings of $55,000 (an ROI of 11 percent for the project), the division manager would likely choose not to undertake the investment. As shown below, the proposed investment would lower the Cookware Division's ROI to 13.95 percent, but it would improve Bastille Company's average ROI to 9.05 percent.

Cookware ROI 13.95% = ($210,000 + $55,000) ÷ ($1,400,000 + $500,000)
Bastille Company ROI 9.05% = ($660,000 + $55,000) ÷ ($500,000 + $7,400,000)

Because it would lower the division's ROI even though it would improve the company's ROI, a division manager who is evaluated on the division's ROI would not undertake the project.

MEASUREMENT PROBLEMS

A third criticism of ROI is the inherent difficulty in measuring both the average invested capital and the actual operating earnings associated with that capital. Many units within an organization share invested capital and often the allocation of capital between those units is arbitrary. For example, if both the Cookware and Fine China divisions share costs associated with a research and development facility and administrative headquarters, how will the invested capital of those activities be allocated between the two divisions? Managers frequently complain that those allocations are arbitrary and should not be included in the evaluation of their business units. Yet if these units were stand-alone businesses, they would have some invested capital in administration and research and development. Organizations constantly struggle with how to make capital allocations in their attempt to evaluate business performance.

CASE IN POINT

Measurement problems also occur when managers do not follow the accounting rules. For example, an SEC enforcement action, settled in 2010, against **Lucent Technologies, Inc.**, stated that nine former officers, executives, and employees were involved in improper revenue recognition. In part, the SEC complaint states: "In their drive to realize revenue, meet internal sales targets and/or obtain sales bonuses," these defendants "violated and circumvented **Lucent**'s internal accounting controls, falsified documents and hid side agreements with customers."

Inflating revenues via improper revenue recognition clearly increases ROI measures, misleading anyone relying on those measures to assess performance. The lesson from **Lucent**'s case is that care must be taken in designing employee reward systems that do not encourage overly aggressive accounting measurement by employees.

Residual Income and Economic Value Added

Learning Objective
LO4 **Calculate and explain residual income (RI) and economic value added (EVA).**

In response to the criticisms leveled at ROI, other financially based business performance measures have been created. Two of these measures, residual income (RI) and economic value added (EVA), are described here. These measures also help managers evaluate the profitability of particular parts of the business related to a specific investment base. But these measures do not suffer from some of the horizon and underinvestment criticisms attributed to ROI.

RESIDUAL INCOME

The amount by which operating earnings exceed a minimum acceptable return on average invested capital is referred to as **residual income.** It is calculated as shown in Exhibit 25–5.

Exhibit 25–5
CALCULATION OF RESIDUAL INCOME

$$\text{Residual Income} = \text{Operating Earnings} - \left\{ \text{Minimum Acceptable Return} \times \text{Invested Capital} \right\}$$

To understand how residual income avoids some of the criticisms associated with ROI, consider the previous example where the manager of the Cookware Division had the opportunity to undertake a new project. The expected operating earnings for the project were \$55,000 on invested capital of \$500,000 (project ROI = 11%). If the minimum acceptable return for the Cookware Division is set at 10 percent and residual income is the performance measure, then the division manager would be motivated to undertake the investment opportunity. Consider the following computations:

Residual Income for Cookware Division

Without the project	= (\$210,000) − .10 (\$1,400,000) = \$70,000
With the project	= (\$210,000 + \$55,000) − .10 (\$1,400,000 + \$500,000) = \$75,000

Although the concept of residual income was developed by **General Motors Corporation** in the 1920s and later refined by **General Electric Company** in the 1950s, historically it has not been widely used in performance measurement plans. Recently, however, consultants have repackaged the residual income concept into economic value added.

ECONOMIC VALUE ADDED

Referred to in the popular press as EVA,[1] **economic value added** is a refinement of the residual income measure. EVA has gained significant popularity as a component of compensation plans. Companies such as **Quaker Oats**, **Herman Miller**, **Eli Lilly**, and **Coca-Cola** have used EVA to measure business performance. EVA is computed as shown in Exhibit 25–6.

$$\text{EVA} = \text{After-Tax Operating Income} - \left\{ \text{Division's Total Assets} - \text{Division's Current Liabilities} \right\} \times \text{Weighted-Average Cost of Capital}$$

Exhibit 25–6
CALCULATION OF ECONOMIC VALUE ADDED

This formula can apply to a division or a total company. The weighted-average cost of capital is a more refined measure of the acceptable minimum return discussed above. It encompasses the average after-tax cost of long-term borrowing and the cost of equity. It is typically measured by the treasurer of the firm. Modifying the EVA computations to fit specific divisions and companies is an art. One consulting firm that measures EVA has more than 150 possible adjustments to reported accounting measures that it uses in determining EVA. Using EVA and residual income concepts in incentive plans motivates managers to eliminate assets that earn less than the minimum required return and invest in those projects that earn more than the minimum required return.

The Balanced Scorecard

A major criticism of ROI, RI, and EVA as performance evaluation tools is that they focus on only one component of the business, financial outcomes. Focusing on financial numbers rather than on supplier quality might motivate the manager of the Cookware Division to unintentionally change to a poor-quality supplier. As discussed in Chapter 19, total quality management includes careful consideration of quality across the entire **value chain.** Exhibit 25–7 shows the value chain for the Cookware Division's product line.

Exhibit 25–7 VALUE CHAIN FOR BASTILLE COMPANY'S COOKWARE DIVISION

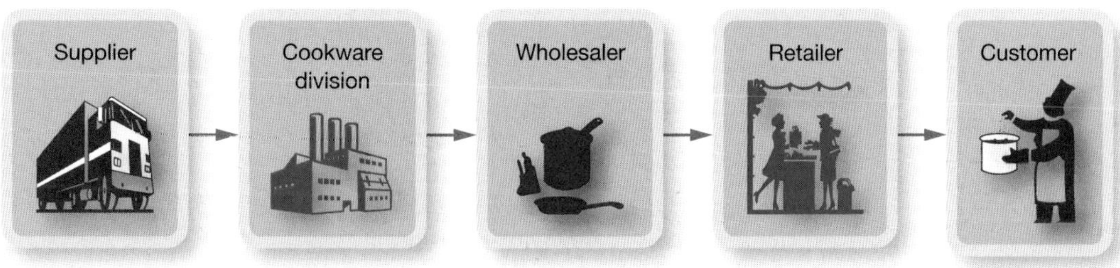

[1] **Stern Stewart & Co.**, a consulting firm, has a trademark on economic value added.

For Bastille Company's cookware line to be successful, all parts of the value chain must add value. Thus, performance measurement systems that ignore the links in the value chain run the risk of a failure somewhere on the chain. That failure could result in the failure of the cookware product. An approach for setting strategic goals and measuring progress toward those goals across the entire value chain has been developed. This approach is referred to as the balanced scorecard.

Learning Objective
LO5 Use the balanced scorecard to identify, evaluate, and reward business performance.

Developed in the early 1990s by two Harvard Business School professors, the **balanced scorecard** is a system for performance measurement that links a company's strategy to specific goals and objectives, provides measures for assessing progress toward those goals, and indicates specific initiatives to achieve those goals. It is a systematic attempt to create a business performance measurement process that integrates objectives across the span of the value chain. The main objective of the balanced scorecard is achieving the organization's strategic goals.

Unlike the DuPont system, which focuses only on the financial measure of ROI, the balanced scorecard looks at firm performance through four lenses, only one of which focuses on financial performance. As identified in Exhibit 25–8, the four lenses include: (1) the traditional financial perspective discussed previously in this chapter; (2) a customer perspective; (3) a business process perspective; and (4) a learning and growth perspective. In Exhibit 25–8 we show the links between the lenses and the firm's strategy. Below we describe each of these

Exhibit 25–8
BALANCED SCORECARD LINKAGES

THE PERFORMANCE LENSES OF THE BALANCED SCORECARD

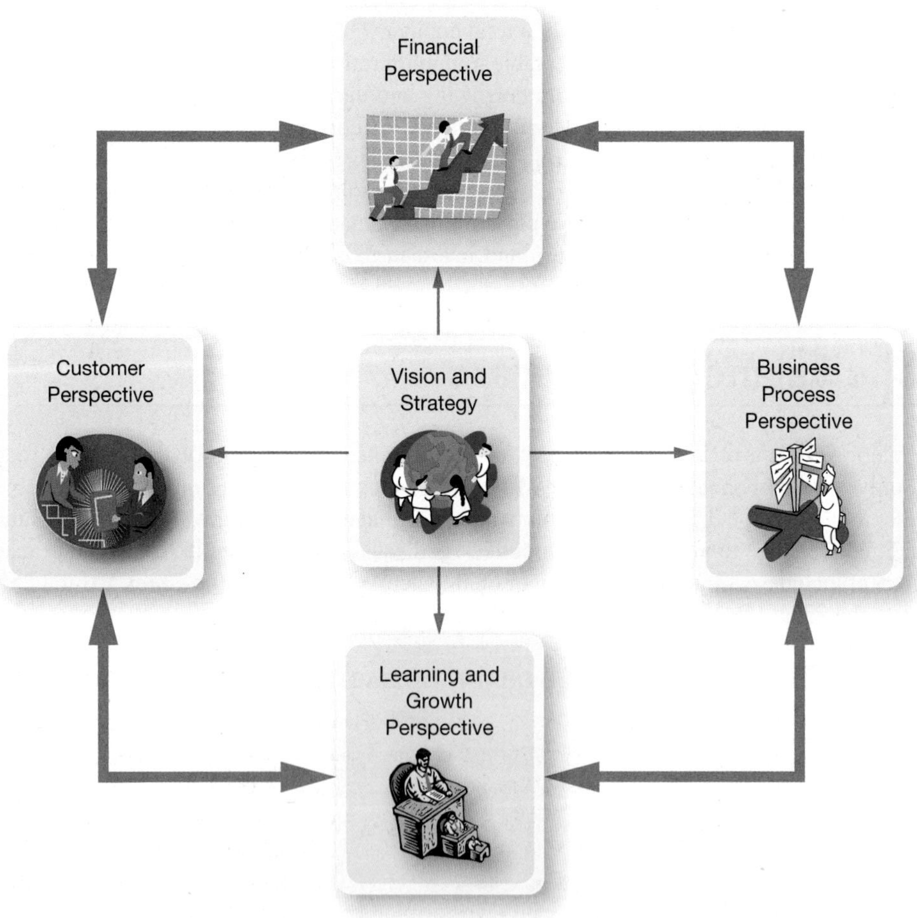

Source: R. S. Kaplan and D. Norton, *The Balanced Scorecard: Translating Strategy into Action.* (Boston: HBS Press, 1997).

lenses, including their associated performance measures. Those related performance measures are shown in Exhibit 25–9.

Exhibit 25–9 BALANCED SCORECARD STRATEGIES AND MATCHING PERFORMANCE MEASURES

Balanced Scorecard Lens	Strategies	Measures
Financial Perspective	1. Improve shareholder perceptions	• Net income • ROI • CT • ROS • EVA • Residual income
	2. Improve credit rating—reduce risk	• Bond ratings
Customer Perspective	1. Improve customer relations—wholesalers and retailers	• Customer retention — Wholesale — Retail • Number of returns • Customer satisfaction
	2. Increase orders from profitable customers	• Market share • Customer profitability
Business Process Perspective	1. Improve supplier relations	• Number quality-certified • Number of vendors • % of on-time deliveries
	2. Improve quality of manufacturing processes	• % machine downtime • Velocity/cycle time • % of orders filled • Scrap as a % of raw materials • Standard cost variances
	3. Improve delivery	• Number of on-time deliveries
Learning and Growth Perspective	1. Improve retention of employees	• Turnover • Employee satisfaction
	2. Improve employee productivity	• Number and cost savings from process improvements • Hours of employee training
	3. Increase new product development	• Number of new patents • % of sales from new products

THE FINANCIAL PERSPECTIVE

Managers use the **financial perspective** lens of the balanced scorecard to view the company through the eyes of creditors and shareholders. This lens helps employees consider the impact of strategic decisions on the traditional financial measures by which shareholders and creditors evaluate business performance. The balance sheet, income statement, and statement of cash flows are the underlying financial measures associated with the financial perspective. As shown in Exhibit 25–9, return on investment, return on sales, capital turnover, residual income, and economic value added are performance measures described earlier in this chapter that are used to evaluate progress toward goals established for the financial perspective.

THE CUSTOMER PERSPECTIVE

The customer perspective lens of the balanced scorecard provides a means for employees to consider their customers' needs and the markets in which their products sell. Through the **customer perspective** lens employees examine how the organization's strategies, products, and services add value for the customer. As shown in Exhibit 25–9, customer retention, customer satisfaction, customer quality perceptions, market share growth, and customer profitability are business performance measures relevant to goals established for the customer perspective.

THE BUSINESS PROCESS PERSPECTIVE

Standard cost variance analyses, just-in-time inventory, and total quality management ideas are embodied in the **business process perspective** lens. This balanced scorecard lens focuses on internal business processes and external business relations with suppliers and distributors. Quality measures such as amounts of scrap, downtime, number of defects, costs of rework, and the number of warranty claims enable assessment of the quality of internal processes. Exhibit 25–9 shows that other internal processes are monitored with measures such as standard cost variances, manufacturing cycle time, percent of on-time deliveries, and percent of orders filled. Finally, relations with suppliers and distributors are assessed with both quality measures (on-time delivery, parts defects per million from suppliers) and profitability measures (profitability per distributor arrangement).

THE LEARNING AND GROWTH PERSPECTIVE

The balanced scorecard also recognizes the importance of intangibles to the strategic goals of organizations by using the **learning and growth perspective** lens. This lens focuses on the people, information systems, and organizational procedures in place for organizational learning and growth. Employee satisfaction, retention, skill, development, and the hours invested in employee training are measures focused on people. This lens also measures the reliability, accuracy, and consistency of the information provided by the organizations' information systems. Without reliability and accuracy, measuring progress toward organizational goal achievement becomes dubious. Exhibit 25–9 shows that the number of patents awarded, the amount of sales from new products, and the money saved from process improvements reflect organizational outcomes showing enhanced learning and growth.

DIFFICULTIES WITH THE BALANCED SCORECARD

Companies using the balanced scorecard have identified several difficulties in using the four lenses described above. First, organizations have difficulty assessing the importance or weights attached to the various perspectives that are part of the scorecard. Second, measuring, quantifying, and evaluating some of the qualitative components that are part of the balanced scorecard present significant technical hurdles. A third difficulty arises from a lack of clarity and sense of direction because of the large number of performance measures used in the four perspectives. Finally, scorecard users suggest that the time and expense required to maintain and operate a fully designed and functioning balanced scorecard system can be significant.

Organizations can avoid some of these difficulties by limiting the number of measures used in each perspective and focusing on critical business issues. In particular, in choosing the measures to be used with the balanced scorecard, management should select those measures that present the best evidence for cause and effect linkages and those that can have a significant impact on achieving the organization's strategy. At any point in time trade-offs are likely to exist between the various strategic goals identified in the balanced scorecard.

YOUR TURN **You as a Purchasing Manager**

Assume that as the manager of purchasing for the BCD Company you have been asked to participate in the design of a balanced scorecard. In particular you have been asked to suggest measures that could be used to evaluate purchasing activities. Having seen the consultants' report, you realize that the measures you suggest will be tied to your bonus each year. Your department has been collecting benchmark information about the suppliers used by other purchasing departments in similar companies. You are aware that your department has been choosing higher-priced suppliers because you believe that the quality of materials provided by these suppliers is superior. Which measures should you suggest?

(See our comments on the Online Learning Center Web site.)

Management Compensation

Early recognition of the importance of incentive systems for employee motivation occurred when **General Motors Corporation** started its bonus plan in 1918. Its specific objectives were to align the managers' goals and objectives with the goals of the corporation. Because **General Motors** decentralized its operating decisions, it had to create a method to let the operating managers know whether their decisions were consistent with those of the overall corporation. Since that time, incentive compensation design has become an art. Multiple consulting companies now provide boards of directors and management with information about how to create and operate incentive compensation plans. We discuss the major compensation design features next.

COMPONENTS OF MANAGEMENT COMPENSATION

Learning Objective **LO6**
Identify and explain the components of management compensation and the trade-offs that compensation designers make.

Fixed Salary Nearly all companies pay fixed salaries to employees. Sometimes union contracts guarantee a minimum fixed salary with an opportunity to earn more through overtime. In addition, many employees are paid a fixed hourly pay rate for a fixed number of hours per week or per month. Most managers receive a fixed salary component as part of their compensation. Guaranteeing a fixed level of compensation that will not be affected by uncontrollable forces reduces employee uncertainty and risk.

Bonuses In contrast to fixed pay, bonuses are typically awarded for meeting or achieving specific goals. Corporations use bonus systems for managers across the organization, not just at the highest levels. At lower levels these bonus plans are designed to let all employees share in company profits during a good year. Many automobile companies give employees bonuses based on profit-sharing results.

Profit center managers receive bonuses typically ranging from 25 percent to 50 percent of their base salaries. These bonus plans take on many forms with different characteristics: Some rely heavily on awards of company stock and others use cash. Some compensation systems provide the bonus in the current period and some provide a bonus that is harvested in future periods. For example, many companies use stock options as part of the bonus compensation. **Stock options** give an employee the right to purchase a prespecified number of company shares at a prespecified price within a certain future time period. Options provide incentives for managers to work toward a stronger market position resulting in increased stock prices. Then the employee can exercise the option and make money on the stock.

Other Types of Incentives In addition to fixed salaries and bonuses of cash and stock options, other types of incentives have become fashionable. For example, many companies pay for life insurance policies for their employees. Automobiles are purchased for key employees. The use of company aircraft for personal use is sometimes awarded. Apartments are sometimes purchased and furnished for high-level executives. Companies pay for financial and tax consulting for employees.

Ethics, Fraud & Corporate Governance

As discussed in this chapter, companies sometimes compensate senior management by providing perquisites (e.g., use of company-owned planes, apartments, luxury stadium boxes, etc.). Perquisites received by senior management must be: (1) authorized by the board of directors (typically via approval by the board's compensation committee), (2) properly disclosed in the proxy statement filed by the company with the Securities and Exchange Commission (SEC), and (3) included in the taxable compensation received by the senior officer.

The Securities and Exchange Commission (SEC) brought an enforcement action against **Tyson Foods** and its former chairman and CEO (Don Tyson). **Tyson Foods** is a processor and marketer of chicken, beef, and pork, and its stock is listed on the New York Stock Exchange.

The SEC alleged that **Tyson Foods** made misleading disclosures of perquisites and personal benefits provided to Don Tyson in proxy statements filed with the Commission. The SEC alleged that **Tyson Foods** provided over $3 million of perquisites and personal benefits to Mr. Tyson, his wife, his daughters, and three individuals with whom he had close personal relationships. Approximately half of the $3 million in perquisites was not approved by **Tyson Foods**'s compensation committee, nor was the compensation committee even informed as to the nature and amount of these perquisites.

The $3 million in perquisites received by Mr. Tyson and his family and friends included:

Nature of Perquisite	Amount
Personal expenses, including purchases of oriental rugs, antiques, vacations, a horse, clothing, jewelry, artwork, and theater tickets	$ 689,016
Personal use of company-owned homes in the English countryside and Cabo San Lucas	$ 464,132
Personal use of company-owned aircraft	$ 426,086
Housekeeping services at five different homes	$ 203,675
Lawn maintenance services at five different homes	$ 84,000
Maintenance of nine different automobiles	$ 46,110
Telephone services	$ 36,554
Purchase of Christmas gift certificates	$ 15,000
Company payments to cover Mr. Tyson's income tax liability on the above perquisites	$1,072,699

Mary L. Schapiro, the 29th Chairman of the U.S. Securities and Exchange Commission © AP Photo/Haraz N. Ghanbari

These types of incentives are called perquisites (perks) and have been very controversial because they occasionally invite abuse by employees. However, companies generally have good reasons for creating and using perks. Those reasons involve hiring and retaining the right type of employee. Large companies compete for the talents of a small pool of top management. In order to attract that talent, they sometimes include "perks" as part of their compensation offers.

The awarding of incentive contracts to employees is typically based on accounting information. The objective of this chapter is to help you to understand the role accounting plays in performance evaluation and employee motivation. To be able to understand this role, you must become familiar with the many design choices that are available when constructing incentive and business performance evaluation systems.

INTERNATIONAL FINANCIAL REPORTING STANDARDS AND MANAGEMENT COMPENSATION

Employee incentive contracts are typically based on accounting information generated from external financial reporting standards. For example, a recent **Home Depot** SEC filing included the following earnings accounting–based performance measures: return on equity, return on capital, return on assets, return on investment, earnings per share, total earnings, and earnings growth.

Convergence with or adoption of IFRS will ultimately require companies to restructure their management incentive contracts. This is because studies have shown that IFRS accounting numbers differ from U.S. GAAP accounting numbers. For example, IFRS-based earnings are, on average, higher than U.S. GAAP earnings and are more variable. Thus, management compensation plans that use IFRS earnings numbers would present a higher risk-return profile than U.S. GAAP-based compensation plans. Managers may be unwilling to undertake the higher risk, or the firm may not want to pay out additional compensation for the higher return. An additional complication is that significant changes to management incentive plans typically require shareholder approval. Thus, adoption of IFRS will be costly for companies by requiring reconsideration of management compensation agreements.

DESIGN CHOICES FOR MANAGEMENT COMPENSATION

Several important design choices must be made when creating incentive compensation systems for managers. Managerial jobs involve multiple tasks and varying degrees of risk. Boards of directors try to design compensation plans that both reward performance across multiple dimensions and reduce the impact on compensation of the various risks that managers face. Compensation designers can choose from a variety of design criteria to develop individual compensation arrangements for managers. We present a few of the more common design choices here.

Choice of Time Horizon The *horizon* choice denotes the emphasis management should place on current performance versus future performance. An important consideration is how to reward managers for doing a good job now while also encouraging them to think about future performance. For an example of this type of choice, consider the contrast between a current cash bonus versus a current bonus of restricted stock options. Both of these bonuses can be based on current performance, but the cash bonus does not encourage a future orientation. The restricted stock option typically is structured so that employees can obtain cash for the options in the future only if they stay with the company during the option strike period and the company's stock price increases. In this case, managers are less likely to trade off increasing current performance at the expense of future performance.

Choice of Fixed versus Variable Bonus Another important concern for compensation designers is whether to use a fixed or variable bonus computation approach. In choosing how to award a bonus, many companies choose either a fixed bonus formula or a variable or more subjective approach. Some firms award a fixed dollar bonus for each percent of ROI above the minimum. This means managers know that if their ROI increases above the minimum, they will earn a fixed dollar amount for each 1 percent. However, one drawback to fixed bonus arrangements is that sometimes unexpected and uncontrollable events occur and these compensation plans are not flexible. In addition, fixed plans do not usually accommodate a complex system like a balanced scorecard.

Choice of Stock- versus Accounting-Based Performance Evaluation Compensation designers also choose to base performance evaluation on accounting information and/or on stock market information. By using stock price information, the managers' incentives are aligned with those of the shareholders. However, one argument against an overemphasis on stock-based compensation is that this approach creates too much risk for managers. Because managers' jobs are tied into the same company as the stock, managers could be more risk averse in their decision making than shareholders would want them to be. Thus, most companies tie incentives not only to stock market information but also to accounting information.

Choice of Rewarding Local versus Companywide Performance The choice of how much emphasis to put on rewarding local performance over rewarding companywide performance is especially controversial. Some companies want their divisions to operate as independent businesses. Other companies want the divisions to cooperate and integrate to maximize total companywide profitability. Under some incentive compensation plans, employees could be motivated to make decisions that improve the performance of their department or division, but might not help the company achieve its overall objectives and goals. Balancing employees' attention on both local goals and companywide goals is a challenging task. Many companies attempt to achieve this balance by combining fixed salary for local performance and bonuses for companywide performance.

Choice of Cooperative versus Competitive Incentive Plans Incentive plans can be designed to allow teams of employees to share equally in performance outcomes or to reward individual performance. A cooperative incentive motivates employees to work together to achieve the best result as a group. These types of incentives are designed to reward everyone for a good outcome regardless of each individual's actual contribution to that outcome. **Herman Miller**, a furniture maker, provides an example of cooperative incentives. At **Herman Miller** all employees are given stock as part of their compensation. When the company as a whole performs well, the stock price increases and employees benefit from the group's efforts.

A competitive incentive, on the other hand, motivates employees to do better jobs than their coworkers. You may be familiar with competitive incentives because scholarships are frequently awarded competitively. Other examples of competitive incentives include promotions. Although many employees may want to be promoted to a better position, when only one position exists only one employee can receive the reward. Likewise, accounting firms can make job offers to only a fixed number of applicants.

GOALS AND REWARDS IN LIFE

As you can see, setting goals, measuring progress toward goal achievement, and designing reward plans that recognize goal achievement are some of the most difficult tasks faced by managers. All of us struggle when determining our goals, both current and future. In deciding on these goals, we keep in mind the rewards we are likely to get as we progress toward goal achievement. Some of these rewards are monetary and are current. Other rewards will occur in the future. Measuring and rewarding goal achievement helps motivate all of us in our daily pursuits.

Concluding Remarks

The focus of this chapter is rewarding business performance using incentive compensation systems to motivate decision makers to align their goals and objectives with those of the organization. We discussed how the DuPont ROI system measures financial performance and why some critics think ROI is flawed. We saw how RI and EVA can correct some of the criticisms of ROI. The balanced scorecard is a broader means for directing, measuring, and rewarding business performance. Finally, we described the components of and design choices for management compensation. In the remaining chapter we will discuss capital budgeting tools. These are financial tools that managers use to decide which major investments to undertake.

END-OF-CHAPTER REVIEW

SUMMARY OF LEARNING OBJECTIVES

LO1 **Explain the importance of incentive systems for motivating performance.** Employees may have goals and objectives that differ from those of the organization. Incentive systems provide a tool that helps align employee goals with those of the organization by drawing attention to the organization's goals, by choosing to measure particular components of performance, and by rewarding employees for the actual outcomes associated with those components of performance being measured.

LO2 **Use the DuPont system to evaluate business performance.** The DuPont system measures return on investment (ROI) by dividing the operating earnings of a product line or division by the average invested capital used in that product line or division. ROI can be broken into two components, return on sales and capital turnover. Return on sales is computed by dividing the operating income by the total sales for the particular business segment or product line. It tells managers the amount of earnings generated from one dollar of sales. Capital turnover is a measure created by dividing sales by the average invested capital to generate those sales. The capital turnover ratio tells managers the amount of sales generated by a dollar of invested capital.

LO3 **Identify and explain the criticisms of using return on investment (ROI) as the only performance measure.** Return on investment provides a systematic method for evaluating a product line or business segment. It is a percent that can be used to compare financial performance across products and/or business segments. ROI can be broken into its component parts to further analyze business performance. Criticisms of ROI include that it motivates short-term decision making, that managers choose to underinvest in projects with acceptable ROIs from the firm's perspective, that it is difficult to match invested capital with related sales and operating earnings, and that ROI focuses only on financial measures and ignores other important components of the value chain.

LO4 **Calculate and explain residual income (RI) and economic value added (EVA).** Residual income is the amount by which operating earnings exceed a minimum acceptable return on the average invested capital. Economic value added is a refinement of the residual income measure that makes many adjustments for items such as taxes, interest, and amortization. Like RI, EVA does not motivate managers to turn down investments expected to earn a return below their current ROI, but above the minimum acceptable return to the firm.

LO5 **Use the balanced scorecard to identify, evaluate, and reward business performance.** The balanced scorecard uses four lenses to consider business performance. These lenses provide financial, business process, customer, and learning and growth perspectives. Each of these perspectives helps to identify goals, strategies to achieve the goals, and measures to assess goal achievement.

LO6 **Identify and explain the components of management compensation and the trade-offs that compensation designers make.** In creating management compensation plans, designers consider multiple characteristics such as fixed salary versus bonuses and the types of bonuses (cash, stock, or stock options). In addition, there are numerous design trade-offs that include choosing the time horizon over which compensation is available, choosing to emphasize local versus global performance, or choosing a cooperative or a competitive incentive scheme.

Key Terms Introduced or Emphasized in Chapter 25

balanced scorecard (p. 1086) A system for performance measurement that links a company's strategy to specific goals, measures that assess progress toward those goals, and specific initiatives to achieve those goals. This systematic business performance measurement process integrates objectives across four business lenses to achieve the organization's strategic goals.

business process perspective (p. 1088) The balanced scorecard lens through which internal business processes, supplier relations, and distributor relations are strategically analyzed and evaluated.

capital turnover (CT) (p. 1081) A measure created by dividing sales by the average invested capital to generate those sales. Capital turnover tells managers the amount of sales generated by a dollar of invested capital.

customer perspective (p. 1088) The balanced scorecard lens through which organizations analyze and measure their customers' needs, expectations, and outcomes that will lead to business success.

DuPont system of performance measurement (p. 1081) A method that analyzes business performance by considering both the earnings per sales dollar and the investment used to generate those sales dollars.

economic value added (EVA) (p. 1085) A specific type of residual income that is computed by multiplying the after-tax weighted-average cost of capital by total assets minus current liabilities and subtracting that product from the after-tax operating income.

financial perspective (p. 1087) The balanced scorecard lens that managers and shareholders (or other financial stakeholders) use to view the organization's business performance.

learning and growth perspective (p. 1088) The balanced scorecard lens that focuses on the people, information systems, and organizational procedures in place for organizational learning and growth.

residual income (RI) (p. 1084) The amount by which operating earnings exceed a minimum acceptable return on the average invested capital. The minimum rate of return represents the opportunity cost of using the invested capital.

return on investment (ROI) (p. 1079) The operating income divided by the average invested capital associated with the generation of that income.

return on sales (ROS) (p. 1081) Computed by dividing the operating income by the total sales for the particular business segment or product line. It tells managers the amount of earnings generated from one dollar of sales.

stock options (p. 1089) An employee receives the right to purchase a prespecified number of shares at a prespecified price within a certain future time period. Options provide incentives for managers to make decisions that help increase stock prices.

value chain (p. 1085) The set of activities necessary to create and distribute a desirable product or service to a customer.

Demonstration Problem

Bergly Automart is a full-service auto dealer with three divisions: the New Car, Used Car, and Service divisions. Budget information for the coming year for these three divisions is shown below. Each division manager's annual evaluation and bonus is based on divisional ROI.

The manager of the New Car Division complains that one reason the sales and resulting earnings for the New Car Division are not higher is the reputation of the Service Division. Because the Service Division does not have the most recent equipment (e.g., a new hydraulic lift) customers buy their new cars from a competitor on the other side of town that has a service department with new equipment, including new lifts that make its service quicker and better. The manager of the New Car Division has requested that other evaluation techniques be considered (such as residual income or a balanced scorecard approach) in an attempt to resolve this problem.

Bergly Automart

	New Car	Used Car	Service
Average investment	$ 5,000,000	$1,000,000	$500,000
Sales revenue	$10,000,000	$5,000,000	$600,000
Cost of goods sold	8,750,000	4,000,000	300,000
Operating expenses	750,000	800,000	175,000
Operating earnings	$ 500,000	$ 200,000	$125,000

Instructions

a. Compute the ROI for each of the divisions and the entire company. Use the DuPont method to analyze its return on sales and capital turnover. Comment on the results

b. Assume the Service Division is considering installing a new hydraulic lift. Upon investigating, the manager of the division finds that the lift would add $100,000 to the division's average invested capital and that the Service Division's operating earnings would increase by $20,000 per year.
   1. What is the ROI of the new hydraulic lift?
   2. What impact does the investment in the hydraulic lift have on the Service Division's ROI?
   3. What is the impact on Bergly Automart's overall ROI? (Assume no change in car sales.)
   4. Would the manager of the Service Division be motivated to undertake such an investment?

c. Compute the residual income for each division if the minimum required rate of return for Bergly Automart is 15 percent. Would the Service Division purchase the hydraulic lift if the performance evaluation were based on the division's residual income and a 10 percent bonus of residual income were awarded? Show calculations to support your answer.

d. What measures might be appropriate for Bergly Automart to use for its divisions if it uses a balanced scorecard to evaluate and reward the division managers?

Solution to the Demonstration Problem

a.

Bergly Automart

Divisions	ROI	Return on Sales	Capital Turnover
New Car	$500,000 ÷ $5,000,000 = 10%	$500,000 ÷ $10,000,000 = 5%	$10,000,000 ÷ $5,000,000 = 200%
Used Car	$200,000 ÷ $1,000,000 = 20%	$200,000 ÷ $5,000,000 = 4%	$5,000,000 ÷ $1,000,000 = 500%
Service	$125,000 ÷ $500,000 = 25%	$125,000 ÷ $600,000 = 20.8%	$600,000 ÷ $500,000 = 120%
Bergly	$825,000 ÷ $6,500,000 = 12.7%	$825,000 ÷ $15,600,000 = 5.3%	$15,600,000 ÷ $6,500,000 = 240%

Return on sales is much lower for the New Car and Used Car divisions than for the Service Division, reflecting the small markups typical for new and used car sales. To offset the lower return on sales, the capital turnover for both new and used cars is higher. The Service Division has a high profit margin with a low turnover. Despite its old equipment, the investment base of the Service Division is still relatively larger than showroom assets for new and used cars.

b. 1. ROI of the hydraulic lift = \$20,000 ÷ \$100,000 = 20%

2. Impact of the lift on the Service Division's ROI: (\$125,000 + \$20,000) ÷ (\$500,000 + \$100,000) = 24%

3. Impact on the Bergly Automart ROI:

   (\$500,000 + \$200,000 + \$125,000 + \$20,000) ÷

   (\$5,000,000 + \$1,000,000 + \$500,000 + \$100,000) = 12.8%

4. Because adding the new lift will lower the Service Division's ROI and presumably lower the bonus received by the Service Division manager, the division manager will not purchase the new lift even though it improves Bergly Automart's ROI.

c.

Divisions	Residual Income without Lift	Bonus
New Car	\$500,000 − (0.15 × \$5,000,000) = (\$250,000)	–0–
Used Car	\$200,000 − (0.15 × \$1,000,000) = \$50,000	\$5,000
Service	\$125,000 − (0.15 × \$500,000) = \$50,000	\$5,000

Service Division residual income after purchasing the lift:

\$145,000 − (0.15 × \$600,00) = \$55,000

The Service Division manager's bonus would increase to \$5,500 and thus, the manager would purchase the lift.

d. Many answers are possible, for example:

Division	Financial	Business Process	Customer	Learning and Growth
New Car	Residual income of both division and company.	• Number of customers processed.	• Customer satisfaction. • Number of retained customers.	• Sales seminars attended. • Accessibility and use of knowledge of new car models.
Used Car	Residual income of both division and company.	• Number of used cars acquired. • Number of customers processed.	• Customer satisfaction. • Number of retained customers.	• Sales seminars attended. • Information on used car market gathered.
Service	Residual income of both division and company.	• Efficiency of services performed. • Number of cars to be serviced in process. • Number of reworks.	• Number of complaints. • Customer satisfaction. • Lost customers.	• Service training time.

Self-Test Questions

The answers to these questions appear on page 1111. There may be more than one response per question.

1. Which of the following are *not* part of the components of the DuPont system for measuring and evaluating business performance?
   - a. Return on sales.
   - b. Residual income.
   - c. Return on investment.
   - d. Capital turnover.
   - e. Number of patents.
2. Premo Pens is a division of InCommunicato, Inc. Premo generates annual revenue of $162,000, operating earnings of $55,000, and has average assets of $400,000. InCommunicato expects its divisions to earn a minimum required return of 12 percent. Which of the following does *not* represent either return on sales, residual income, or return on investment for Premo Pens?
   - a. 13.75%.
   - b. $7,000.
   - c. 34%.
   - d. 40.5%.
   - e. $9,000.
3. Criticisms of return on investment as the only performance measure include:
   - a. ROI focuses on short-term decisions.
   - b. ROI is focused on only one component of the value chain.
   - c. Managers evaluated based only on ROI are sometimes motivated not to make an investment that is in the best interest of the organization as a whole.
   - d. All of the above.
4. Which of the following is not represented in the balanced scorecard?
   - a. A learning and growth perspective.
   - b. The internal business process perspective.
   - c. The government's perspective.
   - d. The customers' perspective.
   - e. The financial perspective.
5. Which of the following is not likely to be included in the typical components of management compensation?
   - a. Company stock options.
   - b. Cash bonuses.
   - c. Free meals.
   - d. Fixed salary.
   - e. Company stock.

ASSIGNMENT MATERIAL Discussion Questions

1. Identify three ways that accounting systems help align the goals of employees and the goals of the organization.
2. Suppose you are interested in opening a new restaurant in your area. What specific activities would you identify as goals for your restaurant?
3. What activities would make up the learning and growth component of the balanced scorecard for a large public accounting firm?
4. Distinguish between the four lenses of the balanced scorecard and provide an example of a business measure for each category for a family-owned grocery store.
5. Assume you are the manager of the finished goods warehouse of a computer manufacturer. Which warehouse-related business measures might help the company achieve its balanced scorecard goals?
6. What are some problems that companies have encountered in using the balanced scorecard?
7. Why is residual income suggested as an improvement over ROI for business measurement?
8. In designing a compensation plan for the manager of the international operations of **Tootsie Roll Industries**, what trade-offs should the company's board of directors consider?
9. How would you expect the components of return on investment to be different for a mostly Internet-based retailer compared to a more traditional bricks-and-mortar retailer (e.g., **Amazon.com** versus **Barnes & Noble**)?
10. Under which circumstances is a fixed salary preferable to a pure bonus compensation system?
11. Exhibit 25–9 identifies balanced scorecard performance measures. Review this exhibit and identify two measures from the customer perspective category that in the short run might be in conflict with some of the measures listed in the financial perspective category. Explain why they might be in conflict.
12. For which perspective of the balanced scorecard would the output from a standard cost system (e.g., variances) provide useful performance measurement information? Explain.
13. Assume sales remain constant from Year 1 to Year 2 and return on sales (ROS) increases from Year 1 to Year 2. Identify two reasons why the return on sales ratio might increase from Year 1 to Year 2.
14. Identify the costs and benefits of a cooperative incentive plan in which a team of individuals equally shares a bonus pool if the team achieves a predetermined goal.
15. Identify the costs and benefits of a competitive incentive plan in which only one individual out of a group receives the bonus if he or she outperforms the others in the group.

Brief Exercises

LO1 LO6 **BRIEF EXERCISE 25.1** Motivating Employee Performance

Marsha's Pet Store employs six employees. Their duties are to sell pets, replenish the stock, keep the pets' cages clean, feed the pets, and maintain good records. Marsha pays a fixed hourly rate and a commission on sales of pets. Lately, Marsha has been finding that the records have not been well maintained and the stock has not been replenished. However, pet sales are good and the pets' cages are clean.

How might Marsha's current reward structure be motivating the employees to pay more attention to the pets than to their other duties?

LO2 LO3 **BRIEF EXERCISE 25.2** Evaluate Business Performance Using ROI

Zylex Corporation has multiple factories across the United States. The upper management at Zylex evaluates each factory based on the capital turnover ratio from the DuPont system. Below is information for the factory in Pennsylvania for the past year.

	Year 2
Sales	$1,000,000
Operating expenses	640,000
Total assets	2,200,000
Accumulated depreciation	220,000

Compute the capital turnover ratio using (1) total assets and (2) assets net of depreciation. Which investment base will the Pennsylvania factory manager prefer and why?

LO2 LO4 **BRIEF EXERCISE 25.3** Comparing ROI and Residual Income

Use the information in Brief Exercise 25.2 to compute the ROI for the Pennsylvania factory using total assets and assets net of depreciation. Now find residual income if the company expects an 18 percent return on total assets. Is the Pennsylvania factory performing up to management's expectations?

LO5 **BRIEF EXERCISE 25.4** Balanced Scorecard

Ricoh Company Ltd., the 74-year-old leading supplier of office automation equipment and electronics, has implemented a balanced scorecard. Match each of the performance indicators from their scorecard below to the four balanced scorecard perspectives (Financial, Customer, Internal Processes, and Learning and Growth).

a. Number of Customer Relationships Managed
b. Hours of Employee Training
c. Customer Service Quality Ratings
d. Revenue Growth
e. Customer's Total Cost of Ownership
f. Asset Utilization
g. Employee's Competitor Knowledge Increased
h. Pounds of Recycled Waste Products

LO2 LO3 **BRIEF EXERCISE 25.5** Computations for the DuPont Model

Saxwell Corporation has many divisions and evaluates them using ROI. The corporation's expected ROI for each division is 12 percent or above.

	Division 1	Division 2
Earnings	$ 750,000	$ 2,000,000
Investment base	5,000,000	20,000,000

Compute the ROI for Divisions 1 and 2. Are the divisions meeting the expected ROI? What other information would you want to know about the investment base before comparing Division 1 and 2 performance?

LO3 **BRIEF EXERCISE 25.6** Criticisms of ROI

Consider the information in Brief Exercise 25.5. Assume that the manager of Division 1 has the opportunity to purchase a new piece of equipment for $1,000,000 that would increase earnings by $130,000 per year. Show the impact of this purchase on Division 1's ROI. Would the manager of Division 1 undertake the investment? Why or why not?

LO2 LO4 **BRIEF EXERCISE 25.7**
Calculate Residual Income

Wellinghouse Industries has established a 10 percent target ROI for its divisions. The following data have been gathered for the Ionia Division's operations for the previous year: Revenues = $30,000,000; Expenses = $28,000,000; Invested capital = $11,200,000. Did the Ionia Division meet the ROI target? What is the Ionia Division's residual income?

LO4 **BRIEF EXERCISE 25.8**
Calculate EVA

The weighted-average cost of capital for Forstone Corporation is 12 percent. Last year one of the divisions of Forstone generated an EVA of $3,720,000, while the division's assets less its current liabilities were $25,600,000. How much after-tax operating income did the division generate?

LO6 **BRIEF EXERCISE 25.9**
Variable versus Fixed Compensation

Compensation for top executives (e.g., CEOs and CFOs) has become more variable over time. For example, recent data show that in large corporations only 20 percent of CFO pay is fixed and 80 percent is variable, based on companywide performance. Explain why you believe this type of reward plan has been chosen for CFOs of large companies.

LO2 **BRIEF EXERCISE 25.10**
Components of ROI

Boris Jasper is the manager of an auto parts division for a large auto parts supplier. The division makes dampers and oil pumps. Identify three things Boris could do to increase the division's ROI in the coming year.

Exercises

LO2 through LO6 **EXERCISE 25.1**
Accounting Terminology

Listed below are eight terms introduced or emphasized in this chapter:

Residual income	Balanced scorecard
Management compensation	Return on investment
Return on sales	Stock options
Business process lens	Capital turnover

Each of the following statements may (or may not) describe one of these terms. For each statement, indicate the term described, or answer "none" if the statement does not correctly describe any of these terms.

a. Tells managers the incremental operating earnings for each additional sales dollar.

b. The focus of this business performance measurement is the sales dollars earned from each invested dollar.

c. A tool used by managers and owners of organizations to align managers' goals with those of the organization.

d. This method considers all costs borne by the consumer from purchase to disposal of a product.

e. A business performance measurement that takes into account the minimum required return on the assets employed.

f. Measures for this category of business performance are associated with eliminating non-value-added costs from the value chain.

g. A method in which a product's selling price is determined by adding a fixed amount to the product's current production cost.

h. This performance evaluation method is criticized for motivating managers, in some instances, to ignore investments that are in the best interest of the company as a whole.

i. An important aspect of this method is the consideration of the many perspectives of the multiple stakeholders in an organization.

LO1 LO5 **EXERCISE 25.2**
Balanced Scorecard Activities

Assume you have just been hired as the management accountant in charge of providing your firm's managers with product information. What activities might you undertake if you were participating in the design of a balanced scorecard?

LO1 **EXERCISE 25.3**
Employee Motivation

In a *Wall Street Journal* quiz about the impact of technology at the office,[2] quiz respondents were requested to say whether a specific activity was unethical. Forty-nine percent of respondents said that using office technology for playing games at work is unethical and 54 percent said that shopping on the Internet at work is unethical. Which performance evaluation and incentive systems would encourage or discourage these behaviors?

[2] Source: *The Wall Street Journal*, October 21, 1999, page B1.

LO2 through LO4

EXERCISE 25.4

ROI versus EVA Measures

Sapsora Company uses ROI to measure the performance of its operating divisions and to reward division managers. A summary of the annual reports from two divisions is shown below. The company's weighted-average cost of capital is 15 percent.

	Division A	Division B
Total assets	$5,600,000	$9,200,000
Current liabilities	800,000	1,200,000
After-tax operating income	960,000	1,440,000
ROI	20%	18%

a. Which division is more profitable?

b. Would EVA more clearly show the relative contribution of the two divisions to the company as a whole? Show the computations.

c. Suppose the manager of Division A was offered a one-year project that would increase his investment base by $100,000 and show a profit of $17,000. Would the manager choose to invest in the new project?

LO2 through LO4

EXERCISE 25.5

Performance and ROI versus Residual Income

An investment center in Shellforth Corporation was asked to identify three proposals for its capital budget. Details of those proposals are:

	Capital Budget Proposals		
	A	B	C
Capital required	$95,000	$40,000	$75,000
Annual operating return	23,000	10,000	10,500

Shellforth uses residual income to evaluate all capital budgeting projects. Its minimum required return is 15 percent.

a. Assume you are the investment center manager. Which project do you prefer? Why?

b. Assume your investment center's current ROI is 20 percent and that the president of Shellforth is thinking about using ROI for the investment center's evaluation. Would your preferences for the projects listed above change? Why?

LO2 LO3

EXERCISE 25.6

Concerns about ROI

Jennifer Baskiter is president and CEO of Plants&More.com, an Internet company that sells plants and flowers. The success of her startup Internet company has motivated her to expand and create two divisions. One division focuses on sales to the general public and the other focuses on business-to-business sales to hotels, restaurants, and other firms that want plants and flowers for their businesses. She is considering using return on investment as a means of evaluating her divisions and their managers. She has hired you as a compensation consultant. What issues or concerns would you raise regarding the use of ROI for evaluating the divisions and their managers?

LO1 LO5 LO6

EXERCISE 25.7

Compensation Choices

You are the manager of the Midwest Region, a 27-restaurant division that is part of the chain "Bites and Bits." The restaurants offer casual dining and compete with such chains in your region as **Olive Garden** and **Outback Steakhouse**. You receive an annual cash bonus of 5 percent of sales when residual income in your region exceeds the required minimum return on invested capital of 15 percent. You are using a similar performance evaluation plan to reward each of the managers in your 27 restaurants.

You are concerned that important performance variables are being overlooked. For example, you have heard complaints from other regions and in your own region that the quality of the food is bad, it is difficult to retain serving staff in the restaurants, and finding a good chef is very difficult. At an upcoming planning meeting for all regional directors, the agenda includes considering the business performance evaluation and compensation plan. What could you say about the current compensation plan and what would you propose to remedy the problems?

LO6 **EXERCISE 25.8** Designing Compensation for Managers

Consider the different responsibilities involved in the following three positions at Vortnoy Corporation: (1) supervisor of the second shift at the Fairfield, Rhode Island, plant, (2) manager for the Northeastern Division, and (3) corporatewide chief financial officer. Use the five design categories for compensation described in this chapter and identify how you would design a compensation arrangement for each of these three positions at Vortnoy Corporation.

LO5 **EXERCISE 25.9** Balanced Scorecard Matching

Match each of the following performance measures with one of the four perspectives of the balanced scorecard (Financial—F, Customer—C, Business Process—B, or Learning and Growth—L).

a. Direct labor efficiency variance.
b. After-tax profits.
c. Customer turnover per sales dollar.
d. Parts per million defects.
e. Employee turnover.
f. Overhead spending variance.
g. Scrap and rework.
h. Residual income.
i. On-time deliveries.
j. Employee satisfaction.
k. Sales per employee.
l. Percent of customer leads turned into sales.
m. Returns and warranty work.

LO2 LO4 **EXERCISE 25.10** City Wide Door ROI and Residual Income

Emily Adams is the manager of City Wide Door, a company specializing in installing and maintaining garage doors of many types. Her associate, Alyssa, has provided Emily with three proposals for different investments in machinery to help expand the business. The minimum required return on investments for City Wide Door is 12 percent.

	Proposal A	Proposal B	Proposal C
Initial investment	$58,600	$75,000	$50,000
Annual operating return	10,000	16,500	13,100

If Emily uses ROI to evaluate investments:

a. Which proposal would be most profitable for the firm?
b. How would the answer change if the company used residual income to evaluate investments?

LO2 through LO4 **EXERCISE 25.11** Using ROI and EVA for Performance Evaluation

The Meikle Division has assets of $600,000, current liabilities of $60,000, and net operating income of $180,000.

a. What is the division's ROI?
b. If the weighted-average cost of capital is 12 percent, what is the division's EVA?
c. How might management behavior be different if EVA were used to evaluate performance rather than ROI?

LO2 LO4 **EXERCISE 25.12** Finding Unknowns

The following information for companies X, Y, and Z is incomplete. Supply the missing data for items (**a**) through (**l**).

	Company X	Company Y	Company Z
Operating income	$220,000	**e.?**	**i.?**
Sales	**a.?**	**f.?**	**j.?**
Invested capital	**b.?**	$6,000,000	$32,000,000
Return on sales	32%	40%	**k.?**
Capital turnover	20%	**g.?**	30%
Return on investment	**c.?**	20%	15%
Minimum acceptable return	10%	12%	**l.?**
Residual income	**d.?**	**h.?**	$960,000

LO5 **EXERCISE 25.13** **Home Depot** Balanced Scorecard Measures

In Appendix A, you will find a table titled "10-Year Summary of Financial and Operating Results" for **Home Depot**. Review the various performance measures listed in the table. Choose at least one measure for each category of the balanced scorecard. Explain why you believe the measure you chose would help **Home Depot** evaluate its performance in the matching category of the balanced scorecard.

LO4 LO5

EXERCISE 25.14
Comparing Division Performance

Salsa Grocery has two divisions. One division, STORES, sells groceries through traditional grocery stores. The second division, CYBER, was formed two years ago and sells groceries through an online grocery ordering service. Data for the past year for the two divisions are as follows:

	STORES	CYBER
Total assets	$120,000,000	$15,000,000
Current liabilities	4,500,000	2,500,000
Net income (loss)	10,000,000	1,000,000
Weighted-average cost of capital	8%	10%

a. Evaluate the two divisions in terms of EVA.

b. Explain why it might be better to evaluate the CYBER division in terms of a balanced scorecard rather than just focusing on EVA.

c. Identify at least one measure from each of the business process and customer perspectives of the balanced scorecard that could be used to evaluate the performance of CYBER.

LO4 LO6

EXERCISE 25.15
Home Depot's ROI and EVA

Use **Home Depot**'s financial information in Appendix A to compute the ROI and EVA for 2008 and 2009. Use Net Earnings from page A-4 to measure earnings or returns and Net Property and Equipment from page A-5 as the invested capital base. Assume the weighted-average cost of capital is 10 percent. Interpret the EVA and ROI numbers for **Home Depot** between 2008 and 2009. Are they improving or declining? Why?

Problem Set A

LO2 through LO4

PROBLEM 25.1A
Empire Hotel

eXcel

The Empire Hotel is a full-service hotel in a large city. Empire is organized into three departments that are treated as investment centers. Budget information for the coming year for these three departments is shown below. The managers of each of the departments are evaluated and bonuses are awarded each year based on ROI.

Empire Hotel

	Hotel Rooms	Restaurants	Health Club—Spa
Average investment	$ 8,000,000	$5,000,000	$1,000,000
Sales revenue	$10,000,000	$2,000,000	$ 600,000
Operating expenses	8,500,000	1,250,000	450,000
Operating earnings	$ 1,500,000	$ 750,000	$ 150,000

Instructions

a. Compute the ROI for each department. Use the DuPont method to analyze the return on sales and capital turnover.

b. Assume the Health Club—Spa is considering installing new exercise equipment. Upon investigating, the manager of the division finds that the equipment would cost $50,000 and that sales revenue would increase by $8,000 per year as a result of the new equipment. What is the ROI of the investment in the new exercise equipment? What impact does the investment in the exercise equipment have on the Health Club—Spa's ROI? Would the manager of the Health Club—Spa be motivated to undertake such an investment?

c. Compute the residual income for each department if the minimum required return for the Empire Hotel is 17 percent. What would be the impact of the investment in (**b**) on the Health Club—Spa's residual income?

LO1 LO5 LO6

PROBLEM 25.2A
Empire Hotel and Balanced Scorecard

Consider the Empire Hotel discussed in Problem 25.1A. The manager of the Restaurants Department complains that sales and resulting earnings for the restaurants are not higher due to the poor reputation of the Hotel Rooms Department. Because the Hotel Rooms Department does not have the best housekeeping staff, the overall reputation of the hotel is slipping. The manager of the Hotel Rooms Department counters that, to keep operating expenses under control and improve ROI, wages for housekeeping have been cut. The manager of the Restaurant Department has requested that other evaluation techniques such as residual income or a balanced scorecard approach be considered in an effort to resolve this problem.

Instructions

Consider which balanced scorecard measures might be useful to the Empire Hotel in evaluating the Hotel Rooms Department. In doing so, identify:

a. The organizational goal that the measure is designed to support.

b. The employee resources and efforts that will be affected by the measurement.

c. How the employees should receive feedback and be rewarded for progress toward achieving the goals.

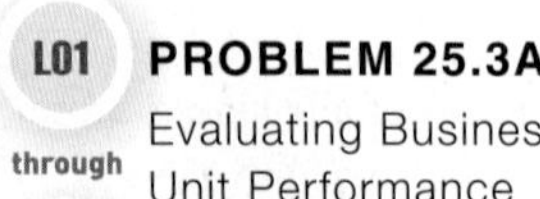

LO1 through LO4 **PROBLEM 25.3A** Evaluating Business Unit Performance

The manager of Healthy Snack Division of Fairfax Industries is evaluated on her division's return on investment and residual income. The company requires that all divisions generate a minimum return on invested assets of 8 percent. Consistent failure to achieve this minimum target is grounds for the dismissal of a division manager. The annual cash bonus paid to division managers is 1 percent of residual income in excess of $100,000. The Snack Division's operating margin for the year was $6.5 million, during which time its average invested capital was $50 million.

Instructions

a. Compute the Snack Division's return on investment and residual income.

b. Will the manager of the Snack Division receive a bonus for her performance? If so, how much will it be?

c. In reporting her investment center's performance for the past 10 years, the manager of the Snack Division accounted for the depreciation of her division's assets by using an accelerated depreciation method allowed for tax purposes. As a result, virtually all of the assets under her control are fully depreciated. Given that the company's other division managers use straight-line depreciation, is her use of an accelerated method ethical? Defend your answer.

LO2 **PROBLEM 25.4A** **Tootsie Roll Industries** Segment Performance Evaluation

Tootsie Roll Industries has two business segments, one for operations in the U.S. and one for operations in Mexico and Canada. The information below (in thousands) comes from a recent annual report. Find the ROI for each segment for each year.

	Year 2		Year 1	
	United States	Mexico and Canada	United States	Mexico and Canada
Sales	$365,920	$27,265	$362,290	$29,465
Net assets	511,743	14,997	489,552	18,909
Net earnings	65,413	975	65,370	317

Instructions

Find and analyze segment ROI by using the DuPont method described in this chapter. Explain the performance difference between the two segments across the two years by using the information from the DuPont breakdown of ROI.

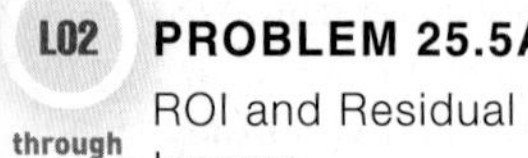

LO2 through LO4 **PROBLEM 25.5A** ROI and Residual Income

Bob Banker is the manager of one location of the Fastwhere Inc. chain, which is a delivery service. Banker's location is currently earning an ROI of 14 percent on existing average capital of $750,000. The minimum required return for Fastwhere Inc. is 12 percent. Banker is considering several additional investment projects, which are independent of existing operations and are independent of each other. The following table lists the projects:

Project	Required Capital	ROI
A–1	$150,000	14.1%
A–2	300,000	20
A–3	250,000	13.5
A–4	400,000	12.5
A–5	500,000	9.8

Instructions

a. Which of the projects would Banker choose for investment if his objective were to maximize his location's ROI?

b. Which projects increase the value of Fastwhere Inc.?

c. Which projects have a negative residual income?

d. Create two rankings for the projects in order of acceptability if Banker is evaluated (1) on ROI and (2) on residual income.

e. On the basis of the projects in the list explain why underinvestment is a problem when using ROI for evaluation purposes.

LO5 LO6

PROBLEM 25.6A
Balanced Scorecard in the Assembly Department

Joyce Biginskor manages the Assembly Department at Valance Autoparts, a parts supplier to large auto companies. Valance has recently adopted a balanced scorecard for the entire company. As a result, the plant manager for each production facility has a set of strategic goals, measurements, and rewards designed to motivate employees to achieve the company's overall goals.

The plant manager has implemented the balanced scorecard throughout each department. The balanced scorecard measures that specifically apply to the Assembly Department are primarily related to business process measures and learning and growth measures. In particular, the assembly line and related employees supervised by Biginskor are evaluated on efficiency measures and learning and growth measures. The learning and growth measures are employee absenteeism, retention, and satisfaction. Operating efficiencies are measured by cycle time, amount of work-in-process inventory, hours of machine downtime, number of defects, cost of rework, and productivity per employee. Biginskor obtains a monthly cash bonus if she can increase the learning and growth measures and reduce inefficiencies in the operations.

During the first year that the balanced scorecard was used at Valance, Biginskor did not earn a bonus. She has been particularly frustrated because whenever she reduces the work-in-process inventory on the shop floor, cycle time increases. When she reduces the hours of machine downtime, the defects increase and employee satisfaction decreases.

The plant manager decides to hire your consulting firm, Consultants Incorporated, to help evaluate the new balanced scorecard performance measurement and compensation scheme.

Instructions

Choose a partner to round out your consulting team and write a memo to the plant manager that explains the problems the manager is encountering in the Assembly Department. In the report identify with bullet points the problems that she is having with the balanced scorecard system and provide suggestions to the plant manager to help remedy the problems.

LO1 LO6

PROBLEM 25.7A
Management Compensation at **Home Depot**

In Schedule 14A recently filed with the SEC, the Leadership Development and Compensation Committee of the **Home Depot** board of directors furnished the information below on executive compensation.

> **Base Salaries:** We provide competitive base salaries that allow us to attract and retain a high performing leadership team.
>
> **Annual Bonus:** All executive officers participate in our Company's Management Incentive Plan ("MIP"). The MIP is designed to motivate and reward executives by aligning pay with annual performance. The MIP is a cash-based bonus plan that rewards executives for the achievement of financial and nonfinancial performance objectives that are established at the beginning of each fiscal year.
>
> **Long-Term Incentives:** To better align the interests of management with long-term stockholder interests, we provide long-term incentives to executive officers. We deliver long-term incentives typically in the form of stock options, a performance shares/cash plan, shares of restricted stock, and deferred shares or deferred stock units. The long-term incentives are designed to reward executives for increasing long-term stockholder value and to retain them at the Company.
>
> **Stock Options:** We provide annual nonqualified stock option grants as part of our long-term incentive compensation under the Omnibus Plan.
>
> **Performance Shares/Units:** Executive officers are eligible to participate in the Company's Long-Term Incentive Plan ("LTIP"). For performance periods beginning before Fiscal 2007, the program rewards management for stockholder returns over a three-year period. Performance is relative to a peer group, offsetting stock appreciation as a result of bear and bull market periods.

Restricted Stock: In Fiscal 2002, we began to grant restricted stock to executive officers to (i) serve as a retention mechanism; (ii) align management and stockholder interests by delivering ownership; and (iii) in some instances offset the less than competitive supplemental executive retirement benefits offered to our executives.

Deferred Shares or Deferred Stock Units: From time to time the Company uses deferred shares or deferred stock units to provide equity compensation to an executive officer that permits such officer to defer receipt of and taxation on such compensation until a future date elected by such officer.

Instructions

In this chapter, five design choice categories for management compensation were described (long versus short horizon; fixed versus variable bonus; stock- versus accounting-based evaluation; local versus companywide orientation; and cooperative versus competitive schemes). For each of **Home Depot**'s executive compensation categories listed above, identify the design choices made by **Home Depot**'s board of directors in constructing that component of the company's management compensation plan.

LO2 through LO4

PROBLEM 25.8A
Performance Measures and Transaction Effects

In the following list, assume each transaction is independent of the others. Each of these transactions occurs in a single division of Hopenstat Incorporated, a multidivision company. Each transaction may impact capital turnover, ROI, and/or residual income. For each transaction, explain how capital turnover, ROI, and/or residual income are affected (increase, decrease, or no effect).

a. During the month of January, management decided to discontinue a research and development project that was scheduled to run throughout the year. The project was not producing the hoped-for results that would lead to a new product.

b. Changes in the production process to a team-based approach during the latter half of the year decreased variable costs per unit of production without the need to purchase new equipment.

c. A large amount of obsolete inventory was written off in the month of April.

d. Newly purchased equipment in June increased the quality of the units produced but had no immediate effect on sales.

e. In August, corporate headquarters lowered the division's target rate of return from 15 percent to 12 percent because of the decreasing cost of debt.

f. The division hired a new chief financial officer to replace its retiring CFO. In order to receive some training for the new job, the newly hired CFO overlapped for six months with the retiring CFO.

LO2 through LO4 LO6

PROBLEM 25.9A
ROI, Residual Income, and Performance Evaluation

Marfar Industries produces metal stamping equipment. The company expanded vertically several years ago by acquiring Bent Press Company, one of its suppliers. Marfar decided to maintain Bent's separate identity and therefore established the Bent Press Division as one of its investment centers.

Marfar evaluates its divisions on the basis of ROI. Management bonuses are also based on ROI. All investments in operating assets are expected to earn a minimum required rate of return of 11 percent.

Bent's ROI has ranged from 14 percent to 17 percent since it was acquired by Marfar. During the past year, Bent had an investment opportunity that would have yielded an estimated rate of return of 13 percent. Bent's management decided against the investment because it believed the investment would decrease the division's overall ROI.

Last year's income statement for the Bent Press Division is given below. The division's operating assets employed were $12,600,000 at the end of the year, which represents a 5 percent increase over the previous year-end balance.

BENT PRESS DIVISION
DIVISIONAL INCOME STATEMENT
FOR THE YEAR ENDED DECEMBER 31

Sales		$31,200,000
Cost of goods sold		16,500,000
Gross margin		14,700,000
Less: Operating expenses:		
Selling expenses	$5,620,000	
Administrative expenses	7,208,000	12,828,000
Net operating income		$ 1,872,000

Instructions

1. Compute the following performance measures for the Bent Press Division:
   a. ROI where the investment base is the average operating assets (based on the beginning of the year plus the end of the year assets) divided by two. Break ROI into both capital turnover and return on sales.
   b. Residual income.
2. Would management of the Bent Press Division have been more likely to accept the investment opportunity it had last year if residual income were used as a performance measure instead of ROI? Explain your answer.
3. The Bent Press Division is a separate investment center within Marfar Industries. Identify the items Bent must be free to control if it is to be evaluated fairly by either the ROI or the residual income performance measures.

(CMA, adapted)

Problem Set B

LO2 through LO4

PROBLEM 25.1B
Triple Creek Golf Complex

The Triple Creek Golf Complex is a three-course complex where each course has its own restaurant and pro shop. Thus, the complex is organized into three departments that are treated as investment centers. Budget information for the coming year for these three departments is shown below. The managers of each of the departments are evaluated and bonuses are awarded each year based on ROI.

Triple Creek Golf Complex

	Golf Courses	Restaurants	Pro Shops
Average investment	$10,000,000	$6,000,000	$1,200,000
Sales revenue	14,000,000	2,500,000	700,000
Operating expenses	10,000,000	1,100,000	500,000
Operating earnings	$ 4,000,000	$1,400,000	$ 200,000

Instructions

a. Compute the ROI for each department. Use the DuPont method to analyze the return on sales and capital turnover.

b. Assume the Pro Shops are considering installing new display cases. Upon investigating, the manager of the division finds that the cases would cost $60,000 and that sales revenue would increase by $10,000 per year as a result of the new cases. What is the ROI of the new cases? What impact does the investment in the display cases have on the Pro Shops' ROI? Would the manager of the Pro Shops be motivated to undertake such an investment?

c. Compute the residual income for each department if the minimum required return for the Triple Creek Golf Complex is 18 percent. What would be the impact of the investment in **b** on the Pro Shops' residual income?

LO1 LO5 LO6

PROBLEM 25.2B
Triple Creek Golf Complex and Balanced Scorecard

Consider the Triple Creek Golf Complex discussed in Problem 25.1B. The manager of the Restaurants Department complains that sales and resulting earnings for the restaurants are not higher due to the poor reputation of the Pro Shops. Because the Pro Shops' staff is apparently rude and uninviting and because the Pro Shops seem shabby and are not tidy, the overall reputation of the total complex is slipping. The manager of the Pro Shops Department counters that, to keep operating expenses under control and improve ROI, staff wages have been cut. The manager of the Restaurant Department has requested that other evaluation techniques such as residual income or a balanced scorecard approach be considered in an effort to resolve this problem.

Instructions

Consider which balanced scorecard measures might be useful to the Triple Creek Golf Complex in evaluating the Pro Shops Department. In doing so, identify:

a. The organizational goal that the measure is designed to support.

b. The employee resources and efforts that will be affected by the measurement.

c. How the employees should receive feedback and be rewarded for progress toward achieving goals.

LO1 through LO4

PROBLEM 25.3B

Evaluating Business Unit Performance

The manager of Wilson's Toy Division is evaluated on her division's return on investment and residual income. The company requires that all divisions generate a minimum return on invested assets of 10 percent. Consistent failure to achieve this minimum target is grounds for the dismissal of a division manager. The annual bonus paid to division managers is 1.5 percent of residual income in excess of $200,000. The Toy Division's operating margin for the year was $10 million, during which time its average invested capital was $75 million.

Instructions

a. Compute the Toy Division's return on investment and residual income.

b. Will the manager of the Toy Division receive a bonus for her performance? If so, how much will it be?

c. What are some advantages and disadvantages of using ROI as a performance measurement criterion?

LO2

PROBLEM 25.4B

Tootsie Roll Industries Segment Performance Evaluation

Tootsie Roll Industries has two business segments, one for operations in the U.S. and one for operations in Mexico and Canada. The information below (in thousands) comes from a recent annual report. Find the ROI for each segment for each year.

	Year 2		Year 1	
	United States	Mexico and Canada	United States	Mexico and Canada
Sales	$387,280	$32,830	$362,373	$30,283
Net assets	293,618	58,098	283,362	5,013
Net earnings	69,230	1,174	65,385	325

Instructions

Find and analyze segment ROI using the DuPont method described in this chapter. Explain the performance difference between the two segments across the two years by using the information from the DuPont breakdown of ROI. How does the fact that **Tootsie Roll** acquired a foreign-based company in August of Year 2 affect your analysis?

LO2 through LO4

PROBLEM 25.5B

ROI and Residual Income

Jan Franks is the manager of one location of the Save Some Inc. chain. Frank's location is currently earning an ROI of 15 percent on existing average capital of $800,000. The minimum required return for Save Some Inc. is 12 percent. Frank is considering several additional investment projects, which are independent of existing operations and are independent of each other. The following table lists the projects:

Project	Required Capital	ROI
A	$200,000	16.2%
B	400,000	15.0
C	300,000	14.0
D	200,000	13.0
E	600,000	10.0

Instructions

a. Which of the above projects would Frank choose for investment if his objective were to maximize his location's ROI?

b. Which projects increase the value of Save Some Inc.?

c. Which projects have a negative residual income?

d. Create two rankings for the projects in the order of acceptability if Frank is evaluated (1) on ROI and (2) on residual income.

e. What are the components of ROI? Explain how the combination of components is useful in evaluating the success of business processes within a firm.

LO5 LO6

PROBLEM 25.6B

Balanced Scorecard in a Restaurant Chain

Sandra Olson manages a restaurant that is part of the Eatwell Chain of restaurants popular in the Southwest. Eatwell has recently adopted a balanced scorecard for the entire company. As a result, the restaurant managers for each individual restaurant have a set of strategic goals, measurements, and rewards designed to motivate their employees to achieve the company's overall goals.

Sandra Olson has implemented the balanced scorecard throughout each part of the restaurant she manages. The balanced scorecard measures that specifically apply to the Kitchen are primarily related to business process measures and learning and growth measures. In particular, the Kitchen employees supervised by Olson are evaluated on efficiency measures and learning and growth measures. The learning and growth measures are employee absenteeism, retention, and satisfaction. Operating efficiencies are measured by time from order placement to order completion, amount of waste and spoiled dinners, number of returned dinners, and productivity per employee. Olson obtains a monthly cash bonus if she can increase the learning and growth measures and reduce inefficiencies in the operations.

During the first year that the balanced scorecard was used at Eatwell, Olson did not earn a bonus for her restaurant. She has been particularly frustrated because whenever she reduces the time from order placement to order completion, spoiled dinners and returned dinners increase and employee satisfaction decreases.

Olson decides to hire your consulting firm, Knowitall Incorporated, to help evaluate the new balanced scorecard performance measurement and compensation scheme.

Instructions

Choose a partner to round out your consulting team and write a memo to Sandra Olson that explains the problems she is encountering in the restaurant and, in particular, in the kitchen. In the report identify with bullet points the problems that she is having with the balanced scorecard system and provide suggestions to help remedy those problems.

LO1 LO6

PROBLEM 25.7B

Management Compensation at **Tootsie Roll Industries**

In a recent Schedule 14A filed with the SEC, the Compensation Committee of the **Tootsie Roll** board of directors furnished the information below on executive compensation.

Executive Compensation Policy: The program is comprised of base salary, annual cash incentive bonuses, annual awards under the Company's CAP, split-dollar insurance plans, and pension, profit-sharing, and excess benefit plans generally available to employees of the Company. The Board of Directors believes that this program will lead to increased shareholder value on a long-term basis.

Base Salary: The Board of Directors annually reviews each executive officer's salary. The Board considers the following with respect to the determination of an individual executive officer's base. . . . The Board of Directors believes that the Company's primary competitors for executive talent are companies with a similar market capitalization and, accordingly, relies on a broad array of companies in various industries for comparative analyses.

Annual Incentives and Other Awards: The annual CAP award and split-dollar life insurance program are principally designed to provide an incentive to executive officers to achieve both short-term and long-term financial and other goals, including strategic objectives. These programs are also designed to provide an incentive for the executive to remain with the Company on a long-term basis. These awards are determined by the Board of Directors based on the performance of the Company and the executive's contribution to the growth and success of the Company.

The Board of Directors considers both achievement of strategic objectives and financial performance measures in determining compensation levels. The following measures of Company performance were considered in the determination of bonuses and awards:

- Earnings per share
- Increase in sales of core brands and total sales
- Return on assets
- Return on equity
- Net earnings as a percentage of sales
- Performance in accomplishing successful acquisitions
- Compliance with the requirements of the Sarbanes-Oxley Act, including the documentation and assessment of internal controls
- Other strategic objectives that may be determined from time to time

The Company has no stock options or other stock-based compensation.

Instructions

In this chapter, five design choice categories for management compensation were described (long versus short horizon; fixed versus variable bonus; stock- versus accounting-based evaluation; local versus companywide orientation; and cooperative versus competitive schemes). For each of **Tootsie Roll**'s executive compensation categories listed above, identify the design choices made by **Tootsie Roll**'s board of directors in constructing that component of the company's management compensation plan.

LO2 through LO4

PROBLEM 25.8B
Performance Measures and Transaction Effects

In the following list, assume each transaction is independent of the others. Each of these transactions occurs in a single division of Frangling International, a multidivision company. Each transaction may impact capital turnover, ROI, and/or residual income. For each transaction, explain how capital turnover, ROI, and/or residual income are affected (increase, decrease, or no effect).

a. During the month of October, management decided to discontinue an advertising campaign that was scheduled to run throughout the holiday season because it was not affecting sales.

b. Additional bad debts were discovered due to poor economic conditions and they were written off during July.

c. During May, the division replaced the CFO at a higher salary than the predecessor.

d. Newly purchased equipment in August increased productive capacity but had no effect on sales.

e. During February the division raised the target rate of return from 10 percent to 12 percent because of an increase in the price of debt.

f. The division's chief information officer left the organization in March and was not replaced at the same salary until September.

LO2 through LO4, LO6

PROBLEM 25.9B
ROI, Residual Income, and Performance Evaluation

Warthers Corporation produces auto parts. The company acquires other companies when they are considered a good strategic fit. Several years ago Warthers acquired Landis Company, a supplier of dashboards. Warthers decided to maintain Landis's separate identity and therefore established the Landis Division as one of its investment centers.

Warthers evaluates its divisions on the basis of ROI. Management bonuses are also based on ROI. All investments in operating assets are expected to earn a minimum required rate of return of 15 percent.

Landis's ROI has ranged from 15 percent to 22 percent since it was acquired by Warthers. During the past year, Landis had an investment opportunity that would have yielded an estimated rate of return of 18 percent. Landis's management decided against the investment because it believed the investment would decrease the division's overall ROI.

Last year's income statement for the Landis Division is given below. The division's operating assets employed were $11,220,000 at the end of the year, which represents a 6 percent increase over the previous year-end balance.

LANDIS DIVISION
DIVISIONAL INCOME STATEMENT
FOR THE YEAR ENDED DECEMBER 31

Sales		$26,200,000
Cost of goods sold		12,500,000
Gross margin		13,700,000
Less: Operating expenses:		
Selling expenses	$5,422,000	
Administrative expenses	6,278,000	11,700,000
Net operating income		$ 2,000,000

Instructions

1. Compute the following performance measures for the Landis Division:

   a. ROI where the investment base is the average operating assets (based on the beginning of the year plus the end of the year assets) divided by two. Break ROI into both capital turnover and return on sales.

   b. Residual income.

2. Would management of the Landis Division have been more likely to accept the investment opportunity it had last year if residual income were used as a performance measure instead of ROI? Explain your answer.
3. Warthers corporate management is reconsidering the design of its division management compensation package. Consider the five compensation design characteristics discussed in this chapter. Which of those design characteristics are consistent with Warthers's current compensation arrangement (i.e., based on ROI)? How do you think the compensation package should be restructured?

(CMA, adapted)

Critical Thinking Cases

LO2 through LO4 LO6

CASE 25.1 Business Performance and Transfer Prices

Wolfe Computer manufactures computers and peripheral equipment. The following data relate to Wolfe's Printer Division for the year just ended:

Contribution margin	$11,000,000
Operating margin	6,000,000
Average total assets	50,000,000

The Printer Division is evaluated as an investment center. Wolfe expects all of its investment centers to earn a minimum annual return of 10 percent on average invested capital. Division managers receive a bonus equal to 1 percent of their division's residual income.

The Printer Division's most popular product is a color printer called the XLC. The division has the capacity to manufacture 30,000 XLCs per year, at a manufacturing cost of $100 per unit. Last year it produced XLCs at full capacity; 25,000 of these printers were sold to independent computer stores for $250 per unit, and the other 5,000 were transferred to Wolfe's Mail-Order Division, which sells them for $300 per unit. Transfers of inventory among units of Wolfe Computer are recorded in the company's accounting records at cost.

As Wolfe's new controller, you are attending a planning meeting of division managers. Kay Green, manager of the Mail-Order Division, has asked for 15,000 XLCs in the coming year. She states, "Net income will increase if the Mail-Order Division sells more XLCs. After all, we get the highest sales price."

David Lee, manager of the Printer Division, replies, "Sorry, Kay, we can't do that. Just look at last year—if we'd supplied you with 15,000 XLCs, we wouldn't have made minimum ROI."

Instructions

a. Compute the Printer Division's ROI and residual income based on last year's data.

b. Evaluate the statements made by Green and Lee. (Show how supplying 15,000 XLCs to Mail-Order would have affected the Printer Division's ROI for last year.)

c. Offer suggestions to resolve this situation. Show how your suggestions would have affected the Printer Division's results last year if they had been in effect then.

d. Do you think that your comments in part **c** might raise an ethical dilemma to be resolved by Wolfe's top management? If so, explain the nature of this potential problem and your personal recommendations about how to resolve it. (Hint: Expect to hear from Lee before the day is over.)

LO1 through LO4

CASE 25.2 Expansion of Big Bertha Sub

Big Bertha Sub Shops has more than 150 locations in the Midwest with approximately 70 percent owner operated through franchise agreements. Big Bertha evaluates its shop managers based on ROI each year and those managers have the right to make menu-related decisions. Big Bertha is offering its locations the opportunity to add toasted sub sandwiches to their menus.

The Indianapolis and Cleveland shops are among the best-managed shops among the Big Bertha locations. Both locations are considering adding toasted sub sandwiches to their menus. Purchase and installation of the necessary equipment to toast subs is $195,000 per sub shop. Additional profit from adding toasted subs to the menu is expected to be $33,600. The current investment bases in the Cleveland and Indianapolis shops are $900,000 and $1,370,000, respectively. Last year, the Cleveland shops' annual revenue and expenses were $880,400 and $739,536, respectively, and the Indianapolis shops' were $1,443,856 and $1,197,344, respectively.

Instructions

a. Find the ROI for both the Cleveland and Indianapolis location for (1) last year's results, (2) the toasted sub addition to the menu, and (3) assuming similar operating profit results next year but adding in proposed menu change.

b. Assume that the cost of capital is 15 percent. Calculate the residual income for both the Cleveland and Indianapolis locations for (1) last year's results, (2) the toasted sub addition to the menu, and (3) assuming similar operating profit results next year but adding in the proposed menu change.

c. Assuming the Cleveland and Indianapolis shops are owned by Big Bertha, will the managers choose to expand the menu to include the toasted subs? Explain. Would your answer change if the two shops were independently franchised units with independent owners?

LO1 LO4 LO5

INTERNET CASE 25.3

EVA

To obtain a better understanding of economic value added, visit the Web site that outlines the EVA philosophy of **Stern Stewart & Company** at:

www.valuebasedmanagement.net/methods_eva.html

In the center of the page find information about usage of the EVA method. List at least four uses of EVA in a company and explain each one.

LO1 LO6

INTERNET CASE 25.4

Tootsie Roll's Incentive Compensation Program

To understand **Tootsie Roll Industries**'s incentive compensation design, access **Tootsie Roll Industries**'s SEC filings at:

http://sec.gov/edgar/searchadgar/companysearch.html

Type **Tootsie Roll** (or its ticker symbol TR) in the company name search space. When the list of SEC filings comes into view, access: form DEF 14A, the proxy statement dated 3/26/2010.

Instructions

a. From the "Summary Compensation Table" on page 16 of the proxy statement, identify the company positions that are eligible for management incentive compensation. What is the ratio of the bonus to the actual salary for each management position in 2009?

b. Pages 11 through 14 of the proxy statement provide detailed information about the incentive compensation program. What are the overall objectives of the program?

c. What type of compensation does the program cover?

d. What measures of company performance were considered in the determination of 2009 bonuses and awards?

Internet sites are time and date sensitive. It is the purpose of these exercises to have you explore the Internet. You may need to use the Yahoo! search engine **http://www.yahoo.com** *(or another favorite search engine) to find a company's current Web address.*

LO6

CASE 25.5

Top Management Compensation and Shareholder Activism at **Pfizer**[3]

Unions and other shareholder groups will blast boardrooms with pay proposals during coming years, hoping to support the Securities and Exchange Commission's push to unmask executive pay, perks, and pension benefits. In particular, some individuals like Henry McKinnell, chairman and CEO of **Pfizer Company**, are front and center. Recent pay studies say he has the fattest retirement package among sitting CEOs of companies in the Standard & Poor's 500 stock list. Estimates suggest that McKinnell, who retired in 2008, gets $6.5 million a year for life. Contrast that with McKinnell's 2006 salary of $2.3 million and **Pfizer**'s simultaneous sluggish performance, and some labor activists see a problem. Other big investors are restless, too. As of early 2006, **Pfizer**'s stock is down 46 percent since McKinnell became CEO several years ago, compared with the 27 percent slide in the Amex drug index. That has led several investors to question the $4 million cash bonus McKinnell got in 2005. Is this really merit pay for performance?

[3] Based on Amy Borrus and Amy Barrett, "Not Your Ordinary Gold Watch," *BusinessWeek* 3970 (February 6, 2006), p. 40.

Instructions

a. Why do you think the **Pfizer** board awarded a $4 million cash bonus to the company's chairman, Henry McKinnell, even though **Pfizer**'s performance, a 46 percent stock price decline, was below the industry average decline of 27 percent?

b. Do you believe performance-based executive compensation can create ethically inappropriate incentives for managers? Explain why or why not.

Answers to Self-Test Questions

1. b, e **2.** d, e **3.** d **4.** c **5.** c

COMPREHENSIVE PROBLEM 6

Utease Corporation

Utease Corporation has many production plants across the midwestern United States. A newly opened plant, the Bellingham plant, produces and sells one product. The plant is treated, for responsibility accounting purposes, as a profit center. The unit standard costs for a production unit, with overhead applied based on direct labor hours, are as follows:

Manufacturing costs (per unit based on expected activity of 24,000 units or 36,000 direct labor hours):	
Direct materials (2 pounds at $20)	$ 40.00
Direct labor (1.5 hours at $90)	135.00
Variable overhead (1.5 hours at $20)	30.00
Fixed overhead (1.5 hours at $30)	45.00
Standard cost per unit	$250.00
Budgeted selling and administrative costs:	
Variable	$ 5 per unit
Fixed	$1,800,000
Expected sales activity: 20,000 units at $425.00 per unit	
Desired ending inventories: 10% of sales	

Assume this is the first year of operations for the Bellingham plant. During the year, the company had the following activity:

Units produced	23,000
Units sold	21,500
Unit selling price	$420
Direct labor hours worked	34,000
Direct labor costs	$3,094,000
Direct materials purchased	50,000 pounds
Direct materials costs	$1,000,000
Direct materials used	50,000 pounds
Actual fixed overhead	$1,080,000
Actual variable overhead	$620,000
Actual selling and administrative costs	$2,000,000

In addition, all over- or underapplied overhead and all product cost variances are adjusted to cost of goods sold.

Instructions

a. Prepare a production budget for the coming year based on the available standards, expected sales, and desired ending inventories.

b. Prepare a budgeted responsibility income statement for the Bellingham plant for the coming year.

c. Find the direct labor variances. Indicate if they are favorable or unfavorable and why they would be considered as such.

d. Find the direct materials variances (materials price variance and quantity variance).

e. Find the total over- or underapplied (both fixed and variable) overhead. Would cost of goods sold be a larger or smaller expense item after the adjustment for over- or underapplied overhead?

f. Calculate the actual plant operating profit for the year.

g. Use a flexible budget to explain the difference between the budgeted operating profit and the actual operating profit for the Bellingham plant for its first year of operations. What part of the difference do you believe is the plant manager's responsibility?

h. Assume Utease Corporation is planning to change its evaluation of business operations in all plants from the profit center format to the investment center format. If the average invested capital at the Bellingham plant is $8,950,000, compute the return on investment (ROI) for the first year of operations. Use the DuPont method of evaluation to compute the return on sales (ROS) and capital turnover (CT) for the plant.

i. Assume that under the investment center evaluation plan the plant manager will be awarded a bonus based on ROI. If the manager has the opportunity in the coming year to invest in new equipment for $500,000 that will generate incremental earnings of $75,000 per year, would the manager undertake the project? Why or why not? What other evaluation tools could Utease use for its plants that might be better?

j. The chief financial officer of Utease Corporation wants to include a charge in each investment center's income statement for corporatewide administrative expenses. Should the Bellingham plant manager's annual bonus be based on plant ROI after deducting the corporatewide administrative fee? Why or why not?

CHAPTER 26

Capital Budgeting

© Library of Congress, Prints & Photographs Division [LC-USZ62-41756]/DAL.

AFTER STUDYING THIS CHAPTER, YOU SHOULD BE ABLE TO:

- **LO1** Explain the nature of capital investment decisions.
- **LO2** Identify nonfinancial factors in capital investment decisions.
- **LO3** Evaluate capital investment proposals using (a) payback period, (b) return on investment, and (c) discounted cash flows.
- **LO4** Discuss the relationship between net present value and an investor's required rate of return.
- **LO5** Explain the behavioral issues involved in capital budgeting and identify how companies try to control the capital budgeting process.

Learning Objectives

GENERAL ELECTRIC COMPANY

GE traces its beginnings to Thomas A. Edison, who established Edison Electric Light Company in 1878. In 1892, a manager of Edison General Electric Company and Thomson-Houston Electric Company created General Electric Company. GE currently operates in more than 100 countries, employs about 300,000 people worldwide, and is one of the most admired companies in the world for its innovativeness, sustainability leadership, and ethical reputation.

Currently, GE has new initiatives under way focused on developing countries. The idea is to take the needs of consumers in developing countries as a starting point for innovation and work backward. The initiatives have been dubbed "reverse innovation." Other terms are "frugal" or "constraint-based" innovation. Frugal innovation is not just about redesigning products; it involves rethinking entire production processes and business models. Companies need to squeeze costs so they can reach many more customers, and accept thin profit margins to gain volume. In order to bring these frugal innovations to market, companies like GE use a process of careful planning called capital budgeting. ■

Capital Investment Decisions

Learning Objective
LO1 Explain the nature of capital investment decisions.

One of the greatest challenges managers face is making capital investment decisions. The term **capital investment** refers broadly to large expenditures made to purchase plant assets, develop new product lines, or acquire subsidiary companies. Such decisions commit financial resources for large periods of time and are difficult, if not impossible, to reverse once the funds are invested. Thus, companies stand to benefit from good capital investments (or suffer from poor ones) for many years.

The process of evaluating and prioritizing capital investment opportunities is called **capital budgeting.** Capital budgeting relies heavily on *estimates of future operating results.* These estimates often involve a considerable degree of uncertainty and should be evaluated accordingly. In addition, many *nonfinancial* factors are taken into consideration.

FINANCIAL AND NONFINANCIAL CONSIDERATIONS

Learning Objective
LO2 Identify nonfinancial factors in capital investment decisions.

Perhaps the most important financial consideration in capital budgeting is the expected effects on *future cash flows* and *future profitability.* But in some cases, nonfinancial considerations are the deciding factor.

Exhibit 26–1 provides a few examples of capital investment proposals in which *nonfinancial* factors may be the primary consideration.

Exhibit 26–1
NONFINANCIAL FACTORS IN CAPITAL EXPENDITURES

Investment Proposal	Nonfinancial Considerations
Pollution control system	Environmental concerns Corporate image
New factory lighting	Better working conditions Product quality
Employee health club	Employee morale Healthier employees
Employee child care facility	Accommodate working parents Enhance scheduling flexibility

We will now address three widely used methods of evaluating the *financial* aspects of capital investment proposals: payback period, return on average investment, and discounting future cash flows.

EVALUATING CAPITAL INVESTMENT PROPOSALS: AN ILLUSTRATION

To illustrate the application of capital budgeting techniques, we will evaluate two investments being considered by the Maine LobStars (commonly referred to as the Stars), a minor league baseball team from Portland, Maine. The first involves the purchase of 10 vending machines for the team's Portland stadium. The second involves the purchase of a new bus to replace the one currently in use.

The Stars' stadium currently has no concession stand for preparing and selling food during games. Steve Wilson, the team's owner, has received several bids for constructing a concession stand under the stadium bleachers. The low bid of $150,000 includes a 1,000-square-foot cement block building, equipped with cash registers, deep fryers, a grill, soda machines, and a walk-in freezer and cooler. Unfortunately, the most that the struggling organization is willing to invest for this purpose is $75,000.

Wilson recently received an alternative proposal from VendiCorp International. VendiCorp sells vending machines that dispense hot and cold sandwiches and drinks. The company has offered to sell 10 vending machines to the Stars for $75,000 ($7,500 each). While the machines are in use, VendiCorp is responsible for keeping them stocked with sandwiches and drinks. At the end of a five-year estimated life, VendiCorp will repurchase the machines for $5,000 ($500 each). VendiCorp will also provide the Stars with an insurance and maintenance contract costing $3,000 per year.

Estimates provided by VendiCorp indicate that the 10 machines will take in $1,875 per ball game. The Stars play 45 home games each season. Thus, the machines have the potential to generate annual revenue of $84,375 ($1,875 per game × 45 games). Of this amount, VendiCorp is to receive $50,625, representing the cost of goods sold (60 percent of sales). The Stars are required to reimburse VendiCorp only for those items that sell. As shown in Exhibit 26–2, the machines are expected to increase the Stars's net income by $10,000 per year.

Exhibit 26–2

INCREASE IN STARS' NET INCOME BECAUSE OF VENDING MACHINES

Estimated Increases in Annual Revenue and Expenses from Vending Machines		
Increase in annual revenue from investment		$84,375
Less: Cost of goods sold (60% of sales paid to VendiCorp)		50,625
Increase in annual gross profit (40% of sales)		$33,750
Less: Cost of maintenance & insurance contract	$ 3,000	
Depreciation [($75,000 − $5,000) ÷ 5 years]	14,000	
Increase in utilities & miscellaneous costs	350	17,350
Increase in annual pretax operating income from investment		$16,400
Less: Additional income taxes (approximately 39%)		6,400
Increase in annual net income from investment		$10,000

Most capital budgeting techniques involve analysis of the *annual net cash flows* pertaining to an investment. Annual net cash flows refer to the excess of cash receipts over cash disbursements in a given year. We may assume in our example that all of the vending machine revenue is received in cash, and that all expenses (other than depreciation) are immediately paid in cash. In other words, the *only difference* between net income and net cash flows relates to depreciation expense.

The annual net cash flows expected to be generated by the vending machines are $24,000, determined as follows:

Increase in annual net income from investment	$10,000
Annual depreciation expense	14,000
Annual net cash flows from investment	$24,000

This computation reflects the fact that depreciation is a *noncash expense*. Because depreciation expense decreases annual net income from an investment, it must be added back to annual net income to find the annual net cash flows.

In our example, the vending machines are expected to increase *both* net income and net cash flows. But the real question is whether these increases *are adequate to justify the required investment.* We will attempt to answer this question using three different capital budgeting techniques.

PAYBACK PERIOD

The **payback period** is the length of time necessary to recover the entire cost of an investment from the resulting annual net cash flows. In our example, the payback period is computed as follows:

$$\frac{\textbf{Amount to Be Invested}}{\textbf{Estimated Annual Net Cash Flows}} = \frac{\$75{,}000}{\$24{,}000} = 3.125 \text{ years}$$

Learning Objective
LO3 Evaluate capital investment proposals using (a) payback period

In the selection among alternative investment opportunities, a short payback period is considered desirable because the more quickly an investment's cost is recovered, the sooner the funds may be put to other use. A short payback period also reduces the risk that changes in economic conditions will prevent full recovery of an investment.

However, the payback period should never be the only factor considered in a major capital budgeting decision because it ignores two important issues. First, it ignores the total profitability and cash flows anticipated over the *entire life* of an investment (in this case, five years). Second, it ignores the *timing* of the future cash flows. We will address this issue in greater depth later in the chapter.

RETURN ON AVERAGE INVESTMENT

Learning Objective
LO3 Evaluate capital investment proposals using (b) return on investment.

The **return on average investment (ROI)** is the average annual net income from an investment expressed as a percentage of the *average* amount invested.[1] The Stars will initially have to invest $75,000 to purchase 10 new vending machines. However, each year depreciation expense will reduce the carrying value of these machines by a total of $14,000. Because the annual net cash flow is expected to exceed net income by this amount, we may view depreciation expense as providing for the *recovery* of the amount originally invested. The amount that the Stars will have invested in the equipment at any given time is represented by the carrying value of the vending machines (their cost less accumulated depreciation).

When straight-line depreciation is used, the carrying value of an asset decreases uniformly over the asset's life. Thus, the average carrying value over the life of an asset is equal to the amount halfway between its original cost and its salvage value. If the salvage value is zero, the average carrying value (or average investment) is simply one-half of the asset's original cost.

Mathematically, the average amount invested over the life of an asset may be determined as follows:

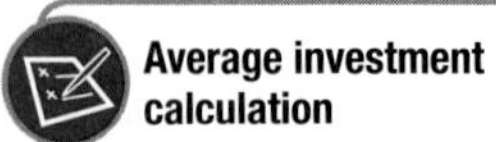

$$\textbf{Average Invesment} = \frac{\textbf{Original Cost + Salvage Value}}{\textbf{2}}$$

Thus, over the life of the 10 new vending machines, the Stars will have an average investment of ($75,000 + $5,000) ÷ 2, or *$40,000.* We may compute the expected return on average investment as follows:

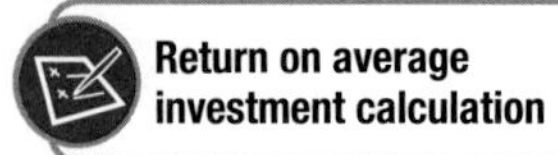

$$\frac{\textbf{Average Estimated Net Income}}{\textbf{Average Investment}} = \frac{\textbf{\$10,000}}{\textbf{\$40,000}} = \textbf{25\%}$$

In deciding whether 25 percent is a satisfactory rate of return, Wilson should consider such factors as the reliability of VendiCorp's forecasts of income and cash flows, the return available from other investment opportunities, and the Stars' cost of capital.[2] In comparing alternative investment opportunities, managers prefer the one with the *lowest risk,* the *highest rate of return,* and the *shortest payback period.*

The concept of return on investment shares a common weakness with the payback method. It fails to consider that the **present value** of an investment depends on the *timing* of its future cash flows. Cash flows received late in the life of an investment, for example, are of *less value* to an investor today than cash flows of equal amount received early in the life of an investment. The return on investment computation simply ignores the question of whether cash receipts will occur early or late in the life of an investment. It also fails to consider whether the purchase price of the investment must be paid in advance or in installments stretching over a period of years. *Discounting* future cash flows is a technique that does take into account cash flow timing issues.

[1] In Chapter 25, ROI is defined as operating income divided by average investment. Operating income rather than net income is frequently used in ROI calculations designed to evaluate *historical* performance. Because interest on the investment and taxes are not controlled by the manager being evaluated, they are not included in the ROI calculations. However, when *future* investment performance is being evaluated, all related cash flows (including nonoperating interest and tax items) must be considered.

[2] A firm's cost of capital refers to the cost of financing investments. In situations where an investment is entirely financed with debt, the cost of capital is the interest rate paid by the firm on borrowed funds. For investments that are financed all or in part with equity, the computation is more complex. Approaches for determining a firm's cost of capital are addressed in a corporate finance course.

DISCOUNTING FUTURE CASH FLOWS

As explained in earlier chapters, the present value of a future cash flow is the amount that a knowledgeable investor would pay today for the right to receive that future amount. Arriving at a present value figure depends on (1) the amount of the future cash flow, (2) the length of time that the investor must wait to receive the cash flow, and (3) the rate of return required by the investor. *Discounting* is the process by which the present value of cash flows (referred to as the **discounted cash flows**) is determined.

The use of present value tables to discount future cash flows is demonstrated in Appendix B (at the end of this text). Those who are not familiar with the concept of present value or with present value tables should read the appendix before continuing with this chapter.

Learning Objective
Evaluate capital investment proposals using (c) discounted cash flows. LO3

For your convenience, the two present value tables presented in the appendix are repeated in this chapter. Exhibit 26–3 shows the present value of a *single lump-sum payment* of $1

Exhibit 26-3

PRESENT VALUE OF $1 PAYABLE IN *n* PERIODS

Present Value of $1 Due in *n* Periods*

Number of Periods (*n*)	Discount Rate 1%	1½%	5%	6%	8%	10%	12%	15%	20%
1	.990	.985	.952	.943	.926	.909	.893	.870	.833
2	.980	.971	.907	.890	.857	.826	.797	.756	.694
3	.971	.956	.864	.840	.794	.751	.712	.658	.579
4	.961	.942	.823	.792	.735	.683	.636	.572	.482
5	.951	.928	.784	.747	.681	.621	.567	.497	.402
6	.942	.915	.746	.705	.630	.564	.507	.432	.335
7	.933	.901	.711	.665	.583	.513	.452	.376	.279
8	.923	.888	.677	.627	.540	.467	.404	.327	.233
9	.914	.875	.645	.592	.500	.424	.361	.284	.194
10	.905	.862	.614	.558	.463	.386	.322	.247	.162
20	.820	.742	.377	.312	.215	.149	.104	.061	.026
24	.788	.700	.310	.247	.158	.102	.066	.035	.013
36	.699	.585	.173	.123	.063	.032	.017	.007	.001

*The present value of $1 is computed by the formula $p = 1/(1 + i)^n$, where p is the present value of $1, i is the discount rate, and n is the number of periods until the future cash flow will occur. Amounts in this table have been rounded to three decimal places and are shown for a limited number of periods and discount rates. Many calculators are programmed to use this formula and can compute present values when the future amount is entered along with values for i and n.

Exhibit 26-4

PRESENT VALUE OF A $1 ANNUITY RECEIVABLE EACH PERIOD FOR *n* PERIODS

Present Value of $1 to Be Received Periodically for *n* Periods

Number of Periods (*n*)	Discount Rate 1%	1½%	5%	6%	8%	10%	12%	15%	20%
1	0.990	0.985	0.952	0.943	0.926	0.909	0.893	0.870	0.833
2	1.970	1.956	1.859	1.833	1.783	1.736	1.690	1.626	1.528
3	2.941	2.912	2.723	2.673	2.577	2.487	2.402	2.283	2.106
4	3.902	3.854	3.546	3.465	3.312	3.170	3.037	2.855	2.589
5	4.853	4.783	4.329	4.212	3.993	3.791	3.605	3.352	2.991
6	5.795	5.697	5.076	4.917	4.623	4.355	4.111	3.784	3.326
7	6.728	6.598	5.786	5.582	5.206	4.868	4.564	4.160	3.605
8	7.652	7.486	6.463	6.210	5.747	5.335	4.968	4.487	3.837
9	8.566	8.361	7.108	6.802	6.247	5.759	5.328	4.772	4.031
10	9.471	9.222	7.722	7.360	6.710	6.145	5.650	5.019	4.192
20	18.046	17.169	12.462	11.470	9.818	8.514	7.469	6.259	4.870
24	21.243	20.030	13.799	12.550	10.529	8.985	7.784	6.434	4.937
36	30.108	27.661	16.547	14.621	11.717	9.677	8.192	6.623	4.993

to be received in n periods (years) in the future. Exhibit 26–4 shows the present value of a $1 *annuity*—that is, $1 to be received *each year* for n consecutive years. For illustrative purposes, both tables have been kept short. They include only selected discount rates and only extend for a limited number of periods. However, they contain the appropriate rates and periods for all of the problem material in this chapter.

The **discount rate** may be viewed as an investor's *required rate of return.* The present value of an investment's future cash flows is the maximum amount that an investor should be willing to pay for the investment and still expect to earn the required rate of return. Therefore, an investment is considered desirable when its cost is less than the present value of its future cash flows. In such cases, the expected rate of return *exceeds* the rate of return required by the investor. Conversely, when the cost of an investment exceeds the present value of its future cash flows, its expected return is *less* than that required by the investor.

The higher the discount rate being used, the lower the resulting present value figure will be. It follows that, the *higher the required rate of return* for a particular investment, the *less* an investor will be willing to pay for the investment. The appropriate discount rate (or required rate of return) for determining the present value of a specific investment depends on the nature of the investment, the alternative investment opportunities available, and the investor's cost of capital.

The required rate of return is adjusted in many companies for a variety of strategic reasons. For example, management may allow a lower required rate of return when there is a strategic necessity to penetrate a new market or to acquire new technology. Also, for certain capital expenditures, such as new technology, estimating the cash flows and the timing of those cash flows can be extremely difficult. Managers know that establishing a high required rate of return will place projects with higher cash flows occurring in the more distant future at a disadvantage. Using a high discount rate for projects where high net cash flows are not received until several years in the future will result in low net present values.

Let us now apply the concept of discounting cash flows to our example. We shall assume that the Stars require a *15 percent* annual rate of return on all capital investments. As shown in Exhibit 26–5, the 10 vending machines are expected to generate annual net cash inflows of $24,000 for five years. Exhibit 26–4 shows that the present value of $1 to be received annually for five years, discounted at 15 percent, is *3.352.* Therefore, the present value of $24,000 received annually for five years is $24,000 × 3.352, or *$80,448.* Notice in Exhibit 26–5 that, even though the total annual cash inflows are $120,000, their present value is only $80,448.

In addition to these annual cash flows, Wilson expects that VendiCorp will repurchase the machines from the Stars at the end of five years for $5,000 (their salvage value). Referring to Exhibit 26–3, we see that the present value of $1 to be received in five years, discounted at 15 percent, is *.497.* Thus, the present value of $5,000 to be received at the end of five years

Exhibit 26–5 **PRESENT VALUE OF CASH FLOWS FOR VENDICORP**

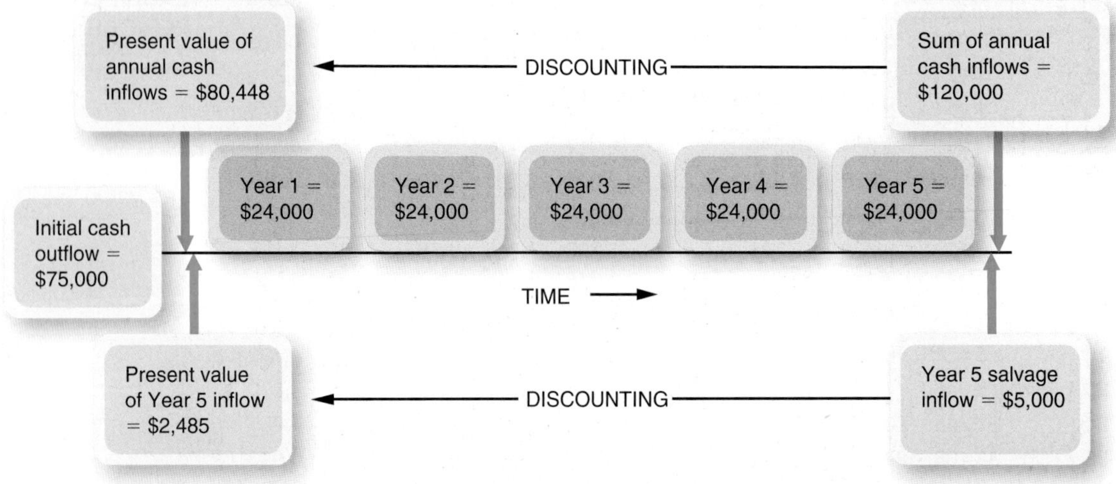

is $5,000 × .497, or *$2,485*. Using the information in Exhibit 26–5, we may now analyze the proposal to invest in the 10 vending machines in the following manner:

Present value of expected annual cash flows ($24,000 × 3.352)	$80,448
Present value of proceeds from disposal ($5,000 × .497)	2,485
Total present value of investment's future cash flows	$82,933
Cost of investment (payable in advance)	75,000
Net present value of proposed investment	$ 7,933

Investment's net present value

This analysis indicates that the present value of the vending machines' future cash flows, discounted at a rate of 15 percent, amounts to *$82,933.* This is the *maximum amount* that the Stars could invest in these machines and still expect to earn the required annual return of 15 percent. As the actual cost of the investment is only $75,000, the machines have the potential to earn a rate of return *in excess* of 15 percent.

Learning Objective LO4
Discuss the relationship between net present value and an investor's required rate of return.

The **net present value** of VendiCorp's proposal is the difference between the total present value of the net cash flows and the cost of the investment. If the net present value is equal to zero, the rate of return is equal to the discount rate. A *positive* net present value means that the investment is expected to provide a rate of return *greater* than the discount rate, whereas a *negative* net present value means that the investment is likely to yield a return *less* than the discount rate. In financial terms, proposals with a positive net present value are considered acceptable and those with a negative net present value are viewed as unacceptable. These relationships are summarized in Exhibit 26–6.

Exhibit 26–6

SUMMARY OF RELATIONSHIPS AMONG NPV, THE DISCOUNT RATE, AND PROJECT ACCEPTABILITY

Net Present Value (NPV)	Interpretation	Action
NPV > Zero	Return exceeds the discount rate.	Accept
NPV = Zero	Return is equal to the discount rate.	Accept
NPV < Zero	Return is less than the discount rate.	Reject

On the basis of our cash flow analysis, purchase of the vending machines appears to be an acceptable proposal. However, there are numerous nonfinancial issues that might be considered before making a decision based *purely on the numbers.*

For instance, all of the revenue and expense estimates used in determining these financial measures were supplied by VendiCorp. It is entirely possible that these estimates may be overly optimistic. Furthermore, Wilson knows nothing about VendiCorp's business reputation. What assurances does he have that VendiCorp will honor its agreement to stock the machines with fresh merchandise before each game, maintain the machines when they break down, and repurchase the machines for $5,000 at the end of five years? Has Wilson obtained bids from other suppliers of vending machines? Or has he considered an arrangement with an outside catering service to provide concessions at the Stars' home ball games? Finally, perhaps there are unrelated investment opportunities to consider, such as investing in a new pitching machine, team uniforms, or new stadium seats.

YOUR TURN **You as a Chief Financial Officer**

You are attending your first meeting with the management team for the Maine LobStars. Your job is to discuss planned capital budgeting projects to get management's approval. Management, including the owner, Steve Wilson, is accustomed to looking at payback period and return on average assets. However, you have also prepared net present value information for management's review. Steve Wilson complains that the net present value information is redundant and unnecessary. How will you respond?

(See our comments on the Online Learning Center Web site.)

REPLACING ASSETS

Many capital investment decisions involve the possible replacement of existing assets. Such decisions involve several decision-making techniques, including identifying *relevant information, incremental analysis,* and *discounting future cash flows.* Careful consideration also should be given to the *income tax effects* of the decision and to *nonfinancial factors.*

Data for an Illustration To illustrate, assume the Maine LobStars own an old bus that transports the team from game to game. This old bus guzzles gas, frequently needs repair, has no air conditioning, and is cramped and uncomfortable. An opportunity arises to purchase another bus that, although used, is larger, in better condition, has air conditioning, and is more fuel efficient.

The financial data in Exhibit 26–7 relate to this capital investment proposal.

Exhibit 26–7

DATA FOR BUS REPLACEMENT ANALYSIS AT MAINE LOBSTARS

Cost of new bus	$65,000
Book value of existing bus	25,000
Current sales value of existing bus	10,000
Estimated annual operating costs (gas, repairs, insurance):	
New bus	18,000
Existing bus	30,000

We will make a simplifying assumption that both buses have a remaining useful life of five years, with no salvage value.

Notice that the old bus has a book value of $25,000, but a current sales value of only $10,000. At first glance, the resulting *$15,000 loss* upon disposal appears to be an argument against replacing the old bus. But the cost of the old bus is a **sunk cost** and therefore is *not relevant* to the decision.

The current book value of the old bus is merely what remains of this sunk cost. If the old bus is sold, its book value is offset against the sale proceeds. But if the old bus is kept, its book value will be recognized as depreciation expense over the next five years. The Stars *cannot avoid* recognizing this cost as expense (or loss) *regardless of which decision is made.* From a present-value standpoint, there actually is some *benefit* to recognizing this sunk cost as a loss in the current period because the related *income tax deduction* will occur now, rather than over the remaining life of the bus.

In deciding whether to replace the old bus, the Stars should determine the present value of the *incremental net cash flows* resulting from this action. This present value may be compared with the cost of the new bus to determine whether the proposal will provide the required rate of return.

Determining the Present Value of Incremental Cash Flows To compute the incremental annual cash flows from acquiring the new bus, we must consider both the annual savings in operating costs and the difference in *annual income taxes.* The Stars's annual income tax expense will be affected by purchasing the new bus because of the difference in annual operating expenses and in the annual deductions for depreciation. (To simplify our computations, we will assume the Stars use straight-line depreciation for tax purposes.)

The data in Exhibit 26–7 show that the new bus is expected to produce a $12,000 annual savings in operating costs. However, annual depreciation on the new bus will be $13,000 ($65,000 ÷ 5 years), whereas annual depreciation on the old bus is only $5,000 ($25,000 ÷ 5 years). This $8,000 increase in depreciation expense means that purchasing the new bus will *increase taxable income* by $4,000 per year ($12,000 annual cost savings, less $8,000 in additional depreciation expense). Assuming a tax rate of 40 percent, purchase of the new bus will *increase annual income tax expense* by *$1,600* ($4,000 × 40%). Thus, the incremental annual net cash flows from purchasing the new bus amount to *$10,400* ($12,000 savings in operating costs, less $1,600 in additional income taxes). Exhibit 26–8 shows the declining present value of each year's annual net cash savings in operating costs if the new bus is purchased.

The Stars require a 15 percent return on capital investments. Referring to the annuity table in Exhibit 26–4, we see that the present value of $1 received annually for five years is *3.352.* Therefore, the $10,400 received annually for five years, discounted at 15 percent, has a present value of *$34,861* ($10,400 × 3.352). In addition to the present value of the *annual* cash flows,

Exhibit 26–8 DECLINING PRESENT VALUES OF THE ANNUAL COST SAVINGS FROM THE NEW LOBSTARS BUS

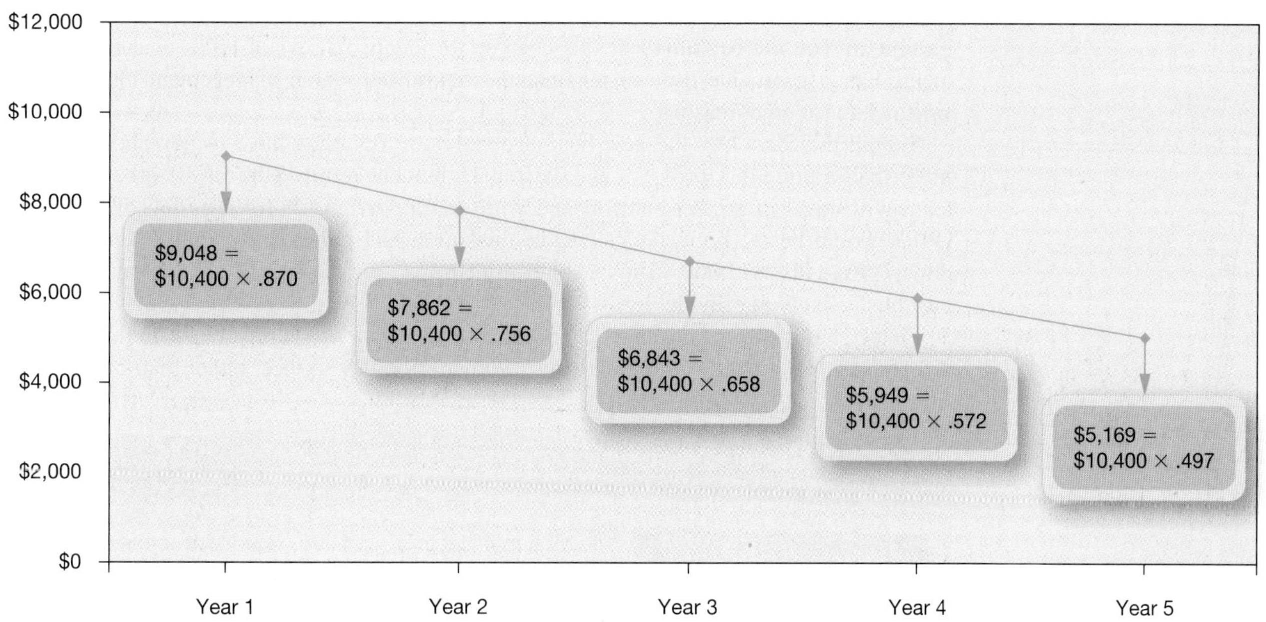

however, we should consider two other factors: the $10,000 sale proceeds from the old bus, and the tax savings resulting from the loss on disposal.

The $10,000 proceeds from the sale will be received immediately and, therefore, have a present value of *$10,000.* The $15,000 loss on disposal results in a $6,000 tax savings at the end of the first year ($15,000 × 40%). The present value of $6,000 one year hence, discounted at 15 percent, is *$5,220* ($6,000 × .870), as determined from Exhibit 26–3.

Summary of Financial Considerations We now can determine the net present value of this proposal as follows:

Present value of incremental annual cash flows	$ 34,861
Present value of proceeds from sale of old bus	10,000
Present value of tax savings from loss on disposal	5,220
Total present value	$ 50,081
Less: Cost of new bus	65,000
Net present value	$(14,919)

This proposal fails to provide the Stars with its required minimum return on capital investments of 15 percent. (***Question:*** What is the most that the Stars could pay for the new bus and earn a 15 percent return? ***Answer:*** $50,081, the present value of the cash flows, discounted at 15 percent.)

YOUR TURN **You as a Transportation Manager**

Assume you manage transportation for the LobStars. You have just seen the proposal for acquiring the new bus with its accompanying financial figures. You know that the operating costs for the new bus will not be $18,000 per year but will more likely be $8,000, $12,000, $20,000, $24,000, and $26,000 for years 1 through 5, respectively. Do you have an ethical responsibility to mention this fact, given that operating costs average $18,000 over five years [($8,000 + $12,000 + $20,000 + $24,000 + $26,000) ÷ 5 = $18,000]?

(See our comments on the Online Learning Center Web site.)

Nonfinancial Considerations Just because a capital investment proposal fails to provide the desired rate of return does not necessarily mean that it should be rejected. In Exhibit 26–1 at the beginning of this chapter we identified several types of capital investments likely to provide little or no financial return, but which management may consider worthwhile for other reasons.

Should the Stars buy the new bus? Probably so. Yes, they have to pay about $15,000 more than a price that provides the desired 15 percent return. But on the other hand, the team will travel in greater comfort and with *greater reliability* for a period of *five years*. (What would be the *opportunity cost* of missing a ball game because the old bus breaks down?) Actually, $15,000 seems a small price to pay for the nonfinancial benefits that the new bus is likely to provide.

Finally, has the team considered all of the available options? Surely, this isn't the only used bus for sale. And what would be the cost of chartering bus service, rather than owning their own bus?

INTERNATIONAL CASE IN POINT

International factors can be important considerations in capital budgeting. For example, when **McDonald's Corporation** invested in Brazil and Russia it had to strategically invest in the infrastructure to make its restaurants successful. Management explained the impact of these needed investments as not surprising when the returns in emerging markets proved to be lower than in established markets. The substantial infrastructure investment required to support restaurant growth is higher in less-developed countries.

BEHAVIORAL CONSIDERATIONS IN CAPITAL BUDGETING

Learning Objective

LO5 Explain the behavioral issues involved in capital budgeting and identify how companies try to control the capital budgeting process.

The accuracy of capital budgets is critically dependent on cash flows and project life-span estimates. However, the estimates created by employees involved in capital budgeting need careful consideration for two reasons. First, because the results of the capital budgeting process have serious implications for employees, their estimates may be overly pessimistic or optimistic. Second, capital budgeting involves estimates from many sources within and outside of the company; thus, there are many opportunities for errors to creep into the process.

Pessimistic or optimistic estimates arise because employees are frequently evaluated on outcomes that clearly depend on the amount and type of capital investments the company chooses. For example, the manager of a profit center is likely to be paid a bonus based on the center's profits each quarter. Assume the profit center's profitability depends on the efficiency of currently operating equipment. In providing data for a capital investment proposal for new equipment, that profit center manager may be overly optimistic about the efficiency of the new equipment and overly pessimistic about the projected efficiency of the current equipment in order to persuade management to acquire new equipment.

Because choices among capital budgeting proposals determine future directions of the firm, careful evaluation and aggregation of data are critical. Most capital budgeting proposals require input from a variety of different individuals. For example, in the case of the LobStars bus decision, estimates of the sales prices of the new and old buses, the operating expenses of the new and old buses, and the life spans of the new and old buses are likely to come from various sources. Operating expense information may come from the accountant, sales prices for old and new buses may be gathered from outside of the organization, and the lifespan estimates may come from the bus mechanic. The reliability of these estimates can be a critical factor in the final choices made among capital budget proposals.

Companies establish internal controls for the capital budgeting process to help guard against overly optimistic or pessimistic estimates and aggregation errors. Many companies use routing forms that require all upper-level managers to sign off on large capital budgeting proposals. A finance department's expertise is used to review and complete analyses about the accuracy of estimates. The largest strategic capital investments ordinarily require approval by the board of directors.

In addition, many companies track capital budget projects as they are implemented. Managers compare the projected expenditures with the actual installation and operating costs to identify weaknesses in their planning processes. Capital budget planners, who know that a **capital budget audit** will be undertaken, will be less likely to be overly optimistic or pessimistic about their estimates. Just as you are careful about planning your expenditures from your checking account because you know the bank audits your balance, capital budget planners are more careful when they know an audit of their proposed investment expenditures will be undertaken.

Concluding Remarks

We now have discussed three methods of evaluating the *financial* aspects of capital investment opportunities. The financial consequences of capital investments are relevant—even if the business has little choice but to make the expenditure.

You probably noticed how income taxes complicated our analysis of decisions about replacing assets. Income taxes *do* complicate business decisions—and in many situations, it is tax considerations that dictate the appropriate course of action. We urge *all* financial decision makers *always to consider the tax consequences* of their actions.

Don't forget that *nonfinancial* considerations drive many business decisions. Businesses must operate in a *socially responsible* manner, which often involves a sacrifice of profitability—especially in the short term. Remember also the concept of *opportunity costs.* There often is a better alternative awaiting discovery by those who are perceptive, innovative, and persistent.

Ethics, Fraud & Corporate Governance

Throughout this text we have emphasized the growing importance of ethics, fraud, and corporate governance to the practice of accounting and the business community. In this final commentary, we discuss recent developments in these three areas.

Most corporations now have codes of business conduct and ethics that they expect all employees to follow. In fact, public companies whose stock is traded on the New York Stock Exchange or on NASDAQ are required to maintain a code of business conduct and ethics. Moreover, many companies provide training related to their code of conduct and ethics and require employees to certify in writing on a yearly basis that they are in compliance with the code. In addition, as discussed earlier in the text, public companies are required to maintain "whistle-blower hotlines" that enable employees to anonymously report to the audit committee their concerns related to questionable accounting or auditing matters. The greater focus on ethics also has affected academia. Proposals that would require accounting students to complete substantial training in ethics are being considered and implemented across the country.

Finally, few business topics have received more attention in recent years than the topic of corporate governance. First, given recent abuses in the area of executive pay, the Securities and Exchange Commission has improved the extent and transparency of the required disclosures surrounding executive compensation. In addition, boards of directors, often prodded by institutional investors and/or hedge funds, are more circumspect in providing lavish compensation packages to senior executives, particularly where these compensation packages are not tied to performance.

Second, shareholder activists continue to press for a greater role in choosing the individuals who serve as directors of public companies. A number of shareholder proposals have been introduced that would require an individual to receive a majority of the shareholder votes cast. Some of these shareholder proposals have passed, and some companies have changed their corporate bylaws or corporate governance guidelines to

(continued)

require director candidates to receive 50 percent or more of the votes cast in order to serve on the board of directors.

Third, corporate boards are being held to a higher standard of performance and accountability. The outside directors are sued personally, and these directors settle their lawsuits by making payments out of their personal assets. The directors at **The Walt Disney Co.** were sued personally based on allegations that they breached their fiduciary duty in overseeing the compensation package, including severance payments, received by a former senior executive of **Disney.** Finally, a growing body of academic research suggests that individuals who serve on the board of a company with financial reporting problems (e.g., fraud, restatements, etc.) are less likely to be appointed to other corporate boards in the future. As a result, the earning capacity of those individuals is reduced, suggesting that this market-based mechanism may complement legal and regulatory efforts to improve the performance of corporate directors in overseeing company management.

A Concluding Comment from the Authors

This book has introduced you to the basic concepts of financial accounting, management accounting, and, to a lesser extent, income taxes. We are confident that you will find this background useful throughout your career. However, we also recommend that you continue your study of accounting with additional courses. We particularly recommend a course in cost accounting and an introductory course in taxation.

We appreciate having the opportunity of addressing you through this text. It is indeed a privilege to share our views of accounting and business with so many students.

The writing of this text has taught us much. All of us have had to challenge, research, verify, and rethink much of what we thought we already knew. We hope the experience of this course proves as rewarding to you.

END-OF-CHAPTER REVIEW

SUMMARY OF LEARNING OBJECTIVES

LO1 **Explain the nature of capital investment decisions.** Capital investment decisions generally refer to projects or proposals that require the purchase of plant assets. These decisions are crucial to the long-run financial health of a business enterprise. Not only do they require that resources be committed for long periods of time, but they are also difficult or impossible to reverse once funds have been invested and a project has begun.

LO2 **Identify nonfinancial factors in capital investment decisions.** Nonfinancial factors may dictate the appropriate course of action. Such factors may include, for example, compliance with laws, corporate image, employee morale, and various aspects of social responsibility. Management must remain alert to such considerations.

LO3 **Evaluate capital investment proposals using (a) payback period, (b) return on investment, and (c) discounted cash flows.** The payback period is the length of time needed to recover the cost of an investment from the resulting net cash flows. However, this type of investment analysis fails to consider the total life and overall profitability of the investment.

Return on average investment expresses the average estimated net income from the investment as a percentage of the average investment. This percentage represents the rate of return earned on the investment. A shortcoming is that average estimated net income ignores the timing of future cash flows. Therefore, no consideration is given to the time value of money.

Discounting future cash flows determines the net present value of an investment proposal. Proposals with a positive net present value usually are considered acceptable, while proposals with a negative net present value are considered unacceptable. This technique considers both the life of the investment and the timing of future cash flows.

LO4 **Discuss the relationship between net present value and an investor's required rate of return.** The discount rate used in determining an investment's net present value may be viewed as the investor's minimum required return for that investment. Thus, when an investment's net present value is positive, its expected rate of return exceeds the minimum return required by the investor. Conversely, a negative net present value suggests that an investment's return potential is less than the minimum return required by the investor.

LO5 **Explain the behavioral issues involved in capital budgeting and identify how companies try to control the capital budgeting process.** Employees may be optimistic or pessimistic in their capital budgeting cash flow estimates because their futures are affected by the selected capital budgeting proposals. Firms audit capital budgeting projects to attempt to control for overly optimistic or pessimistic estimates.

Key Terms Introduced or Emphasized in Chapter 26

capital budget audit (p. 1125) The process where managers compare the projected expenditures with the actual installation and operating costs of a capital budgeting project to identify weaknesses in their planning processes.

capital budgeting (p. 1116) The process of planning and evaluating proposals for investments in plant assets.

capital investments (p. 1116) Large capital expenditures that typically involve the purchase of plant assets.

discount rate (p. 1120) The minimum required rate of return used by an investor to discount future cash flows to their present value.

discounted cash flows (p. 1119) The present value of future cash flows.

net present value (p. 1121) The excess of the present value of the net cash flows expected from an investment over the amount to be invested. Net present value is one method of ranking alternative investment proposals.

payback period (p. 1117) The length of time necessary to recover the cost of an investment through the cash flows generated by that investment. Payback period is one criterion used in making capital budgeting decisions.

present value (p. 1118) The amount of money today that is considered equivalent to a cash inflow or outflow expected to take place in the future. The present value of money is always less than its future amount, since money on hand today can be invested to become the equivalent of a larger amount in the future.

return on average investment (ROI) (p. 1118) The average annual net income from an investment expressed as a percentage of the average amount invested. Return on average investment is one method of ranking alternative investment proposals according to their profitability.

sunk cost (p. 1122) A cost that has been incurred irrevocably by past actions. Sunk costs are irrelevant to decisions regarding future actions.

Demonstration Problem

Grover Contracting, Inc., is considering the purchase of a new cement truck costing $150,000. Grover intends to keep the truck for five years before trading it in on a new one. The truck's estimated salvage value at the end of the five-year period is approximately $25,000. The truck is expected to increase annual income and cash flows by the following amounts:

Year	Increase in Income	Increase in Net Cash Flows
1	$10,000	$ 37,500
2	12,000	37,500
3	14,000	37,500
4	16,000	37,500
5	18,000	37,500
	$70,000	$187,500

Instructions

a. Compute the payback period associated with this investment.

b. Compute the return on average investment of this proposal.

c. Compute the net present value of this investment if Grover requires a minimum return of 12 percent.

d. Comment on your findings.

Solution to the Demonstration Problem

a. The payback period of the investment is computed as follows:

$$\frac{\textbf{Amount to Be Invested}}{\textbf{Estimated Annual Net Cash Flow}} = \frac{\$150{,}000}{\$37{,}500} = \underline{\underline{4 \text{ years}}}$$

b. The return on average investment may be determined in three steps:

Step 1: Compute average investment.

$$\frac{\textbf{Original Cost + Salvage Value}}{2} = \frac{\$150{,}000 + \$25{,}000}{2} = \$87{,}500$$

Step 2: Compute average estimated net income.

$$\frac{\textbf{Total Income}}{\textbf{Estimated Useful Life}} = \frac{\$70{,}000}{5 \text{ years}} = \underline{\underline{\$14{,}000}}$$

Step 3: Compute average return on investment.

$$\frac{\textbf{Average Estimated Net Income}}{\textbf{Average Investment}} = \frac{\$14{,}000}{\$87{,}500} = \underline{\underline{16\%}}$$

c. The net present value of the investment is computed as follows:

Refer to Exhibit 26–3

Present value of salvage value discounted at 12% for 5 years ($25,000 × .567)	$ 14,175
Refer to Exhibit 26–4	
Present value of net cash flows discounted at 12% for 5 years ($37,500 × 3.605)	135,188
Total present value of future cash flows	$149,363
Amount to be invested (payable in advance)	150,000
Net present value of proposed investment	$ (637)

d. Two of the three measures regarding the cement truck investment are encouraging. First, the payback period of four years is less than the truck's estimated life of five years. Second, the return on average investment of 16 percent is greater than Grover's minimum required return of 12 percent. However, a negative net present value of $637 reveals that the truck's return, in present value terms, is actually less than 12 percent. Had the company's minimum required return been 10 percent instead of 12 percent, the net present value of the investment would be positive by $7,688, computed as follows:

Refer to Exhibit 26–3	
Present value of salvage value discounted at 10% for 5 years ($25,000 × .621)	$ 15,525
Refer to Exhibit 26–4	
Present value of net cash flows discounted at 10% for 5 years ($37,500 × 3.791)	142,163
Total present value of future cash flows	$157,688
Amount to be invested (payable in advance)	150,000
Net present value of proposed investment	$ 7,688

Because the net present value of the truck is negative when a discount rate of 12 percent is used and positive when a discount rate of 10 percent is used, we know that the truck's expected return is between 10 percent and 12 percent.

Self-Test Questions

The answers to these questions appear on page 1145.

1. Which of the following capital budgeting measures requires the discounting of an investment's future cash flows?

- **a.** Payback period.
- **b.** Net present value.
- **c.** Return on average investment.
- **d.** All of the above require the discounting of an investment's future cash flows.

2. Which of the following is of least importance in determining whether to replace an old piece of equipment?

- **a.** The incremental costs and revenue associated with the new piece of equipment.
- **b.** The estimated cost of the new piece of equipment.
- **c.** The historical cost of the old piece of equipment.
- **d.** The estimated salvage value of the new piece of equipment.

3. If the net present value of an investment proposal is positive, what conclusions can be drawn? (Identify all correct answers.)

- **a.** The discount rate used is less than the investment's estimated return.
- **b.** The investment's estimated return exceeds the minimum return required by the investor.
- **c.** The discount rate used equals the minimum return required by the investor.
- **d.** The investment generates cash flows with a present value in excess of its cost.

4. Western Mfg. Co. is considering two capital budgeting proposals, each with a 10-year life, and each requiring an initial cash outlay of $50,000. Proposal A shows a higher return on average investment than Proposal B, but Proposal B shows the higher net present value. The most probable explanation is that:

- **a.** Expected cash inflows tend to occur earlier in Proposal B.
- **b.** Total expected cash inflows are greater in Proposal B.
- **c.** The payback period is shorter in Proposal A.
- **d.** The discounted future cash flows approach makes no provision for recovery of the original $50,000 investment.

5. Copy Center is considering replacing its old copying machine, which has a $3,200 book value, with a new one. Discounted cash flow analysis of the proposal to acquire the new machine shows an estimated net present value of $2,800. If the new machine is acquired, the old machine will have no resale value and will be given away. The loss on disposal of the old machine:

- **a.** Is an opportunity cost of purchasing the new machine.
- **b.** Exceeds the net present value of the new machine, indicating that the new machine should not be acquired.
- **c.** Has already been deducted in arriving at the $2,800 net present value of the new machine.
- **d.** Is a sunk cost and is not relevant to the decision at hand, except as it affects the timing of income tax payments.

ASSIGNMENT MATERIAL

Discussion Questions

1. What is *capital budgeting*? Why are capital budgeting decisions crucial to the long-run financial health of a business enterprise?
2. Identify some conditions where upper management might allow some divisions to have a lower required rate of return.
3. What is the major shortcoming of using the payback period as the only criterion in making capital budgeting decisions?
4. Discounting a future cash flow at 15 percent results in a lower present value than does discounting the same cash flow at 10 percent. Explain why.
5. Discounting cash flows takes into consideration one characteristic of the earnings stream that is ignored in the computation of return on average investment. What is this characteristic and why is it important?
6. What nonfinancial considerations should be taken into account regarding a proposal to install a fire sprinkler system in a finished goods warehouse?
7. The present value of an investment depends on the timing of its future cash flows. Explain what this statement means by giving a specific example of two investments that have significant timing differences and discussing the implications of those timing differences.
8. What factors might a company consider in establishing a minimum required return on an investment proposal?
9. A particular investment proposal has a payback period that exceeds the investment's expected life. The investment has no salvage value. Will this proposal's net present value be positive or negative? Explain your answer.
10. Is an investment's average estimated net income used to compute its return on average investment the same thing as the incremental annual cash flows used to compute its net present value? Explain your answer.
11. What can be said about an investment proposal that has a net present value of zero?
12. Depreciation expense does not require payment in cash. However, it is an important consideration in the discounting of an investment's future cash flows. Explain why.
13. What steps can a firm take to ensure that employee estimates of the costs, revenue, and cash flows from a proposed capital investment are not overly optimistic or pessimistic?
14. What are some types of capital investment projects in which nonfinancial factors may outweigh financial factors?
15. Why is it important to consider income tax consequences when deciding whether to replace an asset?

Brief Exercises

LO3 **BRIEF EXERCISE 26.1**
Understanding Payback Period

A company invests $100,000 in plant assets with an estimated 20-year service life and no salvage value. These assets contribute $10,000 to annual net income when depreciation is computed on a straight-line basis. Compute the payback period and explain your computation.

LO3 **BRIEF EXERCISE 26.2**
Using Return on Investment to Evaluate Proposals

Doug's Conveyor Systems, Inc., is considering two investment proposals (1 and 2). Data for the two proposals are presented here:

	1	2
Cost of investment	$98,000	$98,500
Estimated salvage value	12,000	6,500
Average estimated net income	13,000	10,500

Calculate the return on average investment for both proposals.

LO3 LO4 **BRIEF EXERCISE 26.3**
Comparing NPV and Required Rate of Return

A particular investment proposal has a positive net present value of $20 when a discount rate of 8 percent is used. The same proposal has a negative net present value of $2,000 when a discount rate of 10 percent is used. What conclusions can be drawn about the estimated return of this proposal?

LO3 **BRIEF EXERCISE 26.4**

Net Present Value Computations

Landry's Tool Supply Corporation is considering purchasing a machine that costs $56,000 and will produce annual cash flows of $19,000 for six years. The machine will be repurchased at the end of six years for $2,000. What is the net present value of the proposed investment? Landry's requires a 12 percent return on all capital investments.

LO3 **BRIEF EXERCISE 26.5**

Computations for the Payback Period

A company is trying to decide whether to go ahead with an investment opportunity that costs $35,650. The expected incremental cash inflows are $78,000, while the expected incremental cash outflows are $67,500. What is the payback period?

LO1 LO2 **BRIEF EXERCISE 26.6**

Capital Investment Challenges

Some types of capital investments have associated cash flows that are very difficult to estimate, while other types of capital investments have associated cash flows that are very easy to estimate. Name two capital investments, one that has associated cash flows that are easy to estimate and one that has associated cash flows that are difficult to estimate. Explain how these two types of investments differ and why the associated cash flows are easier or more difficult to estimate.

LO3 LO4 **BRIEF EXERCISE 26.7**

Net Present Value and Required Rate of Return

Assume that the required rate of return for investment projects at Rippenstock Corporation is 12 percent. One department has proposed investment in new equipment with a 10-year life span and a present value of expected future annual cash flows of $120,000. The equipment's initial outlay cost is $125,000 and it has a salvage value of $10,000. Will this investment project meet the required rate of return for the company?

LO5 **BRIEF EXERCISE 26.8**

Capital Budgeting Behaviors

Ron Jasper manages a factory for Frombees Inc. A salesperson for new factory equipment has persuaded Ron that the new equipment offered by her company would be less dangerous for the employees and lower the sound level in the factory significantly. Ron believes that employees would be more satisfied with their jobs as a result of reduced danger and lower sound levels. Ron has always said that satisfied employees are more productive. Thus, in making the cash flow estimates for the new equipment, Ron has included increased cash flows from increased productivity. In fact, these estimated increases in productivity are just enough to allow the net present value of the proposal to be positive. Name at least two reasons why the net present value estimates could be optimistic.

LO3 **BRIEF EXERCISE 26.9**

Net Present Value Analysis

The Cook County Authority is considering the purchase of a small plane to transport government officials. It is hoped that the plane will save money on travel costs for government employees. Assume the county requires a 10 percent rate of return. If the plane's cost is $250,000 and it can be sold in five years for $75,000, what minimum annual savings in transportation costs is needed in order to make the plane a good investment?

LO2 **BRIEF EXERCISE 26.10**

Nonfinancial Investment Concerns

Sam's Gardening Centers has multiple stores in the northeastern United States. Sam's is considering investing in an "online" store. In addition to the identifiable cash flows such as increased sales and the initial costs to invest in software and personnel, other nonfinancial considerations may exist. Identify nonfinancial issues that Sam's should consider.

Exercises

LO1 through LO5 **EXERCISE 26.1**

Accounting Terminology

The following are 10 technical accounting terms introduced or emphasized in this chapter:

Net present value	Capital budgeting	Incremental analysis
Discount rate	Payback period	Present value
Sunk cost	Salvage value	Return on average investment
Capital budget audit		

Each of the following statements may (or may not) describe one of these technical terms. For each statement, indicate the accounting term described, or answer "None" if the statement does not correctly describe any of the terms.

a. The examination of differences among revenue, costs, and cash flows under alternative courses of action.

b. A cost incurred in the past that cannot be changed as a result of future actions.

c. The process of planning and evaluating proposals for investments in plant assets.

d. The average annual net income from an investment expressed as a percentage of the average amount invested.

e. The length of time necessary to recover the entire cost of an investment from resulting annual net cash flows.

f. The present value of an investment's expected future cash flows.

g. The amount of money today that is considered equivalent to the cash flows expected to take place in the future.

h. The required rate of return used by an investor to discount future cash flows to their present value.

i. Often an investment's final cash flows to be considered in discounted cash flow analysis.

LO1 through LO3

EXERCISE 26.2

Payback Period

Heartland Paper Company is considering the purchase of a new high-speed cutting machine. Two cutting machine manufacturers have approached Heartland with proposals: (1) Toledo Tools and (2) Akron Industries. Regardless of which vendor Heartland chooses, the following incremental cash flows are expected to be realized:

Year	Incremental Cash Inflows	Incremental Cash Outflows
1	$26,000	$20,000
2	27,000	21,000
3	32,000	26,000
4	35,000	29,000
5	34,000	28,000
6	33,000	27,000

a. If the machine manufactured by Toledo Tools costs $27,000, what is its expected payback period?

b. If the machine manufactured by Akron Industries has a payback period of 66 months, what is its cost?

c. Which of the machines is most attractive based on its respective payback period? Should Heartland base its decision entirely on this criterion? Explain your answer.

LO1 LO3

EXERCISE 26.3

Understanding Return on Average Investment Relationships

Foz Co. is considering four investment proposals (A, B, C, and D). The following table provides data concerning each of these investments:

	A	B	C	D
Investment cost	$44,000	$45,000	$50,000	$?
Estimated salvage value	8,000	5,000	?	4,000
Average estimated net income	6,000	?	5,400	4,500
Return on average investment	?	28%	20%	15%

Solve for the missing information pertaining to each investment proposal.

LO3

EXERCISE 26.4

Discounting Cash Flows

Using the tables in Exhibits 26–3 and 26–4, determine the present value of the following cash flows, discounted at an annual rate of 15 percent:

a. $10,000 to be received 20 years from today.

b. $15,000 to be received annually for 10 years.

c. $10,000 to be received annually for five years, with an additional $12,000 salvage value expected at the end of the fifth year.

d. $30,000 to be received annually for the first three years, followed by $20,000 received annually for the next two years (total of five years in which cash is received).

LO3 **EXERCISE 26.5**
Understanding Net Present Value Relationships

The following information relates to three independent investment decisions, each with a 10-year life and no salvage value:

	A	B	C
Investment cost	$?	$141,250	$80,520
Incremental annual cash inflows	14,000	37,000	19,000
Incremental annual cash outflows	6,000	?	7,000
Discount rate yielding a net present value of zero	10%	12%	?

Using the present value tables in Exhibits 26–3 and 26–4, solve for the missing information pertaining to each investment proposal.

LO1 LO3 **EXERCISE 26.6**
Analyzing a Capital Investment Proposal

Bowman Corporation is considering an investment in special-purpose equipment to enable the company to obtain a four-year government contract for the manufacture of a special item. The equipment costs $300,000 and would have no salvage value when the contract expires at the end of the four years. Estimated annual operating results of the project are as follows:

Revenue from contract sales		$325,000
Expenses other than depreciation	$225,000	
Depreciation (straight-line basis)	75,000	300,000
Increase in net income from contract work		$ 25,000

All revenue and all expenses other than depreciation will be received or paid in cash in the same period as recognized for accounting purposes. Compute the following for Bowman's proposal to undertake the contract work:

a. Payback period.

b. Return on average investment.

c. Net present value of the proposal to undertake contract work, discounted at an annual rate of 12 percent. (Refer to annuity table in Exhibit 26–4.)

LO1 through LO4 **EXERCISE 26.7**
Analyzing a Capital Investment Proposal

Northwest Records is considering the purchase of Seattle Sound, Inc., a small company that promotes and manages "grunge" bands. The terms of the agreement require that Northwest pay the current owners of Seattle Sound $530,000 to purchase the company. Northwest executives estimate that the investment will generate annual net cash flows of $200,000. They do not feel, however, that demand for grunge music will extend beyond four years. Therefore, they plan to liquidate the entire investment in Seattle Sound at its projected book value of $50,000 at the end of the fourth year. Due to the high risk associated with this venture, Northwest requires a minimum rate of return of 20 percent.

a. Compute the payback period for Northwest's proposed investment in Seattle Sound.

b. Compute the net present value of the Seattle Sound proposal, using the tables in Exhibits 26–3 and 26–4.

c. What nonfinancial factors would you recommend that Northwest executives take into consideration regarding this proposal?

LO1 LO3 **EXERCISE 26.8**
Analyzing a Capital Investment Proposal

Pack & Carry is debating whether to invest in new equipment to manufacture a line of high-quality luggage. The new equipment would cost $900,000, with an estimated four-year life and no salvage value. The estimated annual operating results with the new equipment are as follows:

Revenue from sales of new luggage		$975,000
Expenses other than depreciation	$675,000	
Depreciation (straight-line basis)	225,000	(900,000)
Increase in net income from the new line		$ 75,000

All revenue from the new luggage line and all expenses (except depreciation) will be received or paid in cash in the same period as recognized for accounting purposes. You are to compute the following for the investment in the new equipment to produce the new luggage line:

a. Annual cash flows.

b. Payback period.

c. Return on average investment.

d. *Total* present value of the expected future annual cash inflows, discounted at an annual rate of 10 percent.

e. *Net* present value of the proposed investment discounted at 10 percent.

LO1 LO2 LO5

EXERCISE 26.9 Competing Investment Proposals

The division managers of Chester Construction Corporation submit capital investment proposals each year for evaluation at the corporate level. Typically, the total dollar amount requested by the divisional managers far exceeds the company's capital investment budget. Thus, each proposal is first ranked by its estimated net present value as a primary screening criterion.

Jeff Hensel, the manager of Chester's commercial construction division, often overstates the projected cash flows associated with his proposals, and thereby inflates their net present values. He does so because, in his words, "Everybody else is doing it."

a. Assume that all the division managers do overstate cash flow projections in their proposals. What would you do if you were recently promoted to division manager and had to compete for funding under these circumstances?

b. What controls might be implemented to discourage the routine overstatement of capital budgeting estimates by the division managers?

LO1 through LO3 LO5

EXERCISE 26.10 Replacing Existing Equipment

EnterTech has noticed a significant decrease in the profitability of its line of portable CD players. The production manager believes that the source of the trouble is old, inefficient equipment used to manufacture the product. The issue raised, therefore, is whether EnterTech should (1) buy new equipment at a cost of $120,000 or (2) continue using its present equipment.

It is unlikely that demand for these portable CD players will extend beyond a five-year time horizon. EnterTech estimates that both the new equipment and the present equipment will have a remaining useful life of five years and no salvage value.

The new equipment is expected to produce annual cash savings in manufacturing costs of $34,000, before taking into consideration depreciation and taxes. However, management does not believe that the use of new equipment will have any effect on sales volume. Thus, its decision rests entirely on the magnitude of the potential cost savings.

The old equipment has a book value of $100,000. However, it can be sold for only $20,000 if it is replaced. EnterTech has an average tax rate of 40 percent and uses straight-line depreciation for tax purposes. The company requires a minimum return of 12 percent on all investments in plant assets.

a. Compute the net present value of the new machine using the tables in Exhibits 26–3 and 26–4.

b. What nonfinancial factors should EnterTech consider?

c. If the manager of EnterTech is uncertain about the accuracy of the cost savings estimate, what actions could be taken to double-check the estimate?

LO3

EXERCISE 26.11 Gains and Losses on Sale of Equipment

Suppose Concrete Suppliers Inc. sells one of its $155,000 concrete trucks, with an original five-year economic life, at the end of Year 3 after taking three years of straight-line depreciation. Concrete Suppliers has a 40 percent tax rate. If the truck is sold for its book value, there is no tax effect. If Concrete Suppliers sells the truck for more or less than its book value, there is a gain or loss that has a tax effect.

a. Show the effects on cash flow in Year 3 if the sales price is $80,000.

b. Show the effects on cash flow in Year 3 if the sales price is $20,000.

LO3

EXERCISE 26.12 Depreciation and Cash Flow

Refer to Exercise 26.11. Assume Concrete Suppliers Inc. has assembled the following expected annual income statement data for each of its trucks.

Sales	$150,000
Less: Expenses (net of depreciation)	(70,000)
Depreciation	(35,000)
Income before taxes	$ 45,000
Taxes @ 40%	(18,000)
Net income	$ 27,000

Analyze the above income statement data for expected cash flow effects each year.

LO2 LO3 **EXERCISE 26.13**
Net Present Value Computations

The Radiology Department at St. Joseph's Hospital, a not-for-profit, is considering purchasing a magnetic resonance imaging (MRI) machine. The cost to purchase and install an MRI is approximately $2,000,000. Assume St. Joseph's would like a minimum 8 percent return and that the economic life of the MRI is expected to be 10 years, with no salvage value. Assume that if the MRI is installed, the net cash flows are expected to increase by $300,000 per year. Use Exhibit 26–4 for present value factors.

a. Find the NPV of the MRI.

b. Should the hospital acquire the MRI?

c. What nonfinancial considerations might be important to the MRI investment decision?

LO3 **EXERCISE 26.14**
NPV of Uneven Cash Flows

Over the next four years, the City of Inditiny, Massachusetts, is expecting the following cash flows from a federal grant: Year 1—$150,000; Year 2—$220,000; Year 3—$250,000; Year 4—$175,000. The city wants to use the grant as collateral for a loan, but it is unsure about its net present value. What is the net present value of the grant if the rate of return is expected to be 5 percent? What if the rate of return is expected to be 8 percent? Use Exhibit 26–3 for your solution.

LO1 through LO3 **EXERCISE 26.15**
Home Depot's Present Value of Store Closing Costs

The section titled "Impairment of Long-Lived Assets" can be found on page A-11 in the **Home Depot** 2009 financial information in Appendix A. In this section, **Home Depot** explains procedures used to estimate the carrying value of stores closed. Use this section to answer the following questions:

a. Explain how **Home Depot** decides to close a store?

b. What amounts and types or categories of expenses related to the closed stores are recognized?

c. Compute the *tax-related* cash flow impact of the charges to SG&A resulting from the closed stores (assume a 35 percent tax rate).

d. What nonfinancial factors, related to the store closings, are mentioned by **Home Depot**? Name other nonfinancial factors you think are important.

Problem Set A

LO1 through LO4 **PROBLEM 26.1A**
Capital Budgeting and Determination of Annual Net Cash Flows

Toying With Nature wants to take advantage of children's current fascination with dinosaurs by adding several scale-model dinosaurs to its existing product line. Annual sales of the dinosaurs are estimated at 80,000 units at a price of $6 per unit. Variable manufacturing costs are estimated at $2.50 per unit, incremental fixed manufacturing costs (excluding depreciation) at $45,000 annually, and additional selling and general expenses related to the dinosaurs at $55,000 annually.

To manufacture the dinosaurs, the company must invest $350,000 in design molds and special equipment. Since toy fads wane in popularity rather quickly, Toying With Nature anticipates the special equipment will have a three-year service life with only a $20,000 salvage value. Depreciation will be computed on a straight-line basis. All revenue and expenses other than depreciation will be received or paid in cash. The company's combined federal and state income tax rate is 40 percent.

Instructions

a. Prepare a schedule showing the estimated increase in annual net income from the planned manufacture and sale of dinosaur toys.

b. Compute the annual net cash flows expected from this project.

c. Compute for this project the (1) payback period, (2) return on average investment, and (3) net present value, discounted at an annual rate of 15 percent. Round the payback period to the nearest tenth of a year and the return on average investment to the nearest tenth of a percent. Use Exhibits 26–3 and 26–4 where necessary.

LO1 through LO4

PROBLEM 26.2A
Analyzing Capital Investment Proposals

Micro Technology is considering two alternative proposals for modernizing its production facilities. To provide a basis for selection, the cost accounting department has developed the following data regarding the expected annual operating results for the two proposals:

	Proposal 1	Proposal 2
Required investment in equipment	$360,000	$350,000
Estimated service life of equipment	8 years	7 years
Estimated salvage value	$-0-	$14,000
Estimated annual cost savings (net cash flow)	75,000	76,000
Depreciation on equipment (straight-line basis)	45,000	48,000
Estimated increase in annual net income	30,000	28,000

Instructions

a. For each proposal, compute the (1) payback period, (2) return on average investment, and (3) net present value, discounted at an annual rate of 12 percent. (Round the payback period to the nearest tenth of a year and the return on investment to the nearest tenth of a percent.) Use Exhibits 26–3 and 26–4 where necessary.

b. On the basis of your analysis in part **a,** state which proposal you would recommend and explain the reasons for your choice.

LO1 through LO4

PROBLEM 26.3A
Analyzing Capital Investment Proposals

Cartor Industries is evaluating two alternative investment opportunities. The controller of the company has prepared the following analysis of the two investment proposals:

	Proposal A	Proposal B
Required investment in equipment	$220,000	$250,000
Estimated service life of equipment	5 years	6 years
Estimated salvage value	$10,000	$-0-
Estimated annual net cash flow	60,000	60,000
Depreciation on equipment (straight-line basis)	42,000	40,000
Estimated annual net income	18,000	20,000

Instructions

a. For each proposed investment, compute the (1) payback period, (2) return on average investment, and (3) net present value, discounted at an annual rate of 10 percent. (Round the payback period to the nearest tenth of a year and the return on investment to the nearest tenth of a percent.) Use Exhibits 26–3 and 26–4 where necessary.

b. Based on your computations in part **a,** which proposal do you consider to be the better investment? Explain.

LO1 through LO4

PROBLEM 26.4A
Capital Budgeting Using Multiple Models

Marengo is a popular restaurant located in Chilton Resort. Management feels that enlarging the facility to incorporate a large outdoor seating area will enable Marengo to continue to attract existing customers as well as handle large banquet parties that now must be turned away. Two proposals are currently under consideration. Proposal A involves a temporary walled structure and umbrellas used for sun protection; Proposal B entails a more permanent structure with a full awning cover for use even in inclement weather. Although the useful life of each alternative is estimated to be 10 years, Proposal B results in higher salvage value due to the awning protection. The accounting department of Chilton Resort and the manager of Marengo have assembled the following data regarding the two proposals:

	Proposal A	Proposal B
Required investment	$400,000	$500,000
Estimated life of fixtures	10 years	10 years
Estimated salvage value	$20,000	$50,000
Estimated annual net cash flow	80,000	95,000
Depreciation (straight-line basis)	38,000	45,000
Estimated annual net income	?	?

Instructions

a. For each proposal, compute the (1) payback period, (2) return on average investment, and (3) net present value, discounted at management's required rate of return of 15 percent. (Round the payback period to the nearest tenth of a year and the return on investment to the nearest tenth of a percent.) Use Exhibits 26–3 and 26–4 where necessary.

b. On the basis of your analysis in part **a**, state which proposal you would recommend and explain the reasons for your choice.

LO1 through LO4

PROBLEM 26.5A

Capital Budgeting Using Multiple Models

V. S. Yogurt is considering two possible expansion plans. Proposal A involves opening 10 stores in northern California at a total cost of $3,150,000. Under another strategy, Proposal B, V. S. Yogurt would focus on southern California and open six stores for a total cost of $2,500,000. Selected data regarding the two proposals have been assembled by the controller of V. S. Yogurt as follows:

	Proposal A	Proposal B
Required investment	$3,150,000	$2,500,000
Estimated life of store locations	7 years	7 years
Estimated salvage value	$–0–	$400,000
Estimated annual net cash flow	750,000	570,000
Depreciation on equipment (straight-line basis)	450,000	300,000
Estimated annual net income	?	?

Instructions

a. For each proposal, compute the (1) payback period, (2) return on average investment, and (3) net present value, discounted at management's required rate of return of 15 percent. (Round the payback period to the nearest tenth of a year and the return on investment to the nearest tenth of a percent.) Use Exhibits 26–3 and 26–4 where necessary.

b. On the basis of your analysis in part **a,** state which proposal you would recommend and explain the reasoning behind your choice.

LO3

PROBLEM 26.6A

Analyzing a Capital Investment Proposal

Pathways Appliance Company is planning to introduce a built-in blender to its line of small home appliances. Annual sales of the blender are estimated at 12,000 units at a price of $35 per unit. Variable manufacturing costs are estimated at $15 per unit, incremental fixed manufacturing costs (other than depreciation) at $60,000 annually, and incremental selling and general expenses relating to the blenders at $50,000 annually.

To build the blenders, the company must invest $260,000 in molds, patterns, and special equipment. Since the company expects to change the design of the blender every four years, this equipment will have a four-year service life with no salvage value. Depreciation will be computed on a straight-line basis. All revenue and expenses other than depreciation will be received or paid in cash. The company's combined state and federal tax rate is 40 percent.

Instructions

a. Prepare a schedule showing the estimated annual net income from the proposal to manufacture and sell the blenders.

b. Compute the annual net cash flows expected from the proposal.

c. Compute for this proposal the (1) payback period (round to the nearest tenth of a year), (2) return on average investment (round to the nearest tenth of a percent), and (3) net present value, discounted at an annual rate of 15 percent. Use Exhibits 26–3 and 26–4 where necessary.

LO1 through LO4

PROBLEM 26.7A

Considering Financial and Nonfinancial Factors

Doctors Hanson, Dominick, and Borchard are radiologists living in Fargo, North Dakota. They realize that many of the state's small, rural hospitals cannot afford to purchase their own magnetic resonance imaging devices (MRIs). Thus, the doctors are considering whether it would be feasible for them to form a corporation and invest in their own mobile MRI unit. The unit would be transported on a scheduled basis to more than 100 rural hospitals using an 18-wheel tractor-trailer. The cost of a tractor-trailer equipped with MRI equipment is approximately $1,250,000. The estimated life of the investment is eight years, after which time its salvage value is expected to be no more than $100,000.

The doctors anticipate that the investment will generate incremental revenue of $800,000 per year. Incremental expenses (which include depreciation, insurance, fuel, maintenance, their salaries, and income taxes) will average $700,000 per year. Net incremental cash flows will be reinvested back into the corporation. The only difference between incremental cash flows and incremental income is attributable to depreciation expense. The doctors require a minimum return on their investment of 12 percent.

Instructions

a. Compute the payback period of the mobile MRI proposal.

b. Compute the return on average investment of the proposal.

c. Compute the net present value of the proposal using the tables in Exhibits 26–3 and 26–4. Comment on what the actual rate of return might be.

d. What nonfinancial factors should the doctors consider in making this decision?

LO1 through LO4

PROBLEM 26.8A

Analyzing Competing Capital Investment Proposals

Jefferson Mountain is a small ski resort located in central Pennsylvania. In recent years, the resort has experienced two major problems: (1) unusually low annual snowfalls and (2) long lift lines. To remedy these problems, management is considering two investment proposals. The first involves a $125,000 investment in equipment used to make artificial snow. The second involves the $180,000 purchase of a new high-speed chairlift.

The most that the resort can afford to invest at this time is $200,000. Thus, it cannot afford to fund both proposals. Choosing one proposal over the other is somewhat problematic. If the resort funds the snow-making equipment, business will increase, and lift lines will become even longer than they are currently. If it funds the chairlift, lines will be shortened, but there may not be enough natural snow to attract skiers to the mountain.

The following estimates pertain to each of these investment proposals:

	Snow-Making Equipment	Chairlift
Estimated life of investment	20 years	36 years
Estimated incremental annual revenue of investment	$40,000	$54,000
Estimated incremental annual expense of investment (including taxes and depreciation)	15,000	19,000

Neither investment is expected to have any salvage value. Furthermore, the only difference between incremental cash flow and incremental income is attributable to depreciation. Due to inherent risks associated with the ski industry and the resort's high cost of capital, a minimum return on investment of 20 percent is required.

Instructions

a. Compute the payback period of each proposal.

b. Compute the return on average investment of each proposal.

c. Compute the net present value of each proposal using the tables in Exhibits 26–3 and 26–4.

d. What nonfinancial factors should be considered?

e. Which proposal, if either, do you recommend as a capital investment?

LO1 through LO5

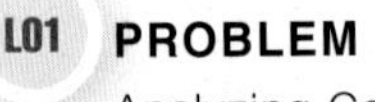

PROBLEM 26.9A

Analyzing Competing Capital Investment Proposals

Sonic, Inc., sells business software. Currently, all of its programs come on disks. Due to their complexity, some of these applications occupy as many as seven disks. Not only are the disks cumbersome for customers to load, they are relatively expensive for Sonic to purchase. The company does not intend to discontinue using disks altogether. However, it does want to reduce its reliance on the disk medium.

Two proposals are being considered. The first is to provide software on computer chips. Doing so requires a $300,000 investment in equipment. The second is to make software available through a computerized "software bank." In essence, programs would be downloaded directly from Sonic using telecommunications technology. Customers would gain access to Sonic's mainframe, specify the program they wish to order, and provide their name, address, and credit card information. The software would then be transferred directly to the customer's hard drive, and copies of the user's manual and registration material would be mailed the same day. This proposal requires an initial investment of $240,000.

The following information pertains to the two proposals. Due to rapidly changing technology, neither proposal is expected to have any salvage value or an estimated life exceeding six years.

	Computer Chip Equipment	Software Bank Installation
Estimated incremental annual revenue of investment. . .	$300,000	$160,000
Estimated incremental annual expense of investment (including taxes and depreciation)	250,000	130,000

The only difference between Sonic's incremental cash flows and its incremental income is attributable to depreciation. A minimum return on investment of 15 percent is required.

Instructions

a. Compute the payback period of each proposal.

b. Compute the return on average investment of each proposal.

c. Compute the net present value of each proposal using the tables in Exhibits 26–3 and 26–4.

d. What nonfinancial factors should be considered?

e. Which of Sonic's employees would most likely underestimate the benefits of investing in the software bank? Why?

f. Which proposal, if either, do you recommend Sonic choose?

Problem Set B

LO1 through LO4

PROBLEM 26.1B
Capital Budgeting and Determination of Annual Net Cash Flows

Monster Toys is considering a new toy monster called Garga. Annual sales of Garga are estimated at 100,000 units at a price of $8 per unit. Variable manufacturing costs are estimated at $3 per unit, incremental fixed manufacturing costs (excluding depreciation) at $60,000 annually, and additional selling and general expenses related to the monsters at $40,000 annually.

To manufacture the monsters, the company must invest $400,000 in design molds and special equipment. Since toy fads wane in popularity rather quickly, Monster Toys anticipates the special equipment will have a three-year service life with only a $10,000 salvage value. Depreciation will be computed on a straight-line basis. All revenue and expenses other than depreciation will be received or paid in cash. The company's combined federal and state income tax rate is 30 percent.

Instructions

a. Prepare a schedule showing the estimated increase in annual net income from the planned manufacture and sale of Garga.

b. Compute the annual net cash flows expected from this project.

c. Compute for this project the (1) payback period, (2) return on average investment, and (3) net present value, discounted at an annual rate of 12 percent. Round the payback period to the nearest tenth of a year and the return on average investment to the nearest tenth of a percent. Use Exhibits 26–3 and 26–4 where necessary.

LO1 through LO4

PROBLEM 26.2B
Analyzing Capital Investment Proposals

Macro Technology is considering two alternative proposals for modernizing its production facilities. To provide a basis for selection, the cost accounting department has developed the following data regarding the expected annual operating results for the two proposals:

	Proposal 1	Proposal 2
Required investment in equipment.	$400,000	$380,000
Estimated service life of equipment	10 years	8 years
Estimated salvage value.	$-0-	$20,000
Estimated annual cost savings (net cash flow).	80,000	82,000
Depreciation on equipment (straight-line basis)	40,000	45,000
Estimated increase in annual net income.	40,000	37,000

Instructions

a. For each proposal, compute the (1) payback period, (2) return on average investment, and (3) net present value, discounted at an annual rate of 15 percent. (Round the payback period to the nearest tenth of a year and the return on investment to the nearest tenth of a percent.) Use Exhibits 26–3 and 26–4 where necessary.

b. On the basis of your analysis in part **a,** state which proposal you would recommend and explain the reasons for your choice.

LO1 through LO4

PROBLEM 26.3B Analyzing Capital Investment Proposals

Flagg Equipment Company is evaluating two alternative investment opportunities. The controller of the company has prepared the following analysis of the two investment proposals:

	Proposal A	Proposal B
Required investment in equipment	$260,000	$280,000
Estimated service life of equipment	6 years	7 years
Estimated salvage value	$20,000	$-0-
Estimated annual net cash flow	82,000	65,000
Depreciation on equipment (straight-line basis)	40,000	40,000
Estimated annual net income	42,000	25,000

Instructions

a. For each proposed investment, compute the (1) payback period, (2) return on average investment, and (3) net present value, discounted at an annual rate of 15 percent. (Round the payback period to the nearest tenth of a year and the return on investment to the nearest tenth of a percent.) Use Exhibits 26–3 and 26–4 where necessary.

b. Based on your analysis in part **a,** which proposal do you consider to be the better investment? Explain.

LO1 through LO4

PROBLEM 26.4B Capital Budgeting Using Multiple Models

Samba is a popular restaurant located in Brazilton Resort. Management feels that enlarging the facility to incorporate a large outdoor seating area will enable Samba to continue to attract existing customers as well as handle large banquet parties that now must be turned away. Two proposals are currently under consideration. Proposal A involves a temporary walled structure and umbrellas used for sun protection; Proposal B entails a more permanent structure with a full awning cover for use even in inclement weather. Although the useful life of each alternative is estimated to be 10 years, Proposal B results in higher salvage value due to the awning protection. The accounting department of Brazilton Resort and the manager of Samba have assembled the following data regarding the two proposals:

	Proposal A	Proposal B
Required investment	$300,000	$310,000
Estimated life of fixtures	10 years	10 years
Estimated salvage value	$10,000	$40,000
Estimated annual net cash flow	75,000	70,000
Depreciation (straight-line basis)	24,000	36,000
Estimated annual net income	?	?

Instructions

a. For each proposal, compute the (1) payback period, (2) return on average investment, and (3) net present value discounted at management's required rate of return of 10 percent. (Round the payback period to the nearest tenth of a year and the return on investment to the nearest tenth of a percent.) Use Exhibits 26–3 and 26–4 where necessary.

b. Based on your analysis in part **a**, which proposal would you recommend? Explain the reasons for your choice.

LO1 through LO4

PROBLEM 26.5B Capital Budgeting Using Multiple Models

I.C. Cream is considering two possible expansion plans. Proposal A involves opening eight stores in northern Alaska at a total cost of $4,000,000. Under another strategy, Proposal B, I.C. Cream would focus on southern Alaska and open five stores for a total cost of $3,000,000. Selected data regarding the two proposals have been assembled by the controller of I.C. Cream as follows:

	Proposal A	Proposal B
Required investment	$4,000,000	$3,000,000
Estimated life of store locations	8 years	8 years
Estimated salvage value	$-0-	$200,000
Estimated annual net cash flow	800,000	700,000
Depreciation on equipment (straight-line basis)	500,000	350,000
Estimated annual net income	?	?

Instructions

a. For each proposal, compute the (1) payback period, (2) return on average investment, and (3) net present value, discounted at management's required rate of return of 12 percent. (Round the payback period to the nearest tenth of a year and the return on investment to the nearest tenth of a percent.) Use Exhibits 26–3 and 26–4 where necessary.

b. On the basis of your analysis in part **a**, state which proposal you would recommend and explain the reasoning behind your choice.

LO3 PROBLEM 26.6B
Analyzing a Capital Investment Proposal

Cafield Appliance Company is planning to introduce a coffee grinder to its line of small home appliances. Annual sales of the grinder are estimated at 15,000 units at a price of $40 per unit. Variable manufacturing costs are estimated at $18 per unit, incremental fixed manufacturing costs (other than depreciation) at $60,000 annually, and incremental selling and general expenses relating to the grinders at $75,000 annually.

To build the grinders, the company must invest $300,000 in molds, patterns, and special equipment. Since the company expects to change the design of the grinder every five years, this equipment will have a five-year service life with no salvage value. Depreciation will be computed on a straight-line basis. All revenue and expenses other than depreciation will be received or paid in cash. The company's combined state and federal tax rate is 30 percent.

Instructions

a. Prepare a schedule showing the estimated annual net income from the proposal to manufacture and sell the grinders.

b. Compute the annual net cash flows expected from the proposal.

c. Compute for this proposal the (1) payback period (round to the nearest tenth of a year), (2) return on average investment (round to the nearest tenth of a percent), and (3) net present value, discounted at an annual rate of 12 percent. Use Exhibits 26–3 and 26–4 where necessary.

LO1 through LO4 PROBLEM 26.7B
Considering Financial and Nonfinancial Factors

Doctors Mowtain, Lawrence, and Curley are radiologists living in Yukville, Maine. They realize that many of the state's small, rural hospitals cannot afford to purchase their own magnetic resonance imaging devices (MRIs). The doctors are considering whether it would be feasible for them to form a corporation and invest in their own MRI unit. The unit would be transported on a scheduled basis to more than 80 rural hospitals using an 18-wheel tractor-trailer. The cost of a tractor-trailer equipped with MRI equipment is approximately $1,500,000. The estimated life of the investment is nine years, after which time its salvage value is expected to be no more than $200,000.

The doctors anticipate that the investment will generate incremental revenue of $900,000 per year. Incremental expenses (which include depreciation, insurance, fuel, maintenance, their salaries, and income taxes) will average $800,000 per year. Net incremental cash flows will be reinvested back into the corporation. The only difference between incremental cash flows and incremental income is attributable to depreciation expense. The doctors require a minimum return on their investment of 15 percent.

Instructions

a. Compute the payback period of the mobile MRI proposal.

b. Compute the return on average investment of the proposal.

c. Compute the net present value of the proposal using the tables in Exhibits 26–3 and 26–4. Comment on what the actual rate of return might be.

d. What nonfinancial factors should the doctors consider in making this decision?

LO1 through LO4 PROBLEM 26.8B
Analyzing Competing Capital Investment Proposals

Jackson Mountain is a small ski resort located in northern Connecticut. In recent years, the resort has experienced two major problems: (1) unusually low annual snowfalls and (2) long lift lines. To remedy these problems, management is considering two investment proposals. The first involves a $225,000 investment in equipment used to make artificial snow. The second involves the $250,000 purchase of a new high-speed chairlift.

The most that the resort can afford to invest at this time is $320,000. Thus, it cannot afford to fund both proposals. Choosing one proposal over the other is somewhat problematic. If the resort funds the snow-making equipment, business will increase, and lift lines will become even longer than they are currently. If it funds the chairlift, lines will be shortened, but there may not be enough natural snow to attract skiers to the mountain.

The following estimates pertain to each of these investment proposals:

	Snow-Making Equipment	Chairlift
Estimated life of investment	10 years	20 years
Estimated incremental annual revenue of investment	$70,000	$70,000
Estimated incremental annual expense of investment (including taxes and depreciation)	20,000	22,000

Neither investment is expected to have any salvage value. Furthermore, the only difference between incremental cash flow and incremental income is attributable to depreciation. Due to inherent risks associated with the ski industry and the resort's high cost of capital, a minimum return on investment of 20 percent is required.

Instructions

a. Compute the payback period of each proposal.

b. Compute the return on average investment of each proposal.

c. Compute the net present value of each proposal using the tables in Exhibits 26–3 and 26–4.

d. What nonfinancial factors should be considered?

e. Which proposal, if either, do you recommend as a capital investment?

LO1 through LO5

PROBLEM 26.9B
Analyzing Competing Capital Investment Proposals

Boom, Inc., sells business software. Currently, all of its programs come on disks. Due to their complexity, some of these applications occupy as many as seven disks. Not only are the disks cumbersome for customers to load, they are relatively expensive for Boom to purchase. The company does not intend to discontinue using disks altogether. However, it does want to reduce its reliance on the disk medium.

Two proposals are being considered. The first is to provide software on memory sticks. Doing so requires a $500,000 investment in duplicating equipment. The second is to make software available through a computerized "program bank." In essence, programs would be downloaded directly from Boom using telecommunications technology. Customers would gain access to Boom's mainframe, specify the program they wish to order, and provide their name, address, and credit card information. The software would then be transferred directly to the customer's hard drive, and copies of the user's manual and registration material would be mailed the same day. The program bank proposal requires an initial investment of $350,000.

The following information pertains to these proposals. Due to rapidly changing technology, neither proposal is expected to have any salvage value or an estimated life exceeding five years.

	Memory Stick Equipment	Program Bank Installation
Estimated incremental annual revenue of investment	$400,000	$260,000
Estimated incremental annual expense of investment (including taxes and depreciation)	260,000	140,000

The only difference between Boom's incremental cash flows and its incremental income is attributable to depreciation. A minimum return on investment of 12 percent is required.

Instructions

a. Compute the payback period of each proposal.

b. Compute the return on average investment of each proposal.

c. Compute the net present value of each proposal using the tables in Exhibits 26–3 and 26–4.

d. What nonfinancial factors should be considered?

e. Which of Boom's employees would most likely underestimate the benefits of investing in the program bank? Why?

f. Which proposal, if either, do you recommend Boom choose?

Critical Thinking Cases

LO2 through LO4

CASE 26.1
How Much Is That Laser in the Window?

The management of Metro Printers is considering a proposal to replace some existing equipment with a new highly efficient laser printer. The existing equipment has a current book value of $2,200,000 and a remaining life (if not replaced) of 10 years. The laser printer has a cost of $1,300,000 and an expected useful life of 10 years. The laser printer would increase the company's annual cash flows by reducing operating costs and by increasing the company's ability to generate revenue. Susan Mills, controller of Metro Printers, has prepared the following estimates of the laser printer's effect on annual earnings and cash flow:

Estimated increase in annual cash flows (before taxes):		
Incremental revenue	$140,000	
Cost savings (other than depreciation)	110,000	$250,000
Reduction in annual depreciation expense:		
Depreciation on existing equipment	$220,000	
Depreciation on laser printer	130,000	90,000
Estimated increase in income before income taxes		$340,000
Increase in annual income taxes (40%)		136,000
Estimated increase in annual net income		$204,000
Estimated increase in annual net cash flows ($250,000 − $136,000)		$114,000

Don Adams, a director of Metro Printers, makes the following observation: "These estimates look fine, but won't we take a huge loss in the current year on the sale of our existing equipment? After the invention of the laser printer, I doubt that our old equipment can be sold for much at all." In response, Mills provides the following information about the expected loss on the sale of the existing equipment:

Book value of existing printing equipment	$2,200,000
Estimated current sales price, net of removal costs	200,000
Estimated loss on sale, before income taxes	$2,000,000
Reduction in current year's income taxes as a result of loss (40%)	800,000
Loss on sale of existing equipment, net of tax savings	$1,200,000

Adams replies, "Good grief, our loss would be almost as great as the cost of the laser itself. Add this $1,200,000 loss to the $1,300,000 cost of the laser, and we're into this new equipment for $2,500,000. I'd go along with a cost of $1,300,000, but $2,500,000 is out of the question."

Instructions

a. Use Exhibits 26–3 and 26–4 to help compute the net present value of the proposal to sell the existing equipment and buy the laser printer, discounted at an annual rate of 15 percent. In your computation, make the following assumptions regarding the timing of cash flows:

1. The purchase price of the laser printer will be paid in cash immediately.
2. The $200,000 sales price of the existing equipment will be received in cash immediately.
3. The income tax benefit from selling the equipment will be realized one year from today.
4. Metro uses straight-line depreciation in its income tax returns as well as its financial statements.
5. The annual net cash flows may be regarded as received at year-end for each of the next 10 years.

b. Is the cost to Metro Printers of acquiring the laser printer $2,500,000, as Adams suggests? Explain fully.

LO1 through LO5

CASE 26.2
Dollars and Cents versus a Sense of Ethics

Grizzly Community Hospital in central Wyoming provides health care services to families living within a 200-mile radius. The hospital is extremely well equipped for a relatively small, community facility. However, it does not have renal dialysis equipment for kidney patients. Those patients requiring dialysis must travel as far as 300 miles to receive care.

Several of the staff physicians have proposed that the hospital invest in a renal dialysis center. The minimum cost required for this expansion is $4.5 million. The physicians estimate that the center will generate revenue of $1.15 million per year for approximately 20 years. Incremental costs, including the salaries of professional staff, will average $850,000 annually. Grizzly is exempt from paying any income taxes. The only difference between annual net income and net cash flows is caused by depreciation expense. The center is not expected to have any salvage value at the end of 20 years.

The administrators of the hospital strongly oppose the proposal for several reasons: (1) they do not believe that it would generate the hospital's minimum required return of 12 percent on capital investments, (2) they do not believe that kidney patients would use the facility even if they could avoid traveling several hundred miles to receive treatment elsewhere, (3) they do not feel that the hospital has enough depth in its professional staff to operate a dialysis center, and (4) they are certain that $4.5 million could be put to better use, such as expanding the hospital's emergency services to include air transport by helicopter.

The issue has resulted in several heated debates between the physicians and the hospital administrators. One physician has even threatened to move out of the area if the dialysis center is not built. Another physician was quoted as saying, "All the administrators are concerned about is the almighty dollar. We are a hospital, not a profit-hungry corporation. It is our ethical responsibility to serve the health care needs of central Wyoming's citizens."

Instructions

Form small groups of four or five persons. Within each group, designate who will play the role of the hospital's physicians and who will play the role of the hospital's administrators. Then engage in a debate from each party's point of view. Be certain to address the following:

a. Financial factors and measures.

b. Nonfinancial factors such as (1) ethical responsibility, (2) quality of care issues, (3) opportunity costs associated with alternative uses of $4.5 million, (4) physician morale, and (5) whether a community hospital should be run like a business.

c. Measures that could be taken to check for overly optimistic or pessimistic estimates.

LO1 LO2 LO5

CASE 26.3
International Investments in Outsourcing

What are the pitfalls to avoid when investing in overseas activities? The following key issues have been identified as important:

- Lower cost offshore does not always mean gains in efficiency.
- Choose your model carefully; either run your own offshore operation or outsource.
- Get your current employees to be supportive, otherwise they can hinder the process.
- Be prepared to invest time and effort because quality control can be challenging.
- Treat your overseas partners as equals in your business dealings.

Instructions

a. Explain how the above list of key issues in offshore investments can have an impact on future cash flows associated with an offshore investment.

b. Discuss the ethical implications of encouraging current employees to help a company shift jobs overseas.

LO1 LO2 LO5

INTERNET CASE 26.4
Capital Investment History

JC Penney Company, founded in the early 1900s, has made many significant capital investment decisions throughout its history. Access the **JC Penney** Web site at the following address:

http://www.jcpenney.net/about/jcp/history.aspx

Locate the **JC Penney** Milestones.

Instructions

a. Identify what you would consider to be a major strategic capital investment decision undertaken by **JC Penney** since 1902.

b. For one such decision, discuss the nonfinancial issues that likely would have been considered.

c. A common capital investment decision undertaken by retailers is whether to invest funds in a store that is earning less than the desired level of profit (in the hopes that the investment will generate higher profits) or close the location altogether. In evaluating both options, which employee groups would you expect to overstate the benefits of additional investment? Which groups would understate the benefits of additional investment?

Internet sites are time and date sensitive. It is the purpose of these exercises to have you explore the Internet. You may need to use the Yahoo! search engine http://www.yahoo.com *(or another favorite search engine) to find a company's current Web address.*

LO5 **CASE 26.5**
Governance and Capital Budgeting Conflicts

Red Robin Gourmet Burgers is an upscale restaurant chain in the Northwest. The chain's former chairman, Michael Snyder, encouraged employees to be "unbridled" in everything they did. Unfortunately, Snyder was too unbridled with his use of some of the company's assets. The company reported the issue to the Securities and Exchange Commission, saying that the chairman's improprieties involved "use of chartered aircraft and travel and entertainment expenses, including charitable donations." After an audit of travel logs, Snyder repaid the company $1.25 million. In addition, Snyder owned a large stake in a company that was on opposite sides of transactions with **Red Robin**, a clear violation of the company's code of ethics governing conflicts of interest. Snyder has since stepped down and the company has moved to improve its corporate governance.

Instructions

a. Explain how governance violations such as those described as taking place at **Red Robin Gourmet Burgers** can have an impact on capital budgeting outcomes.

b. Do you believe that improved corporate governance practices can result in improved returns to capital investments in companies? Explain why or why not.

Answers to Self-Test Questions

1. b **2.** c **3.** a, b, d **4.** a **5.** d

APPENDIX A

Home Depot 2009 Financial Statements

Home Depot Financial Statements Contents

Item 8. Financial Statements and Supplementary Data.

Management's Responsibility for Financial Statements

The financial statements presented in this Annual Report have been prepared with integrity and objectivity and are the responsibility of the management of The Home Depot, Inc. These financial statements have been prepared in conformity with U.S. generally accepted accounting principles and properly reflect certain estimates and judgments based upon the best available information.

The financial statements of the Company have been audited by KPMG LLP, an independent registered public accounting firm. Their accompanying report is based upon an audit conducted in accordance with the standards of the Public Company Accounting Oversight Board (United States).

The Audit Committee of the Board of Directors, consisting solely of independent directors, meets five times a year with the independent registered public accounting firm, the internal auditors and representatives of management to discuss auditing and financial reporting matters. In addition, a telephonic meeting is held prior to each quarterly earnings release. The Audit Committee retains the independent registered public accounting firm and regularly reviews the internal accounting controls, the activities of the independent registered public accounting firm and internal auditors and the financial condition of the Company. Both the Company's independent registered public accounting firm and the internal auditors have free access to the Audit Committee.

Management's Report on Internal Control over Financial Reporting

Our management is responsible for establishing and maintaining adequate internal control over financial reporting, as such term is defined in Rule 13a-15(f) promulgated under the Securities Exchange Act of 1934, as amended (the "Exchange Act"). Under the supervision and with the participation of our management, including our Chief Executive Officer and Chief Financial Officer, we conducted an evaluation of the effectiveness of our internal control over financial reporting as of January 31, 2010 based on the framework in *Internal Control —Integrated Framework* issued by the Committee of Sponsoring Organizations of the Treadway Commission (COSO). Based on our evaluation, our management concluded that our internal control over financial reporting was effective as of January 31, 2010 in providing reasonable assurance regarding the reliability of financial reporting and the preparation of financial statements for external purposes in accordance with U.S. generally accepted accounting principles. The effectiveness of our internal control over financial reporting as of January 31, 2010 has been audited by KPMG LLP, an independent registered public accounting firm, as stated in their report which is included on page 30 in this Form 10-K.

/s/ FRANCIS S. BLAKE

Francis S. Blake
Chairman &
Chief Executive Officer

/s/ CAROL B. TOMÉ

Carol B. Tomé
Chief Financial Officer &
Executive Vice President – Corporate Services

Report of Independent Registered Public Accounting Firm

The Board of Directors and Stockholders
The Home Depot, Inc.:

We have audited the accompanying Consolidated Balance Sheets of The Home Depot, Inc. and subsidiaries as of January 31, 2010 and February 1, 2009, and the related Consolidated Statements of Earnings, Stockholders' Equity and Comprehensive Income, and Cash Flows for each of the fiscal years in the three-year period ended January 31, 2010. These Consolidated Financial Statements are the responsibility of the Company's management. Our responsibility is to express an opinion on these Consolidated Financial Statements based on our audits.

We conducted our audits in accordance with the standards of the Public Company Accounting Oversight Board (United States). Those standards require that we plan and perform the audit to obtain reasonable assurance about whether the financial statements are free of material misstatement. An audit includes examining, on a test basis, evidence supporting the amounts and disclosures in the financial statements. An audit also includes assessing the accounting principles used and significant estimates made by management, as well as evaluating the overall financial statement presentation. We believe that our audits provide a reasonable basis for our opinion.

In our opinion, the Consolidated Financial Statements referred to above present fairly, in all material respects, the financial position of The Home Depot, Inc. and subsidiaries as of January 31, 2010 and February 1, 2009, and the results of their operations and their cash flows for each of the fiscal years in the three-year period ended January 31, 2010, in conformity with U.S. generally accepted accounting principles.

We also have audited, in accordance with the standards of the Public Company Accounting Oversight Board (United States), The Home Depot, Inc.'s internal control over financial reporting as of January 31, 2010, based on criteria established in *Internal Control —Integrated Framework* issued by the Committee of Sponsoring Organizations of the Treadway Commission (COSO), and our report dated March 25, 2010 expressed an unqualified opinion on the effectiveness of the Company's internal control over financial reporting.

/s/ KPMG LLP

Atlanta, Georgia
March 25, 2010

THE HOME DEPOT, INC. AND SUBSIDIARIES

CONSOLIDATED STATEMENTS OF EARNINGS

amounts in millions, except per share data	Fiscal Year Ended[1] January 31, 2010	February 1, 2009	February 3, 2008
NET SALES	**$ 66,176**	$ 71,288	$ 77,349
Cost of Sales	**43,764**	47,298	51,352
GROSS PROFIT	**22,412**	23,990	25,997
Operating Expenses:			
Selling, General and Administrative	**15,902**	17,846	17,053
Depreciation and Amortization	**1,707**	1,785	1,702
Total Operating Expenses	**17,609**	19,631	18755
OPERATING INCOME	**4,803**	4,359	7,242
Interest and Other (Income) Expense:			
Interest and Investment Income	**(18)**	(18)	(74)
Interest Expense	**676**	624	696
Other	**163**	163	—
Interest and Other, net	**821**	769	622
EARNINGS FROM CONTINUING OPERATIONS BEFORE PROVISION FOR INCOME TAXES	**3,982**	3,590	6,620
Provision for Income Taxes	**1,362**	1,278	2,410
EARNINGS FROM CONTINUING OPERATIONS	**2,620**	2,312	4,210
EARNINGS (LOSS) FROM DISCONTINUED OPERATIONS, NET OF TAX	**41**	(52)	185
NET EARNINGS	**$ 2,661**	$ 2,260	$ 4,395
Weighted Average Common Shares	**1,683**	1,682	1,849
BASIC EARNINGS PER SHARE FROM CONTINUING OPERATIONS	**$ 1.56**	$ 1.37	$ 2.28
BASIC EARNINGS (LOSS) PER SHARE FROM DISCONTINUED OPERATIONS	**$ 0.02**	$ (0.03)	$ 0.10
BASIC EARNINGS PER SHARE	**$ 1.58**	$ 1.34	$ 2.38
Diluted Weighted Average Common Shares	**1,692**	1,686	1,856
DILUTED EARNINGS PER SHARE FROM CONTINUING OPERATIONS	**$ 1.55**	$ 1.37	$ 2.27
DILUTED EARNINGS (LOSS) PER SHARE FROM DISCONTINUED OPERATIONS	**$ 0.02**	$ (0.03)	$ 0.10
DILUTED EARNINGS PER SHARE	**$ 1.57**	$ 1.34	$ 2.37

(1) Fiscal years ended January 31, 2010 and February 1, 2009 include 52 weeks. Fiscal year ended February 3, 2008 includes 53 weeks.

See accompanying Notes to Consolidated Financial Statements.

THE HOME DEPOT, INC. AND SUBSIDIARIES

CONSOLIDATED BALANCE SHEETS

amounts in millions, except share and per share data	**January 31, 2010**	**February 1, 2009**
ASSETS		
Current Assets:		
Cash and Cash Equivalents	**$ 1,421**	$ 519
Short-Term Investments	**6**	6
Receivables, net	**964**	972
Merchandise Inventories	**10,188**	10,673
Other Current Assets	**1,321**	1,192
Total Current Assets	**13,900**	13,362
Property and Equipment, at cost:		
Land	**8,451**	8,301
Buildings	**17,391**	16,961
Furniture, Fixtures and Equipment	**9,091**	8,741
Leasehold Improvements	**1,383**	1,359
Construction in Progress	**525**	625
Capital Leases	**504**	490
	37,345	36,477
Less Accumulated Depreciation and Amortization	**11,795**	10,243
Net Property and Equipment	**25,550**	26,234
Notes Receivable	**33**	36
Goodwill	**1,171**	1,134
Other Assets	**223**	398
Total Assets	**$ 40,877**	$ 41,164
LIABILITIES AND STOCKHOLDERS' EQUITY		
Current Liabilities:		
Accounts Payable	**$ 4,863**	$ 4,822
Accrued Salaries and Related Expenses	**1,263**	1,129
Sales Taxes Payable	**362**	337
Deferred Revenue	**1,158**	1,165
Income Taxes Payable	**108**	289
Current Installments of Long-Term Debt	**1,020**	1,767
Other Accrued Expenses	**1,589**	1,644
Total Current Liabilities	**10,363**	11,153
Long-Term Debt, excluding current installments	**8,662**	9,667
Other Long-Term Liabilities	**2,140**	2,198
Deferred Income Taxes	**319**	369
Total Liabilities	**21,484**	23,387
STOCKHOLDERS' EQUITY		
Common Stock, par value $0.05; authorized: 10 billion shares; issued: 1.716 billion shares at January 31, 2010 and 1.707 billion shares at February 1, 2009; outstanding: 1.698 billion shares at January 31, 2010 and 1.696 billion shares at February 1, 2009	**86**	85
Paid-In Capital	**6,304**	6,048
Retained Earnings	**13,226**	12,093
Accumulated Other Comprehensive Income (Loss)	**362**	(77)
Treasury Stock, at cost, 18 million shares at January 31, 2010 and 11 million shares at February 1, 2009	**(585)**	(372)
Total Stockholders' Equity	**19,393**	17,777
Total Liabilities and Stockholders' Equity	**$ 40,877**	$ 41,164

See accompanying Notes to Consolidated Financial Statements.

THE HOME DEPOT, INC. AND SUBSIDIARIES

CONSOLIDATED STATEMENTS OF STOCKHOLDERS' EQUITY AND COMPREHENSIVE INCOME

amounts in millions, except per share data	Common Stock Shares	Common Stock Amount	Paid-In Capital	Retained Earnings	Accumulated Other Comprehensive Income (Loss)	Treasury Stock Shares	Treasury Stock Amount	Stockholders' Equity	Total Comprehensive Income
BALANCE, JANUARY 28, 2007	**2,421**	**$ 121**	**$ 7,930**	**$ 33,052**	**$ 310**	**(451)**	**$(16,383)**	**$ 25,030**	
Cumulative Effect of the Adoption of FIN 48	—	—	—	(111)	—	—	—	(111)	
Net Earnings	—	—	—	4,395	—	—	—	4,395	$ 4,395
Shares Issued Under Employee Stock Plans	12	1	239	—	—	—	—	240	
Tax Effect of Sale of Option Shares by Employees	—	—	4	—	—	—	—	4	
Translation Adjustments	—	—	—	—	455	—	—	455	455
Cash Flow Hedges, net of tax	—	—	—	—	(10)	—	—	(10)	(10)
Stock Options, Awards and Amortization of Restricted Stock	—	—	206	—	—	—		206	
Repurchase of Common Stock	—	—	—	—	—	(292)	(10,815)	(10,815)	
Retirement of Treasury Stock	(735)	(37)	(2,608)	(24,239)	—	735	26,884	—	
Cash Dividends ($0.90 per share)	—	—	—	(1,709)	—	—	—	(1,709)	
Other	—	—	29	—	—	—	—	29	
Comprehensive Income									$ 4,840
BALANCE, FEBRUARY 3, 2008	**1,698**	**$ 85**	**$ 5,800**	**$ 11,388**	**$ 755**	**(8)**	**$ (314)**	**$ 17,714**	
Net Earnings	—	—	—	2,260	—	—	—	2,260	$ 2,260
Shares Issued Under Employee Stock Plans	9	—	68	—	—	—	—	68	
Tax Effect of Sale of Option Shares by Employees	—	—	7	—	—	—	—	7	
Translation Adjustments	—	—	—	—	(831)	—	—	(831)	(831)
Cash Flow Hedges, net of tax	—	—	—	—	(1)	—	—	(1)	(1)
Stock Options, Awards and Amortization of Restricted Stock	—	—	176	—	—	—	—	176	
Repurchase of Common Stock	—	—	—	—	—	(3)	(70)	(70)	
Cash Dividends ($0.90 per share)	—	—	—	(1,521)	—	—	—	(1,521)	
Other	—	—	(3)	(34)	—	—	12	(25)	
Comprehensive Income									$ 1,428
BALANCE, FEBRUARY 1, 2009	**1,707**	**$ 85**	**$ 6,048**	**$ 12,093**	**$ (77)**	**(11)**	**$ (372)**	**$ 17,777**	
Net Earnings	—	—	—	2,661	—	—	—	2,661	$ 2,661
Shares Issued Under Employee Stock Plans	9	1	57	—	—	—	—	58	
Tax Effect of Sale of Option Shares by Employees	—	—	(2)	—	—	—	—	(2)	
Translation Adjustments	—	—	—	—	426	—	—	426	426
Cash Flow Hedges, net of tax	—	—	—	—	11	—	—	11	11
Stock Options, Awards and Amortization of Restricted Stock	—	—	201	—	—	—	—	201	
Repurchase of Common Stock	—	—	—	—	—	(7)	(213)	(213)	
Cash Dividends ($0.90 per share)	—	—	—	(1,525)	—	—	—	(1,525)	
Other	—	—	—	(3)	2	—	—	(1)	2
Comprehensive Income									$ 3,100
BALANCE, JANUARY 31, 2010	**1,716**	**$ 86**	**$ 6,304**	**$ 13,226**	**$ 362**	**(18)**	**$ (585)**	**$ 19,393**	

See accompanying Notes to Consolidated Financial Statements.

THE HOME DEPOT, INC. AND SUBSIDIARIES
CONSOLIDATED STATEMENTS OF CASH FLOWS

amounts in millions	Fiscal Year Ended[1] January 31, 2010	February 1, 2009	February 3, 2008
CASH FLOWS FROM OPERATING ACTIVITIES:			
Net Earnings	**$ 2,661**	$ 2,260	$ 4,395
Reconciliation of Net Earnings to Net Cash Provided by Operating Activities:			
Depreciation and Amortization	**1,806**	1,902	1,906
Impairment Related to Rationalization Charges	**—**	580	—
Impairment of Investment	**163**	163	—
Stock-Based Compensation Expense	**201**	176	207
Changes in Assets and Liabilities, net of the effects of acquisitions and disposition:			
(Increase) Decrease in Receivables, net	**(23)**	121	116
Decrease (Increase) in Merchandise Inventories	**625**	743	(491)
Decrease (Increase) in Other Current Assets	**4**	(7)	109
Increase (Decrease) in Accounts Payable and Accrued Expenses	**59**	(646)	(465)
Decrease in Deferred Revenue	**(21)**	(292)	(159)
(Decrease) Increase in Income Taxes Payable	**(174)**	262	—
Decrease in Deferred Income Taxes	**(227)**	(282)	(348)
(Decrease) Increase in Other Long-Term Liabilities	**(19)**	306	186
Other	**70**	242	271
Net Cash Provided by Operating Activities	**5,125**	5,528	5,727
CASH FLOWS FROM INVESTING ACTIVITIES:			
Capital Expenditures, net of $10, $37 and $19 of non-cash capital expenditures in fiscal 2009, 2008 and 2007, respectively	**(966)**	(1,847)	(3,558)
Proceeds from Sale of Business, net	**—**	—	8,337
Payments for Businesses Acquired, net	**—**	—	(13)
Proceeds from Sales of Property and Equipment	**178**	147	318
Purchases of Investments	**—**	(168)	(11,225)
Proceeds from Sales and Maturities of Investments	**33**	139	10,899
Net Cash (Used in) Provided by Investing Activities	**(755)**	(1,729)	4,758
CASH FLOWS FROM FINANCING ACTIVITIES:			
(Repayments of) Proceeds from Short-Term Borrowings, net	**—**	(1,732)	1,734
Repayments of Long-Term Debt	**(1,774)**	(313)	(20)
Repurchases of Common Stock	**(213)**	(70)	(10,815)
Proceeds from Sales of Common Stock	**73**	84	276
Cash Dividends Paid to Stockholders	**(1,525)**	(1,521)	(1,709)
Other Financing Activities	**(64)**	(128)	(105)
Net Cash Used in Financing Activities	**(3,503)**	(3,680)	(10,639)
Increase (Decrease) in Cash and Cash Equivalents	**867**	119	(154)
Effect of Exchange Rate Changes on Cash and Cash Equivalents	**35**	(45)	(1)
Cash and Cash Equivalents at Beginning of Year	**519**	445	600
Cash and Cash Equivalents at End of Year	**$ 1,421**	$ 519	$ 445
SUPPLEMENTAL DISCLOSURE OF CASH PAYMENTS MADE FOR:			
Interest, net of interest capitalized	**$ 664**	$ 622	$ 672
Income Taxes	**$ 2,082**	$ 1,265	$ 2,524

(1) Fiscal years ended January 31, 2010 and February 1, 2009 include 52 weeks. Fiscal year ended February 3, 2008 includes 53 weeks.

See accompanying Notes to Consolidated Financial Statements.

NOTES TO CONSOLIDATED FINANCIAL STATEMENTS

1. SUMMARY OF SIGNIFICANT ACCOUNTING POLICIES

Business, Consolidation and Presentation

The Home Depot, Inc. and its subsidiaries (the "Company") operate The Home Depot stores, which are full-service, warehouse-style stores averaging approximately 105,000 square feet in size. The stores stock approximately 30,000 to 40,000 different kinds of building materials, home improvement supplies and lawn and garden products that are sold to do-it-yourself customers, do-it-for-me customers and professional customers. At the end of fiscal 2009, the Company was operating 2,244 stores, which included 1,976 The Home Depot stores in the United States, including the Commonwealth of Puerto Rico and the territories of the U.S. Virgin Islands and Guam ("U.S."), 179 The Home Depot stores in Canada, 79 The Home Depot stores in Mexico and 10 The Home Depot stores in China. The Consolidated Financial Statements include the accounts of the Company and its wholly-owned subsidiaries. All significant intercompany transactions have been eliminated in consolidation.

Fiscal Year

The Company's fiscal year is a 52- or 53-week period ending on the Sunday nearest to January 31. Fiscal years ended January 31, 2010 ("fiscal 2009") and February 1, 2009 ("fiscal 2008") include 52 weeks. The fiscal year ended February 3, 2008 ("fiscal 2007") includes 53 weeks.

Use of Estimates

Management of the Company has made a number of estimates and assumptions relating to the reporting of assets and liabilities, the disclosure of contingent assets and liabilities, and reported amounts of revenues and expenses in preparing these financial statements in conformity with U.S. generally accepted accounting principles. Actual results could differ from these estimates.

Fair Value of Financial Instruments

The carrying amounts of Cash and Cash Equivalents, Receivables and Accounts Payable approximate fair value due to the short-term maturities of these financial instruments. The fair value of the Company's investments is discussed under the caption "Short-Term Investments" in this Note 1. The fair value of the Company's Long-Term Debt is discussed in Note 11.

Cash Equivalents

The Company considers all highly liquid investments purchased with original maturities of three months or less to be cash equivalents. The Company's Cash Equivalents are carried at fair market value and consist primarily of high-grade commercial paper, money market funds and U.S. government agency securities.

Short-Term Investments

Short-Term Investments are recorded at fair value based on current market rates and are classified as available-for-sale.

Accounts Receivable

The Company has an agreement with a third-party service provider who directly extends credit to customers, manages the Company's private label credit card program and owns the related receivables. We evaluated the third-party entities holding the receivables under the program and concluded that they should not be consolidated by the Company. The agreement with the third-party service provider expires in 2018, with the Company having the option, but no obligation, to purchase the receivables at the end of the agreement. The deferred interest charges incurred by the Company for its deferred financing programs offered to its customers are included in Cost of Sales. The interchange fees charged to the Company for the customers' use of the cards and the profit sharing with the third-party administrator are included in Selling, General and Administrative expenses ("SG&A"). The sum of the three is referred to by the Company as "the cost of credit" of the private label credit card program.

In addition, certain subsidiaries of the Company extend credit directly to customers in the ordinary course of business. The receivables due from customers were $38 million and $37 million as of January 31, 2010 and February 1, 2009, respectively. The Company's valuation reserve related to accounts receivable was not material to the Consolidated Financial Statements of the Company as of the end of fiscal 2009 or 2008.

Merchandise Inventories

The majority of the Company's Merchandise Inventories are stated at the lower of cost (first-in, first-out) or market, as determined by the retail inventory method. As the inventory retail value is adjusted regularly to reflect market conditions, the inventory valued using the retail method approximates the lower of cost or market. Certain subsidiaries, including retail operations in Canada, Mexico and China, and distribution centers, record Merchandise Inventories at the lower of cost or market, as determined by a cost method. These Merchandise Inventories represent approximately 18% of the total Merchandise Inventories balance. The Company evaluates the inventory valued using a cost method at the end of each quarter to ensure that it is carried at the lower of cost or market. The valuation allowance for Merchandise Inventories valued under a cost method was not material to the Consolidated Financial Statements of the Company as of the end of fiscal 2009 or 2008.

Independent physical inventory counts or cycle counts are taken on a regular basis in each store and distribution center to ensure that amounts reflected in the accompanying Consolidated Financial Statements for Merchandise Inventories are properly stated. During the period between physical inventory counts in stores, the Company accrues for estimated losses related to shrink on a store-by-store basis based on historical shrink results and current trends in the business. Shrink (or in the case of excess inventory, "swell") is the difference between the recorded amount of inventory and the physical inventory. Shrink may occur due to theft, loss, inaccurate records for the receipt of inventory or deterioration of goods, among other things.

Income Taxes

The Company provides for federal, state and foreign income taxes currently payable, as well as for those deferred due to timing differences between reporting income and expenses for financial statement purposes versus tax purposes. Deferred tax assets and liabilities are recognized for the future tax consequences attributable to temporary differences between the financial statement carrying amounts of existing assets and liabilities and their respective tax bases. Deferred tax assets and liabilities are measured using enacted income tax rates expected to apply to taxable income in the years in which those temporary differences are expected to be recovered or settled. The effect of a change in income tax rates is recognized as income or expense in the period that includes the enactment date.

The Company and its eligible subsidiaries file a consolidated U.S. federal income tax return. Non-U.S. subsidiaries and certain U.S. subsidiaries, which are consolidated for financial reporting purposes, are not eligible to be included in the Company's consolidated U.S. federal income tax return. Separate provisions for income taxes have been determined for these entities. The Company intends to reinvest substantially all of the unremitted earnings of its non-U.S. subsidiaries and postpone their remittance indefinitely. Accordingly, no provision for U.S. income taxes for these non-U.S. subsidiaries was recorded in the accompanying Consolidated Statements of Earnings.

Depreciation and Amortization

The Company's Buildings, Furniture, Fixtures and Equipment are recorded at cost and depreciated using the straight-line method over the estimated useful lives of the assets. Leasehold Improvements are amortized using the straight-line method over the original term of the lease or the useful life of the improvement, whichever is shorter. The Company's Property and Equipment is depreciated using the following estimated useful lives:

	Life
Buildings	5–45 years
Furniture, Fixtures and Equipment	3–20 years
Leasehold Improvements	5–45 years

Capitalized Software Costs

The Company capitalizes certain costs related to the acquisition and development of software and amortizes these costs using the straight-line method over the estimated useful life of the software, which is three to six years. These costs are included in Furniture, Fixtures and Equipment in the accompanying Consolidated Balance Sheets. Certain development costs not meeting the criteria for capitalization are expensed as incurred.

Revenues

The Company recognizes revenue, net of estimated returns and sales tax, at the time the customer takes possession of merchandise or receives services. The liability for sales returns is estimated based on historical return levels. When the Company receives payment from customers before the customer has taken possession of the merchandise or the service has been performed, the amount received is recorded as Deferred Revenue in the accompanying Consolidated Balance Sheets until the sale or service is complete. The Company also records Deferred Revenue for the sale of gift cards and recognizes this revenue upon the redemption of gift cards in Net Sales. Gift card breakage income is recognized based upon historical redemption patterns and represents the balance of gift cards for which the Company believes the likelihood of redemption by the customer is remote. During fiscal 2009, 2008 and 2007, the Company recognized $40 million, $37 million and $36 million, respectively, of gift card breakage income. This income is recorded as other income and is included in the accompanying Consolidated Statements of Earnings as a reduction in SG&A.

Services Revenue

Net Sales include services revenue generated through a variety of installation, home maintenance and professional service programs. In these programs, the customer selects and purchases material for a project and the Company provides or arranges professional installation. These programs are offered through the Company's stores. Under certain programs, when the Company provides or arranges the installation of a project and the subcontractor provides material as part of the installation, both the material and labor are included in services revenue. The Company recognizes this revenue when the service for the customer is complete.

All payments received prior to the completion of services are recorded in Deferred Revenue in the accompanying Consolidated Balance Sheets. Services revenue was $2.6 billion, $3.1 billion and $3.5 billion for fiscal 2009, 2008 and 2007, respectively.

Self-Insurance

The Company is self-insured for certain losses related to general liability, product liability, automobile, workers' compensation and medical claims. The expected ultimate cost for claims incurred as of the balance sheet date is not discounted and is recognized as a liability. The expected ultimate cost of claims is estimated based upon analysis of historical data and actuarial estimates.

Prepaid Advertising

Television and radio advertising production costs, along with media placement costs, are expensed when the advertisement first appears. Amounts included in Other Current Assets in the accompanying Consolidated Balance Sheets relating to prepayments of production costs for print and broadcast advertising as well as sponsorship promotions were not material at the end of fiscal 2009 and 2008.

Vendor Allowances

Vendor allowances primarily consist of volume rebates that are earned as a result of attaining certain purchase levels and advertising co-op allowances for the promotion of vendors' products that are typically based on guaranteed minimum amounts with additional amounts being earned for attaining certain purchase levels. These vendor allowances are accrued as earned, with those allowances received as a result of attaining certain purchase levels accrued over the incentive period based on estimates of purchases.

Volume rebates and certain advertising co-op allowances earned are initially recorded as a reduction in Merchandise Inventories and a subsequent reduction in Cost of Sales when the related product is sold. Certain advertising co-op allowances that are reimbursements of specific, incremental and identifiable costs incurred to promote vendors' products are recorded as an offset against advertising expense. In fiscal 2009, 2008 and 2007, gross advertising expense was $897 million, $1.0 billion and $1.2 billion, respectively, and is included in SG&A. Specific, incremental and identifiable advertising co-op allowances were $105 million, $107 million and $120 million for fiscal 2009, 2008 and 2007, respectively, and were recorded as an offset to advertising expense in SG&A.

Cost of Sales

Cost of Sales includes the actual cost of merchandise sold and services performed, the cost of transportation of merchandise from vendors to the Company's stores, locations or customers, the operating cost of the Company's sourcing and distribution network and the cost of deferred interest programs offered through the Company's private label credit card program.

The cost of handling and shipping merchandise from the Company's stores, locations or distribution centers to the customer is classified as SG&A. The cost of shipping and handling, including internal costs and payments to third parties, classified as SG&A was $426 million, $501 million and $571 million in fiscal 2009, 2008 and 2007, respectively.

Impairment of Long-Lived Assets

The Company evaluates its long-lived assets each quarter for indicators of potential impairment. Indicators of impairment include current period losses combined with a history of losses, management's decision to relocate or close a store or other location before the end of its previously estimated useful life, or when changes in other circumstances indicate the carrying amount of an asset may not be recoverable. The evaluation for long-lived assets is performed at the lowest level of identifiable cash flows, which is generally the individual store level.

The assets of a store with indicators of impairment are evaluated by comparing its undiscounted cash flows with its carrying value. The estimate of cash flows includes management's assumptions of cash inflows and outflows directly resulting from the use of those assets in operations, including gross margin on Net Sales, payroll and related items, occupancy costs, insurance allocations and other costs to operate a store. If the carrying value is greater than the undiscounted cash flows, an impairment loss is recognized for the difference between the carrying value and the estimated fair market value. Impairment losses are recorded as a component of SG&A in the accompanying Consolidated Statements of Earnings. When a leased location closes, the Company also recognizes in SG&A the net present value of future lease obligations less estimated sublease income.

As part of its Rationalization Charges, the Company recorded no asset impairment and $84 million of lease obligation costs in fiscal 2009 compared to $580 million of asset impairments and $252 million of lease obligation costs in fiscal 2008. See Note 2 for more details on the Rationalization Charges. The Company also recorded impairments on other closings and relocations in the ordinary course of business, which were not material to the Consolidated Financial Statements in fiscal 2009, 2008 and 2007.

Goodwill and Other Intangible Assets

Goodwill represents the excess of purchase price over the fair value of net assets acquired. The Company does not amortize goodwill, but does assess the recoverability of goodwill in the third quarter of each fiscal year, or more often if indicators warrant, by determining whether the fair value of each reporting unit supports its carrying value. The fair values of the Company's identified reporting units were estimated using the present value of expected future discounted cash flows.

The Company amortizes the cost of other intangible assets over their estimated useful lives, which range from 1 to 20 years, unless such lives are deemed indefinite. Intangible assets with indefinite lives are tested in the third quarter of each fiscal year for impairment, or more often if indicators warrant. The Company recorded no impairment charges for goodwill or other intangible assets for fiscal 2009, 2008 or 2007.

Stock-Based Compensation

The per share weighted average fair value of stock options granted during fiscal 2009, 2008 and 2007 was $6.61, $6.46 and $9.45, respectively. The fair value of these options was determined at the date of grant using the Black-Scholes option-pricing model with the following assumptions:

	Fiscal Year Ended		
	January 31, 2010	**February 1, 2009**	**February 3, 2008**
Risk-free interest rate	**2.3%**	2.9%	4.4%
Assumed volatility	**41.5%**	33.8%	25.5%
Assumed dividend yield	**3.9%**	3.5%	2.4%
Assumed lives of option	**6 years**	6 years	6 years

Derivatives

The Company uses derivative financial instruments from time to time in the management of its interest rate exposure on long-term debt and its exposure on foreign currency fluctuations. The Company accounts for its derivative financial instruments in accordance with the Financial Accounting Standards Board Accounting Standards Codification ("FASB ASC") 815-10. The fair value of the Company's derivative financial instruments is discussed in Note 5.

Comprehensive Income

Comprehensive Income includes Net Earnings adjusted for certain revenues, expenses, gains and losses that are excluded from Net Earnings under U.S. generally accepted accounting principles. Adjustments to Net Earnings and Accumulated Other Comprehensive Income consist primarily of foreign currency translation adjustments.

Foreign Currency Translation

Assets and Liabilities denominated in a foreign currency are translated into U.S. dollars at the current rate of exchange on the last day of the reporting period. Revenues and expenses are generally translated using average exchange rates for the period and equity transactions are translated using the actual rate on the day of the transaction.

Segment Information

The Company operates within a single reportable segment primarily within North America. Net Sales for the Company outside of the U.S. were $7.0 billion for fiscal 2009 and were $7.4 billion for fiscal 2008 and 2007. Long-lived assets outside of the U.S. totaled $3.0 billion and $2.8 billion as of January 31, 2010 and February 1, 2009, respectively.

10-Year Summary of Financial and Operating Results
The Home Depot, Inc. and Subsidiaries

amounts in millions, except where noted	10-Year Compound Annual Growth Rate	2009	2008	2007[1]
STATEMENT OF EARNINGS DATA[2]				
Net sales	5.6%	**$ 66,176**	$ 71,288	$ 77,349
Net sales increase (decrease) (%)	—	**(7.2)**	(7.8)	(2.1)
Earnings before provision for income taxes	0.5	**3,982**	3,590	6,620
Net earnings	1.2	**2,620**	2,312	4,210
Net earnings increase (decrease) (%)	—	**13.3**	(45.1)	(20.1)
Diluted earnings per share ($)	4.5	**1.55**	1.37	2.27
Diluted earnings per share increase (decrease) (%)	—	**13.1**	(39.6)	(11.0)
Diluted weighted average number of common shares	(3.2)	**1,692**	1,686	1,856
Gross margin – % of sales	—	**33.9**	33.7	33.6
Total operating expenses – % of sales	—	**26.6**	27.5	24.3
Interest and other, net – % of sales	—	**1.2**	1.1	0.8
Earnings before provision for income taxes – % of sales	—	**6.0**	5.0	8.6
Net earnings – % of sales	—	**4.0**	3.2	5.4
BALANCE SHEET DATA AND FINANCIAL RATIOS[3]				
Total assets	9.1%	**$ 40,877**	$ 41,164	$ 44,324
Working capital	2.6	**3,537**	2,209	1,968
Merchandise inventories	6.4	**10,188**	10,673	11,731
Net property and equipment	9.6	**25,550**	26,234	27,476
Long-term debt	27.7	**8,662**	9,667	11,383
Stockholders' equity	4.6	**19,393**	17,777	17,714
Book value per share ($)	7.9	**11.42**	10.48	10.48
Long-term debt-to-equity (%)	—	**44.7**	54.4	64.3
Total debt-to-equity (%)	—	**49.9**	64.3	75.8
Current ratio	—	**1.34:1**	1.20:1	1.15:1
Inventory turnover[2]	—	**4.1x**	4.0x	4.2x
Return on invested capital (%)[2]	—	**10.7**	9.5	13.9
STATEMENT OF CASH FLOWS DATA				
Depreciation and amortization	14.6%	**$ 1,806**	$ 1,902	$ 1,906
Capital expenditures	(9.5)	**966**	1,847	3,558
Payments for businesses acquired, net	(100.0)	**—**	—	13
Cash dividends per share ($)	23.3	**0.900**	0.900	0.900
STORE DATA				
Number of stores	9.2%	**2,244**	2,274	2,234
Square footage at fiscal year-end	8.9	**235**	238	235
(Decrease) increase in square footage (%)	—	**(1.3)**	1.3	4.9
Average square footage per store (in thousands)	(0.3)	**105**	105	105
STORE SALES AND OTHER DATA				
Comparable store sales increase (decrease) (%)[4][5]	—	**(6.6)**	(8.7)	(6.7)
Weighted average weekly sales per operating store (in thousands)	(4.3)%	**$ 563**	$ 601	$ 658
Weighted average sales per square foot ($)	(4.1)	**279**	298	332
Number of customer transactions	4.8	**1,274**	1,272	1,336
Average ticket ($)	0.8	**51.76**	55.61	57.48
Number of associates at fiscal year-end[3]	4.6	**317,000**	322,000	331,000

(1) Fiscal years 2007 and 2001 include 53 weeks; all other fiscal years reported include 52 weeks.

(2) Fiscal years 2003 through 2009 include Continuing Operations only. The discontinued operations in fiscal years prior to 2003 were not material. See Note 4 to the Consolidated Financial Statements included in Item 8, "Financial Statements and Supplementary Data."

(3) Amounts for fiscal years 2009, 2008 and 2007 include Continuing Operations only. All amounts in other fiscal years reported include discontinued operations. See Note 4 to the Consolidated Financial Statements included in Item 8, "Financial Statements and Supplementary Data."

amounts in millions, except where noted	2006	2005	2004	2003	2002	2001[1]	2000
STATEMENT OF EARNINGS DATA[2]							
Net sales	$ 79,022	$ 77,019	$ 71,100	$ 63,660	$ 58,247	$ 53,553	$ 45,738
Net sales increase (decrease) (%)	2.6	8.3	11.7	9.3	8.8	17.1	19.0
Earnings before provision for income taxes	8,502	8,967	7,790	6,762	5,872	4,957	4,217
Net earnings	5,266	5,641	4,922	4,253	3,664	3,044	2,581
Net earnings increase (decrease) (%)	(6.6)	14.6	15.7	16.1	20.4	17.9	11.3
Diluted earnings per share ($)	2.55	2.63	2.22	1.86	1.56	1.29	1.10
Diluted earnings per share increase (decrease) (%)	(3.0)	18.5	19.4	19.2	20.9	17.3	10.0
Diluted weighted average number of common shares	2,062	2,147	2,216	2,289	2,344	2,353	2,352
Gross margin – % of sales	33.6	33.7	33.4	31.7	31.1	30.2	29.9
Total operating expenses – % of sales	22.4	21.9	22.4	21.1	21.1	20.9	20.7
Interest and other, net – % of sales	0.5	0.1	—	—	(0.1)	—	—
Earnings before provision for income taxes – % of sales	10.8	11.6	11.0	10.6	10.1	9.3	9.2
Net earnings – % of sales	6.7	7.3	6.9	6.7	6.3	5.7	5.6
BALANCE SHEET DATA AND FINANCIAL RATIOS[3]							
Total assets	$ 52,263	$ 44,405	$ 39,020	$ 34,437	$ 30,011	$ 26,394	$ 21,385
Working capital	5,069	2,563	3,818	3,774	3,882	3,860	3,392
Merchandise inventories	12,822	11,401	10,076	9,076	8,338	6,725	6,556
Net property and equipment	26,605	24,901	22,726	20,063	17,168	15,375	13,068
Long-term debt	11,643	2,672	2,148	856	1,321	1,250	1,545
Stockholders' equity	25,030	26,909	24,158	22,407	19,802	18,082	15,004
Book value per share ($)	12.71	12.67	11.06	9.93	8.38	7.71	6.46
Long-term debt-to-equity (%)	46.5	9.9	8.9	3.8	6.7	6.9	10.3
Total debt-to-equity (%)	46.6	15.2	8.9	6.1	6.7	6.9	10.3
Current ratio	1.39:1	1.20:1	1.37:1	1.40:1	1.48:1	1.59:1	1.77:1
Inventory turnover[2]	4.5x	4.7x	4.9x	5.0x	5.3x	5.4x	5.1x
Return on invested capital (%)[2]	16.8	20.4	19.9	19.2	18.8	18.3	19.6
STATEMENT OF CASH FLOWS DATA							
Depreciation and amortization	$ 1,886	$ 1,579	$ 1,319	$ 1,076	$ 903	$ 764	$ 601
Capital expenditures	3,542	3,881	3,948	3,508	2,749	3,393	3,574
Payments for businesses acquired, net	4,268	2,546	727	215	235	190	26
Cash dividends per share ($)	0.675	0.400	0.325	0.26	0.21	0.17	0.16
STORE DATA							
Number of stores	2,147	2,042	1,890	1,707	1,532	1,333	1,134
Square footage at fiscal year-end	224	215	201	183	166	146	123
(Decrease) increase in square footage (%)	4.2	7.0	9.8	10.2	14.1	18.5	22.6
Average square footage per store (in thousands)	105	105	106	107	108	109	108
STORE SALES AND OTHER DATA							
Comparable store sales increase (decrease) (%)[4][5]	(2.8)	3.1	5.1	3.7	(0.5)	—	4
Weighted average weekly sales per operating store (in thousands)	$ 723	$ 763	$ 766	$ 763	$ 772	$ 812	$ 864
Weighted average sales per square foot ($)	358	377	375	371	370	394	415
Number of customer transactions	1,330	1,330	1,295	1,246	1,161	1,091	937
Average ticket ($)	58.90	57.98	54.89	51.15	49.43	48.64	48.65
Number of associates at fiscal year-end[3]	364,400	344,800	323,100	298,800	280,900	256,300	227,300

(4) *Includes Net Sales at locations open greater than 12 months, including relocated and remodeled stores. Stores become comparable on the Monday following their 365th day of operation. Comparable store sales is intended only as supplemental information and is not a substitute for Net Sales or Net Earnings presented in accordance with generally accepted accounting principles.*

(5) *Comparable store sales in fiscal years prior to 2002 were reported to the nearest percent.*

The Time Value of Money
Future Amounts and Present Values

Learning Objectives

AFTER STUDYING THIS APPENDIX, YOU SHOULD BE ABLE TO:

- **LO1** Explain what is meant by the phrase *time value of money.*
- **LO2** Describe the relationships between *present values* and *future amounts.*
- **LO3** Explain three basic ways in which decision makers apply the time value of money.
- **LO4** Compute future amounts and the investments necessary to accumulate future amounts.
- **LO5** Compute the present values of future cash flows.
- **LO6** Discuss accounting applications of the concept of present value.

The Concept

Learning Objective Explain what is meant by the phrase *time value of money.* LO1

One of the most basic—and important—concepts of investing is the *time value of money.* This concept is based on the idea that an amount of money available today can be safely invested to accumulate to a larger amount in the future. As a result, an amount of money available today is considered to be equivalent in value to a *larger sum* available at a future date.

Learning Objective Describe the relationships between *present values* and *future amounts.* LO2

In our discussion, we will refer to an amount of money available today as a *present value.* In contrast, an amount receivable or payable at a future date will be described as a *future amount.*

To illustrate, assume that you place $500 in a savings account that earns interest at the rate of 8 percent per year. The balance of your account at the end of each of the next four years is illustrated in Exhibit B–1.

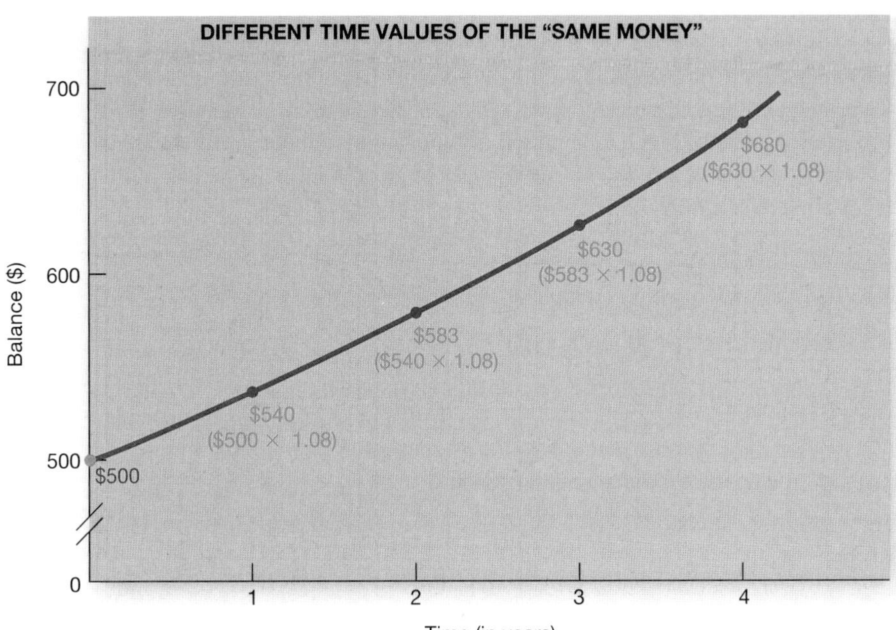

Exhibit B–1

THE VALUES OF MONEY OVER TIME

Future values are bigger, but are they worth more? This is the real issue.

These balances represent different time values of your $500 investment. When you first open the account, your investment has a *present value* of only $500. As time passes, the value of your investment increases to the *future amounts* illustrated in the graph. (Throughout this appendix, present values will be illustrated in red, and future amounts will be shown in blue.)

RELATIONSHIPS BETWEEN PRESENT VALUES AND FUTURE AMOUNTS

The difference between a present value and any future amount is the *interest* that is included in the future amount. We have seen that interest accrues over time. Therefore, the difference between the present value and a future amount depends on *two factors:* (1) the *rate of interest* at which the present value increases and (2) the *length of time* over which interest accumulates. (Notice in our graph, the farther away the future date, the larger the future amount.)

Present Values Change over Time The present value of an investment gradually increases toward the future amount. In fact, when a future date *arrives,* what once was a future amount becomes the present value of the investment. For example, at the end of the first year, $540 will no longer be a future amount—it will be the present value of your savings account.

The Basic Concept (Stated Several Different Ways) Notice that the present value of our savings account is *always less than its future amounts.* This is the basic idea underlying the time value of money. But this idea often is expressed in different ways, including the following:

- A present value is always *less than* a future amount.
- A future amount is always *greater than* a present value.
- A dollar available today is always worth *more* than a dollar that does not become available until a future date.
- A dollar available at a future date is always worth *less* than a dollar that is available today.

Read these statements carefully. All four reflect the idea that a present value is the "equivalent" of a larger number of dollars at a future date. This is what is meant by the time value of money.

COMPOUND INTEREST

The relationships between present values and future amounts assume that the interest earned on the investment is *reinvested,* rather than withdrawn. This concept often is called *compounding the interest.* Compounding has an interesting effect. Reinvesting the interest causes the amount invested to increase each period. This, in turn, causes more interest to be earned in each successive period. Over a long period of time, an investment in which interest is compounded continuously will increase to surprisingly large amounts.

CASE IN POINT

In 1626, Peter Minuit is said to have purchased Manhattan Island from a group of Indians for $24 worth of "beads, cloth, and trinkets." This episode often is portrayed as an incredible bargain—even a steal. But if the Indians had invested this $24 to earn interest at a compound interest rate of 8 percent, they would have more than enough money today to buy the island back—along with everything on it.

APPLICATIONS OF THE TIME VALUE OF MONEY CONCEPT

Learning Objective
LO3 **Explain three basic ways in which decision makers apply the time value of money.**

Investors, accountants, and other decision makers apply the time value of money in three basic ways. These applications are summarized below, along with a typical example.

1. To determine the amount to which an investment will accumulate over time. *Example:* If we invest $5,000 each year and earn an annual rate of return of 10 percent, how much will be accumulated after 10 years?
2. To determine the amount that must be invested every period to accumulate a required future amount. *Example:* We must accumulate a $200 million bond sinking fund over the next 20 years. How much must we deposit into this fund each year, assuming that the fund's assets will be invested to earn an annual rate of return of 8 percent?
3. To determine the present value of cash flows expected to occur in the future. *Example:* Assuming that we require a 15 percent return on our investments, how much can we afford to pay today for new machinery that is expected to reduce production costs by $20,000 per year for the next 10 years?

We will now introduce a framework for answering such questions.

Future Amounts

A future amount is simply the dollar amount to which a present value *will accumulate* over time. As we have stated, the difference between a present value and a related future amount depends on (1) the interest rate and (2) the period of time over which the present value accumulates.

Starting with the present value, we may compute future amounts through a series of multiplications, as illustrated in our graph in Exhibit B–1. But there are faster and easier ways. For example, many financial calculators are programmed to compute future amounts; you merely enter the present value, the interest rate, and the number of periods. Or you may use a *table of future amounts,* such as Table FA–1 in Exhibit B–2.

Exhibit B–2

THE FUTURE VALUE OF $1

Approach to computing future amount

Table FA–1
Future Value of $1 after *n* Periods

Number of Periods (*n*)	Interest Rate								
	1%	1½%	5%	6%	8%	10%	12%	15%	20%
1	1.010	1.015	1.050	1.060	1.080	1.100	1.120	1.150	1.200
2	1.020	1.030	1.103	1.124	1.166	1.210	1.254	1.323	1.440
3	1.030	1.046	1.158	1.191	1.260	1.331	1.405	1.521	1.728
4	1.041	1.061	1.216	1.262	1.360	1.464	1.574	1.749	2.074
5	1.051	1.077	1.276	1.338	1.469	1.611	1.762	2.011	2.488
6	1.062	1.093	1.340	1.419	1.587	1.772	1.974	2.313	2.986
7	1.072	1.110	1.407	1.504	1.714	1.949	2.211	2.660	3.583
8	1.083	1.126	1.477	1.594	1.851	2.144	2.476	3.059	4.300
9	1.094	1.143	1.551	1.689	1.999	2.358	2.773	3.518	5.160
10	1.105	1.161	1.629	1.791	2.159	2.594	3.106	4.046	6.192
20	1.220	1.347	2.653	3.207	4.661	6.727	9.646	16.367	38.338
24	1.270	1.430	3.225	4.049	6.341	9.850	15.179	28.625	79.497
36	1.431	1.709	5.792	8.147	15.968	30.913	59.136	153.152	708.802

THE TABLES APPROACH

Learning Objective
Compute future amounts and the investments necessary to accumulate future amounts. **LO4**

A table of future amounts shows the future amount to which *$1* will accumulate over a given number of periods, assuming that it has been invested to earn any of the illustrated interest rates. We will refer to the amounts shown in the body of this table as *factors,* rather than as dollar amounts.

To find the future amount of a present value *greater* than $1, simply multiply the present value by the factor obtained from the table. The formula for using the table in this manner is:

Future Amount = Present Value × Factor (from Table FA–1)

Using the table to compute the amounts in our graph

Let us demonstrate this approach using the data for our savings account, illustrated in Exhibit B–1. The account started with a present value of $500, invested at an annual interest rate of 8 percent. Thus, the future values of the account in each of the next four years can be computed as follows (rounded to the nearest dollar):

Year	Future Amount	Computation (Using Table FA–1)
1	$540	$500 × 1.080 = $540
2	$583	$500 × 1.166 = $583
3	$630	$500 × 1.260 = $630
4	$680	$500 × 1.360 = $680

Computing a future amount is relatively easy. The more interesting question is: How much must we *invest today* to accumulate a required future amount?

Computing the Required Investment At the beginning of Year 1, Metro Recycling agrees to create a fully funded pension plan for its employees by the end of Year 5. It is estimated that $5 million will be required to fully fund the pension plan. How much must Metro invest in this plan *today* to accumulate the promised $5 million by the end of Year 5, assuming that payments to the fund will be invested to earn an annual return of 8 percent?

Let us repeat our original formula for computing future amounts using Table FA–1:

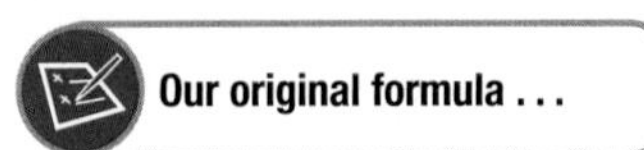

Future Amount = Present Value × Factor (from Table FA–1)

In this situation, we *know* the future amount—$5 million. We are looking for the *present value* which, when invested at an interest rate of 8 percent, will accumulate to $5 million in five years. To determine the *present value,* the formula shown above may be restated as follows:

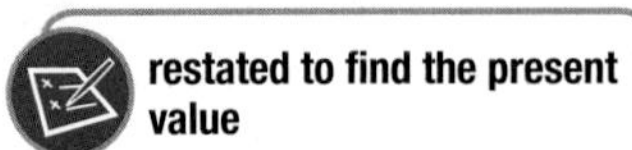

$$\text{Present Value} = \frac{\text{Future Amount}}{\text{Factor (from Table FA–1)}}$$

Referring to Table FA–1, we get a factor of 1.469 at the intersection of five periods and 8 percent interest. Thus, the amount of the required investment at the beginning of Year 1 is $3,403,676 ($5 million ÷ 1.469). Invested at 8 percent, this amount will accumulate to the required $5 million at the end of five years as illustrated in Exhibit B–3.

Exhibit B–3
THE FUTURE AMOUNT OF A SINGLE INVESTMENT

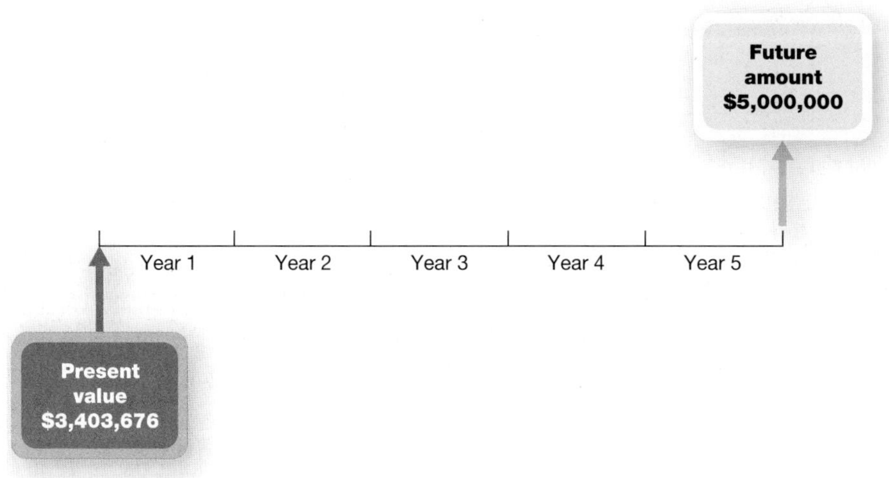

THE FUTURE AMOUNT OF AN ANNUITY

In many situations, an investor will make a *series* of investment payments rather than a single payment. As an example, assume that you plan to deposit $500 into your savings account at the end of each of the next five years. If the account pays annual interest of 8 percent, what will be the balance in your savings account at the end of the fifth year? Tables, such as Table FA–2 in Exhibit B–4, may be used to answer this question. Table FA–2 presents the future amount of an *ordinary annuity of $1,* which is a series of payments of $1 made at the *end* of each of a specified number of periods.

To find the future amount of an ordinary annuity of payments greater than $1, we simply multiply the amount of the periodic payment by the factor appearing in the table, as shown here:

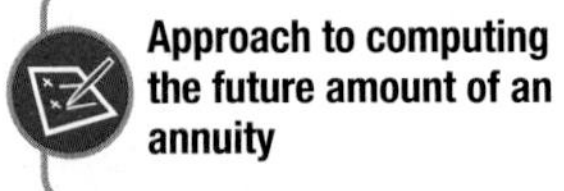

Future Amount of an Annuity = Periodic Payment × Factor (from Table FA–2)

In our example, a factor of 5.867 is obtained from the table at the intersection of five periods and 8 percent interest. If this factor is multiplied by the periodic payment of $500, we find that your savings account will accumulate to a balance of $2,934 ($500 × 5.867) at the end of

Exhibit B–4

FUTURE VALUE OF AN ORDINARY ANNUITY

Table FA–2
Future Amount of $1 Paid Periodically for *n* Periods

Number of Periods (*n*)	Interest Rate								
	1%	1½%	5%	6%	8%	10%	12%	15%	20%
1	1.000	1.000	1.000	1.000	1.000	1.000	1.000	1.000	1.000
2	2.010	2.015	2.050	2.060	2.080	2.100	2.120	2.150	2.200
3	3.030	3.045	3.153	3.184	3.246	3.310	3.374	3.473	3.640
4	4.060	4.091	4.310	4.375	4.506	4.641	4.779	4.993	5.368
5	5.101	5.152	5.526	5.637	5.867	6.105	6.353	6.742	7.442
6	6.152	6.230	6.802	6.975	7.336	7.716	8.115	8.754	9.930
7	7.214	7.323	8.142	8.394	8.923	9.487	10.089	11.067	12.916
8	8.286	8.433	9.549	9.897	10.637	11.436	12.300	13.727	16.499
9	9.369	9.559	11.027	11.491	12.488	13.579	14.776	16.786	20.799
10	10.462	10.703	12.578	13.181	14.487	15.937	17.549	20.304	25.959
20	22.019	23.124	33.066	36.786	45.762	57.275	72.052	102.444	186.688
24	26.974	28.634	44.502	50.816	66.765	88.497	118.155	184.168	392.484
36	43.077	47.276	95.836	119.121	187.102	299.127	484.463	1014.346	3539.009

five years. Therefore, if you invest $500 at the end of each of the next five years in the savings account, you will accumulate $2,934 at the end of the five-year period.

While computing the future amount of an investment is sometimes necessary, many business and accounting problems require us to determine the *amount of the periodic payments* that must be made to accumulate the required future amount.

Computing the Required Periodic Payments

Assume that Ultra Tech Company is required to accumulate $10 million in a *bond sinking fund* to retire bonds payable five years from now. The *bond indenture* requires Ultra Tech to make equal payments to the fund at the end of each of the next five years. What is the amount of the required periodic payment, assuming that the fund will earn 10 percent annual interest? To answer this question, we simply rearrange the following formula for computing the future amount of an annuity:

$$\frac{\text{Future Amount}}{\text{of an Annuity}} = \text{Periodic Payment} \times \text{Factor (from Table FA–2)}$$

Our original formula . . .

In our example, we know that Ultra Tech is required to accumulate a future amount of $10 million. However, we need to know the amount of the periodic payments that, when invested at 10 percent annual interest, will accumulate to that future amount. To make this calculation, the formula may be restated as follows:

$$\text{Periodic Payment} = \frac{\text{Future Amount of an Annuity}}{\text{Factor (from Table FA–2)}}$$

restated to find the amount of the periodic payments

The amount of each required payment, therefore, is $1,638,000 ($10 million ÷ 6.105). If payments of $1,638,000 are made at the end of each of the next five years to a bond sinking fund that earns 10 percent annual interest, the fund will accumulate to $10 million, as shown in Exhibit B–5.

INTEREST PERIODS OF LESS THAN ONE YEAR

In our computations of future amounts, we have assumed that interest is paid (compounded) or payments are made annually. Therefore, in using the tables, we used *annual* periods and an *annual* interest rate. Investment payments or interest payments may be made on a more

Exhibit B–5 FUTURE AMOUNT OF A SERIES OF INVESTMENTS

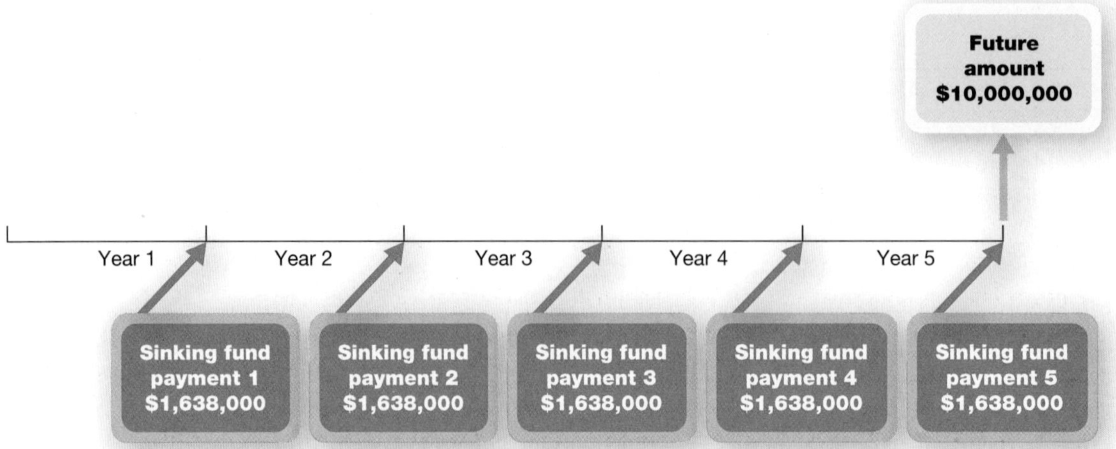

frequent basis, such as monthly, quarterly, or semiannually. Tables FA–1 and FA–2 may be used with any of these payment periods, *but the rate of interest must represent the interest rate for that period.*

As an example, assume that 24 monthly payments are to be made to an investment fund that pays a 12 percent annual interest rate. To determine the future amount of this investment, we would multiply the amount of the monthly payments by the factor from Table FA–2 for 24 periods, using a *monthly* interest rate of 1 percent—the 12 percent annual rate divided by 12 months.

Present Values

Learning Objective
LO5 Compute the present values of future cash flows.

As indicated previously, the present value is *today's* value of funds to be received in the future. While present value has many applications in business and accounting, it is most easily explained in the context of evaluating investment opportunities. In this context, the present value is the amount that a knowledgeable investor would pay *today* for the right to receive an expected future amount of cash. The present value is always *less* than the future amount, because the investor will expect to earn a return on the investment. The amount by which the future cash receipt exceeds its present value represents the investor's profit.

The amount of the profit on a particular investment depends on two factors: (1) the rate of return (called the *discount rate*) required by the investor and (2) the length of time until the future amount will be received. The process of determining the present value of a future cash receipt is called *discounting* the future amount.

To illustrate the computation of present value, assume that an investment is expected to result in a $1,000 cash receipt at the end of one year and that an investor requires a 10 percent return on this investment. We know from our discussion of present and future values that the difference between a present value and a future amount is the return (interest) on the investment. In our example, the future amount would be equal to 110 percent of the original investment, because the investor expects 100 percent of the investment back plus a 10 percent return on the investment. Thus, the investor would be willing to pay *$909* ($1,000 ÷ 1.10) for this investment. This computation may be verified as follows (amounts rounded to the nearest dollar):

Amount to be invested (present value)	$ 909
Required return on investment ($909 × 10%)	91
Amount to be received in one year (future value)	$1,000

As illustrated in Exhibit B–6, if the $1,000 is to be received *two years* in the future, the investor would pay only *$826* for the investment today [($1,000 ÷ 1.10) ÷ 1.10]. This computation may be verified as follows (amounts rounded to the nearest dollar):

Amount to be invested (present value) . . .	$ 826
Required return on investment in first year ($826 × 10%) . . .	83
Amount invested after one year. . .	$ 909
Required return on investment in second year ($909 × 10%) . . .	91
Amount to be received in two years (future value) . . .	$1,000

The amount that our investor would pay today, $826, is the present value of $1,000 to be received two years from now, discounted at an annual rate of 10 percent. The $174 difference between the $826 present value and the $1,000 future amount is the return (interest revenue) to be earned by the investor over the two-year period.

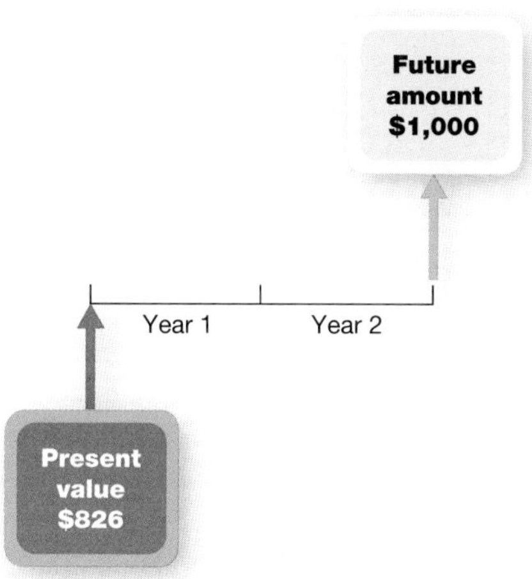

Exhibit B–6

PRESENT VALUE OF $1,000 TO BE RECEIVED IN A SINGLE SUM IN TWO YEARS

USING PRESENT VALUE TABLES

Although we can compute the present value of future amounts by a series of divisions, tables are available that simplify the calculations. We can use a table of present values to find the present value of $1 at a specified discount rate and then multiply that value by the future amount as illustrated in the following formula:

Present Value = Future Amount × Factor (from Table PV–1)

Formula for finding present value

Referring to **Table PV–1** in Exhibit B–7, we find a factor of **.826** at the intersection of two periods and 10 percent interest. If we multiply this factor by the expected future cash receipt of $1,000, we get a present value of *$826* ($1,000 × .826), the same amount computed previously.

WHAT IS THE APPROPRIATE DISCOUNT RATE?

As explained earlier, the *discount rate* may be viewed as the investor's required rate of return. All investments involve some degree of risk that actual future cash flows may turn out to be less than expected. Investors will require a rate of return that justifies taking this risk. In today's market conditions, investors require annual returns of between 2 percent and 6 percent on low-risk investments, such as government bonds and certificates of deposit. For relatively high-risk investments, such as the introduction of a new product line, investors may expect to earn an annual return of perhaps 15 percent or more. When a higher discount rate is used, the present value of the investment will be lower. In other words, as the risk of an investment increases, its value to investors decreases.

Exhibit B–7

PRESENT VALUE OF $1

Table PV–1
Present Values of $1 Due in *n* Periods

Number of Periods (*n*)	Discount Rate								
	1%	1½%	5%	6%	8%	10%	12%	15%	20%
1	.990	.985	.952	.943	.926	.909	.893	.870	.833
2	.980	.971	.907	.890	.857	.826	.797	.756	.694
3	.971	.956	.864	.840	.794	.751	.712	.658	.579
4	.961	.942	.823	.792	.735	.683	.636	.572	.482
5	.951	.928	.784	.747	.681	.621	.567	.497	.402
6	.942	.915	.746	.705	.630	.564	.507	.432	.335
7	.933	.901	.711	.665	.583	.513	.452	.376	.279
8	.923	.888	.677	.627	.540	.467	.404	.327	.233
9	.914	.875	.645	.592	.500	.424	.361	.284	.194
10	.905	.862	.614	.558	.463	.386	.322	.247	.162
20	.820	.742	.377	.312	.215	.149	.104	.061	.026
24	.788	.700	.310	.247	.158	.102	.066	.035	.013
36	.699	.585	.173	.123	.063	.032	.017	.007	.001

THE PRESENT VALUE OF AN ANNUITY

Many investment opportunities are expected to produce annual cash flows for a number of years, instead of one single future cash flow. Let us assume that Camino Company is evaluating an investment that is expected to produce *annual net cash flows of* $10,000 in *each of the next three years.*[1] If Camino Company expects a 12 percent return on this type of investment, it may compute the present value of these cash flows as follows:

Year	Expected New Cash Flows	×	Present Value of $1 Discounted at 12%	=	Present Value of Net Cash Flows
1	$10,000		.893		$ 8,930
2	10,000		.797		7,970
3	10,000		.712		7,120
Total present value of the investment.					$24,020

This analysis indicates that the present value of the expected net cash flows from the investment, discounted at an annual rate of 12 percent, amounts to $24,020. This is the maximum amount that Camino Company could afford to pay for this investment and still expect to earn the 12 percent required rate of return, as shown in Exhibit B–8.

In the preceding analysis, we computed the present value of the investment by separately discounting each period's cash flows, using the appropriate factors from **Table PV–1**. Separately discounting each period's cash flows is necessary only when the cash flows vary in amount from period to period. Since the annual cash flows in our example are *uniform in amount,* there are easier ways to compute the total present value.

Many financial calculators are programmed to compute the present value of an investment after the interest rate, the future cash flows, and the number of periods have been entered.

[1] "Annual net cash flows" normally are the net result of a series of cash receipts and cash payments occurring throughout the year. For convenience, we follow the common practice of assuming that the entire net cash flows for each year occur at *year-end.* This assumption causes relatively little distortion and greatly simplifies computations.

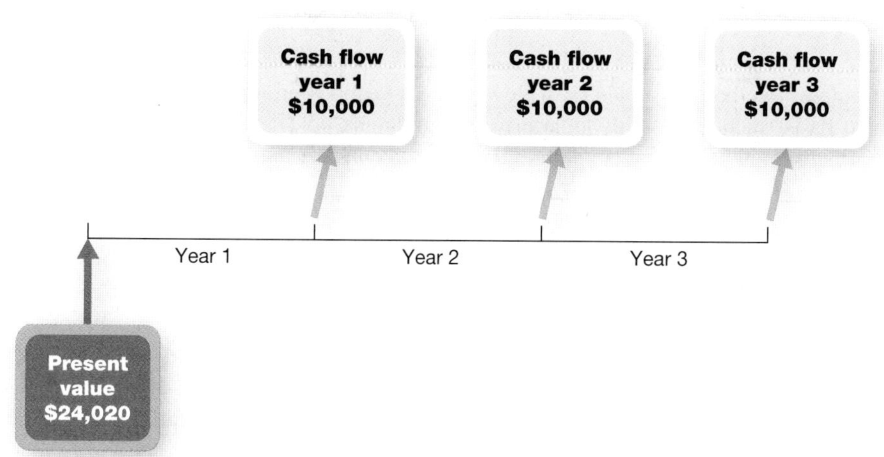

Exhibit B–8

PRESENT VALUE OF THREE $10,000 CASH FLOWS DISCOUNTED AT 12%

Another approach is to refer to a *present value annuity table,* which shows the present value of *$1 to be received each period for a specified number of periods.* An annuity table labeled Table PV–2 appears in Exhibit B–9.[2]

To illustrate the use of Table PV–2, let's return to the example of the investment by Camino Company. That investment was expected to return $10,000 per year for the next three years, and the company's required rate of return was 12 percent per year. Using Table PV–2, we can compute the present value of the investment with the following formula:

Present Value of an Annuity = Periodic Cash Flows × Factor (from Table PV–2)

Formula to find the present value of a series of cash flows 

As illustrated in Table PV–2, the present value of $1 to be received at the end of the next three years, discounted at an annual rate of 12 percent, is **2.402**. If we multiply 2.402 by the expected future annual cash receipt of $10,000, we get a present value of $24,020, which is the same amount produced by the series of calculations made earlier.

Exhibit B–9

PRESENT VALUE OF AN ORDINARY ANNUITY

Table PV–2
Present Values of $1 to Be Received Periodically for *n* Periods

Number of Periods (*n*)	Discount Rate								
	1%	1½%	5%	6%	8%	10%	12%	15%	20%
1	0.990	0.985	0.952	0.943	0.926	0.909	0.893	0.870	0.833
2	1.970	1.956	1.859	1.833	1.783	1.736	1.690	1.626	1.528
3	2.941	2.912	2.723	2.673	2.577	2.487	2.402	2.283	2.106
4	3.902	3.854	3.546	3.465	3.312	3.170	3.037	2.855	2.589
5	4.853	4.783	4.329	4.212	3.993	3.791	3.605	3.352	2.991
6	5.795	5.697	5.076	4.917	4.623	4.355	4.111	3.784	3.326
7	6.728	6.598	5.786	5.582	5.206	4.868	4.564	4.160	3.605
8	7.652	7.486	6.463	6.210	5.747	5.335	4.968	4.487	3.837
9	8.566	8.361	7.108	6.802	6.247	5.759	5.328	4.772	4.031
10	9.471	9.222	7.722	7.360	6.710	6.145	5.650	5.019	4.192
20	18.046	17.169	12.462	11.470	9.818	8.514	7.469	6.259	4.870
24	21.243	20.030	13.799	12.550	10.529	8.985	7.784	6.434	4.937
36	30.108	27.661	16.547	14.621	11.717	9.677	8.192	6.623	4.993

[2] This table is for an *ordinary* annuity, which assumes that the periodic cash flows occur at the *end* of each period.

DISCOUNT PERIODS OF LESS THAN ONE YEAR

The interval between regular periodic cash flows is called the *discount period.* In our preceding examples, we have assumed cash flows once a year. Often, cash flows occur on a more frequent basis, such as monthly, quarterly, or semiannually. The present value tables can be used with discount periods of any length, *but the discount rate must be for that length of time.* For example, if we use **Table PV–2** to find the present value of a series of *quarterly* cash payments, the discount rate must be the *quarterly* rate.

There are many applications of the present value concept in accounting. In the next several pages, we will discuss some of the most important of these applications.

Valuation of Financial Instruments

Learning Objective
LO6 **Discuss accounting applications of the concept of present value.**

Accountants use the phrase *financial instruments* to describe cash, equity investments in another business, and any contracts that call for receipts or payments of cash. (Notice that this phrase applies to all financial assets, as well as most liabilities. In fact, the only common liabilities *not* considered financial instruments are unearned revenue and deferred income taxes.)

Whenever the present value of a financial instrument *differs significantly* from the sum of the expected future cash flows, the instrument is recorded in the accounting records at its *present value*—not at the expected amount of the future cash receipts or payments.

Let us illustrate with a few common examples. Cash appears in the balance sheet at its face amount. This face value *is* a present value—that is, the value of the cash today.

Marketable securities appear in the balance sheet at their *current market values.* These too are present values—representing the amount of cash into which the security can be converted *today.*

Accounts receivable and accounts payable normally appear in the balance sheet at the amounts expected to be collected or paid in the near future. Technically, these are *future amounts,* not present values. But they usually are received or paid within 30 or 60 days. Considering the short periods of time involved, the differences between these future amounts and their present values simply are *not material.*

INTEREST-BEARING RECEIVABLES AND PAYABLES

When a financial instrument calls for the receipt or payment of interest, the difference between the present value and the future amounts *does* become material. Thus, interest-bearing receivables and payables initially are recorded in accounting records at the *present value* of the future cash flows—also called the "principal amount" of the obligation. This present value often is *substantially less* than the sum of the expected future amounts.

Consider, for example, $100 million in 30-year, 9 percent bonds payable issued at par. At the issuance date, the present value of this bond issue is $100 million—the amount of cash received. But the future payments to bondholders are expected to total *$370* million, computed as follows:

Future interest payments ($100 million × 9% × 30 years)	$ 270,000,000
Maturity value of the bonds (due in 30 years)	100,000,000
Sum of the future cash payments	$370,000,000

Thus the $100 million issuance price represents the present value of $370 million in future cash payments to be made over a period of 30 years.

In essence, interest-bearing financial instruments are "automatically" recorded at their present values simply because we do not include future interest charges in the original valuation of the receivable or the liability.

"NON-INTEREST-BEARING" NOTES

On occasion, companies may issue or accept notes that make no mention of interest, or in which the stated interest rates are unreasonably low. If the difference between the present value of such a note and its face amount is *material,* the note initially is recorded at its present value.

To illustrate, assume that on January 1, 2011, Elron Corporation purchases land from U.S. Development Co. As full payment for this land, Elron issues a $300,000 installment note payable, due in three annual installments of $100,000, beginning on December 31, 2011. This note makes *no mention* of interest charges.

Clearly, three annual installments of $100,000 are not the equivalent of $300,000 available today. Elron should use the *present value* of this note—not the face amount—in determining the cost of the land and reporting its liability.

Assume that a realistic interest rate for financing land over a three-year period currently is 10 percent per annum. The present value of Elron's installment note, discounted at 10 percent, is *$248,700* [$100,000, 3-year annuity × **2.487** (from **Table PV–2**) in Exhibit B–9]. Elron should view this $248,700 as the "principal amount" of this installment note payable. The remaining $51,300 ($300,000 − $248,700) represents interest charges included in the installment payments.

Elron should record the purchase of the land and the issuance of this note as follows:[3]

Land	248,700	
Notes Payable		248,700
Purchased land, issuing a 3-year installment note payable with a present value of $248,700.		

(U.S. Development Co. should make similar computations in determining the sales price of the land and the valuation of its note receivable.)

Elron also should prepare an *amortization table* to allocate the amount of each installment payment between interest expense and reduction in the principal amount of this obligation. This table, based on an original unpaid balance of $248,700, three annual payments of $100,000, and an annual interest rate of 10 percent, is illustrated in Exhibit B–10.

Exhibit B–10

AMORTIZATION TABLE FOR A DISCOUNTED NOTE PAYABLE

AMORTIZATION TABLE (3-YEAR, $300,000 INSTALLMENT NOTE PAYABLE, DISCOUNTED AT 10% PER ANNUM)

Interest Period	Payment Date	Annual Payment	Interest Expense (10% of the Last Unpaid Balance)	Reduction in Unpaid Balance	Unpaid Balance
Issue date	Jan. 1, 2011				$248,700
1	Dec. 31, 2011	$100,000	$24,870	$75,130	173,570
2	Dec. 31, 2012	100,000	17,357	82,643	90,927
3	Dec. 31, 2013	100,000	9,073*	90,927	–0–

*In the last period, interest expense is equal to the amount of the final payment minus the remaining unpaid balance. This compensates for the use of a present value table with factors carried to only three decimal places.

The entry at December 31, 2011, to record the first installment payment will be as follows:

Interest Expense	24,870	
Notes Payable	75,130	
Cash		100,000
Made annual payment on installment note payable to U.S. Development Co.		

[3] There is an alternative recording technique that makes use of an account entitled Discount on Notes Payable. This alternative approach produces the same results and will be explained in later accounting courses.

MARKET PRICES OF BONDS

The market price of bonds may be regarded as the *present value* to bondholders of the future principal and interest payments, discounted at the prevailing market rate of interest at the time of issuance. To illustrate, assume that Driscole Corporation issues $1,000,000 of 10-year, 10 percent bonds when the going market rate of interest is 12 percent. Because bond interest is paid semiannually, we must use 20 *semiannual* periods as the life of the bond issue and a 6 percent *semiannual* market rate of interest in our present value calculations. The discounted present value of the bond's future cash flows, discounted for 20 semiannual periods at 6 percent, is $885,500, computed as follows:

Present value of future principal payments:	
$1,000,000 due after 20 semiannual periods, discounted at 6%:	
$1,000,000 × .312 (from Table PV–1)	$312,000
Present value of future interest payments:	
$50,000 per period ($1,000,000 × 10% × ½) for 20 semiannual periods, discounted at 6%: $50,000 × 11.470 (from Table PV–2)	573,500
Expected issuance price of bond issue	$885,500

Note that, because the market rate of interest exceeds the bond's coupon rate, the bonds are issued at a $114,500 discount ($1,000,000 face value − $885,500 issue price). Thus, we know that these bonds were sold to an underwriter at 88.55 (meaning 88.55 percent of their face value).

As illustrated in Chapter 10, the entire amount of the discount is debited to an account titled Discount on Bonds Payable at the time the bonds are issued. The entry to record the issuance of this bond is:

Cash	885,500	
Discount on Bonds Payable.	114,500	
Bonds Payable		1,000,000
Issued 10%, 10-year bonds with $1,000,000 face value to an underwriter at a price of 88.55.		

When the bonds mature in 10 years, Driscole must pay bondholders the *full* $1 million face value of the bond issue, or $114,500 *more* than it received at the time the bonds were issued. As discussed in Chapter 10, the additional $114,500 due at maturity represents a portion of the company's total *interest expense* that must be amortized over the 10-year life of the bond. Thus, Driscole will incur interest expense of $55,725 every six months, computed as follows:

Semiannual interest *payment* (1,000,000 × 10% × ½)	$50,000
Add: Semiannual amortization of bond discount	
([$114,500 ÷ 10 years] × ½)	5,725
Semiannual interest expense	$55,725

The entry to record $55,725 of semiannual interest expense is:

Bond Interest Expense	55,725	
Cash		50,000
Discount on Bonds Payable		5,725
To record semiannual interest expense and to recognize six months' amortization of the $114,500 discount on 10-year bonds payable.		

Notice that, while the amortization of the discount increases semiannual interest expense by $5,725, it does not require an immediate cash outlay. The $114,500 of additional interest expense for the *entire* 10-year period will not be paid until the bonds mature.

CAPITAL LEASES

We briefly discuss capital leases in Chapter 10, but do not illustrate the accounting for these instruments. This appendix gives us an opportunity to explore this topic in greater detail.

A capital lease is regarded as a sale of the leased asset by the lessor to the lessee. At the date of this sale, the lessor recognizes sales revenue equal to the *present value* of the future lease payments receivable, discounted at a realistic rate of interest. The lessee also uses the present value of the future payments to determine the cost of the leased asset and the valuation of the related liability.

To illustrate, assume that, on December 1, Pace Tractor uses a *capital lease* to finance the sale of a tractor to Kelly Grading Co. The tractor was carried in Pace Tractor's perpetual inventory records at a cost of $15,000. Terms of the lease call for Kelly Grading Co. to make *24* monthly payments of *$1,000* each, beginning on December 31. These lease payments include an interest charge of *1 percent* per month. At the end of the 24-month lease, title to the tractor will pass to Kelly Grading Co. at no additional cost.

Accounting by the Lessor (Pace Tractor) Table PV–2 shows that the present value of $1 to be received monthly for 24 months, discounted at 1 percent per month, is **21.243**. Therefore, the present value of the 24 future lease payments is $1,000 × **21.243**, or *$21,243*. Pace Tractor should record this capital lease as a sale of the tractor at a price equal to the present value of the lease payments, as follows:

Lease Payments Receivable (net)	21,243	
Sales		21,243
Financed sale of a tractor to Kelly Grading Co. using a capital lease requiring 24 monthly payments of $1,000. Payments include a 1% monthly interest charge.		
Cost of Goods Sold	15,000	
Inventory		15,000
To record cost of tractor sold under capital lease.		

Notice that the sales price of the tractor is only $21,243, even though the gross amount to be collected from Kelly Grading Co. amounts to $24,000 ($1,000 × 24 payments). The difference between these two amounts, $2,757, will be recognized by Pace Tractor as interest revenue over the term of the lease.

To illustrate the recognition of interest revenue, the entry on December 31 to record collection of the first monthly lease payment (rounded to the nearest dollar) will be:

Cash	1,000	
Interest Revenue		212
Lease Payments Receivable (net)		788
Received first lease payment from Kelly Grading Co.: $1,000 lease payment received, less $212 interest revenue ($21,243 × 1%), equals $788 reduction in lease payments receivable.		

After this first monthly payment is collected, the present value of the lease payments receivable is reduced to $20,455 ($21,243 original balance, less $788). Therefore, the interest revenue earned during the *second* month of the lease (rounded to the nearest dollar) will be *$205* ($20,455 × 1%).[4]

[4] Both Pace Tractor and Kelly Grading Co. would prepare *amortization tables* showing the allocation of each lease payment between interest and the principal amount due.

Accounting by the Lessee (Kelly Grading Co.) Kelly Grading Co. also should use the present value of the lease payments to determine the cost of the tractor and the amount of the related liability, as follows:

Leased Equipment	21,243	
Lease Payments Obligation		21,243
To record acquisition of a tractor through a capital lease from Pace Tractor. Terms call for 24 monthly payments of $1,000, which include a 1% monthly interest charge.		

The entry on December 31 to record the first monthly lease payment (rounded to the nearest dollar) will be:

Interest Expense	212	
Lease Payments Obligation	788	
Cash		1,000
To record first monthly lease payment to Pace Tractor: $1,000 lease payment, less $212 interest expense ($21,243 × 1%), equals $788 reduction in lease payments obligation.		

OBLIGATIONS FOR POSTRETIREMENT BENEFITS

As we explain in Chapter 10, any unfunded obligation for postretirement benefits appears in the balance sheet at the *present value* of the expected future cash outlays to retired employees. The computation of this present value is so complex that it is performed by a professional actuary. But the present value of this obligation normally is far less than the expected future payments, as the cash payments will take place many years in the future.

ASSIGNMENT MATERIAL

Discussion Questions

1. Explain what is meant by the phrase *time value of money.*
2. Explain why the present value of a future amount is always *less* than the future amount.
3. Identify the two factors that determine the difference between the present value and the future amount of an investment.
4. Describe three basic investment applications of the concept of the time value of money.
5. Briefly explain the relationships between present value and (**a**) the length of time until the future cash flow occurs, and (**b**) the discount rate used in determining present value.
6. Define *financial instruments.* Explain the valuation concept used in initially recording financial instruments in financial statements.
7. Are normal accounts receivable and accounts payable financial instruments? Are these items shown in the balance sheet at their present values? Explain.
8. Assuming no change in the expected amount of future cash flows, what factors may cause the present value of a financial instrument to change? Explain fully.

Problems

LO1 LO2 LO4

PROBLEM B.1
Using Future Amount Tables

Use Table FA–1 (in Exhibit B–2) and Table FA–2 (in Exhibit B–4) to determine the future amounts of the following investments:

a. $20,000 is invested for 10 years, at 6 percent interest, compounded annually.

b. $100,000 is to be received five years from today, at 10 percent annual interest.

c. $10,000 is invested in a fund at the end of each of the next 10 years, at 8 percent interest, compounded annually.

d. $50,000 is invested initially, plus $5,000 is invested annually at the end of each of the next three years, at 12 percent interest, compounded annually.

LO3 LO4

PROBLEM B.2
Bond Sinking Fund

Tilman Company is required by a bond indenture to make equal annual payments to a bond sinking fund at the end of each of the next 20 years. The sinking fund will earn 8 percent interest and must accumulate to a total of $500,000 at the end of the 20-year period.

Instructions

a. Calculate the amount of the annual payments.

b. Calculate the total amount of interest that will be earned by the fund over the 20-year period.

c. Make the general journal entry to record redemption of the bond issue at the end of the 20-year period, assuming that the sinking fund is recorded on Tilman's accounting records at $500,000 and bonds payable are recorded at the same amount.

d. What would be the effect of an increase in the rate of return on the required annual payment? Explain.

LO1 LO2 LO5

PROBLEM B.3
Using Present Value Tables

Use Table PV–1 (in Exhibit B–7) and Table PV–2 (in Exhibit B–9) to determine the present values of the following cash flows:

a. $15,000 to be paid annually for 10 years, discounted at an annual rate of 6 percent. Payments are to occur at the end of each year.

b. $9,200 to be received today, assuming that the money will be invested in a two-year certificate of deposit earning 8 percent annually.

c. $300 to be paid monthly for 36 months, with an additional "balloon payment" of $12,000 due at the end of the thirty-sixth month, discounted at a monthly interest rate of 1½ percent. The first payment is to be one month from today.

d. $25,000 to be received annually for the first three years, followed by $15,000 to be received annually for the next two years (total of five years in which collections are received), discounted at an annual rate of 8 percent. Assume collections occur at year-end.

LO3 LO5 LO6

PROBLEM B.4
Present Value and Bond Prices

On June 30 of the current year, Rural Gas & Electric Co. issued $50,000,000 face value, 9 percent, 10-year bonds payable, with interest dates of December 31 and June 30. The bonds were issued at a discount, resulting in an effective *semiannual* interest rate of 5 percent.

Instructions

a. Compute the issue price for the bond that results in an effective semiannual interest rate of 5 percent. (Hint: Discount both the interest payments and the maturity value over 20 semiannual periods.)

b. Prepare a journal entry to record the issuance of the bonds at the sales price you computed in part **a.**

c. Explain why the bonds were issued at a discount.

LO3 LO5 LO6

PROBLEM B.5
Valuation of a Note Payable

On December 1, Showcase Interiors purchased a shipment of furniture from Colonial House by paying $10,500 cash and issuing an installment note payable in the face amount of $28,800. The note is to be paid in 24 monthly installments of $1,200 each. Although the note makes no mention of an interest charge, the rate of interest usually charged to Showcase Interiors in such transactions is 1½ percent per month.

Instructions

a. Compute the present value of the note payable, using a discount rate of 1½ percent per month.

b. Prepare the journal entries in the accounts of Showcase Interiors on:

   1. December 1, to record the purchase of the furniture (debit Inventory).
   2. December 31, to record the first $1,200 monthly payment on the note and to recognize interest expense for one month by the effective interest method. (Round interest expense to the nearest dollar.)

c. Show how the liability for this note would appear in the balance sheet at December 31. (Assume that the note is classified as a current liability.)

LO3 LO5 LO6

PROBLEM B.6

Capital Leases: A Comprehensive Problem

Custom Truck Builders frequently uses long-term lease contracts to finance the sale of its trucks. On November 1, 2011, Custom Truck Builders leased to Interstate Van Lines a truck carried in the perpetual inventory records at $33,520. The terms of the lease call for Interstate Van Lines to make 36 monthly payments of $1,400 each, beginning on November 30, 2011. The present value of these payments, after considering a built-in interest charge of 1 percent per month, is equal to the regular $42,150 sales price of the truck. At the end of the 36-month lease, title to the truck will transfer to Interstate Van Lines.

Instructions

a. Prepare journal entries for 2011 in the accounts of Custom Truck Builders on:

 1. November 1, to record the sale financed by the lease and the related cost of goods sold. (Debit Lease Payments Receivable for the $42,150 present value of the future lease payments.)

 2. November 30, to record receipt of the first $1,400 monthly payment. (Prepare a compound journal entry that allocates the cash receipt between interest revenue and reduction of Lease Payments Receivable. The portion of each monthly payment recognized as interest revenue is equal to 1 percent of the balance of the account Lease Payments Receivable, at the beginning of that month. Round all interest computations to the nearest dollar.)

 3. December 31, to record receipt of the second monthly payment.

b. Prepare journal entries for 2011 in the accounts of Interstate Van Lines on:

 1. November 1, to record acquisition of the leased truck.

 2. November 30, to record the first monthly lease payment. (Determine the portion of the payment representing interest expense in a manner parallel to that described in part **a.**)

 3. December 31, to record the second monthly lease payment.

 4. December 31, to recognize depreciation on the leased truck through year-end. Compute depreciation expense by the straight-line method, using a 10-year service life and an estimated salvage value of $6,150.

c. Compute the net carrying value of the leased truck in the balance sheet of Interstate Van Lines at December 31, 2011.

d. Compute the amount of Interstate Van Lines's lease payment obligation at December 31, 2011.

LO5 LO6

PROBLEM B.7

Valuation of a Note Receivable with an Unrealistic Interest Rate

On December 31, Richland Farms sold a tract of land, which had cost $930,000, to Skyline Developers in exchange for $150,000 cash and a five-year, 4 percent note receivable for $900,000. Interest on the note is payable annually, and the principal amount is due in five years. The accountant for Richland Farms did not notice the unrealistically low interest rate on the note and made the following entry on December 31 to record this sale.

Cash	150,000	
Notes Receivable	900,000	
Land		930,000
Gain on Sale of Land		120,000
Sold land to Skyline Developers in exchange for cash and five-year note with interest due annually.		

Instructions

a. Compute the present value of the note receivable from Skyline Developers at the date of sale, assuming that a realistic rate of interest for this transaction is 12 percent. (Hint: Consider both the annual interest payments and the maturity value of the note.)

b. Prepare the journal entry on December 31 to record the sale of the land correctly. Show supporting computations for the gain or loss on the sale.

c. Explain what effects the error made by Richland Farms's accountant will have on (**1**) the net income in the year of the sale and (**2**) the combined net income of the next five years. Ignore income taxes.

APPENDIX C

Forms of Business Organization

AFTER STUDYING THIS APPENDIX, YOU SHOULD BE ABLE TO:

Learning Objectives

- **LO1** Describe the basic characteristics of a sole proprietorship.
- **LO2** Identify factors to consider in evaluating the profitability and liquidity of a sole proprietorship.
- **LO3** Describe the basic characteristics of a general partnership and of partnerships that limit personal liability.
- **LO4** Describe the basic characteristics of a corporation.
- **LO5** Account for corporate income taxes; explain the effects of these taxes on before-tax profits and losses.
- **LO6** Account for the issuance of capital stock.
- **LO7** Explain the nature of retained earnings, account for dividends, and prepare a statement of retained earnings.
- **LO8** Explain why the financial statements of a corporation are interpreted differently from those of an unincorporated business.
- **LO9** Discuss the principal factors to consider in selecting a form of business organization.
- **LO10** Allocate partnership net income among the partners.

IMPORTANCE OF BUSINESS FORM

The legal form of a business organization is an important consideration not only when the business is first formed but also throughout its operating life. The form of an enterprise affects its ability to raise capital, the relationship between the organization and its owners, and the security of both creditors' and owners' claims. Three primary forms of business organization are generally found in the United States—sole proprietorships, partnerships, and corporations.

Corporations carry out the majority of business activity, and as a result, that form of business organization is the primary focus of this textbook. Sole proprietorships and partnerships are also important, however, because they represent the largest numbers of business organizations in the United States. This appendix supplements the introductory coverage of sole proprietorships and partnerships presented earlier in the text, as well as expanding the coverage of corporations as the dominant form of business organization.

Sole Proprietorships

A **sole proprietorship** is an unincorporated business owned by one person. Proprietorships are the most common form of business organization because they are so easy to start.

Creating a sole proprietorship requires *no authorization* from any governmental agency. Often the business requires little or no investment of capital. For example, a youngster with a paper route, baby-sitting service, or lawn-mowing business is a sole proprietorship. On a larger scale, sole proprietorships are widely used for farms, service businesses, small retail stores, restaurants, and professional practices, such as medicine, law, and public accounting.

A sole proprietorship provides an excellent model for demonstrating accounting principles because it is the simplest form of business organization. But in the business world, you will seldom encounter financial statements for these organizations.

Most sole proprietorships are relatively small businesses with few—if any—financial reporting obligations. Their needs for accounting information consist primarily of data used in daily business operations—the balance in the company's bank account and the amounts receivable and payable. In fact, many sole proprietorships do not prepare formal financial statements unless some special need arises, such as information to support bank loans.

THE CONCEPT OF THE SEPARATE BUSINESS ENTITY

For accounting purposes, and consistent with one of the basic accounting principles, we treat every business organization—including a sole proprietorship—as an entity separate from the other activities of its owner. This enables us to measure the performance of the business separately from the other financial affairs of its owner.

In the eyes of the law, however, a sole proprietorship is *not* an entity separate from its owner. Under the law, the proprietor is the "entity," and a sole proprietorship merely represents some of this individual's financial activities. The fact that a sole proprietorship and its owner legally are one and the same explains many of the distinctive characteristics of this form of organization.

CHARACTERISTICS OF A SOLE PROPRIETORSHIP

Learning Objective **LO1** **Describe the basic characteristics of a sole proprietorship.**

Among the key characteristics of sole proprietorships are:

- *Ease of formation.* (This explains why these organizations are so common.)
- *Business assets actually belong to the proprietor.* Because the business is not a legal entity, it cannot own property. The business assets actually belong to the *proprietor,* not to the business. Therefore, the proprietor may transfer assets in or out of the business *at will.*
- *The business pays no income taxes.* Federal tax laws do not view a sole proprietorship as separate from the other financial activities of its owner. Therefore, the proprietorship *does not* file an income tax return or pay income taxes. Instead, the *owner* must include the income of the business in his or her *personal* federal income tax return.
- *The business pays no salary to the owner.* The owner of a sole proprietorship is not working for a salary. Rather, the owner's compensation consists of the entire net income

(or net loss) of the business. Any money withdrawn from the business by its owner should be recorded in the owner's *drawing* account, *not* recognized as salaries expense.

- *The owner is personally liable for the debts of the business.* This concept, called **unlimited personal liability,** is too important to be treated as just one item in a list. It deserves special attention.

UNLIMITED PERSONAL LIABILITY

The owner of a sole proprietorship is *personally responsible* for all of the company's debts. Thus, a business "mishap," such as personal injuries stemming from business operations, may result in enormous personal liability for the business owner.[1]

Unlimited personal liability is the greatest *disadvantage* to this form of organization. Other forms of business organization provide owners with some means of limiting their personal liability for business debts—but not the sole proprietorship. If business operations entail a risk of substantial liability, the owner should consider another form of business organization.

ACCOUNTING PRACTICES OF SOLE PROPRIETORSHIPS

In the balance sheet of a sole proprietorship, total owner's equity is represented by the balance in the owner's **capital account.** Investments of assets by the owner are recorded by crediting this account. Withdrawals of assets by the owner are recorded by debiting the owner's **drawing account.** At the end of the accounting period, the drawing account and the Income Summary account are closed into the owner's capital account and presented as a single amount.

The only financial reporting obligation of many sole proprietorships is the information that must be included in the owner's personal income tax return. For this reason, some sole proprietorships base their accounting procedures on *income tax rules,* rather than generally accepted accounting principles.

EVALUATING THE FINANCIAL STATEMENTS OF A PROPRIETORSHIP

Learning Objective LO2 Identify factors to consider in evaluating the profitability and liquidity of a sole proprietorship.

The Adequacy of Net Income Sole proprietorships do not recognize any salary expense relating to the owner, nor any interest expense on the capital that the owner has invested in the business. Thus, if the business is to be considered successful, its net income should *at least* provide the owner with reasonable compensation for any personal services and equity capital that the owner has provided to the business.

In addition, the net income of a sole proprietorship should be adequate to compensate the owner for taking significant *risks*. Many small businesses fail. The owner of a sole proprietorship has *unlimited personal liability* for the debts of the business. Therefore, if a sole proprietorship sustains large losses, the owner can lose *much more* than the amount of his or her equity investment.

In summary, the net income of a sole proprietorship should be sufficient to compensate the owner for three factors: (1) personal services rendered to the business, (2) capital invested, and (3) the degree of financial risk that the owner is taking.

Evaluating Liquidity For a business organized as a *corporation,* creditors often base their lending decisions on the relationships between assets and liabilities in the corporation's balance sheet. But if the business is organized as a sole proprietorship, the balance sheet is less useful to creditors.

Remember, the assets listed in the balance sheet are owned by the *proprietor,* not by the business. The owner can transfer assets in and out of the business at will. Also, it is the *owner* who is financially responsible for the company's debts. Therefore, the ability of a sole proprietorship to pay its debts depends on the *financial strength of the owner,* not on the relationships among the assets and liabilities appearing in the company's balance sheet.

[1] Injuries sustained by employees or customers have often resulted in multimillion-dollar liabilities for the business organization. The judgments against a business that result from litigation may exceed available insurance coverage. A sole proprietorship should always carry substantial malpractice and general liability insurance to protect the owner from losing personal assets.

The financial strength of a sole proprietor may be affected by many things that *do not appear* in the financial statements of the business. For example, the owner may have great personal wealth—or overwhelming personal debts.

In summary, creditors of a sole proprietorship should look past the balance sheet of the business. The real issue is the debt-paying ability of the *owner*. Creditors of the business may ask the owner to supply *personal* financial information. They also may investigate the owner's credit history, using such credit-rating agencies as **TRW**.

A Word of Caution In Chapter 1, we discussed several factors that *promote the integrity* of the financial statements of publicly owned companies. Among these safeguards are the structure of internal control, audits by independent accountants, federal securities laws, and the competence and integrity of the professional accountants.

Let us stress that these safeguards apply to the **public information** distributed by publicly owned companies. However, they often *do not* apply to financial information provided by small businesses.

Small businesses may not have the resources—or the need—to establish sophisticated internal control structures. The financial information that they develop usually is *not* audited. Federal securities laws apply only to companies that are publicly owned. And the accounting records of a sole proprietorship often are maintained by the owner, who may have little experience in accounting.

Partnerships

A **partnership** is an unincorporated business owned by two or more *partners*.[2] A partnership often is referred to as a *firm*.

Partnerships are the *least* common form of business organization, but they are widely used for professional practices, such as medicine, law, and public accounting.[3] Partnerships also are used for many small businesses, especially those that are family-owned. Most partnerships are small businesses—but certainly not all.

For accounting purposes, we view a partnership as an entity separate from the other activities of its owners. But under the law, the partnership is *not* separate from its owners. Rather, the law regards the partners as personally—*and jointly*—responsible for the activities of the business.

The assets of a partnership do not belong to the business—they belong jointly to all of the partners. Unless special provisions are made, each partner has unlimited personal liability for the debts of the business. The partnership itself pays no income taxes, but the partners include their respective shares of the firm's income in their *personal* income tax returns.

From a legal standpoint, partnerships have *limited lives*. A partnership ends upon the withdrawal or death of an existing partner. Admission of a new partner terminates the previous partnership and creates a new legal entity. However, this is only a legal distinction. Most partnerships have *continuity of existence* extending beyond the participation of individual partners. Partnership agreements often have provisions that make the retirement of partners and the admission of new partners *routine events* that do not affect the operations of the business.

The term *partnership* actually includes three distinct types of organizations: general partnerships, limited partnerships, and limited liability partnerships. We will begin our discussion with the characteristics of *general partnerships*.

GENERAL PARTNERSHIPS

In a general partnership, each partner has rights and responsibilities similar to those of a sole proprietor. For example, each **general partner** can withdraw cash and other assets from the

Learning Objective LO3
Describe the basic characteristics of a general partnership and of partnerships that limit personal liability.

[2] A partner may be either an individual or a corporation.

[3] Some state laws prohibit professional practices from incorporating. Therefore, professional practices with more than one owner *must* operate as partnerships.

business at will.[4] Also, each partner has the full authority of an owner to negotiate contracts binding upon the business. This concept is called **mutual agency.** Every partner also has *unlimited personal liability* for the debts of the firm.

Combining the characteristics of unlimited personal liability and mutual agency makes a general partnership a potentially risky form of business organization. Assume, for example, that you enter into a general partnership with Tom Jones. You agree to split profits and losses "50–50." While you are on vacation, Jones commits the partnership to a contract that it simply does not have the resources to complete. Your firm's failure to complete the contract causes large financial losses to the customer. The customer sues your firm and is awarded a judgment of $5 million by the court.

Jones has few financial resources and declares personal bankruptcy. The holder of the judgment against your firm can hold *you personally liable for the whole $5 million.* The fact that you and Jones agreed to split everything "50–50" does *not* lessen your personal liability to the partnership's creditors. You may have a legal claim against Jones for his half of this debt, but so what? Jones is bankrupt.

In summary, general partnerships involve the same unlimited personal liability as sole proprietorships. This risk is intensified, however, because you may be held financially responsible for your partner's actions, as well as for your own.

PARTNERSHIPS THAT LIMIT PERSONAL LIABILITY

Over the years, state laws have evolved to allow modified forms of partnerships, including limited partnerships and limited liability partnerships. The purpose of these modified forms of partnerships is to *place limits* on the potential liability of individual partners.

Limited Partnerships A **limited partnership** has one or more general partners and one or more limited partners. The general partners are partners in the traditional sense, with unlimited personal liability for the debts of the business and the right to make managerial decisions.

The **limited partners** are basically passive investors. They share in the profits and losses of the business, but they do not participate actively in management and are *not* personally liable for debts of the business. Thus, if the firm has financial troubles, the losses incurred by the limited partners are limited to the amounts they have invested in the business.

In the past, limited partnerships were widely used for various investment ventures, such as drilling for oil, developing real estate, or making a motion picture. These businesses often lost money—at least in the early years; if they were profitable, the profits came in later years.

For such ventures, the limited partnership concept had great appeal to investors. Limited partners could include their share of any partnership net loss in their personal income tax returns, offsetting taxable income from other sources. And as *limited* partners, their financial risk was limited to the amount of their equity investment.

Recent changes in tax laws have greatly restricted the extent to which limited partners may offset partnership losses against other types of income. For this reason, there are fewer limited partnerships today than in the past. But in many cases, investors today can obtain similar tax benefits if the business venture is organized as an *S Corporation,* a form of business organization discussed later in this appendix.

Limited Liability Partnerships A **limited liability partnership** is a relatively new form of business organization. States traditionally have required professionals, such as doctors, lawyers, and accountants, to organize their practices either as sole proprietorships or as partnerships. The purpose of this requirement was to ensure that these professionals had unlimited liability for their professional activities.

Over the years, many professional partnerships have grown in size. Several public accounting firms, for example, now have thousands of partners and operate in countries all over the

[4] Title to real estate is held in the name of the partnership and, therefore, cannot be sold or withdrawn by any partner at will.

world. Also, lawsuits against professional firms have increased greatly in number and in dollar amount. To prevent these lawsuits from bankrupting innocent partners, the concept of the limited liability partnership has emerged. In this type of partnership, each partner has unlimited personal liability for his or her *own* professional activities, but not for the actions of other partners. Unlike a limited partnership, all of the partners in a limited liability partnership may participate in management of the firm.

ACCOUNTING PRACTICES OF PARTNERSHIPS

In most respects, partnership accounting is similar to that in a sole proprietorship—except there are more owners. As a result, a separate capital account and a separate drawing account are maintained for each partner.

Partnerships, like sole proprietorships, recognize no salaries expense for services provided to the organization by the partners. Amounts paid to partners are recorded in the partner's drawing account.

The statement of owner's equity is replaced by a **statement of partners' equity,** which shows separately the changes in each partner's capital account.[5] A typical statement of partners' equity appears in Exhibit C–1.

Exhibit C–1

STATEMENT OF PARTNERS' EQUITY

Changes in capital accounts during the year

BLAIR AND CROSS
STATEMENT OF PARTNERS' EQUITY
FOR THE YEAR ENDED DECEMBER 31, 2011

	Blair	Cross	Total
Balances, Jan. 1, 2011	$160,000	$160,000	$320,000
Add: Additional Investments	10,000	10,000	20,000
Net Income for the Year	30,000	30,000	60,000
Subtotals	$200,000	$200,000	$400,000
Less: Drawings	24,000	16,000	40,000
Balances, Dec. 31, 2011	$176,000	$184,000	$360,000

Allocating Net Income among the Partners

A special feature of a partnership is the need to *allocate* the firm's net income among its partners. Allocating partnership net income means computing each partner's share of total net income (or loss) and crediting (or debiting) this amount to the partner's capital account.

This allocation of partnership income is simply a bookkeeping entry, made as the Income Summary account is closed into the various partners' capital accounts. It *does not* involve any distributions of cash or other assets to the partners.

The amount that an individual partner *withdraws* during the year may *differ substantially* from the amount of partnership net income allocated to that partner. All partners pay personal income taxes on the amount of partnership income *allocated* to them—*not* on the amount of assets withdrawn.

Partners have great freedom in deciding how to allocate the firm's net income among themselves. In the absence of prior agreement, state laws generally provide for an *equal split* among the partners. But this seldom happens. Partners usually agree in advance how the firm's net income will be allocated.

Various features of partnership accounting, including the allocation of net income, are illustrated later in this appendix.

The Importance of a Partnership Contract

Every partnership needs a carefully written **partnership contract,** prepared before the firm begins operation. This contract is an *agreement among the partners* as to their rights and responsibilities. It spells out the

[5] In firms with a large number of partners, this statement is condensed to show only the changes in *total* partners' equity.

responsibilities of individual partners, how net income will be divided between or among the partners, and the amounts of assets that partners are allowed to withdraw.

A partnership contract does not prevent disputes from arising among the partners, but it does provide a contractual foundation for their resolution.

EVALUATING THE FINANCIAL STATEMENTS OF A PARTNERSHIP

The Adequacy of Net Income The net income of a partnership is similar to that of a sole proprietorship. It represents the partners' compensation for (1) personal services, (2) invested capital, and (3) assumption of the risks of ownership. Also, the reported net income is a pretax amount because the partnership itself pays no income tax.

The services and capital provided by individual partners may vary, as may the degree of financial risk assumed. Therefore, it is quite difficult to evaluate the income of a partnership. Rather, the individual partners must separately evaluate their *respective shares* of the partnership net income in light of their personal contributions to the firm. Some partners may find the partnership quite rewarding, while others may consider their share of the partnership net income inadequate.

Evaluating Liquidity The balance sheet of a partnership is more meaningful than that of a sole proprietorship. This is because there are legal distinctions between partnership assets, which are jointly owned, and the personal assets of individual partners. Another reason is that personal responsibility for business debts may *not* extend to all of the partners.

Creditors should understand the distinctions among the types of partnerships. In a general partnership, all partners have unlimited personal liability for the debts of the business. This situation affords creditors the maximum degree of protection. In a limited partnership, only the *general partners* have personal liability for these obligations. In a limited liability partnership, liability for negligence or malpractice extends only to those partners directly involved.

Corporations

Nearly all large businesses—and many small ones—are organized as corporations. There are many more sole proprietorships than corporations; but in dollar volume of business activity, corporations hold an impressive lead. Because of the dominant role of the corporation in our economy, it is important for everyone interested in business, economics, or politics to have an understanding of corporations and their accounting policies.

WHAT IS A CORPORATION?

Learning Objective
LO4 Describe the basic characteristics of a corporation.

A **corporation** is a *legal entity,* having an existence separate and distinct from that of its owners. The owners of a corporation are called **stockholders** (or shareholders), and their ownership is evidenced by transferable shares of **capital stock.**

A corporation is more difficult and costly to form than other types of organizations. The corporation must obtain a *charter* from the state in which it is formed, and it must receive authorization from that state to issue shares of capital stock. The formation of a corporation usually requires the services of an attorney.

As a separate legal entity, a corporation may own property in its own name. The assets of a corporation belong to the corporation itself, not to the stockholders. A corporation has legal status in court—it may sue and be sued as if it were a person. As a legal entity, a corporation may enter into contracts, is *responsible for its own debts,* and *pays income taxes* on its earnings.

On a daily basis, corporations are run by *salaried professional managers,* not by their stockholders.[6] Thus, the stockholders are primarily investors, rather than active participants in the business.

[6] In many cases, the managers and stockholders are one and the same. That is, managers may own stock, and stockholders may be hired into management roles. Ownership of stock, however, does not *automatically* give the shareholder managerial authority.

The top level of a corporation's professional management is the **board of directors.** These directors are *elected by the stockholders* and are responsible for hiring the other professional managers. In addition, the directors make major policy decisions, including the extent to which profits of the corporation are distributed to stockholders.

The fact that directors are elected by the stockholders means that a stockholder—or group of stockholders—owning more than 50 percent of the company's stock effectively controls the corporation. These controlling stockholders have the voting power to elect the directors, who in turn set company policies and appoint managers and corporate officers.

The transferability of corporate ownership, together with professional management, gives corporations a greater *continuity of existence* than other forms of organization. Individual stockholders may sell, give, or bequeath their shares to someone else without disrupting business operations. Thus, a corporation may continue its business operations *indefinitely,* without regard to changes in ownership.

In Exhibit C–2 we contrast the corporate form of business with a sole proprietorship and a general partnership.

Exhibit C–2

COMPARISON OF BUSINESS ORGANIZATIONS

Characteristics of Forms of Business Organizations

	Sole Proprietorship	General Partnership	Corporation
1. Legal status	Not a separate legal entity	Not a separate legal entity	Separate legal entity
2. Liability of owners for business debts	Personal liability for business debts	Personal liability for partnership debts	No personal liability for corporate debts
3. Accounting status	Separate entity	Separate entity	Separate entity
4. Tax status	Income taxable to owner	Income taxable to partners	Files a corporate tax return and pays income taxes on its earnings
5. Persons with managerial authority	Owner	Every partner	Hires professional managers
6. Continuity of the business	Entity ceases with retirement or death of owner	New partnership is formed with a change in partners	Indefinite existence that is not affected by the exchange of ownership shares

STOCKHOLDERS' LIABILITY FOR DEBTS OF A CORPORATION

The second item in Exhibit C–2—the liability of owners for business debts—deserves special attention. Stockholders in a corporation have *no personal liability* for the debts of the business. If a corporation fails, stockholders' potential losses are limited to the amount of their equity in the business.

To investors in large companies—and to the owners of many small businesses—**limited personal liability** is the *greatest advantage* of the corporate form of business organization.

Creditors, too, should understand that shareholders are not personally liable for the debts of a corporation. Creditors have claims against only the *assets of the corporation,* not the personal assets of the corporation's owners.

WHAT TYPES OF BUSINESSES CHOOSE THE CORPORATE FORM OF ORGANIZATION?

The answer, basically, is *all kinds.*

When we think of corporations, we often think of large, well-known companies such as **IBM**, **Procter & Gamble**, and **AT&T**. Indeed, almost all large businesses are organized as corporations. Limited shareholder liability, transferability of ownership, professional management, and continuity of existence make the corporation the best form of organization for pooling the resources of a great many equity investors.

The stocks of these large corporations are traded (bought and sold by investors) on organized securities markets, such as the New York Stock Exchange and the National Association of Securities Dealers Automated Quotations (NASDAQ). Companies whose shares are traded on these exchanges are said to be **publicly owned corporations** because anyone may purchase their stock.

When you purchase stock through an exchange, you normally are acquiring the shares from *another investor* (stockholder), not from the corporation itself. The existence of organized stock exchanges is what makes the stock in publicly owned corporations readily transferable.

Not all corporations, however, are large and publicly owned. Many small businesses are organized as corporations. In fact, many corporations have *only one stockholder.* Corporations whose ownership shares are not publicly traded are said to be **closely held corporations.**

Generally accepted accounting principles are basically the same for all types of business organizations. Because of the legal characteristics of corporations, however, there are significant differences in the ways these organizations account for income taxes, salaries paid to owners, owners' equity, and distributions of profits to their owners.

ACCOUNTING FOR CORPORATE INCOME TAXES

Learning Objective
LO5 Account for corporate income taxes; explain the effects of these taxes on before-tax profits and losses.

One of the principal differences between a corporation and an *unincorporated business* is that the corporation must pay income taxes on its earnings.

Corporate income taxes usually are payable in four quarterly installments. If the company is to properly "match" income taxes with the related revenue, **income tax expense** should be recognized in the periods in which the taxable income is *earned.* This is accomplished by making an *adjusting entry* at the end of each accounting period.

Total income tax expense for the year cannot be accurately determined until the corporation completes its annual income tax return. But the income tax expense for each accounting period can be *reasonably estimated* by applying the current *tax rate* to the company's *taxable income.* This relationship is summarized below:

$$\textbf{Taxable Income (determined according to tax regulations)} \times \textbf{Tax Rate (set by law)} = \textbf{Income Tax Expense}$$

Taxable income is computed in conformity with *income tax regulations,* not generally accepted accounting principles. In this introductory discussion, we will assume that taxable income is equal to **income before income tax**—a subtotal that often appears in a corporate income statement. Income before income tax is simply total revenue less all expenses *other than* income tax expense.[7]

Tax rates vary depending on the amount of taxable income. Also, Congress may change these rates from one year to the next. For purposes of illustration, we will assume a corporate tax rate of *40 percent* to include the effects of both federal and state income taxes.

To illustrate the recognition of income tax expense, assume that, in November, Warren, Inc., earns income before tax of $50,000. The month-end adjusting entry to recognize the related income tax would be:

Adjusting entry to accrue income taxes for the month

Income Tax Expense	20,000	
Income Tax Payable		20,000
To record estimated income tax expense on income earned in November ($50,000 × 40%).		

[7] In most cases, *income before tax* provides a reasonable approximation of *taxable income,* but differences in the determination of income before income tax and taxable income do exist. We discuss significant differences between these subtotals at various points throughout this textbook, although an in-depth discussion of this topic is deferred to more advanced accounting courses.

Income tax payable is a current liability that will appear in Warren's balance sheet. The presentation of income tax expense in the company's November income statement is illustrated in Exhibit C–3:

Exhibit C–3

CONDENSED INCOME STATEMENT

WARREN, INC. CONDENSED INCOME STATEMENT FOR THE MONTH ENDED NOVEMBER 30, 2011	
Net sales	$550,000
Cost of goods sold	350,000
Gross profit	$200,000
Expenses (other than income taxes—detail not shown)	150,000
Income before income tax	$ 50,000
Income tax expense	20,000
Net income	$ 30,000

Notice income taxes appear separately from other expenses

Income tax expense differs from other business expenses in that income taxes do not help generate revenue. For this reason, income tax is often shown separately from other expenses in the income statement—following a subtotal such as Income (or Loss) Before Income Tax. In an income statement, income tax expense often is termed *provision for income taxes.*

Income Tax in *Unprofitable* Periods What happens to income tax expense when *losses* are incurred? In these situations, the company may recognize a negative amount of income tax expense. The adjusting entry to record income tax in an unprofitable accounting period consists of a *debit* to Income Tax Payable and a *credit* to Income Tax Expense.

"Negative" income tax expense means that the company expects to recover from the government some of the income tax recognized as expense in earlier profitable periods.[8] A negative (credit) balance in the Income Tax Expense account is offset against the amount of the before-tax loss, as shown below:

Partial Income Statement—for an *Unprofitable* Period	
Income (loss) before income tax	$(100,000)
Income tax benefit (recovery of previously recorded tax)	40,000
Net loss	$ (60,000)

Income tax benefit reduces a pretax loss

We have seen that income tax expense *reduces* the amount of before-tax *profits.* Notice now that an income tax *benefit*—representing tax refunds—*reduces the amount of a pretax loss.* Thus, income tax reduces the amounts of *both* profits and losses.

If the Income Taxes Payable account has a *negative (debit) balance* at year-end, it is reclassified in the balance sheet as an *asset,* called "Income Tax Refund Receivable."

SALARIES PAID TO OWNERS

We have made the point that unincorporated businesses record payments to their owners as *drawings,* not as salaries expense. But the owners of a corporation cannot make withdrawals of corporate assets. Also, many of a corporation's employees—perhaps thousands—may also be stockholders. Therefore, corporations make *no distinction* between employees who are stockholders and those who are not. All salaries paid to employees (including employee/stockholders) are recognized by the corporation as *salaries expense.*

[8] Tax refunds are limited to taxes paid in recent years. In this introductory discussion, we assume the company has paid sufficient taxes in prior periods to permit full recovery of any negative tax expense relating to a loss in the current period.

OWNERS' EQUITY IN A CORPORATE BALANCE SHEET

In every form of business organization, there are two basic *sources* of owners' equity: (1) investment by the owners and (2) earnings from profitable operations. State laws require corporations to distinguish in their balance sheets between the amounts of equity arising from each source.

To illustrate, assume the following:

- On January 4, 2009, Mary Foster and several investors started Mary's Cab Co., a closely held corporation, by investing $100,000 cash. In exchange, the corporation issued to these investors 10,000 shares of its capital stock.
- It is now December 31, 2011. Over its three-year life, Mary's Cab Co. has earned total net income of $180,000, of which $60,000 has been distributed to the stockholders as *dividends.*

The stockholders' equity section of the company's 2011 balance sheet follows:

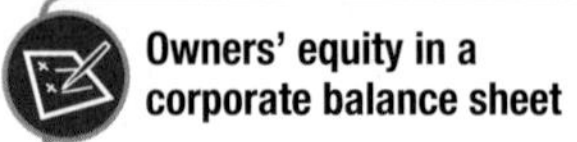

Owners' equity in a corporate balance sheet

Stockholders' equity:	
Capital stock	$100,000
Retained earnings	120,000
Total stockholders' equity	$220,000

The Capital Stock account represents the $100,000 invested in the business by Mary Foster and the other stockholders. This amount often is described as "invested capital," or "paid-in capital."

The $120,000 shown as **retained earnings** represents the *lifetime earnings* of the business, less the amount of cash representing those earnings that has been *distributed to the stockholders as dividends* (that is, $180,000 in net income, less $60,000 in dividends, equals $120,000). Retained earnings often are described as "earned capital."

THE ISSUANCE OF CAPITAL STOCK

Learning Objective
LO6 Account for the issuance of capital stock.

When a corporation receives cash or other assets from its owners, in a sale of capital stock, it records these investment transactions by crediting the Capital Stock account.

For example, the entry made by Mary's Cab Co. to record the issuance of 10,000 shares of capital stock in exchange for $100,000 cash is:

Entry to record issuance of capital stock

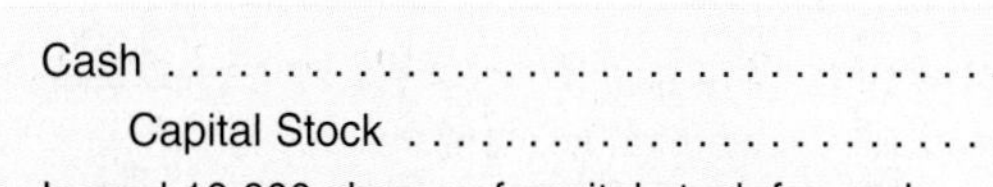

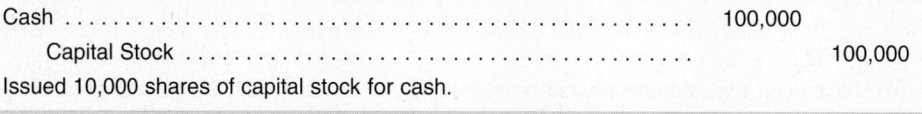

Cash	100,000	
Capital Stock		100,000
Issued 10,000 shares of capital stock for cash.		

RETAINED EARNINGS

Learning Objective
LO7 Explain the nature of retained earnings, account for dividends, and prepare a statement of retained earnings.

Retained earnings represent the owners' equity created through profitable operation of the business. Earning net income causes the balance in the Retained Earnings account to increase. However, many corporations follow a policy of *distributing to their stockholders* some of the resources generated by profitable operations. These distributions are termed **dividends.**

Dividends *reduce* both total assets and stockholders' equity (similar to drawings in an unincorporated business). The reduction in stockholders' equity is reflected by decreasing the balance in the Retained Earnings account. Retained earnings also are reduced by any *net losses* incurred by the business.

Notice that the balance of the Retained Earnings account does *not* represent the net income or net loss of one specific accounting period. Rather, it represents the *cumulative* net income (or net loss) of the business to date, *less* any amounts that have been distributed to the stockholders as dividends. In short, retained earnings represent the earnings that have been *retained* in the corporation. Some of the largest corporations have become large by consistently retaining in the business most of the resources generated by profitable operations.

Remember, retained earnings are *an element of owners' equity.* The owners' equity in a business *does not* represent cash or any other asset. The amount of cash owned by a corporation appears in the *asset section* of the balance sheet, *not* in the stockholders' equity section.

ACCOUNTING FOR DIVIDENDS

The owners of a corporation may not withdraw profits from the business at will. Instead, distributions of cash or other assets to the stockholders must be formally authorized—or *declared*—by the company's board of directors. These formal distributions are termed *dividends.* By law, dividends must be distributed to all stockholders *in proportion to the number of shares owned.*

A dividend is officially declared by the board of directors on one date, and then is paid (distributed) in the near future. To illustrate, assume that on December 1, 2011, the directors of Mary's Cab Co. declare a regular quarterly dividend of 50 cents per share on the 10,000 shares of outstanding capital stock. The board's resolution specifies that the dividend will be paid on December 15 to stockholders of record on December 10.

Two entries are required: one on December 1 to record the *declaration* of the dividend, and the other on December 15 to record payment:

Dec. 1	Dividends	5,000	
	Dividends Payable		5,000
	Declared a dividend of 50 cents per share payable Dec. 15 to stockholders of record on Dec. 10.		
15	Dividends Payable	5,000	
	Cash		5,000
	Paid dividend declared on Dec. 1.		

Entry to record the declaration of a dividend . . .

and the entry to record its payment

Notice that at the *declaration date,* December 1, there is no reduction in assets. But the stockholders' right to receive the dividend is recognized as a liability. This liability is discharged on the *payment date,* December 15, when the dividend checks are actually mailed to stockholders. No entry is required on the date of record, December 10.

At the end of the period, the Dividends account is closed into the Retained Earnings account.

CLOSING ENTRIES AND THE STATEMENT OF RETAINED EARNINGS

Updating the Retained Earnings Account for Profits, Losses, and Dividends To review, the amount of retained earnings is increased by earning net income; it is reduced by incurring net losses and by declaring dividends. In the accounting records, these changes are recorded by *closing* the balances in the Income Summary account and Dividends account into the Retained Earnings account.

To illustrate, assume that at January 1, 2011, Mary's Cab Co. had retained earnings of *$80,000.* During the year, the company earned net income of *$60,000* and paid four quarterly dividends totaling *$20,000.* These entries at December 31 close the Income Summary and Dividends accounts:

Income Summary	60,000	
Retained Earnings		60,000
To close the Income Summary account at the end of a profitable year.		

Net income increases retained earnings

Retained Earnings	20,000	
Dividends		20,000
To close the Dividends account, thereby reducing retained earnings by the amount of dividends declared during the year.		

If the corporation had incurred a *net loss* for the year, the Income Summary account would have had a debit balance. The entry to close the account then would have involved a *debit* to Retained Earnings, which would *reduce* total stockholders' equity, and a *credit* to the Income Summary account.

The Statement of Retained Earnings Corporations prepare a **statement of retained earnings,** summarizing the changes in the amount of retained earnings over the year.[9] A statement of retained earnings for Mary's Cab Co. is in Exhibit C–4. The last line of the statement represents the amount of retained earnings that will appear in the company's year-end balance sheet.

Exhibit C–4
STATEMENT OF RETAINED EARNINGS

MARY'S CAB CO. STATEMENT OF RETAINED EARNINGS FOR THE YEAR ENDED DECEMBER 31, 2011	
Retained earnings, Jan. 1, 2011	$ 80,000
Net income for the year	60,000
Subtotal	$140,000
Less: Dividends	20,000
Retained earnings, Dec. 31, 2011	$120,000

EVALUATING THE FINANCIAL STATEMENTS OF A CORPORATION

Learning Objective
LO8 Explain why the financial statements of a corporation are interpreted differently from those of an unincorporated business.

The Adequacy of Net Income In some respects, the financial statements of a corporation are *easier* to evaluate than those of an unincorporated business. For example, the income of an *unincorporated* business represents compensation to the owners for three distinct factors:

1. Services rendered to the business.
2. Capital invested in the business.
3. The risks of ownership, which often include unlimited personal liability.

But this is *not the case* with a corporation. If stockholders render services to the business, they are compensated with a salary. The corporation recognizes this salary as an expense in the computation of its net income. Therefore, the net income does *not* serve as compensation to the owners for personal services rendered to the business.

Also, stockholders' financial risk of ownership is limited to the amount of their investment. Thus, the net income of a corporation represents simply the *return on the stockholders' financial investment.* The stockholder need only ask, "Is this net income sufficient to compensate me for risking the amount of my investment?" This makes it relatively easy for stockholders to compare the profitability of various corporations in making investment decisions.

Remember also that stockholders *do not* report their respective shares of the corporate net income in their personal income tax returns. However, they must pay personal income taxes on the amount of any dividends received.[10]

Evaluating Liquidity When extending credit to an *unincorporated* business, creditors often look to the liquidity of the individual *owners,* rather than that of the business entity. This is because the owners often are personally liable for the business debts. But in lending funds to a corporation, creditors generally look only to the *business entity* for repayment. Therefore, the financial strength of the business organization becomes much more important when the business is organized as a corporation.

[9] Many corporations instead prepare a *statement of stockholders' equity,* which shows the changes in *all* stockholders' equity accounts over the year. A statement of stockholders' equity is illustrated and discussed in Chapter 12.

[10] An exception to this rule is S Corporations, which we discuss shortly.

Small Corporations and Loan Guarantees Small, closely held corporations often do not have sufficient financial resources to qualify for the credit they need. In such cases, creditors may require one or more of the company's stockholders to personally guarantee (or co-sign) specific debts of the business entity. By co-signing debts of the corporation, the individual stockholders *do become personally liable for the debts if the corporation fails to make payment.*

THE CONCEPT—AND THE PROBLEM—OF "DOUBLE TAXATION"

Unincorporated businesses do not pay income taxes. Instead, each owner pays *personal income taxes* on his or her share of the business net income.

Corporations, in contrast, must pay *corporate income taxes* on their taxable income. In addition, the stockholders must pay *personal income taxes* on the dividends they receive. As a result, corporate earnings may end up being *taxed twice:* once to the corporation as the income is earned and then again to the stockholders when the profits are distributed as dividends.

This concept of taxing a corporation's earnings at two levels is often called **double taxation.** Together, these two levels of taxation can consume as much as *60 percent to 70 percent* of a corporation's before-tax income. Few businesses would be able to raise equity capital if investors indeed expected to face such a high overall tax rate. Therefore, careful **tax planning** is *absolutely essential* in any business organized as a corporation.

There are several ways to avoid the full impact of double taxation. For example, corporations always should pay *salaries* to stockholders who work in the business. These salaries are taxable to the stockholders, but they are expenses of the business and therefore reduce the corporation's taxable income. Also, the taxation of dividends can be avoided entirely if the corporation *retains* its profits, rather than distributing them as dividends.

There are legal limits, however, on the extent to which taxes can be avoided by a corporation retaining its earnings rather than distributing them to stockholders. If a corporation exceeds these limits, it may be required to pay a supplemental tax.

S CORPORATIONS

Tax laws allow many small, closely held corporations a special tax status under Subchapter S of the tax code.[11] Corporations that qualify for this special tax treatment are called **S Corporations.**

S Corporations *do not* pay corporate income taxes; nor do stockholders pay *personal* income taxes on the amounts of dividends received. Instead, each stockholder pays personal income taxes on his or her share of the corporate net income. The net income of an S Corporation is taxed in the same manner as that of a *partnership.*

S Corporation status is most advantageous in the following situations:

- A profitable corporation plans to distribute most of its earnings as dividends. In this case, organization as an S Corporation avoids the problem of *double taxation.*
- A new corporation is expected to incur *net losses* in its early years of operation. Ordinarily, net losses incurred by a corporation have *no effect* on the stockholders' personal income tax returns. But if the business is organized as an S Corporation, stockholders *may* deduct their share of any net business loss in their personal income tax returns.

From a tax standpoint, S Corporation status may greatly benefit the owners of a closely held corporation. Owners of small businesses should consider this form of organization.

S Corporations are a special case, not the norm. Unless we specifically state otherwise, you should assume that all corporations used in our examples and assignment materials are regular corporations, not S Corporations.

[11] An S Corporation must have 75 or fewer stockholders, all of whom are individuals and residents of the United States. Thus, while one corporation generally may own stock in another, it may *not* be a stockholder in an S Corporation.

Learning Objective
LO9 Discuss the principal factors to consider in selecting a form of business organization.

Selecting an Appropriate Form of Business Organization

Anyone planning to start a business should give careful thought to the form of organization. Among the factors most often considered are:

- The personal liability of the owner(s) for business debts.
- Income tax considerations.
- The need to raise large amounts of equity capital.
- The owners' need for flexibility in withdrawing assets from the business.
- Whether all owners are to have managerial authority.
- The need for continuity in business operations, despite future changes in ownership.
- The ease and cost of forming the business.

INCORPORATING AN ESTABLISHED BUSINESS

Often a business starts out as a sole proprietorship or partnership, but as it grows larger, it is reorganized as a closely held corporation. Eventually, the business may "go public," meaning that it issues stock to the general public and its shares are traded on an organized stock exchange.

When an existing business is reorganized as a corporation, the corporation is a *new business entity.* The valuation of the corporation's assets and liabilities is based on their *current market value* when the new entity is established, not on their values in the accounting records of the previous business entity.

Assume, for example, that Devin Ryan has long owned and operated a sole proprietorship called Ryan Engineering. In January, Ryan decides to *incorporate* his business. He obtains a corporate charter and transfers to the new corporation all of the assets used in his sole proprietorship. The new corporation also assumes responsibility for all of the proprietorship's business debts. In exchange for these net assets (assets less liabilities), Ryan receives 20,000 shares of capital stock in the new corporation.

The following table lists the assets, liabilities, and owner's equity of the sole proprietorship at the date the new business is formed. The left-hand column indicates the amounts of these items in the proprietorship's accounting records. The right-hand column indicates the *current market value* of these items on this date. (In each column, owner's equity is equal to total assets less total liabilities.)

	Amount in Proprietorship's Accounting Records	Current Market Value
Cash	$ 30,000	$ 30,000
Accounts Receivable	75,000	60,000
Inventory	10,000	15,000
Land	40,000	100,000
Building	60,000	50,000
Equipment	70,000	80,000
Notes Payable	55,000	55,000
Accounts Payable	20,000	20,000
Owner's Equity	210,000	260,000

The entry to establish a new set of records for the business as a corporation based on the values of the assets received and the liabilities assumed is as follows:

Cash	30,000	
Accounts Receivable	60,000	
Inventory	15,000	
Land	100,000	
Building	50,000	
Equipment	80,000	
Notes Payable		55,000
Accounts Payable		20,000
Capital Stock		260,000
Acquired assets and assumed liabilities of Ryan Engineering; issued 20,000 shares of capital stock in exchange.		

Entries to record the formation of a partnership

A publicly owned corporation receives cash only when it first sells shares of stock to the investing public (called an "initial public offering," or IPO). Future trading of these securities takes place between individual investors and has no direct impact on the company's cash flows. Yet publicly owned corporations are extremely concerned about growth trends in the market value of their outstanding securities.

Why is this? There are several reasons. First, corporations monitor closely the current market value of their securities because current stock performance directly influences the ability to raise equity capital in the future (through new public offerings). Second, poor stock performance often signals that a company is experiencing financial difficulty. This, in turn, often makes it difficult for the company to obtain credit and may even make potential customers reluctant to buy the goods or services it sells. Finally, a growing number of corporations include stock options in their executive compensation plans. If the market price of the company's stock falls below a certain value, these options become worthless. When this happens, key executives often lose motivation to stay with the company and make the decision to take their "intellectual capital" elsewhere.

SUPPLEMENTAL TOPIC

Partnership Accounting—A Closer Look

There are a number of unique aspects of partnership accounting. In this section, we describe opening the accounts of a new partnership, additional investments and withdrawals by owners, allocating partnership net income among the partners, and closing the accounts at year-end.

OPENING THE ACCOUNTS OF A NEW PARTNERSHIP

When a partner contributes assets other than cash, a question always arises as to the value of such assets. The valuations assigned to noncash assets should be their *fair values* at the date of transfer to the partnership. The valuations assigned must be agreed to by all partners.

To illustrate the opening entries for a newly formed partnership, assume that on January 1, 2009, Joan Blair and Richard Cross, who operate competing retail stores, decide to form a partnership by consolidating their two businesses. A capital account is opened for each partner and credited with the agreed valuation of the *net assets* (total assets less total liabilities) that the partner contributes. The journal entries to open the accounts of the partnership of Blair and Cross are as follows:

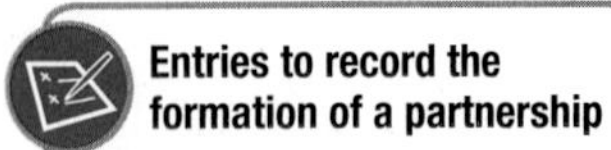

Account	Debit	Credit
Cash	40,000	
Accounts Receivable	60,000	
Inventory	90,000	
Accounts Payable		30,000
Joan Blair, Capital		160,000
To record the investment by Joan Blair in the partnership of Blair and Cross.		
Cash	10,000	
Inventory	60,000	
Land	60,000	
Building	100,000	
Accounts Payable		70,000
Richard Cross, Capital		160,000
To record the investment by Richard Cross in the partnership of Blair and Cross.		

Accounting in a partnership is similar to that in a sole proprietorship, except that separate capital accounts are maintained for each partner. These capital accounts show for each partner the amounts invested, the amounts withdrawn, and the appropriate share of partnership net income. In brief, each partner is provided with a history of his or her equity in the firm.

Separate *drawing accounts* also are maintained for each partner. These drawing accounts are debited to record all withdrawals of cash or other assets, including the use of partnership funds to pay a partner's personal debts.

Additional Investments Assume that after six months of operation the firm is in need of more cash, and the partners make additional investments of $10,000 each on July 1. These additional investments are credited to the capital accounts as shown below:

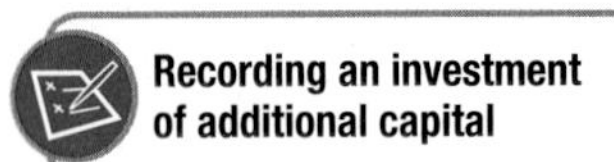

Account	Debit	Credit
Cash	20,000	
Joan Blair, Capital		10,000
Richard Cross, Capital		10,000
To record additional investments.		

Closing the Accounts of a Partnership at Year-End At the end of the accounting period, the balance in the Income Summary account is closed into the partners' capital accounts. The profits or losses of a partnership may be divided among the partners in *any manner agreed upon* by the partners in their partnership agreement.

In our illustration, let us assume that Blair and Cross have agreed to share profits equally. (We will discuss other profit-and-loss sharing arrangements later in this section.) Assuming that the partnership earns net income of $60,000 in the first year of operations, the entry to close the Income Summary account is as follows:

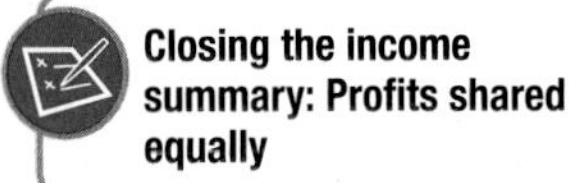

Account	Debit	Credit
Income Summary	60,000	
Joan Blair, Capital		30,000
Richard Cross, Capital		30,000
To divide net income for the year in accordance with partnership agreement to share profits equally.		

The next step in closing the accounts is to transfer the balance of each partner's drawing account to his or her Capital account. Assuming that withdrawals during the year amounted to $24,000 for Blair and $16,000 for Cross, the entry at December 31 to close the drawing accounts is as follows:

Joan Blair, Capital	24,000	
Richard Cross, Capital	16,000	
Joan Blair, Drawing		24,000
Richard Cross, Drawing		16,000
To transfer debit balances in partners' drawing accounts to their respective capital accounts.		

Closing the partners' drawing accounts to their capital accounts

Income Statement for a Partnership The income statement for a partnership differs from that of a sole proprietorship in only one respect: A final section may be added to show the division of the net income between the partners, as illustrated in Exhibit C–5 for the firm of Blair and Cross. The income statement of a partnership is consistent with that of a sole proprietorship in showing no income taxes expense and no salaries relating to services rendered by partners.

Exhibit C–5

INCOME STATEMENT

BLAIR AND CROSS
INCOME STATEMENT
FOR THE YEAR ENDED DECEMBER 31, 2011

Sales		$600,000
Cost of goods sold		400,000
Gross profit on sales		$200,000
Operating expenses:		
Selling expenses	$100,000	
General & administrative expenses	40,000	140,000
Net income		$ 60,000
Division of net income:		
To Joan Blair (50%)	$ 30,000	
To Richard Cross (50%)	30,000	$ 60,000

Statement of Partners' Equity The partners usually want an explanation of the change in their capital accounts from one year-end to the next. The statement of partners' equity for Blair and Cross appears in Exhibit C–6 (this statement also was illustrated in Exhibit C–1):

Exhibit C–6

STATEMENT OF PARTNERS' EQUITY

BLAIR AND CROSS
STATEMENT OF PARTNERS' EQUITY
FOR THE YEAR ENDED DECEMBER 31, 2011

	Blair	Cross	Total
Balances, Jan. 1, 2011	$160,000	$160,000	$320,000
Add: Additional Investments	10,000	10,000	20,000
Net Income for the Year	30,000	30,000	60,000
Subtotals	$200,000	$200,000	$400,000
Less: Drawings	24,000	16,000	40,000
Balances, Dec. 31, 2011	$176,000	$184,000	$360,000

The balance sheet of Blair and Cross would show the capital balance for each partner, as well as the total equity of $360,000.

Learning Objective
LO10 Allocate partnership net income among the partners.

ALLOCATING PARTNERSHIP NET INCOME AMONG THE PARTNERS

Profits earned by partnerships compensate the owners for (1) personal services rendered to the business, (2) capital invested in the business, and (3) assuming the risks of ownership. Recognition of these three factors is helpful in developing an equitable plan for the division of partnership profits.

If one partner devotes full time to the business while another devotes little or no time, the difference in the partners' contributions of time and effort should be reflected in the profit-sharing agreement. If one partner possesses special skills, the profit-sharing agreement should reward this partner's talent. Also, partners may each provide different amounts of capital to the business entity. Again, the differences in the value of the partners' contributions to the business should be reflected in the profit-and-loss sharing agreement.

To recognize the particular contributions of each partner to the business, partnership profit-and-loss sharing agreements often include salary allowances to partners and interest on the balances of partners' capital accounts. These "salaries" and "interest" are *not expenses* of the business; rather, they are *steps in the computation made to divide partnership net income among the partners.*

In the preceding illustrations of the partnership of Blair and Cross, we assumed that the partners invested equal amounts of capital, rendered equal services, and divided net income equally. We are now ready to consider cases in which the partners invest *unequal* amounts of capital and services. Partners can share net income or loss in any manner they choose; however, most profit-sharing agreements fall under one of the following types:

1. A fixed ratio. The fixed ratio method has already been illustrated in the example of the Blair and Cross partnership, in which profits were shared equally, that is, 50 percent and 50 percent. Partners may agree upon any fixed ratio such as 60 percent and 40 percent, or 70 percent and 30 percent.
2. Salary allowances to the partners, with remaining net income or loss divided in a fixed ratio.
3. Interest allowances on partners' capital balances, with remaining net income or loss divided in a fixed ratio.
4. Salary allowances to the partners, interest allowances on partners' capital balances, and remaining net income or loss divided in a fixed ratio.

All these methods of sharing partnership net income are intended to recognize differences in the personal services rendered by partners and in the amounts of capital invested in the firm.

In the illustrations that follow, the assumption is made that beginning balances in the partners' capital accounts are Brooke Adams, $160,000, and Ben Barnes, $40,000. At year-end, the Income Summary account shows a credit balance of $96,000, representing the net income for the year.

Salaries to Partners, with Remainder in a Fixed Ratio Because partners often contribute different amounts of personal services, partnership agreements often provide for partners' salaries as a factor in the division of profits.

For example, assume that Adams and Barnes agree to annual salary allowances of $12,000 for Adams and $60,000 for Barnes. These salaries, which total $72,000 per year, are agreed upon by the partners in advance. Of course, the net income of the business is not likely to be exactly $72,000 in a given year. Therefore, the profit-and-loss sharing agreement should also specify a fixed ratio for dividing any profit or loss remaining after giving consideration to the agreed-upon salary allowances. We will assume that Adams and Barnes agree to divide any remaining profit or loss equally.

The division of the $96,000 in partnership net income between Adams and Barnes is illustrated in the schedule shown in Exhibit C–7. The first step is to allocate to each partner his or her agreed-upon salary allowance. This step allocates $72,000 of the partnership net income. The remaining $24,000 is then divided in the agreed-upon fixed ratio (50–50 in this example).

Exhibit C–7
DISTRIBUTION OF PARTNERSHIP NET INCOME

Division of Partnership Net Income	Adams	Barnes	Net Income
Net income to be divided			$96,000
Salary allowances to partners	$12,000	$60,000	(72,000)
Remaining income after salary allowances			$24,000
Allocated in a fixed ratio:			
Adams (50%)	12,000		
Barnes (50%)		12,000	(24,000)
Total share to each partner	$24,000	$72,000	$ -0-

Profit sharing: Salary allowances and remainder in a fixed ratio

Under this agreement, Adams's share of the $96,000 profit amounts to $24,000 and Barnes's share amounts to $72,000. The entry to close the Income Summary account would be:

Income Summary	96,000	
Brooke Adams, Capital		24,000
Ben Barnes, Capital		72,000
To close the Income Summary account by crediting each partner with agreed-upon salary allowance and dividing the remaining profits equally.		

Notice that the allocation of partnership income is used in this closing entry

The salary allowances used in dividing partnership net income are sometimes misinterpreted, even by the partners. These salary allowances are merely an agreed-upon device for dividing net income; they are *not expenses* of the business and are *not recorded in any ledger account.* A partner is considered an owner of the business, not an employee. In a partnership, the services that a partner renders to the firm are assumed to be rendered in anticipation of earning a share of the profits, not a salary.

The amount of cash or other assets that a partner withdraws from the partnership may be greater than or less than the partner's salary allowance. Even if a partner decides to withdraw an amount of cash equal to his or her "salary allowance," the withdrawal should be recorded by debiting the partner's drawing account, *not by debiting an expense account.* Let us repeat the main point: *"Salary allowances" to partners should not be recorded as expenses of the business.*[12]

Interest Allowances on Partners' Capital, with Remainder in a Fixed Ratio Next we shall assume a business situation in which the partners spend very little time in the business and net income depends primarily on the amount of money invested. The profit-sharing plan then might emphasize invested capital as a basis for the first step in allocating income.

For example, assume that Adams and Barnes had agreed that both partners are to be allowed interest at *15 percent* on their beginning capital balances, with any remaining profit or loss to be divided equally. Net income to be divided is $96,000, and the beginning capital balances are Adams, *$160,000,* and Barnes, *$40,000.* Exhibit C–8 shows the distribution of partnership net income in this case.

[12] Some exceptions to this general rule will be discussed in more advanced accounting courses.

Exhibit C–8

DISTRIBUTION OF PARTNERSHIP NET INCOME

Profit sharing: Interest on capital and remainder in a fixed ratio

Division of Partnership Net Income

	Adams	Barnes	Net Income
Net income to be divided			$96,000
Interest allowances on beginning capital:			
Adams ($160,000 × 15%)	$24,000		
Barnes ($40,000 × 15%)		$ 6,000	
Total allocated as interest allowances			(30,000)
Remaining income after interest allowances			$66,000
Allocated in a fixed ratio:			
Adams (50%)	33,000		
Barnes (50%)		33,000	(66,000)
Total share to each partner	$57,000	$39,000	$ –0–

The entry to close the Income Summary account in this example would be:

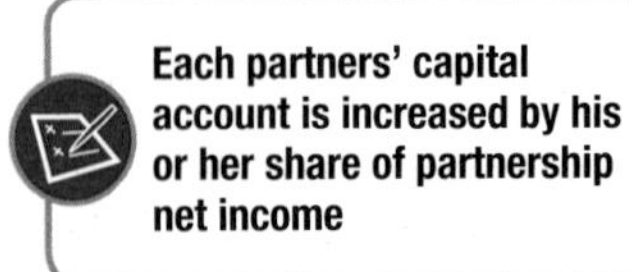

Each partners' capital account is increased by his or her share of partnership net income

Income Summary	96,000	
Brooke Adams, Capital		57,000
Ben Barnes, Capital		39,000
To close the Income Summary account by crediting each partner with interest at 15% on beginning capital and dividing the remaining profits equally.		

Salary Allowances, Interest on Capital, and Remainder in a Fixed Ratio The preceding example took into consideration the difference in amounts of capital provided by Adams and Barnes but ignored any difference in personal services performed. In the next example, we shall assume that the partners agree to a profit-sharing plan providing for salaries and for interest on beginning capital balances. Salary allowances, as before, are authorized at $12,000 for Adams and $60,000 for Barnes. Beginning capital balances are $160,000 for Adams and $40,000 for Barnes. Partners are to be allowed interest at 10 percent on their beginning capital balances, and any profit or loss remaining after authorized salary and interest allowances is to be divided equally. Exhibit C–9 shows the distribution of partnership net income under this agreement.

Exhibit C–9

DISTRIBUTION OF PARTNERSHIP NET INCOME

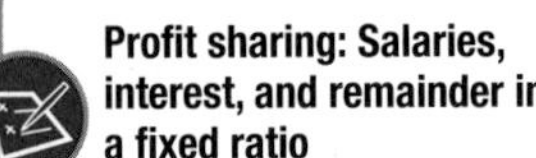

Profit sharing: Salaries, interest, and remainder in a fixed ratio

Division of Partnership Net Income

	Adams	Barnes	Net Income
Net income to be divided			$96,000
Salary allowances to partners	$12,000	$60,000	(72,000)
Income after salary allowances			$24,000
Interest allowances on beginning capital:			
Adams ($160,000 × 10%)	16,000		
Barnes ($40,000 × 10%)		4,000	
Total allocated as interest allowances			(20,000)
Remaining income after salary and interest allowances			$ 4,000
Allocated in a fixed ratio:			
Adams (50%)	2,000		
Barnes (50%)		2,000	(4,000)
Total share to each partner	$30,000	$66,000	$ –0–

The journal entry to close the Income Summary account in this case will be:

Income Summary	96,000	
Brooke Adams, Capital		30,000
Ben Barnes, Capital		66,000
To close the Income Summary account by crediting each partner with authorized salary and interest at 10% on beginning capital, and dividing the remaining profits equally.		

Authorized Salary and Interest Allowance in Excess of Net Income In the preceding example the total of the authorized salaries and interest was $92,000 and the net income to be divided was $96,000. Suppose that the net income had been only $50,000. How should the division have been made?

If the partnership contract provides for salaries and interest on invested capital, these provisions are to be followed even though the net income for the year is *less* than the total of the authorized salaries and interest. If the net income of the firm of Adams and Barnes amounted to only $50,000, this amount would be allocated as shown in Exhibit C–10.

Exhibit C–10

DISTRIBUTION OF PARTNERSHIP NET INCOME

Division of Partnership Net Income

	Adams	Barnes	Net Income
Net income to be divided			$ 50,000
Salary allowances to partners	$12,000	$60,000	(72,000)
Residual loss after salary allowances			$(22,000)
Interest allowances on beginning capital:			
Adams ($160,000 × 10%)	16,000		
Barnes ($40,000 × 10%)		4,000	
Total allocated as interest allowances			(20,000)
Residual loss after salary and interest allowances			$(42,000)
Allocated in a fixed ratio:			
Adams (50%)	(21,000)		
Barnes (50%)		(21,000)	42,000
Total share to each partner	$ 7,000	$43,000	$ -0-

Authorized salary and interest allowances in excess of net income

Unless she is thoroughly familiar with the terms of the partnership contract, Adams certainly will be surprised at her allocation of net income for this accounting period. The allocation formula caused Adams to actually be allocated income of only $7,000 for the period, while Barnes was allocated net income of $43,000. The entry to close the Income Summary will be as follows:

Income Summary	50,000	
Brooke Adams, Capital		7,000
Ben Barnes, Capital		43,000
To close the Income Summary account by crediting each partner with authorized salary and interest at 10% on beginning capital, and dividing the residual loss equally.		

Had the net income of the firm been even less, say, $30,000, Adams would actually have been allocated a *negative* amount, as shown in Exhibit C–11.

Exhibit C–11

DISTRIBUTION OF PARTNERSHIP NET INCOME

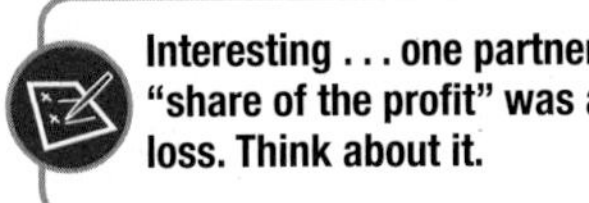

Interesting . . . one partner's "share of the profit" was a loss. Think about it.

Division of Partnership Net Income

	Adams	Barnes	Net Income
Net income to be divided			$ 30,000
Salary allowances to partners	$12,000	$60,000	(72,000)
Residual loss after salary allowances			$(42,000)
Interest allowances on beginning capital:			
Adams ($160,000 × 10%)	16,000		
Barnes ($40,000 × 10%)		4,000	
Total allocated as interest allowances			(20,000)
Residual loss after salary and interest allowances			$(62,000)
Allocated in a fixed ratio:			
Adams (50%)	(31,000)		
Barnes (50%)		(31,000)	62,000
Total share to each partner	$ (3,000)	$33,000	$ -0-

ASSIGNMENT MATERIAL

Discussion Questions

1. Terry Hanson owns Hanson Sporting Goods, a retail store organized as a sole proprietorship. He also owns a home that he purchased for $200,000 but that is worth $250,000 today. (Hanson has a $140,000 mortgage against this house.) Explain how this house and mortgage should be classified in the financial statements of Hanson Sporting Goods.
2. Jane Miller is the proprietor of a small manufacturing business. She is considering the possibility of joining in partnership with Tom Bracken, whom she considers to be thoroughly competent and congenial. Prepare a brief statement outlining the advantages and disadvantages of the potential partnership to Miller.
3. What is meant by the term *mutual agency*?
4. A real estate development business is managed by two experienced developers and is financed by 50 investors from throughout the state. To allow maximum income tax benefits to the investors, the business is organized as a partnership. Explain why this type of business probably would be a limited partnership rather than a regular partnership.
5. What factors should be considered when comparing the net income figure of a partnership to that of a corporation of similar size?
6. Susan Reed is a partner in Computer Works, a retail store. During the current year, she withdraws $45,000 in cash from this business and takes for her personal use inventory costing $3,200. Her share of the partnership net income for the year amounts to $39,000. What amount must Reed report on her personal income tax return?
7. Distinguish between corporations and partnerships in terms of the following characteristics:
   a. Owners' liability for debts of the business.
   b. Transferability of ownership interest.
   c. Continuity of existence.
   d. Federal taxation on income.
8. Explain the meaning of the term *double taxation* as it applies to corporate profits.
9. What factors should be considered in drawing up an agreement as to the way in which income shall be shared by two or more partners?
10. Partner John Young has a choice to make. He has been offered by his partners a choice between no salary allowance and a one-third share in the partnership income or a salary of $16,000 per year and a one-quarter share of residual profits. Write a brief memorandum explaining the factors he should consider in reaching a decision.

PROBLEMS

LO3 LO10

PROBLEM C.1
Partnership Transaction

E-Z Manufacturing Company is a partnership among Yolando Gonzales, Willie Todd, and Linda Yeager. The partnership contract states that partnership profits will be split equally among the three partners. During the current year Gonzales withdrew $25,000, Todd withdrew $23,000, and Yeager withdrew $30,000. Net income of E-Z Manufacturing Company amounted to $180,000.

a. Calculate each partner's share of net income for the period.

b. Describe the effects, if any, that partnership operations would have on the individual tax returns of the partners.

c. Prepare a statement of partners' equity for the year. Assume that partners' capital accounts had beginning balances of $50,000, $60,000, and $40,000 for Gonzales, Todd, and Yeager, respectively.

LO6 LO7

PROBLEM C.2
Analysis of Equity

Shown below are the amounts from the stockholders' equity section of the balance sheets of Wasson Corporation for the years ended December 31, 2010 and 2011.

	2011	2010
Stockholders' equity:		
Capital Stock	$ 50,000	$ 30,000
Retained Earnings	200,000	180,000
Total stockholders' equity	$250,000	$210,000

a. Calculate the amount of additional investment that the stockholders made during 2011.

b. Assuming that the corporation declared and paid $10,000 in dividends during 2011, calculate the amount of *net income* earned by the corporation during 2011.

c. Explain the significance of the $200,000 balance of retained earnings at December 31, 2011.

LO10

PROBLEM C.3
Division of Partnership Income

Guenther and Firmin, both of whom are CPAs, form a partnership, with Guenther investing $100,000 and Firmin, $80,000. They agree to share net income as follows:

1. Salary allowances of $80,000 to Guenther and $50,000 to Firmin.
2. Interest allowances at 15 percent of beginning capital account balances.
3. Any partnership earnings in excess of the amount required to cover the interest and salary allowances to be divided 60 percent to Guenther and 40 percent to Firmin.

The partnership net income for the first year of operations amounted to $247,000 before interest and salary allowances. Show how this $247,000 should be divided between the two partners. Use a three-column schedule of the type illustrated in Exhibit C–9. List on separate lines the amounts of interest, salaries, and the residual amount divided.

LO3

PROBLEM C.4
Analysis of Partnership Accounts

Hot Dog Shack is a fast-food restaurant that is operated as a partnership of three individuals. The three partners share profits equally. The following selected account balances are for the current year before any closing entries are made:

	Debit	Credit
Glen, Capital		55,000
Chow, Capital		60,000
West, Capital		5,000
Glen, Drawing	15,000	
Chow, Drawing	15,000	
West, Drawing	30,000	
Income Summary		90,000

Instructions

On the basis of this information, answer the following questions and show any necessary computations.

a. How much must each of the three partners report on his individual income tax return related to this business?

b. Prepare a Statement of Partners' Equity for the current year ended December 31. Assume that no partner has made an additional investment during the year.

c. Assuming that each of the partners devotes the same amount of time to the business, why might Glen and Chow consider the profit-sharing agreement to be inequitable?

d. Which factors should the partners consider when evaluating whether the profit from the partnership is adequate?

LO6 LO7

PROBLEM C.5

Stockholders' Equity Transactions

The Top Hat, Inc., is a chain of magic shops that is organized as a corporation. During the month of June, the stockholders' equity accounts of The Top Hat were affected by the following events:

June 3 The corporation sold 1,000 shares of capital stock at $20 per share.

June 10 The corporation declared a 25 cents per share dividend on its 20,000 shares of outstanding capital stock, payable on June 23.

June 23 The corporation paid the dividend declared on June 10.

June 30 The Income Summary account showed a credit balance of $60,000; the corporation's accounts are closed monthly.

Instructions

a. Prepare journal entries for each of the above events in the accounts of The Top Hat. Include the entries necessary to close the Income Summary and Dividends accounts.

b. Prepare a statement of retained earnings for June. Assume that the balance of retained earnings on May 31 was $520,000.

LO4 through LO7

PROBLEM C.6

Stockholders' Equity Transactions—More Challenging

William Bost organized Frontier Western Wear, Inc., early in 2010. On January 15, the corporation issued to Bost and other investors 40,000 shares of capital stock at $20 per share.

After the revenue and expense accounts (except Income Tax Expense) were closed into the Income Summary account at the end of 2010, the account showed a before-tax profit of $120,000. The income tax rate for the corporation is 40 percent. No dividends were declared during the year.

On March 15, 2011, the board of directors declared a cash dividend of 50 cents per share, payable on April 15.

Instructions

a. Prepare the journal entries for 2010 to (1) record the issuance of the common stock, (2) record the income tax liability at December 31, and (3) close the Income Tax Expense account.

b. Prepare the journal entries in 2011 for the declaration of the dividend on March 15 and payment of the dividend on April 15.

c. Operations in 2011 resulted in an $18,000 *net loss.* Prepare the journal entries to close the Income Summary and Dividends accounts at December 31, 2011.

d. Prepare the stockholders' equity section of the balance sheet at December 31, 2011. Include a separate supporting schedule showing your determination of retained earnings at that date.

LO6 LO7

PROBLEM C.7

Stockholders' Equity Section

The two cases described below are independent of each other. Each case provides the information necessary to prepare the stockholders' equity section of a corporate balance sheet.

a. Early in 2009, Wesson Corporation was formed with the issuance of 50,000 shares of capital stock at $5 per share. The corporation reported a net loss of $32,000 for 2009, and a net loss of $12,000 in 2010. In 2011 the corporation reported net income of $90,000 and declared a dividend of 50 cents per share.

b. Martin Industries was organized early in 2007 with the issuance of 100,000 shares of capital stock at $10 per share. During the first five years of its existence, the corporation earned a total of $800,000 and paid dividends of 25 cents per share each year on the common stock.

Instructions

Prepare the stockholders' equity section of the corporate balance sheet for each company for the year ending December 31, 2011.

LO1 LO2 LO4 through LO9

PROBLEM C.8

Comparison of Proprietorship with Corporation

S & X Co. is a retail store owned solely by Paul Turner. During the month of November, the equity accounts were affected by the following events:

Nov. 9 Turner invested an additional $15,000 in the business.

Nov. 15 Turner withdrew $1,500 for his salary for the first two weeks of the month.

Nov. 30 Turner withdrew $1,500 for his salary for the second two weeks of the month.

Nov. 30 S & X distributed $1,000 of earnings to Turner.

Instructions

a. Assuming that the business is organized as a sole proprietorship:

  1. Prepare the journal entries to record the above events in the accounts of S & X.

  2. Prepare the closing entries for the month of November. Assume that after closing all of the revenue and expense accounts the Income Summary account has a balance of $5,000.

  Hint: Record the investment in a separate capital account and the withdrawals (salary) in a separate drawing account. Close the drawing account into the capital account as part of the closing entries.

b. Assuming that the business is organized as a corporation:

  1. Prepare the journal entries to record the above events in the accounts of S & X. Assume that the distribution of earnings on November 30 was payment of a dividend that was declared on November 20.

  2. Prepare the closing entries for the month of November. Assume that after closing all of the revenue and expense accounts (except Income Tax Expense) the Income Summary account has a balance of $2,000. Before preparing the closing entries, prepare the entries to accrue income tax expense for the month and to close the Income Tax Expense account to the Income Summary account. Assume that the corporate income tax rate is *30 percent.*

c. Explain the causes of the differences in net income between S & X as a sole proprietorship and S & X as a corporation.

d. Describe the effects of the business operations on Turner's individual income tax return, assuming that the business is organized as (**1**) a sole proprietorship and (**2**) a corporation.

LO10 **PROBLEM C.9**
Formation of a Partnership

The partnership of Avery and Kirk was formed on July 1, when George Avery and Dinah Kirk agreed to invest equal amounts and to share profits and losses equally. The investment by Avery consists of $30,000 cash and an inventory of merchandise valued at $56,000.

Kirk also is to contribute a total of $86,000. However, it is agreed that her contribution will consist of the transfer of both the assets of her business and its liabilities (listed below). A list of the agreed values of the various items as well as their carrying values on Kirk's records follows. Kirk also contributes enough cash to bring her capital account to $86,000.

	Investment by Kirk	
	Balances on Kirk's Records	**Agreed Value**
Accounts Receivable	$81,680	$79,600
Inventory	11,400	12,800
Office Equipment (net)	14,300	9,000
Accounts Payable	24,800	24,800

Instructions

a. Draft entries (in general journal form) to record the investments of Avery and Kirk in the new partnership.

b. Prepare the beginning balance sheet of the partnership (in report form) at the close of business July 1, reflecting the above transfers to the firm.

c. On the following June 30 after one year of operation, the Income Summary account showed a credit balance of $74,000, and the Drawing account for each partner showed a debit balance of $31,000. Prepare journal entries to close the Income Summary account and the Drawing accounts at June 30.

LO10 **PROBLEM C.10**
Sharing Partnership Net Income: Various Methods

A comedy club called Comedy Today was organized as a partnership with Abbott investing $80,000 and Martin investing $120,000. During the first year, net income amounted to $110,000.

Instructions

a. Determine how the $110,000 net income would be divided under each of the following three independent assumptions as to the agreement for sharing profits and losses. Use schedules of the type illustrated in this chapter to show all steps in the division of net income between the partners.

1. Net income is to be divided in a fixed ratio: 40 percent to Abbott and 60 percent to Martin.
2. Interest at 15 percent to be allowed on beginning capital investments and balance to be divided equally.
3. Salaries of $36,000 to Abbott and $56,000 to Martin; interest at 15 percent to be allowed on beginning capital investments; balance to be divided equally.

b. Prepare the journal entry to close the Income Summary account, using the division of net income developed in part **a(3).**

LO10

PROBLEM C.11
Dividing Partnership Profit and Loss

Rothchild Furnishings, Inc., has three partners—Axle, Brandt, and Conrad. At the beginning of the current year their capital balances were: Axle, $180,000; Brandt, $140,000; and Conrad, $80,000. The partnership agreement provides that partners shall receive salary allowances as follows: Axle, $10,000; Brandt, $50,000; and Conrad, $28,000. The partners shall also be allowed 12 percent interest annually on their capital balances. Residual profit or loss is to be divided: Axle, one-half; Brandt, one-third; and Conrad, one-sixth.

Instructions

Prepare separate schedules showing how income will be divided among the three partners in each of the following cases. The figure given in each case is the annual partnership net income or loss to be allocated among the partners. Round calculations to the nearest dollar.

a. Income of $526,000.

b. Income of $95,000.

c. Loss of $32,000.

LO1 LO4 LO5 LO9

PROBLEM C.12
Who Gets the Prime Cut? Tax Planning and Pitfalls

Alan Weber originally started Prime Cuts, a small butcher shop, as a sole proprietorship. Then he began advertising in gift catalogs, and his company quickly grew into a large mail-order business. Now Prime Cuts sends meat and seafood all over the world by overnight mail.

At the beginning of the current year, Weber reorganized Prime Cuts as a corporation—with himself as the sole stockholder. This year, the company earned $1 million before income taxes. (For the current year, the corporate income tax rate is *40 percent.* Weber's *personal* income is taxed at the rate of *45 percent.*)

With respect to salaries and withdrawals of assets, Weber continued the same policies as when the business had been a sole proprietorship. Although he personally runs the business, he draws no salary. He explains, "Why should I draw a salary? Nowadays, I have plenty of income from other sources. Besides, a salary would just reduce the company's profits—which belong to me."

In recent years, Weber had made monthly transfers from the business bank account to his personal bank account of an amount equal to the company's monthly net income. After Prime Cuts became a corporation, he continued making these transfers by declaring monthly dividends.

Instructions

a. Without regard to income taxes, identify several reasons why it might be *advantageous* for Weber to have incorporated this business.

b. Compute the portion of the company's $1 million pretax income that Weber would have retained after income taxes if Prime Cuts *had remained a sole proprietorship.*

c. Compute the portion of this $1 million before-tax income that Weber will retain after income taxes, given that Prime Cuts *is now a corporation.*

d. Explain the meaning of the term *double taxation.*

e. Discuss several ways that Weber legally might have reduced the overall "tax bite" on his company's before-tax earnings.

LO10

PROBLEM C.13
Developing an Equitable Plan for Dividing Partnership Income

Juan Ramirez and Jimmy Smith are considering forming a partnership to engage in the business of aerial photography. Ramirez is a licensed pilot, is currently earning $48,000 a year, and has $50,000 to invest in the partnership. Smith is a professional photographer who is currently earning $30,000 a year. He has recently inherited $70,000, which he plans to invest in the partnership.

Both partners will work full-time in the business. After careful study, they have estimated that expenses are likely to exceed revenue by $10,000 during the first year of operations. In the second year, however, they expect the business to become profitable, with revenue exceeding expenses by an estimated $90,000. (Bear in mind that these estimates of expenses do not include any salaries or interest to the partners.) Under present market conditions, a fair rate of return on capital invested in this type of business is 20 percent.

Instructions

a. On the basis of this information, prepare a brief description of the income-sharing agreement that you would recommend for Ramirez and Smith. Explain the basis for your proposal.

b. Prepare a separate schedule for each of the next two years showing how the estimated amounts of net income would be divided between the two partners under your plan. (Assume that the original capital balances for both partners remain unchanged during the two-year period. This simplifying assumption allows you to ignore the changes that would normally occur in capital accounts as a result of divisions of profits, or from drawings or additional investments.)

c. Write a brief statement explaining the differences in allocation of income to the two partners and defending the results indicated by your income-sharing proposal.

Index

Page numbers followed by n refer to notes.

D

E

J

N

O

P

Q

R

S

T

Y

Z